Contents

Editorial Staff

COLLINS ENGLISH THESAURUS

IN A–Z FORM

HarperCollins*Publishers*

HarperCollins Publishers
PO Box, Glasgow G4 0NB

First Edition 1984
New Edition 1992
Latest Reprint 1995

Standard Edition ISBN 0 00 433635-6

Thumb-indexed Edition ISBN 0 00 470075-9

Typeset by Barbers Ltd,
Wrotham, England

Printed in Great Britain by
HarperCollins Manufacturing

A catalogue record for this book is available from the British Library

COLLINS ENGLISH THESAURUS

IN A–Z FORM

Foreword

When Collins A-Z Thesaurus was first published in 1984 it revolutionized the whole concept of thesauruses. It represented a new idea, a thesaurus in which the material was arranged in a single A-Z listing of main-entry words, with all the alternatives for any word found at the one place where you would be most likely to look it up. The simplicity and practicality of this approach made the book an instant success and it has been a consistent best-seller ever since.

Now, the basic text of this highly successful book has been thoroughly revised and enlarged. This new, bigger edition contains well over 39,000 additional words, derived from the resources of the Collins Dictionaries language-monitoring programme, and the resources of the computerized *Bank of English.*

The words added in this new edition provide a fascinating spectrum of language change since 1984. The basic concepts of our language change very slowly, but the variety of words which are newly added to describe those concepts are legion. So, for instance, the entry *eccentric* has gained a new synonym *off-the-wall; broken-down* has gained *on the fritz; clean,* the synonym *squeaky-clean; clumsy, klutzy; credit, Brownie points; mortifying, cringe-making;* and so on, ad infinitum. Some concepts are so lively that they acquire many new synonyms at one go. One good example of this is our entry for *drunk* where we have added, among others, *bombed, blitzed, bevvied, paralytic, steamboats, steaming, wrecked* and *zonked!*

An entirely new feature in this edition of the thesaurus is the inclusion of antonym lists at many of the main-entry words. As well as being interesting in their own right, antonyms provide you with another way of expressing yourself. For instance, if you wish to say that something is difficult, it can sometimes be effective to use a negative construction and, taking a word from the antonym list, you may think of a phrase such as "by no means straightforward". The antonym lists are as fully detailed as the synonyms and give you a very generous range of opposites at the end of these main entries.

The new edition retains all the virtues of its predecessor, with an enlarged page size and even clearer typography. The use of colour in the text to identify headings and the numbers of the synonym lists helps you to find what you want even more quickly. A wide range of main-entry words - nearly 16,000 - is included, the criterion for selection being that the word or term in question is likely to be looked up as an entry in its own right. If the word which you have in mind does not feature as a main entry (for instance, *gallimaufry*) you can still find synonyms for this concept by trying a more familiar word with the same general meaning (for instance, *jumble* or *hotchpotch*). Terms denoting concrete things are not included as main entries unless they have genuine synonyms or give rise to a figurative use. *Retina*, for example, is not a headword; but *eye* is entered with both literal and figurative senses, while *ear* is given figurative senses only. Having looked up the word which you have in mind, you will find at the one place in the book alternatives for all the possible meanings of it. These are numbered for ease of reference to enable you to find the particular meaning which fits the context you have in mind. All the synonyms given have been chosen as being fully substitutable for the headword in at least one context. Because of this, and because of the range of alternatives given, you can always find the better or more appropriate word that you are searching for.

The name **Thesaurus** came to us from Greek where it meant "treasure, treasury, or store house" and our thesaurus is so named because it is a treasury or store house of words. The English language is particularly rich in synonyms, and this thesaurus will enable you to choose exactly the right word for any occasion, as well as being simply a pleasure for you to browse through, marvelling at the richness and variety of the English language.

Explanatory Notes

1. Under each main entry word, the synonyms are arranged alphabetically. When a word has distinctly separate meanings, separate numbered lists are given for the different senses.

2. Where it is desirable to distinguish between different parts of speech, labels have been added as follows: *n.* (noun), *v.* (verb), *adj.* (adjective), *adv.* (adverb), *pron.* (pronoun), *conj.* (conjunction), *prep.* (preposition), *interj.* (interjection). See entries for *living, loaf, loan, local.*

3. Usually the synonyms for a particular part of speech are grouped together. Thus, in the entry *catch* synonyms for all verb senses are given first, followed by synonyms for all the noun senses. Sometimes, however, noun and verb functions are very closely associated in specific meanings, and where this is the case the synonyms are grouped by meanings, as in the entry for *cover.*

4. When a headword has more than one meaning and can function as more than one part of speech, a new part-of-speech function is shown by a large swung dash (~), as in the entry for *glance* or *grasp.*

5. Much-used phrases appear as main entries; for instance, *act for* comes after *act.* Expressions such as *a priori* or *en route* are also given as main entries within the alphabetical listing. Short idiomatic phrases are entered under their key word and are to be found either at the end of the entry or immediately following the sense with which they are associated. Thus, the phrase *take a dim view* appears as sense 7 of the entry *dim,* since the synonyms in sense 6 most closely approximate to the meaning of the phrase.

6. Plural forms that have a distinctly separate meaning, such as *provisions,* are entered at their own alphabetical position, while those with a less distinct difference, such as *appurtenances,* are given as a separate sense under the singular form, e.g. *appurtenance* ... 2. *Plural* ...

7. The antonym lists which follow many entries are arranged alphabetically, and, where appropriate, treated according to the rules given for synonyms.

8. A label in brackets applies only to the synonym preceding it while one which is not bracketed relates to the whole of that particular sense. Labels have been abbreviated when a readily understandable shortened form exists, such as *Sl.* (Slang), *Inf.* (Informal), and *Fig.* (Figurative).

9. The small swung dash symbol (~) is used to show that a word has been broken merely because it happens to fall at the end of a line, while the conventional sign (-) is used to distinguish a word which is always written with a hyphen, as in the entry for

   disadvantageous adverse, damaging, del~
   eterious, detrimental, harmful, hurtful, ill-
   timed, inconvenient, inexpedient, injuri~
   ous, inopportune, prejudicial, unfavourable

abaft *Nautical* aft, astern, behind

abandon *v.* 1. desert, forsake, jilt, leave, leave behind 2. evacuate, quit, vacate, withdraw from 3. abdicate, cede, give up, relinquish, renounce, resign, surrender, waive, yield 4. desist, discontinue, drop, forgo, kick (*Inf.*) ~*n.* 5. careless freedom, dash, recklessness, unrestraint, wantonness, wild impulse, wildness
Antonyms *v.* claim, continue, defend, hold, keep, maintain, take, uphold ~*n.* control, moderation, restraint

abandoned 1. cast aside, cast away, cast out, derelict, deserted, discarded, dropped, forlorn, forsaken, jilted, left, neglected, outcast, rejected, relinquished, unoccupied, vacant 2. corrupt, debauched, depraved, dissipated, dissolute, profligate, reprobate, sinful, wanton, wicked 3. uncontrolled, uninhibited, unrestrained, wild
Antonyms (*sense 1*) claimed, kept, maintained, occupied (*sense 2*) good, high-principled, honest, moral, pure, reputable, righteous, upright, virtuous, worthy (*sense 3*) conscious, restrained

abandonment 1. dereliction, desertion, forsaking, jilting, leaving 2. evacuation, quitting, withdrawal from 3. abdication, cession, giving up, relinquishment, renunciation, resignation, surrender, waiver 4. desistance, discontinuation, dropping

abase belittle, bring low, cast down, debase, degrade, demean, demote, depress, disgrace, dishonour, downgrade, humble, humiliate, lower, mortify, reduce
Antonyms advance, aggrandize, dignify, elevate, exalt, glorify, honour, prefer, promote, raise, upgrade

abasement belittlement, debasement, degradation, demotion, depression, disgrace, dishonour, downgrading, humbling, humiliation, lowering, mortification, reduction, shame

abash affront, astound, bewilder, chagrin, confound, confuse, discomfit, discompose, disconcert, discountenance, embarrass, faze, humble, humiliate, mortify, perturb, shame

abashed affronted, ashamed, astounded, bewildered, chagrined, confounded, confused, discomfited, discomposed, disconcerted, discountenanced, dismayed, embarrassed, humbled, humiliated, mortified, perturbed, shamefaced, taken aback
Antonyms at ease, blatant, bold, brazen, composed, confident, unashamed, undaunted, undismayed, unperturbed

abashment astonishment, bewilderment, chagrin, confusion, consternation, discomfiture, discomposure, disconcertion, dismay, embarrassment, humiliation, mortification, perturbation, shame

abate 1. alleviate, appease, attenuate, decline, decrease, diminish, dull, dwindle, ease, ebb, fade, lessen, let up, mitigate, moderate, quell, reduce, relax, relieve, sink, slacken, slake, slow, subside, taper off, wane, weaken 2. deduct, discount, subtract
Antonyms add to, amplify, augment, boost, enhance, escalate, increase, intensify, magnify, multiply, strengthen

abatement 1. alleviation, allowance, attenuation, cessation, decline, decrease, diminution, dulling, dwindling, easing, extenuation, fading, lessening, let-up (*Inf.*), mitigation, moderation, quelling, reduction, relief, remission, slackening, slaking, slowing, tapering off, waning, weakening 2. deduction, discount, subtraction

abbey cloister, convent, friary, monastery, nunnery, priory

abbreviate abridge, abstract, clip, compress, condense, contract, curtail, cut, digest, epitomize, précis, reduce, shorten, summarize, trim, truncate
Antonyms amplify, draw out, elongate, expand, extend, increase, lengthen, prolong, protract, spin out, stretch out

abbreviation abridgment, abstract, clipping, compendium, compression, condensation, conspectus, contraction, curtailment, digest, epitome, précis, reduction, résumé, shortening, summary, synopsis, trimming, truncation

abdicate abandon, abjure, abnegate, cede, forgo, give up, quit, relinquish, renounce, resign, retire, step down (*Inf.*), surrender, vacate, waive, yield

abdication abandonment, abjuration, abnegation, cession, giving up, quitting, relinquishment, renunciation, resignation, retiral (*esp. Scot.*), retirement, surrender, waiver, yielding

abdomen belly, breadbasket (*Sl.*), corpora~

tion (*Inf.*), guts (*Sl.*), midriff, midsection, paunch, pot, stomach, tummy (*Inf.*)

abdominal gastric, intestinal, stomachic, stomachical, visceral

abduct carry off, kidnap, make off with, run away with, run off with, seize, snatch (*Sl.*)

abduction carrying off, kidnapping, seizure

aberrant 1. abnormal, anomalous, defective, deviant, divergent, eccentric, irregular, odd, oddball (*Inf.*), off-the-wall (*Sl.*), outré, peculiar, queer, rambling, straying, untypical, wacko (*Sl.*), wandering 2. delusive, delusory, disordered, hallucinatory, illusive, illusory, unstable 3. corrupt, corrupted, degenerate, depraved, deviant, erroneous, perverse, perverted, wrong

aberration 1. aberrancy, abnormality, anomaly, defect, deviation, divergence, eccentricity, irregularity, lapse, oddity, peculiarity, quirk, rambling, straying, wandering 2. delusion, hallucination, illusion, instability, mental disorder, vagary

abet 1. aid, assist, back, condone, connive at, help, promote, sanction, second, succour, support, sustain, uphold 2. egg on, encourage, incite, prompt, spur, urge

abettor 1. accessory, accomplice, assistant, associate, backer, confederate, conniver, cooperator, helper, henchman, second 2. encourager, fomenter, inciter, instigator, prompter

abeyance 1. adjournment, deferral, discontinuation, inactivity, intermission, postponement, recess, reservation, suspense, suspension, waiting 2. **in abeyance** hanging fire, on ice (*Inf.*), pending, shelved, suspended

abeyant adjourned, deferred, discontinued, dormant, inactive, intermitted, latent, postponed, put off, quiescent, reserved, shelved, suspended, waiting

abhor abominate, detest, execrate, hate, loathe, recoil from, regard with repugnance *or* horror, shrink from, shudder at

Antonyms admire, adore, cherish, covet, delight in, desire, enjoy, like, love, relish

abhorrence abomination, animosity, aversion, detestation, disgust, distaste, enmity, execration, hate, hatred, horror, loathing, odium, repugnance, revulsion

abhorrent abominable, detestable, disgusting, distasteful, execrable, hated, hateful, heinous, horrible, horrid, loathsome, obnoxious, obscene, odious, offensive, repellent, repugnant, repulsive, revolting, yucky *or* yukky (*Sl.*)

abide 1. accept, bear, brook, endure, put up with, stand, stomach, submit to, suffer, tolerate 2. dwell, linger, live, lodge, reside, rest, sojourn, stay, stop, tarry, wait 3. continue, endure, last, persist, remain, survive

abide by 1. acknowledge, agree to, comply with, conform to, follow, obey, observe, submit to 2. adhere to, carry out, discharge, fulfil, hold to, keep to, persist in, stand by

abiding constant, continuing, durable, enduring, eternal, everlasting, fast, firm, immortal, immutable, indissoluble, lasting, permanent, persistent, persisting, steadfast, surviving, tenacious, unchanging, unending

Antonyms brief, ephemeral, evanescent, fleeting, momentary, passing, short, short-lived, temporary, transient, transitory

ability adeptness, aptitude, capability, capacity, competence, competency, craft, dexterity, endowment, energy, expertise, expertness, facility, faculty, flair, force, gift, knack, know-how (*Inf.*), potentiality, power, proficiency, qualification, skill, talent

Antonyms inability, incapability, incapacity, incompetence, powerlessness, weakness

abject 1. base, contemptible, cringing, debased, degraded, despicable, dishonourable, fawning, grovelling, humiliating, ignoble, ignominious, low, mean, servile, slavish, sordid, submissive, vile, worthless 2. deplorable, forlorn, hopeless, miserable, outcast, pitiable, wretched

Antonyms august, dignified, distinguished, elevated, eminent, exalted, grand, great, high, lofty, noble, patrician, worthy

abjectness 1. abjection, baseness, contemptibleness, debasement, degradation, dishonour, humbleness, humiliation, ignominy, lowness, meanness, servility, slavishness, sordidness, submissiveness, vileness, worthlessness 2. destitution, forlornness, hopelessness, misery, pitiableness, pitifulness, squalor, wretchedness

abjuration 1. denial, disavowal, disclaiming, disclamation, forswearing, recantation, renunciation, retraction 2. abnegation, abstention, eschewal, rejection, relinquishment, self-denial

abjure 1. deny, disavow, disclaim, forswear, recant, renege on, renounce, retract 2. abandon, abnegate, abstain from, eschew, forsake, give up, kick (*Inf.*), refrain from, reject, relinquish

ablaze 1. afire, aflame, alight, blazing, burning, fiery, flaming, ignited, lighted, on fire 2. aglow, brilliant, flashing, gleaming, glowing, illuminated, incandescent, luminous, radiant, sparkling 3. angry, aroused, enthusiastic, excited, fervent, frenzied, fuming, furious, impassioned, incensed, passionate, raging, stimulated

able accomplished, adept, adequate, adroit, capable, clever, competent, effective, efficient, experienced, expert, fit, fitted, gifted, highly endowed, masterful, masterly, powerful, practised, proficient, qualified, skilful, skilled, strong, talented
Antonyms amateurish, inadequate, incapable, incompetent, ineffective, inefficient, inept, mediocre, unfit, unskilful, weak

able-bodied firm, fit, hale, hardy, healthy, hearty, lusty, powerful, robust, sound, staunch, stout, strapping, strong, sturdy, vigorous
Antonyms ailing, debilitated, feeble, fragile, frail, sickly, tender, weak

ablution bath, bathing, cleansing, lavation, purification, shower, wash, washing

abnegate abandon, abdicate, abjure, abstain from, concede, decline, deny, disallow, eschew, forbear, forgo, forsake, give up, kick (*Inf.*), refrain from, refuse, reject, relinquish, renounce, sacrifice, surrender, yield

abnegation abandonment, abjuration, abstinence, continence, disallowance, eschewal, forbearance, giving up, refusal, rejection, relinquishment, renunciation, sacrifice, self-denial, surrender, temperance

abnormal aberrant, anomalous, atypical, curious, deviant, eccentric, erratic, exceptional, extraordinary, irregular, monstrous, odd, oddball (*Inf.*), off-the-wall (*Sl.*), outré, peculiar, queer, singular, strange, uncommon, unexpected, unnatural, untypical, unusual, wacko (*Sl.*), weird
Antonyms common, conventional, customary, familiar, natural, normal, ordinary, regular, unexceptional, usual

abnormality aberration, anomaly, atypicalness, bizarreness, deformity, deviation, eccentricity, exception, extraordinariness, flaw, irregularity, monstrosity, oddity, peculiarity, queerness, singularity, strangeness, uncommonness, unexpectedness, unnaturalness, untypicalness, unusualness, weirdness

abode domicile, dwelling, dwelling-place, habitat, habitation, home, house, lodging, pad (*Sl.*), quarters, residence

abolish abrogate, annihilate, annul, axe (*Inf.*), blot out, cancel, destroy, do away with, eliminate, end, eradicate, expunge, exterminate, extinguish, extirpate, invalidate, nullify, obliterate, overthrow, overturn, put an end to, quash, repeal, repudiate, rescind, revoke, stamp out, subvert, suppress, terminate, vitiate, void, wipe out
Antonyms authorize, continue, create, establish, found, institute, introduce, legalize, promote, reinstate, reintroduce, restore, revive, sustain

abolition abrogation, annihilation, annulment, blotting out, cancellation, destruction, elimination, end, ending, eradication, expunction, extermination, extinction, extirpation, invalidation, nullification, obliteration, overthrow, overturning, quashing, repeal, repudiation, rescission, revocation, stamping out, subversion, suppression, termination, vitiation, voiding, wiping out, withdrawal

abominable abhorrent, accursed, atrocious, base, contemptible, despicable, detestable, disgusting, execrable, foul, godawful (*Sl.*), hateful, heinous, hellish, horrible, horrid, loathsome, nauseous, obnoxious, obscene, odious, repellent, reprehensible, repugnant, repulsive, revolting, terrible, vile, villainous, wretched, yucky *or* yukky (*Sl.*)
Antonyms admirable, agreeable, charming, commendable, delightful, desirable, good, laudable, likable *or* likeable, lovable, pleasant, pleasing, wonderful

abominate abhor, detest, execrate, hate, loathe, recoil from, regard with repugnance, shudder at
Antonyms admire, adore, cherish, dote on, esteem, idolize, love, revere, treasure, worship

abomination 1. abhorrence, antipathy, aversion, detestation, disgust, distaste, execration, hate, hatred, horror, loathing, odium, repugnance, revulsion 2. anathema, *bête noire,* bugbear, curse, disgrace, evil, horror, plague, shame, torment

aboriginal ancient, autochthonous, earliest, first, indigenous, native, original, primary, primeval, primitive, primordial, pristine

aborigine aboriginal, autochthon, indigene, native, original inhabitant

abort 1. miscarry, terminate (*a pregnancy*) 2. arrest, axe (*Inf.*), call off, check, end, fail, halt, stop, terminate

abortion 1. aborticide, deliberate miscarriage, feticide, miscarriage, termination 2. disappointment, failure, fiasco, misadventure, monstrosity, vain effort

abortive *adj.* 1. bootless, failed, failing, fruitless, futile, idle, ineffectual, miscarried, unavailing, unsuccessful, useless, vain 2. *Biol.* imperfectly developed, incomplete, rudimentary, stunted ~*n.* 3. *Medical* abortifacient

abound be jammed with, be packed with, be plentiful, crowd, flourish, increase, infest, luxuriate, overflow, proliferate, superabound, swarm, swell, teem, thrive

abounding abundant, bountiful, copious, filled, flourishing, flowing, flush, full, lavish, luxuriant, overflowing, plenteous, plentiful, profuse, prolific, rank, replete, rich, superabundant, teeming

about *prep.* 1. anent (*Scot.*), as regards, concerned with, concerning, connected with, dealing with, on, re, referring to, regarding, relating to, relative to, respecting, touching, with respect to 2. adjacent, beside, circa (*used with dates*), close to, near, nearby 3. around, encircling, on all sides, round, surrounding 4. all over, over, through, throughout *~adv.* 5. almost, approaching, approximately, around, close to, more or less, nearing, nearly, roughly 6. from place to place, here and there, hither and thither, to and fro *~adj.* 7. active, around, astir, in motion, present, stirring

about to intending to, on the point of, on the verge *or* brink of, ready to

above *prep.* 1. atop, beyond, exceeding, higher than, on top of, over, upon *~adv.* 2. aloft, atop, in heaven, on high, overhead *~adj.* 3. aforementioned, aforesaid, earlier, foregoing, preceding, previous, prior 4. before, beyond, exceeding, prior to, superior to, surpassing

Antonyms *prep.* below, beneath, under, underneath *~adj.* (*sense 4*) inferior, lesser, less than, lower than, subordinate

aboveboard 1. *adv.* candidly, forthrightly, frankly, honestly, honourably, openly, overtly, straightforwardly, truly, truthfully, uprightly, veraciously, without guile 2. *adj.* candid, fair and square, forthright, frank, guileless, honest, honourable, kosher (*Inf.*), legitimate, on the up and up, open, overt, square, straight, straightforward, true, trustworthy, truthful, upfront (*Inf.*), upright, veracious

Antonyms *adj.* clandestine, crooked, deceitful, deceptive, devious, dishonest, fraudulent, furtive, secret, secretive, shady, sly, sneaky, underhand

abracadabra 1. chant, charm, conjuration, hocus-pocus, incantation, invocation, magic, mumbo jumbo, sorcery, spell, voodoo, witchcraft 2. babble, balderdash, blather, drivel, gibberish, gobbledegook, jabber, jargon, nonsense, pap, twaddle

abrade erase, erode, file, grind, rub off, scour, scrape away, scrape out, wear away, wear down, wear off

abrasion 1. *Medical* chafe, graze, scrape, scratch, scuff, surface injury 2. abrading, chafing, erosion, friction, grating, rubbing, scouring, scraping, scratching, scuffing, wearing away, wearing down

abrasive *adj.* 1. chafing, erosive, frictional, grating, rough, scraping, scratching, scratchy, scuffing 2. annoying, biting, caustic, cutting, galling, grating, hurtful, irritating, nasty, rough, sharp, unpleasant, vitriolic *~n.* 3. abradant, burnisher, grinder, scarifier, scourer

abreast 1. alongside, beside, level, shoulder to shoulder, side by side 2. acquainted, *au courant,* au fait, conversant, familiar, informed, in touch, knowledgeable, up to date

abridge abbreviate, abstract, clip, compress, concentrate, condense, contract, curtail, cut, cut down, decrease, digest, diminish, epitomize, lessen, précis, reduce, shorten, summarize, synopsize (*U.S.*), trim

Antonyms amplify, augment, enlarge, expand, extend, go into detail, lengthen, prolong, protract, spin out, stretch out

abridgment abbreviation, abstract, compendium, condensation, conspectus, contraction, curtailment, cutting, decrease, digest, diminishing, diminution, epitome, lessening, limitation, outline, précis, reduction, restraint, restriction, résumé, shortening, summary, synopsis

abroad 1. beyond the sea, in foreign lands, out of the country, overseas 2. about, at large, away, circulating, current, elsewhere, extensively, far, far and wide, forth, in circulation, out, out-of-doors, outside, publicly, widely, without

abrogate abolish, annul, cancel, countermand, end, invalidate, nullify, obviate, override, quash, repeal, repudiate, rescind, retract, reverse, revoke, scrap (*Inf.*), set aside, void, withdraw

abrogation abolition, annulment, cancellation, countermanding, ending, invalidation, nullification, overriding, quashing, repeal, repudiation, rescission, retraction, reversal, revocation, scrapping (*Inf.*), setting aside, voiding, withdrawal

abrupt 1. blunt, brisk, brusque, curt, direct, discourteous, gruff, impatient, impolite, rough, rude, short, snappish, snappy, terse, unceremonious, uncivil, ungracious 2. precipitous, sharp, sheer, steep, sudden 3. hasty, headlong, hurried, precipitate, quick, sudden, surprising, swift, unanticipated, unexpected, unforeseen 4. broken, disconnected, discontinuous, irregular, jerky, uneven

Antonyms (*sense 1*) civil, courteous, gracious, polite (*sense 2*) gradual (*sense 3*) easy, leisurely, slow, thoughtful, unhurried

abscond bolt, clear out, decamp, disappear, do a bunk (*Brit. sl.*), do a runner (*Sl.*), escape, flee, flit (*Inf.*), fly, fly the coop (*U.S. & Canad. inf.*), make off, run off, skedaddle

(*Inf.*), slip away, sneak away, steal away, take a powder (*U.S. & Canad. sl.*), take it on the lam (*U.S. & Canad. sl.*)

absence 1. absenteeism, nonappearance, nonattendance, truancy 2. default, defect, deficiency, lack, need, nonexistence, omission, privation, unavailability, want 3. absent-mindedness, abstraction, distraction, inattention, preoccupation, reverie

absent *adj.* 1. away, elsewhere, gone, lacking, missing, nonattendant, nonexistent, not present, out, truant, unavailable, wanting 2. absent-minded, absorbed, abstracted, bemused, blank, daydreaming, distracted, dreamy, empty, faraway, heedless, inattentive, musing, oblivious, preoccupied, unaware, unconscious, unheeding, unthinking, vacant, vague ~*v.* 3. **absent oneself** abscond, depart, keep away, play truant, remove, slope off (*Inf.*), stay away, truant, withdraw

Antonyms *adj.* (*sense 1*) attendant, in attendance, present (*sense 2*) alert, attentive, aware, conscious, thoughtful ~*v.* attend, show up (*Inf.*)

absently absent-mindedly, abstractedly, bemusedly, blankly, distractedly, dreamily, emptily, heedlessly, inattentively, obliviously, on automatic pilot, unconsciously, unheedingly, vacantly, vaguely

absent-minded absent, absorbed, abstracted, bemused, distracted, dreaming, dreamy, engrossed, faraway, forgetful, heedless, in a brown study, inattentive, musing, oblivious, preoccupied, unaware, unconscious, unheeding, unthinking

Antonyms alert, awake, observant, on one's toes, on the ball, perceptive, quick, vigilant, wary, wide-awake

absolute 1. arrant, complete, consummate, deep-dyed (*Usu. derogatory*), downright, entire, out-and-out, outright, perfect, pure, sheer, thorough, total, unadulterated, unalloyed, unmitigated, unmixed, unqualified, utter 2. actual, categorical, certain, conclusive, decided, decisive, definite, exact, genuine, infallible, positive, precise, sure, unambiguous, unequivocal, unquestionable 3. absolutist, arbitrary, autarchical, autocratic, autonomous, despotic, dictatorial, full, peremptory, sovereign, supreme, tyrannical, unbounded, unconditional, unlimited, unqualified, unquestionable, unrestrained, unrestricted

absolutely 1. completely, consummately, entirely, fully, perfectly, purely, thoroughly, totally, unmitigatedly, utterly, wholly 2. actually, categorically, certainly, conclusively, decidedly, decisively, definitely, exactly, genuinely, infallibly, positively, precisely, surely, truly, unambiguously, unequivocally, unquestionably 3. arbitrarily, autocratically, autonomously, despotically, dictatorially, fully, peremptorily, sovereignly, supremely, tyrannically, unconditionally, unquestionably, unrestrainedly, without qualification

Antonyms conditionally, fairly, probably, reasonably, somewhat

absoluteness 1. consummateness, entirety, perfection, purity, thoroughness, totality, unmitigatedness, wholeness 2. assuredness, certainty, certitude, conclusiveness, correctness, decidedness, decisiveness, definiteness, exactitude, genuineness, infallibility, positiveness, precision, sureness, surety, truth, unambiguousness, unequivocalness 3. arbitrariness, autonomy, despotism, dictatorialness, fullness, peremptoriness, supremacy, tyranny, unboundedness, unquestionability, unrestrainedness, unrestrictedness

absolution acquittal, amnesty, deliverance, discharge, dispensation, exculpation, exemption, exoneration, forgiveness, freeing, indulgence, liberation, mercy, pardon, release, remission, setting free, shriving, vindication

absolutism absoluteness, arbitrariness, autarchy, authoritarianism, autocracy, despotism, dictatorship, totalitarianism, tyranny

absolutist arbiter, authoritarian, autocrat, despot, dictator, totalitarian, tyrant

absolve acquit, clear, deliver, discharge, exculpate, excuse, exempt, exonerate, forgive, free, let off, liberate, loose, pardon, release, remit, set free, shrive, vindicate

Antonyms blame, censure, charge, condemn, convict, damn, denounce, excoriate, pass sentence on, reprehend, reproach, reprove, sentence, upbraid

absorb 1. assimilate, consume, devour, digest, drink in, exhaust, imbibe, incorporate, ingest, osmose, receive, soak up, suck up, take in 2. captivate, engage, engross, enwrap, fascinate, fill, fill up, fix, hold, immerse, monopolize, occupy, preoccupy, rivet

absorbed 1. captivated, concentrating, engaged, engrossed, fascinated, fixed, held, immersed, involved, lost, occupied, preoccupied, rapt, riveted, wrapped up 2. assimilated, consumed, devoured, digested, exhausted, imbibed, incorporated, received

absorbent absorptive, assimilative, blotting, imbibing, penetrable, permeable, pervious, porous, receptive, spongy

absorbing arresting, captivating, engrossing, fascinating, gripping, interesting, in-

triguing, preoccupying, riveting, spellbinding
Antonyms boring, dreary, dull, humdrum, mind-numbing, monotonous, tedious, tiresome, unexciting

absorption 1. assimilation, consumption, digestion, exhaustion, incorporation, osmosis, soaking up, sucking up 2. captivation, concentration, engagement, fascination, holding, immersion, intentness, involvement, occupation, preoccupation, raptness

abstain avoid, cease, decline, deny (oneself), desist, forbear, forgo, give up, keep from, kick (*Inf.*), refrain, refuse, renounce, shun, stop, withhold
Antonyms abandon oneself, give in, indulge, partake, yield

abstemious abstinent, ascetic, austere, continent, frugal, moderate, self-denying, sober, sparing, temperate
Antonyms greedy, gluttonous, immoderate, incontinent, intemperate, self-indulgent

abstention abstaining, abstinence, avoidance, desistance, eschewal, forbearance, nonindulgence, refraining, refusal, self-control, self-denial, self-restraint

abstinence abstemiousness, asceticism, avoidance, continence, forbearance, moderation, refraining, self-denial, self-restraint, soberness, sobriety, teetotalism, temperance
Antonyms abandon, acquisitiveness, covetousness, excess, gluttony, greediness, indulgence, self-indulgence, wantonness

abstinent abstaining, abstemious, continent, forbearing, moderate, self-controlled, self-denying, self-restraining, sober, temperate

abstract *adj.* 1. abstruse, arcane, complex, conceptual, deep, general, generalized, hypothetical, indefinite, intellectual, nonconcrete, notional, occult, philosophical, profound, recondite, separate, subtle, theoretic, theoretical, unpractical, unrealistic ~*n.* 2. abridgment, compendium, condensation, digest, epitome, essence, outline, précis, recapitulation, résumé, summary, synopsis ~*v.* 3. abbreviate, abridge, condense, digest, epitomize, outline, précis, shorten, summarize, synopsize (*U.S.*) 4. detach, dissociate, extract, isolate, remove, separate, steal, take away, take out, withdraw
Antonyms *adj.* actual, concrete, definite, factual, material, real, specific ~*n.* enlargement, expansion ~*v.* (*sense 4*) add, combine, inject

abstracted 1. absent, absent-minded, bemused, daydreaming, dreamy, faraway, inattentive, preoccupied, remote, withdrawn, woolgathering 2. abbreviated, abridged, condensed, digested, epitomized, shortened, summarized, synopsized (*U.S.*)

abstraction 1. absence, absent-mindedness, bemusedness, dreaminess, inattention, pensiveness, preoccupation, remoteness, woolgathering 2. concept, formula, generality, generalization, hypothesis, idea, notion, theorem, theory, thought

abstruse abstract, arcane, complex, dark, deep, Delphic, enigmatic, esoteric, hidden, incomprehensible, mysterious, mystical, obscure, occult, perplexing, profound, puzzling, recondite, subtle, unfathomable, vague
Antonyms apparent, clear, conspicuous, evident, manifest, open, overt, patent, perceptible, plain, self-evident, transparent, unsubtle

abstruseness arcaneness, complexity, deepness, depth, esotericism, incomprehensibility, mysteriousness, obscurity, occultness, perplexity, profundity, reconditeness, subtlety, vagueness

absurd crazy (*Inf.*), daft (*Inf.*), farcical, foolish, idiotic, illogical, inane, incongruous, irrational, laughable, ludicrous, meaningless, nonsensical, preposterous, ridiculous, senseless, silly, stupid, unreasonable
Antonyms intelligent, logical, prudent, rational, reasonable, sagacious, sensible, smart, wise

absurdity bêtise (*Rare*), craziness (*Inf.*), daftness (*Inf.*), farce, farcicality, farcicalness, folly, foolishness, idiocy, illogicality, illogicalness, incongruity, irrationality, joke, ludicrousness, meaninglessness, nonsense, preposterousness, ridiculousness, senselessness, silliness, stupidity, unreasonableness

abundance 1. affluence, ampleness, bounty, copiousness, exuberance, fullness, heap (*Inf.*), plenitude, plenteousness, plenty, profusion 2. affluence, big bucks (*Inf., chiefly U.S.*), big money, fortune, megabucks (*U.S. & Canad. sl.*), opulence, pretty penny (*Inf.*), riches, tidy sum (*Inf.*), wad (*U.S. & Canad. sl.*), wealth
Antonyms dearth, deficiency, lack, need, paucity, scantiness, scarcity, sparseness

abundant ample, bounteous, bountiful, copious, exuberant, filled, full, lavish, luxuriant, overflowing, plenteous, plentiful, profuse, rank, rich, teeming, well-provided, well-supplied
Antonyms deficient, few, few and far between, inadequate, in short supply, insuf-

ficient, lacking, rare, scant, scanty, scarce, short, sparse

abuse *v.* 1. damage, exploit, harm, hurt, ill-treat, impose upon, injure, maltreat, manhandle, mar, misapply, misuse, oppress, spoil, take advantage of, wrong 2. calumniate, castigate, curse, defame, disparage, insult, inveigh against, libel, malign, revile, scold, slander, smear, swear at, traduce, upbraid, vilify, vituperate ~*n.* 3. damage, exploitation, harm, hurt, ill-treatment, imposition, injury, maltreatment, manhandling, misapplication, misuse, oppression, spoiling, wrong 4. blame, calumniation, castigation, censure, character assassination, contumely, curses, cursing, defamation, derision, disparagement, insults, invective, libel, opprobrium, reproach, revilement, scolding, slander, swearing, tirade, traducement, upbraiding, vilification, vituperation 5. corruption, crime, delinquency, fault, injustice, misconduct, misdeed, offence, sin, wrong, wrongdoing

Antonyms *v.* (*sense 1*) care for, protect (*sense 2*) acclaim, commend, compliment, extol, flatter, praise, respect

abusive 1. calumniating, castigating, censorious, contumelious, defamatory, derisive, disparaging, insulting, invective, libellous, maligning, offensive, opprobrious, reproachful, reviling, rude, scathing, scolding, slanderous, traducing, upbraiding, vilifying, vituperative 2. brutal, cruel, destructive, harmful, hurtful, injurious, rough

Antonyms (*sense 1*) approving, complimentary, eulogistic, flattering, laudatory, panegyrical, praising

abut adjoin, border, impinge, join, meet, touch, verge

abutment brace, bulwark, buttress, pier, prop, strut, support

abutting adjacent, adjoining, bordering, contiguous, joining, meeting, next to, touching, verging

abysmal bottomless, boundless, complete, deep, endless, extreme, immeasurable, incalculable, infinite, profound, thorough, unending, unfathomable, vast

abyss abysm, bottomless depth, chasm, crevasse, fissure, gorge, gulf, pit, void

academic *adj.* 1. bookish, campus, college, collegiate, erudite, highbrow, learned, lettered, literary, scholarly, scholastic, school, studious, university 2. abstract, conjectural, hypothetical, impractical, notional, speculative, theoretical ~*n.* 3. academician, don, fellow, lecturer, master, professor, pupil, scholar, scholastic, schoolman, student, tutor

accede 1. accept, acquiesce, admit, agree, assent, comply, concede, concur, consent, endorse, grant, own, yield 2. assume, attain, come to, enter upon, inherit, succeed, succeed to (*as heir*)

accelerate advance, expedite, forward, further, hasten, hurry, pick up speed, precipitate, quicken, speed, speed up, spur, step up (*Inf.*), stimulate

Antonyms decelerate, delay, hinder, impede, obstruct, slow down

acceleration expedition, hastening, hurrying, quickening, speeding up, spurring, stepping up (*Inf.*), stimulation

accent *n.* 1. beat, cadence, emphasis, force, pitch, rhythm, stress, timbre, tonality 2. articulation, enunciation, inflection, intonation, modulation, pronunciation, tone ~*v.* 3. accentuate, emphasize, stress, underline, underscore

accentuate accent, draw attention to, emphasize, highlight, stress, underline, underscore

Antonyms gloss over, make light of, make little of, minimize, play down, soft-pedal (*Inf.*), underplay

accept 1. acquire, gain, get, have, obtain, receive, secure, take 2. accede, acknowledge, acquiesce, admit, adopt, affirm, agree to, approve, believe, buy (*Sl.*), concur with, consent to, cooperate with, recognize, swallow (*Inf.*) 3. bear, bow to, brook, defer to, put up with, stand, submit to, suffer, take, yield to 4. acknowledge, admit, assume, avow, bear, take on, undertake

Antonyms decline, deny, disown, rebut, refuse, reject, repudiate, spurn

acceptable 1. agreeable, delightful, grateful, gratifying, pleasant, pleasing, welcome 2. adequate, admissible, all right, fair, moderate, passable, satisfactory, so-so (*Inf.*), standard, tolerable

Antonyms unacceptable, unsatisfactory, unsuitable

acceptance 1. accepting, acquiring, gaining, getting, having, obtaining, receipt, securing, taking 2. accedence, accession, acknowledgment, acquiescence, admission, adoption, affirmation, agreement, approbation, approval, assent, belief, compliance, concession, concurrence, consensus, consent, cooperation, credence, O.K. *or* okay (*Inf.*), permission, recognition, stamp *or* seal of approval 3. deference, standing, submission, taking, yielding 4. acknowledgment, admission, assumption, avowal, taking on, undertaking

accepted acceptable, acknowledged, admitted, agreed, agreed upon, approved, authorized, common, confirmed, conventional, customary, established, normal, received, recognized, regular, sanctioned, standard, time-honoured, traditional, universal, usual

Antonyms abnormal, irregular, unconventional, uncustomary, unorthodox, unusual, unwonted

access 1. admission, admittance, approach, avenue, course, door, entering, entrance, entrée, entry, gateway, key, passage, passageway, path, road 2. *Medical* attack, fit, onset, outburst, paroxysm

accessibility 1. approachability, attainability, availability, handiness, nearness, obtainability, possibility, readiness 2. affability, approachability, conversableness, cordiality, friendliness, informality 3. exposedness, openness, susceptibility

accessible 1. achievable, at hand, attainable, available, get-at-able (*Inf.*), handy, near, nearby, obtainable, on hand, possible, reachable, ready 2. affable, approachable, available, conversable, cordial, friendly, informal 3. exposed, liable, open, subject, susceptible, vulnerable, wide-open

Antonyms far-off, hidden, inaccessible, secreted, unapproachable, unavailable, unobtainable, unreachable

accession 1. addition, augmentation, enlargement, extension, increase 2. assumption, attaining to, attainment of, entering upon, succession (*to a throne, dignity, or office*), taking on, taking over 3. accedence, acceptance, acquiescence, agreement, assent, concurrence, consent

accessory *n.* 1. abettor, accomplice, assistant, associate (*in crime*), colleague, confederate, helper, partner 2. accent, accompaniment, addition, add-on, adjunct, adornment, aid, appendage, attachment, component, convenience, decoration, extension, extra, frill, help, supplement, trim, trimming ~*adj.* 3. abetting, additional, aiding, ancillary, assisting in, auxiliary, contributory, extra, secondary, subordinate, supplemental, supplementary

accident 1. blow, calamity, casualty, chance, collision, crash, disaster, misadventure, mischance, misfortune, mishap, pile-up (*Inf.*) 2. chance, fate, fluke, fortuity, fortune, hazard, luck

accidental adventitious, casual, chance, contingent, fortuitous, haphazard, inadvertent, incidental, inessential, nonessential, random, uncalculated, uncertain, unessential, unexpected, unforeseen, unintended, unintentional, unlooked-for, unplanned, unpremeditated, unwitting

Antonyms calculated, designed, expected, foreseen, intended, intentional, planned, prepared

accidentally adventitiously, by accident, by chance, by mistake, casually, fortuitously, haphazardly, inadvertently, incidentally, randomly, unconsciously, undesignedly, unexpectedly, unintentionally, unwittingly

Antonyms by design, consciously, deliberately, designedly, on purpose, wilfully

acclaim 1. *v.* applaud, approve, celebrate, cheer, clap, commend, crack up (*Inf.*), eulogize, exalt, extol, hail, honour, laud, praise, salute, welcome 2. *n.* acclamation, applause, approbation, approval, celebration, cheering, clapping, commendation, eulogizing, exaltation, honour, laudation, plaudits, praise, welcome

Antonyms *n.* bad press, brickbats, censure, criticism, disparagement, fault-finding, flak (*Inf.*), panning (*Inf.*), stick (*Sl.*), vituperation

acclamation acclaim, adulation, approbation, cheer, cheering, cheers, enthusiasm, laudation, loud homage, ovation, plaudit, praise, salutation, shouting, tribute

acclimatization acclimation, accommodation, acculturation, adaptation, adjustment, habituation, inurement, naturalization

acclimatize accommodate, acculture, accustom, adapt, adjust, become seasoned to, get used to, habituate, inure, naturalize

acclivity ascent, hill, rise, rising ground, steep upward slope

accommodate 1. billet, board, cater for, entertain, harbour, house, lodge, put up, quarter, shelter 2. afford, aid, assist, furnish, help, oblige, provide, purvey, serve, supply 3. accustom, adapt, adjust, comply, compose, conform, fit, harmonize, modify, reconcile, settle

accommodating complaisant, considerate, cooperative, friendly, helpful, hospitable, kind, obliging, polite, unselfish, willing

Antonyms disobliging, inconsiderate, rude, uncooperative, unhelpful

accommodation 1. adaptation, adjustment, compliance, composition, compromise, conformity, fitting, harmony, modification, reconciliation, settlement 2. board, digs (*Brit. inf.*), harbouring, house, housing, lodging(s), quartering, quarters, shelter, sheltering 3. aid, assistance, help, provision, service, supply

accompany 1. attend, chaperon, conduct, convoy, escort, go with, squire, usher 2. belong to, coexist with, coincide with, come with, follow, go together with, join with, occur with, supplement

accompanying accessory, added, additional, appended, associate, associated, attached, attendant, complementary, concomitant, concurrent, connected, fellow, joint, related, supplemental, supplementary

accomplice abettor, accessory, ally, assistant, associate, coadjutor, collaborator, colleague, confederate, helper, henchman, partner

accomplish achieve, attain, bring about, bring off (*Inf.*), carry out, complete, conclude, consummate, do, effect, effectuate, execute, finish, fulfil, manage, perform, produce, realize

Antonyms fail, fall short, forsake, give up

accomplished 1. achieved, attained, brought about, carried out, completed, concluded, consummated, done, effected, executed, finished, fulfilled, managed, performed, produced, realized 2. adept, consummate, cultivated, expert, gifted, masterly, polished, practised, proficient, skilful, skilled, talented

Antonyms (*sense 2*) amateurish, incapable, incompetent, inexpert, unestablished, unproven, unrealized, unskilled, untalented

accomplishment 1. achievement, attainment, bringing about, carrying out, completion, conclusion, consummation, doing, effecting, execution, finishing, fulfilment, management, performance, production, realization 2. achievement, act, attainment, coup, deed, exploit, feat, stroke, triumph 3. ability, achievement, art, attainment, capability, craft, gift, proficiency, skill, talent

accord *v.* 1. agree, assent, be in tune (*Inf.*), concur, conform, correspond, fit, harmonize, match, suit, tally 2. allow, bestow, concede, confer, endow, give, grant, present, render, tender, vouchsafe ~*n.* 3. accordance, agreement, concert, concurrence, conformity, congruence, correspondence, harmony, rapport, sympathy, unanimity, unison

Antonyms *v.* (*sense 1*) conflict, contrast, differ, disagree, discord (*sense 2*) hold back, refuse, withhold ~*n.* conflict, contention, disagreement, discord

accordance 1. accord, agreement, assent, concert, concurrence, conformity, congruence, correspondence, harmony, rapport, sympathy, unanimity 2. according, allowance, bestowal, concession, conferment, conferral, endowment, gift, giving, granting, presentation, rendering, tendering

accordingly 1. appropriately, correspondingly, fitly, properly, suitably 2. as a result, consequently, ergo, hence, in consequence, so, therefore, thus

according to 1. commensurate with, in proportion, in relation 2. as believed by, as maintained by, as stated by, in the light of, on the authority of, on the report of 3. after, after the manner of, consistent with, in accordance with, in compliance with, in conformity with, in harmony with, in keeping with, in line with, in obedience to, in step with, in the manner of, obedient to

accost address, approach, buttonhole, confront, greet, hail, halt, salute, solicit (*as a prostitute*), stop

account *n.* 1. chronicle, description, detail, explanation, history, narration, narrative, recital, record, relation, report, statement, story, tale, version 2. *Commerce* balance, bill, book, books, charge, computation, inventory, invoice, ledger, reckoning, register, score, statement, tally 3. advantage, benefit, consequence, distinction, esteem, honour, import, importance, merit, note, profit, rank, repute, significance, standing, use, value, worth 4. basis, cause, consideration, ground, grounds, interest, motive, reason, regard, sake, score ~*v.* 5. appraise, assess, believe, calculate, compute, consider, count, deem, esteem, estimate, explain, gauge, hold, judge, rate, reckon, regard, think, value, weigh

accountability 1. answerability, chargeability, culpability, liability, responsibility 2. comprehensibility, explainability, explicability, intelligibility, understandability

accountable 1. amenable, answerable, charged with, liable, obligated, obliged, responsible 2. comprehensible, explainable, explicable, intelligible, understandable

account for 1. answer for, clarify, clear up, elucidate, explain, illuminate, justify, rationalize 2. destroy, incapacitate, kill, put out of action

accoutre adorn, appoint, array, bedeck, deck, decorate, equip, fit out, furnish, kit out, outfit, provide, supply

accoutrements adornments, appurtenances, array, clothing, decorations, dress, equipage, equipment, fittings, fixtures, furnishings, garb, gear, kit, ornamentation, outfit, paraphernalia, tackle, trappings, trimmings

accredit 1. appoint, authorize, certify, commission, depute, empower, endorse, entrust, guarantee, license, recognize, sanction, vouch for 2. ascribe, assign, attribute, credit

accredited appointed, authorized, certified, commissioned, deputed, deputized, empowered, endorsed, guaranteed, licensed, official, recognized, sanctioned, vouched for

accretion accumulation, addition, augmentation, enlargement, growth, increase, increment, supplement

accrue accumulate, amass, arise, be added, build up, collect, enlarge, ensue, flow, follow, grow, increase, issue, spring up

accumulate accrue, amass, build up, collect, cumulate, gather, grow, hoard, increase, pile up, stockpile, store
Antonyms diffuse, disperse, disseminate, dissipate, distribute, propagate, scatter

accumulation aggregation, augmentation, build-up, collection, conglomeration, gathering, growth, heap, hoard, increase, mass, pile, stack, stock, stockpile, store

accuracy accurateness, authenticity, carefulness, closeness, correctness, exactitude, exactness, faithfulness, faultlessness, fidelity, meticulousness, niceness, nicety, precision, strictness, truth, truthfulness, veracity, verity
Antonyms carelessness, erroneousness, imprecision, inaccuracy, incorrectness, inexactitude, laxity, laxness

accurate authentic, careful, close, correct, exact, faithful, faultless, just, meticulous, nice, precise, proper, regular, right, scrupulous, spot-on (*Brit. inf.*), strict, true, truthful, unerring, veracious
Antonyms careless, defective, faulty, imperfect, imprecise, inaccurate, incorrect, inexact, slovenly, wrong

accurately authentically, carefully, closely, correctly, exactly, faithfully, faultlessly, justly, meticulously, nicely, precisely, properly, regularly, rightly, scrupulously, strictly, truly, truthfully, unerringly, veraciously

accursed 1. bedevilled, bewitched, condemned, cursed, damned, doomed, hopeless, ill-fated, ill-omened, jinxed, luckless, ruined, undone, unfortunate, unlucky, wretched 2. abominable, despicable, detestable, execrable, hateful, hellish, horrible
Antonyms (*sense 1*) blessed, charmed, favoured, fortunate, lucky

accusation allegation, arraignment, attribution, charge, citation, complaint, denunciation, impeachment, imputation, incrimination, indictment, recrimination

accuse allege, arraign, attribute, blame, censure, charge, cite, denounce, impeach, impute, incriminate, indict, recriminate, tax
Antonyms absolve, answer, defend, deny, exonerate, plea, reply, vindicate

accustom acclimatize, acquaint, adapt, discipline, exercise, familiarize, habituate, inure, season, train

accustomed 1. acclimatized, acquainted, adapted, disciplined, exercised, familiar, familiarized, given to, habituated, in the habit of, inured, seasoned, trained, used 2. common, conventional, customary, established, everyday, expected, fixed, general, habitual, normal, ordinary, regular, routine, set, traditional, usual, wonted
Antonyms (*sense 1*) unaccustomed, unfamiliar, unused (*sense 2*) abnormal, infrequent, occasional, odd, peculiar, rare, strange, unaccustomed, uncommon, unfamiliar, unusual

ace *n.* 1. *Cards, dice, etc.* one, single point 2. *Inf.* adept, buff (*Inf.*), champion, dab hand (*Brit. inf.*), expert, genius, hotshot (*Inf.*), master, maven (*U.S.*), star, virtuoso, whiz (*Inf.*), winner, wizard (*Inf.*) ~*adj.* 3. *Inf.* brilliant, champion, excellent, expert, fine, great, masterly, outstanding, superb, virtuoso

acerbic 1. acid, acrid, acrimonious, bitter, brusque, churlish, harsh, nasty, rancorous, rude, severe, sharp, stern, unfriendly, unkind 2. acerb, acetic, acid, acidulous, acrid, astringent, bitter, harsh, sharp, sour, tart, vinegary

acerbity 1. acrimony, asperity, bitterness, brusqueness, churlishness, harshness, nastiness, rancour, rudeness, severity, sharpness, sternness, unfriendliness, unkindness 2. acidity, acidulousness, acridity, acridness, astringency, bitterness, sourness, tartness

ache *v.* 1. hurt, pain, pound, smart, suffer, throb, twinge 2. agonize, eat one's heart out, grieve, mourn, sorrow, suffer 3. covet, crave, desire, eat one's heart out over, hanker, hope, hunger, long, need, pine, thirst, yearn ~*n.* 4. hurt, pain, pang, pounding, smart, smarting, soreness, suffering, throb, throbbing 5. anguish, grief, mourning, sorrow, suffering 6. craving, desire, hankering, hope, hunger, longing, need, pining, thirst, yearning

achievable accessible, accomplishable, acquirable, attainable, feasible, obtainable, possible, practicable, reachable, realizable, winnable, within one's grasp

achieve accomplish, acquire, attain, bring about, carry out, complete, consummate, do, earn, effect, execute, finish, fulfil, gain, get, obtain, perform, procure, reach, realize, win

achievement 1. accomplishment, acquirement, attainment, completion, execution, fulfilment, performance, production, realization 2. accomplishment, act, deed, effort, exploit, feat, stroke

acid 1. acerb, acerbic, acetic, acidulous, acrid, biting, pungent, sharp, sour, tart, vinegarish, vinegary 2. acerbic, biting, bitter, caustic, cutting, harsh, hurtful, mordacious, mordant, pungent, sharp, stinging, trenchant, vitriolic

Antonyms (*sense 1*) alkaline, bland, mild, pleasant, sweet (*sense 2*) benign, bland, gentle, kindly, mild, pleasant, sweet

acidity 1. acerbity, acidulousness, acridity, acridness, bitterness, pungency, sharpness, sourness, tartness, vinegariness, vinegarishness 2. acerbity, acridity, acridness, bitterness, causticity, causticness, harshness, hurtfulness, mordancy, pungency, sharpness, trenchancy

acidulous 1. acerb, acerbic, acetic, acid, bitter, harsh, sharp, sour, tart, vinegarish, vinegary 2. acid, biting, bitter, caustic, cutting, harsh, pungent, sharp, sour, vitriolic

acknowledge 1. accede, accept, acquiesce, admit, allow, concede, confess, declare, grant, own, profess, recognize, yield 2. address, greet, hail, notice, recognize, salute 3. answer, notice, react to, recognize, reply to, respond to, return

Antonyms (*sense 1*) contradict, deny, disclaim, discount, reject, renounce, repudiate (*senses 2 & 3*) deny, disavow, disdain, disregard, ignore, rebut, reject, snub, spurn

acknowledged accepted, accredited, admitted, answered, approved, conceded, confessed, declared, professed, recognized, returned

acknowledgment 1. acceptance, accession, acquiescence, admission, allowing, confession, declaration, profession, realization, yielding 2. addressing, greeting, hail, hailing, notice, recognition, salutation, salute 3. answer, appreciation, Brownie points, credit, gratitude, reaction, recognition, reply, response, return, thanks

acme apex, climax, crest, crown, culmination, height, high point, optimum, peak, pinnacle, summit, top, vertex, zenith

Antonyms bottom, depths, low point, minimum, nadir, rock bottom, zero

acolyte adherent, admirer, altar boy, assistant, attendant, follower, helper

acquaint advise, announce, apprise, disclose, divulge, enlighten, familiarize, inform, let (someone) know, notify, reveal, tell

acquaintance 1. associate, colleague, contact 2. association, awareness, cognizance, companionship, conversance, conversancy, experience, familiarity, fellowship, intimacy, knowledge, relationship, social contact, understanding

Antonyms (*sense 1*) buddy, good friend, intimate, stranger (*sense 2*) ignorance, unfamiliarity

acquainted alive to, apprised of, *au fait*, aware of, cognizant of, conscious of, conversant with, experienced in, familiar with, informed of, in on, knowledgeable about, privy to, versed in

acquiesce accede, accept, agree, allow, approve, assent, bow to, comply, concur, conform, consent, give in, go along with, submit, yield

Antonyms balk at, contest, demur, disagree, dissent, fight, object, protest, refuse, resist, veto

acquiescence acceptance, accession, agreement, approval, assent, compliance, concurrence, conformity, consent, giving in, obedience, submission, yielding

acquiescent acceding, accepting, agreeable, agreeing, approving, assenting, compliant, concurrent, conforming, consenting, obedient, submissive, yielding

acquire achieve, amass, attain, buy, collect, earn, gain, gather, get, obtain, pick up, procure, realize, receive, score (*Sl.*), secure, win

Antonyms be deprived of, forfeit, forgo, give up, lose, relinquish, renounce, surrender, waive

acquirement accomplishment, achievement, acquisition, attainment, gathering, knowledge, learning, mastery, mental gains, qualification, skill

acquisition 1. buy, gain, possession, prize, property, purchase 2. achievement, acquirement, attainment, gaining, learning, obtainment, procurement, pursuit

acquisitive avaricious, avid, covetous, grabbing, grasping, greedy, predatory, rapacious

Antonyms bounteous, bountiful, generous, lavish, liberal, munificent, openhanded, unselfish, unstinting

acquisitiveness avarice, avidity, avidness, covetousness, graspingness, greed, predatoriness, rapaciousness, rapacity

acquit 1. absolve, clear, deliver, discharge, exculpate, exonerate, free, fulfil, liberate, release, relieve, vindicate 2. discharge, pay, pay off, repay, satisfy, settle 3. bear, behave, comport, conduct, perform

Antonyms (*sense 1*) blame, charge, condemn, convict, damn, find guilty, sentence

acquittal absolution, clearance, deliverance, discharge, exculpation, exoneration, freeing, liberation, release, relief, vindication

acquittance acknowledgment, discharge, payment, receipt, release, settlement, settling

acrid 1. acerb, acid, astringent, biting, bitter, burning, caustic, harsh, irritating, pungent, sharp, stinging, vitriolic 2. acrimonious, biting, bitter, caustic, cutting, harsh, mordacious, mordant, nasty, sarcastic, sharp, trenchant, vitriolic

acrimonious acerbic, astringent, biting, bitter, caustic, censorious, churlish, crabbed, cutting, irascible, mordacious, mordant, peevish, petulant, pungent, rancorous, sarcastic, severe, sharp, spiteful, splenetic, tart, testy, trenchant, vitriolic
Antonyms affable, benign, forgiving, good-tempered

acrimony acerbity, asperity, astringency, bitterness, churlishness, harshness, ill will, irascibility, mordancy, peevishness, rancour, sarcasm, spleen, tartness, trenchancy, virulence
Antonyms amity, friendliness, friendship, good feelings, good will, liking, warmth

act *n.* 1. accomplishment, achievement, action, blow, deed, doing, execution, exertion, exploit, feat, move, operation, performance, step, stroke, undertaking 2. bill, decree, edict, enactment, law, measure, ordinance, resolution, statute 3. affectation, attitude, counterfeit, dissimulation, fake, feigning, front, performance, pose, posture, pretence, sham, show, stance 4. performance, routine, show, sketch, turn ~*v.* 5. acquit, bear, behave, carry, carry out, comport, conduct, do, enact, execute, exert, function, go about, make, move, operate, perform, react, serve, strike, take effect, undertake, work 6. affect, assume, counterfeit, dissimulate, feign, imitate, perform, pose, posture, pretend, put on, seem, sham 7. act out, characterize, enact, impersonate, mime, mimic, perform, personate, personify, play, play *or* take the part of, portray, represent

act for cover for, deputize for, fill in for, function in place of, replace, represent, serve, stand in for, substitute for, take the place of

acting *adj.* 1. interim, *pro tem,* provisional, substitute, surrogate, temporary ~*n.* 2. characterization, dramatics, enacting, impersonation, performance, performing, playing, portrayal, portraying, stagecraft, theatre 3. assuming, counterfeiting, dissimulation, feigning, imitating, imitation, imposture, play-acting, posing, posturing, pretence, pretending, putting on, seeming, shamming

action 1. accomplishment, achievement, act, blow, deed, exercise, exertion, exploit, feat, move, operation, performance, step, stroke, undertaking 2. activity, energy, force, liveliness, spirit, vigour, vim, vitality 3. activity, effect, effort, exertion, force, functioning, influence, motion, movement, operation, power, process, work, working 4. battle, combat, conflict, fighting, warfare 5. affray, battle, clash, combat, contest, encounter, engagement, fight, fray, skirmish, sortie 6. case, cause, lawsuit, litigation, proceeding, prosecution, suit

actions bearing, behaviour, comportment, conduct, demeanour, deportment, manners, ways

activate actuate, animate, arouse, energize, galvanize, get going, impel, initiate, kick-start, mobilize, motivate, move, prod, prompt, propel, rouse, set going, set in motion, set off, start, stimulate, stir, switch on, trigger (off), turn on
Antonyms arrest, check, deactivate, halt, impede, stall, stop, terminate, turn off

active 1. acting, astir, at work, doing, effectual, functioning, in action, in force, in operation, live, moving, operative, running, stirring, working 2. bustling, busy, engaged, full, hard-working, involved, occupied, on the go (*Inf.*), on the move, strenuous 3. alert, animated, diligent, energetic, industrious, lively, nimble, on the go (*Inf.*), quick, spirited, sprightly, spry, vibrant, vigorous, vital, vivacious 4. activist, aggressive, ambitious, assertive, committed, devoted, energetic, engaged, enterprising, enthusiastic, forceful, forward, hard-working, industrious, militant, zealous
Antonyms dormant, dull, idle, inactive, inoperative, lazy, sedentary, slow, sluggish, torpid, unimaginative, unoccupied

activity 1. action, activeness, animation, bustle, enterprise, exercise, exertion, hurly-burly, hustle, labour, life, liveliness, motion, movement, stir, work 2. act, avocation, deed, endeavour, enterprise, hobby, interest, job, labour, occupation, pastime, project, pursuit, scheme, task, undertaking, venture, work
Antonyms (*sense 1*) dullness, idleness, immobility, inaction, inactivity, indolence, inertia, lethargy, passivity, sluggishness, torpor

act on, act upon 1. act in accordance with, carry out, comply with, conform to, follow, heed, obey, yield to 2. affect, alter, change, influence, modify, sway, transform

actor 1. actress, dramatic artist, leading man, performer, play-actor, player, Thespian, tragedian, trouper 2. agent, doer, executor, factor, functionary, operative, operator, participant, participator, performer, perpetrator, practitioner, worker

actress actor, dramatic artist, leading lady, performer, play-actor, player, starlet, Thespian, tragedienne, trouper

actual 1. absolute, categorical, certain, concrete, corporeal, definite, factual, indisputable, indubitable, physical, positive, real, substantial, tangible, undeniable, unquestionable 2. authentic, confirmed, genuine, real, realistic, true, truthful, verified 3. current, existent, extant, live, living, present, present-day, prevailing

Antonyms (*senses 1 & 2*) fictitious, hypothetical, made-up, probable, supposed, theoretical, unreal, untrue

actuality 1. corporeality, factuality, materiality, reality, realness, substance, substantiality, truth, verity 2. fact, reality, truth, verity

actually absolutely, as a matter of fact, de facto, essentially, indeed, in fact, in point of fact, in reality, in truth, literally, really, truly, veritably

actuate animate, arouse, cause, dispose, drive, excite, get going, impel, incite, induce, influence, inspire, instigate, motivate, move, prompt, quicken, rouse, set off, spur, stimulate, stir, urge

act up be naughty, carry on, cause trouble, give bother, give trouble, horse around (*Inf.*), malfunction, mess about, misbehave, piss about (*Taboo sl.*), piss around (*Taboo sl.*), play up (*Brit. inf.*)

act upon *see* ACT ON

acumen acuteness, astuteness, cleverness, discernment, ingenuity, insight, intelligence, judgment, keenness, penetration, perception, perspicacity, perspicuity, sagacity, sharpness, shrewdness, smartness, smarts (*Sl., chiefly U.S.*), wisdom, wit

acute 1. astute, canny, clever, discerning, discriminating, incisive, ingenious, insightful, intuitive, keen, observant, penetrating, perceptive, perspicacious, piercing, sensitive, sharp, smart, subtle 2. critical, crucial, dangerous, decisive, essential, grave, important, serious, severe, sudden, urgent, vital 3. cutting, distressing, excruciating, exquisite, fierce, harrowing, intense, overpowering, overwhelming, piercing, poignant, powerful, racking, severe, sharp, shooting, shrill, stabbing, sudden, violent 4. cuspate, needle-shaped, peaked, pointed, sharp, sharpened

Antonyms (*sense 1*) dense, dim, dim-witted, dull, obtuse, slow, stupid, unintelligent (*sense 4*) blunt, blunted, dull, obtuse, unsharpened

acuteness 1 acuity, astuteness, canniness, cleverness, discernment, discrimination, ingenuity, insight, intuition, intuitiveness, keenness, perception, perceptiveness, perspicacity, sensitivity, sharpness, smartness, subtleness, subtlety, wit 2. criticality, criticalness, cruciality, danger, dangerousness, decisiveness, essentiality, gravity, importance, seriousness, severity, suddenness, urgency, vitalness 3. distressingness, exquisiteness, fierceness, intenseness, intensity, poignancy, powerfulness, severity, sharpness, shrillness, suddenness, violence 4. pointedness, sharpness

adage aphorism, apophthegm, axiom, byword, dictum, maxim, motto, precept, proverb, saw, saying

adamant 1. determined, firm, fixed, immovable, inexorable, inflexible, insistent, intransigent, obdurate, relentless, resolute, rigid, set, stiff, stubborn, unbending, uncompromising, unrelenting, unshakable, unyielding 2. adamantine, flinty, hard, impenetrable, indestructible, rock-hard, rocky, steely, stony, tough, unbreakable

Antonyms (*sense 1*) compliant, compromising, easy-going, flexible, lax, pliant, receptive, responsive, susceptible, tensile, tractable, yielding (*sense 2*) bendy, ductile, flexible, pliable, pliant, yielding

adapt acclimatize, accommodate, adjust, alter, apply, change, comply, conform, convert, familiarize, fashion, fit, habituate, harmonize, make, match, modify, prepare, qualify, remodel, shape, suit, tailor

adaptability adaptableness, adjustability, alterability, changeability, compliancy, convertibility, flexibility, malleability, modifiability, plasticity, pliability, pliancy, resilience, variability, versatility

adaptable adjustable, alterable, changeable, compliant, conformable, convertible, easy-going, easy-oasy (*Sl.*), flexible, malleable, modifiable, plastic, pliant, resilient, variable, versatile

adaptation 1. adjustment, alteration, change, conversion, modification, refitting, remodelling, reworking, shift, transformation, variation, version 2. acclimatization, accustomedness, familiarization, habituation, naturalization

add 1 adjoin, affix, amplify, annex, append, attach, augment, enlarge by, include, increase by, supplement 2 add up, compute, count up, reckon, sum up, total, tot up

Antonyms deduct, diminish, lessen, reduce, remove, subtract, take away, take from

addendum addition, adjunct, affix, appendage, appendix, attachment, augmentation, codicil, extension, extra, postscript, supplement

addict 1. dope-fiend (*Sl.*), fiend (*Inf.*), freak (*Inf.*), head (*Sl.*), junkie (*Inf.*), user (*Inf.*) 2. adherent, buff (*Inf.*), devotee, enthusiast, fan, follower, freak (*Inf.*), nut (*Sl.*)

addicted absorbed, accustomed, dedicated, dependent, devoted, disposed, fond, habituated, hooked (*Sl.*), inclined, obsessed, prone

addiction craving, dependence, enslavement, habit, obsession

addition 1. accession, adding, adjoining, affixing, amplification, annexation, attachment, augmentation, enlargement, extension, inclusion, increasing 2. addendum, additive, adjunct, affix, appendage, appendix, extension, extra, gain, increase, increment, supplement 3. adding up, computation, counting up, reckoning, summation, summing up, totalling, totting up 4. **in addition (to)** additionally, also, as well (as), besides, into the bargain, moreover, over and above, to boot, too, withal

Antonyms deduction, detachment, diminution, lessening, reduction, removal, subtraction

additional added, add-on, affixed, appended, extra, fresh, further, increased, more, new, other, over-and-above, spare, supplementary

addle-brained *or* **addle-pated** befuddled, bewildered, confused, daft (*Inf.*), dim-witted, dopey (*Inf.*), dozy (*Brit. inf.*), flustered, foolish, goofy (*Inf.*), halfwitted, mixed-up, muddled, muddleheaded, nonsensical, perplexed, silly, simple, simple-minded, stupid, thick, thickheaded, witless, woolly-minded

addled 1. at sea, befuddled, bewildered, confused, flustered, foolish, mixed-up, muddled, perplexed, silly 2. bad, gone bad, off, rancid, rotten, turned

address *n.* 1. abode, domicile, dwelling, home, house, location, lodging, pad (*Sl.*), place, residence, situation, whereabouts 2. direction, inscription, superscription 3. discourse, disquisition, dissertation, harangue, lecture, oration, sermon, speech, talk 4. adroitness, art, dexterity, discretion, expertness, ingenuity, skilfulness, skill, tact ~*v.* 5. accost, apostrophize, approach, greet, hail, invoke, salute, speak to, talk to 6. discourse, give a speech, give a talk, harangue, lecture, orate, sermonize, speak, spout, talk 7. **address (oneself) to** apply (oneself) to, attend to, concentrate on, devote (oneself) to, engage in, focus on, knuckle down to, look to, take care of, take up, turn to, undertake

adduce advance, allege, cite, designate, mention, name, offer, present, quote

add up 1. add, compute, count, count up, reckon, sum up, total, tot up 2. amount, come to, imply, indicate, mean, reveal, signify 3. be plausible, be reasonable, hold water, make sense, ring true, stand to reason

adept 1. *adj.* able, accomplished, adroit, dexterous, expert, masterful, masterly, practised, proficient, skilful, skilled, versed 2. *n.* buff (*Inf.*), dab hand (*Brit. inf.*), expert, genius, hotshot (*Inf.*), master, maven (*U.S.*), whiz (*Inf.*)

Antonyms *adj.* amateurish, awkward, clumsy, inept, unskilled

adequacy capability, commensurateness, competence, fairness, requisiteness, satisfactoriness, sufficiency, suitability, tolerability

adequate capable, commensurate, competent, enough, fair, passable, requisite, satisfactory, sufficient, suitable, tolerable

Antonyms deficient, inadequate, insufficient, lacking, meagre, scant, short, unsatisfactory, unsuitable

adhere 1. attach, cement, cleave, cling, cohere, fasten, fix, glue, glue on, hold fast, paste, stick, stick fast, unite 2. abide by, be attached, be constant, be devoted, be faithful, be loyal, be true, cleave to, cling, follow, fulfil, heed, keep, keep to, maintain, mind, obey, observe, respect, stand by, support

adherent 1. *n.* admirer, advocate, devotee, disciple, fan, follower, hanger-on, henchman, partisan, protagonist, sectary, supporter, upholder, votary 2. *adj.* adhering, adhesive, clinging, gluey, glutinous, gummy, holding, mucilaginous, sticking, sticky, tacky, tenacious

Antonyms *n.* adversary, antagonist, disputant, dissentient, enemy, foe, opponent, opposer, opposition, rival

adhesion 1. adherence, adhesiveness, attachment, coherence, cohesion, grip, holding fast, sticking, union 2. allegiance, attachment, constancy, devotion, faithfulness, fidelity, fulfilment, heed, loyalty, obedience, observation, respect, support, troth (*Archaic*)

adhesive 1. *adj.* adhering, attaching, clinging, cohesive, gluey, glutinous, gummy, holding, mucilaginous, sticking, sticky, tacky, tenacious 2. *n.* cement, glue, gum, mucilage, paste

adieu congé, farewell, goodbye, leave-taking, parting, valediction

adipose fat, fatty, greasy, obese, oily, oleaginous, sebaceous

adjacent abutting, adjoining, alongside,

beside, bordering, close, contiguous, near, neighbouring, next door, proximate, touching, within sniffing distance (*Inf.*)
Antonyms distant, far away, remote, separated

adjoin abut, add, affix, annex, append, approximate, attach, border, combine, communicate with, connect, couple, impinge, interconnect, join, link, neighbour, touch, unite, verge

adjoining abutting, adjacent, bordering, connecting, contiguous, impinging, interconnecting, joined, joining, near, neighbouring, next door, touching, verging

adjourn defer, delay, discontinue, interrupt, postpone, prorogue, put off, put on the back burner (*Inf.*), recess, stay, suspend, take a rain check on (*U.S. & Canad. inf.*)
Antonyms assemble, continue, convene, gather, open, remain, reopen, stay

adjournment deferment, deferral, delay, discontinuation, interruption, postponement, prorogation, putting off, recess, stay, suspension

adjudge adjudicate, allot, apportion, assign, award, decide, declare, decree, determine, distribute, judge, order, pronounce

adjudicate adjudge, arbitrate, decide, determine, judge, mediate, referee, settle, umpire

adjudication adjudgment, arbitration, conclusion, decision, determination, finding, judgment, pronouncement, ruling, settlement, verdict

adjunct accessory, addendum, addition, add-on, appendage, appurtenance, auxiliary, complement, supplement

adjure 1. appeal to, beg, beseech, entreat, implore, invoke, pray, supplicate 2. charge, command, direct, enjoin, order

adjust acclimatize, accommodate, accustom, adapt, alter, arrange, compose, convert, dispose, fit, fix, harmonize, make conform, measure, modify, order, reconcile, rectify, redress, regulate, remodel, set, settle, suit, tune (up)

adjustable adaptable, alterable, flexible, malleable, modifiable, mouldable, movable, tractable

adjustment 1. adaptation, alteration, arrangement, arranging, fitting, fixing, modification, ordering, rectification, redress, regulation, remodelling, setting, tuning 2. acclimatization, harmonization, orientation, reconciliation, settlement, settling in

ad-lib 1. *v.* busk, extemporize, improvise, make up, speak extemporaneously, speak impromptu, speak off the cuff, vamp, wing it (*Inf.*) 2. *adj.* extemporaneous, extempore, extemporized, impromptu, improvised, made up, off-the-cuff (*Inf.*), unprepared, unrehearsed 3. *adv.* extemporaneously, extempore, impromptu, off the cuff, off the top of one's head (*Inf.*), without preparation, without rehearsal

administer 1. conduct, control, direct, govern, handle, manage, oversee, run, superintend, supervise 2. apply, contribute, dispense, distribute, execute, give, impose, mete out, perform, provide

administration 1. administering, application, conduct, control, direction, dispensation, distribution, execution, governing, government, management, overseeing, performance, provision, running, superintendence, supervision 2. executive, governing body, government, management, ministry, term of office

administrative directorial, executive, governmental, gubernatorial (*Chiefly U.S.*), management, managerial, organizational, regulatory, supervisory

admirable choice, commendable, estimable, excellent, exquisite, fine, laudable, meritorious, praiseworthy, rare, sterling, superior, valuable, wonderful, worthy
Antonyms bad, commonplace, deplorable, disappointing, displeasing, mediocre, worthless

admiration adoration, affection, amazement, appreciation, approbation, approval, astonishment, delight, esteem, pleasure, praise, regard, respect, surprise, veneration, wonder, wonderment

admire 1. adore, appreciate, approve, esteem, idolize, look up to, praise, prize, respect, think highly of, value, venerate, worship 2. appreciate, delight in, marvel at, take pleasure in, wonder at
Antonyms contemn, deride, despise, look down on, look down one's nose at (*Inf.*), misprize, scorn, sneer at, spurn, undervalue

admirer 1. beau, boyfriend, lover, suitor, sweetheart, wooer 2. adherent, buff (*Inf.*), devotee, disciple, enthusiast, fan, follower, partisan, protagonist, supporter, votary, worshipper

admissible acceptable, allowable, allowed, passable, permissible, permitted, tolerable, tolerated
Antonyms disallowed, inadmissible, intolerable, unacceptable

admission 1. acceptance, access, admittance, entrance, entrée, entry, ingress, initiation, introduction 2. acknowledgment, admitting, affirmation, allowance, avowal, concession, confession, declaration, disclosure, divulgence, profession, revelation

admit 1. accept, allow, allow to enter, give access, initiate, introduce, let in, receive, take in 2. acknowledge, affirm, avow, concede, confess, declare, disclose, divulge, own, profess, reveal 3. agree, allow, grant, let, permit, recognize
Antonyms (*sense 1*) exclude, keep out (*senses 2 & 3*) deny, dismiss, forbid, negate, prohibit, reject

admittance acceptance, access, admitting, allowing, entrance, entry, letting in, passage, reception

admix add, alloy, amalgamate, blend, combine, commingle, commix, include, incorporate, intermingle, meld, merge, mingle, mix, put in

admixture 1. alloy, amalgamation, blend, combination, compound, fusion, intermixture, medley, meld 2. component, constituent, element, ingredient

admonish advise, bawl out (*Inf.*), berate, carpet (*Inf.*), caution, censure, check, chew out (*U.S. & Canad. inf.*), chide, counsel, enjoin, exhort, forewarn, give a rocket (*Brit. & N.Z. inf.*), read the riot act, rebuke, reprimand, reprove, scold, tear into (*Inf.*), tear (someone) off a strip (*Brit. inf.*), tell off (*Inf.*), upbraid, warn
Antonyms applaud, commend, compliment, congratulate, praise

admonition advice, berating, caution, chiding, counsel, rebuke, remonstrance, reprimand, reproach, reproof, scolding, telling off (*Inf.*), upbraiding, warning

admonitory admonishing, advisory, cautionary, rebuking, reprimanding, reproachful, reproving, scolding, warning

ado agitation, bother, bustle, commotion, confusion, delay, disturbance, excitement, flurry, fuss, pother, stir, to-do, trouble

adolescence 1. boyhood, girlhood, juvenescence, minority, teens, youth 2. boyishness, childishness, girlishness, immaturity, juvenility, puerility, youthfulness

adolescent 1. *adj.* boyish, girlish, growing, immature, juvenile, puerile, teenage, young, youthful 2. *n.* juvenile, minor, teenager, youngster, youth

adopt 1. accept, appropriate, approve, assume, choose, embrace, endorse, espouse, follow, maintain, ratify, select, support, take on, take over, take up 2. foster, take in
Antonyms (*sense 1*) abandon, abnegate, cast aside, cast off, disavow, disclaim, disown, forswear, give up, reject, renounce, repudiate, spurn, wash one's hands of

adoption 1. acceptance, approbation, appropriation, approval, assumption, choice, embracing, endorsement, espousal, following, maintenance, ratification, selection, support, taking on, taking over, taking up 2. adopting, fosterage, fostering, taking in

adorable appealing, attractive, captivating, charming, cute, darling, dear, delightful, fetching, lovable, pleasing, precious
Antonyms despicable, displeasing, hateful, unlikable *or* unlikeable, unlovable

adoration admiration, esteem, estimation, exaltation, glorification, honour, idolatry, idolization, love, reverence, veneration, worship, worshipping

adore admire, bow to, cherish, dote on, esteem, exalt, glorify, honour, idolize, love, revere, reverence, venerate, worship
Antonyms abhor, abominate, despise, detest, execrate, hate, loathe

adorn array, beautify, bedeck, deck, decorate, embellish, emblazon, enhance, enrich, festoon, garnish, grace, ornament, trim

adornment 1. accessory, decoration, embellishment, festoon, frill, frippery, ornament, trimming 2. beautification, decorating, decoration, embellishment, ornamentation, trimming

adrift 1. afloat, drifting, unanchored, unmoored 2. aimless, directionless, goalless, purposeless 3. amiss, astray, off course, wrong

adroit able, adept, apt, artful, clever, cunning, deft, dexterous, expert, ingenious, masterful, neat, nimble, proficient, quick-witted, skilful, skilled
Antonyms awkward, blundering, bungling, cack-handed (*Inf.*), clumsy, ham-fisted (*Inf.*), inept, inexpert, maladroit, uncoordinated, unhandy, unskilful

adroitness ability, ableness, address, adeptness, aptness, artfulness, cleverness, craft, cunning, deftness, dexterity, expertise, ingeniousness, ingenuity, masterfulness, mastery, nimbleness, proficiency, quick-wittedness, skilfulness, skill

adulation blandishment, bootlicking (*Inf.*), extravagant flattery, fawning, fulsome praise, servile flattery, sycophancy, worship
Antonyms abuse, calumniation, censure, condemnation, disparagement, revilement, ridicule, vilification, vituperation

adulatory blandishing, bootlicking (*Inf.*), fawning, flattering, obsequious, praising, servile, slavish, sycophantic, worshipping

adult 1. *adj.* full grown, fully developed, fully grown, grown-up, mature, of age, ripe 2. *n.* grown *or* grown-up person (man *or* woman), grown-up, person of mature age

adulterate 1. *v.* attenuate, bastardize, contaminate, corrupt, debase, depreciate, deteriorate, devalue, make impure, mix with, thin, vitiate, water down, weaken 2. *adj.*

adulterated, attenuated, bastardized, contaminated, corrupt, debased, depreciated, deteriorated, devalued, mixed, thinned, vitiated, watered down, weakened

adumbrate 1. delineate, indicate, outline, silhouette, sketch, suggest 2. augur, forecast, foreshadow, foretell, portend, predict, prefigure, presage, prognosticate, prophesy 3. bedim, darken, eclipse, obfuscate, obscure, overshadow

adumbration 1. delineation, draft, indication, outline, rough, silhouette, sketch, suggestion 2. augury, forecast, foreshadowing, foretelling, omen, portent, prediction, prefiguration, prefigurement, presage, prognostication, prophecy, sign 3. bedimming, cloud, darkening, darkness, eclipse, eclipsing, obfuscation, obscuring, overshadowing, shadow

advance *v.* 1. accelerate, bring forward, bring up, come forward, elevate, go ahead, go forward, go on, hasten, move onward, move up, press on, proceed, progress, promote, send forward, send up, speed, upgrade 2. benefit, further, grow, improve, multiply, prosper, thrive 3. adduce, allege, cite, offer, present, proffer, put forward, submit, suggest 4. increase (*price*), lend, pay beforehand, raise (*price*), supply on credit *~n.* 5. advancement, development, forward movement, headway, inroad, onward movement, progress 6. advancement, amelioration, betterment, breakthrough, furtherance, gain, growth, improvement, progress, promotion, step 7. appreciation, credit, deposit, down payment, increase (*in price*), loan, prepayment, retainer, rise (*in price*) 8. **advances** approach, approaches, moves, overtures, proposals, proposition *~adj.* 9. beforehand, early, foremost, forward, in front, leading, prior 10. **in advance** ahead, beforehand, earlier, in the forefront, in the lead, in the van, previously
Antonyms *v.* (*sense 1*) demote, hold back, impede, move back, regress, retard, retreat, set back, withdraw (*sense 2*) decrease, diminish, lessen, weaken (*sense 3*) hide, hold back, suppress, withhold (*sense 4*) defer payment, withhold payment

advanced ahead, avant-garde, extreme, foremost, forward, higher, late, leading, precocious, progressive
Antonyms backward, behind, retarded, underdeveloped, undeveloped

advancement 1. advance, forward movement, headway, onward movement, progress 2. advance, amelioration, betterment, gain, growth, improvement, preferment, progress, promotion, rise

advantage aid, ascendancy, asset, assistance, avail, benefit, blessing, boon, convenience, dominance, edge, gain, good, help, interest, lead, precedence, pre-eminence, profit, service, start, superiority, sway, upper hand, use, utility, welfare
Antonyms curse, difficulty, disadvantage, downside, drawback, handicap, hindrance, inconvenience, snag

advantageous 1. dominant, dominating, favourable, superior 2. beneficial, convenient, expedient, helpful, of service, profitable, useful, valuable, worthwhile
Antonyms detrimental, unfavourable, unfortunate, unhelpful, useless

advent appearance, approach, arrival, coming, entrance, occurrence, onset, visitation

adventitious accidental, casual, chance, extraneous, foreign, fortuitous, incidental, nonessential, unexpected

adventure 1. *n.* chance, contingency, enterprise, escapade, experience, exploit, hazard, incident, occurrence, risk, speculation, undertaking, venture 2. *v.* dare, endanger, hazard, imperil, jeopardize, risk, venture

adventurer 1. daredevil, hero, heroine, knight-errant, soldier of fortune, swashbuckler, traveller, venturer, voyager, wanderer 2. charlatan, fortune-hunter, gambler, mercenary, opportunist, rogue, speculator

adventurous adventuresome, audacious, bold, dangerous, daredevil, daring, enterprising, foolhardy, have-a-go (*Inf.*), hazardous, headstrong, intrepid, rash, reckless, risky, temerarious (*Rare*), venturesome
Antonyms careful, cautious, chary, circumspect, hesitant, prudent, tentative, timid, timorous, safe, unadventurous, wary

adversary antagonist, competitor, contestant, enemy, foe, opponent, opposer, rival
Antonyms accomplice, ally, associate, collaborator, colleague, confederate, co-worker, friend, helper, partner, supporter

adverse antagonistic, conflicting, contrary, detrimental, disadvantageous, hostile, inexpedient, inimical, injurious, inopportune, negative, opposing, opposite, reluctant, repugnant, unfavourable, unfortunate, unfriendly, unlucky, unpropitious, unwilling
Antonyms advantageous, auspicious, beneficial, favourable, fortunate, helpful, lucky, opportune, promising, propitious, suitable

adversity affliction, bad luck, calamity, catastrophe, disaster, distress, hardship, hard times, ill-fortune, ill-luck, misery, misfortune, mishap, reverse, sorrow, suffering, trial, trouble, woe, wretchedness

advert *v.* allude, draw attention (to), mention, notice, observe, refer, regard, remark

advertise advise, announce, apprise, blazon, crack up (*Inf.*), declare, display, flaunt, inform, make known, notify, plug (*Inf.*), praise, proclaim, promote, promulgate, publicize, publish, puff, push (*Inf.*), tout

advertisement ad (*Inf.*), advert (*Brit. inf.*), announcement, bill, blurb, circular, commercial, display, notice, placard, plug (*Inf.*), poster, promotion, publicity, puff

advice 1. admonition, caution, counsel, guidance, help, injunction, opinion, recommendation, suggestion, view 2. information, instruction, intelligence, notice, notification, warning, word

advisability appropriateness, aptness, desirability, expediency, fitness, judiciousness, profitability, propriety, prudence, seemliness, soundness, suitability, wisdom

advisable appropriate, apt, desirable, expedient, fit, fitting, judicious, politic, profitable, proper, prudent, recommended, seemly, sensible, sound, suggested, suitable, wise

Antonyms ill-advised, impolitic, improper, imprudent, inappropriate, inexpedient, injudicious, silly, stupid, undesirable, unfitting, unprofitable, unseemly, unsound, unsuitable, unwise

advise 1. admonish, caution, commend, counsel, enjoin, prescribe, recommend, suggest, urge 2. acquaint, apprise, inform, make known, notify, report, tell, warn

adviser aide, authority, coach, confidant, consultant, counsel, counsellor, guide, helper, lawyer, mentor, right-hand man, solicitor, teacher, tutor

advisory advising, consultative, counselling, helping, recommending

advocacy advancement, argument for, backing, campaigning for, championing, defence, encouragement, espousal, justification, pleading for, promotion, promulgation, propagation, proposal, recommendation, spokesmanship, support, upholding, urging

advocate *v.* 1. advise, argue for, campaign for, champion, countenance, defend, encourage, espouse, favour, hold a brief for (*Inf.*), justify, plead for, prescribe, press for, promote, propose, recommend, speak for, support, uphold, urge ~*n.* 2. apologist, apostle, backer, campaigner, champion, counsellor, defender, pleader, promoter, proponent, proposer, speaker, spokesman, supporter, upholder 3. *Law* attorney, barrister, counsel, lawyer, solicitor

Antonyms *v.* contradict, oppose, resist, speak against, take a stand against, take issue with

aegis advocacy, auspices, backing, favour, guardianship, patronage, protection, shelter, sponsorship, support, wing

affability amiability, amicability, approachability, benevolence, benignity, civility, congeniality, cordiality, courtesy, friendliness, geniality, good humour, good nature, graciousness, kindliness, mildness, obligingness, pleasantness, sociability, urbanity, warmth

affable amiable, amicable, approachable, benevolent, benign, civil, congenial, cordial, courteous, friendly, genial, good-humoured, good-natured, gracious, kindly, mild, obliging, pleasant, sociable, urbane, warm

Antonyms brusque, cold, discourteous, distant, haughty, rude, stand-offish, surly, unapproachable, uncivil, unfriendly, ungracious, unpleasant, unsociable

affair 1. activity, business, circumstance, concern, episode, event, happening, incident, interest, matter, occurrence, proceeding, project, question, subject, transaction, undertaking 2. amour, intrigue, liaison, relationship, romance

affect 1. act on, alter, bear upon, change, concern, impinge upon, influence, interest, involve, modify, prevail over, regard, relate to, sway, transform 2. disturb, impress, move, overcome, perturb, stir, touch, upset 3. adopt, aspire to, assume, contrive, counterfeit, feign, imitate, pretend, put on, sham, simulate

affectation act, affectedness, appearance, artificiality, assumed manners, façade, fakery, false display, insincerity, mannerism, pose, pretence, pretension, pretentiousness, sham, show, simulation, unnatural imitation

affected 1. afflicted, altered, changed, concerned, damaged, deeply moved, distressed, hurt, impaired, impressed, influenced, injured, melted, stimulated, stirred, touched, troubled, upset 2. artificial, assumed, camp (*Inf.*), conceited, contrived, counterfeit, feigned, insincere, la-di-da (*Inf.*), mannered, mincing, phoney *or* phony (*Inf.*), pompous, precious, pretended, pretentious, put-on, sham, simulated, spurious, stiff, studied, unnatural

Antonyms (*sense 1*) cured, unaffected, unconcerned, unharmed, uninjured, unmoved, untouched (*sense 2*) genuine, natural, real, unaffected

affecting moving, pathetic, piteous, pitiable, pitiful, poignant, sad, saddening, touching

affection amity, attachment, care, desire, feeling, fondness, friendliness, good will, inclination, kindness, liking, love, passion, propensity, tenderness, warmth

affectionate attached, caring, devoted, doting, fond, friendly, kind, loving, tender, warm, warm-hearted
Antonyms cold, cool, glacial, indifferent, stony, uncaring, undemonstrative, unfeeling, unresponsive

affiance betroth, bind, engage, pledge, promise

affiliate ally, amalgamate, annex, associate, band together, combine, confederate, connect, incorporate, join, unite

affiliation alliance, amalgamation, association, banding together, coalition, combination, confederation, connection, incorporation, joining, league, merging, relationship, union

affinity 1. alliance, analogy, closeness, compatibility, connection, correspondence, kinship, likeness, relation, relationship, resemblance, similarity 2. attraction, fondness, inclination, leaning, liking, partiality, rapport, sympathy
Antonyms (*sense 1*) difference, disparity, dissimilarity (*sense 2*) abhorrence, animosity, antipathy, aversion, dislike, hatred, hostility, loathing, repugnance, revulsion

affirm assert, asseverate, attest, aver, avouch, avow, certify, confirm, declare, maintain, pronounce, ratify, state, swear, testify
Antonyms deny, disallow, rebut, refute, reject, renounce, repudiate, rescind, retract

affirmation assertion, asseveration, attestation, averment, avouchment, avowal, certification, confirmation, declaration, oath, pronouncement, ratification, statement, testimony

affirmative agreeing, approving, assenting, concurring, confirming, consenting, corroborative, favourable, positive
Antonyms denying, disagreeing, disapproving, dissenting, negating, negative

affix add, annex, append, attach, bind, fasten, glue, join, paste, put on, stick, subjoin, tack, tag
Antonyms detach, disconnect, remove, take off, unfasten, unglue

afflict beset, burden, distress, grieve, harass, hurt, oppress, pain, plague, rack, smite, torment, trouble, try, wound

affliction adversity, calamity, cross, curse, depression, disease, distress, grief, hardship, misery, misfortune, ordeal, pain, plague, scourge, sickness, sorrow, suffering, torment, trial, tribulation, trouble, woe, wretchedness

affluence abundance, big bucks (*Inf., chiefly U.S.*), big money, exuberance, fortune, megabucks (*U.S. & Canad. sl.*), opulence, plenty, pretty penny (*Inf.*), profusion, prosperity, riches, tidy sum (*Inf.*), wad (*U.S. & Canad. sl.*), wealth

affluent 1. loaded (*Sl.*), moneyed, opulent, prosperous, rich, wealthy, well-heeled (*Inf.*), well-off, well-to-do 2. abundant, copious, exuberant, plenteous, plentiful
Antonyms (*sense 1*) broke (*Inf.*), destitute, hard-up (*Inf.*), impecunious, impoverished, indigent, penniless, penurious, poor, poverty-stricken, skint (*Brit. sl.*), stony-broke (*Brit. sl.*)

afford 1. bear, spare, stand, sustain 2. bestow, furnish, give, grant, impart, offer, produce, provide, render, supply, yield

affray *bagarre,* brawl, contest, disturbance, dogfight, encounter, feud, fight, fracas, free-for-all (*Inf.*), mêlée, outbreak, quarrel, scrap, scrimmage, scuffle, set-to (*Inf.*), shindig (*Inf.*), shindy (*Inf.*), skirmish, tumult

affront 1. *v.* abuse, anger, annoy, displease, insult, offend, outrage, pique, provoke, slight, vex 2. *n.* abuse, indignity, injury, insult, offence, outrage, provocation, slap in the face (*Inf.*), slight, slur, vexation, wrong

afire 1. ablaze, aflame, alight, blazing, burning, fiery, flaming, ignited, lighted, lit, on fire 2. aglow, aroused, excited, fervent, impassioned, passionate, stimulated

aflame 1. ablaze, afire, alight, blazing, burning, fiery, flaming, ignited, lighted, lit, on fire 2. afire, aroused, excited, fervent, impassioned, passionate, stimulated 3. aglow, flushed, inflamed, red, ruddy

afoot about, abroad, afloat, astir, brewing, circulating, current, going on, hatching, in preparation, in progress, in the wind, on the go (*Inf.*), operating, up (*Inf.*)

afraid 1. alarmed, anxious, apprehensive, cowardly, faint-hearted, fearful, frightened, intimidated, nervous, reluctant, scared, suspicious, timid, timorous 2. regretful, sorry, unhappy
Antonyms audacious, bold, fearless, happy, inapprehensive, indifferent, pleased, unafraid

afresh again, anew, newly, once again, once more, over again

after afterwards, behind, below, following, later, subsequently, succeeding, thereafter
Antonyms before, earlier, in advance, in front, previously, prior to, sooner

aftermath after-effects, consequences, effects, end, outcome, results, sequel, upshot

again 1. afresh, anew, another time, once more 2. also, besides, furthermore, in addition, moreover, on the contrary, on the other hand

against 1. anti (*Inf.*), averse to, contra (*Inf.*), counter, hostile to, in contrast to, in defiance of, in opposition to, in the face of, opposed to, opposing, resisting, versus 2. abutting, close up to, facing, fronting, in contact with, on, opposite to, touching, upon 3. in anticipation of, in expectation of, in preparation for, in provision for

agape 1. gaping, wide, wide open, yawning 2. agog, amazed, astonished, astounded, awestricken, dumbfounded, eager, expectant, flabbergasted, gobsmacked (*Brit. sl.*), spellbound, surprised, thunderstruck

age *n.* 1. date, day(s), duration, epoch, era, generation, lifetime, period, span, time 2. advancing years, decline (*of life*), majority, maturity, old age, senescence, senility, seniority ~*v.* 3. decline, deteriorate, grow old, mature, mellow, ripen

Antonyms *n.* (*sense 2*) adolescence, boyhood, childhood, girlhood, immaturity, juvenescence, salad days, young days, youth

aged age-old, ancient, antiquated, antique, elderly, getting on, grey, hoary, old, senescent, superannuated

Antonyms adolescent, boyish, childish, girlish, immature, juvenile, young, youthful

agency 1. action, activity, auspices, efficiency, force, influence, instrumentality, intercession, intervention, means, mechanism, mediation, medium, operation, power, work 2. bureau, business, department, office, organization

agenda calendar, diary, list, plan, programme, schedule, timetable

agent 1. advocate, deputy, emissary, envoy, factor, go-between, negotiator, rep (*Inf.*), representative, substitute, surrogate 2. actor, author, doer, executor, mover, officer, operative, operator, performer, worker 3. agency, cause, force, instrument, means, power, vehicle

agglomeration accumulation, clump, cluster, collection, heap, lump, mass, pile, stack

agglutinate adhere, attach, bond, cement, fasten, glue, gum, join, solder, stick, unite

aggrandize advance, amplify, augment, dignify, elevate, enlarge, ennoble, enrich, exaggerate, exalt, inflate, intensify, magnify, promote, widen

aggravate 1. exacerbate, exaggerate, heighten, increase, inflame, intensify, magnify, make worse, worsen 2. *Inf.* annoy, be on one's back (*Sl.*), bother, exasperate, gall, get in one's hair (*Inf.*), get on one's nerves (*Inf.*), hassle (*Inf.*), irk, irritate, nark (*Brit., Aust., & N.Z. sl.*), needle (*Inf.*), nettle, pester, piss one off (*Taboo sl.*), provoke, tease, vex

Antonyms (*sense 1*) alleviate, assuage, calm, diminish, ease, improve, lessen, mitigate, smooth (*sense 2*) assuage, calm, pacify, please

aggravation 1. exacerbation, exaggeration, heightening, increase, inflaming, intensification, magnification, worsening 2. *Inf.* annoyance, exasperation, gall, hassle (*Inf.*), irksomeness, irritation, provocation, teasing, vexation

aggregate 1. *v.* accumulate, amass, assemble, collect, combine, heap, mix, pile 2. *n.* accumulation, agglomeration, amount, assemblage, body, bulk, collection, combination, heap, lump, mass, mixture, pile, sum, total, whole 3. *adj.* accumulated, added, assembled, collected, collective, combined, composite, corporate, cumulative, mixed, total

aggression 1. assault, attack, encroachment, injury, invasion, offence, offensive, onslaught, raid 2. aggressiveness, antagonism, belligerence, destructiveness, hostility, pugnacity

aggressive 1. belligerent, destructive, hostile, offensive, pugnacious, quarrelsome 2. assertive, bold, dynamic, energetic, enterprising, forceful, militant, pushing, pushy (*Inf.*), vigorous, zealous

Antonyms friendly, mild, peaceful, quiet, retiring, submissive

aggressor assailant, assaulter, attacker, invader

aggrieved afflicted, distressed, disturbed, harmed, hurt, ill-used, injured, peeved (*Inf.*), saddened, unhappy, woeful, wronged

aghast afraid, amazed, appalled, astonished, astounded, awestruck, confounded, frightened, horrified, horror-struck, shocked, startled, stunned, thunder-struck

agile active, acute, alert, brisk, clever, limber, lissom(e), lithe, lively, nimble, prompt, quick, quick-witted, sharp, sprightly, spry, supple, swift

Antonyms awkward, clumsy, heavy, lumbering, ponderous, slow, slow-moving, stiff, ungainly, unsupple

agility activity, acuteness, alertness, briskness, cleverness, litheness, liveliness, nimbleness, promptitude, promptness, quickness, quick-wittedness, sharpness, sprightliness, spryness, suppleness, swiftness

agitate 1. beat, churn, convulse, disturb, rock, rouse, shake, stir, toss 2. alarm, arouse, confuse, disconcert, disquiet, distract, disturb, excite, faze, ferment, fluster, incite, inflame, perturb, rouse, ruffle, stimulate, trouble, unnerve, upset, work up, worry 3. argue, debate, discuss, dispute, examine, ventilate
Antonyms (*sense 2*) appease, assuage, calm, calm down, mollify, pacify, placate, quiet, quieten, soothe, still, tranquillize

agitation 1. churning, convulsion, disturbance, rocking, shake, shaking, stir, stirring, tossing, turbulence, upheaval 2. alarm, arousal, clamour, commotion, confusion, discomposure, disquiet, distraction, disturbance, excitement, ferment, flurry, fluster, incitement, lather (*Inf.*), outcry, stimulation, trouble, tumult, turmoil, upheaval, upset, worry 3. argument, controversy, debate, discussion, disputation, dispute, ventilation

agitator agent provocateur, demagogue, firebrand, inciter, instigator, rabble-rouser, revolutionary, stirrer (*Inf.*), troublemaker

agog avid, curious, eager, enthralled, enthusiastic, excited, expectant, impatient, in suspense, keen
Antonyms apathetic, incurious, indifferent, unconcerned, uninterested

agonize afflict, be in agony, be in anguish, distress, harrow, labour, pain, rack, strain, strive, struggle, suffer, torment, torture, worry, writhe

agony affliction, anguish, distress, misery, pain, pangs, suffering, throes, torment, torture, woe

agree 1. accede, acquiesce, admit, allow, assent, be of the same mind, comply, concede, concur, consent, engage, grant, permit, see eye to eye, settle 2. accord, answer, chime, coincide, conform, correspond, fit, get on (together), harmonize, match, square, suit, tally
Antonyms contradict, deny, differ, disagree, dispute, dissent, rebut, refute, retract

agreeable 1. acceptable, congenial, delightful, enjoyable, gratifying, likable *or* likeable, pleasant, pleasing, pleasurable, satisfying, to one's liking, to one's taste 2. appropriate, befitting, compatible, consistent, fitting, in keeping, proper, suitable 3. acquiescent, amenable, approving, complying, concurring, consenting, in accord, responsive, sympathetic, well-disposed, willing
Antonyms (*sense 1*) disagreeable, displeasing, horrid, offensive, unlikable *or* unlikeable, unpleasant (*sense 2*) inappropriate, unacceptable, unfitting, unsuitable

agreement 1. accord, accordance, affinity, analogy, compatibility, compliance, concert, concord, concurrence, conformity, congruity, consistency, correspondence, harmony, similarity, suitableness, union, unison 2. arrangement, bargain, compact, contract, covenant, deal (*Inf.*), pact, settlement, treaty, understanding
Antonyms (*sense 1*) altercation, argument, clash, conflict, difference, discord, discrepancy, disparity, dispute, dissent, dissimilarity, diversity, division, falling-out, incompatibility, incongruity, quarrel, row, squabble, strife, tiff, wrangle

agriculture agronomics, agronomy, cultivation, culture, farming, husbandry, tillage

aground ashore, beached, foundered, grounded, high and dry, on the rocks, stranded, stuck

ahead along, at an advantage, at the head, before, forwards, in advance, in front, in the foreground, in the lead, in the vanguard, leading, on, onwards, to the fore, winning

aid *v.* 1. abet, assist, befriend, encourage, favour, help, promote, relieve, second, serve, subsidize, succour, support, sustain ~*n.* 2. assistance, benefit, encouragement, favour, help, promotion, relief, service, succour, support 3. abettor, adjutant, aide, aide-de-camp, assistant, helper, second, supporter
Antonyms *v.* detract from, harm, hinder, hurt, impede, obstruct, oppose, thwart ~*n.* hindrance

ail 1. afflict, annoy, be the matter with, bother, distress, irritate, pain, sicken, trouble, upset, worry 2. be ill, be indisposed, be *or* feel off colour, be sick, be unwell, feel unwell

ailing debilitated, diseased, feeble, ill, indisposed, infirm, invalid, off colour, poorly, sick, sickly, suffering, under the weather (*Inf.*), unsound, unwell, weak

ailment affliction, complaint, disease, disorder, illness, infirmity, malady, sickness

aim 1. *v.* aspire, attempt, design, direct, draw a bead (on), endeavour, intend, level, mean, plan, point, propose, purpose, resolve, seek, set one's sights on, sight, strive, take aim (at), train, try, want, wish 2. *n.* ambition, aspiration, course, design, desire, direction, end, goal, intent, intention, mark, object, objective, plan, purpose, scheme, target, wish

aimless chance, directionless, erratic, frivolous, goalless, haphazard, pointless, purposeless, random, stray, undirected, unguided, unpredictable, vagrant, wayward

Antonyms decided, deliberate, determined, firm, fixed, positive, purposeful, resolute, resolved, settled, single-minded

air *n.* 1. atmosphere, heavens, sky 2. blast, breath, breeze, draught, puff, waft, whiff, wind, zephyr 3. ambience, appearance, atmosphere, aura, bearing, character, demeanour, effect, feeling, flavour, impression, look, manner, mood, quality, style, tone, vibes (*Sl.*) 4. circulation, display, dissemination, exposure, expression, publicity, utterance, vent, ventilation 5. aria, lay, melody, song, tune ~*v.* 6. aerate, expose, freshen, ventilate 7. circulate, communicate, declare, disclose, display, disseminate, divulge, exhibit, expose, express, give vent to, make known, make public, proclaim, publicize, reveal, tell, utter, ventilate, voice

airily 1. animatedly, blithely, breezily, buoyantly, gaily, happily, high-spiritedly, jauntily, light-heartedly 2. daintily, delicately, ethereally, gracefully, lightly

airiness 1. breeziness, draughtiness, freshness, gustiness, lightness, openness, windiness 2. ethereality, immateriality, incorporeality, insubstantiality, lightness, weightlessness 3. animation, blitheness, breeziness, buoyancy, gaiety, happiness, high spirits, jauntiness, light-heartedness, lightness of heart

airing 1. aeration, drying, freshening, ventilation 2. excursion, jaunt, outing, promenade, stroll, walk 3. circulation, display, dissemination, exposure, expression, publicity, utterance, vent, ventilation

airless breathless, close, heavy, muggy, oppressive, stale, stifling, stuffy, suffocating, sultry, unventilated

Antonyms airy, blowy, breezy, draughty, fresh, gusty, light, open, spacious, well-ventilated

airs affectation, affectedness, arrogance, haughtiness, hauteur, pomposity, pretensions, superciliousness, swank (*Inf.*)

airy 1. blowy, breezy, draughty, fresh, gusty, light, lofty, open, spacious, uncluttered, well-ventilated, windy 2. aerial, delicate, ethereal, fanciful, flimsy, illusory, imaginary, immaterial, incorporeal, insubstantial, light, vaporous, visionary, weightless, wispy 3. animated, blithe, buoyant, cheerful, cheery, chirpy (*Inf.*), debonair, frolicsome, gay, genial, graceful, happy, high-spirited, jaunty, light, light-hearted, lively, merry, nonchalant, sprightly, upbeat (*Inf.*)

Antonyms (*sense 1*) airless, close, heavy, muggy, oppressive, stale, stifling, stuffy, suffocating, unventilated (*sense 2*) concrete, corporeal, material, real, realistic, substantial, tangible (*sense 3*) cheerless, dismal, gloomy, glum, melancholy, miserable, morose, sad

aisle alley, corridor, gangway, lane, passage, passageway, path

ajar agape, gaping, open, partly open, unclosed

akin affiliated, alike, allied, analogous, cognate, comparable, congenial, connected, consanguineous, corresponding, kin, kindred, like, parallel, related, similar

alacrity alertness, avidity, briskness, cheerfulness, dispatch, eagerness, enthusiasm, gaiety, hilarity, joyousness, liveliness, promptness, quickness, readiness, speed, sprightliness, willingness, zeal

Antonyms apathy, dullness, inertia, lethargy, reluctance, slowness, sluggishness, unconcern, unwillingness

à la mode all the go (*Inf.*), all the rage (*Inf.*), chic, fashionable, in (*Inf.*), in fashion, in vogue, latest, modish, popular, stylish, the latest rage (*Inf.*), with it (*Inf.*)

alarm *v.* 1. daunt, dismay, distress, frighten, give (someone) a turn (*Inf.*), panic, put the wind up (someone) (*Inf.*), scare, startle, terrify, unnerve 2. alert, arouse, signal, warn ~*n.* 3. anxiety, apprehension, consternation, dismay, distress, fear, fright, nervousness, panic, scare, terror, trepidation, unease, uneasiness 4. alarm-bell, alert, bell, danger signal, distress signal, siren, tocsin, warning 5. *Archaic* call to arms, summons to arms

Antonyms *v.* (*sense 1*) assure, calm, comfort, reassure, relieve, soothe ~*n.* (*sense 3*) calm, calmness, composure, sang-froid, serenity

alarming daunting, dismaying, distressing, disturbing, dreadful, frightening, scaring, shocking, startling, terrifying, unnerving

albeit although, even if, even though, notwithstanding that, tho' (*U.S. or poetic*), though

alcoholic 1. *adj.* brewed, distilled, fermented, hard, inebriant, inebriating, intoxicating, spirituous, strong, vinous 2. *n.* bibber, boozer (*Inf.*), dipsomaniac, drunk, drunkard, hard drinker, inebriate, soak (*Sl.*), sot, sponge (*Inf.*), tippler, toper, tosspot (*Inf.*), wino (*Inf.*)

alcove bay, bower, compartment, corner, cubbyhole, cubicle, niche, nook, recess

alert 1. *adj.* active, agile, attentive, brisk, careful, circumspect, heedful, lively, nimble, observant, on guard, on one's toes, on the ball (*Inf.*), on the lookout, on the watch, perceptive, quick, ready, spirited, sprightly, vigilant, wary, watchful, wide-awake 2. *n.*

alarm, signal, siren, warning 3. *v.* alarm, forewarn, inform, notify, signal, warn
Antonyms *adj.* careless, heedless, inactive, languid, lethargic, listless, oblivious, slow, unaware, unconcerned, unwary *~n.* all clear *~v.* lull

alertness activeness, agility, attentiveness, briskness, carefulness, circumspection, heedfulness, liveliness, nimbleness, perceptiveness, promptitude, quickness, readiness, spiritedness, sprightliness, vigilance, wariness, watchfulness

alias 1. *adv.* also called, also known as, otherwise, otherwise known as 2. *n.* assumed name, *nom de guerre,* nom de plume, pen name, pseudonym, stage name

alibi defence, excuse, explanation, justification, plea, pretext, reason

alien 1. *adj.* adverse, conflicting, contrary, estranged, exotic, foreign, inappropriate, incompatible, incongruous, not native, not naturalized, opposed, outlandish, remote, repugnant, separated, strange, unfamiliar 2. *n.* foreigner, newcomer, outsider, stranger
Antonyms *adj.* affiliated, akin, alike, allied, analogous, cognate, connected, corresponding, kindred, like, parallel, related, similar *~n.* citizen, countryman, dweller, inhabitant, national, resident

alienate 1. break off, disaffect, divert, divorce, estrange, make unfriendly, separate, set against, turn away, withdraw 2. *Law* abalienate, convey, transfer

alienation 1. breaking off, disaffection, diversion, divorce, estrangement, indifference, remoteness, rupture, separation, setting against, turning away, withdrawal 2. *Law* abalienation, conveyance, transfer

alight[1] *v.* come down, come to rest, descend, disembark, dismount, get down, get off, land, light, perch, settle, touch down
Antonyms ascend, climb, float up, fly up, go up, lift off, mount, move up, rise, scale, soar, take off

alight[2] *adj.* 1. ablaze, aflame, blazing, burning, fiery, flaming, flaring, ignited, lighted, lit, on fire 2. bright, brilliant, illuminated, lit up, shining

align 1. arrange in line, coordinate, even, even up, line up, make parallel, order, range, regulate, straighten 2. affiliate, agree, ally, associate, cooperate, join, side, sympathize

alignment 1. adjustment, arrangement, coordination, evening, evening up, line, lining up, order, ranging, regulating, sequence, straightening up 2. affiliation, agreement, alliance, association, cooperation, sympathy, union

alike 1. *adj.* akin, analogous, corresponding, duplicate, equal, equivalent, even, identical, parallel, resembling, similar, the same, uniform 2. *adv.* analogously, correspondingly, equally, evenly, identically, similarly, uniformly
Antonyms *adj.* different, dissimilar, diverse, separate, unlike *~adv.* differently, distinctly, unequally

aliment fare, feed, fodder, food, meat, nourishment, nutriment, nutrition, provender, sustenance, tack (*Inf.*), vittles (*Obs. or dialect*)

alimentary beneficial, nourishing, nutritional, nutritious, nutritive, sustaining, wholesome

alive 1. animate, breathing, having life, in the land of the living (*Inf.*), living, subsisting 2. active, existent, existing, extant, functioning, in existence, in force, operative, unquenched 3. active, alert, animated, awake, brisk, cheerful, chirpy (*Inf.*), eager, energetic, full of life, lively, quick, spirited, sprightly, spry, vigorous, vital, vivacious, zestful
Antonyms (*sense 1*) dead, deceased, departed, expired, extinct, gone, inanimate, lifeless (*sense 2*) extinct, inactive, inoperative, lost (*sense 3*) apathetic, dull, inactive, lifeless, spiritless

alive to alert to, awake to, aware of, cognizant of, eager for, sensible of, sensitive to, susceptible to

alive with abounding in, bristling with, bustling with, buzzing with, crawling with, hopping with, infested with, jumping with, lousy with (*Sl.*), overrun by, packed with, swarming with, teeming with, thronged with

all *adj.* 1. every bit of, the complete, the entire, the sum of, the totality of, the total of, the whole of 2. each, each and every, every, every one of, every single 3. complete, entire, full, greatest, perfect, total, utter *~n.* 4. aggregate, entirety, everything, sum, sum total, total, total amount, totality, utmost, whole, whole amount *~adv.* 5. altogether, completely, entirely, fully, totally, utterly, wholly

allay alleviate, appease, assuage, blunt, calm, check, compose, diminish, dull, ease, lessen, mitigate, moderate, mollify, pacify, quell, quiet, reduce, relax, relieve, smooth, soften, soothe, subdue

allegation accusation, affirmation, assertion, asseveration, averment, avowal, charge, claim, declaration, deposition, plea, profession, statement

allege advance, affirm, assert, asseverate,

aver, avow, charge, claim, declare, depose, maintain, plead, profess, put forward, state
Antonyms abjure, contradict, deny, disagree with, disavow, disclaim, gainsay (*Archaic or literary*), oppose, refute, renounce, repudiate

alleged 1. affirmed, asserted, averred, declared, described, designated, stated 2. doubtful, dubious, ostensible, professed, purported, so-called, supposed, suspect, suspicious

allegiance adherence, constancy, devotion, duty, faithfulness, fealty, fidelity, homage, loyalty, obedience, obligation, troth (*Archaic*)
Antonyms disloyalty, faithlessness, falseness, inconstancy, infidelity, perfidy, treachery, treason, unfaithfulness

allegorical emblematic, figurative, parabolic, symbolic, symbolizing

allegory apologue, emblem, fable, myth, parable, story, symbol, symbolism, tale

allergic 1. affected by, hypersensitive, sensitive, sensitized, susceptible 2. *Inf.* antipathetic, averse, disinclined, hostile, loath, opposed

allergy 1. antipathy, hypersensitivity, sensitivity, susceptibility 2. *Inf.* antipathy, aversion, disinclination, dislike, hostility, loathing, opposition

alleviate abate, allay, assuage, blunt, check, diminish, dull, ease, lessen, lighten, mitigate, moderate, mollify, palliate, quell, quench, quiet, reduce, relieve, slacken, slake, smooth, soften, soothe, subdue

alleviation diminution, dulling, easing, lessening, lightening, mitigation, moderation, palliation, quelling, quenching, reduction, relief, slackening, slaking

alley alleyway, backstreet, lane, passage, passageway, pathway, walk

alliance affiliation, affinity, agreement, association, coalition, combination, compact, concordat, confederacy, confederation, connection, federation, league, marriage, pact, partnership, treaty, union
Antonyms alienation, breach, break, disaffection, dissociation, disunion, disunity, division, rupture, separation, severance, split, split-up

allied affiliated, amalgamated, associated, bound, combined, confederate, connected, hand in glove (*Inf.*), in cahoots (*U.S. inf.*), in league, joined, joint, kindred, leagued, linked, married, related, unified, united, wed

allocate allot, apportion, appropriate, assign, budget, designate, earmark, mete, set aside, share out

allocation allotment, allowance, apportionment, appropriation, grant, lot, measure, portion, quota, ration, share, stint, stipend

allot allocate, apportion, appropriate, assign, budget, designate, earmark, mete, set aside, share out

allotment 1. allocation, allowance, apportionment, appropriation, grant, lot, measure, portion, quota, ration, share, stint, stipend 2. kitchen garden, patch, plot, tract

all-out complete, determined, exhaustive, full, full-scale, maximum, optimum, outright, resolute, supreme, thorough, thoroughgoing, total, undivided, unlimited, unremitting, unrestrained, unstinted, utmost
Antonyms careless, cursory, half-hearted, negligent, off-hand, perfunctory, unenthusiastic

allow 1. acknowledge, acquiesce, admit, concede, confess, grant, own 2. approve, authorize, bear, brook, endure, give leave, let, permit, put up with (*Inf.*), sanction, stand, suffer, tolerate 3. allocate, allot, assign, deduct, give, grant, provide, remit, spare
Antonyms (*sense 1*) contradict, deny, disagree with, gainsay (*Archaic or literary*), oppose (*sense 2*) ban, disallow, forbid, prohibit, proscribe, refuse (*sense 3*) deny, forbid, refuse

allowable acceptable, admissible, all right, appropriate, approved, permissible, sanctionable, sufferable, suitable, tolerable

allowance 1. allocation, allotment, amount, annuity, apportionment, grant, lot, measure, pension, portion, quota, ration, remittance, share, stint, stipend, subsidy 2. admission, concession, sanction, sufferance, toleration 3. concession, deduction, discount, rebate, reduction

allow for arrange for, consider, foresee, keep in mind, make allowances for, make concessions for, make provision for, plan for, provide for, set (something) aside for, take into account, take into consideration

alloy *n.* 1. admixture, amalgam, blend, combination, composite, compound, hybrid, meld, mixture ~*v.* 2. admix, amalgamate, blend, combine, compound, fuse, meld, mix 3. adulterate, debase, devalue, diminish, impair

all right *adj.* 1. acceptable, adequate, average, fair, O.K. *or* okay (*Inf.*), passable, satisfactory, standard, unobjectionable 2. hale, healthy, safe, sound, unharmed, unimpaired, uninjured, well, whole ~*adv.* 3. acceptably, adequately, O.K. *or* okay (*Inf.*),

passably, satisfactorily, unobjectionably, well enough
Antonyms *adj.* (*sense 1*) bad, inadequate, not good enough, not up to scratch (*Inf.*), objectionable, poor, unacceptable, unsatisfactory (*sense 2*) ailing, bad, ill, injured, off colour, out of sorts, poorly, sick, sickly, unhealthy, unwell

allude advert, glance, hint, imply, insinuate, intimate, mention, refer, remark, speak of, suggest, touch upon

allure 1. *v.* attract, beguile, cajole, captivate, charm, coax, decoy, enchant, entice, inveigle, lead on, lure, persuade, seduce, tempt, win over 2. *n.* appeal, attraction, charm, enchantment, enticement, glamour, lure, persuasion, seductiveness, temptation

alluring attractive, beguiling, bewitching, captivating, come-hither, enchanting, fascinating, fetching, glamorous, intriguing, seductive, sexy, tempting
Antonyms abhorrent, off-putting (*Brit. inf.*), repellent, repugnant, repulsive, unattractive

allusion casual remark, glance, hint, implication, indirect reference, innuendo, insinuation, intimation, mention, suggestion

ally 1. *n.* abettor, accessory, accomplice, associate, coadjutor, collaborator, colleague, confederate, co-worker, friend, helper, partner 2. *v.* affiliate, associate, band together, collaborate, combine, confederate, connect, join, join forces, league, marry, unify, unite
Antonyms *n.* adversary, antagonist, competitor, enemy, foe, opponent, rival ~*v.* alienate, disaffect, disunite, divide, drive apart, separate, set at odds

almighty 1. absolute, all-powerful, invincible, omnipotent, supreme, unlimited 2. *Inf.* awful, desperate, enormous, excessive, great, intense, loud, severe, terrible
Antonyms (*sense 1*) helpless, impotent, powerless, weak (*sense 2*) feeble, insignificant, paltry, poor, slight, tame, weak

almost about, all but, approximately, as good as, close to, just about, nearly, not far from, not quite, on the brink of, practically, virtually, well-nigh

alms benefaction, bounty, charity, donation, gift, relief

aloft above, heavenward, higher, high up, in the air, in the sky, on high, overhead, skyward, up, up above, upward

alone 1. abandoned, apart, by itself, by oneself, deserted, desolate, detached, forlorn, forsaken, isolated, lonely, lonesome, only, separate, single, single-handed, sole, solitary, unaccompanied, unaided, unassisted, unattended, uncombined, unconnected, unescorted 2. incomparable, matchless, peerless, singular, unequalled, unique, unparalleled, unsurpassed
Antonyms (*sense 1*) accompanied, aided, among others, assisted, escorted, helped, jointly, together (*sense 2*) equalled, surpassed

aloof 1. chilly, cold, cool, detached, distant, forbidding, formal, haughty, indifferent, remote, reserved, standoffish, supercilious, unapproachable, unfriendly, uninterested, unresponsive, unsociable, unsympathetic 2. above, apart, at a distance, away, distanced, distant
Antonyms (*sense 1*) friendly, gregarious, neighbourly, open, sociable, sympathetic, warm

aloud 1. audibly, clearly, distinctly, intelligibly, out loud, plainly 2. clamorously, loudly, noisily, vociferously

already as of now, at present, before now, by now, by that time, by then, by this time, even now, heretofore, just now, previously

also additionally, along with, and, as well, as well as, besides, further, furthermore, in addition, including, into the bargain, moreover, on top of that, plus, to boot, too

alter adapt, adjust, amend, change, convert, diversify, metamorphose, modify, recast, reform, remodel, reshape, revise, shift, transform, transmute, turn, vary

alteration adaptation, adjustment, amendment, change, conversion, difference, diversification, metamorphosis, modification, reformation, remodelling, reshaping, revision, shift, transformation, transmutation, variance, variation

altercate argue, bicker, clash, contend, controvert, disagree, dispute, dissent, fall out (*Inf.*), quarrel, row, squabble, wrangle

altercation argument, bickering, clash, contention, controversy, disagreement, discord, dispute, dissension, quarrel, row, squabble, wrangle

alternate *v.* 1. act reciprocally, alter, change, fluctuate, follow in turn, follow one another, interchange, intersperse, oscillate, rotate, substitute, take turns, vary ~*adj.* 2. alternating, every other, every second, interchanging, rotating 3. alternative, another, different, second, substitute

alternative 1. *n.* choice, option, other (*of two*), preference, recourse, selection, substitute 2. *adj.* alternate, another, different, other, second, substitute

alternatively as an alternative, by way of alternative, if not, instead, on the other hand, or, otherwise

although albeit, despite the fact that, even if, even supposing, even though, notwithstanding, tho' (*U.S. or poetic*), though, while

altitude elevation, height, loftiness, peak, summit

altogether 1. absolutely, completely, fully, perfectly, quite, thoroughly, totally, utterly, wholly 2. all in all, all things considered, as a whole, collectively, generally, in general, *in toto,* on the whole 3. all told, everything included, in all, in sum, *in toto,* taken together
Antonyms (*sense 1*) halfway, incompletely, in part, in some measure, not fully, partially, relatively, slightly, somewhat, to a certain degree *or* extent, up to a certain point

altruistic benevolent, charitable, considerate, generous, humanitarian, philanthropic, public-spirited, self-sacrificing, unselfish
Antonyms egoistic, egoistical, egotistic, egotistical, greedy, looking out for number one (*Inf.*), mean, self-centred, self-interested, selfish, self-seeking, ungenerous

always aye (*Scot.*), consistently, constantly, continually, eternally, ever, everlastingly, evermore, every time, forever, *in perpetuum,* invariably, perpetually, repeatedly, unceasingly, without exception
Antonyms hardly, hardly ever, infrequently, once in a blue moon, once in a while, only now and then, on rare occasions, rarely, scarcely ever, seldom

amalgam admixture, alloy, amalgamation, blend, combination, composite, compound, fusion, meld, mixture, union

amalgamate alloy, ally, blend, coalesce, combine, commingle, compound, fuse, incorporate, integrate, intermix, meld, merge, mingle, unite
Antonyms disunite, divide, part, separate, split, split up

amalgamation admixture, alliance, alloy, amalgam, amalgamating, blend, coalition, combination, commingling, composite, compound, fusion, incorporation, integration, joining, meld, merger, mingling, mixing, mixture, union

amass accumulate, aggregate, assemble, collect, compile, garner, gather, heap up, hoard, pile up, rake up, scrape together

amateur dabbler, dilettante, layman, nonprofessional

amateurish amateur, bungling, clumsy, crude, inexpert, unaccomplished, unprofessional, unskilful
Antonyms experienced, expert, practised, professional, skilled

amatory amorous, aphrodisiac, erotic, lascivious, libidinous, passionate, romantic, sensual, sexual, sexy, steamy (*Inf.*)

amaze alarm, astonish, astound, bewilder, bowl over (*Inf.*), confound, daze, dumbfound, electrify, flabbergast, shock, stagger, startle, stun, stupefy, surprise

amazement admiration, astonishment, bewilderment, confusion, marvel, perplexity, shock, stupefaction, surprise, wonder

ambassador agent, consul, deputy, diplomat, emissary, envoy, legate, minister, plenipotentiary, representative

ambience air, atmosphere, aura, character, complexion, feel, flavour, impression, milieu, mood, quality, setting, spirit, surroundings, temper, tenor, tone, vibes (*Sl.*), vibrations (*Sl.*)

ambiguity doubt, doubtfulness, dubiety, dubiousness, enigma, equivocacy, equivocality, equivocation, inconclusiveness, indefiniteness, indeterminateness, obscurity, puzzle, tergiversation, uncertainty, unclearness, vagueness

ambiguous cryptic, Delphic, doubtful, dubious, enigmatic, enigmatical, equivocal, inconclusive, indefinite, indeterminate, obscure, oracular, puzzling, uncertain, unclear, vague
Antonyms clear, definite, explicit, obvious, plain, simple, specific, unequivocal, unmistakable, unquestionable

ambition 1. aspiration, avidity, desire, drive, eagerness, enterprise, get-up-and-go (*Inf.*), hankering, longing, striving, yearning, zeal 2. aim, aspiration, desire, dream, end, goal, hope, intent, objective, purpose, wish

ambitious 1. aspiring, avid, desirous, driving, eager, enterprising, hopeful, intent, purposeful, striving, zealous 2. arduous, bold, challenging, demanding, difficult, elaborate, energetic, exacting, formidable, grandiose, hard, impressive, industrious, pretentious, severe, strenuous
Antonyms apathetic, easy, lazy, modest, simple, unambitious, unaspiring

ambivalence clash, conflict, contradiction, doubt, equivocation, fluctuation, hesitancy, indecision, irresolution, opposition, uncertainty, vacillation, wavering

ambivalent clashing, conflicting, contradictory, debatable, doubtful, equivocal, fluctuating, hesitant, inconclusive, in two minds, irresolute, mixed, opposed, uncertain, undecided, unresolved, unsure, vacillating, warring, wavering
Antonyms certain, clear, conclusive, convinced, decided, definite, free from doubt, positive, sure, unwavering

amble dawdle, meander, mosey (*Inf.*), ramble, saunter, stroll, walk, wander

ambush 1. *n.* ambuscade, concealment, cover, hiding, hiding place, lying in wait, retreat, shelter, trap, waylaying 2. *v.* ambuscade, bushwhack (*U.S.*), ensnare, surprise, trap, waylay

ameliorate advance, allay, alleviate, amend, assuage, benefit, better, ease, elevate, improve, meliorate, mend, mitigate, promote, raise, reform, relieve

amenable 1. able to be influenced, acquiescent, agreeable, open, persuadable, responsive, susceptible, tractable 2. accountable, answerable, chargeable, liable, responsible
Antonyms inflexible, intractable, mulish, obdurate, obstinate, pig-headed, recalcitrant, stiff-necked, stubborn, unbending, unyielding

amend alter, ameliorate, better, change, correct, enhance, fix, improve, mend, modify, rectify, reform, remedy, repair, revise

amendment 1. alteration, amelioration, betterment, change, correction, emendation, enhancement, improvement, mending, modification, rectification, reform, remedy, repair, revision 2. addendum, addition, adjunct, alteration, attachment, clarification

amends apology, atonement, compensation, expiation, indemnity, recompense, redress, reparation, requital, restitution, restoration, satisfaction

amenity 1. advantage, comfort, convenience, facility, service 2. affability, agreeableness, amiability, complaisance, courtesy, mildness, pleasantness (*of situation*), politeness, refinement, suavity
Antonyms (*sense 2*) bad manners, discourtesy, impoliteness, incivility, rudeness, ungraciousness

amiability affability, agreeableness, amiableness, attractiveness, benignity, charm, cheerfulness, delightfulness, engagingness, friendliness, friendship, geniality, good humour, good nature, kindliness, kindness, lovableness, pleasantness, pleasingness, sociability, sweetness, sweetness and light (*Inf.*), sweet temper, winsomeness

amiable affable, agreeable, attractive, benign, charming, cheerful, congenial, delightful, engaging, friendly, genial, good-humoured, good-natured, kind, kindly, likable *or* likeable, lovable, obliging, pleasant, pleasing, sociable, sweet-tempered, winning, winsome
Antonyms disagreeable, displeasing, hostile, ill-natured, loathsome, repellent, sour, unfriendly, unpleasant

amicability amiability, amicableness, amity, brotherliness, civility, cordiality, courtesy, fraternity, friendliness, friendship, good will, harmony, kindliness, kindness, neighbourliness, peace, peaceableness, peacefulness, politeness, sociability

amicable amiable, brotherly, civil, cordial, courteous, fraternal, friendly, good-humoured, harmonious, kind, kindly, neighbourly, peaceable, peaceful, polite, sociable
Antonyms antagonistic, bellicose, belligerent, disagreeable, hostile, ill-disposed, impolite, inimical, pugnacious, quarrelsome, uncivil, unfriendly, unkind, unsociable

amid amidst, among, amongst, in the middle of, in the midst of, in the thick of, surrounded by

amiss 1. *adj.* awry, confused, defective, erroneous, fallacious, false, faulty, improper, inaccurate, inappropriate, incorrect, mistaken, out of order, unsuitable, untoward, wrong 2. *adv.* as an insult, as offensive, erroneously, faultily, improperly, inappropriately, incorrectly, mistakenly, out of turn, unsuitably, wrongly
Antonyms *adj.* accurate, appropriate, correct, in order, O.K. *or* okay (*Inf.*), perfect, proper, right, suitable, true ~*adv.* appropriately, correctly, properly, rightly, suitably, well

amity accord, amicability, brotherhood, comity, comradeship, concord, cordiality, fellowship, fraternity, friendliness, friendship, good will, harmony, kindliness, peace, peacefulness, tranquillity, understanding

ammunition armaments, cartridges, explosives, materiel, munitions, powder, rounds, shells, shot, shot and shell

amnesty absolution, condonation, dispensation, forgiveness, general pardon, immunity, oblivion, remission (*of penalty*), reprieve

amok *see* AMUCK

among, amongst 1. amid, amidst, in association with, in the middle of, in the midst of, in the thick of, midst, surrounded by, together with, with 2. between, to each of 3. in the class of, in the company of, in the group of, in the number of, out of 4. by all of, by the joint action of, by the whole of, mutually, with one another

amorous affectionate, amatory, ardent, attached, doting, enamoured, erotic, fond, impassioned, in love, lovesick, loving, lustful, passionate, tender
Antonyms aloof, cold, distant, frigid,

frosty, indifferent, passionless, stand-offish, undemonstrative, unfeeling, unloving

amorphous characterless, formless, inchoate, indeterminate, irregular, nebulous, nondescript, shapeless, unformed, unshaped, unshapen, unstructured, vague
Antonyms definite, distinct, regular, shaped, structured

amount 1. bulk, expanse, extent, lot, magnitude, mass, measure, number, quantity, supply, volume 2. addition, aggregate, entirety, extent, lot, sum, sum total, total, whole 3. full effect, full value, import, result, significance

amount to add up to, aggregate, become, come to, develop into, equal, grow, mean, purport, total

amour affair, *affaire de coeur,* intrigue, liaison, love affair, relationship, romance

ample abounding, abundant, big, bountiful, broad, capacious, commodious, copious, enough and to spare, expansive, extensive, full, generous, great, large, lavish, liberal, plenteous, plentiful, plenty, profuse, rich, roomy, spacious, substantial, unrestricted, voluminous, wide
Antonyms inadequate, insufficient, little, meagre, restricted, scant, skimpy, small, sparse, unsatisfactory

amplification augmentation, boosting, deepening, development, dilation, elaboration, enlargement, expansion, expatiation, extension, fleshing out, heightening, increase, intensification, lengthening, magnification, raising, rounding out, strengthening, stretching, supplementing, widening

amplify augment, boost, deepen, develop, dilate, elaborate, enlarge, expand, expatiate, extend, flesh out, go into detail, heighten, increase, intensify, lengthen, magnify, raise, round out, strengthen, stretch, supplement, widen
Antonyms abbreviate, abridge, boil down, condense, curtail, cut down, decrease, reduce, simplify

amplitude 1. bigness, breadth, bulk, capaciousness, compass, dimension, expanse, extent, greatness, hugeness, largeness, magnitude, mass, range, reach, scope, size, spaciousness, sweep, vastness, width 2. abundance, ampleness, completeness, copiousness, fullness, plenitude, plethora, profusion, richness

amply abundantly, bountifully, capaciously, completely, copiously, extensively, fully, generously, greatly, lavishly, liberally, plenteously, plentifully, profusely, richly, substantially, thoroughly, unstintingly, well, with a blank cheque, with a free hand, without stinting
Antonyms inadequately, insufficiently, meagrely, poorly, scantily, skimpily, sparsely, thinly

amputate curtail, cut off, lop, remove, separate, sever, truncate

amuck, amok berserk, destructively, ferociously, frenziedly, in a frenzy, insanely, madly, maniacally, murderously, savagely, uncontrollably, violently, wildly

amulet charm, fetish, juju, periapt (*Rare*), talisman

amuse beguile, charm, cheer, delight, divert, enliven, entertain, gladden, gratify, interest, occupy, please, recreate, regale, tickle
Antonyms be tedious, bore, jade, pall on, send to sleep, tire, weary

amusement 1. beguilement, cheer, delight, diversion, enjoyment, entertainment, fun, gladdening, gratification, hilarity, interest, jollies (*Sl.*), laughter, merriment, mirth, pleasing, pleasure, recreation, regalement, sport 2. distraction, diversion, entertainment, game, hobby, joke, lark, pastime, prank, recreation, sport
Antonyms boredom, displeasure, monotony, sadness, tedium

amusing charming, cheerful, cheering, comical, delightful, diverting, droll, enjoyable, entertaining, facetious, funny, gladdening, gratifying, humorous, interesting, jocular, laughable, lively, merry, pleasant, pleasing, rib-tickling, witty
Antonyms boring, dead, dull, flat, humdrum, monotonous, stale, tedious, tiresome, unamusing, unexciting, unfunny, uninteresting, wearisome

anaemic ashen, bloodless, characterless, colourless, dull, enervated, feeble, frail, infirm, pale, pallid, sickly, wan, weak
Antonyms blooming, florid, full-blooded, glowing, hearty, radiant, rosy, rosy-cheeked, rubicund, ruddy, sanguine

anaesthetic 1. *n.* analgesic, anodyne, narcotic, opiate, painkiller, sedative, soporific, stupefacient, stupefactive 2. *adj.* analgesic, anodyne, deadening, dulling, narcotic, numbing, opiate, pain-killing, sedative, sleep-inducing, soporific, stupefacient, stupefactive

analogous agreeing, akin, alike, comparable, corresponding, equivalent, homologous, like, parallel, related, resembling, similar
Antonyms contrasting, different, discrepant, disparate, dissimilar, diverse, unlike

analogy agreement, comparison, correlation, correspondence, equivalence, homology, likeness, parallel, relation, resemblance, similarity, similitude

analyse 1. assay, estimate, evaluate, examine, interpret, investigate, judge, research, test, work over 2. anatomize, break down, consider, dissect, dissolve, divide, resolve, separate, study, think through

analysis 1. anatomization, anatomy, assay, breakdown, dissection, dissolution, division, enquiry, examination, investigation, perusal, resolution, scrutiny, separation, sifting, test 2. estimation, evaluation, finding, interpretation, judgment, opinion, reasoning, study

analytic, analytical detailed, diagnostic, discrete, dissecting, explanatory, expository, inquiring, inquisitive, interpretative, interpretive, investigative, logical, organized, problem-solving, questioning, rational, searching, studious, systematic, testing

anarchic chaotic, confused, disordered, disorganized, lawless, misgoverned, misruled, rebellious, revolutionary, rioting, riotous, ungoverned
Antonyms controlled, decorous, disciplined, law-abiding, ordered, peaceable, peaceful, quiet, restrained, well-behaved

anarchist insurgent, nihilist, rebel, revolutionary, terrorist

anarchy chaos, confusion, disorder, disorganization, lawlessness, misgovernment, misrule, rebellion, revolution, riot
Antonyms control, discipline, government, law, law and order, order, peace, rule

anathema 1. ban, condemnation, curse, damnation, denunciation, excommunication, execration, imprecation, malediction, proscription, taboo 2. abomination, bane, *bête noire,* bugbear, enemy, pariah

anathematize abominate, ban, condemn, curse, damn, denounce, excommunicate, execrate, imprecate, proscribe

anatomize analyse, break down, dissect, dissolve, divide, examine, resolve, scrutinize, separate, study

anatomy 1. analysis, dismemberment, dissection, division, enquiry, examination, investigation, study 2. build, composition, frame, framework, make-up, structure

ancestor forebear, forefather, forerunner, precursor, predecessor, progenitor
Antonyms descendant, inheritor, issue, offspring, progeny, successor

ancestry ancestors, antecedents, blood, derivation, descent, extraction, family, forebears, forefathers, genealogy, house, line, lineage, origin, parentage, pedigree, progenitors, race, stock

anchorite eremite, hermit, recluse

ancient aged, age-old, antediluvian, antiquated, antique, archaic, bygone, early, hoary, obsolete, old, olden, old-fashioned, outmoded, out-of-date, primeval, primordial, superannuated, timeworn
Antonyms current, fresh, in vogue, late, modern, modish, new, newfangled, new-fashioned, novel, recent, state-of-the-art, up-to-date, with it (*Inf.*), young

ancillary accessory, additional, auxiliary, contributory, extra, secondary, subordinate, subsidiary, supplementary
Antonyms cardinal, chief, main, major, premier, primary, prime, principal

and along with, also, as well as, furthermore, in addition to, including, moreover, plus, together with

androgynous androgyne, bisexual, epicene, hermaphrodite, hermaphroditic

anecdote reminiscence, short story, sketch, story, tale, urban legend, yarn

anew afresh, again, another time, from scratch, from the beginning, once again, once more, over again

angel 1. archangel, cherub, divine messenger, guardian spirit, seraph, spiritual being 2. *Inf.* beauty, darling, dear, dream, gem, ideal, jewel, paragon, saint, treasure

angelic 1. celestial, cherubic, ethereal, heavenly, seraphic 2. adorable, beatific, beautiful, entrancing, innocent, lovely, pure, saintly, virtuous
Antonyms (*sense 1*) demonic, devilish, diabolic, diabolical, fiendish, hellish, infernal, satanic

anger 1. *n.* annoyance, antagonism, choler, displeasure, exasperation, fury, ill humour, ill temper, indignation, ire, irritability, irritation, outrage, passion, pique, rage, resentment, spleen, temper, vexation, wrath 2. *v.* affront, aggravate (*Inf.*), annoy, antagonize, be on one's back (*Sl.*), displease, enrage, exasperate, excite, fret, gall, get in one's hair (*Inf.*), get on one's nerves (*Inf.*), hassle (*Inf.*), incense, infuriate, irritate, madden, nark (*Brit., Aust., & N.Z. sl.*), nettle, offend, outrage, pique, piss one off (*Taboo sl.*), provoke, rile, vex
Antonyms *n.* acceptance, amiability, approval, calmness, forgiveness, goodwill, gratification, liking, patience, peace, pleasure ~*v.* appease, calm, pacify, placate, please, soothe

angle *n.* 1. bend, corner, crook, crotch, cusp, edge, elbow, intersection, knee, nook, point 2. approach, aspect, outlook, perspective, point of view, position, side, slant, standpoint, viewpoint ~*v.* 3. cast, fish

angle for aim for, be after (*Inf.*), cast about

for, contrive, fish for, hunt, invite, look for, scheme, seek, solicit, try for

angry annoyed, antagonized, choleric, cross, displeased, enraged, exasperated, furious, hacked (off) (*U.S. sl.*), heated, hot, hot under the collar (*Inf.*), ill-tempered, incensed, indignant, infuriated, irascible, irate, ireful, irritable, irritated, mad (*Inf.*), nettled, outraged, passionate, piqued, pissed off (*Taboo sl.*), provoked, raging, resentful, riled, splenetic, tumultuous, uptight (*Inf.*), wrathful

Antonyms agreeable, amiable, calm, congenial, friendly, gratified, happy, loving, mild, peaceful, pleasant, pleased

anguish agony, distress, grief, heartache, heartbreak, misery, pain, pang, sorrow, suffering, throe, torment, torture, woe

anguished afflicted, agonized, brokenhearted, distressed, grief-stricken, suffering, tormented, tortured, wounded, wretched

angular bony, gaunt, lank, lanky, lean, macilent (*Rare*), rangy, rawboned, scrawny, skinny, spare

animadversion blame, censure, comment, condemnation, criticism, knocking (*Inf.*), rebuke, reprehension, reproach, reproof, stick (*Sl.*), strictures

animal *n.* 1. beast, brute, creature 2. *Applied to a person* barbarian, beast, brute, monster, savage, wild man ~*adj.* 3. bestial, bodily, brutish, carnal, fleshly, gross, physical, sensual

animate *v.* 1. activate, embolden, encourage, energize, enliven, excite, fire, gladden, impel, incite, inspire, inspirit, instigate, invigorate, kindle, move, prod, quicken, revive, rouse, spark, spur, stimulate, stir, urge, vitalize, vivify ~*adj.* 2. alive, breathing, live, living, moving 3. gay, lively, spirited, vivacious

Antonyms *v.* check, curb, deaden, deter, devitalize, discourage, dull, inhibit, kill, make lifeless, put a damper on, restrain

animated active, airy, ardent, brisk, buoyant, dynamic, ebullient, elated, energetic, enthusiastic, excited, fervent, gay, lively, passionate, quick, sparky, spirited, sprightly, vibrant, vigorous, vital, vivacious, vivid, zealous, zestful

Antonyms apathetic, boring, dejected, depressed, dull, inactive, lethargic, lifeless, listless, monotonous, passive

animation action, activity, airiness, ardour, brio, briskness, buoyancy, dynamism, ebullience, elation, energy, enthusiasm, excitement, exhilaration, fervour, gaiety, high spirits, life, liveliness, passion, pep, pizzazz *or* pizazz (*Inf.*), sparkle, spirit, sprightliness, verve, vibrancy, vigour, vitality, vivacity, zeal, zest, zing (*Inf.*)

animosity acrimony, animus, antagonism, antipathy, bad blood, bitterness, enmity, hate, hatred, hostility, ill will, malevolence, malice, malignity, rancour, resentment, virulence

Antonyms amity, benevolence, congeniality, friendliness, friendship, goodwill, harmony, kindness, love, rapport, sympathy

animus 1. acrimony, animosity, antagonism, antipathy, bad blood, bitterness, enmity, hate, hatred, hostility, ill will, malevolence, malice, malignity, rancour, resentment, virulence 2. animating force, intention, motive, purpose, will

annals accounts, archives, chronicles, history, journals, memorials, records, registers

anneal case-harden, harden, indurate, steel, strengthen, temper, toughen

annex 1. add, adjoin, affix, append, attach, connect, fasten, join, subjoin, tack, unite 2. acquire, appropriate, arrogate, conquer, expropriate, occupy, seize, take over

Antonyms (*sense 1*) detach, disconnect, disengage, disjoin, disunite, remove, separate, unfasten

annexation annexing, appropriation, arrogation, conquest, expropriation, occupation, seizure, takeover

annexe 1. ell, extension, supplementary building, wing 2. addendum, addition, adjunct, affix, appendix, attachment, supplement

annihilate abolish, destroy, eradicate, erase, exterminate, extinguish, extirpate, liquidate, nullify, obliterate, root out, wipe out

annihilation abolition, destruction, eradication, erasure, extermination, extinction, extinguishing, extirpation, liquidation, nullification, obliteration, rooting out, wiping out

annotate commentate, comment on, elucidate, explain, footnote, gloss, illustrate, interpret, make observations, note

annotation comment, commentary, elucidation, exegesis, explanation, explication, footnote, gloss, illustration, interpretation, note, observation

announce 1. advertise, blow wide open (*Sl.*), broadcast, declare, disclose, divulge, give out, intimate, make known, proclaim, promulgate, propound, publish, report, reveal, tell 2. augur, betoken, foretell, harbinger, herald, portend, presage, signal, signify

Antonyms (*sense 1*) bury, conceal, cover up, hide, hold back, hush, hush up, keep back, keep quiet, keep secret, suppress, withhold

announcement advertisement, broadcast, bulletin, communiqué, declaration, disclosure, divulgence, intimation, proclamation, promulgation, publication, report, revelation, statement

announcer anchor man, broadcaster, commentator, master of ceremonies, newscaster, news reader, reporter

annoy aggravate (*Inf.*), anger, badger, bedevil, be on one's back (*Sl.*), bore, bother, bug (*Inf.*), displease, disturb, exasperate, gall, get (*Inf.*), get in one's hair (*Inf.*), get on one's nerves (*Inf.*), harass, harry, hassle (*Inf.*), incommode, irk, irritate, madden, molest, nark (*Brit., Aust., & N.Z. sl.*), needle (*Inf.*), nettle, peeve, pester, piss one off (*Taboo sl.*), plague, provoke, rile, ruffle, tease, trouble, vex
Antonyms appease, calm, comfort, console, mollify, solace, soothe

annoyance 1. aggravation, anger, bedevilment, bother, displeasure, disturbance, exasperation, harassment, hassle (*Inf.*), irritation, nuisance, provocation, trouble, vexation 2. bind (*Inf.*), bore, bother, drag (*Inf.*), gall, nuisance, pain (*Inf.*), pain in the arse (*Taboo inf.*), pain in the neck (*Inf.*), pest, plague, tease

annoying aggravating, bedevilling, boring, bothersome, displeasing, disturbing, exasperating, galling, harassing, irksome, irritating, maddening, peeving (*Inf.*), provoking, teasing, troublesome, vexatious
Antonyms agreeable, amusing, charming, delightful, diverting, enjoyable, entertaining, gratifying, pleasant

annual once a year, yearlong, yearly

annually by the year, each year, every year, once a year, per annum, per year, year after year, yearly

annul abolish, abrogate, cancel, countermand, declare *or* render null and void, invalidate, negate, nullify, obviate, recall, repeal, rescind, retract, reverse, revoke, void
Antonyms bring back, re-enforce, re-establish, reimpose, reinstate, reintroduce, restore

annulment abolition, abrogation, cancellation, countermanding, invalidation, negation, nullification, recall, repeal, rescindment, rescission, retraction, reversal, revocation, voiding

anodyne 1. *n.* analgesic, narcotic, painkiller, painreliever, palliative 2. *adj.* analgesic, deadening, dulling, narcotic, numbing, pain-killing, pain-relieving, palliative

anoint 1. daub, embrocate, grease, oil, rub, smear, spread over 2. anele (*Archaic*), bless, consecrate, hallow, sanctify

anomalous aberrant, abnormal, atypical, bizarre, deviating, eccentric, exceptional, incongruous, inconsistent, irregular, odd, oddball (*Inf.*), off-the-wall (*Sl.*), outré, peculiar, rare, unusual
Antonyms common, customary, familiar, natural, normal, ordinary, regular, typical, usual

anomaly aberration, abnormality, departure, deviation, eccentricity, exception, incongruity, inconsistency, irregularity, oddity, peculiarity, rarity

anon before long, betimes (*Archaic*), erelong (*Archaic or poetic*), forthwith, presently, promptly, shortly, soon

anonymous 1. incognito, innominate, nameless, unacknowledged, unattested, unauthenticated, uncredited, unidentified, unknown, unnamed, unsigned 2. characterless, nondescript, unexceptional
Antonyms (*sense 1*) accredited, acknowledged, attested, authenticated, credited, identified, known, named, signed

answer *n.* 1. acknowledgment, comeback, counterattack, defence, explanation, plea, reaction, refutation, rejoinder, reply, report, resolution, response, retort, return, riposte, solution, vindication ~*v.* 2. acknowledge, explain, react, refute, rejoin, reply, resolve, respond, retort, return, solve 3. conform, correlate, correspond, do, fill, fit, fulfil, measure up, meet, pass, qualify, satisfy, serve, suffice, suit, work
Antonyms *n.* inquiry, interrogation, query, question ~*v.* (*sense 2*) ask, inquire, interrogate, query, question

answerable 1. accountable, amenable, chargeable, liable, responsible, subject, to blame 2. explainable, refutable, resolvable, solvable

answer back argue, be cheeky, be impertinent, cheek (*Inf.*), contradict, disagree, dispute, rebut, retort, talk back

answer for 1. be accountable for, be answerable for, be chargeable for, be liable for, be responsible for, be to blame for, take the rap for (*Sl.*) 2. atone for, make amends for, pay for, suffer for

answer to 1. be accountable to, be answerable to, be responsible to, be ruled by, obey 2. agree, confirm, correspond, fit, match, meet

antagonism antipathy, competition, conflict, contention, discord, dissension, friction, hostility, opposition, rivalry
Antonyms accord, agreement, amity, friendship, harmony, love, peacefulness, sympathy

antagonist adversary, competitor, contender, enemy, foe, opponent, opposer, rival

antagonistic adverse, antipathetic, at odds, at variance, averse, conflicting, contentious, hostile, ill-disposed, incompatible, in dispute, inimical, opposed, unfriendly

antagonize 1. aggravate (*Inf.*), alienate, anger, annoy, be on one's back (*Sl.*), disaffect, estrange, gall, get in one's hair (*Inf.*), get on one's nerves (*Inf.*), hassle (*Inf.*), insult, irritate, nark (*Brit., Aust., & N.Z. sl.*), offend, piss one off (*Taboo sl.*), repel, rub (someone) up the wrong way (*Inf.*) 2. contend with, counteract, neutralize, oppose, struggle with, work against

Antonyms (*sense 1*) appease, calm, conciliate, disarm, mollify, pacify, placate, propitiate, soothe, win over

antecedent anterior, earlier, foregoing, former, preceding, precursory, preliminary, previous, prior

Antonyms after, coming, consequent, ensuing, following, later, posterior, subsequent, succeeding, successive

antecedents 1. ancestors, ancestry, blood, descent, extraction, family, forebears, forefathers, genealogy, line, progenitors, stock 2. background, history, past

antedate anticipate, come first *or* before, forego, go before, precede, predate

antediluvian 1. prehistoric, primeval, primitive, primordial 2. ancient, antiquated, antique, archaic, obsolete, old-fashioned, out-of-date, out of the ark (*Inf.*), passé

anterior 1. fore, forward, front, frontward 2. antecedent, earlier, foregoing, former, introductory, preceding, previous, prior

anteroom antechamber, foyer, lobby, outer room, reception room, vestibule, waiting room

anthem 1. canticle, chant, chorale, hymn, psalm 2. paean, song of praise

anthology analects, choice, collection, compendium, compilation, digest, garland, miscellany, selection, treasury

anticipate 1. apprehend, await, count upon, expect, forecast, foresee, foretell, hope for, look for, look forward to, predict, prepare for 2. antedate, beat (someone) to it (*Inf.*), forestall, intercept, prevent

anticipation apprehension, awaiting, expectancy, expectation, foresight, foretaste, forethought, hope, preconception, premonition, prescience, presentiment

anticlimax bathos, comedown (*Inf.*), disappointment, letdown

Antonyms climax, culmination, height, highlight, high point, peak, summit, top, zenith

antics buffoonery, capers, clowning, escapades, foolishness, frolics, larks, mischief, monkey tricks, playfulness, pranks, silliness, skylarking, stunts, tomfoolery, tricks

antidote antitoxin, antivenin, corrective, counteragent, countermeasure, cure, neutralizer, nostrum, preventive, remedy, specific

antipathetic abhorrent, antagonistic, averse, disgusting, distasteful, hateful, hostile, incompatible, invidious, loathsome, obnoxious, odious, offensive, repellent, repugnant, repulsive, revolting, yucky *or* yukky (*Sl.*)

antipathy abhorrence, animosity, animus, antagonism, aversion, bad blood, contrariety, disgust, dislike, distaste, enmity, hatred, hostility, ill will, incompatibility, loathing, odium, opposition, rancour, repugnance, repulsion

Antonyms affection, affinity, attraction, bond, empathy, fellow-feeling, good will, harmony, partiality, rapport, sympathy, tie

antiquated 1. antediluvian, antique, archaic, dated, obsolete, old-fashioned, old hat, outmoded, out-of-date, outworn, passé 2. aged, ancient, elderly, hoary, old, superannuated

Antonyms all-singing, all-dancing, current, fashionable, fresh, modern, modish, new, state-of-the-art, stylish, up-to-date, young

antique *adj.* 1. aged, ancient, elderly, old, superannuated 2. archaic, obsolete, old-fashioned, outdated 3. antiquarian, classic, olden, vintage ~*n.* 4. bygone, heirloom, object of virtu, relic

antiquity 1. age, ancientness, elderliness, old age, oldness 2. ancient times, distant past, olden days, time immemorial 3. antique, relic, ruin

antiseptic 1. *adj.* aseptic, clean, germ-free, hygienic, pure, sanitary, sterile, uncontaminated, unpolluted 2. *n.* bactericide, disinfectant, germicide, purifier

Antonyms *adj.* contaminated, dirty, impure, infected, insanitary, polluted, septic, unhygienic

antisocial 1. alienated, asocial, misanthropic, reserved, retiring, uncommunicative, unfriendly, unsociable, withdrawn 2. antagonistic, belligerent, disorderly, disruptive, hostile, menacing, rebellious

Antonyms (*sense 1*) companionable, friendly, gregarious, philanthropic, sociable, social

antithesis 1. antipode, contrary, contrast, converse, inverse, opposite, reverse 2.

contradiction, contraposition, contrariety, contrast, inversion, opposition, reversal

antithetical, antithetic antipodal, contradictory, contrary, contrasted, contrasting, converse, counter, inverse, opposed, opposite, reverse

anxiety angst, apprehension, care, concern, disquiet, disquietude, distress, foreboding, fretfulness, misgiving, nervousness, restlessness, solicitude, suspense, tension, trepidation, unease, uneasiness, watchfulness, worry
Antonyms assurance, calmness, confidence, contentment, relief, security, serenity

anxious 1. apprehensive, careful, concerned, disquieted, distressed, disturbed, fearful, fretful, in suspense, nervous, overwrought, restless, solicitous, taut, tense, troubled, twitchy (*Inf.*), uneasy, unquiet (*Chiefly literary*), watchful, wired (*Sl.*), worried 2. ardent, avid, desirous, eager, expectant, impatient, intent, itching, keen, yearning
Antonyms (*sense 1*) assured, calm, certain, collected, composed, confident, cool, nonchalant, unfazed (*Inf.*), unperturbed (*sense 2*) disinclined, hesitant, loath, nonchalant, reluctant

apace at full speed, expeditiously, posthaste, quickly, rapidly, speedily, swiftly, with dispatch, without delay

apart 1. afar, alone, aloof, aside, away, by itself, by oneself, cut off, distant, distinct, divorced, excluded, independent, independently, isolated, piecemeal, separate, separated, separately, singly, to itself, to oneself, to one side 2. asunder, in bits, in pieces, into parts, to bits, to pieces 3. **apart from** aside from, besides, but, except for, excluding, not counting, other than, save

apartment accommodation, chambers, compartment, flat, living quarters, penthouse, quarters, room, rooms, suite

apathetic cold, cool, emotionless, impassive, indifferent, insensible, listless, passive, phlegmatic, sluggish, stoic, stoical, torpid, unconcerned, unemotional, unfeeling, uninterested, unmoved, unresponsive
Antonyms active, anxious, aroused, bothered, caring, committed, concerned, emotional, enthusiastic, excited, interested, moved, passionate, responsive, troubled, worried, zealous

apathy coldness, coolness, emotionlessness, impassibility, impassivity, indifference, inertia, insensibility, listlessness, nonchalance, passiveness, passivity, phlegm, sluggishness, stoicism, torpor, unconcern, unfeelingness, uninterestedness, unresponsiveness
Antonyms anxiety, attention, concern, emotion, enthusiasm, feeling, interest, zeal

ape affect, caricature, copy, counterfeit, echo, imitate, mimic, mirror, mock, parody, parrot

aperture breach, chink, cleft, crack, eye, eyelet, fissure, gap, hole, interstice, opening, orifice, passage, perforation, rent, rift, slit, slot, space, vent

apex acme, apogee, climax, crest, crown, culmination, height, high point, peak, pinnacle, point, summit, tip, top, vertex, zenith
Antonyms base, bottom, depths, lowest point, nadir, perigee, rock bottom

aphorism adage, apothegm, axiom, dictum, gnome, maxim, precept, proverb, saw, saying

apiece each, for each, from each, individually, respectively, separately, severally, to each
Antonyms all together, as a group, collectively, en masse, overall, together

apish affected, foolish, foppish, imitative, mimicking, silly, stupid, trifling

aplomb balance, calmness, composure, confidence, coolness, equanimity, level-headedness, poise, sang-froid, self-assurance, self-confidence, self-possession, stability
Antonyms awkwardness, chagrin, confusion, discomfiture, discomposure, embarrassment, self-consciousness

apocalyptic ominous, oracular, portentous, prophetic, revelational, vatic

apocryphal doubtful, dubious, equivocal, fictitious, legendary, mythical, questionable, spurious, unauthenticated, uncanonical, unsubstantiated, unverified
Antonyms attested, authentic, authenticated, authorized, canonical, credible, factual, substantiated, true, undisputed, unquestionable, verified

apogee acme, apex, climax, crest, crown, culmination, height, high point, peak, pinnacle, summit, tip, top, vertex, zenith

apologetic contrite, penitent, regretful, remorseful, rueful, sorry

apologist advocate, arguer, champion, defender, justifier, maintainer, pleader, spokesman, supporter, vindicator

apologize ask forgiveness, beg pardon, express regret, say one is sorry, say sorry

apologue allegory, fable, parable, story, tale

apology 1. acknowledgment, confession, defence, excuse, explanation, extenuation, justification, plea, vindication 2. caricature, excuse, imitation, makeshift, mockery, stopgap, substitute, travesty

apostasy backsliding, defection, desertion, disloyalty, faithlessness, falseness, heresy, perfidy, recreance *or* recreancy (*Archaic*), treachery, unfaithfulness

apostate 1. *n.* backslider, defector, deserter, heretic, recreant (*Archaic*), renegade, traitor, turncoat 2. *adj.* backsliding, disloyal, faithless, false, heretical, perfidious, recreant, traitorous, treacherous, unfaithful, untrue

apostatize backslide, defect, desert, renege, turn traitor

apostle 1. evangelist, herald, messenger, missionary, preacher, proselytizer 2. advocate, champion, pioneer, propagandist, propagator, proponent

apothegm adage, aphorism, axiom, dictum, gnome, maxim, precept, proverb, saw, saying

apotheosis deification, elevation, exaltation, glorification, idealization, idolization

apotheosize deify, elevate, exalt, glorify, idealize, idolize

appal alarm, astound, daunt, dishearten, dismay, frighten, harrow, horrify, intimidate, outrage, petrify, scare, shock, terrify, unnerve

appalling alarming, astounding, awful, daunting, dire, disheartening, dismaying, dreadful, fearful, frightening, frightful, ghastly, godawful (*Sl.*), grim, harrowing, hellacious (*U.S. sl.*), hideous, horrible, horrid, horrific, horrifying, intimidating, petrifying, scaring, shocking, terrible, terrifying, unnerving

Antonyms comforting, consolatory, consoling, encouraging, heartening, reassuring

apparatus 1. appliance, contraption (*Inf.*), device, equipment, gear, implements, machine, machinery, materials, means, mechanism, outfit, tackle, tools, utensils 2. bureaucracy, chain of command, hierarchy, network, organization, setup (*Inf.*), structure, system

apparel accoutrements, array (*Poetic*), attire, clothes, clothing, costume, dress, equipment, garb, garments, gear (*Inf.*), habiliments, habit, outfit, raiment (*Archaic or poetic*), robes, trappings, vestments

apparent 1. blatant, clear, conspicuous, discernible, distinct, evident, indubitable, manifest, marked, obvious, open, overt, patent, plain, understandable, unmistakable, visible 2. ostensible, outward, seeming, specious, superficial

Antonyms (*sense 1*) ambiguous, doubtful, dubious, hazy, indefinite, indistinct, obscure, uncertain, unclear, vague (*sense 2*) actual, authentic, bona fide, genuine, honest, intrinsic, real, sincere, true

apparently it appears that, it seems that, on the face of it, ostensibly, outwardly, seemingly, speciously, superficially

apparition 1. appearance, manifestation, materialization, presence, vision, visitation 2. chimera, eidolon, ghost, phantom, revenant, shade (*Literary*), spectre, spirit, spook (*Inf.*), visitant, wraith

appeal *n.* 1. adjuration, application, entreaty, invocation, petition, plea, prayer, request, solicitation, suit, supplication 2. allure, attraction, attractiveness, beauty, charm, engagingness, fascination, interestingness, pleasingness ~*v.* 3. adjure, apply, ask, beg, beseech, call, call upon, entreat, implore, petition, plead, pray, refer, request, resort to, solicit, sue, supplicate 4. allure, attract, charm, engage, entice, fascinate, interest, invite, please, tempt

Antonyms *n.* (*sense 1*) denial, refusal, rejection, repudiation (*sense 2*) repulsiveness ~*v.* (*sense 3*) deny, refuse, reject, repudiate, repulse (*sense 4*) alienate, bore, repulse, revolt

appear 1. arise, arrive, attend, be present, come forth, come into sight, come into view, come out, come to light, crop up (*Inf.*), develop, emerge, issue, loom, materialize, occur, show (*Inf.*), show up (*Inf.*), surface, turn out, turn up 2. look (like *or* as if), occur, seem, strike one as 3. be apparent, be clear, be evident, be manifest, be obvious, be patent, be plain 4. become available, be created, be developed, be invented, be published, come into being, come into existence, come out 5. act, be exhibited, come on, come onstage, enter, perform, play, play a part, take part

Antonyms be doubtful, be unclear, disappear, vanish

appearance 1. advent, appearing, arrival, coming, debut, emergence, introduction, presence, showing up (*Inf.*), turning up 2. air, aspect, bearing, demeanour, expression, face, figure, form, image, look, looks, manner, mien (*Literary*) 3. front, guise, illusion, image, impression, outward show, pretence, semblance

appease allay, alleviate, assuage, blunt, calm, compose, conciliate, diminish, ease, lessen, lull, mitigate, mollify, pacify, placate, quell, quench, quiet, satisfy, soften, soothe, subdue, tranquillize

Antonyms aggravate (*Inf.*), anger, annoy, antagonize, arouse, be on one's back (*Sl.*), disturb, enrage, get in one's hair (*Inf.*), get on one's nerves (*Inf.*), hassle (*Inf.*), incense, inflame, infuriate, irritate, madden, nark (*Brit., Aust., & N.Z. sl.*), piss one off (*Taboo sl.*), provoke, rile, upset

appeasement 1. acceding, accommodation, compromise, concession, conciliation, placation, propitiation 2. abatement, alleviation, assuagement, blunting, easing, lessening, lulling, mitigation, mollification, pacification, quelling, quenching, quieting, satisfaction, softening, solace, soothing, tranquillization

appellation address, description, designation, epithet, name, sobriquet, style, term, title

append add, adjoin, affix, annex, attach, fasten, hang, join, subjoin, tack on, tag on
Antonyms detach, disconnect, disengage, remove, separate, take off

appendage 1. accessory, addendum, addition, adjunct, affix, ancillary, annexe, appendix, appurtenance, attachment, auxiliary, supplement 2. *Zool.* extremity, limb, member, projection, protuberance

appendant *adj.* 1. added, additional, adjoined, affixed, annexed, appended, attached, auxiliary, fastened, joined, subjoined, supplementary, tacked on, tagged on 2. accompanying, associated, attendant, concomitant, connected, consequential, following, related, resulting ~*n.* 3. addition, adjunct, affix, annexe, appendage, appendix, attachment, supplement

appendix addendum, addition, add-on, adjunct, appendage, codicil, postscript, supplement

appertain *Usually with* to apply, bear upon, be characteristic of, be connected, belong, be part of, be pertinent, be proper, be relevant, have to do with, inhere in, pertain, refer, relate, touch upon

appetence, appetency 1. appetite, craving, desire, hankering, hunger, longing, need, yearning 2. bent, drive, inclination, instinct, leaning, penchant, propensity 3. affection, affinity, allurement, attraction, fondness, liking, partiality

appetite appetence, appetency, craving, demand, desire, hankering, hunger, inclination, liking, longing, passion, proclivity, propensity, relish, stomach, taste, willingness, yearning, zeal, zest
Antonyms abhorrence, aversion, disgust, disinclination, dislike, distaste, loathing, repugnance, repulsion, revulsion

appetizer 1. antipasto, canapé, cocktail, hors d'oeuvre, titbit 2. apéritif, cocktail 3. foretaste, sample, taste

appetizing appealing, delicious, inviting, mouthwatering, palatable, savoury, scrumptious (*Inf.*), succulent, tasty, tempting
Antonyms distasteful, nauseating, unappetizing, unpalatable, unsavoury

applaud acclaim, approve, cheer, clap, commend, compliment, crack up (*Inf.*), encourage, eulogize, extol, laud, magnify (*Archaic*), praise
Antonyms blast, boo, censure, condemn, criticize, decry, deprecate, deride, disparage, excoriate, hiss, lambast(e), pan (*Inf.*), put down, ridicule, run down, slag (off) (*Sl.*), tear into (*Inf.*), vilify

applause acclaim, acclamation, accolade, approbation, approval, cheering, cheers, commendation, eulogizing, hand, handclapping, laudation, ovation, plaudit, praise

appliance apparatus, device, gadget, implement, instrument, machine, mechanism, tool

applicable apposite, appropriate, apropos, apt, befitting, fit, fitting, germane, pertinent, relevant, suitable, suited, to the point, to the purpose, useful
Antonyms inapplicable, inappropriate, irrelevant, unsuitable, wrong

applicant aspirant, candidate, claimant, inquirer, petitioner, postulant, suitor, suppliant

application 1. appositeness, exercise, function, germaneness, pertinence, practice, purpose, relevance, use, value 2. appeal, claim, inquiry, petition, request, requisition, solicitation, suit 3. assiduity, attention, attentiveness, commitment, dedication, diligence, effort, hard work, industry, perseverance, study 4. balm, cream, dressing, emollient, lotion, ointment, poultice, salve, unguent

apply 1. administer, assign, bring into play, bring to bear, carry out, employ, engage, execute, exercise, exert, implement, practise, put to use, use, utilize 2. appertain, be applicable, be appropriate, bear upon, be fitting, be relevant, fit, pertain, refer, relate, suit 3. anoint, bring into contact with, cover with, lay on, paint, place, put on, smear, spread on, touch to 4. appeal, claim, inquire, make application, petition, put in, request, requisition, solicit, sue 5. address, be assiduous, be diligent, be industrious, buckle down (*Inf.*), commit, concentrate, dedicate, devote, direct, give, make an effort, pay attention, persevere, study, try, work hard

appoint 1. allot, arrange, assign, choose, decide, designate, determine, establish, fix, set, settle 2. assign, choose, commission, delegate, elect, install, name, nominate, se-

lect 3. command, decree, direct, enjoin, ordain 4. equip, fit out, furnish, provide, supply
Antonyms (*sense 1*) cancel (*sense 2*) discharge, dismiss, fire, give the sack (*Inf.*), sack (*Inf.*) (*sense 4*) dismantle, divest, strip

appointed 1. allotted, arranged, assigned, chosen, decided, designated, determined, established, fixed, set, settled 2. assigned, chosen, commissioned, delegated, elected, installed, named, nominated, selected 3. commanded, decreed, directed, enjoined, ordained 4. equipped, fitted out, furnished, provided, supplied

appointment 1. arrangement, assignation, consultation, date, engagement, interview, meeting, rendezvous, session, tryst (*Archaic*) 2. allotment, assignment, choice, choosing, commissioning, delegation, designation, election, installation, naming, nomination, selection 3. assignment, berth (*Inf.*), job, office, place, position, post, situation, station 4. appointee, candidate, delegate, nominee, office-holder, representative 5. *Usually plural* accoutrements, appurtenances, equipage, fittings, fixtures, furnishings, gear, outfit, paraphernalia, trappings

apportion allocate, allot, assign, deal, dispense, distribute, divide, dole out, measure out, mete out, parcel out, ration out, share

apportionment allocation, allotment, assignment, dealing out, dispensing, distribution, division, doling out, measuring out, meting out, parcelling out, rationing out, sharing

apposite appertaining, applicable, appropriate, apropos, apt, befitting, fitting, germane, pertinent, proper, relevant, suitable, suited, to the point, to the purpose
Antonyms inapplicable, inappropriate, inapt, irrelevant, unsuitable, unsuited

appraisal 1. assessment, estimate, estimation, evaluation, judgment, opinion, recce (*Sl.*), sizing up (*Inf.*) 2. assay, pricing, rating, reckoning, survey, valuation

appraise assay, assess, estimate, evaluate, eye up, gauge, inspect, judge, price, rate, recce (*Sl.*), review, size up (*Inf.*), survey, value

appreciable ascertainable, clear-cut, considerable, definite, detectable, discernible, distinguishable, evident, marked, material, measurable, noticeable, obvious, perceivable, perceptible, pronounced, recognizable, significant, substantial, visible
Antonyms immaterial, imperceptible, inappreciable, indiscernible, indistinguishable, insignificant, invisible, minor, minute, negligible, small, trivial, undetectable, unnoticeable, unsubstantial

appreciate 1. be appreciative, be grateful for, be indebted, be obliged, be thankful for, give thanks for 2. acknowledge, be alive to, be aware (cognizant, conscious) of, comprehend, estimate, know, perceive, realize, recognize, sympathize with, take account of, understand 3. admire, cherish, enjoy, esteem, like, prize, rate highly, regard, relish, respect, savour, treasure, value 4. enhance, gain, grow, improve, increase, inflate, raise the value of, rise
Antonyms (*sense 1*) be ungrateful (*sense 2*) be unaware, misunderstand, underrate (*sense 3*) belittle, disdain, disparage, scorn (*sense 4*) deflate, depreciate, devaluate, fall

appreciation 1. acknowledgment, gratefulness, gratitude, indebtedness, obligation, thankfulness, thanks 2. admiration, appraisal, assessment, awareness, cognizance, comprehension, enjoyment, esteem, estimation, knowledge, liking, perception, realization, recognition, regard, relish, respect, responsiveness, sensitivity, sympathy, understanding, valuation 3. enhancement, gain, growth, improvement, increase, inflation, rise 4. acclamation, criticism, critique, notice, praise, review, tribute
Antonyms (*sense 1*) ingratitude (*sense 2*) antipathy, dislike, ignorance, incomprehension (*sense 3*) decline, depreciation, devaluation, fall

appreciative 1. beholden, grateful, indebted, obliged, thankful 2. admiring, aware, cognizant, conscious, enthusiastic, in the know (*Inf.*), knowledgeable, mindful, perceptive, pleased, regardful, respectful, responsive, sensitive, supportive, sympathetic, understanding

apprehend 1. arrest, bust (*Inf.*), capture, catch, collar (*Inf.*), feel one's collar (*Sl.*), lift (*Sl.*), nab (*Inf.*), nail (*Inf.*), nick (*Sl., chiefly Brit.*), pinch (*Inf.*), run in (*Sl.*), seize, take, take prisoner 2. appreciate, believe, comprehend, conceive, grasp, imagine, know, perceive, realize, recognize, think, understand 3. be afraid of, dread, fear
Antonyms (*sense 1*) discharge, free, let go, liberate, release (*sense 2*) be unaware of, be unconscious of, misapprehend, misconceive, miss, misunderstand

apprehension 1. alarm, anxiety, apprehensiveness, concern, disquiet, doubt, dread, fear, foreboding, misgiving, mistrust, premonition, suspicion, trepidation, unease, uneasiness, worry 2. arrest, capture, catching, seizure, taking 3. awareness, comprehension, grasp, intellect, intelligence, ken, knowledge, perception, under-

standing 4. belief, concept, conception, conjecture, idea, impression, notion, opinion, sentiment, thought, view
Antonyms (*sense 1*) assurance, composure, confidence, nonchalance, serenity, unconcern (*sense 2*) discharge, liberation, release (*sense 3*) incomprehension

apprehensive afraid, alarmed, anxious, concerned, disquieted, doubtful, fearful, foreboding, mistrustful, nervous, suspicious, twitchy (*Inf.*), uneasy, worried
Antonyms assured, at ease, composed, confident, nonchalant, unafraid

apprentice beginner, learner, neophyte, novice, probationer, pupil, student, trainee, tyro
Antonyms ace (*Inf.*), adept, dab hand (*Brit. inf.*), expert, master, past master, pro

apprise acquaint, advise, communicate, enlighten, give notice, inform, make aware, make cognizant, notify, tell, warn

approach *v.* 1. advance, catch up, come close, come near, come to, draw near, gain on, meet, move towards, near, push forward, reach 2. appeal to, apply to, broach the matter with, make advances to, make a proposal to, make overtures to, sound out 3. begin, begin work on, commence, embark on, enter upon, make a start, set about, undertake 4. approximate, be comparable to, be like, come close to, come near to, compare with, resemble ~*n.* 5. access, advance, advent, arrival, avenue, coming, drawing near, entrance, nearing, passage, road, way 6. approximation, likeness, semblance 7. *Often plural* advance, appeal, application, invitation, offer, overture, proposal, proposition 8. attitude, course, manner, means, method, mode, modus operandi, procedure, style, technique, way

approachable 1. accessible, attainable, come-at-able (*Inf.*), get-at-able (*Inf.*), reachable 2. affable, congenial, cordial, friendly, open, sociable
Antonyms (*sense 1*) inaccessible, out of reach, out-of-the-way, remote, un-get-at-able (*Inf.*), unreachable (*sense 2*) aloof, chilly, cool, distant, frigid, remote, reserved, standoffish, unfriendly, unsociable, withdrawn

approbation acceptance, acclaim, applause, approval, assent, commendation, congratulation, encouragement, endorsement, favour, laudation, praise, ratification, recognition, sanction, support
Antonyms blame, censure, condemnation, disapprobation, disapproval, disfavour, dislike, displeasure, dissatisfaction, reproof, stricture

appropriate *adj.* 1. adapted, applicable, apposite, appurtenant, apropos, apt, becoming, befitting, belonging, congruous, correct, felicitous, fit, fitting, germane, meet (*Archaic*), opportune, pertinent, proper, relevant, right, seemly, suitable, to the point, to the purpose, well-suited, well-timed ~*v.* 2. allocate, allot, apportion, assign, devote, earmark, set apart 3. annex, arrogate, assume, commandeer, confiscate, expropriate, impound, pre-empt, seize, take, take over, take possession of, usurp 4. embezzle, filch, misappropriate, pilfer, pocket, steal
Antonyms *adj.* improper, inappropriate, incompatible, incorrect, inopportune, irrelevant, unfitting, unsuitable, untimely ~*v.* cede, donate, give, relinquish, withhold

appropriateness applicability, appositeness, aptness, becomingness, congruousness, correctness, felicitousness, felicity, fitness, fittingness, germaneness, opportuneness, pertinence, properness, relevance, rightness, seemliness, suitability, timeliness, well-suitedness

appropriation 1. allocation, allotment, apportionment, assignment, earmarking, setting apart 2. annexation, arrogation, assumption, commandeering, confiscation, expropriation, impoundment, pre-emption, seizure, takeover, taking, usurpation

approval 1. acquiescence, agreement, assent, authorization, blessing, compliance, concurrence, confirmation, consent, countenance, endorsement, imprimatur, leave, licence, mandate, O.K. *or* okay (*Inf.*), permission, ratification, recommendation, sanction, the go-ahead (*Inf.*), the green light, validation 2. acclaim, admiration, applause, appreciation, approbation, commendation, esteem, favour, good opinion, liking, praise, regard, respect
Antonyms disapproval, dislike, disparagement, displeasure, dissatisfaction, objection

approve 1. acclaim, admire, applaud, appreciate, be pleased with, commend, esteem, favour, have a good opinion of, like, praise, regard highly, respect, think highly of 2. accede to, accept, advocate, agree to, allow, assent to, authorize, bless, concur in, confirm, consent to, countenance, endorse, give the go-ahead (*Inf.*), give the green light, go along with, mandate, O.K. *or* okay (*Inf.*), pass, permit, ratify, recommend, sanction, second, subscribe to, uphold, validate
Antonyms (*sense 1*) blame, censure, condemn, deplore, deprecate, disapprove, dislike, find unacceptable, frown on, look down one's nose at (*Inf.*), object to, take

exception to (*sense 2*) disallow, discountenance, veto

approximate *adj.* 1. almost accurate, almost exact, close, near 2. estimated, inexact, loose, rough 3. analogous, close, comparable, like, near, relative, similar, verging on 4. adjacent, bordering, close together, contiguous, near, nearby, neighbouring ~*v.* 5. approach, border on, come close, come near, reach, resemble, touch, verge on

Antonyms *adj.* (*senses 1 & 2*) accurate, correct, definite, exact, precise, specific

approximately about, almost, around, circa (*used with dates*), close to, generally, in the neighbourhood of, in the region of, in the vicinity of, just about, loosely, more or less, nearly, not far off, relatively, roughly

approximation 1. conjecture, estimate, estimation, guess, guesswork, rough calculation, rough idea 2. approach, correspondence, likeness, resemblance, semblance

appurtenance 1. accessory, accompaniment, adjunct, annexe, appendage, appurtenant, attachment, auxiliary, concomitant, incidental, piece of equipment, subordinate, subsidiary, supplement 2. *Plural* accessories, accompaniments, accoutrements, appendages, equipment, impedimenta, paraphernalia, trappings

appurtenant accessory, appertaining, applicable, appropriate, belonging, concerned, connected, germane, incidental, pertaining, pertinent, proper, related, relating, relevant

a priori 1. deduced, deductive, from cause to effect, inferential 2. conjectural, postulated, postulational, presumptive, self-evident, suppositional, theoretical

apron pinafore, pinny (*Inf.*)

apropos *adj.* 1. applicable, apposite, appropriate, apt, befitting, belonging, correct, fit, fitting, germane, meet (*Archaic*), opportune, pertinent, proper, related, relevant, right, seemly, suitable, to the point, to the purpose ~*adv.* 2. appropriately, aptly, opportunely, pertinently, relevantly, suitably, timely, to the point, to the purpose 3. by the bye, by the way, incidentally, in passing, parenthetically, while on the subject

apropos of *prep.* in respect of, on the subject of, re, regarding, respecting, with reference to, with regard to, with respect to

apt 1. applicable, apposite, appropriate, apropos, befitting, correct, fit, fitting, germane, meet (*Archaic*), pertinent, proper, relevant, seemly, suitable, timely, to the point, to the purpose 2. disposed, given, inclined, liable, likely, of a mind, prone, ready 3. astute, bright, clever, expert, gifted, ingenious, intelligent, prompt, quick, sharp, skilful, smart, talented, teachable

Antonyms (*sense 1*) ill-fitted, ill-suited, ill-timed, improper, inapplicable, inapposite, inappropriate, infelicitous, inopportune, irrelevant, unsuitable, untimely (*sense 3*) awkward, clumsy, dull, gauche, incompetent, inept, inexpert, maladroit, slow, stupid

aptitude 1. bent, disposition, inclination, leaning, predilection, proclivity, proneness, propensity, tendency 2. ability, aptness, capability, capacity, cleverness, faculty, flair, gift, giftedness, intelligence, knack, proficiency, quickness, talent 3. applicability, appositeness, appropriateness, fitness, relevance, suitability, suitableness

aptness 1. applicability, appositeness, appropriateness, becomingness, congruousness, correctness, felicitousness, felicity, fitness, fittingness, germaneness, opportuneness, pertinence, properness, relevance, rightness, seemliness, suitability, timeliness, well-suitedness 2. aptitude, bent, disposition, inclination, leaning, liability, likelihood, likeliness, predilection, proclivity, proneness, propensity, readiness, tendency 3. ability, capability, capacity, cleverness, faculty, fitness, flair, gift, giftedness, intelligence, knack, proficiency, quickness, suitability, talent

arable cultivable, farmable, fecund, fertile, fruitful, ploughable, productive, tillable

arbiter 1. adjudicator, arbitrator, judge, referee, umpire 2. authority, controller, dictator, expert, governor, lord, master, pundit, ruler

arbitrariness 1. capriciousness, fancifulness, inconsistency, randomness, subjectivity, unreasonableness, whimsicality, wilfulness 2. absoluteness, despotism, dictatorialness, dogmatism, domineeringness, high-handedness, imperiousness, magisterialness, overbearingness, peremptoriness, summariness, tyrannicalness, tyrannousness, tyranny, uncontrolledness, unlimitedness, unrestrainedness

arbitrary 1. capricious, chance, discretionary, erratic, fanciful, inconsistent, optional, personal, random, subjective, unreasonable, whimsical, wilful 2. absolute, autocratic, despotic, dictatorial, dogmatic, domineering, high-handed, imperious, magisterial, overbearing, peremptory, summary, tyrannical, tyrannous, uncontrolled, unlimited, unrestrained

Antonyms (*sense 1*) consistent, judicious, logical, objective, rational, reasonable, reasoned, sensible, sound

arbitrate adjudge, adjudicate, decide, determine, judge, mediate, pass judgment, referee, settle, sit in judgment, umpire

arbitration adjudication, arbitrament, decision, determination, judgment, settlement

arbitrator adjudicator, arbiter, judge, referee, umpire

arc arch, bend, bow, crescent, curve, half-moon

arcane cabbalistic, esoteric, hidden, mysterious, occult, recondite, secret

arch[1] *n.* 1. archway, curve, dome, span, vault 2. arc, bend, bow, curvature, curve, hump, semicircle ~*v.* 3. arc, bend, bow, bridge, curve, embow, span

arch[2] 1. accomplished, chief, consummate, expert, finished, first, foremost, greatest, head, highest, lead, leading, main, major, master, pre-eminent, primary, principal, top 2. artful, frolicsome, knowing, mischievous, pert, playful, roguish, saucy, sly, waggish, wily

archaic ancient, antiquated, antique, behind the times, bygone, obsolete, old, olden (*Archaic*), old-fashioned, old hat, outmoded, out of date, passé, primitive, superannuated
Antonyms contemporary, current, fresh, latest, modern, modish, new, newfangled, novel, present, recent, state-of-the-art, up-to-date, up-to-the-minute, with it (*Inf.*)

arched curved, domed, embowed, vaulted

archer bowman (*Archaic*), toxophilite (*Formal*)

archetype classic, exemplar, form, ideal, model, norm, original, paradigm, pattern, prime example, prototype, standard

architect 1. designer, master builder, planner 2. author, contriver, creator, deviser, engineer, founder, instigator, inventor, maker, originator, planner, prime mover, shaper

architecture 1. architectonics, building, construction, design, planning 2. construction, design, framework, make-up, structure, style

archives 1. annals, chronicles, documents, papers, records, registers, rolls 2. museum, record office, registry, repository

arctic 1. far-northern, hyperborean, polar 2. *Inf.* chilly, cold, freezing, frigid, frost-bound, frosty, frozen, gelid, glacial, icy

ardent avid, eager, enthusiastic, fervent, fervid, fierce, fiery, flaming, hot, hot-blooded, impassioned, intense, keen, lusty, passionate, spirited, vehement, warm, warm-blooded, zealous
Antonyms apathetic, cold, cool, frigid, impassive, indifferent, lukewarm, unenthusiastic, unloving

ardour avidity, devotion, eagerness, earnestness, enthusiasm, feeling, fervour, fierceness, fire, heat, intensity, keenness, passion, spirit, vehemence, warmth, zeal

arduous backbreaking, burdensome, difficult, exhausting, fatiguing, formidable, gruelling, hard, harsh, heavy, laborious, onerous, painful, punishing, rigorous, severe, steep, strenuous, taxing, tiring, toilsome, tough, troublesome, trying
Antonyms child's play (*Inf.*), easy, easy-peasy (*Sl.*), effortless, facile, light, no bother, no trouble, painless, simple, undemanding

area 1. district, domain, locality, neighbourhood, patch, plot, realm, region, sector, sphere, stretch, territory, tract, turf (*U.S. sl.*), zone 2. ambit, breadth, compass, expanse, extent, range, scope, size, width 3. arena, department, domain, field, province, realm, sphere, territory 4. part, portion, section, sector 5. sunken space, yard

arena 1. amphitheatre, bowl, coliseum, field, ground, park (*U.S. & Canad.*), ring, stadium, stage 2. area, battlefield, battleground, domain, field, field of conflict, lists, province, realm, scene, scope, sector, sphere, territory, theatre

argot cant, dialect, idiom, jargon, lingo (*Inf.*), parlance, patois, slang, vernacular

argue 1. altercate, bandy words, bicker, disagree, dispute, fall out (*Inf.*), feud, fight, have an argument, quarrel, squabble, wrangle 2. assert, claim, contend, controvert, debate, discuss, dispute, expostulate, hold, maintain, plead, question, reason, remonstrate 3. convince, persuade, prevail upon, talk into, talk round 4. demonstrate, denote, display, evince, exhibit, imply, indicate, manifest, point to, show, suggest

argument 1. altercation, barney (*Inf.*), bickering, clash, controversy, difference of opinion, disagreement, dispute, falling out (*Inf.*), feud, fight, quarrel, row, squabble, wrangle 2. assertion, claim, contention, debate, discussion, dispute, expostulation, plea, pleading, questioning, remonstrance, remonstration 3. argumentation, case, defence, dialectic, ground(s), line of reasoning, logic, polemic, reason, reasoning 4. abstract, gist, outline, plot, story, story line, subject, summary, synopsis, theme
Antonyms (*senses 1 & 2*) accord, agreement, concurrence, rebuttal, refutation, response

argumentative 1. belligerent, combative, contentious, contrary, disputatious, litigious, opinionated, quarrelsome 2. contentious, controversial, disputed, polemic
Antonyms (*sense 1*) accommodating,

amenable, complaisant, compliant, conciliatory, easy-going, obliging

arid 1. barren, desert, dried up, dry, moistureless, parched, sterile, torrid, waterless 2. boring, colourless, dreary, dry, dull, flat, jejune, lifeless, spiritless, tedious, uninspired, uninteresting, vapid

Antonyms (*sense 1*) fertile, fruitful, lush, rich, verdant (*sense 2*) exciting, interesting, lively, sexy (*Inf.*), spirited, stimulating, vivacious

aridity, aridness 1. barrenness, dryness, moisturelessness, parchedness, sterility, waterlessness 2. boredom, colourlessness, dreariness, dryness, dullness, flatness, jejuneness, jejunity, lifelessness, spiritlessness, tediousness, tedium, uninspiredness, uninterestingness, vapidity, vapidness

aright accurately, appropriately, aptly, correctly, duly, exactly, fitly, in due order, justly, properly, rightly, suitably, truly, without error

arise 1. appear, begin, come into being, come to light, commence, crop up (*Inf.*), emanate, emerge, ensue, follow, happen, issue, occur, originate, proceed, result, set in, spring, start, stem 2. get to one's feet, get up, go up, rise, stand up, wake up 3. ascend, climb, lift, mount, move upward, rise, soar, tower

aristocracy body of nobles, elite, gentry, *haut monde,* nobility, noblesse (*Literary*), patricians, patriciate, peerage, ruling class, upper class, upper crust (*Inf.*)

Antonyms commoners, common people, hoi polloi, lower classes, masses, plebeians, plebs, proles (*Derogatory sl., chiefly Brit.*), proletariat, working classes

aristocrat aristo (*Inf.*), grandee, lady, lord, noble, nobleman, noblewoman, patrician, peer, peeress

aristocratic 1. blue-blooded, elite, gentle (*Archaic*), gentlemanly, highborn, lordly, noble, patrician, titled, upper-class, well-born 2. courtly, dignified, elegant, fine, haughty, polished, refined, snobbish, stylish, well-bred

Antonyms (*sense 1*) common, lower-class, plebeian, proletarian, working-class (*sense 2*) boorish, coarse, common, crass, crude, ill-bred, uncouth, unrefined, vulgar

arm[1] *n.* 1. appendage, limb, upper limb 2. bough, branch, department, detachment, division, extension, offshoot, projection, section, sector 3. branch, channel, estuary, firth, inlet, sound, strait, tributary 4. authority, command, force, might, potency, power, strength, sway

arm[2] *v.* 1. *Esp. with weapons* accoutre, array, deck out, equip, furnish, issue with, outfit, provide, rig, supply 2. mobilize, muster forces, prepare for war, take up arms 3. brace, equip, forearm, fortify, gird one's loins, guard, make ready, outfit, prepare, prime, protect, strengthen

armada fleet, flotilla, navy, squadron

armaments ammunition, arms, guns, materiel, munitions, ordnance, weaponry, weapons

armed accoutred, arrayed, carrying weapons, equipped, fitted out, forearmed, fortified, furnished, girded, guarded, in arms, prepared, primed, protected, provided, ready, rigged out, strengthened, supplied, under arms

armistice ceasefire, peace, suspension of hostilities, truce

armour armour plate, covering, protection, sheathing, shield

armoured armour-plated, bombproof, bulletproof, ironclad, mailed, protected, steel-plated

armoury ammunition dump, arms depot, arsenal, magazine, ordnance depot

arms 1. armaments, firearms, guns, instruments of war, ordnance, weaponry, weapons 2. blazonry, crest, escutcheon, heraldry, insignia

army 1. armed force, host (*Archaic*), land forces, legions, military, military force, soldiers, soldiery, troops 2. *Fig.* array, horde, host, multitude, pack, swarm, throng, vast number

aroma bouquet, fragrance, odour, perfume, redolence, savour, scent, smell

aromatic balmy, fragrant, odoriferous, perfumed, pungent, redolent, savoury, spicy, sweet-scented, sweet-smelling

Antonyms acrid, bad-smelling, fetid, foul, foul-smelling, malodorous, niffy (*Brit. sl.*), noisome, offensive, olid, rank, reeking, smelly, stinking, whiffy (*Brit. sl.*)

around *prep.* 1. about, encircling, enclosing, encompassing, environing, on all sides of, on every side of, surrounding 2. about, approximately, circa (*used with dates*), roughly ~*adv.* 3. about, all over, everywhere, here and there, in all directions, on all sides, throughout, to and fro 4. at hand, close, close at hand, close by, near, nearby, nigh (*Archaic or dialect*)

arouse agitate, animate, awaken, call forth, enliven, excite, foment, foster, goad, incite, inflame, instigate, kindle, move, prod, provoke, quicken, rouse, sharpen, spark, spur, stimulate, stir up, summon up, waken, wake up, warm, whet, whip up

Antonyms allay, alleviate, assuage, calm,

dampen, dull, end, lull, pacify, quell, quench, still

arraign accuse, call to account, charge, complain about, denounce, impeach, incriminate, indict, prosecute, take to task

arraignment accusation, charge, complaint, denunciation, impeachment, incrimination, indictment, prosecution

arrange 1. align, array, class, classify, dispose, file, form, group, line up, marshal, order, organize, position, put in order, range, rank, set out, sort, sort out (*Inf.*), systematize, tidy 2. adjust, agree to, come to terms, compromise, construct, contrive, determine, devise, fix up, organize, plan, prepare, project, schedule, settle 3. adapt, instrument, orchestrate, score

Antonyms (*senses 1 & 2*) disarrange, disorganize, disturb, mess up, scatter

arrangement 1. alignment, array, classification, design, display, disposition, form, grouping, line-up, marshalling, order, ordering, organization, ranging, rank, setup (*Inf.*), structure, system 2. *Often plural* adjustment, agreement, compact, compromise, construction, deal, devising, organization, plan, planning, preparation, provision, schedule, settlement, terms 3. adaptation, instrumentation, interpretation, orchestration, score, version

arrant absolute, atrocious, blatant, complete, deep-dyed (*Usu. derogatory*), downright, egregious, extreme, flagrant, gross, infamous, monstrous, notorious, out-and-out, outright, rank, thorough, thoroughgoing, undisguised, unmitigated, utter, vile

array *n.* 1. arrangement, collection, display, disposition, exhibition, formation, line-up, marshalling, muster, order, parade, show, supply 2. *Poetic* apparel, attire, clothes, dress, finery, garb, garments, raiment (*Archaic or poetic*), regalia ~*v.* 3. align, arrange, display, dispose, draw up, exhibit, form up, group, line up, marshal, muster, order, parade, place in order, range, set in line (*Military*), show 4. accoutre, adorn, apparel (*Archaic*), attire, bedeck, caparison, clothe, deck, decorate, dress, equip, festoon, fit out, garb, get ready, outfit, robe, supply, wrap

arrest *v.* 1. apprehend, bust (*Inf.*), capture, catch, collar (*Inf.*), detain, feel one's collar (*Sl.*), lay hold of, lift (*Sl.*), nab (*Inf.*), nail (*Inf.*), nick (*Sl., chiefly Brit.*), pinch (*Inf.*), run in (*Sl.*), seize, take, take into custody, take prisoner 2. block, check, delay, end, halt, hinder, hold, inhibit, interrupt, obstruct, restrain, retard, slow, stall, stay, stop, suppress 3. absorb, catch, engage, engross, fascinate, grip, hold, intrigue, occupy ~*n.* 4. apprehension, bust (*Inf.*), capture, cop (*Sl.*), detention, seizure 5. blockage, check, delay, end, halt, hindrance, inhibition, interruption, obstruction, restraint, stalling, stay, stoppage, suppression

Antonyms *v.* (*sense 1*) free, let go, release, set free (*sense 2*) accelerate, encourage, precipitate, promote, quicken, speed up ~*n.* (*sense 4*) freeing, release (*sense 5*) acceleration, encouragement, precipitation, promotion, quickening

arresting conspicuous, engaging, extraordinary, impressive, noticeable, outstanding, remarkable, striking, stunning, surprising

Antonyms inconspicuous, unimpressive, unnoticeable, unremarkable

arrival 1. advent, appearance, arriving, coming, entrance, happening, occurrence, taking place 2. arriver, caller, comer, entrant, incomer, newcomer, visitant, visitor

arrive 1. appear, attain, befall, come, enter, get to, happen, occur, reach, show up (*Inf.*), take place, turn up 2. *Inf.* achieve recognition, become famous, make good, make it (*Inf.*), make the grade (*Inf.*), reach the top, succeed

Antonyms (*sense 1*) depart, disappear, exit, go, go away, leave, retire, take (one's) leave, vanish, withdraw

arrogance bluster, conceit, conceitedness, contemptuousness, disdainfulness, haughtiness, hauteur, high-handedness, imperiousness, insolence, loftiness, lordliness, overweeningness, pomposity, pompousness, presumption, pretension, pretentiousness, pride, scornfulness, superciliousness, swagger, uppishness (*Brit. inf.*)

Antonyms bashfulness, diffidence, humility, meekness, modesty, politeness, shyness

arrogant assuming, blustering, conceited, contemptuous, disdainful, haughty, high and mighty (*Inf.*), high-handed, imperious, insolent, lordly, overbearing, overweening, pompous, presumptuous, pretentious, proud, scornful, supercilious, swaggering, uppish (*Brit. inf.*)

Antonyms bashful, deferential, diffident, humble, modest, polite, servile, shy, unassuming

arrogate appropriate, assume, claim unduly, commandeer, demand, expropriate, presume, seize, usurp

arrogation appropriation, assumption, commandeering, demand, expropriation, presumption, seizure, usurpation

arrow 1. bolt, dart, flight, quarrel, reed (*Archaic*), shaft (*Archaic*) 2. indicator, pointer

arsenal ammunition dump, armoury, arms

depot, magazine, ordnance depot, stock, stockpile, store, storehouse, supply

art 1. adroitness, aptitude, artifice (*Archaic*), artistry, craft, craftsmanship, dexterity, expertise, facility, ingenuity, knack, knowledge, mastery, method, profession, skill, trade, virtuosity 2. artfulness, artifice, astuteness, craftiness, cunning, deceit, duplicity, guile, trickery, wiliness

artful adept, adroit, clever, crafty, cunning, deceitful, designing, dexterous, foxy, ingenious, intriguing, masterly, politic, proficient, resourceful, scheming, sharp, shrewd, skilful, sly, smart, subtle, tricky, wily

Antonyms artless, clumsy, frank, ingenuous, open, simple, straightforward, unadept, unskilled, untalented

article 1. commodity, item, object, piece, substance, thing, unit 2. composition, discourse, essay, feature, item, paper, piece, story, treatise 3. branch, clause, count, detail, division, head, heading, item, matter, paragraph, part, particular, passage, piece, point, portion, section

articulate *adj.* 1. clear, coherent, comprehensible, eloquent, expressive, fluent, intelligible, lucid, meaningful, understandable, vocal, well-spoken *~v.* 2. enounce, enunciate, express, pronounce, say, speak, state, talk, utter, verbalize, vocalize, voice 3. connect, couple, fit together, hinge, join, joint

Antonyms *adj.* dumb, faltering, halting, hesitant, incoherent, incomprehensible, indistinct, mumbled, mute, poorly-spoken, silent, speechless, stammering, stuttering, tongue-tied, unclear, unintelligible, voiceless

articulation 1. delivery, diction, enunciation, expression, pronunciation, saying, speaking, statement, talking, utterance, verbalization, vocalization, voicing 2. connection, coupling, hinge, joint, jointing, juncture

artifice 1. contrivance, device, dodge, expedient, hoax, machination, manoeuvre, ruse, stratagem, subterfuge, tactic, trick, wile 2. artfulness, chicanery, craft, craftiness, cunning, deception, duplicity, guile, scheming, slyness, trickery 3. adroitness, cleverness, deftness, facility, finesse, ingenuity, invention, inventiveness, skill

artificer 1. artisan, craftsman, mechanic 2. architect, builder, contriver, creator, designer, deviser, inventor, maker, originator

artificial 1. man-made, manufactured, non-natural, plastic, synthetic 2. bogus, counterfeit, ersatz, fake, imitation, mock, phoney *or* phony (*Inf.*), sham, simulated, specious, spurious 3. affected, assumed, contrived, false, feigned, forced, hollow, insincere, meretricious, phoney *or* phony (*Inf.*), pretended, spurious, unnatural

Antonyms authentic, frank, genuine, honest, natural, sincere, true, unaffected

artillery battery, big guns, cannon, cannonry, gunnery, ordnance

artisan artificer, craftsman, handicraftsman, journeyman, mechanic, skilled workman, technician

artistic aesthetic, beautiful, creative, cultivated, cultured, decorative, elegant, exquisite, graceful, imaginative, ornamental, refined, sensitive, sophisticated, stylish, tasteful

Antonyms inartistic, inelegant, tasteless, unattractive, untalented

artistry accomplishment, art, artistic ability, brilliance, craft, craftsmanship, creativity, finesse, flair, genius, mastery, proficiency, sensibility, skill, style, talent, taste, touch, virtuosity, workmanship

artless 1. candid, direct, fair, frank, genuine, guileless, honest, open, plain, sincere, straightforward, true, undesigning, upfront (*Inf.*) 2. humble, natural, plain, pure, simple, unadorned, unaffected, uncontrived, unpretentious 3. awkward, bungling, clumsy, crude, incompetent, inept, maladroit, primitive, rude, unskilled, untalented 4. childlike, ingenuous, innocent, jejune, naive, trustful, trusting, unsophisticated

Antonyms (*sense 1*) artful, crafty, cunning, designing, dishonest, false, insincere (*sense 2*) affected, artificial, unnatural (*sense 3*) aesthetic, artful, artistic, crafty, cunning, sophisticated (*sense 4*) sophisticated, suspicious

as *conj.* 1. at the time that, during the time that, just as, when, while 2. in the manner that, in the way that, like 3. that which, what 4. because, considering that, seeing that, since 5. in the same manner with, in the same way that, like 6. for instance, like, such as *~prep.* 7. being, in the character of, in the role of, under the name of 8. **as for** as regards, in reference to, on the subject of, with reference to, with regard to, with respect to 9. **as it were** in a manner of speaking, in a way, so to say, so to speak

ascend climb, float up, fly up, go up, lift off, mount, move up, rise, scale, slope upwards, soar, take off, tower

Antonyms alight, descend, dip, drop, fall, go down, incline, move down, plummet, plunge, sink, slant, slope, subside, tumble

ascendancy, ascendency authority, command, control, dominance, domination, dominion, hegemony, influence, mas-

tery, power, predominance, pre-eminence, prevalence, reign, rule, sovereignty, superiority, supremacy, sway, upper hand
Antonyms inferiority, servility, subjection, subordination, weakness

ascendant, ascendent *adj.* 1. ascending, climbing, going upwards, mounting, rising 2. authoritative, commanding, controlling, dominant, influential, powerful, predominant, pre-eminent, prevailing, ruling, superior, supreme, uppermost ~*n.* 3. **in the ascendant** ascending, climbing, commanding, dominant, dominating, flourishing, growing, increasing, mounting, on the rise, on the way up, prevailing, rising, supreme, up-and-coming, uppermost, winning

ascension ascent, climb, mounting, moving upwards, rise, rising

ascent 1. ascending, ascension, clambering, climb, climbing, mounting, rise, rising, scaling, upward movement 2. acclivity, gradient, incline, ramp, rise, rising ground, upward slope

ascertain confirm, determine, discover, establish, ferret out, find out, fix, identify, learn, make certain, settle, suss (out) (*Sl.*), verify

ascetic 1. *n.* abstainer, anchorite, hermit, monk, nun, recluse, self-denier 2. *adj.* abstemious, abstinent, austere, celibate, frugal, harsh, plain, puritanical, rigorous, self-denying, self-disciplined, severe, Spartan, stern
Antonyms *n.* hedonist, sensualist, voluptuary ~*adj.* abandoned, comfortable, luxurious, self-indulgent, sensuous, voluptuous

asceticism abstemiousness, abstinence, austerity, celibacy, frugality, harshness, mortification of the flesh, plainness, puritanism, rigorousness, rigour, self-abnegation, self-denial, self-discipline, self-mortification

ascribe assign, attribute, charge, credit, impute, put down, refer, set down

ashamed abashed, bashful, blushing, chagrined, conscience-stricken, crestfallen, discomfited, distressed, embarrassed, guilty, humbled, humiliated, mortified, prudish, reluctant, remorseful, shamefaced, sheepish, shy, sorry
Antonyms gratified, honoured, pleased, proud, satisfied, unashamed, vain

ashen anaemic, ashy, colourless, grey, leaden, livid, pale, pallid, pasty, wan, white
Antonyms blooming, blushing, florid, flushed, glowing, radiant, red, reddish, rosy, rosy-cheeked, rubicund, ruddy

ashore aground, landwards, on dry land, on land, on the beach, on the shore, shorewards, to the shore

aside 1. *adv.* alone, alongside, apart, away, beside, in isolation, in reserve, on one side, out of mind, out of the way, privately, separately, to one side, to the side 2. *n.* departure, digression, excursion, excursus, interpolation, interposition, parenthesis, tangent

asinine braindead (*Inf.*), brainless, daft (*Inf.*), dunderheaded, fatuous, foolish, goofy (*Inf.*), gormless (*Brit. inf.*), half-witted, idiotic, imbecile, imbecilic, inane, moronic, obstinate, senseless, silly, stupid, thickheaded, thick-witted
Antonyms brainy (*Inf.*), bright, clever, intelligent, quick-witted, sage, sane, sensible, sharp, smart, wise

ask 1. inquire, interrogate, query, question, quiz 2. appeal, apply, beg, beseech, claim, crave, demand, entreat, implore, petition, plead, pray, request, seek, solicit, sue, supplicate 3. bid, invite, summon
Antonyms (*sense 1*) answer, reply, respond

askance 1. awry, indirectly, obliquely, out of the corner of one's eye, sideways, with a side glance 2. disapprovingly, distrustfully, doubtfully, dubiously, mistrustfully, sceptically, suspiciously

askew *adv./adj.* aslant, awry, cockeyed (*Inf.*), crooked, crookedly, lopsided, oblique, obliquely, off-centre, skewwhiff (*Brit. inf.*), to one side
Antonyms aligned, even, in line, level, right, square, straight, true

asleep crashed out (*Sl.*), dead to the world (*Inf.*), dormant, dozing, fast asleep, napping, sleeping, slumbering, snoozing (*Inf.*), sound asleep

aspect 1. air, appearance, attitude, bearing, condition, countenance, demeanour, expression, look, manner, mien (*Literary*) 2. bearing, direction, exposure, outlook, point of view, position, prospect, scene, situation, view 3. angle, facet, feature, side

asperity acerbity, acrimony, bitterness, churlishness, crabbedness, crossness, harshness, irascibility, irritability, moroseness, peevishness, roughness, ruggedness, severity, sharpness, sourness, sullenness

asperse abuse, calumniate, cast aspersions (on), defame, detract, disparage, reproach, slander, slur, smear, traduce, vilify, vituperate

aspersion abuse, calumny, censure, character assassination, defamation, detraction, disparagement, obloquy, reproach, slander, slur, smear, traducement, vilification, vituperation

asphyxiate choke, smother, stifle, strangle, strangulate, suffocate, throttle

aspirant 1. *n.* applicant, aspirer, candidate, hopeful, postulant, seeker, suitor 2. *adj.* ambitious, aspiring, eager, endeavouring, hopeful, longing, striving, wishful

aspiration aim, ambition, craving, desire, dream, eagerness, endeavour, goal, hankering, hope, longing, object, objective, wish, yearning

aspire aim, be ambitious, be eager, crave, desire, dream, hanker, hope, long, pursue, seek, wish, yearn

aspiring *adj.* ambitious, aspirant, eager, endeavouring, hopeful, longing, striving, wishful, would-be

ass 1. donkey, jennet, moke (*Sl.*) 2. airhead (*Sl.*), berk (*Brit. sl.*), blockhead, bonehead (*Sl.*), charlie (*Brit. inf.*), coot, daftie (*Inf.*), dickhead (*Sl.*), dipstick (*Brit. sl.*), divvy (*Brit. sl.*), dolt, dope (*Inf.*), dork (*Sl.*), dunce, dweeb (*U.S. sl.*), fool, fuckwit (*Taboo sl.*), geek (*Sl.*), gonzo (*Sl.*), halfwit, idiot, jackass, jerk (*Sl., chiefly U.S. & Canad.*), nerd *or* nurd (*Sl.*), nincompoop, ninny, nitwit (*Inf.*), numskull *or* numbskull, oaf, pillock (*Brit. sl.*), plank (*Brit. sl.*), plonker (*Sl.*), prat (*Sl.*), prick (*Derogatory sl.*), schmuck (*U.S. sl.*), simpleton, twerp *or* twirp (*Inf.*), twit (*Inf., chiefly Brit.*), wally (*Sl.*)

assail 1. assault, attack, belabour, beset, charge, encounter, fall upon, invade, lay into (*Inf.*), maltreat, set about, set upon 2. abuse, berate, blast, criticize, impugn, lambast(e), malign, put down, revile, tear into (*Inf.*), vilify

assailant aggressor, assailer, assaulter, attacker, invader

assassin eliminator (*Sl.*), executioner, hatchet man (*Sl.*), hit man (*Sl.*), killer, liquidator, murderer, slayer

assassinate blow away (*Sl., chiefly U.S.*), eliminate (*Sl.*), hit (*Sl.*), kill, liquidate, murder, slay, take out (*Sl.*)

assault 1. *n.* aggression, attack, charge, incursion, inroad, invasion, offensive, onset, onslaught, storm, storming, strike 2. *v.* assail, attack, belabour, beset, charge, fall upon, invade, lay into (*Inf.*), set about, set upon, storm, strike at

Antonyms *n.* defence, protection, resistance ~*v.* defend, protect, resist

assay *v.* 1. analyse, appraise, assess, evaluate, examine, inspect, investigate, prove, test, try, weigh ~*n.* 2. *Archaic* attempt, endeavour, essay, stab (*Inf.*), try, venture 3. analysis, examination, inspection, investigation, test, trial

assemblage accumulation, aggregation, assembly, body, collection, company, conclave, congregation, convocation, crowd, flock, gathering, group, mass, meeting, multitude, rally, throng

assemble 1. accumulate, amass, bring together, call together, collect, come together, congregate, convene, convoke, flock, forgather, gather, marshal, meet, muster, rally, round up, summon 2. build up, connect, construct, erect, fabricate, fit together, join, make, manufacture, piece together, put together, set up

Antonyms adjourn, break up (*Inf.*), disassemble, disband, dismiss, disperse, distribute, divide, scatter, take apart

assembly 1. accumulation, aggregation, assemblage, body, collection, company, conclave, conference, congregation, congress, convocation, council, crowd, diet, flock, gathering, group, house, mass, meeting, multitude, rally, synod, throng 2. building up, connecting, construction, erection, fabrication, fitting together, joining, manufacture, piecing together, putting together, setting up

assent 1. *v.* accede, accept, acquiesce, agree, allow, approve, comply, concur, consent, fall in with, go along with, grant, permit, sanction, subscribe 2. *n.* acceptance, accession, accord, acquiescence, agreement, approval, compliance, concurrence, consent, permission, sanction

Antonyms *v.* deny, differ, disagree, dissent, object, protest, rebut, reject, retract ~*n.* denial, disagreement, disapproval, dissension, dissent, objection, refusal

assert 1. affirm, allege, asseverate, attest, aver, avouch (*Archaic*), avow, contend, declare, maintain, predicate, profess, pronounce, state, swear 2. claim, defend, insist upon, press, put forward, stand up for, stress, uphold, vindicate 3. **assert oneself** exert one's influence, make one's presence felt, put oneself forward

Antonyms (*senses 1 & 2*) deny, disavow, disclaim, rebut, refute, retract

assertion 1. affirmation, allegation, asseveration, attestation, avowal, contention, declaration, predication, profession, pronouncement, statement 2. defence, insistence, maintenance, stressing, vindication

assertive aggressive, confident, decided, decisive, demanding, dogmatic, domineering, emphatic, feisty (*Inf., chiefly U.S. & Canad.*), firm, forceful, forward, insistent, overbearing, positive, pushy (*Inf.*), self-assured, strong-willed

Antonyms backward, bashful, diffident, hesitant, insecure, meek, modest, reserved, retiring, self-conscious, self-effacing, sheepish, shrinking, shy, timid, timorous, unassertive, unobtrusive

assess 1. appraise, compute, determine, estimate, evaluate, eye up, fix, gauge, judge, rate, size up (*Inf.*), value, weigh 2. demand, evaluate, fix, impose, levy, rate, tax, value

assessment 1. appraisal, computation, determination, estimate, estimation, evaluation, judgment, rating, valuation 2. charge, demand, duty, evaluation, fee, impost, levy, rate, rating, tariff, tax, taxation, toll, valuation

asset 1. advantage, aid, benefit, blessing, boon, help, resource, service 2. *Plural* capital, estate, funds, goods, holdings, means, money, possessions, property, reserves, resources, valuables, wealth
Antonyms (*sense 1*) burden, disadvantage, drag, drawback, encumbrance, handicap, hindrance, impediment, liability, millstone, minus (*Inf.*), nuisance

asseverate affirm, assert, attest, aver, avouch (*Archaic*), avow, declare, maintain, predicate, profess, pronounce, protest, state, swear

asseveration affirmation, assertion, attestation, averment, avowal, declaration, predication, profession, pronouncement, protestation, statement, vow

assiduity application, assiduousness, attentiveness, constancy, diligence, indefatigability, industriousness, industry, laboriousness, perseverance, persistence, sedulity, sedulousness, steadiness, studiousness, tirelessness

assiduous attentive, constant, diligent, hard-working, indefatigable, industrious, laborious, persevering, persistent, sedulous, steady, studious, unflagging, untiring, unwearied
Antonyms careless, idle, inattentive, indolent, lax, lazy, negligent, slack

assign 1. appoint, choose, delegate, designate, name, nominate, select 2. allocate, allot, apportion, consign, distribute, give, give out, grant, make over 3. appoint, appropriate, determine, fix, set apart, stipulate 4. accredit, ascribe, attribute, put down

assignation 1. clandestine meeting, illicit meeting, rendezvous, secret meeting, tryst (*Archaic*) 2. allocation, allotment, appointment, apportionment, appropriation, ascription, assignment, attribution, choice, consignment, delegation, designation, determination, distribution, giving, grant, nomination, selection, specification, stipulation

assignment 1. appointment, charge, commission, duty, job, mission, position, post, responsibility, task 2. allocation, allotment, appointment, apportionment, appropriation, ascription, assignation (*Law, chiefly Scot.*), attribution, choice, consignment, delegation, designation, determination, distribution, giving, grant, nomination, selection, specification, stipulation

assimilate 1. absorb, digest, imbibe (*Literary*), incorporate, ingest, learn, take in 2. acclimatize, accommodate, acculturate, accustom, adapt, adjust, become like, become similar, blend in, conform, fit, homogenize, intermix, mingle

assist abet, aid, back, benefit, boost, collaborate, cooperate, encourage, expedite, facilitate, further, help, promote, reinforce, relieve, second, serve, succour, support, sustain, work for, work with
Antonyms frustrate, hamper, handicap, hinder, hold back, hold up, impede, obstruct, resist, thwart, work against

assistance abetment, aid, backing, benefit, boost, collaboration, cooperation, encouragement, furtherance, help, helping hand, promotion, reinforcement, relief, service, succour, support, sustenance
Antonyms hindrance, obstruction, opposition, resistance

assistant abettor, accessory, accomplice, aide, aider, ally, associate, auxiliary, backer, coadjutor (*Rare*), collaborator, colleague, confederate, cooperator, helper, helpmate, henchman, partner, protagonist, right-hand man, second, supporter

associate *v.* 1. affiliate, ally, combine, confederate, conjoin, connect, correlate, couple, identify, join, league, link, lump together, mix, pair, relate, think of together, unite, yoke 2. accompany, befriend, be friends, consort, fraternize, hang about, hang out (*Inf.*), hobnob, mingle, mix, run around (*Inf.*) ~*n.* 3. ally, collaborator, colleague, companion, compeer, comrade, confederate, confrère, co-worker, follower, friend, mate, partner
Antonyms (*sense 1*) detach, disconnect, dissociate, distance, distinguish, divorce, isolate, segregate, separate, set apart (*sense 2*) be alienated, avoid, be estranged, break off, part company

association 1. affiliation, alliance, band, clique, club, coalition, combine, company, confederacy, confederation, cooperative, corporation, federation, fraternity, group, league, order, organization, partnership, society, syndicate, union 2. affinity, companionship, comradeship, familiarity, fellowship, fraternization, friendship, intimacy, liaison, partnership, relations, relationship 3. blend, bond, combination, concomitance, connection, correlation, identification, joining, juxtaposition, linkage, linking, lumping together, mixing, mixture, pairing, relation, tie, union, yoking

assort arrange, array, categorize, classify, dispose, distribute, file, grade, group, range, rank, sort, type

assorted 1. different, diverse, diversified, heterogeneous, manifold, miscellaneous, mixed, motley, sundry, varied, variegated, various 2. arranged, arrayed, categorized, classified, disposed, filed, graded, grouped, ranged, ranked, sorted, typed
Antonyms (*sense 1*) alike, homogeneous, identical, like, same, similar, uniform, unvaried

assortment 1. array, choice, collection, diversity, farrago, hotchpotch, jumble, medley, *mélange,* miscellany, mishmash, mixed bag (*Inf.*), mixture, potpourri, salmagundi, selection, variety 2. arrangement, categorizing, classification, disposition, distribution, filing, grading, grouping, ranging, ranking, sorting, typing

assuage 1. allay, alleviate, calm, ease, lessen, lighten, mitigate, moderate, palliate, quench, relieve, soothe, temper 2. appease, calm, lull, mollify, pacify, quiet, relax, satisfy, soften, soothe, still, tranquillize
Antonyms (*sense 1*) aggravate, exacerbate, heighten, increase, intensify, worsen (*sense 2*) aggravate, embitter, enrage, infuriate, madden, provoke

assume 1. accept, believe, expect, fancy, guess (*Inf., chiefly U.S. & Canad.*), imagine, infer, presume, presuppose, suppose, surmise, suspect, take for granted, think 2. adopt, affect, counterfeit, feign, imitate, impersonate, mimic, pretend to, put on, sham, simulate 3. accept, acquire, attend to, begin, don, embark upon, embrace, enter upon, put on, set about, shoulder, take on, take over, take responsibility for, take up, undertake 4. acquire, appropriate, arrogate, commandeer, expropriate, pre-empt, seize, take, take over, usurp
Antonyms (*sense 1*) know, prove (*senses 3 & 4*) give up, hand over, leave, put aside, relinquish

assumed 1. affected, bogus, counterfeit, fake, false, feigned, fictitious, imitation, made-up, make-believe, phoney *or* phony (*Inf.*), pretended, pseudonymous, sham, simulated, spurious 2. accepted, expected, hypothetical, presumed, presupposed, supposed, surmised, taken for granted 3. appropriated, arrogated, pre-empted, seized, usurped
Antonyms (*senses 1 & 2*) actual, authentic, known, natural, positive, real, stated, true

assuming *adj.* arrogant, bold, conceited, disdainful, domineering, egotistic, forward, haughty, imperious, overbearing, presumptuous, pushy (*Inf.*), rude

assumption 1. acceptance, belief, conjecture, expectation, fancy, guess, hypothesis, inference, postulate, postulation, premise, premiss, presumption, presupposition, supposition, surmise, suspicion, theory 2. acceptance, acquisition, adoption, embracing, entering upon, putting on, shouldering, takeover, taking on, taking up, undertaking 3. acquisition, appropriation, arrogation, expropriation, pre-empting, seizure, takeover, taking, usurpation 4. arrogance, conceit, imperiousness, presumption, pride, self-importance

assurance 1. affirmation, assertion, declaration, guarantee, oath, pledge, profession, promise, protestation, vow, word, word of honour 2. assertiveness, assuredness, boldness, certainty, certitude, confidence, conviction, coolness, courage, faith, firmness, nerve, poise, positiveness, security, self-confidence, self-reliance, sureness 3. arrogance, brass neck (*Brit. inf.*), chutzpah (*U.S. & Canad. inf.*), effrontery, gall (*Inf.*), impudence, neck (*Inf.*), nerve (*Inf.*), presumption
Antonyms (*sense 1*) falsehood, lie (*sense 2*) apprehension, diffidence, distrust, doubt, self-doubt, self-effacement, shyness, timidity, uncertainty

assure 1. comfort, convince, embolden, encourage, hearten, persuade, reassure, soothe 2. affirm, attest, certify, confirm, declare confidently, give one's word to, guarantee, pledge, promise, swear, vow 3. clinch, complete, confirm, ensure, guarantee, make certain, make sure, seal, secure

assured 1. beyond doubt, clinched, confirmed, dependable, ensured, fixed, guaranteed, indubitable, irrefutable, made certain, sealed, secure, settled, sure, unquestionable 2. assertive, audacious, bold, brazen, certain, complacent, confident, overconfident, poised, positive, pushy (*Inf.*), self-assured, self-confident, self-possessed, sure of oneself
Antonyms (*sense 1*) ambiguous, doubtful, indefinite, questionable, uncertain, unconfirmed, unsettled, unsure (*sense 2*) bashful, diffident, hesitant, retiring, self-conscious, self-effacing, timid

astir active, afoot, awake, in motion, on the

go (*Inf.*), on the move (*Inf.*), out of bed, roused, up and about, up and around

astonish amaze, astound, bewilder, confound, daze, dumbfound, flabbergast (*Inf.*), stagger, stun, stupefy, surprise

astonishing amazing, astounding, bewildering, breathtaking, brilliant, impressive, sensational (*Inf.*), staggering, striking, stunning, stupefying, surprising, wondrous (*Archaic or literary*)
Antonyms anticipated, expected, foreseen

astonishment amazement, awe, bewilderment, confusion, consternation, stupefaction, surprise, wonder, wonderment

astound amaze, astonish, bewilder, confound, daze, dumbfound, flabbergast (*Inf.*), overwhelm, stagger, stun, stupefy, surprise

astounding amazing, astonishing, bewildering, breathtaking, brilliant, impressive, sensational (*Inf.*), staggering, striking, stunning, stupefying, surprising, wondrous (*Archaic or literary*)

astray *adj./adv.* 1. adrift, afield, amiss, lost, off, off course, off the mark, off the right track, off the subject 2. into error, into sin, to the bad, wrong

astringent 1. acerbic, austere, caustic, exacting, grim, hard, harsh, rigid, rigorous, severe, stern, strict, stringent 2. contractile, contractive, styptic

astronaut cosmonaut, spaceman, space pilot, space traveller, spacewoman

astute adroit, artful, bright, calculating, canny, clever, crafty, cunning, discerning, foxy, insightful, intelligent, keen, knowing, penetrating, perceptive, politic, sagacious, sharp, shrewd, sly, subtle, wily
Antonyms dull, ingenuous, naive, slow, straightforward, stupid, unintelligent, unknowing

astuteness acumen, adroitness, artfulness, brightness, canniness, cleverness, craftiness, cunning, discernment, foxiness, insight, intelligence, keenness, knowledge, penetration, perceptiveness, sagacity, sharpness, shrewdness, slyness, smarts (*Sl., chiefly U.S.*), subtlety, suss (*Sl.*), wiliness

asunder *adv./adj.* apart, in pieces, into pieces, rent, to bits, to pieces, torn, to shreds

asylum 1. harbour, haven, preserve, refuge, retreat, safety, sanctuary, shelter 2. *Old-fashioned* funny farm (*Facetious*), hospital, institution, laughing academy (*U.S. sl.*), loony bin (*Sl.*), madhouse (*Inf.*), mental hospital, nuthouse (*Sl.*), psychiatric hospital, rubber room (*U.S. sl.*)

atheism disbelief, freethinking, godlessness, heathenism, infidelity, irreligion, nonbelief, paganism, scepticism, unbelief

atheist disbeliever, freethinker, heathen, infidel, irreligionist, nonbeliever, pagan, sceptic, unbeliever

athlete competitor, contender, contestant, games player, gymnast, player, runner, sportsman, sportswoman

athletic 1. *adj.* able-bodied, active, brawny, energetic, fit, herculean, husky (*Inf.*), lusty, muscular, powerful, robust, sinewy, strapping, strong, sturdy, vigorous, well-proportioned 2. *pl. n.* contests, exercises, games of strength, gymnastics, races, sports, track and field events
Antonyms (*sense 1*) delicate, feeble, frail, puny, sickly, weedy (*Inf.*)

atmosphere 1. aerosphere, air, heavens, sky 2. air, ambience, aura, character, climate, environment, feel, feeling, flavour, mood, quality, spirit, surroundings, tone, vibes (*Sl.*)

atom bit, crumb, dot, fragment, grain, iota, jot, mite, molecule, morsel, mote, particle, scintilla (*Rare*), scrap, shred, speck, spot, tittle, trace, whit

atone 1. *With* **for** answer for, compensate, do penance for, make amends for, make redress, make reparation for, make up for, pay for, recompense, redress 2. appease, expiate, make expiation for, propitiate, reconcile, redeem

atonement amends, compensation, expiation, payment, penance, propitiation, recompense, redress, reparation, restitution, satisfaction

atrocious 1. barbaric, brutal, cruel, diabolical, fiendish, flagrant, godawful (*Sl.*), heinous, hellacious (*U.S. sl.*), infamous, infernal, inhuman, monstrous, nefarious, ruthless, savage, vicious, villainous, wicked 2. appalling, detestable, execrable, grievous, horrible, horrifying, shocking, terrible
Antonyms admirable, civilized, fine, generous, gentle, good, honourable, humane, kind, merciful, tasteful

atrocity 1. abomination, act of savagery, barbarity, brutality, crime, cruelty, enormity, evil, horror, monstrosity, outrage, villainy 2. atrociousness, barbarity, barbarousness, brutality, cruelty, enormity, fiendishness, grievousness, heinousness, horror, infamy, inhumanity, monstrousness, nefariousness, ruthlessness, savagery, shockingness, viciousness, villainousness, wickedness

atrophy 1. *n.* decay, decaying, decline, degeneration, deterioration, diminution, shrivelling, wasting, wasting away, withering 2. *v.* decay, decline, degenerate, deteriorate, diminish, dwindle, fade, shrink, shrivel, waste, waste away, wilt, wither

attach 1. add, adhere, affix, annex, append, bind, connect, couple, fasten, fix, join, link, make fast, secure, stick, subjoin, tie, unite 2. accompany, affiliate, associate, become associated with, combine, enlist, join, join forces with, latch on to, sign on with, sign up with, unite with 3. ascribe, assign, associate, attribute, connect, impute, invest with, lay, place, put 4. allocate, allot, appoint, assign, consign, designate, detail, earmark, second, send

Antonyms detach, disconnect, dissociate, loosen, remove, retire, separate, untie, withdraw

attached 1. affectionate towards, devoted, fond of, full of regard for, possessive 2. accompanied, engaged, married, partnered, spoken for

attachment 1. adapter, bond, clamp, connection, connector, coupling, fastener, fastening, joint, junction, link, tie 2. affection, affinity, attraction, bond, devotion, fidelity, fondness, friendship, liking, love, loyalty, partiality, possessiveness, predilection, regard, tenderness 3. accessory, accoutrement, adapter, addition, add-on, adjunct, appendage, appurtenance, auxiliary, extension, extra, fitting, fixture, supplement, supplementary part

Antonyms (*sense 2*) animosity, antipathy, aversion, disinclination, distaste, hatred, hostility, loathing

attack *n.* 1. aggression, assault, charge, foray, incursion, inroad, invasion, offensive, onset, onslaught, raid, rush, strike 2. abuse, blame, calumny, censure, character assassination, criticism, denigration, impugnment, stick (*Sl.*), vilification 3. access, bout, convulsion, fit, paroxysm, seizure, spasm, spell, stroke ~*v.* 4. assail, assault, charge, fall upon, invade, lay into (*Inf.*), raid, rush, set about, set upon, storm, strike (at) 5. abuse, berate, blame, blast, censure, criticize, excoriate, impugn, lambast(e), malign, put down, revile, tear into (*Inf.*), vilify

Antonyms *n.* defence, retreat, support, vindication, withdrawal ~*v.* defend, guard, protect, retreat, support, sustain, vindicate, withdraw

attacker aggressor, assailant, assaulter, intruder, invader, raider

attain accomplish, achieve, acquire, arrive at, bring off, complete, earn, effect, fulfil, gain, get, grasp, obtain, procure, reach, realize, reap, score (*Sl.*), secure, win

attainable accessible, accomplishable, achievable, at hand, feasible, gettable, graspable, likely, obtainable, possible, potential, practicable, probable, procurable, reachable, realizable, within reach

Antonyms impossible, impracticable, improbable, inaccessible, out of reach, unattainable, unfeasible, unlikely, unobtainable, unprocurable, unreachable

attainment 1. accomplishment, achievement, acquirement, acquisition, arrival at, completion, feat, fulfilment, gaining, getting, obtaining, procurement, reaching, realization, reaping, winning 2. ability, accomplishment, achievement, art, capability, competence, gift, mastery, proficiency, skill, talent

attempt 1. *n.* assault, attack, bid, crack (*Inf.*), effort, endeavour, essay, experiment, go (*Inf.*), shot (*Inf.*), stab (*Inf.*), trial, try, undertaking, venture 2. *v.* endeavour, essay, experiment, have a crack (go (*Inf.*), shot (*Inf.*), stab (*Inf.*)) (*Inf.*), seek, strive, tackle, take on, try, try one's hand at, undertake, venture

attend 1. appear, be at, be here, be present, be there, frequent, go to, haunt, make one (*Archaic*), put in an appearance, show oneself, show up (*Inf.*), turn up, visit 2. care for, look after, mind, minister to, nurse, take care of, tend 3. follow, hear, hearken (*Archaic*), heed, listen, look on, mark, mind, note, notice, observe, pay attention, pay heed, regard, take to heart, watch 4. accompany, arise from, be associated with, be connected with, be consequent on, follow, go hand in hand with, issue from, occur with, result from 5. *With* **to** apply oneself to, concentrate on, devote oneself to, get to work on, look after, occupy oneself with, see to, take care of 6. accompany, chaperon, companion, convoy, escort, guard, squire, usher 7. be in the service of, serve, wait upon, work for

Antonyms (*sense 1*) be absent, miss, play truant (*sense 2*) neglect (*senses 3 & 5*) discount, disregard, ignore, neglect (*sense 4*) dissociate

attendance 1. appearance, attending, being there, presence 2. audience, crowd, gate, house, number present, turnout

attendant 1. *n.* aide, assistant, auxiliary, chaperon, companion, custodian, escort, flunky, follower, guard, guide, helper, lackey, menial, servant, steward, underling, usher, waiter 2. *adj.* accessory, accompanying, associated, concomitant, consequent, related

attention 1. concentration, consideration, contemplation, deliberation, heed, heedfulness, intentness, mind, scrutiny, thinking, thought, thoughtfulness 2. awareness, consciousness, consideration, notice, observation, recognition, regard 3. care, concern, looking after, ministration, treatment 4. *Often plural* assiduities, care, civility, compliment, consideration, courtesy, deference, gallantry, mindfulness, politeness, regard, respect, service

Antonyms carelessness, discourtesy, disregard, disrespect, distraction, impoliteness, inattention, laxity, laxness, negligence, thoughtlessness, unconcern

attentive 1. alert, awake, careful, concentrating, heedful, intent, listening, mindful, observant, regardful, studious, watchful 2. accommodating, civil, conscientious, considerate, courteous, devoted, gallant, gracious, kind, obliging, polite, respectful, thoughtful

Antonyms absent-minded, careless, distracted, dreamy, heedless, inattentive, neglectful, negligent, preoccupied, remiss, thoughtless, unheeding, unmindful

attenuate *v.* 1. adulterate, contract, decrease, devaluate, dilute, diminish, enervate, enfeeble, lessen, lower, reduce, sap, water down, weaken 2. draw out, elongate, extend, lengthen, make fine, make slender, rarefy, refine, slim, spin out, stretch out, thin *~adj. Also* **attenuated** 3. adulterated, contracted, decreased, devalued, dilute, diluted, diminished, enervated, enfeebled, lessened, lowered, reduced, sapped, watered down, weakened 4. drawn out, elongated, extended, lengthened, rarefied, refined, slender, slimmed, spun out, stretched out, thinned

attest adjure, affirm, assert, authenticate, aver, bear out, bear witness, certify, confirm, corroborate, declare, demonstrate, display, evince, exhibit, give evidence, invoke, manifest, prove, ratify, seal, show, substantiate, swear, testify, verify, vouch for, warrant, witness

Antonyms contradict, controvert, deny, disprove, gainsay (*Archaic or literary*), give the lie to, prove false, rebut, refute

attic[1] *adj.* chaste, classical, correct, elegant, graceful, polished, pure, refined, simple, tasteful

attic[2] *n.* garret, loft

attire 1. *n.* accoutrements, apparel, array (*Poetic*), clothes, clothing, costume, dress, garb, garments, gear (*Inf.*), habiliments, habit, outfit, raiment (*Archaic or poetic*), robes, uniform, vestment, wear 2. *v.* accoutre, apparel (*Archaic*), array, clothe, costume, deck out, dress, equip, fit out, garb, get ready, rig out, robe, turn out

attitude 1. approach, disposition, frame of mind, mood, opinion, outlook, perspective, point of view, position, posture, stance, standing, view 2. air, aspect, bearing, carriage, condition, demeanour, manner, mien (*Literary*), pose, position, posture, stance

attract allure, appeal to, bewitch, captivate, charm, decoy, draw, enchant, endear, engage, entice, fascinate, incline, induce, interest, invite, lure, pull (*Inf.*), tempt

Antonyms disgust, give one the creeps (*Inf.*), put one off, repel, repulse, revolt, turn one off (*Inf.*)

attraction allure, appeal, attractiveness, bait, captivation, charm, come-on (*Inf.*), draw, enchantment, endearment, enticement, fascination, inducement, interest, invitation, lure, magnetism, pull (*Inf.*), temptation, temptingness

attractive agreeable, alluring, appealing, beautiful, captivating, charming, comely, engaging, enticing, fair, fascinating, fetching, glamorous, good-looking, gorgeous, handsome, interesting, inviting, likable *or* likeable, lovely, magnetic, pleasant, pleasing, prepossessing, pretty, seductive, tempting, winning, winsome

Antonyms disagreeable, displeasing, distasteful, offensive, repulsive, ugly, unappealing, unbecoming, uninviting, unlikable *or* unlikeable, unpleasant, unsightly

attribute 1. *v.* apply, ascribe, assign, blame, charge, credit, impute, lay at the door of, put down to, refer, set down to, trace to 2. *n.* aspect, character, characteristic, facet, feature, idiosyncrasy, indication, mark, note, peculiarity, point, property, quality, quirk, sign, symbol, trait, virtue

attrition 1. abrasion, chafing, erosion, friction, grinding, rubbing, scraping, wear, wearing away, wearing down 2. attenuation, debilitation, harassment, harrying, thinning out, weakening, wearing down

attune acclimatize, accord, accustom, adapt, adjust, coordinate, familiarize, harmonize, modulate, regulate, set, tune

auburn chestnut-coloured, copper-coloured, henna, nutbrown, reddish-brown, russet, rust-coloured, tawny, Titian red

au courant abreast of, acquainted, *au fait,* conversant, enlightened, in the know, in the swim, knowledgeable, up-to-date, well-informed, well up

audacious 1. adventurous, bold, brave, courageous, daredevil, daring, dauntless, death-defying, enterprising, fearless, intrepid, rash, reckless, risky, valiant, venturesome 2. assuming, brazen, cheeky, defiant, disrespectful, forward, fresh (*Inf.*), impertinent, impudent, insolent, pert, presumptuous, rude, sassy (*U.S. inf.*), shameless

Antonyms (*sense 1*) careful, cautious, cowardly, frightened, guarded, prudent, timid, unadventurous, unenterprising (*sense 2*) deferential, gracious, tactful, unassuming

audacity 1. adventurousness, audaciousness, boldness, bravery, courage, daring, dauntlessness, enterprise, fearlessness, front, guts (*Inf.*), intrepidity, nerve, rashness, recklessness, valour, venturesomeness 2. audaciousness, brass neck (*Brit. inf.*), cheek, chutzpah (*U.S. & Canad. inf.*), defiance, disrespectfulness, effrontery, forwardness, gall (*Inf.*), impertinence, impudence, insolence, neck (*Inf.*), nerve, pertness, presumption, rudeness, shamelessness

audible clear, detectable, discernible, distinct, hearable, perceptible

Antonyms faint, imperceptible, inaudible, indistinct, low, out of earshot

audience 1. assemblage, assembly, congregation, crowd, gallery, gathering, house, listeners, onlookers, spectators, turnout, viewers 2. devotees, fans, following, market, public 3. consultation, hearing, interview, meeting, reception

audit *Accounting* 1. *n.* balancing, check, checking, examination, inspection, investigation, review, scrutiny, verification 2. *v.* balance, check, examine, go over, go through, inspect, investigate, review, scrutinize, verify

au fait abreast of, *au courant,* clued-up (*Inf.*), conversant, expert, familiar, fully informed, in the know, in touch, knowledgeable, on the ball (*Inf.*), well-acquainted, well up

augment add to, amplify, boost, build up, dilate, enhance, enlarge, expand, extend, grow, heighten, increase, inflate, intensify, magnify, multiply, raise, reinforce, strengthen, swell

Antonyms contract, curtail, cut down, decrease, diminish, lessen, lower, reduce, shrink

augmentation accession, addition, amplification, boost, build-up, dilation, enhancement, enlargement, expansion, extension, growth, heightening, increase, inflation, intensification, magnification, multiplication, reinforcement, rise, strengthening, swelling

augur 1. *n.* auspex, diviner, haruspex, oracle, prophet, seer, soothsayer 2. *v.* be an omen of, bespeak (*Archaic*), betoken, bode, foreshadow, harbinger, herald, portend, predict, prefigure, presage, promise, prophesy, signify

augury 1. divination, prediction, prophecy, soothsaying, sortilege 2. auspice, forerunner, forewarning, harbinger, herald, omen, portent, precursor, presage, prognostication, promise, prophecy, sign, token, warning

august dignified, exalted, glorious, grand, high-ranking, imposing, impressive, kingly, lofty, magnificent, majestic, monumental, noble, regal, solemn, stately, superb

aura air, ambience, aroma, atmosphere, emanation, feel, feeling, mood, odour, quality, scent, suggestion, tone, vibes (*Sl.*), vibrations (*Sl.*)

auspice *n.* 1. *Usually plural* advocacy, aegis, authority, backing, care, championship, charge, control, countenance, guidance, influence, patronage, protection, sponsorship, supervision, support 2. augury, indication, omen, portent, prognostication, prophecy, sign, token, warning

auspicious bright, encouraging, favourable, felicitous, fortunate, happy, hopeful, lucky, opportune, promising, propitious, prosperous, rosy, timely

Antonyms bad, black, discouraging, ill-omened, inauspicious, infelicitous, ominous, unfavourable, unfortunate, unlucky, unpromising, unpropitious

austere 1. cold, exacting, forbidding, formal, grave, grim, hard, harsh, inflexible, rigorous, serious, severe, solemn, stern, stiff, strict, stringent, unfeeling, unrelenting 2. abstemious, abstinent, ascetic, chaste, continent, economical, exacting, puritanical, rigid, self-denying, self-disciplined, sober, solemn, Spartan, strait-laced, strict, unrelenting 3. bleak, economical, harsh, plain, severe, simple, spare, Spartan, stark, subdued, unadorned, unornamented

Antonyms abandoned, affable, cheerful, comfortable, convivial, flexible, free-and-easy, genial, immoral, indulgent, jovial, kindly, loose, luxurious, permissive, sweet

austerity 1. coldness, exactingness, forbiddingness, formality, gravity, grimness, hardness, harshness, inflexibility, rigour, seriousness, severity, solemnity, sternness, stiffness, strictness 2. abstemiousness, abstinence, asceticism, chasteness, chastity, continence, economy, exactingness, puritanism, rigidity, self-denial, self-discipline, sobriety, solemnity, Spartanism, strictness 3. economy, plainness, severity, simplicity, spareness, Spartanism, starkness

authentic accurate, actual, authoritative, bona fide, certain, dependable, factual, faithful, genuine, legitimate, original, pure, real, reliable, simon-pure (*Rare*), true, true-to-life, trustworthy, valid, veritable

Antonyms counterfeit, fake, false, fictitious, fraudulent, hypothetical, imitation, misleading, mock, spurious, supposed, synthetic, unfaithful, unreal, untrue

authenticate attest, authorize, avouch, certify, confirm, endorse, guarantee, validate, verify, vouch for, warrant
Antonyms annul, invalidate, render null and void

authenticity accuracy, actuality, authoritativeness, certainty, dependability, factualness, faithfulness, genuineness, legitimacy, purity, realness, reliability, trustworthiness, truth, truthfulness, validity, veritableness, verity

author architect, composer, creator, designer, doer, fabricator, father, founder, framer, initiator, inventor, maker, mover, originator, parent, planner, prime mover, producer, writer

authoritarian 1. *adj.* absolute, autocratic, despotic, dictatorial, disciplinarian, doctrinaire, dogmatic, domineering, harsh, imperious, rigid, severe, strict, tyrannical, unyielding 2. *n.* absolutist, autocrat, despot, dictator, disciplinarian, tyrant
Antonyms *adj.* broad-minded, democratic, flexible, indulgent, lenient, liberal, permissive, tolerant

authoritative 1. accurate, authentic, definitive, dependable, factual, faithful, learned, reliable, scholarly, sound, true, trustworthy, truthful, valid, veritable 2. assertive, autocratic, commanding, confident, decisive, dictatorial, dogmatic, dominating, imperative, imperious, imposing, lordly, masterly, peremptory, self-assured 3. approved, authorized, commanding, legitimate, official, sanctioned, sovereign
Antonyms (*sense 1*) deceptive, undependable, unreliable (*sense 2*) humble, subservient, timid, weak (*sense 3*) unauthorized, unofficial, unsanctioned

authority 1. ascendancy, charge, command, control, direction, domination, dominion, force, government, influence, jurisdiction, might, power, prerogative, right, rule, say-so, strength, supremacy, sway, weight 2. **the authorities** administration, government, management, officialdom, police, powers that be, the establishment 3. authorization, justification, licence, permission, permit, sanction, say-so, warrant 4. arbiter, bible, connoisseur, expert, judge, master, professional, scholar, specialist, textbook 5. attestation, avowal, declaration, evidence, profession, say-so, statement, testimony, word

authorization 1. ability, authority, power, right, say-so, strength 2. approval, credentials, leave, licence, permission, permit, sanction, say-so, warrant

authorize 1. accredit, commission, empower, enable, entitle, give authority 2. accredit, allow, approve, confirm, countenance, give authority for, give leave, license, permit, ratify, sanction, vouch for, warrant
Antonyms ban, debar, disallow, exclude, forbid, outlaw, preclude, prohibit, proscribe, rule out, veto

autocracy absolution, despotism, dictatorship, tyranny

autocrat absolutist, despot, dictator, tyrant

autocratic absolute, all-powerful, despotic, dictatorial, domineering, imperious, tyrannical, tyrannous, unlimited

automatic 1. automated, mechanical, mechanized, push-button, robot, self-acting, self-activating, self-moving, self-propelling, self-regulating 2. habitual, kneejerk, mechanical, perfunctory, routine, unconscious 3. instinctive, instinctual, involuntary, mechanical, natural, reflex, spontaneous, unconscious, unwilled 4. assured, certain, inescapable, inevitable, necessary, routine, unavoidable
Antonyms (*sense 1*) done by hand, hand-operated, human, manual, physical (*senses 2 & 3*) conscious, deliberate, intentional, voluntary

autonomous free, independent, self-determining, self-governing, self-ruling, sovereign

autonomy freedom, home rule, independence, self-determination, self-government, self-rule, sovereignty
Antonyms dependency, foreign rule, subjection

autopsy dissection, necropsy, postmortem, postmortem examination

auxiliary 1. *adj.* accessory, aiding, ancillary, assisting, back-up, emergency, fall-back, helping, reserve, secondary, subsidiary, substitute, supplementary, supporting 2. *n.* accessory, accomplice, ally, assistant, associate, companion, confederate, helper, henchman, partner, protagonist, reserve, subordinate, supporter
Antonyms *adj.* cardinal, chief, essential, first, leading, main, primary, prime, principal

avail *v.* 1. aid, assist, be effective, benefit, be of advantage, be of use, be useful, help, profit, serve, work 2. **avail oneself of** employ, exploit, have recourse to, make the most of, make use of, profit from, take advantage of, turn to account, use, utilize *~n.* 3. advantage, aid, assistance, benefit, effectiveness, efficacy, good, help, profit, purpose, service, use, usefulness, utility

available accessible, applicable, at hand, at one's disposal, attainable, convenient, free, handy, obtainable, on hand, on tap, ready, ready for use, to hand, vacant
Antonyms busy, engaged, inaccessible, in use, occupied, spoken for, taken, unattainable, unavailable, unobtainable

avalanche 1. landslide, landslip, snowslide, snow-slip 2. barrage, deluge, flood, inundation, torrent

avant-garde *adj.* experimental, far-out (*Sl.*), ground-breaking, innovative, innovatory, pioneering, progressive, unconventional, way-out (*Inf.*)
Antonyms conservative, conventional, hidebound, reactionary, traditional

avarice acquisitiveness, close-fistedness, covetousness, cupidity, graspingness, greed, greediness, meanness, miserliness, niggardliness, parsimony, penny-pinching, penuriousness, rapacity, stinginess
Antonyms benevolence, bountifulness, extravagance, generosity, largess *or* largesse, liberality, unselfishness

avaricious acquisitive, close-fisted, covetous, grasping, greedy, mean, miserable, miserly, niggardly, parsimonious, penny-pinching, penurious, rapacious, stingy, tight-arsed (*Taboo sl.*), tight as a duck's arse (*Taboo sl.*), tight-assed (*U.S. taboo sl.*)

avenge even the score for, get even for (*Inf.*), hit back, punish, repay, requite, retaliate, revenge, take satisfaction for, take vengeance

avenue access, alley, approach, boulevard, channel, course, drive, driveway, entrance, entry, pass, passage, path, pathway, road, route, street, thoroughfare, way

aver affirm, allege, assert, asseverate, avouch, avow, declare, maintain, proclaim, profess, pronounce, protest, say, state, swear

average *n.* 1. common run, mean, medium, midpoint, norm, normal, par, rule, run, run of the mill, standard 2. **on average** as a rule, for the most part, generally, normally, typically, usually ~*adj.* 3. banal, common, commonplace, fair, general, indifferent, mediocre, middling, moderate, normal, not bad, ordinary, passable, regular, run-of-the-mill, so-so (*Inf.*), standard, tolerable, typical, undistinguished, unexceptional, usual 4. intermediate, mean, median, medium, middle ~*v.* 5. balance out to, be on average, do on average, even out to, make on average
Antonyms *adj.* abnormal, awful, bad, different, exceptional, great, maximum, memorable, minimum, notable, outstanding, remarkable, special, terrible, unusual

averse antipathetic, backward, disinclined, hostile, ill-disposed, indisposed, inimical, loath, opposed, reluctant, unfavourable, unwilling
Antonyms agreeable, amenable, disposed, eager, favourable, inclined, keen, sympathetic, willing

aversion abhorrence, animosity, antipathy, detestation, disgust, disinclination, dislike, distaste, hate, hatred, horror, hostility, indisposition, loathing, odium, opposition, reluctance, repugnance, repulsion, revulsion, unwillingness
Antonyms desire, inclination, liking, love, willingness

avert 1. turn, turn aside, turn away 2. avoid, fend off, forestall, frustrate, preclude, prevent, stave off, ward off

aviation aeronautics, flight, flying, powered flight

aviator aeronaut, airman, flier, pilot

avid 1. ardent, devoted, eager, enthusiastic, fanatical, fervent, intense, keen, passionate, zealous 2. acquisitive, athirst, avaricious, covetous, grasping, greedy, hungry, insatiable, rapacious, ravenous, thirsty, voracious
Antonyms (*sense 1*) apathetic, impassive, indifferent, lukewarm, unenthusiastic

avidity 1. ardour, devotion, eagerness, enthusiasm, fervour, keenness, zeal 2. acquisitiveness, avarice, covetousness, cupidity, desire, graspingness, greediness, hankering, hunger, insatiability, longing, rapacity, ravenousness, thirst, voracity

avocation 1. diversion, hobby, occupation, pastime, recreation 2. business, calling, employment, job, occupation, profession, pursuit, trade, vocation, work

avoid avert, body-swerve (*Scot.*), bypass, circumvent, dodge, duck (out of) (*Inf.*), elude, escape, eschew, evade, fight shy of, keep aloof from, keep away from, prevent, refrain from, shirk, shun, sidestep, steer clear of
Antonyms approach, confront, contact, face, find, invite, pursue, seek out, solicit

avoidance body swerve (*Scot.*), circumvention, dodging, eluding, escape, eschewal, evasion, keeping away from, prevention, refraining, shirking, shunning, steering clear of

avouch acknowledge, affirm, allege, assert, asseverate, aver, avow, declare, guarantee, maintain, proclaim, profess, pronounce, state, swear, vouch for

avow acknowledge, admit, affirm, allege, assert, asseverate, aver, confess, declare, maintain, own, proclaim, profess, recognize, state, swear

avowal acknowledgment, admission, affirmation, allegation, assertion, asseveration, averment, confession, declaration, maintenance, oath, owning, proclamation, profession, recognition, statement

avowed acknowledged, admitted, confessed, declared, open, professed, self-proclaimed, sworn

await 1. abide, anticipate, expect, look for, look forward to, stay for, wait for 2. attend, be in readiness for, be in store for, be prepared for, be ready for, wait for

awake *v.* 1. awaken, rouse, wake, wake up 2. activate, alert, animate, arouse, awaken, call forth, enliven, excite, fan, incite, kindle, provoke, revive, stimulate, stir up, vivify ~*adj.* 3. alert, alive, aroused, attentive, awakened, aware, conscious, heedful, not sleeping, observant, on guard, on the alert, on the lookout, vigilant, wakeful, waking, watchful, wide-awake
Antonyms *adj.* asleep, crashed out (*Sl.*), dead to the world (*Inf.*), dormant, dozing, inattentive, napping, sleeping, unaware, unconscious

awaken activate, alert, animate, arouse, awake, call forth, enliven, excite, fan, incite, kindle, provoke, revive, rouse, stimulate, stir up, vivify, wake

awakening *n.* activation, animating, arousal, awaking, birth, enlivening, incitement, kindling, provocation, revival, rousing, stimulation, stirring up, vivification, waking, waking up

award *v.* 1. accord, adjudge, allot, apportion, assign, bestow, confer, decree, distribute, endow, gift, give, grant, hand out, present, render ~*n.* 2. adjudication, allotment, bestowal, conferment, conferral, decision, decree, endowment, gift, hand-out, order, presentation, stipend 3. decoration, gift, grant, prize, trophy, verdict

aware acquainted, alive to, appreciative, apprised, attentive, *au courant,* clued-up (*Inf.*), cognizant, conscious, conversant, enlightened, familiar, hip (*Sl.*), informed, knowing, knowledgeable, mindful, sensible, sentient, wise (*Sl.*)
Antonyms ignorant, insensible, oblivious, unaware, unfamiliar with, unknowledgeable

awareness acquaintance, appreciation, attention, cognizance, consciousness, enlightenment, familiarity, knowledge, mindfulness, perception, realization, recognition, sensibility, sentience, understanding

away *adv.* 1. abroad, elsewhere, from here, from home, hence, off 2. apart, at a distance, far, remote 3. aside, out of the way, to one side 4. continuously, incessantly, interminably, relentlessly, repeatedly, uninterruptedly, unremittingly ~*adj.* 5. abroad, absent, elsewhere, gone, not at home, not here, not present, not there, out ~*interj.* 6. beat it (*Sl.*), begone, be off, bugger off (*Taboo sl.*), fuck off (*Offens. taboo sl.*), get lost (*Inf.*), get out, go, go away, on your bike (*Sl.*), on your way

awe 1. *n.* admiration, amazement, astonishment, dread, fear, horror, respect, reverence, terror, veneration, wonder 2. *v.* amaze, astonish, cow, daunt, frighten, horrify, impress, intimidate, stun, terrify
Antonyms *n.* arrogance, boldness, contempt, disrespect, fearlessness, irreverence, scorn

awe-inspiring amazing, astonishing, awesome, breathtaking, daunting, fearsome, impressive, intimidating, magnificent, striking, stunning (*Inf.*), wonderful, wondrous (*Archaic or literary*)
Antonyms bland, boring, dull, flat, humdrum, insipid, prosaic, tame, tedious, unimpressive, uninspiring, vapid

awesome alarming, amazing, astonishing, awe-inspiring, awful, breathtaking, daunting, dreadful, fearful, fearsome, formidable, frightening, horrible, horrifying, imposing, impressive, intimidating, magnificent, majestic, overwhelming, redoubtable, shocking, solemn, striking, stunning, stupefying, terrible, terrifying, wonderful, wondrous (*Archaic or literary*)

awe-stricken, awe-struck afraid, amazed, astonished, awed, awe-inspired, cowed, daunted, dumbfounded, fearful, frightened, horrified, impressed, intimidated, shocked, struck dumb, stunned, terrified, wonder-stricken, wonder-struck

awful 1. abysmal, alarming, appalling, deplorable, dire, distressing, dreadful, fearful, frightful, ghastly, godawful (*Sl.*), gruesome, harrowing, hellacious (*U.S. sl.*), hideous, horrendous, horrible, horrid, horrific, horrifying, nasty, shocking, terrible, tremendous, ugly, unpleasant, unsightly 2. *Archaic* amazing, awe-inspiring, awesome, dread, fearsome, majestic, portentous, solemn
Antonyms (*sense 1*) amazing, brilliant, excellent, fabulous (*Inf.*), fantastic, great (*Inf.*), magnificent, marvellous, miraculous, sensational (*Inf.*), smashing (*Inf.*), super (*Inf.*), superb, terrific, tremendous, wonderful

awfully 1. badly, disgracefully, disreputably, dreadfully, inadequately, reprehensibly, shoddily, unforgivably, unpleasantly, wickedly, woefully, wretchedly 2. *Inf.* badly, dreadfully, exceedingly, exceptionally, excessively, extremely, greatly, immensely, quite, terribly, very, very much

awhile briefly, for a little while, for a moment, for a short time, for a while

awkward 1. all thumbs, artless, blundering, bungling, clownish, clumsy, coarse, gauche, gawky, graceless, ham-fisted, ham-handed, ill-bred, inelegant, inept, inexpert, lumbering, maladroit, oafish, rude, skill-less, stiff, uncoordinated, uncouth, ungainly, ungraceful, unpolished, unrefined, unskilful, unskilled 2. cumbersome, difficult, inconvenient, troublesome, unhandy, unmanageable, unwieldy 3. compromising, cringe-making (*Brit. inf.*), delicate, difficult, embarrassed, embarrassing, ill at ease, inconvenient, inopportune, painful, perplexing, sticky (*Inf.*), thorny, ticklish, troublesome, trying, uncomfortable, unpleasant, untimely 4. annoying, bloody-minded (*Brit. inf.*), difficult, disobliging, exasperating, hard to handle, intractable, irritable, perverse, prickly, stubborn, touchy, troublesome, trying, uncooperative, unhelpful, unpredictable, vexatious, vexing 5. chancy (*Inf.*), dangerous, difficult, hazardous, perilous, risky

Antonyms (*sense 1*) adept, adroit, dexterous, graceful, skilful (*sense 2*) convenient, easy, handy (*sense 3*) comfortable, pleasant

awkwardness 1. artlessness, clownishness, clumsiness, coarseness, gaucheness, gaucherie, gawkiness, gracelessness, ill-breeding, inelegance, ineptness, inexpertness, maladroitness, oafishness, rudeness, skill-lessness, stiffness, uncoordination, uncouthness, ungainliness, unskilfulness, unskilledness 2. cumbersomeness, difficulty, inconvenience, troublesomeness, unhandiness, unmanageability, unwieldiness 3. delicacy, difficulty, discomfort, embarrassment, inconvenience, inopportuneness, painfulness, perplexingness, stickiness (*Inf.*), thorniness, ticklishness, unpleasantness, untimeliness 4. bloody-mindedness (*Brit. inf.*), difficulty, disobligingness, intractability, irritability, perversity, prickliness, stubbornness, touchiness, uncooperativeness, unhelpfulness, unpredictability 5. chanciness (*Inf.*), danger, difficulty, hazardousness, peril, perilousness, risk, riskiness

awry *adv./adj.* amiss, askew, asymmetrical, cockeyed (*Inf.*), crooked, crookedly, misaligned, obliquely, off-centre, off course, out of line, out of true, skew-whiff (*Inf.*), to one side, twisted, uneven, unevenly, wrong

axe *n.* 1. adze, chopper, hatchet 2. **an axe to grind** grievance, personal consideration, pet subject, private ends, private purpose, ulterior motive 3. **the axe** *Inf.* cancellation, cutback, discharge, dismissal, termination, the boot (*Sl.*), the chop (*Sl.*), the (old) heave-ho (*Inf.*), the order of the boot (*Sl.*), the sack (*Inf.*), wind-up ~*v.* 4. chop, cut down, fell, hew 5. *Inf.* cancel, cut back, discharge, dismiss, dispense with, eliminate, fire (*Inf.*), get rid of, oust, relegate, remove, sack (*Inf.*), terminate, throw out, turn off (*Inf.*), wind up

axiom adage, aphorism, apophthegm, dictum, fundamental, gnome, maxim, postulate, precept, principle, truism

axiomatic 1. absolute, accepted, apodictic, assumed, certain, fundamental, given, granted, indubitable, manifest, presupposed, self-evident, understood, unquestioned 2. aphoristic, apophthegmatic, epigrammatic, gnomic, pithy, terse

axis 1. axle, centre line, pivot, shaft, spindle 2. alliance, bloc, coalition, compact, entente, league, pact

axle arbor, axis, mandrel, pin, pivot, rod, shaft, spindle

azure blue, cerulean, clear blue, sky-blue, sky-coloured, ultramarine

B

babble 1. *v.* blab, burble, cackle, chatter, gabble, gibber, gurgle, jabber, mumble, murmur, mutter, prate, prattle, rabbit (on) (*Brit. inf.*), run off at the mouth (*Sl.*), waffle (*Inf., chiefly Brit.*) 2. *n.* burble, clamour, drivel, gabble, gibberish, murmur, waffle (*Inf., chiefly Brit.*)

babe 1. ankle-biter (*Aust. sl.*), baby, bairn (*Scot.*), child, infant, nursling, rug rat (*Sl.*), sprog (*Sl.*), suckling 2. babe in arms, ingénue, innocent

babel bedlam, clamour, confusion, din, disorder, hubbub, hullabaloo, hurly-burly, pandemonium, tumult, turmoil, uproar

baby 1. *n.* ankle-biter (*Aust. sl.*), babe, bairn (*Scot.*), child, infant, newborn child, rug rat (*Sl.*), sprog (*Sl.*) 2. *adj.* diminutive, dwarf, little, midget, mini, miniature, minute, pygmy *or* pigmy, small, teensy-weensy, teeny-weeny, tiny, wee 3. *v.* coddle, cosset, humour, indulge, mollycoddle, overindulge, pamper, pet, spoil, spoon-feed

babyish baby, childish, foolish, immature, infantile, juvenile, namby-pamby, puerile, silly, sissy, soft (*Inf.*), spoiled
Antonyms adult, grown-up, mature, of age

bacchanal 1. carouser, debauchee, drunkard, reveller, roisterer, winebibber 2. debauch, debauchery, orgy, revel, revelry

back *v.* 1. abet, advocate, assist, champion, countenance, encourage, endorse, espouse, favour, finance, promote, sanction, second, side with, sponsor, subsidize, support, sustain, underwrite 2. backtrack, go back, move back, regress, retire, retreat, reverse, turn tail, withdraw ~*n.* 3. backside, end, far end, hind part, hindquarters, posterior, rear, reverse, stern, tail end ~*adj.* 4. end, hind, hindmost, posterior, rear, tail 5. *From an earlier time* delayed, earlier, elapsed, former, overdue, past, previous 6. **behind one's back** covertly, deceitfully, secretly, sneakily, surreptitiously
Antonyms *v.* (*sense 1*) attack, combat, hinder, thwart, undermine, weaken (*sense 2*) advance, approach, move forward, progress ~*n.* face, fore, front, head ~*adj.* advance, fore, front, future, late

backbite abuse, bad-mouth (*Sl., chiefly U.S. & Canad.*), calumniate, defame, denigrate, detract, knock (*Inf.*), libel, malign, revile, rubbish (*Inf.*), slag (off) (*Sl.*), slander, traduce, vilify, vituperate

backbiting abuse, aspersion, bitchiness (*Sl.*), calumniation, calumny, cattiness (*Inf.*), defamation, denigration, detraction, disparagement, gossip, malice, scandalmongering, slander, spite, spitefulness, vilification, vituperation

backbone 1. *Medical* spinal column, spine, vertebrae, vertebral column 2. bottle (*Brit. sl.*), character, courage, determination, firmness, fortitude, grit, hardihood, mettle, moral fibre, nerve, pluck, resolution, resolve, stamina, steadfastness, strength of character, tenacity, toughness, will, willpower 3. basis, foundation, mainstay, support

backbreaking arduous, crushing, exhausting, gruelling, hard, killing, laborious, punishing, strenuous, toilsome, wearing, wearying

back down accede, admit defeat, back-pedal, concede, give in, surrender, withdraw, yield

backer advocate, angel (*Inf.*), benefactor, patron, promoter, second, sponsor, subscriber, supporter, underwriter, well-wisher

backfire boomerang, disappoint, fail, flop (*Inf.*), miscarry, rebound, recoil

background breeding, circumstances, credentials, culture, education, environment, experience, grounding, history, milieu, preparation, qualifications, tradition, upbringing

backhanded ambiguous, double-edged, equivocal, indirect, ironic, oblique, sarcastic, sardonic, two-edged

backing abetment, accompaniment, advocacy, aid, assistance, championing, encouragement, endorsement, espousal, funds, grant, moral support, patronage, promotion, sanction, seconding, sponsorship, subsidy, support

backlash backfire, boomerang, counteraction, counterblast, kickback, reaction, recoil, repercussion, resentment, resistance, response, retaliation, retroaction

backlog accumulation, build-up, excess, hoard, reserve, reserves, resources, stock, supply

back out abandon, cancel, chicken out

(*Inf.*), cop out (*Sl.*), give up, go back on, recant, renege, resign, retreat, withdraw

backslide fall from grace, go astray, go wrong, lapse, regress, relapse, renege, retrogress, revert, sin, slip, stray, weaken

backslider apostate, deserter, recidivist, recreant, renegade, reneger, turncoat

back up aid, assist, bolster, confirm, corroborate, reinforce, second, stand by, substantiate, support

backward *adj.* 1. bashful, diffident, hesitating, late, reluctant, shy, sluggish, tardy, unwilling, wavering 2. behind, behindhand, braindead (*Inf.*), dense, dozy (*Brit. inf.*), dull, obtuse, retarded, slow, stupid, subnormal, underdeveloped, undeveloped ~*adv.* 3. aback, behind, in reverse, rearward
Antonyms *adj.* advanced, ahead, bold, brash, eager, forward, pushy (*Inf.*), willing ~*adv.* correctly, forward, frontward, properly

backwoods 1. *adj.* agrestic, hick (*Inf., chiefly U.S. & Canad.*), isolated, remote, rustic, uncouth 2. *n.* back of beyond, middle of nowhere, outback, sticks (*Inf.*)

bacteria bacilli, bugs (*Sl.*), germs, microbes, microorganisms, pathogens, viruses

bad 1. chickenshit (*U.S. sl.*), defective, deficient, duff (*Brit. inf.*), erroneous, fallacious, faulty, imperfect, inadequate, incorrect, inferior, of a sort *or* of sorts, pathetic, poor, poxy (*Sl.*), substandard, unsatisfactory 2. damaging, dangerous, deleterious, detrimental, harmful, hurtful, injurious, ruinous, unhealthy 3. base, corrupt, criminal, delinquent, evil, immoral, mean, sinful, vile, villainous, wicked, wrong 4. disobedient, mischievous, naughty, unruly 5. decayed, mouldy, off, putrid, rancid, rotten, sour, spoiled 6. disastrous, distressing, grave, harsh, painful, serious, severe, terrible 7. ailing, diseased, ill, sick, unwell 8. apologetic, conscience-stricken, contrite, guilty, regretful, remorseful, sad, sorry, upset 9. adverse, discouraged, discouraging, distressed, distressing, gloomy, grim, melancholy, troubled, troubling, unfortunate, unpleasant 10. **not bad** all right, average, fair, fair to middling (*Inf.*), moderate, O.K. *or* okay (*Inf.*), passable, respectable, so-so (*Inf.*), tolerable
Antonyms (*sense 1*) adequate, fair, satisfactory (*sense 2*) agreeable, beneficial, good, healthful, safe, sound, wholesome (*sense 3*) ethical, fine, first-rate, good, moral, righteous, virtuous (*sense 4*) biddable, docile, good, obedient, well-behaved

bad blood acrimony, anger, animosity, antagonism, dislike, enmity, feud, hatred, ill feeling, ill will, malevolence, malice, rancour, resentment

badge brand, device, emblem, identification, insignia, mark, sign, stamp, token

badger bend someone's ear (*Inf.*), bully, chivvy, goad, harass, harry, hound, importune, nag, pester, plague, torment

badinage banter, chaff, drollery, mockery, persiflage, pleasantry, raillery, repartee, teasing, waggery, wordplay

badly 1. carelessly, defectively, erroneously, faultily, imperfectly, inadequately, incorrectly, ineptly, poorly, shoddily, wrong, wrongly 2. unfavourably, unfortunately, unsuccessfully 3. criminally, evilly, immorally, improperly, naughtily, shamefully, unethically, wickedly 4. acutely, deeply, desperately, exceedingly, extremely, gravely, greatly, intensely, painfully, seriously, severely
Antonyms ably, competently, correctly, ethically, morally, properly, righteously, rightly, satisfactorily, splendidly, well

bad manners boorishness, churlishness, coarseness, discourtesy, disrespect, impoliteness, incivility, inconsideration, indelicacy, rudeness, unmannerliness
Antonyms civility, cordiality, courteousness, courtesy, good manners, graciousness, politeness, urbanity

baffle 1. amaze, astound, bewilder, confound, confuse, daze, disconcert, dumbfound, elude, flummox, mystify, nonplus, perplex, puzzle, stump, stun 2. balk, check, defeat, foil, frustrate, hinder, thwart, upset
Antonyms (*sense 1*) clarify, clear up, elucidate, explain, explicate, interpret, make plain, shed *or* throw light upon, spell out

bag *v.* 1. balloon, bulge, droop, sag, swell 2. acquire, capture, catch, gain, get, kill, land, shoot, take, trap

baggage accoutrements, bags, belongings, equipment, gear, impedimenta, luggage, paraphernalia, suitcases, things

baggy billowing, bulging, droopy, floppy, ill-fitting, loose, oversize, roomy, sagging, seated, slack
Antonyms close, close-fitting, constricted, cramped, narrow, snug, stretched, taut, tight, tight-fitting

bail[1] *n.* bond, guarantee, guaranty, pledge, security, surety, warranty

bail[2], **bale** *v.* dip, drain off, ladle, scoop

bail out, bale out 1. aid, help, relieve, rescue 2. escape, quit, retreat, withdraw

bait *n.* 1. allurement, attraction, bribe, decoy, enticement, inducement, lure, snare, temptation ~*v.* 2. aggravate (*Inf.*), annoy, be on one's back (*Sl.*), bother, gall, get in one's hair (*Inf.*), get on one's nerves (*Inf.*), harass, hassle (*Inf.*), hound, irk, irritate, nark (*Brit., Aust., & N.Z. sl.*), needle (*Inf.*), persecute, piss one off (*Taboo sl.*), provoke, tease, torment, wind up (*Brit. sl.*) 3. allure, beguile, entice, lure, seduce, tempt

baked arid, desiccated, dry, parched, scorched, seared, sun-baked, torrid

balance *v.* 1. level, match, parallel, poise, stabilize, steady 2. adjust, compensate for, counteract, counterbalance, counterpoise, equalize, equate, make up for, neutralize, offset 3. assess, compare, consider, deliberate, estimate, evaluate, weigh 4. calculate, compute, settle, square, tally, total *~n.* 5. correspondence, equilibrium, equipoise, equity, equivalence, evenness, parity, symmetry 6. composure, equanimity, poise, self-control, self-possession, stability, steadiness 7. difference, remainder, residue, rest, surplus
Antonyms *v.* outweigh, overbalance, upset *~n.* disproportion, instability, shakiness, unbalance, uncertainty

balanced disinterested, equitable, even-handed, fair, impartial, just, unbiased, unprejudiced
Antonyms biased, distorted, jaundiced, lopsided, one-sided, partial, predisposed, prejudiced, slanted, unfair, warped, weighted

balance sheet account, budget, credits and debits, ledger, report, statement

balcony 1. terrace, veranda 2. gallery, gods, upper circle

bald 1. baldheaded, baldpated, depilated, glabrous (*Biol.*), hairless 2. barren, bleak, exposed, naked, stark, treeless, uncovered 3. bare, blunt, direct, downright, forthright, outright, plain, severe, simple, straight, straightforward, unadorned, unvarnished, upfront (*Inf.*)

balderdash balls (*Taboo sl.*), bilge (*Inf.*), bosh (*Inf.*), bull (*Sl.*), bullshit (*Taboo sl.*), bunk (*Inf.*), bunkum *or* buncombe (*Chiefly U.S.*), claptrap (*Inf.*), cobblers (*Brit. taboo sl.*), crap (*Sl.*), drivel, eyewash (*Inf.*), garbage (*Inf.*), gibberish, guff (*Sl.*), hogwash, hokum (*Sl., chiefly U.S. & Canad.*), horsefeathers (*U.S. sl.*), hot air (*Inf.*), moonshine, nonsense, pap, piffle (*Inf.*), poppycock (*Inf.*), rot, rubbish, shit (*Taboo sl.*), tommyrot, tosh (*Sl., chiefly Brit.*), trash, tripe (*Inf.*), twaddle

baldness 1. alopecia (*Pathology*), baldheadedness, baldpatedness, glabrousness (*Biol.*), hairlessness 2. barrenness, bleakness, nakedness, sparseness, starkness, treelessness 3. austerity, bluntness, plainness, severity, simplicity, spareness

bale *see* BAIL[2]

baleful calamitous, deadly, evil, harmful, hurtful, injurious, maleficent, malevolent, malignant, menacing, mournful, noxious, ominous, pernicious, ruinous, sad, sinister, venomous, woeful
Antonyms beneficial, benevolent, benign, friendly, good, healthy, salubrious

bale out *see* BAIL OUT

balk 1. demur, dodge, evade, flinch, hesitate, jib, recoil, refuse, resist, shirk, shrink from 2. baffle, bar, check, counteract, defeat, disconcert, foil, forestall, frustrate, hinder, obstruct, prevent, thwart
Antonyms (*sense 1*) accede, accept, acquiesce, comply, relent, submit, yield (*sense 2*) abet, advance, aid, assist, further, help, promote, support, sustain

balky intractable, obstinate, stubborn, uncooperative, unmanageable, unpredictable, unruly

ball 1. drop, globe, globule, orb, pellet, sphere, spheroid 2. ammunition, bullet, grapeshot, pellet, shot, slug

ballast balance, counterbalance, counterweight, equilibrium, sandbag, stability, stabilizer, weight

balloon *v.* belly, billow, bloat, blow up, dilate, distend, enlarge, expand, inflate, puff out, swell

ballot election, poll, polling, vote, voting

ballyhoo 1. babble, commotion, fuss, hubbub, hue and cry, hullabaloo, noise, racket, to-do 2. advertising, build-up, hype, promotion, propaganda, publicity

balm 1. balsam, cream, embrocation, emollient, lotion, ointment, salve, unguent 2. anodyne, comfort, consolation, curative, palliative, restorative, solace

balmy 1. clement, mild, pleasant, summery, temperate 2. *Also* **barmy** crackpot (*Inf.*), crazy, daft (*Inf.*), foolish, goofy (*Inf.*), idiotic, insane, loony (*Sl.*), loopy (*Inf.*), nuts (*Sl.*), nutty (*Sl.*), odd, off one's trolley (*Sl.*), out to lunch (*Inf.*), silly, stupid, up the pole (*Inf.*)
Antonyms (*sense 1*) annoying, discomforting, harsh, inclement, intense, irksome, rough, stormy

bamboozle 1. cheat, con (*Inf.*), deceive, defraud, delude, dupe, fool, hoax, hoodwink, skin (*Sl.*), swindle, trick 2. baffle, befuddle, confound, confuse, mystify, perplex, puzzle, stump

ban 1. *v.* banish, bar, black, blackball, block, boycott, debar, disallow, disqualify, exclude, forbid, interdict, outlaw, prohibit, proscribe, restrict, suppress 2. *n.* block, boycott, censorship, embargo, interdict,

interdiction, prohibition, proscription, restriction, stoppage, suppression, taboo
Antonyms *v.* allow, approve, authorize, let, permit, sanction *~n.* allowance, approval, permission, sanction

banal clichéd, cliché-ridden, commonplace, everyday, hackneyed, humdrum, mundane, old hat, ordinary, pedestrian, platitudinous, stale, stereotyped, stock, threadbare, tired, trite, unimaginative, unoriginal, vapid
Antonyms challenging, distinctive, fresh, imaginative, interesting, new, novel, original, stimulating, unique, unusual

banality bromide (*Inf.*), cliché, commonplace, platitude, triteness, trite phrase, triviality, truism, vapidity

band[1] *n.* bandage, belt, binding, bond, chain, cord, fetter, fillet, ligature, manacle, ribbon, shackle, strap, strip, tie

band[2] *n.* 1. assembly, association, bevy, body, camp, clique, club, company, coterie, crew (*Inf.*), gang, horde, party, posse (*Inf.*), society, troop 2. combo, ensemble, group, orchestra *~v.* 3. affiliate, ally, consolidate, federate, gather, group, join, merge, unite
Antonyms *v.* cleave, disperse, disunite, divide, part, segregate, separate, split, sunder

bandage 1. *n.* compress, dressing, gauze, plaster 2. *v.* bind, cover, dress, swathe

bandit brigand, crook, desperado, footpad, freebooter, gangster, gunman, highwayman, hijacker, marauder, outlaw, pirate, racketeer, robber, thief

bandy 1. *v.* barter, exchange, interchange, pass, shuffle, swap, throw, toss, trade 2. *adj.* bandy-legged, bent, bowed, bow-legged, crooked, curved

bane affliction, *bête noire,* blight, burden, calamity, curse, despair, destruction, disaster, downfall, misery, nuisance, pest, plague, ruin, scourge, torment, trial, trouble, woe
Antonyms blessing, comfort, consolation, joy, pleasure, relief, solace, support

baneful baleful, calamitous, deadly, deleterious, destructive, disastrous, fatal, harmful, hurtful, injurious, maleficent, noxious, pernicious, pestilential, ruinous, venomous

bang *n.* 1. boom, burst, clang, clap, clash, detonation, explosion, peal, pop, report, shot, slam, thud, thump 2. belt (*Inf.*), blow, box, bump, cuff, hit, knock, punch, smack, stroke, wallop (*Inf.*), whack *~v.* 3. bash (*Inf.*), beat, belt (*Inf.*), bump, clatter, crash, hammer, knock, pound, pummel, rap, slam, strike, thump 4. boom, burst, clang, detonate, drum, echo, explode, peal, resound, thump, thunder *~adv.* 5. abruptly, hard, headlong, noisily, precisely, slap, smack, straight, suddenly

banish 1. deport, drive away, eject, evict, exclude, excommunicate, exile, expatriate, expel, ostracize, outlaw, shut out, transport 2. ban, cast out, discard, dislodge, dismiss, dispel, eliminate, eradicate, get rid of, oust, remove, shake off
Antonyms accept, admit, embrace, hail, invite, offer hospitality to, receive, welcome

banishment deportation, exile, expatriation, expulsion, proscription, transportation

banisters balusters, balustrade, handrail, rail, railing

bank[1] 1. *n.* accumulation, depository, fund, hoard, repository, reserve, reservoir, savings, stock, stockpile, store, storehouse 2. *v.* deal with, deposit, keep, save, transact business with

bank[2] *n.* 1. banking, embankment, heap, mass, mound, pile, ridge 2. brink, edge, margin, shore, side *~v.* 3. amass, heap, mass, mound, pile, stack 4. camber, cant, heel, incline, pitch, slant, slope, tilt, tip

bank[3] *n.* array, file, group, line, rank, row, sequence, series, succession, tier, train

bank on assume, believe in, count on, depend on, lean on, look to, rely on, trust

bankrupt broke (*Inf.*), depleted, destitute, exhausted, failed, impoverished, insolvent, lacking, ruined, spent
Antonyms in the money (*Inf.*), on the up and up, prosperous, solvent, sound, wealthy

bankruptcy disaster, exhaustion, failure, indebtedness, insolvency, lack, liquidation, ruin

banner banderole, burgee, colours, ensign, fanion, flag, gonfalon, pennant, pennon, standard, streamer

banquet dinner, feast, meal, repast, revel, treat

banter 1. *v.* chaff, deride, jeer, jest, joke, josh (*Sl., chiefly U.S. & Canad.*), kid (*Inf.*), make fun of, rib (*Inf.*), ridicule, taunt, tease, twit 2. *n.* badinage, chaff, chaffing, derision, jeering, jesting, joking, kidding (*Inf.*), mockery, persiflage, pleasantry, raillery, repartee, ribbing (*Inf.*), ridicule, wordplay

baptism 1. christening, immersion, purification, sprinkling 2. beginning, debut, dedication, initiation, introduction, launching, rite of passage

baptize 1. besprinkle, cleanse, immerse, purify 2. admit, enrol, initiate, recruit 3. call, christen, dub, name, title

bar *n.* 1. batten, crosspiece, paling, palisade, pole, rail, rod, shaft, stake, stick 2. barricade, barrier, block, deterrent, hindrance, impediment, obstacle, obstruction, rail, railing, stop 3. boozer (*Brit., Aust., & N.Z. inf.*), canteen, counter, inn, lounge, pub (*Inf., chiefly Brit.*), public house, saloon, taproom, tavern, watering hole (*Facetious sl.*) 4. bench, court, courtroom, dock, law court 5. *Law* barristers, body of lawyers, counsel, court, judgment, tribunal ~*v.* 6. barricade, bolt, fasten, latch, lock, secure 7. ban, black, blackball, exclude, forbid, hinder, keep out, obstruct, prevent, prohibit, restrain

Antonyms (*sense 2*) aid, benefit, help (*sense 7*) accept, admit, allow, clear, let, open, permit, receive

barb 1. bristle, point, prickle, prong, quill, spike, spur, thorn 2. affront, cut, dig, gibe, insult, rebuff, sarcasm, scoff, sneer

barbarian *n.* 1. brute, hooligan, lout, lowbrow, ned (*Sl.*), ruffian, savage, vandal, yahoo 2. bigot, boor, ignoramus, illiterate, lowbrow, philistine ~*adj.* 3. boorish, crude, lowbrow, philistine, primitive, rough, uncouth, uncultivated, uncultured, unsophisticated, vulgar, wild

Antonyms *adj.* civil, civilized, cultured, genteel, highbrow, refined, sophisticated, urbane, well-mannered

barbaric 1. primitive, rude, uncivilized, wild 2. barbarous, boorish, brutal, coarse, crude, cruel, fierce, inhuman, savage, uncouth, vulgar

Antonyms civilized, cultivated, cultured, gentlemanly, gracious, humane, refined, sophisticated, urbane

barbarism 1. coarseness, crudity, savagery, uncivilizedness 2. atrocity, barbarity, enormity, outrage 3. corruption, misusage, misuse, solecism, vulgarism

barbarity brutality, cruelty, inhumanity, ruthlessness, savagery, viciousness

barbarous 1. barbarian, brutish, primitive, rough, rude, savage, uncivilized, uncouth, wild 2. barbaric, brutal, cruel, ferocious, heartless, inhuman, monstrous, ruthless, vicious 3. coarse, crude, ignorant, uncultured, unlettered, unrefined, vulgar

barbed 1. hooked, jagged, prickly, pronged, spiked, spiny, thorny, toothed 2. acid, acrid, catty (*Inf.*), critical, cutting, hostile, hurtful, nasty, pointed, scathing, unkind

bare 1. buck naked (*Sl.*), denuded, exposed, in the raw (*Inf.*), naked, naked as the day one was born (*Inf.*), nude, peeled, shorn, stripped, unclad, unclothed, uncovered, undressed, without a stitch on (*Inf.*) 2. barren, blank, empty, lacking, mean, open, poor, scanty, scarce, unfurnished, vacant, void, wanting 3. austere, bald, basic, cold, essential, hard, literal, plain, severe, sheer, simple, spare, spartan, stark, unadorned, unembellished, unvarnished

Antonyms abundant, adorned, attired, clad, clothed, concealed, covered, dressed, full, hidden, plentiful, profuse, well-stocked

barefaced 1. audacious, bold, brash, brazen, impudent, insolent, shameless 2. bald, blatant, flagrant, glaring, manifest, naked, obvious, open, palpable, patent, transparent, unconcealed

Antonyms concealed, covered, hidden, inconspicuous, masked, obscured, secret, tucked away, unseen

barely almost, hardly, just, only just, scarcely

Antonyms amply, completely, fully, profusely

bargain *n.* 1. agreement, arrangement, business, compact, contract, convention, engagement, negotiation, pact, pledge, promise, stipulation, transaction, treaty, understanding 2. (cheap) purchase, discount, giveaway, good buy, good deal, good value, reduction, snip (*Inf.*), steal (*Inf.*) ~*v.* 3. agree, contract, covenant, negotiate, promise, stipulate, transact 4. barter, buy, deal, haggle, sell, trade, traffic

bargain for anticipate, contemplate, expect, foresee, imagine, look for, plan for

bargain on assume, bank on, count on, depend on, plan on, rely on

barge canal boat, flatboat, lighter, narrow boat, scow

barge in break in, burst in, butt in, infringe, interrupt, intrude, muscle in (*Inf.*)

barge into bump into, cannon into, collide with, hit, push, shove

bark[1] 1. *n.* casing, cortex (*Anat., bot.*), covering, crust, husk, rind, skin 2. *v.* abrade, flay, rub, scrape, shave, skin, strip

bark[2] 1. *n./v.* bay, growl, howl, snarl, woof, yap, yelp 2. ~*v. Fig.* bawl, bawl at, berate, bluster, growl, shout, snap, snarl, yell

barmy 1. *Also* **balmy** crackpot (*Inf.*), crazy, daft (*Inf.*), dippy, doolally (*Sl.*), foolish, goofy (*Inf.*), idiotic, insane, loony (*Sl.*), loopy (*Inf.*), nuts (*Sl.*), nutty (*Sl.*), odd, off one's trolley (*Sl.*), out to lunch (*Inf.*), silly, stupid, up the pole (*Inf.*) 2. fermenting, foamy, frothy, spumy, yeasty

Antonyms (*sense 1*) all there (*Inf.*), in one's right mind, of sound mind, rational, reasonable, sane, sensible

baroque bizarre, convoluted, elaborate, extravagant, flamboyant, florid, grotesque, ornate, overdecorated, rococo

barracks billet, camp, cantonment, casern, encampment, garrison, quarters

barrage 1. battery, bombardment, cannonade, curtain of fire, fusillade, gunfire, salvo, shelling, volley 2. assault, attack, burst, deluge, hail, mass, onslaught, plethora, profusion, rain, storm, stream, torrent

barred 1. banded, crosshatched, lined, marked, ribbed, ridged, streaked, striped, veined 2. banned, excluded, forbidden, outlawed, prohibited, proscribed, taboo

barren 1. childless, infecund, infertile, sterile, unprolific 2. arid, desert, desolate, dry, empty, unfruitful, unproductive, waste 3. boring, dull, flat, fruitless, lacklustre, stale, uninformative, uninspiring, uninstructive, uninteresting, unrewarding, useless, vapid
Antonyms fecund, fertile, fruitful, instructive, interesting, lush, productive, profitable, rich, useful

barricade 1. *n.* barrier, blockade, bulwark, fence, obstruction, palisade, rampart, stockade 2. *v.* bar, block, blockade, defend, fortify, obstruct, protect, shut in

barrier 1. bar, barricade, block, blockade, boundary, ditch, fence, fortification, obstacle, obstruction, pale, railing, rampart, stop, wall 2. *Fig.* check, difficulty, drawback, handicap, hindrance, hurdle, impediment, limitation, obstacle, restriction, stumbling block

barter bargain, exchange, haggle, sell, swap, trade, traffic

base[1] *n.* 1. bed, bottom, foot, foundation, groundwork, pedestal, rest, stand, support 2. basis, core, essence, essential, fundamental, heart, key, origin, principle, root, source 3. camp, centre, headquarters, home, post, settlement, starting point, station ~*v.* 4. build, construct, depend, derive, establish, found, ground, hinge, locate, station
Antonyms (*sense 1*) apex, crest, crown, peak, summit, top, vertex

base[2] 1. abject, contemptible, corrupt, depraved, despicable, dishonourable, disreputable, evil, ignoble, immoral, infamous, scandalous, shameful, sordid, vile, villainous, vulgar, wicked 2. downtrodden, grovelling, low, lowly, mean, menial, miserable, paltry, pitiful, poor, servile, slavish, sorry, subservient, worthless, wretched 3. adulterated, alloyed, counterfeit, debased, fake, forged, fraudulent, impure, inferior, pinchbeck, spurious
Antonyms admirable, good, honest, honourable, just, lofty, moral, noble, pure, rare, righteous, unalloyed, upright, valuable, virtuous

baseless groundless, unconfirmed, uncorroborated, unfounded, ungrounded, unjustifiable, unjustified, unsubstantiated, unsupported
Antonyms authenticated, confirmed, corroborated, proven, substantiated, supported, validated, verified, well-founded

baseness 1. contemptibility, degradation, depravation, depravity, despicability, disgrace, ignominy, infamy, notoriety, obloquy, turpitude 2. lowliness, meanness, misery, poverty, servility, slavishness, subservience, vileness, worthlessness, wretchedness 3. adulteration, debasement, fraudulence, phoneyness *or* phoniness (*Inf.*), pretence, speciousness, spuriousness

bash 1. *v.* belt (*Inf.*), biff (*Sl.*), break, chin (*Sl.*), crash, crush, deck (*Sl.*), hit, lay one on (*Sl.*), punch, slosh (*Brit. sl.*), smash, sock (*Sl.*), strike, wallop (*Inf.*) 2. *n.* attempt, crack (*Inf.*), go (*Inf.*), shot (*Inf.*), stab (*Inf.*), try

bashful abashed, blushing, confused, constrained, coy, diffident, easily embarrassed, nervous, overmodest, reserved, reticent, retiring, self-conscious, self-effacing, shamefaced, sheepish, shrinking, shy, timid, timorous
Antonyms aggressive, arrogant, bold, brash, conceited, confident, egoïstic, fearless, forward, immodest, impudent, intrepid, pushy (*Inf.*), self-assured

bashfulness constraint, coyness, diffidence, embarrassment, hesitation, modesty, reserve, self-consciousness, sheepishness, shyness, timidity, timorousness

basic bog-standard (*Inf.*), central, elementary, essential, fundamental, indispensable, inherent, intrinsic, key, necessary, primary, radical, underlying, vital
Antonyms complementary, minor, peripheral, secondary, supplementary, supporting, trivial, unessential

basically at bottom, at heart, *au fond,* essentially, firstly, fundamentally, inherently, in substance, intrinsically, mostly, primarily, radically

basics brass tacks (*Inf.*), core, essentials, facts, fundamentals, hard facts, necessaries, nitty-gritty (*Inf.*), nuts and bolts (*Inf.*), practicalities, principles, rudiments

basis 1. base, bottom, footing, foundation, ground, groundwork, support 2. chief ingredient, core, essential, fundamental, heart, premise, principal element, principle, theory

bask 1. laze, lie in, loll, lounge, relax, sunbathe, swim in, toast oneself, warm oneself 2. delight in, enjoy, indulge oneself, luxuriate, relish, revel, savour, take pleasure, wallow

bass deep, deep-toned, grave, low, low-pitched, resonant, sonorous

bastard 1. *n.* illegitimate (child), love child, natural child, whoreson (*Archaic*) 2. *adj.* adulterated, baseborn, counterfeit, false, illegitimate, imperfect, impure, inferior, irregular, misbegotten, sham, spurious

bastardize adulterate, cheapen, corrupt, debase, defile, degrade, demean, devalue, distort, pervert

bastion bulwark, citadel, defence, fastness, fortress, mainstay, prop, rock, stronghold, support, tower of strength

bat bang, hit, punch, rap, smack, strike, swat, thump, wallop (*Inf.*), whack

batch accumulation, aggregation, amount, assemblage, bunch, collection, crowd, group, lot, pack, quantity, set

bath 1. *n.* ablution, cleansing, douche, douse, scrubbing, shower, soak, soaping, sponging, tub, wash, washing 2. *v.* bathe, clean, douse, lave (*Archaic*), scrub down, shower, soak, soap, sponge, tub, wash

bathe 1. *v.* cleanse, cover, dunk, flood, immerse, moisten, rinse, soak, steep, suffuse, wash, wet 2. *n.* dip, dook (*Scot.*), swim, wash

bathetic anticlimactic, mawkish, sentimental

bathing costume bathing suit, bikini, swimming costume, swimsuit, trunks

bathos anticlimax, false pathos, letdown, mawkishness, sentimentality

baton club, crook, mace, rod, sceptre, staff, stick, truncheon, wand

battalion army, brigade, company, contingent, division, force, horde, host, legion, multitude, regiment, squadron, throng

batten[1] board up, clamp down, cover up, fasten, fasten down, fix, nail down, secure, tighten

batten[2] fatten, flourish, gain, grow, increase, prosper, thrive, wax

batter 1. assault, bash (*Inf.*), beat, belabour, break, buffet, clobber (*Sl.*), dash against, lambast(e), lash, pelt, pound, pummel, smash, smite, thrash, wallop (*Inf.*) 2. bruise, crush, deface, demolish, destroy, disfigure, hurt, injure, mangle, mar, maul, ruin, shatter, shiver, total (*Sl.*), trash (*Sl.*)

battered beaten, beat-up (*Inf.*), broken-down, bruised, crushed, damaged, dilapidated, injured, ramshackle, squashed, weather-beaten

battery 1. chain, ring, sequence, series, set, suite 2. assault, attack, beating, mayhem, onslaught, physical violence, thumping 3. artillery, cannon, cannonry, gun emplacements, guns

battle *n.* 1. action, attack, combat, encounter, engagement, fight, fray, hostilities, skirmish, war, warfare 2. agitation, campaign, clash, conflict, contest, controversy, crusade, debate, disagreement, dispute, head-to-head, strife, struggle ~*v.* 3. agitate, argue, clamour, combat, contend, contest, dispute, feud, fight, strive, struggle, war

Antonyms *n.* accord, agreement, armistice, ceasefire, concord, entente, peace, suspension of hostilities, truce

battle-axe ballbreaker (*Sl.*), disciplinarian, fury, harridan, scold, shrew, tartar, termagant, virago, vixen

battle cry catchword, motto, slogan, war cry, war whoop, watchword

battlefield battleground, combat zone, field, field of battle, front

battlement barbican, bartizan, bastion, breastwork, bulwark, crenellation, fortification, parapet, rampart

battleship capital ship, gunboat, man-of-war, ship of the line, warship

batty barking (*Sl.*), barking mad (*Sl.*), barmy (*Sl.*), bats (*Sl.*), bonkers (*Sl., chiefly Brit.*), cracked (*Sl.*), crackers (*Brit. sl.*), crackpot (*Inf.*), cranky (*Inf.*), crazy, daft (*Inf.*), dotty (*Sl., chiefly Brit.*), eccentric, insane, loony (*Sl.*), loopy (*Inf.*), lunatic, mad, not the full shilling (*Inf.*), nuts (*Sl.*), nutty (*Sl.*), odd, oddball (*Inf.*), off one's rocker (*Sl.*), off one's trolley (*Sl.*), off-the-wall (*Sl.*), outré, out to lunch (*Inf.*), peculiar, potty (*Brit. inf.*), queer (*Inf.*), screwy (*Inf.*), touched, up the pole (*Inf.*), wacko (*Sl.*)

bauble bagatelle, gewgaw, gimcrack, kickshaw, knick-knack, plaything, toy, trifle, trinket

baulk *see* BALK

bawd brothel-keeper, madam, pimp, procuress, prostitute, whore, working girl (*Facetious sl.*)

bawdy blue, coarse, dirty, erotic, gross, indecent, indecorous, indelicate, lascivious, lecherous, lewd, libidinous, licentious, lustful, obscene, prurient, ribald, risqué, rude, salacious, smutty, steamy (*Inf.*), suggestive, vulgar

Antonyms chaste, clean, decent, good, modest, moral, respectable, seemly, undefiled, upright, virtuous

bawl 1. bellow, call, clamour, halloo, howl, roar, shout, vociferate, yell 2. blubber, cry, sob, squall, wail, weep

bay[1] bight, cove, gulf, inlet, natural harbour, sound

bay[2] alcove, compartment, embrasure, niche, nook, opening, recess

bay[3] 1. bark, bell, clamour, cry, growl, howl, yelp 2. **at bay** caught, cornered, trapped

bayonet *v.* impale, knife, run through, spear, stab, stick, transfix

bays chaplet, garland, glory, laurel crown, praise, prize, renown, trophy

bazaar 1. exchange, market, marketplace, mart 2. bring-and-buy, fair, fête, sale of work

be 1. be alive, breathe, exist, inhabit, live 2. befall, come about, come to pass, happen, occur, take place, transpire (*Inf.*) 3. abide, continue, endure, last, obtain, persist, prevail, remain, stand, stay, survive

beach coast, lido, littoral, margin, plage, sands, seaboard (*Chiefly U.S.*), seashore, seaside, shingle, shore, strand, water's edge

beachcomber forager, loafer, scavenger, scrounger, tramp, vagabond, vagrant, wanderer

beached abandoned, aground, ashore, deserted, grounded, high and dry, marooned, stranded, wrecked

beacon beam, bonfire, flare, lighthouse, pharos, rocket, sign, signal, signal fire, smoke signal, watchtower

bead blob, bubble, dot, drop, droplet, globule, pellet, pill, spherule

beads chaplet, choker, necklace, necklet, pearls, pendant, rosary

beak 1. bill, mandible, neb (*Archaic or dialect*), nib 2. nose, proboscis, snout 3. *Naut.* bow, prow, ram, rostrum, stem

beaked curved, hooked, pointed, sharp

beam *n.* 1. girder, joist, plank, rafter, spar, support, timber 2. bar, emission, gleam, glimmer, glint, glow, radiation, ray, shaft, streak, stream ~*v.* 3. broadcast, emit, glare, gleam, glitter, glow, radiate, shine, transmit 4. grin, laugh, smile

beaming 1. beautiful, bright, brilliant, flashing, gleaming, glistening, glittering, radiant, scintillating, shining, sparkling 2. cheerful, grinning, happy, joyful, smiling, sunny

bear 1. bring, carry, convey, hump (*Brit. sl.*), move, take, tote (*Inf.*), transport 2. cherish, entertain, exhibit, harbour, have, hold, maintain, possess, shoulder, support, sustain, uphold, weigh upon 3. abide, admit, allow, brook, endure, permit, put up with (*Inf.*), stomach, suffer, tolerate, undergo 4. beget, breed, bring forth, develop, engender, generate, give birth to, produce, yield
Antonyms abandon, cease, desert, discontinue, drop, give up, leave, put down, quit, relinquish, shed

bearable admissible, endurable, manageable, passable, sufferable, supportable, sustainable, tolerable
Antonyms insufferable, insupportable, intolerable, oppressive, too much (*Inf.*), unacceptable, unbearable, unendurable

beard 1. *n.* bristles, five-o'clock shadow, stubble, whiskers 2. *v.* brave, confront, dare, defy, face, oppose, tackle

bearded bewhiskered, bristly, bushy, hairy, hirsute, shaggy, stubbly, unshaven, whiskered

beardless 1. barefaced, clean-shaven, hairless, smooth, smooth-faced 2. callow, fresh, green, immature, inexperienced

bear down 1. burden, compress, encumber, press down, push, strain, weigh down 2. advance on, approach, attack, close in, converge on, move in

bearer 1. agent, carrier, conveyor, messenger, porter, runner, servant 2. beneficiary, consignee, payee

bearing 1. air, aspect, attitude, behaviour, carriage, demeanour, deportment, manner, mien, posture 2. *Naut.* course, direction, point of compass 3. application, connection, import, pertinence, reference, relation, relevance, significance
Antonyms (*sense 3*) inappositeness, inappropriateness, inaptness, inconsequence, irrelevance, irrelevancy, non sequitur

bearings aim, course, direction, location, orientation, position, situation, track, way, whereabouts

bearish 1. churlish, clumsy, gruff, rough, sullen, surly 2. *Stock Exchange* declining, falling, slumping

bear on affect, appertain to, belong to, concern, involve, pertain to, refer to, relate to, touch upon

bear out confirm, corroborate, endorse, justify, prove, substantiate, support, uphold, vindicate

bear up bear the brunt, carry on, endure, grin and bear it (*Inf.*), persevere, suffer, withstand

bear with be patient, forbear, make allowances, put up with (*Inf.*), suffer, tolerate, wait

beast 1. animal, brute, creature 2. barbarian, brute, fiend, ghoul, monster, ogre, sadist, savage, swine

beastly 1. animal, barbarous, bestial, brutal, brutish, coarse, cruel, depraved, inhuman, monstrous, repulsive, sadistic, savage 2. awful, disagreeable, foul, horrid, mean, nasty, rotten, shitty (*Taboo sl.*), terrible, unpleasant

Antonyms agreeable, fine, good, humane, pleasant, sensitive

beat *v.* 1. bang, batter, belt (*Inf.*), break, bruise, buffet, cane, chin (*Sl.*), clobber (*Sl.*), cudgel, deck (*Sl.*), drub, flog, hit, knock, lambast(e), lash, lay one on (*Sl.*), lick (*Inf.*), maul, pelt, pound, punch, strike, thrash, thwack, whip 2. best, blow out of the water (*Sl.*), clobber (*Sl.*), conquer, defeat, excel, lick (*Inf.*), master, outdo, outrun, outstrip, overcome, overwhelm, run rings around (*Inf.*), subdue, surpass, tank (*Sl.*), undo, vanquish, wipe the floor with (*Inf.*) 3. fashion, forge, form, hammer, model, shape, work 4. flap, flutter, palpitate, pound, pulsate, pulse, quake, quiver, shake, throb, thump, tremble, vibrate 5. **beat it** bugger off (*Taboo sl.*), depart, exit, fuck off (*Offens. taboo sl.*), get lost (*Inf.*), go away, hook it (*Sl.*), hop it (*Sl.*), leave, piss off (*Taboo sl.*), scarper (*Brit. sl.*), scram (*Inf.*), shoo, skedaddle (*Inf.*), vamoose (*Sl., chiefly U.S.*) ~*n.* 6. belt (*Inf.*), blow, hit, lash, punch, shake, slap, strike, swing, thump 7. flutter, palpitation, pulsation, pulse, throb 8. accent, cadence, measure (*Prosody*), metre, rhythm, stress, time 9. circuit, course, path, rounds, route, way ~*adj.* 10. *Sl.* clapped out (*Aust. & N.Z. inf.*), exhausted, fatigued, tired, wearied, worn out, zonked (*Sl.*)

beaten 1. baffled, cowed, defeated, disappointed, disheartened, frustrated, overcome, overwhelmed, thwarted, vanquished 2. forged, formed, hammered, shaped, stamped, worked 3. much travelled, trampled, trodden, well-trodden, well-used, worn 4. blended, foamy, frothy, mixed, stirred, whipped, whisked

beatific blessed, blissful, divine, ecstatic, enraptured, exalted, glorious, heavenly, joyful, rapt, rapturous, serene, sublime

beating 1. belting (*Inf.*), caning, chastisement, corporal punishment, flogging, pasting (*Sl.*), slapping, smacking, thrashing, whipping 2. conquest, defeat, downfall, overthrow, pasting (*Sl.*), rout, ruin

beatitude beatification, blessedness, bliss, ecstasy, exaltation, felicity, happiness, holy joy, saintliness

beat up assault, attack, batter, beat the living daylights out of (*Inf.*), clobber (*Sl.*), do over (*Brit., Aust., & N.Z. sl.*), duff up (*Brit. sl.*), fill in (*Brit. sl.*), knock about *or* around, lambast(e), put the boot in (*Sl.*), thrash

beau 1. admirer, boyfriend, escort, fancy man (*Sl.*), fiancé, guy (*Inf.*), leman (*Archaic*), lover, suitor, swain, sweetheart 2. cavalier, coxcomb, dandy, fop, gallant, ladies' man, popinjay, swell (*Inf.*)

beautiful alluring, appealing, attractive, charming, comely, delightful, drop-dead (*Sl.*), exquisite, fair, fine, glamorous, good-looking, gorgeous, graceful, handsome, lovely, pleasing, radiant, ravishing, stunning (*Inf.*)

Antonyms awful, bad, hideous, repulsive, terrible, ugly, unattractive, unpleasant, unsightly

beautify adorn, array, bedeck, deck, decorate, embellish, enhance, festoon, garnish, gild, glamorize, grace, ornament

beauty 1. allure, attractiveness, bloom, charm, comeliness, elegance, exquisiteness, fairness, glamour, grace, handsomeness, loveliness, pulchritude, seemliness, symmetry 2. belle, charmer, cracker (*Sl.*), goddess, good-looker, lovely (*Sl.*), stunner (*Inf.*), Venus 3. advantage, asset, attraction, benefit, blessing, boon, excellence, feature, good thing

Antonyms detraction, disadvantage, flaw, repulsiveness, ugliness, unpleasantness, unseemliness

beaver away exert oneself, graft (*Inf.*), hammer away, peg away, persevere, persist, plug away (*Inf.*), slog, work

becalmed motionless, settled, still, stranded, stuck

because as, by reason of, in that, on account of, owing to, since, thanks to

beck gesture, nod, signal, summons, wave

beckon 1. bid, gesticulate, gesture, motion, nod, signal, summon, wave at 2. allure, attract, call, coax, draw, entice, invite, lure, pull, tempt

becloud bedim, befog, complicate, confuse, darken, muddle, obfuscate, obscure, overcast, screen, veil

become 1. alter to, be transformed into, change into, develop into, evolve into, grow into, mature into, metamorphose into, ripen into 2. embellish, enhance, fit, flatter, grace, harmonize, ornament, set off, suit

becoming 1. attractive, comely, enhancing, flattering, graceful, neat, pretty, tasteful 2. appropriate, befitting, *comme il faut,* compatible, congruous, decent, decorous, fit, fitting, in keeping, meet (*Archaic*), proper, seemly, suitable, worthy

Antonyms improper, ugly, unattractive, unbecoming, unfit, unsuitable, unworthy

bed *n.* 1. bedstead, berth, bunk, cot, couch, divan, pallet 2. area, border, garden, patch, plot, row, strip 3. base, bottom, foundation, groundwork, substratum ~*v.* 4. base, embed, establish, fix, found, implant, insert, plant, settle, set up

bedaub besmear, smear, smirch, soil, spatter, splash, stain

bedazzle amaze, astound, bewilder, blind, captivate, confuse, daze, dazzle, dumbfound, enchant, overwhelm, stagger, stun

bedclothes bedding, bed linen, blankets, coverlets, covers, duvets, eiderdowns, pillowcases, pillows, quilts, sheets

bed down lie, retire, settle down, sleep, turn in (*Inf.*)

bedeck adorn, array, bedight (*Archaic*), bedizen (*Archaic*), decorate, embellish, festoon, garnish, ornament, trim

bedevil afflict, aggravate (*Inf.*), annoy, be on one's back (*Sl.*), confound, distress, fret, frustrate, get in one's hair (*Inf.*), get on one's nerves (*Inf.*), harass, hassle (*Inf.*), irk, irritate, pester, plague, torment, torture, trouble, vex, worry

bedew besprinkle, dampen, drench, moisten, shower, soak, spray, sprinkle, water, wet

bedim becloud, bedarken, cloak, cloud, darken, dim, obscure, overcast, shade, shadow

bedlam chaos, clamour, commotion, confusion, furore, hubbub, hullabaloo, madhouse (*Inf.*), noise, pandemonium, tumult, turmoil, uproar

bedraggled dirty, dishevelled, disordered, drenched, dripping, messy, muddied, muddy, sodden, soiled, stained, sullied, unkempt, untidy

bedridden confined, confined to bed, flat on one's back, incapacitated, laid up (*Inf.*)

bedrock 1. bed, bottom, foundation, nadir, rock bottom, substratum, substructure 2. basics, basis, core, essentials, fundamentals, roots

beef 1. *Inf.* brawn, flesh, heftiness, muscle, physique, robustness, sinew, strength 2. *Sl.* complaint, criticism, dispute, grievance, gripe (*Inf.*), grouch (*Inf.*), grouse, grumble, objection, protest, protestation

beefy *Inf.* 1. brawny, bulky, burly, hulking, muscular, stalwart, stocky, strapping, sturdy, thickset 2. chubby, corpulent, fat, fleshy, heavy, obese, overweight, paunchy, plump, podgy, portly, pudgy, rotund

Antonyms feeble, frail, puny, scrawny, skinny, weak

beetle, beetling *adj.* hanging over, jutting, leaning over, overhanging, pendent, projecting, prominent, protruding, sticking out, swelling over

befall bechance, betide, chance, come to pass, ensue, fall, follow, happen, materialize, occur, supervene, take place, transpire (*Inf.*)

befitting apposite, appropriate, becoming, fit, fitting, meet (*Archaic*), proper, right, seemly, suitable

Antonyms improper, inappropriate, irrelevant, unbecoming, unfit, unsuitable, wrong

befog becloud, blur, confuse, darken, fuzz, make hazy (indistinct, vague), muddle, obfuscate, obscure

befool bamboozle (*Inf.*), beguile, cheat, cozen, delude, dupe, fool, hoax, hoodwink, humbug, impose on, mislead, outwit, trick

before 1. *adv.* ahead, earlier, formerly, in advance, in front, previously, sooner 2. *prep.* earlier than, in advance of, in front of, in the presence of, prior to

Antonyms *adv.* after, afterwards, behind, later, subsequently, thereafter ~*prep.* after, behind, following, succeeding

beforehand ahead of time, already, before, before now, earlier, in advance, in anticipation, previously, sooner

befriend advise, aid, assist, back, benefit, encourage, favour, help, patronize, side with, stand by, succour, support, sustain, uphold, welcome

befuddle baffle, bewilder, confuse, daze, disorient, intoxicate, muddle, puzzle, stupefy

Antonyms clarify, clear up, elucidate, explicate, illuminate, interpret, make clear, make plain, resolve, simplify, throw *or* shed light on

befuddled confused, dazed, fuddled, groggy (*Inf.*), inebriated, intoxicated, muddled, woozy (*Inf.*)

beg 1. beseech, crave, desire, entreat, implore, importune, petition, plead, pray, request, solicit, supplicate 2. blag (*Sl.*), cadge, call for alms, mooch (*Sl.*), scrounge, seek charity, solicit charity, sponge on, touch (someone) for (*Sl.*) 3. *As in* **beg the question** avoid, dodge, duck (*Inf.*), equivocate, eschew, evade, fend off, flannel (*Brit. inf.*), hedge, parry, shirk, shun, sidestep

Antonyms (*sense 1*) apportion, award, bestow, commit, confer, contribute, donate, give, grant, impart, present (*sense 2*) claim, demand, exact, extort, insist on

beget 1. breed, father, generate, get, procreate, propagate, sire 2. bring, bring about, cause, create, effect, engender, give rise to, occasion, produce, result in

beggar *n.* 1. bag lady (*Chiefly U.S.*), bum (*Inf.*), cadger, mendicant, scrounger (*Inf.*), sponger (*Inf.*), supplicant, tramp, vagrant 2. bankrupt, down-and-out, pauper, starveling ~*v.* 3. *As in* **beggar description** baffle, challenge, defy, surpass

beggarly abject, base, contemptible, des~

picable, destitute, impoverished, inadequate, indigent, low, meagre, mean, miserly, needy, niggardly, pitiful, poor, poverty-stricken, stingy, vile, wretched

beggary bankruptcy, destitution, indigence, need, pauperism, poverty, vagrancy, want, wretchedness

begin 1. commence, embark on, inaugurate, initiate, instigate, institute, prepare, set about, set on foot, start 2. appear, arise, be born, come into being, come into existence, commence, crop up (*Inf.*), dawn, emerge, happen, originate, spring, start
Antonyms cease, complete, end, finish, stop, terminate

beginner amateur, apprentice, cub, fledgling, freshman, greenhorn (*Inf.*), initiate, learner, neophyte, novice, recruit, starter, student, tenderfoot, trainee, tyro
Antonyms authority, expert, master, old hand, old stager, old-timer, past master, past mistress, pro (*Inf.*), professional, trouper, veteran

beginning 1. birth, commencement, inauguration, inception, initiation, onset, opening, opening move, origin, outset, overture, preface, prelude, rise, rudiments, source, start, starting point 2. embryo, fount, fountainhead, germ, root, seed
Antonyms (*sense 1*) closing, completion, conclusion, end, ending, finish, termination

begrime besmirch, blacken, dirty, muddy, smear, smirch, soil, spatter, stain, sully, tarnish

begrudge be jealous, be reluctant, be stingy, envy, grudge, resent

beguile 1. befool, cheat, deceive, delude, dupe, fool, hoodwink, impose on, mislead, trick 2. amuse, charm, cheer, delight, distract, divert, engross, entertain, occupy, solace, tickle the fancy of
Antonyms alarm, alert, enlighten, put right

beguiling alluring, attractive, bewitching, captivating, charming, diverting, enchanting, entertaining, enthralling, interesting, intriguing

behalf account, advantage, benefit, defence, good, interest, part, profit, sake, side, support

behave 1. act, function, operate, perform, run, work 2. act correctly, conduct oneself properly, mind one's manners
Antonyms act up (*Inf.*), be bad, be insubordinate, be naughty, carry on (*Inf.*), get up to mischief (*Inf.*), misbehave, muck about (*Brit. sl.*)

behaviour 1. actions, bearing, carriage, comportment, conduct, demeanour, deportment, manner, manners, ways 2. action, functioning, operation, performance

behest bidding, charge, command, commandment, decree, dictate, direction, expressed desire, injunction, instruction, mandate, order, precept, wish

behind *prep.* 1. after, at the back of, at the rear of, following, later than 2. at the bottom of, causing, initiating, instigating, responsible for 3. backing, for, in agreement, on the side of, supporting *~adv.* 4. after, afterwards, following, in the wake (of), next, subsequently 5. behindhand, in arrears, in debt, overdue *~n.* 6. arse (*Taboo sl.*), ass (*U.S. & Canad. taboo sl.*), bottom, bum (*Brit. sl.*), buns (*U.S. sl.*), butt (*U.S. & Canad. inf.*), buttocks, derrière (*Euphemistic*), jacksy (*Brit. sl.*), posterior, rump, seat, tail (*Inf.*)
Antonyms (*sense 1*) earlier than, in advance of, in front of, in the presence of, prior to (*sense 4*) ahead, earlier, formerly, in advance, previously, sooner

behindhand backward, behind time, dilatory, late, remiss, slow, tardy

behind the times antiquated, dated, *démodé,* obsolete, old-fashioned, old hat, outmoded, out of date, passé
Antonyms advanced, avant-garde, experimental, far-out (*Sl.*), ground-breaking, innovative, pioneering, progressive, trendy (*Brit. inf.*), unconventional, way-out (*Inf.*)

behold 1. *v.* check, check out (*Inf.*), clock (*Brit. sl.*), consider, contemplate, discern, eye, eyeball (*U.S. sl.*), get a load of (*Inf.*), look at, observe, perceive, recce (*Sl.*), regard, scan, survey, take a dekko at (*Brit. sl.*), view, watch, witness 2. *interj.* lo, look, mark, observe, see, watch

beholden bound, grateful, indebted, obligated, obliged, owing, under obligation

behove be advisable, befit, be fitting, be incumbent upon, be necessary, benefit, be obligatory, beseem, be wise

beige biscuit, buff, *café au lait,* camel, cinnamon, coffee, cream, ecru, fawn, khaki, mushroom, neutral, oatmeal, sand, tan

being 1. actuality, animation, existence, life, living, reality 2. entity, essence, nature, soul, spirit, substance 3. animal, beast, body, creature, human being, individual, living thing, mortal, thing
Antonyms nihility, nonbeing, nonexistence, nothingness, nullity, oblivion

belabour 1. batter, beat, clobber (*Sl.*), flog, lambast(e), thrash, whip 2. attack, berate, blast, castigate, censure, criticize, excoriate, flay, lambast(e), lay into (*Inf.*), put down, tear into (*Inf.*)

belated behindhand, behind time, delayed, late, overdue, tardy

belch 1. burp (*Inf.*), eruct, eructate, hiccup 2. discharge, disgorge, emit, erupt, give off, gush, spew forth, vent, vomit

beleaguer 1. assail, beset, besiege, blockade, encompass, environ, hem in, surround 2. aggravate (*Inf.*), annoy, badger, be on one's back (*Sl.*), bother, get in one's hair (*Inf.*), get on one's nerves (*Inf.*), harass, hassle (*Inf.*), pester, vex

beleaguered badgered, beset, besieged, bothered, harassed, nagged, persecuted, plagued, put upon, set upon, vexed

belie 1. confute, contradict, deny, disprove, gainsay (*Archaic or literary*), give the lie to, negate, rebut, repudiate 2. conceal, deceive, disguise, falsify, gloss over, mislead, misrepresent

belief 1. admission, assent, assurance, confidence, conviction, credit, feeling, impression, judgment, notion, opinion, persuasion, presumption, reliance, theory, trust, view 2. credence, credo, creed, doctrine, dogma, faith, ideology, principles, tenet
Antonyms disbelief, distrust, doubt, dubiety, incredulity, mistrust, scepticism

believable acceptable, authentic, credible, creditable, imaginable, likely, plausible, possible, probable, reliable, trustworthy, verisimilar
Antonyms doubtful, dubious, fabulous, implausible, incredible, questionable, unacceptable, unbelievable

believe 1. accept, be certain of, be convinced of, buy (*Sl.*), count on, credit, depend on, have faith in, hold, place confidence in, presume true, rely on, swallow (*Inf.*), swear by, trust 2. assume, conjecture, consider, gather, guess (*Inf., chiefly U.S. & Canad.*), imagine, judge, maintain, postulate, presume, reckon, speculate, suppose, think
Antonyms disbelieve, distrust, doubt, know, question

believer adherent, convert, devotee, disciple, follower, proselyte, protagonist, supporter, upholder, zealot
Antonyms agnostic, atheist, disbeliever, doubting Thomas, infidel, sceptic, unbeliever

belittle decry, deprecate, depreciate, deride, derogate, detract, diminish, disparage, downgrade, minimize, scoff at, scorn, sneer at, underestimate, underrate, undervalue
Antonyms boast about, elevate, exalt, magnify, praise, vaunt

bellicose aggressive, antagonistic, belligerent, combative, defiant, hawkish, hostile, jingoistic, militaristic, provocative, pugnacious, quarrelsome, sabre-rattling, warlike, warloving, warmongering

belligerence aggressiveness, animosity, antagonism, combativeness, hostility, pugnacity, unfriendliness

belligerent 1. *adj.* aggressive, antagonistic, argumentative, bellicose, combative, contentious, hostile, litigious, pugnacious, quarrelsome, unfriendly, warlike, warring 2. *n.* combatant, fighter, warring nation
Antonyms amicable, benign, conciliatory, friendly, harmonious, nonviolent, without hostility

bellow bell, bawl, call, clamour, cry, howl, roar, scream, shout, shriek, yell

belly 1. *n.* abdomen, breadbasket (*Sl.*), corporation (*Inf.*), gut, insides (*Inf.*), paunch, potbelly, stomach, tummy, vitals 2. *v.* billow, bulge, fill, spread, swell, swell out

belong 1. *With* **to** be at the disposal of, be held by, be owned by, be the property of 2. *With* **to** be affiliated to, be allied to, be a member of, be associated with, be included in 3. attach to, be connected with, be fitting, be part of, fit, go with, have as a proper place, pertain to, relate to

belonging acceptance, affiliation, affinity, association, attachment, fellowship, inclusion, kinship, loyalty, rapport, relationship

belongings accoutrements, chattels, effects, gear, goods, paraphernalia, personal property, possessions, stuff, things

beloved admired, adored, cherished, darling, dear, dearest, loved, pet, precious, prized, revered, sweet, treasured, worshipped

below *adv.* 1. beneath, down, lower, under, underneath *~prep.* 2. inferior, lesser, lesser than, subject, subordinate, unworthy of 3. **below par** below average, imperfect, inferior, off colour, off form, poor, second-rate, unfit

belt 1. band, cincture, cummerbund, girdle, girth, sash, waistband 2. *Geog.* area, district, layer, region, stretch, strip, tract, zone 3. **below the belt** cowardly, foul, not playing the game (*Inf.*), unfair, unjust, unscrupulous, unsporting, unsportsmanlike

bemoan bewail, deplore, express sorrow, grieve for, lament, moan over, mourn, regret, rue, weep for

bemuse amaze, bewilder, confuse, daze, flummox, muddle, nonplus, overwhelm, perplex, puzzle, stun

bemused absent-minded, at sea, bewildered, confused, dazed, engrossed, flummoxed, fuddled, half-drunk, muddled, nonplussed, perplexed, preoccupied, stunned, stupefied, tipsy

bench 1. form, pew, seat, settle, stall 2. board, counter, table, trestle table, workbench, worktable 3. court, courtroom, judge, judges, judiciary, magistrate, magistrates, tribunal

benchmark criterion, example, gauge, level, measure, model, norm, par, reference, reference point, standard, touchstone, yardstick

bend *v.* 1. arc, arch, bow, buckle, contort, crouch, curve, deflect, diverge, flex, incline, incurvate, lean, stoop, swerve, turn, twist, veer, warp 2. compel, direct, influence, mould, persuade, shape, subdue, submit, sway, yield ~*n.* 3. angle, arc, arch, bow, corner, crook, curve, hook, loop, turn, twist, zigzag

beneath 1. *adv.* below, in a lower place, underneath 2. *prep.* below, inferior to, less than, lower than, unbefitting, underneath, unworthy of
Antonyms (*sense 2*) above, atop, beyond, exceeding, higher than, on top of, over, upon

benediction beatitude, *benedictus,* benison, blessing, consecration, favour, grace, gratitude, invocation, orison, prayer, thankfulness, thanksgiving

benefaction 1. beneficence, benevolence, charity, generosity, largess *or* largesse, liberality, munificence, philanthropy 2. alms, bequest, boon, charity, contribution, donation, endowment, gift, grant, gratuity, hand-out, largess *or* largesse, legacy, offering, present, stipend

benefactor angel (*Inf.*), backer, contributor, donor, helper, patron, philanthropist, promoter, sponsor, subscriber, subsidizer, supporter, well-wisher

benefice Church living, emolument, incumbency, office, prebend, preferment, sinecure, stipend

beneficence 1. altruism, benevolence, compassion, generosity, goodness, good will, helpfulness, kindness, largess *or* largesse, liberality, love, unselfishness, virtue 2. aid, benefaction, bestowal, donation, gift, hand-out, largess *or* largesse, present, relief, succour

beneficent benevolent, benign, bounteous, bountiful, charitable, generous, helpful, kind, liberal, munificent, princely

beneficial advantageous, benign, expedient, favourable, gainful, healthful, helpful, profitable, salubrious, salutary, serviceable, useful, valuable, wholesome
Antonyms detrimental, disadvantageous, harmful, pernicious, useless

beneficiary assignee, heir, inheritor, legatee, payee, receiver, recipient, successor

benefit 1. *n.* advantage, aid, asset, assistance, avail, betterment, blessing, boon, favour, gain, good, help, interest, profit, use 2. *v.* advance, advantage, aid, ameliorate, assist, avail, better, enhance, further, improve, profit, promote, serve
Antonyms *n.* damage, detriment, disadvantage, downside, harm, impairment, injury, loss ~*v.* damage, deprive, detract from, harm, impair, injure, worsen

benevolence altruism, charity, compassion, fellow feeling, generosity, goodness, good will, humanity, kind-heartedness, kindness, sympathy
Antonyms ill will, malevolence, selfishness, stinginess, unkindness

benevolent affable, altruistic, beneficent, benign, bounteous, bountiful, caring, charitable, compassionate, considerate, generous, humane, humanitarian, kind, kind-hearted, liberal, philanthropic, tender-hearted, warm-hearted, well-disposed

benighted backward, crude, ignorant, illiterate, primitive, uncivilized, uncultivated, unenlightened

benign 1. affable, amiable, complaisant, friendly, generous, genial, gracious, kind, kindly, liberal, obliging, sympathetic 2. balmy, gentle, healthful, mild, refreshing, temperate, warm, wholesome 3. advantageous, auspicious, beneficial, encouraging, favourable, good, lucky, propitious, salutary 4. *Medical* curable, harmless, limited, remediable, slight, superficial
Antonyms bad, disobliging, harsh, hateful, inhumane, malicious, malign, severe, stern, unfavourable, unkind, unlucky, unpleasant, unsympathetic

bent *adj.* 1. angled, arched, bowed, crooked, curved, hunched, stooped, twisted 2. *With* **on** determined, disposed, fixed, inclined, insistent, predisposed, resolved, set ~*n.* 3. ability, aptitude, bag (*Sl.*), cup of tea (*Inf.*), facility, faculty, flair, forte, inclination, knack, leaning, penchant, preference, proclivity, propensity, talent, tendency
Antonyms (*sense 1*) aligned, erect, even, horizontal, in line, level, perpendicular, plumb, smooth, square, straight, true, upright, vertical

benumb anaesthetize, chill, deaden, freeze, numb, paralyse, shock, stun, stupefy

benumbed anaesthetized, dazed, deadened, frozen, immobilized, insensible, insensitive, numb, paralysed, stunned, stupefied, unfeeling, unresponsive

bequeath bestow, commit, endow, entrust, give, grant, hand down, impart, leave to by will, pass on, transmit, will

bequest bequeathal, bestowal, dower, endowment, estate, gift, heritage, inheritance, legacy, settlement, trust

berate bawl out (*Inf.*), blast, carpet (*Inf.*), castigate, censure, chew out (*U.S. & Canad. inf.*), chide, criticize, excoriate, give a rocket (*Brit. & N.Z. inf.*), lambast(e), put down, rail at, read the riot act, rebuke, reprimand, reproach, reprove, revile, scold, tear into (*Inf.*), tear (someone) off a strip (*Brit. inf.*), tell off (*Inf.*), upbraid, vituperate
Antonyms acclaim, admire, applaud, approve, cheer, commend, compliment, congratulate, extol, laud, praise

bereave afflict, deprive of kindred, dispossess, divest, make destitute, strip, take away from, widow

bereavement affliction, death, deprivation, loss, misfortune, tribulation

bereft cut off, deprived, destitute, devoid, lacking, minus, parted from, robbed of, shorn, wanting

berserk amok, ape (*Sl.*), apeshit (*Sl.*), crazy, enraged, frantic, frenzied, insane, mad, maniacal, manic, rabid, raging, uncontrollable, violent, wild

berth *n.* 1. bed, billet, bunk, cot (*Naut.*), hammock 2. anchorage, dock, harbour, haven, pier, port, quay, slip, wharf 3. appointment, employment, job, living, position, post, situation ~*v.* 4. *Naut.* anchor, dock, drop anchor, land, moor, tie up

beseech adjure, ask, beg, call upon, crave, entreat, implore, importune, petition, plead, pray, solicit, sue, supplicate

beset 1. assail, attack, besiege, encircle, enclose, encompass, environ, hem in, surround 2. *Fig.* badger, bedevil, embarrass, entangle, harass, perplex, pester, plague

besetting habitual, harassing, inveterate, persistent, prevalent, troublesome

beside 1. abreast of, adjacent to, alongside, at the side of, close to, near, nearby, neighbouring, next door to, next to, overlooking 2. **beside oneself** apoplectic, berserk, crazed, delirious, demented, deranged, desperate, distraught, frantic, frenzied, insane, mad, out of one's mind, unbalanced, uncontrolled, unhinged

besides 1. *adv.* also, as well, further, furthermore, in addition, moreover, otherwise, too, what's more 2. *prep.* apart from, barring, excepting, excluding, in addition to, other than, over and above, without

beside the point extraneous, immaterial, inapplicable, inapposite, inappropriate, inconsequent, irrelevant, neither here nor there, unconnected
Antonyms admissible, applicable, apposite, appropriate, appurtenant, apt, fitting, germane, pertinent, relevant, significant, to the point

besiege 1. beleaguer, beset, blockade, confine, encircle, encompass, environ, hedge in, hem in, invest (*Rare*), lay siege to, shut in, surround 2. badger, bend someone's ear (*Inf.*), bother, harass, harry, hassle (*Inf.*), hound, importune, nag, pester, plague, trouble

besmirch daub, defame, dishonour, slander, smear, smirch, soil, stain, sully, tarnish

besotted 1. befuddled, bevvied (*Dialect*), blitzed (*Sl.*), blotto (*Sl.*), bombed (*Sl.*), drunk, intoxicated, legless (*Inf.*), lit up (*Sl.*), out of it (*Sl.*), out to it (*Aust. & N.Z. sl.*), paralytic (*Inf.*), pissed (*Taboo sl.*), smashed (*Sl.*), steamboats (*Sl.*), steaming (*Sl.*), stupefied, wasted (*Sl.*), wrecked (*Sl.*), zonked (*Sl.*) 2. doting, hypnotized, infatuated, smitten, spellbound 3. confused, foolish, muddled, witless

bespatter bedaub, befoul, begrime, besmirch, besprinkle, muddy, smear, spatter, splatter, sully

bespeak 1. engage, order beforehand, prearrange, solicit 2. betoken, denote, display, evidence, evince, exhibit, foretell, imply, indicate, predict, proclaim, reveal, show, signify, suggest, testify to

best *adj.* 1. chief, finest, first, first-class, first-rate, foremost, highest, leading, most excellent, outstanding, perfect, pre-eminent, principal, superlative, supreme, unsurpassed 2. advantageous, apt, correct, golden, most desirable, most fitting, right 3. greatest, largest, most ~*adv.* 4. advantageously, attractively, excellently, most fortunately 5. extremely, greatly, most deeply, most fully, most highly ~*n.* 6. choice, cream, elite, favourite, finest, first, flower, pick, prime, top 7. hardest, highest endeavour, utmost ~*v.* 8. beat, blow out of the water (*Sl.*), conquer, defeat, get the better of, lick (*Inf.*), master, outclass, outdo, run rings around (*Inf.*), surpass, tank (*Sl.*), thrash, triumph over, trounce, undo, wipe the floor with (*Inf.*)

bestial animal, barbaric, barbarous, beastlike, beastly, brutal, brutish, carnal, degraded, depraved, gross, inhuman, low, savage, sensual, sordid, vile

bestir activate, actuate, animate, awaken, exert, get going, incite, motivate, rouse, set off, stimulate, stir up, trouble

bestow accord, allot, apportion, award, commit, confer, donate, entrust, give, grant, hand out, honour with, impart, lavish, present, render to

Antonyms acquire, attain, come by, earn, gain, get, make, net, obtain, procure, secure

bestride bestraddle, bridge, dominate, extend, mount, span, step over, straddle, tower over

bet 1. *n.* ante, gamble, hazard, long shot, pledge, risk, speculation, stake, venture, wager 2. *v.* chance, gamble, hazard, pledge, punt (*Chiefly Brit.*), put money on, risk, speculate, stake, venture, wager

bête noire abomination, anathema, aversion, bane, bugbear, curse, pet hate

bethink cogitate, consider, ponder, recall, recollect, reconsider, reflect, remember, review, take thought

betide bechance, befall, chance, come to pass, crop up (*Inf.*), ensue, happen, occur, overtake, supervene, take place, transpire (*Inf.*)

betimes anon, beforehand, before long, erelong (*Archaic or poetic*), early, first thing, in good time, punctually, seasonably, soon

betoken augur, bespeak, bode, declare, denote, evidence, indicate, manifest, mark, portend, presage, prognosticate, promise, represent, signify, suggest, typify

betray 1. be disloyal (treacherous, unfaithful), break one's promise, break with, double-cross (*Inf.*), inform on *or* against, sell down the river (*Inf.*), sell out (*Inf.*), shop (*Sl., chiefly Brit.*) 2. blurt out, disclose, divulge, evince, expose, give away, lay bare, let slip, manifest, reveal, show, tell, tell on, uncover, unmask 3. beguile, corrupt, deceive, delude, dupe, ensnare, entrap, lead astray, mislead, undo 4. abandon, desert, forsake, jilt, walk out on

betrayal 1. deception, disloyalty, double-cross (*Inf.*), double-dealing, duplicity, falseness, perfidy, sell-out (*Inf.*), treachery, treason, trickery, unfaithfulness 2. blurting out, disclosure, divulgence, giving away, revelation, telling

Antonyms (*sense 1*) allegiance, constancy, devotion, faithfulness, fealty, fidelity, loyalty, steadfastness, trustiness, trustworthiness (*sense 2*) guarding, keeping, keeping secret, preserving, safeguarding

betrayer apostate, conspirator, deceiver, renegade, traitor

betroth affiance, contract, engage to marry, pledge in marriage, plight, plight one's troth, promise

betrothal affiancing, betrothing, engagement, espousal (*Archaic*), marriage compact, plight, promise, troth, vow

better *adj.* 1. bigger, excelling, finer, fitter, greater, higher quality, larger, more appropriate (desirable, expert, fitting, suitable, useful, valuable), preferable, superior, surpassing, worthier 2. cured, fitter, fully recovered, healthier, improving, less ill, mending, more healthy, on the mend (*Inf.*), progressing, recovering, stronger, well 3. bigger, greater, larger, longer ~*adv.* 4. in a more excellent manner, in a superior way, more advantageously (attractively, competently, completely, effectively, thoroughly), to a greater degree ~*v.* 5. advance, ameliorate, amend, correct, enhance, forward, further, improve, meliorate, mend, promote, raise, rectify, reform 6. beat, cap (*Inf.*), clobber (*Sl.*), exceed, excel, improve on *or* upon, lick (*Inf.*), outdo, outstrip, run rings around (*Inf.*), surpass, top ~*n.* 7. **get the better of** beat, best, defeat, get the upper hand, outdo, outsmart (*Inf.*), outwit, prevail over, score off, surpass, triumph over, worst

Antonyms *adj.* inferior, lesser, smaller, substandard, worse ~*adv.* worse ~*v.* depress, devaluate, go downhill, impoverish, lessen, lower, weaken, worsen

betterment amelioration, edification, improvement, melioration

between amidst, among, betwixt, halfway, in the middle of, mid

bevel 1. *n.* angle, bezel, cant, chamfer, diagonal, mitre, oblique, slant, slope 2. *v.* cant, chamfer, cut at an angle, mitre

beverage bevvy (*Dialect*), draught, drink, libation (*Facetious*), liquid, liquor, potable, potation, refreshment

bevy 1. band, bunch (*Inf.*), collection, company, crowd, gathering, group, pack, troupe 2. covey, flight, flock

bewail bemoan, cry over, deplore, express sorrow, grieve for, keen, lament, moan, mourn, regret, repent, rue, wail, weep over

beware avoid, be careful (cautious, wary), guard against, heed, look out, mind, refrain from, shun, steer clear of, take heed, watch out

bewilder baffle, befuddle, bemuse, confound, confuse, daze, flummox, mix up, mystify, nonplus, perplex, puzzle, stupefy

bewildered at sea, awed, baffled, bamboozled (*Inf.*), confused, disconcerted, dizzy, flummoxed, giddy, mystified, nonplussed, perplexed, puzzled, speechless, startled, stunned, surprised, taken aback, uncertain

bewitch absorb, allure, attract, beguile, captivate, charm, enchant, enrapture, entrance, fascinate, hypnotize, ravish, spellbind

Antonyms disgust, give one the creeps (*Inf.*), make one sick, offend, repel, repulse, sicken, turn off (*Inf.*)

bewitched charmed, enchanted, entranced, mesmerized, possessed, spellbound, transformed, under a spell, unrecognizable

beyond above, apart from, at a distance, away from, before, farther, out of range, out of reach, outwith (*Scot.*), over, past, remote, superior to, yonder

bias *n.* 1. bent, bigotry, favouritism, inclination, intolerance, leaning, narrow-mindedness, one-sidedness, partiality, penchant, predilection, predisposition, prejudice, proclivity, proneness, propensity, tendency, turn, unfairness 2. angle, cross, diagonal line, slant ~*v.* 3. distort, influence, predispose, prejudice, slant, sway, twist, warp, weight
Antonyms (*sense 1*) equality, equity, fairness, impartiality, neutrality, objectivity, open-mindedness

biased distorted, embittered, jaundiced, one-sided, partial, predisposed, prejudiced, slanted, swayed, twisted, warped, weighted

bicker argue, disagree, dispute, fight, quarrel, row (*Inf.*), scrap (*Inf.*), spar, squabble, wrangle
Antonyms accord, acquiesce, agree, assent, concur, cooperate, get on, harmonize

bid *v.* 1. offer, proffer, propose, submit, tender 2. call, greet, say, tell, wish 3. ask, call, charge, command, desire, direct, enjoin, instruct, invite, require, solicit, summon, tell ~*n.* 4. advance, amount, offer, price, proposal, proposition, submission, sum, tender 5. attempt, crack (*Inf.*), effort, endeavour, go (*Inf.*), stab (*Inf.*), try, venture

biddable amenable, complaisant, cooperative, docile, obedient, teachable, tractable
Antonyms awkward, difficult, disobedient, intractable, petulant, querulous, refractory, unruly

bidding 1. beck, behest, call, canon, charge, command, demand, direction, injunction, instruction, invitation, order, request, summons 2. auction, offer, offers, proposal, tender

big 1. bulky, burly, colossal, considerable, elephantine, enormous, extensive, gigantic, great, huge, hulking, humongous *or* humungous (*U.S. sl.*), immense, large, mammoth, massive, ponderous, prodigious, sizable, spacious, substantial, vast, voluminous 2. big-time (*Inf.*), eminent, important, influential, leading, main, major league (*Inf.*), momentous, paramount, powerful, prime, principal, prominent, serious, significant, valuable, weighty 3. adult, elder, grown, grown-up, mature 4. altruistic, benevolent, generous, gracious, heroic, magnanimous, noble, princely, unselfish 5. arrogant, boastful, bragging, conceited, haughty, inflated, pompous, pretentious, proud
Antonyms (*senses 1 & 3*) diminutive, immature, insignificant, little, mini, miniature, petite, pint-sized (*Inf.*), pocket-sized, pygmy *or* pigmy, small, tiny, wee, young (*sense 2*) humble, ignoble, insignificant, minor, modest, ordinary, unimportant, unknown

bigot dogmatist, fanatic, persecutor, sectarian, zealot

bigoted biased, dogmatic, illiberal, intolerant, narrow-minded, obstinate, opinionated, prejudiced, sectarian, twisted, warped
Antonyms broad-minded, equitable, open-minded, tolerant, unbiased, unbigoted, unprejudiced

bigotry bias, discrimination, dogmatism, fanaticism, ignorance, injustice, intolerance, mindlessness, narrow-mindedness, pig-ignorance (*Sl.*), prejudice, provincialism, racialism, racism, sectarianism, sexism, unfairness
Antonyms broad-mindedness, forbearance, open-mindedness, permissiveness, tolerance

bigwig big cheese (*Sl., old-fashioned*), big gun (*Inf.*), big noise (*Inf.*), big shot (*Inf.*), celeb (*Inf.*), celebrity, dignitary, heavyweight (*Inf.*), mogul, nob (*Sl.*), notability, notable, panjandrum, personage, somebody, V.I.P.
Antonyms cipher, lightweight (*Inf.*), nobody, nonentity, nothing, zero

bile anger, bitterness, churlishness, ill humour, irascibility, irritability, nastiness, peevishness, rancour, spleen

bilious 1. liverish, nauseated, out of sorts, queasy, sick 2. bad-tempered, cantankerous, crabby, cross, crotchety, edgy, grouchy (*Inf.*), grumpy, ill-humoured, ill-tempered, irritable, nasty, peevish, ratty (*Brit. & N.Z. inf.*), short-tempered, testy, tetchy, touchy

bilk bamboozle (*Inf.*), cheat, con (*Inf.*), cozen, deceive, defraud, do (*Sl.*), fleece, rook (*Sl.*), skin (*Sl.*), stiff (*Sl.*), swindle, trick

bill[1] *n.* 1. account, charges, invoice, note of charge, reckoning, score, statement, tally 2. advertisement, broadsheet, bulletin, circular, handbill, handout, leaflet, notice, placard, playbill, poster 3. agenda, card, catalogue, inventory, list, listing, programme, roster, schedule, syllabus 4. measure, piece of legislation, projected law, proposal ~*v.* 5. charge, debit, figure, invoice, reckon, record 6. advertise, announce, give advance notice of, post

bill[2] beak, mandible, neb (*Archaic or dialect*), nib

billet 1. *n.* accommodation, barracks, lodging, quarters 2. *v.* accommodate, berth, quarter, station

billow *n.* 1. breaker, crest, roller, surge, swell, tide, wave 2. cloud, deluge, flood, outpouring, rush, surge, wave ~*v.* 3. balloon, belly, puff up, rise up, roll, surge, swell

billowy heaving, rippling, rolling, surging, swelling, swirling, undulating, waving, wavy

bind *v.* 1. attach, fasten, glue, hitch, lash, paste, rope, secure, stick, strap, tie, tie up, truss, wrap 2. compel, constrain, engage, force, necessitate, obligate, oblige, prescribe, require 3. confine, detain, hamper, hinder, restrain, restrict 4. bandage, cover, dress, encase, swathe, wrap 5. border, edge, finish, hem, trim ~*n.* 6. *Inf.* bore, difficulty, dilemma, drag (*Inf.*), hot water (*Inf.*), nuisance, pain in the arse (*Taboo inf.*), predicament, quandary, spot (*Inf.*), tight spot
Antonyms (*senses 1 & 3*) free, loosen, release, unbind, undo, unfasten, untie

binding *adj.* compulsory, conclusive, imperative, indissoluble, irrevocable, mandatory, necessary, obligatory, unalterable
Antonyms discretionary, free, noncompulsory, optional, uncompelled, unconstrained, unforced, voluntary

binge beano (*Brit. sl.*), bender (*Inf.*), blind (*Sl.*), bout, feast, fling, jag (*Sl.*), orgy, spree

biography account, curriculum vitae, CV, life, life history, life story, memoir, memoirs, profile, record

birth 1. childbirth, delivery, nativity, parturition 2. beginning, emergence, fountainhead, genesis, origin, rise, source 3. ancestry, background, blood, breeding, derivation, descent, extraction, forebears, genealogy, line, lineage, nobility, noble extraction, parentage, pedigree, race, stock, strain
Antonyms (*senses 1 & 2*) death, demise, end, extinction, passing, passing away *or* on

bisect bifurcate, cross, cut across, cut in half, cut in two, divide in two, halve, intersect, separate, split, split down the middle

bisexual AC/DC (*Sl.*), ambidextrous (*Sl.*), androgyne, androgynous, bi (*Sl.*), epicene, gynandromorphic *or* gynandromorphous (*Entomology*), gynandrous, hermaphrodite, hermaphroditic, monoclinous (*Bot.*), swinging both ways (*Sl.*)

bishopric diocese, episcopacy, episcopate, primacy, see

bit[1] 1. atom, chip, crumb, fragment, grain, iota, jot, mite, morsel, mouthful, part, piece, remnant, scrap, segment, slice, small piece, speck, tittle, whit 2. instant, jiffy (*Inf.*), little while, minute, moment, period, second, spell, tick (*Brit. inf.*), time

bit[2] 1. brake, check, curb, restraint, snaffle 2. **take the bit in** *or* **between one's teeth** defy, disobey, get stuck into (*Inf.*), get to grips with, rebel, resist, revolt, run amok, rush into, set about

bitchy backbiting, catty (*Inf.*), cruel, malicious, mean, nasty, rancorous, shrewish, snide, spiteful, venomous, vicious, vindictive, vixenish
Antonyms charitable, generous, gracious, kindly, magnanimous, nice

bite *v.* 1. champ, chew, clamp, crunch, crush, cut, gnaw, grip, hold, masticate, nibble, nip, pierce, pinch, rend, seize, snap, tear, wound 2. burn, corrode, eat away, eat into, erode, smart, sting, tingle, wear away ~*n.* 3. itch, nip, pinch, prick, smarting, sting, tooth marks, wound 4. food, light meal, morsel, mouthful, piece, refreshment, snack, taste 5. edge, kick (*Inf.*), piquancy, punch (*Inf.*), pungency, spice

biting 1. bitter, blighting, cold, cutting, freezing, harsh, nipping, penetrating, piercing, sharp 2. caustic, cutting, incisive, mordacious, mordant, sarcastic, scathing, severe, sharp, stinging, trenchant, vitriolic, withering

bitter 1. acerb, acid, acrid, astringent, sharp, sour, tart, unsweetened, vinegary 2. acrimonious, begrudging, crabbed, embittered, hostile, morose, rancorous, resentful, sore, sour, sullen, with a chip on one's shoulder 3. calamitous, cruel, dire, distressing, galling, grievous, harsh, heartbreaking, merciless, painful, poignant, ruthless, savage, vexatious 4. biting, fierce, freezing, intense, severe, stinging
Antonyms appreciative, balmy, bland, fortunate, friendly, gentle, grateful, happy, mellow, mild, pleasant, sugary, sweet, thankful

bitterness 1. acerbity, acidity, sharpness, sourness, tartness, vinegariness 2. animosity, grudge, hostility, pique, rancour, resentment 3. acrimoniousness, asperity, sarcasm, venom, virulence

bizarre abnormal, comical, curious, eccentric, extraordinary, fantastic, freakish, grotesque, ludicrous, odd, oddball (*Inf.*), offbeat, off-the-wall (*Sl.*), outlandish, outré, peculiar, queer, ridiculous, rum (*Brit. sl.*), strange, unusual, wacko (*Sl.*), way-out (*Inf.*), weird, zany
Antonyms common, customary, normal, ordinary, regular, routine, standard, typical

blab blow wide open (*Sl.*), blurt out, disclose, divulge, gossip, let slip, reveal, shop (*Sl., chiefly Brit.*), sing (*Sl., chiefly U.S.*), spill one's guts (*Sl.*), tattle, tell, tell all, tell on

blabber 1. *n.* busybody, gossip, informer, rumour-monger, scandalmonger, talebearer, tattler, telltale 2. *v.* blather, blether (*Scot.*), chatter, gab (*Inf.*), jabber, prattle

blabbermouth bigmouth (*Sl.*), blatherskite, flibbertigibbet, gossip, loudmouth (*Inf.*), motormouth (*Sl.*), windbag (*Sl.*)

black *adj.* 1. coal-black, dark, dusky, ebony, inky, jet, murky, pitchy, raven, sable, starless, stygian, swarthy 2. *Fig.* atrocious, depressing, dismal, distressing, doleful, foreboding, funereal, gloomy, hopeless, horrible, lugubrious, mournful, ominous, sad, sombre 3. dingy, dirty, filthy, grimy, grubby, soiled, sooty, stained 4. angry, furious, hostile, menacing, resentful, sullen, threatening 5. bad, evil, iniquitous, nefarious, villainous, wicked ~*v.* 6. ban, bar, blacklist, boycott, ~*n.* 7. **in the black** in credit, in funds, solvent, without debt
Antonyms amicable, bright, cheerful, friendly, good, happy, honourable, illuminated, light, lighted, lit, moonlit, moral, pleased, pure, sunny, warm, white, whitish

blackball *v.* ban, bar, blacklist, debar, drum out, exclude, expel, ostracize, oust, repudiate, snub, vote against

blacken 1. befoul, begrime, cloud, darken, grow black, make black, smudge, soil 2. bad-mouth (*Sl., chiefly U.S. & Canad.*), calumniate, decry, defame, defile, denigrate, dishonour, knock (*Inf.*), malign, rubbish (*Inf.*), slag (off) (*Sl.*), slander, smear, smirch, stain, sully, taint, tarnish, traduce, vilify

blackguard bad egg (*Old-fashioned inf.*), bastard (*Offensive*), blighter (*Brit. inf.*), bounder (*Old-fashioned Brit. sl.*), bugger (*Taboo sl.*), miscreant, rascal, rogue, scoundrel, scumbag (*Sl.*), shit (*Taboo sl.*), son-of-a-bitch (*Sl., chiefly U.S. & Canad.*), swine, villain, wretch

blacklist *v.* ban, bar, blackball, boycott, debar, exclude, expel, ostracize, preclude, proscribe, reject, repudiate, snub, vote against

black magic black art, diabolism, necromancy, sorcery, voodoo, witchcraft, wizardry

blackmail 1. *n.* bribe, exaction, extortion, hush money (*Sl.*), intimidation, milking, pay-off (*Inf.*), protection (*Inf.*), ransom, shakedown (*U.S. sl.*), slush fund 2. *v.* bleed (*Inf.*), bribe, coerce, compel, demand, exact, extort, force, hold to ransom, milk, squeeze, threaten

blackness darkness, duskiness, gloom, inkiness, melanism, murkiness, nigrescence, nigritude (*Rare*), swarthiness
Antonyms brightness, brilliance, effulgence, incandescence, lambency, light, lightness, luminescence, luminosity, phosphorescence, radiance

blackout *n.* 1. coma, faint, loss of consciousness, oblivion, swoon, syncope (*Pathology*), unconsciousness 2. power cut, power failure 3. censorship, noncommunication, radio silence, secrecy, suppression, withholding news

black out *v.* 1. conceal, cover, darken, eclipse, obfuscate, shade 2. collapse, faint, flake out (*Inf.*), lose consciousness, pass out, swoon

black sheep disgrace, dropout, ne'er-do-well, outcast, prodigal, renegade, reprobate, wastrel

blamable answerable, blameworthy, culpable, deserving of censure, faulty, guilty, in the wrong, liable, reprehensible, reproachable, reprovable, responsible

blame *n.* 1. accountability, culpability, fault, guilt, incrimination, liability, onus, rap (*Sl.*), responsibility 2. accusation, castigation, censure, charge, complaint, condemnation, criticism, recrimination, reproach, reproof, stick (*Sl.*) ~*v.* 3. accuse, admonish, blast, censure, charge, chide, condemn, criticize, disapprove, express disapprobation, find fault with, hold responsible, lambast(e), put down, reprehend, reproach, reprove, tax, tear into (*Inf.*), upbraid
Antonyms *n.* absolution, acclaim, alibi, Brownie points, commendation, credit, excuse, exoneration, honour, praise, tribute, vindication ~*v.* absolve, acclaim, acquit, approve of, clear, commend, compliment, excuse, exonerate, forgive, praise, vindicate

blameless above suspicion, clean, faultless, guiltless, immaculate, impeccable, innocent, in the clear, irreproachable, perfect, squeaky-clean, stainless, unblemished, unimpeachable, unoffending, unspotted, unsullied, untarnished, upright, virtuous
Antonyms at fault, censurable, culpable, guilty, reprovable, responsible, to blame

blameworthy discreditable, disreputable, indefensible, inexcusable, iniquitous, reprehensible, reproachable, shameful

blanch become *or* grow white, become pallid, bleach, blench, drain, fade, pale, turn pale, wan, whiten

bland 1. boring, dull, flat, humdrum, insipid, monotonous, tasteless, tedious, undistinctive, unexciting, uninspiring, uninteresting, unstimulating, vapid, weak 2. affable, amiable, congenial, courteous, debo-

nair, friendly, gentle, gracious, smooth, suave, unemotional, urbane 3. balmy, calm, mild, mollifying, nonirritant *or* non-irritating (*Medical*), soft, soothing, temperate
Antonyms (*sense 1*) distinctive, exciting, inspiring, interesting, rousing, stimulating, turbulent, volatile (*sense 3*) annoying, harsh, irritating, rough, severe

blandishments blarney, cajolery, coaxing, compliments, fawning, flattery, ingratiation, inveiglement, soft soap (*Inf.*), soft words, sweet talk (*Inf.*), wheedling, winning caresses

blank *adj.* 1. bare, clean, clear, empty, plain, spotless, uncompleted, unfilled, unmarked, void, white 2. deadpan, dull, empty, expressionless, hollow, impassive, inane, lifeless, poker-faced (*Inf.*), vacant, vacuous, vague 3. at a loss, at sea, bewildered, confounded, confused, disconcerted, dumbfounded, flummoxed, muddled, nonplussed, uncomprehending 4. absolute, complete, outright, thorough, unqualified, utter ~*n.* 5. emptiness, empty space, gap, nothingness, space, tabula rasa, vacancy, vacuity, vacuum, void
Antonyms alert, busy, completed, expressive, filled in, full, intelligent, interested, lively, marked, productive, profitable, rewarding, significant, thoughtful, useful, valuable

blanket *n.* 1. afghan, cover, coverlet, rug 2. carpet, cloak, coat, coating, covering, envelope, film, layer, mantle, sheet, wrapper, wrapping ~*adj.* 3. across-the-board, all-inclusive, comprehensive, overall, sweeping, wide-ranging ~*v.* 4. cloak, cloud, coat, conceal, cover, eclipse, hide, mask, obscure, suppress, surround

blankness abstraction, fatuity, inanity, indifference, no recollection, obliviousness, vacancy, vacuity

blare blast, boom, clamour, clang, honk, hoot, peal, resound, roar, scream, sound out, toot, trumpet

blarney blandishment, cajolery, coaxing, exaggeration, flattery, honeyed words, overpraise, soft soap (*Inf.*), spiel, sweet talk (*Inf.*), wheedling

blasé apathetic, bored, cloyed, glutted, indifferent, jaded, lukewarm, nonchalant, offhand, satiated, surfeited, unconcerned, unexcited, uninterested, unmoved, weary, world-weary
Antonyms affected, caring, enthusiastic, excited, interested, responsive, stimulated

blaspheme abuse, anathematize, curse, damn, desecrate, execrate, profane, revile, swear

blasphemous godless, impious, irreligious, irreverent, profane, sacrilegious, ungodly
Antonyms devout, God-fearing, godly, pious, religious, respectful, reverent, reverential

blasphemy cursing, desecration, execration, impiety, impiousness, indignity (*to God*), irreverence, profanation, profaneness, profanity, sacrilege, swearing

blast *n./v.* 1. blare, blow, clang, honk, peal, scream, toot, wail ~*n.* 2. bang, blow-up, burst, crash, detonation, discharge, eruption, explosion, outburst, salvo, volley 3. gale, gust, squall, storm, strong breeze, tempest ~*v.* 4. blow up, break up, burst, demolish, destroy, explode, ruin, shatter 5. blight, kill, shrivel, wither 6. attack, castigate, criticize, flay, lambast(e), put down, rail at, tear into (*Inf.*)

blasted blighted, desolated, destroyed, devastated, ravaged, ruined, shattered, spoiled, wasted, withered

blastoff *n.* discharge, expulsion, firing, launch, launching, lift-off, projection, shot

blatant 1. bald, brazen, conspicuous, flagrant, flaunting, glaring, naked, obtrusive, obvious, ostentatious, outright, overt, prominent, pronounced, sheer, unmitigated 2. clamorous, deafening, ear-splitting, harsh, loud, noisy, piercing, strident
Antonyms agreeable, cultured, dignified, hidden, inconspicuous, quiet, refined, soft, subtle, tasteful, unnoticeable, unobtrusive, well-mannered

blather claptrap (*Inf.*), drivel, gibberish, gobbledegook, jabber, jabbering, moonshine, pap, twaddle

blaze *n.* 1. bonfire, conflagration, fire, flame, flames 2. beam, brilliance, flare, flash, glare, gleam, glitter, glow, light, radiance 3. blast, burst, eruption, flare-up, fury, outbreak, outburst, rush, storm, torrent ~*v.* 4. beam, burn, fire, flame, flare, flash, glare, gleam, glow, shine 5. boil, explode, flare up, fume, seethe

blazon broadcast, celebrate, flourish, make known, proclaim, renown, trumpet

bleach blanch, etiolate, fade, grow pale, lighten, peroxide, wash out, whiten

bleached achromatic, etiolated, faded, lightened, peroxided, stone-washed, washed-out

bleak 1. bare, barren, chilly, cold, desolate, exposed, gaunt, open, raw, unsheltered, weather-beaten, windswept, windy 2. cheerless, comfortless, depressing, discouraging, disheartening, dismal, dreary, gloomy, grim, hopeless, joyless, sombre, unpromising

Antonyms cheerful, cosy, encouraging, promising, protected, sheltered, shielded

bleary blurred, blurry, dim, fogged, foggy, fuzzy, hazy, indistinct, misty, murky, rheumy, watery

bleed 1. exude, flow, gush, lose blood, ooze, run, seep, shed blood, spurt, trickle, weep 2. deplete, drain, draw *or* take blood, exhaust, extort, extract, fleece, leech, milk, phlebotomize (*Medical*), reduce, sap, squeeze 3. ache, agonize, feel for, grieve, pity, suffer, sympathize

blemish 1. *n.* blot, blotch, blur, defect, demerit, disfigurement, disgrace, dishonour, fault, flaw, imperfection, mark, scar, smirch, smudge, speck, spot, stain, taint 2. *v.* blot, blotch, blur, damage, deface, disfigure, flaw, impair, injure, mar, mark, smirch, smudge, spoil, spot, stain, sully, taint, tarnish

Antonyms *n.* enhancement, improvement, ornament, perfection, purity, refinement ~*v.* correct, enhance, improve, perfect, purify, refine, restore

blench cower, cringe, falter, flinch, hesitate, quail, quake, quiver, recoil, shrink, shudder, shy, start, wince

blend *v.* 1. amalgamate, coalesce, combine, compound, fuse, intermix, meld, merge, mingle, mix, synthesize, unite 2. complement, fit, go well, go with, harmonize, suit ~*n.* 3. alloy, amalgam, amalgamation, combination, composite, compound, concoction, fusion, meld, mix, mixture, synthesis, union

bless 1. anoint, consecrate, dedicate, exalt, extol, give thanks to, glorify, hallow, invoke happiness on, magnify, ordain, praise, sanctify, thank 2. bestow, endow, favour, give, grace, grant, provide

Antonyms (*sense 1*) accuse, anathematize, curse, damn, excommunicate, execrate, fulminate, imprecate (*sense 2*) afflict, blight, burden, curse, destroy, doom, plague, scourge, torment, trouble, vex

blessed 1. adored, beatified, divine, hallowed, holy, revered, sacred, sanctified 2. endowed, favoured, fortunate, granted, jammy (*Brit. sl.*), lucky 3. blissful, contented, glad, happy, joyful, joyous

blessedness beatitude, bliss, blissfulness, content, felicity, happiness, heavenly joy, pleasure, sanctity, state of grace, *summum bonum*

blessing 1. benediction, benison, commendation, consecration, dedication, grace, invocation, thanksgiving 2. approbation, approval, backing, concurrence, consent, favour, good wishes, leave, permission, regard, sanction, support 3. advantage, benefit, boon, bounty, favour, gain, gift, godsend, good fortune, help, kindness, profit, service, windfall

Antonyms condemnation, curse, damage, deprivation, disadvantage, disapproval, disfavour, drawback, harm, malediction, misfortune, objection, reproof

blight *n.* 1. canker, decay, disease, fungus, infestation, mildew, pest, pestilence, rot 2. affliction, bane, contamination, corruption, curse, evil, plague, pollution, scourge, woe ~*v.* 3. blast, destroy, injure, nip in the bud, ruin, shrivel, taint with mildew, wither 4. *Fig.* annihilate, crush, dash, disappoint, frustrate, mar, nullify, ruin, spoil, undo, wreck

Antonyms *n.* benefaction, blessing, boon, bounty, favour, godsend, help, service

blind *adj.* 1. destitute of vision, eyeless, sightless, stone-blind, unseeing, unsighted, visionless 2. *Fig.* careless, heedless, ignorant, inattentive, inconsiderate, indifferent, indiscriminate, injudicious, insensitive, morally darkened, neglectful, oblivious, prejudiced, thoughtless, unaware of, unconscious of, uncritical, undiscerning, unmindful of, unobservant, unreasoning 3. hasty, impetuous, irrational, mindless, rash, reckless, senseless, uncontrollable, uncontrolled, unthinking, violent, wild 4. closed, concealed, dark, dead-end, dim, hidden, leading nowhere, obscured, obstructed, without exit ~*n.* 5. camouflage, cloak, cover, façade, feint, front, mask, masquerade, screen, smoke screen

Antonyms *adj.* alive to, attentive, aware, concerned, conscious, discerning, heedful, knowledgeable, noticeable, observant, obvious, open, seeing, sighted

blindly 1. aimlessly, at random, confusedly, frantically, indiscriminately, instinctively, madly, purposelessly, wildly 2. carelessly, heedlessly, impulsively, inconsiderately, passionately, recklessly, regardlessly, senselessly, thoughtlessly, unreasonably, wilfully

blink 1. bat, flutter, glimpse, nictate, nictitate, peer, squint, wink 2. flash, flicker, gleam, glimmer, scintillate, shine, sparkle, twinkle, wink 3. *Fig.* condone, connive at, disregard, ignore, overlook, pass by, turn a blind eye to 4. **on the blink** *Sl.* faulty, malfunctioning, not working (properly), on the fritz (*U.S. sl.*), out of action, out of order, playing up

bliss beatitude, blessedness, blissfulness, ecstasy, euphoria, felicity, gladness, happiness, heaven, joy, paradise, rapture

Antonyms affliction, anguish, distress, grief, heartbreak, misery, mourning, regret, sadness, sorrow, unhappiness, woe, wretchedness

blissful cock-a-hoop, delighted, ecstatic, elated, enchanted, enraptured, euphoric, happy, heavenly (*Inf.*), in ecstasies, joyful, joyous, over the moon (*Inf.*), rapt, rapturous

blister abscess, blain, bleb, boil, bubble, canker, carbuncle, cyst, furuncle (*Pathology*), pimple, pustule, sore, swelling, ulcer, welt, wen

blithe 1. animated, buoyant, carefree, cheerful, cheery, chirpy (*Inf.*), debonair, gay, genial, gladsome (*Archaic*), happy, jaunty, light-hearted, merry, mirthful, sprightly, sunny, upbeat (*Inf.*), vivacious 2. careless, casual, heedless, indifferent, nonchalant, thoughtless, unconcerned, untroubled

Antonyms concerned, dejected, depressed, gloomy, kind-hearted, melancholy, morose, preoccupied, sad, thoughtful, unhappy

blitz assault, attack, blitzkrieg, bombardment, offensive, onslaught, raid, strike

blizzard blast, gale, snowstorm, squall, storm, tempest

bloat balloon, blow up, dilate, distend, enlarge, expand, inflate, puff up, swell

Antonyms contract, deflate, shrink, shrivel, wither, wrinkle

blob ball, bead, bubble, dab, dewdrop, drop, droplet, glob, globule, lump, mass, pearl, pellet, pill

bloc alliance, axis, cabal, clique, coalition, combine, entente, faction, group, league, ring, schism, union, wing

block *n.* 1. bar, brick, cake, chunk, cube, hunk, ingot, lump, mass, piece, square 2. bar, barrier, blockage, hindrance, impediment, jam, obstacle, obstruction, occlusion, stoppage ~*v.* 3. bung up (*Inf.*), choke, clog, close, obstruct, plug, stop up 4. arrest, bar, check, deter, halt, hinder, impede, obstruct, stop, thwart

Antonyms *v.* (*sense 3*) clear, open, unblock, unclog (*sense 4*) advance, aid, expedite, facilitate, foster, further, lend support to, promote, push, support

blockade barricade, barrier, block, closure, encirclement, hindrance, impediment, obstacle, obstruction, restriction, siege, stoppage

blockage block, blocking, impediment, obstruction, occlusion, stoppage, stopping up

blockhead berk (*Brit. sl.*), bonehead (*Sl.*), charlie (*Brit. inf.*), chump (*Inf.*), coot, dickhead (*Sl.*), dipstick (*Brit. sl.*), divvy (*Brit. sl.*), dolt, dork (*Sl.*), dullard, dunce, dweeb (*U.S. sl.*), fool, fuckwit (*Taboo sl.*), geek (*Sl.*), gonzo (*Sl.*), idiot, ignoramus, jerk (*Sl., chiefly U.S. & Canad.*), nerd *or* nurd (*Sl.*), noodle, numskull *or* numbskull, pillock (*Brit. sl.*), plank (*Brit. sl.*), plonker (*Sl.*), prat (*Sl.*), prick (*Derogatory sl.*), schmuck (*U.S. sl.*), thickhead, twit (*Inf., chiefly Brit.*), wally (*Sl.*)

block out chart, map out, outline, plan, sketch

bloke bastard (*Inf.*), bod (*Inf.*), body, boy, bugger (*Sl.*), chap, character (*Inf.*), customer (*Inf.*), fellow, guy (*Inf.*), individual, man, person, punter (*Inf.*)

blond, blonde fair, fair-haired, fair-skinned, flaxen, golden-haired, light, light-coloured, light-complexioned, tow-headed

blood 1. gore, lifeblood, vital fluid 2. ancestry, birth, consanguinity, descendants, descent, extraction, family, kindred, kinship, lineage, noble extraction, relations 3. *Fig.* anger, disposition, feeling, passion, spirit, temper

bloodcurdling appalling, chilling, dreadful, fearful, frightening, hair-raising, horrendous, horrifying, scaring, spine-chilling, terrifying

bloodless 1. cold, languid, lifeless, listless, passionless, spiritless, torpid, unemotional, unfeeling 2. anaemic, ashen, chalky, colourless, pale, pallid, pasty, sallow, sickly, wan

bloodshed blood bath, bloodletting, butchery, carnage, gore, killing, massacre, murder, slaughter, slaying

bloodthirsty barbarous, brutal, cruel, ferocious, inhuman, murderous, ruthless, savage, vicious, warlike

bloody 1. bleeding, blood-soaked, blood-spattered, bloodstained, gaping, raw, unstaunched 2. cruel, ferocious, fierce, sanguinary, savage

bloom *n.* 1. blossom, blossoming, bud, efflorescence, flower, opening (*of flowers*) 2. *Fig.* beauty, blush, flourishing, flush, freshness, glow, health, heyday, lustre, perfection, prime, radiance, rosiness, vigour ~*v.* 3. blossom, blow, bud, burgeon, open, sprout 4. develop, fare well, flourish, grow, prosper, succeed, thrive, wax

Antonyms (*sense 2*) bloodlessness, paleness, pallor, wanness, whiteness (*senses 3 & 4*) decay, decline, die, droop, fade, fail, languish, perish, shrink, shrivel, wane, waste, wilt, wither

blossom *n.* 1. bloom, bud, floret, flower, flowers ~*v.* 2. bloom, burgeon, flower 3. *Fig.* bloom, develop, flourish, grow, mature, progress, prosper, thrive

blot *n.* 1. blotch, mark, patch, smear, smudge, speck, splodge, spot 2. blemish, blur, defect, demerit, disgrace, fault, flaw, scar, smirch, spot, stain, taint ~*v.* 3. bespatter, disfigure, disgrace, mark, smirch, smudge, spoil, spot, stain, sully, tarnish 4. absorb, dry, soak up, take up 5. **blot out** cancel, darken, destroy, efface, erase, expunge, obliterate, obscure, shadow

blotch blemish, blot, mark, patch, scar, smirch, smudge, smutch, splash, splodge, spot, stain

blotchy blemished, macular, patchy, reddened, scurvy, spotty, uneven

blow[1] *v.* 1. blast, breathe, exhale, fan, pant, puff, waft 2. flow, rush, stream, whirl 3. bear, buffet, drive, fling, flutter, sweep, waft, whirl, whisk 4. blare, mouth, pipe, play, sound, toot, trumpet, vibrate ~*n.* 5. blast, draught, flurry, gale, gust, puff, strong breeze, tempest, wind

blow[2] *n.* 1. bang, bash (*Inf.*), belt (*Inf.*), buffet, clomp (*Sl.*), clout (*Inf.*), clump (*Sl.*), knock, punch, rap, slosh (*Brit. sl.*), smack, sock (*Sl.*), stroke, thump, wallop (*Inf.*), whack 2. *Fig.* affliction, bolt from the blue, bombshell, bummer (*Sl.*), calamity, catastrophe, comedown (*Inf.*), disappointment, disaster, jolt, misfortune, reverse, setback, shock, upset

blowout 1. blast, detonation, eruption, explosion 2. break, burst, escape, flat, flat tyre, fuse, leak, puncture, rupture, tear 3. beano (*Brit. sl.*), binge (*Inf.*), carousal, carouse, feast, party, rave (*Brit. sl.*), rave-up (*Brit. sl.*), spree

blow out 1. extinguish, put out, snuff 2. burst, erupt, explode, rupture, shatter

blow over be forgotten, cease, die down, disappear, end, finish, pass, pass away, subside, vanish

blow up 1. bloat, distend, enlarge, expand, fill, inflate, puff up, pump up, swell 2. blast, bomb, burst, detonate, dynamite, explode, go off, rupture, shatter 3. enlarge, enlarge on, exaggerate, heighten, magnify, overstate 4. *Inf.* become angry, become enraged, blow a fuse (*Sl., chiefly U.S.*), crack up (*Inf.*), erupt, fly off the handle (*Inf.*), go off the deep end (*Inf.*), go up the wall (*Sl.*), hit the roof (*Inf.*), lose one's temper, rage, see red (*Inf.*)

blowy blustery, breezy, draughty, exposed, fresh, stormy, well-ventilated, windy

blowzy, blowsy 1. bedraggled, dishevelled, frowzy, slatternly, slipshod, sloppy, slovenly, sluttish, tousled, unkempt, untidy 2. florid, red-faced, ruddy

bludgeon *n.* 1. club, cosh (*Brit.*), cudgel, shillelagh, truncheon ~*v.* 2. beat, beat up, club, cosh (*Brit.*), cudgel, knock down, strike 3. browbeat, bulldoze (*Inf.*), bully, coerce, dragoon, force, hector, railroad (*Inf.*), steamroller

blue 1. azure, cerulean, cobalt, cyan, navy, sapphire, sky-coloured, ultramarine 2. *Fig.* dejected, depressed, despondent, dismal, downcast, down-hearted, down in the dumps (*Inf.*), fed up, gloomy, glum, low, melancholy, sad, unhappy 3. *Inf.* bawdy, dirty, indecent, lewd, naughty, near the knuckle (*Inf.*), obscene, risqué, smutty, vulgar

Antonyms (*sense 2*) blithe, cheerful, cheery, chirpy (*Inf.*), elated, genial, happy, jolly, merry, optimistic, sunny (*sense 3*) decent, respectable

blueprint design, draft, layout, norm, outline, pattern, pilot scheme, plan, project, prototype, scheme, sketch

blues dejection, depression, despondency, doldrums, dumps (*Inf.*), gloom, gloominess, glumness, low spirits, melancholy, moodiness, the hump (*Brit. inf.*)

bluff[1] 1. *v.* deceive, defraud, delude, fake, feign, humbug, lie, mislead, pretend, sham 2. *n.* bluster, boast, braggadocio, bragging, bravado, deceit, deception, fake, feint, fraud, humbug, idle boast, lie, mere show, pretence, sham, show, subterfuge

bluff[2] *n.* 1. bank, cliff, crag, escarpment, headland, peak, precipice, promontory, ridge, scarp ~*adj.* 2. abrupt, blunt, blustering, downright, frank, genial, good-natured, hearty, open, outspoken, plain-spoken 3. abrupt, perpendicular, precipitous, sheer, steep, towering

Antonyms (*sense 2*) delicate, diplomatic, discreet, judicious, sensitive, tactful, thoughtful

blunder *n.* 1. error, fault, inaccuracy, mistake, oversight, slip, slip-up (*Inf.*) 2. bloomer (*Brit. inf.*), boob (*Brit. sl.*), boo-boo (*Inf.*), clanger (*Inf.*), faux pas, gaffe, gaucherie, howler (*Inf.*), impropriety, indiscretion, mistake ~*v.* 3. bodge (*Inf.*), botch, bungle, err, slip up (*Inf.*) 4. bumble, confuse, flounder, misjudge, stumble

Antonyms *n.* accuracy, achievement, correctness, success ~*v.* be correct, be exact, get it right, go alertly

blunt *adj.* 1. dull, dulled, edgeless, pointless, rounded, unsharpened 2. *Fig.* bluff, brusque, discourteous, downright, explicit, forthright, frank, impolite, outspoken, plain-spoken, rude, straightforward, tactless, trenchant, uncivil, unpolished, upfront (*Inf.*) ~*v.* 3. dampen, deaden, dull, numb, soften, take the edge off, water down, weaken

Antonyms *adj.* acute, courteous, diplomatic, keen, pointed, sensitive, sharp, sub~

tle, tactful ~*v.* animate, put an edge on, sharpen, stimulate, vitalize

blur *v.* 1. becloud, bedim, befog, cloud, darken, dim, fog, make hazy, make indistinct, make vague, mask, obscure, soften 2. blot, smear, smudge, spot, stain ~*n.* 3. blear, blurredness, cloudiness, confusion, dimness, fog, haze, indistinctness, obscurity 4. blot, smear, smudge, spot, stain

blurred bleary, blurry, faint, foggy, fuzzy, hazy, ill-defined, indistinct, lacking definition, misty, nebulous, out of focus, unclear, vague

blurt out babble, blab, cry, disclose, exclaim, gush, reveal, run off at the mouth (*Sl.*), spill, spill one's guts (*Sl.*), spill the beans (*Inf.*), spout (*Inf.*), sputter, tattle, tell all, utter suddenly

blush 1. *v.* colour, crimson, flush, redden, turn red, turn scarlet 2. *n.* colour, flush, glow, pink tinge, reddening, rosiness, rosy tint, ruddiness

Antonyms *v.* blanch, blench, drain, fade, pale, turn pale, whiten

bluster 1. *v.* boast, brag, bulldoze, bully, domineer, hector, rant, roar, roister, storm, swagger, swell, vaunt 2. *n.* bluff, boasting, boisterousness, bombast, bragging, bravado, crowing, swagger, swaggering

blustery blusterous, boisterous, gusty, inclement, squally, stormy, tempestuous, violent, wild

board *n.* 1. panel, piece of timber, plank, slat, timber 2. daily meals, food, meals, provisions, victuals 3. advisers, advisory group, committee, conclave, council, directorate, directors, panel, trustees ~*v.* 4. embark, embus, enplane, enter, entrain, mount 5. accommodate, feed, house, lodge, put up, quarter, room

Antonyms (*sense 4*) alight, arrive, disembark, dismount, get off, go ashore, land

boast *v.* 1. blow one's own trumpet, bluster, brag, crow, exaggerate, puff, strut, swagger, talk big (*Sl.*), vaunt 2. be proud of, congratulate oneself on, exhibit, flatter oneself, possess, pride oneself on, show off ~*n.* 3. avowal, brag, gasconade (*Rare*), rodomontade (*Literary*), swank (*Inf.*), vaunt 4. gem, joy, pride, pride and joy, source of pride, treasure

Antonyms *v.* cover up, depreciate, disavow, disclaim ~*n.* disavowal, disclaimer

boastful bragging, cocky, conceited, crowing, egotistical, puffed-up, swaggering, swanky (*Inf.*), swollen-headed, vainglorious, vaunting

Antonyms deprecating, humble, modest, self-belittling, self-effacing, unassuming

bob bounce, duck, hop, jerk, leap, nod, oscillate, quiver, skip, waggle, weave, wobble

bob up appear, arise, emerge, materialize, pop up, rise, spring up, surface, turn up

bode augur, betoken, forebode, foreshadow, foretell, forewarn, impart, omen, portend, predict, presage, prophesy, signify, threaten

bodiless disembodied, ghostly, immaterial, incorporeal, insubstantial, spectral, spiritual, supernatural

bodily 1. *adj.* actual, carnal, corporal, corporeal, fleshly, material, physical, substantial, tangible 2. *adv.* altogether, as a body, as a group, collectively, completely, en masse, entirely, fully, totally, wholly

body 1. build, figure, form, frame, physique, shape, torso, trunk 2. cadaver, carcass, corpse, dead body, relics, remains, stiff (*Sl.*) 3. being, creature, human, human being, individual, mortal, person 4. bulk, essence, main part, mass, material, matter, substance 5. association, band, bloc, collection, company, confederation, congress, corporation, society 6. crowd, horde, majority, mass, mob, multitude, throng 7. consistency, density, firmness, richness, solidity, substance

boffin authority, brain(s) (*Inf.*), brainbox, egghead, genius, intellect, intellectual, inventor, mastermind, maven (*U.S.*), planner, thinker, virtuoso, wizard

bog fen, marsh, marshland, mire, morass, moss (*Scot. & Northern English dialect*), peat bog, quagmire, slough, swamp, wetlands

bog down delay, halt, impede, sink, slow down, slow up, stall, stick

bogey 1. apparition, bogeyman, goblin, hobgoblin, imp, spectre, spirit, spook (*Inf.*), sprite 2. *bête noire,* bugaboo, bugbear, nightmare

boggle 1. be alarmed (confused, surprised, taken aback), shy, stagger, startle, take fright 2. demur, dither (*Chiefly Brit.*), doubt, equivocate, falter, hang back, hesitate, hover, jib, shillyshally (*Inf.*), shrink from, vacillate, waver

boggy fenny, marshy, miry, muddy, oozy, quaggy, soft, spongy, swampy, waterlogged, yielding

bogus artificial, counterfeit, dummy, ersatz, fake, false, forged, fraudulent, imitation, phoney *or* phony (*Inf.*), pseudo (*Inf.*), sham, spurious

Antonyms actual, authentic, genuine, real, true

bohemian 1. *adj.* alternative, artistic, arty (*Inf.*), avant-garde, eccentric, exotic, left bank, nonconformist, oddball (*Inf.*), offbeat, off-the-wall (*Sl.*), outré, unconventional, unorthodox, way-out (*Inf.*) 2. *n.* beatnik, dropout, hippie, iconoclast, nonconformist

Antonyms *adj.* bourgeois, conservative, conventional, square (*Inf.*), straight (*Sl.*), straight-laced, stuffy

boil[1] *v.* 1. agitate, bubble, churn, effervesce, fizz, foam, froth, seethe 2. be angry, be indignant, blow a fuse (*Sl., chiefly U.S.*), crack up (*Inf.*), fly off the handle (*Inf.*), foam at the mouth (*Inf.*), fulminate, fume, go off the deep end (*Inf.*), go up the wall (*Sl.*), rage, rave, see red (*Inf.*), storm

boil[2] *n.* blain, blister, carbuncle, furuncle (*Pathology*), gathering, pustule, tumour, ulcer

boil down come down, condense, decrease, reduce, summarize

boiling 1. baking, blistering, hot, roasting, scorching, tropical, very hot 2. angry, cross, enraged, fuming, furious, incensed, indignant, infuriated

boisterous 1. bouncy, clamorous, disorderly, impetuous, loud, noisy, obstreperous, riotous, rollicking, rowdy, rumbustious, unrestrained, unruly, uproarious, vociferous, wild 2. blustery, gusty, raging, rough, squally, stormy, tempestuous, tumultuous, turbulent

Antonyms calm, controlled, peaceful, quiet, restrained, self-controlled, subdued

bold 1. adventurous, audacious, brave, courageous, daring, dauntless, enterprising, fearless, gallant, gritty, heroic, intrepid, lion-hearted, valiant, valorous 2. barefaced, brash, brazen, cheeky, confident, feisty (*Inf., chiefly U.S. & Canad.*), forward, fresh (*Inf.*), impudent, insolent, pert, pushy (*Inf.*), rude, sassy (*U.S. inf.*), saucy, shameless 3. bright, colourful, conspicuous, eye-catching, flashy, forceful, lively, loud, prominent, pronounced, showy, spirited, striking, strong, vivid

Antonyms conservative, cool, courteous, cowardly, dull, faint-hearted, fearful, meek, modest, ordinary, pale, polite, retiring, shy, soft, tactful, timid, timorous, unimaginative

bolster aid, assist, augment, boost, brace, buoy up, buttress, cushion, help, hold up, maintain, pillow, prop, reinforce, shore up, stay, strengthen, support

bolt *n.* 1. bar, catch, fastener, latch, lock, sliding bar 2. peg, pin, rivet, rod 3. bound, dart, dash, escape, flight, rush, spring, sprint 4. arrow, dart, missile, projectile, shaft, thunderbolt ~*v.* 5. bar, fasten, latch, lock, secure 6. cram, devour, gobble, gorge, gulp, guzzle, stuff, swallow whole, wolf 7. abscond, bound, dash, decamp, do a runner (*Sl.*), escape, flee, fly, fly the coop (*U.S. & Canad. inf.*), hurtle, jump, leap, make a break (for it), run, run for it, rush, skedaddle (*Inf.*), spring, sprint, take a powder (*U.S. & Canad. sl.*), take it on the lam (*U.S. & Canad. sl.*)

bomb 1. *n.* bombshell, charge, device, explosive, grenade, mine, missile, projectile, rocket, shell, torpedo 2. *v.* attack, blow up, bombard, destroy, shell, strafe, torpedo

bombard 1. assault, blast, blitz, bomb, cannonade, fire upon, open fire, pound, shell, strafe 2. assail, attack, barrage, batter, beset, besiege, harass, hound, pester

bombardment assault, attack, barrage, blitz, bombing, cannonade, fire, flak, fusillade, shelling, strafe

bombast bluster, brag, braggadocio, extravagant boasting, fustian, gasconade (*Rare*), grandiloquence, grandiosity, magniloquence, pomposity, rant, rodomontade (*Literary*)

bombastic declamatory, fustian, grandiloquent, grandiose, high-flown, histrionic, inflated, magniloquent, pompous, ranting, turgid, verbose, windy, wordy

bona fide actual, authentic, genuine, honest, kosher (*Inf.*), lawful, legal, legitimate, real, true

Antonyms bogus, counterfeit, ersatz, fake, false, imitation, phoney *or* phony (*Inf.*), sham

bond *n.* 1. band, binding, chain, cord, fastening, fetter, ligature, link, manacle, shackle, tie 2. affiliation, affinity, attachment, connection, link, relation, tie, union 3. agreement, compact, contract, covenant, guarantee, obligation, pledge, promise, word ~*v.* 4. bind, connect, fasten, fix together, fuse, glue, gum, paste

bondage captivity, confinement, duress, enslavement, enthralment, imprisonment, serfdom, servitude, slavery, subjection, subjugation, thraldom, vassalage, yoke

bonny 1. beautiful, comely, fair, handsome, lovely, pretty, sweet 2. bouncing, buxom, chubby, fine, plump, rounded, shapely 3. blithe, cheerful, cheery, gay, joyful, merry, sunny, winsome

bonus benefit, bounty, commission, dividend, extra, gift, gratuity, hand-out, honorarium, icing on the cake, perk (*Brit. inf.*), plus, premium, prize, reward

bon viveur *bon vivant,* epicure, epicurean, foodie, gastronome, gourmet, hedonist, luxurist, pleasure-seeker, voluptuary

Antonyms abstainer, ascetic, celibate, self-denier

bony angular, emaciated, gangling, gaunt,

lanky, lean, macilent (*Rare*), rawboned, scrawny, skinny, thin

booby berk (*Brit. sl.*), blockhead, charlie (*Brit. inf.*), coot, dickhead (*Sl.*), dimwit (*Inf.*), dipstick (*Brit. sl.*), divvy (*Brit. sl.*), dork (*Sl.*), duffer (*Inf.*), dunce, dweeb (*U.S. sl.*), fool, fuckwit (*Taboo sl.*), geek (*Sl.*), gonzo (*Sl.*), goof (*Inf.*), idiot, jerk (*Sl., chiefly U.S. & Canad.*), lamebrain (*Inf.*), muggins (*Brit. sl.*), nerd *or* nurd (*Sl.*), nitwit (*Inf.*), numskull *or* numbskull, oaf, pillock (*Brit. sl.*), plank (*Brit. sl.*), plonker (*Sl.*), prat (*Sl.*), prick (*Derogatory sl.*), schmuck (*U.S. sl.*), simpleton, twit (*Inf., chiefly Brit.*), wally (*Sl.*)

book *n.* 1. hardback, manual, paperback, publication, roll, scroll, textbook, title, tome, tract, volume, work 2. album, diary, exercise book, jotter, notebook, pad ~*v.* 3. arrange for, bill, charter, engage, line up, make reservations, organize, procure, programme, reserve, schedule 4. enrol, enter, insert, list, log, mark down, note, post, put down, record, register, write down

bookish academic, donnish, erudite, intellectual, learned, literary, pedantic, scholarly, studious, well-read

boom *v.* 1. bang, blast, crash, explode, resound, reverberate, roar, roll, rumble, thunder 2. develop, expand, flourish, gain, grow, increase, intensify, prosper, spurt, strengthen, succeed, swell, thrive ~*n.* 3. bang, blast, burst, clap, crash, explosion, roar, rumble, thunder 4. advance, boost, development, expansion, gain, growth, improvement, increase, jump, push, spurt, upsurge, upswing, upturn

Antonyms *v.* (*sense 2*) crash, fail, fall, slump ~*n.* (*sense 4*) bust (*Inf.*), collapse, crash, decline, depression, downturn, failure, hard times, recession, slump

boomerang backfire, come back, come home to roost, rebound, recoil, return, reverse, ricochet

boon 1. *n.* advantage, benefaction, benefit, blessing, donation, favour, gift, godsend, grant, gratuity, hand-out, present, windfall 2. *adj.* close, intimate, special

boor barbarian, brute, bumpkin, churl, clodhopper (*Inf.*), clodpole, hayseed (*U.S. & Canad. inf.*), hick (*Inf., chiefly U.S. & Canad.*), lout, oaf, peasant, philistine, redneck (*U.S. sl.*), vulgarian

boorish awkward, barbaric, bearish, churlish, clownish, coarse, crude, gross, gruff, hick (*Inf., chiefly U.S. & Canad.*), ill-bred, loutish, lubberly, oafish, rude, rustic, uncivilized, uncouth, uneducated, unrefined, vulgar

Antonyms cultured, gallant, genteel, polite, refined, sophisticated, urbane

boost *n.* 1. encouragement, help, hype, improvement, praise, promotion 2. heave, hoist, lift, push, raise, shove, thrust 3. addition, expansion, improvement, increase, increment, jump, rise ~*v.* 4. advance, advertise, assist, crack up (*Inf.*), encourage, foster, further, hype, improve, inspire, plug (*Inf.*), praise, promote, support, sustain 5. elevate, heave, hoist, lift, push, raise, shove, thrust 6. add to, amplify, develop, enlarge, expand, heighten, hoick, increase, jack up, magnify, raise

Antonyms *n.* condemnation, criticism, cut-back, decline, decrease, deterioration, fall, knock (*Inf.*), reduction ~*v.* condemn, criticize, cut, decrease, diminish, drop, hinder, hold back, knock (*Inf.*), lessen, let down, lower, moderate, pare, reduce, scale down

boot *v.* 1. drive, drop-kick, kick, knock, punt, shove 2. *Inf.* dismiss, eject, expel, give the bum's rush (*Sl.*), give the heave *or* push (*Inf.*), kick out, kiss off (*Sl., chiefly U.S. & Canad.*), oust, relegate, sack (*Inf.*), show one the door, throw out, throw out on one's ear (*Inf.*)

bootless fruitless, futile, ineffective, profitless, unavailing, unsuccessful, useless, vain

bootlicker ass-kisser (*U.S. & Canad. taboo sl.*), brown-noser (*Taboo sl.*), fawner, flatterer, flunky, lackey, spaniel, sycophant, toady, yes man

booty boodle (*Sl., chiefly U.S.*), gains, haul, loot, pillage, plunder, prey, spoil, spoils, swag (*Sl.*), takings, winnings

border *n.* 1. bound, boundary, bounds, brim, brink, confine, confines, edge, flange, hem, limit, limits, lip, margin, pale, rim, skirt, verge 2. borderline, boundary, frontier, line, march ~*v.* 3. bind, decorate, edge, fringe, hem, rim, trim

borderline *adj.* ambivalent, doubtful, equivocal, indecisive, indefinite, indeterminate, inexact, marginal, unclassifiable

border on 1. abut, adjoin, connect, contact, impinge, join, march, neighbour, touch, verge on 2. approach, approximate, be like, be similar to, come close to, come near, echo, match, parallel, resemble

bore[1] 1. *v.* burrow, drill, gouge out, mine, penetrate, perforate, pierce, sink, tunnel 2. *n.* borehole, calibre, drill hole, hole, shaft, tunnel

bore[2] 1. *v.* annoy, be tedious, bother, exhaust, fatigue, jade, pall on, pester, send to sleep, tire, trouble, vex, wear out, weary, worry 2. *n.* bother, drag (*Inf.*), dullard, dull

person, headache (*Inf.*), nuisance, pain (*Inf.*), pain in the arse (*Taboo inf.*), pain in the neck (*Inf.*), pest, tiresome person, wearisome talker, yawn (*Inf.*)
Antonyms *v.* amuse, divert, engross, excite, fascinate, hold the attention of, interest, stimulate

boredom apathy, doldrums, dullness, ennui, flatness, irksomeness, monotony, sameness, tedium, tediousness, weariness, world-weariness
Antonyms amusement, entertainment, excitement, interest, stimulation

boring dead, dull, flat, ho-hum (*Inf.*), humdrum, insipid, mind-numbing, monotonous, repetitious, routine, stale, tedious, tiresome, tiring, unexciting, uninteresting, unvaried, wearisome

borrow 1. blag (*Sl.*), cadge, mooch (*Sl.*), scrounge (*Inf.*), take and return, take on loan, touch (someone) for (*Sl.*), use temporarily 2. acquire, adopt, appropriate, copy, filch, imitate, obtain, pilfer, pirate, plagiarize, simulate, steal, take, use, usurp
Antonyms advance, give, lend, loan, provide, return, supply

bosom *n.* 1. breast, bust, chest 2. affections, emotions, feelings, heart, sentiments, soul, spirit, sympathies 3. centre, circle, core, midst, protection, shelter *~adj.* 4. boon, cherished, close, confidential, intimate, very dear

boss[1] 1. *n.* administrator, big cheese (*Sl., old-fashioned*), chief, director, employer, executive, foreman, gaffer (*Inf., chiefly Brit.*), governor (*Inf.*), head, kingpin, leader, manager, master, Mister Big (*Sl., chiefly U.S.*), numero uno (*Inf.*), overseer, owner, superintendent, supervisor 2. *v.* administrate, command, control, direct, employ, manage, oversee, run, superintend, supervise, take charge

boss[2] knob, nub, nubble, point, protuberance, stud, tip

boss around bully, dominate, domineer, oppress, order, overbear, push around (*Sl.*), put upon, tyrannize

bossy arrogant, authoritarian, autocratic, despotic, dictatorial, domineering, hectoring, high-handed, imperious, lordly, overbearing, tyrannical

botch 1. *v.* balls up (*Taboo sl.*), blunder, bodge (*Inf.*), bungle, butcher, cobble, cock up (*Brit. sl.*), fuck up (*Offens. taboo sl.*), fumble, mar, mend, mess, mismanage, muff, patch, screw up (*Inf.*), spoil 2. *n.* balls-up (*Taboo sl.*), blunder, bungle, bungling, cock-up (*Brit. sl.*), failure, fuck-up (*Offens. taboo sl.*), fumble, hash, mess, miscarriage, pig's breakfast (*Inf.*), pig's ear (*Inf.*)

bother 1. *v.* alarm, annoy, bend someone's ear (*Inf.*), concern, dismay, distress, disturb, gall, harass, hassle (*Inf.*), inconvenience, irritate, molest, nag, nark (*Brit., Aust., & N.Z. sl.*), pester, plague, put out, trouble, upset, vex, worry 2. *n.* aggravation, annoyance, bustle, difficulty, flurry, fuss, gall, hassle (*Inf.*), inconvenience, irritation, molestation, nuisance, perplexity, pest, problem, strain, trouble, vexation, worry
Antonyms *v.* aid, assist, facilitate, further, help, relieve, succour, support *~n.* advantage, aid, benefit, comfort, convenience, help, service, use

bothersome aggravating, annoying, distressing, exasperating, inconvenient, irritating, tiresome, troublesome, vexatious, vexing
Antonyms appropriate, beneficial, commodious, convenient, handy, helpful, serviceable, useful

bottleneck block, blockage, congestion, hold-up, impediment, jam, obstacle, obstruction, snarl-up (*Inf., chiefly Brit.*)

bottle up check, contain, curb, keep back, restrict, shut in, suppress, trap

bottom *n.* 1. base, basis, bed, deepest part, depths, floor, foot, foundation, groundwork, lowest part, pedestal, support 2. lower side, sole, underneath, underside 3. arse (*Taboo sl.*), ass (*U.S. & Canad. taboo sl.*), backside, behind (*Inf.*), bum (*Brit. sl.*), buns (*U.S. sl.*), butt (*U.S. & Canad. inf.*), buttocks, derrière (*Euphemistic*), fundament, jacksy (*Brit. sl.*), posterior, rear, rear end, rump, seat, tail (*Inf.*) 4. base, basis, cause, core, essence, ground, heart, mainspring, origin, principle, root, source, substance *~adj.* 5. base, basement, basic, fundamental, ground, last, lowest, undermost
Antonyms *n.* cover, crown, height, lid, peak, summit, surface, top *~adj.* higher, highest, top, upper

bottomless boundless, deep, fathomless, immeasurable, inexhaustible, infinite, unfathomable, unlimited

bounce *v.* 1. bob, bound, bump, jounce, jump, leap, rebound, recoil, resile, ricochet, spring, thump 2. *Sl.* boot out (*Inf.*), eject, fire (*Inf.*), kick out (*Inf.*), oust, relegate, throw out *~n.* 3. bound, elasticity, give, rebound, recoil, resilience, spring, springiness 4. animation, brio, dynamism, energy, go (*Inf.*), life, liveliness, pep, vigour, vitality, vivacity, zip (*Inf.*)

bouncing blooming, bonny, healthy, robust, thriving, vigorous

bound[1] *adj.* 1. cased, fastened, fixed, pinioned, secured, tied, tied up 2. certain, destined, doomed, fated, sure 3. beholden, committed, compelled, constrained, duty-bound, forced, obligated, obliged, pledged, required

bound[2] *v./n.* bob, bounce, caper, frisk, gambol, hurdle, jump, leap, lope, pounce, prance, skip, spring, vault

bound[3] *n.* 1. *Usually plural* border, boundary, confine, edge, extremity, fringe, limit, line, march, margin, pale, periphery, rim, termination, verge 2. **out of bounds** banned, barred, forbidden, off-limits (*Chiefly U.S. military*), prohibited, taboo ~*v.* 3. circumscribe, confine, define, delimit, demarcate, encircle, enclose, hem in, limit, restrain, restrict, surround, terminate

boundary barrier, border, borderline, bounds, brink, confines, edge, extremity, fringe, frontier, limits, march, margin, pale, precinct, termination, verge

boundless endless, illimitable, immeasurable, immense, incalculable, inexhaustible, infinite, limitless, measureless, unbounded, unconfined, unending, unlimited, untold, vast

Antonyms bounded, confined, limited, little, restricted, small

bountiful 1. abundant, ample, bounteous, copious, exuberant, lavish, luxuriant, plenteous, plentiful, prolific 2. beneficent, bounteous, generous, liberal, magnanimous, munificent, open-handed, princely, prodigal, unstinting

bounty 1. almsgiving, assistance, beneficence, benevolence, charity, generosity, kindness, largess *or* largesse, liberality, open-handedness, philanthropy 2. bonus, donation, gift, grant, gratuity, largess *or* largesse, meed (*Archaic*), premium, present, recompense, reward

bouquet 1. boutonniere, bunch of flowers, buttonhole, corsage, garland, nosegay, posy, spray, wreath 2. aroma, fragrance, perfume, redolence, savour, scent

bourgeois conventional, hidebound, materialistic, middle-class, traditional

bourn 1. *Archaic* border, boundary, confine, destination, goal, limit 2. *Chiefly southern Brit.* brook, burn, rill, rivulet, stream, torrent 3. *Fig.* death

bout 1. course, fit, period, round, run, session, spell, spree, stint, stretch, term, time, turn 2. battle, boxing match, competition, contest, encounter, engagement, fight, head-to-head, match, set-to, struggle

bovine dense, dozy (*Brit. inf.*), dull, slow, sluggish, stolid, stupid, thick

bow[1] *v.* 1. bend, bob, droop, genuflect, incline, make obeisance, nod, stoop 2. accept, acquiesce, comply, concede, defer, give in, kowtow, relent, submit, succumb, surrender, yield 3. cast down, conquer, crush, depress, overpower, subdue, subjugate, vanquish, weigh down ~*n.* 4. bending, bob, genuflexion, inclination, kowtow, nod, obeisance, salaam

bow[2] *Naut.* beak, fore, head, prow, stem

bowdlerize blue-pencil, censor, clean up, expurgate, mutilate

bowels 1. entrails, guts, innards (*Inf.*), insides (*Inf.*), intestines, viscera, vitals 2. belly, core, deep, depths, hold, inside, interior 3. *Archaic* compassion, mercifulness, mercy, pity, sympathy, tenderness

bower alcove, arbour, grotto, leafy shelter, shady recess, summerhouse

bowl 1. *n.* basin, deep dish, vessel 2. *v.* fling, hurl, pitch, revolve, roll, rotate, spin, throw, trundle, whirl

bowl over 1. amaze, astonish, astound, dumbfound, stagger, startle, stun, surprise 2. bring down, fell, floor, knock down, overthrow, overturn

bow out abandon, back out, cop out (*Sl.*), get out, give up, pull out, quit, resign, retire, step down (*Inf.*), withdraw

box[1] 1. *n.* ark (*Dialect*), carton, case, casket, chest, container, kist (*Scot. & Northern English dialect*), pack, package, portmanteau, receptacle, trunk 2. *v.* pack, package, wrap

box[2] *v.* 1. exchange blows, fight, spar 2. belt (*Inf.*), buffet, butt, chin (*Sl.*), clout (*Inf.*), cuff, deck (*Sl.*), hit, lay one on (*Sl.*), punch, slap, sock (*Sl.*), strike, thwack, wallop (*Inf.*), whack ~*n.* 3. belt (*Inf.*), blow, buffet, clout (*Inf.*), cuff, punch, slap, stroke, thumping, wallop (*Inf.*)

boxer fighter, prizefighter, pugilist, sparrer, sparring partner

box in cage, confine, contain, coop up, enclose, hem in, isolate, shut in, surround, trap

boxing fisticuffs, prizefighting, pugilism, sparring, the fight game (*Inf.*), the ring

boy fellow, junior, lad, schoolboy, stripling, youngster, youth

boycott ban, bar, black, blackball, blacklist, embargo, exclude, ostracize, outlaw, prohibit, proscribe, refrain from, refuse, reject, spurn

Antonyms accept, advocate, back, champion, defend, espouse, help, patronize, promote, support, welcome

boyfriend admirer, beau, date, follower, leman (*Archaic*), lover, man, steady, suitor, swain, sweetheart, toy boy, young man

boyish adolescent, childish, immature, innocent, juvenile, puerile, young, youthful

brace 1. *n.* bolster, bracer, bracket, buttress, prop, reinforcement, stanchion, stay, strut, support, truss 2. *v.* bandage, bind, bolster, buttress, fasten, fortify, hold up, prop, reinforce, shove, shove up, steady, strap, strengthen, support, tie, tighten

bracing brisk, chilly, cool, crisp, energizing, exhilarating, fortifying, fresh, invigorating, lively, refreshing, restorative, reviving, rousing, stimulating, tonic, vigorous
Antonyms debilitating, draining, enervating, exhausting, fatiguing, sapping, soporific, taxing, tiring, weakening

brackish bitter, briny, saline, salt, salty, undrinkable
Antonyms clean, clear, fresh, pure, sweet, unpolluted

brag blow one's own trumpet, bluster, boast, crow, swagger, talk big (*Sl.*), vaunt

braggart bigmouth (*Sl.*), bluffer, blusterer, boaster, brag, braggadocio, bragger, hot dog (*Chiefly U.S.*), show-off (*Inf.*), swaggerer, swashbuckler

braid entwine, interlace, intertwine, interweave, lace, plait, ravel, twine, weave

brain brainbox, egghead (*Inf.*), genius, highbrow, intellect, intellectual, mastermind, prodigy, pundit, sage, scholar

brainless braindead (*Inf.*), foolish, idiotic, inane, inept, mindless, senseless, stupid, thoughtless, unintelligent, witless

brains capacity, intellect, intelligence, mind, nous (*Brit. sl.*), reason, sagacity, savvy (*Sl.*), sense, shrewdness, smarts (*Sl., chiefly U.S.*), suss (*Sl.*), understanding, wit

brainwashing alteration, conditioning, indoctrination, persuasion, re-education

brainy bright, brilliant, clever, intelligent, smart

brake 1. *n.* check, constraint, control, curb, rein, restraint 2. *v.* check, decelerate, halt, moderate, reduce speed, slacken, slow, stop

branch 1. arm, bough, limb, offshoot, prong, ramification, shoot, spray, sprig 2. chapter, department, division, local office, office, part, section, subdivision, subsection, wing

branch out add to, develop, diversify, enlarge, expand, extend, increase, multiply, proliferate, ramify, spread out

brand *n.* 1. cast, class, grade, kind, make, quality, sort, species, type, variety 2. emblem, hallmark, label, mark, marker, sign, stamp, symbol, trademark 3. blot, disgrace, infamy, mark, reproach, slur, smirch, stain, stigma, taint ~*v.* 4. burn, burn in, label, mark, scar, stamp 5. censure, denounce, discredit, disgrace, expose, mark, stigmatize

brandish display, exhibit, flaunt, flourish, parade, raise, shake, swing, wield

brash 1. audacious, foolhardy, hasty, impetuous, impulsive, indiscreet, precipitate, rash, reckless 2. bold, brazen, cocky, forward, heedless, impertinent, impudent, insolent, pushy (*Inf.*), rude
Antonyms careful, cautious, polite, prudent, reserved, respectful, thoughtful, timid, uncertain

brass audacity, brass neck (*Brit. inf.*), cheek, chutzpah (*U.S. & Canad. inf.*), effrontery, front, gall, impertinence, impudence, insolence, neck (*Inf.*), nerve (*Inf.*), presumption, rudeness

brassy 1. barefaced, bold, brash, brazen, forward, impudent, insolent, loud-mouthed, pert, pushy (*Inf.*), saucy 2. blatant, flashy, garish, gaudy, hard, jazzy (*Inf.*), loud, obtrusive, showy, vulgar 3. blaring, cacophonous, dissonant, grating, harsh, jangling, jarring, loud, noisy, piercing, raucous, shrill, strident
Antonyms discreet, low-key, modest, played down, quiet, restrained, subdued, toned down, understated

brat cub, guttersnipe, jackanapes, kid (*Inf.*), puppy (*Inf.*), rascal, spoilt child, urchin, whippersnapper, youngster

bravado bluster, boast, boastfulness, boasting, bombast, brag, braggadocio, fanfaronade (*Rare*), swagger, swaggering, swashbuckling, vaunting

brave 1. *adj.* ballsy (*Taboo sl.*), bold, courageous, daring, dauntless, fearless, gallant, gritty, heroic, intrepid, plucky, resolute, undaunted, valiant, valorous 2. *v.* bear, beard, challenge, confront, dare, defy, endure, face, stand up to, suffer, tackle, withstand
Antonyms *adj.* afraid, chickenshit (*U.S. sl.*), cowardly, craven, faint-hearted, fearful, frightened, scared, shrinking, timid ~*v.* give in to, retreat from, surrender to

bravery balls (*Taboo sl.*), ballsiness (*Taboo sl.*), boldness, bravura, courage, daring, dauntlessness, doughtiness, fearlessness, fortitude, gallantry, grit, guts (*Inf.*), hardihood, hardiness, heroism, indomitability, intrepidity, mettle, pluck, pluckiness, spirit, spunk (*Inf.*), valour
Antonyms cowardice, faint-heartedness, fearfulness, fright, timidity

bravo assassin, bandit, brigand, cutthroat, desperado, hired killer, murderer, villain

bravura animation, audacity, boldness, brilliance, brio, daring, dash, display, élan, energy, exhibitionism, ostentation, panache, punch (*Inf.*), spirit, verve, vigour, virtuosity

brawl 1. *n.* affray (*Law*), altercation, argument, *bagarre,* battle, broil, clash, disorder, dispute, donnybrook, fight, fracas, fray, free-for-all (*Inf.*), melee *or* mêlée, punch-up (*Brit. inf.*), quarrel, row (*Inf.*), ruckus (*Inf.*), rumpus, scrap (*Inf.*), scrimmage, scuffle, shindig (*Inf.*), shindy (*Inf.*), skirmish, squabble, tumult, uproar, wrangle 2. *v.* altercate, argue, battle, dispute, fight, quarrel, row (*Inf.*), scrap (*Inf.*), scuffle, tussle, wrangle, wrestle

brawn beef (*Inf.*), beefiness (*Inf.*), brawniness, flesh, might, muscle, muscles, muscularity, power, robustness, strength, vigour

brawny athletic, beefy (*Inf.*), bulky, burly, fleshy, hardy, hefty (*Inf.*), herculean, husky (*Inf.*), lusty, muscular, powerful, Ramboesque, robust, sinewy, stalwart, strapping, strong, sturdy, thewy, thickset, vigorous, well-built, well-knit
Antonyms frail, scrawny, skinny, thin, undeveloped, weak, weakly, weedy (*Inf.*), wimpish *or* wimpy (*Inf.*)

bray 1. *v.* bell, bellow, blare, heehaw, hoot, roar, screech, trumpet 2. *n.* bawl, bell, bellow, blare, cry, harsh sound, heehaw, hoot, roar, screech, shout

brazen *adj.* 1. audacious, barefaced, bold, brash, brassy (*Inf.*), defiant, forward, immodest, impudent, insolent, pert, pushy (*Inf.*), saucy, shameless, unabashed, unashamed 2. brass, brassy, bronze, metallic ~*v.* 3. *With* **out** be impenitent, be unashamed, confront, defy, outface, outstare, persevere, stare out
Antonyms (*sense 1*) cautious, decorous, diffident, mannerly, modest, reserved, respectful, reticent, secret, shy, stealthy, timid

breach 1. aperture, break, chasm, cleft, crack, fissure, gap, hole, opening, rent, rift, rupture, split 2. contravention, disobedience, infraction, infringement, noncompliance, nonobservance, offence, transgression, trespass, violation 3. alienation, difference, disaffection, disagreement, dissension, division, estrangement, falling-out (*Inf.*), parting of the ways, quarrel, schism, separation, severance, variance
Antonyms (*sense 2*) adherence to, attention, compliance, discharge, fulfilment, heeding, honouring, observation, performance

bread 1. aliment, diet, fare, food, necessities, nourishment, nutriment, provisions, subsistence, sustenance, viands, victuals 2. *Sl.* ackers (*Sl.*), brass (*Northern English dialect*), cash, dibs (*Sl.*), dosh (*Brit. & Aust. sl.*), dough (*Sl.*), finance, funds, money, necessary (*Inf.*), needful (*Inf.*), rhino (*Brit. sl.*), shekels (*Inf.*), silver, spondulicks (*Sl.*), tin (*Sl.*)

breadth 1. beam (*of a ship*), broadness, latitude, span, spread, wideness, width 2. amplitude, area, compass, comprehensiveness, dimension, expanse, extensiveness, extent, magnitude, measure, range, reach, scale, scope, size, space, spread, sweep, vastness 3. broad-mindedness, freedom, latitude, liberality, open-mindedness, openness, permissiveness

break *v.* 1. batter, burst, crack, crash, demolish, destroy, disintegrate, divide, fracture, fragment, part, rend, separate, sever, shatter, shiver, smash, snap, splinter, split, tear, total (*Sl.*), trash (*Sl.*) 2. breach, contravene, disobey, disregard, infract (*Law*), infringe, renege on, transgress, violate 3. cow, cripple, demoralize, dispirit, enervate, enfeeble, impair, incapacitate, subdue, tame, undermine, weaken 4. abandon, cut, discontinue, give up, interrupt, pause, rest, stop, suspend 5. bust (*Inf.*), degrade, demote, discharge, dismiss, humiliate, impoverish, make bankrupt, reduce, ruin 6. announce, come out, disclose, divulge, impart, inform, let out, make public, proclaim, reveal, tell 7. *Of a record, etc.* beat, better, cap (*Inf.*), exceed, excel, go beyond, outdo, outstrip, surpass, top 8. appear, burst out, come forth suddenly, emerge, erupt, happen, occur 9. cut and run (*Inf.*), dash, escape, flee, fly, get away, hook it (*Sl.*), run away 10. cushion, diminish, lessen, lighten, moderate, reduce, soften, weaken ~*n.* 11. breach, cleft, crack, division, fissure, fracture, gap, gash, hole, opening, rent, rift, rupture, split, tear 12. breather (*Inf.*), entr'acte, halt, hiatus, interlude, intermission, interruption, interval, let-up (*Inf.*), lull, pause, recess, respite, rest, suspension 13. alienation, breach, disaffection, dispute, divergence, estrangement, rift, rupture, schism, separation, split 14. *Inf.* advantage, chance, fortune, opening, opportunity, stroke of luck
Antonyms (*sense 1*) attach, bind, connect, fasten, join, repair, unite (*sense 2*) abide by, adhere to, conform, discharge, follow, obey, observe

breakable brittle, crumbly, delicate, flimsy, fragile, frail, frangible, friable
Antonyms durable, indestructible, infrangible, lasting, nonbreakable, resistant, rugged, shatterproof, solid, strong, toughened, unbreakable

breakaway *adj.* dissenting, heretical, rebel, schismatic, seceding, secessionist

break away 1. decamp, escape, flee, fly, hook it (*Sl.*), make a break for it, make a run for it (*Inf.*), make off, run away 2. break with, detach, part company, secede, separate

breakdown 1. collapse, crackup (*Inf.*), disintegration, disruption, failure, mishap, stoppage 2. analysis, categorization, classification, detailed list, diagnosis, dissection, itemization

break down be overcome, collapse, conk out (*Inf.*), crack up (*Inf.*), fail, give way, go kaput (*Inf.*), go to pieces, seize up, stop, stop working

breaker billow, comber, roller, wave, whitecap, white horse

break-in breaking and entering, burglary, invasion, robbery

break in 1. barge in, burst in, butt in, interfere, interject, interpose, interrupt, intervene, intrude, put one's two cents in (*U.S. sl.*) 2. break and enter, burgle, invade, rob 3. accustom, condition, get used to, habituate, initiate, prepare, tame, train

break into begin, burst into, burst out, commence, dissolve into, give way to, launch into

break off 1. detach, divide, part, pull off, separate, sever, snap off, splinter 2. cease, desist, discontinue, end, finish, halt, pause, stop, suspend, terminate

break out 1. appear, arise, begin, commence, emerge, happen, occur, set in, spring up, start 2. abscond, bolt, break loose, burst out, escape, flee, get free 3. burst out, erupt

breakthrough advance, development, discovery, find, finding, gain, improvement, invention, leap, progress, quantum leap, step forward

break through achieve, burst through, crack it (*Inf.*), cut it (*Inf.*), emerge, get past, pass, penetrate, shine forth, succeed

break-up breakdown, breaking, crackup (*Inf.*), disintegration, dispersal, dissolution, divorce, ending, parting, rift, separation, split, splitting, termination, wind-up

break up adjourn, disband, dismantle, disperse, disrupt, dissolve, divide, divorce, end, part, scatter, separate, sever, split, stop, suspend, terminate

breakwater groyne, jetty, mole, sea wall, spur

break with break away from, depart from, ditch (*Sl.*), drop (*Inf.*), jilt, part company, reject, renounce, repudiate, separate from

breast 1. boob (*Sl.*), bosom, bust, chest, front, teat, thorax, tit (*Sl.*), udder 2. being, conscience, core, emotions, feelings, heart, seat of the affections, sentiments, soul, thoughts

breath 1. air, animation, breathing, exhalation, gasp, gulp, inhalation, pant, respiration, wheeze 2. aroma, niff (*Brit. sl.*), odour, smell, vapour, whiff 3. break, breather, breathing-space, instant, moment, pause, respite, rest, second 4. faint breeze, flutter, gust, puff, sigh, slight movement, waft, zephyr 5. hint, murmur, suggestion, suspicion, undertone, whisper 6. animation, energy, existence, life, lifeblood, life force, vitality

breathe 1. draw in, gasp, gulp, inhale and exhale, pant, puff, respire, wheeze 2. imbue, impart, infuse, inject, inspire, instil, transfuse 3. articulate, express, murmur, say, sigh, utter, voice, whisper

breather break, breathing space, breath of air, halt, pause, recess, respite, rest

breathless 1. choking, exhausted, gasping, gulping, out of breath, panting, short-winded, spent, wheezing, winded 2. agog, anxious, astounded, avid, eager, excited, flabbergasted (*Inf.*), gobsmacked (*Brit. sl.*), on tenterhooks, open-mouthed, thunderstruck, with bated breath

breathtaking amazing, astonishing, awe-inspiring, awesome, brilliant, exciting, heart-stirring, impressive, magnificent, moving, overwhelming, sensational, striking, stunning (*Inf.*), thrilling, wondrous (*Archaic or literary*)

breech arse (*Taboo sl.*), ass (*U.S. & Canad. taboo sl.*), backside (*Inf.*), behind (*Inf.*), bum (*Brit. sl.*), buns (*U.S. sl.*), butt (*U.S. & Canad. inf.*), buttocks, derrière (*Euphemistic*), fundament, jacksy (*Brit. sl.*), posterior, rump, seat, tail (*Inf.*)

breed *v.* 1. bear, beget, bring forth, engender, generate, hatch, multiply, originate, procreate, produce, propagate, reproduce 2. bring up, cultivate, develop, discipline, educate, foster, instruct, nourish, nurture, raise, rear 3. arouse, bring about, cause, create, generate, give rise to, induce, make, occasion, originate, produce, stir up ~*n.* 4. brand, class, extraction, family, ilk, kind, line, lineage, pedigree, progeny, race, sort, species, stamp, stock, strain, type, variety

breeding 1. ancestry, cultivation, development, lineage, nurture, raising, rearing, reproduction, training, upbringing 2. civility, conduct, courtesy, cultivation, culture, gentility, manners, polish, refinement, sophistication, urbanity

breeze 1. *n.* air, breath of wind, capful of wind, current of air, draught, flurry, gust, light wind, puff of air, waft, whiff, zephyr 2. *v.* flit, glide, hurry, move briskly, pass, sail, sally, sweep, trip

breezy 1. airy, blowing, blowy, blusterous, blustery, fresh, gusty, squally, windy 2. airy, animated, blithe, buoyant, carefree, casual, cheerful, chirpy (*Inf.*), debonair, easy-going, free and easy, genial, informal, jaunty, light, light-hearted, lively, sparkling, sparky, spirited, sprightly, sunny, upbeat (*Inf.*), vivacious
Antonyms calm, depressed, dull, heavy, lifeless, mournful, oppressive, sad, serious, windless

brevity 1. conciseness, concision, condensation, crispness, curtness, economy, pithiness, succinctness, terseness 2. briefness, ephemerality, impermanence, shortness, transience, transitoriness
Antonyms (*sense 1*) circuity, diffuseness, discursiveness, long-windedness, prolixity, rambling, redundancy, tautology, tediousness, verbiage, verboseness, verbosity, wordiness

brew *v.* 1. boil, ferment, infuse (*tea*), make (*beer*), prepare by fermentation, seethe, soak, steep, stew 2. breed, concoct, contrive, develop, devise, excite, foment, form, gather, hatch, plan, plot, project, scheme, start, stir up *~n.* 3. beverage, blend, concoction, distillation, drink, fermentation, infusion, liquor, mixture, preparation

bribe 1. *n.* allurement, backhander (*Sl.*), boodle (*Sl., chiefly U.S.*), corrupting gift, enticement, graft (*Inf.*), hush money (*Sl.*), incentive, inducement, kickback (*U.S.*), pay-off (*Inf.*), payola (*Inf.*), reward for treachery, sop, sweetener (*Sl.*) 2. *v.* buy off, corrupt, get at, grease the palm *or* hand of (*Sl.*), influence by gifts, lure, oil the palm of (*Inf.*), pay off (*Inf.*), reward, square, suborn

bribery buying off, corruption, graft (*Inf.*), inducement, palm-greasing (*Sl.*), payola (*Inf.*), protection, subornation

bric-a-brac baubles, bibelots, curios, gewgaws, kickshaws, knick-knacks, objects of virtu, *objets d'art,* ornaments, trinkets

bridal bride's, conjugal, connubial, hymeneal, marital, marriage, matrimonial, nuptial, spousal, wedding

bridge *n.* 1. arch, flyover, overpass, span, viaduct 2. band, bond, connection, link, tie *~v.* 3. arch over, attach, bind, connect, couple, cross, cross over, extend across, go over, join, link, reach across, span, traverse, unite
Antonyms *v.* cleave, come apart, disjoin, divide, keep apart, separate, sever, split, sunder, widen

bridle *v.* 1. check, constrain, control, curb, govern, keep in check, master, moderate, rein, repress, restrain, subdue 2. be indignant, bristle, draw (oneself) up, get angry, get one's back up, raise one's hackles, rear up *~n.* 3. check, control, curb, rein, restraint, trammels

brief *adj.* 1. compendious, compressed, concise, crisp, curt, laconic, limited, pithy, short, succinct, terse, thumbnail, to the point 2. ephemeral, fast, fleeting, hasty, little, momentary, quick, quickie (*Inf.*), short, short-lived, swift, temporary, transitory 3. abrupt, blunt, brusque, curt, sharp, short, surly *~n.* 4. abridgment, abstract, digest, epitome, outline, précis, sketch, summary, synopsis 5. argument, case, contention, data, defence, demonstration *~v.* 6. advise, clue in (*Inf.*), explain, fill in (*Inf.*), gen up (*Brit. inf.*), give (someone) a rundown, give (someone) the gen (*Brit. inf.*), inform, instruct, prepare, prime, put (someone) in the picture (*Inf.*)
Antonyms *adj.* circuitous, detailed, diffuse, extensive, lengthy, long, long-drawn-out, long-winded, protracted

briefing conference, directions, guidance, information, instruction, instructions, meeting, preamble, preparation, priming, rundown

briefly abruptly, briskly, casually, concisely, cursorily, curtly, fleetingly, hastily, hurriedly, in a few words, in a nutshell, in brief, in outline, in passing, momentarily, precisely, quickly, shortly, temporarily

brigade band, body, camp, company, contingent, corps, crew, force, group, organization, outfit, party, squad, team, troop, unit

brigand bandit, desperado, footpad (*Archaic*), freebooter, gangster, highwayman, marauder, outlaw, plunderer, robber, ruffian

bright 1. beaming, blazing, brilliant, dazzling, effulgent, flashing, gleaming, glistening, glittering, glowing, illuminated, intense, lambent, luminous, lustrous, radiant, resplendent, scintillating, shimmering, shining, sparkling, twinkling, vivid 2. clear, clement, cloudless, fair, limpid, lucid, pellucid, pleasant, sunny, translucent, transparent, unclouded 3. acute, astute, aware, brainy, brilliant, clear-headed, clever, ingenious, intelligent, inventive, keen, quick, quick-witted, sharp, smart, wide-awake 4. auspicious, encouraging, excellent, favourable, golden, good, hopeful, optimistic, palmy, promising, propitious, prosperous, rosy 5. cheerful, chirpy (*Inf.*), gay, genial, glad, happy, jolly, joyful, joyous, light-hearted, lively, merry, sparky, upbeat (*Inf.*), vivacious 6. distinguished, famous, glori-

ous, illustrious, magnificent, outstanding, remarkable, splendid
Antonyms (*senses 1 & 2*) cloudy, dark, dim, dusky, gloomy, grey, overcast, poorly lit (*sense 3*) dense, dim, dim-witted (*Inf.*), dull, dumb (*Inf.*), foolish, idiotic, ignorant, retarded, simple, slow, stupid, thick, unintelligent, witless

brighten 1. clear up, enliven, gleam, glow, illuminate, lighten, light up, make brighter, shine 2. become cheerful, buck up (*Inf.*), buoy up, cheer, encourage, enliven, gladden, hearten, make happy, perk up
Antonyms (*sense 1*) becloud, blacken, cloud over *or* up, dim, dull, obscure, overshadow, shade, shadow (*sense 2*) become angry, become gloomy, blacken, cloud, deject, depress, dispirit, look black, sadden

brilliance, brilliancy 1. blaze, brightness, dazzle, effulgence, gleam, glitter, intensity, luminosity, lustre, radiance, refulgence, resplendence, sheen, sparkle, vividness 2. acuity, aptitude, braininess, cleverness, distinction, excellence, genius, giftedness, greatness, inventiveness, talent, wisdom 3. éclat, gilt, glamour, gorgeousness, grandeur, illustriousness, magnificence, pizzazz *or* pizazz (*Inf.*), splendour
Antonyms darkness, dimness, dullness, folly, idiocy, inanity, incompetence, ineptitude, obscurity, paleness, silliness, simple-mindedness, stupidity, thickness

brilliant 1. ablaze, bright, coruscating, dazzling, glittering, glossy, intense, luminous, lustrous, radiant, refulgent, resplendent, scintillating, shining, sparkling, vivid 2. celebrated, eminent, exceptional, famous, glorious, illustrious, magnificent, notable, outstanding, splendid, superb 3. accomplished, acute, astute, brainy, clever, discerning, expert, gifted, intellectual, intelligent, inventive, masterly, penetrating, profound, quick, talented
Antonyms (*sense 1*) dark, dim, dull, gloomy, obscure (*senses 2 & 3*) dim, dull, ordinary, run-of-the-mill, simple, slow, stupid, unaccomplished, unexceptional, untalented

brim 1. *n.* border, brink, circumference, edge, flange, lip, margin, rim, skirt, verge 2. *v.* fill, fill up, hold no more, overflow, run over, spill, well over

brimful brimming, filled, flush, full, level with, overflowing, overfull, packed, running over

brindled mottled, patched, speckled, spotted, streaked, tabby

brine pickling solution, saline solution, salt water, sea water, the sea

bring 1. accompany, bear, carry, conduct, convey, deliver, escort, fetch, gather, guide, import, lead, take, transfer, transport, usher 2. cause, contribute to, create, effect, engender, inflict, occasion, produce, result in, wreak 3. compel, convince, dispose, force, induce, influence, make, move, persuade, prevail on *or* upon, prompt, sway 4. command, earn, fetch, gross, net, produce, return, sell for, yield

bring about accomplish, achieve, bring to pass, cause, compass, create, effect, effectuate, generate, give rise to, make happen, manage, occasion, produce, realize

bring down abase, cut down, drop, fell, floor, lay low, level, lower, overthrow, overturn, pull down, reduce, shoot down, undermine, upset

bring in accrue, bear, be worth, fetch, gross, produce, profit, realize, return, yield

bring off accomplish, achieve, bring home the bacon (*Inf.*), bring to pass, carry off, carry out, crack it (*Inf.*), cut it (*Inf.*), discharge, execute, perform, pull off, succeed

bring up 1. breed, develop, educate, form, nurture, raise, rear, support, teach, train 2. advance, allude to, broach, introduce, mention, move, propose, put forward, submit

brink border, boundary, brim, edge, fringe, frontier, limit, lip, margin, point, rim, skirt, threshold, verge

brisk 1. active, agile, alert, animated, bustling, busy, energetic, lively, nimble, no-nonsense, quick, sparky, speedy, sprightly, spry, vigorous, vivacious 2. biting, bracing, crisp, exhilarating, fresh, invigorating, keen, nippy, refreshing, sharp, snappy, stimulating
Antonyms boring, dull, enervating, heavy, lazy, lethargic, slow, sluggish, tiring, unenergetic, wearisome

briskly actively, apace, brusquely, coolly, decisively, efficiently, energetically, firmly, incisively, nimbly, pdq (*Sl.*), posthaste, promptly, pronto (*Inf.*), quickly, rapidly, readily, smartly, vigorously

bristle *n.* 1. barb, hair, prickle, spine, stubble, thorn, whisker ~*v.* 2. horripilate, prickle, rise, stand on end, stand up 3. be angry, be infuriated, be maddened, bridle, flare up, get one's dander up (*Sl.*), rage, see red, seethe, spit (*Inf.*) 4. *With* **with** abound, be alive, be thick, crawl, hum, swarm, teem

bristly bearded, bewhiskered, hairy, prickly, rough, stubbly, unshaven, whiskered

brittle 1. breakable, crisp, crumbling, crumbly, delicate, fragile, frail, frangible, friable, shatterable, shivery 2. curt, edgy, irritable, nervous, prim, stiff, stilted, tense, wired (*Sl.*)

Antonyms durable, elastic, flexible, infrangible, nonbreakable, resistant, rugged, shatterproof, strong, sturdy, toughened

broach 1. approach, bring up, hint at, introduce, mention, open up, propose, raise the subject, speak of, suggest, talk of, touch on 2. crack, draw off, open, pierce, puncture, start, tap, uncork

broad 1. ample, beamy (*of a ship*), capacious, expansive, extensive, generous, large, roomy, spacious, vast, voluminous, wide, widespread 2. all-embracing, catholic, comprehensive, encyclopedic, far-reaching, general, global, inclusive, nonspecific, sweeping, undetailed, universal, unlimited, wide, wide-ranging 3. *As in* **broad daylight** clear, full, obvious, open, plain, straightforward, undisguised 4. broad-minded, liberal, open, permissive, progressive, tolerant, unbiased 5. blue, coarse, gross, improper, indecent, indelicate, near the knuckle (*Inf.*), unrefined, vulgar

Antonyms close, confined, constricted, cramped, limited, meagre, narrow, restricted, tight

broadcast *v.* 1. air, beam, cable, put on the air, radio, relay, show, televise, transmit 2. advertise, announce, circulate, disseminate, make public, proclaim, promulgate, publish, report, spread ~*n.* 3. programme, show, telecast, transmission

broaden augment, develop, enlarge, expand, extend, fatten, increase, open up, spread, stretch, supplement, swell, widen

Antonyms circumscribe, constrain, diminish, narrow, reduce, restrict, simplify, tighten

broad-minded catholic, cosmopolitan, dispassionate, flexible, free-thinking, indulgent, liberal, open-minded, permissive, responsive, tolerant, unbiased, unbigoted, undogmatic, unprejudiced

Antonyms biased, bigoted, closed-minded, dogmatic, inflexible, intolerant, narrow-minded, prejudiced, uncharitable

broadside abuse, assault, attack, battering, bombardment, censure, criticism, denunciation, diatribe, philippic, stick (*Sl.*)

brochure advertisement, booklet, circular, folder, handbill, hand-out, leaflet, mailshot, pamphlet

broil 1. *n.* affray, altercation, *bagarre,* brawl, brouhaha, dispute, feud, fracas, fray, quarrel, scrimmage, shindig (*Inf.*), shindy (*Inf.*), skirmish, strife, wrangle 2. *v.* brawl, dispute, quarrel, scrimmage, wrangle

broke bankrupt, bust (*Inf.*), cleaned out (*Sl.*), dirt-poor (*Inf.*), down and out, flat broke (*Inf.*), impoverished, insolvent, on one's uppers, penniless, penurious, ruined, short, skint (*Brit. sl.*), stony-broke (*Brit. sl.*), without two pennies to rub together (*Inf.*)

Antonyms affluent, comfortable, flush (*Inf.*), in the money (*Inf.*), prosperous, rich, solvent, wealthy, well-to-do

broken 1. burst, demolished, destroyed, fractured, fragmented, rent, ruptured, separated, severed, shattered, shivered 2. defective, exhausted, feeble, imperfect, kaput (*Inf.*), not functioning, out of order, ruined, run-down, spent, weak 3. disconnected, discontinuous, disturbed, erratic, fragmentary, incomplete, intermittent, interrupted, spasmodic 4. beaten, browbeaten, crippled, crushed, defeated, demoralized, humbled, oppressed, overpowered, subdued, tamed, vanquished 5. dishonoured, disobeyed, disregarded, forgotten, ignored, infringed, isolated, retracted, traduced, transgressed 6. disjointed, halting, hesitating, imperfect, stammering

broken-down collapsed, dilapidated, in disrepair, inoperative, kaput (*Inf.*), not functioning, not in working order, old, on the blink (*Sl.*), on the fritz (*U.S. sl.*), out of commission, out of order, worn out

brokenhearted crestfallen, desolate, despairing, devastated, disappointed, disconsolate, grief-stricken, heartbroken, heartsick, inconsolable, miserable, mournful, prostrated, sorrowful, wretched

broker agent, dealer, factor, go-between, intermediary, middleman, negotiator

bromide banality, cliché, commonplace, hackneyed saying, platitude, stereotype, trite remark, truism

bronze brownish, chestnut, copper, copper-coloured, metallic brown, reddish-brown, reddish-tan, rust, tan

brood *v.* 1. agonize, dwell upon, eat one's heart out, fret, meditate, mope, mull over, muse, ponder, repine, ruminate, think upon 2. cover, hatch, incubate, set, sit upon ~*n.* 3. breed, chicks, children, clutch, family, hatch, infants, issue, litter, offspring, progeny, young

brook[1] beck, burn, gill (*Dialect*), rill, rivulet, runnel (*Literary*), stream, streamlet, watercourse

brook[2] abide, accept, allow, bear, countenance, endure, put up with (*Inf.*), stand, stomach, suffer, support, swallow, thole (*Dialect*), tolerate, withstand

brothel bagnio, bawdy house (*Archaic*), bordello, cathouse (*U.S. sl.*), house of ill fame, house of ill repute, house of prostitution, knocking shop (*Sl.*), red-light district, stews (*Archaic*), whorehouse

brother 1. blood brother, kin, kinsman, relation, relative, sibling 2. associate, chum (*Inf.*), cock (*Brit. inf.*), colleague, companion, compeer, comrade, confrère, fellow member, mate, pal (*Inf.*), partner 3. cleric, friar, monk, regular, religious

brotherhood 1. brotherliness, camaraderie, companionship, comradeship, fellowship, friendliness, kinship 2. alliance, association, clan, clique, community, coterie, fraternity, guild, league, order, society, union

brotherly affectionate, altruistic, amicable, benevolent, cordial, fraternal, friendly, kind, neighbourly, philanthropic, sympathetic

brow 1. air, appearance, aspect, bearing, countenance, eyebrow, face, forehead, front, mien, temple 2. brim, brink, crest, crown, edge, peak, rim, summit, tip, top, verge

browbeat badger, bulldoze (*Inf.*), bully, coerce, cow, domineer, dragoon, hector, intimidate, lord it over, oppress, overawe, overbear, threaten, tyrannize

Antonyms beguile, cajole, coax, entice, flatter, inveigle, lure, manoeuvre, seduce, sweet-talk (*Inf.*), tempt, wheedle

brown 1. *adj.* auburn, bay, brick, bronze, bronzed, browned, brunette, chestnut, chocolate, coffee, dark, donkey brown, dun, dusky, fuscous, ginger, hazel, rust, sunburnt, tan, tanned, tawny, toasted, umber 2. *v.* cook, fry, grill, sauté, seal, sear

browned off cheesed off (*Brit. sl.*), discontented, discouraged, disgruntled, disheartened, fed up, pissed off (*Taboo sl.*), sick as a parrot (*Inf.*), weary

brown study absorption, abstractedness, abstraction, contemplation, meditation, musing, preoccupation, reflection, reverie, rumination

browse 1. dip into, examine cursorily, flip through, glance at, leaf through, look round, look through, peruse, scan, skim, survey 2. crop, eat, feed, graze, nibble, pasture

bruise *v.* 1. blacken, blemish, contuse, crush, damage, deface, discolour, injure, mar, mark, pound, pulverize 2. displease, grieve, hurt, injure, insult, offend, pain, sting, wound ~*n.* 3. black-and-blue mark, black mark, blemish, contusion, discoloration, injury, mark, swelling

brunt burden, force, full force, impact, pressure, shock, strain, stress, thrust, violence

brush[1] *n.* 1. besom, broom, sweeper 2. clash, conflict, confrontation, encounter, fight, fracas, scrap (*Inf.*), set-to (*Inf.*), skirmish, slight engagement, spot of bother (*Inf.*), tussle ~*v.* 3. buff, clean, paint, polish, sweep, wash 4. caress, contact, flick, glance, graze, kiss, scrape, stroke, sweep, touch

brush[2] *n.* brushwood, bushes, copse, scrub, shrubs, thicket, undergrowth, underwood

brush aside discount, dismiss, disregard, have no time for, ignore, kiss off (*Sl., chiefly U.S. & Canad.*), override, sweep aside

brush-off *n.* cold shoulder, cut, dismissal, go-by (*Sl.*), kiss-off (*Sl., chiefly U.S. & Canad.*), knock-back (*Sl.*), rebuff, refusal, rejection, repudiation, repulse, slight, snub, the (old) heave-ho (*Inf.*)

brush off *v.* cold-shoulder, cut, deny, disdain, dismiss, disown, disregard, ignore, kiss off (*Sl., chiefly U.S. & Canad.*), put down, rebuff, refuse, reject, repudiate, scorn, slight, snub, spurn

brush up bone up on (*Inf.*), cram, go over, polish up, read up, refresh one's memory, relearn, revise, study

brusque abrupt, blunt, curt, discourteous, gruff, hasty, impolite, sharp, short, surly, tart, terse, unmannerly

Antonyms accommodating, civil, courteous, gentle, patient, polite, well-mannered

brutal 1. barbarous, bloodthirsty, cruel, ferocious, heartless, inhuman, merciless, pitiless, remorseless, ruthless, savage, uncivilized, vicious 2. animal, beastly, bestial, brute, brutish, carnal, coarse, crude, sensual 3. bearish, callous, gruff, harsh, impolite, insensitive, rough, rude, severe, uncivil, unfeeling, unmannerly

Antonyms civilized, gentle, humane, kind, merciful, polite, refined, sensitive, soft-hearted

brutality atrocity, barbarism, barbarity, bloodthirstiness, brutishness, cruelty, ferocity, inhumanity, ruthlessness, savageness, savagery, viciousness

brutally barbarically, barbarously, brutishly, callously, cruelly, ferociously, fiercely, hardheartedly, heartlessly, in cold blood, inhumanly, meanly, mercilessly, murderously, pitilessly, remorselessly, ruthlessly, savagely, unkindly, viciously

brute *n.* 1. animal, beast, creature, wild animal 2. barbarian, beast, devil, fiend, ghoul, monster, ogre, sadist, savage, swine ~*adj.* 3. bodily, carnal, fleshly, instinctive, mindless, physical, senseless, unthinking 4. bestial, coarse, depraved, gross, sensual

brutish barbarian, boorish, coarse, crass, crude, cruel, gross, loutish, savage, stupid, subhuman, swinish, uncouth, vulgar

bubble *n.* 1. air ball, bead, blister, blob, drop, droplet, globule, vesicle 2. bagatelle, delusion, fantasy, illusion, toy, trifle, vanity ~*v.* 3. boil, effervesce, fizz, foam, froth, percolate, seethe, sparkle 4. babble, burble, gurgle, murmur, purl, ripple, trickle, trill

bubbles effervescence, fizz, foam, froth, head, lather, spume, suds

bubbly 1. carbonated, curly, effervescent, fizzy, foamy, frothy, lathery, sparkling, sudsy 2. animated, bouncy, elated, excited, happy, lively, merry, sparky

buccaneer corsair, freebooter, pirate, privateer, sea-rover

buck *n.* 1. *Archaic* beau, blade, blood, coxcomb, dandy, fop, gallant, popinjay, spark ~*v.* 2. bound, jerk, jump, leap, prance, spring, start, vault 3. dislodge, throw, unseat 4. *Inf.* cheer, encourage, gladden, gratify, hearten, inspirit, please

buckle *n.* 1. catch, clasp, clip, fastener, hasp 2. bulge, contortion, distortion, kink, warp ~*v.* 3. catch, clasp, close, fasten, hook, secure 4. bend, bulge, cave in, collapse, contort, crumple, distort, fold, twist, warp

buckle down apply oneself, exert oneself, launch into, pitch in, put one's shoulder to the wheel, set to

buck up 1. get a move on, hasten, hurry up, shake a leg, speed up 2. brighten, cheer up, encourage, hearten, inspirit, perk up, rally, take heart

bucolic agrarian, agrestic, agricultural, country, pastoral, rural, rustic

bud 1. *n.* embryo, germ, shoot, sprout 2. *v.* burgeon, burst forth, develop, grow, pullulate, shoot, sprout

budding beginning, burgeoning, developing, embryonic, fledgling, flowering, germinal, growing, incipient, nascent, potential, promising

budge 1. dislodge, give way, inch, move, propel, push, remove, roll, shift, slide, stir 2. bend, change, convince, give way, influence, persuade, sway, yield

budget 1. *n.* allocation, allowance, cost, finances, financial statement, fiscal estimate, funds, means, resources 2. *v.* allocate, apportion, cost, cost out, estimate, plan, ration

buff[1] 1. *adj.* sandy, straw, tan, yellowish, yellowish-brown 2. *n.* **in the buff** bare, buck naked (*Sl.*), in one's birthday suit (*Inf.*), in the altogether (*Inf.*), in the raw (*Inf.*), naked, nude, unclad, unclothed, with bare skin, without a stitch on (*Inf.*) 3. *v.* brush, burnish, polish, rub, shine, smooth

buff[2] *Inf.* addict, admirer, aficionado, connoisseur, devotee, enthusiast, expert, fan, fiend (*Inf.*), freak (*Inf.*), grandmaster, hotshot (*Inf.*), maven (*U.S.*), whiz (*Inf.*)

buffer bulwark, bumper, cushion, fender, intermediary, safeguard, screen, shield, shock absorber

buffet[1] *n.* café, cafeteria, cold table, counter, cupboard, refreshment-counter, salad bar, sideboard, snack bar

buffet[2] 1. *v.* bang, batter, beat, box, bump, clobber (*Sl.*), cuff, flail, knock, lambast(e), pound, pummel, punch, push, rap, shove, slap, strike, thump, wallop (*Inf.*) 2. *n.* bang, blow, box, bump, cuff, jolt, knock, push, rap, shove, slap, smack, thump, wallop (*Inf.*)

buffoon clown, comedian, comic, droll, fool, harlequin, jester, joker, merry-andrew, silly billy (*Inf.*), wag

buffoonery clowning, drollery, jesting, nonsense, silliness, tomfoolery, waggishness

bug *n.* 1. *Inf.* bacterium, disease, germ, infection, microorganism, virus 2. craze, fad, mania, obsession, rage 3. blemish, catch, defect, error, failing, fault, flaw, glitch, gremlin, imperfection, snarl-up (*Inf., chiefly Brit.*), virus ~*v.* 4. *Inf.* aggravate (*Inf.*), annoy, badger, be on one's back (*Sl.*), bother, disturb, gall, get in one's hair (*Inf.*), get on one's nerves (*Inf.*), get on one's wick (*Brit. sl.*), harass, hassle (*Inf.*), irk, irritate, nark (*Brit., Aust., & N.Z. sl.*), needle (*Inf.*), nettle, pester, piss one off (*Taboo sl.*), plague, vex 5. eavesdrop, listen in, spy, tap, wiretap

bugbear anathema, bane, *bête noire,* bogey, bugaboo, devil, dread, fiend, horror, nightmare, pet hate

build *v.* 1. assemble, construct, erect, fabricate, form, make, put up, raise 2. base, begin, constitute, establish, formulate, found, inaugurate, initiate, institute, originate, set up, start 3. accelerate, amplify, augment, develop, enlarge, escalate, extend, improve, increase, intensify, strengthen ~*n.* 4. body, figure, form, frame, physique, shape, structure

Antonyms *v.* contract, debilitate, decline, decrease, demolish, dilute, dismantle, end, finish, harm, impair, lower, reduce, relinquish, sap, suspend, tear down, weaken

building 1. domicile, dwelling, edifice, fabric, house, pile, structure 2. architecture, construction, erection, fabricating, raising

build-up 1. accumulation, development, enlargement, escalation, expansion, gain, growth, increase 2. ballyhoo (*Inf.*), hype, plug (*Inf.*), promotion, publicity, puff 3. accretion, accumulation, heap, load, mass, stack, stockpile, store

build up 1. add to, amplify, augment, develop, enhance, expand, extend, fortify, heighten, improve, increase, intensify, reinforce, strengthen 2. advertise, boost, plug (*Inf.*), promote, publicize, spotlight

built-in essential, implicit, in-built, included, incorporated, inherent, inseparable, integral, part and parcel of

bulbous bloated, bulging, convex, rounded, swelling, swollen

bulge *n.* 1. bump, hump, lump, projection, protrusion, protuberance, swelling 2. boost, increase, intensification, rise, surge ~*v.* 3. bag, dilate, distend, enlarge, expand, project, protrude, puff out, sag, stand out, stick out, swell, swell out

Antonyms bowl, cave, cavity, concavity, crater, dent, depression, hole, hollow, indentation, pit, trough

bulk *n.* 1. amplitude, bigness, dimensions, immensity, largeness, magnitude, massiveness, size, substance, volume, weight 2. better part, body, generality, lion's share, main part, majority, major part, mass, most, nearly all, plurality, preponderance ~*v.* 3. **bulk large** be important, carry weight, dominate, loom, loom large, preponderate, stand out, threaten

bulky big, colossal, cumbersome, elephantine, enormous, ginormous (*Inf.*), heavy, huge, hulking, humongous *or* humungous (*U.S. sl.*), immense, mammoth, massive, massy, mega (*Sl.*), ponderous, substantial, unmanageable, unwieldy, very large, voluminous, weighty

Antonyms convenient, handy, manageable, neat, slim, small, wieldy

bulldoze 1. demolish, flatten, level, raze 2. drive, force, propel, push, shove, thrust 3. browbeat, bully, coerce, cow, dragoon, hector, intimidate, railroad (*Inf.*)

bullet ball, missile, pellet, projectile, shot, slug

bulletin account, announcement, communication, communiqué, dispatch, message, news flash, notification, report, statement

bull-headed headstrong, inflexible, mulish, obstinate, pig-headed, stiff-necked, stubborn, stupid, tenacious, uncompromising, unyielding, wilful

bullish assured, bold, confident, expectant, improving, positive, rising

bully 1. *n.* big bully, browbeater, bully boy, coercer, intimidator, oppressor, persecutor, ruffian, tormentor, tough 2. *v.* bluster, browbeat, bulldoze (*Inf.*), bullyrag, coerce, cow, domineer, hector, intimidate, oppress, overbear, persecute, push around (*Sl.*), ride roughshod over, swagger, terrorize, tyrannize 3. *adj.* admirable, excellent, fine, nifty (*Inf.*), radical (*Inf.*), very good 4. *interj.* bravo, capital, good, grand, great, well done

bulwark 1. bastion, buttress, defence, embankment, fortification, outwork, partition, rampart, redoubt 2. buffer, guard, mainstay, safeguard, security, support

bumbling awkward, blundering, botching, bungling, clumsy, incompetent, inefficient, inept, lumbering, maladroit, muddled, stumbling

Antonyms able, brisk, capable, competent, efficient, equal, fit

bump *v.* 1. bang, collide (with), crash, hit, knock, slam, smash into, strike 2. bounce, jar, jerk, jolt, jostle, jounce, rattle, shake 3. budge, dislodge, displace, move, remove, shift ~*n.* 4. bang, blow, collision, crash, hit, impact, jar, jolt, knock, rap, shock, smash, thud, thump 5. bulge, contusion, hump, knob, knot, lump, node, nodule, protuberance, swelling

bumper *adj.* abundant, bountiful, excellent, exceptional, jumbo (*Inf.*), massive, mega (*Sl.*), prodigal, spanking (*Inf.*), teeming, unusual, whacking (*Inf., chiefly Brit.*), whopping (*Inf.*)

bump into chance upon, come across, encounter, happen upon, light upon, meet, meet up with, run across, run into

bumpkin boor, clodhopper, clown, country bumpkin, hayseed (*U.S. & Canad. inf.*), hick (*Inf., chiefly U.S. & Canad.*), hillbilly, lout, lubber, oaf, peasant, rustic, yokel

bump off assassinate, blow away (*Sl., chiefly U.S.*), dispatch, do away with, do in (*Sl.*), eliminate, finish off, kill, knock off (*Sl.*), liquidate, murder, remove, rub out (*U.S. sl.*), take out (*Sl.*), wipe out (*Inf.*)

bumptious arrogant, boastful, brash, cocky, conceited, egotistic, forward, full of oneself, impudent, overbearing, overconfident, presumptuous, pushy (*Inf.*), self-assertive, showy, swaggering, vainglorious, vaunting

bumpy bone-breaking, bouncy, choppy, irregular, jarring, jerky, jolting, jolty, knobby, lumpy, pitted, potholed, rough, rutted, uneven

bunch *n.* 1. assortment, batch, bouquet, bundle, clump, cluster, collection, heap, lot, mass, number, parcel, pile, quantity, sheaf, spray, stack, tuft 2. band, bevy, crew (*Inf.*), crowd, flock, gang, gathering, group, knot, mob, multitude, party, posse (*Inf.*), swarm, team, troop ~*v.* 3. assemble, bundle, cluster, collect, congregate, cram together, crowd, flock, group, herd, huddle, mass, pack

bundle *n.* 1. accumulation, assortment, batch, bunch, collection, group, heap, mass, pile, quantity, stack 2. bag, bale, box, carton, crate, pack, package, packet, pallet, parcel, roll ~*v.* 3. bale, bind, fasten, pack, package, palletize, tie, tie together, tie up, truss, wrap 4. *With* **out, off, into,** *etc.* hurry, hustle, push, rush, shove, throw, thrust

5. *With* **up** clothe warmly, muffle up, swathe, wrap up

bungle blow (*Sl.*), blunder, bodge (*Inf.*), botch, butcher, cock up (*Brit. sl.*), foul up, fuck up (*Offens. taboo sl.*), fudge, louse up (*Sl.*), make a mess of, mar, mess up, miscalculate, mismanage, muff, ruin, screw up (*Inf.*), spoil

Antonyms accomplish, achieve, carry off, effect, fulfil, succeed, triumph

bungler blunderer, botcher, butcher, butterfingers (*Inf.*), duffer (*Inf.*), fumbler, incompetent, lubber, muddler, muff

bungling awkward, blundering, botching, cack-handed (*Inf.*), clumsy, ham-fisted (*Inf.*), ham-handed (*Inf.*), incompetent, inept, maladroit, unskilful

bunk[1] *v.* abscond, beat it (*Sl.*), bolt, clear out (*Inf.*), cut and run (*Inf.*), decamp, do a bunk (*Brit. sl.*), do a runner (*Sl.*), flee, fly the coop (*U.S. & Canad. inf.*), run for it (*Inf.*), scram (*Inf.*), skedaddle (*Inf.*), take a powder (*U.S. & Canad. sl.*), take it on the lam (*U.S. & Canad. sl.*)

bunk[2], **bunkum** balderdash, balls (*Taboo sl.*), baloney (*Inf.*), bilge (*Inf.*), bosh (*Inf.*), bullshit (*Taboo sl.*), cobblers (*Brit. taboo sl.*), crap (*Sl.*), eyewash (*Inf.*), garbage (*Inf.*), guff (*Sl.*), havers (*Scot.*), hogwash, hokum (*Sl., chiefly U.S. & Canad.*), hooey (*Sl.*), horsefeathers (*U.S. sl.*), hot air (*Inf.*), moonshine, nonsense, piffle (*Inf.*), poppycock (*Inf.*), rot, rubbish, shit (*Taboo sl.*), stuff and nonsense, tarradiddle, tomfoolery, tommyrot, tosh (*Sl., chiefly Brit.*), trash, tripe (*Inf.*), truck (*Inf.*), twaddle

buoy 1. *n.* beacon, float, guide, marker, signal 2. *v. With* **up** boost, cheer, cheer up, encourage, hearten, keep afloat, lift, raise, support, sustain

buoyancy 1. floatability, lightness, weightlessness 2. animation, bounce (*Inf.*), cheerfulness, cheeriness, good humour, high spirits, liveliness, pep, spiritedness, sunniness, zing (*Inf.*)

buoyant 1. afloat, floatable, floating, light, weightless 2. animated, blithe, bouncy, breezy, bright, carefree, cheerful, chirpy (*Inf.*), debonair, genial, happy, jaunty, joyful, light-hearted, lively, peppy (*Inf.*), sparky, sunny, upbeat (*Inf.*), vivacious

Antonyms (*sense 2*) cheerless, depressed, despairing, dull, forlorn, gloomy, glum, hopeless, melancholy, moody, morose, pessimistic, sad, sullen, unhappy

burden *n.* 1. affliction, anxiety, care, clog, encumbrance, grievance, load, millstone, obstruction, onus, responsibility, sorrow, strain, stress, trial, trouble, weight, worry 2. *Naut.* cargo, freight, lading, tonnage ~*v.* 3. bother, encumber, handicap, load, oppress, overload, overwhelm, saddle with, strain, tax, weigh down, worry

burdensome crushing, difficult, exacting, heavy, irksome, onerous, oppressive, taxing, troublesome, trying, weighty

bureau 1. desk, writing desk 2. agency, branch, department, division, office, service

bureaucracy 1. administration, authorities, civil service, corridors of power, directorate, government, ministry, officials, officialdom, the system 2. bumbledom, officialdom, officialese, red tape, regulations

bureaucrat administrator, apparatchik, civil servant, functionary, mandarin, minister, office-holder, officer, official, public servant

burglar cat burglar, filcher, housebreaker, picklock, pilferer, robber, sneak thief, thief

burglary break-in, breaking and entering, filching, housebreaking, larceny, pilferage, robbery, stealing, theft, thieving

burial burying, entombment, exequies, funeral, inhumation, interment, obsequies, sepulture

burial ground cemetery, churchyard, God's acre, golgotha (*Rare*), graveyard, necropolis

buried 1. coffined, consigned to the grave, entombed, interred, laid to rest 2. dead and buried, dead and gone, in the grave, long gone, pushing up the daisies, six feet under 3. covered, forgotten, hidden, repressed, sunk in oblivion, suppressed 4. cloistered, concealed, hidden, private, sequestered, tucked away 5. caught up, committed, concentrating, devoted, engrossed, immersed, intent, lost, occupied, preoccupied, rapt

burlesque 1. *n.* caricature, mock, mockery, parody, satire, send-up (*Brit. inf.*), spoof (*Inf.*), takeoff (*Inf.*), travesty 2. *adj.* caricatural, comic, farcical, hudibrastic, ironical, ludicrous, mock, mock-heroic, mocking, parodic, satirical, travestying 3. *v.* ape, caricature, exaggerate, imitate, lampoon, make fun of, mock, parody, ridicule, satirize, send up (*Brit. inf.*), spoof (*Inf.*), take off (*Inf.*), take the piss out of (*Taboo sl.*), travesty

burly beefy (*Inf.*), big, brawny, bulky, hefty, hulking, muscular, powerful, Ramboesque, stocky, stout, strapping, strong, sturdy, thickset, well-built

Antonyms lean, puny, scraggy, scrawny, slight, spare, thin, weak, weedy (*Inf.*), wimpish *or* wimpy (*Inf.*)

burn 1. be ablaze, be on fire, blaze, flame, flare, flash, flicker, glow, smoke 2. brand, calcine, char, ignite, incinerate, kindle, light, parch, reduce to ashes, scorch, set on fire, shrivel, singe, toast, wither **3.** bite, hurt, pain, smart, sting, tingle **4.** be excited (angry, aroused, inflamed, passionate), blaze, desire, fume, seethe, simmer, smoulder, yearn **5.** consume, eat up, expend, use

burning **1.** blazing, fiery, flaming, flashing, gleaming, glowing, hot, illuminated, scorching, smouldering **2.** all-consuming, ardent, eager, earnest, fervent, fervid, flaming, frantic, frenzied, impassioned, intense, passionate, vehement, zealous **3.** acrid, biting, caustic, irritating, painful, piercing, prickling, pungent, reeking, smarting, stinging, tingling **4.** acute, compelling, critical, crucial, essential, important, pressing, significant, urgent, vital
Antonyms apathetic, calm, cool, cooling, faint, indifferent, mild, numbing, passive, soothing

burnish **1.** *v.* brighten, buff, furbish, glaze, polish, rub up, shine, smooth **2.** *n.* gloss, lustre, patina, polish, sheen, shine
Antonyms *v.* abrade, graze, scratch, scuff

burrow **1.** *n.* den, hole, lair, retreat, shelter, tunnel **2.** *v.* delve, dig, excavate, hollow out, scoop out, tunnel

burst *v.* **1.** blow up, break, crack, disintegrate, explode, fly open, fragment, puncture, rend asunder, rupture, shatter, shiver, split, tear apart **2.** barge, break, break out, erupt, gush forth, run, rush, spout ~*n.* **3.** bang, blast, blasting, blowout, blow-up, breach, break, crack, discharge, explosion, rupture, split **4.** eruption, fit, gush, gust, outbreak, outburst, outpouring, rush, spate, spurt, surge, torrent ~*adj.* **5.** flat, punctured, rent, ruptured, split

bury **1.** consign to the grave, entomb, inearth, inhume, inter, lay to rest, sepulchre **2.** conceal, cover, cover up, enshroud, hide, secrete, shroud, stash (*Inf.*), stow away **3.** drive in, embed, engulf, implant, sink, submerge **4.** absorb, engage, engross, immerse, interest, occupy
Antonyms (*senses 1 & 2*) bring to light, dig up, discover, disinter, dredge up, exhume, expose, find, reveal, turn up, uncover, unearth

bush **1.** hedge, plant, shrub, shrubbery, thicket **2.** backwoods, brush, scrub, scrubland, the wild, woodland

bushy bristling, bristly, fluffy, fuzzy, luxuriant, rough, shaggy, spreading, stiff, thick, unruly, wiry

busily actively, assiduously, briskly, carefully, diligently, earnestly, energetically, industriously, intently, purposefully, speedily, strenuously

business **1.** calling, career, craft, employment, function, job, line, métier, occupation, profession, pursuit, trade, vocation, work **2.** company, concern, corporation, enterprise, establishment, firm, organization, venture **3.** bargaining, commerce, dealings, industry, manufacturing, merchandising, selling, trade, trading, transaction **4.** affair, assignment, concern, duty, function, issue, matter, point, problem, question, responsibility, subject, task, topic

businesslike correct, efficient, matter-of-fact, methodical, orderly, organized, practical, professional, regular, routine, systematic, thorough, well-ordered, workaday
Antonyms careless, disorderly, disorganized, frivolous, impractical, inefficient, irregular, sloppy, unprofessional, unsystematic, untidy

businessman, businesswoman capitalist, employer, entrepreneur, executive, financier, *homme d'affaires,* industrialist, merchant, tradesman, tycoon

bust[1] bosom, breast, chest, torso

bust[2] *v.* **1.** break, burst, fracture, rupture **2.** bankrupt, break, crash, fail, impoverish, ruin **3.** arrest, catch, collar (*Inf.*), cop (*Sl.*), feel one's collar (*Sl.*), lift (*Sl.*), nab (*Inf.*), nail (*Inf.*), raid, search ~*adj.* **4.** **go bust** become insolvent, be ruined, break, fail, go bankrupt ~*n.* **5.** arrest, capture, cop (*Sl.*), raid, search, seizure

bustle **1.** *v.* beetle, bestir, dash, flutter, fuss, hasten, hurry, rush, scamper, scramble, scurry, scuttle, stir, tear **2.** *n.* activity, ado, agitation, commotion, excitement, flurry, fuss, haste, hurly-burly, hurry, pother, stir, to-do, tumult
Antonyms *v.* be indolent, idle, laze, lie around, loaf, loiter, loll, relax, rest, take it easy ~*n.* inaction, inactivity, quiet, quietness, stillness, tranquillity

bustling active, astir, busy, buzzing, crowded, energetic, eventful, full, humming, hustling, lively, rushing, stirring, swarming, teeming, thronged

busy *adj.* **1.** active, assiduous, brisk, diligent, employed, engaged, engrossed, hard at work, industrious, in harness, occupied, on duty, persevering, slaving, working **2.** active, energetic, exacting, full, hectic, hustling, lively, on the go (*Inf.*), restless, strenuous, tireless, tiring **3.** fussy, inquisitive, interfering, meddlesome, meddling, nosy, officious, prying, snoopy, stirring, troublesome ~*v.* **4.** absorb, employ, engage, engross, immerse, interest, occupy
Antonyms (*senses 1 & 2*) idle, inactive, indolent, lackadaisical, lazy, off duty, relaxed, shiftless, slothful, unoccupied

busybody eavesdropper, gossip, intriguer, intruder, meddler, nosy parker (*Inf.*), pry, scandalmonger, snoop, snooper, stirrer (*Inf.*), troublemaker

but *conj.* 1. further, however, moreover, nevertheless, on the contrary, on the other hand, still, yet 2. bar, barring, except, excepting, excluding, notwithstanding, save, with the exception of ~*adv.* 3. just, merely, only, simply, singly, solely

butcher *n.* 1. destroyer, killer, murderer, slaughterer, slayer ~*v.* 2. carve, clean, cut, cut up, dress, joint, prepare, slaughter 3. assassinate, cut down, destroy, exterminate, kill, liquidate, massacre, put to the sword, slaughter, slay 4. bodge (*Inf.*), botch, destroy, mess up, mutilate, ruin, spoil, wreck

butchery blood bath, blood-letting, bloodshed, carnage, killing, massacre, mass murder, murder, slaughter

butt[1] 1. haft, handle, hilt, shaft, shank, stock 2. base, end, fag end (*Inf.*), foot, leftover, stub, tail, tip

butt[2] Aunt Sally, dupe, laughing stock, mark, object, point, subject, target, victim

butt[3] *v./n.* 1. *With* or *of the head or horns* buck, buffet, bump, bunt, jab, knock, poke, prod, punch, push, ram, shove, thrust ~*v.* 2. abut, join, jut, meet, project, protrude 3. *With* **in** *or* **into** chip in (*Inf.*), cut in, interfere, interrupt, intrude, meddle, put one's oar in, put one's two cents in (*U.S. sl.*), stick one's nose in

butt[4] barrel, cask, pipe

butter up blarney, brown-nose (*Taboo sl.*), cajole, coax, fawn on *or* upon, flatter, honey up, kiss (someone's) ass (*U.S. sl.*), oil one's tongue, pander to, soft-soap, suck up to (*Inf.*), wheedle

buttocks arse (*Taboo sl.*), ass (*U.S. & Canad. taboo sl.*), backside (*Inf.*), behind (*Inf.*), bottom, bum (*Brit. sl.*), buns (*U.S. sl.*), butt (*U.S. & Canad. inf.*), derrière (*Euphemistic*), fundament, gluteus maximus (*Anat.*), haunches, hindquarters, jacksy (*Brit. sl.*), nates (*Technical name*), posterior, rear, rump, seat, tail (*Inf.*)

buttonhole *v. Fig.* accost, bore, catch, detain in talk, grab, importune, persuade importunately, take aside, waylay

buttress 1. *n.* abutment, brace, mainstay, pier, prop, reinforcement, shore, stanchion, stay, strut, support 2. *v.* augment, back up, bolster, brace, prop, prop up, reinforce, shore, shore up, strengthen, support, sustain, uphold

buxom ample, bosomy, busty, comely, curvaceous, debonair, fresh-looking, full-bosomed, healthy, hearty, jocund, jolly, lively, lusty, merry, plump, robust, sprightly, voluptuous, well-rounded, winsome

Antonyms delicate, frail, slender, slight, slim, svelte, sylphlike, thin, trim

buy *v.* 1. acquire, get, invest in, obtain, pay for, procure, purchase, score (*Sl.*), shop for 2. *Often with* **off** bribe, corrupt, fix (*Inf.*), grease someone's palm (*Sl.*), square, suborn ~*n.* 3. acquisition, bargain, deal, purchase

Antonyms *v.* auction, barter, retail, sell, vend

buzz *n.* 1. bombilation *or* bombination (*Literary*), buzzing, drone, hiss, hum, murmur, purr, ring, ringing, sibilation, susurration *or* susurrus (*Literary*), whir, whisper 2. dirt (*U.S. sl.*), gen (*Brit. inf.*), gossip, hearsay, latest (*Inf.*), news, report, rumour, scandal, whisper ~*v.* 3. bombilate *or* bombinate (*Literary*), drone, fizzle, hum, murmur, reverberate, ring, sibilate, susurrate (*Literary*), whir, whisper, whizz 4. chatter, gossip, natter, rumour, tattle

by *prep.* 1. along, beside, by way of, close to, near, next to, over, past, via 2. through, through the agency of, under the aegis of ~*adv.* 3. aside, at hand, away, beyond, close, handy, in reach, near, past, to one side

by and by before long, erelong (*Archaic or poetic*), eventually, in a while, in the course of time, one day, presently, soon

bygone ancient, antiquated, departed, erstwhile, extinct, forgotten, former, gone by, lost, of old, of yore, olden, one-time, past, past recall, previous, sunk in oblivion

Antonyms coming, forthcoming, future, prospective, to be, to come

bypass avoid, body-swerve (*Scot.*), circumvent, depart from, detour round, deviate from, get round, go round, ignore, neglect, outflank, pass round

Antonyms abut, adjoin, come together, connect, converge, cross, intersect, join, link, meet, touch, unite

bystander eyewitness, looker-on, observer, onlooker, passer-by, spectator, viewer, watcher, witness

Antonyms contributor, partaker, participant, party

byword adage, aphorism, apophthegm, dictum, epithet, gnome, maxim, motto, precept, proverb, saw, saying, slogan

C

cab hackney, hackney carriage, minicab, taxi, taxicab

cabal camp, caucus, clique, coalition, combination, conclave, confederacy, conspiracy, coterie, faction, intrigue, junta, league, machination, party, plot, scheme, schism, set

cabbalistic cryptic, dark, esoteric, fanciful, mysterious, mystic, mystical, obscure, occult, secret

cabin 1. berth, bothy, chalet, cot, cottage, crib, hovel, hut, lodge, shack, shanty, shed 2. berth, compartment, deckhouse, quarters, room

cabinet 1. case, chiffonier, closet, commode, cupboard, dresser, escritoire, locker 2. administration, assembly, council, counsellors, ministry 3. apartment, boudoir, chamber (*Archaic*)

cache 1. *n.* accumulation, fund, garner (*Archaic*), hiding place, hoard, nest egg, repository, reserve, stash (*Inf.*), stockpile, store, storehouse, supply, treasury 2. *v.* bury, conceal, hide, put away, secrete, stash (*Inf.*), store

cackle babble, blather, chatter, chuckle, cluck, crow, gabble, gibber, giggle, jabber, prattle, snicker, snigger, titter

cacophonous discordant, dissonant, grating, harsh, inharmonious, jarring, raucous, strident

cacophony caterwauling, discord, disharmony, dissonance, stridency

cad bounder (*Old-fashioned Brit. sl.*), churl, cur, dastard (*Archaic*), heel (*Sl.*), knave, rat (*Inf.*), rotter (*Sl., chiefly Brit.*), scumbag (*Sl.*)

cadaverous ashen, blanched, bloodless, corpselike, deathlike, deathly, emaciated, exsanguinous, gaunt, ghastly, haggard, hollow-eyed, pale, pallid, wan

caddish despicable, ill-bred, low, ungentlemanly, unmannerly
Antonyms gentlemanly, honourable, laudable, mannerly, pleasant, praiseworthy

cadence 1. beat, lilt, measure (*Prosody*), metre, pulse, rhythm, swing, tempo, throb 2. accent, inflection, intonation, modulation

cadre core, framework, hard core, infrastructure, key group, nucleus

café cafeteria, coffee bar, coffee shop, lunchroom, restaurant, snack bar, tearoom

cage 1. *v.* confine, coop up, fence in, immure, impound, imprison, incarcerate, lock up, mew, pound, restrain, shut up 2. *n.* corral (*U.S.*), enclosure, pen, pound

cagey, cagy careful, cautious, chary, discreet, guarded, noncommittal, shrewd, wary, wily
Antonyms careless, dull, imprudent, indiscreet, reckless, stolid, unthinking, unwary

caitiff 1. *n.* coward, knave, miscreant, rascal, rogue, scoundrel, traitor, vagabond, villain, wretch 2. *adj.* base, cowardly, craven, dastardly, ignoble

cajole beguile, coax, decoy, dupe, entice, entrap, flatter, inveigle, lure, manoeuvre, mislead, seduce, sweet-talk (*Inf.*), tempt, wheedle

cajolery beguilement, blandishments, blarney, coaxing, enticement, flattery, inducement(s), inveigling, persuasion, soft soap (*Inf.*), sweet talk (*Inf.*), wheedling

cake 1. *v.* bake, cement, coagulate, congeal, consolidate, dry, encrust, harden, inspissate (*Archaic*), ossify, solidify, thicken 2. *n.* bar, block, cube, loaf, lump, mass, slab

calamitous blighting, cataclysmic, catastrophic, deadly, devastating, dire, disastrous, fatal, pernicious, ruinous, tragic, woeful
Antonyms advantageous, beneficial, favourable, fortunate, good, helpful

calamity adversity, affliction, cataclysm, catastrophe, disaster, distress, downfall, hardship, misadventure, mischance, misfortune, mishap, reverse, ruin, scourge, tragedy, trial, tribulation, woe, wretchedness
Antonyms advantage, benefit, blessing, boon, good fortune, good luck, help

calculate 1. adjust, compute, consider, count, determine, enumerate, estimate, figure, gauge, judge, rate, reckon, value, weigh, work out 2. aim, design, intend, plan

calculated considered, deliberate, intended, intentional, planned, premeditated, purposeful
Antonyms haphazard, hasty, heedless, hurried, impetuous, impulsive, rash, spon-

taneous, unintentional, unplanned, unpremeditated

calculating canny, cautious, contriving, crafty, cunning, designing, devious, Machiavellian, manipulative, politic, scheming, sharp, shrewd, sly
Antonyms blunt, direct, downright, frank, guileless, honest, open, outspoken, sincere, undesigning

calculation 1. answer, computation, estimate, estimation, figuring, forecast, judgment, reckoning, result 2. caution, circumspection, contrivance, deliberation, discretion, foresight, forethought, planning, precaution

calibre 1. bore, diameter, gauge, measure 2. *Fig.* ability, capacity, distinction, endowment, faculty, force, gifts, merit, parts, quality, scope, stature, strength, talent, worth

call *v.* 1. announce, arouse, awaken, cry, cry out, hail, halloo, proclaim, rouse, shout, waken, yell 2. assemble, bid, collect, contact, convene, convoke, gather, invite, muster, rally, summon 3. give (someone) a bell (*Brit. sl.*), phone, ring up (*Inf., chiefly Brit.*), telephone 4. christen, denominate, describe as, designate, dub, entitle, label, name, style, term 5. announce, appoint, declare, decree, elect, ordain, order, proclaim, set apart 6. consider, estimate, judge, regard, think ~*n.* 7. cry, hail, scream, shout, signal, whoop, yell 8. announcement, appeal, command, demand, invitation, notice, order, plea, request, ring (*Inf., chiefly Brit.*), summons, supplication, visit 9. cause, claim, excuse, grounds, justification, need, occasion, reason, right, urge
Antonyms (*sense 1*) be quiet, be silent, murmur, mutter, speak softly, whisper (*senses 2 & 5*) call off, cancel, dismiss, disperse, excuse, release (*sense 7*) murmur, mutter, whisper (*sense 8*) dismissal, release

call for 1. demand, entail, involve, necessitate, need, occasion, require, suggest 2. collect, fetch, pick up, uplift (*Scot.*)

calling business, career, employment, life's work, line, métier, mission, occupation, profession, province, pursuit, trade, vocation, walk of life, work
Antonyms affliction, avocation, curse, dislike, hobby

call on 1. drop in on, look in on, look up, see, visit 2. appeal to, ask, bid, call upon, entreat, invite, invoke, request, summon, supplicate

callous apathetic, case-hardened, cold, hard-bitten, hard-boiled (*Inf.*), hardened, hardhearted, harsh, heartless, indifferent, indurated (*Rare*), insensate, insensible, insensitive, inured, obdurate, soulless, thick-skinned, torpid, uncaring, unfeeling, unresponsive, unsusceptible, unsympathetic
Antonyms caring, compassionate, considerate, gentle, sensitive, soft, sympathetic, tender, understanding

callow green, guileless, immature, inexperienced, jejune, juvenile, naive, puerile, raw, unfledged, unsophisticated, untried

calm *adj.* 1. balmy, halcyon, mild, pacific, peaceful, placid, quiet, restful, serene, smooth, still, tranquil, windless 2. collected, composed, cool, dispassionate, equable, impassive, imperturbable, relaxed, sedate, self-possessed, undisturbed, unemotional, unexcitable, unexcited, unfazed (*Inf.*), unflappable (*Inf.*), unmoved, unruffled ~*v.* 3. hush, mollify, placate, quieten, relax, soothe ~*n.* 4. calmness, hush, peace, peacefulness, quiet, repose, serenity, stillness
Antonyms *adj.* agitated, aroused, discomposed, disturbed, emotional, excited, fierce, frantic, heated, perturbed, rough, shaken, stormy, troubled, wild, worried ~*v.* aggravate, agitate, arouse, disturb, excite, irritate, stir ~*n.* agitation, disturbance, wildness

calmness 1. calm, composure, equability, hush, motionlessness, peace, peacefulness, placidity, quiet, repose, restfulness, serenity, smoothness, stillness, tranquillity 2. composure, cool (*Sl.*), coolness, dispassion, equanimity, impassivity, imperturbability, poise, sang-froid, self-possession

calumniate asperse, backbite, bad-mouth (*Sl., chiefly U.S. & Canad.*), blacken, defame, denigrate, detract, knock (*Inf.*), lampoon, libel, malign, misrepresent, revile, rubbish (*Inf.*), slag (off) (*Sl.*), slander, stigmatize, traduce, vilify, vilipend (*Rare*)

calumnious abusive, aspersive, backbiting, defamatory, derogatory, detractive, insulting, libellous, lying, slanderous, vituperative

calumny abuse, aspersion, backbiting, calumniation, defamation, denigration, derogation, detraction, evil-speaking, insult, libel, lying, misrepresentation, obloquy, revilement, slander, smear, stigma, vilification, vituperation

camaraderie brotherhood, brotherliness, companionability, companionship, comradeship, esprit de corps, fellowship, fraternization, good-fellowship, togetherness

camouflage 1. *n.* blind, cloak, concealment, cover, deceptive markings, disguise, false appearance, front, guise, mask, masquerade, mimicry, protective colouring, screen, subterfuge 2. *v.* cloak, conceal, cov-

er, disguise, hide, mask, obfuscate, obscure, screen, veil
Antonyms *v.* bare, display, exhibit, expose, reveal, show, uncover, unmask, unveil

camp[1] bivouac, camping ground, camp site, cantonment (*Mil.*), encampment, tents

camp[2] affected, artificial, camped up (*Inf.*), campy (*Inf.*), effeminate, mannered, ostentatious, poncy (*Sl.*), posturing

campaign attack, crusade, drive, expedition, jihad (*Rare*), movement, offensive, operation, push

canaille hoi polloi, masses, mob, plebs, populace, proletariat, rabble, ragtag, riffraff, scum, vulgar herd

cancel 1. abolish, abort, abrogate, annul, blot out, call off, countermand, cross out, delete, do away with, efface, eliminate, erase, expunge, obliterate, obviate, quash, repeal, repudiate, rescind, revoke 2. balance out, compensate for, counterbalance, make up for, neutralize, nullify, obviate, offset, redeem

cancellation abandoning, abandonment, abolition, annulment, deletion, elimination, quashing, repeal, revocation

cancer blight, canker, carcinoma (*Pathol.*), corruption, evil, growth, malignancy, pestilence, rot, sickness, tumour

candid 1. blunt, downright, fair, forthright, frank, free, guileless, impartial, ingenuous, just, open, outspoken, plain, sincere, straightforward, truthful, unbiased, unequivocal, unprejudiced, upfront (*Inf.*) 2. impromptu, informal, uncontrived, unposed
Antonyms biased, complimentary, diplomatic, flattering, kind, subtle

candidate applicant, aspirant, claimant, competitor, contender, contestant, entrant, nominee, possibility, runner, solicitant, suitor

candour artlessness, directness, fairness, forthrightness, frankness, guilelessness, honesty, impartiality, ingenuousness, naïveté, openness, outspokenness, simplicity, sincerity, straightforwardness, truthfulness, unequivocalness
Antonyms bias, cunning, deceit, diplomacy, dishonesty, flattery, insincerity, prejudice, subtlety

canker 1. *v.* blight, consume, corrode, corrupt, embitter, envenom, inflict, poison, pollute, rot, rust, waste away 2. *n.* bane, blight, blister, cancer, corrosion, corruption, infection, lesion, rot, scourge, sore, ulcer

cannon 1. artillery piece, big gun, field gun, gun, mortar 2. *Plural* artillery, battery, big guns, cannonry, field guns, guns, ordnance

cannonade barrage, battery, bombardment, broadside, pounding, salvo, shelling, volley

canny acute, artful, astute, careful, cautious, circumspect, clever, judicious, knowing, perspicacious, prudent, sagacious, sharp, shrewd, subtle, wise, worldly-wise
Antonyms bumbling, inept, lumpen (*Inf.*), obtuse, unskilled

canon catalogue, criterion, dictate, formula, list, precept, principle, regulation, roll, rule, standard, statute, yardstick

canonical accepted, approved, authoritative, authorized, orthodox, recognized, sanctioned

canopy awning, baldachin, covering, shade, sunshade, tester

cant *n.* 1. affected piety, humbug, hypocrisy, insincerity, lip service, pious platitudes, pretence, pretentiousness, sanctimoniousness, sham holiness 2. argot, jargon, lingo, slang, vernacular ~*v.* 3. angle, bevel, incline, rise, slant, slope, tilt

cantankerous bad-tempered, captious, choleric, contrary, crabby, cranky (*U.S., Canad., & Irish inf.*), crotchety (*Inf.*), crusty, difficult, disagreeable, grouchy (*Inf.*), grumpy, ill-humoured, irascible, irritable, liverish, peevish, perverse, quarrelsome, ratty (*Brit. & N.Z. inf.*), testy, tetchy
Antonyms agreeable, amiable, breezy, cheerful, complaisant, congenial, genial, good-natured, happy, kindly, merry, placid, pleasant, vivacious

canter *n.* amble, dogtrot, easy gait, jog, lope

canting hypocritical, insincere, Janus-faced, sanctimonious, two-faced

canvass *v.* 1. analyse, campaign, electioneer, examine, inspect, investigate, poll, scan, scrutinize, sift, solicit, solicit votes, study, ventilate 2. agitate, debate, discuss, dispute ~*n.* 3. examination, investigation, poll, scrutiny, survey, tally

canyon coulee (*U.S.*), gorge, gulch (*U.S.*), gulf, gully, ravine

cap *v.* beat, better, clobber (*Sl.*), complete, cover, crown, eclipse, exceed, excel, finish, lick (*Inf.*), outdo, outstrip, overtop, run rings around (*Inf.*), surpass, top, transcend

capability ability, capacity, competence, facility, faculty, means, potential, potentiality, power, proficiency, qualification(s), wherewithal
Antonyms inability, incompetence, inefficiency, ineptitude, powerlessness

capable able, accomplished, adapted, adept, adequate, apt, clever, competent, efficient, experienced, fitted, gifted, intelli-

gent, masterly, proficient, qualified, skilful, suited, susceptible, talented
Antonyms incapable, incompetent, ineffective, inept, inexpert, unqualified, unskilled

capacious ample, broad, comfortable, commodious, comprehensive, expansive, extended, extensive, generous, liberal, roomy, sizable, spacious, substantial, vast, voluminous, wide
Antonyms confined, constricted, cramped, enclosed, incommodious, insubstantial, limited, narrow, poky, restricted, small, tight, tiny, uncomfortable, ungenerous

capacity 1. amplitude, compass, dimensions, extent, magnitude, range, room, scope, size, space, volume 2. ability, aptitude, aptness, brains, capability, cleverness, competence, competency, efficiency, facility, faculty, forte, genius, gift, intelligence, power, readiness, strength 3. appointment, function, office, position, post, province, role, service, sphere

cape chersonese (*Poetic*), head, headland, ness (*Archaic*), peninsula, point, promontory

caper 1. *v.* bounce, bound, cavort, dance, frisk, frolic, gambol, hop, jump, leap, romp, skip, spring, trip 2. *n.* antic, dido (*Inf.*), escapade, gambol, high jinks, hop, jape, jest, jump, lark (*Inf.*), leap, mischief, practical joke, prank, revel, shenanigan (*Inf.*), sport, stunt

capital *adj.* 1. cardinal, central, chief, controlling, essential, foremost, important, leading, main, major, overruling, paramount, pre-eminent, primary, prime, principal, prominent, vital 2. excellent, fine, first, first-rate, prime, splendid, sterling, superb, world-class ~*n.* 3. assets, cash, finance, finances, financing, funds, investment(s), means, money, principal, property, resources, stock, wealth, wherewithal

capitalism free enterprise, *laissez faire,* private enterprise, private ownership

capitulate come to terms, give in, give up, relent, submit, succumb, surrender, yield
Antonyms beat, conquer, crush, defeat, get the better of, lick (*Inf.*), overcome, overpower, subdue, subjugate, vanquish

capitulation accedence, submission, surrender, yielding

caprice changeableness, fad, fancy, fickleness, fitfulness, freak, humour, impulse, inconstancy, notion, quirk, vagary, whim, whimsy

capricious changeful, crotchety (*Inf.*), erratic, fanciful, fickle, fitful, freakish, impulsive, inconstant, mercurial, odd, queer, quirky, unpredictable, variable, wayward, whimsical
Antonyms consistent, constant, certain, decisive, determined, firm, resolute, responsible, stable, unchangeable, unmoveable, unwavering

capsize invert, keel over, overturn, tip over, turn over, turn turtle, upset

capsule 1. bolus, lozenge, pill, tablet, troche (*Medical*) 2. case, pericarp (*Bot.*), pod, receptacle, seed vessel, sheath, shell, vessel

captain boss, chief, chieftain, commander, head, leader, master, number one (*Inf.*), officer, (senior) pilot, skipper

captious 1. carping, cavilling, censorious, critical, deprecating, disparaging, fault-finding, hypercritical, nagging, nit-picking (*Inf.*) 2. acrimonious, cantankerous, crabbed, cross, irritable, peevish, ratty (*Brit. & N.Z. inf.*), testy, tetchy, touchy

captivate absorb, allure, attract, beguile, bewitch, charm, dazzle, enamour, enchant, enrapture, enslave, ensnare, enthral, entrance, fascinate, hypnotize, infatuate, lure, mesmerize, ravish, seduce, win
Antonyms alienate, disenchant, disgust, repel, repulse

captive 1. *n.* bondservant, convict, detainee, hostage, internee, prisoner, prisoner of war, slave 2. *adj.* caged, confined, enslaved, ensnared, imprisoned, incarcerated, locked up, penned, restricted, subjugated

captivity bondage, confinement, custody, detention, durance (*Archaic*), duress, enthralment, imprisonment, incarceration, internment, restraint, servitude, slavery, thraldom, vassalage

capture 1. *v.* apprehend, arrest, bag, catch, collar (*Inf.*), feel one's collar (*Sl.*), lift (*Sl.*), nab (*Inf.*), nail (*Inf.*), secure, seize, take, take into custody, take prisoner 2. *n.* apprehension, arrest, catch, imprisonment, seizure, taking, taking captive, trapping
Antonyms *v.* free, let go, let out, liberate, release, set free, turn loose

car 1. auto (*U.S.*), automobile, jalopy (*Inf.*), machine, motor, motorcar, vehicle 2. buffet car, cable car, coach, dining car, (railway) carriage, sleeping car, van

carafe decanter, flagon, flask, jug, pitcher

carcass body, cadaver (*Medical*), corpse, corse (*Archaic*), dead body, framework, hulk, remains, shell, skeleton

cardinal capital, central, chief, essential, first, foremost, fundamental, greatest, highest, important, key, leading, main, paramount, pre-eminent, primary, prime, principal

Antonyms dispensable, least important, lowest, secondary, subordinate, unessential

care 1. affliction, anxiety, burden, concern, disquiet, hardship, interest, perplexity, pressure, responsibility, solicitude, stress, tribulation, trouble, vexation, woe, worry 2. attention, carefulness, caution, circumspection, consideration, direction, forethought, heed, management, meticulousness, pains, prudence, regard, vigilance, watchfulness 3. charge, control, custody, guardianship, keeping, management, ministration, protection, supervision, ward
Antonyms (*sense 1*) pleasure, relaxation (*sense 2*) abandon, carelessness, heedlessness, inattention, indifference, laxity, laxness, neglect, negligence, unconcern

career *n.* 1. calling, employment, life work, livelihood, occupation, pursuit, vocation 2. course, passage, path, procedure, progress, race, walk ~*v.* 3. barrel (along) (*Inf., chiefly U.S. & Canad.*), bolt, burn rubber (*Inf.*), dash, hurtle, race, rush, speed, tear

care for 1. attend, foster, look after, mind, minister to, nurse, protect, provide for, tend, watch over 2. be fond of, desire, enjoy, find congenial, like, love, prize, take to, want

carefree airy, blithe, breezy, buoyant, careless, cheerful, cheery, chirpy (*Inf.*), easy-going, happy, happy-go-lucky, insouciant, jaunty, light-hearted, lightsome (*Archaic*), radiant, sunny, untroubled
Antonyms blue, careworn, cheerless, dejected, depressed, desolate, despondent, down, gloomy, melancholy, miserable, sad, unhappy, worried

careful 1. accurate, attentive, cautious, chary, circumspect, conscientious, discreet, fastidious, heedful, painstaking, precise, prudent, punctilious, scrupulous, thoughtful, thrifty 2. alert, concerned, judicious, mindful, particular, protective, solicitous, vigilant, wary, watchful
Antonyms abandoned, careless, casual, inaccurate, inattentive, inexact, neglectful, negligent, reckless, remiss, slovenly, thoughtless, unconcerned, untroubled

careless 1. absent-minded, cursory, forgetful, hasty, heedless, incautious, inconsiderate, indiscreet, negligent, perfunctory, regardless, remiss, thoughtless, unconcerned, unguarded, unmindful, unthinking 2. inaccurate, irresponsible, lackadaisical, neglectful, offhand, slapdash, slipshod, sloppy (*Inf.*) 3. artless, casual, nonchalant, unstudied
Antonyms accurate, alert, anxious, attentive, careful, cautious, concerned, correct, neat, on the ball (*Inf.*), orderly, painstaking, tidy, wary, watchful

carelessness inaccuracy, inattention, inconsiderateness, indiscretion, irresponsibility, laxity, laxness, neglect, negligence, omission, remissness, slackness, sloppiness (*Inf.*), thoughtlessness

caress 1. *v.* cuddle, embrace, fondle, hug, kiss, nuzzle, pet, stroke 2. *n.* cuddle, embrace, fondling, hug, kiss, pat, stroke

caretaker 1. *n.* concierge, curator, custodian, janitor, keeper, porter, superintendent, warden, watchman 2. *adj.* holding, interim, short-term, temporary

cargo baggage, consignment, contents, freight, goods, lading, load, merchandise, shipment, tonnage, ware

caricature 1. *n.* burlesque, cartoon, distortion, farce, lampoon, mimicry, parody, pasquinade, satire, send-up (*Brit. inf.*), takeoff (*Inf.*), travesty 2. *v.* burlesque, distort, lampoon, mimic, mock, parody, ridicule, satirize, send up (*Brit. inf.*), take off (*Inf.*)

carnage blood bath, bloodshed, butchery, havoc, holocaust, massacre, mass murder, murder, shambles, slaughter

carnal 1. amorous, animal, erotic, fleshly, impure, lascivious, lecherous, lewd, libidinous, licentious, lustful, prurient, randy (*Inf., chiefly Brit.*), raunchy (*Sl.*), salacious, sensual, sensuous, sexual, sexy (*Inf.*), steamy (*Inf.*), unchaste, voluptuous, wanton 2. bodily, corporeal, earthly, human, mundane, natural, physical, profane, secular, sublunary, temporal, unregenerate, unspiritual, worldly

carnality bestiality, corporeality, fleshliness, lechery, lust, lustfulness, prurience, salaciousness, sensuality, voluptuousness, worldliness

carnival celebration, fair, festival, fête, fiesta, gala, holiday, jamboree, jubilee, Mardi Gras, merrymaking, revelry

carol canticle, canzonet, chorus, ditty, hymn, lay, noel, song, strain

carouse bend the elbow (*Inf.*), bevvy (*Dialect*), booze (*Inf.*), drink, imbibe, make merry, quaff, roister, wassail

carp beef (*Sl.*), cavil, censure, complain, criticize, find fault, hypercriticize, knock (*Inf.*), kvetch (*U.S. sl.*), nag, pick holes, quibble, reproach
Antonyms admire, applaud, approve, commend, compliment, extol, laud (*Literary*), pay tribute to, praise, sing the praises of, speak highly of

carpenter cabinet-maker, joiner, woodworker

carping captious, cavilling, critical, fault-finding, grouchy (*Inf.*), hard to please, hypercritical, nagging, nit-picking (*Inf.*), picky (*Inf.*), reproachful

carriage 1. carrying, conveyance, conveying, delivery, freight, transport, transportation 2. cab, coach, conveyance, vehicle 3. *Fig.* air, bearing, behaviour, comportment, conduct, demeanour, deportment, gait, manner, mien, posture, presence

carry 1. bear, bring, conduct, convey, fetch, haul, hump (*Brit. sl.*), lift, lug, move, relay, take, tote (*Inf.*), transfer, transmit, transport 2. accomplish, capture, effect, gain, secure, win 3. drive, impel, influence, motivate, spur, urge 4. bear, bolster, hold up, maintain, shoulder, stand, suffer, support, sustain, underpin, uphold 5. broadcast, communicate, display, disseminate, give, offer, publish, release, stock

carry on 1. continue, endure, keep going, last, maintain, perpetuate, persevere, persist 2. administer, manage, operate, run 3. *Inf.* create (*Sl.*), make a fuss, misbehave

carry out accomplish, achieve, carry through, consummate, discharge, effect, execute, fulfil, implement, perform, realize

carton box, case, container, pack, package, packet

cartoon animated cartoon, animated film, animation, caricature, comic strip, lampoon, parody, satire, sketch, takeoff (*Inf.*)

cartridge 1. capsule, case, cassette, container, cylinder, magazine 2. charge, round, shell

carve chip, chisel, cut, divide, engrave, etch, fashion, form, grave (*Archaic*), hack, hew, incise, indent, inscribe, mould, sculpt, sculpture, slash, slice, whittle

cascade 1. *n.* avalanche, cataract, deluge, falls, flood, fountain, outpouring, shower, torrent, waterfall 2. *v.* descend, flood, gush, overflow, pitch, plunge, pour, spill, surge, tumble

case 1. box, cabinet, canister, capsule, carton, cartridge, casket, chest, compact, container, crate, holder, receptacle, shell, suitcase, tray, trunk 2. capsule, casing, cover, covering, envelope, folder, integument, jacket, sheath, wrapper, wrapping 3. circumstance(s), condition, context, contingency, dilemma, event, plight, position, predicament, situation, state 4. example, illustration, instance, occasion, occurrence, specimen 5. *Law* action, cause, dispute, lawsuit, proceedings, process, suit, trial

cash ackers (*Sl.*), banknotes, brass (*Northern English dialect*), bread (*Sl.*), bullion, change, coin, coinage, currency, dibs (*Sl.*), dosh (*Brit. & Aust. sl.*), dough (*Sl.*), funds, money, necessary (*Inf.*), needful (*Inf.*), notes, payment, ready (*Inf.*), ready money, resources, rhino (*Brit. sl.*), shekels (*Inf.*), silver, specie, spondulicks (*Sl.*), tin (*Sl.*), wherewithal

cashier 1. *n.* accountant, bank clerk, banker, bursar, clerk, purser, teller, treasurer 2. *v.* break, cast off, discard, discharge, dismiss, drum out, expel

casket ark (*Dialect*), box, case, chest, coffer, jewel box, kist (*Scot. & Northern English dialect*)

cast *v.* 1. chuck (*Inf.*), drive, drop, fling, hurl, impel, launch, lob, pitch, project, shed, shy, sling, throw, thrust, toss 2. bestow, deposit, diffuse, distribute, emit, give, radiate, scatter, shed, spread 3. allot, appoint, assign, choose, name, pick, select 4. add, calculate, compute, figure, forecast, reckon, total 5. form, found, model, mould, set, shape ~*n.* 6. fling, lob, throw, thrust, toss 7. air, appearance, complexion, demeanour, look, manner, mien, semblance, shade, stamp, style, tinge, tone, turn 8. actors, characters, company, dramatis personae, players, troupe

cast down deject, depress, desolate, discourage, dishearten, dispirit

caste class, estate, grade, lineage, order, race, rank, social order, species, station, status, stratum

castigate bawl out (*Inf.*), beat, berate, blast, cane, carpet (*Inf.*), censure, chasten, chastise, chew out (*U.S. & Canad. inf.*), correct, criticize, discipline, dress down (*Inf.*), excoriate, flail, flay, flog, give a rocket (*Brit. & N.Z. inf.*), haul over the coals (*Inf.*), lambast(e), lash, put down, read the riot act, rebuke, reprimand, scold, scourge, tear into (*Inf.*), tear (someone) off a strip (*Brit. inf.*), whip

castle chateau, citadel, donjon, fastness, fortress, keep, mansion, palace, peel, stronghold, tower

castrate emasculate, geld, neuter, unman

casual 1. accidental, chance, contingent, fortuitous, incidental, irregular, occasional, random, serendipitous, uncertain, unexpected, unforeseen, unintentional, unpremeditated 2. apathetic, blasé, cursory, indifferent, informal, insouciant, lackadaisical, nonchalant, offhand, perfunctory, relaxed, unconcerned 3. informal, non-dressy, sporty

Antonyms (*sense 1*) arranged, expected, deliberate, fixed, foreseen, intentional, planned, premeditated (*sense 2*) committed, concerned, direct, enthusiastic, passionate, serious, systematic (*sense 3*) dressy, ceremonial, formal

casualties dead, fatalities, losses, missing, wounded

casualty 1. loss, sufferer, victim 2. accident, calamity, catastrophe, chance, contingency, disaster, misadventure, misfortune, mishap

casuistry chicanery, equivocation, oversubtleness, sophism, sophistry, speciousness

cat feline, grimalkin, malkin (*Archaic*), moggy (*Sl.*), mouser, puss (*Inf.*), pussy (*Inf.*), tabby

cataclysm calamity, catastrophe, collapse, convulsion, debacle, disaster, upheaval

catacomb crypt, ossuary, tomb, vault

catalogue 1. *n.* directory, gazetteer, index, inventory, list, record, register, roll, roster, schedule 2. *v.* accession, alphabetize, classify, file, index, inventory, list, register, tabulate

catapult 1. *n.* ballista, sling, slingshot (*U.S.*), trebuchet 2. *v.* heave, hurl, hurtle, pitch, plunge, propel, shoot, toss

cataract 1. cascade, deluge, downpour, falls, Niagara, rapids, torrent, waterfall 2. *Medical* opacity (*of the eye*)

catastrophe 1. adversity, affliction, blow, bummer (*Sl.*), calamity, cataclysm, devastation, disaster, failure, fiasco, ill, meltdown (*Inf.*), mischance, misfortune, mishap, reverse, tragedy, trial, trouble 2. conclusion, culmination, curtain, debacle, dénouement, end, finale, termination, upshot, winding-up

catcall 1. *v.* boo, deride, gibe, give the bird to (*Inf.*), hiss, jeer, whistle 2. *n.* boo, gibe, hiss, jeer, raspberry, whistle

catch *v.* 1. apprehend, arrest, capture, clutch, ensnare, entangle, entrap, feel one's collar (*Sl.*), get, grab, grasp, grip, lay hold of, lift (*Sl.*), nab (*Inf.*), nail (*Inf.*), seize, snare, snatch, take 2. detect, discover, expose, find out, surprise, take unawares, unmask 3. bewitch, captivate, charm, delight, enchant, enrapture, fascinate 4. contract, develop, get, go down with, incur, succumb to, suffer from 5. apprehend, discern, feel, follow, get, grasp, hear, perceive, recognize, sense, take in, twig (*Brit. inf.*) ~*n.* 6. bolt, clasp, clip, fastener, hasp, hook, hook and eye, latch, sneck, snib (*Scot.*) 7. disadvantage, drawback, fly in the ointment, hitch, snag, stumbling block, trap, trick

Antonyms *v.* (*sense 1*) drop, free, give up, liberate, loose, release (*sense 3*) alienate, bore, disenchant, disgust, fail to interest, repel (*sense 4*) avert, avoid, escape, ward off ~*n.* (*sense 7*) advantage, benefit, bonus, boon, reward

catching 1. communicable, contagious, infectious, infective, transferable, transmittable 2. attractive, captivating, charming, enchanting, fascinating, fetching, taking, winning

Antonyms (*sense 1*) incommunicable, non-catching, non-contagious, non-infectious, non-transmittable

catch on comprehend, find out, grasp, see, see through, twig (*Brit. inf.*), understand

catchword byword, motto, password, refrain, slogan, watchword

catchy captivating, haunting, memorable, popular

catechize cross-examine, drill, examine, grill (*Inf.*), interrogate, question

catechumen convert, disciple, initiate, learner, neophyte, novice, probationer, tyro

categorical absolute, direct, downright, emphatic, explicit, express, positive, unambiguous, unconditional, unequivocal, unqualified, unreserved

Antonyms conditional, hesitant, indefinite, qualified, questionable, uncertain, vague

category class, classification, department, division, grade, grouping, head, heading, list, order, rank, section, sort, type

cater furnish, outfit, provide, provision, purvey, supply, victual

cater to coddle, feed, gratify, humour, indulge, minister to, mollycoddle, pamper, pander to, spoil

caterwaul bawl, howl, scream, screech, shriek, squall, wail, yowl

catharsis abreaction, cleansing, lustration, purgation, purging, purification, release

catholic all-embracing, all-inclusive, broad-minded, charitable, comprehensive, eclectic, ecumenical, general, global, liberal, tolerant, unbigoted, universal, unsectarian, whole, wide, world-wide

Antonyms bigoted, exclusive, illiberal, limited, narrow-minded, parochial, sectarian

cattle beasts, bovines, cows, kine (*Archaic*), livestock, neat (*Archaic*), stock

catty backbiting, bitchy (*Inf.*), ill-natured, malevolent, malicious, mean, rancorous, shrewish, snide, spiteful, venomous

Antonyms benevolent, charitable, compassionate, considerate, generous, kind, pleasant

caucus assembly, conclave, congress, convention, get-together (*Inf.*), meeting, parley, session

cause *n.* 1. agent, beginning, creator, genesis, mainspring, maker, origin, originator, prime mover, producer, root, source, spring

2. account, agency, aim, basis, consideration, end, grounds, incentive, inducement, motivation, motive, object, purpose, reason 3. attempt, belief, conviction, enterprise, ideal, movement, purpose, undertaking ~*v.* 4. begin, bring about, compel, create, effect, engender, generate, give rise to, incite, induce, lead to, motivate, occasion, precipitate, produce, provoke, result in

Antonyms *n.* consequence, effect, end, outcome, result ~*v.* deter, foil, inhibit, prevent, stop

caustic 1. acrid, astringent, biting, burning, corroding, corrosive, keen, mordant, vitriolic 2. acrimonious, cutting, mordacious, pungent, sarcastic, scathing, severe, stinging, trenchant, virulent, vitriolic

Antonyms agreeable, bland, gentle, healing, kind, loving, mild, pleasant, pleasing, soft, soothing, sweet, temperate

caution *n.* 1. alertness, care, carefulness, circumspection, deliberation, discretion, forethought, heed, heedfulness, prudence, vigilance, watchfulness 2. admonition, advice, counsel, injunction, warning ~*v.* 3. admonish, advise, tip off, urge, warn

Antonyms *n.* carelessness, daring, imprudence, rashness, recklessness ~*v.* dare

cautious alert, cagey (*Inf.*), careful, chary, circumspect, discreet, guarded, heedful, judicious, prudent, tentative, vigilant, wary, watchful

Antonyms adventurous, bold, careless, daring, foolhardy, heedless, impetuous, inattentive, incautious, indiscreet, madcap, rash, reckless, unguarded, unheedful, venturesome, venturous

cavalcade array, march-past, parade, procession, spectacle, train

cavalier *n.* 1. chevalier, equestrian, horseman, knight, royalist 2. beau, blade (*Archaic*), escort, gallant, gentleman ~*adj.* 3. arrogant, condescending, curt, disdainful, haughty, insolent, lofty, lordly, offhand, scornful, supercilious

cavalry horse, horsemen, mounted troops

Antonyms foot soldiers, infantrymen

cave cavern, cavity, den, grotto, hollow

caveat admonition, caution, warning

cavern cave, hollow, pothole

cavernous 1. concave, deep-set, hollow, sunken, yawning 2. echoing, resonant, reverberant, sepulchral

cavil beef (*Sl.*), carp, censure, complain, find fault, hypercriticize, kvetch (*U.S. sl.*), object, quibble

cavilling captious, carping, censorious, critical, fault-finding, hypercritical, nitpicking (*Inf.*), quibbling

cavity crater, dent, gap, hole, hollow, pit

cavort caper, caracole, frisk, frolic, gambol, prance, romp, sport

cease break off, bring *or* come to an end, conclude, culminate, desist, die away, discontinue, end, fail, finish, halt, leave off, refrain, stay, stop, terminate

Antonyms begin, commence, continue, initiate, start

ceaseless constant, continual, continuous, endless, eternal, everlasting, incessant, indefatigable, interminable, never-ending, nonstop, perennial, perpetual, unending, unremitting, untiring

Antonyms broken, erratic, intermittent, irregular, occasional, periodic, spasmodic, sporadic

cede abandon, abdicate, allow, concede, convey, grant, hand over, make over, relinquish, renounce, resign, step down (*Inf.*), surrender, transfer, yield

celebrate bless, commemorate, commend, crack up (*Inf.*), drink to, eulogize, exalt, extol, glorify, honour, keep, laud, observe, perform, praise, proclaim, publicize, rejoice, reverence, solemnize, toast

celebrated acclaimed, distinguished, eminent, famed, famous, glorious, illustrious, lionized, notable, outstanding, popular, pre-eminent, prominent, renowned, revered, well-known

Antonyms dishonoured, forgotten, insignificant, obscure, trivial, unacclaimed, undistinguished, unknown, unnotable, unpopular

celebration 1. beano (*Brit. sl.*), carousal, festival, festivity, gala, jollification, jubilee, junketing, merrymaking, party, rave (*Brit. sl.*), rave-up (*Brit. sl.*), revelry 2. anniversary, commemoration, honouring, observance, performance, remembrance, solemnization

celebrity 1. big name, big shot (*Inf.*), bigwig (*Inf.*), celeb (*Inf.*), dignitary, lion, luminary, megastar (*Inf.*), name, personage, personality, star, superstar, V.I.P. 2. distinction, éclat, eminence, fame, glory, honour, notability, popularity, pre-eminence, prestige, prominence, renown, reputation, repute, stardom

Antonyms has-been, nobody, obscurity, unknown

celerity dispatch, expedition, fleetness, haste, promptness, quickness, rapidity, speed, swiftness, velocity, vivacity

celestial angelic, astral, divine, elysian, empyrean (*Poetic*), eternal, ethereal, godlike, heavenly, immortal, seraphic, spiritual, sublime, supernatural

celibacy chastity, continence, purity, singleness, virginity

cell 1. cavity, chamber, compartment, cubicle, dungeon, stall 2. caucus, coterie, group, nucleus, unit

cement 1. *v.* attach, bind, bond, cohere, combine, glue, gum, join, plaster, seal, solder, stick together, unite, weld 2. *n.* adhesive, binder, glue, gum, paste, plaster, sealant

cemetery burial ground, churchyard, God's acre, graveyard, necropolis

censor blue-pencil, bowdlerize, cut, expurgate

censorious captious, carping, cavilling, condemnatory, disapproving, disparaging, fault-finding, hypercritical, scathing, severe

censurable at fault, blamable, blameworthy, chargeable, contemptible, culpable, faulty, guilty, reprehensible, scandalous

censure 1. *v.* abuse, bawl out (*Inf.*), berate, blame, blast, carpet (*Inf.*), castigate, chew out (*U.S. & Canad. inf.*), chide, condemn, criticize, denounce, excoriate, give (someone) a rocket (*Brit. & N.Z. inf.*), lambast(e), put down, read the riot act, rebuke, reprehend, reprimand, reproach, reprove, scold, tear into (*Inf.*), tear (someone) off a strip (*Brit. inf.*), upbraid 2. *n.* blame, castigation, condemnation, criticism, disapproval, dressing down (*Inf.*), obloquy, rebuke, remonstrance, reprehension, reprimand, reproach, reproof, stick (*Sl.*), stricture

Antonyms *v.* applaud, commend, compliment, laud (*Literary*) ~*n.* approval, commendation, compliment, encouragement

central chief, essential, focal, fundamental, inner, interior, key, main, mean, median, mid, middle, primary, principal

Antonyms exterior, minor, outer, outermost, secondary, subordinate, subsidiary

centralize amalgamate, compact, concentrate, concentre, condense, converge, incorporate, rationalize, streamline, unify

centre 1. *n.* bull's-eye, core, crux, focus, heart, hub, kernel, mid, middle, midpoint, nucleus, pivot 2. *v.* cluster, concentrate, converge, focus, revolve

Antonyms *n.* border, boundary, brim, circumference, edge, fringe, limit, lip, margin, perimeter, periphery, rim ~*v.* bestrew, diffuse, disseminate, fling, scatter, spread, sprinkle, strew, toss

centrepiece cynosure, epergne, focus, highlight, hub, star

centrifugal diffusive, divergent, diverging, efferent, radial, radiating

ceremonial 1. *adj.* formal, liturgical, ritual, ritualistic, solemn, stately 2. *n.* ceremony, formality, rite, ritual, solemnity

Antonyms casual, informal, relaxed, simple

ceremonious civil, courteous, courtly, deferential, dignified, exact, formal, precise, punctilious, ritual, solemn, starchy (*Inf.*), stately, stiff

ceremony 1. commemoration, function, observance, parade, rite, ritual, service, show, solemnities 2. ceremonial, decorum, etiquette, form, formal courtesy, formality, niceties, pomp, propriety, protocol

certain 1. assured, confident, convinced, positive, satisfied, sure 2. ascertained, conclusive, incontrovertible, indubitable, irrefutable, known, plain, true, undeniable, undoubted, unequivocal, unmistakable, valid 3. bound, definite, destined, fated, ineluctable, inescapable, inevitable, inexorable, sure 4. decided, definite, established, fixed, settled 5. assured, constant, dependable, reliable, stable, staunch, steady, trustworthy, unfailing, unquestionable 6. express, individual, particular, precise, special, specific

Antonyms disputable, doubtful, dubious, equivocal, fallible, indefinite, questionable, uncertain, unconvinced, undecided, unlikely, unreliable, unsettled, unsure

certainty 1. assurance, authoritativeness, certitude, confidence, conviction, faith, indubitableness, inevitability, positiveness, sureness, trust, validity 2. fact, reality, sure thing (*Inf.*), surety, truth

Antonyms disbelief, doubt, indecision, qualm, scepticism, uncertainty, unsureness

certificate authorization, credential(s), diploma, document, licence, testimonial, voucher, warrant

certify ascertain, assure, attest, authenticate, aver, avow, confirm, corroborate, declare, endorse, guarantee, notify, show, testify, validate, verify, vouch, witness

certitude assurance, certainty, confidence, conviction

cessation abeyance, arrest, break, ceasing, discontinuance, ending, entr'acte, halt, halting, hiatus, intermission, interruption, interval, let-up (*Inf.*), pause, recess, remission, respite, rest, standstill, stay, stoppage, suspension, termination, time off

cession abandonment, abnegation, capitulation, ceding, conceding, concession, conveyance, grant, relinquishment, renunciation, surrender, yielding

chafe abrade, anger, annoy, exasperate, fret, fume, gall, grate, incense, inflame, irritate, nark (*Brit., Aust., & N.Z. sl.*), offend, pro~

voke, rage, rasp, rub, ruffle, scrape, scratch, vex, worry

Antonyms allay, alleviate, appease, assuage, calm, conciliate, mollify, pacify, placate, please, soothe

chaff *n.* 1. dregs, glumes, hulls, husks, refuse, remains, rubbish, trash, waste 2. badinage, banter, joking, josh (*Sl., chiefly U.S. & Canad.*), persiflage, raillery, teasing *~v.* 3. banter, deride, jeer, josh (*Sl., chiefly U.S. & Canad.*), mock, rib (*Inf.*), ridicule, scoff, take the piss out of (*Taboo sl.*), taunt, tease

chagrin 1. *n.* annoyance, discomfiture, discomposure, displeasure, disquiet, dissatisfaction, embarrassment, fretfulness, humiliation, ill-humour, irritation, mortification, peevishness, spleen, vexation 2. *v.* annoy, discomfit, discompose, displease, disquiet, dissatisfy, embarrass, humiliate, irk, irritate, mortify, peeve, vex

chain *v.* 1. bind, confine, enslave, fetter, gyve (*Archaic*), handcuff, manacle, restrain, shackle, tether, trammel, unite *~n.* 2. bond, coupling, fetter, link, manacle, shackle, union 3. concatenation, progression, sequence, series, set, string, succession, train

chairman chairperson, chairwoman, director, master of ceremonies, president, presider, speaker, spokesman, toastmaster

chalk up accumulate, achieve, attain, credit, enter, gain, log, mark, record, register, score, tally, win

challenge 1. *v.* accost, arouse, beard, brave, call out, claim, confront, dare, defy, demand, dispute, face off (*Sl.*), impugn, investigate, object to, provoke, question, require, stimulate, summon, tackle, tax, test, throw down the gauntlet, try 2. *n.* confrontation, dare, defiance, face-off (*Sl.*), interrogation, provocation, question, summons to contest, test, trial, ultimatum

chamber 1. apartment, bedroom, cavity, compartment, cubicle, enclosure, hall, hollow, room 2. assembly, council, legislative body, legislature

champion 1. *n.* backer, challenger, conqueror, defender, guardian, hero, nonpareil, patron, protector, title holder, upholder, victor, vindicator, warrior, winner 2. *v.* advocate, back, defend, encourage, espouse, fight for, promote, stick up for (*Inf.*), support, uphold

chance *n.* 1. liability, likelihood, occasion, odds, opening, opportunity, possibility, probability, prospect, scope, time, window 2. accident, casualty, coincidence, contingency, destiny, fate, fortuity, fortune, luck, misfortune, peril, providence 3. gamble, hazard, jeopardy, risk, speculation, uncertainty *~v.* 4. befall, betide, come about, come to pass, fall out, happen, occur 5. endanger, gamble, go out on a limb, hazard, jeopardize, risk, stake, try, venture, wager *~adj.* 6. accidental, casual, contingent, fortuitous, inadvertent, incidental, random, serendipitous, unforeseeable, unforeseen, unintentional, unlooked-for

Antonyms *n.* certainty, design, impossibility, improbability, intention, surety, unlikelihood *~adj.* arranged, deliberate, designed, expected, foreseen, intentional, planned

chancy dangerous, dicey (*Inf., chiefly Brit.*), dodgy (*Brit., Aust., & N.Z. sl.*), hazardous, perilous, problematical, risky, speculative, uncertain

Antonyms certain, reliable, safe, secure, sound, stable, sure

change *v.* 1. alter, convert, diversify, fluctuate, metamorphose, moderate, modify, mutate, reform, remodel, reorganize, restyle, shift, transform, transmute, vacillate, vary, veer 2. alternate, barter, convert, displace, exchange, interchange, remove, replace, substitute, swap (*Inf.*), trade, transmit *~n.* 3. alteration, difference, innovation, metamorphosis, modification, mutation, permutation, revolution, transformation, transition, transmutation, vicissitude 4. conversion, exchange, interchange, substitution, trade 5. break (*Inf.*), departure, diversion, novelty, variation, variety

Antonyms *v.* hold, keep, remain, stay *~n.* constancy, invariability, monotony, permanence, stability, uniformity

changeable capricious, changeful, chequered, erratic, fickle, fitful, fluid, inconstant, irregular, kaleidoscopic, labile (*Chem.*), mercurial, mobile, mutable, protean, shifting, temperamental, uncertain, uneven, unpredictable, unreliable, unsettled, unstable, unsteady, vacillating, variable, versatile, volatile, wavering

Antonyms constant, invariable, irreversible, regular, reliable, stable, steady, unchangeable

changeless abiding, consistent, constant, eternal, everlasting, fixed, immovable, immutable, permanent, perpetual, regular, reliable, resolute, settled, stationary, steadfast, steady, unalterable, unchanging, uniform, unvarying

channel *n.* 1. canal, chamber, conduit, duct, fluting, furrow, groove, gutter, main, passage, route, strait 2. *Fig.* approach, artery, avenue, course, means, medium, path, route, way *~v.* 3. conduct, convey, direct, guide, transmit

chant 1. *n.* carol, chorus, melody, psalm,

song 2. *v.* carol, chorus, croon, descant, intone, recite, sing, warble

chaos anarchy, bedlam, confusion, disorder, disorganization, entropy, lawlessness, pandemonium, tumult
Antonyms neatness, orderliness, organization, tidiness

chaotic anarchic, confused, deranged, disordered, disorganized, lawless, purposeless, rampageous, riotous, topsy-turvy, tumultuous, uncontrolled

chap bloke (*Brit. inf.*), character, cove (*Sl.*), customer (*Inf.*), dude (*U.S. & Canad. inf.*), fellow, guy (*Inf.*), individual, person, sort, type

chaperon 1. *n.* companion, duenna, escort, governess 2. *v.* accompany, attend, escort, protect, safeguard, shepherd, watch over

chaplet bouquet, coronal, garland, wreath

chapter clause, division, episode, part, period, phase, section, stage, topic

char carbonize, cauterize, scorch, sear, singe

character 1. attributes, bent, calibre, cast, complexion, constitution, disposition, individuality, kidney, make-up, marked traits, nature, personality, quality, reputation, temper, temperament, type 2. honour, integrity, rectitude, strength, uprightness 3. card (*Inf.*), eccentric, nut (*Sl.*), oddball (*Inf.*), odd bod (*Inf.*), oddity, original, queer fish (*Brit. inf.*), wacko (*Sl.*) 4. cipher, device, emblem, figure, hieroglyph, letter, logo, mark, rune, sign, symbol, type 5. part, persona, portrayal, role 6. fellow, guy (*Inf.*), individual, person, sort, type

characteristic 1. *adj.* distinctive, distinguishing, idiosyncratic, individual, peculiar, representative, singular, special, specific, symbolic, symptomatic, typical 2. *n.* attribute, faculty, feature, idiosyncrasy, mark, peculiarity, property, quality, quirk, trait
Antonyms rare, uncharacteristic, unrepresentative, unusual

characterize brand, distinguish, identify, indicate, inform, mark, represent, stamp, typify

charade fake, farce, pantomime, parody, pretence, travesty

charge *v.* 1. accuse, arraign, blame, impeach, incriminate, indict, involve ~*n.* 2. accusation, allegation, imputation, indictment ~*v.* 3. assail, assault, attack, rush, storm ~*n.* 4. assault, attack, onset, onslaught, rush, sortie ~*v.* 5. afflict, burden, commit, entrust, tax ~*n.* 6. burden, care, concern, custody, duty, office, responsibility, safekeeping, trust, ward 7. amount, cost, damage (*Inf.*), expenditure, expense, outlay, payment, price, rate ~*v.* 8. fill, instil, lade, load, suffuse 9. bid, command, demand, enjoin, exhort, instruct, order, require ~*n.* 10. canon, command, demand, dictate, direction, exhortation, injunction, instruction, mandate, order, precept
Antonyms *v.* (*sense 1*) absolve, acquit, clear, exonerate, pardon ~*n.* (*sense 2*) absolution, acquittal, clearance, exoneration, pardon, reprieve ~*v.* (*sense 3*) retreat, withdraw ~*n.* (*sense 4*) retreat, withdrawal

charitable 1. beneficent, benevolent, bountiful, eleemosynary, generous, kind, lavish, liberal, philanthropic 2. broad-minded, considerate, favourable, forgiving, gracious, humane, indulgent, kindly, lenient, magnanimous, sympathetic, tolerant, understanding
Antonyms inconsiderate, mean, stingy, strict, uncharitable, unforgiving, ungenerous, unkind, unsympathetic

charity 1. alms-giving, assistance, benefaction, contributions, donations, endowment, fund, gift, hand-out, largess *or* largesse, philanthropy, relief 2. affection, Agape, altruism, benevolence, benignity, bountifulness, bounty, compassion, fellow feeling, generosity, goodness, good will, humanity, indulgence, love, pity, tenderheartedness
Antonyms (*sense 1*) miserliness, selfishness, stinginess, uncharitableness (*sense 2*) hatred, ill will, intolerance, malice

charlatan cheat, con man (*Inf.*), fake, fraud, impostor, mountebank, phoney *or* phony (*Inf.*), pretender, quack, sham, swindler

charm *v.* 1. absorb, allure, attract, beguile, bewitch, cajole, captivate, delight, enamour, enchant, enrapture, entrance, fascinate, mesmerize, please, ravish, win, win over ~*n.* 2. allure, allurement, appeal, attraction, desirability, enchantment, fascination, magic, magnetism, sorcery, spell 3. amulet, fetish, good-luck piece, lucky piece, periapt (*Rare*), talisman, trinket
Antonyms *v.* alienate, repel, repulse ~*n.* (*sense 2*) repulsiveness, unattractiveness

charming appealing, attractive, bewitching, captivating, delectable, delightful, engaging, eye-catching, fetching, irresistible, likable *or* likeable, lovely, pleasant, pleasing, seductive, winning, winsome
Antonyms disgusting, horrid, repulsive, unappealing, unattractive, unlikable *or* unlikeable, unpleasant, unpleasing

chart 1. *n.* blueprint, diagram, graph, map, plan, table, tabulation 2. *v.* delineate, draft, graph, map out, outline, plot, shape, sketch

charter 1. *n.* bond, concession, contract, deed, document, franchise, indenture, licence, permit, prerogative, privilege, right

2. *v.* authorize, commission, employ, hire, lease, rent, sanction

chary 1. careful, cautious, circumspect, guarded, heedful, leery (*Sl.*), prudent, reluctant, scrupulous, slow, suspicious, uneasy, wary 2. careful (*Brit.*), frugal, niggardly, parsimonious, thrifty

chase 1. *v.* course, drive, drive away, expel, follow, hound, hunt, pursue, put to flight, run after, track 2. *n.* hunt, hunting, pursuit, race, venery (*Archaic*)

chasm abyss, alienation, breach, cavity, cleft, crater, crevasse, fissure, gap, gorge, gulf, hiatus, hollow, opening, ravine, rent, rift, split, void

chassis anatomy, bodywork, frame, framework, fuselage, skeleton, substructure

chaste austere, decent, decorous, elegant, immaculate, incorrupt, innocent, modest, moral, neat, pure, quiet, refined, restrained, simple, unaffected, uncontaminated, undefiled, unsullied, vestal, virginal, virtuous, wholesome

Antonyms blemished, corrupt, dirty, dishonourable, gaudy, immoral, impure, married, ornate, promiscuous, self-indulgent, tainted, unchaste, unclean, unrestrained, wanton

chasten afflict, castigate, chastise, correct, cow, curb, discipline, humble, humiliate, repress, soften, subdue, tame

chastise beat, berate, castigate, censure, correct, discipline, flog, lash, lick (*Inf.*), punish, scold, scourge, upbraid, whip

Antonyms caress, commend, compliment, congratulate, cuddle, embrace, fondle, hug, praise, reward

chastity celibacy, continence, innocence, maidenhood, modesty, purity, virginity, virtue

Antonyms debauchery, immorality, lewdness, licentiousness, profligacy, promiscuity, wantonness

chat 1. *n.* chatter, chinwag (*Brit. inf.*), confab (*Inf.*), gossip, heart-to-heart, natter, talk, tête-à-tête 2. *v.* chatter, chew the rag *or* fat (*Sl.*), gossip, jaw (*Sl.*), natter, rabbit (on) (*Brit. inf.*), talk

chatter *n./v.* babble, blather, chat, gab (*Inf.*), gossip, jabber, natter, prate, prattle, rabbit (on) (*Brit. inf.*), tattle, twaddle

chatty colloquial, familiar, friendly, gossipy, informal, newsy (*Inf.*), talkative

Antonyms aloof, cold, distant, formal, hostile, quiet, reserved, shy, silent, standoffish, taciturn, timid, unfriendly, unsociable

cheap 1. bargain, cheapo (*Inf.*), cut-price, economical, economy, inexpensive, keen, low-cost, low-priced, reasonable, reduced, sale 2. bush-league (*Aust. & N.Z. inf.*), chickenshit (*U.S. sl.*), common, crappy (*Sl.*), dime-a-dozen (*Inf.*), inferior, paltry, piss-poor (*U.S. taboo sl.*), poor, poxy (*Sl.*), second-rate, shoddy, tatty, tawdry, tinhorn (*U.S. sl.*), two-bit (*U.S. & Canad. sl.*), worthless 3. base, contemptible, despicable, low, mean, scurvy, sordid, vulgar

Antonyms (*sense 1*) costly, dear, expensive, pricey (*Inf.*), steep (*senses 2 & 3*) admirable, charitable, decent, elegant, generous, good, high-class, honourable, superior, tasteful, valuable

cheapen belittle, debase, degrade, demean, denigrate, depreciate, derogate, devalue, discredit, disparage, lower

cheat *v.* 1. bamboozle (*Inf.*), beguile, bilk, con (*Inf.*), cozen, deceive, defraud, diddle (*Inf.*), do (*Inf.*), double-cross (*Inf.*), dupe, finagle (*Inf.*), fleece, fool, gull (*Archaic*), hoax, hoodwink, kid (*Inf.*), mislead, rip off (*Sl.*), skin (*Sl.*), stiff (*Sl.*), sting (*Inf.*), swindle, take for a ride (*Inf.*), take in (*Inf.*), thwart, trick, victimize 2. baffle, check, defeat, deprive, foil, frustrate, prevent, thwart ~*n.* 3. artifice, deceit, deception, fraud, imposture, rip-off (*Sl.*), scam (*Sl.*), sting (*Inf.*), swindle, trickery 4. charlatan, cheater, chiseller (*Inf.*), con man (*Inf.*), deceiver, dodger, double-crosser (*Inf.*), impostor, knave (*Archaic*), rogue, shark, sharper, swindler, trickster

check *v.* 1. check out (*Inf.*), compare, confirm, enquire into, examine, inspect, investigate, look at, look over, make sure, monitor, note, probe, research, scrutinize, study, take a dekko at (*Brit. sl.*), test, tick, verify, vet, work over 2. arrest, bar, bridle, control, curb, delay, halt, hinder, impede, inhibit, limit, nip in the bud, obstruct, pause, rein, repress, restrain, retard, stop, thwart 3. admonish, bawl out (*Inf.*), blame, carpet (*Inf.*), chew out (*U.S. & Canad. inf.*), chide, give (someone) a rocket (*Brit. & N.Z. inf.*), give (someone) a row (*Inf.*), rate, read the riot act, rebuff, rebuke, reprimand, reprove, scold, tear into (*Inf.*), tear (someone) off a strip (*Brit. inf.*), tell off (*Inf.*) ~*n.* 4. examination, inspection, investigation, research, scrutiny, test 5. constraint, control, curb, damper, hindrance, impediment, inhibition, limitation, obstacle, obstruction, rein, restraint, stoppage 6. blow, disappointment, frustration, rejection, reverse, setback

Antonyms *v.* (*sense 1*) disregard, ignore, neglect, overlook, pass over, pay no attention to (*sense 2*) accelerate, advance, begin, encourage, further, give free rein, help, release, start

cheek audacity, brass neck (*Brit. inf.*), brazenness, chutzpah (*U.S. & Canad. inf.*), disrespect, effrontery, front, gall (*Inf.*), impertinence, impudence, insolence, lip (*Sl.*), neck (*Inf.*), nerve, sauce (*Inf.*), temerity

cheeky audacious, disrespectful, fresh (*Inf.*), forward, impertinent, impudent, insolent, insulting, lippy (*U.S. & Canad. sl.*), pert, sassy (*U.S. inf.*), saucy
Antonyms civil, complaisant, courteous, decorous, deferential, mannerly, polite, respectful, well-behaved, well-mannered

cheer *v.* 1. animate, brighten, buoy up, cheer up, comfort, console, elate, elevate, encourage, enliven, exhilarate, gladden, hearten, incite, inspirit, solace, uplift, warm 2. acclaim, applaud, clap, hail, hurrah ~*n.* 3. animation, buoyancy, cheerfulness, comfort, gaiety, gladness, glee, hopefulness, joy, liveliness, merriment, merry-making, mirth, optimism, solace 4. acclamation, applause, ovation, plaudits
Antonyms *v.* (*sense 1*) darken, depress, discourage, dishearten, sadden (*sense 2*) blow a raspberry, boo, hiss, jeer, ridicule

cheerful animated, blithe, bright, bucked (*Inf.*), buoyant, cheery, chirpy (*Inf.*), contented, enlivening, enthusiastic, gay, genial, glad, gladsome (*Archaic*), happy, hearty, jaunty, jolly, joyful, light-hearted, lightsome (*Archaic*), merry, optimistic, pleasant, sparkling, sprightly, sunny, upbeat (*Inf.*)
Antonyms cheerless, dejected, depressed, depressing, despondent, dismal, down, downcast, down in the dumps (*Inf.*), dull, gloomy, lifeless, melancholy, miserable, morose, pensive, sad, unhappy, unpleasant

cheerfulness buoyancy, exuberance, gaiety, geniality, gladness, good cheer, good humour, high spirits, jauntiness, joyousness, light-heartedness

cheering auspicious, bright, comforting, encouraging, heartening, promising, propitious

cheerless austere, bleak, comfortless, dark, dejected, depressed, desolate, despondent, disconsolate, dismal, dolorous, drab, dreary, dull, forlorn, funereal, gloomy, grim, joyless, melancholy, miserable, mournful, sad, sombre, sorrowful, sullen, unhappy, woebegone, woeful
Antonyms cheerful, cheery, elated, happy, jolly, joyful, light-hearted, merry

cheer up brighten, buck up (*Inf.*), comfort, encourage, enliven, gladden, hearten, jolly along (*Inf.*), perk up, rally, take heart

cheery breezy, carefree, cheerful, chirpy (*Inf.*), genial, good-humoured, happy, jovial, lively, pleasant, sunny, upbeat (*Inf.*)

chef d'oeuvre brainchild, crowning achievement, *magnum opus*, masterpiece, masterwork

chemical compound, drug, potion, synthetic

cherish care for, cleave to, cling to, comfort, cosset, encourage, entertain, foster, harbour, hold dear, nourish, nurse, nurture, prize, shelter, support, sustain, treasure
Antonyms abandon, desert, despise, disdain, dislike, forsake, hate, neglect

cherubic adorable, angelic, heavenly, innocent, lovable, seraphic, sweet

chest ark (*Dialect*), box, case, casket, coffer, crate, kist (*Scot. & Northern English dialect*), strongbox, trunk

chew 1. bite, champ, crunch, gnaw, grind, masticate, munch 2. *Fig. Usually with* over consider, deliberate upon, meditate, mull (over), muse on, ponder, reflect upon, ruminate, weigh

chic elegant, fashionable, modish, sexy (*Inf.*), smart, stylish, trendy (*Brit. inf.*), up-to-date
Antonyms dinosaur, inelegant, naff (*Brit. sl.*), old-fashioned, out-moded, out-of-date, passé, shabby, unfashionable

chicanery artifice, cheating, chicane, deception, deviousness, dodge, double-dealing, duplicity, intrigue, sharp practice, skulduggery (*Inf.*), sophistry, stratagems, subterfuge, trickery, underhandedness, wiles, wire-pulling (*Chiefly U.S.*)

chide admonish, bawl out (*Inf.*), berate, blame, blast, carpet (*Inf.*), censure, check, chew out (*U.S. & Canad. inf.*), criticize, find fault, give (someone) a rocket (*Brit. & N.Z. inf.*), give (someone) a row (*Inf.*), lambast(e), lecture, put down, read the riot act, rebuke, reprehend, reprimand, reproach, reprove, scold, tear into (*Inf.*), tear (someone) off a strip (*Brit. inf.*), tell off (*Inf.*), upbraid

chief 1. *adj.* big-time (*Inf.*), capital, cardinal, central, especial, essential, foremost, grand, highest, key, leading, main, major league (*Inf.*), most important, outstanding, paramount, predominant, pre-eminent, premier, prevailing, primary, prime, principal, superior, supreme, uppermost, vital 2. *n.* boss (*Inf.*), captain, chieftain, commander, director, governor, head, leader, lord, manager, master, principal, ringleader, ruler, superintendent, suzerain
Antonyms *adj.* least, minor, subordinate, subsidiary ~*n.* follower, subject, subordinate

chiefly above all, especially, essentially, in general, in the main, largely, mainly, most~

ly, on the whole, predominantly, primarily, principally, usually

child ankle-biter (*Aust. sl.*), babe, baby, bairn (*Scot.*), brat, chit, descendant, infant, issue, juvenile, kid (*Inf.*), little one, minor, nipper (*Inf.*), nursling, offspring, progeny, rug rat (*Sl.*), sprog (*Sl.*), suckling, toddler, tot, wean (*Scot.*), youngster

childbirth accouchement, child-bearing, confinement, delivery, labour, lying-in, parturition, travail

childhood boyhood, girlhood, immaturity, infancy, minority, schooldays, youth

childish boyish, foolish, frivolous, girlish, immature, infantile, juvenile, puerile, silly, simple, trifling, weak, young
Antonyms adult, grown-up, manly, mature, sensible, sophisticated, womanly

childlike artless, credulous, guileless, ingenuous, innocent, naive, simple, trustful, trusting, unfeigned

chill *adj.* 1. biting, bleak, chilly, cold, freezing, frigid, parky (*Brit. inf.*), raw, sharp, wintry 2. *Fig.* aloof, cool, depressing, distant, frigid, hostile, stony, unfriendly, ungenial, unresponsive, unwelcoming ~*v.* 3. congeal, cool, freeze, refrigerate 4. *Fig.* dampen, deject, depress, discourage, dishearten, dismay ~*n.* 5. bite, cold, coldness, coolness, crispness, frigidity, nip, rawness, sharpness

chilly 1. blowy, breezy, brisk, cool, crisp, draughty, fresh, nippy, parky (*Brit. inf.*), penetrating, sharp 2. frigid, hostile, unfriendly, unresponsive, unsympathetic, unwelcoming
Antonyms (*sense 1*) balmy, hot, mild, scorching, sunny, sweltering, warm (*sense 2*) affable, chummy (*Inf.*), congenial, cordial, friendly, responsive, sociable, sympathetic, warm, welcoming

chime boom, clang, dong, jingle, peal, ring, sound, strike, tinkle, tintinnabulate, toll

chimera bogy, delusion, dream, fantasy, figment, hallucination, ignis fatuus, illusion, monster, monstrosity, snare, spectre, will-o'-the-wisp

chimerical delusive, fabulous, fanciful, fantastic, hallucinatory, illusive, illusory, imaginary, quixotic, unfounded, unreal, vain, visionary, wild

china ceramics, crockery, porcelain, pottery, service, tableware, ware

chink aperture, cleft, crack, cranny, crevice, cut, fissure, flaw, gap, opening, rift

chip 1. *n.* dent, flake, flaw, fragment, nick, notch, paring, scrap, scratch, shard, shaving, sliver, wafer 2. *v.* chisel, damage, gash, nick, whittle

chip in contribute, donate, go Dutch (*Inf.*), interpose, interrupt, pay, subscribe

chirp cheep, chirrup, peep, pipe, tweet, twitter, warble

chivalrous bold, brave, courageous, courteous, courtly, gallant, gentlemanly, heroic, high-minded, honourable, intrepid, knightly, magnanimous, true, valiant
Antonyms boorish, cowardly, cruel, dishonourable, disloyal, rude, uncourtly, ungallant, unmannerly

chivalry courage, courtesy, courtliness, gallantry, gentlemanliness, knight-errantry, knighthood, politeness

chivvy annoy, badger, bend someone's ear (*Inf.*), bug (*Inf.*), harass, hassle (*Inf.*), hound, nag, pester, plague, pressure (*Inf.*), prod, torment

choice 1. *n.* alternative, discrimination, election, option, pick, preference, say, selection, variety 2. *adj.* bad (*Sl.*), best, crucial (*Sl.*), dainty, def (*Sl.*), elect, elite, excellent, exclusive, exquisite, hand-picked, nice, precious, prime, prize, rare, select, special, superior, uncommon, unusual, valuable

choke asphyxiate, bar, block, bung, clog, close, congest, constrict, dam, gag, obstruct, occlude, overpower, smother, stifle, stop, strangle, suffocate, suppress, throttle

choleric angry, bad-tempered, cross, fiery, hasty, hot, hot-tempered, ill-tempered, irascible, irritable, passionate, petulant, quick-tempered, ratty (*Brit. & N.Z. inf.*), testy, tetchy, touchy

choose adopt, cull, designate, desire, elect, espouse, fix on, opt for, pick, predestine, prefer, see fit, select, settle upon, single out, take, wish
Antonyms decline, dismiss, exclude, forgo, leave, refuse, reject, throw aside

choosy discriminating, exacting, faddy, fastidious, finicky, fussy, particular, picky (*Inf.*), selective
Antonyms easy (*Inf.*), easy to please, indiscriminate, undemanding, unselective

chop 1. *v.* axe, cleave, cut, fell, hack, hew, lop, sever, shear, slash, truncate 2. *n.* **the chop** *Sl.* dismissal, one's cards, sacking (*Inf.*), termination, the axe (*Inf.*), the boot (*Sl.*), the (old) heave-ho (*Inf.*), the order of the boot (*Sl.*), the sack (*Inf.*)

choppy blustery, broken, rough, ruffled, squally, tempestuous
Antonyms calm, smooth, windless

chop up cube, dice, divide, fragment, mince

chore burden, duty, errand, fag (*Inf.*), job, task

chortle cackle, chuckle, crow, guffaw

chorus 1. choir, choristers, ensemble, singers, vocalists 2. burden, refrain, response, strain 3. accord, concert, harmony, unison

christen baptize, call, designate, dub, name, style, term, title

chronic 1. confirmed, deep-rooted, deep-seated, habitual, incessant, incurable, ineradicable, ingrained, inveterate, persistent 2. *Inf.* abysmal, appalling, atrocious, awful, dreadful
Antonyms infrequent, occasional, temporary

chronicle 1. *n.* account, annals, diary, history, journal, narrative, record, register, story 2. *v.* enter, narrate, put on record, record, recount, register, relate, report, set down, tell

chronicler annalist, diarist, historian, historiographer, narrator, recorder, reporter, scribe

chronological consecutive, historical, in sequence, ordered, progressive, sequential
Antonyms haphazard, intermittent, irregular, out-of-order, random

chubby buxom, flabby, fleshy, plump, podgy, portly, rotund, round, stout, tubby
Antonyms lean, skinny, slender, slight, slim, sylphlike, thin

chuck cast, discard, fling, heave, hurl, pitch, shy, sling, throw, toss

chuckle chortle, crow, exult, giggle, laugh, snigger, titter

chum cock (*Brit. inf.*), companion, comrade, crony, friend, mate (*Inf.*), pal (*Inf.*)

chummy affectionate, buddy-buddy (*Sl., chiefly U.S. & Canad.*), close, friendly, intimate, matey *or* maty (*Brit. inf.*), pally (*Inf.*), palsy-walsy (*Inf.*), thick (*Inf.*)

chunk block, dollop (*Inf.*), hunk, lump, mass, piece, portion, slab, wad, wodge (*Brit. inf.*)

chunky beefy (*Inf.*), dumpy, stocky, stubby, thickset

churl 1. boor, lout, oaf 2. bumpkin, clodhopper (*Inf.*), clown, hayseed (*U.S. & Canad. inf.*), hick (*Inf., chiefly U.S. & Canad.*), hillbilly, peasant, rustic, yokel 3. curmudgeon, miser, niggard, skinflint

churlish 1. boorish, brusque, crabbed, harsh, ill-tempered, impolite, loutish, morose, oafish, rude, sullen, surly, uncivil, uncouth, unmannerly, vulgar 2. close-fisted, illiberal, inhospitable, mean, miserly, niggardly, unneighbourly, unsociable
Antonyms admirable, agreeable, amiable, civil, courteous, cultivated, generous, good-tempered, mannerly, noble, pleasant, polite, well-bred

churlishness boorishness, crassness, crudeness, loutishness, oafishness, rudeness, surliness, uncouthness

churn agitate, beat, boil, convulse, foam, froth, seethe, stir up, swirl, toss

chute channel, gutter, incline, ramp, runway, slide, slope, trough

cicerone courier, dragoman, escort, guide, mentor, pilot

cigarette cancer stick (*Sl.*), ciggy (*Inf.*), coffin nail (*Sl.*), fag (*Brit. sl.*), gasper (*Sl.*), smoke

cinema big screen (*Inf.*), films, flicks (*Sl.*), motion pictures, movies, pictures

cipher 1. nil, nothing, nought, zero 2. nobody, nonentity 3. character, digit, figure, number, numeral, symbol 4. code, cryptograph 5. device, logo, mark, monogram

circa about, approximately, around, in the region of, roughly

circle *n.* 1. band, circumference, coil, cordon, cycle, disc, globe, lap, loop, orb, perimeter, periphery, revolution, ring, round, sphere, turn 2. area, bounds, circuit, compass, domain, enclosure, field, orbit, province, range, realm, region, scene, sphere 3. assembly, class, clique, club, company, coterie, crowd, fellowship, fraternity, group, order, school, set, society ~*v.* 4. belt, circumnavigate, circumscribe, coil, compass, curve, encircle, enclose, encompass, envelop, gird, hem in, pivot, revolve, ring, rotate, surround, tour, whirl

circuit 1. area, compass, course, journey, lap, orbit, perambulation, revolution, round, route, tour, track 2. boundary, bounding line, bounds, circumference, compass, district, limit, pale, range, region, tract

circuitous ambagious (*Archaic*), devious, indirect, labyrinthine, meandering, oblique, rambling, roundabout, tortuous, winding
Antonyms as the crow flies, direct, straight, undeviating, unswerving

circuitousness deviousness, indirectness, obliqueness, rambling, roundaboutness, tortuousness

circulate 1. broadcast, diffuse, disseminate, distribute, issue, make known, promulgate, propagate, publicize, publish, spread 2. flow, gyrate, radiate, revolve, rotate

circulation 1. currency, dissemination, distribution, spread, transmission, vogue 2. circling, flow, motion, rotation

circumference border, boundary, bounds, circuit, edge, extremity, fringe, limits, outline, pale, perimeter, periphery, rim, verge

circumlocution beating about the

bush (*Inf.*), diffuseness, discursiveness, euphemism, indirectness, periphrasis, prolixity, redundancy, wordiness

circumscribe bound, confine, define, delimit, delineate, demarcate, encircle, enclose, encompass, environ, hem in, limit, mark off, restrain, restrict, straiten, surround

circumspect attentive, canny, careful, cautious, deliberate, discreet, discriminating, guarded, heedful, judicious, observant, politic, prudent, sagacious, sage, vigilant, wary, watchful
Antonyms bold, careless, daring, foolhardy, heedless, imprudent, rash, venturous

circumspection canniness, care, caution, chariness, deliberation, discretion, prudence, wariness

circumstance accident, condition, contingency, detail, element, event, fact, factor, happening, incident, item, occurrence, particular, position, respect, situation

circumstances life style, means, position, resources, situation, state, state of affairs, station, status, times

circumstantial conjectural, contingent, detailed, founded on circumstances, hearsay, incidental, indirect, inferential, particular, presumptive, provisional, specific

circumvent beguile, bypass, deceive, dupe, elude, ensnare, entrap, evade, hoodwink, mislead, outflank, outgeneral, outwit, overreach, sidestep, steer clear of, thwart, trick

circumvention chicanery, deceit, deception, dodge, duplicity, evasion, fraud, guile, imposition, imposture, trickery, wiles

cistern basin, reservoir, sink, tank, vat

citadel bastion, fastness, fortification, fortress, keep, stronghold, tower

citation 1. commendation, excerpt, illustration, passage, quotation, quote, reference, source 2. award, commendation, mention

cite 1. adduce, advance, allude to, enumerate, evidence, extract, mention, name, quote, specify 2. *Law* call, subpoena, summon

citizen burgess, burgher, denizen, dweller, freeman, inhabitant, ratepayer, resident, subject, townsman

city 1. *n.* conurbation, megalopolis, metropolis, municipality 2. *adj.* civic, metropolitan, municipal, urban

civic borough, communal, community, local, municipal, public

civil 1. civic, domestic, home, interior, municipal, political 2. accommodating, affable, civilized, complaisant, courteous, courtly, obliging, polished, polite, refined, urbane, well-bred, well-mannered
Antonyms (*sense 1*) military, religious, state (*sense 2*) discourteous, ill-mannered, impolite, rude, uncivil, unfriendly, ungracious, unpleasant

civility affability, amiability, breeding, complaisance, cordiality, courteousness, courtesy, good manners, graciousness, politeness, politesse, tact, urbanity

civilization 1. advancement, cultivation, culture, development, education, enlightenment, progress, refinement, sophistication 2. community, nation, people, polity, society 3. customs, mores, way of life

civilize cultivate, educate, enlighten, humanize, improve, polish, refine, sophisticate, tame

civilized cultured, educated, enlightened, humane, polite, sophisticated, tolerant, urbane
Antonyms barbarous, green, ignorant, naive, primitive, simple, uncivilized, uncultivated, uncultured, undeveloped, uneducated, unenlightened, unsophisticated, untutored, wild

claim 1. *v.* allege, ask, assert, call for, challenge, collect, demand, exact, hold, insist, maintain, need, pick up, profess, require, take, uphold 2. *n.* affirmation, allegation, application, assertion, call, demand, petition, pretension, privilege, protestation, request, requirement, right, title

claimant applicant, petitioner, pretender, suppliant, supplicant

clairvoyant 1. *adj.* extrasensory, fey, oracular, prescient, prophetic, psychic, second-sighted, sibylline, telepathic, vatic, visionary 2. *n.* augur, diviner, fortune-teller, haruspex, oracle, prophet, prophetess, seer, sibyl, soothsayer, telepath, telepathist, visionary

clamber claw, climb, scale, scrabble, scramble, shin

clammy close, damp, dank, drizzly, moist, pasty, slimy, sticky, sweating, sweaty

clamorous blaring, deafening, insistent, lusty, noisy, riotous, strident, tumultuous, uproarious, vehement, vociferous

clamour agitation, babel, blare, brouhaha, commotion, din, exclamation, hubbub, hullabaloo, noise, outcry, racket, shout, shouting, uproar, vociferation

clamp 1. *n.* bracket, fastener, grip, press, vice 2. *v.* brace, clinch, fasten, fix, impose, make fast, secure

clan band, brotherhood, clique, coterie, faction, family, fraternity, gens, group, house, order, race, schism, sect, sept, set, society, sodality, tribe

clandestine cloak-and-dagger, closet, concealed, covert, fraudulent, furtive, hidden, private, secret, sly, stealthy, surreptitious, underground, underhand, under-the-counter

clang 1. *v.* bong, chime, clank, clash, jangle, resound, reverberate, ring, toll 2. *n.* clangour, ding-dong, knell, reverberation

clannish cliquish, exclusive, insular, narrow, sectarian, select, unfriendly

clap 1. acclaim, applaud, cheer 2. bang, pat, punch, slap, strike gently, thrust, thwack, wallop (*Inf.*), whack

Antonyms (*sense 1*) blow a raspberry, boo, catcall, hiss, jeer

claptrap affectation, balls (*Taboo sl.*), bilge (*Inf.*), blarney, bombast, bosh (*Inf.*), bull (*Sl.*), bullshit (*Taboo sl.*), bunk (*Inf.*), bunkum *or* buncombe (*Chiefly U.S.*), cobblers (*Brit. taboo sl.*), crap (*Sl.*), drivel, eyewash (*Inf.*), flannel (*Brit. inf.*), garbage (*Inf.*), guff (*Sl.*), hogwash, hokum (*Sl., chiefly U.S. & Canad.*), horsefeathers (*U.S. sl.*), hot air (*Inf.*), humbug, insincerity, moonshine, nonsense, pap, piffle (*Inf.*), poppycock (*Inf.*), rodomontade (*Literary*), rot, rubbish, shit (*Taboo sl.*), tommyrot, tosh (*Sl., chiefly Brit.*), tripe (*Inf.*)

clarification elucidation, explanation, exposition, illumination, interpretation, simplification

clarify 1. clear up, elucidate, explain, explicate, illuminate, interpret, make plain, resolve, simplify, throw *or* shed light on 2. cleanse, purify, refine

clarion *adj.* blaring, clear, inspiring, loud, ringing, stirring, strident

clarity clearness, comprehensibility, definition, explicitness, intelligibility, limpidity, lucidity, obviousness, precision, simplicity, transparency

Antonyms cloudiness, complexity, complication, dullness, haziness, imprecision, intricacy, murkiness, obscurity

clash *v.* 1. bang, clang, clank, clatter, crash, jangle, jar, rattle 2. conflict, cross swords, feud, grapple, quarrel, war, wrangle ~*n.* 3. brush, collision, conflict, confrontation, difference of opinion, disagreement, fight, showdown (*Inf.*)

clasp *v.* 1. attack, clutch, concatenate, connect, embrace, enfold, fasten, grapple, grasp, grip, hold, hug, press, seize, squeeze ~*n.* 2. brooch, buckle, catch, clip, fastener, fastening, grip, hasp, hook, pin, press stud, snap 3. embrace, grasp, grip, hold, hug

class 1. *n.* caste, category, classification, collection, denomination, department, division, genre, genus, grade, group, grouping, kind, league, order, rank, set, sort, species, sphere, stamp, status, type, value 2. *v.* brand, categorize, classify, codify, designate, grade, group, label, rank, rate

classic *adj.* 1. best, consummate, finest, first-rate, masterly, world-class 2. archetypal, definitive, exemplary, ideal, master, model, paradigmatic, quintessential, standard 3. characteristic, regular, standard, time-honoured, typical, usual 4. abiding, ageless, deathless, enduring, immortal, lasting, undying ~*n.* 5. exemplar, masterpiece, masterwork, model, paradigm, prototype, standard

Antonyms *adj.* inferior, modern, poor, second-rate, terrible, unrefined, unrepresentative ~*n.* trash

classical 1. chaste, elegant, harmonious, pure, refined, restrained, symmetrical, understated, well-proportioned 2. Attic, Augustan, Grecian, Greek, Hellenic, Latin, Roman

classification analysis, arrangement, cataloguing, categorization, codification, grading, sorting, taxonomy

classify arrange, catalogue, categorize, codify, dispose, distribute, file, grade, pigeonhole, rank, sort, systematize, tabulate

classy elegant, exclusive, high-class, high-toned, posh (*Inf., chiefly Brit.*), ritzy (*Sl.*), select, stylish, superior, swanky (*Inf.*), swish (*Inf., chiefly Brit.*), top-drawer, up-market

clause 1. article, chapter, condition, paragraph, part, passage, section 2. heading, item, point, provision, proviso, rider, specification, stipulation

claw 1. *n.* nail, nipper, pincer, talon, tentacle, unguis 2. *v.* dig, graze, lacerate, mangle, maul, rip, scrabble, scrape, scratch, tear

clean *adj.* 1. faultless, flawless, fresh, hygienic, immaculate, impeccable, laundered, pure, sanitary, spotless, squeaky-clean, unblemished, unsoiled, unspotted, unstained, unsullied, washed 2. antiseptic, clarified, decontaminated, natural, purified, sterile, sterilized, unadulterated, uncontaminated, unpolluted 3. chaste, decent, exemplary, good, honourable, impeccable, innocent, moral, pure, respectable, undefiled, upright, virtuous 4. delicate, elegant, graceful, neat, simple, tidy, trim, uncluttered 5. complete, conclusive, decisive, entire, final, perfect, thorough, total, unimpaired, whole ~*v.* 6. bath, cleanse, deodorize, disinfect, do up, dust, launder, lave, mop, purge, purify, rinse, sanitize, scour, scrub, sponge, swab, sweep, vacuum, wash, wipe

Antonyms *adj.* (*sense 1*) dirty, filthy, mucky, scuzzy (*Sl., chiefly U.S.*), soiled, sullied, unwashed (*sense 2*) adulterated, contaminated, infected, polluted (*sense 3*) dishonourable, immoral, impure, indecent, unchaste (*sense 4*) chaotic, disorderly, disorganized, higgledy-piggledy (*Inf.*), shambolic (*Inf.*), untidy ~*v.* adulterate, defile, dirty, disorder, disorganize, infect, mess up, pollute, soil, stain

clean-cut chiselled, clear, definite, etched, neat, outlined, sharp, trim, well-defined

cleanse absolve, clean, clear, lustrate, purge, purify, rinse, scour, scrub, wash

cleanser detergent, disinfectant, purifier, scourer, soap, soap powder, solvent

clear[1] *adj.* 1. bright, cloudless, fair, fine, halcyon, light, luminous, shining, sunny, unclouded, undimmed 2. apparent, articulate, audible, blatant, coherent, comprehensible, conspicuous, definite, distinct, evident, explicit, express, incontrovertible, intelligible, lucid, manifest, obvious, palpable, patent, perceptible, plain, pronounced, recognizable, unambiguous, unequivocal, unmistakable, unquestionable 3. empty, free, open, smooth, unhampered, unhindered, unimpeded, unlimited, unobstructed 4. crystalline, glassy, limpid, pellucid, see-through, translucent, transparent 5. certain, convinced, decided, definite, positive, resolved, satisfied, sure 6. clean, guiltless, immaculate, innocent, pure, sinless, stainless, unblemished, undefiled, untarnished, untroubled

Antonyms (*sense 1*) cloudy, dark, dull, foggy, hazy, misty, murky, overcast, stormy (*sense 2*) ambiguous, confused, doubtful, equivocal, hidden, inarticulate, inaudible, incoherent, indistinct, inexplicit, obscured, unrecognizable (*sense 3*) barricaded, blocked, closed, engaged, hampered, impeded, obstructed (*sense 4*) cloudy, muddy, non-translucent, non-transparent, opaque, turbid

clear[2] *v.* 1. clean, cleanse, erase, purify, refine, sweep away, tidy (up), wipe 2. break up, brighten, clarify, lighten 3. absolve, acquit, excuse, exonerate, justify, vindicate 4. emancipate, free, liberate, set free 5. disengage, disentangle, extricate, free, loosen, open, rid, unblock, unclog, unload, unpack 6. jump, leap, miss, pass over, vault 7. acquire, earn, gain, make, reap, secure

Antonyms (*sense 3*) accuse, blame, charge, condemn, convict, find guilty

clearance 1. authorization, consent, endorsement, go-ahead (*Inf.*), green light, leave, O.K. *or* okay (*Inf.*), permission, sanction 2. allowance, gap, headroom, margin 3. depopulation, emptying, evacuation, eviction, removal, unpeopling, withdrawal

clear-cut definite, explicit, plain, precise, specific, straightforward, unambiguous, unequivocal

clearing dell, glade

clearly beyond doubt, distinctly, evidently, incontestably, incontrovertibly, markedly, obviously, openly, overtly, undeniably, undoubtedly

clearness audibility, brightness, clarity, coherence, distinctness, glassiness, intelligibility, lucidity, luminosity, transparency

clear out 1. empty, exhaust, get rid of, sort, tidy up 2. beat it (*Sl.*), decamp, depart, hook it (*Sl.*), leave, make oneself scarce, retire, slope off, take oneself off, withdraw

clear up 1. answer, clarify, elucidate, explain, resolve, solve, straighten out, unravel 2. order, rearrange, tidy (up)

cleave[1] abide by, adhere, agree, attach, be devoted to, be true, cling, cohere, hold, remain, stand by, stick

cleave[2] crack, dissever, disunite, divide, hew, open, part, rend, rive, sever, slice, split, sunder, tear asunder

cleft 1. *n.* breach, break, chasm, chink, crack, cranny, crevice, fissure, fracture, gap, opening, rent, rift 2. *adj.* cloven, parted, rent, riven, ruptured, separated, split, sundered, torn

clemency compassion, forbearance, forgiveness, humanity, indulgence, kindness, leniency, mercifulness, mercy, mildness, moderation, pity, quarter, soft-heartedness, tenderness

clement 1. compassionate, forbearing, forgiving, gentle, humane, indulgent, kind, kind-hearted, lenient, merciful, mild, soft-hearted, tender 2. balmy, calm, fair, fine, mild, temperate

clergy churchmen, clergymen, clerics, ecclesiastics, first estate, holy orders, ministry, priesthood, the cloth

clergyman chaplain, cleric, curate, divine, father, man of God, man of the cloth, minister, padre, parson, pastor, priest, rabbi, rector, reverend (*Inf.*), vicar

clerical 1. ecclesiastical, pastoral, priestly, sacerdotal 2. book-keeping, clerkish, clerkly, office, secretarial, stenographic

clever able, adroit, apt, astute, brainy (*Inf.*), bright, canny, capable, cunning, deep, dexterous, discerning, expert, gifted, ingenious, intelligent, inventive, keen, knowing, knowledgeable, quick, quick-witted, ra~

tional, resourceful, sagacious, sensible, shrewd, skilful, smart, talented, witty
Antonyms awkward, boring, clumsy, dense, dull, ham-fisted (*Inf.*), inept, inexpert, maladroit, slow, stupid, thick, unaccomplished, unimaginative, witless

cleverness ability, adroitness, astuteness, brains, brightness, canniness, dexterity, flair, gift, gumption (*Brit. inf.*), ingenuity, intelligence, nous (*Brit. sl.*), quickness, quick wits, resourcefulness, sagacity, sense, sharpness, shrewdness, smartness, smarts (*Sl., chiefly U.S.*), suss (*Sl.*), talent, wit

cliché banality, bromide, chestnut (*Inf.*), commonplace, hackneyed phrase, old saw, platitude, stereotype, truism

click *n./v.* 1. beat, clack, snap, tick ~*v.* 2. *Inf.* become clear, come home (to), fall into place, make sense 3. *Sl.* be compatible, be on the same wavelength, feel a rapport, get on, go over, hit it off (*Inf.*), make a hit, succeed, take to each other

client applicant, buyer, consumer, customer, dependant, habitué, patient, patron, protégé, shopper

clientele business, clients, customers, following, market, patronage, regulars, trade

cliff bluff, crag, escarpment, face, overhang, precipice, rock face, scar, scarp

climactic climactical, critical, crucial, decisive, paramount, peak

climate 1. clime, country, region, temperature, weather 2. ambience, disposition, feeling, mood, temper, tendency, trend

climax 1. *n.* acme, apogee, crest, culmination, head, height, highlight, high spot (*Inf.*), *ne plus ultra*, pay-off (*Inf.*), peak, summit, top, zenith 2. *v.* come to a head, culminate, peak

climb ascend, clamber, mount, rise, scale, shin up, soar, top

climb down 1. descend, dismount 2. back down, eat crow (*U.S. inf.*), eat one's words, retract, retreat

clinch 1. assure, cap, conclude, confirm, decide, determine, seal, secure, set the seal on, settle, sew up (*Inf.*), verify 2. bolt, clamp, fasten, fix, make fast, nail, rivet, secure 3. clutch, cuddle, embrace, grasp, hug, squeeze

cling adhere, attach to, be true to, clasp, cleave to, clutch, embrace, fasten, grasp, grip, hug, stick, twine round

clinical analytic, antiseptic, cold, detached, disinterested, dispassionate, emotionless, impersonal, objective, scientific, unemotional

clip[1] 1. *v.* crop, curtail, cut, cut short, dock, pare, prune, shear, shorten, snip, trim 2. *n./v.* *Inf.* belt (*Inf.*), blow, box, clout (*Inf.*), cuff, knock, punch, skelp (*Dialect*), smack, thump, wallop (*Inf.*), whack 3. *n.* *Inf.* gallop, lick (*Inf.*), rate, speed, velocity

clip[2] *v.* attach, fasten, fix, hold, pin, staple

clipping cutting, excerpt, extract, piece

clique cabal, circle, clan, coterie, crew (*Inf.*), crowd, faction, gang, group, mob, pack, posse (*Inf.*), schism, set

cloak 1. *v.* camouflage, conceal, cover, disguise, hide, mask, obscure, screen, veil 2. *n.* blind, cape, coat, cover, front, mantle, mask, pretext, shield, wrap

clodhopper booby, boor, bumpkin, clown, galoot (*Sl., chiefly U.S.*), loon (*Inf.*), lout, oaf, yokel

clog 1. *v.* block, burden, bung, congest, dam up, hamper, hinder, impede, jam, obstruct, occlude, shackle, stop up 2. *n.* burden, dead weight, drag, encumbrance, hindrance, impediment, obstruction

cloistered cloistral, confined, hermitic, insulated, reclusive, restricted, secluded, sequestered, sheltered, shielded, shut off, withdrawn
Antonyms extrovert, genial, gregarious, outgoing, public, sociable, social

close[1] *v.* 1. bar, block, bung, choke, clog, confine, cork, fill, lock, obstruct, plug, seal, secure, shut, shut up, stop up 2. axe (*Inf.*), cease, complete, conclude, culminate, discontinue, end, finish, mothball, shut down, terminate, wind up 3. come together, connect, couple, fuse, grapple, join, unite
Antonyms (*sense 1*) clear, free, open, release, unblock, unclog, uncork, unstop, widen (*sense 2*) begin, commence, initiate, open, start (*sense 3*) disconnect, disjoin, disunite, divide, part, separate, split, uncouple

close[2] 1. adjacent, adjoining, approaching, at hand, handy, hard by, imminent, impending, near, nearby, neighbouring, nigh, proximate, upcoming, within sniffing distance (*Inf.*) 2. compact, congested, cramped, cropped, crowded, dense, impenetrable, jam-packed, packed, short, solid, thick, tight 3. accurate, conscientious, exact, faithful, literal, precise, strict 4. alert, assiduous, attentive, careful, concentrated, detailed, dogged, earnest, fixed, intense, intent, keen, minute, painstaking, rigorous, searching, thorough 5. attached, confidential, dear, devoted, familiar, inseparable, intimate, loving 6. airless, confined, frowsty, fuggy, heavy, humid, muggy, oppressive, stale, stifling, stuffy, suffocating, sweltering, thick, unventilated 7. hidden, private, reticent, retired, secluded, secret, secretive,

taciturn, uncommunicative, unforthcoming 8. illiberal, mean, mingy (*Brit. inf.*), miserly, near, niggardly, parsimonious, penurious, stingy, tight as a duck's arse (*Taboo sl.*), tight-fisted, ungenerous
Antonyms (*sense 1*) distant, far, far away, far off, future, outlying, remote (*sense 2*) dispersed, empty, free, loose, penetrable, porous, uncongested, uncrowded (*sense 5*) alienated, aloof, chilly, cold, cool, distant, indifferent, standoffish, unfriendly (*sense 6*) airy, fresh, refreshing, roomy, spacious (*sense 8*) charitable, extravagant, generous, lavish, liberal, magnanimous, unstinting

close[3] cessation, completion, conclusion, culmination, denouement, end, ending, finale, finish, termination

closed 1. fastened, locked, out of business, out of service, sealed, shut 2. concluded, decided, ended, finished, over, resolved, settled, terminated 3. exclusive, restricted
Antonyms (*sense 1*) ajar, open, unclosed, unfastened, unlocked, unsealed

closure 1. cessation, closing, conclusion, end, finish, stoppage 2. bung, cap, lid, plug, seal, stopper 3. *In a deliberative assembly* cloture, guillotine

clot 1. clotting, coagulation, curdling, embolism, embolus, gob, lump, mass, occlusion, thrombus 2. ass, berk (*Brit. sl.*), buffoon, charlie (*Brit. inf.*), coot, dickhead (*Sl.*), dipstick (*Brit. sl.*), divvy (*Brit. sl.*), dolt, dope (*Inf.*), dork (*Sl.*), dunderhead, dweeb (*U.S. sl.*), fathead (*Inf.*), fool, fuckwit (*Taboo sl.*), geek (*Sl.*), gonzo (*Sl.*), idiot, jerk (*Sl., chiefly U.S. & Canad.*), nerd *or* nurd (*Sl.*), nincompoop, nit (*Inf.*), nitwit (*Inf.*), numskull *or* numbskull, pillock (*Brit. sl.*), plank (*Brit. sl.*), plonker (*Sl.*), prat (*Sl.*), prick (*Derogatory sl.*), schmuck (*U.S. sl.*), twerp *or* twirp (*Inf.*), twit (*Inf., chiefly Brit.*), wally (*Sl.*) 3. coagulate, coalesce, congeal, curdle, jell, thicken

cloth dry goods, fabric, material, stuff, textiles

clothe accoutre, apparel, array, attire, bedizen (*Archaic*), caparison, cover, deck, doll up (*Sl.*), drape, dress, endow, enwrap, equip, fit out, garb, get ready, habit, invest, outfit, rig, robe, swathe
Antonyms disrobe, divest, expose, strip, strip off, unclothe, uncover, undress

clothes, clothing apparel, attire, clobber (*Brit. sl.*), costume, dress, duds (*Inf.*), ensemble, garb, garments, gear (*Inf.*), get-up (*Inf.*), glad rags (*Inf.*), habits, outfit, raiment (*Archaic or poetic*), rigout (*Inf.*), togs (*Inf.*), vestments, vesture, wardrobe, wear

cloud *n.* 1. billow, darkness, fog, gloom, haze, mist, murk, nebula, nebulosity, obscurity, vapour 2. crowd, dense mass, flock, horde, host, multitude, shower, swarm, throng ~*v.* 3. becloud, darken, dim, eclipse, obfuscate, obscure, overcast, overshadow, shade, shadow, veil 4. confuse, disorient, distort, impair, muddle

cloudy blurred, confused, dark, dim, dismal, dull, dusky, emulsified, gloomy, hazy, indistinct, leaden, louring *or* lowering, muddy, murky, nebulous, obscure, opaque, overcast, sombre, sullen, sunless
Antonyms bright, clear, distinct, fair, obvious, plain, sunny, uncloudy

clout 1. *v.* box, chin (*Sl.*), clobber (*Sl.*), cuff, deck (*Sl.*), hit, lay one on (*Sl.*), punch, skelp (*Dialect*), sock (*Sl.*), strike, thump, wallop (*Inf.*), wham 2. *n.* authority, bottom, influence, power, prestige, pull, standing, weight

cloven bisected, cleft, divided, split

clown *n.* 1. buffoon, comedian, dolt, fool, harlequin, jester, joker, merry-andrew, mountebank, pierrot, prankster, punchinello 2. boor, clodhopper (*Inf.*), hind (*Obsolete*), peasant, swain (*Archaic*), yahoo, yokel ~*v.* 3. act the fool, act the goat, jest, mess about, piss about (*Taboo sl.*), piss around (*Taboo sl.*)

clownish 1. comic, foolish, galumphing (*Inf.*), nonsensical, slapstick, zany 2. awkward, boorish, churlish, clumsy, ill-bred, rough, rude, rustic, uncivil, ungainly, vulgar

cloy disgust, glut, gorge, nauseate, sate, satiate, sicken, surfeit, weary

cloying excessive, nauseating, oversweet, sickly, treacly

club 1. *n.* bat, bludgeon, cosh (*Brit.*), cudgel, stick, truncheon 2. *v.* bash, baste, batter, beat, bludgeon, clobber (*Sl.*), clout (*Inf.*), cosh (*Brit.*), hammer, pommel (*Rare*), pummel, strike 3. *n.* association, circle, clique, company, fraternity, group, guild, lodge, order, set, society, sodality, union

clue evidence, hint, indication, inkling, intimation, lead, pointer, sign, suggestion, suspicion, tip, tip-off, trace

clump 1. *n.* bunch, bundle, cluster, mass, shock 2. *v.* bumble, clomp, lumber, plod, stamp, stomp, stump, thud, thump, tramp

clumsy accident-prone, awkward, blundering, bumbling, bungling, butterfingered (*Inf.*), cack-handed (*Inf.*), gauche, gawky, ham-fisted (*Inf.*), ham-handed (*Inf.*), heavy, ill-shaped, inept, inexpert, klutzy (*U.S. & Canad. sl.*), lumbering, maladroit, ponderous, uncoordinated, uncouth, ungainly, unhandy, unskilful, unwieldy
Antonyms adept, adroit, competent, deft,

dexterous, expert, graceful, handy, proficient, skilful

cluster 1. *n.* assemblage, batch, bunch, clump, collection, gathering, group, knot 2. *v.* assemble, bunch, collect, flock, gather, group

clutch catch (up), clasp, cling to, embrace, fasten, grab, grapple, grasp, grip, seize, snatch

clutches claws, control, custody, grasp, grip, hands, keeping, possession, power, sway

clutter 1. *n.* confusion, disarray, disorder, hotchpotch, jumble, litter, mess, muddle, untidiness 2. *v.* litter, scatter, strew
Antonyms *n.* neatness, order, organization, tidiness ~*v.* arrange, order, organize, straighten, tidy

coach *n.* 1. bus, car, carriage, charabanc, vehicle 2. handler, instructor, teacher, trainer, tutor ~*v.* 3. cram, drill, exercise, instruct, prepare, train, tutor

coagulate clot, congeal, curdle, jell, thicken

coalesce amalgamate, blend, cohere, combine, come together, commingle, commix, consolidate, fraternize, fuse, incorporate, integrate, meld, merge, mix, unite

coalition affiliation, alliance, amalgam, amalgamation, association, bloc, combination, compact, confederacy, confederation, conjunction, fusion, integration, league, merger, union

coarse 1. boorish, brutish, coarse-grained, foul-mouthed, gruff, loutish, rough, rude, uncivil 2. bawdy, earthy, immodest, impolite, improper, impure, indelicate, inelegant, mean, offensive, raunchy (*Sl.*), ribald, rude, smutty, vulgar 3. coarse-grained, crude, homespun, impure, rough-hewn, unfinished, unpolished, unprocessed, unpurified, unrefined
Antonyms (*senses 1 & 2*) civilized, cultured, elegant, fine, genteel, inoffensive, pleasant, polished, polite, proper, refined, sophisticated, urbane, well-bred, well-mannered (*sense 3*) fine-grained, polished, purified, refined, smooth, soft

coarsen anaesthetize, blunt, callous, deaden, desensitize, dull, harden, indurate, roughen

coarseness bawdiness, boorishness, crudity, earthiness, indelicacy, offensiveness, poor taste, ribaldry, roughness, smut, smuttiness, uncouthness, unevenness

coast 1. *n.* beach, border, coastline, littoral, seaboard, seaside, shore, strand 2. *v.* cruise, drift, freewheel, get by, glide, sail, taxi

coat *n.* 1. fleece, fur, hair, hide, pelt, skin, wool 2. coating, covering, layer, overlay ~*v.* 3. Artex (*Trademark*), apply, cover, plaster, smear, spread

coating blanket, coat, covering, dusting, film, finish, glaze, lamination, layer, membrane, patina, sheet, skin, varnish, veneer

coax allure, beguile, cajole, decoy, entice, flatter, inveigle, persuade, prevail upon, soft-soap (*Inf.*), soothe, sweet-talk (*Inf.*), talk into, wheedle
Antonyms browbeat, bully, coerce, force, harass, intimidate, pressurize, threaten

cobble botch, bungle, clout, mend, patch, tinker

cock 1. *n.* chanticleer, cockerel, rooster 2. *v.* perk up, prick, raise, stand up

cockeyed absurd, askew, asymmetrical, awry, crazy, crooked, lopsided, ludicrous, nonsensical, preposterous, skewwhiff (*Brit. inf.*), squint (*Inf.*)

cocksure arrogant, brash, bumptious, cocky, hubristic, overconfident, presumptuous

cocky arrogant, brash, cocksure, conceited, egotistical, lordly, swaggering, swollen-headed, vain
Antonyms hesitant, lacking confidence, modest, self-effacing, uncertain, unsure

cocoon cushion, envelop, insulate, pad, protect, swaddle, swathe, wrap

coddle baby, cosset, humour, indulge, mollycoddle, nurse, pamper, pet, spoil, wet-nurse (*Inf.*)

code 1. cipher, cryptograph 2. canon, convention, custom, ethics, etiquette, manners, maxim, regulations, rules, system

codify catalogue, classify, collect, condense, digest, organize, summarize, systematize, tabulate

coerce browbeat, bulldoze (*Inf.*), bully, compel, constrain, dragoon, drive, force, intimidate, press-gang, pressurize, railroad (*Inf.*)

coercion browbeating, bullying, compulsion, constraint, duress, force, intimidation, pressure, strong-arm tactics (*Inf.*), threats

coeval coetaneous (*Rare*), coexistent, contemporaneous, contemporary, synchronous

coffer ark (*Dialect*), case, casket, chest, kist (*Scot. & Northern English dialect*), repository, strongbox, treasure chest, treasury

coffers assets, capital, finances, funds, means, reserves, treasury, vaults

cogency conviction, force, potency, power, strength

cogent compelling, conclusive, convincing, effective, forceful, forcible, influential, irresistible, potent, powerful, strong, urgent, weighty

cogitate consider, contemplate, deliberate, meditate, mull over, muse, ponder, reflect, ruminate, think

cogitation consideration, contemplation, deliberation, meditation, reflection, rumination, thought

cognate affiliated, akin, alike, allied, analogous, associated, connected, kindred, related, similar

cognition apprehension, awareness, comprehension, discernment, insight, intelligence, perception, reasoning, understanding

cognizance acknowledgment, apprehension, cognition, knowledge, notice, perception, percipience, recognition, regard

cognizant acquainted, aware, clued-up (*Inf.*), conscious, conversant, familiar, informed, knowledgeable, versed

cohere 1. adhere, bind, cling, coalesce, combine, consolidate, fuse, glue, hold, stick, unite 2. agree, be connected, be consistent, correspond, hang together, harmonize, hold good, hold water, square

coherence agreement, comprehensibility, concordance, congruity, connection, consistency, consonance, correspondence, intelligibility, rationality, union, unity

coherent articulate, comprehensible, consistent, intelligible, logical, lucid, meaningful, orderly, organized, rational, reasoned, systematic
Antonyms confusing, disjointed, illogical, incomprehensible, inconsistent, meaningless, rambling, unintelligible, vague

cohort 1. band, company, contingent, legion, regiment, squadron, troop 2. *Chiefly U.S.* accomplice, assistant, comrade, follower, henchman, mate, myrmidon, partner, protagonist, sidekick (*Sl.*), supporter

coil convolute, curl, entwine, loop, snake, spiral, twine, twist, wind, wreathe, writhe

coin 1. *v.* conceive, create, fabricate, forge, formulate, frame, invent, make up, mint, mould, originate, think up 2. *n.* cash, change, copper, dosh (*Brit. & Aust. sl.*), money, silver, specie

coincide 1. be concurrent, coexist, occur simultaneously, synchronize 2. accord, harmonize, match, quadrate, square, tally 3. acquiesce, agree, concur, correspond
Antonyms be inconsistent, be unlike, contradict, differ, disagree, diverge, divide, part, separate

coincidence 1. accident, chance, eventuality, fluke, fortuity, happy accident, luck, stroke of luck 2. concomitance, concurrence, conjunction, correlation, correspondence, synchronism

coincident coinciding, concomitant, concurring, consonant, contemporaneous, coordinate, correspondent, synchronous

coincidental 1. accidental, casual, chance, fluky (*Inf.*), fortuitous, unintentional, unplanned 2. coincident, concomitant, concurrent, simultaneous, synchronous
Antonyms (*sense 1*) calculated, deliberate, done on purpose, intentional, planned, prearranged

coitus coition, congress, copulation, coupling, mating, nookie (*Sl.*), rumpy-pumpy (*Sl.*), sexual intercourse, the other (*Inf.*), union

cold *adj.* 1. arctic, biting, bitter, bleak, brumal, chill, chilly, cool, freezing, frigid, frosty, frozen, gelid, harsh, icy, inclement, parky (*Brit. inf.*), raw, wintry 2. benumbed, chilled, chilly, freezing, frozen to the marrow, numbed, shivery 3. aloof, apathetic, cold-blooded, dead, distant, frigid, glacial, indifferent, inhospitable, lukewarm, passionless, phlegmatic, reserved, spiritless, standoffish, stony, undemonstrative, unfeeling, unmoved, unresponsive, unsympathetic ~*n.* 4. chill, chilliness, coldness, frigidity, frostiness, iciness, inclemency
Antonyms (*sense 1*) balmy, heated, hot, mild, sunny, warm (*sense 3*) alive, animated, caring, compassionate, conscious, demonstrative, emotional, friendly, loving, open, passionate, responsive, spirited, sympathetic, warm

cold-blooded barbarous, brutal, callous, cruel, dispassionate, heartless, inhuman, merciless, pitiless, Ramboesque, ruthless, savage, steely, stony-hearted, unemotional, unfeeling, unmoved
Antonyms caring, charitable, civilized, concerned, emotional, feeling, friendly, humane, involved, kind, kind-hearted, merciful, open, passionate, sensitive, warm

cold-hearted callous, detached, frigid, hardhearted, harsh, heartless, indifferent, inhuman, insensitive, stony-hearted, uncaring, unfeeling, unkind, unsympathetic

collaborate 1. cooperate, coproduce, join forces, participate, team up, work together 2. collude, conspire, cooperate, fraternize

collaboration alliance, association, concert, cooperation, partnership, teamwork

collaborator 1. associate, colleague, confederate, co-worker, partner, team-mate 2. collaborationist, fraternizer, quisling, traitor, turncoat

collapse 1. *v.* break down, cave in, come to nothing, crack up (*Inf.*), crumple, fail, faint, fall, fold, founder, give way, subside 2. *n.*

breakdown, cave-in, disintegration, downfall, exhaustion, failure, faint, flop, prostration, subsidence

collar *v.* apprehend, appropriate, capture, catch, grab, lay hands on, nab (*Inf.*), nail (*Inf.*), seize

collate adduce, analogize, collect, compare, compose, gather (*Printing*)

collateral *n.* 1. assurance, deposit, guarantee, pledge, security, surety *~adj.* 2. concurrent, confirmatory, corroborative, indirect, not lineal, parallel, related, supporting 3. ancillary, auxiliary, secondary, subordinate

colleague aider, ally, assistant, associate, auxiliary, coadjutor (*Rare*), collaborator, companion, comrade, confederate, confrère, fellow worker, helper, partner, team-mate, workmate

collect 1. accumulate, aggregate, amass, assemble, gather, heap, hoard, save, stockpile 2. assemble, cluster, congregate, convene, converge, flock together, rally 3. acquire, muster, obtain, raise, secure, solicit
Antonyms disperse, distribute, scatter, spread, strew

collected calm, composed, confident, cool, placid, poised, sedate, self-possessed, serene, together (*Sl.*), unfazed (*Inf.*), unperturbable, unperturbed, unruffled
Antonyms agitated, distressed, emotional, excitable, irritable, nervous, perturbed, ruffled, shaky, troubled, twitchy (*Inf.*), unpoised, unsteady

collection 1. accumulation, anthology, compilation, congeries, heap, hoard, mass, pile, set, stockpile, store 2. assemblage, assembly, assortment, cluster, company, congregation, convocation, crowd, gathering, group 3. alms, contribution, offering, offertory

collective aggregate, combined, common, composite, concerted, cooperative, corporate, cumulative, joint, shared, unified, united
Antonyms divided, individual, piecemeal, split, uncombined, uncooperative

collide clash, come into collision, conflict, crash, meet head-on

collision 1. accident, bump, crash, impact, pile-up (*Inf.*), prang (*Inf.*), smash 2. clash, clashing, conflict, confrontation, encounter, opposition, skirmish

colloquial conversational, demotic, everyday, familiar, idiomatic, informal, vernacular

colloquy confabulation, conference, conversation, debate, dialogue, discourse, discussion, talk

collude abet, be in cahoots (*Inf.*), collaborate, complot, connive, conspire, contrive, intrigue, machinate, plot, scheme

collusion cahoots (*Inf.*), complicity, connivance, conspiracy, craft, deceit, fraudulent artifice, intrigue, secret understanding

colonist colonial, colonizer, frontiersman, homesteader (*U.S.*), immigrant, pioneer, planter, settler

colonize open up, people, pioneer, populate, settle

colonnade arcade, cloisters, covered walk, peristyle, portico

colony community, dependency, dominion, outpost, possession, province, satellite state, settlement, territory

colossal Brobdingnagian, elephantine, enormous, gargantuan, gigantic, ginormous (*Inf.*), herculean, huge, humongous *or* humungous (*U.S. sl.*), immense, mammoth, massive, monstrous, monumental, mountainous, prodigious, titanic, vast
Antonyms average, diminutive, little, miniature, minute, ordinary, pygmy *or* pigmy, slight, small, tiny, weak, wee

colour *n.* 1. colorant, coloration, complexion, dye, hue, paint, pigment, pigmentation, shade, tincture, tinge, tint 2. animation, bloom, blush, brilliance, flush, glow, liveliness, rosiness, ruddiness, vividness 3. *Fig.* appearance, disguise, excuse, façade, false show, guise, plea, pretence, pretext, semblance *~v.* 4. colourwash, dye, paint, stain, tinge, tint 5. *Fig.* disguise, distort, embroider, exaggerate, falsify, garble, gloss over, misrepresent, pervert, prejudice, slant, taint 6. blush, burn, crimson, flush, go crimson, redden

colourful 1. bright, brilliant, Day-glo (*Trademark*), intense, jazzy (*Inf.*), kaleidoscopic, motley, multicoloured, psychedelic, rich, variegated, vibrant, vivid 2. characterful, distinctive, graphic, interesting, lively, picturesque, rich, stimulating, unusual, vivid
Antonyms (*sense 1*) colourless, dark, drab, dreary, dull, faded, pale, washed out (*sense 2*) boring, characterless, dull, flat, lifeless, monotonous, unexciting, uninteresting, unvaried

colourless 1. achromatic, achromic, anaemic, ashen, bleached, drab, faded, neutral, sickly, wan, washed out 2. characterless, dreary, insipid, lacklustre, tame, uninteresting, unmemorable, vacuous, vapid
Antonyms (*sense 1*) blooming, flushed, glowing, healthy, radiant, robust, ruddy (*sense 2*) animated, bright, colourful, com-

pelling, distinctive, exciting, interesting, unusual

colours 1. banner, emblem, ensign, flag, standard 2. *Fig.* aspect, breed, character, identity, nature, stamp, strain

coltish frisky, frolicsome, lively, playful, romping, skittish, sportive, unruly

column 1. cavalcade, file, line, list, procession, queue, rank, row, string, train 2. caryatid, obelisk, pilaster, pillar, post, shaft, support, upright

columnist correspondent, critic, editor, gossip columnist, journalist, journo (*Sl.*), reporter, reviewer

coma drowsiness, insensibility, lethargy, oblivion, somnolence, stupor, torpor, trance, unconsciousness

comatose drowsy, drugged, insensible, lethargic, sleepy, sluggish, somnolent, soporose (*Medical*), stupefied, torpid, unconscious

comb *v.* 1. arrange, curry, dress, groom, untangle 2. *Of flax, wool, etc.* card, hackle, hatchel, heckle, tease, teasel, teazle 3. *Fig.* go through with a fine-tooth comb, hunt, rake, ransack, rummage, scour, screen, search, sift, sweep

combat 1. *n.* action, battle, conflict, contest, encounter, engagement, fight, skirmish, struggle, war, warfare 2. *v.* battle, contend, contest, cope, defy, do battle with, engage, fight, oppose, resist, strive, struggle, withstand

Antonyms *n.* agreement, armistice, peace, surrender, truce ~*v.* accept, acquiesce, declare a truce, give up, make peace, support, surrender

combatant 1. *n.* adversary, antagonist, belligerent, contender, enemy, fighter, fighting man, gladiator, opponent, serviceman, soldier, warrior 2. *adj.* battling, belligerent, combating, conflicting, contending, fighting, opposing, warring

combative aggressive, antagonistic, bellicose, belligerent, contentious, militant, pugnacious, quarrelsome, truculent, warlike

Antonyms nonaggressive, nonbelligerent, nonviolent, pacific, pacifist, peaceable, peaceful, peace-loving

combination 1. amalgam, amalgamation, blend, coalescence, composite, connection, meld, mix, mixture 2. alliance, association, cabal, cartel, coalition, combine, compound, confederacy, confederation, consortium, conspiracy, federation, merger, syndicate, unification, union

combine amalgamate, associate, bind, blend, bond, compound, connect, cooperate, fuse, incorporate, integrate, join (together), link, marry, meld, merge, mix, pool, put together, synthesize, unify, unite

Antonyms detach, dissociate, dissolve, disunite, divide, part, separate, sever

combustible explosive, flammable, incendiary, inflammable

come 1. advance, appear, approach, arrive, become, draw near, enter, happen, materialize, move, move towards, near, occur, originate, show up (*Inf.*), turn out, turn up (*Inf.*) 2. appear, arrive, attain, enter, materialize, reach, show up (*Inf.*), turn up (*Inf.*) 3. fall, happen, occur, take place 4. arise, emanate, emerge, end up, flow, issue, originate, result, turn out 5. extend, reach 6. be available (made, offered, on offer, produced)

come about arise, befall, come to pass, happen, occur, result, take place, transpire (*Inf.*)

come across bump into (*Inf.*), chance upon, discover, encounter, find, happen upon, hit upon, light upon, meet, notice, stumble upon, unearth

come along develop, improve, mend, perk up, pick up, progress, rally, recover, recuperate

come apart break, come unstuck, crumble, disintegrate, fall to pieces, give way, separate, split, tear

come at 1. attain, discover, find, grasp, reach 2. assail, assault, attack, charge, fall upon, fly at, go for, light into, rush, rush at

comeback 1. rally, rebound, recovery, resurgence, return, revival, triumph 2. rejoinder, reply, response, retaliation, retort, riposte

come back reappear, recur, re-enter, return

come between alienate, divide, estrange, interfere, meddle, part, separate, set at odds

come by acquire, get, lay hold of, obtain, procure, score (*Sl.*), secure, take possession of, win

come clean acknowledge, admit, confess, make a clean breast of, own up, reveal, sing (*Sl., chiefly U.S.*), spill one's guts (*Sl.*)

comedian card (*Inf.*), clown, comic, funny man, humorist, jester, joker, laugh (*Inf.*), wag, wit

comedown anticlimax, blow, decline, deflation, demotion, disappointment, humiliation, letdown, reverse

come down 1. decline, degenerate, descend, deteriorate, fall, go downhill, reduce, worsen 2. choose, decide, favour, recommend

come down on bawl out (*Inf.*), blast, carpet (*Inf.*), chew out (*U.S. & Canad. inf.*), criticize, dress down (*Inf.*), give (someone) a rocket (*Brit. & N.Z. inf.*), jump on (*Inf.*), lambast(e), put down, read the riot act, rebuke, reprimand, tear into (*Inf.*), tear (someone) off a strip (*Brit. inf.*)

come down to amount to, boil down to, end up as, result in

come down with ail, be stricken with, catch, contract, fall ill, fall victim to, get, sicken, take, take sick

comedy chaffing, drollery, facetiousness, farce, fun, hilarity, humour, jesting, joking, light entertainment, sitcom (*Inf.*), slapstick, wisecracking, witticisms
Antonyms high drama, melancholy, melodrama, opera, sadness, seriousness, serious play, soap opera, solemnity, tragedy

come forward offer one's services, present *or* proffer oneself, volunteer

come in appear, arrive, cross the threshold, enter, finish, reach, show up (*Inf.*)

come in for acquire, bear the brunt of, endure, get, receive, suffer

comely 1. attractive, beautiful, becoming, blooming, bonny, buxom, fair, good-looking, graceful, handsome, lovely, pleasing, pretty, wholesome, winsome 2. *Archaic* decent, decorous, fit, fitting, proper, seemly, suitable
Antonyms affected, disagreeable, distasteful, faded, homely, improper, indecorous, mumsy, plain, repulsive, ugly, unattractive, unbecoming, unfitting, unnatural, unpleasant, unseemly

come off go off, happen, occur, succeed, take place, transpire (*Inf.*)

come on 1. advance, develop, improve, make headway, proceed, progress 2. appear, begin, take place

come out 1. appear, be published (announced, divulged, issued, released, reported, revealed) 2. conclude, end, result, terminate

come out with acknowledge, come clean, declare, disclose, divulge, lay open, own, own up, say

come round 1. accede, acquiesce, allow, concede, grant, mellow, relent, yield 2. come to, rally, recover, regain consciousness, revive 3. call, drop in, pop in, stop by, visit

come through 1. accomplish, achieve, prevail, succeed, triumph 2. endure, survive, weather the storm, withstand

come up arise, crop up, happen, occur, rise, spring up, turn up

comeuppance chastening, deserts, due reward, dues, merit, punishment, recompense, requital, retribution

come up to admit of comparison with, approach, compare with, equal, match, measure up to, meet, resemble, rival, stand *or* bear comparison with

come up with advance, create, discover, furnish, offer, present, produce, propose, provide, submit, suggest

comfort *v.* 1. alleviate, assuage, cheer, commiserate with, compassionate (*Archaic*), console, ease, encourage, enliven, gladden, hearten, inspirit, invigorate, reassure, refresh, relieve, solace, soothe, strengthen ~*n.* 2. aid, alleviation, cheer, compensation, consolation, ease, encouragement, enjoyment, help, relief, satisfaction, succour, support 3. cosiness, creature comforts, ease, luxury, opulence, snugness, wellbeing
Antonyms *v.* aggravate (*Inf.*), agitate, annoy, bother, depress, discomfort, distress, excite, hassle (*Inf.*), irk, irritate, rile, ruffle, sadden, trouble ~*n.* aggravation, annoyance, discouragement, displeasure, hassle (*Inf.*), inconvenience, irritation

comfortable 1. adequate, agreeable, ample, commodious, convenient, cosy, delightful, easy, enjoyable, homely, loose, loose-fitting, pleasant, relaxing, restful, roomy, snug 2. at ease, contented, gratified, happy, relaxed, serene 3. affluent, prosperous, well-off, well-to-do
Antonyms (*sense 1*) disagreeable, inadequate, skin-tight, tight, tight-fitting, uncomfortable, unpleasant (*sense 2*) distressed, disturbed, ill at ease, miserable, nervous, on tenterhooks, tense, troubled, uncomfortable, uneasy

comforting cheering, consolatory, consoling, encouraging, heart-warming, inspiriting, reassuring, soothing
Antonyms alarming, dismaying, disturbing, perplexing, upsetting, worrying

comfortless 1. bleak, cheerless, cold, desolate, dismal, dreary 2. disconsolate, forlorn, inconsolable, miserable, sick at heart, woebegone, wretched

comic 1. *adj.* amusing, comical, droll, facetious, farcical, funny, humorous, jocular, joking, light, rich, waggish, witty 2. *n.* buffoon, clown, comedian, funny man, humorist, jester, wag, wit
Antonyms depressing, melancholy, pathetic, sad, serious, solemn, touching, tragic

comical absurd, amusing, comic, diverting, droll, entertaining, farcical, funny, hilarious, humorous, laughable, ludicrous, priceless, ridiculous, risible, side-splitting, silly, whimsical

coming *adj.* 1. approaching, at hand, due, en route, forthcoming, future, imminent, impending, in store, in the wind, near, next, nigh, upcoming 2. aspiring, future, promising, up-and-coming ~*n.* 3. accession, advent, approach, arrival

command *v.* 1. bid, charge, compel, demand, direct, enjoin, order, require 2. administer, control, dominate, govern, handle, head, lead, manage, reign over, rule, supervise, sway ~*n.* 3. behest, bidding, canon, commandment, decree, demand, direction, directive, edict, fiat, injunction, instruction, mandate, order, precept, requirement, ultimatum 4. authority, charge, control, direction, domination, dominion, government, grasp, management, mastery, power, rule, supervision, sway, upper hand
Antonyms (*sense 1*) appeal (to), ask, beg, beseech, plead, request, supplicate (*sense 2*) be inferior, be subordinate, follow

commandeer appropriate, confiscate, expropriate, hijack, requisition, seize, sequester, sequestrate, usurp

commander boss, captain, chief, C in C, C.O., commander-in-chief, commanding officer, director, head, leader, officer, ruler

commanding 1. advantageous, controlling, decisive, dominant, dominating, superior 2. assertive, authoritative, autocratic, compelling, forceful, imposing, impressive, peremptory
Antonyms retiring, shrinking, shy, submissive, timid, unassertive, unimposing, weak

commemorate celebrate, honour, immortalize, keep, memorialize, observe, pay tribute to, remember, salute, solemnize
Antonyms disregard, forget, ignore, omit, overlook, pass over, take no notice of

commemoration ceremony, honouring, memorial service, observance, remembrance, tribute

commemorative celebratory, dedicatory, in honour, in memory, in remembrance, memorial

commence begin, embark on, enter upon, inaugurate, initiate, open, originate, start
Antonyms bring *or* come to an end, cease, complete, conclude, desist, end, finish, halt, stop, terminate, wind up

commend 1. acclaim, applaud, approve, compliment, crack up (*Inf.*), eulogize, extol, praise, recommend, speak highly of 2. commit, confide, consign, deliver, entrust, hand over, yield
Antonyms (*sense 1*) attack, blast, censure, condemn, criticize, denounce, disapprove, knock (*Inf.*), lambast(e), put down, slam, tear into (*Inf.*) (*sense 2*) hold back, keep, keep back, retain, withdraw, withhold

commendable admirable, creditable, deserving, estimable, exemplary, laudable, meritorious, praiseworthy, worthy

commendation acclaim, acclamation, approbation, approval, Brownie points, credit, encomium, encouragement, good opinion, panegyric, praise, recommendation

commensurate adequate, appropriate, coextensive, comparable, compatible, consistent, corresponding, due, equivalent, fit, fitting, in accord, proportionate, sufficient

comment *v.* 1. animadvert, interpose, mention, note, observe, opine, point out, remark, say, utter 2. annotate, criticize, elucidate, explain, interpret ~*n.* 3. animadversion, observation, remark, statement 4. annotation, commentary, criticism, elucidation, explanation, exposition, illustration, note

commentary analysis, critique, description, exegesis, explanation, narration, notes, review, treatise, voice-over

commentator 1. commenter, reporter, special correspondent, sportscaster 2. annotator, critic, expositor, interpreter, scholiast

commerce 1. business, dealing, exchange, merchandising, trade, traffic 2. communication, dealings, intercourse, relations, socializing

commercial 1. business, mercantile, profit-making, sales, trade, trading 2. in demand, marketable, popular, profitable, saleable 3. exploited, materialistic, mercenary, monetary, pecuniary, profit-making, venal

commingle amalgamate, blend, combine, commix, intermingle, intermix, join, meld, mingle, unite

commiserate compassionate (*Archaic*), condole, console, feel for, pity, sympathize

commiseration compassion, condolence, consolation, fellow feeling, pity, sympathy

commission *n.* 1. appointment, authority, charge, duty, employment, errand, function, mandate, mission, task, trust, warrant 2. allowance, brokerage, compensation, cut, fee, percentage, rake-off (*Sl.*), royalties 3. board, body of commissioners, commissioners, committee, delegation, deputation, representative ~*v.* 4. appoint, authorize, contract, delegate, depute, empower, engage, nominate, order, select, send

commit 1. carry out, do, enact, execute, perform, perpetrate 2. commend, confide, consign, deliver, deposit, engage, entrust, give, hand over 3. align, bind, compromise, endanger, make liable, obligate, pledge, rank 4. confine, imprison, put in custody
Antonyms (*sense 1*) omit (*sense 2*) receive,

withhold (*sense 3*) disavow, vacillate, waver (*sense 4*) free, let out, release, set free

commitment 1. duty, engagement, liability, obligation, responsibility, tie 2. adherence, dedication, devotion, involvement, loyalty 3. assurance, guarantee, pledge, promise, undertaking, vow, word
Antonyms disavowal, indecisiveness, negation, vacillation, wavering

commodious ample, capacious, comfortable, convenient, expansive, extensive, large, loose, roomy, spacious

commodities goods, merchandise, produce, products, stock, wares

common 1. average, commonplace, conventional, customary, daily, everyday, familiar, frequent, general, habitual, humdrum, obscure, ordinary, plain, regular, routine, run-of-the-mill, simple, standard, stock, usual, workaday 2. accepted, general, popular, prevailing, prevalent, universal, widespread 3. collective, communal, community, popular, public, social 4. coarse, hackneyed, inferior, low, pedestrian, plebeian, stale, trite, undistinguished, vulgar
Antonyms (*sense 1*) abnormal, distinguished, famous, formal, important, infrequent, noble, outstanding, rare, scarce, sophisticated, strange, superior, uncommon, unknown, unpopular, unusual (*sense 3*) personal, private (*sense 4*) cultured, gentle, refined, sensitive

commonplace 1. *adj.* banal, common, customary, everyday, humdrum, mundane, obvious, ordinary, pedestrian, stale, threadbare, trite, uninteresting, widespread, worn out 2. *n.* banality, cliché, platitude, truism
Antonyms *adj.* exciting, extraordinary, infrequent, interesting, new, novel, original, rare, strange, uncommon, unfamiliar, unique, unusual

common-sense, common-sensical *adj.* astute, down-to-earth, hard-headed, judicious, level-headed, matter-of-fact, practical, realistic, reasonable, sane, sensible, shrewd, sound
Antonyms airy-fairy (*Inf.*), daft (*Inf.*), foolish, impractical, irrational, unrealistic, unreasonable, unthinking, unwise

common sense good sense, gumption (*Brit. inf.*), horse sense, level-headedness, mother wit, native intelligence, nous (*Brit. sl.*), practicality, prudence, reasonableness, smarts (*Sl., chiefly U.S.*), sound judgment, soundness, wit

commotion ado, agitation, brouhaha, bustle, disorder, disturbance, excitement, ferment, furore, fuss, hubbub, hullabaloo, hurly-burly, perturbation, racket, riot, rumpus, to-do, tumult, turmoil, upheaval, uproar

communal collective, communistic, community, general, joint, neighbourhood, public, shared
Antonyms exclusive, individual, personal, private, single, unshared

commune[1] *v.* 1. communicate, confer, confide in, converse, discourse, discuss, parley 2. contemplate, meditate, muse, ponder, reflect

commune[2] *n.* collective, community, cooperative, kibbutz

communicable catching, contagious, infectious, taking, transferable, transmittable

communicate acquaint, announce, be in contact, be in touch, connect, convey, correspond, declare, disclose, disseminate, divulge, impart, inform, make known, pass on, phone, proclaim, publish, report, reveal, ring up (*Inf., chiefly Brit.*), signify, spread, transmit, unfold
Antonyms conceal, cover up, hold back, hush up, keep back, keep secret, keep under wraps, repress, sit on (*Inf.*), suppress, whitewash (*Inf.*), withhold

communication 1. connection, contact, conversation, correspondence, dissemination, intercourse, link, transmission 2. announcement, disclosure, dispatch, information, intelligence, message, news, report, statement, word

communications 1. routes, transport, travel 2. information technology, media, publicity, public relations, telecommunications

communicative candid, chatty, conversable, expansive, forthcoming, frank, informative, loquacious, open, outgoing, talkative, unreserved, voluble
Antonyms quiet, reserved, reticent, secretive, taciturn, uncommunicative, uninformative, untalkative

communion 1. accord, affinity, agreement, closeness, communing, concord, consensus, converse, fellowship, harmony, intercourse, participation, rapport, sympathy, togetherness, unity 2. *Church* Eucharist, Lord's Supper, Mass, Sacrament

communiqué announcement, bulletin, dispatch, news flash, official communication, report

communism Bolshevism, collectivism, Marxism, socialism, state socialism

communist Bolshevik, collectivist, Marxist, Red (*Inf.*), socialist

community 1. association, body politic, brotherhood, commonwealth, company, district, general public, locality, people, populace, population, public, residents, society, state 2. affinity, agreement, identity, likeness, sameness, similarity

commute 1. barter, exchange, interchange, substitute, switch, trade 2. *Law: of penalties, etc.* alleviate, curtail, mitigate, modify, reduce, remit, shorten, soften

commuter 1. *n.* daily traveller, straphanger (*Inf.*), suburbanite 2. *adj.* suburban

compact[1] *adj.* 1. close, compressed, condensed, dense, firm, impenetrable, impermeable, pressed together, solid, thick 2. brief, compendious, concise, epigrammatic, laconic, pithy, pointed, succinct, terse, to the point ~*v.* 3. compress, condense, cram, pack down, stuff, tamp

Antonyms *adj.* (*sense 1*) dispersed, large, loose, roomy, scattered, spacious, sprawling (*sense 2*) circumlocutory, garrulous, lengthy, long-winded, prolix, rambling, verbose, wordy ~*v.* disperse, loosen, separate

compact[2] *n.* agreement, alliance, arrangement, bargain, bond, concordat, contract, covenant, deal, entente, pact, stipulation, treaty, understanding

companion 1. accomplice, ally, associate, buddy (*Inf.*), colleague, comrade, confederate, consort, crony, friend, mate (*Inf.*), partner 2. aide, assistant, attendant, chaperon, duenna, escort, squire 3. complement, counterpart, fellow, match, mate, twin

companionable affable, congenial, conversable, convivial, cordial, familiar, friendly, genial, gregarious, neighbourly, outgoing, sociable

companionship amity, camaraderie, company, comradeship, conviviality, esprit de corps, fellowship, fraternity, friendship, rapport, togetherness

company 1. assemblage, assembly, band, bevy, body, camp, circle, collection, community, concourse, convention, coterie, crew, crowd, ensemble, gathering, group, league, party, set, throng, troop, troupe, turnout 2. association, business, concern, corporation, establishment, firm, house, partnership, syndicate 3. callers, companionship, fellowship, guests, party, presence, society, visitors

comparable 1. a match for, as good as, commensurate, equal, equivalent, in a class with, on a par, proportionate, tantamount 2. akin, alike, analogous, cognate, corresponding, related, similar

Antonyms different, dissimilar, incommensurable, incomparable, unequal

comparative approximate, by comparison, qualified, relative

compare 1. *With* **with** balance, collate, contrast, juxtapose, set against, weigh 2. *With* **to** correlate, equate, identify with, liken, parallel, resemble 3. *Be the equal of* approach, approximate to, bear comparison, be in the same class as, be on a par with, come up to, compete with, equal, hold a candle to, match, vie

comparison 1. collation, contrast, distinction, juxtaposition 2. analogy, comparability, correlation, likeness, resemblance, similarity

compartment 1. alcove, bay, berth, booth, carrel, carriage, cell, chamber, cubbyhole, cubicle, locker, niche, pigeonhole, section 2. area, category, department, division, section, subdivision

compass *n.* 1. area, bound, boundary, circle, circuit, circumference, enclosure, extent, field, limit, range, reach, realm, round, scope, sphere, stretch, zone ~*v.* 2. beset, besiege, blockade, circumscribe, encircle, enclose, encompass, environ, hem in, invest (*Rare*), surround 3. accomplish, achieve, attain, bring about, effect, execute, fulfil, perform, procure, realize

compassion charity, clemency, commiseration, compunction, condolence, fellow feeling, heart, humanity, kindness, mercy, pity, quarter, ruth (*Archaic*), soft-heartedness, sorrow, sympathy, tender-heartedness, tenderness

Antonyms apathy, cold-heartedness, indifference, mercilessness, unconcern

compassionate benevolent, charitable, humane, humanitarian, indulgent, kind-hearted, kindly, lenient, merciful, pitying, sympathetic, tender, tender-hearted, understanding

Antonyms callous, harsh, heartless, inhumane, pitiless, uncaring, unfeeling, unmerciful, unsympathetic

compatibility affinity, agreement, amity, concord, congeniality, empathy, harmony, like-mindedness, rapport, single-mindedness, sympathy

compatible accordant, adaptable, agreeable, congenial, congruent, congruous, consistent, consonant, harmonious, in harmony, in keeping, like-minded, reconcilable, suitable

Antonyms contradictory, inappropriate, inapt, incompatible, unfitting, unharmonious, unsuitable

compatriot countryman, fellow citizen, fellow countryman

compel bulldoze (*Inf.*), coerce, constrain, dragoon, drive, enforce, exact, force, hustle (*Sl.*), impel, make, necessitate, oblige, railroad (*Inf.*), restrain, squeeze, urge

compelling 1. cogent, conclusive, convincing, forceful, irrefutable, powerful, telling, weighty 2. enchanting, enthralling, gripping, hypnotic, irresistible, mesmeric, spellbinding 3. binding, coercive, imperative, overriding, peremptory, pressing, unavoidable, urgent
Antonyms (*sense 1*) boring, dull, humdrum, monotonous, ordinary, repetitious, tiresome, uneventful, uninteresting, wearisome

compendious abbreviated, abridged, brief, comprehensive, concise, condensed, contracted, short, succinct, summarized, summary, synoptic

compensate 1. atone, indemnify, make good, make restitution, recompense, refund, reimburse, remunerate, repay, requite, reward, satisfy 2. balance, cancel (out), counteract, counterbalance, countervail, make amends, make up for, offset, redress

compensation amends, atonement, damages, indemnification, indemnity, meed (*Archaic*), payment, recompense, reimbursement, remuneration, reparation, requital, restitution, reward, satisfaction

compete be in the running, challenge, contend, contest, emulate, fight, pit oneself against, rival, strive, struggle, vie

competence ability, adequacy, appropriateness, capability, capacity, competency, craft, expertise, fitness, proficiency, skill, suitability
Antonyms inability, inadequacy, incompetence

competent able, adapted, adequate, appropriate, capable, clever, endowed, equal, fit, pertinent, proficient, qualified, sufficient, suitable
Antonyms cowboy (*Inf.*), inadequate, incapable, incompetent, inexperienced, inexpert, undependable, unqualified, unskilled

competition 1. contention, contest, emulation, one-upmanship (*Inf.*), opposition, rivalry, strife, struggle 2. championship, contest, event, head-to-head, puzzle, quiz, tournament 3. challengers, field, opposition, rivals

competitive aggressive, ambitious, antagonistic, at odds, combative, cutthroat, dog-eat-dog, emulous, opposing, rival, vying

competitor adversary, antagonist, challenger, competition, contestant, emulator, opponent, opposition, rival

compilation accumulation, anthology, assemblage, assortment, collection, treasury

compile accumulate, amass, anthologize, collect, cull, garner, gather, marshal, organize, put together

complacency contentment, gratification, pleasure, satisfaction, self-satisfaction, smugness

complacent contented, gratified, pleased, pleased with oneself, satisfied, self-assured, self-contented, self-righteous, self-satisfied, serene, smug, unconcerned
Antonyms discontent, dissatisfied, insecure, rude, troubled, uneasy, unsatisfied

complain beef (*Sl.*), bellyache (*Sl.*), bemoan, bewail, bitch (*Sl.*), bleat, carp, deplore, find fault, fuss, grieve, gripe (*Inf.*), groan, grouch (*Inf.*), grouse, growl, grumble, kick up a fuss (*Inf.*), kvetch (*U.S. sl.*), lament, moan, whine, whinge (*Inf.*)

complaint 1. accusation, annoyance, beef (*Sl.*), bitch (*Sl.*), charge, criticism, dissatisfaction, fault-finding, grievance, gripe (*Inf.*), grouch (*Inf.*), grouse, grumble, lament, moan, plaint, protest, remonstrance, trouble, wail 2. affliction, ailment, disease, disorder, illness, indisposition, malady, sickness, upset

complaisance accommodativeness, acquiescence, agreeableness, compliance, deference, obligingness

complaisant accommodating, amiable, compliant, conciliatory, deferential, obliging, polite, solicitous

complement *n.* 1. companion, completion, consummation, correlative, counterpart, finishing touch, rounding-off, supplement 2. aggregate, capacity, entirety, quota, total, totality, wholeness ~*v.* 3. cap (*Inf.*), complete, crown, round off, set off

complementary companion, completing, correlative, corresponding, fellow, interdependent, interrelating, matched, reciprocal
Antonyms contradictory, different, incompatible, incongruous, uncomplementary

complete *adj.* 1. all, entire, faultless, full, intact, integral, plenary, unabridged, unbroken, undivided, unimpaired, whole 2. accomplished, achieved, concluded, ended, finished 3. absolute, consummate, deep-dyed (*Usu. derogatory*), dyed-in-the-wool, outright, perfect, thorough, thoroughgoing, total, utter ~*v.* 4. accomplish, achieve, cap, close, conclude, crown, discharge, do, end, execute, fill in, finalize, finish, fulfil, perfect, perform, realize, round off, settle, terminate, wrap up (*Inf.*)
Antonyms *adj.* deficient, imperfect, incomplete, inconclusive, partial, spoilt, unaccomplished, unfinished, unsettled ~*v.* begin, commence, initiate, mar, spoil, start

completely absolutely, altogether, down to

the ground, en masse, entirely, from A to Z, from beginning to end, fully, heart and soul, hook, line and sinker, in full, *in toto,* perfectly, quite, root and branch, solidly, thoroughly, totally, utterly, wholly

completion accomplishment, attainment, close, conclusion, consummation, culmination, end, expiration, finalization, fruition, fulfilment, realization

complex *adj.* 1. circuitous, complicated, convoluted, Daedalian (*Literary*), intricate, involved, knotty, labyrinthine, mingled, mixed, tangled, tortuous 2. composite, compound, compounded, heterogeneous, manifold, multifarious, multiple ~*n.* 3. aggregate, composite, network, organization, scheme, structure, synthesis, system 4. fixation, fixed idea, *idée fixe,* obsession, phobia, preoccupation

Antonyms (*sense 1*) clear, easy, easy-peasy (*Sl.*), elementary, obvious, simple, straightforward, uncomplicated

complexion 1. colour, colouring, hue, pigmentation, skin, skin tone 2. appearance, aspect, cast, character, countenance, disposition, guise, light, look, make-up, nature, stamp

complexity complication, convolution, elaboration, entanglement, intricacy, involvement, multiplicity, ramification

compliance acquiescence, agreement, assent, complaisance, concession, concurrence, conformity, consent, deference, obedience, observance, passivity, submission, submissiveness, yielding

Antonyms defiance, disobedience, noncompliance, nonconformity, opposition, refusal, resistance, revolt

complicate confuse, entangle, interweave, involve, make intricate, muddle, ravel, snarl up

Antonyms clarify, clear up, disentangle, elucidate, explain, facilitate, simplify, spell out, unsnarl

complicated 1. Byzantine (*of attitudes, etc.*), complex, convoluted, elaborate, interlaced, intricate, involved, labyrinthine 2. difficult, involved, perplexing, problematic, puzzling, troublesome

Antonyms clear, easy, easy-peasy (*Sl.*), simple, straightforward, uncomplicated, undemanding, understandable, uninvolved, user-friendly

complication 1. combination, complexity, confusion, entanglement, intricacy, mixture, web 2. aggravation, difficulty, drawback, embarrassment, factor, obstacle, problem, snag

complicity abetment, collaboration, collusion, concurrence, connivance

compliment 1. *n.* admiration, bouquet, commendation, congratulations, courtesy, eulogy, favour, flattery, honour, praise, tribute 2. *v.* commend, congratulate, crack up (*Inf.*), extol, felicitate, flatter, laud, pay tribute to, praise, salute, sing the praises of, speak highly of, wish joy to

Antonyms *n.* complaint, condemnation, criticism, disparagement, insult, reproach ~*v.* blast, condemn, criticize, decry, disparage, insult, lambast(e), put down, reprehend, reproach, tear into (*Inf.*)

complimentary 1. appreciative, approving, commendatory, congratulatory, eulogistic, flattering, laudatory, panegyrical 2. courtesy, donated, free, free of charge, gratis, gratuitous, honorary, on the house

Antonyms (*sense 1*) abusive, critical, disparaging, fault-finding, insulting, scathing, uncomplimentary, unflattering

compliments good wishes, greetings, regards, remembrances, respects, salutation

comply abide by, accede, accord, acquiesce, adhere to, agree to, conform to, consent to, defer, discharge, follow, fulfil, obey, observe, perform, respect, satisfy, submit, yield

Antonyms break, defy, disobey, disregard, fight, ignore, oppose, refuse to obey, reject, repudiate, resist, spurn, violate

component 1. *n.* constituent, element, ingredient, item, part, piece, unit 2. *adj.* composing, constituent, inherent, intrinsic

comport 1. accord, agree, coincide, correspond, fit, harmonize, square, suit, tally 2. acquit, act, bear, behave, carry, conduct, demean

compose 1. build, compound, comprise, constitute, construct, fashion, form, make, make up, put together 2. contrive, create, devise, frame, imagine, indite, invent, produce, write 3. adjust, arrange, reconcile, regulate, resolve, settle 4. appease, assuage, calm, collect, control, pacify, placate, quell, quiet, soothe, still, tranquillize

Antonyms (*sense 1*) bulldoze, demolish, destroy, dismantle, obliterate, raze (*sense 4*) agitate, disturb, excite, perturb, trouble, unsettle, upset

composed at ease, calm, collected, confident, cool, imperturbable, laid-back (*Inf.*), level-headed, poised, relaxed, sedate, self-possessed, serene, together (*Sl.*), tranquil, unfazed (*Inf.*), unflappable, unruffled, unworried

Antonyms agitated, anxious, disturbed, excited, nervous, ruffled, twitchy (*Inf.*), uncontrolled, uneasy, unpoised, upset

composite 1. *adj.* blended, combined, complex, compound, conglomerate, mixed, synthesized 2. *n.* amalgam, blend, compound, conglomerate, fusion, meld, synthesis

composition 1. arrangement, configuration, constitution, design, form, formation, layout, make-up, organization, structure 2. compilation, creation, fashioning, formation, formulation, invention, making, mixture, production 3. creation, essay, exercise, literary work, opus, piece, study, treatise, work, writing 4. arrangement, balance, concord, consonance, harmony, placing, proportion, symmetry

compost humus, mulch, organic fertilizer

composure aplomb, calm, calmness, collectedness, cool (*Sl.*), coolness, dignity, ease, equanimity, imperturbability, placidity, poise, sang-froid, sedateness, self-assurance, self-possession, serenity, tranquillity
Antonyms agitation, discomposure, excitability, impatience, nervousness, perturbation, uneasiness

compound *v.* 1. amalgamate, blend, coalesce, combine, concoct, fuse, intermingle, meld, mingle, mix, synthesize, unite 2. add to, aggravate, augment, complicate, exacerbate, heighten, intensify, magnify, worsen 3. *Used of a dispute, difference, etc.* adjust, arrange, compose, settle ~*n.* 4. alloy, amalgam, blend, combination, composite, composition, conglomerate, fusion, medley, meld, mixture, synthesis ~*adj.* 5. complex, composite, conglomerate, intricate, multiple, not simple
Antonyms *v.* decrease, divide, lessen, minimize, moderate, modify, part, segregate ~*n.* element ~*adj.* pure, simple, single, unmixed

comprehend 1. apprehend, assimilate, conceive, discern, fathom, grasp, know, make out, perceive, see, take in, understand 2. comprise, contain, embody, embrace, enclose, encompass, include, involve, take in
Antonyms (*sense 1*) get (it) wrong, get the wrong end of the stick, misapprehend, misconceive, misconstrue, misinterpret, miss the point of, mistake, misunderstand, pervert

comprehensible clear, coherent, conceivable, explicit, graspable, intelligible, plain, understandable, user-friendly

comprehension 1. conception, discernment, grasp, intelligence, judgment, knowledge, perception, realization, sense, understanding 2. compass, domain, field, limits, province, range, reach, scope
Antonyms (*sense 1*) incomprehension, misapprehension, misunderstanding, unawareness

comprehensive all-embracing, all-inclusive, blanket, broad, catholic, complete, encyclopedic, exhaustive, extensive, full, inclusive, sweeping, thorough, umbrella, wide
Antonyms incomplete, limited, narrow, restricted, specialized, specific

compress abbreviate, compact, concentrate, condense, constrict, contract, cram, crowd, crush, knit, press, pucker, shorten, squash, squeeze, summarize, wedge

compressed abridged, compact, compacted, concentrated, concise, consolidated, constricted, flattened, reduced, shortened, squashed, squeezed

compression condensation, consolidation, constriction, crushing, pressure, squeezing, wedging

comprise 1. be composed of, comprehend, consist of, contain, embrace, encompass, include, take in 2. compose, constitute, form, make up

compromise *v.* 1. adjust, agree, arbitrate, compose, compound, concede, give and take, go fifty-fifty (*Inf.*), meet halfway, settle, strike a balance ~*n.* 2. accommodation, accord, adjustment, agreement, concession, give-and-take, half measures, middle ground, settlement, trade-off ~*v.* 3. discredit, dishonour, embarrass, endanger, expose, hazard, imperil, implicate, jeopardize, prejudice, weaken
Antonyms *v.* argue, assure, boost, contest, differ, disagree, enhance, support ~*n.* contention, controversy, difference, disagreement, dispute, quarrel

compulsion 1. coercion, constraint, demand, duress, force, obligation, pressure, urgency 2. drive, necessity, need, obsession, preoccupation, urge

compulsive besetting, compelling, driving, irresistible, obsessive, overwhelming, uncontrollable, urgent

compulsory binding, *de rigueur,* forced, imperative, mandatory, obligatory, required, requisite
Antonyms discretionary, non-obligatory, non-requisite, optional, unimperative, unnecessary, voluntary

compunction contrition, misgiving, penitence, qualm, regret, reluctance, remorse, repentance, sorrow, stab *or* sting of conscience

compute add up, calculate, cast up, cipher, count, enumerate, estimate, figure, figure out, measure, rate, reckon, sum, tally, total

comrade ally, associate, buddy (*Inf.*), cock (*Brit. inf.*), colleague, companion, compatriot, compeer, confederate, co-worker, crony, fellow, friend, mate (*Inf.*), pal (*Inf.*), partner

con 1. *v.* bamboozle (*Inf.*), bilk, cheat, cozen, deceive, defraud, diddle (*Inf.*), double-cross (*Inf.*), dupe, gull (*Archaic*), hoax, hoodwink, humbug, inveigle, kid (*Inf.*), mislead, rip off (*Sl.*), rook (*Sl.*), skin (*Sl.*), stiff (*Sl.*), sting (*Inf.*), swindle, trick 2. *n.* bluff, canard, deception, fraud, scam (*Sl.*), sting (*Inf.*), swindle, trick

concatenation chain, connection, interlocking, linking, nexus, sequence, series, succession

concave cupped, depressed, excavated, hollow, hollowed, incurved, indented, scooped, sunken
Antonyms bulging, convex, curving, protuberant, rounded

conceal bury, camouflage, cover, disguise, dissemble, hide, keep dark, keep secret, mask, obscure, screen, secrete, shelter, stash (*Inf.*)
Antonyms disclose, display, divulge, expose, lay bare, reveal, show, uncover, unmask, unveil

concealed covered, hidden, inconspicuous, masked, obscured, screened, secret, secreted, tucked away, unseen

concealment camouflage, cover, disguise, hideaway, hide-out, hiding, secrecy
Antonyms disclosure, display, exposure, give-away, leak, revelation, showing, uncovering

concede 1. accept, acknowledge, admit, allow, confess, grant, own 2. cede, give up, hand over, relinquish, surrender, yield
Antonyms (*sense 1*) contest, deny, disclaim, dispute, protest, refute, reject (*sense 2*) beat, conquer, defeat, fight to the bitter end, make a stand

conceit 1. amour-propre, arrogance, complacency, egotism, narcissism, pride, self-importance, self-love, swagger, vainglory, vanity 2. *Archaic* belief, fancy, fantasy, idea, image, imagination, judgment, notion, opinion, quip, thought, vagary, whim, whimsy

conceited arrogant, bigheaded (*Inf.*), cocky, egotistical, immodest, narcissistic, overweening, puffed up, self-important, stuck up (*Inf.*), swollen-headed, vain, vainglorious
Antonyms humble, modest, self-effacing, unassuming

conceivable believable, credible, imaginable, possible, thinkable
Antonyms inconceivable, incredible, unbelievable, unimaginable, unthinkable

conceive 1. appreciate, apprehend, believe, comprehend, envisage, fancy, grasp, imagine, realize, suppose, understand 2. contrive, create, design, develop, devise, form, formulate, produce, project, purpose, think up 3. become impregnated, become pregnant

concentrate 1. be engrossed in, consider closely, focus attention on, give all one's attention to, put one's mind to, rack one's brains 2. bring to bear, centre, cluster, converge, focus 3. accumulate, cluster, collect, congregate, gather, huddle
Antonyms (*sense 1*) disregard, let one's mind wander, lose concentration, pay no attention to, pay no heed to (*senses 2 & 3*) deploy, diffuse, disperse, dissipate, scatter, spread out

concentrated 1. all-out (*Inf.*), deep, hard, intense, intensive 2. boiled down, condensed, evaporated, reduced, rich, thickened, undiluted

concentration 1. absorption, application, heed, single-mindedness 2. bringing to bear, centralization, centring, combination, compression, consolidation, convergence, focusing, intensification 3. accumulation, aggregation, cluster, collection, convergence, horde, mass
Antonyms (*sense 1*) absent-mindedness, disregard, distraction, inattention (*senses 2 & 3*) diffusion, dispersion, scattering, spreading-out

concept abstraction, conception, conceptualization, hypothesis, idea, image, impression, notion, theory, view

conception 1. concept, design, idea, image, notion, plan 2. beginning, birth, formation, inception, initiation, invention, launching, origin, outset 3. appreciation, clue, comprehension, impression, inkling, perception, picture, understanding 4. fertilization, germination, impregnation, insemination

concern *v.* 1. affect, apply to, bear on, be relevant to, interest, involve, pertain to, regard, touch ~*n.* 2. affair, business, charge, deportment, field, interest, involvement, job, matter, mission, occupation, responsibility, task, transaction 3. bearing, importance, interest, reference, relation, relevance ~*v.* 4. bother, disquiet, distress, disturb, make anxious, make uneasy, perturb, trouble, worry ~*n.* 5. anxiety, apprehension, attention, burden, care, consideration, disquiet, disquietude, distress, heed, responsibility, solicitude, worry 6. business, company, corporation, enterprise, establishment, firm, house, organization

concerned 1. active, implicated, interested, involved, mixed up, privy to 2. anxious, bothered, distressed, disturbed, exercised,

troubled, uneasy, upset, worried 3. attentive, caring, interested, solicitous
Antonyms aloof, carefree, detached, indifferent, neglectful, unconcerned, uninterested, untroubled, without a care

concerning about, anent (*Scot.*), apropos of, as regards, as to, in the matter of, on the subject of, re, regarding, relating to, respecting, touching, with reference to

concert *n.* 1. accord, agreement, concord, concordance, harmony, unanimity, union, unison 2. **in concert** concertedly, in collaboration, in league, in unison, jointly, shoulder to shoulder, together, unanimously

concerted agreed upon, collaborative, combined, coordinated, joint, planned, prearranged, united
Antonyms disunited, separate, uncontrived, uncooperative, unplanned

concession 1. acknowledgment, admission, assent, confession, surrender, yielding 2. adjustment, allowance, boon, compromise, grant, indulgence, permit, privilege, sop

conciliate appease, disarm, mediate, mollify, pacify, placate, propitiate, reconcile, restore harmony, soothe, win over

conciliation appeasement, disarming, mollification, pacification, placation, propitiation, reconciliation, soothing

conciliatory appeasing, disarming, irenic, mollifying, pacific, peaceable, placatory, propitiative

concise brief, compact, compendious, compressed, condensed, epigrammatic, laconic, pithy, short, succinct, summary, synoptic, terse, to the point
Antonyms diffuse, discursive, garrulous, lengthy, long-winded, prolix, rambling, verbose, wordy

conclave assembly, cabinet, conference, congress, council, parley, secret *or* private meeting, session

conclude 1. bring down the curtain, cease, close, come to an end, complete, draw to a close, end, finish, round off, terminate, wind up 2. assume, decide, deduce, gather, infer, judge, reckon (*Inf.*), sum up, suppose, surmise 3. accomplish, bring about, carry out, clinch, decide, determine, effect, establish, fix, pull off, resolve, settle, work out
Antonyms (*sense 1*) begin, commence, extend, initiate, open, protract, start

conclusion 1. close, completion, end, finale, finish, result, termination 2. consequence, culmination, issue, outcome, result, sequel, upshot 3. agreement, conviction, decision, deduction, inference, judgment, opinion, resolution, settlement, verdict 4. **in conclusion** finally, in closing, lastly, to sum up

conclusive clinching, convincing, decisive, definite, definitive, final, irrefutable, ultimate, unanswerable, unarguable
Antonyms contestable, disputable, doubtful, dubious, impeachable, inconclusive, indecisive, indefinite, questionable, refutable, unconvincing, vague

concoct brew, contrive, cook up (*Inf.*), design, devise, fabricate, formulate, hatch, invent, make up, manufacture, mature, plot, prepare, project, think up, trump up

concoction blend, brew, combination, compound, contrivance, creation, mixture, preparation

concomitant accompanying, associative, attendant, coexistent, coincidental, collateral, complementary, concurrent, contemporaneous, contributing, coterminous, synchronous

concord 1. accord, agreement, amity, concert, consensus, consonance, friendship, good understanding, good will, harmony, peace, rapport, unanimity, unison 2. agreement, compact, concordat, convention, entente, protocol, treaty

concourse 1. assemblage, assembly, collection, confluence, convergence, crowd, crush, gathering, meeting, multitude, rout (*Archaic*), throng 2. entrance, foyer, gathering *or* meeting place, hall, lounge, rallying point

concrete *adj.* 1. actual, definite, explicit, factual, material, real, sensible, specific, substantial, tangible 2. calcified, compact, compressed, conglomerated, consolidated, firm, petrified, solid, solidified ~*n.* 3. cement (*Not in technical usage*), concretion
Antonyms (*sense 1*) abstract, immaterial, indefinite, insubstantial, intangible, notional, theoretical, unspecified, vague

concubine courtesan, kept woman, leman (*Archaic*), mistress, odalisque, paramour

concupiscence appetite, desire, horniness (*Sl.*), lasciviousness, lechery, libidinousness, libido, lickerishness (*Archaic*), lust, lustfulness, randiness (*Inf., chiefly Brit.*)

concupiscent horny (*Sl.*), lascivious, lecherous, lewd, libidinous, lickerish (*Archaic*), lustful, randy (*Inf., chiefly Brit.*)

concur accede, accord, acquiesce, agree, approve, assent, coincide, combine, consent, cooperate, harmonize, join

concurrent 1. coexisting, coincident, concerted, concomitant, contemporaneous, simultaneous, synchronous 2. confluent, convergent, converging, uniting 3. agreeing, at one, compatible, consentient, consistent, cooperating, harmonious, in agreement, in rapport, like-minded, of the same mind

concussion clash, collision, crash, impact, jarring, jolt, jolting, shaking, shock

condemn 1. blame, censure, damn, denounce, disapprove, excoriate, reprehend, reproach, reprobate, reprove, upbraid 2. convict, damn, doom, pass sentence on, proscribe, sentence

Antonyms (*sense 1*) acclaim, applaud, approve, commend, compliment, condone, praise (*sense 2*) acquit, free, liberate

condemnation 1. blame, censure, denouncement, denunciation, disapproval, reproach, reprobation, reproof, stricture 2. conviction, damnation, doom, judgment, proscription, sentence

condemnatory accusatory, accusing, censorious, critical, damnatory, denunciatory, disapproving, proscriptive, reprobative, scathing

condensation 1. abridgment, contraction, digest, précis, synopsis 2. condensate, deliquescence, distillation, liquefaction, precipitate, precipitation 3. compression, concentration, consolidation, crystallization, curtailment, reduction

condense 1. abbreviate, abridge, compact, compress, concentrate, contract, curtail, encapsulate, epitomize, précis, shorten, summarize 2. boil down, coagulate, concentrate, decoct, precipitate (*Chem.*), reduce, solidify, thicken

Antonyms (*sense 1*) elaborate, enlarge, expand, expatiate, increase, lengthen, pad out, spin out (*sense 2*) dilute, make thinner, thin (out), water down, weaken

condensed 1. abridged, compressed, concentrated, curtailed, shortened, shrunken, slimmed down, summarized 2. boiled down, clotted, coagulated, concentrated, precipitated (*Chem.*), reduced, thickened

condescend 1. be courteous, bend, come down off one's high horse (*Inf.*), deign, humble *or* demean oneself, lower oneself, see fit, stoop, submit, unbend (*Inf.*), vouchsafe 2. patronize, talk down to

condescending disdainful, lofty, lordly, patronizing, snobbish, snooty (*Inf.*), supercilious, superior, toffee-nosed (*Sl., chiefly Brit.*)

condescension 1. airs, disdain, haughtiness, loftiness, lordliness, patronizing attitude, superciliousness, superiority 2. affability, civility, courtesy, deference, favour, graciousness, humiliation, obeisance

condign *Used esp. of a punishment* adequate, appropriate, deserved, fitting, just, meet (*Archaic*), merited, richly-deserved, suitable

condition *n.* 1. case, circumstances, plight, position, predicament, shape, situation, state, state of affairs, *status quo* 2. arrangement, article, demand, limitation, modification, prerequisite, provision, proviso, qualification, requirement, requisite, restriction, rider, rule, stipulation, terms 3. fettle, fitness, health, kilter, order, shape, state of health, trim 4. ailment, complaint, infirmity, malady, problem, weakness 5. caste, class, estate, grade, order, position, rank, status, stratum *~v.* 6. accustom, adapt, educate, equip, habituate, inure, make ready, prepare, ready, tone up, train, work out

conditional contingent, dependent, limited, provisional, qualified, subject to, with reservations

Antonyms absolute, categorical, unconditional, unrestricted

conditioned acclimatized, accustomed, adapted, adjusted, familiarized, habituated, inured, made ready, prepared, seasoned, trained, used

conditioning *n.* 1. grooming, preparation, readying, training 2. accustoming, familiarization, hardening, inurement, reorientation, seasoning *~adj.* 3. astringent, toning

conditions circumstances, environment, milieu, situation, surroundings, way of life

condole commiserate, compassionate (*Archaic*), console, feel for, sympathize

condolence commiseration, compassion, consolation, fellow feeling, pity, sympathy

condom flunky (*Sl.*), Frenchie (*Sl.*), French letter (*Sl.*), French tickler (*Sl.*), rubber (*U.S. sl.*), rubber johnny (*Brit. sl.*), scumbag (*U.S. sl.*), sheath

condone disregard, excuse, forgive, let pass, look the other way, make allowance for, overlook, pardon, turn a blind eye to, wink at

Antonyms censure, condemn, denounce, disapprove, punish

conduce advance, aid, avail, contribute, lead, promote, tend

conducive calculated to produce, contributive, contributory, favourable, helpful, leading, productive of, promotive, tending

conduct *n.* 1. administration, control, direction, guidance, leadership, management, organization, running, supervision *~v.* 2. administer, carry on, control, direct, govern, handle, lead, manage, organize, preside over, regulate, run, supervise 3. accompany, attend, chair, convey, escort, guide, pilot, preside over, steer, usher *~n.* 4. attitude, bearing, behaviour, carriage, comportment, demeanour, deportment, manners, mien

(*Literary*), ways ~*v.* 5. acquit, act, behave, carry, comport, deport

conduit canal, channel, duct, main, passage, pipe, tube

confab, confabulation *n.* chat, chinwag (*Brit. inf.*), conversation, discussion, gossip, natter, powwow, session, talk

confabulate *v.* chat, converse, discuss, gossip, natter, talk

confederacy alliance, bund, coalition, compact, confederation, conspiracy, covenant, federation, league, union

confederate 1. *adj.* allied, associated, combined, federal, federated, in alliance 2. *n.* abettor, accessory, accomplice, ally, associate, colleague, partner 3. *v.* ally, amalgamate, associate, band together, combine, federate, merge, unite

confer 1. accord, award, bestow, give, grant, hand out, present, vouchsafe 2. consult, converse, deliberate, discourse, parley, talk

conference colloquium, congress, consultation, convention, convocation, discussion, forum, meeting, seminar, symposium, teach-in

confess 1. acknowledge, admit, allow, blurt out, come clean (*Inf.*), concede, confide, disclose, divulge, grant, make a clean breast of, own, own up, recognize, sing (*Sl., chiefly U.S.*), spill one's guts (*Sl.*) 2. affirm, assert, attest, aver, confirm, declare, evince, manifest, profess, prove, reveal

Antonyms button one's lips, conceal, cover, deny, hide, hush up, keep mum, keep secret, keep under wraps, repudiate, suppress, withhold

confession acknowledgment, admission, avowal, disclosure, divulgence, exposure, revelation, unbosoming

confidant, confidante alter ego, bosom friend, close friend, crony, familiar, intimate

confide 1. admit, breathe, confess, disclose, divulge, impart, reveal, whisper 2. commend, commit, consign, entrust

confidence 1. belief, credence, dependence, faith, reliance, trust 2. aplomb, assurance, boldness, courage, firmness, nerve, self-possession, self-reliance 3. **in confidence** between you and me (and the gatepost), confidentially, in secrecy, privately

Antonyms (*sense 1*) disbelief, distrust, doubt, misgiving, mistrust (*sense 2*) apprehension, fear, self-doubt, shyness, uncertainty

confident 1. certain, convinced, counting on, positive, satisfied, secure, sure 2. assured, bold, dauntless, fearless, self-assured, self-reliant

Antonyms (*sense 1*) doubtful, dubious, not sure, tentative, uncertain, unconvinced, unsure (*sense 2*) afraid, hesitant, insecure, jittery, lacking confidence, mousy, nervous, scared, self-doubting, unsure

confidential 1. classified, hush-hush (*Inf.*), intimate, off the record, private, privy, secret 2. faithful, familiar, trusted, trustworthy, trusty

confidentially behind closed doors, between ourselves, in camera, in confidence, in secret, personally, privately, sub rosa

configuration arrangement, cast, conformation, contour, figure, form, outline, shape

confine 1. *v.* bind, bound, cage, circumscribe, enclose, hem in, hold back, immure, imprison, incarcerate, intern, keep, limit, repress, restrain, restrict, shut up, straiten 2. *n.* border, boundary, frontier, limit, precinct

confined 1. enclosed, limited, restricted 2. in childbed, in childbirth, lying-in

confinement 1. custody, detention, imprisonment, incarceration, internment, porridge (*Sl.*) 2. *accouchement,* childbed, childbirth, labour, lying-in, parturition, time, travail

confines boundaries, bounds, circumference, edge, limits, pale, precincts

confirm 1. assure, buttress, clinch, establish, fix, fortify, reinforce, settle, strengthen 2. approve, authenticate, bear out, corroborate, endorse, ratify, sanction, substantiate, validate, verify

confirmation 1. authentication, corroboration, evidence, proof, substantiation, testimony, validation, verification 2. acceptance, agreement, approval, assent, endorsement, ratification, sanction

Antonyms (*sense 1*) contradiction, denial, disavowal, repudiation (*sense 2*) annulment, cancellation, disapproval, refusal, rejection

confirmed chronic, dyed-in-the-wool, habitual, hardened, ingrained, inured, inveterate, long-established, rooted, seasoned

confiscate appropriate, commandeer, expropriate, impound, seize, sequester, sequestrate

Antonyms free, give, give back, hand back, release, return, restore

confiscation appropriation, expropriation, forfeiture, impounding, seizure, sequestration, takeover

conflagration blaze, fire, holocaust, inferno, wildfire

conflict *n.* 1. battle, clash, collision, com-

bat, contention, contest, encounter, engagement, fight, fracas, head-to-head, set-to (*Inf.*), strife, war, warfare 2. antagonism, bad blood, difference, disagreement, discord, dissension, divided loyalties, friction, hostility, interference, opposition, strife, variance ~*v.* 3. be at variance, clash, collide, combat, contend, contest, differ, disagree, fight, interfere, strive, struggle
Antonyms *n.* accord, agreement, harmony, peace, treaty, truce ~*v.* agree, coincide, harmonize, reconcile

conflicting antagonistic, clashing, contradictory, contrary, discordant, inconsistent, opposed, opposing, paradoxical
Antonyms accordant, agreeing, compatible, congruous, consistent, harmonious, similar, unopposing

confluence 1. concurrence, conflux, convergence, junction 2. assemblage, assembly, concourse, concurrence, crowd, host, meeting, multitude, union

conform 1. adapt, adjust, comply, fall in with, follow, follow the crowd, obey, run with the pack, yield 2. accord, agree, assimilate, correspond, harmonize, match, square, suit, tally

conformation anatomy, arrangement, build, configuration, form, framework, outline, shape, structure

conformist *n.* Babbitt (*U.S.*), conventionalist, stick-in-the-mud (*Inf.*), traditionalist, yes man

conformity 1. allegiance, Babbittry (*U.S.*), compliance, conventionality, observance, orthodoxy 2. affinity, agreement, conformance, congruity, consonance, correspondence, harmony, likeness, resemblance, similarity

confound 1. amaze, astonish, astound, baffle, bewilder, confuse, dumbfound, flabbergast (*Inf.*), flummox, mix up, mystify, nonplus, perplex, startle, surprise 2. annihilate, contradict, demolish, destroy, explode, overthrow. overwhelm, refute, ruin

confront accost, beard, brave, bring face to face with, challenge, defy, encounter, face, face off (*Sl.*), face up to, oppose, stand up to, tackle
Antonyms avoid, body-swerve (*Scot.*), circumvent, dodge, evade, flee, give a wide berth to, keep clear of, sidestep, steer clear of

confrontation conflict, contest, crisis, encounter, face-off (*Sl.*), head-to-head, set-to (*Inf.*), showdown (*Inf.*)

confuse 1. baffle, bemuse, bewilder, darken, faze, flummox, mystify, nonplus, obscure, perplex, puzzle 2. blend, confound, disarrange, disorder, intermingle, involve, jumble, mingle, mistake, mix up, muddle, ravel, snarl up (*Inf.*), tangle 3. abash, addle, demoralize, discomfit, discompose, disconcert, discountenance, disorient, embarrass, fluster, mortify, nonplus, rattle (*Inf.*), shame, throw off balance, unnerve, upset

confused 1. at a loss, at sea, at sixes and sevens, baffled, bewildered, dazed, discombobulated (*Inf., chiefly U.S. & Canad.*), disorganized, disorientated, flummoxed, muddled, muzzy (*U.S. inf.*), nonplussed, not with it (*Inf.*), perplexed, puzzled, taken aback, thrown off balance, upset 2. at sixes and sevens, chaotic, disarranged, disarrayed, disordered, disorderly, disorganized, higgledy-piggledy (*Inf.*), hugger-mugger (*Archaic*), in disarray, jumbled, mistaken, misunderstood, mixed up, out of order, topsy-turvy, untidy
Antonyms arranged, aware, enlightened, informed, in order, on the ball (*Inf.*), ordered, orderly, organized, tidy, with it (*Inf.*)

confusing ambiguous, baffling, complicated, contradictory, disconcerting, inconsistent, misleading, muddling, perplexing, puzzling, unclear
Antonyms clear, definite, explicit, plain, simple, straightforward, uncomplicated, understandable

confusion 1. befuddlement, bemusement, bewilderment, disorientation, mystification, perplexity, puzzlement 2. bustle, chaos, clutter, commotion, disarrangement, disarray, disorder, disorganization, hodgepodge (*U.S.*), hotchpotch, jumble, mess, muddle, pig's breakfast (*Inf.*), shambles, state, tangle, turmoil, untidiness, upheaval 3. abashment, chagrin, demoralization, discomfiture, distraction, embarrassment, fluster, perturbation
Antonyms (*sense 1*) clarification, composure, enlightenment, explanation, solution (*sense 2*) arrangement, neatness, order, organization, tidiness

confute controvert, disprove, invalidate, oppugn, overthrow, prove false, rebut, refute, set aside

congeal benumb, clot, coagulate, condense, curdle, freeze, gelatinize, harden, jell, set, solidify, stiffen, thicken

congenial adapted, affable, agreeable, companionable, compatible, complaisant, favourable, fit, friendly, genial, kindly, kindred, like-minded, pleasant, pleasing, suitable, sympathetic, well-suited

congenital 1. constitutional, inborn, inbred, inherent, innate, natural 2. *Inf.* complete, deep-dyed (*Usu. derogatory*), inveterate, thorough, utter

congested blocked-up, clogged, crammed,

crowded, jammed, overcrowded, overfilled, overflowing, packed, stuffed, stuffed-up, teeming
Antonyms clear, empty, free, half-full, uncongested, uncrowded, unhampered, unhindered, unimpeded, unobstructed

congestion bottleneck, clogging, crowding, jam, mass, overcrowding, snarl-up (*Inf., chiefly Brit.*), surfeit

conglomerate 1. *adj.* amassed, clustered, composite, heterogeneous, massed 2. *v.* accumulate, agglomerate, aggregate, cluster, coalesce, snowball 3. *n.* agglomerate, aggregate, multinational

conglomeration accumulation, aggregation, assortment, combination, composite, hotchpotch, mass, medley, miscellany, mishmash, potpourri

congratulate compliment, felicitate, wish joy to

congratulations best wishes, compliments, felicitations, good wishes, greetings

congregate assemble, collect, come together, concentrate, convene, converge, convoke, flock, forgather, gather, mass, meet, muster, rally, rendezvous, throng
Antonyms break up, dispel, disperse, dissipate, part, scatter, separate, split up

congregation assembly, brethren, crowd, fellowship, flock, host, laity, multitude, parish, parishioners, throng

congress assembly, chamber of deputies, conclave, conference, convention, convocation, council, delegates, diet, house, legislative assembly, legislature, meeting, parliament, representatives

congruence accord, agreement, coincidence, compatibility, concurrence, conformity, congruity, consistency, correspondence, harmony, identity

congruous appropriate, apt, becoming, compatible, concordant, congruent, consistent, consonant, correspondent, corresponding, fit, meet, seemly, suitable

conic, conical cone-shaped, conoid, funnel-shaped, pointed, pyramidal, tapered, tapering

conjectural academic, hypothetical, speculative, supposed, suppositional, surmised, tentative, theoretical

conjecture 1. *v.* assume, fancy, guess, hypothesize, imagine, infer, suppose, surmise, suspect, theorize 2. *n.* assumption, conclusion, fancy, guess, guesstimate (*Inf.*), guesswork, hypothesis, inference, notion, presumption, shot in the dark, speculation, supposition, surmise, theorizing, theory

conjugal bridal, connubial, hymeneal, marital, married, matrimonial, nuptial, spousal, wedded

conjunction association, coincidence, combination, concurrence, juxtaposition, union

conjuncture combination, concurrence, connection, crisis, crossroads, crucial point, emergency, exigency, juncture, pass, predicament, stage, turning point

conjure 1. juggle, play tricks 2. bewitch, call upon, cast a spell, charm, enchant, fascinate, invoke, raise, rouse, summon up 3. adjure, appeal to, beg, beseech, crave, entreat, implore, importune, pray, supplicate

conjurer, conjuror magician, miracle-worker, sorcerer, thaumaturge (*Rare*), wizard

conjure up bring to mind, contrive, create, evoke, produce as by magic, recall, recollect

connect affix, ally, associate, cohere, combine, couple, fasten, join, link, relate, unite
Antonyms detach, disconnect, dissociate, divide, part, separate, sever, unfasten

connected 1. affiliated, akin, allied, associated, banded together, bracketed, combined, coupled, joined, linked, related, united 2. *Of speech* coherent, comprehensible, consecutive, intelligible

connection 1. alliance, association, attachment, coupling, fastening, junction, link, tie, union 2. affiliation, affinity, association, bond, commerce, communication, correlation, correspondence, intercourse, interrelation, liaison, link, marriage, relation, relationship, relevance, tie-in 3. context, frame of reference, reference 4. acquaintance, ally, associate, contact, friend, sponsor 5. kin, kindred, kinsman, kith, relation, relative

connivance abetment, abetting, collusion, complicity, conspiring, tacit consent

connive 1. cabal, collude, conspire, cook up (*Inf.*), intrigue, plot, scheme 2. *With* at abet, aid, be an accessory to, be a party to, be in collusion with, blink at, disregard, lend oneself to, let pass, look the other way, overlook, pass by, shut one's eyes to, turn a blind eye to, wink at

connoisseur aficionado, appreciator, arbiter, authority, buff (*Inf.*), cognoscente, devotee, expert, judge, maven (*U.S.*), savant, specialist, whiz (*Inf.*)

connotation association, colouring, implication, nuance, significance, suggestion, undertone

connote betoken, hint at, imply, indicate, intimate, involve, signify, suggest

connubial conjugal, marital, married, matrimonial, nuptial, wedded

conquer 1. beat, blow out of the water (*Sl.*), checkmate, clobber (*Sl.*), crush, defeat, discomfit, get the better of, humble, lick (*Inf.*), master, overcome, overpower, overthrow, prevail, quell, rout, run rings around (*Inf.*), subdue, subjugate, succeed, surmount, tank (*Sl.*), triumph, undo, vanquish, wipe the floor with (*Inf.*) 2. acquire, annex, obtain, occupy, overrun, seize, win
Antonyms (*sense 1*) be defeated, capitulate, give in, give up, lose, quit, submit, surrender, throw in the towel, yield

conqueror champion, conquistador, defeater, hero, lord, master, subjugator, vanquisher, victor, winner

conquest 1. defeat, discomfiture, mastery, overthrow, pasting (*Sl.*), rout, triumph, vanquishment, victory 2. acquisition, annexation, appropriation, coup, invasion, occupation, subjection, subjugation, takeover 3. captivation, enchantment, enthralment, enticement, seduction 4. acquisition, adherent, admirer, catch, fan, feather in one's cap, follower, prize, supporter, worshipper

consanguinity affinity, blood-relationship, family tie, kin, kindred, kinship

conscience 1. moral sense, principles, scruples, sense of right and wrong, still small voice 2. **in all conscience** assuredly, certainly, fairly, honestly, in truth, rightly, truly

conscience-stricken ashamed, compunctious, contrite, disturbed, guilty, penitent, remorseful, repentant, sorry, troubled

conscientious 1. careful, diligent, exact, faithful, meticulous, painstaking, particular, punctilious, thorough 2. high-minded, high-principled, honest, honourable, incorruptible, just, moral, responsible, scrupulous, straightforward, strict, upright
Antonyms careless, irresponsible, negligent, remiss, slack, thoughtless, unconscientious, unprincipled, unreliable, unscrupulous, untrustworthy

conscious 1. alert, alive to, awake, aware, clued-up (*Inf.*), cognizant, percipient, responsive, sensible, sentient, wise to (*Sl.*) 2. calculated, deliberate, intentional, knowing, premeditated, rational, reasoning, reflective, responsible, self-conscious, studied, wilful
Antonyms (*sense 1*) ignorant, insensible, oblivious, unaware, unconscious (*sense 2*) accidental, uncalculated, unintended, unintentional, unplanned, unpremeditated, unwitting

consciousness apprehension, awareness, knowledge, realization, recognition, sensibility

consecrate dedicate, devote, exalt, hallow, ordain, sanctify, set apart, venerate

consecutive chronological, following, in sequence, in turn, running, sequential, seriatim, succeeding, successive, uninterrupted

consensus agreement, assent, common consent, concord, concurrence, general agreement, harmony, unanimity, unity

consent 1. *v.* accede, acquiesce, agree, allow, approve, assent, comply, concede, concur, permit, yield 2. *n.* acquiescence, agreement, approval, assent, compliance, concession, concurrence, go-ahead (*Inf.*), O.K. *or* okay (*Inf.*), permission, sanction
Antonyms *v.* decline, demur, disagree, disapprove, dissent, refuse, resist ~*n.* disagreement, disapproval, dissent, refusal, unwillingness

consequence 1. effect, end, event, issue, outcome, repercussion, result, sequel, upshot 2. account, concern, import, importance, interest, moment, note, portent, significance, value, weight 3. bottom, distinction, eminence, notability, rank, repute, standing, status 4. **in consequence** as a result, because, following

consequent ensuing, following, resultant, resulting, sequential, subsequent, successive

consequential 1. eventful, far-reaching, grave, important, momentous, serious, significant, weighty 2. arrogant, bumptious, conceited, inflated, pompous, pretentious, self-important, supercilious, vainglorious 3. consequent, indirect, resultant

consequently accordingly, ergo, hence, necessarily, subsequently, therefore, thus

conservation custody, economy, guardianship, husbandry, maintenance, preservation, protection, safeguarding, safekeeping, saving, upkeep

conservative 1. *adj.* cautious, conventional, die-hard, guarded, hidebound, middle-of-the-road, moderate, quiet, reactionary, right-wing, sober, tory, traditional 2. *n.* middle-of-the-roader, moderate, reactionary, right-winger, stick-in-the-mud (*Inf.*), tory, traditionalist
Antonyms *adj.* imaginative, innovative, liberal, progressive, radical ~*n.* changer, innovator, progressive, radical

conservatory glasshouse, greenhouse, hothouse

conserve go easy on, hoard, husband, keep, nurse, preserve, protect, save, store up, take care of, use sparingly
Antonyms be extravagant, blow (*Sl.*), dissipate, fritter away, misspend, misuse,

spend, spend like water, squander, use up, waste

consider 1. chew over, cogitate, consult, contemplate, deliberate, discuss, examine, eye up, meditate, mull over, muse, ponder, reflect, revolve, ruminate, study, think about, turn over in one's mind, weigh, work over 2. believe, deem, hold to be, judge, rate, regard as, think 3. bear in mind, care for, keep in view, make allowance for, reckon with, regard, remember, respect, take into account

considerable 1. abundant, ample, appreciable, comfortable, goodly, great, large, lavish, marked, much, noticeable, plentiful, reasonable, sizable, substantial, tidy, tolerable 2. distinguished, important, influential, noteworthy, renowned, significant, venerable
Antonyms insignificant, insubstantial, meagre, ordinary, paltry, small, unimportant, unremarkable

considerably appreciably, greatly, markedly, noticeably, remarkably, significantly, substantially, very much

considerate attentive, charitable, circumspect, concerned, discreet, forbearing, kind, kindly, mindful, obliging, patient, tactful, thoughtful, unselfish
Antonyms heedless, inconsiderate, selfish, thoughtless

consideration 1. analysis, attention, cogitation, contemplation, deliberation, discussion, examination, perusal, reflection, regard, review, scrutiny, study, thought 2. concern, factor, issue, point 3. concern, considerateness, friendliness, kindliness, kindness, respect, solicitude, tact, thoughtfulness 4. fee, payment, perquisite, recompense, remuneration, reward, tip 5. **take into consideration** bear in mind, make allowance for, take into account, weigh

considering all in all, all things considered, insomuch as, in the light of, in view of

consign commend to, commit, convey, deliver, deposit with, entrust, hand over, relegate, ship (*cargo*), transfer, transmit

consignment 1. *Act of consigning* assignment, committal, dispatch, distribution, entrusting, handing over, relegation, sending, shipment, transmittal 2. *Something consigned* batch, delivery, goods, shipment

consist 1. *With* **of** amount to, be composed of, be made up of, comprise, contain, embody, include, incorporate, involve 2. *With* **in** be expressed by, be found *or* contained in, inhere, lie, reside

consistency 1. compactness, density, firmness, thickness, viscosity 2. accordance, agreement, coherence, compatibility, congruity, correspondence, harmony 3. constancy, evenness, regularity, steadfastness, steadiness, uniformity

consistent 1. constant, dependable, persistent, regular, steady, true to type, unchanging, undeviating 2. accordant, agreeing, all of a piece, coherent, compatible, congruous, consonant, harmonious, logical
Antonyms (*sense 1*) changing, deviating, erratic, inconsistent, irregular (*sense 2*) contradictory, contrary, discordant, incompatible, incongruous, inconsistent, inharmonious

consolation alleviation, assuagement, cheer, comfort, ease, easement, encouragement, help, relief, solace, succour, support

console assuage, calm, cheer, comfort, encourage, express sympathy for, relieve, solace, soothe
Antonyms aggravate (*Inf.*), agitate, annoy, discomfort, distress, hassle (*Inf.*), hurt, sadden, torment, trouble, upset

consolidate 1. amalgamate, cement, combine, compact, condense, conjoin, federate, fuse, harden, join, solidify, thicken, unite 2. fortify, reinforce, secure, stabilize, strengthen

consolidation alliance, amalgamation, association, compression, condensation, federation, fortification, fusion, reinforcement, strengthening

consonance accord, agreement, concord, conformity, congruence, congruity, consistency, correspondence, harmony, suitableness, unison

consonant accordant, according, compatible, concordant, congruous, consistent, correspondent, harmonious, in agreement, suitable

consort *n.* 1. associate, companion, fellow, husband, partner, significant other (*U.S. inf.*), spouse (*of a reigning monarch*), wife ~*v.* 2. associate, fraternize, go around with, hang about, around *or* out with, keep company, mingle, mix 3. accord, agree, correspond, harmonize, square, tally

conspectus abstract, compendium, digest, epitome, outline, précis, résumé, summary, survey, syllabus, synopsis

conspicuous 1. apparent, blatant, clear, discernible, easily seen, evident, manifest, noticeable, obvious, patent, perceptible, visible 2. celebrated, distinguished, eminent, famous, illustrious, notable, outstanding, prominent, remarkable, signal, striking 3. blatant, flagrant, flashy, garish, glaring, showy
Antonyms (*sense 1*) concealed, hidden, imperceptible, inconspicuous, indiscern~

ible, invisible, obscure, unnoticeable (*sense 2*) humble, inconspicuous, insignificant, ordinary, unacclaimed, undistinguished, unmemorable, unnotable

conspiracy cabal, collusion, confederacy, frame-up (*Sl.*), intrigue, league, machination, plot, scheme, treason

conspirator cabalist, conspirer, intriguer, plotter, schemer, traitor

conspire 1. cabal, confederate, contrive, devise, hatch treason, intrigue, machinate, manoeuvre, plot, scheme 2. combine, concur, conduce, contribute, cooperate, tend, work together

constancy decision, determination, devotion, fidelity, firmness, fixedness, permanence, perseverance, regularity, resolution, stability, steadfastness, steadiness, tenacity, uniformity

constant 1. continual, even, firm, fixed, habitual, immovable, immutable, invariable, permanent, perpetual, regular, stable, steadfast, steady, unalterable, unbroken, uniform, unvarying 2. ceaseless, continual, continuous, endless, eternal, everlasting, incessant, interminable, never-ending, nonstop, perpetual, persistent, relentless, sustained, uninterrupted, unrelenting, unremitting 3. determined, dogged, persevering, resolute, unflagging, unshaken, unwavering 4. attached, dependable, devoted, faithful, loyal, stalwart, staunch, tried-and-true, true, trustworthy, trusty, unfailing

Antonyms (*senses 1 & 2*) changeable, changing, deviating, erratic, inconstant, intermittent, irregular, occasional, random, uneven, unstable, unsustained, variable (*sense 4*) disloyal, fickle, irresolute, undependable

constantly all the time, always, aye (*Scot.*), continually, continuously, endlessly, everlastingly, incessantly, interminably, invariably, morning, noon and night, night and day, nonstop, perpetually, persistently, relentlessly

Antonyms (every) now and then, every so often, from time to time, intermittently, irregularly, now and again, occasionally, off and on, periodically, sometimes

consternation alarm, amazement, anxiety, awe, bewilderment, confusion, dismay, distress, dread, fear, fright, horror, panic, shock, terror, trepidation

constituent *adj.* 1. basic, component, elemental, essential, integral *~n.* 2. component, element, essential, factor, ingredient, part, principle, unit 3. elector, voter

constitute 1. compose, comprise, create, enact, establish, fix, form, found, make, make up, set up 2. appoint, authorize, commission, delegate, depute, empower, name, nominate, ordain

constitution 1. composition, establishment, formation, organization 2. build, character, composition, disposition, form, habit, health, make-up, nature, physique, structure, temper, temperament

constitutional *adj.* 1. congenital, inborn, inherent, intrinsic, organic 2. chartered, statutory, vested *~n.* 3. airing, stroll, turn, walk

constrain 1. bind, coerce, compel, drive, force, impel, necessitate, oblige, pressure, pressurize, urge 2. chain, check, confine, constrict, curb, hem in, rein, restrain, straiten

constrained embarrassed, forced, guarded, inhibited, reserved, reticent, subdued, unnatural

constraint 1. coercion, compulsion, force, necessity, pressure, restraint 2. bashfulness, diffidence, embarrassment, inhibition, repression, reservation, restraint, timidity 3. check, curb, damper, deterrent, hindrance, limitation, rein, restriction

constrict choke, compress, contract, cramp, inhibit, limit, narrow, pinch, restrict, shrink, squeeze, strangle, strangulate, tighten

constriction blockage, compression, constraint, cramp, impediment, limitation, narrowing, pressure, reduction, restriction, squeezing, stenosis (*Pathology*), stricture, tightness

construct assemble, build, compose, create, design, elevate, engineer, erect, establish, fabricate, fashion, form, formulate, found, frame, make, manufacture, organize, put up, raise, set up, shape

Antonyms bulldoze, demolish, destroy, devastate, dismantle, flatten, knock down, level, pull down, raze, tear down

construction 1. assembly, building, composition, creation, edifice, erection, fabric, fabrication, figure, form, formation, shape, structure 2. explanation, inference, interpretation, reading, rendering

constructive helpful, positive, practical, productive, useful, valuable

Antonyms destructive, futile, ineffective, limp-wristed, negative, unhelpful, unproductive, useless, vain, worthless

construe analyse, deduce, explain, expound, interpret, parse, read, render, take, translate

consult 1. ask, ask advice of, commune, compare notes, confer, consider, debate, deliberate, interrogate, question, refer to, take counsel, turn to 2. consider, have regard for, regard, respect, take account of, take into consideration

consultant adviser, authority, specialist

consultation appointment, conference, council, deliberation, dialogue, discussion, examination, hearing, interview, meeting, seminar, session

consume 1. absorb, deplete, dissipate, drain, eat up, employ, exhaust, expend, finish up, fritter away, lavish, lessen, spend, squander, use, use up, utilize, vanish, waste, wear out 2. devour, eat, eat up, gobble (up), guzzle, polish off (*Inf.*), put away, swallow 3. annihilate, decay, demolish, destroy, devastate, lay waste, ravage 4. *Often passive* absorb, devour, dominate, eat up, engross, monopolize, obsess, preoccupy

consumer buyer, customer, purchaser, shopper, user

consuming absorbing, compelling, devouring, engrossing, excruciating, gripping, immoderate, overwhelming, tormenting

consummate 1. *v.* accomplish, achieve, carry out, compass, complete, conclude, crown, effectuate, end, finish, perfect, perform 2. *adj.* absolute, accomplished, complete, conspicuous, deep-dyed (*Usu. derogatory*), finished, matchless, perfect, polished, practised, skilled, superb, supreme, total, transcendent, ultimate, unqualified, utter

Antonyms *v.* begin, commence, conceive, get under way, inaugurate, initiate, originate, start

consummation achievement, completion, culmination, end, fulfilment, perfection, realization

consumption 1. consuming, decay, decrease, depletion, destruction, diminution, dissipation, drain, exhaustion, expenditure, loss, use, using up, utilization, waste 2. *Medical* atrophy, emaciation, phthisis, T.B., tuberculosis

contact *n.* 1. association, communication, connection 2. approximation, contiguity, junction, juxtaposition, touch, union 3. acquaintance, connection ~*v.* 4. approach, call, communicate with, get *or* be in touch with, get hold of, phone, reach, ring (up) (*Inf., chiefly Brit.*), speak to, write to

contagion 1. contamination, corruption, infection, pestilence, plague, pollution, taint 2. communication, passage, spread, transference, transmittal

contagious catching, communicable, epidemic, epizootic (*Veterinary medicine*), infectious, pestiferous, pestilential, spreading, taking (*Inf.*), transmissible

contain 1. accommodate, enclose, have capacity for, hold, incorporate, seat 2. comprehend, comprise, embody, embrace, include, involve 3. control, curb, hold back, hold in, repress, restrain, stifle

container holder, receptacle, repository, vessel

contaminate adulterate, befoul, corrupt, defile, deprave, infect, pollute, radioactivate, smirch, soil, stain, sully, taint, tarnish, vitiate

Antonyms clean, cleanse, decontaminate, deodorize, disinfect, fumigate, purify, sanitize, sterilize

contamination adulteration, contagion, corruption, decay, defilement, dirtying, filth, foulness, impurity, infection, poisoning, pollution, radioactivation, rottenness, taint

contemn despise, disdain, disregard, hold cheap, neglect, scorn, slight, spurn, treat with contempt

contemplate 1. brood over, consider, deliberate, meditate, meditate on, mull over, muse over, observe, ponder, reflect upon, revolve *or* turn over in one's mind, ruminate (upon), study 2. behold, check out (*Inf.*), examine, eye, eye up, gaze at, inspect, recce (*Sl.*), regard, scrutinize, stare at, survey, view, weigh 3. aspire to, consider, design, envisage, expect, foresee, have in view *or* in mind, intend, mean, plan, propose, think of

contemplation 1. cogitation, consideration, deliberation, meditation, musing, pondering, reflection, reverie, rumination, thought 2. examination, gazing at, inspection, looking at, observation, recce (*Sl.*), scrutiny, survey, viewing

contemplative deep *or* lost in thought, in a brown study, intent, introspective, meditative, musing, pensive, rapt, reflective, ruminative, thoughtful

contemporary *adj.* 1. coetaneous (*Rare*), coeval, coexistent, coexisting, concurrent, contemporaneous, synchronous 2. à la mode, current, happening (*Inf.*), in fashion, latest, modern, newfangled, present, present-day, recent, trendy (*Brit. inf.*), ultramodern, up-to-date, up-to-the-minute, with it (*Inf.*) ~*n.* 3. compeer, fellow, peer

Antonyms *adj.* antecedent, antique, early, obsolete, old, old-fashioned, out-of-date, passé, succeeding

contempt 1. condescension, contumely, derision, despite (*Archaic*), disdain, disregard, disrespect, mockery, neglect, scorn, slight 2. *A state of contempt* disgrace, dishonour, humiliation, shame

Antonyms admiration, esteem, honour, liking, regard, respect

contemptible abject, base, cheap, degenerate, despicable, detestable, ignominious, low, low-down (*Inf.*), mean, measly, paltry, pitiful, scurvy, shabby, shameful, vile, worthless
Antonyms admirable, attractive, honourable, laudable, pleasant, praiseworthy

contemptuous arrogant, cavalier, condescending, contumelious, derisive, disdainful, haughty, high and mighty, insolent, insulting, scornful, sneering, supercilious, withering
Antonyms civil, courteous, deferential, gracious, humble, mannerly, obsequious, polite, respectful

contend 1. clash, compete, contest, cope, emulate, grapple, jostle, litigate, skirmish, strive, struggle, vie 2. affirm, allege, argue, assert, aver, avow, debate, dispute, hold, maintain

content[1] 1. *v.* appease, delight, gladden, gratify, humour, indulge, mollify, placate, please, reconcile, sate, satisfy, suffice 2. *n.* comfort, contentment, ease, gratification, peace, peace of mind, pleasure, satisfaction 3. *adj.* agreeable, at ease, comfortable, contented, fulfilled, satisfied, willing to accept

content[2] 1. burden, essence, gist, ideas, matter, meaning, significance, substance, text, thoughts 2. capacity, load, measure, size, volume

contented at ease, at peace, cheerful, comfortable, complacent, content, glad, gratified, happy, pleased, satisfied, serene, thankful
Antonyms annoyed, discontented, displeased, dissatisfied, pissed off (*Taboo sl.*), troubled, uncomfortable, uneasy

contention 1. competition, contest, discord, dispute, dissension, enmity, feuding, hostility, rivalry, row, strife, struggle, wrangling 2. affirmation, allegation, argument, assertion, asseveration, belief, claim, declaration, ground, idea, maintaining, opinion, position, profession, stand, thesis, view

contentious argumentative, bickering, captious, cavilling, combative, controversial, cross, disputatious, factious, litigious, peevish, perverse, pugnacious, quarrelsome, querulous, wrangling

contentment comfort, complacency, content, contentedness, ease, equanimity, fulfilment, gladness, gratification, happiness, peace, pleasure, repletion, satisfaction, serenity
Antonyms discomfort, discontent, discontentment, displeasure, dissatisfaction, uneasiness, unhappiness

contents 1. constituents, elements, ingredients, load 2. chapters, divisions, subject matter, subjects, themes, topics

contest *n.* 1. competition, game, head-to-head, match, tournament, trial 2. affray, altercation, battle, combat, conflict, controversy, debate, discord, dispute, encounter, fight, shock, struggle ~*v.* 3. compete, contend, fight, fight over, strive, vie 4. argue, call in *or* into question, challenge, debate, dispute, doubt, litigate, object to, oppose, question

contestant aspirant, candidate, competitor, contender, entrant, participant, player

context 1. background, connection, frame of reference, framework, relation 2. ambience, circumstances, conditions, situation

contiguous abutting, adjacent, adjoining, beside, bordering, conterminous, in contact, juxtaposed, juxtapositional, near, neighbouring, next, next door to, touching

continence abstinence, asceticism, celibacy, chastity, moderation, self-control, self-restraint, temperance

continent abstemious, abstinent, ascetic, austere, celibate, chaste, self-restrained, sober

contingency accident, chance, emergency, event, eventuality, fortuity, happening, incident, juncture, possibility, uncertainty

contingent *adj.* 1. *With* **on** *or* **upon** conditional, controlled by, dependent, subject to 2. accidental, casual, fortuitous, haphazard, random, uncertain ~*n.* 3. batch, body, bunch (*Inf.*), deputation, detachment, group, mission, quota, section, set

continual constant, continuous, endless, eternal, everlasting, frequent, incessant, interminable, oft-repeated, perpetual, recurrent, regular, repeated, repetitive, unceasing, uninterrupted, unremitting
Antonyms broken, ceasing, erratic, fluctuating, fragmentary, infrequent, intermittent, interrupted, irregular, occasional, periodic, spasmodic, sporadic, terminable

continually all the time, always, aye (*Scot.*), constantly, endlessly, eternally, everlastingly, forever, incessantly, interminably, nonstop, persistently, repeatedly

continuance continuation, duration, period, protraction, term

continuation 1. addition, extension, furtherance, postscript, sequel, supplement 2. maintenance, perpetuation, prolongation, resumption

continue 1. abide, carry on, endure, last, live on, persist, remain, rest, stay, stay on, survive 2. go on, keep at, keep on, keep the ball rolling, keep up, maintain, persevere, persist in, prolong, pursue, stick at, stick

to, sustain 3. draw out, extend, lengthen, project, prolong, reach 4. carry on, pick up where one left off, proceed, recommence, resume, return to, take up
Antonyms (*sense 1*) abdicate, leave, quit, resign, retire, step down (*senses 2 & 4*) break off, call it a day, cease, discontinue, give up, leave off, pack in (*Brit. inf.*), quit, stop

continuing enduring, in progress, lasting, ongoing, sustained

continuity cohesion, connection, flow, interrelationship, progression, sequence, succession, whole

continuous connected, constant, continued, extended, prolonged, unbroken, unceasing, undivided, uninterrupted
Antonyms broken, disconnected, ending, inconstant, intermittent, interrupted, occasional, passing, severed, spasmodic

contort convolute, deform, distort, gnarl, knot, misshape, twist, warp, wrench, writhe

contour curve, figure, form, lines, outline, profile, relief, shape, silhouette

contraband 1. *n.* black-marketing, bootlegging, moonshine (*U.S.*), rum-running, smuggling, trafficking 2. *adj.* banned, black-market, bootleg, bootlegged, forbidden, hot (*Inf.*), illegal, illicit, interdicted, prohibited, smuggled, unlawful

contract *v.* 1. abbreviate, abridge, compress, condense, confine, constrict, curtail, dwindle, epitomize, knit, lessen, narrow, pucker, purse, reduce, shrink, shrivel, tighten, wither, wrinkle 2. agree, arrange, bargain, clinch, close, come to terms, commit oneself, covenant, engage, enter into, negotiate, pledge, stipulate 3. acquire, be afflicted with, catch, develop, get, go down with, incur ~*n.* 4. agreement, arrangement, bargain, bond, commission, commitment, compact, concordat, convention, covenant, deal (*Inf.*), engagement, pact, settlement, stipulation, treaty, understanding
Antonyms (*sense 1*) broaden, develop, distend, enlarge, expand, grow, increase, inflate, multiply, spread, stretch, swell, widen (*sense 2*) decline, disagree, refuse, turn down (*sense 3*) avert, avoid, escape, ward off

contraction abbreviation, compression, constriction, diminution, drawing in, elision, narrowing, reduction, shortening, shrinkage, shrivelling, tensing, tightening

contradict be at variance with, belie, challenge, contravene, controvert, counter, counteract, deny, dispute, gainsay (*Archaic or literary*), impugn, negate, oppose, rebut
Antonyms affirm, agree, authenticate, confirm, defend, endorse, support, verify

contradiction conflict, confutation, contravention, denial, incongruity, inconsistency, negation, opposite

contradictory antagonistic, antithetical, conflicting, contrary, discrepant, incompatible, inconsistent, irreconcilable, opposed, opposite, paradoxical, repugnant

contraption apparatus, contrivance, device, gadget, instrument, mechanism, rig

contrary *adj.* 1. adverse, antagonistic, clashing, contradictory, counter, discordant, hostile, inconsistent, inimical, opposed, opposite, paradoxical 2. awkward, balky, cantankerous, cussed (*Inf.*), difficult, disobliging, froward, intractable, obstinate, perverse, stroppy (*Brit. sl.*), thrawn (*Northern English dialect*), unaccommodating, wayward, wilful ~*n.* 3. antithesis, converse, opposite, reverse 4. **on the contrary** conversely, in contrast, not at all, on the other hand, quite the opposite *or* reverse
Antonyms (*sense 1*) accordant, congruous, consistent, harmonious, in agreement, parallel, unopposed (*sense 2*) accommodating, agreeable, amiable, cooperative, eager to please, helpful, obliging, tractable, willing

contrast 1. *n.* comparison, contrariety, difference, differentiation, disparity, dissimilarity, distinction, divergence, foil, opposition 2. *v.* compare, differ, differentiate, distinguish, oppose, set in opposition, set off

contravene 1. break, disobey, go against, infringe, transgress, violate 2. conflict with, contradict, counteract, cross, go against, hinder, interfere, oppose, refute, thwart

contretemps accident, calamity, difficulty, misfortune, mishap, mistake, predicament

contribute 1. add, afford, bestow, chip in (*Inf.*), donate, furnish, give, provide, subscribe, supply 2. be conducive, be instrumental, be partly responsible for, conduce, help, lead, tend

contribution addition, bestowal, donation, gift, grant, input, offering, stipend, subscription

contributor 1. backer, bestower, conferrer, donor, giver, patron, subscriber, supporter 2. correspondent, freelance, freelancer, journalist, journo (*Sl.*), reporter

contrite chastened, conscience-stricken, humble, in sackcloth and ashes, penitent, regretful, remorseful, repentant, sorrowful, sorry

contrition compunction, humiliation, penitence, remorse, repentance, self-reproach, sorrow

contrivance 1. artifice, design, dodge, expedient, fabrication, formation, intrigue, inventiveness, machination, measure, plan, plot, project, ruse, scheme, stratagem, trick 2. apparatus, appliance, contraption, device, equipment, gadget, gear, implement, instrument, invention, machine, mechanism

contrive 1. concoct, construct, create, design, devise, engineer, fabricate, frame, improvise, invent, manufacture, wangle (*Inf.*) 2. arrange, bring about, effect, hit upon, manage, manoeuvre, plan, plot, scheme, succeed

contrived artificial, elaborate, forced, laboured, overdone, planned, recherché, strained, unnatural
Antonyms genuine, natural, relaxed, spontaneous, unaffected, unconstrained, unfeigned, unforced, unpretentious

control *v.* 1. administer, boss (*Inf.*), call the tune, command, conduct, direct, dominate, govern, handle, have charge of, hold the purse strings, lead, manage, manipulate, oversee, pilot, reign over, rule, steer, superintend, supervise 2. bridle, check, constrain, contain, curb, hold back, limit, master, rein in, repress, restrain, subdue 3. *Used of a machine, an experiment, etc.* counteract, determine, monitor, regulate, verify ~*n.* 4. authority, charge, command, direction, discipline, government, guidance, jurisdiction, management, mastery, oversight, rule, superintendence, supervision, supremacy 5. brake, check, curb, limitation, regulation, restraint

controls console, control panel, dash, dashboard, dials, instruments

controversial at issue, contended, contentious, controvertible, debatable, disputable, disputed, open to question, polemic, under discussion

controversy altercation, argument, contention, debate, discussion, dispute, dissension, polemic, quarrel, row, squabble, strife, wrangle, wrangling

controvert 1. challenge, contradict, counter, deny, oppose, refute 2. argue, contest, debate, discuss, dispute, wrangle

contumacious haughty, headstrong, insubordinate, intractable, intransigent, obdurate, obstinate, perverse, pig-headed, rebellious, recalcitrant, refractory, stiff-necked, stubborn

contumacy contempt, contrariety, delinquency, disobedience, haughtiness, insubordination, intransigence, obstinacy, perverseness, pig-headedness, rebelliousness, recalcitrance, refractoriness, stubbornness

contumelious contemptuous, disdainful, insolent, insulting, scornful, sneering, sniffy (*Inf.*), supercilious, withering

contumely abuse, affront, arrogance, contempt, derision, disdain, humiliation, indignity, insolence, insult, obloquy, opprobrium, rudeness, scorn, superciliousness

contusion bruise, discoloration, injury, knock, swelling

conundrum brain-teaser (*Inf.*), enigma, poser, problem, puzzle, riddle, teaser

convalescence improvement, recovery, recuperation, rehabilitation, return to health

convalescent *adj.* getting better, improving, mending, on the mend, recovering, recuperating

convene assemble, bring together, call, come together, congregate, convoke, gather, meet, muster, rally, summon

convenience 1. accessibility, appropriateness, availability, fitness, handiness, opportuneness, serviceability, suitability, usefulness, utility 2. *A convenient time or situation* chance, leisure, opportunity, spare moment, spare time 3. accommodation, advantage, benefit, comfort, ease, enjoyment, satisfaction, service, use 4. *A useful device* amenity, appliance, comfort, facility, help, labour-saving device
Antonyms discomfort, hardship, inconvenience, uselessness

convenient 1. adapted, appropriate, beneficial, commodious, fit, fitted, handy, helpful, labour-saving, opportune, seasonable, serviceable, suitable, suited, timely, useful, well-timed 2. accessible, at hand, available, close at hand, handy, just round the corner, nearby, within reach
Antonyms awkward, distant, inaccessible, inconvenient, out-of-the-way, unsuitable, useless

convent convent school, nunnery, religious community

convention 1. assembly, conference, congress, convocation, council, delegates, meeting, representatives 2. code, custom, etiquette, formality, practice, propriety, protocol, tradition, usage 3. agreement, bargain, compact, concordat, contract, pact, protocol, stipulation, treaty

conventional 1. accepted, common, correct, customary, decorous, expected, formal, habitual, normal, ordinary, orthodox, prevailing, prevalent, proper, regular, ritual, standard, traditional, usual, wonted 2. banal, bourgeois, commonplace, hackneyed, hidebound, pedestrian, prosaic, routine, run-of-the-mill, stereotyped, unoriginal

Antonyms abnormal, off-the-wall (*Sl.*), uncommon, unconventional, unorthodox

converge coincide, combine, come together, concentrate, focus, gather, join, meet, merge, mingle

convergence approach, blending, coincidence, concentration, concurrence, confluence, conflux, conjunction, junction, meeting, merging, mingling

conversant *Usually with* **with** acquainted, *au fait*, experienced, familiar, knowledgeable, practised, proficient, skilled, versed, well-informed, well up in (*Inf.*)

conversation chat, chinwag (*Brit. inf.*), colloquy, communication, communion, confab (*Inf.*), confabulation, conference, converse, dialogue, discourse, discussion, exchange, gossip, intercourse, powwow, talk, tête-à-tête

conversational chatty, colloquial, communicative, informal

converse[1] *v.* 1. chat, commune, confer, discourse, exchange views 2. *Obsolete* associate, consort ~*n.* 3. chat, communication, conference, conversation, dialogue, talk

converse[2] 1. *n.* antithesis, contrary, obverse, opposite, other side of the coin, reverse 2. *adj.* contrary, counter, opposite, reverse, reversed, transposed

conversion 1. change, metamorphosis, transfiguration, transformation, transmogrification (*Jocular*), transmutation 2. adaptation, alteration, modification, reconstruction, remodelling, reorganization 3. change of heart, proselytization, rebirth, reformation, regeneration

convert[1] *v.* 1. alter, change, interchange, metamorphose, transform, transmogrify (*Jocular*), transmute, transpose, turn 2. adapt, apply, appropriate, modify, remodel, reorganize, restyle, revise 3. baptize, bring to God, convince, proselytize, reform, regenerate, save

convert[2] *n.* catechumen, disciple, neophyte, proselyte

convertible adaptable, adjustable, exchangeable, interchangeable

convex bulging, gibbous, outcurved, protuberant, rounded

Antonyms concave, cupped, depressed, excavated, hollowed, indented, sunken

convey 1. bear, bring, carry, conduct, fetch, forward, grant, guide, move, send, support, transmit, transport 2. communicate, disclose, impart, make known, relate, reveal, tell 3. *Law* bequeath, cede, deliver, demise, devolve, grant, lease, transfer, will

conveyance 1. carriage, movement, transfer, transference, transmission, transport, transportation 2. transport, vehicle

convict 1. *v.* condemn, find guilty, imprison, pronounce guilty, sentence 2. *n.* con (*Sl.*), criminal, culprit, felon, jailbird, lag (*Sl.*), malefactor, prisoner, villain

conviction 1. assurance, certainty, certitude, confidence, earnestness, fervour, firmness, reliance 2. belief, creed, faith, opinion, persuasion, principle, tenet, view

convince assure, bring round, gain the confidence of, persuade, prevail upon, prove to, satisfy, sway, win over

convincing cogent, conclusive, credible, impressive, incontrovertible, likely, persuasive, plausible, powerful, probable, telling, verisimilar

Antonyms beyond belief, dubious, far-fetched, implausible, improbable, inconclusive, incredible, unconvincing, unlikely

convivial back-slapping, cheerful, festive, friendly, fun-loving, gay, genial, hearty, hilarious, jolly, jovial, lively, merry, mirthful, partyish (*Inf.*), sociable

conviviality bonhomie, cheer, cordiality, festivity, gaiety, geniality, good fellowship, jollification, jollity, joviality, liveliness, merrymaking, mirth, sociability

convocation assemblage, assembly, conclave, concourse, congregation, congress, convention, council, diet, meeting, synod

convoke assemble, call together, collect, convene, gather, muster, summon

convolution coil, coiling, complexity, contortion, curlicue, helix, intricacy, involution, loop, sinuosity, sinuousness, spiral, tortuousness, twist, undulation, winding

convoy 1. *n.* armed guard, attendance, attendant, escort, guard, protection 2. *v.* accompany, attend, escort, guard, pilot, protect, shepherd, usher

convulse agitate, churn up, derange, disorder, disturb, shake, shatter, twist, work

convulsion 1. agitation, commotion, disturbance, furore, shaking, tumult, turbulence, upheaval 2. contortion, contraction, cramp, fit, paroxysm, seizure, spasm, throe (*Rare*), tremor

convulsive churning, fitful, jerky, paroxysmal, spasmodic, sporadic, violent

cook up concoct, contrive, devise, dream up, fabricate, improvise, invent, manufacture, plot, prepare, scheme, trump up

cool *adj.* 1. chilled, chilling, chilly, coldish, nippy, refreshing 2. calm, collected, composed, deliberate, dispassionate, imperturbable, laid-back (*Inf.*), level-headed, placid, quiet, relaxed, sedate, self-controlled, self-possessed, serene, together

(*Sl.*), unemotional, unexcited, unfazed (*Inf.*), unruffled 3. aloof, apathetic, distant, frigid, incurious, indifferent, lukewarm, offhand, reserved, standoffish, uncommunicative, unconcerned, unenthusiastic, unfriendly, uninterested, unresponsive, unwelcoming 4. audacious, bold, brazen, cheeky, impertinent, impudent, presumptuous, shameless 5. *Inf.* cosmopolitan, elegant, sophisticated, urbane ~*v.* 6. chill, cool off, freeze, lose heat, refrigerate 7. abate, allay, assuage, calm (down), dampen, lessen, moderate, quiet, temper ~*n.* 8. *Sl.* calmness, composure, control, poise, self-control, self-discipline, self-possession, temper

Antonyms *adj.* (*sense 1*) lukewarm, moderately hot, sunny, tepid, warm (*sense 2*) agitated, delirious, excited, impassioned, nervous, overwrought, perturbed, tense, troubled, twitchy (*Inf.*) (*sense 3*) amiable, chummy (*Inf.*), cordial, friendly, outgoing, receptive, responsive, sociable, warm ~*v.* (*sense 6*) heat, reheat, take the chill off, thaw, warm, warm up

coop 1. *n.* box, cage, enclosure, hutch, pen, pound 2. *v.* cage, confine, immure, impound, imprison, pen, pound, shut up

cooperate abet, aid, assist, collaborate, combine, concur, conduce, conspire, contribute, coordinate, go along with, help, join forces, pitch in, play ball (*Inf.*), pool resources, pull together, work together

Antonyms conflict, contend with, fight, hamper, hamstring, hinder, impede, obstruct, oppose, prevent, put the mockers on (*Inf.*), resist, struggle against, stymie, thwart

cooperation assistance, collaboration, combined effort, concert, concurrence, esprit de corps, give-and-take, helpfulness, participation, responsiveness, teamwork, unity

Antonyms discord, dissension, hindrance, opposition, rivalry

cooperative 1. accommodating, helpful, obliging, responsive, supportive 2. coactive, collective, combined, concerted, coordinated, joint, shared, unified, united

coordinate 1. *v.* correlate, harmonize, integrate, match, mesh, organize, relate, synchronize, systematize 2. *adj.* coequal, correlative, correspondent, equal, equivalent, parallel, tantamount

cope 1. carry on, get by (*Inf.*), hold one's own, make out (*Inf.*), make the grade, manage, rise to the occasion, struggle through, survive 2. **cope with** contend, deal, dispatch, encounter, grapple, handle, struggle, tangle, tussle, weather, wrestle

copious abundant, ample, bounteous, bountiful, extensive, exuberant, full, generous, lavish, liberal, luxuriant, overflowing, plenteous, plentiful, profuse, rich, superabundant

copiousness abundance, amplitude, bountifulness, bounty, cornucopia, exuberance, fullness, horn of plenty, lavishness, luxuriance, plentifulness, plenty, richness, superabundance

cop-out alibi, dodge, fraud, pretence, pretext

cop out abandon, desert, dodge, quit, renege, renounce, revoke, skip, skive (*Brit. sl.*), withdraw

copulate ball (*Taboo sl., chiefly U.S.*), bonk (*Inf.*), fuck (*Taboo sl.*), have intercourse, have sex, hump (*Taboo sl.*), screw (*Taboo sl.*), shag (*Taboo sl., chiefly Brit.*)

copulation carnal knowledge, coition, coitus, congress, coupling, love, lovemaking, mating, nookie (*Sl.*), rumpy-pumpy (*Sl.*), sex, sex act, sexual intercourse, the other (*Inf.*), venery (*Archaic*)

copy *n.* 1. archetype, carbon copy, counterfeit, duplicate, facsimile, fake, fax, forgery, image, imitation, likeness, model, pattern, photocopy, Photostat (*Trademark*), print, replica, replication, representation, reproduction, transcription, Xerox (*Trademark*) ~*v.* 2. counterfeit, duplicate, photocopy, Photostat (*Trademark*), replicate, reproduce, transcribe, Xerox (*Trademark*) 3. ape, echo, emulate, follow, follow suit, follow the example of, imitate, mimic, mirror, parrot, repeat, simulate

Antonyms *n.* model, original, pattern, prototype, the real thing ~*v.* create, originate

coquet dally, flirt, lead on, make eyes at, philander, tease, toy, trifle, vamp (*Inf.*)

coquettish amorous, arch, come-hither (*Inf.*), coy, dallying, flighty, flirtatious, flirty, inviting, teasing

cord 1. line, rope, string, twine 2. bond, connection, link, tie

cordial affable, affectionate, agreeable, cheerful, congenial, earnest, friendly, genial, heartfelt, hearty, invigorating, sociable, warm, warm-hearted, welcoming, wholehearted

Antonyms aloof, cold, distant, formal, frigid, reserved, unfriendly, ungracious

cordiality affability, amiability, friendliness, geniality, heartiness, sincerity, warmth, wholeheartedness

cordon 1. *n.* barrier, chain, line, ring 2. *v.* **cordon off** close off, encircle, enclose, fence off, isolate, picket, separate, surround

core centre, crux, essence, gist, heart, kernel, nub, nucleus, pith

corner *n.* 1. angle, bend, crook, joint 2. cavity, cranny, hideaway, hide-out, hidey-hole (*Inf.*), hole, niche, nook, recess, retreat 3. hole (*Inf.*), hot water (*Inf.*), pickle (*Inf.*), predicament, spot (*Inf.*), tight spot ~*v.* 4. bring to bay, run to earth, trap 5. *As in* **corner the market** dominate, engross, hog (*Sl.*), monopolize

cornerstone 1. quoin 2. basis, bedrock, key, premise, starting point

corny banal, commonplace, dull, feeble, hackneyed, maudlin, mawkish, old-fashioned, old hat, sentimental, stale, stereotyped, trite

corollary conclusion, consequence, deduction, induction, inference, result, sequel, upshot

corporal anatomical, bodily, carnal, corporeal (*Archaic*), fleshly, material, physical, somatic

corporate allied, collaborative, collective, combined, communal, joint, merged, pooled, shared, united

corporation 1. association, corporate body, society 2. civic authorities, council, municipal authorities, town council 3. *Inf.* beer belly (*Inf.*), paunch, pod, pot, potbelly, spare tyre, spread (*Inf.*)

corporeal bodily, fleshy, human, material, mortal, physical, substantial

corps band, body, company, contingent, crew, detachment, division, regiment, squad, squadron, team, troop, unit

corpse body, cadaver, carcass, remains, stiff (*Sl.*)

corpulence beef (*Inf.*), blubber, burliness, *embonpoint,* fatness, fleshiness, obesity, plumpness, portliness, rotundity, stoutness, tubbiness

corpulent beefy (*Inf.*), bulky, burly, fat, fattish, fleshy, large, lusty, obese, overweight, plump, portly, roly-poly, rotund, stout, tubby, well-padded
Antonyms anorexic, bony, emaciated, gaunt, scrawny, skin and bones (*Inf.*), skinny, slim, thin, thin as a rake, underweight

corpus body, collection, compilation, complete works, entirety, *oeuvre,* whole

correct *v.* 1. adjust, amend, cure, emend, improve, rectify, redress, reform, regulate, remedy, right 2. admonish, chasten, chastise, chide, discipline, punish, reprimand, reprove ~*adj.* 3. accurate, equitable, exact, faultless, flawless, just, O.K. *or* okay (*Inf.*), precise, regular, right, strict, true 4. acceptable, appropriate, diplomatic, fitting, kosher (*Inf.*), O.K. *or* okay (*Inf.*), proper, seemly, standard
Antonyms *v.* (*sense 1*) damage, harm, impair, ruin, spoil (*sense 2*) compliment, excuse, praise ~*adj.* (*sense 3*) false, inaccurate, incorrect, untrue, wrong (*sense 4*) improper, inappropriate, unacceptable, unfitting, unsuitable

correction 1. adjustment, alteration, amendment, emendation, improvement, modification, rectification, righting 2. admonition, castigation, chastisement, discipline, punishment, reformation, reproof

corrective *adj.* 1. palliative, rehabilitative, remedial, restorative, therapeutic 2. disciplinary, penal, punitive, reformatory

correctly accurately, aright, perfectly, precisely, properly, right, rightly

correctness 1. accuracy, exactitude, exactness, faultlessness, fidelity, preciseness, precision, regularity, truth 2. *bon ton,* civility, decorum, good breeding, propriety, seemliness

correlate associate, compare, connect, coordinate, correspond, equate, interact, parallel, tie in

correlation alternation, correspondence, equivalence, interaction, interchange, interdependence, interrelationship, reciprocity

correspond 1. accord, agree, be consistent, coincide, complement, conform, correlate, dovetail, fit, harmonize, match, square, tally 2. communicate, exchange letters, keep in touch, write
Antonyms be at variance, be dissimilar, be inconsistent, belie, be unlike, differ, disagree, diverge, vary

correspondence 1. agreement, analogy, coincidence, comparability, comparison, concurrence, conformity, congruity, correlation, fitness, harmony, match, relation, similarity 2. communication, letters, mail, post, writing

correspondent *n.* 1. letter writer, pen friend *or* pal 2. contributor, gazetteer (*Archaic*), journalist, journo (*Sl.*), reporter, special correspondent ~*adj.* 3. analogous, comparable, like, parallel, reciprocal, similar

corresponding analogous, answering, complementary, correlative, correspondent, equivalent, identical, interrelated, matching, reciprocal, similar, synonymous

corridor aisle, alley, hallway, passage, passageway

corroborate authenticate, back up, bear out, confirm, document, endorse, establish, ratify, substantiate, support, sustain, validate

Antonyms contradict, disprove, invalidate, negate, rebut, refute

corrode canker, consume, corrupt, deteriorate, eat away, erode, gnaw, impair, oxidize, rust, waste, wear away

corrosive 1. acrid, biting, caustic, consuming, corroding, erosive, virulent, vitriolic, wasting, wearing 2. caustic, cutting, incisive, mordant, sarcastic, trenchant, venomous, vitriolic

corrugated channelled, creased, crinkled, fluted, furrowed, grooved, puckered, ridged, rumpled, wrinkled

corrupt *adj.* 1. bent (*Sl.*), bribable, crooked (*Inf.*), dishonest, fraudulent, rotten, shady (*Inf.*), unethical, unprincipled, unscrupulous, venal 2. abandoned, debased, defiled, degenerate, demoralized, depraved, dishonoured, dissolute, profligate, vicious ~*v.* 3. bribe, buy off, debauch, demoralize, deprave, entice, fix (*Inf.*), grease (someone's) palm (*Sl.*), lure, pervert, square, suborn, subvert ~*adj.* 4. adulterated, altered, contaminated, decayed, defiled, distorted, doctored, falsified, infected, polluted, putrescent, putrid, rotten, tainted ~*v.* 5. adulterate, contaminate, debase, defile, doctor, infect, putrefy, spoil, taint, tamper with, vitiate

Antonyms *adj.* (*senses 1 & 2*) ethical, honest, honourable, moral, noble, principled, righteous, scrupulous, straight, undefiled, upright, virtuous ~*v.* (*sense 3*) correct, purify, reform

corruption 1. breach of trust, bribery, bribing, crookedness (*Inf.*), demoralization, dishonesty, extortion, fiddling (*Inf.*), fraud, fraudulency, graft (*Inf.*), jobbery, profiteering, shadiness, shady dealings (*Inf.*), unscrupulousness, venality 2. baseness, decadence, degeneration, degradation, depravity, evil, immorality, impurity, iniquity, perversion, profligacy, sinfulness, turpitude, vice, viciousness, wickedness 3. adulteration, debasement, decay, defilement, distortion, doctoring, falsification, foulness, infection, pollution, putrefaction, putrescence, rot, rottenness

corsair buccaneer, freebooter, picaroon (*Archaic*), pirate, rover, sea rover

corset 1. belt, bodice, corselet, foundation garment, girdle, panty girdle, stays (*Rare*) 2. *Fig.* check, curb, limitation, restriction

cortege cavalcade, entourage, procession, retinue, suite, train

cosmetic *adj.* beautifying, nonessential, superficial, surface, touching-up

cosmic grandiose, huge, immense, infinite, limitless, measureless, universal, vast

cosmonaut astronaut, spaceman, space pilot

cosmopolitan 1. *adj.* broad-minded, catholic, open-minded, sophisticated, universal, urbane, well-travelled, worldly, worldly-wise 2. *n.* cosmopolite, jetsetter, man *or* woman of the world, sophisticate

Antonyms *adj.* hidebound, illiberal, insular, limited, narrow-minded, parochial, provincial, restricted, rustic, unsophisticated

cosmos 1. creation, macrocosm, universe, world 2. harmony, order, structure

cosset baby, coddle, cosher (*Irish*), mollycoddle, pamper, pet, wrap up in cotton wool (*Inf.*)

cost *n.* 1. amount, charge, damage (*Inf.*), expenditure, expense, figure, outlay, payment, price, rate, worth 2. damage, deprivation, detriment, expense, harm, hurt, injury, loss, penalty, sacrifice, suffering ~*v.* 3. come to, command a price of, sell at, set (someone) back (*Inf.*) 4. *Fig.* do disservice to, harm, hurt, injure, lose, necessitate

costly 1. dear, excessive, exorbitant, expensive, extortionate, highly-priced, steep (*Inf.*), stiff, valuable 2. gorgeous, lavish, luxurious, opulent, precious, priceless, rich, splendid, sumptuous 3. *Entailing loss or sacrifice* catastrophic, damaging, deleterious, disastrous, harmful, loss-making, ruinous, sacrificial

Antonyms (*sense 1*) cheap, cheapo (*Inf.*), dirt-cheap, economical, fair, inexpensive, low-priced, reasonable, reduced

costs 1. budget, expenses, outgoings 2. **at all costs** at any price, no matter what, regardless, without fail

costume apparel, attire, clothing, dress, ensemble, garb, get-up (*Inf.*), livery, national dress, outfit, robes, uniform

cosy comfortable, comfy (*Inf.*), cuddled up, homely, intimate, secure, sheltered, snug, snuggled down, tucked up, warm

coterie cabal, camp, circle, clique, gang, group, outfit (*Inf.*), posse (*Inf.*), set

cottage but-and-ben (*Scot.*), cabin, chalet, cot, hut, lodge, shack

couch 1. *v.* express, frame, phrase, set forth, utter, word 2. *n.* bed, chaise longue, chesterfield, daybed, divan, ottoman, settee, sofa

cough 1. *n.* bark, frog *or* tickle in one's throat, hack 2. *v.* bark, clear one's throat, hack, hawk, hem

cough up ante up (*Inf., chiefly U.S.*), come across, deliver, fork out (*Sl.*), give up, hand over, shell out (*Inf.*), surrender

council assembly, board, cabinet, chamber,

committee, conclave, conference, congress, convention, convocation, diet, governing body, house, ministry, panel, parliament, synod

counsel *n.* 1. admonition, advice, caution, consideration, consultation, deliberation, direction, forethought, guidance, information, recommendation, suggestion, warning 2. advocate, attorney, barrister, lawyer, legal adviser, solicitor ~*v.* 3. admonish, advise, advocate, caution, exhort, instruct, prescribe, recommend, urge, warn

count *v.* 1. add (up), calculate, cast up, check, compute, enumerate, estimate, number, reckon, score, tally, tot up 2. consider, deem, esteem, impute, judge, look upon, rate, regard, think 3. carry weight, cut any ice (*Inf.*), enter into consideration, matter, rate, signify, tell, weigh 4. include, number among, take into account *or* consideration ~*n.* 5. calculation, computation, enumeration, numbering, poll, reckoning, sum, tally

countenance *n.* 1. appearance, aspect, expression, face, features, look, mien, physiognomy, visage 2. aid, approval, assistance, backing, endorsement, favour, sanction, support ~*v.* 3. abet, aid, approve, back, champion, condone, encourage, endorse, help, sanction, support 4. brook, endure, put up with (*Inf.*), stand for (*Inf.*), tolerate

counter 1. *adv.* against, at variance with, contrarily, contrariwise, conversely, in defiance of, versus 2. *adj.* adverse, against, conflicting, contradictory, contrary, contrasting, obverse, opposed, opposing, opposite 3. *v.* answer, hit back, meet, offset, parry, resist, respond, retaliate, return, ward off

Antonyms *adv./adj.* accordant, in agreement, parallel, similar ~*v.* accept, give in, surrender, take, yield

counteract annul, check, contravene, counterbalance, countervail, cross, defeat, foil, frustrate, hinder, invalidate, negate, neutralize, obviate, offset, oppose, resist, thwart

counterbalance balance, compensate, counterpoise, countervail, make up for, offset, set off

counterfeit 1. *v.* copy, fabricate, fake, feign, forge, imitate, impersonate, pretend, sham, simulate 2. *adj.* bogus, copied, ersatz, faked, false, feigned, forged, fraudulent, imitation, phoney *or* phony (*Inf.*), pseud (*Inf.*), pseudo (*Inf.*), sham, simulated, spurious, suppositious 3. *n.* copy, fake, forgery, fraud, imitation, phoney *or* phony (*Inf.*), reproduction, sham

Antonyms authentic, genuine, good, original, real, the real thing

countermand annul, cancel, override, repeal, rescind, retract, reverse, revoke

counterpane bedcover, bedspread, cover, coverlet, quilt

counterpart complement, copy, correlative, duplicate, equal, fellow, match, mate, opposite number, supplement, tally, twin

countless endless, immeasurable, incalculable, infinite, innumerable, legion, limitless, measureless, multitudinous, myriad, numberless, uncounted, untold

Antonyms finite, limited, restricted

count on *or* **upon** bank on, believe (in), depend on, lean on, pin one's faith on, reckon on, rely on, take for granted, take on trust, trust

count out disregard, except, exclude, leave out, leave out of account, pass over

countrified agrestic, Arcadian, bucolic, cracker-barrel (*U.S.*), homespun, idyllic, pastoral, picturesque, provincial, rural, rustic

country *n.* 1. commonwealth, kingdom, nation, people, realm, sovereign state, state 2. fatherland, homeland, motherland, nationality, native land, *patria* 3. land, part, region, terrain, territory 4. citizenry, citizens, community, electors, grass roots, inhabitants, nation, people, populace, public, society, voters 5. backwoods, boondocks (*U.S. sl.*), countryside, farmland, green belt, outback (*Aust. & N.Z.),* outdoors, provinces, rural areas, sticks (*Inf.*), the back of beyond, the middle of nowhere, wide open spaces (*Inf.*) ~*adj.* 6. agrestic, agrarian, Arcadian, bucolic, georgic (*Literary*), landed, pastoral, provincial, rural, rustic

Antonyms *n.* (*sense 5*) city, metropolis, town ~*adj.* city, cosmopolitan, sophisticated, urban, urbane

countryman 1. bumpkin, country dweller, farmer, hayseed (*U.S. & Canad. inf.*), hick (*Inf., chiefly U.S. & Canad.*), hind (*Obsolete*), husbandman, peasant, provincial, rustic, swain, yokel 2. compatriot, fellow citizen

countryside country, farmland, green belt, outback (*Aust. & N.Z),* outdoors, panorama, sticks (*Inf.*), view, wide open spaces (*Inf.*)

count up add, reckon up, sum, tally, total

county 1. *n.* province, shire 2. *adj.* green-wellie, huntin', shootin', and fishin' (*Inf.*), plummy (*Inf.*), tweedy, upper-class, upper-crust (*Inf.*)

coup accomplishment, action, deed, exploit,

feat, manoeuvre, masterstroke, stratagem, stroke, stroke of genius, stunt, *tour de force*

coup de grâce clincher (*Inf.*), comeuppance (*Sl.*), deathblow, final blow, kill, knockout blow, mercy stroke, mortal blow, quietus

coup d'état coup, overthrow, palace revolution, putsch, rebellion, seizure of power, takeover

couple 1. *n.* brace, duo, item, pair, span (*of horses or oxen*), twain (*Archaic*), twosome 2. *v.* buckle, clasp, conjoin, connect, hitch, join, link, marry, pair, unite, wed, yoke

coupon card, certificate, detachable portion, slip, ticket, token, voucher

courage balls (*Taboo sl.*), ballsiness (*Taboo sl.*), boldness, bottle (*Brit. sl.*), bravery, daring, dauntlessness, fearlessness, firmness, fortitude, gallantry, grit, guts (*Inf.*), hardihood, heroism, intrepidity, lion-heartedness, mettle, nerve, pluck, resolution, spunk (*Inf.*), valour

Antonyms cowardice, faint-heartedness, fear, timidity

courageous audacious, ballsy (*Taboo sl.*), bold, brave, daring, dauntless, fearless, gallant, gritty, hardy, heroic, indomitable, intrepid, lion-hearted, plucky, resolute, stalwart, stouthearted, valiant, valorous

Antonyms chicken (*Sl.*), chicken-hearted, chickenshit (*U.S. sl.*), cowardly, craven, dastardly, faint-hearted, gutless (*Inf.*), lily-livered, pusillanimous, scared, spineless, timid, timorous, yellow (*Inf.*)

courier 1. bearer, carrier, emissary, envoy, herald, messenger, pursuivant (*Historical*), runner 2. guide, representative

course *n.* 1. advance, advancement, continuity, development, flow, furtherance, march, movement, order, progress, progression, sequence, succession, unfolding 2. channel, direction, line, orbit, passage, path, road, route, tack, track, trail, trajectory, way 3. duration, lapse, passage, passing, sweep, term, time 4. behaviour, conduct, manner, method, mode, plan, policy, procedure, programme, regimen 5. cinder track, circuit, lap, race, racecourse, round 6. classes, course of study, curriculum, lectures, programme, schedule, studies ~*v.* 7. dash, flow, gush, move apace, race, run, scud, scurry, speed, stream, surge, tumble 8. chase, follow, hunt, pursue 9. **in due course** eventually, finally, in the course of time, in the end, in time, sooner or later 10. **of course** certainly, definitely, indubitably, naturally, obviously, undoubtedly, without a doubt

court *n.* 1. cloister, courtyard, piazza, plaza, quad (*Inf.*), quadrangle, square, yard 2. hall, manor, palace 3. attendants, cortege, entourage, retinue, royal household, suite, train 4. bar, bench, court of justice, lawcourt, seat of judgment, tribunal 5. addresses, attention, homage, respects, suit ~*v.* 6. chase, date, go (out) with, go steady with (*Inf.*), keep company with, make love to, pay court to, pay one's addresses to, pursue, run after, serenade, set one's cap at, sue (*Archaic*), take out, walk out with, woo 7. cultivate, curry favour with, fawn upon, flatter, pander to, seek, solicit 8. attract, bring about, incite, invite, prompt, provoke, seek

courteous affable, attentive, ceremonious, civil, courtly, elegant, gallant, gracious, mannerly, polished, polite, refined, respectful, urbane, well-bred, well-mannered

Antonyms discourteous, disrespectful, ill-mannered, impolite, insolent, rude, uncivil, ungracious, unkind

courtesan call girl, demimondaine, *fille de joie*, harlot, hetaera, kept woman, mistress, paramour, prostitute, scarlet woman, whore, working girl (*Facetious sl.*)

courtesy 1. affability, civility, courteousness, courtliness, elegance, gallantness, gallantry, good breeding, good manners, graciousness, polish, politeness, urbanity 2. benevolence, consent, consideration, favour, generosity, indulgence, kindness

courtier attendant, follower, henchman, liegeman, pursuivant (*Historical*), squire, train-bearer

courtliness affability, breeding, ceremony, chivalrousness, correctness, courtesy, decorum, elegance, formality, gallantry, gentility, graciousness, politeness, politesse, propriety, refinement, stateliness, urbanity

courtly affable, aristocratic, ceremonious, chivalrous, civil, decorous, dignified, elegant, flattering, formal, gallant, highbred, lordly, obliging, polished, refined, stately, urbane

courtship courting, engagement, keeping company, pursuit, romance, suit, wooing

courtyard area, enclosure, peristyle, playground, quad, quadrangle, yard

cove[1] anchorage, bay, bayou, creek, firth *or* frith (*Scot.*), inlet, sound

cove[2] bloke (*Brit. inf.*), chap, character, customer, fellow, type

covenant *n.* 1. arrangement, bargain, commitment, compact, concordat, contract, convention, pact, promise, stipulation, treaty, trust 2. bond, deed ~*v.* 3. agree, bargain, contract, engage, pledge, stipulate, undertake

cover *v.* 1. camouflage, cloak, conceal, cover up, curtain, disguise, eclipse, enshroud, hide, hood, house, mask, obscure, screen, secrete, shade, shroud, veil ~*n.* 2. cloak, cover-up, disguise, façade, front, mask, pretence, screen, smoke screen, veil, window-dressing ~*v.* 3. defend, guard, protect, reinforce, shelter, shield, watch over ~*n.* 4. camouflage, concealment, defence, guard, hiding place, protection, refuge, sanctuary, shelter, shield, undergrowth, woods ~*v.* 5. canopy, clothe, coat, daub, dress, encase, envelop, invest, layer, mantle, overlay, overspread, put on, wrap ~*n.* 6. binding, canopy, cap, case, clothing, coating, covering, dress, envelope, jacket, lid, sheath, top, wrapper ~*v.* 7. comprehend, comprise, consider, contain, deal with, embody, embrace, encompass, examine, include, incorporate, involve, provide for, refer to, survey, take account of 8. double for, fill in for, relieve, stand in for, substitute, take over, take the rap for (*Sl.*) 9. describe, detail, investigate, narrate, recount, relate, report, tell of, write up 10. balance, compensate, counterbalance, insure, make good, make up for, offset ~*n.* 11. compensation, indemnity, insurance, payment, protection, reimbursement ~*v.* 12. cross, pass through *or* over, range, travel over, traverse 13. engulf, flood, overrun, submerge, wash over

Antonyms *v.* exclude, exhibit, expose, omit, reveal, show, unclothe, uncover, unmask, unwrap ~*n.* base, bottom

coverage analysis, description, reportage, reporting, treatment

covering 1. *n.* blanket, casing, clothing, coating, cover, housing, layer, overlay, protection, shelter, top, wrap, wrapper, wrapping 2. *adj.* accompanying, descriptive, explanatory, introductory

covert 1. *adj.* clandestine, concealed, disguised, dissembled, hidden, private, secret, sly, stealthy, surreptitious, underhand, unsuspected, veiled 2. *n.* brush (*Archaic*), bushes, coppice, shrubbery, thicket, undergrowth, underwood

cover-up complicity, concealment, conspiracy, front, smoke screen, whitewash (*Inf.*)

cover up 1. conceal, cover one's tracks, feign ignorance, hide, hush up, keep dark, keep secret, keep silent about, keep under one's hat (*Inf.*), repress, stonewall, suppress, whitewash (*Inf.*) 2. Artex (*Trademark*), coat, cover, encrust, envelop, hide, plaster, slather (*U.S. sl.*), swathe

covet aspire to, begrudge, crave, desire, envy, fancy (*Inf.*), hanker after, have one's eye on, long for, lust after, thirst for, yearn for

covetous acquisitive, avaricious, close-fisted, envious, grasping, greedy, jealous, mercenary, rapacious, yearning

covey bevy, brood, cluster, flight, flock, group, nye *or* nide (*of pheasants*)

cow awe, browbeat, bully, daunt, dishearten, dismay, frighten, intimidate, overawe, psych out (*Inf.*), scare, subdue, terrorize, unnerve

coward caitiff (*Archaic*), chicken (*Sl.*), craven, dastard (*Archaic*), faint-heart, funk (*Inf.*), poltroon, recreant (*Archaic*), renegade, scaredy-cat (*Inf.*), skulker, sneak, wimp (*Inf.*), yellow-belly (*Sl.*)

cowardly abject, base, caitiff (*Archaic*), chicken (*Sl.*), chicken-hearted, chickenshit (*U.S. sl.*), craven, dastardly, faint-hearted, fearful, gutless (*Inf.*), lily-livered, pusillanimous, recreant (*Archaic*), scared, shrinking, soft, spineless, timorous, weak, weak-kneed (*Inf.*), white-livered, yellow (*Inf.*)

Antonyms audacious, bold, brave, courageous, daring, dauntless, doughty, intrepid, plucky, valiant

cowboy broncobuster (*U.S.*), cattleman, cowhand, cowpuncher (*U.S. inf.*), drover, gaucho (*S. American*), herder, herdsman, rancher, ranchero (*U.S.*), stockman, wrangler (*U.S.*)

cower cringe, crouch, draw back, fawn, flinch, grovel, quail, shrink, skulk, sneak, tremble, truckle

coxcomb beau, Beau Brummell, dandy, dude (*U.S. & Canad. inf.*), exquisite, fop, macaroni (*Obsolete*), peacock, popinjay, poser (*Inf.*), prig, puppy, spark (*Rare*), swell (*Inf.*)

coy arch, backward, bashful, coquettish, demure, evasive, flirtatious, kittenish, modest, overmodest, prudish, reserved, retiring, self-effacing, shrinking, shy, skittish, timid

Antonyms bold, brash, brass-necked (*Brit. inf.*), brassy (*Inf.*), brazen, flip (*Inf.*), forward, impertinent, impudent, pert, pushy (*Inf.*), saucy, shameless

coyness affectation, archness, backwardness, bashfulness, coquettishness, demureness, diffidence, evasiveness, modesty, primness, prissiness (*Inf.*), prudery, prudishness, reserve, shrinking, shyness, skittishness, timidity

cozen bilk, cheat, circumvent, con (*Inf.*), deceive, diddle (*Inf.*), double-cross (*Inf.*), dupe, gull (*Archaic*), hoodwink, impose on, inveigle, stiff (*Sl.*), swindle, take advantage of, take for a ride (*Inf.*), victimize

crabbed 1. acrid, acrimonious, captious, churlish, cross, cynical, difficult, fretful, harsh, ill-tempered, irritable, morose, perverse, petulant, prickly, ratty (*Brit. & N.Z. inf.*), sour, splenetic, surly, tart, testy, tetchy, tough, trying 2. *Of handwriting* awkward, cramped, hieroglyphical, illegible, indecipherable, laboured, squeezed, unreadable

crabby acid, awkward, bad-tempered, cross, crotchety (*Inf.*), grouchy (*Inf.*), ill-humoured, irritable, mardy (*Dialect*), misanthropic, nasty-tempered, prickly, ratty (*Brit. & N.Z. inf.*), snappish, snappy, sour, surly, testy, tetchy, unsociable

crack *v.* 1. break, burst, chip, chop, cleave, crackle, craze, fracture, rive, snap, splinter, split ~*n.* 2. breach, break, chink, chip, cleft, cranny, crevice, fissure, fracture, gap, interstice, rift ~*v.* 3. burst, crash, detonate, explode, pop, ring, snap ~*n.* 4. burst, clap, crash, explosion, pop, report, snap ~*v.* 5. break down, collapse, give way, go to pieces, lose control, succumb, yield ~*v./n.* 6. *Inf.* buffet, clip (*Inf.*), clout (*Inf.*), cuff, slap, thump, wallop (*Inf.*), whack ~*v.* 7. decipher, fathom, get the answer to, solve, work out ~*n.* 8. *Inf.* attempt, go (*Inf.*), opportunity, stab (*Inf.*), try 9. *Sl.* dig, funny remark, gag (*Inf.*), insult, jibe, joke, quip, smart-alecky remark, wisecrack, witticism ~*adj.* 10. *Sl.* ace, choice, elite, excellent, first-class, first-rate, hand-picked, superior, world-class

crackbrained cracked (*Sl.*), crackers (*Brit. sl.*), crackpot (*Inf.*), crazy (*Inf.*), idiotic, insane, loopy (*Inf.*), lunatic, off one's trolley (*Sl.*), out to lunch (*Inf.*), up the pole (*Inf.*)

crackdown clampdown, crushing, repression, suppression

cracked 1. broken, chipped, crazed, damaged, defective, faulty, fissured, flawed, imperfect, split 2. *Sl.* bats (*Sl.*), batty (*Sl.*), crackbrained, crackpot (*Inf.*), crazy (*Inf.*), daft (*Inf.*), eccentric, insane, loony (*Sl.*), loopy (*Inf.*), nuts (*Sl.*), nutty (*Sl.*), oddball (*Inf.*), off one's head *or* nut (*Sl.*), off one's trolley (*Sl.*), off-the-wall (*Sl.*), out of one's mind, outré, out to lunch (*Inf.*), round the bend (*Sl.*), touched, up the pole (*Inf.*), wacko (*Sl.*)

cracked up blown up, exaggerated, hyped (up), overpraised, overrated, puffed up

crack up break down, collapse, come apart at the seams (*Inf.*), freak out (*Inf.*), go ape (*Sl.*), go apeshit (*Sl.*), go berserk, go crazy (*Inf.*), go off one's rocker (*Sl.*), go out of one's mind, go to pieces, have a breakdown, throw a wobbly (*Sl.*)

cradle *n.* 1. bassinet, cot, crib, Moses basket 2. *Fig.* beginning, birthplace, fount, fountainhead, origin, source, spring, wellspring ~*v.* 3. hold, lull, nestle, nurse, rock, support 4. nourish, nurture, tend, watch over

craft 1. ability, aptitude, art, artistry, cleverness, dexterity, expertise, expertness, ingenuity, knack, know-how (*Inf.*), skill, technique, workmanship 2. artfulness, artifice, contrivance, craftiness, cunning, deceit, duplicity, guile, ruse, scheme, shrewdness, stratagem, subterfuge, subtlety, trickery, wiles 3. business, calling, employment, handicraft, handiwork, line, occupation, pursuit, trade, vocation, work 4. aircraft, barque, boat, plane, ship, spacecraft, vessel

craftiness artfulness, astuteness, canniness, cunning, deviousness, duplicity, foxiness, guile, shrewdness, slyness, subtlety, trickiness, wiliness

craftsman artificer, artisan, maker, master, skilled worker, smith, technician, wright

craftsmanship artistry, expertise, mastery, technique, workmanship

crafty artful, astute, calculating, canny, cunning, deceitful, designing, devious, duplicitous, foxy, fraudulent, guileful, insidious, knowing, scheming, sharp, shrewd, sly, subtle, tricksy, tricky, wily

Antonyms candid, ethical, frank, honest, ingenuous, innocent, naive, open, simple

crag aiguille, bluff, peak, pinnacle, rock, tor

craggy broken, cragged, jagged, jaggy (*Scot.*), precipitous, rock-bound, rocky, rough, rugged, stony, uneven

cram 1. compact, compress, crowd, crush, fill to overflowing, force, jam, overcrowd, overfill, pack, pack in, press, ram, shove, squeeze, stuff 2. glut, gorge, gormandize, guzzle, overeat, overfeed, pig out (*Sl.*), put *or* pack away, satiate, stuff 3. *Inf.* bone up on (*Inf.*), con, grind, mug up (*Sl.*), revise, study, swot, swot up

cramp[1] *v.* check, circumscribe, clog, confine, constrain, encumber, hamper, hamstring, handicap, hinder, impede, inhibit, obstruct, restrict, shackle, stymie, thwart

cramp[2] *n.* ache, contraction, convulsion, crick, pain, pang, shooting pain, spasm, stiffness, stitch, twinge

cramped 1. awkward, circumscribed, closed in, confined, congested, crowded, hemmed in, jammed in, narrow, overcrowded, packed, restricted, squeezed, uncomfortable 2. *Esp. of handwriting* crabbed, indecipherable, irregular, small

Antonyms (*sense 1*) capacious, commodious, large, open, roomy, sizable, spacious, uncongested, uncrowded

crank case (*Inf.*), character (*Inf.*), freak

(*Inf.*), kook (*U.S. & Canad. inf.*), nut (*Sl.*), oddball (*Inf.*), odd fish (*Inf.*), queer fish (*Brit. inf.*), rum customer (*Brit. sl.*), screwball (*Sl., chiefly U.S. & Canad.*), wacko (*Sl.*), weirdo *or* weirdie (*Inf.*)

cranky bizarre, capricious, eccentric, erratic, freakish, freaky (*Sl.*), funny (*Inf.*), idiosyncratic, odd, oddball (*Inf.*), off-the-wall (*Sl.*), outré, peculiar, queer, quirky, rum (*Brit. sl.*), strange, wacko (*Sl.*), wacky (*Sl.*)

cranny breach, chink, cleft, crack, crevice, fissure, gap, hole, interstice, nook, opening, rift

crash *n.* 1. bang, boom, clang, clash, clatter, clattering, din, racket, smash, smashing, thunder ~*v.* 2. break, break up, dash to pieces, disintegrate, fracture, fragment, shatter, shiver, smash, splinter 3. come a cropper (*Inf.*), dash, fall, fall headlong, give way, hurtle, lurch, overbalance, pitch, plunge, precipitate oneself, sprawl, topple 4. bang, bump (into), collide, crash-land (*an aircraft*), drive into, have an accident, hit, hurtle into, plough into, run together, wreck ~*n.* 5. accident, bump, collision, jar, jolt, pile-up (*Inf.*), prang (*Inf.*), smash, smash-up, thud, thump, wreck 6. bankruptcy, collapse, debacle, depression, downfall, failure, ruin, smash ~*v.* 7. be ruined, collapse, fail, fold, fold up, go broke (*Inf.*), go bust (*Inf.*), go to the wall, go under, smash ~*adj.* 8. *Of a course of studies, etc.* emergency, intensive, immediate, round-the-clock, speeded-up, telescoped, urgent

crass asinine, blundering, boorish, bovine, coarse, dense, doltish, gross, indelicate, insensitive, lumpish, oafish, obtuse, stupid, unrefined, witless

Antonyms brainy (*Inf.*), bright, clever, elegant, intelligent, polished, refined, sensitive, sharp, smart

crassness asininity, boorishness, coarseness, denseness, doltishness, grossness, indelicacy, insensitivity, oafishness, stupidity, tactlessness, vulgarity

crate 1. *n.* box, case, container, packing case, tea chest 2. *v.* box, case, encase, enclose, pack, pack up

crater depression, dip, hollow, shell hole

crave 1. be dying for, cry out for (*Inf.*), desire, eat one's heart out over, fancy (*Inf.*), hanker after, hope for, hunger after, long for, lust after, need, pant for, pine for, require, sigh for, thirst for, want, yearn for 2. ask, beg, beseech, entreat, implore, petition, plead for, pray for, seek, solicit, supplicate

craven 1. *adj.* abject, caitiff (*Archaic*), chicken-hearted, chickenshit (*U.S. sl.*), cowardly, dastardly, fearful, lily-livered, mean-spirited, niddering (*Archaic*), pusillanimous, scared, timorous, weak, yellow (*Inf.*) 2. *n.* base fellow (*Archaic*), caitiff (*Archaic*), coward, dastard (*Archaic*), niddering (*Archaic*), poltroon, recreant (*Archaic*), renegade, wheyface, yellow-belly (*Sl.*)

craving appetite, cacoethes, desire, hankering, hope, hunger, longing, lust, thirst, urge, yearning, yen (*Inf.*)

craw crop, gizzard, gullet, maw, stomach, throat

crawl 1. advance slowly, creep, drag, go on all fours, inch, move at a snail's pace, move on hands and knees, pull *or* drag oneself along, slither, worm one's way, wriggle, writhe 2. be overrun (alive, full of, lousy) (*Sl.*), swarm, teem 3. abase oneself, brown-nose (*Taboo sl.*), cringe, fawn, grovel, humble oneself, kiss ass (*U.S. & Canad. taboo sl.*), pander to, toady, truckle

Antonyms (*sense 1*) dart, dash, fly, hasten, hurry, race, run, rush, sprint, step on it (*Inf.*), walk

craze 1. *n.* enthusiasm, fad, fashion, infatuation, mania, mode, novelty, passion, preoccupation, rage, the latest (*Inf.*), thing, trend, vogue 2. *v.* bewilder, confuse, dement, derange, distemper, drive mad, enrage, infatuate, inflame, madden, make insane, send crazy *or* berserk, unbalance, unhinge

crazy 1. *Inf.* a bit lacking upstairs (*Inf.*), barking (*Sl.*), barking mad (*Sl.*), barmy (*Sl.*), batty (*Sl.*), berserk, bonkers (*Sl., chiefly Brit.*), cracked (*Sl.*), crackpot (*Inf.*), crazed, cuckoo (*Inf.*), daft (*Inf.*), delirious, demented, deranged, idiotic, insane, loopy (*Inf.*), lunatic, mad, mad as a hatter, mad as a March hare, maniacal, mental (*Sl.*), not all there (*Inf.*), not the full shilling (*Inf.*), nuts (*Sl.*), nutty (*Sl.*), nutty as a fruitcake (*Sl.*), off one's head (*Sl.*), off one's trolley (*Sl.*), off-the-wall (*Sl.*), of unsound mind, out to lunch (*Inf.*), potty (*Brit. inf.*), round the bend (*Sl.*), touched, unbalanced, unhinged, up the pole (*Inf.*) 2. bizarre, eccentric, fantastic, odd, oddball, outrageous, peculiar, ridiculous, rum (*Brit. sl.*), silly, strange, wacko (*Sl.*), weird 3. absurd, bird-brained (*Inf.*), cockeyed (*Inf.*), derisory, fatuous, foolhardy, foolish, half-baked (*Inf.*), idiotic, ill-conceived, impracticable, imprudent, inane, inappropriate, irresponsible, ludicrous, nonsensical, potty (*Brit. inf.*), preposterous, puerile, quixotic, senseless, short-sighted, unrealistic, unwise, unworkable, wild 4. *Inf.* ardent, beside oneself, devoted, eager, enamoured, enthusiastic, fanatical, hysterical, infatu-

ated, into (*Inf.*), mad, passionate, smitten, very keen, wild (*Inf.*), zealous
Antonyms (*sense 1*) all there (*Inf.*), *compos mentis,* down-to-earth, in one's right mind, intelligent, mentally sound, practical, prudent, rational, reasonable, sane, sensible, smart, wise (*sense 2*) common, conventional, normal, ordinary, orthodox, regular, usual (*sense 3*) appropriate, brilliant, feasible, possible, practicable, prudent, realistic, responsible, sensible, wise, workable (*sense 4*) cool, indifferent, uncaring, unenthusiastic, uninterested

creak *v.* grate, grind, groan, rasp, scrape, scratch, screech, squeak, squeal

creaky creaking, grating, rasping, raspy, rusty, squeaking, squeaky, unoiled

cream *n.* 1. cosmetic, emulsion, essence, liniment, lotion, oil, ointment, paste, salve, unguent 2. best, *crème de la crème,* elite, flower, pick, prime ~*adj.* 3. off-white, yellowish-white

creamy buttery, creamed, lush, milky, oily, rich, smooth, soft, velvety

crease 1. *v.* corrugate, crimp, crinkle, crumple, double up, fold, pucker, ridge, ruck up, rumple, screw up, wrinkle 2. *n.* bulge, corrugation, fold, groove, line, overlap, pucker, ridge, ruck, tuck, wrinkle

create 1. beget, bring into being *or* existence, coin, compose, concoct, design, develop, devise, dream up (*Inf.*), form, formulate, generate, give birth to, give life to, hatch, initiate, invent, make, originate, produce, spawn 2. appoint, constitute, establish, found, install, invest, make, set up 3. bring about, cause, lead to, occasion
Antonyms annihilate, close, demolish, destroy

creation 1. conception, formation, generation, genesis, making, procreation, siring 2. constitution, development, establishment, formation, foundation, inception, institution, laying down, origination, production, setting up 3. achievement, brainchild (*Inf.*), *chef-d'oeuvre,* concept, concoction, handiwork, invention, *magnum opus, pièce de résistance,* production 4. all living things, cosmos, life, living world, natural world, nature, universe, world

creative artistic, clever, fertile, gifted, imaginative, ingenious, inspired, inventive, original, productive, stimulating, visionary

creativity cleverness, fecundity, fertility, imagination, imaginativeness, ingenuity, inspiration, inventiveness, originality, productivity, talent

creator architect, author, begetter, designer, father, framer, God, initiator, inventor, maker, originator, prime mover

creature 1. animal, beast, being, brute, critter (*U.S. dialect*), dumb animal, living thing, lower animal, quadruped 2. body, character, fellow, human being, individual, man, mortal, person, soul, wight (*Archaic*), woman 3. dependant, hanger-on, hireling, instrument (*Inf.*), lackey, minion, puppet, retainer, tool, wretch

credence acceptance, assurance, belief, certainty, confidence, credit, dependence, faith, reliance, trust

credentials attestation, authorization, card, certificate, deed, diploma, docket, letter of recommendation *or* introduction, letters of credence, licence, missive, passport, recommendation, reference(s), testament, testimonial, title, voucher, warrant

credibility believability, believableness, integrity, plausibility, reliability, tenability, trustworthiness

credible 1. believable, conceivable, imaginable, likely, plausible, possible, probable, reasonable, supposable, tenable, thinkable, verisimilar 2. dependable, honest, reliable, sincere, trustworthy, trusty
Antonyms (*sense 1*) doubtful, implausible, inconceivable, incredible, questionable, unbelievable, unlikely (*sense 2*) dishonest, insincere, not dependable, unreliable, untrustworthy

credit *n.* 1. acclaim, acknowledgment, approval, Brownie points, commendation, fame, glory, honour, kudos, merit, praise, recognition, thanks, tribute 2. character, clout (*Inf.*), esteem, estimation, good name, influence, position, prestige, regard, reputation, repute, standing, status 3. belief, confidence, credence, faith, reliance, trust 4. *As in* **be a credit to** feather in one's cap, honour, source of satisfaction *or* pride 5. **on credit** by deferred payment, by instalments, on account, on hire-purchase, on (the) H.P., on the slate (*Inf.*), on tick (*Inf.*) ~*v.* 6. *With* **with** accredit, ascribe to, assign to, attribute to, chalk up to (*Inf.*), impute to, refer to 7. accept, bank on, believe, buy (*Sl.*), depend on, fall for, have faith in, rely on, swallow (*Inf.*), trust

creditable admirable, commendable, deserving, estimable, exemplary, honourable, laudable, meritorious, praiseworthy, reputable, respectable, worthy

credulity blind faith, credulousness, gullibility, naiveté, silliness, simplicity, stupidity

credulous born yesterday (*Inf.*), dupable, green, gullible, naive, overtrusting, trustful, uncritical, unsuspecting, unsuspicious
Antonyms cynical, incredulous, sceptical, suspecting, unbelieving, wary

creed articles of faith, belief, canon, catechism, confession, credo, doctrine, dogma, persuasion, principles, profession (*of faith*), tenet

creek 1. bay, bight, cove, firth *or* frith (*Scot.*), inlet 2. *U.S., Canad. & Aust.* bayou, brook, rivulet, runnel, stream, streamlet, tributary, watercourse

creep *v.* 1. crawl, crawl on all fours, glide, insinuate, slither, squirm, worm, wriggle, writhe 2. approach unnoticed, skulk, slink, sneak, steal, tiptoe 3. crawl, dawdle, drag, edge, inch, proceed at a snail's pace 4. bootlick (*Inf.*), brown-nose (*Taboo sl.*), cower, cringe, fawn, grovel, kiss (someone's) ass (*U.S. & Canad. taboo sl.*), kowtow, pander to, scrape, suck up to (*Inf.*), toady, truckle ~*n.* 5. *Sl.* ass-kisser (*U.S. & Canad. taboo sl.*), bootlicker (*Inf.*), brownnoser (*Taboo sl.*), sneak, sycophant, toady 6. **give one the creeps** *or* **make one's flesh creep** disgust, frighten, horrify, make one flinch (quail, shrink, squirm, wince), make one's hair stand on end (*Inf.*), repel, repulse, scare, terrify, terrorize

creeper climber, climbing plant, rambler, runner, trailing plant, vine (*Chiefly U.S.*)

creepy awful, direful, disgusting, disturbing, eerie, forbidding, frightening, ghoulish, goose-pimply (*Inf.*), gruesome, hair-raising, horrible, macabre, menacing, nightmarish, ominous, scary (*Inf.*), sinister, terrifying, threatening, unpleasant, weird

crepitate crack, crackle, rattle, snap

crescent *n.* 1. half-moon, meniscus, new moon, old moon, sickle, sickle-shape ~*adj.* 2. arched, bow-shaped, curved, falcate, semicircular, sickle-shaped 3. *Archaic* growing, increasing, waxing

Crescent, the Islam, Mohammedanism, Muslim Empire, Turkey

crest 1. apex, crown, head, height, highest point, peak, pinnacle, ridge, summit, top 2. aigrette, caruncle (*Zoology*), cockscomb, comb, crown, mane, panache, plume, tassel, topknot, tuft 3. *Heraldry* badge, bearings, charge, device, emblem, insignia, symbol

crestfallen chapfallen, dejected, depressed, despondent, disappointed, disconsolate, discouraged, disheartened, downcast, downhearted, sick as a parrot (*Inf.*)

Antonyms cock-a-hoop, elated, encouraged, exuberant, happy, in seventh heaven, joyful, on cloud nine (*Inf.*), over the moon (*Inf.*)

crevasse abyss, bergschrund, chasm, cleft, crack, fissure

crevice chink, cleft, crack, cranny, fissure, fracture, gap, hole, interstice, opening, rent, rift, slit, split

crew 1. hands, (ship's) company, (ship's) complement 2. company, corps, gang, party, posse, squad, team, working party 3. *Inf.* assemblage, band, bunch (*Inf.*), camp, company, crowd, gang, herd, horde, lot, mob, pack, posse (*Inf.*), set, swarm, troop

crib *n.* 1. bassinet, bed, cot, cradle 2. bin, box, bunker, manger, rack, stall 3. *Inf.* key, translation, trot (*U.S. sl.*) ~*v.* 4. *Inf.* cheat, pass off as one's own work, pilfer, pirate, plagiarize, purloin, steal 5. box up, cage, confine, coop, coop up, enclose, fence, imprison, limit, pen, rail, restrict, shut in

crick 1. *n.* convulsion, cramp, spasm, twinge 2. *v.* jar, rick, wrench

crime 1. atrocity, fault, felony, job (*Inf.*), malfeasance, misdeed, misdemeanour, offence, outrage, transgression, trespass, unlawful act, violation, wrong 2. corruption, delinquency, guilt, illegality, iniquity, lawbreaking, malefaction, misconduct, sin, unrighteousness, vice, villainy, wickedness, wrong, wrongdoing

criminal *n.* 1. con (*Sl.*), con man (*Inf.*), convict, crook (*Inf.*), culprit, delinquent, evildoer, felon, jailbird, lag (*Sl.*), lawbreaker, malefactor, offender, sinner, transgressor, villain ~*adj.* 2. bent (*Sl.*), corrupt, crooked (*Inf.*), culpable, felonious, illegal, illicit, immoral, indictable, iniquitous, lawless, nefarious, peccant (*Rare*), under-the-table, unlawful, unrighteous, vicious, villainous, wicked, wrong 3. *Inf.* deplorable, foolish, preposterous, ridiculous, scandalous, senseless

Antonyms commendable, honest, honourable, innocent, law-abiding, lawful, legal, right

criminality corruption, culpability, delinquency, depravity, guiltiness, illegality, sinfulness, turpitude, villainy, wickedness

cringe 1. blench, cower, dodge, draw back, duck, flinch, quail, quiver, recoil, shrink, shy, start, tremble, wince 2. bend, bootlick (*Inf.*), bow, brown-nose (*Taboo sl.*), crawl, creep, crouch, fawn, grovel, kiss ass (*U.S. & Canad. taboo sl.*), kneel, kowtow, pander to, sneak, stoop, toady, truckle

crinkle *n./v.* 1. cockle, crimp, crimple, crumple, curl, fold, pucker, ruffle, rumple, scallop, twist, wrinkle 2. crackle, hiss, rustle, swish, whisper

crinkly buckled, cockled, curly, fluted, frizzy, furrowed, gathered, kinky, knit, puckered, ruffled, scalloped, wrinkled

cripple *v.* 1. debilitate, disable, enfeeble, hamstring, incapacitate, lame, maim, mutilate, paralyse, weaken 2. bring to a stand-

still, cramp, damage, destroy, halt, impair, put out of action, ruin, spoil, vitiate
Antonyms advance, aid, assist, assist the progress of, ease, expedite, facilitate, further, help, promote

crippled bedridden, deformed, disabled, enfeebled, handicapped, housebound, incapacitated, laid up (*Inf.*), lame, paralysed

crisis 1. climacteric, climax, confrontation, critical point, crunch (*Inf.*), crux, culmination, height, moment of truth, point of no return, turning point 2. catastrophe, critical situation, dilemma, dire straits, disaster, emergency, exigency, extremity, meltdown (*Inf.*), mess, panic stations (*Inf.*), plight, predicament, quandary, strait, trouble

crisp 1. brittle, crispy, crumbly, crunchy, firm, fresh, unwilted 2. bracing, brisk, fresh, invigorating, refreshing 3. brief, brusque, clear, incisive, pithy, short, succinct, tart, terse 4. clean-cut, neat, orderly, smart, snappy, spruce, tidy, trig (*Archaic or dialect*), well-groomed, well-pressed
Antonyms (*sense 1*) drooping, droopy, flaccid, floppy, limp, soft, wilted, withered (*sense 2*) balmy, clement, mild, pleasant, warm

criterion bench mark, canon, gauge, measure, norm, par, principle, proof, rule, standard, test, touchstone, yardstick

critic 1. analyst, arbiter, authority, commentator, connoisseur, expert, expositor, judge, pundit, reviewer 2. attacker, carper, caviller, censor, censurer, detractor, fault-finder, knocker (*Inf.*), Momus, reviler, vilifier

critical 1. captious, carping, cavilling, censorious, derogatory, disapproving, disparaging, fault-finding, nagging, niggling, nit-picking (*Inf.*), scathing 2. accurate, analytical, diagnostic, discerning, discriminating, fastidious, judicious, penetrating, perceptive, precise 3. all-important, crucial, dangerous, deciding, decisive, grave, hairy (*Sl.*), high-priority, momentous, perilous, pivotal, precarious, pressing, psychological, risky, serious, urgent, vital
Antonyms appreciative, approving, complimentary, permissive, safe, secure, settled, uncritical, undiscriminating, unimportant

criticism 1. animadversion, bad press, brickbats (*Inf.*), censure, character assassination, critical remarks, disapproval, disparagement, fault-finding, flak (*Inf.*), knocking (*Inf.*), panning (*Inf.*), slam (*Sl.*), slating (*Inf.*), stick (*Sl.*), stricture 2. analysis, appraisal, appreciation, assessment, comment, commentary, critique, elucidation, evaluation, judgment, notice, review

criticize 1. animadvert on *or* upon, blast, carp, censure, condemn, disapprove of, disparage, excoriate, find fault with, give (someone *or* something) a bad press, knock (*Inf.*), lambast(e), nag at, pan (*Inf.*), pass strictures upon, pick to pieces, put down, slam (*Sl.*), slate (*Inf.*), tear into (*Inf.*) 2. analyse, appraise, assess, comment upon, evaluate, give an opinion, judge, pass judgment on, review
Antonyms commend, compliment, extol, laud (*Literary*), praise

critique analysis, appraisal, assessment, commentary, essay, examination, review, treatise

croak *v.* 1. caw, gasp, grunt, squawk, utter *or* speak harshly (huskily, throatily), wheeze 2. *Inf.* complain, groan, grouse, grumble, moan, murmur, mutter, repine 3. *Sl.* buy it (*U.S. sl.*), check out (*U.S. sl.*), die, expire, go belly-up (*Sl.*), hop the twig (*Inf.*), kick it (*Sl.*), kick the bucket (*Inf.*), pass away, peg it (*Inf.*), peg out (*Inf.*), perish, pop one's clogs (*Inf.*)

crone beldam (*Archaic*), gammer (*Dialect*), hag, old bag (*Derogatory sl.*), old bat (*Sl.*), witch

crony accomplice, ally, associate, buddy (*Inf.*), china (*Brit. sl.*), chum (*Inf.*), cock (*Brit. inf.*), colleague, companion, comrade, friend, mate (*Inf.*), pal (*Inf.*), sidekick (*Sl.*)

crook 1. *n. Inf.* cheat, chiseller (*Inf.*), criminal, knave (*Archaic*), lag (*Sl.*), racketeer, robber, rogue, shark, swindler, thief, villain 2. *v.* angle, bend, bow, curve, flex, hook

crooked 1. anfractuous, bent, bowed, crippled, curved, deformed, deviating, disfigured, distorted, hooked, irregular, meandering, misshapen, out of shape, tortuous, twisted, twisting, warped, winding, zigzag 2. angled, askew, asymmetric, at an angle, awry, lopsided, off-centre, skewwhiff (*Brit. inf.*), slanted, slanting, squint, tilted, to one side, uneven, unsymmetrical 3. *Inf.* bent (*Sl.*), corrupt, crafty, criminal, deceitful, dishonest, dishonourable, dubious, fraudulent, illegal, knavish, nefarious, questionable, shady (*Inf.*), shifty, treacherous, underhand, under-the-table, unlawful, unprincipled, unscrupulous
Antonyms (*sense 1*) flat, straight (*sense 3*) ethical, fair, honest, honourable, lawful, legal, straight, upright

croon breathe, hum, purr, sing, warble

crop *n.* 1. fruits, gathering, harvest, produce, reaping, season's growth, vintage, yield ~*v.* 2. clip, curtail, cut, dock, lop, mow, pare, prune, reduce, shear, shorten, snip, top, trim 3. bring home, bring in, collect, garner, gather, harvest, mow, pick, reap 4. browse, graze, nibble

crop up appear, arise, emerge, happen, occur, spring up, turn up

cross *adj.* 1. angry, annoyed, cantankerous, captious, churlish, crotchety (*Inf.*), crusty, disagreeable, fractious, fretful, grouchy (*Inf.*), grumpy, hacked (off) (*U.S. sl.*), ill-humoured, ill-tempered, impatient, in a bad mood, irascible, irritable, liverish, out of humour, peeved (*Inf.*), peevish, pettish, petulant, pissed off (*Taboo sl.*), put out, querulous, ratty (*Brit. & N.Z. inf.*), shirty (*Sl., chiefly Brit.*), short, snappish, snappy, splenetic, sullen, surly, testy, tetchy, vexed, waspish ~*v.* 2. bridge, cut across, extend over, ford, meet, pass over, ply, span, traverse, zigzag 3. crisscross, intersect, intertwine, lace, lie athwart of 4. blend, crossbreed, cross-fertilize, cross-pollinate, hybridize, interbreed, intercross, mix, mongrelize 5. block, deny, foil, frustrate, hinder, impede, interfere, obstruct, oppose, resist, thwart ~*n.* 6. affliction, burden, grief, load, misery, misfortune, trial, tribulation, trouble, woe, worry 7. crucifix, rood 8. crossing, crossroads, intersection, junction 9. amalgam, blend, combination, crossbreed, cur, hybrid, hybridization, mixture, mongrel, mutt (*Sl.*) ~*adj.* 10. crosswise, intersecting, oblique, transverse 11. adverse, contrary, opposed, opposing, unfavourable 12. *Involving an interchange* opposite, reciprocal
Antonyms (*sense 1*) affable, agreeable, calm, cheerful, civil, congenial, even-tempered, genial, good-humoured, good-natured, nice, placid, pleasant, sweet

cross-examine catechize, grill (*Inf.*), interrogate, pump, question, quiz

cross-grained awkward, cantankerous, crabby, difficult, disobliging, ill-natured, morose, peevish, perverse, refractory, stubborn, truculent, wayward

cross out *or* **off** blue-pencil, cancel, delete, eliminate, strike off *or* out

crosspatch bear, crank (*U.S., Canad., & Irish inf.*), curmudgeon, grump (*Inf.*), killjoy, scold, shrew, sorehead (*Inf., chiefly U.S.*), sourpuss (*Inf.*)

crosswise, crossways across, aslant, at an angle, athwart, at right angles, awry, crisscross, diagonally, from side to side, on the bias, over, sideways, transversely

crotch crutch, groin

crotchet caprice, fad, fancy, quirk, vagary, whim, whimsy

crotchety awkward, bad-tempered, cantankerous, contrary, crabby, cross, crusty, curmudgeonly, difficult, disagreeable, fractious, grumpy, irritable, liverish, obstreperous, peevish, ratty (*Brit. & N.Z. inf.*), surly, testy, tetchy

crouch 1. bend down, bow, duck, hunch, kneel, squat, stoop 2. abase oneself, cower, cringe, fawn, grovel, pander to, truckle

crow bluster, boast, brag, drool, exult, flourish, gloat, glory in, strut, swagger, triumph, vaunt

crowd *n.* 1. army, assembly, bevy, company, concourse, flock, herd, horde, host, mass, mob, multitude, pack, press, rabble, swarm, throng, troupe 2. bunch (*Inf.*), circle, clique, group, lot, set 3. attendance, audience, gate, house, spectators ~*v.* 4. cluster, congregate, cram, flock, forgather, gather, huddle, mass, muster, press, push, stream, surge, swarm, throng 5. bundle, congest, cram, pack, pile, squeeze 6. batter, butt, elbow, jostle, shove 7. **the crowd** hoi polloi, masses, mob, people, populace, proletariat, public, rabble, rank and file, riffraff, vulgar herd

crowded busy, congested, cramped, crushed, full, huddled, jam-packed, mobbed, overflowing, packed, populous, swarming, teeming, thronged

crown *n.* 1. chaplet, circlet, coronal (*Poetic*), coronet, diadem, tiara 2. bays, distinction, garland, honour, kudos, laurels, laurel wreath, prize, trophy 3. emperor, empress, king, monarch, monarchy, queen, *rex*, royalty, ruler, sovereign, sovereignty 4. acme, apex, crest, head, perfection, pinnacle, summit, tip, top, ultimate, zenith ~*v.* 5. adorn, dignify, festoon, honour, invest, reward 6. be the climax *or* culmination of, cap, complete, consummate, finish, fulfil, perfect, put the finishing touch to, round off, surmount, terminate, top 7. *Sl.* belt (*Inf.*), biff (*Sl.*), box, cuff, hit over the head, punch

crowning *adj.* climactic, consummate, culminating, final, paramount, sovereign, supreme, ultimate

crucial 1. central, critical, decisive, pivotal, psychological, searching, testing, trying 2. *Inf.* essential, high-priority, important, momentous, pressing, urgent, vital

crucify 1. execute, harrow, persecute, rack, torment, torture 2. *Sl.* lampoon, pan (*Inf.*), ridicule, tear to pieces, wipe the floor with (*Inf.*)

crude 1. boorish, coarse, crass, dirty, gross, indecent, lewd, obscene, smutty, tactless, tasteless, uncouth, vulgar 2. natural, raw, unmilled, unpolished, unprepared, unprocessed, unrefined 3. clumsy, makeshift, outline, primitive, rough, rough-hewn, rude, rudimentary, sketchy, undeveloped, unfinished, unformed, unpolished

Antonyms (*sense 1*) genteel, polished, refined, subtle, tasteful (*sense 2*) fine, fine-grained, polished, prepared, processed, refined

crudely bluntly, clumsily, coarsely, impolitely, indecently, pulling no punches (*Inf.*), roughly, rudely, sketchily, tastelessly, vulgarly

crudity 1. coarseness, crudeness, impropriety, indecency, indelicacy, lewdness, loudness, lowness, obscenity, obtrusiveness, smuttiness, vulgarity 2. clumsiness, crudeness, primitiveness, roughness, rudeness

cruel 1. atrocious, barbarous, bitter, bloodthirsty, brutal, brutish, callous, cold-blooded, depraved, excruciating, fell (*Archaic*), ferocious, fierce, flinty, grim, hard, hard-hearted, harsh, heartless, hellish, implacable, inclement, inexorable, inhuman, inhumane, malevolent, murderous, painful, poignant, Ramboesque, ravening, raw, relentless, remorseless, sadistic, sanguinary, savage, severe, spiteful, stony-hearted, unfeeling, unkind, unnatural, vengeful, vicious 2. merciless, pitiless, ruthless, unrelenting

Antonyms benevolent, caring, compassionate, gentle, humane, kind, merciful, sympathetic, warm-hearted

cruelly 1. barbarously, brutally, brutishly, callously, ferociously, fiercely, heartlessly, in cold blood, mercilessly, pitilessly, sadistically, savagely, spitefully, unmercifully, viciously 2. bitterly, deeply, fearfully, grievously, monstrously, mortally, severely

cruelty barbarity, bestiality, bloodthirstiness, brutality, brutishness, callousness, depravity, ferocity, fiendishness, hard-heartedness, harshness, heartlessness, inhumanity, mercilessness, murderousness, ruthlessness, sadism, savagery, severity, spite, spitefulness, venom, viciousness

cruise *v.* 1. coast, sail, voyage 2. coast, drift, keep a steady pace, travel along ~*n.* 3. boat trip, sail, sea trip, voyage

crumb atom, bit, grain, mite, morsel, particle, scrap, shred, sliver, snippet, *soupçon*, speck

crumble 1. bruise, crumb, crush, fragment, granulate, grind, pound, powder, pulverize, triturate 2. break up, collapse, come to dust, decay, decompose, degenerate, deteriorate, disintegrate, fall apart, go to pieces, go to wrack and ruin, moulder, perish, tumble down

crumbly brashy, brittle, friable, powdery, rotted, short (*of pastry*)

crummy bush-league (*Aust. & N.Z. inf.*), cheap, chickenshit (*U.S. sl.*), contemptible, crappy (*Sl.*), dime-a-dozen (*Inf.*), duff (*Brit. inf.*), half-baked (*Inf.*), inferior, lousy (*Sl.*), miserable, of a sort *or* of sorts, piss-poor (*Taboo sl.*), poor, poxy (*Sl.*), rotten (*Inf.*), rubbishy, second-rate, shitty (*Taboo sl.*), shoddy, third-rate, tinhorn (*U.S. sl.*), trashy, two-bit (*U.S. & Canad. sl.*), useless, weak, worthless

crumple 1. crease, crush, pucker, rumple, screw up, wrinkle 2. break down, cave in, collapse, fall, give way, go to pieces

crunch 1. *v.* champ, chew noisily, chomp, grind, masticate, munch 2. *n.* *Inf.* crisis, critical point, crux, emergency, hour of decision, moment of truth, test

crusade campaign, cause, drive, holy war, jihad, movement, push

crusader advocate, campaigner, champion, reformer

crush *v.* 1. bray, break, bruise, comminute, compress, contuse, crease, crumble, crumple, crunch, mash, pound, pulverize, rumple, smash, squeeze, wrinkle 2. conquer, extinguish, overcome, overpower, overwhelm, put down, quell, stamp out, subdue, vanquish 3. abash, browbeat, chagrin, dispose of, humiliate, mortify, put down (*Sl.*), quash, shame 4. embrace, enfold, hug, press, squeeze ~*n.* 5. crowd, huddle, jam, party

crust caking, coat, coating, concretion, covering, film, incrustation, layer, outside, scab, shell, skin, surface

crusty 1. brittle, crisp, crispy, friable, hard, short, well-baked, well-done 2. brusque, cantankerous, captious, choleric, crabby, cross, curt, gruff, ill-humoured, irritable, peevish, prickly, ratty (*Brit. & N.Z. inf.*), short, short-tempered, snappish, snarling, splenetic, surly, testy, tetchy, touchy

crux core, decisive point, essence, heart, nub

cry *v.* 1. bawl, bewail, blubber, boohoo, greet (*Scot. or archaic*), howl one's eyes out, keen, lament, mewl, pule, shed tears, snivel, sob, wail, weep, whimper, whine, whinge (*Inf.*), yowl ~*n.* 2. bawling, blubbering, crying, greet (*Scot. or archaic*), howl, keening, lament, lamentation, plaint (*Archaic*), snivel, snivelling, sob, sobbing, sorrowing, wailing, weep, weeping ~*v.* 3. bawl, bell, bellow, call, call out, ejaculate, exclaim, hail, halloo, holler (*Inf.*), howl, roar, scream, screech, shout, shriek, sing out, vociferate, whoop, yell ~*n.* 4. bawl, bell, bellow, call, ejaculation, exclamation, holler (*Inf.*), hoot, howl, outcry, roar, scream, screech, shriek, squawk, whoop, yell, yelp, yoo-hoo ~*v.* 5. advertise, announce, bark

(*Inf.*), broadcast, bruit, hawk, noise, proclaim, promulgate, publish, trumpet ~*n.* 6. announcement, barking (*Inf.*), noising, proclamation, publication ~*v.* 7. beg, beseech, clamour, entreat, implore, plead, pray ~*n.* 8. appeal, entreaty, petition, plea, prayer, supplication

Antonyms (*sense 1*) chortle, chuckle, giggle, laugh, snicker, snigger, twitter (*sense 4*) drone, mumble, murmur, mutter, speak in hushed tones, speak softly, utter indistinctly, whisper

cry down asperse, bad-mouth (*Sl., chiefly U.S. & Canad.*), belittle, decry, denigrate, disparage, knock (*Inf.*), rubbish (*Inf.*), run down, slag (off) (*Sl.*)

cry off back out, beg off, cop out (*Sl.*), excuse oneself, quit, withdraw, withdraw from

crypt catacomb, tomb, undercroft, vault

cryptic abstruse, ambiguous, apocryphal, arcane, cabbalistic, coded, dark, Delphic, enigmatic, equivocal, esoteric, hidden, mysterious, obscure, occult, oracular, perplexing, puzzling, recondite, secret, vague, veiled

crystallize appear, coalesce, form, harden, materialize, take shape

cub 1. offspring, whelp, young 2. babe (*Inf.*), beginner, fledgling, greenhorn (*Inf.*), lad, learner, puppy, recruit, tenderfoot, trainee, whippersnapper, youngster

cubbyhole 1. den, hideaway, hole, snug 2. compartment, niche, pigeonhole, recess, slot

cuddle canoodle (*Sl.*), clasp, cosset, embrace, fondle, hug, nestle, pet, snuggle

cuddly buxom, cuddlesome, curvaceous, huggable, lovable, plump, soft, warm

cudgel 1. *n.* bastinado, baton, bludgeon, club, cosh (*Brit.*), shillelagh, stick, truncheon 2. *v.* bang, baste, batter, beat, bludgeon, cane, cosh (*Brit.*), drub, maul, pound, pummel, thrash, thump, thwack

cue catchword, hint, key, nod, prompting, reminder, sign, signal, suggestion

cuff[1] 1. *v.* bat (*Inf.*), beat, belt (*Inf.*), biff (*Sl.*), box, buffet, clap, clobber (*Sl.*), clout (*Inf.*), knock, lambast(e), pummel, punch, slap, smack, thump, whack 2. *n.* belt (*Inf.*), biff (*Sl.*), box, buffet, clout (*Inf.*), knock, punch, rap, slap, smack, thump, whack

cuff[2] **off the cuff** ad lib, extempore, impromptu, improvised, offhand, off the top of one's head, on the spur of the moment, spontaneous, spontaneously, unrehearsed

cul-de-sac blind alley, dead end

cull 1. choose, pick, pluck, select, sift, thin, thin out, winnow 2. amass, collect, gather, glean, pick up

culminate climax, close, come to a climax, come to a head, conclude, end, end up, finish, rise to a crescendo, terminate, wind up

culmination acme, apex, apogee, climax, completion, conclusion, consummation, crown, crowning touch, finale, height, *ne plus ultra*, peak, perfection, pinnacle, punch line, summit, top, zenith

culpability answerability, blame, blameworthiness, fault, guilt, liability, responsibility

culpable answerable, at fault, blamable, blameworthy, censurable, found wanting, guilty, in the wrong, liable, reprehensible, sinful, to blame, wrong

Antonyms blameless, clean (*Sl.*), guiltless, innocent, in the clear, not guilty, squeaky-clean

culprit criminal, delinquent, evildoer, felon, guilty party, malefactor, miscreant, offender, person responsible, rascal, sinner, transgressor, villain, wrongdoer

cult 1. body, church, clique, denomination, faction, faith, following, party, religion, school, sect 2. admiration, craze, devotion, idolization, reverence, veneration, worship

cultivate 1. bring under cultivation, farm, fertilize, harvest, plant, plough, prepare, tend, till, work 2. ameliorate, better, bring on, cherish, civilize, develop, discipline, elevate, enrich, foster, improve, polish, promote, refine, train 3. aid, devote oneself to, encourage, forward, foster, further, help, patronize, promote, pursue, support 4. associate with, butter up, consort with, court, dance attendance upon, run after, seek out, seek someone's company *or* friendship, take trouble *or* pains with

cultivation 1. agronomy, farming, gardening, husbandry, planting, ploughing, tillage, tilling, working 2. breeding, civility, civilization, culture, discernment, discrimination, education, enlightenment, gentility, good taste, learning, letters, manners, polish, refinement, sophistication, taste 3. advancement, advocacy, development, encouragement, enhancement, fostering, furtherance, help, nurture, patronage, promotion, support 4. devotion to, pursuit, study

cultural artistic, broadening, civilizing, developmental, edifying, educational, educative, elevating, enlightening, enriching, humane, humanizing, liberal, liberalizing

culture 1. civilization, customs, life style, mores, society, stage of development, the arts, way of life 2. accomplishment, breeding, education, elevation, enlightenment, erudition, gentility, good taste, improvement, polish, politeness, refinement, sophistication, urbanity 3. agriculture, agronomy, cultivation, farming, husbandry

cultured accomplished, advanced, educated, enlightened, erudite, genteel, highbrow, knowledgeable, polished, refined, scholarly, urbane, versed, well-bred, well-informed, well-read
Antonyms coarse, common, inelegant, uncultivated, uneducated, unpolished, unrefined, vulgar

culvert channel, conduit, drain, gutter, watercourse

cumbersome awkward, bulky, burdensome, clumsy, cumbrous, embarrassing, heavy, hefty (*Inf.*), incommodious, inconvenient, oppressive, unmanageable, unwieldy, weighty
Antonyms compact, convenient, easy to use, handy, manageable, practical, serviceable, wieldy

cumulative accruing, accumulative, aggregate, amassed, collective, heaped, increasing, snowballing

cunning *adj.* 1. artful, astute, canny, crafty, devious, foxy, guileful, knowing, Machiavellian, sharp, shifty, shrewd, subtle, tricky, wily ~*n.* 2. artfulness, astuteness, craftiness, deceitfulness, deviousness, foxiness, guile, shrewdness, slyness, trickery, wiliness ~*adj.* 3. adroit, deft, dexterous, imaginative, ingenious, skilful ~*n.* 4. ability, adroitness, art, artifice, cleverness, craft, deftness, dexterity, finesse, ingenuity, skill, subtlety
Antonyms *adj.* artless, dull, ethical, frank, honest, ingenuous, maladroit ~*n.* candour, clumsiness, ingenuousness, sincerity

cup beaker, cannikin, chalice, cupful, demitasse, draught, drink, goblet, potion, teacup, trophy

cupboard ambry (*Obsolete*), cabinet, closet, locker, press

Cupid amoretto, Eros, god of love, love

cupidity acquisitiveness, avarice, avidity, covetousness, graspingness, greed, greediness, hunger, itching, longing, rapaciousness, rapacity, voracity, yearning

cupola dome, onion dome

cur 1. canine, hound, mongrel, mutt (*Sl.*), stray 2. bad egg (*Old-fashioned inf.*), bastard (*Offensive*), blackguard, bugger (*Taboo sl.*), cocksucker (*Taboo sl.*), coward, good-for-nothing, heel (*Sl.*), rat (*Inf.*), rotter (*Sl., chiefly Brit.*), scoundrel, scumbag (*Sl.*), shit (*Taboo sl.*), son-of-a-bitch (*Sl., chiefly U.S. & Canad.*), villain, wretch

curative alleviative, corrective, healing, healthful, health-giving, medicinal, remedial, restorative, salutary, therapeutic, tonic

curb 1. *v.* bite back, bridle, check, constrain, contain, control, hinder, impede, inhibit, moderate, muzzle, repress, restrain, restrict, retard, subdue, suppress 2. *n.* brake, bridle, check, control, deterrent, limitation, rein, restraint

curdle clot, coagulate, condense, congeal, curd, solidify, thicken, turn sour
Antonyms deliquesce, dissolve, liquefy, melt, soften, thaw

cure *v.* 1. alleviate, correct, ease, heal, help, make better, mend, rehabilitate, relieve, remedy, restore, restore to health ~*n.* 2. alleviation, antidote, corrective, healing, medicine, nostrum, panacea, recovery, remedy, restorative, specific, treatment ~*v.* 3. dry, kipper, pickle, preserve, salt, smoke

cure-all catholicon, elixir, *elixir vitae,* nostrum, panacea

curio antique, bibelot, bygone, collector's item, knick-knack, trinket

curiosity 1. inquisitiveness, interest, nosiness (*Inf.*), prying, snooping (*Inf.*) 2. celebrity, freak, marvel, novelty, oddity, phenomenon, rarity, sight, spectacle, wonder 3. bibelot, bygone, curio, knickknack, *objet d'art,* trinket

curious 1. inquiring, inquisitive, interested, puzzled, questioning, searching 2. inquisitive, meddling, nosy (*Inf.*), peeping, peering, prying, snoopy (*Inf.*) 3. bizarre, exotic, extraordinary, marvellous, mysterious, novel, odd, peculiar, puzzling, quaint, queer, rare, rum (*Brit. sl.*), singular, strange, unconventional, unexpected, unique, unorthodox, unusual, wonderful
Antonyms (*senses 1 & 2*) incurious, indifferent, uninquisitive, uninterested (*sense 3*) common, everyday, familiar, ordinary

curl 1. *v.* bend, coil, convolute, corkscrew, crimp, crinkle, crisp, curve, entwine, frizz, loop, meander, ripple, spiral, turn, twine, twirl, twist, wind, wreathe, writhe 2. *n.* coil, curlicue, kink, ringlet, spiral, twist, whorl

curly corkscrew, crimped, crimpy, crinkly, crisp, curled, curling, frizzy, fuzzy, kinky, permed, spiralled, waved, wavy, winding

curmudgeon bear, bellyacher (*Sl.*), churl, crosspatch (*Inf.*), grouch (*Inf.*), grouser, grumbler, grump (*Inf.*), malcontent, sourpuss (*Inf.*)

currency 1. bills, coinage, coins, dosh (*Brit. & Aust. sl.*), medium of exchange, money, notes 2. acceptance, circulation, exposure, popularity, prevalence, publicity, transmission, vogue

current *adj.* 1. accepted, circulating, common, common knowledge, customary, general, going around, in circulation, in progress, in the air, in the news, ongoing, popular, present, prevailing, prevalent, rife, topical, widespread 2. contemporary, fashionable, happening (*Inf.*), in, in fashion, in vogue, now (*Inf.*), present-day, sexy (*Inf.*), trendy (*Brit. inf.*), up-to-date, up-to-the-minute ~*n.* 3. course, draught, flow, jet, progression, river, stream, tide, tideway, undertow 4. atmosphere, drift, feeling, inclination, mood, tendency, trend, undercurrent, vibes (*Sl.*)

Antonyms (*sense 2*) archaic, obsolete, old-fashioned, outmoded, out-of-date, passé, past

curse *n.* 1. blasphemy, expletive, oath, obscenity, swearing, swearword 2. anathema, ban, denunciation, evil eye, excommunication, execration, hoodoo (*Inf.*), imprecation, jinx, malediction, malison (*Archaic*) 3. affliction, bane, burden, calamity, cross, disaster, evil, hardship, misfortune, ordeal, plague, scourge, torment, tribulation, trouble, vexation ~*v.* 4. be foul-mouthed, blaspheme, cuss (*Inf.*), swear, take the Lord's name in vain, turn the air blue (*Inf.*), use bad language 5. accurse, anathematize, damn, excommunicate, execrate, fulminate, imprecate 6. afflict, blight, burden, destroy, doom, plague, scourge, torment, trouble, vex

cursed 1. accursed, bedevilled, blighted, cast out, confounded, damned, doomed, excommunicate, execrable, fey (*Scot.*), foredoomed, ill-fated, star-crossed, unholy, unsanctified, villainous 2. abominable, damnable, detestable, devilish, fell (*Archaic*), fiendish, hateful, infamous, infernal, loathsome, odious, pernicious, pestilential, vile

cursory brief, careless, casual, desultory, hasty, hurried, offhand, passing, perfunctory, rapid, slapdash, slight, summary, superficial

curt abrupt, blunt, brief, brusque, concise, gruff, offhand, pithy, rude, sharp, short, snappish, succinct, summary, tart, terse, unceremonious, uncivil, ungracious

curtail abbreviate, abridge, contract, cut, cut back, cut short, decrease, dock, lessen, lop, pare down, reduce, retrench, shorten, trim, truncate

curtailment abbreviation, abridgment, contraction, cutback, cutting, cutting short, docking, retrenchment, truncation

curtain 1. *n.* drape (*Chiefly U.S.*), hanging 2. *v.* conceal, drape, hide, screen, shroud, shut off, shutter, veil

curvaceous bosomy, buxom, comely, curvy, shapely, voluptuous, well-rounded, well-stacked (*Brit. sl.*)

curvature arching, bend, curve, curving, curvity, deflection, flexure, incurvation

curve 1. *v.* arc, arch, bend, bow, coil, hook, inflect, spiral, swerve, turn, twist, wind 2. *n.* arc, bend, camber, curvature, half-moon, loop, trajectory, turn

curved arced, arched, bent, bowed, crooked, humped, rounded, serpentine, sinuous, sweeping, turned, twisted

cushion 1. *n.* beanbag, bolster, hassock, headrest, pad, pillow, scatter cushion, squab 2. *v.* bolster, buttress, cradle, dampen, deaden, muffle, pillow, protect, soften, stifle, support, suppress

cushy comfortable, easy, jammy (*Brit. sl.*), soft, undemanding

custodian caretaker, curator, guardian, keeper, overseer, protector, superintendent, warden, warder, watchdog, watchman

custody 1. aegis, auspices, care, charge, custodianship, guardianship, keeping, observation, preservation, protection, safekeeping, supervision, trusteeship, tutelage, ward, watch 2. arrest, confinement, detention, durance (*Archaic*), duress, imprisonment, incarceration

custom 1. habit, habitude (*Rare*), manner, mode, procedure, routine, way, wont 2. convention, etiquette, fashion, form, formality, matter of course, observance, observation, policy, practice, praxis, ritual, rule, style, tradition, unwritten law, usage, use 3. customers, patronage, trade

customarily as a rule, commonly, generally, habitually, in the ordinary way, normally, ordinarily, regularly, traditionally, usually

customary accepted, accustomed, acknowledged, common, confirmed, conventional, established, everyday, familiar, fashionable, general, habitual, normal, ordinary, popular, regular, routine, traditional, usual, wonted

Antonyms exceptional, infrequent, irregular, occasional, rare, uncommon, unusual

customer buyer, client, consumer, habitué, patron, prospect, purchaser, regular (*Inf.*), shopper

customs duty, import charges, tariff, taxes, toll

cut *v.* 1. chop, cleave, divide, gash, incise, lacerate, nick, notch, penetrate, pierce, score, sever, slash, slice, slit, wound 2. carve, chip, chisel, chop, engrave, fashion, form, inscribe, saw, sculpt, sculpture, shape, whittle 3. clip, dock, fell, gather, hack, harvest, hew, lop, mow, pare, prune, reap, saw down, shave, trim **4.** contract, cut back, decrease, ease up on, lower, rationalize, reduce, slash, slim (down) **5.** abbreviate, abridge, condense, curtail, delete, edit out, excise, precis, shorten **6.** *Often with* **through, off,** *or* **across** bisect, carve, cleave, cross, dissect, divide, interrupt, intersect, part, segment, sever, slice, split, sunder **7.** avoid, cold-shoulder, freeze (someone) out (*Inf.*), grieve, hurt, ignore, insult, look straight through (someone), pain, put down, send to Coventry, slight, snub, spurn, sting, turn one's back on, wound *~n.* **8.** gash, graze, groove, incision, laceration, nick, rent, rip, slash, slit, stroke, wound **9.** cutback, decrease, decrement, diminution, economy, fall, lowering, reduction, saving **10.** *Inf.* chop (*Sl.*), division, kickback (*Chiefly U.S.*), percentage, piece, portion, rake-off (*Sl.*), section, share, slice **11.** configuration, fashion, form, look, mode, shape, style **12.** **a cut above** *Inf.* better than, higher than, more efficient (capable, competent, reliable, trustworthy, useful) than, superior to **13.** **cut and dried** *Inf.* automatic, fixed, organized, prearranged, predetermined, settled, sorted out (*Inf.*)

Antonyms (*sense 5*) add to, augment, enlarge, expand, extend, fill out, increase (*sense 7*) accept gladly, embrace, greet, hail, receive, welcome with open arms

cut along dash (off), fly, go, hurry (away), leave, press on

cutback cut, decrease, economy, lessening, reduction, retrenchment

cut back check, curb, decrease, economize, lessen, lower, prune, reduce, retrench, slash, trim

cut down **1.** fell, hew, level, lop, raze **2.** *Sometimes with* **on** decrease, lessen, lower, reduce **3.** blow away (*Sl., chiefly U.S.*), dispatch, kill, massacre, mow down, slaughter, slay (*Archaic*), take out (*Sl.*) **4.** **cut (someone) down to size** abash, humiliate, make (someone) look small, take the wind out of (someone's) sails

cute appealing, attractive, charming, delightful, engaging, lovable, sweet, winning, winsome

cut in break in, butt in, interpose, interrupt, intervene, intrude, move in (*Inf.*)

cut off **1.** disconnect, intercept, interrupt, intersect **2.** bring to an end, discontinue, halt, obstruct, suspend **3.** isolate, separate, sever **4.** disinherit, disown, renounce

cut out **1.** cease, delete, extract, give up, kick (*Inf.*), refrain from, remove, sever, stop **2.** *Inf.* displace, eliminate, exclude, oust, supersede, supplant

cut out for adapted, adequate, competent, designed, equipped, fitted, qualified, suitable, suited

cut-price bargain, cheap, cheapo (*Inf.*), cut-rate (*Chiefly U.S.*), reduced, sale

cutpurse footpad (*Archaic*), mugger (*Inf.*), pickpocket, robber, thief

cut short abort, break off, bring to an end, check, halt, interrupt, leave unfinished, postpone, stop, terminate

cutthroat *n.* **1.** assassin, bravo, butcher, executioner, heavy (*Sl.*), hit man (*Sl.*), homicide, killer, liquidator, murderer, slayer (*Archaic*), thug *~adj.* **2.** barbarous, bloodthirsty, bloody, cruel, death-dealing, ferocious, homicidal, murderous, savage, thuggish, violent **3.** competitive, dog-eat-dog, fierce, relentless, ruthless, unprincipled

cutting *adj.* **1.** biting, bitter, chill, keen, numbing, penetrating, piercing, raw, sharp, stinging **2.** acid, acrimonious, barbed, bitter, caustic, hurtful, malicious, mordacious, pointed, sarcastic, sardonic, scathing, severe, trenchant, vitriolic, wounding

Antonyms (*sense 1*) balmy, pleasant, soothing (*sense 2*) consoling, flattering, kind, mild

cut up *v.* **1.** carve, chop, dice, divide, mince, slice **2.** injure, knife, lacerate, slash, wound **3.** *Inf.* blast, criticize, crucify (*Sl.*), give (someone *or* something) a rough ride, lambast(e), pan (*Inf.*), put down, ridicule, slate (*Inf.*), tear into (*Inf.*), vilify *~adj.* **4.** *Inf.* agitated, dejected, desolated, distressed, disturbed, heartbroken, stricken, upset, wretched

cycle aeon, age, circle, era, period, phase, revolution, rotation, round (*of years*)

cyclone hurricane, tempest, tornado, twister (*U.S. inf.*), typhoon, whirlwind

cynic doubter, misanthrope, misanthropist, pessimist, sceptic, scoffer

cynical contemptuous, derisive, distrustful, ironic, misanthropic, misanthropical, mocking, mordacious, pessimistic, sarcastic, sardonic, sceptical, scoffing, scornful, sneering, unbelieving

Antonyms credulous, green, gullible, hopeful, optimistic, trustful, trusting, unsceptical, unsuspecting

cynicism disbelief, doubt, misanthropy, pessimism, sarcasm, sardonicism, scepticism

cynosure attraction, centre, centre of attention, focus, focus of attention, leading light (*Inf.*), point (of attraction), shining example

cyst bleb, blister, growth, sac, vesicle, wen

D

dab *v.* 1. blot, daub, pat, stipple, swab, tap, touch, wipe ~*n.* 2. bit, dollop (*Inf.*), drop, fleck, pat, smidgen *or* smidgin (*Inf., chiefly U.S. & Canad.*), smudge, speck, spot 3. flick, pat, peck, smudge, stroke, tap, touch

dabble 1. dip, guddle (*Scot.*), moisten, paddle, spatter, splash, sprinkle, wet 2. dally, dip into, play at, potter, tinker, trifle (with)

dabbler amateur, dilettante, potterer, tinkerer, trifler

dab hand ace (*Inf.*), adept, buff (*Inf.*), dabster (*Dialect*), expert, hotshot (*Inf.*), maven (*U.S.*), past master, whiz (*Inf.*), wizard

daft 1. absurd, asinine, crackpot (*Inf.*), crazy, dopey (*Inf.*), foolish, giddy, goofy (*Inf.*), idiotic, inane, loopy (*Inf.*), off one's trolley (*Sl.*), out to lunch (*Inf.*), scatty (*Brit. inf.*), silly, simple, stupid, up the pole (*Inf.*), witless 2. barking (*Sl.*), barking mad (*Sl.*), crackers (*Brit. sl.*), crazy, demented, deranged, insane, lunatic, mental (*Sl.*), not the full shilling (*Inf.*), nuts (*Sl.*), nutty (*Sl.*), touched, unhinged 3. *With* **about** besotted by, crazy (*Inf.*), doting, dotty (*Sl., chiefly Brit.*), infatuated by, mad, nuts (*Sl.*), nutty (*Inf.*), potty (*Brit. inf.*), sweet on

dagger 1. bayonet, dirk, poniard, skean, stiletto 2. **at daggers drawn** at enmity, at loggerheads, at odds, at war, on bad terms, up in arms 3. **look daggers** frown, glare, glower, look black, lour *or* lower, scowl

daily *adj.* 1. circadian, diurnal, everyday, quotidian 2. common, commonplace, day-to-day, everyday, ordinary, quotidian, regular, routine ~*adv.* 3. constantly, day after day, day by day, every day, often, once a day, per diem, regularly

dainty *adj.* 1. charming, delicate, elegant, exquisite, fine, graceful, neat, petite, pretty 2. choice, delectable, delicious, palatable, savoury, tasty, tender, toothsome 3. choosy, fastidious, finical, finicky, fussy, mincing, nice, particular, picky (*Inf.*), refined, scrupulous ~*n.* 4. *bonne bouche,* delicacy, fancy, sweetmeat, titbit
Antonyms awkward, clumsy, coarse, gauche, inelegant, maladroit, uncouth, ungainly

dale bottom, coomb, dell, dingle, glen, strath (*Scot.*), vale, valley

dalliance *n.* 1. dabbling, dawdling, delay, dilly-dallying (*Inf.*), frittering, frivolling (*Inf.*), idling, loafing, loitering, playing, pottering, procrastination, toying, trifling 2. *Archaic* amorous play, coquetry, flirtation

dally 1. dawdle, delay, dilly-dally (*Inf.*), fool (about *or* around), fritter away, hang about, linger, loiter, procrastinate, tarry, waste time, while away 2. *Often with* **with** caress, flirt, fondle, fool (about *or* around), frivol (*Inf.*), lead on, play, play fast and loose (*Inf.*), tamper, tease, toy, trifle
Antonyms hasten, hurry (up), make haste, push forward *or* on, run, step on it (*Inf.*)

dam 1. *n.* barrage, barrier, embankment, hindrance, obstruction, wall 2. *v.* barricade, block, block up, check, choke, confine, hold back, hold in, obstruct, restrict

damage *n.* 1. destruction, detriment, devastation, harm, hurt, impairment, injury, loss, mischief, mutilation, suffering 2. *Inf.* bill, charge, cost, expense, total 3. *Plural* compensation, fine, indemnity, reimbursement, reparation, satisfaction ~*v.* 4. deface, harm, hurt, impair, incapacitate, injure, mar, mutilate, ruin, spoil, tamper with, undo, weaken, wreck
Antonyms *n.* gain, improvement, reparation ~*v.* better, fix, improve, mend, repair

damages compensation, fine, indemnity, reimbursement, reparation, satisfaction

damaging deleterious, detrimental, disadvantageous, harmful, hurtful, injurious, prejudicial, ruinous
Antonyms advantageous, favourable, healthful, helpful, profitable, salutary, useful, valuable, wholesome

dame baroness, dowager, *grande dame,* lady, matron (*Archaic*), noblewoman, peeress

damn *v.* 1. blast, castigate, censure, condemn, criticize, denounce, denunciate, excoriate, inveigle against, lambast(e), pan (*Inf.*), put down, slam (*Sl.*), slate (*Inf.*), tear into (*Inf.*) 2. abuse, anathematize, blaspheme, curse, execrate, imprecate, revile, swear 3. condemn, doom, sentence ~*n.* 4. brass farthing, hoot, iota, jot, tinker's curse *or* damn (*Sl.*), two hoots, whit 5. **not give a damn** be indifferent, not care, not mind
Antonyms (*sense 1*) acclaim, admire, applaud, approve, cheer, compliment, congratulate, extol, honour, laud, praise (*sense

2) adore, bless, exalt, glorify, magnify (*Archaic*), pay homage to

damnable abominable, accursed, atrocious, culpable, cursed, despicable, detestable, execrable, hateful, horrible, offensive, wicked

Antonyms admirable, commendable, creditable, excellent, exemplary, fine, honourable, laudable, meritorious, praiseworthy, worthy

damnation anathema, ban, condemnation, consigning to perdition, damning, denunciation, doom, excommunication, objurgation, proscription, sending to hell

damned 1. accursed, anathematized, condemned, doomed, infernal, lost, reprobate, unhappy 2. *Sl.* confounded, despicable, detestable, hateful, infamous, infernal, loathsome, revolting

damning accusatorial, condemnatory, damnatory, dooming, implicating, implicative, incriminating

damp *n.* 1. clamminess, dampness, dankness, dew, drizzle, fog, humidity, mist, moisture, mugginess, vapour ~*adj.* 2. clammy, dank, dewy, dripping, drizzly, humid, misty, moist, muggy, sodden, soggy, sopping, vaporous, wet ~*v.* 3. dampen, moisten, wet 4. *Fig.* allay, check, chill, cool, curb, dash, deaden, deject, depress, diminish, discourage, dispirit, dull, inhibit, moderate, restrain, stifle ~*n.* 5. *Fig.* check, chill, cold water (*Inf.*), curb, damper, discouragement, gloom, restraint, wet blanket (*Inf.*)

Antonyms *n.* aridity, dryness ~*adj.* arid, dry, watertight ~*v.* encourage, hearten, inspire

dampen 1. bedew, besprinkle, make damp, moisten, spray, wet 2. *Fig.* check, dash, deaden, depress, deter, dishearten, dismay, dull, lessen, moderate, muffle, reduce, restrain, smother, stifle

damper chill, cloud, cold water (*Inf.*), curb, discouragement, gloom, hindrance, kill-joy, pall, restraint, wet blanket (*Inf.*)

dance 1. *v.* bob up and down, caper, cut a rug (*Inf.*), frolic, gambol, hop, jig, prance, rock, skip, spin, sway, swing, trip, whirl 2. *n.* ball, dancing party, disco, discotheque, hop (*Inf.*), knees-up (*Brit. inf.*), social

dandle amuse, caress, cradle, cuddle, dance, fondle, give a knee ride, pet, rock, toss, toy (with)

dandy 1. *n.* beau, blade (*Archaic*), blood (*Rare*), buck (*Archaic*), coxcomb, dude (*U.S. & Canad. inf.*), exquisite (*Obsolete*), fop, macaroni (*Obsolete*), man about town, peacock, popinjay, swell (*Inf.*), toff (*Brit. sl.*) 2. *adj. Inf.* capital, excellent, fine, first-rate, great, splendid

danger endangerment, hazard, insecurity, jeopardy, menace, peril, pitfall, precariousness, risk, threat, venture, vulnerability

dangerous alarming, breakneck, chancy (*Inf.*), exposed, hairy (*Sl.*), hazardous, insecure, menacing, nasty, parlous (*Archaic*), perilous, precarious, risky, threatening, treacherous, ugly, unchancy (*Scot.*), unsafe, vulnerable

Antonyms harmless, innocuous, O.K. *or* okay (*Inf.*), out of danger, out of harm's way, protected, safe, safe and sound, secure

dangerously 1. alarmingly, carelessly, daringly, desperately, harmfully, hazardously, perilously, precariously, recklessly, riskily, unsafely, unsecurely 2. critically, gravely, seriously, severely

dangle *v.* 1. depend, flap, hang, hang down, sway, swing, trail 2. brandish, entice, flaunt, flourish, lure, tantalize, tempt, wave

dangling disconnected, drooping, hanging, loose, swaying, swinging, trailing, unconnected

dank chilly, clammy, damp, dewy, dripping, moist, slimy, soggy

dapper active, brisk, chic, dainty, natty (*Inf.*), neat, nice, nimble, smart, soigné *or* soignée, spruce, spry, stylish, trig (*Archaic or dialect*), trim, well-groomed, well turned out

Antonyms disarrayed, dishevelled, dowdy, frowzy, ill-groomed, rumpled, slobby (*Inf.*), sloppy (*Inf.*), slovenly, unkempt, untidy

dapple *v.* bespeckle, dot, fleck, freckle, mottle, speckle, spot, stipple

dappled brindled, checkered, flecked, freckled, mottled, piebald, pied, speckled, spotted, stippled, variegated

dare *v.* 1. challenge, defy, goad, provoke, taunt, throw down the gauntlet 2. adventure, brave, endanger, gamble, hazard, make bold, presume, risk, stake, venture ~*n.* 3. challenge, defiance, provocation, taunt

daredevil 1. *n.* adventurer, desperado, exhibitionist, hot dog (*Chiefly U.S.*), madcap, show-off (*Inf.*), stunt man 2. *adj.* adventurous, audacious, bold, daring, death-defying, madcap, reckless

daring 1. *adj.* adventurous, audacious, ballsy (*Taboo sl.*), bold, brave, daredevil, fearless, game (*Inf.*), have-a-go (*Inf.*), impulsive, intrepid, plucky, rash, reckless, valiant, venturesome 2. *n.* audacity, balls (*Taboo sl.*), ballsiness (*Taboo sl.*), boldness, bottle (*Brit. sl.*), bravery, courage, derring-do (*Archaic*), fearlessness, grit, guts (*Inf.*), intrepidity, nerve (*Inf.*), pluck, rashness, spirit, spunk (*Inf.*), temerity

Antonyms *adj.* anxious, careful, cautious, cowardly, faint-hearted, fearful, timid, wary, uncourageous ~*n.* anxiety, caution, cowardice, fear, timidity

dark *adj.* 1. black, brunette, dark-skinned, dusky, ebony, sable, swarthy 2. cloudy, darksome (*Literary*), dim, dingy, indistinct, murky, overcast, pitch-black, pitchy, shadowy, shady, sunless, unlit 3. abstruse, arcane, concealed, cryptic, deep, Delphic, enigmatic, hidden, mysterious, mystic, obscure, occult, puzzling, recondite, secret 4. bleak, cheerless, dismal, doleful, drab, gloomy, grim, joyless, morbid, morose, mournful, sombre 5. benighted, ignorant, uncultivated, unenlightened, unlettered 6. atrocious, damnable, evil, foul, hellish, horrible, infamous, infernal, nefarious, satanic, sinful, sinister, vile, wicked 7. angry, dour, forbidding, frowning, glowering, glum, ominous, scowling, sulky, sullen, threatening ~*n.* 8. darkness, dimness, dusk, gloom, murk, murkiness, obscurity, semi-darkness 9. evening, night, nightfall, night-time, twilight 10. *Fig.* concealment, ignorance, secrecy

Antonyms (*sense 1*) blond, blonde, fair, fair-haired, flaxen-haired, light, light-complexioned, towheaded (*senses 2 & 4*) bright, cheerful, clear, genial, glad, hopeful, pleasant, sunny

darken 1. becloud, blacken, cloud up *or* over, deepen, dim, eclipse, make dark, make darker, make dim, obscure, overshadow, shade, shadow 2. become angry, become gloomy, blacken, cast a pall over, cloud, deject, depress, dispirit, grow troubled, look black, sadden

Antonyms (*sense 1*) brighten, clear up, enliven, gleam, glow, illuminate, lighten, light up, make bright, shine (*sense 2*) become cheerful, cheer, encourage, gladden, hearten, make happy, perk up

darkling 1. *adj.* black, dark, darksome (*Literary*), dim, dusky, gloomy, pitchy, shadowy, tenebrous 2. *adv.* at *or* by night, in the dark, in the dead of night, in the night

darkness 1. blackness, dark, dimness, dusk, duskiness, gloom, murk, murkiness, nightfall, obscurity, shade, shadiness, shadows 2. *Fig.* blindness, concealment, ignorance, mystery, privacy, secrecy, unawareness

darling *n.* 1. beloved, dear, dearest, love, sweetheart, truelove 2. apple of one's eye, blue-eyed boy, fair-haired boy (*U.S.*), favourite, pet, spoilt child ~*adj.* 3. adored, beloved, cherished, dear, precious, treasured 4. adorable, attractive, captivating, charming, cute, enchanting, lovely, sweet

darn 1. *v.* cobble up, mend, patch, repair, sew up, stitch 2. *n.* invisible repair, mend, patch, reinforcement

dart 1. bound, dash, flash, flit, fly, race, run, rush, scoot, shoot, spring, sprint, start, tear, whistle, whiz 2. cast, fling, hurl, launch, propel, send, shoot, sling, throw

dash *v.* 1. break, crash, destroy, shatter, shiver, smash, splinter 2. cast, fling, hurl, slam, sling, throw 3. barrel (along) (*Inf., chiefly U.S. & Canad.*), bolt, bound, burn rubber (*Inf.*), dart, fly, haste, hasten, hurry, race, run, rush, speed, spring, sprint, tear 4. abash, chagrin, confound, dampen, disappoint, discomfort, discourage 5. blight, foil, frustrate, ruin, spoil, thwart, undo ~*n.* 6. bolt, dart, haste, onset, race, run, rush, sortie, sprint, spurt 7. brio, élan, flair, flourish, panache, spirit, style, verve, vigour, vivacity 8. bit, drop, flavour, hint, little, pinch, smack, *soupçon,* sprinkling, suggestion, tinge, touch

Antonyms *v.* crawl, dawdle, enhance, improve, walk ~*n.* lot, much

dashing 1. bold, daring, debonair, exuberant, gallant, lively, plucky, spirited, swashbuckling 2. dapper, dazzling, elegant, flamboyant, jaunty, showy, smart, sporty, stylish, swish (*Inf., chiefly Brit.*)

Antonyms boring, dreary, dull, lacklustre, stolid, unexciting, uninteresting

dastard *n.* caitiff (*Archaic*), coward, craven, niddering (*Archaic*), poltroon, recreant (*Archaic*), renegade, sneak, traitor, worm

dastardly *adj.* abject, base, caitiff (*Archaic*), contemptible, cowardly, craven, despicable, faint-hearted, low, mean, niddering (*Archaic*), recreant (*Archaic*), sneaking, sneaky, spiritless, underhand, vile, weak-kneed (*Inf.*)

data details, documents, dope (*Inf.*), facts, figures, info (*Inf.*), information, input, materials, statistics

date *n.* 1. age, epoch, era, period, stage, time 2. appointment, assignation, engagement, meeting, rendezvous, tryst 3. escort, friend, partner, steady (*Inf.*) 4. **out of date** antiquated, archaic, dated, obsolete, old, old-fashioned, passé 5. **to date** now, so far, up to now, up to the present, up to this point, yet 6. **up-to-date** à la mode, contemporary, current, fashionable, modern, trendy (*Brit. inf.*), up-to-the-minute ~*v.* 7. assign a date to, determine the date of, fix the period of, put a date on 8. bear a date, belong to, come from, exist from, originate in 9. become obsolete, be dated, obsolesce, show one's age

dated antiquated, archaic, *démodé,* obsolete, old-fashioned, old hat, out, outdated, outmoded, out of date, passé, unfashionable, untrendy (*Brit. inf.*)
Antonyms à la mode, all the rage, chic, cool (*Inf.*), current, hip (*Sl.*), in vogue, latest, modern, modish, popular, stylish, trendy (*Brit. inf.*), up-to-date

daub *v.* 1. coat, cover, paint, plaster, slap on (*Inf.*), smear 2. bedaub, begrime, besmear, blur, deface, dirty, grime, smirch, smudge, spatter, splatter, stain, sully ~*n.* 3. blot, blotch, smear, smirch, splodge, splotch, spot, stain

daunt 1. alarm, appal, cow, dismay, frighten, frighten off, intimidate, overawe, scare, subdue, terrify 2. deter, discourage, dishearten, dispirit, put off, shake
Antonyms cheer, comfort, encourage, hearten, inspire, inspirit, reassure, spur, support

daunted *adj.* alarmed, cowed, demoralized, deterred, discouraged, disillusioned, dismayed, dispirited, downcast, frightened, hesitant, intimidated, overcome, put off, unnerved

dauntless bold, brave, courageous, daring, doughty, fearless, gallant, gritty, heroic, indomitable, intrepid, lion-hearted, resolute, stouthearted, undaunted, unflinching, valiant, valorous

dawdle dally, delay, dilly-dally (*Inf.*), fritter away, hang about, idle, lag, loaf, loiter, potter, trail, waste time
Antonyms fly, get a move on (*Inf.*), hasten, hurry, lose no time, make haste, rush, scoot, step on it (*Inf.*)

dawdler laggard, lingerer, loiterer, slowcoach (*Brit. inf.*), slowpoke (*U.S. & Canad. inf.*), snail, tortoise

dawn *n.* 1. aurora (*Poetic*), cockcrow, crack of dawn, dawning, daybreak, daylight, dayspring (*Poetic*), morning, sunrise, sunup ~*v.* 2. break, brighten, gleam, glimmer, grow light, lighten ~*n.* 3. advent, beginning, birth, dawning, emergence, genesis, inception, onset, origin, outset, rise, start, unfolding ~*v.* 4. appear, begin, develop, emerge, initiate, open, originate, rise, unfold 5. come into one's head, come to mind, cross one's mind, flash across one's mind, hit, occur, register (*Inf.*), strike

day 1. daylight, daylight hours, daytime, twenty-four hours, working day 2. age, ascendancy, cycle, epoch, era, generation, height, heyday, period, prime, time, zenith 3. date, particular day, point in time, set time, time 4. **call it a day** *Inf.* end, finish, knock off (*Inf.*), leave off, pack it in (*Sl.*), pack up (*Inf.*), shut up shop, stop 5. **day after day** continually, monotonously, persistently, regularly, relentlessly 6. **day by day** daily, gradually, progressively, steadily

daybreak break of day, cockcrow, crack of dawn, dawn, dayspring (*Poetic*), first light, morning, sunrise, sunup

daydream *n.* 1. dream, imagining, musing, reverie, stargazing, vision, woolgathering 2. castle in the air *or* in Spain, dream, fancy, fantasy, figment of the imagination, fond hope, pipe dream, wish ~*v.* 3. dream, envision, fancy, fantasize, hallucinate, imagine, muse, stargaze

daydreamer castle-builder, dreamer, fantast, pipe dreamer, visionary, Walter Mitty, wishful thinker, woolgatherer

daylight 1. light of day, sunlight, sunshine 2. broad day, daylight hours, daytime 3. full view, light of day, openness, public attention

daze *v.* 1. benumb, numb, paralyse, shock, stun, stupefy 2. amaze, astonish, astound, befog, bewilder, blind, confuse, dazzle, dumbfound, flabbergast (*Inf.*), flummox, nonplus, perplex, stagger, startle, surprise ~*n.* 3. bewilderment, confusion, distraction, shock, stupor, trance, trancelike state

dazed at sea, baffled, bemused, bewildered, confused, disorientated, dizzy, dopey (*Sl.*), flabbergasted (*Inf.*), flummoxed, fuddled, groggy (*Inf.*), light-headed, muddled, nonplussed, numbed, perplexed, punch-drunk, shocked, staggered, stunned, stupefied, woozy (*Inf.*)

dazzle *v.* 1. bedazzle, blind, blur, confuse, daze 2. amaze, astonish, awe, bowl over (*Inf.*), fascinate, hypnotize, impress, overawe, overpower, overwhelm, strike dumb, stupefy ~*n.* 3. brilliance, éclat, flash, glitter, magnificence, razzle-dazzle (*Sl.*), razzmatazz (*Sl.*), sparkle, splendour

dazzling brilliant, drop-dead (*Sl.*), glittering, glorious, radiant, ravishing, scintillating, sensational (*Inf.*), shining, sparkling, splendid, stunning, sublime, superb, virtuoso
Antonyms dull, ordinary, tedious, unexceptional, unexciting, uninspiring, uninteresting, unmemorable, unremarkable

dead *adj.* 1. deceased, defunct, departed, extinct, gone, inanimate, late, lifeless, passed away, perished 2. apathetic, callous, cold, dull, frigid, glassy, glazed, indifferent, inert, lukewarm, numb, paralysed, spiritless, torpid, unresponsive, wooden 3. barren, inactive, inoperative, not working, obsolete, stagnant, sterile, still, unemployed, unprofitable, useless 4. boring, dead-and-alive, dull, flat, ho-hum (*Inf.*), insipid, stale, tasteless, uninteresting, vapid 5. *Fig.*

absolute, complete, downright, entire, outright, thorough, total, unqualified, utter 6. *Inf.* dead beat (*Inf.*), exhausted, spent, tired, worn out ~*n.* 7. depth, middle, midst ~*adv.* 8. absolutely, completely, directly, entirely, exactly, totally

Antonyms active, alive, animate, animated, effective, existing, in use, lively, living, operative, productive, responsive, vivacious, working

deaden abate, alleviate, anaesthetize, benumb, blunt, check, cushion, damp, dampen, diminish, dull, hush, impair, lessen, muffle, mute, numb, paralyse, quieten, reduce, smother, stifle, suppress, weaken

deadlock cessation, dead heat, draw, full stop, halt, impasse, stalemate, standoff, standstill, tie

deadly 1. baleful, baneful, dangerous, death-dealing, deathly, destructive, fatal, lethal, malignant, mortal, noxious, pernicious, poisonous, venomous 2. cruel, grim, implacable, mortal, ruthless, savage, unrelenting 3. ashen, deathlike, deathly, ghastly, ghostly, pallid, wan, white 4. accurate, effective, exact, on target, precise, sure, true, unerring, unfailing 5. *Inf.* boring, dull, ho-hum (*Inf.*), mind-numbing, monotonous, tedious, uninteresting, wearisome

deadpan *adj.* blank, empty, expressionless, impassive, inexpressive, inscrutable, poker-faced, straight-faced

deaf *adj.* 1. hard of hearing, stone deaf, without hearing 2. indifferent, oblivious, unconcerned, unhearing, unmoved

deafen din, drown out, make deaf, split *or* burst the eardrums

deafening booming, dinning, ear-piercing, ear-splitting, intense, overpowering, piercing, resounding, ringing, thunderous

deal *v.* 1. *With* **with** attend to, cope with, handle, manage, oversee, see to, take care of, treat 2. *With* **with** concern, consider, treat (of) 3. *With* **with** act, behave, conduct oneself 4. bargain, buy and sell, do business, negotiate, sell, stock, trade, traffic, treat (with) ~*n.* 5. *Inf.* agreement, arrangement, bargain, contract, pact, transaction, understanding ~*v.* 6. allot, apportion, assign, bestow, dispense, distribute, divide, dole out, give, mete out, reward, share ~*n.* 7. amount, degree, distribution, extent, portion, quantity, share, transaction 8. cut and shuffle, distribution, hand, round, single game

dealer chandler, marketer, merchandiser, merchant, purveyor, supplier, trader, tradesman, wholesaler

dealings business, business relations, commerce, trade, traffic, transactions, truck

dear *adj.* 1. beloved, cherished, close, darling, esteemed, familiar, favourite, intimate, precious, prized, respected, treasured 2. at a premium, costly, expensive, high-priced, overpriced, pricey (*Inf.*) ~*n.* 3. angel, beloved, darling, loved one, precious, treasure ~*adv.* 4. at a heavy cost, at a high price, at great cost, dearly

Antonyms cheap, common, disliked, hated, inexpensive, worthless

dearly 1. extremely, greatly, profoundly, very much 2. affectionately, devotedly, fondly, lovingly, tenderly 3. at a heavy cost, at a high price, at great cost, dear

dearth absence, deficiency, exiguousness, famine, inadequacy, insufficiency, lack, need, paucity, poverty, scantiness, scarcity, shortage, sparsity, want

death 1. bereavement, cessation, curtains (*Inf.*), decease, demise, departure, dissolution, dying, end, exit, expiration, loss, passing, quietus, release 2. annihilation, destruction, downfall, eradication, extermination, extinction, finish, grave, obliteration, ruin, ruination, undoing

Antonyms beginning, birth, emergence, genesis, growth, origin, rise, source

deathless eternal, everlasting, immortal, imperishable, incorruptible, timeless, undying

Antonyms corporeal, earthly, ephemeral, human, mortal, passing, temporal, transient, transitory

deathly 1. cadaverous, deathlike, gaunt, ghastly, grim, haggard, pale, pallid, wan 2. deadly, extreme, fatal, intense, mortal, terrible

debacle catastrophe, collapse, defeat, devastation, disaster, downfall, fiasco, havoc, overthrow, reversal, rout, ruin, ruination

debar bar, black, blackball, deny, exclude, hinder, interdict, keep out, obstruct, preclude, prevent, prohibit, refuse admission to, restrain, segregate, shut out, stop

debase 1. abase, cheapen, degrade, demean, devalue, disgrace, dishonour, drag down, humble, humiliate, lower, reduce, shame 2. adulterate, bastardize, contaminate, corrupt, defile, depreciate, impair, pollute, taint, vitiate

Antonyms elevate, enhance, exalt, improve, purify, uplift

debased 1. adulterated, depreciated, devalued, impure, lowered, mixed, polluted, reduced 2. abandoned, base, corrupt, debauched, degraded, depraved, fallen, low, perverted, sordid, vile

Antonyms chaste, decent, ethical, good,

honourable, incorruptible, innocent, moral, pure, upright, virtuous

debasement 1. adulteration, contamination, depreciation, devaluation, pollution, reduction 2. abasement, baseness, corruption, degradation, depravation, perversion

debatable arguable, borderline, controversial, disputable, doubtful, dubious, iffy (*Inf.*), in dispute, moot, open to question, problematical, questionable, uncertain, undecided, unsettled

debate *v.* 1. argue, contend, contest, controvert, discuss, dispute, question, wrangle ~*n.* 2. altercation, argument, contention, controversy, discussion, disputation, dispute, polemic, row ~*v.* 3. cogitate, consider, deliberate, meditate upon, mull over, ponder, reflect, revolve, ruminate, weigh ~*n.* 4. cogitation, consideration, deliberation, meditation, reflection

debauch *v.* 1. corrupt, demoralize, deprave, lead astray, pervert, pollute, seduce, subvert, vitiate 2. deflower, ravish, ruin, seduce, violate ~*n.* 3. bacchanalia, bender (*Inf.*), binge (*Inf.*), bout, carousal, carouse, fling, orgy, saturnalia, spree

debauched *adj.* abandoned, corrupt, debased, degenerate, degraded, depraved, dissipated, dissolute, immoral, licentious, perverted, pervy (*Sl.*), profligate, sleazy, wanton

debauchee libertine, Lothario, playboy, profligate, rake, roué, sensualist, wanton

debauchery carousal, depravity, dissipation, dissoluteness, excess, gluttony, incontinence, indulgence, intemperance, lewdness, licentiousness, lust, orgy, overindulgence, revel

debilitate devitalize, enervate, enfeeble, exhaust, incapacitate, prostrate, relax, sap, undermine, weaken, wear out

Antonyms animate, brighten, energize, enliven, excite, fire, invigorate, pep up, perk up, rouse, stimulate, vitalize, wake up

debility decrepitude, enervation, enfeeblement, exhaustion, faintness, feebleness, frailty, incapacity, infirmity, languor, malaise, sickliness, weakness

debonair affable, buoyant, charming, cheerful, courteous, dashing, elegant, jaunty, light-hearted, refined, smooth, sprightly, suave, urbane, well-bred

debouch come forth, come out, come out in the open, disembogue, emerge, issue, sally, sortie

debrief 1. cross-examine, examine, interrogate, probe, question, quiz 2. describe, detail, report

debris bits, brash, detritus, dross, fragments, litter, pieces, remains, rubbish, rubble, ruins, waste, wreck, wreckage

debt 1. arrears, bill, claim, commitment, debit, due, duty, liability, obligation, score 2. **in debt** accountable, beholden, in arrears, in hock (*Inf., chiefly U.S.*), in the red (*Inf.*), liable, owing, responsible

debtor borrower, defaulter, insolvent, mortgagor

debunk cut down to size, deflate, disparage, expose, lampoon, mock, puncture, ridicule, show up

debut beginning, bow, coming out, entrance, first appearance, inauguration, initiation, introduction, launching, presentation

decadence corruption, debasement, decay, decline, degeneration, deterioration, dissipation, dissolution, fall, perversion, retrogression

decadent corrupt, debased, debauched, decaying, declining, degenerate, degraded, depraved, dissolute, immoral, self-indulgent

Antonyms decent, ethical, good, high-minded, honourable, incorruptible, moral, principled, proper, upright, upstanding, virtuous

decamp 1. abscond, bolt, desert, do a bunk (*Brit. sl.*), do a runner (*Sl.*), escape, flee, flit (*Inf.*), fly, fly the coop (*U.S. & Canad. inf.*), hightail (*Inf., chiefly U.S.*), hook it (*Sl.*), make off, run away, scarper (*Brit. sl.*), skedaddle (*Inf.*), sneak off, steal away, take a powder (*U.S. & Canad. sl.*), take it on the lam (*U.S. & Canad. sl.*) 2. break up camp, evacuate, march off, move off, strike camp, vacate

decant drain, draw off, pour out, tap

decapitate behead, execute, guillotine

decay *v.* 1. atrophy, crumble, decline, degenerate, deteriorate, disintegrate, dissolve, dwindle, moulder, shrivel, sink, spoil, wane, waste away, wear away, wither 2. corrode, decompose, mortify, perish, putrefy, rot ~*n.* 3. atrophy, collapse, decadence, decline, degeneracy, degeneration, deterioration, dying, fading, failing, wasting, withering 4. caries, cariosity, decomposition, gangrene, mortification, perishing, putrefaction, putrescence, putridity, rot, rotting

Antonyms *v.* expand, flourish, flower, grow, increase ~*n.* growth

decayed bad, carious, carrion, corroded, decomposed, perished, putrefied, putrid, rank, rotten, spoiled, wasted, withered

decaying crumbling, deteriorating, disintegrating, gangrenous, perishing, putrefacient, rotting, wasting away, wearing away

decease 1. *n.* death, demise, departure, dissolution, dying, release 2. *v.* buy it (*U.S. sl.*), cease, check out (*U.S. sl.*), croak (*Sl.*), die, expire, go belly-up (*Sl.*), kick it (*Sl.*), kick the bucket (*Sl.*), pass away *or* on *or* over, peg it (*Inf.*), peg out (*Inf.*), perish, pop one's clogs (*Inf.*)

deceased *adj.* dead, defunct, departed, expired, finished, former, gone, late, lifeless, lost

deceit 1. artifice, cheating, chicanery, craftiness, cunning, deceitfulness, deception, dissimulation, double-dealing, duplicity, fraud, fraudulence, guile, hypocrisy, imposition, pretence, slyness, treachery, trickery, underhandedness 2. artifice, blind, cheat, chicanery, deception, duplicity, fake, feint, fraud, imposture, misrepresentation, pretence, ruse, scam (*Sl.*), sham, shift, sting (*Inf.*), stratagem, subterfuge, swindle, trick, wile
Antonyms candour, frankness, honesty, openness, sincerity, truthfulness

deceitful counterfeit, crafty, deceiving, deceptive, designing, dishonest, disingenuous, double-dealing, duplicitous, fallacious, false, fraudulent, guileful, hypocritical, illusory, insincere, knavish (*Archaic*), sneaky, treacherous, tricky, two-faced, underhand, untrustworthy

deceive 1. bamboozle (*Inf.*), beguile, betray, cheat, con (*Inf.*), cozen, delude, disappoint, double-cross (*Inf.*), dupe, ensnare, entrap, fool, hoax, hoodwink, impose upon, kid (*Inf.*), lead (someone) on (*Inf.*), mislead, outwit, pull a fast one (*Sl.*), pull the wool over (someone's) eyes, stiff (*Sl.*), sting (*Inf.*), swindle, take for a ride (*Inf.*), take in (*Inf.*), trick 2. **be deceived by** be made a fool of, be taken in (by), be the dupe of, bite, fall for, fall into a trap, swallow (*Inf.*), swallow hook, line, and sinker (*Inf.*), take the bait

deceiver betrayer, charlatan, cheat, chiseller (*Inf.*), con man (*Inf.*), cozener, crook (*Inf.*), deluder, dissembler, double-dealer, fake, fraud, hypocrite, impostor, inveigler, mountebank, pretender, sharper, swindler, trickster

decency appropriateness, civility, correctness, courtesy, decorum, etiquette, fitness, good form, good manners, modesty, propriety, respectability, seemliness

decent 1. appropriate, becoming, befitting, chaste, comely, *comme il faut,* decorous, delicate, fit, fitting, modest, nice, polite, presentable, proper, pure, respectable, seemly, suitable 2. acceptable, adequate, ample, average, competent, fair, passable, reasonable, satisfactory, sufficient, tolerable 3. accommodating, courteous, friendly, generous, gracious, helpful, kind, obliging, thoughtful
Antonyms awkward, clumsy, discourteous, immodest, improper, inadequate, incorrect, indecent, inept, unsatisfactory, unseemly, unsuitable

deception 1. craftiness, cunning, deceit, deceitfulness, deceptiveness, dissimulation, duplicity, fraud, fraudulence, guile, hypocrisy, imposition, insincerity, legerdemain, treachery, trickery 2. artifice, bluff, canard, cheat, decoy, feint, fraud, hoax, hokum (*Sl., chiefly U.S. & Canad.*), illusion, imposture, leg-pull (*Brit. inf.*), lie, pork pie (*Brit. sl.*), porky (*Brit. sl.*), ruse, sham, snare, stratagem, subterfuge, trick, wile
Antonyms artlessness, candour, fidelity, frankness, honesty, openness, scrupulousness, straightforwardness, trustworthiness, truthfulness

deceptive ambiguous, deceitful, delusive, dishonest, fake, fallacious, false, fraudulent, illusory, misleading, mock, specious, spurious, unreliable

decide adjudge, adjudicate, choose, come to a conclusion, commit oneself, conclude, decree, determine, elect, end, make a decision, make up one's mind, purpose, reach *or* come to a decision, resolve, settle
Antonyms be indecisive, be unable to decide, blow hot and cold (*Inf.*), dither (*Chiefly Brit.*), falter, fluctuate, hesitate, hum and haw, seesaw, shillyshally (*Inf.*), swither (*Scot.*), vacillate

decided 1. absolute, categorical, certain, clear-cut, definite, distinct, express, indisputable, positive, pronounced, unambiguous, undeniable, undisputed, unequivocal, unquestionable 2. assertive, decisive, deliberate, determined, emphatic, firm, resolute, strong-willed, unfaltering, unhesitating
Antonyms doubtful, dubious, hesitant, indecisive, irresolute, questionable, undetermined, weak

decidedly absolutely, certainly, clearly, decisively, distinctly, downright, positively, unequivocally, unmistakably

deciding chief, conclusive, critical, crucial, decisive, determining, influential, prime, principal, significant

decipher construe, crack, decode, deduce, explain, figure out (*Inf.*), interpret, make out, read, reveal, solve, suss (out) (*Sl.*), understand, unfold, unravel

decision 1. arbitration, conclusion, finding, judgment, outcome, resolution, result, ruling, sentence, settlement, verdict 2. decisiveness, determination, firmness, purpose, purposefulness, resoluteness, resolution, resolve, strength of mind *or* will

decisive 1. absolute, conclusive, critical, crucial, definite, definitive, fateful, final, influential, momentous, positive, significant 2. decided, determined, firm, forceful, incisive, resolute, strong-minded, trenchant

Antonyms doubtful, hesitant, hesitating, indecisive, in two minds (*Inf.*), irresolute, pussy-footing (*Inf.*), uncertain, undecided, vacillating

deck *v.* 1. adorn, apparel (*Archaic*), array, attire, beautify, bedeck, bedight (*Archaic*), bedizen (*Archaic*), clothe, decorate, dress, embellish, festoon, garland, grace, ornament, trim 2. **deck up *or* out** doll up (*Sl.*), get ready, prettify, pretty up, prink, rig out, tog up *or* out, trick out

declaim 1. harangue, hold forth, lecture, orate, perorate, proclaim, rant, recite, speak, spiel (*Inf.*) 2. **declaim against** attack, decry, denounce, inveigh, rail

declamation address, harangue, lecture, oration, rant, recitation, speech, tirade

declamatory bombastic, discursive, grandiloquent, high-flown, incoherent, inflated, magniloquent, orotund, pompous, rhetorical, stagy, stilted, theatrical, turgid

declaration 1. acknowledgment, affirmation, assertion, attestation, averment, avowal, deposition, disclosure, protestation, revelation, statement, testimony 2. announcement, edict, manifesto, notification, proclamation, profession, promulgation, pronouncement, pronunciamento

declarative, declaratory affirmative, definite, demonstrative, enunciatory, explanatory, expository, expressive, positive

declare 1. affirm, announce, assert, asseverate, attest, aver, avow, certify, claim, confirm, maintain, proclaim, profess, pronounce, state, swear, testify, utter, validate 2. confess, convey, disclose, make known, manifest, reveal, show

declension 1. decadence, decay, decline, degeneracy, descent, deterioration, diminution, fall 2. inflection, variation

declination decline, declivity, descent, deviation, dip, divergence, inclination, obliquity, slope

decline *v.* 1. abstain, avoid, deny, forgo, refuse, reject, say 'no', send one's regrets, turn down 2. decrease, diminish, drop, dwindle, ebb, fade, fail, fall, fall off, flag, lessen, shrink, sink, wane ~*n.* 3. abatement, diminution, downturn, drop, dwindling, falling off, lessening, recession, slump ~*v.* 4. decay, degenerate, deteriorate, droop, languish, pine, weaken, worsen ~*n.* 5. decay, decrepitude, degeneration, deterioration, enfeeblement, failing, senility, weakening, worsening 6. *Archaic* consumption, phthisis, tuberculosis ~*v.* 7. descend, dip, sink, slant, slope ~*n.* 8. declivity, hill, incline, slope

Antonyms *v.* accept, agree, consent, improve, increase, rise ~*n.* improvement, rise, upswing

declivity brae (*Scot.*), declination, descent, incline, slant, slope

decompose 1. break up, crumble, decay, fall apart, fester, putrefy, rot, spoil 2. analyse, atomize, break down, break up, decompound, disintegrate, dissect, dissolve, distil, separate

decomposition atomization, breakdown, corruption, decay, disintegration, dissolution, division, putrefaction, putrescence, putridity, rot

décor colour scheme, decoration, furnishing style, ornamentation

decorate 1. adorn, beautify, bedeck, deck, embellish, enrich, festoon, grace, ornament, trim 2. colour, do up (*Inf.*), furbish, paint, paper, renovate, wallpaper 3. cite, honour, pin a medal on

decoration 1. adornment, beautification, elaboration, embellishment, enrichment, garnishing, ornamentation, trimming 2. arabesque, bauble, cartouch(e), curlicue, falderal, festoon, flounce, flourish, frill, furbelow, garnish, ornament, scroll, spangle, trimmings, trinket 3. award, badge, colours, emblem, garter, medal, order, ribbon, star

decorative adorning, arty-crafty, beautifying, enhancing, fancy, nonfunctional, ornamental, pretty

decorous appropriate, becoming, befitting, comely, *comme il faut,* correct, decent, dignified, fit, fitting, mannerly, polite, proper, refined, sedate, seemly, staid, suitable, well-behaved

Antonyms inapposite, inappropriate, malapropos, out of keeping, unbefitting, undignified, unseemly

decorum behaviour, breeding, courtliness, decency, deportment, dignity, etiquette, gentility, good grace, good manners, gravity, politeness, politesse, propriety, protocol, punctilio, respectability, seemliness

Antonyms bad manners, churlishness, impoliteness, impropriety, indecorum, rudeness, unseemliness

decoy 1. *n.* attraction, bait, ensnarement, enticement, inducement, lure, pretence, trap 2. *v.* allure, bait, deceive, ensnare, entice, entrap, inveigle, lure, seduce, tempt

decrease 1. *v.* abate, contract, curtail, cut

down, decline, diminish, drop, dwindle, ease, fall off, lessen, lower, peter out, reduce, shrink, slacken, subside, wane 2. *n.* abatement, contraction, cutback, decline, diminution, downturn, dwindling, ebb, falling off, lessening, loss, reduction, shrinkage, subsidence
Antonyms *v.* enlarge, expand, extend, increase ~*n.* expansion, extension, growth

decree 1. *n.* act, canon, command, demand, dictum, edict, enactment, law, mandate, order, ordinance, precept, proclamation, regulation, ruling, statute 2. *v.* command, decide, demand, determine, dictate, enact, establish, lay down, ordain, order, prescribe, proclaim, pronounce, rule

decrepit 1. aged, crippled, debilitated, doddering, effete, feeble, frail, incapacitated, infirm, superannuated, wasted, weak 2. antiquated, battered, beat-up (*Inf.*), broken-down, deteriorated, dilapidated, ramshackle, rickety, run-down, tumble-down, weather-beaten, worn-out

decrepitude 1. debility, dotage, feebleness, incapacity, infirmity, invalidity, old age, senility, wasting, weakness 2. decay, degeneration, deterioration, dilapidation

decry abuse, asperse, belittle, blame, blast, censure, condemn, criticize, cry down, denounce, depreciate, derogate, detract, devalue, discredit, disparage, excoriate, lambast(e), put down, rail against, run down, tear into (*Inf.*), traduce, underestimate, underrate, undervalue

dedicate 1. commit, devote, give over to, pledge, surrender 2. address, assign, inscribe, offer 3. bless, consecrate, hallow, sanctify, set apart

dedicated committed, devoted, enthusiastic, given over to, purposeful, single-minded, sworn, wholehearted, zealous
Antonyms indifferent, uncaring, uncommitted, unconcerned, uninterested, unresponsive

dedication 1. adherence, allegiance, commitment, devotedness, devotion, faithfulness, loyalty, single-mindedness, wholeheartedness 2. address, inscription, message 3. consecration, hallowing, sanctification
Antonyms apathy, coolness, indifference, insensibility, torpor, unconcern, uninterestedness

deduce conclude, derive, draw, gather, glean, infer, reason, take to mean, understand

deducible derivable, inferable, to be inferred, traceable

deduct decrease by, knock off (*Inf.*), reduce by, remove, subtract, take away, take from, take off, take out, withdraw
Antonyms add, add to, enlarge

deduction 1. assumption, conclusion, consequence, corollary, finding, inference, reasoning, result 2. abatement, allowance, decrease, diminution, discount, reduction, subtraction, withdrawal

deed 1. achievement, act, action, exploit, fact, feat, performance, reality, truth 2. *Law* contract, document, indenture, instrument, title, title deed, transaction

deem account, believe, conceive, consider, esteem, estimate, hold, imagine, judge, reckon, regard, suppose, think

deep *adj.* 1. abyssal, bottomless, broad, far, profound, unfathomable, wide, yawning 2. abstract, abstruse, arcane, esoteric, hidden, mysterious, obscure, recondite, secret 3. acute, discerning, learned, penetrating, sagacious, wise 4. artful, astute, canny, cunning, designing, devious, insidious, knowing, scheming, shrewd 5. extreme, grave, great, intense, profound, unqualified 6. absorbed, engrossed, immersed, lost, preoccupied, rapt 7. *Of a colour* dark, intense, rich, strong, vivid 8. *Of a sound* bass, booming, full-toned, low, low-pitched, resonant, sonorous ~*n.* 9. *Usually preceded by* the briny (*Inf.*), high seas, main, ocean, sea 10. culmination, dead, middle, mid point ~*adv.* 11. deeply, far down, far into, late
Antonyms high, light, pale, shallow, sharp, simple, superficial

deepen 1. dig out, dredge, excavate, hollow, scoop out, scrape out 2. grow, increase, intensify, magnify, reinforce, strengthen

deeply 1. completely, gravely, profoundly, seriously, severely, thoroughly, to the heart, to the quick 2. acutely, affectingly, distressingly, feelingly, intensely, mournfully, movingly, passionately, sadly

deep-rooted *or* **deep-seated** confirmed, entrenched, fixed, ineradicable, ingrained, inveterate, rooted, settled, subconscious, unconscious
Antonyms eradicable, exterior, external, on the surface, peripheral, shallow, skin-deep, slight, superficial, surface

deface blemish, deform, destroy, disfigure, impair, injure, mar, mutilate, obliterate, spoil, sully, tarnish, total (*Sl.*), trash (*Sl.*), vandalize

defacement blemish, damage, destruction, disfigurement, distortion, impairment, injury, mutilation, vandalism

de facto 1. *adv.* actually, in effect, in fact, in reality, really 2. *adj.* actual, existing, real

defalcation default, deficiency, deficit,

embezzlement, fraud, misappropriation, shortage

defamation aspersion, calumny, character assassination, denigration, disparagement, libel, obloquy, opprobrium, scandal, slander, slur, smear, traducement, vilification

defamatory abusive, calumnious, contumelious, denigrating, derogatory, disparaging, injurious, insulting, libellous, slanderous, vilifying, vituperative

defame asperse, bad-mouth (*Sl., chiefly U.S. & Canad.*), belie, besmirch, blacken, calumniate, cast a slur on, cast aspersions on, denigrate, detract, discredit, disgrace, dishonour, disparage, knock (*Inf.*), libel, malign, rubbish (*Inf.*), slag (off) (*Sl.*), slander, smear, speak evil of, stigmatize, traduce, vilify, vituperate

default 1. *n.* absence, defect, deficiency, dereliction, failure, fault, lack, lapse, neglect, nonpayment, omission, want 2. *v.* bilk, defraud, dodge, evade, fail, levant (*Brit.*), neglect, rat (*Inf.*), swindle, welsh (*Sl.*)

defaulter delinquent, embezzler, levanter (*Brit.*), nonpayer, offender, peculator, welsher (*Sl.*)

defeat *v.* 1. beat, blow out of the water (*Sl.*), clobber (*Sl.*), conquer, crush, lick (*Inf.*), master, overpower, overthrow, overwhelm, quell, repulse, rout, run rings around (*Inf.*), subdue, subjugate, tank (*Sl.*), undo, vanquish, wipe the floor with (*Inf.*) 2. baffle, balk, confound, disappoint, discomfit, foil, frustrate, get the better of, ruin, thwart ~*n.* 3. beating, conquest, debacle, overthrow, pasting (*Sl.*), repulse, rout, trouncing, vanquishment 4. disappointment, discomfiture, failure, frustration, rebuff, repulse, reverse, setback, thwarting

Antonyms *v.* bow, lose, submit, succumb, surrender, yield ~*n.* success, triumph, victory

defeated balked, beaten, bested, checkmated, conquered, crushed, licked (*Inf.*), overcome, overpowered, overwhelmed, routed, thrashed, thwarted, trounced, vanquished, worsted

Antonyms conquering, dominant, glorious, successful, triumphal, triumphant, undefeated, victorious, winning

defeatist 1. *n.* pessimist, prophet of doom, quitter, submitter, yielder 2. *adj.* pessimistic

defecate crap (*Taboo sl.*), egest, empty, evacuate (*Physiol.*), excrete, move, open the bowels, pass a motion, shit (*Taboo sl.*), void excrement

defecation egestion, elimination, emptying *or* opening of the bowels, evacuation (*Physiol.*), excrement, excretion, motion, movement, voiding excrement

defect *n.* 1. blemish, blotch, error, failing, fault, flaw, foible, imperfection, mistake, spot, taint, want 2. absence, default, deficiency, frailty, inadequacy, lack, shortcoming, weakness ~*v.* 3. abandon, apostatize, break faith, change sides, desert, go over, rebel, revolt, tergiversate, walk out on (*Inf.*)

defection abandonment, apostasy, backsliding, dereliction, desertion, rebellion, revolt

defective 1. broken, deficient, faulty, flawed, imperfect, inadequate, incomplete, insufficient, not working, out of order, scant, short 2. abnormal, mentally deficient, retarded, subnormal

Antonyms adequate, intact, normal, perfect, whole, working

defector apostate, deserter, rat (*Inf.*), recreant (*Archaic*), renegade, runagate (*Archaic*), tergiversator, turncoat

defence 1. armament, cover, deterrence, guard, immunity, protection, resistance, safeguard, security, shelter 2. barricade, bastion, buckler, bulwark, buttress, fastness, fortification, rampart, shield 3. apologia, apology, argument, excuse, exoneration, explanation, extenuation, justification, plea, vindication 4. *Law* alibi, case, declaration, denial, plea, pleading, rebuttal, testimony

defenceless endangered, exposed, helpless, naked, powerless, unarmed, unguarded, unprotected, vulnerable, wide open

Antonyms free from harm, guarded, out of harm's way, protected, safe, safe and sound, secure

defend 1. cover, fortify, guard, keep safe, preserve, protect, safeguard, screen, secure, shelter, shield, ward off, watch over 2. assert, champion, endorse, espouse, justify, maintain, plead, speak up for, stand by, stand up for, stick up for (*Inf.*), support, sustain, uphold, vindicate

defendant appellant, defence, litigant, offender, prisoner at the bar, respondent, the accused

defender 1. bodyguard, escort, guard, protector 2. advocate, champion, patron, sponsor, supporter, vindicator

defensible 1. holdable, impregnable, safe, secure, unassailable 2. justifiable, pardonable, permissible, plausible, tenable, valid, vindicable

Antonyms faulty, inexcusable, insupportable, unforgivable, unjustifiable, unpardonable, untenable, wrong

defensive averting, defending, on the defensive, opposing, protective, safeguarding, uptight (*Inf.*), watchful, withstanding

defensively at bay, in defence, in self-defence, on guard, on the defensive, suspiciously

defer[1] adjourn, delay, hold over, postpone, procrastinate, prorogue, protract, put off, put on ice, put on the back burner (*Inf.*), set aside, shelve, suspend, table, take a rain check on (*U.S. & Canad. inf.*)

defer[2] accede, bow, capitulate, comply, give in, give way to, respect, submit, yield

deference 1. acquiescence, capitulation, complaisance, compliance, obedience, obeisance, submission, yielding 2. attention, civility, consideration, courtesy, esteem, homage, honour, obeisance, politeness, regard, respect, reverence, thoughtfulness, veneration

Antonyms (*sense 1*) disobedience, insubordination, noncompliance, nonobservance, revolt (*sense 2*) contempt, discourtesy, dishonour, disregard, disrespect, impertinence, impoliteness, impudence, incivility, insolence, irreverence, lack of respect, rudeness

deferential civil, complaisant, considerate, courteous, dutiful, ingratiating, obedient, obeisant, obsequious, polite, regardful, respectful, reverential, submissive

deferment, deferral adjournment, delay, moratorium, postponement, putting off, stay, suspension

defiance challenge, confrontation, contempt, contumacy, disobedience, disregard, insolence, insubordination, opposition, provocation, rebelliousness, recalcitrance, spite

Antonyms accordance, acquiescence, compliance, deference, obedience, observance, regard, respect, subservience

defiant aggressive, audacious, bold, challenging, contumacious, daring, disobedient, insolent, insubordinate, mutinous, provocative, rebellious, recalcitrant, refractory, truculent

Antonyms cowardly, meek, obedient, respectful, submissive

deficiency 1. defect, demerit, failing, fault, flaw, frailty, imperfection, shortcoming, weakness 2. absence, dearth, deficit, inadequacy, insufficiency, lack, scantiness, scarcity, shortage

Antonyms abundance, adequacy, sufficient, superfluity, surfeit

deficient 1. defective, faulty, flawed, impaired, imperfect, incomplete, inferior, unsatisfactory, weak 2. exiguous, inadequate, insufficient, lacking, meagre, pathetic, scant, scanty, scarce, short, skimpy, wanting

deficit arrears, default, deficiency, loss, shortage, shortfall

defile[1] *v.* 1. befoul, contaminate, corrupt, dirty, make foul, pollute, smear, smirch, soil, taint, tarnish, vitiate 2. besmirch, debase, degrade, disgrace, dishonour, smirch, stain, sully 3. desecrate, profane, treat sacrilegiously 4. abuse, deflower, molest, rape, ravish, seduce, violate

defile[2] *n.* gorge, gully, pass, passage, ravine, way through

defiled besmirched, desecrated, dishonoured, impure, polluted, profaned, ravished, spoilt, tainted, unclean

Antonyms chaste, clean, immaculate, innocent, spotless, uncontaminated, uncorrupted, undefiled, unstained, unsullied, untainted

defilement contamination, corruption, debasement, degradation, depravity, desecration, disgrace, pollution, sullying, violation

definable apparent, definite, describable, determinable, explicable, perceptible, specific

define 1. characterize, describe, designate, detail, determine, explain, expound, interpret, specify, spell out 2. bound, circumscribe, delimit, delineate, demarcate, limit, mark out, outline

definite 1. clear, clear-cut, clearly defined, determined, exact, explicit, express, fixed, marked, obvious, particular, precise, specific 2. assured, certain, decided, guaranteed, positive, settled, sure

Antonyms confused, fuzzy, general, hazy, ill-defined, imprecise, indefinite, indeterminate, indistinct, inexact, loose, obscure, uncertain, unclear, undetermined, vague

definitely absolutely, beyond any doubt, categorically, certainly, clearly, decidedly, easily, far and away, finally, indubitably, obviously, plainly, positively, surely, undeniably, unequivocally, unmistakably, unquestionably, without doubt, without fail, without question

definition 1. clarification, description, elucidation, explanation, exposition, statement of meaning 2. delimitation, delineation, demarcation, determination, fixing, outlining, settling 3. clarity, contrast, distinctness, focus, precision, sharpness

definitive absolute, authoritative, complete, conclusive, decisive, exhaustive, final, perfect, reliable, ultimate

deflate 1. collapse, contract, empty, exhaust, flatten, puncture, shrink, void 2. chasten, dash, debunk (*Inf.*), disconcert, dispirit, humble, humiliate, mortify, put

down (*Sl.*), squash, take the wind out of (someone's) sails 3. *Economics* decrease, depreciate, depress, devalue, diminish, reduce
Antonyms aerate, amplify, balloon, bloat, blow up, boost, dilate, distend, enlarge, exaggerate, expand, increase, inflate, puff up *or* out, pump up, swell

deflect bend, deviate, diverge, glance off, ricochet, shy, sidetrack, slew, swerve, turn, turn aside, twist, veer, wind

deflection aberration, bend, declination, deviation, divergence, drift, refraction, swerve, veer

deflower 1. assault, force, molest, rape, ravish, ruin, seduce, violate 2. defile, desecrate, despoil, harm, mar, spoil, violate

deform 1. buckle, contort, distort, gnarl, malform, mangle, misshape, twist, warp 2. cripple, deface, disfigure, injure, maim, mar, mutilate, ruin, spoil

deformed 1. bent, blemished, crippled, crooked, disfigured, distorted, maimed, malformed, mangled, marred, misbegotten, misshapen 2. depraved, gross, offensive, perverted, twisted, warped

deformity 1. abnormality, defect, disfigurement, distortion, irregularity, malformation, misproportion, misshapenness, ugliness 2. corruption, depravity, grossness, hatefulness, vileness

defraud beguile, bilk, cheat, con (*Inf.*), cozen, delude, diddle (*Inf.*), do (*Sl.*), dupe, embezzle, fleece, gull (*Archaic*), gyp (*Sl.*), outwit, pilfer, pull a fast one on (*Inf.*), rip off (*Sl.*), rob, rook (*Sl.*), skin (*Sl.*), stiff (*Sl.*), swindle, trick

defray clear, cover, discharge, foot the bill, liquidate, meet, pay, settle

defrayal, defrayment clearance, discharge, liquidation, payment, settlement

deft able, adept, adroit, agile, clever, dexterous, expert, handy, neat, nimble, proficient, skilful
Antonyms awkward, bumbling, cack-handed (*Inf.*), clumsy, gauche, inept, maladroit, unskilful

defunct 1. dead, deceased, departed, extinct, gone 2. a dead letter, bygone, expired, inoperative, invalid, nonexistent, not functioning, obsolete, out of commission

defy 1. beard, brave, challenge, confront, contemn, dare, despise, disregard, face, flout, hurl defiance at, provoke, scorn, slight, spurn 2. baffle, defeat, elude, foil, frustrate, repel, repulse, resist, thwart, withstand

degeneracy 1. corruption, decadence, degradation, depravity, dissoluteness, immorality, inferiority, meanness, poorness, turpitude 2. debasement, decay, decline, decrease, depravation, deterioration

degenerate 1. *adj.* base, corrupt, debased, debauched, decadent, degenerated, degraded, depraved, deteriorated, dissolute, fallen, immoral, low, mean, perverted, pervy (*Sl.*) 2. *v.* decay, decline, decrease, deteriorate, fall off, lapse, regress, retrogress, rot, sink, slip, worsen

degeneration debasement, decline, degeneracy, descent, deterioration, dissipation, dissolution, regression

degradation 1. abasement, debasement, decadence, decline, degeneracy, degeneration, demotion, derogation, deterioration, downgrading, perversion 2. discredit, disgrace, dishonour, humiliation, ignominy, mortification, shame

degrade 1. cheapen, corrupt, debase, demean, deteriorate, discredit, disgrace, dishonour, humble, humiliate, impair, injure, pervert, shame, vitiate 2. break, cashier, demote, depose, downgrade, lower, reduce to inferior rank 3. adulterate, dilute, doctor, mix, thin, water, water down, weaken
Antonyms dignify, elevate, enhance, ennoble, honour, improve, promote, raise

degraded abandoned, base, corrupt, debased, debauched, decadent, depraved, despicable, disgraced, disreputable, dissolute, low, mean, profligate, sordid, vicious, vile

degrading cheapening, contemptible, debasing, demeaning, disgraceful, dishonourable, humiliating, infra dig (*Inf.*), lowering, shameful, undignified, unworthy

degree 1. class, grade, level, order, position, rank, standing, station, status 2. division, extent, gradation, grade, interval, limit, mark, measure, notch, point, rung, scale, stage, step, unit 3. ambit, calibre, extent, intensity, level, measure, proportion, quality, quantity, range, rate, ratio, scale, scope, severity, standard 4. **by degrees** bit by bit, gently, gradually, imperceptibly, inch by inch, little by little, slowly, step by step

dehydrate desiccate, drain, dry out, dry up, evaporate, exsiccate, parch

deification apotheosis, elevation, ennoblement, exaltation, glorification, idolization

deify apotheosize, elevate, ennoble, enthrone, exalt, extol, glorify, idealize, idolize, immortalize, venerate, worship

deign condescend, consent, deem worthy, lower oneself, see fit, stoop, think fit

deity celestial being, divine being, divinity, god, goddess, godhead, idol, immortal, supreme being

deject cast down, dampen, daunt, demoralize, depress, discourage, dishearten, dismay, dispirit

dejected blue, cast down, crestfallen, depressed, despondent, disconsolate, disheartened, dismal, doleful, down, downcast, downhearted, gloomy, glum, low, low-spirited, melancholy, miserable, morose, sad, sick as a parrot (*Inf.*), woebegone, wretched
Antonyms blithe, cheerful, chirpy (*Inf.*), encouraged, genial, happy, joyous, light-hearted, upbeat (*Inf.*)

dejection blues, depression, despair, despondency, doldrums, downheartedness, dumps (*Inf.*), gloom, gloominess, heavy-heartedness, low spirits, melancholy, sadness, sorrow, the hump (*Brit. inf.*), unhappiness

de jure according to the law, by right, legally, rightfully

delay *v.* 1. defer, hold over, postpone, procrastinate, prolong, protract, put off, put on the back burner (*Inf.*), shelve, stall, suspend, table, take a rain check on (*U.S. & Canad. inf.*), temporize ~*n.* 2. deferment, postponement, procrastination, stay, suspension ~*v.* 3. arrest, bog down, check, detain, halt, hinder, hold back, hold up, impede, obstruct, retard, set back, slow up, stop ~*n.* 4. check, detention, hindrance, hold-up, impediment, interruption, interval, obstruction, setback, stoppage, wait ~*v.* 5. dawdle, dilly-dally (*Inf.*), drag, lag, linger, loiter, tarry ~*n.* 6. dawdling, dilly-dallying (*Inf.*), lingering, loitering, tarrying
Antonyms accelerate, advance, dispatch, expedite, facilitate, forward, hasten, hurry, precipitate, press, promote, quicken, rush, speed (up), urge

delectable adorable, agreeable, appetizing, charming, dainty, delicious, delightful, enjoyable, enticing, gratifying, inviting, luscious, lush, pleasant, pleasurable, satisfying, scrumptious (*Inf.*), tasty, toothsome, yummy (*Sl.*)
Antonyms awful, disagreeable, disgusting, distasteful, dreadful, horrible, horrid, nasty, offensive, terrible, unappetizing, unpleasant, yucky *or* yukky (*Sl.*)

delectation amusement, delight, diversion, enjoyment, entertainment, gratification, happiness, jollies (*Sl.*), pleasure, refreshment, relish, satisfaction

delegate *n.* 1. agent, ambassador, commissioner, deputy, envoy, legate, representative, vicar ~*v.* 2. accredit, appoint, authorize, commission, depute, designate, empower, mandate 3. assign, consign, devolve, entrust, give, hand over, pass on, relegate, transfer

delegation 1. commission, contingent, deputation, embassy, envoys, legation, mission 2. assignment, commissioning, committal, deputizing, devolution, entrustment, relegation

delete blot out, blue-pencil, cancel, cross out, cut out, dele, edit, edit out, efface, erase, excise, expunge, obliterate, remove, rub out, strike out

deleterious bad, damaging, destructive, detrimental, harmful, hurtful, injurious, pernicious, prejudicial, ruinous

deliberate *v.* 1. cogitate, consider, consult, debate, discuss, meditate, mull over, ponder, reflect, think, weigh ~*adj.* 2. calculated, conscious, considered, designed, intentional, planned, prearranged, premeditated, purposeful, studied, thoughtful, wilful 3. careful, cautious, circumspect, heedful, measured, methodical, ponderous, prudent, slow, thoughtful, unhurried, wary
Antonyms (*sense 2*) accidental, inadvertent, unconscious, unintended, unpremeditated, unthinking (*sense 3*) fast, haphazard, hasty, heedless, hurried, impetuous, impulsive, rash

deliberately by design, calculatingly, consciously, determinedly, emphatically, in cold blood, intentionally, knowingly, on purpose, pointedly, resolutely, studiously, wilfully, wittingly

deliberation 1. calculation, care, carefulness, caution, circumspection, cogitation, consideration, coolness, forethought, meditation, prudence, purpose, reflection, speculation, study, thought, wariness 2. conference, consultation, debate, discussion

delicacy 1. accuracy, daintiness, elegance, exquisiteness, fineness, lightness, nicety, precision, subtlety 2. debility, flimsiness, fragility, frailness, frailty, infirmity, slenderness, tenderness, weakness 3. discrimination, fastidiousness, finesse, purity, refinement, sensibility, sensitiveness, sensitivity, tact, taste 4. *bonne bouche,* dainty, luxury, relish, savoury, titbit, treat

delicate 1. ailing, debilitated, flimsy, fragile, frail, sickly, slender, slight, tender, weak 2. choice, dainty, delicious, elegant, exquisite, fine, graceful, savoury, tender 3. faint, muted, pastel, soft, subdued, subtle 4. accurate, deft, detailed, minute, precise, skilled 5. considerate, diplomatic, discreet, sensitive, tactful 6. critical, difficult, precarious, sensitive, sticky (*Inf.*), ticklish, touchy 7. careful, critical, discriminating,

fastidious, nice, prudish, pure, refined, scrupulous, squeamish
Antonyms bright, careless, coarse, crude, harsh, healthy, inconsiderate, indelicate, insensitive, rough, strong, unrefined

delicately carefully, daintily, deftly, elegantly, exquisitely, fastidiously, finely, gracefully, lightly, precisely, sensitively, skilfully, softly, subtly, tactfully

delicious 1. ambrosial, appetizing, choice, dainty, delectable, luscious, mouthwatering, nectareous, palatable, savoury, scrumptious (*Inf.*), tasty, toothsome, yummy (*Sl.*) 2. agreeable, charming, delightful, enjoyable, entertaining, exquisite, pleasant, pleasing
Antonyms disagreeable, distasteful, unpleasant

delight *n.* 1. ecstasy, enjoyment, felicity, gladness, gratification, happiness, jollies (*Sl.*), joy, pleasure, rapture, transport ~*v.* 2. amuse, charm, cheer, divert, enchant, gratify, please, ravish, rejoice, satisfy, thrill 3. *With* **in** appreciate, enjoy, feast on, glory in, indulge in, like, love, luxuriate in, relish, revel in, savour
Antonyms *n.* disapprobation, disfavour, dislike, displeasure, dissatisfaction, distaste ~*v.* disgust, displease, dissatisfy, gall, irk, offend, upset, vex

delighted captivated, charmed, cock-a-hoop, ecstatic, elated, enchanted, gladdened, happy, joyous, jubilant, overjoyed, over the moon (*Inf.*), pleased, rapt, thrilled

delightful agreeable, amusing, captivating, charming, congenial, delectable, enchanting, engaging, enjoyable, entertaining, fascinating, gratifying, heavenly, pleasant, pleasing, pleasurable, rapturous, ravishing, thrilling
Antonyms disagreeable, displeasing, distasteful, horrid, nasty, unpleasant

delimit bound, define, demarcate, determine, fix, mark (out)

delineate characterize, chart, contour, depict, describe, design, draw, figure, map out, outline, paint, picture, portray, render, sketch, trace

delineation account, chart, depiction, description, design, diagram, drawing, outline, picture, portrait, portrayal, representation, tracing

delinquency crime, fault, misbehaviour, misconduct, misdeed, misdemeanour, offence, wrongdoing

delinquent criminal, culprit, defaulter, juvenile delinquent, lawbreaker, malefactor, miscreant, offender, villain, wrongdoer, young offender

delirious 1. crazy, demented, deranged, incoherent, insane, light-headed, mad, raving, unhinged 2. beside oneself, carried away, corybantic, ecstatic, excited, frantic, frenzied, hysterical, wild
Antonyms calm, clear-headed, coherent, *compos mentis,* in one's right mind, lucid, rational, sane, sensible

delirium 1. aberration, derangement, hallucination, insanity, lunacy, madness, raving 2. ecstasy, fever, frenzy, fury, hysteria, passion, rage

deliver 1. bear, bring, carry, cart, convey, distribute, transport 2. cede, commit, give up, grant, hand over, make over, relinquish, resign, surrender, transfer, turn over, yield 3. acquit, discharge, emancipate, free, liberate, loose, ransom, redeem, release, rescue, save 4. announce, declare, give, give forth, present, proclaim, pronounce, publish, read, utter 5. administer, aim, deal, direct, give, inflict, launch, strike, throw 6. discharge, dispense, feed, give forth, provide, purvey, release, supply

deliverance emancipation, escape, liberation, ransom, redemption, release, rescue, salvation

delivery 1. consignment, conveyance, dispatch, distribution, handing over, surrender, transfer, transmission, transmittal 2. articulation, elocution, enunciation, intonation, speech, utterance 3. *Medical* childbirth, confinement, labour, parturition 4. deliverance, escape, liberation, release, rescue

delude bamboozle (*Inf.*), beguile, cheat, con (*Inf.*), cozen, deceive, dupe, fool, gull (*Archaic*), hoax, hoodwink, impose on, kid (*Inf.*), lead up the garden path (*Inf.*), misguide, mislead, take in (*Inf.*), trick

deluge *n.* 1. cataclysm, downpour, flood, inundation, overflowing, spate, torrent 2. *Fig.* avalanche, barrage, flood, rush, spate, torrent ~*v.* 3. douse, drench, drown, flood, inundate, soak, submerge, swamp 4. *Fig.* engulf, inundate, overload, overrun, overwhelm, swamp

delusion deception, error, fallacy, false impression, fancy, hallucination, illusion, misapprehension, misbelief, misconception, mistake, phantasm, self-deception

delusive chimerical, deceptive, fallacious, illusive, illusory, misleading, specious, spurious

de luxe choice, costly, elegant, exclusive, expensive, gorgeous, grand, luxurious, opulent, palatial, plush (*Inf.*), rich, select, special, splendid, splendiferous (*Facetious*), sumptuous, superior

delve burrow, dig into, examine, explore, ferret out, investigate, look into, probe, ransack, research, rummage, search, unearth

demagogue agitator, firebrand, haranguer, rabble-rouser, soapbox orator

demand *v.* 1. ask, challenge, inquire, interrogate, question, request 2. call for, cry out for, entail, involve, necessitate, need, require, take, want 3. claim, exact, expect, insist on, order ~*n.* 4. bidding, charge, inquiry, interrogation, order, question, request, requisition 5. call, claim, market, necessity, need, requirement, want 6. **in demand** fashionable, in vogue, needed, popular, requested, sought after
Antonyms *v.* come up with, contribute, furnish, give, grant, produce, provide, supply, yield

demanding 1. challenging, difficult, exacting, exhausting, exigent, hard, taxing, tough, trying, wearing 2. clamorous, imperious, importunate, insistent, nagging, pressing, urgent
Antonyms a piece of cake (*Inf.*), child's play (*Inf.*), easy, easy-peasy (*Sl.*), effortless, facile, no bother, painless, simple, straightforward, uncomplicated, undemanding

demarcate define, delimit, determine, differentiate, distinguish between, fix, mark, separate

demarcation 1. bound, boundary, confine, enclosure, limit, margin, pale 2. delimitation, differentiation, distinction, division, separation

demean abase, debase, degrade, descend, humble, lower, stoop

demeanour air, bearing, behaviour, carriage, comportment, conduct, deportment, manner, mien

demented barking (*Sl.*), barking mad (*Sl.*), crackbrained, crackpot (*Inf.*), crazed, crazy, daft (*Inf.*), deranged, distraught, dotty (*Sl., chiefly Brit.*), foolish, frenzied, idiotic, insane, loopy (*Inf.*), lunatic, mad, maniacal, manic, *non compos mentis,* not the full shilling (*Inf.*), off one's trolley (*Sl.*), out to lunch (*Inf.*), unbalanced, unhinged, up the pole (*Inf.*)
Antonyms all there (*Inf.*), *compos mentis,* in one's right mind, lucid, mentally sound, normal, of sound mind, rational, reasonable, sensible, sound

demise *n.* 1. death, decease, departure, expiration 2. collapse, dissolution, downfall, end, failure, fall, ruin, termination 3. *Law* alienation, conveyance, transfer, transmission ~*v.* 4. *Law* bequeath, convey, grant, leave, transfer, will

democracy commonwealth, government by the people, representative government, republic

democratic autonomous, egalitarian, popular, populist, representative, republican, self-governing

demolish 1. bulldoze, destroy, dismantle, flatten, knock down, level, overthrow, pulverize, raze, ruin, tear down, total (*Sl.*), trash (*Sl.*) 2. *Fig.* annihilate, blow out of the water (*Sl.*), defeat, destroy, lick (*Inf.*), master, overthrow, overturn, tank (*Sl.*), undo, wipe the floor with (*Inf.*), wreck 3. consume, devour, eat, gobble up, put away
Antonyms build, construct, create, repair, restore, strengthen

demolition bulldozing, destruction, explosion, knocking down, levelling, razing, wrecking

demon 1. devil, evil spirit, fiend, ghoul, goblin, malignant spirit 2. *Fig.* devil, fiend, ghoul, monster, rogue, villain 3. ace (*Inf.*), addict, fanatic, fiend, go-getter (*Inf.*), master, wizard 4. daemon, daimon, genius, guardian spirit, ministering angel, numen

demonic, demoniac, demoniacal 1. devilish, diabolic, diabolical, fiendish, hellish, infernal, satanic 2. crazed, frantic, frenetic, frenzied, furious, hectic, like one possessed, mad, maniacal, manic

demonstrable attestable, axiomatic, certain, evident, evincible, incontrovertible, indubitable, irrefutable, obvious, palpable, positive, provable, self-evident, undeniable, unmistakable, verifiable

demonstrate 1. display, establish, evidence, evince, exhibit, indicate, manifest, prove, show, testify to 2. describe, explain, illustrate, make clear, show how, teach 3. march, parade, picket, protest, rally

demonstration 1. affirmation, confirmation, display, evidence, exhibition, expression, illustration, manifestation, proof, substantiation, testimony, validation 2. description, explanation, exposition, presentation, test, trial 3. march, mass lobby, parade, picket, protest, rally, sit-in

demonstrative 1. affectionate, effusive, emotional, expansive, expressive, gushing, loving, open, unreserved, unrestrained 2. evincive, explanatory, expository, illustrative, indicative, symptomatic
Antonyms (*sense 1*) aloof, cold, contained, distant, formal, impassive, reserved, restrained, stiff, unaffectionate, undemonstrative, unemotional, unresponsive

demoralization 1. agitation, crushing, devitalization, discomfiture, enervation, lowering *or* loss of morale, panic, perturbation, trepidation, unmanning, weakening 2. cor~

ruption, debasement, depravation, lowering, perversion, vitiation

demoralize 1. cripple, daunt, deject, depress, disconcert, discourage, dishearten, dispirit, enfeeble, psych out (*Inf.*), rattle (*Inf.*), sap, shake, undermine, unnerve, weaken 2. corrupt, debase, debauch, deprave, lower, pervert, vitiate

Antonyms (*sense 1*) boost, cheer, egg on, encourage, hearten, spur

demoralized 1. broken, crushed, depressed, discouraged, disheartened, dispirited, downcast, sick as a parrot (*Inf.*), subdued, unmanned, unnerved, weakened 2. bad, base, corrupt, degenerate, depraved, dissolute, immoral, low, reprobate, sinful, wicked

demote declass, degrade, disrate (*Naval*), downgrade, kick downstairs (*Sl.*), lower in rank, relegate

Antonyms advance, elevate, kick upstairs (*Inf.*), prefer, raise, upgrade

demulcent calming, easing, emollient, lenitive, mild, mollifying, relieving, sedative, softening, soothing

demur 1. *v.* balk, cavil, disagree, dispute, doubt, hesitate, object, pause, protest, refuse, take exception, waver 2. *n.* compunction, demurral, demurrer, dissent, hesitation, misgiving, objection, protest, qualm, scruple

demure 1. decorous, diffident, grave, modest, reserved, reticent, retiring, sedate, shy, sober, staid, unassuming 2. affected, bashful, coy, priggish, prim, prissy (*Inf.*), prudish, strait-laced

Antonyms brash, brazen, forward, immodest, impudent, shameless

den 1. cave, cavern, haunt, hide-out, hole, lair, shelter 2. cloister, cubbyhole, hideaway, retreat, sanctuary, sanctum, snuggery, study

denial adjuration, contradiction, disavowal, disclaimer, dismissal, dissent, negation, prohibition, rebuff, refusal, rejection, renunciation, repudiation, repulse, retraction, veto

Antonyms acknowledgment, admission, affirmation, avowal, confession, declaration, disclosure, divulgence, profession, revelation

denigrate asperse, bad-mouth (*Sl., chiefly U.S. & Canad.*), belittle, besmirch, blacken, calumniate, decry, defame, disparage, impugn, knock (*Inf.*), malign, revile, rubbish (*Inf.*), run down, slag (off) (*Sl.*), slander, vilify

Antonyms acclaim, admire, approve, cheer, compliment, eulogize, extol, honour, laud, praise

denigration aspersion, backbiting, defamation, detraction, disparagement, obloquy, scandal, scurrility, slander, vilification

denizen citizen, dweller, inhabitant, occupant, resident

denominate call, christen, designate, dub, entitle, name, phrase, style, term

denomination 1. belief, communion, creed, persuasion, religious group, school, sect 2. grade, size, unit, value 3. body, category, class, classification, group 4. appellation, designation, label, name, style, term, title

denotation designation, indication, meaning, signification, specification

denote betoken, designate, express, imply, import, indicate, mark, mean, show, signify, typify

dénouement climax, conclusion, culmination, finale, outcome, resolution, solution, termination, upshot

denounce accuse, arraign, attack, brand, castigate, censure, condemn, declaim against, decry, denunciate, excoriate, impugn, proscribe, revile, stigmatize, vilify

dense 1. close, close-knit, compact, compressed, condensed, heavy, impenetrable, opaque, solid, substantial, thick, thickset 2. blockish, braindead (*Inf.*), crass, dozy (*Brit. inf.*), dull, obtuse, slow, slow-witted, stolid, stupid, thick, thick-witted

Antonyms alert, bright, clever, intelligent, light, quick, scattered, sparse, thin, transparent

density 1. body, bulk, closeness, compactness, consistency, crowdedness, denseness, impenetrability, mass, solidity, thickness, tightness 2. crassness, dullness, obtuseness, slowness, stolidity, stupidity, thickness

dent 1. *n.* chip, concavity, crater, depression, dimple, dip, hollow, impression, indentation, pit 2. *v.* depress, dint, gouge, hollow, imprint, make a dent in, make concave, press in, push in

denude bare, divest, expose, lay bare, strip, uncover

denunciate castigate, condemn, curse, damn, denounce, stigmatize, vituperate

denunciation accusation, castigation, censure, character assassination, condemnation, criticism, denouncement, fulmination, incrimination, invective, obloquy, stick (*Sl.*), stigmatization

denunciatory accusatory, censorious, comminatory, condemnatory, fulminatory, incriminatory, recriminatory, reproachful

deny 1. contradict, disagree with, disprove, gainsay (*Archaic or literary*), oppose, re-

buff, rebut, refute 2. abjure, disavow, discard, disclaim, disown, recant, renege, renounce, repudiate, retract, revoke 3. begrudge, decline, disallow, forbid, negative, refuse, reject, turn down, veto, withhold
Antonyms accept, acknowledge, admit, affirm, agree, allow, concede, confirm, grant, let, permit, receive, recognize

deodorant air freshener, antiperspirant, deodorizer, disinfectant, fumigant

deodorize aerate, disinfect, freshen, fumigate, purify, refresh, ventilate

depart 1. absent (oneself), decamp, disappear, escape, exit, go, go away, hook it (*Sl.*), leave, migrate, quit, remove, retire, retreat, set forth, slope off, start out, take (one's) leave, vanish, withdraw 2. deviate, differ, digress, diverge, stray, swerve, turn aside, vary, veer
Antonyms arrive, remain, show up (*Inf.*), stay, turn up

departed dead, deceased, expired, late

department 1. district, division, province, region, sector 2. branch, bureau, division, office, section, station, subdivision, unit 3. area, domain, function, line, province, realm, responsibility, speciality, sphere

departure 1. exit, exodus, going, going away, leave-taking, leaving, removal, retirement, withdrawal 2. abandonment, branching off, deviation, digression, divergence, variation, veering 3. branching out, change, difference, innovation, novelty, shift
Antonyms advent, appearance, arrival, coming, entrance, return

depend 1. bank on, build upon, calculate on, confide in, count on, lean on, reckon on, rely upon, trust in, turn to 2. be based on, be contingent on, be determined by, be subject to, be subordinate to, hang on, hinge on, rest on, revolve around

dependable faithful, reliable, reputable, responsible, staunch, steady, sure, trustworthy, trusty, unfailing
Antonyms irresponsible, undependable, unreliable, unstable, untrustworthy

dependant *n.* child, client, hanger-on, henchman, minion, minor, protégé, relative, retainer, subordinate, vassal

dependence, dependency 1. assurance, belief, confidence, expectation, faith, hope, reliance, trust 2. addiction, attachment, helplessness, need, subordination, subservience, vulnerability, weakness

dependent *adj.* 1. counting on, defenceless, helpless, immature, reliant, relying on, vulnerable, weak 2. conditional, contingent, depending, determined by, liable to, relative, subject to 3. feudal, subject, subordinate, tributary
Antonyms autarkic, autonomous, independent, self-determining, self-governing, self-reliant

depict 1. delineate, draw, illustrate, limn, outline, paint, picture, portray, render, reproduce, sculpt, sketch 2. characterize, describe, detail, narrate, outline, sketch

depiction delineation, description, drawing, illustration, image, likeness, outline, picture, portrayal, representation, sketch

deplete bankrupt, consume, decrease, drain, empty, evacuate, exhaust, expend, impoverish, lessen, milk, reduce, use up
Antonyms add to, augment, enhance, expand, increase, raise, step up (*Inf.*), swell

depleted consumed, decreased, depreciated, devoid of, drained, emptied, exhausted, lessened, out of, reduced, short of, spent, used (up), wasted, weakened, worn out

depletion attenuation, consumption, decrease, deficiency, diminution, drain, dwindling, exhaustion, expenditure, lessening, lowering, reduction, using up

deplorable 1. calamitous, dire, disastrous, distressing, grievous, heartbreaking, lamentable, melancholy, miserable, pitiable, regrettable, sad, unfortunate, wretched 2. blameworthy, disgraceful, dishonourable, disreputable, execrable, opprobrious, reprehensible, scandalous, shameful
Antonyms A1 *or* A-one (*Inf.*), admirable, bad (*Sl.*), brilliant, excellent, fantastic, great (*Inf.*), laudable, marvellous, notable, outstanding, praiseworthy, super (*Inf.*), superb

deplore 1. bemoan, bewail, grieve for, lament, mourn, regret, rue, sorrow over 2. abhor, censure, condemn, denounce, deprecate, disapprove of, excoriate, object to

deploy arrange, dispose, extend, position, redistribute, set out, set up, spread out, station, use, utilize

deport 1. banish, exile, expatriate, expel, extradite, oust 2. *Used reflexively* acquit, act, bear, behave, carry, comport, conduct, hold

deportation banishment, eviction, exile, expatriation, expulsion, extradition, transportation

deportment air, appearance, aspect, bearing, behaviour, carriage, cast, comportment, conduct, demeanour, manner, mien, posture, stance

depose 1. break, cashier, degrade, demote, dethrone, dismiss, displace, downgrade, oust, remove from office 2. *Law* avouch, declare, make a deposition, testify

deposit *v.* 1. drop, lay, locate, place, precipitate, put, settle, sit down 2. amass, bank, consign, entrust, hoard, lodge, save, store *~n.* 3. down payment, instalment, money (*in bank*), part payment, pledge, retainer, security, stake, warranty 4. accumulation, alluvium, deposition, dregs, lees, precipitate, sediment, silt

depositary fiduciary (*Law*), guardian, steward, trustee

deposition 1. dethronement, dismissal, displacement, ousting, removal 2. *Law* affidavit, declaration, evidence, sworn statement, testimony

depository depot, repository, safe-deposit box, store, storehouse, warehouse

depot 1. depository, repository, storehouse, warehouse 2. *Military* arsenal, dump 3. bus station, garage, terminus

deprave brutalize, corrupt, debase, debauch, degrade, demoralize, lead astray, pervert, seduce, subvert, vitiate

depraved abandoned, corrupt, debased, debauched, degenerate, degraded, dissolute, evil, immoral, lascivious, lewd, licentious, perverted, pervy (*Sl.*), profligate, shameless, sinful, vicious, vile, wicked

Antonyms chaste, decent, ethical, good, honourable, innocent, moral, principled, proper, pure, upright, virtuous, wholesome

depravity baseness, contamination, corruption, criminality, debasement, debauchery, degeneracy, depravation, evil, immorality, iniquity, profligacy, sinfulness, turpitude, vice, viciousness, vitiation, wickedness

deprecate 1. condemn, deplore, disapprove of, frown on, object to, protest against, take exception to 2. belittle, depreciate, detract, disparage

deprecatory 1. censuring, condemnatory, disapproving, opprobrious, reproachful 2. apologetic, contrite, penitent, regretful, remorseful, rueful

depreciate 1. decrease, deflate, devaluate, devalue, lessen, lose value, lower, reduce 2. belittle, decry, denigrate, deride, detract, disparage, look down on, ridicule, run down, scorn, sneer at, traduce, underestimate, underrate, undervalue

Antonyms (*sense 1*) add to, augment, appreciate, enhance, enlarge, expand, grow, increase, rise (*sense 2*) admire, appreciate, cherish, esteem, like, prize, rate highly, regard, respect, value

depreciation 1. deflation, depression, devaluation, drop, fall, slump 2. belittlement, deprecation, derogation, detraction, disparagement, pejoration

depredation desolation, despoiling, destruction, devastation, harrying, laying waste, marauding, pillage, plunder, ransacking, rapine, ravaging, robbery, spoliation, theft

depredator despoiler, destroyer, looter, marauder, pillager, plunderer, raider, ransacker, ravager, rifler, sacker

depress 1. cast down, chill, damp, daunt, deject, desolate, discourage, dishearten, dispirit, make despondent, oppress, sadden, weigh down 2. debilitate, devitalize, drain, enervate, exhaust, lower, sap, slow up, weaken 3. cheapen, depreciate, devaluate, devalue, diminish, downgrade, impair, lessen, lower, reduce 4. flatten, level, lower, press down, push down

Antonyms cheer, elate, hearten, heighten, increase, lift, raise, strengthen, uplift

depressed 1. blue, crestfallen, dejected, despondent, discouraged, dispirited, down, downcast, downhearted, down in the dumps (*Inf.*), fed up, glum, low, low-spirited, melancholy, moody, morose, pessimistic, sad, unhappy 2. concave, hollow, indented, recessed, set back, sunken 3. *Of an area, circumstances* deprived, destitute, disadvantaged, distressed, grey, needy, poor, poverty-stricken, run-down 4. cheapened, depreciated, devalued, impaired, weakened

depressing black, bleak, daunting, dejecting, depressive, discouraging, disheartening, dismal, dispiriting, distressing, dreary, funereal, gloomy, harrowing, heartbreaking, hopeless, melancholy, sad, saddening, sombre

depression 1. dejection, despair, despondency, dolefulness, downheartedness, dumps (*Inf.*), gloominess, hopelessness, low spirits, melancholia, melancholy, sadness, the blues, the hump (*Brit. inf.*) 2. *Commerce* dullness, economic decline, hard *or* bad times, inactivity, lowness, recession, slump, stagnation 3. bowl, cavity, concavity, dent, dimple, dip, excavation, hollow, impression, indentation, pit, sag, sink, valley

deprivation 1. denial, deprival, dispossession, divestment, expropriation, removal, withdrawal, withholding 2. destitution, detriment, disadvantage, distress, hardship, need, privation, want

deprive bereave, despoil, dispossess, divest, expropriate, rob, strip, wrest

deprived bereft, denuded, destitute, disadvantaged, forlorn, in need, in want, lacking, necessitous, needy, poor

Antonyms born with a silver spoon in one's mouth, favoured, fortunate, golden, happy, having a charmed life, lucky, prosperous, sitting pretty (*Inf.*), successful, well-off

depth 1. abyss, deepness, drop, extent, measure, profoundness, profundity 2. *Fig.* astuteness, discernment, insight, penetration, profoundness, profundity, sagacity, wisdom 3. abstruseness, complexity, obscurity, reconditeness 4. intensity, richness, strength 5. *Often plural* abyss, bowels of the earth, deepest (furthest, innermost, most intense, remotest) part, middle, midst, slough of despond 6. **in depth** comprehensively, extensively, intensively, thoroughly

Antonyms (*sense 1*) apex, apogee, crest, crown, height, peak, pinnacle, summit, top, vertex, zenith (*sense 2*) *Fig.* emptiness, lack of depth *or* substance, superficiality, triviality

deputation 1. commission, delegates, delegation, deputies, embassy, envoys, legation 2. appointment, assignment, commission, designation, nomination

depute *v.* accredit, appoint, authorize, charge, commission, delegate, empower, entrust, mandate

deputize 1. commission, delegate, depute 2. act for, stand in for, take the place of, understudy

deputy 1. *n.* agent, ambassador, commissioner, delegate, legate, lieutenant, nuncio, proxy, representative, second-in-command, substitute, surrogate, vicegerent 2. *adj.* assistant, depute (*Scot.*), subordinate

derange 1. confound, confuse, disarrange, disarray, discompose, disconcert, disorder, displace, disturb, ruffle, unsettle, upset 2. craze, dement (*Rare*), drive mad, madden, make insane, unbalance, unhinge

deranged barking (*Sl.*), barking mad (*Sl.*), berserk, crackpot (*Inf.*), crazed, crazy, delirious, demented, distracted, frantic, frenzied, insane, irrational, loopy (*Inf.*), lunatic, mad, maddened, not the full shilling (*Inf.*), off one's trolley (*Sl.*), out to lunch (*Inf.*), unbalanced, unhinged, up the pole (*Inf.*)

Antonyms all there (*Inf.*), calm, *compos mentis,* in one's right mind, lucid, mentally sound, normal, of sound mind

derangement 1. confusion, disarrangement, disarray, disorder, disturbance, irregularity, jumble, muddle 2. aberration, alienation, delirium, dementia, hallucination, insanity, loss of reason, lunacy, madness, mania

derelict *adj.* 1. abandoned, deserted, dilapidated, discarded, forsaken, neglected, ruined 2. careless, irresponsible, lax, negligent, remiss, slack ~*n.* 3. bag lady (*Chiefly U.S.*), bum (*Inf.*), down-and-out, good-for-nothing, ne'er-do-well, outcast, tramp, vagrant, wastrel

dereliction 1. delinquency, evasion, failure, faithlessness, fault, neglect, negligence, nonperformance, remissness 2. abandonment, abdication, desertion, forsaking, relinquishment, renunciation

deride chaff, contemn, detract, disdain, disparage, flout, gibe, insult, jeer, knock (*Inf.*), mock, pooh-pooh, ridicule, scoff, scorn, sneer, take the piss out of (*Taboo sl.*), taunt

de rigueur *comme il faut,* conventional, correct, decent, decorous, done, fitting, necessary, proper, required, right, the done thing

derision contempt, contumely, disdain, disparagement, disrespect, insult, laughter, mockery, raillery, ridicule, satire, scoffing, scorn, sneering

derisive contemptuous, jeering, mocking, ridiculing, scoffing, scornful, taunting

derisory contemptible, insulting, laughable, ludicrous, outrageous, preposterous, ridiculous

derivable attributable, deducible, determinable, extractable, inferable, obtainable, traceable

derivation 1. acquiring, deriving, extraction, getting, obtaining 2. ancestry, basis, beginning, descent, etymology, foundation, genealogy, origin, root, source

derivative *adj.* 1. acquired, borrowed, derived, inferred, obtained, procured, transmitted 2. copied, imitative, plagiaristic, plagiarized, rehashed, secondary, second-hand, uninventive, unoriginal ~*n.* 3. by-product, derivation, descendant, offshoot, outgrowth, spin-off

Antonyms *adj.* archetypal, authentic, first-hand, genuine, master, original, prototypical, seminal

derive 1. collect, deduce, draw, elicit, extract, follow, gain, gather, get, glean, infer, obtain, procure, receive, trace 2. *With* **from** arise, descend, emanate, flow, issue, originate, proceed, spring from, stem from

derogate 1. cheapen, compromise, depreciate, detract, devaluate, diminish, disparage, lessen, run down 2. *Of oneself* decline, degenerate, degrade, descend, deteriorate, deviate from, retrogress, stoop

derogatory belittling, damaging, defamatory, depreciative, detracting, discreditable, dishonouring, disparaging, injurious, offensive, slighting, uncomplimentary, unfavourable, unflattering

Antonyms appreciative, complimentary, flattering, fulsome, laudatory

descant *v.* 1. amplify, animadvert, comment on, dilate, discourse, discuss, enlarge, expatiate ~*n.* 2. animadversion, commentary, criticism, discourse, discussion, dissertation 3. counterpoint, decoration, melody, song, tune

descend 1. alight, dismount, drop, fall, go down, move down, plummet, plunge, sink, subside, tumble 2. dip, gravitate, incline, slant, slope 3. be handed down, be passed down, derive, issue, originate, proceed, spring 4. abase oneself, condescend, degenerate, deteriorate, lower oneself, stoop 5. *Often with* **on** arrive, assail, assault, attack, come in force, invade, pounce, raid, swoop

Antonyms ascend, climb, go up, mount, rise, scale, soar

descent 1. coming down, drop, fall, plunge, swoop 2. declination, declivity, dip, drop, incline, slant, slope 3. ancestry, extraction, family tree, genealogy, heredity, lineage, origin, parentage 4. debasement, decadence, decline, degradation, deterioration 5. assault, attack, foray, incursion, invasion, pounce, raid, swoop

describe 1. characterize, define, depict, detail, explain, express, illustrate, narrate, portray, recount, relate, report, specify, tell 2. delineate, draw, mark out, outline, trace

description 1. account, characterization, delineation, depiction, detail, explanation, narration, narrative, portrayal, report, representation, sketch 2. brand, breed, category, class, genre, genus, ilk, kidney, kind, order, sort, species, type, variety

descriptive circumstantial, depictive, detailed, explanatory, expressive, graphic, illustrative, pictorial, picturesque, vivid

descry behold, detect, discern, discover, distinguish, espy, make out, mark, notice, observe, perceive, recognize, see, sight, spy out

desecrate abuse, blaspheme, commit sacrilege, contaminate, defile, despoil, dishonour, pervert, pollute, profane, violate

Antonyms esteem, exalt, glorify, hallow, prize, respect, revere, value, venerate, worship

desecration blasphemy, debasement, defilement, impiety, profanation, sacrilege, violation

desert[1] 1. *n.* solitude, waste, wasteland, wilderness, wilds 2. *adj.* arid, bare, barren, desolate, infertile, lonely, solitary, uncultivated, uninhabited, unproductive, untilled, waste, wild

desert[2] *v.* abandon, abscond, betray, decamp, defect, forsake, give up, go over the hill (*Military sl.*), jilt, leave, leave high and dry, leave (someone) in the lurch, leave stranded, maroon, quit, rat (on) (*Inf.*), relinquish, renounce, resign, run out on (*Inf.*), strand, throw over, vacate, walk out on (*Inf.*)

Antonyms be a source of strength to, look after, maintain, provide for, succour, sustain, take care of

desert[3] *n.* 1. *Often plural* comeuppance (*Sl.*), due, guerdon (*Poetic*), meed (*Archaic*), payment, recompense, requital, retribution, return, reward, right 2. excellence, merit (*or* demerit), virtue, worth

deserted abandoned, bereft, cast off, derelict, desolate, empty, forlorn, forsaken, godforsaken, isolated, left in the lurch, left stranded, lonely, neglected, solitary, unfriended, unoccupied, vacant

deserter absconder, apostate, defector, escapee, fugitive, rat (*Inf.*), renegade, runaway, traitor, truant

desertion abandonment, absconding, apostasy, betrayal, defection, departure, dereliction, escape, evasion, flight, forsaking, relinquishment, truancy

deserve be entitled to, be worthy of, earn, gain, justify, merit, procure, rate, warrant, win

deserved appropriate, condign, due, earned, fair, fitting, just, justifiable, justified, meet (*Archaic*), merited, proper, right, rightful, suitable, warranted, well-earned

deserving commendable, estimable, laudable, meritorious, praiseworthy, righteous, worthy

Antonyms not deserving of, not good enough, not worth, undeserving, unworthy

desiccate dehydrate, drain, dry, evaporate, exsiccate, parch

desiccated 1. dehydrated, dried, dry, powdered 2. cold, dead, dry, dry-as-dust, dull, empty, inanimate, inert, lifeless, passionless, spiritless

desideratum aim, aspiration, dream, essential, goal, heart's desire, hope, ideal, lack, need, objective, *sine qua non*, want, wish

design *v.* 1. delineate, describe, draft, draw, outline, plan, sketch, trace ~*n.* 2. blueprint, delineation, draft, drawing, model, outline, plan, scheme, sketch ~*v.* 3. conceive, create, fabricate, fashion, invent, originate, think up ~*n.* 4. arrangement, configuration, construction, figure, form, motif, organization, pattern, shape, style ~*v.* 5. aim, contrive, destine, devise, intend, make, mean, plan, project, propose, purpose, scheme, tailor ~*n.* 6. enterprise, plan, project, schema, scheme, undertaking 7. aim, end, goal, intent, intention, meaning, object, objective, point, purport, purpose, target, view 8. *Often plural* conspiracy, evil intentions, intrigue, machination, plot, scheme

designate 1. call, christen, dub, entitle, label, name, nominate, style, term 2. allot, appoint, assign, choose, delegate, depute, nominate, select 3. characterize, define, denote, describe, earmark, indicate, pinpoint, show, specify, stipulate

designation 1. denomination, description, epithet, label, mark, name, title 2. appointment, classification, delegation, indication, selection, specification

designedly by design, calculatedly, deliberately, intentionally, knowingly, on purpose, purposely, studiously, wilfully, wittingly

designer 1. architect, artificer, couturier, creator, deviser, inventor, originator, stylist 2. conniver, conspirator, intriguer, plotter, schemer

designing artful, astute, conniving, conspiring, crafty, crooked (*Inf.*), cunning, deceitful, devious, intriguing, Machiavellian, plotting, scheming, sharp, shrewd, sly, treacherous, tricky, unscrupulous, wily

desirability advantage, benefit, merit, profit, usefulness, value, worth

desirable 1. advantageous, advisable, agreeable, beneficial, covetable, eligible, enviable, good, pleasing, preferable, profitable, worthwhile 2. adorable, alluring, attractive, fascinating, fetching, glamorous, seductive, sexy (*Inf.*)

Antonyms disagreeable, distasteful, unacceptable, unappealing, unattractive, undesirable, unpleasant, unpopular, unsexy (*Inf.*)

desire *v.* 1. aspire to, covet, crave, desiderate, fancy, hanker after, hope for, long for, set one's heart on, thirst for, want, wish for, yearn for ~*n.* 2. appetite, aspiration, craving, hankering, hope, longing, need, thirst, want, wish, yearning, yen (*Inf.*) ~*v.* 3. ask, entreat, importune, petition, request, solicit ~*n.* 4. appeal, entreaty, importunity, petition, request, solicitation, supplication 5. appetite, concupiscence, lasciviousness, lechery, libido, lust, lustfulness, passion

desired accurate, appropriate, correct, exact, expected, express, fitting, necessary, particular, proper, required, right

desirous ambitious, anxious, aspiring, avid, craving, desiring, eager, hopeful, hoping, keen, longing, ready, willing, wishing, yearning

Antonyms averse, disinclined, grudging, indisposed, loath, opposed, reluctant, unenthusiastic, unwilling

desist abstain, break off, cease, discontinue, end, forbear, give over (*Inf.*), give up, have done with, kick (*Inf.*), leave off, pause, refrain from, remit, stop, suspend

desolate *adj.* 1. bare, barren, bleak, desert, dreary, godforsaken, ruined, solitary, unfrequented, uninhabited, waste, wild ~*v.* 2. depopulate, despoil, destroy, devastate, lay low, lay waste, pillage, plunder, ravage, ruin ~*adj.* 3. abandoned, bereft, cheerless, comfortless, companionless, dejected, depressing, despondent, disconsolate, dismal, downcast, forlorn, forsaken, gloomy, lonely, melancholy, miserable, wretched ~*v.* 4. daunt, deject, depress, discourage, dishearten, dismay, distress, grieve

Antonyms *adj.* cheerful, happy, inhabited, joyous, light-hearted, populous ~*v.* cheer, develop, encourage, hearten, nourish

desolation 1. destruction, devastation, havoc, ravages, ruin, ruination 2. barrenness, bleakness, desolateness, forlornness, isolation, loneliness, solitariness, solitude, wildness 3. anguish, dejection, despair, distress, gloom, gloominess, melancholy, misery, sadness, unhappiness, woe, wretchedness

despair *v.* 1. despond, give up, lose heart, lose hope ~*n.* 2. anguish, dejection, depression, desperation, despondency, disheartenment, gloom, hopelessness, melancholy, misery, wretchedness 3. burden, cross, hardship, ordeal, pain, trial, tribulation

despairing anxious, broken-hearted, dejected, depressed, desperate, despondent, disconsolate, dismal, downcast, frantic, grief-stricken, hopeless, inconsolable, melancholy, miserable, suicidal, wretched

despatch *see* DISPATCH

desperado bandit, criminal, cutthroat, gangster, gunman, heavy (*Sl.*), hoodlum (*Chiefly U.S.*), lawbreaker, mugger (*Inf.*), outlaw, ruffian, thug, villain

desperate 1. audacious, dangerous, daring, death-defying, determined, foolhardy, frantic, furious, hasty, hazardous, headstrong, impetuous, madcap, precipitate, rash, reckless, risky, violent, wild 2. acute, critical, dire, drastic, extreme, great, urgent, very grave 3. despairing, despondent, forlorn, hopeless, inconsolable, irrecoverable, irremediable, irretrievable, wretched

desperately 1. badly, dangerously, gravely, perilously, seriously, severely 2. appallingly, fearfully, frightfully, hopelessly, shockingly

desperation 1. defiance, foolhardiness, frenzy, heedlessness, impetuosity, madness, rashness, recklessness 2. agony, anguish, anxiety, despair, despondency, distraction, heartache, hopelessness, misery, pain, sorrow, torture, trouble, unhappiness, worry

despicable abject, base, beyond contempt, cheap, contemptible, degrading, detestable, disgraceful, disreputable, hateful, ignominious, infamous, low, mean, pitiful, reprehensible, scurvy, shameful, sordid, vile, worthless, wretched
Antonyms admirable, estimable, ethical, exemplary, good, honest, honourable, moral, noble, praiseworthy, righteous, upright, virtuous, worthy

despise abhor, contemn, deride, detest, disdain, disregard, flout, loathe, look down on, neglect, revile, scorn, slight, spurn, undervalue
Antonyms admire, adore, be fond of, be keen on, cherish, dig (*Sl.*), esteem, fancy (*Inf.*), love, relish, revel in, take to

despite against, even with, in contempt of, in defiance of, in spite of, in the face of, in the teeth of, notwithstanding, regardless of, undeterred by

despoil denude, deprive, destroy, devastate, dispossess, divest, loot, pillage, plunder, ravage, rifle, rob, strip, total (*Sl.*), trash (*Sl.*), vandalize, wreak havoc upon, wreck

despoliation depredation, despoilment, destruction, devastation, havoc, looting, pillage, plunder, ruin, vandalism, wreckage

despond be cast down, be depressed, despair, give up, lose heart, lose hope, mourn, sorrow

despondency dejection, depression, despair, desperation, disconsolateness, discouragement, dispiritedness, downheartedness, gloom, hopelessness, low spirits, melancholy, misery, sadness, the hump (*Brit. inf.*), wretchedness

despondent blue, dejected, depressed, despairing, disconsolate, discouraged, disheartened, dismal, dispirited, doleful, down, downcast, downhearted, gloomy, glum, hopeless, in despair, low, low-spirited, melancholy, miserable, morose, sad, sick as a parrot (*Inf.*), sorrowful, woebegone, wretched
Antonyms buoyant, cheerful, cheery, chirpy (*Inf.*), genial, happy, hopeful, glad, joyful, light-hearted, optimistic, upbeat (*Inf.*)

despot autocrat, dictator, monocrat, oppressor, tyrant

despotic absolute, arbitrary, arrogant, authoritarian, autocratic, dictatorial, domineering, imperious, monocratic, oppressive, tyrannical, unconstitutional

despotism absolutism, autarchy, autocracy, dictatorship, monocracy, oppression, totalitarianism, tyranny

destination 1. harbour, haven, journey's end, landing-place, resting-place, station, stop, terminus 2. aim, ambition, design, end, goal, intention, object, objective, purpose, target

destine allot, appoint, assign, consecrate, decree, design, devote, doom, earmark, fate, intend, mark out, ordain, predetermine, preordain, purpose, reserve

destined 1. bound, certain, designed, doomed, fated, foreordained, ineluctable, inescapable, inevitable, intended, meant, ordained, predestined, unavoidable 2. assigned, booked, bound for, directed, en route, heading, on the road to, routed, scheduled

destiny cup, divine decree, doom, fate, fortune, karma, kismet, lot, portion

destitute 1. dirt-poor (*Inf.*), distressed, down and out, flat broke (*Inf.*), impecunious, impoverished, indigent, insolvent, moneyless, necessitous, needy, on one's uppers, on the breadline (*Inf.*), penniless, penurious, poor, poverty-stricken, short, without two pennies to rub together (*Inf.*) 2. bereft of, deficient in, depleted, deprived of, devoid of, drained, empty of, in need of, lacking, wanting, without

destitution beggary, dire straits, distress, impecuniousness, indigence, neediness, pauperism, pennilessness, penury, privation, utter poverty, want
Antonyms affluence, fortune, good fortune, life of luxury, luxury, plenty, prosperity, riches, wealth

destroy annihilate, blow to bits, break down, crush, demolish, desolate, devastate, dismantle, dispatch, eradicate, extinguish, extirpate, gut, kill, ravage, raze, ruin, shatter, slay, smash, torpedo, total (*Sl.*), trash (*Sl.*), waste, wipe out, wreck

destruction annihilation, crushing, demolition, devastation, downfall, end, eradication, extermination, extinction, havoc, liquidation, massacre, overthrow, overwhelming, ruin, ruination, shattering, slaughter, undoing, wreckage, wrecking

destructive 1. baleful, baneful, calamitous, cataclysmic, catastrophic, damaging, deadly, deleterious, detrimental, devastating, fatal, harmful, hurtful, injurious, lethal, maleficent, noxious, pernicious, ruinous 2. adverse, antagonistic, contrary, derogatory, discouraging, discrediting, disparaging, hostile, invalidating, negative, opposed, undermining, vicious

desultory aimless, capricious, cursory, disconnected, discursive, disorderly, erratic, fitful, haphazard, inconsistent, inconstant, inexact, irregular, loose, maundering, off and on, rambling, random, roving, spasmodic, unmethodical, unsettled, unsystematic, vague

detach cut off, disconnect, disengage, disentangle, disjoin, disunite, divide, free, isolate, loosen, remove, segregate, separate, sever, tear off, unbridle, uncouple, unfasten, unhitch
Antonyms attach, bind, connect, fasten

detached 1. disconnected, discrete, disjoined, divided, free, loosened, separate, severed, unconnected 2. aloof, disinterested, dispassionate, impartial, impersonal, neutral, objective, reserved, unbiased, uncommitted, uninvolved, unprejudiced
Antonyms biased, concerned, interested, involved, partisan, prejudiced

detachment 1. aloofness, coolness, indifference, nonchalance, remoteness, unconcern 2. disinterestedness, fairness, impartiality, neutrality, nonpartisanship, objectivity 3. disconnection, disengagement, disjoining, separation, severing 4. *Military* body, detail, force, party, patrol, squad, task force, unit

detail *n.* 1. aspect, component, count, element, fact, factor, feature, item, particular, point, respect, specific, technicality 2. *Plural* fine points, minutiae, niceties, particulars, parts, trivia, trivialities 3. **in detail** comprehensively, exhaustively, inside out, item by item, point by point, thoroughly 4. *Military* assignment, body, detachment, duty, fatigue, force, party, squad ~*v.* 5. catalogue, delineate, depict, describe, enumerate, individualize, itemize, narrate, particularize, portray, recite, recount, rehearse, relate, specify, tabulate 6. allocate, appoint, assign, charge, commission, delegate, detach, send

detailed blow-by-blow, circumstantial, comprehensive, elaborate, exact, exhaustive, full, intricate, itemized, meticulous, minute, particular, particularized, specific, thorough
Antonyms brief, compact, concise, condensed, limited, pithy, short, slight, succinct, summary, superficial, terse

detain 1. check, delay, hinder, hold up, impede, keep, keep back, retard, slow up (*or* down), stay, stop 2. arrest, confine, hold, intern, restrain

detect 1. ascertain, catch, descry, distinguish, identify, note, notice, observe, recognize, scent, spot 2. catch, disclose, discover, expose, find, reveal, track down, uncover, unmask

detection discovery, exposé, exposure, ferreting out, revelation, tracking down, uncovering, unearthing, unmasking

detective bizzy (*Sl.*), C.I.D. man, constable, cop (*Sl.*), copper (*Sl.*), dick (*Sl., chiefly U.S.*), gumshoe (*U.S. sl.*), investigator, private eye, private investigator, sleuth (*Inf.*), tec (*Sl.*)

detention confinement, custody, delay, hindrance, holding back, imprisonment, incarceration, keeping in, porridge (*Sl.*), quarantine, restraint, withholding
Antonyms acquittal, discharge, emancipation, freedom, liberation, liberty, release

deter caution, check, damp, daunt, debar, discourage, dissuade, frighten, hinder, inhibit from, intimidate, prevent, prohibit, put off, restrain, stop, talk out of

detergent 1. *n.* cleaner, cleanser 2. *adj.* abstergent, cleaning, cleansing, detersive, purifying

deteriorate 1. corrupt, debase, decline, degenerate, degrade, deprave, depreciate, go downhill (*Inf.*), go to pot, go to the dogs (*Inf.*), impair, injure, lower, slump, spoil, worsen 2. be the worse for wear (*Inf.*), crumble, decay, decline, decompose, disintegrate, ebb, fade, fall apart, lapse, retrogress, weaken, wear away
Antonyms advance, ameliorate, get better, improve, upgrade

deterioration atrophy, corrosion, debasement, decline, degeneration, degradation, *dégringolade*, depreciation, descent, dilapidation, disintegration, downturn, drop, fall, lapse, retrogression, slump, vitiation, worsening

determinable answerable, ascertainable, assessable, definable, describable, discoverable

determinate absolute, certain, conclusive, decided, decisive, defined, definite, definitive, determined, distinct, established, explicit, express, fixed, limited, positive, precise, quantified, settled, specified

determination 1. backbone, constancy, conviction, dedication, doggedness, drive, firmness, fortitude, indomitability, perseverance, persistence, resoluteness, resolution, resolve, single-mindedness, steadfastness, tenacity, willpower 2. conclusion, decision, judgment, purpose, resolve, result, settlement, solution, verdict
Antonyms doubt, hesitancy, hesitation, indecision, instability, irresolution, vacillation

determine 1. arbitrate, conclude, decide, end, finish, fix upon, ordain, regulate, settle, terminate 2. ascertain, certify, check, detect, discover, find out, learn, verify, work out 3. choose, decide, elect, establish, fix, make up one's mind, purpose, resolve 4. affect, condition, control, decide, dictate, direct, govern, impel, impose, incline, induce, influence, lead, modify, regulate, rule, shape

determined bent on, constant, dogged, firm, fixed, immovable, intent, persevering, persistent, purposeful, resolute, set on, single-minded, stalwart, steadfast, strong-minded, strong-willed, tenacious, unflinching, unwavering

determining conclusive, critical, crucial, deciding, decisive, definitive, essential, final, important, settling

deterrent *n.* check, curb, defensive measures, determent, discouragement, disincentive, hindrance, impediment, obstacle, restraint
Antonyms bait, carrot (*Inf.*), enticement, incentive, inducement, lure, motivation, spur, stimulus

detest abhor, abominate, despise, dislike intensely, execrate, feel aversion (disgust, hostility, repugnance) towards, hate, loathe, recoil from
Antonyms adore, cherish, dig (*Sl.*), dote on, love, relish

detestable abhorred, abominable, accursed, despicable, disgusting, execrable, hateful, heinous, loathsome, obnoxious, obscene, odious, offensive, repugnant, repulsive, revolting, shocking, vile, yucky *or* yukky (*Sl.*)

detestation 1. abhorrence, abomination, animosity, animus, antipathy, aversion, disgust, dislike, execration, hatred, hostility, loathing, odium, repugnance, revulsion 2. abomination, anathema, bête noire, hate

dethrone depose, oust, uncrown, unseat

detonate blast, blow up, discharge, explode, fulminate, set off, touch off, trigger

detonation bang, blast, blow-up, boom, discharge, explosion, fulmination, report

detour bypass, byway, circuitous route, deviation, diversion, indirect course, roundabout way

detract 1. devaluate, diminish, lessen, lower, reduce, take away from 2. deflect, distract, divert, shift
Antonyms add to, augment, boost, complement, enhance, improve, reinforce, strengthen

detraction abuse, aspersion, belittlement, calumny, defamation, denigration, deprecation, disparagement, innuendo, insinuation, misrepresentation, muckraking, running down, scandalmongering, scurrility, slander, traducement, vituperation

detractor backbiter, belittler, defamer, denigrator, derogator (*Rare*), disparager, muckraker, scandalmonger, slanderer, traducer

detriment damage, disadvantage, disservice, harm, hurt, impairment, injury, loss, mischief, prejudice

detrimental adverse, baleful, damaging, deleterious, destructive, disadvantageous, harmful, inimical, injurious, mischievous, pernicious, prejudicial, unfavourable
Antonyms advantageous, beneficial, efficacious, favourable, good, helpful, salutary

detritus debris, fragments, litter, remains, rubbish, waste

de trop in the way, redundant, superfluous, surplus, unnecessary, unwanted, unwelcome

devastate 1. demolish, desolate, despoil, destroy, lay waste, level, pillage, plunder, ravage, raze, ruin, sack, spoil, total (*Sl.*), trash (*Sl.*), waste, wreck 2. *Inf.* chagrin, confound, discomfit, discompose, disconcert, floor (*Inf.*), nonplus, overpower, overwhelm, take aback

devastating caustic, cutting, deadly, destructive, effective, incisive, keen, mordant, overpowering, overwhelming, ravishing, sardonic, satirical, savage, stunning, trenchant, vitriolic, withering

devastation demolition, depredation, desolation, destruction, havoc, pillage, plunder, ravages, ruin, ruination, spoliation

develop 1. advance, blossom, cultivate, evolve, flourish, foster, grow, mature, progress, promote, prosper, ripen 2. amplify, augment, broaden, dilate upon, elaborate, enlarge, expand, unfold, work out 3. acquire, begin, breed, commence, contract, establish, form, generate, invent, originate, pick up, start 4. be a direct result of, break out, come about, ensue, follow, happen, result

development 1. advance, advancement, evolution, expansion, growth, improvement, increase, maturity, progress, progression, spread, unfolding, unravelling 2. change, circumstance, event, happening, incident, issue, occurrence, outcome, phenomenon, result, situation, turn of events, upshot

deviant 1. *adj.* aberrant, abnormal, bent (*Sl.*), deviate, devious, freaky (*Sl.*), heretical, kinky (*Sl.*), perverse, perverted, pervy (*Sl.*), queer (*Inf., derogatory*), sick (*Inf.*), twisted, warped, wayward 2. *n.* deviate, freak, misfit, odd type, pervert, queer (*Inf., derogatory*)
Antonyms conventional, normal, orthodox, straight, straightforward

deviate avert, bend, deflect, depart, differ, digress, diverge, drift, err, meander, part, stray, swerve, turn, turn aside, vary, veer, wander

deviation aberration, alteration, change, deflection, departure, digression, discrepancy, disparity, divergence, fluctuation, inconsistency, irregularity, shift, variance, variation

device 1. apparatus, appliance, contraption, contrivance, gadget, gimmick, gismo *or* gizmo (*Sl., chiefly U.S. & Canad.*), implement, instrument, invention, tool, utensil 2. artifice, design, dodge, expedient, gambit, improvisation, manoeuvre, plan, ploy, project, purpose, ruse, scheme, shift, stratagem, strategy, stunt, trick, wile 3. badge, colophon, crest, design, emblem, figure, insignia, logo, motif, motto, symbol, token

devil 1. *Sometimes cap.* Apollyon, archfiend, Beelzebub, Belial, Clootie (*Scot.*), demon, fiend, Lucifer, Old Harry (*Inf.*), Old Nick (*Inf.*), Old Scratch (*Inf.*), Prince of Darkness, Satan 2. beast, brute, demon, fiend, ghoul, monster, ogre, rogue, savage, terror, villain 3. imp, monkey (*Inf.*), pickle (*Brit. inf.*), rascal, rogue, scamp, scoundrel 4. beggar, creature, thing, unfortunate, wretch 5. demon, enthusiast, fiend, go-getter (*Inf.*)

devilish accursed, atrocious, damnable, detestable, diabolic, diabolical, execrable, fiendish, hellish, infernal, satanic, wicked

devil-may-care careless, casual, easy-going, flippant, happy-go-lucky, heedless, insouciant, nonchalant, reckless, swaggering, swashbuckling, unconcerned

devilment devilry, knavery, mischief, mischievousness, naughtiness, rascality, roguery, roguishness

devilry, deviltry 1. devilment, jiggery-pokery (*Inf., chiefly Brit.*), knavery, mischief, mischievousness, monkey-business (*Inf.*), rascality, roguery 2. cruelty, evil, malevolence, malice, vice, viciousness, villainy, wickedness 3. black magic, diablerie, diabolism, sorcery

devious 1. calculating, crooked (*Inf.*), deceitful, dishonest, double-dealing, evasive, indirect, insidious, insincere, not straightforward, scheming, sly, surreptitious, treacherous, tricky, underhand, wily 2. circuitous, confusing, crooked, deviating, erratic, excursive, indirect, misleading, rambling, roundabout, tortuous, wandering

Antonyms blunt, candid, direct, downright, forthright, frank, honest, straight, straightforward, undeviating, unswerving

devise arrange, conceive, concoct, construct, contrive, design, dream up, form, formulate, frame, imagine, invent, plan, plot, prepare, project, scheme, think up, work out

devitalize cripple, debilitate, enervate, enfeeble, exhaust, reduce, sap, undermine, weaken

devoid barren, bereft, deficient, denuded, destitute, empty, free from, lacking, sans (*Archaic*), vacant, void, wanting, without

devolution decentralization, delegation

devolve 1. be transferred, commission, consign, delegate, depute, entrust, fall upon *or* to, rest with, transfer 2. *Law* alienate, be handed down, convey

devote allot, apply, appropriate, assign, commit, concern oneself, consecrate, dedicate, enshrine, give, occupy oneself, pledge, reserve, set apart

devoted ardent, caring, committed, concerned, constant, dedicated, devout, faithful, fond, loving, loyal, staunch, steadfast, true

Antonyms disloyal, inconstant, indifferent, uncommitted, undedicated, unfaithful

devotee addict, adherent, admirer, aficionado, buff (*Inf.*), disciple, enthusiast, fan, fanatic, follower, supporter, votary

devotion 1. adherence, allegiance, commitment, consecration, constancy, dedication, faithfulness, fidelity, loyalty 2. adoration, devoutness, godliness, holiness, piety, prayer, religiousness, reverence, sanctity, spirituality, worship 3. affection, ardour, attachment, earnestness, fervour, fondness, intensity, love, passion, zeal 4. *Plural* church service, divine office, prayers, religious observance

Antonyms (*sense 1*) carelessness, disregard, inattention, indifference, laxity, laxness, neglect, thoughtlessness (*sense 2*) derision, disrespect, impiety, irreverence

devotional devout, holy, pious, religious, reverential, sacred, solemn, spiritual

devour 1. bolt, consume, cram, dispatch, eat, gobble, gorge, gulp, guzzle, pig out on (*Sl.*), polish off (*Inf.*), stuff, swallow, wolf 2. annihilate, consume, destroy, ravage, spend, waste, wipe out 3. absorb, appreciate, be engrossed by, be preoccupied, delight in, drink in, enjoy, feast on, go through, read compulsively *or* voraciously, relish, revel in, take in

devouring consuming, excessive, flaming, insatiable, intense, overwhelming, passionate, powerful

devout 1. godly, holy, orthodox, pious, prayerful, pure, religious, reverent, saintly 2. ardent, deep, devoted, earnest, fervent, genuine, heartfelt, intense, passionate, profound, serious, sincere, zealous

Antonyms impious, indifferent, irreligious, irreverent, passive, sacrilegious

devoutly fervently, heart and soul, profoundly, sincerely, with all one's heart

dexterity 1. adroitness, artistry, craft, deftness, effortlessness, expertise, facility, finesse, handiness, knack, mastery, neatness, nimbleness, proficiency, skill, smoothness, touch 2. ability, address, adroitness, aptitude, aptness, art, cleverness, expertness, ingenuity, readiness, skilfulness, tact

Antonyms clumsiness, gaucheness, inability, incapacity, incompetence, ineptitude, uselessness

dexterous able, active, acute, adept, adroit, agile, apt, clever, deft, expert, handy, ingenious, masterly, neat, nimble, nimble-fingered, proficient, prompt, quick, skilful

diabolic 1. demoniac, demonic, devilish, fiendish, hellish, infernal, satanic 2. atrocious, cruel, evil, fiendish, monstrous, nefarious, vicious, villainous, wicked

diabolical appalling, atrocious, damnable, difficult, disastrous, dreadful, excruciating, fiendish, hellacious (*U.S. sl.*), hellish, nasty, outrageous, shocking, tricky, unpleasant, vile

diadem circlet, coronet, crown, tiara

diagnose analyse, determine, distinguish, identify, interpret, investigate, pinpoint, pronounce, recognize

diagnosis 1. analysis, examination, investigation, scrutiny 2. conclusion, interpretation, opinion, pronouncement

diagnostic demonstrative, distinctive, distinguishing, idiosyncratic, indicative, particular, peculiar, recognizable, symptomatic

diagonal *adj.* angled, cater-cornered (*U.S. inf.*), cornerways, cross, crossways, crosswise, oblique, slanting

diagonally aslant, at an angle, cornerwise, crosswise, obliquely, on the bias, on the cross

diagram chart, drawing, figure, layout, outline, plan, representation, sketch

dialect accent, idiom, jargon, language, lingo (*Inf.*), localism, patois, pronunciation, provincialism, speech, tongue, vernacular

dialectal dialect, idiomatic, local, nonstandard, regional, restricted, vernacular

dialectic 1. *adj.* analytic, argumentative, dialectical, logical, polemical, rational, rationalistic 2. *n. Often plural* argumentation, contention, discussion, disputation, logic, polemics, ratiocination, reasoning

dialogue 1. colloquy, communication, confabulation, conference, conversation, converse, discourse, discussion, duologue, interlocution 2. conversation, lines, script, spoken part

diametric, diametrical antipodal, antithetical, conflicting, contrary, contrasting, counter, opposed, opposite

diametrically absolutely, completely, entirely, utterly

diaphanous chiffon, clear, cobwebby, delicate, filmy, fine, gauzy, gossamer, light, pellucid, seethrough, sheer, thin, translucent, transparent

diary appointment book, chronicle, daily record, day-to-day account, engagement book, Filofax (*Trademark*), journal

diarrhoea *n.* dysentery, gippy tummy, holiday tummy, looseness, Montezuma's revenge (*Inf.*), Spanish tummy, the runs, the skits (*Inf.*), the skitters (*Inf.*), the trots (*Inf.*)

diatribe abuse, castigation, criticism, denunciation, disputation, harangue, invective, philippic, reviling, stream of abuse, stricture, tirade, verbal onslaught, vituperation

dicey chancy (*Inf.*), dangerous, difficult, hairy (*Sl.*), risky, ticklish, tricky

dicky *adj.* fluttery, queer, shaky, unreliable, unsound, unsteady, weak

dictate *v.* 1. read out, say, speak, transmit, utter 2. command, decree, demand, direct, enjoin, establish, impose, lay down, ordain, order, prescribe, pronounce ~*n.* 3. behest, bidding, command, decree, demand, direction, edict, fiat, injunction, mandate, order, ordinance, requirement, statute, ultimatum, word 4. canon, code, dictum, law, precept, principle, rule

dictator absolute ruler, autocrat, despot, oppressor, tyrant

dictatorial 1. absolute, arbitrary, autocratic, despotic, totalitarian, tyrannical, unlimited, unrestricted 2. authoritarian, bossy (*Inf.*), dogmatical, domineering, imperious, iron-handed, magisterial, oppressive, overbearing

Antonyms constitutional, democratic, egalitarian, humble, restricted, servile, suppliant, tolerant

dictatorship absolute rule, absolutism, authoritarianism, autocracy, despotism, reign of terror, totalitarianism, tyranny

diction 1. expression, language, phraseology, phrasing, style, usage, vocabulary, wording 2. articulation, delivery, elocution, enunciation, fluency, inflection, intonation, pronunciation, speech

dictionary concordance, encyclopedia, glossary, lexicon, vocabulary, wordbook

dictum 1. canon, command, decree, demand, dictate, edict, fiat, order, pronouncement 2. adage, axiom, gnome, maxim, precept, proverb, saw, saying

didactic edifying, educational, enlightening, homiletic, instructive, moral, moralizing, pedagogic, pedantic, preceptive

die 1. breathe one's last, buy it (*U.S. sl.*), check out (*U.S. sl.*), croak (*Sl.*), decease, depart, expire, finish, give up the ghost, go belly-up (*Sl.*), hop the twig (*Sl.*), kick it (*Sl.*), kick the bucket (*Sl.*), pass away, peg it (*Inf.*), peg out (*Inf.*), perish, pop one's clogs (*Inf.*), snuff it (*Sl.*) 2. decay, decline, disappear, dwindle, ebb, end, fade, lapse, pass, sink, subside, vanish, wane, wilt, wither 3. break down, fade out *or* away, fail, fizzle out, halt, lose power, peter out, run down, stop 4. ache, be eager, desire, hunger, languish, long, pine for, swoon, yearn 5. *Usually with* **of** be overcome, collapse, succumb to

Antonyms be born, begin, build, come to life, exist, flourish, grow, increase, live, survive

die-hard 1. *n.* fanatic, intransigent, old fogy, reactionary, stick-in-the-mud (*Inf.*), ultraconservative, zealot 2. *adj.* dyed-in-the-wool, immovable, inflexible, intransigent, reactionary, ultraconservative, uncompromising, unreconstructed (*Chiefly U.S.*)

diet[1] *n.* 1. abstinence, dietary, fast, regime, regimen 2. aliment, comestibles, commons, edibles, fare, food, nourishment, nutriment, provisions, rations, subsistence, sustenance, viands, victuals ~*v.* 3. abstain, eat sparingly, fast, lose weight, reduce, slim

Antonyms *v.* get fat, glut, gobble, gormandize, guzzle, indulge, overindulge, pig out (*Sl.*), stuff oneself

diet[2] chamber, congress, convention, council, legislative assembly, legislature, meeting, parliament, sitting

dieter calorie counter, faster, reducer, slimmer, weight watcher

differ 1. be dissimilar, be distinct, contradict, contrast, depart from, diverge, run counter to, stand apart, vary 2. clash, contend, debate, demur, disagree, dispute, dissent, oppose, take issue

Antonyms accord, acquiesce, agree, assent, coincide, concur, cooperate, harmonize

difference 1. alteration, change, contrast, deviation, differentiation, discrepancy, disparity, dissimilarity, distinction, distinctness, divergence, diversity, unlikeness, variation, variety 2. distinction, exception, idiosyncrasy, particularity, peculiarity, singularity 3. argument, clash, conflict, contention, contrariety, contretemps, controversy, debate, disagreement, discordance, dispute, quarrel, row, set-to (*Inf.*), strife, tiff, wrangle 4. balance, remainder, rest, result

Antonyms (*senses 1, 2 & 3*) affinity, agreement, comparability, concordance, conformity, congruence, likeness, relation, resemblance, sameness, similarity, similitude

different 1. altered, at odds, at variance, changed, clashing, contrasting, deviating, discrepant, disparate, dissimilar, divergent, diverse, inconsistent, opposed, unlike 2. another, discrete, distinct, individual, other, separate 3. assorted, divers (*Archaic*), diverse, manifold, many, miscellaneous, multifarious, numerous, several, some, sundry, varied, various 4. another story, atypical, bizarre, distinctive, extraordinary, out of the ordinary, peculiar, rare, singular, something else, special, strange, uncommon, unconventional, unique, unusual

differential 1. *adj.* diacritical, discriminative, distinctive, distinguishing 2. *n.* amount of difference, difference, discrepancy, disparity

differentiate 1. contrast, discern, discriminate, distinguish, make a distinction, mark off, separate, set off *or* apart, tell apart 2. adapt, alter, change, convert, make different, modify, transform

difficult 1. arduous, burdensome, demanding, formidable, hard, laborious, no picnic (*Inf.*), onerous, painful, strenuous, toilsome, uphill, wearisome 2. abstract, abstruse, baffling, complex, complicated, delicate, enigmatical, intricate, involved, knotty, obscure, perplexing, problematical, thorny, ticklish 3. demanding, fastidious, fractious, fussy, hard to please, intractable, obstreperous, perverse, refractory, rigid, tiresome, troublesome, trying, unaccommodating, unamenable, unmanageable 4. dark, full of hardship, grim, hard, straitened, tough, trying

Antonyms accommodating, amenable, cooperative, easy, easy-peasy (*Sl.*), light, manageable, obvious, plain, pleasant, simple, straightforward, uncomplicated

difficulty 1. arduousness, awkwardness, hardship, laboriousness, labour, pain, painfulness, strain, strenuousness, tribulation 2. deep water, dilemma, distress, embarrassment, fix (*Inf.*), hot water (*Inf.*), jam (*Inf.*), mess, perplexity, pickle (*Inf.*), plight, predicament, quandary, spot (*Inf.*), straits, tight spot, trial, trouble 3. *Often* *plural* complication, hassle (*Inf.*), hindrance, hurdle, impediment, objection, obstacle, opposition, pitfall, problem, protest, snag, stumbling block

diffidence backwardness, bashfulness, constraint, doubt, fear, hesitancy, hesitation, humility, insecurity, lack of self-confidence, meekness, modesty, reluctance, reserve, self-consciousness, sheepishness, shyness, timidity, timidness, timorousness, unassertiveness

Antonyms assurance, boldness, confidence, courage, firmness, self-confidence, self-possession

diffident backward, bashful, constrained, distrustful, doubtful, hesitant, insecure, meek, modest, reluctant, reserved, self-conscious, self-effacing, sheepish, shrinking, shy, suspicious, timid, timorous, unassertive, unassuming, unobtrusive, unsure, withdrawn

diffuse *adj.* 1. circumlocutory, copious, diffusive, digressive, discursive, long-winded, loose, maundering, meandering, prolix, rambling, vague, verbose, waffling (*Inf.*), wordy 2. dispersed, scattered, spread out, unconcentrated ~*v.* 3. circulate, dispel, dispense, disperse, disseminate, dissipate, distribute, propagate, scatter, spread

Antonyms *adj.* apposite, brief, compendious, concentrated, concise, succinct, terse, to the point

diffusion 1. circulation, dispersal, dispersion, dissemination, dissipation, distribution, expansion, propaganda, propagation, scattering, spread 2. circuitousness, diffuseness, digressiveness, discursiveness, long-windedness, prolixity, rambling, verbiage, verbosity, wandering, wordiness

dig *v.* 1. break up, burrow, delve, excavate, gouge, grub, hoe, hollow out, mine, penetrate, pierce, quarry, scoop, till, tunnel, turn over 2. drive, jab, poke, prod, punch, thrust 3. delve, dig down, go into, investigate, probe, research, search 4. *With* **out** *or* **up** bring to light, come across, come up with, discover, expose, extricate, find, retrieve, root (*Inf.*), rootle, uncover, unearth 5. *Inf.* appreciate, enjoy, follow, groove (*Dated sl.*), like, understand ~*n.* 6. jab, poke, prod, punch, thrust 7. barb, crack (*Sl.*), cutting remark, gibe, insult, jeer, quip, sneer, taunt, wisecrack (*Inf.*)

digest *v.* 1. absorb, assimilate, concoct, dissolve, incorporate, macerate 2. absorb, assimilate, con, consider, contemplate, grasp, master, meditate, ponder, study, take in, understand 3. arrange, classify, codify, dispose, methodize, systematize, tabulate 4. abridge, compress, condense, reduce, shorten, summarize ~*n.* 5. abridgment, abstract, compendium, condensation, epitome, précis, résumé, summary, synopsis

digestion absorption, assimilation, conversion, incorporation, ingestion, transformation

dig in 1. defend, entrench, establish, fortify, maintain 2. *Inf.* begin, set about, start eating, tuck in (*Inf.*)

dignified august, decorous, distinguished, exalted, formal, grave, honourable, imposing, lofty, lordly, noble, reserved, solemn, stately, upright

Antonyms crass, inelegant, unbecoming, undignified, unseemly, vulgar

dignify adorn, advance, aggrandize, distinguish, elevate, ennoble, exalt, glorify, grace, honour, promote, raise

dignitary *n.* bigwig (*Inf.*), celeb (*Inf.*), high-up (*Inf.*), notability, notable, personage, pillar of society (the church, the state), public figure, V.I.P., worthy

dignity 1. courtliness, decorum, grandeur, gravity, hauteur, loftiness, majesty, nobility, propriety, solemnity, stateliness 2. elevation, eminence, excellence, glory, greatness, honour, importance, nobleness, rank, respectability, standing, station, status 3. *amour-propre,* pride, self-esteem, self-importance, self-possession, self-regard, self-respect

digress be diffuse, depart, deviate, diverge, drift, expatiate, get off the point *or* subject, go off at a tangent, meander, ramble, stray, turn aside, wander

digression apostrophe, aside, departure, detour, deviation, divergence, diversion, footnote, obiter dictum, parenthesis, straying, wandering

digressive anecdotal, circuitous, circumlocutory, diffuse, discursive, divergent, drifting, episodic, excursive, meandering, rambling

dilapidated battered, beat-up (*Inf.*), broken-down, crumbling, decayed, decaying, decrepit, fallen in, falling apart, gone to rack and ruin, in ruins, neglected, ramshackle, rickety, ruined, ruinous, run-down, shabby, shaky, tumbledown, uncared for, worn-out

dilapidation collapse, decay, demolition, destruction, deterioration, disintegration, disrepair, dissolution, downfall, ruin, waste, wear and tear

dilate 1. broaden, distend, enlarge, expand, extend, puff out, stretch, swell, widen 2. amplify, be profuse, be prolix, descant, detail, develop, dwell on, enlarge, expand, expatiate, expound, spin out

Antonyms compress, constrict, contract, narrow, shrink

dilation broadening, dilatation, distension, enlargement, expansion, extension, increase, spread

dilatory backward, behindhand, dallying, delaying, laggard, lingering, loitering, procrastinating, putting off, slack, slow, sluggish, snail-like, tardy, tarrying, time-wasting

Antonyms on-the-ball (*Inf.*), prompt, punctual, sharp (*Inf.*)

dilemma 1. difficulty, embarrassment, fix (*Inf.*), jam (*Inf.*), mess, perplexity, pickle (*Inf.*), plight, predicament, problem, puzzle, quandary, spot (*Inf.*), strait, tight corner *or* spot 2. **on the horns of a dilemma** between a rock and a hard place (*Inf.*), between Scylla and Charybdis, between the devil and the deep blue sea

dilettante aesthete, amateur, dabbler, nonprofessional, trifler

diligence activity, application, assiduity, assiduousness, attention, attentiveness, care, constancy, earnestness, heedfulness, industry, intentness, laboriousness, perseverance, sedulousness

diligent active, assiduous, attentive, busy, careful, conscientious, constant, earnest, hard-working, indefatigable, industrious, laborious, painstaking, persevering, persistent, sedulous, studious, tireless

Antonyms careless, dilatory, inconstant, indifferent, lazy

dilly-dally dally, dawdle, delay, dither (*Chiefly Brit.*), falter, fluctuate, hesitate, hover, linger, loiter, potter, procrastinate, shillyshally (*Inf.*), trifle, vacillate, waver

dilute *v.* 1. adulterate, cut, make thinner, thin (out), water down, weaken 2. *Fig.* attenuate, decrease, diffuse, diminish, lessen, mitigate, reduce, temper, weaken

Antonyms concentrate, condense, intensify, strengthen, thicken

diluted adulterated, cut, dilute, thinned, watered down, watery, weak, weakened, wishy-washy (*Inf.*)

dim *adj.* 1. caliginous (*Archaic*), cloudy, dark, darkish, dusky, grey, overcast, poorly lit, shadowy, tenebrous, unilluminated 2. bleary, blurred, faint, fuzzy, ill-defined, indistinct, obscured, shadowy, unclear 3. braindead (*Inf.*), dense, doltish, dozy (*Brit. inf.*), dull, dumb (*Inf.*), obtuse, slow, slow on the uptake (*Inf.*), stupid, thick 4. confused, hazy, imperfect, indistinct, intangible, obscure, remote, shadowy, vague 5. dingy, dull, feeble, lacklustre, muted, opaque, pale, sullied, tarnished, weak 6. dashing, depressing, discouraging, gloomy, sombre, unfavourable, unpromising 7. **take a dim view** be displeased, be sceptical, disapprove, look askance, reject, suspect, take exception, view with disfavour ~*v.* 8. bedim, blur, cloud, darken, dull, fade, lower, obscure, tarnish, turn down

Antonyms (*sense 1*) bright, clear, cloudless, fair, limpid, pleasant, sunny, unclouded (*sense 2*) bright, brilliant, clear, distinct, limpid, palpable (*sense 3*) acute, astute, aware, brainy, bright, clever, intelligent, keen, quick-witted, sharp, smart

dimension *Often plural* 1. amplitude, bulk, capacity, extent, measurement, proportions, size, volume 2. bigness, extent, greatness, importance, largeness, magnitude, measure, range, scale, scope

diminish 1. abate, contract, curtail, cut, decrease, lessen, lower, reduce, retrench, shrink, weaken 2. decline, die out, dwindle, ebb, fade away, peter out, recede, shrivel, slacken, subside, wane 3. belittle, cheapen, demean, depreciate, devalue

Antonyms amplify, augment, enhance, enlarge, expand, grow, heighten, increase

diminution abatement, contraction, curtailment, cut, cutback, decay, decline, decrease, deduction, lessening, reduction, retrenchment, weakening

diminutive *adj.* bantam, Lilliputian, little, midget, mini, miniature, minute, petite, pocket(-sized), pygmy *or* pigmy, small, teensy-weensy, teeny-weeny, tiny, undersized, wee

Antonyms big, colossal, enormous, giant, gigantic, great, immense, jumbo (*Inf.*), king-size, massive (*Inf.*)

dimwit blockhead, bonehead (*Sl.*), booby, dullard, dunce, dunderhead, ignoramus, lamebrain (*Inf.*), nitwit (*Inf.*), numskull *or* numbskull

din 1. *n.* babel, clamour, clangour, clash, clatter, commotion, crash, hubbub, hullabaloo, noise, outcry, pandemonium, racket, row, shout, uproar 2. *v. Usually with* **into** drum into, go on at, hammer into, inculcate, instil, instruct, teach

Antonyms *n.* calm, calmness, hush, peace, quiet, quietness, silence, tranquillity

dine 1. banquet, chow down (*Sl.*), eat, feast, lunch, sup 2. *Often with* **on, off** *or* **upon** consume, eat, feed on

dingle dale, dell, glen, hollow, vale, valley

dingy bedimmed, colourless, dark, dim, dirty, discoloured, drab, dreary, dull, dusky, faded, gloomy, grimy, murky, obscure, seedy, shabby, soiled, sombre, tacky (*Inf.*)

dinky cute, dainty, mini, miniature, natty (*Inf.*), neat, petite, small, trim

dinner banquet, beanfeast (*Brit. inf.*), blowout (*Sl.*), collation, feast, main meal, meal, refection, repast, spread (*Inf.*)

dint 1. *As in* **by dint of** force, means, power, use, virtue 2. blow, dent, depression, indentation, stroke

dip *v.* 1. bathe, douse, duck, dunk, immerse, plunge, rinse, souse 2. decline, descend, disappear, droop, drop (down), fade, fall, lower, sag, set, sink, slope, slump, subside, tilt 3. ladle, scoop, spoon 4. *With* **in** *or* **into** browse, dabble, glance at, peruse, play at, run over, sample, skim, try 5. *With* **in** *or* **into** draw upon, reach into ~*n.* 6. douche, drenching, ducking, immersion, plunge, soaking 7. bathe, dive, plunge, swim 8. concoction, dilution, infusion, mixture, preparation, solution, suspension 9. basin, concavity, depression, hole, hollow, incline, slope 10. decline, drop, fall, lowering, sag, slip, slump

diplomacy 1. international negotiation, statecraft, statesmanship 2. artfulness, craft, delicacy, discretion, finesse, savoir-faire, skill, subtlety, tact
Antonyms awkwardness, clumsiness, ineptness, tactlessness, thoughtlessness

diplomat conciliator, go-between, mediator, moderator, negotiator, politician, public relations expert, tactician

diplomatic adept, discreet, polite, politic, prudent, sensitive, subtle, tactful
Antonyms impolitic, insensitive, rude, tactless, thoughtless, undiplomatic, unsubtle

dire 1. alarming, appalling, awful, calamitous, cataclysmic, catastrophic, cruel, disastrous, godawful (*Sl.*), horrible, horrid, ruinous, terrible, woeful 2. dismal, dreadful, fearful, gloomy, grim, ominous, portentous 3. critical, crucial, crying, desperate, drastic, exigent, extreme, pressing, urgent

direct[1] *v.* 1. administer, advise, conduct, control, dispose, govern, guide, handle, lead, manage, mastermind, oversee, preside over, regulate, rule, run, superintend, supervise 2. bid, charge, command, demand, dictate, enjoin, instruct, order 3. guide, indicate, lead, point in the direction of, point the way, show 4. address, aim, cast, fix, focus, intend, level, mean, point, train, turn 5. address, label, mail, route, send, superscribe

direct[2] *adj.* 1. candid, downright, frank, honest, man-to-man, matter-of-fact, open, outspoken, plain-spoken, sincere, straight, straightforward, upfront (*Inf.*) 2. absolute, blunt, categorical, downright, explicit, express, plain, point-blank, unambiguous, unequivocal 3. nonstop, not crooked, shortest, straight, through, unbroken, undeviating, uninterrupted 4. face-to-face, first-hand, head-on, immediate, personal
Antonyms ambiguous, circuitous, crooked, devious, indirect, mediated, sly, subtle

direction 1. administration, charge, command, control, government, guidance, leadership, management, order, oversight, superintendence, supervision 2. aim, bearing, course, line, path, road, route, track, way 3. bent, bias, current, drift, end, leaning, orientation, proclivity, tack, tendency, tenor, trend 4. address, label, mark, superscription

directions briefing, guidance, guidelines, indication, instructions, plan, recommendation, regulations

directive *n.* charge, command, decree, dictate, edict, fiat, imperative, injunction, instruction, mandate, notice, order, ordinance, regulation, ruling

directly 1. by the shortest route, exactly, in a beeline, precisely, straight, unswervingly, without deviation 2. as soon as possible, at once, dead, due, forthwith, immediately, in a second, instantaneously, instantly, pdq (*Sl.*), posthaste, presently, promptly, pronto (*Inf.*), quickly, right away, soon, speedily, straightaway 3. candidly, face-to-face, honestly, in person, openly, overtly, personally, plainly, point-blank, straightforwardly, truthfully, unequivocally, without prevarication

directness bluntness, candour, forthrightness, frankness, honesty, outspokenness, sincerity, straightforwardness

director administrator, boss (*Inf.*), chairman, chief, controller, executive, governor, head, leader, manager, organizer, principal, producer, supervisor

direful appalling, awful, calamitous, dire, dreadful, fearful, ghastly, gloomy, godawful (*Sl.*), horrible, horrid, shocking, terrible

dirge coronach (*Scot. & Irish*), dead march, elegy, funeral song, lament, requiem, threnody

dirt 1. crap (*Sl.*), crud (*Sl.*), dust, excrement, filth, grime, grot (*Sl.*), impurity, mire, muck, mud, shit (*Taboo sl.*), slime, smudge, stain, tarnish 2. clay, earth, loam, soil 3. indecency, obscenity, pornography, sleaze, smut

dirty *adj.* 1. begrimed, filthy, foul, grimy, grotty (*Sl.*), grubby, grungy (*Sl., chiefly U.S.*), messy, mucky, muddy, nasty, polluted, scuzzy (*Sl., chiefly U.S.*), soiled, sullied, unclean 2. blue, indecent, obscene, off-colour, pornographic, risqué, salacious, sleazy, smutty, vulgar 3. clouded, dark, dull, miry, muddy, not clear 4. corrupt, crooked, dishonest, fraudulent, illegal, treacherous, unfair, unscrupulous, unsporting 5. base, beggarly, contemptible, cowardly, despicable, ignominious, low, low-down (*Inf.*), mean, nasty, scurvy, shabby, sordid, squalid, vile 6. angry, annoyed, bitter, indignant, offended, resentful, scorching 7. *Of weather* gusty, louring *or* lowering, rainy, squally, stormy ~*v.* 8. begrime, blacken, defile, foul, mess up, muddy, pollute, smear, smirch, smudge, soil, spoil, stain, sully

Antonyms *adj.* clean, decent, honest, moral, pleasant, pure, reputable, respectable, upright ~*v.* clean, tidy up

disability 1. affliction, ailment, complaint, defect, disablement, disorder, handicap, impairment, infirmity, malady 2. disqualification, impotency, inability, incapacity, incompetency, unfitness, weakness

disable 1. cripple, damage, debilitate, enfeeble, hamstring, handicap, immobilize, impair, incapacitate, paralyse, prostrate, put out of action, render *hors de combat,* render inoperative, unfit, unman, weaken 2. disenable, disqualify, invalidate, render *or* declare incapable

disabled bedridden, crippled, handicapped, incapacitated, infirm, lame, maimed, mangled, mutilated, paralysed, weak, weakened, wrecked

Antonyms able-bodied, fit, hale, healthy, hearty, robust, sound, strong, sturdy

disabuse correct, enlighten, free from error, open the eyes of, set right, set straight, shatter (someone's) illusions, undeceive

disadvantage 1. damage, detriment, disservice, harm, hurt, injury, loss, prejudice 2. *Often plural* burden, downside, drawback, flaw, fly in the ointment (*Inf.*), handicap, hardship, hindrance, impediment, inconvenience, liability, minus (*Inf.*), nuisance, privation, snag, trouble, weakness, weak point 3. **at a disadvantage** boxed in, cornered, handicapped, in a corner, vulnerable

Antonyms advantage, aid, benefit, convenience, gain, help, merit, profit

disadvantaged deprived, discriminated against, handicapped, impoverished, struggling, underprivileged

disadvantageous adverse, damaging, deleterious, detrimental, harmful, hurtful, ill-timed, inconvenient, inexpedient, injurious, inopportune, prejudicial, unfavourable

disaffect alienate, antagonize, disunite, divide, estrange, repel

disaffected alienated, antagonistic, discontented, disloyal, dissatisfied, estranged, hostile, mutinous, rebellious, seditious, uncompliant, unsubmissive

disaffection alienation, animosity, antagonism, antipathy, aversion, breach, disagreement, discontent, dislike, disloyalty, dissatisfaction, estrangement, hostility, ill will, repugnance, resentment, unfriendliness

disagree 1. be discordant, be dissimilar, conflict, contradict, counter, depart, deviate, differ, diverge, run counter to, vary 2. argue, bicker, clash, contend, contest, debate, differ (in opinion), dispute, dissent, fall out (*Inf.*), have words (*Inf.*), object, oppose, quarrel, take issue with, wrangle 3. be injurious, bother, discomfort, distress, hurt, make ill, nauseate, sicken, trouble, upset

Antonyms accord, agree, coincide, concur, get on (together), harmonize

disagreeable 1. bad-tempered, brusque, churlish, contrary, cross, difficult, disobliging, ill-natured, irritable, nasty, peevish, ratty (*Brit. & N.Z. inf.*), rude, surly, tetchy, unfriendly, ungracious, unlikable *or* unlikeable, unpleasant 2. disgusting, displeasing, distasteful, horrid, nasty, objectionable, obnoxious, offensive, repellent, repugnant, repulsive, uninviting, unpalatable, unpleasant, unsavoury, yucky *or* yukky (*Sl.*)

Antonyms agreeable, congenial, delightful, enjoyable, friendly, good-natured, lovely, nice, pleasant

disagreement 1. difference, discrepancy, disparity, dissimilarity, dissimilitude, divergence, diversity, incompatibility, incongruity, unlikeness, variance 2. altercation, argument, clash, conflict, debate, difference, discord, dispute, dissent, division, falling out, misunderstanding, quarrel, row, squabble, strife, wrangle 3. **in disagreement** at daggers drawn, at loggerheads, at odds, at variance, disunited, in conflict, in disharmony

Antonyms accord, agreement, assent, consensus, correspondence, harmony, similarity, unison, unity

disallow 1. abjure, disavow, disclaim, dismiss, disown, rebuff, refuse, reject, repudiate 2. ban, boycott, cancel, embargo, forbid, prohibit, proscribe, veto

disappear 1. abscond, be lost to view, depart, drop out of sight, ebb, escape, evanesce, fade away, flee, fly, go, pass, recede, retire, vanish from sight, wane, withdraw 2. cease, cease to be known, die out, dissolve, end, evaporate, expire, fade, leave no trace, melt away, pass away, perish, vanish

Antonyms appear, arrive, materialize, reappear

disappearance departure, desertion, disappearing, disappearing trick, eclipse, evanescence, evaporation, fading, flight, going, loss, melting, passing, vanishing, vanishing point

disappoint 1. chagrin, dash, deceive, delude, disenchant, disgruntle, dishearten, disillusion, dismay, dissatisfy, fail, let down, sadden, vex 2. baffle, balk, defeat, disconcert, foil, frustrate, hamper, hinder, thwart

disappointed balked, cast down, depressed, despondent, discontented, discouraged, disenchanted, disgruntled, disillusioned, dissatisfied, distressed, downhearted, foiled, frustrated, let down, saddened, thwarted, upset

Antonyms content, contented, fulfilled, happy, pleased, satisfied

disappointing depressing, disagreeable, disconcerting, discouraging, failing, inadequate, inferior, insufficient, lame, pathetic, sad, second-rate, sorry, unexpected, unhappy, unsatisfactory, unworthy, upsetting

disappointment 1. chagrin, discontent, discouragement, disenchantment, disillusionment, displeasure, dissatisfaction, distress, failure, frustration, ill-success, mortification, regret, unfulfilment 2. blow, calamity, disaster, failure, fiasco, letdown, miscarriage, misfortune, setback, washout (*Inf.*)

disapprobation blame, censure, condemnation, disapproval, disfavour, dislike, displeasure, dissatisfaction, reproof, stricture

disapproval censure, condemnation, criticism, denunciation, deprecation, disapprobation, displeasure, dissatisfaction, objection, reproach, stick (*Sl.*)

disapprove 1. *Often with* of blame, censure, condemn, deplore, deprecate, discountenance, dislike, find unacceptable, frown on, look down one's nose at (*Inf.*), object to, reject, take exception to 2. disallow, set aside, spurn, turn down, veto

Antonyms applaud, approve, commend, compliment, endorse, give the go-ahead (to) (*Inf.*), like, O.K. *or* okay (*Inf.*)

disarm 1. disable, render defenceless, unarm 2. deactivate, demilitarize, demobilize, disband 3. persuade, set at ease, win over

disarmament arms limitation, arms reduction, de-escalation, demilitarization, demobilization

disarming charming, irresistible, likable *or* likeable, persuasive, winning

disarrange confuse, derange, discompose, disorder, disorganize, disturb, jumble (up), mess (up), scatter, shake (up), shuffle, unsettle, untidy

disarray 1. confusion, discomposure, disharmony, dismay, disorder, disorderliness, disorganization, disunity, indiscipline, unruliness, upset 2. chaos, clutter, dishevelment, hodgepodge (*U.S.*), hotchpotch, jumble, mess, mix-up, muddle, pig's breakfast (*Inf.*), shambles, state, tangle, untidiness

Antonyms arrangement, harmony, method, neatness, order, orderliness, organization, pattern, plan, regularity, symmetry, system, tidiness

disassemble deconstruct, dismantle, dismount, knock down, strike, take apart, take down

disaster accident, act of God, adversity, blow, bummer (*Sl.*), calamity, cataclysm, catastrophe, misadventure, mischance, misfortune, mishap, reverse, ruin, ruination, stroke, tragedy, trouble

disastrous adverse, calamitous, cataclysmal, cataclysmic, catastrophic, destructive, detrimental, devastating, dire, dreadful, fatal, hapless, harmful, ill-fated, ill-starred, ruinous, terrible, tragic, unfortunate, unlucky, unpropitious, untoward

disavow abjure, contradict, deny, disclaim, disown, forswear, gainsay (*Archaic or literary*), rebut, reject, repudiate, retract

disavowal abjuration, contradiction, denial, disclaimer, gainsaying (*Archaic or literary*), recantation, rejection, renunciation, repudiation, retraction

disband break up, demobilize, dismiss, disperse, dissolve, go (their) separate ways, let go, part company, scatter, send home, separate

disbelief distrust, doubt, dubiety, incredulity, mistrust, scepticism, unbelief

Antonyms belief, credence, credulity, faith, trust

disbelieve discount, discredit, give no credence to, mistrust, not accept, not buy (*Sl.*), not credit, not swallow (*Inf.*), reject, repudiate, scoff at, suspect

disbeliever agnostic, atheist, doubter, doubting Thomas, questioner, sceptic, scoffer

Antonyms adherent, believer, devotee, disciple, follower, proselyte, supporter, upholder, zealot

disbelievingly askance, cynically, doubtingly, incredulously, mistrustfully, quizzically, sceptically, suspiciously, with a pinch of salt

disburden alleviate, diminish, discharge, disencumber, ease, free, lighten, relieve, take a load off one's mind, unburden, unload

disburse expend, fork out (*Sl.*), lay out, pay out, shell out (*Inf.*), spend

disbursement disposal, expenditure, outlay, payment, spending

discard abandon, axe (*Inf.*), cast aside, chuck (*Inf.*), dispense with, dispose of, ditch (*Sl.*), drop, dump (*Inf.*), get rid of, jettison, junk (*Inf.*), reject, relinquish, remove, repudiate, scrap, shed, throw away *or* out

Antonyms hang *or* hold on to, hold back, keep, reserve, retain, save

discern 1. behold, catch sight of, descry, discover, espy, make out, notice, observe, perceive, recognize, see, suss (out) (*Sl.*) 2. detect, determine, differentiate, discriminate, distinguish, judge, make a distinction, pick out

discernible apparent, appreciable, clear, detectable, discoverable, distinct, distinguishable, noticeable, observable, obvious, perceptible, plain, recognizable, visible

discerning acute, astute, clear-sighted, critical, discriminating, ingenious, intelligent, judicious, knowing, penetrating, perceptive, percipient, perspicacious, piercing, sagacious, sensitive, sharp, shrewd, subtle, wise

discernment acumen, acuteness, astuteness, awareness, clear-sightedness, cleverness, discrimination, ingenuity, insight, intelligence, judgment, keenness, penetration, perception, perceptiveness, percipience, perspicacity, sagacity, sharpness, shrewdness, understanding

discharge *v.* 1. absolve, acquit, allow to go, clear, exonerate, free, liberate, pardon, release, set free *~n.* 2. acquittal, clearance, exoneration, liberation, pardon, release, remittance *~v.* 3. cashier, discard, dismiss, eject, expel, fire (*Inf.*), give (someone) the sack (*Inf.*), oust, remove, sack (*Inf.*) *~n.* 4. congé, demobilization, dismissal, ejection, the boot (*Sl.*), the (old) heave-ho (*Inf.*), the order of the boot (*Sl.*), the sack (*Inf.*) *~v.* 5. detonate, explode, fire, let off, set off, shoot *~n.* 6. blast, burst, detonation, discharging, explosion, firing, fusillade, report, salvo, shot, volley *~v.* 7. disembogue, dispense, emit, empty, excrete, exude, give off, gush, leak, ooze, pour forth, release, void *~n.* 8. emission, emptying, excretion, flow, ooze, pus, secretion, seepage, suppuration, vent, voiding *~v.* 9. disburden, lighten, off-load, remove, unburden, unload *~n.* 10. disburdening, emptying, unburdening, unloading *~v.* 11. accomplish, carry out, do, execute, fulfil, observe, perform *~n.* 12. accomplishment, achievement, execution, fulfilment, observance, performance *~v.* 13. clear, honour, meet, pay, relieve, satisfy, settle, square up *~n.* 14. payment, satisfaction, settlement

disciple adherent, apostle, believer, catechumen, convert, devotee, follower, learner, partisan, proselyte, pupil, student, supporter, votary

Antonyms guru, leader, master, swami, teacher

disciplinarian authoritarian, despot, drill sergeant, hard master, martinet, stickler, strict teacher, taskmaster, tyrant

discipline *n.* 1. drill, exercise, method, practice, regimen, regulation, training 2. conduct, control, orderliness, regulation, restraint, self-control, strictness 3. castigation, chastisement, correction, punishment 4. area, branch of knowledge, course, curriculum, field of study, speciality, subject *~v.* 5. break in, bring up, check, control, drill, educate, exercise, form, govern, instruct, inure, prepare, regulate, restrain, train 6. castigate, chasten, chastise, correct, penalize, punish, reprimand, reprove

disclaim abandon, abjure, abnegate, decline, deny, disaffirm, disallow, disavow, disown, forswear, rebut, reject, renege, renounce, repudiate, retract

disclaimer abjuration, contradiction, denial, disavowal, rejection, renunciation, repudiation, retraction

disclose 1. blow wide open (*Sl.*), broadcast, communicate, confess, divulge, impart, leak, let slip, make known, make public, publish, relate, reveal, spill one's guts about (*Sl.*), spill the beans about (*Inf.*), tell, unveil, utter 2. bring to light, discover, exhibit, expose, lay bare, reveal, show, uncover, unveil

Antonyms conceal, cover, dissemble, hide, keep dark, keep secret, mask, obscure, secrete, veil

disclosure acknowledgment, admission, announcement, broadcast, confession, declaration, discovery, divulgence, exposé, exposure, leak, publication, revelation, uncovering

discoloration blemish, blot, blotch, mark, patch, smirch, splotch, spot, stain

discolour fade, mar, mark, rust, soil, stain, streak, tarnish, tinge

discomfit 1. abash, confound, confuse, demoralize, discompose, disconcert, embarrass, faze, flurry, fluster, perplex, perturb, rattle (*Inf.*), ruffle, take aback, unnerve, unsettle, worry 2. baffle, balk, beat, checkmate, defeat, foil, frustrate, outwit, overcome, thwart, trump, worst

discomfiture 1. abashment, chagrin, confusion, demoralization, discomposure, embarrassment, humiliation, shame, unease 2. beating, defeat, disappointment, failure, frustration, overthrow, rout, ruin, undoing

discomfort 1. *n.* ache, annoyance, disquiet, distress, gall, hardship, hurt, inquietude, irritation, malaise, nuisance, pain, soreness, trouble, uneasiness, unpleasantness, vexation 2. *v.* discomfit, discompose, disquiet, distress, disturb, embarrass, make uncomfortable

Antonyms *n.* comfort, ease, reassurance, solace ~*v.* alleviate, assuage, comfort, ease, reassure, solace, soothe

discommode annoy, bother, burden, disquiet, disturb, harass, hassle (*Inf.*), incommode, inconvenience, molest, put out, trouble

discompose agitate, annoy, bewilder, confuse, discomfit, disconcert, displease, disturb, embarrass, faze, flurry, fluster, fret, hassle (*Inf.*), irritate, nettle, perplex, perturb, provoke, rattle (*Inf.*), ruffle, unnerve, unsettle, upset, vex, worry

discomposure agitation, anxiety, confusion, discomfiture, disquiet, disquietude, distraction, disturbance, embarrassment, fluster, inquietude, malaise, nervousness, perturbation, trepidation, uneasiness

disconcert 1. abash, agitate, bewilder, discompose, disturb, faze, flummox, flurry, fluster, nonplus, perplex, perturb, put out of countenance, rattle (*Inf.*), ruffle, shake up (*Inf.*), take aback, throw off balance, trouble, unbalance, unnerve, unsettle, upset, worry 2. baffle, balk, confuse, defeat, disarrange, frustrate, hinder, put off, thwart, undo

disconcerted annoyed, at sea, bewildered, caught off balance, confused, distracted, disturbed, embarrassed, fazed, flummoxed, flurried, flustered, mixed-up, nonplussed, out of countenance, perturbed, rattled (*Inf.*), ruffled, shook up (*Inf.*), taken aback, thrown (*Inf.*), troubled, unsettled, upset

disconcerting alarming, awkward, baffling, bewildering, bothersome, confusing, dismaying, distracting, disturbing, embarrassing, off-putting (*Brit. inf.*), perplexing, upsetting

disconnect cut off, detach, disengage, divide, part, separate, sever, take apart, uncouple

disconnected confused, disjointed, garbled, illogical, incoherent, irrational, jumbled, mixed-up, rambling, uncoordinated, unintelligible, wandering

disconnection cessation, cut-off, cutting off, discontinuation, discontinuity, interruption, separation, severance, stoppage, suspension

disconsolate crushed, dejected, desolate, despairing, dismal, forlorn, gloomy, grief-stricken, heartbroken, hopeless, inconsolable, melancholy, miserable, sad, unhappy, woeful, wretched

discontent *n.* discontentment, displeasure, dissatisfaction, envy, fretfulness, regret, restlessness, uneasiness, unhappiness, vexation

discontented brassed off (*Brit. sl.*), cheesed off (*Brit. sl.*), complaining, disaffected, disgruntled, displeased, dissatisfied, exasperated, fed up, fretful, miserable, pissed off (*Taboo sl.*), unhappy, vexed, with a chip on one's shoulder (*Inf.*)

Antonyms cheerful, content, contented, happy, pleased, satisfied

discontinuance adjournment, cessation, discontinuation, disjunction, intermission, interruption, separation, stop, stoppage, stopping, suspension, termination

discontinue abandon, axe (*Inf.*), break off, cease, drop, end, finish, give up, halt, interrupt, kick (*Inf.*), leave off, pause, put an end to, quit, refrain from, stop, suspend, terminate

discontinued abandoned, ended, finished, given up *or* over, halted, no longer made, terminated

discontinuity disconnectedness, disconnection, disjointedness, disruption, disunion, incoherence, interruption, lack of coherence, lack of unity

discontinuous broken, disconnected, fitful, intermittent, interrupted, irregular, spasmodic

discord 1. clashing, conflict, contention, difference, disagreement, discordance, dispute, dissension, disunity, division, friction, incompatibility, lack of concord, opposition, row, rupture, strife, variance, wrangling 2. cacophony, din, disharmony, dissonance, harshness, jangle, jarring, racket, tumult

Antonyms accord, agreement, concord, euphony, friendship, harmony, melody, peace, tunefulness, understanding, unison, unity

discordant 1. at odds, clashing, conflicting, contradictory, contrary, different, disagreeing, divergent, incompatible, incongruous, inconsistent, opposite 2. cacophonous, dissonant, grating, harsh, inharmonious, jangling, jarring, shrill, strident, unmelodious

discount *v.* 1. brush off (*Sl.*), disbelieve, disregard, ignore, leave out of account, overlook, pass over 2. deduct, lower, mark down, rebate, reduce, take off ~*n.* 3. abatement, allowance, concession, cut, cut price, deduction, drawback, percentage (*Inf.*), rebate, reduction

discountenance *v.* 1. abash, chagrin, confuse, discompose, disconcert, embarrass, humiliate, put down (*Sl.*), shame 2. condemn, disapprove, discourage, disfavour, frown on, object to, oppose, resist, take exception to, veto

discourage 1. abash, awe, cast down, cow, damp, dampen, dash, daunt, deject, demoralize, depress, dishearten, dismay, dispirit, frighten, intimidate, overawe, psych out (*Inf.*), put a damper on, scare, unman, unnerve 2. check, curb, deprecate, deter, discountenance, disfavour, dissuade, divert from, hinder, inhibit, prevent, put off, restrain, talk out of, throw cold water on (*Inf.*)
Antonyms bid, countenance, embolden, encourage, hearten, inspire, urge, welcome

discouraged crestfallen, dashed, daunted, deterred, disheartened, dismayed, dispirited, downcast, down in the mouth, glum, pessimistic, put off, sick as a parrot (*Inf.*)

discouragement 1. cold feet (*Inf.*), dejection, depression, despair, despondency, disappointment, discomfiture, dismay, downheartedness, hopelessness, loss of confidence, low spirits, pessimism 2. constraint, curb, damper, deterrent, disincentive, hindrance, impediment, obstacle, opposition, rebuff, restraint, setback

discouraging dampening, daunting, depressing, disappointing, disheartening, dispiriting, off-putting (*Brit. inf.*), unfavourable, unpropitious

discourse *n.* 1. chat, communication, conversation, converse, dialogue, discussion, seminar, speech, talk 2. address, disquisition, dissertation, essay, homily, lecture, oration, sermon, speech, talk, treatise ~*v.* 3. confer, converse, debate, declaim, discuss, expatiate, hold forth, speak, talk

discourteous abrupt, bad-mannered, boorish, brusque, curt, disrespectful, ill-bred, ill-mannered, impolite, insolent, offhand, rude, uncivil, uncourteous, ungentlemanly, ungracious, unmannerly
Antonyms civil, courteous, courtly, gracious, mannerly, polite, respectful, well-mannered

discourtesy 1. bad manners, disrespectfulness, ill-breeding, impertinence, impoliteness, incivility, insolence, rudeness, ungraciousness, unmannerliness 2. affront, cold shoulder, insult, rebuff, slight, snub

discover 1. bring to light, come across, come upon, dig up, find, light upon, locate, turn up, uncover, unearth 2. ascertain, descry, detect, determine, discern, disclose, espy, find out, get wise to (*Inf.*), learn, notice, perceive, realize, recognize, reveal, see, spot, suss (out) (*Sl.*), turn up, uncover 3. conceive, contrive, design, devise, invent, originate, pioneer

discoverer author, explorer, founder, initiator, inventor, originator, pioneer

discovery 1. ascertainment, detection, disclosure, espial, exploration, finding, introduction, locating, location, origination, revelation, uncovering 2. bonanza, breakthrough, coup, find, findings, godsend, innovation, invention, secret

discredit *v.* 1. blame, bring into disrepute, censure, defame, degrade, detract from, disgrace, dishonour, disparage, reproach, slander, slur, smear, vilify ~*n.* 2. aspersion, censure, disgrace, dishonour, disrepute, ignominy, ill-repute, imputation, odium, reproach, scandal, shame, slur, smear, stigma ~*v.* 3. challenge, deny, disbelieve, discount, dispute, distrust, doubt, mistrust, question ~*n.* 4. distrust, doubt, mistrust, question, scepticism, suspicion
Antonyms *v.* acclaim, applaud, commend, honour, laud, pay tribute to, praise ~*n.* acclaim, acknowledgment, approval, commendation, credit, honour, merit, praise

discreditable blameworthy, degrading, disgraceful, dishonourable, humiliating, ignominious, improper, infamous, reprehensible, scandalous, shameful, unprincipled, unworthy

discredited brought into disrepute, debunked, discarded, exploded, exposed, obsolete, outworn, refuted, rejected

discreet careful, cautious, circumspect, considerate, diplomatic, discerning, guarded, judicious, politic, prudent, reserved, sagacious, sensible, tactful, wary
Antonyms incautious, indiscreet, injudicious, rash, tactless, undiplomatic, unthinking, unwise

discrepancy conflict, contrariety, difference, disagreement, discordance, disparity, dissimilarity, dissonance, divergence, incongruity, inconsistency, variance, variation

discrepant at variance, conflicting, contradictory, contrary, differing, disagreeing, discordant, incompatible, incongruous, inconsistent

discrete detached, disconnected, discontinuous, distinct, individual, separate, unattached

discretion 1. acumen, care, carefulness, caution, circumspection, consideration, diplomacy, discernment, good sense, heedfulness, judgment, judiciousness, maturity,

prudence, sagacity, tact, wariness 2. choice, disposition, inclination, liking, mind, option, pleasure, predilection, preference, responsibility, volition, will, wish
Antonyms carelessness, indiscretion, insensitivity, rashness, tactlessness, thoughtlessness

discretionary arbitrary (*Law*), elective, nonmandatory, open, open to choice, optional, unrestricted

discriminate 1. disfavour, favour, show bias, show prejudice, single out, treat as inferior, treat differently, victimize 2. assess, differentiate, discern, distinguish, draw a distinction, evaluate, segregate, separate, sift, tell the difference

discriminating acute, astute, critical, cultivated, discerning, fastidious, keen, particular, refined, selective, sensitive, tasteful
Antonyms careless, desultory, general, hit or miss (*Inf.*), indiscriminate, random, undiscriminating, unselective, unsystematic

discrimination 1. bias, bigotry, favouritism, inequity, intolerance, prejudice, unfairness 2. acumen, acuteness, clearness, discernment, insight, judgment, keenness, penetration, perception, refinement, sagacity, subtlety, taste

discriminatory, discriminative 1. biased, favouring, inequitable, one-sided, partial, partisan, preferential, prejudiced, prejudicial, unjust, weighted 2. analytical, astute, differentiating, discerning, discriminating, perceptive, perspicacious

discursive circuitous, desultory, diffuse, digressive, erratic, long-winded, loose, meandering, prolix, rambling, roundabout, roving

discuss argue, confer, consider, consult with, converse, debate, deliberate, examine, exchange views on, get together, go into, reason about, review, sift, talk about, thrash out, ventilate, weigh up the pros and cons

discussion analysis, argument, colloquy, confabulation, conference, consideration, consultation, conversation, debate, deliberation, dialogue, discourse, examination, exchange, review, scrutiny, seminar, symposium

disdain 1. *v.* belittle, contemn, deride, despise, disregard, look down on, look down one's nose at (*Inf.*), misprize, pooh-pooh, reject, scorn, slight, sneer at, spurn, undervalue 2. *n.* arrogance, contempt, contumely, derision, dislike, haughtiness, hauteur, indifference, scorn, sneering, snobbishness, superciliousness

disdainful aloof, arrogant, contemptuous, derisive, haughty, high and mighty (*Inf.*), hoity-toity (*Inf.*), insolent, proud, scornful, sneering, supercilious, superior

disease 1. affliction, ailment, complaint, condition, disorder, ill health, illness, indisposition, infection, infirmity, malady, sickness, upset 2. *Fig.* blight, cancer, canker, contagion, contamination, disorder, malady, plague

diseased ailing, infected, rotten, sick, sickly, tainted, unhealthy, unsound, unwell, unwholesome

disembark alight, arrive, get off, go ashore, land, step out of

disembodied bodiless, ghostly, immaterial, incorporeal, intangible, phantom, spectral, spiritual, unbodied

disembowel draw, eviscerate, gut, paunch

disenchant break the spell, bring (someone) down to earth, destroy (someone's) illusions, disabuse, disillusion, open (someone's) eyes, undeceive

disenchanted blasé, cynical, disappointed, disillusioned, indifferent, jaundiced, let down, out of love, sick of, soured, undeceived

disenchantment disappointment, disillusion, disillusionment, revulsion, rude awakening

disencumber disburden, discharge, disembarrass, disembroil, extricate, lighten, unburden, unhamper, unload

disengage 1. disentangle, ease, extricate, free, liberate, loosen, release, set free, unbridle, unloose, untie 2. detach, disconnect, disjoin, disunite, divide, separate, undo, withdraw

disengaged 1. apart, detached, free, loose, out of gear, released, separate, unattached, unconnected, uncoupled 2. at ease, at leisure, free, not busy, uncommitted, unoccupied, vacant

disengagement detachment, disconnection, disentanglement, division, separation, withdrawal

disentangle 1. detach, disconnect, disengage, extricate, free, loose, separate, sever, unfold, unravel, unsnarl, untangle, untwist 2. clarify, clear (up), resolve, simplify, sort out, work out

disfavour 1. disapprobation, disapproval, dislike, displeasure 2. *As in* **fall into disfavour** bad books (*Inf.*), discredit, disesteem, disgrace, doghouse (*Inf.*), shame, unpopularity 3. bad turn, discourtesy, disservice

disfigure blemish, damage, deface, deform, disfeature, distort, injure, maim, make ugly, mar, mutilate, scar

disfigurement blemish, defacement, defect, deformity, distortion, impairment, injury, mutilation, scar, spot, stain

disgorge 1. barf (*U.S. sl.*), belch, chuck (up) (*Sl., chiefly U.S.*), chunder (*Sl., chiefly Aust.*), discharge, do a technicolour yawn (*Sl.*), eject, empty, expel, regurgitate, spew, spit up, spout, throw up, toss one's cookies (*U.S. sl.*), upchuck (*U.S. sl.*), vomit 2. cede, give up, relinquish, renounce, resign, surrender, yield

disgrace *n.* 1. baseness, degradation, dishonour, disrepute, ignominy, infamy, odium, opprobrium, shame 2. aspersion, blemish, blot, defamation, reproach, scandal, slur, stain, stigma 3. contempt, discredit, disesteem, disfavour, obloquy ~*v.* 4. abase, bring shame upon, defame, degrade, discredit, disfavour, dishonour, disparage, humiliate, reproach, shame, slur, stain, stigmatize, sully, taint
Antonyms *n.* credit, esteem, favour, grace, honour, repute ~*v.* credit, grace, honour

disgraced branded, degraded, discredited, dishonoured, humiliated, in disgrace, in the doghouse (*Inf.*), mortified, shamed, stigmatized

disgraceful blameworthy, contemptible, degrading, detestable, discreditable, dishonourable, disreputable, ignominious, infamous, low, mean, opprobrious, scandalous, shameful, shocking, unworthy

disgruntled annoyed, cheesed off (*Brit. sl.*), discontented, displeased, dissatisfied, grumpy, hacked (off) (*U.S. sl.*), huffy, irritated, malcontent, peeved, peevish, petulant, pissed off (*Taboo sl.*), put out, sulky, sullen, testy, vexed

disguise *v.* 1. camouflage, cloak, conceal, cover, hide, mask, screen, secrete, shroud, veil 2. deceive, dissemble, dissimulate, fake, falsify, fudge, gloss over, misrepresent ~*n.* 3. camouflage, cloak, costume, cover, get-up (*Inf.*), mask, screen, veil 4. deception, dissimulation, façade, front, pretence, semblance, trickery, veneer

disguised camouflaged, cloaked, covert, fake, false, feigned, incognito, in disguise, masked, pretend, undercover, unrecognizable

disgust 1. *v.* cause aversion, displease, fill with loathing, gross out (*U.S. sl.*), nauseate, offend, outrage, put off, repel, revolt, sicken, turn one's stomach 2. *n.* abhorrence, abomination, antipathy, aversion, detestation, dislike, distaste, hatefulness, hatred, loathing, nausea, odium, repugnance, repulsion, revulsion
Antonyms *v.* delight, impress, please ~*n.* liking, love, pleasure, satisfaction, taste

disgusted appalled, nauseated, offended, outraged, repelled, repulsed, scandalized, sick and tired of (*Inf.*), sickened, sick of (*Inf.*)

disgusting abominable, cringe-making (*Brit. inf.*), detestable, distasteful, foul, gross, grotty (*Sl.*), hateful, loathsome, nasty, nauseating, nauseous, objectionable, obnoxious, odious, offensive, repellent, repugnant, revolting, shameless, sickening, stinking, vile, vulgar, yucky *or* yukky (*Sl.*)

dish *n.* 1. bowl, plate, platter, salver 2. fare, food, recipe ~*v.* 3. *Sl.* finish, muck up (*Sl.*), ruin, spoil, torpedo, wreck

disharmony clash, conflict, disaccord, discord, discordance, dissonance, friction, inharmoniousness

dishearten cast down, crush, damp, dampen, dash, daunt, deject, depress, deter, discourage, dismay, dispirit, put a damper on
Antonyms buck up (*Inf.*), cheer up, encourage, hearten, lift, perk up, rally

disheartened crestfallen, crushed, daunted, dejected, depressed, disappointed, discouraged, dismayed, dispirited, downcast, downhearted, sick as a parrot (*Inf.*)

dishevelled bedraggled, blowzy, disarranged, disarrayed, disordered, frowzy, hanging loose, messy, ruffled, rumpled, tousled, uncombed, unkempt, untidy
Antonyms chic, dapper, neat, smart, soigné *or* soignée, spick-and-span, spruce, tidy, trim, well-groomed

dishonest bent (*Sl.*), cheating, corrupt, crafty, crooked (*Inf.*), deceitful, deceiving, deceptive, designing, disreputable, double-dealing, false, fraudulent, guileful, knavish (*Archaic*), lying, mendacious, perfidious, shady (*Inf.*), swindling, treacherous, unfair, unprincipled, unscrupulous, untrustworthy, untruthful
Antonyms honest, honourable, law-abiding, lawful, principled, true, trustworthy, upright

dishonesty cheating, chicanery, corruption, craft, criminality, crookedness, deceit, duplicity, falsehood, falsity, fraud, fraudulence, graft (*Inf.*), improbity, mendacity, perfidy, sharp practice, stealing, treachery, trickery, unscrupulousness, wiliness

dishonour *v.* 1. abase, blacken, corrupt, debase, debauch, defame, degrade, discredit, disgrace, shame, sully 2. defile, deflower, pollute, rape, ravish, seduce ~*n.* 3. abasement, degradation, discredit, disfavour, disgrace, disrepute, ignominy, infamy, obloquy, odium, opprobrium, reproach, scandal, shame 4. abuse, affront, discourtesy, indignity, insult, offence, outrage, slight
Antonyms *v.* esteem, exalt, respect, revere,

worship ~*n.* decency, goodness, honour, integrity, morality, principles, rectitude

dishonourable 1. base, contemptible, despicable, discreditable, disgraceful, ignoble, ignominious, infamous, scandalous, shameful 2. blackguardly, corrupt, disreputable, shameless, treacherous, unprincipled, unscrupulous, untrustworthy

dish out allocate, distribute, dole out, hand out, inflict, mete out

dish-shaped concave, cupped, cup-shaped, depressed, hollow, hollowed out, incurvate, incurved, pushed in, scooped, scooped out, scyphiform, sunken

dish up hand out, ladle, prepare, present, produce, scoop, serve, spoon

disillusion *v.* break the spell, bring down to earth, disabuse, disenchant, open the eyes of, shatter one's illusions, undeceive

disillusioned disabused, disappointed, disenchanted, enlightened, indifferent, out of love, sadder and wiser, undeceived

disincentive damper, determent, deterrent, discouragement, dissuasion, impediment

disinclination alienation, antipathy, aversion, demur, dislike, hesitance, lack of desire, lack of enthusiasm, loathness, objection, opposition, reluctance, repugnance, resistance, unwillingness

disinclined antipathetic, averse, balking, hesitating, indisposed, loath, not in the mood, opposed, reluctant, resistant, unwilling

disinfect clean, cleanse, decontaminate, deodorize, fumigate, purify, sanitize, sterilize

Antonyms contaminate, defile, infect, poison, pollute, taint, vitiate

disinfectant antiseptic, germicide, sanitizer, sterilizer

disingenuous artful, cunning, deceitful, designing, dishonest, duplicitous, feigned, guileful, insidious, insincere, shifty, sly, two-faced, uncandid, underhanded, unfair, wily

disinherit cut off, cut off without a penny, disown, dispossess, oust, repudiate

disintegrate break apart, break up, crumble, disunite, fall apart, fall to pieces, reduce to fragments, separate, shatter, splinter

disinter 1. dig up, disentomb, exhume, unearth 2. bring to light, disclose, discover, expose, uncover, unearth

disinterest candidness, detachment, disinterestedness, dispassionateness, equity, fairness, impartiality, justice, neutrality, unbiasedness

disinterested candid, detached, dispassionate, equitable, even-handed, free from self-interest, impartial, impersonal, neutral, outside, unbiased, uninvolved, unprejudiced, unselfish

Antonyms biased, involved, partial, prejudiced, selfish

disjointed 1. aimless, confused, disconnected, disordered, fitful, incoherent, loose, rambling, spasmodic, unconnected 2. disconnected, dislocated, displaced, disunited, divided, separated, split

dislikable, dislikeable detestable, displeasing, distasteful, hatable, nasty, objectionable, odious, unattractive, unlikable *or* unlikeable, unpleasant

dislike 1. *n.* animosity, animus, antagonism, antipathy, aversion, detestation, disapprobation, disapproval, disgust, disinclination, displeasure, distaste, enmity, hatred, hostility, loathing, odium, repugnance 2. *v.* abhor, abominate, be averse to, despise, detest, disapprove, disfavour, disrelish, hate, have no taste *or* stomach for, loathe, not be able to bear *or* abide, object to, scorn, shun

Antonyms *n.* admiration, attraction, delight, esteem, inclination, liking ~*v.* esteem, favour, like

dislocate 1. disorder, displace, disrupt, disturb, misplace, shift 2. disarticulate, disconnect, disengage, disjoint, disunite, luxate (*Medical*), put out of joint, unhinge

dislocation 1. disarray, disorder, disorganization, disruption, disturbance, misplacement 2. disarticulation, disconnection, disengagement, luxation (*Medical*), unhinging

dislodge dig out, disentangle, displace, disturb, eject, extricate, force out, knock loose, oust, remove, uproot

disloyal apostate, disaffected, faithless, false, perfidious, seditious, subversive, traitorous, treacherous, treasonable, two-faced, unfaithful, unpatriotic, untrustworthy

Antonyms constant, dependable, dutiful, faithful, loyal, steadfast, true, trustworthy, trusty

disloyalty betrayal of trust, breach of trust, breaking of faith, deceitfulness, double-dealing, falseness, falsity, inconstancy, infidelity, perfidy, Punic faith, treachery, treason, unfaithfulness

dismal black, bleak, cheerless, dark, depressing, despondent, discouraging, dolorous, dreary, forlorn, funereal, gloomy, gruesome, lonesome, louring *or* lowering, lugubrious, melancholy, sad, sombre, sorrowful

Antonyms bright, cheerful, cheery, glad, happy, joyful, light-hearted, sunny

dismantle demolish, disassemble, dismount, raze, strike, strip, take apart, take to pieces, unrig

dismay *v.* 1. affright, alarm, appal, distress, fill with consternation, frighten, horrify, paralyse, scare, terrify, unnerve 2. daunt, disappoint, discourage, dishearten, disillusion, dispirit, put off ~*n.* 3. agitation, alarm, anxiety, apprehension, consternation, distress, dread, fear, fright, horror, panic, terror, trepidation 4. chagrin, disappointment, discouragement, disillusionment, upset

dismember amputate, anatomize, cut into pieces, disjoint, dislimb, dislocate, dissect, divide, mutilate, rend, sever

dismiss 1. axe (*Inf.*), cashier, discharge, fire (*Inf.*), give notice to, kiss off (*Sl., chiefly U.S. & Canad.*), lay off, oust, remove, sack (*Inf.*), send packing (*Inf.*) 2. disband, disperse, dissolve, free, let go, release, send away 3. banish, discard, dispel, disregard, drop, lay aside, pooh-pooh, put out of one's mind, reject, relegate, repudiate, set aside, shelve, spurn

dismissal 1. adjournment, congé, end, freedom to depart, permission to go, release 2. discharge, expulsion, kiss-off (*Sl., chiefly U.S. & Canad.*), marching orders (*Inf.*), notice, one's books *or* cards (*Inf.*), removal, the boot (*Sl.*), the (old) heave-ho (*Inf.*), the order of the boot (*Sl.*), the push (*Sl.*), the sack (*Inf.*)

dismount alight, descend, get down, get off, light

disobedience indiscipline, infraction, insubordination, mutiny, noncompliance, nonobservance, recalcitrance, revolt, unruliness, waywardness

disobedient contrary, contumacious, defiant, disorderly, froward, insubordinate, intractable, mischievous, naughty, noncompliant, nonobservant, obstreperous, refractory, undisciplined, unruly, wayward, wilful

Antonyms biddable, compliant, dutiful, manageable, obedient, submissive, well-behaved

disobey contravene, defy, disregard, flout, go counter to, ignore, infringe, overstep, rebel, refuse to obey, resist, transgress, violate

disoblige 1. annoy, bother, discommode, disturb, inconvenience, put out, trouble, upset 2. affront, displease, insult, offend, slight

disobliging awkward, bloody-minded (*Brit. inf.*), cussed (*Inf.*), disagreeable, discourteous, ill-disposed, rude, unaccommodating, uncivil, uncooperative, unhelpful, unobliging, unpleasant

disorder *n.* 1. chaos, clutter, confusion, derangement, disarray, disorderliness, disorganization, hodgepodge (*U.S.*), hotchpotch, irregularity, jumble, mess, muddle, pig's breakfast (*Inf.*), shambles, state, untidiness 2. *bagarre,* brawl, clamour, commotion, disturbance, fight, fracas, hubbub, hullabaloo, quarrel, riot, rumpus, scrimmage, shindig (*Inf.*), shindy (*Inf.*), tumult, turbulence, turmoil, unrest, unruliness, upheaval, uproar 3. *Medical* affliction, ailment, complaint, disease, illness, indisposition, malady, sickness ~*v.* 4. clutter, confound, confuse, derange, disarrange, discompose, disorganize, disturb, jumble, make hay of, mess up, mix up, muddle, scatter, unsettle, upset

disordered all over the place, confused, deranged, disarranged, disarrayed, dislocated, disorganized, displaced, higgledy-piggledy (*Inf.*), in a mess, in confusion, jumbled, misplaced, muddled, out of kelter, out of place, untidy

disorderly 1. chaotic, confused, disorganized, higgledy-piggledy (*Inf.*), indiscriminate, irregular, jumbled, messy, shambolic (*Inf.*), unsystematic, untidy 2. boisterous, disruptive, indisciplined, lawless, obstreperous, rebellious, refractory, riotous, rowdy, stormy, tumultuous, turbulent, ungovernable, unlawful, unmanageable, unruly

Antonyms arranged, neat, orderly, organized, tidy

disorganization chaos, confusion, derangement, disarray, disjointedness, disorder, disruption, incoherence, unconnectedness

disorganize break up, confuse, derange, destroy, disarrange, discompose, disorder, disrupt, disturb, jumble, make a shambles of, muddle, turn topsy-turvy, unsettle, upset

disorganized chaotic, confused, disordered, haphazard, jumbled, muddled, shuffled, unmethodical, unorganized, unsystematic

disorientate, disorient cause to lose one's bearings, confuse, dislocate, mislead, perplex, upset

disorientated, disoriented adrift, all at sea, astray, bewildered, confused, lost, mixed up, not adjusted, off-beam, off-course, out of joint, perplexed, unbalanced, unhinged, unsettled, unstable

disown abandon, abnegate, cast off, deny, disallow, disavow, disclaim, rebut, refuse to acknowledge *or* recognize, reject, renounce, repudiate, retract

disparage asperse, bad-mouth (*Sl., chiefly U.S. & Canad.*), belittle, blast, criticize, decry, defame, degrade, denigrate, deprecate, depreciate, deride, derogate, detract from, discredit, disdain, dismiss, knock (*Inf.*), lambast(e), malign, minimize, put down, ridicule, rubbish (*Inf.*), run down, scorn, slag (off) (*Sl.*), slander, tear into (*Inf.*), traduce, underestimate, underrate, undervalue, vilify

disparagement aspersion, belittlement, condemnation, contempt, contumely, criticism, debasement, degradation, denunciation, depreciation, derision, derogation, detraction, discredit, disdain, impairment, lessening, prejudice, reproach, ridicule, scorn, slander, underestimation

disparate at odds, at variance, contrary, contrasting, different, discordant, discrepant, dissimilar, distinct, diverse, unlike

disparity difference, discrepancy, disproportion, dissimilarity, dissimilitude, distinction, gap, imbalance, incongruity, inequality, unevenness, unlikeness

dispassion candidness, detachment, disinterestedness, impartiality, neutrality, objectivity

dispassionate 1. calm, collected, composed, cool, imperturbable, moderate, quiet, serene, sober, temperate, unemotional, unexcitable, unexcited, unfazed (*Inf.*), unmoved, unruffled 2. candid, detached, disinterested, fair, impartial, impersonal, indifferent, neutral, objective, unbiased, uninvolved, unprejudiced
Antonyms (*sense 1*) ardent, emotional, excited, fervent, impassioned, intense, passionate (*sense 2*) biased, concerned, interested, involved, partial, prejudiced

dispatch, despatch *v.* 1. accelerate, consign, dismiss, express, forward, hasten, hurry, quicken, remit, send, transmit 2. conclude, discharge, dispose of, expedite, finish, make short work of (*Inf.*), perform, settle 3. assassinate, blow away (*Sl., chiefly U.S.*), bump off (*Sl.*), butcher, eliminate (*Sl.*), execute, finish off, kill, murder, put an end to, slaughter, slay, take out (*Sl.*) ~*n.* 4. alacrity, celerity, expedition, haste, precipitateness, promptitude, promptness, quickness, rapidity, speed, swiftness 5. account, bulletin, communication, communiqué, document, instruction, item, letter, message, missive, news, piece, report, story

dispel allay, banish, chase away, dismiss, disperse, dissipate, drive away, eliminate, expel, resolve, rout, scatter

dispensable disposable, expendable, inessential, needless, nonessential, superfluous, unnecessary, unrequired, useless
Antonyms crucial, essential, important, indispensable, necessary, requisite, vital

dispensation 1. allotment, appointment, apportionment, bestowal, conferment, consignment, dealing out, disbursement, distribution, endowment, supplying 2. award, dole, part, portion, quota, share 3. administration, direction, economy, management, plan, regulation, scheme, stewardship, system 4. exception, exemption, immunity, indulgence, licence, permission, privilege, relaxation, relief, remission, reprieve

dispense 1. allocate, allot, apportion, assign, deal out, disburse, distribute, dole out, mete out, share 2. measure, mix, prepare, supply 3. administer, apply, carry out, direct, discharge, enforce, execute, implement, operate, undertake 4. except, excuse, exempt, exonerate, let off (*Inf.*), release, relieve, reprieve 5. *With* **with** abstain from, do without, forgo, give up, omit, relinquish, waive 6. *With* **with** abolish, brush aside, cancel, dispose of, disregard, do away with, get rid of, ignore, pass over, render needless, shake off

disperse 1. broadcast, circulate, diffuse, disseminate, dissipate, distribute, scatter, spread, strew 2. break up, disappear, disband, dismiss, dispel, dissolve, rout, scatter, send off, separate, vanish
Antonyms amass, assemble, collect, concentrate, congregate, convene, gather, muster, pool

dispersion broadcast, circulation, diffusion, dispersal, dissemination, dissipation, distribution, scattering, spread

dispirit cast down, damp, dampen, dash, deject, depress, deter, discourage, dishearten, disincline, sadden

dispirited crestfallen, dejected, depressed, despondent, discouraged, disheartened, down, downcast, gloomy, glum, in the doldrums, low, morose, sad, sick as a parrot (*Inf.*)

displace 1. derange, disarrange, disturb, misplace, move, shift, transpose 2. cashier, depose, discard, discharge, dismiss, fire (*Inf.*), remove, sack (*Inf.*) 3. crowd out, oust, replace, succeed, supersede, supplant, take the place of 4. dislocate, dislodge, dispossess, eject, evict, force out, unsettle

display *v.* 1. betray, demonstrate, disclose, evidence, evince, exhibit, expose, manifest, open, open to view, present, reveal, show, unveil 2. expand, extend, model, open out, spread out, stretch out, unfold, unfurl 3. boast, flash (*Inf.*), flaunt, flourish, parade, show off, vaunt ~*n.* 4. array, demonstration, exhibition, exposition, exposure, manifestation, presentation, revelation,

show 5. flourish, ostentation, pageant, parade, pomp, show, spectacle
Antonyms *v.* conceal, cover, hide, keep dark, keep secret, mask, secrete, veil

displease aggravate (*Inf.*), anger, annoy, disgust, dissatisfy, exasperate, gall, hassle (*Inf.*), incense, irk, irritate, nark (*Brit., Aust., & N.Z. sl.*), nettle, offend, pique, piss one off (*Taboo sl.*), provoke, put out, rile, upset, vex

displeasure anger, annoyance, disapprobation, disapproval, disfavour, disgruntlement, dislike, dissatisfaction, distaste, indignation, irritation, offence, pique, resentment, vexation, wrath
Antonyms approval, endorsement, pleasure, satisfaction

disport 1. amuse, beguile, cheer, delight, divert, entertain, make merry 2. caper, frisk, frolic, gambol, play, revel, romp, sport

disposable 1. biodegradable, compostable, decomposable, nonreturnable, paper, throwaway 2. at one's service, available, consumable, expendable, free for use, spendable

disposal 1. clearance, discarding, dumping (*Inf.*), ejection, jettisoning, parting with, relinquishment, removal, riddance, scrapping, throwing away 2. arrangement, array, dispensation, disposition, distribution, grouping, placing, position 3. assignment, bequest, bestowal, consignment, conveyance, dispensation, gift, settlement, transfer 4. *As in* **at one's disposal** authority, conduct, control, determination, direction, discretion, government, management, ordering, regulation, responsibility

dispose 1. adjust, arrange, array, determine, distribute, fix, group, marshal, order, place, put, range, rank, regulate, set, settle, stand 2. actuate, adapt, bias, condition, incline, induce, influence, lead, motivate, move, predispose, prompt, tempt

disposed apt, given, inclined, liable, likely, of a mind to, predisposed, prone, ready, subject, tending towards

dispose of 1. deal with, decide, determine, end, finish with, settle 2. bestow, give, make over, part with, sell, transfer 3. bin (*Inf.*), chuck (*Inf.*), destroy, discard, dump (*Inf.*), get rid of, jettison, junk (*Inf.*), scrap, throw out *or* away, unload

disposition 1. character, constitution, make-up, nature, spirit, temper, temperament 2. bent, bias, habit, inclination, leaning, predisposition, proclivity, proneness, propensity, readiness, tendency 3. adjustment, arrangement, classification, disposal, distribution, grouping, ordering, organization, placement 4. control, direction, disposal, management, regulation

dispossess deprive, dislodge, divest, drive out, eject, evict, expel, oust, strip, take away, turn out

dispraise 1. *v.* animadvert on *or* upon, blame, blast, censure, condemn, criticize, disapprove, disparage, lambast(e), put down, reproach, reprove, tear into (*Inf.*) 2. *n.* blame, censure, depreciation, discredit, disgrace, dishonour, disparagement, opprobrium, reproach, shame

disproof confutation, counterargument, denial, disproval, invalidation, negation, rebuttal, refutation

disproportion asymmetry, discrepancy, disparity, imbalance, inadequacy, inequality, insufficiency, lopsidedness, unevenness, unsuitableness
Antonyms balance, congruity, harmony, proportion, symmetry

disproportionate excessive, incommensurate, inordinate, out of proportion, too much, unbalanced, unequal, uneven, unreasonable

disprove confute, contradict, controvert, discredit, expose, give the lie to, invalidate, negate, prove false, rebut, refute
Antonyms ascertain, bear out, confirm, evince, prove, show, substantiate, verify

disputable arguable, controversial, debatable, doubtful, dubious, iffy (*Inf.*), moot, open to discussion, questionable, uncertain

disputant adversary, antagonist, arguer, contender, contestant, debater, opponent

disputation argumentation, controversy, debate, dispute, dissension, polemics

disputatious argumentative, cantankerous, captious, cavilling, contentious, dissentious, litigious, polemical, pugnacious, quarrelsome

dispute *v.* 1. altercate, argue, brawl, clash, contend, debate, discuss, quarrel, row, spar, squabble, wrangle 2. challenge, contest, contradict, controvert, deny, doubt, impugn, question, rebut ~*n.* 3. altercation, argument, *bagarre,* brawl, conflict, disagreement, discord, disturbance, feud, friction, quarrel, shindig (*Inf.*), shindy (*Inf.*), strife, wrangle 4. argument, contention, controversy, debate, discussion, dissension

disqualification 1. disability, disablement, incapacitation, incapacity, unfitness 2. debarment, disenablement, disentitlement, elimination, exclusion, incompetence, ineligibility, rejection

disqualified debarred, eliminated, ineligible, knocked out, out of the running

disqualify 1. disable, incapacitate, invalidate, unfit (*Rare*) 2. ban, debar, declare ineligible, disentitle, preclude, prohibit, rule out

disquiet 1. *n.* alarm, angst, anxiety, concern, disquietude, distress, disturbance, fear, foreboding, fretfulness, nervousness, restlessness, trepidation, trouble, uneasiness, unrest, worry 2. *v.* agitate, annoy, bother, concern, discompose, distress, disturb, fret, harass, hassle (*Inf.*), incommode, make uneasy, perturb, pester, plague, trouble, unsettle, upset, vex, worry

disquieting annoying, bothersome, disconcerting, distressing, disturbing, harrowing, irritating, perturbing, troubling, unnerving, unsettling, upsetting, vexing, worrying

disquisition discourse, dissertation, essay, exposition, lecture, paper, thésis, treatise

disregard *v.* 1. brush aside *or* away, discount, disobey, ignore, laugh off, leave out of account, make light of, neglect, overlook, pass over, pay no attention to, pay no heed to, take no notice of, turn a blind eye to 2. brush off (*Sl.*), cold-shoulder, contemn, despise, disdain, disparage, slight, snub ~*n.* 3. brushoff (*Sl.*), contempt, disdain, disrespect, heedlessness, ignoring, inattention, indifference, neglect, negligence, oversight, slight, the cold shoulder
Antonyms *v.* attend, heed, listen to, mind, note, pay attention to, regard, respect, take into consideration, take notice of

disrelish 1. *v.* be averse to, be turned off by (*Inf.*), disfavour, dislike, loathe, regard with distaste 2. *n.* antipathy, aversion, disfavour, disgust, disinclination, dislike, distaste, loathing, repugnance

disrepair 1. collapse, decay, deterioration, dilapidation, ruination 2. **in disrepair** broken, bust (*Inf.*), decayed, decrepit, kaput (*Inf.*), not functioning, on the blink (*Sl.*), out of commission, out of order, worn-out

disreputable 1. base, contemptible, derogatory, discreditable, disgraceful, dishonourable, disorderly, ignominious, infamous, louche, low, mean, notorious, opprobrious, scandalous, shady (*Inf.*), shameful, shocking, unprincipled, vicious, vile 2. bedraggled, dilapidated, dingy, dishevelled, down at heel, scruffy, seedy, shabby, threadbare, worn
Antonyms decent, reputable, respectable, respected, upright, worthy

disrepute discredit, disesteem, disfavour, disgrace, dishonour, ignominy, ill favour, ill repute, infamy, obloquy, shame, unpopularity

disrespect contempt, discourtesy, dishonour, disregard, impertinence, impoliteness, impudence, incivility, insolence, irreverence, lack of respect, lese-majesty, rudeness, unmannerliness
Antonyms esteem, regard, respect

disrespectful bad-mannered, cheeky, contemptuous, discourteous, ill-bred, impertinent, impolite, impudent, insolent, insulting, irreverent, misbehaved, rude, uncivil

disrobe bare, denude, divest, doff, remove, shed, strip, take off, unclothe, uncover, undress

disrupt 1. agitate, confuse, disorder, disorganize, disturb, spoil, throw into disorder, upset 2. break up *or* into, interfere with, interrupt, intrude, obstruct, unsettle, upset

disruption confusion, disarray, disorder, disorderliness, disturbance, interference, interruption, stoppage

disruptive confusing, disorderly, distracting, disturbing, obstreperous, troublemaking, troublesome, unruly, unsettling, upsetting
Antonyms biddable, cooperative, docile, obedient, well-behaved

dissatisfaction annoyance, chagrin, disappointment, discomfort, discontent, dislike, dismay, displeasure, distress, exasperation, frustration, irritation, regret, resentment, unhappiness

dissatisfied disappointed, discontented, disgruntled, displeased, fed up, frustrated, not satisfied, unfulfilled, ungratified, unhappy, unsatisfied
Antonyms content, contented, pleased, satisfied

dissatisfy annoy, disappoint, discontent, disgruntle, displease, give cause for complaint, irritate, leave dissatisfied, not pass muster, not suffice, put out, vex

dissect 1. anatomize, cut up *or* apart, dismember, lay open 2. analyse, break down, explore, inspect, investigate, research, scrutinize, study

dissection 1. anatomization, anatomy, autopsy, dismemberment, necropsy, postmortem (examination) 2. analysis, breakdown, examination, inspection, investigation, research, scrutiny

dissemble 1. camouflage, cloak, conceal, cover up, disguise, dissimulate, hide, mask 2. affect, counterfeit, falsify, feign, pretend, sham, simulate

dissembler charlatan, con man (*Inf.*), deceiver, dissimulator, feigner, fraud, hypocrite, impostor, pretender, trickster, whited sepulchre

disseminate broadcast, circulate, diffuse, disperse, dissipate, distribute, proclaim, promulgate, propagate, publicize, publish, scatter, sow, spread

dissemination broadcasting, circulation, diffusion, distribution, promulgation, propagation, publication, publishing, spread

dissension conflict, conflict of opinion, contention, difference, disagreement, discord, discordance, dispute, dissent, friction, quarrel, row, strife, variance

dissent 1. *v.* decline, differ, disagree, object, protest, refuse, withhold assent *or* approval 2. *n.* difference, disagreement, discord, dissension, dissidence, nonconformity, objection, opposition, refusal, resistance
Antonyms *v.* agree, assent, concur ~*n.* accord, assent, agreement, concurrence, consensus

dissenter disputant, dissident, nonconformist, objector, protestant

dissentient *adj.* conflicting, differing, disagreeing, dissenting, dissident, opposing, protesting

dissertation critique, discourse, disquisition, essay, exposition, thesis, treatise

disservice bad turn, disfavour, harm, ill turn, injury, injustice, unkindness, wrong
Antonyms courtesy, good turn, indulgence, kindness, obligement (*Scot. or archaic*), service

dissever cleave, disunite, divorce, part, rend, rift, separate, sever, sunder

dissidence difference of opinion, disagreement, discordance, dispute, dissent, feud, rupture, schism

dissident 1. *adj.* differing, disagreeing, discordant, dissentient, dissenting, heterodox, nonconformist, schismatic 2. *n.* agitator, dissenter, protestor, rebel, recusant

dissimilar different, disparate, divergent, diverse, heterogeneous, manifold, mismatched, not alike, not capable of comparison, not similar, unlike, unrelated, various
Antonyms alike, comparable, congruous, corresponding, in agreement, much the same, resembling, uniform

dissimilarity difference, discrepancy, disparity, dissimilitude, distinction, divergence, heterogeneity, incomparability, nonuniformity, unlikeness, unrelatedness

dissimilitude difference, discrepancy, disparity, dissimilarity, diversity, heterogeneity, incomparability, nonuniformity, unlikeness, unrelatedness

dissimulate camouflage, cloak, conceal, disguise, dissemble, feign, hide, mask, pretend

dissimulation concealment, deceit, deception, dissembling, double-dealing, duplicity, feigning, hypocrisy, play-acting, pretence, sham, wile

dissipate 1. burn up, consume, deplete, expend, fritter away, indulge oneself, lavish, misspend, run through, spend, squander, waste 2. disappear, dispel, disperse, dissolve, drive away, evaporate, scatter, vanish

dissipated 1. abandoned, debauched, dissolute, intemperate, profligate, rakish, self-indulgent 2. consumed, destroyed, exhausted, scattered, squandered, wasted

dissipation 1. abandonment, debauchery, dissoluteness, drunkenness, excess, extravagance, indulgence, intemperance, lavishness, prodigality, profligacy, squandering, wantonness, waste 2. amusement, distraction, diversion, entertainment, gratification 3. disappearance, disintegration, dispersion, dissemination, dissolution, scattering, vanishing

dissociate 1. break off, disband, disrupt, part company, quit 2. detach, disconnect, distance, divorce, isolate, segregate, separate, set apart

dissociation break, detachment, disconnection, disengagement, distancing, disunion, division, divorce, isolation, segregation, separation, severance

dissolute abandoned, corrupt, debauched, degenerate, depraved, dissipated, immoral, lax, lewd, libertine, licentious, loose, profligate, rakish, unrestrained, vicious, wanton, wild
Antonyms chaste, clean-living, good, moral, squeaky-clean, upright, virtuous

dissolution 1. breaking up, disintegration, division, divorce, parting, resolution, separation 2. death, decay, decomposition, demise, destruction, dispersal, extinction, overthrow, ruin 3. adjournment, conclusion, disbandment, discontinuation, dismissal, end, ending, finish, suspension, termination 4. corruption, debauchery, dissipation, intemperance, wantonness 5. disappearance, evaporation, liquefaction, melting, solution
Antonyms (*senses 1*) alliance, amalgamation, coalition, combination, unification, union

dissolve 1. deliquesce, flux, fuse, liquefy, melt, soften, thaw 2. crumble, decompose, diffuse, disappear, disintegrate, disperse, dissipate, dwindle, evanesce, evaporate, fade, melt away, perish, vanish, waste away 3. axe (*Inf.*), break up, destroy, discontinue, dismiss, end, overthrow, ruin, suspend, terminate, wind up 4. break into *or* up, collapse, disorganize, disunite, divorce, loose, resolve into, separate, sever

dissonance 1. cacophony, discord, discordance, harshness, jangle, jarring, unmelodiousness, want of harmony 2. difference, disagreement, discord, discrepancy, disparity, dissension, incongruity, inconsistency, variance

dissonant 1. cacophonous, discordant, grating, harsh, inharmonious, jangling, jarring, out of tune, raucous, strident, tuneless, unmelodious 2. anomalous, at variance, different, differing, disagreeing, discrepant, dissentient, incompatible, incongruous, inconsistent, irreconcilable, irregular

dissuade advise against, deter, discourage, disincline, divert, expostulate, persuade not to, put off, remonstrate, talk out of, urge not to, warn

Antonyms bring round (*Inf.*), coax, convince, persuade, sway, talk into

dissuasion caution, damper, determent, deterrence, deterrent, discouragement, disincentive, expostulation, hindrance, remonstrance, setback

dissuasive admonitory, cautionary, discouraging, disincentive, dissuading, monitory, off-putting (*Brit. inf.*), remonstrative, warning

distance *n.* 1. absence, extent, gap, interval, lapse, length, range, reach, remoteness, remove, separation, space, span, stretch, width 2. aloofness, coldness, coolness, frigidity, reserve, restraint, stiffness 3. **go the distance** bring to an end, complete, finish, see through, stay the course 4. **keep one's distance** avoid, be aloof (indifferent, reserved), keep (someone) at arm's length, shun 5. **in the distance** afar, far away, far off, on the horizon, yonder ~*v.* 6. dissociate oneself, put in proportion, separate oneself 7. leave behind, outdistance, outdo, outrun, outstrip, pass

distant 1. abroad, afar, far, faraway, far-flung, far-off, outlying, out-of-the-way, remote, removed 2. apart, disparate, dispersed, distinct, scattered, separate 3. aloof, ceremonious, cold, cool, formal, haughty, reserved, restrained, reticent, standoffish, stiff, unapproachable, unfriendly, withdrawn 4. faint, indirect, indistinct, obscure, slight, uncertain

Antonyms (*senses 1 & 2*) adjacent, adjoining, at hand, close, handy, imminent, near, nearby, neighbouring, nigh, proximate, within sniffing distance (*Inf.*) (*sense 3*) close, friendly, intimate, warm

distaste abhorrence, antipathy, aversion, detestation, disfavour, disgust, disinclination, dislike, displeasure, disrelish, dissatisfaction, horror, loathing, odium, repugnance, revulsion

distasteful abhorrent, disagreeable, displeasing, loathsome, nauseous, objectionable, obnoxious, obscene, offensive, repugnant, repulsive, undesirable, uninviting, unpalatable, unpleasant, unsavoury

Antonyms agreeable, charming, enjoyable, pleasing, pleasurable

distend balloon, bloat, bulge, dilate, enlarge, expand, increase, inflate, puff, stretch, swell, widen

distended bloated, dilated, enlarged, expanded, inflated, puffy, stretched, swollen, tumescent

distension dilatation, dilation, enlargement, expansion, extension, inflation, intumescence, spread

distil condense, draw out, evaporate, express, extract, press out, purify, rectify, refine, sublimate, vaporize

distillation elixir, essence, extract, quintessence, spirit

distinct 1. apparent, blatant, clear, clear-cut, decided, definite, evident, lucid, manifest, marked, noticeable, obvious, palpable, patent, plain, recognizable, sharp, unambiguous, unmistakable, well-defined 2. detached, different, discrete, dissimilar, individual, separate, unconnected

Antonyms common, connected, fuzzy, identical, indefinite, indistinct, obscure, similar, unclear, vague

distinction 1. differentiation, discernment, discrimination, penetration, perception, separation 2. contrast, difference, differential, division, separation 3. characteristic, distinctiveness, feature, individuality, mark, particularity, peculiarity, quality 4. account, celebrity, consequence, credit, eminence, excellence, fame, greatness, honour, importance, merit, name, note, prominence, quality, rank, renown, reputation, repute, superiority, worth

distinctive characteristic, different, distinguishing, extraordinary, idiosyncratic, individual, original, peculiar, singular, special, typical, uncommon, unique

Antonyms common, ordinary, run-of-the-mill, typical

distinctly clearly, decidedly, definitely, evidently, manifestly, markedly, noticeably, obviously, palpably, patently, plainly, precisely, sharply

distinctness 1. clarity, lucidity, obviousness, plainness, sharpness, vividness 2. detachment, difference, discreteness, disparateness, dissimilarity, dissociation, distinctiveness, individuality, separation

distinguish 1. ascertain, decide, determine,

differentiate, discriminate, judge, tell apart, tell between, tell the difference 2. categorize, characterize, classify, individualize, make distinctive, mark, separate, set apart, single out 3. discern, know, make out, perceive, pick out, recognize, see, tell 4. celebrate, dignify, honour, immortalize, make famous, signalize

distinguishable clear, conspicuous, discernible, evident, manifest, noticeable, obvious, perceptible, plain, recognizable, well-marked

distinguished 1. acclaimed, celebrated, conspicuous, eminent, famed, famous, illustrious, notable, noted, renowned, well-known 2. conspicuous, extraordinary, marked, outstanding, signal, striking
Antonyms common, inelegant, inferior, undistinguished, unknown

distinguishing characteristic, different, differentiating, distinctive, individualistic, marked, peculiar, typical

distort 1. bend, buckle, contort, deform, disfigure, misshape, twist, warp, wrench, wrest 2. bias, colour, falsify, garble, misrepresent, pervert, slant, twist

distortion 1. bend, buckle, contortion, crookedness, deformity, malformation, twist, twistedness, warp 2. bias, colouring, falsification, misrepresentation, perversion, slant

distract 1. divert, draw away, sidetrack, turn aside 2. amuse, beguile, engross, entertain, occupy 3. agitate, bewilder, confound, confuse, derange, discompose, disconcert, disturb, harass, madden, perplex, puzzle, torment, trouble

distracted 1. agitated, at sea, bemused, bewildered, confounded, confused, flustered, harassed, in a flap (*Inf.*), perplexed, puzzled, troubled 2. crazy, deranged, desperate, distraught, frantic, frenzied, grief-stricken, insane, mad, overwrought, raving, wild

distracting bewildering, bothering, confusing, disconcerting, dismaying, disturbing, off-putting (*Brit. inf.*), perturbing

distraction 1. abstraction, agitation, bewilderment, commotion, confusion, discord, disorder, disturbance 2. amusement, beguilement, diversion, divertissement, entertainment, pastime, recreation 3. disturbance, diversion, interference, interruption 4. aberration, alienation, delirium, derangement, desperation, frenzy, hallucination, incoherence, insanity, mania

distrait absent, absent-minded, abstracted, distracted, forgetful, inattentive, oblivious, preoccupied, unaware

distraught agitated, anxious, beside oneself, crazed, desperate, distracted, distressed, frantic, hysterical, mad, out of one's mind, overwrought, raving, wild, worked-up, wrought-up

distress *n.* 1. affliction, agony, anguish, anxiety, desolation, discomfort, grief, heartache, misery, pain, sadness, sorrow, suffering, torment, torture, woe, worry, wretchedness 2. adversity, calamity, destitution, difficulties, hardship, indigence, misfortune, need, poverty, privation, straits, trial, trouble ~*v.* 3. afflict, agonize, bother, disturb, grieve, harass, harrow, pain, perplex, sadden, torment, trouble, upset, worry, wound

distressed 1. afflicted, agitated, anxious, distracted, distraught, saddened, tormented, troubled, upset, worried, wretched 2. destitute, indigent, needy, poor, poverty-stricken, straitened

distressing affecting, afflicting, distressful, disturbing, grievous, harrowing, heart-breaking, hurtful, lamentable, nerve-racking, painful, sad, upsetting, worrying

distribute 1. administer, allocate, allot, apportion, assign, deal, dispense, dispose, divide, dole out, give, measure out, mete, share 2. circulate, convey, deliver, hand out, pass round 3. diffuse, disperse, disseminate, scatter, spread, strew 4. arrange, assort, categorize, class, classify, file, group

distribution 1. allocation, allotment, apportionment, dispensation, division, dole, partition, sharing 2. circulation, diffusion, dispersal, dispersion, dissemination, propagation, scattering, spreading 3. arrangement, assortment, classification, disposition, grouping, location, organization, placement 4. *Commerce* dealing, delivery, handling, mailing, marketing, trading, transport, transportation

district area, community, locale, locality, neighbourhood, parish, quarter, region, sector, vicinity, ward

distrust 1. *v.* be sceptical of, be suspicious of, be wary of, disbelieve, discredit, doubt, misbelieve, mistrust, question, smell a rat (*Inf.*), suspect, wonder about 2. *n.* disbelief, doubt, dubiety, lack of faith, misgiving, mistrust, qualm, question, scepticism, suspicion, wariness
Antonyms *v.* believe, depend, have confidence, have faith, trust ~*n.* confidence, faith, reliance, trust

distrustful chary, cynical, disbelieving, distrusting, doubtful, doubting, dubious, leery (*Sl.*), mistrustful, sceptical, suspicious, uneasy, wary

disturb 1. bother, butt in on, disrupt, interfere with, interrupt, intrude on, pester, rouse, startle 2. confuse, derange, disar-

range, disorder, disorganize, muddle, unsettle 3. agitate, alarm, annoy, confound, discompose, distract, distress, excite, fluster, harass, hassle (*Inf.*), perturb, ruffle, shake, trouble, unnerve, unsettle, upset, worry
Antonyms calm, compose, lull, pacify, quiet, quieten, reassure, relax, relieve, settle, soothe

disturbance 1. agitation, annoyance, bother, confusion, derangement, disorder, distraction, hindrance, interruption, intrusion, molestation, perturbation, upset 2. bother (*Inf.*), brawl, commotion, disorder, fracas, fray, hubbub, riot, ruckus (*Inf.*), ruction (*Inf.*), shindig (*Inf.*), shindy (*Inf.*), tumult, turmoil, upheaval, uproar

disturbed 1. *Psychiatry* disordered, maladjusted, neurotic, troubled, unbalanced, upset 2. agitated, anxious, apprehensive, bothered, concerned, disquieted, nervous, troubled, uneasy, upset, worried
Antonyms balanced, calm, collected, self-possessed, unfazed (*Inf.*), untroubled

disturbing agitating, alarming, disconcerting, discouraging, dismaying, disquieting, distressing, frightening, harrowing, perturbing, startling, threatening, troubling, unsettling, upsetting, worrying

disunion 1. abstraction, detachment, disconnection, disjunction, division, partition, separation, severance 2. alienation, breach, disagreement, discord, dissension, dissidence, estrangement, feud, rupture, schism, split

disunite 1. detach, disband, disconnect, disengage, disjoin, disrupt, divide, part, segregate, separate, sever, split, sunder 2. alienate, embroil, estrange, set at odds, set at variance

disunity alienation, breach, disagreement, discord, discordance, dissension, dissent, estrangement, rupture, schism, split, variance

disuse abandonment, decay, desuetude, discontinuance, idleness, neglect, non-employment, nonuse
Antonyms application, employment, practice, service, usage, use

ditch *n.* 1. channel, drain, dyke, furrow, gully, moat, trench, watercourse ~*v.* 2. dig, drain, excavate, gouge, trench 3. *Sl.* abandon, axe (*Inf.*), bin (*Inf.*), chuck (*Inf.*), discard, dispose of, drop, dump (*Inf.*), get rid of, jettison, junk (*Inf.*), scrap, throw out *or* overboard

dither 1. *v.* faff about (*Brit. inf.*), falter, haver, hesitate, oscillate, shillyshally (*Inf.*), swither (*Scot.*), teeter, vacillate, waver 2. *n.* bother, flap (*Inf.*), fluster, flutter, pother, stew (*Inf.*), tiz-woz (*Inf.*), tizzy (*Inf.*), twitter (*Inf.*)
Antonyms *v.* come to a conclusion, conclude, decide, make a decision, make up one's mind, reach *or* come to a decision, resolve, settle

diurnal circadian, daily, daytime, everyday, quotidian, regular

dive *v.* 1. descend, dip, disappear, drop, duck, fall, go underwater, jump, leap, nose-dive, pitch, plummet, plunge, submerge, swoop ~*n.* 2. dash, header (*Inf.*), jump, leap, lunge, nose dive, plunge, spring 3. *Sl.* honky-tonk (*U.S. sl.*), joint (*Sl.*), sleazy bar

diverge 1. bifurcate, branch, divaricate, divide, fork, part, radiate, separate, split, spread 2. be at odds, be at variance, conflict, differ, disagree, dissent 3. depart, deviate, digress, meander, stray, turn aside, wander

divergence branching out, deflection, departure, deviation, difference, digression, disparity, divagation, ramification, separation, varying

divergent conflicting, deviating, different, differing, disagreeing, dissimilar, diverging, diverse, separate, variant

divers different, manifold, many, multifarious, numerous, several, some, sundry, varied, various

diverse 1. assorted, diversified, manifold, miscellaneous, of every description, several, sundry, varied, various 2. different, differing, discrete, disparate, dissimilar, distinct, divergent, separate, unlike, varying

diversify alter, assort, branch out, change, expand, mix, modify, spread out, transform, variegate, vary

diversion 1. alteration, change, deflection, departure, detour, deviation, digression, variation 2. amusement, beguilement, delight, distraction, divertissement, enjoyment, entertainment, game, gratification, jollies (*Sl.*), pastime, play, pleasure, recreation, relaxation, sport

diversity assortment, difference, dissimilarity, distinctiveness, divergence, diverseness, diversification, heterogeneity, medley, multiplicity, range, unlikeness, variance, variegation, variety

divert 1. avert, deflect, redirect, switch, turn aside 2. amuse, beguile, delight, entertain, gratify, recreate, regale 3. detract, distract, draw *or* lead away from, lead astray, sidetrack

diverted 1. changed, deflected, made use of, rebudgeted, rechannelled, reclassified, redirected, taken over, turned aside 2. amused, entertained, taken out of oneself, tickled

diverting amusing, beguiling, enjoyable, entertaining, fun, humorous, pleasant

divest 1. denude, disrobe, doff, remove, strip, take off, unclothe, undress 2. deprive, despoil, dispossess, strip

divide 1. bisect, cleave, cut (up), detach, disconnect, part, partition, segregate, separate, sever, shear, split, subdivide, sunder 2. allocate, allot, apportion, deal out, dispense, distribute, divvy (up) (*Inf.*), dole out, measure out, portion, share 3. alienate, break up, cause to disagree, come between, disunite, estrange, set *or* pit against one another, set at variance *or* odds, sow dissension, split 4. arrange, categorize, classify, grade, group, put in order, separate, sort
Antonyms (*sense 1*) combine, come together, connect, join, knit, marry, splice, unite

dividend bonus, cut (*Inf.*), divvy (*Inf.*), extra, gain, plus, portion, share, surplus

divination augury, clairvoyance, divining, foretelling, fortune-telling, prediction, presage, prognostication, prophecy, soothsaying, sortilege

divine *adj.* 1. angelic, celestial, godlike, heavenly, holy, spiritual, superhuman, supernatural 2. consecrated, holy, religious, sacred, sanctified, spiritual 3. beatific, blissful, exalted, mystical, rapturous, supreme, transcendent, transcendental, transmundane 4. *Inf.* beautiful, excellent, glorious, marvellous, perfect, splendid, superlative, wonderful ~*n.* 5. churchman, clergyman, cleric, ecclesiastic, minister, pastor, priest, reverend ~*v.* 6. apprehend, conjecture, deduce, discern, foretell, guess, infer, intuit, perceive, prognosticate, suppose, surmise, suspect, understand 7. *Of water or minerals* dowse

diviner 1. astrologer, augur, oracle, prophet, seer, sibyl, soothsayer 2. *Of water or minerals* dowser

divinity 1. deity, divine nature, godhead, godhood, godliness, holiness, sanctity 2. daemon, deity, genius, god, goddess, guardian spirit, spirit 3. religion, religious studies, theology

divisible dividable, fractional, separable, splittable

division 1. bisection, cutting up, detaching, dividing, partition, separation, splitting up 2. allotment, apportionment, distribution, sharing 3. border, boundary, demarcation, divide, divider, dividing line, partition 4. branch, category, class, compartment, department, group, head, part, portion, section, sector, segment 5. breach, difference of opinion, disagreement, discord, disunion, estrangement, feud, rupture, split, variance
Antonyms (*sense 5*) accord, agreement, concord, harmony, peace, union, unity

divisive alienating, damaging, detrimental, discordant, disruptive, estranging, inharmonious, pernicious, troublesome, unsettling

divorce 1. *n.* annulment, breach, break, decree nisi, dissolution, disunion, rupture, separation, severance, split-up 2. *v.* annul, disconnect, dissociate, dissolve (*marriage*), disunite, divide, part, separate, sever, split up, sunder

divulge betray, blow wide open (*Sl.*), communicate, confess, declare, disclose, exhibit, expose, impart, leak, let slip, make known, proclaim, promulgate, publish, reveal, spill (*Inf.*), spill one's guts about (*Sl.*), tell, uncover
Antonyms conceal, hide, keep secret

divvy 1. *n.* cut (*Inf.*), dividend, percentage, portion, quota, share, whack (*Inf.*) 2. *v.* *Sometimes with* **up** apportion, cut, distribute, divide, parcel out, share (out), split

dizzy 1. faint, giddy, light-headed, off balance, reeling, shaky, staggering, swimming, vertiginous, weak at the knees, wobbly, woozy (*Inf.*) 2. at sea, befuddled, bemused, bewildered, confused, dazed, dazzled, muddled 3. lofty, steep, vertiginous 4. *Inf.* capricious, fickle, flighty, foolish, frivolous, giddy, light-headed, scatterbrained, silly

do *v.* 1. accomplish, achieve, act, carry out, complete, conclude, discharge, end, execute, perform, produce, transact, undertake, work 2. answer, be adequate, be enough, be of use, be sufficient, pass muster, satisfy, serve, suffice, suit 3. arrange, be responsible for, fix, get ready, look after, make, make ready, organize, prepare, see to, take on 4. decipher, decode, figure out, puzzle out, resolve, solve, work out 5. adapt, render, translate, transpose 6. bear oneself, behave, carry oneself, comport oneself, conduct oneself 7. fare, get along, get on, make out, manage, proceed 8. bring about, cause, create, effect, produce 9. *Of a play, etc.* act, give, perform, present, produce, put on 10. *Inf.* cover, explore, journey through *or* around, look at, stop in, tour, travel, visit 11. *Inf.* cheat, con (*Inf.*), cozen, deceive, defraud, diddle (*Inf.*), dupe, fleece, hoax, skin (*Sl.*), stiff (*Sl.*), swindle, take (someone) for a ride (*Inf.*), trick ~*n.* 12. *Inf.* affair, event, function, gathering, occasion, party 13. **do's and don'ts** *Inf.* code, customs, etiquette, instructions, regulations, rules, standards

do away with 1. blow away (*Sl., chiefly*

U.S.), bump off (*Sl.*), destroy, do in (*Sl.*), exterminate, kill, liquidate, murder, slay, take out (*Sl.*) 2. abolish, axe (*Inf.*), chuck (*Inf.*), discard, discontinue, eliminate, get rid of, junk (*Inf.*), put an end to, remove

docile amenable, biddable, compliant, ductile, manageable, obedient, pliant, submissive, teachable (*Rare*), tractable
Antonyms difficult, intractable, obstreperous, troublesome, trying, uncooperative, unmanageable

docility amenability, biddableness, compliance, ductility, manageability, meekness, obedience, pliancy, submissiveness, tractability

dock[1] *n.* 1. harbour, pier, quay, waterfront, wharf ~*v.* 2. anchor, berth, drop anchor, land, moor, put in, tie up 3. *Of spacecraft* couple, hook up, join, link up, rendezvous, unite

dock[2] 1. clip, crop, curtail, cut off, cut short, diminish, lessen, shorten 2. decrease, deduct, diminish, lessen, reduce, subtract, withhold
Antonyms (*sense 2*) augment, boost, increase, raise

docket 1. *n.* bill, certificate, chit, chitty, counterfoil, label, receipt, tab, tag, tally, ticket 2. *v.* catalogue, file, index, label, mark, register, tab, tag, ticket

doctor *n.* 1. general practitioner, G.P., medic (*Inf.*), medical practitioner, physician ~*v.* 2. apply medication to, give medical treatment to, treat 3. botch, cobble, do up (*Inf.*), fix, mend, patch up, repair 4. alter, change, disguise, falsify, fudge, misrepresent, pervert, tamper with 5. add to, adulterate, cut, dilute, mix with, spike, water down

doctrinaire *adj.* 1. biased, dogmatic, fanatical, inflexible, insistent, opinionated, rigid 2. hypothetical, ideological, impractical, speculative, theoretical, unpragmatic, unrealistic

doctrine article, article of faith, belief, canon, concept, conviction, creed, dogma, opinion, precept, principle, teaching, tenet

document 1. *n.* certificate, instrument, legal form, paper, record, report 2. *v.* authenticate, back up, certify, cite, corroborate, detail, give weight to, instance, particularize, substantiate, support, validate, verify

dodder quake, quaver, quiver, shake, shamble, shiver, shuffle, stagger, sway, teeter, totter, tremble

doddering aged, decrepit, doddery, faltering, feeble, floundering, infirm, senile, shaky, shambling, tottery, trembly, unsteady, weak

doddle cakewalk (*Inf.*), child's play (*Inf.*), cinch (*Sl.*), easy-peasy (*Sl.*), no sweat (*Sl.*), picnic (*Inf.*), piece of cake (*Inf.*), pushover (*Sl.*)

dodge *v.* 1. body-swerve (*Scot.*), dart, duck, shift, sidestep, swerve, turn aside 2. avoid, body-swerve (*Scot.*), deceive, elude, equivocate, evade, fend off, flannel (*Brit. inf.*), fudge, get out of, hedge, parry, shirk, shuffle, trick ~*n.* 3. contrivance, device, feint, flannel (*Brit. inf.*), machination, ploy, ruse, scheme, stratagem, subterfuge, trick, wheeze (*Brit. sl.*), wile

dodger evader, shifty so-and-so, shirker, slacker, slippery one, slyboots, trickster

dodgy chancy (*Inf.*), dangerous, delicate, dicey (*Inf., chiefly Brit.*), dicky (*Brit. inf.*), difficult, problematic(al), risky, ticklish, tricky, uncertain, unreliable

doer achiever, active person, activist, bustler, dynamo, go-getter (*Inf.*), live wire (*Sl.*), organizer, powerhouse (*Sl.*), wheeler-dealer (*Inf.*)

doff 1. *Of a hat* lift, raise, remove, take off, tip, touch 2. *Of clothing* cast off, discard, remove, shed, slip off, slip out of, take off, throw off, undress

do for defeat, destroy, finish (off), kill, ruin, shatter, slay, undo

dog *n.* 1. bitch, canine, cur, hound, man's best friend, mongrel, mutt (*Sl.*), pooch (*Sl.*), pup, puppy, tyke 2. *Inf.* beast, blackguard, cur, heel (*Sl.*), knave (*Archaic*), scoundrel, villain 3. **dog-eat-dog** cutthroat, ferocious, fierce, ruthless, vicious, with no holds barred 4. **go to the dogs** *Inf.* degenerate, deteriorate, go down the drain, go to pot, go to ruin ~*v.* 5. haunt, hound, plague, pursue, shadow, tail (*Inf.*), track, trail, trouble

dogged determined, firm, immovable, indefatigable, obstinate, persevering, persistent, pertinacious, resolute, single-minded, staunch, steadfast, steady, stiff-necked, stubborn, tenacious, unflagging, unshakable, unyielding
Antonyms doubtful, half-hearted, hesitant, irresolute, undetermined, unsteady

doggedness bulldog tenacity, determination, endurance, obstinacy, perseverance, persistence, pertinacity, relentlessness, resolution, single-mindedness, steadfastness, steadiness, stubbornness, tenaciousness, tenacity

doggo lie doggo be in hiding, go to earth, keep a low profile, keep one's head down, keep out of the public eye, stay out of sight

dogma article, article of faith, belief, credo, creed, doctrine, opinion, precept, principle, teachings, tenet

dogmatic 1. arbitrary, arrogant, assertive,

categorical, dictatorial, doctrinaire, downright, emphatic, imperious, magisterial, obdurate, opinionated, overbearing, peremptory 2. authoritative, canonical, categorical, doctrinal, ex cathedra, oracular, positive

dogmatism arbitrariness, arrogance, dictatorialness, imperiousness, opinionatedness, peremptoriness, positiveness, presumption

dogsbody drudge, general factotum, maid *or* man of all work, menial, skivvy (*Chiefly Brit.*), slave

do in 1. blow away (*Sl., chiefly U.S.*), butcher, dispatch, eliminate (*Sl.*), execute, kill, liquidate, murder, slaughter, slay, take out (*Sl.*) 2. exhaust, fag (*Inf.*), fatigue, knacker (*Sl.*), shatter (*Inf.*), tire, wear out, weary

doing achievement, act, action, carrying out *or* through, deed, execution, exploit, handiwork, implementation, performance

doings actions, affairs, concerns, dealings, deeds, events, exploits, goings-on (*Inf.*), handiwork, happenings, proceedings, transactions

doldrums apathy, blues, boredom, depression, dullness, dumps (*Inf.*), ennui, gloom, inertia, lassitude, listlessness, malaise, stagnation, tedium, the hump (*Brit. inf.*), torpor

dole *n.* 1. allowance, alms, benefit, donation, gift, grant, gratuity, modicum, parcel, pittance, portion, quota, share 2. allocation, allotment, apportionment, dispensation, distribution, division ~*v.* 3. *Usually with* **out** administer, allocate, allot, apportion, assign, deal, dispense, distribute, divide, give, hand out, mete, share

doleful cheerless, depressing, dismal, distressing, dolorous, down in the mouth, dreary, forlorn, funereal, gloomy, lugubrious, melancholy, mournful, painful, pitiful, rueful, sad, sombre, sorrowful, woebegone, woeful, wretched

doll up deck out, dress up (like a dog's dinner), get ready, gussy up (*Sl.*), preen, primp, prink, tart up (*Sl.*), titivate, trick out

dolorous anguished, dismal, distressing, doleful, grievous, harrowing, heart-rending, melancholy, miserable, mournful, painful, rueful, sad, sorrowful, woebegone, woeful, wretched

dolour anguish, distress, grief, heartache, heartbreak, heaviness of heart, misery, ruth (*Archaic*), sadness, sorrow, suffering

dolt ass, berk (*Brit. sl.*), blockhead, booby, charlie (*Brit. inf.*), chump (*Inf.*), clot (*Brit. inf.*), coot, dimwit (*Inf.*), dipstick (*Brit. sl.*), dope (*Inf.*), dork (*Sl.*), dullard, dunce, dweeb (*U.S. sl.*), fool, fuckwit (*Taboo sl.*), geek (*Sl.*), gonzo (*Sl.*), idiot, ignoramus, jerk (*Sl., chiefly U.S. & Canad.*), lamebrain (*Inf.*), nerd *or* nurd (*Sl.*), nitwit (*Inf.*), numskull *or* numbskull, oaf, plank (*Brit. sl.*), plonker (*Sl.*), prat (*Sl.*), prick (*Derogatory sl.*), schmuck (*U.S. sl.*), simpleton, thickhead, twit (*Inf., chiefly Brit.*), wally (*Sl.*)

doltish asinine, boneheaded (*Sl.*), brainless, clottish (*Brit. inf.*), dense, dim-witted (*Inf.*), dopey (*Inf.*), dumb (*Inf.*), foolish, goofy (*Inf.*), halfwitted, idiotic, inane, mindless, silly, stupid

domain 1. demesne, dominion, empire, estate, kingdom, lands, policies (*Scot.*), province, realm, region, territory 2. area, authority, bailiwick, concern, department, discipline, field, jurisdiction, orbit, power, realm, scope, speciality, sphere, sway

domestic *adj.* 1. domiciliary, family, home, household, private 2. domesticated, home-loving, homely, housewifely, stay-at-home 3. domesticated, house, house-trained, pet, tame, trained 4. indigenous, internal, native, not foreign ~*n.* 5. char (*Inf.*), charwoman, daily, daily help, help, maid, servant, woman (*Inf.*)

domesticate 1. break, gentle, house-train, tame, train 2. acclimatize, accustom, familiarize, habituate, naturalize

domesticated 1. *Of plants or animals* broken (in), naturalized, tame, tamed 2. *Of people* domestic, home-loving, homely, house-trained (*Jocular*), housewifely

Antonyms feral, ferocious, savage, unbroken, undomesticated, untamed, wild

domesticity domestication, home life, home-lovingness, homemaking, housekeeping, housewifery

domicile abode, dwelling, habitation, home, house, legal residence, mansion, pad (*Sl.*), residence, residency, settlement

dominance ascendancy, authority, command, control, domination, government, mastery, paramountcy, power, rule, supremacy, sway

dominant 1. ascendant, assertive, authoritative, commanding, controlling, governing, leading, presiding, ruling, superior, supreme 2. chief, influential, main, outstanding, paramount, predominant, pre-eminent, prevailing, prevalent, primary, principal, prominent

Antonyms ancillary, auxiliary, inferior, junior, lesser, lower, minor, secondary, subservient, subsidiary

dominate 1. control, direct, domineer, govern, have the upper hand over, have the whip hand over, keep under one's thumb, lead, lead by the nose (*Inf.*), master, monopolize, overbear, rule, tyrannize 2. bestride, loom over, overlook, stand head and shoulders above, stand over, survey, tower above 3. detract from, eclipse, outshine, overrule, overshadow, predominate, prevail over

domination 1. ascendancy, authority, command, control, influence, mastery, power, rule, superiority, supremacy, sway 2. despotism, dictatorship, oppression, repression, subjection, subordination, suppression, tyranny

domineer bluster, boss around *or* about (*Inf.*), browbeat, bully, hector, intimidate, lord (it) over, menace, overbear, ride roughshod over, swagger, threaten, tyrannize

domineering arrogant, authoritarian, autocratic, bossy (*Inf.*), coercive, despotic, dictatorial, high-handed, imperious, iron-handed, magisterial, masterful, oppressive, overbearing, tyrannical
Antonyms meek, obsequious, servile, shy, submissive, subservient

dominion 1. ascendancy, authority, command, control, domination, government, jurisdiction, mastery, power, rule, sovereignty, supremacy, sway 2. country, domain, empire, kingdom, patch, province, realm, region, territory, turf (*U.S. sl.*)

don clothe oneself in, dress in, get into, pull on, put on, slip on *or* into

donate bequeath, bestow, chip in (*Inf.*), contribute, gift, give, hand out, make a gift of, present, subscribe

donation alms, benefaction, boon, contribution, gift, grant, gratuity, hand-out, largess *or* largesse, offering, present, stipend, subscription

done *adj.* 1. accomplished, completed, concluded, consummated, ended, executed, finished, over, perfected, realized, terminated, through 2. cooked, cooked enough, cooked sufficiently, cooked to a turn, ready 3. depleted, exhausted, finished, spent, used up 4. acceptable, conventional, *de rigueur,* proper 5. *Inf.* cheated, conned (*Inf.*), duped, taken for a ride (*Inf.*), tricked ~*interj.* 6. agreed, it's a bargain, O.K. *or* okay (*Inf.*), settled, you're on (*Inf.*) 7. **done for** *Inf.* beaten, broken, dashed, defeated, destroyed, doomed, finished, foiled, lost, ruined, undone, wrecked 8. **done in** *or* **up** *Inf.* all in (*Sl.*), bushed (*Inf.*), clapped out (*Aust. & N.Z. inf.*), dead (*Inf.*), dead beat (*Inf.*), dog-tired (*Inf.*), exhausted, fagged out (*Inf.*), knackered (*Sl.*), on one's last legs, ready to drop, tired out, worn out, worn to a frazzle (*Inf.*), zonked (*Sl.*) 9. **have done with** be through with, desist, end relations with, finish with, give up, throw over, wash one's hands of

donnish bookish, erudite, formalistic, pedagogic, pedantic, precise, scholarly, scholastic

donor almsgiver, benefactor, contributor, donator, giver, grantor (*Law*), philanthropist
Antonyms assignee, beneficiary, inheritor, legatee, payee, receiver, recipient

doom *n.* 1. catastrophe, death, destiny, destruction, downfall, fate, fortune, lot, portion, ruin 2. condemnation, decision, decree, judgment, sentence, verdict 3. Armageddon, Doomsday, end of the world, Judgment Day, the Last Day, the Last Judgment, the last trump ~*v.* 4. condemn, consign, damn, decree, destine, foreordain, judge, predestine, preordain, sentence, threaten

doomed bedevilled, bewitched, condemned, cursed, fated, hopeless, ill-fated, ill-omened, luckless, star-crossed

door 1. doorway, egress, entrance, entry, exit, ingress, opening 2. **lay at the door of** blame, censure, charge, hold responsible, impute to 3. **out of doors** alfresco, in the air, out, outdoors, outside 4. **show someone the door** ask to leave, boot out (*Inf.*), bounce (*Sl.*), eject, oust, show out

do out of balk, bilk, cheat, con (*Inf.*), cozen, deprive, diddle (*Inf.*), swindle, trick

dope *n.* 1. drugs, narcotic, opiate 2. berk (*Brit. sl.*), blockhead, charlie (*Brit. inf.*), coot, dickhead (*Sl.*), dimwit (*Inf.*), dipstick (*Brit. sl.*), divvy (*Brit. sl.*), dolt, dork (*Sl.*), dunce, dweeb (*U.S. sl.*), fool, fuckwit (*Taboo sl.*), geek (*Sl.*), gonzo (*Sl.*), idiot, jerk (*Sl., chiefly U.S. & Canad.*), lamebrain (*Inf.*), nerd *or* nurd (*Sl.*), nitwit (*Inf.*), numskull *or* numbskull, oaf, pillock (*Brit. sl.*), plank (*Brit. sl.*), plonker (*Sl.*), prat (*Sl.*), prick (*Derogatory sl.*), schmuck (*U.S. sl.*), simpleton, twit (*Inf., chiefly Brit.*), wally (*Sl.*) 3. details, facts, gen (*Brit. inf.*), info (*Inf.*), information, inside information, lowdown (*Inf.*), news, tip ~*v.* 4. anaesthetize, doctor, drug, inject, knock out, narcotize, sedate, stupefy

dopey, dopy 1. asinine, dense, dozy (*Brit. inf.*), dumb (*Inf.*), foolish, goofy (*Inf.*), idiotic, senseless, silly, simple, slow, stupid, thick 2. dazed, drowsy, drugged, groggy (*Inf.*), muzzy, stupefied, woozy (*Inf.*)

dormant asleep, comatose, fallow, hibernating, inactive, inert, inoperative, latent, quiescent, sleeping, sluggish, slumbering, suspended, torpid

Antonyms active, alert, aroused, awake, awakened, conscious, wakeful, wide-awake

dose dosage, draught, drench, measure, portion, potion, prescription, quantity

dot *n.* **1.** atom, circle, dab, fleck, full stop, iota, jot, mark, mite, mote, point, speck, speckle, spot **2. on the dot** exactly, on time, precisely, promptly, punctually, to the minute *~v.* **3.** dab, dabble, fleck, speckle, spot, sprinkle, stipple, stud

dotage **1.** decrepitude, feebleness, imbecility, old age, second childhood, senility, weakness **2.** doting, foolish fondness, infatuation

dote on *or* **upon** admire, adore, hold dear, idolize, lavish affection on, prize, treasure

doting adoring, devoted, fond, foolish, indulgent, lovesick

dotty **1.** batty (*Sl.*), crackpot (*Inf.*), crazy, eccentric, feeble-minded, loopy (*Inf.*), oddball (*Inf.*), off one's trolley (*Sl.*), off-the-wall (*Sl.*), outré, out to lunch (*Inf.*), peculiar, potty (*Brit. inf.*), touched, up the pole (*Inf.*), wacko (*Sl.*) **2.** *With* **about** crazy (*Inf.*), daft (*Inf.*), fond of, keen on

double *adj.* **1.** binate (*Botany*), coupled, doubled, dual, duplicate, in pairs, paired, twice, twin, twofold **2.** deceitful, dishonest, false, hypocritical, insincere, Janus-faced, knavish (*Archaic*), perfidious, treacherous, two-faced, vacillating *~v.* **3.** duplicate, enlarge, fold, grow, increase, magnify, multiply, plait, repeat *~n.* **4.** clone, copy, counterpart, dead ringer (*Sl.*), Doppelgänger, duplicate, fellow, impersonator, lookalike, mate, replica, ringer (*Sl.*), spitting image (*Inf.*), twin **5. at** *or* **on the double** at full speed, briskly, immediately, in double-quick time, pdq (*Sl.*), posthaste, quickly, without delay

double back backtrack, circle, dodge, loop, retrace one's steps, return, reverse

double-cross betray, cheat, cozen, defraud, hoodwink, mislead, swindle, trick, two-time (*Inf.*)

double-dealer betrayer, cheat, con man (*Inf.*), cozener, deceiver, dissembler, double-crosser (*Inf.*), fraud, hypocrite, rogue, swindler, traitor, two-timer (*Inf.*)

double-dealing **1.** *n.* bad faith, betrayal, cheating, deceit, deception, dishonesty, duplicity, foul play, hypocrisy, mendacity, perfidy, treachery, trickery, two-timing (*Inf.*) **2.** *adj.* cheating, crooked (*Inf.*), deceitful, dishonest, duplicitous, fraudulent, hypocritical, lying, perfidious, sneaky, swindling, treacherous, tricky, two-faced, two-timing (*Inf.*), underhanded, untrustworthy, wily

double entendre ambiguity, double meaning, innuendo, play on words, pun

doublet **1.** jacket, jerkin, vest, waistcoat **2.** couple, pair, set, two

doubly again, as much again, even more, in double measure, once more, over again, twice, twofold

doubt *v.* **1.** discredit, distrust, fear, lack confidence in, misgive, mistrust, query, question, suspect *~n.* **2.** apprehension, disquiet, distrust, fear, incredulity, lack of faith, misgiving, mistrust, qualm, scepticism, suspicion *~v.* **3.** be dubious, be uncertain, demur, fluctuate, hesitate, scruple, vacillate, waver *~n.* **4.** dubiety, hesitancy, hesitation, indecision, irresolution, lack of conviction, suspense, uncertainty, vacillation **5.** ambiguity, confusion, difficulty, dilemma, perplexity, problem, quandary **6. no doubt** admittedly, assuredly, certainly, doubtless, doubtlessly, probably, surely

Antonyms *v.* accept, believe, buy (*Sl.*), have faith in, swallow (*Inf.*), trust *~n.* belief, certainty, confidence, conviction, trust

doubter agnostic, disbeliever, doubting Thomas, questioner, sceptic, unbeliever

doubtful **1.** ambiguous, debatable, dodgy (*Brit., Aust., & N.Z. inf.*), dubious, equivocal, hazardous, iffy (*Inf.*), inconclusive, indefinite, indeterminate, obscure, precarious, problematic(al), questionable, unclear, unconfirmed, unsettled, vague **2.** distrustful, hesitating, in two minds (*Inf.*), irresolute, leery (*Sl.*), perplexed, sceptical, suspicious, tentative, uncertain, unconvinced, undecided, unresolved, unsettled, unsure, vacillating, wavering **3.** disreputable, dodgy (*Brit., Aust., & N.Z. inf.*), dubious, questionable, shady (*Inf.*), suspect, suspicious

Antonyms certain, decided, definite, indubitable, positive, resolute

doubtless **1.** assuredly, certainly, clearly, indisputably, of course, precisely, surely, truly, undoubtedly, unquestionably, without doubt **2.** apparently, most likely, ostensibly, presumably, probably, seemingly, supposedly

doughty bold, brave, courageous, daring, dauntless, fearless, gallant, gritty, hardy, heroic, intrepid, redoubtable, resolute, stouthearted, valiant, valorous

dour **1.** dismal, dreary, forbidding, gloomy, grim, morose, sour, sullen, unfriendly **2.** austere, hard, inflexible, obstinate, rigid, rigorous, severe, strict, uncompromising, unyielding

Antonyms carefree, cheerful, cheery, chirpy (*Inf.*), genial, good-humoured, happy, jovial, pleasant, sunny

douse, dowse **1.** drench, duck, dunk, im~

merse, plunge into water, saturate, soak, souse, steep, submerge 2. blow out, extinguish, put out, smother, snuff (out)

dovetail *v.* 1. fit, fit together, interlock, join, link, mortise, tenon, unite 2. accord, agree, coincide, conform, correspond, harmonize, match, tally

dowdy dingy, drab, frowzy, frumpish, frumpy, ill-dressed, old-fashioned, scrubby (*Brit. inf.*), shabby, slovenly, tacky (*U.S. inf.*), unfashionable
Antonyms chic, dressy, fashionable, neat, smart, spruce, trim, well-dressed

dower 1. dowry, inheritance, legacy, portion, provision, share 2. endowment, faculty, gift, talent

do without abstain from, dispense with, forgo, get along without, give up, kick (*Inf.*), manage without

down *adj.* 1. blue, dejected, depressed, disheartened, dismal, downcast, low, miserable, sad, sick as a parrot (*Inf.*), unhappy ~*v.* 2. bring down, fell, floor, knock down, overthrow, prostrate, subdue, tackle, throw, trip 3. *Inf.* drain, drink (down), gulp, put away, swallow, toss off ~*n.* 4. decline, descent, drop, dropping, fall, falling, reverse 5. **have a down on** *Inf.* be antagonistic *or* hostile to, be anti (*Inf.*), bear a grudge towards, be contra (*Inf.*), be prejudiced against, be set against, feel ill will towards, have it in for (*Sl.*) 6. **down with** away with, get rid of, kick out (*Inf.*), oust, push out

down and out 1. *adj.* derelict, destitute, dirt-poor (*Inf.*), flat broke (*Inf.*), impoverished, penniless, ruined, short, without two pennies to rub together (*Inf.*) 2. **down-and-out** *n.* bag lady (*Chiefly U.S.*), beggar, bum (*Inf.*), derelict, dosser (*Brit. sl.*), loser, outcast, pauper, tramp, vagabond, vagrant

downcast cheerless, crestfallen, daunted, dejected, depressed, despondent, disappointed, disconsolate, discouraged, disheartened, dismal, dismayed, dispirited, miserable, sad, sick as a parrot (*Inf.*), unhappy
Antonyms cheerful, cheery, chirpy (*Inf.*), contented, elated, genial, happy, joyful, light-hearted, optimistic

downfall 1. breakdown, collapse, comedown, comeuppance (*Sl.*), debacle, descent, destruction, disgrace, fall, overthrow, ruin, undoing 2. cloudburst, deluge, downpour, rainstorm

downgrade 1. degrade, demote, humble, lower *or* reduce in rank, take down a peg (*Inf.*) 2. decry, denigrate, detract from, disparage, run down
Antonyms advance, ameliorate, better, elevate, enhance, improve, promote, raise, upgrade

downhearted blue, chapfallen, crestfallen, dejected, depressed, despondent, discouraged, disheartened, dismayed, dispirited, downcast, low-spirited, sad, sick as a parrot (*Inf.*), sorrowful, unhappy

downpour cloudburst, deluge, flood, inundation, rainstorm, torrential rain

downright 1. absolute, arrant, blatant, categorical, clear, complete, deep-dyed (*Usu. derogatory*), explicit, out-and-out, outright, plain, positive, simple, thoroughgoing, total, undisguised, unequivocal, unqualified, utter 2. blunt, candid, forthright, frank, honest, open, outspoken, plain, sincere, straightforward, straight-from-the-shoulder, upfront (*Inf.*)

down-to-earth common-sense, hard-headed, matter-of-fact, mundane, no-nonsense, plain-spoken, practical, realistic, sane, sensible, unsentimental

downtrodden abused, afflicted, distressed, exploited, helpless, oppressed, subjugated, subservient, tyrannized

downward *adj.* declining, descending, earthward, heading down, sliding, slipping

downy feathery, fleecy, fluffy, plumate (*Zool., Bot.*), silky, soft, velvety, woolly

dowse *see* DOUSE

doze 1. *v.* catnap, drop off (*Inf.*), drowse, kip (*Brit. sl.*), nap, nod, nod off (*Inf.*), sleep, sleep lightly, slumber, snooze (*Inf.*), zizz (*Brit. inf.*) 2. *n.* catnap, forty winks (*Inf.*), kip (*Brit. sl.*), little sleep, nap, shuteye (*Sl.*), siesta, snooze (*Inf.*), zizz (*Brit. inf.*)

dozy 1. dozing, drowsy, half asleep, nodding, sleepy 2. *Inf.* daft (*Inf.*), goofy (*Inf.*), not all there, senseless, silly, simple, slow, slow-witted, stupid, witless

drab cheerless, colourless, dingy, dismal, dreary, dull, flat, gloomy, grey, lacklustre, shabby, sombre, uninspired, vapid
Antonyms bright, cheerful, colourful, jazzy (*Inf.*), vibrant, vivid

draft *v.* 1. compose, delineate, design, draw, draw up, formulate, outline, plan, sketch ~*n.* 2. abstract, delineation, outline, plan, preliminary form, rough, sketch, version 3. bill (*of exchange*), cheque, order, postal order

drag *v.* 1. draw, hale, haul, lug, pull, tow, trail, tug, yank 2. crawl, creep, go slowly, inch, limp along, shamble, shuffle 3. dawdle, draggle, lag behind, linger, loiter, straggle, trail behind 4. *With* **on** *or* **out** draw out, extend, keep going, lengthen, persist, prolong, protract, spin out, stretch out 5. **drag one's feet** *Inf.* block, hold back, obstruct, procrastinate, stall *~n.* 6. *Sl.* annoyance, bore, bother, nuisance, pain (*Inf.*), pain in the arse (*Taboo inf.*), pest

dragging boring, dull, going slowly, humdrum, mind-numbing, monotonous, tedious, tiresome, wearisome

draggle 1. befoul, bemire, besmirch, drabble, trail 2. dally, dawdle, dilly-dally (*Inf.*), lag, straggle, trail behind

dragoon *v.* browbeat, bully, coerce, compel, constrain, drive, force, impel, intimidate, railroad (*Inf.*), strong-arm (*Inf.*)

drain *v.* 1. bleed, draw off, dry, empty, evacuate, milk, pump off *or* out, remove, tap, withdraw 2. consume, deplete, dissipate, empty, exhaust, sap, strain, tax, use up, weary 3. discharge, effuse, exude, flow out, leak, ooze, seep, trickle, well out 4. drink up, finish, gulp down, quaff, swallow *~n.* 5. channel, conduit, culvert, ditch, duct, outlet, pipe, sewer, sink, trench, watercourse 6. depletion, drag, exhaustion, expenditure, reduction, sap, strain, withdrawal 7. **down the drain** gone, gone for good, lost, ruined, wasted

drainage bilge (water), seepage, sewage, sewerage, waste

dram drop, glass, measure, shot (*Inf.*), slug, snifter (*Inf.*), snort (*Sl.*), tot

drama 1. dramatization, play, show, stage play, stage show, theatrical piece 2. acting, dramatic art, dramaturgy, stagecraft, theatre, Thespian art 3. crisis, dramatics, excitement, histrionics, scene, spectacle, theatrics, turmoil

dramatic 1. dramaturgic, dramaturgical, theatrical, Thespian 2. breathtaking, climactic, electrifying, emotional, exciting, melodramatic, sensational, shock-horror (*Facetious*), startling, sudden, suspenseful, tense, thrilling 3. affecting, effective, expressive, impressive, moving, powerful, striking, vivid

Antonyms ordinary, run-of-the-mill, undramatic, unexceptional, unmemorable

dramatist dramaturge, playwright, screenwriter, scriptwriter

dramatize act, exaggerate, lay it on (thick) (*Sl.*), make a performance of, overdo, overstate, play-act, play to the gallery

drape 1. adorn, array, cloak, cover, fold, swathe, wrap 2. dangle, droop, drop, hang, lean over, let fall, suspend

drastic desperate, dire, extreme, forceful, harsh, radical, severe, strong

draught 1. *Of air* current, flow, influx, movement, puff 2. dragging, drawing, haulage, pulling, traction 3. cup, dose, drench, drink, potion, quantity

draw *v.* 1. drag, haul, pull, tow, tug 2. delineate, depict, design, map out, mark out, outline, paint, portray, sketch, trace 3. deduce, derive, get, infer, make, take 4. allure, attract, bring forth, call forth, elicit, engage, entice, evoke, induce, influence, invite, persuade 5. extort, extract, pull out, take out 6. attenuate, elongate, extend, lengthen, stretch 7. breathe in, drain, inhale, inspire, puff, pull, respire, suck 8. compose, draft, formulate, frame, prepare, write 9. choose, pick, select, single out, take *~n.* 10. *Inf.* attraction, enticement, lure, pull (*Inf.*) 11. dead heat, deadlock, impasse, stalemate, tie

drawback defect, deficiency, detriment, difficulty, disadvantage, downside, fault, flaw, fly in the ointment (*Inf.*), handicap, hindrance, hitch, impediment, imperfection, nuisance, obstacle, snag, stumbling block, trouble

Antonyms advantage, asset, benefit, gain, help, service, use

draw back recoil, retract, retreat, shrink, start back, withdraw

drawing cartoon, delineation, depiction, illustration, outline, picture, portrayal, representation, sketch, study

drawl *v. Of speech sounds* drag out, draw out, extend, lengthen, prolong, protract

drawling dragging, drawly, droning, dull, twanging, twangy

drawn fatigued, fraught, haggard, harassed, harrowed, pinched, sapped, strained, stressed, taut, tense, tired, worn

draw on employ, exploit, extract, fall back on, have recourse to, make use of, rely on, take from, use

draw out drag out, extend, lengthen, make longer, prolong, prolongate, protract, spin out, stretch, string out

Antonyms curtail, cut, cut short, dock, pare down, reduce, shorten, trim, truncate

draw up 1. bring to a stop, halt, pull up, run in, stop, stop short 2. compose, draft, formulate, frame, prepare, write out

dread 1. *v.* anticipate with horror, cringe at, fear, have cold feet (*Inf.*), quail, shrink from, shudder, tremble 2. *n.* affright, alarm, apprehension, aversion, awe, dismay, fear, fright, funk (*Inf.*), heebie-jeebies (*Sl.*), horror, terror, trepidation 3. *adj.* alarming, awe-inspiring, awful, dire, dreaded, dreadful, frightening, frightful, horrible, terrible, terrifying

dreadful alarming, appalling, awful, dire, distressing, fearful, formidable, frightful, ghastly, godawful (*Sl.*), grievous, hellacious (*U.S. sl.*), hideous, horrendous, horrible, monstrous, shocking, terrible, tragic, tremendous

dream *n.* 1. daydream, delusion, fantasy, hallucination, illusion, imagination, pipe dream, reverie, speculation, trance, vagary, vision 2. ambition, aspiration, design, desire, goal, hope, notion, thirst, wish 3. beauty, delight, gem, joy, marvel, pleasure, treasure ~*v.* 4. build castles in the air *or* in Spain, conjure up, daydream, envisage, fancy, fantasize, hallucinate, have dreams, imagine, stargaze, think, visualize

dreamer daydreamer, Don Quixote, fantasist, fantasizer, fantast, idealist, romancer, theorizer, utopian, visionary, Walter Mitty

dreamland cloud-cuckoo-land, cloudland, dream world, fairyland, fantasy, illusion, land of dreams, land of make-believe, land of Nod, never-never land (*Inf.*), sleep

dreamlike chimerical, hallucinatory, illusory, phantasmagoric, phantasmagorical, surreal, trancelike, unreal, unsubstantial, visionary

dream up concoct, contrive, cook up (*Inf.*), create, devise, hatch, imagine, invent, spin, think up

dreamy 1. airy-fairy, dreamlike, fanciful, imaginary, impractical, quixotic, speculative, surreal, vague, visionary 2. chimerical, dreamlike, fantastic, intangible, misty, phantasmagoric, phantasmagorical, shadowy, unreal 3. absent, abstracted, daydreaming, faraway, in a reverie, musing, pensive, preoccupied, with one's head in the clouds 4. calming, gentle, lulling, relaxing, romantic, soothing

Antonyms common-sense, down-to-earth, feet-on-the-ground, practical, pragmatic, realistic, unromantic

dreary 1. bleak, cheerless, comfortless, depressing, dismal, doleful, downcast, drear, forlorn, funereal, gloomy, glum, joyless, lonely, lonesome, melancholy, mournful, sad, solitary, sombre, sorrowful, wretched 2. boring, colourless, drab, dull, ho-hum (*Inf.*), humdrum, lifeless, mind-numbing, monotonous, routine, tedious, uneventful, uninteresting, wearisome

Antonyms bright, cheerful, happy, interesting, joyful

dredge up dig up, discover, drag up, draw up, fish up, raise, rake up, uncover, unearth

dreg bit, drop, mite, particle, piece, remnant, scrap

dregs 1. deposit, draff, dross, grounds, lees, residue, residuum, scourings, scum, sediment, trash, waste 2. *Sl.* *canaille,* down-and-outs, good-for-nothings, outcasts, rabble, ragtag and bobtail, riffraff, scum

drench 1. *v.* drown, duck, flood, imbrue, inundate, saturate, soak, souse, steep, wet 2. *n. Veterinary* dose, physic, purge

dress *n.* 1. costume, ensemble, frock, garment, get-up (*Inf.*), gown, outfit, rigout (*Inf.*), robe, suit 2. apparel, attire, clothes, clothing, costume, garb, garments, gear (*Inf.*), guise, habiliment, raiment (*Archaic or poetic*), togs, vestment ~*v.* 3. attire, change, clothe, don, garb, put on, robe, slip on *or* into 4. adorn, apparel (*Archaic*), array, bedeck, deck, decorate, drape, embellish, festoon, furbish, ornament, rig, trim 5. adjust, align, arrange, comb (out), dispose, do (up), fit, get ready, groom, prepare, set, straighten 6. bandage, bind up, plaster, treat

Antonyms (*sense 3*) disrobe, divest oneself of, peel off (*Sl.*), shed, strip, take off one's clothes

dress down bawl out (*Inf.*), berate, carpet (*Inf.*), castigate, chew out (*U.S. & Canad. inf.*), give a rocket (*Brit. & N.Z. inf.*), haul over the coals, read the riot act, rebuke, reprimand, reprove, scold, tear into (*Inf.*), tear (someone) off a strip (*Brit. inf.*), tell off (*Inf.*), upbraid

dressmaker couturier, modiste, seamstress, sewing woman, tailor

dress up 1. doll up (*Sl.*), dress for dinner, dress formally, put on one's best bib and tucker (*Inf.*), put on one's glad rags (*Inf.*) 2. disguise, play-act, put on fancy dress, wear a costume 3. beautify, do oneself up, embellish, gild, improve, titivate, trick out *or* up

dressy classy (*Sl.*), elaborate, elegant, formal, ornate, ritzy (*Sl.*), smart, stylish, swish (*Inf., chiefly Brit.*)

dribble 1. drip, drop, fall in drops, leak, ooze, run, seep, trickle 2. drip saliva, drivel, drool, slaver, slobber

driblet bit, dash, drop, droplet, fragment, gobbet, morsel, piece, scrap, speck, sprinkling

drift *v.* 1. be carried along, coast, float, go (aimlessly), meander, stray, waft, wander 2. accumulate, amass, bank up, drive, gather, pile up ~*n.* 3. accumulation, bank, heap, mass, mound, pile 4. course, current, direction, flow, impulse, movement, rush, sweep, trend 5. *Fig.* aim, design, direction, gist, implication, import, intention, meaning, object, purport, scope, significance, tendency, tenor, thrust

drifter bag lady (*Chiefly U.S.*), beachcomber, bum (*Inf.*), hobo (*U.S.*), itinerant, rolling stone, tramp, vagabond, vagrant, wanderer

drill *v.* 1. coach, discipline, exercise, instruct, practise, rehearse, teach, train ~*n.*

2. discipline, exercise, instruction, practice, preparation, repetition, training ~*v.* 3. bore, penetrate, perforate, pierce, puncture, sink in ~*n.* 4. bit, borer, boring-tool, gimlet, rotary tool

drink *v.* 1. absorb, drain, gulp, guzzle, imbibe, partake of, quaff, sip, suck, sup, swallow, swig (*Inf.*), swill, toss off, wash down, wet one's whistle (*Inf.*) 2. bend the elbow (*Inf.*), bevvy (*Dialect*), booze (*Inf.*), carouse, go on a binge *or* bender (*Inf.*), hit the bottle (*Inf.*), indulge, pub-crawl (*Inf., chiefly Brit.*), revel, tipple, tope, wassail ~*n.* 3. beverage, liquid, potion, refreshment, thirst quencher 4. alcohol, booze (*Inf.*), hooch *or* hootch (*Inf., chiefly U.S. & Canad.*), liquor, spirits, the bottle (*Inf.*) 5. cup, draught, glass, gulp, noggin, sip, snifter (*Inf.*), swallow, swig (*Inf.*), taste, tipple 6. **the drink** *Inf.* the briny (*Inf.*), the deep, the main, the ocean, the sea

drinkable drinking, fit to drink, potable

drinker alcoholic, bibber, boozer (*Inf.*), dipsomaniac, drunk, drunkard, guzzler, inebriate, lush (*Sl.*), soak (*Sl.*), sot, sponge (*Inf.*), tippler, toper, wino (*Inf.*)

drink in absorb, assimilate, be all ears (*Inf.*), be fascinated by, be rapt, hang on (someone's) words, hang on the lips of, pay attention

drinking bout bacchanalia, bender (*Inf.*), bevvy (*Dialect*), binge (*Inf.*), celebration, debauch, orgy, pub-crawl (*Inf., chiefly Brit.*), spree, wassail

drink to pledge, pledge the health of, salute, toast

drip *v.* 1. dribble, drizzle, drop, exude, filter, plop, splash, sprinkle, trickle ~*n.* 2. dribble, dripping, drop, leak, trickle 3. *Inf.* milksop, mummy's boy (*Inf.*), namby-pamby, ninny, softy (*Inf.*), weakling, weed (*Inf.*), wet (*Brit. inf.*)

drive *v.* 1. herd, hurl, impel, propel, push, send, urge 2. direct, go, guide, handle, manage, motor, operate, ride, steer, travel 3. actuate, coerce, compel, constrain, dragoon, force, goad, harass, impel, motivate, oblige, overburden, overwork, press, prick, prod, prompt, railroad (*Inf.*), rush, spur 4. dash, dig, plunge, hammer, ram, sink, stab, thrust ~*n.* 5. excursion, hurl (*Scot.*), jaunt, journey, outing, ride, run, spin (*Inf.*), trip, turn 6. action, advance, appeal, campaign, crusade, effort, push (*Inf.*), surge 7. ambition, effort, energy, enterprise, get-up-and-go (*Inf.*), initiative, motivation, pep, pressure, push (*Inf.*), vigour, zip (*Inf.*)

drive at aim, allude to, get at, have in mind, hint at, imply, indicate, insinuate, intend, intimate, mean, refer to, signify, suggest

drivel *v.* 1. dribble, drool, slaver, slobber 2. babble, blether, gab (*Inf.*), gas (*Inf.*), maunder, prate, ramble, waffle (*Inf., chiefly Brit.*) ~*n.* 3. balderdash, balls (*Taboo sl.*), bilge (*Inf.*), blah (*Sl.*), bosh (*Inf.*), bull (*Sl.*), bullshit (*Taboo sl.*), bunk (*Inf.*), bunkum *or* buncombe (*Chiefly U.S.*), cobblers (*Brit. taboo sl.*), crap (*Sl.*), dross, eyewash (*Inf.*), fatuity, garbage (*Inf.*), gibberish, guff (*Sl.*), hogwash, hokum (*Sl., chiefly U.S. & Canad.*), horsefeathers (*U.S. sl.*), hot air (*Inf.*), moonshine, nonsense, pap, piffle (*Inf.*), poppycock (*Inf.*), prating, rot, rubbish, shit (*Taboo sl.*), stuff, tommyrot, tosh (*Sl., chiefly Brit.*), tripe (*Inf.*), twaddle, waffle (*Inf., chiefly Brit.*) 4. saliva, slaver, slobber

driveller 1. drooler, slaverer, slobberer, splutterer, sputterer 2. babbler, blatherskite, prater, prattler, rambler, twaddler, waffler (*Inf., chiefly Brit.*), windbág (*Sl.*)

driving compelling, dynamic, energetic, forceful, galvanic, sweeping, vigorous, violent

drizzle 1. *n.* fine rain, Scotch mist, smir (*Scot.*) 2. *v.* mizzle (*Dialect*), rain, shower, spot *or* spit with rain, spray, sprinkle

droll amusing, clownish, comic, comical, diverting, eccentric, entertaining, farcical, funny, humorous, jocular, laughable, ludicrous, odd, oddball (*Inf.*), off-the-wall (*Sl.*), quaint, ridiculous, risible, waggish, whimsical

drollery absurdity, archness, buffoonery, comicality, farce, fun, humour, jocularity, pleasantry, waggishness, whimsicality, wit

drone[1] *n.* couch potato (*Sl.*), idler, leech, loafer, lounger, parasite, scrounger (*Inf.*), skiver (*Brit. sl.*), sluggard, sponger (*Inf.*)

drone[2] *v.* 1. buzz, hum, purr, thrum, vibrate, whirr 2. *Often with* **on** be boring, chant, drawl, intone, prose about, speak monotonously, spout, talk interminably ~*n.* 3. buzz, hum, murmuring, purr, thrum, vibration, whirr, whirring

drool 1. *Often with* **over** dote on, fondle, gloat over, gush, make much of, pet, rave (*Inf.*), slobber over, spoil 2. dribble, drivel, salivate, slaver, slobber, water at the mouth

droop 1. bend, dangle, drop, fall down, hang (down), sag, sink 2. decline, diminish, fade, faint, flag, languish, slump, wilt, wither 3. despond, falter, give in, give up, give way, lose heart *or* hope

droopy 1. drooping, flabby, floppy, languid, languorous, lassitudinous, limp, pendulous, sagging, stooped, wilting 2. blue, dejected, disheartened, dispirited, doleful, downcast, down (in the dumps) (*Inf.*), sick as a parrot (*Inf.*)

drop *n.* 1. bead, bubble, driblet, drip, droplet, globule, pearl, tear 2. dab, dash, mouthful, nip, pinch, shot (*Inf.*), sip, spot, taste, tot, trace, trickle 3. abyss, chasm, declivity, descent, fall, plunge, precipice, slope 4. cut, decline, decrease, deterioration, downturn, fall-off, lowering, reduction, slump ~*v.* 5. dribble, drip, fall in drops, trickle 6. decline, depress, descend, diminish, dive, droop, fall, lower, plummet, plunge, sink, tumble 7. abandon, axe (*Inf.*), cease, desert, discontinue, forsake, give up, kick (*Inf.*), leave, quit, relinquish, remit, terminate 8. *Inf.* disown, ignore, jilt, reject, renounce, repudiate, throw over 9. *Sometimes with* **off** deposit, leave, let off, set down, unload

drop in (on) blow in (*Inf.*), call, call in, go and see, look in (on), look up, pop in (*Inf.*), roll up (*Inf.*), stop, turn up, visit

drop off 1. decline, decrease, diminish, dwindle, fall off, lessen, slacken 2. allow to alight, deliver, leave, let off, set down 3. *Inf.* catnap, doze (off), drowse, fall asleep, have forty winks (*Inf.*), nod (off), snooze (*Inf.*)

drop out abandon, back out, cop out (*Sl.*), forsake, give up, leave, quit, renege, stop, withdraw

dross crust, debris, dregs, impurity, lees, recrement, refuse, remains, scoria, scum, waste

drought 1. aridity, dehydration, drouth (*Scot.*), dryness, dry spell, dry weather, parchedness 2. dearth, deficiency, insufficiency, lack, need, scarcity, shortage, want
Antonyms abundance, deluge, downpour, flood, flow, inundation, outpouring, profusion, rush, stream, torrent

drove collection, company, crowd, flock, gathering, herd, horde, mob, multitude, press, swarm, throng

drown 1. deluge, drench, engulf, flood, go down, go under, immerse, inundate, sink, submerge, swamp 2. *Fig.* deaden, engulf, muffle, obliterate, overcome, overpower, overwhelm, stifle, swallow up, wipe out

drowse 1. *v.* be drowsy, be lethargic, be sleepy, doze, drop off (*Inf.*), kip (*Brit. sl.*), nap, nod, sleep, slumber, snooze (*Inf.*), zizz (*Brit. inf.*) 2. *n.* doze, forty winks (*Inf.*), kip (*Brit. sl.*), nap, sleep, slumber, zizz (*Brit. inf.*)

drowsy 1. comatose, dazed, dopey (*Sl.*), dozy, drugged, half asleep, heavy, lethargic, nodding, sleepy, somnolent, tired, torpid 2. dreamy, lulling, restful, sleepy, soothing, soporific
Antonyms alert, awake, full of beans (*Inf.*), lively, perky

drub 1. bang, beat, birch, cane, clobber (*Sl.*), club, cudgel, flog, hit, knock, lambast(e), pound, pummel, punch, strike, thrash, thump, whack 2. beat, best, blow out of the water (*Sl.*), defeat, hammer (*Inf.*), lick (*Inf.*), master, outclass, overcome, rout, run rings around (*Inf.*), tank (*Sl.*), trounce, undo, vanquish, wipe the floor with (*Inf.*), worst

drubbing beating, clobbering (*Sl.*), defeat, flogging, hammering (*Inf.*), licking (*Inf.*), pasting (*Sl.*), pounding, pummelling, thrashing, trouncing, walloping (*Inf.*), whipping

drudge 1. *n.* dogsbody (*Inf.*), factotum, hack, maid *or* man of all work, menial, plodder, scullion (*Archaic*), servant, skivvy (*Chiefly Brit.*), slave, toiler, worker 2. *v.* grind (*Inf.*), keep one's nose to the grindstone, labour, moil (*Archaic or dialect*), plod, plug away (*Inf.*), slave, toil, work

drudgery chore, donkey-work, fag (*Inf.*), grind (*Inf.*), hack work, hard work, labour, menial labour, skivvying (*Brit.*), slavery, slog, sweat (*Inf.*), sweated labour, toil

drug *n.* 1. medicament, medication, medicine, physic, poison, remedy 2. dope (*Sl.*), narcotic, opiate, stimulant ~*v.* 3. administer a drug, dope (*Sl.*), dose, medicate, treat 4. anaesthetize, deaden, knock out, numb, poison, stupefy

drug addict *n.* acid head (*Inf.*), crack-head (*Inf.*), dope-fiend (*Sl.*), head (*Inf.*), hophead (*Inf.*), junkie (*Inf.*), tripper (*Inf.*)

drugged bombed (*Sl.*), comatose, doped (*Sl.*), dopey (*Sl.*), flying (*Sl.*), high (*Inf.*), on a trip (*Inf.*), out of it (*Sl.*), out of one's mind (*Sl.*), out to it (*Aust. & N.Z. sl.*), smashed (*Sl.*), spaced out (*Sl.*), stoned (*Sl.*), stupefied, turned on (*Sl.*), under the influence (*Inf.*), wasted (*Sl.*), wrecked (*Sl.*), zonked (*Sl.*)

drum *v.* 1. beat, pulsate, rap, reverberate, tap, tattoo, throb 2. *With* **into** din into, drive home, hammer away, harp on, instil, reiterate

drum out cashier, discharge, dismiss, disown, drive out, expel, oust, outlaw

drum up attract, bid for, canvass, obtain, petition, round up, solicit

drunk 1. *adj.* bacchic, bevvied (*Dialect*), blitzed (*Sl.*), blotto (*Sl.*), bombed (*Sl.*), canned (*Sl.*), drunken, flying (*Sl.*), fu' (*Scot.*), fuddled, half seas over (*Inf.*), inebriated, intoxicated, legless (*Inf.*), lit up (*Sl.*), loaded (*Sl., chiefly U.S. & Canad.*), maudlin, merry (*Brit. inf.*), muddled, out of it (*Sl.*), out to it (*Aust. & N.Z. sl.*), paralytic

(*Inf.*), pickled (*Inf.*), pie-eyed (*Sl.*), pissed (*Taboo sl.*), plastered (*Sl.*), sloshed (*Sl.*), smashed (*Sl.*), soaked (*Inf.*), steamboats (*Sl.*), steaming (*Sl.*), stewed (*Sl.*), stoned (*Sl.*), tanked up (*Sl.*), tiddly (*Sl., chiefly Brit.*), tight (*Inf.*), tipsy, tired and emotional (*Euphemistic*), under the influence (*Inf.*), wasted (*Sl.*), well-oiled (*Sl.*), wrecked (*Sl.*), zonked (*Sl.*) 2. *n.* boozer (*Inf.*), drunkard, inebriate, lush (*Sl.*), soak (*Sl.*), sot, toper, wino (*Inf.*)

drunkard alcoholic, carouser, dipsomaniac, drinker, drunk, lush (*Sl.*), soak (*Sl.*), sot, tippler, toper, wino (*Inf.*)

drunken 1. bevvied (*Dialect*), bibulous, blitzed (*Sl.*), blotto (*Sl.*), bombed (*Sl.*), boozing (*Inf.*), drunk, flying (*Sl.*), (gin-) sodden, inebriate, intoxicated, legless (*Inf.*), lit up (*Sl.*), out of it (*Sl.*), out to it (*Aust. & N.Z. sl.*), paralytic (*Inf.*), pissed (*Taboo sl.*), red-nosed, smashed (*Sl.*), sottish, steamboats (*Sl.*), steaming (*Sl.*), tippling, toping, under the influence (*Inf.*), wasted (*Sl.*), wrecked (*Sl.*), zonked (*Sl.*) 2. bacchanalian, bacchic, boozy (*Inf.*), debauched, dionysian, dissipated, orgiastic, riotous, saturnalian

drunkenness alcoholism, bibulousness, dipsomania, inebriety, insobriety, intemperance, intoxication, sottishness, tipsiness

dry *adj.* 1. arid, barren, dehydrated, desiccated, dried up, juiceless, moistureless, parched, sapless, thirsty, torrid, waterless 2. *Fig.* boring, dreary, dull, ho-hum (*Inf.*), monotonous, plain, tedious, tiresome, uninteresting 3. *Fig.* cutting, deadpan, droll, keen, low-key, quietly humorous, sarcastic, sharp, sly ~*v.* 4. dehumidify, dehydrate, desiccate, drain, make dry, parch, sear 5. *With* **out** *or* **up** become dry, become unproductive, harden, mummify, shrivel up, wilt, wither, wizen

Antonyms *adj.* (*sense 1*) damp, humid, moist, wet (*sense 2*) entertaining, interesting, lively ~*v.* moisten, wet

dryness aridity, aridness, dehumidification, dehydration, drought, thirst, thirstiness

dual binary, coupled, double, duplex, duplicate, matched, paired, twin, twofold

duality biformity, dichotomy, doubleness, dualism, duplexity, polarity

dub 1. bestow, confer, confer knighthood upon, entitle, knight 2. call, christen, denominate, designate, label, name, nickname, style, term

dubiety doubt, doubtfulness, dubiosity, incertitude, indecision, misgiving, mistrust, qualm, scepticism, uncertainty

dubious 1. doubtful, hesitant, iffy (*Inf.*), leery (*Sl.*), sceptical, uncertain, unconvinced, undecided, unsure, wavering 2. ambiguous, debatable, dodgy (*Brit., Aust., & N.Z. inf.*), doubtful, equivocal, indefinite, indeterminate, obscure, problematic(al), unclear, unsettled 3. dodgy (*Brit., Aust., & N.Z. inf.*), fishy (*Inf.*), questionable, shady (*Inf.*), suspect, suspicious, undependable, unreliable, untrustworthy

Antonyms certain, definite, dependable, obvious, positive, reliable, sure, trustworthy

dubitable debatable, doubtable, doubtful, dubious, iffy (*Inf.*), in doubt, more than doubtful, open to doubt, problematic(al), questionable, unconvincing

duck 1. bend, bob, bow, crouch, dodge, drop, lower, stoop 2. dip, dive, douse, dunk, immerse, plunge, souse, submerge, wet 3. *Inf.* avoid, body-swerve (*Scot.*), dodge, escape, evade, shirk, shun, sidestep

duct blood vessel, canal, channel, conduit, funnel, passage, pipe, tube

ductile 1. extensible, flexible, malleable, plastic, pliable, pliant, tensile 2. amenable, biddable, compliant, docile, manageable, tractable, yielding

dud 1. *n.* failure, flop (*Inf.*), washout (*Inf.*) 2. *adj.* broken, bust (*Inf.*), duff (*Brit. inf.*), failed, inoperative, kaput (*Inf.*), not functioning, valueless, worthless

dudgeon 1. *Archaic* indignation, ire, resentment, umbrage, wrath 2. **in high dudgeon** angry, fuming, indignant, offended, resentful, vexed

due *adj.* 1. in arrears, outstanding, owed, owing, payable, unpaid 2. appropriate, becoming, bounden, deserved, fit, fitting, just, justified, merited, obligatory, proper, requisite, right, rightful, suitable, well-earned 3. adequate, ample, enough, plenty of, sufficient 4. expected, expected to arrive, scheduled ~*n.* 5. comeuppance (*Sl.*), deserts, merits, prerogative, privilege, right(s) ~*adv.* 6. dead, direct, directly, exactly, straight, undeviatingly

duel *n.* 1. affair of honour, single combat 2. clash, competition, contest, encounter, engagement, fight, head-to-head, rivalry ~*v.* 3. clash, compete, contend, contest, fight, rival, struggle, vie with

dues charge, charges, contribution, fee, levy, membership fee

duff bad, counterfeit, dud (*Inf.*), fake, false, not working, useless, worthless

duffer blunderer, booby, bungler, clod, clot (*Brit. inf.*), galoot (*Sl., chiefly U.S.*), lubber, lummox (*Inf.*), oaf

dulcet agreeable, charming, delightful, euphonious, harmonious, honeyed, mellifluent, mellifluous, melodious, musical, pleasant, pleasing, soothing, sweet

dull *adj.* 1. braindead (*Inf.*), dense, dim, dim-witted (*Inf.*), doltish, dozy (*Brit. inf.*), obtuse, slow, stolid, stupid, thick, unintelligent 2. apathetic, blank, callous, dead, empty, heavy, indifferent, insensible, insensitive, lifeless, listless, passionless, slow, sluggish, unresponsive, unsympathetic, vacuous 3. banal, boring, commonplace, dozy, dreary, dry, flat, ho-hum (*Inf.*), humdrum, mind-numbing, monotonous, plain, prosaic, run-of-the-mill, tedious, tiresome, unimaginative, uninteresting, vapid 4. blunt, blunted, dulled, edgeless, not keen, not sharp, unsharpened 5. cloudy, dim, dismal, gloomy, leaden, opaque, overcast, turbid 6. depressed, inactive, slack, slow, sluggish, torpid, uneventful 7. drab, faded, feeble, indistinct, lacklustre, muffled, murky, muted, sombre, subdued, subfusc, toned-down ~*v.* 8. dampen, deject, depress, discourage, dishearten, dispirit, sadden 9. allay, alleviate, assuage, blunt, lessen, mitigate, moderate, palliate, paralyse, relieve, soften, stupefy, take the edge off 10. cloud, darken, dim, fade, obscure, stain, sully, tarnish

Antonyms *adj.* active, bright, clever, distinct, exciting, intelligent, interesting, lively, sharp

dullard blockhead, clod, dimwit (*Inf.*), dolt, dope (*Inf.*), dunce, lamebrain (*Inf.*), nitwit (*Inf.*), numskull *or* numbskull, oaf

duly 1. accordingly, appropriately, befittingly, correctly, decorously, deservedly, fittingly, properly, rightfully, suitably 2. at the proper time, on time, punctually

dumb 1. at a loss for words, inarticulate, mum, mute, silent, soundless, speechless, tongue-tied, voiceless, wordless 2. *Inf.* asinine, braindead (*Inf.*), dense, dim-witted (*Inf.*), dozy (*Brit. inf.*), dull, foolish, obtuse, stupid, thick, unintelligent

Antonyms (*sense 2*) articulate, bright, clever, intelligent, quick-witted, smart

dumbfound, dumfound amaze, astonish, astound, bewilder, bowl over (*Inf.*), confound, confuse, flabbergast (*Inf.*), flummox, nonplus, overwhelm, stagger, startle, stun, take aback

dumbfounded, dumfounded amazed, astonished, astounded, at sea, bewildered, bowled over (*Inf.*), breathless, confounded, confused, dumb, flabbergasted (*Inf.*), flummoxed, gobsmacked (*Brit. sl.*), knocked for six (*Inf.*), knocked sideways (*Inf.*), nonplussed, overcome, overwhelmed, speechless, staggered, startled, stunned, taken aback, thrown, thunderstruck

dummy *n.* 1. figure, form, lay figure, manikin, mannequin, model 2. copy, counterfeit, duplicate, imitation, sham, substitute 3. *Sl.* berk (*Brit. sl.*), blockhead, charlie (*Brit. inf.*), coot, dickhead (*Sl.*), dimwit (*Inf.*), dipstick (*Brit. sl.*), divvy (*Brit. sl.*), dolt, dork (*Sl.*), dullard, dunce, dweeb (*U.S. sl.*), fool, fuckwit (*Taboo sl.*), geek (*Sl.*), gonzo (*Sl.*), jerk (*Sl., chiefly U.S. & Canad.*), lamebrain (*Inf.*), nerd *or* nurd (*Sl.*), nitwit (*Inf.*), numskull *or* numbskull, oaf, pillock (*Brit. sl.*), plank (*Brit. sl.*), plonker (*Sl.*), prat (*Sl.*), prick (*Derogatory sl.*), schmuck (*U.S. sl.*), simpleton, wally (*Sl.*) ~*adj.* 4. artificial, bogus, fake, false, imitation, mock, phoney *or* phony (*Inf.*), sham, simulated 5. mock, practice, simulated, trial

dump *v.* 1. deposit, drop, fling down, let fall, throw down 2. coup (*Scot.*), discharge, dispose of, ditch (*Sl.*), empty out, get rid of, jettison, scrap, throw away *or* out, tip, unload ~*n.* 3. junkyard, refuse heap, rubbish heap, rubbish tip, tip 4. *Inf.* hole (*Inf.*), hovel, joint (*Sl.*), mess, pigsty, shack, shanty, slum

dumps blues, dejection, depression, despondency, dolour, gloom, gloominess, low spirits, melancholy, mopes, sadness, the hump (*Brit. inf.*), unhappiness, woe

dumpy chubby, chunky, fubsy (*Archaic or dialect*), homely, plump, podgy, pudgy, roly-poly, short, squab, squat, stout, tubby

dun *v.* beset, importune, pester, plague, press, urge

dunce ass, blockhead, bonehead (*Sl.*), dimwit (*Inf.*), dolt, donkey, duffer (*Inf.*), dullard, dunderhead, goose (*Inf.*), halfwit, ignoramus, lamebrain (*Inf.*), loon (*Inf.*), moron, nincompoop, nitwit (*Inf.*), numskull *or* numbskull, oaf, simpleton, thickhead

dungeon cage, cell, donjon, lockup, oubliette, prison, vault

dupe *n.* 1. fall guy (*Inf.*), gull, mug (*Brit. sl.*), pigeon (*Sl.*), pushover (*Sl.*), sap (*Sl.*), simpleton, sucker (*Sl.*), victim 2. cat's-paw, instrument, pawn, puppet, stooge (*Sl.*), tool ~*v.* 3. bamboozle (*Inf.*), beguile, cheat, con (*Inf.*), cozen, deceive, defraud, delude, gull (*Archaic*), hoax, hoodwink, humbug, kid (*Inf.*), outwit, overreach, rip off (*Sl.*), swindle, trick

duplicate 1. *adj.* corresponding, identical, matched, matching, twin, twofold 2. *n.* carbon copy, clone, copy, double, facsimile, fax, likeness, lookalike, match, mate, photocopy, Photostat (*Trademark*), replica, reproduction, ringer (*Sl.*), twin, Xerox (*Trademark*) 3. *v.* clone, copy, double, echo, fax, photocopy, Photostat (*Trademark*), repeat, replicate, reproduce, Xerox (*Trademark*)

duplicity artifice, chicanery, deceit, deception, dishonesty, dissimulation, double-dealing, falsehood, fraud, guile, hypocrisy, perfidy
Antonyms candour, honesty, straightforwardness

durability constancy, durableness, endurance, imperishability, lastingness, permanence, persistence

durable abiding, constant, dependable, enduring, fast, firm, fixed, hard-wearing, lasting, long-lasting, permanent, persistent, reliable, resistant, sound, stable, strong, sturdy, substantial, tough
Antonyms breakable, brittle, delicate, fragile, impermanent, perishable, weak

duration continuance, continuation, extent, length, period, perpetuation, prolongation, span, spell, stretch, term, time

duress 1. coercion, compulsion, constraint, pressure, threat 2. captivity, confinement, constraint, hardship, imprisonment, incarceration, restraint

dusk 1. dark, evening, eventide, gloaming (*Scot. or poetic*), nightfall, sundown, sunset, twilight 2. *Poetic* darkness, gloom, murk, obscurity, shade, shadowiness
Antonyms aurora (*Poetic*), cockcrow, dawn, dawning, daybreak, daylight, morning, sunlight, sunup

dusky 1. dark, dark-complexioned, dark-hued, sable, swarthy 2. caliginous (*Archaic*), cloudy, crepuscular, darkish, dim, gloomy, murky, obscure, overcast, shadowy, shady, tenebrous, twilight, twilit, veiled

dust *n.* 1. fine fragments, grime, grit, particles, powder, powdery dirt 2. dirt, earth, ground, soil 3. *Inf.* commotion, disturbance, fuss, racket, row 4. **bite the dust** *Inf.* die, drop dead, expire, fall in battle, pass away, perish 5. **lick the dust** *Inf.* be servile, bootlick (*Inf.*), demean oneself, grovel, kowtow, toady 6. **throw dust in the eyes of** con (*Sl.*), confuse, deceive, fool, have (someone) on, hoodwink, mislead, take in (*Inf.*) ~*v.* 7. cover, dredge, powder, scatter, sift, spray, spread, sprinkle

dust-up argument, brush, conflict, encounter, fight, fracas, punch-up (*Brit. inf.*), quarrel, scrap (*Inf.*), set-to (*Inf.*), shindig (*Inf.*), skirmish, tussle

dusty 1. dirty, grubby, sooty, unclean, undusted, unswept 2. chalky, crumbly, friable, granular, powdery, sandy

dutiful compliant, conscientious, deferential, devoted, docile, duteous (*Archaic*), filial, obedient, punctilious, respectful, reverential, submissive
Antonyms disobedient, disrespectful, insubordinate, remiss, uncaring

duty 1. assignment, business, calling, charge, engagement, function, mission, obligation, office, onus, province, responsibility, role, service, task, work 2. allegiance, deference, loyalty, obedience, respect, reverence 3. customs, due, excise, impost, levy, tariff, tax, toll 4. **do duty for** stand in, substitute, take the place of 5. **be the duty of** behove (*Archaic*), be incumbent upon, belong to, be (someone's) pigeon (*Brit. inf.*), be up to (*Inf.*), devolve upon, pertain to, rest with 6. **off duty** at leisure, free, off, off work, on holiday 7. **on duty** at work, busy, engaged

dwarf *n.* 1. bantam, homunculus, hop-o'-my-thumb, Lilliputian, manikin, midget, pygmy *or* pigmy, Tom Thumb 2. gnome, goblin ~*adj.* 3. baby, bonsai, diminutive, dwarfed, Lilliputian, miniature, petite, pocket, small, teensy-weensy, teeny-weeny, tiny, undersized ~*v.* 4. dim, diminish, dominate, minimize, overshadow, tower above *or* over 5. check, cultivate by bonsai, lower, retard, stunt

dwarfish diminutive, dwarfed, low, miniature, minute, pint-size (*Inf.*), pygmaean, pygmy *or* pigmy, runtish, runty, short, small, stunted, teensy-weensy, teeny-weeny, tiny, undersized

dwell abide, establish oneself, hang out (*Inf.*), inhabit, live, lodge, quarter, remain, reside, rest, settle, sojourn, stay, stop

dwelling abode, domicile, dwelling house, establishment, habitation, home, house, lodging, pad (*Sl.*), quarters, residence

dwell on *or* **upon** be engrossed in, continue, elaborate, emphasize, expatiate, harp on, linger over, tarry over

dwindle abate, contract, decay, decline, decrease, die away (down, out), diminish, ebb, fade, fall, grow less, lessen, peter out, pine, shrink, shrivel, sink, subside, taper off, wane, waste away, weaken, wither
Antonyms advance, amplify, develop, dilate, enlarge, escalate, expand, grow, heighten, increase, magnify, multiply, swell, wax

dye 1. *n.* colorant, colour, colouring, pigment, stain, tinge, tint 2. *v.* colour, pigment, stain, tincture, tinge, tint

dyed-in-the-wool complete, confirmed, deep-dyed (*Usu. derogatory*), deep-rooted, die-hard, entrenched, established, inveterate, through-and-through

dying at death's door, ebbing, expiring, fading, failing, final, going, *in extremis,* moribund, mortal, passing, perishing, sinking

dynamic active, driving, electric, energetic, forceful, go-ahead, go-getting (*Inf.*), high-powered, lively, magnetic, powerful, vigorous, vital, zippy (*Inf.*)

Antonyms apathetic, couldn't-care-less (*Inf.*), impassive, inactive, listless, sluggish, torpid, undynamic, unenergetic

dynamism brio, drive, energy, enterprise, forcefulness, get-up-and-go (*Inf.*), go (*Inf.*), initiative, liveliness, pep, push (*Inf.*), vigour, zap (*Sl.*), zip (*Inf.*)

dynasty ascendancy, dominion, empire, government, house, regime, rule, sovereignty, sway

E

each 1. *adj.* every 2. *pron.* each and every one, each one, every one, one and all 3. *adv.* apiece, for each, from each, individually, per capita, per head, per person, respectively, singly, to each

eager agog, anxious, ardent, athirst, avid, earnest, enthusiastic, fervent, fervid, greedy, hot, hungry, impatient, intent, keen, longing, raring, vehement, yearning, zealous
Antonyms apathetic, blasé, impassive, indifferent, lazy, nonchalant, opposed, unambitious, unconcerned, unenthusiastic, unimpressed, uninterested

eagerness ardour, avidity, earnestness, enthusiasm, fervour, greediness, heartiness, hunger, impatience, impetuosity, intentness, keenness, longing, thirst, vehemence, yearning, zeal

ear *Fig.* 1. attention, consideration, hearing, heed, notice, regard 2. appreciation, discrimination, musical perception, sensitivity, taste

early *adj.* 1. advanced, forward, premature, untimely 2. primeval, primitive, primordial, undeveloped, young ~*adv.* 3. ahead of time, beforehand, betimes (*Archaic*), in advance, in good time, prematurely, too soon
Antonyms (*sense 2*) developed, mature, ripe, seasoned (*sense 3*) behind, belated, late, overdue, tardy

earmark 1. *v.* allocate, designate, flag, keep back, label, mark out, reserve, set aside, tag 2. *n.* attribute, characteristic, feature, hallmark, label, quality, signature, stamp, tag, token, trademark, trait

earn 1. bring in, collect, draw, gain, get, gross, make, net, obtain, procure, realize, reap, receive 2. acquire, attain, be entitled to, be worthy of, deserve, merit, rate, warrant, win

earnest *adj.* 1. close, constant, determined, firm, fixed, grave, intent, resolute, resolved, serious, sincere, solemn, stable, staid, steady, thoughtful 2. ardent, devoted, eager, enthusiastic, fervent, fervid, heartfelt, impassioned, keen, passionate, purposeful, urgent, vehement, warm, zealous ~*n.* 3. determination, reality, resolution, seriousness, sincerity, truth 4. assurance, deposit, down payment, earnest money (*Law*), foretaste, guarantee, pledge, promise, security, token
Antonyms *adj.* apathetic, couldn't-care-less, flippant, frivolous, half-hearted, indifferent, insincere, light, slack, trifling, unconcerned, unenthusiastic, uninterested, unstable ~*n.* apathy, indifference, unconcern

earnestness ardour, determination, devotion, eagerness, enthusiasm, fervour, gravity, intentness, keenness, passion, purposefulness, resolution, seriousness, sincerity, urgency, vehemence, warmth, zeal

earnings emolument, gain, income, pay, proceeds, profits, receipts, remuneration, return, reward, salary, stipend, takings, wages

earth 1. globe, orb, planet, sphere, terrestrial sphere, world 2. clay, clod, dirt, ground, land, loam, mould, sod, soil, topsoil, turf

earthenware ceramics, crockery, crocks, pots, pottery, terra cotta

earthiness bawdiness, coarseness, crudeness, crudity, lustiness, naturalness, ribaldry, robustness, uninhibitedness

earthly 1. mundane, sublunary, tellurian, telluric, terrene, terrestrial, worldly 2. human, material, mortal, non-spiritual, profane, secular, temporal, worldly 3. base, carnal, fleshly, gross, low, materialistic, physical, sensual, sordid, vile 4. *Inf.* conceivable, feasible, imaginable, likely, possible, practical
Antonyms ethereal, heavenly, immaterial, immortal, otherwordly, spiritual, supernatural, unearthly

earthy bawdy, coarse, crude, down-to-earth, homely, lusty, natural, raunchy (*Sl.*), ribald, robust, rough, simple, uninhibited, unrefined, unsophisticated

ease *n.* 1. affluence, calmness, comfort, content, contentment, enjoyment, happiness, leisure, peace, peace of mind, quiet, quietude, relaxation, repose, rest, restfulness, serenity, tranquillity 2. easiness, effortlessness, facility, readiness, simplicity 3. flexibility, freedom, informality, liberty, naturalness, unaffectedness, unconstraint, unreservedness 4. aplomb, composure, insouciance, nonchalance, poise, relaxedness ~*v.* 5. abate, allay, alleviate, appease, assuage, calm, comfort, disburden, lessen, lighten, mitigate, moderate, mollify, pacify, palliate, quiet, relax, relent, relieve, slacken, soothe, still, tranquillize 6. aid, assist, expedite, facilitate, forward, further, lessen the labour of, make easier, simplify, smooth, speed up 7. edge, guide, inch, manoeuvre, move carefully, slide, slip, squeeze, steer

Antonyms *n.* agitation, arduousness, awkwardness, clumsiness, concern, constraint, difficulty, discomfort, disturbance, effort, exertion, formality, hardship, irritation, pain, poverty, tension, toil, tribulation ~*v.* aggravate, discomfort, exacerbate, hinder, irritate, make nervous, make uneasy, retard, worsen

easeful calm, comfortable, easy, peaceful, quiet, reposeful, restful, soothing, tranquil

easily 1. comfortably, effortlessly, facilely, readily, simply, smoothly, with ease, without difficulty, without trouble 2. absolutely, beyond question, by far, certainly, clearly, definitely, doubtlessly, far and away, indisputably, indubitably, plainly, surely, undeniably, undoubtedly, unequivocally, unquestionably, without a doubt 3. almost certainly, probably, well

easy 1. a piece of cake (*Inf.*), a pushover (*Sl.*), child's play (*Inf.*), clear, easy-peasy (*Sl.*), effortless, facile, light, no bother, not difficult, no trouble, painless, simple, smooth, straightforward, uncomplicated, undemanding 2. calm, carefree, comfortable, contented, cushy (*Inf.*), easeful, leisurely, peaceful, pleasant, quiet, relaxed, satisfied, serene, tranquil, undisturbed, untroubled, unworried, well-to-do 3. flexible, indulgent, lenient, liberal, light, mild, permissive, tolerant, unburdensome, unoppressive 4. affable, casual, easy-going, friendly, gentle, graceful, gracious, informal, laid-back (*Inf.*), mild, natural, open, pleasant, relaxed, smooth, tolerant, unaffected, unceremonious, unconstrained, undemanding, unforced, unpretentious 5. accommodating, amenable, biddable, compliant, docile, gullible, manageable, pliant, soft, submissive, suggestible, susceptible, tractable, trusting, yielding 6. comfortable, gentle, leisurely, light, mild, moderate, temperate, undemanding, unexacting, unhurried

Antonyms affected, anxious, arduous, complex, demanding, dictatorial, difficult, exacting, exhausting, forced, formal, formidable, hard, harsh, impossible, inflexible, insecure, intolerant, onerous, poor, rigid, self-conscious, stern, stiff, stressful, strict, uncomfortable, unnatural, unyielding, worried

easy-going amenable, calm, carefree, casual, complacent, easy, easy-oasy (*Sl.*), even-tempered, flexible, happy-go-lucky, indulgent, insouciant, laid-back (*Inf.*), lenient, liberal, mild, moderate, nonchalant, permissive, placid, relaxed, serene, tolerant, unconcerned, uncritical, undemanding, unhurried

Antonyms anxious, edgy, fussy, hung-up (*Sl.*), intolerant, irritated, nervy (*Brit. inf.*), on edge, strict, tense, uptight (*Inf.*)

eat 1. chew, consume, devour, gobble, ingest, munch, scoff (*Sl.*), swallow 2. break bread, chow down (*Sl.*), dine, feed, have a meal, take food, take nourishment 3. corrode, crumble, decay, dissolve, erode, rot, waste away, wear away 4. **eat one's words** abjure, recant, rescind, retract, take (statement) back

eatable comestible (*Rare*), digestible, edible, esculent, fit to eat, good, harmless, palatable, wholesome

eavesdrop bug (*Inf.*), listen in, monitor, overhear, snoop (*Inf.*), spy, tap

eavesdropper listener, monitor, snooper (*Inf.*), spy

ebb *v.* 1. abate, fall away, fall back, flow back, go out, recede, retire, retreat, retrocede, sink, subside, wane, withdraw ~*n.* 2. ebb tide, going out, low tide, low water, reflux, regression, retreat, retrocession, subsidence, wane, waning, withdrawal ~*v.* 3. decay, decline, decrease, degenerate, deteriorate, diminish, drop, dwindle, fade away, fall away, flag, lessen, peter out, shrink, sink, slacken, weaken ~*n.* 4. decay, decline, decrease, degeneration, deterioration, diminution, drop, dwindling, fading away, flagging, lessening, petering out, shrinkage, sinking, slackening, weakening

ebullience 1. brio, buoyancy, effervescence, effusiveness, elation, enthusiasm, excitement, exhilaration, exuberance, high spirits, vivacity, zest 2. boiling, bubbling, ebullition, effervescence, ferment, fermentation, foam, froth, frothing, seething

ebullient 1. buoyant, effervescent, effusive, elated, enthusiastic, excited, exhilarated, exuberant, frothy, gushing, in high spirits, irrepressible, vivacious, zestful 2. boiling, bubbling, effervescent, foaming, frothing, seething

ebullition 1. boiling, bubbling, effervescence, fermentation, frothing, outburst, overflow, seething 2. access, fit, outbreak, outburst, overflow, paroxysm, spasm, storm, throe (*Rare*)

eccentric 1. *adj.* aberrant, abnormal,

anomalous, bizarre, capricious, erratic, freakish, idiosyncratic, irregular, odd, oddball (*Inf.*), off-the-wall (*Sl.*), outlandish, outré, peculiar, queer (*Inf.*), quirky, rum (*Brit. sl.*), singular, strange, uncommon, unconventional, wacko (*Sl.*), weird, whimsical 2. *n.* card (*Inf.*), case (*Inf.*), character (*Inf.*), crank (*Inf.*), freak (*Inf.*), kook (*U.S. & Canad. inf.*), nonconformist, nut (*Sl.*), oddball (*Inf.*), odd fish (*Inf.*), oddity, queer fish (*Brit. inf.*), rum customer (*Brit. sl.*), screwball (*Sl., chiefly U.S. & Canad.*), wacko (*Sl.*), weirdo *or* weirdie (*Inf.*)
Antonyms *adj.* average, conventional, normal, ordinary, regular, run-of-the-mill, straightforward, typical

eccentricity aberration, abnormality, anomaly, bizarreness, caprice, capriciousness, foible, freakishness, idiosyncrasy, irregularity, nonconformity, oddity, oddness, outlandishness, peculiarity, queerness (*Inf.*), quirk, singularity, strangeness, unconventionality, waywardness, weirdness, whimsicality, whimsicalness

ecclesiastic 1. *n.* churchman, clergyman, cleric, divine, holy man, man of the cloth, minister, parson, pastor, priest 2. *adj. Also* **ecclesiastical** church, churchly, clerical, divine, holy, pastoral, priestly, religious, spiritual

echelon degree, grade, level, office, place, position, rank, tier

echo *v.* 1. repeat, resound, reverberate 2. ape, copy, imitate, mirror, parallel, parrot, recall, reflect, reiterate, reproduce, resemble, ring, second *~n.* 3. answer, repetition, reverberation 4. copy, imitation, mirror image, parallel, reflection, reiteration, reproduction, ringing 5. allusion, evocation, hint, intimation, memory, reminder, suggestion, trace 6. *Often plural* aftereffect, aftermath, consequence, repercussion

echoic imitative, onomatopoeic

éclat 1. brilliance, effect, success 2. display, lustre, ostentation, pomp, show, showmanship, splendour 3. celebrity, distinction, fame, glory, renown 4. acclaim, acclamation, applause, approval, plaudits

eclectic all-embracing, broad, catholic, comprehensive, dilettantish, diverse, diversified, general, heterogeneous, liberal, manifold, many-sided, multifarious, selective, varied, wide-ranging

eclipse *v.* 1. blot out, cloud, darken, dim, extinguish, obscure, overshadow, shroud, veil 2. exceed, excel, outdo, outshine, surpass, transcend *~n.* 3. darkening, dimming, extinction, obscuration, occultation, shading 4. decline, diminution, failure, fall, loss

eclogue bucolic, georgic, idyll, pastoral

economic 1. business, commercial, financial, industrial, mercantile, trade 2. money-making, productive, profitable, profit-making, remunerative, solvent, viable 3. bread-and-butter (*Inf.*), budgetary, financial, fiscal, material, monetary, pecuniary 4. *Inf. Also* **economical** cheap, fair, inexpensive, low, low-priced, modest, reasonable

economical 1. cost-effective, efficient, money-saving, sparing, time-saving, unwasteful, work-saving 2. careful, economizing, frugal, prudent, saving, scrimping, sparing, thrifty 3. *Also* **economic** cheap, fair, inexpensive, low, low-priced, modest, reasonable
Antonyms exorbitant, expensive, extravagant, generous, imprudent, lavish, loss-making, profligate, spendthrift, uneconomical, unprofitable, unthrifty, wasteful

economize be economical, be frugal, be sparing, cut back, husband, retrench, save, scrimp, tighten one's belt
Antonyms be extravagant, push the boat out (*Inf.*), spend, splurge, squander

economy frugality, husbandry, parsimony, providence, prudence, restraint, retrenchment, saving, sparingness, thrift, thriftiness

ecstasy bliss, delight, elation, enthusiasm, euphoria, exaltation, fervour, frenzy, joy, rapture, ravishment, rhapsody, seventh heaven, trance, transport
Antonyms affliction, agony, anguish, distress, hell, misery, pain, suffering, torment, torture

ecstatic blissful, cock-a-hoop, delirious, elated, enraptured, enthusiastic, entranced, euphoric, fervent, frenzied, in exaltation, in transports of delight, joyful, joyous, on cloud nine (*Inf.*), overjoyed, over the moon (*Inf.*), rapturous, rhapsodic, transported

ecumenical catholic, general, unifying, universal, worldwide

eddy 1. *n.* counter-current, counterflow, swirl, tideway, undertow, vortex, whirlpool 2. *v.* swirl, whirl

edge *n.* 1. border, bound, boundary, brim, brink, contour, flange, fringe, limit, line, lip, margin, outline, perimeter, periphery, rim, side, threshold, verge 2. acuteness, animation, bite, effectiveness, force, incisiveness, interest, keenness, point, pungency, sharpness, sting, urgency, zest 3. advantage, ascendancy, dominance, lead, superiority, upper hand 4. **on edge** apprehensive, eager, edgy, excited, ill at ease, impatient, irritable, keyed up, nervous, on tenterhooks, tense, tetchy, twitchy (*Inf.*), uptight (*Inf.*), wired (*Sl.*) ~*v.* 5. bind, border, fringe, hem, rim, shape, trim 6. creep, ease, inch, sidle, steal, work, worm 7. hone, sharpen, strop, whet

edgy anxious, ill at ease, irascible, irritable, keyed up, nervous, nervy (*Brit. inf.*), on edge, restive, tense, tetchy, touchy, twitchy (*Inf.*), uptight (*Inf.*), wired (*Sl.*)

edible comestible (*Rare*), digestible, eatable, esculent, fit to eat, good, harmless, palatable, wholesome
Antonyms baneful, harmful, indigestible, inedible, noxious, pernicious, poisonous, uneatable

edict act, canon, command, decree, demand, dictate, dictum, enactment, fiat, injunction, law, mandate, manifesto, order, ordinance, proclamation, pronouncement, pronunciamento, regulation, ruling, statute, ukase (*Rare*)

edification education, elevation, enlightenment, guidance, improvement, information, instruction, nurture, schooling, teaching, tuition, uplifting

edifice building, construction, erection, fabric (*Rare*), habitation, house, pile, structure

edify educate, elevate, enlighten, guide, improve, inform, instruct, nurture, school, teach, uplift

edit 1. adapt, annotate, censor, check, condense, correct, emend, polish, redact, rephrase, revise, rewrite 2. assemble, compose, put together, rearrange, reorder, select

edition copy, impression, issue, number, printing, programme (*TV, Radio*), version, volume

educate civilize, coach, cultivate, develop, discipline, drill, edify, enlighten, exercise, foster, improve, indoctrinate, inform, instruct, mature, rear, school, teach, train, tutor

educated 1. coached, informed, instructed, nurtured, schooled, taught, tutored 2. civilized, cultivated, cultured, enlightened, experienced, informed, knowledgeable, learned, lettered, literary, polished, refined, tasteful
Antonyms (*sense 1*) ignorant, illiterate, uneducated, unlettered, unread, unschooled, untaught (*sense 2*) benighted, lowbrow, philistine, uncultivated, uncultured, uneducated

education breeding, civilization, coaching, cultivation, culture, development, discipline, drilling, edification, enlightenment, erudition, improvement, indoctrination, instruction, knowledge, nurture, scholarship, schooling, teaching, training, tuition, tutoring

educational cultural, didactic, edifying, educative, enlightening, heuristic, improving, informative, instructive

educative didactic, edifying, educational, enlightening, heuristic, improving, informative, instructive

educator coach, edifier, educationalist *or* educationist, instructor, pedagogue, schoolmaster, schoolmistress, schoolteacher, teacher, trainer, tutor

educe 1. come out, develop, evolve 2. bring forth, bring out, derive, draw out, elicit, evoke, extract 3. *Logic* conclude, deduce, infer

eerie awesome, creepy (*Inf.*), eldritch (*Poetic*), fearful, frightening, ghostly, mysterious, scary (*Inf.*), spectral, spooky (*Inf.*), strange, uncanny, unearthly, uneasy, weird

efface 1. annihilate, blot out, cancel, cross out, delete, destroy, dim, eradicate, erase, excise, expunge, extirpate, obliterate, raze, rub out, wipe out 2. *Of oneself* be modest (bashful, diffident, retiring, timid, unassertive), humble, lower, make inconspicuous, withdraw

effect *n.* 1. aftermath, conclusion, consequence, event, fruit, issue, outcome, result, upshot 2. clout (*Inf.*), effectiveness, efficacy, efficiency, fact, force, influence, power, reality, strength, use, validity, vigour, weight 3. drift, essence, impact, import, impression, meaning, purport, purpose, sense, significance, tenor 4. action, enforcement, execution, force, implementation, operation 5. **in effect** actually, effectively, essentially, for practical purposes, in actuality, in fact, in reality, in truth, really, to all intents and purposes, virtually 6. **take effect** become operative, begin, come into force, produce results, work ~*v.* 7. accomplish, achieve, actuate, bring about, carry out, cause, complete, consummate, create, effectuate, execute, fulfil, give rise to, initiate, make, perform, produce

effective 1. able, active, adequate, capable, competent, effectual, efficacious, efficient, energetic, operative, productive, serviceable, useful 2. cogent, compelling, convincing, emphatic, forceful, forcible, impressive, moving, persuasive, potent, powerful, striking, telling 3. active, actual, current, in effect, in execution, in force, in operation, operative, real
Antonyms feeble, futile, inactive, inadequate, incompetent, ineffective, ineffectual, inefficient, inoperative, insufficient, powerless, tame, unimpressive, unproductive, useless, vain, weak, worthless

effectiveness bottom, capability, clout (*Inf.*), cogency, effect, efficacy, efficiency, force, influence, potency, power, strength, success, use, validity, vigour, weight

effects belongings, chattels, furniture, gear, goods, movables, paraphernalia, possessions, property, things, trappings

effectual 1. capable, effective, efficacious, efficient, forcible, influential, potent, powerful, productive, serviceable, successful, telling, useful 2. authoritative, binding, in force, lawful, legal, licit (*Rare*), sound, valid

effectuate accomplish, achieve, bring about, carry out *or* through, cause, complete, create, do, effect, execute, fulfil, make, perform, procure, produce

effeminacy delicacy, femininity, softness, tenderness, unmanliness, weakness, womanishness, womanliness

effeminate camp (*Inf.*), delicate, feminine, poofy (*Sl.*), sissy, soft, tender, unmanly, weak, wimpish *or* wimpy (*Inf.*), womanish, womanlike, womanly
Antonyms butch (*Sl.*), he-man (*Inf.*), macho, manly, virile

effervesce bubble, ferment, fizz, foam, froth, sparkle

effervescence 1. bubbling, ferment, fermentation, fizz, foam, foaming, froth, frothing, sparkle 2. animation, brio, buoyancy, ebullience, enthusiasm, excitedness, excitement, exhilaration, exuberance, gaiety, high spirits, liveliness, pizzazz *or* pizazz (*Inf.*), vim (*Sl.*), vitality, vivacity, zing (*Inf.*)

effervescent 1. bubbling, bubbly, carbonated, fermenting, fizzing, fizzy, foaming, foamy, frothing, frothy, sparkling 2. animated, bubbly, buoyant, ebullient, enthusiastic, excited, exhilarated, exuberant, gay, in high spirits, irrepressible, lively, merry, vital, vivacious, zingy (*Inf.*)
Antonyms boring, dull, flat, flavourless, insipid, jejune, lacklustre, lifeless, spiritless, stale, unexciting, vapid, watery, weak

effete 1. corrupt, debased, decadent, decayed, decrepit, degenerate, dissipated, enervated, enfeebled, feeble, ineffectual, overrefined, spoiled, weak 2. burnt out, drained, enervated, exhausted, played out, spent, used up, wasted, worn out 3. barren, fruitless, infecund, infertile, sterile, unfruitful, unproductive, unprolific

efficacious active, adequate, capable, competent, effective, effectual, efficient, energetic, operative, potent, powerful, productive, serviceable, successful, useful
Antonyms abortive, futile, ineffective, ineffectual, inefficacious, unavailing, unproductive, unsuccessful, useless

efficacy ability, capability, competence, effect, effectiveness, efficaciousness, efficiency, energy, force, influence, potency, power, strength, success, use, vigour, virtue, weight

efficiency ability, adeptness, capability, competence, economy, effectiveness, efficacy, power, productivity, proficiency, readiness, skilfulness, skill

efficient able, adept, businesslike, capable, competent, economic, effective, effectual, organized, powerful, productive, proficient, ready, skilful, well-organized, workmanlike
Antonyms cowboy (*Inf.*), disorganized, incompetent, ineffectual, inefficient, inept, slipshod, sloppy, unbusinesslike, unproductive, wasteful

effigy dummy, figure, guy, icon, idol, image, likeness, picture, portrait, representation, statue

effluence discharge, effluent, effluvium, efflux, emanation, emission, exhalation, flow, issue, outflow, outpouring, secretion

effluent *n.* 1. effluvium, pollutant, sewage, waste 2. discharge, effluence, efflux, emanation, emission, exhalation, flow, issue, outflow, outpouring ~*adj.* 3. discharged, emanating, emitted, outflowing

effluvium exhalation, exhaust, fumes, mephitis, miasma, niff (*Brit. sl.*), odour, pong (*Brit. inf.*), reek, smell, stench, stink

effort 1. application, endeavour, energy, exertion, force, labour, pains, power, strain, stress, stretch, striving, struggle, toil, travail (*Literary*), trouble, work 2. attempt, endeavour, essay, go (*Inf.*), shot (*Inf.*), stab (*Inf.*), try 3. accomplishment, achievement, act, creation, deed, feat, job, product, production

effortless easy, easy-peasy (*Sl.*), facile, painless, simple, smooth, uncomplicated, undemanding, untroublesome
Antonyms demanding, difficult, formidable, hard, onerous, uphill

effrontery arrogance, assurance, audacity, boldness, brashness, brass (*Inf.*), brass neck (*Brit. inf.*), brazenness, cheek (*Inf.*), cheekiness, chutzpah (*U.S. & Canad. inf.*), disrespect, front, gall (*Inf.*), impertinence, impudence, incivility, insolence, neck (*Inf.*), nerve, presumption, rudeness, shamelessness, temerity

effulgence blaze, brightness, brilliance, dazzle, fire, flame, fluorescence, glow, incandescence, luminosity, lustre, radiance, refulgence (*Literary*), resplendence, shine, splendour, vividness

effulgent beaming, blazing, bright, brilliant, dazzling, flaming, fluorescent, fulgent (*Poetic*), glowing, incandescent, lucent, luminous, lustrous, radiant, refulgent (*Literary*), resplendent, shining, splendid, vivid

effusion 1. discharge, effluence, efflux, emission, gush, issue, outflow, outpouring, shedding, stream 2. address, outpouring, speech, talk, utterance, writing

effusive demonstrative, ebullient, enthusiastic, expansive, extravagant, exuberant, free-flowing, fulsome, gushing, lavish, overflowing, profuse, talkative, unreserved, unrestrained, wordy

egg on encourage, exhort, goad, incite, prod, prompt, push, spur, urge
Antonyms deter, discourage, dissuade, hold back, put off, talk out of

egocentric egoistic, egoistical, egotistic, egotistical, self-centred, selfish

egoism egocentricity, egomania, egotism, narcissism, self-absorption, self-centredness, self-importance, self-interest, selfishness, self-love, self-regard, self-seeking

egoist egomaniac, egotist, narcissist, self-seeker

egoistic, egoistical egocentric, egomaniacal, egotistic, egotistical, full of oneself, narcissistic, self-absorbed, self-centred, self-important, self-seeking

egotism conceitedness, egocentricity, egoism, egomania, narcissism, self-admiration, self-centredness, self-conceit, self-esteem, self-importance, self-love, self-praise, superiority, vainglory, vanity

egotist bighead (*Inf.*), blowhard (*Inf.*), boaster, braggadocio, braggart, egoist, egomaniac, self-admirer, swaggerer

egotistic, egotistical boasting, bragging, conceited, egocentric, egoistic, egoistical, egomaniacal, full of oneself, narcissistic, opinionated, self-admiring, self-centred, self-important, superior, vain, vainglorious

egregious arrant, enormous, flagrant, glaring, grievous, gross, heinous, infamous, insufferable, intolerable, monstrous, notorious, outrageous, rank, scandalous, shocking

egress departure, emergence, escape, exit, exodus, issue, outlet, passage out, vent, way out, withdrawal

ejaculate 1. discharge, eject, emit, spurt 2. blurt out, burst out, cry out, exclaim, shout

ejaculation 1. cry, exclamation, shout 2. discharge, ejection, emission, spurt

eject 1. cast out, discharge, disgorge, emit, expel, spew, spout, throw out, vomit 2. banish, boot out (*Inf.*), bounce (*Sl.*), deport, dispossess, drive out, evacuate, evict, exile, expel, give the bum's rush (*Sl.*), oust, relegate, remove, show one the door, throw out, throw out on one's ear (*Inf.*), turn out 3. discharge, dislodge, dismiss, fire (*Inf.*), get rid of, kick out (*Inf.*), oust, sack (*Inf.*), throw out

ejection 1. casting out, disgorgement, expulsion, spouting, throwing out 2. banishment, deportation, dispossession, evacuation, eviction, exile, expulsion, ouster (*Law*), removal 3. discharge, dislodgement, dismissal, firing (*Inf.*), sacking (*Inf.*), the boot (*Sl.*), the sack (*Inf.*)

eke out 1. be economical with, be frugal with, be sparing with, economize on, husband, stretch out 2. add to, enlarge, increase, make up (with), supplement

elaborate *adj.* 1. careful, detailed, exact, intricate, laboured, minute, painstaking, perfected, precise, skilful, studied, thorough 2. complex, complicated, decorated, detailed, extravagant, fancy, fussy, involved, ornamented, ornate, ostentatious, showy ~*v.* 3. add detail, amplify, complicate, decorate, develop, devise, embellish, enhance, enlarge, expand (upon), flesh out, garnish, improve, ornament, polish, produce, refine, work out
Antonyms *adj.* basic, minimal, modest, plain, simple, unadorned, unembellished, unfussy ~*v.* abbreviate, condense, put in a nutshell, reduce to essentials, simplify, streamline, summarize, truncate

élan animation, brio, dash, esprit, flair, impetuosity, panache, spirit, style, verve, vigour, vivacity, zest

elapse glide by, go, go by, lapse, pass, pass by, roll by, roll on, slip away, slip by

elastic 1. ductile, flexible, plastic, pliable, pliant, resilient, rubbery, springy, stretchable, stretchy, supple, tensile, yielding 2. accommodating, adaptable, adjustable, complaisant, compliant, flexible, supple, tolerant, variable, yielding 3. bouncy, buoyant, irrepressible, resilient
Antonyms firm, immovable, inflexible, intractable, obdurate, resolute, rigid, set, stiff, strict, stringent, unyielding

elasticity 1. ductileness, ductility, flexibility, give (*Inf.*), plasticity, pliability, pliancy, pliantness, resilience, rubberiness, springiness, stretch, stretchiness, suppleness 2. adaptability, adjustability, complaisance, compliantness, flexibility, suppleness, tolerance, variability 3. bounce (*Inf.*), buoyancy, irrepressibility, resilience

elated animated, blissful, cheered, cock-a-hoop, delighted, ecstatic, elevated, euphoric, excited, exhilarated, exultant, gleeful, in high spirits, joyful, joyous, jubilant, over-

joyed, over the moon (*Inf.*), proud, puffed up, rapt, roused
Antonyms dejected, depressed, discouraged, dispirited, downcast, down in the dumps (*Inf.*), miserable, sad, unhappy, woebegone

elation bliss, delight, ecstasy, euphoria, exaltation, exhilaration, exultation, glee, high spirits, joy, joyfulness, joyousness, jubilation, rapture

elbow *n.* 1. angle, bend, corner, joint, turn 2. **at one's elbow** at hand, close by, handy, near, to hand, within reach 3. **out at elbow(s)** beggarly, down at heel, impoverished, in rags, ragged, seedy, shabby, tattered 4. **rub elbows with** associate, fraternize, hang out (*Inf.*), hobnob, mingle, mix, socialize 5. **up to the elbows** absorbed, busy, engaged, engrossed, immersed, occupied, tied up, up to the ears, wrapped up ~*v.* 6. bump, crowd, hustle, jostle, knock, nudge, push, shoulder, shove

elbowroom freedom, latitude, leeway, play, room, scope, space

elder *adj.* 1. ancient, earlier born, first-born, older, senior ~*n.* 2. older person, senior 3. *Presbyterianism* church official, office bearer, presbyter

elect 1. *v.* appoint, choose, decide upon, designate, determine, opt for, pick, pick out, prefer, select, settle on, vote 2. *adj.* choice, chosen, elite, hand-picked, picked, preferred, select, selected

election appointment, choice, choosing, decision, determination, judgment, preference, selection, vote, voting

elector chooser, constituent, selector, voter

electric *Fig.* charged, dynamic, exciting, rousing, stimulating, stirring, tense, thrilling

electrify *Fig.* amaze, animate, astonish, astound, excite, fire, galvanize, invigorate, jolt, rouse, shock, startle, stimulate, stir, take one's breath away, thrill
Antonyms be tedious, bore, fatigue, jade, send to sleep, weary

eleemosynary almsgiving, altruistic, benevolent, charitable, philanthropic

elegance, elegancy 1. beauty, courtliness, dignity, exquisiteness, gentility, grace, gracefulness, grandeur, luxury, polish, politeness, refinement, sumptuousness 2. discernment, distinction, propriety, style, taste

elegant 1. à la mode, artistic, beautiful, chic, choice, comely, courtly, cultivated, delicate, exquisite, fashionable, fine, genteel, graceful, handsome, luxurious, modish, nice, polished, refined, stylish, sumptuous, tasteful 2. appropriate, apt, clever, effective, ingenious, neat, simple
Antonyms (*sense 1*) awkward, clumsy, coarse, gauche, graceless, inelegant, misshapen, plain, tasteless, tawdry, ugly, uncouth, undignified, ungraceful, unrefined

elegiac dirgeful, funereal, keening, lamenting, melancholy, mournful, nostalgic, plaintive, sad, threnodial, threnodic, valedictory

elegy coronach (*Scot. & Irish*), dirge, keen, lament, plaint (*Archaic*), requiem, threnody

element 1. basis, component, constituent, essential factor, factor, feature, hint, ingredient, member, part, section, subdivision, trace, unit 2. domain, environment, field, habitat, medium, milieu, sphere

elemental 1. basic, elementary, essential, fundamental, original, primal, primitive, primordial 2. atmospheric, meteorological, natural

elementary 1. clear, easy, facile, plain, rudimentary, simple, straightforward, uncomplicated 2. basic, bog-standard (*Inf.*), elemental, fundamental, initial, introductory, original, primary, rudimentary
Antonyms advanced, complex, complicated, higher, highly-developed, progressive, secondary, sophisticated

elements 1. basics, essentials, foundations, fundamentals, principles, rudiments 2. atmospheric conditions, atmospheric forces, powers of nature, weather

elephantine bulky, clumsy, enormous, heavy, huge, hulking, humongous *or* humungous (*U.S. sl.*), immense, laborious, lumbering, massive, monstrous, ponderous, weighty

elevate 1. heighten, hoist, lift, lift up, raise, uplift, upraise 2. advance, aggrandize, exalt, prefer, promote, upgrade 3. animate, boost, brighten, buoy up, cheer, elate, excite, exhilarate, hearten, lift up, perk up, raise, rouse, uplift 4. augment, boost, heighten, increase, intensify, magnify, swell

elevated 1. dignified, exalted, grand, high, high-flown, high-minded, inflated, lofty, noble, sublime 2. animated, bright, cheerful, cheery, elated, excited, exhilarated, gleeful, in high spirits, overjoyed
Antonyms (*sense 1*) humble, lowly, modest, simple

elevation 1. altitude, height 2. acclivity, eminence, height, hill, hillock, mountain, rise, rising ground 3. exaltedness, grandeur, loftiness, nobility, nobleness, sublimity 4. advancement, aggrandizement, exaltation, preferment, promotion, upgrading

elfin arch, charming, elfish, elflike, elvish, frolicsome, impish, mischievous, playful, prankish, puckish, sprightly

elicit bring forth, bring out, bring to light, call forth, cause, derive, draw out, educe, evoke, evolve, exact, extort, extract, give rise to, obtain, wrest

eligible acceptable, appropriate, desirable, fit, preferable, proper, qualified, suitable, suited, worthy
Antonyms inappropriate, ineligible, unacceptable, unqualified, unsuitable, unsuited

eliminate 1. cut out, dispose of, do away with, eradicate, exterminate, get rid of, remove, stamp out, take out 2. axe (*Inf.*), dispense with, disregard, drop, eject, exclude, expel, ignore, knock out, leave out, omit, put out, reject, throw out 3. *Sl.* annihilate, blow away (*Sl., chiefly U.S.*), bump off (*Sl.*), kill, liquidate, murder, rub out (*U.S. sl.*), slay, take out (*Sl.*), terminate, waste (*Inf.*)

elite 1. *n.* aristocracy, best, cream, *crème de la crème,* elect, flower, gentry, high society, nobility, pick, upper class 2. *adj.* aristocratic, best, choice, crack (*Sl.*), elect, exclusive, first-class, noble, pick, selected, upper-class
Antonyms *n.* dregs, hoi polloi, rabble, riff-raff

elixir 1. cure-all, nostrum, panacea, sovereign remedy 2. concentrate, essence, extract, pith, principle, quintessence 3. mixture, potion, solution, syrup, tincture

elliptical 1. oval 2. abstruse, ambiguous, concentrated, concise, condensed, cryptic, laconic, obscure, recondite, terse

elocution articulation, declamation, delivery, diction, enunciation, oratory, pronunciation, public speaking, rhetoric, speech, speechmaking, utterance, voice production

elongate draw out, extend, lengthen, make longer, prolong, protract, stretch

elope abscond, bolt, decamp, disappear, escape, leave, run away, run off, slip away, steal away

eloquence expression, expressiveness, fluency, forcefulness, oratory, persuasiveness, rhetoric, way with words

eloquent 1. articulate, fluent, forceful, graceful, moving, persuasive, silver-tongued, stirring, well-expressed 2. expressive, meaningful, pregnant, revealing, suggestive, telling, vivid
Antonyms faltering, halting, hesitant, inarticulate, speechless, stumbling, tongue-tied, wordless

elsewhere abroad, absent, away, hence (*Archaic*), in *or* to another place, not here, not present, somewhere else

elucidate annotate, clarify, clear up, explain, explicate, expound, gloss, illuminate, illustrate, interpret, make plain, shed *or* throw light upon, spell out, unfold

elucidation annotation, clarification, comment, commentary, explanation, explication, exposition, gloss, illumination, illustration, interpretation

elude 1. avoid, body-swerve (*Scot.*), circumvent, dodge, duck (*Inf.*), escape, evade, flee, get away from, outrun, shirk, shun 2. baffle, be beyond (someone), confound, escape, foil, frustrate, puzzle, stump, thwart

elusive 1. difficult to catch, shifty, slippery, tricky 2. baffling, fleeting, indefinable, intangible, puzzling, subtle, transient, transitory 3. ambiguous, deceitful, deceptive, elusory, equivocal, evasive, fallacious, fraudulent, illusory, misleading, oracular, unspecific

Elysian blessed, blissful, celestial, charming, delightful, enchanting, glorious, happy, heavenly, paradisiac, paradisiacal, ravishing, seraphic

emaciated atrophied, attenuate, attenuated, cadaverous, gaunt, haggard, lank, lean, macilent (*Rare*), meagre, pinched, scrawny, skeletal, thin, undernourished, wasted

emaciation atrophy, attenuation, gauntness, haggardness, leanness, meagreness, scrawniness, thinness, wasting away

emanate 1. arise, come forth, derive, emerge, flow, issue, originate, proceed, spring, stem 2. discharge, emit, exhale, give off, give out, issue, radiate, send forth

emanation 1. arising, derivation, emergence, flow, origination, proceeding 2. discharge, effluent, efflux, effusion, emission, exhalation, radiation

emancipate deliver, discharge, disencumber, disenthral, enfranchise, free, liberate, manumit, release, set free, unbridle, unchain, unfetter, unshackle
Antonyms bind, capture, enchain, enslave, enthral, fetter, shackle, subjugate, yoke

emancipation deliverance, discharge, enfranchisement, freedom, liberation, liberty, manumission, release
Antonyms bondage, captivity, confinement, detention, enthralment, imprisonment, servitude, slavery, thraldom

emasculate 1. castrate, geld 2. cripple, debilitate, deprive of force, enervate, impoverish, soften, weaken

embalm 1. mummify, preserve 2. *Of memories* cherish, consecrate, conserve, enshrine, immortalize, store, treasure 3. *Poetic* make fragrant, perfume, scent

embargo 1. *n.* ban, bar, barrier, block, blockage, boycott, check, hindrance, impediment, interdict, interdiction, prohibition, proscription, restraint, restriction, stoppage 2. *v.* ban, bar, block, boycott, check, impede, interdict, prohibit, proscribe, restrict, stop

embark 1. board ship, go aboard, put on board, take on board, take ship 2. *With* **on** *or* **upon** begin, broach, commence, engage, enter, initiate, launch, plunge into, set about, set out, start, take up, undertake
Antonyms (*sense 1*) alight, arrive, get off, go ashore, land, step out of

embarrass abash, chagrin, confuse, discomfit, discompose, disconcert, discountenance, distress, faze, fluster, mortify, put out of countenance, shame, show up (*Inf.*)

embarrassing awkward, blush-making, compromising, cringe-making (*Brit. inf.*), discomfiting, disconcerting, distressing, humiliating, mortifying, sensitive, shameful, shaming, touchy, tricky, uncomfortable

embarrassment 1. awkwardness, bashfulness, chagrin, confusion, discomfiture, discomposure, distress, humiliation, mortification, self-consciousness, shame, showing up (*Inf.*) 2. bind (*Inf.*), difficulty, mess, pickle (*Inf.*), predicament, scrape (*Inf.*) 3. excess, overabundance, superabundance, superfluity, surfeit, surplus

embed dig in, drive in, fix, hammer in, implant, plant, ram in, root, set, sink

embellish adorn, beautify, bedeck, deck, decorate, dress up, elaborate, embroider, enhance, enrich, exaggerate, festoon, garnish, gild, grace, ornament, tart up (*Sl.*), varnish

embellishment adornment, decoration, elaboration, embroidery, enhancement, enrichment, exaggeration, gilding, ornament, ornamentation, trimming

embers ashes, cinders, live coals

embezzle abstract, appropriate, defalcate (*Law*), filch, have one's hand in the till (*Inf.*), misapply, misappropriate, misuse, peculate, pilfer, purloin, rip off (*Sl.*), steal

embezzlement abstraction, appropriation, defalcation (*Law*), filching, fraud, larceny, misapplication, misappropriation, misuse, peculation, pilferage, pilfering, purloining, stealing, theft, thieving

embitter 1. alienate, anger, disaffect, disillusion, envenom, make bitter *or* resentful, poison, sour 2. aggravate, exacerbate, exasperate, worsen

emblazon 1. adorn, blazon, colour, decorate, embellish, illuminate, ornament, paint 2. crack up (*Inf.*), extol, glorify, laud (*Literary*), praise, proclaim, publicize, publish, trumpet

emblem badge, crest, device, figure, image, insignia, mark, representation, sigil (*Rare*), sign, symbol, token, type

emblematic, emblematical figurative, representative, symbolic

embodiment 1. bodying forth, epitome, example, exemplar, exemplification, expression, incarnation, incorporation, manifestation, personification, realization, reification, representation, symbol, type 2. bringing together, codification, collection, combination, comprehension, concentration, consolidation, inclusion, incorporation, integration, organization, systematization

embody 1. body forth, concretize, exemplify, express, incarnate, incorporate, manifest, personify, realize, reify, represent, stand for, symbolize, typify 2. bring together, codify, collect, combine, comprehend, comprise, concentrate, consolidate, contain, include, incorporate, integrate, organize, systematize

embolden animate, cheer, encourage, fire, hearten, inflame, inspirit, invigorate, nerve, reassure, rouse, stimulate, stir, strengthen, vitalize

embrace *v.* 1. clasp, cuddle, encircle, enfold, grasp, hold, hug, seize, squeeze, take *or* hold in one's arms 2. accept, adopt, avail oneself of, espouse, grab, make use of, receive, seize, take up, welcome 3. comprehend, comprise, contain, cover, deal with, embody, enclose, encompass, include, involve, provide for, subsume, take in, take into account ~*n.* 4. canoodle (*Sl.*), clasp, clinch (*Sl.*), cuddle, hug, squeeze

embroil complicate, compromise, confound, confuse, disorder, disturb, encumber, enmesh, ensnare, entangle, implicate, incriminate, involve, mire, mix up, muddle, perplex, trouble

embryo beginning, germ, nucleus, root, rudiment

embryonic beginning, early, germinal, immature, inchoate, incipient, primary, rudimentary, seminal, undeveloped
Antonyms advanced, developed, progressive

emend amend, correct, edit, improve, rectify, redact, revise

emendation amendment, correction, editing, improvement, rectification, redaction, revision

emerge 1. appear, arise, become visible, come forth, come into view, come out, come

up, emanate, issue, proceed, rise, spring up, surface 2. become apparent, become known, come out, come to light, crop up, develop, materialize, transpire, turn up
Antonyms depart, disappear, enter, fade, fall, recede, retreat, sink, submerge, vanish from sight, wane, withdraw

emergence advent, apparition, appearance, arrival, coming, dawn, development, disclosure, emanation, issue, materialization, rise

emergency crisis, danger, difficulty, exigency, extremity, necessity, panic stations (*Inf.*), pass, pinch, plight, predicament, quandary, scrape (*Inf.*), strait

emergent appearing, budding, coming, developing, rising

emetic vomitive, vomitory

emigrate migrate, move, move abroad, remove

emigration departure, exodus, migration, removal

eminence 1. celebrity, dignity, distinction, esteem, fame, greatness, illustriousness, importance, notability, note, pre-eminence, prestige, prominence, rank, renown, reputation, repute, superiority 2. elevation, height, high ground, hill, hillock, knoll, rise, summit

eminent big-time (*Inf.*), celebrated, conspicuous, distinguished, elevated, esteemed, exalted, famous, grand, great, high, high-ranking, illustrious, important, major league (*Inf.*), notable, noted, noteworthy, outstanding, paramount, pre-eminent, prestigious, prominent, renowned, signal, superior, well-known
Antonyms anonymous, commonplace, infamous, lowly, ordinary, undistinguished, unheard-of, unimportant, unknown, unremarkable, unsung

eminently conspicuously, exceedingly, exceptionally, extremely, greatly, highly, notably, outstandingly, prominently, remarkably, signally, strikingly, surpassingly, well

emissary agent, ambassador, courier, delegate, deputy, envoy, go-between, herald, legate, messenger, representative, scout, secret agent, spy

emission diffusion, discharge, ejaculation, ejection, emanation, exhalation, exudation, issuance, issue, radiation, shedding, transmission, utterance, venting

emit breathe forth, cast out, diffuse, discharge, eject, emanate, exhale, exude, give off, give out, give vent to, issue, radiate, send forth, send out, shed, throw out, transmit, utter, vent
Antonyms absorb, assimilate, consume, devour, digest, drink in, incorporate, ingest, receive, soak up, suck up, take in

emollient 1. *adj.* assuaging, assuasive, balsamic, demulcent, lenitive, mollifying, softening, soothing 2. *n.* balm, lenitive, liniment, lotion, moisturizer, oil, ointment, salve

emolument benefit, compensation, earnings, fee, gain, hire, pay, payment, profits, recompense, remuneration, return, reward, salary, stipend, wages

emotion agitation, ardour, excitement, feeling, fervour, passion, perturbation, sensation, sentiment, vehemence, warmth

emotional 1. demonstrative, excitable, feeling, hot-blooded, passionate, responsive, sensitive, sentimental, susceptible, temperamental, tender, warm 2. affecting, emotive, exciting, heart-warming, moving, pathetic, poignant, sentimental, stirring, tear-jerking (*Inf.*), thrilling, touching 3. ardent, enthusiastic, fervent, fervid, fiery, flaming, heated, impassioned, passionate, roused, stirred, zealous
Antonyms apathetic, cold, detached, dispassionate, insensitive, phlegmatic, undemonstrative, unemotional, unenthusiastic, unexcitable, unfeeling, unmoved, unruffled, unsentimental

emotionless blank, cold, cold-blooded, cool, detached, distant, frigid, glacial, impassive, indifferent, remote, toneless, undemonstrative, unemotional, unfeeling

emotive 1. argumentative, controversial, delicate, sensitive, touchy 2. affecting, emotional, exciting, heart-warming, moving, pathetic, poignant, sentimental, stirring, tear-jerking (*Inf.*), thrilling, touching 3. ardent, emotional, enthusiastic, fervent, fervid, fiery, heated, impassioned, passionate, roused, stirred, zealous

emphasis accent, accentuation, attention, decidedness, force, importance, impressiveness, insistence, intensity, moment, positiveness, power, pre-eminence, priority, prominence, significance, strength, stress, underscoring, weight

emphasize accent, accentuate, dwell on, give priority to, highlight, insist on, lay stress on, play up, press home, put the accent on, stress, underline, underscore, weight
Antonyms gloss over, make light of, make little of, minimize, play down, soft-pedal (*Inf.*), underplay

emphatic absolute, categorical, certain, decided, definite, direct, distinct, earnest, energetic, forceful, forcible, important, impressive, insistent, marked, momentous, positive, powerful, pronounced, resound-

ing, significant, striking, strong, telling, unequivocal, unmistakable, vigorous
Antonyms commonplace, equivocal, hesitant, insignificant, tame, tentative, uncertain, undecided, unremarkable, unsure, weak

empire 1. commonwealth, domain, imperium (*Rare*), kingdom, realm 2. authority, command, control, dominion, government, power, rule, sovereignty, supremacy, sway

empirical, empiric experiential, experimental, first-hand, observed, practical, pragmatic
Antonyms academic, assumed, conjectural, hypothetical, putative, speculative, theoretic, theoretical

emplace insert, place, position, put, put in place, set up, station

emplacement 1. location, lodgment, platform, position, site, situation, station 2. placement, placing, positioning, putting in place, setting up, stationing

employ *v.* 1. commission, engage, enlist, hire, retain, take on 2. engage, fill, keep busy, make use of, occupy, spend, take up, use up 3. apply, bring to bear, exercise, exert, make use of, ply, put to use, use, utilize ~*n.* 4. employment, engagement, hire, service

employed active, busy, engaged, in a job, in employment, in work, occupied, working
Antonyms idle, jobless, laid off, on the dole (*Brit. inf.*), out of a job, out of work, redundant, unoccupied

employee hand, job-holder, staff member, wage-earner, worker, workman

employer boss (*Inf.*), business, company, establishment, firm, gaffer (*Inf., chiefly Brit.*), organization, outfit (*Inf.*), owner, patron, proprietor

employment 1. engagement, enlistment, hire, retaining, taking on 2. application, exercise, exertion, use, utilization 3. avocation (*Archaic*), business, calling, craft, employ, job, line, métier, occupation, profession, pursuit, service, trade, vocation, work

emporium bazaar, market, mart, shop, store, warehouse

empower allow, authorize, commission, delegate, enable, entitle, license, permit, qualify, sanction, warrant

emptiness 1. bareness, blankness, desertedness, desolation, destitution, vacancy, vacuum, void, waste 2. aimlessness, banality, barrenness, frivolity, futility, hollowness, inanity, ineffectiveness, meaninglessness, purposelessness, senselessness, silliness, unreality, unsatisfactoriness, unsubstantiality, vainness, valuelessness, vanity, worthlessness 3. cheapness, hollowness, idleness, insincerity, triviality, trivialness 4. absentness, blankness, expressionlessness, unintelligence, vacancy, vacantness, vacuity, vacuousness 5. *Inf.* desire, hunger, ravening

empty *adj.* 1. bare, blank, clear, deserted, desolate, destitute, hollow, unfurnished, uninhabited, unoccupied, untenanted, vacant, void, waste 2. aimless, banal, bootless, frivolous, fruitless, futile, hollow, inane, ineffective, meaningless, purposeless, senseless, silly, unreal, unsatisfactory, unsubstantial, vain, valueless, worthless 3. cheap, hollow, idle, insincere, trivial 4. absent, blank, expressionless, unintelligent, vacant, vacuous 5. *Inf.* famished, hungry, ravenous, starving (*Inf.*), unfed, unfilled ~*v.* 6. clear, consume, deplete, discharge, drain, dump, evacuate, exhaust, gut, pour out, unburden, unload, use up, vacate, void
Antonyms *adj.* busy, fulfilled, full, inhabited, interesting, meaningful, occupied, packed, purposeful, satisfying, serious, significant, stuffed, useful, valuable, worthwhile ~*v.* cram, fill, pack, replenish, stock, stuff

empty-headed brainless, dizzy (*Inf.*), featherbrained, flighty, frivolous, giddy, goofy (*Inf.*), harebrained, inane, scatterbrained, silly, skittish, vacuous

empyrean, empyreal aerial, airy, celestial, ethereal, heavenly, refined, skylike, sublime

emulate challenge, compete with, contend with, copy, echo, follow, follow suit, follow the example of, imitate, mimic, rival, take after, vie with

emulation challenge, competition, contention, contest, copying, envy, following, imitation, jealousy, mimicry, rivalry, strife

emulous aspiring, competitive, contending, imitative, vying

enable allow, authorize, capacitate, commission, empower, entitle, facilitate, fit, license, permit, prepare, qualify, sanction, warrant
Antonyms bar, block, hinder, impede, obstruct, prevent, stop, thwart

enact 1. authorize, command, decree, establish, legislate, ordain, order, pass, proclaim, ratify, sanction 2. act, act out, appear as, depict, perform, personate, play, play the part of, portray, represent

enactment 1. authorization, command, commandment, decree, dictate, edict, law, legislation, order, ordinance, proclamation, ratification, regulation, statute 2. acting, depiction, performance, personation, play-acting, playing, portrayal, representation

enamour absorb, bewitch, captivate, charm, enchant, endear, enrapture, entrance, fascinate, infatuate

enamoured bewitched, captivated, charmed, crazy about (*Inf.*), enchanted, enraptured, entranced, fascinated, fond, infatuated, in love, nuts on *or* about (*Sl.*), smitten, swept off one's feet, taken, wild about (*Inf.*)

encampment base, bivouac, camp, camping ground, campsite, cantonment, quarters, tents

encapsulate, incapsulate abridge, compress, condense, digest, epitomize, précis, summarize, sum up

enchain bind, enslave, fetter, hold, hold fast, manacle, pinion, put in irons, shackle

enchant beguile, bewitch, captivate, cast a spell on, charm, delight, enamour, enrapture, enthral, fascinate, hypnotize, mesmerize, ravish, spellbind

enchanter conjurer, magician, magus, necromancer, sorcerer, spellbinder, warlock, witch, wizard

enchanting alluring, appealing, attractive, bewitching, captivating, charming, delightful, endearing, entrancing, fascinating, lovely, pleasant, ravishing, winsome

enchantment 1. allure, allurement, beguilement, bliss, charm, delight, fascination, hypnotism, mesmerism, rapture, ravishment, transport 2. charm, conjuration, incantation, magic, necromancy, sorcery, spell, witchcraft, wizardry

enchantress 1. conjurer, lamia, magician, necromancer, sorceress, spellbinder, witch 2. charmer, *femme fatale,* seductress, siren, vamp (*Inf.*)

encircle begird (*Poetic*), circle, circumscribe, compass, enclose, encompass, enfold, envelop, environ, gird in, girdle, hem in, ring, surround

enclose, inclose 1. bound, circumscribe, cover, encase, encircle, encompass, environ, fence, hedge, hem in, impound, pen, pound, shut in, wall in, wrap 2. include, insert, put in, send with 3. comprehend, contain, embrace, hold, include, incorporate

encomium acclaim, · acclamation, applause, compliment, eulogy, homage, laudation, panegyric, praise, tribute

encompass 1. circle, circumscribe, encircle, enclose, envelop, environ, girdle, hem in, ring, surround 2. bring about, cause, contrive, devise, effect, manage 3. admit, comprehend, comprise, contain, cover, embody, embrace, hold, include, incorporate, involve, subsume, take in

encounter *v.* 1. bump into (*Inf.*), chance upon, come upon, confront, experience, face, happen on *or* upon, meet, run across, run into (*Inf.*) 2. attack, clash with, combat, come into conflict with, contend, cross swords with, do battle with, engage, face off (*Sl.*), fight, grapple with, strive, struggle ~*n.* 3. brush, confrontation, meeting, rendezvous 4. action, battle, clash, collision, combat, conflict, contest, dispute, engagement, face-off (*Sl.*), fight, head-to-head, run-in (*Inf.*), set to (*Inf.*), skirmish

encourage 1. animate, buoy up, cheer, comfort, console, embolden, hearten, incite, inspire, inspirit, rally, reassure, rouse, stimulate 2. abet, advance, advocate, aid, boost, egg on, favour, forward, foster, further, help, promote, prompt, spur, strengthen, succour, support, urge

Antonyms daunt, depress, deter, discourage, dishearten, dispirit, dissuade, hinder, inhibit, intimidate, prevent, retard, scare, throw cold water on (*Inf.*)

encouragement advocacy, aid, boost, cheer, consolation, favour, help, incitement, inspiration, inspiritment, promotion, reassurance, security blanket (*Inf.*), stimulation, stimulus, succour, support, urging

encouraging bright, cheerful, cheering, comforting, good, heartening, hopeful, promising, reassuring, rosy, satisfactory, stimulating

Antonyms daunting, depressing, disappointing, discouraging, disheartening, dispiriting, offputting (*Inf.*), unfavourable, unpropitious

encroach appropriate, arrogate, impinge, infringe, intrude, invade, make inroads, overstep, trench, trespass, usurp

encroachment appropriation, arrogation, impingement, incursion, infringement, inroad, intrusion, invasion, trespass, usurpation, violation

encumber burden, clog, cramp, embarrass, hamper, handicap, hinder, impede, incommode, inconvenience, make difficult, obstruct, oppress, overload, retard, saddle, slow down, trammel, weigh down

encumbrance burden, clog, difficulty, drag, embarrassment, handicap, hindrance, impediment, inconvenience, liability, load, millstone, obstacle, obstruction

encyclopedic all-embracing, all-encompassing, all-inclusive, complete, comprehensive, exhaustive, thorough, universal, vast, wide-ranging

end *n.* 1. bound, boundary, edge, extent, extreme, extremity, limit, point, terminus, tip 2. attainment, cessation, close, closure, completion, conclusion, consequence, consummation, culmination, denouement, ending, expiration, expiry, finale, finish, issue, outcome, resolution, result, sequel, stop, termination, upshot, wind-up 3. aim, aspiration, design, drift, goal, intent, intention, object, objective, point, purpose, reason 4. part, piece, portion, responsibility, share, side 5. bit, butt, fragment, leftover, oddment, remainder, remnant, scrap, stub, tag end, tail end 6. annihilation, death, demise, destruction, dissolution, doom, extermination, extinction, ruin, ruination 7. **the end** *Sl.* beyond endurance, insufferable, intolerable, the final blow, the last straw, the limit (*Inf.*), the worst, too much (*Inf.*), unbearable, unendurable ~*v.* 8. axe (*Inf.*), bring to an end, cease, close, complete, conclude, culminate, dissolve, expire, finish, resolve, stop, terminate, wind up 9. abolish, annihilate, destroy, exterminate, extinguish, kill, put to death, ruin

Antonyms *n.* beginning, birth, commencement, inception, launch, opening, origin, outset, prelude, source, start ~*v.* begin, come into being, commence, initiate, launch, originate, start

endanger compromise, hazard, imperil, jeopardize, put at risk, put in danger, risk, threaten

Antonyms defend, guard, preserve, protect, safeguard, save, secure

endear attach, attract, bind, captivate, charm, engage, win

endearing adorable, attractive, captivating, charming, cute, engaging, lovable, sweet, winning, winsome

endearment 1. affectionate utterance, loving word, sweet nothing 2. affection, attachment, fondness, love

endeavour 1. *n.* aim, attempt, crack (*Inf.*), effort, enterprise, essay, go (*Inf.*), shot (*Inf.*), stab (*Inf.*), trial, try, undertaking, venture 2. *v.* aim, aspire, attempt, bend over backwards (*Inf.*), break one's neck (*Inf.*), bust a gut (*Inf.*), do one's best, do one's damnedest (*Inf.*), essay, give it one's all (*Inf.*), give it one's best shot (*Inf.*), go for broke (*Sl.*), go for it (*Inf.*), have a go (crack, (*Inf.*) shot, (*Inf.*) stab, (*Inf.*)) (*Inf.*), knock oneself out (*Inf.*), labour, make an all-out effort (*Inf.*), make an effort, rupture oneself (*Inf.*), strive, struggle, take pains, try, undertake

ending catastrophe, cessation, close, completion, conclusion, consummation, culmination, denouement, end, finale, finish, resolution, termination, wind-up

Antonyms birth, commencement, inauguration, inception, onset, opening, origin, preface, source, start, starting point

endless 1. boundless, ceaseless, constant, continual, eternal, everlasting, immortal, incessant, infinite, interminable, limitless, measureless, perpetual, unbounded, unbroken, undying, unending, uninterrupted, unlimited 2. interminable, monotonous, overlong 3. continuous, unbroken, undivided, whole

Antonyms bounded, brief, circumscribed, finite, limited, passing, restricted, temporary, terminable, transient, transitory

endorse, indorse 1. advocate, affirm, approve, authorize, back, champion, confirm, espouse, favour, prescribe, promote, ratify, recommend, sanction, subscribe to, support, sustain, vouch for, warrant 2. countersign, sign, superscribe, undersign

endorsement, indorsement 1. comment, countersignature, qualification, signature, superscription 2. advocacy, affirmation, approbation, approval, authorization, backing, championship, confirmation, espousal, favour, fiat, O.K. *or* okay (*Inf.*), promotion, ratification, recommendation, sanction, seal of approval, subscription to, support, warrant

endow award, bequeath, bestow, confer, donate, endue, enrich, favour, finance, fund, furnish, give, grant, invest, leave, make over, provide, purvey, settle on, supply, will

endowment 1. award, benefaction, bequest, bestowal, boon, donation, fund, gift, grant, hand-out, income, largess *or* largesse, legacy, presentation, property, provision, revenue, stipend 2. *Often plural* ability, aptitude, attribute, capability, capacity, faculty, flair, genius, gift, power, qualification, quality, talent

endue, indue endow, fill, furnish, invest, provide, supply

end up 1. become eventually, finish as, finish up, pan out (*Inf.*), turn out to be 2. arrive finally, come to a halt, fetch up (*Inf.*), finish up, stop, wind up

endurable acceptable, bearable, sufferable, supportable, sustainable, tolerable

Antonyms insufferable, insupportable, intolerable, too much (*Inf.*), unbearable, unendurable

endurance 1. bearing, fortitude, patience, perseverance, persistence, pertinacity, resignation, resolution, stamina, staying power, strength, submission, sufferance, tenacity, toleration 2. continuation, continuity, durability, duration, immutability, lastingness, longevity, permanence, stability

endure 1. bear, brave, cope with, experience, go through, stand, stick it out (*Inf.*), suffer, support, sustain, take it (*Inf.*), thole

(*Scot.*), undergo, weather, withstand 2. abide, allow, bear, brook, countenance, permit, put up with, stand, stick (*Sl.*), stomach, submit to, suffer, swallow, take patiently, tolerate 3. abide, be durable, continue, hold, last, live, live on, persist, prevail, remain, stand, stay, survive, wear well

enduring abiding, continuing, durable, eternal, firm, immortal, immovable, imperishable, lasting, living, long-lasting, perennial, permanent, persistent, persisting, prevailing, remaining, steadfast, steady, surviving, unfaltering, unwavering
Antonyms brief, ephemeral, fleeting, momentary, passing, short, short-lived, temporary, transient, transitory

enemy adversary, antagonist, competitor, foe, opponent, rival, the opposition, the other side
Antonyms ally, confederate, friend, supporter

energetic active, animated, brisk, dynamic, forceful, forcible, high-powered, indefatigable, lively, potent, powerful, spirited, strenuous, strong, tireless, vigorous, zippy (*Inf.*)
Antonyms debilitated, dull, enervated, inactive, lazy, lethargic, lifeless, listless, slow, sluggish, torpid, weak

energize 1. activate, animate, enliven, inspirit, invigorate, liven up, motivate, pep up, quicken, stimulate, vitalize 2. activate, electrify, kick-start, start up, switch on, turn on

energy activity, animation, ardour, brio, drive, efficiency, élan, exertion, fire, force, forcefulness, get-up-and-go (*Inf.*), go (*Inf.*), intensity, life, liveliness, pep, pluck, power, spirit, stamina, strength, strenuousness, verve, vigour, vim (*Sl.*), vitality, vivacity, zeal, zest, zip (*Inf.*)

enervate 1. *v.* debilitate, devitalize, enfeeble, exhaust, fatigue, incapacitate, paralyse, prostrate, sap, tire, unnerve, wash out, weaken, wear out 2. *adj.* debilitated, devitalized, done in (*Inf.*), enervated, enfeebled, exhausted, fatigued, feeble, incapacitated, limp, paralysed, prostrate, prostrated, rundown, sapped, spent, tired, undermined, unnerved, washed out, weak, weakened, worn out

enervation debilitation, debility, enfeeblement, exhaustedness, exhaustion, fatigue, feebleness, impotence, incapacity, infirmity, lassitude, paralysis, powerlessness, prostration, tiredness, weakening, weakness

enfeeble debilitate, deplete, devitalize, diminish, exhaust, fatigue, render feeble, sap, undermine, unhinge, unnerve, weaken, wear out

enfold, infold clasp, embrace, enclose, encompass, envelop, enwrap, fold, hold, hug, shroud, swathe, wrap, wrap up

enforce administer, apply, carry out, coerce, compel, constrain, exact, execute, implement, impose, insist on, oblige, prosecute, put in force, put into effect, reinforce, require, urge

enforced compelled, compulsory, constrained, dictated, imposed, involuntary, necessary, ordained, prescribed, required, unavoidable, unwilling

enforcement 1. administration, application, carrying out, exaction, execution, implementation, imposition, prosecution, reinforcement 2. coercion, compulsion, constraint, insistence, obligation, pressure, requirement

enfranchise 1. give the vote to, grant suffrage to, grant the franchise to, grant voting rights to 2. emancipate, free, liberate, manumit, release, set free

enfranchisement 1. giving the vote, granting suffrage *or* the franchise, granting voting rights 2. emancipation, freedom, freeing, liberating, liberation, manumission, release, setting free

engage 1. appoint, commission, employ, enlist, enrol, hire, retain, take on 2. bespeak, book, charter, hire, lease, prearrange, rent, reserve, secure 3. absorb, busy, engross, grip, involve, occupy, preoccupy, tie up 4. allure, arrest, attach, attract, captivate, catch, charm, draw, enamour, enchant, fascinate, fix, gain, win 5. embark on, enter into, join, partake, participate, practise, set about, take part, undertake 6. affiance, agree, betroth (*Archaic*), bind, commit, contract, covenant, guarantee, obligate, oblige, pledge, promise, undertake, vouch, vow 7. *Military* assail, attack, combat, come to close quarters with, encounter, face off (*Sl.*), fall on, fight with, give battle to, join battle with, meet, take on 8. activate, apply, bring into operation, energize, set going, switch on 9. dovetail, interact, interconnect, interlock, join, mesh
Antonyms (*sense 1*) axe (*Inf.*), discharge, dismiss, fire (*Inf.*), give notice to, lay off, oust, remove, sack (*Inf.*)

engaged 1. affianced, betrothed (*Archaic*), pledged, promised, spoken for 2. absorbed, busy, committed, employed, engrossed, in use, involved, occupied, preoccupied, tied up, unavailable
Antonyms available, fancy-free, free, unattached, uncommitted, unengaged

engagement 1. assurance, betrothal,

bond, compact, contract, oath, obligation, pact, pledge, promise, troth (*Archaic*), undertaking, vow, word 2. appointment, arrangement, commitment, date, meeting 3. commission, employment, gig (*Inf.*), job, post, situation, stint, work 4. action, battle, combat, conflict, confrontation, contest, encounter, face-off (*Sl.*), fight

engaging agreeable, appealing, attractive, captivating, charming, enchanting, fascinating, fetching (*Inf.*), likable *or* likeable, lovable, pleasant, pleasing, winning, winsome

Antonyms disagreeable, objectionable, obnoxious, offensive, repulsive, unattractive, unlikable *or* unlikeable, unlovely, unpleasant

engender 1. beget, breed, bring about, cause, create, excite, foment, generate, give rise to, hatch, incite, induce, instigate, lead to, make, occasion, precipitate, produce, provoke 2. beget, breed, bring forth, father, generate, give birth to, procreate, propagate, sire, spawn

engine 1. machine, mechanism, motor 2. agency, agent, apparatus, appliance, contrivance, device, implement, instrument, means, tool, weapon

engineer 1. *n.* architect, contriver, designer, deviser, director, inventor, manager, manipulator, originator, planner, schemer 2. *v.* bring about, cause, concoct, contrive, control, create, devise, effect, encompass, finagle (*Inf.*), manage, manoeuvre, mastermind, originate, plan, plot, scheme, wangle (*Inf.*)

engorge bolt, cram, devour, eat, fill, glut, gobble, gorge, gulp, guzzle, pig out (*Sl.*), satiate, stuff, wolf

engraft, ingraft graft, implant, incorporate, inculcate, infix, infuse, ingrain, instil

engrain *see* INGRAIN

engrave 1. carve, chase, chisel, cut, enchase (*Rare*), etch, grave (*Archaic*), inscribe 2. impress, imprint, print 3. embed, fix, impress, imprint, infix, ingrain, lodge

engraving 1. carving, chasing, chiselling, cutting, dry point, enchasing (*Rare*), etching, inscribing, inscription 2. block, carving, etching, inscription, plate, woodcut 3. etching, impression, print

engross 1. absorb, arrest, engage, engulf, hold, immerse, involve, occupy, preoccupy 2. corner, monopolize, sew up (*U.S.*)

engrossed absorbed, captivated, caught up, deep, enthralled, fascinated, gripped, immersed, intent, intrigued, lost, preoccupied, rapt, riveted

engrossing absorbing, captivating, compelling, enthralling, fascinating, gripping, interesting, intriguing, riveting

engulf, ingulf absorb, bury, consume, deluge, drown, encompass, engross, envelop, flood (out), immerse, inundate, overrun, overwhelm, plunge, submerge, swallow up, swamp

enhance add to, augment, boost, complement, elevate, embellish, exalt, heighten, improve, increase, intensify, lift, magnify, raise, reinforce, strengthen, swell

Antonyms debase, decrease, depreciate, devalue, diminish, lower, minimize, reduce, spoil

enigma conundrum, mystery, problem, puzzle, riddle, teaser

enigmatic, enigmatical ambiguous, cryptic, Delphic, doubtful, equivocal, incomprehensible, indecipherable, inexplicable, inscrutable, mysterious, obscure, oracular, perplexing, puzzling, recondite, sphinxlike, uncertain, unfathomable, unintelligible

Antonyms clear, comprehensible, simple, straightforward, uncomplicated

enjoin 1. advise, bid, call upon, charge, command, counsel, demand, direct, instruct, order, prescribe, require, urge, warn 2. *Law* ban, bar, disallow, forbid, interdict, place an injunction on, preclude, prohibit, proscribe, restrain

enjoy 1. appreciate, be entertained by, be pleased with, delight in, like, rejoice in, relish, revel in, take joy in, take pleasure in *or* from 2. be blessed *or* favoured with, experience, have, have the benefit of, have the use of, own, possess, reap the benefits of, use 3. **enjoy oneself** have a ball (*Inf.*), have a good time, have fun, make merry

Antonyms (*sense 1*) abhor, despise, detest, dislike, hate, have no taste *or* stomach for, loathe

enjoyable agreeable, amusing, delectable, delicious, delightful, entertaining, gratifying, pleasant, pleasing, pleasurable, satisfying, to one's liking

Antonyms despicable, disagreeable, displeasing, hateful, loathsome, obnoxious, offensive, repugnant, unenjoyable, unpleasant, unsatisfying, unsavoury

enjoyment 1. amusement, delectation, delight, diversion, entertainment, fun, gladness, gratification, gusto, happiness, indulgence, joy, pleasure, recreation, relish, satisfaction, zest 2. advantage, benefit, exercise, ownership, possession, use

enkindle 1. fire, ignite, kindle, light, put a match to, put to the torch, set ablaze, set alight, set fire to, set on fire 2. arouse, awake, excite, foment, incite, inflame, inspire, provoke, stir

enlarge 1. add to, amplify, augment, blow

up (*Inf.*), broaden, diffuse, dilate, distend, elongate, expand, extend, grow, heighten, increase, inflate, lengthen, magnify, make *or* grow larger, multiply, stretch, swell, wax, widen 2. amplify, descant, develop, dilate, elaborate, expand, expatiate, give details
Antonyms abbreviate, abridge, compress, condense, curtail, decrease, diminish, lessen, narrow, reduce, shorten, shrink, trim, truncate

enlighten advise, apprise, cause to understand, civilize, counsel, edify, educate, inform, instruct, make aware, teach

enlightened aware, broad-minded, civilized, cultivated, educated, informed, knowledgeable, liberal, literate, open-minded, reasonable, refined, sophisticated
Antonyms ignorant, narrow-minded, short-sighted, small-minded, unaware, uneducated, unenlightened

enlightenment awareness, broad-mindedness, civilization, comprehension, cultivation, edification, education, information, insight, instruction, knowledge, learning, literacy, open-mindedness, refinement, sophistication, teaching, understanding, wisdom

enlist engage, enrol, enter (into), gather, join, join up, muster, obtain, procure, recruit, register, secure, sign up, volunteer

enliven animate, brighten, buoy up, cheer, cheer up, excite, exhilarate, fire, gladden, hearten, inspire, inspirit, invigorate, pep up, perk up, quicken, rouse, spark, stimulate, vitalize, vivify, wake up
Antonyms chill, dampen, deaden, depress, put a damper on, repress, subdue

en masse all at once, all together, as a group, as a whole, as one, ensemble, in a group (body, mass), together

enmesh catch, embroil, ensnare, entangle, implicate, incriminate, involve, net, snare, snarl, tangle, trammel, trap

enmity acrimony, animosity, animus, antagonism, antipathy, aversion, bad blood, bitterness, hate, hatred, hostility, ill will, malevolence, malice, malignity, rancour, spite, venom
Antonyms affection, amity, cordiality, friendliness, friendship, geniality, goodwill, harmony, love, warmth

ennoble aggrandize, dignify, elevate, enhance, exalt, glorify, honour, magnify, raise

ennui boredom, dissatisfaction, lassitude, listlessness, tedium, the doldrums

enormity 1. atrociousness, atrocity, depravity, disgrace, evilness, heinousness, monstrousness, nefariousness, outrageousness, turpitude, viciousness, vileness, villainy, wickedness 2. abomination, atrocity, crime, disgrace, evil, horror, monstrosity, outrage, villainy 3. *Inf.* enormousness, greatness, hugeness, immensity, magnitude, massiveness, vastness

enormous 1. astronomic, Brobdingnagian, colossal, elephantine, excessive, gargantuan, gigantic, gross, huge, humongous *or* humungous (*U.S. sl.*), immense, jumbo (*Inf.*), mammoth, massive, monstrous, mountainous, prodigious, titanic, tremendous, vast 2. *Archaic* abominable, atrocious, depraved, disgraceful, evil, heinous, monstrous, nefarious, odious, outrageous, vicious, vile, villainous, wicked
Antonyms diminutive, dwarf, infinitesimal, insignificant, Lilliputian, little, meagre, microscopic, midget, minute, petite, pint-sized (*Inf.*), small, tiny, trivial, wee

enough 1. *adj.* abundant, adequate, ample, plenty, sufficient 2. *n.* abundance, adequacy, ample supply, plenty, right amount, sufficiency 3. *adv.* abundantly, adequately, amply, fairly, moderately, passably, reasonably, satisfactorily, sufficiently, tolerably

enquire 1. ask, query, question, request information, seek information 2. *Also* **inquire** conduct an inquiry, examine, explore, inspect, investigate, look into, make inquiry, probe, research, scrutinize, search

enquiry 1. query, question 2. *Also* **inquiry** examination, exploration, inquest, inspection, investigation, probe, research, scrutiny, search, study, survey

enrage aggravate (*Inf.*), anger, exasperate, gall, incense, incite, inflame, infuriate, irritate, madden, make one's blood boil, make one see red (*Inf.*), nark (*Brit., Aust., & N.Z. sl.*), provoke
Antonyms appease, assuage, calm, conciliate, mollify, pacify, placate, soothe

enraged aggravated (*Inf.*), angered, angry, boiling mad, cross, exasperated, fuming, furious, incensed, inflamed, infuriated, irate, irritated, livid (*Inf.*), mad (*Inf.*), raging, raging mad, wild

enrapture absorb, beguile, bewitch, captivate, charm, delight, enamour, enchant, enthral, entrance, fascinate, ravish, spellbind, transport

enrich 1. make rich, make wealthy 2. aggrandize, ameliorate, augment, cultivate, develop, endow, enhance, improve, refine, supplement 3. adorn, decorate, embellish, grace, ornament

enrol 1. chronicle, inscribe, list, note, record 2. accept, admit, engage, enlist, join up, matriculate, recruit, register, sign up *or* on, take on

enrolment acceptance, admission, engagement, enlistment, matriculation, recruitment, registration

en route in transit, on *or* along the way, on the road

ensconce 1. curl up, establish, install, nestle, settle, snuggle up 2. conceal, cover, hide, protect, screen, shelter, shield

ensemble *n.* 1. aggregate, assemblage, collection, entirety, set, sum, total, totality, whole, whole thing 2. costume, get-up (*Inf.*), outfit, suit 3. band, cast, chorus, company, group, supporting cast, troupe ~*adv.* 4. all at once, all together, as a group, as a whole, at once, at the same time, en masse, in concert

enshrine apotheosize, cherish, consecrate, dedicate, embalm, exalt, hallow, preserve, revere, sanctify, treasure

enshroud cloak, cloud, conceal, cover, enclose, enfold, envelop, enwrap, hide, obscure, pall, shroud, veil, wrap

ensign badge, banner, colours, flag, jack, pennant, pennon, standard, streamer

enslave bind, dominate, enchain, enthral, reduce to slavery, subjugate, yoke

ensnare catch, embroil, enmesh, entangle, entrap, net, snare, snarl, trap

ensue arise, attend, be consequent on, befall, come after, come next, come to pass (*Archaic*), derive, flow, follow, issue, proceed, result, stem, succeed, supervene, turn out *or* up

Antonyms antecede, come first, forerun, go ahead of, go before, introduce, lead, pave the way, precede, usher

ensure, insure 1. certify, confirm, effect, guarantee, make certain, make sure, secure, warrant 2. guard, make safe, protect, safeguard, secure

entail bring about, call for, cause, demand, encompass, give rise to, impose, involve, lead to, necessitate, occasion, require, result in

entangle 1. catch, compromise, embroil, enmesh, ensnare, entrap, foul, implicate, involve, knot, mat, mix up, ravel, snag, snare, tangle, trammel, trap 2. bewilder, complicate, confuse, jumble, mix up, muddle, perplex, puzzle, snarl, twist

Antonyms (*sense 1*) detach, disconnect, disengage, disentangle, extricate, free, loose, separate, sever, unfold, unravel, unsnarl, untangle, untwist (*sense 2*) clarify, clear (up), resolve, simplify, work out

entanglement 1. complication, confusion, ensnarement, entrapment, imbroglio (*Obsolete*), involvement, jumble, knot, mesh, mess, mix-up, muddle, snare, snarl-up (*Inf., chiefly Brit.*), tangle, toils, trap 2. difficulty, embarrassment, imbroglio, involvement, liaison, predicament, tie

entente *Also* **entente cordiale** agreement, arrangement, compact, deal, friendship, pact, treaty, understanding

enter 1. arrive, come *or* go in *or* into, insert, introduce, make an entrance, pass into, penetrate, pierce 2. become a member of, begin, commence, commit oneself to, embark upon, enlist, enrol, join, participate in, set about, set out on, sign up, start, take part in, take up 3. inscribe, list, log, note, record, register, set down, take down 4. offer, present, proffer, put forward, register, submit, tender

Antonyms depart, drop out, exit, go, issue from, leave, pull out, resign, retire, take one's leave, withdraw

enterprise 1. adventure, effort, endeavour, essay, operation, plan, programme, project, undertaking, venture 2. activity, adventurousness, alertness, audacity, boldness, daring, dash, drive, eagerness, energy, enthusiasm, get-up-and-go (*Inf.*), gumption (*Inf.*), initiative, pep, push (*Inf.*), readiness, resource, resourcefulness, spirit, vigour, zeal 3. business, company, concern, establishment, firm, operation

enterprising active, adventurous, alert, audacious, bold, daring, dashing, eager, energetic, enthusiastic, go-ahead, intrepid, keen, ready, resourceful, spirited, stirring, up-and-coming, venturesome, vigorous, zealous

entertain 1. amuse, charm, cheer, delight, divert, occupy, please, recreate (*Rare*), regale 2. accommodate, be host to, harbour, have company, have guests *or* visitors, lodge, put up, show hospitality to, treat 3. cherish, cogitate on, conceive, consider, contemplate, foster, harbour, hold, imagine, keep in mind, maintain, muse over, ponder, support, think about, think over

entertaining amusing, charming, cheering, delightful, diverting, funny, humorous, interesting, pleasant, pleasing, pleasurable, recreative (*Rare*), witty

entertainment amusement, cheer, distraction, diversion, enjoyment, fun, good time, leisure activity, pastime, play, pleasure, recreation, satisfaction, sport, treat

enthral absorb, beguile, captivate, charm, enchant, enrapture, entrance, fascinate, grip, hold spellbound, hypnotize, intrigue, mesmerize, ravish, rivet, spellbind

enthralling beguiling, captivating, charming, compelling, compulsive, enchanting, entrancing, fascinating, gripping, hypnotizing, intriguing, mesmerizing, riveting, spellbinding

enthusiasm 1. ardour, avidity, devotion, eagerness, earnestness, excitement, fervour, frenzy, interest, keenness, passion, relish, vehemence, warmth, zeal, zest 2. craze, fad (*Inf.*), hobby, hobbyhorse, interest, mania, passion, rage

enthusiast admirer, aficionado, buff (*Inf.*), devotee, fan, fanatic, fiend (*Inf.*), follower, freak (*Inf.*), lover, supporter, zealot

enthusiastic ardent, avid, devoted, eager, earnest, ebullient, excited, exuberant, fervent, fervid, forceful, hearty, keen, lively, passionate, spirited, unqualified, unstinting, vehement, vigorous, warm, wholehearted, zealous
Antonyms apathetic, blasé, bored, cool, dispassionate, half-hearted, indifferent, nonchalant, unconcerned, unenthusiastic, uninterested

entice allure, attract, beguile, cajole, coax, decoy, draw, inveigle, lead on, lure, persuade, prevail on, seduce, tempt, wheedle

enticement allurement, attraction, bait, blandishments, cajolery, coaxing, come-on (*Inf.*), decoy, inducement, inveiglement, lure, persuasion, seduction, temptation

entire 1. complete, full, gross, total, whole 2. absolute, full, outright, thorough, total, undiminished, unmitigated, unreserved, unrestricted 3. intact, perfect, sound, unbroken, undamaged, unmarked, unmarred, whole, without a scratch 4. continuous, integrated, unbroken, undivided, unified

entirely 1. absolutely, altogether, completely, fully, in every respect, perfectly, thoroughly, totally, unreservedly, utterly, wholly, without exception, without reservation 2. exclusively, only, solely
Antonyms incompletely, moderately, partially, partly, piecemeal, slightly, somewhat, to a certain extent *or* degree

entirety 1. absoluteness, completeness, fullness, totality, undividedness, unity, wholeness 2. aggregate, sum, total, unity, whole

entitle 1. accredit, allow, authorize, empower, enable, enfranchise, fit for, license, make eligible, permit, qualify for, warrant 2. call, characterize, christen, denominate, designate, dub, label, name, style, term, title

entity 1. being, body, creature, existence, individual, object, organism, presence, quantity, substance, thing 2. essence, essential nature, quiddity (*Philosophy*), quintessence, real nature

entomb bury, inhume, inter, inurn, lay to rest, sepulchre

entombment burial, inhumation, interment, inurnment, sepulture

entourage 1. associates, attendants, companions, company, cortege, court, escort, followers, following, retainers, retinue, staff, suite, train 2. ambience, environment, environs, milieu, surroundings

entrails bowels, guts, innards (*Inf.*), insides (*Inf.*), intestines, offal, viscera

entrance[1] *n.* 1. access, avenue, door, doorway, entry, gate, ingress, inlet, opening, passage, portal, way in 2. appearance, arrival, coming in, entry, ingress, introduction 3. access, admission, admittance, entrée, entry, ingress, permission to enter 4. beginning, commencement, debut, initiation, introduction, outset, start
Antonyms departure, egress, exit, exodus, leave-taking, outlet, way out

entrance[2] *v.* 1. absorb, bewitch, captivate, charm, delight, enchant, enrapture, enthral, fascinate, gladden, ravish, spellbind, transport 2. hypnotize, mesmerize, put in a trance
Antonyms bore, disenchant, irritate, offend, put off, turn off (*Inf.*)

entrant 1. beginner, convert, initiate, neophyte, newcomer, new member, novice, probationer, tyro 2. candidate, competitor, contestant, entry, participant, player

entrap 1. capture, catch, ensnare, net, snare, trap 2. allure, beguile, decoy, embroil, enmesh, ensnare, entangle, entice, implicate, inveigle, involve, lead on, lure, seduce, trick

entreat appeal to, ask, ask earnestly, beg, beseech, conjure, crave, enjoin, exhort, implore, importune, petition, plead with, pray, request, supplicate

entreaty appeal, earnest request, exhortation, importunity, petition, plea, prayer, request, solicitation, suit, supplication

entrench, intrench 1. construct defences, dig in, dig trenches, fortify 2. anchor, dig in, embed, ensconce, establish, fix, implant, ingrain, install, lodge, plant, root, seat, set, settle 3. encroach, impinge, infringe, interlope, intrude, make inroads, trespass

entrenched, intrenched deep-rooted, deep-seated, firm, fixed, indelible, ineradicable, ingrained, rooted, set, unshakable, well-established

entre nous between ourselves, between the two of us, between you and me, confidentially, in confidence, off the record, privately

entrepreneur businessman, businesswoman, contractor, director, financier, impresario, industrialist, magnate, tycoon

entrust, intrust assign, authorize, charge, commend, commit, confide, consign, delegate, deliver, give custody of, hand over, invest, trust, turn over

entry 1. appearance, coming in, entering, entrance, initiation, introduction 2. access, avenue, door, doorway, entrance, gate, ingress, inlet, opening, passage, passageway, portal, way in 3. access, admission, entrance, entrée, free passage, permission to enter 4. account, item, jotting, listing, memo, memorandum, minute, note, record, registration 5. attempt, candidate, competitor, contestant, effort, entrant, participant, player, submission
Antonyms departure, egress, exit, leave, leave-taking, withdrawal

entwine, intwine braid, embrace, encircle, entwist (*Archaic*), interlace, intertwine, interweave, knit, plait, ravel, surround, twine, twist, weave, wind
Antonyms disentangle, extricate, free, separate, straighten out, undo, unravel, untangle, unwind

enumerate 1. cite, detail, itemize, list, mention, name, quote, recapitulate, recite, recount, rehearse, relate, specify, spell out, tell 2. add up, calculate, compute, count, number, reckon, sum up, tally, total

enunciate 1. articulate, enounce, pronounce, say, sound, speak, utter, vocalize, voice 2. declare, proclaim, promulgate, pronounce, propound, publish, state

envelop blanket, cloak, conceal, cover, embrace, encase, encircle, enclose, encompass, enfold, engulf, enwrap, hide, obscure, sheathe, shroud, surround, swaddle, swathe, veil, wrap

envelope case, casing, coating, cover, covering, jacket, sheath, shell, skin, wrapper, wrapping

envenom 1. contaminate, infect, poison, taint 2. acerbate, aggravate (*Inf.*), embitter, enrage, exacerbate, exasperate, incense, inflame, irritate, madden, provoke, sour

enviable advantageous, blessed, covetable, desirable, favoured, fortunate, lucky, much to be desired, privileged
Antonyms disagreeable, painful, thankless, uncomfortable, undesirable, unenviable, unpleasant

envious begrudging, covetous, green-eyed, green with envy, grudging, jaundiced, jealous, malicious, resentful, spiteful

environ beset, besiege, encircle, enclose, encompass, engird, envelop, gird, hem, invest (*Rare*), ring, surround

environment atmosphere, background, conditions, context, domain, element, habitat, locale, medium, milieu, scene, setting, situation, surroundings, territory

environmentalist conservationist, ecologist, friend of the earth, green

environs district, locality, neighbourhood, outskirts, precincts, purlieus, suburbs, surrounding area, vicinity

envisage 1. conceive (of), conceptualize, contemplate, fancy, imagine, picture, think up, visualize 2. anticipate, envision, foresee, predict, see

envision anticipate, conceive of, contemplate, envisage, foresee, predict, see, visualize

envoy agent, ambassador, courier, delegate, deputy, diplomat, emissary, intermediary, legate, messenger, minister, plenipotentiary, representative

envy 1. *n.* covetousness, enviousness, grudge, hatred, ill will, jealousy, malice, malignity, resentfulness, resentment, spite, the green-eyed monster (*Inf.*) 2. *v.* be envious (of), begrudge, be jealous (of), covet, grudge, resent

ephemeral brief, evanescent, fleeting, flitting, fugacious, fugitive, impermanent, momentary, passing, short, short-lived, temporary, transient, transitory
Antonyms abiding, durable, enduring, eternal, immortal, lasting, long-lasting, persisting, steadfast

epicene *adj.* 1. androgyne, androgynous, bisexual, gynandrous, hermaphrodite, hermaphroditic 2. asexual, neuter, sexless 3. camp (*Inf.*), effeminate, unmanly, weak, womanish ~*n.* 4. androgyne, bisexual, gynandromorph, hermaphrodite

epicure 1. *bon vivant,* epicurean, foodie, gastronome, gourmet 2. glutton, gourmand, hedonist, sensualist, sybarite, voluptuary

epicurean 1. *adj.* gluttonous, gourmandizing, hedonistic, libertine, luscious, lush, luxurious, pleasure-seeking, self-indulgent, sensual, sybaritic, voluptuous 2. *n. bon vivant,* epicure, foodie, gastronome, gourmet

epidemic 1. *adj.* general, pandemic, prevailing, prevalent, rampant, rife, sweeping, wide-ranging, widespread 2. *n.* contagion, growth, outbreak, plague, rash, spread, upsurge, wave

epigram aphorism, *bon mot,* quip, witticism

epigrammatic concise, laconic, piquant, pithy, pointed, pungent, sharp, short, succinct, terse, witty

epilogue afterword, coda, concluding speech, conclusion, postscript
Antonyms exordium, foreword, introduction, preamble, preface, prelude, prologue

episode 1. adventure, affair, business, circumstance, escapade, event, experience, happening, incident, matter, occurrence 2. chapter, instalment, part, passage, scene, section

episodic anecdotal, digressive, disconnected, discursive, disjointed, intermittent, irregular, occasional, picaresque, rambling, sporadic, wandering

epistle communication, letter, message, missive, note

epithet appellation, description, designation, moniker *or* monicker (*Sl.*), name, nickname, sobriquet, tag, title

epitome 1. archetype, embodiment, essence, exemplar, norm, personification, quintessence, representation, type, typical example 2. abbreviation, abridgment, abstract, compendium, condensation, conspectus, contraction, digest, précis, résumé, summary, syllabus, synopsis

epitomize 1. embody, exemplify, illustrate, incarnate, personify, represent, symbolize, typify 2. abbreviate, abridge, abstract, condense, contract, curtail, cut, encapsulate, précis, reduce, shorten, summarize, synopsize

epoch age, date, era, period, time

equable 1. agreeable, calm, composed, easy-going, even-tempered, imperturbable, level-headed, placid, serene, temperate, unexcitable, unfazed (*Inf.*), unflappable (*Inf.*), unruffled 2. consistent, constant, even, regular, smooth, stable, steady, temperate, tranquil, unchanging, uniform, unvarying

Antonyms changeable, excitable, fitful, inconsistent, irregular, nervous, temperamental, uneven, unpredictable, unstable, volatile

equal *adj.* 1. alike, commensurate, equivalent, identical, like, one and the same, proportionate, tantamount, the same, uniform 2. balanced, corresponding, egalitarian, even, evenly balanced, evenly matched, evenly proportioned, fifty-fifty (*Inf.*), level pegging (*Brit. inf.*), matched, regular, symmetrical, uniform, unvarying 3. able, adequate, capable, competent, fit, good enough, ready, strong enough, suitable, up to 4. egalitarian, equable, even-handed, fair, impartial, just, unbiased ~*n.* 5. brother, compeer, counterpart, equivalent, fellow, match, mate, parallel, peer, rival, twin ~*v.* 6. agree with, amount to, balance, be equal to, be even with, be level with, be tantamount to, come up to, correspond to, equalize, equate, even, level, match, parallel, rival, square with, tally with, tie with

Antonyms *adj.* different, disproportionate, dissimilar, diverse, inadequate, inequitable, irregular, unbalanced, unequal, uneven, unlike, unmatched ~*v.* be different, be unequal, disagree

equality balance, coequality, correspondence, egalitarianism, equal opportunity, equatability, equivalence, evenness, fairness, identity, likeness, parity, sameness, similarity, uniformity

Antonyms bias, discrimination, disparity, imparity, inequality, lack of balance, prejudice, unevenness, unfairness

equalize balance, equal, equate, even up, level, make equal, match, regularize, smooth, square, standardize

equanimity aplomb, calm, calmness, composure, coolness, imperturbability, level-headedness, peace, phlegm, placidity, poise, presence of mind, sang-froid, self-possession, serenity, steadiness, tranquillity

equate agree, balance, be commensurate, compare, correspond with *or* to, equalize, liken, make *or* be equal, match, offset, pair, parallel, square, tally, think of together

equation agreement, balancing, comparison, correspondence, equality, equalization, equating, equivalence, likeness, match, pairing, parallel

equestrian 1. *adj.* in the saddle, mounted, on horseback 2. *n.* cavalier (*Archaic*), horseman, knight, rider

equilibrate balance, ballast, compensate (for), counterbalance, counterpoise, countervail, equipoise, even up, neutralize, offset

equilibrium 1. balance, counterpoise, equipoise, evenness, rest, stability, steadiness, symmetry 2. calm, calmness, collectedness, composure, coolness, equanimity, poise, self-possession, serenity, stability, steadiness

equip accoutre, arm, array, attire, deck out, dress, endow, fit out, fit up, furnish, kit out, outfit, prepare, provide, rig, stock, supply

equipage 1. carriage, coach 2. accoutrements, apparatus, baggage, equipment, gear, materiel, munitions, stores

equipment accoutrements, apparatus, appurtenances, baggage, equipage, furnishings, furniture, gear, materiel, outfit, paraphernalia, rig, stuff, supplies, tackle, tools

equipoise *n.* 1. balance, equilibrium, even balance, evenness, stability, steadiness, symmetry 2. ballast, counterbalance, counterpoise, counterweight, offset ~*v.* 3. balance, ballast, compensate (for), counterbalance, counterpoise, countervail, equilibrate, neutralize, offset

equitable candid, disinterested, dispassionate, due, even-handed, fair, honest, impartial, just, nondiscriminatory, proper, proportionate, reasonable, right, rightful, unbiased, unprejudiced

equity disinterestedness, equitableness, even-handedness, fair-mindedness, fairness, fair play, honesty, impartiality, integrity, justice, reasonableness, rectitude, righteousness, uprightness
Antonyms bias, discrimination, injustice, partiality, preference, prejudice, unfairness

equivalence agreement, alikeness, conformity, correspondence, equality, evenness, identity, interchangeableness, likeness, match, parallel, parity, sameness, similarity, synonymy

equivalent 1. *adj.* alike, commensurate, comparable, correspondent, corresponding, equal, even, homologous, interchangeable, of a kind, same, similar, synonymous, tantamount 2. *n.* correspondent, counterpart, equal, match, opposite number, parallel, peer, twin
Antonyms *adj.* different, dissimilar, incomparable, unequal, unlike

equivocal ambiguous, ambivalent, doubtful, dubious, evasive, indefinite, indeterminate, misleading, oblique, obscure, oracular, prevaricating, questionable, suspicious, uncertain, vague
Antonyms absolute, certain, clear, clear-cut, decisive, definite, evident, explicit, incontrovertible, indubitable, manifest, plain, positive, straight, unambiguous, unequivocal

equivocate avoid the issue, beat about the bush (*Inf.*), dodge, evade, fence, flannel (*Brit. inf.*), fudge, hedge, parry, prevaricate, pussyfoot (*Inf.*), quibble, shuffle, sidestep, tergiversate, waffle (*Inf., chiefly Brit.*)

equivocation ambiguity, double talk, doubtfulness, evasion, hedging, prevarication, quibbling, shuffling, tergiversation, waffle (*Inf., chiefly Brit.*), weasel words (*Inf., chiefly U.S.*)

era aeon, age, cycle, date, day *or* days, epoch, generation, period, stage, time

eradicate abolish, annihilate, deracinate, destroy, efface, eliminate, erase, excise, expunge, exterminate, extinguish, extirpate, obliterate, remove, root out, stamp out, uproot, weed out, wipe out

eradication abolition, annihilation, deracination, destruction, effacement, elimination, erasure, expunction, extermination, extinction, extirpation, obliteration, removal

erase blot, cancel, delete, efface, excise, expunge, obliterate, remove, rub out, scratch out, wipe out

erect *adj.* 1. elevated, firm, perpendicular, pricked-up, raised, rigid, standing, stiff, straight, upright, vertical ~*v.* 2. build, construct, elevate, lift, mount, pitch, put up, raise, rear, set up, stand up 3. create, establish, form, found, initiate, institute, organize, set up
Antonyms *adj.* bent, flaccid, horizontal, leaning, limp, prone, recumbent, relaxed, supine ~*v.* demolish, destroy, dismantle, raze, tear down

erection 1. assembly, building, construction, creation, elevation, establishment, fabrication, manufacture 2. building, construction, edifice, pile, structure

erelong *Archaic or poetic* before long, early, quickly, shortly, soon, speedily

eremite anchorite, hermit, recluse, solitary

ergo accordingly, consequently, for that reason, hence, in consequence, so, then, therefore, thus

erode abrade, consume, corrode, destroy, deteriorate, disintegrate, eat away, grind down, spoil, wear down *or* away

erosion abrasion, attrition, consumption, corrasion, corrosion, destruction, deterioration, disintegration, eating away, grinding down, spoiling, wear, wearing down *or* away

erotic amatory, aphrodisiac, carnal, erogenous, lustful, rousing, seductive, sensual, sexy (*Inf.*), steamy (*Inf.*), stimulating, suggestive, titillating, voluptuous

err 1. be inaccurate, be incorrect, be in error, blunder, go astray, go wrong, make a mistake, misapprehend, miscalculate, misjudge, mistake, slip up (*Inf.*) 2. be out of order, deviate, do wrong, fall, go astray, lapse, misbehave, offend, sin, transgress, trespass

errand charge, commission, job, message, mission, task

errant 1. *Archaic* itinerant, journeying, peripatetic, rambling, roaming, roving, wandering 2. aberrant, deviant, erring, offending, sinning, straying, wayward, wrong

erratic 1. aberrant, abnormal, capricious, changeable, desultory, eccentric, fitful, inconsistent, inconstant, irregular, irregular, shifting, uneven, unpredictable, unreliable, unstable, variable, wayward 2. directionless, meandering, planetary, wandering
Antonyms certain, consistent, constant, dependable, invariable, natural, normal, predictable, regular, reliable, stable, steady, straight, unchanging, undeviating

erroneous amiss, fallacious, false, faulty, flawed, inaccurate, incorrect, inexact, in-

valid, mistaken, spurious, unfounded, unsound, untrue, wrong
Antonyms accurate, correct, factual, faultless, flawless, precise, right, true, veracious

error 1. bloomer (*Brit. inf.*), blunder, boner (*Sl.*), boob (*Brit. sl.*), delusion, erratum, fallacy, fault, flaw, howler (*Inf.*), inaccuracy, misapprehension, miscalculation, misconception, mistake, oversight, slip, solecism 2. delinquency, deviation, fault, lapse, misdeed, offence, sin, transgression, trespass, wrong, wrongdoing

ersatz artificial, bogus, counterfeit, fake, imitation, phoney *or* phony (*Inf.*), pretended, sham, simulated, spurious, substitute, synthetic

erstwhile bygone, ex (*Inf.*), former, late, old, once, one-time, past, previous, quondam, sometime

erudite cultivated, cultured, educated, knowledgeable, learned, lettered, literate, scholarly, well-educated, well-read
Antonyms ignorant, illiterate, shallow, uneducated, uninformed, unlettered, unschooled, untaught, unthinking

erudition education, knowledge, learning, letters, lore, scholarship

erupt 1. be ejected, belch forth, blow up, break out, burst forth, burst into, burst out, discharge, explode, flare up, gush, pour forth, spew forth *or* out, spit out, spout, throw off, vent, vomit 2. *Medical* appear, break out

eruption 1. discharge, ejection, explosion, flare-up, outbreak, outburst, sally, venting 2. *Medical* inflammation, outbreak, rash

escalate amplify, ascend, be increased, enlarge, expand, extend, grow, heighten, increase, intensify, magnify, mount, raise, rise, step up
Antonyms abate, contract, decrease, descend, diminish, fall, lessen, limit, lower, shrink, wane, wind down

escapade adventure, antic, caper, fling, lark (*Inf.*), mischief, prank, romp, scrape (*Inf.*), spree, stunt, trick

escape *v.* 1. abscond, bolt, break free *or* out, decamp, do a bunk (*Brit. sl.*), do a runner (*Sl.*), flee, fly, fly the coop (*U.S. & Canad. inf.*), get away, hook it (*Sl.*), make *or* effect one's escape, make one's getaway, run away *or* off, skedaddle (*Inf.*), skip, slip away, take a powder (*U.S. & Canad. sl.*), take it on the lam (*U.S. & Canad. sl.*) ~*n.* 2. bolt, break, break-out, decampment, flight, getaway ~*v.* 3. avoid, body-swerve (*Scot.*), circumvent, dodge, duck, elude, evade, pass, shun, slip ~*n.* 4. avoidance, circumvention, elusion, evasion ~*v.* 5. discharge, drain, emanate, exude, flow, gush, issue, leak, pour forth, seep, spurt ~*n.* 6. discharge, drain, effluence, efflux, emanation, emission, gush, leak, leakage, outflow, outpour, seepage, spurt ~*v.* 7. baffle, be beyond (someone), be forgotten by, elude, puzzle, stump ~*n.* 8. distraction, diversion, pastime, recreation, relief

eschew abandon, abjure, abstain from, avoid, elude, fight shy of, forgo, forswear, give up, have nothing to do with, keep *or* steer clear of, kick (*Inf.*), refrain from, renounce, shun, swear off

escort *n.* 1. bodyguard, company, convoy, cortege, entourage, guard, protection, retinue, safeguard, train 2. attendant, beau, chaperon, companion, guide, partner, protector, squire (*Rare*) ~*v.* 3. accompany, chaperon, conduct, convoy, guard, guide, lead, partner, protect, shepherd, squire, usher

esculent eatable, edible, fit to eat, palatable, wholesome

esoteric abstruse, arcane, cabbalistic, cryptic, hidden, inner, inscrutable, mysterious, mystic, mystical, obscure, occult, private, recondite, secret

especial 1. chief, distinguished, exceptional, extraordinary, marked, notable, noteworthy, outstanding, principal, signal, special, uncommon, unusual 2. exclusive, express, individual, particular, peculiar, personal, private, singular, special, specific, unique

especially 1. chiefly, conspicuously, exceptionally, extraordinarily, largely, mainly, markedly, notably, outstandingly, principally, remarkably, signally, specially, strikingly, supremely, uncommonly, unusually 2. exclusively, expressly, particularly, peculiarly, singularly, specifically, uniquely

espionage counter-intelligence, intelligence, spying, surveillance, undercover work

espousal 1. adoption, advocacy, backing, championing, championship, defence, embracing, maintenance, promotion, support, taking up 2. *Archaic* affiancing, betrothal, betrothing (*Archaic*), engagement, espousing (*Archaic*), marriage, nuptials, plighting, wedding

espouse 1. adopt, advocate, back, champion, defend, embrace, maintain, promote, stand up for, support, take up 2. *Archaic* betroth (*Archaic*), marry, take as spouse, take to wife, wed

esprit animation, brio, élan, liveliness, quickness, sparkle, spirit, sprightliness, verve, vitality, vivacity, wit, zest

espy behold, catch a glimpse of, catch sight of, descry, detect, discern, discover, glimpse, make out, notice, observe, perceive, sight, spot, spy

essay[1] article, composition, discourse, disquisition, dissertation, paper, piece, tract, treatise

essay[2] 1. *n.* aim, attempt, bid, crack (*Inf.*), effort, endeavour, exertion, experiment, go (*Inf.*), shot (*Inf.*), stab (*Inf.*), struggle, test, trial, try, undertaking, venture 2. *v.* aim, attempt, endeavour, have a go (bash (*Inf.*), crack (*Inf.*), shot (*Inf.*)) (*Inf.*), put to the test, strive, take on, test, try, try out, undertake

essence 1. being, core, crux, entity, heart, kernel, life, lifeblood, meaning, nature, pith, principle, quiddity, quintessence, significance, soul, spirit, substance 2. concentrate, distillate, elixir, extract, spirits, tincture 3. *Rare* cologne, fragrance, perfume, scent 4. **in essence** basically, essentially, fundamentally, in effect, in substance, in the main, materially, substantially, to all intents and purposes, virtually 5. **of the essence** crucial, essential, indispensable, of the utmost importance, vital, vitally important

essential *adj.* 1. crucial, important, indispensable, necessary, needed, requisite, vital 2. basic, cardinal, constitutional, elemental, elementary, fundamental, inherent, innate, intrinsic, key, main, principal, radical 3. absolute, complete, ideal, perfect, quintessential 4. concentrated, distilled, extracted, rectified, refined, volatile ~*n.* 5. basic, fundamental, must, necessity, prerequisite, principle, requisite, rudiment, *sine qua non,* vital part

Antonyms accessory, dispensable, expendable, extra, extraneous, incidental, inessential, lesser, minor, nonessential, option, secondary, superfluous, surplus, trivial, unimportant, unnecessary

establish 1. base, constitute, create, decree, enact, ensconce, entrench, fix, form, found, ground, implant, inaugurate, install, institute, organize, plant, root, secure, settle, set up, start 2. authenticate, certify, confirm, corroborate, demonstrate, prove, ratify, show, substantiate, validate, verify

establishment 1. creation, enactment, formation, foundation, founding, inauguration, installation, institution, organization, setting up 2. business, company, concern, corporation, enterprise, firm, house, institute, institution, organization, outfit (*Inf.*), setup (*Inf.*), structure, system 3. building, factory, house, office, plant, quarters 4. abode, domicile, dwelling, home, house, household, pad (*Sl.*), residence 5. **the Establishment** established order, institutionalized authority, ruling class, the powers that be, the system

estate 1. area, demesne, domain, holdings, lands, manor, property 2. *Property law* assets, belongings, effects, fortune, goods, possessions, property, wealth 3. caste, class, order, rank 4. condition, lot, period, place, position, quality, rank, situation, standing, state, station, status

esteem *v.* 1. admire, be fond of, cherish, honour, like, love, prize, regard highly, respect, revere, reverence, think highly of, treasure, value, venerate 2. *Formal* account, believe, calculate, consider, deem, estimate, hold, judge, rate, reckon, regard, think, view ~*n.* 3. admiration, Brownie points, consideration, credit, estimation, good opinion, honour, regard, respect, reverence, veneration

estimable admirable, esteemed, excellent, good, honourable, honoured, meritorious, reputable, respectable, respected, valuable, valued, worthy

estimate *v.* 1. appraise, assess, calculate roughly, evaluate, gauge, guess, judge, number, reckon, value 2. assess, believe, conjecture, consider, form an opinion, guess, judge, rank, rate, reckon, surmise, think ~*n.* 3. appraisal, appraisement, approximate calculation, assessment, evaluation, guess, guesstimate (*Inf.*), judgment, reckoning, valuation 4. appraisal, appraisement, assessment, belief, conjecture, educated guess, estimation, judgment, opinion, surmise, thought(s)

estimation 1. appraisal, appreciation, assessment, belief, consideration, considered opinion, estimate, evaluation, judgment, opinion, view 2. admiration, Brownie points, credit, esteem, good opinion, honour, regard, respect, reverence, veneration

estrange alienate, antagonize, disaffect, disunite, divide, drive apart, lose *or* destroy the affection of, make hostile, part, separate, set at odds, withdraw, withhold

Antonyms ally, associate, coalesce, couple, fuse, join, link, marry, unite

estrangement alienation, antagonization, breach, break-up, disaffection, dissociation, disunity, division, hostility, parting, separation, split, withdrawal, withholding

estuary creek, firth, fjord, inlet, mouth

et cetera and others, and so forth, and so on, and the like, and the rest, et al.

etch carve, corrode, cut, eat into, engrave, furrow, impress, imprint, incise, ingrain, inscribe, stamp

etching carving, engraving, impression, imprint, inscription, print

eternal 1. abiding, ceaseless, constant, deathless, endless, everlasting, immortal, infinite, interminable, never-ending, perennial, perpetual, sempiternal (*Literary*), timeless, unceasing, undying, unending, unremitting, without end 2. deathless, enduring, everlasting, immortal, immutable, imperishable, indestructible, lasting, permanent

Antonyms changing, ephemeral, evanescent, finite, fleeting, infrequent, irregular, mortal, occasional, perishable, random, rare, temporal, transient, transitory

eternity 1. age, ages, endlessness, for ever, immortality, infinitude, infinity, perpetuity, timelessness, time without end 2. *Theology* heaven, paradise, the afterlife, the hereafter, the next world

ethereal 1. dainty, delicate, exquisite, fine, insubstantial, light, rarefied, refined, subtle, tenuous 2. aerial, airy, fairy, impalpable, intangible, light, rarefied 3. celestial, empyreal, heavenly, spiritual, sublime, unearthly, unworldly

ethical conscientious, correct, decent, fair, fitting, good, honest, honourable, just, moral, principled, proper, right, righteous, upright, virtuous

Antonyms dishonourable, disreputable, immoral, improper, indecent, low-down (*Inf.*), underhand, unethical, unfair, unscrupulous, unseemly

ethics conscience, moral code, morality, moral philosophy, moral values, principles, rules of conduct, standards

ethnic cultural, folk, indigenous, national, native, racial, traditional

ethos attitude, beliefs, character, disposition, ethic, spirit, tenor

etiolated achromatic, blanched, bleached, colourless, faded, pale, wan, washed out, white, whitened

etiquette civility, code, convention, courtesy, customs, decorum, formalities, good *or* proper behaviour, manners, politeness, politesse, propriety, protocol, rules, usage

eulogize acclaim, applaud, commend, compliment, crack up (*Inf.*), cry up, exalt, extol, glorify, laud, magnify (*Archaic*), panegyrize, pay tribute to, praise, sing *or* sound the praises of

eulogy acclaim, acclamation, accolade, applause, commendation, compliment, encomium, exaltation, glorification, laudation, paean, panegyric, plaudit, praise, tribute

euphonic, euphonious canorous (*Rare*), clear, consonant, dulcet, harmonious, mellifluous, mellow, melodic, melodious, musical, pleasing to the ear, silvery, sweet-toned, tuneful

euphony consonance, harmony, mellifluousness, mellowness, melodiousness, melody, music, musicality, tunefulness, unison

euphoria bliss, ecstasy, elation, exaltation, exhilaration, exultation, glee, high spirits, intoxication, joy, joyousness, jubilation, rapture, transport

Antonyms depression, despair, despondency, dolefulness, downheartedness, dumps (*Inf.*), gloominess, hopelessness, low spirits, melancholia, melancholy, sadness, the blues

evacuate 1. abandon, clear, decamp, depart, desert, forsake, leave, move out, pull out, quit, relinquish, remove, vacate, withdraw 2. crap (*Taboo sl.*), defecate, discharge, eject, eliminate, empty, excrete, expel, shit (*Taboo sl.*), void

evade 1. avoid, body-swerve (*Scot.*), circumvent, decline, dodge, duck, elude, escape, escape the clutches of, eschew, get away from, shirk, shun, sidestep, steer clear of 2. balk, circumvent, cop out (*Sl.*), equivocate, fence, fend off, flannel (*Brit. inf.*), fudge, hedge, parry, prevaricate, quibble, waffle (*Inf., chiefly Brit.*)

Antonyms brave, confront, encounter, face, meet, meet face to face

evaluate appraise, assay, assess, calculate, estimate, gauge, judge, rank, rate, reckon, size up (*Inf.*), value, weigh

evaluation appraisal, assessment, calculation, estimate, estimation, judgment, opinion, rating, valuation

evanesce clear, disappear, disperse, dissolve, evaporate, fade, melt, vanish

evanescence brevity, briefness, ephemerality, ephemeralness, fleetingness, fugaciousness, fugacity, impermanence, momentariness, transience, transitoriness

evanescent brief, ephemeral, fading, fleeting, fugacious, fugitive, impermanent, momentary, passing, short-lived, transient, transitory, vanishing

evangelical, evangelistic crusading, missionary, propagandizing, proselytizing, zealous

evaporate 1. dehydrate, desiccate, dry, dry up, vaporize 2. dematerialize, disappear, dispel, disperse, dissipate, dissolve, evanesce, fade, fade away, melt, melt away, vanish

evaporation 1. dehydration, desiccation, drying, drying up, vaporization 2. dematerialization, disappearance, dispelling, dispersal, dissipation, dissolution, evanescence, fading, fading away, melting, melting away, vanishing

evasion artifice, avoidance, circumvention, cop-out (*Sl.*), cunning, dodge, elusion, equivocation, escape, evasiveness, excuse, fudging, obliqueness, pretext, prevarication, ruse, shift, shirking, shuffling, sophism, sophistry, subterfuge, trickery, waffle (*Inf., chiefly Brit.*)

evasive cagey (*Inf.*), casuistic, casuistical, cunning, deceitful, deceptive, devious, dissembling, elusive, elusory, equivocating, indirect, misleading, oblique, prevaricating, shifty, shuffling, slippery, sophistical, tricky
Antonyms candid, direct, frank, guileless, honest, open, straight, straightforward, truthful, unequivocating

eve 1. day before, night before, vigil 2. brink, edge, point, threshold, verge

even *adj.* 1. flat, flush, horizontal, level, parallel, plane, plumb, smooth, steady, straight, true, uniform 2. constant, metrical, regular, smooth, steady, unbroken, uniform, uninterrupted, unvarying, unwavering 3. calm, composed, cool, equable, equanimous, even-tempered, imperturbable, peaceful, placid, serene, stable, steady, tranquil, undisturbed, unexcitable, unruffled, well-balanced 4. coequal, commensurate, comparable, drawn, equal, equalized, equally balanced, fifty-fifty (*Inf.*), identical, level, level pegging (*Brit. inf.*), like, matching, neck and neck, on a par, parallel, similar, square, the same, tied, uniform 5. balanced, disinterested, dispassionate, equitable, fair, fair and square, impartial, just, unbiased, unprejudiced 6. **get even (with)** *Inf.* be revenged *or* revenge oneself, even the score, give tit for tat, pay back, reciprocate, repay, requite, return like for like, settle the score, take an eye for an eye, take vengeance ~*adv.* 7. all the more, much, still, yet 8. despite, disregarding, in spite of, notwithstanding 9. **even as** at the same time as, at the time that, during the time that, exactly as, just as, while, whilst 10. **even so** all the same, be that as it may, despite (that), however, in spite of (that), nevertheless, nonetheless, notwithstanding (that), still, yet ~*v.* 11. *Often followed by* **out** *or* **up** align, balance, become level, equal, equalize, flatten, level, match, regularize, smooth, square, stabilize, steady 12. **even the score** be revenged *or* revenge oneself, equalize, get even (*Inf.*), give tit for tat, pay (someone) back, reciprocate, repay, requite, return like for like, settle the score, take an eye for an eye, take vengeance
Antonyms (*senses 1 & 2*) asymmetrical, awry, broken, bumpy, changeable, changing, curving, different, fluctuating, irregular, odd, rough, twisting, undulating, uneven, variable, wavy (*sense 3*) agitated, changeable, emotional, excitable, quick-tempered, unpredictable (*sense 4*) disproportionate, ill-matched, imbalanced, irregular, unequal, uneven (*sense 5*) biased, partial, prejudiced, unbalanced, unequal, unfair

even-handed balanced, disinterested, equitable, fair, fair and square, impartial, just, unbiased, unprejudiced

evening crepuscule, dusk, e'en (*Archaic or poetic*), eve, even (*Archaic*), eventide (*Archaic or poetic*), gloaming (*Scot. or poetic*), twilight, vesper (*Archaic*)

event 1. adventure, affair, business, circumstance, escapade, episode, experience, fact, happening, incident, matter, milestone, occasion, occurrence 2. conclusion, consequence, effect, end, issue, outcome, result, termination, upshot 3. bout, competition, contest, game, tournament 4. **at all events** at any rate, come what may, in any case, in any event, regardless, whatever happens

even-tempered calm, composed, cool, cool-headed, equable, imperturbable, level-headed, peaceful, placid, serene, steady, tranquil, unexcitable, unruffled
Antonyms emotional, excitable, hasty, highly-strung, hot-headed, hot-tempered, irascible, quick-tempered, temperamental, touchy, volatile

eventful active, busy, consequential, critical, crucial, decisive, dramatic, exciting, fateful, full, historic, important, lively, memorable, momentous, notable, noteworthy, remarkable, significant
Antonyms commonplace, dull, humdrum, insignificant, ordinary, trivial, uneventful, unexceptional, unexciting, unimportant, uninteresting, unremarkable

eventual concluding, consequent, ensuing, final, future, later, overall, prospective, resulting, ultimate

eventuality case, chance, contingency, event, likelihood, possibility, probability

eventually after all, at the end of the day, finally, in the course of time, in the end, in the long run, one day, some day, some time, sooner or later, ultimately, when all is said and done

eventuate be a consequence, be consequent, come about, come to pass (*Archaic*), ensue, follow, issue, result

ever 1. at all, at any time (period, point), by any chance, in any case, on any occasion 2.

always, at all times, aye (*Scot.*), constantly, continually, endlessly, eternally, everlastingly, evermore, for ever, incessantly, perpetually, relentlessly, to the end of time, unceasingly, unendingly

everlasting 1. abiding, deathless, endless, eternal, immortal, imperishable, indestructible, infinite, interminable, never-ending, perpetual, timeless, undying 2. ceaseless, constant, continual, continuous, endless, incessant, interminable, never-ending, unceasing, uninterrupted, unremitting

Antonyms brief, ephemeral, fleeting, impermanent, passing, short-lived, temporary, transient, transitory

evermore always, eternally, ever, for ever, *in perpetuum*, to the end of time

every all, each, each one, the whole number

everybody all and sundry, each one, each person, everyone, every person, one and all, the whole world

everyday 1. daily, quotidian 2. accustomed, banal, common, common or garden (*Inf.*), commonplace, conventional, customary, dull, familiar, frequent, habitual, informal, mundane, ordinary, routine, run-of-the-mill, stock, unexceptional, unimaginative, usual, wonted, workaday

Antonyms best, exceptional, exciting, extraordinary, incidental, individual, infrequent, interesting, irregular, now and then, occasional, original, outlandish, periodic, special, uncommon, unusual

everyone all and sundry, each one, each person, everybody, every person, one and all, the whole world

everything all, each thing, the aggregate, the entirety, the lot, the sum, the total, the whole caboodle (*Inf.*), the whole lot

everywhere all around, all over, far and wide *or* near, high and low, in each place, in every place, omnipresent, the world over, to *or* in all places, ubiquitous, ubiquitously

evict boot out (*Inf.*), chuck out (*Inf.*), dislodge, dispossess, eject, expel, kick out (*Inf.*), oust, put out, remove, show the door (to), throw on to the streets, throw out, turf out (*Inf.*), turn out

eviction clearance, dislodgement, dispossession, ejection, expulsion, ouster (*Law*), removal

evidence 1. *n.* affirmation, attestation, averment, confirmation, corroboration, data, declaration, demonstration, deposition, grounds, indication, manifestation, mark, proof, sign, substantiation, testimony, token, witness 2. *v.* demonstrate, denote, display, evince, exhibit, indicate, manifest, prove, reveal, show, signify, testify to, witness

evident apparent, blatant, clear, conspicuous, incontestable, incontrovertible, indisputable, manifest, noticeable, obvious, palpable, patent, perceptible, plain, tangible, unmistakable, visible

Antonyms ambiguous, concealed, doubtful, dubious, hidden, imperceptible, obscure, questionable, secret, uncertain, unclear, unknown, vague

evidently 1. clearly, doubtless, doubtlessly, incontestably, incontrovertibly, indisputably, manifestly, obviously, patently, plainly, undoubtedly, unmistakably, without question 2. apparently, it seems, it would seem, ostensibly, outwardly, seemingly, to all appearances

evil *adj.* 1. bad, base, corrupt, depraved, heinous, immoral, iniquitous, maleficent, malevolent, malicious, malignant, nefarious, reprobate, sinful, vicious, vile, villainous, wicked, wrong ~*n.* 2. badness, baseness, corruption, curse, depravity, heinousness, immorality, iniquity, maleficence, malignity, sin, sinfulness, turpitude, vice, viciousness, villainy, wickedness, wrong, wrongdoing ~*adj.* 3. baneful (*Archaic*), calamitous, catastrophic, deleterious, destructive, detrimental, dire, disastrous, harmful, hurtful, inauspicious, injurious, mischievous, painful, pernicious, ruinous, sorrowful, unfortunate, unlucky, woeful ~*n.* 4. affliction, calamity, catastrophe, disaster, harm, hurt, ill, injury, mischief, misery, misfortune, pain, ruin, sorrow, suffering, woe ~*adj.* 5. foul, mephitic, noxious, offensive, pestilential, putrid, unpleasant, vile

evince attest, bespeak, betoken, demonstrate, display, establish, evidence, exhibit, express, indicate, make clear, make evident, manifest, reveal, show, signify

evoke 1. arouse, awaken, call, excite, give rise to, induce, recall, rekindle, stimulate, stir up, summon up 2. call forth, educe (*Rare*), elicit, produce, provoke 3. arouse, call, call forth, conjure up, invoke, raise, summon

Antonyms contain, hold in check, inhibit, muffle, repress, restrain, smother, stifle, suppress

evolution development, enlargement, evolvement, expansion, growth, increase, maturation, progress, progression, unfolding, unrolling, working out

evolve develop, disclose, educe, elaborate, enlarge, expand, grow, increase, mature, open, progress, unfold, unroll, work out

exacerbate aggravate (*Inf.*), embitter, enrage, envenom, exasperate, excite, inflame, infuriate, intensify, irritate, madden, provoke, vex, worsen

exact *adj.* 1. accurate, careful, correct, definite, explicit, express, faithful, faultless, identical, literal, methodical, orderly, particular, precise, right, specific, true, unequivocal, unerring, veracious, very 2. careful, exacting, meticulous, painstaking, punctilious, rigorous, scrupulous, severe, strict ~*v.* 3. call for, claim, command, compel, demand, extort, extract, force, impose, insist upon, require, squeeze, wrest, wring

Antonyms *adj.* approximate, careless, imprecise, inaccurate, incorrect, indefinite, inexact, loose, rough, slovenly

exacting demanding, difficult, hard, harsh, imperious, oppressive, painstaking, rigid, rigorous, severe, stern, strict, stringent, taxing, tough, unsparing

Antonyms easy, easy-peasy (*Sl.*), effortless, no bother, simple, undemanding

exaction compulsion, contribution, demand, extortion, imposition, oppression, rapacity, requirement, requisition, shakedown (*U.S. sl.*), squeeze (*Inf.*), tribute

exactitude accuracy, carefulness, correctness, exactness, faithfulness, faultlessness, nicety, orderliness, painstakingness, preciseness, precision, promptitude, regularity, rigorousness, rigour, scrupulousness, strictness, truth, unequivocalness, veracity

exactly *adv.* 1. accurately, carefully, correctly, definitely, explicitly, faithfully, faultlessly, literally, methodically, precisely, rigorously, scrupulously, severely, strictly, truly, truthfully, unequivocally, unerringly, veraciously 2. absolutely, bang, explicitly, expressly, indeed, in every respect, just, particularly, precisely, quite, specifically 3. **not exactly** *Ironical* by no means, certainly not, hardly, in no manner, in no way, not at all, not by any means, not quite, not really ~*interj.* 4. absolutely, assuredly, as you say, certainly, indeed, just so, of course, precisely, quite, quite so, spot-on (*Brit. inf.*), truly

exactness accuracy, carefulness, correctness, exactitude, faithfulness, faultlessness, nicety, orderliness, painstakingness, preciseness, precision, promptitude, regularity, rigorousness, rigour, scrupulousness, strictness, truth, unequivocalness, veracity

Antonyms imprecision, inaccuracy, incorrectness, inexactness, unfaithfulness

exaggerate amplify, embellish, embroider, emphasize, enlarge, exalt, hyperbolize, inflate, lay it on thick (*Inf.*), magnify, make a federal case of (*U.S. inf.*), make a production (out) of (*Inf.*), overdo, overemphasize, overestimate, overstate

exaggerated amplified, exalted, excessive, extravagant, highly coloured, hyped, hyperbolic, inflated, overblown, overdone, overestimated, overstated, over the top (*Inf.*), pretentious, tall (*Inf.*)

exaggeration amplification, embellishment, emphasis, enlargement, exaltation, excess, extravagance, hyperbole, inflation, magnification, overemphasis, overestimation, overstatement, pretension, pretentiousness

Antonyms litotes, meiosis, restraint, underplaying, understatement

exalt 1. advance, aggrandize, dignify, elevate, ennoble, honour, promote, raise, upgrade 2. acclaim, apotheosize, applaud, bless, crack up (*Inf.*), extol, glorify, idolize, laud, magnify (*Archaic*), pay homage to, pay tribute to, praise, reverence, set on a pedestal, worship 3. animate, arouse, electrify, elevate, excite, fire the imagination (of), heighten, inspire, inspirit, stimulate, uplift 4. delight, elate, exhilarate, fill with joy, thrill

exaltation 1. advancement, aggrandizement, dignity, elevation, eminence, ennoblement, grandeur, high rank, honour, loftiness, prestige, promotion, rise, upgrading 2. acclaim, acclamation, apotheosis, applause, blessing, extolment, glorification, glory, homage, idolization, laudation, lionization, magnification, panegyric, plaudits, praise, reverence, tribute, worship 3. animation, elevation, excitement, inspiration, stimulation, uplift 4. bliss, delight, ecstasy, elation, exhilaration, exultation, joy, joyousness, jubilation, rapture, transport

exalted 1. august, dignified, elevated, eminent, grand, high, high-ranking, honoured, lofty, prestigious 2. elevated, high-minded, ideal, intellectual, lofty, noble, sublime, superior, uplifting 3. *Inf.* elevated, exaggerated, excessive, inflated, overblown, pretentious 4. animated, blissful, cock-a-hoop, ecstatic, elated, elevated, excited, exhilarated, exultant, in high spirits, in seventh heaven, inspired, inspirited, joyous, jubilant, on cloud nine (*Inf.*), over the moon (*Inf.*), rapturous, stimulated, transported, uplifted

examination analysis, assay, catechism, checkup, exploration, inquiry, inquisition, inspection, interrogation, investigation, observation, perusal, probe, questioning, quiz, recce (*Sl.*), research, review, scrutiny, search, study, survey, test, trial

examine 1. analyse, appraise, assay, check,

check out, consider, explore, go over *or* through, inspect, investigate, look over, peruse, ponder, pore over, probe, recce (*Sl.*), research, review, scan, scrutinize, sift, study, survey, take stock of, test, vet, weigh, work over 2. catechize, cross-examine, grill (*Inf.*), inquire, interrogate, question, quiz

example 1. case, case in point, exemplification, illustration, instance, sample, specimen 2. archetype, exemplar, ideal, illustration, model, norm, paradigm, paragon, pattern, precedent, prototype, standard 3. admonition, caution, lesson, warning 4. **for example** as an illustration, by way of illustration, e.g., *exempli gratia,* for instance, to cite an instance, to illustrate

exasperate aggravate (*Inf.*), anger, annoy, bug (*Inf.*), embitter, enrage, exacerbate, excite, gall, get (*Inf.*), get in one's hair (*Inf.*), get on one's nerves (*Inf.*), hassle (*Inf.*), incense, inflame, infuriate, irk, irritate, madden, nark (*Brit., Aust., & N.Z. sl.*), needle (*Inf.*), nettle, peeve (*Inf.*), pique, piss one off (*Taboo sl.*), provoke, rankle, rile (*Inf.*), rouse, try the patience of, vex
Antonyms appease, assuage, calm, conciliate, mollify, pacify, placate, soothe

exasperation aggravation (*Inf.*), anger, annoyance, exacerbation, fury, ire (*Literary*), irritation, passion, pique, provocation, rage, vexation, wrath

excavate burrow, cut, delve, dig, dig out, dig up, gouge, hollow, mine, quarry, scoop, trench, tunnel, uncover, unearth

excavation burrow, cavity, cut, cutting, dig, diggings, ditch, dugout, hole, hollow, mine, pit, quarry, shaft, trench, trough

exceed 1. beat, be superior to, better, cap (*Inf.*), eclipse, excel, go beyond, outdistance, outdo, outreach, outrun, outshine, outstrip, overtake, pass, run rings around (*Inf.*), surmount, surpass, top, transcend 2. go beyond the bounds of, go over the limit of, go over the top, overstep

exceeding enormous, exceptional, excessive, extraordinary, great, huge, pre-eminent, superior, superlative, surpassing, vast

exceedingly enormously, especially, exceptionally, excessively, extraordinarily, extremely, greatly, highly, hugely, inordinately, superlatively, surpassingly, unusually, vastly, very

excel 1. beat, be superior, better, cap (*Inf.*), eclipse, exceed, go beyond, outdo, outrival, outshine, pass, run rings around (*Inf.*), surmount, surpass, top, transcend 2. be good, be master of, be proficient, be skilful, be talented, predominate, shine, show talent, take precedence

excellence distinction, eminence, fineness, goodness, greatness, high quality, merit, perfection, pre-eminence, purity, superiority, supremacy, transcendence, virtue, worth

excellent A1 *or* A-one (*Inf.*), admirable, boffo (*Sl.*), brill (*Inf.*), brilliant, capital, champion, chillin' (*U.S. sl.*), choice, cracking (*Brit. inf.*), crucial (*Sl.*), def (*Sl.*), distinguished, estimable, exemplary, exquisite, fine, first-class, first-rate, good, great, jim-dandy (*Sl.*), mean (*Sl.*), mega (*Sl.*), meritorious, notable, noted, outstanding, prime, select, sovereign, sterling, superb, superior, superlative, tiptop, top-notch (*Inf.*), topping (*Brit. sl.*), world-class, worthy
Antonyms abysmal, bad, dreadful, faulty, imperfect, incompetent, inexpert, inferior, lousy (*Sl.*), mediocre, piss-poor (*Taboo sl.*), poor, rotten (*Inf.*), second-class, second-rate, substandard, terrible, unskilled

except 1. *prep. Also* **except for** apart from, bar, barring, besides, but, excepting, excluding, exclusive of, omitting, other than, save (*Archaic*), saving, with the exception of 2. *v.* ban, bar, disallow, exclude, leave out, omit, pass over, reject, rule out

exception 1. debarment, disallowment, excepting, exclusion, leaving out, omission, passing over, rejection 2. anomaly, departure, deviation, freak, inconsistency, irregularity, oddity, peculiarity, quirk, special case 3. **take exception** be offended, be resentful, demur, disagree, object, quibble, take offence, take umbrage

exceptionable disagreeable, inappropriate, objectionable, unacceptable, unbearable, undesirable, unsatisfactory, unwelcome

exceptional 1. aberrant, abnormal, anomalous, atypical, deviant, extraordinary, inconsistent, irregular, odd, peculiar, rare, singular, special, strange, uncommon, unusual 2. excellent, extraordinary, marvellous, notable, outstanding, phenomenal, prodigious, remarkable, special, superior
Antonyms average, awful, bad, common, customary, familiar, lousy (*Sl.*), mediocre, normal, ordinary, regular, second-rate, straightforward, typical, unexceptional, unremarkable, usual

excerpt 1. *n.* citation, extract, fragment, part, passage, pericope, piece, portion, quotation, section, selection 2. *v.* cite, cull, extract, pick out, quote, select, take

excess *n.* 1. glut, leftover, overabundance, overdose, overflow, overload, plethora, remainder, superabundance, superfluity, surfeit, surplus, too much 2. debauchery, dissipation, dissoluteness, exorbitance, extravagance, immoderation, intemperance, overindulgence, prodigality, unrestraint ~*adj.* 3. extra, leftover, redundant, remaining, residual, spare, superfluous, surplus

Antonyms (*sense 1*) dearth, deficiency, insufficiency, lack, shortage, want (*sense 2*) moderation, restraint, self-control, self-discipline, self-restraint, temperance

excessive disproportionate, enormous, exaggerated, exorbitant, extravagant, extreme, immoderate, inordinate, intemperate, needless, O.T.T. (*Sl.*), overdone, overmuch, over the top (*Sl.*), prodigal, profligate, superfluous, too much, unconscionable, undue, unreasonable

exchange *v.* 1. bandy, barter, change, commute, convert into, interchange, reciprocate, swap (*Inf.*), switch, trade, truck ~*n.* 2. barter, dealing, interchange, quid pro quo, reciprocity, substitution, swap (*Inf.*), switch, tit for tat, trade, traffic, truck 3. Bourse, market

excise[1] customs, duty, impost, levy, surcharge, tariff, tax, toll

excise[2] 1. cross out, cut, delete, destroy, eradicate, erase, expunge, exterminate, extirpate, strike out 2. cut off *or* out, extract, remove

excision deletion, destruction, eradication, extermination, extirpation, removal

excitable edgy, emotional, hasty, highly strung, hot-headed, hot-tempered, irascible, mercurial, nervous, passionate, quick-tempered, sensitive, susceptible, temperamental, testy, touchy, uptight (*Inf.*), violent, volatile

Antonyms calm, cool, cool-headed, even-tempered, imperturbable, laid-back (*Inf.*), placid, unexcitable, unruffled

excite agitate, animate, arouse, awaken, discompose, disturb, electrify, elicit, evoke, fire, foment, galvanize, incite, inflame, inspire, instigate, kindle, move, provoke, quicken, rouse, stimulate, stir up, thrill, titillate, waken, whet

excited aflame, agitated, animated, aroused, awakened, discomposed, disturbed, enthusiastic, feverish, flurried, high (*Inf.*), hot and bothered (*Inf.*), moved, nervous, overwrought, roused, stimulated, stirred, thrilled, tumultuous, wild, worked up

excitement 1. action, activity, ado, adventure, agitation, animation, commotion, discomposure, elation, enthusiasm, ferment, fever, flurry, furore, heat, kicks (*Inf.*), passion, perturbation, thrill, tumult, warmth 2. impulse, incitement, instigation, motivation, motive, provocation, stimulation, stimulus, urge

exciting dramatic, electrifying, exhilarating, inspiring, intoxicating, moving, provocative, rip-roaring (*Inf.*), rousing, sensational, sexy (*Inf.*), stimulating, stirring, thrilling, titillating

Antonyms boring, dreary, dull, flat, humdrum, mind-numbing, monotonous, unexciting, uninspiring, uninteresting

exclaim call, call out, cry, cry out, declare, ejaculate, proclaim, shout, utter, vociferate, yell

exclamation call, cry, ejaculation, expletive, interjection, outcry, shout, utterance, vociferation, yell

exclude 1. ban, bar, black, blackball, boycott, debar, disallow, embargo, forbid, interdict, keep out, ostracize, prohibit, proscribe, refuse, shut out, veto 2. count out, eliminate, except, ignore, leave out, omit, pass over, preclude, reject, repudiate, rule out, set aside 3. bounce (*Sl.*), drive out, eject, evict, expel, force out, get rid of, oust, remove, throw out

Antonyms accept, admit, allow, count, include, let in, permit, receive, welcome

exclusion 1. ban, bar, boycott, debarment, embargo, forbiddance, interdict, nonadmission, preclusion, prohibition, proscription, refusal, veto 2. elimination, exception, omission, rejection, repudiation 3. eviction, expulsion, removal

exclusive 1. absolute, complete, entire, full, only, private, single, sole, total, undivided, unique, unshared, whole 2. aristocratic, chic, choice, clannish, classy (*Sl.*), cliquish, closed, discriminative, elegant, fashionable, high-toned, limited, narrow, posh (*Inf., chiefly Brit.*), private, restricted, restrictive, ritzy (*Sl.*), select, selfish, snobbish, swish (*Inf., chiefly Brit.*), top-drawer, up-market 3. confined, limited, peculiar, restricted, unique 4. debarring, except for, excepting, excluding, leaving aside, not counting, omitting, restricting, ruling out

Antonyms common, communal, inclusive, nonexclusive, open, partial, popular, public, shared, sociable, unrestricted

excogitate conceive, contemplate, contrive, deliberate, devise, evolve, frame, invent, mull over, ponder, ruminate, think out *or* up, weigh, work out

excommunicate anathematize, ban, banish, cast out, denounce, eject, exclude, expel, proscribe, remove, repudiate, unchurch

excoriate 1. abrade, flay, gall, peel, scarify, scrape, scratch, skin, strip 2. attack, bawl out (*Inf.*), berate, blast, carpet (*Inf.*), castigate, censure, chastise, chew out (*U.S. & Canad. inf.*), condemn, criticize, denounce, flay, give a rocket (*Brit. & N.Z. inf.*), lambast(e), put down, read the riot act, rebuke, reproach, reprove, revile, scold, slam (*Sl.*), tear into (*Inf.*), tear (someone) off a strip (*Brit. inf.*), upbraid, vilify

excrescence 1. *Medical* growth, lump, swelling, tumour, wart 2. knob, lump, outgrowth, process, projection, prominence, protrusion, protuberance

excrete crap (*Taboo sl.*), defecate, discharge, egest, eject, eliminate, evacuate, expel, exude, shit (*Taboo sl.*), void

excruciate afflict, agonize, harrow, rack, torment, torture

excruciating acute, agonizing, burning, exquisite, extreme, harrowing, insufferable, intense, piercing, racking, searing, severe, tormenting, torturous, unbearable, unendurable, violent

exculpate absolve, acquit, clear, discharge, dismiss, excuse, exonerate, free, justify, pardon, release, vindicate

excursion 1. airing, day trip, expedition, jaunt, journey, outing, pleasure trip, ramble, tour, trip 2. detour, deviation, digression, episode, excursus, wandering

excursive devious, diffusive, digressive, discursive, episodic, errant, rambling, roaming, roving, wandering

excusable allowable, defensible, forgivable, justifiable, minor, pardonable, permissible, slight, understandable, venial, warrantable

excuse *v.* 1. absolve, acquit, bear with, exculpate, exonerate, extenuate, forgive, indulge, make allowances for, overlook, pardon, pass over, tolerate, turn a blind eye to, wink at 2. apologize for, condone, defend, explain, justify, mitigate, vindicate 3. absolve, discharge, exempt, free, let off, liberate, release, relieve, spare *~n.* 4. apology, defence, explanation, grounds, justification, mitigation, plea, pretext, reason, vindication 5. cop-out (*Sl.*), disguise, evasion, expedient, makeshift, pretence, pretext, semblance, shift, subterfuge 6. *Inf.* apology, makeshift, mockery, substitute, travesty

Antonyms *v.* accuse, arraign, blame, censure, charge, chasten, chastise, criticize, compel, condemn, convict, correct, hold responsible, indict, oblige, punish, sentence *~n.* (*sense 4*) accusation, charge, imputation, indictment

execrable abhorrent, abominable, accursed, atrocious, cringe-making (*Brit. inf.*), damnable, deplorable, despicable, detestable, disgusting, foul, hateful, heinous, horrible, loathsome, nauseous, obnoxious, obscene, odious, offensive, repulsive, revolting, sickening, vile, yucky *or* yukky (*Sl.*)

execrate abhor, abominate, anathematize, condemn, curse, damn, denounce, deplore, despise, detest, excoriate, hate, imprecate, loathe, revile, slam (*Sl.*), vilify

execration abhorrence, abomination, anathema, condemnation, contempt, curse, damnation, detestation, excoriation, hate, hatred, imprecation, loathing, malediction, odium, vilification

execute 1. behead, electrocute, guillotine, hang, kill, put to death, shoot 2. accomplish, achieve, administer, bring off, carry out, complete, consummate, discharge, do, effect, enact, enforce, finish, fulfil, implement, perform, prosecute, put into effect, realize, render 3. *Law* deliver, seal, serve, sign, validate

execution 1. accomplishment, achievement, administration, carrying out, completion, consummation, discharge, effect, enactment, enforcement, implementation, operation, performance, prosecution, realization, rendering 2. capital punishment, hanging, killing 3. delivery, manner, mode, performance, rendition, style, technique 4. *Law* warrant, writ

executioner 1. hangman, headsman 2. assassin, exterminator, hit man (*Sl.*), killer, liquidator, murderer, slayer

executive *n.* 1. administrator, director, manager, official 2. administration, directorate, directors, government, hierarchy, leadership, management *~adj.* 3. administrative, controlling, decision-making, directing, governing, managerial

exemplar 1. criterion, epitome, example, ideal, model, paradigm, paragon, pattern, standard 2. example, exemplification, illustration, instance, prototype, specimen, type

exemplary 1. admirable, commendable, correct, estimable, excellent, fine, good, honourable, ideal, laudable, meritorious, model, praiseworthy, punctilious, sterling 2. admonitory, cautionary, monitory, warning 3. characteristic, illustrative, representative, typical

exemplify demonstrate, depict, display, embody, evidence, exhibit, illustrate, instance, manifest, represent, serve as an example of, show

exempt 1. *v.* absolve, discharge, except, excuse, exonerate, free, grant immunity, let off, liberate, release, relieve, spare 2. *adj.* absolved, clear, discharged, excepted, excused, favoured, free, immune, liberated,

not liable, not subject, privileged, released, spared
Antonyms *adj.* accountable, answerable, chargeable, liable, obligated, responsible, subject

exemption absolution, discharge, dispensation, exception, exoneration, freedom, immunity, privilege, release

exercise *v.* 1. apply, bring to bear, employ, enjoy, exert, practise, put to use, use, utilize, wield 2. discipline, drill, habituate, inure, practise, train, work out 3. afflict, agitate, annoy, burden, distress, disturb, occupy, pain, perturb, preoccupy, trouble, try, vex, worry ~*n.* 4. action, activity, discipline, drill, drilling, effort, labour, toil, training, work, work-out 5. accomplishment, application, discharge, employment, enjoyment, exertion, fulfilment, implementation, practice, use, utilization 6. drill, lesson, practice, problem, schooling, schoolwork, task, work

exert 1. bring into play, bring to bear, employ, exercise, expend, make use of, put forth, use, utilize, wield 2. **exert oneself** apply oneself, bend over backwards (*Inf.*), break one's neck (*Inf.*), bust a gut (*Inf.*), do one's best, do one's damnedest (*Inf.*), endeavour, give it one's all (*Inf.*), give it one's best shot (*Inf.*), go for broke (*Sl.*), go for it (*Inf.*), knock oneself out (*Inf.*), labour, make an all-out effort (*Inf.*), make an effort, rupture oneself (*Inf.*), spare no effort, strain, strive, struggle, toil, try hard, work

exertion action, application, attempt, effort, employment, endeavour, exercise, industry, labour, pains, strain, stretch, struggle, toil, travail (*Literary*), trial, use, utilization

exhalation breath, breathing out, discharge, effluvium, emanation, emission, evaporation, exhaust, expiration, fog, fume, mist, smoke, steam, vapour

exhale breathe, breathe out, discharge, eject, emanate, emit, evaporate, expel, give off, issue, respire, steam

exhaust 1. bankrupt, cripple, debilitate, disable, drain, enervate, enfeeble, fatigue, impoverish, prostrate, sap, tire, tire out, weaken, wear out 2. consume, deplete, dissipate, expend, finish, run through, spend, squander, use up, waste 3. drain, dry, empty, strain, void 4. be emitted, discharge, emanate, escape, issue

exhausted 1. all in (*Sl.*), beat (*Sl.*), clapped out (*Aust. & N.Z. inf.*), crippled, dead (*Inf.*), dead beat (*Inf.*), dead tired, debilitated, disabled, dog-tired (*Inf.*), done in (*Inf.*), drained, enervated, enfeebled, fatigued, jaded, knackered (*Sl.*), out on one's feet (*Inf.*), prostrated, ready to drop, sapped, spent, tired out, wasted, weak, worn out, zonked (*Sl.*) 2. at an end, consumed, depleted, dissipated, done, expended, finished, gone, spent, squandered, used up, wasted 3. bare, drained, dry, empty, void
Antonyms active, animated, conserved, enlivened, invigorated, kept, preserved, refreshed, rejuvenated, replenished, restored, revived, stimulated

exhausting arduous, backbreaking, crippling, debilitating, difficult, draining, enervating, fatiguing, gruelling, hard, laborious, punishing, sapping, strenuous, taxing, testing, tiring

exhaustion 1. debilitation, enervation, fatigue, feebleness, lassitude, prostration, tiredness, weariness 2. consumption, depletion, emptying

exhaustive all-embracing, all-inclusive, all-out (*Inf.*), complete, comprehensive, encyclopedic, extensive, far-reaching, full, full-scale, in-depth, intensive, sweeping, thorough, thoroughgoing, total
Antonyms casual, cursory, desultory, incomplete, perfunctory, sketchy, superficial

exhibit 1. *v.* air, demonstrate, disclose, display, evidence, evince, expose, express, flaunt, indicate, make clear *or* plain, manifest, offer, parade, present, put on view, reveal, show 2. *n.* display, exhibition, illustration, model, show

exhibition airing, demonstration, display, exhibit, expo (*Inf.*), exposition, fair, manifestation, performance, presentation, representation, show, showing, spectacle

exhilarate animate, cheer, delight, elate, enliven, exalt, gladden, inspirit, invigorate, lift, pep *or* perk up, rejoice, stimulate, thrill

exhilarating breathtaking, cheering, enlivening, exalting, exciting, exhilarant, exhilarative, exhilaratory, gladdening, invigorating, stimulating, thrilling, vitalizing

exhilaration animation, cheerfulness, delight, elation, exaltation, excitement, gaiety, gladness, gleefulness, high spirits, hilarity, joy, joyfulness, liveliness, mirth, sprightliness, vivacity
Antonyms dejection, depression, despondency, gloom, low spirits, melancholy, misery, sadness

exhort admonish, advise, beseech, bid, call upon, caution, counsel, encourage, enjoin, entreat, goad, incite, persuade, press, prompt, spur, urge, warn

exhortation admonition, advice, beseeching, bidding, caution, counsel, encouragement, enjoinder (*Rare*), entreaty, goading, incitement, lecture, persuasion, sermon, urging, warning

exhume dig up, disentomb, disinter, unbury, unearth
Antonyms bury, entomb, inearth, inhume, inter

exigency, exigence 1. acuteness, constraint, criticalness, demandingness, difficulty, distress, emergency, imperativeness, necessity, needfulness, pressingness, pressure, stress, urgency 2. constraint, demand, necessity, need, requirement, wont 3. crisis, difficulty, emergency, extremity, fix (*Inf.*), hardship, jam (*Inf.*), juncture, panic stations (*Inf.*), pass, pickle (*Inf.*), pinch, plight, predicament, quandary, scrape (*Inf.*), strait

exigent 1. acute, constraining, critical, crucial, imperative, importunate, insistent, necessary, needful, pressing, urgent 2. arduous, demanding, difficult, exacting, hard, harsh, rigorous, severe, stiff, strict, stringent, taxing, tough

exiguous bare, meagre, negligible, paltry, scanty, skimpy, slender, spare, sparse

exile *n.* 1. banishment, deportation, expatriation, expulsion, ostracism, proscription, separation 2. deportee, émigré, expatriate, outcast, refugee ~*v.* 3. banish, deport, drive out, eject, expatriate, expel, ostracize, oust, proscribe

exist 1. abide, be, be extant, be living, be present, breathe, continue, endure, happen, last, live, obtain, occur, prevail, remain, stand, survive 2. eke out a living, get along *or* by, stay alive, subsist, survive

existence 1. actuality, animation, being, breath, continuance, continuation, duration, endurance, life, subsistence, survival 2. being, creature, entity, thing 3. creation, life, reality, the world

existent abiding, around, current, enduring, existing, extant, in existence, living, obtaining, present, prevailing, remaining, standing, surviving

exit *n.* 1. door, egress, gate, outlet, passage out, vent, way out 2. adieu, departure, evacuation, exodus, farewell, going, goodbye, leave-taking, retirement, retreat, withdrawal 3. death, decease, demise, expiry, passing away ~*v.* 4. bid farewell, depart, go away, go offstage (*Theatre*), go out, issue, leave, retire, retreat, say goodbye, take one's leave, withdraw
Antonyms (*sense 1*) entrance, entry, ingress, inlet, opening, way in (*sense 4*) arrive, come *or* go in *or* into, enter, make an entrance

exodus departure, evacuation, exit, flight, going out, leaving, migration, retirement, retreat, withdrawal

exonerate 1. absolve, acquit, clear, discharge, dismiss, exculpate, excuse, justify, pardon, vindicate 2. discharge, dismiss, except, excuse, exempt, free, let off, liberate, release, relieve

exoneration 1. absolution, acquittal, amnesty, discharge, dismissal, exculpation, justification, pardon, vindication 2. deliverance, discharge, dismissal, exception, exemption, freeing, liberation, release, relief

exorbitance excess, excessiveness, extravagance, extremeness, immoderateness, immoderation, inordinateness, preposterousness, unreasonableness

exorbitant enormous, excessive, extortionate, extravagant, extreme, immoderate, inordinate, outrageous, preposterous, ridiculous, unconscionable, undue, unreasonable, unwarranted
Antonyms cheap, fair, moderate, reasonable

exorcise adjure, cast out, deliver (from), drive out, expel, purify

exorcism adjuration, casting out, deliverance, driving out, expulsion, purification

exordium beginning, foreword, introduction, opening, opening remarks, preamble, preface, prelude, proem, prolegomenon, prologue

exotic 1. alien, external, extraneous, extrinsic, foreign, imported, introduced, naturalized, not native 2. bizarre, colourful, curious, different, extraordinary, fascinating, glamorous, mysterious, outlandish, peculiar, strange, striking, unfamiliar, unusual
Antonyms (*sense 2*) conventional, familiar, ordinary, pedestrian, plain, run-of-the-mill, unmemorable, unremarkable

expand 1. amplify, augment, bloat, blow up, broaden, develop, dilate, distend, enlarge, extend, fatten, fill out, grow, heighten, increase, inflate, lengthen, magnify, multiply, prolong, protract, swell, thicken, wax, widen 2. diffuse, open (out), outspread, spread (out), stretch (out), unfold, unfurl, unravel, unroll 3. amplify, develop, dilate, elaborate, embellish, enlarge, expatiate, expound, flesh out, go into detail
Antonyms abbreviate, close, condense, contract, decrease, reduce, shorten, shrink

expanse area, breadth, extent, field, plain, range, space, stretch, sweep, tract

expansion amplification, augmentation, development, diffusion, dilatation, distension, enlargement, expanse, growth, increase, inflation, magnification, multiplication, opening out, spread, swelling, unfolding, unfurling

expansive 1. dilating, distending, elastic, enlargeable, expanding, extendable, inflatable, stretching, stretchy, swelling 2. all-embracing, broad, comprehensive, extensive, far-reaching, inclusive, thorough, voluminous, wide, wide-ranging, widespread 3. affable, communicative, easy, effusive, free, friendly, garrulous, genial, loquacious, open, outgoing, sociable, talkative, unreserved, warm

expatiate amplify, descant, develop, dilate, dwell on, elaborate, embellish, enlarge, expound, go into detail

expatriate 1. *adj.* banished, emigrant, émigré, exiled, refugee 2. *n.* emigrant, émigré, exile 3. *v.* banish, exile, expel, ostracize, proscribe

expect 1. assume, believe, calculate, conjecture, forecast, foresee, imagine, presume, reckon, suppose, surmise, think, trust 2. anticipate, await, bargain for, contemplate, envisage, hope for, look ahead to, look for, look forward to, predict, watch for 3. call for, count on, demand, insist on, look for, rely upon, require, want, wish

expectancy 1. anticipation, assumption, belief, conjecture, expectation, hope, looking forward, prediction, presumption, probability, supposition, surmise, suspense, waiting 2. likelihood, outlook, prospect

expectant 1. anticipating, anxious, apprehensive, awaiting, eager, expecting, hopeful, in suspense, ready, watchful 2. enceinte, expecting (*Inf.*), gravid, pregnant

expectation 1. assumption, assurance, belief, calculation, confidence, conjecture, forecast, likelihood, presumption, probability, supposition, surmise, trust 2. anticipation, apprehension, chance, expectancy, fear, hope, looking forward, outlook, possibility, prediction, promise, prospect, suspense 3. demand, insistence, reliance, requirement, trust, want, wish

expecting enceinte, expectant, gravid, in the club (*Brit. sl.*), in the family way (*Inf.*), pregnant, with child

expediency, expedience 1. advantageousness, advisability, appropriateness, aptness, benefit, convenience, desirability, effectiveness, fitness, helpfulness, judiciousness, meetness, practicality, pragmatism, profitability, properness, propriety, prudence, suitability, usefulness, utilitarianism, utility 2. contrivance, device, expedient, makeshift, manoeuvre, means, measure, method, resort, resource, scheme, shift, stopgap, stratagem, substitute

expedient 1. *adj.* advantageous, advisable, appropriate, beneficial, convenient, desirable, effective, fit, helpful, judicious, meet, opportune, politic, practical, pragmatic, profitable, proper, prudent, suitable, useful, utilitarian, worthwhile 2. *n.* contrivance, device, expediency, makeshift, manoeuvre, means, measure, method, resort, resource, scheme, shift, stopgap, stratagem, substitute

Antonyms *adj.* detrimental, disadvantageous, futile, harmful, ill-advised, impractical, imprudent, inadvisable, inappropriate, ineffective, inexpedient, unwise, wrong

expedite accelerate, advance, assist, dispatch, facilitate, forward, hasten, hurry, precipitate, press, promote, quicken, rush, speed (up), urge

Antonyms block, curb, decelerate, delay, handicap, hold up, obstruct, restrict, slow up *or* down

expedition 1. enterprise, excursion, exploration, journey, mission, quest, safari, tour, trek, trip, undertaking, voyage 2. company, crew, explorers, team, travellers, voyagers, wayfarers 3. alacrity, celerity, dispatch, expeditiousness, haste, hurry, promptness, quickness, rapidity, readiness, speed, swiftness

expeditious active, alert, brisk, diligent, efficient, fast, hasty, immediate, instant, nimble, prompt, quick, rapid, ready, speedy, swift

expel 1. belch, cast out, discharge, dislodge, drive out, eject, remove, spew, throw out 2. ban, banish, bar, black, blackball, discharge, dismiss, drum out, evict, exclude, exile, expatriate, give the bum's rush (*Sl.*), oust, proscribe, relegate, send packing, show one the door, throw out, throw out on one's ear (*Inf.*), turf out (*Inf.*)

Antonyms (*sense 2*) admit, allow to enter, give access, let in, receive, take in, welcome

expend consume, disburse, dissipate, employ, exhaust, fork out (*Sl.*), go through, lay out (*Inf.*), pay out, shell out (*Inf.*), spend, use (up)

expendable dispensable, inessential, nonessential, replaceable, unimportant, unnecessary

Antonyms crucial, essential, indispensable, key, necessary, vital

expenditure application, charge, consumption, cost, disbursement, expense, outgoings, outlay, output, payment, spending, use

expense charge, consumption, cost, disbursement, expenditure, loss, outlay, output, payment, sacrifice, spending, toll, use

expensive costly, dear, excessive, exorbitant, extravagant, high-priced, inordinate, lavish, overpriced, rich, steep (*Inf.*), stiff

Antonyms bargain, budget, cheap, cut-price, economical, inexpensive, low-cost, low-priced, reasonable

experience *n.* 1. contact, doing, evidence, exposure, familiarity, involvement, know-how (*Inf.*), knowledge, observation, participation, practice, proof, training, trial, understanding 2. adventure, affair, encounter, episode, event, happening, incident, occurrence, ordeal, test, trial ~*v.* 3. apprehend, become familiar with, behold, encounter, endure, face, feel, go through, have, know, live through, meet, observe, participate in, perceive, sample, sense, suffer, sustain, taste, try, undergo

experienced 1. accomplished, adept, capable, competent, expert, familiar, knowledgeable, master, practised, professional, qualified, seasoned, skilful, tested, trained, tried, veteran, well-versed 2. knowing, mature, sophisticated, wise, worldly, worldly-wise

Antonyms apprentice, green, incompetent, inexperienced, new, unqualified, unskilled, untrained, untried

experiment 1. *n.* assay, attempt, examination, experimentation, investigation, procedure, proof, research, test, trial, trial and error, trial run, venture 2. *v.* assay, examine, investigate, put to the test, research, sample, test, try, verify

experimental empirical, exploratory, pilot, preliminary, probationary, provisional, speculative, tentative, test, trial, trial-and-error

expert 1. *n.* ace (*Inf.*), adept, authority, buff (*Inf.*), connoisseur, dab hand (*Brit. inf.*), hotshot (*Inf.*), master, maven (*U.S.*), past master, pro (*Inf.*), professional, specialist, virtuoso, whiz (*Inf.*), wizard 2. *adj.* able, adept, adroit, apt, clever, deft, dexterous, experienced, facile, handy, knowledgeable, master, masterly, practised, professional, proficient, qualified, skilful, skilled, trained, virtuoso

Antonyms *n.* amateur, dabbler, ham, layman, nonprofessional, novice ~*adj.* amateurish, cack-handed (*Inf.*), clumsy, incompetent, inexperienced, unpractised, unqualified, unskilled, untrained

expertise ableness, adroitness, aptness, cleverness, command, craft, deftness, dexterity, expertness, facility, judgment, knack, know-how (*Inf.*), knowledge, masterliness, mastery, proficiency, skilfulness, skill

expertness ableness, adroitness, aptness, command, craft, deftness, dexterity, expertise, facility, judgment, know-how (*Inf.*), knowledge, masterliness, mastery, proficiency, skilfulness, skill

expiate atone for, do penance for, make amends for, redeem, redress

expiation amends, atonement, penance, redemption, redress, shrift (*Archaic*)

expiration 1. cessation, close, conclusion, end, expiry, finis, finish, termination 2. death, decease, demise, departure

expire 1. cease, close, come to an end, conclude, end, finish, lapse, run out, stop, terminate 2. breathe out, emit, exhale, expel 3. buy it (*U.S. sl.*), check out (*U.S. sl.*), croak (*Sl.*), decease, depart, die, go belly-up (*Sl.*), kick it (*Sl.*), kick the bucket (*Inf.*), pass away *or* on, peg it (*Inf.*), peg out (*Inf.*), perish, pop one's clogs (*Inf.*)

explain 1. clarify, clear up, define, demonstrate, describe, disclose, elucidate, explicate (*Formal*), expound, illustrate, interpret, make clear *or* plain, resolve, solve, teach, unfold 2. account for, excuse, give an explanation for, give a reason for, justify

explanation 1. clarification, definition, demonstration, description, elucidation, explication, exposition, illustration, interpretation, resolution 2. account, answer, cause, excuse, justification, meaning, mitigation, motive, reason, sense, significance, vindication

explanatory demonstrative, descriptive, elucidatory, explicative, expository, illuminative, illustrative, interpretive, justifying

explicable accountable, definable, explainable, intelligible, interpretable, justifiable, resolvable, understandable

explicate 1. clarify, clear up, elucidate, explain, expound, interpret, make clear *or* explicit, make plain, unfold, untangle 2. construct, develop, devise, evolve, formulate, work out

explicit absolute, categorical, certain, clear, definite, direct, distinct, exact, express, frank, open, outspoken, patent, plain, positive, precise, specific, stated, straightforward, unambiguous, unequivocal, unqualified, unreserved, upfront (*Inf.*)

Antonyms ambiguous, cryptic, general, implicit, implied, indefinite, indirect, inexact, obscure, oracular, suggested, uncertain, vague

explode 1. blow up, burst, detonate, discharge, erupt, go off, set off, shatter, shiver 2. belie, debunk, discredit, disprove, give the lie to, invalidate, refute, repudiate

exploit *n.* 1. accomplishment, achievement, adventure, attainment, deed, escapade, feat, stunt ~*v.* 2. abuse, impose upon, manipulate, milk, misuse, play on *or* upon, take advantage of 3. capitalize on, cash in on (*Inf.*), make capital out of, make use of, profit by *or* from, put to use, turn to account, use, use to advantage, utilize

exploration 1. analysis, examination, inquiry, inspection, investigation, probe, research, scrutiny, search, study 2. expedition, recce (*Sl.*), reconnaissance, survey, tour, travel, trip

exploratory analytic, experimental, fact-finding, investigative, probing, searching, trial

explore 1. analyse, examine, inquire into, inspect, investigate, look into, probe, prospect, research, scrutinize, search, work over 2. case (*Sl.*), have *or* take a look around, range over, recce (*Sl.*), reconnoitre, scout, survey, tour, travel, traverse

explosion 1. bang, blast, burst, clap, crack, detonation, discharge, outburst, report 2. eruption, fit, outbreak, outburst, paroxysm

explosive 1. unstable, volatile 2. fiery, stormy, touchy, vehement, violent 3. charged, dangerous, hazardous, overwrought, perilous, tense, ugly

exponent 1. advocate, backer, champion, defender, promoter, propagandist, proponent, spokesman, spokeswoman, supporter, upholder 2. commentator, demonstrator, elucidator, expositor, expounder, illustrator, interpreter 3. example, exemplar, illustration, indication, model, norm, sample, specimen, type 4. executant, interpreter, performer, player, presenter

expose 1. display, exhibit, manifest, present, put on view, reveal, show, uncover, unveil 2. air, betray, blow wide open (*Sl.*), bring to light, denounce, detect, disclose, divulge, lay bare, let out, make known, reveal, show up, smoke out, uncover, unearth, unmask 3. endanger, hazard, imperil, jeopardize, lay open, leave open, make vulnerable, risk, subject 4. *With* **to** acquaint with, bring into contact with, familiarize with, introduce to, make conversant with

Antonyms conceal, cover, hide, keep secret, mask, protect, screen, shelter, shield

exposé disclosure, divulgence, exposure, revelation, uncovering

exposed 1. bare, exhibited, laid bare, made manifest, made public, on display, on show, on view, revealed, shown, unconcealed, uncovered, unveiled 2. open, open to the elements, unprotected, unsheltered 3. in danger, in peril, laid bare, laid open, left open, liable, open, susceptible, vulnerable

exposition 1. account, commentary, critique, description, elucidation, exegesis, explanation, explication, illustration, interpretation, presentation 2. demonstration, display, exhibition, expo (*Inf.*), fair, presentation, show

expository descriptive, elucidative, exegetic, explanatory, explicative, explicatory, hermeneutic, illustrative, interpretive

expostulate argue (with), dissuade, protest, reason (with), remonstrate (with)

exposure 1. baring, display, exhibition, manifestation, presentation, publicity, revelation, showing, uncovering, unveiling 2. airing, betrayal, denunciation, detection, disclosure, divulgence, divulging, exposé, revelation, unmasking 3. danger, hazard, jeopardy, risk, vulnerability 4. acquaintance, contact, conversancy, experience, familiarity, introduction, knowledge 5. aspect, frontage, location, outlook, position, setting, view

expound describe, elucidate, explain, explicate (*Formal*), illustrate, interpret, set forth, spell out, unfold

express *v.* 1. articulate, assert, asseverate, communicate, couch, declare, enunciate, phrase, pronounce, put, put across, put into words, say, speak, state, tell, utter, verbalize, voice, word 2. bespeak, convey, denote, depict, designate, disclose, divulge, embody, evince, exhibit, indicate, intimate, make known, manifest, represent, reveal, show, signify, stand for, symbolize, testify 3. extract, force out, press out, squeeze out *~adj.* 4. accurate, categorical, certain, clear, definite, direct, distinct, exact, explicit, outright, plain, pointed, precise, unambiguous 5. clearcut, especial, particular, singular, special 6. direct, fast, high-speed, nonstop, quick, quickie (*Inf.*), rapid, speedy, swift

expression 1. announcement, assertion, asseveration, communication, declaration, enunciation, mention, pronouncement, speaking, statement, utterance, verbalization, voicing 2. demonstration, embodiment, exhibition, indication, manifestation, representation, show, sign, symbol, token 3. air, appearance, aspect, countenance, face, look, mien (*Literary*) 4. choice of words, delivery, diction, emphasis, execution, intonation, language, phraseology, phrasing, speech, style, wording 5. idiom, locution, phrase, remark, set phrase, term, turn of phrase, word

expressionless blank, deadpan, dull, empty, inscrutable, poker-faced (*Inf.*), straight-faced, vacuous, wooden

expressive 1. eloquent, emphatic, energetic, forcible, lively, mobile, moving, poignant, striking, strong, sympathetic, telling, vivid 2. allusive, demonstrative, indicative,

meaningful, pointed, pregnant, revealing, significant, suggestive, thoughtful
Antonyms blank, dead-pan, dull, empty, impassive, inscrutable, poker-faced (*Inf.*), straight-faced, vacuous, wooden

expressly 1. especially, exactly, intentionally, on purpose, particularly, precisely, purposely, specially, specifically 2. absolutely, categorically, clearly, decidedly, definitely, distinctly, explicitly, in no uncertain terms, manifestly, outright, plainly, pointedly, positively, unambiguously, unequivocally, unmistakably

expropriate appropriate, arrogate, assume, commandeer, confiscate, impound, requisition, seize, take, take over

expulsion banishment, debarment, discharge, dislodgment, dismissal, ejection, eviction, exclusion, exile, expatriation, extrusion, proscription, removal

expunge abolish, annihilate, annul, blot out, cancel, delete, destroy, efface, eradicate, erase, excise, exterminate, extinguish, extirpate, obliterate, raze, remove, strike out, wipe out

expurgate blue-pencil, bowdlerize, censor, clean up (*Inf.*), cut, purge, purify

exquisite 1. beautiful, dainty, delicate, elegant, fine, lovely, precious 2. attractive, beautiful, charming, comely, lovely, pleasing, striking 3. admirable, choice, consummate, delicious, excellent, fine, flawless, incomparable, matchless, outstanding, peerless, perfect, rare, select, splendid, superb, superlative 4. appreciative, consummate, cultivated, discerning, discriminating, fastidious, impeccable, meticulous, polished, refined, selective, sensitive 5. acute, excruciating, intense, keen, piercing, poignant, sharp
Antonyms flawed, ill-favoured, imperfect, ugly, unattractive, unlovely, unsightly

extant existent, existing, in existence, living, remaining, subsisting, surviving, undestroyed

extemporaneous, extemporary 1. ad-lib, extempore, free, impromptu, improvisatory, improvised, made-up, offhand, off-the-cuff (*Inf.*), spontaneous, unplanned, unpremeditated, unprepared, unrehearsed 2. expedient, improvised, makeshift, on-the-spot, temporary

extempore *adv./adj.* ad lib, extemporaneous, extemporary, freely, impromptu, improvised, offhand, off the cuff (*Inf.*), off the top of one's head, on the spot, spontaneously, unplanned, unpremeditated, unprepared

extemporize ad-lib, busk, improvise, make up, play (it) by ear, vamp, wing it (*Inf.*)

extend 1. carry on, continue, drag out, draw out, elongate, lengthen, make longer, prolong, protract, spin out, spread out, stretch, unfurl, unroll 2. carry on, continue, go on, last, take 3. amount to, attain, go as far as, reach, spread 4. add to, amplify, augment, broaden, develop, dilate, enhance, enlarge, expand, increase, spread, supplement, widen 5. advance, bestow, confer, give, grant, hold out, impart, offer, present, proffer, put forth, reach out, stretch out, yield
Antonyms abbreviate, abridge, condense, contract, curtail, cut, decrease, limit, reduce, restrict, shorten, take back, withdraw

extended 1. continued, drawn-out, elongated, enlarged, lengthened, long, prolonged, protracted, spread (out), stretched out, unfolded, unfurled, unrolled 2. broad, comprehensive, enlarged, expanded, extensive, far-reaching, large-scale, sweeping, thorough, wide, widespread 3. conferred, outstretched, proffered, stretched out

extension 1. amplification, augmentation, broadening, continuation, delay, development, dilatation, distension, elongation, enlargement, expansion, extent, increase, lengthening, postponement, prolongation, protraction, spread, stretching, widening 2. addendum, addition, adjunct, add-on, annexe, appendage, appendix, branch, ell, supplement, wing

extensive all-inclusive, broad, capacious, commodious, comprehensive, expanded, extended, far-flung, far-reaching, general, great, huge, humongous *or* humungous (*U.S. sl.*), large, large-scale, lengthy, long, pervasive, prevalent, protracted, spacious, sweeping, thorough, universal, vast, voluminous, wholesale, wide, widespread
Antonyms circumscribed, confined, constricted, limited, narrow, restricted, tight

extent 1. ambit, bounds, compass, play, range, reach, scope, sphere, sweep 2. amount, amplitude, area, breadth, bulk, degree, duration, expanse, expansion, length, magnitude, measure, quantity, size, stretch, term, time, volume, width

extenuate 1. decrease, diminish, excuse, lessen, make allowances for, minimize, mitigate, moderate, palliate, play down, qualify, reduce, soften, temper, weaken 2. discount, make light of, underestimate, underrate, undervalue

extenuating justifying, mitigating, moderating, qualifying, serving as an excuse

exterior *n.* 1. appearance, aspect, coating, covering, façade, face, finish, outside, shell, skin, surface *~adj.* 2. external, outer, outermost, outside, outward, superficial,

surface 3. alien, exotic, external, extraneous, extrinsic, foreign, outside
Antonyms *n.* inner, inside, interior *~adj.* domestic, inherent, inside, interior, internal, intrinsic

exterminate abolish, annihilate, destroy, eliminate, eradicate, extirpate

external 1. apparent, exterior, outer, outermost, outside, outward, superficial, surface, visible 2. alien, exotic, exterior, extramural, extraneous, extrinsic, foreign, independent, outside
Antonyms inherent, inner, inside, interior, internal, intrinsic

extinct 1. dead, defunct, gone, lost, vanished 2. doused, extinguished, inactive, out, quenched, snuffed out 3. abolished, defunct, ended, obsolete, terminated, void
Antonyms active, existing, extant, flourishing, living, surviving, thriving

extinction abolition, annihilation, death, destruction, dying out, eradication, excision, extermination, extirpation, obliteration, oblivion

extinguish 1. blow out, douse, put out, quench, smother, snuff out, stifle 2. abolish, annihilate, destroy, eliminate, end, eradicate, erase, expunge, exterminate, extirpate, kill, obscure, remove, suppress, wipe out

extirpate abolish, annihilate, deracinate, destroy, eliminate, eradicate, erase, excise, expunge, exterminate, extinguish, pull up by the roots, remove, root out, uproot, wipe out

extol acclaim, applaud, celebrate, commend, crack up (*Inf.*), cry up, eulogize, exalt, glorify, laud, magnify (*Archaic*), panegyrize, pay tribute to, praise, sing the praises of

extort blackmail, bleed (*Inf.*), bully, coerce, exact, extract, force, squeeze, wrest, wring

extortion 1. blackmail, coercion, compulsion, demand, exaction, force, oppression, rapacity, shakedown (*U.S. sl.*) 2. enormity, exorbitance, expensiveness, overcharging

extortionate 1. excessive, exorbitant, extravagant, immoderate, inflated, inordinate, outrageous, preposterous, sky-high, unreasonable 2. blood-sucking (*Inf.*), exacting, grasping, hard, harsh, oppressive, rapacious, rigorous, severe, usurious
Antonyms (*sense 1*) fair, inexpensive, moderate, modest, reasonable

extra *adj.* 1. accessory, added, additional, add-on, ancillary, auxiliary, fresh, further, more, new, other, supplemental, supplementary 2. excess, extraneous, inessential, leftover, needless, redundant, reserve, spare, supererogatory, superfluous, supernumerary, surplus, unnecessary, unneeded, unused *~n.* 3. accessory, addendum, addition, add-on, adjunct, affix, appendage, appurtenance, attachment, bonus, complement, extension, supernumerary, supplement *~adv.* 4. especially, exceptionally, extraordinarily, extremely, particularly, remarkably, uncommonly, unusually
Antonyms *adj.* (*sense 2*) compulsory, essential, mandatory, necessary, needed, obligatory, required, requisite, vital *~n.* essential, must, necessity, precondition, prerequisite, requirement, requisite

extract *v.* 1. draw, extirpate, pluck out, pull, pull out, remove, take out, uproot, withdraw 2. bring out, derive, draw, elicit, evoke, exact, gather, get, glean, obtain, reap, wrest, wring 3. deduce, derive, develop, educe, elicit, evolve 4. distil, draw out, express, obtain, press out, separate out, squeeze, take out 5. abstract, choose, cite, copy out, cull, cut out, quote, select *~n.* 6. concentrate, decoction, distillate, distillation, essence, juice 7. abstract, citation, clipping, cutting, excerpt, passage, quotation, selection

extraction 1. drawing, extirpation, pulling, removal, taking out, uprooting, withdrawal 2. derivation, distillation, separation 3. ancestry, birth, blood, derivation, descent, family, lineage, origin, parentage, pedigree, race, stock

extraneous 1. accidental, additional, adventitious, extra, incidental, inessential, needless, nonessential, peripheral, redundant, superfluous, supplementary, unessential, unnecessary, unneeded 2. beside the point, immaterial, impertinent, inadmissible, inapplicable, inapposite, inappropriate, inapt, irrelevant, off the subject, unconnected, unrelated 3. adventitious, alien, exotic, external, extrinsic, foreign, out of place, strange

extraordinary amazing, bizarre, curious, exceptional, fantastic, marvellous, notable, odd, outstanding, particular, peculiar, phenomenal, rare, remarkable, singular, special, strange, surprising, uncommon, unfamiliar, unheard-of, unique, unprecedented, unusual, unwonted, weird, wonderful, wondrous (*Archaic or literary*)
Antonyms banal, common, commonplace, customary, everyday, ordinary, unexceptional, unremarkable, usual

extravagance 1. improvidence, lavishness, overspending, prodigality, profligacy, profusion, squandering, waste, wastefulness 2. absurdity, dissipation, exaggeration, excess, exorbitance, folly, immoderation, outrageousness, preposterousness, recklessness, unreasonableness, unrestraint, wildness

extravagant 1. excessive, improvident, imprudent, lavish, prodigal, profligate, spendthrift, wasteful 2. absurd, exaggerated, excessive, exorbitant, fanciful, fantastic, foolish, immoderate, inordinate, O.T.T. (*Sl.*), outrageous, over the top (*Sl.*), preposterous, reckless, unreasonable, unrestrained, wild 3. fancy, flamboyant, flashy, garish, gaudy, grandiose, ornate, ostentatious, pretentious, showy 4. costly, excessive, exorbitant, expensive, extortionate, inordinate, overpriced, steep (*Inf.*), unreasonable

Antonyms careful, close, conservative, down-to-earth, economical, frugal, miserly, moderate, prudent, realistic, reasonable, restrained, sensible, sober, sparing, thrifty, tight-fisted (*Inf.*)

extravaganza display, flight of fancy, pageant, show, spectacle, spectacular

extreme *adj.* 1. acute, great, greatest, high, highest, intense, maximum, severe, supreme, ultimate, utmost, uttermost, worst 2. downright, egregious, exaggerated, exceptional, excessive, extraordinary, extravagant, fanatical, immoderate, inordinate, intemperate, O.T.T. (*Sl.*), out-and-out, outrageous, over the top (*Sl.*), radical, remarkable, sheer, uncommon, unconventional, unreasonable, unusual, utter, zealous 3. dire, Draconian, drastic, harsh, radical, rigid, severe, stern, strict, unbending, uncompromising 4. faraway, far-off, farthest, final, last, most distant, outermost, remotest, terminal, ultimate, utmost, uttermost ~*n.* 5. acme, apex, apogee, boundary, climax, consummation, depth, edge, end, excess, extremity, height, limit, maximum, minimum, nadir, pinnacle, pole, termination, top, ultimate, zenith

Antonyms *adj.* average, common, mild, moderate, modest, nearest, ordinary, reasonable, traditional, unremarkable

extremely acutely, awfully (*Inf.*), exceedingly, exceptionally, excessively, extraordinarily, greatly, highly, inordinately, intensely, markedly, quite, severely, terribly, to *or* in the extreme, ultra, uncommonly, unusually, utterly, very

extremist die-hard, fanatic, radical, ultra, zealot

extremity 1. acme, apex, apogee, border, bound, boundary, brim, brink, edge, end, extreme, frontier, limit, margin, maximum, minimum, nadir, pinnacle, pole, rim, terminal, termination, terminus, tip, top, ultimate, verge, zenith 2. acuteness, climax, consummation, depth, excess, height 3. adversity, crisis, dire straits, disaster, emergency, exigency, hardship, pinch, plight, setback, trouble 4. *Plural* fingers and toes, hands and feet, limbs

extricate clear, deliver, disembarrass, disengage, disentangle, free, get out, get (someone) off the hook (*Sl.*), liberate, release, relieve, remove, rescue, withdraw, wriggle out of

extrinsic alien, exotic, exterior, external, extraneous, foreign, imported, outside, superficial

extrovert amiable, exuberant, gregarious, hearty, out-going, sociable, social

Antonyms introspective, introverted, inward-looking, self-contained, withdrawn

extrude eject, expel, force out, press out, squeeze out, thrust out

exuberance 1. animation, brio, buoyancy, cheerfulness, eagerness, ebullience, effervescence, energy, enthusiasm, excitement, exhilaration, high spirits, life, liveliness, pep, spirit, sprightliness, vigour, vitality, vivacity, zest 2. effusiveness, exaggeration, excessiveness, fulsomeness, lavishness, prodigality, superfluity 3. abundance, copiousness, lavishness, lushness, luxuriance, plenitude, profusion, rankness, richness, superabundance, teemingness

exuberant 1. animated, buoyant, cheerful, chirpy (*Inf.*), eager, ebullient, effervescent, elated, energetic, enthusiastic, excited, exhilarated, full of life, high-spirited, in high spirits, lively, sparkling, spirited, sprightly, upbeat (*Inf.*), vigorous, vivacious, zestful 2. effusive, exaggerated, excessive, fulsome, lavish, overdone, prodigal, superfluous 3. abundant, copious, lavish, lush, luxuriant, overflowing, plenteous, plentiful, profuse, rank, rich, superabundant, teeming

Antonyms (*sense 1*) apathetic, dull, lifeless, subdued, unenthusiastic

exude 1. bleed, discharge, emanate, emit, excrete, filter through, issue, leak, ooze, secrete, seep, sweat, trickle, weep, well forth 2. display, emanate, exhibit, manifest, radiate, show

exult 1. be delighted, be elated, be in high spirits, be joyful, be jubilant, be overjoyed, celebrate, jubilate, jump for joy, make merry, rejoice 2. boast, brag, crow, drool, gloat, glory (in), revel, take delight in, taunt, triumph, vaunt

exultant cock-a-hoop, delighted, elated, exulting, flushed, gleeful, joyful, joyous, jubilant, overjoyed, over the moon (*Inf.*), rapt, rejoicing, revelling, transported, triumphant

exultation 1. celebration, delight, elation, glee, high spirits, joy, joyousness, jubilation, merriness, rejoicing, transport 2. boasting, bragging, crowing, gloating, glory, glorying, revelling, triumph

eye *n.* 1. eyeball, optic (*Inf.*), orb (*Poetic*), peeper (*Sl.*) 2. appreciation, discernment, discrimination, judgment, perception, recognition, taste 3. *Often plural* belief, judgment, mind, opinion, point of view, viewpoint 4. **keep an** *or* **one's eye on** guard, keep in view, keep tabs on (*Inf.*), keep under surveillance, look after, look out for, monitor, observe, pay attention to, regard, scrutinize, supervise, survey, watch, watch over 5. **an eye for an eye** justice, reprisal, requital, retaliation, retribution, revenge, vengeance 6. **lay, clap** *or* **set eyes on** behold, come across, encounter, meet, notice, observe, run into, see 7. **see eye to eye** accord, agree, back, be in unison, coincide, concur, fall in, get on, go along, harmonize, jibe (*Inf.*), subscribe to 8. **up to one's eyes** busy, caught up, engaged, flooded out, fully occupied, inundated, overwhelmed, up to here, up to one's elbows, wrapped up in ~*v.* 9. check, check out (*Inf.*), clock (*Brit. sl.*), contemplate, eyeball (*U.S. sl.*), gaze at, get a load of (*Inf.*), glance at, have *or* take a look at, inspect, look at, peruse, recce (*Sl.*), regard, scan, scrutinize, stare at, study, survey, take a dekko at (*Brit. sl.*), view, watch 10. eye up, give (someone) the (glad) eye, leer at, make eyes at, ogle

eye-catching arresting, attractive, captivating, showy, spectacular, striking

eyeful 1. butcher's (*Brit. sl.*), gander (*Inf.*), gaze, glance, look, shufti (*Brit. sl.*), sight, view 2. beauty, dazzler, knockout (*Inf.*), show, sight, sight for sore eyes (*Inf.*), spectacle, stunner (*Inf.*), vision

eyesight observation, perception, range of vision, sight, vision

eyesore atrocity, blemish, blight, blot, disfigurement, disgrace, horror, mess, monstrosity, sight (*Inf.*), ugliness

eyewitness bystander, looker-on, observer, onlooker, passer-by, spectator, viewer, watcher, witness

F

Fabian attritional, cautious, circumspect, cunctative *or* cunctatory (*Rare*), delaying, procrastinating

fable 1. allegory, apologue, legend, myth, parable, story, tale 2. fabrication, fairy story (*Inf.*), falsehood, fantasy, fib, fiction, figment, invention, lie, romance, tall story (*Inf.*), untruth, urban legend, white lie, yarn (*Inf.*)
Antonyms actuality, certainty, fact, reality, truth, verity

fabled fabulous, famed, famous, fictional, legendary, mythical, storied

fabric 1. cloth, material, stuff, textile, web 2. constitution, construction, foundations, framework, infrastructure, make-up, organization, structure

fabricate 1. assemble, build, construct, erect, fashion, form, frame, make, manufacture, shape 2. coin, concoct, devise, fake, falsify, feign, forge, form, invent, make up, trump up

fabrication 1. assemblage, assembly, building, construction, erection, manufacture, production 2. cock-and-bull story (*Inf.*), concoction, fable, fairy story (*Inf.*), fake, falsehood, fiction, figment, forgery, invention, lie, pork pie (*Brit. sl.*), porky (*Brit. sl.*), myth, untruth

fabulous 1. amazing, astounding, breathtaking, fictitious, immense, inconceivable, incredible, legendary, phenomenal, unbelievable 2. *Inf.* brilliant, fantastic (*Inf.*), magic (*Inf.*), marvellous, out-of-this-world (*Inf.*), sensational (*Inf.*), spectacular, superb, wonderful 3. apocryphal, fantastic, fictitious, imaginary, invented, legendary, made-up, mythical, unreal
Antonyms actual, common, commonplace, credible, genuine, natural, ordinary, real

façade appearance, exterior, face, front, frontage, guise, mask, pretence, semblance, show, veneer

face *n.* 1. clock (*Brit. sl.*), countenance, dial (*Brit. sl.*), features, kisser (*Sl.*), lineaments, mug (*Sl.*), phiz *or* phizog (*Sl.*), physiognomy, visage 2. appearance, aspect, expression, frown, grimace, look, *moue,* pout, scowl, smirk 3. air, appearance, disguise, display, exterior, façade, front, mask, pretence, semblance, show 4. authority, dignity, honour, image, prestige, reputation, self-respect, standing, status 5. *Inf.* assurance, audacity, boldness, brass neck (*Brit. inf.*), cheek (*Inf.*), chutzpah (*U.S. & Canad. inf.*), confidence, effrontery, front, gall (*Inf.*), impudence, neck (*Inf.*), nerve, presumption, sauce (*Inf.*) 6. aspect, cover, exterior, facet, front, outside, right side, side, surface 7. **face to face** *à deux,* confronting, eyeball to eyeball, in confrontation, opposite, tête-à-tête, vis-à-vis 8. **fly in the face of** act in defiance of, defy, disobey, go against, oppose, rebel against, snap one's fingers at (*Inf.*) 9. **on the face of it** apparently, at first sight, seemingly, to all appearances, to the eye 10. **pull** (*or* **make**) **a long face** frown, grimace, knit one's brows, look black (disapproving, displeased, put out, stern), lour *or* lower, pout, scowl, sulk 11. **show one's face** approach, be seen, come, put in *or* make an appearance, show up (*Inf.*), turn up 12. **to one's face** directly, in one's presence, openly, straight ~*v.* 13. be confronted by, brave, come up against, confront, cope with, deal with, defy, encounter, experience, face off (*Sl.*), meet, oppose, tackle 14. be opposite, front onto, give towards *or* onto, look onto, overlook 15. clad, coat, cover, dress, finish, level, line, overlay, sheathe, surface, veneer

face-lift 1. cosmetic surgery, plastic surgery 2. renovation, restoration

facer difficulty, dilemma, how-do-you-do (*Inf.*), poser, problem, puzzle, teaser

facet angle, aspect, face, part, phase, plane, side, slant, surface

facetious amusing, comical, droll, flippant, frivolous, funny, humorous, jesting, jocose, jocular, merry, playful, pleasant, tongue in cheek, unserious, waggish, witty
Antonyms earnest, genuine, grave, lugubrious, pensive, sedate, serious, sincere, sober, thoughtful

face up to accept, acknowledge, come to terms with, confront, cope with, deal with, meet head-on, tackle

facile 1. adept, adroit, dexterous, easy, effortless, fluent, light, proficient, quick, ready, simple, skilful, smooth, uncomplicated 2. cursory, glib, hasty, shallow, slick, superficial
Antonyms awkward, careful, clumsy, dif-

ficult, intractable, maladroit, slow, thoughtful, unskilful

facilitate assist the progress of, ease, expedite, forward, further, help, make easy, promote, smooth the path of, speed up
Antonyms delay, encumber, frustrate, hamper, handicap, hinder, hold up *or* back, impede, obstruct, prevent, restrain, thwart

facility 1. ability, adroitness, craft, dexterity, ease, efficiency, effortlessness, expertness, fluency, gift, knack, proficiency, quickness, readiness, skilfulness, skill, smoothness, talent 2. *Often plural* advantage, aid, amenity, appliance, convenience, equipment, means, opportunity, resource
Antonyms awkwardness, clumsiness, difficulty, hardship, ineptness, maladroitness, pains

facing 1. *adj.* fronting, opposite, partnering 2. *n.* cladding, coating, façade, false front, front, overlay, plaster, reinforcement, revetment, stucco, surface, trimming, veneer

facsimile carbon, carbon copy, copy, duplicate, fax (*Trademark*), photocopy, Photostat (*Trademark*), print, replica, reproduction, transcript, Xerox (*Trademark*)

fact 1. act, deed, event, *fait accompli,* happening, incident, occurrence, performance 2. actuality, certainty, gospel (truth), naked truth, reality, truth 3. circumstance, detail, feature, item, particular, point, specific 4. **in fact** actually, indeed, in point of fact, in reality, in truth, really, truly
Antonyms delusion, fable, fabrication, falsehood, fiction, invention, lie, tall story, untruth, yarn (*Inf.*)

faction 1. bloc, cabal, camp, caucus, clique, coalition, combination, confederacy, contingent, coterie, division, gang, ginger group, group, junta, lobby, minority, party, pressure group, schism, section, sector, set, splinter group 2. conflict, disagreement, discord, disharmony, dissension, disunity, division, divisiveness, friction, infighting, rebellion, sedition, strife, tumult, turbulence
Antonyms (*sense 2*) accord, agreement, amity, assent, concord, consensus, friendship, goodwill, harmony, peace, rapport, unanimity, unity

factious conflicting, contentious, disputatious, dissident, divisive, insurrectionary, litigious, malcontent, mutinous, partisan, rebellious, refractory, rival, sectarian, seditious, troublemaking, tumultuous, turbulent, warring

factitious affected, artificial, assumed, counterfeited, engineered, fabricated, fake, false, imitation, insincere, made-up, manufactured, mock, phoney *or* phony (*Inf.*), pinchbeck, put-on, sham, simulated, spurious, synthetic, unnatural, unreal

factor 1. aspect, cause, circumstance, component, consideration, determinant, element, influence, item, part, point, thing 2. *Scot.* agent, deputy, estate manager, middleman, reeve, steward

factory manufactory (*Obsolete*), mill, plant, works

factotum Girl Friday, handyman, jack of all trades, Man Friday, man of all work, odd job man

facts data, details, gen (*Brit. inf.*), info (*Inf.*), information, the lowdown (*Inf.*), the score (*Inf.*), the whole story

factual accurate, authentic, circumstantial, close, correct, credible, exact, faithful, genuine, literal, matter-of-fact, objective, precise, real, sure, true, true-to-life, unadorned, unbiased, veritable
Antonyms embellished, fanciful, fictitious, fictive, figurative, imaginary, unreal

faculties capabilities, intelligence, powers, reason, senses, wits

faculty 1. ability, adroitness, aptitude, bent, capability, capacity, cleverness, dexterity, facility, gift, knack, power, propensity, readiness, skill, talent, turn 2. branch of learning, department, discipline, profession, school, teaching staff (*Chiefly U.S.*) 3. authorization, licence, prerogative, privilege, right
Antonyms (*sense 1*) failing, inability, shortcoming, unskilfulness, weak point, weakness

fad affectation, craze, fancy, fashion, mania, mode, rage, trend, vogue, whim

fade 1. blanch, bleach, blench, dim, discolour, dull, grow dim, lose colour, lose lustre, pale, wash out 2. decline, die away, die out, dim, disappear, disperse, dissolve, droop, dwindle, ebb, etiolate, evanesce, fail, fall, flag, languish, melt away, perish, shrivel, vanish, vanish into thin air, wane, waste away, wilt, wither

faded bleached, dim, discoloured, dull, etiolated, indistinct, lustreless, pale, washed out

fading declining, decreasing, disappearing, dying, on the decline, vanishing

faeces bodily waste, droppings, dung, excrement, excreta, ordure, stools

fag[1] *n.* bind (*Inf.*), bore, bother, chore, drag (*Inf.*), inconvenience, irritation, nuisance, pain in the arse (*Taboo inf.*)

fag[2] bender (*Sl.*), catamite, dyke (*Sl.*), fairy (*Sl.*), gay, homo (*Inf.*), homosexual, lesbian, nancy boy (*Sl.*), poof (*Sl.*), poofter (*Sl.*), queen (*Sl.*), queer (*Inf., derogatory*), woofter (*Sl.*)

fagged out all in (*Sl.*), beat (*Sl.*), clapped out (*Aust. & N.Z. inf.*), exhausted, fatigued, jaded, jiggered (*Inf.*), knackered (*Sl.*), on one's last legs (*Inf.*), wasted, weary, worn out, zonked (*Sl.*)

fail 1. be defeated, be found lacking *or* wanting, be in vain, be unsuccessful, break down, come a cropper (*Inf.*), come to grief, come to naught, come to nothing, fall, fall short, fall short of, fall through, fizzle out (*Inf.*), flop (*Inf.*), founder, go astray, go belly-up (*Sl.*), go down, go down like a lead balloon (*Inf.*), go up in smoke, meet with disaster, miscarry, misfire, miss, not make the grade (*Inf.*), run aground, turn out badly 2. abandon, break one's word, desert, disappoint, forget, forsake, let down, neglect, omit 3. be on one's last legs (*Inf.*), cease, conk out (*Inf.*), cut out, decline, die, disappear, droop, dwindle, fade, give out, give up, gutter, languish, peter out, sicken, sink, stop working, wane, weaken 4. become insolvent, close down, crash, fold (*Inf.*), go bankrupt, go broke (*Inf.*), go bust (*Inf.*), go into receivership, go out of business, go to the wall, go under, smash 5. **without fail** conscientiously, constantly, dependably, like clockwork, punctually, regularly, religiously, without exception
Antonyms bloom, flourish, grow, pass, prosper, strengthen, succeed, thrive, triumph

failing 1. *n.* blemish, blind spot, defect, deficiency, drawback, error, failure, fault, flaw, foible, frailty, imperfection, lapse, miscarriage, misfortune, shortcoming, weakness 2. *prep.* in default of, in the absence of, lacking
Antonyms (*sense 1*) advantage, asset, forte, metier, speciality, strength, strong suit

failure 1. abortion, breakdown, collapse, defeat, downfall, fiasco, frustration, lack of success, miscarriage, overthrow, wreck 2. black sheep, dead duck (*Sl.*), disappointment, dud (*Inf.*), flop (*Inf.*), incompetent, loser, ne'er-do-well, no-good, no-hoper (*Chiefly Aust.*), nonstarter, washout (*Inf.*) 3. default, deficiency, dereliction, neglect, negligence, nonobservance, nonperformance, nonsuccess, omission, remissness, shortcoming, stoppage 4. breakdown, decay, decline, deterioration, failing, loss 5. bankruptcy, crash, downfall, folding (*Inf.*), insolvency, ruin
Antonyms adequacy, care, effectiveness, fortune, observance, prosperity, strengthening, success, triumph

fain *adv.* 1. as lief (*Rare*), as soon, cheerfully, eagerly, gladly, willingly ~*adj.* 2. anxious, eager, glad, well-pleased 3. compelled, constrained, with no alternative but

faint *adj.* 1. bleached, delicate, dim, distant, dull, faded, faltering, feeble, hazy, hushed, ill-defined, indistinct, light, low, muffled, muted, soft, subdued, thin, vague, whispered 2. feeble, remote, slight, unenthusiastic, weak 3. dizzy, drooping, enervated, exhausted, faltering, fatigued, giddy, languid, lethargic, light-headed, muzzy, vertiginous, weak, woozy (*Inf.*) 4. faint-hearted, lily-livered, spiritless, timid, timorous ~*v.* 5. black out, collapse, fade, fail, flake out (*Inf.*), keel over (*Inf.*), languish, lose consciousness, pass out, swoon (*Literary*), weaken ~*n.* 6. blackout, collapse, swoon (*Literary*), syncope (*Pathology*), unconsciousness
Antonyms *adj.* bold, brave, bright, clear, conspicuous, courageous, distinct, energetic, fresh, hearty, loud, powerful, strong, vigorous

faint-hearted chickenshit (*U.S. sl.*), cowardly, diffident, half-arsed, half-assed (*U.S. & Canad. sl.*), half-hearted, irresolute, spineless, timid, timorous, weak, yellow

faintly 1. feebly, in a whisper, indistinctly, softly, weakly 2. a little, dimly, slightly, somewhat
Antonyms audacious, bold, brave, courageous, daring, dauntless, fearless, game (*Inf.*), intrepid, plucky, stouthearted

faintness dimness, dizziness, feebleness, giddiness, indistinctness, languor, loss of strength, shakiness, weakness

fair[1] *adj.* 1. above board, according to the rules, clean, disinterested, dispassionate, equal, equitable, even-handed, honest, honourable, impartial, just, lawful, legitimate, objective, on the level (*Inf.*), proper, square, trustworthy, unbiased, unprejudiced, upright 2. blond, blonde, fair-haired, flaxen-haired, light, light-complexioned, tow-haired, towheaded 3. adequate, all right, average, decent, mediocre, middling, moderate, not bad, O.K. *or* okay (*Inf.*), passable, reasonable, respectable, satisfactory, so-so (*Inf.*), tolerable 4. beauteous, beautiful, bonny, comely, handsome, lovely, pretty, well-favoured 5. bright, clear, clement, cloudless, dry, favourable, fine, sunny, sunshiny, unclouded
Antonyms (*sense 1*) bad, biased, bigoted, discriminatory, dishonest, inequitable, partial, partisan, prejudiced, one-sided, unfair, unjust (*sense 4*) homely, plain, ugly

fair[2] *n.* bazaar, carnival, expo (*Inf.*), exposition, festival, fête, gala, market, show

fair-and-square above board, correct, honest, just, kosher (*Inf.*), on the level (*Inf.*), straight

fairly 1. adequately, moderately, pretty well, quite, rather, reasonably, somewhat, tolerably 2. deservedly, equitably, honestly, impartially, justly, objectively, properly, without fear or favour 3. absolutely, in a manner of speaking, positively, really, veritably

fair-minded disinterested, even-handed, impartial, just, open-minded, unbiased, unprejudiced

fairness decency, disinterestedness, equitableness, equity, impartiality, justice, legitimacy, rightfulness, uprightness

fairy brownie, elf, hob, leprechaun, peri, pixie, Robin Goodfellow, sprite

fairy tale *or* **fairy story** 1. folk tale, romance 2. cock-and-bull story (*Inf.*), fabrication, fantasy, fiction, invention, lie, pork pie (*Brit. sl.*), porky (*Brit. sl.*), tall story, untruth

faith 1. assurance, confidence, conviction, credence, credit, dependence, reliance, trust 2. belief, church, communion, creed, denomination, dogma, persuasion, religion 3. allegiance, constancy, faithfulness, fealty, fidelity, loyalty, troth (*Archaic*), truth, truthfulness 4. *As in* **keep faith, in good faith** honour, pledge, promise, sincerity, vow, word, word of honour
Antonyms agnosticism, apprehension, denial, disbelief, distrust, doubt, incredulity, infidelity, misgiving, mistrust, rejection, scepticism, suspicion, uncertainty

faithful 1. attached, constant, dependable, devoted, immovable, loyal, reliable, staunch, steadfast, true, true-blue, trusty, truthful, unswerving, unwavering 2. accurate, close, exact, just, precise, strict, true 3. **the faithful** adherents, believers, brethren, communicants, congregation, followers, the elect
Antonyms disloyal, doubting, faithless, false, false-hearted, fickle, inconstant, perfidious, recreant (*Archaic*), traitorous, treacherous, unbelieving, unfaithful, unreliable, untrue, untrustworthy, untruthful

faithfulness 1. adherence, constancy, dependability, devotion, fealty, fidelity, loyalty, trustworthiness 2. accuracy, closeness, exactness, justice, strictness, truth

faithless disloyal, doubting, false, false-hearted, fickle, inconstant, perfidious, recreant (*Archaic*), traitorous, treacherous, unbelieving, unfaithful, unreliable, untrue, untrustworthy, untruthful

faithlessness betrayal, disloyalty, fickleness, inconstancy, infidelity, perfidy, treachery, unfaithfulness

fake 1. *v.* affect, assume, copy, counterfeit, fabricate, feign, forge, pretend, put on, sham, simulate 2. *n.* charlatan, copy, forgery, fraud, hoax, imitation, impostor, mountebank, phoney *or* phony (*Inf.*), reproduction, sham 3. *adj.* affected, artificial, assumed, counterfeit, false, forged, imitation, mock, phoney *or* phony (*Inf.*), pinchbeck, pseudo (*Inf.*), reproduction, sham
Antonyms *adj.* actual, authentic, bona fide, faithful, genuine, honest, legitimate, real, true, veritable

faker fake, fraud, humbug, impostor, phoney *or* phony (*Inf.*), pretender, sham

fall *v.* 1. be precipitated, cascade, collapse, crash, descend, dive, drop, drop down, go head over heels, keel over, nose-dive, pitch, plummet, plunge, settle, sink, stumble, subside, topple, trip, trip over, tumble 2. abate, become lower, decline, decrease, depreciate, diminish, drop, dwindle, ebb, fall off, flag, go down, lessen, slump, subside 3. be overthrown, be taken, capitulate, give in *or* up, give way, go out of office, pass into enemy hands, resign, succumb, surrender, yield 4. be a casualty, be killed, be lost, be slain, die, meet one's end, perish 5. become, befall, chance, come about, come to pass, fall out, happen, occur, take place 6. **fall foul of** brush with, come into conflict with, cross swords with, have trouble with, make an enemy of 7. **fall in love (with)** become attached to, become enamoured of, become fond of, become infatuated (with), be smitten by, conceive an affection for, fall (for), lose one's heart (to), take a fancy to 8. fall away, incline, incline downwards, slope 9. backslide, err, go astray, lapse, offend, sin, transgress, trespass, yield to temptation ~*n.* 10. descent, dive, drop, nose dive, plummet, plunge, slip, spill, tumble 11. cut, decline, decrease, diminution, dip, drop, dwindling, falling off, lessening, lowering, reduction, slump 12. capitulation, collapse, death, defeat, destruction, downfall, failure, overthrow, resignation, ruin, surrender 13. declivity, descent, downgrade, incline, slant, slope 14. degradation, failure, lapse, sin, slip, transgression
Antonyms (*sense 1*) ascend, climb, go up, increase, mount, rise, scale, soar, wax (*sense 2*) advance, appreciate, climb, escalate, extend, heighten, increase (*senses 3 & 4*) endure, hold out, prevail, survive, triumph

fallacious deceptive, delusive, delusory, erroneous, false, fictitious, illogical, illusory, incorrect, misleading, mistaken, sophistic, sophistical, spurious, untrue, wrong

fallacy casuistry, deceit, deception, delusion, error, falsehood, faultiness, flaw, illusion, inconsistency, misapprehension, misconception, mistake, sophism, sophistry, untruth

fall apart break up, crumble, disband, disintegrate, disperse, dissolve, fall to bits, go *or* come to pieces, lose cohesion, shatter

fall asleep doze off, drop off (*Inf.*), go to sleep, nod off (*Inf.*)

fall back draw back, recede, recoil, retire, retreat, withdraw

fall back on call upon, employ, have recourse to, make use of, press into service, resort to

fall behind be in arrears, drop back, get left behind, lag, lose one's place, trail

fall down disappoint, fail, fail to make the grade, fall short, go wrong, prove unsuccessful

fallen *adj.* 1. collapsed, decayed, flat, on the ground, ruinous, sunken 2. disgraced, dishonoured, immoral, loose, lost, ruined, shamed, sinful, unchaste 3. dead, killed, lost, perished, slain, slaughtered

fall for 1. become infatuated with, desire, fall in love with, lose one's head over, succumb to the charms of 2. accept, be deceived (duped, fooled, taken in) by, buy (*Sl.*), give credence to, swallow (*Inf.*)

fallible erring, frail, ignorant, imperfect, mortal, prone to error, uncertain, weak
Antonyms divine, faultless, impeccable, infallible, omniscient, perfect, superhuman, unerring, unimpeachable

fall in cave in, collapse, come down about one's ears, sink

falling off *n.* deceleration, decline, decrease, deterioration, downward trend, drop, slackening, slowing down, slump, waning, worsening

fall in with accept, agree with, assent, concur with, cooperate with, go along with, support

fall on *or* **fall upon** assail, assault, attack, belabour, descend upon, lay (pitch (*Inf.*), tear (*Inf.*)) into (*Inf.*), set upon *or* about, snatch

fall out 1. altercate, argue, clash, differ, disagree, fight, quarrel, squabble 2. chance, come to pass, happen, occur, pan out (*Inf.*), result, take place, turn out

fallow dormant, idle, inactive, inert, resting, uncultivated, undeveloped, unplanted, untilled, unused

falls cascade, cataract, force (*Northern English dialect*), linn (*Scot.*), rapids, waterfall

fall short be deficient (lacking, wanting), fail, miss, prove inadequate

fall through come to nothing, fail, fizzle out (*Inf.*), miscarry

fall to 1. apply oneself to, begin, commence, set about, start 2. be up to, come down to, devolve upon

false 1. concocted, erroneous, faulty, fictitious, improper, inaccurate, incorrect, inexact, invalid, mistaken, unfounded, unreal, wrong 2. lying, mendacious, truthless, unreliable, unsound, untrue, untrustworthy, untruthful 3. artificial, bogus, counterfeit, ersatz, fake, feigned, forged, imitation, mock, pretended, sham, simulated, spurious, synthetic 4. deceitful, deceiving, deceptive, delusive, fallacious, fraudulent, hypocritical, misleading, trumped up 5. dishonest, dishonourable, disloyal, double-dealing, duplicitous, faithless, false-hearted, hypocritical, perfidious, treacherous, treasonable, two-faced, unfaithful, untrustworthy 6. **play (someone) false** betray, cheat, deceive, double-cross, give the Judas kiss to, sell down the river (*Inf.*), stab in the back
Antonyms authentic, bona fide, correct, exact, faithful, genuine, honest, kosher (*Inf.*), loyal, real, right, sincere, sound, true, trustworthy, valid

falsehood 1. deceit, deception, dishonesty, dissimulation, inveracity (*Rare*), mendacity, perjury, prevarication, untruthfulness 2. fabrication, fib, fiction, lie, misstatement, pork pie (*Brit. sl.*), porky (*Brit. sl.*), story, untruth

falsification adulteration, deceit, dissimulation, distortion, forgery, misrepresentation, perversion, tampering with

falsify alter, belie, cook (*Sl.*), counterfeit, distort, doctor, fake, forge, garble, misrepresent, misstate, pervert, tamper with

falsity 1. deceit, deceptiveness, dishonesty, double-dealing, duplicity, fraudulence, hypocrisy, inaccuracy, mendacity, perfidy, treachery, unreality, untruth 2. cheating, deception, fraud, lie, pork pie (*Brit. sl.*), porky (*Brit. sl.*)

falter break, hesitate, shake, speak haltingly, stammer, stumble, stutter, totter, tremble, vacillate, waver
Antonyms continue, endure, keep going, last, persevere, persist, proceed, stand firm, stick at, survive

faltering broken, hesitant, irresolute, stammering, tentative, timid, uncertain, weak

fame celebrity, credit, eminence, glory, honour, illustriousness, name, prominence,

public esteem, renown, reputation, repute, stardom
Antonyms disgrace, dishonour, disrepute, ignominy, infamy, oblivion, obscurity, shame

famed acclaimed, celebrated, recognized, renowned, widely-known

familiar 1. accustomed, common, common or garden (*Inf.*), conventional, customary, domestic, everyday, frequent, household, mundane, ordinary, recognizable, repeated, routine, stock, well-known 2. **familiar with** abreast of, acquainted with, at home with, *au courant, au fait,* aware of, conscious of, conversant with, introduced, knowledgeable, no stranger to, on speaking terms with, versed in, well up in 3. amicable, buddy-buddy (*Sl., chiefly U.S. & Canad.*), chummy (*Inf.*), close, confidential, cordial, easy, free, free-and-easy, friendly, hail-fellow-well-met, informal, intimate, near, open, palsy-walsy (*Inf.*), relaxed, unceremonious, unconstrained, unreserved 4. bold, disrespectful, forward, impudent, intrusive, overfree, presuming, presumptuous
Antonyms aloof, cold, detached, distant, formal, ignorant, infrequent, unaccustomed, unacquainted, uncommon, unfamiliar, unfriendly, uninformed, unknown, unskilled, unusual

familiarity 1. acquaintance, acquaintanceship, awareness, experience, grasp, understanding 2. absence of reserve, closeness, ease, fellowship, freedom, friendliness, friendship, informality, intimacy, naturalness, openness, sociability, unceremoniousness 3. boldness, disrespect, forwardness, liberties, liberty, presumption
Antonyms constraint, decorum, distance, formality, ignorance, inexperience, propriety, reserve, respect, unfamiliarity

familiarize accustom, bring into common use, coach, get to know (about), habituate, instruct, inure, make conversant, make used to, prime, school, season, train

family 1. brood, children, descendants, folk (*Inf.*), household, issue, kin, kindred, kinsfolk, kinsmen, kith and kin, ménage, offspring, one's nearest and dearest, one's own flesh and blood, people, progeny, relations, relatives 2. ancestors, ancestry, birth, blood, clan, descent, dynasty, extraction, forebears, forefathers, genealogy, house, line, lineage, parentage, pedigree, race, sept, stemma, stirps, strain, tribe 3. class, classification, genre, group, kind, network, subdivision, system

family tree ancestry, extraction, genealogy, line, lineage, line of descent, pedigree, stemma, stirps

famine dearth, destitution, hunger, scarcity, starvation

famished ravening, ravenous, ready to eat a horse (*Inf.*), starved, starving, voracious

famous acclaimed, celebrated, conspicuous, distinguished, eminent, excellent, far-famed, glorious, honoured, illustrious, legendary, lionized, much-publicized, notable, noted, prominent, remarkable, renowned, signal, well-known
Antonyms forgotten, mediocre, obscure, uncelebrated, undistinguished, unexceptional, unknown, unremarkable

fan[1] *v.* 1. *Often fig.* add fuel to the flames, agitate, arouse, enkindle, excite, impassion, increase, provoke, rouse, stimulate, stir up, whip up, work up 2. air-condition, air-cool, blow, cool, refresh, ventilate, winnow (*Rare*) ~*n.* 3. air conditioner, blade, blower, propeller, punkah (*In India*), vane, ventilator

fan[2] adherent, admirer, aficionado, buff (*Inf.*), devotee, enthusiast, fiend (*Inf.*), follower, freak (*Inf.*), groupie (*Sl.*), lover, rooter (*U.S.*), supporter, zealot

fanatic *n.* activist, addict, bigot, buff (*Inf.*), devotee, enthusiast, extremist, militant, visionary, zealot

fanatical bigoted, burning, enthusiastic, extreme, fervent, frenzied, immoderate, mad, obsessive, overenthusiastic, passionate, rabid, visionary, wild, zealous

fanaticism bigotry, dedication, devotion, enthusiasm, extremism, immoderation, infatuation, madness, monomania, obsessiveness, overenthusiasm, single-mindedness, zeal, zealotry

fancier aficionado, amateur, breeder, connoisseur, expert

fanciful capricious, chimerical, curious, extravagant, fabulous, fairy-tale, fantastic, ideal, imaginary, imaginative, mythical, poetic, romantic, unreal, visionary, whimsical, wild
Antonyms conventional, dry, dull, literal, matter of fact, ordinary, pedestrian, predictable, routine, sensible, sober, unimaginative, uninspired

fancy *v.* 1. be inclined to think, believe, conceive, conjecture, guess (*Inf., chiefly U.S. & Canad.*), imagine, infer, reckon, suppose, surmise, think, think likely 2. be attracted to, crave, desire, dream of, hanker after, have a yen for, hope for, long for, relish, thirst for, wish for, would like, yearn for 3. *Inf.* be attracted to, be captivated by, desire, favour, go for, have an eye for, like, lust after, prefer, take a liking to, take to ~*n.* 4. caprice, desire, humour, idea, impulse, inclination, notion, thought, urge,

whim 5. fondness, hankering, inclination, liking, partiality, predilection, preference, relish, thirst 6. conception, image, imagination, impression 7. chimera, daydream, delusion, dream, fantasy, nightmare, phantasm, vision *~adj.* 8. baroque, decorated, decorative, elaborate, elegant, embellished, extravagant, fanciful, intricate, ornamental, ornamented, ornate 9. capricious, chimerical, delusive, fanciful, fantastic, far-fetched, illusory, whimsical
Antonyms (*sense 5*) aversion, disinclination, dislike (*sense 8*) basic, cheap, common, inferior, ordinary, plain, simple, unadorned, undecorated

fanfare ballyhoo, fanfaronade, flourish, trump (*Archaic*), trumpet call, tucket (*Archaic*)

fang tooth, tusk

fan out disperse, lay out, open out, space out, spread, spread out, unfurl

fantasize build castles in the air, daydream, dream, envision, give free rein to the imagination, hallucinate, imagine, invent, live in a dream world, romance, see visions

fantastic 1. comical, eccentric, exotic, fanciful, freakish, grotesque, imaginative, odd, oddball (*Inf.*), off-the-wall (*Sl.*), outlandish, outré, peculiar, phantasmagorical, quaint, queer, rococo, strange, unreal, weird, whimsical 2. ambitious, chimerical, extravagant, far-fetched, grandiose, illusory, ludicrous, ridiculous, unrealistic, visionary, wild 3. absurd, capricious, implausible, incredible, irrational, mad, preposterous, unlikely 4. *Inf.* enormous, extreme, great, overwhelming, severe, tremendous 5. *Inf.* boffo (*Sl.*), brill (*Inf.*), chillin' (*U.S. sl.*), cracking (*Brit. inf.*), crucial (*Sl.*), def (*Sl.*), excellent, first-rate, jim-dandy (*Sl.*), marvellous, mean (*Sl.*), mega (*Sl.*), out of this world (*Inf.*), sensational (*Inf.*), sovereign, superb, topping (*Brit. sl.*), wonderful, world-class
Antonyms common, credible, everyday, moderate, normal, ordinary, poor, rational, realistic, sensible, typical

fantasy, phantasy 1. creativity, fancy, imagination, invention, originality 2. apparition, daydream, delusion, dream, fancy, figment of the imagination, flight of fancy, hallucination, illusion, mirage, nightmare, pipe dream, reverie, vision

far *adv.* 1. afar, a good way, a great distance, a long way, deep, miles 2. considerably, decidedly, extremely, greatly, incomparably, much, very much 3. **by far** by a long chalk (*Inf.*), by a long shot, by a long way, easily, far and away, immeasurably, incomparably, to a great degree, very much 4. **far and wide** broadly, everywhere, extensively, far and near, here, there, and everywhere, widely, worldwide 5. **so far** thus far, to date, until now, up to now, up to the present *~adj.* 6. distant, faraway, far-flung, far-off, far-removed, long, outlying, out-of-the-way, remote, removed
Antonyms adjacent, adjoining, alongside, at close quarters, beside, bordering, close, contiguous, near, nearby, neighbouring, proximate, within sniffing distance (*Inf.*)

faraway 1. beyond the horizon, distant, far, far-flung, far-off, far-removed, outlying, remote 2. absent, abstracted, distant, dreamy, lost

farce 1. broad comedy, buffoonery, burlesque, comedy, satire, slapstick 2. absurdity, joke, mockery, nonsense, parody, ridiculousness, sham, travesty

farcical absurd, amusing, comic, custard-pie, derisory, diverting, droll, funny, laughable, ludicrous, nonsensical, preposterous, ridiculous, risible, slapstick

fare *n.* 1. charge, passage money, price, ticket money, transport cost 2. passenger, pick-up (*Inf.*), traveller 3. commons, diet, eatables, feed, food, meals, menu, nosebag (*Sl.*), provisions, rations, sustenance, table, tack (*Inf.*), victuals, vittles (*Obs. or dialect*) *~v.* 4. do, get along, get on, make out, manage, prosper 5. *Used impersonally* go, happen, pan out (*Inf.*), proceed, turn out

farewell adieu, adieux *or* adieus, departure, goodbye, leave-taking, parting, sendoff (*Inf.*), valediction

far-fetched doubtful, dubious, fantastic, hard to swallow (*Inf.*), implausible, improbable, incredible, preposterous, strained, unbelievable, unconvincing, unlikely, unnatural, unrealistic
Antonyms acceptable, authentic, believable, credible, feasible, imaginable, likely, plausible, possible, probable, realistic, reasonable

farm 1. *n.* acreage, acres, croft (*Scot.*), farmstead, grange, holding, homestead, land, plantation, ranch (*Chiefly North American*), smallholding, station (*Aust. & N.Z.*) 2. *v.* bring under cultivation, cultivate, operate, plant, practise husbandry, till the soil, work

farmer agriculturist, agronomist, husbandman, smallholder, yeoman

farming agriculture, agronomy, husbandry

far-out advanced, avant-garde, bizarre, off-the-wall (*Sl.*), outlandish, outré, unconventional, weird, wild

farrago gallimaufry, hash, hodgepodge, hotchpotch, jumble, medley, *mélange*, miscellany, mishmash, mixed bag, mixture, potpourri, salmagundi

far-reaching broad, extensive, important, momentous, pervasive, significant, sweeping, widespread

far-sighted acute, canny, cautious, discerning, far-seeing, judicious, politic, prescient, provident, prudent, sage, shrewd, wise

fascinate absorb, allure, beguile, bewitch, captivate, charm, delight, enamour, enchant, engross, enrapture, enravish, enthral, entrance, hold spellbound, hypnotize, infatuate, intrigue, mesmerize, ravish, rivet, spellbind, transfix
Antonyms alienate, bore, disenchant, disgust, irritate, jade, put one off, sicken, turn one off (*Inf.*)

fascinated absorbed, beguiled, bewitched, captivated, charmed, engrossed, enthralled, entranced, hooked on, hypnotized, infatuated, smitten, spellbound, under a spell

fascinating alluring, bewitching, captivating, compelling, enchanting, engaging, engrossing, enticing, gripping, intriguing, irresistible, ravishing, riveting, seductive
Antonyms boring, dull, mind-numbing, unexciting, uninteresting

fascination allure, attraction, charm, enchantment, glamour, lure, magic, magnetism, pull, sorcery, spell

fascism *n.* absolutism, authoritarianism, autocracy, dictatorship, Hitlerism, totalitarianism

fashion *n.* 1. convention, craze, custom, fad, latest, latest style, look, mode, prevailing taste, rage, style, trend, usage, vogue 2. attitude, demeanour, manner, method, mode, style, way 3. appearance, configuration, cut, figure, form, guise (*Archaic*), line, make, model, mould, pattern, shape, stamp 4. description, kind, sort, stamp, type 5. beau monde, fashionable society, high society, jet set 6. **after a fashion** in a manner of speaking, in a way, moderately, somehow, somehow or other, to a degree, to some extent ~*v.* 7. construct, contrive, create, design, forge, form, make, manufacture, mould, shape, work 8. accommodate, adapt, adjust, fit, suit, tailor

fashionable à la mode, all the go (*Inf.*), all the rage, chic, cool (*Sl.*), current, customary, genteel, happening (*Inf.*), hip (*Sl.*), in (*Inf.*), in vogue, latest, modern, modish, popular, prevailing, smart, stylish, trendsetting, trendy (*Brit. inf.*), up-to-date, up-to-the-minute, usual, voguish (*Inf.*), with it (*Inf.*)
Antonyms behind the times, dated, frumpy, obsolete, old-fashioned, old-hat, outmoded, out of date, uncool (*Sl.*), unfashionable, unpopular, unstylish, untrendy (*Brit. inf.*)

fast[1] *adj.* 1. accelerated, brisk, fleet, flying, hasty, hurried, mercurial, nippy (*Brit. inf.*), quick, quickie (*Inf.*), rapid, speedy, swift, winged ~*adv.* 2. apace, hastily, hell for leather (*Inf.*), hotfoot, hurriedly, in haste, like a bat out of hell (*Sl.*), like a flash, like a shot (*Inf.*), pdq (*Sl.*), posthaste, presto, quickly, rapidly, speedily, swiftly, with all haste ~*adj.* 3. close, constant, fastened, firm, fixed, fortified, immovable, impregnable, lasting, loyal, permanent, secure, sound, stalwart, staunch, steadfast, tight, unwavering ~*adv.* 4. deeply, firmly, fixedly, securely, soundly, tightly ~*adj.* 5. dissipated, dissolute, extravagant, gadabout (*Inf.*), giddy, immoral, intemperate, licentious, loose, profligate, promiscuous, rakish, reckless, self-indulgent, wanton, wild ~*adv.* 6. extravagantly, intemperately, loosely, promiscuously, rakishly, recklessly, wildly 7. **pull a fast one** bamboozle (*Inf.*), cheat, con (*Inf.*), deceive, defraud, hoodwink, put one over on (*Inf.*), swindle, take advantage of, take for a ride (*Inf.*), trick
Antonyms (*sense 1*) leisurely, plodding, slow, slow moving, unhurried (*sense 2*) at a snail's pace, at one's leisure, gradually, leisurely, slowly, steadily, unhurriedly (*sense 3*) inconstant, irresolute, unfaithful, unreliable, unstable, wavering, weak

fast[2] 1. *v.* abstain, deny oneself, go hungry, go without food, practise abstention, refrain from food *or* eating 2. *n.* abstinence, fasting

fasten 1. affix, anchor, attach, bind, bolt, chain, connect, fix, grip, join, lace, link, lock, make fast, make firm, seal, secure, tie, unite 2. *Fig.* aim, bend, concentrate, direct, fix, focus, rivet

fastidious choosey, choosy, critical, dainty, difficult, discriminating, finicky, fussy, hard to please, hypercritical, meticulous, nice, overdelicate, overnice, particular, pernickety, picky (*Inf.*), punctilious, squeamish
Antonyms careless, casual, disorderly, easygoing, lenient, slack, slipshod, sloppy, slovenly, unsystematic

fat *adj.* 1. beefy (*Inf.*), broad in the beam (*Inf.*), corpulent, elephantine, fleshy, gross, heavy, obese, overweight, plump, podgy, portly, roly-poly, rotund, solid, stout, tubby 2. adipose, fatty, greasy, lipid, oily, oleaginous, suety 3. affluent, cushy (*Sl.*), fertile, flourishing, fruitful, jammy (*Brit. sl.*), lucrative, lush, productive, profitable, prosperous, remunerative, rich, thriving ~*n.* 4.

adipose tissue, beef (*Inf.*), blubber, bulk, cellulite, corpulence, fatness, flab, flesh, obesity, overweight, paunch, weight problem
Antonyms angular, barren, bony, empty, gaunt, lank, lean, poor, scanty, scarce, scrawny, skinny, slender, slight, slim, spare, thin, unproductive, unprofitable, unrewarding

fatal 1. deadly, destructive, final, incurable, killing, lethal, malignant, mortal, pernicious, terminal 2. baleful, baneful, calamitous, catastrophic, disastrous, lethal, ruinous 3. critical, crucial, decisive, destined, determining, doomed, fateful, final, foreordained, inevitable, predestined
Antonyms beneficial, benign, harmless, inconsequential, innocuous, inoffensive, minor, non-lethal, non-toxic, salutary, vitalizing, wholesome

fatalism acceptance, determinism, necessitarianism, passivity, predestinarianism, resignation, stoicism

fatality casualty, deadliness, death, disaster, fatal accident, lethalness, loss, mortality

fate 1. chance, destiny, divine will, fortune, kismet, nemesis, predestination, providence, weird (*Archaic*) 2. cup, fortune, horoscope, lot, portion, stars 3. end, future, issue, outcome, upshot 4. death, destruction, doom, downfall, end, ruin

fated destined, doomed, foreordained, ineluctable, inescapable, inevitable, marked down, predestined, pre-elected, preordained, sure, written

fateful 1. critical, crucial, decisive, important, portentous, significant 2. deadly, destructive, disastrous, fatal, lethal, ominous, ruinous
Antonyms inconsequential, insignificant, nugatory, ordinary, unimportant

Fates Providence, the Norns, the Three Sisters, the Weird Sisters

fathead ass, berk (*Brit. sl.*), booby, charlie (*Brit. inf.*), coot, dickhead (*Sl.*), dimwit (*Inf.*), dipstick (*Brit. sl.*), divvy (*Brit. sl.*), dope (*Inf.*), dork (*Sl.*), dunderhead, dweeb (*U.S. sl.*), fool, fuckwit (*Taboo sl.*), geek (*Sl.*), gonzo (*Sl.*), goose, idiot, imbecile, jackass, jerk (*Sl., chiefly U.S. & Canad.*), lamebrain (*Inf.*), nerd *or* nurd (*Sl.*), nincompoop, nitwit (*Inf.*), numskull *or* numbskull, pillock (*Brit. sl.*), plank (*Brit. sl.*), plonker (*Sl.*), prat (*Sl.*), prick (*Derogatory sl.*), schmuck (*U.S. sl.*), twerp *or* twirp (*Inf.*), twit (*Inf., chiefly Brit.*), wally (*Sl.*)

father *n.* 1. begetter, dad (*Inf.*), daddy (*Inf.*), governor (*Inf.*), old boy (*Inf.*), old man (*Inf.*), pa (*Inf.*), papa (*Old-fashioned inf.*), pater, paterfamilias, patriarch, pop (*Inf.*), sire 2. ancestor, forebear, forefather, predecessor, progenitor 3. architect, author, creator, founder, inventor, maker, originator, prime mover 4. city father, elder, leader, patriarch, patron, senator 5. abbé, confessor, curé, padre (*Inf.*), pastor, priest ~*v.* 6. beget, get, procreate, sire 7. create, engender, establish, found, institute, invent, originate

fatherland homeland, land of one's birth, land of one's fathers, motherland, native land, old country

fatherly affectionate, benevolent, benign, forbearing, indulgent, kind, kindly, paternal, patriarchal, protective, supportive, tender

fathom 1. divine, estimate, gauge, measure, penetrate, plumb, probe, sound 2. comprehend, get to the bottom of, grasp, interpret, understand

fathomless abysmal, bottomless, deep, immeasurable, impenetrable, incomprehensible, profound, unfathomable, unplumbed

fatigue 1. *v.* drain, drain of energy, exhaust, fag (out) (*Inf.*), jade, knacker (*Sl.*), overtire, poop (*Inf.*), take it out of (*Inf.*), tire, weaken, wear out, weary, whack (*Brit. inf.*) 2. *n.* debility, ennui, heaviness, languor, lethargy, listlessness, overtiredness, tiredness
Antonyms *n.* alertness, animation, energy, freshness, get-up-and-go (*Inf.*), go, indefatigability, life, vigour, zest ~*v.* refresh, rejuvenate, relieve, rest, revive, stimulate

fatigued all in (*Sl.*), bushed (*Inf.*), clapped out (*Aust. & N.Z. inf.*), dead beat (*Inf.*), exhausted, fagged (out) (*Inf.*), jaded, jiggered (*Inf.*), knackered (*Sl.*), overtired, tired, tired out, wasted, weary, whacked (*Brit. inf.*), zonked (*Sl.*)

fatness beef (*Inf.*), bulkiness, corpulence, *embonpoint,* flab, flesh, fleshiness, girth, grossness, heaviness, obesity, overweight, podginess, rotundity, size, stoutness, weight, weight problem

fatten 1. broaden, coarsen, expand, gain weight, grow fat, put on weight, spread, swell, thicken, thrive 2. *Often with* **up** bloat, build up, cram, distend, feed, feed up, nourish, overfeed, stuff

fatty adipose, fat, greasy, oily, oleaginous, rich

fatuity absurdity, bêtise (*Rare*), brainlessness, daftness (*Inf.*), denseness, fatuousness, folly, foolishness, idiocy, imbecility, insanity, ludicrousness, lunacy, mindlessness, stupidity

fatuous absurd, asinine, brainless, dense, dull, foolish, idiotic, inane, ludicrous, lunatic, mindless, moronic, puerile, silly, stupid, vacuous, weak-minded, witless

fault *n.* 1. blemish, defect, deficiency, demerit, drawback, failing, flaw, imperfection, infirmity, lack, shortcoming, snag, weakness, weak point 2. blunder, boob (*Brit. sl.*), error, error of judgment, inaccuracy, indiscretion, lapse, mistake, negligence, offence, omission, oversight, slip, slip-up 3. accountability, culpability, liability, responsibility 4. delinquency, frailty, lapse, misconduct, misdeed, misdemeanour, offence, peccadillo, sin, transgression, trespass, wrong 5. **at fault** answerable, blamable, culpable, guilty, in the wrong, responsible, to blame 6. **find fault with** carp at, complain, criticize, pick holes in, pull to pieces, quibble, take to task 7. **to a fault** excessively, immoderately, in the extreme, needlessly, out of all proportion, overly (*U.S.*), overmuch, preposterously, ridiculously, unduly ~*v.* 8. blame, call to account, censure, criticize, find fault with, find lacking, hold (someone) accountable (responsible, to blame), impugn

Antonyms (*sense 1*) asset, attribute, credit, goodness, merit, perfection, strength, virtue

fault-finding 1. *n.* carping, hairsplitting, nagging, niggling, nit-picking (*Inf.*) 2. *adj.* captious, carping, censorious, critical, hypercritical, pettifogging

Antonyms complimentary, easily pleased, indiscriminate, uncritical, undiscerning, unexacting, unfussy, unperceptive

faultless 1. accurate, classic, correct, exemplary, faithful, flawless, foolproof, impeccable, model, perfect, unblemished 2. above reproach, blameless, guiltless, immaculate, impeccable, innocent, irreproachable, pure, sinless, spotless, stainless, unblemished, unspotted, unsullied

faulty bad, blemished, broken, damaged, defective, erroneous, fallacious, flawed, impaired, imperfect, imprecise, inaccurate, incorrect, invalid, malfunctioning, not working, out of order, unsound, weak, wrong

faux pas bloomer (*Brit. inf.*), blunder, boob (*Brit. sl.*), breach of etiquette, clanger (*Inf.*), gaffe, gaucherie, impropriety, indiscretion, solecism

favour *n.* 1. approbation, approval, backing, bias, championship, espousal, esteem, favouritism, friendliness, good opinion, good will, grace, kindness, kind regard, partiality, patronage, promotion, support 2. benefit, boon, courtesy, good turn, indulgence, kindness, obligement (*Scot. or Archaic*), service 3. **in favour of** all for (*Inf.*), backing, for, on the side of, pro, supporting, to the benefit of 4. gift, keepsake, love-token, memento, present, souvenir, token 5. badge, decoration, knot, ribbons, rosette ~*v.* 6. be partial to, esteem, have in one's good books, indulge, pamper, pull strings for (*Inf.*), reward, side with, smile upon, spoil, treat with partiality, value 7. advocate, approve, back, be in favour of, champion, choose, commend, countenance, encourage, espouse, fancy, incline towards, like, opt for, patronize, prefer, single out, support 8. abet, accommodate, advance, aid, assist, befriend, do a kindness to, facilitate, help, oblige, promote, succour 9. *Inf.* be the image *or* picture of, look like, resemble, take after 10. ease, extenuate, spare

Antonyms *n.* animosity, antipathy, disapproval, disfavour, disservice, harm, ill will, injury, malevolence, wrong ~*v.* disapprove, disdain, dislike, inconvenience, object to, oppose, thwart

favourable 1. advantageous, appropriate, auspicious, beneficial, convenient, encouraging, fair, fit, good, helpful, hopeful, opportune, promising, propitious, suitable, timely 2. affirmative, agreeable, amicable, approving, benign, encouraging, enthusiastic, friendly, kind, positive, reassuring, sympathetic, understanding, welcoming, well-disposed

Antonyms disadvantageous, disapproving, ill-disposed, inauspicious, unfavourable, unfriendly, unhelpful, unpromising, unsympathetic, useless

favourably 1. advantageously, auspiciously, conveniently, fortunately, opportunely, profitably, to one's advantage, well 2. agreeably, approvingly, enthusiastically, genially, graciously, helpfully, in a kindly manner, positively, with approval (approbation, cordiality), without prejudice

favoured 1. best-liked, chosen, favourite, pet, preferred, recommended, selected, singled out 2. advantaged, blessed, elite, jammy (*Brit. sl.*), lucky, privileged

favourite 1. *adj.* best-loved, choice, dearest, esteemed, favoured, preferred 2. *n.* beloved, blue-eyed boy (*Inf.*), choice, darling, dear, idol, pet, pick, preference, teacher's pet, the apple of one's eye

favouritism bias, jobs for the boys (*Inf.*), nepotism, one-sidedness, partiality, partisanship, preference, preferential treatment

Antonyms equality, equity, evenhandedness, fairness, impartiality, neutrality, objectivity, open-mindedness

fawn[1] *adj.* beige, buff, greyish-brown, neutral

fawn[2] *v. Often with* **on** *or* **upon** be obsequious, be servile, bow and scrape, brown-nose (*Taboo sl.*), court, crawl, creep, cringe, curry favour, dance attendance, flatter, grovel, ingratiate oneself, kiss ass (*U S. & Canad. taboo sl.*), kneel, kowtow, lick (someone's) boots, pander to, pay court, toady, truckle

fawning abject, bootlicking (*Inf.*), bowing and scraping, crawling, cringing, deferential, flattering, grovelling, obsequious, prostrate, servile, slavish, sycophantic

fealty allegiance, devotion, faith, faithfulness, fidelity, homage, loyalty, obeisance, submission, troth (*Archaic*)

fear *n.* 1. alarm, apprehensiveness, awe, blue funk (*Inf.*), consternation, cravenness, dismay, dread, fright, horror, panic, qualms, terror, timidity, tremors, trepidation 2. *bête noire,* bogey, bugbear, horror, nightmare, phobia, spectre 3. agitation, anxiety, apprehension, concern, disquietude, distress, doubt, foreboding(s), misgiving(s), solicitude, suspicion, unease, uneasiness, worry 4. awe, reverence, veneration, wonder ~*v.* 5. apprehend, be apprehensive (afraid, frightened, scared), be in a blue funk (*Inf.*), dare not, dread, have a horror of, have a phobia about, have butterflies in one's stomach (*Inf.*), have qualms, live in dread of, shake in one's shoes, shudder at, take fright, tremble at 6. anticipate, apprehend, be afraid, expect, foresee, suspect 7. *With* **for** be anxious (concerned, distressed) about, be disquieted over, feel concern for, tremble for, worry about 8. respect, revere, reverence, stand in awe of, venerate

fearful 1. afraid, alarmed, anxious, apprehensive, diffident, faint-hearted, frightened, hellacious (*U.S. sl.*), hesitant, intimidated, jittery (*Inf.*), jumpy, nervous, nervy (*Brit. inf.*), panicky, pusillanimous, scared, shrinking, tense, timid, timorous, uneasy, wired (*Sl.*) 2. appalling, atrocious, awful, dire, distressing, dreadful, frightful, ghastly, grievous, grim, gruesome, hair-raising, harrowing, hideous, horrendous, horrible, horrific, monstrous, shocking, terrible, unspeakable
Antonyms (*sense 1*) ballsy (*Taboo sl.*), bold, brave, confident, courageous, daring, dauntless, doughty, gallant, game (*Inf.*), gutsy (*Sl.*), heroic, indomitable, intrepid, lion-hearted, plucky, unabashed, unafraid, undaunted, unflinching, valiant, valorous

fearfully 1. apprehensively, diffidently, in fear and trembling, nervously, timidly, timorously, uneasily, with many misgivings *or* forebodings, with one's heart in one's mouth 2. awfully, exceedingly, excessively, frightfully, terribly, tremendously, very

fearless ballsy (*Taboo sl.*), bold, brave, confident, courageous, daring, dauntless, doughty, gallant, game (*Inf.*), gutsy (*Sl.*), heroic, indomitable, intrepid, lion-hearted, plucky, unabashed, unafraid, undaunted, unflinching, valiant, valorous

fearlessness balls (*Taboo sl.*), ballsiness (*Taboo sl.*), boldness, bravery, confidence, courage, dauntlessness, guts (*Inf.*), indomitability, intrepidity, lion-heartedness, nerve, pluckiness

fearsome alarming, appalling, awe-inspiring, awesome, awful, baleful, daunting, dismaying, formidable, frightening, hair-raising, hellacious (*U.S. sl.*), horrendous, horrifying, menacing, unnerving

feasibility expediency, practicability, usefulness, viability, workability

feasible achievable, attainable, likely, possible, practicable, realizable, reasonable, viable, workable
Antonyms impossible, impracticable, inconceivable, unreasonable, untenable, unviable, unworkable

feast *n.* 1. banquet, barbecue, beanfeast (*Brit. inf.*), beano (*Brit. sl.*), blowout (*Sl.*), carousal, carouse, dinner, entertainment, festive board, jollification, junket, repast, revels, slap-up meal (*Brit. inf.*), spread (*Inf.*), treat 2. celebration, festival, fête, gala day, holiday, holy day, saint's day 3. delight, enjoyment, gratification, pleasure, treat ~*v.* 4. eat one's fill, eat to one's heart's content, fare sumptuously, gorge, gormandize, indulge, overindulge, pig out (*Sl.*), stuff, stuff one's face (*Sl.*), wine and dine 5. entertain, hold a reception for, kill the fatted calf for, regale, treat, wine and dine 6. delight, gladden, gratify, rejoice, thrill

feat accomplishment, achievement, act, attainment, deed, exploit, performance

feathers down, plumage, plumes

feathery downy, feathered, fluffy, plumate *or* plumose (*Bot. & Zool.*), plumed, plumy, wispy

feature *n.* 1. aspect, attribute, characteristic, facet, factor, hallmark, mark, peculiarity, point, property, quality, trait 2. attraction, crowd puller (*Inf.*), draw, highlight, innovation, main item, special, special attraction, speciality, specialty 3. article, column, comment, item, piece, report, story ~*v.* 4. accentuate, call attention to, emphasize, give prominence to, give the full works (*Sl.*), headline, play up, present, promote, set off, spotlight, star

featured given prominence, headlined,

highlighted, in the public eye, presented, promoted, recommended, specially presented, starred

features countenance, face, lineaments, physiognomy

featuring calling attention to, displaying, drawing attention to, giving a star role, giving prominence to, giving the full works (*Sl.*), highlighting, making the main attraction, presenting, promoting, pushing, recommending, showing, showing off, starring, turning the spotlight on

febrile delirious, fevered, feverish, fiery, flushed, hot, inflamed, pyretic (*Medical*)

feckless aimless, feeble, futile, hopeless, incompetent, ineffectual, irresponsible, shiftless, useless, weak, worthless

fecund fertile, fructiferous, fruitful, productive, prolific, teeming

fecundity fertility, fructiferousness, fruitfulness, productiveness

federate *v.* amalgamate, associate, combine, confederate, integrate, syndicate, unify, unite

federation alliance, amalgamation, association, *Bund,* coalition, combination, confederacy, copartnership, entente, federacy, league, syndicate, union

fed up (with) annoyed, blue, bored, brassed off (*Brit. sl.*), browned-off (*Inf.*), depressed, discontented, dismal, dissatisfied, down, gloomy, glum, hacked (off) (*U.S. sl.*), pissed off (*Taboo sl.*), sick and tired of (*Inf.*), tired of, weary of

fee account, bill, charge, compensation, emolument, hire, honorarium, meed (*Archaic*), pay, payment, recompense, remuneration, reward, toll

feeble 1. debilitated, delicate, doddering, effete, enervated, enfeebled, etiolated, exhausted, failing, faint, frail, infirm, languid, powerless, puny, shilpit (*Scot.*), sickly, weak, weakened, weedy (*Inf.*) 2. flat, flimsy, inadequate, incompetent, indecisive, ineffective, ineffectual, inefficient, insignificant, insufficient, lame, paltry, pathetic, poor, slight, tame, thin, unconvincing, weak

Antonyms ardent, effective, energetic, forceful, hale, healthy, hearty, lusty, robust, stalwart, strong, sturdy, successful, vigorous

feeble-minded addle-pated, bone-headed (*Sl.*), braindead (*Inf.*), deficient, dim-witted (*Inf.*), dozy (*Brit. inf.*), dull, dumb (*Inf.*), half-witted, idiotic, imbecilic, lacking, moronic, obtuse, retarded, simple, slow on the uptake, slow-witted, soft in the head (*Inf.*), stupid, vacant, weak-minded

Antonyms astute, aware, bright, clear-headed, clever, intelligent, keen, quick-witted, smart

feebleness 1. debility, delicacy, effeteness, enervation, etiolation, exhaustion, frailness, frailty, incapacity, infirmity, lack of strength, languor, lassitude, sickliness, weakness 2. flimsiness, inadequacy, incompetence, indecisiveness, ineffectualness, insignificance, insufficiency, lameness, weakness

feed *v.* 1. cater for, nourish, provide for, provision, supply, sustain, victual, wine and dine 2. *Sometimes with* **on** devour, eat, exist on, fare, graze, live on, nurture, partake of, pasture, subsist, take nourishment 3. augment, bolster, encourage, foster, fuel, minister to, strengthen, supply ~*n.* 4. fodder, food, forage, pasturage, provender, silage 5. *Inf.* feast, meal, nosh (*Sl.*), nosh-up (*Brit. sl.*), repast, spread (*Inf.*), tuck-in (*Inf.*)

feel *v.* 1. caress, finger, fondle, handle, manipulate, maul, paw, run one's hands over, stroke, touch 2. be aware of, be sensible of, endure, enjoy, experience, go through, have, have a sensation of, know, notice, observe, perceive, suffer, take to heart, undergo 3. explore, fumble, grope, sound, test, try 4. be convinced, feel in one's bones, have a hunch, have the impression, intuit, sense 5. believe, be of the opinion that, consider, deem, hold, judge, think 6. appear, resemble, seem, strike one as 7. *With* **for** be moved by, be sorry for, bleed for, commiserate, compassionate, condole with, empathize, feel compassion for, pity, sympathize with 8. **feel like** could do with, desire, fancy, feel inclined, feel the need for, feel up to, have the inclination, want ~*n.* 9. finish, surface, texture, touch 10. air, ambience, atmosphere, feeling, impression, quality, sense, vibes (*Sl.*)

feeler 1. antenna, tentacle, whisker 2. advance, approach, probe, trial balloon

feeling 1. feel, perception, sensation, sense, sense of touch, touch 2. apprehension, consciousness, hunch, idea, impression, inkling, notion, presentiment, sense, suspicion 3. affection, ardour, emotion, fervour, fondness, heat, intensity, passion, sentiment, sentimentality, warmth 4. appreciation, compassion, concern, empathy, pity, sensibility, sensitivity, sympathy, understanding 5. inclination, instinct, opinion, point of view, view 6. air, ambience, atmosphere, aura, feel, mood, quality, vibes (*Sl.*) 7. **bad feeling** anger, dislike, distrust, enmity, hostility, upset

feelings ego, emotions, self-esteem, sensitivities, susceptibilities

feign act, affect, assume, counterfeit, devise, dissemble, fabricate, fake, forge, give the appearance of, imitate, make a show of, pretend, put on, sham, simulate

feigned affected, artificial, assumed, counterfeit, ersatz, fabricated, fake, false, imitation, insincere, pretended, pseudo (*Inf.*), sham, simulated, spurious

feint *n.* artifice, blind, bluff, distraction, dodge, expedient, gambit, manoeuvre, mock attack, play, pretence, ruse, stratagem, subterfuge, wile

felicitate compliment, congratulate, wish joy to

felicitous apposite, appropriate, apropos, apt, fitting, happy, inspired, neat, opportune, pat, propitious, suitable, timely, well-chosen, well-timed

felicity 1. blessedness, bliss, blissfulness, delectation, ecstasy, happiness, joy 2. applicability, appropriateness, aptness, becomingness, effectiveness, grace, propriety, suitability, suitableness

feline 1. catlike, leonine 2. graceful, sinuous, sleek, slinky, smooth, stealthy

fell[1] *v.* cut, cut down, demolish, flatten, floor, hew, knock down, level, prostrate, raze, strike down

fell[2] *adj.* 1. barbarous, bloody, cruel, ferocious, fierce, grim, implacable, inhuman, malicious, malignant, merciless, murderous, pitiless, relentless, ruthless, sanguinary, savage, vicious 2. baneful, deadly, destructive, fatal, malign, mortal, noxious, pernicious, pestilential, ruinous

fellow *n.* 1. bloke (*Brit. inf.*), boy, chap (*Inf.*), character, customer (*Inf.*), guy (*Inf.*), individual, man, person, punter (*Inf.*) 2. associate, colleague, companion, compeer, comrade, co-worker, equal, friend, member, partner, peer 3. brother, counterpart, double, duplicate, match, mate, twin ~*adj.* 4. affiliated, akin, allied, associate, associated, co-, like, related, similar

fellow feeling compassion, empathy, pity, sympathy, understanding

fellowship 1. amity, brotherhood, camaraderie, communion, companionability, companionship, familiarity, fraternization, intercourse, intimacy, kindliness, sociability 2. association, brotherhood, club, fraternity, guild, league, order, sisterhood, society, sodality

feminine 1. delicate, gentle, girlish, graceful, ladylike, modest, soft, tender, womanly 2. camp (*Inf.*), effeminate, effete, unmanly, unmasculine, weak, womanish
Antonyms Amazonian, butch, indelicate, manly, mannish, masculine, rough, unfeminine, unladylike, unwomanly, virile

femininity delicacy, feminineness, gentleness, girlishness, muliebrity, softness, womanhood, womanliness

femme fatale charmer, Circe, enchantress, seductress, siren, vamp (*Inf.*)

fen bog, holm (*Dialect*), marsh, morass, moss (*Scot.*), quagmire, slough, swamp

fence *n.* 1. barbed wire, barricade, barrier, defence, guard, hedge, paling, palisade, railings, rampart, shield, stockade, wall 2. **on the fence** between two stools, irresolute, uncertain, uncommitted, undecided, vacillating ~*v.* 3. *Often with* **in** *or* **off** bound, circumscribe, confine, coop, defend, encircle, enclose, fortify, guard, hedge, impound, pen, pound, protect, restrict, secure, separate, surround 4. beat about the bush, cavil, dodge, equivocate, evade, flannel (*Brit. inf.*), hedge, parry, prevaricate, quibble, shift, stonewall, tergiversate

fencing *Fig.* beating about the bush, double talk, equivocation, evasiveness, hedging, parrying, prevarication, quibbling, stonewalling, tergiversation, weasel words (*Inf., chiefly U.S.*)

fend for look after, make do, make provision for, provide for, shift for, support, sustain, take care of

fend off avert, beat off, deflect, drive back, hold *or* keep at bay, keep off, parry, repel, repulse, resist, stave off, turn aside, ward off

feral 1. unbroken, uncultivated, undomesticated, untamed, wild 2. bestial, brutal, fell, ferocious, fierce, savage, vicious

ferment *v.* 1. boil, brew, bubble, concoct, effervesce, foam, froth, heat, leaven, rise, seethe, work ~*n.* 2. bacteria, barm, fermentation agent, leaven, leavening, mother, mother-of-vinegar, yeast ~*v.* 3. *Fig.* agitate, boil, excite, fester, foment, heat, incite, inflame, provoke, rouse, seethe, smoulder, stir up ~*n.* 4. *Fig.* agitation, brouhaha, commotion, disruption, excitement, fever, frenzy, furore, glow, heat, hubbub, imbroglio, state of unrest, stew, stir, tumult, turbulence, turmoil, unrest, uproar
Antonyms *n.* calmness, hush, peacefulness, quiet, restfulness, stillness, tranquillity

ferocious 1. feral, fierce, predatory, rapacious, ravening, savage, violent, wild 2. barbaric, barbarous, bloodthirsty, brutal, brutish, cruel, merciless, pitiless, relentless, ruthless, tigerish, vicious
Antonyms calm, docile, gentle, mild, subdued, submissive, tame

ferocity barbarity, bloodthirstiness, brutality, cruelty, ferociousness, fierceness, inhumanity, rapacity, ruthlessness, sav~ageness, savagery, viciousness, wildness

ferret out bring to light, dig up, disclose, discover, drive out, elicit, get at, nose out, root out, run to earth, search out, smell out, trace, track down, unearth

ferry 1. *n.* ferryboat, packet, packet boat 2. *v.* carry, chauffeur, convey, run, ship, shut~tle, transport

fertile abundant, fat, fecund, flowering, flowing with milk and honey, fruit-bearing, fruitful, generative, luxuriant, plenteous, plentiful, productive, prolific, rich, teem~ing, yielding
Antonyms barren, dry, impotent, infe~cund, infertile, poor, sterile, unfruitful, un~imaginative, uninventive, unproductive

fertility abundance, fecundity, fruitfulness, luxuriance, productiveness, richness

fertilization 1. implantation, impregnation, insemination, pollination, procreation, propagation 2. dressing, manuring, mulch~ing, top dressing

fertilize 1. fecundate, fructify, impregnate, inseminate, make fruitful, make pregnant, pollinate 2. compost, dress, enrich, feed, manure, mulch, top-dress

fertilizer compost, dressing, dung, guano, manure, marl

fervent, fervid animated, ardent, devout, eager, earnest, ecstatic, emotional, enthu~siastic, excited, fiery, flaming, heartfelt, impassioned, intense, perfervid (*Literary*), vehement, warm, zealous
Antonyms apathetic, cold, cool, detached, dispassionate, frigid, impassive, unfeeling, unimpassioned

fervour animation, ardour, eagerness, ear~nestness, enthusiasm, excitement, ferven~cy, intensity, passion, vehemence, warmth, zeal

fester 1. become inflamed, decay, gather, maturate, putrefy, suppurate, ulcerate 2. *Fig.* aggravate, chafe, gall, intensify, irk, rankle, smoulder

festering 1. gathering, inflamed, maturat~ing, poisonous, purulent, pussy, septic, suppurating, ulcerated 2. black-hearted, smouldering, venomous, vicious, virulent

festival 1. anniversary, commemoration, feast, fête, fiesta, holiday, holy day, saint's day 2. carnival, celebration, entertainment, festivities, fête, field day, gala, jubilee, treat

festive back-slapping, carnival, celebra~tory, cheery, Christmassy, convivial, festal, gala, gay, gleeful, happy, hearty, holiday, jolly, jovial, joyful, joyous, jubilant, light-hearted, merry, mirthful, sportive
Antonyms depressing, drab, dreary, fu~nereal, gloomy, lugubrious, mournful, sad

festivity 1. amusement, conviviality, fun, gaiety, jollification, joviality, joyfulness, merriment, merrymaking, mirth, pleasure, revelry, sport 2. *Often plural* beano (*Brit. sl.*), carousal, celebration, entertainment, festival, festive event, festive proceedings, fun and games, jollification, party, rave (*Brit. sl.*), rave-up (*Brit. sl.*)

festoon 1. *n.* chaplet, garland, lei, swag, swathe, wreath 2. *v.* array, bedeck, berib~bon, deck, decorate, drape, garland, hang, swathe, wreathe

fetch 1. bring, carry, conduct, convey, de~liver, escort, get, go for, lead, obtain, re~trieve, transport 2. draw forth, elicit, give rise to, produce 3. bring in, earn, go for, make, realize, sell for, yield

fetching alluring, attractive, captivating, charming, cute, enchanting, enticing, fas~cinating, intriguing, sweet, taking, winsome

fetch up arrive, come, end up, finish up, halt, land, reach, stop, turn up

fête, fete 1. *n.* bazaar, fair, festival, gala, garden party, sale of work 2. *v.* bring out the red carpet for (someone), entertain re~gally, hold a reception for (someone), hon~our, kill the fatted calf for (someone), lion~ize, make much of, treat, wine and dine

fetid corrupt, foul, malodorous, mephitic, noisome, noxious, offensive, olid, rancid, rank, reeking, stinking

fetish 1. amulet, cult object, talisman 2. fixation, *idée fixe*, mania, obsession, thing (*Inf.*)

fetter *v.* bind, chain, confine, curb, encum~ber, gyve (*Archaic*), hamper, hamstring, hobble, hold captive, manacle, put a strait~jacket on, restrain, restrict, shackle, strait~en, tie, tie up, trammel

fetters *n.* 1. bilboes, bonds, chains, gyves (*Archaic*), irons, leg irons, manacles, shackles 2. bondage, captivity, check, curb, hindrance, obstruction, restraint

feud 1. *n.* argument, bad blood, bickering, broil, conflict, contention, disagreement, discord, dissension, enmity, estrangement, faction, falling out, grudge, hostility, quar~rel, row, rivalry, strife, vendetta 2. *v.* be at daggers drawn, be at odds, bicker, brawl, clash, contend, dispute, duel, fall out, quarrel, row, squabble, war

fever *Fig.* agitation, delirium, ecstasy, ex~citement, ferment, fervour, flush, frenzy, heat, intensity, passion, restlessness, tur~moil, unrest

fevered burning, feverish, flushed, hectic, hot, on fire, pyretic (*Medical*)

feverish 1. burning, febrile, fevered, flaming, flushed, hectic, hot, inflamed, pyretic (*Medical*) 2. agitated, desperate, distracted, excited, frantic, frenetic, frenzied, impatient, obsessive, overwrought, restless
Antonyms calm, collected, composed, cool, dispassionate, nonchalant, offhand, serene, tranquil, unfazed (*Inf.*), unemotional, unexcitable, unruffled

few *adj.* 1. hardly any, inconsiderable, infrequent, insufficient, meagre, negligible, not many, rare, scant, scanty, scarce, scarcely any, scattered, sparse, sporadic, thin 2. **few and far between** at great intervals, hard to come by, infrequent, in short supply, irregular, rare, scarce, scattered, seldom met with, uncommon, unusual, widely spaced ~*pron.* 3. handful, scarcely any, scattering, small number, some
Antonyms abundant, bounteous, divers (*Archaic*), inexhaustible, manifold, many, multifarious, plentiful, sundry

fiancé, fiancée betrothed, intended, prospective spouse, wife- *or* husband-to-be

fiasco balls-up (*Taboo sl.*), catastrophe, cock-up (*Brit. sl.*), debacle, disaster, failure, flap (*Inf.*), fuck-up (*Offens. taboo sl.*), mess, rout, ruin, washout (*Inf.*)

fiat 1. authorization, permission, sanction, warrant 2. canon, command, decree, demand, dictate, dictum, edict, mandate, order, ordinance, precept, proclamation, ukase

fib *n.* fiction, lie, pork pie (*Brit. sl.*), porky (*Brit. sl.*), prevarication, story, untruth, white lie, whopper (*Inf.*)

fibre 1. fibril, filament, pile, staple, strand, texture, thread, wisp 2. *Fig.* essence, nature, quality, spirit, substance 3. *Fig. As in* **moral fibre** resolution, stamina, strength, strength of character, toughness

fickle blowing hot and cold, capricious, changeable, faithless, fitful, flighty, inconstant, irresolute, mercurial, mutable, quicksilver, temperamental, unfaithful, unpredictable, unstable, unsteady, vacillating, variable, volatile
Antonyms changeless, constant, faithful, firm, invariable, loyal, reliable, resolute, settled, stable, staunch, steadfast, true, trustworthy

fickleness capriciousness, fitfulness, flightiness, inconstancy, mutability, unfaithfulness, unpredictability, unsteadiness, volatility

fiction 1. fable, fantasy, legend, myth, novel, romance, story, storytelling, tale, urban legend, work of imagination, yarn (*Inf.*) 2. cock and bull story (*Inf.*), concoction, fabrication, falsehood, fancy, fantasy, figment of the imagination, imagination, improvisation, invention, lie, pork pie (*Brit. sl.*), porky (*Brit. sl.*), tall story, untruth

fictional imaginary, invented, legendary, made-up, nonexistent, unreal

fictitious apocryphal, artificial, assumed, bogus, counterfeit, fabricated, false, fanciful, feigned, imaginary, imagined, improvised, invented, made-up, make-believe, mythical, spurious, unreal, untrue
Antonyms actual, authentic, genuine, legitimate, real, true, truthful, veracious, veritable

fiddle *v.* 1. *Often with* **with** fidget, finger, interfere with, mess about *or* around, play, tamper with, tinker, toy, trifle 2. *Inf.* cheat, cook the books (*Inf.*), diddle (*Inf.*), finagle (*Inf.*), fix, gerrymander, graft (*Inf.*), manoeuvre, racketeer, sting (*Inf.*), swindle, wangle (*Inf.*) ~*n.* 3. violin 4. **fit as a fiddle** blooming, hale and hearty, healthy, in fine fettle, in good form, in good shape, in rude health, in the pink, sound, strong 5. *Inf.* fix, fraud, graft (*Inf.*), piece of sharp practice, racket, scam (*Sl.*), sting (*Inf.*), swindle, wangle (*Inf.*)

fiddling futile, insignificant, nickel-and-dime (*U.S. sl.*), pettifogging, petty, trifling, trivial

fidelity 1. allegiance, constancy, dependability, devotedness, devotion, faith, faithfulness, fealty, integrity, lealty (*Archaic or Scot.*), loyalty, staunchness, troth (*Archaic*), true-heartedness, trustworthiness 2. accuracy, adherence, closeness, correspondence, exactitude, exactness, faithfulness, preciseness, precision, scrupulousness
Antonyms disloyalty, faithlessness, falseness, inaccuracy, inexactness, infidelity, perfidiousness, treachery, unfaithfulness, untruthfulness

fidget 1. *v.* be like a cat on hot bricks (*Inf.*), bustle, chafe, fiddle (*Inf.*), fret, jiggle, jitter (*Inf.*), move restlessly, squirm, twitch, worry 2. *n. Usually* **the fidgets** fidgetiness, jitters (*Inf.*), nervousness, restlessness, unease, uneasiness

fidgety impatient, jerky, jittery (*Inf.*), jumpy, nervous, on edge, restive, restless, twitchy (*Inf.*), uneasy

field *n.* 1. grassland, green, greensward (*Archaic or literary*), lea (*Poetic*), mead (*Archaic*), meadow, pasture 2. applicants, candidates, competition, competitors, contestants, entrants, possibilities, runners 3. area, bailiwick, bounds, confines, department, discipline, domain, environment, limits, line, metier, pale, province, purview, range, scope, speciality, specialty, sphere of influence (activity, interest, study), territory ~*v.* 4. catch, pick up, retrieve, return, stop 5. *Fig.* deal with, deflect, handle, turn aside

fiend 1. demon, devil, evil spirit, hellhound 2. barbarian, beast, brute, degenerate, ghoul, monster, ogre, savage 3. *Inf.* addict, enthusiast, fanatic, freak (*Inf.*), maniac

fiendish accursed, atrocious, black-hearted, cruel, demoniac, devilish, diabolical, hellish, implacable, infernal, inhuman, malevolent, malicious, malignant, monstrous, satanic, savage, ungodly, unspeakable, wicked

fierce 1. baleful, barbarous, brutal, cruel, dangerous, fell (*Archaic*), feral, ferocious, fiery, menacing, murderous, passionate, savage, threatening, tigerish, truculent, uncontrollable, untamed, vicious, wild 2. blustery, boisterous, furious, howling, inclement, powerful, raging, stormy, strong, tempestuous, tumultuous, uncontrollable, violent 3. cutthroat, intense, keen, relentless, strong
Antonyms affectionate, calm, civilized, cool, docile, domesticated, gentle, harmless, kind, mild, peaceful, submissive, tame, temperate, tranquil

fiercely ferociously, frenziedly, furiously, in a frenzy, like cat and dog, menacingly, passionately, savagely, tempestuously, tigerishly, tooth and nail, uncontrolledly, viciously, with bared teeth, with no holds barred

fierceness 1. ferocity, fieriness, mercilessness, ruthlessness, savageness, viciousness, wildness 2. bluster, destructiveness, roughness, storminess, tempestuousness, turbulence, violence 3. avidity, fervidness, fervour, intensity, passion, relentlessness, strength

fiery 1. ablaze, afire, aflame, blazing, burning, flaming, glowing, in flames, on fire, red-hot 2. choleric, excitable, fierce, hotheaded, impetuous, irascible, irritable, passionate, peppery, violent 3. burning, febrile, fevered, feverish, flushed, heated, hot, inflamed

fight *v.* 1. assault, battle, bear arms against, box, brawl, carry on war, clash, close, combat, come to blows, conflict, contend, cross swords, do battle, engage, engage in hostilities, exchange blows, feud, go to war, grapple, joust, row, scrap (*Inf.*), spar, struggle, take the field, take up arms against, tilt, tussle, wage war, war, wrestle 2. contest, defy, dispute, make a stand against, oppose, resist, stand up to, strive, struggle, withstand 3. argue, bicker, dispute, fall out (*Inf.*), squabble, wrangle 4. carry on, conduct, engage in, prosecute, wage 5. **fight shy of** avoid, duck out of (*Inf.*), keep aloof from, keep at arm's length, shun, steer clear of ~*n.* 6. action, affray (*Law*), altercation, *bagarre,* battle, bout, brawl, brush, clash, combat, conflict, contest, dispute, dissension, dogfight, duel, encounter, engagement, exchange of blows, fracas, fray, free-for-all (*Inf.*), head-to-head, hostilities, joust, melee *or* mêlée, passage of arms, riot, row, rumble (*U.S. & N.Z. sl.*), scrap (*Inf.*), scrimmage, scuffle, set-to (*Inf.*), shindig (*Inf.*), shindy (*Inf.*), skirmish, sparring match, struggle, tussle, war 7. *Fig.* belligerence, gameness, mettle, militancy, pluck, resistance, spirit, will to resist

fight back 1. defend oneself, give tit for tat, hit back, put up a fight, reply, resist, retaliate 2. bottle up, contain, control, curb, hold back, hold in check, restrain

fight down bottle up, control, curb, hold back, repress, restrain, suppress

fighter 1. fighting man, man-at-arms, soldier, warrior 2. boxer, bruiser (*Inf.*), prize fighter, pugilist 3. antagonist, battler, belligerent, combatant, contender, contestant, disputant, militant

fighting 1. *adj.* aggressive, argumentative, bellicose, belligerent, combative, contentious, disputatious, hawkish, martial, militant, pugnacious, sabre-rattling, truculent, warlike 2. *n.* battle, bloodshed, blows struck, combat, conflict, hostilities, warfare

fight off beat off, keep *or* hold at bay, repel, repress, repulse, resist, stave off, ward off

figment creation, fable, fabrication, falsehood, fancy, fiction, improvisation, invention, production

figurative 1. allegorical, emblematical, metaphorical, representative, symbolical, typical 2. descriptive, fanciful, florid, flowery, ornate, pictorial, poetical, tropical (*Rhetoric*)
Antonyms accurate, exact, factual, faithful, literal, prosaic, simple, true, unpoetical, unvarnished

figure *n.* 1. character, cipher, digit, number, numeral, symbol 2. amount, cost, price, sum, total, value 3. form, outline, shadow, shape, silhouette 4. body, build, chassis (*Sl.*), frame, physique, proportions, shape, torso 5. depiction, design, device, diagram, drawing, emblem, illustration, motif, pattern, representation, sketch 6. celebrity, character, dignitary, force, leader, notability, notable, personage, personality, presence, somebody, worthy ~*v.* 7. *Often with*

up add, calculate, compute, count, reckon, sum, tally, tot up, work out 8. *Usually with* **in** act, appear, be conspicuous, be featured, be included, be mentioned, contribute to, feature, have a place in, play a part 9. **it figures** it follows, it goes without saying, it is to be expected

figured adorned, decorated, embellished, marked, ornamented, patterned, variegated

figurehead cipher, dummy, front man (*Inf.*), leader in name only, man of straw, mouthpiece, name, nonentity, puppet, straw man (*Chiefly U.S.*), titular *or* nominal head, token

figure of speech conceit, image, trope, turn of phrase

figure out 1. calculate, compute, reckon, work out 2. comprehend, decipher, fathom, make head or tail of (*Inf.*), make out, resolve, see, suss (out) (*Sl.*), understand

filament cilium (*Biol. & Zool.*), fibre, fibril, pile, staple, strand, string, thread, wire, wisp

filch abstract, cabbage (*Brit. sl.*), crib (*Inf.*), embezzle, half-inch (*Old-fashioned sl.*), lift (*Inf.*), misappropriate, nick (*Sl., chiefly Brit.*), pilfer, pinch (*Inf.*), purloin, rip off (*Sl.*), snaffle (*Brit. inf.*), steal, swipe (*Sl.*), take, thieve, walk off with

file[1] *v.* abrade, burnish, furbish, polish, rasp, refine, rub, rub down, scrape, shape, smooth

file[2] *n.* 1. case, data, documents, dossier, folder, information, portfolio ~*v.* 2. document, enter, pigeonhole, put in place, record, register, slot in (*Inf.*) ~*n.* 3. column, line, list, queue, row, string ~*v.* 4. march, parade, troop

filibuster *n.* 1. *Chiefly U.S., with reference to legislation* delay, hindrance, obstruction, postponement, procrastination ~*v.* 2. *Chiefly U.S., with reference to legislation* delay, hinder, obstruct, prevent, procrastinate, put off ~*n.* 3. adventurer, buccaneer, corsair, freebooter, pirate, sea robber, sea rover, soldier of fortune

filigree lace, lacework, lattice, tracery, wirework

fill 1. brim over, cram, crowd, furnish, glut, gorge, inflate, pack, pervade, replenish, sate, satiate, satisfy, stock, store, stuff, supply, swell 2. charge, imbue, impregnate, overspread, pervade, saturate, suffuse 3. block, bung, close, cork, plug, seal, stop 4. assign, carry out, discharge, engage, execute, fulfil, hold, occupy, officiate, perform, take up 5. **one's fill** all one wants, ample, a sufficiency, enough, plenty, sufficient

Antonyms diminish, drain, empty, exhaust, shrink, subside, vacate, void

fill in 1. answer, complete, fill out (*U.S.*), fill up 2. *Inf.* acquaint, apprise, bring up to date, give the facts *or* background, inform, put wise (*Sl.*) 3. deputize, replace, represent, stand in, sub, substitute, take the place of

filling 1. *n.* contents, filler, innards (*Inf.*), inside, insides, padding, stuffing, wadding 2. *adj.* ample, heavy, satisfying, square, substantial

fillip *n.* goad, incentive, prod, push, spice, spur, stimulus, zest

film *n.* 1. coat, coating, covering, dusting, gauze, integument, layer, membrane, pellicle, scum, skin, tissue 2. blur, cloud, haze, haziness, mist, mistiness, opacity, veil 3. flick (*Sl.*), motion picture, movie (*U.S. inf.*) ~*v.* 4. photograph, shoot, take, video, videotape 5. *Often with* **over** blear, blur, cloud, dull, haze, mist, veil

filmy 1. chiffon, cobwebby, delicate, diaphanous, fine, finespun, flimsy, floaty, fragile, gauzy, gossamer, insubstantial, seethrough, sheer, transparent 2. bleared, bleary, blurred, blurry, cloudy, dim, hazy, membranous, milky, misty, opalescent, opaque, pearly

filter *v.* 1. clarify, filtrate, purify, refine, screen, sieve, sift, strain, winnow 2. *Often with* **through** *or* **out** dribble, escape, exude, leach, leak, ooze, penetrate, percolate, seep, trickle, well ~*n.* 3. gauze, membrane, mesh, riddle, sieve, strainer

filth 1. carrion, contamination, crap (*Sl.*), crud (*Sl.*), defilement, dirt, dung, excrement, excreta, faeces, filthiness, foul matter, foulness, garbage, grime, grot (*Sl.*), muck, nastiness, ordure, pollution, putrefaction, putrescence, refuse, sewage, shit (*Taboo sl.*), slime, sludge, squalor, uncleanness 2. corruption, dirty-mindedness, impurity, indecency, obscenity, pornography, smut, vileness, vulgarity

filthy 1. dirty, faecal, feculent, foul, nasty, polluted, putrid, scummy, scuzzy (*Sl., chiefly U.S.*), slimy, squalid, unclean, vile 2. begrimed, black, blackened, grimy, grubby, miry, mucky, muddy, mud-encrusted, scuzzy (*Sl., chiefly U.S.*), smoky, sooty, unwashed 3. bawdy, coarse, corrupt, depraved, dirty-minded, foul, foul-mouthed, impure, indecent, lewd, licentious, obscene, pornographic, smutty, suggestive 4. base, contemptible, despicable, low, mean, offensive, scurvy, vicious, vile

final 1. closing, concluding, end, eventual, last, last-minute, latest, terminal, terminating, ultimate 2. absolute, conclusive,

decided, decisive, definite, definitive, determinate, finished, incontrovertible, irrevocable, settled
Antonyms earliest, first, initial, introductory, maiden, opening, original, precursory, prefatory, premier, preparatory

finale climax, close, conclusion, crowning glory, culmination, dénouement, epilogue, finis, last act
Antonyms commencement, exordium, foreword, intro (*Inf.*), lead-in, opening, overture, preamble, preface, preliminaries, prelude, proem, prolegomenon, prologue

finality certitude, conclusiveness, decidedness, decisiveness, definiteness, inevitableness, irrevocability, resolution, unavoidability

finalize agree, clinch, complete, conclude, decide, settle, sew up (*Inf.*), tie up, work out, wrap up (*Inf.*)

finally 1. at last, at length, at long last, at the last, at the last moment, eventually, in the end, in the long run, lastly, ultimately, when all is said and done 2. in conclusion, in summary, to conclude 3. beyond the shadow of a doubt, completely, conclusively, convincingly, decisively, for all time, for ever, for good, inescapably, inexorably, irrevocably, once and for all, permanently

finance 1. *n.* accounts, banking, business, commerce, economics, financial affairs, investment, money, money management 2. *v.* back, bankroll (*U.S.*), float, fund, guarantee, pay for, provide security for, set up in business, subsidize, support, underwrite

finances affairs, assets, capital, cash, financial condition, funds, money, resources, wherewithal

financial budgeting, economic, fiscal, monetary, money, pecuniary

financing *n.* costs, expenditure, expense(s), funding, operating expenses, outlay

find *v.* 1. catch sight of, chance upon, come across, come up with, descry, discover, encounter, espy, expose, ferret out, hit upon, lay one's hand on, light upon, locate, meet, recognize, run to earth, spot, stumble upon, track down, turn up, uncover, unearth 2. achieve, acquire, attain, earn, gain, get, obtain, procure, win 3. get back, recover, regain, repossess, retrieve 4. arrive at, ascertain, become aware, detect, discover, experience, learn, note, notice, observe, perceive, realise, remark 5. be responsible for, bring, contribute, cough up (*Inf.*), furnish, provide, purvey, supply ~*n.* 6. acquisition, asset, bargain, catch, discovery, good buy
Antonyms (*sense 1*) lose, mislay, misplace, miss, overlook

finding award, conclusion, decision, decree, judgment, pronouncement, recommendation, verdict

find out 1. detect, discover, learn, note, observe, perceive, realize 2. bring to light, catch, detect, disclose, expose, reveal, rumble (*Brit. inf.*), suss (out) (*Sl.*), uncover, unmask

fine[1] *adj.* 1. accomplished, admirable, beautiful, choice, excellent, exceptional, exquisite, first-class, first-rate, great, magnificent, masterly, ornate, outstanding, rare, select, showy, skilful, splendid, sterling, superior, supreme, world-class 2. balmy, bright, clear, clement, cloudless, dry, fair, pleasant, sunny 3. dainty, delicate, elegant, expensive, exquisite, fragile, quality 4. abstruse, acute, critical, discriminating, fastidious, hairsplitting, intelligent, keen, minute, nice, precise, quick, refined, sensitive, sharp, subtle, tasteful, tenuous 5. delicate, diaphanous, fine-grained, flimsy, gauzy, gossamer, light, lightweight, powdered, powdery, pulverized, sheer, slender, small, thin 6. clear, pure, refined, solid, sterling, unadulterated, unalloyed, unpolluted 7. attractive, bonny, good-looking, handsome, lovely, smart, striking, stylish, well-favoured 8. acceptable, agreeable, all right, convenient, good, hunky-dory (*Inf.*), O.K. *or* okay (*Inf.*), satisfactory, suitable 9. brilliant, cutting, honed, keen, polished, razor-sharp, sharp
Antonyms (*sense 1*) indifferent, inferior, poor, second rate, substandard (*sense 2*) cloudy, dull, overcast, unpleasant (*senses 3 & 4*) blunt, coarse, crude, dull, heavy, rough, uncultured, unfinished, unrefined

fine[2] 1. *v.* amerce (*Archaic*), mulct, penalize, punish 2. *n.* amercement (*Obsolete*), damages, forfeit, penalty, punishment

finery best bib and tucker (*Inf.*), decorations, frippery, gear (*Inf.*), gewgaws, glad rags (*Inf.*), ornaments, showiness, splendour, Sunday best, trappings, trinkets

finesse *n.* 1. adeptness, adroitness, artfulness, cleverness, craft, delicacy, diplomacy, discretion, know-how (*Inf.*), polish, quickness, savoir-faire, skill, sophistication, subtlety, tact 2. artifice, bluff, feint, manoeuvre, ruse, stratagem, trick, wile ~*v.* 3. bluff, manipulate, manoeuvre

finger *v.* 1. feel, fiddle with (*Inf.*), handle, manipulate, maul, meddle with, paw (*Inf.*), play about with, touch, toy with 2. **put one's finger on** bring to mind, discover, find out, hit the nail on the head, hit upon, identify, indicate, locate, pin down, place, recall, remember

finicky choosy (*Inf.*), critical, dainty, difficult, fastidious, finicking, fussy, hard to please, nit-picking (*Inf.*), overnice, over~particular, particular, picky (*Inf.*), scrupulous, squeamish

finish *v.* 1. accomplish, achieve, bring to a close *or* conclusion, carry through, cease, close, complete, conclude, culminate, deal with, discharge, do, end, execute, finalize, fulfil, get done, get out of the way, make short work of, put the finishing touch(es) to, round off, settle, stop, terminate, wind up, wrap up (*Inf.*) 2. *Sometimes with* **up** *or* **off** consume, deplete, devour, dispatch, dispose of, drain, drink, eat, empty, exhaust, expend, spend, use, use up 3. *Often with* **off** administer *or* give the coup de grâce, annihilate, best, bring down, defeat, destroy, dispose of, drive to the wall, exterminate, get rid of, kill, overcome, overpower, put an end to, rout, ruin, worst ~*n.* 4. cessation, close, closing, completion, conclusion, culmination, dénouement, end, ending, finale, last stage(s), termination, winding up (*Inf.*), wind-up 5. annihilation, bankruptcy, curtains (*Inf.*), death, defeat, end, end of the road, liquidation, ruin ~*v.* 6. elaborate, perfect, polish, refine ~*n.* 7. cultivation, culture, elaboration, perfection, polish, refinement, sophistication ~*v.* 8. coat, face, gild, lacquer, polish, smooth off, stain, texture, veneer, wax ~*n.* 9. appearance, grain, lustre, patina, polish, shine, smoothness, surface, texture

Antonyms *v.* begin, commence, create, embark on, instigate, start, undertake ~*n.* beginning, birth, commencement, conception, genesis, inauguration, inception, instigation, preamble, preface, prologue

finished 1. accomplished, classic, consummate, cultivated, elegant, expert, flawless, impeccable, masterly, perfected, polished, professional, proficient, refined, skilled, smooth, urbane 2. accomplished, achieved, closed, complete, completed, concluded, done, ended, entire, final, finalized, full, in the past, over, over and done with, sewed up (*Inf.*), shut, terminated, through, tied up, wrapped up (*Inf.*) 3. done, drained, empty, exhausted, gone, played out (*Inf.*), spent, used up 4. bankrupt, defeated, devastated, done for (*Inf.*), doomed, gone, liquidated, lost, ruined, through, undone, washed up (*Inf., chiefly U.S.*), wiped out, wound up, wrecked

Antonyms basic, begun, coarse, crude, imperfect, inartistic, incomplete, inelegant, inexperienced, raw, rough, unfinished, unrefined, unskilled, unsophisticated

finite bounded, circumscribed, conditioned, delimited, demarcated, limited, restricted, subject to limitations, terminable

Antonyms boundless, endless, eternal, everlasting, immeasurable, infinite, interminable, limitless, perpetual, unbounded

fire *n.* 1. blaze, combustion, conflagration, flames, inferno 2. barrage, bombardment, cannonade, flak, fusillade, hail, salvo, shelling, sniping, volley 3. *Fig.* animation, ardour, brio, burning passion, dash, eagerness, élan, enthusiasm, excitement, fervency, fervour, force, heat, impetuosity, intensity, life, light, lustre, passion, pizzazz *or* pizazz (*Inf.*), radiance, scintillation, sparkle, spirit, splendour, verve, vigour, virtuosity, vivacity 4. **hanging fire** delayed, in abeyance, pending, postponed, put back, put off, shelved, suspended, undecided 5. **on fire a.** ablaze, aflame, alight, blazing, burning, fiery, flaming, in flames **b.** ardent, eager, enthusiastic, excited, inspired, passionate ~*v.* 6. enkindle, ignite, kindle, light, put a match to, set ablaze, set aflame, set alight, set fire to, set on fire 7. detonate, discharge, eject, explode, hurl, launch, let off, loose, pull the trigger, set off, shell, shoot, touch off 8. *Fig.* animate, arouse, electrify, enliven, excite, galvanize, impassion, incite, inflame, inspire, inspirit, irritate, quicken, rouse, stir 9. *Inf.* cashier, discharge, dismiss, give marching orders, kiss off (*Sl., chiefly U.S. & Canad.*), make redundant, sack (*Inf.*), show the door

firebrand *Fig.* agitator, demagogue, fomenter, incendiary, instigator, rabble-rouser, soapbox orator, tub-thumper

fireworks 1. illuminations, pyrotechnics 2. *Fig.* fit of rage, hysterics, paroxysms, rage, rows, storm, temper, trouble, uproar

firm[1] *adj.* 1. close-grained, compact, compressed, concentrated, congealed, dense, hard, inelastic, inflexible, jelled, jellified, rigid, set, solid, solidified, stiff, unyielding 2. anchored, braced, cemented, embedded, fast, fastened, fixed, immovable, motionless, riveted, robust, rooted, secure, secured, stable, stationary, steady, strong, sturdy, taut, tight, unfluctuating, unmoving, unshakable 3. adamant, constant, definite, fixed, immovable, inflexible, obdurate, resolute, resolved, set on, settled, stalwart, staunch, steadfast, strict, true, unalterable, unbending, unfaltering, unflinching, unshakable, unshaken, unswerving, unwavering, unyielding

Antonyms flabby, flaccid, flimsy, inconstant, insecure, irresolute, limp, loose, shaky, soft, unreliable, unstable, unsteady, wavering

firm[2] *n.* association, business, company, concern, conglomerate, corporation, enter~

prise, house, organization, outfit (*Inf.*), partnership

firmament empyrean (*Poetic*), heaven, heavens, sky, the blue, the skies, vault, vault of heaven, welkin (*Archaic*)

firmly 1. enduringly, immovably, like a rock, motionlessly, securely, steadily, tightly, unflinchingly, unshakably 2. determinedly, resolutely, staunchly, steadfastly, strictly, through thick and thin, unchangeably, unwaveringly, with a rod of iron, with decision

firmness 1. compactness, density, fixedness, hardness, inelasticity, inflexibility, resistance, rigidity, solidity, stiffness 2. immovability, soundness, stability, steadiness, strength, tautness, tensile strength, tension, tightness 3. constancy, fixedness, fixity of purpose, inflexibility, obduracy, resolution, resolve, staunchness, steadfastness, strength of will, strictness

first *adj.* 1. chief, foremost, head, highest, leading, pre-eminent, prime, principal, ruling 2. earliest, initial, introductory, maiden, opening, original, premier, primeval, primitive, primordial, pristine 3. basic, cardinal, elementary, fundamental, key, primary, rudimentary ~*adv.* 4. at the beginning, at the outset, before all else, beforehand, firstly, initially, in the first place, to begin with, to start with ~*n.* 5. *As in* **from the first** beginning, commencement, inception, introduction, outset, start, starting point, word 'go' (*Inf.*)

firsthand direct, straight from the horse's mouth

first-rate admirable, A1 *or* A-one (*Inf.*), boffo (*Sl.*), brill (*Inf.*), chillin' (*U.S. sl.*), crack (*Sl.*), cracking (*Brit. inf.*), crucial (*Sl.*), def (*Sl.*), elite, excellent, exceptional, exclusive, first class, jim-dandy (*Sl.*), mean (*Sl.*), mega (*Sl.*), outstanding, prime, second to none, sovereign, superb, superlative, tiptop, top, topnotch (*Inf.*), topping (*Brit. sl.*), tops (*Sl.*), world-class

fiscal budgetary, economic, financial, monetary, money, pecuniary

fish for angle for, elicit, hint at, hope for, hunt for, invite, look for, search for, seek, solicit

fish out extract, extricate, find, haul out, produce, pull out

fishy 1. *Inf.* dodgy (*Brit., Aust., & N.Z. inf.*), doubtful, dubious, funny (*Inf.*), implausible, improbable, odd, queer, questionable, rum (*Brit. sl.*), suspect, suspicious, unlikely 2. blank, deadpan, dull, expressionless, glassy, glassy-eyed, inexpressive, lacklustre, lifeless, vacant, wooden 3. fishlike, piscatorial, piscatory, piscine

fission breaking, cleavage, division, parting, rending, rupture, schism, scission, splitting

fissure breach, break, chink, cleavage, cleft, crack, cranny, crevice, fault, fracture, gap, hole, interstice, opening, rent, rift, rupture, slit, split

fit[1] *adj.* 1. able, adapted, adequate, apposite, appropriate, apt, becoming, capable, competent, convenient, correct, deserving, equipped, expedient, fitted, fitting, good enough, meet (*Archaic*), prepared, proper, qualified, ready, right, seemly, suitable, trained, well-suited, worthy 2. able-bodied, hale, healthy, in good condition, in good shape, in good trim, robust, strapping, toned up, trim, well ~*v.* 3. accord, agree, be consonant, belong, concur, conform, correspond, dovetail, go, interlock, join, match, meet, suit, tally 4. *Often with* **out** *or* **up** accommodate, accoutre, arm, equip, fit out, kit out, outfit, prepare, provide, rig out 5. adapt, adjust, alter, arrange, dispose, fashion, modify, place, position, shape

Antonyms (*sense 1*) amiss, ill-fitted, ill-suited, improper, inadequate, inappropriate, unfit, unprepared, unseemly, unsuitable, untimely (*sense 2*) flabby, in poor condition, out of shape, out of trim, unfit, unhealthy

fit[2] *n.* 1. attack, bout, convulsion, paroxysm, seizure, spasm 2. caprice, fancy, humour, mood, whim 3. bout, burst, outbreak, outburst, spell 4. **by fits and starts** erratically, fitfully, intermittently, irregularly, on and off, spasmodically, sporadically, unsystematically

fitful broken, desultory, disturbed, erratic, flickering, fluctuating, haphazard, impulsive, inconstant, intermittent, irregular, spasmodic, sporadic, uneven, unstable, variable

Antonyms constant, equable, even, orderly, predictable, regular, steady, systematic, unchanging, uniform

fitfully desultorily, erratically, in fits and starts, in snatches, intermittently, interruptedly, irregularly, off and on, spasmodically, sporadically

fitness 1. adaptation, applicability, appropriateness, aptness, competence, eligibility, pertinence, preparedness, propriety, qualifications, readiness, seemliness, suitability 2. good condition, good health, health, robustness, strength, vigour

fitted 1. adapted, cut out for, equipped, fit, qualified, right, suitable, tailor-made 2. *Often with* **with** accoutred, appointed, armed, equipped, furnished, outfitted, provided, rigged out, set up, supplied 3. built-in, permanent

fitting 1. *adj.* apposite, appropriate, becoming, *comme il faut,* correct, decent, decorous, desirable, meet (*Archaic*), proper, right, seemly, suitable 2. *n.* accessory, attachment, component, connection, part, piece, unit
Antonyms ill-suited, improper, unfitting, unseemly, unsuitable

fittings accessories, accoutrements, appointments, appurtenances, conveniences, equipment, extras, furnishings, furniture, trimmings

fix *v.* 1. anchor, embed, establish, implant, install, locate, place, plant, position, root, set, settle 2. attach, bind, cement, connect, couple, fasten, glue, link, make fast, pin, secure, stick, tie 3. agree on, appoint, arrange, arrive at, conclude, decide, define, determine, establish, limit, name, resolve, set, settle, specify 4. adjust, correct, mend, patch up, put to rights, regulate, repair, see to, sort 5. congeal, consolidate, harden, rigidify, set, solidify, stiffen, thicken 6. direct, focus, level at, rivet 7. *Inf.* bribe, fiddle (*Inf.*), influence, manipulate, manoeuvre, pull strings (*Inf.*), rig 8. *Sl.* cook (someone's) goose (*Inf.*), get even with (*Inf.*), get revenge on, pay back, settle (someone's) hash (*Inf.*), sort (someone) out (*Inf.*), take retribution on, wreak vengeance on ~*n.* 9. *Inf.* difficult situation, difficulty, dilemma, embarrassment, hole (*Sl.*), hot water (*Inf.*), jam (*Inf.*), mess, pickle (*Inf.*), plight, predicament, quandary, spot (*Inf.*), ticklish situation, tight spot

fixation complex, hang-up (*Inf.*), *idée fixe,* infatuation, mania, obsession, preoccupation, thing (*Inf.*)

fixed 1. anchored, attached, established, immovable, made fast, permanent, rigid, rooted, secure, set 2. intent, level, resolute, steady, unbending, unblinking, undeviating, unflinching, unwavering 3. agreed, arranged, decided, definite, established, planned, resolved, settled 4. going, in working order, mended, put right, repaired, sorted 5. *Inf.* framed, manipulated, packed, put-up, rigged
Antonyms bending, inconstant, mobile, motile, moving, pliant, unfixed, varying, wavering

fixity doggedness, intentness, perseverance, persistence, stability, steadiness

fix up 1. agree on, arrange, fix, organize, plan, settle, sort out 2. *Often with* **with** accommodate, arrange for, bring about, furnish, lay on, provide

fizz bubble, effervesce, fizzle, froth, hiss, sparkle, sputter

fizzle out abort, collapse, come to nothing, die away, end in disappointment, fail, fall through, fold (*Inf.*), miss the mark, peter out

fizzy bubbling, bubbly, carbonated, effervescent, gassy, sparkling

flab beef (*Inf.*), fat, flabbiness, flesh, fleshiness, heaviness, overweight, plumpness, slackness, weight

flabbergasted abashed, amazed, astonished, astounded, bowled over (*Inf.*), confounded, dazed, disconcerted, dumbfounded, gobsmacked (*Brit. sl.*), nonplussed, overcome, overwhelmed, rendered speechless, speechless, staggered, struck dumb, stunned

flabbiness bloatedness, flaccidity, limpness, looseness, pendulousness, slackness

flabby 1. baggy, drooping, flaccid, floppy, hanging, lax, limp, loose, pendulous, sagging, slack, sloppy, toneless, unfit, yielding 2. effete, enervated, feeble, impotent, ineffective, ineffectual, nerveless, spineless, weak, wimpish *or* wimpy (*Inf.*)
Antonyms firm, hard, solid, strong, taut, tense, tight, tough

flaccid drooping, flabby, lax, limp, loose, nerveless, slack, soft, weak

flaccidity flabbiness, limpness, looseness, nervelessness, slackness, softness

flag[1] *v.* abate, decline, die, droop, ebb, fade, fail, faint, fall, fall off, feel the pace, languish, peter out, pine, sag, sink, slump, succumb, taper off, wane, weaken, weary, wilt

flag[2] *n.* 1. banderole, banner, colours, ensign, gonfalon, jack, pennant, pennon, standard, streamer ~*v.* 2. *Sometimes with* **down** hail, salute, signal, warn, wave 3. docket, indicate, label, mark, note, tab

flagellate beat, castigate, chastise, flay, flog, lambast(e), lash, scourge, thrash, whip

flagellation beating, flogging, lashing, thrashing, whipping

flagging declining, decreasing, deteriorating, ebbing, fading, failing, faltering, giving up, sinking, slowing down, tiring, waning, weakening, wilting

flagrancy blatancy, enormity, heinousness, infamy, insolence, ostentation, outrageousness, public display, shamelessness

flagrant arrant, atrocious, awful, barefaced, blatant, bold, brazen, crying, dreadful, egregious, enormous, flagitious, flaunting, glaring, heinous, immodest, infamous, notorious, open, ostentatious, out-and-out, outrageous, scandalous, shameless, undisguised
Antonyms delicate, faint, implied, indirect, insinuated, slight, subtle, understated

flagstone block, flag, paving stone, slab

flail *v.* beat, thrash, thresh, windmill

flair 1. ability, accomplishment, aptitude, faculty, feel, genius, gift, knack, mastery, talent 2. chic, dash, discernment, elegance, panache, style, stylishness, taste

flak *Fig.* abuse, bad press, brickbats (*Inf.*), censure, complaints, condemnation, criti~cism, disapprobation, disapproval, dispar~agement, fault-finding, hostility, opposi~tion, stick (*Sl.*)

flake 1. *n.* disk, lamina, layer, peeling, scale, shaving, sliver, squama (*Biol.*), wafer 2. *v.* blister, chip, desquamate, peel (off), scale (off)

flake out collapse, faint, keel over, lose consciousness, pass out, swoon (*Literary*)

flamboyant 1. actorly, baroque, camp (*Inf.*), elaborate, extravagant, florid, ornate, ostentatious, over the top (*Inf.*), rich, roco~co, showy, theatrical 2. brilliant, colourful, dashing, dazzling, exciting, glamorous, glitzy (*Sl.*), swashbuckling

flame *v.* 1. blaze, burn, flare, flash, glare, glow, shine ~*n.* 2. blaze, brightness, fire, light 3. *Fig.* affection, ardour, enthusiasm, fervency, fervour, fire, intensity, keenness, passion, warmth 4. *Inf.* beau, beloved, boy~friend, girlfriend, heart-throb (*Brit.*), lady~love, lover, sweetheart

flameproof fire-resistant, incombustible, nonflammable, non-inflammable

flaming 1. ablaze, afire, blazing, brilliant, burning, fiery, glowing, ignited, in flames, raging, red, red-hot 2. angry, ardent, aroused, frenzied, hot, impassioned, in~tense, raging, scintillating, vehement, vivid

flammable combustible, ignitable, incen~diary, inflammable

flank *n.* 1. ham, haunch, hip, loin, quarter, side, thigh 2. side, wing ~*v.* 3. border, bound, edge, fringe, line, screen, skirt, wall

flannel *Fig.* 1. *n.* baloney (*Inf.*), blarney, equivocation, flattery, hedging, prevarica~tion, soft soap (*Inf.*), sweet talk (*U.S. inf.*), waffle (*Inf., chiefly Brit.*), weasel words (*Inf., chiefly U.S.*) 2. *v.* blarney, butter up, equivocate, flatter, hedge, prevaricate, pull the wool over (someone's) eyes, soft-soap (*Inf.*), sweet-talk (*Inf.*), waffle (*Inf., chiefly Brit.*)

flap *v.* 1. agitate, beat, flail, flutter, shake, swing, swish, thrash, thresh, vibrate, wag, wave ~*n.* 2. bang, banging, beating, flutter, shaking, swinging, swish, waving ~*v.* 3. *Inf.* dither (*Chiefly Brit.*), fuss, panic ~*n.* 4. *Inf.* agitation, commotion, fluster, panic, state (*Inf.*), stew (*Inf.*), sweat (*Inf.*), tizzy (*Inf.*), twitter (*Inf.*) 5. apron, cover, fly, fold, lapel, lappet, overlap, skirt, tab, tail

flare *v.* 1. blaze, burn up, dazzle, flicker, flutter, glare, waver 2. *Often with* **out** broaden, spread out, widen ~*n.* 3. blaze, burst, dazzle, flame, flash, flicker, glare

flare up blaze, blow one's top (*Inf.*), boil over, break out, explode, fire up, fly off the handle (*Inf.*), lose control, lose one's cool (*Inf.*), lose one's temper, throw a tantrum

flash *v.* 1. blaze, coruscate, flare, flicker, glare, gleam, glint, glisten, glitter, light, scintillate, shimmer, sparkle, twinkle ~*n.* 2. blaze, burst, coruscation, dazzle, flare, flicker, gleam, ray, scintillation, shaft, shimmer, spark, sparkle, streak, twinkle ~*v.* 3. barrel (along) (*Inf., chiefly U.S. & Canad.*), bolt, burn rubber (*Inf.*), dart, dash, fly, race, shoot, speed, sprint, streak, sweep, whistle, zoom ~*n.* 4. instant, jiffy (*Inf.*), moment, second, shake, split second, trice, twinkling, twinkling of an eye, two shakes of a lamb's tail (*Inf.*) ~*v.* 5. display, exhibit, expose, flaunt, flourish, show ~*n.* 6. burst, demonstration, display, manifes~tation, outburst, show, sign, touch ~*adj.* 7. *Inf.* cheap, glamorous, naff (*Brit. sl.*), os~tentatious, tacky (*Inf.*), tasteless, vulgar

flashy brash, cheap, cheap and nasty, flam~boyant, flaunting, garish, gaudy, glittery, glitzy (*Sl.*), in poor taste, jazzy (*Inf.*), loud, meretricious, naff (*Brit. sl.*), ostentatious, over the top (*Inf.*), showy, snazzy (*Inf.*), tacky (*Inf.*), tasteless, tawdry, tinselly

Antonyms downbeat, low-key, modest, natural, plain, unaffected, understated

flat[1] *adj.* 1. even, horizontal, level, levelled, low, planar, plane, smooth, unbroken 2. laid low, lying full length, outstretched, prone, prostrate, reclining, recumbent, su~pine 3. boring, dead, dull, flavourless, ho-hum (*Inf.*), insipid, jejune, lacklustre, life~less, monotonous, pointless, prosaic, spir~itless, stale, tedious, uninteresting, vapid, watery, weak 4. absolute, categorical, di~rect, downright, explicit, final, fixed, out-and-out, peremptory, plain, positive, straight, unconditional, unequivocal, un~mistakable, unqualified 5. blown out, burst, collapsed, deflated, empty, punc~tured ~*n.* 6. *Often plural* lowland, marsh, mud flat, plain, shallow, shoal, strand, swamp ~*adv.* 7. absolutely, categorically, completely, exactly, point blank, precisely, utterly 8. **flat out** all out, at full gallop, at full speed, at full tilt, for all one is worth, hell for leather (*Inf.*), posthaste, under full steam

Antonyms (*sense 1*) broken, hilly, irregu~lar, rolling, rough, rugged, slanting, sloping, uneven, up and down (*sense 2*) on end, perpendicular, straight, upright, vertical (*sense 3*) bubbly, effervescent, exciting, fizzy, palatable, sparkling, tasty, zestful

flat[2] apartment, rooms

flatly absolutely, categorically, completely, positively, unhesitatingly

flatness 1. evenness, horizontality, levelness, smoothness, uniformity 2. dullness, emptiness, insipidity, monotony, staleness, tedium, vapidity

flatten 1. compress, even out, iron out, level, plaster, raze, roll, smooth off, squash, trample 2. bowl over, crush, fell, floor, knock down, knock off one's feet, prostrate, subdue

flatter 1. blandish, butter up, cajole, compliment, court, fawn, flannel (*Brit. inf.*), humour, inveigle, lay it on (thick) (*Sl.*), pander to, praise, puff, soft-soap (*Inf.*), sweet-talk (*Inf.*), wheedle 2. become, do something for, enhance, set off, show to advantage, suit

flattering 1. becoming, effective, enhancing, kind, well-chosen 2. adulatory, complimentary, fawning, fulsome, gratifying, honeyed, honey-tongued, ingratiating, laudatory, sugary

Antonyms (*sense 1*) not shown in the best light, not shown to advantage, plain, unattractive, unbecoming, unflattering (*sense 2*) blunt, candid, honest, straight, uncomplimentary, warts and all

flattery adulation, blandishment, blarney, cajolery, false praise, fawning, flannel (*Brit. inf.*), fulsomeness, honeyed words, obsequiousness, servility, soft-soap (*Inf.*), sweet-talk (*Inf.*), sycophancy, toadyism

flatulence 1. borborygmus (*Medical*), eructation, wind 2. *Fig.* boasting, bombast, claptrap, empty words, fanfaronade (*Rare*), fustian, hot air (*Inf.*), pomposity, prolixity, rodomontade, twaddle

flatulent *Fig.* bombastic, inflated, long-winded, pompous, pretentious, prolix, swollen, tedious, turgid, wordy

flaunt boast, brandish, display, disport, exhibit, flash about, flourish, make an exhibition of, make a (great) show of, parade, show off, sport (*Inf.*), vaunt

flaunting brazen, flamboyant, gaudy, ostentatious, pretentious

flavour *n.* 1. aroma, essence, extract, flavouring, odour, piquancy, relish, savour, seasoning, smack, tang, taste, zest, zing (*Inf.*) 2. aspect, character, essence, feel, feeling, property, quality, soupçon, stamp, style, suggestion, tinge, tone, touch ~*v.* 3. ginger up, imbue, infuse, lace, leaven, season, spice

Antonyms (*sense 1*) blandness, flatness, insipidity, odourlessness, tastelessness, vapidity

flavouring essence, extract, spirit, tincture, zest

flaw 1. blemish, defect, disfigurement, failing, fault, imperfection, scar, speck, spot, weakness, weak spot 2. breach, break, cleft, crack, crevice, fissure, fracture, rent, rift, scission, split, tear

flawed blemished, broken, chipped, cracked, damaged, defective, erroneous, faulty, imperfect, unsound

flawless 1. faultless, impeccable, perfect, spotless, unblemished, unsullied 2. intact, sound, unbroken, undamaged, whole

flay 1. excoriate, skin 2. *Fig.* castigate, excoriate, execrate, give a tongue-lashing, pull to pieces (*Inf.*), revile, slam (*Sl.*), tear a strip off, tear into (*Inf.*), upbraid

fleabite drop in the ocean, nothing, piddling amount, pinprick, trifle

flea-bitten crawling, decrepit, fetid, flea-ridden, frowsty, grotty (*Sl.*), grubby, infested, insalubrious, lousy, mean, mucky, pediculous (*Medical*), run-down, scabby, scruffy, scurfy, sleazy, slummy, sordid, squalid, tatty, unhygienic

fleck 1. *v.* bespeckle, besprinkle, dapple, dot, dust, mark, mottle, speckle, spot, stipple, streak, variegate 2. *n.* dot, mark, pinpoint, speck, speckle, spot, streak

fledgling 1. chick, nestling 2. apprentice, beginner, learner, neophyte, newcomer, novice, rookie (*Inf.*), trainee, tyro

flee abscond, avoid, beat a hasty retreat, bolt, cut and run (*Inf.*), decamp, depart, do a runner (*Sl.*), escape, fly, fly the coop (*U.S. & Canad. inf.*), get away, hook it (*Sl.*), leave, make a quick exit, make off, make oneself scarce (*Inf.*), make one's escape, make one's getaway, run away, scarper (*Brit. sl.*), shun, skedaddle (*Inf.*), slope off, split (*Sl.*), take a powder (*U.S. & Canad. sl.*), take flight, take it on the lam (*U.S. & Canad. sl.*), take off (*Inf.*), take to one's heels, vanish

fleece 1. *Fig.* bleed (*Inf.*), cheat, con (*Inf.*), cozen, defraud, despoil, diddle (*Inf.*), mulct, overcharge, plunder, rifle, rip off (*Sl.*), rob, rook (*Sl.*), skin (*Sl.*), soak (*U.S. & Canad. sl.*), steal, stiff (*Sl.*), swindle, take for a ride (*Inf.*), take to the cleaners (*Sl.*) 2. clip, shear

fleecy downy, fluffy, shaggy, soft, woolly

fleet[1] *n.* argosy, armada, flotilla, naval force, navy, sea power, squadron, task force, vessels, warships

fleet[2] *adj.* fast, flying, mercurial, meteoric,

nimble, nimble-footed, quick, rapid, speedy, swift, winged

fleeting brief, ephemeral, evanescent, flitting, flying, fugacious, fugitive, here today, gone tomorrow, momentary, passing, short, short-lived, temporary, transient, transitory
Antonyms abiding, continuing, durable, enduring, eternal, imperishable, lasting, long-lasting, long-lived, permanent

fleetness celerity, lightning speed, nimble-footedness, nimbleness, quickness, rapidity, speed, speediness, swiftness, velocity

flesh 1. beef (*Inf.*), body, brawn, fat, fatness, food, meat, tissue, weight 2. animality, body, carnality, flesh and blood, human nature, physicality, physical nature, sensuality 3. homo sapiens, humankind, human race, living creatures, man, mankind, mortality, people, race, stock, world 4. **one's own flesh and blood** blood, family, kin, kindred, kinsfolk, kith and kin, relations, relatives

fleshiness chubbiness, corpulence, flabbiness, heaviness, obesity, plumpness, stoutness

fleshly 1. animal, bodily, carnal, erotic, lascivious, lecherous, lustful, sensual 2. corporal, corporeal, earthly, human, material, mundane, of this world, physical, secular, terrestrial, worldly

fleshy ample, beefy (*Inf.*), brawny, chubby, chunky, corpulent, fat, hefty, meaty, obese, overweight, plump, podgy, stout, tubby, well-padded

flex *v.* angle, bend, contract, crook, curve, tighten

flexibility adaptability, adjustability, complaisance, elasticity, give (*Inf.*), pliability, pliancy, resilience, springiness, tensility

flexible 1. bendable, ductile, elastic, limber, lissom(e), lithe, mouldable, plastic, pliable, pliant, springy, stretchy, supple, tensile, whippy, willowy, yielding 2. adaptable, adjustable, discretionary, open, variable 3. amenable, biddable, complaisant, compliant, docile, gentle, manageable, responsive, tractable
Antonyms absolute, determined, fixed, immovable, inexorable, inflexible, intractable, obdurate, rigid, staunch, stiff, tough, unyielding

flick *v.* 1. dab, fillip, flip, hit, jab, peck, rap, strike, tap, touch 2. *With* **through** browse, flip, glance, skim, skip, thumb ~*n.* 3. fillip, flip, jab, peck, rap, tap, touch

flicker *v.* 1. flare, flash, glimmer, gutter, shimmer, sparkle, twinkle 2. flutter, quiver, vibrate, waver ~*n.* 3. flare, flash, gleam, glimmer, spark 4. atom, breath, drop, glimmer, iota, spark, trace, vestige

flickering fitful, guttering, twinkling, unsteady, wavering

flight[1] 1. flying, mounting, soaring, winging 2. *Of air travel* journey, trip, voyage 3. aerial navigation, aeronautics, air transport, aviation, flying 4. cloud, flock, formation, squadron, swarm, unit, wing

flight[2] 1. departure, escape, exit, exodus, fleeing, getaway, retreat, running away 2. **put to flight** chase off, disperse, drive off, rout, scare off, scatter, send packing, stampede 3. **take (to) flight** abscond, beat a retreat, bolt, decamp, do a bunk (*Brit. sl.*), do a runner (*Sl.*), flee, fly the coop (*U.S. & Canad. inf.*), light out (*Inf.*), make a hasty retreat, run away *or* off, skedaddle (*Inf.*), take a powder (*U.S. & Canad. sl.*), take it on the lam (*U.S. & Canad. sl.*), withdraw hastily

flightiness capriciousness, fickleness, flippancy, frivolity, giddiness, irresponsibility, levity, lightness, mercurialness, volatility

flighty capricious, changeable, dizzy, fickle, frivolous, giddy, harebrained, impetuous, impulsive, irresponsible, light-headed, mercurial, scatterbrained, skittish, thoughtless, unbalanced, unstable, unsteady, volatile, wild

flimsy 1. delicate, fragile, frail, gimcrack, insubstantial, makeshift, rickety, shaky, shallow, slight, superficial, unsubstantial 2. chiffon, gauzy, gossamer, light, sheer, thin, transparent 3. feeble, frivolous, implausible, inadequate, pathetic, poor, thin, transparent, trivial, unconvincing, unsatisfactory, weak
Antonyms durable, heavy, robust, serious, solid, sound, stout, strong, sturdy, substantial

flinch baulk, blench, cower, cringe, draw back, duck, flee, quail, recoil, retreat, shirk, shrink, shy away, start, swerve, wince, withdraw

fling *v.* 1. cast, catapult, chuck (*Inf.*), heave, hurl, jerk, let fly, lob (*Inf.*), pitch, precipitate, propel, send, shy, sling, throw, toss ~*n.* 2. cast, lob, pitch, shot, throw, toss 3. bash, beano (*Brit. sl.*), binge (*Inf.*), bit of fun, good time, indulgence, party, rave (*Brit. sl.*), rave-up (*Brit. sl.*), spree 4. attempt, bash (*Inf.*), crack (*Inf.*), gamble, go (*Inf.*), shot (*Inf.*), stab (*Inf.*), trial, try, venture, whirl (*Inf.*)

flinty adamant, cruel, hard, hard-hearted, harsh, heartless, inflexible, obdurate, pitiless, steely, stern, stony, unfeeling, unmerciful, unyielding

flip *v./n.* cast, flick, jerk, pitch, snap, spin, throw, toss, twist

flippancy cheek (*Inf.*), cheekiness, disrespectfulness, frivolity, impertinence, irreverence, levity, pertness, sauciness

flippant cheeky, disrespectful, flip (*Inf.*), frivolous, glib, impertinent, impudent, irreverent, offhand, pert, rude, saucy, superficial
Antonyms gracious, mannerly, polite, respectful, serious, sincere, solicitous, well-mannered

flirt *v.* 1. chat up (*Inf.*), coquet, dally, lead on, make advances, make eyes at, philander 2. *Usually with* with consider, dabble in, entertain, expose oneself to, give a thought to, play with, toy with, trifle with ~*n.* 3. coquette, heart-breaker, philanderer, tease, trifler, wanton

flirtation coquetry, dalliance, intrigue, philandering, teasing, toying, trifling

flirtatious amorous, arch, come-hither, come-on (*Inf.*), coquettish, coy, enticing, flirty, provocative, sportive, teasing

flirting amorous play, chatting up (*Inf.*), coquetry, dalliance, sport

flit dart, flash, fleet, flutter, fly, pass, skim, speed, whisk, wing

float *v.* 1. be *or* lie on the surface, be buoyant, displace water, hang, hover, poise, rest on water, stay afloat 2. bob, drift, glide, move gently, sail, slide, slip along 3. get going, launch, promote, push off, set up
Antonyms (*senses 1 & 2*) dip, drown, founder, go down, settle, sink, submerge (*sense 3*) abolish, annul, cancel, dissolve, terminate

floating 1. afloat, buoyant, buoyed up, nonsubmersible, ocean-going, sailing, swimming, unsinkable 2. fluctuating, free, migratory, movable, unattached, uncommitted, unfixed, variable, wandering

flock *v.* 1. collect, congregate, converge, crowd, gather, group, herd, huddle, mass, throng, troop ~*n.* 2. colony, drove, flight, gaggle, herd, skein 3. assembly, bevy, collection, company, congregation, convoy, crowd, gathering, group, herd, host, mass, multitude, throng

flog 1. beat, castigate, chastise, flagellate, flay, lambast(e), lash, scourge, thrash, trounce, whack, whip 2. drive, oppress, overexert, overtax, overwork, punish, push, strain, tax

flogging beating, caning, flagellation, hiding (*Inf.*), horsewhipping, lashing, scourging, thrashing, trouncing, whipping

flood *v.* 1. brim over, deluge, drown, immerse, inundate, overflow, pour over, submerge, swamp 2. engulf, flow, gush, overwhelm, rush, surge, swarm, sweep 3. choke, fill, glut, oversupply, saturate ~*n.* 4. deluge, downpour, flash flood, freshet, inundation, overflow, spate, tide, torrent 5. abundance, flow, glut, multitude, outpouring, profusion, rush, stream, torrent

floor 1. *n.* level, stage, storey, tier 2. *v. Fig.* baffle, beat, bewilder, bowl over (*Inf.*), bring up short, confound, conquer, defeat, discomfit, disconcert, dumbfound, faze, knock down, nonplus, overthrow, perplex, prostrate, puzzle, stump, throw (*Inf.*)

flop *v.* 1. collapse, dangle, droop, drop, fall, hang limply, sag, slump, topple, tumble 2. *Inf.* bomb (*U.S. & Canad. sl.*), close, come to nothing, fail, fall flat, fall short, fold (*Inf.*), founder, go belly-up (*Sl.*), go down like a lead balloon (*Inf.*), misfire ~*n.* 3. *Inf.* cockup (*Brit. sl.*), debacle, disaster, failure, fiasco, loser, nonstarter, washout (*Inf.*)
Antonyms *v.* flourish, make a hit, make it (*Inf.*), prosper, succeed, triumph, work ~*n.* hit, success, triumph

floppy baggy, droopy, flaccid, flapping, flip-flop, hanging, limp, loose, pendulous, sagging, soft

floral flower-patterned, flowery

florescence blooming, blossoming, development, flourishing, flowering, fruition, maturity

florid 1. blowzy, flushed, high-coloured, high-complexioned, rubicund, ruddy 2. baroque, busy, embellished, euphuistic, figurative, flamboyant, flowery, fussy, grandiloquent, high-flown, ornate, over-elaborate
Antonyms anaemic, bare, bloodless, dull, pale, pallid, pasty, plain, unadorned, wan, washed out

flossy downy, feathery, fluffy, satiny, silky, soft

flotsam debris, detritus, jetsam, junk, odds and ends, sweepings, wreckage

flounce *v.* bounce, fling, jerk, spring, stamp, storm, throw, toss

flounder *v.* be in the dark, blunder, fumble, grope, muddle, plunge, struggle, stumble, thrash, toss, tumble, wallow

flourish *v.* 1. bear fruit, be in one's prime, be successful, be vigorous, bloom, blossom, boom, burgeon, develop, do well, flower, get ahead, get on, go great guns (*Sl.*), go up in the world, grow, grow fat, increase, prosper, succeed, thrive 2. brandish, display, flaunt, flutter, shake, sweep, swing, swish, twirl, vaunt, wag, wave, wield ~*n.* 3. brandishing, dash, display, fanfare, parade, shaking, show, showy gesture, twirling, wave 4. cur~

licue, decoration, embellishment, ornamentation, plume, sweep
Antonyms decline, diminish, dwindle, fade, fail, grow less, pine, shrink, wane

flourishing blooming, burgeoning, doing well, going strong, in the pink, in top form, lush, luxuriant, mushrooming, on the up and up (*Inf.*), prospering, rampant, successful, thriving

flout defy, deride, gibe at, insult, jeer at, laugh in the face of, mock, outrage, ridicule, scoff at, scorn, scout (*Archaic*), show contempt for, sneer at, spurn, take the piss out of (*Taboo sl.*), taunt, treat with disdain
Antonyms attend, esteem, heed, honour, mind, note, pay attention to, regard, respect, revere, value

flow *v.* 1. circulate, course, glide, gush, move, pour, purl, ripple, roll, run, rush, slide, surge, sweep, swirl, whirl 2. cascade, deluge, flood, inundate, issue, overflow, pour, run, run out, spew, spill, spurt, squirt, stream, teem, well forth 3. arise, emanate, emerge, issue, pour, proceed, result, spring ~*n.* 4. course, current, drift, flood, flux, gush, issue, outflow, outpouring, spate, stream, tide, tideway, undertow 5. abundance, deluge, effusion, emanation, outflow, outpouring, plenty, plethora, succession, train

flower *n.* 1. bloom, blossom, efflorescence 2. *Fig.* best, choicest part, cream, elite, freshness, greatest *or* finest point, height, pick, vigour ~*v.* 3. bloom, blossom, blow, burgeon, effloresce, flourish, mature, open, unfold

flowering *adj.* abloom, blooming, blossoming, florescent, in bloom, in blossom, in flower, open, out, ready

flowery baroque, embellished, euphuistic, fancy, figurative, florid, high-flown, ornate, overwrought, rhetorical
Antonyms austere, bare, basic, modest, muted, plain, restrained, simple, spartan, unadorned, unembellished

flowing 1. falling, gushing, rolling, rushing, smooth, streaming, sweeping 2. continuous, cursive, easy, fluent, smooth, unbroken, uninterrupted 3. abounding, brimming over, flooded, full, overrun, prolific, rich, teeming

fluctuate alter, alternate, change, ebb and flow, go up and down, hesitate, oscillate, rise and fall, seesaw, shift, swing, undulate, vacillate, vary, veer, waver

fluctuation alternation, change, fickleness, inconstancy, instability, oscillation, shift, swing, unsteadiness, vacillation, variation, wavering

fluency articulateness, assurance, command, control, ease, facility, glibness, readiness, slickness, smoothness, volubility

fluent articulate, easy, effortless, facile, flowing, glib, natural, ready, smooth, smooth-spoken, voluble, well-versed
Antonyms faltering, halting, hesitant, hesitating, inarticulate, stammering, stumbling, terse, tongue-tied

fluff 1. *n.* down, dust, dustball, fuzz, lint, nap, oose (*Scot.*), pile 2. *v. Inf.* bungle, cock up (*Brit. sl.*), foul up (*Inf.*), fuck up (*Offens. taboo sl.*), make a mess off, mess up (*Inf.*), muddle, screw up (*Inf.*), spoil

fluffy downy, feathery, fleecy, flossy, fuzzy, gossamer, silky, soft

fluid *adj.* 1. aqueous, flowing, in solution, liquefied, liquid, melted, molten, running, runny, watery 2. adaptable, adjustable, changeable, flexible, floating, fluctuating, indefinite, mercurial, mobile, mutable, protean, shifting 3. easy, elegant, feline, flowing, graceful, sinuous, smooth ~*n.* 4. liquid, liquor, solution
Antonyms *adj.* definite, firm, fixed, hard, immobile, immutable, rigid, set, solid

fluke accident, blessing, break, chance, chance occurrence, coincidence, fortuity, freak, lucky break, quirk, quirk of fate, serendipity, stroke, stroke of luck, windfall

fluky 1. accidental, coincidental, fortuitous, lucky 2. at the mercy of events, chancy, incalculable, uncertain, variable

flummox baffle, bamboozle (*Inf.*), bewilder, bring up short, defeat, fox, mystify, nonplus, perplex, stump, stymie

flummoxed at a loss, at sea, baffled, bewildered, foxed, mystified, nonplussed, stumped, stymied

flunky 1. assistant, drudge, hanger-on, menial, minion, slave, toady, tool, underling, yes man 2. footman, lackey, manservant, valet

flurry *n.* 1. *Fig.* ado, agitation, bustle, commotion, disturbance, excitement, ferment, flap, fluster, flutter, furore, fuss, hurry, stir, to-do, tumult, whirl 2. flaw, gust, squall 3. burst, outbreak, spell, spurt ~*v.* 4. agitate, bewilder, bother, bustle, confuse, disconcert, disturb, faze, fluster, flutter, fuss, hassle (*Inf.*), hurry, hustle, rattle (*Inf.*), ruffle, unnerve, unsettle, upset

flush[1] *v.* 1. blush, burn, colour, colour up, crimson, flame, glow, go red, redden, suffuse ~*n.* 2. bloom, blush, colour, freshness, glow, redness, rosiness ~*v.* 3. cleanse, douche, drench, eject, expel, flood, hose down, rinse out, swab, syringe, wash out

flush[2] *adj.* 1. even, flat, level, plane, square, true 2. abundant, affluent, full, generous, lavish, liberal, overflowing, prodigal 3. *Inf.* in funds, in the money (*Inf.*), moneyed, rich, rolling (*Sl.*), wealthy, well-heeled (*Inf.*), well-off, well-supplied ~*adv.* 4. even with, hard against, in contact with, level with, squarely, touching

flush[3] *v.* discover, disturb, drive out, put to flight, rouse, start, uncover

flushed 1. blushing, burning, crimson, embarrassed, feverish, glowing, hot, red, rosy, rubicund, ruddy 2. *Often with* **with** ablaze, animated, aroused, elated, enthused, excited, exhilarated, high (*Inf.*), inspired, intoxicated, thrilled

fluster 1. *v.* agitate, bother, bustle, confound, confuse, disturb, excite, flurry, hassle (*Inf.*), heat, hurry, make nervous, perturb, rattle (*Inf.*), ruffle, throw off balance, unnerve, upset 2. *n.* agitation, bustle, commotion, disturbance, dither (*Chiefly Brit.*), flap (*Inf.*), flurry, flutter, furore, perturbation, ruffle, state (*Inf.*), turmoil

fluted channelled, corrugated, furrowed, grooved

flutter *v.* 1. agitate, bat, beat, flap, flicker, flit, flitter, fluctuate, hover, palpitate, quiver, ripple, ruffle, shiver, tremble, vibrate, waver ~*n.* 2. palpitation, quiver, quivering, shiver, shudder, tremble, tremor, twitching, vibration 3. agitation, commotion, confusion, dither (*Chiefly Brit.*), excitement, flurry, fluster, perturbation, state (*Inf.*), state of nervous excitement, tremble, tumult

flux alteration, change, flow, fluctuation, fluidity, instability, modification, motion, mutability, mutation, transition, unrest

fly[1] *v.* 1. flit, flutter, hover, mount, sail, soar, take to the air, take wing, wing 2. aviate, be at the controls, control, manoeuvre, operate, pilot 3. display, flap, float, flutter, show, wave 4. elapse, flit, glide, pass, pass swiftly, roll on, run its course, slip away 5. barrel (along) (*Inf., chiefly U.S. & Canad.*), be off like a shot (*Inf.*), bolt, burn rubber (*Inf.*), career, dart, dash, hare (*Brit. inf.*), hasten, hurry, race, rush, scamper, scoot, shoot, speed, sprint, tear, whiz (*Inf.*), zoom 6. abscond, avoid, beat a retreat, clear out (*Inf.*), cut and run (*Inf.*), decamp, disappear, do a runner (*Sl.*), escape, flee, fly the coop (*U.S. & Canad. inf.*), get away, hasten away, hightail (*Inf., chiefly U.S.*), light out (*Inf.*), make a getaway, make a quick exit, make one's escape, run, run for it, run from, show a clean pair of heels, shun, skedaddle (*Inf.*), take a powder (*U.S. & Canad. sl.*), take flight, take it on the lam (*U.S. & Canad. sl.*), take off, take to one's heels 7. **fly in the ointment** difficulty, drawback, flaw, hitch, problem, rub, small problem, snag 8. **fly off the handle** blow one's top, explode, flip one's lid (*Sl.*), fly into a rage, have a tantrum, hit *or* go through the roof (*Inf.*), let fly (*Inf.*), lose one's cool (*Sl.*), lose one's temper 9. **let fly** a. burst forth, give free reign, keep nothing back, lash out, let (someone) have it, lose one's temper, tear into (*Inf.*), vent b. cast, chuck (*Inf.*), fire, fling, heave, hurl, hurtle, launch, let off, lob (*Inf.*), shoot, sling, throw

fly[2] *adj.* astute, canny, careful, knowing, nobody's fool, not born yesterday, on the ball (*Inf.*), sharp, shrewd, smart, wide-awake

fly at assail, assault, attack, belabour, fall upon, get stuck into (*Inf.*), go for, have a go at (*Inf.*), lay about, pitch into (*Inf.*), rush at

fly-by-night *adj.* 1. cowboy (*Inf.*), dubious, questionable, shady, undependable, unreliable, untrustworthy 2. brief, here today, gone tomorrow, impermanent, short-lived

flying *adj.* 1. brief, fleeting, fugacious, hasty, hurried, rushed, short-lived, transitory 2. express, fast, fleet, mercurial, mobile, rapid, speedy, winged 3. airborne, flapping, floating, fluttering, gliding, hovering, in the air, soaring, streaming, volitant, waving, wind-borne, winging

foam 1. *n.* bubbles, froth, head, lather, spray, spume, suds 2. *v.* boil, bubble, effervesce, fizz, froth, lather

foamy bubbly, foaming, frothy, lathery, spumescent, sudsy

fob off 1. appease, deceive, equivocate with, flannel (*Brit. inf.*), give (someone) the runaround (*Inf.*), put off, stall 2. dump, foist, get rid of, inflict, palm off, pass off, unload

focus *n.* 1. bull's eye, centre, centre of activity, centre of attraction, core, cynosure, focal point, headquarters, heart, hub, meeting place, target 2. **in focus** clear, distinct, sharp-edged, sharply defined 3. **out of focus** blurred, fuzzy, ill-defined, indistinct, muzzy, unclear ~*v.* 4. aim, bring to bear, centre, concentrate, converge, direct, fix, join, meet, pinpoint, rivet, spotlight, zero in (*Inf.*), zoom in

fodder feed, food, foodstuff, forage, provender, rations, tack (*Inf.*), victuals, vittles (*Obs. or dialect*)

foe adversary, antagonist, enemy, foeman (*Archaic*), opponent, rival

Antonyms ally, companion, comrade, confederate, friend, partner

fog *n.* 1. gloom, miasma, mist, murk, murkiness, peasouper (*Inf.*), smog 2. *Fig.* blindness, confusion, daze, haze, mist, obscurity, perplexity, stupor, trance ~*v.* 3. becloud, bedim, befuddle, bewilder, blind, cloud, confuse, darken, daze, dim, muddle, obfuscate, obscure, perplex, stupefy 4. cloud, mist over *or* up, steam up

foggy 1. blurred, brumous (*Rare*), cloudy, dim, grey, hazy, indistinct, misty, murky, nebulous, obscure, smoggy, soupy, vaporous 2. *Fig.* befuddled, bewildered, clouded, cloudy, confused, dark, dazed, dim, indistinct, muddled, obscure, stupefied, stupid, unclear, vague

Antonyms accurate, alert, awake, bright, clear, decisive, distinct, lucid, palpable, sharp, shrewd, undimmed

fogy, fogey anachronism, antique (*Inf.*), back number (*Inf.*), dinosaur, dodo (*Inf.*), fossil (*Inf.*), fuddy-duddy (*Inf.*), relic, square (*Inf.*), stick-in-the-mud (*Inf.*)

foible defect, failing, fault, idiosyncrasy, imperfection, infirmity, peculiarity, quirk, weakness, weak point

foil[1] *v.* baffle, balk, check, checkmate, circumvent, counter, defeat, disappoint, elude, frustrate, nip in the bud, nullify, outwit, put a spoke in (someone's) wheel (*Brit.*), stop, thwart

foil[2] antithesis, background, complement, contrast, setting

foist fob off, get rid of, impose, insert, insinuate, interpolate, introduce, palm off, pass off, put over, sneak in, unload

fold *v.* 1. bend, crease, crumple, dog-ear, double, double over, gather, intertwine, overlap, pleat, tuck, turn under ~*n.* 2. bend, crease, double thickness, folded portion, furrow, knife-edge, layer, overlap, pleat, turn, wrinkle ~*v.* 3. do up, enclose, enfold, entwine, envelop, wrap, wrap up 4. *Inf.* be ruined, close, collapse, crash, fail, go bankrupt, go belly-up (*Sl.*), go bust (*Inf.*), go down like a lead balloon (*Inf.*), go to the wall, go under, shut down

folder binder, envelope, file, portfolio

folk clan, ethnic group, family, kin, kindred, people, race, tribe

follow 1. come after, come next, step into the shoes of, succeed, supersede, supplant, take the place of 2. chase, dog, hound, hunt, pursue, run after, shadow, stalk, tail (*Inf.*), track, trail 3. accompany, attend, bring up the rear, come *or* go with, come after, escort, tag along, tread on the heels of 4. act in accordance with, be guided by, comply, conform, give allegiance to, heed, mind, note, obey, observe, regard, watch 5. appreciate, catch, catch on (*Inf.*), comprehend, fathom, get, get the picture, grasp, keep up with, realize, see, take in, understand 6. arise, be consequent, develop, emanate, ensue, flow, issue, proceed, result, spring, supervene 7. adopt, copy, emulate, imitate, live up to, pattern oneself upon, take as example 8. be a devotee *or* supporter of, be devoted to, be interested in, cultivate, keep abreast of, support

Antonyms abandon, avoid, desert, disobey, elude, escape, flout, forsake, give up, guide, ignore, lead, precede, reject, renounce, shun, steer

follower 1. adherent, admirer, apostle, backer, believer, convert, devotee, disciple, fan, fancier, habitué, henchman, partisan, protagonist, pupil, representative, supporter, votary, worshipper 2. attendant, companion, hanger-on, helper, henchman, lackey, minion, retainer (*History*), sidekick (*Sl.*)

Antonyms (*sense 1*) guru, leader, mentor, teacher, tutor, svengali, swami (*sense 2*) antagonist, contender, enemy, foe, opponent, rival

following 1. *adj.* coming, consequent, consequential, ensuing, later, next, specified, subsequent, succeeding, successive 2. *n.* audience, circle, clientele, coterie, entourage, fans, patronage, public, retinue, suite, support, supporters, train

follow through bring to a conclusion, complete, conclude, consummate, pursue, see through

follow up 1. check out, find out about, investigate, look into, make inquiries, pursue, research 2. consolidate, continue, make sure, reinforce

folly absurdity, bêtise (*Rare*), daftness (*Inf.*), fatuity, foolishness, idiocy, imbecility, imprudence, indiscretion, irrationality, lunacy, madness, nonsense, preposterousness, rashness, recklessness, silliness, stupidity

Antonyms judgment, level-headedness, moderation, prudence, rationality, reason, sanity, sense, wisdom

foment abet, agitate, arouse, brew, encourage, excite, fan the flames, foster, goad, incite, instigate, promote, provoke, quicken, raise, rouse, sow the seeds of, spur, stimulate, stir up, whip up

fomenter agitator, demagogue, firebrand, incendiary, inciter, instigator, rabble-rouser, stirrer (*Inf.*), troublemaker

fond 1. *With* **of** addicted to, attached to, enamoured of, have a liking (fancy, taste, soft spot) for, hooked on, into (*Inf.*), keen on, partial to, predisposed towards 2. adoring, affectionate, amorous, caring, devoted, doting, indulgent, loving, tender, warm 3. absurd, credulous, deluded, delusive, delusory, empty, foolish, indiscreet, naive, overoptimistic, vain

Antonyms (*senses 1 & 2*) aloof, austere, averse, disinterested, indifferent, rational, sensible, unaffectionate, unconcerned, undemonstrative

fondle caress, cuddle, dandle, pat, pet, stroke

fondly 1. affectionately, dearly, indulgently, lovingly, possessively, tenderly, with affection 2. credulously, foolishly, naively, stupidly, vainly

fondness 1. attachment, fancy, liking, love, partiality, penchant, predilection, preference, soft spot, susceptibility, taste, weakness 2. affection, attachment, devotion, kindness, love, tenderness
Antonyms antagonism, antipathy, aversion, coldness, contempt, dislike, enmity, harshness, hatred, hostility, loathing, repugnance, repulsion

food 1. aliment, board, bread, chow (*Inf.*), comestibles, commons, cooking, cuisine, diet, eatables (*Sl.*), eats (*Sl.*), edibles, fare, feed, foodstuffs, grub (*Sl.*), larder, meat, menu, nosebag (*Sl.*), nosh (*Sl.*), nourishment, nutriment, nutrition, pabulum (*Rare*), provender, provisions, rations, refreshment, scoff (*Sl.*), stores, subsistence, sustenance, table, tack (*Inf.*), tuck (*Inf.*), viands, victuals, vittles (*Obs. or dialect*) 2. *Cattle, etc.* feed, fodder, forage, provender

foodie *bon vivant, bon viveur,* connoisseur, epicure, gastronome, gourmet

fool *n.* 1. ass, berk (*Brit. sl.*), bird-brain (*Inf.*), blockhead, bonehead (*Sl.*), charlie (*Brit. inf.*), chump (*Inf.*), clodpate (*Archaic*), clot (*Brit. inf.*), coot, dickhead (*Sl.*), dimwit (*Inf.*), dipstick (*Brit. sl.*), divvy (*Brit. sl.*), dolt, dope (*Inf.*), dork (*Sl.*), dunce, dunderhead, dweeb (*U.S. sl.*), fathead (*Inf.*), fuckwit (*Taboo sl.*), geek (*Sl.*), gonzo (*Sl.*), goose (*Inf.*), halfwit, idiot, ignoramus, illiterate, imbecile (*Inf.*), jackass, jerk (*Sl., chiefly U.S. & Canad.*), lamebrain (*Inf.*), loon, mooncalf, moron, nerd *or* nurd (*Sl.*), nincompoop, ninny, nit (*Inf.*), nitwit (*Inf.*), numskull *or* numbskull, oaf, pillock (*Brit. sl.*), plank (*Brit. sl.*), plonker (*Sl.*), prat (*Sl.*), prick (*Derogatory sl.*), sap (*Sl.*), schmuck (*U.S. sl.*), silly, simpleton, twerp *or* twirp (*Inf.*), twit (*Inf., chiefly Brit.*), wally (*Sl.*) 2. butt, chump (*Inf.*), dupe, easy mark (*Inf.*), fall guy (*Inf.*), greenhorn (*Inf.*), gull (*Archaic*), laughing stock, mug (*Brit. sl.*), stooge (*Sl.*), sucker (*Sl.*) 3. buffoon, clown, comic, harlequin, jester, merry-andrew, motley, pierrot, punchinello 4. **act** *or* **play the fool** act up, be silly, cavort, clown, cut capers, frolic, lark about (*Inf.*), mess about, piss about (*Taboo sl.*), piss around (*Taboo sl.*), play the goat, show off (*Inf.*) ~*v.* 5. bamboozle, beguile, bluff, cheat, con (*Inf.*), deceive, delude, dupe, gull (*Archaic*), have (someone) on, hoax, hoodwink, kid (*Inf.*), make a fool of, mislead, play a trick on, put one over on (*Inf.*), stiff (*Sl.*), take in, trick 6. act the fool, cut capers, feign, jest, joke, kid (*Inf.*), make believe, piss about (*Taboo sl.*), piss around (*Taboo sl.*), pretend, tease 7. *With* **with, around with,** *or* **about with** fiddle (*Inf.*), meddle, mess, monkey, piss about (*Taboo sl.*), piss around (*Taboo sl.*), play, tamper, toy, trifle
Antonyms (*senses 1 & 2*) expert, genius, master, sage, savant, scholar, wise man

fool around *or* **about** dawdle, footle (*Inf.*), hang around, idle, kill time, lark, mess about, play about, waste time

foolery antics, capers, carry-on (*Inf., chiefly Brit.*), childishness, clowning, folly, fooling, horseplay, larks, mischief, monkey tricks (*Inf.*), nonsense, practical jokes, pranks, shenanigans (*Inf.*), silliness, tomfoolery

foolhardy adventurous, bold, hot-headed, impetuous, imprudent, incautious, irresponsible, madcap, precipitate, rash, reckless, temerarious, venturesome, venturous
Antonyms alert, careful, cautious, chary, circumspect, heedful, judicious, prudent, shrewd, solicitous, thoughtful, wary, watchful

fooling *n.* bluffing, buffoonery, clownishness, farce, joking, kidding (*Inf.*), mockery, nonsense, pretence, shamming, skylarking (*Inf.*), teasing, tricks, trifling

foolish 1. absurd, asinine, ill-advised, ill-considered, ill-judged, imprudent, inane, incautious, indiscreet, injudicious, nonsensical, senseless, short-sighted, silly, unintelligent, unreasonable, unwise 2. braindead (*Inf.*), brainless, crackpot (*Inf.*), crazy, daft (*Inf.*), doltish, fatuous, goofy (*Inf.*), half-baked (*Inf.*), half-witted, harebrained, idiotic, imbecilic, inane, loopy (*Inf.*), ludicrous, mad, moronic, potty (*Brit. inf.*), ridiculous, senseless, silly, simple, stupid, weak, witless
Antonyms bright, cautious, clever, commonsensical, intelligent, judicious, prudent, rational, sagacious, sane, sensible, sharp, smart, sound, thoughtful, wise

foolishly absurdly, idiotically, ill-advisedly, imprudently, incautiously, indiscreetly, injudiciously, like a fool, mistakenly, short-sightedly, stupidly, unwisely, without due consideration

foolishness 1. absurdity, bêtise (*Rare*), folly, idiocy, imprudence, inanity, indiscretion, irresponsibility, silliness, stupidity, weakness 2. bunk (*Inf.*), bunkum *or* buncombe (*Chiefly U.S.*), carrying-on (*Inf.,* chiefly Brit.), claptrap (Inf.), foolery, nonsense, rigmarole, rubbish

foolproof certain, guaranteed, infallible, never-failing, safe, sure-fire (Inf.), unassailable, unbreakable

footing 1. basis, establishment, foot-hold, foundation, ground, groundwork, installation, settlement 2. condition, grade, position, rank, relations, relationship, standing, state, status, terms

footling fiddling, fussy, hairsplitting, immaterial, insignificant, irrelevant, minor, nickel-and-dime (U.S. sl.), niggly, petty, pointless, silly, time-wasting, trifling, trivial, unimportant

footslog hike, hoof it (Sl.), march, plod, tramp, trudge, yomp (Sl.)

footstep 1. footfall, step, tread 2. footmark, footprint, trace, track

fop beau, Beau Brummel, clotheshorse, coxcomb (Archaic), dandy, exquisite (Obsolete), fashion plate, macaroni (Obsolete), peacock, popinjay, smoothie *or* smoothy (Sl.), swell

foppish coxcombical, dandified, dandyish, dapper, dressy (Inf.), finical, natty (Inf.), preening, prinking, spruce, vain

forage 1. *n. Cattle, etc.* feed, fodder, food, foodstuffs, provender 2. *v.* cast about, explore, hunt, look round, plunder, raid, ransack, rummage, scavenge, scour, scrounge (Inf.), search, seek

foray depredation, descent, incursion, inroad, invasion, irruption, raid, reconnaissance, sally, sortie, swoop

forbear abstain, avoid, cease, decline, desist, eschew, hold back, keep from, omit, pause, refrain, resist the temptation to, restrain oneself, stop, withhold

forbearance 1. indulgence, leniency, lenity, longanimity (Rare), long-suffering, mildness, moderation, patience, resignation, restraint, self-control, temperance, tolerance 2. abstinence, avoidance, refraining

Antonyms anger, impatience, impetuosity, intolerance, irritability, shortness

forbearing clement, easy, forgiving, indulgent, lenient, long-suffering, merciful, mild, moderate, patient, tolerant

forbid ban, debar, disallow, exclude, hinder, inhibit, interdict, outlaw, preclude, prohibit, proscribe, rule out, veto

Antonyms allow, approve, authorize, bid, endorse, grant, let, license, O.K. *or* okay (Inf.), order, permit, sanction

forbidden banned, outlawed, out of bounds, prohibited, proscribed, taboo, *verboten*, vetoed

forbidding 1. abhorrent, disagreeable, odious, offensive, off-putting (Brit. inf.), repellent, repulsive 2. baleful, daunting, foreboding, frightening, grim, hostile, menacing, ominous, sinister, threatening, unfriendly

Antonyms alluring, attractive, beguiling, enticing, inviting, magnetic, tempting, welcoming, winning

force *n.* 1. dynamism, energy, impact, impulse, life, might, momentum, muscle, potency, power, pressure, stimulus, strength, stress, vigour 2. arm-twisting (Inf.), coercion, compulsion, constraint, duress, enforcement, pressure, violence 3. bite, cogency, effect, effectiveness, efficacy, influence, persuasiveness, power, punch (Inf.), strength, validity, weight 4. drive, emphasis, fierceness, intensity, persistence, vehemence, vigour 5. army, battalion, body, corps, detachment, division, host, legion, patrol, regiment, squad, squadron, troop, unit 6. **in force a.** binding, current, effective, in operation, on the statute book, operative, valid, working **b.** all together, in full strength, in great numbers ~*v.* 7. bring pressure to bear upon, coerce, compel, constrain, dragoon, drive, impel, impose, make, necessitate, obligate, oblige, overcome, press, press-gang, pressure, pressurize, put the squeeze on (Inf.), railroad (Inf.), strong-arm (Inf.), urge 8. blast, break open, prise, propel, push, thrust, use violence on, wrench, wrest 9. drag, exact, extort, wring

Antonyms *n.* debility, enervation, feebleness, fragility, frailty, impotence, ineffectiveness, irresolution, powerlessness, weakness ~*v.* coax, convince, induce, persuade, prevail, talk into

forced 1. compulsory, conscripted, enforced, involuntary, mandatory, obligatory, slave, unwilling 2. affected, artificial, contrived, false, insincere, laboured, stiff, strained, unnatural, wooden

Antonyms easy, natural, simple, sincere, spontaneous, unforced, unpretending, voluntary

forceful cogent, compelling, convincing, dynamic, effective, persuasive, pithy, potent, powerful, telling, vigorous, weighty

Antonyms enervated, exhausted, faint, feeble, frail, powerless, spent, weak

forcible 1. active, cogent, compelling, effective, efficient, energetic, forceful, impressive, mighty, potent, powerful, strong, telling, valid, weighty 2. aggressive, armed, coercive, compulsory, drastic, violent

forcibly against one's will, by force, by main

force, compulsorily, under compulsion, under protest, willy-nilly

forebear ancestor, father, forefather, forerunner, predecessor, progenitor

forebode augur, betoken, foreshadow, foreshow, foretell, foretoken, forewarn, indicate, portend, predict, presage, prognosticate, promise, vaticinate (*Rare*), warn of

foreboding 1. anxiety, apprehension, apprehensiveness, chill, dread, fear, misgiving, premonition, presentiment 2. augury, foreshadowing, foretoken, omen, portent, prediction, presage, prognostication, sign, token, warning

forecast 1. *v.* anticipate, augur, calculate, divine, estimate, foresee, foretell, plan, predict, prognosticate, prophesy, vaticinate (*Rare*) 2. *n.* anticipation, conjecture, foresight, forethought, guess, outlook, planning, prediction, prognosis, projection, prophecy

forefather ancestor, father, forebear, forerunner, predecessor, primogenitor, procreator, progenitor

forefront centre, fore, foreground, front, lead, prominence, spearhead, van, vanguard

forego *see* FORGO

foregoing above, antecedent, anterior, former, preceding, previous, prior

foreground centre, forefront, front, limelight, prominence

foreign 1. alien, borrowed, distant, exotic, external, imported, outlandish, outside, overseas, remote, strange, unfamiliar, unknown 2. extraneous, extrinsic, incongruous, irrelevant, unassimilable, uncharacteristic, unrelated

Antonyms applicable, characteristic, customary, domestic, familiar, intrinsic, native, pertinent, relevant, suited, well-known

foreigner alien, immigrant, incomer, newcomer, outlander, stranger

foreknowledge clairvoyance, foresight, forewarning, precognition, prescience, prevision, prior knowledge

foremost chief, first, front, headmost, highest, inaugural, initial, leading, paramount, pre-eminent, primary, prime, principal, supreme

foreordain doom, fate, foredoom, prearrange, predestine, predetermine, preordain, reserve

forerunner 1. ancestor, announcer, envoy, forebear, foregoer, harbinger, herald, precursor, predecessor, progenitor, prototype 2. augury, foretoken, indication, omen, portent, premonition, prognostic, sign, token

foresee anticipate, divine, envisage, forebode, forecast, foretell, predict, prophesy, vaticinate (*Rare*)

foreshadow adumbrate, augur, betoken, bode, forebode, imply, indicate, portend, predict, prefigure, presage, promise, prophesy, signal

foresight anticipation, care, caution, circumspection, far-sightedness, forethought, precaution, premeditation, preparedness, prescience, prevision (*Rare*), provision, prudence

Antonyms carelessness, hindsight, imprudence, inconsideration, lack of foresight, neglect, retrospection, thoughtlessness, unpreparedness

forestall anticipate, balk, circumvent, frustrate, head off, hinder, intercept, nip in the bud, obviate, parry, preclude, prevent, provide against, thwart

forestry arboriculture, dendrology (*Bot.*), silviculture, woodcraft, woodmanship

foretaste *n.* example, foretoken, indication, prelude, preview, sample, trailer, warning, whiff

foretell adumbrate, augur, bode, forebode, forecast, foreshadow, foreshow, forewarn, portend, predict, presage, prognosticate, prophesy, signify, soothsay, vaticinate (*Rare*)

forethought anticipation, far-sightedness, foresight, precaution, providence, provision, prudence

Antonyms carelessness, imprudence, impulsiveness, inconsideration, neglect, unpreparedness

foretoken *v.* augur, forebode, foreshadow, foreshow, give notice of, give warning of, portend, presage, signify, warn of

forever 1. always, evermore, for all time, for good and all (*Inf.*), for keeps, in perpetuity, till Doomsday, till the cows come home (*Inf.*), till the end of time, world without end 2. all the time, constantly, continually, endlessly, eternally, everlastingly, incessantly, interminably, perpetually, unremittingly

forewarn admonish, advise, alert, apprise, caution, dissuade, give fair warning, put on guard, put on the qui vive, tip off

foreword introduction, preamble, preface, preliminary, prolegomenon, prologue

forfeit 1. *n.* amercement (*Obsolete*), damages, fine, forfeiture, loss, mulct, penalty 2. *v.* be deprived of, be stripped of, give up, lose, relinquish, renounce, surrender

forfeiture confiscation, giving up, loss, relinquishment, sequestration (*Law*), surrender

forge *v.* 1. construct, contrive, create, devise, fabricate, fashion, form, frame, hammer out, invent, make, mould, shape, work 2. coin, copy, counterfeit, fake, falsify, feign, imitate

forger coiner, counterfeiter, falsifier

forgery 1. coining, counterfeiting, falsification, fraudulence, fraudulent imitation 2. counterfeit, fake, falsification, imitation, phoney *or* phony (*Inf.*), sham

forget 1. consign to oblivion, dismiss from one's mind, let bygones be bygones, let slip from the memory 2. leave behind, lose sight of, omit, overlook
Antonyms bring to mind, mind, recall, recollect, remember, retain

forgetful absent-minded, apt to forget, careless, dreamy, heedless, inattentive, lax, neglectful, negligent, oblivious, slapdash, slipshod, unmindful
Antonyms attentive, careful, mindful, retentive, unforgetful, unforgetting

forgetfulness absent-mindedness, abstraction, carelessness, dreaminess, heedlessness, inattention, lapse of memory, laxity, laxness, oblivion, obliviousness, woolgathering

forgive absolve, accept (someone's) apology, acquit, bear no malice, condone, excuse, exonerate, let bygones be bygones, let off (*Inf.*), pardon, remit
Antonyms blame, censure, charge, condemn, find fault with, reproach, reprove

forgiveness absolution, acquittal, amnesty, condonation, exoneration, mercy, overlooking, pardon, remission

forgiving clement, compassionate, forbearing, humane, lenient, magnanimous, merciful, mild, soft-hearted, tolerant

forgo, forego abandon, abjure, cede, do without, give up, kick (*Inf.*), leave alone *or* out, relinquish, renounce, resign, sacrifice, surrender, waive, yield

forgotten blotted out, buried, bygone, consigned to oblivion, gone (clean) out of one's mind, left behind *or* out, lost, obliterated, omitted, past, past recall, unremembered

fork *v.* bifurcate, branch, branch off, diverge, divide, go separate ways, part, split

forked angled, bifurcate(d), branched, branching, divided, pronged, split, tined, zigzag

forlorn abandoned, bereft, cheerless, comfortless, deserted, desolate, destitute, disconsolate, forgotten, forsaken, friendless, helpless, homeless, hopeless, lonely, lost, miserable, pathetic, pitiable, pitiful, unhappy, woebegone, wretched
Antonyms busy, cheerful, happy, hopeful, optimistic, thriving

form[1] *v.* 1. assemble, bring about, build, concoct, construct, contrive, create, devise, establish, fabricate, fashion, forge, found, invent, make, manufacture, model, mould, produce, put together, set up, shape, stamp 2. arrange, combine, design, dispose, draw up, frame, organize, pattern, plan, think up 3. accumulate, appear, become visible, come into being, crystallize, grow, materialize, rise, settle, show up (*Inf.*), take shape 4. acquire, contract, cultivate, develop, get into (*Inf.*), pick up 5. compose, comprise, constitute, make, make up, serve as 6. bring up, discipline, educate, instruct, rear, school, teach, train

form[2] *n.* 1. appearance, cast, configuration, construction, cut, fashion, formation, model, mould, pattern, shape, stamp, structure 2. anatomy, being, body, build, figure, frame, outline, person, physique, shape, silhouette 3. arrangement, character, description, design, guise, kind, manifestation, manner, method, mode, order, practice, semblance, sort, species, stamp, style, system, type, variety, way 4. format, framework, harmony, order, orderliness, organization, plan, proportion, structure, symmetry 5. condition, fettle, fitness, good condition, good spirits, health, shape, trim 6. **off form** below par, not in the pink (*Inf.*), not up to the mark, out of condition, stale, under the weather (*Inf.*), unfit 7. behaviour, ceremony, conduct, convention, custom, done thing, etiquette, formality, manners, procedure, protocol, ritual, rule 8. application, document, paper, sheet 9. class, grade, rank

formal 1. approved, ceremonial, explicit, express, fixed, lawful, legal, methodical, official, prescribed, *pro forma,* regular, rigid, ritualistic, set, solemn, strict 2. affected, aloof, ceremonious, conventional, correct, exact, precise, prim, punctilious, reserved, starched, stiff, unbending
Antonyms casual, easy-going, informal, laid-back (*Inf.*), relaxed, unceremonious, unofficial

formality 1. ceremony, convention, conventionality, custom, form, gesture, matter of form, procedure, red tape, rite, ritual 2. ceremoniousness, correctness, decorum, etiquette, politesse, protocol, punctilio

format appearance, arrangement, construction, form, layout, look, make-up, plan, style, type

formation 1. accumulation, compilation,

composition, constitution, crystallization, development, establishment, evolution, forming, generation, genesis, manufacture, organization, production 2. arrangement, configuration, design, disposition, figure, grouping, pattern, rank, structure

formative 1. impressionable, malleable, mouldable, pliant, sensitive, susceptible 2. determinative, developmental, influential, moulding, shaping

former 1. antecedent, anterior, *ci-devant*, earlier, erstwhile, ex-, late, one-time, previous, prior, quondam, whilom (*Archaic*) 2. ancient, bygone, departed, long ago, long gone, of yore, old, old-time, past 3. above, aforementioned, aforesaid, first mentioned, foregoing, preceding

Antonyms coming, current, ensuing, following, future, latter, modern, present, present-day, subsequent, succeeding

formerly aforetime (*Archaic*), already, at one time, before, heretofore, lately, once, previously

formidable 1. appalling, baleful, dangerous, daunting, dismaying, dreadful, fearful, frightful, horrible, intimidating, menacing, shocking, terrifying, threatening 2. arduous, challenging, colossal, difficult, mammoth, onerous, overwhelming, staggering, toilsome 3. awesome, great, impressive, indomitable, mighty, powerful, puissant, redoubtable, terrific, tremendous

Antonyms cheering, comforting, easy, encouraging, genial, heartening, pleasant, reassuring

formless amorphous, disorganized, inchoate, incoherent, indefinite, nebulous, shapeless, unformed, vague

formula 1. form of words, formulary, rite, ritual, rubric 2. blueprint, method, modus operandi, precept, prescription, principle, procedure, recipe, rule, way

formulate 1. codify, define, detail, express, frame, give form to, particularize, set down, specify, systematize 2. coin, develop, devise, evolve, forge, invent, map out, originate, plan, work out

forsake 1. abandon, cast off, desert, disown, jettison, jilt, leave, leave in the lurch, quit, repudiate, throw over 2. abdicate, forgo, forswear, give up, have done with, kick (*Inf.*), relinquish, renounce, set aside, surrender, turn one's back on, yield

forsaken abandoned, cast off, deserted, destitute, disowned, forlorn, friendless, ignored, isolated, jilted, left behind, left in the lurch, lonely, marooned, outcast, solitary

forswear 1. abandon, abjure, drop (*Inf.*), forgo, forsake, give up, renounce, swear off 2. deny, disavow, disclaim, disown, recant, reject, repudiate, retract 3. lie, perjure oneself, renege, swear falsely

fort 1. blockhouse, camp, castle, citadel, fastness, fortification, fortress, garrison, redoubt, station, stronghold 2. **hold the fort** carry on, keep things moving, keep things on an even keel, maintain the status quo, stand in, take over the reins

forte gift, long suit (*Inf.*), métier, speciality, strength, strong point, talent

Antonyms Achilles heel, chink in one's armour, defect, failing, imperfection, shortcoming, weak point

forth ahead, away, forward, into the open, onward, out, out of concealment, outward

forthcoming 1. approaching, coming, expected, future, imminent, impending, prospective, upcoming 2. accessible, at hand, available, in evidence, obtainable, on tap (*Inf.*), ready 3. chatty, communicative, expansive, free, informative, open, sociable, talkative, unreserved

forthright above-board, blunt, candid, direct, downright, frank, open, outspoken, plain-spoken, straightforward, straight from the shoulder (*Inf.*), upfront (*Inf.*)

Antonyms dishonest, furtive, secret, secretive, sneaky, underhand, untruthful

forthwith at once, directly, immediately, instantly, quickly, right away, straightaway, *tout de suite*, without delay

fortification 1. bastion, bulwark, castle, citadel, defence, fastness, fort, fortress, keep, protection, stronghold 2. embattlement, reinforcement, strengthening

fortify 1. augment, brace, buttress, embattle, garrison, protect, reinforce, secure, shore up, strengthen, support 2. brace, cheer, confirm, embolden, encourage, hearten, invigorate, reassure, stiffen, strengthen, sustain

Antonyms debilitate, demoralize, dilute, dishearten, impair, reduce, sap the strength of, weaken

fortitude backbone, braveness, courage, dauntlessness, determination, endurance, fearlessness, firmness, grit, guts (*Inf.*), hardihood, intrepidity, patience, perseverance, pluck, resolution, staying power, stoutheartedness, strength, strength of mind, valour

fortress castle, citadel, fastness, fort, redoubt, stronghold

fortuitous 1. accidental, arbitrary, casual, chance, contingent, incidental, random, unforeseen, unplanned 2. fluky (*Inf.*), fortunate, happy, lucky, providential, serendipitous

fortunate 1. born with a silver spoon in

one's mouth, bright, favoured, golden, happy, having a charmed life, in luck, jammy (*Brit. sl.*), lucky, prosperous, rosy, sitting pretty (*Inf.*), successful, well-off 2. advantageous, auspicious, convenient, encouraging, expedient, favourable, felicitous, fortuitous, helpful, opportune, profitable, promising, propitious, providential, timely
Antonyms disastrous, hapless, ill-fated, ill-starred, miserable, poor, unfortunate, unhappy, unlucky, unsuccessful, wretched

fortunately by a happy chance, by good luck, happily, luckily, providentially

fortune 1. affluence, big bucks (*Inf., chiefly U.S.*), big money, gold mine, megabucks (*U.S. & Canad. sl.*), opulence, possessions, pretty penny (*Inf.*), property, prosperity, riches, tidy sum (*Inf.*), treasure, wad (*U.S. & Canad. sl.*), wealth 2. accident, chance, contingency, destiny, fate, fortuity, hap (*Archaic*), hazard, kismet, luck, providence 3. *Often plural* adventures, circumstances, destiny, doom, expectation, experience(s), history, life, lot, portion, star, success 4. bomb (*Brit. sl.*), bundle (*Sl.*), king's ransom, mint, packet (*Sl.*), pile (*Inf.*), wealth
Antonyms (*sense 1*) destitution, hardship, indigence, penury, poverty, privation

forward *adj.* 1. advanced, advancing, early, forward-looking, onward, precocious, premature, progressive, well-developed 2. advance, first, fore, foremost, front, head, leading 3. assuming, bare-faced, bold, brash, brass-necked (*Brit. inf.*), brazen, brazen-faced, cheeky, confident, familiar, fresh (*Inf.*), impertinent, impudent, overassertive, overweening, pert, presuming, presumptuous, pushy (*Inf.*), sassy (*U.S. inf.*) ~*adv.* 4. *Also* **forwards** ahead, forth, on, onward 5. into consideration, into prominence, into the open, into view, out, to light, to the fore, to the surface ~*v.* 6. advance, aid, assist, back, encourage, expedite, favour, foster, further, hasten, help, hurry, promote, speed, support 7. *Commerce* dispatch, freight, post, route, send, send on, ship, transmit
Antonyms *adj.* backward, diffident, modest, regressive, retiring, shy ~*adv.* backward(s) ~*v.* bar, block, hinder, hold up, impede, obstruct, retard, thwart

forward-looking dynamic, enlightened, enterprising, go-ahead, go-getting (*Inf.*), liberal, modern, progressive, reforming

forwardness boldness, brashness, brazenness, cheek (*Inf.*), cheekiness, chutzpah (*U.S. & Canad. inf.*), impertinence, impudence, overconfidence, pertness, presumption

fossilized 1. dead, dead as a dodo, extinct, inflexible, ossified, petrified, prehistoric 2. anachronistic, antediluvian, antiquated, archaistic, behind the times, *démodé*, obsolete, out of the ark (*Inf.*), passé, superannuated

foster 1. cultivate, encourage, feed, foment, nurture, promote, stimulate, support, uphold 2. bring up, mother, nurse, raise, rear, take care of 3. accommodate, cherish, entertain, harbour, nourish, sustain
Antonyms combat, curb, curtail, hold out against, inhibit, oppose, resist, restrain, subdue, suppress, withstand

foul *adj.* 1. contaminated, dirty, disgusting, fetid, filthy, grotty (*Sl.*), grungy (*Sl., chiefly U.S.*), impure, loathsome, malodorous, mephitic, nasty, nauseating, noisome, offensive, olid, polluted, putrid, rank, repulsive, revolting, rotten, scuzzy (*Sl., chiefly U.S.*), squalid, stinking, sullied, tainted, unclean, yucky *or* yukky (*Sl.*) 2. abusive, blasphemous, blue, coarse, dirty, filthy, foul-mouthed, gross, indecent, lewd, low, obscene, profane, scatological, scurrilous, smutty, vulgar 3. abhorrent, abominable, base, despicable, detestable, disgraceful, dishonourable, egregious, hateful, heinous, infamous, iniquitous, nefarious, notorious, offensive, scandalous, shameful, shitty (*Taboo sl.*), vicious, vile, wicked 4. crooked, dirty, dishonest, fraudulent, inequitable, shady (*Inf.*), underhand, unfair, unjust, unscrupulous, unsportsmanlike 5. bad, blustery, disagreeable, foggy, murky, rainy, rough, stormy, wet, wild ~*v.* 6. begrime, besmear, besmirch, contaminate, defile, dirty, pollute, smear, smirch, soil, stain, sully, taint 7. block, catch, choke, clog, ensnare, entangle, jam, snarl, twist
Antonyms *adj.* admirable, attractive, clean, clear, decent, fair, fragrant, fresh, pleasant, pure, respectable, spotless, undefiled ~*v.* clean, cleanse, clear, honour, purge, purify, sanitize

foul-mouthed abusive, blasphemous, coarse, Fescennine (*Rare*), obscene, offensive, profane

foul play chicanery, corruption, crime, deception, dirty work, double-dealing, duplicity, fraud, perfidy, roguery, sharp practice, skulduggery, treachery, villainy

foul up bodge (*Inf.*), botch, bungle, cock up (*Brit. sl.*), fuck up (*Offens. taboo sl.*), make a mess of, mismanage, muck up (*Sl.*), put a spanner in the works (*Brit. inf.*), spoil

found 1. bring into being, constitute, construct, create, endow, erect, establish, fix, inaugurate, institute, organize, originate, plant, raise, settle, set up, start 2. base, bottom, build, ground, rest, root, sustain

foundation 1. base, basis, bedrock, bottom, footing, groundwork, substructure, underpinning 2. endowment, establishment, inauguration, institution, organization, setting up, settlement

founder[1] *n.* architect, author, beginner, benefactor, builder, constructor, designer, establisher, father, framer, generator, initiator, institutor, inventor, maker, organizer, originator, patriarch

founder[2] *v.* 1. be lost, go down, go to the bottom, sink, submerge 2. *Fig.* abort, break down, collapse, come to grief, come to nothing, fail, fall through, go belly-up (*Sl.*), go down like a lead balloon (*Inf.*), miscarry, misfire 3. collapse, fall, go lame, lurch, sprawl, stagger, stumble, trip

foundling orphan, outcast, stray, waif

fountain 1. font, fount, jet, reservoir, spout, spray, spring, well 2. *Fig.* beginning, cause, commencement, derivation, fount, fountainhead, genesis, origin, rise, source, wellhead, wellspring

fountainhead *fons et origo,* fount, inspiration, mainspring, origin, source, spring, well, wellspring

foursquare 1. *adv.* firmly, resolutely, squarely 2. *adj.* firm, firmly-based, immovable, resolute, solid, steady, strong, unyielding

foxy artful, astute, canny, crafty, cunning, devious, guileful, knowing, sharp, shrewd, sly, tricky, wily

foyer antechamber, anteroom, entrance hall, lobby, reception area, vestibule

fracas affray (*Law*), aggro (*Sl.*), *bagarre,* brawl, disturbance, donnybrook, fight, free-for-all (*Inf.*), melee *or* mêlée, quarrel, riot, row, rumpus, scrimmage, scuffle, shindig (*Inf.*), shindy (*Inf.*), skirmish, trouble, uproar

fractious awkward, captious, crabby, cross, fretful, froward, grouchy (*Inf.*), irritable, peevish, pettish, petulant, querulous, ratty (*Brit. & N.Z. inf.*), recalcitrant, refractory, testy, tetchy, touchy, unruly

Antonyms affable, agreeable, amiable, biddable, complaisant, genial, good-natured, good-tempered, tractable

fracture 1. *n.* breach, break, cleft, crack, fissure, gap, opening, rent, rift, rupture, schism, split 2. *v.* break, crack, rupture, splinter, split

fragile breakable, brittle, dainty, delicate, feeble, fine, flimsy, frail, frangible, infirm, slight, weak

Antonyms durable, elastic, flexible, hardy, lasting, reliable, resilient, robust, strong, sturdy, tough

fragility brittleness, delicacy, feebleness, frailty, frangibility, infirmity, weakness

fragment 1. *n.* bit, chip, fraction, morsel, oddment, part, particle, piece, portion, remnant, scrap, shiver, sliver 2. *v.* break, break up, come apart, come to pieces, crumble, disintegrate, disunite, divide, shatter, shiver, splinter, split, split up

Antonyms *v.* bond, combine, compound, fuse, join together, link, marry, merge, synthesize, unify

fragmentary bitty, broken, disconnected, discrete, disjointed, incoherent, incomplete, partial, piecemeal, scattered, scrappy, sketchy, unsystematic

fragrance aroma, balm, bouquet, fragrancy, perfume, redolence, scent, smell, sweet odour

Antonyms effluvium, miasma, niff (*Brit. sl.*), offensive smell, pong (*Brit. inf.*), reek, smell, stink, whiff (*Brit. sl.*)

fragrant ambrosial, aromatic, balmy, odoriferous, odorous, perfumed, redolent, sweet-scented, sweet-smelling

Antonyms fetid, foul-smelling, malodorous, niffy (*Brit. sl.*), noisome, olid, pongy (*Brit. inf.*), reeking, smelling, smelly, stinking

frail breakable, brittle, decrepit, delicate, feeble, flimsy, fragile, frangible, infirm, insubstantial, puny, slight, tender, unsound, vulnerable, weak, wispy

Antonyms hale, healthy, robust, sound, stalwart, strong, sturdy, substantial, tough, vigorous

frailty 1. fallibility, feebleness, frailness, infirmity, peccability, puniness, susceptibility, weakness 2. blemish, defect, deficiency, failing, fault, flaw, foible, imperfection, peccadillo, shortcoming, vice, weak point

Antonyms asset, fortitude, might, robustness, strength, strong point, virtue

frame *v.* 1. assemble, build, constitute, construct, fabricate, fashion, forge, form, institute, invent, make, manufacture, model, mould, put together, set up 2. block out, compose, conceive, concoct, contrive, cook up, devise, draft, draw up, form, formulate, hatch, map out, plan, shape, sketch 3. case, enclose, mount, surround ~*n.* 4. casing, construction, fabric, form, framework, scheme, shell, structure, system 5. anatomy, body, build, carcass, morphology, physique, skeleton 6. mount, mounting, setting 7. **frame of mind** attitude, disposition, fettle, humour, mood, outlook, spirit, state, temper

frame-up fabrication, fit-up (*Sl.*), put-up job, trumped-up charge

framework core, fabric, foundation, frame, frame of reference, groundwork, plan, schema, shell, skeleton, structure, the bare bones

franchise authorization, charter, exemption, freedom, immunity, prerogative, privilege, right, suffrage, vote

frank artless, blunt, candid, direct, downright, forthright, free, honest, ingenuous, open, outright, outspoken, plain, plain-spoken, sincere, straightforward, straight from the shoulder (*Inf.*), transparent, truthful, unconcealed, undisguised, unreserved, unrestricted, upfront (*Inf.*)
Antonyms artful, crafty, cunning, evasive, indirect, inscrutable, reserved, reticent, secretive, shifty, shy, underhand

frankly 1. candidly, honestly, in truth, to be honest 2. bluntly, directly, freely, openly, overtly, plainly, straight, without reserve

frankness absence of reserve, bluntness, candour, forthrightness, ingenuousness, openness, outspokenness, plain speaking, truthfulness

frantic at one's wits' end, berserk, beside oneself, desperate, distracted, distraught, fraught (*Inf.*), frenetic, frenzied, furious, hectic, mad, overwrought, raging, raving, uptight (*Inf.*), wild
Antonyms calm, collected, composed, cool, laid-back, poised, self-possessed, together (*Sl.*), unfazed (*Inf.*), unruffled

fraternity association, brotherhood, camaraderie, circle, clan, club, companionship, company, comradeship, fellowship, guild, kinship, league, order, set, sodality, union

fraternize associate, concur, consort, cooperate, go around with, hang out (*Inf.*), hobnob, keep company, mingle, mix, socialize, sympathize, unite
Antonyms avoid, eschew, keep away from, shun, steer clear of

fraud 1. artifice, canard, cheat, chicane, chicanery, craft, deceit, deception, double-dealing, duplicity, guile, hoax, humbug, imposture, scam (*Sl.*), sharp practice, spuriousness, sting (*Inf.*), stratagems, swindling, treachery, trickery 2. bluffer, charlatan, cheat, counterfeit, double-dealer, fake, forgery, hoax, hoaxer, impostor, mountebank, phoney *or* phony (*Inf.*), pretender, quack, sham, swindler
Antonyms (*sense 1*) fairness, good faith, honesty, integrity, probity, rectitude, trustworthiness, virtue

fraudulent counterfeit, crafty, criminal, crooked (*Inf.*), deceitful, deceptive, dishonest, double-dealing, duplicitous, false, knavish, phoney *or* phony (*Inf.*), sham, spurious, swindling, treacherous
Antonyms above board, genuine, honest, honourable, lawful, principled, reputable, true, trustworthy, upright

fraught 1. *With* **with** abounding, accompanied, attended, bristling, charged, filled, full, heavy, laden, replete, stuffed 2. *Inf.* agitated, anxious, difficult, distracted, distressed, distressing, emotionally charged, emotive, hag-ridden, strung-up, tense, tricky, trying, uptight (*Inf.*), wired (*Sl.*)

fray[1] *n.* affray (*Law*), *bagarre,* battle, battle royal, brawl, broil, clash, combat, conflict, disturbance, donnybrook, fight, melee *or* mêlée, quarrel, riot, row, ruckus (*Inf.*), rumble (*U.S. & N.Z. sl.*), rumpus, scrimmage, scuffle, set-to (*Inf.*), shindig (*Inf.*), shindy (*Inf.*), skirmish

fray[2] *v.* become threadbare, chafe, fret, rub, wear, wear away, wear thin

frayed frazzled, out at elbows, ragged, tattered, threadbare, worn

freak *n.* 1. aberration, abnormality, abortion, anomaly, grotesque, malformation, monster, monstrosity, mutant, oddity, queer fish (*Brit. inf.*), *rara avis,* sport (*Biol.*), teratism, weirdo *or* weirdie (*Inf.*) 2. caprice, crotchet, fad, fancy, folly, humour, irregularity, quirk, turn, twist, vagary, whim, whimsy 3. *Sl.* addict, aficionado, buff (*Inf.*), devotee, enthusiast, fan, fanatic, fiend (*Inf.*), nut (*Sl.*) ~*adj.* 4. aberrant, abnormal, atypical, bizarre, erratic, exceptional, fluky (*Inf.*), fortuitous, odd, queer, unaccountable, unexpected, unforeseen, unparalleled, unpredictable, unusual

freakish 1. arbitrary, capricious, changeable, erratic, fanciful, fitful, humorous, odd, unpredictable, vagarious (*Rare*), wayward, whimsical 2. aberrant, abnormal, fantastic, freaky (*Sl.*), grotesque, malformed, monstrous, odd, outlandish, *outré,* preternatural, strange, teratoid (*Biol.*), unconventional, weird

freaky abnormal, bizarre, crazy, far-out (*Sl.*), freakish, odd, queer, rum (*Brit. sl.*), strange, unconventional, weird, wild

free *adj.* 1. buckshee (*Brit. sl.*), complimentary, for free (*Inf.*), for nothing, free of charge, gratis, gratuitous, on the house, unpaid, without charge 2. at large, at liberty, footloose, independent, liberated, loose, off the hook (*Sl.*), on the loose, uncommitted, unconstrained, unengaged, unfettered, unrestrained 3. able, allowed, clear, disengaged, loose, open, permitted, unattached, unengaged, unhampered, unimpeded, unobstructed, unregulated, unrestricted, untrammelled 4. *With* **of** above, beyond, deficient in, devoid of, exempt from, immune to, lacking (in), not liable to, safe from, sans (*Archaic*), unaffected by, unencumbered by, untouched by, without 5. autarchic, autonomous, democratic, emancipated, independent, self-governing, self-ruling, sovereign 6. at leisure, available, empty, extra, idle, not tied down, spare, unemployed, uninhabited, unoccupied, unused, vacant 7. casual, easy, familiar, forward, frank, free and easy, informal, laid-back (*Inf.*), lax, liberal, loose, natural, open, relaxed, spontaneous, unbidden, unceremonious, unconstrained, unforced, uninhibited 8. big (*Inf.*), bounteous, bountiful, charitable, eager, generous, hospitable, lavish, liberal, munificent, open-handed, prodigal, unsparing, unstinting, willing 9. **free and easy** casual, easy-going, informal, laid-back (*Inf.*), lax, lenient, liberal, relaxed, tolerant, unceremonious ~*adv.* 10. at no cost, for love, gratis, without charge 11. abundantly, copiously, freely, idly, loosely ~*v.* 12. deliver, discharge, disenthrall, emancipate, let go, let out, liberate, loose, manumit, release, set at liberty, set free, turn loose, unbridle, uncage, unchain, unfetter, unleash, untie 13. clear, cut loose, deliver, disengage, disentangle, exempt, extricate, ransom, redeem, relieve, rescue, rid, unburden, undo, unshackle

Antonyms (*senses 2 & 3*) bound, captive, confined, dependent, fettered, immured, incarcerated, occupied, restrained, restricted, secured (*sense 7*) constrained, formal, official, stiff, unnatural (*sense 8*) close, mean, mingy (*Inf.*), stingy, tight, ungenerous (*senses 12 & 13*) confine, imprison, incarcerate, inhibit, limit, restrain, restrict, straiten

freebooter bandit, brigand, buccaneer, cateran (*Scot.*), highwayman, looter, marauder, pillager, pirate, plunderer, raider, reiver (*Dialect*), robber, rover

freedom 1. autonomy, deliverance, emancipation, home rule, independence, liberty, manumission, release, self-government 2. exemption, immunity, impunity, privilege 3. ability, blank cheque, carte blanche, discretion, elbowroom, facility, flexibility, free rein, latitude, leeway, licence, opportunity, play, power, range, scope 4. abandon, candour, directness, ease, familiarity, frankness, informality, ingenuousness, lack of restraint *or* reserve, openness, unconstraint 5. boldness, brazenness, disrespect, forwardness, impertinence, laxity, licence, overfamiliarity, presumption

Antonyms bondage, captivity, caution, dependence, imprisonment, limitation, respectfulness, restraint, restriction, servitude, slavery, thraldom

free-for-all affray (*Law*), *bagarre*, brawl, donnybrook, dust-up (*Inf.*), fight, fracas, melee *or* mêlée, riot, row, scrimmage, shindig (*Inf.*), shindy (*Inf.*)

free hand *n.* authority, blank cheque, carte blanche, discretion, freedom, latitude, liberty, scope

freely 1. of one's own accord, of one's own free will, spontaneously, voluntarily, willingly, without prompting 2. candidly, frankly, openly, plainly, unreservedly, without reserve 3. as you please, unchallenged, without let or hindrance, without restraint 4. abundantly, amply, bountifully, copiously, extravagantly, lavishly, liberally, like water, open-handedly, unstintingly, with a free hand 5. cleanly, easily, loosely, readily, smoothly

freethinker agnostic, deist, doubter, infidel, sceptic, unbeliever

freewheel coast, drift, float, glide, relax one's efforts, rest on one's oars

freeze 1. benumb, chill, congeal, glaciate, harden, ice over *or* up, stiffen 2. fix, hold up, inhibit, peg, stop, suspend

freezing arctic, biting, bitter, chill, chilled, cutting, frost-bound, frosty, glacial, icy, numbing, parky (*Brit. inf.*), penetrating, polar, raw, Siberian, wintry

freight *n.* 1. carriage, conveyance, shipment, transportation 2. bales, bulk, burden, cargo, consignment, contents, goods, haul, lading, load, merchandise, payload, tonnage

French Gallic

frenetic demented, distraught, excited, fanatical, frantic, frenzied, hyped up (*Sl.*), insane, mad, maniacal, obsessive, overwrought, unbalanced, wild

frenzied agitated, all het up (*Inf.*), convulsive, distracted, distraught, excited, feverish, frantic, frenetic, furious, hysterical, mad, maniacal, rabid, uncontrolled, wild

frenzy 1. aberration, agitation, delirium, derangement, distraction, fury, hysteria, insanity, lunacy, madness, mania, paroxysm, passion, rage, seizure, transport, turmoil 2. bout, burst, convulsion, fit, outburst, paroxysm, spasm

Antonyms calm, collectedness, composure, coolness, sanity

frequency constancy, frequentness, periodicity, prevalence, recurrence, repetition

frequent[1] *adj.* common, constant, continual, customary, everyday, familiar, habitual, incessant, numerous, persistent, recurrent, recurring, reiterated, repeated, usual

Antonyms few, few and far between, infrequent, occasional, rare, scanty, sporadic

frequent[2] *v.* attend, be a regular customer of, be found at, hang out at (*Inf.*), haunt, patronize, resort, visit
Antonyms avoid, keep away, shun, spurn

frequenter client, fan, habitué, haunter, patron, regular, regular customer, regular visitor

frequently commonly, customarily, habitually, many a time, many times, much, not infrequently, oft (*Archaic or poetic*), often, oftentimes (*Archaic*), over and over again, repeatedly, thick and fast, very often
Antonyms hardly ever, infrequently, occasionally, once in a blue moon (*Inf.*), rarely, seldom

fresh 1. different, latest, modern, modernistic, new, new-fangled, novel, original, recent, this season's, unconventional, unusual, up-to-date 2. added, additional, auxiliary, extra, further, more, other, renewed, supplementary 3. bracing, bright, brisk, clean, clear, cool, crisp, invigorating, pure, refreshing, spanking, sparkling, stiff, sweet, unpolluted 4. alert, bouncing, bright, bright-eyed and bushy-tailed (*Inf.*), chipper (*Inf.*), energetic, full of vim and vigour (*Inf.*), invigorated, keen, like a new man, lively, refreshed, rested, restored, revived, sprightly, spry, vigorous, vital 5. blooming, clear, fair, florid, glowing, good, hardy, healthy, rosy, ruddy, wholesome 6. dewy, undimmed, unfaded, unwearied, unwithered, verdant, vivid, young 7. artless, callow, green, inexperienced, natural, new, raw, uncultivated, untrained, untried, youthful 8. crude, green, natural, raw, uncured, undried, unprocessed, unsalted 9. *Inf.* bold, brazen, cheeky, disrespectful, familiar, flip (*Inf.*), forward, impudent, insolent, pert, presumptuous, sassy (*U.S. inf.*), saucy, smart-alecky (*Inf.*)
Antonyms dull, exhausted, experienced, impure, musty, old, ordinary, pallid, preserved, salted, sickly, stale, stereotyped, tinned, trite, warm, weary, well-mannered

freshen 1. enliven, freshen up, liven up, refresh, restore, revitalize, rouse, spruce up, titivate 2. air, purify, ventilate

freshness 1. innovativeness, inventiveness, newness, novelty, originality 2. bloom, brightness, cleanness, clearness, dewiness, glow, shine, sparkle, vigour, wholesomeness

fret[1] 1. affront, agonize, anguish, annoy, brood, chagrin, goad, grieve, harass, irritate, lose sleep over, provoke, ruffle, torment, upset *or* distress oneself, worry 2. agitate, bother, distress, disturb, gall, irk, nag, nettle, peeve (*Inf.*), pique, rankle with, rile, trouble, vex

fret[2] abrade, chafe, erode, fray, gall, rub, wear, wear away

fretful captious, complaining, cross, crotchety (*Inf.*), edgy, fractious, irritable, out of sorts, peevish, petulant, querulous, ratty (*Brit. & N.Z. inf.*), short-tempered, splenetic, testy, tetchy, touchy, uneasy

friable brittle, crisp, crumbly, powdery, pulverizable

friction 1. abrasion, attrition, chafing, erosion, fretting, grating, irritation, rasping, resistance, rubbing, scraping, wearing away 2. animosity, antagonism, bad blood, bad feeling, bickering, conflict, disagreement, discontent, discord, disharmony, dispute, dissension, hostility, incompatibility, opposition, resentment, rivalry, wrangling

friend 1. Achates, alter ego, boon companion, bosom friend, buddy (*Inf.*), china (*Brit. sl.*), chum (*Inf.*), cock (*Brit. inf.*), companion, comrade, confidant, crony, familiar, intimate, mate (*Inf.*), pal, partner, playmate, soul mate 2. adherent, advocate, ally, associate, backer, benefactor, partisan, patron, protagonist, supporter, well-wisher
Antonyms adversary, antagonist, competitor, enemy, foe, opponent, rival

friendless abandoned, alienated, all alone, alone, cut off, deserted, estranged, forlorn, forsaken, isolated, lonely, lonesome, ostracized, shunned, solitary, unattached, with no one to turn to, without a friend in the world, without ties

friendliness affability, amiability, companionability, congeniality, conviviality, geniality, kindliness, mateyness *or* matiness (*Brit. inf.*), neighbourliness, open arms, sociability, warmth

friendly affable, affectionate, amiable, amicable, attached, attentive, auspicious, beneficial, benevolent, benign, buddy-buddy (*Sl., chiefly U.S. & Canad.*), chummy (*Inf.*), close, clubby, companionable, comradely, conciliatory, confiding, convivial, cordial, familiar, favourable, fond, fraternal, genial, good, helpful, intimate, kind, kindly, matey *or* maty (*Brit. inf.*), neighbourly, on good terms, on visiting terms, outgoing, palsy-walsy (*Inf.*), peaceable, propitious, receptive, sociable, sympathetic, thick (*Inf.*), welcoming, well-disposed
Antonyms antagonistic, belligerent, cold, contentious, distant, inauspicious, sinister, uncongenial, unfriendly

friendship affection, affinity, alliance, amity, attachment, benevolence, closeness, concord, familiarity, fondness, friendliness, good-fellowship, good will, harmony, intimacy, love, rapport, regard
Antonyms animosity, antagonism, an~

tipathy, aversion, conflict, enmity, hatred, hostility, resentment, strife, unfriendliness

fright 1. alarm, apprehension, (blue) funk (*Inf.*), cold sweat, consternation, dismay, dread, fear, fear and trembling, horror, panic, quaking, scare, shock, terror, the shivers, trepidation 2. *Inf.* eyesore, frump, mess (*Inf.*), scarecrow, sight (*Inf.*)
Antonyms boldness, bravery, courage, pluck, valor

frighten affright (*Archaic*), alarm, appal, cow, daunt, dismay, freeze one's blood, intimidate, make one's blood run cold, make one's hair stand on end (*Inf.*), make (someone) jump out of his skin (*Inf.*), petrify, put the wind up (someone) (*Inf.*), scare, scare (someone) stiff, scare the living daylights out of (someone) (*Inf.*), shock, startle, terrify, terrorize, throw into a fright, throw into a panic, unman, unnerve
Antonyms allay, assuage, calm, comfort, encourage, hearten, reassure, soothe

frightened abashed, affrighted (*Archaic*), afraid, alarmed, cowed, dismayed, frozen, in a cold sweat, in a panic, in fear and trepidation, numb with fear, panicky, petrified, scared, scared shitless (*Taboo sl.*), scared stiff, shit-scared (*Taboo sl.*), startled, terrified, terrorized, terror-stricken, unnerved

frightening alarming, appalling, baleful, bloodcurdling, daunting, dismaying, dreadful, fearful, fearsome, hair-raising, horrifying, intimidating, menacing, scary (*Inf.*), shocking, spooky (*Inf.*), terrifying, unnerving

frightful 1. alarming, appalling, awful, dire, dread, dreadful, fearful, ghastly, godawful (*Sl.*), grim, grisly, gruesome, harrowing, hellacious (*U.S. sl.*), hideous, horrendous, horrible, horrid, lurid, macabre, petrifying, shocking, terrible, terrifying, traumatic, unnerving, unspeakable 2. annoying, awful, disagreeable, dreadful, extreme, great, insufferable, terrible, terrific, unpleasant
Antonyms attractive, beautiful, calming, lovely, moderate, nice, pleasant, slight, soothing

frigid 1. arctic, chill, cold, cool, frost-bound, frosty, frozen, gelid, glacial, hyperboreal, icy, Siberian, wintry 2. aloof, austere, cold-hearted, forbidding, formal, icy, lifeless, passionless, passive, repellent, rigid, stiff, unapproachable, unbending, unfeeling, unloving, unresponsive
Antonyms ardent, cordial, friendly, hospitable, hot, impassioned, passionate, responsive, sensual, stifling, sweltering, warm

frigidity aloofness, austerity, chill, cold-heartedness, coldness, frostiness, iciness, impassivity, lack of response, lifelessness, passivity, touch-me-not attitude, unapproachability, unresponsiveness, wintriness

frill *n.* flounce, furbelow, gathering, purfle, ruche, ruching, ruff, ruffle, tuck

frills additions, affectation(s), bits and pieces, decoration(s), dressing up, embellishment(s), extras, fanciness, fandangles, finery, frilliness, frippery, fuss, gewgaws, jazz (*Sl.*), mannerisms, nonsense, ornamentation, ostentation, superfluities, tomfoolery, trimmings

frilly fancy, flouncy, frothy, lacy, ruched, ruffled

fringe *n.* 1. binding, border, edging, hem, tassel, trimming 2. borderline, edge, limits, march, marches, margin, outskirts, perimeter, periphery *~adj.* 3. unconventional, unofficial, unorthodox *~v.* 4. border, edge, enclose, skirt, surround, trim

fringed befringed, bordered, edged, margined, outlined, overhung

frippery 1. fanciness, finery, flashiness, foppery, frilliness, frills, fussiness, gaudiness, glad rags (*Inf.*), meretriciousness, nonsense, ostentation, pretentiousness, showiness, tawdriness 2. adornment, bauble, decoration, fandangle, gewgaw, knick-knack, ornament, toy, trinket

frisk 1. bounce, caper, cavort, curvet, dance, frolic, gambol, hop, jump, play, prance, rollick, romp, skip, sport, trip 2. *Inf.* check, inspect, run over, search, shake down (*U.S. sl.*)

frisky bouncy, coltish, frolicsome, full of beans (*Inf.*), full of joie de vivre, high-spirited, in high spirits, kittenish, lively, playful, rollicking, romping, spirited, sportive
Antonyms demure, dull, lacklustre, pensive, sedate, stodgy, stolid, wooden

fritter (away) dally away, dissipate, fool away, idle (away), misspend, run through, spend like water, squander, waste

frivolity childishness, flightiness, flippancy, flummery, folly, frivolousness, fun, gaiety, giddiness, jest, levity, light-heartedness, lightness, nonsense, puerility, shallowness, silliness, superficiality, trifling, triviality
Antonyms earnestness, gravity, humourlessness, importance, sedateness, seriousness, significance, soberness, sobriety

frivolous 1. childish, dizzy, empty-headed, flighty, flip (*Inf.*), flippant, foolish, giddy, idle, ill-considered, juvenile, light-minded, nonserious, puerile, silly, superficial 2. extravagant, footling (*Inf.*), impractical, light, minor, nickel-and-dime (*U.S. sl.*), niggling,

paltry, peripheral, petty, pointless, shallow, trifling, trivial, unimportant
Antonyms earnest, important, mature, practical, responsible, sensible, serious, solemn, vital

frizzle crisp, fry, hiss, roast, scorch, sizzle, sputter

frizzy corrugated, crimped, crisp, frizzed, tight-curled, wiry

frolic *v.* 1. caper, cavort, cut capers, frisk, gambol, lark, make merry, play, rollick, romp, sport ~*n.* 2. antic, escapade, gambado, gambol, game, lark, prank, revel, romp, spree 3. amusement, drollery, fun, fun and games, gaiety, high jinks, merriment, skylarking (*Inf.*), sport

frolicsome coltish, frisky, gay, kittenish, lively, merry, playful, rollicking, sportive, sprightly, wanton (*Archaic*)

front *n.* 1. anterior, exterior, façade, face, facing, foreground, forepart, frontage, obverse 2. beginning, fore, forefront, front line, head, lead, top, van, vanguard 3. air, appearance, aspect, bearing, countenance, demeanour, expression, exterior, face, manner, mien, show 4. blind, cover, cover-up, disguise, façade, mask, pretext, show 5. **in front** ahead, before, first, in advance, in the lead, in the van, leading, preceding, to the fore ~*adj.* 6. first, foremost, head, headmost, lead, leading, topmost ~*v.* 7. face (onto), look over *or* onto, overlook
Antonyms (*senses 1 & 2*) aft, back, back end, behind, hindmost, nethermost, rear

frontier borderland, borderline, bound, boundary, confines, edge, limit, marches, perimeter, verge

frost freeze, freeze-up, hoarfrost, Jack Frost, rime

frosty 1. chilly, cold, frozen, hoar (*Rare*), ice-capped, icicled, icy, parky (*Brit. inf.*), rimy, wintry 2. discouraging, frigid, off-putting (*Brit. inf.*), standoffish, unenthusiastic, unfriendly, unwelcoming

froth 1. *n.* bubbles, effervescence, foam, head, lather, scum, spume, suds 2. *v.* bubble over, come to a head, effervesce, fizz, foam, lather

frothy 1. foaming, foamy, spumescent, spumous, spumy, sudsy 2. *Fig.* empty, frilly, frivolous, light, petty, slight, trifling, trivial, trumpery, unnecessary, unsubstantial, vain

frown 1. give a dirty look, glare, glower, knit one's brows, look daggers, lour *or* lower, scowl 2. *With* **on** *or* **upon** disapprove of, discountenance, discourage, dislike, look askance at, not take kindly to, show disapproval *or* displeasure, take a dim view of, view with disfavour

frowsty close, fuggy, fusty, ill-smelling, musty, stale, stuffy

frowzy blowzy, dirty, draggletailed (*Archaic*), frumpish, messy, slatternly, sloppy, slovenly, sluttish, ungroomed, unkempt, untidy, unwashed

frozen 1. arctic, chilled, chilled to the marrow, frigid, frosted, icebound, ice-cold, ice-covered, icy, numb 2. fixed, pegged (*of prices*), petrified, rooted, stock-still, stopped, suspended, turned to stone

frugal abstemious, careful, cheeseparing, economical, meagre, niggardly, parsimonious, penny-wise, provident, prudent, saving, sparing, thrifty
Antonyms excessive, extravagant, imprudent, lavish, luxurious, prodigal, profligate, spendthrift, wasteful

frugality carefulness, conservation, economizing, economy, good management, husbandry, moderation, providence, thrift, thriftiness

fruit 1. crop, harvest, produce, product, yield 2. advantage, benefit, consequence, effect, outcome, profit, result, return, reward

fruitful 1. fecund, fertile, fructiferous 2. abundant, copious, flush, plenteous, plentiful, productive, profuse, prolific, rich, spawning 3. advantageous, beneficial, effective, gainful, productive, profitable, rewarding, successful, useful, well-spent, worthwhile
Antonyms barren, fruitless, futile, ineffectual, infertile, pointless, scarce, sterile, unfruitful, unproductive, useless, vain

fruition actualization, attainment, completion, consummation, enjoyment, fulfilment, materialization, maturation, maturity, perfection, realization, ripeness

fruitless abortive, barren, bootless, futile, idle, ineffectual, in vain, pointless, profitless, to no avail, to no effect, unavailing, unfruitful, unproductive, unprofitable, unprolific, unsuccessful, useless, vain
Antonyms abundant, effective, fecund, fertile, fruitful, productive, profitable, prolific, useful

fruity 1. full, mellow, resonant, rich 2. *Inf.* bawdy, blue, hot, indecent, indelicate, juicy, near the knuckle (*Inf.*), racy, ripe, risqué, salacious, sexy, smutty, spicy (*Inf.*), suggestive, titillating, vulgar

frumpish, frumpy badly-dressed, dated, dingy, dowdy, drab, dreary, mumsy, out of date

frustrate 1. baffle, balk, block, check, circumvent, confront, counter, defeat, disappoint, foil, forestall, inhibit, neutralize,

nullify, render null and void, stymie, thwart 2. depress, discourage, dishearten
Antonyms advance, cheer, encourage, endorse, forward, further, hearten, promote, satisfy, stimulate

frustrated carrying a chip on one's shoulder (*Inf.*), disappointed, discontented, discouraged, disheartened, embittered, foiled, irked, resentful, sick as a parrot (*Inf.*)

frustration 1. blocking, circumvention, contravention, curbing, failure, foiling, nonfulfilment, nonsuccess, obstruction, thwarting 2. annoyance, disappointment, dissatisfaction, grievance, irritation, resentment, vexation

fuddled bevvied (*Dialect*), blitzed (*Sl.*), blotto (*Sl.*), bombed (*Sl.*), confused, drunk, flying (*Sl.*), inebriated, intoxicated, legless (*Inf.*), lit up (*Sl.*), muddled, muzzy, out of it (*Sl.*), out to it (*Aust. & N.Z. sl.*), paralytic (*Inf.*), pissed (*Taboo sl.*), smashed (*Sl.*), sozzled (*Inf.*), steamboats (*Sl.*), steaming (*Sl.*), stupefied, tipsy, wasted (*Sl.*), woozy (*Inf.*), wrecked (*Sl.*), zonked (*Sl.*)

fuddy-duddy *n.* back number (*Inf.*), conservative, dinosaur, dodo (*Inf.*), fossil, museum piece, (old) fogy, square (*Inf.*), stick-in-the-mud (*Inf.*), stuffed shirt (*Inf.*)

fudge *v.* avoid, cook (*Sl.*), dodge, equivocate, evade, fake, falsify, flannel (*Brit. inf.*), hedge, misrepresent, patch up, shuffle, slant, stall

fuel 1. *n. Fig.* ammunition, encouragement, fodder, food, incitement, material, means, nourishment, provocation 2. *v.* charge, fan, feed, fire, incite, inflame, nourish, stoke up, sustain

fug fetidity, fetor, frowst, frowstiness, fustiness, reek, stale air, staleness, stink

fuggy airless, fetid, foul, frowsty, noisome, noxious, stale, stuffy, suffocating, unventilated

fugitive 1. *n.* deserter, escapee, refugee, runagate (*Archaic*), runaway 2. *adj.* brief, ephemeral, evanescent, fleeing, fleeting, flitting, flying, fugacious, momentary, passing, short, short-lived, temporary, transient, transitory, unstable

fulfil accomplish, achieve, answer, bring to completion, carry out, complete, comply with, conclude, conform to, discharge, effect, execute, fill, finish, keep, meet, obey, observe, perfect, perform, realise, satisfy
Antonyms disappoint, dissatisfy, fail in, fail to meet, fall short of, neglect

fulfilment accomplishment, achievement, attainment, carrying out *or* through, completion, consummation, crowning, discharge, discharging, effecting, end, implementation, observance, perfection, realization

full 1. brimful, brimming, complete, entire, filled, gorged, intact, loaded, replete, sated, satiated, satisfied, saturated, stocked, sufficient 2. abundant, adequate, all-inclusive, ample, broad, comprehensive, copious, detailed, exhaustive, extensive, generous, maximum, plenary, plenteous, plentiful, thorough, unabridged 3. chock-a-block, chock-full, crammed, crowded, in use, jammed, occupied, packed, taken 4. clear, deep, distinct, loud, resonant, rich, rounded 5. baggy, balloonlike, buxom, capacious, curvaceous, large, loose, plump, puffy, rounded, voluminous, voluptuous 6. **in full** completely, in its entirety, in total, *in toto,* without exception 7. **to the full** completely, entirely, fully, thoroughly, to the utmost, without reservation
Antonyms abridged, blank, devoid, empty, exhausted, faint, incomplete, limited, partial, restricted, thin, tight, vacant, void

full-blooded ballsy (*Taboo sl.*), gutsy (*Sl.*), hearty, lusty, mettlesome, red-blooded, vigorous, virile

full-bodied fruity, full-flavoured, heady, heavy, mellow, redolent, rich, strong, well-matured

full-grown adult, developed, full-fledged, grown-up, in one's prime, marriageable, mature, nubile, of age, ripe
Antonyms adolescent, green, premature, undeveloped, unfledged, unformed, unripe, untimely, young

fullness 1. abundance, adequateness, ampleness, copiousness, fill, glut, plenty, profusion, repletion, satiety, saturation, sufficiency 2. broadness, completeness, comprehensiveness, entirety, extensiveness, plenitude, totality, vastness, wealth, wholeness 3. clearness, loudness, resonance, richness, strength 4. curvaceousness, dilation, distension, enlargement, roundness, swelling, tumescence, voluptuousness

full-scale all-encompassing, all-out, comprehensive, exhaustive, extensive, full-dress, in-depth, major, proper, sweeping, thorough, thoroughgoing, wide-ranging

fully 1. absolutely, altogether, completely, entirely, every inch, from first to last, heart and soul, in all respects, intimately, perfectly, positively, thoroughly, totally, utterly, wholly 2. abundantly, adequately, amply, comprehensively, enough, plentifully, satisfactorily, sufficiently 3. at least, quite, without (any) exaggeration, without a word of a lie (*Inf.*)

fully-fledged experienced, mature, professional, proficient, qualified, senior, time-served, trained

fulminate animadvert upon, berate, blast, castigate, censure, criticize, curse, denounce, denunciate, excoriate, execrate, fume, inveigh against, lambast(e), protest against, put down, rage, rail against, reprobate, tear into (*Inf.*), thunder, upbraid, vilify, vituperate

fulmination condemnation, denunciation, diatribe, excoriation, invective, obloquy, philippic, reprobation, tirade

fulsome adulatory, cloying, excessive, extravagant, fawning, gross, immoderate, ingratiating, inordinate, insincere, nauseating, overdone, saccharine, sickening, smarmy (*Brit. inf.*), sycophantic, unctuous

fumble 1. bumble, feel around, flounder, grope, paw (*Inf.*), scrabble 2. bodge (*Inf.*), botch, bungle, cock up (*Brit. sl.*), fuck up (*Offens. taboo sl.*), make a hash of (*Inf.*), mess up, misfield, mishandle, mismanage, muff, spoil

fume *Fig.* 1. *v.* blow a fuse (*Sl., chiefly U.S.*), boil, chafe, champ at the bit (*Inf.*), crack up (*Inf.*), fly off the handle (*Inf.*), get hot under the collar (*Inf.*), get steamed up about (*Sl.*), go off the deep end (*Inf.*), go up the wall (*Sl.*), rage, rant, rave, see red (*Inf.*), seethe, smoulder, storm 2. *n.* agitation, dither (*Chiefly Brit.*), fit, fret, fury, passion, rage, stew (*Inf.*), storm

fumes effluvium, exhalation, exhaust, gas, haze, miasma, pollution, reek, smog, smoke, stench, vapour

fumigate clean out *or* up, cleanse, disinfect, purify, sanitize, sterilize

fuming all steamed up (*Sl.*), angry, at boiling point (*Inf.*), enraged, foaming at the mouth, in a rage, incensed, raging, roused, seething, up in arms

fun *n.* 1. amusement, cheer, distraction, diversion, enjoyment, entertainment, frolic, gaiety, good time, high jinks, jollification, jollity, joy, junketing, living it up, merriment, merrymaking, mirth, pleasure, recreation, romp, sport, treat, whoopee (*Inf.*) 2. buffoonery, clowning, foolery, game, horseplay, jesting, jocularity, joking, nonsense, play, playfulness, skylarking (*Inf.*), sport, teasing, tomfoolery 3. **in** *or* **for fun** facetiously, for a joke, for a laugh, in jest, jokingly, light-heartedly, mischievously, playfully, roguishly, teasingly, tongue in cheek, with a gleam *or* twinkle in one's eye, with a straight face 4. **make fun of** deride, hold up to ridicule, lampoon, laugh at, make a fool of, make game of, make sport of, make the butt of, mock, parody, poke fun at, rag, rib (*Inf.*), ridicule, satirize, scoff at, send up (*Brit. inf.*), sneer at, take off, take the piss out of (*Taboo sl.*), taunt ~*adj.* 5. amusing, convivial, diverting, enjoyable, entertaining, lively, witty

Antonyms (*sense 1*) depression, desolation, despair, distress, gloom, grief, melancholy, misery, sadness, sorrow, unhappiness, woe

function *n.* 1. activity, business, capacity, charge, concern, duty, employment, exercise, job, mission, occupation, office, operation, part, post, province, purpose, raison d'être, responsibility, role, situation, task ~*v.* 2. act, act the part of, behave, be in commission, be in operation *or* action, be in running order, do duty, go, officiate, operate, perform, run, serve, serve one's turn, work ~*n.* 3. affair, do (*Inf.*), gathering, reception, social occasion

functional hard-wearing, operative, practical, serviceable, useful, utilitarian, utility, working

functionary dignitary, employee, office bearer, office holder, officer, official

fund *n.* 1. capital, endowment, fall-back, foundation, kitty, pool, reserve, stock, store, supply 2. hoard, mine, repository, reserve, reservoir, source, storehouse, treasury, vein ~*v.* 3. capitalize, endow, finance, float, pay for, promote, stake, subsidize, support

fundamental 1. *adj.* basic, bog-standard (*Inf.*), cardinal, central, constitutional, crucial, elementary, essential, first, important, indispensable, integral, intrinsic, key, necessary, organic, primary, prime, principal, radical, rudimentary, underlying, vital 2. *n.* axiom, basic, cornerstone, essential, first principle, law, principle, rudiment, rule, *sine qua non*

Antonyms advanced, back-up, extra, incidental, lesser, secondary, subsidiary, superfluous

fundamentally at bottom, at heart, basically, essentially, intrinsically, primarily, radically

funds 1. ackers (*Sl.*), brass (*Northern English dialect*), bread (*Sl.*), capital, cash, dibs (*Sl.*), dosh (*Brit. & Aust. sl.*), dough (*Sl.*), finance, hard cash, money, necessary (*Inf.*), needful (*Inf.*), ready money, resources, rhino (*Brit. sl.*), savings, shekels (*Inf.*), silver, spondulicks (*Sl.*), the ready (*Inf.*), the wherewithal, tin (*Sl.*) 2. **in funds** flush (*Inf.*), in the black, solvent, well-off, well-supplied

funeral burial, inhumation, interment, obsequies

funereal dark, deathlike, depressing, dirgelike, dismal, dreary, gloomy, grave, lamenting, lugubrious, mournful, sad, sepulchral, solemn, sombre, woeful

funk 1. *v.* chicken out of (*Inf.*), dodge, duck out of (*Inf.*), flinch from, recoil from, take fright, turn tail 2. **be in a (blue) funk** be in a cold sweat, be in a panic, be scared stiff, be sick with fear, cower, dread, fear, quail, quake, quiver, shake at the knees, shrink, tremble, tremble in one's boots

funnel *v.* channel, conduct, convey, direct, filter, move, pass, pour

funny *adj.* 1. absurd, amusing, a scream (card (*Inf.*), caution (*Inf.*)) (*Inf.*), comic, comical, diverting, droll, entertaining, facetious, farcical, hilarious, humorous, jocose, jocular, jolly, killing (*Inf.*), laughable, ludicrous, rich, ridiculous, riotous, risible, side-splitting, silly, slapstick, waggish, witty 2. curious, dubious, mysterious, odd, peculiar, perplexing, puzzling, queer, remarkable, rum (*Brit. sl.*), strange, suspicious, unusual, weird ~*n.* 3. *Inf.* crack (*Sl.*), jest, joke, play on words, pun, quip, wisecrack, witticism

Antonyms (*sense 1*) grave, humourless, melancholy, serious, sober, solemn, stern, unfunny

furbish brighten, burnish, polish, renovate, restore, rub, shine, smarten up, spruce up

furious 1. angry, beside oneself, boiling, cross, enraged, frantic, frenzied, fuming, incensed, infuriated, in high dudgeon, livid (*Inf.*), mad, maddened, on the warpath (*Inf.*), raging, up in arms, wrathful, wroth (*Archaic*) 2. agitated, boisterous, fierce, impetuous, intense, savage, stormy, tempestuous, tumultuous, turbulent, ungovernable, unrestrained, vehement, violent, wild

Antonyms calm, dispassionate, impassive, imperturbable, mild, placated, pleased, serene, tranquil

furnish 1. appoint, decorate, equip, fit (out, up), outfit, provide, provision, purvey, rig, stock, store, supply 2. afford, bestow, endow, give, grant, hand out, offer, present, provide, reveal, supply

furniture appliances, appointments, chattels, effects, equipment, fittings, furnishings, goods, household goods, movable property, movables, possessions, things (*Inf.*)

furore 1. commotion, disturbance, excitement, flap (*Inf.*), frenzy, fury, hullabaloo, outburst, outcry, stir, to-do, uproar 2. craze, enthusiasm, mania, rage

furrow 1. *n.* channel, corrugation, crease, crow's-foot, fluting, groove, hollow, line, rut, seam, trench, wrinkle 2. *v.* corrugate, crease, draw together, flute, knit, seam, wrinkle

further 1. *adj.* additional, extra, fresh, more, new, other, supplementary 2. *adv.* additionally, also, as well as, besides, furthermore, in addition, moreover, on top of, over and above, to boot, what's more, yet 3. *v.* advance, aid, assist, champion, contribute to, encourage, expedite, facilitate, forward, foster, hasten, help, lend support to, patronize, plug (*Inf.*), promote, push, speed, succour, work for

Antonyms *v.* foil, frustrate, hinder, impede, obstruct, oppose, prevent, retard, stop, thwart

furtherance advancement, advocacy, backing, boosting, carrying-out, championship, promotion, prosecution, pursuit

furthermore additionally, as well, besides, further, in addition, into the bargain, moreover, not to mention, to boot, too, what's more

furthest extreme, farthest, furthermost, most distant, outermost, outmost, remotest, ultimate, uttermost

furtive clandestine, cloaked, conspiratorial, covert, hidden, secret, secretive, skulking, slinking, sly, sneaking, sneaky, stealthy, surreptitious, underhand, under-the-table

Antonyms above-board, candid, forthright, frank, open, public, straightforward, undisguised, unreserved

fury 1. anger, frenzy, impetuosity, ire, madness, passion, rage, wrath 2. ferocity, fierceness, force, intensity, power, savagery, severity, tempestuousness, turbulence, vehemence, violence 3. bacchante, hag, hellcat, shrew, spitfire, termagant, virago, vixen

Antonyms calm, calmness, composure, equanimity, hush, peace, peacefulness, serenity, stillness, tranquillity

fuse *v.* agglutinate, amalgamate, blend, coalesce, combine, commingle, dissolve, federate, integrate, intermingle, intermix, join, meld, melt, merge, run together, smelt, solder, unite, weld

Antonyms diffuse, dispense, disseminate, dissipate, disunite, scatter, separate, spread, strew

fusillade barrage, broadside, burst, fire, hail, outburst, salvo, volley

fusion alloy, amalgam, amalgamation, blend, blending, coalescence, commingling, commixture, federation, integration, liquefaction, meld, merger, merging, mixture, smelting, synthesis, union, uniting, welding

fuss *n.* 1. ado, agitation, bother, bustle, commotion, confusion, excitement, fidget, flap (*Inf.*), flurry, fluster, flutter, hurry, palaver, pother, stir, storm in a teacup (*Brit.*), to-do, upset, worry 2. altercation, argument, bother, complaint, difficulty, display, furore, hassle (*Inf.*), objection, row, squabble, trouble, unrest, upset ~*v.* 3. bustle, chafe, fidget, flap (*Inf.*), fret, fume, get in a stew (*Inf.*), get worked up, labour over, make a meal of (*Inf.*), make a thing of (*Inf.*), niggle, take pains, worry

fusspot fidget, fussbudget (*U.S.*), nit-picker (*Inf.*), old woman, perfectionist, worrier

fussy 1. choosy (*Inf.*), dainty, difficult, discriminating, exacting, faddish, faddy, fastidious, finicky, hard to please, nit-picking (*Inf.*), old-maidish, old womanish, overparticular, particular, pernickety, picky (*Inf.*), squeamish 2. busy, cluttered, overdecorated, overelaborate, overembellished, overworked, rococo

fustiness airlessness, dampness, frowstiness, fug, mouldiness, mustiness, smell of decay, staleness, stuffiness

fusty 1. airless, damp, frowsty, ill-smelling, malodorous, mildewed, mildewy, mouldering, mouldy, musty, rank, stale, stuffy 2. antediluvian, antiquated, archaic, old-fashioned, old-fogyish, outdated, out-of-date, out of the ark (*Inf.*), passé

futile 1. abortive, barren, bootless, empty, forlorn, fruitless, hollow, ineffectual, in vain, nugatory, profitless, sterile, to no avail, unavailing, unproductive, unprofitable, unsuccessful, useless, vain, valueless, worthless 2. idle, pointless, trifling, trivial, unimportant

Antonyms constructive, effective, fruitful, profitable, purposeful, significant, successful, useful, valuable, worthwhile

futility 1. bootlessness, emptiness, fruitlessness, hollowness, ineffectiveness, uselessness 2. pointlessness, triviality, unimportance, vanity

future 1. *n.* expectation, hereafter, outlook, prospect, time to come 2. *adj.* approaching, coming, destined, eventual, expected, fated, forthcoming, impending, in the offing, later, prospective, subsequent, to be, to come, ultimate, unborn

Antonyms *adj.* bygone, erstwhile, ex-, former, late, past, preceding, previous, quondam

fuzz down, fibre, floss, fluff, hair, lint, nap, pile

fuzzy 1. down-covered, downy, flossy, fluffy, frizzy, linty, napped, woolly 2. bleary, blurred, distorted, faint, ill-defined, indistinct, muffled, out of focus, shadowy, unclear, unfocused, vague

Antonyms clear, defined, detailed, distinct, in focus, precise

G

gab 1. *v.* babble, blabber, blather, buzz, chatter, gossip, jabber, jaw (*Sl.*), prattle, rabbit (*Brit. inf.*), run off at the mouth (*Sl.*), spout, talk, waffle (*Inf., chiefly Brit.*), yak (*Sl.*) 2. *n.* blab, blarney, blather, chat, chatter, chitchat, conversation, gossip, loquacity, palaver, small talk, talk, tête-à-tête, tittle-tattle, tongue-wagging, waffle (*Inf., chiefly Brit.*), yackety-yak (*Sl.*), yak (*Sl.*)

gabble 1. *v.* babble, blab, blabber, cackle, chatter, gaggle, gibber, gush, jabber, prattle, rabbit (*Brit. inf.*), rattle, run off at the mouth (*Sl.*), splutter, spout, sputter, waffle (*Inf., chiefly Brit.*) 2. *n.* babble, blabber, cackling, chatter, drivel, gibberish, jargon, pap, prattle, twaddle, waffle (*Inf., chiefly Brit.*)

gabby chatty, effusive, garrulous, glib, gossiping, gushing, long-winded, loquacious, mouthy, prattling, prolix, talkative, verbose, voluble, windy, wordy

gad (about *or* around) gallivant, ramble, range, roam, rove, run around, stravaig (*Scot., & northern English dialect*), stray, traipse (*Inf.*), wander

gadabout gallivanter, pleasure-seeker, rambler, rover, wanderer

gadget appliance, contraption (*Inf.*), contrivance, device, gimmick, gizmo (*Sl., chiefly U.S.*), instrument, invention, novelty, thing, tool

gaffe bloomer (*Inf.*), blunder, boob (*Brit. sl.*), boo-boo (*Inf.*), clanger (*Inf.*), faux pas, gaucherie, howler, indiscretion, mistake, slip, solecism

gaffer 1. granddad, greybeard, old boy (*Inf.*), old fellow, old man, old-timer (*U.S.*) 2. *Inf.* boss (*Inf.*), foreman, ganger, manager, overseer, superintendent, supervisor

gag[1] *v.* 1. curb, muffle, muzzle, quiet, silence, stifle, still, stop up, suppress, throttle 2. *Sl.* barf (*Sl.*), disgorge, heave, puke (*Sl.*), retch, spew, throw up (*Inf.*), vomit 3. *Sl.* choke, gasp, pant, struggle for breath

gag[2] crack (*Sl.*), funny (*Inf.*), hoax, jest, joke, wisecrack (*Inf.*), witticism

gage *n.* 1. bond, deposit, earnest, guarantee, pawn, pledge, security, surety, token 2. challenge, dare, defiance, gauntlet, glove

gaiety 1. animation, blitheness, blitheness (*Literary*), cheerfulness, effervescence, elation, exhilaration, glee, good humour, high spirits, hilarity, *joie de vivre,* jollity, joviality, joyousness, light-heartedness, liveliness, merriment, mirth, sprightliness, vivacity 2. celebration, conviviality, festivity, fun, jollification, merrymaking, revelry, revels 3. brightness, brilliance, colour, colourfulness, gaudiness, glitter, show, showiness, sparkle
Antonyms despondency, gloom, melancholy, misery, sadness

gaily 1. blithely, cheerfully, gleefully, happily, joyfully, light-heartedly, merrily 2. brightly, brilliantly, colourfully, flamboyantly, flashily, gaudily, showily

gain *v.* 1. achieve, acquire, advance, attain, bag, build up, capture, collect, enlist, gather, get, glean, harvest, improve, increase, net, obtain, pick up, procure, profit, realize, reap, score (*Sl.*), secure, win, win over 2. acquire, bring in, clear, earn, get, make, net, obtain, produce, realize, win, yield 3. *Usually with* **on a.** approach, catch up with, close with, get nearer, narrow the gap, overtake **b.** draw *or* pull away from, get farther away, leave behind, outdistance, recede, widen the gap 4. arrive at, attain, come to, get to, reach 5. **gain time** delay, procrastinate, stall, temporize, use delaying tactics ~*n.* 6. accretion, achievement, acquisition, advance, advancement, advantage, attainment, benefit, dividend, earnings, emolument, growth, headway, improvement, income, increase, increment, lucre, proceeds, produce, profit, progress, return, rise, winnings, yield
Antonyms *v.* fail, forfeit, lose, worsen ~*n.* damage, forfeiture, injury, loss, privation

gainful advantageous, beneficial, expedient, fruitful, lucrative, moneymaking, paying, productive, profitable, remunerative, rewarding, useful, worthwhile

gains booty, earnings, gainings, pickings, prize, proceeds, profits, revenue, takings, winnings

gainsay contradict, contravene, controvert, deny, disaffirm, disagree with, dispute, rebut, retract
Antonyms agree with, back, confirm, support

gait bearing, carriage, pace, step, stride, tread, walk

gala 1. *n.* beano (*Brit. sl.*), carnival, celebration, festival, festivity, fête, jamboree, pageant, party, rave (*Brit. sl.*), rave-up (*Brit. sl.*) 2. *adj.* celebratory, convivial, festal, festive, gay, jovial, joyful, merry

gale 1. blast, cyclone, hurricane, squall, storm, tempest, tornado, typhoon 2. *Inf.* burst, eruption, explosion, fit, howl, outbreak, outburst, peal, shout, shriek

gall[1] 1. *Inf.* brass (*Inf.*), brass neck (*Brit. inf.*), brazenness, cheek (*Inf.*), chutzpah (*U.S. & Canad. inf.*), effrontery, impertinence, impudence, insolence, neck (*Inf.*), nerve (*Inf.*), sauciness 2. acrimony, animosity, animus, antipathy, bad blood, bile, bitterness, enmity, hostility, malevolence, malice, malignity, rancour, sourness, spite, spleen, venom

gall[2] *n.* 1. abrasion, chafe, excoriation, raw spot, scrape, sore, sore spot, wound 2. aggravation (*Inf.*), annoyance, bother, botheration (*Inf.*), exasperation, harassment, irritant, irritation, nuisance, pest, provocation, vexation ~*v.* 3. abrade, bark, chafe, excoriate, fret, graze, irritate, rub raw, scrape, skin 4. aggravate (*Inf.*), annoy, be on one's back (*Sl.*), bother, exasperate, fret, get in one's hair (*Inf.*), get on one's nerves (*Inf.*), harass, hassle (*Inf.*), irk, irritate, nag, nark (*Brit., Aust., & N.Z. sl.*), nettle, peeve (*Inf.*), pester, piss one off (*Taboo sl.*), plague, provoke, rankle, rile (*Inf.*), rub up the wrong way, ruffle, vex

gallant *adj.* 1. bold, brave, courageous, daring, dashing, dauntless, doughty, fearless, game (*Inf.*), heroic, high-spirited, honourable, intrepid, lion-hearted, manful, manly, mettlesome, noble, plucky, valiant, valorous 2. attentive, chivalrous, courteous, courtly, gentlemanly, gracious, magnanimous, noble, polite 3. august, dignified, elegant, glorious, grand, imposing, lofty, magnificent, noble, splendid, stately ~*n.* 4. admirer, beau, boyfriend, escort, leman (*Archaic*), lover, paramour, suitor, wooer 5. beau, blade (*Archaic*), buck (*Inf.*), dandy, fop, ladies' man, lady-killer (*Inf.*), man about town, man of fashion 6. adventurer, cavalier, champion, daredevil, hero, knight, man of mettle, *preux chevalier*

Antonyms churlish, cowardly, discourteous, fearful, ignoble, ill-mannered, impolite, rude

gallantry 1. audacity, boldness, bravery, courage, courageousness, daring, dauntlessness, derring-do (*Archaic*), fearlessness, heroism, intrepidity, manliness, mettle, nerve, pluck, prowess, spirit, valiance, valour 2. attentiveness, chivalry, courteousness, courtesy, courtliness, elegance, gentlemanliness, graciousness, nobility, politeness

Antonyms churlishness, cowardice, discourtesy, irresolution, rudeness, ungraciousness

galling aggravating (*Inf.*), annoying, bitter, bothersome, exasperating, harassing, humiliating, irksome, irritating, nettlesome, plaguing, provoking, rankling, vexatious, vexing

gallivant gad about, ramble, range, roam, rove, run around, stravaig (*Scot., & northern English dialect*), stray, traipse (*Inf.*), wander

gallop barrel (along) (*Inf., chiefly U.S. & Canad.*), bolt, career, dart, dash, fly, hasten, hie (*Archaic*), hurry, race, run, rush, scud, shoot, speed, sprint, tear along, zoom

galore à gogo (*Inf.*), all over the place, aplenty, everywhere, in abundance, in great quantity, in numbers, in profusion, to spare

galvanize arouse, awaken, electrify, excite, fire, inspire, invigorate, kick-start, jolt, move, prod, provoke, quicken, shock, spur, startle, stimulate, stir, thrill, vitalize, wake

gamble *v.* 1. back, bet, game, have a flutter (*Inf.*), lay *or* make a bet, play, punt, stake, try one's luck, wager 2. back, chance, hazard, put one's faith *or* trust in, risk, speculate, stake, stick one's neck out (*Inf.*), take a chance, venture ~*n.* 3. chance, leap in the dark, lottery, risk, speculation, uncertainty, venture 4. bet, flutter (*Inf.*), punt, wager

Antonyms (*sense 3*) certainty, foregone conclusion, safe bet, sure thing

gambol 1. *v.* caper, cavort, curvet, cut a caper, frisk, frolic, hop, jump, prance, rollick, skip 2. *n.* antic, caper, frolic, gambado, hop, jump, prance, skip, spring

game[1] *n.* 1. amusement, distraction, diversion, entertainment, frolic, fun, jest, joke, lark, merriment, pastime, play, recreation, romp, sport 2. competition, contest, event, head-to-head, match, meeting, round, tournament 3. adventure, business, enterprise, line, occupation, plan, proceeding, scheme, undertaking 4. chase, prey, quarry, wild animals 5. *Inf.* design, device, plan, plot, ploy, scheme, stratagem, strategy, tactic, trick 6. **make (a) game of** deride, make a fool of, make a laughing stock, make fun of, make sport of, mock, poke fun at, ridicule, send up (*Brit. inf.*)

Antonyms business, chore, duty, job, labour, toil, work

game[2] *adj.* 1. ballsy (*Taboo sl.*), bold, brave, courageous, dauntless, dogged, fearless, feisty (*Inf., chiefly U.S. & Canad.*), gallant, gritty, have-a-go (*Inf.*), heroic, intrepid,

persevering, persistent, plucky, resolute, spirited, unflinching, valiant, valorous 2. desirous, disposed, eager, inclined, interested, prepared, ready, willing
Antonyms cowardly, fearful, irresolute

game[3] *adj.* bad, crippled, deformed, disabled, gammy (*Brit. sl.*), incapacitated, injured, lame, maimed

gamesome coltish, frisky, frolicsome, gay, lively, merry, playful, rollicking, sportive, vivacious

gamin guttersnipe, mudlark (*Sl.*), ragamuffin, street Arab, (street) urchin, waif

gammon 1. *v.* beguile, cheat, cozen, deceive, dupe, gull (*Archaic*), hoax, hoodwink, humbug, kid (*Inf.*), trick 2. *n.* deceit, deception, humbug, imposition, nonsense, trick

gamut area, catalogue, compass, field, range, scale, scope, series, sweep

gang band, bevy, camp, circle, clique, club, company, coterie, crew (*Inf.*), crowd, group, herd, horde, lot, mob, pack, party, posse (*Sl.*), ring, set, shift, squad, team, troupe

gangling, gangly angular, awkward, lanky, loose-jointed, rangy, rawboned, skinny, spindly, tall

gangster bandit, brigand, crook (*Inf.*), desperado, gang member, heavy (*Sl.*), hood (*U.S. sl.*), hoodlum (*Chiefly U.S.*), mobster (*U.S. sl.*), racketeer, robber, ruffian, thug, tough

gaol *see* JAIL

gap 1. blank, breach, break, chink, cleft, crack, cranny, crevice, discontinuity, divide, entr'acte, hiatus, hole, interlude, intermission, interruption, interstice, interval, lacuna, lull, opening, pause, recess, rent, respite, rift, space, vacuity, void 2. difference, disagreement, disparity, divergence, inconsistency

gape 1. gawk, gawp (*Brit. sl.*), goggle, stare, wonder 2. crack, open, split, yawn

gaping broad, cavernous, great, open, vast, wide, wide open, yawning

garb *n.* 1. apparel, array, attire, clothes, clothing, costume, dress, garment, gear (*Sl.*), habiliment, habit, outfit, raiment (*Archaic*), robes, uniform, vestments, wear 2. cut, fashion, look, mode, style 3. appearance, aspect, attire, covering, guise, outward form ~*v.* 4. apparel, attire, clothe, cover, dress, rig out, robe

garbage 1. bits and pieces, debris, detritus, junk, litter, odds and ends, rubbish, scraps 2. dreck (*Sl., chiefly U.S.*), dross, filth, muck, offal, refuse, rubbish, scourings, slops, sweepings, swill, trash (*Chiefly U.S.*), waste 3. balderdash, balls (*Taboo sl.*), bilge (*Inf.*), bosh (*Inf.*), bull (*Sl.*), bullshit (*Taboo sl.*), bunkum *or* buncombe (*Chiefly U.S.*), claptrap (*Inf.*), cobblers (*Brit. taboo sl.*), codswallop (*Brit. sl.*), crap (*Sl.*), drivel, eyewash (*Inf.*), flapdoodle (*Sl.*), gibberish, guff (*Sl.*), havers (*Scot.*), hogwash, hokum (*Sl., chiefly U.S. & Canad.*), horsefeathers (*U.S. sl.*), hot air (*Inf.*), moonshine, nonsense, pap, piffle (*Inf.*), poppycock (*Inf.*), rot, shit (*Taboo sl.*), stuff and nonsense, tommyrot, tosh (*Inf.*), tripe (*Inf.*), twaddle

garble 1. confuse, jumble, mix up 2. corrupt, distort, doctor, falsify, misinterpret, misquote, misreport, misrepresent, misstate, mistranslate, mutilate, pervert, slant, tamper with, twist
Antonyms clarify, decipher, make intelligible

gargantuan big, Brobdingnagian, colossal, elephantine, enormous, giant, gigantic, huge, humongous *or* humungous (*U.S. sl.*), immense, mammoth, massive, monstrous, monumental, mountainous, prodigious, titanic, towering, tremendous, vast
Antonyms little, meagre, miniature, paltry, puny, pygmy *or* pigmy, small, tiny

garish brash, brassy, brummagem, cheap, flash (*Inf.*), flashy, flaunting, gaudy, glaring, glittering, loud, meretricious, naff (*Brit. sl.*), raffish, showy, tacky (*Inf.*), tasteless, tawdry, vulgar
Antonyms conservative, elegant, modest, plain, refined, sedate, sombre, unobtrusive

garland 1. *n.* bays, chaplet, coronal, crown, festoon, honours, laurels, wreath 2. *v.* adorn, crown, deck, festoon, wreathe

garments apparel, array, articles of clothing, attire, clothes, clothing, costume, dress, duds (*Inf.*), garb, gear (*Sl.*), habiliment, habit, outfit, raiment (*Archaic*), robes, togs, uniform, vestments, wear

garner 1. *v.* accumulate, amass, assemble, collect, deposit, gather, hoard, husband, lay in *or* up, put by, reserve, save, stockpile, store, stow away, treasure 2. *n. Literary* depository, granary, store, storehouse, vault

garnish 1. *v.* adorn, beautify, bedeck, deck, decorate, embellish, enhance, festoon, grace, ornament, set off, trim 2. *n.* adornment, decoration, embellishment, enhancement, festoon, garniture, ornament, ornamentation, trim, trimming
Antonyms denude, spoil, strip

garniture accessories, adornment, appendages, appurtenances, decoration, embellishment, furniture, garnish, ornamentation, ornaments, trimmings

garrison *n.* 1. armed force, command, detachment, troops, unit 2. base, camp, encampment, fort, fortification, fortress, post, station, stronghold ~*v.* 3. assign, mount, position, post, put on duty, station 4. defend, guard, man, occupy, protect, supply with troops

garrulity 1. babble, babbling, chatter, chattering, chattiness, effusiveness, gabbiness (*Inf.*), garrulousness, gift of the gab (*Inf.*), glibness, loquacity, mouthiness, prating, prattle, talkativeness, verbosity, volubility 2. diffuseness, long-windedness, prolixity, prosiness, verbosity, windiness, wordiness

garrulous 1. babbling, chattering, chatty, effusive, gabby (*Inf.*), glib, gossiping, gushing, loquacious, mouthy, prating, prattling, talkative, verbose, voluble 2. diffuse, gassy (*Sl.*), long-winded, prolix, prosy, verbose, windy, wordy
Antonyms concise, reserved, reticent, succinct, taciturn, terse, tight-lipped, uncommunicative

gash 1. *v.* cleave, cut, gouge, incise, lacerate, rend, slash, slit, split, tear, wound 2. *n.* cleft, cut, gouge, incision, laceration, rent, slash, slit, split, tear, wound

gasp 1. *v.* blow, catch one's breath, choke, fight for breath, gulp, pant, puff 2. *n.* blow, ejaculation, exclamation, gulp, pant, puff

gate access, barrier, door, doorway, egress, entrance, exit, gateway, opening, passage, port (*Scot.*), portal

gather 1. accumulate, amass, assemble, bring *or* get together, collect, congregate, convene, flock, forgather, garner, group, heap, hoard, marshal, mass, muster, pile up, round up, stack up, stockpile 2. assume, be led to believe, conclude, deduce, draw, hear, infer, learn, make, surmise, understand 3. clasp, draw, embrace, enfold, hold, hug 4. crop, cull, garner, glean, harvest, pick, pluck, reap, select 5. build, deepen, enlarge, expand, grow, heighten, increase, intensify, rise, swell, thicken, wax 6. fold, pleat, pucker, ruffle, shirr, tuck
Antonyms diffuse, disperse, dissipate, scatter, separate

gathering 1. assemblage, assembly, company, conclave, concourse, congregation, congress, convention, convocation, crowd, flock, get-together (*Inf.*), group, knot, meeting, muster, party, rally, throng, turnout 2. accumulation, acquisition, aggregate, collecting, collection, concentration, gain, heap, hoard, mass, pile, procuring, roundup, stock, stockpile 3. *Inf.* abscess, boil, carbuncle, pimple, pustule, sore, spot, tumour, ulcer

gauche awkward, clumsy, graceless, ignorant, ill-bred, ill-mannered, inelegant, inept, insensitive, lacking in social graces, maladroit, tactless, uncultured, unpolished, unsophisticated
Antonyms elegant, gracious, polished, polite, refined, sophisticated, tasteful, well-mannered

gaucherie 1. awkwardness, bad taste, clumsiness, gaucheness, gracelessness, ignorance, ill-breeding, inelegance, ineptness, insensitivity, lack of polish, maladroitness, tactlessness, unsophisticatedness 2. bloomer (*Inf.*), blunder, boob (*Sl.*), breach of etiquette, clanger (*Inf.*), faux pas, gaffe, indiscretion, mistake, slip, solecism

gaudy brash, bright, brilliant, brummagem, flash (*Inf.*), flashy, florid, garish, gay, glaring, loud, meretricious, naff (*Brit. sl.*), ostentatious, raffish, showy, tacky (*Inf.*), tasteless, tawdry, vulgar
Antonyms colourless, conservative, dull, elegant, modest, quiet, refined, sedate, subtle, tasteful

gauge *v.* 1. ascertain, calculate, check, compute, count, determine, measure, weigh 2. adjudge, appraise, assess, estimate, evaluate, guess, judge, rate, reckon, value ~*n.* 3. basis, criterion, example, exemplar, guide, guideline, indicator, measure, meter, model, par, pattern, rule, sample, standard, test, touchstone, yardstick 4. bore, capacity, degree, depth, extent, height, magnitude, measure, scope, size, span, thickness, width

gaunt 1. angular, attenuated, bony, cadaverous, emaciated, haggard, lank, lean, macilent (*Rare*), meagre, pinched, rawboned, scraggy, scrawny, skeletal, skinny, spare, thin, wasted 2. bare, bleak, desolate, dismal, dreary, forbidding, forlorn, grim, harsh
Antonyms active, chubby, corpulent, fat, inviting, lush, luxurious, obese, plump, stout, well-fed

gauzy delicate, diaphanous, filmy, flimsy, gossamer, insubstantial, light, see-through, sheer, thin, translucent, transparent

gawk 1. *n.* boor, churl, clod, clodhopper (*Inf.*), dolt, dunderhead, galoot (*Sl.*), ignoramus, lout, lubber, lummox (*Inf.*), oaf 2. *v.* gape, gawp (*Sl.*), gaze open-mouthed, goggle, stare

gawky awkward, clownish, clumsy, gauche, loutish, lumbering, lumpish, maladroit, oafish, uncouth, ungainly
Antonyms elegant, graceful, self-assured, well-coordinated

gay *adj.* 1. homosexual, lesbian, poofy (*Offens. sl.*), queer (*Offens. sl.*) 2. animated, blithe, carefree, cheerful, debonair, glad, gleeful, happy, hilarious, insouciant, jolly, jovial, joyful, joyous, light-hearted, lively, merry, sparkling, sunny, vivacious 3. bright, brilliant, colourful, flamboyant, flashy, fresh, garish, gaudy, rich, showy, vivid 4. convivial, festive, frivolous, frolicsome, fun-loving, gamesome, merry, playful, pleasure-seeking, rakish, rollicking, sportive, waggish ~*n.* 5. dyke (*Offens. sl.*), faggot (*U.S. offens. sl.*), fairy (*Offens. sl.*), homosexual, invert, lesbian, poof (*Offens. sl.*), queer (*Offens. sl.*)

Antonyms (*senses 1 & 5*) heterosexual, straight (*sense 2*) cheerless, colourless, conservative, drab, dull, grave, grim, melancholy, miserable, sad, sedate, serious, sober, solemn, sombre, unhappy

gaze 1. *v.* contemplate, eyeball (*U.S. sl.*), gape, look, look fixedly, regard, stare, view, watch, wonder 2. *n.* fixed look, look, stare

gazette journal, newspaper, news-sheet, organ, paper, periodical

gear *n.* 1. cog, cogwheel, gearwheel, toothed wheel 2. cogs, gearing, machinery, mechanism, works 3. accessories, accoutrements, apparatus, equipment, harness, instruments, outfit, paraphernalia, rigging, supplies, tackle, tools, trappings 4. baggage, belongings, effects, kit, luggage, stuff, things 5. *Sl.* apparel, array, attire, clothes, clothing, costume, dress, garb, garments, habit, outfit, rigout (*Inf.*), togs, wear ~*v.* 6. adapt, adjust, equip, fit, rig, suit, tailor

gelatinous gluey, glutinous, gummy, jelly-like, mucilaginous, sticky, viscid, viscous

gelid arctic, chilly, cold, freezing, frigid, frosty, frozen, glacial, ice-cold, icy, polar

Antonyms hot, red-hot, scorching, sweltering, torrid

gem 1. jewel, precious stone, semiprecious stone, stone 2. flower, jewel, masterpiece, pearl, pick, prize, treasure

genealogy ancestry, blood line, derivation, descent, extraction, family tree, line, lineage, pedigree, progeniture, stemma, stirps, stock, strain

general 1. accepted, broad, common, extensive, popular, prevailing, prevalent, public, universal, widespread 2. accustomed, conventional, customary, everyday, habitual, normal, ordinary, regular, typical, usual 3. approximate, ill-defined, imprecise, inaccurate, indefinite, inexact, loose, undetailed, unspecific, vague 4. across-the-board, all-inclusive, blanket, broad, catholic, collective, comprehensive, encyclopedic, generic, indiscriminate, miscellaneous, panoramic, sweeping, total, universal

Antonyms definite, distinctive, exact, exceptional, extraordinary, individual, infrequent, particular, peculiar, precise, rare, special, specific, unusual

generality 1. abstract principle, generalization, loose statement, sweeping statement, vague notion 2. acceptedness, commonness, extensiveness, popularity, prevalence, universality 3. approximateness, impreciseness, indefiniteness, inexactness, lack of detail, looseness, vagueness 4. breadth, catholicity, comprehensiveness, miscellaneity, sweepingness, universality

generally 1. almost always, as a rule, by and large, conventionally, customarily, for the most part, habitually, in most cases, largely, mainly, normally, on average, on the whole, ordinarily, regularly, typically, usually 2. commonly, extensively, popularly, publicly, universally, widely 3. approximately, broadly, chiefly, for the most part, in the main, largely, mainly, mostly, on the whole, predominantly, principally

Antonyms especially, individually, occasionally, particularly, rarely, unusually

generate beget, breed, bring about, cause, create, engender, form, give rise to, initiate, make, originate, procreate, produce, propagate, spawn, whip up

Antonyms annihilate, crush, destroy, end, extinguish, kill, terminate

generation 1. begetting, breeding, creation, engenderment, formation, genesis, origination, procreation, production, propagation, reproduction 2. age group, breed, crop 3. age, day, days, epoch, era, period, time, times

generic all-encompassing, blanket, collective, common, comprehensive, general, inclusive, sweeping, universal, wide

Antonyms individual, particular, precise, specific

generosity 1. beneficence, benevolence, bounteousness, bounty, charity, kindness, largess *or* largesse, liberality, munificence, open-handedness 2. disinterestedness, goodness, high-mindedness, magnanimity, nobleness, unselfishness

generous 1. beneficent, benevolent, bounteous, bountiful, charitable, free, hospitable, kind, lavish, liberal, munificent, open-handed, princely, prodigal, ungrudging, unstinting 2. big-hearted, disinterested, good, high-minded, lofty, magnanimous, noble, unselfish 3. abundant, ample, copious, full, lavish, liberal, overflowing, plentiful, rich, unstinting

Antonyms avaricious, cheap, close-fisted, greedy, mean, minimal, miserly, parsimonious, scanty, selfish, small, stingy, tight, tiny

genesis beginning, birth, commencement,

creation, dawn, engendering, formation, generation, inception, origin, outset, propagation, root, source, start
Antonyms completion, conclusion, end, finish, termination

genial affable, agreeable, amiable, cheerful, cheery, congenial, convivial, cordial, easy-going, enlivening, friendly, glad, good-natured, happy, hearty, jolly, jovial, joyous, kind, kindly, merry, pleasant, sunny, warm, warm-hearted
Antonyms cheerless, cool, discourteous, frigid, morose, rude, sardonic, sullen, unfriendly, ungracious, unpleasant

geniality affability, agreeableness, amiability, cheerfulness, cheeriness, congenialness, conviviality, cordiality, friendliness, gladness, good cheer, good nature, happiness, heartiness, jollity, joviality, joy, joyousness, kindliness, kindness, mirth, pleasantness, sunniness, warm-heartedness, warmth

genitals genitalia, loins, private parts, pudenda, reproductive organs, sex organs

genius 1. adept, buff (*Inf.*), brain (*Inf.*), brainbox, expert, hotshot (*Inf.*), intellect (*Inf.*), maestro, master, master-hand, mastermind, maven (*U.S.*), virtuoso, whiz (*Inf.*) 2. ability, aptitude, bent, brilliance, capacity, creative power, endowment, faculty, flair, gift, inclination, knack, propensity, talent, turn
Antonyms dolt, dunce, fool, half-wit, idiot, imbecile, nincompoop, simpleton

genre brand, category, character, class, fashion, genus, group, kind, school, sort, species, stamp, style, type

genteel aristocratic, civil, courteous, courtly, cultivated, cultured, elegant, fashionable, formal, gentlemanly, ladylike, mannerly, polished, polite, refined, respectable, sophisticated, stylish, urbane, well-bred, well-mannered
Antonyms discourteous, ill-bred, impolite, inelegant, low-bred, natural, plebeian, rude, unaffected, uncultured, unmannerly, unpolished, unrefined

gentility 1. breeding, civility, courtesy, courtliness, cultivation, culture, decorum, elegance, etiquette, formality, good breeding, good manners, mannerliness, polish, politeness, propriety, refinement, respectability, sophistication, urbanity 2. blue blood, gentle birth, good family, high birth, nobility, rank 3. aristocracy, elite, gentlefolk, gentry, nobility, nobles, ruling class, upper class

gentle 1. amiable, benign, bland, compassionate, dove-like, humane, kind, kindly, lenient, meek, merciful, mild, pacific, peaceful, placid, quiet, soft, sweet-tempered, tender 2. balmy, calm, clement, easy, light, low, mild, moderate, muted, placid, quiet, serene, slight, smooth, soft, soothing, temperate, tranquil, untroubled 3. easy, gradual, imperceptible, light, mild, moderate, slight, slow 4. biddable, broken, docile, manageable, placid, tame, tractable 5. *Archaic* aristocratic, civil, courteous, cultured, elegant, genteel, gentlemanlike, gentlemanly, high-born, ladylike, noble, polished, polite, refined, upper-class, well-born, well-bred
Antonyms aggressive, cruel, fierce, hard, harsh, heartless, impolite, powerful, rough, savage, sharp, strong, sudden, unkind, unmanageable, violent, wild

gentlemanly civil, civilized, courteous, cultivated, debonair, gallant, genteel, gentlemanlike, honourable, mannerly, noble, obliging, polished, polite, refined, reputable, suave, urbane, well-bred, well-mannered

gentry aristocracy, elite, gentility, gentlefolk, nobility, nobles, ruling class, upper class, upper crust (*Inf.*)

genuine 1. actual, authentic, bona fide, honest, legitimate, natural, original, pure, real, sound, sterling, true, unadulterated, unalloyed, veritable 2. artless, candid, earnest, frank, heartfelt, honest, sincere, unaffected, unfeigned
Antonyms affected, artificial, bogus, counterfeit, fake, false, feigned, fraudulent, hypocritical, imitation, insincere, phoney, sham, simulated, spurious

genus breed, category, class, genre, group, kind, order, race, set, sort, type

germ 1. bacterium, bug (*Inf.*), microbe, microorganism, virus 2. beginning, bud, cause, embryo, origin, root, rudiment, seed, source, spark 3. bud, egg, embryo, nucleus, ovule, ovum, seed, spore, sprout

germane akin, allied, apposite, appropriate, apropos, apt, cognate, connected, fitting, kindred, material, pertinent, proper, related, relevant, suitable, to the point *or* purpose
Antonyms extraneous, foreign, immaterial, inappropriate, irrelevant, unrelated

germinate bud, develop, generate, grow, originate, pullulate, shoot, sprout, swell, vegetate

gestation development, evolution, incubation, maturation, pregnancy, ripening

gesticulate gesture, indicate, make a sign, motion, sign, signal, wave

gesture 1. *n.* action, gesticulation, indication, motion, sign, signal 2. *v.* gesticulate, indicate, motion, sign, signal, wave

get 1. achieve, acquire, attain, bag, bring, come by, come into possession of, earn, fall heir to, fetch, gain, glean, inherit, make, net, obtain, pick up, procure, realize, reap, receive, score (*Sl.*), secure, succeed to, win 2. be afflicted with, become infected with, be smitten by, catch, come down with, contract, fall victim to, take 3. arrest, capture, collar (*Inf.*), grab, lay hold of, nab (*Inf.*), nail (*Inf.*), seize, take, trap 4. become, come to be, grow, turn, wax 5. catch, comprehend, fathom, follow, hear, notice, perceive, see, suss (out) (*Sl.*), take in, understand, work out 6. arrive, come, make it (*Inf.*), reach 7. arrange, contrive, fix, manage, succeed, wangle (*Inf.*) 8. coax, convince, induce, influence, persuade, prevail upon, sway, talk into, wheedle, win over 9. communicate with, contact, get in touch with, reach 10. *Inf.* affect, arouse, excite, have an effect on, impress, move, stimulate, stir, touch 11. *Inf.* annoy, bother, bug (*Inf.*), gall, get (someone's) goat (*Sl.*), irk, irritate, nark (*Brit., Aust., & N.Z. sl.*), pique, rub (someone) up the wrong way, upset, vex 12. baffle, confound, mystify, nonplus, perplex, puzzle, stump

get across 1. cross, ford, negotiate, pass over, traverse 2. bring home to, communicate, convey, get (something) through to, impart, make clear *or* understood, put over, transmit

get ahead 1. advance, be successful, cut it (*Inf.*), do well, flourish, get on, make good, progress, prosper, succeed, thrive 2. excel, leave behind, outdo, outmanoeuvre, overtake, surpass

get along 1. agree, be compatible, be friendly, get on, harmonize, hit it off (*Inf.*) 2. cope, develop, fare, get by (*Inf.*), make out (*Inf.*), manage, progress, shift 3. be off, depart, go, go away, leave, move off, slope off

get at 1. acquire, attain, come to grips with, gain access to, get, get hold of, reach 2. hint, imply, intend, lead up to, mean, suggest 3. annoy, attack, be on one's back (*Sl.*), blame, carp, criticize, find fault with, hassle (*Inf.*), irritate, nag, nark (*Brit., Aust., & N.Z. sl.*), pick on, taunt 4. bribe, buy off, corrupt, influence, suborn, tamper with

getaway break, break-out, decampment, escape, flight

get away abscond, break free, break out, decamp, depart, disappear, escape, flee, leave, make good one's escape, slope off

get back 1. recoup, recover, regain, repossess, retrieve 2. arrive home, come back *or* home, return, revert, revisit 3. *With* **at** be avenged, get even with, give tit for tat, hit back, retaliate, settle the score with, take vengeance on

get by 1. circumvent, get ahead of, go around, go past, overtake, pass, round 2. *Inf.* contrive, cope, exist, fare, get along, make both ends meet, manage, subsist, survive

get down 1. alight, bring down, climb down, descend, disembark, dismount, get off, lower, step down 2. bring down, depress, dishearten, dispirit

get in alight, appear, arrive, collect, come, embark, enter, include, infiltrate, insert, interpose, land, mount, penetrate

get off 1. alight, depart, descend, disembark, dismount, escape, exit, leave 2. detach, remove, shed, take off

get on 1. ascend, board, climb, embark, mount 2. advance, cope, cut it (*Inf.*), fare, get along, make out (*Inf.*), manage, progress, prosper, succeed 3. agree, be compatible, be friendly, concur, get along, harmonize, hit it off (*Inf.*)

get out alight, break out, clear out (*Inf.*), decamp, escape, evacuate, extricate oneself, free oneself, leave, vacate, withdraw

get out of avoid, body-swerve (*Scot.*), dodge, escape, evade, shirk

get over 1. cross, ford, get across, pass, pass over, surmount, traverse 2. come round, get better, mend, pull through, rally, recover from, revive, survive 3. defeat, get the better of, master, overcome, shake off 4. communicate, convey, get *or* put across, impart, make clear *or* understood

get round 1. bypass, circumvent, edge, evade, outmanoeuvre, skirt 2. *Inf.* cajole, coax, convert, persuade, prevail upon, talk round, wheedle, win over

get together accumulate, assemble, collect, congregate, convene, converge, gather, join, meet, muster, rally, unite

get up arise, ascend, climb, increase, mount, rise, scale, stand

gewgaw bagatelle, bauble, bijou, gaud, gimcrack, kickshaw, knick-knack, novelty, plaything, toy, trifle, trinket

ghastly ashen, cadaverous, deathlike, deathly pale, dreadful, frightful, godawful (*Sl.*), grim, grisly, gruesome, hideous, horrendous, horrible, horrid, livid, loathsome, pale, pallid, repellent, shocking, spectral, terrible, terrifying, wan
Antonyms appealing, attractive, beautiful, blooming, charming, healthy, lovely, pleasing

ghost 1. apparition, eidolon, manes, phantasm, phantom, revenant, shade (*Literary*), soul, spectre, spirit, spook (*Inf.*), wraith 2.

glimmer, hint, possibility, semblance, shadow, suggestion, trace

ghostly eerie, ghostlike, illusory, insubstantial, phantasmal, phantom, spectral, spooky (*Inf.*), supernatural, uncanny, unearthly, weird, wraithlike

ghoulish disgusting, grisly, gruesome, macabre, morbid, sick (*Inf.*), unwholesome

giant 1. *n.* behemoth, colossus, Hercules, leviathan, monster, ogre, titan 2. *adj.* Brobdingnagian, colossal, elephantine, enormous, gargantuan, gigantic, huge, humongous *or* humungous (*U.S. sl.*), immense, jumbo (*Inf.*), large, mammoth, monstrous, prodigious, titanic, vast
Antonyms (*sense 2*) dwarf, Lilliputian, miniature, pygmy *or* pigmy, tiny

gibber babble, blab, blabber, blather, cackle, chatter, gabble, jabber, prattle, rabbit (*Brit. inf.*), waffle (*Inf., chiefly Brit.*)

gibberish babble, balderdash, balls (*Taboo sl.*), bilge (*Inf.*), blather, bosh (*Inf.*), bull (*Sl.*), bullshit (*Taboo sl.*), bunkum *or* buncombe (*Chiefly U.S.*), cobblers (*Brit. taboo sl.*), crap (*Sl.*), double talk, drivel, eyewash (*Inf.*), gabble, garbage (*Inf.*), gobbledegook (*Inf.*), guff (*Sl.*), hogwash, hokum (*Sl., chiefly U.S. & Canad.*), horsefeathers (*U.S. sl.*), hot air (*Inf.*), jabber, jargon, moonshine, mumbo jumbo, nonsense, pap, piffle (*Inf.*), poppycock (*Inf.*), prattle, shit (*Taboo sl.*), tommyrot, tosh (*Sl., chiefly Brit.*), tripe (*Inf.*), twaddle, yammer (*Inf.*)

gibbous bulging, convex, crookbacked, humpbacked, humped, hunchbacked, hunched, protuberant, rounded

gibe, jibe 1. *v.* deride, flout, jeer, make fun of, mock, poke fun at, ridicule, scoff, scorn, sneer, take the piss out of (*Sl.*), taunt, twit 2. *n.* barb, crack (*Sl.*), cutting remark, derision, dig, jeer, mockery, ridicule, sarcasm, scoffing, sneer, taunt

giddiness dizziness, faintness, light-headedness, vertigo

giddy 1. dizzy, dizzying, faint, light-headed, reeling, unsteady, vertiginous 2. capricious, careless, changeable, changeful, erratic, fickle, flighty, frivolous, heedless, impulsive, inconstant, irresolute, irresponsible, reckless, scatterbrained, silly, thoughtless, unbalanced, unstable, unsteady, vacillating, volatile, wild
Antonyms calm, constant, determined, earnest, resolute, serious, steady

gift 1. benefaction, bequest, bonus, boon, bounty, contribution, donation, grant, gratuity, hand-out, largess *or* largesse, legacy, offering, present 2. ability, aptitude, attribute, bent, capability, capacity, endowment, faculty, flair, genius, knack, power, talent, turn

gifted able, accomplished, adroit, brilliant, capable, clever, expert, ingenious, intelligent, masterly, skilled, talented
Antonyms amateur, backward, dull, incapable, inept, retarded, slow, talentless, unskilled

gigantic Brobdingnagian, colossal, Cyclopean, elephantine, enormous, gargantuan, giant, herculean, huge, humongous *or* humungous (*U.S. sl.*), immense, mammoth, monstrous, prodigious, stupendous, titanic, tremendous, vast
Antonyms diminutive, insignificant, little, miniature, puny, small, tiny, weak

giggle *v./n.* cackle, chortle, chuckle, laugh, snigger, tee-hee, titter, twitter

gild adorn, beautify, bedeck, brighten, coat, deck, dress up, embellish, embroider, enhance, enrich, garnish, grace, ornament

gimcrack 1. *adj.* cheap, rubbishy, shoddy, tawdry, trashy 2. *n.* bauble, gewgaw, kickshaw, plaything, toy, trinket

gimmick contrivance, device, dodge, gadget, gambit, gizmo (*Sl., chiefly U.S.*), ploy, scheme, stratagem, stunt, trick

gingerly 1. *adv.* carefully, cautiously, charily, circumspectly, daintily, delicately, fastidiously, hesitantly, reluctantly, squeamishly, suspiciously, timidly, warily 2. *adj.* careful, cautious, chary, circumspect, dainty, delicate, fastidious, hesitant, reluctant, squeamish, suspicious, timid, wary
Antonyms boldly, carelessly, confidently, rashly

gird[1] 1. belt, bind, girdle 2. blockade, encircle, enclose, encompass, enfold, engird, environ, hem in, pen, ring, surround 3. brace, fortify, make ready, prepare, ready, steel

gird[2] deride, gibe, jeer, make fun of, mock, poke fun at, ridicule, scoff, scorn, sneer, taunt

girdle 1. *n.* band, belt, cincture, cummerbund, fillet, sash, waistband 2. *v.* bind, bound, encircle, enclose, encompass, engird, environ, gird, hem, ring, surround

girl bird (*Sl.*), chick (*Sl.*), colleen (*Irish*), damsel (*Archaic*), daughter, female child, lass, lassie (*Inf.*), maid (*Archaic*), maiden (*Archaic*), miss, wench

girth bulk, circumference, measure, size

gist core, drift, essence, force, idea, import, marrow, meaning, nub, pith, point, quintessence, sense, significance, substance

give 1. accord, administer, allow, award, bestow, commit, confer, consign, contribute, deliver, donate, entrust, furnish, grant, hand over *or* out, make over, permit, present, provide, purvey, supply, vouchsafe 2. announce, be a source of, communicate, emit, impart, issue, notify, pronounce, publish, render, transmit, utter 3. demonstrate, display, evidence, indicate, manifest, offer, proffer, provide, set forth, show 4. allow, cede, concede, devote, grant, hand over, lend, relinquish, surrender, yield 5. cause, do, engender, lead, make, occasion, perform, produce 6. bend, break, collapse, fall, recede, retire, sink

Antonyms accept, get, hold, keep, receive, take, withdraw

give away betray, disclose, divulge, expose, inform on, leak, let out, let slip, reveal, shop (*Sl., chiefly Brit.*), uncover

give in admit defeat, capitulate, collapse, comply, concede, quit, submit, succumb, surrender, yield

given addicted, apt, disposed, inclined, liable, likely, prone

give off discharge, emit, exhale, exude, produce, release, send out, smell of, throw out, vent

give out 1. discharge, emit, exhale, exude, produce, release, send out, smell of, throw out, vent 2. announce, broadcast, communicate, disseminate, impart, make known, notify, publish, transmit, utter

give up abandon, capitulate, cease, cede, cut out, desist, despair, forswear, hand over, kick (*Inf.*), leave off, quit, relinquish, renounce, resign, step down (*Inf.*), stop, surrender, throw in the towel, waive

glacial 1. arctic, biting, bitter, chill, chilly, cold, freezing, frigid, frosty, frozen, gelid, icy, piercing, polar, raw, wintry 2. antagonistic, cold, frigid, hostile, icy, inimical, unfriendly

glad 1. blithesome (*Literary*), cheerful, chuffed (*Sl.*), contented, delighted, gay, gleeful, gratified, happy, jocund, jovial, joyful, overjoyed, pleased, willing 2. animated, cheerful, cheering, cheery, delightful, felicitous, gratifying, joyous, merry, pleasant, pleasing

Antonyms depressed, discontented, displeased, melancholy, miserable, sad, sorrowful, unhappy

gladden cheer, delight, elate, enliven, exhilarate, gratify, hearten, please, rejoice

gladly cheerfully, freely, gaily, gleefully, happily, jovially, joyfully, joyously, lief (*Rare*), merrily, readily, willingly, with (a) good grace, with pleasure

Antonyms dolefully, grudgingly, reluctantly, sadly, unenthusiastically, unwillingly

gladness animation, blitheness, cheerfulness, delight, felicity, gaiety, glee, happiness, high spirits, hilarity, jollity, joy, joyousness, mirth, pleasure

glamorous alluring, attractive, beautiful, bewitching, captivating, charming, dazzling, elegant, enchanting, entrancing, exciting, fascinating, glittering, glitzy (*Sl.*), glossy, lovely, prestigious, smart

Antonyms colourless, dull, unattractive, unexciting, unglamorous

glamour allure, appeal, attraction, beauty, bewitchment, charm, enchantment, fascination, magnetism, prestige, ravishment, witchery

glance *v.* 1. check, check out (*Inf.*), clock (*Brit. inf.*), gaze, glimpse, look, peek, peep, scan, take a dekko at (*Brit. sl.*), view 2. flash, gleam, glimmer, glint, glisten, glitter, reflect, shimmer, shine, twinkle 3. bounce, brush, graze, rebound, ricochet, skim 4. *With* **over, through,** *etc.* browse, dip into, flip through, leaf through, riffle through, run over *or* through, scan, skim through, thumb through ~*n.* 5. brief look, butcher's (*Brit. sl.*), dekko (*Sl.*), gander (*Inf.*), glimpse, look, peek, peep, quick look, shufti (*Brit. sl.*), squint, view 6. flash, gleam, glimmer, glint, reflection, sparkle, twinkle 7. allusion, passing mention, reference

Antonyms (*sense 1*) peruse, scrutinize, study (*sense 5*) examination, good look, inspection, perusal

glare *v.* 1. frown, give a dirty look, glower, look daggers, lour *or* lower, scowl, stare angrily 2. blaze, dazzle, flame, flare ~*n.* 3. angry stare, black look, dirty look, frown, glower, lour *or* lower, scowl 4. blaze, brilliance, dazzle, flame, flare, glow 5. flashiness, floridness, gaudiness, loudness, meretriciousness, showiness, tawdriness

glaring 1. audacious, blatant, conspicuous, egregious, flagrant, gross, manifest, obvious, open, outrageous, outstanding, overt, patent, rank, unconcealed, visible 2. blazing, bright, dazzling, flashy, florid, garish, glowing, loud

Antonyms concealed, hidden, inconspicuous, obscure, soft, subdued, subtle

glassy 1. clear, glossy, icy, shiny, slick, slippery, smooth, transparent 2. blank, cold, dazed, dull, empty, expressionless, fixed, glazed, lifeless, vacant

glaze 1. *v.* burnish, coat, enamel, furbish, gloss, lacquer, polish, varnish 2. *n.* coat, enamel, finish, gloss, lacquer, lustre, patina, polish, shine, varnish

gleam *n.* 1. beam, flash, glimmer, glow, ray, sparkle 2. brightness, brilliance, coruscation, flash, gloss, lustre, sheen, splendour

3. flicker, glimmer, hint, inkling, ray, suggestion, trace ~*v.* 4. coruscate, flare, flash, glance, glimmer, glint, glisten, glitter, glow, scintillate, shimmer, shine, sparkle

glean accumulate, amass, collect, cull, garner, gather, harvest, learn, pick, pick up, reap, select

glee cheerfulness, delight, elation, exhilaration, exuberance, exultation, fun, gaiety, gladness, hilarity, jocularity, jollity, joviality, joy, joyfulness, joyousness, liveliness, merriment, mirth, sprightliness, triumph, verve
Antonyms depression, gloom, melancholy, misery, sadness

gleeful cheerful, chirpy (*Inf.*), cock-a-hoop, delighted, elated, exuberant, exultant, gay, gratified, happy, jocund, jovial, joyful, joyous, jubilant, merry, mirthful, overjoyed, over the moon (*Inf.*), pleased, rapt, triumphant

glib artful, easy, fast-talking, fluent, garrulous, insincere, plausible, quick, ready, slick, slippery, smooth, smooth-tongued, suave, talkative, voluble
Antonyms halting, hesitant, implausible, sincere, tongue-tied

glide coast, drift, float, flow, fly, roll, run, sail, skate, skim, slide, slip, soar

glimmer *v.* 1. blink, flicker, gleam, glisten, glitter, glow, shimmer, shine, sparkle, twinkle ~*n.* 2. blink, flicker, gleam, glow, ray, shimmer, sparkle, twinkle 3. flicker, gleam, grain, hint, inkling, ray, suggestion, trace

glimpse 1. *n.* brief view, butcher's (*Brit. sl.*), gander (*Inf.*), glance, look, peek, peep, quick look, shufti (*Brit. sl.*), sight, sighting, squint 2. *v.* catch sight of, clock (*Brit. inf.*), descry, espy, sight, spot, spy, view

glint 1. *v.* flash, gleam, glimmer, glitter, shine, sparkle, twinkle 2. *n.* flash, gleam, glimmer, glitter, shine, sparkle, twinkle, twinkling

glisten coruscate, flash, glance, glare, gleam, glimmer, glint, glitter, scintillate, shimmer, shine, sparkle, twinkle

glitter *v.* 1. coruscate, flare, flash, glare, gleam, glimmer, glint, glisten, scintillate, shimmer, shine, sparkle, twinkle ~*n.* 2. beam, brightness, brilliance, flash, glare, gleam, lustre, radiance, scintillation, sheen, shimmer, shine, sparkle 3. display, gaudiness, gilt, glamour, pageantry, show, showiness, splendour, tinsel

gloaming dusk, eventide (*Archaic*), half-light, nightfall, twilight

gloat crow, drool, exult, glory, relish, revel in, rub it in (*Inf.*), triumph, vaunt

global 1. international, pandemic, planetary, universal, world, worldwide 2. all-encompassing, all-inclusive, all-out, comprehensive, encyclopedic, exhaustive, general, thorough, total, unbounded, unlimited
Antonyms (*sense 2*) limited, narrow, parochial, restricted, sectional

globe ball, earth, orb, planet, round, sphere, world

globular globate, globelike, globoid, globose, globous, globulous, orbicular, round, spherical, spheroid

globule bead, bubble, drop, droplet, particle, pearl, pellet

gloom 1. blackness, cloud, cloudiness, dark, darkness, dimness, dullness, dusk, duskiness, gloominess, murk, murkiness, obscurity, shade, shadow, twilight 2. blues, dejection, depression, desolation, despair, despondency, downheartedness, low spirits, melancholy, misery, sadness, sorrow, the hump (*Brit. inf.*), unhappiness, woe
Antonyms brightness, cheerfulness, daylight, delight, happiness, high spirits, jollity, joy, light, mirth, radiance

gloomy 1. black, crepuscular, dark, dim, dismal, dreary, dull, dusky, murky, obscure, overcast, shadowy, sombre, Stygian, tenebrous 2. bad, black, cheerless, comfortless, depressing, disheartening, dismal, dispiriting, dreary, funereal, joyless, sad, saddening, sombre 3. blue, chapfallen, cheerless, crestfallen, dejected, despondent, dismal, dispirited, down, downcast, downhearted, down in the dumps (*Inf.*), down in the mouth, glum, in low spirits, melancholy, miserable, moody, morose, pessimistic, sad, saturnine, sullen
Antonyms blithe, bright, brilliant, cheerful, chirpy (*Inf.*), happy, high-spirited, jolly, jovial, light, merry, radiant, sunny, upbeat (*Inf.*)

glorify 1. add lustre to, adorn, aggrandize, augment, dignify, elevate, enhance, ennoble, illuminate, immortalize, lift up, magnify, raise 2. adore, apotheosize, beatify, bless, canonize, deify, enshrine, exalt, honour, idolize, pay homage to, revere, sanctify, venerate, worship 3. celebrate, crack up (*Inf.*), cry up (*Inf.*), eulogize, extol, hymn, laud, lionize, magnify, panegyrize, praise, sing *or* sound the praises of
Antonyms condemn, debase, defile, degrade, desecrate, dishonour, humiliate, mock

glorious 1. celebrated, distinguished, elevated, eminent, excellent, famed, famous, grand, honoured, illustrious, magnificent, majestic, noble, noted, renowned, sublime, triumphant 2. beautiful, bright, brilliant,

dazzling, divine, effulgent, gorgeous, radiant, resplendent, shining, splendid, splendiferous (*Facetious*), superb **3.** *Inf.* delightful, enjoyable, excellent, fine, gorgeous, great, heavenly (*Inf.*), marvellous, pleasurable, splendid, splendiferous (*Facetious*), wonderful
Antonyms awful, dreary, dull, gloomy, horrible, minor, ordinary, trivial, unimportant, unimpressive, unknown, unpleasant

glory *n.* **1.** celebrity, dignity, distinction, eminence, exaltation, fame, honour, illustriousness, immortality, kudos, praise, prestige, renown **2.** adoration, benediction, blessing, gratitude, homage, laudation, praise, thanksgiving, veneration, worship **3.** éclat, grandeur, greatness, magnificence, majesty, nobility, pageantry, pomp, splendour, sublimity, triumph **4.** beauty, brilliance, effulgence, gorgeousness, lustre, radiance, resplendence ~*v.* **5.** boast, crow, drool, exult, gloat, pride oneself, relish, revel, take delight, triumph
Antonyms blasphemy, condemnation, disgrace, dishonour, disrepute, infamy, shame, triviality, ugliness

gloss[1] *n.* **1.** brightness, brilliance, burnish, gleam, lustre, polish, sheen, shine, varnish, veneer **2.** appearance, façade, front, mask, semblance, show, surface ~*v.* **3.** burnish, finish, furbish, glaze, lacquer, polish, shine, varnish, veneer **4.** camouflage, conceal, cover up, disguise, hide, mask, smooth over, veil, whitewash (*Inf.*)

gloss[2] **1.** *n.* annotation, comment, commentary, elucidation, explanation, footnote, interpretation, note, scholium, translation **2.** *v.* annotate, comment, construe, elucidate, explain, interpret, translate

glossy bright, brilliant, burnished, glassy, glazed, lustrous, polished, sheeny, shining, shiny, silken, silky, sleek, smooth
Antonyms drab, dull, mat *or* matt, subfusc

glow *n.* **1.** burning, gleam, glimmer, incandescence, lambency, light, luminosity, phosphorescence **2.** brightness, brilliance, effulgence, radiance, splendour, vividness **3.** ardour, earnestness, enthusiasm, excitement, fervour, gusto, impetuosity, intensity, passion, vehemence, warmth **4.** bloom, blush, flush, reddening, rosiness ~*v.* **5.** brighten, burn, gleam, glimmer, redden, shine, smoulder **6.** be suffused, blush, colour, fill, flush, radiate, thrill, tingle
Antonyms chill, coolness, dullness, greyness, half-heartedness, iciness, indifference, paleness, pallor, wanness

glower 1. *v.* frown, give a dirty look, glare, look daggers, lour *or* lower, scowl **2.** *n.* angry stare, black look, dirty look, frown, glare, lour *or* lower, scowl

glowing 1. aglow, beaming, bright, flaming, florid, flushed, lambent, luminous, radiant, red, rich, ruddy, suffused, vibrant, vivid, warm **2.** adulatory, complimentary, ecstatic, enthusiastic, eulogistic, laudatory, panegyrical, rave (*Inf.*), rhapsodic
Antonyms colourless, cool, cruel, dispassionate, dull, grey, pale, pallid, scathing, unenthusiastic, wan

glue 1. *n.* adhesive, cement, gum, mucilage, paste **2.** *v.* affix, agglutinate, cement, fix, gum, paste, seal, stick

glum chapfallen, churlish, crabbed, crestfallen, crusty, dejected, doleful, down, gloomy, gruff, grumpy, huffy, ill-humoured, low, moody, morose, pessimistic, saturnine, sour, sulky, sullen, surly
Antonyms cheerful, cheery, chirpy (*Inf.*), jolly, joyful, merry, upbeat (*Inf.*)

glut *n.* **1.** excess, overabundance, oversupply, plethora, saturation, superabundance, superfluity, surfeit, surplus ~*v.* **2.** cram, fill, gorge, overfeed, satiate, stuff **3.** choke, clog, deluge, flood, inundate, overload, oversupply, saturate
Antonyms dearth, lack, paucity, scarcity, shortage, want

glutinous adhesive, cohesive, gluey, gooey, gummy, mucilaginous, sticky, viscid, viscous

glutton gannet (*Sl.*), gobbler, gorger, gormandizer, gourmand, pig (*Inf.*)

gluttonous gormandizing, greedy, hoggish, insatiable, piggish, rapacious, ravenous, voracious

gluttony gormandizing, gourmandism, greed, greediness, piggishness, rapacity, voraciousness, voracity

gnarled contorted, knotted, knotty, knurled, leathery, rough, rugged, twisted, weather-beaten, wrinkled

gnaw 1. bite, chew, munch, nibble, worry **2.** consume, devour, eat away *or* into, erode, fret, wear away *or* down **3.** distress, fret, harry, haunt, nag, plague, prey on one's mind, trouble, worry

go *v.* **1.** advance, decamp, depart, fare (*Archaic*), journey, leave, make for, move, move out, pass, proceed, repair, set off, slope off, travel, withdraw **2.** function, move, operate, perform, run, work **3.** connect, extend, fit, give access, lead, reach, run, span, spread, stretch **4.** avail, concur, conduce, contribute, incline, lead to, serve, tend, work towards **5.** develop, eventuate, fall out, fare, happen, pan out (*Inf.*), proceed, result, turn out, work out **6.** accord, agree, blend, chime, complement, correspond, fit, harmonize, match, suit 7. buy it (*U.S. sl.*), check out (*U.S. sl.*), croak (*Sl.*), die, expire, give up the ghost, go belly-up (*Sl.*), kick it (*Sl.*), kick the bucket (*Sl.*), pass away, peg it (*Inf.*), peg out (*Inf.*), perish, pop one's clogs (*Inf.*) 8. elapse, expire, flow, lapse, pass, slip away ~*n.* 9. attempt, bid, crack (*Inf.*), effort, essay, shot (*Inf.*), stab (*Inf.*), try, turn, whack (*Inf.*), whirl (*Inf.*) 10. *Inf.* activity, animation, brio, drive, energy, force, get-up-and-go (*Inf.*), life, oomph (*Inf.*), pep, spirit, verve, vigour, vitality, vivacity

Antonyms (*sense 1*) arrive, halt, reach, remain, stay, stop (*sense 2*) break (down), fail, malfunction, stop

go about 1. circulate, move around, pass around, wander 2. approach, begin, set about, tackle, undertake 3. busy *or* occupy oneself with, devote oneself to

goad 1. *n.* impetus, incentive, incitement, irritation, motivation, pressure, spur, stimulation, stimulus, urge 2. *v.* annoy, arouse, be on one's back (*Sl.*), drive, egg on, exhort, harass, hassle (*Inf.*), hound, impel, incite, instigate, irritate, lash, nark (*Brit., Aust., & N.Z. sl.*), prick, prod, prompt, propel, spur, stimulate, sting, urge, worry

go-ahead 1. *n. Inf.* assent, authorization, consent, green light, leave, O.K. *or* okay (*Inf.*), permission 2. *adj.* ambitious, enterprising, go-getting (*Inf.*), pioneering, progressive, up-and-coming

go ahead advance, begin, continue, go forward, go on, proceed, progress

goal aim, ambition, design, destination, end, intention, limit, mark, object, objective, purpose, target

go along 1. acquiesce, agree, assent, concur, cooperate, follow 2. accompany, carry on, escort, join, keep up, move, pass, travel

go at argue, attack, blame, blast, criticize, impugn, lambast(e), put down, set about, tear into (*Inf.*)

go away decamp, depart, exit, hook it (*Sl.*), leave, move out, recede, slope off, withdraw

gob blob, chunk, clod, gobbet, hunk, lump, piece, wad, wodge (*Brit. inf.*)

go back 1. retrocede, return, revert 2. change one's mind, desert, forsake, renege, repudiate, retract

gobble bolt, cram, devour, gorge, gulp, guzzle, pig out on (*U.S. & Canad. sl.*), stuff, swallow, wolf

gobbledegook babble, cant, double talk, gabble, gibberish, hocus-pocus, jabber, jargon, mumbo jumbo, nonsense, officialese, rigmarole, twaddle

go-between agent, broker, dealer, factor, intermediary, liaison, mediator, medium, middleman

go by 1. elapse, exceed, flow on, move onward, pass, proceed 2. adopt, be guided by, follow, heed, judge from, observe, take as guide

godforsaken abandoned, backward, bleak, deserted, desolate, dismal, dreary, forlorn, gloomy, lonely, neglected, remote, wretched

godless atheistic, depraved, evil, impious, irreligious, profane, ungodly, unprincipled, unrighteous, wicked

godlike celestial, deific, deiform, divine, heavenly, superhuman, transcendent

godly devout, god-fearing, good, holy, pious, religious, righteous, saintly

go down 1. be beaten, collapse, decline, decrease, drop, fall, founder, go under, lose, set, sink, submerge, submit, suffer defeat 2. be commemorated (recalled, recorded, remembered)

godsend blessing, boon, manna, stroke of luck, windfall

go far advance, be successful, cut it (*Inf.*), do well, get ahead (*Inf.*), get on (*Inf.*), make a name for oneself, progress, succeed

go for 1. clutch at, fetch, obtain, reach, seek, stretch for 2. admire, be attracted to, be fond of, choose, favour, hold with, like, prefer 3. assail, assault, attack, launch oneself at, rush upon, set about *or* upon, spring upon

goggle gape, gawk, gawp (*Sl.*), peer, rubberneck (*Sl.*), stare

go in (for) adopt, embrace, engage in, enter, espouse, practise, pursue, take up, undertake

going-over 1. analysis, check, examination, inspection, investigation, perusal, recce (*Sl.*), review, scrutiny, study, survey 2. beating, buffeting, doing (*Inf.*), drubbing, pasting (*Sl.*), thrashing, thumping, whipping 3. castigation, chastisement, chiding, dressing-down (*Inf.*), lecture, rebuke, reprimand, row, scolding, talking-to (*Inf.*), tongue-lashing

go into 1. begin, develop, enter, participate in, undertake 2. analyse, consider, delve into, discuss, examine, inquire into, investigate, look into, probe, pursue, research, review, scrutinize, study, work over

golden 1. blond *or* blonde, bright, brilliant, flaxen, resplendent, shining, yellow 2. best, blissful, delightful, flourishing, glorious, happy, joyful, joyous, precious, prosperous, rich, successful 3. advantageous, auspicious, excellent, favourable, opportune, promising, propitious, rosy, valuable

Antonyms (*sense 1*) black, brunette, dark,

dull (*sense 2*) poorest, sad, unfavourable, worst (*sense 3*) black, dark, sad, unfavourable, untimely, wretched

gone 1. elapsed, ended, finished, over, past 2. absent, astray, away, lacking, lost, missing, vanished 3. dead, deceased, defunct, departed, extinct, no more 4. consumed, done, finished, spent, used up

good *adj.* 1. acceptable, admirable, agreeable, bad (*Sl.*), capital, choice, commendable, crucial (*Sl.*), excellent, fine, first-class, first-rate, great, hunky-dory (*Inf.*), pleasant, pleasing, positive, precious, satisfactory, splendid, super (*Inf.*), superior, tiptop, valuable, wicked (*Sl.*), world-class, worthy 2. admirable, estimable, ethical, exemplary, honest, honourable, moral, praiseworthy, right, righteous, trustworthy, upright, virtuous, worthy 3. able, accomplished, adept, adroit, capable, clever, competent, dexterous, efficient, expert, first-rate, proficient, reliable, satisfactory, serviceable, skilled, sound, suitable, talented, thorough, useful 4. adequate, advantageous, auspicious, beneficial, convenient, favourable, fit, fitting, healthy, helpful, opportune, profitable, propitious, salubrious, salutary, suitable, useful, wholesome 5. eatable, fit to eat, sound, uncorrupted, untainted, whole 6. altruistic, approving, beneficent, benevolent, charitable, friendly, gracious, humane, kind, kind-hearted, kindly, merciful, obliging, well-disposed 7. authentic, bona fide, dependable, genuine, honest, legitimate, proper, real, reliable, sound, true, trustworthy, valid 8. decorous, dutiful, mannerly, obedient, orderly, polite, proper, seemly, well-behaved, well-mannered 9. agreeable, cheerful, congenial, convivial, enjoyable, gratifying, happy, pleasant, pleasing, pleasurable, satisfying 10. adequate, ample, complete, considerable, entire, extensive, full, large, long, sizable, solid, substantial, sufficient, whole 11. best, fancy, finest, newest, nicest, precious, smartest, special, valuable 12. *Of weather* balmy, bright, calm, clear, clement, cloudless, fair, halcyon, mild, sunny, sunshiny, tranquil ~*n.* 13. advantage, avail, behalf, benefit, gain, interest, profit, service, use, usefulness, welfare, wellbeing, worth 14. excellence, goodness, merit, morality, probity, rectitude, right, righteousness, uprightness, virtue, worth 15. **for good** finally, for ever, irrevocably, never to return, once and for all, permanently, *sine die*

Antonyms *adj.* (*sense 1*) awful, bad, boring, disagreeable, dull, inadequate, rotten, tedious, unpleasant (*sense 2*) bad, base, corrupt, dishonest, dishonourable, evil, immoral, improper, sinful (*sense 3*) bad, incompetent, inefficient, unsatisfactory, unskilled (*sense 4*) inappropriate, unbecoming, unbefitting, unfavourable, unfitting, unsuitable, useless (*sense 5*) bad, decayed, mouldy, off, rotten, unsound (*sense 6*) cruel, evil, mean (*Inf.*), selfish, unkind, vicious, wicked (*sense 7*) counterfeit, false, fraudulent, invalid, phoney (*sense 8*) ill-mannered, mischievous, naughty, rude, unkind (*sense 10*) scant, short ~*n.* (*sense 13*) detriment, disadvantage, failure, ill-fortune, loss (*sense 14*) badness, baseness, corruption, cruelty, dishonesty, evil, immorality, meanness, wickedness

goodbye adieu, farewell, leave-taking, parting

good-for-nothing 1. *n.* black sheep, idler, layabout, ne'er-do-well, profligate, rapscallion, scapegrace, skiver (*Brit. sl.*), waster, wastrel 2. *adj.* feckless, idle, irresponsible, useless, worthless

good-humoured affable, amiable, cheerful, congenial, genial, good-tempered, happy, pleasant

good-looking attractive, comely, fair, handsome, personable, pretty, well-favoured

goodly 1. ample, considerable, large, significant, sizable, substantial, tidy (*Inf.*) 2. agreeable, attractive, comely, desirable, elegant, fine, good-looking, graceful, handsome, personable, pleasant, pleasing, well-favoured

good-natured agreeable, benevolent, friendly, good-hearted, helpful, kind, kindly, tolerant, warm-hearted, well-disposed, willing to please

goodness 1. excellence, merit, quality, superiority, value, worth 2. beneficence, benevolence, friendliness, generosity, good will, graciousness, humaneness, kind-heartedness, kindliness, kindness, mercy, obligingness 3. honesty, honour, integrity, merit, morality, probity, rectitude, righteousness, uprightness, virtue 4. advantage, benefit, nourishment, nutrition, salubriousness, wholesomeness

Antonyms badness, corruption, detriment, disadvantage, dishonesty, evil, immorality, wickedness, worthlessness

goods 1. appurtenances, belongings, chattels, effects, furnishings, furniture, gear, movables, paraphernalia, possessions, property, things, trappings 2. commodities, merchandise, stock, stuff, wares

good will amity, benevolence, favour, friendliness, friendship, heartiness, kindliness, zeal

gooey 1. gluey, glutinous, mucilaginous, soft, sticky, tacky, viscous 2. maudlin, mawkish, sentimental, slushy (*Inf.*), syrupy (*Inf.*), tear-jerking (*Inf.*)

go off 1. blow up, detonate, explode, fire 2. happen, occur, take place 3. decamp, depart, go away, hook it (*Sl.*), leave, move out, part, quit, slope off 4. *Inf.* go bad, go stale, rot

go on 1. continue, endure, happen, last, occur, persist, proceed, stay 2. blether, carry on, chatter, prattle, rabbit (*Brit. inf.*), ramble on, waffle (*Inf., chiefly Brit.*), witter (on) (*Inf.*)

go out 1. depart, exit, leave 2. be extinguished, die out, expire, fade out

go over 1. examine, inspect, rehearse, reiterate, review, revise, study, work over 2. peruse, read, scan, skim

gore[1] *n.* blood, bloodshed, butchery, carnage, slaughter

gore[2] *v.* impale, pierce, spit, stab, transfix, wound

gorge[1] *n.* canyon, cleft, clough (*Dialect*), defile, fissure, pass, ravine

gorge[2] *v.* bolt, cram, devour, feed, fill, glut, gobble, gormandize, gulp, guzzle, overeat, pig out (*U.S. & Canad. sl.*), raven, sate, satiate, stuff, surfeit, swallow, wolf

gorgeous 1. beautiful, brilliant, dazzling, drop-dead (*Sl.*), elegant, glittering, grand, luxuriant, magnificent, opulent, ravishing, resplendent, showy, splendid, splendiferous (*Facetious*), stunning (*Inf.*), sumptuous, superb 2. *Inf.* attractive, bright, delightful, enjoyable, exquisite, fine, glorious, good, good-looking, lovely, pleasing

Antonyms cheap, dismal, dreary, dull, gloomy, homely, plain, repulsive, shabby, shoddy, sombre, ugly, unattractive, unsightly

gory blood-soaked, bloodstained, bloodthirsty, bloody, ensanguined (*Literary*), murderous, sanguinary

gospel 1. certainty, fact, the last word, truth, verity 2. credo, creed, doctrine, message, news, revelation, tidings

gossamer *adj.* airy, delicate, diaphanous, fine, flimsy, gauzy, light, sheer, silky, thin, transparent

gossip *n.* 1. blether, chinwag (*Brit. inf.*), chitchat, clishmaclaver (*Scot.*), dirt (*U.S. sl.*), gen (*Brit. inf.*), hearsay, idle talk, jaw (*Sl.*), latest (*Inf.*), newsmongering (*Old-fashioned*), prattle, scandal, small talk, tittle-tattle 2. babbler, blatherskite, blether, busybody, chatterbox (*Inf.*), chatterer, flibbertigibbet, gossipmonger, newsmonger (*Old-fashioned*), prattler, quidnunc, scandalmonger, tattler, telltale ~*v.* 3. blather, blether, chat, gabble, jaw (*Sl.*), prate, prattle, tattle

go through 1. bear, brave, endure, experience, suffer, tolerate, undergo, withstand 2. consume, exhaust, squander, use 3. check, examine, explore, hunt, look, search, work over

go together 1. accord, agree, fit, harmonize, make a pair, match 2. *Inf.* court, date (*Inf., chiefly U.S.*), escort, go out with, go steady with (*Inf.*)

gouge 1. *v.* chisel, claw, cut, dig (out), gash, hollow (out), incise, scoop, score, scratch 2. *n.* cut, furrow, gash, groove, hollow, incision, notch, scoop, score, scratch, trench

go under default, die, drown, fail, fold (*Inf.*), founder, go down, sink, submerge, succumb

gourmet *bon vivant,* connoisseur, epicure, foodie (*Inf.*), gastronome

govern 1. administer, be in power, command, conduct, control, direct, guide, handle, hold sway, lead, manage, order, oversee, pilot, reign, rule, steer, superintend, supervise 2. bridle, check, contain, control, curb, direct, discipline, get the better of, hold in check, inhibit, master, regulate, restrain, subdue, tame 3. decide, determine, guide, influence, rule, sway, underlie

government 1. administration, authority, dominion, execution, governance, law, polity, rule, sovereignty, state, statecraft 2. administration, executive, ministry, powers-that-be, regime 3. authority, command, control, direction, domination, guidance, management, regulation, restraint, superintendence, supervision, sway

governmental administrative, bureaucratic, executive, ministerial, official, political, sovereign, state

governor administrator, boss (*Inf.*), chief, commander, comptroller, controller, director, executive, head, leader, manager, overseer, ruler, superintendent, supervisor

go with accompany, agree, blend, complement, concur, correspond, fit, harmonize, match, suit

go without abstain, be denied, be deprived of, deny oneself, do without, go short, lack, want

gown costume, dress, frock, garb, garment, habit, robe

grab bag, capture, catch (up), catch *or* take hold of, clutch, grasp, grip, latch on to, nab (*Inf.*), nail (*Inf.*), pluck, seize, snap up, snatch

grace *n.* 1. attractiveness, beauty, charm, comeliness, ease, elegance, finesse, grace~

fulness, loveliness, pleasantness, poise, polish, refinement, shapeliness, tastefulness 2. benefaction, beneficence, benevolence, favour, generosity, goodness, good will, kindliness, kindness 3. breeding, consideration, cultivation, decency, decorum, etiquette, mannerliness, manners, propriety, tact 4. charity, clemency, compassion, forgiveness, indulgence, leniency, lenity, mercy, pardon, quarter, reprieve 5. benediction, blessing, prayer, thanks, thanksgiving ~*v.* 6. adorn, beautify, bedeck, deck, decorate, dignify, distinguish, elevate, embellish, enhance, enrich, favour, garnish, glorify, honour, ornament, set off
Antonyms *n.* awkwardness, bad manners, clumsiness, condemnation, disfavour, harshness, ill will, inelegance, stiffness, tactlessness, tastelessness, ugliness, ungainliness ~*v.* desecrate, dishonour, insult, ruin, spoil

graceful agile, beautiful, becoming, charming, comely, easy, elegant, fine, flowing, gracile (*Rare*), natural, pleasing, smooth, symmetrical, tasteful
Antonyms awkward, clumsy, gawky, inelegant, plain, ponderous, stiff, ugly, ungainly, ungraceful

graceless 1. barbarous, boorish, coarse, crude, ill-mannered, improper, indecorous, rude, shameless, unmannerly, unsophisticated, vulgar 2. awkward, clumsy, forced, gauche, gawky, inelegant, loutish, rough, uncouth, ungainly, untutored

Graces, the Charities

gracious accommodating, affable, amiable, beneficent, benevolent, benign, benignant, charitable, chivalrous, civil, compassionate, considerate, cordial, courteous, courtly, friendly, hospitable, indulgent, kind, kindly, lenient, loving, merciful, mild, obliging, pleasing, polite, well-mannered
Antonyms brusque, cold, discourteous, gruff, haughty, impolite, mean, remote, rude, surly, unfriendly, ungracious, unpleasant

gradation 1. array, progression, sequence, series, succession 2. degree, grade, level, mark, measurement, notch, place, point, position, rank, stage, step 3. arrangement, classification, grouping, ordering, sorting

grade *n.* 1. brand, category, class, condition, degree, echelon, group, level, mark, notch, order, place, position, quality, rank, rung, size, stage, station, step 2. **make the grade** *Inf.* come through with flying colours, come up to scratch (*Inf.*), measure up, measure up to expectations, pass muster, prove acceptable, succeed, win through 3. acclivity, bank, declivity, gradient, hill, incline, rise, slope ~*v.* 4. arrange, brand, class, classify, evaluate, group, order, range, rank, rate, sort, value

gradient acclivity, bank, declivity, grade, hill, incline, rise, slope

gradual continuous, even, gentle, graduated, moderate, piecemeal, progressive, regular, slow, steady, successive, unhurried
Antonyms abrupt, broken, instantaneous, overnight, sudden

gradually bit by bit, by degrees, drop by drop, evenly, gently, little by little, moderately, piece by piece, piecemeal, progressively, slowly, steadily, step by step, unhurriedly

graduate *v.* 1. calibrate, grade, mark off, measure out, proportion, regulate 2. arrange, classify, grade, group, order, range, rank, sort

graft 1. *n.* bud, implant, scion, shoot, splice, sprout 2. *v.* affix, implant, ingraft, insert, join, splice, transplant

grain 1. cereals, corn 2. grist, kernel, seed 3. atom, bit, crumb, fragment, granule, iota, jot, mite, modicum, molecule, morsel, mote, ounce, particle, piece, scintilla (*Rare*), scrap, scruple, spark, speck, suspicion, trace, whit 4. fibre, nap, pattern, surface, texture, weave 5. character, disposition, humour, inclination, make-up, temper

grand 1. ambitious, august, dignified, elevated, eminent, exalted, fine, glorious, gorgeous, grandiose, great, haughty, illustrious, imposing, impressive, large, lofty, lordly, luxurious, magnificent, majestic, monumental, noble, opulent, ostentatious, palatial, pompous, pretentious, princely, regal, splendid, splendiferous (*Facetious*), stately, striking, sublime, sumptuous, superb 2. admirable, excellent, fine, first-class, first-rate, great (*Inf.*), hunky-dory (*Inf.*), marvellous (*Inf.*), outstanding, smashing (*Inf.*), splendid, splendiferous (*Facetious*), super (*Inf.*), superb, terrific (*Inf.*), very good, wonderful, world-class 3. big-time (*Inf.*), chief, head, highest, lead, leading, main, major league (*Inf.*), pre-eminent, principal, supreme
Antonyms awful, bad, base, chickenshit (*U.S. sl.*), common, contemptible, crappy (*Sl.*), inferior, insignificant, little, mean, petty, poor, poxy (*Sl.*), secondary, small, terrible, trivial, undignified, unimportant, unimposing, worthless

grandeur augustness, dignity, greatness, importance, loftiness, magnificence, majesty, nobility, pomp, splendour, state, stateliness, sublimity
Antonyms commonness, inferiority, insig~

nificance, lowliness, pettiness, smallness, triviality, unimportance

grandiloquent bombastic, flowery, fustian, high-flown, high-sounding, inflated, magniloquent, orotund, pompous, pretentious, rhetorical

grandiose 1. affected, ambitious, bombastic, extravagant, flamboyant, high-flown, ostentatious, pompous, pretentious, showy 2. ambitious, grand, imposing, impressive, lofty, magnificent, majestic, monumental, stately

Antonyms down-to-earth, humble, modest, small-scale, unpretentious

grant *v.* 1. accede to, accord, acknowledge, admit, agree to, allocate, allot, allow, assign, award, bestow, cede, concede, confer, consent to, donate, give, hand out, impart, permit, present, vouchsafe, yield 2. *Law* assign, convey, transfer, transmit *~n.* 3. admission, allocation, allotment, allowance, award, benefaction, bequest, boon, bounty, concession, donation, endowment, gift, hand-out, present, stipend, subsidy

granular crumbly, grainy, granulated, gravelly, gritty, rough, sandy

granulate crumble, crush, crystallize, grind, levigate (*Chemistry*), pound, powder, pulverize, triturate

granule atom, crumb, fragment, grain, iota, jot, molecule, particle, scrap, speck

graphic 1. clear, descriptive, detailed, explicit, expressive, forcible, illustrative, lively, lucid, picturesque, striking, telling, vivid, well-drawn 2. delineated, diagrammatic, drawn, illustrative, pictorial, representational, seen, visible, visual

Antonyms (*sense 1*) generalized, imprecise, impressionistic, unspecific, vague, woolly

grapple 1. catch, clasp, clutch, come to grips, fasten, grab, grasp, grip, hold, hug, lay *or* take hold, make fast, seize, wrestle 2. address oneself to, attack, battle, clash, combat, confront, contend, cope, deal with, do battle, encounter, engage, face, fight, struggle, tackle, take on, tussle, wrestle

grasp *v.* 1. catch (up), clasp, clinch, clutch, grab, grapple, grip, hold, lay *or* take hold of, seize, snatch 2. catch *or* get the drift of, catch on, comprehend, follow, get, realize, see, take in, understand *~n.* 3. clasp, clutches, embrace, grip, hold, possession, tenure 4. capacity, compass, control, extent, mastery, power, range, reach, scope, sway, sweep 5. awareness, comprehension, ken, knowledge, mastery, perception, realization, understanding

grasping acquisitive, avaricious, close-fisted, covetous, greedy, mean, miserly, niggardly, penny-pinching (*Inf.*), rapacious, selfish, stingy, tight-arsed (*Taboo sl.*), tight as a duck's arse (*Sl.*), tight-assed (*U.S. taboo sl.*), tightfisted, usurious, venal

Antonyms altruistic, generous, unselfish

grate *v.* 1. mince, pulverize, shred, triturate 2. creak, grind, rasp, rub, scrape, scratch 3. aggravate (*Inf.*), annoy, chafe, exasperate, fret, gall, get one down, get on one's nerves (*Inf.*), irk, irritate, jar, nark (*Brit., Aust., & N.Z. sl.*), nettle, peeve, rankle, rub one up the wrong way, set one's teeth on edge, vex

grateful 1. appreciative, beholden, indebted, obliged, thankful 2. acceptable, agreeable, favourable, gratifying, nice, pleasing, refreshing, restful, satisfactory, satisfying, welcome

gratification delight, enjoyment, fruition, fulfilment, glee, indulgence, joy, kick *or* kicks (*Inf.*), pleasure, recompense, relish, reward, satisfaction, thrill

Antonyms control, denial, disappointment, discipline, dissatisfaction, frustration, pain, restraint, sorrow

gratify cater to, delight, favour, feed, fulfil, give pleasure, gladden, humour, indulge, pander to, please, recompense, requite, satisfy, thrill

grating[1] *adj.* annoying, disagreeable, discordant, displeasing, grinding, harsh, irksome, irritating, jarring, offensive, rasping, raucous, scraping, squeaky, strident, unpleasant, vexatious

Antonyms agreeable, calming, mellifluous, musical, pleasing, soft, soothing

grating[2] grate, grid, gridiron, grille, lattice, trellis

gratis buckshee (*Brit. sl.*), for nothing, free, freely, free of charge, gratuitously, on the house, unpaid

gratitude appreciation, gratefulness, indebtedness, obligation, recognition, sense of obligation, thankfulness, thanks

Antonyms ingratitude, ungratefulness, unthankfulness

gratuitous 1. buckshee (*Brit. sl.*), complimentary, free, spontaneous, unasked-for, unpaid, unrewarded, voluntary 2. assumed, baseless, causeless, groundless, irrelevant, needless, superfluous, uncalled-for, unfounded, unjustified, unmerited, unnecessary, unprovoked, unwarranted, wanton

Antonyms compulsory, involuntary, justifiable, paid, provoked, relevant, well-founded

gratuity baksheesh, benefaction, bonus, boon, bounty, donation, gift, largess *or* largesse, perquisite, *pourboire,* present, recompense, reward, tip

grave[1] *n.* burying place, crypt, last resting

place, mausoleum, pit, sepulchre, tomb, vault

grave[2] 1. dignified, dour, dull, earnest, gloomy, grim-faced, heavy, leaden, long-faced, muted, quiet, sage (*Obsolete*), sedate, serious, sober, solemn, sombre, staid, subdued, thoughtful, unsmiling 2. acute, critical, crucial, dangerous, exigent, hazardous, important, life-and-death, momentous, of great consequence, perilous, pressing, serious, severe, significant, threatening, urgent, vital, weighty

Antonyms carefree, exciting, flippant, frivolous, happy, insignificant, joyous, merry, mild, trifling, undignified, unimportant

graveyard boneyard (*Inf.*), burial ground, cemetery, charnel house, churchyard, God's acre (*Literary*), necropolis

gravitas gravity, seriousness, solemnity

gravitate 1. *With* **to** *or* **towards** be influenced (attracted, drawn, pulled), incline, lean, move, tend 2. be precipitated, descend, drop, fall, precipitate, settle, sink

gravity 1. acuteness, consequence, exigency, hazardousness, importance, moment, momentousness, perilousness, pressingness, seriousness, severity, significance, urgency, weightiness 2. demureness, dignity, earnestness, gloom, gravitas, grimness, reserve, sedateness, seriousness, sobriety, solemnity, thoughtfulness

Antonyms flippancy, frivolity, gaiety, happiness, inconsequentiality, insignificance, joy, levity, merriment, thoughtlessness, triviality, unimportance

graze[1] browse, crop, feed, pasture

graze[2] *v.* 1. brush, glance off, kiss, rub, scrape, shave, skim, touch 2. abrade, bark, chafe, scrape, scratch, skin ~*n.* 3. abrasion, scrape, scratch

greasy 1. fatty, oily, slick, slimy, slippery 2. fawning, glib, grovelling, ingratiating, oily, slick, smarmy (*Brit. inf.*), smooth, sycophantish, toadying, unctuous

great 1. big, bulky, colossal, elephantine, enormous, extensive, gigantic, huge, humongous *or* humungous (*U.S. sl.*), immense, large, mammoth, prodigious, stupendous, tremendous, vast, voluminous 2. extended, lengthy, long, prolonged, protracted 3. big-time (*Inf.*), capital, chief, grand, head, lead, leading, main, major, major league (*Inf.*), paramount, primary, principal, prominent, superior 4. considerable, decided, excessive, extravagant, extreme, grievous, high, inordinate, prodigious, pronounced, strong 5. consequential, critical, crucial, grave, heavy, important, momentous, serious, significant, weighty 6. celebrated, distinguished, eminent, exalted, excellent, famed, famous, glorious, illustrious, notable, noteworthy, outstanding, prominent, remarkable, renowned, superb, superlative, talented, world-class 7. august, chivalrous, dignified, distinguished, exalted, fine, glorious, grand, heroic, high-minded, idealistic, impressive, lofty, magnanimous, noble, princely, sublime 8. active, devoted, enthusiastic, keen, zealous 9. able, adept, adroit, crack (*Sl.*), expert, good, masterly, proficient, skilful, skilled 10. *Inf.* admirable, boffo (*Sl.*), brill (*Inf.*), chillin' (*U.S. sl.*), cracking (*Brit. inf.*), crucial (*Sl.*), def (*Inf.*), excellent, fantastic (*Inf.*), fine, first-rate, good, hunky-dory (*Inf.*), jim-dandy (*Sl.*), marvellous (*Inf.*), mean (*Sl.*), mega (*Sl.*), sovereign, superb, terrific (*Inf.*), topping (*Brit. sl.*), tremendous (*Inf.*), wonderful 11. absolute, arrant, complete, consummate, downright, egregious, flagrant, out-and-out, perfect, positive, thoroughgoing, thundering (*Inf.*), total, unmitigated, unqualified, utter

Antonyms average, bad, base, diminutive, hateful, ignoble, inconsequential, inconsiderable, inferior, inhumane, insignificant, little, mean, mild, petty, poor, secondary, second-rate, small, terrible, trivial, undistinguished, unimportant, unkind, unnotable, unskilled, weak

greatly abundantly, by leaps and bounds, by much, considerably, enormously, exceedingly, extremely, highly, hugely, immensely, markedly, mightily, much, notably, powerfully, remarkably, tremendously, vastly, very much

greatness 1. bulk, enormity, hugeness, immensity, largeness, length, magnitude, mass, prodigiousness, size, vastness 2. amplitude, force, high degree, intensity, potency, power, strength 3. gravity, heaviness, import, importance, moment, momentousness, seriousness, significance, urgency, weight 4. celebrity, distinction, eminence, fame, glory, grandeur, illustriousness, lustre, note, renown 5. chivalry, dignity, disinterestedness, generosity, grandeur, heroism, high-mindedness, idealism, loftiness, majesty, nobility, nobleness, stateliness, sublimity

greed, greediness 1. edacity, esurience, gluttony, gormandizing, hunger, insatiableness, ravenousness, voracity 2. acquisitiveness, avarice, avidity, covetousness, craving, cupidity, desire, eagerness, graspingness, longing, rapacity, selfishness

Antonyms altruism, benevolence, generosity, largess *or* largesse, munificence, self-restraint, unselfishness

greedy 1. edacious, esurient, gluttonous, gormandizing, hoggish, hungry, insatiable, piggish, ravenous, voracious 2. acquisitive, avaricious, avid, covetous, craving, desirous, eager, grasping, hungry, impatient, rapacious, selfish
Antonyms altruistic, apathetic, benevolent, full, generous, indifferent, munificent, self-restrained, unselfish

Greek 1. *n.* Hellene 2. *adj.* Hellenic

green *adj.* 1. blooming, budding, flourishing, fresh, grassy, leafy, new, undecayed, verdant, verdurous 2. fresh, immature, new, raw, recent, unripe 3. conservationist, ecological, environment-friendly, non-polluting 4. callow, credulous, gullible, ignorant, immature, inexperienced, inexpert, ingenuous, innocent, naive, new, raw, unpolished, unpractised, unskilful, unsophisticated, untrained, unversed, wet behind the ears (*Inf.*) 5. covetous, envious, grudging, jealous, resentful 6. ill, nauseous, pale, sick, unhealthy, wan 7. immature, pliable, supple, tender, undried, unseasoned, young ~*n.* 8. common, grassplot, lawn, sward, turf

greenhorn apprentice, beginner, ignoramus, ingénue, learner, naïf, neophyte, newcomer, novice, raw recruit, simpleton, tyro

green light approval, authorization, blessing, clearance, confirmation, go-ahead (*Inf.*), imprimatur, O.K. *or* okay (*Inf.*), permission, sanction

greet accost, address, compliment, hail, meet, nod to, receive, salute, tip one's hat to, welcome

greeting 1. address, hail, reception, salutation, salute, welcome 2. *Plural* best wishes, compliments, devoirs, good wishes, regards, respects, salutations

gregarious affable, companionable, convivial, cordial, friendly, outgoing, sociable, social
Antonyms antisocial, reserved, solitary, standoffish, unsociable, withdrawn

grey 1. ashen, bloodless, colourless, livid, pale, pallid, wan 2. cheerless, cloudy, dark, depressing, dim, dismal, drab, dreary, dull, foggy, gloomy, misty, murky, overcast, sunless 3. anonymous, characterless, colourless, dull, indistinct, neutral, unclear, unidentifiable 4. aged, ancient, elderly, experienced, hoary, mature, old, venerable

grief 1. affliction, agony, anguish, bereavement, dejection, distress, grievance, hardship, heartache, heartbreak, misery, mournfulness, mourning, pain, regret, remorse, sadness, sorrow, suffering, trial, tribulation, trouble, woe 2. **come to grief** *Inf.* come unstuck, fail, meet with disaster, miscarry
Antonyms cheer, comfort, consolation, delight, gladness, happiness, joy, rejoicing, solace

grief-stricken afflicted, agonized, broken, brokenhearted, crushed, desolate, despairing, devastated, heartbroken, inconsolable, overwhelmed, sorrowful, sorrowing, woebegone, wretched

grievance affliction, beef (*Sl.*), complaint, damage, distress, grief, gripe (*Inf.*), hardship, injury, injustice, protest, resentment, sorrow, trial, tribulation, trouble, unhappiness, wrong

grieve 1. ache, bemoan, bewail, complain, deplore, lament, mourn, regret, rue, sorrow, suffer, wail, weep 2. afflict, agonize, break the heart of, crush, distress, hurt, injure, make one's heart bleed, pain, sadden, wound
Antonyms cheer, comfort, console, ease, gladden, please, rejoice, solace

grievous 1. afflicting, calamitous, damaging, distressing, dreadful, grave, harmful, heavy, hurtful, injurious, lamentable, oppressive, painful, severe, wounding 2. appalling, atrocious, deplorable, dreadful, egregious, flagrant, glaring, heinous, intolerable, lamentable, monstrous, offensive, outrageous, shameful, shocking, unbearable 3. agonized, grief-stricken, heart-rending, mournful, pitiful, sorrowful, tragic
Antonyms delightful, glad, happy, insignificant, joyous, mild, pleasant, trivial, unimportant

grim cruel, ferocious, fierce, forbidding, formidable, frightful, ghastly, godawful (*Sl.*), grisly, gruesome, hard, harsh, hideous, horrible, horrid, implacable, merciless, morose, relentless, resolute, ruthless, severe, shocking, sinister, stern, sullen, surly, terrible, unrelenting, unyielding
Antonyms amiable, attractive, benign, cheerful, easy, genial, gentle, happy, kind, pleasant, soft, sympathetic

grimace 1. *n.* face, frown, mouth, scowl, sneer, wry face 2. *v.* frown, lour *or* lower, make a face *or* faces, mouth, scowl, sneer

grime dirt, filth, grot (*Sl.*), smut, soot

grimy begrimed, besmeared, besmirched, dirty, filthy, foul, grubby, scuzzy (*Sl.*), smutty, soiled, sooty, unclean

grind *v.* 1. abrade, comminute, crush, granulate, grate, kibble, mill, pound, powder, pulverize, triturate 2. file, polish, sand, sharpen, smooth, whet 3. gnash, grate, grit, scrape 4. *With* **down** afflict, harass, hold down, hound, oppress, persecute, plague, trouble, tyrannize (over) ~*n.* 5. *Inf.* chore, drudgery, hard work, labour, sweat (*Inf.*), task, toil

grip *n.* 1. clasp, handclasp (*U.S.*), purchase 2. clutches, comprehension, control, domination, grasp, hold, influence, keeping, mastery, perception, possession, power, tenure, understanding 3. **come** *or* **get to grips (with)** close with, confront, contend with, cope with, deal with, encounter, face up to, grapple with, grasp, handle, meet, tackle, take on, undertake ~*v.* 4. clasp, clutch, grasp, hold, latch on to, seize, take hold of 5. absorb, catch up, compel, engross, enthral, entrance, fascinate, hold, involve, mesmerize, rivet, spellbind

gripe *v.* 1. *Inf.* beef (*Sl.*), bellyache (*Sl.*), bitch (*Sl.*), bleat, carp, complain, groan, grouch (*Inf.*), grouse, grumble, kvetch (*U.S. sl.*), moan, nag, whine 2. ache, compress, cramp, hurt, pain, pinch, press, squeeze ~*n.* 3. *Often plural* ache, aching, affliction, colic, cramps, distress, griping, pain, pang, pinching, stomachache, twinge 4. *Inf.* beef (*Sl.*), complaint, grievance, groan, grouch (*Inf.*), grouse, grumble, moan, objection, protest

gripping compelling, compulsive, engrossing, enthralling, entrancing, exciting, fascinating, riveting, spellbinding, thrilling, unputdownable (*Inf.*)

grisly abominable, appalling, awful, dreadful, frightful, ghastly, grim, gruesome, hellacious (*U.S. sl.*), hideous, horrible, horrid, macabre, shocking, sickening, terrible, terrifying

Antonyms agreeable, attractive, charming, innocuous, nice, pleasant

grit *n.* 1. dust, gravel, pebbles, sand 2. backbone, balls (*Taboo sl.*), courage, determination, doggedness, fortitude, gameness, guts (*Inf.*), hardihood, mettle, nerve, perseverance, pluck, resolution, spirit, tenacity, toughness ~*v.* 3. clench, gnash, grate, grind

gritty 1. abrasive, dusty, grainy, granular, gravelly, rasping, rough, sandy 2. ballsy (*Taboo sl.*), brave, courageous, determined, dogged, feisty (*Inf., chiefly U.S. & Canad.*), game, hardy, mettlesome, plucky, resolute, spirited, steadfast, tenacious, tough

grizzle fret, girn (*Scot.*), pule, snivel, whimper, whine, whinge (*Inf.*)

grizzled canescent, grey, grey-haired, grey-headed, greying, griseous, grizzly, hoary

groan *n.* 1. cry, moan, sigh, whine 2. *Inf.* beef (*Sl.*), complaint, gripe (*Inf.*), grouse, grumble, objection, protest ~*v.* 3. cry, moan, sigh, whine 4. *Inf.* beef (*Sl.*), bemoan, bitch (*Sl.*), complain, gripe (*Inf.*), grouse, grumble, lament, object

groggy befuddled, confused, dazed, dizzy, faint, muzzy, punch-drunk, reeling, shaky, staggering, stunned, stupefied, unsteady, weak, wobbly, woozy (*Inf.*)

groom *n.* 1. currier (*Rare*), hostler *or* ostler (*Archaic*), stableboy, stableman ~*v.* 2. clean, dress, get up (*Inf.*), preen, primp, smarten up, spruce up, tidy, turn out 3. brush, clean, curry, rub down, tend 4. coach, drill, educate, make ready, nurture, prepare, prime, ready, train

groove channel, cut, cutting, flute, furrow, gutter, hollow, indentation, rebate, rut, score, trench

grope cast about, feel, finger, fish, flounder, fumble, grabble, scrabble, search

gross *adj.* 1. big, bulky, corpulent, dense, fat, great, heavy, hulking, large, lumpish, massive, obese, overweight, thick 2. aggregate, before deductions, before tax, entire, total, whole 3. coarse, crude, improper, impure, indecent, indelicate, lewd, low, obscene, offensive, ribald, rude, sensual, smutty, unseemly, vulgar 4. apparent, arrant, blatant, downright, egregious, flagrant, glaring, grievous, heinous, manifest, obvious, outrageous, plain, rank, serious, shameful, sheer, shocking, unmitigated, unqualified, utter 5. boorish, callous, coarse, crass, dull, ignorant, imperceptive, insensitive, tasteless, uncultured, undiscriminating, unfeeling, unrefined, unsophisticated ~*v.* 6. bring in, earn, make, rake in (*Inf.*), take

Antonyms *adj.* cultivated, decent, delicate, elegant, little, net, partial, petite, proper, pure, qualified, refined, slim, small, svelte, thin ~*v.* clear, net

grossness 1. bigness, bulkiness, corpulence, fatness, greatness, heaviness, lumpishness, obesity, thickness 2. bestiality, coarseness, crudity, impurity, indecency, indelicacy, licentiousness, obscenity, offensiveness, ribaldry, rudeness, sensuality, smut, smuttiness, unseemliness, vulgarity 3. blatancy, egregiousness, flagrancy, grievousness, obviousness, rankness, seriousness, shamefulness 4. coarseness, crassness, ignorance, insensitivity, lack of taste, pig-ignorance (*Sl.*), tastelessness

grotesque absurd, bizarre, deformed, distorted, extravagant, fanciful, fantastic, freakish, incongruous, ludicrous, malformed, misshapen, odd, outlandish, preposterous, ridiculous, strange, unnatural, weird, whimsical

Antonyms average, classic, graceful, natural, normal, realistic

grouch *v.* 1. beef (*Sl.*), bellyache (*Sl.*), bitch (*Sl.*), bleat, carp, complain, find fault, gripe

(*Inf.*), grouse, grumble, kvetch (*U.S. sl.*), moan, whine, whinge (*Inf.*) ~*n.* 2. beef (*Sl.*), complaint, grievance, gripe (*Inf.*), grouse, grumble, moan, objection, protest 3. complainer, crab (*Inf.*), crosspatch (*Inf.*), curmudgeon, faultfinder, grouser, grumbler, malcontent, moaner, whiner

grouchy cantankerous, cross, discontented, grumbling, grumpy, huffy, ill-tempered, irascible, irritable, liverish, peevish, petulant, querulous, ratty (*Brit. & N.Z. inf.*), sulky, surly, testy, tetchy

ground *n.* 1. clod, dirt, dry land, dust, earth, field, land, loam, mould, sod, soil, terra firma, terrain, turf 2. *Often plural* area, country, district, domain, estate, fields, gardens, habitat, holding, land, property, realm, terrain, territory, tract 3. *Usually plural* account, argument, base, basis, call, cause, excuse, factor, foundation, inducement, justification, motive, occasion, premise, pretext, rationale, reason 4. *Usually plural* deposit, dregs, grouts, lees, sediment, settlings 5. arena, field, park (*Inf.*), pitch, stadium ~*v.* 6. base, establish, fix, found, set, settle 7. acquaint with, coach, familiarize with, inform, initiate, instruct, prepare, teach, train, tutor

groundless baseless, chimerical, empty, false, idle, illusory, imaginary, unauthorized, uncalled-for, unfounded, unjustified, unprovoked, unsupported, unwarranted
Antonyms justified, logical, proven, real, reasonable, substantial, supported, true, well-founded

groundwork base, basis, cornerstone, footing, foundation, fundamentals, preliminaries, preparation, spadework, underpinnings

group *n.* 1. aggregation, assemblage, association, band, batch, bevy, bunch, camp, category, circle, class, clique, clump, cluster, collection, company, congregation, coterie, crowd, faction, formation, gang, gathering, organization, pack, party, posse (*Sl.*), set, troop ~*v.* 2. arrange, assemble, associate, assort, bracket, class, classify, dispose, gather, marshal, order, organize, put together, range, sort 3. associate, band together, cluster, congregate, consort, fraternize, gather, get together

grouse 1. *v.* beef (*Sl.*), bellyache (*Sl.*), bitch (*Sl.*), bleat, carp, complain, find fault, gripe (*Inf.*), grouch (*Inf.*), grumble, kvetch (*U.S. sl.*), moan, whine, whinge (*Inf.*) 2. *n.* beef (*Sl.*), complaint, grievance, gripe (*Inf.*), grouch (*Inf.*), grumble, moan, objection, protest

grove brake, coppice, copse, covert, plantation, spinney, thicket, wood, woodland

grovel abase oneself, bootlick (*Inf.*), bow and scrape, brown-nose (*Taboo sl.*), cower, crawl, creep, cringe, crouch, demean oneself, fawn, flatter, humble oneself, kiss ass (*Taboo sl.*), kowtow, pander to, sneak, toady
Antonyms be proud, domineer, face, hold one's head high, intimidate

grow 1. develop, enlarge, expand, extend, fill out, get bigger, get taller, heighten, increase, multiply, spread, stretch, swell, thicken, widen 2. develop, flourish, germinate, shoot, spring up, sprout, vegetate 3. arise, issue, originate, spring, stem 4. advance, expand, flourish, improve, progress, prosper, succeed, thrive 5. become, come to be, develop (into), get, turn, wax 6. breed, cultivate, farm, nurture, produce, propagate, raise
Antonyms decline, decrease, die, diminish, dwindle, fail, lessen, shrink, subside, wane

grown-up 1. *adj.* adult, fully-grown, mature, of age 2. *n.* adult, man, woman

growth 1. aggrandizement, augmentation, development, enlargement, evolution, expansion, extension, growing, heightening, increase, multiplication, proliferation, stretching, thickening, widening 2. crop, cultivation, development, germination, produce, production, shooting, sprouting, vegetation 3. advance, advancement, expansion, improvement, progress, prosperity, rise, success 4. *Medicine* excrescence, lump, tumour
Antonyms decline, decrease, dwindling, failure, lessening, retreat, shrinkage, slackening, subsiding

grub *v.* 1. burrow, dig up, probe, pull up, root (*Inf.*), rootle (*Brit.*), search for, uproot 2. ferret, forage, hunt, rummage, scour, search, uncover, unearth 3. drudge, grind (*Inf.*), labour, plod, slave, slog, sweat, toil ~*n.* 4. caterpillar, larva, maggot 5. *Sl.* eats (*Sl.*), feed, food, nosebag (*Sl.*), nosh (*Sl.*), rations, sustenance, tack (*Inf.*), victuals, vittles (*Obs. or dialect*)

grubby besmeared, dirty, filthy, frowzy, grimy, manky (*Scot. dialect*), mean, messy, mucky, scruffy, scuzzy (*Sl.*), seedy, shabby, slovenly, smutty, soiled, sordid, squalid, unkempt, untidy, unwashed

grudge 1. *n.* animosity, animus, antipathy, aversion, bitterness, dislike, enmity, grievance, hard feelings, hate, ill will, malevolence, malice, pique, rancour, resentment, spite, venom 2. *v.* begrudge, be reluctant, complain, covet, envy, hold back, mind, resent, stint
Antonyms *n.* appreciation, goodwill, lik-

ing, thankfulness ~*v.* be glad for, celebrate, welcome

gruelling arduous, backbreaking, brutal, crushing, demanding, difficult, exhausting, fatiguing, fierce, grinding, hard, harsh, laborious, punishing, severe, stiff, strenuous, taxing, tiring, trying
Antonyms cushy (*Inf.*), easy, enjoyable, light, pleasant, undemanding

gruesome abominable, awful, fearful, ghastly, grim, grisly, hellacious (*U.S. sl.*), hideous, horrendous, horrible, horrid, horrific, horrifying, loathsome, macabre, obscene, repugnant, repulsive, shocking, spine-chilling, terrible
Antonyms appealing, benign, cheerful, pleasant, sweet

gruff 1. bad-tempered, bearish, blunt, brusque, churlish, crabbed, crusty, curt, discourteous, grouchy (*Inf.*), grumpy, ill-humoured, ill-natured, impolite, rough, rude, sour, sullen, surly, uncivil, ungracious, unmannerly 2. croaking, guttural, harsh, hoarse, husky, low, rasping, rough, throaty
Antonyms courteous, good-tempered, gracious, kind, mellifluous, pleasant, polite, smooth, sweet

grumble *v.* 1. beef (*Sl.*), bellyache (*Sl.*), bitch (*Sl.*), bleat, carp, complain, find fault, gripe (*Inf.*), grouch (*Inf.*), grouse, kvetch (*U.S. sl.*), moan, repine, whine, whinge (*Inf.*) 2. growl, gurgle, murmur, mutter, roar, rumble ~*n.* 3. beef (*Sl.*), complaint, grievance, gripe (*Inf.*), grouch (*Inf.*), grouse, moan, objection, protest 4. growl, gurgle, murmur, muttering, roar, rumble

grumpy cantankerous, crabbed, cross, crotchety (*Inf.*), edgy, grouchy (*Inf.*), grumbling, huffy, ill-tempered, irritable, liverish, peevish, petulant, querulous, ratty (*Brit. & N.Z. inf.*), sulky, sullen, surly, testy, tetchy

guarantee 1. *n.* assurance, bond, certainty, collateral, covenant, earnest, guaranty, pledge, promise, security, surety, undertaking, warranty, word, word of honour 2. *v.* answer for, assure, certify, ensure, insure, maintain, make certain, pledge, promise, protect, secure, stand behind, swear, vouch for, warrant

guarantor backer, bailsman (*Rare*), bondsman (*Law*), guarantee, sponsor, supporter, surety, underwriter, voucher, warrantor

guaranty 1. agreement, assurance, bond, contract, covenant, guarantee, insurance, oath, pledge, promise, undertaking, warrant, warranty, word 2. bail, bond, collateral, deposit, earnest, gage, pawn, pledge, security, token

guard *v.* 1. cover, defend, escort, keep, mind, oversee, patrol, police, preserve, protect, safeguard, save, screen, secure, shelter, shield, supervise, tend, watch, watch over ~*n.* 2. custodian, defender, lookout, picket, protector, sentinel, sentry, warder, watch, watchman 3. convoy, escort, patrol 4. buffer, bulwark, bumper, defence, pad, protection, rampart, safeguard, screen, security, shield 5. attention, care, caution, heed, vigilance, wariness, watchfulness 6. **off (one's) guard** napping, unprepared, unready, unwary, with one's defences down 7. **on (one's) guard** alert, cautious, circumspect, on the alert, on the lookout, on the qui vive, prepared, ready, vigilant, wary, watchful

guarded cagey (*Inf.*), careful, cautious, circumspect, discreet, leery (*Sl.*), noncommittal, prudent, reserved, restrained, reticent, suspicious, wary

guardian attendant, champion, curator, custodian, defender, escort, guard, keeper, preserver, protector, trustee, warden, warder

guerrilla freedom fighter, irregular, member of the underground *or* resistance, partisan, underground fighter

guess *v.* 1. conjecture, estimate, fathom, hypothesize, penetrate, predict, solve, speculate, work out 2. believe, conjecture, dare say, deem, divine, fancy, hazard, imagine, judge, reckon, suppose, surmise, suspect, think ~*n.* 3. conjecture, feeling, hypothesis, judgment, notion, prediction, reckoning, speculation, supposition, surmise, suspicion, theory
Antonyms *v.* be certain, be sure, know, prove, show ~*n.* certainty, fact

guesswork conjecture, estimation, presumption, speculation, supposition, surmise, suspicion, theory

guest boarder, caller, company, lodger, visitant, visitor

guff balderdash, balls (*Taboo sl.*), bilge (*Inf.*), bosh (*Inf.*), bull (*Sl.*), bullshit (*Taboo sl.*), bunkum *or* buncombe (*Chiefly U.S.*), cobblers (*Brit. taboo sl.*), crap (*Sl.*), drivel, empty talk, eyewash (*Inf.*), garbage (*Inf.*), guff (*Sl.*), hogwash, hokum (*Sl., chiefly U.S. & Canad.*), horsefeathers (*U.S. sl.*), hot air (*Inf.*), humbug, moonshine, nonsense, pap, piffle (*Inf.*), poppycock (*Inf.*), rot, rubbish, shit (*Taboo sl.*), tommyrot, tosh (*Sl., chiefly Brit.*), tripe (*Inf.*)

guidance advice, auspices, conduct, control, counsel, counselling, direction, government, help, instruction, intelligence, leadership, management, teaching

guide *v.* 1. accompany, attend, conduct, convoy, direct, escort, lead, pilot, shepherd, show the way, steer, usher 2. command, control, direct, handle, manage, manoeuvre, steer 3. advise, counsel, educate, govern, influence, instruct, oversee, regulate, rule, superintend, supervise, sway, teach, train ~*n.* 4. adviser, attendant, chaperon, cicerone, conductor, controller, counsellor, director, dragoman, escort, leader, mentor, monitor, pilot, steersman, teacher, usher 5. criterion, example, exemplar, ideal, inspiration, lodestar, master, model, par, paradigm, standard 6. beacon, clue, guiding light, key, landmark, lodestar, mark, marker, pointer, sign, signal, signpost 7. catalogue, directory, guidebook, handbook, instructions, key, manual, vade mecum

guild association, brotherhood, club, company, corporation, fellowship, fraternity, league, lodge, order, organization, society, union

guile art, artfulness, artifice, cleverness, craft, craftiness, cunning, deceit, deception, duplicity, gamesmanship (*Inf.*), knavery, ruse, sharp practice, slyness, treachery, trickery, trickiness, wiliness
Antonyms candour, frankness, honesty, sincerity, truthfulness

guileful artful, clever, crafty, cunning, deceitful, duplicitous, foxy, sly, sneaky, treacherous, tricky, underhand, wily

guileless above-board, artless, candid, frank, genuine, honest, ingenuous, innocent, naive, natural, open, simple, simple-minded, sincere, straightforward, truthful, undesigning, unsophisticated, upfront (*Inf.*)

guilt 1. blame, blameworthiness, criminality, culpability, delinquency, guiltiness, iniquity, misconduct, responsibility, sinfulness, wickedness, wrong, wrongdoing 2. bad conscience, contrition, disgrace, dishonour, guiltiness, guilty conscience, infamy, regret, remorse, self-condemnation, self-reproach, shame, stigma
Antonyms blamelessness, honour, innocence, pride, righteousness, self-respect, sinlessness, virtue

guiltless blameless, clean (*Sl.*), clear, immaculate, impeccable, innocent, irreproachable, pure, sinless, spotless, squeaky-clean, unimpeachable, unsullied, untainted, untarnished

guilty 1. at fault, blameworthy, convicted, criminal, culpable, delinquent, erring, evil, felonious, iniquitous, offending, reprehensible, responsible, sinful, to blame, wicked, wrong 2. ashamed, conscience-stricken, contrite, hangdog, regretful, remorseful, rueful, shamefaced, sheepish, sorry
Antonyms blameless, innocent, moral, proud, righteous, virtuous

guise air, appearance, aspect, behaviour, demeanour, disguise, dress, façade, face, fashion, form, front, mask, mode, pretence, semblance, shape, show

gulf 1. bay, bight, sea inlet 2. abyss, breach, chasm, cleft, gap, opening, rent, rift, separation, split, void, whirlpool

gull 1. *n.* babe in arms (*Inf.*), chump (*Inf.*), dupe, easy mark (*Sl.*), fool, gudgeon (*Sl.*), mug (*Sl.*), sap (*Sl.*), simpleton, sucker (*Sl.*) 2. *v.* beguile, cheat, con (*Sl.*), cozen, deceive, defraud, dupe, hoax, put one over on (*Inf.*), rook (*Sl.*), skin (*Sl.*), stiff (*Sl.*), swindle, take in (*Inf.*), trick

gullet craw, crop, maw, oesophagus, throat

gullibility credulity, innocence, naiveté, simplicity, trustingness

gullible born yesterday, credulous, easily taken in, foolish, green, innocent, naive, silly, simple, trusting, unsceptical, unsophisticated, unsuspecting
Antonyms cynical, sophisticated, suspicious, untrusting, worldly

gully channel, ditch, gutter, watercourse

gulp *v.* 1. bolt, devour, gobble, guzzle, knock back (*Inf.*), quaff, swallow, swig (*Inf.*), swill, toss off, wolf 2. choke, gasp, stifle, swallow ~*n.* 3. draught, mouthful, swallow, swig (*Inf.*)

gum 1. *n.* adhesive, cement, exudate, glue, mucilage, paste, resin 2. *v.* affix, cement, clog, glue, paste, stick, stiffen

gummy adhesive, gluey, sticky, tacky, viscid

gumption ability, acumen, astuteness, cleverness, common sense, discernment, enterprise, get-up-and-go (*Inf.*), horse sense, initiative, mother wit, nous (*Brit. sl.*), resourcefulness, sagacity, savvy (*Sl.*), shrewdness, spirit, wit(s)

gunman assassin, bandit, bravo, desperado, gangster, gunslinger (*U.S. sl.*), heavy (*Sl.*), hit man (*Sl.*), killer, mobster (*U.S. sl.*), murderer, terrorist, thug

gurgle 1. *v.* babble, bubble, burble, crow, lap, murmur, plash, purl, ripple, splash 2. *n.* babble, murmur, purl, ripple

guru authority, guiding light, leader, maharishi, mahatma, master, mentor, sage, swami, teacher, tutor

gush *v.* 1. burst, cascade, flood, flow, issue, jet, pour, run, rush, spout, spurt, stream 2. babble, blather, chatter, effervesce, effuse, enthuse, jabber, overstate, spout ~*n.* 3. burst, cascade, flood, flow, issue, jet, outburst, outflow, rush, spout, spurt, stream, torrent **4.** babble, blather, chatter, effusion, exuberance

gushy cloying, effusive, emotional, excessive, fulsome, gushing, mawkish, overdone, overenthusiastic, sentimental

gust *n.* **1.** blast, blow, breeze, flurry, gale, puff, rush, squall **2.** burst, eruption, explosion, fit, gale, outburst, paroxysm, passion, storm, surge ~*v.* **3.** blast, blow, puff, squall

gusto appetite, appreciation, brio, delight, enjoyment, enthusiasm, exhilaration, fervour, liking, pleasure, relish, savour, verve, zeal, zest

Antonyms apathy, coolness, disinterest, distaste, inertia

gusty blowy, blustering, blustery, breezy, inclement, squally, stormy, tempestuous, windy

gut *n.* **1.** *Often plural* belly, bowels, entrails, innards (*Inf.*), insides (*Inf.*), intestines, inwards, paunch, stomach, viscera **2.** *Plural Inf.* audacity, backbone, boldness, bottle (*Sl.*), courage, daring, forcefulness, grit, hardihood, mettle, nerve, pluck, spirit, spunk (*Inf.*), willpower ~*v.* **3.** clean, disembowel, draw, dress, eviscerate **4.** clean out, despoil, empty, pillage, plunder, ransack, ravage, rifle, sack, strip ~*adj.* **5.** *Inf.* basic, deep-seated, emotional, heartfelt, innate, instinctive, intuitive, involuntary, natural, spontaneous, unthinking, visceral

gutless abject, chicken (*Sl.*), chickenshit (*U.S. sl.*), cowardly, craven, faint-hearted, feeble, irresolute, lily-livered, spineless, submissive, timid, weak

Antonyms bold, brave, courageous, determined, resolute

gutsy ballsy (*Taboo sl.*), bold, brave, courageous, determined, feisty (*Inf., chiefly U.S. & Canad.*), gallant, game (*Inf.*), gritty, have-a-go (*Inf.*), indomitable, mettlesome, plucky, resolute, spirited, staunch

gutter channel, conduit, ditch, drain, duct, pipe, sluice, trench, trough, tube

guttersnipe gamin, mudlark (*Sl.*), ragamuffin, street Arab, street urchin, waif

guttural deep, gravelly, gruff, hoarse, husky, low, rasping, rough, thick, throaty

guy **1.** *n. Inf.* bloke (*Brit. inf.*), cat (*Sl.*), chap, fellow, lad, man, person, youth **2.** *v.* caricature, make (a) game of, make fun of, mock, poke fun at, rib (*Inf.*), ridicule, send up (*Brit inf.*), take off (*Inf.*), take the piss out of (*Sl.*)

guzzle bolt, carouse, cram, devour, drink, gobble, gorge, gormandize, knock back (*Inf.*), pig out (*U.S. & Canad. sl.*), quaff, stuff (oneself), swill, tope, wolf

Gypsy, Gipsy Bohemian, nomad, rambler, roamer, Romany, rover, traveller, vagabond, vagrant, wanderer

gyrate circle, pirouette, revolve, rotate, spin, spiral, twirl, whirl

gyration convolution, pirouette, revolution, rotation, spin, spinning, spiral, whirl, whirling

H

habiliment apparel, array, attire, clothes, clothing, costume, dress, garb, garment, habit, raiment (*Archaic or poetic*), robes, uniform, vestments

habit *n.* 1. bent, custom, disposition, manner, mannerism, practice, proclivity, propensity, quirk, tendency, way 2. convention, custom, mode, practice, routine, rule, second nature, tradition, usage, wont 3. constitution, disposition, frame of mind, make-up, nature 4. addiction, dependence, fixation, obsession, weakness 5. apparel, dress, garb, garment, habiliment, riding dress ~*v.* 6. array, attire, clothe, dress, equip

habitat abode, element, environment, home, home ground, locality, natural home, surroundings, terrain, territory

habitation 1. abode, domicile, dwelling, dwelling house, home, house, living quarters, lodging, pad (*Sl.*), quarters, residence 2. inhabitance, inhabitancy, occupancy, occupation, tenancy

habitual 1. accustomed, common, customary, familiar, fixed, natural, normal, ordinary, regular, routine, standard, traditional, usual, wonted 2. chronic, confirmed, constant, established, frequent, hardened, ingrained, inveterate, persistent, recurrent
Antonyms abnormal, exceptional, extraordinary, infrequent, irregular, occasional, rare, strange, uncommon, unusual

habituate acclimatize, accustom, break in, condition, discipline, familiarize, harden, inure, make used to, school, season, train

habituated acclimatized, accustomed, adapted, broken in, conditioned, disciplined, familiarized, hardened, inured, schooled, seasoned, trained, used (to)
Antonyms unaccustomed, unfamiliar, unused (to)

habitué constant customer, frequenter, frequent visitor, regular (*Inf.*), regular patron

hack[1] *v.* 1. chop, cut, gash, hew, kick, lacerate, mangle, mutilate, notch, slash ~*n.* 2. chop, cut, gash, notch, slash ~*v./n.* 3. *Inf.* bark, cough, rasp

hack[2] *adj.* 1. banal, mediocre, pedestrian, poor, stereotyped, tired, undistinguished, uninspired, unoriginal ~*n.* 2. Grub Street writer, literary hack, penny-a-liner, scribbler 3. drudge, plodder, slave 4. crock, hired horse, horse, jade, nag, poor old tired horse

hackles **make one's hackles rise** anger, annoy, bridle at, cause resentment, get one's dander up (*Sl.*), infuriate, make one see red (*Inf.*)

hackneyed banal, clichéd, common, commonplace, overworked, pedestrian, played out (*Inf.*), run-of-the-mill, stale, stereotyped, stock, threadbare, timeworn, tired, trite, unoriginal, worn-out
Antonyms fresh, imaginative, new, novel, original, striking, unusual

Hades hell, infernal regions, lower world, nether regions, realm of Pluto, (the) inferno, underworld

hag ballbreaker (*Sl.*), beldam (*Archaic*), crone, fury, harridan, Jezebel, shrew, termagant, virago, vixen, witch

haggard careworn, drawn, emaciated, gaunt, ghastly, hollow-eyed, pinched, shrunken, thin, wan, wasted, wrinkled
Antonyms bright-eyed, brisk, energetic, fresh, hale, robust, sleek, vigorous

haggle 1. bargain, barter, beat down, chaffer, dicker (*Chiefly U.S.*), higgle, palter 2. bicker, dispute, quarrel, squabble, wrangle

hail[1] *Fig.* 1. *n.* barrage, bombardment, pelting, rain, shower, storm, volley 2. *v.* barrage, batter, beat down upon, bombard, pelt, rain, rain down on, shower, storm, volley

hail[2] 1. acclaim, acknowledge, applaud, cheer, exalt, glorify, greet, honour, salute, welcome 2. accost, address, call, flag down, halloo, shout to, signal to, sing out, speak to, wave down 3. *With* **from** be a native of, be born in, come from, originate in
Antonyms (*sense 1*) boo, condemn, criticize, hiss, insult, jeer (*sense 2*) avoid, cut (*Inf.*), ignore, snub

hair 1. head of hair, locks, mane, mop, shock, tresses 2. **by a hair** by a fraction of an inch, by a hair's-breadth, by a narrow margin, by a split second, by a whisker, by the skin of one's teeth 3. **get in one's hair** aggravate (*Inf.*), annoy, exasperate, be on one's back (*Sl.*), get on one's nerves (*Inf.*), harass, hassle (*Inf.*), irritate, nark (*Brit., Aust., & N.Z. sl.*), pester, piss one off (*Taboo sl.*), plague 4. **let one's hair down** chill out (*Sl., chiefly U.S.*), let it all hang out

(*Inf.*), let off steam (*Inf.*), let oneself go, relax, veg out (*Sl., chiefly U.S.*) 5. **not turn a hair** keep one's cool (*Sl.*), keep one's hair on (*Brit. inf.*), not bat an eyelid, remain calm 6. **split hairs** cavil, find fault, overrefine, pettifog, quibble

hairdo coiffure, cut, haircut, hairstyle, style

hairless bald, baldheaded, beardless, clean-shaven, depilated, glabrous *or* glabrate (*Biol.*), shorn, tonsured

hair-raising alarming, bloodcurdling, breathtaking, creepy, exciting, frightening, horrifying, petrifying, scary, shocking, spine-chilling, startling, terrifying, thrilling

hair's-breadth 1. *n.* fraction, hair, jot, narrow margin, whisker 2. *adj.* close, hazardous, narrow

hairsplitting *adj.* captious, carping, cavilling, fault-finding, fine, finicky, nice, niggling, nit-picking (*Inf.*), overrefined, pettifogging, quibbling, subtle

hairy 1. bearded, bewhiskered, bushy, fleecy, furry, hirsute, pileous (*Biol.*), pilose (*Biol.*), shaggy, stubbly, unshaven, woolly 2. *Sl.* dangerous, difficult, hazardous, perilous, risky, scaring

halcyon 1. calm, gentle, mild, pacific, peaceful, placid, quiet, serene, still, tranquil, undisturbed, unruffled 2. *Fig.* carefree, flourishing, golden, happy, palmy, prosperous

hale able-bodied, blooming, fit, flourishing, healthy, hearty, in fine fettle, in the pink, robust, sound, strong, vigorous, well

half 1. *n.* bisection, division, equal part, fifty per cent, fraction, hemisphere, portion, section 2. *adj.* divided, fractional, halved, incomplete, limited, moderate, partial 3. *adv.* after a fashion, all but, barely, inadequately, incompletely, in part, partially, partly, pretty nearly, slightly 4. **by half** considerably, excessively, very much

half-baked 1. brainless, crackpot (*Inf.*), crazy, foolish, harebrained, inane, loopy (*Inf.*), senseless, silly, stupid 2. ill-conceived, ill-judged, impractical, poorly planned, short-sighted, unformed, unthought out *or* through

half-hearted apathetic, cool, half-arsed, half-assed (*U.S. & Canad. sl.*), indifferent, lacklustre, listless, lukewarm, neutral, passive, perfunctory, spiritless, tame, unenthusiastic, uninterested

Antonyms ambitious, animated, avid, concerned, determined, eager, emotional, energetic, enthusiastic, excited, spirited, warm, wholehearted, zealous

halfway *adv.* 1. midway, to *or* in the middle, to the midpoint 2. incompletely, moderately, nearly, partially, partly, rather 3. **meet halfway** accommodate, come to terms, compromise, concede, give and take, strike a balance, trade off ~*adj.* 4. central, equidistant, intermediate, mid, middle, midway 5. imperfect, incomplete, moderate, partial, part-way

halfwit airhead (*Sl.*), berk (*Brit. sl.*), charlie (*Brit. inf.*), coot, dickhead (*Sl.*), dimwit (*Inf.*), dipstick (*Brit. sl.*), divvy (*Brit. sl.*), dolt, dork (*Sl.*), dullard, dunce, dunderhead, dweeb (*U.S. sl.*), fool, fuckwit (*Taboo sl.*), geek (*Sl.*), gonzo (*Sl.*), idiot, imbecile (*Inf.*), jerk (*Sl., chiefly U.S. & Canad.*), lamebrain (*Inf.*), mental defective, moron, nerd *or* nurd (*Sl.*), nitwit (*Inf.*), numskull *or* numbskull, oaf, pillock (*Brit. sl.*), plank (*Brit. sl.*), plonker (*Sl.*), prat (*Sl.*), prick (*Derogatory sl.*), schmuck (*U.S. sl.*), simpleton, twit (*Inf., chiefly Brit.*), wally (*Sl.*)

half-witted addle-brained, barmy (*Sl.*), batty (*Sl.*), crazy, doltish (*Inf.*), dull, dull-witted, feeble-minded, flaky (*U.S. sl.*), foolish, goofy (*Inf.*), ho-hum, idiotic, moronic, nerdish *or* nurdish (*Sl.*), obtuse, silly, simple, simple-minded, stupid

hall 1. corridor, entrance hall, entry, foyer, hallway, lobby, passage, passageway, vestibule 2. assembly room, auditorium, chamber, concert hall, meeting place

hallmark 1. authentication, device, endorsement, mark, seal, sign, signet, stamp, symbol 2. badge, emblem, indication, sure sign, telltale sign

halloo call, cry, hail, holla, shout

hallow bless, consecrate, dedicate, devote, enshrine, glorify, magnify (*Archaic*), respect, revere, reverence, sanctify, venerate

hallowed beatified, blessed, consecrated, dedicated, holy, honoured, inviolable, revered, sacred, sacrosanct, sanctified

hallucinate daydream, envision, fantasize, freak out (*Inf.*), have hallucinations, imagine, trip (*Inf.*)

hallucination aberration, apparition, delusion, dream, fantasy, figment of the imagination, illusion, mirage, phantasmagoria, vision

halo aura, aureole *or* aureola, corona, halation (*Photog.*), nimbus, radiance, ring of light

halt[1] *v.* 1. break off, call it a day, cease, close down, come to an end, desist, draw up, pull up, rest, stand still, stop, wait 2. arrest, block, bring to an end, check, curb, cut short, end, hold back, impede, obstruct, staunch, stem, terminate ~*n.* 3. arrest, break, close, end, impasse, interruption, pause, stand, standstill, stop, stoppage, termination

Antonyms *v.* aid, begin, boost, commence, continue, encourage, forward, go ahead, maintain, proceed, resume, start ~*n.* beginning, commencement, continuation, resumption, start

halt[2] *v.* **1.** be defective, falter, hobble, limp, stumble **2.** be unsure, boggle, dither (*Chiefly Brit.*), haver, hesitate, pause, stammer, swither (*Scot.*), think twice, waver ~*adj.* **3.** *Archaic* crippled, lame, limping

halting awkward, faltering, hesitant, imperfect, laboured, stammering, stumbling, stuttering

halve **1.** *v.* bisect, cut in half, divide equally, reduce by fifty per cent, share equally, split in two **2.** *n. Plural* **by halves** imperfectly, incompletely, scrappily, skimpily

hammer *v.* **1.** bang, beat, drive, hit, knock, lambast(e), strike, tap **2.** beat out, fashion, forge, form, make, shape **3.** *Often with* **into** din into, drive home, drub into, drum into, grind into, impress upon, instruct, repeat **4.** *Often with* **away (at)** beaver away (*Brit. inf.*), drudge, grind, keep on, peg away (*Chiefly Brit.*), persevere, persist, plug away (*Inf.*), pound away, stick at, work **5.** *Inf.* beat, blow out of the water (*Sl.*), clobber (*Sl.*), defeat, drub, lick (*Inf.*), master, run rings around (*Inf.*), slate (*Inf.*), tank (*Sl.*), thrash, trounce, undo, wipe the floor with (*Inf.*), worst

hammer out accomplish, bring about, come to a conclusion, complete, excogitate, finish, form a resolution, make a decision, negotiate, produce, settle, sort out, thrash out, work out

hamper *v.* bind, cramp, curb, embarrass, encumber, entangle, fetter, frustrate, hamstring, handicap, hinder, hold up, impede, interfere with, obstruct, prevent, restrain, restrict, slow down, thwart, trammel

Antonyms aid, assist, boost, encourage, expedite, forward, further, help, promote, speed

hamstring **1.** cripple, disable, hock, injure, lame **2.** balk, foil, frustrate, prevent, ruin, stop, thwart

hamstrung at a loss, crippled, disabled, helpless, *hors de combat,* incapacitated, paralysed

hand *n.* **1.** fist, hook, meathook (*Sl.*), mitt (*Sl.*), palm, paw (*Inf.*) **2.** agency, direction, influence, part, participation, share **3.** aid, assistance, help, support **4.** artificer, artisan, craftsman, employee, hired man, labourer, operative, worker, workman **5.** calligraphy, chirography, handwriting, longhand, penmanship, script **6.** clap, ovation, round of applause **7.** ability, art, artistry, skill **8. at** *or* **on hand** approaching, available, close, handy, imminent, near, nearby, on tap (*Inf.*), ready, within reach **9. from hand to mouth** by necessity, improvidently, in poverty, insecurely, on the breadline (*Inf.*), precariously, uncertainly **10. hand in glove** allied, in cahoots (*Inf.*), in league, in partnership **11. hand over fist** by leaps and bounds, easily, steadily, swiftly **12. in hand a.** in order, receiving attention, under control **b.** available for use, in reserve, put by, ready ~*v.* **13.** deliver, hand over, pass **14.** aid, assist, conduct, convey, give, guide, help, lead, present, transmit

handbook Baedeker, guide, guidebook, instruction book, manual, vade mecum

handcuff **1.** *v.* fetter, manacle, shackle **2.** *n. Plural* bracelets (*Sl.*), cuffs (*Inf.*), fetters, manacles, shackles

hand down *or* **on** bequeath, give, grant, pass on *or* down, transfer, will

handful few, small number, small quantity, smattering, sprinkling

Antonyms a lot, crowd, heaps, horde, large number, large quantity, loads (*Inf.*), masses (*Inf.*), mob, plenty, scores, stacks

handicap *n.* **1.** barrier, block, disadvantage, drawback, encumbrance, hindrance, impediment, limitation, millstone, obstacle, restriction, shortcoming, stumbling block **2.** advantage, edge, head start, odds, penalty, upper hand **3.** defect, disability, impairment ~*v.* **4.** burden, encumber, hamper, hamstring, hinder, hold back, impede, limit, place at a disadvantage, restrict, retard

Antonyms *n.* (*sense 1*) advantage, asset, benefit, boost, edge ~*v.* aid, assist, benefit, boost, forward, further, help, promote

handicraft art, artisanship, craft, craftsmanship, handiwork, skill, workmanship

handily **1.** adroitly, capably, cleverly, deftly, dexterously, expertly, proficiently, skilfully **2.** accessibly, advantageously, conveniently, helpfully, readily, suitably

handiness **1.** accessibility, availability, closeness, convenience, practicality, proximity, usefulness, workability **2.** adroitness, aptitude, cleverness, deftness, dexterity, efficiency, expertise, knack, proficiency, skill

handiwork **1.** craft, handicraft, handwork **2.** achievement, artefact, creation, design, invention, product, production, result

handle *n.* **1.** grip, haft, handgrip, helve, hilt, knob, stock ~*v.* **2.** feel, finger, fondle, grasp, hold, maul, paw (*Inf.*), pick up, poke, touch **3.** control, direct, guide, manage, manipulate, manoeuvre, operate, steer, use, wield **4.** administer, conduct, cope with, deal with, manage, supervise, take care of, treat

5. discourse, discuss, treat 6. carry, deal in, market, sell, stock, trade, traffic in

handling administration, approach, conduct, direction, management, manipulation, running, treatment

hand-me-down *adj.* cast-off, handed down, inherited, passed on, reach-me-down (*Inf.*), second-hand, used, worn

hand-out 1. alms, charity, dole 2. bulletin, circular, free sample, leaflet, literature (*Inf.*), mailshot, press release

hand out deal out, disburse, dish out (*Inf.*), dispense, disseminate, distribute, give out, mete

hand over deliver, donate, fork out *or* up (*Sl.*), present, release, surrender, transfer, turn over, yield

hand-picked choice, chosen, elect, elite, recherché, select, selected
Antonyms haphazard, indiscriminate, random, run-of-the-mill, wholesale

hands 1. authority, care, charge, command, control, custody, disposal, guardianship, keeping, possession, power, supervision 2. **hands down** easily, effortlessly, with no contest, with no trouble

handsome 1. admirable, attractive, becoming, comely, dishy (*Inf., chiefly Brit.*), elegant, fine, good-looking, gorgeous, graceful, majestic, personable, stately, well-proportioned 2. abundant, ample, bountiful, considerable, generous, gracious, large, liberal, magnanimous, plentiful, sizable
Antonyms base, cheap, inelegant, meagre, mean, miserly, selfish, small, stingy, tasteless, ugly, unattractive, ungenerous, unprepossessing, unsightly

handsomely abundantly, amply, bountifully, generously, liberally, magnanimously, munificently, plentifully, richly

handwriting calligraphy, chirography, fist, hand, longhand, penmanship, scrawl, script

handy 1. accessible, at *or* on hand, available, close, convenient, near, nearby, within reach 2. convenient, easy to use, helpful, manageable, neat, practical, serviceable, useful, user-friendly 3. adept, adroit, clever, deft, dexterous, expert, nimble, proficient, ready, skilful, skilled
Antonyms awkward, clumsy, ham-fisted, inaccessible, incompetent, inconvenient, inept, inexpert, maladroit, out of the way, unaccomplished, unavailable, unskilful, unskilled, unwieldy, useless

hang *v.* 1. be pendent, dangle, depend, droop, incline, suspend 2. execute, gibbet, send to the gallows, string up (*Inf.*) 3. adhere, cling, hold, rest, stick 4. attach, cover, deck, decorate, drape, fasten, fix, furnish 5. be poised, drift, float, hover, remain, swing 6. bend downward, bend forward, bow, dangle, drop, incline, lean over, let droop, loll, lower, sag, trail 7. **hang fire** be slow, be suspended, delay, hang back, procrastinate, stall, stick, vacillate ~*n.* 8. **get the hang of** comprehend, get the knack *or* technique, grasp, understand

hang about *or* **around** 1. dally, linger, loiter, roam, tarry, waste time 2. associate with, frequent, hang out (*Inf.*), haunt, resort

hang back be backward, be reluctant, demur, hesitate, hold back, recoil

hangdog *adj.* abject, browbeaten, cowed, cringing, defeated, downcast, furtive, guilty, shamefaced, sneaking, wretched

hanger-on dependant, follower, freeloader (*Sl.*), lackey, leech, ligger (*Sl.*), minion, parasite, sponger (*Inf.*), sycophant

hanging *adj.* 1. dangling, drooping, flapping, flopping, floppy, loose, pendent, suspended, swinging, unattached, unsupported 2. undecided, unresolved, unsettled, up in the air (*Inf.*) 3. beetle, beetling, jutting, overhanging, projecting, prominent

hang on 1. carry on, continue, endure, go on, hold on, hold out, persevere, persist, remain 2. cling, clutch, grasp, grip, hold fast 3. be conditional upon, be contingent on, be dependent on, be determined by, depend on, hinge, rest, turn on 4. *Also* **hang onto, hang upon** be rapt, give ear, listen attentively 5. *Inf.* hold on, hold the line, remain, stop, wait

hang-out den, dive (*Sl.*), haunt, home, joint (*Sl.*), resort

hangover aftereffects, crapulence, head (*Inf.*), morning after (*Inf.*)

hang over be imminent, impend, loom, menace, threaten

hang-up block, difficulty, inhibition, obsession, preoccupation, problem, thing (*Inf.*)

hank coil, length, loop, piece, roll, skein

hanker *With* **for** *or* **after** covet, crave, desire, eat one's heart out over, hope, hunger, itch, long, lust, pine, thirst, want, wish, yearn, yen (*Inf.*)

hankering craving, desire, hope, hunger, itch, longing, pining, thirst, urge, wish, yearning, yen (*Inf.*)

hanky-panky chicanery, deception, devilry, funny business (*Inf.*), jiggery-pokery (*Inf., chiefly Brit.*), knavery, machinations, mischief, monkey business (*Inf.*), shenanigans (*Inf.*), subterfuge, trickery

haphazard 1. accidental, arbitrary, chance, fluky (*Inf.*), random 2. aimless, careless,

casual, disorderly, disorganized, hit or miss (*Inf.*), indiscriminate, slapdash, slipshod, unmethodical, unsystematic
Antonyms arranged, careful, considered, deliberate, methodical, orderly, organized, planned, systematic, thoughtful

hapless cursed, ill-fated, ill-starred, jinxed, luckless, miserable, unfortunate, unhappy, unlucky, wretched

happen 1. appear, arise, come about, come off (*Inf.*), come to pass, crop up (*Inf.*), develop, ensue, eventuate, follow, materialize, occur, present itself, result, take place, transpire (*Inf.*) 2. become of, befall, betide 3. chance, fall out, have the fortune to be, pan out (*Inf.*), supervene, turn out

happening accident, adventure, affair, case, chance, episode, escapade, event, experience, incident, occasion, occurrence, phenomenon, proceeding, scene

happen on *or* **upon** chance upon, come upon, discover unexpectedly, find, hit upon, light upon, stumble on, turn up

happily 1. agreeably, contentedly, delightedly, enthusiastically, freely, gladly, heartily, lief (*Rare*), willingly, with pleasure 2. blithely, cheerfully, gaily, gleefully, joyfully, joyously, merrily 3. auspiciously, favourably, fortunately, luckily, opportunely, propitiously, providentially, seasonably 4. appropriately, aptly, felicitously, gracefully, successfully

happiness beatitude, blessedness, bliss, cheer, cheerfulness, cheeriness, contentment, delight, ecstasy, elation, enjoyment, exuberance, felicity, gaiety, gladness, high spirits, joy, jubilation, light-heartedness, merriment, pleasure, prosperity, satisfaction, wellbeing
Antonyms annoyance, bane, depression, despondency, distress, grief, low spirits, misery, misfortune, sadness, sorrow, unhappiness

happy 1. blessed, blest, blissful, blithe, cheerful, cock-a-hoop, content, contented, delighted, ecstatic, elated, glad, gratified, jolly, joyful, joyous, jubilant, merry, overjoyed, over the moon (*Inf.*), pleased, rapt, sunny, thrilled, walking on air (*Inf.*) 2. advantageous, appropriate, apt, auspicious, befitting, convenient, enviable, favourable, felicitous, fortunate, lucky, opportune, promising, propitious, satisfactory, seasonable, successful, timely, well-timed
Antonyms depressed, despondent, discontented, displeased, down in the dumps, forlorn, gloomy, inapt, joyless, melancholy, miserable, mournful, sad, sombre, sorrowful, sorry, unfortunate, unhappy, unlucky

happy-go-lucky blithe, carefree, casual, devil-may-care, easy-going, heedless, improvident, insouciant, irresponsible, light-hearted, nonchalant, unconcerned, untroubled
Antonyms careworn, cheerless, gloomy, melancholy, morose, sad, serious, unhappy

harangue 1. *n.* address, declamation, diatribe, exhortation, lecture, oration, philippic, screed, speech, spiel (*Inf.*), tirade 2. *v.* address, declaim, exhort, hold forth, lecture, rant, spout (*Inf.*)

harass annoy, badger, bait, beleaguer, be on one's back (*Sl.*), bother, chivvy (*Brit.*), devil (*Inf.*), disturb, exasperate, exhaust, fatigue, harry, hassle (*Inf.*), hound, perplex, persecute, pester, plague, tease, tire, torment, trouble, vex, weary, worry

harassed careworn, distraught, harried, hassled (*Inf.*), plagued, strained, tormented, troubled, under pressure, under stress, vexed, worried

harassment aggravation (*Inf.*), annoyance, badgering, bedevilment, bother, hassle (*Inf.*), irritation, molestation, nuisance, persecution, pestering, torment, trouble, vexation

harbinger forerunner, foretoken, herald, indication, messenger, omen, portent, precursor, sign

harbour *n.* 1. anchorage, destination, haven, port 2. asylum, covert, haven, refuge, retreat, sanctuary, sanctum, security, shelter ~*v.* 3. conceal, hide, lodge, protect, provide refuge, relieve, secrete, shelter, shield 4. believe, brood over, cherish, cling to, entertain, foster, hold, imagine, maintain, nurse, nurture, retain

hard *adj.* 1. compact, dense, firm, impenetrable, inflexible, rigid, rocklike, solid, stiff, stony, strong, tough, unyielding 2. arduous, backbreaking, burdensome, exacting, exhausting, fatiguing, formidable, Herculean, laborious, rigorous, strenuous, toilsome, tough, uphill, wearying 3. baffling, complex, complicated, difficult, intricate, involved, knotty, perplexing, puzzling, tangled, thorny, unfathomable 4. callous, cold, cruel, exacting, grim, hardhearted, harsh, implacable, obdurate, pitiless, ruthless, severe, stern, strict, stubborn, unfeeling, unjust, unkind, unrelenting, unsparing, unsympathetic 5. calamitous, dark, disagreeable, disastrous, distressing, grievous, grim, intolerable, painful, unpleasant 6. driving, fierce, forceful, heavy, powerful, strong, violent 7. *Of feelings or words* acrimonious, angry, antagonistic, bitter, hostile, rancorous, resentful 8. *Of truth or facts* actual, bare, cold, definite, indisputable, plain, undeniable, unvarnished, verified

~*adv.* 9. energetically, fiercely, forcefully, forcibly, heavily, intensely, powerfully, severely, sharply, strongly, vigorously, violently, with all one's might, with might and main 10. assiduously, determinedly, diligently, doggedly, earnestly, industriously, intently, persistently, steadily, strenuously, untiringly 11. agonizingly, badly, distressingly, harshly, laboriously, painfully, roughly, severely, with difficulty 12. bitterly, hardly, keenly, rancorously, reluctantly, resentfully, slowly, sorely
Antonyms *adj.* agreeable, amiable, careless, clear, direct, easy, easy-peasy (*Sl.*), flexible, friendly, gentle, good, humane, kind, lazy, lenient, light, malleable, merciful, mild, permissive, pleasant, pliable, simple, soft, straightforward, uncomplicated, weak ~*adv.* calmly, easily, gently, lazily, lightly, loosely, mildly, serenely, softly, weakly

hard and fast binding, immutable, incontrovertible, inflexible, invariable, rigid, set, strict, stringent, unalterable

hard-bitten *or* **hard-boiled** case-hardened, cynical, down-to-earth, hard-headed, hard-nosed (*Inf.*), matter-of-fact, practical, realistic, shrewd, tough, unsentimental
Antonyms benign, compassionate, gentle, humane, idealistic, merciful, mild, romantic, sympathetic

hard-core 1. dedicated, die-hard, dyed-in-the-wool, extreme, intransigent, obstinate, rigid, staunch, steadfast 2. explicit, obscene

harden 1. anneal, bake, cake, freeze, set, solidify, stiffen 2. brace, buttress, fortify, gird, indurate, nerve, reinforce, steel, strengthen, toughen 3. accustom, brutalize, case-harden, habituate, inure, season, train

hardened 1. chronic, fixed, habitual, incorrigible, inveterate, irredeemable, reprobate, set, shameless 2. accustomed, habituated, inured, seasoned, toughened
Antonyms infrequent, irregular, occasional, rare, unaccustomed

hard-favoured *or* **hard-featured** austere, coarse-featured, forbidding, grim visaged, ill-favoured, severe, ugly

hard-headed astute, cool, hard-boiled (*Inf.*), level-headed, practical, pragmatic, realistic, sensible, shrewd, tough, unsentimental
Antonyms idealistic, impractical, sentimental, unrealistic

hardhearted callous, cold, cruel, hard, heartless, indifferent, inhuman, insensitive, intolerant, merciless, pitiless, stony, uncaring, unfeeling, unkind, unsympathetic
Antonyms compassionate, forgiving, gentle, humane, kind, loving, merciful, sensitive, soft-hearted, sympathetic, understanding, warm, warm-hearted

hard-hitting critical, no holds barred, pulling no punches, strongly worded, tough, uncompromising, unsparing, vigorous

hardihood 1. backbone, boldness, bottle (*Brit. sl.*), bravery, courage, daring, determination, firmness, grit, guts (*Inf.*), intrepidity, mettle, nerve, pluck, resolution, spirit, spunk (*Inf.*), strength 2. assurance, audacity, effrontery, foolhardiness, impertinence, impetuousness, rashness, recklessness, temerity

hardiness boldness, courage, fortitude, intrepidity, resilience, resolution, robustness, ruggedness, sturdiness, toughness, valour

hardline definite, inflexible, intransigent, tough, uncompromising, undeviating, unyielding

hardly almost not, barely, by no means, faintly, infrequently, just, not at all, not quite, no way, only, only just, scarcely, with difficulty
Antonyms abundantly, amply, by all means, certainly, completely, easily, fully, indubitably, more than, really, truly, undoubtedly, well over

hard-pressed harried, hotly pursued, in difficulties, pushed (*Inf.*), under attack, under pressure, up against it (*Inf.*), with one's back to the wall

hardship adversity, affliction, austerity, burden, calamity, destitution, difficulty, fatigue, grievance, labour, misery, misfortune, need, oppression, persecution, privation, suffering, toil, torment, trial, tribulation, trouble, want
Antonyms aid, blessing, boon, comfort, ease, good fortune, happiness, help, prosperity, relief

hard up bankrupt, broke (*Inf.*), bust (*Inf.*), cleaned out (*Sl.*), dirt-poor (*Inf.*), down and out, flat broke (*Inf.*), impecunious, impoverished, in the red (*Inf.*), on one's uppers (*Inf.*), out of pocket, penniless, poor, short, short of cash *or* funds, skint (*Brit. sl.*), without two pennies to rub together (*Inf.*)
Antonyms affluent, comfortable (*Inf.*), fortunate, loaded (*Sl.*), rich, wealthy, well-heeled (*Inf.*), well-off

hard-wearing durable, resilient, rugged, stout, strong, tough, well-made

hard-working assiduous, busy, conscientious, diligent, energetic, indefatigable, industrious, sedulous, zealous

Antonyms careless, dilatory, inconstant, indifferent, lazy

hardy 1. firm, fit, hale, healthy, hearty, in fine fettle, lusty, robust, rugged, sound, stalwart, stout, strong, sturdy, tough, vigorous 2. bold, brave, courageous, daring, feisty (*Inf., chiefly U.S. & Canad.*), gritty, heroic, intrepid, manly, plucky, resolute, stouthearted, valiant, valorous 3. audacious, brazen, foolhardy, headstrong, impudent, rash, reckless

Antonyms delicate, faint-hearted, feeble, fragile, frail, sickly, soft, weak, weedy (*Inf.*), wimpish *or* wimpy (*Inf.*)

harebrained asinine, careless, empty-headed, flighty, foolish, giddy, half-baked (*Inf.*), harum-scarum, heedless, inane, mindless, rash, reckless, scatterbrained, unstable, unsteady, wild

hark attend, give ear, give heed, hear, hearken (*Archaic*), listen, mark, notice, pay attention

hark back look back, recall, recollect, regress, remember, revert, think back

harlot call girl, fallen woman, hussy, loose woman, pro (*Sl.*), prostitute, scrubber (*Brit. & Aust. sl.*), slag (*Brit. sl.*), streetwalker, strumpet, tart (*Inf.*), tramp (*Sl.*), whore, working girl (*Facetious sl.*)

harm *n.* 1. abuse, damage, detriment, disservice, hurt, ill, impairment, injury, loss, mischief, misfortune 2. evil, immorality, iniquity, sin, sinfulness, vice, wickedness, wrong *~v.* 3. abuse, blemish, damage, hurt, ill-treat, ill-use, impair, injure, maltreat, mar, molest, ruin, spoil, wound

Antonyms *n.* aid, assistance, benefit, blessing, boon, gain, good, goodness, help, improvement, reparation, righteousness *~v.* aid, alleviate, ameliorate, assist, benefit, better, cure, heal, help, improve, repair

harmful baleful, baneful, damaging, deleterious, destructive, detrimental, disadvantageous, evil, hurtful, injurious, maleficent, noxious, pernicious

Antonyms beneficial, good, harmless, healthy, helpful, innocuous, safe, wholesome

harmless gentle, innocent, innocuous, innoxious, inoffensive, nontoxic, not dangerous, safe, unobjectionable

Antonyms dangerous, destructive, harmful, unhealthy, unsafe, unwholesome

harmonious 1. agreeable, compatible, concordant, congruous, consonant, coordinated, correspondent, dulcet, euphonic, euphonious, harmonic, harmonizing, matching, mellifluous, melodious, musical, sweet-sounding, symphonious (*Literary*), tuneful 2. agreeable, amicable, compatible, concordant, congenial, cordial, *en rapport*, fraternal, friendly, in accord, in harmony, in unison, of one mind, sympathetic

Antonyms cacophonous, contrasting, discordant, grating, harsh, incompatible, inconsistent, unfriendly, unlike, unmelodious

harmonize accord, adapt, agree, arrange, attune, be in unison, be of one mind, blend, chime with, cohere, compose, coordinate, correspond, match, reconcile, suit, tally, tone in with

harmony 1. accord, agreement, amicability, amity, assent, compatibility, concord, conformity, consensus, cooperation, friendship, good will, like-mindedness, peace, rapport, sympathy, unanimity, understanding, unity 2. balance, compatibility, concord, congruity, consistency, consonance, coordination, correspondence, fitness, parallelism, suitability, symmetry 3. euphony, melodiousness, melody, tune, tunefulness, unison

Antonyms antagonism, cacophony, conflict, contention, disagreement, dissension, hostility, incongruity, inconsistency, opposition, unsuitability

harness *n.* 1. equipment, gear, tack, tackle, trappings 2. **in harness** active, at work, busy, in action, working *~v.* 3. couple, hitch up, put in harness, saddle, yoke 4. apply, channel, control, employ, exploit, make productive, mobilize, render useful, turn to account, utilize

harp *With* **on** *or* **upon** dwell on, go on, labour, press, reiterate, renew, repeat

harping *n.* nagging, reiteration, repetition

harridan ballbreaker (*Sl.*), battle-axe (*Inf.*), nag, scold, shrew, tartar, termagant, virago, witch, Xanthippe

harried agitated, anxious, beset, bothered, distressed, hag-ridden, harassed, hard-pressed, hassled (*Inf.*), plagued, tormented, troubled, worried

harrow *v. Fig.* agonize, distress, harass, lacerate, perturb, rack, rend, tear, torment, torture, vex, wound, wring

harrowing agonizing, alarming, chilling, distressing, disturbing, excruciating, frightening, heartbreaking, heart-rending, nerve-racking, painful, racking, scaring, terrifying, tormenting, traumatic

harry 1. annoy, badger, bedevil, be on one's back (*Sl.*), bother, chivvy, disturb, fret, get in one's hair (*Inf.*), harass, hassle (*Inf.*), molest, persecute, pester, plague, tease, torment, trouble, vex, worry 2. depredate (*Rare*), despoil, devastate, pillage, plunder, raid, ravage, rob, sack

harsh 1. coarse, croaking, crude, discordant,

dissonant, glaring, grating, guttural, jarring, rasping, raucous, rough, strident, unmelodious 2. abusive, austere, bitter, bleak, brutal, comfortless, cruel, dour, Draconian, drastic, grim, hard, pitiless, punitive, relentless, ruthless, severe, sharp, Spartan, stern, stringent, unfeeling, unkind, unpleasant, unrelenting
Antonyms agreeable, gentle, harmonious, kind, loving, mellifluous, merciful, mild, pleasant, smooth, soft, soothing, sweet

harshly brutally, cruelly, grimly, roughly, severely, sharply, sternly, strictly

harshness acerbity, acrimony, asperity, austerity, bitterness, brutality, churlishness, coarseness, crudity, hardness, ill-temper, rigour, roughness, severity, sourness, sternness

harum-scarum careless, erratic, giddy, haphazard, harebrained, hasty, ill-considered, impetuous, imprudent, inconstant, irresponsible, precipitate, rash, reckless, scatterbrained, scatty (*Brit. inf.*), wild

harvest *n.* 1. harvesting, harvest-time, ingathering, reaping 2. crop, produce, yield 3. *Fig.* consequence, effect, fruition, product, result, return ~*v.* 4. gather, mow, pick, pluck, reap 5. accumulate, acquire, amass, collect, garner

hash 1. balls-up (*Taboo sl.*), cock-up (*Brit. sl.*), confusion, fuck-up (*Offens. taboo sl.*), hodgepodge (*U.S.*), hotchpotch, jumble, mess, mishmash, mix-up, muddle, pig's breakfast (*Inf.*), pig's ear (*Inf.*), shambles, state 2. **make a hash of** *Inf.* bodge (*Inf.*), botch, bungle, cock up (*Brit. sl.*), fuck up (*Offens. taboo sl.*), jumble, mess up, mishandle, mismanage, mix, muddle

hassle *n.* 1. altercation, argument, bickering, disagreement, dispute, fight, quarrel, row, squabble, tussle, wrangle 2. bother, difficulty, inconvenience, problem, struggle, trial, trouble, upset ~*v.* 3. annoy, badger, be on one's back (*Sl.*), bother, bug (*Inf.*), get in one's hair (*Inf.*), get on one's nerves (*Inf.*), harass, harry, hound, pester

haste 1. alacrity, briskness, celerity, dispatch, expedition, fleetness, nimbleness, promptitude, quickness, rapidity, rapidness, speed, swiftness, urgency, velocity 2. bustle, hastiness, helter-skelter, hurry, hustle, impetuosity, precipitateness, rashness, recklessness, rush
Antonyms calmness, care, delay, deliberation, leisureliness, slowness, sluggishness, sureness

hasten 1. barrel (along) (*Inf., chiefly U.S. & Canad.*), beetle, bolt, burn rubber (*Inf.*), dash, fly, haste, hurry (up), make haste, race, run, rush, scurry, scuttle, speed, sprint, step on it (*Inf.*), tear (along) 2. accelerate, advance, dispatch, expedite, goad, hurry (up), precipitate, press, push forward, quicken, speed (up), step up (*Inf.*), urge
Antonyms crawl, creep, dawdle, decelerate, delay, hinder, impede, move slowly, retard, slow, slow down

hastily 1. apace, double-quick, fast, hotfoot, pdq (*Sl.*), posthaste, promptly, pronto (*Inf.*), quickly, rapidly, speedily, straightaway 2. heedlessly, hurriedly, impetuously, impulsively, on the spur of the moment, precipitately, rashly, recklessly, too quickly

hasty 1. brisk, eager, expeditious, fast, fleet, hurried, prompt, rapid, speedy, swift, urgent 2. brief, cursory, fleeting, passing, perfunctory, rushed, short, superficial 3. foolhardy, headlong, heedless, impetuous, impulsive, indiscreet, precipitate, rash, reckless, thoughtless, unduly quick 4. brusque, excited, fiery, hot-headed, hot-tempered, impatient, irascible, irritable, passionate, quick-tempered, snappy
Antonyms careful, cautious, detailed, dispassionate, leisurely, long, protracted, slow, thorough, thoughtful

hatch 1. breed, bring forth, brood, incubate 2. *Fig.* conceive, concoct, contrive, cook up (*Inf.*), design, devise, dream up (*Inf.*), manufacture, plan, plot, project, scheme, think up, trump up

hatchet man assassin, bravo, calumniator, cutthroat, debunker, defamer, destroyer, detractor, gunman, heavy (*Sl.*), hired assassin, hit man (*Sl.*), killer, murderer, smear campaigner, thug, traducer

hate *v.* 1. abhor, abominate, be hostile to, be repelled by, be sick of, despise, detest, dislike, execrate, have an aversion to, loathe, recoil from 2. be loath, be reluctant, be sorry, be unwilling, dislike, feel disinclined, have no stomach for, shrink from ~*n.* 3. abhorrence, abomination, animosity, animus, antagonism, antipathy, aversion, detestation, dislike, enmity, execration, hatred, hostility, loathing, odium
Antonyms *v.* be fond of, cherish, dote on, enjoy, esteem, fancy, like, love, relish, treasure, wish ~*n.* affection, amity, devotion, fondness, goodwill, liking, love

hateful abhorrent, abominable, despicable, detestable, disgusting, execrable, forbidding, foul, heinous, horrible, loathsome, obnoxious, obscene, odious, offensive, repellent, repugnant, repulsive, revolting, vile
Antonyms affectionate, attractive, beautiful, charming, desirable, devoted, friendly,

good, kind, likable *or* likeable, lovable, loving, pleasant, wonderful

hatred abomination, animosity, animus, antagonism, antipathy, aversion, detestation, dislike, enmity, execration, hate, ill will, odium, repugnance, revulsion
Antonyms affection, amity, attachment, devotion, fondness, friendliness, good will, liking, love

haughtiness airs, aloofness, arrogance, conceit, contempt, contemptuousness, disdain, hauteur, insolence, loftiness, pomposity, pride, snobbishness, superciliousness

haughty arrogant, assuming, conceited, contemptuous, disdainful, high, high and mighty (*Inf.*), hoity-toity (*Inf.*), imperious, lofty, overweening, proud, scornful, snobbish, snooty (*Inf.*), stuck-up (*Inf.*), supercilious, uppish (*Brit. inf.*)
Antonyms humble, meek, mild, modest, self-effacing, subservient, wimpish *or* wimpy (*Inf.*)

haul *v.* 1. drag, draw, hale, heave, lug, pull, tow, trail, tug 2. carry, cart, convey, hump (*Brit. sl.*), move, transport ~*n.* 3. drag, heave, pull, tug 4. booty, catch, find, gain, harvest, loot, spoils, takings, yield

haunt *v.* 1. visit, walk 2. beset, come back, obsess, plague, possess, prey on, recur, stay with, torment, trouble, weigh on 3. frequent, hang around *or* about, repair, resort, visit ~*n.* 4. den, gathering place, hangout (*Inf.*), meeting place, rendezvous, resort, stamping ground

haunted 1. cursed, eerie, ghostly, jinxed, possessed, spooky (*Inf.*) 2. obsessed, plagued, preoccupied, tormented, troubled, worried

haunting disturbing, eerie, evocative, indelible, nostalgic, persistent, poignant, recurrent, recurring, unforgettable

hauteur affectedness, airs, arrogance, contempt, dignity, disdain, haughtiness, loftiness, pride, snobbishness, stateliness, superciliousness

have 1. hold, keep, obtain, occupy, own, possess, retain 2. accept, acquire, gain, get, obtain, procure, receive, secure, take 3. comprehend, comprise, contain, embody, include, take in 4. endure, enjoy, experience, feel, meet with, suffer, sustain, undergo 5. *Sl.* cheat, deceive, dupe, fool, outwit, stiff (*Sl.*), swindle, take in (*Inf.*), trick 6. *Usually* **have to** be bound, be compelled, be forced, be obliged, have got to, must, ought, should 7. allow, consider, entertain, permit, put up with (*Inf.*), think about, tolerate 8. bear, beget, bring forth, bring into the world, deliver, give birth to 9. **have had it** *Inf.* be defeated, be exhausted, be finished, be out, be past it (*Inf.*), be pooped (*U.S. sl.*), be stonkered (*Sl.*)

haven 1. anchorage, harbour, port, roads (*Nautical*) 2. *Fig.* asylum, refuge, retreat, sanctuary, sanctum, shelter

have on 1. be clothed in, be dressed in, wear 2. be committed to, be engaged to, have on the agenda, have planned 3. *Of a person* deceive, kid (*Inf.*), play a joke on, tease, trick, wind up (*Brit. sl.*)

havoc 1. carnage, damage, desolation, despoliation, destruction, devastation, rack and ruin, ravages, ruin, slaughter, waste, wreck 2. *Inf.* chaos, confusion, disorder, disruption, mayhem, shambles 3. **play havoc (with)** bring into chaos, confuse, demolish, destroy, devastate, disorganize, disrupt, wreck

hawk *v.* 1. bark (*Inf.*), cry, market, peddle, sell, tout (*Inf.*), vend 2. *Often with* **about** bandy about (*Inf.*), bruit about, buzz, noise abroad, put about, retail, rumour

hawker barrow boy (*Brit.*), cheap-jack (*Inf.*), colporteur, crier, huckster, pedlar, vendor

haywire 1. *Of things* chaotic, confused, disarranged, disordered, disorganized, mixed up, on the blink (*Sl.*), out of commission, out of order, shambolic (*Inf.*), tangled, topsy-turvy 2. *Of people* crazy, erratic, mad, wild

hazard *n.* 1. danger, endangerment, imperilment, jeopardy, peril, pitfall, risk, threat 2. accident, chance, coincidence, fluke, luck, misfortune, mishap, stroke of luck ~*v.* 3. chance, dare, gamble, risk, stake 4. advance, conjecture, offer, presume, proffer, speculate, submit, suppose, throw out, venture, volunteer 5. endanger, expose, imperil, jeopardize, risk, threaten

hazardous 1. dangerous, dicey (*Inf., chiefly Brit.*), difficult, fraught with danger, hairy (*Sl.*), insecure, perilous, precarious, risky, unsafe 2. chancy (*Inf.*), haphazard, precarious, uncertain, unpredictable
Antonyms reliable, safe, secure, sound, stable, sure

haze cloud, dimness, film, fog, mist, obscurity, smog, smokiness, steam, vapour

hazy 1. blurry, cloudy, dim, dull, faint, foggy, misty, nebulous, obscure, overcast, smoky, veiled 2. *Fig.* fuzzy, ill-defined, indefinite, indistinct, loose, muddled, muzzy, nebulous, uncertain, unclear, vague
Antonyms bright, certain, clear, detailed, light, sunny, well-defined

head *n.* 1. bean (*U.S. & Canad. sl.*), conk (*Sl.*), cranium, crown, loaf (*Sl.*), noddle (*Inf., chiefly Brit.*), noggin, nut (*Sl.*), pate, skull 2. boss (*Inf.*), captain, chief, chieftain, commander, director, headmaster, headmistress, head teacher, leader, manager, master, principal, superintendent, supervisor 3. apex, crest, crown, height, peak, pitch, summit, tip, top, vertex 4. cutting edge, first place, fore, forefront, front, van, vanguard 5. beginning, commencement, origin, rise, source, start 6. ability, aptitude, brain, brains (*Inf.*), capacity, faculty, flair, intellect, intelligence, mentality, mind, talent, thought, understanding 7. branch, category, class, department, division, heading, section, subject, topic 8. climax, conclusion, crisis, culmination, end, turning point 9. *Geog.* cape, foreland, headland, point, promontory 10. **go to one's head** dizzy, excite, intoxicate, make conceited, puff up 11. **head over heels** completely, intensely, thoroughly, uncontrollably, utterly, wholeheartedly 12. **put (our, their,** *etc.*) **heads together** *Inf.* confab (*Inf.*), confabulate, confer, consult, deliberate, discuss, palaver, powwow, talk over ~*adj.* 13. arch, chief, first, foremost, front, highest, leading, main, pre-eminent, premier, prime, principal, supreme, topmost ~*v.* 14. be *or* go first, cap, crown, lead, lead the way, precede, top 15. be in charge of, command, control, direct, govern, guide, lead, manage, rule, run, supervise 16. *Often with* **for** aim, go to, make a beeline for, make for, point, set off for, set out, start towards, steer, turn

headache 1. cephalalgia (*Medical*), head (*Inf.*), migraine, neuralgia 2. *Inf.* bane, bother, inconvenience, nuisance, problem, trouble, vexation, worry

headfirst 1. *adj./adv.* diving, headlong, head-on 2. ~*adv.* carelessly, hastily, head over heels, precipitately, rashly, recklessly

heading 1. caption, headline, name, rubric, title 2. category, class, division, section

headland bill, bluff, cape, cliff, foreland, head, mull (*Scot.*), point, promontory

headlong 1. *adj./adv.* headfirst, headforemost, head-on 2. ~*adj.* breakneck, dangerous, hasty, impetuous, impulsive, inconsiderate, precipitate, reckless, thoughtless 3. ~*adv.* hastily, heedlessly, helter-skelter, hurriedly, pell-mell, precipitately, rashly, thoughtlessly, wildly

head off 1. block off, cut off, deflect, divert, intercept, interpose, intervene 2. avert, fend off, forestall, parry, prevent, stop, ward off

headstrong contrary, foolhardy, froward, heedless, imprudent, impulsive, intractable, mulish, obstinate, perverse, pigheaded, rash, reckless, self-willed, stiff-necked, stubborn, ungovernable, unruly, wilful

Antonyms cautious, impressionable, manageable, pliant, subservient, tractable

headway 1. advance, improvement, progress, progression, way 2. **make headway** advance, come *or* get on, cover ground, develop, gain, gain ground, make strides, progress

heady 1. inebriating, intoxicating, potent, spirituous, strong 2. exciting, exhilarating, intoxicating, overwhelming, stimulating, thrilling 3. hasty, impetuous, impulsive, inconsiderate, precipitate, rash, reckless, thoughtless

heal 1. cure, make well, mend, regenerate, remedy, restore, treat 2. alleviate, ameliorate, compose, conciliate, harmonize, patch up, reconcile, settle, soothe

Antonyms aggravate, exacerbate, harm, hurt, inflame, injure, make worse, reopen, wound

healing 1. analeptic, curative, medicinal, remedial, restorative, restoring, sanative, therapeutic 2. assuaging, comforting, emollient, gentle, lenitive, mild, mitigative, palliative, soothing

health 1. fitness, good condition, haleness, healthiness, robustness, salubrity, soundness, strength, vigour, wellbeing 2. condition, constitution, fettle, form, shape, state, tone

Antonyms (*sense 1*) debility, disease, frailty, illness, sickness, weakness

healthful beneficial, bracing, good for one, health-giving, healthy, invigorating, nourishing, nutritious, salubrious, salutary, wholesome

healthy 1. active, blooming, fit, flourishing, hale, hale and hearty, hardy, hearty, in fine feather, in fine fettle, in fine form, in good condition, in good shape (*Inf.*), in the pink, physically fit, robust, sound, strong, sturdy, vigorous, well 2. beneficial, bracing, good for one, healthful, health-giving, hygienic, invigorating, nourishing, nutritious, salubrious, salutary, wholesome

Antonyms ailing, debilitated, delicate, diseased, feeble, fragile, frail, ill, infirm, poorly (*Inf.*), sick, sickly, unfit, unhealthy, unsound, unwell, unwholesome, weak, weedy (*Inf.*)

heap *n.* 1. accumulation, aggregation, collection, hoard, lot, mass, mound, mountain, pile, stack, stockpile, store 2. *Often plural Inf.* abundance, a lot, great deal, lashings (*Brit. inf.*), load(s) (*Inf.*), lots (*Inf.*), mass, mint, ocean(s), oodles (*Inf.*), plenty, pot(s) (*Inf.*), quantities, stack(s), tons ~*v.* 3. accumulate, amass, augment, bank, collect, gather, hoard, increase, mound, pile, stack, stockpile, store 4. assign, bestow, burden, confer, load, shower upon

hear 1. attend, be all ears (*Inf.*), catch, eavesdrop, give attention, hark, hearken (*Archaic*), heed, listen in, listen to, overhear 2. ascertain, be informed, be told of, discover, find out, gather, get wind of (*Inf.*), hear tell (*Dialect*), learn, pick up, understand 3. *Law* examine, investigate, judge, try

hearing 1. audition, auditory, ear, perception 2. audience, audition, chance to speak, interview 3. auditory range, earshot, hearing distance, range, reach, sound 4. industrial tribunal, inquiry, investigation, review, trial

hearsay buzz, dirt (*U.S. sl.*), gossip, grapevine (*Inf.*), idle talk, mere talk, *on dit,* report, rumour, scuttlebutt (*Sl., chiefly U.S.*), talk, talk of the town, tittle-tattle, word of mouth

heart 1. character, disposition, emotion, feeling, inclination, nature, sentiment, soul, sympathy, temperament 2. affection, benevolence, compassion, concern, humanity, love, pity, tenderness, understanding 3. balls (*Taboo sl.*), boldness, bravery, courage, fortitude, guts (*Inf.*), mettle, mind, nerve, pluck, purpose, resolution, spirit, spunk (*Inf.*), will 4. central part, centre, core, crux, essence, hub, kernel, marrow, middle, nucleus, pith, quintessence, root 5. **at heart** *au fond,* basically, essentially, fundamentally, in essence, in reality, really, truly 6. **by heart** by memory, by rote, off pat, parrot-fashion (*Inf.*), pat, word for word 7. **eat one's heart out** agonize, brood, grieve, mope, mourn, pine, regret, repine, sorrow 8. **from (the bottom of) one's heart** deeply, devoutly, fervently, heart and soul, heartily, sincerely, with all one's heart 9. **heart and soul** absolutely, completely, devotedly, entirely, gladly, wholeheartedly 10. **take heart** be comforted, be encouraged, be heartened, brighten up, buck up (*Inf.*), cheer up, perk up, revive

heartache affliction, agony, anguish, bitterness, despair, distress, grief, heartbreak, heartsickness, pain, remorse, sorrow, suffering, torment, torture

heartbreak anguish, desolation, despair, grief, misery, pain, sorrow, suffering

heartbreaking agonizing, bitter, desolating, disappointing, distressing, grievous, harrowing, heart-rending, pitiful, poignant, sad, tragic

Antonyms cheerful, cheery, comic, glorious, happy, jolly, joyful, joyous, lighthearted

heartbroken brokenhearted, crestfallen, crushed, dejected, desolate, despondent, disappointed, disconsolate, disheartened, dismal, dispirited, downcast, grieved, heartsick, miserable, sick as a parrot (*Inf.*)

Antonyms cheerful, cock-a-hoop, elated, exuberant, happy, in seventh heaven, joyful, joyous, on cloud nine, over the moon (*Inf.*)

hearten animate, assure, buck up (*Inf.*), buoy up, cheer, comfort, console, embolden, encourage, incite, inspire, inspirit, raise someone's spirits, reassure, revivify, rouse, stimulate

heartfelt ardent, cordial, deep, devout, earnest, fervent, genuine, hearty, honest, profound, sincere, unfeigned, warm, wholehearted

Antonyms false, feigned, flippant, fraudulent, frivolous, half-hearted, hypocritical, insincere, phoney *or* phony (*Inf.*), pretended, put on, reserved, unenthusiastic, unimpassioned

heartily 1. cordially, deeply, feelingly, genuinely, profoundly, sincerely, unfeignedly, warmly 2. eagerly, earnestly, enthusiastically, resolutely, vigorously, zealously 3. absolutely, completely, thoroughly, totally, very

heartless brutal, callous, cold, cold-blooded, cold-hearted, cruel, hard, hard-hearted, harsh, inhuman, merciless, pitiless, uncaring, unfeeling, unkind

Antonyms compassionate, generous, humane, kind, merciful, sensitive, sympathetic, warm-hearted

heart-rending affecting, distressing, harrowing, heartbreaking, moving, pathetic, piteous, pitiful, poignant, sad, tragic

heartsick dejected, despondent, dispirited, downcast, heartsore, heavy-hearted, sick at heart

heart-to-heart 1. *adj.* candid, intimate, open, personal, sincere, unreserved 2. *n.* cosy chat, tête-à-tête

heart-warming 1. gratifying, pleasing, rewarding, satisfying 2. affecting, cheering, encouraging, heartening, moving, touching, warming

hearty 1. affable, ardent, back-slapping, cordial, eager, ebullient, effusive, enthusiastic, friendly, generous, genial, jovial, unreserved, warm 2. earnest, genuine, heartfelt, honest, real, sincere, true, unfeigned, wholehearted 3. active, energetic, hale, hardy, healthy, robust, sound, strong, vigorous, well 4. ample, filling, nourishing, sizable, solid, square, substantial

Antonyms cold, cool, delicate, feeble, frail, half-hearted, insincere, mild, sickly, unhealthy, weak

heat *n.* 1. calefaction, fever, fieriness, high temperature, hotness, hot spell, sultriness, swelter, torridity, warmness, warmth 2. *Fig.* agitation, ardour, earnestness, excitement, fervour, fever, fury, impetuosity, intensity, passion, vehemence, violence, warmth, zeal ~*v.* 3. become warm, chafe, flush, glow, grow hot, make hot, reheat, warm up 4. animate, excite, impassion, inflame, inspirit, rouse, stimulate, stir, warm

Antonyms *n.* calmness, cold, coldness, composure, coolness ~*v.* chill, cool, cool off, freeze

heated angry, bitter, excited, fierce, fiery, frenzied, furious, impassioned, intense, passionate, raging, stormy, tempestuous, vehement, violent

Antonyms calm, civilized, dispassionate, friendly, half-hearted, mellow, mild, peaceful, quiet, rational, reasoned, serene, subdued, unemotional, unfazed (*Inf.*), unruffled

heathen *n.* 1. idolater, idolatress, infidel, pagan, unbeliever 2. barbarian, philistine, savage ~*adj.* 3. godless, heathenish, idolatrous, infidel, irreligious, pagan 4. barbaric, philistine, savage, uncivilized, unenlightened

heave 1. drag (up), elevate, haul (up), heft (*Inf.*), hoist, lever, lift, pull (up), raise, tug 2. cast, fling, hurl, pitch, send, sling, throw, toss 3. breathe heavily, groan, puff, sigh, sob, suspire (*Archaic*), utter wearily 4. billow, breathe, dilate, exhale, expand, palpitate, pant, rise, surge, swell, throb 5. barf (*U.S. sl.*), be sick, chuck (up) (*Sl., chiefly U.S.*), chunder (*Sl., chiefly Aust.*), do a technicolour yawn (*Sl.*), gag, retch, spew, throw up (*Inf.*), toss one's cookies (*U.S. sl.*), upchuck (*U.S. sl.*), vomit

heaven 1. abode of God, bliss, Elysium *or* Elysian fields (*Greek myth*), happy hunting ground (*Amerind legend*), hereafter, life everlasting, life to come, next world, nirvana (*Buddhism, Hinduism*), paradise, Valhalla (*Norse myth*), Zion (*Christianity*) 2. *Usually plural* empyrean (*Poetic*), ether, firmament, sky, welkin (*Archaic*) 3. *Fig.* bliss, dreamland, ecstasy, enchantment, felicity, happiness, paradise, rapture, seventh heaven, sheer bliss, transport, utopia

heavenly 1. *Inf.* alluring, beautiful, blissful, delightful, divine (*Inf.*), entrancing, exquisite, glorious, lovely, rapturous, ravishing, sublime, wonderful 2. angelic, beatific, blessed, blest, celestial, cherubic, divine, empyrean (*Poetic*), extraterrestrial, godlike, holy, immortal, paradisaical, seraphic, superhuman, supernal (*Literary*), supernatural

Antonyms (*sense 1*) abominable, appalling, awful, bad, depressing, dire, disagreeable, dreadful, dreary, dull, frightful, gloomy, grim, hellacious (*U.S. sl.*), horrid, horrible, lousy (*Sl.*), miserable, rotten (*Inf.*), terrible, unpleasant, vile (*sense 2*) earthly, human, secular, worldly

heavily 1. awkwardly, clumsily, ponderously, weightily 2. laboriously, painfully, with difficulty 3. completely, decisively, roundly, thoroughly, utterly 4. dejectedly, dully, gloomily, sluggishly, woodenly 5. closely, compactly, densely, fast, hard, thick, thickly 6. deep, deeply, profoundly, sound, soundly 7. a great deal, considerably, copiously, excessively, frequently, to excess, very much

heaviness 1. gravity, heftiness, ponderousness, weight 2. arduousness, burdensomeness, grievousness, onerousness, oppressiveness, severity, weightiness 3. deadness, dullness, languor, lassitude, numbness, sluggishness, torpor 4. dejection, depression, despondency, gloom, gloominess, glumness, melancholy, sadness, seriousness

heavy 1. bulky, hefty, massive, ponderous, portly, weighty 2. burdensome, difficult, grievous, hard, harsh, intolerable, laborious, onerous, oppressive, severe, tedious, vexatious, wearisome 3. apathetic, drowsy, dull, inactive, indolent, inert, listless, slow, sluggish, stupid, torpid, wooden 4. crestfallen, dejected, depressed, despondent, disconsolate, downcast, gloomy, grieving, melancholy, sad, sorrowful 5. complex, deep, difficult, grave, profound, serious, solemn, weighty 6. abundant, considerable, copious, excessive, large, profuse 7. burdened, encumbered, laden, loaded, oppressed, weighted 8. boisterous, rough, stormy, tempestuous, turbulent, violent, wild 9. dull, gloomy, leaden, louring *or* lowering, overcast

Antonyms agile, alert, bearable, brisk, calm, cheerful, compact, easy, exciting, gentle, handy, happy, inconsequential, joyful, light, mild, moderate, quick, slight, small, soft, sparse, trivial, unimportant, weak

heavy-handed 1. awkward, bungling, clumsy, graceless, ham-fisted (*Inf.*), ham-handed (*Inf.*), inept, inexpert, like a bull in a china shop (*Inf.*), maladroit, unhandy 2. bungling, inconsiderate, insensitive, tactless, thoughtless 3. autocratic, domineering, harsh, oppressive, overbearing

Antonyms adept, adroit, competent, considerate, considered, dexterous, diplomatic, effectual, efficient, gentle, graceful, intelligent, prudent, sensible, skilful, smart, smooth, submissive, subservient, suitable, tactful, well-advised, well-thought-out, wise

heavy-hearted crushed, depressed, despondent, discouraged, disheartened, dismal, downcast, downhearted, forlorn, heartsick, melancholy, miserable, morose, mournful, sad, sick as a parrot (*Inf.*), sorrowful

heckle bait, barrack (*Inf.*), boo, disrupt, interrupt, jeer, pester, shout down, taunt

hectic animated, boisterous, chaotic, excited, fevered, feverish, flurrying, flustering, frantic, frenetic, frenzied, furious, heated, riotous, rumbustious, tumultuous, turbulent, wild

Antonyms calm, peaceful, relaxing, tranquil

hector bluster, boast, browbeat, bully, bullyrag, harass, huff and puff, intimidate, menace, provoke, ride roughshod over, roister, threaten, worry

hedge *n.* 1. hedgerow, quickset 2. barrier, boundary, screen, windbreak 3. compensation, counterbalance, guard, insurance cover, protection ~*v.* 4. border, edge, enclose, fence, surround 5. block, confine, hem in (about, around), hinder, obstruct, restrict 6. beg the question, be noncommittal, dodge, duck, equivocate, evade, flannel (*Brit. inf.*), prevaricate, pussyfoot (*Inf.*), quibble, sidestep, temporize, waffle (*Inf., chiefly Brit.*) 7. cover, fortify, guard, insure, protect, safeguard, shield

hedonism 1. epicureanism, epicurism, sybaritism 2. dolce vita, gratification, luxuriousness, pleasure-seeking, pursuit of pleasure, self-indulgence, sensualism, sensuality

hedonist 1. epicure, epicurean, sybarite 2. *bon vivant,* pleasure seeker, sensualist, voluptuary

hedonistic 1. epicurean, sybaritic 2. luxurious, pleasure-seeking, self-indulgent, voluptuous

heed 1. *n.* attention, care, caution, consideration, ear, heedfulness, mind, note, notice, regard, respect, thought, watchfulness 2. *v.* attend, bear in mind, be guided by, consider, follow, give ear to, listen to, mark, mind, note, obey, observe, pay attention to, regard, take notice of, take to heart

Antonyms *n.* carelessness, disregard, inattention, laxity, laxness, neglect, thoughtlessness ~*v.* be inattentive to, discount, disobey, disregard, flout, ignore, neglect, overlook, reject, shun, turn a deaf ear to

heedful attentive, careful, cautious, chary, circumspect, mindful, observant, prudent, vigilant, wary, watchful

heedless careless, foolhardy, imprudent, inattentive, incautious, neglectful, negligent, oblivious, precipitate, rash, reckless, thoughtless, unmindful, unobservant, unthinking

Antonyms attentive, aware, careful, cautious, concerned, heedful, mindful, observant, thoughtful, vigilant, wary, watchful

heel[1] *n.* 1. crust, end, remainder, rump, stub, stump 2. *Sl.* blackguard, bounder (*Old-fashioned Brit. sl.*), cad (*Brit inf.*), cocksucker (*Taboo sl.*), rotter (*Sl., chiefly Brit.*), scally (*Northwest English dialect*), scoundrel, scumbag (*Sl.*), swine 3. **down at heel** dowdy, impoverished, out at elbows, run-down, seedy, shabby, slipshod, slovenly, worn 4. **take to one's heels** escape, flee, hook it (*Sl.*), run away *or* off, show a clean pair of heels, skedaddle (*Inf.*), take flight, vamoose (*Sl., chiefly U.S.*) 5. **well-heeled** affluent, flush (*Inf.*), moneyed, prosperous, rich, wealthy, well-off, well-to-do

heel[2] cant, careen, incline, keel over, lean over, list, tilt

hefty 1. beefy (*Inf.*), big, brawny, burly, hulking, husky (*Inf.*), massive, muscular, Ramboesque, robust, strapping, strong 2. forceful, heavy, powerful, thumping (*Sl.*), vigorous 3. ample, awkward, bulky, colossal, cumbersome, heavy, large, massive, ponderous, substantial, tremendous, unwieldy, weighty

Antonyms agile, diminutive, feeble, frail, inconsequential, ineffectual, infinitesimal, insignificant, light, little, mild, minute, narrow, petty, pocket-sized, scanty, short, slight, slim, small, soft, thin, tiny, trivial, weak, weedy (*Inf.*), wimpish *or* wimpy (*Inf.*)

height 1. altitude, elevation, highness, loftiness, stature, tallness 2. apex, apogee, crest, crown, elevation, hill, mountain, peak, pinnacle, summit, top, vertex, zenith 3. acme, dignity, eminence, exaltation, grandeur, loftiness, prominence 4. climax, culmination, extremity, limit, maximum, *ne plus ultra,* ultimate, utmost degree, uttermost

Antonyms abyss, base, bottom, canyon, chasm, depth, lowland, lowness, low point, minimum, moderation, nadir, ravine, shortness, smallness, tininess, triviality, valley

heighten 1. add to, aggravate, amplify, augment, enhance, improve, increase, intensify, magnify, sharpen, strengthen 2. el~

evate, enhance, ennoble, exalt, magnify, raise, uplift

heinous abhorrent, abominable, atrocious, awful, evil, execrable, flagrant, grave, hateful, hideous, infamous, iniquitous, monstrous, nefarious, odious, outrageous, revolting, shocking, unspeakable, vicious, villainous

heir beneficiary, heiress (*Fem.*), inheritor, inheritress *or* inheritrix (*Fem.*), next in line, scion, successor

hell 1. Abaddon, abode of the damned, abyss, Acheron (*Greek myth*), bottomless pit, fire and brimstone, Gehenna (*New Testament, Judaism*), Hades (*Greek myth*), hellfire, infernal regions, inferno, lower world, nether world, Tartarus (*Greek myth*), underworld 2. affliction, agony, anguish, martyrdom, misery, nightmare, ordeal, suffering, torment, trial, wretchedness 3. **hell for leather** at the double, full-tilt, headlong, hotfoot, hurriedly, like a bat out of hell (*Sl.*), pell-mell, posthaste, quickly, speedily, swiftly

hellbent bent, determined, fixed, intent, resolved, set, settled

hellish 1. damnable, damned, demoniacal, devilish, diabolical, fiendish, infernal 2. abominable, accursed, atrocious, barbarous, cruel, detestable, execrable, inhuman, monstrous, nefarious, vicious, wicked
Antonyms admirable, agreeable, benevolent, delightful, fine, gentle, good, harmless, honourable, humane, innocuous, kind, merciful, noble, pleasant, virtuous, wonderful

helm 1. *Nautical* rudder, steering gear, tiller, wheel 2. *Fig.* command, control, direction, leadership, rule 3. **at the helm** at the wheel, directing, in charge, in command, in control, in the driving seat, in the saddle

help *v.* 1. abet, aid, assist, back, befriend, cooperate, encourage, lend a hand, promote, relieve, save, second, serve, stand by, succour, support 2. alleviate, ameliorate, cure, ease, facilitate, heal, improve, mitigate, relieve, remedy, restore 3. abstain, avoid, control, eschew, forbear, hinder, keep from, prevent, refrain from, resist, shun, withstand ~*n.* 4. advice, aid, assistance, avail, benefit, cooperation, guidance, helping hand, promotion, service, support, use, utility 5. assistant, employee, hand, helper, worker 6. balm, corrective, cure, relief, remedy, restorative, salve, succour
Antonyms *v.* aggravate, bar, block, discourage, fight, foil, frustrate, harm, hinder, hurt, impede, injure, irritate, make worse, obstruct, oppose ~*n.* aggravation, bane, block, discouragement, hindrance, irritant, obstruction, opposition

helper abettor, adjutant, aide, aider, ally, assistant, attendant, auxiliary, coadjutor, collaborator, colleague, deputy, helpmate, henchman, mate, partner, protagonist, right-hand man, second, subsidiary, supporter

helpful 1. advantageous, beneficial, constructive, favourable, fortunate, practical, productive, profitable, serviceable, timely, useful 2. accommodating, beneficent, benevolent, caring, considerate, cooperative, friendly, kind, neighbourly, supportive, sympathetic

helping *n.* dollop (*Inf.*), piece, plateful, portion, ration, serving

helpless 1. abandoned, defenceless, dependent, destitute, exposed, forlorn, unprotected, vulnerable 2. debilitated, disabled, feeble, impotent, incapable, incompetent, infirm, paralysed, powerless, unfit, weak
Antonyms able, capable, competent, equipped, fit, hardy, healthy, hearty, invulnerable, mighty, powerful, robust, safe, secure, solid, strong, sturdy, thriving, tough, well-protected

helpmate assistant, associate, companion, consort, helper, helpmeet, husband, partner, significant other (*U.S. inf.*), spouse, support, wife

helter-skelter 1. *adv.* carelessly, hastily, headlong, hurriedly, pell-mell, rashly, recklessly, wildly 2. *adj.* anyhow, confused, disordered, haphazard, higgledy-piggledy (*Inf.*), hit-or-miss, jumbled, muddled, random, topsy-turvy

hem 1. *n.* border, edge, fringe, margin, trimming 2. *v. Usually with* **in** beset, border, circumscribe, confine, edge, enclose, environ, hedge in, restrict, shut in, skirt, surround

hem and haw falter, fumble, hesitate, pause, stammer, stutter

hence ergo, for this reason, on that account, therefore, thus

henceforth from now on, from this day forward, hence, hereafter, hereinafter, in the future

henchman aide, associate, attendant, bodyguard, cohort (*Chiefly U.S.*), crony, follower, heavy (*Sl.*), minder (*Sl.*), minion, myrmidon, right-hand man, satellite, sidekick (*Sl.*), subordinate, supporter

henpeck browbeat, bully, carp, cavil, chide, criticize, domineer, find fault, harass, hector, intimidate, nag, niggle, pester, pick at, scold, torment

henpecked browbeaten, bullied, cringing, dominated, led by the nose, meek, subject, subjugated, timid, treated like dirt
Antonyms aggressive, assertive, bossy (*Inf.*), dominating, domineering, forceful, macho, overbearing, Ramboesque, self-assertive, spirited, wilful

herald *n.* 1. bearer of tidings, crier, messenger 2. forerunner, harbinger, indication, omen, precursor, sign, signal, token ~*v.* 3. advertise, announce, broadcast, proclaim, publicize, publish, trumpet 4. foretoken, harbinger, indicate, pave the way, portend, precede, presage, promise, show, usher in

herculean 1. arduous, demanding, difficult, exhausting, formidable, gruelling, hard, heavy, laborious, onerous, prodigious, strenuous, toilsome, tough 2. athletic, brawny, husky (*Inf.*), mighty, muscular, powerful, rugged, sinewy, stalwart, strapping, strong, sturdy 3. colossal, elephantine, enormous, gigantic, great, huge, humongous *or* humungous (*U.S. sl.*), large, mammoth, massive, titanic

herd *n.* 1. assemblage, collection, crowd, crush, drove, flock, horde, mass, mob, multitude, press, swarm, throng 2. mob, populace, rabble, riffraff, the hoi polloi, the masses, the plebs ~*v.* 3. assemble, associate, collect, congregate, flock, gather, huddle, muster, rally 4. drive, force, goad, guide, lead, shepherd, spur

herdsman cowherd, cowman, drover, grazier, stockman

hereafter 1. *adv.* after this, from now on, hence, henceforth, henceforward, in future 2. *n.* afterlife, future life, life after death, next world, the beyond

hereditary 1. family, genetic, inborn, inbred, inheritable, transmissible 2. ancestral, bequeathed, handed down, inherited, patrimonial, traditional, transmitted, willed

heredity congenital traits, constitution, genetic make-up, genetics, inheritance

heresy apostasy, dissidence, error, heterodoxy, iconoclasm, impiety, revisionism, schism, unorthodoxy

heretic apostate, dissenter, dissident, nonconformist, renegade, revisionist, schismatic, sectarian, separatist

heretical freethinking, heterodox, iconoclastic, idolatrous, impious, revisionist, schismatic, unorthodox

heritage bequest, birthright, endowment, estate, inheritance, legacy, lot, patrimony, portion, share, tradition

hermetic, hermetical airtight, sealed, shut

hermit anchoret, anchorite, eremite, monk, recluse, solitary, stylite

hero 1. celeb (*Inf.*), celebrity, champion, conqueror, exemplar, great man, heart-throb (*Brit.*), idol, man of the hour, megastar (*Inf.*), popular figure, star, superstar, victor 2. lead actor, leading man, male lead, principal male character, protagonist

heroic 1. bold, brave, courageous, daring, dauntless, doughty, fearless, gallant, intrepid, lion-hearted, stouthearted, undaunted, valiant, valorous 2. classical, Homeric, legendary, mythological 3. classic, elevated, epic, exaggerated, extravagant, grand, grandiose, high-flown, inflated
Antonyms (*sense 1*) base, chicken (*Sl.*), cowardly, craven, faint-hearted, ignoble, irresolute, mean, timid (*sense 3*) lowbrow, simple, unadorned

heroine 1. celeb (*Inf.*), celebrity, goddess, ideal, megastar (*Inf.*), woman of the hour 2. diva, female lead, lead actress, leading lady, prima donna, principal female character, protagonist

heroism boldness, bravery, courage, courageousness, daring, fearlessness, fortitude, gallantry, intrepidity, prowess, spirit, valour

hero worship admiration, adoration, adulation, idealization, idolization, putting on a pedestal, veneration

hesitant diffident, doubtful, half-arsed, half-assed (*U.S. & Canad. sl.*), half-hearted, halting, hanging back, hesitating, irresolute, lacking confidence, reluctant, sceptical, shy, timid, uncertain, unsure, vacillating, wavering
Antonyms arrogant, avid, clear, confident, definite, determined, dogmatic, eager, enthusiastic, firm, forceful, keen, positive, resolute, self-assured, spirited, sure, unhesitating, unwavering

hesitate 1. be uncertain, delay, dither (*Chiefly Brit.*), doubt, haver (*Brit.*), pause, shillyshally (*Inf.*), swither (*Scot.*), vacillate, wait, waver 2. balk, be reluctant, be unwilling, boggle, demur, hang back, scruple, shrink from, think twice 3. falter, fumble, hem and haw, stammer, stumble, stutter
Antonyms (*sense 1*) be confident, be decisive, be firm, continue, decide (*sense 2*) be determined, resolve, welcome

hesitation 1. delay, doubt, dubiety, hesitancy, indecision, irresolution, uncertainty, vacillation 2. demurral, misgiving(s), qualm(s), reluctance, scruple(s), unwillingness 3. faltering, fumbling, hemming and hawing, stammering, stumbling, stuttering

heterodox dissident, heretical, iconoclastic, revisionist, schismatic, unorthodox, unsound

heterogeneous assorted, contrary, contrasted, different, discrepant, disparate, dissimilar, divergent, diverse, diversified, incongruous, manifold, miscellaneous, mixed, motley, opposed, unlike, unrelated, varied

hew 1. axe, chop, cut, hack, lop, split 2. carve, fashion, form, make, model, sculpt, sculpture, shape, smooth

heyday bloom, flowering, pink, prime, prime of life, salad days

hiatus aperture, blank, breach, break, chasm, discontinuity, entr'acte, gap, interruption, interval, lacuna, lapse, opening, respite, rift, space

hibernate hole up, lie dormant, overwinter, remain torpid, sleep snug, vegetate, winter

hidden abstruse, clandestine, close, concealed, covered, covert, cryptic, dark, hermetic, hermetical, masked, mysterious, mystic, mystical, obscure, occult, recondite, secret, shrouded, ulterior, unrevealed, unseen, veiled

hide[1] 1. cache, conceal, go into hiding, go to ground, go underground, hole up, lie low, secrete, stash (*Inf.*), take cover 2. blot out, bury, camouflage, cloak, conceal, cover, disguise, eclipse, mask, obscure, screen, shelter, shroud, veil 3. hush up, keep secret, suppress, withhold
Antonyms admit, bare, confess, disclose, display, divulge, exhibit, expose, find, flaunt, reveal, show, uncover, unveil

hide[2] fell, pelt, skin

hideaway haven, hide-out, hiding place, nest, refuge, retreat, sanctuary, sequestered nook

hidebound brassbound, conventional, narrow, narrow-minded, rigid, set, set in one's ways, strait-laced, ultraconservative
Antonyms broad-minded, flexible, liberal, open, receptive, tolerant, unconventional, unorthodox

hideous 1. ghastly, grim, grisly, grotesque, gruesome, monstrous, repulsive, revolting, ugly, unsightly 2. abominable, appalling, awful, detestable, disgusting, dreadful, godawful (*Sl.*), horrendous, horrible, horrid, loathsome, macabre, obscene, odious, shocking, sickening, terrible, terrifying
Antonyms appealing, beautiful, captivating, charming, entrancing, lovely, pleasant, pleasing

hide-out den, hideaway, hiding place, lair, secret place, shelter

hiding *n.* beating, caning, drubbing, flogging, larruping (*Brit. dialect*), lathering (*Inf.*), licking (*Inf.*), spanking, tanning (*Sl.*), thrashing, walloping (*Inf.*), whaling, whipping

hierarchy grading, pecking order, ranking

hieroglyphic *adj.* enigmatical, figurative, indecipherable, obscure, runic, symbolical

higgledy-piggledy 1. *adv.* all over the place, all over the shop (*Inf.*), anyhow, any old how, confusedly, disorderly, haphazard, helter-skelter, pell-mell, topsy-turvy 2. *adj.* haphazard, helter-skelter, indiscriminate, jumbled, muddled, pell-mell, topsy-turvy

high *adj.* 1. elevated, lofty, soaring, steep, tall, towering 2. excessive, extraordinary, extreme, great, intensified, sharp, strong 3. arch, big-time (*Inf.*), chief, consequential, distinguished, eminent, exalted, important, influential, leading, major league (*Inf.*), notable, powerful, prominent, ruling, significant, superior 4. arrogant, boastful, bragging, despotic, domineering, haughty, lofty, lordly, ostentatious, overbearing, proud, tyrannical, vainglorious 5. capital, extreme, grave, important, serious 6. boisterous, bouncy (*Inf.*), cheerful, elated, excited, exhilarated, exuberant, joyful, lighthearted, merry, strong, tumultuous, turbulent 7. *Inf.* delirious, euphoric, freaked out (*Inf.*), hyped up (*Sl.*), inebriated, intoxicated, on a trip (*Inf.*), spaced out (*Sl.*), stoned (*Sl.*), tripping (*Inf.*), turned on (*Sl.*), zonked (*Sl.*) 8. costly, dear, exorbitant, expensive, high-priced, steep (*Inf.*), stiff 9. acute, high-pitched, penetrating, piercing, piping, sharp, shrill, soprano, strident, treble 10. extravagant, grand, lavish, luxurious, rich 11. gamy, niffy (*Brit. sl.*), pongy (*Brit. inf.*), strong-flavoured, tainted, whiffy (*Brit. sl.*) 12. **high and dry** abandoned, bereft, destitute, helpless, stranded 13. **high and low** all over, everywhere, exhaustively, far and wide, in every nook and cranny 14. **high and mighty** *Inf.* arrogant, cavalier, conceited, disdainful, haughty, imperious, overbearing, self-important, snobbish, stuck-up (*Inf.*), superior ~*adv.* 15. aloft, at great height, far up, way up ~*n.* 16. apex, crest, height, peak, record level, summit, top 17. *Inf.* delirium, ecstasy, euphoria, intoxication, trip (*Inf.*)
Antonyms (*sense 1*) dwarfed, low, short, stunted (*sense 2*) average, low, mild, moderate, reduced, restrained, routine, suppressed (*sense 3*) average, common, degraded, ignoble, inconsequential, insignificant, low, lowly, low-ranking, menial, routine, secondary, undistinguished, unimportant (*sense 6*) angry, dejected, depressed, gloomy, low, melancholy, sad

(*sense 9*) alto, bass, deep, gruff, low, low-pitched

highborn aristocratic, blue-blooded, gentle (*Archaic*), noble, patrician, pedigreed, thoroughbred, well-born

highbrow 1. *n.* aesthete, Brahmin (*U.S.*), brain (*Inf.*), brainbox (*Sl.*), egghead (*Inf.*), intellectual, mastermind, savant, scholar 2. *adj.* bookish, brainy (*Inf.*), cultivated, cultured, deep, highbrowed, intellectual, sophisticated
Antonyms *n.* idiot, ignoramus, illiterate, imbecile (*Inf.*), lowbrow, moron, philistine ~*adj.* ignorant, lowbrow, philistine, shallow, uncultivated, uninformed, unintellectual, unlearned, unsophisticated

high-class A1 *or* A-one (*Inf.*), choice, classy (*Sl.*), elite, exclusive, first-rate, high-quality, high-toned, posh (*Inf., chiefly Brit.*), ritzy (*Sl.*), select, superior, swish (*Inf., chiefly Brit.*), tip-top, top-drawer, top-flight, tops (*Sl.*), U (*Brit. inf.*), up-market, upper-class
Antonyms cheap, cheapo (*Inf.*), common, inferior, mediocre, ordinary, run-of-the-mill

highfalutin, highfaluting big, bombastic, florid, grandiose, high-flown, high-sounding, lofty, magniloquent, pompous, pretentious, supercilious, swanky (*Inf.*)

high-flown elaborate, exaggerated, extravagant, florid, grandiose, high-falutin (*Inf.*), inflated, lofty, magniloquent, overblown, pretentious
Antonyms down-to-earth, moderate, modest, practical, pragmatic, realistic, reasonable, restrained, sensible, simple, straightforward, unpretentious

high-handed arbitrary, autocratic, bossy (*Inf.*), despotic, dictatorial, domineering, imperious, inconsiderate, oppressive, overbearing, peremptory, self-willed, tyrannical, wilful

high jinks fun and games, horseplay, jollity, junketing, merrymaking, revelry, skylarking (*Inf.*), sport, spree

highland *n.* heights, hill country, hills, mesa, mountainous region, plateau, tableland, uplands

highlight 1. *n.* best part, climax, feature, focal point, focus, high point, high spot, main feature, memorable part, peak 2. *v.* accent, accentuate, bring to the fore, emphasize, feature, focus attention on, give prominence to, play up, set off, show up, spotlight, stress, underline
Antonyms *n.* disappointment, low point ~*v.* de-emphasize, gloss over, neglect, overlook, play down

highly 1. decidedly, eminently, exceptionally, extraordinarily, extremely, greatly, immensely, supremely, tremendously, vastly, very, very much 2. appreciatively, approvingly, enthusiastically, favourably, warmly, well

highly strung easily upset, edgy, excitable, irascible, irritable, nervous, nervy (*Brit. inf.*), neurotic, restless, sensitive, stressed, taut, temperamental, tense, tetchy, twitchy (*Inf.*), wired (*Sl.*)
Antonyms calm, collected, easy-going, even-tempered, laid-back (*Inf.*), placid, relaxed, serene, unfazed (*Inf.*)

high-minded elevated, ethical, fair, good, honourable, idealistic, magnanimous, moral, noble, principled, pure, righteous, upright, virtuous, worthy
Antonyms dishonest, dishonourable, unethical, unfair

high-powered aggressive, driving, dynamic, effective, energetic, enterprising, fast-track, forceful, go-ahead, go-getting (*Inf.*), highly capable, vigorous

high-pressure *Of salesmanship* aggressive, bludgeoning, coercive, compelling, forceful, high-powered, importunate, insistent, intensive, persistent, persuasive, pushy (*Inf.*)

high-priced costly, dear, excessive, exorbitant, expensive, extortionate, high, steep (*Inf.*), stiff, unreasonable

high-sounding affected, artificial, bombastic, extravagant, flamboyant, florid, grandiloquent, grandiose, high-flown, imposing, magniloquent, ostentatious, overblown, pompous, pretentious, stilted, strained

high-speed brisk, express, fast, hotted-up (*Inf.*), quick, rapid, souped-up (*Inf.*), streamlined, swift

high-spirited animated, boisterous, bold, bouncy, daring, dashing, ebullient, effervescent, energetic, exuberant, frolicsome, full of life, fun-loving, gallant, lively, mettlesome, sparky, spirited, spunky (*Inf.*), vibrant, vital, vivacious

high spirits abandon, boisterousness, exhilaration, exuberance, good cheer, hilarity, *joie de vivre,* rare good humour

hijack commandeer, expropriate, seize, skyjack, take over

hike *v.* 1. back-pack, hoof it (*Sl.*), leg it (*Inf.*), ramble, tramp, walk 2. *Usually with* **up** hitch up, jack up, lift, pull up, raise ~*n.* 3. journey on foot, march, ramble, tramp, trek, walk

hilarious amusing, comical, convivial, entertaining, exhilarated, funny, gay, happy, humorous, jolly, jovial, joyful, joyous, merry, mirthful, noisy, rollicking, side-splitting, uproarious

Antonyms dull, gloomy, quiet, sad, sedate, serious

hilarity amusement, boisterousness, cheerfulness, conviviality, exhilaration, exuberance, gaiety, glee, high spirits, jollification, jollity, joviality, joyousness, laughter, levity, merriment, mirth

hill 1. brae (*Scot.*), down (*Archaic*), elevation, eminence, fell, height, hillock, hilltop, knoll, mound, mount, prominence, tor 2. drift, heap, hummock, mound, pile, stack 3. acclivity, brae (*Scot.*), climb, gradient, incline, rise, slope

hillock barrow, hummock, knap (*Dialect*), knoll, monticule, mound, tump (*Western Brit. dialect*)

hilt 1. grip, haft, handgrip, handle, helve 2. **to the hilt** completely, entirely, fully, totally, wholly

hind after, back, caudal (*Anat.*), hinder, posterior, rear

hinder arrest, block, check, debar, delay, deter, encumber, frustrate, hamper, hamstring, handicap, hold up *or* back, impede, interrupt, obstruct, oppose, prevent, retard, slow down, stop, stymie, thwart, trammel

Antonyms accelerate, advance, aid, benefit, encourage, expedite, facilitate, further, help, hurry, promote, quicken, speed, support

hindmost concluding, final, furthest, furthest behind, last, most remote, rearmost, terminal, trailing, ultimate

hindrance bar, barrier, block, check, deterrent, difficulty, drag, drawback, encumbrance, handicap, hitch, impediment, interruption, limitation, obstacle, obstruction, restraint, restriction, snag, stoppage, stumbling block, trammel

Antonyms advancement, advantage, aid, asset, assistance, benefit, boon, boost, encouragement, furtherance, help, support

hinge *v.* be contingent, be subject to, depend, hang, pivot, rest, revolve around, turn

hint *n.* 1. allusion, clue, implication, indication, inkling, innuendo, insinuation, intimation, mention, reminder, suggestion, tip-off, word to the wise 2. advice, help, pointer, suggestion, tip, wrinkle (*Inf.*) 3. breath, dash, *soupçon,* speck, suggestion, suspicion, taste, tinge, touch, trace, undertone, whiff, whisper ~*v.* 4. allude, cue, imply, indicate, insinuate, intimate, let it be known, mention, prompt, suggest, tip off

hip *adj.* aware, clued-up (*Inf.*), fashionable, in, informed, in on, knowledgeable, onto, trendy (*Brit. inf.*), wise (*Sl.*), with it (*Inf.*)

hippie beatnik, bohemian, dropout, flower child

hire *v.* 1. appoint, commission, employ, engage, sign up, take on 2. charter, engage, lease, let, rent ~*n.* 3. charge, cost, fee, price, rent, rental

hirsute bearded, bewhiskered, bristly, hairy, hispid (*Biol.*), shaggy, unshaven

hiss *n.* 1. buzz, hissing, sibilance, sibilation 2. boo, catcall, contempt, derision, jeer, raspberry ~*v.* 3. rasp, shrill, sibilate, wheeze, whirr, whistle, whiz 4. blow a raspberry, boo, catcall, condemn, damn, decry, deride, hoot, jeer, mock, revile, ridicule

historian annalist, biographer, chronicler, historiographer, recorder

historic celebrated, consequential, epoch-making, extraordinary, famous, momentous, notable, outstanding, red-letter, remarkable, significant

Antonyms ordinary, uncelebrated, unimportant, unknown

historical actual, archival, attested, authentic, chronicled, documented, factual, real, verifiable

Antonyms contemporary, current, fabulous, fictional, legendary, mythical, present-day

history 1. account, annals, autobiography, biography, chronicle, memoirs, narration, narrative, recapitulation, recital, record, relation, saga, story 2. ancient history, antiquity, bygone times, days of old, days of yore, olden days, the good old days, the old days, the past, yesterday, yesteryear

histrionic actorly, actressy, affected, artificial, bogus, camp (*Inf.*), dramatic, forced, insincere, melodramatic, sensational, theatrical, unnatural

histrionics dramatics, performance, scene, staginess, tantrums, temperament, theatricality

hit *v.* 1. bang, bash (*Inf.*), batter, beat, belt (*Inf.*), chin (*Sl.*), clip (*Inf.*), clobber (*Sl.*), clout (*Inf.*), cuff, deck (*Sl.*), flog, knock, lambast(e), lay one on (*Sl.*), lob, punch, slap, smack, smite (*Archaic*), sock (*Sl.*), strike, swat, thump, wallop (*Inf.*), whack 2. bang into, bump, clash with, collide with, crash against, meet head-on, run into, smash into 3. accomplish, achieve, arrive at, attain, gain, reach, secure, strike, touch 4. affect, damage, devastate, impinge on, influence, leave a mark on, make an impact *or* impression on, move, overwhelm, touch ~*n.* 5. belt (*Inf.*), blow, bump, clash, clout (*Inf.*), collision, cuff, impact, knock, rap, shot, slap, smack, stroke, swipe (*Inf.*), wallop (*Inf.*) 6. *Inf.* sellout, sensation, smash (*Inf.*), success, triumph, winner

hitch *v.* 1. attach, connect, couple, fasten, harness, join, make fast, tether, tie, unite, yoke 2. *Often with* **up** hoick, jerk, pull, tug, yank 3. *Inf.* hitchhike, thumb a lift ~*n.* 4. catch, check, delay, difficulty, drawback, hassle (*Inf.*), hindrance, hold-up, impediment, mishap, obstacle, problem, snag, stoppage, trouble

hither close, closer, here, near, nearer, nigh (*Archaic*), over here, to this place

hitherto heretofore, previously, so far, thus far, till now, until now, up to now

hit off 1. capture, catch, impersonate, mimic, represent, take off (*Inf.*) 2. **hit it off** *Inf.* be on good terms, click (*Sl.*), get on (well) with, take to, warm to

hit on *or* **upon** arrive at, chance upon, come upon, discover, guess, invent, light upon, realize, strike upon, stumble on, think up

hit or miss aimless, casual, cursory, disorganized, haphazard, indiscriminate, perfunctory, random, undirected, uneven
Antonyms arranged, deliberate, organized, planned, systematic

hit out (at) assail, attack, castigate, condemn, denounce, inveigh against, lash out, rail against, strike out at

hive 1. cluster, colony, swarm 2. *Fig.* centre, heart, hub, powerhouse (*Sl.*)

hoard 1. *n.* accumulation, cache, fall-back, fund, heap, mass, pile, reserve, stockpile, store, supply, treasure-trove 2. *v.* accumulate, amass, buy up, cache, collect, deposit, garner, gather, hive, lay up, put away, put by, save, stash away (*Inf.*), stockpile, store, treasure

hoarder collector, magpie (*Brit.*), miser, niggard, saver, squirrel (*Inf.*), tight-arse (*Taboo sl.*), tight-ass (*U.S. taboo sl.*)

hoarse croaky, discordant, grating, gravelly, growling, gruff, guttural, harsh, husky, rasping, raucous, rough, throaty
Antonyms harmonious, mellifluous, mellow, melodious, smooth

hoary 1. frosty, grey, grey-haired, grizzled, hoar, silvery, white, white-haired 2. aged, ancient, antiquated, antique, old, venerable

hoax 1. *n.* canard, cheat, con (*Inf.*), deception, fast one (*Inf.*), fraud, imposture, joke, practical joke, prank, ruse, spoof (*Inf.*), swindle, trick 2. *v.* bamboozle (*Inf.*), befool, bluff, con (*Sl.*), deceive, delude, dupe, fool, gammon (*Brit. inf.*), gull (*Archaic*), hoodwink, hornswoggle (*Sl.*), kid (*Inf.*), swindle, take in (*Inf.*), take (someone) for a ride (*Inf.*), trick, wind up (*Brit. sl.*)

hoaxer bamboozler (*Inf.*), hoodwinker, humbug, joker, practical joker, prankster, spoofer (*Inf.*), trickster

hobble 1. dodder, falter, halt, limp, shamble, shuffle, stagger, stumble, totter 2. clog, fasten, fetter, hamstring, restrict, shackle, tie

hobby diversion, favourite occupation, (leisure) activity, leisure pursuit, pastime, relaxation, sideline

hobgoblin apparition, bogey, goblin, hob, imp, spectre, spirit, sprite

hobnob associate, consort, fraternize, hang about, hang out (*Inf.*), keep company, mingle, mix, socialize

hocus-pocus 1. artifice, cheat, chicanery, deceit, deception, delusion, hoax, humbug, imposture, swindle, trickery 2. abracadabra, cant, gibberish, gobbledegook (*Inf.*), hokum (*Sl., chiefly U.S. & Canad.*), jargon, mumbo jumbo, nonsense, rigmarole 3. conjuring, jugglery, legerdemain, prestidigitation, sleight of hand

hoggish brutish, dirty, filthy, gluttonous, greedy, gross, mean, piggish, rapacious, ravenous, selfish, sordid, squalid, swinish, unclean

hogwash balderdash, balls (*Taboo sl.*), bilge (*Inf.*), bosh (*Inf.*), bull (*Sl.*), bullshit (*Taboo sl.*), bunk (*Inf.*), bunkum *or* buncombe (*Chiefly U.S.*), cobblers (*Brit. taboo sl.*), crap (*Sl.*), drivel, eyewash (*Inf.*), garbage (*Inf.*), guff (*Sl.*), hokum (*Sl., chiefly U.S. & Canad.*), hooey (*Sl.*), horsefeathers (*U.S. sl.*), hot air (*Inf.*), moonshine, nonsense, pap, piffle (*Inf.*), poppycock (*Inf.*), rot, rubbish, shit (*Taboo sl.*), tommyrot, tosh (*Sl., chiefly Brit.*), trash, tripe (*Inf.*), twaddle

hoiden *see* HOYDEN

hoi polloi admass, *canaille,* commonalty, riffraff, the (common) herd, the common people, the great unwashed (*Inf. & derogatory*), the lower orders, the masses, the plebs, the populace, the proles (*Derogatory sl., chiefly Brit.*), the proletariat, the rabble, the third estate, the underclass

hoist 1. *v.* elevate, erect, heave, lift, raise, rear, upraise 2. *n.* crane, elevator, lift, tackle, winch

hoity-toity arrogant, conceited, disdainful, haughty, high and mighty (*Inf.*), lofty, overweening, proud, scornful, snobbish, snooty (*Inf.*), stuck-up (*Inf.*), supercilious, toffee-nosed (*Sl., chiefly Brit.*), uppish (*Brit. inf.*)

hold *v.* 1. have, keep, maintain, occupy, own, possess, retain 2. adhere, clasp, cleave, clinch, cling, clutch, cradle, embrace, enfold, grasp, grip, stick 3. arrest, bind, check, confine, curb, detain, impound, imprison, pound, restrain, stay, stop, suspend 4. assume, believe, consider, deem, entertain, esteem, judge, maintain, presume, reckon, regard, think, view **5.** continue, endure, last, persevere, persist, remain, resist, stay, wear **6.** assemble, call, carry on, celebrate, conduct, convene, have, officiate at, preside over, run, solemnize **7.** bear, brace, carry, prop, shoulder, support, sustain, take **8.** accommodate, comprise, contain, have a capacity for, seat, take **9.** apply, be in force, be the case, exist, hold good, operate, remain true, remain valid, stand up **10. hold one's own** do well, hold fast, hold out, keep one's head above water, keep pace, keep up, maintain one's position, stand firm, stand one's ground, stay put, stick to one's guns (*Inf.*) *~n.* **11.** clasp, clutch, grasp, grip **12.** anchorage, foothold, footing, leverage, prop, purchase, stay, support, vantage **13.** ascendancy, authority, clout (*Inf.*), control, dominance, dominion, influence, mastery, pull (*Inf.*), sway

Antonyms bestow, break, call off, cancel, come undone, deny, disavow, disclaim, free, give, give up, give way, hand over, let go, let loose, loosen, offer, postpone, put down, refute, reject, release, turn over

hold back 1. check, control, curb, inhibit, rein, repress, restrain, suppress **2.** desist, forbear, keep back, refuse, withhold

holder 1. bearer, custodian, incumbent, keeper, occupant, owner, possessor, proprietor, purchaser **2.** case, container, cover, housing, receptacle, sheath

hold forth declaim, descant, discourse, go on, harangue, lecture, orate, preach, speak, speechify, spiel (*Inf.*), spout (*Inf.*)

holdings assets, estate, investments, land interests, possessions, property, resources, securities, stocks and shares

hold off 1. avoid, defer, delay, keep from, postpone, put off, refrain **2.** fend off, keep off, rebuff, repel, repulse, stave off

hold out 1. extend, give, offer, present, proffer **2.** carry on, continue, endure, hang on, last, persevere, persist, stand fast, withstand

hold over adjourn, defer, delay, postpone, put off, suspend, waive

hold-up 1. bottleneck, delay, difficulty, hitch, obstruction, setback, snag, stoppage, traffic jam, trouble, wait **2.** burglary, mugging (*Inf.*), robbery, steaming (*Inf.*), stick-up (*Sl., chiefly U.S.*), theft

hold up 1. delay, detain, hinder, impede, retard, set back, slow down, stop **2.** bolster, brace, buttress, jack up, prop, shore up, support, sustain **3.** mug (*Inf.*), rob, stick up (*Sl., chiefly U.S.*), waylay **4.** display, exhibit, flaunt, present, show **5.** bear up, endure, last, survive, wear

hold with agree to *or* with, approve of, be in favour of, countenance, subscribe to, support, take kindly to

Antonyms be against, disagree with, disapprove of, hold out against, oppose

hole 1. aperture, breach, break, crack, fissure, gap, opening, orifice, outlet, perforation, puncture, rent, split, tear, vent **2.** cave, cavern, cavity, chamber, depression, excavation, hollow, pit, pocket, scoop, shaft **3.** burrow, covert, den, earth, lair, nest, retreat, shelter **4.** *Inf.* dive (*Sl.*), dump (*Inf.*), hovel, joint (*Sl.*), slum **5.** *Inf.* cell, dungeon, oubliette, prison **6.** defect, discrepancy, error, fallacy, fault, flaw, inconsistency, loophole **7.** *Sl.* dilemma, fix (*Inf.*), hot water (*Inf.*), imbroglio, jam (*Inf.*), mess, predicament, quandary, scrape (*Inf.*), spot (*Inf.*), tangle, tight spot **8. pick holes in** asperse, bad-mouth (*Sl., chiefly U.S. & Canad.*), cavil, crab (*Inf.*), criticize, denigrate, disparage, disprove, find fault, knock (*Inf.*), niggle, pull to pieces, put down, rubbish (*Inf.*), run down, slag (off) (*Sl.*), slate (*Inf.*)

hole-and-corner backstairs, clandestine, furtive, secret, secretive, sneaky (*Inf.*), stealthy, surreptitious, underhand, under the counter (*Inf.*)

Antonyms above-board, candid, frank, open, public

hole up go to earth, hibernate, hide, shelter, take cover, take refuge

holiday 1. break, leave, recess, time off, vacation **2.** anniversary, bank holiday, celebration, feast, festival, festivity, fête, gala, public holiday, saint's day

holier-than-thou goody-goody (*Inf.*), pietistic, pietistical, priggish, religiose, sanctimonious, self-righteous, self-satisfied, smug, squeaky-clean, unctuous

holiness blessedness, devoutness, divinity, godliness, piety, purity, religiousness, righteousness, sacredness, saintliness, sanctity, spirituality, virtuousness

holler *v./n.* bawl, bellow, call, cheer, clamour, cry, hail, halloo, hollo, hurrah, huzzah (*Archaic*), roar, shout, whoop, yell

hollow *adj.* **1.** empty, not solid, unfilled, vacant, void **2.** cavernous, concave, deep-set, depressed, indented, sunken **3.** deep, dull, expressionless, flat, low, muffled, muted, reverberant, rumbling, sepulchral, toneless **4.** empty, fruitless, futile, meaningless, pointless, Pyrrhic, specious, unavailing, useless, vain, worthless **5.** empty, famished, hungry, ravenous, starved **6.** artificial, cynical, deceitful, faithless, false, flimsy, hollow-hearted, hypocritical, insincere, treacherous, unsound, weak **7. beat (someone) hollow** *Inf.* defeat, hammer (*Inf.*), outdo, overcome, rout, thrash, trounce, worst ~*n.* 8. basin, bowl, cave, cavern, cavity, concavity, crater, cup, den, dent, depression, dimple, excavation, hole, indentation, pit, trough 9. bottom, dale, dell, dingle, glen, valley ~*v.* 10. channel, dig, dish, excavate, furrow, gouge, groove, pit, scoop

Antonyms *adj.* (*sense 1*) full, occupied, solid (*sense 2*) convex, rounded (*sense 3*) expressive, vibrant (*sense 4*) gratifying, meaningful, pleasing, satisfying, valuable, worthwhile (*sense 6*) genuine ~*n.* (*sense 8*) bump, mound, projection (*sense 9*) bluff, height, hill, knoll, mountain, rise

holocaust annihilation, carnage, conflagration, destruction, devastation, fire, genocide, inferno, massacre, mass murder

holy 1. devout, divine, faithful, god-fearing, godly, hallowed, pious, pure, religious, righteous, saintly, sublime, virtuous 2. blessed, consecrated, dedicated, hallowed, sacred, sacrosanct, sanctified, venerable, venerated

Antonyms blasphemous, corrupt, desecrated, earthly, evil, human, immoral, impious, irreligious, sacrilegious, secular, sinful, unconsecrated, unhallowed, unholy, unsanctified, wicked, worldly

homage 1. admiration, adoration, adulation, awe, deference, devotion, duty, esteem, honour, respect, reverence, worship 2. allegiance, devotion, faithfulness, fealty, fidelity, loyalty, obeisance, service, tribute, troth (*Archaic*)

Antonyms condemnation, contempt, disdain, disregard, disrespect, irreverence, scorn

home *n.* 1. abode, domicile, dwelling, dwelling place, habitation, house, pad (*Sl.*), residence 2. birthplace, family, fireside, hearth, homestead, home town, household 3. abode, element, environment, habitat, habitation, haunt, home ground, range, stamping ground, territory 4. **at home a.** available, in, present **b.** at ease, comfortable, familiar, relaxed **c.** entertaining, giving a party, having guests, receiving **d.** *As a noun* party, reception, soirée 5. **at home in, on,** *or* **with** conversant with, familiar with, knowledgeable, proficient, skilled, well-versed 6. **bring home to** drive home, emphasize, impress upon, make clear, press home ~*adj.* 7. central, domestic, familiar, family, household, inland, internal, local, national, native

homeland country of origin, fatherland, mother country, motherland, native land

homeless 1. *adj.* abandoned, destitute, displaced, dispossessed, down-and-out, exiled, forlorn, forsaken, outcast, unsettled 2. *n.* **the homeless** dossers (*Brit. sl.*), squatters, vagrants

homelike cheerful, comfortable, cosy, easy, familiar, homy, informal, intimate, relaxing, snug

homely comfortable, comfy (*Inf.*), cosy, domestic, downhome (*Sl., chiefly U.S.*), everyday, familiar, friendly, homelike, homespun, homy, informal, modest, natural, ordinary, plain, simple, unaffected, unassuming, unpretentious, welcoming

Antonyms affected, elaborate, elegant, grand, ostentatious, pretentious, refined, regal, sophisticated, splendid

Homeric epic, grand, heroic, imposing, impressive

homespun artless, coarse, homely, homemade, inelegant, plain, rough, rude, rustic, unpolished, unsophisticated

homicidal deadly, death-dealing, lethal, maniacal, mortal, murderous

homicide 1. bloodshed, killing, manslaughter, murder, slaying 2. killer, murderer, slayer

homily address, discourse, lecture, preaching, preachment, sermon

homogeneity analogousness, comparability, consistency, correspondence, identicalness, oneness, sameness, similarity, uniformity

homogeneous akin, alike, analogous, cognate, comparable, consistent, identical, kindred, similar, uniform, unvarying

Antonyms different, disparate, dissimilar, divergent, diverse, heterogeneous, manifold, mixed, unlike, unrelated, varied, various, varying

homologous analogous, comparable, correspondent, corresponding, like, parallel, related, similar

homosexual *adj.* bent (*Sl.*), camp (*Inf.*), gay, homoerotic, lesbian, queer (*Inf., derogatory*), sapphic

homy comfortable, comfy (*Inf.*), congenial, cosy, domestic, familiar, friendly, informal, intimate, pleasant, warm

hone *v.* edge, file, grind, point, polish, sharpen, strop, whet

honest 1. conscientious, decent, ethical, high-minded, honourable, law-abiding, reliable, reputable, scrupulous, trustworthy, trusty, truthful, upright, veracious, virtuous 2. above board, authentic, bona fide, genuine, honest to goodness, on the level (*Inf.*), on the up and up, proper, real, straight, true 3. equitable, fair, fair and square, impartial, just 4. candid, direct, forthright, frank, ingenuous, open, out-

right, plain, sincere, straightforward, undisguised, unfeigned, upfront (*Inf.*)
Antonyms bad, corrupt, counterfeit, crooked, deceitful, disguised, dishonest, false, fraudulent, guilty, illegitimate, immoral, insincere, secretive, treacherous, unethical, unfair, unfaithful, unlawful, unprincipled, unreliable, unrighteous, unscrupulous, untrustworthy, untruthful

honestly 1. by fair means, cleanly, ethically, honourably, in good faith, lawfully, legally, legitimately, on the level (*Inf.*), with clean hands 2. candidly, frankly, in all sincerity, in plain English, plainly, straight (out), to one's face, truthfully

honesty 1. faithfulness, fidelity, honour, incorruptibility, integrity, morality, probity, rectitude, reputability, scrupulousness, straightness, trustworthiness, truthfulness, uprightness, veracity, virtue 2. bluntness, candour, equity, even-handedness, fairness, frankness, genuineness, openness, outspokenness, plainness, sincerity, straightforwardness

honeyed agreeable, alluring, cajoling, dulcet, enticing, flattering, mellow, melodious, seductive, soothing, sweet, sweetened, unctuous

honorary complimentary, ex officio, formal, *honoris causa,* in name *or* title only, nominal, titular, unofficial, unpaid

honour *n.* 1. credit, dignity, distinction, elevation, eminence, esteem, fame, glory, high standing, prestige, rank, renown, reputation, repute 2. acclaim, accolade, adoration, Brownie points, commendation, deference, homage, kudos, praise, recognition, regard, respect, reverence, tribute, veneration 3. decency, fairness, goodness, honesty, integrity, morality, principles, probity, rectitude, righteousness, trustworthiness, uprightness 4. compliment, credit, favour, pleasure, privilege, source of pride *or* satisfaction 5. chastity, innocence, modesty, purity, virginity, virtue ~*v.* 6. admire, adore, appreciate, esteem, exalt, glorify, hallow, prize, respect, revere, reverence, value, venerate, worship 7. be as good as (*Inf.*), be faithful to, be true to, carry out, discharge, fulfil, keep, live up to, observe 8. acclaim, celebrate, commemorate, commend, compliment, crack up (*Inf.*), decorate, dignify, exalt, glorify, laud, lionize, praise 9. accept, acknowledge, cash, clear, credit, pass, pay, take
Antonyms *n.* condemnation, contempt, degradation, disfavour, disgrace, dishonesty, dishonour, disrepute, disrespect, infamy, insincerity, insult, lowness, meanness, scorn, shame, slight, unscrupulousness ~*v.* condemn, defame, degrade, dishonour, disobey, insult, offend, refuse, scorn, slight

honourable 1. ethical, fair, high-minded, honest, just, moral, principled, true, trustworthy, trusty, upright, upstanding, virtuous 2. distinguished, eminent, great, illustrious, noble, notable, noted, prestigious, renowned, venerable 3. creditable, estimable, proper, reputable, respectable, respected, right, righteous, virtuous

honours adornments, awards, decorations, dignities, distinctions, laurels, titles

hoodwink bamboozle (*Inf.*), befool, cheat, con (*Inf.*), cozen, deceive, delude, dupe, fool, gull (*Archaic*), hoax, impose, kid (*Inf.*), lead up the garden path (*Inf.*), mislead, pull a fast one on (*Inf.*), rook (*Sl.*), swindle, trick

hook *n.* 1. catch, clasp, fastener, hasp, holder, link, lock, peg 2. noose, snare, springe, trap 3. **by hook or by crook** by any means, by fair means or foul, somehow, somehow or other, someway 4. **hook, line, and sinker** *Inf.* completely, entirely, thoroughly, through and through, totally, utterly, wholly 5. **off the hook** *Sl.* acquitted, cleared, exonerated, in the clear, let off, under no obligation, vindicated ~*v.* 6. catch, clasp, fasten, fix, hasp, secure 7. catch, enmesh, ensnare, entrap, snare, trap

hooked 1. aquiline, beaked, beaky, bent, curved, falcate (*Biol.*), hamate (*Rare*), hooklike, hook-shaped, unciform (*Anat., etc.*), uncinate (*Biol.*) 2. addicted to, devoted to, enamoured of, obsessed with, taken with, turned on (*Sl.*)

hooligan casual, lager lout, delinquent, hoodlum (*Chiefly U.S.*), ned (*Sl.*), rowdy, ruffian, tough, vandal, yob *or* yobbo (*Brit. sl.*)

hoop band, circlet, girdle, loop, ring, wheel

hoot *n.* 1. call, cry, toot 2. boo, catcall, hiss, jeer, yell 3. *Inf.* card (*Inf.*), caution (*Inf.*), laugh (*Inf.*), scream (*Inf.*) ~*v.* 4. boo, catcall, condemn, decry, denounce, execrate, hiss, howl down, jeer, yell at 5. cry, scream, shout, shriek, toot, whoop, yell

hop 1. *v.* bound, caper, dance, jump, leap, skip, spring, vault, trip 2. *n.* bounce, bound, jump, leap, skip, spring, step, vault

hope 1. *n.* ambition, anticipation, assumption, belief, confidence, desire, dream, expectancy, expectation, faith, longing 2. *v.* anticipate, aspire, await, believe, contemplate, count on, desire, expect, foresee, long, look forward to, rely, trust
Antonyms despair, distrust, doubt, dread, hopelessness

hopeful 1. anticipating, assured, buoyant, confident, expectant, looking forward to,

optimistic, sanguine 2. auspicious, bright, cheerful, encouraging, heartening, promising, propitious, reassuring, rosy
Antonyms (*sense 1*) cheerless, dejected, despairing, hopeless, pessimistic (*sense 2*) depressing, discouraging, disheartening, unpromising

hopefully 1. confidently, expectantly, optimistically, sanguinely 2. *Inf.* all being well, conceivably, expectedly, feasibly, probably

hopeless 1. defeatist, dejected, demoralized, despairing, desperate, despondent, disconsolate, downhearted, forlorn, in despair, pessimistic, woebegone 2. helpless, incurable, irremediable, irreparable, irreversible, lost, past remedy, remediless 3. forlorn, futile, impossible, impracticable, pointless, unachievable, unattainable, useless, vain 4. *Inf.* inadequate, incompetent, ineffectual, inferior, no good, pathetic, poor, useless (*Inf.*)
Antonyms (*sense 1*) assured, cheerful, confident, expectant, happy, heartened, hopeful, optimistic, uplifted (*sense 2*) curable, encouraging, favourable, heartening, promising, reassuring, remediable

horde band, crew, crowd, drove, gang, host, mob, multitude, pack, press, swarm, throng, troop

horizon 1. field of vision, skyline, vista 2. ambit, compass, ken, perspective, prospect, purview, range, realm, scope, sphere, stretch

horrible 1. abhorrent, abominable, appalling, awful, dreadful, fearful, frightful, ghastly, grim, grisly, gruesome, heinous, hellacious (*U.S. sl.*), hideous, horrid, loathsome, obscene, repulsive, revolting, shameful, shocking, terrible, terrifying 2. *Inf.* awful, beastly (*Inf.*), cruel, disagreeable, dreadful, ghastly (*Inf.*), horrid, mean, nasty, terrible, unkind, unpleasant
Antonyms agreeable, appealing, attractive, charming, delightful, enchanting, fetching, lovely, pleasant, wonderful

horrid 1. awful, disagreeable, disgusting, dreadful, horrible, nasty, obscene, offensive, terrible, unpleasant, yucky *or* yukky (*Sl.*) 2. abominable, alarming, appalling, formidable, frightening, hair-raising, harrowing, hideous, horrific, odious, repulsive, revolting, shocking, terrifying, terrorizing 3. *Inf.* beastly (*Inf.*), cruel, mean, nasty, unkind

horrific appalling, awful, dreadful, frightening, frightful, ghastly, grim, grisly, hellacious (*U.S. sl.*), horrendous, horrifying, shocking, terrifying

horrify 1. affright, alarm, frighten, intimidate, petrify, scare, terrify, terrorize 2. appal, disgust, dismay, gross out (*U.S. sl.*), outrage, shock, sicken
Antonyms comfort, delight, enchant, encourage, gladden, hearten, please, reassure, soothe

horror 1. alarm, apprehension, awe, consternation, dismay, dread, fear, fright, panic, terror 2. abhorrence, abomination, antipathy, aversion, detestation, disgust, hatred, loathing, odium, repugnance, revulsion
Antonyms affinity, approval, attraction, delight, liking, love

horror-struck *or* **horror-stricken** aghast, appalled, awe-struck, frightened to death, horrified, petrified, scared out of one's wits, shocked

horse around *or* **about** clown, fool about *or* around, misbehave, play the fool, roughhouse (*Sl.*)

horseman cavalier, cavalryman, dragoon, equestrian, horse-soldier, rider

horseplay buffoonery, clowning, fooling around, high jinks, pranks, romping, rough-and-tumble, roughhousing (*Sl.*), skylarking (*Inf.*)

horse sense common sense, gumption (*Brit. inf.*), judgment, mother wit, nous (*Brit. sl.*), practicality

hospitable 1. amicable, bountiful, cordial, friendly, generous, genial, gracious, kind, liberal, sociable, welcoming 2. accessible, amenable, open-minded, receptive, responsive, tolerant
Antonyms (*sense 1*) inhospitable, parsimonious (*sense 2*) inhospitable, intolerant, narrow-minded, unapproachable, unreceptive

hospitality cheer, conviviality, cordiality, friendliness, heartiness, hospitableness, neighbourliness, sociability, warmth, welcome

host[1] *n.* 1. entertainer, innkeeper, landlord, master of ceremonies, proprietor 2. anchor man, compere (*Brit.*), presenter ~*v.* 3. compere (*Brit.*), front (*Inf.*), introduce, present

host[2] army, array, drove, horde, legion, multitude, myriad, swarm, throng

hostage captive, gage, pawn, pledge, prisoner, security, surety

hostile 1. antagonistic, anti (*Inf.*), bellicose, belligerent, contrary, ill-disposed, inimical, malevolent, opposed, opposite, rancorous, unkind, warlike 2. adverse, alien, inhospitable, unfriendly, unpropitious, unsympathetic, unwelcoming
Antonyms affable, agreeable, amiable, approving, congenial, cordial, friendly, kind, peaceful, sympathetic, warm

hostilities conflict, fighting, state of war, war, warfare
Antonyms alliance, peace, treaty, truce
hostility abhorrence, animosity, animus, antagonism, antipathy, aversion, detestation, enmity, hatred, ill will, malevolence, malice, opposition, resentment, unfriendliness
Antonyms agreement, amity, approval, congeniality, cordiality, friendliness, good will, sympathy
hot 1. blistering, boiling, burning, fiery, flaming, heated, piping hot, roasting, scalding, scorching, searing, steaming, sultry, sweltering, torrid, warm 2. acrid, biting, peppery, piquant, pungent, sharp, spicy 3. *Fig.* animated, ardent, excited, fervent, fervid, fierce, fiery, flaming, impetuous, inflamed, intense, irascible, lustful, passionate, raging, stormy, touchy, vehement, violent 4. fresh, just out, latest, new, recent, up to the minute 5. approved, favoured, in demand, in vogue, popular, sought-after 6. close, following closely, in hot pursuit, near
Antonyms (*sense 1*) chilly, cold, cool, freezing, frigid, frosty, icy, parky (*Brit. inf.*) (*sense 2*) mild (*sense 3*) apathetic, calm, dispassionate, half-hearted, indifferent, mild, moderate (*sense 4*) old, stale, trite (*sense 5*) out of favour, unpopular (*sense 6*) cold
hot air blather, blether, bombast, bosh (*Inf.*), bunkum *or* buncombe (*Chiefly U.S.*), claptrap (*Inf.*), empty talk, gas (*Inf.*), guff (*Sl.*), rant, tall talk (*Inf.*), verbiage, wind
hotbed breeding ground, den, forcing house, nest, nursery, seedbed
hot-blooded ardent, excitable, fervent, fiery, heated, impulsive, passionate, rash, spirited, temperamental, wild
Antonyms apathetic, calm, cold, cool, frigid, impassive, restrained, unenthusiastic
hotchpotch conglomeration, farrago, gallimaufry, hash, hodgepodge (*U.S.*), jumble, medley, *mélange,* mess, miscellany, mishmash, mixture, olio, olla podrida, potpourri
hotfoot hastily, helter-skelter, hurriedly, pell-mell, posthaste, quickly, speedily
hothead daredevil, desperado, hotspur, madcap, tearaway
hot-headed fiery, foolhardy, hasty, hot-tempered, impetuous, precipitate, quick-tempered, rash, reckless, unruly, volatile
hothouse 1. *n.* conservatory, glasshouse, greenhouse 2. *adj.* coddled, dainty, delicate, exotic, fragile, frail, overprotected, pampered, sensitive
hound *v.* 1. chase, drive, give chase, hunt, hunt down, pursue 2. badger, goad, harass, harry, impel, persecute, pester, prod, provoke
house *n.* 1. abode, building, domicile, dwelling, edifice, habitation, home, homestead, pad (*Sl.*), residence 2. family, household, ménage 3. ancestry, clan, dynasty, family tree, kindred, line, lineage, race, tribe 4. business, company, concern, establishment, firm, organization, outfit (*Inf.*), partnership 5. assembly, Commons, legislative body, parliament 6. hotel, inn, public house, tavern 7. **on the house** for nothing, free, gratis, without expense ~*v.* 8. accommodate, billet, board, domicile, harbour, lodge, put up, quarter, take in 9. contain, cover, keep, protect, sheathe, shelter, store
household 1. *n.* family, home, house, ménage 2. *adj.* domestic, domiciliary, family, ordinary, plain
householder homeowner, occupant, resident, tenant
housekeeping home economy, homemaking (*U.S.*), housecraft, household management, housewifery
housing 1. accommodation, dwellings, homes, houses 2. case, casing, container, cover, covering, enclosure, sheath
hovel cabin, den, hole, hut, shack, shanty, shed
hover 1. be suspended, drift, float, flutter, fly, hang, poise 2. hang about, linger, wait nearby 3. alternate, dither (*Chiefly Brit.*), falter, fluctuate, haver (*Brit.*), oscillate, pause, seesaw, swither (*Scot. dialect*), vacillate, waver
however after all, anyhow, be that as it may, but, even though, nevertheless, nonetheless, notwithstanding, on the other hand, still, though, yet
howl 1. *n.* bawl, bay, bell, bellow, clamour, cry, groan, hoot, outcry, roar, scream, shriek, ululation, wail, yelp, yowl 2. *v.* bawl, bell, bellow, cry, cry out, lament, quest (*used of hounds*), roar, scream, shout, shriek, ululate, wail, weep, yell, yelp
howler bloomer (*Brit. inf.*), blunder, boner (*Sl.*), boob (*Brit. sl.*), booboo (*Inf.*), bull (*Sl.*), clanger (*Inf.*), error, malapropism, mistake, schoolboy howler
hoyden, hoiden romp (*Archaic*), tomboy
hoydenish, hoidenish boisterous, bold, ill-mannered, inelegant, rackety, uncouth, unfeminine, ungenteel, unladylike, unruly
hub centre, core, focal point, focus, heart, middle, nerve centre, pivot
hubbub babel, bedlam, brouhaha, clamour, confusion, din, disorder, disturbance, hue and cry, hullabaloo, hurly-burly, noise,

pandemonium, racket, riot, ruckus (*Inf.*), ruction (*Inf.*), rumpus, tumult, uproar

huckster barker (*Inf.*), hawker, pedlar, pitchman (*U.S.*), salesman, vendor

huddle *n.* 1. confusion, crowd, disorder, heap, jumble, mass, mess, muddle 2. *Inf.* confab (*Inf.*), conference, discussion, meeting, powwow ~*v.* 3. cluster, converge, crowd, flock, gather, press, throng 4. crouch, cuddle, curl up, hunch up, make oneself small, nestle, snuggle

hue 1. colour, dye, shade, tincture, tinge, tint, tone 2. aspect, cast, complexion, light

hue and cry brouhaha, clamour, furore, hullabaloo, much ado, outcry, ruction (*Inf.*), rumpus, uproar

huff *n.* 1. anger, bad mood, bate (*Brit. sl.*), miff (*Inf.*), passion, pet, pique, rage, temper 2. **in a huff** angered, annoyed, exasperated, hacked (off) (*U.S. sl.*), hurt, in high dudgeon, irked, miffed (*Inf.*), nettled, peeved, piqued, pissed off (*Taboo sl.*), provoked, put out (*Inf.*), riled (*Inf.*), vexed ~*v.* 3. blow, exhale, puff

huffish, huffy angry, crabbed, cross, crotchety (*Inf.*), crusty, curt, disgruntled, edgy, grumpy, irritable, moody, moping, offended, peevish, pettish, petulant, querulous, ratty (*Brit. & N.Z. inf.*), resentful, shirty (*Sl., chiefly Brit.*), short, snappy, sulky, sullen, surly, testy, tetchy, touchy, waspish
Antonyms amiable, calm, cheerful, friendly, gay, good-humoured, happy, pleasant, sunny

hug *v.* 1. clasp, cuddle, embrace, enfold, hold close, squeeze, take in one's arms 2. cling to, follow closely, keep close, stay near 3. cherish, cling, hold onto, nurse, retain ~*n.* 4. bear hug, clasp, clinch (*Sl.*), embrace, squeeze

huge Brobdingnagian, bulky, colossal, elephantine, enormous, extensive, gargantuan, giant, gigantic, ginormous (*Inf.*), great, humongous *or* humungous (*U.S. sl.*), immense, jumbo (*Inf.*), large, mammoth, massive, mega (*Sl.*), monumental, mountainous, prodigious, stupendous, titanic, tremendous, vast
Antonyms insignificant, little, microscopic, minute, petty, puny, small, tiny

huggermugger confusion, disarray, disorder, disorganization, guddle (*Scot.*), hodgepodge (*U.S.*), hotchpotch, huddle, jumble, mess, muddle, pig's breakfast (*Inf.*), shambles, state

hulk 1. derelict, frame, hull, shell, shipwreck, wreck 2. lout, lubber, lump (*Inf.*), oaf

hulking awkward, bulky, clumsy, cumbersome, gross, lubberly, lumbering, lumpish, massive, oafish, overgrown, ponderous, ungainly, unwieldy

hull *n.* 1. body, casing, covering, frame, framework, skeleton 2. husk, peel, pod, rind, shell, shuck, skin ~*v.* 3. husk, peel, shell, shuck, skin, trim

hullabaloo babel, bedlam, brouhaha, clamour, commotion, confusion, din, disturbance, furore, hubbub, hue and cry, hurly-burly, noise, outcry, pandemonium, racket, ruckus (*Inf.*), ruction (*Inf.*), rumpus, to-do, tumult, turmoil, upheaval, uproar

hum 1. bombinate *or* bombilate (*Literary*), buzz, croon, drone, mumble, murmur, purr, sing, throb, thrum, vibrate, whir 2. be active, be busy, bustle, buzz, move, pulsate, pulse, stir, vibrate

human *adj.* 1. anthropoid, fleshly, manlike, mortal 2. approachable, compassionate, considerate, fallible, forgivable, humane, kind, kindly, natural, understandable, understanding, vulnerable ~*n.* 3. body, child, creature, human being, individual, man, mortal, person, soul, wight (*Archaic*), woman
Antonyms *adj.* (*sense 1*) animal, nonhuman (*sense 2*) beastly, brutish, cruel, inhuman, unsympathetic ~*n.* animal, god, nonhuman

humane benevolent, benign, charitable, clement, compassionate, forbearing, forgiving, gentle, good, good-natured, kind, kind-hearted, kindly, lenient, merciful, mild, sympathetic, tender, understanding
Antonyms barbarous, brutal, cruel, inhuman, inhumane, ruthless, uncivilized, unkind, unmerciful, unsympathetic

humanitarian 1. *adj.* altruistic, beneficent, benevolent, charitable, compassionate, humane, philanthropic, public-spirited 2. *n.* altruist, benefactor, Good Samaritan, philanthropist

humanitarianism beneficence, benevolence, charity, generosity, good will, humanism, philanthropy

humanities classical studies, classics, liberal arts, literae humaniores

humanity 1. flesh, Homo sapiens, humankind, human race, man, mankind, men, mortality, people 2. human nature, humanness, mortality 3. benevolence, benignity, brotherly love, charity, compassion, fellow feeling, kind-heartedness, kindness, mercy, philanthropy, sympathy, tenderness, tolerance, understanding

humanize civilize, cultivate, educate, enlighten, improve, mellow, polish, reclaim, refine, soften, tame

humble *adj.* 1. meek, modest, self-effacing,

submissive, unassuming, unostentatious, unpretentious 2. common, commonplace, insignificant, low, low-born, lowly, mean, modest, obscure, ordinary, plebeian, poor, simple, undistinguished, unimportant, unpretentious 3. courteous, deferential, obliging, obsequious, polite, respectful, servile, subservient ~*v.* 4. abase, abash, break, bring down, chagrin, chasten, crush, debase, degrade, demean, disgrace, humiliate, lower, mortify, put down (*Sl.*), reduce, shame, sink, subdue, take down a peg (*Inf.*) 5. **humble oneself** abase oneself, eat crow (*U.S. inf.*), eat humble pie, go on bended knee, grovel, swallow one's pride

Antonyms *adj.* (*senses 1 & 3*) arrogant, assuming, conceited, haughty, immodest, lordly, ostentatious, overbearing, pompous, presumptuous, pretentious, proud, snobbish, superior, vain (*sense 2*) aristocratic, distinguished, elegant, famous, glorious, high, important, rich, significant, superior, wealthy ~*v.* elevate, exalt, magnify, raise

humbly cap in hand, deferentially, diffidently, meekly, modestly, obsequiously, on bended knee, respectfully, servilely, submissively, subserviently, unassumingly

humbug *n.* 1. bluff, canard, cheat, deceit, deception, dodge, feint, fraud, hoax, imposition, imposture, ruse, sham, swindle, trick, trickery, wile 2. charlatan, cheat, con man (*Inf.*), faker, fraud, impostor, phoney *or* phony (*Inf.*), quack, swindler, trickster 3. baloney (*Inf.*), cant, charlatanry, claptrap (*Inf.*), eyewash (*Inf.*), gammon (*Brit. inf.*), hypocrisy, nonsense, quackery, rubbish ~*v.* 4. bamboozle (*Inf.*), befool, beguile, cheat, con (*Inf.*), cozen, deceive, delude, dupe, fool, gull (*Archaic*), hoax, hoodwink, impose, mislead, swindle, take in (*Inf.*), trick

humdrum banal, boring, commonplace, dreary, dull, ho-hum (*Inf.*), mind-numbing, monotonous, mundane, ordinary, repetitious, routine, tedious, tiresome, uneventful, uninteresting, unvaried, wearisome

Antonyms dramatic, entertaining, exciting, extraordinary, interesting, lively, sexy (*Inf.*), stimulating

humid clammy, damp, dank, moist, muggy, steamy, sticky, sultry, watery, wet

Antonyms arid, dry, sunny, torrid

humidity clamminess, damp, dampness, dankness, dew, humidness, moistness, moisture, mugginess, sogginess, wetness

humiliate abase, abash, bring low, chagrin, chasten, crush, debase, degrade, discomfit, disgrace, embarrass, humble, make (someone) eat humble pie, mortify, put down (*Sl.*), shame, subdue, take down a peg (*Inf.*)

Antonyms elevate, honour, magnify, make proud

humiliating cringe-making (*Brit. inf.*), crushing, degrading, disgracing, embarrassing, humbling, ignominious, mortifying, shaming

humiliation abasement, affront, chagrin, condescension, degradation, disgrace, dishonour, embarrassment, humbling, ignominy, indignity, loss of face, mortification, put-down, resignation, self-abasement, shame, submission, submissiveness

humility diffidence, humbleness, lack of pride, lowliness, meekness, modesty, self-abasement, servility, submissiveness, unpretentiousness

Antonyms arrogance, conceit, disdain, haughtiness, pomposity, presumption, pretentiousness, pride, snobbishness, superciliousness, superiority, vanity

hummock hillock, hump, knoll, mound

humorist card (*Inf.*), comedian, comic, eccentric, funny man, jester, joker, wag, wit

humorous amusing, comic, comical, droll, entertaining, facetious, farcical, funny, hilarious, jocose, jocular, laughable, ludicrous, merry, playful, pleasant, side-splitting, waggish, whimsical, witty

Antonyms earnest, grave, sad, serious, sober, solemn

humour *n.* 1. amusement, comedy, drollery, facetiousness, fun, funniness, jocularity, ludicrousness, wit 2. comedy, farce, gags (*Inf.*), jesting, jests, jokes, joking, pleasantry, wisecracks (*Inf.*), wit, witticisms, wittiness 3. disposition, frame of mind, mood, spirits, temper 4. bent, bias, fancy, freak, mood, propensity, quirk, vagary, whim ~*v.* 5. accommodate, cosset, favour, feed, flatter, go along with, gratify, indulge, mollify, pamper, pander to, spoil

Antonyms *n.* gravity, grief, melancholy, sadness, seriousness, sobriety, solemnity, sorrow ~*v.* aggravate, excite, oppose, rouse, stand up to

hump *n.* 1. bulge, bump, hunch, knob, lump, mound, projection, protrusion, protuberance, swelling 2. **the hump** *Brit. inf.* megrims (*Rare*), the blues, the doldrums, the dumps (*Inf.*), the grumps (*Inf.*), the mopes, the sulks ~*v.* 3. arch, curve, form a hump, hunch, lift, tense 4. *Sl.* carry, heave, hoist, lug, shoulder

hunch 1. *n.* feeling, idea, impression, inkling, intuition, premonition, presentiment, suspicion 2. *v.* arch, bend, crouch, curve, draw in, huddle, hump, squat, stoop, tense

hunchback crookback (*Rare*), crouch-back

(*Archaic*), humpback, kyphosis (*Pathol.*), Quasimodo

hunchbacked gibbous, humpbacked, humped, malformed, misshapen, stooped

hunger *n.* 1. appetite, emptiness, esurience, famine, hungriness, ravenousness, starvation, voracity 2. appetence, appetite, craving, desire, greediness, itch, lust, thirst, yearning, yen (*Inf.*) ~*v.* 3. crave, desire, hanker, hope, itch, long, pine, starve, thirst, want, wish, yearn

hungry 1. empty, famished, famishing, hollow, peckish (*Inf., chiefly Brit.*), ravenous, sharp-set, starved, starving, voracious 2. athirst, avid, covetous, craving, desirous, eager, greedy, keen, yearning

hunk block, chunk, gobbet, lump, mass, piece, slab, wedge, wodge (*Brit. inf.*)

hunt *v.* 1. chase, gun for, hound, pursue, stalk, track, trail 2. ferret about, forage, go in quest of, look, look high and low, rummage through, scour, search, seek, try to find ~*n.* 3. chase, hunting, investigation, pursuit, quest, search

hunted careworn, desperate, distraught, gaunt, haggard, harassed, harried, persecuted, stricken, terror-stricken, tormented, worn

hurdle *n.* 1. barricade, barrier, block, fence, hedge, wall 2. barrier, block, complication, difficulty, handicap, hindrance, impediment, obstacle, obstruction, snag, stumbling block

hurl cast, chuck (*Inf.*), fire, fling, heave, launch, let fly, pitch, project, propel, send, shy, sling, throw, toss

hurly-burly bedlam, brouhaha, chaos, commotion, confusion, disorder, furore, hubbub, pandemonium, tumult, turbulence, turmoil, upheaval, uproar

Antonyms composure, order, organization, tidiness

hurricane cyclone, gale, storm, tempest, tornado, twister (*U.S. inf.*), typhoon, willy-willy (*Aust.*), windstorm

hurried breakneck, brief, cursory, hasty, hectic, perfunctory, precipitate, quick, quickie (*Inf.*), rushed, short, slapdash, speedy, superficial, swift

hurry *v.* 1. barrel (along) (*Inf., chiefly U.S. & Canad.*), burn rubber (*Inf.*), dash, fly, get a move on (*Inf.*), lose no time, make haste, rush, scoot, scurry, step on it (*Inf.*) 2. accelerate, expedite, goad, hasten, hustle, push on, quicken, speed (up), urge ~*n.* 3. bustle, celerity, commotion, dispatch, expedition, flurry, haste, precipitation, promptitude, quickness, rush, speed, urgency

Antonyms *v.* crawl, creep, dawdle, delay, move slowly, retard, slow, slow down ~*n.* calmness, slowness

hurt *v.* 1. bruise, damage, disable, harm, impair, injure, mar, spoil, wound 2. ache, be sore, be tender, burn, pain, smart, sting, throb 3. afflict, aggrieve, annoy, cut to the quick, distress, grieve, pain, sadden, sting, upset, wound ~*n.* 4. discomfort, distress, pain, pang, soreness, suffering 5. bruise, sore, wound 6. damage, detriment, disadvantage, harm, injury, loss, mischief, wrong ~*adj.* 7. bruised, cut, damaged, grazed, harmed, injured, scarred, scraped, scratched, wounded 8. aggrieved, crushed, injured, miffed (*Inf.*), offended, pained, piqued, rueful, sad, wounded

Antonyms *v.* aid, alleviate, benefit, calm, compensate, compliment, console, cure, forward, heal, heighten, help, increase, please, relieve, repair, restore, soothe ~*n.* delight, happiness, joy, pleasure, pride, satisfaction ~*adj.* alleviated, assuaged, calmed, consoled, healed, placated, relieved, repaired, restored, soothed

hurtful cruel, cutting, damaging, destructive, detrimental, disadvantageous, distressing, harmful, injurious, maleficent, malicious, mean, mischievous, nasty, pernicious, prejudicial, spiteful, unkind, upsetting, wounding

hurtle barrel (along) (*Inf., chiefly U.S. & Canad.*), burn rubber (*Inf.*), charge, crash, fly, go hell for leather (*Inf.*), plunge, race, rush, rush headlong, scoot, scramble, shoot, speed, spurt, stampede, tear

husband *v.* budget, conserve, economize, hoard, manage thriftily, save, store, use sparingly

Antonyms be extravagant, fritter away, spend, splash out (*Inf., chiefly Brit.*), squander

husbandry 1. agriculture, agronomy, cultivation, farming, land management, tillage 2. careful management, economy, frugality, good housekeeping, thrift

hush *v.* 1. mute, muzzle, quieten, shush, silence, still, suppress 2. allay, appease, calm, compose, mollify, soothe ~*n.* 3. calm, peace, peacefulness, quiet, silence, still (*Poetic*), stillness, tranquillity

hush-hush classified, confidential, restricted, secret, top-secret

hush up conceal, cover up, keep dark, keep secret, sit on (*Inf.*), smother, squash, suppress

husk bark, chaff, covering, glume, hull, rind, shuck

huskiness dryness, harshness, hoarseness, raspingness, roughness

husky 1. croaking, croaky, gruff, guttural,

harsh, hoarse, rasping, raucous, rough, throaty 2. *Inf.* beefy (*Inf.*), brawny, burly, hefty, muscular, powerful, Ramboesque, rugged, stocky, strapping, thickset

hussy baggage (*Inf., old-fashioned*), floozy (*Sl.*), jade, minx, quean (*Archaic*), scrubber (*Brit. & Aust. sl.*), slut, strumpet, tart (*Inf.*), tramp (*Sl.*), trollop, wanton, wench (*Archaic*)

hustle bustle, crowd, elbow, force, haste, hasten, hurry, impel, jog, jostle, push, rush, shove, thrust

hut cabin, den, hovel, lean-to, refuge, shanty, shed, shelter

hybrid *n.* amalgam, composite, compound, cross, crossbreed, half-blood, half-breed, mixture, mongrel, mule

hygiene cleanliness, hygienics, sanitary measures, sanitation

hygienic aseptic, clean, disinfected, germ-free, healthy, pure, salutary, sanitary, sterile
Antonyms dirty, filthy, germ-ridden, harmful, insanitary, polluted, unhealthy, unhygienic, unwholesome

hymn anthem, canticle, carol, chant, doxology, paean, psalm, song of praise

hype ballyhoo (*Inf.*), brouhaha, build-up, plugging (*Inf.*), promotion, publicity, puffing, racket, razzmatazz (*Sl.*)

hyperbole amplification, enlargement, exaggeration, magnification, overstatement

hypercritical captious, carping, cavilling, censorious, fault-finding, finicky, fussy, hairsplitting, niggling, overcritical, overexacting, overscrupulous, pernickety (*Inf.*), strict

hypnotic mesmeric, mesmerizing, narcotic, opiate, sleep-inducing, somniferous, soothing, soporific, spellbinding

hypnotize 1. mesmerize, put in a trance, put to sleep 2. absorb, entrance, fascinate, magnetize, spellbind

hypochondria hypochondriasis, valetudinarianism

hypochondriac *adj./n.* valetudinarian

hypocrisy cant, deceit, deceitfulness, deception, dissembling, duplicity, falsity, imposture, insincerity, pharisaism, phariseeism, phoneyness *or* phoniness (*Inf.*), pretence, sanctimoniousness, speciousness, two-facedness
Antonyms honesty, sincerity, truthfulness

hypocrite charlatan, deceiver, dissembler, fraud, Holy Willie, impostor, Pecksniff, pharisee, phoney *or* phony (*Inf.*), pretender, Tartuffe, whited sepulchre

hypocritical canting, deceitful, deceptive, dissembling, duplicitous, false, fraudulent, hollow, insincere, Janus-faced, pharisaical, phoney *or* phony (*Inf.*), sanctimonious, specious, spurious, two-faced

hypothesis assumption, postulate, premise, premiss, proposition, supposition, theory, thesis

hypothetical academic, assumed, conjectural, imaginary, putative, speculative, supposed, theoretical
Antonyms actual, confirmed, established, known, proven, real, true

hysteria agitation, delirium, frenzy, hysterics, madness, panic, unreason

hysterical 1. berserk, beside oneself, convulsive, crazed, distracted, distraught, frantic, frenzied, mad, overwrought, raving, uncontrollable 2. *Inf.* comical, farcical, hilarious, screaming, side-splitting, uproarious, wildly funny
Antonyms calm, composed, grave, melancholy, poised, sad, self-possessed, serious, unfazed (*Inf.*)

I

ice 1. **break the ice** begin, initiate the proceedings, kick off (*Inf.*), lead the way, make a start, start *or* set the ball rolling (*Inf.*), take the plunge (*Inf.*) 2. **on thin ice** at risk, in jeopardy, open to attack, out on a limb, sticking one's neck out (*Inf.*), unsafe, vulnerable

ice-cold arctic, biting, bitter, chilled to the bone *or* marrow, freezing, frozen, glacial, icy, raw, refrigerated, shivering

iconoclast critic, dissident, heretic, radical, rebel

iconoclastic denunciatory, dissentient, impious, innovative, irreverent, questioning, radical, rebellious, subversive

icy 1. arctic, biting, bitter, chill, chilling, chilly, cold, freezing, frost-bound, frosty, frozen over, ice-cold, parky (*Brit. inf.*), raw 2. glacial, glassy, like a sheet of glass, rimy, slippery, slippy (*Inf. or dialect*) 3. *Fig.* aloof, cold, distant, forbidding, frigid, frosty, glacial, hostile, indifferent, steely, stony, unfriendly, unwelcoming
Antonyms (*sense 1*) blistering, boiling, hot, sizzling, warm (*sense 3*) cordial, friendly, gracious, warm

idea 1. abstraction, concept, conception, conclusion, fancy, impression, judgment, perception, thought, understanding 2. belief, conviction, doctrine, interpretation, notion, opinion, teaching, view, viewpoint 3. approximation, clue, estimate, guess, hint, impression, inkling, intimation, notion, suspicion 4. aim, end, import, intention, meaning, object, objective, plan, purpose, *raison d'être,* reason, sense, significance 5. design, hypothesis, plan, recommendation, scheme, solution, suggestion, theory 6. archetype, essence, form, pattern

ideal *n.* 1. archetype, criterion, epitome, example, exemplar, last word, model, nonpareil, paradigm, paragon, pattern, perfection, prototype, standard, standard of perfection 2. *Often plural* moral value, principle, standard ~*adj.* 3. archetypal, classic, complete, consummate, model, optimal, perfect, quintessential, supreme 4. abstract, conceptual, hypothetical, intellectual, mental, notional, theoretical, transcendental 5. fanciful, imaginary, impractical, ivory-tower, unattainable, unreal, Utopian, visionary
Antonyms *adj.* (*sense 3*) deficient, flawed, impaired, imperfect, unsuitable (*sense 5*) actual, factual, literal, mundane, ordinary, real

idealist *n.* dreamer, romantic, Utopian, visionary

idealistic impracticable, optimistic, perfectionist, quixotic, romantic, starry-eyed, Utopian, visionary
Antonyms down-to-earth, practical, pragmatic, realistic, sensible

idealization ennoblement, exaltation, glorification, magnification, worship

idealize apotheosize, deify, ennoble, exalt, glorify, magnify, put on a pedestal, romanticize, worship

ideally all things being equal, if one had one's way, in a perfect world, under the best of circumstances

idée fixe bee in one's bonnet, fixation, fixed idea, hobbyhorse, monomania, obsession, one-track mind (*Inf.*), preoccupation, thing (*Inf.*)

identical alike, corresponding, duplicate, equal, equivalent, indistinguishable, interchangeable, like, matching, selfsame, the same, twin
Antonyms different, disparate, distinct, diverse, separate, unlike

identifiable ascertainable, detectable, discernible, distinguishable, known, noticeable, recognizable, unmistakable

identification 1. cataloguing, classifying, establishment of identity, labelling, naming, pinpointing, recognition 2. association, connection, empathy, fellow feeling, involvement, rapport, relationship, sympathy 3. credentials, ID, identity card, letters of introduction, papers

identify 1. catalogue, classify, diagnose, flag, label, make out, name, pick out, pinpoint, place, put one's finger on (*Inf.*), recognize, single out, spot, tag 2. *Often with* **with** ally, associate, empathize, feel for, put in the same category, put oneself in the place *or* shoes of, relate to, respond to, see through another's eyes, think of in connection (with)

identity 1. distinctiveness, existence, individuality, oneness, particularity, personality, self, selfhood, singularity, uniqueness

2. accord, correspondence, empathy, rapport, sameness, unanimity, unity

ideology articles of faith, belief(s), creed, dogma, ideas, philosophy, principles, tenets, *Weltanschauung,* world view

idiocy abject stupidity, asininity, cretinism, fatuity, fatuousness, foolishness, imbecility, inanity, insanity, lunacy, senselessness, tomfoolery
Antonyms acumen, sagacity, sanity, sense, soundness, wisdom

idiom 1. expression, locution, phrase, set phrase, turn of phrase 2. jargon, language, mode of expression, parlance, style, talk, usage, vernacular

idiomatic dialectal, native, vernacular

idiosyncrasy affectation, characteristic, eccentricity, habit, mannerism, oddity, peculiarity, personal trait, quirk, singularity, trick

idiosyncratic distinctive, individual, individualistic, peculiar

idiot airhead (*Sl.*), ass, berk (*Brit. sl.*), blockhead, booby, charlie (*Brit. inf.*), coot, cretin, dickhead (*Sl.*), dimwit (*Inf.*), dipstick (*Brit. sl.*), divvy (*Brit. sl.*), dork (*Sl.*), dunderhead, dweeb (*U.S. sl.*), fool, fuckwit (*Taboo sl.*), geek (*Sl.*), gonzo (*Sl.*), halfwit, imbecile, jerk (*Sl., chiefly U.S. & Canad.*), lamebrain (*Inf.*), mooncalf, moron, nerd *or* nurd (*Sl.*), nincompoop, nitwit (*Inf.*), numskull *or* numbskull, oaf, pillock (*Brit. sl.*), plank (*Brit. sl.*), plonker (*Sl.*), prat (*Sl.*), prick (*Derogatory sl.*), schmuck (*U.S. sl.*), simpleton, twit (*Inf., chiefly Brit.*), wally (*Sl.*)

idiotic asinine, braindead (*Inf.*), crackpot (*Inf.*), crazy, daft (*Inf.*), dumb (*Inf.*), fatuous, foolhardy, foolish, halfwitted, harebrained, imbecile, imbecilic, inane, insane, loopy (*Inf.*), lunatic, moronic, senseless, stupid, unintelligent
Antonyms brilliant, commonsensical, intelligent, sensible, thoughtful, wise

idle *adj.* 1. dead, empty, gathering dust, inactive, jobless, mothballed, out of action *or* operation, out of work, redundant, stationary, ticking over, unemployed, unoccupied, unused, vacant 2. indolent, lackadaisical, lazy, shiftless, slothful, sluggish 3. frivolous, insignificant, irrelevant, nugatory, superficial, trivial, unhelpful, unnecessary 4. abortive, bootless, fruitless, futile, groundless, ineffective, of no avail, otiose, pointless, unavailing, unproductive, unsuccessful, useless, vain, worthless ~*v.* 5. *Often with* **away** dally, dawdle, fool, fritter, hang out (*Inf.*), kill time, laze, loiter, lounge, potter, waste, while 6. bob off (*Brit. sl.*), coast, drift, mark time, shirk, sit back and do nothing, skive (*Brit. sl.*), slack, slow down, take it easy, vegetate, veg out (*Sl.*)
Antonyms (*senses 1 & 2*) active, busy, employed, energetic, functional, industrious, occupied, operative, working (*sense 3*) important, meaningful (*sense 4*) advantageous, effective, fruitful, profitable, useful, worthwhile

idleness 1. inaction, inactivity, leisure, time on one's hands, unemployment 2. hibernation, inertia, laziness, shiftlessness, sloth, sluggishness, torpor, vegetating 3. dilly-dallying (*Inf.*), lazing, loafing, pottering, skiving (*Brit. sl.*), time-wasting, trifling

idler clock-watcher, couch potato (*Sl.*), dawdler, deadbeat (*Inf., chiefly U.S. & Canad.*), dodger, drone, laggard, layabout, lazybones, loafer, lounger, malingerer, shirker, skiver (*Brit. sl.*), slacker, sloth, slouch (*Inf.*), slugabed, sluggard, time-waster, Weary Willie (*Inf.*)

idling *adj.* dawdling, drifting, loafing, pottering, resting, resting on one's oars, taking it easy, ticking over

idol 1. deity, god, graven image, image, pagan symbol 2. *Fig.* beloved, darling, favourite, hero, pet, pin-up (*Sl.*), superstar

idolater 1. heathen, idol-worshipper, pagan 2. admirer, adorer, devotee, idolizer, votary, worshipper

idolatrous adoring, adulatory, reverential, uncritical, worshipful

idolatry adoration, adulation, apotheosis, deification, exaltation, glorification, hero worship, idolizing

idolize admire, adore, apotheosize, bow down before, deify, dote upon, exalt, glorify, hero-worship, look up to, love, revere, reverence, venerate, worship, worship to excess

idyllic arcadian, charming, halcyon, heavenly, ideal, idealized, out of this world, pastoral, peaceful, picturesque, rustic, unspoiled

if 1. *conj.* admitting, allowing, assuming, granting, in case, on condition that, on the assumption that, provided, providing, supposing, though, whenever, wherever, whether 2. *n.* condition, doubt, hesitation, stipulation, uncertainty

iffy chancy (*Inf.*), conditional, doubtful, in the lap of the gods, problematical, uncertain, undecided, unpredictable, up in the air

ignis fatuus bubble, chimera, delusion, illusion, mirage, phantasm, self-deception, will-o'-the-wisp

ignite burn, burst into flames, catch fire, fire, flare up, inflame, kindle, light, put a match to (*Inf.*), set alight, set fire to, take fire, touch off

ignoble 1. abject, base, contemptible, craven, dastardly, degenerate, degraded, despicable, disgraceful, dishonourable, heinous, infamous, low, mean, petty, shabby, shameless, unworthy, vile, wretched 2. baseborn (*Archaic*), common, humble, lowborn (*Rare*), lowly, mean, of humble birth, peasant, plebeian, vulgar

ignominious abject, despicable, discreditable, disgraceful, dishonourable, disreputable, humiliating, indecorous, inglorious, mortifying, scandalous, shameful, sorry, undignified
Antonyms creditable, honourable, reputable, worthy

ignominy bad odour, contempt, discredit, disgrace, dishonour, disrepute, humiliation, infamy, mortification, obloquy, odium, opprobrium, reproach, shame, stigma
Antonyms credit, honour, repute

ignoramus ass, blockhead, bonehead (*Sl.*), dolt, donkey, duffer (*Inf.*), dullard, dunce, fool, illiterate, lowbrow, numskull *or* numbskull, simpleton

ignorance 1. greenness, inexperience, innocence, nescience (*Literary*), oblivion, unawareness, unconsciousness, unfamiliarity 2. benightedness, blindness, illiteracy, lack of education, mental darkness, unenlightenment, unintelligence
Antonyms (*sense 2*) comprehension, enlightenment, insight, intelligence, knowledge, understanding, wisdom

ignorant 1. benighted, blind to, inexperienced, innocent, in the dark about, oblivious, unaware, unconscious, unenlightened, uninformed, uninitiated, unknowing, unschooled, unwitting 2. green, illiterate, naive, unaware, uncultivated, uneducated, unknowledgeable, unlearned, unlettered, unread, untaught, untrained, untutored 3. crass, crude, gross, half-baked (*Inf.*), insensitive, rude, shallow, superficial, uncomprehending, unscholarly
Antonyms astute, aware, brilliant, conscious, cultured, educated, informed, knowledgeable, learned, literate, sagacious, wise

ignore be oblivious to, bury one's head in the sand, cold-shoulder, cut (*Inf.*), discount, disregard, give the cold shoulder to, neglect, overlook, pass over, pay no attention to, reject, send (someone) to Coventry, shut one's eyes to, take no notice of, turn a blind eye to, turn a deaf ear to, turn one's back on
Antonyms acknowledge, heed, note, pay attention to, recognize, regard

ilk brand, breed, character, class, description, disposition, kidney, kind, sort, stamp, style, type, variety

ill *adj.* 1. ailing, dicky (*Brit. inf.*), diseased, funny (*Inf.*), indisposed, infirm, laid up (*Inf.*), not up to snuff (*Inf.*), off-colour, on the sick list (*Inf.*), out of sorts (*Inf.*), poorly (*Inf.*), queasy, queer, seedy (*Inf.*), sick, under the weather (*Inf.*), unhealthy, unwell, valetudinarian 2. bad, damaging, deleterious, detrimental, evil, foul, harmful, iniquitous, injurious, ruinous, unfortunate, unlucky, vile, wicked, wrong 3. acrimonious, adverse, antagonistic, cantankerous, cross, harsh, hateful, hostile, hurtful, inimical, malevolent, malicious, sullen, surly, unfriendly, unkind 4. disturbing, foreboding, inauspicious, ominous, sinister, threatening, unfavourable, unhealthy, unlucky, unpromising, unpropitious, unwholesome *~n.* 5. affliction, hardship, harm, hurt, injury, misery, misfortune, pain, trial, tribulation, trouble, unpleasantness, woe 6. ailment, complaint, disease, disorder, illness, indisposition, infirmity, malady, malaise, sickness 7. abuse, badness, cruelty, damage, depravity, destruction, evil, ill usage, malice, mischief, suffering, wickedness *~adv.* 8. badly, hard, inauspiciously, poorly, unfavourably, unfortunately, unluckily 9. barely, by no means, hardly, insufficiently, scantily 10. *As in* **ill-gotten** criminally, dishonestly, foully, fraudulently, illegally, illegitimately, illicitly, unlawfully, unscrupulously
Antonyms *adj.* (*sense 1*) hale, healthy, strong, well (*sense 2*) favourable, good (*sense 3*) generous, kind *~n.* good, honour, kindness *~adv.* easily, well

ill-advised foolhardy, foolish, ill-considered, ill-judged, impolitic, imprudent, inappropriate, incautious, indiscreet, injudicious, misguided, overhasty, rash, reckless, short-sighted, thoughtless, unseemly, unwise, wrong-headed
Antonyms appropriate, cautious, discreet, judicious, politic, prudent, seemly, sensible, wise

ill-assorted incompatible, incongruous, inharmonious, mismatched, uncongenial, unsuited

ill at ease anxious, awkward, disquieted, disturbed, edgy, faltering, fidgety, hesitant, nervous, on edge, on pins and needles (*Inf.*), on tenterhooks, out of place, restless, self-conscious, strange, tense, twitchy (*Inf.*), uncomfortable, uneasy, unquiet, unrelaxed, unsettled, unsure, wired (*Sl.*)

Antonyms at ease, comfortable, easy, quiet, relaxed, settled, sure

ill-bred bad-mannered, boorish, churlish, coarse, crass, discourteous, ill-mannered, impolite, indelicate, rude, uncivil, uncivilized, uncouth, ungallant, ungentlemanly, unladylike, unmannerly, unrefined, vulgar
Antonyms civil, courteous, delicate, mannerly, refined, urbane, well-bred

ill-considered careless, hasty, heedless, improvident, imprudent, injudicious, overhasty, precipitate, rash, unwise

ill-defined blurred, dim, fuzzy, indistinct, nebulous, shadowy, unclear, vague, woolly
Antonyms apparent, clear, conspicuous, distinct, evident, manifest, obvious, plain

ill-disposed against, antagonistic, anti (*Inf.*), antipathetic, averse, disobliging, down on (*Inf.*), hostile, inimical, opposed, uncooperative, unfriendly, unwelcoming
Antonyms cooperative, friendly, obliging, welcoming, well-disposed

illegal actionable (*Law*), banned, black-market, bootleg, criminal, felonious, forbidden, illicit, lawless, outlawed, prohibited, proscribed, unauthorized, unconstitutional, under-the-counter, under-the-table, unlawful, unlicensed, unofficial, wrongful
Antonyms lawful, legal, licit, permissible

illegality crime, criminality, felony, illegitimacy, illicitness, lawlessness, unlawfulness, wrong, wrongness

illegible crabbed, faint, hard to make out, hieroglyphic, indecipherable, obscure, scrawled, undecipherable, unreadable
Antonyms clear, decipherable, legible, plain, readable

illegitimacy 1. illegality, illicitness, irregularity, unconstitutionality, unlawfulness 2. bastardism, bastardy

illegitimate 1. illegal, illicit, improper, unauthorized, unconstitutional, under-the-table, unlawful, unsanctioned 2. baseborn (*Archaic*), bastard, born on the wrong side of the blanket, born out of wedlock, fatherless, misbegotten (*Literary*), natural, spurious (*Rare*) 3 illogical, incorrect, invalid, spurious, unsound
Antonyms (*sense 1*) authorized, constitutional, lawful, legal, legitimate, proper, sanctioned

ill-fated blighted, doomed, hapless, ill-omened, ill-starred, luckless, star-crossed, unfortunate, unhappy, unlucky

ill-favoured hideous, no oil painting (*Inf.*), plain, repulsive, ugly, unattractive, unlovely, unprepossessing, unsightly

ill feeling animosity, animus, antagonism, bad blood, bitterness, disgruntlement, dissatisfaction, dudgeon (*Archaic*), enmity, frustration, hard feelings, hostility, ill will, indignation, offence, rancour, resentment
Antonyms amity, benevolence, favour, friendship, good will, satisfaction

ill-founded baseless, empty, groundless, idle, unjustified, unproven, unreliable, unsubstantiated, unsupported

ill humour (bad) mood, (bad) temper, bate (*Brit. sl.*), crabbiness, crossness, disagreeableness, grumpiness, irascibility, irritability, moodiness, moroseness, petulance, pique, sharpness, spleen, sulkiness, sulks, tartness, testiness

ill-humoured acrimonious, bad-tempered, crabbed, crabby, cross, disagreeable, grumpy, huffy, impatient, irascible, irritable, like a bear with a sore head (*Inf.*), liverish, mardy (*Dialect*), moody, morose, out of sorts, out of temper, petulant, ratty (*Brit. & N.Z. inf.*), sharp, snappish, snappy, sulky, sullen, tart, testy, tetchy, thin-skinned, touchy, waspish
Antonyms affable, agreeable, amiable, charming, congenial, delightful, genial, good-humoured, good-natured, pleasant

illiberal 1. bigoted, hidebound, intolerant, narrow-minded, prejudiced, reactionary, small-minded, uncharitable, ungenerous 2. close-fisted, mean, miserly, niggardly, parsimonious, selfish, sordid, stingy, tight, tight-arsed (*Taboo sl.*), tight as a duck's arse (*Taboo sl.*), tight-assed (*U.S. taboo sl.*), tightfisted, ungenerous
Antonyms (*sense 1*) broad-minded, charitable, generous, liberal, open-minded, right-on (*Inf.*), tolerant

illicit 1. black-market, bootleg, contraband, criminal, felonious, illegal, illegitimate, prohibited, unauthorized, unlawful, unlicensed 2. clandestine, forbidden, furtive, guilty, immoral, improper, wrong
Antonyms above-board, lawful, legal, legitimate, licit, permissible, proper

illimitable boundless, eternal, immeasurable, immense, infinite, limitless, unbounded, unending, unlimited, vast, without end

illiteracy benightedness, ignorance, illiterateness, lack of education

illiterate benighted, ignorant, uncultured, uneducated, unlettered, untaught, untutored
Antonyms cultured, educated, lettered, literate, taught, tutored

ill-judged foolish, ill-advised, ill-considered, injudicious, misguided, overhasty, rash, short-sighted, unwise, wrong-headed

ill-mannered badly behaved, boorish, churlish, coarse, discourteous, ill-behaved,

ill-bred, impolite, insolent, loutish, rude, uncivil, uncouth, unmannerly
Antonyms civil, courteous, cultivated, mannerly, polished, polite, refined, well-mannered

ill-natured bad-tempered, catty (*Inf.*), churlish, crabbed, cross, cross-grained, disagreeable, disobliging, malevolent, malicious, mean, nasty, perverse, petulant, spiteful, sulky, sullen, surly, unfriendly, unkind, unpleasant
Antonyms agreeable, amiable, cheerful, congenial, friendly, good-natured, kind, obliging, pleasant

illness affliction, ailment, attack, complaint, disability, disease, disorder, ill health, indisposition, infirmity, malady, malaise, poor health, sickness

illogical absurd, fallacious, faulty, inconclusive, inconsistent, incorrect, invalid, irrational, meaningless, senseless, sophistical, specious, spurious, unreasonable, unscientific, unsound
Antonyms coherent, consistent, correct, logical, rational, reasonable, scientific, sound, valid

ill-starred doomed, ill-fated, ill-omened, inauspicious, star-crossed, unfortunate, unhappy, unlucky

ill temper annoyance, bad temper, crossness, curtness, impatience, irascibility, irritability, petulance, sharpness, spitefulness, tetchiness

ill-tempered annoyed, bad-tempered, choleric, cross, curt, grumpy, ill-humoured, impatient, irascible, irritable, liverish, ratty (*Brit. & N.Z. inf.*), sharp, spiteful, testy, tetchy, touchy
Antonyms benign, cheerful, good-natured, mild-mannered, patient, pleasant, sweet-tempered

ill-timed awkward, inappropriate, inconvenient, inept, inopportune, unseasonable, untimely, unwelcome
Antonyms appropriate, convenient, opportune, seasonable, timely, well-timed

ill-treat abuse, damage, handle roughly, harass, harm, harry, ill-use, injure, knock about *or* around, maltreat, mishandle, misuse, oppress, wrong

ill-treatment abuse, damage, harm, ill-use, injury, mistreatment, misuse, rough handling

illuminate 1. brighten, illumine (*Literary*), irradiate, light, light up 2. clarify, clear up, elucidate, enlighten, explain, explicate, give insight into, instruct, interpret, make clear, shed light on 3. adorn, decorate, illustrate, ornament
Antonyms (*sense 1*) black out, darken, dim, obscure, overshadow (*sense 2*) befog, cloud, dull, obfuscate, overcast, shade, veil

illuminating enlightening, explanatory, helpful, informative, instructive, revealing
Antonyms confusing, obscuring, puzzling, unhelpful

illumination 1. beam, brightening, brightness, light, lighting, lighting up, lights, radiance, ray 2. awareness, clarification, edification, enlightenment, insight, inspiration, instruction, perception, revelation, understanding

illuminations decorations, fairy lights, lights

illusion 1. chimera, daydream, fantasy, figment of the imagination, hallucination, ignis fatuus, mirage, mockery, phantasm, semblance, will-o'-the-wisp 2. deception, delusion, error, fallacy, false impression, fancy, misapprehension, misconception
Antonyms actuality, reality, truth

illusory *or* **illusive** apparent, Barmecide, beguiling, chimerical, deceitful, deceptive, delusive, fallacious, false, hallucinatory, misleading, mistaken, seeming, sham, unreal, untrue
Antonyms authentic, down-to-earth, factual, genuine, real, reliable, solid, true

illustrate 1. bring home, clarify, demonstrate, elucidate, emphasize, exemplify, exhibit, explain, explicate, instance, interpret, make clear, make plain, point up, show 2. adorn, decorate, depict, draw, ornament, picture, sketch

illustrated decorated, embellished, graphic, illuminated, pictorial, picture, pictured, with illustrations

illustration 1. analogy, case, case in point, clarification, demonstration, elucidation, example, exemplification, explanation, instance, interpretation, specimen 2. adornment, decoration, figure, picture, plate, sketch

illustrative delineative, descriptive, diagrammatic, explanatory, explicatory, expository, graphic, illustrational, interpretive, pictorial, representative, sample, typical

illustrious brilliant, celebrated, distinguished, eminent, exalted, famed, famous, glorious, great, noble, notable, noted, prominent, remarkable, renowned, resplendent, signal, splendid
Antonyms humble, ignoble, infamous, lowly, meek, notorious, obscure, unassuming

ill will acrimony, animosity, animus, antagonism, antipathy, aversion, bad blood, dislike, enmity, envy, grudge, hard feelings, hatred, hostility, malevolence, malice, no

love lost, rancour, resentment, spite, unfriendliness, venom
Antonyms amiability, amity, charity, congeniality, cordiality, friendship, good will

image 1. appearance, effigy, figure, icon, idol, likeness, picture, portrait, reflection, representation, statue 2. chip off the old block (*Inf.*), counterpart, (dead) ringer (*Sl.*), Doppelgänger, double, facsimile, replica, similitude, spit (*Inf., chiefly Brit.*), spitting image *or* spit and image (*Inf.*) 3. conceit, concept, conception, figure, idea, impression, mental picture, perception, trope

imaginable believable, comprehensible, conceivable, credible, likely, plausible, possible, supposable, thinkable, under the sun, within the bounds of possibility
Antonyms impossible, incomprehensible, inconceivable, incredible, unbelievable, unimaginable, unlikely, unthinkable

imaginary assumed, chimerical, dreamlike, fancied, fanciful, fictional, fictitious, hallucinatory, hypothetical, ideal, illusive, illusory, imagined, invented, legendary, made-up, mythological, nonexistent, phantasmal, shadowy, supposed, suppositious, supposititious, unreal, unsubstantial, visionary
Antonyms actual, factual, genuine, known, proven, real, substantial, tangible, true

imagination 1. creativity, enterprise, fancy, ingenuity, insight, inspiration, invention, inventiveness, originality, resourcefulness, vision, wit, wittiness 2. chimera, conception, idea, ideality, illusion, image, invention, notion, supposition, unreality

imaginative clever, creative, dreamy, enterprising, fanciful, fantastic, ingenious, inspired, inventive, original, poetical, visionary, vivid, whimsical
Antonyms literal, mundane, ordinary, uncreative, unimaginative, uninspired, unoriginal, unpoetical, unromantic

imagine 1. conceive, conceptualize, conjure up, create, devise, dream up (*Inf.*), envisage, fantasize, form a mental picture of, frame, invent, picture, plan, project, scheme, see in the mind's eye, think of, think up, visualize 2. apprehend, assume, believe, conjecture, deduce, deem, fancy, gather, guess (*Inf., chiefly U.S. & Canad.*), infer, realize, suppose, surmise, suspect, take for granted, take it, think

imbalance bias, disproportion, inequality, lack of proportion, lopsidedness, partiality, top-heaviness, unevenness, unfairness

imbecile 1. *n.* berk (*Brit. sl.*), bungler, charlie (*Brit. inf.*), coot, cretin, dickhead (*Sl.*), dipstick (*Brit. sl.*), divvy (*Brit. sl.*), dolt, dork (*Sl.*), dotard, dweeb (*U.S. sl.*), fool, fuckwit (*Taboo sl.*), geek (*Sl.*), gonzo (*Sl.*), halfwit, idiot, jerk (*Sl., chiefly U.S. & Canad.*), moron, nerd *or* nurd (*Sl.*), numskull *or* numbskull, pillock (*Brit. sl.*), plank (*Brit. sl.*), plonker (*Sl.*), prat (*Sl.*), prick (*Derogatory sl.*), schmuck (*U.S. sl.*), thickhead, tosser (*Brit. sl.*), twit (*Inf., chiefly Brit.*), wally (*Sl.*) 2. *adj.* asinine, braindead (*Inf.*), fatuous, feeble-minded, foolish, idiotic, imbecilic, inane, ludicrous, moronic, simple, stupid, thick, witless

imbecility asininity, childishness, cretinism, fatuity, foolishness, idiocy, inanity, incompetency, stupidity
Antonyms comprehension, intelligence, perspicacity, reasonableness, sagacity, sense, soundness, wisdom

imbibe 1. consume, drink, knock back (*Inf.*), quaff, sink (*Inf.*), suck, swallow, swig (*Inf.*) 2. *Literary* absorb, acquire, assimilate, gain, gather, ingest, receive, take in

imbroglio complexity, complication, embarrassment, entanglement, involvement, misunderstanding, quandary

imbue 1. *Fig.* bathe, impregnate, inculcate, infuse, instil, permeate, pervade, saturate, steep 2. colour, dye, ingrain, stain, suffuse, tinge, tint

imitate affect, ape, burlesque, caricature, copy, counterfeit, do (*Inf.*), do an impression of, duplicate, echo, emulate, follow, follow in the footsteps of, follow suit, impersonate, mimic, mirror, mock, parody, personate, repeat, send up (*Brit. inf.*), simulate, spoof (*Inf.*), take a leaf out of (someone's) book, take off (*Inf.*), travesty

imitation *n.* 1. aping, copy, counterfeit, counterfeiting, duplication, echoing, likeness, mimicry, resemblance, simulation 2. fake, forgery, impersonation, impression, mockery, parody, reflection, replica, reproduction, sham, substitution, takeoff (*Inf.*), travesty ~*adj.* 3. artificial, dummy, ersatz, man-made, mock, phoney *or* phony (*Inf.*), pseudo (*Inf.*), repro, reproduction, sham, simulated, synthetic
Antonyms *adj.* authentic, genuine, original, real, true, valid

imitative copied, copycat (*Inf.*), copying, derivative, echoic, mimetic, mimicking, mock, onomatopoeic, parrotlike, plagiarized, pseudo (*Inf.*), put-on, second-hand, simulated, unoriginal

imitator aper, copier, copycat (*Inf.*), echo, epigone (*Rare*), follower, impersonator, impressionist, mimic, parrot, shadow

immaculate 1. clean, impeccable, neat, neat as a new pin, spick-and-span, spruce,

squeaky-clean, trim, unexceptionable 2. above reproach, faultless, flawless, guiltless, impeccable, incorrupt, innocent, perfect, pure, sinless, spotless, squeaky-clean, stainless, unblemished, uncontaminated, undefiled, unpolluted, unsullied, untarnished, virtuous
Antonyms contaminated, corrupt, dirty, filthy, impeachable, impure, polluted, stained, tainted, unclean

immanent congenital, inborn, indigenous, indwelling, inherent, innate, internal, intrinsic, mental, natural, subjective

immaterial 1. a matter of indifference, extraneous, impertinent, inapposite, inconsequential, inconsiderable, inessential, insignificant, irrelevant, of little account, of no consequence, of no importance, trifling, trivial, unimportant, unnecessary 2. airy, disembodied, ethereal, ghostly, incorporeal, metaphysical, spiritual, unembodied, unsubstantial
Antonyms (*sense 1*) crucial, essential, germane, important, material, relevant, significant, substantial (*sense 2*) earthly, physical, real, tangible

immature 1. adolescent, crude, green, imperfect, premature, raw, undeveloped, unfinished, unfledged, unformed, unripe, unseasonable, untimely, young 2. babyish, callow, childish, inexperienced, infantile, jejune, juvenile, puerile, wet behind the ears (*Inf.*)
Antonyms adult, developed, fully-fledged, mature, mellow, responsible, ripe

immaturity 1. crudeness, crudity, greenness, imperfection, rawness, unpreparedness, unripeness 2. babyishness, callowness, childishness, inexperience, juvenility, puerility

immeasurable bottomless, boundless, endless, illimitable, immense, incalculable, inestimable, inexhaustible, infinite, limitless, measureless, unbounded, unfathomable, unlimited, vast
Antonyms bounded, calculable, estimable, exhaustible, fathomable, finite, limited, measurable

immediate 1. instant, instantaneous 2. adjacent, close, contiguous, direct, near, nearest, next, primary, proximate, recent 3. actual, current, existing, extant, on hand, present, pressing, up to date, urgent
Antonyms delayed, distant, far, late, later, leisurely, postponed, remote, slow, tardy

immediately 1. at once, before you could say Jack Robinson (*Inf.*), directly, forthwith, instantly, now, posthaste, promptly, pronto (*Inf.*), right away, right now, straight away, this instant, this very minute, *tout de suite*, unhesitatingly, without delay, without hesitation 2. at first hand, closely, directly, nearly

immemorial age-old, ancient, archaic, fixed, long-standing, of yore, olden (*Archaic*), rooted, time-honoured, traditional

immense Brobdingnagian, colossal, elephantine, enormous, extensive, giant, gigantic, ginormous (*Inf.*), great, huge, humongous *or* humungous (*U.S. sl.*), illimitable, immeasurable, infinite, interminable, jumbo (*Inf.*), large, mammoth, massive, mega (*Sl.*), monstrous, monumental, prodigious, stupendous, titanic, tremendous, vast
Antonyms infinitesimal, little, microscopic, minuscule, minute, puny, small, tiny

immensity bulk, enormity, expanse, extent, greatness, hugeness, infinity, magnitude, massiveness, scope, size, sweep, vastness

immerse 1. bathe, dip, douse, duck, dunk, plunge, sink, submerge, submerse 2. *Fig.* absorb, busy, engage, engross, involve, occupy, take up

immersed *Fig.* absorbed, bound up, buried, busy, consumed, deep, engrossed, in a brown study, involved, mesmerized, occupied, rapt, spellbound, taken up, wrapped up

immersion 1. baptism, bathe, dip, dipping, dousing, ducking, dunking, plunging, submerging 2. *Fig.* absorption, concentration, involvement, preoccupation

immigrant incomer, newcomer, settler

imminent at hand, brewing, close, coming, fast-approaching, forthcoming, gathering, impending, in the air, in the offing, looming, menacing, near, nigh (*Archaic*), on the horizon, on the way, threatening, upcoming
Antonyms delayed, distant, far-off, remote

immobile at a standstill, at rest, fixed, frozen, immobilized, immotile, immovable, like a statue, motionless, rigid, riveted, rooted, stable, static, stationary, stiff, still, stock-still, stolid, unmoving
Antonyms active, mobile, movable, on the move, pliant, portable, vigorous

immobility absence of movement, firmness, fixity, immovability, inertness, motionlessness, stability, steadiness, stillness

immobilize bring to a standstill, cripple, disable, freeze, halt, lay up (*Inf.*), paralyse, put out of action, render inoperative, stop, transfix

immoderate egregious, enormous, exaggerated, excessive, exorbitant, extravagant, extreme, inordinate, intemperate, O.T.T. (*Sl.*), over the odds (*Inf.*), over the top (*Sl.*),

profligate, steep (*Inf.*), uncalled-for, unconscionable, uncontrolled, undue, unjustified, unreasonable, unrestrained, unwarranted, wanton
Antonyms controlled, judicious, mild, moderate, reasonable, restrained, temperate

immoderation excess, exorbitance, extravagance, intemperance, lack of restraint *or* balance, overindulgence, prodigality, unrestraint

immodest 1. bawdy, coarse, depraved, flirtatious, gross, immoral, improper, impure, indecent, indecorous, indelicate, lewd, obscene, revealing, titillating, unchaste 2. bold, bold as brass, brass-necked (*Brit. inf.*), brazen, forward, fresh (*Inf.*), impudent, pushy (*Inf.*), shameless, unblushing

immodesty 1. bawdiness, coarseness, impurity, indecorousness, indelicacy, lewdness, obscenity 2. audacity, balls (*Taboo sl.*), boldness, brass neck (*Brit. inf.*), forwardness, gall (*Inf.*), impudence, shamelessness, temerity
Antonyms (*sense 1*) decency, decorousness, delicacy, modesty, restraint, sobriety

immolate kill, sacrifice

immolation offering up, sacrifice, slaughter

immoral abandoned, bad, corrupt, debauched, degenerate, depraved, dishonest, dissolute, evil, impure, indecent, iniquitous, lewd, licentious, nefarious, obscene, of easy virtue, pornographic, profligate, reprobate, sinful, unchaste, unethical, unprincipled, vicious, vile, wicked, wrong
Antonyms conscientious, good, honourable, inoffensive, law-abiding, moral, pure, upright, virtuous

immorality badness, corruption, debauchery, depravity, dissoluteness, evil, iniquity, licentiousness, profligacy, sin, turpitude, vice, wickedness, wrong
Antonyms goodness, honesty, lawfulness, morality, purity

immorally corruptly, degenerately, dishonestly, dissolutely, evilly, sinfully, unethically, unrighteously, wickedly

immortal *adj.* 1. abiding, constant, death-defying, deathless, endless, enduring, eternal, everlasting, imperishable, incorruptible, indestructible, lasting, perennial, perpetual, sempiternal (*Literary*), timeless, undying, unfading ~*n.* 2. god, goddess, Olympian 3. genius, great (*Usually plural*), hero, paragon
Antonyms *adj.* ephemeral, fading, fleeting, mortal, passing, perishable, temporary, transitory

immortality 1. deathlessness, endlessness, eternity, everlasting life, incorruptibility, indestructibility, perpetuity, timelessness 2. celebrity, fame, glorification, gloriousness, glory, greatness, renown

immortalize apotheosize, celebrate, commemorate, enshrine, eternalize, eternize, exalt, glorify, memorialize, perpetuate, solemnize

immovable 1. fast, firm, fixed, immutable, jammed, rooted, secure, set, stable, stationary, stuck, unbudgeable 2. adamant, constant, impassive, inflexible, obdurate, resolute, steadfast, stony-hearted, unchangeable, unimpressionable, unshakable, unshaken, unwavering, unyielding
Antonyms (*sense 2*) changeable, flexible, impressionable, movable, shakable, wavering, yielding

immune clear, exempt, free, insusceptible, invulnerable, let off (*Inf.*), not affected, not liable, not subject, proof (against), protected, resistant, safe, unaffected
Antonyms exposed, liable, prone, susceptible, unprotected, vulnerable

immunity 1. amnesty, charter, exemption, exoneration, franchise, freedom, indemnity, invulnerability, liberty, licence, prerogative, privilege, release, right 2. immunization, protection, resistance
Antonyms (*sense 1*) exposure, liability, openness, proneness, susceptibility, vulnerability

immunize inoculate, protect, safeguard, vaccinate

immure cage, cloister, confine, enclose, imprison, incarcerate, jail, shut in *or* up, wall up *or* in

immutability agelessness, changelessness, constancy, durability, invariability, permanence, stability, unalterableness, unchangeableness

immutable abiding, ageless, changeless, constant, enduring, fixed, fixed as the laws of the Medes and Persians, immovable, inflexible, invariable, permanent, perpetual, sacrosanct, stable, steadfast, unalterable, unchangeable

imp brat, demon, devil, gamin, minx, pickle (*Brit. inf.*), rascal, rogue, scamp, sprite, urchin

impact *n.* 1. bang, blow, bump, collision, concussion, contact, crash, force, jolt, knock, shock, smash, stroke, thump 2. brunt, burden, consequences, effect, full force, impression, influence, meaning, power, repercussions, significance, thrust, weight ~*v.* 3. clash, collide, crash, crush, hit, strike

impair blunt, damage, debilitate, decrease, deteriorate, diminish, enervate, enfeeble,

harm, hinder, injure, lessen, mar, reduce, spoil, undermine, vitiate, weaken, worsen
Antonyms ameliorate, amend, better, enhance, facilitate, improve, strengthen
impaired damaged, defective, faulty, flawed, imperfect, unsound
impale lance, pierce, run through, skewer, spear, spike, spit, stick, transfix
impalpable airy, delicate, disembodied, fine, imperceptible, incorporeal, indistinct, insubstantial, intangible, shadowy, tenuous, thin, unsubstantial
impart 1. communicate, convey, disclose, discover, divulge, make known, pass on, relate, reveal, tell 2. accord, afford, bestow, confer, contribute, give, grant, lend, offer, yield
impartial detached, disinterested, equal, equitable, even-handed, fair, just, neutral, nondiscriminating, nonpartisan, objective, open-minded, unbiased, unprejudiced, without fear or favour
Antonyms biased, bigoted, influenced, partial, prejudiced, swayed, unfair, unjust
impartiality detachment, disinterest, disinterestedness, dispassion, equality, equity, even-handedness, fairness, lack of bias, neutrality, nonpartisanship, objectivity, open-mindedness
Antonyms bias, favouritism, partiality, partisanship, subjectivity, unfairness
impassable blocked, closed, impenetrable, obstructed, pathless, trackless, unnavigable
impasse blind alley (*Inf.*), dead end, deadlock, stalemate, standoff, standstill
impassioned animated, ardent, blazing, excited, fervent, fervid, fiery, flaming, furious, glowing, heated, inflamed, inspired, intense, passionate, rousing, stirring, vehement, violent, vivid, warm, worked up
Antonyms apathetic, cool, impassive, indifferent, objective, reasoned
impassive aloof, apathetic, callous, calm, composed, cool, dispassionate, emotionless, impassible (*Rare*), imperturbable, indifferent, inscrutable, insensible, insusceptible, phlegmatic, poker-faced (*Inf.*), reserved, self-contained, serene, stoical, stolid, unconcerned, unemotional, unexcitable, unfazed (*Inf.*), unfeeling, unimpressible, unmoved, unruffled
impassivity aloofness, calmness, composure, dispassion, impassiveness, imperturbability, indifference, inscrutability, insensibility, nonchalance, phlegm, stoicism, stolidity
impatience 1. haste, hastiness, heat, impetuosity, intolerance, irritability, irritableness, quick temper, rashness, shortness, snappiness, vehemence, violence 2. agitation, anxiety, avidity, disquietude, eagerness, edginess, fretfulness, nervousness, restiveness, restlessness, uneasiness
Antonyms (*sense 2*) calm, composure, control, forbearance, patience, restraint, serenity, tolerance
impatient 1. abrupt, brusque, curt, demanding, edgy, hasty, hot-tempered, indignant, intolerant, irritable, quick-tempered, snappy, sudden, testy, vehement, violent 2. agog, athirst, chafing, eager, fretful, headlong, impetuous, like a cat on hot bricks (*Inf.*), restless, straining at the leash
Antonyms (*sense 1*) calm, composed, cool, easy-going, imperturbable, patient, quiet, serene, tolerant
impeach 1. accuse, arraign, blame, censure, charge, criminate (*Rare*), denounce, indict, tax 2. call into question, cast aspersions on, cast doubt on, challenge, disparage, impugn, question
impeachment accusation, arraignment, indictment
impeccable above suspicion, blameless, exact, exquisite, faultless, flawless, immaculate, incorrupt, innocent, irreproachable, perfect, precise, pure, sinless, stainless, unblemished, unerring, unimpeachable
Antonyms blameworthy, corrupt, cursory, defective, deficient, faulty, flawed, shallow, sinful, superficial
impecunious broke (*Inf.*), cleaned out (*Sl.*), destitute, dirt-poor (*Inf.*), down and out, flat broke (*Inf.*), indigent, insolvent, penniless, poverty-stricken, short, skint (*Brit. sl.*), stony (*Brit. sl.*), strapped (*Sl.*), without two pennies to rub together (*Inf.*)
Antonyms affluent, prosperous, rich, wealthy, well-off, well-to-do
impede bar, block, brake, check, clog, curb, delay, disrupt, hamper, hinder, hold up, obstruct, restrain, retard, slow (down), stop, throw a spanner in the works (*Brit. inf.*), thwart
Antonyms advance, aid, assist, further, help, promote
impediment bar, barrier, block, check, clog, curb, defect, difficulty, encumbrance, hindrance, obstacle, obstruction, snag, stumbling block
Antonyms advantage, aid, assistance, benefit, encouragement, relief, support
impedimenta accoutrements, baggage, belongings, effects, equipment, gear, junk (*Inf.*), luggage, movables, odds and ends, paraphernalia, possessions, stuff, things, trappings, traps
impel actuate, chivy, compel, constrain,

drive, force, goad, incite, induce, influence, inspire, instigate, motivate, move, oblige, power, prod, prompt, propel, push, require, spur, stimulate, urge
Antonyms check, discourage, dissuade, rebuff, repulse, restrain

impending approaching, brewing, coming, forthcoming, gathering, hovering, imminent, in the offing, looming, menacing, near, nearing, on the horizon, threatening, upcoming

impenetrable 1. dense, hermetic, impassable, impermeable, impervious, inviolable, solid, thick, unpierceable 2. arcane, baffling, cabbalistic, dark, enigmatic, enigmatical, hidden, incomprehensible, indiscernible, inexplicable, inscrutable, mysterious, obscure, unfathomable, unintelligible
Antonyms (*sense 1*) accessible, enterable, passable, penetrable, pierceable, vulnerable (*sense 2*) clear, explicable, obvious, soluble, understandable

impenitence hardheartedness, impenitency, incorrigibility, obduracy, stubbornness

impenitent defiant, hardened, hardhearted, incorrigible, obdurate, recidivistic, relentless, remorseless, unabashed, unashamed, uncontrite, unreformed, unrepentant

imperative 1. compulsory, crucial, essential, exigent, indispensable, insistent, obligatory, pressing, urgent, vital 2. authoritative, autocratic, commanding, dictatorial, domineering, high-handed, imperious, lordly, magisterial, peremptory
Antonyms (*sense 1*) avoidable, discretional, nonessential, optional, unimportant, unnecessary

imperceptible faint, fine, gradual, impalpable, inappreciable, inaudible, indiscernible, indistinguishable, infinitesimal, insensible, invisible, microscopic, minute, shadowy, slight, small, subtle, teensy-weensy, teeny-weeny, tiny, undetectable, unnoticeable
Antonyms audible, detectable, discernible, distinguishable, noticeable, perceptible, visible

imperceptibly by a hair's-breadth, inappreciably, indiscernibly, invisibly, little by little, slowly, subtly, unnoticeably, unobtrusively, unseen

imperceptive impercipient, insensitive, obtuse, superficial, unappreciative, unaware, undiscerning, unobservant, unseeing

imperfect broken, damaged, defective, deficient, faulty, flawed, immature, impaired, incomplete, inexact, limited, partial, patchy, rudimentary, sketchy, undeveloped, unfinished
Antonyms complete, developed, exact, finished, flawless, perfect

imperfection blemish, defect, deficiency, failing, fallibility, fault, flaw, foible, frailty, inadequacy, incompleteness, infirmity, insufficiency, peccadillo, scar, shortcoming, stain, taint, weakness, weak point
Antonyms adequacy, completeness, consummation, excellence, faultlessness, flawlessness, perfection, sufficiency

imperial 1. kingly, majestic, princely, queenly, regal, royal, sovereign 2. august, exalted, grand, great, high, imperious, lofty, magnificent, noble, superior, supreme

imperil endanger, expose, hazard, jeopardize, risk
Antonyms care for, guard, protect, safeguard, secure

imperious arrogant, authoritative, autocratic, bossy (*Inf.*), commanding, despotic, dictatorial, domineering, exacting, haughty, high-handed, imperative, lordly, magisterial, overbearing, overweening, tyrannical, tyrannous

imperishable abiding, enduring, eternal, everlasting, immortal, indestructible, perennial, permanent, perpetual, undying, unfading, unforgettable
Antonyms destructible, dying, fading, forgettable, mortal, perishable

impermanent brief, elusive, ephemeral, evanescent, fleeting, fly-by-night (*Inf.*), flying, fugacious, fugitive, here today, gone tomorrow (*Inf.*), inconstant, momentary, mortal, passing, perishable, short-lived, temporary, transient, transitory

impermeable hermetic, impassable, impenetrable, impervious, nonporous, proof, resistant

impersonal aloof, bureaucratic, businesslike, cold, detached, dispassionate, formal, inhuman, neutral, remote
Antonyms friendly, intimate, outgoing, personal, warm

impersonate act, ape, caricature, do (*Inf.*), do an impression of, enact, imitate, masquerade as, mimic, parody, pass oneself off as, personate, pose as (*Inf.*), take off (*Inf.*)

impersonation caricature, imitation, impression, mimicry, parody, takeoff (*Inf.*)

impertinence assurance, audacity, backchat (*Inf.*), boldness, brass neck (*Brit. inf.*), brazenness, cheek (*Inf.*), chutzpah (*U.S. & Canad. inf.*), disrespect, effrontery, forwardness, front, impudence, incivility, insolence, neck (*Inf.*), nerve (*Inf.*), pertness, presumption, rudeness, sauce (*Inf.*)

impertinent 1. bold, brazen, cheeky (*Inf.*),

discourteous, disrespectful, flip (*Inf.*), forward, fresh (*Inf.*), impolite, impudent, insolent, interfering, lippy (*U.S. & Canad. sl.*), pert, presumptuous, rude, sassy (*U.S. inf.*), saucy (*Inf.*), uncivil, unmannerly **2.** inapplicable, inappropriate, incongruous, irrelevant
Antonyms (*sense 1*) mannerly, polite, respectful (*sense 2*) appropriate, germane, important, pertinent, relevant, vital

imperturbable calm, collected, complacent, composed, cool, equanimous, nerveless, sedate, self-possessed, serene, stoi-cal, tranquil, undisturbed, unexcitable, unfazed (*Inf.*), unflappable (*Inf.*), unmoved, unruffled
Antonyms agitated, excitable, frantic, jittery (*Inf.*), nervous, panicky, ruffled, touchy, upset

impervious **1.** hermetic, impassable, impenetrable, impermeable, imperviable, invulnerable, resistant, sealed **2.** closed to, immune, invulnerable, proof against, unaffected by, unmoved by, unreceptive, unswayable, untouched by

impetuosity haste, hastiness, impulsiveness, precipitancy, precipitateness, rashness, vehemence, violence

impetuous ardent, eager, fierce, furious, hasty, headlong, impassioned, impulsive, passionate, precipitate, rash, spontaneous, spur-of-the-moment, unbridled, unplanned, unpremeditated, unreflecting, unrestrained, unthinking, vehement, violent
Antonyms cautious, leisurely, mild, slow, wary

impetuously helter-skelter, impulsively, in the heat of the moment, on the spur of the moment, passionately, rashly, recklessly, spontaneously, unthinkingly, vehemently, without thinking

impetus **1.** catalyst, goad, impulse, impulsion, incentive, motivation, push, spur, stimulus **2.** energy, force, momentum, power

impiety godlessness, iniquity, irreligion, irreverence, profaneness, profanity, sacrilege, sinfulness, ungodliness, unholiness, unrighteousness, wickedness
Antonyms devoutness, godliness, holiness, piety, respect, reverence, righteousness

impinge **1.** encroach, invade, make inroads, obtrude, trespass, violate **2.** affect, bear upon, have a bearing on, influence, infringe, relate to, touch, touch upon **3.** clash, collide, dash, strike

impious blasphemous, godless, iniquitous, irreligious, irreverent, profane, sacrilegious, sinful, ungodly, unholy, unrighteous, wicked
Antonyms devout, godly, holy, pious, religious, reverent, righteous

impish devilish, elfin, mischievous, prankish, puckish, rascally, roguish, sportive, waggish

implacability implacableness, inexorability, inflexibility, intractability, mercilessness, pitilessness, relentlessness, ruthlessness, unforgivingness, vengefulness

implacable cruel, inexorable, inflexible, intractable, merciless, pitiless, rancorous, relentless, remorseless, ruthless, unappeasable, unbending, uncompromising, unforgiving, unrelenting, unyielding
Antonyms appeasable, flexible, lenient, merciful, reconcilable, relenting, tolerant, yielding

implant **1.** inculcate, infix, infuse, inseminate, instil, sow **2.** embed, fix, graft, ingraft, insert, place, plant, root, sow

implausible dubious, far-fetched, flimsy, improbable, incredible, suspect, unbelievable, unconvincing, unlikely, unreasonable, weak

implement **1.** *n.* agent, apparatus, appliance, device, gadget, instrument, tool, utensil **2.** *v.* bring about, carry out, complete, effect, enforce, execute, fulfil, perform, put into action *or* effect, realize
Antonyms *v.* delay, hamper, hinder, impede, weaken

implementation accomplishment, carrying out, discharge, effecting, enforcement, execution, fulfilment, performance, performing, realization

implicate associate, compromise, concern, embroil, entangle, imply, include, incriminate, inculpate, involve, mire, tie up with
Antonyms acquit, disentangle, dissociate, eliminate, exclude, exculpate, rule out

implicated incriminated, involved, suspected, under suspicion

implication **1.** association, connection, entanglement, incrimination, involvement **2.** conclusion, inference, innuendo, meaning, overtone, presumption, ramification, significance, signification, suggestion

implicit **1.** contained, implied, inferred, inherent, latent, tacit, taken for granted, undeclared, understood, unspoken **2.** absolute, constant, entire, firm, fixed, full, steadfast, total, unhesitating, unqualified, unreserved, unshakable, unshaken, wholehearted
Antonyms (*sense 1*) declared, explicit, expressed, obvious, patent, spoken, stated

implicitly absolutely, completely, firmly,

unconditionally, unhesitatingly, unreservedly, utterly, without reservation

implied hinted at, implicit, indirect, inherent, insinuated, suggested, tacit, undeclared, unexpressed, unspoken, unstated

implore beg, beseech, conjure, crave, entreat, go on bended knee to, importune, plead with, pray, solicit, supplicate

imply 1. connote, give (someone) to understand, hint, insinuate, intimate, signify, suggest 2. betoken, denote, entail, evidence, import, include, indicate, involve, mean, point to, presuppose

impolite bad-mannered, boorish, churlish, discourteous, disrespectful, ill-bred, ill-mannered, indecorous, indelicate, insolent, loutish, rough, rude, uncivil, uncouth, ungallant, ungentlemanly, ungracious, unladylike, unmannerly, unrefined
Antonyms courteous, decorous, gallant, gracious, mannerly, polite, refined, respectful, well-bred

impoliteness bad manners, boorishness, churlishness, discourtesy, disrespect, incivility, indelicacy, insolence, rudeness, unmannerliness
Antonyms civility, courtesy, delicacy, mannerliness, politeness, respect

impolitic ill-advised, ill-judged, imprudent, indiscreet, inexpedient, injudicious, maladroit, misguided, undiplomatic, untimely, unwise
Antonyms diplomatic, discreet, expedient, judicious, politic, prudent, timely, wise

import *n.* 1. bearing, drift, gist, implication, intention, meaning, message, purport, sense, significance, thrust 2. bottom, consequence, importance, magnitude, moment, significance, substance, weight ~*v.* 3. bring in, introduce, land

importance 1. concern, consequence, import, interest, moment, momentousness, significance, substance, value, weight 2. bottom, distinction, eminence, esteem, influence, mark, pre-eminence, prestige, prominence, standing, status, usefulness, worth

important 1. far-reaching, grave, large, material, meaningful, momentous, of substance, primary, salient, serious, signal, significant, substantial, urgent, weighty 2. big-time (*Inf.*), eminent, foremost, high-level, high-ranking, influential, leading, major league (*Inf.*), notable, noteworthy, of note, outstanding, powerful, pre-eminent, prominent, seminal 3. *Usually with* **to** basic, essential, of concern *or* interest, relevant, valuable, valued
Antonyms inconsequential, insignificant, minor, needless, negligible, secondary, trivial, undistinctive, unimportant, unnecessary

importunate burning, clamant, clamorous, demanding, dogged, earnest, exigent, insistent, persistent, pertinacious, pressing, solicitous, troublesome, urgent

importune badger, beset, besiege, dun, entreat, harass, hound, lay siege to, pester, plague, press, solicit

importunity cajolery, dunning, entreaties, insistence, persistence, pressing, solicitations, urging

impose 1. decree, establish, exact, fix, institute, introduce, lay, levy, ordain, place, promulgate, put, set 2. appoint, charge with, dictate, enforce, enjoin, inflict, prescribe, saddle (someone) with 3. *With* **on** *or* **upon** butt in, encroach, foist, force oneself, gate-crash (*Inf.*), horn in (*Inf.*), intrude, obtrude, presume, take liberties, trespass 4. *With* **on** *or* **upon** a. abuse, exploit, play on, take advantage of, use b. con (*Inf.*), deceive, dupe, hoodwink, pull the wool over (somebody's) eyes, trick

imposing august, commanding, dignified, effective, grand, impressive, majestic, stately, striking
Antonyms insignificant, mean, modest, ordinary, petty, poor, unimposing

imposition 1. application, decree, introduction, laying on, levying, promulgation 2. cheek (*Inf.*), encroachment, intrusion, liberty, presumption 3. artifice, cheating, con (*Inf.*), deception, dissimulation, fraud, hoax, imposture, stratagem, trickery 4. burden, charge, constraint, duty, levy, tax

impossibility hopelessness, impracticability, inability, inconceivability

impossible 1. beyond one, beyond the bounds of possibility, hopeless, impracticable, inconceivable, not to be thought of, out of the question, unachievable, unattainable, unobtainable, unthinkable 2. absurd, inadmissible, insoluble, intolerable, ludicrous, outrageous, preposterous, unacceptable, unanswerable, ungovernable, unreasonable, unsuitable, unworkable
Antonyms (*sense 1*) conceivable, imaginable, likely, plausible, possible, reasonable

impostor charlatan, cheat, deceiver, fake, fraud, hypocrite, impersonator, knave (*Archaic*), phoney *or* phony (*Inf.*), pretender, quack, rogue, sham, trickster

imposture artifice, canard, cheat, con trick (*Inf.*), counterfeit, deception, fraud, hoax, impersonation, imposition, quackery, swindle, trick

impotence disability, enervation, feebleness, frailty, helplessness, inability, inad-

equacy, incapacity, incompetence, ineffectiveness, inefficacy, inefficiency, infirmity, paralysis, powerlessness, uselessness, weakness
Antonyms ability, adequacy, competence, effectiveness, efficacy, efficiency, powerfulness, strength, usefulness

impotent disabled, emasculate, enervated, feeble, frail, helpless, incapable, incapacitated, incompetent, ineffective, infirm, nerveless, paralysed, powerless, unable, unmanned, weak
Antonyms able, capable, competent, effective, manned, potent, powerful, strong

impoverish 1. bankrupt, beggar, break, ruin 2. deplete, diminish, drain, exhaust, pauperize, reduce, sap, use up, wear out

impoverished 1. bankrupt, destitute, distressed, impecunious, indigent, in reduced *or* straitened circumstances, necessitous, needy, on one's uppers, penurious, poverty-stricken, ruined, straitened 2. barren, denuded, depleted, drained, empty, exhausted, played out, reduced, spent, sterile, worn out
Antonyms (*sense 1*) affluent, rich, wealthy, well-off (*sense 2*) fecund, fertile, productive

impracticability futility, hopelessness, impossibility, impracticality, unsuitableness, unworkability, uselessness

impracticable 1. impossible, out of the question, unachievable, unattainable, unfeasible, unworkable 2. awkward, impractical, inapplicable, inconvenient, unserviceable, unsuitable, useless
Antonyms feasible, possible, practicable, practical, serviceable, suitable

impractical 1. impossible, impracticable, inoperable, nonviable, unrealistic, unserviceable, unworkable, visionary, wild 2. idealistic, romantic, starry-eyed, unbusinesslike, unrealistic, visionary
Antonyms (*sense 1*) possible, practical, serviceable, viable, workable (*sense 2*) down-to-earth, realistic, sensible

impracticality hopelessness, impossibility, inapplicability, romanticism, unworkability

imprecation anathema, blasphemy, curse, denunciation, execration, malediction, profanity, vilification

imprecise ambiguous, blurred round the edges, careless, equivocal, estimated, fluctuating, hazy, ill-defined, inaccurate, indefinite, indeterminate, inexact, inexplicit, loose, rough, sloppy (*Inf.*), vague, wide of the mark, woolly
Antonyms accurate, careful, definite, determinate, exact, explicit, precise

impregnable immovable, impenetrable, indestructible, invincible, invulnerable, secure, strong, unassailable, unbeatable, unconquerable, unshakable
Antonyms destructible, exposed, insecure, movable, open, pregnable, shakable, vulnerable

impregnate 1. fill, imbrue (*Rare*), imbue, infuse, percolate, permeate, pervade, saturate, seep, soak, steep, suffuse 2. fecundate, fertilize, fructify, get with child, inseminate, make pregnant

impress 1. affect, excite, grab (*Inf.*), influence, inspire, make an impression, move, stir, strike, sway, touch 2. *Often with* **on** *or* **upon** bring home to, emphasize, fix, inculcate, instil into, stress 3. emboss, engrave, imprint, indent, mark, print, stamp

impression 1. effect, feeling, impact, influence, reaction, sway 2. **make an impression** arouse comment, be conspicuous, cause a stir, excite notice, find favour, make a hit (*Inf.*), make an impact, stand out 3. belief, concept, conviction, fancy, feeling, funny feeling (*Inf.*), hunch, idea, memory, notion, opinion, recollection, sense, suspicion 4. brand, dent, hollow, impress, imprint, indentation, mark, outline, stamp, stamping 5. edition, imprinting, issue, printing 6. imitation, impersonation, parody, send-up (*Brit. inf.*), take-off (*Inf.*)

impressionability ingenuousness, receptiveness, receptivity, sensitivity, suggestibility, susceptibility, vulnerability

impressionable feeling, gullible, ingenuous, open, receptive, responsive, sensitive, suggestible, susceptible, vulnerable
Antonyms blasé, hardened, insensitive, jaded, unresponsive

impressive affecting, exciting, forcible, moving, powerful, stirring, striking, touching
Antonyms ordinary, unimposing, unimpressive, uninspiring, unmemorable, weak

imprint 1. *n.* impression, indentation, mark, print, sign, stamp 2. *v.* engrave, establish, etch, fix, impress, print, stamp

imprison confine, constrain, detain, immure, incarcerate, intern, jail, lock up, put away, put under lock and key, send down (*Inf.*), send to prison
Antonyms discharge, emancipate, free, liberate, release

imprisoned behind bars, captive, confined, immured, incarcerated, in irons, in jail, inside (*Sl.*), interned, jailed, locked up, put away, under lock and key

imprisonment confinement, custody, detention, durance (*Archaic*), duress, incarceration, internment, porridge (*Sl.*)

improbability doubt, doubtfulness, dubiety, uncertainty, unlikelihood

improbable doubtful, dubious, fanciful, far-fetched, implausible, questionable, unbelievable, uncertain, unconvincing, unlikely, weak
Antonyms certain, convincing, doubtless, likely, plausible, probable, reasonable

improbity chicanery, crookedness (*Inf.*), dishonesty, faithlessness, fraud, knavery, unfairness, unscrupulousness, villainy

impromptu 1. *adj.* ad-lib, extemporaneous, extempore, extemporized, improvised, offhand, off the cuff (*Inf.*), spontaneous, unpremeditated, unprepared, unrehearsed, unscripted, unstudied 2. *adv.* ad lib, off the cuff (*Inf.*), off the top of one's head (*Inf.*), on the spur of the moment, spontaneously, without preparation
Antonyms *adj.* considered, planned, premeditated, prepared, rehearsed

improper 1. impolite, indecent, indecorous, indelicate, off-colour, risqué, smutty, suggestive, unbecoming, unfitting, unseemly, untoward, vulgar 2. ill-timed, inapplicable, inapposite, inappropriate, inapt, incongruous, infelicitous, inopportune, malapropos, out of place, uncalled-for, unfit, unseasonable, unsuitable, unsuited, unwarranted 3. abnormal, erroneous, false, inaccurate, incorrect, irregular, wrong
Antonyms (*sense 1*) becoming, decent, decorous, delicate, fitting, proper, seemly (*sense 2*) apposite, appropriate, apt, felicitous, opportune, seasoned, suitable

impropriety 1. bad taste, immodesty, incongruity, indecency, indecorum, unsuitability, vulgarity 2. bloomer (*Brit. inf.*), blunder, faux pas, gaffe, gaucherie, mistake, slip, solecism
Antonyms (*sense 1*) decency, decorum, delicacy, modesty, propriety, suitability

improve 1. advance, ameliorate, amend, augment, better, correct, face-lift, help, mend, polish, rectify, touch up, upgrade 2. develop, enhance, gain strength, increase, look up (*Inf.*), make strides, perk up, pick up, progress, rally, reform, rise, take a turn for the better (*Inf.*), take on a new lease of life (*Inf.*) 3. convalesce, gain ground, gain strength, grow better, make progress, mend, recover, recuperate, turn the corner 4. clean up one's act (*Inf.*), get it together (*Inf.*), get one's act together (*Inf.*), pull one's socks up (*Brit. inf.*), reform, shape up (*Inf.*), turn over a new leaf
Antonyms damage, harm, impair, injure, mar, worsen

improvement 1. advancement, amelioration, amendment, augmentation, betterment, correction, face-lift, gain, rectification 2. advance, development, enhancement, furtherance, increase, progress, rally, recovery, reformation, rise, upswing

improvidence carelessness, extravagance, heedlessness, imprudence, negligence, prodigality, profligacy, short-sightedness, thriftlessness, wastefulness

improvident careless, heedless, imprudent, inconsiderate, negligent, prodigal, profligate, reckless, shiftless, short-sighted, spendthrift, thoughtless, thriftless, uneconomical, unthrifty, wasteful
Antonyms careful, considerate, economical, heedful, provident, prudent, thrifty

improvisation ad-lib, ad-libbing, expedient, extemporizing, impromptu, invention, makeshift, spontaneity

improvise 1. ad-lib, busk, coin, extemporize, invent, play it by ear (*Inf.*), speak off the cuff (*Inf.*), vamp, wing it (*Inf.*) 2. concoct, contrive, devise, make do, throw together

improvised ad-lib, extemporaneous, extempore, extemporized, makeshift, off the cuff (*Inf.*), spontaneous, spur-of-the-moment, unprepared, unrehearsed

imprudence carelessness, folly, foolhardiness, foolishness, heedlessness, improvidence, inadvisability, incaution, incautiousness, inconsideration, indiscretion, irresponsibility, rashness, recklessness, temerity

imprudent careless, foolhardy, foolish, heedless, ill-advised, ill-considered, ill-judged, impolitic, improvident, incautious, inconsiderate, indiscreet, injudicious, irresponsible, overhasty, rash, reckless, temerarious, unthinking, unwise
Antonyms careful, cautious, considerate, discreet, judicious, politic, provident, prudent, responsible, wise

impudence assurance, audacity, backchat (*Inf.*), boldness, brass neck (*Brit. inf.*), brazenness, bumptiousness, cheek (*Inf.*), chutzpah (*U.S. & Canad. inf.*), effrontery, face (*Inf.*), front, impertinence, insolence, lip (*Sl.*), neck (*Inf.*), nerve (*Inf.*), pertness, presumption, rudeness, sauciness, shamelessness

impudent audacious, bold, bold-faced, brazen, bumptious, cheeky (*Inf.*), cocky (*Inf.*), forward, fresh (*Inf.*), immodest, impertinent, insolent, lippy (*U.S. & Canad. sl.*), pert, presumptuous, rude, sassy (*U.S. inf.*), saucy (*Inf.*), shameless
Antonyms courteous, modest, polite, re-

spectful, retiring, self-effacing, timid, well-behaved

impugn assail, attack, call into question, cast aspersions upon, cast doubt upon, challenge, criticize, dispute, gainsay (*Archaic or literary*), oppose, question, resist, traduce

impulse 1. catalyst, force, impetus, momentum, movement, pressure, push, stimulus, surge, thrust 2. *Fig.* caprice, drive, feeling, incitement, inclination, influence, instinct, motive, notion, passion, resolve, urge, whim, wish

impulsive devil-may-care, emotional, hasty, headlong, impetuous, instinctive, intuitive, passionate, precipitate, quick, rash, spontaneous, unconsidered, unpredictable, unpremeditated
Antonyms arresting, calculating, cautious, considered, cool, deliberate, halting, planned, premeditated, rehearsed, restrained

impunity dispensation, exemption, freedom, immunity, liberty, licence, nonliability, permission, security

impure 1. admixed, adulterated, alloyed, debased, mixed, unrefined 2. contaminated, defiled, dirty, filthy, foul, infected, polluted, sullied, tainted, unclean, unwholesome, vitiated 3. carnal, coarse, corrupt, gross, immodest, immoral, indecent, indelicate, lascivious, lewd, licentious, lustful, obscene, prurient, ribald, salacious, smutty, unchaste, unclean
Antonyms (*sense 2*) clean, immaculate, spotless, squeaky-clean, undefiled, unsullied (*sense 3*) chaste, decent, delicate, modest, moral, pure, wholesome

impurity 1. admixture, adulteration, mixture 2. befoulment, contamination, defilement, dirtiness, filth, foulness, infection, pollution, taint, uncleanness 3. *Often plural* bits, contaminant, dirt, dross, foreign body, foreign matter, grime, marks, pollutant, scum, spots, stains 4. carnality, coarseness, corruption, grossness, immodesty, immorality, indecency, lasciviousness, lewdness, licentiousness, obscenity, prurience, salaciousness, smuttiness, unchastity, vulgarity

imputable accreditable, ascribable, attributable, chargeable, referable, traceable

imputation accusation, ascription, aspersion, attribution, blame, censure, charge, insinuation, reproach, slander, slur

impute accredit, ascribe, assign, attribute, credit, lay at the door of, refer, set down to

inability disability, disqualification, impotence, inadequacy, incapability, incapacity, incompetence, ineptitude, powerlessness
Antonyms ability, adequacy, capability, capacity, competence, potential, power, talent

inaccessible impassable, out of reach, out of the way, remote, unapproachable, unattainable, un-get-at-able (*Inf.*), unreachable
Antonyms accessible, approachable, attainable, reachable

inaccuracy 1. erroneousness, imprecision, incorrectness, inexactness, unfaithfulness, unreliability 2. blunder, boob (*Brit. sl.*), corrigendum, defect, erratum, error, fault, howler (*Inf.*), literal (*Printing*), miscalculation, mistake, slip, typo (*Inf., printing*)

inaccurate careless, defective, discrepant, erroneous, faulty, imprecise, incorrect, in error, inexact, mistaken, out, unfaithful, unreliable, unsound, wide of the mark, wild, wrong
Antonyms accurate, correct, exact, precise, reliable, sound

inaccurately carelessly, clumsily, imprecisely, inexactly, unfaithfully, unreliably

inaction dormancy, idleness, immobility, inactivity, inertia, rest, torpidity, torpor

inactive 1. abeyant, dormant, idle, immobile, inert, inoperative, jobless, kicking one's heels, latent, mothballed, out of service, out of work, unemployed, unoccupied, unused 2. dull, indolent, lazy, lethargic, low-key (*Inf.*), passive, quiet, sedentary, slothful, slow, sluggish, somnolent, torpid
Antonyms (*sense 1*) employed, mobile, occupied, operative, running, used, working (*sense 2*) active, busy, diligent, energetic, industrious, vibrant

inactivity 1. dormancy, hibernation, immobility, inaction, passivity, unemployment 2. dilatoriness, *dolce far niente,* dullness, heaviness, indolence, inertia, inertness, lassitude, laziness, lethargy, quiescence, sloth, sluggishness, stagnation, torpor, vegetation
Antonyms action, activeness, bustle, employment, exertion, mobility, movement

inadequacy 1. dearth, deficiency, inadequateness, incompleteness, insufficiency, meagreness, paucity, poverty, scantiness, shortage, skimpiness 2. defectiveness, faultiness, inability, inaptness, incapacity, incompetence, incompetency, ineffectiveness, inefficacy, unfitness, unsuitableness 3. defect, failing, imperfection, lack, shortage, shortcoming, weakness

inadequate 1. defective, deficient, faulty, imperfect, incommensurate, incomplete, insubstantial, insufficient, meagre, niggardly, scant, scanty, short, sketchy, skimpy, sparse 2. found wanting, inapt, in-

capable, incompetent, not up to scratch (*Inf.*), unequal, unfitted, unqualified
Antonyms (*sense 1*) adequate, ample, complete, perfect, satisfactory, substantial, sufficient (*sense 2*) apt, capable, competent, equal, fit, qualified

inadequately imperfectly, insufficiently, meagrely, poorly, scantily, sketchily, skimpily, sparsely, thinly

inadmissible immaterial, improper, inappropriate, incompetent, irrelevant, unacceptable, unallowable, unqualified, unreasonable

inadvertence, inadvertency blunder, carelessness, error, heedlessness, inattention, inconsideration, inobservance, mistake, neglect, negligence, oversight, remissness, thoughtlessness

inadvertent accidental, careless, chance, heedless, negligent, thoughtless, unheeding, unintended, unintentional, unplanned, unpremeditated, unthinking, unwitting

inadvertently 1. carelessly, heedlessly, in an unguarded moment, negligently, thoughtlessly, unguardedly, unthinkingly 2. accidentally, by accident, by mistake, involuntarily, mistakenly, unintentionally, unwittingly
Antonyms carefully, consciously, deliberately, heedfully, intentionally

inadvisable ill-advised, impolitic, imprudent, inexpedient, injudicious, unwise

inalienable absolute, entailed (*Law*), inherent, inviolable, non-negotiable, non-transferable, sacrosanct, unassailable, untransferable

inane asinine, daft (*Inf.*), devoid of intelligence, empty, fatuous, frivolous, futile, goofy (*Inf.*), idiotic, imbecilic, mindless, puerile, senseless, silly, stupid, trifling, unintelligent, vacuous, vain, vapid, worthless
Antonyms meaningful, profound, sensible, serious, significant, weighty, worthwhile

inanimate cold, dead, defunct, extinct, inactive, inert, insensate, insentient, lifeless, quiescent, soulless, spiritless
Antonyms active, alive, animate, lively, living, moving

inanity asininity, bêtise (*Rare*), daftness (*Inf.*), emptiness, fatuity, folly, frivolity, imbecility, puerility, senselessness, silliness, vacuity, vapidity, worthlessness

inapplicable inapposite, inappropriate, inapt, irrelevant, unsuitable, unsuited
Antonyms applicable, apposite, appropriate, apt, fitting, pertinent, relevant, suitable

inapposite impertinent, inapplicable, inappropriate, infelicitous, irrelevant, out of place, unfit, unsuitable

inappreciable imperceptible, infinitesimal, insignificant, minuscule, negligible

inappropriate disproportionate, ill-fitted, ill-suited, ill-timed, improper, incongruous, malapropos, out of place, tasteless, unbecoming, unbefitting, unfit, unfitting, unseemly, unsuitable, untimely
Antonyms appropriate, becoming, congruous, fitting, proper, seemly, suitable, timely

inapt 1. ill-fitted, ill-suited, inapposite, inappropriate, infelicitous, unsuitable, unsuited 2. awkward, clumsy, dull, gauche, incompetent, inept, inexpert, maladroit, slow, stupid
Antonyms (*sense 1*) apposite, appropriate, apt, felicitous, fitting, suitable, suited

inaptitude awkwardness, clumsiness, incompetence, maladroitness, unfitness, unreadiness, unsuitableness

inarticulate 1. blurred, incoherent, incomprehensible, indistinct, muffled, mumbled, unclear, unintelligible 2. dumb, mute, silent, speechless, tongue-tied, unspoken, unuttered, unvoiced, voiceless, wordless 3. faltering, halting, hesitant, poorly spoken
Antonyms (*senses 1 & 3*) articulate, clear, coherent, comprehensible, intelligible, well-spoken

inattention absent-mindedness, carelessness, daydreaming, disregard, forgetfulness, heedlessness, inadvertence, inattentiveness, indifference, neglect, preoccupation, thoughtlessness, woolgathering

inattentive absent-minded, careless, distracted, distrait, dreamy, heedless, inadvertent, neglectful, negligent, preoccupied, regardless, remiss, slapdash, slipshod, thoughtless, unheeding, unmindful, unobservant, vague
Antonyms attentive, aware, careful, considerate, heeding, mindful, observant, thoughtful

inaudible indistinct, low, mumbling, out of earshot, stifled, unheard
Antonyms audible, clear, discernible, distinct, perceptible

inaugural dedicatory, first, initial, introductory, maiden, opening

inaugurate 1. begin, commence, get under way, initiate, institute, introduce, kick off (*Inf.*), launch, originate, set in motion, set up, usher in 2. induct, install, instate, invest 3. commission, dedicate, open, ordain

inauguration 1. initiation, institution, launch, launching, opening, setting up 2. induction, installation, investiture

inauspicious bad, black, discouraging, ill-

omened, ominous, unfavourable, unfortunate, unlucky, unpromising, unpropitious, untoward
Antonyms auspicious, encouraging, favourable, fortunate, good, lucky, promising, propitious

inborn congenital, connate, hereditary, inbred, ingrained, inherent, inherited, innate, instinctive, intuitive, native, natural

inbred constitutional, deep-seated, ingrained, inherent, innate, native, natural

incalculable boundless, countless, enormous, immense, incomputable, inestimable, infinite, innumerable, limitless, measureless, numberless, uncountable, untold, vast, without number

incandescent brilliant, glowing, luminous, phosphorescent, radiant, red-hot, shining, white-hot

incantation abracadabra, chant, charm, conjuration, formula, hex (*U.S. & Canad. inf.*), invocation, spell

incapable 1. feeble, inadequate, incompetent, ineffective, inept, inexpert, insufficient, not equal to, not up to, unfit, unfitted, unqualified, weak 2. helpless, impotent, powerless, unable, unfit 3. *With* of impervious, not admitting of, not susceptible to, resistant
Antonyms (*sense 1*) adequate, capable, competent, efficient, expert, fit, qualified, sufficient

incapacitate cripple, disable, disqualify, immobilize, lay up (*Inf.*), paralyse, prostrate, put out of action (*Inf.*), scupper (*Brit. sl.*), unfit (*Rare*)

incapacitated disqualified, *hors de combat,* immobilized, indisposed, laid up (*Inf.*), out of action (*Inf.*), unfit

incapacity disqualification, feebleness, impotence, inability, inadequacy, incapability, incompetency, ineffectiveness, powerlessness, unfitness, weakness

incapsulate *see* ENCAPSULATE

incarcerate commit, confine, coop up, detain, gaol, immure, impound, imprison, intern, jail, lock up, put under lock and key, restrain, restrict, send down (*Brit.*), throw in jail

incarceration bondage, captivity, confinement, detention, imprisonment, internment, porridge (*Sl.*), restraint

incarnate 1. in bodily form, in human form, in the flesh, made flesh 2. embodied, personified, typified

incarnation avatar, bodily form, embodiment, epitome, exemplification, impersonation, manifestation, personification, type

incautious careless, hasty, heedless, ill-advised, ill-judged, improvident, imprudent, impulsive, inconsiderate, indiscreet, injudicious, negligent, precipitate, rash, reckless, thoughtless, unguarded, unthinking, unwary
Antonyms careful, cautious, considerate, discreet, guarded, heedful, judicious, prudent, thoughtful, wary

incautiously imprudently, impulsively, indiscreetly, precipitately, rashly, recklessly, thoughtlessly, unthinkingly

incendiary *adj.* 1. dissentious, inflammatory, provocative, rabble-rousing, seditious, subversive ~*n.* 2. arsonist, firebug (*Inf.*), fire raiser, pyromaniac 3. agitator, demagogue, firebrand, insurgent, rabble-rouser, revolutionary

incense[1] *v.* anger, enrage, exasperate, excite, gall, get one's hackles up, inflame, infuriate, irritate, madden, make one's blood boil (*Inf.*), make one see red (*Inf.*), make one's hackles rise, nark (*Brit., Aust., & N.Z. sl.*), provoke, raise one's hackles, rile (*Inf.*)

incense[2] *n.* aroma, balm, bouquet, fragrance, perfume, redolence, scent

incensed angry, cross, enraged, exasperated, fuming, furious, indignant, infuriated, irate, ireful (*Literary*), mad (*Inf.*), maddened, on the warpath (*Inf.*), steamed up (*Sl.*), up in arms, wrathful

incentive bait, carrot (*Inf.*), encouragement, enticement, goad, impetus, impulse, inducement, lure, motivation, motive, spur, stimulant, stimulus
Antonyms deterrent, discouragement, disincentive, dissuasion, warning

inception beginning, birth, commencement, dawn, inauguration, initiation, kick-off (*Inf.*), origin, outset, rise, start
Antonyms completion, conclusion, end, ending, finish, termination

incessant ceaseless, constant, continual, continuous, endless, eternal, everlasting, interminable, never-ending, nonstop, perpetual, persistent, relentless, unbroken, unceasing, unending, unrelenting, unremitting
Antonyms infrequent, intermittent, occasional, periodic, rare, sporadic

incessantly all the time, ceaselessly, constantly, continually, endlessly, eternally, everlastingly, interminably, nonstop, perpetually, persistently, without a break

inchoate 1. beginning, inceptive, incipient, nascent 2. elementary, embryonic, formless, immature, imperfect, rudimentary, undeveloped, unformed

incidence amount, degree, extent, frequency, occurrence, prevalence, rate

incident 1. adventure, circumstance, episode, event, fact, happening, matter, occasion, occurrence 2. brush, clash, commotion, confrontation, contretemps, disturbance, mishap, scene, skirmish

incidental 1. accidental, casual, chance, fortuitous, odd, random 2. *With* to accompanying, attendant, by-the-way, concomitant, contingent, contributory, related 3. ancillary, minor, nonessential, occasional, secondary, subordinate, subsidiary
Antonyms (*sense 3*) crucial, essential, important, necessary, vital

incidentally 1. accidentally, by chance, casually, fortuitously 2. by the bye, by the way, in passing, parenthetically

incidentals contingencies, extras, minutiae, odds and ends

incinerate burn up, carbonize, char, consume by fire, cremate, reduce to ashes

incipient beginning, commencing, developing, embryonic, inceptive, inchoate, nascent, originating, starting

incise carve, chisel, cut (into), engrave, etch, inscribe

incision cut, gash, notch, opening, slash, slit

incisive 1. acute, keen, penetrating, perspicacious, piercing, trenchant 2. acid, biting, caustic, cutting, mordacious, mordant, sarcastic, sardonic, satirical, severe, sharp, vitriolic
Antonyms (*sense 1*) dense, dull, superficial, vague, woolly

incisiveness 1. keenness, penetration, perspicacity, sharpness, trenchancy 2. acidity, pungency, sarcasm

incite agitate for *or* against, animate, drive, egg on, encourage, excite, foment, goad, impel, inflame, instigate, prod, prompt, provoke, put up to, rouse, set on, spur, stimulate, stir up, urge, whip up
Antonyms dampen, deter, discourage, dishearten, dissuade, restrain

incitement agitation, encouragement, goad, impetus, impulse, inducement, instigation, motivation, motive, prompting, provocation, spur, stimulus

incivility bad manners, boorishness, discourteousness, discourtesy, disrespect, ill-breeding, impoliteness, rudeness, unmannerliness
Antonyms civility, courteousness, courtesy, good manners, mannerliness, politeness, respect

inclemency 1. bitterness, boisterousness, rawness, rigour, roughness, severity, storminess 2. callousness, cruelty, harshness, mercilessness, severity, tyranny, unfeelingness

inclement 1. bitter, boisterous, foul, harsh, intemperate, rigorous, rough, severe, stormy, tempestuous 2. callous, cruel, draconian, harsh, intemperate, merciless, pitiless, rigorous, severe, tyrannical, unfeeling, unmerciful
Antonyms (*sense 1*) balmy, calm, clement, fine, mild, pleasant, temperate (*sense 2*) compassionate, gentle, humane, kind, merciful, tender

inclination 1. affection, aptitude, bent, bias, desire, disposition, fancy, fondness, leaning, liking, partiality, penchant, predilection, predisposition, prejudice, proclivity, proneness, propensity, stomach, taste, tendency, thirst, turn, turn of mind, wish 2. bending, bow, bowing, nod 3. angle, bend, bending, deviation, gradient, incline, leaning, pitch, slant, slope, tilt
Antonyms (*sense 1*) antipathy, aversion, disinclination, dislike, revulsion

incline *v.* 1. be disposed *or* predisposed, bias, influence, persuade, predispose, prejudice, sway, tend, turn 2. bend, bow, lower, nod, nutate (*Rare*), stoop 3. bend, bevel, cant, deviate, diverge, heel, lean, slant, slope, tend, tilt, tip, veer ~*n.* 4. acclivity, ascent, declivity, descent, dip, grade, gradient, ramp, rise, slope

inclined apt, disposed, given, liable, likely, minded, of a mind (*Inf.*), predisposed, prone, willing

inclose *see* ENCLOSE

include 1. comprehend, comprise, contain, cover, embody, embrace, encompass, incorporate, involve, subsume, take in, take into account 2. add, allow for, build in, count, enter, insert, introduce, number among
Antonyms eliminate, exclude, leave out, omit, rule out

including as well as, containing, counting, inclusive of, plus, together with, with

inclusion addition, incorporation, insertion
Antonyms exception, exclusion, omission, rejection

inclusive across-the-board, all-embracing, all in, all together, blanket, catch-all (*Chiefly U.S.*), comprehensive, full, general, global, *in toto*, overall, sweeping, umbrella, without exception
Antonyms confined, exclusive, limited, narrow, restricted, unique

incognito disguised, in disguise, under an assumed name, unknown, unrecognized

incoherence disconnectedness, disjointedness, inarticulateness, unintelligibility

incoherent confused, disconnected, dis~

jointed, disordered, inarticulate, inconsistent, jumbled, loose, muddled, rambling, stammering, stuttering, unconnected, uncoordinated, unintelligible, wandering, wild
Antonyms coherent, connected, intelligible, logical, rational

incombustible fireproof, flameproof, noncombustible, nonflammable, noninflammable

income earnings, gains, interest, means, pay, proceeds, profits, receipts, revenue, salary, takings, wages

incoming approaching, arriving, entering, homeward, landing, new, returning, succeeding
Antonyms departing, exiting, leaving, outgoing

incommensurate disproportionate, inadequate, inequitable, insufficient, unequal

incommode annoy, be a trouble to, bother, disturb, embarrass, get in one's hair (*Inf.*), give (someone) bother *or* trouble, hassle (*Inf.*), hinder, impede, inconvenience, irk, put out, put (someone) to trouble, trouble, upset, vex

incommodious awkward, confined, cramped, inconvenient, narrow, restricted, small, uncomfortable

incommunicable indescribable, ineffable, inexpressible, unspeakable, unutterable

incomparable beyond compare, inimitable, matchless, paramount, peerless, superlative, supreme, transcendent, unequalled, unmatched, unparalleled, unrivalled

incomparably beyond compare, by far, easily, eminently, far and away, immeasurably

incompatibility antagonism, conflict, discrepancy, disparateness, incongruity, inconsistency, irreconcilability, uncongeniality

incompatible antagonistic, antipathetic, conflicting, contradictory, discordant, discrepant, disparate, ill-assorted, incongruous, inconsistent, inconsonant, irreconcilable, mismatched, uncongenial, unsuitable, unsuited
Antonyms alike, appropriate, compatible, congenial, consistent, harmonious, reconcilable, suitable, suited

incompetence inability, inadequacy, incapability, incapacity, incompetency, ineffectiveness, ineptitude, ineptness, insufficiency, skill-lessness, unfitness, uselessness

incompetent bungling, cowboy (*Inf.*), floundering, incapable, incapacitated, ineffectual, inept, inexpert, insufficient, skill-less, unable, unfit, unfitted, unskilful, useless
Antonyms able, capable, competent, expert, fit, proficient, skilful

incomplete broken, defective, deficient, fragmentary, imperfect, insufficient, lacking, partial, short, unaccomplished, undeveloped, undone, unexecuted, unfinished, wanting
Antonyms accomplished, complete, developed, finished, perfect, unified, whole

incomprehensible above one's head, all Greek to (*Inf.*), baffling, beyond comprehension, beyond one's grasp, enigmatic, impenetrable, inconceivable, inscrutable, mysterious, obscure, opaque, perplexing, puzzling, unfathomable, unimaginable, unintelligible, unthinkable
Antonyms apparent, clear, comprehensible, conceivable, evident, intelligible, manifest, obvious, understandable

inconceivable beyond belief, impossible, incomprehensible, incredible, mind-boggling (*Inf.*), not to be thought of, out of the question, staggering (*Inf.*), unbelievable, unheard-of, unimaginable, unknowable, unthinkable
Antonyms believable, comprehensible, conceivable, credible, imaginable, likely, plausible, possible, reasonable

inconclusive ambiguous, indecisive, indeterminate, open, uncertain, unconvincing, undecided, unsettled, up in the air (*Inf.*), vague

incongruity conflict, discrepancy, disparity, inappropriateness, inaptness, incompatibility, inconsistency, inharmoniousness, unsuitability

incongruous absurd, conflicting, contradictory, contrary, disconsonant, discordant, extraneous, improper, inappropriate, inapt, incoherent, incompatible, inconsistent, out of keeping, out of place, unbecoming, unsuitable, unsuited
Antonyms appropriate, becoming, compatible, consistent, harmonious, suitable, suited

inconsequential immaterial, inconsiderable, insignificant, measly, minor, negligible, nickel-and-dime (*U.S. sl.*), of no significance, paltry, petty, trifling, trivial, unimportant

inconsiderable exiguous, inconsequential, insignificant, light, minor, negligible, petty, slight, small, small-time (*Inf.*), trifling, trivial, unimportant

inconsiderate careless, indelicate, insensitive, intolerant, rude, self-centred, self-

ish, tactless, thoughtless, uncharitable, ungracious, unkind, unthinking
Antonyms attentive, careful, considerate, gracious, kind, sensitive, tactful, thoughtful, tolerant

inconsistency 1. contrariety, disagreement, discrepancy, disparity, divergence, incompatibility, incongruity, inconsonance, paradox, variance 2. fickleness, instability, unpredictability, unreliability, unsteadiness

inconsistent 1. at odds, at variance, conflicting, contradictory, contrary, discordant, discrepant, incoherent, incompatible, in conflict, incongruous, inconstant, irreconcilable, out of step 2. capricious, changeable, erratic, fickle, inconstant, irregular, uneven, unpredictable, unstable, unsteady, vagarious (*Rare*), variable
Antonyms (*sense 1*) coherent, compatible, homogenous, orderly, reconcilable, uniform (*sense 2*) consistent, constant, predictable, reliable, stable, steady, unchanging

inconsistently contradictorily, differently, eccentrically, erratically, inequably, randomly, unequally, unfairly, unpredictably, variably

inconsolable brokenhearted, desolate, despairing, heartbroken, heartsick, prostrate with grief, sick at heart

inconspicuous camouflaged, hidden, insignificant, modest, muted, ordinary, plain, quiet, retiring, unassuming, unnoticeable, unobtrusive, unostentatious
Antonyms conspicuous, noticeable, obtrusive, obvious, significant, visible

inconstant blowing hot and cold (*Inf.*), capricious, changeable, changeful, erratic, fickle, fluctuating, inconsistent, irresolute, mercurial, mutable, temperamental, uncertain, undependable, uneven, unreliable, unsettled, unstable, unsteady, vacillating, vagarious (*Rare*), variable, volatile, wavering, wayward

incontestable beyond doubt, beyond question, certain, incontrovertible, indisputable, indubitable, irrefutable, self-evident, sure, undeniable, unquestionable

incontinent 1. unbridled, unchecked, uncontrollable, uncontrolled, ungovernable, ungoverned, unrestrained 2. debauched, lascivious, lecherous, lewd, loose, lustful, profligate, promiscuous, unchaste, wanton

incontrovertible beyond dispute, certain, established, incontestable, indisputable, indubitable, irrefutable, positive, sure, undeniable, unquestionable, unshakable

inconvenience *n.* 1. annoyance, awkwardness, bother, difficulty, disadvantage, disruption, disturbance, downside, drawback, fuss, hassle (*Inf.*), hindrance, nuisance, trouble, uneasiness, upset, vexation 2. awkwardness, cumbersomeness, unfitness, unhandiness, unsuitableness, untimeliness, unwieldiness ~*v.* 3. bother, discommode, disrupt, disturb, give (someone) bother *or* trouble, hassle (*Inf.*), irk, make (someone) go out of his way, put out, put to trouble, trouble, upset

inconvenient 1. annoying, awkward, bothersome, disadvantageous, disturbing, embarrassing, inopportune, tiresome, troublesome, unseasonable, unsuitable, untimely, vexatious 2. awkward, cumbersome, difficult, unhandy, unmanageable, unwieldy
Antonyms (*sense 1*) convenient, handy, opportune, seasonable, suitable, timely

incorporate absorb, amalgamate, assimilate, blend, coalesce, combine, consolidate, embody, fuse, include, integrate, meld, merge, mix, subsume, unite

incorporation absorption, amalgamation, assimilation, blend, coalescence, federation, fusion, inclusion, integration, merger, unifying

incorrect erroneous, false, faulty, flawed, improper, inaccurate, inappropriate, inexact, mistaken, out, specious, unfitting, unsuitable, untrue, wide of the mark (*Inf.*), wrong
Antonyms accurate, correct, exact, faultless, fitting, flawless, right, suitable, true

incorrectness erroneousness, error, fallacy, faultiness, impreciseness, imprecision, impropriety, inaccuracy, inexactness, speciousness, unsoundness, unsuitability, wrongness

incorrigible hardened, hopeless, incurable, intractable, inveterate, irredeemable, unreformed

incorruptibility honesty, honour, integrity, justness, uprightness

incorruptible 1. above suspicion, honest, honourable, just, straight, trustworthy, unbribable, upright 2. everlasting, imperishable, undecaying

increase *v.* 1. add to, advance, aggrandize, amplify, augment, boost, build up, develop, dilate, enhance, enlarge, escalate, expand, extend, grow, heighten, inflate, intensify, magnify, mount, multiply, proliferate, prolong, raise, snowball, spread, step up (*Inf.*), strengthen, swell, wax ~*n.* 2. addition, augmentation, boost, development, enlargement, escalation, expansion, extension, gain, growth, increment, intensification, rise, upsurge, upturn 3. **on the increase** developing, escalating, expanding, growing, increasing, multiplying, on the rise, proliferating, spreading

Antonyms *v.* abate, abbreviate, abridge, condense, curtail, decline, decrease, deflate, diminish, dwindle, lessen, reduce, shorten, shrink

increasingly more and more, progressively, to an increasing extent

incredible 1. absurd, beyond belief, far-fetched, implausible, impossible, improbable, inconceivable, preposterous, unbelievable, unimaginable, unthinkable 2. *Inf.* ace (*Inf.*), amazing, astonishing, astounding, awe-inspiring, brilliant, def (*Sl.*), extraordinary, far-out (*Sl.*), great, marvellous, mega (*Sl.*), prodigious, rad (*Inf.*), sensational (*Inf.*), superhuman, wonderful

incredulity disbelief, distrust, doubt, scepticism, unbelief

incredulous disbelieving, distrustful, doubtful, doubting, dubious, mistrustful, sceptical, suspicious, unbelieving, unconvinced

Antonyms believing, credulous, gullible, naive, trusting, unsuspecting

increment accretion, accrual, accrument, addition, advancement, augmentation, enlargement, gain, increase, step (up), supplement

incriminate accuse, arraign, blacken the name of, blame, charge, impeach, implicate, inculpate, indict, involve, point the finger at (*Inf.*), stigmatize

inculcate drill, drum into, hammer into (*Inf.*), implant, impress, indoctrinate, infuse, instil

inculpate accuse, blame, censure, charge, drag into (*Inf.*), impeach, implicate, incriminate, involve

incumbent binding, compulsory, mandatory, necessary, obligatory

incur arouse, bring (upon oneself), contract, draw, earn, expose oneself to, gain, induce, lay oneself open to, meet with, provoke

incurable *adj.* 1. dyed-in-the-wool, hopeless, incorrigible, inveterate 2. fatal, inoperable, irrecoverable, irremediable, remediless, terminal

incurious apathetic, indifferent, pococurante, unconcerned, uninquiring, uninterested

incursion foray, infiltration, inroad, invasion, irruption, penetration, raid

indebted beholden, grateful, in debt, obligated, obliged, under an obligation

indecency bawdiness, coarseness, crudity, foulness, grossness, immodesty, impropriety, impurity, indecorum, indelicacy, lewdness, licentiousness, obscenity, outrageousness, pornography, smut, smuttiness, unseemliness, vileness, vulgarity

Antonyms decency, decorum, delicacy, modesty, propriety, purity, seemliness

indecent 1. blue, coarse, crude, dirty, filthy, foul, gross, immodest, improper, impure, indelicate, lewd, licentious, pornographic, salacious, scatological, smutty, vile 2. ill-bred, improper, in bad taste, indecorous, offensive, outrageous, tasteless, unbecoming, unseemly, vulgar

Antonyms decent, decorous, delicate, modest, proper, pure, respectable, seemly, tasteful

indecipherable crabbed, illegible, indistinguishable, unintelligible, unreadable

indecision ambivalence, dithering (*Chiefly Brit.*), doubt, hesitancy, hesitation, indecisiveness, irresolution, shilly-shallying (*Inf.*), uncertainty, vacillation, wavering

indecisive 1. dithering (*Chiefly Brit.*), doubtful, faltering, hesitating, in two minds (*Inf.*), irresolute, pussyfooting (*Inf.*), tentative, uncertain, undecided, undetermined, vacillating, wavering 2. inconclusive, indefinite, indeterminate, unclear, undecided

Antonyms (*sense 1*) certain, decided, determined, positive, resolute, unhesitating (*sense 2*) clear, conclusive, decisive, definite, determinate, final

indecorous boorish, churlish, coarse, ill-bred, immodest, impolite, improper, indecent, rude, tasteless, uncivil, uncouth, undignified, unmannerly, unseemly, untoward

indeed actually, certainly, doubtlessly, in point of fact, in truth, positively, really, strictly, to be sure, truly, undeniably, undoubtedly, verily (*Archaic*), veritably

indefatigable assiduous, diligent, dogged, inexhaustible, patient, persevering, pertinacious, relentless, sedulous, tireless, unflagging, unremitting, untiring, unwearied, unwearying

indefensible faulty, inexcusable, insupportable, unforgivable, unjustifiable, unpardonable, untenable, unwarrantable, wrong

Antonyms defensible, excusable, forgivable, justifiable, legitimate, pardonable, supportable, tenable, warrantable

indefinable dim, hazy, impalpable, indescribable, indistinct, inexpressible, nameless, obscure, unrealized, vague

indefinite ambiguous, confused, doubtful, equivocal, evasive, general, ill-defined, imprecise, indeterminate, indistinct, inexact, loose, obscure, oracular, uncertain, unclear, undefined, undetermined, unfixed, unknown, unlimited, unsettled, vague

Antonyms certain, clear, definite, determinate, distinct, exact, fixed, settled, specific

indefinitely ad infinitum, continually, endlessly, for ever, *sine die*

indelible enduring, indestructible, ineffaceable, ineradicable, inexpungible, inextirpable, ingrained, lasting, permanent
Antonyms eradicable, erasable, impermanent, removable, short-lived, temporary, washable

indelicacy bad taste, coarseness, crudity, grossness, immodesty, impropriety, indecency, obscenity, offensiveness, rudeness, smuttiness, suggestiveness, tastelessness, vulgarity

indelicate blue, coarse, crude, embarrassing, gross, immodest, improper, indecent, indecorous, low, near the knuckle (*Inf.*), obscene, off-colour, offensive, risqué, rude, suggestive, tasteless, unbecoming, unseemly, untoward, vulgar
Antonyms becoming, decent, decorous, delicate, modest, proper, refined, seemly

indemnify 1. endorse, guarantee, insure, protect, secure, underwrite 2. compensate, pay, reimburse, remunerate, repair, repay, requite, satisfy

indemnity 1. guarantee, insurance, protection, security 2. compensation, redress, reimbursement, remuneration, reparation, requital, restitution, satisfaction 3. *Law* exemption, immunity, impunity, privilege

indent *v.* 1. ask for, order, request, requisition 2. cut, dint, mark, nick, notch, pink, scallop, score, serrate

indentation bash (*Inf.*), cut, dent, depression, dimple, dip, hollow, jag, nick, notch, pit

independence autarchy, autonomy, freedom, home rule, liberty, self-determination, self-government, self-reliance, self-rule, self-sufficiency, separation, sovereignty
Antonyms bondage, dependence, subjection, subjugation, subordination, subservience

independent 1. absolute, free, liberated, separate, unconnected, unconstrained, uncontrolled, unrelated 2. autarchic, autarchical, autonomous, decontrolled, nonaligned, self-determining, self-governing, separated, sovereign 3. bold, individualistic, liberated, self-contained, self-reliant, self-sufficient, self-supporting, unaided, unconventional
Antonyms (*sense 2*) aligned, controlled, dependent, restrained, subject, submissive, subordinate, subservient, subsidiary

independently alone, autonomously, by oneself, individually, on one's own, separately, solo, unaided

indescribable beggaring description, beyond description, beyond words, incommunicable, indefinable, ineffable, inexpressible, unutterable

indestructible abiding, durable, enduring, everlasting, immortal, imperishable, incorruptible, indelible, indissoluble, lasting, nonperishable, permanent, unbreakable, unfading
Antonyms breakable, corruptible, destructible, fading, impermanent, mortal, perishable

indeterminate imprecise, inconclusive, indefinite, inexact, uncertain, undefined, undetermined, unfixed, unspecified, unstipulated, vague
Antonyms certain, clear, conclusive, definite, determinate, exact, fixed, precise, specified, stipulated

index 1. clue, guide, indication, mark, sign, symptom, token 2. director, forefinger, hand, indicator, needle, pointer

indicate 1. add up to (*Inf.*), bespeak, be symptomatic of, betoken, denote, evince, imply, manifest, point to, reveal, show, signify, suggest 2. designate, point out, point to, specify 3. display, express, mark, read, record, register, show

indicated advisable, called-for, desirable, necessary, needed, recommended, suggested

indication clue, evidence, explanation, forewarning, hint, index, inkling, intimation, manifestation, mark, note, omen, portent, sign, signal, suggestion, symptom, warning

indicative exhibitive, indicatory, indicial, pointing to, significant, suggestive, symptomatic

indicator display, gauge, guide, index, mark, marker, meter, pointer, sign, signal, signpost, symbol

indict accuse, arraign, charge, impeach, prosecute, serve with a summons, summon, summons, tax

indictment accusation, allegation, charge, impeachment, prosecution, summons

indifference 1. absence of feeling, aloofness, apathy, callousness, carelessness, coldness, coolness, detachment, disregard, heedlessness, inattention, lack of interest, negligence, nonchalance, stoicalness, unconcern 2. disinterestedness, dispassion, equity, impartiality, neutrality, objectivity 3. insignificance, irrelevance, triviality, unimportance
Antonyms (*sense 1*) attention, care, com-

mitment, concern, enthusiasm, heed, regard

indifferent 1. aloof, apathetic, callous, careless, cold, cool, detached, distant, heedless, impervious, inattentive, regardless, uncaring, unconcerned, unimpressed, uninterested, unmoved, unresponsive, unsympathetic 2. immaterial, insignificant, of no consequence, unimportant 3. average, fair, mediocre, middling, moderate, ordinary, passable, perfunctory, so-so (*Inf.*), undistinguished, uninspired 4. disinterested, dispassionate, equitable, impartial, neutral, nonaligned, nonpartisan, objective, unbiased, uninvolved, unprejudiced
Antonyms (*sense 1*) avid, compassionate, concerned, eager, enthusiastic, interested, keen, responsive, sensitive, susceptible, sympathetic (*sense 3*) excellent, exceptional, fine, first-class, notable, remarkable

indigence destitution, distress, necessity, need, penury, poverty, privation, want

indigenous 1. aboriginal, autochthonous, home-grown, native, original 2. congenital, connate, inborn, inbred, inherent, innate

indigent destitute, dirt-poor (*Inf.*), down and out, flat broke (*Inf.*), impecunious, impoverished, in want, necessitous, needy, on one's uppers (*Inf.*), penniless, penurious, poor, poverty-stricken, short, straitened, without two pennies to rub together (*Inf.*)
Antonyms affluent, prosperous, rich, wealthy, well-off, well-to-do

indigestion dyspepsia, dyspepsy, heartburn, upset stomach

indignant angry, annoyed, disgruntled, exasperated, fuming (*Inf.*), furious, hacked (off) (*U.S. sl.*), heated, huffy (*Inf.*), in a huff, incensed, in high dudgeon, irate, livid (*Inf.*), mad (*Inf.*), miffed (*Inf.*), narked (*Brit., Aust., & N.Z. sl.*), peeved (*Inf.*), pissed off (*Taboo sl.*), provoked, resentful, riled, scornful, seeing red (*Inf.*), sore (*Inf.*), up in arms (*Inf.*), wrathful

indignation anger, exasperation, fury, ire (*Literary*), pique, rage, resentment, righteous anger, scorn, umbrage, wrath

indignity abuse, affront, contumely, dishonour, disrespect, humiliation, injury, insult, obloquy, opprobrium, outrage, reproach, slap in the face (*Inf.*), slight, snub

indirect 1. backhanded, circuitous, circumlocutory, crooked, devious, long-drawn-out, meandering, oblique, periphrastic, rambling, roundabout, tortuous, wandering, winding, zigzag 2. ancillary, collateral, contingent, incidental, secondary, subsidiary, unintended
Antonyms (*sense 1*) clear-cut, direct, straight, straightforward, undeviating, uninterrupted (*sense 2*) direct, explicit, express, intended

indirectly by implication, circumlocutorily, in a roundabout way, obliquely, periphrastically, second-hand

indiscernible hidden, impalpable, imperceptible, indistinct, indistinguishable, invisible, unapparent, undiscernible
Antonyms apparent, clear, discernible, distinct, distinguishable, perceptible, visible

indiscreet foolish, hasty, heedless, ill-advised, ill-considered, ill-judged, impolitic, imprudent, incautious, injudicious, naive, rash, reckless, tactless, undiplomatic, unthinking, unwise
Antonyms cautious, diplomatic, discreet, judicious, politic, prudent, tactful, wise

indiscretion bloomer (*Brit. inf.*), boob (*Brit. sl.*), error, faux pas, folly, foolishness, gaffe, gaucherie, imprudence, mistake, rashness, recklessness, slip, slip of the tongue, tactlessness

indiscriminate 1. aimless, careless, desultory, general, hit or miss (*Inf.*), random, sweeping, uncritical, undiscriminating, unmethodical, unselective, unsystematic, wholesale 2. chaotic, confused, haphazard, higgledy-piggledy (*Inf.*), jumbled, mingled, miscellaneous, mixed, mongrel, motley, promiscuous, undistinguishable
Antonyms (*sense 1*) deliberate, discriminating, exclusive, methodical, selective, systematic

indispensable crucial, essential, imperative, key, necessary, needed, needful, requisite, vital
Antonyms dispensable, disposable, nonessential, superfluous, unimportant, unnecessary

indisposed 1. ailing, confined to bed, ill, laid up (*Inf.*), on the sick list (*Inf.*), poorly (*Inf.*), sick, unwell 2. averse, disinclined, loath, reluctant, unwilling
Antonyms (*sense 1*) fine, fit, hardy, healthy, sound, well

indisposition 1. ailment, ill health, illness, sickness 2. aversion, disinclination, dislike, distaste, hesitancy, reluctance, unwillingness

indisputable absolute, beyond doubt, certain, evident, incontestable, incontrovertible, indubitable, irrefutable, positive, sure, unassailable, undeniable, unquestionable
Antonyms assailable, disputable, doubtful, indefinite, questionable, refutable, uncertain, vague

indissoluble abiding, binding, enduring, eternal, fixed, imperishable, incorruptible, indestructible, inseparable, lasting, permanent, solid, unbreakable

indistinct ambiguous, bleary, blurred, confused, dim, doubtful, faint, fuzzy, hazy, ill-defined, indefinite, indeterminate, indiscernible, indistinguishable, misty, muffled, obscure, out of focus, shadowy, unclear, undefined, unintelligible, vague, weak
Antonyms clear, defined, determinate, discernible, distinct, distinguishable, evident, intelligible

indistinguishable 1. alike, identical, like as two peas in a pod (*Inf.*), (the) same, twin 2. imperceptible, indiscernible, invisible, obscure

individual 1. *adj.* characteristic, discrete, distinct, distinctive, exclusive, identical, idiosyncratic, own, particular, peculiar, personal, personalized, proper, respective, separate, several, single, singular, special, specific, unique 2. *n.* being, body (*Inf.*), character, creature, mortal, party, person, personage, soul, type, unit
Antonyms *adj.* collective, common, conventional, general, indistinct, ordinary, universal

individualism egocentricity, egoism, freethinking, independence, originality, self-direction, self-interest, self-reliance

individualist freethinker, independent, loner, lone wolf, maverick, nonconformist, original

individualistic 1. characteristic, distinctive, idiosyncratic, individual, original, particular, special, typical, unique 2. egocentric, egoistic, independent, self-reliant

individuality character, discreteness, distinction, distinctiveness, originality, peculiarity, personality, separateness, singularity, uniqueness

individually apart, independently, one at a time, one by one, personally, separately, severally, singly

indoctrinate brainwash, drill, ground, imbue, initiate, instruct, school, teach, train

indoctrination brainwashing, drilling, grounding, inculcation, instruction, schooling, training

indolence faineance, faineancy, heaviness, idleness, inactivity, inertia, inertness, languidness, languor, laziness, lethargy, shirking, skiving (*Brit. sl.*), slacking, sloth, sluggishness, torpidity, torpor

indolent fainéant, idle, inactive, inert, lackadaisical, languid, lazy, lethargic, listless, lumpish, slack, slothful, slow, sluggish, torpid, workshy
Antonyms active, assiduous, busy, conscientious, diligent, energetic, industrious, vigorous

indomitable bold, invincible, resolute, staunch, steadfast, unbeatable, unconquerable, unflinching, untameable, unyielding
Antonyms cowardly, faltering, feeble, shrinking, wavering, weak, yielding

indorse *see* ENDORSE

indorsement *see* ENDORSEMENT

indubitable certain, evident, incontestable, incontrovertible, indisputable, irrefutable, obvious, sure, unarguable, undeniable, undoubted, unquestionable, veritable

induce 1. actuate, convince, draw, encourage, get, impel, incite, influence, instigate, move, persuade, press, prevail upon, prompt, talk into 2. bring about, cause, effect, engender, generate, give rise to, lead to, occasion, produce, set in motion, set off
Antonyms curb, deter, discourage, dissuade, hinder, prevent, restrain, stop, suppress

inducement attraction, bait, carrot (*Inf.*), cause, come-on (*Inf.*), consideration, encouragement, impulse, incentive, incitement, influence, lure, motive, reward, spur, stimulus, urge

induct inaugurate, initiate, install, introduce, invest, swear in

induction 1. inauguration, initiation, installation, institution, introduction, investiture 2. conclusion, generalization, inference

indulge 1. cater to, feed, give way to, gratify, pander to, regale, satiate, satisfy, treat oneself to, yield to 2. *With* in bask in, give free rein to, give oneself up to, luxuriate in, revel in, wallow in 3. baby, coddle, cosset, favour, foster, give in to, go along with, humour, mollycoddle, pamper, pet, spoil

indulgence 1. excess, fondness, immoderation, intemperance, intemperateness, kindness, leniency, pampering, partiality, permissiveness, profligacy, profligateness, spoiling 2. appeasement, fulfilment, gratification, satiation, satisfaction 3. extravagance, favour, luxury, privilege, treat 4. courtesy, forbearance, good will, patience, tolerance, understanding
Antonyms (*sense 1*) moderation, strictness, temperance, temperateness

indulgent compliant, easy-going, favourable, fond, forbearing, gentle, gratifying, kind, kindly, lenient, liberal, mild, permissive, tender, tolerant, understanding
Antonyms austere, demanding, harsh, intolerant, rigorous, stern, strict, stringent, unmerciful

industrialist baron, big businessman, boss, capitalist, captain of industry, financier, magnate, manufacturer, producer, tycoon

industrious active, assiduous, busy, conscientious, diligent, energetic, hard-working, laborious, persevering, persistent, productive, purposeful, sedulous, steady, tireless, zealous
Antonyms idle, indolent, lackadaisical, lazy, shiftless, slothful

industriously assiduously, conscientiously, diligently, doggedly, hard, like a Trojan, nose to the grindstone (*Inf.*), perseveringly, sedulously, steadily, without slacking

industry 1. business, commerce, commercial enterprise, manufacturing, production, trade 2. activity, application, assiduity, determination, diligence, effort, labour, perseverance, persistence, tirelessness, toil, vigour, zeal

inebriate *v.* 1. intoxicate, make drunk, stupefy 2. animate, arouse, carry away, excite, exhilarate, fire, stimulate ~*n.* 3. alcoholic, boozer (*Inf.*), dipsomaniac, drunk, drunkard, heavy drinker, lush (*Sl.*), soak (*Sl.*), sot, toper

inebriated befuddled, bevvied (*Dialect*), blind drunk, blitzed (*Sl.*), blotto (*Sl.*), bombed (*Sl.*), drunk, flying (*Sl.*), fou *or* fu' (*Scot.*), half-cut (*Inf.*), half seas over (*Inf.*), high (*Inf.*), high as a kite (*Inf.*), inebriate, in one's cups, intoxicated, legless (*Inf.*), lit up (*Sl.*), merry (*Brit. inf.*), out of it (*Sl.*), out to it (*Aust. & N.Z. sl.*), paralytic (*Inf.*), pie-eyed (*Sl.*), pissed (*Taboo sl.*), plastered (*Sl.*), smashed (*Sl.*), sozzled (*Inf.*), steamboats (*Sl.*), steaming (*Sl.*), stoned (*Sl.*), the worse for drink, three sheets in the wind (*Inf.*), tight (*Inf.*), tipsy, under the influence (*Inf.*), under the weather (*Inf.*), wasted (*Sl.*), wrecked (*Sl.*), zonked (*Sl.*)

inebriation crapulence, drunkenness, inebriety, insobriety, intemperance, intoxication, sottishness

ineffable beyond words, incommunicable, indefinable, indescribable, inexpressible, unspeakable, unutterable

ineffective barren, bootless, feeble, fruitless, futile, idle, impotent, inadequate, ineffectual, inefficacious, inefficient, unavailing, unproductive, useless, vain, weak, worthless
Antonyms effective, efficacious, efficient, fruitful, potent, productive, useful, worthwhile

ineffectual abortive, bootless, emasculate, feeble, fruitless, futile, idle, impotent, inadequate, incompetent, ineffective, inefficacious, inefficient, inept, lame, powerless, unavailing, useless, vain, weak

inefficacious abortive, futile, ineffective, ineffectual, unavailing, unproductive, unsuccessful

inefficacy futility, inadequacy, ineffectiveness, ineffectuality, nonsuccess, unproductiveness, uselessness

inefficiency carelessness, disorganization, incompetence, muddle, slackness, sloppiness

inefficient cowboy (*Inf.*), disorganized, feeble, incapable, incompetent, ineffectual, inefficacious, inept, inexpert, slipshod, sloppy, wasteful, weak
Antonyms able, capable, competent, effective, efficient, expert, organized, skilled

inelegant awkward, clumsy, coarse, crass, crude, gauche, graceless, indelicate, laboured, rough, uncouth, uncultivated, ungainly, ungraceful, unpolished, unrefined

ineligible disqualified, incompetent (*Law*), objectionable, ruled out, unacceptable, undesirable, unequipped, unfit, unfitted, unqualified, unsuitable

inept 1. awkward, bumbling, bungling, cack-handed (*Inf.*), clumsy, cowboy (*Inf.*), gauche, incompetent, inexpert, maladroit, unhandy, unskilful, unworkmanlike 2. absurd, improper, inappropriate, inapt, infelicitous, malapropos, meaningless, out of place, pointless, ridiculous, unfit, unsuitable
Antonyms able, adroit, appropriate, apt, competent, dexterous, efficient, effectual, germane, qualified, sensible, skilful, suitable, talented

ineptitude 1. clumsiness, gaucheness, incapacity, incompetence, inexpertness, unfitness, unhandiness 2. absurdity, inappropriateness, pointlessness, uselessness

inequality bias, difference, disparity, disproportion, diversity, imparity, irregularity, lack of balance, preferentiality, prejudice, unevenness

inequitable biased, discriminatory, one-sided, partial, partisan, preferential, prejudiced, unfair, unjust
Antonyms even-handed, fair, impartial, just, unbiased, unprejudiced

inequity bias, discrimination, injustice, one-sidedness, prejudice, unfairness, unjustness

inert dead, dormant, dull, idle, immobile, inactive, inanimate, indolent, lazy, leaden, lifeless, motionless, passive, quiescent, slack, slothful, sluggish, slumberous (*Chiefly poetic*), static, still, torpid, unmoving, unreactive, unresponsive
Antonyms active, alive, animated, energetic, living, mobile, moving, reactive, responsive, vital

inertia apathy, deadness, disinclination to move, drowsiness, dullness, idleness, immobility, inactivity, indolence, languor,

lassitude, laziness, lethargy, listlessness, passivity, sloth, sluggishness, stillness, stupor, torpor, unresponsiveness
Antonyms action, activity, animation, brio, energy, liveliness, vigour, vitality

inescapable certain, destined, fated, ineluctable, ineludible (*Rare*), inevitable, inexorable, sure, unavoidable

inessential 1. *adj.* dispensable, extraneous, extrinsic, needless, optional, redundant, spare, superfluous, surplus, uncalled-for, unnecessary 2. *n.* accessory, extra, extravagance, luxury, makeweight, superfluity, trimming

inestimable beyond price, immeasurable, incalculable, invaluable, precious, priceless, prodigious

inevitable assured, certain, decreed, destined, fixed, ineluctable, inescapable, inexorable, necessary, ordained, settled, sure, unavoidable, unpreventable
Antonyms avoidable, escapable, evadable, preventable, uncertain

inevitably as a necessary consequence, as a result, automatically, certainly, necessarily, of necessity, perforce, surely, unavoidably, willy-nilly

inexact imprecise, inaccurate, incorrect, indefinite, indeterminate, off

inexcusable indefensible, inexpiable, outrageous, unforgivable, unjustifiable, unpardonable, unwarrantable
Antonyms defensible, excusable, forgivable, justifiable, pardonable

inexhaustible 1. bottomless, boundless, endless, illimitable, infinite, limitless, measureless, never-ending, unbounded 2. indefatigable, tireless, undaunted, unfailing, unflagging, untiring, unwearied, unwearying
Antonyms (*sense 1*) bounded, exhaustible, finite, limitable, limited, measurable (*sense 2*) daunted, enervated, failing, flagging, tiring, wearied

inexorable adamant, cruel, hard, harsh, immovable, implacable, ineluctable, inescapable, inflexible, merciless, obdurate, pitiless, relentless, remorseless, severe, unappeasable, unbending, unrelenting, unyielding
Antonyms bending, flexible, lenient, movable, relenting, yielding

inexorably implacably, inevitably, irresistibly, relentlessly, remorselessly, unrelentingly

inexpedient disadvantageous, ill-advised, ill-considered, ill-judged, impolitic, impractical, improper, imprudent, inadvisable, inappropriate, indiscreet, injudicious, misguided, unadvisable, undesirable, undiplomatic, unsuitable, unwise

inexpensive bargain, budget, cheap, economical, low-cost, low-priced, modest, reasonable
Antonyms costly, dear, exorbitant, expensive, high-priced, pricey, uneconomical

inexperience callowness, greenness, ignorance, newness, rawness, unexpertness, unfamiliarity

inexperienced amateur, callow, fresh, green, immature, new, raw, unaccustomed, unacquainted, unfamiliar, unfledged, unpractised, unschooled, unseasoned, unskilled, untrained, untried, unused, unversed, wet behind the ears (*Inf.*)
Antonyms experienced, familiar, knowledgeable, practised, seasoned, skilled, trained, versed

inexpert amateurish, awkward, bungling, cack-handed (*Inf.*), clumsy, inept, maladroit, skill-less, unhandy, unpractised, unprofessional, unskilful, unskilled, unworkmanlike

inexplicable baffling, beyond comprehension, enigmatic, incomprehensible, inscrutable, insoluble, mysterious, mystifying, strange, unaccountable, unfathomable, unintelligible
Antonyms comprehensible, explainable, explicable, fathomable, intelligible, soluble, understandable

inexpressible incommunicable, indefinable, indescribable, ineffable, unspeakable, unutterable

inexpressive bland, blank, cold, dead, deadpan, emotionless, empty, expressionless, impassive, inanimate, inscrutable, lifeless, stony, vacant

inextinguishable enduring, eternal, immortal, imperishable, indestructible, irrepressible, undying, unquenchable, unsuppressible

inextricably indissolubly, indistinguishably, inseparably, intricately, irretrievably, totally

infallibility 1. faultlessness, impeccability, irrefutability, omniscience, perfection, supremacy, unerringness 2. dependability, reliability, safety, sureness, trustworthiness

infallible 1. faultless, impeccable, omniscient, perfect, unerring, unimpeachable 2. certain, dependable, foolproof, reliable, sure, sure-fire (*Inf.*), trustworthy, unbeatable, unfailing
Antonyms (*sense 1*) errant, fallible, human, imperfect, mortal (*sense 2*) doubtful, dubious, uncertain, undependable, unreliable, unsure

infamous abominable, atrocious, base, detestable, disgraceful, dishonourable, disreputable, egregious, flagitious, hateful, heinous, ignominious, ill-famed, iniquitous, loathsome, monstrous, nefarious, notorious, odious, opprobrious, outrageous, scandalous, scurvy, shameful, shocking, vile, villainous, wicked
Antonyms esteemed, glorious, honourable, noble, reputable, virtuous

infamy abomination, atrocity, discredit, disgrace, dishonour, disrepute, ignominy, notoriety, obloquy, odium, opprobrium, outrageousness, scandal, shame, stigma, villainy

infancy 1. babyhood, early childhood 2. beginnings, cradle, dawn, early stages, emergence, inception, origins, outset, start
Antonyms (*sense 2*) close, conclusion, death, end, expiration, finish, termination

infant 1. *n.* ankle-biter (*Aust. sl.*), babe, baby, bairn (*Scot.*), child, little one, neonate, newborn child, rug rat (*Sl.*), sprog (*Sl.*), suckling, toddler, tot, wean (*Scot.*) 2. *adj.* baby, dawning, developing, early, emergent, growing, immature, initial, nascent, newborn, unfledged, young

infantile babyish, childish, immature, puerile, tender, weak, young
Antonyms adult, developed, mature

infatuate befool, beguile, besot, bewitch, captivate, delude, enchant, enrapture, enravish, fascinate, make a fool of, mislead, obsess, stupefy, sweep one off one's feet, turn (someone's) head

infatuated beguiled, besotted, bewitched, captivated, carried away, crazy about (*Inf.*), enamoured, enraptured, fascinated, head over heels in love with, inflamed, intoxicated, obsessed, possessed, smitten (*Inf.*), spellbound, swept off one's feet, under the spell of

infatuation crush (*Inf.*), fixation, folly, foolishness, madness, obsession, passion, thing (*Inf.*)

infect affect, blight, contaminate, corrupt, defile, influence, poison, pollute, spread to *or* among, taint, touch, vitiate

infection contagion, contamination, corruption, defilement, poison, pollution, septicity, virus

infectious catching, communicable, contagious, contaminating, corrupting, defiling, infective, pestilential, poisoning, polluting, spreading, transmittable, virulent, vitiating

infelicity 1. inappropriateness, inaptness, incongruity, unsuitability, wrongness 2. bad luck, misery, misfortune, sadness, unhappiness, woe, wretchedness

infer conclude, conjecture, deduce, derive, gather, presume, read between the lines, surmise, understand

inference assumption, conclusion, conjecture, consequence, corollary, deduction, illation (*Rare*), presumption, reading, surmise

inferior *adj.* 1. junior, lesser, lower, menial, minor, secondary, subordinate, subsidiary, under, underneath 2. bad, bush-league (*Aust. & N.Z. inf.*), chickenshit (*U.S. sl.*), crappy (*Sl.*), dime-a-dozen (*Inf.*), duff (*Brit. inf.*), imperfect, indifferent, low-grade, mean, mediocre, of a sort *or* of sorts, piss-poor (*Taboo sl.*), poor, poorer, poxy (*Sl.*), second-class, second-rate, shoddy, substandard, tinhorn (*U.S. sl.*), two-bit (*U.S. & Canad. sl.*), worse ~*n.* 3. junior, menial, subordinate, underling
Antonyms (*sense 1*) greater, higher, senior, superior, top (*sense 2*) excellent, fine, first-class

inferiority 1. badness, deficiency, imperfection, inadequacy, insignificance, meanness, mediocrity, shoddiness, unimportance, worthlessness 2. abasement, inferior status *or* standing, lowliness, subordination, subservience
Antonyms advantage, ascendancy, dominance, eminence, excellence, superiority

infernal 1. chthonian, Hadean, hellish, lower, nether, Plutonian, Stygian, Tartarean (*Literary*), underworld 2. accursed, damnable, damned, demonic, devilish, diabolical, fiendish, hellish, malevolent, malicious, satanic
Antonyms angelic, celestial, glorious, godlike, heavenly, seraphic

infertile barren, infecund, nonproductive, sterile, unfruitful, unproductive
Antonyms fecund, fertile, fruitful, generative, productive

infertility barrenness, infecundity, sterility, unfruitfulness, unproductiveness

infest beset, flood, invade, overrun, penetrate, permeate, ravage, swarm, throng

infested alive, beset, crawling, lousy (*Sl.*), overrun, pervaded, plagued, ravaged, ridden, swarming, teeming

infidel atheist, freethinker, Gentile, giaour (*Turkish*), heathen, heretic, pagan, sceptic, unbeliever

infidelity 1. adultery, bad faith, betrayal, cheating (*Inf.*), disloyalty, duplicity, faithlessness, false-heartedness, falseness, perfidy, unfaithfulness 2. apostasy, disbelief, irreligion, scepticism, treachery, unbelief

infiltrate creep in, filter through, insinuate oneself, penetrate, percolate, permeate, pervade, sneak in (*Inf.*), work *or* worm one's way into

infinite absolute, all-embracing, bottomless, boundless, enormous, eternal, everlasting, illimitable, immeasurable, immense, inestimable, inexhaustible, interminable, limitless, measureless, never-ending, numberless, perpetual, stupendous, total, unbounded, uncounted, untold, vast, wide, without end, without number
Antonyms bounded, circumscribed, finite, limited, measurable, restricted

infinitesimal atomic, inappreciable, insignificant, microscopic, minuscule, minute, negligible, teensy-weensy, teeny, teeny-weeny, tiny, unnoticeable, wee
Antonyms enormous, great, huge, infinite, large, vast

infinity boundlessness, endlessness, eternity, immensity, infinitude, perpetuity, vastness

infirm 1. ailing, debilitated, decrepit, doddering, doddery, enfeebled, failing, feeble, frail, lame, weak 2. faltering, indecisive, insecure, irresolute, shaky, unsound, unstable, vacillating, wavering, weak, wobbly
Antonyms (*sense 1*) healthy, hearty, robust, sound, strong, sturdy, vigorous

infirmity 1. debility, decrepitude, deficiency, feebleness, frailty, ill health, imperfection, sickliness, vulnerability 2. ailment, defect, disorder, failing, fault, malady, sickness, weakness
Antonyms health, soundness, stability, strength, vigour

infix 1. engraft, fasten, implant, insert, inset, introduce, place, set 2. drum into, entrench, impress, inculcate, ingrain, instil

inflame 1. agitate, anger, arouse, embitter, enrage, exasperate, excite, fire, foment, heat, ignite, impassion, incense, infuriate, intoxicate, kindle, madden, provoke, rile, rouse, stimulate 2. aggravate, exacerbate, exasperate, fan, increase, intensify, worsen
Antonyms allay, calm, cool, discourage, extinguish, pacify, quench, quiet, soothe, suppress

inflamed angry, chafing, festering, fevered, heated, hot, infected, red, septic, sore, swollen

inflammable combustible, flammable, incendiary

inflammation burning, heat, painfulness, rash, redness, sore, soreness, tenderness

inflammatory anarchic, demagogic, explosive, fiery, incendiary, inflaming, instigative, insurgent, intemperate, provocative, rabble-rousing, rabid, riotous, seditious

inflate aerate, aggrandize, amplify, balloon, bloat, blow up, boost, dilate, distend, enlarge, escalate, exaggerate, expand, increase, puff up *or* out, pump up, swell
Antonyms collapse, compress, contract, deflate, diminish, lessen, shrink

inflated bombastic, exaggerated, grandiloquent, ostentatious, overblown, swollen

inflation aggrandizement, blowing up, distension, enhancement, enlargement, escalation, expansion, extension, increase, intensification, puffiness, rise, spread, swelling, tumefaction

inflect 1. intonate, modulate 2. *Gram.* conjugate, decline 3. arch, bend, bow, crook, curve, flex, round

inflection 1. accentuation, bend, bow, crook, curvature, intonation, modulation 2. *Gram.* conjugation, declension 3. angle, arc, arch

inflexibility 1. hardness, immovability, inelasticity, rigidity, stiffness, stringency 2. fixity, intransigence, obduracy, obstinacy, steeliness

inflexible 1. adamant, brassbound, dyed-in-the-wool, firm, fixed, hard and fast, immovable, immutable, implacable, inexorable, intractable, iron, obdurate, obstinate, relentless, resolute, rigorous, set, set in one's ways, steadfast, steely, stiff-necked, strict, stringent, stubborn, unadaptable, unbending, unchangeable, uncompromising, unyielding 2. hard, hardened, inelastic, nonflexible, rigid, stiff, taut
Antonyms elastic, flexible, irresolute, lissom(e), movable, pliable, pliant, supple, variable, yielding

inflict administer, apply, deliver, exact, impose, levy, mete *or* deal out, visit, wreak

infliction 1. administration, exaction, imposition, perpetration, wreaking 2. affliction, penalty, punishment, trouble, visitation, worry

influence *n.* 1. agency, ascendancy, authority, control, credit, direction, domination, effect, guidance, magnetism, mastery, power, pressure, rule, spell, sway, weight 2. bottom, clout (*Inf.*), connections, good offices, hold, importance, leverage, power, prestige, pull (*Inf.*), weight ~*v.* 3. act *or* work upon, affect, arouse, bias, control, count, direct, dispose, guide, impel, impress, incite, incline, induce, instigate, lead to believe, manipulate, modify, move, persuade, predispose, prompt, rouse, sway 4. bring pressure to bear upon, carry weight with, make oneself felt, pull strings (*Inf.*)

influential authoritative, controlling, effective, efficacious, forcible, guiding, important, instrumental, leading, meaningful, momentous, moving, persuasive, potent, powerful, significant, telling, weighty

Antonyms impotent, ineffective, ineffectual, powerless, unimportant, uninfluential, unpersuasive, weak

influx arrival, convergence, flow, incursion, inflow, inrush, inundation, invasion, rush

infold *see* ENFOLD

inform 1. acquaint, advise, apprise, clue in (*Inf.*), communicate, enlighten, give (someone) to understand, instruct, leak to, let know, make conversant (with), notify, put (someone) in the picture (*Inf.*), send word to, teach, tell, tip off 2. *Often with* **against** *or* **on** betray, blab, blow the whistle on (*Inf.*), clype (*Scot.*), denounce, grass (*Brit. sl.*), incriminate, inculpate, nark (*Brit., Aust., & N.Z. sl.*), peach (*Sl.*), rat (*Inf.*), shop (*Sl., chiefly Brit.*), sing (*Sl., chiefly U.S.*), snitch (*Sl.*), spill one's guts (*Sl.*), squeal (*Sl.*), tell all, tell on (*Inf.*) 3. animate, characterize, illuminate, imbue, inspire, permeate, suffuse, typify

informal casual, colloquial, cosy, easy, familiar, natural, relaxed, simple, unceremonious, unconstrained, unofficial

Antonyms ceremonious, constrained, conventional, formal, official, stiff

informality casualness, ease, familiarity, lack of ceremony, naturalness, relaxation, simplicity

information advice, blurb, counsel, data, dope (*Inf.*), facts, gen (*Brit. inf.*), info (*Inf.*), inside story, instruction, intelligence, knowledge, latest (*Inf.*), lowdown (*Inf.*), material, message, news, notice, report, tidings, word

informative chatty, communicative, edifying, educational, enlightening, forthcoming, gossipy, illuminating, instructive, newsy, revealing

informed abreast, acquainted, *au courant, au fait,* briefed, conversant, enlightened, erudite, expert, familiar, genned up (*Brit. inf.*), in the know (*Inf.*), knowledgeable, learned, posted, primed, reliable, up, up to date, versed, well-read

informer accuser, betrayer, grass (*Brit. sl.*), Judas, nark (*Brit., Aust., & N.Z. sl.*), sneak, squealer (*Sl.*), stool pigeon

infraction breach, breaking, contravention, infringement, nonfulfilment, transgression, trespass, violation

infrequent few and far between, occasional, rare, sporadic, uncommon, unusual

Antonyms common, customary, frequent, habitual, often, regular, usual

infringe 1. break, contravene, disobey, transgress, violate 2. *With* **on** *or* **upon** encroach, intrude, trespass

infringement breach, contravention, infraction, noncompliance, nonobservance, transgression, trespass, violation

infuriate anger, be like a red rag to a bull, enrage, exasperate, gall, get one's back up, get one's goat (*Sl.*), incense, irritate, madden, make one's blood boil, make one see red (*Inf.*), make one's hackles rise, nark (*Brit., Aust., & N.Z. sl.*), provoke, raise one's hackles, rile

Antonyms appease, calm, mollify, pacify, placate, propitiate, soothe

infuriating aggravating (*Inf.*), annoying, exasperating, galling, irritating, maddening, mortifying, pestilential, provoking, vexatious

infuse 1. breathe into, engraft, impart to, implant, inculcate, inspire, instil, introduce 2. brew, macerate, soak, steep

ingenious adroit, bright, brilliant, clever, crafty, creative, dexterous, fertile, inventive, masterly, original, ready, resourceful, shrewd, skilful, subtle

Antonyms artless, clumsy, unimaginative, uninventive, unoriginal, unresourceful, unskilful

ingenuity adroitness, cleverness, faculty, flair, genius, gift, ingeniousness, inventiveness, knack, originality, resourcefulness, sharpness, shrewdness, skill, turn

Antonyms clumsiness, dullness, incompetence, ineptitude, ineptness

ingenuous artless, candid, childlike, frank, guileless, honest, innocent, naive, open, plain, simple, sincere, trustful, trusting, unreserved, unsophisticated, unstudied

Antonyms artful, crafty, devious, insincere, reserved, sly, sophisticated, subtle, wily

ingenuousness artlessness, candour, frankness, guilelessness, innocence, naivety, openness, trustingness, unsuspiciousness

Antonyms artfulness, craftiness, insincerity, slyness, sophistication, subterfuge, subtlety

inglorious discreditable, disgraceful, dishonourable, disreputable, failed, humiliating, ignoble, ignominious, infamous, obscure, shameful, unheroic, unknown, unsuccessful, unsung

ingraft *see* ENGRAFT

ingrain embed, entrench, fix, imbue, implant, impress, imprint, instil, root

ingrained brassbound, constitutional, deep-rooted, deep-seated, fixed, fundamental, hereditary, inborn, inbred, inbuilt, indelible, ineradicable, inherent, in the blood, intrinsic, inveterate, rooted

ingratiate be a yes man, blandish, brown-nose (*Taboo sl.*), crawl, curry favour, fawn, flatter, get in with, get on the right side of, grovel, insinuate oneself, kiss (someone's) ass (*U.S. & Canad. taboo sl.*), lick (someone's) boots, pander to, play up to, rub (someone) up the right way (*Inf.*), seek the favour (of someone), suck up to (*Inf.*), toady, worm oneself into (someone's) favour

ingratiating bootlicking (*Inf.*), crawling, fawning, flattering, humble, obsequious, servile, sycophantic, timeserving, toadying, unctuous

ingratitude thanklessness, unappreciativeness, ungratefulness

Antonyms appreciation, gratefulness, gratitude, thankfulness, thanks, thanksgiving

ingredient component, constituent, element, part

ingress access, admission, admittance, door, entrance, entrée, entry, right of entry, way in

ingulf *see* ENGULF

inhabit abide, dwell, live, lodge, make one's home, occupy, people, populate, possess, reside, take up residence in, tenant

inhabitant aborigine, citizen, denizen, dweller, indigene, indweller, inmate, native, occupant, occupier, resident, tenant

inhabited colonized, developed, held, occupied, peopled, populated, settled, tenanted

inhalation breath, breathing, inhaling, inspiration

inhale breathe in, draw in, gasp, respire, suck in

Antonyms blow, breathe out, exhale, expire

inharmonious antipathetic, cacophonous, clashing, discordant, dissonant, grating, harsh, incompatible, inconsonant, jangling, jarring, strident, tuneless, unharmonious, unmelodious, unmusical

inherent basic, congenital, connate, essential, hereditary, inborn, inbred, inbuilt, ingrained, inherited, innate, instinctive, intrinsic, native, natural

Antonyms alien, extraneous, extrinsic, imposed, superficial, supplementary

inherit accede to, be bequeathed, be left, come into, fall heir to, succeed to

inheritance bequest, birthright, heritage, legacy, patrimony

inheritor beneficiary, heir, legatee, recipient, successor

inhibit arrest, bar, bridle, check, constrain, cramp (someone's) style (*Inf.*), curb, debar, discourage, forbid, frustrate, hinder, hold back *or* in, impede, obstruct, prevent, prohibit, restrain, stop

Antonyms abet, allow, encourage, further, let, permit, support

inhibited constrained, frustrated, guarded, repressed, reserved, reticent, self-conscious, shy, subdued, uptight (*Inf.*), withdrawn

Antonyms free, natural, outgoing, relaxed, spontaneous, uninhibited, unreserved

inhibition bar, block, check, embargo, hang-up (*Inf.*), hindrance, interdict, mental blockage, obstacle, prohibition, reserve, restraint, restriction, reticence, self-consciousness, shyness

inhospitable 1. cool, uncongenial, unfriendly, ungenerous, unkind, unreceptive, unsociable, unwelcoming, xenophobic 2. bare, barren, bleak, desolate, empty, forbidding, godforsaken, hostile, lonely, sterile, unfavourable, uninhabitable

Antonyms (*sense 1*) amicable, friendly, generous, genial, gracious, hospitable, sociable, welcoming

inhuman animal, barbaric, barbarous, bestial, brutal, cold-blooded, cruel, diabolical, fiendish, heartless, merciless, pitiless, remorseless, ruthless, savage, unfeeling, vicious

Antonyms charitable, compassionate, feeling, humane, merciful, sensitive, tender, warmhearted

inhumane brutal, cruel, heartless, pitiless, uncompassionate, unfeeling, unkind, unsympathetic

inhumanity atrocity, barbarism, brutality, brutishness, cold-bloodedness, cold-heartedness, cruelty, hardheartedness, heartlessness, pitilessness, ruthlessness, unkindness, viciousness

inhumation burial, entombment, interment, sepulture

inhume bury, entomb, inter, lay to rest, sepulchre

inimical adverse, antagonistic, antipathetic, contrary, destructive, disaffected, harmful, hostile, hurtful, ill-disposed, injurious, noxious, opposed, oppugnant (*Rare*), pernicious, repugnant, unfavourable, unfriendly, unwelcoming

Antonyms affable, amicable, congenial, favourable, friendly, good, helpful, kindly, sympathetic, welcoming

inimitable consummate, incomparable, matchless, nonpareil, peerless, supreme, unequalled, unexampled, unique, unmatched, unparalleled, unrivalled, unsurpassable

iniquitous abominable, accursed, atrocious, base, criminal, evil, heinous, immoral, infamous, nefarious, reprehensible, reprobate, sinful, unjust, unrighteous, vicious, wicked

iniquity abomination, baseness, crime, evil, evildoing, heinousness, infamy, injustice, misdeed, offence, sin, sinfulness, unrighteousness, wickedness, wrong, wrongdoing
Antonyms fairness, goodness, honesty, integrity, justice, morality, righteousness, uprightness, virtue

initial *adj.* beginning, commencing, early, first, inaugural, inceptive, inchoate, incipient, introductory, opening, primary
Antonyms closing, concluding, ending, final, last, terminal, ultimate

initially at *or* in the beginning, at first, at the outset, at the start, first, firstly, in the early stages, originally, primarily, to begin with

initiate *v.* 1. begin, break the ice, commence, get under way, inaugurate, institute, kick off (*Inf.*), kick-start, launch, lay the foundations of, open, originate, pioneer, set going, set in motion, set the ball rolling, start 2. coach, familiarize with, indoctrinate, induct, instate, instruct, introduce, invest, teach, train ~*n.* 3. beginner, convert, entrant, learner, member, novice, probationer, proselyte, tyro

initiation admission, commencement, debut, enrolment, entrance, inauguration, inception, induction, installation, instatement, introduction, investiture

initiative 1. advantage, beginning, commencement, first move, first step, lead 2. ambition, drive, dynamism, enterprise, get-up-and-go (*Inf.*), inventiveness, leadership, originality, push (*Inf.*), resource, resourcefulness

inject 1. inoculate, jab (*Inf.*), shoot (*Inf.*), vaccinate 2. bring in, infuse, insert, instil, interject, introduce

injection 1. inoculation, jab (*Inf.*), shot (*Inf.*), vaccination, vaccine 2. dose, infusion, insertion, interjection, introduction

injudicious foolish, hasty, ill-advised, ill-judged, ill-timed, impolitic, imprudent, incautious, inconsiderate, indiscreet, inexpedient, rash, unthinking, unwise
Antonyms cautious, considerate, discreet, expedient, judicious, polite, prudent, well-timed, wise

injunction admonition, command, dictate, exhortation, instruction, mandate, order, precept, ruling

injure abuse, blemish, blight, break, damage, deface, disable, harm, hurt, impair, maltreat, mar, ruin, spoil, tarnish, undermine, vitiate, weaken, wound, wrong

injured 1. broken, disabled, hurt, lamed, undermined, weakened, wounded 2. cut to the quick, disgruntled, displeased, hurt, long-suffering, put out, reproachful, stung, unhappy, upset, wounded 3. abused, blackened, blemished, defamed, ill-treated, maligned, maltreated, offended, tarnished, vilified, wronged

injurious adverse, bad, baneful (*Archaic*), corrupting, damaging, deleterious, destructive, detrimental, disadvantageous, harmful, hurtful, iniquitous, maleficent, mischievous, noxious, pernicious, ruinous, slanderous, unconducive, unhealthy, unjust, wrongful

injury abuse, damage, detriment, disservice, evil, grievance, harm, hurt, ill, injustice, mischief, ruin, wound, wrong

injustice bias, discrimination, favouritism, inequality, inequity, iniquity, one-sidedness, oppression, partiality, partisanship, prejudice, unfairness, unjustness, unlawfulness, wrong
Antonyms equality, equity, fairness, impartiality, justice, lawfulness, rectitude, right

inkling clue, conception, faintest *or* foggiest idea, glimmering, hint, idea, indication, intimation, notion, suggestion, suspicion, whisper

inland *adj.* domestic, interior, internal, upcountry

inlet arm (of the sea), bay, bight, cove, creek, entrance, firth *or* frith (*Scot.*), ingress, passage, sea loch (*Scot.*)

inmost *or* **innermost** basic, buried, central, deep, deepest, essential, intimate, personal, private, secret

innards 1. entrails, guts, insides (*Inf.*), intestines, inwards, viscera, vitals 2. guts (*Inf.*), mechanism, works

innate congenital, connate, constitutional, essential, inborn, inbred, indigenous, ingrained, inherent, inherited, instinctive, intrinsic, intuitive, native, natural
Antonyms accidental, acquired, affected, assumed, cultivated, fostered, incidental, learned, nurtured, unnatural

inner 1. central, essential, inside, interior, internal, intestinal, inward, middle 2. esoteric, hidden, intimate, personal, private, repressed, secret, unrevealed 3. emotional, mental, psychological, spiritual
Antonyms (*sense 1*) exterior, external, outer, outside, outward (*sense 2*) exposed, obvious, overt, revealed, surface, unconcealed, unrepressed, visible

innkeeper host, hostess, hotelier, landlady, landlord, mine host, publican

innocence 1. blamelessness, chastity, clean hands, guiltlessness, incorruptibility, probity, purity, righteousness, sinlessness, stainlessness, uprightness, virginity, virtue 2. harmlessness, innocuousness, innoxiousness, inoffensiveness 3. artlessness, credulousness, freshness, guilelessness, gullibility, inexperience, ingenuousness, naiveté, simplicity, unsophistication, unworldliness 4. ignorance, lack of knowledge, nescience (*Literary*), unawareness, unfamiliarity

Antonyms (*sense 1*) corruption, guilt, impurity, offensiveness, sinfulness, wrongness (*sense 3*) artfulness, cunning, disingenuousness, guile, wiliness, worldliness

innocent *adj.* 1. blameless, clear, faultless, guiltless, honest, in the clear, not guilty, uninvolved, unoffending 2. chaste, immaculate, impeccable, incorrupt, pristine, pure, righteous, sinless, spotless, stainless, unblemished, unsullied, upright, virgin, virginal 3. *With* **of** clear of, empty of, free from, ignorant, lacking, nescient, unacquainted with, unaware, unfamiliar with, untouched by 4. harmless, innocuous, inoffensive, unmalicious, unobjectionable, well-intentioned, well-meant 5. artless, childlike, credulous, frank, guileless, gullible, ingenuous, naive, open, simple, unsuspicious, unworldly, wet behind the ears (*Inf.*) ~*n.* 6. babe (in arms) (*Inf.*), child, greenhorn (*Inf.*), ingénue (*fem.*)

Antonyms (*sense 1*) blameworthy, culpable, dishonest, guilty, responsible (*sense 2*) corrupt, immoral, impure, sinful, wrong (*sense 4*) evil, harmful, iniquitous, malicious, offensive, wicked (*sense 5*) artful, disingenuous, sophisticated, worldly

innocuous harmless, innocent, innoxious, inoffensive, safe, unobjectionable

innovation alteration, change, departure, introduction, modernism, modernization, newness, novelty, variation

innuendo aspersion, hint, implication, imputation, insinuation, intimation, overtone, suggestion, whisper

innumerable beyond number, countless, incalculable, infinite, many, multitudinous, myriad, numberless, numerous, unnumbered, untold

Antonyms calculable, computable, finite, limited, measurable, numbered

inoffensive harmless, humble, innocent, innocuous, innoxious, mild, neutral, nonprovocative, peaceable, quiet, retiring, unobjectionable, unobtrusive, unoffending

Antonyms abrasive, harmful, irksome, irritating, malicious, objectionable, offensive, provocative

inoperable impracticable, impractical, nonviable, unrealistic, unworkable

inoperative broken, broken-down, defective, *hors de combat,* ineffective, ineffectual, inefficacious, invalid, nonactive, null and void, on the fritz (*U.S. sl.*), out of action, out of commission, out of order, out of service, unserviceable, unworkable, useless

inopportune ill-chosen, ill-timed, inappropriate, inauspicious, inconvenient, malapropos, mistimed, unfavourable, unfortunate, unpropitious, unseasonable, unsuitable, untimely

Antonyms appropriate, auspicious, convenient, favourable, fortunate, opportune, seasonable, suitable, timely, well-timed

inordinate disproportionate, excessive, exorbitant, extravagant, immoderate, intemperate, preposterous, unconscionable, undue, unreasonable, unrestrained, unwarranted

Antonyms inhibited, moderate, reasonable, restrained, rightful, sensible, temperate

inorganic artificial, chemical, man-made, mineral

inquest inquiry, inquisition, investigation, probe

inquietude anxiety, apprehension, disquiet, disquietude, jumpiness, nervousness, restlessness, the jitters (*Inf.*), trepidation, unease, uneasiness, worry

inquire 1. examine, explore, inspect, investigate, look into, make inquiries, probe, research, scrutinize, search 2. *Also* **enquire** ask, query, question, request information, seek information

inquiring analytical, curious, doubtful, inquisitive, interested, investigative, nosy (*Inf.*), outward-looking, probing, questioning, searching, wondering

inquiry 1. examination, exploration, inquest, interrogation, investigation, probe, research, scrutiny, search, study, survey 2. *Also* **enquiry** query, question

inquisition cross-examination, examination, grilling (*Inf.*), inquest, inquiry, investigation, question, quizzing, third degree (*Inf.*)

inquisitive curious, inquiring, intrusive, nosy (*Inf.*), nosy-parkering (*Inf.*), peering, probing, prying, questioning, scrutinizing, snooping (*Inf.*), snoopy (*Inf.*)

Antonyms apathetic, incurious, indifferent, unconcerned, uninterested, unquestioning

inroad 1. advance, encroachment, foray, incursion, intrusion, invasion, irruption, onslaught, raid 2. **make inroads upon** consume, eat away, eat up *or* into, encroach upon, use up

insalubrious injurious, insanitary, noxious, unhealthful, unhealthy, unwholesome

insane 1. barking (*Sl.*), barking mad (*Sl.*), crackpot (*Inf.*), crazed, crazy, demented, deranged, loopy (*Inf.*), mad, mentally disordered, mentally ill, *non compos mentis,* not the full shilling (*Inf.*), off one's trolley (*Sl.*), of unsound mind, out of one's mind, out to lunch (*Inf.*), unhinged, up the pole (*Inf.*) 2. barking (*Sl.*), barking mad (*Sl.*), barmy (*Sl.*), batty (*Sl.*), bonkers (*Sl., chiefly Brit.*), cracked (*Sl.*), crackers (*Brit. sl.*), cuckoo (*Inf.*), loony (*Sl.*), loopy (*Inf.*), mental (*Sl.*), nuts (*Sl.*), nutty (*Sl.*), off one's chump (*Sl.*), off one's head (*Sl.*), off one's nut (*Sl.*), off one's rocker (*Sl.*), round the bend (*Inf.*), round the twist (*Inf.*), screwy (*Inf.*) 3. bizarre, daft (*Inf.*), fatuous, foolish, idiotic, impractical, inane, irrational, irresponsible, lunatic, preposterous, senseless, stupid
Antonyms logical, lucid, normal, practical, rational, reasonable, reasoned, sane, sensible, sound

insanitary contaminated, dirtied, dirty, disease-ridden, feculent, filthy, impure, infected, infested, insalubrious, noxious, polluted, unclean, unhealthy, unhygienic
Antonyms clean, healthy, hygienic, pure, salubrious, unpolluted

insanity 1. aberration, craziness, delirium, dementia, frenzy, madness, mental derangement, mental disorder, mental illness 2. folly, irresponsibility, lunacy, preposterousness, senselessness, stupidity
Antonyms logic, lucidity, normality, rationality, reason, sanity, sense, soundness, wisdom

insatiable gluttonous, greedy, insatiate, intemperate, quenchless, rapacious, ravenous, unappeasable, unquenchable, voracious
Antonyms appeasable, limited, quenchable, satiable, temperate

inscribe 1. carve, cut, engrave, etch, impress, imprint 2. engross, enlist, enrol, enter, record, register, write 3. address, dedicate

inscription dedication, engraving, label, legend, lettering, saying, words

inscrutable 1. blank, deadpan, enigmatic, impenetrable, poker-faced (*Inf.*), sphinxlike, unreadable 2. hidden, incomprehensible, inexplicable, mysterious, undiscoverable, unexplainable, unfathomable, unintelligible
Antonyms clear, comprehensible, evident, explainable, explicable, intelligible, lucid, manifest, obvious, open, palpable, patent, penetrable, plain, readable, revealing, transparent, understandable

insecure 1. afraid, anxious, uncertain, unconfident, unsure 2. dangerous, defenceless, exposed, hazardous, ill-protected, open to attack, perilous, unguarded, unprotected, unsafe, unshielded, vulnerable 3. built upon sand, flimsy, frail, insubstantial, loose, on thin ice, precarious, rickety, rocky, shaky, unreliable, unsound, unstable, unsteady, weak, wobbly
Antonyms (*sense 1*) assured, certain, confident, decisive, secure (*senses 2 & 3*) firm, protected, reliable, safe, secure, sound, stable, steady, substantial, sure

insecurity 1. anxiety, fear, uncertainty, unsureness, worry 2. danger, defencelessness, hazard, peril, risk, uncertainty, vulnerability, weakness 3. dubiety, frailness, instability, precariousness, shakiness, uncertainty, unreliability, unsteadiness, weakness
Antonyms (*sense 1*) assurance, certainty, confidence, security (*senses 2 & 3*) dependability, firmness, reliability, safety, security, stability, steadiness

insensate 1. anaesthetized, dead, inanimate, inert, insensible, insentient, lifeless, numbed, out (*Inf.*), unconscious 2. hardened, imperceptive, impercipient, indifferent, insensitive, inured, obtuse, stolid, thick-skinned, thoughtless, unfeeling, unperceiving 3. brainless, fatuous, foolish, mindless, senseless, stupid, thoughtless, unreasonable, witless

insensibility 1. apathy, callousness, dullness, indifference, inertia, insensitivity, lethargy, thoughtlessness, torpor 2. inertness, numbness, unconsciousness

insensible 1. anaesthetized, benumbed, dull, inert, insensate, numbed, senseless, stupid, torpid 2. apathetic, callous, cold, deaf, hard-hearted, impassive, impervious, indifferent, oblivious, unaffected, unaware, unconscious, unfeeling, unmindful, unmoved, unresponsive, unsusceptible, untouched 3. imperceivable, imperceptible, minuscule, negligible, unnoticeable
Antonyms (*sense 2*) affected, aware, conscious, feeling, mindful, responsive, sensible

insensibly by degrees, gradually, imperceptibly, invisibly, little by little, slightly, unnoticeably

insensitive 1. callous, crass, hardened, imperceptive, indifferent, obtuse, tactless, thick-skinned, tough, uncaring, unconcerned, unfeeling, unresponsive, unsusceptible 2. *With* to dead to, immune to, imper-

vious to, nonreactive, proof against, unaffected by, unmoved by
Antonyms (*sense 1*) caring, concerned, perceptive, responsive, sensitive, sentient, susceptible, tactful, tender

inseparable 1. conjoined, inalienable, indissoluble, indivisible, inseverable 2. bosom, close, devoted, intimate

insert embed, enter, implant, infix, interject, interpolate, interpose, introduce, place, pop in (*Inf.*), put, set, stick in, tuck in, work in
Antonyms delete, extract, pull out, remove, take out, withdraw

insertion addition, implant, inclusion, insert, inset, interpolation, introduction, supplement

inside *n.* 1. contents, inner part, interior 2. *Often plural Inf.* belly, bowels, entrails, gut, guts, innards (*Inf.*), internal organs, stomach, viscera, vitals *~adv.* 3. indoors, under cover, within *~adj.* 4. inner, innermost, interior, internal, intramural, inward 5. classified, confidential, esoteric, exclusive, internal, limited, private, restricted, secret
Antonyms (*sense 4*) exterior, external, extramural, outer, outermost, outside, outward

insidious artful, crafty, crooked, cunning, deceitful, deceptive, designing, disingenuous, duplicitous, guileful, intriguing, Machiavellian, slick, sly, smooth, sneaking, stealthy, subtle, surreptitious, treacherous, tricky, wily
Antonyms artless, conspicuous, forthright, harmless, honest, ingenuous, obvious, open, sincere, straightforward, upright

insight acumen, awareness, comprehension, discernment, intuition, intuitiveness, judgment, observation, penetration, perception, perspicacity, understanding, vision

insightful astute, discerning, knowledgeable, observant, penetrating, perceptive, perspicacious, sagacious, shrewd, understanding, wise

insignia badge, crest, decoration, distinguishing mark, earmark, emblem, ensign, symbol

insignificance immateriality, inconsequence, irrelevance, meaninglessness, negligibility, paltriness, pettiness, triviality, unimportance, worthlessness
Antonyms consequence, importance, matter, meaningfulness, relevance, significance, weight, worth

insignificant flimsy, immaterial, inconsequential, inconsiderable, irrelevant, meagre, meaningless, measly, minor, negligible, nickel-and-dime (*U.S. sl.*), nondescript, nonessential, not worth mentioning, nugatory, of no account (consequence, moment), paltry, petty, scanty, trifling, trivial, unimportant, unsubstantial
Antonyms consequential, considerable, essential, important, meaningful, momentous, relevant, significant, substantial, vital, weighty

insincere deceitful, deceptive, devious, dishonest, disingenuous, dissembling, dissimulating, double-dealing, duplicitous, evasive, faithless, false, hollow, hypocritical, Janus-faced, lying, mendacious, perfidious, pretended, two-faced, unfaithful, untrue, untruthful
Antonyms direct, earnest, faithful, genuine, honest, sincere, straightforward, true, truthful

insincerity deceitfulness, deviousness, dishonesty, disingenuousness, dissimulation, duplicity, faithlessness, hypocrisy, lip service, mendacity, perfidy, pretence, untruthfulness
Antonyms directness, faithfulness, honesty, sincerity, truthfulness

insinuate 1. allude, hint, imply, indicate, intimate, suggest 2. infiltrate, infuse, inject, instil, introduce 3. curry favour, get in with, ingratiate, worm *or* work one's way in

insinuation 1. allusion, aspersion, hint, implication, innuendo, slur, suggestion 2. infiltration, infusion, ingratiating, injection, instillation, introduction

insipid 1. anaemic, banal, bland, characterless, colourless, drab, dry, dull, flat, ho-hum (*Inf.*), jejune, lifeless, limp, pointless, prosaic, prosy, spiritless, stale, stupid, tame, tedious, trite, unimaginative, uninteresting, vapid, weak, wearisome, wishy-washy (*Inf.*) 2. bland, flavourless, savourless, tasteless, unappetizing, watered down, watery, wishy-washy (*Inf.*)
Antonyms (*sense 1*) colourful, engaging, exciting, interesting, lively, provocative, spirited, stimulating (*sense 2*) appetizing, fiery, palatable, piquant, pungent, savoury, tasteful

insipidity, insipidness 1. banality, colourlessness, dullness, flatness, lack of imagination, pointlessness, staleness, tameness, tediousness, triteness, uninterestingness, vapidity 2. blandness, flavourlessness, lack of flavour, tastelessness
Antonyms (*sense 1*) animation, character, dynamism, gaiety, liveliness, spirit, vitality, vivacity

insist 1. be firm, brook no refusal, demand, lay down the law, not take no for an answer, persist, press (someone), require, stand firm, stand one's ground, take *or* make a stand, urge 2. assert, asseverate, aver, claim, contend, hold, maintain, reiterate, repeat, swear, urge, vow

insistence assertion, contention, demands, emphasis, importunity, insistency, persistence, pressing, reiteration, stress, urging

insistent demanding, dogged, emphatic, exigent, forceful, importunate, incessant, peremptory, persevering, persistent, pressing, unrelenting, urgent

insobriety crapulence, drunkenness, inebriety, intemperance, intoxication

insolence abuse, audacity, backchat (*Inf.*), boldness, cheek (*Inf.*), chutzpah (*U.S. & Canad. inf.*), contemptuousness, contumely, disrespect, effrontery, front, gall (*Inf.*), impertinence, impudence, incivility, insubordination, offensiveness, pertness, rudeness, sauce (*Inf.*), uncivility

Antonyms civility, courtesy, deference, esteem, mannerliness, politeness, respect, submission

insolent abusive, bold, brazen-faced, contemptuous, fresh (*Inf.*), impertinent, impudent, insubordinate, insulting, pert, rude, saucy, uncivil

Antonyms civil, courteous, deferential, mannerly, polite, respectful, submissive

insoluble baffling, impenetrable, indecipherable, inexplicable, mysterious, mystifying, obscure, unaccountable, unfathomable, unsolvable

Antonyms accountable, comprehensible, explicable, fathomable, penetrable, soluble, solvable

insolvency bankruptcy, failure, liquidation, ruin

insolvent bankrupt, broke (*Inf.*), failed, gone bust (*Inf.*), gone to the wall, in queer street (*Inf.*), in receivership, in the hands of the receivers, on the rocks (*Inf.*), ruined

insomnia sleeplessness, wakefulness

insouciance airiness, breeziness, carefreeness, jauntiness, light-heartedness, nonchalance

insouciant airy, breezy, buoyant, carefree, casual, free and easy, gay, happy-go-lucky, jaunty, light-hearted, nonchalant, sunny, unconcerned, untroubled, unworried

inspect audit, check, check out (*Inf.*), examine, eyeball (*U.S. sl.*), give (something *or* someone) the once-over (*Inf.*), go over *or* through, investigate, look over, oversee, recce (*Sl.*), research, scan, scrutinize, search, superintend, supervise, survey, take a dekko at (*Brit. sl.*), vet, work over

inspection check, checkup, examination, investigation, look-over, once-over (*Inf.*), recce (*Sl.*), review, scan, scrutiny, search, superintendence, supervision, surveillance, survey

inspector censor, checker, critic, examiner, investigator, overseer, scrutineer, scrutinizer, superintendent, supervisor

inspiration 1. arousal, awakening, encouragement, influence, muse, spur, stimulus 2. afflatus, creativity, elevation, enthusiasm, exaltation, genius, illumination, insight, revelation, stimulation

Antonyms depressant, deterrent, discouragement, disenchantment

inspire 1. animate, be responsible for, encourage, enliven, fire *or* touch the imagination of, galvanize, hearten, imbue, influence, infuse, inspirit, instil, rouse, spark off, spur, stimulate 2. arouse, enkindle, excite, give rise to, produce, quicken, rouse, stir

Antonyms daunt, deflate, depress, discourage, disenchant, dishearten, dispirit

inspired 1. brilliant, dazzling, enthralling, exciting, impressive, memorable, of genius, outstanding, superlative, thrilling, wonderful 2. *Of a guess* instinctive, instinctual, intuitive 3. aroused, elated, enthused, exalted, exhilarated, galvanized, possessed, stimulated, stirred up, uplifted

inspiring affecting, encouraging, exciting, exhilarating, heartening, moving, rousing, stimulating, stirring, uplifting

Antonyms boring, depressing, discouraging, disheartening, dispiriting, dull, uninspiring

inspirit animate, cheer, embolden, encourage, enliven, exhilarate, fire, galvanize, give hope to, hearten, incite, inspire, invigorate, move, nerve, put (new) heart into, rouse, stimulate

instability capriciousness, changeableness, disequilibrium, fickleness, fitfulness, fluctuation, fluidity, frailty, imbalance, impermanence, inconstancy, insecurity, irresolution, mutability, oscillation, precariousness, restlessness, shakiness, transience, unpredictability, unsteadiness, vacillation, variability, volatility, wavering, weakness

Antonyms balance, constancy, equilibrium, permanence, predictability, resolution, security, stability, steadiness, strength

install, instal 1. fix, lay, lodge, place, position, put in, set up, station 2. establish, inaugurate, induct, instate, institute, introduce, invest, set up 3. ensconce, position, settle

installation 1. establishment, fitting, instalment, placing, positioning, setting up 2. inauguration, induction, instatement, investiture 3. equipment, machinery, plant, system 4. *Military* base, establishment, post, station

instalment chapter, division, episode, part, portion, repayment, section

instance *n.* 1. case, case in point, example, illustration, occasion, occurrence, precedent, situation, time 2. application, behest, demand, entreaty, importunity, impulse, incitement, insistence, instigation, pressure, prompting, request, solicitation, urging ~*v.* 3. adduce, cite, mention, name, quote, specify

instant *n.* 1. flash, jiffy (*Inf.*), moment, second, shake (*Inf.*), split second, tick (*Brit. inf.*), trice, twinkling, twinkling of an eye (*Inf.*), two shakes of a lamb's tail (*Inf.*) 2. **on the instant** forthwith, immediately, instantly, now, right away, without delay 3. juncture, moment, occasion, point, time ~*adj.* 4. direct, immediate, instantaneous, on-the-spot, prompt, quick, quickie (*Inf.*), split-second, urgent 5. convenience, fast, precooked, ready-mixed 6. burning, exigent, imperative, importunate, pressing, urgent

instantaneous direct, immediate, instant, on-the-spot

instantaneously at once, forthwith, immediately, in a fraction of a second, instantly, in the same breath, in the twinkling of an eye (*Inf.*), like greased lightning (*Inf.*), on the instant, on the spot, posthaste, promptly, pronto (*Inf.*), quick as lightning, straight away, then and there

instantly at once, directly, forthwith, immediately, instantaneously, instanter (*Law*), now, on the spot, posthaste, pronto (*Inf.*), right away, right now, straight away, there and then, this minute, *tout de suite*, without delay

instate establish, inaugurate, induct, install, invest, put in office

instead 1. alternatively, in lieu, in preference, on second thoughts, preferably, rather 2. *With* of as an alternative *or* equivalent to, in lieu of, in place of, rather than

instigate actuate, bring about, encourage, foment, get going, impel, incite, influence, initiate, kick-start, kindle, move, persuade, prod, prompt, provoke, rouse, set off, set on, spur, start, stimulate, stir up, trigger, urge, whip up

Antonyms discourage, repress, restrain, stop, suppress

instigation behest, bidding, encouragement, incentive, incitement, prompting, urging

instigator agitator, firebrand, fomenter, goad, incendiary, inciter, leader, mischief-maker, motivator, prime mover, ringleader, spur, stirrer (*Inf.*), troublemaker

instil, instill engender, engraft, imbue, implant, impress, inculcate, infix, infuse, insinuate, introduce

instinct aptitude, faculty, feeling, gift, gut feeling (*Inf.*), gut reaction (*Inf.*), impulse, intuition, knack, natural inclination, predisposition, proclivity, sixth sense, talent, tendency, urge

instinctive automatic, inborn, inherent, innate, instinctual, intuitional, intuitive, involuntary, mechanical, native, natural, reflex, spontaneous, unlearned, unpremeditated, unthinking, visceral

Antonyms acquired, calculated, considered, learned, mindful, premeditated, thinking, voluntary, willed

instinctively automatically, by instinct, intuitively, involuntarily, naturally, without thinking

institute[1] *v.* appoint, begin, bring into being, commence, constitute, enact, establish, fix, found, induct, initiate, install, introduce, invest, launch, ordain, organize, originate, pioneer, put into operation, set in motion, settle, set up, start

Antonyms abandon, abolish, cancel, cease, discontinue, end, stop, suspend, terminate

institute[2] *n.* 1. academy, association, college, conservatory, foundation, guild, institution, school, seat of learning, seminary, society 2. custom, decree, doctrine, dogma, edict, law, maxim, precedent, precept, principle, regulation, rule, tenet

institution 1. constitution, creation, enactment, establishment, formation, foundation, initiation, introduction, investiture, investment, organization 2. academy, college, establishment, foundation, hospital, institute, school, seminary, society, university 3. convention, custom, fixture, law, practice, ritual, rule, tradition

institutional 1. accepted, bureaucratic, conventional, established, establishment (*Inf.*), formal, organized, orthodox, societal 2. cheerless, clinical, cold, drab, dreary, dull, forbidding, formal, impersonal, monotonous, regimented, routine, uniform, unwelcoming

instruct 1. bid, charge, command, canon, direct, enjoin, order, tell 2. coach, discipline, drill, educate, enlighten, ground, guide, inform, school, teach, train, tutor 3. acquaint, advise, apprise, brief, counsel, inform, notify, tell

instruction 1. apprenticeship, coaching, discipline, drilling, education, enlightenment, grounding, guidance, information, lesson(s), preparation, schooling, teaching, training, tuition, tutelage 2. briefing, command, demand, direction, directive, injunction, mandate, order, ruling

instructions advice, directions, guidance, information, key, orders, recommendations, rules

instructive cautionary, didactic, edifying, educational, enlightening, helpful, illuminating, informative, instructional, revealing, useful

instructor adviser, coach, demonstrator, exponent, guide, handler, master, mentor, mistress, pedagogue, preceptor (*Rare*), schoolmaster, schoolmistress, teacher, trainer, tutor

instrument 1. apparatus, appliance, contraption (*Inf.*), contrivance, device, gadget, implement, mechanism, tool, utensil 2. agency, agent, channel, factor, force, means, mechanism, medium, organ, vehicle 3. *Inf.* cat's-paw, dupe, pawn, puppet, tool

instrumental active, assisting, auxiliary, conducive, contributory, helpful, helping, influential, involved, of help *or* service, subsidiary, useful

instrumentality agency, assistance, good offices, intercession, intervention, mediation, medium, vehicle

insubordinate contumacious, defiant, disobedient, disorderly, fractious, insurgent, mutinous, rebellious, recalcitrant, refractory, riotous, seditious, turbulent, undisciplined, ungovernable, unruly
Antonyms compliant, deferential, disciplined, docile, obedient, orderly, submissive, subservient

insubordination defiance, disobedience, indiscipline, insurrection, mutinousness, mutiny, rebellion, recalcitrance, revolt, riotousness, sedition, ungovernability
Antonyms acquiescence, compliance, deference, discipline, docility, obedience, submission, subordination

insubstantial 1. feeble, flimsy, frail, poor, slight, tenuous, thin, weak 2. chimerical, ephemeral, false, fanciful, idle, illusory, imaginary, immaterial, incorporeal, unreal
Antonyms (*sense 1*) firm, solid, strong, substantial, weighty

insufferable detestable, dreadful, enough to test the patience of a saint, enough to try the patience of Job, impossible, insupportable, intolerable, more than flesh and blood can stand, outrageous, past bearing, too much, unbearable, unendurable, unspeakable
Antonyms appealing, attractive, bearable, charming, disarming, pleasant

insufficiency dearth, deficiency, inadequacy, inadequateness, lack, paucity, poverty, scantiness, scarcity, shortage, short supply, want

insufficient deficient, inadequate, incapable, incommensurate, incompetent, lacking, scant, short, unfitted, unqualified
Antonyms adequate, ample, commensurate, competent, enough, plentiful, qualified, sufficient

insular *Fig.* blinkered, circumscribed, closed, contracted, cut off, illiberal, inward-looking, isolated, limited, narrow, narrow-minded, parish-pump, parochial, petty, prejudiced, provincial
Antonyms broad-minded, cosmopolitan, experienced, liberal, open-minded, tolerant, worldly

insulate *Fig.* close off, cocoon, cushion, cut off, isolate, protect, sequester, shield, wrap up in cotton wool

insult 1. *n.* abuse, affront, aspersion, contumely, indignity, insolence, offence, outrage, put-down, rudeness, slap in the face (*Inf.*), slight, snub 2. *v.* abuse, affront, call names, give offence to, injure, miscall (*Dialect*), offend, outrage, put down, revile, slag (off) (*Sl.*), slander, slight, snub
Antonyms *n.* compliment, flattery, honour ~*v.* flatter, please, praise

insulting abusive, affronting, contemptuous, degrading, disparaging, insolent, offensive, rude, scurrilous, slighting
Antonyms complimentary, deferential, flattering, laudatory, respectful

insuperable impassable, insurmountable, invincible, unconquerable
Antonyms conquerable, possible, surmountable

insupportable 1. insufferable, intolerable, past bearing, unbearable, unendurable 2. indefensible, unjustifiable, untenable

insurance assurance, cover, coverage, guarantee, indemnification, indemnity, protection, provision, safeguard, security, something to fall back on (*Inf.*), warranty

insure assure, cover, guarantee, indemnify, underwrite, warrant

insurgent 1. *n.* insurrectionist, mutineer, rebel, resister, revolter, revolutionary, revolutionist, rioter 2. *adj.* disobedient, insubordinate, insurrectionary, mutinous, rebellious, revolting, revolutionary, riotous, seditious

insurmountable hopeless, impassable, impossible, insuperable, invincible, overwhelming, unconquerable

insurrection coup, insurgency, mutiny, putsch, rebellion, revolt, revolution, riot, rising, sedition, uprising

insusceptible immovable, immune, indifferent, insensible, insensitive, proof against, unimpressible, unmoved, unresponsive

intact all in one piece, complete, entire, perfect, scatheless, sound, together, unbroken, undamaged, undefiled, unharmed, unhurt, unimpaired, uninjured, unscathed, untouched, unviolated, virgin, whole
Antonyms broken, damaged, harmed, impaired, injured

intangible airy, dim, elusive, ethereal, evanescent, impalpable, imperceptible, incorporeal, indefinite, invisible, shadowy, unreal, unsubstantial, vague

integral 1. basic, component, constituent, elemental, essential, fundamental, indispensable, intrinsic, necessary, requisite 2. complete, entire, full, intact, undivided, whole
Antonyms fractional, inessential, unimportant, unnecessary

integrate accommodate, amalgamate, assimilate, blend, coalesce, combine, fuse, harmonize, incorporate, intermix, join, knit, meld, merge, mesh, unite
Antonyms disperse, divide, segregate, separate

integration amalgamation, assimilation, blending, combining, commingling, fusing, harmony, incorporation, mixing, unification

integrity 1. candour, goodness, honesty, honour, incorruptibility, principle, probity, purity, rectitude, righteousness, uprightness, virtue 2. coherence, cohesion, completeness, soundness, unity, wholeness
Antonyms (*sense 1*) corruption, deceit, dishonesty, disrepute, duplicity, faultiness, flimsiness, fragility, immorality, uncertainty, unsoundness

intellect 1. brains (*Inf.*), intelligence, judgment, mind, reason, sense, understanding 2. *Inf.* brain (*Inf.*), egghead (*Inf.*), genius, intellectual, intelligence, mind, thinker

intellectual 1. *adj.* bookish, cerebral, highbrow, intelligent, mental, rational, scholarly, studious, thoughtful 2. *n.* academic, egghead (*Inf.*), highbrow, thinker
Antonyms *adj.* ignorant, illiterate, material, physical, stupid, unintellectual, unlearned ~*n.* idiot, moron

intelligence 1. acumen, alertness, aptitude, brain power, brains (*Inf.*), brightness, capacity, cleverness, comprehension, discernment, grey matter (*Inf.*), intellect, mind, nous (*Brit. sl.*), penetration, perception, quickness, reason, smarts (*Sl., chiefly U.S.*), understanding 2. advice, data, disclosure, facts, findings, gen (*Brit. inf.*), information, knowledge, low-down (*Inf.*), news, notice, notification, report, rumour, tidings, tip-off, word
Antonyms (*sense 1*) dullness, ignorance, stupidity (*sense 2*) concealment, misinformation

intelligent acute, alert, apt, brainy (*Inf.*), bright, clever, discerning, enlightened, instructed, knowing, penetrating, perspicacious, quick, quick-witted, rational, sharp, smart, thinking, well-informed
Antonyms dim-witted, dull, foolish, ignorant, obtuse, stupid, unintelligent

intelligentsia eggheads (*Inf.*), highbrows, illuminati, intellectuals, literati, masterminds, the learned

intelligibility clarity, clearness, comprehensibility, distinctness, explicitness, lucidity, plainness, precision, simplicity

intelligible clear, comprehensible, distinct, lucid, open, plain, understandable
Antonyms confused, garbled, incomprehensible, puzzling, unclear, unintelligible

intemperance crapulence, excess, extravagance, immoderation, inebriation, insobriety, intoxication, overindulgence, unrestraint

intemperate excessive, extravagant, extreme, immoderate, incontinent, inordinate, intoxicated, O.T.T. (*Sl.*), over the top (*Sl.*), passionate, prodigal, profligate, self-indulgent, severe, tempestuous, unbridled, uncontrollable, ungovernable, unrestrained, violent, wild
Antonyms continent, disciplined, moderate, restrained, self-controlled, temperate

intend 1. aim, be resolved *or* determined, contemplate, determine, have in mind *or* view, mean, meditate, plan, propose, purpose, scheme 2. *Often with* **for** aim, consign, design, destine, earmark, mark out, mean, set apart

intended 1. *adj.* betrothed, destined, future, planned, proposed 2. *n. Inf.* betrothed, fiancé, fiancée, future wife *or* husband, husband- *or* wife-to-be

intense 1. acute, agonizing, close, concentrated, deep, drastic, excessive, exquisite, extreme, fierce, forceful, great, harsh, intensive, powerful, profound, protracted, severe, strained, unqualified 2. ardent, burning, consuming, eager, earnest, energetic, fanatical, fervent, fervid, fierce, flaming, forcible, heightened, impassioned, keen, passionate, speaking, vehement
Antonyms (*sense 1*) easy, gentle, mild, moderate, relaxed, slight (*sense 2*) casual, cool, indifferent, subdued, weak

intensely deeply, extremely, fiercely, passionately, profoundly, strongly

intensify add fuel to the flames (*Inf.*), add

to, aggravate, augment, boost, concentrate, deepen, emphasize, enhance, escalate, exacerbate, heighten, increase, magnify, quicken, redouble, reinforce, set off, sharpen, step up (*Inf.*), strengthen, whet
Antonyms damp down, decrease, dilute, diminish, dull, lessen, minimize, weaken

intensity ardour, concentration, depth, earnestness, emotion, energy, excess, extremity, fanaticism, fervency, fervour, fierceness, fire, force, intenseness, keenness, passion, potency, power, severity, strain, strength, tension, vehemence, vigour

intensive all-out, comprehensive, concentrated, demanding, exhaustive, in-depth, thorough, thoroughgoing
Antonyms apathetic, careless, feeble, hit-or-miss, superficial, weakened

intent *adj.* 1. absorbed, alert, attentive, committed, concentrated, determined, eager, earnest, engrossed, fixed, industrious, intense, occupied, piercing, preoccupied, rapt, resolute, resolved, steadfast, steady, watchful, wrapped up 2. bent, hell-bent (*Inf.*), set ~*n.* 3. aim, design, end, goal, intention, meaning, object, objective, plan, purpose 4. **to all intents and purposes** as good as, practically, virtually
Antonyms *adj.* (*sense 1*) casual, indifferent, irresolute, unsteady, wavering ~*n.* chance, fortune

intention aim, design, end, end in view, goal, idea, intent, meaning, object, objective, point, purpose, scope, target, view

intentional calculated, deliberate, designed, done on purpose, intended, meant, planned, prearranged, preconcerted, premeditated, purposed, studied, wilful
Antonyms accidental, inadvertent, unintentional, unplanned

intentionally by design, deliberately, designedly, on purpose, wilfully

intently attentively, closely, fixedly, hard, keenly, searchingly, steadily, watchfully

inter bury, entomb, inhume, inurn, lay to rest, sepulchre

intercede advocate, arbitrate, interpose, intervene, mediate, plead, speak

intercept arrest, block, catch, check, cut off, deflect, head off, interrupt, obstruct, seize, stop, take

intercession advocacy, entreaty, good offices, intervention, mediation, plea, pleading, prayer, solicitation, supplication

intercessor advocate, arbitrator, go-between, interceder, intermediary, mediator, middleman, negotiator, pleader

interchange 1. *v.* alternate, bandy, barter, exchange, reciprocate, swap (*Inf.*), switch, trade 2. *n.* alternation, crossfire, exchange, give and take, intersection, junction, reciprocation

interchangeable commutable, equivalent, exchangeable, identical, reciprocal, synonymous, the same, transposable

intercourse 1. association, commerce, communication, communion, connection, contact, converse, correspondence, dealings, intercommunication, trade, traffic, truck 2. carnal knowledge, coition, coitus, congress, copulation, intimacy, nookie (*Sl.*), rumpy-pumpy (*Sl.*), sex (*Inf.*), sexual act, sexual intercourse, sexual relations, the other (*Inf.*)

interdict 1. *v.* ban, bar, debar, disallow, forbid, outlaw, prevent, prohibit, proscribe, veto 2. *n.* ban, disallowance, interdiction, prohibition, taboo, veto

interest *n.* 1. affection, attention, attentiveness, attraction, concern, curiosity, notice, regard, suspicion, sympathy 2. concern, consequence, importance, moment, note, relevance, significance, weight 3. activity, diversion, hobby, leisure activity, pastime, preoccupation, pursuit, relaxation 4. advantage, benefit, gain, good, profit 5. **in the interest of** for the sake of, on behalf of, on the part of, profitable to, to the advantage of 6. authority, claim, commitment, influence, investment, involvement, participation, portion, right, share, stake 7. *Often plural* affair, business, care, concern, matter ~*v.* 8. amuse, arouse one's curiosity, attract, divert, engross, fascinate, hold the attention of, intrigue, move, touch 9. affect, concern, engage, involve
Antonyms *n.* (*sense 1*) boredom, coolness, disinterest, dispassion, disregard, unconcern (*sense 2*) inconsequence, insignificance, irrelevance, worthlessness ~*v.* bore, burden, irk, repel, tire, weary

interested 1. affected, attentive, attracted, curious, drawn, excited, fascinated, intent, into (*Inf.*), keen, moved, responsive, stimulated 2. biased, concerned, implicated, involved, partial, partisan, predisposed, prejudiced
Antonyms (*sense 1*) apathetic, bored, detached, inattentive, indifferent, unconcerned, uninterested, wearied

interesting absorbing, amusing, appealing, attractive, compelling, curious, engaging, engrossing, entertaining, gripping, intriguing, pleasing, provocative, stimulating, suspicious, thought-provoking, unusual
Antonyms boring, dull, mind-numbing, tedious, uninteresting

interfere 1. butt in, get involved, intermed~

dle, intervene, intrude, meddle, poke one's nose in (*Inf.*), put one's two cents in (*U.S. sl.*), stick one's oar in (*Inf.*), tamper 2. *Often with* **with** be a drag upon (*Inf.*), block, clash, collide, conflict, cramp, frustrate, get in the way of, hamper, handicap, hinder, impede, inhibit, obstruct, trammel

interference 1. intermeddling, intervention, intrusion, meddlesomeness, meddling, prying 2. clashing, collision, conflict, impedance, obstruction, opposition

interim 1. *adj.* acting, caretaker, improvised, intervening, makeshift, pro tem, provisional, stopgap, temporary 2. *n.* entr'acte, interregnum, interval, meantime, meanwhile, respite

interior *adj.* 1. inner, inside, internal, inward 2. *Geog.* central, inland, remote, upcountry 3. *Politics* domestic, home 4. hidden, inner, intimate, mental, personal, private, secret, spiritual ~*n.* 5. bosom, centre, contents, core, heart, innards (*Inf.*), inside 6. *Geog.* centre, heartland, upcountry
Antonyms (*sense 1*) exposed, exterior, external, outer, outside, outward

interject interpolate, interpose, interrupt with, introduce, put in, throw in

interjection cry, ejaculation, exclamation, interpolation, interposition

interlace braid, cross, entwine, interlock, intersperse, intertwine, interweave, interwreathe, knit, plait, reticulate, twine

interlink interconnect, interlock, intertwine, interweave, knit, link, mesh

interloper gate-crasher (*Inf.*), intermeddler, intruder, meddler, trespasser, uninvited guest, unwanted visitor

interlude break, breathing space, delay, entr'acte, episode, halt, hiatus, intermission, interval, pause, respite, rest, spell, stop, stoppage, wait

intermediary *n.* agent, broker, entrepreneur, go-between, mediator, middleman

intermediate halfway, in-between (*Inf.*), intermediary, interposed, intervening, mean, mid, middle, midway, transitional

interment burial, burying, funeral, inhumation, sepulture

interminable boundless, ceaseless, dragging, endless, everlasting, immeasurable, infinite, limitless, long, long-drawn-out, long-winded, never-ending, perpetual, protracted, unbounded, unlimited, wearisome
Antonyms bounded, finite, limited, measurable, restricted, temporary

intermingle amalgamate, blend, combine, commingle, commix, fuse, interlace, intermix, interweave, meld, merge, mix

intermission break, cessation, entr'acte, interlude, interruption, interval, let-up (*Inf.*), lull, pause, recess, respite, rest, stop, stoppage, suspense, suspension

intermittent broken, discontinuous, fitful, irregular, occasional, periodic, punctuated, recurrent, recurring, spasmodic, sporadic, stop-go (*Inf.*)
Antonyms continuous, steady, unceasing

intern confine, detain, hold, hold in custody

internal 1. inner, inside, interior, intimate, private, subjective 2. civic, domestic, home, in-house, intramural
Antonyms (*sense 1*) exposed, exterior, external, outer, outermost, outside, revealed, unconcealed

international cosmopolitan, ecumenical (*Rare*), global, intercontinental, universal, worldwide

internecine bloody, deadly, destructive, exterminating, exterminatory, fatal, mortal, ruinous

interplay give-and-take, interaction, meshing, reciprocation, reciprocity

interpolate add, insert, intercalate, introduce

interpolation addition, aside, insert, insertion, intercalation, interjection, introduction

interpose 1. come *or* place between, intercede, interfere, intermediate, intervene, intrude, mediate, step in 2. insert, interject, interrupt (with), introduce, put forth

interpret adapt, clarify, construe, decipher, decode, define, elucidate, explain, explicate, expound, make sense of, paraphrase, read, render, solve, spell out, take, throw light on, translate, understand

interpretation analysis, clarification, construction, diagnosis, elucidation, exegesis, explanation, explication, exposition, meaning, performance, portrayal, reading, rendering, rendition, sense, signification, translation, understanding, version

interpreter annotator, commentator, exponent, scholiast, translator

interrogate ask, catechize, cross-examine, cross-question, enquire, examine, give (someone) the third degree (*Inf.*), grill (*Inf.*), inquire, investigate, pump, put the screws on (*Inf.*), question, quiz

interrogation cross-examination, cross-questioning, enquiry, examination, grilling (*Inf.*), inquiry, inquisition, probing, questioning, third degree (*Inf.*)

interrogative curious, inquiring, inquisitive, inquisitorial, questioning, quizzical

interrupt barge in (*Inf.*), break, break in, break off, break (someone's) train of thought, butt in, check, cut, cut off, cut short, delay, disconnect, discontinue, disjoin, disturb, disunite, divide, heckle, hinder, hold up, interfere (with), intrude, lay aside, obstruct, punctuate, separate, sever, stay, stop, suspend

interrupted broken, cut off, disconnected, discontinuous, disturbed, incomplete, intermittent, uneven

interruption break, cessation, disconnection, discontinuance, disruption, dissolution, disturbance, disuniting, division, halt, hiatus, hindrance, hitch, impediment, intrusion, obstacle, obstruction, pause, separation, severance, stop, stoppage, suspension

intersect bisect, crisscross, cross, cut, cut across, divide, meet

intersection crossing, crossroads, interchange, junction

intersperse bestrew, interlard, intermix, pepper, scatter, sprinkle

interstice aperture, chink, cleft, crack, cranny, crevice, fissure, gap, interval, opening, rift, slit, space, vent

intertwine braid, convolute, cross, entwine, interlace, interweave, interwreathe, inweave, link, reticulate, twist

interval break, delay, distance, entr'acte, gap, hiatus, interim, interlude, intermission, meantime, meanwhile, opening, pause, period, playtime, respite, rest, season, space, spell, term, time, wait

intervene 1. arbitrate, intercede, interfere, interpose oneself, intrude, involve oneself, mediate, put one's two cents in (*U.S. sl.*), step in (*Inf.*), take a hand (*Inf.*) 2. befall, come to pass, ensue, happen, occur, succeed, supervene, take place

intervention agency, intercession, interference, interposition, intrusion, mediation

interview 1. *n.* audience, conference, consultation, dialogue, evaluation, meeting, oral (examination), press conference, talk 2. *v.* examine, interrogate, question, sound out, talk to

interviewer examiner, interlocutor, interrogator, investigator, questioner, reporter

interweave blend, braid, crisscross, cross, interlace, intertwine, interwreathe, inweave, reticulate, splice

interwoven blended, connected, entwined, inmixed, interconnected, interlaced, interlocked, intermingled, knit

intestinal abdominal, coeliac, duodenal, gut (*Inf.*), inner, stomachic, visceral

intestines bowels, entrails, guts, innards (*Inf.*), insides (*Inf.*), internal organs, viscera, vitals

intimacy closeness, confidence, confidentiality, familiarity, fraternization, understanding

Antonyms alienation, aloofness, coldness, detachment, distance, estrangement, remoteness, separation

intimate[1] *adj.* 1. bosom, cherished, close, confidential, dear, friendly, near, nearest and dearest, thick (*Inf.*), warm 2. confidential, personal, private, privy, secret 3. deep, detailed, exhaustive, experienced, first-hand, immediate, in-depth, penetrating, personal, profound, thorough 4. comfy (*Inf.*), cosy, friendly, informal, snug, tête-à-tête, warm ~*n.* 5. bosom friend, buddy (*Inf.*), china (*Brit. sl.*), chum (*Inf.*), close friend, cock (*Brit. inf.*), comrade, confidant, confidante, (constant) companion, crony, familiar, friend, mate (*Inf.*), mucker (*Brit. sl.*), pal

Antonyms *n.* (*sense 1*) distant, remote, superficial (*sense 2*) known, open, public ~*n.* enemy, foe, stranger

intimate[2] *v.* allude, announce, communicate, declare, drop a hint, give (someone) to understand, hint, impart, imply, indicate, insinuate, let it be known, make known, remind, state, suggest, tip (someone) the wink (*Brit. inf.*), warn

intimately 1. affectionately, closely, confidentially, confidingly, familiarly, personally, tenderly, very well, warmly 2. fully, in detail, inside out, thoroughly, through and through, to the core, very well

intimation 1. allusion, hint, indication, inkling, insinuation, reminder, suggestion, warning 2. announcement, communication, declaration, notice

intimidate affright (*Archaic*), alarm, appal, browbeat, bully, coerce, cow, daunt, dishearten, dismay, dispirit, frighten, lean on (*Inf.*), overawe, scare, scare off (*Inf.*), subdue, terrify, terrorize, threaten, twist someone's arm (*Inf.*)

intimidation arm-twisting (*Inf.*), browbeating, bullying, coercion, fear, menaces, pressure, terror, terrorization, threat(s)

intolerable beyond bearing, excruciating, impossible, insufferable, insupportable, more than flesh and blood can stand, not to be borne, painful, unbearable, unendurable

Antonyms bearable, endurable, painless, possible, sufferable, supportable, tolerable

intolerance bigotry, chauvinism, discrimination, dogmatism, fanaticism, illiberality, impatience, jingoism, narrow-mindedness, narrowness, prejudice, racialism, racism, xenophobia

Antonyms broad-mindedness, liberality, open-mindedness, patience, tolerance, understanding

intolerant bigoted, chauvinistic, dictatorial, dogmatic, fanatical, illiberal, impatient, narrow, narrow-minded, one-sided, prejudiced, racialist, racist, small-minded, uncharitable, xenophobic
Antonyms broad-minded, charitable, lenient, liberal, open-minded, patient, tolerant, understanding

intonation 1. accentuation, cadence, inflection, modulation, tone 2. chant, incantation

intone chant, croon, intonate, recite, sing

in toto as a whole, completely, entirely, in its entirety, totally, unabridged, uncut, wholly

intoxicate 1. addle, befuddle, fuddle, go to one's head, inebriate, put (someone) under the table (*Inf.*), stupefy 2. *Fig.* elate, excite, exhilarate, inflame, make one's head spin, stimulate

intoxicated 1. bevvied (*Dialect*), blitzed (*Sl.*), blotto (*Sl.*), bombed (*Sl.*), canned (*Sl.*), cut (*Brit. sl.*), drunk, drunken, flying (*Sl.*), fuddled, half seas over (*Brit. inf.*), high (*Inf.*), inebriated, in one's cups (*Inf.*), legless (*Inf.*), lit up (*Sl.*), out of it (*Sl.*), out to it (*Aust. & N.Z. sl.*), paralytic (*Inf.*), pissed (*Taboo sl.*), plastered (*Sl.*), smashed (*Sl.*), sozzled (*Inf.*), steamboats (*Sl.*), steaming (*Sl.*), stewed (*Sl.*), stiff (*Sl.*), stoned (*Sl.*), the worse for drink, three sheets in the wind (*Inf.*), tight (*Inf.*), tipsy, under the influence, wasted (*Sl.*), wrecked (*Sl.*), zonked (*Sl.*) 2. *Fig.* dizzy, elated, enraptured, euphoric, excited, exhilarated, high (*Inf.*), infatuated, sent (*Sl.*), stimulated

intoxicating 1. alcoholic, inebriant, intoxicant, spirituous, strong 2. *Fig.* exciting, exhilarating, heady, sexy (*Inf.*), stimulating, thrilling

intoxication 1. drunkenness, inebriation, inebriety, insobriety, tipsiness 2. *Fig.* delirium, elation, euphoria, exaltation, excitement, exhilaration, infatuation

intractability awkwardness, cantankerousness, contrariness, incorrigibility, indiscipline, indocility, mulishness, obduracy, obstinacy, perverseness, perversity, pigheadedness, stubbornness, uncooperativeness, ungovernability, waywardness

intractable awkward, bull-headed, cantankerous, contrary, difficult, fractious, headstrong, incurable, insoluble, intransigent, obdurate, obstinate, perverse, pig-headed, refractory, self-willed, stiff-necked, stubborn, unbending, uncooperative, undisciplined, ungovernable, unmanageable, unruly, unyielding, wayward, wild, wilful

intransigent hardline, immovable, intractable, obdurate, obstinate, stiff-necked, stubborn, tenacious, tough, unbending, unbudgeable, uncompromising, unyielding
Antonyms acquiescent, compliant, compromising, flexible, open-minded

intrenched *see* ENTRENCHED

intrepid audacious, bold, brave, courageous, daring, dauntless, doughty, fearless, gallant, game (*Inf.*), have-a-go (*Inf.*), heroic, lion-hearted, nerveless, plucky, resolute, stalwart, stouthearted, unafraid, undaunted, unflinching, valiant, valorous
Antonyms afraid, cautious, cowardly, craven, daunted, faint-hearted, fearful, flinching, irresolute, timid

intrepidity audacity, boldness, bravery, courage, daring, dauntlessness, doughtiness, fearlessness, fortitude, gallantry, guts (*Inf.*), heroism, lion-heartedness, nerve, pluck, prowess, spirit, stoutheartedness, valour

intricacy complexity, complication, convolutions, elaborateness, entanglement, intricateness, involution, involvement, knottiness, obscurity

intricate baroque, Byzantine, complex, complicated, convoluted, daedal (*Literary*), difficult, elaborate, fancy, involved, knotty, labyrinthine, obscure, perplexing, rococo, sophisticated, tangled, tortuous
Antonyms clear, easy, obvious, plain, simple, straightforward

intrigue *v.* 1. arouse the curiosity of, attract, charm, fascinate, interest, pique, rivet, tickle one's fancy, titillate 2. connive, conspire, machinate, manoeuvre, plot, scheme *~n.* 3. cabal, chicanery, collusion, conspiracy, double-dealing, knavery, machination, manipulation, manoeuvre, plot, ruse, scheme, sharp practice, stratagem, trickery, wile 4. affair, amour, intimacy, liaison, romance

intriguing beguiling, compelling, diverting, exciting, fascinating, interesting, tantalizing, titillating

intrinsic basic, built-in, central, congenital, constitutional, elemental, essential, fundamental, genuine, inborn, inbred, inherent, native, natural, radical, real, true, underlying
Antonyms acquired, added, appended, artificial, extraneous, extrinsic, incidental

intrinsically as such, at heart, basically, by definition, constitutionally, essentially, fundamentally, in itself, per se

introduce 1. acquaint, do the honours, familiarize, make known, make the introduction, present 2. begin, bring in, commence, establish, found, inaugurate, initiate, institute, launch, organize, pioneer, set up, start, usher in 3. advance, air, bring up, broach, moot, offer, propose, put forward, recommend, set forth, submit, suggest, ventilate 4. announce, lead into, lead off, open, preface 5. add, inject, insert, interpolate, interpose, put in, throw in (*Inf.*)

introduction 1. baptism, debut, establishment, first acquaintance, inauguration, induction, initiation, institution, launch, pioneering, presentation 2. commencement, exordium, foreword, intro (*Inf.*), lead-in, opening, opening passage, opening remarks, overture, preamble, preface, preliminaries, prelude, proem, prolegomena, prolegomenon, prologue 3. addition, insertion, interpolation
Antonyms (*sense 1*) completion, elimination, termination (*sense 2*) afterward, conclusion, end, epilogue (*sense 3*) extraction, removal, withdrawal

introductory early, elementary, first, inaugural, initial, initiatory, opening, precursory, prefatory, preliminary, preparatory, starting
Antonyms closing, concluding, final, last, terminating

introspection brooding, heart-searching, introversion, self-analysis, self-examination

introspective brooding, contemplative, inner-directed, introverted, inward-looking, meditative, pensive, subjective

introverted indrawn, inner-directed, introspective, inward-looking, self-centred, self-contained, withdrawn

intrude butt in, encroach, infringe, interfere, interrupt, meddle, obtrude, push in, put one's two cents in (*U.S. sl.*), thrust oneself in *or* forward, trespass, violate

intruder burglar, gate-crasher (*Inf.*), infiltrator, interloper, invader, prowler, raider, snooper (*Inf.*), squatter, thief, trespasser

intrusion encroachment, infringement, interference, interruption, invasion, trespass, violation

intrusive disturbing, forward, impertinent, importunate, interfering, invasive, meddlesome, nosy (*Inf.*), officious, presumptuous, pushy (*Inf.*), uncalled-for, unwanted

intrust *see* ENTRUST

intuition discernment, hunch, insight, instinct, perception, presentiment, sixth sense

intuitive innate, instinctive, instinctual, involuntary, spontaneous, unreflecting, untaught

intwine *see* ENTWINE

inundate deluge, drown, engulf, flood, glut, immerse, overflow, overrun, overwhelm, submerge, swamp

inundation deluge, flood, overflow, tidal wave, torrent

inure accustom, anneal, case-harden, desensitize, familiarize, habituate, harden, strengthen, temper, toughen, train

invade 1. assail, assault, attack, burst in, descend upon, encroach, infringe, make inroads, occupy, raid, violate 2. infect, infest, overrun, overspread, penetrate, permeate, pervade, swarm over

invader aggressor, alien, attacker, looter, plunderer, raider, trespasser

invalid[1] 1. *adj.* ailing, bedridden, disabled, feeble, frail, ill, infirm, poorly (*Inf.*), sick, sickly, valetudinarian, weak 2. *n.* convalescent, patient, valetudinarian

invalid[2] *adj.* baseless, fallacious, false, ill-founded, illogical, inoperative, irrational, not binding, nugatory, null, null and void, unfounded, unscientific, unsound, untrue, void, worthless
Antonyms logical, operative, rational, solid, sound, true, valid, viable

invalidate abrogate, annul, cancel, nullify, overrule, overthrow, quash, render null and void, rescind, undermine, undo, weaken
Antonyms authorize, empower, ratify, sanction, strengthen, validate

invalidism chronic illness, valetudinarianism

invalidity fallaciousness, fallacy, falsity, illogicality, inconsistency, irrationality, sophism, speciousness, unsoundness

invaluable beyond price, costly, inestimable, precious, priceless, valuable
Antonyms cheap, rubbishy, valueless, worthless

invariable changeless, consistent, constant, fixed, immutable, inflexible, regular, rigid, set, unalterable, unchangeable, unchanging, unfailing, uniform, unvarying, unwavering
Antonyms alterable, changeable, changing, differing, flexible, inconsistent, irregular, uneven, variable, varying

invariably always, consistently, customarily, day in, day out, ever, every time, habitually, inevitably, on every occasion, perpetually, regularly, unfailingly, without exception

invasion 1. aggression, assault, attack, foray, incursion, inroad, irruption, offensive, onslaught, raid 2. breach, encroachment, infiltration, infraction, infringement, intrusion, overstepping, usurpation, violation

invective abuse, berating, billingsgate, castigation, censure, contumely, denunciation, diatribe, obloquy, philippic(s), reproach, revilement, sarcasm, tirade, tongue-lashing, vilification, vituperation

inveigh berate, blame, castigate, censure, condemn, denounce, excoriate, expostulate, lambast(e), rail, recriminate, reproach, sound off, tongue-lash, upbraid, vituperate

inveigle allure, bamboozle (*Inf.*), beguile, cajole, coax, con (*Sl.*), decoy, ensnare, entice, entrap, lead on, lure, manipulate, manoeuvre, persuade, seduce, sweet-talk (*Inf.*), wheedle

invent 1. coin, come up with (*Inf.*), conceive, contrive, create, design, devise, discover, dream up (*Inf.*), formulate, imagine, improvise, originate, think up 2. concoct, cook up (*Inf.*), fabricate, feign, forge, make up, manufacture, trump up

invention 1. brainchild (*Inf.*), contraption, contrivance, creation, design, development, device, discovery, gadget, instrument 2. coinage, creativeness, creativity, genius, imagination, ingenuity, inspiration, inventiveness, originality, resourcefulness 3. deceit, fabrication, fake, falsehood, fantasy, fib (*Inf.*), fiction, figment *or* product of (someone's) imagination, forgery, lie, prevarication, sham, story, tall story (*Inf.*), untruth, yarn

inventive creative, fertile, gifted, groundbreaking, imaginative, ingenious, innovative, inspired, original, resourceful
Antonyms imitative, pedestrian, trite, unimaginative, uninspired, uninventive

inventor architect, author, coiner, creator, designer, father, framer, maker, originator

inventory *n.* account, catalogue, file, list, record, register, roll, roster, schedule, stock book

inverse *adj.* contrary, converse, inverted, opposite, reverse, reversed, transposed

inversion antipode, antithesis, contraposition, contrariety, contrary, opposite, reversal, transposal, transposition

invert capsize, introvert, intussuscept (*Pathol.*), invaginate (*Pathol.*), overset, overturn, reverse, transpose, turn inside out, turn turtle, turn upside down, upset, upturn

invest 1. advance, devote, lay out, put in, sink, spend 2. endow, endue, provide, supply 3. authorize, charge, empower, license, sanction, vest 4. adopt, consecrate, enthrone, establish, inaugurate, induct, install, ordain 5. *Mil.* beleaguer, beset, besiege, enclose, lay siege to, surround 6. *Archaic* array, bedeck, bedizen (*Archaic*), clothe, deck, drape, dress, robe

investigate consider, enquire into, examine, explore, go into, inquire into, inspect, look into, make enquiries, probe, put to the test, recce (*Sl.*), research, scrutinize, search, sift, study, work over

investigation analysis, enquiry, examination, exploration, fact finding, hearing, inquest, inquiry, inspection, probe, recce (*Sl.*), research, review, scrutiny, search, study, survey

investigative fact-finding, inspecting, investigating, research, researching

investigator dick (*Sl., chiefly U.S.*), examiner, gumshoe (*U.S. sl.*), inquirer, (private) detective, private eye (*Inf.*), researcher, reviewer, sleuth *or* sleuthhound (*Inf.*)

investiture admission, enthronement, inauguration, induction, installation, instatement, investing, investment, ordination

investment 1. asset, investing, speculation, transaction, venture 2. ante (*Inf.*), contribution, stake 3. *Mil.* beleaguering, besieging, blockading, siege, surrounding

inveterate chronic, confirmed, deep-dyed (*Usu. derogatory*), deep-rooted, deep-seated, dyed-in-the-wool, entrenched, established, habitual, hard-core, hardened, incorrigible, incurable, ineradicable, ingrained, long-standing, obstinate

invidious discriminatory, envious (*Obsolete*), hateful, obnoxious, odious, offensive, repugnant, slighting, undesirable
Antonyms benevolent, desirable, generous, gratifying, kind, pleasant, pleasing

invigorate animate, brace, buck up (*Inf.*), energize, enliven, exhilarate, fortify, freshen (up), galvanize, harden, liven up, nerve, pep up, perk up, put new heart into, quicken, refresh, rejuvenate, revitalize, stimulate, strengthen

invigorating bracing, energizing, exhilarating, fresh, healthful, refreshing, rejuvenating, rejuvenative, restorative, salubrious, stimulating, tonic, uplifting

invincible impregnable, indestructible, indomitable, inseparable, insuperable, invulnerable, unassailable, unbeatable, unconquerable, unsurmountable, unyielding
Antonyms assailable, beatable, conquerable, defenceless, fallible, powerless, unprotected, vulnerable, weak, yielding

inviolability holiness, inalienability, inviolacy, invulnerability, sacredness, sanctity

inviolable hallowed, holy, inalienable, sacred, sacrosanct, unalterable

inviolate entire, intact, pure, sacred, stainless, unbroken, undefiled, undisturbed, unhurt, unpolluted, unstained, unsullied, untouched, virgin, whole

Antonyms abused, broken, defiled, polluted, stained, sullied, touched, violated

invisible 1. imperceptible, indiscernible, out of sight, unperceivable, unseen 2. concealed, disguised, hidden, inappreciable, inconspicuous, infinitesimal, microscopic
Antonyms (*sense 1*) discernible, distinct, obvious, perceptible, seen, visible

invitation 1. asking, begging, bidding, call, invite (*Inf.*), request, solicitation, summons, supplication 2. allurement, challenge, come-on (*Inf.*), coquetry, enticement, glad eye (*Inf.*), incitement, inducement, open door, overture, provocation, temptation

invite 1. ask, beg, bid, call, request, request the pleasure of (someone's) company, solicit, summon 2. allure, ask for (*Inf.*), attract, bring on, court, draw, encourage, entice, lead, leave the door open to, provoke, solicit, tempt, welcome

inviting alluring, appealing, attractive, beguiling, captivating, delightful, engaging, enticing, fascinating, intriguing, magnetic, mouthwatering, pleasing, seductive, tempting, warm, welcoming, winning
Antonyms disagreeable, offensive, off-putting (*Brit. inf.*), repellent, unappealing, unattractive, undesirable, uninviting, unpleasant

invocation appeal, beseeching, entreaty, petition, prayer, supplication

invoke 1. adjure, appeal to, beg, beseech, call upon, conjure, entreat, implore, petition, pray, solicit, supplicate 2. apply, call in, have recourse to, implement, initiate, put into effect, resort to, use

involuntary 1. compulsory, forced, obligatory, reluctant, unwilling 2. automatic, blind, conditioned, instinctive, instinctual, reflex, spontaneous, unconscious, uncontrolled, unintentional, unthinking
Antonyms (*sense 1*) optional, unconstrained, volitional, voluntary, willing (*sense 2*) calculated, deliberate, intentional, planned, purposed, wilful

involve 1. entail, imply, mean, necessitate, presuppose, require 2. affect, associate, compromise, concern, connect, draw in, implicate, incriminate, inculpate, mix up (*Inf.*), touch 3. comprehend, comprise, contain, cover, embrace, include, incorporate, number among, take in 4. absorb, bind, commit, engage, engross, grip, hold, preoccupy, rivet, wrap up 5. complicate, embroil, enmesh, entangle, link, mire, mix up, snarl up, tangle

involved 1. Byzantine, complex, complicated, confusing, convoluted, difficult, elaborate, intricate, knotty, labyrinthine, sophisticated, tangled, tortuous 2. caught (up), concerned, implicated, in on (*Inf.*), mixed up in *or* with, occupied, participating, taking part
Antonyms (*sense 1*) easy, easy-peasy (*Sl.*), elementary, simple, simplified, straightforward, uncomplicated, unsophisticated

involvement 1. association, commitment, concern, connection, dedication, interest, participation, responsibility 2. complexity, complication, difficulty, embarrassment, entanglement, imbroglio, intricacy, problem, ramification

invulnerability impenetrability, inviolability, safety, security, strength, unassailability, untouchability

invulnerable impenetrable, indestructible, insusceptible, invincible, proof against, safe, secure, unassailable
Antonyms assailable, defenceless, insecure, susceptible, unprotected, vulnerable, weak

inward *adj.* 1. entering, inbound, incoming, inflowing, ingoing, inpouring, penetrating 2. confidential, hidden, inmost, inner, innermost, inside, interior, internal, personal, private, privy, secret
Antonyms (*sense 2*) exterior, external, open, outer, outermost, outside, outward, public

inwardly at heart, deep down, in one's head, in one's inmost heart, inside, privately, secretly, to oneself, within

iota atom, bit, grain, hint, jot, mite, particle, scintilla (*Rare*), scrap, speck, tittle, trace, whit

irascibility asperity, bad temper, cantankerousness, choler, crossness, edginess, fieriness, ill temper, impatience, irritability, irritation, petulance, shortness, snappishness, testiness, touchiness, uncertain temper

irascible cantankerous, choleric, crabbed, cross, hasty, hot-tempered, irritable, narky (*Brit. sl.*), peppery, petulant, quick-tempered, ratty (*Brit. & N.Z. inf.*), short-tempered, testy, tetchy, touchy

irate angered, angry, annoyed, cross, enraged, exasperated, fuming (*Inf.*), furious, hacked (off) (*U.S. sl.*), incensed, indignant, infuriated, irritated, livid, mad (*Inf.*), piqued, pissed off (*Taboo sl.*), provoked, riled, up in arms, worked up, wrathful, wroth (*Archaic*)

ire anger, annoyance, choler, displeasure, exasperation, fury, indignation, passion, rage, wrath

iridescent nacreous, opalescent, opaline, pearly, polychromatic, prismatic, rainbow-coloured, shimmering, shot

Irish green, Hibernian

irk aggravate (*Inf.*), annoy, be on one's back (*Sl.*), bug (*Inf.*), gall, get in one's hair (*Inf.*), get on one's nerves (*Inf.*), irritate, miff (*Inf.*), nark (*Brit., Aust., & N.Z. sl.*), nettle, peeve (*Inf.*), piss one off (*Taboo sl.*), provoke, put one's nose out of joint (*Inf.*), put out (*Inf.*), rile, rub one up the wrong way (*Inf.*), ruffle, vex

irksome aggravating, annoying, boring, bothersome, burdensome, disagreeable, exasperating, irritating, tedious, tiresome, troublesome, uninteresting, unwelcome, vexatious, vexing, wearisome
Antonyms agreeable, enjoyable, gratifying, interesting, pleasant, pleasing, welcome

iron *adj.* 1. chalybeate, ferric, ferrous, irony 2. *Fig.* adamant, cruel, hard, heavy, immovable, implacable, indomitable, inflexible, obdurate, rigid, robust, steel, steely, strong, tough, unbending, unyielding
Antonyms (*sense 2*) bending, easy, flexible, light, malleable, pliable, soft, weak, yielding

ironic, ironical 1. double-edged, mocking, mordacious, sarcastic, sardonic, satirical, scoffing, sneering, wry 2. incongruous, paradoxical

iron out clear up, eliminate, eradicate, erase, expedite, get rid of, harmonize, put right, reconcile, resolve, settle, simplify, smooth over, sort out, straighten out, unravel

irons bonds, chains, fetters, gyves (*Archaic*), manacles, shackles

irony 1. mockery, sarcasm, satire 2. contrariness, incongruity, paradox

irradiate brighten, cast light upon, enlighten, illume (*Poetic*), illuminate, illumine, lighten, light up, shine upon

irrational 1. absurd, crackpot (*Inf.*), crazy, foolish, illogical, injudicious, loopy (*Inf.*), nonsensical, preposterous, silly, unreasonable, unreasoning, unsound, unthinking, unwise 2. aberrant, brainless, crazy, demented, insane, mindless, muddle-headed, raving, senseless, unstable, wild
Antonyms (*sense 1*) circumspect, judicious, logical, rational, reasonable, sensible, sound, wise

irrationality absurdity, brainlessness, illogicality, insanity, lack of judgment, lunacy, madness, preposterousness, senselessness, unreasonableness, unsoundness

irreconcilable 1. hardline, implacable, inexorable, inflexible, intransigent, unappeasable, uncompromising 2. clashing, conflicting, diametrically opposed, incompatible, incongruous, inconsistent, opposed

irrecoverable gone for ever, irreclaimable, irredeemable, irremediable, irreparable, irretrievable, lost, unregainable, unsalvageable, unsavable

irrefutable apodeictic, apodictic, beyond question, certain, incontestable, incontrovertible, indisputable, indubitable, invincible, irrefragable, irresistible, sure, unanswerable, unassailable, undeniable, unquestionable

irregular *adj.* 1. desultory, disconnected, eccentric, erratic, fitful, fluctuating, fragmentary, haphazard, inconstant, intermittent, nonuniform, occasional, out of order, patchy, random, shifting, spasmodic, sporadic, uncertain, uneven, unmethodical, unpunctual, unsteady, unsystematic, variable, wavering 2. abnormal, anomalous, capricious, disorderly, eccentric, exceptional, extraordinary, immoderate, improper, inappropriate, inordinate, odd, peculiar, queer, quirky, rum (*Brit. sl.*), unconventional, unofficial, unorthodox, unsuitable, unusual 3. asymmetrical, broken, bumpy, craggy, crooked, elliptic, elliptical, holey, jagged, lopsided, lumpy, pitted, ragged, rough, serrated, unequal, uneven, unsymmetrical ~*n.* 4. guerrilla, partisan, volunteer
Antonyms (*sense 1*) certain, invariable, methodical, punctual, reliable, steady, systematic (*sense 2*) appropriate, conventional, normal, orthodox, proper, regular, usual (*sense 3*) balanced, equal, even, regular, smooth, symmetrical

irregularity 1. asymmetry, bumpiness, crookedness, jaggedness, lack of symmetry, lopsidedness, lumpiness, patchiness, raggedness, roughness, spottiness, unevenness 2. aberration, abnormality, anomaly, breach, deviation, eccentricity, freak, malfunction, malpractice, oddity, peculiarity, singularity, unconventionality, unorthodoxy 3. confusion, desultoriness, disorderliness, disorganization, haphazardness, lack of method, randomness, uncertainty, unpunctuality, unsteadiness

irregularly anyhow, by fits and starts, disconnectedly, eccentrically, erratically, fitfully, haphazardly, in snatches, intermittently, jerkily, now and again, occasionally, off and on, out of sequence, spasmodically, unevenly, unmethodically, unpunctually

irrelevance, irrelevancy inappositeness, inappropriateness, inaptness, inconsequence, non sequitur
Antonyms appositeness, appropriateness, aptness, consequence, pertinence, point, relevance, suitability

irrelevant beside the point, extraneous,

immaterial, impertinent, inapplicable, inapposite, inappropriate, inapt, inconsequent, neither here nor there, unconnected, unrelated
Antonyms applicable, apposite, appropriate, apt, connected, fitting, pertinent, related, relevant, suitable

irreligious 1. agnostic, atheistic, freethinking, godless, pagan, sceptical, unbelieving 2. blasphemous, iconoclastic, impious, irreverent, profane, sacrilegious, sinful, undevout, ungodly, unholy, unrighteous, wicked

irremediable beyond redress, deadly, fatal, final, hopeless, incurable, irrecoverable, irredeemable, irreparable, irreversible, mortal, remediless, terminal

irreparable beyond repair, incurable, irrecoverable, irremediable, irreplaceable, irretrievable, irreversible

irreplaceable indispensable, invaluable, priceless, unique, vital

irrepressible boisterous, bubbling over, buoyant, ebullient, effervescent, insuppressible, uncontainable, uncontrollable, unmanageable, unquenchable, unrestrainable, unstoppable

irreproachable beyond reproach, blameless, faultless, guiltless, impeccable, inculpable, innocent, irreprehensible, irreprovable, perfect, pure, unblemished, unimpeachable

irresistible 1. compelling, imperative, overmastering, overpowering, overwhelming, potent, urgent 2. ineluctable, inescapable, inevitable, inexorable, unavoidable 3. alluring, beckoning, enchanting, fascinating, ravishing, seductive, tempting

irresolute doubtful, fickle, half-arsed, half-assed (*U.S. & Canad. sl.*), half-hearted, hesitant, hesitating, indecisive, infirm, in two minds, tentative, undecided, undetermined, unsettled, unstable, unsteady, vacillating, wavering, weak
Antonyms decisive, determined, firm, fixed, resolute, resolved, settled, stable, stalwart, steadfast, steady, strong

irresolution dithering (*Chiefly Brit.*), faint-heartedness, half-heartedness, hesitancy, hesitation, indecisiveness, infirmity (of purpose), shillyshallying (*Inf.*), uncertainty, vacillation, wavering

irrespective of apart from, despite, discounting, in spite of, notwithstanding, regardless of, without reference to, without regard to

irresponsible careless, featherbrained, flighty, giddy, harebrained, harum-scarum, ill-considered, immature, reckless, scatterbrained, shiftless, thoughtless, undependable, unreliable, untrustworthy, wild
Antonyms careful, dependable, level-headed, mature, reliable, responsible, sensible, trustworthy

irreverence cheek (*Inf.*), cheekiness (*Inf.*), chutzpah (*U.S. & Canad. inf.*), derision, disrespect, flippancy, impertinence, impudence, lack of respect, mockery, sauce (*Inf.*)

irreverent cheeky (*Inf.*), contemptuous, derisive, disrespectful, flip (*Inf.*), flippant, fresh (*Inf.*), iconoclastic, impertinent, impious, impudent, mocking, sassy (*U.S. inf.*), saucy, tongue-in-cheek
Antonyms awed, deferential, meek, pious, respectful, reverent, submissive

irreversible final, incurable, irreparable, irrevocable, unalterable

irrevocable changeless, fated, fixed, immutable, invariable, irremediable, irretrievable, irreversible, predestined, predetermined, settled, unalterable, unchangeable, unreversible

irrigate flood, inundate, moisten, water, wet

irritability bad temper, ill humour, impatience, irascibility, peevishness, petulance, prickliness, testiness, tetchiness, touchiness
Antonyms bonhomie, cheerfulness, complacence, good humour, patience

irritable bad-tempered, cantankerous, choleric, crabbed, crabby, cross, crotchety (*Inf.*), dyspeptic, edgy, exasperated, fiery, fretful, hasty, hot, ill-humoured, ill-tempered, irascible, narky (*Brit. sl.*), out of humour, oversensitive, peevish, petulant, prickly, ratty (*Brit. & N.Z. inf.*), snappish, snappy, snarling, tense, testy, tetchy, touchy
Antonyms agreeable, calm, cheerful, complacent, composed, even-tempered, good-natured, imperturbable, patient, unexcitable

irritate 1. aggravate (*Inf.*), anger, annoy, bother, drive one up the wall (*Sl.*), enrage, exasperate, fret, gall, get in one's hair (*Inf.*), get one's back up, get one's hackles up, get on one's nerves (*Inf.*), harass, incense, inflame, infuriate, nark (*Brit., Aust., & N.Z. sl.*), needle (*Inf.*), nettle, offend, pester, piss one off (*Taboo sl.*), provoke, raise one's hackles, rankle with, rub up the wrong way (*Inf.*), ruffle, try one's patience, vex 2. aggravate, chafe, fret, inflame, intensify, pain, rub
Antonyms (*sense 1*) calm, comfort, gratify, mollify, placate, please, soothe

irritated angry, annoyed, bothered, cross, displeased, exasperated, flustered, hacked (off) (*U.S. sl.*), harassed, impatient, irritable, nettled, out of humour, peeved (*Inf.*), piqued, pissed off (*Taboo sl.*), put out, ruffled, vexed

irritating aggravating (*Inf.*), annoying, displeasing, disquieting, disturbing, galling, infuriating, irksome, maddening, nagging, pestilential, provoking, thorny, troublesome, trying, upsetting, vexatious, worrisome

Antonyms agreeable, assuaging, calming, comforting, mollifying, pleasant, pleasing, quieting, soothing

irritation 1. anger, annoyance, crossness, displeasure, exasperation, ill humour, ill temper, impatience, indignation, irritability, resentment, shortness, snappiness, testiness, vexation, wrath 2. aggravation (*Inf.*), annoyance, drag (*Inf.*), gall, goad, irritant, nuisance, pain (*Inf.*), pain in the arse (*Taboo inf.*), pain in the neck (*Inf.*), pest, provocation, tease, thorn in one's flesh

Antonyms (*sense 1*) calm, composure, ease, pleasure, quietude, satisfaction, serenity, tranquillity

irrupt break in, burst in, crash in (*Inf.*), invade, rush in, storm in

irruption breaking in, foray, forcible entry, incursion, inroad, intrusion, invasion, raid

isolate cut off, detach, disconnect, divorce, insulate, quarantine, segregate, separate, sequester, set apart

isolated 1. backwoods, hidden, incommunicado, in the middle of nowhere, lonely, off the beaten track, outlying, out-of-the-way, remote, retired, secluded, unfrequented 2. abnormal, anomalous, exceptional, freak, random, single, solitary, special, unique, unrelated, untypical, unusual

isolation aloofness, detachment, disconnection, exile, insularity, insulation, loneliness, quarantine, remoteness, retirement, seclusion, segregation, self-sufficiency, separation, solitude, withdrawal

issue *n.* 1. affair, argument, concern, controversy, matter, matter of contention, point, point in question, problem, question, subject, topic 2. **at issue** at variance, controversial, in disagreement, in dispute, to be decided, under discussion, unsettled 3. **take issue** challenge, disagree, dispute, object, oppose, raise an objection, take exception 4. conclusion, consequence, culmination, effect, end, finale, outcome, pay-off (*Inf.*), result, termination, upshot 5. copy, edition, impression, instalment, number, printing 6. circulation, delivery, dispersion, dissemination, distribution, granting, issuance, issuing, publication, sending out, supply, supplying 7. children, descendants, heirs, offspring, progeny, scions, seed (*Chiefly biblical*) ~*v.* 8. announce, broadcast, circulate, deliver, distribute, emit, give out, promulgate, publish, put in circulation, put out, release 9. arise, be a consequence of, come forth, emanate, emerge, flow, originate, proceed, rise, spring, stem

Antonyms *n.* (*sense 4*) beginning, cause, inception, start (*sense 6*) cancellation, recall (*sense 7*) parent, sire ~*v.* cause, revoke, withdraw

itch *v.* 1. crawl, irritate, prickle, tickle, tingle 2. ache, burn, crave, hanker, hunger, long, lust, pant, pine, yearn ~*n.* 3. irritation, itchiness, prickling, tingling 4. craving, desire, hankering, hunger, longing, lust, passion, restlessness, yearning, yen (*Inf.*)

itching agog, aquiver, atremble, avid, burning, consumed with curiosity, eager, impatient, inquisitive, longing, mad keen (*Inf.*), raring, spoiling for

itchy eager, edgy, fidgety, impatient, restive, restless, unsettled

item 1. article, aspect, component, consideration, detail, entry, matter, particular, point, thing 2. account, article, bulletin, dispatch, feature, note, notice, paragraph, piece, report

itemize count, detail, document, enumerate, instance, inventory, list, number, particularize, record, set out, specify

iterate go over, recap (*Inf.*), recapitulate, reiterate, repeat, restate

itinerant *adj.* ambulatory, Gypsy, journeying, migratory, nomadic, peripatetic, roaming, roving, travelling, unsettled, vagabond, vagrant, wandering, wayfaring

Antonyms established, fixed, resident, rooted, settled, stable

itinerary 1. circuit, journey, line, programme, route, schedule, timetable, tour 2. Baedeker, guide, guidebook

ivory tower cloister, refuge, remoteness, retreat, sanctum, seclusion, splendid isolation, unreality, world of one's own

ivory-towered 1. cloistered, far from the madding crowd, remote, retired, sequestered, sheltered, withdrawn 2. academic, airy-fairy (*Inf.*), idealistic, quixotic, unrealizable, visionary

J

jab *v./n.* dig, lunge, nudge, poke, prod, punch, stab, tap, thrust

jabber babble, blather, blether, chatter, drivel, gabble, mumble, prate, rabbit (on) (*Brit. inf.*), ramble, run off at the mouth (*Sl.*), tattle, waffle (*Inf., chiefly Brit.*), yap (*Inf.*)

jackass berk (*Brit. sl.*), blockhead, charlie (*Brit. inf.*), coot, dickhead (*Sl.*), dimwit (*Inf.*), dipstick (*Brit. sl.*), divvy (*Brit. sl.*), dolt, dork (*Sl.*), dweeb (*U.S. sl.*), fool, fuckwit (*Taboo sl.*), geek (*Sl.*), gonzo (*Sl.*), idiot, imbecile, jerk (*Sl., chiefly U.S. & Canad.*), lamebrain (*Inf.*), nerd *or* nurd (*Sl.*), nincompoop, ninny, nitwit (*Inf.*), numskull *or* numbskull, oaf, pillock (*Brit. sl.*), plank (*Brit. sl.*), plonker (*Sl.*), prat (*Sl.*), prick (*Derogatory sl.*), schmuck (*U.S. sl.*), simpleton, twit (*Inf., chiefly Brit.*), wally (*Sl.*)

jacket case, casing, coat, covering, envelope, folder, sheath, skin, wrapper, wrapping

jackpot award, bonanza, kitty, pool, pot, prize, reward, winnings

jack up 1. elevate, heave, hoist, lift, lift up, raise, rear 2. accelerate, augment, boost, escalate, increase, inflate, put up, raise

jade harridan, hussy, nag, shrew, slattern, slut, trollop, vixen, wench

jaded 1. clapped out (*Aust. & N.Z. inf.*), exhausted, fagged (out) (*Inf.*), fatigued, spent, tired, tired-out, weary, zonked (*Sl.*) 2. bored, cloyed, dulled, glutted, gorged, sated, satiated, surfeited, tired
Antonyms eager, enthusiastic, fresh, keen, life-loving, naive, refreshed

jag[1] notch, point, projection, protuberance, snag, spur, tooth

jag[2] binge (*Inf.*), bout, carouse, carousal, fit, orgy, period, spell, spree

jagged barbed, broken, cleft, craggy, denticulate, indented, notched, pointed, ragged, ridged, rough, serrated, snaggy, spiked, toothed, uneven
Antonyms glassy, level, regular, rounded, smooth

jail, gaol 1. *n.* borstal, brig (*Chiefly U.S.*), can (*Sl.*), clink (*Sl.*), cooler (*Sl.*), inside (*Sl.*), jailhouse (*Southern U.S.*), jug (*Sl.*), lockup, nick (*Brit. sl.*), penitentiary (*U.S.*), poky *or* pokey (*U.S. & Canad. sl.*), prison, quod (*Sl.*), reformatory, slammer (*Sl.*), stir (*Sl.*) 2. *v.* confine, detain, immure, impound, imprison, incarcerate, lock up, send down

jailer, gaoler captor, guard, keeper, screw (*Sl.*), turnkey (*Archaic*), warden, warder

jam *v.* 1. cram, crowd, crush, force, pack, press, ram, squeeze, stuff, throng, wedge 2. block, cease, clog, congest, halt, obstruct, stall, stick ~*n.* 3. crowd, crush, horde, mass, mob, multitude, pack, press, swarm, throng 4. bind, dilemma, fix (*Inf.*), hole (*Sl.*), hot water, pickle (*Inf.*), plight, predicament, quandary, scrape (*Inf.*), spot (*Inf.*), strait, tight spot, trouble

jamboree beano (*Brit. sl.*), carnival, carousal, carouse, celebration, festival, festivity, fête, frolic, jubilee, merriment, party, rave (*Brit. sl.*), rave-up (*Brit. sl.*), revelry, spree

jangle 1. *v.* chime, clank, clash, clatter, jingle, rattle, vibrate 2. *n.* cacophony, clang, clangour, clash, din, dissonance, jar, racket, rattle, reverberation
Antonyms (*sense 2*) harmoniousness, mellifluousness, quiet, silence

janitor caretaker, concierge, custodian, doorkeeper, porter

jar[1] amphora, carafe, container, crock, flagon, jug, pitcher, pot, receptacle, urn, vase, vessel

jar[2] *v.* 1. bicker, clash, contend, disagree, interfere, oppose, quarrel, wrangle 2. agitate, convulse, disturb, grate, irritate, jolt, offend, rasp, rattle (*Inf.*), rock, shake, vibrate 3. annoy, clash, discompose, gall, get on one's nerves (*Inf.*), grate, grind, irk, irritate, nark (*Brit., Aust., & N.Z. sl.*), nettle, piss one off (*Taboo sl.*) ~*n.* 4. agitation, altercation, bickering, disagreement, discord, grating, irritation, jolt, quarrel, rasping, wrangling

jargon 1. argot, cant, dialect, idiom, lingo (*Inf.*), parlance, patois, slang, tongue, usage 2. balderdash, bunkum *or* buncombe (*Chiefly U.S.*), drivel, gabble, gibberish, gobbledegook, mumbo jumbo, nonsense, palaver, rigmarole, twaddle

jaundiced 1. cynical, preconceived, sceptical 2. biased, bigoted, bitter, distorted, envious, hostile, jealous, partial, prejudiced, resentful, spiteful, suspicious
Antonyms credulous, ingenuous, naive,

open-minded, optimistic, trusting, unbiased

jaunt airing, excursion, expedition, outing, promenade, ramble, stroll, tour, trip

jaunty airy, breezy, buoyant, carefree, dapper, gay, high-spirited, lively, perky, self-confident, showy, smart, sparky, sprightly, spruce, trim
Antonyms dignified, dull, lifeless, sedate, serious, staid

jaw *v.* 1. babble, chat, chatter, gossip, lecture, spout, talk 2. abuse, censure, criticize, revile, scold ~*n.* 3. chat, chinwag (*Brit. inf.*), conversation, gabfest (*Inf., chiefly U.S. & Canad.*), gossip, natter, talk

jaws abyss, aperture, entrance, gates, ingress, maw, mouth, opening, orifice

jazz up animate, enhance, enliven, heighten, improve

jazzy animated, fancy, flashy, gaudy, lively, smart, snazzy (*Inf.*), spirited, vivacious, wild, zestful

jealous 1. covetous, desirous, emulous, envious, green, green-eyed, grudging, intolerant, invidious, resentful, rival 2. anxious, apprehensive, attentive, guarded, mistrustful, protective, solicitous, suspicious, vigilant, wary, watchful, zealous
Antonyms carefree, indifferent, satisfied, trusting

jealousy covetousness, distrust, envy, heart-burning, ill-will, mistrust, possessiveness, resentment, spite, suspicion

jeer 1. *v.* banter, barrack, cock a snook at (*Brit.*), contemn (*Formal*), deride, flout, gibe, heckle, hector, knock (*Inf.*), mock, ridicule, scoff, sneer, taunt 2. *n.* abuse, aspersion, boo, catcall, derision, gibe, hiss, hoot, obloquy, ridicule, scoff, sneer, taunt
Antonyms (*sense 1*) acclaim, applaud, cheer, clap, praise (*sense 2*) adulation, applause, cheers, encouragement, praise

jejune 1. childish, immature, juvenile, naive, pointless, puerile, senseless, silly, simple, unsophisticated 2. banal, colourless, dry, dull, inane, insipid, prosaic, uninteresting, vapid, wishy-washy (*Inf.*)

jell 1. congeal, harden, set, solidify, thicken 2. come together, crystallize, finalize, form, materialize, take shape

jeopardize chance, endanger, expose, gamble, hazard, imperil, risk, stake, venture

jeopardy danger, endangerment, exposure, hazard, insecurity, liability, peril, pitfall, precariousness, risk, venture, vulnerability

jeremiad complaint, groan, keen, lament, lamentation, moan, plaint, wail

jerk *v./n.* jolt, lurch, pull, throw, thrust, tug, tweak, twitch, wrench, yank

jerky bouncy, bumpy, convulsive, fitful, jolting, jumpy, rough, shaky, spasmodic, tremulous, twitchy, uncontrolled
Antonyms flowing, frictionless, gliding, smooth

jerry-built cheap, defective, faulty, flimsy, ramshackle, rickety, shabby, slipshod, thrown together, unsubstantial
Antonyms sturdy, substantial, well-built, well-constructed

jest 1. *n.* banter, bon mot, crack (*Sl.*), fun, gag (*Inf.*), hoax, jape, joke, josh (*Sl., chiefly U.S. & Canad.*), play, pleasantry, prank, quip, sally, sport, wisecrack (*Inf.*), witticism 2. *v.* banter, chaff, deride, gibe, jeer, joke, josh (*Sl., chiefly U.S. & Canad.*), kid (*Inf.*), mock, quip, scoff, sneer, tease

jester 1. comedian, comic, humorist, joker, quipster, wag, wit 2. buffoon, clown, fool, harlequin, madcap, mummer, pantaloon, prankster, zany

jet[1] *adj.* black, coal-black, ebony, inky, pitch-black, raven, sable

jet[2] *n.* 1. flow, fountain, gush, spout, spray, spring, stream 2. atomizer, nose, nozzle, rose, spout, sprayer, sprinkler ~*v.* 3. flow, gush, issue, rush, shoot, spew, spout, squirt, stream, surge 4. fly, soar, zoom

jettison abandon, discard, dump, eject, expel, heave, scrap, throw overboard, unload

jetty breakwater, dock, groyne, mole, pier, quay, wharf

jewel 1. brilliant, gemstone, ornament, precious stone, rock (*Sl.*), sparkler (*Inf.*), trinket 2. charm, find, gem, humdinger (*Sl.*), masterpiece, paragon, pearl, prize, rarity, treasure, wonder

jewellery finery, gems, jewels, ornaments, precious stones, regalia, treasure, trinkets

Jezebel harlot, harridan, hussy, jade, virago, wanton, witch

jib balk, recoil, refuse, retreat, shrink, stop short

jibe *see* GIBE

jiffy flash, instant, moment, second, split second, trice, twinkling

jig *v.* bob, bounce, caper, jiggle, jounce, prance, shake, skip, twitch, wiggle, wobble

jiggle agitate, bounce, fidget, jerk, jig, jog, joggle, shake, shimmy, twitch, wiggle

jilt *v.* abandon, betray, break with, coquette, deceive, desert, disappoint, discard, ditch (*Sl.*), drop, forsake, reject, throw over

jingle *v.* 1. chime, clatter, clink, jangle, rattle, ring, tinkle, tintinnabulate ~*n.* 2. clang, clangour, clink, rattle, reverberation, ringing, tinkle 3. chorus, ditty, doggerel, limerick, melody, song, tune

jinx 1. *n.* black magic, curse, evil eye, hex

(*U.S. & Canad. inf.*), hoodoo (*Inf.*), nemesis, plague, voodoo 2. *v.* bewitch, curse, hex (*U.S. & Canad. inf.*)

jitters anxiety, fidgets, heebie-jeebies (*Sl.*), nerves, nervousness, tenseness, the shakes (*Inf.*), the willies (*Inf.*)

jittery agitated, anxious, fidgety, hyper (*Inf.*), jumpy, nervous, quivering, shaky, trembling, twitchy (*Inf.*), wired (*Sl.*),
Antonyms calm, composed, laid-back (*Inf.*), relaxed, together (*Sl.*), unfazed (*Inf.*), unflustered

job 1. affair, assignment, charge, chore, concern, contribution, duty, enterprise, errand, function, pursuit, responsibility, role, stint, task, undertaking, venture, work 2. activity, business, calling, capacity, career, craft, employment, function, livelihood, métier, occupation, office, position, post, profession, situation, trade, vocation 3. allotment, assignment, batch, commission, consignment, contract, lot, output, piece, portion, product, share

jobless idle, inactive, out of work, unemployed, unoccupied

jockey *v.* 1. bamboozle, cheat, con (*Inf.*), deceive, dupe, fool, hoax, hoodwink, trick 2. cajole, engineer, finagle (*Inf.*), ingratiate, insinuate, manage, manipulate, manoeuvre, negotiate, trim, wheedle

jocose blithe, comical, droll, facetious, funny, humorous, jesting, jocular, jovial, joyous, merry, mischievous, playful, pleasant, sportive, teasing, waggish, witty

jocular amusing, comical, droll, facetious, frolicsome, funny, humorous, jesting, jocose, jocund, joking, jolly, jovial, playful, roguish, sportive, teasing, waggish, whimsical, witty
Antonyms earnest, humourless, serious, solemn

jog 1. activate, arouse, nudge, prod, prompt, push, remind, shake, stimulate, stir, suggest 2. bounce, jar, jerk, jiggle, joggle, jolt, jostle, jounce, rock, shake 3. canter, dogtrot, lope, run, trot 4. lumber, plod, traipse (*Inf.*), tramp, trudge

joie de vivre ebullience, enjoyment, enthusiasm, gaiety, gusto, joy, joyfulness, pleasure, relish, zest
Antonyms apathy, depression, distaste

join 1. accompany, add, adhere, annex, append, attack, cement, combine, connect, couple, fasten, knit, link, marry, splice, tie, unite, yoke 2. affiliate with, associate with, enlist, enrol, enter, sign up 3. adjoin, border, border on, butt, conjoin, extend, meet, reach, touch, verge on
Antonyms detach, disconnect, disengage, disentangle, divide, leave, part, quit, resign, separate, sever, unfasten

joint *n.* 1. articulation, connection, hinge, intersection, junction, juncture, knot, nexus, node, seam, union ~*adj.* 2. collective, combined, communal, concerted, consolidated, cooperative, joined, mutual, shared, united ~*v.* 3. connect, couple, fasten, fit, join, unite 4. carve, cut up, dismember, dissect, divide, segment, sever, sunder

jointly as one, collectively, in common, in conjunction, in league, in partnership, mutually, together, unitedly
Antonyms individually, separately, singly

joke *n.* 1. frolic, fun, gag (*Inf.*), jape, jest, josh (*Sl., chiefly U.S. & Canad.*), lark, play, prank, pun, quip, quirk, sally, sport, whimsy, wisecrack (*Inf.*), witticism, yarn 2. buffoon, butt, clown, laughing stock, simpleton, target ~*v.* 3. banter, chaff, deride, frolic, gambol, jest, josh (*Sl., chiefly U.S. & Canad.*), kid (*Inf.*), mock, quip, ridicule, taunt, tease, wind up (*Brit. sl.*)

joker buffoon, clown, comedian, comic, humorist, jester, kidder (*Inf.*), prankster, trickster, wag, wit

jolly blithesome, carefree, cheerful, chirpy (*Inf.*), convivial, festive, frolicsome, funny, gay, genial, gladsome (*Archaic*), hilarious, jocund, jovial, joyful, joyous, jubilant, merry, mirthful, playful, sportive, sprightly, upbeat (*Inf.*)
Antonyms doleful, gaunt, grave, lugubrious, miserable, morose, saturnine, serious, solemn

jolt *v.* 1. jar, jerk, jog, jostle, knock, push, shake, shove 2. astonish, discompose, disturb, perturb, stagger, startle, stun, surprise, upset ~*n.* 3. bump, jar, jerk, jog, jump, lurch, quiver, shake, start 4. blow, bolt from the blue, bombshell, reversal, setback, shock, surprise, thunderbolt

jostle bump, butt, crowd, elbow, hustle, jog, joggle, jolt, press, push, scramble, shake, shove, squeeze, throng, thrust

jot 1. *n.* ace, atom, bit, detail, fraction, grain, iota, mite, morsel, particle, scintilla, scrap, smidgen *or* smidgin (*Inf., chiefly U.S. & Canad.*), speck, tittle, trifle, whit 2. *v.* list, note, note down, record, register, scribble, tad (*Inf., chiefly U.S.*), tally

journal 1. chronicle, daily, gazette, magazine, monthly, newspaper, paper, periodical, record, register, review, tabloid, weekly 2. chronicle, commonplace book, daybook, diary, log, record

journalist broadcaster, columnist, commentator, contributor, correspondent, hack, journo (*Sl.*), newsman, newspaperman, pressman, reporter, scribe (*Inf.*), stringer

journey 1. *n.* excursion, expedition, jaunt, odyssey, outing, passage, peregrination, pilgrimage, progress, ramble, tour, travel, trek, trip, voyage 2. *v.* fare, fly, go, peregrinate, proceed, ramble, range, roam, rove, tour, travel, traverse, trek, voyage, wander, wend

joust 1. *n.* combat, duel, encounter, engagement, lists, match, passage of arms, set-to, tilt, tournament, tourney 2. *v.* break a lance, cross swords, engage, enter the lists, fight, tilt, trade blows

jovial airy, animated, blithe, buoyant, cheery, convivial, cordial, gay, glad, happy, hilarious, jocose, jocund, jolly, jubilant, merry, mirthful
Antonyms antisocial, doleful, grumpy, morose, solemn, unfriendly

joviality fun, gaiety, glee, hilarity, jollity, merriment, mirth

joy 1. bliss, delight, ecstasy, elation, exaltation, exultation, felicity, festivity, gaiety, gladness, glee, hilarity, pleasure, rapture, ravishment, satisfaction, transport 2. charm, delight, gem, jewel, pride, prize, treasure, treat, wonder
Antonyms bane, despair, grief, misery, sorrow, tribulation, unhappiness

joyful blithesome, cock-a-hoop, delighted, elated, enraptured, glad, gladsome (*Archaic*), gratified, happy, jocund, jolly, jovial, jubilant, light-hearted, merry, over the moon (*Inf.*), pleased, rapt, satisfied

joyless cheerless, dejected, depressed, dismal, dispirited, downcast, dreary, gloomy, miserable, sad, unhappy

joyous cheerful, festive, heartening, joyful, merry, rapturous

jubilant cock-a-hoop, elated, enraptured, euphoric, excited, exuberant, exultant, glad, joyous, overjoyed, over the moon (*Inf.*), rejoicing, rhapsodic, thrilled, triumphal, triumphant
Antonyms despondent, doleful, downcast, melancholy, sad, sorrowful

jubilation celebration, ecstasy, elation, excitement, exultation, festivity, jamboree, joy, jubilee, triumph

jubilee carnival, celebration, festival, festivity, fête, gala, holiday

Judas betrayer, deceiver, renegade, traitor, turncoat

judge *n.* 1. adjudicator, arbiter, arbitrator, moderator, referee, umpire 2. appraiser, arbiter, assessor, authority, connoisseur, critic, evaluator, expert 3. beak (*Brit. sl.*), justice, magistrate ~*v.* 4. adjudge, adjudicate, arbitrate, ascertain, conclude, decide, determine, discern, distinguish, mediate, referee, umpire 5. appraise, appreciate, assess, consider, criticize, esteem, estimate, evaluate, examine, rate, review, value 6. adjudge, condemn, decree, doom, find, pass sentence, pronounce sentence, rule, sentence, sit, try

judgment 1. acumen, common sense, discernment, discrimination, intelligence, penetration, percipience, perspicacity, prudence, sagacity, sense, shrewdness, smarts (*Sl., chiefly U.S.*), taste, understanding, wisdom 2. arbitration, award, conclusion, decision, decree, determination, finding, order, result, ruling, sentence, verdict 3. appraisal, assessment, belief, conviction, deduction, diagnosis, estimate, finding, opinion, valuation, view 4. damnation, doom, fate, misfortune, punishment, retribution

judicial 1. judiciary, juridical, legal, official 2. discriminating, distinguished, impartial, judgelike, magisterial, magistral

judicious acute, astute, careful, cautious, circumspect, considered, diplomatic, discerning, discreet, discriminating, enlightened, expedient, informed, politic, prudent, rational, reasonable, sagacious, sage, sane, sapient, sensible, shrewd, skilful, sober, sound, thoughtful, well-advised, well-judged, wise
Antonyms imprudent, indiscreet, injudicious, tactless, thoughtless

jug carafe, container, crock, ewer, jar, pitcher, urn, vessel

juggle alter, change, disguise, doctor (*Inf.*), falsify, fix (*Inf.*), manipulate, manoeuvre, misrepresent, modify, tamper with

juice extract, fluid, liquid, liquor, nectar, sap, secretion, serum

juicy 1. lush, moist, sappy, succulent, watery 2. colourful, interesting, provocative, racy, risqué, sensational, spicy (*Inf.*), suggestive, vivid

jumble 1. *v.* confound, confuse, disarrange, dishevel, disorder, disorganize, entangle, mistake, mix, muddle, ravel, shuffle, tangle 2. *n.* chaos, clutter, confusion, disarrangement, disarray, disorder, farrago, gallimaufry, hodgepodge, hotchpotch (*U.S.*), litter, medley, *mélange,* mess, miscellany, mishmash, mixture, muddle, pig's breakfast (*Inf.*)

jumbo elephantine, giant, gigantic, ginormous (*Inf.*), huge, humongous *or* humungous (*U.S. sl.*), immense, large, mega (*Inf.*), oversized
Antonyms baby, dwarf, micro, mini, pocket, tiny, wee

jump *v.* 1. bounce, bound, caper, clear, gambol, hop, hurdle, leap, skip, spring, vault 2. flinch, jerk, recoil, start, wince 3. avoid, digress, evade, miss, omit, overshoot, skip, switch 4. advance, ascend, boost, escalate, gain, hike, increase, mount, rise, surge ~*n.* 5. bound, buck, caper, hop, leap, skip, spring, vault 6. barricade, barrier, fence, hurdle, impediment, obstacle, rail 7. breach, break, gap, hiatus, interruption, lacuna, space 8. advance, augmentation, boost, increase, increment, rise, upsurge, upturn 9. jar, jerk, jolt, lurch, shock, start, swerve, twitch, wrench

jumper jersey, pullover, sweater, woolly

jumpy agitated, anxious, apprehensive, fidgety, hyper (*Inf.*), jittery (*Inf.*), nervous, on edge, restless, shaky, tense, timorous, twitchy (*Inf.*), wired (*Sl.*)
Antonyms calm, composed, laid-back (*Inf.*), nerveless, together (*Sl.*), unfazed (*Inf.*), unflustered

junction alliance, combination, connection, coupling, joint, juncture, linking, seam, union

juncture 1. conjuncture, contingency, crisis, crux, emergency, exigency, moment, occasion, point, predicament, strait, time 2. bond, connection, convergence, edge, intersection, junction, link, seam, weld

junior inferior, lesser, lower, minor, secondary, subordinate, younger
Antonyms elder, higher-ranking, older, senior, superior

junk clutter, debris, dreck (*Sl., chiefly U.S.*), leavings, litter, oddments, odds and ends, refuse, rubbish, rummage, scrap, trash, waste

junta assembly, cabal, camp, clique, combination, confederacy, convocation, coterie, council, crew, faction, gang, league, party, ring, schism, set

jurisdiction 1. authority, command, control, dominion, influence, power, prerogative, rule, say, sway 2. area, bounds, circuit, compass, district, dominion, field, orbit, province, range, scope, sphere, zone

just *adj.* 1. blameless, conscientious, decent, equitable, fair, fairminded, good, honest, honourable, impartial, lawful, pure, right, righteous, unbiased, upright, virtuous 2. accurate, correct, exact, faithful, normal, precise, proper, regular, sound, true 3. appropriate, apt, condign, deserved, due, fitting, justified, legitimate, merited, proper, reasonable, rightful, suitable, well-deserved ~*adv.* 4. absolutely, completely, entirely, exactly, perfectly, precisely 5. hardly, lately, only now, recently, scarcely 6. at most, but, merely, no more than, nothing but, only, simply, solely
Antonyms *adj.* corrupt, devious, dishonest, inappropriate, inequitable, prejudiced, undeserved, unfair, unfit, unjust, unlawful, unreasonable, untrue

just about all but, almost, around, close to, nearly, not quite, practically, well-nigh

justice 1. equity, fairness, honesty, impartiality, integrity, justness, law, legality, legitimacy, reasonableness, rectitude, right 2. amends, compensation, correction, penalty, recompense, redress, reparation 3. judge, magistrate
Antonyms dishonesty, favouritism, inequity, injustice, partiality, unfairness, unlawfulness, unreasonableness, untruth, wrong

justifiable acceptable, defensible, excusable, fit, lawful, legitimate, proper, reasonable, right, sound, tenable, understandable, valid, vindicable, warrantable, well-founded
Antonyms arbitrary, capricious, indefensible, inexcusable, unreasonable, unwarranted

justification 1. absolution, apology, approval, defence, exculpation, excuse, exoneration, explanation, extenuation, plea, rationalization, vindication 2. basis, defence, grounds, plea, reason, warrant

justify absolve, acquit, approve, confirm, defend, establish, exculpate, excuse, exonerate, explain, legalize, legitimize, maintain, substantiate, support, sustain, uphold, validate, vindicate, warrant

justly accurately, correctly, equally, equitably, fairly, honestly, impartially, lawfully, properly

jut bulge, extend, impend, overhang, poke, project, protrude, stick out

juvenile 1. *n.* adolescent, boy, child, girl, infant, minor, youth 2. *adj.* babyish, boyish, callow, childish, girlish, immature, inexperienced, infantile, jejune, puerile, undeveloped, unsophisticated, young, youthful
Antonyms *n.* adult, grown-up ~*adj.* adult, grown-up, mature, responsible

juxtaposition adjacency, closeness, contact, contiguity, nearness, propinquity, proximity, vicinity

K

kaleidoscopic 1. changeable, fluctuating, fluid, many-coloured, mobile, motley, mutable, unstable, variegated 2. complex, complicated, confused, convoluted, disordered, intricate, jumbled, varied

kamikaze *adj.* foolhardy, self-destructive, suicidal

kaput broken, dead, defunct, destroyed, extinct, finished, ruined, undone, wrecked

keel over black out (*Inf.*), capsize, collapse, faint, founder, overturn, pass out, swoon (*Literary*), topple over, upset

keen[1] 1. ardent, avid, devoted to, eager, earnest, ebullient, enthusiastic, fervid, fierce, fond of, impassioned, intense, into (*Inf.*), zealous 2. acid, acute, biting, caustic, cutting, edged, finely honed, incisive, penetrating, piercing, pointed, razorlike, sardonic, satirical, sharp, tart, trenchant, vitriolic 3. astute, brilliant, canny, clever, discerning, discriminating, perceptive, perspicacious, quick, sagacious, sapient, sensitive, shrewd, wise
Antonyms (*sense 1*) apathetic, half-hearted, indifferent, laodicean, lukewarm, unenthusiastic, uninterested (*sense 2*) blunt, dull (*sense 3*) dull, obtuse, unperceptive

keen[2] 1. *v.* bewail, grieve, lament, mourn, wail, weep 2. *n.* coronach (*Scot. & Irish*), dirge, lament, lamentation, mourning, wailing, weeping

keenness 1. ardour, avidity, avidness, diligence, eagerness, earnestness, ebullience, enthusiasm, fervour, impatience, intensity, passion, zeal, zest 2. acerbity, harshness, incisiveness, mordancy, penetration, pungency, rigour, severity, sharpness, sternness, trenchancy, unkindness, virulence 3. astuteness, canniness, cleverness, discernment, insight, sagacity, sapience, sensitivity, shrewdness, wisdom

keep *v.* 1. conserve, control, hold, maintain, possess, preserve, retain 2. accumulate, amass, carry, deal in, deposit, furnish, garner, heap, hold, pile, place, stack, stock, store, trade in 3. care for, defend, guard, look after, maintain, manage, mind, operate, protect, safeguard, shelter, shield, tend, watch over 4. board, feed, foster, maintain, nourish, nurture, provide for, provision, subsidize, support, sustain, victual 5. accompany, associate with, consort with, fraternize with 6. arrest, block, check, constrain, control, curb, delay, detain, deter, hamper, hamstring, hinder, hold, hold back, impede, inhibit, keep back, limit, obstruct, prevent, restrain, retard, shackle, stall, withhold 7. adhere to, celebrate, commemorate, comply with, fulfil, hold, honour, obey, observe, perform, respect, ritualize, solemnize ~*n.* 8. board, food, livelihood, living, maintenance, means, nourishment, subsistence, support 9. castle, citadel, donjon, dungeon, fastness, stronghold, tower
Antonyms abandon, discard, disregard, expedite, free, give up, ignore, liberate, lose, release, speed

keep at be steadfast, carry on, complete, continue, drudge, endure, finish, grind, labour, last, maintain, persevere, persist, remain, slave, stay, stick, toil

keep back 1. check, constrain, control, curb, delay, hold back, limit, prohibit, restrain, restrict, retard, withhold 2. censor, conceal, hide, reserve, suppress, withhold

keeper attendant, caretaker, curator, custodian, defender, gaoler, governor, guard, guardian, jailer, overseer, preserver, steward, superintendent, warden, warder

keeping 1. aegis, auspices, care, charge, custody, guardianship, keep, maintenance, patronage, possession, protection, safekeeping, trust 2. accord, agreement, balance, compliance, conformity, congruity, consistency, correspondence, harmony, observance, proportion

keep on carry on, continue, endure, last, persevere, persist, prolong, remain

keepsake emblem, favour, memento, relic, remembrance, reminder, souvenir, symbol, token

keep up balance, compete, contend, continue, emulate, keep pace, maintain, match, persevere, preserve, rival, sustain, vie

keg barrel, cask, drum, firkin, hogshead, tun, vat

ken 1. compass, field, range, scope, sight, view, vision 2. acquaintance, awareness, cognisance, comprehension, knowledge, notice, understanding

kerchief babushka, headscarf, headsquare, scarf, square

kernel core, essence, germ, gist, grain, marrow, nub, pith, seed, substance

key *n.* 1. latchkey, opener 2. *Fig.* answer, clue, cue, explanation, guide, indicator, interpretation, lead, means, pointer, sign, solution, translation ~*adj.* 3. basic, chief, crucial, decisive, essential, fundamental, important, leading, main, major, pivotal, principal
Antonyms (*sense 3*) minor, secondary, subsidiary, superficial

key in enter, input, keyboard, type

keynote centre, core, essence, gist, heart, kernel, marrow, pith, substance, theme

keystone basis, core, cornerstone, crux, fundament, ground, linchpin, mainspring, motive, principle, quoin, root, source, spring

kick *v.* 1. boot, punt 2. *Fig.* complain, gripe (*Inf.*), grumble, object, oppose, protest, rebel, resist, spurn 3. *Inf.* abandon, desist from, give up, leave off, quit, stop ~*n.* 4. force, intensity, pep, power, punch, pungency, snap (*Inf.*), sparkle, strength, tang, verve, vitality, zest 5. buzz (*Sl.*), enjoyment, excitement, fun, gratification, jollies (*Sl.*), pleasure, stimulation, thrill

kickback bribe, cut (*Inf.*), gift, graft (*Inf.*), payment, payoff, recompense, reward, share, sop, sweetener (*Sl.*)

kickoff *n.* beginning, commencement, opening, outset, start

kick off *v.* begin, commence, get under way, initiate, kick-start, open, start

kick out discharge, dismiss, eject, evict, expel, kiss off (*Sl., chiefly U.S. & Canad.*), get rid of, give the bum's rush (*Sl.*), oust, reject, remove, sack (*Inf.*), show one the door, throw out on one's ear (*Inf.*), toss out

kid 1. *n.* ankle-biter (*Aust. sl.*), baby, bairn, boy, child, girl, infant, lad, lass, little one, rug rat (*Sl.*), sprog (*Sl.*), stripling, teenager, tot, youngster, youth 2. *v.* bamboozle, beguile, cozen, delude, fool, gull (*Archaic*), hoax, hoodwink, jest, joke, mock, plague, pretend, rag (*Brit.*), ridicule, tease, trick, wind up (*Brit. sl.*)

kidnap abduct, capture, hijack, hold to ransom, remove, seize, steal

kill 1. annihilate, assassinate, blow away (*Sl., chiefly U.S.*), bump off (*Sl.*), butcher, destroy, dispatch, do away with, do in (*Sl.*), eradicate, execute, exterminate, extirpate, knock off (*Sl.*), liquidate, massacre, murder, neutralize, obliterate, slaughter, slay, take out (*Sl.*), take (someone's) life, waste (*Inf.*) 2. *Fig.* cancel, cease, deaden, defeat, extinguish, halt, quash, quell, ruin, scotch, smother, stifle, still, stop, suppress, veto

killer assassin, butcher, cutthroat, destroyer, executioner, exterminator, gunman, hit man (*Sl.*), liquidator, murderer, slaughterer, slayer

killing *n.* 1. bloodshed, carnage, execution, extermination, fatality, homicide, manslaughter, massacre, murder, slaughter, slaying 2. *Inf.* bomb (*Sl.*), bonanza, cleanup (*Inf.*), coup, gain, profit, success, windfall ~*adj.* 3. deadly, death-dealing, deathly, fatal, lethal, mortal, murderous 4. *Inf.* debilitating, enervating, exhausting, fatiguing, punishing, tiring 5. *Inf.* absurd, amusing, comical, hilarious, ludicrous, uproarious

kill-joy dampener, damper, spoilsport, wet blanket (*Inf.*)

kin *n.* 1. affinity, blood, connection, consanguinity, extraction, kinship, lineage, relationship, stock 2. connections, family, kindred, kinsfolk, kinsmen, kith, people, relations, relatives ~*adj.* 3. akin, allied, close, cognate, consanguine, consanguineous, kindred, near, related

kind[1] 1. *n.* brand, breed, class, family, genus, ilk, race, set, sort, species, stamp, variety 2. character, description, essence, habit, manner, mould, nature, persuasion, sort, style, temperament, type

kind[2] *adj.* affectionate, amiable, amicable, beneficent, benevolent, benign, bounteous, charitable, clement, compassionate, congenial, considerate, cordial, courteous, friendly, generous, gentle, good, gracious, humane, indulgent, kind-hearted, kindly, lenient, loving, mild, neighbourly, obliging, philanthropic, propitious, sympathetic, tender-hearted, thoughtful, understanding
Antonyms cruel, hard-hearted, harsh, heartless, merciless, severe, unkind, unsympathetic, vicious

kind-hearted altruistic, amicable, compassionate, considerate, generous, good-natured, gracious, helpful, humane, kind, sympathetic, tender-hearted
Antonyms cold, cold-hearted, cruel, hard-hearted, harsh, heartless, selfish, severe, unkind, unsympathetic

kindle 1. fire, ignite, inflame, light, set fire to 2. *Fig.* agitate, animate, arouse, awaken, bestir, enkindle, exasperate, excite, foment, incite, induce, inflame, inspire, provoke, rouse, sharpen, stimulate, stir, thrill
Antonyms douse, extinguish, quell, quench

kindliness amiability, beneficence, benevolence, benignity, charity, compassion, friendliness, gentleness, humanity, kind-heartedness, kindness, sympathy

kindly 1. *adj.* affable, beneficial, benevolent, benign, compassionate, cordial, favourable, genial, gentle, good-natured, hearty, helpful, kind, mild, pleasant, polite, sympathetic, warm 2. *adv.* agreeably, cordially, graciously, politely, tenderly, thoughtfully
Antonyms *adj.* cruel, harsh, malevolent, malicious, mean, severe, spiteful, unkindly, unsympathetic ~*adv.* cruelly, harshly, malevolently, maliciously, meanly, spitefully, unkindly, unsympathetically

kindness 1. affection, amiability, beneficence, benevolence, charity, clemency, compassion, decency, fellow-feeling, generosity, gentleness, goodness, good will, grace, hospitality, humanity, indulgence, kindliness, magnanimity, patience, philanthropy, tenderness, tolerance, understanding 2. aid, assistance, benefaction, bounty, favour, generosity, good deed, help, service
Antonyms (*sense 1*) animosity, callousness, cold-heartedness, cruelty, hard-heartedness, heartlessness, ill will, inhumanity, malevolence, malice, misanthropy, viciousness

kindred *n.* 1. affinity, consanguinity, relationship 2. connections, family, flesh, kin, kinsfolk, kinsmen, lineage, relations, relatives ~*adj.* 3. affiliated, akin, allied, cognate, congenial, corresponding, kin, like, matching, related, similar

king crowned head, emperor, majesty, monarch, overlord, prince, ruler, sovereign

kingdom 1. dominion, dynasty, empire, monarchy, realm, reign, sovereignty 2. commonwealth, county, division, nation, province, state, territory, tract 3. area, domain, field, province, sphere, territory

kingly 1. imperial, monarchical, regal, royal, sovereign 2. august, glorious, grand, grandiose, imposing, majestic, noble, splendid, stately

kink 1. bend, coil, corkscrew, crimp, entanglement, frizz, knot, tangle, twist, wrinkle 2. cramp, crick, pang, pinch, spasm, stab, tweak, twinge 3. complication, defect, difficulty, flaw, hitch, imperfection, knot, tangle 4. crotchet, eccentricity, fetish, foible, idiosyncrasy, quirk, singularity, vagary, whim

kinky 1. bizarre, eccentric, odd, oddball (*Inf.*), off-the-wall (*Sl.*), outlandish, outré, peculiar, queer, quirky, strange, unconventional, wacko (*Sl.*), weird 2. degenerated, depraved, deviant, licentious, perverted, pervy (*Sl.*), unnatural, warped 3. coiled, crimped, curled, curly, frizzled, frizzy, tangled, twisted

kinsfolk connections, family, kin, kindred, kinsmen, relations, relatives

kinship 1. blood relationship, consanguinity, kin, relation, ties of blood 2. affinity, alliance, association, bearing, connection, correspondence, relationship, similarity

kinsman blood relative, fellow clansman, fellow tribesman, relation, relative

kiosk bookstall, booth, counter, newsstand, stall, stand

kismet destiny, fate, fortune, karma, lot, portion, preordination, Providence

kiss *v.* 1. buss (*Archaic*), canoodle (*Sl.*), greet, neck (*Inf.*), osculate, peck (*Inf.*), salute, smooch (*Inf.*) 2. brush, caress, glance, graze, scrape, touch ~*n.* 3. buss (*Archaic*), osculation, peck (*Inf.*), smacker (*Sl.*)

kit accoutrements, apparatus, effects, equipment, gear, impedimenta, implements, instruments, outfit, paraphernalia, provisions, rig, supplies, tackle, tools, trappings, utensils

kitchen cookhouse, galley, kitchenette

kit out *or* **up** accoutre, arm, deck out, equip, fit out, fix up, furnish, outfit, provide with, supply

kittenish coquettish, coy, flirtatious, frisky, frolicsome, funloving, playful, sportive

knack ability, adroitness, aptitude, bent, capacity, dexterity, expertise, expertness, facility, flair, forte, genius, gift, handiness, ingenuity, propensity, quickness, skilfulness, skill, talent, trick
Antonyms awkwardness, clumsiness, disability, ineptitude

knave blackguard, bounder (*Old-fashioned Brit. sl.*), cheat, cocksucker (*Taboo sl.*), rapscallion, rascal, reprobate, rogue, rotter (*Sl., chiefly Brit.*), scally (*Northwest English dialect*), scallywag (*Inf.*), scamp, scapegrace, scoundrel, scumbag (*Sl.*), swindler, varlet (*Archaic*), villain

knavery chicanery, corruption, deceit, deception, dishonesty, double-dealing, duplicity, fraud, imposture, rascality, roguery, trickery, villainy

knavish deceitful, deceptive, dishonest, dishonourable, fraudulent, lying, rascally, roguish, scoundrelly, tricky, unprincipled, unscrupulous, villainous
Antonyms honest, honourable, noble, principled, trustworthy

knead blend, form, manipulate, massage, mould, press, rub, shape, squeeze, stroke, work

kneel bow, bow down, curtsey, curtsy, genuflect, get down on one's knees, kowtow, make obeisance, stoop

knell 1. *v.* announce, chime, herald, peal,

resound, ring, sound, toll 2. *n.* chime, peal, ringing, sound, toll

knickers bloomers, briefs, drawers, panties, smalls, underwear

knick-knack bagatelle, bauble, bibelot, bric-a-brac, gewgaw, gimcrack, kickshaw, plaything, trifle, trinket

knife 1. *n.* blade, cutter, cutting tool 2. *v.* cut, impale, lacerate, pierce, slash, stab, wound

knightly chivalrous, courageous, courtly, gallant, gracious, heroic, noble, valiant

knit 1. affix, ally, bind, connect, contract, fasten, heal, interlace, intertwine, join, link, loop, mend, secure, tie, unite, weave 2. crease, furrow, knot, wrinkle, pucker

knob boss, bulk, bump, bunch, hump, knot, knurl, lump, nub, projection, protrusion, protuberance, snag, stud, swell, swelling, tumour

knock *v.* 1. belt (*Inf.*), buffet, chin (*Sl.*), clap, cuff, deck (*Sl.*), hit, lay one on (*Sl.*), punch, rap, slap, smack, smite (*Archaic*), strike, thump, thwack ~*n.* 2. belt (*Inf.*), blow, box, clip, clout (*Inf.*), cuff, hammering, rap, slap, smack, thump ~*v.* 3. *Inf.* abuse, asperse, belittle, carp, cavil, censure, condemn, criticize, deprecate, disparage, find fault, lambast(e), run down, slag (off) (*Sl.*), slam (*Sl.*) ~*n.* 4. blame, censure, condemnation, criticism, defeat, failure, heat (*Sl., chiefly U.S. & Canad.*), rebuff, rejection, reversal, setback, slagging (off) (*Sl.*), stick (*Sl.*), stricture

knock about *or* **around** 1. ramble, range, roam, rove, traipse, travel, wander 2. abuse, batter, beat up (*Inf.*), bruise, buffet, clobber (*Sl.*), damage, hit, hurt, lambast(e), maltreat, manhandle, maul, mistreat, strike, wound

knock down batter, clout (*Inf.*), demolish, destroy, fell, floor, level, pound, raze, smash, wallop (*Inf.*), wreck

knock off 1. clock off, clock out, complete, conclude, finish, stop work, terminate 2. blag (*Sl.*), cabbage (*Brit. sl.*), filch, nick (*Sl., chiefly Brit.*), pilfer, pinch, purloin, rob, steal, thieve 3. assassinate, blow away (*Sl., chiefly U.S.*), bump off (*Sl.*), do away with, do in (*Sl.*), kill, liquidate, murder, slay, take out (*Sl.*), waste (*Inf.*)

knockout 1. *coup de grâce,* kayo (*Sl.*), KO *or* K.O. (*Sl.*) 2. hit, sensation, smash, smash-hit, stunner (*Inf.*), success, triumph, winner

Antonyms (*sense 2*) failure, flop (*Inf.*), turkey (*Inf.*)

knoll barrow, hill, hillock, hummock, mound, swell

knot *v.* 1. bind, complicate, entangle, knit, loop, secure, tether, tie, weave ~*n.* 2. bond, bow, braid, connection, joint, ligature, loop, rosette, tie 3. aggregation, bunch, clump, cluster, collection, heap, mass, pile, tuft 4. assemblage, band, circle, clique, company, crew (*Inf.*), crowd, gang, group, mob, pack, set, squad

knotty 1. bumpy, gnarled, knobby, knotted, nodular, rough, rugged 2. baffling, complex, complicated, difficult, hard, intricate, mystifying, perplexing, problematical, puzzling, thorny, tricky, troublesome

know 1. apprehend, comprehend, experience, fathom, feel certain, ken (*Scot.*), learn, notice, perceive, realize, recognize, see, undergo, understand 2. associate with, be acquainted with, be familiar with, fraternize with, have dealings with, have knowledge of, recognize 3. differentiate, discern, distinguish, identify, make out, perceive, recognize, see, tell

Antonyms be ignorant, be unfamiliar with, misunderstand

know-how ability, adroitness, aptitude, capability, craft, dexterity, experience, expertise, faculty, flair, ingenuity, knack, knowledge, proficiency, savoir-faire, skill, talent

knowing 1. astute, clever, clued-up (*Inf.*), competent, discerning, experienced, expert, intelligent, qualified, skilful, well-informed 2. acute, cunning, eloquent, expressive, meaningful, perceptive, sagacious, shrewd, significant 3. aware, conscious, deliberate, intended, intentional

Antonyms accidental, ignorant, ingenuous, naive, obtuse, unintentional

knowingly consciously, deliberately, intentionally, on purpose, purposely, wilfully, wittingly

knowledge 1. education, enlightenment, erudition, instruction, intelligence, learning, scholarship, schooling, science, tuition, wisdom 2. ability, apprehension, cognition, comprehension, consciousness, discernment, grasp, judgment, recognition, understanding 3. acquaintance, cognizance, familiarity, information, intimacy, notice

Antonyms ignorance, illiteracy, misunderstanding, unawareness, unfamiliarity

knowledgeable 1. acquainted, *au courant, au fait,* aware, clued-up (*Inf.*), cognizant, conscious, conversant, experienced, familiar, in the know (*Inf.*), understanding, well-informed 2. educated, erudite, intelligent, learned, lettered, scholarly

known acknowledged, admitted, avowed, celebrated, common, confessed, familiar, famous, manifest, noted, obvious, patent, plain, popular, published, recognized, well-known

Antonyms closet (*Inf.*), concealed, hidden, secret, unfamiliar, unknown, unrecognized, unrevealed

knuckle under *v.* accede, acquiesce, capitulate, give in, give way, submit, succumb, surrender, yield

Antonyms be defiant, hold out (against), kick up (a fuss *or* stink), rebel, resist

knurl bulb, bulge, burl, gnarl, knot, lump, node, protuberance, ridge

kowtow **1.** bow, genuflect, kneel **2.** brown-nose (*Taboo sl.*), court, cringe, fawn, flatter, grovel, kiss (someone's) ass (*U.S. & Canad. taboo sl.*), pander to, suck up to (*Sl.*), toady, truckle

kudos acclaim, applause, distinction, esteem, fame, glory, honour, laudation, notability, plaudits, praise, prestige, regard, renown, repute

L

label *n.* 1. docket (*Chiefly Brit.*), flag, marker, sticker, tag, tally, ticket 2. characterization, classification, description, epithet 3. brand, company, mark, trademark ~*v.* 4. docket (*Chiefly Brit.*), flag, mark, stamp, sticker, tag, tally 5. brand, call, characterize, class, classify, define, describe, designate, identify, name

laborious 1. arduous, backbreaking, burdensome, difficult, exhausting, fatiguing, hard, herculean, onerous, strenuous, tiresome, tiring, toilsome, tough, uphill, wearing, wearisome 2. assiduous, diligent, hard-working, indefatigable, industrious, painstaking, persevering, sedulous, tireless, unflagging 3. *Of literary style, etc.* forced, laboured, not fluent, ponderous, strained
Antonyms easy, easy-peasy (*Sl.*), effortless, light, natural, simple

labour *n.* 1. industry, toil, work 2. employees, hands, labourers, workers, work force, workmen 3. donkey-work, drudgery, effort, exertion, grind (*Inf.*), industry, pains, painstaking, sweat (*Inf.*), toil, travail 4. chore, job, task, undertaking 5. childbirth, contractions, delivery, labour pains, pains, parturition, throes, travail ~*v.* 6. drudge, endeavour, grind (*Inf.*), peg along *or* away (*Chiefly Brit.*), plod, plug along *or* away (*Inf.*), slave, strive, struggle, sweat (*Inf.*), toil, travail, work 7. *Usually with* **under** be a victim of, be burdened by, be disadvantaged, suffer 8. dwell on, elaborate, make a federal case of (*U.S. inf.*), make a production (out) of (*Inf.*), overdo, overemphasize, strain 9. *Of a ship* heave, pitch, roll, toss
Antonyms *n.* ease, idleness, leisure, relaxation, repose, respite, rest ~*v.* relax, rest

laboured 1. awkward, difficult, forced, heavy, stiff, strained 2. affected, contrived, overdone, overwrought, ponderous, studied, unnatural

labourer blue-collar worker, drudge, hand, labouring man, manual worker, navvy (*Brit. inf.*), unskilled worker, worker, working man, workman

labyrinth coil, complexity, complication, convolution, entanglement, intricacy, jungle, knotty problem, maze, perplexity, puzzle, riddle, snarl, tangle, windings

labyrinthine Byzantine, complex, confused, convoluted, Daedalian, Gordian, intricate, involved, knotty, mazelike, mazy, perplexing, puzzling, tangled, tortuous, winding

lace *n.* 1. filigree, netting, openwork, tatting 2. bootlace, cord, shoelace, string, thong, tie ~*v.* 3. attach, bind, close, do up, fasten, intertwine, interweave, thread, tie, twine 4. add to, fortify, mix in, spike

lace into assail, attack, belabour, berate, castigate, flay, lay into (*Inf.*), light into (*Inf.*), set about, vituperate

lacerate 1. claw, cut, gash, jag, maim, mangle, rend, rip, slash, tear, wound 2. *Fig.* afflict, distress, harrow, rend, torment, torture, wound

laceration cut, gash, injury, mutilation, rent, rip, slash, tear, wound

lachrymose crying, dolorous, lugubrious, mournful, sad, tearful, weeping, weepy (*Inf.*), woeful

lack 1. *n.* absence, dearth, deficiency, deprivation, destitution, insufficiency, need, privation, scantiness, scarcity, shortage, shortcoming, shortness, want 2. *v.* be deficient in, be short of, be without, miss, need, require, want
Antonyms *n.* abundance, adequacy, excess, plentifulness, sufficiency, surplus ~*v.* enjoy, have, own, possess

lackadaisical 1. apathetic, dull, enervated, half-arsed, half-assed (*U.S. & Canad. sl.*), half-hearted, indifferent, languid, languorous, lethargic, limp, listless, spiritless 2. abstracted, dreamy, idle, indolent, inert, lazy
Antonyms ambitious, diligent, excited, inspired, spirited

lackey 1. ass-kisser (*U.S. & Canad. taboo sl.*), brown-noser (*Taboo sl.*), creature, fawner, flatterer, flunky, hanger-on, instrument, menial, minion, parasite, pawn, sycophant, toady, tool, yes man 2. attendant, flunky, footman, manservant, valet, varlet (*Archaic*)

lacking defective, deficient, flawed, impaired, inadequate, minus (*Inf.*), missing, needing, sans (*Archaic*), wanting, without

lacklustre boring, dim, drab, dry, dull, flat, leaden, lifeless, lustreless, muted, prosaic, sombre, unimaginative, uninspired, vapid

laconic brief, compact, concise, crisp, curt,

pithy, sententious, short, succinct, terse, to the point
Antonyms long-winded, loquacious, rambling, verbose, voluble, wordy

lacuna blank, break, gap, hiatus, omission, space, void

lacy delicate, filigree, fine, frilly, gauzy, gossamer, lacelike, meshy, netlike, open, sheer

lad boy, chap (*Inf.*), fellow, guy (*Inf.*), juvenile, kid (*Inf.*), laddie (*Scot.*), schoolboy, shaver (*Inf.*), stripling, youngster, youth

laden burdened, charged, encumbered, fraught, full, hampered, loaded, oppressed, taxed, weighed down, weighted

la-di-da affected, conceited, highfalutin (*Inf.*), mannered, mincing, overrefined, posh (*Inf., chiefly Brit.*), precious, pretentious, snobbish, snooty (*Inf.*), stuck-up (*Inf.*), toffee-nosed (*Sl., chiefly Brit.*), too-too

lady-killer Casanova, Don Juan, heartbreaker, ladies' man, libertine, Lothario, philanderer, rake, roué, wolf (*Inf.*), womanizer

ladylike courtly, cultured, decorous, elegant, genteel, modest, polite, proper, refined, respectable, well-bred
Antonyms discourteous, ill-bred, ill-mannered, impolite, rude, uncultured, unladylike, unmannerly, unrefined

lag 1. be behind, dawdle, delay, drag (behind), drag one's feet (*Inf.*), hang back, idle, linger, loiter, saunter, straggle, tarry, trail 2. decrease, diminish, ebb, fail, fall off, flag, lose strength, slacken, wane

laggard dawdler, idler, lingerer, loafer, loiterer, lounger, saunterer, skiver (*Brit. sl.*), slowcoach (*Brit. inf.*), slowpoke (*U.S. & Canad. inf.*), sluggard, snail, straggler

laid-back at ease, casual, easy-going, easy-oasy (*Sl.*), free and easy, relaxed, together (*Sl.*), unflappable (*Inf.*), unhurried
Antonyms edgy, jittery (*Inf.*), jumpy, keyed-up, nervous, on edge, tense, twitchy (*Inf.*), uptight (*Inf.*), wound-up (*Inf.*)

laid up bedridden, disabled, housebound, ill, immobilized, incapacitated, injured, on the sick list, out of action (*Inf.*), sick

lair 1. burrow, den, earth, form, hole, nest, resting place 2. *Inf.* den, hide-out, refuge, retreat, sanctuary

laissez faire *n.* free enterprise, free trade, individualism, live and let live, nonintervention

lam batter, beat, hit, knock, lambast(e), pelt, pound, strike, thrash

lambast(e) 1. beat, bludgeon, cosh (*Brit.*), cudgel, drub, flog, strike, thrash, whip 2. bawl out (*Inf.*), berate, carpet (*Inf.*), castigate, censure, chew out (*U.S. & Canad. inf.*), excoriate, flay, give a rocket (*Brit. & N.Z. inf.*), read the riot act, rebuke, reprimand, scold, tear into (*Inf.*), tear (someone) off a strip (*Brit. inf.*), upbraid

lambent 1. dancing, flickering, fluttering, licking, touching, twinkling 2. gleaming, glistening, glowing, luminous, lustrous, radiant, refulgent, shimmering 3. *Of wit or humour* brilliant, light, sparkling

lamblike 1. gentle, meek, mild, passive, peaceable, submissive 2. artless, childlike, guileless, innocent, naive, simple, trusting

lame 1. crippled, defective, disabled, game, halt (*Archaic*), handicapped, hobbling, limping 2. *Fig.* feeble, flimsy, inadequate, insufficient, pathetic, poor, thin, unconvincing, unsatisfactory, weak

lament *v.* 1. bemoan, bewail, complain, deplore, grieve, mourn, regret, sorrow, wail, weep ~*n.* 2. complaint, keening, lamentation, moan, moaning, plaint, ululation, wail, wailing 3. coronach (*Scot. & Irish*), dirge, elegy, monody, requiem, threnody

lamentable 1. deplorable, distressing, grievous, harrowing, mournful, regrettable, sorrowful, tragic, unfortunate, woeful 2. low, meagre, mean, miserable, pitiful, poor, unsatisfactory, wretched

lamentation dirge, grief, grieving, keening, lament, moan, mourning, plaint, sobbing, sorrow, ululation, wailing, weeping

laminate 1. coat, cover, face, foliate, layer, stratify, veneer 2. exfoliate, flake, separate, split

lampoon 1. *n.* burlesque, caricature, parody, pasquinade, satire, send-up (*Brit. inf.*), skit, squib, takeoff (*Inf.*) 2. *v.* burlesque, caricature, make fun of, mock, parody, pasquinade, ridicule, satirize, send up (*Brit. inf.*), squib, take off (*Inf.*)

land *n.* 1. dry land, earth, ground, terra firma 2. dirt, ground, loam, soil 3. countryside, farming, farmland, rural districts 4. acres, estate, grounds, property, real property, realty 5. country, district, fatherland, motherland, nation, province, region, territory, tract ~*v.* 6. alight, arrive, berth, come to rest, debark, disembark, dock, touch down 7. *Sometimes with* **up** arrive, bring, carry, cause, end up, lead, turn up, wind up 8. *Inf.* acquire, gain, get, obtain, score (*Sl.*), secure, win

landlord 1. host, hotelier, hotel-keeper, innkeeper 2. freeholder, lessor, owner, proprietor

landmark 1. feature, monument 2. crisis, milestone, turning point, watershed 3. benchmark, boundary, cairn, milepost, signpost

landscape countryside, outlook, panorama, prospect, scene, scenery, view, vista

landslide 1. *n.* avalanche, landslip, rockfall 2. *adj.* decisive, overwhelming, runaway

language 1. communication, conversation, discourse, expression, interchange, parlance, speech, talk, utterance, verbalization, vocalization 2. argot, cant, dialect, idiom, jargon, lingo (*Inf.*), lingua franca, patois, speech, terminology, tongue, vernacular, vocabulary 3. diction, expression, phraseology, phrasing, style, wording

languid 1. drooping, faint, feeble, languorous, limp, pining, sickly, weak, weary 2. indifferent, lackadaisical, languorous, lazy, listless, spiritless, unenthusiastic, uninterested 3. dull, heavy, inactive, inert, lethargic, sluggish, torpid
Antonyms active, energetic, strong, tireless, vigorous

languish 1. decline, droop, fade, fail, faint, flag, sicken, waste, weaken, wilt, wither 2. *Often with* **for** desire, eat one's heart out over, hanker, hunger, long, pine, sigh, want, yearn 3. be abandoned, be disregarded, be neglected, rot, suffer, waste away 4. brood, despond, grieve, repine, sorrow
Antonyms bloom, flourish, prosper, thrive

languishing 1. declining, deteriorating, drooping, droopy, fading, failing, flagging, sickening, sinking, wasting away, weak, weakening, wilting, withering 2. dreamy, longing, lovelorn, lovesick, melancholic, nostalgic, pensive, pining, soulful, tender, wistful, woebegone, yearning

languor 1. apathy, debility, enervation, ennui, faintness, fatigue, feebleness, frailty, heaviness, inertia, lassitude, lethargy, listlessness, torpor, weakness, weariness 2. dreaminess, drowsiness, indolence, laziness, lotus-eating, relaxation, sleepiness, sloth 3. calm, hush, lull, oppressiveness, silence, stillness

lank 1. dull, lifeless, limp, long, lustreless, straggling 2. attenuated, emaciated, gaunt, lanky, lean, rawboned, scraggy, scrawny, skinny, slender, slim, spare, thin

lanky angular, bony, gangling, gaunt, loose-jointed, rangy, rawboned, scraggy, scrawny, spare, tall, thin, weedy (*Inf.*)
Antonyms brawny, burly, chubby, fat, muscular, plump, portly, rotund, rounded, short, sinewy, stocky, stout

lap[1] 1. *n.* circle, circuit, course, distance, loop, orbit, round, tour 2. *v.* cover, enfold, envelop, fold, swaddle, swathe, turn, twist, wrap

lap[2] 1. gurgle, plash, purl, ripple, slap, splash, swish, wash 2. drink, lick, sip, sup

lapse *n.* 1. error, failing, fault, indiscretion, mistake, negligence, omission, oversight, slip 2. break, gap, intermission, interruption, interval, lull, passage, pause 3. backsliding, decline, descent, deterioration, drop, fall, relapse ~*v.* 4. decline, degenerate, deteriorate, drop, fail, fall, sink, slide, slip 5. become obsolete, become void, end, expire, run out, stop, terminate

lapsed 1. discontinued, ended, expired, finished, invalid, out of date, run out, unrenewed 2. backsliding, lacking faith, nonpractising

larceny burglary, misappropriation, pilfering, purloining, robbery, stealing, theft

large 1. big, bulky, colossal, considerable, elephantine, enormous, giant, gigantic, ginormous (*Inf.*), goodly, great, huge, humongous *or* humungous (*U.S. sl.*), immense, jumbo (*Inf.*), king-size, man-size, massive, mega (*Sl.*), monumental, sizable, substantial, tidy (*Inf.*), vast 2. abundant, ample, broad, capacious, comprehensive, copious, extensive, full, generous, grand, grandiose, liberal, plentiful, roomy, spacious, sweeping, wide 3. **at large a.** at liberty, free, on the loose, on the run, roaming, unconfined **b.** as a whole, chiefly, generally, in general, in the main, mainly **c.** at length, considerably, exhaustively, greatly, in full detail
Antonyms brief, inconsiderable, infinitesimal, little, minute, narrow, petty, scanty, scarce, short, slender, slight, slim, small, sparse, thin, tiny, trivial

large-hearted big-hearted, compassionate, good, good-hearted, kind, kind-hearted, large-souled, magnanimous, sympathetic, understanding

largely as a rule, by and large, chiefly, considerably, extensively, generally, mainly, mostly, predominantly, primarily, principally, to a great extent, widely

large-scale broad, extensive, far-reaching, global, sweeping, vast, wholesale, wide, wide-ranging

largess, largesse 1. alms-giving, benefaction, bounty, charity, generosity, liberality, munificence, open-handedness, philanthropy 2. bequest, bounty, donation, endowment, gift, grant, present

lark 1. *n.* antic, caper, escapade, fling, frolic, fun, gambol, game, jape, mischief, prank, revel, rollick, romp, skylark, spree 2. *v.* caper, cavort, cut capers, frolic, gambol, have fun, make mischief, play, rollick, romp, sport

lascivious 1. horny (*Sl.*), lecherous, lewd, libidinous, licentious, lustful, prurient, randy (*Inf., chiefly Brit.*), salacious, sensual, unchaste, voluptuous, wanton 2.

bawdy, blue, coarse, crude, dirty, indecent, obscene, offensive, pornographic, ribald, scurrilous, smutty, suggestive, vulgar

lash[1] *n.* 1. blow, hit, stripe, stroke, swipe (*Inf.*) ~*v.* 2. beat, birch, chastise, flagellate, flog, horsewhip, lam (*Sl.*), lambast(e), scourge, thrash, whip 3. beat, buffet, dash, drum, hammer, hit, knock, lambast(e), larrup (*Dialect*), pound, punch, smack, strike 4. attack, belabour, berate, blast, castigate, censure, criticize, flay, lambast(e), lampoon, put down, ridicule, satirize, scold, tear into (*Inf.*), upbraid

lash[2] bind, fasten, join, make fast, rope, secure, strap, tie

lass bird (*Sl.*), chick (*Sl.*), colleen (*Irish*), damsel, girl, lassie (*Inf.*), maid, maiden, miss, schoolgirl, wench (*Facetious*), young woman

lassitude apathy, drowsiness, dullness, enervation, ennui, exhaustion, fatigue, heaviness, inertia, languor, lethargy, listlessness, prostration, sluggardliness, sluggishness, tiredness, torpor, weariness

last[1] *adj.* 1. aftermost, at the end, hindmost, rearmost 2. latest, most recent 3. closing, concluding, extreme, final, furthest, remotest, terminal, ultimate, utmost ~*adv.* 4. after, behind, bringing up the rear, in *or* at the end, in the rear ~*n.* 5. close, completion, conclusion, end, ending, finale, finish, termination 6. **at last** at length, eventually, finally, in conclusion, in the end, ultimately

Antonyms (*sense 1*) first, foremost, leading (*sense 3*) earliest, first, initial, introductory, opening

last[2] *v.* abide, carry on, continue, endure, hold on, hold out, keep, keep on, persist, remain, stand up, survive, wear

Antonyms cease, depart, die, end, expire, fade, fail, stop, terminate

last-ditch all-out (*Inf.*), desperate, final, frantic, heroic, straining, struggling

lasting abiding, continuing, deep-rooted, durable, enduring, eternal, indelible, lifelong, long-standing, long-term, perennial, permanent, perpetual, unceasing, undying, unending

Antonyms ephemeral, fleeting, momentary, passing, short-lived, transient, transitory

lastly after all, all in all, at last, finally, in conclusion, in the end, to conclude, to sum up, ultimately

last word, the 1. final say, finis, summation, ultimatum 2. best, cream, *crème de la crème,* crown, epitome, *ne plus ultra,* perfection, quintessence, ultimate 3. *dernier cri,* fashion, latest, newest, rage, vogue

latch 1. *n.* bar, bolt, catch, clamp, fastening, hasp, hook, lock, sneck (*Dialect*) 2. *v.* bar, bolt, fasten, lock, make fast, secure, sneck (*Dialect*)

late *adj.* 1. behind, behindhand, belated, delayed, last-minute, overdue, slow, tardy, unpunctual 2. advanced, fresh, modern, new, recent 3. dead, deceased, defunct, departed, ex-, former, old, past, preceding, previous ~*adv.* 4. at the last minute, behindhand, behind time, belatedly, dilatorily, slowly, tardily, unpunctually

Antonyms *adj.* (*sense 1*) beforehand, early, prompt, punctual, seasoned, timely (*sense 2*) old (*sense 3*) alive, existing ~*adv.* beforehand, early, in advance

lately in recent times, just now, latterly, not long ago, of late, recently

lateness advanced hour, belatedness, delay, late date, retardation, tardiness, unpunctuality

latent concealed, dormant, hidden, inherent, invisible, lurking, potential, quiescent, secret, undeveloped, unexpressed, unrealized, unseen, veiled

Antonyms apparent, conspicuous, developed, evident, expressed, manifest, obvious, realized

later *adv.* after, afterwards, by and by, in a while, in time, later on, next, subsequently, thereafter

lateral edgeways, flanking, side, sideward, sideways

latest *adj.* current, fashionable, happening (*Inf.*), in, modern, most recent, newest, now, up-to-date, up-to-the-minute, with it (*Inf.*)

lather *n.* 1. bubbles, foam, froth, soap, soapsuds, suds 2. *Inf.* dither (*Chiefly Brit.*), fever, flap (*Inf.*), fluster, fuss, pother, state (*Inf.*), stew (*Inf.*), sweat, tizzy (*Inf.*), twitter (*Inf.*) ~*v.* 3. foam, froth, soap 4. *Inf.* beat, cane, drub, flog, lambast(e), strike, thrash, whip

lathery bubbly, foamy, frothy, soapy, sudsy

latitude 1. breadth, compass, extent, range, reach, room, scope, space, span, spread, sweep, width 2. elbowroom, freedom, indulgence, laxity, leeway, liberty, licence, play, unrestrictedness

latter closing, concluding, last, last-mentioned, later, latest, modern, recent, second

Antonyms antecedent, earlier, foregoing, former, preceding, previous, prior

latterly hitherto, lately, of late, recently

lattice fretwork, grating, grid, grille, latticework, mesh, network, openwork, reticulation, tracery, trellis, web

laud acclaim, approve, celebrate, crack up (*Inf.*), extol, glorify, honour, magnify (*Archaic*), praise, sing *or* sound the praises of

laudable admirable, commendable, creditable, estimable, excellent, meritorious, of note, praiseworthy, worthy
Antonyms base, blameworthy, contemptible, ignoble, lowly, unworthy

laudatory acclamatory, adulatory, approbatory, approving, commendatory, complimentary, eulogistic, panegyrical

laugh *v.* 1. be convulsed (*Inf.*), be in stitches, bust a gut (*Inf.*), chortle, chuckle, crack up (*Inf.*), crease up (*Inf.*), giggle, guffaw, roar with laughter, snigger, split one's sides, titter 2. **laugh at** belittle, deride, jeer, lampoon, make a mock of, make fun of, mock, ridicule, scoff at, take the mickey (out of) (*Inf.*), taunt ~*n.* 3. belly laugh (*Inf.*), chortle, chuckle, giggle, guffaw, roar *or* shriek of laughter, snigger, titter 4. *Inf.* card (*Inf.*), caution (*Inf.*), clown, comedian, comic, entertainer, hoot (*Inf.*), humorist, joke, lark, scream (*Inf.*), wag, wit

laughable 1. absurd, derisive, derisory, ludicrous, nonsensical, preposterous, ridiculous, worthy of scorn 2. amusing, comical, diverting, droll, farcical, funny, hilarious, humorous, mirthful, risible

laughing stock Aunt Sally (*Brit.*), butt, everybody's fool, fair game, figure of fun, target, victim

laugh off brush aside, dismiss, disregard, ignore, minimize, pooh-pooh, shrug off

laughter 1. cachinnation, chortling, chuckling, giggling, guffawing, laughing, tittering 2. amusement, glee, hilarity, merriment, mirth

launch 1. cast, discharge, dispatch, fire, project, propel, send off, set afloat, set in motion, throw 2. begin, commence, embark upon, inaugurate, initiate, instigate, introduce, open, start

laurels acclaim, awards, bays, Brownie points, commendation, credit, distinction, fame, glory, honour, kudos, praise, prestige, recognition, renown, reward

lavatory bathroom, bog (*Sl.*), can (*U.S. & Canad. sl.*), cloakroom (*Brit.*), crapper (*Taboo sl.*), Gents, head(s) (*Nautical sl.*), john (*Sl., chiefly U.S. & Canad.*), khazi (*Sl.*), Ladies, latrine, little boy's room (*Inf.*), little girl's room (*Inf.*), loo (*Brit. inf.*), *pissoir*, powder room, (public) convenience, toilet, washroom, water closet, W.C.

lavish *adj.* 1. abundant, copious, exuberant, lush, luxuriant, opulent, plentiful, profuse, prolific, sumptuous 2. bountiful, effusive, free, generous, liberal, munificent, open-handed, unstinting 3. exaggerated, excessive, extravagant, immoderate, improvident, intemperate, prodigal, thriftless, unreasonable, unrestrained, wasteful, wild ~*v.* 4. deluge, dissipate, expend, heap, pour, shower, spend, squander, waste
Antonyms *adj.* cheap, frugal, meagre, miserly, parsimonious, scanty, sparing, stingy, thrifty, tight-fisted ~*v.* begrudge, economize, stint, withhold

law 1. charter, code, constitution, jurisprudence 2. act, canon, code, command, commandment, covenant, decree, demand, edict, enactment, order, ordinance, rule, statute 3. axiom, canon, criterion, formula, precept, principle, regulation, standard 4. **lay down the law** dictate, dogmatize, emphasize, pontificate

law-abiding compliant, dutiful, good, honest, honourable, lawful, obedient, orderly, peaceable, peaceful

lawbreaker convict, criminal, crook (*Inf.*), culprit, delinquent, felon (*Formerly criminal law*), miscreant, offender, sinner, transgressor, trespasser, violater, villain, wrongdoer

lawful allowable, authorized, constitutional, just, legal, legalized, legitimate, licit, permissible, proper, rightful, valid, warranted
Antonyms banned, forbidden, illegal, illegitimate, illicit, prohibited, unauthorized, unlawful

lawless anarchic, chaotic, disorderly, insubordinate, insurgent, mutinous, rebellious, reckless, riotous, seditious, ungoverned, unrestrained, unruly, wild
Antonyms civilized, compliant, disciplined, law-abiding, lawful, legitimate, licit, obedient, orderly, regimented, restrained, well-governed

lawlessness anarchy, chaos, disorder, mobocracy, mob rule, ochlocracy, reign of terror

lawsuit action, argument, case, cause, contest, dispute, industrial tribunal, litigation, proceedings, prosecution, suit, trial

lawyer advocate, attorney, barrister, counsel, counsellor, legal adviser, solicitor

lax 1. careless, casual, easy-going, easy-oasy (*Sl.*), lenient, neglectful, negligent, overindulgent, remiss, slack, slapdash, slipshod 2. broad, general, imprecise, inaccurate, indefinite, inexact, nonspecific, shapeless, vague 3. flabby, flaccid, loose, slack, soft, yielding
Antonyms (*sense 1*) conscientious, disciplined, firm, heedful, moral, rigid, scrupulous, severe, stern, strict, stringent (*sense 3*) firm, rigid

laxative aperient, cathartic, physic (*Rare*), purgative, purge, salts

lay[1] 1. deposit, establish, leave, place, plant, posit, put, set, set down, settle, spread 2. arrange, dispose, locate, organize, position, set out 3. bear, deposit, produce 4. advance, bring forward, lodge, offer, present, put forward, submit 5. allocate, allot, ascribe, assign, attribute, charge, impute 6. concoct, contrive, design, devise, hatch, plan, plot, prepare, work out 7. apply, assess, burden, charge, encumber, impose, saddle, tax 8. bet, gamble, give odds, hazard, risk, stake, wager 9. allay, alleviate, appease, assuage, calm, quiet, relieve, soothe, still, suppress 10. **lay bare** disclose, divulge, explain, expose, reveal, show, unveil 11. **lay hands on** a. acquire, get, get hold of, grab, grasp, seize b. assault, attack, beat up, lay into (*Inf.*), set on c. discover, find, unearth d. *Christianity* bless, confirm, consecrate, ordain 12. **lay hold of** get, get hold of, grab, grasp, grip, seize, snatch

lay[2] 1. laic, laical, nonclerical, secular 2. amateur, inexpert, nonprofessional, nonspecialist

lay[3] ballad, lyric, ode, poem, song

layabout beachcomber, couch potato (*Sl.*), good-for-nothing, idler, laggard, loafer, lounger, ne'er-do-well, shirker, skiver (*Brit. sl.*), slubberdegullion (*Archaic*), vagrant, wastrel

lay aside abandon, cast aside, dismiss, postpone, put aside, put off, reject, shelve

lay away accumulate, collect, hoard, keep, lay aside, lay in, salt away, save, stash (*Inf.*), stockpile, store

lay down 1. discard, drop, give, give up, relinquish, surrender, yield 2. affirm, assume, establish, formulate, ordain, postulate, prescribe, stipulate

layer 1. bed, ply, row, seam, stratum, thickness, tier 2. blanket, coat, coating, cover, covering, film, mantle, sheet

lay in accumulate, amass, build up, collect, hoard, stockpile, stock up, store (up)

lay into assail, attack, belabour, hit out at, lambast(e), let fly at, pitch into (*Inf.*), set about

layman amateur, lay person, nonprofessional, outsider

lay-off discharge, dismissal, unemployment

lay off 1. discharge, dismiss, drop, let go, make redundant, oust, pay off 2. *Inf.* cease, desist, give it a rest (*Inf.*), give over (*Inf.*), give up, leave alone, leave off, let up, quit, stop

lay on 1. cater (for), furnish, give, provide, purvey, supply 2. **lay it on** *Sl.* butter up, exaggerate, flatter, overdo it, overpraise, soft-soap (*Inf.*)

layout arrangement, design, draft, formation, geography, outline, plan

lay out 1. arrange, design, display, exhibit, plan, spread out 2. *Inf.* disburse, expend, fork out (*Sl.*), invest, pay, shell out (*Inf.*), spend 3. *Inf.* kayo (*Sl.*), knock for six (*Inf.*), knock out, knock unconscious, KO *or* K.O. (*Sl.*)

lay up 1. accumulate, amass, garner, hoard, keep, preserve, put away, save, store up, treasure 2. *Inf.* confine (to bed), hospitalize, incapacitate

laze 1. hang around, idle, loaf, loll, lounge, stand around 2. *Often with* **away** fool away, fritter away, kill time, pass time, veg out (*Sl., chiefly U.S.*), waste time, while away the hours

laziness dilatoriness, do-nothingness, faineance, faineancy, idleness, inactivity, indolence, lackadaisicalness, slackness, sloth, slothfulness, slowness, sluggishness, tardiness

lazy 1. idle, inactive, indolent, inert, remiss, shiftless, slack, slothful, slow, workshy 2. drowsy, languid, languorous, lethargic, sleepy, slow-moving, sluggish, somnolent, torpid

Antonyms active, assiduous, diligent, energetic, industrious, quick, stimulated

lazybones loafer, lounger, shirker, skiver (*Brit. sl.*), sleepyhead, slugabed, sluggard

leach drain, extract, filter, filtrate, lixiviate (*Chem.*), percolate, seep, strain

lead *v.* 1. conduct, escort, guide, pilot, precede, show the way, steer, usher 2. cause, dispose, draw, incline, induce, influence, persuade, prevail, prompt 3. command, direct, govern, head, manage, preside over, supervise 4. be ahead (of), blaze a trail, come first, exceed, excel, outdo, outstrip, surpass, transcend 5. experience, have, live, pass, spend, undergo 6. bring on, cause, conduce, contribute, produce, result in, serve, tend ~*n.* 7. advance, advantage, cutting edge, edge, first place, margin, precedence, primacy, priority, start, supremacy, van, vanguard 8. direction, example, guidance, leadership, model 9. clue, guide, hint, indication, suggestion, tip, trace 10. leading role, principal, protagonist, star part, title role ~*adj.* 11. chief, first, foremost, head, leading, main, most important, premier, primary, prime, principal

leaden 1. burdensome, crushing, cumbersome, heavy, inert, lead, onerous, oppressive 2. humdrum, laboured, plodding, sluggish, stiff, stilted, wooden 3. dismal, dreary, dull, gloomy, languid, lifeless, listless, spiritless 4. dingy, grey, greyish, lacklustre, louring *or* lowering, lustreless, overcast, sombre

leader bellwether, boss (*Inf.*), captain, chief, chieftain, commander, conductor, counsellor, director, guide, head, number one, principal, ringleader, ruler, superior
Antonyms adherent, disciple, follower, hanger-on, henchman, sidekick (*Sl.*), supporter

leadership 1. administration, direction, directorship, domination, guidance, management, running, superintendency 2. authority, command, control, influence, initiative, pre-eminence, supremacy, sway

leading chief, dominant, first, foremost, governing, greatest, highest, main, number one, outstanding, pre-eminent, primary, principal, ruling, superior
Antonyms following, hindmost, incidental, inferior, lesser, minor, secondary, subordinate, superficial

lead off begin, commence, get going, get under way, inaugurate, initiate, kick off (*Inf.*), open, set out, start, start the ball rolling (*Inf.*)

lead on beguile, deceive, draw on, entice, inveigle, lure, seduce, string along (*Inf.*), tempt

lead up to approach, intimate, introduce, make advances, make overtures, pave the way, prepare for, prepare the way, work round to

leaf *n.* 1. blade, bract, flag, foliole, frond, needle, pad 2. folio, page, sheet 3. **turn over a new leaf** amend, begin anew, change, change one's ways, improve, reform ~*v.* 4. bud, green, put out leaves, turn green 5. browse, flip, glance, riffle, skim, thumb (through)

leaflet advert (*Brit. inf.*), bill, booklet, brochure, circular, handbill, mailshot, pamphlet

leafy bosky (*Literary*), green, in foliage, leafed, leaved, shaded, shady, springlike, summery, verdant, wooded

league *n.* 1. alliance, association, band, coalition, combination, combine, compact, confederacy, confederation, consortium, federation, fellowship, fraternity, group, guild, order, partnership, union 2. ability group, category, class, level 3. **in league (with)** allied, collaborating, hand in glove, in cahoots (*Inf.*), leagued ~*v.* 4. ally, amalgamate, associate, band, collaborate, combine, confederate, join forces, unite

leak *n.* 1. aperture, chink, crack, crevice, fissure, hole, opening, puncture 2. drip, leakage, leaking, oozing, percolation, seepage 3. disclosure, divulgence ~*v.* 4. discharge, drip, escape, exude, ooze, pass, percolate, seep, spill, trickle 5. blow wide open (*Sl.*), disclose, divulge, give away, let slip, let the cat out of the bag, make known, make public, pass on, reveal, spill the beans (*Inf.*), tell

leaky cracked, holey, leaking, not watertight, perforated, porous, punctured, split, waterlogged

lean[1] *v.* 1. be supported, prop, recline, repose, rest 2. bend, heel, incline, slant, slope, tilt, tip 3. be disposed to, be prone to, favour, gravitate towards, have a propensity, prefer, tend 4. confide, count on, depend, have faith in, rely, trust

lean[2] *adj.* 1. angular, bony, emaciated, gaunt, lank, macilent (*Rare*), rangy, scraggy, scrawny, skinny, slender, slim, spare, thin, unfatty, wiry 2. bare, barren, inadequate, infertile, meagre, pitiful, poor, scanty, sparse, unfruitful, unproductive
Antonyms abundant, ample, brawny, burly, fat, fertile, full, obese, plentiful, plump, portly, profuse, rich

leaning aptitude, bent, bias, disposition, inclination, liking, partiality, penchant, predilection, proclivity, proneness, propensity, taste, tendency

leap *v.* 1. bounce, bound, caper, cavort, frisk, gambol, hop, jump, skip, spring 2. *Fig.* arrive at, come to, form hastily, hasten, hurry, jump, reach, rush 3. clear, jump (over), vault 4. advance, become prominent, escalate, gain attention, increase, rocket, soar, surge ~*n.* 5. bound, caper, frisk, hop, jump, skip, spring, vault 6. escalation, increase, rise, surge, upsurge, upswing

learn 1. acquire, attain, become able, grasp, imbibe, master, pick up 2. commit to memory, con (*Archaic*), get off pat, get (something) word-perfect, learn by heart, memorize 3. ascertain, detect, determine, discern, discover, find out, gain, gather, hear, suss (out) (*Sl.*), understand

learned academic, cultured, erudite, experienced, expert, highbrow, intellectual, lettered, literate, scholarly, skilled, versed, well-informed, well-read
Antonyms ignorant, illiterate, uneducated, unlearned

learner 1. apprentice, beginner, neophyte, novice, tyro 2. disciple, pupil, scholar, student, trainee
Antonyms (*sense 1*) adept, expert, grandmaster, master, maven, pastmaster, virtuoso, wizard (*sense 2*) coach, instructor, mentor, teacher, tutor

learning acquirements, attainments, culture, education, erudition, information, knowledge, letters, literature, lore, research, scholarship, schooling, study, tuition, wisdom

lease *v.* charter, hire, let, loan, rent

leash *n.* 1. lead, rein, tether 2. check, control, curb, hold, restraint ~*v.* 3. fasten, secure, tether, tie up 4. check, control, curb, hold back, restrain, suppress

least feeblest, fewest, last, lowest, meanest, minimum, minutest, poorest, slightest, smallest, tiniest

leathery coriaceous, durable, hard, hardened, leatherlike, leathern (*Archaic*), rough, rugged, tough, wrinkled

leave[1] *v.* 1. abandon, abscond, decamp, depart, desert, disappear, do a bunk (*Brit. sl.*), exit, flit (*Inf.*), forsake, go, go away, hook it (*Sl.*), move, pull out, quit, relinquish, retire, set out, slope off, take off (*Inf.*), withdraw 2. forget, lay down, leave behind, mislay 3. cause, deposit, generate, produce, result in 4. abandon, cease, desert, desist, drop, evacuate, forbear, give up, refrain, relinquish, renounce, stop, surrender 5. allot, assign, cede, commit, consign, entrust, give over, refer 6. bequeath, demise, devise (*Law*), hand down, transmit, will

Antonyms appear, arrive, assume, come, continue, emerge, hold, persist, remove, retain, stay

leave[2] *n.* 1. allowance, authorization, concession, consent, dispensation, freedom, liberty, permission, sanction 2. furlough, holiday, leave of absence, sabbatical, time off, vacation 3. adieu, departure, farewell, goodbye, leave-taking, parting, retirement, withdrawal

Antonyms (*sense 1*) denial, prohibition, refusal, rejection (*sense 2*) duty (*sense 3*) arrival, stay

leaven *n.* 1. barm, ferment, leavening, yeast 2. *Fig.* catalyst, influence, inspiration ~*v.* 3. ferment, lighten, raise, work 4. *Fig.* elevate, imbue, inspire, permeate, pervade, quicken, stimulate, suffuse

leave off abstain, break off, cease, desist, discontinue, end, give over (*Inf.*), give up, halt, kick (*Inf.*), knock off (*Inf.*), refrain, stop

leave out bar, cast aside, count out, disregard, except, exclude, ignore, neglect, omit, overlook, reject

leave-taking departure, farewell, going, goodbye, leaving, parting, sendoff (*Inf.*), valediction

leavings bits, dregs, fragments, leftovers, orts (*Archaic or dialect*), pieces, refuse, remains, remnants, residue, scraps, spoil, sweepings, waste

lecher adulterer, Casanova, debauchee, dirty old man (*Sl.*), Don Juan, fornicator, goat (*Inf.*), lech *or* letch (*Inf.*), libertine, profligate, rake, roué, satyr, seducer, sensualist, wanton, wolf (*Inf.*), womanizer

lecherous carnal, concupiscent, goatish (*Archaic or literary*), lascivious, lewd, libidinous, licentious, lubricious (*U.S. sl.*), lubricous, lustful, prurient, randy (*Inf., chiefly Brit.*), raunchy (*Sl.*), ruttish, salacious, unchaste, wanton

Antonyms prim, proper, prudish, puritanical, strait-laced, virginal, virtuous

lechery carnality, concupiscence, debauchery, lasciviousness, lecherousness, leching (*Inf.*), lewdness, libertinism, libidinousness, licentiousness, lubricity, lust, lustfulness, profligacy, prurience, rakishness, randiness (*Inf., chiefly Brit.*), salaciousness, sensuality, wantonness, womanizing

lecture *n.* 1. address, discourse, disquisition, harangue, instruction, lesson, speech, talk ~*v.* 2. address, discourse, expound, give a talk, harangue, hold forth, speak, spout, talk, teach ~*n.* 3. castigation, censure, chiding, dressing-down (*Inf.*), going-over (*Inf.*), heat (*Sl., chiefly U.S. & Canad.*), rebuke, reprimand, reproof, scolding, talking-to (*Inf.*), telling off (*Inf.*), wigging (*Brit. sl.*) ~*v.* 4. admonish, bawl out (*Inf.*), berate, carpet (*Inf.*), castigate, censure, chew out (*U.S. & Canad. inf.*), chide, give a rocket (*Brit. & N.Z. inf.*), rate, read the riot act, reprimand, reprove, scold, tear into (*Inf.*), tear (someone) off a strip (*Brit. inf.*), tell off (*Inf.*)

ledge mantle, projection, ridge, shelf, sill, step

lee cover, protection, refuge, screen, shade, shadow, shelter, shield

leech *Fig.* bloodsucker (*Inf.*), freeloader (*Sl.*), hanger-on, ligger (*Sl.*), parasite, sponger (*Inf.*), sycophant

leer *n./v.* drool, eye, gloat, goggle, grin, ogle, smirk, squint, stare, wink

leery careful, cautious, chary, distrustful, doubting, dubious, on one's guard, sceptical, shy, suspicious, uncertain, unsure, wary

lees deposit, dregs, grounds, precipitate, refuse, sediment, settlings

leeway elbowroom, latitude, margin, play, room, scope, space

left *adj.* 1. larboard (*Nautical*), left-hand, port, sinistral 2. *Of politics* leftist, left-wing, liberal, progressive, radical, socialist

left-handed 1. awkward, cack-handed (*Inf.*), careless, clumsy, fumbling, gauche, maladroit 2. ambiguous, backhanded, double-edged, enigmatic, equivocal, indirect, ironic, sardonic

leftover *n.* 1. legacy, remainder, residue, surplus, survivor 2. *Plural* leavings, oddments, odds and ends, remains, remnants, scraps *~adj.* 3. excess, extra, remaining, surplus, uneaten, unused, unwanted

leg *n.* 1. limb, lower limb, member, pin (*Inf.*), stump (*Inf.*) 2. brace, prop, support, upright 3. lap, part, portion, section, segment, stage, stretch 4. **a leg up** assistance, boost, help, helping hand, push, support 5. **not have a leg to stand on** *Inf.* be defenceless, be full of holes, be illogical, be invalid, be undermined, be vulnerable, lack support 6. **on one's (its) last legs** about to break down, about to collapse, at death's door, dying, exhausted, failing, giving up the ghost, worn out 7. **pull someone's leg** *Inf.* chaff, deceive, fool, kid (*Inf.*), make fun of, tease, trick, wind up (*Brit. sl.*) 8. **shake a leg** *Sl.* a. get a move on (*Inf.*), get cracking (*Inf.*), hasten, hurry, look lively (*Inf.*), rush, stir one's stumps b. boogie (*Sl.*), dance, get down (*Inf., chiefly U.S.*), hoof it (*Sl.*), trip the light fantastic 9. **stretch one's legs** exercise, go for a walk, move about, promenade, stroll, take a walk, take the air *~v.* 10. **leg it** *Inf.* go on foot, hotfoot, hurry, run, skedaddle (*Inf.*), walk

legacy 1. bequest, devise (*Law*), estate, gift, heirloom, inheritance 2. birthright, endowment, heritage, inheritance, patrimony, throwback, tradition

legal 1. allowable, allowed, authorized, constitutional, lawful, legalized, legitimate, licit, permissible, proper, rightful, sanctioned, valid 2. forensic, judicial, juridical

legalistic contentious, disputatious, hairsplitting, literal, litigious, narrow, narrow-minded, polemical, strict

legality accordance with the law, admissibleness, lawfulness, legitimacy, permissibility, rightfulness, validity

legalize allow, approve, authorize, decriminalize, legitimate, legitimatize, license, permit, sanction, validate

legate ambassador, delegate, depute (*Scot.*), deputy, emissary, envoy, messenger, nuncio

legatee beneficiary, heir, inheritor, recipient

legation consulate, delegation, diplomatic mission, embassy, envoys, ministry, representation

legend 1. fable, fiction, folk tale, myth, narrative, saga, story, tale, urban legend 2. celeb (*Inf.*), celebrity, luminary, marvel, megastar (*Inf.*), phenomenon, prodigy, spectacle, wonder 3. caption, device, inscription, motto 4. cipher, code, key, table of symbols

legendary 1. apocryphal, fabled, fabulous, fanciful, fictitious, mythical, romantic, storied, traditional 2. celebrated, famed, famous, illustrious, immortal, renowned, well-known

Antonyms (*sense 1*) factual, genuine, historical (*sense 2*) unknown

legerdemain 1. prestidigitation, sleight of hand 2. artfulness, artifice, chicanery, contrivance, craftiness, cunning, deception, feint, hocus-pocus, manipulation, manoeuvring, subterfuge, trickery

legibility clarity, decipherability, ease of reading, legibleness, neatness, plainness, readability, readableness

legible clear, decipherable, distinct, easily read, easy to read, neat, plain, readable

legion *n.* 1. army, brigade, company, division, force, troop 2. drove, horde, host, mass, multitude, myriad, number, throng *~adj.* 3. countless, multitudinous, myriad, numberless, numerous, very many

legislate codify, constitute, enact, establish, make laws, ordain, pass laws, prescribe, put in force

legislation 1. codification, enactment, lawmaking, prescription, regulation 2. act, bill, charter, law, measure, regulation, ruling, statute

legislative *adj.* congressional, judicial, juridical, jurisdictive, lawgiving, lawmaking, ordaining, parliamentary

legislator lawgiver, lawmaker, parliamentarian

legislature assembly, chamber, congress, diet, house, lawmaking body, parliament, senate

legitimate *adj.* 1. acknowledged, authentic, authorized, genuine, kosher (*Inf.*), lawful, legal, legit (*Sl.*), licit, proper, real, rightful, sanctioned, statutory, true 2. admissible, correct, just, justifiable, logical, reasonable, sensible, valid, warranted, well-founded *~v.* 3. authorize, legalize, legitimatize, legitimize, permit, pronounce lawful, sanction

Antonyms *adj.* false, fraudulent, illegal, illegitimate, unfair, unfounded, unjustified, unlawful, unreasonable, unsound

legitimatize, legitimize authorize, legalize, legitimate, permit, pronounce lawful, sanction

leisure 1. breathing space, ease, freedom, free time, holiday, liberty, opportunity, pause, quiet, recreation, relaxation, respite, rest, retirement, spare moments, spare time, time off, vacation 2. **at leisure** a. available, free, not booked up, on holiday, unengaged, unoccupied b. *Also* **at one's**

leisure at an unhurried pace, at one's convenience, deliberately, in one's own (good) time, unhurriedly, when it suits one, when one gets round to it (*Inf.*), without hurry

Antonyms business, duty, employment, labour, obligation, occupation, work

leisurely 1. *adj.* comfortable, easy, gentle, laid-back (*Inf.*), lazy, relaxed, restful, slow, unhurried 2. *adv.* at one's convenience, at one's leisure, comfortably, deliberately, easily, indolently, lazily, lingeringly, slowly, unhurriedly, without haste

Antonyms *adj.* brisk, fast, hasty, hectic, hurried, quick, rapid, rushed ~*adv.* briskly, hastily, hurriedly, quickly, rapidly

leitmotif *All with* **recurrent** *or* **recurring** air, convention, device, idea, melody, motif, phrase, strain, theme

lend 1. accommodate one with, advance, loan 2. add, afford, bestow, confer, contribute, furnish, give, grant, hand out, impart, present, provide, supply 3. **lend an ear** give ear, hearken (*Archaic*), heed, listen, take notice 4. **lend a hand** aid, assist, give a (helping) hand, help, help out 5. **lend itself to** be adaptable, be appropriate, be serviceable, fit, present opportunities of, suit 6. **lend oneself to** agree, consent, cooperate, countenance, espouse, support

length 1. *Of linear extent* distance, extent, longitude, measure, reach, span 2. *Of time* duration, period, space, span, stretch, term 3. measure, piece, portion, section, segment 4. elongation, extensiveness, lengthiness, protractedness 5. **at length a.** completely, fully, in depth, in detail, thoroughly, to the full **b.** for ages, for a long time, for hours, interminably **c.** at last, at long last, eventually, finally, in the end

lengthen continue, draw out, elongate, expand, extend, increase, make longer, prolong, protract, spin out, stretch

Antonyms abbreviate, abridge, curtail, cut, cut down, diminish, shorten, trim

lengthy diffuse, drawn-out, extended, interminable, lengthened, long, long-drawn-out, long-winded, overlong, prolix, prolonged, protracted, tedious, verbose, very long

Antonyms brief, concise, condensed, limited, short, succinct, terse, to the point

leniency, lenience clemency, compassion, forbearance, gentleness, indulgence, lenity, mercy, mildness, moderation, pity, quarter, tenderness, tolerance

lenient clement, compassionate, forbearing, forgiving, gentle, indulgent, kind, merciful, mild, sparing, tender, tolerant

Antonyms harsh, merciless, rigid, rigorous, severe, stern, strict, stringent

lenitive alleviative, assuaging, calming, easing, mitigative, mollifying, palliative, relieving, soothing

leper lazar (*Archaic*), outcast, pariah, untouchable

lesbian 1. *n.* butch (*Sl.*), dyke (*Sl.*), sapphist, tribade 2. *adj.* butch (*Sl.*), gay, homosexual, sapphic, tribadic

lesion abrasion, bruise, contusion, hurt, impairment, injury, sore, trauma (*Pathol.*), wound

less *adj.* 1. shorter, slighter, smaller 2. inferior, minor, secondary, subordinate ~*adv.* 3. barely, little, meagrely, to a smaller extent ~*prep.* 4. excepting, lacking, minus, subtracting, without

lessen abate, abridge, contract, curtail, decrease, de-escalate, degrade, die down, diminish, dwindle, ease, erode, grow less, impair, lighten, lower, minimize, moderate, narrow, reduce, relax, shrink, slacken, slow down, weaken, wind down

Antonyms add to, augment, boost, enhance, enlarge, expand, increase, magnify, multiply, raise

lessening abatement, contraction, curtailment, decline, decrease, de-escalation, diminution, dwindling, ebbing, erosion, let-up (*Inf.*), minimization, moderation, petering out, reduction, shrinkage, slackening, slowing down, waning, weakening

lesser inferior, less important, lower, minor, secondary, slighter, subordinate, under-

Antonyms greater, higher, major, primary, superior

lesson 1. class, coaching, instruction, period, schooling, teaching, tutoring 2. assignment, drill, exercise, homework, lecture, practice, reading, recitation, task 3. deterrent, example, exemplar, message, model, moral, precept 4. admonition, censure, chiding, punishment, rebuke, reprimand, reproof, scolding, warning

let[1] *v.* 1. allow, authorize, entitle, give leave, give permission, give the go-ahead (green light, O.K. *or* okay (*Inf.*)) (*Inf.*), grant, permit, sanction, suffer (*Archaic*), tolerate, warrant 2. hire, lease, rent 3. allow, cause, enable, grant, make, permit

let[2] *n.* constraint, hindrance, impediment, interference, obstacle, obstruction, prohibition, restriction

letdown anticlimax, bitter pill, blow, comedown (*Inf.*), disappointment, disgruntlement, disillusionment, frustration, setback, washout (*Inf.*)

let down disappoint, disenchant, disillusion, dissatisfy, fail, fall short, leave in the lurch, leave stranded

lethal baneful, dangerous, deadly, deathly, destructive, devastating, fatal, mortal, murderous, noxious, pernicious, poisonous, virulent
Antonyms harmless, healthy, innocuous, safe, wholesome

lethargic apathetic, comatose, debilitated, drowsy, dull, enervated, heavy, inactive, indifferent, inert, languid, lazy, listless, sleepy, slothful, slow, sluggish, somnolent, stupefied, torpid
Antonyms active, alert, animated, energetic, responsive, spirited, stimulated, vigorous

lethargy apathy, drowsiness, dullness, hebetude (*Rare*), inaction, indifference, inertia, languor, lassitude, listlessness, sleepiness, sloth, slowness, sluggishness, stupor, torpidity, torpor
Antonyms animation, brio, energy, life, liveliness, spirit, verve, vigour, vim, vitality, vivacity, zeal, zest

let in admit, allow to enter, give access to, greet, include, incorporate, receive, take in, welcome

let off 1. detonate, discharge, emit, explode, exude, fire, give off, leak, release 2. absolve, discharge, dispense, excuse, exempt, exonerate, forgive, pardon, release, spare

let on 1. admit, disclose, divulge, give away, make known, reveal, say 2. act, counterfeit, dissemble, dissimulate, feign, make believe, make out, pretend, profess, simulate

let out 1. emit, give vent to, produce 2. discharge, free, let go, liberate, release 3. betray, blow wide open (*Sl.*), disclose, leak, let fall, let slip, make known, reveal

letter 1. character, sign, symbol 2. acknowledgment, answer, billet (*Archaic*), communication, dispatch, epistle, line, message, missive, note, reply 3. **to the letter** accurately, exactly, literally, precisely, strictly, word for word

lettered accomplished, cultivated, cultured, educated, erudite, informed, knowledgeable, learned, literate, scholarly, versed, well-educated, well-read

letters belles-lettres, culture, erudition, humanities, learning, literature, scholarship

let-up abatement, break, cessation, interval, lessening, lull, pause, recess, remission, respite, slackening

let up abate, decrease, diminish, ease (up), moderate, relax, slacken, stop, subside

levee ceremony, entertainment, gathering, party, reception

level *adj.* 1. consistent, even, flat, horizontal, plain, plane, smooth, uniform 2. aligned, balanced, commensurate, comparable, equal, equivalent, even, flush, in line, neck and neck, on a line, on a par, proportionate 3. calm, equable, even, even-tempered, stable, steady ~*v.* 4. even off *or* out, flatten, make flat, plane, smooth 5. bulldoze, demolish, destroy, devastate, equalize, flatten, knock down, lay low, pull down, raze, smooth, tear down, wreck 6. aim, beam, direct, focus, point, train 7. *Inf.* be above board, be frank, be honest, be open, be straightforward, be up front (*Sl.*), come clean (*Inf.*), keep nothing back ~*n.* 8. altitude, elevation, height, vertical position 9. achievement, degree, grade, position, rank, stage, standard, standing, status 10. bed, floor, layer, storey, stratum, zone 11. flat surface, horizontal, plain, plane 12. **on the level** *Inf.* above board, fair, genuine, honest, open, sincere, square, straight, straightforward, up front (*Sl.*)
Antonyms *adj.* (*sense 1*) bumpy, hilly, slanted, tilted, uneven, vertical, warped (*sense 2*) above, below ~*v.* (*sense 5*) build, erect, raise, roughen

level-headed balanced, calm, collected, composed, cool, dependable, even-tempered, reasonable, sane, self-possessed, sensible, steady, together (*Sl.*), unflappable (*Inf.*)

lever 1. *n.* bar, crowbar, handle, handspike, jemmy 2. *v.* force, jemmy, move, prise, pry (*U.S.*), purchase, raise

leverage ascendancy, authority, clout (*Inf.*), influence, pull (*Inf.*), purchasing power, rank, weight

leviathan behemoth, colossus, hulk, mammoth, monster, Titan, whale

levity buoyancy, facetiousness, fickleness, flightiness, flippancy, frivolity, giddiness, light-heartedness, light-mindedness, silliness, skittishness, triviality
Antonyms earnestness, gravity, seriousness, solemnity

levy *v.* 1. charge, collect, demand, exact, gather, impose, tax 2. call, call up, conscript, mobilize, muster, press, raise, summon ~*n.* 3. assessment, collection, exaction, gathering, imposition 4. assessment, duty, excise, fee, imposition, impost, tariff, tax, toll

lewd bawdy, blue, dirty, impure, indecent, lascivious, libidinous, licentious, loose, lustful, obscene, pornographic, profligate, salacious, smutty, unchaste, vile, vulgar, wanton, wicked

lewdness bawdiness, carnality, crudity, debauchery, depravity, impurity, indecency, lasciviousness, lechery, licentiousness, lubricity, obscenity, pornography, profligacy, salaciousness, smut, smuttiness, unchastity, vulgarity, wantonness

lexicon dictionary, glossary, vocabulary, wordbook, word list

liabilities accounts payable, debts, expenditure, obligations

liability 1. accountability, answerability, culpability, duty, obligation, onus, responsibility 2. arrear, debit, debt, indebtedness, obligation 3. burden, disadvantage, drag, drawback, encumbrance, handicap, hindrance, impediment, inconvenience, millstone, minus (*Inf.*), nuisance 4. likelihood, probability, proneness, susceptibility, tendency

liable 1. accountable, amenable, answerable, bound, chargeable, obligated, responsible 2. exposed, open, subject, susceptible, vulnerable 3. apt, disposed, inclined, likely, prone, tending 4. **render oneself liable to** expose oneself to, incur, lay oneself open to, run the risk of

liaison 1. communication, connection, contact, go-between, hook-up, interchange, intermediary 2. affair, amour, entanglement, illicit romance, intrigue, love affair, romance

liar fabricator, falsifier, fibber, perjurer, prevaricator, storyteller (*Inf.*)

libel 1. *n.* aspersion, calumny, defamation, denigration, obloquy, slander, smear, vituperation 2. *v.* blacken, calumniate, defame, derogate, drag (someone's) name through the mud, malign, revile, slander, slur, smear, traduce, vilify

libellous aspersive, calumniatory, calumnious, defamatory, derogatory, false, injurious, malicious, maligning, scurrilous, slanderous, traducing, untrue, vilifying, vituperative

liberal 1. advanced, humanistic, latitudinarian, libertarian, progressive, radical, reformist, right-on (*Inf.*) 2. altruistic, beneficent, bounteous, bountiful, charitable, free-handed, generous, kind, open-handed, open-hearted, prodigal, unstinting 3. advanced, broad-minded, catholic, enlightened, high-minded, humanitarian, indulgent, magnanimous, permissive, right-on (*Inf.*), tolerant, unbiased, unbigoted, unprejudiced 4. abundant, ample, bountiful, copious, handsome, lavish, munificent, plentiful, profuse, rich 5. broad, flexible, free, general, inexact, lenient, loose, not close, not literal, not strict

Antonyms biased, bigoted, cheap, conservative, fixed, inadequate, inflexible, intolerant, left-wing, limited, literal, prejudiced, reactionary, right-wing, skimpy, small, stingy, strict

liberalism freethinking, humanitarianism, latitudinarianism, libertarianism, progressivism, radicalism

liberality 1. altruism, beneficence, benevolence, bounty, charity, free-handedness, generosity, kindness, largess *or* largesse, munificence, open-handedness, philanthropy 2. breadth, broad-mindedness, candour, catholicity, impartiality, latitude, liberalism, libertarianism, magnanimity, permissiveness, progressivism, toleration

liberalize ameliorate, broaden, ease, expand, extend, loosen, mitigate, moderate, modify, relax, slacken, soften, stretch

liberate deliver, discharge, disenthral, emancipate, free, let loose, let out, manumit, redeem, release, rescue, set free

Antonyms confine, detain, immure, imprison, incarcerate, intern, jail, lock up, put away

liberation deliverance, emancipation, enfranchisement, freedom, freeing, liberating, liberty, manumission, redemption, release, unfettering, unshackling

liberator deliverer, emancipator, freer, manumitter, redeemer, rescuer, saviour

libertine 1. *n.* debauchee, lech *or* letch (*Inf.*), lecher, loose liver, profligate, rake, reprobate, roué, seducer, sensualist, voluptuary, womanizer 2. *adj.* abandoned, corrupt, debauched, decadent, degenerate, depraved, dissolute, immoral, licentious, profligate, rakish, reprobate, voluptuous, wanton

liberty 1. autonomy, emancipation, freedom, immunity, independence, liberation, release, self-determination, sovereignty 2. authorization, with a blank cheque, carte blanche, dispensation, exemption, franchise, freedom, leave, licence, permission, prerogative, privilege, right, sanction 3. *Often plural* disrespect, familiarity, forwardness, impertinence, impropriety, impudence, insolence, overfamiliarity, presumption, presumptuousness 4. **at liberty** free, not confined, on the loose, unlimited, unoccupied, unrestricted

Antonyms captivity, compulsion, constraint, duress, enslavement, imprisonment, restraint, restriction, slavery, tyranny

libidinous carnal, concupiscent, debauched, impure, incontinent, lascivious, lecherous, lickerish (*Archaic*), loose, lustful, prurient, randy (*Inf., chiefly Brit.*), ruttish, salacious, sensual, unchaste, wanton, wicked

libretto book, lines, lyrics, script, words

licence *n.* 1. authority, authorization, carte blanche, certificate, charter, dispensation, entitlement, exemption, immunity, leave, liberty, permission, permit, privilege, right, warrant 2. freedom, independence, latitude, liberty, self-determination 3. abandon, anarchy, disorder, excess, immoderation, impropriety, indulgence, irresponsibility, lawlessness, laxity, profligacy, unruliness
Antonyms constraint, denial, moderation, prohibition, restraint, restriction, strictness

license *v.* accredit, allow, authorize, certify, commission, empower, entitle, permit, sanction, warrant
Antonyms ban, debar, disallow, forbid, outlaw, prohibit, proscribe, rule out, veto

licentious abandoned, debauched, disorderly, dissolute, immoral, impure, lascivious, lax, lewd, libertine, libidinous, lubricious, lubricous, lustful, profligate, promiscuous, sensual, uncontrollable, uncontrolled, uncurbed, unruly, wanton
Antonyms chaste, law-abiding, lawful, moral, principled, proper, scrupulous, virtuous

licentiousness abandon, debauchery, dissipation, dissoluteness, lechery, lewdness, libertinism, libidinousness, lubricity, lust, lustfulness, profligacy, promiscuity, prurience, salaciousness, salacity, wantonness

lick *v.* 1. brush, lap, taste, tongue, touch, wash 2. *Of flames* dart, flick, flicker, ignite, kindle, play over, ripple, touch 3. *Inf.* a. blow out of the water (*Sl.*), clobber (*Sl.*), defeat, master, overcome, rout, run rings around (*Inf.*), tank (*Sl.*), trounce, undo, vanquish, wipe the floor with (*Inf.*) b. beat, clobber (*Sl.*), flog, lambast(e), slap, spank, strike, thrash, wallop (*Inf.*) c. beat, best, blow out of the water (*Sl.*), clobber (*Sl.*), excel, outdo, outstrip, run rings around (*Inf.*), surpass, tank (*Sl.*), top, wipe the floor with (*Inf.*) ~*n.* 4. bit, brush, dab, little, sample, speck, stroke, taste, touch 5. *Inf.* clip (*Inf.*), pace, rate, speed

licking 1. beating, drubbing, flogging, hiding (*Inf.*), spanking, tanning (*Sl.*), thrashing, whipping 2. beating, defeat, drubbing, pasting (*Sl.*), trouncing

lie[1] 1. *v.* dissimulate, equivocate, fabricate, falsify, fib, forswear oneself, invent, misrepresent, perjure, prevaricate, tell a lie, tell untruths 2. *n.* deceit, fabrication, falsehood, falsification, falsity, fib, fiction, invention, mendacity, pork pie (*Brit. sl.*), porky (*Brit. sl.*), prevarication, untruth, white lie

lie[2] *v.* 1. be prone, be prostrate, be recumbent, be supine, couch, loll, lounge, recline, repose, rest, sprawl, stretch out 2. be, be buried, be found, be interred, be located, belong, be placed, be situated, exist, extend, remain 3. *Usually with* **on** *or* **upon** burden, oppress, press, rest, weigh 4. *Usually with* **in** be present, consist, dwell, exist, inhere, pertain 5. **lie low** conceal oneself, go to earth, go underground, hide, hide away, hide out, hole up, keep a low profile, keep out of sight, lurk, skulk, take cover

liege chieftain, feudal lord, master, overlord, seigneur, sovereign, superior, suzerain

lieu place, room, stead

life 1. animation, being, breath, entity, growth, sentience, viability, vitality 2. being, career, continuance, course, duration, existence, lifetime, span, time 3. human, human being, individual, mortal, person, soul 4. autobiography, biography, career, confessions, history, life story, memoirs, story 5. behaviour, conduct, life style, way of life 6. the human condition, the times, the world, this mortal coil, trials and tribulations, vicissitudes 7. activity, animation, brio, energy, get-up-and-go (*Inf.*), go (*Inf.*), high spirits, liveliness, oomph (*Inf.*), pep, sparkle, spirit, verve, vigour, vitality, vivacity, zest 8. animating spirit, *élan vital,* essence, heart, lifeblood, soul, spirit, vital spark 9. creatures, living beings, living things, organisms, wildlife 10. **come to life** awaken, become animate, revive, rouse, show signs of life 11. **for dear life** *Inf.* desperately, for all one is worth, intensely, quickly, urgently, vigorously

lifeblood animating force, driving force, essence, guts (*Inf.*), heart, inspiration, life, stimulus, vital spark

lifeless 1. cold, dead, deceased, defunct, extinct, inanimate, inert 2. bare, barren, desert, empty, sterile, uninhabited, unproductive, waste 3. cold, colourless, dull, flat, heavy, hollow, lacklustre, lethargic, listless, passive, pointless, slow, sluggish, spent, spiritless, static, stiff, torpid, wooden 4. comatose, dead to the world (*Inf.*), in a faint, inert, insensate, insensible, out cold, out for six, unconscious
Antonyms active, alive, animate, animated, live, lively, living, spirited, vital

lifelike authentic, exact, faithful, graphic, natural, photographic, real, realistic, true-to-life, undistorted, vivid

lifelong constant, deep-rooted, enduring, for all one's life, for life, lasting, lifetime, long-lasting, long-standing, perennial, permanent, persistent

lifetime all one's born days, career, course, day(s), existence, life span, one's natural life, period, span, time

life work business, calling, career, interest, mission, occupation, profession, purpose, pursuit, vocation, work

lift *v.* 1. bear aloft, buoy up, draw up, elevate, heft (*Inf.*), hoist, pick up, raise, raise high, rear, upheave, uplift, upraise 2. advance, ameliorate, boost, dignify, elevate, enhance, exalt, improve, promote, raise, upgrade 3. annul, cancel, countermand, end, relax, remove, rescind, revoke, stop, terminate 4. ascend, be dispelled, climb, disappear, disperse, dissipate, mount, rise, vanish 5. *Inf.* appropriate, blag (*Sl.*), cabbage (*Brit. sl.*), copy, crib (*Inf.*), half-inch (*Old-fashioned sl.*), nick (*Sl., chiefly Brit.*), pilfer, pinch (*Inf.*), pirate, plagiarize, pocket, purloin, steal, take, thieve ~*n.* 6. car ride, drive, ride, run, transport 7. boost, encouragement, fillip, pick-me-up, reassurance, shot in the arm (*Inf.*), uplift 8. elevator (*Chiefly U.S.*)

Antonyms *v.* (*sense 1*) dash, depress, drop, hang, lower (*sense 3*) establish, impose (*sense 4*) descend, drop, fall, lower ~*n.* (*sense 7*) blow, letdown

ligature band, bandage, binding, bond, connection, ligament, link, tie

light[1] *n.* 1. blaze, brightness, brilliance, effulgence, flash, glare, gleam, glint, glow, illumination, incandescence, lambency, luminescence, luminosity, lustre, phosphorescence, radiance, ray, refulgence, scintillation, shine, sparkle 2. beacon, bulb, candle, flare, lamp, lantern, lighthouse, star, taper, torch, windowpane 3. broad day, cockcrow, dawn, daybreak, daylight, daytime, morn (*Poetic*), morning, sun, sunbeam, sunrise, sunshine 4. *Fig.* angle, approach, aspect, attitude, context, interpretation, point of view, slant, vantage point, viewpoint 5. awareness, comprehension, elucidation, explanation, illustration, information, insight, knowledge, understanding 6. example, exemplar, guiding light, model, paragon, shining example 7. flame, lighter, match 8. **bring to light** disclose, discover, expose, reveal, show, uncover, unearth, unveil 9. **come to light** appear, be disclosed, be discovered, be revealed, come out, transpire, turn up 10. **in (the) light of** bearing in mind, because of, considering, in view of, taking into account, with knowledge of 11. **shed** *or* **throw light on** clarify, clear up, elucidate, explain, simplify ~*adj.* 12. aglow, bright, brilliant, glowing, illuminated, luminous, lustrous, shining, sunny, well-lighted, well-lit 13. bleached, blond, faded, fair, light-hued, light-toned, pale, pastel ~*v.* 14. fire, ignite, inflame, kindle, set a match to 15. brighten, clarify, floodlight, flood with light, illuminate, illumine, irradiate, lighten, light up, put on, switch on, turn on 16. animate, brighten, cheer, irradiate, lighten

Antonyms *n.* cloud, dark, darkness, dusk, mystery, obscurity, shade, shadow ~*adj.* dark, deep, dim, dusky, gloomy ~*v.* cloud, darken, douse, dull, extinguish, put out, quench

light[2] *adj.* 1. airy, buoyant, delicate, easy, flimsy, imponderous, insubstantial, lightsome, lightweight, portable, slight, underweight 2. faint, gentle, indistinct, mild, moderate, slight, soft, weak 3. inconsequential, inconsiderable, insignificant, minute, scanty, slight, small, thin, tiny, trifling, trivial, unsubstantial, wee 4. cushy (*Inf.*), easy, effortless, manageable, moderate, simple, undemanding, unexacting, untaxing 5. agile, airy, graceful, light-footed, lithe, nimble, sprightly, sylphlike 6. amusing, diverting, entertaining, frivolous, funny, gay, humorous, light-hearted, pleasing, superficial, trifling, trivial, witty 7. airy, animated, blithe, carefree, cheerful, cheery, fickle, frivolous, gay, lively, merry, sunny 8. dizzy, giddy, light-headed, reeling, unsteady, volatile 9. digestible, frugal, modest, not heavy, not rich, restricted, small 10. crumbly, friable, loose, porous, sandy, spongy ~*v.* 11. alight, land, perch, settle 12. *With* **on** *or* **upon** chance, come across, discover, encounter, find, happen upon, hit upon, stumble on

Antonyms *adj.* burdensome, clumsy, deep, forceful, hard, heavy, intense, profound, rich, serious, sombre, strenuous, strong, substantial, weighty

lighten[1] become light, brighten, flash, gleam, illuminate, irradiate, light up, make bright, shine

lighten[2] 1. disburden, ease, make lighter, reduce in weight, unload 2. allay, alleviate, ameliorate, assuage, ease, facilitate, lessen, mitigate, reduce, relieve 3. brighten, buoy up, cheer, elate, encourage, gladden, hearten, inspire, lift, perk up, revive

Antonyms (*sense 1*) burden, encumber, handicap (*sense 2*) aggravate, heighten, increase, intensify, make worse, worsen (*sense 3*) depress, oppress, sadden, weigh down

light-fingered crafty, crooked (*Inf.*), dishonest, furtive, pilfering, pinching (*Inf.*), shifty, sly, stealing, thieving, underhand

light-footed agile, buoyant, graceful, lithe, nimble, sprightly, spry, swift, tripping, winged

light-headed 1. bird-brained (*Inf.*), featherbrained, fickle, flighty, flippant, foolish, frivolous, giddy, inane, rattle-brained (*Sl.*), shallow, silly, superficial, trifling 2. delirious, dizzy, faint, giddy, hazy, vertiginous, woozy (*Inf.*)

light-hearted blithe, blithesome (*Literary*), bright, carefree, cheerful, chirpy (*Inf.*), effervescent, frolicsome, gay, genial, glad, gleeful, happy-go-lucky, insouciant, jocund, jolly, jovial, joyful, joyous, merry, playful, sunny, untroubled, upbeat (*Inf.*)
Antonyms cheerless, dejected, depressed, despondent, gloomy, heavy-hearted, melancholy, morose, sad

light into assail, attack, belabour, clobber (*Sl.*), flail, flay, go at hammer and tongs, lambast(e), lay into (*Inf.*), let fly at, pitch into (*Inf.*), sail into (*Inf.*), set about, tear into (*Inf.*)

lightless caliginous (*Archaic*), dark, dim, dusky, gloomy, inky, jet black, murky, pitch-black, pitch-dark, pitchy, Stygian, sunless, tenebrous, unilluminated, unlighted, unlit

lightly 1. airily, delicately, faintly, gently, gingerly, slightly, softly, timidly 2. moderately, sparingly, sparsely, thinly 3. easily, effortlessly, readily, simply 4. breezily, carelessly, flippantly, frivolously, heedlessly, indifferently, slightingly, thoughtlessly
Antonyms abundantly, arduously, awkwardly, carefully, earnestly, firmly, forcefully, heavily, ponderously, seriously, slowly, thickly, with difficulty

light out abscond, depart, do a bunk (*Brit. sl.*), do a runner (*Sl.*), escape, fly the coop (*U.S. & Canad. inf.*), make off, quit, run away, scarper (*Brit. sl.*), skedaddle (*Inf.*), take a powder (*U.S. & Canad. sl.*), take it on the lam (*U.S. & Canad. sl.*)

lightweight *adj.* inconsequential, insignificant, nickel-and-dime (*U.S. sl.*), of no account, paltry, petty, slight, trifling, trivial, unimportant, worthless
Antonyms important, momentous, serious, significant, substantial, weighty

likable, likeable agreeable, amiable, appealing, attractive, charming, engaging, friendly, genial, nice, pleasant, pleasing, sympathetic, winning, winsome

like[1] 1. *adj.* akin, alike, allied, analogous, approximating, cognate, corresponding, equivalent, identical, parallel, relating, resembling, same, similar 2. *n.* counterpart, equal, fellow, match, parallel, twin
Antonyms *adj.* contrasted, different, dissimilar, divergent, diverse, opposite, unlike ~*n.* opposite

like[2] *v.* 1. adore (*Inf.*), be fond of, be keen on, be partial to, delight in, dig (*Sl.*), enjoy, go for, love, relish, revel in 2. admire, appreciate, approve, cherish, esteem, hold dear, prize, take a shine to (*Inf.*), take to 3. care to, choose, choose to, desire, fancy, feel inclined, prefer, select, want, wish ~*n.* 4. *Usually plural* cup of tea (*Inf.*), favourite, liking, partiality, predilection, preference
Antonyms *v.* abominate, despise, detest, dislike, hate, loathe

likelihood chance, good chance, liability, likeliness, possibility, probability, prospect, reasonableness, strong possibility

likely *adj.* 1. anticipated, apt, disposed, expected, in a fair way, inclined, liable, on the cards, possible, probable, prone, tending, to be expected 2. **be *or* seem likely** be in the running for, bid fair, incline towards, promise, stand a good chance, suggest, tend 3. believable, credible, feasible, plausible, reasonable, verisimilar 4. acceptable, agreeable, appropriate, befitting, fit, pleasing, proper, qualified, suitable 5. fair, favourite, hopeful, odds-on, promising, up-and-coming ~*adv.* 6. doubtlessly, in all probability, like as not (*Inf.*), like enough (*Inf.*), no doubt, presumably, probably

like-minded agreeing, compatible, *en rapport,* harmonious, in accord, in harmony, of one mind, of the same mind, unanimous

liken compare, equate, juxtapose, match, parallel, relate, set beside

likeness 1. affinity, correspondence, resemblance, similarity, similitude 2. copy, counterpart, delineation, depiction, effigy, facsimile, image, model, photograph, picture, portrait, replica, representation, reproduction, study 3. appearance, form, guise, semblance

likewise 1. also, besides, further, furthermore, in addition, moreover, too 2. in like manner, in the same way, similarly

liking affection, affinity, appreciation, attraction, bent, bias, desire, fondness, inclination, love, partiality, penchant, predilection, preference, proneness, propensity, soft spot, stomach, taste, tendency, thirst, weakness
Antonyms abhorrence, aversion, dislike, hatred, loathing, repugnance

Lilliputian 1. *n.* dwarf, homunculus, hop-o'-my-thumb, manikin, midget, pygmy *or* pigmy, Tom Thumb 2. *adj.* baby, bantam, diminutive, dwarf, little, mini, miniature, minuscule, petite, pocket-sized, pygmy *or* pigmy, small, teensy-weensy, teeny, teeny-weeny, tiny, wee

lilt beat, cadence, rhythm, sway, swing

lily-livered abject, chicken (*Sl.*), chicken-hearted, chickenshit (*U.S. sl.*), cowardly, craven, faint-hearted, fearful, gutless (*Inf.*), pusillanimous, scared, spineless, timid, timorous, yellow (*Inf.*), yellow-bellied (*Sl.*)

lily-white 1. milk-white, pure white, white, white as snow, white-skinned 2. *Inf.* chaste, impeccable, innocent, irreproachable, pure, spotless, unsullied, untainted, untarnished, virgin, virtuous

limb 1. appendage, arm, extension, extremity, leg, member, part, wing 2. bough, branch, offshoot, projection, spur

limber *adj.* 1. elastic, flexible, plastic, pliable, pliant, supple 2. agile, graceful, lissom(e), lithe, loose-jointed, loose-limbed, supple ~*v.* 3. *With* **up** exercise, get ready, loosen up, prepare, warm up

limelight attention, celebrity, fame, glare of publicity, prominence, public eye, publicity, public notice, recognition, stardom, the spotlight

limit *n.* 1. bound, breaking point, cutoff point, deadline, end, end point, furthest bound, greatest extent, termination, the bitter end, ultimate, utmost 2. *Often plural* border, boundary, confines, edge, end, extent, frontier, pale, perimeter, periphery, precinct 3. ceiling, check, curb, limitation, maximum, obstruction, restraint, restriction 4. **the limit** *Inf.* enough, it (*Inf.*), the end, the last straw ~*v.* 5. bound, check, circumscribe, confine, curb, delimit, demarcate, fix, hem in, hinder, ration, restrain, restrict, specify, straiten

limitation block, check, condition, constraint, control, curb, disadvantage, drawback, impediment, obstruction, qualification, reservation, restraint, restriction, snag

limited 1. bounded, checked, circumscribed, confined, constrained, controlled, curbed, defined, finite, fixed, hampered, hemmed in, restricted 2. cramped, diminished, inadequate, insufficient, minimal, narrow, reduced, restricted, scant, short, unsatisfactory

Antonyms boundless, limitless, unlimited, unrestricted

limitless boundless, countless, endless, illimitable, immeasurable, immense, inexhaustible, infinite, measureless, never-ending, numberless, unbounded, uncalculable, undefined, unending, unlimited, untold, vast

limp[1] 1. *v.* falter, halt (*Archaic*), hobble, hop, shamble, shuffle 2. *n.* hobble, lameness

limp[2] *adj.* 1. drooping, flabby, flaccid, flexible, floppy, lax, limber, loose, pliable, relaxed, slack, soft 2. debilitated, enervated, exhausted, lethargic, spent, tired, weak, worn out

Antonyms (*sense 1*) firm, hard, rigid, solid, stiff, taut, tense, unyielding (*sense 2*) hardy, powerful, robust, strong, sturdy, tough

limpid 1. bright, clear, crystal-clear, crystalline, pellucid, pure, translucent, transparent 2. clear, comprehensible, intelligible, lucid, perspicuous, unambiguous 3. calm, peaceful, placid, quiet, serene, still, tranquil, unruffled, untroubled

line[1] *n.* 1. band, bar, channel, dash, groove, mark, rule, score, scratch, streak, stripe, stroke, underline 2. crease, crow's foot, furrow, mark, wrinkle 3. border, borderline, boundary, demarcation, edge, frontier, limit, mark 4. configuration, contour, features, figure, outline, profile, silhouette 5. cable, cord, filament, rope, strand, string, thread, wire, wisp 6. axis, course, direction, path, route, track, trajectory 7. approach, avenue, belief, course, course of action, ideology, method, policy, position, practice, procedure, scheme, system 8. activity, area, bag (*Sl.*), business, calling, department, employment, field, forte, interest, job, occupation, profession, province, pursuit, specialization, trade, vocation 9. column, crocodile (*Brit.*), file, procession, queue, rank, row, sequence, series 10. ancestry, breed, family, lineage, race, stock, strain, succession 11. card, letter, message, note, postcard, report, word 12. clue, hint, indication, information, lead 13. *Military* disposition, firing line, formation, front, front line, position, trenches 14. **draw the line** lay down the law, object, prohibit, put one's foot down, restrict, set a limit 15. **in line a.** in alignment, in a row, plumb, straight, true **b.** in accord, in agreement, in conformity, in harmony, in step 16. **in line for** a candidate for, being considered for, due for, in the running for, next in succession to, on the short list for ~*v.* 17. crease, cut, draw, furrow, inscribe, mark, rule, score, trace, underline 18. border, bound, edge, fringe, rank, rim, skirt, verge

line[2] *v.* ceil, cover, face, fill, interline

lineage ancestry, birth, breed, descendants, descent, extraction, family, forebears, forefathers, genealogy, heredity, house, line, offspring, pedigree, progeny, stirps, stock, succession

lineaments configuration, countenance, face, features, line, outline, phiz *or* phizog (*Sl., chiefly Brit.*), physiognomy, trait, visage

lined 1. feint, ruled 2. furrowed, wizened, worn, wrinkled

lines 1. appearance, configuration, contour, cut, outline, shape, style 2. convention, example, model, pattern, plan, principle, procedure 3. part, script, words

line-up arrangement, array, row, selection, team

line up 1. fall in, form ranks, queue up 2. assemble, come up with, lay on, obtain, organize, prepare, procure, produce, secure 3. align, arrange, array, marshal, order, range, regiment, straighten

linger 1. hang around, loiter, remain, stay, stop, tarry, wait 2. dally, dawdle, delay, idle, lag, procrastinate, take one's time 3. cling to life, die slowly, hang on, last, survive 4. abide, continue, endure, persist, remain, stay

lingering dragging, long-drawn-out, persistent, protracted, remaining, slow

lingo argot, cant, dialect, idiom, jargon, language, patois, speech, talk, tongue, vernacular

liniment balm, balsam, cream, embrocation, emollient, lotion, ointment, salve, unguent

link *n.* 1. component, constituent, division, element, member, part, piece 2. affiliation, affinity, association, attachment, bond, connection, joint, knot, liaison, relationship, tie, tie-up, vinculum *~v.* 3. attach, bind, connect, couple, fasten, join, tie, unite, yoke 4. associate, bracket, connect, identify, relate

Antonyms *v.* detach, disconnect, divide, separate, sever, split, sunder

lion *Fig.* 1. brave man, champion, conqueror, fighter, hero, warrior 2. big name, celeb (*Inf.*), celebrity, idol, luminary, megastar (*Inf.*), notable, prodigy, star, superstar, V.I.P., wonder 3. **beard the lion in his den** brave, confront, court destruction, defy danger, face, stand up to, tempt providence

lion-hearted bold, brave, courageous, daring, dauntless, heroic, intrepid, resolute, stalwart, valiant, valorous

Antonyms chicken-hearted, chickenshit (*U.S. sl.*), cowardly, craven, faint-hearted, gutless (*Inf.*), lily-livered, pusillanimous, spineless, timorous, wimpish *or* wimpy (*Inf.*), yellow (*Inf.*)

lionize acclaim, adulate, aggrandize, celebrate, crack up (*Inf.*), eulogize, exalt, fête, glorify, hero-worship, honour, idolize, make much of, mob, sing *or* sound the praises of

lip 1. brim, brink, edge, flange, margin, rim 2. *Sl.* backchat (*Inf.*), cheek (*Inf.*), effrontery, impertinence, insolence, rudeness, sauce (*Inf.*) 3. *Music* control, embouchure 4. **smack *or* lick one's lips** anticipate, delight in, drool over, enjoy, gloat over, relish, savour, slaver over

liquefaction deliquescence, dissolution, dissolving, fusion, melting, thawing

liquefy deliquesce, dissolve, flux, fuse, liquesce, liquidize, melt, run, thaw

liquid *n.* 1. fluid, juice, liquor, solution *~adj.* 2. aqueous, flowing, fluid, liquefied, melted, molten, running, runny, thawed, wet 3. bright, brilliant, clear, limpid, shining, translucent, transparent 4. dulcet, fluent, mellifluent, mellifluous, melting, smooth, soft, sweet 5. *Of assets* convertible, negotiable

liquidate 1. clear, discharge, honour, pay, pay off, settle, square 2. abolish, annul, cancel, dissolve, terminate 3. cash, convert to cash, realize, sell off, sell up 4. annihilate, blow away (*Sl., chiefly U.S.*), bump off (*Sl.*), destroy, dispatch, do away with, do in (*Sl.*), eliminate, exterminate, finish off, get rid of, kill, murder, remove, rub out (*U.S. sl.*), silence, take out (*Sl.*), wipe out (*Inf.*)

liquor 1. alcohol, booze (*Inf.*), drink, grog, hard stuff (*Inf.*), hooch *or* hootch (*Inf., chiefly U.S. & Canad.*), intoxicant, juice (*Inf.*), spirits, strong drink 2. broth, extract, gravy, infusion, juice, liquid, stock

lissom(e) agile, flexible, graceful, light, limber, lithe, loose-jointed, loose-limbed, nimble, pliable, pliant, supple, willowy

list[1] 1. *n.* catalogue, directory, file, index, inventory, invoice, leet (*Scot.*), listing, record, register, roll, schedule, series, syllabus, tabulation, tally 2. *v.* bill, book, catalogue, enrol, enter, enumerate, file, index, itemize, note, record, register, schedule, set down, tabulate, write down

list[2] 1. *v.* cant, careen, heel, heel over, incline, lean, tilt, tip 2. *n.* cant, leaning, slant, tilt

listen 1. attend, be all ears, be attentive, give ear, hang on (someone's) words, hark, hear, hearken (*Archaic*), keep one's ears open, lend an ear, pin back one's ears (*Inf.*), prick up one's ears 2. concentrate, do as one is told, give heed to, heed, mind, obey, observe, pay attention, take notice

listless apathetic, enervated, heavy, impassive, inattentive, indifferent, indolent, inert, languid, languishing, lethargic, lifeless, limp, lymphatic, mopish, sluggish, spiritless, supine, torpid, vacant

Antonyms active, alert, attentive, energetic, lively, sparky, spirited, wide-awake

listlessness apathy, enervation, ennui, inattention, indifference, indolence, inertia, languidness, languor, lethargy, lifelessness, sluggishness, spiritlessness, supineness, torpidity

litany 1. invocation, petition, prayer, supplication 2. account, catalogue, enumeration, list, recital, recitation, refrain, repetition, tale

literacy ability, articulacy, articulateness, cultivation, education, knowledge, learning, proficiency, scholarship

literal 1. accurate, close, exact, faithful, strict, verbatim, word for word 2. boring, colourless, down-to-earth, dull, factual, matter-of-fact, prosaic, prosy, unimaginative, uninspired 3. actual, bona fide, genuine, gospel, plain, real, simple, true, unexaggerated, unvarnished

literally actually, exactly, faithfully, plainly, precisely, really, simply, strictly, to the letter, truly, verbatim, word for word

literary bookish, erudite, formal, learned, lettered, literate, scholarly, well-read

literate cultivated, cultured, educated, erudite, informed, knowledgeable, learned, lettered, scholarly, well-informed, well-read

literature 1. belles-lettres, letters, lore, writings, written works 2. brochure, information, leaflet, mailshot, pamphlet

lithe flexible, limber, lissom(e), loose-jointed, loose-limbed, pliable, pliant, supple

litigant claimant, contestant, disputant, litigator, party, plaintiff

litigate contest at law, file a suit, go to court, go to law, institute legal proceedings, press charges, prosecute, sue

litigation action, case, contending, disputing, lawsuit, process, prosecution

litigious argumentative, belligerent, contentious, disputatious, quarrelsome

litter *n.* 1. debris, detritus, fragments, garbage (*Chiefly U.S.*), grot (*Sl.*), muck, refuse, rubbish, shreds 2. clutter, confusion, disarray, disorder, jumble, mess, scatter, untidiness 3. brood, family, offspring, progeny, young 4. bedding, couch, floor cover, mulch, straw-bed 5. palanquin, stretcher ~*v.* 6. clutter, derange, disarrange, disorder, mess up, scatter, strew

little *adj.* 1. diminutive, dwarf, elfin, infinitesimal, Lilliputian, mini, miniature, minute, petite, pygmy *or* pigmy, short, slender, small, teensy-weensy, teeny-weeny, tiny, wee 2. babyish, immature, infant, junior, undeveloped, young 3. hardly any, insufficient, meagre, measly, scant, skimpy, small, sparse 4. brief, fleeting, hasty, passing, short, short-lived 5. inconsiderable, insignificant, minor, negligible, paltry, trifling, trivial, unimportant 6. base, cheap, illiberal, mean, narrow-minded, petty, small-minded ~*adv.* 7. barely, hardly, not much, not quite, only just 8. hardly ever, not often, rarely, scarcely, seldom 9. **little by little** bit by bit, by degrees, gradually, imperceptibly, piecemeal, progressively, slowly, step by step ~*n.* 10. bit, dab, dash, fragment, hint, modicum, particle, pinch, small amount, snippet, speck, spot, tad (*Inf., chiefly U.S.*), taste, touch, trace, trifle

Antonyms *adj.* abundant, ample, big, colossal, considerable, enormous, giant, ginormous (*Inf.*), grave, great, huge, immense, important, large, long, major, mega (*Sl.*), momentous, much, plentiful, serious, significant ~*adv.* always, certainly, much, surely ~*n.* lot, many, much

liturgical ceremonial, eucharistic, formal, ritual, sacramental, solemn

liturgy celebration, ceremony, form of worship, formula, rite, ritual, sacrament, service, services, worship

livable 1. adequate, comfortable, fit (for human habitation), habitable, inhabitable, satisfactory 2. acceptable, bearable, endurable, passable, sufferable, supportable, tolerable, worth living, worthwhile 3. *With* **with** companionable, compatible, congenial, easy, easy to live with, harmonious, sociable

live[1] *v.* 1. be, be alive, breathe, draw breath, exist, have life 2. be permanent, be remembered, last, persist, prevail, remain alive 3. *Sometimes with* **in** abide, dwell, hang out (*Inf.*), inhabit, lodge, occupy, reside, settle, stay (*Chiefly Scot.*) 4. abide, continue, earn a living, endure, fare, feed, get along, lead, make ends meet, pass, remain, subsist, support oneself, survive 5. be happy, enjoy life, flourish, luxuriate, make the most of life, prosper, thrive 6. **live it up** *Inf.* celebrate, enjoy oneself, have a ball (*Inf.*), have fun, make whoopee (*Inf.*), paint the town red, push the boat out (*Brit. inf.*), revel

live[2] *adj.* 1. alive, animate, breathing, existent, living, quick (*Archaic*), vital 2. active, burning, controversial, current, hot, pertinent, pressing, prevalent, topical, unsettled, vital 3. *Inf.* active, alert, brisk, dynamic, earnest, energetic, lively, sparky, vigorous, vivid, wide-awake 4. active, alight, blazing, burning, connected, glowing, hot, ignited, smouldering, switched on

livelihood employment, job, living, maintenance, means, (means of) support, occupation, (source of) income, subsistence, sustenance, work

liveliness activity, animation, boisterousness, brio, briskness, dynamism, energy, gaiety, quickness, smartness, spirit, sprightliness, vitality, vivacity

livelong complete, dragged out, entire,

everlasting, full, long-drawn-out, unbroken, whole

lively 1. active, agile, alert, brisk, chipper (*Inf.*), chirpy (*Inf.*), energetic, full of pep (*Inf.*), keen, nimble, perky, quick, sprightly, spry, vigorous 2. animated, blithe, blithesome, cheerful, chirpy (*Inf.*), frisky, frolicsome, gay, merry, sparkling, sparky, spirited, upbeat (*Inf.*), vivacious 3. astir, bustling, busy, buzzing, crowded, eventful, moving, stirring 4. bright, colourful, exciting, forceful, invigorating, racy, refreshing, stimulating, vivid

Antonyms apathetic, debilitated, disabled, dull, inactive, lifeless, listless, slow, sluggish, torpid

liven animate, brighten, buck up (*Inf.*), enliven, hot up (*Inf.*), pep up, perk up, put life into, rouse, stir, vitalize, vivify

liverish 1. bilious, queasy, sick 2. crotchety (*Inf.*), crusty, disagreeable, fratchy (*Inf.*), grumpy, ill-humoured, irascible, irritable, peevish, ratty (*Brit. & N.Z. inf.*), snappy, splenetic, tetchy

livery attire, clothing, costume, dress, garb, raiment (*Archaic or poetic*), regalia, suit, uniform, vestments

live wire ball of fire (*Inf.*), dynamo, go-getter (*Inf.*), hustler (*U.S. & Canad. sl.*), life and soul of the party, self-starter

livid 1. angry, black-and-blue, bruised, contused, discoloured, purple 2. ashen, blanched, bloodless, doughy, greyish, leaden, pale, pallid, pasty, wan, waxen 3. *Inf.* angry, beside oneself, boiling, cross, enraged, exasperated, fuming, furious, incensed, indignant, infuriated, mad (*Inf.*), outraged

Antonyms (*sense 3*) assuaged, blissful, content, delighted, enchanted, forgiving, happy, mollified, overjoyed, pleased

living *adj.* 1. active, alive, animated, breathing, existing, in the land of the living (*Inf.*), lively, quick (*Archaic*), strong, vigorous, vital 2. active, contemporary, continuing, current, developing, extant, in use, ongoing, operative, persisting ~*n.* 3. animation, being, existence, existing, life, subsistence 4. life style, mode of living, way of life 5. job, livelihood, maintenance, (means of) support, occupation, (source of) income, subsistence, sustenance, work 6. *Church of England* benefice, incumbency, stipend 7. **the living** flesh and blood, the quick (*Archaic*)

Antonyms *adj.* (*sense 1*) dead, deceased, defunct, departed, expired, late, lifeless, perished (*sense 2*) obsolescent, obsolete, out-of-date, vanishing

load *n.* 1. bale, cargo, consignment, freight, lading, shipment 2. affliction, burden, encumbrance, incubus, millstone, onus, oppression, pressure, trouble, weight, worry ~*v.* 3. cram, fill, freight, heap, lade, pack, pile, stack, stuff 4. burden, encumber, hamper, oppress, saddle with, trouble, weigh down, worry 5. *Of firearms* charge, make ready, prepare to fire, prime 6. **load the dice** fix, rig, set up

loaded 1. burdened, charged, freighted, full, laden, weighted 2. biased, distorted, weighted 3. artful, insidious, manipulative, prejudicial, tricky 4. at the ready, charged, primed, ready to shoot *or* fire 5. *Sl.* affluent, flush (*Inf.*), moneyed, rich, rolling (*Sl.*), wealthy, well-heeled (*Inf.*), well off, well-to-do

loaf[1] *n.* 1. block, cake, cube, lump, slab 2. *Sl.* block (*Inf.*), chump (*Brit. sl.*), gumption (*Brit. inf.*), head, noddle (*Inf., chiefly Brit.*), nous (*Brit. sl.*), sense

loaf[2] *v.* 1. be indolent, idle, laze, lie around, loiter, loll, lounge around, take it easy 2. *With* **away** fritter away, kill time, pass time, veg out (*Sl., chiefly U.S.*), waste time, while away the hours

loafer bum (*Inf.*), couch potato (*Sl.*), drone (*Brit.*), idler, layabout, lazybones (*Inf.*), lounger, ne'er-do-well, shirker, skiver (*Brit. sl.*), time-waster, wastrel

loan 1. *n.* accommodation, advance, allowance, credit, mortgage, touch (*Sl.*) 2. *v.* accommodate, advance, allow, credit, lend, let out

loath, loth against, averse, backward, counter, disinclined, indisposed, opposed, reluctant, resisting, unwilling

Antonyms anxious, avid, desirous, eager, enthusiastic, keen, willing

loathe abhor, abominate, despise, detest, dislike, execrate, feel repugnance towards, find disgusting, hate, have a strong aversion to, not be able to bear *or* abide

loathing abhorrence, abomination, antipathy, aversion, detestation, disgust, execration, hatred, horror, odium, repugnance, repulsion, revulsion

loathsome abhorrent, abominable, detestable, disgusting, execrable, hateful, horrible, nasty, nauseating, obnoxious, obscene, odious, offensive, repugnant, repulsive, revolting, vile, yucky *or* yukky (*Sl.*)

Antonyms adorable, attractive, charming, delightful, enchanting, engaging, fetching, likable *or* likeable, lovable, lovely

lob *v.* fling, launch, lift, loft, pitch, shy (*Inf.*), throw, toss

lobby *n.* 1. corridor, entrance hall, foyer, hall, hallway, passage, passageway, porch, vestibule 2. pressure group ~*v.* 3. bring pressure to bear, campaign for, exert influence, influence, persuade, press for, pressure, promote, pull strings (*Brit. inf.*), push for, solicit votes, urge

local *adj.* 1. community, district, neighbourhood, parish, provincial, regional 2. confined, limited, narrow, parish pump, parochial, provincial, restricted, small-town ~*n.* 3. character (*Inf.*), inhabitant, local yokel (*Disparaging*), native, resident

locale locality, location, locus, place, position, scene, setting, site, spot, venue

locality 1. area, district, neck of the woods (*Inf.*), neighbourhood, region, vicinity 2. locale, location, place, position, scene, setting, site, spot

localize 1. circumscribe, concentrate, confine, contain, delimit, delimitate, limit, restrain, restrict 2. ascribe, assign, narrow down, pinpoint, specify

locate 1. come across, detect, discover, find, lay one's hands on, pin down, pinpoint, run to earth, track down, unearth 2. establish, fix, place, put, seat, set, settle, situate

location bearings, locale, locus, place, point, position, site, situation, spot, venue, whereabouts

lock[1] *n.* 1. bolt, clasp, fastening, padlock ~*v.* 2. bolt, close, fasten, latch, seal, secure, shut, sneck (*Dialect*) 3. clench, engage, entangle, entwine, join, link, mesh, unite 4. clasp, clutch, embrace, encircle, enclose, grapple, grasp, hug, press

lock[2] curl, ringlet, strand, tress, tuft

lock out ban, bar, debar, exclude, keep out, refuse admittance to, shut out

lockup can (*Sl.*), cell, cooler (*Sl.*), gaol, jail, jug (*Sl.*), police cell

lock up cage, confine, detain, imprison, incarcerate, jail, put behind bars, shut up

locomotion action, headway, motion, movement, moving, progress, progression, travel, travelling

locution 1. collocation, expression, idiom, phrase, term, turn of speech, wording 2. accent, articulation, diction, inflection, intonation, manner of speech, phrasing, style

lodestar beacon, guide, model, par, pattern, signal, standard

lodestone beacon, focal point, focus, lodestar, magnet

lodge *n.* 1. cabin, chalet, cottage, gatehouse, house, hunting lodge, hut, shelter 2. assemblage, association, branch, chapter, club, group, society 3. den, haunt, lair, retreat ~*v.* 4. accommodate, billet, board, entertain, harbour, put up, quarter, room, shelter, sojourn, stay, stop 5. become fixed, catch, come to rest, imbed, implant, stick 6. deposit, file, lay, place, put, put on record, register, set, submit

lodger boarder, guest, paying guest, P.G., resident, roomer, tenant

lodging *Often plural* abode, accommodation, apartments, boarding, digs (*Brit. inf.*), dwelling, habitation, quarters, residence, rooms, shelter

lofty 1. elevated, high, raised, sky-high, soaring, tall, towering 2. dignified, distinguished, elevated, exalted, grand, illustrious, imposing, majestic, noble, renowned, stately, sublime, superior 3. arrogant, condescending, disdainful, haughty, high and mighty (*Inf.*), lordly, patronizing, proud, snooty (*Inf.*), supercilious, toffee-nosed (*Sl., chiefly Brit.*)

Antonyms debased, degraded, dwarfed, friendly, humble, low, lowly, mean, modest, short, stunted, unassuming, warm

log *n.* 1. block, bole, chunk, piece of timber, stump, trunk ~*v.* 2. chop, cut, fell, hew ~*n.* 3. account, chart, daybook, journal, listing, logbook, record, tally ~*v.* 4. book, chart, make a note of, note, record, register, report, set down, tally

loggerhead **at loggerheads** at daggers drawn, at each other's throats, at enmity, at odds, estranged, feuding, in dispute, opposed, quarrelling

logic 1. argumentation, deduction, dialectics, ratiocination, science of reasoning, syllogistic reasoning 2. good reason, good sense, reason, sense, sound judgment 3. chain of thought, coherence, connection, link, rationale, relationship

logical 1. clear, cogent, coherent, consistent, deducible, pertinent, rational, reasonable, relevant, sound, valid, well-organized 2. judicious, most likely, necessary, obvious, plausible, reasonable, sensible, wise

Antonyms illogical, implausible, instinctive, irrational, unlikely, unorganized, unreasonable

logistics coordination, engineering, management, masterminding, orchestration, organization, plans, strategy

loiter dally, dawdle, delay, dilly-dally (*Inf.*), hang about *or* around, idle, lag, linger, loaf, loll, saunter, skulk, stroll

loll 1. flop, lean, loaf, lounge, recline, relax, slouch, slump, sprawl 2. dangle, droop, drop, flap, flop, hang, hang loosely, sag

lone by oneself, deserted, isolated, lonesome, one, only, separate, separated, single, sole, solitary, unaccompanied

loneliness aloneness, desertedness, desolation, dreariness, forlornness, isolation, lonesomeness, seclusion, solitariness, solitude

lonely 1. abandoned, destitute, estranged, forlorn, forsaken, friendless, lonesome, outcast 2. alone, apart, by oneself, companionless, isolated, lone, single, solitary, withdrawn 3. deserted, desolate, godforsaken, isolated, off the beaten track (*Inf.*), out-of-the-way, remote, secluded, sequestered, solitary, unfrequented, uninhabited

Antonyms (*sense 1*) accompanied, befriended, popular, together (*sense 2*) bustling, crowded, frequented, populous, teeming

loner hermit, individualist, lone wolf, maverick, misanthrope, outsider, recluse, solitary

lonesome cheerless, companionless, deserted, desolate, dreary, forlorn, friendless, gloomy, isolated, lone, lonely

long[1] *adj.* 1. elongated, expanded, extended, extensive, far-reaching, lengthy, spread out, stretched 2. dragging, interminable, late, lengthy, lingering, long-drawn-out, prolonged, protracted, slow, sustained, tardy

Antonyms abbreviated, abridged, brief, compressed, contracted, little, momentary, quick, short, short-lived, small

long[2] *v.* covet, crave, desire, dream of, eat one's heart out over, hanker, hunger, itch, lust, pine, want, wish, yearn

long-drawn-out dragged out, interminable, lengthy, marathon, overextended, overlong, prolonged, protracted, spun out

long-headed acute, astute, discerning, far-sighted, penetrating, perceptive, sagacious, shrewd, wise

longing 1. *n.* ambition, aspiration, coveting, craving, desire, hankering, hope, hungering, itch, thirst, urge, wish, yearning, yen (*Inf.*) 2. *adj.* anxious, ardent, avid, craving, desirous, eager, hungry, languishing, pining, wishful, wistful, yearning

Antonyms *n.* abhorrence, antipathy, apathy, disgust, indifference, loathing, revulsion, unconcern *~adj.* apathetic, cold, disgusted, hateful, indifferent, loathing, unconcerned, uninterested

long-lived enduring, full of years, longevous, long-lasting, old as Methuselah

long-standing abiding, enduring, established, fixed, hallowed by time, long-established, long-lasting, long-lived, time-honoured

long-suffering easygoing, forbearing, forgiving, patient, resigned, stoical, tolerant, uncomplaining

long-winded diffuse, discursive, garrulous, lengthy, long-drawn-out, overlong, prolix, prolonged, rambling, repetitious, tedious, verbose, wordy

Antonyms brief, concise, crisp, curt, laconic, pithy, sententious, short, succinct, terse, to the point

look *v.* 1. behold (*Archaic*), check, check out (*Inf.*), clock (*Brit. sl.*), consider, contemplate, examine, eye, eyeball (*U.S. sl.*), feast one's eyes upon, gaze, get a load of (*Inf.*), glance, inspect, observe, peep, recce (*Sl.*), regard, scan, scrutinize, see, study, survey, take a dekko at (*Brit. sl.*), take a gander at (*Inf.*), view, watch 2. appear, display, evidence, exhibit, look like, make clear, manifest, present, seem, seem to be, show, strike one as 3. face, front, front on, give onto, overlook 4. anticipate, await, expect, hope, reckon on 5. forage, hunt, search, seek 6. gape, gawk, gawp (*Brit. sl.*), glower, goggle, rubberneck (*Sl.*), ogle, stare 7. **look like** be the image of, favour, make one think of, put one in mind of, remind one of, resemble, take after *~n.* 8. butcher's (*Brit. sl.*), examination, eyeful (*Inf.*), gander (*Inf.*), gaze, glance, glimpse, inspection, look-see (*Sl.*), observation, once-over (*Inf.*), peek, recce (*Sl.*), review, shufti (*Brit. sl.*), sight, squint (*Inf.*), survey, view 9. air, appearance, aspect, bearing, cast, complexion, countenance, demeanour, effect, expression, face, fashion, guise, manner, mien (*Literary*), semblance

look after attend to, care for, guard, keep an eye on, mind, nurse, protect, sit with, supervise, take care of, take charge of, tend, watch

lookalike clone, dead ringer (*Sl.*), double, exact match, living image, replica, ringer (*Sl.*), spit (*Inf., chiefly Brit.*), spit and image (*Inf.*), spitting image (*Inf.*), twin

look down on *or* **upon** contemn, despise, disdain, hold in contempt, look down one's nose at (*Inf.*), misprize, scorn, sneer, spurn, treat with contempt, turn one's nose up (at) (*Inf.*)

look forward to anticipate, await, count on, count the days until, expect, hope for, long for, look for, wait for

look into check out, delve into, examine, explore, follow up, go into, inquire about, inspect, investigate, look over, make enquiries, make inquiries, probe, research, scrutinize, study

lookout 1. guard, qui vive, readiness, vigil, watch 2. guard, sentinel, sentry, vedette (*Military*), watchman 3. beacon, citadel, observation post, observatory, post, tower, watchtower 4. *Inf.* business, concern, funeral (*Inf.*), pigeon (*Brit. inf.*), worry 5. chances, future, likelihood, outlook, prospect, view

look out be alert, be careful, be on guard, be

on the qui vive, be vigilant, beware, keep an eye out, keep one's eyes open (peeled, skinned), pay attention, watch out

look over cast an eye over, check, check out (*Inf.*), examine, eyeball (*U.S. sl.*), flick through, inspect, look through, monitor, peruse, scan, take a dekko at (*Brit. sl.*), view, work over

look up 1. find, hunt for, research, search for, seek out, track down 2. ameliorate, come along, get better, improve, perk up, pick up, progress, shape up (*Inf.*), show improvement 3. *With* **to** admire, defer to, esteem, have a high opinion of, honour, regard highly, respect, revere 4. call (on), drop in on (*Inf.*), go to see, look in on, pay a visit to, visit

loom 1. appear, become visible, be imminent, bulk, emerge, hover, impend, menace, take shape, threaten 2. dominate, hang over, mount, overhang, overshadow, overtop, rise, soar, tower

loop 1. *n.* bend, circle, coil, convolution, curl, curve, eyelet, hoop, kink, loophole, noose, ring, spiral, twirl, twist, whorl 2. *v.* bend, braid, circle, coil, connect, curl, curve round, encircle, fold, join, knot, roll, spiral, turn, twist, wind round

loophole 1. aperture, knothole, opening, slot 2. *Fig.* avoidance, escape, evasion, excuse, let-out, means of escape, plea, pretence, pretext, subterfuge

loose *adj.* 1. floating, free, insecure, movable, released, unattached, unbound, unconfined, unfastened, unfettered, unrestricted, unsecured, untied, wobbly 2. baggy, easy, hanging, loosened, not fitting, not tight, relaxed, slack, slackened, sloppy 3. diffuse, disconnected, disordered, ill-defined, imprecise, inaccurate, indefinite, indistinct, inexact, rambling, random, vague 4. abandoned, debauched, disreputable, dissipated, dissolute, fast, immoral, lewd, libertine, licentious, profligate, promiscuous, unchaste, wanton 5. careless, heedless, imprudent, lax, negligent, rash, thoughtless, unmindful ~*v.* 6. detach, disconnect, disengage, ease, free, let go, liberate, loosen, release, set free, slacken, unbind, unbridle, undo, unfasten, unleash, unloose, untie

Antonyms *adj.* (*sense 1*) bound, curbed, fastened, fettered, restrained, secured, tethered, tied (*sense 2*) tight (*sense 3*) accurate, clear, concise, exact, precise (*sense 4*) chaste, disciplined, moral, virtuous ~*v.* bind, cage, capture, fasten, fetter, imprison, tether

loose-jointed *or* **loose-limbed** agile, elastic, flexible, limber, lissom(e), lithe, pliable, pliant, supple

loosen 1. detach, let out, separate, slacken, unbind, undo, unloose, unstick, untie, work free, work loose 2. deliver, free, let go, liberate, release, set free 3. *Often with* **up** ease up *or* off, go easy (*Inf.*), lessen, let up, lighten up (*Sl.*), mitigate, moderate, relax, soften, weaken

loot 1. *n.* booty, goods, haul, plunder, prize, spoils, swag (*Sl.*) 2. *v.* despoil, pillage, plunder, raid, ransack, ravage, rifle, rob, sack

lop chop, clip, crop, curtail, cut, detach, dock, hack, prune, sever, shorten, trim, truncate

lope bound, canter, gallop, lollop, spring, stride

lopsided askew, asymmetrical, awry, cockeyed, crooked, disproportionate, off balance, one-sided, out of shape, out of true, skewwhiff (*Brit. inf.*), squint, tilting, unbalanced, unequal, uneven, warped

loquacious babbling, blathering, chattering, chatty, gabby (*Inf.*), garrulous, gassy (*Inf.*), gossipy, talkative, voluble, wordy

loquacity babbling, chattering, chattiness, effusiveness, gabbling, garrulity, gassiness (*Inf.*), talkativeness, volubility

lord 1. commander, governor, king, leader, liege, master, monarch, overlord, potentate, prince, ruler, seigneur, sovereign, superior 2. earl, noble, nobleman, peer, viscount 3. **lord it over** act big (*Sl.*), be overbearing, boss around (*Inf.*), domineer, order around, play the lord, pull rank, put on airs, swagger

Lord, Our *or* **The** Christ, God, Jehovah, Jesus Christ, the Almighty

lordly 1. arrogant, condescending, despotic, dictatorial, disdainful, domineering, haughty, high and mighty (*Inf.*), high-handed, hoity-toity (*Inf.*), imperious, lofty, overbearing, patronizing, proud, stuck-up (*Inf.*), supercilious, toffee-nosed (*Sl., chiefly Brit.*), tyrannical 2. aristocratic, dignified, exalted, gracious, grand, imperial, lofty, majestic, noble, princely, regal, stately

lore 1. beliefs, doctrine, experience, folk-wisdom, mythos, saws, sayings, teaching, traditional wisdom, traditions, wisdom 2. erudition, knowhow (*Inf.*), knowledge, learning, letters, scholarship

lose 1. be deprived of, displace, drop, fail to keep, forget, mislay, misplace, miss, suffer loss 2. capitulate, default, fail, fall short, forfeit, lose out on (*Inf.*), miss, pass up (*Inf.*), yield 3. be defeated, be the loser, be worsted, come a cropper (*Inf.*), come to grief, get the worst of, lose out, suffer defeat, take a licking (*Inf.*) 4. consume, deplete, dissipate, drain, exhaust, expend, lavish, misspend, squander, use up, waste 5. confuse, miss, stray from, wander from 6. lap, leave behind, outdistance, outrun, outstrip, overtake, pass 7. dodge, duck, elude, escape, evade, give someone the slip, shake off, slip away, throw off

loser also-ran, dud (*Inf.*), failure, flop (*Inf.*), lemon (*Sl.*), no-hoper (*Aust. sl.*), underdog, washout (*Inf.*)

loss 1. bereavement, deprivation, disappearance, drain, failure, forfeiture, losing, misfortune, mislaying, privation, squandering, waste 2. cost, damage, defeat, destruction, detriment, disadvantage, harm, hurt, impairment, injury, ruin 3. *Plural* casualties, dead, death toll, fatalities, number killed (captured, injured, missing, wounded) 4. *Sometimes plural* debit, debt, deficiency, deficit, depletion, losings, shrinkage 5. **at a loss** at one's wits' end, baffled, bewildered, confused, helpless, nonplussed, perplexed, puzzled, stuck (*Inf.*), stumped
Antonyms acquisition, advantage, finding, gain, preservation, recovery, reimbursement, restoration, saving, winning

lost 1. disappeared, forfeited, mislaid, misplaced, missed, missing, strayed, vanished, wayward 2. adrift, astray, at sea, disoriented, off-course, off-track 3. baffled, bewildered, clueless (*Sl.*), confused, helpless, ignorant, mystified, perplexed, puzzled 4. abolished, annihilated, demolished, destroyed, devastated, eradicated, exterminated, obliterated, perished, ruined, wasted, wiped out, wrecked 5. absent, absorbed, abstracted, distracted, dreamy, engrossed, entranced, preoccupied, rapt, spellbound, taken up 6. consumed, dissipated, frittered away, misapplied, misdirected, misspent, misused, squandered, wasted 7. bygone, dead, extinct, forgotten, gone, lapsed, obsolete, out-of-date, past, unremembered 8. abandoned, corrupt, damned, depraved, dissolute, fallen, irreclaimable, licentious, profligate, unchaste, wanton

lot 1. assortment, batch, bunch (*Inf.*), collection, consignment, crowd, group, quantity, set 2. accident, chance, destiny, doom, fate, fortune, hazard, plight, portion 3. allowance, cut (*Inf.*), parcel, part, percentage, piece, portion, quota, ration, share 4. **a lot** *or* **lots** abundance, a great deal, heap(s), large amount, load(s) (*Inf.*), masses (*Inf.*), numbers, ocean(s), oodles (*Inf.*), piles (*Inf.*), plenty, quantities, reams (*Inf.*), scores, stack(s) 5. **draw lots** choose, cut for aces, cut straws (*Inf.*), decide, pick, select, spin a coin, toss up 6. **throw in one's lot with** ally *or* align oneself with, join, join forces with, join fortunes with, make common cause with, support

loth *see* LOATH

lotion balm, cream, embrocation, liniment, salve, solution

lottery 1. draw, raffle, sweepstake 2. chance, gamble, hazard, risk, toss-up (*Inf.*), venture

loud 1. blaring, blatant, boisterous, booming, clamorous, deafening, ear-piercing, ear-splitting, forte (*Music*), high-sounding, noisy, obstreperous, piercing, resounding, rowdy, sonorous, stentorian, strident, strong, thundering, tumultuous, turbulent, vehement, vociferous 2. *Fig.* brash, brassy, flamboyant, flashy, garish, gaudy, glaring, lurid, naff (*Brit. sl.*), ostentatious, showy, tacky (*Inf.*), tasteless, tawdry, vulgar 3. brash, brazen, coarse, crass, crude, loud-mouthed (*Inf.*), offensive, raucous, vulgar
Antonyms (*sense 1*) gentle, inaudible, low, low-pitched, quiet, silent, soft, soundless, subdued (*sense 2*) conservative, dull, sober, sombre (*sense 3*) quiet, reserved, retiring, shy, unassuming

loudly at full volume, at the top of one's voice, clamorously, deafeningly, fortissimo (*Music*), lustily, noisily, shrilly, uproariously, vehemently, vigorously, vociferously

loudmouth bigmouth (*Sl.*), blowhard (*Inf.*), blusterer, brag, braggadocio, braggart, bullshit artist (*Taboo sl.*), bullshitter (*Taboo sl.*), gasbag (*Inf.*), swaggerer, windbag (*Sl.*)

lounge *v.* 1. laze, lie about, loaf, loiter, loll, recline, relax, saunter, sprawl, take it easy 2. dawdle, fritter time away, hang out (*Inf.*), idle, kill time, pass time idly, potter, veg out (*Sl., chiefly U.S.*), waste time

lour, lower 1. be brewing, blacken, cloud up *or* over, darken, loom, menace, threaten 2. frown, give a dirty look, glare, glower, look daggers, look sullen, scowl

louring, lowering 1. black, clouded, cloudy, dark, darkening, forbidding, foreboding, gloomy, grey, heavy, menacing, ominous, overcast, threatening 2. brooding, forbidding, frowning, glowering, grim, scowling, sullen, surly

lousy 1. *Sl.* base, contemptible, despicable, dirty, hateful, low, mean, rotten (*Inf.*), shitty (*Taboo sl.*), vicious, vile 2. *Sl.* awful, bad, bush-league (*Aust. & N.Z. inf.*), chickenshit (*U.S. sl.*), dime-a-dozen (*Inf.*), duff (*Inf.*), inferior, miserable, no good, of a sort *or* of sorts, piss-poor (*Taboo sl.*), poor, poxy (*Sl.*), rotten (*Inf.*), second-rate, shitty (*Taboo sl.*), shoddy, slovenly, terrible, tinhorn (*U.S. sl.*), two-bit (*U.S. & Canad. sl.*) 3. lice-infected, lice-infested, lice-ridden, pedicular, pediculous 4. **lousy with** *Sl.* **a.** amply supplied with, not short of, rolling in (*Sl.*), well-supplied with **b.** alive with, overrun by, swarming with, teeming with

lout bear, boor, bumpkin, churl, clod, clumsy idiot, dolt, gawk, lubber, lummox (*Inf.*), ned (*Sl.*), oaf, yahoo, yob *or* yobbo (*Brit. sl.*)

loutish boorish, bungling, churlish, clod-hopping (*Inf.*), coarse, doltish, gawky, gross, ill-bred, ill-mannered, lubberly, lumpen (*Inf.*), lumpish, oafish, rough, stolid, swinish, uncouth, unmannerly

lovable adorable, amiable, attractive, captivating, charming, cuddly, cute, delightful, enchanting, endearing, engaging, fetching (*Inf.*), likable *or* likeable, lovely, pleasing, sweet, winning, winsome

Antonyms abhorrent, abominable, detestable, hateful, loathsome, obnoxious, odious, offensive, revolting

love *v.* 1. adore, adulate, be attached to, be in love with, cherish, dote on, have affection for, hold dear, idolize, prize, think the world of, treasure, worship 2. appreciate, delight in, desire, enjoy, fancy, have a weakness for, like, relish, savour, take pleasure in 3. canoodle (*Sl.*), caress, cuddle, embrace, fondle, kiss, neck (*Inf.*), pet ~*n.* 4. adoration, adulation, affection, amity, ardour, attachment, devotion, fondness, friendship, infatuation, liking, passion, rapture, regard, tenderness, warmth 5. delight, devotion, enjoyment, fondness, inclination, liking, partiality, relish, soft spot, taste, weakness 6. angel, beloved, darling, dear, dearest, dear one, inamorata, inamorato, leman (*Archaic*), loved one, lover, sweet, sweetheart, truelove 7. **for love** for nothing, freely, free of charge, gratis, pleasurably, without payment 8. **for love or money** by any means, ever, under any conditions 9. **in love** besotted, charmed, enamoured, enraptured, infatuated, smitten 10. **fall in love (with)** bestow one's affections on, be taken with, fall for, lose one's heart (to), take a shine to (*Inf.*)

Antonyms *v.* (*senses 1 & 2*) abhor, abominate, detest, dislike, hate, scorn ~*n.* (*senses 4 & 5*) abhorrence, abomination, animosity, antagonism, antipathy, aversion, bitterness, detestation, disgust, dislike, hate, hatred, hostility, ill will, incompatibility, loathing, malice, repugnance, resentment, scorn (*sense 6*) enemy, foe

love affair 1. affair, *affaire de coeur,* amour, intrigue, liaison, relationship, romance 2. appreciation, devotion, enthusiasm, love, mania, passion

loveless 1. disliked, forsaken, friendless, lovelorn, unappreciated, uncherished, unloved, unvalued 2. cold, cold-hearted, frigid, hard, heartless, icy, insensitive, unfeeling, unfriendly, unloving, unresponsive

lovelorn crossed in love, jilted, languishing, lovesick, mooning, moping, pining, slighted, spurned, unrequited, yearning

lovely 1. admirable, adorable, amiable, attractive, beautiful, charming, comely, exquisite, graceful, handsome, pretty, sweet, winning 2. agreeable, captivating, delightful, enchanting, engaging, enjoyable, gratifying, nice, pleasant, pleasing

Antonyms abhorrent, detestable, hateful, hideous, loathsome, odious, repellent, repugnant, revolting, ugly, unattractive

lovemaking act of love, carnal knowledge, coition, coitus, copulation, intercourse, intimacy, mating, nookie (*Sl.*), rumpy-pumpy (*Sl.*), sexual intercourse, sexual relations, sexual union *or* congress, the other (*Inf.*)

lover admirer, beau, beloved, boyfriend, fancy man (*Sl.*), fancy woman (*Sl.*), fiancé, fiancée, flame (*Inf.*), girlfriend, inamorata, inamorato, leman (*Archaic*), mistress, paramour, suitor, swain (*Archaic*), sweetheart, toy boy

lovesick desiring, languishing, longing, lovelorn, pining, yearning

loving affectionate, amorous, ardent, cordial, dear, demonstrative, devoted, doting, fond, friendly, kind, solicitous, tender, warm, warm-hearted

Antonyms aloof, cold, contemptuous, cruel, detached, distasteful, hateful, hostile, indifferent, mean, unconcerned, unloving, scornful

low[1] 1. fubsy (*Archaic or dialect*), little, short, small, squat, stunted 2. deep, depressed, ground-level, low-lying, shallow, subsided, sunken 3. depleted, insignificant, little, meagre, measly, paltry, reduced, scant, small, sparse, trifling 4. deficient, inadequate, inferior, low-grade, mediocre, pathetic, poor, puny, second-rate, shoddy, substandard, worthless 5. coarse, common, crude, disgraceful, dishonourable, disreputable, gross, ill-bred, obscene, rough, rude, unbecoming, undignified, unrefined, vulgar 6. humble, lowborn, lowly, meek, obscure, plain, plebeian, poor, simple, unpretentious 7. blue, brassed off (*Brit. sl.*), dejected, depressed, despondent, disheartened, dismal, down, downcast, down in the dumps (*Inf.*), fed up, forlorn, gloomy, glum, miserable, morose, sad, sick as a parrot (*Inf.*), unhappy 8. debilitated, dying, exhausted, feeble, frail, ill, prostrate, reduced, sinking, stricken, weak 9. gentle,

hushed, muffled, muted, quiet, soft, subdued, whispered 10. cheap, economical, inexpensive, moderate, modest, reasonable 11. abject, base, contemptible, dastardly, degraded, depraved, despicable, ignoble, mean, menial, nasty, scurvy, servile, sordid, unworthy, vile, vulgar
Antonyms admirable, alert, brave, cheerful, elated, elevated, eminent, energetic, enthusiastic, exalted, fine, grand, happy, high, high-ranking, honourable, important, laudable, lofty, loud, noisy, praiseworthy, significant, strong, superior, tall, towering, worthy

low[2] 1. *v.* bellow, moo 2. *n.* bellow, bellowing, lowing, moo, mooing

lowdown *Inf.* dope (*Inf.*), gen (*Brit. inf.*), info (*Inf.*), information, inside story, intelligence

low-down base, cheap (*Inf.*), contemptible, despicable, low, mean, nasty, reprehensible, scurvy, ugly, underhand

lower[1] *adj.* 1. inferior, junior, lesser, low-level, minor, secondary, second-class, smaller, subordinate, under 2. curtailed, decreased, diminished, lessened, pared down, reduced ~*v.* 3. depress, drop, fall, let down, make lower, sink, submerge, take down 4. abase, belittle, condescend, debase, degrade, deign, demean, devalue, disgrace, downgrade, humble, humiliate, stoop 5. abate, curtail, cut, decrease, diminish, lessen, minimize, moderate, prune, reduce, slash 6. soften, tone down
Antonyms *adj.* enlarged, higher, increased ~*v.* amplify, augment, boost, elevate, enlarge, extend, hoist, increase, inflate, lift, magnify, raise

lower[2] *see* LOUR

lowering *see* LOURING

low-grade bad, bush-league (*Aust. & N.Z. inf.*), chickenshit (*U.S. sl.*), dime-a-dozen (*Inf.*), duff (*Inf.*), inferior, not good enough, not up to snuff (*Inf.*), of a sort *or* of sorts, piss-poor (*Taboo sl.*), poor, poxy (*Sl.*), second-rate, substandard, tinhorn (*U.S. sl.*), two-bit (*U.S. & Canad. sl.*)

low-key low-pitched, muffled, muted, played down, quiet, restrained, subdued, toned down, understated

lowly 1. ignoble, inferior, lowborn, mean, obscure, plebeian, proletarian, subordinate 2. docile, dutiful, gentle, humble, meek, mild, modest, submissive, unassuming 3. average, common, homespun, modest, ordinary, plain, poor, simple, unpretentious

low-minded coarse, crude, dirty, disgusting, filthy, foul, gross, indecent, obscene, rude, smutty, uncouth, vulgar

low-spirited apathetic, blue, brassed off (*Brit. sl.*), dejected, depressed, despondent, dismal, down, down-hearted, down in the dumps (*Inf.*), fed up, gloomy, heavy-hearted, low, miserable, moody, sad, unhappy

loyal attached, constant, dependable, devoted, dutiful, faithful, immovable, patriotic, staunch, steadfast, tried and true, true, true-blue, true-hearted, trustworthy, trusty, unswerving, unwavering
Antonyms disloyal, false, perfidious, traitorous, treacherous, unfaithful, untrustworthy

loyalty allegiance, constancy, dependability, devotion, faithfulness, fealty, fidelity, patriotism, reliability, staunchness, steadfastness, troth (*Archaic*), true-heartedness, trueness, trustiness, trustworthiness

lozenge cough drop, jujube, pastille, tablet, troche

lubberly *adj.* awkward, blundering, bungling, churlish, clodhopping (*Inf.*), clownish, clumsy, coarse, crude, doltish, gawky, heavy-handed, loutish, lumbering, lumpen (*Inf.*), lumpish, oafish, uncouth, ungainly

lubricate grease, make slippery, make smooth, oil, oil the wheels, smear, smooth the way

lucid 1. clear, clear-cut, comprehensible, crystal clear, distinct, evident, explicit, intelligible, limpid, obvious, pellucid, plain, transparent 2. beaming, bright, brilliant, effulgent, gleaming, luminous, radiant, resplendent, shining 3. clear, crystalline, diaphanous, glassy, limpid, pellucid, pure, translucent, transparent 4. all there, clear-headed, *compos mentis,* in one's right mind, rational, reasonable, sane, sensible, sober, sound
Antonyms (*sense 1*) ambiguous, confused, equivocal, incomprehensible, indistinct, muddled, unclear, unintelligible, vague (*sense 2*) dull (*sense 3*) unclear (*sense 4*) confused, irrational, muddled, unclear, unperceptive, vague

luck 1. accident, chance, destiny, fate, fortuity, fortune, hap (*Archaic*), hazard 2. advantage, blessing, break (*Inf.*), fluke, godsend, good fortune, good luck, prosperity, serendipity, stroke, success, windfall

luckily 1. favourably, fortunately, happily, opportunely, propitiously, providentially 2. as it chanced, as luck would have it, by chance, fortuitously

luckless calamitous, cursed, disastrous, doomed, hapless, hopeless, ill-fated, ill-starred, jinxed, star-crossed, unfortunate, unhappy, unlucky, unpropitious, unsuccessful

lucky 1. advantageous, blessed, charmed,

favoured, fortunate, jammy (*Brit. sl.*), prosperous, serendipitous, successful 2. adventitious, auspicious, fortuitous, opportune, propitious, providential, timely
Antonyms bad, detrimental, ominous, unfavourable, unfortunate, unhappy, unlucky, unpromising, untimely

lucrative advantageous, fat, fruitful, gainful, high-income, money-making, paying, productive, profitable, remunerative, well-paid

lucre gain, mammon, money, pelf, profit, riches, spoils, wealth

lucubration 1. brainwork, grind (*Inf.*), meditation, study 2. dissertation, opus, production, treatise

ludicrous absurd, burlesque, comic, comical, crazy, droll, farcical, funny, incongruous, laughable, nonsensical, odd, outlandish, preposterous, ridiculous, silly, zany
Antonyms grave, logical, sad, sensible, serious, solemn

lug carry, drag, haul, heave, hump (*Brit. sl.*), pull, tow, yank

luggage baggage, bags, cases, gear, impedimenta, paraphernalia, suitcases, things, trunks

lugubrious dirgelike, dismal, doleful, dreary, funereal, gloomy, melancholy, morose, mournful, sad, serious, sombre, sorrowful, woebegone, woeful

lukewarm 1. blood-warm, tepid, warm 2. *Fig.* apathetic, cold, cool, half-arsed, half-assed (*U.S. & Canad. sl.*), half-hearted, indifferent, laodicean, phlegmatic, unconcerned, unenthusiastic, uninterested, unresponsive

lull *v.* 1. allay, calm, compose, hush, lullaby, pacify, quell, quiet, rock to sleep, soothe, still, subdue, tranquillize 2. abate, cease, decrease, diminish, dwindle, ease off, let up, moderate, quieten down, slacken, subside, wane ~*n.* 3. calm, calmness, hush, let-up (*Inf.*), pause, quiet, respite, silence, stillness, tranquillity

lullaby berceuse, cradlesong

lumber[1] 1. *n.* castoffs, clutter, discards, jumble, junk, refuse, rubbish, trash, trumpery, white elephants 2. *v. Brit. sl.* burden, encumber, impose upon, land, load, saddle

lumber[2] *v.* clump, lump along, plod, shamble, shuffle, stump, trudge, trundle, waddle

lumbering awkward, blundering, bovine, bumbling, clumsy, elephantine, heavy, heavy-footed, hulking, lubberly, overgrown, ponderous, ungainly, unwieldy

luminary big name, celeb (*Inf.*), celebrity, dignitary, leading light, lion, megastar (*Inf.*), notable, personage, somebody, star, V.I.P., worthy

luminescent effulgent, fluorescent, glowing, luminous, phosphorescent, radiant, shining

luminous 1. bright, brilliant, glowing, illuminated, lighted, lit, luminescent, lustrous, radiant, resplendent, shining, vivid 2. clear, evident, intelligible, lucid, obvious, perspicuous, plain, transparent

lump[1] *n.* 1. ball, bunch, cake, chunk, clod, cluster, dab, gob, gobbet, group, hunk, mass, nugget, piece, spot, wedge 2. bulge, bump, growth, hump, protrusion, protuberance, swelling, tumescence, tumour ~*v.* 3. agglutinate, aggregate, batch, bunch, coalesce, collect, combine, conglomerate, consolidate, group, mass, pool, unite

lump[2] *v.* bear, brook, endure, put up with, stand, suffer, take, thole (*Northern English dialect*), tolerate

lumpish awkward, bungling, clumsy, doltish, elephantine, gawky, heavy, lethargic, lumbering, oafish, obtuse, puddingy, stolid, stupid, ungainly

lumpy bumpy, clotted, curdled, full of lumps, grainy, granular, knobbly, uneven

lunacy 1. dementia, derangement, idiocy, insanity, madness, mania, psychosis 2. aberration, absurdity, craziness, folly, foolhardiness, foolishness, idiocy, imbecility, madness, senselessness, stupidity, tomfoolery
Antonyms prudence, reason, sanity, sense

lunatic 1. *adj.* barking (*Sl.*), barking mad (*Sl.*), barmy (*Sl.*), bonkers (*Sl., chiefly Brit.*), crackbrained, crackpot (*Inf.*), crazy, daft, demented, deranged, insane, irrational, loopy (*Inf.*), mad, maniacal, not the full shilling (*Inf.*), nuts (*Sl.*), off one's trolley (*Sl.*), out to lunch (*Inf.*), psychotic, unhinged, up the pole (*Inf.*) 2. *n.* headbanger (*Inf.*), headcase (*Inf.*), loony (*Sl.*), madman, maniac, nut (*Sl.*), nutcase (*Sl.*), nutter (*Brit. sl.*), psychopath

lunge 1. *n.* charge, cut, jab, pass, pounce, spring, stab, swing, swipe (*Inf.*), thrust 2. *v.* bound, charge, cut, dash, dive, fall upon, hit at, jab, leap, pitch into (*Inf.*), plunge, poke, pounce, set upon, stab, strike at, thrust

lurch 1. heave, heel, lean, list, pitch, rock, roll, tilt, wallow 2. reel, stagger, stumble, sway, totter, weave

lure 1. *v.* allure, attract, beckon, decoy, draw, ensnare, entice, inveigle, invite, lead on, seduce, tempt 2. *n.* allurement, attraction, bait, carrot (*Inf.*), come-on (*Inf.*), decoy, enticement, inducement, magnet, siren song, temptation

lurid 1. exaggerated, graphic, melodramatic, sensational, shock-horror (*Facetious*), shocking, startling, unrestrained, vivid, yellow (*of journalism*) 2. disgusting, ghastly, gory, grim, grisly, gruesome, macabre, revolting, savage, violent 3. ashen, ghastly, pale, pallid, sallow, wan 4. bloody, fiery, flaming, glaring, glowering, intense, livid, overbright, sanguine
Antonyms (*senses 1 & 2*) breezy, bright, carefree, controlled, factual, jaunty, light-hearted, mild (*sense 4*) pale, pastel, watery

lurk conceal oneself, crouch, go furtively, hide, lie in wait, move with stealth, prowl, skulk, slink, sneak, snoop

luscious appetizing, delectable, delicious, honeyed, juicy, mouth-watering, palatable, rich, savoury, scrumptious (*Inf.*), succulent, sweet, toothsome, yummy (*Sl.*)

lush 1. abundant, dense, flourishing, green, lavish, overgrown, prolific, rank, teeming, verdant 2. fresh, juicy, ripe, succulent, tender 3. elaborate, extravagant, grand, lavish, luxurious, opulent, ornate, palatial, plush (*Inf.*), ritzy (*Sl.*), sumptuous

lust *n.* 1. carnality, concupiscence, lasciviousness, lechery, lewdness, libido, licentiousness, pruriency, randiness (*Inf., chiefly Brit.*), salaciousness, sensuality, the hots (*Sl.*), wantonness 2. appetence, appetite, avidity, covetousness, craving, cupidity, desire, greed, longing, passion, thirst ~*v.* 3. be consumed with desire for, covet, crave, desire, hunger for *or* after, lech after (*Inf.*), need, slaver over, want, yearn

lustful carnal, concupiscent, craving, hankering, horny (*Sl.*), hot-blooded, lascivious, lecherous, lewd, libidinous, licentious, passionate, prurient, randy (*Inf., chiefly Brit.*), raunchy (*Sl.*), sensual, sexy (*Inf.*), unchaste, wanton

lustily forcefully, hard, loudly, powerfully, strongly, vigorously, with all one's might, with might and main

lustre 1. burnish, gleam, glint, glitter, gloss, glow, sheen, shimmer, shine, sparkle 2. brightness, brilliance, dazzle, lambency, luminousness, radiance, resplendence 3. distinction, fame, glory, honour, illustriousness, prestige, renown

lustreless colourless, dingy, drab, dull, faded, flat, lacklustre, lifeless, matt, pale, tarnished, unpolished, washed out

lustrous bright, burnished, dazzling, gleaming, glistening, glossy, glowing, luminous, radiant, shimmering, shining, shiny, sparkling

lusty brawny, energetic, hale, healthy, hearty, in fine fettle, powerful, Rambo-esque, red-blooded (*Inf.*), robust, rugged, stalwart, stout, strapping, strong, sturdy, vigorous, virile

luxuriant 1. abundant, ample, copious, excessive, lavish, plenteous, plentiful, prodigal, profuse, superabundant 2. baroque, corinthian, decorated, elaborate, extravagant, fancy, festooned, flamboyant, florid, flowery, ornate, rococo, sumptuous 3. dense, exuberant, fecund, fertile, flourishing, fruitful, lush, overflowing, productive, prolific, rank, rich, riotous, teeming, thriving
Antonyms barren, meagre, plain, scanty, simple, sparse, thin, unadorned

luxuriate 1. bask, delight, enjoy, flourish, indulge, relish, revel, wallow 2. abound, bloom, burgeon, flourish, grow, prosper, thrive 3. be in clover, have the time of one's life, live in luxury, live the life of Riley, take it easy, wanton

luxurious 1. comfortable, costly, de luxe, expensive, lavish, magnificent, opulent, plush (*Inf.*), rich, ritzy (*Sl.*), splendid, sumptuous, well-appointed 2. epicurean, pampered, pleasure-loving, self-indulgent, sensual, sybaritic, voluptuous
Antonyms ascetic, austere, deprived, economical, plain, poor, sparing, Spartan, squalid, thrifty

luxury 1. affluence, hedonism, opulence, richness, splendour, sumptuousness, voluptuousness 2. bliss, comfort, delight, enjoyment, gratification, indulgence, pleasure, satisfaction, wellbeing 3. extra, extravagance, frill, indulgence, nonessential, treat
Antonyms austerity, burden, deprivation, destitution, difficulty, discomfort, hardship, infliction, misery, necessity, need, poverty, privation, want

lying 1. *n.* deceit, dishonesty, dissimulation, double-dealing, duplicity, fabrication, falsity, fibbing, guile, mendacity, perjury, prevarication, untruthfulness 2. *adj.* deceitful, dishonest, dissembling, double-dealing, false, guileful, mendacious, perfidious, treacherous, two-faced, untruthful
Antonyms *adj.* candid, forthright, frank, honest, reliable, sincere, straight, straightforward, truthful, veracious

lyric *adj.* 1. *Of poetry* expressive, lyrical, melodic, musical, songlike 2. *Of a voice* clear, dulcet, flowing, graceful, light, silvery ~*n.* 3. *Plural* book, libretto, text, the words, words of a song

lyrical carried away, ecstatic, effusive, emotional, enthusiastic, expressive, impassioned, inspired, poetic, rapturous, rhapsodic

M

macabre cadaverous, deathlike, deathly, dreadful, eerie, frightening, frightful, ghastly, ghostly, ghoulish, grim, grisly, gruesome, hideous, horrid, morbid, unearthly, weird
Antonyms appealing, beautiful, charming, delightful, lovely, pleasant

macerate mash, pulp, soak, soften, steep

machiavellian amoral, artful, astute, crafty, cunning, cynical, deceitful, designing, double-dealing, foxy, intriguing, opportunist, perfidious, scheming, shrewd, sly, underhand, unscrupulous, wily

machinate conspire, contrive, design, devise, engineer, hatch, intrigue, invent, manoeuvre, plan, plot, scheme

machination artifice, cabal, conspiracy, design, device, dodge, intrigue, manoeuvre, plot, ploy, ruse, scheme, stratagem, trick

machine 1. apparatus, appliance, contraption, contrivance, device, engine, instrument, mechanism, tool 2. agency, machinery, organization, party, setup (*Inf.*), structure, system 3. *Fig.* agent, automaton, mechanical man, puppet, robot, zombie

machinery 1. apparatus, equipment, gear, instruments, mechanism, tackle, tools, works 2. agency, channels, machine, organization, procedure, structure, system

mad 1. aberrant, bananas (*Sl.*), barking (*Sl.*), barking mad (*Sl.*), barmy (*Sl.*), batty (*Sl.*), bonkers (*Sl., chiefly Brit.*), crackers (*Brit. sl.*), crackpot (*Inf.*), crazed, crazy (*Inf.*), cuckoo (*Inf.*), delirious, demented, deranged, distracted, flaky (*U.S. sl.*), frantic, frenzied, insane, loony (*Sl.*), loopy (*Inf.*), lunatic, mental (*Sl.*), *non compos mentis,* not the full shilling (*Inf.*), nuts (*Sl.*), nutty (*Sl.*), off one's chump (*Sl.*), off one's head (*Sl.*), off one's nut (*Sl.*), off one's rocker (*Sl.*), off one's trolley (*Sl.*), of unsound mind, out of one's mind, out to lunch (*Inf.*), psychotic, rabid, raving, round the bend (*Brit. sl.*), round the twist (*Brit. sl.*), screwy (*Inf.*), unbalanced, unhinged, unstable, up the pole (*Inf.*) 2. absurd, asinine, daft (*Inf.*), foolhardy, foolish, imprudent, inane, irrational, ludicrous, nonsensical, preposterous, senseless, unreasonable, unsafe, unsound, wild 3. *Inf.* angry, ape (*Sl.*), apeshit (*Sl.*), berserk, cross, enraged, exasperated, fuming, furious, in a wax (*Inf., chiefly Brit.*), incensed, infuriated, irate, irritated, livid (*Inf.*), raging, resentful, seeing red (*Inf.*), wild, wrathful 4. ardent, avid, crazy, daft (*Inf.*), devoted, dotty (*Sl., chiefly Brit.*), enamoured, enthusiastic, fanatical, fond, hooked, impassioned, infatuated, in love with, keen, nuts (*Sl.*), wild, zealous 5. abandoned, agitated, boisterous, ebullient, energetic, excited, frenetic, frenzied, gay, riotous, uncontrolled, unrestrained, wild 6. **like mad** *Inf.* energetically, enthusiastically, excitedly, furiously, madly, quickly, rapidly, speedily, unrestrainedly, violently, wildly, with might and main
Antonyms appeased, calm, composed, cool, mollified, nonchalant, rational, sane, sensible, sound, uncaring

madcap 1. *adj.* crackpot (*Inf.*), crazy, foolhardy, hare-brained, heedless, hot-headed, ill-advised, imprudent, impulsive, lively, rash, reckless, thoughtless, wild 2. *n.* daredevil, hothead, tearaway, wild man

madden aggravate (*Inf.*), annoy, craze, derange, drive one crazy (off one's head (*Sl.*), out of one's mind, round the bend (*Brit. sl.*), round the twist (*Brit. sl.*), to distraction (*Inf.*)), enrage, exasperate, gall, get one's hackles up, incense, inflame, infuriate, irritate, make one's blood boil, make one see red (*Inf.*), make one's hackles rise, nark (*Brit., Aust., & N.Z. sl.*), piss one off (*Taboo sl.*), provoke, raise one's hackles, unhinge, upset, vex
Antonyms appease, calm, mollify, pacify, soothe

made-up fabricated, false, fictional, imaginary, invented, make-believe, mythical, specious, trumped-up, unreal, untrue

madhouse 1. funny farm (*Facetious*), insane asylum, laughing academy (*U.S. sl.*), loony bin (*Sl.*), lunatic asylum, mental hospital, mental institution, nuthouse (*Sl.*), psychiatric hospital, rubber room (*U.S. sl.*) 2. Babel, bedlam, chaos, pandemonium, turmoil, uproar

madly 1. crazily, deliriously, dementedly, distractedly, frantically, frenziedly, hysterically, insanely, rabidly 2. absurdly, foolishly, irrationally, ludicrously, nonsensically, senselessly, unreasonably, wildly 3. energetically, excitedly, furiously, hastily, hotfoot, hurriedly, like mad (*Inf.*), quickly, rapidly, recklessly, speedily, violently, wildly 4. *Inf.* desperately, devotedly, exceedingly, excessively, extremely, intensely, passionately, to distraction

madman *or* **madwoman** headbanger (*Inf.*), headcase (*Inf.*), loony (*Sl.*), lunatic, maniac, mental case (*Sl.*), nut (*Sl.*), nutcase (*Sl.*), nutter (*Brit. sl.*), psycho (*Sl.*), psychopath, psychotic

madness 1. aberration, craziness, delusion, dementia, derangement, distraction, insanity, lunacy, mania, mental illness, psychopathy, psychosis 2. absurdity, daftness (*Inf.*), folly, foolhardiness, foolishness, idiocy, nonsense, preposterousness, wildness 3. anger, exasperation, frenzy, fury, ire, rage, raving, wildness, wrath 4. ardour, craze, enthusiasm, fanaticism, fondness, infatuation, keenness, passion, rage, zeal 5. abandon, agitation, excitement, frenzy, furore, intoxication, riot, unrestraint, uproar

maelstrom 1. vortex, whirlpool 2. bedlam, chaos, confusion, disorder, pandemonium, tumult, turmoil, upheaval, uproar

maestro expert, genius, master, virtuoso

magazine 1. journal, pamphlet, paper, periodical 2. ammunition dump, arsenal, depot, powder room (*Obsolete*), store, storehouse, warehouse

magic *n.* 1. black art, enchantment, necromancy, occultism, sorcery, sortilege, spell, theurgy, witchcraft, wizardry 2. conjuring, hocus-pocus, illusion, jiggery-pokery (*Inf., chiefly Brit.*), jugglery, legerdemain, prestidigitation, sleight of hand, trickery 3. allurement, charm, enchantment, fascination, glamour, magnetism, power ~*adj.* 4. *Also* **magical** bewitching, charismatic, charming, enchanting, entrancing, fascinating, magnetic, marvellous, miraculous, sorcerous, spellbinding

magician 1. archimage (*Rare*), conjurer, conjuror, enchanter, enchantress, illusionist, necromancer, sorcerer, thaumaturge (*Rare*), theurgist, warlock, witch, wizard 2. genius, marvel, miracle-worker, spellbinder, virtuoso, wizard, wonder-worker

magisterial arrogant, assertive, authoritative, bossy (*Inf.*), commanding, dictatorial, domineering, high-handed, imperious, lordly, masterful, overbearing, peremptory
Antonyms deferential, diffident, humble, servile, shy, submissive, subservient, wimpish *or* wimpy (*Inf.*)

magistrate bailie (*Scot.*), J.P., judge, justice, justice of the peace, provost (*Scot.*)

magnanimity beneficence, big-heartedness, bountifulness, charitableness, generosity, high-mindedness, largess *or* largesse, munificence, nobility, open-handedness, selflessness, unselfishness

magnanimous beneficent, big, big-hearted, bountiful, charitable, free, generous, great-hearted, handsome, high-minded, kind, kindly, munificent, noble, open-handed, selfless, ungrudging, unselfish, unstinting
Antonyms miserly, petty, resentful, selfish, small, unforgiving, vindictive

magnate 1. baron, big cheese (*Sl., old-fashioned*), big noise (*Inf.*), big shot (*Inf.*), big wheel (*Sl.*), bigwig (*Inf.*), captain of industry, chief, fat cat (*Sl., chiefly U.S.*), leader, mogul, Mister Big (*Sl., chiefly U.S.*), nabob (*Inf.*), notable, plutocrat, tycoon, V.I.P. 2. aristo (*Inf.*), aristocrat, baron, bashaw, grandee, magnifico, merchant, noble, notable, personage, prince

magnetic alluring, attractive, captivating, charismatic, charming, enchanting, entrancing, fascinating, hypnotic, irresistible, mesmerizing, seductive
Antonyms disagreeable, offensive, repellent, repulsive, unappealing, unattractive, unlikable *or* unlikeable, unpleasant

magnetism allure, appeal, attraction, attractiveness, captivatingness, charisma, charm, draw, drawing power, enchantment, fascination, hypnotism, magic, mesmerism, power, pull, seductiveness, spell

magnification aggrandizement, amplification, augmentation, blow-up (*Inf.*), boost, build-up, deepening, dilation, enhancement, enlargement, exaggeration, expansion, heightening, increase, inflation, intensification

magnificence brilliance, éclat, glory, gorgeousness, grandeur, luxuriousness, luxury, majesty, nobility, opulence, pomp, resplendence, splendour, stateliness, sublimity, sumptuousness

magnificent august, brilliant, elegant, elevated, exalted, excellent, fine, glorious, gorgeous, grand, grandiose, imposing, impressive, lavish, luxurious, majestic, noble, opulent, outstanding, princely, regal, resplendent, rich, splendid, splendiferous (*Facetious*), stately, striking, sublime, sumptuous, superb, superior, transcendent
Antonyms bad, humble, ignoble, lowly, mean, modest, ordinary, petty, poor, trivial, undistinguished, unimposing

magnifico 1. aristo (*Inf.*), aristocrat, grandee, lord, magnate, noble, patrician, seigneur 2. bashaw, big cheese (*Sl., old-fashioned*), big noise (*Inf.*), big shot (*Inf.*), big wheel (*Sl.*), bigwig (*Inf.*), mogul, nabob (*Inf.*), notable, personage, V.I.P.

magnify 1. aggrandize, amplify, augment,

blow up (*Inf.*), boost, build up, deepen, dilate, enlarge, expand, heighten, increase, intensify 2. aggravate, blow up, blow up out of all proportion, dramatize, enhance, exaggerate, inflate, make a federal case of (*U.S. inf.*), make a mountain out of a molehill, make a production (out) of (*Inf.*), overdo, overemphasize, overestimate, overplay, overrate, overstate
Antonyms belittle, decrease, deflate, deprecate, diminish, disparage, lessen, lower, minimize, reduce, shrink, understate

magniloquence bombast, fustian, grandiloquence, loftiness, pomposity, pretentiousness, turgidity

magniloquent bombastic, declamatory, elevated, exalted, grandiloquent, high-flown, high-sounding, lofty, orotund, overblown, pompous, pretentious, rhetorical, sonorous, stilted, turgid

magnitude 1. consequence, eminence, grandeur, greatness, importance, mark, moment, note, significance, weight 2. amount, amplitude, bigness, bulk, capacity, dimensions, enormity, expanse, extent, hugeness, immensity, intensity, largeness, mass, measure, proportions, quantity, size, space, strength, vastness, volume
Antonyms insignificance, meanness, smallness, triviality, unimportance

maid 1. damsel, girl, lass, lassie (*Inf.*), maiden, miss, nymph (*Poetic*), wench 2. abigail (*Archaic*), handmaiden (*Archaic*), housemaid, maidservant, servant, serving-maid

maiden *n.* 1. damsel, girl, lass, lassie (*Inf.*), maid, miss, nymph (*Poetic*), virgin, wench ~*adj.* 2. chaste, intact, pure, undefiled, unmarried, unwed, virgin, virginal 3. first, inaugural, initial, initiatory, introductory 4. fresh, new, unbroached, untapped, untried, unused

maidenly chaste, decent, decorous, demure, gentle, girlish, modest, pure, reserved, undefiled, unsullied, vestal, virginal, virtuous
Antonyms brazen, corrupt, defiled, depraved, dirty, immodest, immoral, impure, indecent, loose, promiscuous, shameless, sinful, unchaste, wanton, wicked

mail *n.* 1. correspondence, letters, packages, parcels, post 2. post, postal service, postal system ~*v.* 3. dispatch, forward, post, send, send by mail *or* post

maim cripple, disable, hamstring, hurt, impair, incapacitate, injure, lame, mangle, mar, mutilate, put out of action, wound

main *adj.* 1. capital, cardinal, central, chief, critical, crucial, essential, foremost, head, leading, necessary, outstanding, paramount, particular, predominant, pre-eminent, premier, primary, prime, principal, special, supreme, vital 2. absolute, brute, direct, downright, entire, mere, pure, sheer, undisguised, utmost, utter ~*n.* 3. cable, channel, conduit, duct, line, pipe 4. effort, force, might, potency, power, puissance, strength 5. **in** *or* **for the main** for the most part, generally, in general, mainly, mostly, on the whole
Antonyms *adj.* auxiliary, dependent, insignificant, least, lesser, minor, secondary, subordinate, trivial, unimportant

mainly above all, chiefly, first and foremost, for the most part, generally, in general, in the main, largely, mostly, most of all, on the whole, overall, predominantly, primarily, principally, substantially, to the greatest extent, usually

mainspring cause, driving force, generator, impulse, incentive, inspiration, motivation, motive, origin, prime mover, source

mainstay anchor, backbone, bulwark, buttress, chief support, linchpin, pillar, prop

maintain 1. care for, carry on, conserve, continue, finance, keep, keep up, look after, nurture, perpetuate, preserve, prolong, provide, retain, supply, support, sustain, take care of, uphold 2. affirm, allege, assert, asseverate, aver, avow, claim, contend, declare, hold, insist, profess, state 3. advocate, argue for, back, champion, defend, fight for, justify, plead for, stand by, take up the cudgels for, uphold, vindicate
Antonyms (*sense 1*) abolish, break off, conclude, discontinue, drop, end, finish, give up, relinquish, suspend, terminate (*sense 2*) disavow (*sense 3*) abandon, desert

maintenance 1. care, carrying-on, conservation, continuance, continuation, keeping, nurture, perpetuation, preservation, prolongation, provision, repairs, retainment, supply, support, sustainment, sustention, upkeep 2. aliment, alimony, allowance, food, keep, livelihood, living, subsistence, support, sustenance, upkeep

majestic august, awesome, dignified, elevated, exalted, grand, grandiose, imperial, imposing, impressive, kingly, lofty, magnificent, monumental, noble, pompous, princely, regal, royal, splendid, splendiferous (*Facetious*), stately, sublime, superb
Antonyms humble, ignoble, lowly, mean, modest, ordinary, unassuming, undistinguished, unimposing

majesty augustness, awesomeness, dignity, exaltedness, glory, grandeur, imposingness, impressiveness, kingliness, loftiness, magnificence, nobility, pomp, queenliness, royalty, splendour, state, stateliness, sublimity

Antonyms disgrace, meanness, shame, triviality

major 1. better, bigger, chief, elder, greater, head, higher, larger, lead, leading, main, most, senior, superior, supreme, uppermost 2. critical, crucial, grave, great, important, mega (*Sl.*), notable, outstanding, pre-eminent, radical, serious, significant, vital, weighty
Antonyms auxiliary, inconsequential, insignificant, lesser, minor, secondary, smaller, subordinate, trivial, unimportant

majority 1. best part, bulk, greater number, mass, more, most, plurality, preponderance, superiority 2. adulthood, manhood, maturity, seniority, womanhood

make *v.* 1. assemble, build, compose, constitute, construct, create, fabricate, fashion, forge, form, frame, manufacture, mould, originate, produce, put together, shape, synthesize 2. accomplish, beget, bring about, cause, create, effect, engender, generate, give rise to, lead to, occasion, produce 3. cause, coerce, compel, constrain, dragoon, drive, force, impel, induce, oblige, press, pressurize, prevail upon, railroad (*Inf.*), require 4. appoint, assign, create, designate, elect, install, invest, nominate, ordain 5. draw up, enact, establish, fix, form, frame, pass 6. add up to, amount to, compose, constitute, embody, form, represent 7. act, carry out, do, effect, engage in, execute, perform, practise, prosecute 8. calculate, estimate, gauge, judge, reckon, suppose, think 9. acquire, clear, earn, gain, get, net, obtain, realize, secure, take in, win 10. arrive at, arrive in time for, attain, catch, get to, meet, reach 11. **make it** *Inf.* arrive (*Inf.*), be successful, come through, crack it (*Inf.*), cut it (*Inf.*), get on, get somewhere, prosper, pull through, succeed, survive *~n.* 12. brand, build, character, composition, constitution, construction, cut, designation, form, kind, make-up, mark, model, shape, sort, structure, style, type, variety 13. cast of mind, character, disposition, frame of mind, humour, kidney, make-up, nature, stamp, temper, temperament

make as if *or* **though** act as if *or* though, affect, feign, feint, give the impression that, make a show of, pretend

make away 1. abscond, beat a hasty retreat, clear out (*Inf.*), cut and run (*Inf.*), decamp, depart, do a runner (*Sl.*), flee, fly, fly the coop (*U.S. & Canad. inf.*), hook it (*Sl.*), make off, run away *or* off, run for it (*Inf.*), scoot, skedaddle (*Inf.*), slope off, take a powder (*U.S. & Canad. sl.*), take it on the lam (*U.S. & Canad. sl.*), take to one's heels 2. *With* **with** abduct, cabbage (*Brit. sl.*), carry off, filch, kidnap, knock off (*Sl.*), make off with, nab (*Inf.*), nick (*Sl., chiefly Brit.*), pilfer, pinch (*Inf.*), purloin, steal, swipe (*Sl.*) 3. *With* **with** blow away (*Sl., chiefly U.S.*), bump off (*Sl.*), destroy, dispose of, do away with, do in (*Sl.*), eliminate, get rid of, kill, murder, rub out (*U.S. sl.*)

make-believe 1. *n.* charade, dream, fantasy, imagination, play-acting, pretence, unreality 2. *adj.* dream, fantasized, fantasy, imaginary, imagined, made-up, mock, pretend, pretended, sham, unreal
Antonyms *n.* actuality, fact, reality, truthfulness *~adj.* authentic, genuine, real, unfeigned

make believe act as if *or* though, dream, enact, fantasize, imagine, play, play-act, pretend

make do cope, get along *or* by, improvise, manage, muddle through, scrape along *or* by

make for 1. aim for, be bound for, head for *or* towards, proceed towards, steer (a course) for 2. assail, assault, attack, fall on, fly at, go for, have a go at (*Inf.*), lunge at, set upon 3. be conducive to, conduce to, contribute to, facilitate, favour, promote

make off 1. abscond, beat a hasty retreat, bolt, clear out (*Inf.*), cut and run (*Inf.*), decamp, do a runner (*Sl.*), flee, fly, fly the coop (*U.S. & Canad. inf.*), hook it (*Sl.*), make away, run away *or* off, run for it (*Inf.*), skedaddle (*Inf.*), slope off, take a powder (*U.S. & Canad. sl.*), take it on the lam (*U.S. & Canad. sl.*), take to one's heels 2. *With* **with** abduct, cabbage (*Brit. sl.*), carry off, filch, kidnap, knock off (*Sl.*), make away with, nab (*Inf.*), nick (*Sl., chiefly Brit.*), pilfer, pinch (*Inf.*), purloin, run away *or* off with, steal, swipe (*Sl.*)

make out 1. descry, detect, discern, discover, distinguish, espy, perceive, recognize, see 2. comprehend, decipher, fathom, follow, grasp, perceive, realize, see, suss (out) (*Sl.*), understand, work out 3. complete, draw up, fill in *or* out, inscribe, write (out) 4. demonstrate, describe, prove, represent, show 5. assert, claim, let on, make as if *or* though, pretend 6. fare, get on, manage, prosper, succeed, thrive

maker author, builder, constructor, director, fabricator, framer, manufacturer, producer

Maker Creator, God

makeshift 1. *adj.* expedient, jury (*Chiefly nautical*), make-do, provisional, rough and ready, stopgap, substitute, temporary 2. *n.* expedient, shift, stopgap, substitute

make-up 1. cosmetics, face (*Inf.*), greasepaint (*Theatre*), *maquillage,* paint (*Inf.*), powder, war paint (*Inf., humorous*) 2. arrangement, assembly, composition, configuration, constitution, construction, form, format, formation, organization, structure 3. build, cast of mind, character, constitution, disposition, figure, frame of mind, make, nature, stamp, temper, temperament

make up 1. compose, comprise, constitute, form 2. coin, compose, concoct, construct, cook up (*Inf.*), create, devise, dream up, fabricate, formulate, frame, hatch, invent, manufacture, originate, trump up, write 3. complete, fill, meet, supply 4. *With* for atone, balance, compensate, make amends, offset, recompense, redeem, redress, requite 5. bury the hatchet, call it quits, come to terms, compose, forgive and forget, make peace, mend, reconcile, settle, shake hands 6. **make up one's mind** choose, come to a decision, decide, determine, make a decision, reach a decision, resolve, settle 7. **make up to** *Inf.* chat up (*Inf.*), court, curry favour with, flirt with, make overtures to, woo

making 1. assembly, building, composition, construction, creation, fabrication, forging, manufacture, production 2. **in the making** budding, coming, emergent, growing, nascent, potential

makings 1. beginnings, capability, capacity, ingredients, materials, potentiality, potential(s), qualities 2. earnings, income, proceeds, profits, returns, revenue, takings

maladjusted alienated, disturbed, estranged, hung-up (*Sl.*), neurotic, unstable

maladministration blundering, bungling, corruption, dishonesty, incompetence, inefficiency, malfeasance (*Law*), malpractice, misgovernment, mismanagement, misrule

maladroit 1. awkward, bungling, cack-handed (*Inf.*), clumsy, hamfisted *or* -handed (*Inf.*), inept, inexpert, unhandy, unskilful 2. gauche, inconsiderate, inelegant, insensitive, tactless, thoughtless, undiplomatic, untoward

malady affliction, ailment, complaint, disease, disorder, ill, illness, indisposition, infirmity, sickness

malaise angst, anxiety, depression, discomfort, disquiet, doldrums, enervation, illness, lassitude, melancholy, sickness, unease, weakness

malapropos 1. *adj.* ill-timed, impertinent, inapposite, inappropriate, inapt, inopportune, misapplied, out of place, unseemly, unsuitable 2. *adv.* impertinently, inappositely, inappropriately, inaptly, inopportunely, out of turn, unseasonably, unsuitably, untimely 3. *n.* blunder, faux pas, gaffe, malapropism, solecism

malcontent 1. *adj.* disaffected, discontented, disgruntled, disgusted, dissatisfied, dissentious, factious, ill-disposed, rebellious, resentful, restive, unhappy, unsatisfied 2. *n.* agitator, complainer, fault-finder, grouch (*Inf.*), grouser, grumbler, mischief-maker, rebel, stirrer (*Inf.*), troublemaker

male manful, manlike, manly, masculine, virile

Antonyms camp (*Inf.*), effeminate, female, feminine, unmanly, wimpish *or* wimpy (*Inf.*), womanish, womanly

malediction anathema, curse, damnation, damning, denunciation, execration, imprecation, malison (*Archaic*)

malefactor convict, criminal, crook (*Inf.*), culprit, delinquent, evildoer, felon, lawbreaker, miscreant, offender, outlaw, transgressor, villain, wrongdoer

maleficent baleful, deleterious, destructive, detrimental, evil, harmful, hurtful, injurious, malign, malignant, noxious, pernicious

malevolence hate, hatred, ill will, malice, maliciousness, malignity, rancour, spite, spitefulness, vengefulness, vindictiveness

malevolent baleful, evil-minded, hateful (*Archaic*), hostile, ill-natured, maleficent, malicious, malign, malignant, pernicious, rancorous, spiteful, vengeful, vicious, vindictive

Antonyms amiable, benevolent, benign, friendly, gracious, kind, warm-hearted

malformation crookedness, deformity, distortion, misshape, misshapenness

malformed abnormal, contorted, crooked, deformed, distorted, irregular, misshapen, twisted

malfunction 1. *v.* break down, develop a fault, fail, go wrong 2. *n.* breakdown, defect, failure, fault, flaw, glitch, impairment

malice animosity, animus, bad blood, bitterness, enmity, evil intent, hate, hatred, ill will, malevolence, maliciousness, malignity, rancour, spite, spitefulness, spleen, vengefulness, venom, vindictiveness

malicious baleful, bitchy (*Inf.*), bitter, catty (*Inf.*), evil-minded, hateful, ill-disposed, ill-natured, injurious, malevolent, malignant, mischievous, pernicious, rancorous, resentful, shrewish, spiteful, vengeful, vicious

Antonyms amiable, benevolent, friendly, kind, warm-hearted

malign 1. *adj.* bad, baleful, baneful, deleterious, destructive, evil, harmful, hostile, hurtful, injurious, maleficent, malevolent,

malignant, pernicious, vicious, wicked **2.** *v.* abuse, asperse, bad-mouth (*Sl., chiefly U.S. & Canad.*), blacken (someone's name), calumniate, defame, denigrate, derogate, disparage, do a hatchet job on (*Inf.*), harm, injure, knock (*Inf.*), libel, revile, rubbish (*Inf.*), run down, slag (off) (*Sl.*), slander, smear, speak ill of, traduce, vilify
Antonyms *adj.* agreeable, amiable, beneficial, benevolent, benign, friendly, good, harmless, honourable, innocuous, kind, moral, virtuous, warm-hearted, wholesome ~*v.* commend, compliment, extol, praise

malignant **1.** baleful, bitter, destructive, harmful, hostile, hurtful, inimical, injurious, maleficent, malevolent, malicious, malign, of evil intent, pernicious, spiteful, vicious **2.** *Medical* cancerous, dangerous, deadly, evil, fatal, irremediable, metastatic, uncontrollable, virulent
Antonyms (*sense 1*) amicable, benign, friendly, kind, warm-hearted (*sense 2*) benign

malignity **1.** animosity, animus, bad blood, bitterness, evil, hate, hatred, hostility, ill will, malevolence, malice, maliciousness, rancour, spite, vengefulness, venom, viciousness, vindictiveness, wickedness **2.** balefulness, deadliness, destructiveness, harmfulness, hurtfulness, perniciousness, virulence

malleable **1.** ductile, plastic, soft, tensile, workable **2.** adaptable, biddable, compliant, governable, impressionable, manageable, pliable, tractable

malodorous evil-smelling, fetid, foul-smelling, mephitic, nauseating, niffy (*Brit. sl.*), noisome, offensive, olid, putrid, rank, reeking, smelly, stinking

malpractice **1.** abuse, dereliction, misbehaviour, misconduct, mismanagement, negligence **2.** abuse, misdeed, offence, transgression

maltreat abuse, bully, damage, handle roughly, harm, hurt, ill-treat, injure, mistreat

maltreatment abuse, bullying, harm, ill-treatment, ill-usage, injury, mistreatment, rough handling

mammoth Brobdingnagian, colossal, elephantine, enormous, gargantuan, giant, gigantic, ginormous (*Inf.*), huge, humongous *or* humungous (*U.S. sl.*), immense, jumbo (*Inf.*), massive, mega (*Sl.*), mighty, monumental, mountainous, prodigious, stupendous, titanic, vast
Antonyms diminutive, insignificant, little, miniature, minute, puny, small, tiny, trivial

man *n.* **1.** bloke (*Brit. inf.*), chap (*Inf.*), gentleman, guy (*Inf.*), male **2.** adult, being, body, human, human being, individual, one, person, personage, somebody, soul **3.** Homo sapiens, humanity, humankind, human race, mankind, mortals, people **4.** attendant, employee, follower, hand, hireling, liegeman, manservant, retainer, servant, soldier, subject, subordinate, valet, vassal, worker, workman **5.** beau, boyfriend, husband, lover, partner, significant other (*U.S. inf.*), spouse **6.** **to a man** bar none, every one, one and all, unanimously, without exception ~*v.* **7.** crew, fill, furnish with men, garrison, occupy, people, staff

manacle **1.** *n.* bond, chain, fetter, gyve (*Archaic*), handcuff, iron, shackle, tie **2.** *v.* bind, chain, check, clap *or* put in irons, confine, constrain, curb, fetter, hamper, handcuff, inhibit, put in chains, restrain, shackle, tie one's hands

manage **1.** administer, be in charge (of), command, concert, conduct, direct, govern, handle, manipulate, oversee, preside over, rule, run, superintend, supervise **2.** accomplish, arrange, bring about *or* off, contrive, cope with, crack it (*Inf.*), cut it (*Inf.*), deal with, effect, engineer, succeed **3.** control, dominate, govern, guide, handle, influence, manipulate, operate, pilot, ply, steer, train, use, wield **4.** carry on, cope, fare, get along, get by (*Inf.*), get on, make do, make out, muddle through, shift, survive
Antonyms bodge (*Inf.*), botch, fail, follow, make a mess of, mismanage, muff, spoil, starve

manageable amenable, compliant, controllable, convenient, docile, easy, governable, handy, submissive, tamable, tractable, user-friendly, wieldy
Antonyms demanding, difficult, disobedient, hard, headstrong, obstinate, refractory, stubborn, ungovernable, unruly, unyielding, wild

management **1.** administration, board, bosses (*Inf.*), directorate, directors, employers, executive(s) **2.** administration, care, charge, command, conduct, control, direction, governance, government, guidance, handling, manipulation, operation, rule, running, superintendence, supervision

manager administrator, boss (*Inf.*), comptroller, conductor, controller, director, executive, gaffer (*Inf., chiefly Brit.*), governor, head, organizer, overseer, proprietor, superintendent, supervisor

mandate authority, authorization, bidding, charge, command, commission, decree, directive, edict, fiat, injunction, instruction, order, precept, sanction, warrant

mandatory binding, compulsory, obligatory, required, requisite
Antonyms discretionary, nonbinding, noncompulsory, nonobligatory, optional, unnecessary, voluntary

manful bold, brave, courageous, daring, determined, gallant, hardy, heroic, indomitable, intrepid, manly, noble, powerful, resolute, stalwart, stout, stout-hearted, strong, valiant, vigorous

manfully boldly, bravely, courageously, desperately, determinedly, gallantly, hard, heroically, intrepidly, like a Trojan, like one possessed, like the devil, nobly, powerfully, resolutely, stalwartly, stoutly, strongly, to the best of one's ability, valiantly, vigorously, with might and main

mangle butcher, cripple, crush, cut, deform, destroy, disfigure, distort, hack, lacerate, maim, mar, maul, mutilate, rend, ruin, spoil, tear, total (*Sl.*), trash (*Sl.*), wreck

mangy dirty, grungy (*Sl., chiefly U.S.*), mean, moth-eaten, scabby (*Inf.*), scruffy, scuzzy (*Sl., chiefly U.S.*), seedy, shabby, shoddy, squalid
Antonyms attractive, choice, clean, de luxe, fine, splendid, spotless, superb, tidy, well-dressed, well-kempt, well-kept

manhandle 1. handle roughly, knock about *or* around, maul, paw (*Inf.*), pull, push, rough up 2. carry, haul, heave, hump (*Brit. sl.*), lift, manoeuvre, pull, push, shove, tug

manhood bravery, courage, determination, firmness, fortitude, hardihood, manfulness, manliness, masculinity, maturity, mettle, resolution, spirit, strength, valour, virility

mania 1. aberration, craziness, delirium, dementia, derangement, disorder, frenzy, insanity, lunacy, madness 2. cacoethes, craving, craze, desire, enthusiasm, fad (*Inf.*), fetish, fixation, obsession, partiality, passion, preoccupation, rage, thing (*Inf.*)

maniac 1. headbanger (*Inf.*), headcase (*Inf.*), loony (*Sl.*), lunatic, madman, madwoman, nutcase (*Sl.*), nutter (*Brit. sl.*), psycho (*Sl.*), psychopath 2. enthusiast, fan, fanatic, fiend (*Inf.*), freak (*Inf.*)

maniacal *or* **manic** berserk, crazed, crazy, demented, deranged, frenzied, insane, lunatic, mad, nutty (*Sl.*), psychotic, raving, unbalanced, wild

manifest 1. *adj.* apparent, blatant, clear, conspicuous, distinct, evident, glaring, noticeable, obvious, open, palpable, patent, plain, unmistakable, visible 2. *v.* declare, demonstrate, display, establish, evince, exhibit, expose, express, make plain, prove, reveal, set forth, show
Antonyms *adj.* concealed, disguised, hidden, inconspicuous, indistinct, masked, suppressed, unapparent, vague, veiled ~*vb.* conceal, cover, cover up, deny, hide, mask, obscure, refute

manifestation appearance, demonstration, disclosure, display, exhibition, exposure, expression, indication, instance, mark, materialization, revelation, show, sign, symptom, token

manifold abundant, assorted, copious, diverse, diversified, many, multifarious, multifold, multiple, multiplied, multitudinous, numerous, varied, various

manipulate 1. employ, handle, operate, ply, use, wield, work 2. conduct, control, direct, engineer, guide, influence, manoeuvre, negotiate, steer

mankind Homo sapiens, humanity, humankind, human race, man, people

manliness boldness, bravery, courage, fearlessness, firmness, hardihood, heroism, independence, intrepidity, machismo, manfulness, manhood, masculinity, mettle, resolution, stoutheartedness, valour, vigour, virility

manly bold, brave, butch (*Sl.*), courageous, daring, dauntless, fearless, gallant, hardy, heroic, macho, male, manful, masculine, muscular, noble, powerful, Ramboesque, red-blooded (*Inf.*), resolute, robust, stout-hearted, strapping, strong, valiant, valorous, vigorous, virile, well-built
Antonyms camp (*Inf.*), cowardly, craven, delicate, effeminate, faint-hearted, feeble, feminine, frail, ignoble, irresolute, sickly, soft, timid, unmanly, weak, wimpish *or* wimpy (*Inf.*), womanish

man-made artificial, ersatz, manufactured, plastic (*Sl.*), synthetic

manner 1. air, appearance, aspect, bearing, behaviour, comportment, conduct, demeanour, deportment, look, mien (*Literary*), presence, tone 2. approach, custom, fashion, form, genre, habit, line, means, method, mode, practice, procedure, process, routine, style, tack, tenor, usage, way, wont 3. brand, breed, category, form, kind, nature, sort, type, variety

mannered affected, artificial, posed, pretentious, pseudo (*Inf.*), put-on, stilted
Antonyms genuine, honest, natural, real, sincere, unaffected, unpretentious

mannerism characteristic, foible, habit, idiosyncrasy, peculiarity, quirk, trait, trick

mannerly civil, civilized, courteous, decorous, genteel, gentlemanly, gracious, ladylike, polished, polite, refined, respectful, well-behaved, well-bred, well-mannered
Antonyms boorish, discourteous, disre-

spectful, ill-mannered, impertinent, impolite, impudent, insolent, rude, unmannerly

manners 1. bearing, behaviour, breeding, carriage, comportment, conduct, demeanour, deportment 2. ceremony, courtesy, decorum, etiquette, formalities, good form, polish, politeness, politesse, proprieties, protocol, refinement, social graces, the done thing

manoeuvrable fast-moving, handleable, manipulatable, mobile, responsive, versatile

manoeuvre *n.* 1. action, artifice, dodge, intrigue, machination, move, movement, plan, plot, ploy, ruse, scheme, stratagem, subterfuge, tactic, trick 2. deployment, evolution, exercise, movement, operation ~*v.* 3. contrive, devise, engineer, intrigue, machinate, manage, manipulate, plan, plot, pull strings, scheme, wangle (*Inf.*) 4. deploy, exercise, move 5. direct, drive, guide, handle, navigate, negotiate, pilot, steer

mansion abode, dwelling, habitation, hall, manor, residence, seat, villa

mantle *n.* 1. *Archaic* cape, cloak, hood, shawl, wrap 2. blanket, canopy, cloud, cover, covering, curtain, envelope, pall, screen, shroud, veil ~*v.* 3. blanket, cloak, cloud, cover, disguise, envelop, hide, mask, overspread, screen, shroud, veil, wrap

manual 1. *adj.* done by hand, hand-operated, human, physical 2. *n.* bible, enchiridion (*Rare*), guide, guidebook, handbook, instructions, workbook

manufacture *v.* 1. assemble, build, compose, construct, create, fabricate, forge, form, make, mass-produce, mould, process, produce, put together, shape, turn out 2. concoct, cook up (*Inf.*), devise, fabricate, hatch, invent, make up, think up, trump up ~*n.* 3. assembly, construction, creation, fabrication, making, mass-production, produce, production

manufacturer builder, constructor, creator, fabricator, factory-owner, industrialist, maker, producer

manumission deliverance, emancipation, enfranchisement, freeing, liberation, release, unchaining

manumit deliver, emancipate, enfranchise, free, liberate, release, set free, unchain

manure compost, droppings, dung, excrement, fertilizer, muck, ordure

many *adj.* 1. abundant, copious, countless, divers (*Archaic*), frequent, innumerable, manifold, multifarious, multifold, multitudinous, myriad, numerous, profuse, sundry, umpteen (*Inf.*), varied, various ~*n.* 2. a horde, a lot, a mass, a multitude, a thousand and one, heaps (*Inf.*), large numbers, lots (*Inf.*), piles (*Inf.*), plenty, scores, tons (*Inf.*), umpteen (*Inf.*) 3. **the many** crowd, hoi polloi, majority, masses, multitude, people, rank and file

mar blemish, blight, blot, damage, deface, detract from, disfigure, harm, hurt, impair, injure, maim, mangle, mutilate, ruin, scar, spoil, stain, sully, taint, tarnish, vitiate

Antonyms adorn, ameliorate, better, embellish, improve, ornament

maraud despoil, forage, foray, harry, loot, pillage, plunder, raid, ransack, ravage, reive (*Dialect*), sack

marauder bandit, brigand, buccaneer, cateran (*Scot.*), corsair, freebooter, mosstrooper, outlaw, pillager, pirate, plunderer, raider, ravager, reiver (*Dialect*), robber

march *v.* 1. file, footslog, pace, parade, stalk, stride, strut, tramp, tread, walk ~*n.* 2. hike, routemarch, tramp, trek, walk 3. demo (*Inf.*), demonstration, parade, procession 4. gait, pace, step, stride 5. advance, development, evolution, progress, progression 6. **on the march** advancing, afoot, astir, en route, marching, on one's way, on the way, proceeding, progressing, under way

marches borderland, borders, boundaries, confines, frontiers, limits, marchlands

margin 1. border, bound, boundary, brim, brink, confine, edge, limit, perimeter, periphery, rim, side, verge 2. allowance, compass, elbowroom, extra, latitude, leeway, play, room, scope, space, surplus

marginal 1. bordering, borderline, on the edge, peripheral 2. insignificant, low, minimal, minor, negligible, slight, small

marijuana bhang, cannabis, charas, dope (*Sl.*), ganja, grass (*Sl.*), hash (*Sl.*), hashish, hemp, kif, leaf (*Sl.*), mary jane (*U.S. sl.*), pot (*Sl.*), sinsemilla, smoke (*Inf.*), stuff (*Sl.*), tea (*U.S. sl.*), weed (*Sl.*)

marine maritime, nautical, naval, ocean-going, oceanic, pelagic, saltwater, sea, seafaring, seagoing, thalassic

mariner bluejacket, gob (*U.S. sl.*), hand, Jack Tar, matelot (*Sl., chiefly Brit..*), navigator, sailor, salt, sea dog, seafarer, seafaring man, seaman, tar

marital conjugal, connubial, married, matrimonial, nuptial, spousal, wedded

maritime 1. marine, nautical, naval, oceanic, sea, seafaring 2. coastal, littoral, seaside

mark *n.* 1. blemish, blot, blotch, bruise, dent, impression, line, nick, pock, scar, scratch, smirch, smudge, splotch, spot, stain, streak 2. badge, blaze, brand, characteristic, device, earmark, emblem, evidence, feature, flag, hallmark, impression, incision, index, indication, label, note, print, proof, seal, sign, signet, stamp, symbol, symptom, token 3. criterion, level, measure, norm, par, standard, yardstick 4. aim, end, goal, object, objective, purpose, target 5. consequence, dignity, distinction, eminence, fame, importance, influence, notability, note, notice, prestige, quality, regard, standing 6. footmark, footprint, sign, trace, track, trail, vestige 7. **make one's mark** achieve recognition, be a success, find a place in the sun, get on in the world, make a success of oneself, make good, make it (*Inf.*), make something of oneself, prosper, succeed ~*v.* 8. blemish, blot, blotch, brand, bruise, dent, impress, imprint, nick, scar, scratch, smirch, smudge, splotch, stain, streak 9. brand, characterize, flag, identify, label, stamp 10. betoken, denote, distinguish, evince, exemplify, illustrate, show 11. attend, hearken (*Archaic*), mind, note, notice, observe, pay attention, pay heed, regard, remark, watch 12. appraise, assess, correct, evaluate, grade

marked apparent, blatant, clear, considerable, conspicuous, decided, distinct, evident, manifest, notable, noted, noticeable, obvious, outstanding, patent, prominent, pronounced, remarkable, salient, signal, striking

Antonyms concealed, doubtful, dubious, hidden, imperceptible, inconspicuous, indistinct, insignificant, obscure, unclear, unnoticeable, vague

markedly clearly, considerably, conspicuously, decidedly, distinctly, evidently, greatly, manifestly, notably, noticeably, obviously, outstandingly, patently, remarkably, signally, strikingly, to a great extent

market 1. *n.* bazaar, fair, mart 2. *v.* offer for sale, retail, sell, vend

marketable in demand, merchantable, salable, sought after, vendible, wanted

marksman, -woman crack shot (*Inf.*), deadeye (*Inf., chiefly U.S.*), dead shot (*Inf.*), good shot, sharpshooter

maroon abandon, cast ashore, cast away, desert, leave, leave high and dry (*Inf.*), strand

marriage 1. espousal, match, matrimony, nuptial rites, nuptials, wedding, wedding ceremony, wedlock 2. alliance, amalgamation, association, confederation, coupling, link, merger, union

married 1. hitched (*Sl.*), joined, one, spliced (*Inf.*), united, wed, wedded 2. conjugal, connubial, husbandly, marital, matrimonial, nuptial, spousal, wifely

marrow core, cream, essence, gist, heart, kernel, pith, quick, quintessence, soul, spirit, substance

marry 1. become man and wife, espouse, get hitched (*Sl.*), get spliced (*Inf.*), take the plunge (*Inf.*), take to wife, tie the knot (*Inf.*), walk down the aisle (*Inf.*), wed, wive (*Archaic*) 2. ally, bond, join, knit, link, match, merge, splice, tie, unify, unite, yoke

marsh bog, fen, morass, moss (*Scot. & northern English dialect*), quagmire, slough, swamp

marshal 1. align, arrange, array, assemble, collect, deploy, dispose, draw up, gather, group, line up, muster, order, organize, rank 2. conduct, escort, guide, lead, shepherd, usher

marshy boggy, fenny, miry, quaggy, spongy, swampy, waterlogged, wet

martial bellicose, belligerent, brave, heroic, military, soldierly, warlike

martinet disciplinarian, drillmaster, stickler

martyrdom agony, anguish, ordeal, persecution, suffering, torment, torture

Antonyms bliss, ecstasy, happiness, joy

marvel 1. *v.* be amazed, be awed, be filled with surprise, gape, gaze, goggle, wonder 2. *n.* genius, miracle, phenomenon, portent, prodigy, whiz (*Inf.*), wonder

marvellous 1. amazing, astonishing, astounding, breathtaking, brilliant, extraordinary, miraculous, phenomenal, prodigious, remarkable, sensational (*Inf.*), singular, spectacular, stupendous, wondrous (*Archaic or literary*) 2. difficult *or* hard to believe, fabulous, fantastic, implausible, improbable, incredible, surprising, unbelievable, unlikely 3. *Inf.* bad (*Sl.*), boffo (*Sl.*), brill (*Inf.*), chillin' (*U.S. sl.*), colossal, cracking (*Brit. inf.*), crucial (*Sl.*), def (*Sl.*), excellent, fabulous (*Inf.*), fantastic (*Inf.*), glorious, great (*Inf.*), jim-dandy (*Sl.*), magnificent, mean (*Sl.*), mega (*Sl.*), sensational (*Inf.*), smashing (*Inf.*), splendid, sovereign, stupendous, super (*Inf.*), superb, terrific (*Inf.*), topping (*Brit. sl.*), wicked (*Inf.*), wonderful

Antonyms awful, bad, believable, commonplace, credible, everyday, ordinary, terrible

masculine 1. male, manful, manlike, manly, mannish, virile 2. bold, brave, butch (*Sl.*), gallant, hardy, macho, muscular, powerful, Ramboesque, red-blooded (*Inf.*), resolute, robust, stout-hearted, strapping, strong, vigorous, well-built

mask *n.* 1. domino, false face, visor, vizard (*Archaic*) 2. blind, camouflage, cloak, concealment, cover, cover-up, disguise, façade, front, guise, screen, semblance, show, veil, veneer ~*v.* 3. camouflage, cloak, conceal, cover, disguise, hide, obscure, screen, veil

masquerade *n.* 1. costume ball, fancy dress party, mask, masked ball, masked party, mummery, revel 2. costume, disguise, domino 3. cloak, cover, cover-up, deception, disguise, dissimulation, front (*Inf.*), guise, imposture, mask, pose, pretence, put-on (*Sl.*), screen, subterfuge ~*v.* 4. disguise, dissemble, dissimulate, impersonate, mask, pass oneself off, pose, pretend (to be)

mass *n.* 1. block, chunk, concretion, hunk, lump, piece 2. aggregate, body, collection, entirety, sum, sum total, totality, whole 3. accumulation, aggregation, assemblage, batch, bunch, collection, combination, conglomeration, heap, load, lot, pile, quantity, stack 4. assemblage, band, body, bunch (*Inf.*), crowd, group, horde, host, lot, mob, number, throng, troop 5. body, bulk, greater part, lion's share, majority, preponderance 6. bulk, dimension, greatness, magnitude, size 7. **the masses** commonalty, common people, crowd, hoi polloi, multitude ~*adj.* 8. extensive, general, indiscriminate, large-scale, pandemic, popular, wholesale, widespread ~*v.* 9. accumulate, amass, assemble, collect, congregate, forgather, gather, mob, muster, rally, swarm, throng

massacre 1. *n.* annihilation, blood bath, butchery, carnage, extermination, holocaust, killing, mass slaughter, murder, slaughter 2. *v.* annihilate, blow away (*Sl., chiefly U.S.*), butcher, cut to pieces, exterminate, kill, mow down, murder, slaughter, slay, take out (*Sl.*), wipe out

massage 1. *n.* acupressure, kneading, manipulation, reflexology, rubbing, rub-down, shiatsu 2. *v.* knead, manipulate, rub, rub down

massive big, bulky, colossal, elephantine, enormous, extensive, gargantuan, gigantic, ginormous (*Inf.*), great, heavy, hefty, huge, hulking, humongous *or* humungous (*U.S. sl.*), immense, imposing, impressive, mammoth, mega (*Sl.*), monster, monumental, ponderous, solid, substantial, titanic, vast, weighty, whacking (*Inf.*), whopping (*Inf.*)
Antonyms frail, light, little, minute, petty, slight, small, thin, tiny, trivial

master *n.* 1. boss (*Inf.*), captain, chief, commander, controller, director, employer, governor, head, lord, manager, overlord, overseer, owner, principal, ruler, skipper (*Inf.*), superintendent 2. ace (*Inf.*), adept, dab hand (*Brit. inf.*), doyen, expert, genius, grandmaster, maestro, maven (*U.S.*), past master, pro (*Inf.*), virtuoso, wizard 3. guide, guru, instructor, pedagogue, preceptor, schoolmaster, spiritual leader, swami, teacher, tutor ~*adj.* 4. adept, crack (*Inf.*), expert, masterly, proficient, skilful, skilled 5. chief, controlling, foremost, grand, great, leading, main, predominant, prime, principal ~*v.* 6. acquire, become proficient in, get the hang of (*Inf.*), grasp, learn 7. bridle, check, conquer, curb, defeat, lick (*Inf.*), overcome, overpower, quash, quell, subdue, subjugate, suppress, tame, triumph over, vanquish 8. command, control, direct, dominate, govern, manage, regulate, rule
Antonyms *n.* (*sense 1*) crew, servant, slave, subject (*sense 2*) amateur, novice (*sense 3*) student ~*adj.* (*sense 4*) amateurish, clumsy, incompetent, inept, novice, unaccomplished, unskilled, untalented (*sense 5*) lesser, minor ~*v.* (*sense 7*) give in, surrender, yield

masterful 1. adept, adroit, clever, consummate, crack (*Inf.*), deft, dexterous, excellent, expert, exquisite, fine, finished, first-rate, masterly, skilful, skilled, superior, superlative, supreme, world-class 2. arrogant, authoritative, bossy (*Inf.*), despotic, dictatorial, domineering, high-handed, imperious, magisterial, overbearing, overweening, peremptory, self-willed, tyrannical
Antonyms (*sense 1*) amateurish, clumsy, incompetent, inept, unaccomplished, unskilled, untalented (*sense 2*) irresolute, meek, spineless, weak, wimpish *or* wimpy (*Inf.*)

masterly adept, adroit, clever, consummate, crack (*Inf.*), dexterous, excellent, expert, exquisite, fine, finished, first-rate, masterful, skilful, skilled, superior, superlative, supreme, world-class

mastermind 1. *v.* be the brains behind (*Inf.*), conceive, devise, direct, manage, organize, plan 2. *n.* architect, authority, brain(s) (*Inf.*), brainbox, director, engineer, genius, intellect, manager, organizer, planner, virtuoso

masterpiece *chef d'oeuvre,* classic, jewel, magnum opus, master work, *pièce de résistance, tour de force*

mastery 1. command, comprehension, familiarity, grasp, knowledge, understanding 2. ability, acquirement, attainment, cleverness, deftness, dexterity, expertise, finesse, know-how (*Inf.*), proficiency, prowess, skill, virtuosity 3. ascendancy, authority, command, conquest, control, domination, dominion, pre-eminence, rule, superiority, supremacy, sway, triumph, upper hand, victory, whip hand

masticate champ, chew, crunch, eat, munch

masturbation autoeroticism, onanism, playing with oneself (*Sl.*), self-abuse

match *n.* 1. bout, competition, contest, game, head-to-head, test, trial 2. competitor, counterpart, equal, equivalent, peer, rival 3. companion, complement, counterpart, equal, equivalent, fellow, mate, tally 4. copy, dead ringer (*Sl.*), double, duplicate, equal, lookalike, replica, ringer (*Sl.*), spit (*Inf., chiefly Brit.*), spit and image (*Inf.*), spitting image (*Inf.*), twin 5. affiliation, alliance, combination, couple, duet, item (*Inf.*), marriage, pair, pairing, partnership, union ~*v.* 6. ally, combine, couple, join, link, marry, mate, pair, unite, yoke 7. accompany, accord, adapt, agree, blend, coordinate, correspond, fit, go with, harmonize, suit, tally, tone with 8. compare, compete, contend, emulate, equal, measure up to, oppose, pit against, rival, vie

matching analogous, comparable, coordinating, corresponding, double, duplicate, equal, equivalent, identical, like, paired, parallel, same, toning, twin
Antonyms different, disparate, dissimilar, distinct, divergent, diverse, nonparallel, other, unequal, unlike

matchless consummate, exquisite, incomparable, inimitable, peerless, perfect, superlative, supreme, unequalled, unique, unmatched, unparalleled, unrivalled, unsurpassed
Antonyms average, cheaper, common, commonplace, comparable, equalled, everyday, excelled, inferior, lesser, mediocre, ordinary, second-class, surpassed

mate *n.* 1. better half (*Humorous*), husband, partner, significant other (*U.S. inf.*), spouse, wife 2. *Inf.* buddy (*Inf.*), china (*Brit. sl.*), chum (*Inf.*), cock (*Brit. inf.*), comrade, crony, friend, pal (*Inf.*) 3. associate, colleague, companion, compeer, co-worker, fellow-worker 4. assistant, helper, subordinate 5. companion, double, fellow, match, twin ~*v.* 6. breed, copulate, couple, pair 7. marry, match, wed 8. couple, join, match, pair, yoke

material *n.* 1. body, constituents, element, matter, stuff, substance 2. data, evidence, facts, information, notes, work 3. cloth, fabric, stuff ~*adj.* 4. bodily, concrete, corporeal, fleshly, nonspiritual, palpable, physical, substantial, tangible, worldly 5. consequential, essential, grave, important, indispensable, key, meaningful, momentous, serious, significant, vital, weighty 6. applicable, apposite, apropos, germane, pertinent, relevant

materialize appear, come about, come into being, come to pass, happen, occur, take place, take shape, turn up

materially considerably, essentially, gravely, greatly, much, seriously, significantly, substantially
Antonyms barely, hardly, insignificantly, little, scarcely, superficially, unsubstantially

materiel accoutrements, apparatus, equipment, gear, hardware, machinery, materials, stores, supplies, tackle, tools

maternal motherly

maternity motherhood, motherliness

matrimonial conjugal, connubial, hymeneal, marital, married, nuptial, spousal, wedded, wedding

matrimony marital rites, marriage, nuptials, wedding ceremony, wedlock

matrix forge, mould, origin, source, womb

matted knotted, tangled, tousled, uncombed

matter *n.* 1. body, material, stuff, substance 2. affair, business, concern, episode, event, incident, issue, occurrence, proceeding, question, situation, subject, thing, topic, transaction 3. amount, quantity, sum 4. argument, context, purport, sense, subject, substance, text, thesis 5. consequence, import, importance, moment, note, significance, weight 6. complication, difficulty, distress, problem, trouble, upset, worry 7. *Medical* discharge, purulence, pus, secretion ~*v.* 8. be important, be of consequence, carry weight, count, have influence, make a difference, mean something, signify

matter-of-fact deadpan, down-to-earth, dry, dull, emotionless, flat, lifeless, mundane, plain, prosaic, sober, unembellished, unimaginative, unsentimental, unvarnished

mature 1. *adj.* adult, complete, fit, full-blown, full-grown, fully fledged, grown, grown-up, matured, mellow, of age, perfect, prepared, ready, ripe, ripened, seasoned 2. *v.* age, become adult, bloom, blossom, come of age, develop, grow up, maturate, mellow, perfect, reach adulthood, ripen, season
Antonyms adolescent, childish, green, immature, incomplete, juvenile, puerile, undeveloped, unfinished, unperfected, unripe, young, youthful

maturity adulthood, completion, experience, full bloom, full growth, fullness, majority, manhood, maturation, matureness, perfection, ripeness, wisdom, womanhood
Antonyms childishness, excitability, immaturity, imperfection, incompletion, irre-

sponsibility, juvenility, puerility, youthfulness

maudlin lachrymose, mawkish, mushy (*Inf.*), overemotional, sentimental, slushy (*Inf.*), soppy (*Brit. inf.*), tearful, weepy (*Inf.*)

maul 1. abuse, handle roughly, ill-treat, manhandle, molest, paw 2. batter, beat, beat up (*Inf.*), claw, knock about *or* around, lacerate, lambast(e), mangle, pummel, rough up, thrash

maunder 1. dawdle, dilly-dally (*Inf.*), drift, idle, loaf, meander, mooch (*Sl.*), potter, ramble, straggle, stray, traipse (*Inf.*) 2. babble, blather, blether, chatter, gabble, prattle, rabbit (on) (*Brit. inf.*), ramble, rattle on, waffle (*Inf., chiefly Brit.*), witter (*Inf.*)

maw craw, crop, gullet, jaws, mouth, stomach, throat

mawkish 1. emotional, feeble, gushy (*Inf.*), maudlin, mushy (*Inf.*), schmaltzy (*Sl.*), sentimental, slushy (*Inf.*), soppy (*Brit. inf.*) 2. disgusting, flat, foul, insipid, jejune, loathsome, nauseous, offensive, stale, vapid

maxim adage, aphorism, apophthegm, axiom, byword, dictum, gnome, motto, proverb, rule, saw, saying

maximum 1. *n.* apogee, ceiling, crest, extremity, height, most, peak, pinnacle, summit, top, upper limit, utmost, uttermost, zenith 2. *adj.* greatest, highest, maximal, most, paramount, supreme, topmost, utmost

Antonyms bottom, least, lowest, minimum

maybe it could be, mayhap (*Archaic*), peradventure (*Archaic*), perchance (*Archaic*), perhaps, possibly

mayhem chaos, commotion, confusion, destruction, disorder, fracas, havoc, trouble, violence

maze 1. convolutions, intricacy, labyrinth, meander 2. *Fig.* bewilderment, confusion, imbroglio, mesh, perplexity, puzzle, snarl, tangle, uncertainty, web

mazy baffling, bewildering, confused, confusing, intricate, labyrinthine, perplexing, puzzling, serpentine, twisting, twisting and turning, winding

meadow field, grassland, lea (*Poetic*), ley, pasture

meagre 1. deficient, exiguous, inadequate, insubstantial, little, measly, paltry, pathetic, poor, puny, scanty, scrimpy, short, skimpy, slender, slight, small, spare, sparse 2. bony, emaciated, gaunt, hungry, lank, lean, scraggy, scrawny, skinny, starved, thin, underfed 3. barren, infertile, poor, unfruitful, unproductive, weak

mealy-mouthed afraid, equivocal, euphemistic, hesitant, indirect, mincing, overdelicate, prim, reticent

mean[1] *v.* 1. betoken, connote, convey, denote, drive at, express, hint at, imply, indicate, purport, represent, say, signify, spell, stand for, suggest, symbolize 2. aim, aspire, contemplate, design, desire, have in mind, intend, plan, propose, purpose, set out, want, wish 3. design, destine, fate, fit, make, match, predestine, preordain, suit 4. bring about, cause, engender, entail, give rise to, involve, lead to, necessitate, produce, result in 5. adumbrate, augur, betoken, foreshadow, foretell, herald, portend, presage, promise

mean[2] *adj.* 1. beggarly, close, mercenary, mingy (*Brit. inf.*), miserly, near (*Inf.*), niggardly, parsimonious, penny-pinching, penurious, selfish, skimpy, stingy, tight, tight-arsed (*Taboo sl.*), tight as a duck's arse (*Taboo sl.*), tight-assed (*U.S. taboo sl.*), tight-fisted, ungenerous 2. bad-tempered, cantankerous, churlish, disagreeable, hostile, ill-tempered, malicious, nasty, rude, sour, unfriendly, unpleasant 3. abject, base, callous, contemptible, degenerate, degraded, despicable, disgraceful, dishonourable, hard-hearted, ignoble, low-minded, narrow-minded, petty, scurvy, shabby, shameful, sordid, vile, wretched 4. beggarly, contemptible, down-at-heel, grungy (*Sl., chiefly U.S.*), insignificant, miserable, paltry, petty, poor, run-down, scruffy, scuzzy (*Sl., chiefly U.S.*), seedy, shabby, sordid, squalid, tawdry, wretched 5. base, baseborn (*Archaic*), common, humble, ignoble, inferior, low, lowborn, lowly, menial, modest, obscure, ordinary, plebeian, proletarian, servile, undistinguished, vulgar

Antonyms agreeable, altruistic, attractive, big, bountiful, choice, compassionate, consequential, deluxe, excellent, first-rate, generous, gentle, good, high, honourable, humane, important, kind, liberal, munificent, noble, pleasing, praiseworthy, princely, prodigal, significant, superb, superior, sympathetic, unselfish, warm-hearted

mean[3] 1. *n.* average, balance, compromise, happy medium, median, middle, middle course *or* way, mid-point, norm 2. *adj.* average, intermediate, medial, median, medium, middle, middling, normal, standard

meander 1. *v.* ramble, snake, stravaig (*Scot. & northern English dialect*), stray, stroll, turn, wander, wind, zigzag 2. *n.* bend, coil, curve, loop, turn, twist, zigzag

meandering anfractuous, circuitous, convoluted, indirect, roundabout, serpentine, snaking, tortuous, wandering, winding
Antonyms direct, straight, straightforward, undeviating

meaning *n.* 1. connotation, denotation, drift, explanation, gist, implication, import, interpretation, message, purport, sense, significance, signification, substance, upshot, value 2. aim, design, end, goal, idea, intention, object, plan, point, purpose, trend 3. effect, efficacy, force, point, thrust, use, usefulness, validity, value, worth *~adj.* 4. eloquent, expressive, meaningful, pointed, pregnant, speaking, suggestive

meaningful 1. important, material, purposeful, relevant, serious, significant, useful, valid, worthwhile 2. eloquent, expressive, meaning, pointed, pregnant, speaking, suggestive
Antonyms inconsequential, insignificant, meaningless, senseless, superficial, trivial, unimportant, useless, worthless

meaningless aimless, empty, futile, hollow, inane, inconsequential, insignificant, insubstantial, nonsensical, nugatory, pointless, purposeless, senseless, trifling, trivial, useless, vain, valueless, worthless
Antonyms clear, coherent, comprehensible, consequential, decipherable, deep, evident, important, intelligible, legible, meaningful, obvious, purposeful, sensible, significant, understandable, useful, valuable, worthwhile

meanness 1. minginess (*Brit. inf.*), miserliness, niggardliness, parsimony, penuriousness, selfishness, stinginess, tightfistedness 2. bad temper, cantankerousness, churlishness, disagreeableness, hostility, ill temper, malice, maliciousness, nastiness, rudeness, sourness, unfriendliness, unpleasantness 3. abjectness, baseness, degeneracy, degradation, despicableness, disgracefulness, dishonourableness, low-mindedness, narrow-mindedness, pettiness, scurviness, shabbiness, shamefulness, sordidness, vileness, wretchedness 4. beggarliness, contemptibleness, insignificance, paltriness, pettiness, poorness, scruffiness, seediness, shabbiness, sordidness, squalor, tawdriness, wretchedness 5. baseness, humbleness, lowliness, obscurity, servility

means 1. agency, avenue, channel, course, expedient, instrument, measure, medium, method, mode, process, way 2. affluence, capital, estate, fortune, funds, income, money, property, resources, riches, substance, wealth, wherewithal 3. **by all means** absolutely, certainly, definitely, doubtlessly, of course, positively, surely 4. **by means of** by dint of, by way of, through, using, utilizing, via, with the aid of 5. **by no means** absolutely not, definitely not, in no way, not at all, not in the least, not in the slightest, not the least bit, no way, on no account

meantime, meanwhile at the same time, concurrently, for now, for the duration, for the moment, for then, in the interim, in the interval, in the intervening time, in the meantime, in the meanwhile, simultaneously

measly beggarly, contemptible, meagre, mean, mingy (*Brit. inf.*), miserable, miserly, niggardly, paltry, pathetic, petty, pitiful, poor, puny, scanty, skimpy, stingy, ungenerous

measurable assessable, computable, determinable, gaugeable, material, mensurable, perceptible, quantifiable, quantitative, significant

measure *n.* 1. allotment, allowance, amount, amplitude, capacity, degree, extent, magnitude, portion, proportion, quantity, quota, range, ration, reach, scope, share, size 2. gauge, metre, rule, scale, yardstick 3. method, standard, system 4. criterion, example, model, norm, par, standard, test, touchstone, yardstick 5. bounds, control, limit, limitation, moderation, restraint 6. act, action, course, deed, expedient, manoeuvre, means, procedure, proceeding, step 7. act, bill, enactment, law, resolution, statute 8. beat, cadence, foot, metre, rhythm, verse 9. **for good measure** as a bonus, besides, in addition, into the bargain, to boot *~v.* 10. appraise, assess, calculate, calibrate, compute, determine, estimate, evaluate, gauge, judge, mark out, quantify, rate, size, sound, survey, value, weigh 11. adapt, adjust, calculate, choose, fit, judge, tailor

measured 1. exact, gauged, modulated, precise, predetermined, quantified, regulated, standard, verified 2. dignified, even, leisurely, regular, sedate, slow, solemn, stately, steady, unhurried 3. calculated, considered, deliberate, grave, planned, premeditated, reasoned, sober, studied, well thought-out

measureless beyond measure, boundless, endless, immeasurable, immense, incalculable, inestimable, infinite, limitless, unbounded, vast

measurement 1. appraisal, assessment, calculation, calibration, computation, estimation, evaluation, judgment, mensuration, metage, survey, valuation 2. amount, amplitude, area, capacity, depth, dimension, extent, height, length, magnitude, size, volume, weight, width

measure off circumscribe, delimit, demarcate, determine, fix, lay down, limit, mark out, pace out

measure out allot, apportion, assign, deal out, dispense, distribute, divide, dole out, issue, mete out, parcel out, pour out, share out

measure up (to) be adequate, be capable, be equal to, be fit, be suitable, be suited, come up to scratch (*Inf.*), come up to standard, compare, cut the mustard (*U.S. sl.*), equal, fit *or* fill the bill, fulfil the expectations, make the grade (*Inf.*), match, meet, rival

meat 1. aliment, cheer, chow (*Inf.*), comestibles, eats (*Sl.*), fare, flesh, food, grub (*Sl.*), nosh (*Sl.*), nourishment, nutriment, provender, provisions, rations, subsistence, sustenance, viands, victuals 2. core, essence, gist, heart, kernel, marrow, nub, nucleus, pith, point, substance

meaty 1. hearty, nourishing, rich, substantial 2. beefy (*Inf.*), brawny, burly, fleshy, heavily built, heavy, husky (*Inf.*), muscular, Ramboesque, solid, strapping, sturdy 3. interesting, meaningful, pithy, profound, rich, significant, substantial

mechanical 1. automated, automatic, machine-driven 2. automatic, cold, cursory, dead, emotionless, habitual, impersonal, instinctive, involuntary, lacklustre, lifeless, machine-like, matter-of-fact, perfunctory, routine, spiritless, unconscious, unfeeling, unthinking
Antonyms (*sense 1*) manual (*sense 2*) conscious, genuine, sincere, thinking, voluntary, warm, wholehearted

mechanism 1. apparatus, appliance, contrivance, device, instrument, machine, structure, system, tool 2. action, components, gears, innards (*Inf.*), machinery, motor, workings, works 3. agency, execution, functioning, means, medium, method, operation, performance, procedure, process, system, technique, workings

meddle butt in, interfere, intermeddle, interpose, intervene, intrude, pry, put one's oar in, put one's two cents in (*U.S. sl.*), stick one's nose in (*Inf.*), tamper

meddlesome interfering, intermeddling, intruding, intrusive, meddling, mischievous, officious, prying

mediate act as middleman, arbitrate, bring to an agreement, bring to terms, conciliate, intercede, interpose, intervene, make peace between, moderate, reconcile, referee, resolve, restore harmony, settle, step in (*Inf.*), umpire

mediation arbitration, conciliation, good offices, intercession, interposition, intervention, reconciliation

mediator advocate, arbiter, arbitrator, go-between, honest broker, interceder, intermediary, judge, middleman, moderator, negotiator, peacemaker, referee, umpire

medicable curable, healable, remediable, treatable

medicinal analeptic, curative, healing, medical, remedial, restorative, roborant, sanatory, therapeutic

medicine cure, drug, medicament, medication, nostrum, physic, remedy

medieval 1. Gothic 2. *Inf.* antediluvian, antiquated, antique, archaic, old-fashioned, primitive, unenlightened

mediocre average, banal, commonplace, fair to middling (*Inf.*), indifferent, inferior, insignificant, mean, medium, middling, ordinary, passable, pedestrian, run-of-the-mill, second-rate, so-so (*Inf.*), tolerable, undistinguished, uninspired
Antonyms distinctive, distinguished, excellent, extraordinary, fine, incomparable, superb, superior, unexcelled, unique, unrivalled, unsurpassed

mediocrity 1. commonplaceness, indifference, inferiority, insignificance, ordinariness, poorness, unimportance 2. cipher, lightweight (*Inf.*), nobody, nonentity, second-rater

meditate 1. be in a brown study, cogitate, consider, contemplate, deliberate, muse, ponder, reflect, ruminate, study, think 2. consider, contemplate, design, devise, have in mind, intend, mull over, plan, purpose, scheme, think over

meditation brown study, cerebration, cogitation, concentration, contemplation, musing, pondering, reflection, reverie, ruminating, rumination, study, thought

meditative cogitative, contemplative, deliberative, pensive, reflective, ruminative, studious, thoughtful

medium *adj.* 1. average, fair, intermediate, mean, medial, median, mediocre, middle, middling, midway ~*n.* 2. average, centre, compromise, mean, middle, middle course (ground, path, way), midpoint 3. agency, avenue, channel, form, instrument, instrumentality, means, mode, organ, vehicle, way 4. atmosphere, conditions, element, environment, habitat, influences, milieu, setting, surroundings 5. channeller, spiritist, spiritualist
Antonyms *adj.* distinctive, extraordinary,

extreme, uncommon, unique, unusual, utmost

medley assortment, confusion, farrago, gallimaufry, hodgepodge, hotchpotch, jumble, *mélange,* miscellany, mishmash, mixed bag (*Inf.*), mixture, olio, omnium-gatherum, pastiche, patchwork, potpourri, salmagundi

meek 1. deferential, docile, forbearing, gentle, humble, long-suffering, mild, modest, patient, peaceful, soft, submissive, unassuming, unpretentious, yielding 2. acquiescent, compliant, resigned, spineless, spiritless, tame, timid, unresisting, weak, weak-kneed (*Inf.*), wimpish *or* wimpy (*Inf.*)
Antonyms arrogant, bold, bossy, domineering, feisty (*Inf., chiefly U.S. & Canad.*), forward, immodest, overbearing, presumptuous, pretentious, proud, self-assertive, spirited, wilful

meekness 1. deference, docility, forbearance, gentleness, humbleness, humility, long-suffering, lowliness, mildness, modesty, patience, peacefulness, resignation, softness, submission, submissiveness 2. acquiescence, compliance, resignation, spinelessness, spiritlessness, tameness, timidity, weakness

meet 1. bump into, chance on, come across, confront, contact, encounter, find, happen on, run across, run into 2. abut, adjoin, come together, connect, converge, cross, intersect, join, link up, touch, unite 3. answer, carry out, come up to, comply, cope with, discharge, equal, fulfil, gratify, handle, match, measure up, perform, satisfy 4. assemble, collect, come together, congregate, convene, forgather, gather, muster, rally 5. bear, encounter, endure, experience, face, go through, suffer, undergo
Antonyms (*sense 1*) avoid, elude, escape, miss (*sense 2*) diverge (*sense 3*) fail, fall short, renege (*sense 4*) adjourn, disperse, scatter

meeting 1. assignation, confrontation, encounter, engagement, introduction, rendezvous, tryst (*Archaic*) 2. assembly, audience, company, conclave, conference, congregation, congress, convention, convocation, gathering, get-together (*Inf.*), meet, powwow, rally, reunion, session 3. concourse, confluence, conjunction, convergence, crossing, intersection, junction, union

melancholy 1. *n.* blues, dejection, depression, despondency, gloom, gloominess, low spirits, misery, pensiveness, sadness, sorrow, the hump (*Brit. inf.*), unhappiness, woe 2. *adj.* blue, dejected, depressed, despondent, disconsolate, dismal, dispirited, doleful, down, downcast, downhearted, down in the dumps (*Inf.*), down in the mouth, gloomy, glum, heavy-hearted, joyless, low, low-spirited, lugubrious, melancholic, miserable, moody, mournful, pensive, sad, sombre, sorrowful, unhappy, woebegone, woeful
Antonyms *n.* delight, gladness, happiness, joy, pleasure ~*adj.* blithe, bright, cheerful, gay, glad, happy, jolly, joyful, joyous, light-hearted, lively, merry, sunny

mélange assortment, confusion, farrago, gallimaufry, hodge-podge, hotch-potch, jumble, medley, miscellany, mishmash, mix, mixed bag (*Inf.*), mixture, olio, omnium-gatherum, pastiche, potpourri, salmagundi

melee, mêlée affray (*Law*), *bagarre,* battle royal, brawl, broil, donnybrook, fight, fracas, fray, free-for-all (*Inf.*), ruckus (*Inf.*), ruction (*Inf.*), rumpus, scrimmage, scuffle, set-to (*Inf.*), shindig (*Inf.*), shindy (*Inf.*), skirmish, stramash (*Scot.*), tussle

mellifluous, mellifluent dulcet, euphonious, honeyed, mellow, silvery, smooth, soft, soothing, sweet, sweet-sounding

mellow *adj.* 1. delicate, full-flavoured, juicy, mature, perfect, rich, ripe, soft, sweet, well-matured 2. dulcet, euphonic, full, mellifluous, melodious, rich, rounded, smooth, sweet, tuneful, well-tuned 3. cheerful, cordial, elevated, expansive, genial, half-tipsy, happy, jolly, jovial, merry (*Brit. inf.*), relaxed ~*v.* 4. develop, improve, mature, perfect, ripen, season, soften, sweeten
Antonyms *adj.* green, harsh, immature, raw, sour, unripe ~*v.* brutalize, harden

melodious concordant, dulcet, euphonic, euphonious, harmonious, melodic, musical, silvery, sweet-sounding, sweet-toned, tuneful
Antonyms cacophonous, discordant, grating, harsh, unharmonious, unmelodic, unmelodious, unmusical, untuneful

melodramatic actressy, blood-and-thunder, extravagant, hammy (*Inf.*), histrionic, overdramatic, overemotional, sensational, stagy, theatrical

melody 1. air, descant, music, refrain, song, strain, theme, tune 2. euphony, harmony, melodiousness, music, musicality, tunefulness

melt 1. deliquesce, diffuse, dissolve, flux, fuse, liquefy, soften, thaw 2. *Often with* **away** disappear, disperse, dissolve, evanesce, evaporate, fade, vanish 3. disarm, mollify, relax, soften, touch

member 1. associate, fellow, representative 2. appendage, arm, component, constituent, element, extremity, leg, limb, organ, part, portion

membership 1. associates, body, fellows, members 2. belonging, enrolment, fellowship, participation

memento keepsake, memorial, relic, remembrance, reminder, souvenir, token, trophy

memoir account, biography, essay, journal, life, monograph, narrative, record, register

memoirs 1. autobiography, diary, experiences, journals, life, life story, memories, recollections, reminiscences 2. annals, chronicles, records, transactions

memorable catchy, celebrated, distinguished, extraordinary, famous, historic, illustrious, important, impressive, momentous, notable, noteworthy, remarkable, signal, significant, striking, unforgettable
Antonyms commonplace, forgettable, insignificant, ordinary, trivial, undistinguished, unimportant, unimpressive, unmemorable

memorial *adj.* 1. commemorative, monumental ~*n.* 2. cairn, memento, monument, plaque, record, remembrance, souvenir 3. address, memorandum, petition, statement

memorize commit to memory, con (*Archaic*), get by heart, learn, learn by heart, learn by rote, remember

memory 1. recall, recollection, remembrance, reminiscence, retention 2. commemoration, honour, remembrance 3. celebrity, fame, glory, name, renown, reputation, repute

menace *v.* 1. alarm, bode ill, browbeat, bully, frighten, impend, intimidate, loom, lour *or* lower, terrorize, threaten, utter threats to ~*n.* 2. commination, intimidation, scare, threat, warning 3. danger, hazard, jeopardy, peril 4. *Inf.* annoyance, nuisance, pest, plague, troublemaker

menacing alarming, baleful, dangerous, forbidding, frightening, intimidating, intimidatory, looming, louring *or* lowering, minacious, minatory, ominous, threatening
Antonyms auspicious, encouraging, favourable, promising

mend *v.* 1. cure, darn, fix, heal, patch, rectify, refit, reform, remedy, renew, renovate, repair, restore, retouch 2. ameliorate, amend, better, correct, emend, improve, rectify, reform, revise 3. convalesce, get better, heal, recover, recuperate ~*n.* 4. darn, patch, repair, stitch 5. **on the mend** convalescent, convalescing, getting better, improving, recovering, recuperating

mendacious deceitful, deceptive, dishonest, duplicitous, fallacious, false, fraudulent, insincere, lying, perfidious, perjured, untrue, untruthful
Antonyms genuine, honest, true, truthful

mendacity deceit, deceitfulness, dishonesty, distortion, duplicity, falsehood, falsification, fraudulence, insincerity, inveracity, lie, lying, mendaciousness, misrepresentation, perfidy, perjury, untruth, untruthfulness

mendicant 1. *adj.* begging 2. *n.* beggar, pauper

menial *adj.* 1. boring, dull, humdrum, low-status, routine, unskilled 2. abject, base, degrading, demeaning, fawning, grovelling, humble, ignoble, ignominious, low, lowly, mean, obsequious, servile, slavish, sorry, subservient, sycophantic, vile ~*n.* 3. attendant, dogsbody (*Inf.*), domestic, drudge, flunky, labourer, lackey, serf, servant, skivvy (*Chiefly Brit.*), slave, underling, varlet (*Archaic*), vassal
Antonyms *adj.* aristocratic, autocratic, bossy, dignified, domineering, elevated, haughty, high, noble, overbearing, proud ~*n.* boss, chief, commander, lord, master, superior

menstruation catamenia (*Physiology*), courses (*Physiology*), flow (*Inf.*), menses, menstrual cycle, monthly (*Inf.*), period, the curse (*Inf.*)

mensuration assessment, calculation, calibration, computation, estimation, measurement, measuring, metage, survey, surveying

mental 1. cerebral, intellectual 2. deranged, disturbed, insane, lunatic, mad, mentally ill, psychiatric, psychotic, unbalanced, unstable

mentality 1. brainpower, brains, comprehension, grey matter (*Inf.*), intellect, intelligence quotient, I.Q., mental age, mind, rationality, understanding, wit 2. attitude, cast of mind, character, disposition, frame of mind, make-up, outlook, personality, psychology, turn of mind, way of thinking

mentally in one's head, intellectually, in the mind, inwardly, psychologically, rationally, subjectively

mention *v.* 1. acknowledge, adduce, allude to, bring up, broach, call attention to, cite, communicate, declare, disclose, divulge, hint at, impart, intimate, make known, name, point out, recount, refer to, report, reveal, speak about *or* of, state, tell, touch upon 2. **not to mention** as well as, besides, not counting, to say nothing of ~*n.* 3. acknowledgment, citation, recognition, tribute 4. allusion, announcement, indication, notification, observation, reference, remark

mentor adviser, coach, counsellor, guide, guru, instructor, teacher, tutor

menu bill of fare, carte du jour, tariff (*Chiefly Brit.*)

mephitic baleful, baneful, evil- *or* ill-smelling, fetid, foul, foul-smelling, malodorous, miasmal, miasmatic, miasmic, noisome, noxious, olid, pestilential, poisonous, putrid, stinking

mercantile commercial, marketable, trade, trading

mercenary *adj.* 1. acquisitive, avaricious, bribable, covetous, grasping, greedy, money-grubbing (*Inf.*), sordid, venal 2. bought, hired, paid, venal ~*n.* 3. condottiere (*Hist.*), free companion (*Hist.*), freelance (*Hist.*), hireling, soldier of fortune

Antonyms altruistic, benevolent, generous, idealistic, liberal, munificent, philanthropic, unselfish

merchandise 1. *n.* commodities, goods, produce, products, staples, stock, stock in trade, truck, vendibles, wares 2. *v.* buy and sell, deal in, distribute, do business in, market, retail, sell, trade, traffic in, vend

merchant broker, dealer, purveyor, retailer, salesman, seller, shopkeeper, supplier, trader, tradesman, trafficker, vendor, wholesaler

merchantable marketable, salable, tradable, vendible

merciful beneficent, benignant, clement, compassionate, forbearing, forgiving, generous, gracious, humane, kind, lenient, liberal, mild, pitying, soft, sparing, sympathetic, tender-hearted

Antonyms cruel, hard-hearted, inhumane, merciless, pitiless, uncompassionate, unfeeling

merciless barbarous, callous, cruel, fell (*Archaic*), hard, hard-hearted, harsh, heartless, implacable, inexorable, inhumane, pitiless, relentless, ruthless, severe, unappeasable, unfeeling, unforgiving, unmerciful, unpitying, unsparing, unsympathetic

mercurial active, capricious, changeable, erratic, fickle, flighty, gay, impulsive, inconstant, irrepressible, light-hearted, lively, mobile, quicksilver, spirited, sprightly, temperamental, unpredictable, unstable, variable, volatile

Antonyms consistent, constant, dependable, reliable, stable, steady, unchanging

mercy 1. benevolence, charity, clemency, compassion, favour, forbearance, forgiveness, grace, kindness, leniency, pity, quarter 2. benison (*Archaic*), blessing, boon, godsend, piece of luck, relief 3. at the mercy of defenceless against, exposed to, in the clutches of, in the power of, naked before, open to, prey to, subject to, threatened by, unprotected against, vulnerable to

Antonyms brutality, cruelty, harshness, inhumanity, pitilessness, severity

mere *adj.* absolute, bare, common, complete, entire, nothing more than, plain, pure, pure and simple, sheer, simple, stark, unadulterated, unmitigated, unmixed, utter

meretricious 1. flashy, garish, gaudy, plastic (*Sl.*), showy, tawdry, tinsel, trashy 2. bogus, counterfeit, deceitful, false, hollow, insincere, phoney *or* phony (*Inf.*), put-on, sham, specious, spurious

merge amalgamate, be swallowed up by, become lost in, blend, coalesce, combine, consolidate, converge, fuse, incorporate, intermix, join, meet, meld, melt into, mingle, mix, tone with, unite

Antonyms detach, diverge, divide, part, separate, sever

merger amalgamation, coalition, combination, consolidation, fusion, incorporation, union

meridian acme, apex, apogee, climax, crest, culmination, high noon, high-water mark, peak, pinnacle, summit, zenith

merit *n.* 1. advantage, asset, excellence, good, goodness, integrity, quality, strong point, talent, value, virtue, worth, worthiness 2. claim, credit, desert, due, right ~*v.* 3. be entitled to, be worthy of, deserve, earn, have a claim to, have a right to, have coming to one, incur, rate, warrant

merited appropriate, condign, deserved, earned, entitled, just, justified, rightful, rightly due, warranted

meritorious admirable, commendable, creditable, deserving, excellent, exemplary, good, honourable, laudable, praiseworthy, right, righteous, virtuous, worthy

Antonyms discreditable, dishonourable, ignoble, unchivalrous, undeserving, unexceptional, ungenerous, unpraiseworthy

merriment amusement, conviviality, festivity, frolic, fun, gaiety, glee, hilarity, jocularity, jollity, joviality, laughter, levity, liveliness, merrymaking, mirth, revelry, sport

merry 1. blithe, blithesome, carefree, cheerful, chirpy (*Inf.*), convivial, festive, frolicsome, fun-loving, gay, genial, glad, gleeful, happy, jocund, jolly, joyful, joyous, light-hearted, mirthful, rollicking, sportive, upbeat (*Inf.*), vivacious 2. amusing, comic, comical, facetious, funny, hilarious, humorous, jocular, mirthful 3. *Brit. inf.* elevated (*Inf.*), happy, mellow, squiffy (*Brit. inf.*), tiddly (*Sl., chiefly Brit.*), tipsy 4.

make merry carouse, celebrate, enjoy oneself, feast, frolic, have a good time, have fun, make whoopee (*Inf.*), revel
Antonyms dejected, dismal, gloomy, miserable, sad, unhappy

merrymaking beano (*Brit. sl.*), carousal, carouse, celebration, conviviality, festivity, fun, gaiety, jollification, merriment, party, rave (*Brit. sl.*), rave-up (*Brit. sl.*), revelry

mesh *n.* 1. net, netting, network, plexus, reticulation, tracery, web 2. entanglement, snare, tangle, toils, trap, web ~*v.* 3. catch, enmesh, ensnare, entangle, net, snare, tangle, trap 4. combine, come together, connect, coordinate, dovetail, engage, fit together, harmonize, interlock, knit

mesmerize absorb, captivate, enthral, entrance, fascinate, grip, hold spellbound, hypnotize, magnetize, spellbind

mess *n.* 1. balls-up (*Taboo sl.*), bodge (*Inf.*), botch, chaos, clutter, cock-up (*Brit. sl.*), confusion, dirtiness, disarray, disorder, disorganization, fuck-up (*Offens. taboo sl.*), grot (*Sl.*), hash, hodgepodge (*U.S.*), hotchpotch, jumble, litter, mishmash, pig's breakfast (*Inf.*), shambles, state, turmoil, untidiness 2. difficulty, dilemma, fine kettle of fish (*Inf.*), fix (*Inf.*), hot water (*Inf.*), imbroglio, jam (*Inf.*), mix-up, muddle, perplexity, pickle (*Inf.*), plight, predicament, spot (*Inf.*), stew (*Inf.*), tight spot ~*v.* 3. *Often with* **up** befoul, besmirch, botch, bungle, clutter, cock up (*Brit. sl.*), dirty, disarrange, dishevel, foul, fuck up (*Offens. taboo sl.*), litter, make a hash of (*Inf.*), muck up (*Brit. sl.*), muddle, pollute, scramble 4. *Often with* **with** fiddle (*Inf.*), interfere, meddle, play, tamper, tinker

mess about *or* **around** 1. amuse oneself, dabble, fool (about *or* around), footle (*Inf.*), muck about (*Inf.*), piss about *or* around (*Taboo sl.*), play about *or* around, potter, trifle 2. fiddle (*Inf.*), fool (about *or* around), interfere, meddle, piss about *or* around (*Taboo sl.*), play, tamper, tinker, toy

message 1. bulletin, communication, communiqué, dispatch, intimation, letter, memorandum, missive, note, notice, tidings, word 2. idea, import, meaning, moral, point, purport, theme 3. commission, errand, job, mission, task 4. **get the message** catch on (*Inf.*), comprehend, get it, get the point, see, take the hint, twig (*Brit. inf.*), understand

messenger agent, bearer, carrier, courier, delivery boy, emissary, envoy, errand-boy, go-between, harbinger, herald, runner

messy chaotic, cluttered, confused, dirty, dishevelled, disordered, disorganized, grubby, littered, muddled, scuzzy (*Sl., chiefly U.S.*), shambolic (*Inf.*), sloppy (*Inf.*), slovenly, unkempt, untidy
Antonyms clean, meticulous, neat, ordered, orderly, shipshape, smart, squeaky-clean, tidy

metamorphose alter, be reborn, change, convert, mutate, remake, remodel, reshape, transfigure, transform, translate, transmogrify (*Jocular*), transmute, transubstantiate

metamorphosis alteration, change, changeover, conversion, mutation, rebirth, transfiguration, transformation, translation, transmogrification (*Jocular*), transmutation, transubstantiation

metaphor allegory, analogy, emblem, figure of speech, image, symbol, trope

metaphorical allegorical, emblematic, emblematical, figurative, symbolic, tropical (*Rhetoric*)

metaphysical 1. basic, esoteric, essential, eternal, fundamental, general, ideal, intellectual, philosophical, profound, speculative, spiritual, subjective, universal 2. abstract, abstruse, deep, high-flown, oversubtle, recondite, theoretical, transcendental 3. immaterial, impalpable, incorporeal, intangible, spiritual, supernatural, unreal, unsubstantial

mete *v.* administer, allot, apportion, assign, deal, dispense, distribute, divide, dole, measure, parcel, portion, ration, share

meteoric brief, brilliant, dazzling, ephemeral, fast, flashing, fleeting, momentary, overnight, rapid, spectacular, speedy, sudden, swift, transient
Antonyms gradual, lengthy, long, prolonged, slow, steady, unhurried

method 1. approach, arrangement, course, fashion, form, manner, mode, modus operandi, plan, practice, procedure, process, programme, routine, rule, scheme, style, system, technique, way 2. design, form, order, orderliness, organization, pattern, planning, purpose, regularity, structure, system

methodical businesslike, deliberate, disciplined, efficient, meticulous, neat, ordered, orderly, organized, painstaking, planned, precise, regular, structured, systematic, tidy, well-regulated
Antonyms casual, chaotic, confused, disordered, disorderly, haphazard, irregular, random, unmethodical

meticulous detailed, exact, fastidious, fussy, microscopic, painstaking, particular, perfectionist, precise, punctilious, scrupulous, strict, thorough
Antonyms careless, haphazard, imprecise, inexact, loose, negligent, slapdash, sloppy

métier 1. calling, craft, line, occupation, profession, pursuit, trade, vocation 2. forte, long suit (*Inf.*), speciality, specialty, strong point, strong suit

metropolis capital, city

mettle 1. ardour, balls (*Taboo sl.*), boldness, bottle (*Brit. sl.*), bravery, courage, daring, fire, fortitude, gallantry, gameness, grit, guts (*Inf.*), hardihood, heart, indomitability, life, nerve, pluck, resolution, resolve, spirit, spunk (*Inf.*), valour, vigour 2. calibre, character, disposition, kidney, make-up, nature, quality, stamp, temper, temperament

mettlesome ardent, bold, brisk, courageous, daring, dashing, feisty (*Inf., chiefly U.S. & Canad.*), fiery, frisky, game (*Inf.*), have-a-go (*Inf.*), high-spirited, lively, mettled, plucky, sprightly, valiant, vigorous

mewl blubber, cry, grizzle (*Inf., chiefly Brit.*), pule, snivel, whimper, whine, whinge (*Inf.*)

miasma effluvium, fetor, mephitis, niff (*Brit. sl.*), odour, pollution, reek, smell, stench

miasmal fetid, foul, insalubrious, malodorous, mephitic, niffy (*Brit. sl.*), noisome, noxious, olid, polluted, putrid, reeking, smelly, stinking, unwholesome

microbe bacillus, bacterium, bug (*Inf.*), germ, microorganism, virus

microscopic imperceptible, infinitesimal, invisible, minuscule, minute, negligible, teensy-weensy, teeny-weeny, tiny
Antonyms enormous, gigantic, ginormous (*Inf.*), great, huge, immense, large, vast

midday noon, noonday, noontide, noontime, twelve noon, twelve o'clock

middle *adj.* 1. central, halfway, inner, inside, intermediate, intervening, mean, medial, median, medium, mid ~*n.* 2. centre, focus, halfway point, heart, inside, mean, midpoint, midsection, midst, thick 3. midriff, midsection, waist

middleman broker, distributor, entrepreneur, go-between, intermediary

middling adequate, all right, average, fair, indifferent, mediocre, medium, moderate, modest, O.K. *or* okay (*Inf.*), ordinary, passable, run-of-the-mill, so-so (*Inf.*), tolerable, unexceptional, unremarkable

midget 1. *n.* dwarf, gnome, homuncule, homunculus, manikin, pygmy *or* pigmy, shrimp (*Inf.*), Tom Thumb 2. *adj.* baby, dwarf, Lilliputian, little, miniature, pocket, pygmy *or* pigmy, small, teensy-weensy, teeny-weeny, tiny

midnight dead of night, middle of the night, the witching hour, twelve o'clock (at night)

midst 1. bosom, centre, core, depths, heart, hub, interior, middle, thick 2. **in the midst of** amidst, among, during, enveloped by, in the middle of, in the thick of, surrounded by

midway betwixt and between, halfway, in the middle

mien air, appearance, aspect, aura, bearing, carriage, countenance, demeanour, deportment, look, manner, presence

miffed aggrieved, annoyed, displeased, hacked (off) (*U.S. sl.*), hurt, in a huff, irked, irritated, narked (*Brit., Aust., & N.Z. sl.*), nettled, offended, piqued, pissed off (*Taboo sl.*), put out, resentful, upset, vexed

might 1. ability, capability, capacity, clout (*Inf.*), efficacy, efficiency, energy, force, potency, power, prowess, puissance, strength, sway, valour, vigour 2. **(with) might and main** as hard as one can, as hard as possible, forcefully, full blast, full force, lustily, manfully, mightily, vigorously, with all one's might *or* strength

mightily 1. decidedly, exceedingly, extremely, greatly, highly, hugely, intensely, much, very, very much 2. energetically, forcefully, lustily, manfully, powerfully, strongly, vigorously, with all one's might and main, with all one's strength

mighty 1. doughty, forceful, hardy, indomitable, lusty, manful, potent, powerful, puissant, Ramboesque, robust, stalwart, stout, strapping, strong, sturdy, vigorous 2. bulky, colossal, elephantine, enormous, gigantic, ginormous (*Inf.*), grand, great, huge, humongous *or* humungous (*U.S. sl.*), immense, large, massive, mega (*Sl.*), monumental, prodigious, stupendous, titanic, towering, tremendous, vast
Antonyms feeble, impotent, small, tiny, unimposing, unimpressive, weak, weedy (*Inf.*), wimpish *or* wimpy (*Inf.*)

migrant 1. *n.* drifter, emigrant, gypsy, immigrant, itinerant, nomad, rover, tinker, transient, traveller, vagrant, wanderer 2. *adj.* drifting, gypsy, immigrant, itinerant, migratory, nomadic, roving, shifting, transient, travelling, vagrant, wandering

migrate drift, emigrate, journey, move, roam, rove, shift, travel, trek, voyage, wander

migration emigration, journey, movement, roving, shift, travel, trek, voyage, wandering

migratory gypsy, itinerant, migrant, nomadic, peripatetic, roving, shifting, transient, travelling, unsettled, vagrant, wandering

mild 1. amiable, balmy, bland, calm, clem~

ent, compassionate, docile, easy, easy-going, easy-oasy (*Sl.*), equable, forbearing, forgiving, gentle, indulgent, kind, meek, mellow, merciful, moderate, pacific, peaceable, placid, pleasant, serene, smooth, soft, temperate, tender, tranquil, warm 2. demulcent, emollient, lenitive, mollifying, soothing
Antonyms (*sense 1*) bitter, cold, fierce, harsh, rough, stormy, unkind, unpleasant, violent, wild (*sense 2*) harsh, powerful, severe, sharp, strong

mildness blandness, calmness, clemency, docility, forbearance, gentleness, indulgence, kindness, leniency, lenity, meekness, mellowness, moderation, placidity, smoothness, softness, temperateness, tenderness, tranquillity, warmth

milieu background, element, environment, locale, location, *mise en scène,* scene, setting, sphere, surroundings

militant *adj.* 1. active, aggressive, assertive, combative, Ramboesque, vigorous 2. belligerent, combating, contending, embattled, fighting, in arms, warring ~*n.* 3. activist, partisan 4. belligerent, combatant, fighter, gladiator, warrior
Antonyms concessive, pacific, pacifist, peaceful

military 1. *adj.* armed, martial, soldierlike, soldierly, warlike 2. *n.* armed forces, army, forces, services

militate 1. *With* **against** be detrimental to, conflict with, contend, count, counter, counteract, oppose, resist, tell, weigh 2. *With* **for** advance, aid, further, help, promote

militia fencibles (*History*), National Guard (*U.S.*), reserve(s), Territorial Army (*Brit.*), trainband (*History*), yeomanry (*History*)

milk *v.* 1. drain, draw off, express, extract, let out, press, siphon, tap 2. bleed, drain, exploit, extract, impose on, pump, take advantage of, use, wring

milk-and-water feeble, innocuous, insipid, jejune, nerdy *or* nurdy (*Sl.*), vapid, weak, weedy (*Inf.*), wimpish *or* wimpy (*Inf.*), wishy-washy (*Inf.*)
Antonyms effective, energetic, forceful, healthy, Ramboesque, strong

milksop chinless wonder (*Brit. inf.*), coward, dastard (*Archaic*), jessie (*Scot. sl.*), namby-pamby, sissy, weakling, wimp (*Inf.*)

milky alabaster, clouded, cloudy, milk-white, opaque, white, whitish

mill *n.* 1. factory, foundry, plant, shop, works 2. crusher, grinder 3. **run of the mill** average, commonplace, everyday, fair, middling, ordinary, routine, unexceptional, unremarkable ~*v.* 4. comminute, crush, granulate, grate, grind, pound, powder, press, pulverize 5. crowd, seethe, swarm, throng

millstone 1. grindstone, quernstone 2. affliction, burden, dead weight, drag, encumbrance, load, weight

mime 1. *n.* dumb show, gesture, mummery, pantomime 2. *v.* act out, gesture, pantomime, represent, simulate

mimic *v.* 1. ape, caricature, do (*Inf.*), imitate, impersonate, parody, take off (*Inf.*) 2. echo, look like, mirror, resemble, simulate, take on the appearance of ~*n.* 3. caricaturist, copycat (*Inf.*), imitator, impersonator, impressionist, parodist, parrot ~*adj.* 4. echoic, imitation, imitative, make-believe, mimetic, mock, sham, simulated

mimicry apery, burlesque, caricature, copying, imitating, imitation, impersonation, impression, mimicking, mockery, parody, take-off (*Inf.*)

minatory baleful, dangerous, menacing, minacious, minatorial, threatening

mince 1. chop, crumble, cut, grind, hash 2. diminish, euphemize, extenuate, hold back, moderate, palliate, soften, spare, tone down, weaken 3. attitudinize, give oneself airs, ponce (*Sl.*), pose, posture

mincing affected, camp (*Inf.*), dainty, effeminate, foppish, lah-di-dah (*Inf.*), nice, niminy-piminy, poncy (*Sl.*), precious, pretentious, sissy

mind *n.* 1. brain(s) (*Inf.*), grey matter (*Inf.*), intellect, intelligence, mentality, ratiocination, reason, sense, spirit, understanding, wits 2. memory, recollection, remembrance 3. brain, head, imagination, psyche 4. brain (*Inf.*), brainbox, genius, intellect, intellectual, thinker 5. attitude, belief, feeling, judgment, opinion, outlook, point of view, sentiment, thoughts, view, way of thinking 6. bent, desire, disposition, fancy, inclination, intention, leaning, notion, purpose, tendency, urge, will, wish 7. attention, concentration, thinking, thoughts 8. judgment, marbles (*Inf.*), mental balance, rationality, reason, sanity, senses, wits 9. **in *or* of two minds** dithering (*Chiefly Brit.*), hesitant, shillyshallying (*Inf.*), swithering (*Scot.*), uncertain, undecided, unsure, vacillating, wavering 10. **make up one's mind** choose, come to a decision, decide, determine, reach a decision, resolve 11. **bear *or* keep in mind** be cognizant of, be mindful of, remember, take note of ~*v.* 12. be affronted, be bothered, care, disapprove, dislike, look askance at, object, resent, take offence 13. adhere to, attend, comply with, follow, heed, listen to, mark, note, notice, obey, observe, pay attention, pay heed to, regard, respect, take heed, watch **14.** be sure, ensure, make certain **15.** attend to, guard, have charge of, keep an eye on, look after, take care of, tend, watch **16.** be careful, be cautious, be on (one's) guard, be wary, take care, watch **17. never mind** disregard, do not concern yourself, don't bother, don't give (it) a second thought, forget (it), it does not matter, it's none of your business, it's nothing to do with you, pay no attention

mindful alert, alive to, attentive, aware, careful, chary, cognizant, conscious, heedful, regardful, respectful, sensible, thoughtful, wary, watchful
Antonyms heedless, inattentive, incautious, mindless, oblivious, thoughtless, unaware

mindless 1. asinine, braindead (*Inf.*), brutish, careless, foolish, forgetful, gratuitous, heedless, idiotic, imbecilic, inane, inattentive, moronic, neglectful, negligent, oblivious, obtuse, stupid, thoughtless, unintelligent, unmindful, unthinking, witless **2.** automatic, brainless, mechanical
Antonyms attentive, aware, considerate, intelligent, mindful, reasonable, reasoning, sane, sensitive, thinking

mind out be careful, be on one's guard, beware, keep one's eyes open, look out, pay attention, take care, watch

mind's eye head, imagination, memory, mind, recollection, remembrance

mine *n.* **1.** coalfield, colliery, deposit, excavation, lode, pit, shaft, vein **2.** abundance, fund, hoard, reserve, source, stock, store, supply, treasury, wealth **3.** sap, trench, tunnel *~v.* **4.** delve, dig for, dig up, excavate, extract, hew, quarry, unearth **5.** lay mines in *or* under, sow with mines **6.** sap, subvert, tunnel, undermine, weaken

miner coalminer, collier (*Brit.*), pitman (*Brit.*)

mingle 1. alloy, blend, coalesce, combine, commingle, compound, intermingle, intermix, interweave, join, marry, meld, merge, mix, unite **2.** associate, circulate, consort, fraternize, hang about *or* around, hang out (*Inf.*), hobnob, rub shoulders (*Inf.*), socialize
Antonyms avoid, detach, dissociate, dissolve, divide, estrange, part, separate

miniature *adj.* baby, diminutive, dwarf, Lilliputian, little, midget, mini, minuscule, minute, pocket, pygmy *or* pigmy, reduced, scaled-down, small, teensy-weensy, teeny-weeny, tiny, toy, wee
Antonyms big, enlarged, enormous, giant, gigantic, ginormous (*Inf.*), great, huge, immense, large, mega (*Sl.*), oversize

minimal least, least possible, littlest, minimum, nominal, slightest, smallest, token

minimize 1. abbreviate, attenuate, curtail, decrease, diminish, miniaturize, prune, reduce, shrink **2.** belittle, decry, deprecate, depreciate, discount, disparage, make light *or* little of, play down, underestimate, underrate
Antonyms augment, boast about, elevate, enhance, enlarge, exalt, expand, extend, heighten, increase, magnify, praise, vaunt

minimum 1. *n.* bottom, depth, least, lowest, nadir, slightest **2.** *adj.* least, least possible, littlest, lowest, minimal, slightest, smallest
Antonyms greatest, highest, largest, maximum, most

minion bootlicker (*Inf.*), creature, darling, dependant, favourite, flatterer, flunky, follower, hanger-on, henchman, hireling, lackey, lickspittle, myrmidon, parasite, pet, sycophant, toady, underling, yes man

minister *n.* **1.** chaplain, churchman, clergyman, cleric, divine, ecclesiastic, padre (*Inf.*), parson, pastor, preacher, priest, rector, vicar **2.** administrator, ambassador, cabinet member, delegate, diplomat, envoy, executive, office-holder, official, plenipotentiary **3.** agent, aide, assistant, lieutenant, servant, subordinate, underling *~v.* **4.** accommodate, administer, answer, attend, be solicitous of, cater to, pander to, serve, take care of, tend

ministration aid, assistance, favour, help, patronage, relief, service, succour, support

ministry 1. administration, bureau, cabinet, council, department, government, office **2.** holy orders, the church, the priesthood, the pulpit

minor inconsequential, inconsiderable, inferior, insignificant, junior, lesser, light, negligible, nickel-and-dime (*U.S. sl.*), paltry, petty, secondary, slight, small, smaller, subordinate, trifling, trivial, unimportant, younger
Antonyms appreciable, consequential, considerable, essential, grand, great, heavy, important, major, profound, serious, significant, substantial, superior, vital, weighty

minstrel bard, harper, jongleur, musician, singer, songstress, troubadour

mint *n.* **1.** bomb (*Brit. sl.*), bundle (*Sl.*), fortune, heap (*Inf.*), King's ransom, million, packet (*Sl.*), pile (*Inf.*) *~adj.* **2.** brand-new, excellent, first-class, fresh, perfect, unblemished, undamaged, untarnished *~v.* **3.** cast, coin, make, produce, punch, stamp, strike **4.** coin, construct, devise, fabricate, fashion, forge, invent, make up, produce, think up

minuscule diminutive, fine, infinitesimal, Lilliputian, little, microscopic, miniature, minute, teensy-weensy, teeny-weeny, tiny, very small

minute[1] *n.* 1. sixtieth of an hour, sixty seconds 2. flash, instant, jiffy (*Inf.*), moment, second, shake (*Inf.*), tick (*Brit. inf.*), trice 3. **any minute** any moment, any second, any time, at any time, before long, very soon 4. **up to the minute** all the rage, in, latest, modish, (most) fashionable, newest, now (*Inf.*), smart, stylish, trendiest, trendy (*Brit. inf.*), up to date, vogue, with it (*Inf.*)

minute[2] *adj.* 1. diminutive, fine, infinitesimal, Lilliputian, little, microscopic, miniature, minuscule, slender, small, teensy-weensy, teeny-weeny, tiny 2. inconsiderable, negligible, paltry, petty, picayune (*U.S.*), piddling (*Inf.*), puny, slight, trifling, trivial, unimportant 3. close, critical, detailed, exact, exhaustive, meticulous, painstaking, precise, punctilious

Antonyms (*senses 1 & 2*) enormous, generous, gigantic, ginormous (*Inf.*), grand, great, huge, immense, important, major, mega (*Sl.*), monstrous, significant, vital (*sense 3*) careless, haphazard, imprecise, inexact, loose, quick, rough, superficial

minutely closely, critically, exactly, exhaustively, in detail, meticulously, painstakingly, precisely, with a fine-tooth comb

minutes memorandum, notes, proceedings, record(s), transactions, transcript

minutiae details, finer points, niceties, particulars, subtleties, trifles, trivia

minx baggage (*Inf., old-fashioned*), coquette, flirt, hoyden, hussy, jade, tomboy, wanton

miracle marvel, phenomenon, prodigy, thaumaturgy, wonder

miraculous amazing, astonishing, astounding, extraordinary, incredible, inexplicable, magical, marvellous, phenomenal, preternatural, prodigious, superhuman, supernatural, thaumaturgic, unaccountable, unbelievable, wonderful, wondrous (*Archaic or literary*)

Antonyms awful, bad, banal, common, commonplace, everyday, normal, ordinary, run-of-the-mill, terrible, unexceptional, unremarkable, usual

mirage hallucination, illusion, optical illusion, phantasm

mire *n.* 1. bog, marsh, morass, quagmire, swamp 2. dirt, grot (*Sl.*), muck, mud, ooze, slime 3. **in the mire** encumbered, entangled, in difficulties, in trouble ~*v.* 4. bog down, flounder, sink, stick in the mud 5. begrime, besmirch, bespatter, cake, dirty, muddy, soil 6. catch up, enmesh, entangle, involve

mirror *n.* 1. glass, looking-glass, reflector, speculum 2. copy, double, image, likeness, reflection, replica, representation, twin ~*v.* 3. copy, depict, echo, emulate, follow, reflect, represent, show

mirth amusement, cheerfulness, festivity, frolic, fun, gaiety, gladness, glee, hilarity, jocularity, jollity, joviality, joyousness, laughter, levity, merriment, merrymaking, pleasure, rejoicing, revelry, sport

mirthful amused, amusing, blithe, cheerful, cheery, festive, frolicsome, funny, gay, glad, gladsome (*Archaic*), happy, hilarious, jocund, jolly, jovial, laughable, light-hearted, merry, playful, sportive, uproarious, vivacious

Antonyms dejected, depressed, despondent, dismal, gloomy, grave, lugubrious, melancholy, miserable, morose, sad, saturnine, sedate, serious, solemn, sombre, sorrowful, unhappy

misadventure accident, bad break (*Inf.*), bad luck, bummer (*Sl.*), calamity, catastrophe, debacle, disaster, failure, ill fortune, ill luck, mischance, misfortune, mishap, reverse, setback

misanthrope cynic, egoist, egotist, mankind-hater, misanthropist

misanthropic antisocial, cynical, egoistic, inhumane, malevolent, unfriendly, unsociable

misanthropy cynicism, egoism, hatred of mankind, inhumanity, malevolence

misapply abuse, misappropriate, misemploy, misuse, pervert

misapprehend get hold of the wrong end of the stick, get the wrong idea *or* impression, misconceive, misconstrue, misinterpret, misread, mistake, misunderstand

misapprehension delusion, error, fallacy, false belief, false impression, misconception, misconstruction, misinterpretation, misreading, mistake, misunderstanding, wrong idea *or* impression

misappropriate cabbage (*Brit. sl.*), defalcate (*Law*), embezzle, misapply, misspend, misuse, peculate, pocket, steal, swindle

misbegotten 1. dishonest, disreputable, ill-gotten, illicit, purloined, shady (*Inf.*), stolen, unlawful, unrespectable 2. abortive, hare-brained, ill-advised, ill-conceived, poorly thought-out 3. *Literary* bastard, born out of wedlock, illegitimate, natural, spurious (*Rare*)

misbehave act up (*Inf.*), be bad, be insub~

ordinate, be naughty, carry on (*Inf.*), get up to mischief (*Inf.*), muck about (*Brit. sl.*)
Antonyms act correctly, be good, behave, conduct oneself properly, mind one's manners, mind one's p's and q's, toe the line

misbehaviour acting up (*Inf.*), bad behaviour, impropriety, incivility, indiscipline, insubordination, mischief, misconduct, misdeeds, misdemeanour, monkey business (*Inf.*), naughtiness, rudeness, shenanigans (*Inf.*)

misbelief delusion, error, fallacy, false belief, heresy, unorthodoxy

miscalculate blunder, calculate wrongly, err, get (it) wrong, go wrong, make a mistake, misjudge, overestimate, overrate, slip up, underestimate, underrate

miscarriage 1. miss (*Inf.*), spontaneous abortion 2. botch (*Inf.*), breakdown, error, failure, misadventure, mischance, misfire, mishap, mismanagement, nonsuccess, perversion, thwarting, undoing

miscarry 1. abort 2. come to grief, come to nothing, fail, fall through, gang agley (*Scot.*), go amiss, go astray, go awry, go wrong, misfire

miscellaneous assorted, confused, diverse, diversified, farraginous, heterogeneous, indiscriminate, jumbled, manifold, many, mingled, mixed, motley, multifarious, multiform, promiscuous, sundry, varied, various

miscellany anthology, assortment, collection, diversity, farrago, gallimaufry, hotchpotch, jumble, medley, *mélange,* mixed bag, mixture, omnium-gatherum, potpourri, salmagundi, variety

mischance accident, bad break (*Inf.*), bad luck, bummer (*Sl.*), calamity, contretemps, disaster, ill chance, ill fortune, ill luck, infelicity, misadventure, misfortune, mishap

mischief 1. devilment, impishness, misbehaviour, monkey business (*Inf.*), naughtiness, pranks, roguery, roguishness, shenanigans (*Inf.*), trouble, waywardness 2. devil, imp, monkey, nuisance, pest, rascal, rogue, scallywag (*Inf.*), scamp, tyke (*Inf.*), villain 3. damage, detriment, disadvantage, disruption, evil, harm, hurt, injury, misfortune, trouble

mischievous 1. arch, bad, badly behaved, exasperating, frolicsome, impish, naughty, playful, puckish, rascally, roguish, sportive, teasing, troublesome, vexatious, wayward 2. bad, damaging, deleterious, destructive, detrimental, evil, harmful, hurtful, injurious, malicious, malignant, pernicious, sinful, spiteful, troublesome, vicious, wicked

misconceive fail to understand, get the wrong idea (about), misapprehend, misconstrue, misjudge, mistake, misunderstand

misconception delusion, error, fallacy, misapprehension, misconstruction, mistaken belief, misunderstanding, wrong end of the stick, wrong idea

misconduct 1. *n.* delinquency, dereliction, immorality, impropriety, malfeasance (*Law*), malpractice, malversation (*Rare*), misbehaviour, misdemeanour, mismanagement, naughtiness, rudeness, transgression, unethical behaviour, wrongdoing 2. *v.* behave badly, botch (up), bungle, err, make a mess of, misdirect, mismanage, sin

misconstruction false interpretation, misapprehension, misinterpretation, misreading, mistake, mistaken *or* false impression, misunderstanding, wrong idea

misconstrue get a false impression, make a wrong interpretation, misapprehend, misconceive, misinterpret, misjudge, misread, mistake, mistranslate, misunderstand, take the wrong way (*Inf.*)

miscreant 1. *n.* blackguard, caitiff (*Archaic*), criminal, evildoer, knave (*Archaic*), malefactor, rascal, reprobate, rogue, scally (*Northwest English dialect*), scoundrel, sinner, vagabond, villain, wrongdoer 2. *adj.* corrupt, criminal, depraved, evil, iniquitous, nefarious, rascally, reprehensible, reprobate, scoundrelly, unprincipled, vicious, villainous, wicked

misdeed crime, fault, misconduct, misdemeanour, offence, sin, transgression, trespass, villainy, wrong

misdemeanour fault, infringement, misbehaviour, misconduct, misdeed, offence, peccadillo, transgression, trespass

miser cheapskate (*Inf.*), churl (*Archaic*), curmudgeon, hunks (*Rare*), niggard, penny-pincher (*Inf.*), screw (*Sl.*), Scrooge, skinflint, tight-arse (*Taboo sl.*), tight-ass (*U.S. taboo sl.*), tightwad (*U.S. & Canad. sl.*)

miserable 1. afflicted, broken-hearted, crestfallen, dejected, depressed, desolate, despondent, disconsolate, dismal, distressed, doleful, down, downcast, down in the mouth (*Inf.*), forlorn, gloomy, heartbroken, melancholy, mournful, sorrowful, unhappy, woebegone, wretched 2. destitute, dirt-poor (*Inf.*), down and out, flat broke (*Inf.*), impoverished, indigent, meagre, needy, penniless, poor, poverty-stricken, scanty, short, without two pennies to rub together (*Inf.*) 3. abject, bad, contemptible, deplorable, despicable, detestable, disgraceful, lamentable, low, mean, pathetic, piteous, pitiable, scurvy, shabby, shameful,

sordid, sorry, squalid, vile, worthless, wretched
Antonyms admirable, cheerful, comfortable, good, happy, respectable, rich

miserliness avarice, cheeseparing, churlishness, close- *or* tightfistedness, covetousness, graspingness, meanness, minginess (*Brit. inf.*), nearness, niggardliness, parsimony, penny-pinching (*Inf.*), penuriousness, stinginess

miserly avaricious, beggarly, close, close-fisted, covetous, grasping, illiberal, mean, mingy (*Brit. inf.*), near, niggardly, parsimonious, penny-pinching (*Inf.*), penurious, sordid, stingy, tight-arsed (*Taboo sl.*), tight as a duck's arse (*Taboo sl.*), tight-assed (*U.S. taboo sl.*), tightfisted, ungenerous
Antonyms charitable, extravagant, generous, prodigal, unselfish

misery 1. agony, anguish, depression, desolation, despair, discomfort, distress, gloom, grief, hardship, melancholy, sadness, sorrow, suffering, torment, torture, unhappiness, woe, wretchedness 2. affliction, bitter pill (*Inf.*), burden, calamity, catastrophe, curse, disaster, hardship, load, misfortune, ordeal, sorrow, trial, tribulation, trouble, woe 3. destitution, indigence, need, penury, poverty, privation, sordidness, squalor, want, wretchedness 4. *Brit. inf.* grouch (*Inf.*), killjoy, moaner, pessimist, prophet of doom, sourpuss (*Inf.*), spoilsport, wet blanket (*Inf.*)
Antonyms comfort, contentment, ease, enjoyment, happiness, joy, luxury, pleasure

misfire fail, fail to go off, fall through, go phut (*Inf.*), go wrong, miscarry

misfit eccentric, fish out of water (*Inf.*), nonconformist, oddball (*Inf.*), square peg (in a round hole) (*Inf.*)

misfortune 1. bad luck, evil fortune, hard luck, ill luck, infelicity 2. accident, adversity, affliction, blow, bummer (*Sl.*), calamity, disaster, evil chance, failure, hardship, harm, loss, misadventure, mischance, misery, mishap, reverse, setback, stroke of bad luck, tragedy, trial, tribulation, trouble
Antonyms fortune, good luck, relief

misgiving anxiety, apprehension, distrust, doubt, dubiety, hesitation, qualm, reservation, scruple, suspicion, trepidation, uncertainty, unease, worry

misguided deluded, erroneous, foolish, ill-advised, imprudent, injudicious, labouring under a delusion *or* misapprehension, misled, misplaced, mistaken, uncalled-for, unreasonable, unwarranted, unwise

mishandle bodge (*Inf.*), botch, bungle, make a hash of (*Inf.*), make a mess of, mess up (*Inf.*), mismanage, muff, screw (up) (*Inf.*)

mishap accident, adversity, bad luck, calamity, contretemps, disaster, evil chance, evil fortune, hard luck, ill fortune, ill luck, infelicity, misadventure, mischance, misfortune

mishmash farrago, gallimaufry, hash, hotchpotch, jumble, medley, potpourri, salmagundi

misinform deceive, give (someone) a bum steer (*Inf., chiefly U.S.*), give (someone) duff gen (*Brit. inf.*), misdirect, misguide, mislead

misinterpret distort, falsify, get wrong, misapprehend, misconceive, misconstrue, misjudge, misread, misrepresent, mistake, misunderstand, pervert

misjudge be wrong about, get the wrong idea about, miscalculate, overestimate, overrate, underestimate, underrate

mislay be unable to find, be unable to put *or* lay one's hand on, forget the whereabouts of, lose, lose track of, misplace, miss

mislead beguile, bluff, deceive, delude, fool, give (someone) a bum steer (*Inf., chiefly U.S.*), hoodwink, lead astray, misdirect, misguide, misinform, pull the wool over (someone's) eyes (*Inf.*), take in (*Inf.*)

misleading ambiguous, casuistical, confusing, deceitful, deceptive, delusive, delusory, disingenuous, evasive, false, sophistical, specious, spurious, tricky (*Inf.*), unstraightforward
Antonyms candid, clear, correct, direct, explicit, frank, genuine, honest, obvious, open, plain, simple, sincere, straightforward, true, truthful

mismanage be incompetent, be inefficient, bodge (*Inf.*), botch, bungle, make a hash of (*Inf.*), make a mess of, maladminister, mess up, misconduct, misdirect, misgovern, mishandle

mismatched clashing, discordant, disparate, ill-assorted, incompatible, incongruous, irregular, misallied, unreconcilable, unsuited

misplace 1. be unable to find, be unable to put *or* lay one's hand on, forget the whereabouts of, lose, lose track of, misfile, mislay, miss, put in the wrong place 2. place unwisely, place wrongly

misprint corrigendum, erratum, literal, mistake, printing error, typo (*Inf.*), typographical error

misprize disparage, fail to appreciate, hold cheap, look down on, set no store by, slight, underestimate, underrate, undervalue

misquote distort, falsify, garble, mangle,

misreport, misrepresent, misstate, muddle, pervert, quote *or* take out of context, twist

misrepresent belie, disguise, distort, falsify, garble, misinterpret, misstate, pervert, twist

misrule 1. bad government, maladministration, misgovernment, mismanagement 2. anarchy, chaos, confusion, disorder, lawlessness, tumult, turmoil

miss[1] *v.* 1. avoid, be late for, blunder, err, escape, evade, fail, fail to grasp, fail to notice, forego, lack, leave out, let go, let slip, lose, miscarry, mistake, omit, overlook, pass over, pass up, skip, slip, trip 2. feel the loss of, hunger for, long for, need, pine for, want, wish, yearn for ~*n.* 3. blunder, error, failure, fault, loss, mistake, omission, oversight, want

miss[2] damsel, girl, lass, lassie (*Inf.*), maid, maiden, schoolgirl, spinster, young lady

misshapen contorted, crippled, crooked, deformed, distorted, grotesque, ill-made, ill-proportioned, malformed, twisted, ugly, ungainly, unshapely, unsightly, warped, wry

missile projectile, rocket, weapon

missing absent, astray, gone, lacking, left behind, left out, lost, mislaid, misplaced, not present, nowhere to be found, unaccounted-for, wanting

Antonyms accounted for, at hand, available, here, in attendance, on hand, present, there, to hand

mission 1. aim, assignment, business, calling, charge, commission, duty, errand, goal, job, office, operation, purpose, pursuit, quest, task, trust, undertaking, vocation, work 2. commission, delegation, deputation, embassy, legation, ministry, task force

missionary apostle, converter, evangelist, preacher, propagandist, proselytizer

missive communication, dispatch, epistle, letter, memorandum, message, note, report

misspent dissipated, idle, imprudent, misapplied, prodigal, profitless, squandered, thrown away, wasted

Antonyms active, fruitful, industrious, meaningful, profitable, unwasted, useful, worthwhile

misstate distort, falsify, garble, give a false impression, misquote, misreport, misrepresent, pervert, twist

misstep bad move, blunder, error, false step, faux pas, gaffe, indiscretion, lapse, mistake, slip, slip-up (*Inf.*), stumble, trip, wrong move

mist 1. *n.* cloud, condensation, dew, drizzle, film, fog, haar (*Eastern Brit.*), haze, smog, smur *or* smir (*Scot.*), spray, steam, vapour 2. *v.* becloud, befog, blur, cloud, film, fog, obscure, steam (up)

mistake *n.* 1. bloomer (*Brit. inf.*), blunder, boob (*Brit. sl.*), boo-boo (*Inf.*), clanger (*Inf.*), erratum, error, error of judgment, false move, fault, faux pas, gaffe, goof (*Inf.*), howler (*Inf.*), inaccuracy, miscalculation, misconception, misstep, misunderstanding, oversight, slip, slip-up (*Inf.*), solecism ~*v.* 2. get wrong, misapprehend, misconceive, misconstrue, misinterpret, misjudge, misread, misunderstand 3. accept as, confound, confuse with, misinterpret as, mix up with, take for 4. be wide of *or* be off the mark, be wrong, blunder, boob (*Brit. sl.*), drop a clanger (*Inf.*), err, goof (*Inf.*), miscalculate, misjudge, put one's foot in it (*Inf.*), slip up (*Inf.*)

mistaken barking up the wrong tree (*Inf.*), erroneous, fallacious, false, faulty, inaccurate, inappropriate, incorrect, in the wrong, labouring under a misapprehension, misguided, misinformed, misled, off target, off the mark, unfounded, unsound, wide of the mark, wrong

Antonyms accurate, correct, logical, right, sound, true

mistakenly by mistake, erroneously, fallaciously, falsely, inaccurately, inappropriately, incorrectly, in error, misguidedly, wrongly

mistimed badly timed, ill-timed, inconvenient, inopportune, unseasonable, unsynchronized, untimely

mistreat abuse, brutalize, handle roughly, harm, ill-treat, ill-use, injure, knock about *or* around, maltreat, manhandle, maul, misuse, molest, rough up, wrong

mistreatment abuse, brutalization, harm, ill-treatment, ill-usage, injury, maltreatment, manhandling, mauling, misuse, molestation, rough handling, roughing up, unkindness

mistress concubine, doxy (*Archaic*), fancy woman (*Sl.*), floozy (*Sl.*), girlfriend, inamorata, kept woman, ladylove (*Rare*), lover, paramour

mistrust 1. *v.* apprehend, beware, be wary of, distrust, doubt, fear, have doubts about, suspect 2. *n.* apprehension, distrust, doubt, dubiety, fear, misgiving, scepticism, suspicion, uncertainty, wariness

mistrustful apprehensive, cautious, chary, cynical, distrustful, doubtful, dubious, fearful, hesitant, leery (*Sl.*), nervous, sceptical, suspicious, uncertain, wary

Antonyms certain, definite, positive, sure, unafraid

misty bleary, blurred, cloudy, dark, dim,

foggy, fuzzy, hazy, indistinct, murky, nebulous, obscure, opaque, overcast, unclear, vague
Antonyms bright, clear, distinct, lucid, obvious, plain, sunny, well-defined

misunderstand get (it) wrong, get the wrong end of the stick, get the wrong idea (about), misapprehend, misconceive, misconstrue, mishear, misinterpret, misjudge, misread, miss the point (of), mistake

misunderstanding 1. error, false impression, misapprehension, misconception, misconstruction, misinterpretation, misjudgment, misreading, mistake, mix-up, wrong idea 2. argument, breach, conflict, difference, difficulty, disagreement, discord, dissension, falling-out (*Inf.*), quarrel, rift, rupture, squabble, variance

misunderstood misconstrued, misheard, misinterpreted, misjudged, misread, unappreciated, unrecognized

misuse *n.* 1. abuse, barbarism, catachresis, corruption, desecration, dissipation, malapropism, misapplication, misemployment, misusage, perversion, profanation, solecism, squandering, waste 2. abuse, cruel treatment, exploitation, harm, ill-treatment, ill-usage, inhumane treatment, injury, maltreatment, manhandling, mistreatment, rough handling ~*v.* 3. abuse, corrupt, desecrate, dissipate, misapply, misemploy, pervert, profane, prostitute, squander, waste 4. abuse, brutalize, exploit, handle roughly, harm, ill-treat, ill-use, injure, maltreat, manhandle, maul, mistreat, molest, wrong
Antonyms *v.* appreciate, cherish, honour, prize, respect, treasure, use

mitigate abate, allay, appease, assuage, blunt, calm, check, diminish, dull, ease, extenuate, lessen, lighten, moderate, modify, mollify, pacify, palliate, placate, quiet, reduce the force of, remit, soften, soothe, subdue, take the edge off, temper, tone down, tranquillize, weaken
Antonyms aggravate, augment, enhance, heighten, increase, intensify, strengthen

mitigation abatement, allaying, alleviation, assuagement, diminution, easement, extenuation, moderation, mollification, palliation, relief, remission

mix *v.* 1. alloy, amalgamate, associate, blend, coalesce, combine, commingle, commix, compound, cross, fuse, incorporate, intermingle, interweave, join, jumble, meld, merge, mingle, put together, unite 2. associate, come together, consort, fraternize, hang out (*Inf.*), hobnob, join, mingle, socialize ~*n.* 3. alloy, amalgam, assortment, blend, combination, compound, fusion, medley, meld, mixture

mixed 1. alloyed, amalgamated, blended, combined, composite, compound, fused, incorporated, joint, mingled, united 2. assorted, cosmopolitan, diverse, diversified, heterogeneous, manifold, miscellaneous, motley, varied 3. crossbred, hybrid, interbred, interdenominational, mongrel 4. ambivalent, equivocal, indecisive, uncertain
Antonyms homogeneous, isolated, pure, straight, unmixed

mixed-up at sea, bewildered, confused, distraught, disturbed, maladjusted, muddled, perplexed, puzzled, upset

mixture admixture, alloy, amalgam, amalgamation, association, assortment, blend, brew, combine, composite, compound, concoction, conglomeration, cross, fusion, hotchpotch, jumble, medley, *mélange*, meld, miscellany, mix, potpourri, salmagundi, union, variety

mix-up confusion, disorder, fankle (*Scot.*), jumble, mess, mistake, misunderstanding, muddle, snarl-up (*Inf., chiefly Brit.*), tangle

mix up 1. blend, combine, commix, mix 2. confound, confuse, muddle 3. bewilder, confuse, disturb, fluster, muddle, perplex, puzzle, throw into confusion, unnerve, upset 4. embroil, entangle, implicate, involve, rope in

moan *n.* 1. groan, lament, lamentation, sigh, sob, sough, wail, whine 2. *Inf.* beef (*Sl.*), bitch (*Sl.*), complaint, gripe (*Inf.*), grouch (*Inf.*), grouse, grumble, kvetch (*U.S. sl.*), protest, whine ~*v.* 3. bemoan, bewail, deplore, grieve, groan, keen, lament, mourn, sigh, sob, sough, whine 4. *Inf.* beef (*Sl.*), bitch (*Sl.*), bleat, carp, complain, gripe (*Inf.*), groan, grouch (*Inf.*), grouse, grumble, moan and groan, whine, whinge (*Inf.*)

mob *n.* 1. assemblage, body, collection, crowd, drove, flock, gang, gathering, herd, horde, host, mass, multitude, pack, press, swarm, throng 2. class, company, crew (*Inf.*), gang, group, lot, set, troop 3. *canaille*, commonalty, great unwashed (*Inf. & derogatory*), hoi polloi, masses, rabble, riffraff, scum ~*v.* 4. crowd around, jostle, overrun, set upon, surround, swarm around 5. cram into, crowd, crowd into, fill, fill to overflowing, jam, pack

mobile 1. ambulatory, itinerant, locomotive, migrant, motile, movable, moving, peripatetic, portable, travelling, wandering 2. animated, changeable, ever-changing, expressive

mobilize activate, animate, call to arms, call up, get *or* make ready, marshal, muster, organize, prepare, put in motion, rally, ready

mock *v.* 1. chaff, deride, flout, insult, jeer, laugh at, laugh to scorn, make fun of, poke fun at, ridicule, scoff, scorn, show contempt for, sneer, take the mickey (out of) (*Inf.*), take the piss (out of) (*Taboo sl.*), taunt, tease, wind up (*Brit. sl.*) 2. ape, burlesque, caricature, counterfeit, do (*Inf.*), imitate, lampoon, mimic, parody, satirize, send up (*Brit. inf.*), take off (*Inf.*), travesty 3. belie, cheat, deceive, delude, disappoint, dupe, elude, fool, let down, mislead 4. defeat, defy, disappoint, foil, frustrate, thwart ~*n.* 5. banter, derision, gibe, jeering, mockery, ridicule, scorn, sneer, sneering 6. Aunt Sally (*Brit.*), butt, dupe, fool, jest, laughing stock, sport, travesty 7. counterfeit, fake, forgery, fraud, imitation, phoney *or* phony (*Inf.*), sham ~*adj.* 8. artificial, bogus, counterfeit, dummy, ersatz, fake, faked, false, feigned, forged, fraudulent, imitation, phoney *or* phony (*Inf.*), pretended, pseudo (*Inf.*), sham, spurious

Antonyms *v.* encourage, praise, respect, revere ~*adj.* authentic, genuine, natural, real, sincere, true, unfeigned

mockery 1. contempt, contumely, derision, disdain, disrespect, gibes, insults, jeering, ridicule, scoffing, scorn 2. burlesque, caricature, deception, farce, imitation, lampoon, laughing stock, mimicry, parody, pretence, send-up (*Brit. inf.*), sham, spoof (*Inf.*), take-off (*Inf.*), travesty 3. apology, disappointment, farce, joke, letdown

mocking contemptuous, contumelious, derisive, derisory, disdainful, disrespectful, insulting, irreverent, sarcastic, sardonic, satiric, satirical, scoffing, scornful, taunting

mode 1. approach, condition, course, custom, fashion, form, manner, method, plan, practice, procedure, process, quality, rule, state, style, system, technique, vein, way 2. craze, fashion, look, rage, style, trend, vogue

model *n.* 1. copy, dummy, facsimile, image, imitation, miniature, mock-up, replica, representation 2. archetype, design, epitome, example, exemplar, gauge, ideal, lodestar, mould, norm, original, par, paradigm, paragon, pattern, prototype, standard, type 3. poser, sitter, subject 4. mannequin 5. configuration, design, form, kind, mark, mode, stamp, style, type, variety, version ~*v.* 6. base, carve, cast, design, fashion, form, mould, pattern, plan, sculpt, shape, stamp 7. display, show off, sport (*Inf.*), wear ~*adj.* 8. copy, dummy, facsimile, imitation, miniature 9. archetypal, exemplary, ideal, illustrative, paradigmatic, perfect, standard, typical

Antonyms *adj.* (*sense 9*) deficient, flawed, impaired, imperfect

moderate *adj.* 1. calm, controlled, cool, deliberate, equable, gentle, judicious, limited, middle-of-the-road, mild, modest, peaceable, reasonable, restrained, sober, steady, temperate 2. average, fair, fairish, fair to middling (*Inf.*), indifferent, mediocre, medium, middling, ordinary, passable, so-so (*Inf.*), unexceptional ~*v.* 3. abate, allay, appease, assuage, calm, control, curb, decrease, diminish, ease, lessen, mitigate, modulate, pacify, play down, quiet, regulate, relax, repress, restrain, soften, soft-pedal (*Inf.*), subdue, tame, temper, tone down 4. arbitrate, chair, judge, mediate, preside, referee, take the chair

Antonyms *adj.* (*sense 1*) extreme, intemperate, ruffled, unreasonable, wild (*sense 2*) excessive, expensive, extreme, immoderate, inordinate, unusual ~*v.* heighten, increase, intensify

moderately fairly, gently, in moderation, passably, quite, rather, reasonably, slightly, somewhat, to a degree, tolerably, to some extent, within limits, within reason

moderation 1. calmness, composure, coolness, equanimity, fairness, judiciousness, justice, justness, mildness, moderateness, reasonableness, restraint, sedateness, temperance 2. **in moderation** moderately, within limits, within reason

modern contemporary, current, fresh, late, latest, neoteric (*Rare*), new, newfangled, novel, present, present-day, recent, twentieth-century, up-to-date, up-to-the-minute, with it (*Inf.*)

Antonyms ancient, antiquated, archaic, former, obsolete, old, old-fashioned, old hat, outmoded, passé, past, square (*Inf.*), uncool (*Sl.*)

modernity contemporaneity, currency, freshness, innovation, newness, novelty, recentness

modernize bring into the twentieth century, bring up to date, face-lift, make over, rejuvenate, remake, remodel, renew, renovate, revamp, update

modest 1. bashful, blushing, coy, demure, diffident, discreet, humble, meek, quiet, reserved, reticent, retiring, self-conscious, self-effacing, shy, simple, unassuming, unpretentious 2. fair, limited, middling, moderate, ordinary, small, unexceptional

modesty bashfulness, coyness, decency, demureness, diffidence, discreetness, humbleness, humility, lack of pretension, meekness, propriety, quietness, reserve,

reticence, self-effacement, shyness, simplicity, timidity, unobtrusiveness, unpretentiousness
Antonyms arrogance, assurance, boastfulness, boldness, conceit, confidence, egotism, extravagance, forwardness, haughtiness, immodesty, indecency, ostentation, presumption, pretentiousness, pride, showiness, vanity

modicum atom, bit, crumb, dash, drop, fragment, grain, inch, iota, little, mite, ounce, particle, pinch, scrap, shred, small amount, speck, tad (*Inf., chiefly U.S.*), tinge, touch

modification adjustment, alteration, change, modulation, mutation, qualification, refinement, reformation, restriction, revision, variation

modify 1. adapt, adjust, alter, change, convert, recast, redo, refashion, reform, remodel, reorganize, reshape, revise, rework, transform, vary 2. abate, ease, lessen, limit, lower, moderate, qualify, reduce, relax, restrain, restrict, soften, temper, tone down

modish à la mode, all the rage, chic, contemporary, current, fashionable, hip (*Sl.*), in, now (*Inf.*), smart, stylish, trendy (*Brit. inf.*), up-to-the-minute, vogue, voguish, with it (*Inf.*)

modulate adjust, attune, balance, harmonize, inflect, regulate, tone, tune, vary

modus operandi method, operation, practice, praxis, procedure, process, system, technique, way

mogul baron, bashaw, big cheese (*Sl., old-fashioned*), big gun (*Inf.*), big noise (*Inf.*), big shot (*Inf.*), big wheel (*Sl.*), lord, magnate, nabob (*Inf.*), notable, personage, potentate, tycoon, V.I.P.

moiety fifty percent, half, part, piece, portion, share

moist clammy, damp, dampish, dank, dewy, dripping, drizzly, humid, not dry, rainy, soggy, wet, wettish

moisten bedew, damp, dampen, humidify, lick, moisturize, soak, water, wet

moisture damp, dampness, dankness, dew, humidity, liquid, perspiration, sweat, water, wateriness, wetness

mole breakwater, dike, dyke, embankment, groyne, jetty, pier, sea wall

molecule atom, iota, jot, mite, mote, particle, speck

molest 1. abuse, afflict, annoy, badger, beset, bother, bug (*Inf.*), disturb, harass, harry, hector, irritate, persecute, pester, plague, tease, torment, upset, vex, worry 2. abuse, accost, assail, attack, harm, hurt, ill-treat, injure, interfere with, maltreat, manhandle

mollify 1. appease, calm, compose, conciliate, pacify, placate, propitiate, quell, quiet, soothe, sweeten 2. abate, allay, assuage, blunt, curb, cushion, ease, lessen, lull, mitigate, moderate, modify, relieve, soften, temper, tone down, tranquillize

mollycoddle 1. *v.* baby, coddle, cosset, indulge, pamper, pet, ruin, spoil 2. *n.* baby, chinless wonder (*Brit. inf.*), crybaby, milksop, milquetoast (*U.S.*), namby-pamby, sissy, weakling

moment 1. flash, instant, jiffy (*Inf.*), minute, no time, second, shake (*Inf.*), split second, tick (*Brit. inf.*), trice, twinkling, two shakes (*Inf.*), two shakes of a lamb's tail (*Inf.*) 2. hour, instant, juncture, point, point in time, stage, time 3. concern, consequence, gravity, import, importance, seriousness, significance, substance, value, weight, weightiness, worth

momentarily briefly, for a moment (little while, minute, second, short time, short while), for an instant, for the nonce, temporarily

momentary brief, ephemeral, evanescent, fleeting, flying, fugitive, hasty, passing, quick, short, short-lived, temporary, transitory
Antonyms lasting, lengthy, long-lived, permanent

momentous consequential, critical, crucial, decisive, earth-shaking (*Inf.*), fateful, grave, historic, important, of moment, pivotal, serious, significant, vital, weighty
Antonyms inconsequential, insignificant, trifling, trivial, unimportant

momentum drive, energy, force, impetus, power, propulsion, push, strength, thrust

monarch crowned head, emperor, empress, king, potentate, prince, princess, queen, ruler, sovereign

monarchy 1. absolutism, autocracy, despotism, kingship, monocracy, royalism, sovereignty 2. empire, kingdom, principality, realm

monastery abbey, cloister, convent, friary, house, nunnery, priory, religious community

monastic ascetic, austere, celibate, cenobitic, cloistered, cloistral, coenobitic, contemplative, conventual, eremitic, hermit-like, monachal, monkish, recluse, reclusive, secluded, sequestered, withdrawn

monetary budgetary, capital, cash, financial, fiscal, pecuniary

money 1. ackers (*Sl.*), banknotes, brass (*Northern English dialect*), bread (*Sl.*), capital, cash, coin, currency, dibs (*Sl.*), dosh (*Brit. & Aust. sl.*), dough (*Sl.*), filthy lucre (*Facetious*), funds, gelt (*Sl., chiefly U.S.*), green (*Sl.*), hard cash, legal tender, lolly (*Brit. sl.*), loot (*Inf.*), mazuma (*Sl., chiefly U.S.*), megabucks (*U.S. & Canad. sl.*), moolah (*Sl.*), necessary (*Inf.*), needful (*Inf.*), pelf (*Contemptuous*), readies (*Inf.*), rhino (*Brit. sl.*), riches, shekels (*Inf.*), silver, specie, spondulicks (*Sl.*), the ready (*Inf.*), the wherewithal, tin (*Sl.*), wealth 2. **in the money** affluent, flush (*Inf.*), in clover (*Inf.*), loaded (*Sl.*), on Easy Street (*Inf.*), prosperous, rich, rolling (*Sl.*), wealthy, well-heeled (*Inf.*), well-off, well-to-do

moneyed, monied affluent, flush (*Inf.*), loaded (*Sl.*), prosperous, rich, wealthy, well-heeled (*Inf.*), well-off, well-to-do

moneymaking *adj.* gainful, going, lucrative, paying, profitable, remunerative, successful, thriving

mongrel 1. *n.* bigener (*Biol.*), cross, crossbreed, half-breed, hybrid, mixed breed 2. *adj.* bastard, crossbred, half-breed, hybrid, of mixed breed

monitor 1. *n.* guide, invigilator, overseer, prefect (*Brit.*), supervisor, watchdog 2. *v.* check, follow, keep an eye on, keep track of, observe, oversee, record, scan, supervise, survey, watch

monitory admonishing, admonitory, cautionary, cautioning, reproving, warning

monk brother, friar (*loosely*), monastic, religious

monkey *n.* 1. primate, simian 2. devil, imp, mischief maker, pickle (*Brit. inf.*), rascal, rogue, scamp 3. *Sl.* ass, butt, dupe, fool, laughing stock 4. **make a monkey of** make a fool of, make (someone) a laughing stock, make fun of, make (someone) look foolish (ridiculous, silly), play a trick on, ridicule ~*v.* 5. fiddle (*Inf.*), fool, interfere, meddle, mess, play, tamper, tinker, trifle

monkey business 1. carry-on (*Inf., chiefly Brit.*), clowning, mischief, monkey tricks, pranks, shenanigans (*Inf.*), skylarking (*Inf.*), tomfoolery 2. chicanery, dishonesty, funny business, hanky-panky (*Inf.*), skulduggery (*Inf.*), trickery

monolithic colossal, giant, gigantic, huge, immovable, impenetrable, imposing, intractable, massive, monumental, solid, substantial, undifferentiated, undivided, unitary

monologue harangue, lecture, sermon, soliloquy, speech

monomania bee in one's bonnet (*Inf.*), fanaticism, fixation, hobbyhorse, *idée fixe*, obsession, one-track mind (*Inf.*)

monopolize control, corner, corner the market in, dominate, engross, exercise *or* have a monopoly of, hog (*Sl.*), keep to oneself, take over, take up

monotonous all the same, boring, colourless, droning, dull, flat, ho-hum (*Inf.*), humdrum, mind-numbing, plodding, repetitious, repetitive, samey (*Inf.*), soporific, tedious, tiresome, toneless, unchanging, uniform, uninflected, unvaried, wearisome
Antonyms animated, enjoyable, entertaining, enthralling, exciting, exhilarating, interesting, lively, sexy (*Inf.*), stimulating

monotony boredom, colourlessness, dullness, flatness, humdrumness, monotonousness, repetitiveness, repetitiousness, routine, sameness, tediousness, tedium, tiresomeness, uniformity, wearisomeness

monster *n.* 1. barbarian, beast, bogeyman, brute, demon, devil, fiend, ghoul, ogre, savage, villain 2. abortion, freak, lusus naturae, miscreation, monstrosity, mutant, teratism 3. behemoth, Brobdingnagian, colossus, giant, leviathan, mammoth, titan ~*adj.* 4. Brobdingnagian, colossal, elephantine, enormous, gargantuan, giant, gigantic, ginormous (*Inf.*), huge, humongous *or* humungous (*U.S. sl.*), immense, jumbo (*Inf.*), mammoth, massive, mega (*Sl.*), monstrous, stupendous, titanic, tremendous

monstrosity 1. abortion, eyesore, freak, horror, lusus naturae, miscreation, monster, mutant, ogre, teratism 2. abnormality, atrocity, dreadfulness, evil, frightfulness, heinousness, hellishness, hideousness, horror, loathsomeness, obscenity

monstrous 1. abnormal, dreadful, enormous, fiendish, freakish, frightful, grotesque, gruesome, hellish, hideous, horrendous, horrible, miscreated, obscene, teratoid, terrible, unnatural 2. atrocious, cruel, devilish, diabolical, disgraceful, egregious, evil, fiendish, foul, heinous, horrifying, infamous, inhuman, intolerable, loathsome, odious, outrageous, satanic, scandalous, shocking, vicious, villainous 3. colossal, elephantine, enormous, gargantuan, giant, gigantic, ginormous (*Inf.*), great, huge, humongous *or* humungous (*U.S. sl.*), immense, mammoth, massive, mega (*Sl.*), prodigious, stupendous, titanic, towering, tremendous, vast
Antonyms (*sense 1*) appealing, attractive, beautiful, delightful, lovely, natural, normal, ordinary, pleasant (*sense 2*) admirable, decent, fine, good, honourable, humane, kind, merciful, mild (*sense 3*) diminutive, insignificant, little, meagre, miniature, minute, puny, slight, small, tiny

month four weeks, moon, thirty days

monument 1. cairn, cenotaph, commemoration, gravestone, headstone, marker, mausoleum, memorial, obelisk, pillar, shrine, statue, tombstone 2. memento, record, remembrance, reminder, testament, token, witness

monumental 1. awe-inspiring, awesome, classic, enduring, enormous, epoch-making, historic, immortal, important, lasting, majestic, memorable, outstanding, prodigious, significant, stupendous, unforgettable 2. commemorative, cyclopean, funerary, memorial, monolithic, statuary 3. *Inf.* catastrophic, colossal, egregious, gigantic, great, horrible, immense, indefensible, massive, staggering, terrible, tremendous, unforgivable, whopping (*Inf.*)
Antonyms (*sense 1*) ephemeral, inconsequential, insignificant, modest, negligible, ordinary, trivial, undistinguished, unimportant, unimpressive, unremarkable (*sense 3*) average, insignificant, mild, petty, slight, small, tiny, trivial

mood 1. disposition, frame of mind, humour, spirit, state of mind, temper, tenor, vein 2. bad temper, bate (*Brit. sl.*), blues, depression, doldrums, dumps (*Inf.*), fit of pique, grumps (*Inf.*), low spirits, melancholy, sulk, the hump (*Brit. inf.*), the sulks 3. **in the mood** disposed (towards), eager, favourable, inclined, interested, in the (right) frame of mind, keen, minded, willing

moody 1. angry, broody, cantankerous, crabbed, crabby, crestfallen, cross, crotchety (*Inf.*), crusty, curt, dismal, doleful, dour, downcast, down in the dumps (*Inf.*), down in the mouth (*Inf.*), frowning, gloomy, glum, huffish, huffy, ill-humoured, ill-tempered, in a huff, in the doldrums, introspective, irascible, irritable, lugubrious, melancholy, miserable, mopish, mopy, morose, offended, out of sorts (*Inf.*), pensive, petulant, piqued, sad, saturnine, short-tempered, splenetic, sulky, sullen, temperamental, testy, tetchy, touchy, waspish, wounded 2. capricious, changeable, erratic, faddish, fickle, fitful, flighty, impulsive, inconstant, mercurial, temperamental, unpredictable, unstable, unsteady, volatile
Antonyms (*sense 1*) amiable, cheerful, compatible, gay, happy, optimistic (*sense 2*) constant, stable, steady

moon *n.* 1. satellite 2. **once in a blue moon** almost never, hardly ever, rarely, very seldom ~*v.* 3. daydream, idle, languish, mooch (*Sl.*), mope, waste time

moonshine 1. moonbeams, moonlight 2. *U.S.* bootleg, hooch *or* hootch (*Inf., chiefly U.S. & Canad.*), poteen 3. blather, blether, bosh (*Inf.*), bunk (*Inf.*), bunkum *or* buncombe (*Chiefly U.S.*), claptrap (*Inf.*), foolish talk, gas (*Inf.*), guff (*Sl.*), havers (*Scot.*), hogwash, hot air (*Inf.*), nonsense, piffle (*Inf.*), rubbish, stuff and nonsense, tarradiddle, tosh (*Sl., chiefly Brit.*), tripe (*Inf.*), twaddle

moor[1] fell (*Brit.*), heath, moorland, muir (*Scot.*)

moor[2] anchor, berth, dock, fasten, fix, lash, make fast, secure, tie up

moot 1. *adj.* arguable, at issue, contestable, controversial, debatable, disputable, doubtful, open, open to debate, undecided, unresolved, unsettled 2. *v.* bring up, broach, introduce, propose, put forward, suggest, ventilate

mop *n.* 1. sponge, squeegee, swab 2. mane, shock, tangle, thatch ~*v.* 3. clean, soak up, sponge, swab, wash, wipe

mope be apathetic, be dejected, be down in the mouth (*Inf.*), be gloomy, brood, eat one's heart out, fret, go about like a half-shut knife (*Inf.*), hang around, idle, languish, moon, pine, pout, sulk, waste time, wear a long face

mop up 1. clean up, mop, soak up, sponge, swab, wash, wipe 2. *Military* account for, clean out, clear, eliminate, finish off, neutralize, pacify, round up, secure

moral *adj.* 1. ethical 2. blameless, chaste, decent, ethical, good, high-minded, honest, honourable, incorruptible, innocent, just, meritorious, noble, principled, proper, pure, right, righteous, upright, upstanding, virtuous ~*n.* 3. lesson, meaning, message, point, significance 4. adage, aphorism, apophthegm, epigram, gnome, maxim, motto, proverb, saw, saying
Antonyms amoral, dishonest, dishonourable, immoral, improper, sinful, unethical, unfair, unjust, wrong

morale confidence, esprit de corps, heart, mettle, self-esteem, spirit, temper

morality 1. chastity, decency, ethicality, ethicalness, goodness, honesty, integrity, justice, principle, rectitude, righteousness, rightness, uprightness, virtue 2. conduct, ethics, habits, ideals, manners, moral code, morals, mores, philosophy, principles, standards

morals behaviour, conduct, ethics, habits, integrity, manners, morality, mores, principles, scruples, standards

morass 1. bog, fen, marsh, marshland, moss (*Scot. & northern English dialect*), quagmire, slough, swamp 2. chaos, confusion, jam (*Inf.*), mess, mix-up, muddle, quagmire, tangle

moratorium freeze, halt, postponement, respite, standstill, stay, suspension

morbid 1. brooding, funereal, ghoulish, gloomy, grim, melancholy, pessimistic, sick, sombre, unhealthy, unwholesome 2. dreadful, ghastly, grisly, gruesome, hideous, horrid, macabre 3. ailing, deadly, diseased, infected, malignant, pathological, sick, sickly, unhealthy, unsound
Antonyms bright, cheerful, happy, healthy, salubrious, wholesome

mordant 1. acerbic, acid, acrimonious, astringent, biting, caustic, cutting, edged, harsh, incisive, mordacious, pungent, sarcastic, scathing, sharp, stinging, trenchant, venomous, vitriolic, waspish 2. acid, acidic, caustic, corrosive, pungent, vitriolic

more 1. *adj.* added, additional, extra, fresh, further, new, other, spare, supplementary 2. *adv.* better, further, longer, to a greater extent

moreover additionally, also, as well, besides, further, furthermore, in addition, into the bargain, likewise, to boot, too, what is more, withal (*Literary*)

morgue mortuary

moribund 1. at death's door, breathing one's last, doomed, dying, fading fast, failing, (having) one foot in the grave, *in extremis,* near death, near the end, on one's deathbed, on one's last legs 2. at a standstill, declining, forceless, obsolescent, on its last legs, on the way out, stagnant, stagnating, standing still, waning, weak

morning a.m., break of day, dawn, daybreak, forenoon, morn (*Poetic*), morrow (*Archaic*), sunrise

moron airhead (*Sl.*), ass, berk (*Brit. sl.*), blockhead, bonehead (*Sl.*), charlie (*Brit. inf.*), coot, cretin, dickhead (*Sl.*), dimwit (*Inf.*), dipstick (*Brit. sl.*), divvy (*Brit. sl.*), dolt, dope (*Inf.*), dork (*Sl.*), dummy (*Sl.*), dunce, dunderhead, dweeb (*U.S. sl.*), fool, fuckwit (*Taboo sl.*), geek (*Sl.*), gonzo (*Sl.*), halfwit, idiot, imbecile, jerk (*Sl., chiefly U.S. & Canad.*), lamebrain (*Inf.*), mental defective, muttonhead (*Sl.*), nerd *or* nurd (*Sl.*), nitwit (*Inf.*), numskull *or* numbskull, oaf, pillock (*Brit. sl.*), plank (*Brit. sl.*), plonker (*Sl.*), prat (*Sl.*), prick (*Derogatory sl.*), schmuck (*U.S. sl.*), simpleton, thickhead, tosser (*Brit. sl.*), twit (*Inf., chiefly Brit.*), wally (*Sl.*)

moronic asinine, Boeotian, braindead (*Inf.*), brainless, cretinous, daft (*Inf.*), dimwitted (*Inf.*), doltish, foolish, gormless (*Brit. inf.*), halfwitted, idiotic, imbecilic, mentally defective, mindless, muttonheaded (*Sl.*), retarded, simple, stupid, thick, unintelligent

morose blue, churlish, crabbed, crabby, cross, crusty, depressed, dour, down, down in the dumps (*Inf.*), gloomy, glum, grouchy (*Inf.*), gruff, ill-humoured, ill-natured, ill-tempered, in a bad mood, low, melancholy, miserable, moody, mournful, perverse, pessimistic, saturnine, sour, sulky, sullen, surly, taciturn
Antonyms amiable, blithe, cheerful, chirpy (*Inf.*), friendly, gay, genial, good-humoured, good-natured, happy, pleasant, sweet

morsel bit, bite, crumb, fraction, fragment, grain, mouthful, nibble, part, piece, scrap, segment, slice, snack, soupçon, tad (*Inf., chiefly U.S.*), taste, titbit

mortal *adj.* 1. corporeal, earthly, ephemeral, human, impermanent, passing, sublunary, temporal, transient, worldly 2. deadly, death-dealing, destructive, fatal, killing, lethal, murderous, terminal 3. bitter, deadly, implacable, irreconcilable, out-and-out, remorseless, sworn, to the death, unrelenting 4. agonizing, awful, dire, enormous, extreme, grave, great, intense, severe, terrible ~*n.* 5. being, body, earthling, human, human being, individual, man, person, woman

mortality 1. ephemerality, humanity, impermanence, temporality, transience 2. bloodshed, carnage, death, destruction, fatality, killing, loss of life

mortification 1. abasement, annoyance, chagrin, discomfiture, dissatisfaction, embarrassment, humiliation, loss of face, shame, vexation 2. abasement, chastening, control, denial, discipline, subjugation 3. *Medical* corruption, festering, gangrene, necrosis, putrescence

mortified 1. abashed, affronted, annoyed, ashamed, chagrined, chastened, confounded, crushed, deflated, discomfited, displeased, embarrassed, given a showing-up (*Inf.*), humbled, humiliated, made to eat humble pie (*Inf.*), put down, put out (*Inf.*), put to shame, rendered speechless, shamed, vexed 2. abased, chastened, conquered, controlled, crushed, disciplined, subdued 3. *Of flesh* decayed, gangrenous, necrotic, rotted

mortify 1. abase, abash, affront, annoy, chagrin, chasten, confound, crush, deflate, disappoint, discomfit, displease, embarrass, humble, humiliate, make (someone) eat humble pie (*Inf.*), put down, put to shame, shame, take (someone) down a peg (*Inf.*), vex 2. abase, chasten, control, deny, discipline, subdue 3. *Of flesh* become gangrenous, corrupt, deaden, die, fester, gangrene, necrose, putrefy

mortuary funeral home (*U.S.*), funeral parlour, morgue

mostly above all, almost entirely, as a rule, chiefly, customarily, for the most part, generally, largely, mainly, most often, on the whole, particularly, predominantly, primarily, principally, usually

mote atom, grain, mite, particle, speck, spot

moth-eaten antiquated, decayed, decrepit, dilapidated, grungy (*Sl., chiefly U.S.*), obsolete, outdated, outworn, ragged, scuzzy (*Sl., chiefly U.S.*), seedy, shabby, stale, tattered, threadbare, worn-out

mother *n.* 1. dam, ma (*Inf.*), mater, mom (*U.S. inf.*), mum (*Brit. inf.*), mummy (*Brit. inf.*), old lady (*Inf.*), old woman (*Inf.*) ~*adj.* 2. connate, inborn, innate, native, natural ~*v.* 3. bear, bring forth, drop, give birth to, produce 4. care for, cherish, nurse, nurture, protect, raise, rear, tend 5. baby, fuss over, indulge, pamper, spoil

motherly affectionate, caring, comforting, fond, gentle, kind, loving, maternal, protective, sheltering, tender, warm

mother wit brains, common sense, gumption (*Brit. inf.*), horse sense, judgment, native intelligence, savvy (*Sl.*), smarts (*Sl., chiefly U.S.*)

motif 1. concept, idea, leitmotiv, subject, theme 2. decoration, design, form, ornament, shape

motion *n.* 1. action, change, flow, kinesics, locomotion, mobility, motility, move, movement, passage, passing, progress, travel 2. gesticulation, gesture, sign, signal, wave 3. proposal, proposition, recommendation, submission, suggestion 4. **in motion** afoot, functioning, going, in progress, moving, on the go (*Inf.*), on the move (*Inf.*), operational, travelling, under way, working ~*v.* 5. beckon, direct, gesticulate, gesture, nod, signal, wave

motionless at a standstill, at rest, calm, fixed, frozen, halted, immobile, inanimate, inert, lifeless, paralysed, standing, static, stationary, still, stock-still, transfixed, unmoved, unmoving

Antonyms active, agitated, animated, frantic, lively, mobile, moving, restless, travelling

motivate actuate, arouse, bring, cause, draw, drive, get going, give incentive to, impel, induce, inspire, inspirit, instigate, lead, move, persuade, prod, prompt, provoke, set off, set on, stimulate, stir, trigger

motivation 1. ambition, desire, drive, hunger, inspiration, interest, wish 2. impulse, incentive, incitement, inducement, inspiration, instigation, motive, persuasion, reason, spur, stimulus

motive 1. *n.* cause, design, ground(s), incentive, incitement, inducement, influence, inspiration, intention, mainspring, motivation, object, occasion, purpose, rationale, reason, spur, stimulus, thinking 2. *adj.* activating, driving, impelling, motivating, moving, operative, prompting

motley 1. assorted, disparate, dissimilar, diversified, heterogeneous, mingled, miscellaneous, mixed, unlike, varied 2. chequered, multicoloured, particoloured, polychromatic, polychrome, polychromous, rainbow, variegated

Antonyms (*sense 1*) homogeneous, similar, uniform (*sense 2*) monochromatic, plain, self-coloured, solid

mottled blotchy, brindled, chequered, dappled, flecked, freckled, marbled, piebald, pied, speckled, spotted, stippled, streaked, tabby, variegated

motto adage, byword, cry, dictum, formula, gnome, maxim, precept, proverb, rule, saw, saying, slogan, watchword

mould[1] *n.* 1. cast, die, form, matrix, pattern, shape, stamp 2. brand, build, configuration, construction, cut, design, fashion, form, format, frame, kind, line, make, pattern, shape, stamp, structure, style 3. calibre, character, ilk, kidney, kind, nature, quality, sort, stamp, type ~*v.* 4. carve, cast, construct, create, fashion, forge, form, make, model, sculpt, shape, stamp, work 5. affect, control, direct, form, influence, make, shape

mould[2] blight, fungus, mildew, mouldiness, mustiness

mould[3] dirt, earth, humus, loam, soil

moulder crumble, decay, decompose, disintegrate, perish, rot, waste

mouldy bad, blighted, decaying, fusty, mildewed, musty, rotten, rotting, spoiled, stale

mound 1. bing (*Scot.*), drift, heap, pile, stack 2. bank, dune, embankment, hill, hillock, knoll, rise 3. *Archaeology* barrow, tumulus 4. bulwark, earthwork, motte (*History*), rampart

mount *v.* 1. ascend, clamber up, climb, escalade, go up, make one's way up, scale 2. bestride, climb onto, climb up on, get astride, get (up) on, jump on 3. arise, ascend, rise, soar, tower 4. accumulate, build, escalate, grow, increase, intensify, multiply, pile up, swell 5. display, frame, set, set off 6. exhibit, get up (*Inf.*), prepare, produce, put on, stage 7. *Military* deliver, launch, prepare, ready, set in motion, stage 8. emplace, fit, install, place, position, put in place, set up ~*n.* 9. backing, base, fixture, foil, frame, mounting, setting, stand, support 10. horse, steed (*Literary*)

Antonyms (*sense 1*) descend, drop, go down, make one's way down (*sense 2*) climb down from, climb off, dismount, get down from, get off, jump off (*sense 4*) contract, decline, decrease, diminish, dwindle, fall, lessen, lower, reduce, shrink, wane

mountain 1. alp, ben (*Scot.*), elevation, eminence, fell (*Brit.*), height, mount, Munro, peak 2. abundance, heap, mass, mound, pile, stack, ton

mountainous 1. alpine, high, highland, rocky, soaring, steep, towering, upland 2. daunting, enormous, gigantic, great, huge, hulking, immense, mammoth, mighty, monumental, ponderous, prodigious

Antonyms (*sense 2*) diminutive, insignificant, little, minute, petty, puny, small, tiny, trivial, weak

mountebank charlatan, cheat, chiseller (*Inf.*), confidence trickster, con man (*Inf.*), fake, fraud, impostor, phoney *or* phony (*Inf.*), pretender, quack, rogue, swindler

mourn bemoan, bewail, deplore, grieve, keen, lament, miss, rue, sorrow, wail, wear black, weep

mournful 1. afflicting, calamitous, deplorable, distressing, grievous, harrowing, lamentable, melancholy, painful, piteous, plaintive, sad, sorrowful, tragic, unhappy, woeful 2. brokenhearted, cheerless, desolate, disconsolate, dismal, downcast, funereal, gloomy, grief-stricken, grieving, heartbroken, heavy, heavy-hearted, joyless, lugubrious, melancholy, miserable, rueful, sad, sombre, unhappy, woeful

Antonyms (*sense 1*) agreeable, cheerful, fortunate, happy, lucky, pleasant, satisfying (*sense 2*) bright, cheerful, chirpy (*Inf.*), genial, happy, jolly, joyful, light-hearted, sunny, upbeat (*Inf.*)

mourning 1. bereavement, grief, grieving, keening, lamentation, weeping, woe 2. black, sackcloth and ashes, weeds, widow's weeds

mousy, mousey 1. brownish, colourless, drab, dull, indeterminate, plain 2. diffident, ineffectual, quiet, self-effacing, shy, timid, timorous, unassertive

mouth *n.* 1. chops (*Sl.*), gob (*Sl., esp. Brit.*), jaws, lips, maw, trap (*Sl.*), yap (*Sl.*) 2. *Inf.* boasting, braggadocio, bragging, empty talk, gas (*Inf.*), hot air (*Sl.*), idle talk 3. *Inf.* backchat (*Inf.*), cheek (*Inf.*), impudence, insolence, lip (*Sl.*), rudeness, sauce (*Inf.*) 4. aperture, cavity, crevice, door, entrance, gateway, inlet, lips, opening, orifice, rim 5. face, grimace, *moue*, pout, wry face 6. **down in *or* at the mouth** blue, crestfallen, dejected, depressed, disheartened, dispirited, down, downcast, down in the dumps (*Inf.*), in low spirits, melancholy, miserable, sad, sick as a parrot (*Inf.*), unhappy

mouthful bit, bite, drop, forkful, little, morsel, sample, sip, spoonful, sup, swallow, taste

mouthpiece 1. agent, delegate, representative, spokesman, spokeswoman 2. journal, organ, periodical, publication

movable detachable, mobile, not fixed, portable, portative, transferable, transportable

movables belongings, chattels, effects, furniture, gear, goods, possessions, property, stuff (*Inf.*), things (*Inf.*)

move *v.* 1. advance, budge, change position, drift, go, march, proceed, progress, shift, stir, walk 2. carry, change, shift, switch, transfer, transport, transpose 3. change residence, flit (*Scot. & northern English dialect*), go away, leave, migrate, move house, quit, relocate, remove 4. activate, drive, impel, motivate, operate, prod, propel, push, set going, shift, shove, start, turn 5. actuate, affect, agitate, cause, excite, give rise to, impel, impress, incite, induce, influence, inspire, instigate, lead, make an impression on, motivate, persuade, prompt, rouse, stimulate, touch, urge 6. advocate, propose, put forward, recommend, suggest, urge ~*n.* 7. act, action, deed, manoeuvre, measure, motion, movement, ploy, shift, step, stratagem, stroke, turn 8. change of address, flit (*Scot. & northern English dialect*), flitting (*Scot. & northern English dialect*), migration, relocation, removal, shift, transfer 9. **get a move on** get cracking (*Inf.*), get going, hurry (up), make haste, shake a leg (*Inf.*), speed up, step on it (*Inf.*), stir oneself 10. **on the move** *Inf.* a. in transit, journeying, moving, on the road (*Inf.*), on the run, on the wing, travelling, under way, voyaging b. active, advancing, astir, going forward, moving, progressing, stirring, succeeding

Antonyms (*sense 5*) deter, discourage, dissuade, prevent, stop

movement 1. act, action, activity, advance, agitation, change, development, displacement, exercise, flow, gesture, manoeuvre, motion, move, moving, operation, progress, progression, shift, steps, stir, stirring, transfer 2. camp, campaign, crusade, drive, faction, front, group, grouping, organization, party 3. current, drift, flow, swing, tendency, trend 4. action, innards (*Inf.*), machinery, mechanism, workings, works 5. *Music* division, part, passage, section 6. beat, cadence, measure (*Prosody*), metre, pace, rhythm, swing, tempo

movie 1. feature, film, flick (*Sl.*), motion

picture, moving picture (*U.S.*), picture 2. *Plural* cinema, film, films, flicks (*Sl.*), pictures (*Inf.*), silver screen (*Inf.*)

moving 1. affecting, arousing, emotional, emotive, exciting, impelling, impressive, inspiring, pathetic, persuasive, poignant, stirring, touching 2. mobile, motile, movable, portable, running, unfixed 3. dynamic, impelling, inspirational, motivating, propelling, stimulating, stimulative
Antonyms (*sense 1*) unemotional, unexciting, unimpressive, uninspiring (*sense 2*) fixed, immobile, immovable, stationary, still, unmoving

mow crop, cut, scythe, shear, trim

mow down blow away (*Sl., chiefly U.S.*), butcher, cut down, cut to pieces, massacre, shoot down, slaughter

much 1. *adj.* abundant, a lot of, ample, considerable, copious, great, plenteous, plenty of, sizeable, substantial 2. *adv.* a great deal, a lot, considerably, decidedly, exceedingly, frequently, greatly, indeed, often, regularly 3. *n.* a good deal, a great deal, a lot, an appreciable amount, heaps (*Inf.*), loads (*Inf.*), lots (*Inf.*), plenty
Antonyms *adj.* inadequate, insufficient, little, scant ~*adv.* barely, hardly, infrequently, irregularly, not a lot, not much, occasionally, only just, rarely, scarcely, seldom, slightly ~*n.* hardly anything, little, next to nothing, not a lot, not much, practically nothing, very little

muck 1. crap (*Taboo sl.*), dung, manure, ordure, shit (*Taboo sl.*) 2. crap (*Sl.*), crud (*Sl.*), dirt, filth, grot (*Sl.*), gunge (*Inf.*), gunk (*Inf.*), mire, mud, ooze, scum, sewage, shit (*Taboo sl.*), slime, sludge 3. **make a muck of** *Sl.* blow (*Sl.*), botch, bungle, cock up (*Brit. sl.*), fuck up (*Offens. taboo sl.*), make a mess of, mar, mess up, muff, ruin, screw up (*Inf.*), spoil

muck up blow (*Sl.*), bodge (*Inf.*), botch, bungle, cock up (*Brit. sl.*), fuck up (*Offens. taboo sl.*), make a mess of, make a muck of (*Sl.*), mar, mess up, muff, ruin, screw up (*Inf.*), spoil

mucky begrimed, bespattered, dirty, filthy, grimy, messy, mud-caked, muddy, soiled, sticky

mucous glutinous, gummy, mucilaginous, slimy, viscid, viscous

mud clay, dirt, mire, ooze, silt, slime, sludge

muddle *v.* 1. confuse, disarrange, disorder, disorganize, jumble, make a mess of, mess, mix up, ravel, scramble, spoil, tangle 2. befuddle, bewilder, confound, confuse, daze, disorient, perplex, stupefy ~*n.* 3. chaos, clutter, confusion, daze, disarray, disorder, disorganization, fankle (*Scot.*), hodgepodge (*U.S.*), hotchpotch, jumble, mess, mix-up, perplexity, pig's breakfast (*Inf.*), plight, predicament, ravel, tangle

muddle along *or* **through** cope, get along, get by (*Inf.*), make it, manage, manage somehow, scrape by

muddled 1. chaotic, confused, disarrayed, disordered, disorganized, higgledy-piggledy (*Inf.*), jumbled, messy, mixed-up, scrambled, tangled 2. at sea, befuddled, bewildered, confused, dazed, disoriented, perplexed, stupefied, vague 3. confused, incoherent, loose, muddleheaded, unclear, woolly
Antonyms clear, exact, orderly, organized, precise

muddy *adj.* 1. bespattered, boggy, clarty (*Scot., & northern English dialect*), dirty, grimy, marshy, miry, mucky, mud-caked, quaggy, soiled, swampy 2. blurred, dingy, dull, flat, lustreless, smoky, unclear, washed-out 3. cloudy, dirty, foul, impure, opaque, turbid 4. confused, fuzzy, hazy, indistinct, muddled, unclear, vague, woolly ~*v.* 5. begrime, bespatter, cloud, dirty, smear, smirch, soil

muff *v.* bodge (*Inf.*), botch, bungle, cock up (*Brit. sl.*), fluff (*Inf.*), fuck up (*Offens. taboo sl.*), make a mess of, make a muck of (*Inf.*), mess up, mismanage, screw up (*Inf.*), spoil

muffle 1. cloak, conceal, cover, disguise, envelop, hood, mask, shroud, swaddle, swathe, wrap up 2. deaden, dull, gag, hush, muzzle, quieten, silence, soften, stifle, suppress

muffled dim, dull, faint, indistinct, muted, stifled, strangled, subdued, suppressed

mug[1] beaker, cup, flagon, jug, pot, tankard, toby jug

mug[2] clock (*Brit. sl.*), countenance, dial (*Sl.*), face, features, kisser (*Sl.*), mush (*Brit. sl.*), phiz *or* phizog (*Brit. sl.*), puss (*Sl.*), visage

mug[3] *n.* 1. charlie (*Brit. inf.*), chump (*Inf.*), gull (*Archaic*), easy *or* soft touch (*Sl.*), fool, innocent, mark (*Sl.*), muggins (*Brit. sl.*), simpleton, sucker (*Sl.*) ~*v.* 2. assail, assault, attack, beat up, do over (*Brit., Aust., & N.Z. sl.*), duff up (*Brit. sl.*), hold up, lay into (*Inf.*), put the boot in (*Sl.*), rob, set about *or* upon, steam (*Inf.*)

muggy clammy, close, damp, humid, moist, oppressive, sticky, stuffy, sultry

mug up bone up on (*Inf.*), burn the midnight oil (*Inf.*), cram (*Inf.*), get up (*Inf.*), study, swot (*Brit. inf.*)

mulish bull-headed, cross-grained, difficult, headstrong, inflexible, intractable, intransigent, obstinate, perverse, pig-headed, recalcitrant, refractory, rigid, self-willed, stiff-necked, stubborn, unreasonable, wilful

mull consider, contemplate, deliberate, examine, meditate, muse on, ponder, reflect on, review, ruminate, study, think about, think over, turn over in one's mind, weigh

multifarious different, diverse, diversified, legion, manifold, many, miscellaneous, multiform, multiple, multitudinous, numerous, sundry, varied, variegated

multiple collective, manifold, many, multitudinous, numerous, several, sundry, various

multiplicity abundance, array, diversity, heaps (*Inf.*), host, loads (*Inf.*), lot, lots (*Inf.*), mass, myriad, number, oodles (*Inf.*), piles (*Inf.*), profusion, scores, stacks, tons, variety

multiply accumulate, augment, breed, build up, expand, extend, increase, proliferate, propagate, reproduce, spread
Antonyms abate, decline, decrease, diminish, lessen, reduce

multitude 1. army, assemblage, assembly, collection, concourse, congregation, crowd, great number, horde, host, legion, lot, lots (*Inf.*), mass, mob, myriad, sea, swarm, throng 2. commonalty, common people, herd, hoi polloi, mob, populace, proletariat, public, rabble

multitudinous abounding, abundant, considerable, copious, countless, great, infinite, innumerable, legion, manifold, many, myriad, numerous, profuse, teeming, very numerous

mum 1. closemouthed, dumb, mute, quiet, secretive, silent, tight-lipped, uncommunicative, unforthcoming 2. **mum's the word** don't let on, don't tell a soul, keep quiet, keep silent, keep (something) secret, keep (something) to oneself, keep (something) under one's hat, play dumb, say nothing, tell no-one

mumbo jumbo 1. abracadabra, chant, charm, conjuration, hocus-pocus, incantation, magic, rite, ritual, spell, superstition 2. cant, claptrap (*Inf.*), double talk, gibberish, gobbledegook (*Inf.*), humbug, jargon, nonsense, rigmarole

mumsy dowdy, drab, fogyish, frumpish *or* frumpy, homely, old-fashioned, plain, square (*Inf.*), unfashionable, unglamorous, unsophisticated
Antonyms attractive, beautiful, chic, elegant, fashionable, glamorous, modern, modish, smart, sophisticated, well-dressed

munch champ, chew, chomp, crunch, masticate, scrunch

mundane 1. banal, commonplace, day-to-day, everyday, humdrum, ordinary, prosaic, routine, workaday 2. earthly, fleshly, human, material, mortal, secular, sublunary, temporal, terrestrial, worldly
Antonyms (*sense 1*) dramatic, exciting, extraordinary, imaginative, interesting, novel, original, special, uncommon, unusual (*sense 2*) ethereal, heavenly, spiritual, unworldly

municipal borough, city, civic, community, public, town, urban

municipality borough, burgh (*Scot.*), city, district, town, township, urban community

munificence beneficence, benevolence, big-heartedness, bounteousness, bounty, generosity, generousness, largess *or* largesse, liberality, magnanimousness, open-handedness, philanthropy

munificent beneficent, benevolent, big-hearted, bounteous, bountiful, free-handed, generous, lavish, liberal, magnanimous, open-handed, philanthropical, princely, rich, unstinting
Antonyms cheap, mean, miserly, parsimonious, small, stingy

murder *n.* 1. assassination, bloodshed, butchery, carnage, homicide, killing, manslaughter, massacre, slaying 2. *Inf.* agony, an ordeal, a trial, danger, difficulty, hell (*Inf.*), misery, trouble ~*v.* 3. assassinate, blow away (*Sl., chiefly U.S.*), bump off (*Sl.*), butcher, destroy, dispatch, do in (*Inf.*), do to death, eliminate (*Sl.*), hit (*Sl.*), kill, massacre, rub out (*U.S. sl.*), slaughter, slay, take out (*Sl.*), take the life of, waste (*Inf.*) 4. abuse, butcher, destroy, mangle, mar, misuse, ruin, spoil 5. *Inf.* beat decisively, blow out of the water (*Sl.*), cream (*Sl., chiefly U.S.*), defeat utterly, drub, hammer (*Inf.*), lick (*Inf.*), make mincemeat of (*Inf.*), slaughter, tank (*Sl.*), thrash, wipe the floor with (*Inf.*)

murderer assassin, butcher, cutthroat, hit man (*Sl.*), homicide, killer, slaughterer, slayer

murderous 1. barbarous, bloodthirsty, bloody, brutal, cruel, deadly, death-dealing, destructive, devastating, fatal, fell (*Archaic*), ferocious, internecine, lethal, sanguinary, savage, slaughterous, withering 2. *Inf.* arduous, dangerous, difficult, exhausting, harrowing, hellish (*Inf.*), killing (*Inf.*), sapping, strenuous, unpleasant

murky cheerless, cloudy, dark, dim, dismal, dreary, dull, dusky, foggy, gloomy, grey, impenetrable, misty, nebulous, obscure, overcast
Antonyms bright, cheerful, clear, distinct, sunny

murmur *n.* 1. babble, buzzing, drone, humming, mumble, muttering, purr, rumble, susurrus (*Literary*), undertone, whisper, whispering ~*v.* 2. babble, buzz, drone, hum, mumble, mutter, purr, rumble, speak in an undertone, whisper ~*n.* 3. beef (*Sl.*), complaint, gripe (*Inf.*), grouse, grumble, moan (*Inf.*), word ~*v.* 4. beef (*Sl.*), carp, cavil, complain, gripe (*Inf.*), grouse, grumble, moan (*Inf.*)

muscle *n.* 1. muscle tissue, sinew, tendon, thew 2. brawn, clout (*Inf.*), force, forcefulness, might, potency, power, stamina, strength, sturdiness, weight ~*v.* 3. **muscle in** *Inf.* butt in, elbow one's way in, force one's way in, impose oneself

muscular athletic, beefy (*Inf.*), brawny, husky (*Inf.*), lusty, powerful, powerfully built, Ramboesque, robust, sinewy, stalwart, strapping, strong, sturdy, thickset, vigorous, well-knit

muse be in a brown study, be lost in thought, brood, cogitate, consider, contemplate, deliberate, dream, meditate, mull over, ponder, reflect, ruminate, speculate, think, think over, weigh

mush 1. dough, mash, pap, paste, pulp 2. *Inf.* corn (*Inf.*), mawkishness, schmaltz (*Sl.*), sentimentality, slush (*Inf.*)

mushroom *v.* boom, burgeon, expand, flourish, grow rapidly, increase, luxuriate, proliferate, shoot up, spread, spring up, sprout

mushy 1. doughy, pappy, paste-like, pulpy, semi-liquid, semi-solid, slushy, soft, squashy, squelchy, squidgy (*Inf.*) 2. *Inf.* corny (*Sl.*), maudlin, mawkish, saccharine, schmaltzy (*Sl.*), sentimental, sloppy (*Inf.*), slushy (*Inf.*), sugary, syrupy, weepy, wet (*Brit. inf.*)

musical dulcet, euphonic, euphonious, harmonious, lilting, lyrical, melodic, melodious, sweet-sounding, tuneful
Antonyms discordant, grating, harsh, unmelodious, unmusical

musing *n.* absent-mindedness, abstraction, brown study, cerebration, cogitation, contemplation, day-dreaming, dreaming, introspection, meditation, reflection, reverie, rumination, thinking, woolgathering

must[1] *n.* duty, essential, fundamental, imperative, necessary thing, necessity, obligation, prerequisite, requirement, requisite, *sine qua non*

must[2] *n.* decay, fetor, fustiness, mildew, mould, mouldiness, mustiness, rot

muster *v.* 1. assemble, call together, call up, collect, come together, congregate, convene, convoke, enrol, gather, group, marshal, meet, mobilize, rally, round up, summon ~*n.* 2. assemblage, assembly, collection, concourse, congregation, convention, convocation, gathering, meeting, mobilization, rally, roundup 3. **pass muster** be *or* come up to scratch, be acceptable, fill the bill (*Inf.*), make the grade, measure up, qualify

musty 1. airless, dank, decayed, frowsty, fusty, mildewed, mildewy, mouldy, old, smelly, stale, stuffy 2. ancient, antediluvian, antiquated, banal, clichéd, dull, hackneyed, hoary, moth-eaten, obsolete, old-fashioned, stale, threadbare, trite, worn-out
Antonyms (*sense 2*) current, exciting, fashionable, fresh, imaginative, interesting, lively, modern, modish, new, novel, original, unusual, up-to-date, with it (*Inf.*)

mutability alteration, change, evolution, metamorphosis, transition, variation, vicissitude

mutable adaptable, alterable, changeable, changing, fickle, flexible, immutable, inconsistent, inconstant, irresolute, uncertain, undependable, unreliable, unsettled, unstable, unsteady, vacillating, variable, volatile, wavering

mutation 1. alteration, change, deviation, evolution, metamorphosis, modification, transfiguration, transformation, variation 2. anomaly, deviant, mutant

mute 1. *adj.* aphasiac, aphasic, aphonic, dumb, mum, silent, speechless, unexpressed, unspeaking, unspoken, voiceless, wordless 2. *v.* dampen, deaden, lower, moderate, muffle, soften, soft-pedal, subdue, tone down, turn down

mutilate 1. amputate, butcher, cripple, cut to pieces, cut up, damage, disable, disfigure, dismember, hack, injure, lacerate, lame, maim, mangle 2. adulterate, bowdlerize, butcher, censor, cut, damage, distort, expurgate, hack, mar, spoil

mutinous bolshie (*Brit. inf.*), contumacious, disobedient, insubordinate, insurgent, rebellious, refractory, revolutionary, riotous, seditious, subversive, turbulent, ungovernable, unmanageable, unruly

mutiny 1. *n.* defiance, disobedience, insubordination, insurrection, rebellion, refusal to obey orders, resistance, revolt, revolution, riot, rising, strike, uprising 2. *v.* be insubordinate, defy authority, disobey, rebel, refuse to obey orders, resist, revolt, rise up, strike

mutt 1. berk (*Brit. sl.*), charlie (*Brit. inf.*), coot, dickhead (*Sl.*), dipstick (*Brit. sl.*), divvy (*Brit. sl.*), dolt, dork (*Sl.*), dunderhead, dweeb (*U.S. sl.*), fool, fuckwit (*Taboo sl.*), geek (*Sl.*), gonzo (*Sl.*), idiot, ignoramus, imbecile (*Inf.*), jerk (*Sl., chiefly U.S. & Canad.*), moron, nerd *or* nurd (*Sl.*), num~

skull *or* numbskull, pillock (*Brit. sl.*), plank (*Brit. sl.*), plonker (*Sl.*), prat (*Sl.*), prick (*Derogatory sl.*), schmuck (*U.S. sl.*), thickhead, twit (*Inf., chiefly Brit.*), wally (*Sl.*) 2. cur, dog, mongrel

mutter complain, grouch (*Inf.*), grouse, grumble, mumble, murmur, rumble

mutual common, communal, correlative, interactive, interchangeable, interchanged, joint, reciprocal, reciprocated, requited, returned, shared

muzzle *n.* 1. jaws, mouth, nose, snout 2. gag, guard ~*v.* 3. censor, choke, curb, gag, restrain, silence, stifle, suppress

myopic near-sighted, short-sighted

myriad 1. *adj.* a thousand and one, countless, immeasurable, incalculable, innumerable, multitudinous, untold 2. *n.* a million, army, a thousand, flood, horde, host, millions, mountain, multitude, scores, sea, swarm, thousands

mysterious abstruse, arcane, baffling, concealed, covert, cryptic, curious, dark, Delphic, enigmatic, furtive, hidden, impenetrable, incomprehensible, inexplicable, inscrutable, insoluble, mystical, mystifying, obscure, perplexing, puzzling, recondite, secret, secretive, sphinxlike, strange, uncanny, unfathomable, unknown, veiled, weird

Antonyms apparent, clear, intelligible, manifest, open, plain

mystery conundrum, enigma, problem, puzzle, question, riddle, secrecy, secret, teaser

mystic, mystical abstruse, arcane, cabalistic, cryptic, enigmatical, esoteric, hidden, inscrutable, metaphysical, mysterious, nonrational, occult, otherworldly, paranormal, preternatural, supernatural, transcendental

mystify baffle, bamboozle (*Inf.*), beat (*Sl.*), befog, bewilder, confound, confuse, elude, escape, flummox, nonplus, perplex, puzzle, stump

mystique awe, charisma, charm, fascination, glamour, magic, spell

myth 1. allegory, fable, fairy story, fiction, folk tale, legend, parable, saga, story, tradition, urban legend 2. delusion, fancy, fantasy, figment, illusion, imagination, superstition, tall story

mythical 1. allegorical, chimerical, fabled, fabulous, fairy-tale, legendary, mythological, storied 2. fabricated, fanciful, fantasy, fictitious, imaginary, invented, made-up, make-believe, nonexistent, pretended, unreal, untrue

mythological fabulous, folkloric, heroic, legendary, mythic, mythical, traditional

mythology folklore, folk tales, legend, lore, mythos, myths, stories, tradition

N

nab apprehend, arrest, capture, catch, collar (*Inf.*), feel one's collar (*Sl.*), grab, lift (*Sl.*), nail (*Inf.*), nick (*Sl., chiefly Brit.*), seize, snatch

nabob billionaire, Croesus, millionaire, multimillionaire

nadir bottom, depths, lowest point, minimum, rock bottom, zero
Antonyms acme, apex, climax, crest, height, high point, peak, pinnacle, summit, top, vertex, zenith

nag[1] 1. *v.* annoy, badger, bend someone's ear (*Inf.*), be on one's back (*Sl.*), berate, chivvy, goad, harass, harry, hassle (*Inf.*), henpeck, irritate, nark (*Brit., Aust., & N.Z. sl.*), pester, plague, provoke, scold, torment, upbraid, vex, worry 2. *n.* harpy, scold, shrew, tartar, termagant, virago

nag[2] hack, horse, jade, plug (*U.S.*)

nagging continuous, critical, distressing, irritating, painful, persistent, scolding, shrewish, worrying

naiad nymph, Oceanid (*Greek myth.*), sprite, undine, water nymph

nail *v.* attach, beat, fasten, fix, hammer, join, pin, secure, tack

naive 1. artless, candid, childlike, confiding, frank, guileless, ingenuous, innocent, jejune, natural, open, simple, trusting, unaffected, unpretentious, unsophisticated, unworldly 2. callow, credulous, gullible, green, unsuspicious
Antonyms artful, disingenuous, experienced, sly, sophisticated, urbane, worldly, worldly-wise

naiveté, naivety 1. artlessness, candour, frankness, guilelessness, inexperience, ingenuousness, innocence, naturalness, openness, simplicity 2. callowness, credulity, gullibility

naked 1. bare, buck naked (*Sl.*), denuded, disrobed, divested, exposed, in one's birthday suit (*Inf.*), in the altogether (*Inf.*), in the buff (*Inf.*), in the raw (*Inf.*), naked as the day one was born (*Inf.*), nude, starkers (*Inf.*), stripped, unclothed, unconcealed, uncovered, undraped, undressed, without a stitch on (*Inf.*) 2. blatant, evident, manifest, open, overt, patent, plain, simple, stark, unadorned, undisguised, unexaggerated, unmistakable, unqualified, unvarnished 3. defenceless, helpless, insecure, unarmed, unguarded, unprotected, vulnerable
Antonyms clothed, concealed, covered, dressed, wrapped up

nakedness 1. baldness, bareness, nudity, undress 2. openness, plainness, simplicity, starkness

namby-pamby anaemic, colourless, feeble, insipid, mawkish, prim, prissy (*Inf.*), sentimental, spineless, vapid, weak, weedy (*Inf.*), wimpish *or* wimpy (*Inf.*), wishy-washy (*Inf.*)

name *n.* 1. appellation, cognomen, denomination, designation, epithet, handle (*Sl.*), moniker *or* monicker (*Sl.*), nickname, sobriquet, term, title 2. distinction, eminence, esteem, fame, honour, note, praise, renown, repute 3. character, credit, reputation ~*v.* 4. baptize, call, christen, denominate, dub, entitle, label, style, term 5. appoint, choose, cite, classify, commission, designate, flag, identify, mention, nominate, select, specify

named 1. baptized, called, christened, denominated, dubbed, entitled, known as, labelled, styled, termed 2. appointed, chosen, cited, classified, commissioned, designated, identified, mentioned, nominated, picked, selected, singled out, specified

nameless 1. anonymous, innominate, undesignated, unnamed, untitled 2. incognito, obscure, undistinguished, unheard-of, unknown, unsung 3. abominable, horrible, indescribable, ineffable, inexpressible, unmentionable, unspeakable, unutterable

namely i.e., specifically, that is to say, to wit, viz.

nap[1] 1. *v.* catnap, doze, drop off (*Inf.*), drowse, kip (*Brit. sl.*), nod, nod off (*Inf.*), rest, sleep, snooze (*Inf.*), zizz (*Brit. inf.*) 2. *n.* catnap, forty winks (*Inf.*), kip (*Brit. sl.*), rest, shuteye (*Sl.*), siesta, sleep, zizz (*Brit. inf.*)

nap[2] down, fibre, grain, pile, shag, weave

narcissism egotism, self-admiration, self-love, vanity

narcotic 1. *n.* anaesthetic, analgesic, anodyne, drug, opiate, painkiller, sedative, tranquillizer 2. *adj.* analgesic, calming, dulling, hypnotic, Lethean, numbing, painkilling, sedative, somnolent, soporific, stupefacient, stupefactive, stupefying

nark aggravate (*Inf.*), annoy, bother, bug, exasperate, gall, get on one's nerves (*Inf.*), irk, irritate, miff (*Inf.*), nettle, peeve, pique, piss one off (*Taboo sl.*), provoke, rile

narrate chronicle, describe, detail, recite, recount, rehearse, relate, repeat, report, set forth, tell, unfold

narration description, explanation, reading, recital, rehearsal, relation, storytelling, telling, voice-over (*in film*)

narrative account, chronicle, detail, history, report, statement, story, tale

narrator annalist, author, bard, chronicler, commentator, raconteur, reciter, relater, reporter, storyteller, writer

narrow *adj.* 1. circumscribed, close, confined, constricted, contracted, cramped, incapacious, limited, meagre, near, pinched, restricted, scanty, straitened, tight 2. biased, bigoted, dogmatic, illiberal, intolerant, narrow-minded, partial, prejudiced, reactionary, small-minded 3. attenuated, fine, slender, slim, spare, tapering, thin 4. exclusive, select 5. *Inf.* avaricious, close (*Inf.*), mean, mercenary, niggardly, ungenerous ~*v.* 6. circumscribe, constrict, diminish, limit, reduce, simplify, straiten, tighten
Antonyms ample, big, broad, broad-minded, generous, liberal, open, receptive, spacious, tolerant, wide

narrowly 1. barely, by a whisker *or* hair's-breadth, just, only just, scarcely 2. carefully, closely, painstakingly, scrutinizingly

narrow-minded biased, bigoted, conservative, hidebound, illiberal, insular, intolerant, opinionated, parochial, petty, prejudiced, provincial, reactionary, short-sighted, small-minded, strait-laced
Antonyms broad-minded, catholic, cosmopolitan, freethinking, indulgent, open-minded, permissive, tolerant, unprejudiced

narrows channel, gulf, passage, sound, straits

nascent beginning, budding, dawning, developing, evolving, incipient

nastiness 1. defilement, dirtiness, filth, filthiness, foulness, impurity, pollution, squalor, uncleanliness 2. indecency, licentiousness, obscenity, pollution, porn (*Inf.*), pornography, ribaldry, smuttiness 3. disagreeableness, malice, meanness, offensiveness, spitefulness, unpleasantness

nasty 1. dirty, disagreeable, disgusting, filthy, foul, grotty (*Sl.*), horrible, loathsome, malodorous, mephitic, nauseating, noisome, objectionable, obnoxious, odious, offensive, polluted, repellent, repugnant, sickening, unappetizing, unpleasant, vile, yucky *or* yukky (*Sl.*) 2. blue, foul, gross, impure, indecent, lascivious, lewd, licentious, obscene, pornographic, ribald, smutty 3. abusive, annoying, bad-tempered, despicable, disagreeable, distasteful, malicious, mean, spiteful, unpleasant, vicious, vile 4. bad, critical, dangerous, painful, serious, severe
Antonyms admirable, agreeable, clean, decent, enjoyable, kind, nice, pleasant, sweet

nation commonwealth, community, country, people, population, race, realm, society, state, tribe

national *adj.* 1. civil, countrywide, governmental, nationwide, public, state, widespread 2. domestic, internal, social ~*n.* 3. citizen, inhabitant, native, resident, subject

nationalism allegiance, chauvinism, fealty, jingoism, loyalty, nationality, patriotism

nationalistic chauvinistic, jingoistic, loyal, patriotic, xenophobic

nationality birth, ethnic group, nation, race

nationwide countrywide, general, national, overall, widespread

native *adj.* 1. built-in, congenital, endemic, hereditary, inborn, inbred, indigenous, ingrained, inherent, inherited, innate, instinctive, intrinsic, inveterate, natal, natural 2. genuine, original, real 3. domestic, home, home-grown, home-made, indigenous, local, mother, vernacular 4. aboriginal, autochthonous ~*n.* 5. aborigine, autochthon, citizen, countryman, dweller, inhabitant, national, resident

nativity 1. birth, delivery, parturition 2. crèche, manger scene
Antonyms (*sense 1*) death, demise, dying, expiration

natter 1. *v.* blather, blether, chatter, gabble, gossip, jabber, jaw (*Sl.*), palaver, prate, prattle, rabbit (on) (*Brit. inf.*), talk, talk idly, witter (*Inf.*) 2. *n.* blather, blether, chat, chinwag (*Brit. inf.*), chitchat, confabulation, conversation, gab (*Inf.*), gabble, gabfest (*Inf., chiefly U.S. & Canad.*), gossip, jabber, jaw (*Sl.*), palaver, prattle, talk

natty chic, crucial (*Sl.*), dapper, elegant, fashionable, neat, smart, snazzy (*Inf.*), spruce, stylish, trendy (*Brit. inf.*), trim, well-dressed, well-turned-out

natural 1. common, everyday, legitimate, logical, normal, ordinary, regular, typical, usual 2. characteristic, congenital, essential, inborn, indigenous, inherent, innate, instinctive, intuitive, natal, native 3. artless, candid, frank, genuine, ingenuous, open, real, simple, spontaneous, unaffected, unpretentious, unsophisticated, unstudied **4.** organic, plain, pure, unbleached, unmixed, unpolished, unrefined, whole

Antonyms (*sense 1*) abnormal, irregular, out of the ordinary, strange, untypical (*sense 3*) affected, artificial, assumed, counterfeit, feigned, phoney *or* phony (*Inf.*), unnatural (*sense 4*) manufactured, processed, synthetic, unnatural

naturalism factualism, realism, verisimilitude

naturalist 1. biologist, botanist, ecologist, zoologist **2.** factualist, realist

naturalistic factualistic, kitchen sink, lifelike, photographic, realistic, real-life, representational, true-to-life, warts and all (*Inf.*)

naturalize acclimate, acclimatize, acculturate, accustom, adapt, adopt, domesticate, enfranchise, familiarize, grant citizenship, habituate

naturally 1. *adv.* as anticipated, customarily, genuinely, informally, normally, simply, spontaneously, typically, unaffectedly, unpretentiously **2.** *interj.* absolutely, as a matter of course, certainly, of course

naturalness 1. artlessness, candidness, frankness, genuineness, ingenuousness, openness, realism, simpleness, simplicity, spontaneousness, unaffectedness, unpretentiousness, unsophisticatedness, unstudiedness **2.** plainness, pureness, purity, wholeness

nature 1. attributes, character, complexion, constitution, essence, features, make-up, quality, traits **2.** category, description, kind, sort, species, style, type, variety **3.** cosmos, creation, earth, environment, universe, world **4.** disposition, humour, mood, outlook, temper, temperament **5.** country, countryside, landscape, natural history, scenery

naturist nudist

naught nil, nothing, nothingness, nought, zero

naughty 1. annoying, bad, disobedient, exasperating, fractious, impish, misbehaved, mischievous, perverse, playful, refractory, roguish, sinful, teasing, wayward, wicked, worthless **2.** bawdy, blue, improper, lewd, obscene, off-colour, ribald, risqué, smutty, vulgar

Antonyms good, obedient, polite, proper, seemly, well-behaved, well-mannered

nausea 1. biliousness, qualm(s), queasiness, retching, sickness, squeamishness, vomiting **2.** abhorrence, aversion, disgust, loathing, odium, repugnance, revulsion

nauseate disgust, gross out (*U.S. sl.*), horrify, offend, repel, repulse, revolt, sicken, turn one's stomach

nauseous abhorrent, detestable, disgusting, distasteful, loathsome, nauseating, offensive, repugnant, repulsive, revolting, sickening, yucky *or* yukky (*Sl.*)

nautical marine, maritime, naval, oceanic, seafaring, seagoing, yachting

naval marine, maritime, nautical, oceanic

navel 1. bellybutton (*Inf.*), omphalos (*Literary*), umbilicus **2.** central point, centre, hub, middle

navigable 1. clear, negotiable, passable, traversable, unobstructed **2.** controllable, dirigible, sailable, steerable

navigate con (*Nautical*), cross, cruise, direct, drive, guide, handle, journey, manoeuvre, pilot, plan, plot, sail, skipper, steer, voyage

navigation cruising, helmsmanship, pilotage, sailing, seamanship, steering, voyaging

navigator mariner, pilot, seaman

navvy ganger, labourer, worker, workman

navy argosy (*Archaic*), armada, fleet, flotilla, warships

near *adj.* **1.** adjacent, adjoining, alongside, at close quarters, beside, bordering, close, close by, contiguous, nearby, neighbouring, nigh, proximate, touching, within sniffing distance (*Inf.*) **2.** approaching, forthcoming, imminent, impending, in the offing, looming, near-at-hand, next, on the cards (*Inf.*), upcoming **3.** akin, allied, attached, connected, dear, familiar, intimate, related **4.** *Inf.* close-fisted, mean, miserly, niggardly, parsimonious, stingy, tightfisted, ungenerous

Antonyms (*senses 1, 2 & 3*) distant, far, faraway, far-flung, far-off, far-removed, long, outlying, out-of-the-way, remote, removed

nearby 1. *adj.* adjacent, adjoining, convenient, handy, neighbouring **2.** *adv.* at close quarters, close at hand, not far away, proximate, within reach, within sniffing distance (*Inf.*)

nearing advancing, approaching, approximating, coming, imminent, impending, upcoming

nearly *adv.* about, all but, almost, approaching, approximately, as good as, closely, just about, not quite, practically, roughly, virtually, well-nigh

nearness 1. accessibility, availability, closeness, contiguity, handiness, juxtaposition, propinquity, proximity, vicinity **2.** immediacy, imminence **3.** dearness, familiarity, intimacy **4.** *Inf.* meanness, niggardliness, parsimony, stinginess

near-sighted myopic, short-sighted

near thing close shave (*Inf.*), narrow escape, near miss

neat 1. accurate, dainty, fastidious, methodical, nice, orderly, shipshape, smart, spick-and-span, spruce, straight, systematic, tidy, trim, uncluttered 2. adept, adroit, agile, apt, clever, deft, dexterous, efficient, effortless, elegant, expert, graceful, handy, nimble, practised, precise, skilful, stylish, well-judged 3. *Of alcoholic drinks* pure, straight, undiluted, unmixed
Antonyms (*senses 1 & 2*) awful, bad, clumsy, cluttered, disarrayed, disorderly, disorganized, incompetent, inefficient, inelegant, messy, slobby (*Inf.*), sloppy (*Inf.*), terrible, untidy

neaten arrange, clean up, groom, put to rights, straighten out *or* up, tidy, tidy up, trig (*Archaic or dialect*), trim

neatly 1. accurately, daintily, fastidiously, methodically, nicely, smartly, sprucely, systematically, tidily 2. adeptly, adroitly, agilely, aptly, cleverly, deftly, dexterously, efficiently, effortlessly, elegantly, expertly, gracefully, handily, nimbly, precisely, skilfully, stylishly

neatness 1. accuracy, daintiness, fastidiousness, methodicalness, niceness, nicety, orderliness, smartness, spruceness, straightness, tidiness, trimness 2. adeptness, adroitness, agility, aptness, cleverness, deftness, dexterity, efficiency, effortlessness, elegance, expertness, grace, gracefulness, handiness, nimbleness, preciseness, precision, skilfulness, skill, style, stylishness

nebulous ambiguous, amorphous, cloudy, confused, dim, hazy, imprecise, indefinite, indeterminate, indistinct, misty, murky, obscure, shadowy, shapeless, uncertain, unclear, unformed, vague

necessarily accordingly, automatically, axiomatically, by definition, certainly, compulsorily, consequently, incontrovertibly, ineluctably, inevitably, inexorably, irresistibly, naturally, *nolens volens,* of course, of necessity, perforce, undoubtedly, willy-nilly

necessary 1. compulsory, *de rigueur,* essential, imperative, indispensable, mandatory, needed, needful, obligatory, required, requisite, vital 2. certain, fated, inescapable, inevitable, inexorable, unavoidable
Antonyms dispensable, expendable, inessential, nonessential, superfluous, unnecessary

necessitate call for, coerce, compel, constrain, demand, entail, force, impel, make necessary, oblige, require

necessities essentials, exigencies, fundamentals, indispensables, needs, requirements

necessitous destitute, distressed, impecunious, impoverished, indigent, needy, penniless, penurious, poor, poverty-stricken

necessity 1. demand, exigency, indispensability, need, needfulness, requirement 2. desideratum, essential, fundamental, necessary, need, prerequisite, requirement, requisite, *sine qua non,* want 3. destitution, extremity, indigence, need, penury, poverty, privation 4. compulsion, destiny, fate, inevitability, inexorableness, obligation

necromancer black magician, diviner, enchanter, enchantress, magician, sorcerer, sorceress, warlock, witch, wizard

necromancy black art, black magic, demonology, divination, enchantment, magic, sorcery, thaumaturgy (*Rare*), voodoo, witchcraft, witchery, wizardry

necropolis burial ground, cemetery, churchyard, God's acre, graveyard

need *v.* 1. call for, demand, entail, have occasion to *or* for, lack, miss, necessitate, require, want ~*n.* 2. longing, requisite, want, wish 3. deprivation, destitution, distress, extremity, impecuniousness, inadequacy, indigence, insufficiency, lack, neediness, paucity, penury, poverty, privation, shortage 4. emergency, exigency, necessity, obligation, urgency, want 5. demand, desideratum, essential, requirement, requisite

needed called for, desired, lacked, necessary, required, wanted

needful essential, indispensable, necessary, needed, required, requisite, stipulated, vital

needle *v.* aggravate (*Inf.*), annoy, bait, be on one's back (*Sl.*), gall, get in one's hair (*Inf.*), get on one's nerves (*Inf.*), goad, harass, hassle (*Inf.*), irk, irritate, nag, nark (*Brit., Aust., & N.Z. sl.*), nettle, pester, piss one off (*Taboo sl.*), prick, prod, provoke, rile, ruffle, spur, sting, taunt

needless causeless, dispensable, excessive, expendable, gratuitous, groundless, nonessential, pointless, redundant, superfluous, uncalled-for, undesired, unnecessary, unwanted, useless
Antonyms beneficial, essential, obligatory, required, useful

needlework embroidery, fancywork, needlecraft, sewing, stitching, tailoring

needy deprived, destitute, dirt-poor (*Inf.*), disadvantaged, impecunious, impoverished, indigent, on the breadline (*Inf.*), penniless, poor, poverty-stricken, underprivileged
Antonyms affluent, comfortable, mon~

eyed, prosperous, rich, wealthy, well-off, well-to-do

ne'er-do-well black sheep, good-for-nothing, idler, layabout, loafer, loser, skiver (*Brit. sl.*), wastrel

nefarious abominable, atrocious, base, criminal, depraved, detestable, dreadful, evil, execrable, foul, heinous, horrible, infamous, infernal, iniquitous, monstrous, odious, opprobrious, shameful, sinful, vicious, vile, villainous, wicked
Antonyms admirable, good, honest, honourable, just, noble, praiseworthy, upright, virtuous

negate 1. abrogate, annul, cancel, countermand, invalidate, neutralize, nullify, obviate, repeal, rescind, retract, reverse, revoke, void, wipe out 2. contradict, deny, disallow, disprove, gainsay (*Archaic or literary*), oppose, rebut, refute
Antonyms affirm, assert, attest, avouch, avow, certify, confirm, declare, maintain, pronounce, ratify, state, swear, testify

negation 1. antithesis, antonym, contradiction, contrary, converse, counterpart, denial, disavowal, disclaimer, inverse, opposite, rejection, renunciation, reverse 2. opposition, proscription, refusal, repudiation, veto 3. cancellation, neutralization, nullification 4. blank, nonexistence, nothingness, nullity, vacuity, void

negative *adj.* 1. contradictory, contrary, denying, dissenting, opposing, recusant, refusing, rejecting, resisting 2. annulling, counteractive, invalidating, neutralizing, nullifying 3. antagonistic, colourless, contrary, cynical, gloomy, jaundiced, neutral, pessimistic, uncooperative, unenthusiastic, uninterested, unwilling, weak ~*n.* 4. contradiction, denial, refusal
Antonyms *adj.* affirmative, approving, assenting, cheerful, concurring, enthusiastic, optimistic, positive

negativeness, negativity 1. contradiction, contradictoriness, contrariness, denial, dissent, opposition, recusancy, refusal, rejection, resistance 2. antagonism, colourlessness, contrariness, cynicism, gloom, neutrality, pessimism, uncooperativeness, uninterestedness, unwillingness, weakness

neglect *v.* 1. contemn, discount, disdain, disregard, ignore, leave alone, overlook, pass by, rebuff, scorn, slight, spurn 2. be remiss, evade, forget, let slide, omit, pass over, procrastinate, shirk, skimp ~*n.* 3. disdain, disregard, disrespect, heedlessness, inattention, indifference, slight, unconcern 4. carelessness, default, dereliction, failure, forgetfulness, laxity, laxness, neglectfulness, negligence, oversight, remissness, slackness, slovenliness
Antonyms *v.* appreciate, attend to, notice, observe, regard, remember, value ~*n.* attention, care, consideration, notice, regard, respect

neglected 1. abandoned, derelict, overgrown 2. disregarded, unappreciated, underestimated, undervalued

neglectful careless, disregardful, heedless, inattentive, indifferent, lax, negligent, remiss, thoughtless, uncaring, unmindful

negligence carelessness, default, dereliction, disregard, failure, forgetfulness, heedlessness, inadvertence, inattention, inattentiveness, indifference, laxity, laxness, neglect, omission, oversight, remissness, shortcoming, slackness, thoughtlessness

negligent careless, cursory, disregardful, forgetful, heedless, inadvertent, inattentive, indifferent, neglectful, nonchalant, offhand, regardless, remiss, slack, slapdash, slipshod, thoughtless, unmindful, unthinking
Antonyms attentive, careful, considerate, mindful, painstaking, rigorous, thorough, thoughtful

negligible imperceptible, inconsequential, insignificant, minor, minute, nickel-and-dime (*U.S. sl.*), petty, small, trifling, trivial, unimportant
Antonyms important, noteworthy, significant, vital

negotiable debatable, discussable *or* discussible, transactional, transferable, variable

negotiate 1. adjudicate, arbitrate, arrange, bargain, conciliate, confer, consult, contract, deal, debate, discuss, handle, manage, mediate, parley, settle, transact, work out 2. clear, cross, get over, get past, get round, pass, pass through, surmount

negotiation arbitration, bargaining, debate, diplomacy, discussion, mediation, transaction, wheeling and dealing (*Inf.*)

negotiator adjudicator, ambassador, arbitrator, delegate, diplomat, honest broker, intermediary, mediator, moderator

neighbourhood community, confines, district, environs, locale, locality, precincts, proximity, purlieus, quarter, region, surroundings, vicinity

neighbouring abutting, adjacent, adjoining, bordering, connecting, contiguous, near, nearby, nearest, next, surrounding
Antonyms distant, far, far-off, remote

neighbourly amiable, civil, companionable, considerate, friendly, genial, harmonious, helpful, hospitable, kind, obliging, sociable, social, well-disposed

nemesis destiny, destruction, fate, retribution, vengeance

neologism buzz word (*Inf.*), coinage, new phrase, new word, nonce word, vogue word

neophyte amateur, apprentice, beginner, catechumen, disciple, learner, novice, novitiate, probationer, proselyte, pupil, recruit, student, trainee, tyro

ne plus ultra acme, culmination, extreme, perfection, the last word, ultimate, uttermost point

nerve *n.* 1. balls (*Taboo sl.*), ballsiness (*Taboo sl.*), bottle (*Brit. sl.*), bravery, coolness, courage, daring, determination, endurance, energy, fearlessness, firmness, force, fortitude, gameness, grit, guts (*Inf.*), hardihood, intrepidity, mettle, might, pluck, resolution, spirit, spunk (*Inf.*), steadfastness, vigour, will 2. *Inf.* audacity, boldness, brass (*Inf.*), brass neck (*Brit. inf.*), brazenness, cheek (*Inf.*), chutzpah (*U.S. & Canad. inf.*), effrontery, front, gall, impertinence, impudence, insolence, neck (*Inf.*), sauce (*Inf.*), temerity ~*v.* 3. brace, embolden, encourage, fortify, hearten, invigorate, steel, strengthen

nerveless 1. calm, collected, composed, controlled, cool, impassive, imperturbable, self-possessed, unemotional 2. afraid, cowardly, debilitated, enervated, feeble, nervous, spineless, timid, weak

nerve-racking annoying, difficult, distressing, frightening, harassing, harrowing, maddening, stressful, tense, trying, worrying

nerves anxiety, fretfulness, heebie-jeebies (*Sl.*), imbalance, nervousness, strain, stress, tension, worry

nervous agitated, anxious, apprehensive, edgy, excitable, fearful, fidgety, flustered, hesitant, highly strung, hyper (*Inf.*), hysterical, jittery (*Inf.*), jumpy, nervy (*Brit. inf.*), neurotic, on edge, ruffled, shaky, tense, timid, timorous, twitchy (*Inf.*), uneasy, uptight (*Inf.*), weak, wired (*Sl.*), worried

Antonyms bold, calm, cool, confident, constant, equable, even, laid-back (*Inf.*), peaceful, relaxed, steady, together (*Sl.*), unfazed (*Inf.*)

nervous breakdown breakdown, collapse, crack-up (*Inf.*), nervous disorder, neurasthenia (*Obsolete*)

nervousness agitation, anxiety, disquiet, excitability, fluster, perturbation, tension, timidity, touchiness, tremulousness, worry

nervy agitated, anxious, excitable, fidgety, jittery (*Inf.*), jumpy, nervous, on edge, restless, tense, twitchy (*Inf.*), wired (*Sl.*)

nescience 1. ignorance, lack of knowledge, obliviousness, unawareness, unconsciousness, unenlightenment 2. agnosticism, doubt, irreligion, unbelief

nescient 1. ignorant, oblivious, unaware, unconscious, unenlightened, unknowing, unknowledgeable 2. agnostic, doubting, irreligious, unbelieving

nest 1. den, haunt, hideaway, refuge, resort, retreat, snuggery 2. breeding-ground, den, hotbed

nest egg cache, deposit, fall-back, fund(s), reserve, savings, store

nestle cuddle, curl up, huddle, nuzzle, snuggle

nestling 1. chick, fledgling 2. babe, babe in arms, baby, infant, suckling

net[1] 1. *n.* lacework, lattice, mesh, netting, network, openwork, reticulum, tracery, web 2. *v.* bag, capture, catch, enmesh, ensnare, entangle, nab (*Inf.*), trap

net[2]**, nett** *adj.* 1. after taxes, clear, final, take-home 2. closing, conclusive, final ~*v.* 3. accumulate, bring in, clear, earn, gain, make, realize, reap

nether basal, below, beneath, bottom, inferior, lower, Stygian, under, underground

nether world Avernus, Hades, hell, infernal regions, nether regions, underworld

nettle aggravate (*Inf.*), annoy, chafe, exasperate, fret, gall, get on one's nerves (*Inf.*), goad, harass, hassle (*Inf.*), incense, irritate, nark (*Brit., Aust., & N.Z. sl.*), pique, piss one off (*Taboo sl.*), provoke, ruffle, sting, tease, vex

nettled aggrieved, angry, annoyed, chafed, cross, exasperated, galled, goaded, hacked (off) (*U.S. sl.*), harassed, huffy, incensed, irritable, irritated, peeved, peevish, piqued, pissed off (*Taboo sl.*), provoked, put out, ratty (*Brit. & N.Z. inf.*), riled, ruffled, stung, teased, tetchy, touchy, vexed

network arrangement, channels, circuitry, complex, convolution, grid, grill, interconnections, labyrinth, maze, mesh, net, nexus, organization, plexus, structure, system, tracks, web

neurosis abnormality, affliction, derangement, deviation, instability, maladjustment, mental disturbance, mental illness, obsession, phobia, psychological *or* emotional disorder

neurotic abnormal, anxious, compulsive, deviant, disordered, distraught, disturbed, hyper (*Inf.*), maladjusted, manic, nervous, obsessive, overwrought, twitchy (*Inf.*), unhealthy, unstable

Antonyms calm, laid-back (*Inf.*), level-headed, normal, rational, sane, stable, together (*Sl.*), well-adjusted, well-balanced

neuter *v.* castrate, doctor (*Inf.*), dress, emasculate, fix (*Inf.*), geld, spay

neutral 1. disinterested, dispassionate, even-handed, impartial, indifferent, nonaligned, nonbelligerent, noncombatant, noncommittal, nonpartisan, sitting on the fence, unaligned, unbiased, uncommitted, undecided, uninvolved, unprejudiced 2. achromatic, colourless, dull, expressionless, indeterminate, indistinct, indistinguishable, intermediate, toneless, undefined

Antonyms active, belligerent, biased, decided, interested, interfering, partial, participating, positive, prejudiced

neutrality detachment, disinterestedness, impartiality, nonalignment, noninterference, noninterventionism, noninvolvement, nonpartisanship

neutralize cancel, compensate for, counteract, counterbalance, frustrate, invalidate, negate, nullify, offset, undo

never at no time, not at all, not on your life (*Inf.*), not on your nelly (*Brit. sl.*), no way, on no account, under no circumstances

Antonyms always, aye (*Scot.*), constantly, continually, every time, forever, perpetually, without exception

never-ending boundless, ceaseless, constant, continual, continuous, eternal, everlasting, incessant, interminable, nonstop, perpetual, persistent, relentless, unbroken, unceasing, unchanging, uninterrupted, unremitting

never-never hire-purchase (*Brit.*), H.P. (*Brit.*)

nevertheless but, even so, (even) though, however, nonetheless, notwithstanding, regardless, still, yet

new 1. advanced, all-singing, all-dancing, contemporary, current, different, fresh, happening (*Inf.*), latest, modern, modernistic, modish, newfangled, novel, original, recent, state-of-the-art, topical, ultramodern, unfamiliar, unknown, unused, unusual, up-to-date, virgin 2. added, extra, more, supplementary 3. altered, changed, improved, modernized, redesigned, renewed, restored

Antonyms aged, ancient, antiquated, antique, experienced, hackneyed, old, old-fashioned, outmoded, passé, stale, trite

newcomer alien, arrival, beginner, foreigner, immigrant, incomer, Johnny-come-lately (*Inf.*), novice, outsider, parvenu, settler, stranger

newfangled all-singing, all-dancing, contemporary, fashionable, gimmicky, modern, new, new-fashioned, novel, state-of-the-art, recent

Antonyms antiquated, dated, obsolete, old-fashioned, outmoded, out-of-date, passé

newly anew, freshly, just, lately, latterly, recently

newness freshness, innovation, novelty, oddity, originality, strangeness, unfamiliarity, uniqueness

news account, advice, bulletin, communiqué, dirt (*U.S. sl.*), disclosure, dispatch, exposé, gen (*Brit. inf.*), gossip, hearsay, information, intelligence, latest (*Inf.*), leak, news flash, release, report, revelation, rumour, scandal, statement, story, tidings, word

newsworthy arresting, important, interesting, notable, noteworthy, remarkable, significant, stimulating

next *adj.* 1. consequent, ensuing, following, later, subsequent, succeeding 2. adjacent, adjoining, closest, nearest, neighbouring ~*adv.* 3. afterwards, closely, following, later, subsequently, thereafter

next world afterlife, afterworld, heaven, hereafter, nirvana, paradise

nexus bond, connection, joining, junction, link, tie

nibble 1. *n.* bite, crumb, morsel, peck, snack, *soupçon*, taste, titbit 2. *v.* bite, eat, gnaw, munch, nip, peck, pick at

nice 1. agreeable, amiable, attractive, charming, commendable, courteous, delightful, friendly, good, kind, likable *or* likeable, pleasant, pleasurable, polite, prepossessing, refined, well-mannered 2. dainty, fine, neat, tidy, trim 3. accurate, careful, critical, delicate, discriminating, exact, exacting, fastidious, fine, meticulous, precise, rigorous, scrupulous, strict, subtle 4. cultured, genteel, refined, respectable, virtuous, well-bred

Antonyms awful, careless, coarse, crude, disagreeable, dreadful, ill-bred, mean, miserable, rough, shabby, sloppy (*Inf.*), unfriendly, unkind, unpleasant, vague, vulgar

nicely 1. acceptably, agreeably, amiably, attractively, charmingly, commendably, courteously, delightfully, kindly, likably, pleasantly, pleasingly, pleasurably, politely, prepossessingly, well 2. daintily, finely, neatly, tidily, trimly 3. accurately, carefully, critically, delicately, exactingly, exactly, fastidiously, finely, meticulously, precisely, rigorously, scrupulously, strictly, subtly 4. genteelly, respectably, virtuously

Antonyms carelessly, sloppily (*Inf.*), unattractively, unfortunately, unpleasantly

niceness 1. agreeableness, amiability, at~

tractiveness, charm, courtesy, delightfulness, friendliness, good manners, goodness, kindness, likableness *or* likeableness, pleasantness, pleasurableness, politeness, refinement 2. daintiness, fineness, neatness, tidiness, trimness 3. accuracy, care, carefulness, criticalness, delicacy, discrimination, exactingness, exactitude, exactness, fastidiousness, fineness, meticulosity, meticulousness, preciseness, precision, rigorousness, rigour, scrupulosity, scrupulousness, strictness, subtleness, subtlety 4. gentility, good breeding, refinement, respectability, virtue

nicety 1. accuracy, exactness, fastidiousness, finesse, meticulousness, minuteness, precision 2. daintiness, delicacy, discrimination, distinction, nuance, refinement, subtlety

niche 1. alcove, corner, hollow, nook, opening, recess 2. calling, pigeonhole (*Inf.*), place, position, slot (*Inf.*), vocation

nick[1] chip, cut, damage, dent, mark, notch, scar, score, scratch, snick

nick[2] finger (*Sl.*), knock off (*Sl.*), pilfer, pinch (*Inf.*), snitch (*Sl.*), steal, swipe (*Sl.*)

nickname diminutive, epithet, familiar name, handle (*Sl.*), label, pet name, moniker *or* monicker (*Sl.*), sobriquet

nifty agile, apt, attractive, chic, clever, deft, enjoyable, excellent, neat, pleasing, quick, sharp, smart, spruce, stylish

niggard cheapskate (*Inf.*), cheeseparer, churl (*Archaic*), meanie *or* meany (*Inf., chiefly Brit.*), miser, penny-pincher (*Inf.*), screw (*Sl.*), Scrooge, skinflint, tight-arse (*Taboo sl.*), tight-ass (*U.S. taboo sl.*)

niggardliness 1. avarice, avariciousness, closeness, covetousness, frugality, grudgingness, meanness, mercenariness, miserliness, nearness (*Inf.*), parsimony, penuriousness, sordidness, sparingness, stinginess, thrift, tightfistedness, ungenerousness 2. beggarliness, inadequacy, insufficiency, meagreness, meanness, miserableness, paltriness, scantiness, skimpiness, smallness, wretchedness

niggardly 1. avaricious, close, covetous, frugal, grudging, mean, mercenary, miserly, near (*Inf.*), parsimonious, penurious, Scroogelike, sordid, sparing, stinging, stingy, tight-arse (*Taboo sl.*), tight-arsed (*Taboo sl.*), tight as a duck's arse (*Taboo sl.*), tight-ass (*U.S. taboo sl.*), tight-assed (*U.S. taboo sl.*), tightfisted, ungenerous 2. beggarly, inadequate, insufficient, meagre, mean, measly, miserable, paltry, scant, scanty, skimpy, small, wretched
Antonyms abundant, ample, bountiful, copious, generous, handsome, lavish, liberal, munificent, plentiful, prodigal, profuse

niggle 1. carp, cavil, criticize, find fault, fuss 2. annoy, irritate, rankle, worry

niggler carper, caviller, fault-finder, fusspot (*Brit. inf.*), nag, nit-picker (*Inf.*), pettifogger, quibbler

niggling 1. cavilling, finicky, fussy, insignificant, minor, nit-picking (*Inf.*), pettifogging, petty, picky (*Inf.*), piddling (*Inf.*), quibbling, trifling, unimportant 2. gnawing, irritating, persistent, troubling, worrying

nigh 1. *adj.* adjacent, adjoining, approximate, at hand, bordering, close, contiguous, imminent, impending, near, next, upcoming 2. *adv.* about, almost, approximately, close, near, practically

night dark, darkness, dead of night, hours of darkness, night-time, night watches

night and day all the time, ceaselessly, constantly, continually, continuously, day in, day out, endlessly, incessantly, interminably, unremittingly

nightfall crepuscule, dusk, eve (*Archaic*), evening, eventide, gloaming (*Scot. or poetic*), sundown, sunset, twilight, vespers
Antonyms aurora (*Poetic*), cockcrow, dawn, dawning, daybreak, daylight, morning, sunrise

nightly *adv./adj.* 1. each night, every night, night after night, nights (*Inf.*) ~*adv.* 2. after dark, at night, by night, in the night, nights (*Inf.*), nocturnally ~*adj.* 3. night-time, nocturnal

nightmare 1. bad dream, hallucination, incubus, succubus 2. horror, ordeal, torment, trial, tribulation

nightmarish agonizing, alarming, creepy (*Inf.*), disturbing, frightening, harrowing, horrible, Kafkaesque, scaring, terrifying, unreal

nihilism 1. abnegation, agnosticism, atheism, denial, disbelief, nonbelief, rejection, renunciation, repudiation, scepticism 2. blank, emptiness, negation, nonexistence, nothingness, nullity, oblivion 3. anarchy, disorder, lawlessness, terrorism

nihilist 1. agnostic, atheist, cynic, disbeliever, nonbeliever, pessimist, sceptic 2. agitator, anarchist, extremist, revolutionary, terrorist

nil duck, love, naught, *nihil,* none, nothing, zero, zilch (*Sl.*)

nimble active, agile, alert, brisk, deft, dexterous, lively, nippy (*Brit. inf.*), pdq (*Sl.*), proficient, prompt, quick, quick-witted, ready, smart, sprightly, spry, swift

Antonyms awkward, clumsy, dull, heavy, inactive, indolent, lethargic, slow

nimbleness adroitness, agility, alacrity, alertness, dexterity, finesse, grace, lightness, nippiness (*Brit. inf.*), skill, smartness, sprightliness, spryness

nimbly actively, acutely, agilely, alertly, briskly, deftly, dexterously, easily, fast, fleetly, hotfoot, pdq (*Sl.*), posthaste, proficiently, promptly, pronto (*Inf.*), quickly, quick-wittedly, readily, sharply, smartly, speedily, spryly, swiftly

nimbus ambience, atmosphere, aura, aureole, cloud, corona, glow, halo, irradiation

nincompoop berk (*Brit. sl.*), blockhead, charlie (*Brit. inf.*), coot, dickhead (*Sl.*), dimwit (*Inf.*), dipstick (*Brit. sl.*), divvy (*Sl.*), dolt, dork (*Sl.*), dunce, dweeb (*U.S. sl.*), fool, fuckwit (*Taboo sl.*), geek (*Sl.*), gonzo (*Sl.*), idiot, jerk (*Sl., chiefly U.S. & Canad.*), lamebrain (*Inf.*), nerd *or* nurd (*Sl.*), ninny, nitwit (*Inf.*), noodle, numskull *or* numbskull, oaf, pillock (*Brit. sl.*), plank (*Brit. sl.*), plonker (*Sl.*), prat (*Sl.*), prick (*Derogatory sl.*), schmuck (*U.S. sl.*), simpleton, twit (*Inf., chiefly Brit.*), wally (*Sl.*)

nip[1] *v.* 1. bite, catch, clip, compress, grip, nibble, pinch, snag, snap, snip, squeeze, tweak, twitch 2. check, frustrate, thwart

nip[2] *n.* dram, draught, drop, finger, mouthful, peg (*Brit.*), portion, shot (*Inf.*), sip, snifter (*Inf.*), *soupçon,* sup, swallow, taste

nipper 1. claw, pincer 2. *Inf.* ankle-biter (*Aust. sl.*), baby, boy, child, girl, infant, kid (*Inf.*), little one, rug rat (*Sl.*), sprog (*Sl.*), tot

nipple boob (*Sl.*), breast, dug, mamilla, pap, papilla, teat, tit, udder

nippy 1. biting, chilly, nipping, sharp, stinging 2. *Brit. inf.* active, agile, fast, nimble, pdq (*Sl.*), quick, spry

nirvana bliss, joy, paradise, peace, serenity, tranquillity

nit-picking captious, carping, cavilling, finicky, fussy, hairsplitting, pedantic, pettifogging, quibbling

nitty-gritty basics, brass tacks (*Inf.*), core, crux, essence, essentials, facts, fundamentals, gist, heart of the matter, reality, substance

nitwit (*Inf.*), dickhead (*Sl.*), dimwit (*Inf.*), dipstick (*Brit. sl.*), divvy (*Sl.*), dork (*Sl.*), dummy (*Sl.*), fool, fuckwit (*Taboo sl.*), geek (*Sl.*), halfwit, lamebrain (*Inf.*), nincompoop, ninny, oaf, plank (*Brit. sl.*), simpleton

nob aristo (*Inf.*), aristocrat, big shot (*Inf.*), bigwig (*Inf.*), celeb (*Inf.*), fat cat (*Sl., chiefly U.S.*), nabob (*Inf.*), toff (*Brit. sl.*), V.I.P.

nobble 1. disable, handicap, incapacitate, weaken 2. bribe, get at, influence, intimidate, outwit, win over 3. filch, knock off (*Sl.*), nick (*Sl., chiefly Brit.*), pilfer, pinch (*Inf.*), purloin, snitch (*Sl.*), steal, swipe (*Sl.*) 4. get hold of, grab, take

nobbly nubby, projecting, protruding, protuberant, ridged, rough

nobility 1. aristocracy, elite, high society, lords, nobles, patricians, peerage, ruling class, upper class 2. dignity, eminence, excellence, grandeur, greatness, illustriousness, loftiness, magnificence, majesty, nobleness, stateliness, sublimity, superiority, worthiness 3. honour, incorruptibility, integrity, uprightness, virtue

noble *n.* 1. aristo (*Inf.*), aristocrat, lord, nobleman, peer ~*adj.* 2. aristocratic, blue-blooded, gentle (*Archaic*), highborn, lordly, patrician, titled 3. august, dignified, distinguished, elevated, eminent, excellent, grand, great, imposing, impressive, lofty, splendid, stately, superb 4. generous, honourable, magnanimous, upright, virtuous, worthy

Antonyms *n.* commoner, peasant, serf ~*adj.* base, contemptible, dishonest, humble, ignoble, insignificant, lowborn, lowly, mean, modest, peasant, plain, plebeian, selfish, vulgar

nobody 1. no-one 2. cipher, lightweight (*Inf.*), menial, nonentity, nothing (*Inf.*)

Antonyms big noise (*Inf.*), big shot (*Sl.*), celeb (*Inf.*), celebrity, megastar (*Inf.*), personage, star, superstar, V.I.P.

nocturnal night, nightly, night-time, of the night

nod *v.* 1. acknowledge, bob, bow, dip, duck, gesture, indicate, nutate (*Rare*), salute, signal 2. agree, assent, concur, show agreement 3. be sleepy, doze, droop, drowse, kip (*Brit. sl.*), nap, sleep, slump, zizz (*Brit. inf.*) ~*n.* 4. acknowledgment, beck, gesture, greeting, indication, salute, sign, signal

node bud, bump, burl, growth, knob, knot, lump, nodule, protuberance, swelling

noggin 1. gill, quarter-pint 2. cup, dram, mug, nip, tot 3. *Inf.* bean (*U.S. & Canad. sl.*), block (*Inf.*), bonce (*Brit. sl.*), conk (*Sl.*), dome (*Sl.*), head, napper (*Sl.*), noddle (*Inf., chiefly Brit.*), nut (*Sl.*)

no go futile, hopeless, impossible, not on (*Inf.*), vain

noise 1. *n.* babble, blare, clamour, clatter, commotion, cry, din, fracas, hubbub, outcry, pandemonium, racket, row, sound, talk, tumult, uproar 2. *v.* advertise, bruit, circulate, gossip, publicize, repeat, report, rumour

noiseless hushed, inaudible, mute, muted, quiet, silent, soundless, still

noisome 1. bad, baneful (*Archaic*), deleterious, harmful, hurtful, injurious, mischievous, pernicious, pestiferous, pestilential, poisonous, unhealthy, unwholesome 2. disgusting, fetid, foul, malodorous, mephitic, niffy (*Brit. sl.*), noxious, offensive, olid, putrid, reeking, smelly, stinking

noisy boisterous, cacophonous, chattering, clamorous, deafening, ear-splitting, loud, obstreperous, piercing, riotous, strident, tumultuous, turbulent, uproarious, vociferous

Antonyms hushed, quiet, silent, still, subdued, tranquil, tuneful

nomad drifter, itinerant, migrant, rambler, rover, vagabond, wanderer

nomadic itinerant, migrant, migratory, pastoral, peripatetic, roaming, roving, travelling, vagrant, wandering

nom de plume alias, assumed name, nom de guerre, pen name, pseudonym

nomenclature classification, codification, locution, phraseology, taxonomy, terminology, vocabulary

nominal 1. formal, ostensible, pretended, professed, puppet, purported, self-styled, so-called, *soi-disant,* supposed, theoretical, titular 2. inconsiderable, insignificant, minimal, small, symbolic, token, trifling, trivial

nominate appoint, assign, choose, commission, designate, elect, elevate, empower, name, present, propose, recommend, select, submit, suggest, term

nomination appointment, choice, designation, election, proposal, recommendation, selection, suggestion

nominee aspirant, candidate, contestant, entrant, favourite, protégé, runner

nonaligned impartial, neutral, uncommitted, undecided

nonchalance calm, composure, cool (*Sl.*), equanimity, imperturbability, indifference, sang-froid, self-possession, unconcern

nonchalant airy, apathetic, blasé, calm, careless, casual, collected, cool, detached, dispassionate, indifferent, insouciant, laid-back (*Inf.*), offhand, unconcerned, unemotional, unfazed (*Inf.*), unperturbed

Antonyms anxious, caring, concerned, involved, worried

noncombatant civilian, neutral, nonbelligerent

noncommittal ambiguous, careful, cautious, circumspect, discreet, equivocal, evasive, guarded, indefinite, neutral, politic, reserved, tactful, temporizing, tentative, unrevealing, vague, wary

non compos mentis crazy, deranged, insane, mentally ill, of unsound mind, unbalanced, unhinged

Antonyms all there (*Inf.*) *compos mentis* in one's right mind, lucid, mentally sound, rational, sane

nonconformist dissenter, dissentient, eccentric, heretic, iconoclast, individualist, maverick, protester, radical, rebel

Antonyms Babbitt (*U.S.*), conventionalist, stick-in-the-mud (*Inf.*), traditionalist, yes man

nonconformity dissent, eccentricity, heresy, heterodoxy, unconventionality

nondescript characterless, common or garden (*Inf.*), commonplace, dull, featureless, indeterminate, mousy, ordinary, unclassifiable, unclassified, undistinguished, unexceptional, uninspiring, uninteresting, unmemorable, unremarkable, vague

Antonyms distinctive, extraordinary, memorable, remarkable, unique, unusual

none bugger all (*Sl.*), f.a. (*Brit. sl.*), fuck all (*Taboo sl.*), nil, nobody, no-one, no part, not a bit, not any, nothing, not one, sweet F.A. (*Brit. sl.*), sweet Fanny Adams (*Brit. sl.*), zero

nonentity cipher, lightweight (*Inf.*), mediocrity, nobody, small fry, unimportant person

nonessential dispensable, excessive, expendable, extraneous, inessential, peripheral, superfluous, unimportant, unnecessary

Antonyms appropriate, essential, important, indispensable, significant, vital

nonetheless despite that, even so, however, in spite of that, nevertheless, yet

nonexistent chimerical, fancied, fictional, hallucinatory, hypothetical, illusory, imaginary, imagined, insubstantial, legendary, missing, mythical, unreal

Antonyms actual, existent, existing, genuine, real, true, veritable

nonpareil 1. *n.* ideal, nonesuch (*Archaic*), paragon, perfection 2. *adj.* incomparable, matchless, peerless, supreme, unequalled, unique, unmatched, unparalleled, unrivalled, unsurpassed

nonpartisan detached, impartial, independent, neutral, nonpolitical, objective, unaffiliated, unbiased, unprejudiced

nonplus astonish, astound, baffle, bewilder, confound, confuse, discomfit, disconcert, discountenance, dismay, dumbfound, embarrass, faze, flummox, mystify, perplex, puzzle, stump, stun, take aback

nonsense absurdity, balderdash, balls (*Taboo sl.*), bilge (*Inf.*), blather, bombast, bosh (*Inf.*), bull (*Sl.*), bullshit (*Taboo sl.*), bunk (*Inf.*), bunkum *or* buncombe (*Chiefly*

U.S.), claptrap (*Inf.*), cobblers (*Brit. taboo sl.*), crap (*Sl.*), double Dutch (*Brit. inf.*), drivel, eyewash (*Inf.*), fatuity, folly, foolishness, garbage (*Inf.*), gibberish, guff (*Sl.*), hogwash, hokum (*Sl., chiefly U.S. & Canad.*), horsefeathers (*U.S. sl.*), hot air (*Inf.*), idiocy, inanity, jest, ludicrousness, moonshine, pap, piffle (*Inf.*), poppycock (*Inf.*), ridiculousness, rot, rubbish, senselessness, shit (*Taboo sl.*), silliness, stuff, stupidity, tommyrot, tosh (*Sl., chiefly Brit.*), trash, tripe (*Inf.*), twaddle, waffle (*Inf., chiefly Brit.*)
Antonyms fact, reality, reason, sense, seriousness, truth, wisdom

nonsensical absurd, asinine, crazy, foolish, inane, incomprehensible, irrational, ludicrous, meaningless, ridiculous, senseless, silly

nonstop 1. *adj.* ceaseless, constant, continuous, direct, endless, incessant, interminable, relentless, steady, unbroken, unending, unfaltering, uninterrupted, unremitting 2. *adv.* ceaselessly, constantly, continuously, directly, endlessly, incessantly, interminably, relentlessly, steadily, unbrokenly, unendingly, unfalteringly, uninterruptedly, unremittingly, without stopping
Antonyms *adj.* broken, discontinuous, fitful, intermittent, irregular, occasional, periodic, punctuated, recurrent, spasmodic, sporadic, stop-go (*Inf.*)

nonviolent nonbelligerent, pacifist, peaceable, peaceful

nook alcove, cavity, corner, cranny, crevice, cubbyhole, hide-out, inglenook (*Brit.*), niche, opening, recess, retreat

noon high noon, midday, noonday, noontide, noontime, twelve noon

norm average, benchmark, criterion, mean, measure, model, par, pattern, rule, standard, type, yardstick

normal 1. accustomed, acknowledged, average, common, conventional, habitual, natural, ordinary, popular, regular, routine, run-of-the-mill, standard, typical, usual 2. rational, reasonable, sane, well-adjusted
Antonyms abnormal, exceptional, irregular, peculiar, rare, remarkable, singular, uncommon, unnatural, unusual

normality 1. accustomedness, averageness, commonness, commonplaceness, conventionality, habitualness, naturalness, ordinariness, popularity, regularity, routineness, typicality, usualness 2. adjustment, balance, rationality, reason, sanity

normally as a rule, commonly, habitually, ordinarily, regularly, typically, usually

normative controlling, normalizing, prescriptive, regularizing, regulating, standardizing

north 1. *adj.* Arctic, boreal, northerly, northern, polar 2. *adv.* northerly, northward(s)

North Star lodestar, Polaris, Pole Star

nose *n.* 1. beak, bill, conk (*Sl.*), hooter (*Sl.*), neb (*Archaic or dialect*), proboscis, schnozzle (*Sl., chiefly U.S.*), snitch (*Sl.*), snout (*Sl.*) ~*v.* 2. detect, scent, search (for), smell, sniff 3. ease forward, nudge, nuzzle, push, shove 4. meddle, pry, snoop (*Inf.*)

nose dive dive, drop, plummet, plunge

nosegay bouquet, posy

nosh 1. *n.* aliment, chow (*Inf.*), comestibles, eats (*Sl.*), fare, feed, food, grub (*Sl.*), meal, nosebag (*Sl.*), repast, scoff (*Sl.*), sustenance, tack (*Inf.*), viands, victuals, vittles (*Obs. or dialect*) 2. *v.* consume, eat, scoff (*Sl.*)

nostalgia homesickness, longing, pining, regret, regretfulness, remembrance, reminiscence, wistfulness, yearning

nostalgic emotional, homesick, longing, maudlin, regretful, sentimental, wistful

nostrum cure, cure-all, drug, elixir, medicine, panacea, patent medicine, potion, quack medicine, remedy, sovereign cure, specific, treatment

nosy, nosey curious, eavesdropping, inquisitive, interfering, intrusive, meddlesome, prying, snooping (*Inf.*)

notability 1. celebrity, distinction, eminence, esteem, fame, renown 2. celeb (*Inf.*), celebrity, dignitary, megastar (*Inf.*), notable, personage, V.I.P., worthy

notable 1. *adj.* celebrated, conspicuous, distinguished, eminent, evident, extraordinary, famous, manifest, marked, memorable, noteworthy, noticeable, notorious, outstanding, pre-eminent, pronounced, rare, remarkable, renowned, striking, uncommon, unusual, well-known 2. *n.* celeb (*Inf.*), celebrity, dignitary, megastar (*Inf.*), notability, personage, V.I.P., worthy
Antonyms anonymous, concealed, hidden, imperceptible, obscure, unknown, vague

notably conspicuously, distinctly, especially, markedly, noticeably, outstandingly, particularly, remarkably, signally, strikingly, uncommonly

notation 1. characters, code, script, signs, symbols, system 2. jotting, notating, note, noting, record

notch *n.* 1. cleft, cut, incision, indentation, mark, nick, score 2. *Inf.* cut (*Inf.*), degree, grade, level, step ~*v.* 3. cut, indent, mark, nick, score, scratch

notch up achieve, gain, make, register, score

note *n.* 1. annotation, comment, communication, epistle, gloss, jotting, letter, memo, memorandum, message, minute, record, remark, reminder 2. indication, mark, sign, symbol, token 3. heed, notice, observation, regard 4. celebrity, character, consequence, distinction, eminence, fame, prestige, renown, reputation ~*v.* 5. denote, designate, indicate, mark, mention, notice, observe, perceive, record, register, remark, see

notebook commonplace book, diary, exercise book, Filofax (*Trademark*), jotter, journal, memorandum book, notepad, record book

noted acclaimed, celebrated, conspicuous, distinguished, eminent, famous, illustrious, notable, notorious, prominent, recognized, renowned, well-known
Antonyms infamous, obscure, undistinguished, unknown

notes impressions, jottings, outline, record, report, sketch

noteworthy exceptional, extraordinary, important, notable, outstanding, remarkable, significant, unusual
Antonyms commonplace, insignificant, normal, ordinary, pedestrian, run-of-the-mill, unexceptional, unremarkable

nothing bagatelle, cipher, emptiness, naught, nobody, nonentity, nonexistence, nothingness, nought, nullity, trifle, void, zero

nothingness 1. nihility, nonbeing, nonexistence, nullity, oblivion 2. insignificance, unimportance, worthlessness

notice *v.* 1. detect, discern, distinguish, heed, mark, mind, note, observe, perceive, remark, see, spot ~*n.* 2. cognizance, consideration, heed, interest, note, observation, regard 3. advice, announcement, communication, instruction, intelligence, intimation, news, notification, order, warning 4. advertisement, comment, criticism, poster, review, sign 5. attention, civility, respect
Antonyms *v.* disregard, ignore, neglect, over-look ~*n.* disregard, ignorance, neglect, omission, oversight

noticeable appreciable, blatant, clear, conspicuous, distinct, evident, manifest, observable, obvious, perceptible, plain, striking, unmistakable

notification advice, alert, announcement, declaration, information, intelligence, message, notice, notifying, publication, statement, telling, warning

notify acquaint, advise, alert, announce, apprise, declare, inform, publish, tell, warn

notion 1. apprehension, belief, concept, conception, idea, impression, inkling, judgment, knowledge, opinion, sentiment, understanding, view 2. caprice, desire, fancy, impulse, inclination, whim, wish

notional abstract, conceptual, fanciful, hypothetical, ideal, imaginary, speculative, theoretical, unreal, visionary
Antonyms actual, factual, genuine, real

notoriety dishonour, disrepute, infamy, obloquy, opprobrium, scandal

notorious 1. dishonourable, disreputable, infamous, opprobrious, scandalous 2. blatant, flagrant, glaring, obvious, open, overt, patent, undisputed

notoriously 1. dishonourably, disreputably, infamously, opprobriously, scandalously 2. blatantly, flagrantly, glaringly, notably, obviously, openly, overtly, particularly, patently, spectacularly, undisputedly

notwithstanding although, despite, (even) though, however, nevertheless, nonetheless, though, yet

nought naught, nil, nothing, nothingness, zero

nourish 1. attend, feed, furnish, nurse, nurture, supply, sustain, tend 2. comfort, cultivate, encourage, foster, maintain, promote, support

nourishing alimentative, beneficial, healthful, health-giving, nutritious, nutritive, wholesome

nourishment aliment, diet, food, nutriment, nutrition, sustenance, tack (*Inf.*), viands, victuals, vittles (*Obs. or dialect*)

nouveau riche arriviste, new-rich, parvenu, upstart

novel 1. *adj.* different, fresh, ground-breaking, innovative, new, original, rare, singular, strange, uncommon, unfamiliar, unusual 2. *n.* fiction, narrative, romance, story, tale
Antonyms *adj.* ancient, common, customary, familiar, habitual, old-fashioned, ordinary, run-of-the-mill, traditional, usual

novelty 1. freshness, innovation, newness, oddity, originality, strangeness, surprise, unfamiliarity, uniqueness 2. bagatelle, bauble, curiosity, gadget, gewgaw, gimcrack, gimmick, knick-knack, memento, souvenir, trifle, trinket

novice amateur, apprentice, beginner, convert, learner, neophyte, newcomer, novitiate, probationer, proselyte, pupil, trainee, tyro
Antonyms ace, doyen, expert, grandmaster, master, maven, old hand, professional, teacher

novitiate 1. apprenticeship, probation, training 2. novice

now 1. at once, immediately, instanter (*Law*), instantly, presently (*Scot. & U.S.*), promptly, straightaway 2. any more, at the moment, nowadays, these days 3. **now and then** *or* **again** at times, from time to time, infrequently, intermittently, occasionally, on and off, once in a while, on occasion, sometimes, sporadically

nowadays any more, at the moment, in this day and age, now, these days, today

noxious baneful (*Archaic*), corrupting, deadly, deleterious, destructive, detrimental, foul, harmful, hurtful, injurious, insalubrious, noisome, pernicious, pestilential, poisonous, unhealthy, unwholesome
Antonyms innocuous, innoxious, inoffensive, nontoxic, not dangerous, safe, unobjectionable

nuance degree, distinction, gradation, hint, nicety, refinement, shade, shadow, subtlety, suggestion, suspicion, tinge, touch, trace

nub 1. core, crux, essence, gist, heart, kernel, nucleus, pith, point 2. bulge, bump, knob, knot, lump, node, protuberance, swelling

nubile marriageable, ripe (*Inf.*)

nucleus basis, centre, core, focus, heart, kernel, nub, pivot

nude *au naturel*, bare, buck naked (*Sl.*), disrobed, exposed, in one's birthday suit (*Inf.*), in the altogether (*Inf.*), in the buff (*Inf.*), in the raw (*Inf.*), naked, naked as the day one was born (*Inf.*), starkers (*Inf.*), stark-naked, stripped, unclad, unclothed, uncovered, undraped, undressed, without a stitch on (*Inf.*)
Antonyms attired, clothed, covered, dressed

nudge *v.* bump, dig, elbow, jog, poke, prod, push, shove, touch

nudity bareness, dishabille, nakedness, nudism, undress

nugatory 1. insignificant, trifling, trivial, valueless, worthless 2. bootless, futile, ineffectual, inoperative, invalid, null and void, unavailing, useless, vain

nugget chunk, clump, hunk, lump, mass, piece

nuisance annoyance, bore, bother, drag (*Inf.*), gall, hassle (*Inf.*), inconvenience, infliction, irritation, offence, pain in the arse (*Taboo inf.*), pest, plague, problem, trouble, vexation
Antonyms benefit, blessing, delight, happiness, joy, pleasure, satisfaction

null characterless, ineffectual, inoperative, invalid, nonexistent, null and void, powerless, useless, vain, valueless, void, worthless

nullify abolish, abrogate, annul, bring to naught, cancel, counteract, countervail, invalidate, negate, neutralize, obviate, quash, rebut, render null and void, repeal, rescind, revoke, veto, void
Antonyms authorize, confirm, endorse, ratify, validate

nullity characterlessness, ineffectualness, invalidity, nonexistence, powerlessness, uselessness, valuelessness, voidness, worthlessness

numb 1. *adj.* benumbed, dead, deadened, frozen, immobilized, insensible, insensitive, paralysed, stupefied, torpid, unfeeling 2. *v.* benumb, deaden, dull, freeze, immobilize, paralyse, stun, stupefy
Antonyms *adj.* feeling, responsive, sensitive, sentient

number *n.* 1. character, count, digit, figure, integer, numeral, sum, total, unit 2. aggregate, amount, collection, company, crowd, horde, many, multitude, quantity, throng 3. copy, edition, imprint, issue, printing ~*v.* 4. account, add, calculate, compute, count, enumerate, include, reckon, tell, total
Antonyms *n.* insufficiency, lack, scantiness, scarcity, shortage, want ~*v.* conjecture, guess, theorize

numbered categorized, contained, counted, designated, fixed, included, limited, limited in number, specified, totalled

numberless countless, endless, infinite, innumerable, multitudinous, myriad, unnumbered, untold

numbness deadness, dullness, insensibility, insensitivity, paralysis, stupefaction, torpor, unfeelingness

numeral character, cipher, digit, figure, integer, number, symbol

numerous abundant, copious, many, plentiful, profuse, several
Antonyms few, not many, scarcely any

numinous awe-inspiring, divine, heavenly, holy, mysterious, religious, spiritual, supernatural

numskull, numbskull berk (*Brit. sl.*), blockhead, bonehead (*Sl.*), buffoon, charlie (*Brit. inf.*), clot (*Brit. inf.*), coot, dickhead (*Sl.*), dimwit (*Inf.*), dipstick (*Brit. sl.*), divvy (*Sl.*), dolt, dope (*Inf.*), dork (*Sl.*), dullard, dummy (*Sl.*), dunce, dunderhead, dweeb (*U.S. sl.*), fathead (*Inf.*), fool, fuckwit (*Taboo sl.*), geek (*Sl.*), gonzo (*Sl.*), jerk (*Sl., chiefly U.S. & Canad.*), lamebrain (*Inf.*), nerd *or* nurd (*Sl.*), nitwit (*Inf.*), oaf, pillock (*Brit. sl.*), plank (*Brit. sl.*), plonker (*Sl.*), prat (*Sl.*), prick (*Derogatory sl.*), schmuck (*U.S. sl.*), simpleton, thickhead, twit (*Inf.*), wally (*Sl.*)

nuncio ambassador, envoy, legate, messenger

nunnery abbey, cloister, convent, house, monastery

nuptial *adj.* bridal, conjugal, connubial, epithalamial (*Poetic*), hymeneal (*Poetic*), marital, matrimonial, wedded, wedding

nuptials espousal (*Archaic*), marriage, matrimony, wedding

nurse *v.* 1. care for, look after, minister to, tend, treat 2. breast-feed, feed, nourish, nurture, suckle, wet-nurse 3. *Fig.* cherish, cultivate, encourage, foster, harbour, keep alive, preserve, promote, succour, support

nurture *n.* 1. diet, food, nourishment 2. development, discipline, education, instruction, rearing, training, upbringing ~*v.* 3. feed, nourish, nurse, support, sustain, tend 4. bring up, cultivate, develop, discipline, educate, instruct, rear, school, train
Antonyms *v.* deprive, disregard, ignore, neglect, overlook

nut 1. kernel, pip, seed, stone 2. *Sl.* brain, head, mind, reason, senses 3. *Sl.* crackpot (*Inf.*), crank (*Inf.*), eccentric, headbanger (*Inf.*), headcase (*Inf.*), loony (*Sl.*), lunatic, madman, maniac, nutcase (*Sl.*), nutter (*Brit. sl.*), oddball (*Inf.*), psycho (*Sl.*), wacko (*Sl.*)

nutriment aliment, diet, food, foodstuff, nourishment, nutrition, subsistence, support, sustenance

nutrition food, nourishment, nutriment, sustenance

nutritious alimental, alimentative, beneficial, healthful, health-giving, invigorating, nourishing, nutritive, strengthening, wholesome

nuts bananas (*Sl.*), barking (*Sl.*), barking mad (*Sl.*), batty (*Sl.*), crazy (*Inf.*), demented, deranged, eccentric, insane, irrational, loony (*Sl.*), loopy (*Inf.*), mad, not the full shilling (*Inf.*), nutty (*Sl.*), off one's trolley (*Sl.*), out to lunch (*Inf.*), psycho (*Sl.*), psychopathic, up the pole (*Inf.*)

nuts and bolts basics, details, essentials, fundamentals, nitty-gritty (*Inf.*), practicalities

nuzzle burrow, cuddle, fondle, nestle, nudge, pet, snuggle

nymph damsel, dryad, girl, hamadryad, lass, maid, maiden, naiad, Oceanid (*Greek myth.*), oread, sylph

O

oaf airhead (*Sl.*), berk (*Brit. sl.*), blockhead, bonehead (*Sl.*), booby, brute, charlie (*Brit. inf.*), clod, coot, dickhead (*Sl.*), dipstick (*Brit. sl.*), divvy (*Brit. sl.*), dolt, dork (*Sl.*), dullard, dummy (*Sl.*), dunce, dweeb (*U.S. sl.*), fool, fuckwit (*Taboo sl.*), galoot (*Sl., chiefly U.S.*), gawk, geek (*Sl.*), goon, gonzo (*Sl.*), gorilla (*Inf.*), halfwit, idiot, imbecile, jerk (*Sl., chiefly U.S. & Canad.*), lout, lummox (*Inf.*), moron, nerd *or* nurd (*Sl.*), nincompoop, nitwit (*Inf.*), numskull *or* numbskull, pillock (*Brit. sl.*), plank (*Brit. sl.*), plonker (*Sl.*), prat (*Sl.*), sap (*Sl.*), schmuck (*U.S. sl.*), simpleton, twit (*Inf., chiefly Brit.*), wally (*Sl.*)
Antonyms brain (*Inf.*), egghead (*Inf.*), genius, intellect, smart aleck (*Inf.*), wiseacre

oafish blockish, Boeotian, boneheaded (*Sl.*), bovine, brutish, dense, dim, dim-witted (*Inf.*), doltish, dozy (*Brit. inf.*), dull, dumb (*Inf.*), heavy, loutish, lubberly, lumbering, moronic, obtuse, slow on the uptake (*Inf.*), stupid, thick
Antonyms acute, brainy (*Inf.*), bright, clever, intelligent, quick-witted, sharp, smart

oasis *Fig.* haven, island, refuge, resting place, retreat, sanctuary, sanctum

oath 1. affirmation, avowal, bond, pledge, promise, sworn statement, vow, word 2. blasphemy, curse, cuss (*Inf.*), expletive, imprecation, malediction, profanity, strong language, swearword

obdurate adamant, callous, dogged, firm, fixed, hard, hard-hearted, harsh, immovable, implacable, indurate (*Rare*), inexorable, inflexible, iron, mulish, obstinate, perverse, pig-headed, proof against persuasion, relentless, stiff-necked, stubborn, unbending, unfeeling, unimpressible, unrelenting, unshakable, unyielding
Antonyms amenable, biddable, compliant, flexible, malleable, pliant, soft-hearted, submissive, tender, tractable, yielding

obedience accordance, acquiescence, agreement, compliance, conformability, deference, docility, dutifulness, duty, observance, respect, reverence, submission, submissiveness, subservience, tractability
Antonyms defiance, disobedience, insubordination, obstinacy, recalcitrance, stubbornness, wilfulness

obedient acquiescent, amenable, biddable, compliant, deferential, docile, duteous, dutiful, law-abiding, observant, regardful, respectful, submissive, subservient, tractable, under control, well-trained, yielding
Antonyms arrogant, contrary, disobedient, disrespectful, intractable, obdurate, obstinate, rebellious, stubborn, undutiful, ungovernable, unmanageable, unruly, wayward

obeisance bending of the knee, bow, curtsy *or* curtsey, deference, genuflection, homage, kowtow, respect, reverence, salaam, salutation

obelisk column, monolith, monument, needle, pillar, shaft

obese corpulent, Falstaffian, fat, fleshy, gross, heavy, outsize, overweight, paunchy, plump, podgy, portly, roly-poly, rotund, stout, tubby, well-upholstered (*Inf.*)
Antonyms emaciated, gaunt, lean, scraggy, skeletal, skinny, slender, thin

obesity beef (*Inf.*), bulk, corpulence, *embonpoint,* fatness, fleshiness, grossness, overweight, portliness, stoutness, tubbiness, weight problem
Antonyms emaciation, gauntness, leanness, skinniness, slenderness, thinness

obey 1. abide by, act upon, adhere to, be ruled by, carry out, comply, conform, discharge, do what is expected, embrace, execute, follow, fulfil, heed, keep, mind, observe, perform, respond, serve 2. bow to, come to heel, do what one is told, get into line, give in, give way, knuckle under (*Inf.*), submit, succumb, surrender (to), take orders from, toe the line, yield
Antonyms contravene, defy, disobey, disregard, ignore, rebel, transgress, violate

obfuscate befog, bewilder, cloud, confuse, darken, obscure, perplex

object[1] *n.* 1. article, body, entity, fact, item, phenomenon, reality, thing 2. aim, butt, focus, recipient, target, victim 3. design, end, end in view, end purpose, goal, idea, intent, intention, motive, objective, point, purpose, reason

object[2] *v.* argue against, demur, expostulate, oppose, protest, raise objections, take exception

Antonyms accept, acquiesce, admire, agree, approve, assent, compliment, comply, concur, consent, like, relish, welcome

objection cavil, censure, counter-argument, demur, doubt, exception, niggle (*Inf.*), opposition, protest, remonstrance, scruple

Antonyms acceptance, affirmation, agreement, approbation, assent, concession, endorsement, support

objectionable abhorrent, deplorable, disagreeable, dislikable *or* dislikeable, displeasing, distasteful, exceptionable, indecorous, insufferable, intolerable, noxious, obnoxious, offensive, regrettable, repugnant, unacceptable, undesirable, unpleasant, unseemly, unsociable

Antonyms acceptable, agreeable, desirable, likable *or* likeable, pleasant, pleasing, welcome

objective 1. *adj.* detached, disinterested, dispassionate, equitable, even-handed, fair, impartial, impersonal, judicial, just, open-minded, unbiased, uncoloured, unemotional, uninvolved, unprejudiced 2. *n.* aim, ambition, aspiration, design, end, end in view, goal, intention, mark, object, purpose, target

Antonyms (*sense 1*) abstract, biased, personal, prejudiced, subjective, theoretical, unfair, unjust

objectively disinterestedly, dispassionately, even-handedly, impartially, with an open mind, with objectivity *or* impartiality, without fear or favour

objectivity detachment, disinterest, disinterestedness, dispassion, equitableness, impartiality, impersonality

Antonyms bent, bias, partiality, predisposition, prejudice, subjectivity

obligation 1. accountability, accountableness, burden, charge, compulsion, duty, liability, must, onus, requirement, responsibility, trust 2. agreement, bond, commitment, contract, debt, engagement, promise, understanding 3. **under an obligation** beholden, duty-bound, grateful, honour-bound, indebted, in (someone's) debt, obligated, obliged, owing a favour, thankful

obligatory binding, coercive, compulsory, *de rigueur*, enforced, essential, imperative, mandatory, necessary, required, requisite, unavoidable

Antonyms discretionary, elective, noncompulsory, optional, voluntary

oblige 1. bind, coerce, compel, constrain, dragoon, force, impel, make, necessitate, obligate, railroad (*Inf.*), require 2. accommodate, benefit, do (someone) a favour *or* a kindness, favour, gratify, indulge, please, put oneself out for, serve

Antonyms (*sense 2*) bother, discommode, disoblige, disrupt, inconvenience, put out, trouble

obliged 1. appreciative, beholden, grateful, gratified, indebted, in (someone's) debt, thankful 2. bound, compelled, forced, required, under an obligation, under compulsion, without any option

obliging accommodating, agreeable, amiable, civil, complaisant, considerate, cooperative, courteous, eager to please, friendly, good-natured, helpful, kind, polite, willing

Antonyms discourteous, disobliging, inconsiderate, rude, sullen, surly, unaccommodating, uncooperative, unhelpful, unobliging

oblique 1. angled, aslant, at an angle, inclined, slanted, slanting, sloped, sloping, tilted 2. backhanded, circuitous, circumlocutory, evasive, implied, indirect, roundabout, sidelong

Antonyms (*sense 2*) blunt, candid, direct, downright, forthright, frank, open, straightforward

obliquely 1. aslant, aslope, at an angle, diagonally, slantwise 2. circuitously, evasively, in a roundabout manner *or* way, indirectly, not in so many words

obliterate annihilate, blot out, cancel, delete, destroy, destroy root and branch, efface, eradicate, erase, expunge, extirpate, root out, wipe off the face of the earth, wipe out

Antonyms build, construct, create, establish, form, formulate, generate, make

obliteration annihilation, deletion, effacement, elimination, eradication, erasure, expunction, extirpation, wiping (blotting, rooting, sponging) out

Antonyms building, construction, creation, establishment, formation, generation, making

oblivion 1. abeyance, disregard, forgetfulness, insensibility, neglect, obliviousness, unawareness, unconsciousness, (waters of) Lethe 2. blackness, darkness, eclipse, extinction, limbo, nothingness, obscurity, void

Antonyms (*sense 1*) awareness, consciousness, perception, realization, recognition, sensibility

oblivious blind, careless, deaf, disregardful, forgetful, heedless, ignorant, inattentive, insensible, neglectful, negligent, regardless, unaware, unconcerned, unconscious, unmindful, unobservant

Antonyms alert, attentive, aware, conscious, heedful, mindful, observant, watchful

obloquy 1. abuse, animadversion, aspersion, attack, bad press, blame, calumny, censure, character assassination, contumely, criticism, defamation, detraction, invective, opprobrium, reproach, slander, vilification, stick (*Sl.*) 2. discredit, disfavour, disgrace, dishonour, humiliation, ignominy, ill fame, ill repute, infamy, odium, shame, stigma

obnoxious abhorrent, abominable, detestable, disagreeable, disgusting, dislikable *or* dislikeable, foul, hateable, hateful, horrid, insufferable, loathsome, nasty, nauseating, objectionable, obscene, odious, offensive, repellent, reprehensible, repugnant, repulsive, revolting, sickening, unpleasant
Antonyms agreeable, amiable, charming, congenial, delightful, likable *or* likeable, pleasant, pleasing

obscene 1. bawdy, blue, coarse, dirty, disgusting, Fescennine (*Rare*), filthy, foul, gross, immodest, immoral, improper, impure, indecent, lewd, licentious, loose, offensive, pornographic, prurient, ribald, salacious, scabrous, shameless, smutty, suggestive, unchaste, unwholesome 2. *Fig.* atrocious, evil, heinous, loathsome, outrageous, shocking, sickening, vile, wicked
Antonyms (*sense 1*) chaste, decent, decorous, inoffensive, modest, proper, pure, refined, respectable, seemly

obscenity 1. bawdiness, blueness, coarseness, dirtiness, filthiness, foulness, grossness, immodesty, impurity, lewdness, licentiousness, pornography, prurience, salacity, smuttiness, suggestiveness, vileness 2. four-letter word, impropriety, indecency, indelicacy, profanity, smut, swearword, vulgarism 3. abomination, affront, atrocity, blight, evil, offence, outrage, vileness, wrong
Antonyms (*sense 1*) chastity, decency, decorum, delicacy, innocence, modesty, propriety, purity

obscure *adj.* 1. abstruse, ambiguous, arcane, concealed, confusing, cryptic, deep, Delphic, doubtful, enigmatic, esoteric, hazy, hidden, incomprehensible, indefinite, intricate, involved, mysterious, occult, opaque, recondite, unclear, vague 2. blurred, clouded, cloudy, dim, dusky, faint, gloomy, indistinct, murky, obfuscated, shadowy, shady, sombre, tenebrous, unlit, veiled 3. humble, inconspicuous, inglorious, little-known, lowly, minor, nameless, out-of-the-way, remote, undistinguished, unheard-of, unhonoured, unimportant, unknown, unnoted, unseen, unsung *~v.* 4. conceal, cover, disguise, hide, muddy, obfuscate, screen, throw a veil over, veil 5. adumbrate, bedim, befog, block, block out, blur, cloak, cloud, darken, dim, dull, eclipse, mask, overshadow, shade, shroud
Antonyms *adj.* (*senses 1 & 2*) apparent, bright, clear, conspicuous, definite, distinct, evident, explicit, intelligible, lucid, manifest, obvious, plain, prominent, sharp, significant, straightforward, transparent, unmistakable, well-defined (*sense 3*) celebrated, distinguished, eminent, familiar, famous, illustrious, important, major, prominent, renowned, well-known, widely-known *~v.* brighten, clarify, disclose, explain, explicate, expose, interpret, reveal, show, uncover, unmask, unveil

obscurity 1. abstruseness, ambiguity, complexity, impenetrableness, incomprehensibility, intricacy, reconditeness, vagueness 2. darkness, dimness, dusk, duskiness, gloom, haze, haziness, indistinctness, murkiness, shadowiness, shadows 3. inconspicuousness, ingloriousness, insignificance, lowliness, namelessness, nonrecognition, unimportance
Antonyms (*sense 1*) clarity, clearness, comprehensibility, explicitness, lucidity, obviousness, transparency

obsequies burial, burial service, exequies, funeral, funeral rites, last offices

obsequious abject, cringing, deferential, fawning, flattering, grovelling, ingratiating, mealy-mouthed, menial, servile, slavish, smarmy (*Brit. inf.*), submissive, sycophantic, toadying, unctuous

obsequiously abjectly, cringingly, deferentially, fawningly, ingratiatingly, on one's knees, servilely, slavishly, smarmily (*Brit. inf.*), sycophantically, unctuously

observable apparent, appreciable, blatant, clear, detectable, discernible, evident, noticeable, obvious, open, patent, perceivable, perceptible, recognizable, visible

observance 1. adherence to, attention, carrying out, celebration, compliance, discharge, fulfilment, heeding, honouring, notice, observation, performance 2. ceremonial, ceremony, custom, fashion, form, formality, practice, rite, ritual, service, tradition
Antonyms (*sense 1*) disdain, disregard, evasion, heedlessness, inattention, neglect, nonobservance, omission, oversight

observant alert, attentive, eagle-eyed, heedful, mindful, obedient, perceptive, quick, sharp-eyed, submissive, vigilant, watchful, wide-awake
Antonyms distracted, dreamy, heedless, inattentive, indifferent, negligent, preoccupied, unobservant

observation 1. attention, cognition, con~

sideration, examination, experience, information, inspection, knowledge, monitoring, notice, review, scrutiny, study, surveillance, watching 2. annotation, comment, finding, note, obiter dictum, opinion, pronouncement, reflection, remark, thought, utterance

observe 1. detect, discern, discover, espy, note, notice, perceive, see, spot, witness 2. check, check out (*Inf.*), clock (*Brit. sl.*), contemplate, eyeball (*U.S. sl.*), get a load of (*Inf.*), keep an eye on (*Inf.*), keep under observation, look at, monitor, pay attention to, recce (*Sl.*), regard, scrutinize, study, survey, take a dekko at (*Brit. sl.*), view, watch 3. animadvert, comment, declare, mention, note, opine, remark, say, state 4. abide by, adhere to, comply, conform to, follow, fulfil, heed, honour, keep, mind, obey, perform, respect 5. celebrate, commemorate, keep, remember, solemnize
Antonyms (*sense 4*) disregard, ignore, miss, neglect, omit, overlook, violate

observer beholder, bystander, commentator, eyewitness, looker-on, onlooker, spectator, spotter, viewer, watcher, witness

obsess bedevil, be on one's mind, be uppermost in one's thoughts, consume, dominate, engross, grip, haunt, monopolize, plague, possess, preoccupy, prey on one's mind, rule, torment

obsessed beset, dominated, gripped, hag-ridden, haunted, hung up on (*Sl.*), immersed in, infatuated, in the grip of, preoccupied, troubled
Antonyms aloof, apathetic, detached, disinterested, impassive, indifferent, uncaring, unconcerned

obsession bee in one's bonnet (*Inf.*), complex, enthusiasm, fetish, fixation, hang-up (*Inf.*), *idée fixe,* infatuation, mania, phobia, preoccupation, ruling passion, thing (*Inf.*)

obsessive besetting, compulsive, consuming, fixed, gripping, haunting, tormenting, unforgettable

obsolescent ageing, declining, dying out, not with it (*Inf.*), on the decline, on the wane, on the way out, past its prime, waning

obsolete anachronistic, ancient, antediluvian, antiquated, antique, archaic, bygone, dated, *démodé,* discarded, disused, extinct, musty, old, old-fashioned, old hat, out, outmoded, out of date, out of fashion, out of the ark (*Inf.*), outworn, passé, superannuated, *vieux jeu*
Antonyms à la mode, contemporary, current, fashionable, in, in vogue, modern, new, present day, trendy (*Brit. inf.*), up-to-date

obstacle bar, barrier, block, check, difficulty, hindrance, hitch, hurdle, impediment, interference, interruption, obstruction, snag, stumbling block
Antonyms advantage, aid, asset, assistance, benefit, crutch, help, support

obstinacy doggedness, firmness, inflexibility, intransigence, mulishness, obduracy, perseverance, persistence, pertinacity, pig-headedness, resoluteness, stubbornness, tenacity, wilfulness
Antonyms compliance, cooperativeness, docility, flexibility, meekness, submissiveness, tractability

obstinate contumacious, determined, dogged, firm, headstrong, immovable, inflexible, intractable, intransigent, mulish, opinionated, persistent, pertinacious, perverse, pig-headed, recalcitrant, refractory, self-willed, steadfast, stiff-necked, strong-minded, stubborn, tenacious, unyielding, wilful
Antonyms amenable, biddable, complaisant, compliant, docile, flexible, irresolute, manageable, obedient, submissive, tractable, undecided, wavering

obstreperous boisterous, clamorous, disorderly, loud, noisy, out of control, out of hand, rackety, rambunctious (*Inf.*), rampaging, raucous, restive, riotous, rip-roaring (*Inf.*), roistering, roisterous, rough, rowdy, stroppy (*Brit. sl.*), tempestuous, tumultuous, turbulent, uncontrolled, undisciplined, unmanageable, unruly, uproarious, vociferous, wild
Antonyms calm, controlled, disciplined, docile, gentle, orderly, peaceful, placid, quiet

obstruct arrest, bar, barricade, block, bring to a standstill, bung, check, choke, clog, cumber, curb, cut off, frustrate, get in the way of, hamper, hamstring, hide, hinder, hold up, impede, inhibit, interfere with, interrupt, mask, obscure, prevent, restrict, retard, shield, shut off, slow down, stop, thwart, trammel
Antonyms abet, advance, aid, assist, encourage, favour, further, help, promote, support

obstruction bar, barricade, barrier, block, blockage, check, difficulty, hindrance, impediment, obstacle, occlusion, snag, stop, stoppage, trammel
Antonyms aid, assistance, cooperation, encouragement, favour, furtherance, help, support

obstructive awkward, blocking, delaying, hindering, inhibiting, preventative, restrictive, stalling, uncooperative, unhelpful

Antonyms cooperative, encouraging, favourable, helpful, obliging, supportive

obtain 1. achieve, acquire, attain, come by, earn, gain, get, get hold of, get one's hands on, procure, score (*Sl.*), secure 2. be in force, be prevalent, be the case, exist, hold, prevail, stand
Antonyms (*sense 1*) forfeit, forgo, give up, hand over, lose, relinquish, renounce, surrender

obtainable achievable, at hand, attainable, available, on tap (*Inf.*), procurable, ready, realizable, to be had

obtrusive 1. forward, importunate, interfering, intrusive, meddling, nosy, officious, prying, pushy (*Inf.*) 2. blatant, noticeable, obvious, prominent, protruding, protuberant, sticking out
Antonyms (*sense 1*) bashful, decorous, diffident, modest, reserved, reticent, retiring, shy, unassuming (*sense 2*) concealed, covert, hidden, inconspicuous, low-key, muted, unnoticeable, unobtrusive

obtrusively blatantly, bluntly, boldly, crassly, importunately, obviously, officiously, pushily

obtuse 1. boneheaded (*Sl.*), dense, dopey (*Inf.*), dull, dull-witted, dumb (*Inf.*), heavy, imperceptive, insensitive, muttonheaded (*Sl.*), retarded, slow, slow on the uptake (*Inf.*), stolid, stupid, thick, thick-skinned, uncomprehending, unintelligent 2. blunt, rounded
Antonyms (*sense 1*) astute, bright, clever, keen, quick, sensitive, sharp, shrewd, smart

obviate anticipate, avert, counter, counteract, do away with, preclude, prevent, remove, render unnecessary

obvious apparent, blatant, clear, clear as a bell, conspicuous, distinct, evident, indisputable, manifest, much in evidence, noticeable, open, overt, palpable, patent, perceptible, plain, plain as the nose on your face (*Inf.*), pronounced, recognizable, right under one's nose (*Inf.*), self-evident, self-explanatory, staring one in the face (*Inf.*), sticking out a mile (*Inf.*), straightforward, transparent, unconcealed, undeniable, undisguised, unmistakable, unsubtle, visible
Antonyms ambiguous, concealed, dark, hidden, imperceptible, inconspicuous, indistinct, invisible, obscure, unapparent, unclear, vague

obviously certainly, clearly, distinctly, manifestly, of course, palpably, patently, plainly, undeniably, unmistakably, unquestionably, without doubt

occasion *n.* 1. chance, convenience, incident, moment, occurrence, opening, opportunity, time, window 2. affair, celebration, event, experience, happening, occurrence 3. call, cause, excuse, ground(s), inducement, influence, justification, motive, prompting, provocation, reason ~*v.* 4. bring about, cause, create, effect, elicit, engender, evoke, generate, give rise to, induce, influence, inspire, lead to, move, originate, persuade, produce, prompt, provoke

occasional casual, desultory, incidental, infrequent, intermittent, irregular, odd, rare, sporadic, uncommon
Antonyms customary, constant, continual, frequent, habitual, incessant, regular, routine, usual

occasionally at intervals, at times, (every) now and then, every so often, from time to time, irregularly, now and again, off and on, on and off, once in a while, on occasion, periodically, sometimes
Antonyms constantly, continually, continuously, frequently, habitually, often, regularly, routinely

occlude block, bung, choke, clog, close, fill, hinder, obstruct, plug, seal, shut, stop up

occult abstruse, arcane, cabbalistic, concealed, esoteric, hidden, invisible, magical, mysterious, mystic, mystical, obscure, preternatural, recondite, secret, supernatural, unknown, unrevealed, veiled
Antonyms apparent, blatant, evident, exposed, manifest, obvious, open, overt, plain, revealed, visible

occultism black magic, diabolism, magic, sorcery, supernaturalism, the black arts, witchcraft

occupancy habitation, holding, inhabitancy, occupation, possession, residence, tenancy, tenure, term, use

occupant addressee, denizen, holder, incumbent, indweller, inhabitant, inmate, lessee, occupier, resident, tenant, user

occupation 1. activity, business, calling, craft, employment, job, line (of work), post, profession, pursuit, trade, vocation, walk of life, work 2. control, holding, occupancy, possession, residence, tenancy, tenure, use 3. conquest, foreign rule, invasion, seizure, subjugation

occupied 1. busy, employed, engaged, hard at it (*Inf.*), tied up (*Inf.*), working 2. engaged, full, in use, taken, unavailable 3. full, inhabited, lived-in, peopled, settled, tenanted
Antonyms (*sense 3*) deserted, empty, tenantless, uninhabited, unoccupied, untenanted, vacant, void

occupy 1. *Often passive* absorb, amuse, busy, divert, employ, engage, engross, entertain, hold the attention of, immerse, in-

terest, involve, keep busy *or* occupied, monopolize, preoccupy, take up, tie up **2.** be established in, be in residence in, dwell in, ensconce oneself in, establish oneself in, inhabit, live in, own, possess, reside in, stay in (*Scot.*), tenant **3.** cover, fill, hold, permeate, pervade, take up, use, utilize **4.** capture, garrison, hold, invade, keep, overrun, seize, take over, take possession of
Antonyms abandon, depart, desert, evacuate, quit, retreat, vacate, withdraw

occur 1. arise, befall, betide, chance, come about, come off (*Inf.*), come to pass (*Archaic*), crop up (*Inf.*), eventuate, happen, materialize, result, take place, turn up (*Inf.*) **2.** appear, be found, be met with, be present, develop, exist, manifest itself, obtain, show itself **3.** *With* **to** come to mind, come to one, cross one's mind, dawn on, enter one's head, spring to mind, strike one, suggest (offer, present) itself

occurrence 1. adventure, affair, circumstance, episode, event, happening, incident, instance, proceeding, transaction **2.** appearance, development, existence, manifestation, materialization

odd 1. abnormal, atypical, bizarre, curious, deviant, different, eccentric, exceptional, extraordinary, fantastic, freak, freakish, freaky (*Sl.*), funny, irregular, kinky (*Inf.*), oddball (*Inf.*), off-the-wall (*Sl.*), outlandish, out of the ordinary, outré, peculiar, quaint, queer, rare, remarkable, rum (*Brit. sl.*), singular, strange, uncanny, uncommon, unconventional, unusual, wacko (*Sl.*), weird, whimsical **2.** casual, fragmentary, incidental, irregular, miscellaneous, occasional, periodic, random, seasonal, sundry, varied, various **3.** leftover, lone, remaining, single, solitary, spare, surplus, unconsumed, uneven, unmatched, unpaired
Antonyms common, customary, even, familiar, habitual, matched, natural, normal, ordinary, paired, permanent, regular, steady, typical, unexceptional, unremarkable, usual

oddity 1. abnormality, anomaly, eccentricity, freak, idiosyncrasy, irregularity, kink, peculiarity, phenomenon, quirk, rarity **2.** card (*Inf.*), crank (*Inf.*), fish out of water, maverick, misfit, nut (*Sl.*), oddball (*Inf.*), odd bird (*Inf.*), odd fish (*Brit. inf.*), rara avis, screwball (*Sl., chiefly U.S. & Canad.*), wacko (*Sl.*), weirdo *or* weirdie (*Inf.*) **3.** abnormality, bizarreness, eccentricity, extraordinariness, freakishness, incongruity, oddness, outlandishness, peculiarity, queerness, singularity, strangeness, unconventionality, unnaturalness

odd man out exception, freak, maverick, misfit, nonconformist, outsider

oddment bit, butt, end, end of a line, fag end, fragment, leftover, off cut, remnant, scrap, shred, sliver, snippet, stub, tail end

odds 1. advantage, allowance, edge, lead, superiority **2.** balance, chances, likelihood, probability **3.** *Brit.* difference, disparity, dissimilarity, distinction **4. at odds** at daggers drawn, at loggerheads, at sixes and sevens, at variance, in conflict, in disagreement, in opposition to, not in keeping, on bad terms, out of line

odds and ends bits, bits and pieces, debris, leavings, litter, oddments, remnants, rubbish, scraps, sundry *or* miscellaneous items

odious abhorrent, abominable, detestable, disgusting, execrable, foul, hateful, horrible, horrid, loathsome, obnoxious, obscene, offensive, repellent, repugnant, repulsive, revolting, unpleasant, vile, yucky *or* yukky (*Sl.*)
Antonyms agreeable, charming, congenial, delightful, enchanting, enjoyable, pleasant, pleasing, winsome

odium abhorrence, antipathy, censure, condemnation, detestation, disapprobation, disapproval, discredit, disfavour, disgrace, dishonour, dislike, disrepute, execration, hatred, infamy, obloquy, opprobrium, reprobation, shame

odorous aromatic, balmy, fragrant, odoriferous, perfumed, redolent, scented, sweet-smelling

odour 1. aroma, bouquet, essence, fragrance, niff (*Brit. sl.*), perfume, redolence, scent, smell, stench, stink **2.** air, atmosphere, aura, emanation, flavour, quality, spirit

odyssey crusade, journey, peregrination, pilgrimage, quest, trek, voyage

off *adj.* **1.** absent, cancelled, finished, gone, inoperative, postponed, unavailable **2.** bad, below par, disappointing, disheartening, displeasing, low-quality, mortifying, poor, quiet, slack, substandard, unrewarding, unsatisfactory **3.** bad, decomposed, high, mouldy, rancid, rotten, sour, turned *~adv.* **4.** apart, aside, away, elsewhere, out

off and on (every) now and again, every once in a while, from time to time, intermittently, now and then, occasionally, on and off, sometimes, sporadically

offbeat bizarre, Bohemian, eccentric, far-out (*Sl.*), freaky (*Sl.*), idiosyncratic, kinky (*Inf.*), novel, oddball (*Inf.*), off-the-wall (*Sl.*), *outré,* rum (*Brit. sl.*), strange, uncommon, unconventional, unorthodox, unusual, wacko (*Sl.*), way-out (*Inf.*), weird

Antonyms common, conventional, normal, ordinary, orthodox, run-of-the-mill, stereotyped, traditional, unoriginal, usual

off colour ill, not up to par, off form, out of sorts, peaky, peely-wally (*Scot.*), poorly (*Inf.*), queasy, run down, sick, under par, under the weather (*Inf.*), unwell, washed out

offence 1. breach of conduct, crime, delinquency, fault, lapse, misdeed, misdemeanour, peccadillo, sin, transgression, trespass, wrong, wrongdoing 2. affront, displeasure, harm, hurt, indignity, injury, injustice, insult, outrage, put-down (*Sl.*), slight, snub 3. anger, annoyance, displeasure, hard feelings, huff, indignation, ire (*Literary*), needle (*Inf.*), pique, resentment, umbrage, wounded feelings, wrath 4. **take offence** be disgruntled, be offended, get riled, go into a huff, resent, take the huff, take the needle (*Inf.*), take umbrage

offend 1. aggravate (*Inf.*), affront, annoy, disgruntle, displease, fret, gall, give offence, hurt (someone's) feelings, insult, irritate, miff (*Inf.*), nark (*Brit., Aust., & N.Z. sl.*), outrage, pain, pique, piss one off (*Taboo sl.*), provoke, put down, put (someone's) back up, rile, slight, snub, tread on (someone's) toes (*Inf.*), upset, vex, wound 2. be disagreeable to, disgust, gross out (*U.S. sl.*), make (someone) sick, nauseate, repel, repulse, sicken, turn (someone) off (*Inf.*)

Antonyms (*sense 1*) appease, assuage, conciliate, delight, mollify, placate, please, soothe

offended affronted, disgruntled, displeased, huffy, in a huff, miffed (*Inf.*), outraged, pained, piqued, put out (*Inf.*), resentful, smarting, stung, upset

offender criminal, crook, culprit, delinquent, lawbreaker, malefactor, miscreant, sinner, transgressor, villain, wrongdoer

offensive *adj.* 1. abusive, annoying, detestable, discourteous, displeasing, disrespectful, embarrassing, impertinent, insolent, insulting, irritating, objectionable, rude, uncivil, unmannerly 2. abominable, detestable, disagreeable, disgusting, grisly, loathsome, nasty, nauseating, noisome, obnoxious, odious, repellent, revolting, sickening, unpalatable, unpleasant, unsavoury, vile, yucky *or* yukky (*Sl.*) 3. aggressive, attacking, invading ~*n.* 4. attack, drive, onslaught, push (*Inf.*) 5. **on the offensive** advancing, aggressive, attacking, invading, invasive, on the warpath (*Inf.*)

Antonyms *adj.* agreeable, attractive, captivating, charming, civil, conciliatory, courteous, defensive, deferential, delightful, pleasant, polite, respectful ~*n.* defensive

offer *v.* 1. bid, extend, give, hold out, proffer, put on the market, put under the hammer, put up for sale, tender 2. afford, furnish, make available, place at (someone's) disposal, present, provide, purvey, show 3. advance, extend, move, propose, put forth, put forward, submit, suggest 4. be at (someone's) service, come forward, offer one's services, volunteer ~*n.* 5. attempt, bid, endeavour, essay, overture, proposal, proposition, submission, suggestion, tender

Antonyms (*sense 1*) recant, refuse, retract, revoke, take back, withdraw, withhold

offering contribution, donation, gift, handout, oblation (*in religious contexts*), present, sacrifice, subscription, widow's mite

off form below par, having lost one's touch, not at one's best, not up to scratch (*Inf.*), on a bad day, out of practice, out of training, unpractised

offhand 1. *adj.* abrupt, aloof, brusque, careless, casual, cavalier, couldn't-care-less, curt, glib, informal, offhanded, perfunctory, take-it-or-leave-it (*Inf.*), unceremonious, unconcerned, uninterested 2. *adv.* ad lib, extempore, impromptu, just like that (*Inf.*), off the cuff (*Inf.*), off the top of one's head (*Inf.*), without preparation

Antonyms attentive, careful, grave, intent, planned, premeditated, prepared, responsible, serious, thoughtful

office 1. appointment, business, capacity, charge, commission, duty, employment, function, obligation, occupation, place, post, responsibility, role, service, situation, station, trust, work 2. *Plural* advocacy, aegis, aid, auspices, backing, favour, help, intercession, intervention, mediation, patronage, recommendation, referral, support, word

officer agent, appointee, bureaucrat, dignitary, executive, functionary, office-holder, official, public servant, representative

official 1. *adj.* accredited, authentic, authoritative, authorized, bona fide, certified, endorsed, ex cathedra, ex officio, formal, legitimate, licensed, proper, sanctioned, straight from the horse's mouth (*Inf.*) 2. *n.* agent, bureaucrat, executive, functionary, office bearer, officer, representative

Antonyms (*sense 1*) casual, doubtful, dubious, informal, unauthorized, unofficial, unreliable

officiate chair, conduct, emcee (*Inf.*), manage, oversee, preside, serve, superintend

officious bustling, dictatorial, forward, im~

pertinent, inquisitive, interfering, intrusive, meddlesome, meddling, mischievous, obtrusive, opinionated, overbusy, overzealous, pragmatical (*Rare*), pushy (*Inf.*), self-important
Antonyms aloof, detached, indifferent, reserved, reticent, retiring, shy, taciturn, unforthcoming, withdrawn

offing in the offing close at hand, coming up, hovering, imminent, in prospect, in the immediate future, in the wings, on the horizon, on the way, upcoming

off key discordant, dissonant, inharmonious, jarring, out of keeping, out of tune

off-load disburden, discharge, dump, get rid of, jettison, lighten, shift, take off, transfer, unburden, unload, unship

off-putting daunting, discomfiting, disconcerting, discouraging, dismaying, dispiriting, disturbing, formidable, frustrating, intimidating, unnerving, unsettling, upsetting

offset 1. *v.* balance out, cancel out, compensate for, counteract, counterbalance, counterpoise, countervail, make up for, neutralize 2. *n.* balance, compensation, counterbalance, counterweight, equipoise

offshoot adjunct, appendage, branch, by-product, development, limb, outgrowth, spin-off, sprout

offspring brood, child, children, descendant, descendants, family, fry, heir, heirs, issue, kids (*Inf.*), progeny, scion, seed (*Chiefly biblical*), spawn, successor, successors, young
Antonyms ancestor, begetter, forebear, forefather, forerunner, parent, predecessor, procreator, progenitor

often again and again, frequently, generally, many a time, much, oft (*Archaic or poetic*), oftentimes (*Archaic*), ofttimes (*Archaic*), over and over again, repeatedly, time after time, time and again
Antonyms hardly ever, infrequently, irregularly, never, now and then, occasionally, rarely, scarely, seldom

ogle eye up (*Inf.*), gawp at (*Brit. sl.*), give the glad eye (*Inf.*), give the once-over (*Inf.*), lech *or* letch after (*Inf.*), leer, make sheep's eyes at (*Inf.*)

ogre bogey, bogeyman, bugbear, demon, devil, giant, monster, spectre

oil *v.* grease, lubricate

oily 1. fatty, greasy, oiled, oleaginous, smeary, swimming 2. flattering, fulsome, glib, hypocritical, obsequious, plausible, servile, smarmy (*Brit. inf.*), smooth, unctuous

ointment balm, cerate, cream, embrocation, emollient, liniment, lotion, salve, unguent

O.K., okay 1. *adj.* acceptable, accurate, adequate, all right, approved, convenient, correct, fair, fine, good, in order, middling, not bad (*Inf.*), passable, permitted, satisfactory, so-so (*Inf.*), tolerable 2. *n.* agreement, approbation, approval, assent, authorization, consent, endorsement, go-ahead (*Inf.*), green light, permission, sanction, say-so (*Inf.*), seal of approval 3. *v.* agree to, approve, authorize, consent to, endorse, entitle, give one's consent to, give the go-ahead (green light, thumbs up (*Inf.*)), pass, rubber-stamp (*Inf.*), sanction, say yes to 4. *interj.* agreed, all right, right, roger, very good, very well, yes
Antonyms (*sense 1*) displeasing, inaccurate, inadequate, incorrect, not up to scratch (*Inf.*), poor, unacceptable, unsatisfactory, unsuitable

old 1. advanced in years, aged, ancient, decrepit, elderly, full of years, getting on, grey, grey-haired, grizzled, hoary, mature, over the hill (*Inf.*), past one's prime, patriarchal, senescent, senile, venerable 2. antediluvian, antiquated, antique, cast-off, crumbling, dated, decayed, done, hackneyed, obsolete, old-fashioned, outdated, outmoded, out of date, passé, stale, superannuated, timeworn, unfashionable, unoriginal, worn-out 3. aboriginal, antique, archaic, bygone, early, immemorial, of old, of yore, olden (*Archaic*), original, primeval, primitive, primordial, pristine, remote 4. age-old, experienced, familiar, hardened, long-established, of long standing, practised, skilled, time-honoured, traditional, versed, veteran, vintage 5. earlier, erstwhile, ex-, former, one-time, previous, quondam
Antonyms current, fashionable, immature, juvenile, modern, modish, new, novel, recent, up-to-date, young, youthful

old age advancing years, age, agedness, Anno Domini (*Inf.*), autumn *or* evening of one's life, declining years, dotage, senescence, senility, Third Age
Antonyms adolescence, childhood, early life, immaturity, juvenescence, young days, youth

old-fashioned ancient, antiquated, archaic, behind the times, corny (*Sl.*), dated, dead, *démodé*, fusty, musty, not with it (*Inf.*), obsolescent, obsolete, oldfangled, (old-)fogyish, old hat, old-time, outdated, outmoded, out of date, out of style, out of the ark (*Inf.*), passé, past, square (*Inf.*), superannuated, unfashionable
Antonyms chic, contemporary, current,

fashionable, happening (*Inf.*), modern, modish, trendy (*Brit. inf.*), up-to-date, voguish, with it (*Inf.*)

old hand expert, old soldier, old-timer, one of the old school, past master, veteran

old man elder, elder statesman, father, gaffer, grandfather, greybeard, O.A.P. (*Brit.*), old codger (*Inf.*), old stager, oldster (*Inf.*), old-timer (*U.S.*), papa (*Old-fashioned inf.*), patriarch, senior citizen

old-time ancient, antique, bygone, former, old-fashioned, past, vintage

old womanish finicky, fussy, niggly, old-maidish (*Inf.*), overcautious, overparticular, pernickety (*Inf.*), prim, prudish, strait-laced, timid, timorous

old-world archaic, ceremonious, chivalrous, courtly, gallant, old-fashioned, picturesque, quaint, traditional

oleaginous adipose, fat, fatty, greasy, oily, sebaceous, unguinous (*Obsolete*)

Olympian elevated, exalted, glorious, godlike, lofty, majestic, rarefied, splendid, sublime

omen augury, foreboding, foretoken, indication, portent, premonition, presage, prognostic, prognostication, sign, straw in the wind, warning, writing on the wall

ominous baleful, dark, fateful, forbidding, foreboding, inauspicious, menacing, minatory, portentous, premonitory, sinister, threatening, unpromising, unpropitious
Antonyms auspicious, encouraging, favourable, promising, propitious

omission default, exclusion, failure, forgetfulness, gap, lack, leaving out, neglect, noninclusion, oversight
Antonyms addition, inclusion, incorporation, insertion

omit disregard, drop, eliminate, exclude, fail, forget, give (something) a miss (*Inf.*), leave out, leave (something) undone, let (something) slide, miss (out), neglect, overlook, pass over, skip
Antonyms add, enter, include, incorporate, insert, put in

omnipotence divine right, invincibility, mastery, sovereignty, supremacy, supreme power, undisputed sway
Antonyms frailty, impotence, inability, inferiority, powerlessness, vulnerability, weakness

omnipotent all-powerful, almighty, supreme
Antonyms feeble, frail, impotent, incapable, inferior, powerless, vulnerable, weak

omniscient all-knowing, all-seeing, all-wise

on and off discontinuously, (every) now and again, fitfully, from time to time, intermittently, now and then, off and on, on occasion, sometimes, spasmodically

once 1. at one time, formerly, in the old days, in the past, in times gone by, in times past, long ago, once upon a time, previously 2. **at once a.** directly, forthwith, immediately, instantly, now, right away, straight away, straightway (*Archaic*), this (very) minute, without delay, without hesitation **b.** at *or* in one go (*Inf.*), at the same time, simultaneously, together 3. **once and for all** conclusively, decisively, finally, for all time, for good, for the last time, permanently, positively, with finality 4. **once in a while** at intervals, at times, every now and then, from time to time, now and again, occasionally, once in a blue moon (*Inf.*), on occasion, sometimes

oncoming advancing, approaching, forthcoming, imminent, impending, looming, onrushing, upcoming

one-horse backwoods, inferior, minor, obscure, petty, quiet, sleepy, slow, small, small-time (*Inf.*), tinpot (*Brit. inf.*), unimportant

onerous backbreaking, burdensome, crushing, demanding, difficult, exacting, exhausting, exigent, formidable, grave, hard, heavy, laborious, oppressive, responsible, taxing, weighty
Antonyms cushy (*Inf.*), easy, effortless, facile, light, painless, simple, trifling, undemanding, unexacting, untaxing

one-sided biased, coloured, discriminatory, inequitable, lopsided, partial, partisan, prejudiced, unequal, unfair, unjust
Antonyms equal, equitable, fair, impartial, just, unbiased, uncoloured, unprejudiced

one-time erstwhile, ex-, former, late, previous, quondam, sometime

ongoing advancing, continuous, current, developing, evolving, extant, growing, in progress, progressing, successful, unfinished, unfolding

onlooker bystander, eyewitness, looker-on, observer, spectator, viewer, watcher, witness

only 1. *adv.* at most, barely, exclusively, just, merely, purely, simply 2. *adj.* exclusive, individual, lone, one and only, single, sole, solitary, unique

onomatopoeic echoic, imitative, onomatopoetic

onrush charge, flood, flow, onset, onslaught, push, rush, stampede, stream, surge

onset 1. assault, attack, charge, onrush, onslaught 2. beginning, inception, kick-off (*Inf.*), outbreak, start

Antonyms (*sense 2*) conclusion, culmination, end, ending, finish, outcome, termination, wind-up

onslaught assault, attack, blitz, charge, offensive, onrush, onset
Antonyms defensive, escape, flight, recession, retreat, rout, stampede, withdrawal

onus burden, liability, load, obligation, responsibility, task
Antonyms easement, exemption, exoneration, liberation, pardon, release, relief, remission

onward, onwards *adv.* ahead, beyond, forth, forward, in front, on

ooze 1. *v.* bleed, discharge, drain, dribble, drip, drop, emit, escape, exude, filter, leach, leak, overflow with, percolate, seep, strain, sweat, weep 2. *n.* alluvium, mire, muck, mud, silt, slime, sludge

oozy dewy, dripping, miry, moist, mucky, slimy, sloppy, sludgy, sweaty, weeping

opacity cloudiness, density, dullness, filminess, impermeability, milkiness, murkiness, obscurity, opaqueness

opalescent iridescent, lustrous, nacreous, opaline, pearly, prismatic, rainbow-hued, shot

opaque 1. clouded, cloudy, dim, dull, filmy, hazy, impenetrable, lustreless, muddied, muddy, murky, obfuscated, turbid 2. abstruse, baffling, cryptic, difficult, enigmatic, incomprehensible, obscure, unclear, unfathomable, unintelligible
Antonyms bright, clear, crystal clear, limpid, lucid, pellucid, transparent, transpicuous

open *adj.* 1. agape, ajar, expanded, extended, gaping, revealed, spread out, unbarred, unclosed, uncovered, unfastened, unfolded, unfurled, unlocked, unobstructed, unsealed, yawning 2. airy, bare, clear, exposed, extensive, free, navigable, not built-up, passable, rolling, spacious, sweeping, uncluttered, uncrowded, unenclosed, unfenced, unsheltered, wide, wide-open 3. accessible, available, free, general, nondiscriminatory, public, unconditional, unengaged, unoccupied, unqualified, unrestricted, vacant 4. apparent, avowed, barefaced, blatant, clear, conspicuous, downright, evident, flagrant, frank, manifest, noticeable, obvious, overt, plain, unconcealed, undisguised, visible 5. arguable, debatable, moot, undecided, unresolved, unsettled, up in the air, yet to be decided 6. disinterested, free, impartial, objective, receptive, unbiased, uncommitted, unprejudiced 7. *With* **to** an easy target for, at the mercy of, defenceless against, disposed, exposed, liable, susceptible, vulnerable 8. artless, candid, fair, frank, guileless, honest, ingenuous, innocent, natural, sincere, transparent, unreserved 9. filigree, fretted, holey, honeycombed, lacy, loose, openwork, porous, spongy 10. bounteous, bountiful, generous, liberal, munificent, prodigal 11. exposed, undefended, unfortified, unprotected ~*v.* 12. begin, begin business, commence, get *or* start the ball rolling, inaugurate, initiate, kick off (*Inf.*), launch, put up one's plate, set in motion, set up shop, start 13. clear, crack, throw wide, unbar, unblock, unclose, uncork, uncover, undo, unfasten, unlock, unseal, untie, unwrap 14. expand, spread (out), unfold, unfurl, unroll 15. come apart, crack, rupture, separate, split 16. disclose, divulge, exhibit, explain, lay bare, pour out, show, uncover
Antonyms *adj.* (*senses 1 & 2*) bounded, closed, concealed, confined, covered, crowded, enclosed, fastened, limited, locked, obstructed, restricted, sealed, shut (*senses 3 & 4*) covert, disguised, hidden, inaccessible, private, protected, restricted, secret, veiled (*sense 6*) biased, partial, prejudiced (*senses 7 & 11*) defended, protected (*sense 8*) artful, cunning, introverted, reserved, secretive, sly, withdrawn ~*v.* (*sense 12*) close, conclude, end, finish, terminate (*sense 13*) block, close, fasten, lock, obstruct, seal, shut (*sense 14*) fold

open-air alfresco, outdoor

open-and-shut foregone, noncontroversial, obvious, simple, straightforward

open-handed bountiful, free, generous, lavish, liberal, munificent, prodigal, unstinting
Antonyms avaricious, close-fisted, grasping, grudging, mean, miserly, parsimonious, penny-pinching (*Inf.*), stingy, tight-fisted

opening *n.* 1. aperture, breach, break, chink, cleft, crack, fissure, gap, hole, interstice, orifice, perforation, rent, rupture, slot, space, split, vent 2. break (*Inf.*), chance, look-in (*Inf.*), occasion, opportunity, place, vacancy, window 3. beginning, birth, commencement, dawn, inauguration, inception, initiation, kickoff (*Inf.*), launch, launching, onset, opening move, outset, overture, start ~*adj.* 4. beginning, commencing, early, first, inaugural, initial, initiatory, introductory, maiden, primary
Antonyms (*sense 1*) blockage, cessation, closing, closure, obstruction, occlusion, plug, seal, stoppage (*sense 3*) close, completion, conclusion, culmination, ending, finale, finish, termination, winding up (*Inf.*)

openly 1. candidly, face to face, forthrightly,

frankly, overtly, plainly, straight from the shoulder (*Inf.*), unhesitatingly, unreservedly 2. blatantly, brazenly, flagrantly, in full view, in public, publicly, shamelessly, unabashedly, unashamedly, wantonly, without pretence

Antonyms covertly, furtively, in camera, privately, quietly, secretly, slyly, surreptitiously

open-minded broad, broad-minded, catholic, dispassionate, enlightened, free, impartial, liberal, reasonable, receptive, tolerant, unbiased, undogmatic, unprejudiced

Antonyms assertive, biased, bigoted, dogmatic, intolerant, narrow-minded, opinionated, pig-headed, prejudiced, uncompromising

operate 1. act, be in action, function, go, perform, run, work 2. be in charge of, handle, manage, manoeuvre, use, work 3. perform surgery

Antonyms (*sense 1*) break down, conk out (*Inf.*), cut out (*Inf.*), fail, falter, halt, seize up, stall, stop

operation 1. action, affair, course, exercise, motion, movement, performance, procedure, process, use, working 2. **in operation** effective, functioning, going, in action, in force, operative 3. activity, agency, effect, effort, force, influence, instrumentality, manipulation 4. affair, business, deal, enterprise, proceeding, transaction, undertaking 5. assault, campaign, exercise, manoeuvre 6. surgery

operational functional, going, in working order, operative, prepared, ready, usable, viable, workable, working

Antonyms broken, ineffective, inoperative, kaput (*Inf.*), nonfunctional, on the blink (*Sl.*), out of order

operative *adj.* 1. active, current, effective, efficient, functional, functioning, in force, in operation, operational, serviceable, standing, workable 2. crucial, important, indicative, influential, key, relevant, significant ~*n.* 3. artisan, employee, hand, labourer, machinist, mechanic, worker

Antonyms (*sense 1*) ineffective, inefficient, inoperative, nonfunctional, powerless, unusable, unworkable

operator 1. conductor, driver, handler, mechanic, operative, practitioner, skilled employee, technician, worker 2. administrator, contractor, dealer, director, manager, speculator, trader 3. *Inf.* Machiavellian, machinator, manipulator, mover, shyster (*Sl., chiefly U.S.*), smart aleck (*Inf.*), wheeler-dealer (*Inf.*), wirepuller, worker

opiate anodyne, bromide, downer (*Sl.*), drug, narcotic, nepenthe, pacifier, sedative, soporific, tranquillizer

opine believe, conceive, conclude, conjecture, declare, give as one's opinion, judge, presume, say, suggest, suppose, surmise, think, venture, volunteer, ween (*Poetic*)

opinion 1. assessment, belief, conception, conjecture, estimation, feeling, idea, impression, judgment, mind, notion, persuasion, point of view, sentiment, theory, view 2. **be of the opinion** be convinced, believe, be under the impression, conclude, consider, hold, judge, reckon, suppose, surmise, think 3. **matter of opinion** debatable point, matter of judgment, moot point, open question, open to debate, up to the individual

opinionated adamant, biased, bigoted, bull-headed, cocksure, dictatorial, doctrinaire, dogmatic, inflexible, obdurate, obstinate, overbearing, pig-headed, prejudiced, self-assertive, single-minded, stubborn, uncompromising

Antonyms broad-minded, compliant, compromising, dispassionate, flexible, open-minded, receptive, tolerant, unbiased, unbigoted, unprejudiced

opponent adversary, antagonist, challenger, competitor, contestant, disputant, dissentient, enemy, foe, opposer, rival, the opposition

Antonyms accomplice, ally, associate, colleague, friend, helper, mate, supporter

opportune advantageous, appropriate, apt, auspicious, convenient, favourable, felicitous, fit, fitting, fortunate, happy, lucky, proper, propitious, seasonable, suitable, timely, well-timed

Antonyms inappropriate, inconvenient, inopportune, unfavourable, unfortunate, unsuitable, untimely

opportunism expediency, exploitation, Machiavellianism, making hay while the sun shines (*Inf.*), pragmatism, realism, *Realpolitik,* striking while the iron is hot (*Inf.*), trimming, unscrupulousness

opportunity break (*Inf.*), chance, convenience, hour, look-in (*Inf.*), moment, occasion, opening, scope, time, window

oppose 1. bar, block, check, combat, confront, contradict, counter, counterattack, defy, face, fight, fly in the face of, hinder, obstruct, prevent, resist, speak against, stand up to, take a stand against, take issue with, take on, thwart, withstand 2. compare, contrast, counterbalance, match, pit *or* set against, play off

Antonyms advance, advocate, aid, back, defend, espouse, help, promote, support

opposed against, antagonistic, anti (*Inf.*),

antipathetic, antithetical, at daggers drawn, averse, clashing, conflicting, contra (*Inf.*), contrary, dissentient, hostile, incompatible, inimical, in opposition, opposing, opposite

opposing antagonistic, antipathetic, clashing, combatant, conflicting, contrary, enemy, hostile, incompatible, irreconcilable, opposed, opposite, rival, warring

opposite *adj.* 1. corresponding, facing, fronting 2. adverse, antagonistic, antithetical, conflicting, contradictory, contrary, contrasted, diametrically opposed, different, differing, diverse, hostile, inconsistent, inimical, irreconcilable, opposed, reverse, unlike ~*n.* 3. antithesis, contradiction, contrary, converse, inverse, reverse, the other extreme, the other side of the coin (*Inf.*)

Antonyms (*sense 2*) alike, consistent, corresponding, identical, like, matching, same, similar, uniform

opposition 1. antagonism, competition, contrariety, counteraction, disapproval, hostility, obstruction, obstructiveness, prevention, resistance, unfriendliness 2. antagonist, competition, foe, opponent, other side, rival

Antonyms (*sense 1*) agreement, approval, collaboration, concurrence, cooperation, correspondence, friendliness, responsiveness

oppress 1. afflict, burden, depress, dispirit, harass, lie *or* weigh heavy upon, sadden, take the heart out of, torment, vex 2. abuse, crush, harry, maltreat, overpower, overwhelm, persecute, rule with an iron hand, subdue, subjugate, suppress, trample underfoot, tyrannize over, wrong

Antonyms deliver, emancipate, free, liberate, loose, release, set free, unburden

oppressed abused, browbeaten, burdened, disadvantaged, downtrodden, enslaved, harassed, henpecked, maltreated, misused, prostrate, slave, subject, troubled, tyrannized, underprivileged

Antonyms advantaged, exalted, favoured, honoured, liberated, privileged

oppression abuse, brutality, calamity, cruelty, hardship, harshness, injury, injustice, iron hand, maltreatment, misery, persecution, severity, subjection, suffering, tyranny

Antonyms benevolence, clemency, compassion, goodness, humaneness, justice, kindness, mercy, sympathy, tenderness

oppressive 1. brutal, burdensome, cruel, despotic, grinding, harsh, heavy, inhuman, onerous, overbearing, overwhelming, repressive, severe, tyrannical, unjust 2. airless, close, heavy, muggy, overpowering, stifling, stuffy, suffocating, sultry, torrid

Antonyms (*sense 1*) encouraging, gentle, humane, just, lenient, merciful, propitious, soft

oppressor autocrat, bully, despot, harrier, intimidator, iron hand, persecutor, scourge, slave-driver, taskmaster, tormentor, tyrant

opprobrious 1. abusive, calumniatory, contemptuous, contumelious, damaging, defamatory, hateful, insolent, insulting, invective, offensive, scandalous, scurrilous, vitriolic, vituperative 2. abominable, contemptible, despicable, dishonourable, disreputable, hateful, ignominious, infamous, notorious, reprehensible, shameful

opprobrium calumny, censure, contumely, discredit, disfavour, disgrace, dishonour, disrepute, ignominy, ill repute, infamy, obloquy, odium, reproach, scurrility, shame, slur, stigma

oppugn argue, assail, attack, call into question, cast doubt on, combat, dispute, oppose, resist, withstand

opt (for) choose, decide (on), elect, exercise one's discretion (in favour of), go for, make a selection, plump for, prefer

Antonyms decide against, dismiss, eliminate, exclude, preclude, reject, rule out, turn down

optimistic 1. disposed to take a favourable view, idealistic, seen through rose-coloured spectacles, Utopian 2. assured, bright, buoyant, buoyed up, cheerful, confident, encouraged, expectant, hopeful, positive, sanguine

Antonyms bleak, cynical, despairing, despondent, downhearted, fatalistic, gloomy, glum, hopeless, pessimistic, resigned

optimum *adj.* A1 *or* A-one (*Inf.*), best, choicest, flawless, highest, ideal, most favourable *or* advantageous, optimal, peak, perfect, superlative

Antonyms inferior, least, lowest, minimal, poorest, worst

option alternative, choice, election, preference, selection

optional discretionary, elective, extra, noncompulsory, open, possible, up to the individual, voluntary

Antonyms compulsory, de rigeur, mandatory, obligatory, required

opulence 1. affluence, big bucks (*Inf., chiefly U.S.*), big money, easy circumstances, Easy Street (*Inf.*), fortune, lavishness, luxuriance, luxury, megabucks (*U.S. & Canad. sl.*), plenty, pretty penny (*Inf.*), prosperity, riches, richness, sumptuousness, tidy sum (*Inf.*), wad (*U.S. & Canad. sl.*), wealth 2. abundance, copiousness, cor~

nucopia, fullness, profusion, richness, superabundance
Antonyms dearth, impecuniousness, indigence, lack, paucity, penury, poverty, privation, scantiness, scarcity, want

opulent 1. affluent, lavish, luxurious, moneyed, prosperous, rich, sumptuous, wealthy, well-heeled (*Inf.*), well-off, well-to-do 2. abundant, copious, lavish, luxuriant, plentiful, profuse, prolific
Antonyms (*sense 1*) broke (*Inf.*), destitute, down and out, indigent, moneyless, needy, on the rocks, penurious, poor, poverty-stricken

opus brainchild, composition, creation, *oeuvre,* piece, production, work

oracle 1. augur, Cassandra, prophet, seer, sibyl, soothsayer 2. answer, augury, divination, divine utterance, prediction, prognostication, prophecy, revelation, vision 3. adviser, authority, guru, high priest, horse's mouth, mastermind, mentor, pundit, source, wizard

oracular 1. auspicious, foreboding, haruspical, mantic, ominous, portentous, prescient, prophetic, pythonic, sibylline, vatic (*Rare*) 2. authoritative, dictatorial, dogmatic, grave, positive, sage, significant, venerable, wise 3. ambiguous, arcane, cryptic, Delphic, equivocal, mysterious, obscure, two-edged

oral spoken, verbal, viva voce, vocal

orate declaim, discourse, hold forth, make a speech, pontificate, speak, speechify, talk

oration address, declamation, discourse, harangue, homily, lecture, speech, spiel (*Inf.*)

orator Cicero, declaimer, lecturer, public speaker, rhetorician, speaker, spellbinder, spieler (*Inf.*)

oratorical bombastic, Ciceronian, declamatory, eloquent, grandiloquent, high-flown, magniloquent, rhetorical, silver-tongued, sonorous

oratory declamation, elocution, eloquence, grandiloquence, public speaking, rhetoric, speechifying, speech-making, spieling (*Inf.*)

orb ball, circle, globe, ring, round, sphere

orbit *n.* 1. circle, circumgyration, course, cycle, ellipse, path, revolution, rotation, track, trajectory 2. *Fig.* ambit, compass, course, domain, influence, range, reach, scope, sphere, sphere of influence, sweep ~*v.* 3. circle, circumnavigate, encircle, revolve around

orchestrate 1. arrange, score 2. arrange, concert, coordinate, integrate, organize, present, put together, set up, stage-manage

ordain 1. anoint, appoint, call, consecrate, destine, elect, frock, invest, nominate 2. fate, foreordain, intend, predestine, predetermine 3. decree, demand, dictate, enact, enjoin, establish, fix, lay down, legislate, order, prescribe, pronounce, rule, set, will

ordeal affliction, agony, anguish, hardship, nightmare, suffering, test, torture, trial, tribulation(s), trouble(s)
Antonyms bliss, delight, elation, enjoyment, gladness, happiness, joy, pleasure

order *n.* 1. arrangement, harmony, method, neatness, orderliness, organization, pattern, plan, propriety, regularity, symmetry, system, tidiness 2. arrangement, array, categorization, classification, codification, disposal, disposition, grouping, layout, line, line-up, ordering, placement, progression, sequence, series, setup (*Inf.*), structure, succession 3. **in order a.** arranged, in sequence, neat, orderly, shipshape, tidy **b.** acceptable, appropriate, called for, correct, fitting, O.K. *or* okay (*Inf.*), right, suitable 4. **out of order a.** broken, broken-down, bust (*Inf.*), gone haywire (*Inf.*), gone phut (*Inf.*), in disrepair, inoperative, kaput (*Inf.*), nonfunctional, not working, on the blink (*Sl.*), on the fritz (*U.S. sl.*), out of commission, U/S (*Inf.*), wonky (*Brit. sl.*) **b.** improper, indecorous, not cricket (*Inf.*), not done, not on (*Inf.*), out of place, out of turn, uncalled-for, wrong 5. calm, control, discipline, law, law and order, peace, quiet, tranquillity 6. caste, class, degree, grade, hierarchy, pecking order (*Inf.*), position, rank, status 7. breed, cast, class, family, genre, genus, ilk, kind, sort, species, subclass, taxonomic group, tribe, type 8. behest, canon, command, decree, dictate, direction, directive, injunction, instruction, law, mandate, ordinance, precept, regulation, rule, say-so (*Inf.*), stipulation 9. application, booking, commission, request, requisition, reservation 10. association, brotherhood, community, company, fraternity, guild, league, lodge, organization, sect, sisterhood, society, sodality, union ~*v.* 11. adjure, bid, charge, command, decree, demand, direct, enact, enjoin, instruct, ordain, prescribe, require 12. apply for, authorize, book, call for, contract for, engage, prescribe, request, reserve, send away for 13. adjust, align, arrange, catalogue, class, classify, conduct, control, dispose, group, lay out, manage, marshal, neaten, organize, put to rights, regulate, set in order, sort out, systematize, tabulate, tidy
Antonyms *n.* (*senses 1 & 2*) chaos, clutter, confusion, disarray, disorder, jumble, mess, muddle, pandemonium, shambles ~*v.* (*sense 13*) clutter, confuse, disarrange, dis-

order, disturb, jumble up, mess up, mix up, muddle, scramble

orderly *adj.* 1. businesslike, in apple-pie order (*Inf.*), in order, methodical, neat, regular, scientific, shipshape, systematic, systematized, tidy, trim, well-organized, well-regulated 2. controlled, decorous, disciplined, law-abiding, nonviolent, peaceable, quiet, restrained, well-behaved

Antonyms chaotic, disorderly, disorganized, higgledy-piggledy (*Inf.*), messy, riotous, sloppy, uncontrolled, undisciplined, unsystematic

ordinance 1. canon, command, decree, dictum, edict, enactment, fiat, law, order, precept, regulation, rule, ruling, statute 2. ceremony, institution, observance, practice, rite, ritual, sacrament, usage

ordinarily as a rule, commonly, customarily, generally, habitually, in general, in the general run (of things), in the usual way, normally, usually

Antonyms hardly ever, infrequently, occasionally, rarely, scarcely, seldom, uncommonly

ordinary 1. accustomed, banal, common, customary, established, everyday, habitual, humdrum, mundane, normal, prevailing, quotidian, regular, routine, settled, standard, stock, typical, usual, wonted 2. common or garden (*Inf.*), conventional, familiar, homespun, household, humble, modest, plain, prosaic, run-of-the-mill, simple, unmemorable, unpretentious, unremarkable, workaday 3. average, commonplace, fair, indifferent, inferior, mean, mediocre, pedestrian, second-rate, stereotyped, undistinguished, unexceptional, uninspired, unremarkable 4. **out of the ordinary** atypical, distinguished, exceptional, exciting, extraordinary, high-calibre, imaginative, important, impressive, inspired, noteworthy, outstanding, rare, remarkable, significant, special, striking, superior, uncommon, unusual

Antonyms consequential, distinguished, exceptional, extraordinary, important, impressive, inspired, notable, novel, outstanding, rare, significant, superior, uncommon, unconventional, unique, unusual

ordnance arms, artillery, big guns, cannon, guns, materiel, munitions, weapons

organ 1. device, implement, instrument, tool 2. element, member, part, process, structure, unit 3. agency, channel, forum, journal, means, medium, mouthpiece, newspaper, paper, periodical, publication, vehicle, voice

organic 1. animate, biological, biotic, live, living, natural 2. integrated, methodical, ordered, organized, structured, systematic 3. anatomical, constitutional, fundamental, inherent, innate, integral, structural

organism animal, being, body, creature, entity, living thing, structure

organization 1. assembling, assembly, construction, coordination, direction, disposal, formation, forming, formulation, making, management, methodology, organizing, planning, regulation, running, standardization, structuring 2. arrangement, chemistry, composition, configuration, conformation, constitution, design, format, framework, grouping, make-up, method, organism, pattern, plan, structure, system, unity, whole 3. association, body, combine, company, concern, confederation, consortium, corporation, federation, group, institution, league, outfit (*Inf.*), syndicate

organize arrange, be responsible for, catalogue, classify, codify, constitute, construct, coordinate, dispose, establish, form, frame, get going, get together, group, lay the foundations of, lick into shape, look after, marshal, pigeonhole, put in order, put together, run, see to (*Inf.*), set up, shape, straighten out, systematize, tabulate, take care of

Antonyms confuse, derange, disorganize, disrupt, jumble, mix up, muddle, scramble, upset

orgiastic abandoned, bacchanalian, bacchic, debauched, depraved, Dionysian, dissolute, frenetic, riotous, Saturnalian, wanton, wild

orgy 1. bacchanal, bacchanalia, carousal, carouse, debauch, revel, revelry, Saturnalia 2. binge (*Inf.*), bout, excess, indulgence, overindulgence, splurge, spree, surfeit

orient *v.* acclimatize, adapt, adjust, align, familiarize, find one's feet (*Inf.*), get one's bearings, get the lie of the land, orientate

orientation 1. bearings, coordination, direction, location, position, sense of direction 2. acclimatization, adaptation, adjustment, assimilation, breaking in, familiarization, introduction, settling in

orifice aperture, cleft, hole, mouth, opening, perforation, pore, rent, vent

origin 1. base, basis, cause, derivation, *fons et origo*, font (*Poetic*), fount, fountain, fountainhead, occasion, provenance, root, roots, source, spring, wellspring 2. beginning, birth, commencement, creation, dawning, early stages, emergence, foundation, genesis, inauguration, inception, launch, origination, outset, start 3. ancestry, beginnings, birth, descent, extraction, family, heritage, lineage, parentage, pedigree, stirps, stock

Antonyms conclusion, culmination, death, end, expiry, finale, finish, outcome, termination

original *adj.* 1. aboriginal, autochthonous, commencing, earliest, early, embryonic, first, infant, initial, introductory, opening, primary, primitive, primordial, pristine, rudimentary, starting 2. creative, fertile, fresh, ground-breaking, imaginative, ingenious, innovative, innovatory, inventive, new, novel, resourceful, seminal, unconventional, unprecedented, untried, unusual 3. archetypal, authentic, first, first-hand, genuine, master, primary, prototypical ~*n.* 4. archetype, master, model, paradigm, pattern, precedent, prototype, standard, type 5. anomaly, card (*Inf.*), case (*Inf.*), character, eccentric, nonconformist, nut (*Sl.*), oddball (*Inf.*), oddity, queer fish (*Brit. inf.*), wacko (*Sl.*), weirdo *or* weirdie (*Inf.*)
Antonyms *adj.* antiquated, banal, borrowed, commonplace, conventional, copied, familiar, final, last, latest, normal, old, old-fashioned, ordinary, secondary, stale, standard, stock, traditional, typical, unimaginative, unoriginal, usual ~*n.* copy, imitation, replica, reproduction

originality boldness, break with tradition, cleverness, creativeness, creative spirit, creativity, daring, freshness, imagination, imaginativeness, individuality, ingenuity, innovation, innovativeness, inventiveness, new ideas, newness, novelty, resourcefulness, unconventionality, unorthodoxy
Antonyms conformity, conventionality, imitativeness, normality, orthodoxy, regularity, staleness, traditionalism

originally at first, at the outset, at the start, by origin (birth, derivation), first, initially, in the beginning, in the first place, to begin with

originate 1. arise, be born, begin, come, derive, emanate, emerge, flow, issue, proceed, result, rise, spring, start, stem 2. bring about, conceive, create, develop, discover, evolve, form, formulate, generate, give birth to, inaugurate, initiate, institute, introduce, invent, launch, pioneer, produce, set in motion, set up
Antonyms cease, conclude, culminate, end, expire, finish, terminate, wind up

originator architect, author, creator, father, founder, generator, innovator, inventor, maker, mother, pioneer, prime mover

ornament *n.* 1. accessory, adornment, bauble, decoration, embellishment, festoon, frill, furbelow, garnish, gewgaw, knick-knack, trimming, trinket 2. flower, honour, jewel, leading light, pride, treasure ~*v.* 3. adorn, beautify, bedizen (*Archaic*), brighten, deck, decorate, dress up, embellish, festoon, garnish, gild, grace, prettify, prink, trim

ornamental attractive, beautifying, decorative, embellishing, for show, showy

ornamentation adornment, decoration, elaboration, embellishment, embroidery, frills, ornateness

ornate aureate, baroque, beautiful, bedecked, busy, convoluted, decorated, elaborate, elegant, fancy, florid, flowery, fussy, high-wrought, ornamented, overelaborate, rococo
Antonyms austere, bare, basic, ordinary, plain, severe, simple, spartan, stark, subdued, unadorned, unfussy

orthodox accepted, approved, conformist, conventional, correct, customary, doctrinal, established, kosher (*Inf.*), official, received, sound, traditional, true, well-established
Antonyms eccentric, heretical, liberal, nonconformist, novel, off-the-wall (*Sl.*), original, radical, unconventional, unorthodox, unusual

orthodoxy authenticity, authoritativeness, authority, conformism, conformity, conventionality, devotion, devoutness, faithfulness, inflexibility, received wisdom, soundness, traditionalism
Antonyms flexibility, heresy, heterodoxy, impiety, nonconformism, nonconformity, unconventionality

oscillate fluctuate, seesaw, sway, swing, vacillate, vary, vibrate, waver
Antonyms commit oneself, decide, determine, purpose, resolve, settle

oscillation fluctuation, instability, seesawing, swing, vacillation, variation, wavering

ossified bony, fixed, fossilized, frozen, hardened, indurated (*Rare*), inflexible, petrified, rigid, rigidified, solid

ossify fossilize, freeze, harden, indurate (*Rare*), petrify, solidify, stiffen

ostensible alleged, apparent, avowed, exhibited, manifest, outward, plausible, pretended, professed, purported, seeming, so-called, specious, superficial, supposed

ostensibly apparently, for the ostensible purpose of, on the face of it, on the surface, professedly, seemingly, supposedly, to all intents and purposes

ostentation affectation, boasting, display, exhibitionism, flamboyance, flashiness, flaunting, flourish, pageantry, parade, pomp, pretension, pretentiousness, show, showiness, showing off (*Inf.*), swank (*Inf.*), vaunting, window-dressing
Antonyms humility, inconspicuousness, modesty, plainness, reserve, simplicity, unpretentiousness

ostentatious boastful, brash, conspicuous, crass, dashing, extravagant, flamboyant, flash (*Inf.*), flashy, flaunted, gaudy, loud, obtrusive, pompous, pretentious, showy, swanky (*Inf.*), vain, vulgar
Antonyms conservative, inconspicuous, low-key, modest, plain, reserved, simple, sombre

ostracism avoidance, banishment, boycott, cold-shouldering, exclusion, exile, expulsion, isolation, rejection
Antonyms acceptance, admission, approval, inclusion, invitation, reception, welcome

ostracize avoid, banish, blackball, blacklist, boycott, cast out, cold-shoulder, exclude, excommunicate, exile, expatriate, expel, give (someone) the cold shoulder, reject, send to Coventry, shun, snub
Antonyms accept, admit, approve, embrace, greet, include, invite, receive, welcome

other *adj.* 1. added, additional, alternative, auxiliary, extra, further, more, spare, supplementary 2. contrasting, different, dissimilar, distinct, diverse, remaining, separate, unrelated, variant

otherwise *adv.* 1. if not, or else, or then 2. any other way, contrarily, differently

ounce atom, crumb, drop, grain, iota, particle, scrap, shred, speck, trace, whit

oust depose, disinherit, dislodge, displace, dispossess, eject, evict, expel, relegate, throw out, topple, turn out, unseat

out *adj.* 1. impossible, not allowed, not on (*Inf.*), ruled out, unacceptable 2. abroad, absent, away, elsewhere, gone, not at home, outside 3. antiquated, behind the times, dated, dead, *démodé,* old-fashioned, old hat, passé, square (*Inf.*), unfashionable 4. at an end, cold, dead, doused, ended, exhausted, expired, extinguished, finished, used up
Antonyms (*sense 3*) à la mode, fashionable, in, in fashion, latest, modern, trendy (*Brit. inf.*), up-to-date, with it (*Inf.*)

out-and-out absolute, arrant, complete, consummate, deep-dyed (*Usu. derogatory*), downright, dyed-in-the-wool, outright, perfect, thoroughgoing, total, unmitigated, unqualified, utter

outbreak burst, epidemic, eruption, explosion, flare-up, flash, outburst, rash, spasm, upsurge

outburst access, attack, discharge, eruption, explosion, fit of temper, flare-up, gush, outbreak, outpouring, paroxysm, spasm, storm, surge

outcast *n.* castaway, derelict, displaced person, exile, leper, pariah, *persona non grata,* refugee, reprobate, untouchable, vagabond, wretch

outclass be a cut above (*Inf.*), beat, eclipse, exceed, excel, leave *or* put in the shade, leave standing (*Inf.*), outdistance, outdo, outrank, outshine, outstrip, overshadow, run rings around (*Inf.*), surpass

outcome aftereffect, aftermath, conclusion, consequence, end, end result, issue, payoff (*Inf.*), result, sequel, upshot

outcry clamour, commotion, complaint, cry, exclamation, howl, hue and cry, hullabaloo, noise, outburst, protest, scream, screech, uproar, yell

outdated antiquated, antique, archaic, behind the times, *démodé,* obsolete, old-fashioned, outmoded, out of date, out of style, passé, unfashionable
Antonyms à la mode, all the rage, contemporary, current, fashionable, in vogue, modern, modish, stylish, trendy (*Brit. inf.*), up-to-date, with it (*Inf.*)

outdistance leave behind, leave standing (*Inf.*), lose, outrun, outstrip, shake off

outdo beat, be one up on, best, eclipse, exceed, excel, get the better of, go one better than (*Inf.*), outclass, outdistance, outfox, outjockey, outmanoeuvre, outshine, outsmart (*Inf.*), overcome, run rings around (*Inf.*), surpass, top, transcend

outdoor alfresco, open-air, out-of-door(s), outside
Antonyms indoor, inside, interior, within

outer exposed, exterior, external, outlying, outside, outward, peripheral, remote, superficial, surface
Antonyms central, closer, inner, inside, interior, internal, inward, nearer

outface beard, brave, confront, defy, look straight in the eye, outstare, square up to, stare down, stare out (of countenance)

outfit *n.* 1. accoutrements, clothes, costume, ensemble, garb, gear (*Inf.*), get-up (*Inf.*), kit, rigout (*Inf.*), suit, togs (*Inf.*), trappings 2. *Inf.* clique, company, corps, coterie, crew, firm, *galère,* group, organization, set, setup (*Inf.*), squad, team, unit ~*v.* 3. accoutre, appoint, equip, fit out, furnish, kit out, provision, stock, supply, turn out

outfitter clothier, costumier, couturier, dressmaker, haberdasher (*U.S.*), modiste, tailor

outflow discharge, drainage, ebb, effluence, efflux, effusion, emanation, emergence, gush, issue, jet, outfall, outpouring, rush, spout

outgoing 1. departing, ex-, former, last, leaving, past, retiring, withdrawing 2. approachable, communicative, cordial, de~

monstrative, easy, expansive, extrovert, friendly, genial, gregarious, informal, open, sociable, sympathetic, unreserved, warm
Antonyms (*sense 1*) arriving, entering, incoming (*sense 2*) austere, cold, indifferent, reserved, retiring, withdrawn

outgoings costs, expenditure, expenses, outlay, overheads

outgrowth 1. bulge, excrescence, node, offshoot, outcrop, process, projection, protuberance, shoot, sprout 2. by-product, consequence, derivative, development, emergence, issue, product, result, spin-off, yield

outing excursion, expedition, jaunt, pleasure trip, spin (*Inf.*), trip

outlandish alien, barbarous, bizarre, eccentric, exotic, fantastic, far-out (*Sl.*), foreign, freakish, grotesque, *outré,* preposterous, queer, strange, unheard-of, weird
Antonyms banal, commonplace, everyday, familiar, humdrum, mundane, normal, ordinary, usual, well-known

outlast endure beyond, outlive, outstay, outwear, survive

outlaw 1. *n.* bandit, brigand, desperado, fugitive, highwayman, marauder, outcast, pariah, robber 2. *v.* ban, banish, bar, condemn, disallow, embargo, exclude, forbid, interdict, make illegal, prohibit, proscribe, put a price on (someone's) head
Antonyms (*sense 2*) allow, approve, authorize, consent, endorse, legalise, permit, sanction, support

outlay *n.* cost, disbursement, expenditure, expenses, investment, outgoings, spending

outlet 1. avenue, channel, duct, egress, exit, means of expression, opening, orifice, release, safety valve, vent, way out 2. market, shop, store

outline *n.* 1. draft, drawing, frame, framework, layout, lineament(s), plan, rough, skeleton, sketch, tracing 2. bare facts, main features, recapitulation, résumé, rough idea, rundown, summary, synopsis, thumbnail sketch 3. configuration, contour, delineation, figure, form, profile, shape, silhouette ~*v.* 4. adumbrate, delineate, draft, plan, rough out, sketch (in), summarize, trace

outlive come through, endure beyond, live through, outlast, survive

outlook 1. angle, attitude, frame of mind, perspective, point of view, slant, standpoint, viewpoint, views 2. expectations, forecast, future, prospect 3. aspect, panorama, prospect, scene, view, vista

outlying backwoods, distant, far-flung, in the middle of nowhere, outer, out-of-the-way, peripheral, provincial, remote

outmanoeuvre circumvent, get the better of, outdo, outflank, outfox, outgeneral, outjockey, outsmart (*Inf.*), outwit, run rings round (*Inf.*), steal a march on (*Inf.*)

outmoded anachronistic, antediluvian, antiquated, antique, archaic, behind the times, bygone, dated, *démodé,* fossilized, obsolescent, obsolete, olden (*Archaic*), oldfangled, old-fashioned, old-time, out, out of date, out of style, outworn, passé, square (*Inf.*), superannuated, superseded, unfashionable, unusable
Antonyms all the rage, fashionable, fresh, in vogue, latest, modern, modish, new, recent, usable

out of date antiquated, archaic, dated, discarded, elapsed, expired, extinct, invalid, lapsed, obsolete, old-fashioned, outmoded, outworn, passé, stale, superannuated, superseded, unfashionable
Antonyms contemporary, current, fashionable, in, new, now (*Inf.*), trendy (*Brit. inf.*), up to date, valid

out-of-the-way 1. distant, far-flung, inaccessible, isolated, lonely, obscure, off the beaten track, outlying, remote, secluded, unfrequented 2. abnormal, curious, exceptional, extraordinary, odd, outlandish, out of the ordinary, peculiar, strange, uncommon, unusual
Antonyms (*sense 1*) accessible, close, convenient, frequented, handy, near, nearby, proximate, reachable, within sniffing distance (*Inf.*)

out of work idle, jobless, laid off, on the dole (*Brit.*), out of a job, redundant, unemployed

outpouring cascade, debouchment, deluge, effluence, efflux, effusion, emanation, flow, flux, issue, outflow, spate, spurt, stream, torrent

output achievement, manufacture, outturn (*Rare*), product, production, productivity, yield

outrage *n.* 1. atrocity, barbarism, enormity, evil, inhumanity 2. abuse, affront, desecration, indignity, injury, insult, offence, profanation, rape, ravishing, shock, violation, violence 3. anger, fury, hurt, indignation, resentment, shock, wrath ~*v.* 4. affront, incense, infuriate, madden, make one's blood boil, offend, scandalize, shock 5. abuse, defile, desecrate, injure, insult, maltreat, rape, ravage, ravish, violate

outrageous 1. abominable, atrocious, barbaric, beastly, egregious, flagrant, heinous, horrible, infamous, inhuman, iniquitous, nefarious, scandalous, shocking, unspeakable, villainous, violent, wicked 2. disgraceful, excessive, exorbitant, extravagant,

immoderate, offensive, O.T.T. (*Sl.*), over the top (*Sl.*), preposterous, scandalous, shocking, steep (*Inf.*), unreasonable
Antonyms equitable, fair, just, mild, minor, moderate, reasonable, tolerable, trivial

outré bizarre, eccentric, extravagant, fantastic, freakish, freaky (*Sl.*), grotesque, indecorous, kinky (*Inf.*), odd, off-the-wall (*Sl.*), outlandish, rum (*Brit. sl.*), unconventional, way-out (*Inf.*), weird

outrider advance guard, advance man, attendant, bodyguard, escort, guard, harbinger, herald, precursor, scout, squire

outright *adj.* 1. absolute, arrant, complete, consummate, deep-dyed (*Usu. derogatory*), downright, out-and-out, perfect, pure, thorough, thoroughgoing, total, unconditional, undeniable, unmitigated, unqualified, utter, wholesale 2. definite, direct, flat, straightforward, unequivocal, unqualified ~*adv.* 3. absolutely, completely, explicitly, openly, overtly, straightforwardly, thoroughly, to the full, without hesitation, without restraint 4. at once, cleanly, immediately, instantaneously, instantly, on the spot, straight away, there and then, without more ado

outrun beat, escape, exceed, excel, get away from, leave behind, lose, outdistance, outdo, outpace, outstrip, shake off, surpass

outset beginning, commencement, early days, inauguration, inception, kickoff (*Inf.*), onset, opening, start, starting point
Antonyms closing, completion, conclusion, consummation, end, finale, finish, termination

outshine be head and shoulders above, be superior to, eclipse, leave *or* put in the shade, outclass, outdo, outstrip, overshadow, surpass, top, transcend, upstage

outside *adj.* 1. exterior, external, extramural, extraneous, extreme, out, outdoor, outer, outermost, outward, surface 2. distant, faint, marginal, negligible, remote, slight, slim, small, unlikely ~*n.* 3. exterior, façade, face, front, skin, surface, topside
Antonyms (*sense 1*) in, indoor, inner, innermost, inside, interior, internal, intramural, inward

outsider alien, foreigner, incomer, interloper, intruder, newcomer, nonmember, odd man out, outlander, stranger

outskirts borders, boundary, edge, environs, faubourgs, periphery, purlieus, suburbia, suburbs, vicinity

outsmart deceive, dupe, get the better of, go one better than (*Inf.*), make a fool of (*Inf.*), outfox, outjockey, outmanoeuvre, outperform, outthink, outwit, pull a fast one on (*Inf.*), put one over on (*Inf.*), run rings round (*Inf.*), trick

outspoken abrupt, blunt, candid, direct, downright, explicit, forthright, frank, free, free-spoken, open, plain-spoken, round, unceremonious, undissembling, unequivocal, unreserved
Antonyms diplomatic, gracious, judicious, reserved, reticent, tactful

outspread 1. *adj.* expanded, extended, fanlike, fanned out, flared, open, opened up, outstretched, unfolded, unfurled, wide-open 2. *v.* expand, extend, fan out, open, open wide, outstretch, spread out, unfold, unfurl

outstanding 1. celebrated, distinguished, eminent, excellent, exceptional, great, important, impressive, meritorious, pre-eminent, special, superior, superlative, well-known 2. arresting, conspicuous, eye-catching, marked, memorable, notable, noteworthy, prominent, salient, signal, striking 3. due, ongoing, open, owing, payable, pending, remaining, uncollected, unpaid, unresolved, unsettled
Antonyms (*senses 1 & 2*) dull, inferior, insignificant, mediocre, ordinary, pedestrian, run-of-the-mill, unexceptional, unimpressive

outstrip beat, better, eclipse, exceed, excel, get ahead of, leave behind, leave standing (*Inf.*), lose, outclass, outdistance, outdo, outpace, outperform, outrun, outshine, overtake, run rings around (*Inf.*), shake off, surpass, top, transcend

outward *adj.* apparent, evident, exterior, external, noticeable, observable, obvious, ostensible, outer, outside, perceptible, superficial, surface, visible
Antonyms inner, inside, interior, internal, invisible, inward, obscure, unnoticeable

outwardly apparently, as far as one can see, externally, officially, on the face of it, on the surface, ostensibly, professedly, seemingly, superficially, to all appearances, to all intents and purposes, to the eye

outweigh cancel (out), compensate for, eclipse, make up for, outbalance, overcome, override, predominate, preponderate, prevail over, take precedence over, tip the scales

outwit cheat, circumvent, deceive, defraud, dupe, get the better of, gull (*Archaic*), make a fool *or* monkey of, outfox, outjockey, outmanoeuvre, outsmart (*Inf.*), outthink, put one over on (*Inf.*), run rings round (*Inf.*), swindle, take in (*Inf.*)

outworn abandoned, antiquated, behind the times, defunct, discredited, disused, exhausted, hackneyed, obsolete, outdated,

outmoded, out of date, overused, rejected, stale, superannuated, threadbare, tired, worn-out
Antonyms credited, fresh, modish, new, recent, up to date, used

oval *adj.* egg-shaped, ellipsoidal, elliptical, ovate, oviform, ovoid

ovation acclaim, acclamation, applause, cheering, cheers, clapping, laudation, plaudits, tribute
Antonyms abuse, booing, catcalls, derision, heckling, jeers, jibes, mockery, ridicule

over *adj.* 1. accomplished, ancient history (*Inf.*), at an end, by, bygone, closed, completed, concluded, done (with), ended, finished, gone, past, settled, up (*Inf.*) *~adj./adv.* 2. beyond, extra, in addition, in excess, left over, remaining, superfluous, surplus, unused *~prep.* 3. above, on, on top of, superior to, upon 4. above, exceeding, in excess of, more than *~adv.* 5. above, aloft, on high, overhead 6. **over and above** added to, as well as, besides, in addition to, let alone, not to mention, on top of, plus 7. **over and over (again)** ad nauseam, again and again, frequently, often, repeatedly, time and again

overabundance embarrassment of riches, excess, glut, oversupply, plethora, profusion, superabundance, superfluity, surfeit, surplus, too much of a good thing

overact exaggerate, ham *or* ham up (*Inf.*), overdo, overplay

overall 1. *adj.* all-embracing, blanket, complete, comprehensive, general, global, inclusive, long-range, long-term, total, umbrella 2. *adv.* generally speaking, in general, in (the) large, in the long term, on the whole

overawe abash, alarm, browbeat, cow, daunt, frighten, intimidate, scare, terrify
Antonyms bolster, buoy up, cheer up, comfort, console, hearten, reassure

overbalance capsize, keel over, lose one's balance, lose one's footing, overset, overturn, slip, take a tumble, tip over, topple over, tumble, turn turtle, upset

overbearing arrogant, autocratic, bossy (*Inf.*), cavalier, despotic, dictatorial, dogmatic, domineering, haughty, high-handed, imperious, lordly, magisterial, officious, oppressive, overweening, peremptory, supercilious, superior, tyrannical
Antonyms deferential, humble, modest, self-effacing, submissive, unassertive, unassuming

overblown 1. disproportionate, excessive, fulsome, immoderate, inflated, overdone, undue 2. aureate, bombastic, euphuistic, florid, flowery, fustian, grandiloquent, magniloquent, pompous, turgid, windy

overcast clouded, clouded over, cloudy, darkened, dismal, dreary, dull, grey, hazy, leaden, louring *or* lowering, murky, sombre, sunless, threatening
Antonyms bright, brilliant, clear, cloudless, fine, sunny, unclouded

overcharge 1. cheat, clip (*Sl.*), diddle (*Inf.*), do (*Sl.*), fleece, rip off (*Sl.*), rook (*Sl.*), short-change, skin (*Sl.*), sting (*Inf.*), surcharge 2. burden, oppress, overburden, overload, overtask, overtax, strain, surfeit 3. *Literary* embellish, embroider, exaggerate, hyperbolize, lay it on thick (*Inf.*), overstate

overcome 1. *v.* beat, best, be victorious, blow out of the water (*Sl.*), clobber (*Sl.*), come out on top (*Inf.*), conquer, crush, defeat, get the better of, lick (*Inf.*), master, overpower, overthrow, overwhelm, prevail, render incapable (helpless, powerless), rise above, subdue, subjugate, surmount, survive, tank (*Sl.*), triumph over, undo, vanquish, weather, wipe the floor with (*Inf.*), worst 2. *adj.* affected, at a loss for words, bowled over (*Inf.*), overwhelmed, speechless, swept off one's feet, unable to continue, visibly moved

overconfident brash, cocksure, foolhardy, hubristic, overweening, presumptuous, riding for a fall (*Inf.*), uppish (*Brit. inf.*)
Antonyms cautious, diffident, doubtful, hesitant, insecure, timid, timorous, uncertain, unsure

overcritical captious, carping, cavilling, fault-finding, hairsplitting, hard to please, hypercritical, nit-picking (*Inf.*), overparticular, pedantic, pernickety (*Inf.*), picky (*Inf.*)
Antonyms easily pleased, easy-going, laid-back (*Inf.*), lenient, tolerant, uncritical, undemanding, unfussy

overcrowded choked, congested, crammed full, hoatching (*Scot.*), jam-packed, like the Black Hole of Calcutta, overloaded, overpopulated, packed (out), swarming
Antonyms abandoned, deserted, desolate, empty, forsaken, unoccupied, vacant

overdo 1. be intemperate, belabour, carry too far, do to death (*Inf.*), exaggerate, gild the lily, go overboard (*Inf.*), go to extremes, lay it on thick (*Inf.*), not know when to stop, overindulge, overplay, overreach, overstate, overuse, overwork, run riot 2. **overdo it** bite off more than one can chew, burn the candle at both ends (*Inf.*), drive oneself, fatigue, go too far, have too many irons in the fire, overburden, overload, overtax one's strength, overtire, overwork, strain *or* overstrain oneself, wear oneself out

Antonyms (*sense 1*) belittle, disparage, minimize, play down, underplay, under~ rate, understate, underuse, undervalue

overdone 1. beyond all bounds, exaggerat~ ed, excessive, fulsome, hyped, immoderate, inordinate, overelaborate, preposterous, too much, undue, unnecessary 2. burnt, burnt to a cinder, charred, dried up, overcooked, spoiled

Antonyms (*sense 1*) belittled, minimized, moderated, played down, underdone, underplayed, understated

overdue behindhand, behind schedule, be~ hind time, belated, late, long delayed, not before time (*Inf.*), owing, tardy, unpunctual

Antonyms ahead of time, beforehand, ear~ ly, in advance, in good time, punctual

overeat binge (*Inf.*), eat like a horse (*Inf.*), gorge, gormandize, guzzle, make a pig of oneself (*Inf.*), overindulge, pack away (*Sl.*), pig away (*Sl.*), pig out (*Sl.*), stuff, stuff oneself

overemphasize belabour, blow up out of all proportion, lay too much stress on, make a big thing of (*Inf.*), make a federal case of (*U.S. inf.*), make a mountain out of a molehill (*Inf.*), make a production (out) of (*Inf.*), make something out of nothing, make too much of, overdramatize, overstress

Antonyms belittle, downplay, make light of, minimize, play down, underplay, under~ rate, understate

overexert burn the candle at both ends (*Inf.*), do too much, drive (oneself), fatigue, knock (oneself) out, overstrain, overtax, overtire, overwork, push (oneself) too hard, strain, wear out, work to death

overflow *v.* 1. bubble (brim, fall, pour, run, slop, well) over, discharge, pour out, run with, shower, spill, spray, surge 2. cover, deluge, drown, flood, inundate, soak, sub~ merge, swamp ~*n.* 3. discharge, flash flood, flood, flooding, inundation, overabun~ dance, spill, spilling over, surplus

overflowing abounding, bountiful, brim~ ful, copious, plentiful, profuse, rife, superabundant, swarming, teeming, thronged

Antonyms deficient, inadequate, insuffi~ cient, lacking, missing, scarce, wanting

overhang *v.* beetle, bulge, cast a shadow, extend, impend, jut, loom, project, pro~ trude, stick out, threaten

overhaul *v.* 1. check, do up (*Inf.*), examine, inspect, recondition, re-examine, repair, restore, service, survey ~*n.* 2. check, check~ up, examination, going-over (*Inf.*), inspec~ tion, reconditioning, service ~*v.* 3. catch up with, draw level with, get ahead of, over~ take, pass

overhead 1. *adv.* above, aloft, atop, in the sky, on high, skyward, up above, upward 2. *adj.* aerial, overhanging, roof, upper

Antonyms (*sense 1*) below, beneath, downward, underfoot, underneath

overheads burden, oncosts, operating cost(s), running cost(s)

overheated agitated, fiery, flaming, im~ passioned, inflamed, overexcited, roused

Antonyms calm, collected, composed, cool, dispassionate, unemotional, unexcit~ ed, unfazed (*Inf.*), unruffled

overindulge be immoderate *or* intemper~ ate, drink *or* eat too much, have a binge (*Inf.*), live it up (*Inf.*), make a pig of oneself (*Inf.*), overdo it, pig out (*Sl.*)

overindulgence excess, immoderation, in~ temperance, overeating, surfeit

overjoyed cock-a-hoop, delighted, deliri~ ously happy, elated, euphoric, happy as a lark, in raptures, joyful, jubilant, on cloud nine (*Inf.*), only too happy, over the moon (*Inf.*), rapt, rapturous, thrilled, tickled pink (*Inf.*), transported

Antonyms crestfallen, dejected, disap~ pointed, downcast, heartbroken, miserable, sad, unhappy, woebegone

overlay 1. *v.* adorn, blanket, cover, inlay, laminate, ornament, overspread, superim~ pose, veneer 2. *n.* adornment, appliqué, covering, decoration, ornamentation, ve~ neer

overload burden, encumber, oppress, over~ burden, overcharge, overtax, saddle (with), strain, weigh down

overlook 1. disregard, fail to notice, forget, ignore, leave out of consideration, leave undone, miss, neglect, omit, pass, slight, slip up on 2. blink at, condone, disregard, excuse, forgive, let bygones be bygones, let one off with, let pass, let ride, make allow~ ances for, pardon, turn a blind eye to, wink at 3. afford a view of, command a view of, front on to, give upon, have a view of, look over *or* out on

Antonyms (*sense 1*) discern, heed, mark, note, notice, observe, perceive, regard, spot

overly exceedingly, excessively, immoder~ ately, inordinately, over, too, unduly, very much

overpower beat, clobber (*Sl.*), conquer, crush, defeat, get the upper hand over, im~ mobilize, knock out, lick (*Inf.*), master, overcome, overthrow, overwhelm, quell, subdue, subjugate, vanquish

overpowering compelling, extreme, force~ ful, invincible, irrefutable, irresistible, nauseating, overwhelming, powerful, sickening, strong, suffocating, telling, unbearable, uncontrollable

overrate assess too highly, exaggerate, make too much of, overestimate, overpraise, overprize, oversell, overvalue, rate too highly, think *or* expect too much of, think too highly of

overreach 1. **overreach oneself** be hoist with one's own petard, bite off more than one can chew, defeat one's own ends, go too far, have one's schemes rebound (backfire, boomerang) on one, try to be too clever 2. cheat, circumvent, deceive, defraud, dupe, gull (*Archaic*), outsmart (*Inf.*), outwit, swindle, trick, victimize

override annul, cancel, countermand, discount, disregard, ignore, nullify, outweigh, overrule, quash, reverse, ride roughshod over, set aside, supersede, take no account of, trample underfoot, upset, vanquish

overriding cardinal, compelling, determining, dominant, final, major, number one, overruling, paramount, pivotal, predominant, prevailing, primary, prime, ruling, supreme, ultimate

Antonyms immaterial, inconsequential, insignificant, irrelevant, minor, negligible, paltry, petty, trifling, trivial, unimportant

overrule 1. alter, annul, cancel, countermand, disallow, invalidate, make null and void, outvote, override, overturn, recall, repeal, rescind, reverse, revoke, rule against, set aside, veto 2. bend to one's will, control, direct, dominate, govern, influence, prevail over, sway

Antonyms (*sense 1*) allow, approve, consent to, endorse, pass, permit, sanction

overrun 1. cut to pieces, invade, massacre, occupy, overwhelm, put to flight, rout, swamp 2. choke, infest, inundate, overflow, overgrow, permeate, ravage, spread like wildfire, spread over, surge over, swarm over 3. exceed, go beyond, overshoot, run over *or* on

overseer boss (*Inf.*), chief, foreman, gaffer (*Inf., chiefly Brit.*), manager, master, super (*Inf.*), superintendent, superior, supervisor

overshadow 1. dominate, dwarf, eclipse, excel, leave *or* put in the shade, outshine, outweigh, render insignificant by comparison, rise above, steal the limelight from, surpass, take precedence over, throw into the shade, tower above 2. adumbrate, becloud, bedim, cloud, darken, dim, obfuscate, obscure, veil 3. blight, cast a gloom upon, mar, ruin, spoil, take the edge off, take the pleasure *or* enjoyment out of, temper

oversight 1. blunder, carelessness, delinquency, error, fault, inattention, lapse, laxity, mistake, neglect, omission, slip 2. administration, care, charge, control, custody, direction, handling, inspection, keeping, management, superintendence, supervision, surveillance

overt apparent, blatant, manifest, observable, obvious, open, patent, plain, public, unconcealed, undisguised, visible

Antonyms concealed, covert, disguised, hidden, hush-hush (*Inf.*), invisible, secret, surreptitious, underhand

overtake 1. catch up with, do better than, draw level with, get past, leave behind, outdistance, outdo, outstrip, overhaul, pass 2. befall, catch unprepared, come upon, engulf, happen, hit, overwhelm, strike, take by surprise

overthrow *v.* 1. abolish, beat, bring down, conquer, crush, defeat, depose, dethrone, do away with, master, oust, overcome, overpower, overwhelm, subdue, subjugate, topple, unseat, vanquish 2. bring to ruin, demolish, destroy, knock down, level, overturn, put an end to, raze, ruin, subvert, upend, upset ~*n.* 3. defeat, deposition, destruction, dethronement, discomfiture, disestablishment, displacement, dispossession, downfall, end, fall, ousting, prostration, rout, ruin, subjugation, subversion, suppression, undoing, unseating

Antonyms *v.* defend, guard, keep, maintain, preserve, protect, restore, support, uphold ~*n.* defence, preservation, protection

overtone association, connotation, flavour, hint, implication, innuendo, intimation, nuance, sense, suggestion, undercurrent

overture 1. *Often plural* advance, approach, conciliatory move, invitation, offer, opening move, proposal, proposition, signal, tender 2. *Music* introduction, opening, prelude

Antonyms afterword, close, coda, epilogue, finale, rebuke, rejection, withdrawal

overturn 1. capsize, keel over, knock over *or* down, overbalance, reverse, spill, tip over, topple, tumble, upend, upset, upturn 2. abolish, annul, bring down, countermand, depose, destroy, invalidate, obviate, overthrow, repeal, rescind, reverse, set aside, unseat

overused cliché'd, hackneyed, platitudinous, played out, stale, stereotyped, threadbare, tired, unoriginal, worn (out)

overweening 1. arrogant, cavalier, cocksure, cocky, conceited, egotistical, haughty, high and mighty (*Inf.*), high-handed, insolent, lordly, opinionated, pompous, presumptuous, proud, self-confident, supercilious, uppish (*Brit. inf.*), vain, vaing: lori-

ous 2. blown up out of all proportion, excessive, extravagant, immoderate
Antonyms (*sense 1*) deferential, diffident, hesitant, modest, self-conscious, self-effacing, timid, unassuming, unobtrusive

overweight *adj.* ample, bulky, buxom, chubby, chunky, corpulent, fat, fleshy, gross, heavy, hefty, huge, massive, obese, on the plump side, outsize, plump, podgy, portly, stout, tubby (*Inf.*), well-padded (*Inf.*), well-upholstered (*Inf.*)
Antonyms emaciated, gaunt, lean, pinched, scraggy, scrawny, skinny, thin, underweight

overwhelm 1. bury, crush, deluge, engulf, flood, inundate, snow under, submerge, swamp 2. bowl over (*Inf.*), confuse, devastate, knock (someone) for six (*Inf.*), overcome, overpower, prostrate, render speechless, stagger 3. crush, cut to pieces, destroy, massacre, overpower, overrun, rout

overwhelming breathtaking, crushing, devastating, invincible, irresistible, overpowering, shattering, stunning, towering, uncontrollable, vast, vastly superior
Antonyms commonplace, incidental, insignificant, negligible, paltry, resistible, trivial, unimportant

overwork be a slave-driver *or* hard taskmaster to, burden, burn the midnight oil, drive into the ground, exhaust, exploit, fatigue, oppress, overstrain, overtax, overuse, prostrate, strain, sweat (*Inf.*), wear out, weary, work one's fingers to the bone

overwrought 1. agitated, beside oneself, distracted, excited, frantic, in a state (tizzy (*Inf.*), twitter (*Inf.*)) (*Inf.*), keyed up, on edge, overexcited, overworked, stirred, strung up (*Inf.*), tense, uptight (*Inf.*), wired (*Sl.*), worked up (*Inf.*), wound up (*Inf.*) 2. baroque, busy, contrived, florid, flowery, fussy, overdone, overelaborate, overembellished, overornate, rococo
Antonyms (*sense 1*) calm, collected, controlled, cool, dispassionate, emotionless, impassive, self-contained, unfazed (*Inf.*), unmoved

owe be beholden to, be in arrears, be in debt, be obligated *or* indebted, be under an obligation to

owing *adj.* due, outstanding, overdue, owed, payable, unpaid, unsettled

owing to *prep.* as a result of, because of, on account of

own *adj.* 1. individual, particular, personal, private 2. **on one's own** alone, by oneself, by one's own efforts, independently, isolated, left to one's own devices, off one's own bat, on one's tod (*Brit. sl.*), singly, (standing) on one's own two feet, unaided, unassisted 3. **hold one's own** compete, keep going, keep one's end up, keep one's head above water, maintain one's position ~*v.* 4. be in possession of, be responsible for, enjoy, have, hold, keep, possess, retain 5. **own up (to)** admit, come clean (about) (*Inf.*), confess, make a clean breast of, tell the truth (about) 6. acknowledge, admit, allow, allow to be valid, avow, concede, confess, disclose, go along with, grant, recognize

owner holder, landlord, lord, master, mistress, possessor, proprietor, proprietress, proprietrix

ownership dominion, possession, proprietary rights, proprietorship, right of possession, title

P

pace *n.* 1. gait, measure, step, stride, tread, walk 2. clip (*Inf.*), lick (*Inf.*), momentum, motion, movement, progress, rate, speed, tempo, time, velocity ~*v.* 3. march, patrol, pound, stride, walk back and forth, walk up and down 4. count, determine, mark out, measure, step

pacific 1. appeasing, conciliatory, diplomatic, irenic, pacificatory, peacemaking, placatory, propitiatory 2. dovelike, dovish, friendly, gentle, mild, nonbelligerent, nonviolent, pacifist, peaceable, peace-loving 3. at peace, calm, halcyon, peaceful, placid, quiet, serene, smooth, still, tranquil, unruffled
Antonyms aggressive, antagonistic, belligerent, hostile, nonconciliatory, pugnacious, Ramboesque, unforgiving, unfriendly, violent, warlike

pacifist conchie (*Inf.*), conscientious objector, dove, passive resister, peace lover, peacemonger, peacenik (*Inf.*), satyagrahi

pacify 1. allay, ameliorate, appease, assuage, calm, compose, conciliate, make peace, moderate, mollify, placate, pour oil on troubled waters, propitiate, quiet, restore harmony, smooth down *or* over, smooth one's ruffled feathers, soften, soothe, still, tranquillize 2. chasten, crush, impose peace, put down, quell, repress, silence, subdue, tame

pack *n.* 1. back pack, bale, bundle, burden, fardel (*Archaic*), kit, kitbag, knapsack, load, package, packet, parcel, rucksack, truss 2. assemblage, band, bunch, collection, company, crew, crowd, deck, drove, flock, gang, group, herd, lot, mob, set, troop ~*v.* 3. batch, bundle, burden, load, package, packet, store, stow 4. charge, compact, compress, cram, crowd, fill, jam, mob, press, ram, stuff, tamp, throng, wedge 5. *With* **off** bundle out, dismiss, hustle out, send someone about his business, send away, send packing (*Inf.*)

package *n.* 1. box, carton, container, packet, parcel 2. amalgamation, combination, entity, unit, whole ~*v.* 3. batch, box, pack, packet, parcel (up), wrap, wrap up

packed brimful, chock-a-block, chock-full, congested, cram-full, crammed, crowded, filled, full, hoatching (*Scot.*), jammed, jam-packed, loaded *or* full to the gunwales, overflowing, overloaded, packed like sardines, seething, swarming
Antonyms deserted, empty, uncongested, uncrowded

packet 1. bag, carton, container, package, parcel, poke (*Dialect*), wrapper, wrapping 2. *Sl.* a bob or two (*Brit. inf.*), big bucks (*Inf., chiefly U.S.*), big money, bomb (*Brit. sl.*), bundle (*Sl.*), fortune, king's ransom (*Inf.*), lot(s), megabucks (*U.S. & Canad. sl.*), mint, pile (*Inf.*), pot(s) (*Inf.*), pretty penny (*Inf.*), tidy sum (*Inf.*), wad (*U.S. & Canad. sl.*)

pack in 1. attract, cram, draw, fill to capacity, squeeze in 2. *Brit. inf.* cease, chuck (*Inf.*), desist, give up *or* over, jack in, kick (*Inf.*), leave off, stop

pack up 1. put away, store, tidy up 2. *Inf.* call it a day (*Inf.*), finish, give up, pack in (*Brit. inf.*) 3. break down, conk out (*Inf.*), fail, give out, stall, stop

pact agreement, alliance, arrangement, bargain, bond, compact, concord, concordat, contract, convention, covenant, deal, league, protocol, treaty, understanding

pad[1] *n.* 1. buffer, cushion, protection, stiffening, stuffing, wad 2. block, jotter, notepad, tablet, writing pad 3. foot, paw, sole 4. *Sl.* apartment, flat, hang-out (*Inf.*), home, place, quarters, room ~*v.* 5. cushion, fill, line, pack, protect, shape, stuff 6. *Often with* **out** amplify, augment, eke, elaborate, fill out, flesh out, inflate, lengthen, protract, spin out, stretch

pad[2] *v.* 1. creep, go barefoot, pussyfoot (*Inf.*), sneak, steal 2. hike, march, plod, traipse (*Inf.*), tramp, trek, trudge, walk

padding 1. filling, packing, stuffing, wadding 2. hot air (*Inf.*), prolixity, verbiage, verbosity, waffle (*Inf., chiefly Brit.*), wordiness

paddle[1] 1. *n.* oar, scull, sweep 2. *v.* oar, propel, pull, row, scull

paddle[2] dabble, plash, slop, splash (about), stir, wade

paddy bate (*Brit. sl.*), fit of temper, paddywhack (*Brit. inf.*), passion, rage, tantrum, temper, tiff, wax (*Inf., chiefly Brit.*)

paean 1. anthem, hymn, psalm, thanksgiving 2. encomium, eulogy, hymn of praise, ovation, panegyric, rave review (*Inf.*)

pagan 1. *n.* Gentile, heathen, idolater, infidel, polytheist, unbeliever 2. *adj.* Gentile, heathen, heathenish, idolatrous, infidel, irreligious, polytheistic

page[1] *n.* 1. folio, leaf, sheet, side 2. chapter, episode, epoch, era, event, incident, period, phase, point, stage, time ~*v.* 3. foliate, number, paginate

page[2] 1. *n.* attendant, bellboy (*U.S.*), footboy, pageboy, servant, squire 2. *v.* announce, call, call out, preconize, seek, send for, summon

pageant display, extravaganza, parade, procession, ritual, show, spectacle, tableau

pageantry display, drama, extravagance, glamour, glitter, grandeur, magnificence, parade, pomp, show, showiness, spectacle, splash (*Inf.*), splendour, state, theatricality

pain *n.* 1. ache, cramp, discomfort, hurt, irritation, pang, smarting, soreness, spasm, suffering, tenderness, throb, throe (*Rare*), trouble, twinge 2. affliction, agony, anguish, bitterness, distress, grief, hardship, heartache, misery, suffering, torment, torture, tribulation, woe, wretchedness 3. *Inf.* aggravation, annoyance, bore, bother, drag (*Inf.*), gall, headache (*Inf.*), irritation, nuisance, pain in the arse (*Taboo inf.*), pain in the neck (*Inf.*), pest, vexation ~*v.* 4. ail, chafe, discomfort, harm, hurt, inflame, injure, smart, sting, throb 5. afflict, aggrieve, agonize, cut to the quick, disquiet, distress, grieve, hurt, sadden, torment, torture, vex, worry, wound 6. *Inf.* annoy, exasperate, gall, harass, irritate, nark (*Brit., Aust., & N.Z. sl.*), rile, vex

pained aggrieved, anguished, distressed, hurt, injured, miffed (*Inf.*), offended, reproachful, stung, unhappy, upset, worried, wounded

painful 1. afflictive, disagreeable, distasteful, distressing, grievous, saddening, unpleasant 2. aching, agonizing, excruciating, harrowing, hurting, inflamed, raw, smarting, sore, tender, throbbing 3. arduous, difficult, hard, laborious, severe, tedious, troublesome, trying, vexatious 4. *Inf.* abysmal, awful, dire, dreadful, excruciating, extremely bad, godawful, terrible

Antonyms (*sense 1*) agreeable, enjoyable, pleasant, satisfying (*sense 2*) comforting, painless, relieving, soothing (*sense 3*) a piece of cake (*Inf.*), easy, effortless, interesting, short, simple, straightforward, undemanding

painfully alarmingly, clearly, deplorably, distressingly, dreadfully, excessively, markedly, sadly, unfortunately, woefully

painkiller anaesthetic, analgesic, anodyne, drug, palliative, remedy, sedative

painless easy, effortless, fast, no trouble, pain-free, quick, simple, trouble-free

pains 1. assiduousness, bother, care, diligence, effort, industry, labour, special attention, trouble 2. birth-pangs, childbirth, contractions, labour

painstaking assiduous, careful, conscientious, diligent, earnest, exacting, hard-working, industrious, meticulous, persevering, punctilious, scrupulous, sedulous, strenuous, thorough, thoroughgoing

Antonyms careless, half-hearted, haphazard, heedless, lazy, negligent, slapdash, slipshod, thoughtless

paint *n.* 1. colour, colouring, dye, emulsion, pigment, stain, tint 2. *Inf.* cosmetics, face (*Inf.*), greasepaint, make-up, *maquillage*, war paint (*Inf.*) ~*v.* 3. catch a likeness, delineate, depict, draw, figure, picture, portray, represent, sketch 4. apply, coat, colour, cover, daub, decorate, slap on (*Inf.*) 5. bring to life, capture, conjure up a vision, depict, describe, evoke, make one see, portray, put graphically, recount, tell vividly 6. **paint the town red** *Inf.* carouse, celebrate, go on a binge (*Inf.*), go on a spree, go on the town, live it up (*Inf.*), make merry, make whoopee (*Inf.*), revel

pair 1. *n.* brace, combination, couple, doublet, duo, match, matched set, span, twins, two of a kind, twosome, yoke 2. *v.* bracket, couple, join, marry, match, match up, mate, pair off, put together, team, twin, wed, yoke

pal boon companion, buddy (*Inf.*), chum (*Inf.*), cock (*Brit. inf.*), companion, comrade, crony, friend, mate (*Inf.*)

palatable 1. appetizing, delectable, delicious, luscious, mouthwatering, savoury, tasty, toothsome 2. acceptable, agreeable, attractive, enjoyable, fair, pleasant, satisfactory

Antonyms (*sense 1*) bland, flat, insipid, stale, tasteless, unappetizing, unpalatable

palate 1. appetite, heart, stomach, taste 2. appreciation, enjoyment, gusto, liking, relish, zest

palatial de luxe, gorgeous, grand, grandiose, illustrious, imposing, luxurious, magnificent, majestic, opulent, plush (*Inf.*), regal, spacious, splendid, splendiferous (*Facetious*), stately, sumptuous

palaver *n.* 1. business (*Inf.*), carry-on (*Inf., chiefly Brit.*), performance (*Inf.*), procedure, rigmarole, song and dance (*Brit. inf.*), to-do 2. babble, blather, blether, chatter, hubbub, natter (*Brit.*), prattle, tongue-wagging, yak (*Sl.*) 3. colloquy, confab (*Inf.*), conference, discussion, get-together (*Inf.*), parley, powwow, session ~*v.* 4. confab (*Inf.*), confer, discuss, go into a huddle (*Inf.*), parley, powwow, put heads together 5. blather, blether, chatter, gabble, jabber, jaw (*Sl.*), natter (*Brit.*), prattle, yak (*Sl.*)

pale[1] *adj.* 1. anaemic, ashen, ashy, bleached, bloodless, colourless, faded, light, pallid, pasty, sallow, wan, washed-out, white, whitish 2. dim, faint, feeble, inadequate, poor, thin, weak ~*v.* 3. become pale, blanch, go white, lose colour, whiten 4. decrease, dim, diminish, dull, fade, grow dull, lessen, lose lustre

Antonyms (*sense 1*) blooming, florid, flushed, glowing, rosy-cheeked, rubicund, ruddy, sanguine

pale[2] *n.* 1. paling, palisade, picket, post, slat, stake, upright 2. barricade, barrier, fence, palisade, railing 3. border, boundary, bounds, confines, district, limits, region, territory 4. **beyond the pale** barbaric, forbidden, improper, inadmissible, indecent, irregular, not done, out of line, unacceptable, unseemly, unspeakable, unsuitable

palisade bulwark, defence, enclosure, fence, paling, stockade

pall[1] *n.* 1. cloud, mantle, shadow, shroud, veil 2. check, damp, damper, dismay, gloom, melancholy

pall[2] *v.* become dull *or* tedious, bore, cloy, glut, jade, satiate, sicken, surfeit, tire, weary

palliate 1. abate, allay, alleviate, assuage, diminish, ease, mitigate, moderate, mollify, relax, relieve, soften, soothe, temper 2. cloak, conceal, cover, excuse, extenuate, gloss over, hide, lessen, minimize, paper over the cracks (*Inf.*), varnish, whitewash (*Inf.*)

palliative 1. *adj.* alleviative, anodyne, assuasive, calmative, calming, demulcent, lenitive, mitigative, mitigatory, mollifying, soothing 2. *n.* analgesic, anodyne, calmative, demulcent, drug, lenitive, painkiller, sedative, tranquillizer

pallid 1. anaemic, ashen, ashy, cadaverous, colourless, pale, pasty, sallow, wan, waxen, wheyfaced, whitish 2. anaemic, bloodless, colourless, insipid, lifeless, spiritless, sterile, tame, tired, uninspired, vapid

pallor ashen hue, bloodlessness, lack of colour, paleness, pallidness, wanness, whiteness

pally affectionate, buddy-buddy (*Sl., chiefly U.S. & Canad.*), chummy (*Inf.*), close, familiar, friendly, intimate, palsy-walsy (*Inf.*), thick as thieves (*Inf.*)

palm[1] 1. hand, hook, meathook (*Sl.*), mitt (*Sl.*), paw (*Inf.*) 2. **in the palm of one's hand** at one's mercy, in one's clutches (control, power) 3. **grease someone's palm** *Sl.* bribe, buy, corrupt, fix (*Inf.*), give a backhander (*Sl.*), induce, influence, pay off (*Inf.*), square, suborn

palm[2] *Fig.* bays, crown, fame, glory, honour, laurels, merit, prize, success, triumph, trophy, victory

palm off 1. *With* **on** *or* **with** fob off, foist off, pass off 2. *With* **on** foist on, force upon, impose upon, take advantage of, thrust upon, unload upon

palmy flourishing, fortunate, glorious, golden, halcyon, happy, joyous, luxurious, prosperous, thriving, triumphant

palpable 1. apparent, blatant, clear, conspicuous, evident, manifest, obvious, open, patent, plain, unmistakable, visible 2. concrete, material, real, solid, substantial, tangible, touchable

palpitate beat, flutter, pitapat, pitter-patter, pound, pulsate, pulse, quiver, shiver, throb, tremble, vibrate

palsied arthritic, atonic (*Pathol.*), crippled, debilitated, disabled, helpless, paralysed, paralytic, rheumatic, sclerotic, shaking, shaky, spastic, trembling

palter 1. be evasive, deceive, double-talk, equivocate, flannel (*Brit. inf.*), fudge, hedge, mislead, prevaricate, shuffle, tergiversate, trifle 2. bargain, barter, chaffer, dicker (*Chiefly U.S.*), haggle, higgle

paltry base, beggarly, chickenshit (*U.S. sl.*), contemptible, crappy (*Sl.*), derisory, despicable, inconsiderable, insignificant, low, meagre, mean, measly, Mickey Mouse (*Sl.*), minor, miserable, nickel-and-dime (*U.S. sl.*), petty, picayune (*U.S.*), piddling (*Inf.*), pitiful, poor, poxy (*Sl.*), puny, slight, small, sorry, trifling, trivial, twopenny-halfpenny (*Brit. inf.*), unimportant, worthless, wretched

Antonyms consequential, considerable, essential, grand, important, major, mega (*Sl.*), significant, valuable

pamper baby, cater to one's every whim, coddle, cosset, fondle, gratify, humour, indulge, mollycoddle, pander to, pet, spoil

pamphlet booklet, brochure, circular, folder, leaflet, tract

pan[1] *n.* 1. container, pot, saucepan, vessel ~*v.* 2. look for, search for, separate, sift out, wash 3. *Inf.* blast, censure, criticize, flay, hammer (*Brit. inf.*), knock (*Inf.*), lambast(e), put down, roast (*Inf.*), rubbish (*Inf.*), slam (*Sl.*), slag (off) (*Sl.*), slate (*Inf.*), tear into (*Inf.*), throw brickbats at (*Inf.*)

pan[2] *v.* follow, move, scan, sweep, swing, track, traverse

panacea catholicon, cure-all, elixir, nostrum, sovereign remedy, universal cure

panache a flourish, brio, dash, élan, flair, flamboyance, spirit, style, swagger, verve

pandemonium babel, bedlam, chaos, clamour, commotion, confusion, din, hubbub, hue and cry, hullabaloo, racket, ruckus (*Inf.*), ruction (*Inf.*), rumpus, tumult, turmoil, uproar
Antonyms arrangement, calm, hush, order, peace, peacefulness, quietude, repose, stillness, tranquillity

pander 1. *v. With* to cater to, gratify, indulge, play up to (*Inf.*), please, satisfy 2. *n.* go-between, mack (*Sl.*), pimp, ponce (*Sl.*), procurer, white-slaver, whoremaster (*Archaic*)

panegyric accolade, commendation, encomium, eulogy, homage, paean, praise, tribute

panegyrical commendatory, complimentary, encomiastic, eulogistic, favourable, flattering, glowing, laudatory

pang ache, agony, anguish, discomfort, distress, gripe, pain, prick, spasm, stab, sting, stitch, throe (*Rare*), twinge, wrench

panic 1. *n.* agitation, alarm, consternation, dismay, fear, fright, horror, hysteria, scare, terror 2. *v.* become hysterical, be terror-stricken, go to pieces, lose one's bottle (*Brit. sl.*), lose one's nerve, overreact 3. alarm, put the wind up (someone) (*Inf.*), scare, startle, terrify, unnerve

panicky afraid, agitated, distressed, fearful, frantic, frenzied, frightened, hysterical, in a flap (*Inf.*), in a tizzy (*Inf.*), jittery (*Inf.*), nervous, windy (*Sl.*), worked up, worried
Antonyms calm, collected, composed, confident, cool, imperturbable, self-controlled, together (*Sl.*), unexcitable, unfazed (*Inf.*), unflappable, unruffled

panic-stricken *or* **panic-struck** aghast, agitated, alarmed, appalled, fearful, frenzied, frightened, frightened out of one's wits, frightened to death, horrified, horror-stricken, hysterical, in a cold sweat (*Inf.*), panicky, petrified, scared, scared shitless (*Taboo sl.*), scared stiff, shit-scared (*Taboo sl.*), startled, terrified, terror-stricken, unnerved

panoply array, attire, dress, garb, get-up (*Inf.*), insignia, raiment (*Archaic or poetic*), regalia, show, trappings, turnout

panorama 1. bird's-eye view, prospect, scenery, scenic view, view, vista 2. overall picture, overview, perspective, survey

panoramic all-embracing, bird's-eye, comprehensive, extensive, far-reaching, general, inclusive, overall, scenic, sweeping, wide

pan out come out, come to pass (*Archaic*), culminate, eventuate, happen, result, turn out, work out

pant *v.* 1. blow, breathe, gasp, heave, huff, palpitate, puff, throb, wheeze 2. *Fig.* ache, covet, crave, desire, eat one's heart out over, hanker after, hunger, long, pine, set one's heart on, sigh, thirst, want, yearn ~*n.* 3. gasp, huff, puff, wheeze

panting *adj.* 1. breathless, gasping, out of breath, out of puff, puffed, puffed out, puffing, short of breath, winded 2. agog, all agog, anxious, champing at the bit (*Inf.*), eager, impatient, raring to go

pants 1. *Brit.* boxer shorts, briefs, drawers, knickers, panties, underpants, Y-fronts (*Trademark*) 2. *U.S.* slacks, trousers

pap 1. baby food, mash, mush, pulp 2. drivel, rubbish, trash, trivia

paper *n.* 1. *Often plural* certificate, deed, documents, instrument, record 2. *Plural* archive, diaries, documents, dossier, file, letters, records 3. daily, blat, gazette, journal, news, newspaper, organ, rag (*Inf.*) 4. analysis, article, assignment, composition, critique, dissertation, essay, examination, monograph, report, script, study, thesis, treatise 5. **on paper** ideally, in the abstract, in theory, theoretically ~*adj.* 6. cardboard, disposable, flimsy, insubstantial, paper-thin, papery, thin ~*v.* 7. cover with paper, hang, line, paste up, wallpaper

papery flimsy, fragile, frail, insubstantial, light, lightweight, paperlike, paper-thin, thin

par *n.* 1. average, level, mean, median, norm, standard, usual 2. balance, equal footing, equality, equilibrium, equivalence, parity 3. **above par** excellent, exceptional, first-rate (*Inf.*), outstanding, superior 4. **below par** a. below average, bush-league (*Aust. & N.Z. inf.*), dime-a-dozen (*Inf.*), inferior, lacking, not up to scratch (*Inf.*), poor, second-rate, substandard, tinhorn (*U.S. sl.*), two-bit (*U.S. & Canad. sl.*), wanting b. not oneself, off colour (*Chiefly Brit.*), off form, poorly (*Inf.*), sick, under the weather (*Inf.*), unfit, unhealthy 5. **par for the course** average, expected, ordinary, predictable, standard, typical, usual 6. **on a par** equal, much the same, the same, well-matched 7. **up to par** acceptable, adequate, good enough, passable, satisfactory, up to scratch (*Inf.*), up to the mark

parable allegory, exemplum, fable, lesson, moral tale, story

parabolic allegorical, figurative, metaphoric, symbolic

parade *n.* 1. array, cavalcade, ceremony, column, march, pageant, procession, review, spectacle, train 2. array, display, exhibition, flaunting, ostentation, pomp, show, spectacle, vaunting ~*v.* 3. defile, march, process 4. air, brandish, display, exhibit, flaunt, make a show of, show, show off (*Inf.*), strut, swagger, vaunt

paradigm archetype, example, exemplar, ideal, model, norm, original, pattern, prototype

paradise 1. City of God, divine abode, Elysian fields, garden of delights (*Islam*), heaven, heavenly kingdom, Olympus (*Poetic*), Promised Land, Zion (*Christianity*) 2. Eden, Garden of Eden 3. bliss, delight, felicity, heaven, seventh heaven, utopia

paradisiacal blessed, blissful, celestial, divine, Elysian, glorious, golden, heavenly, out of this world (*Inf.*), utopian

paradox absurdity, ambiguity, anomaly, contradiction, enigma, inconsistency, mystery, oddity, puzzle

paradoxical absurd, ambiguous, baffling, confounding, contradictory, enigmatic, equivocal, illogical, impossible, improbable, inconsistent, oracular, puzzling, riddling

paragon apotheosis, archetype, criterion, cynosure, epitome, exemplar, ideal, jewel, masterpiece, model, nonesuch (*Archaic*), nonpareil, norm, paradigm, pattern, prototype, quintessence, standard

paragraph clause, item, notice, part, passage, portion, section, subdivision

parallel *adj.* 1. aligned, alongside, coextensive, equidistant, side by side 2. akin, analogous, complementary, correspondent, corresponding, like, matching, resembling, similar, uniform ~*n.* 3. analogue, complement, corollary, counterpart, duplicate, equal, equivalent, likeness, match, twin 4. analogy, comparison, correlation, correspondence, likeness, parallelism, resemblance, similarity ~*v.* 5. agree, be alike, chime with, compare, complement, conform, correlate, correspond, equal, keep pace (with), match
Antonyms *adj.* different, dissimilar, divergent, non-parallel, unlike ~*n.* difference, dissimilarity, divergence, opposite, reverse ~*v.* be unlike, differ, diverge

paralyse 1. cripple, debilitate, disable, incapacitate, lame 2. anaesthetize, arrest, benumb, freeze, halt, immobilize, numb, petrify, stop dead, stun, stupefy, transfix

paralysis 1. immobility, palsy, paresis (*Pathol.*) 2. arrest, breakdown, halt, shutdown, stagnation, standstill, stoppage

paralytic *adj.* 1. crippled, disabled, immobile, immobilized, incapacitated, lame, numb, palsied, paralysed 2. *Inf.* bevvied (*Dialect*), blitzed (*Sl.*), blotto (*Sl.*), bombed (*Sl.*), canned (*Sl.*), drunk, flying (*Sl.*), inebriated, intoxicated, legless (*Inf.*), lit up (*Sl.*), out of it (*Sl.*), out to it (*Aust. & N.Z. sl.*), pie-eyed (*Sl.*), pissed (*Taboo sl.*), plastered (*Sl.*), sloshed (*Sl.*), smashed (*Sl.*), steamboats (*Sl.*), steaming (*Sl.*), stewed (*Sl.*), stoned (*Sl.*), tired and emotional (*Euphemistic*), wasted (*Sl.*), wrecked (*Sl.*), zonked (*Sl.*)

parameter constant, criterion, framework, guideline, limit, limitation, restriction, specification

paramount capital, cardinal, chief, dominant, eminent, first, foremost, main, outstanding, predominant, pre-eminent, primary, prime, principal, superior, supreme
Antonyms inferior, insignificant, least, minor, negligible, secondary, slight, subordinate, trifling, unimportant

paramour beau, concubine, courtesan, fancy man (*Sl.*), fancy woman (*Sl.*), inamorata, inamorato, kept woman, lover, mistress

paraphernalia accoutrements, apparatus, appurtenances, baggage, belongings, clobber (*Brit. sl.*), effects, equipage, equipment, gear, impedimenta, material, stuff, tackle, things, trappings

paraphrase 1. *n.* interpretation, rehash, rendering, rendition, rephrasing, restatement, rewording, translation, version 2. *v.* express in other words *or* one's own words, interpret, rehash, render, rephrase, restate, reword

parasite bloodsucker (*Inf.*), cadger, drone (*Brit.*), hanger-on, leech, scrounger (*Inf.*), sponge (*Inf.*), sponger (*Inf.*)

parasitic, parasitical bloodsucking (*Inf.*), cadging, leechlike, scrounging (*Inf.*), sponging (*Inf.*)

parcel *n.* 1. bundle, carton, pack, package, packet 2. band, batch, bunch, collection, company, crew, crowd, gang, group, lot, pack 3. piece of land, plot, property, tract ~*v.* 4. *Often with* **up** do up, pack, package, tie up, wrap 5. *Often with* **out** allocate, allot, apportion, carve up, deal out, dispense, distribute, divide, dole out, mete out, portion, share out, split up

parch blister, burn, dehydrate, desiccate, dry up, evaporate, make thirsty, scorch, sear, shrivel, wither

parched arid, dehydrated, dried out *or* up, drouthy (*Scot.*), dry, scorched, shrivelled, thirsty, torrid, waterless, withered

parching *adj.* baking, blistering, burning, dry, drying, hot, roasting (*Inf.*), scorching, searing, sweltering, withering

pardon 1. *v.* absolve, acquit, amnesty, condone, exculpate, excuse, exonerate, forgive, free, let off (*Inf.*), liberate, overlook, release,

remit, reprieve 2. *n.* absolution, acquittal, allowance, amnesty, condonation, discharge, excuse, exoneration, forgiveness, grace, indulgence, mercy, release, remission, reprieve
Antonyms *v.* admonish, blame, castigate, censure, chasten, chastise, condemn, discipline, excoriate, fine, penalize, punish, rebuke *~n.* condemnation, guilt, penalty, punishment, redress, retaliation, retribution, revenge, vengeance

pardonable allowable, condonable, excusable, forgivable, minor, not serious, permissible, understandable, venial

pare 1. clip, cut, peel, shave, skin, trim 2. crop, cut, cut back, decrease, dock, lop, prune, reduce, retrench, shear

parent 1. begetter, father, guardian, mother, procreator, progenitor, sire 2. architect, author, cause, creator, forerunner, origin, originator, prototype, root, source, wellspring

parentage ancestry, birth, derivation, descent, extraction, family, line, lineage, origin, paternity, pedigree, race, stirps, stock

parenthetic, parenthetical bracketed, by-the-way, explanatory, extraneous, extrinsic, incidental, in parenthesis, inserted, interposed, qualifying

parenthetically by the bye, by the way, by way of explanation, incidentally, in parenthesis, in passing

pariah exile, leper, outcast, outlaw, undesirable, unperson, untouchable

paring *n.* clipping, flake, fragment, peel, peeling, rind, shaving, shred, skin, slice, sliver, snippet

parish church, churchgoers, community, congregation, flock, fold, parishioners

parity 1. consistency, equality, equal terms, equivalence, par, parallelism, quits (*Inf.*), uniformity, unity 2. affinity, agreement, analogy, conformity, congruity, correspondence, likeness, resemblance, sameness, similarity, similitude

park 1. *n.* estate, garden, grounds, parkland, pleasure garden, recreation ground, woodland 2. *v.* leave, manoeuvre, position, station

parlance idiom, jargon, language, lingo (*Inf.*), manner of speaking, phraseology, -speak, speech, talk, tongue

parley 1. *n.* colloquy, confab (*Inf.*), conference, congress, council, dialogue, discussion, meeting, palaver, powwow, seminar, talk(s) 2. *v.* confabulate, confer, deliberate, discuss, negotiate, palaver, powwow, speak, talk

parliament 1. assembly, congress, convocation, council, diet, legislature, senate, talking shop (*Inf.*) 2. **Parliament** Houses of Parliament, Mother of Parliaments, the House, the House of Commons and the House of Lords, Westminster

parliamentary congressional, deliberative, governmental, lawgiving, lawmaking, legislative

parlour best room, drawing room, front room, lounge, reception room, sitting room

parlous chancy (*Inf.*), dangerous, desperate, difficult, dire, hairy (*Sl.*), hazardous, perilous, risky

parochial insular, inward-looking, limited, narrow, narrow-minded, parish-pump, petty, provincial, restricted, small-minded
Antonyms all-embracing, broad, broad-minded, cosmopolitan, international, liberal, national, universal, world-wide

parodist burlesquer, caricaturist, humorist, impressionist, ironist, lampooner, mimic, mocker, pasquinader, satirist

parody *n.* 1. burlesque, caricature, imitation, lampoon, satire, send-up (*Brit. inf.*), skit, spoof (*Inf.*), takeoff (*Inf.*) 2. apology, caricature, farce, mockery, travesty *~v.* 3. burlesque, caricature, do a takeoff of (*Inf.*), lampoon, mimic, poke fun at, satirize, send up (*Brit. inf.*), spoof (*Inf.*), take off (*Inf.*), take the piss out of (*Taboo sl.*), travesty

paroxysm attack, convulsion, eruption, fit, flare-up (*Inf.*), outburst, seizure, spasm

parrot *n.* 1. *Fig.* copycat (*Inf.*), imitator, (little) echo, mimic 2. **parrot-fashion** *Inf.* by rote, mechanically, mindlessly *~v.* 3. copy, echo, imitate, mimic, reiterate, repeat

parry 1. block, deflect, fend off, hold at bay, rebuff, repel, repulse, stave off, ward off 2. avoid, circumvent, dodge, duck (*Inf.*), evade, fence, fight shy of, shun, sidestep

parsimonious cheeseparing, close, close-fisted, frugal, grasping, mean, mingy (*Brit. inf.*), miserable, miserly, near (*Inf.*), niggardly, penny-pinching (*Inf.*), penurious, saving, scrimpy, skinflinty, sparing, stingy, stinting, tight-arse (*Taboo sl.*), tight-arsed (*Taboo sl.*), tight as a duck's arse (*Taboo sl.*), tight-ass (*U.S. taboo sl.*), tight-assed (*U.S. taboo sl.*), tightfisted
Antonyms extravagant, generous, lavish, munificent, open-handed, spendthrift, wasteful

parsimony frugality, meanness, minginess (*Brit. inf.*), miserliness, nearness (*Inf.*), niggardliness, penny-pinching (*Inf.*), stinginess, tightness

parson churchman, clergyman, cleric, divine, ecclesiastic, incumbent, man of God, man of the cloth, minister, pastor, preacher, priest, rector, reverend (*Inf.*), vicar

part *n.* 1. bit, fraction, fragment, lot, particle, piece, portion, scrap, section, sector, segment, share, slice 2. branch, component, constituent, department, division, element, ingredient, limb, member, module, organ, piece, unit 3. behalf, cause, concern, faction, interest, party, side 4. bit, business, capacity, charge, duty, function, involvement, office, place, responsibility, role, say, share, task, work 5. *Theat.* character, lines, role 6. *Often plural* airt (*Scot.*), area, district, neck of the woods (*Inf.*), neighbourhood, quarter, region, territory, vicinity 7. **for the most part** chiefly, generally, in the main, largely, mainly, mostly, on the whole, principally 8. **in good part** cheerfully, cordially, good-naturedly, well, without offence 9. **in part** a little, in some measure, partially, partly, slightly, somewhat, to a certain extent, to some degree 10. **on the part of** for the sake of, in support of, in the name of, on behalf of 11. **take part in** associate oneself with, be instrumental in, be involved in, have a hand in, join in, partake in, participate in, play a part in, put one's twopence-worth in, take a hand in ~*v.* 12. break, cleave, come apart, detach, disconnect, disjoin, dismantle, disunite, divide, rend, separate, sever, split, tear 13. break up, depart, go, go away, go (their) separate ways, leave, part company, quit, say goodbye, separate, split up, take one's leave, withdraw 14. **part with** abandon, discard, forgo, give up, let go of, relinquish, renounce, sacrifice, surrender, yield
Antonyms *n.* (*senses 1 & 2*) bulk, entirety, mass, totality, whole ~*v.* (*sense 12*) adhere, close, combine, hold, join, stick, unite (*sense 13*) appear, arrive, come, gather, remain, show up (*Inf.*), stay, turn up

partake 1. *With* **in** engage, enter into, participate, share, take part 2. *With* **of** consume, eat, receive, share, take 3. *With* **of** evince, evoke, have the quality of, show, suggest

partial 1. fragmentary, imperfect, incomplete, limited, uncompleted, unfinished 2. biased, discriminatory, influenced, interested, one-sided, partisan, predisposed, prejudiced, tendentious, unfair, unjust 3. **be partial to** be fond of, be keen on, be taken with, care for, have a liking (soft spot, weakness) for
Antonyms (*sense 1*) complete, entire, finished, full, total, whole (*sense 2*) impartial, objective, unbiased, unprejudiced

partiality 1. bias, favouritism, partisanship, predisposition, preference, prejudice 2. affinity, bag (*Sl.*), cup of tea (*Inf.*), fondness, inclination, liking, love, penchant, predilection, predisposition, preference, proclivity, taste, weakness
Antonyms (*sense 1*) disinterest, equity, fairness, impartiality, objectivity (*sense 2*) abhorrence, antipathy, aversion, disgust, disinclination, dislike, distaste, loathing, revulsion

partially fractionally, halfway, incompletely, in part, moderately, not wholly, partly, piecemeal, somewhat, to a certain extent *or* degree

participant associate, contributor, member, partaker, participator, party, shareholder

participate be a participant, be a party to, engage in, enter into, get in on the act, have a hand in, join in, partake, perform, share, take part
Antonyms abstain, boycott, forgo, forsake, forswear, opt out, pass up, refrain from, take no part of

participation assistance, contribution, involvement, joining in, partaking, partnership, sharing in, taking part

particle atom, bit, crumb, grain, iota, jot, mite, molecule, mote, piece, scrap, shred, speck, tittle, whit

particular *adj.* 1. distinct, exact, express, peculiar, precise, special, specific 2. especial, exceptional, marked, notable, noteworthy, remarkable, singular, uncommon, unusual 3. blow-by-blow, circumstantial, detailed, itemized, minute, painstaking, precise, selective, thorough 4. choosy (*Inf.*), critical, dainty, demanding, discriminating, exacting, fastidious, finicky, fussy, meticulous, nice (*Rare*), overnice, pernickety (*Inf.*), picky (*Inf.*) ~*n.* 5. *Usually plural* circumstance, detail, fact, feature, item, specification 6. **in particular** distinctly, especially, exactly, expressly, particularly, specifically
Antonyms (*sense 1*) general, imprecise, indefinite, indistinct, inexact, unspecified, vague (*sense 4*) casual, easy, easy to please, indiscriminate, negligent, slack, sloppy, uncritical

particularity 1. *Often plural* circumstance, detail, fact, instance, item, point 2. carefulness, choosiness (*Inf.*), fastidiousness, fussiness, meticulousness 3. accuracy, detail, precision, thoroughness 4. characteristic, distinctiveness, feature, idiosyncrasy, individuality, peculiarity, property, singularity, trait

particularize detail, enumerate, itemize, specify, spell out, stipulate

particularly 1. decidedly, especially, exceptionally, markedly, notably, outstandingly, peculiarly, singularly, surprisingly, un~

commonly, unusually 2. distinctly, especially, explicitly, expressly, in particular, specifically

parting *n.* 1. adieu, departure, farewell, going, goodbye, leave-taking, valediction 2. breaking, detachment, divergence, division, partition, rift, rupture, separation, split ~*adj.* 3. departing, farewell, final, last, valedictory

partisan *n.* 1. adherent, backer, champion, devotee, disciple, follower, stalwart, supporter, upholder, votary ~*adj.* 2. biased, factional, interested, one-sided, partial, prejudiced, sectarian, tendentious ~*n.* 3. guerrilla, irregular, resistance fighter, underground fighter ~*adj.* 4. guerrilla, irregular, resistance, underground
Antonyms *n.* adversary, contender, critic, detractor, foe, knocker (*Inf.*), leader, opponent, rival ~*adj.* bipartisan, broad-minded, disinterested, impartial, non-partisan, unbiased, unprejudiced

partition *n.* 1. dividing, division, segregation, separation, severance, splitting 2. barrier, divider, room divider, screen, wall 3. allotment, apportionment, distribution, portion, rationing out, share ~*v.* 4. apportion, cut up, divide, parcel out, portion, section, segment, separate, share, split up, subdivide 5. divide, fence off, screen, separate, wall off

partly halfway, incompletely, in part, in some measure, not fully, partially, relatively, slightly, somewhat, to a certain degree *or* extent, up to a certain point
Antonyms completely, entirely, fully, in full, totally, wholly

partner 1. accomplice, ally, associate, bedfellow, collaborator, colleague, companion, comrade, confederate, copartner, helper, mate, participant, team-mate 2. bedfellow, consort, helpmate, her indoors (*Brit. sl.*), husband, mate, significant other (*U.S. inf.*), spouse, wife

partnership 1. companionship, connection, cooperation, copartnership, fellowship, interest, participation, sharing 2. alliance, association, combine, company, conglomerate, cooperative, corporation, firm, house, society, union

parts 1. ability, accomplishments, attributes, calibre, capabilities, endowments, faculties, genius, gifts, intellect, intelligence, talents 2. bits and pieces, components, spare parts, spares

party 1. at-home, bash (*Inf.*), beano (*Brit. sl.*), celebration, do (*Inf.*), festivity, function, gathering, get-together (*Inf.*), knees-up (*Brit. inf.*), rave (*Brit. sl.*), rave-up (*Brit. sl.*), reception, shindig (*Inf.*), social, social gathering, soirée 2. band, body, bunch (*Inf.*), company, crew, detachment (*Military*), gang, gathering, group, squad, team, unit 3. alliance, association, cabal, camp, clique, coalition, combination, confederacy, coterie, faction, grouping, league, schism, set, side 4. individual, person, somebody, someone 5. *Law* contractor (*Law*), defendant, litigant, participant, plaintiff

parvenu 1. *n.* arriviste, *nouveau riche,* social climber, upstart 2. *adj. nouveau riche,* upstart

pass[1] *v.* 1. depart, elapse, flow, go, go by *or* past, lapse, leave, move, move onwards, proceed, roll, run 2. beat, exceed, excel, go beyond, outdistance, outdo, outstrip, surmount, surpass, transcend 3. answer, come up to scratch (*Inf.*), do, get through, graduate, pass muster, qualify, succeed, suffice, suit 4. beguile, devote, employ, experience, fill, occupy, spend, suffer, undergo, while away 5. befall, come up, develop, fall out, happen, occur, take place 6. convey, deliver, exchange, give, hand, kick, let have, reach, send, throw, transfer, transmit 7. accept, adopt, approve, authorize, decree, enact, establish, legislate, ordain, ratify, sanction, validate 8. declare, deliver, express, pronounce, utter 9. disregard, ignore, miss, neglect, not heed, omit, overlook, skip (*Inf.*) 10. crap (*Taboo sl.*), defecate, discharge, eliminate, empty, evacuate, excrete, expel, shit (*Taboo sl.*), void 11. blow over, cease, die, disappear, dissolve, dwindle, ebb, end, evaporate, expire, fade, go, melt away, terminate, vanish, wane 12. *With* **for** *or* **as** be accepted as, be mistaken for, be regarded as, be taken for, impersonate, serve as
Antonyms (*sense 1*) bring *or* come to a standstill, cease, halt, pause, stop (*senses 2 & 3*) be inadequate, be inferior to, be unsuccessful, come a cropper (*Inf.*), fail, lose, suffer defeat (*sense 7*) ban, disallow, invalidate, overrule, prohibit, refuse, reject, veto (*sense 9*) acknowledge, heed, note, notice, observe, pay attention to

pass[2] *n.* 1. canyon, col, defile, gap, gorge, ravine 2. authorization, identification, identity card, licence, passport, permission, permit, safe-conduct, ticket, warrant 3. *Inf.* advances, approach, overture, play (*Inf.*), proposition, suggestion 4. condition, juncture, pinch, plight, predicament, situation, stage, state, state of affairs, straits 5. feint, jab, lunge, push, swing, thrust

passable 1. acceptable, adequate, admissible, allowable, all right, average, fair, fair enough, mediocre, middling, moderate, not too bad, ordinary, presentable, so-so (*Inf.*),

tolerable, unexceptional 2. clear, crossable, navigable, open, traversable, unobstructed
Antonyms (*sense 1*) A1 *or* A-one (*Inf.*), exceptional, extraordinary, first-class, inadequate, inadmissible, marvellous, outstanding, superb, tops (*Sl.*), unacceptable, unsatisfactory (*sense 2*) blocked, closed, impassable, obstructed, sealed off, unnavigable

passably after a fashion, fairly, moderately, pretty much, rather, relatively, somewhat, tolerably, well enough

passage 1. alley, avenue, channel, course, lane, opening, path, road, route, thoroughfare, way 2. corridor, doorway, entrance, entrance hall, exit, hall, hallway, lobby, passageway, vestibule 3. clause, excerpt, extract, paragraph, piece, quotation, reading, section, sentence, text, verse 4. crossing, journey, tour, trek, trip, voyage 5. advance, change, conversion, flow, motion, movement, passing, progress, progression, transit, transition 6. allowance, authorization, freedom, permission, right, safe-conduct, visa, warrant 7. acceptance, enactment, establishment, legalization, legislation, passing, ratification

passageway aisle, alley, corridor, cut, entrance, exit, hall, hallway, lane, lobby, passage, wynd (*Scot.*)

pass away buy it (*U.S. sl.*), check out (*U.S. sl.*), croak (*Sl.*), decease, depart (this life), die, expire, go belly-up (*Sl.*), kick it (*Sl.*), kick the bucket (*Sl.*), pass on, pass over, peg it (*Inf.*), peg out (*Inf.*), pop one's clogs (*Inf.*), shuffle off this mortal coil, snuff it (*Inf.*)

pass by 1. go past, leave, move past, pass 2. disregard, miss, neglect, not choose, overlook, pass over

passé antiquated, dated, *démodé*, obsolete, old-fashioned, old hat, outdated, outmoded, out-of-date, outworn, unfashionable

passenger fare, hitchhiker, pillion rider, rider, traveller

passer-by bystander, onlooker, witness

passing *adj.* 1. brief, ephemeral, fleeting, momentary, short, short-lived, temporary, transient, transitory 2. casual, cursory, glancing, hasty, quick, shallow, short, slight, superficial 3. **in passing** accidentally, by the bye, by the way, en passant, incidentally, on the way ~*n.* 4. death, decease, demise, end, finish, loss, termination

passion 1. animation, ardour, eagerness, emotion, excitement, feeling, fervour, fire, heat, intensity, joy, rapture, spirit, transport, warmth, zeal, zest 2. adoration, affection, ardour, attachment, concupiscence, desire, fondness, infatuation, itch, keenness, love, lust, the hots (*Sl.*) 3. bug (*Inf.*), craving, craze, enthusiasm, fancy, fascination, idol, infatuation, mania, obsession 4. anger, fit, flare-up (*Inf.*), frenzy, fury, indignation, ire, outburst, paroxysm, rage, resentment, storm, vehemence, wrath
Antonyms apathy, calmness, coldness, coolness, frigidity, hate, indifference, unconcern

passionate 1. amorous, ardent, aroused, desirous, erotic, hot, loving, lustful, sensual, sexy (*Inf.*), steamy (*Inf.*), wanton 2. animated, ardent, eager, emotional, enthusiastic, excited, fervent, fervid, fierce, flaming, frenzied, heartfelt, impassioned, impetuous, impulsive, intense, strong, vehement, warm, wild, zealous 3. choleric, excitable, fiery, hot-headed, hot-tempered, irascible, irritable, peppery, quick-tempered, stormy, tempestuous, violent
Antonyms (*sense 1*) cold, frigid, passionless, unloving, unresponsive (*sense 2*) apathetic, calm, cold, half-hearted, indifferent, languorous, nonchalant, subdued, unemotional, unenthusiastic (*sense 3*) agreeable, calm, easy-going, even-tempered, nonviolent, placid, unexcitable

passionless 1. apathetic, cold, cold-blooded, cold-hearted, emotionless, frigid, icy, indifferent, uncaring, unfeeling, unloving, unresponsive 2. calm, detached, dispassionate, impartial, impassive, neutral, restrained, unemotional, uninvolved

passive acquiescent, compliant, docile, enduring, inactive, inert, lifeless, long-suffering, nonviolent, patient, quiescent, receptive, resigned, submissive, unassertive, uninvolved, unresisting
Antonyms active, alive, assertive, bossy (*Inf.*), defiant, domineering, energetic, feisty (*Inf., chiefly U.S. & Canad.*), impatient, involved, lively, rebellious, spirited, violent, zippy (*Inf.*)

pass off 1. counterfeit, fake, feign, make a pretence of, palm off 2. come to an end, die away, disappear, fade out, vanish 3. emit, evaporate, give off, send forth, vaporize 4. be completed, go off, happen, occur, take place, turn out 5. dismiss, disregard, ignore, pass by, wink at

pass out 1. *Inf.* become unconscious, black out (*Inf.*), drop, faint, flake out (*Inf.*), keel over (*Inf.*), lose consciousness, swoon (*Literary*) 2. deal out, distribute, dole out, hand out

pass over discount, disregard, forget, ignore, not dwell on, omit, overlook, pass by, take no notice of

pass up abstain, decline, forgo, give (something) a miss (*Inf.*), ignore, let go, let slip, miss, neglect, refuse, reject

password countersign, key word, open sesame, signal, watchword

past *adj.* 1. accomplished, completed, done, elapsed, ended, extinct, finished, forgotten, gone, over, over and done with, spent 2. ancient, bygone, early, erstwhile, foregoing, former, late, long-ago, olden, preceding, previous, prior, quondam, recent ~*n.* 3. **the past** antiquity, days gone by, days of yore, former times, good old days, history, long ago, olden days, old times, times past, yesteryear (*Literary*) 4. background, experience, history, life, past life ~*adv.* 5. across, beyond, by, on, over ~*prep.* 6. after, beyond, farther than, later than, outside, over, subsequent to

Antonyms *adj.* arrived, begun, coming, future, now, present ~*n.* future, now, present, time to come, today, tomorrow

paste 1. *n.* adhesive, cement, glue, gum, mucilage 2. *v.* cement, fasten, fix, glue, gum, stick

pastel *adj.* delicate, light, muted, pale, soft, soft-hued

Antonyms bright, deep, rich, strong, vibrant, vivid

pastiche blend, farrago, gallimaufry, hotchpotch, medley, *mélange,* miscellany, mixture, motley

pastille cough drop, jujube, lozenge, tablet, troche (*Medical*)

pastime activity, amusement, distraction, diversion, entertainment, game, hobby, leisure, play, recreation, relaxation, sport

past master ace (*Inf.*), artist, dab hand (*Brit. inf.*), expert, old hand, virtuoso, wizard

pastor churchman, clergyman, divine, ecclesiastic, minister, parson, priest, rector, vicar

pastoral *adj.* 1. agrestic, Arcadian, bucolic, country, georgic (*Literary*), idyllic, rural, rustic, simple 2. clerical, ecclesiastical, ministerial, priestly

pasture grass, grassland, grazing, grazing land, lea (*Poetic*), meadow, pasturage, shieling (*Scot.*)

pasty *adj.* 1. doughy, glutinous, mucilaginous, starchy, sticky 2. anaemic, pale, pallid, sallow, sickly, unhealthy, wan, wheyfaced

pat[1] *v.* 1. caress, dab, fondle, pet, slap, stroke, tap, touch ~*n.* 2. clap, dab, light blow, slap, stroke, tap 3. cake, dab, lump, portion, small piece

pat[2] *adv.* 1. exactly, faultlessly, flawlessly, off pat, perfectly, precisely 2. aptly, bang, dead on, fittingly, just right, opportunely, plumb (*Inf.*), relevantly, seasonably ~*adj.* 3. apposite, apropos, apt, felicitous, fitting, happy, neat, pertinent, relevant, spot-on (*Brit. inf.*), suitable, to the point 4. automatic, easy, facile, glib, ready, simplistic, slick, smooth

patch *n.* 1. piece of material, reinforcement 2. bit, scrap, shred, small piece, spot, stretch 3. area, ground, land, plot, tract ~*v.* 4. cover, fix, mend, reinforce, repair, sew up 5. *With* **up** bury the hatchet, conciliate, make friends, placate, restore, settle, settle differences, smooth

patchwork confusion, hash, hotchpotch, jumble, medley, mishmash, mixture, pastiche

patchy bitty, erratic, fitful, inconstant, irregular, random, sketchy, spotty, uneven, variable, varying

Antonyms constant, even, regular, unbroken, unvarying

patent 1. *adj.* apparent, blatant, clear, conspicuous, downright, evident, flagrant, glaring, indisputable, manifest, obvious, open, palpable, transparent, unconcealed, unequivocal, unmistakable 2. *n.* copyright, invention, licence

paternal 1. benevolent, concerned, fatherlike, fatherly, protective, solicitous, vigilant 2. patrilineal, patrimonial

paternity 1. fatherhood, fathership 2. descent, extraction, family, lineage, parentage 3. authorship, derivation, origin, source

path 1. footpath, footway, pathway, towpath, track, trail, walkway (*Chiefly U.S.*) 2. avenue, course, direction, passage, procedure, road, route, track, walk, way

pathetic 1. affecting, distressing, harrowing, heartbreaking, heart-rending, melting, moving, pitiable, plaintive, poignant, sad, tender, touching 2. deplorable, feeble, inadequate, lamentable, meagre, measly, miserable, paltry, petty, pitiful, poor, puny, sorry, wet (*Brit. inf.*), woeful 3. *Sl.* chickenshit (*U.S. sl.*), crappy (*Sl.*), crummy (*Sl.*), poxy (*Sl.*), rubbishy, trashy, uninteresting, useless, worthless

Antonyms (*sense 1*) amusing, comical, droll, entertaining, funny, laughable, ludicrous, ridiculous

pathfinder discoverer, explorer, guide, pioneer, scout, trailblazer

pathless impassable, impenetrable, trackless, uncharted, unexplored, untrodden, waste, wild

pathos pitiableness, pitifulness, plaintiveness, poignancy, sadness

patience 1. calmness, composure, cool (*Sl.*), equanimity, even temper, forbear-

ance, imperturbability, restraint, serenity, sufferance, tolerance, toleration 2. constancy, diligence, endurance, fortitude, long-suffering, perseverance, persistence, resignation, stoicism, submission
Antonyms (*sense 1*) agitation, exasperation, excitement, impatience, irritation, nervousness, passion, restlessness (*sense 2*) irresolution, vacillation

patient *adj.* 1. calm, composed, enduring, long-suffering, persevering, persistent, philosophical, quiet, resigned, self-possessed, serene, stoical, submissive, uncomplaining, untiring 2. accommodating, even-tempered, forbearing, forgiving, indulgent, lenient, mild, tolerant, understanding ~*n.* 3. case, invalid, sick person, sufferer

patois 1. dialect 2. argot, cant, jargon, lingo (*Inf.*), patter, slang, vernacular

patriarch 1. father, paterfamilias, sire 2. elder, grandfather, greybeard, old man

patrician 1. *n.* aristo (*Inf.*), aristocrat, noble, nobleman, peer 2. *adj.* aristocratic, blue-blooded, gentle (*Archaic*), highborn, high-class, lordly, noble

patrimony bequest, birthright, heritage, inheritance, legacy, portion, share

patriot chauvinist, flag-waver (*Inf.*), jingo, lover of one's country, loyalist, nationalist

patriotic chauvinistic, flag-waving (*Inf.*), jingoistic, loyal, nationalistic

patriotism flag-waving (*Inf.*), jingoism, love of one's country, loyalty, nationalism

patrol *n.* 1. guarding, policing, protecting, rounds, safeguarding, vigilance, watching 2. garrison, guard, patrolman, sentinel, watch, watchman ~*v.* 3. cruise, guard, inspect, keep guard, keep watch, make the rounds, police, pound, range, safeguard, walk the beat

patron 1. advocate, angel (*Inf.*), backer, benefactor, champion, defender, friend, guardian, helper, philanthropist, protagonist, protector, sponsor, supporter 2. buyer, client, customer, frequenter, habitué, shopper

patronage 1. aid, assistance, backing, benefaction, championship, encouragement, espousal, help, promotion, sponsorship, support 2. business, clientele, commerce, custom, trade, trading, traffic 3. condescension, deigning, disdain, patronizing, stooping

patronize 1. be lofty with, look down on, talk down to, treat as inferior, treat condescendingly, treat like a child 2. assist, back, befriend, foster, fund, help, maintain, promote, sponsor, subscribe to, support 3. be a customer *or* client of, buy from, deal with, do business with, frequent, shop at, trade with

patronizing condescending, contemptuous, disdainful, gracious, haughty, lofty, snobbish, stooping, supercilious, superior, toffee-nosed (*Sl., chiefly Brit.*)
Antonyms deferential, humble, obsequious, respectful, servile

patter[1] *v.* 1. scurry, scuttle, skip, tiptoe, trip, walk lightly 2. beat, pat, pelt, pitapat, pitter-patter, rat-a-tat, spatter, tap ~*n.* 3. pattering, pitapat, pitter-patter, tapping

patter[2] *n.* 1. line, monologue, pitch, spiel (*Inf.*) 2. chatter, gabble, jabber, nattering, prattle, yak (*Sl.*) 3. argot, cant, jargon, lingo (*Inf.*), patois, slang, vernacular ~*v.* 4. babble, blab, chatter, hold forth, jabber, prate, rattle off, rattle on, spiel (*Inf.*), spout (*Inf.*), tattle

pattern *n.* 1. arrangement, decoration, decorative design, design, device, figure, motif, ornament 2. arrangement, method, order, orderliness, plan, sequence, system 3. kind, shape, sort, style, type, variety 4. design, diagram, guide, instructions, original, plan, stencil, template 5. archetype, criterion, cynosure, example, exemplar, guide, model, norm, original, par, paradigm, paragon, prototype, sample, specimen, standard ~*v.* 6. copy, emulate, follow, form, imitate, model, mould, order, shape, style 7. decorate, design, trim

paucity dearth, deficiency, fewness, insufficiency, lack, meagreness, paltriness, poverty, rarity, scantiness, scarcity, shortage, slenderness, slightness, smallness, sparseness, sparsity

paunch abdomen, beer-belly (*Inf.*), belly, corporation (*Inf.*), pot, potbelly, spare tyre (*Brit. sl.*), spread (*Inf.*)

pauper bankrupt, beggar, down-and-out, have-not, indigent, insolvent, mendicant, poor person

pauperism beggary, destitution, impecuniousness, indigence, mendicancy, need, neediness, pennilessness, penury, poverty, privation, want

pauperize bankrupt, beggar, break, bust (*Inf.*), cripple financially, impoverish, reduce to beggary, ruin

pause 1. *v.* break, cease, delay, deliberate, desist, discontinue, halt, have a breather (*Inf.*), hesitate, interrupt, rest, stop briefly, take a break, wait, waver 2. *n.* break, breather (*Inf.*), caesura, cessation, delay, discontinuance, entr'acte, gap, halt, hesitation, interlude, intermission, interruption, interval, let-up (*Inf.*), lull, respite, rest, stay, stoppage, wait
Antonyms *v.* advance, continue, proceed,

progress ~*n.* advancement, continuance, progression

pave asphalt, concrete, cover, flag, floor, macadamize, surface, tar, tile

paw *v.* grab, handle roughly, manhandle, maul, molest

pawn[1] 1. *v.* deposit, gage (*Archaic*), hazard, hock (*Inf., chiefly U.S.*), mortgage, pledge, pop (*Inf.*), stake, wager 2. *n.* assurance, bond, collateral, gage, guarantee, guaranty, pledge, security

pawn[2] *n.* cat's-paw, creature, dupe, instrument, plaything, puppet, stooge (*Sl.*), tool, toy

pay *v.* 1. clear, compensate, cough up (*Inf.*), discharge, foot, give, honour, liquidate, meet, offer, recompense, reimburse, remit, remunerate, render, requite, reward, settle, square up 2. be advantageous, benefit, be worthwhile, repay, serve 3. bestow, extend, give, grant, hand out, present, proffer, render 4. *Often with* **for** answer for, atone, be punished, compensate, get one's deserts, make amends, suffer, suffer the consequences 5. bring in, produce, profit, return, yield 6. be profitable, be remunerative, make a return, make money, provide a living 7. avenge oneself for, get even with (*Inf.*), get revenge on, pay back, punish, reciprocate, repay, requite, settle a score ~*n.* 8. allowance, compensation, earnings, emoluments, fee, hand-out, hire, income, meed (*Archaic*), payment, recompense, reimbursement, remuneration, reward, salary, stipend, takings, wages

payable due, mature, obligatory, outstanding, owed, owing, receivable, to be paid

pay back 1. get even with (*Inf.*), get one's own back, hit back, reciprocate, recompense, retaliate, settle a score 2. refund, reimburse, repay, return, settle up, square

payment 1. defrayal, discharge, outlay, paying, remittance, settlement 2. advance, deposit, instalment, portion, premium, remittance 3. fee, hire, remuneration, reward, wage

payoff *n.* 1. conclusion, day of reckoning, final reckoning, judgment, retribution, reward, settlement 2. *Inf.* climax, clincher (*Inf.*), consequence, culmination, finale, moment of truth, outcome, punch line, result, the crunch (*Inf.*), upshot

pay off 1. discharge, dismiss, fire, lay off, let go, sack (*Inf.*) 2. clear, discharge, liquidate, pay in full, settle, square 3. be effective (profitable, successful), succeed, work 4. get even with (*Inf.*), pay back, retaliate, settle a score 5. *Inf.* bribe, buy off, corrupt, get at, grease the palm of (*Sl.*), oil (*Inf.*), suborn

pay out 1. cough up (*Inf.*), disburse, expend, fork out *or* over *or* up (*Sl.*), lay out (*Inf.*), shell out (*Inf.*), spend 2. get even with (*Inf.*), pay back, retaliate, settle a score

peace 1. accord, agreement, amity, concord, harmony 2. armistice, cessation of hostilities, conciliation, pacification, treaty, truce 3. calm, composure, contentment, placidity, relaxation, repose, serenity 4. calm, calmness, hush, peacefulness, quiet, quietude, repose, rest, silence, stillness, tranquillity

peaceable 1. amiable, amicable, conciliatory, dovish, friendly, gentle, inoffensive, mild, nonbelligerent, pacific, peaceful, peace-loving, placid, unwarlike 2. balmy, calm, peaceful, quiet, restful, serene, still, tranquil, undisturbed

peaceful 1. amicable, at peace, free from strife, friendly, harmonious, nonviolent, on friendly *or* good terms, without hostility 2. calm, gentle, placid, quiet, restful, serene, still, tranquil, undisturbed, unruffled, untroubled 3. conciliatory, irenic, pacific, peaceable, peace-loving, placatory, unwarlike

Antonyms agitated, antagonistic, belligerent, bitter, disquieted, disturbed, hostile, loud, nervous, noisy, Ramboesque, raucous, restless, unfriendly, upset, violent, warlike, warring, wartime

peacemaker appeaser, arbitrator, conciliator, mediator, pacifier, peacemonger

peak *n.* 1. aiguille, apex, brow, crest, pinnacle, point, summit, tip, top 2. acme, apogee, climax, crown, culmination, high point, maximum point, *ne plus ultra,* zenith ~*v.* 3. be at its height, climax, come to a head, culminate, reach its highest point, reach the zenith

peaky emaciated, ill, in poor shape, off colour, pale, peelie-wally (*Scot.*), pinched, poorly (*Inf.*), sick, sickly, under the weather (*Inf.*), unwell, wan

peal 1. *n.* blast, carillon, chime, clamour, clang, clap, crash, resounding, reverberation, ring, ringing, roar, rumble, sound, tintinnabulation 2. *v.* chime, crack, crash, resonate, resound, reverberate, ring, roar, roll, rumble, sound, tintinnabulate, toll

peasant 1. churl (*Archaic*), countryman, hind (*Obsolete*), rustic, son of the soil, swain (*Archaic*) 2. *Inf.* boor, churl, country bumpkin, hayseed (*U.S. & Canad. inf.*), hick (*Inf., chiefly U.S. & Canad.*), lout, provincial, yokel

peccadillo error, indiscretion, infraction, lapse, misdeed, misdemeanour, petty offence, slip, trifling fault

peck *v./n.* bite, dig, hit, jab, kiss, nibble, pick, poke, prick, strike, tap

peculate appropriate, defalcate (*Law*), defraud, embezzle, misapply, misappropriate, pilfer, purloin, rob, steal

peculiar 1. abnormal, bizarre, curious, eccentric, exceptional, extraordinary, far-out (*Sl.*), freakish, funny, odd, offbeat, off-the-wall (*Sl.*), outlandish, out-of-the-way, outré, quaint, queer, singular, strange, uncommon, unconventional, unusual, wacko (*Sl.*), weird 2. appropriate, characteristic, distinct, distinctive, distinguishing, endemic, idiosyncratic, individual, local, particular, personal, private, restricted, special, specific, unique
Antonyms (*sense 1*) commonplace, conventional, expected, familiar, ordinary, usual (*sense 2*) common, general, indistinctive, unspecific

peculiarity 1. abnormality, bizarreness, eccentricity, foible, freakishness, idiosyncrasy, mannerism, oddity, odd trait, queerness, quirk 2. attribute, characteristic, distinctiveness, feature, mark, particularity, property, quality, singularity, speciality, trait

pecuniary commercial, financial, fiscal, monetary

pedagogue dogmatist, dominie (*Scot.*), educator, instructor, master, mistress, pedant, schoolmaster, schoolmistress, teacher

pedant casuist, doctrinaire, dogmatist, hairsplitter, literalist, nit-picker (*Inf.*), pedagogue, pettifogger, precisian, quibbler, scholastic, sophist

pedantic abstruse, academic, bookish, didactic, donnish, erudite, formal, fussy, hairsplitting, nit-picking (*Inf.*), overnice, particular, pedagogic, picky (*Inf.*), pompous, precise, priggish, punctilious, scholastic, schoolmasterly, sententious, stilted

pedantry bookishness, finicality, hairsplitting, overnicety, pedagogism, pettifoggery, pomposity, punctiliousness, quibbling, sophistry, stuffiness

peddle flog (*Sl.*), hawk, huckster, market, push (*Inf.*), sell, sell door to door, trade, vend

pedestal 1. base, dado (*Architect.*), foot, foundation, mounting, pier, plinth, socle, stand, support 2. **put on a pedestal** apotheosize, deify, dignify, ennoble, exalt, glorify, idealize, worship

pedestrian 1. *n.* footslogger, foot-traveller, walker 2. *adj.* banal, boring, commonplace, dull, flat, ho-hum (*Inf.*), humdrum, mediocre, mundane, ordinary, plodding, prosaic, run-of-the-mill, unimaginative, uninspired, uninteresting
Antonyms *n.* driver *~adj.* exciting, fascinating, imaginative, important, interesting, noteworthy, outstanding, remarkable, significant

pedigree 1. *n.* ancestry, blood, breed, derivation, descent, extraction, family, family tree, genealogy, heritage, line, lineage, race, stemma, stirps, stock 2. *adj.* full-blooded, purebred, thoroughbred

pedlar cheap-jack (*Inf.*), colporteur, door-to-door salesman, duffer (*Dialect*), hawker, huckster, seller, vendor

peek 1. *v.* glance, keek (*Scot.*), look, peep, peer, snatch a glimpse, sneak a look, spy, squinny, take *or* have a gander (*Inf.*), take a look 2. *n.* blink, butcher's (*Brit. sl.*), gander (*Inf.*), glance, glim (*Scot.*), glimpse, keek (*Scot.*), look, look-see (*Sl.*), peep, shufti (*Brit. sl.*)

peel 1. *v.* decorticate, desquamate, flake off, pare, scale, skin, strip off 2. *n.* epicarp, exocarp, peeling, rind, skin

peep[1] *v.* 1. keek (*Scot.*), look from hiding, look surreptitiously, peek, peer, sneak a look, spy, steal a look 2. appear briefly, emerge, peer out, show partially *~n.* 3. butcher's (*Brit. sl.*), gander (*Inf.*), glim (*Scot.*), glimpse, keek (*Scot.*), look, look-see (*Sl.*), peek, shufti (*Brit. sl.*)

peep[2] *v./n.* cheep, chirp, chirrup, pipe, squeak, tweet, twitter

peephole aperture, chink, crack, crevice, fissure, hole, keyhole, opening, pinhole, slit, spyhole

peer[1] *n.* 1. aristo (*Inf.*), aristocrat, baron, count, duke, earl, lord, marquess, marquis, noble, nobleman, viscount 2. coequal, compeer, equal, fellow, like, match

peer[2] *v.* 1. gaze, inspect, peep, scan, scrutinize, snoop, spy, squinny, squint 2. appear, become visible, emerge, peep out

peerage aristocracy, lords and ladies, nobility, peers, titled classes

peerless beyond compare, excellent, incomparable, matchless, nonpareil, outstanding, second to none, superlative, unequalled, unique, unmatched, unparalleled, unrivalled, unsurpassed
Antonyms commonplace, inferior, mediocre, ordinary, poor, second-rate

peeve 1. *v.* annoy, bother, bug (*Inf.*), exasperate, gall, get (*Inf.*), get one's goat (*Sl.*), get on one's nerves (*Inf.*), irk, irritate, nark (*Brit., Aust., & N.Z. sl.*), nettle, pique, piss one off (*Taboo sl.*), provoke, rile, rub (up) the wrong way, vex 2. *n.* annoyance, bother, gripe (*Inf.*), nuisance, pest, sore point, vexation

peeved annoyed, exasperated, galled, hacked (off) (*U.S. sl.*), irked, irritated, nettled, piqued, pissed off (*Taboo sl.*), put out, riled, sore, upset, vexed

peevish acrimonious, cantankerous, captious, childish, churlish, crabbed, cross, crotchety (*Inf.*), crusty, fractious, fretful, grumpy, huffy, ill-natured, ill-tempered, irritable, liverish, pettish, petulant, querulous, ratty (*Brit. & N.Z. inf.*), short-tempered, shrewish, snappy, splenetic, sulky, sullen, surly, testy, tetchy, touchy, waspish, whingeing (*Inf.*)
Antonyms affable, agreeable, cheerful, cheery, easy-going, even-tempered, genial, good-natured, happy, merry, pleasant, sweet

peg *v.* 1. attach, fasten, fix, join, make fast, secure 2. *With* **along** *or* **away** apply oneself to, beaver away (*Brit. inf.*), keep at it, keep going, keep on, persist, plod along, plug away at (*Inf.*), stick to it, work at, work away 3. *Of prices, etc.* control, fix, freeze, limit, set

pejorative belittling, debasing, deprecatory, depreciatory, derogatory, detractive, detractory, disparaging, negative, slighting, uncomplimentary, unpleasant

pell-mell 1. *adv.* full tilt, hastily, heedlessly, helter-skelter, hurriedly, impetuously, posthaste, precipitously, rashly, recklessly 2. *adj.* chaotic, confused, disordered, disorganized, haphazard, tumultuous 3. *n.* anarchy, chaos, confusion, disarray, disorder, ferment, helter-skelter, pandemonium, tumult, turmoil, upheaval

pellucid 1. bright, clear, crystalline, glassy, limpid, translucent, transparent 2. clear, comprehensible, limpid, lucid, perspicuous, plain, straightforward, unambiguous

pelt[1] *v.* 1. assail, batter, beat, belabour, bombard, cast, hurl, pepper, pummel, shower, sling, strike, thrash, throw, wallop (*Inf.*) 2. barrel (along) (*Inf., chiefly U.S. & Canad.*), belt (*Sl.*), burn rubber (*Inf.*), career, charge, dash, hurry, run fast, rush, shoot, speed, tear, whiz (*Inf.*) 3. bucket down (*Inf.*), pour, rain cats and dogs (*Inf.*), rain hard, teem

pelt[2] *n.* coat, fell, hide, skin

pen[1] *v.* commit to paper, compose, draft, draw up, jot down, write

pen[2] 1. *n.* cage, coop, enclosure, fold, hutch, pound, sty 2. *v.* cage, confine, coop up, enclose, fence in, hedge, hem in, hurdle, impound, mew (up), pound, shut up *or* in

penal corrective, disciplinary, penalizing, punitive, retributive

penalize award a penalty against (*Sport*), correct, discipline, handicap, impose a penalty on, inflict a handicap on, punish, put at a disadvantage

penalty disadvantage, fine, forfeit, forfeiture, handicap, mulct, price, punishment, retribution

penance 1. atonement, mortification, penalty, punishment, reparation, sackcloth and ashes 2. **do penance** accept punishment, atone, make amends, make reparation, mortify oneself, show contrition, suffer

penchant affinity, bent, bias, disposition, fondness, inclination, leaning, liking, partiality, predilection, predisposition, proclivity, proneness, propensity, taste, tendency, turn

pendent *adj.* dangling, drooping, hanging, pendulous, suspended, swinging

pending awaiting, forthcoming, hanging fire, imminent, impending, in the balance, in the offing, undecided, undetermined, unsettled, up in the air

pendulous dangling, drooping, hanging, pendent, sagging, swaying, swinging

penetrable accessible, clear, comprehensible, fathomable, intelligible, open, passable, permeable, pervious, porous

penetrate 1. bore, enter, go through, impale, perforate, pierce, prick, probe, stab 2. diffuse, enter, get in, infiltrate, permeate, pervade, seep, suffuse 3. *Fig.* affect, become clear, be understood, come across, get through to, impress, touch 4. *Fig.* comprehend, decipher, discern, fathom, figure out (*Inf.*), get to the bottom of, grasp, suss (out) (*Sl.*), understand, unravel, work out

penetrating 1. biting, carrying, harsh, intrusive, pervasive, piercing, pungent, sharp, shrill, stinging, strong 2. *Fig.* acute, astute, critical, discerning, discriminating, incisive, intelligent, keen, perceptive, perspicacious, profound, quick, sagacious, searching, sharp, sharp-witted, shrewd
Antonyms (*sense 1*) blunt, dull, mild, sweet (*sense 2*) apathetic, dull, indifferent, obtuse, shallow, stupid, uncomprehending, unperceptive

penetration 1. entrance, entry, incision, inroad, invasion, perforation, piercing, puncturing 2. acuteness, astuteness, discernment, insight, keenness, perception, perspicacity, sharpness, shrewdness, wit

penis chopper (*Brit. sl.*), cock (*Taboo sl.*), dick (*Taboo sl.*), dong (*Sl.*), John Thomas (*Taboo sl.*), joystick (*Sl.*), knob (*Brit. taboo sl.*), member, organ, pecker (*U.S. & Canad. taboo sl.*), phallus, pizzle (*Archaic & dialect*), plonker (*Sl.*), prick (*Taboo sl.*), schlong (*U.S. sl.*), tadger (*Brit. sl.*), tool

(*Taboo sl.*), wang (*U.S. sl.*), whang (*U.S. sl.*), weenie (*U.S. sl.*), winkle (*Brit. sl.*)

penitence compunction, contrition, regret, remorse, repentance, ruefulness, self-reproach, shame, sorrow

penitent *adj.* abject, apologetic, atoning, conscience-stricken, contrite, regretful, remorseful, repentant, rueful, sorrowful, sorry

Antonyms callous, impenitent, remorseless, unrepentant

penmanship calligraphy, chirography, fist (*Inf.*), hand, handwriting, longhand, script, writing

pen name allonym, nom de plume, pseudonym

pennant banderole, banner, burgee (*Nautical*), ensign, flag, jack, pennon, streamer

penniless bankrupt, broke (*Inf.*), cleaned out (*Sl.*), destitute, dirt-poor (*Inf.*), down and out, flat broke (*Inf.*), impecunious, impoverished, indigent, moneyless, necessitous, needy, on one's uppers, penurious, poor, poverty-stricken, ruined, short, skint (*Brit. sl.*), stony-broke (*Brit. sl.*), strapped (*Sl.*), without a penny to one's name, without two pennies to rub together (*Inf.*)

Antonyms affluent, filthy rich, loaded (*Sl.*), rich, rolling (*Sl.*), wealthy, well-heeled (*Inf.*)

penny-pincher meany (*Inf.*), miser, niggard, pinchpenny, screw (*Sl.*), Scrooge, skinflint, tight-arse (*Taboo sl.*), tight-ass (*U.S. taboo sl.*)

penny-pinching *adj.* cheeseparing, close, frugal, mean, mingy (*Brit. inf.*), miserly, near (*Inf.*), niggardly, scrimping, Scrooge-like, stingy, tight-arse (*Taboo sl.*), tight-arsed (*Taboo sl.*), tight as a duck's arse (*Taboo sl.*), tight-ass (*U.S. taboo sl.*), tight-assed (*U.S. taboo sl.*), tightfisted

Antonyms generous, kind, liberal, munificent, prodigal, unstinting

pennyworth bit, crumb, jot, little, mite, modicum, particle, scrap, small amount, tittle

pension allowance, annuity, benefit, superannuation

pensioner O.A.P., retired person, senior citizen

pensive blue (*Inf.*), cogitative, contemplative, dreamy, grave, in a brown study (*Inf.*), meditative, melancholy, mournful, musing, preoccupied, reflective, ruminative, sad, serious, sober, solemn, sorrowful, thoughtful, wistful

Antonyms active, carefree, cheerful, frivolous, gay, happy, joyous, light-hearted

pent-up bottled up, bridled, checked, constrained, curbed, held back, inhibited, repressed, smothered, stifled, suppressed

penurious 1. cheeseparing, close, close-fisted, frugal, grudging, mean, miserly, near (*Inf.*), niggardly, parsimonious, skimping, stingy, tight-arse (*Taboo sl.*), tight-arsed (*Taboo sl.*), tight as a duck's arse (*Taboo sl.*), tight-ass (*U.S. taboo sl.*), tight-assed (*U.S. taboo sl.*), tightfisted, ungenerous 2. destitute, down and out, impecunious, impoverished, indigent, needy, penniless, poor, poverty-stricken 3. beggarly, deficient, inadequate, meagre, miserable, miserly, paltry, poor, scanty

penury 1. beggary, destitution, indigence, need, pauperism, poverty, privation, straitened circumstances, want 2. dearth, deficiency, lack, paucity, scantiness, scarcity, shortage, sparseness

people *n.* 1. human beings, humanity, humans, mankind, men and women, mortals, persons 2. citizens, clan, community, family, folk, inhabitants, nation, population, public, race, tribe 3. commonalty, crowd, general public, grass roots, hoi polloi, masses, mob, multitude, plebs, populace, rabble, rank and file, the herd ~*v.* 4. colonize, inhabit, occupy, populate, settle

pep 1. *n.* animation, brio, energy, get-up-and-go (*Inf.*), gusto, high spirits, life, liveliness, spirit, verve, vigour, vim (*Sl.*), vitality, vivacity, zip (*Inf.*) 2. *v. With* **up** animate, enliven, exhilarate, inspire, invigorate, jazz up (*Inf.*), quicken, stimulate, vitalize, vivify

pepper *v.* 1. flavour, season, spice 2. bespeckle, dot, fleck, spatter, speck, sprinkle, stipple, stud 3. bombard, pelt, riddle, scatter, shower

peppery 1. fiery, highly seasoned, hot, piquant, pungent, spicy 2. choleric, hot-tempered, irascible, irritable, quick-tempered, snappish, testy, touchy, vitriolic, waspish 3. astringent, biting, caustic, incisive, sarcastic, sharp, stinging, trenchant, vitriolic

Antonyms (*sense 1*) bland, insipid, mild, tasteless, vapid

perceive 1. be aware of, behold, descry, discern, discover, distinguish, espy, make out, note, notice, observe, recognize, remark, see, spot 2. appreciate, apprehend, comprehend, conclude, deduce, feel, gather, get (*Inf.*), grasp, know, learn, realize, see, sense, suss (out) (*Sl.*), understand

perceptible apparent, appreciable, blatant, clear, conspicuous, detectable, discernible, distinct, evident, noticeable, observable, obvious, palpable, perceivable, recognizable, tangible, visible

Antonyms concealed, hidden, imperceptible, inconspicuous, indiscernible, invisible, unapparent, undetectable, unnoticeable

perception apprehension, awareness, conception, consciousness, discernment, feeling, grasp, idea, impression, insight, notion, observation, recognition, sensation, sense, taste, understanding

perceptive acute, alert, astute, aware, discerning, insightful, intuitive, observant, penetrating, percipient, perspicacious, quick, responsive, sensitive, sharp

Antonyms dull, indifferent, insensitive, obtuse, slow-witted, stupid, thick

perch 1. *n.* branch, pole, post, resting place, roost 2. *v.* alight, balance, land, rest, roost, settle, sit on

perchance by chance, for all one knows, haply (*Archaic*), maybe, mayhap (*Archaic*), peradventure (*Archaic*), perhaps, possibly, probably

percipience acuity, alertness, astuteness, awareness, discernment, insight, intuition, penetration, perception, perspicacity, sagacity, sensitivity, understanding

percipient alert, alive, astute, aware, discerning, discriminating, intelligent, penetrating, perceptive, perspicacious, quick-witted, sharp, wide-awake

percolate drain, drip, exude, filter, filtrate, leach, ooze, penetrate, perk (*of coffee, inf.*), permeate, pervade, seep, strain, transfuse

percussion blow, brunt, bump, clash, collision, concussion, crash, impact, jolt, knock, shock, smash, thump

perdition condemnation, damnation, destruction, doom, downfall, everlasting punishment, hell, hellfire, ruin

peregrination 1. expedition, exploration, journey, odyssey, tour, trek, trip, voyage 2. globetrotting, roaming, roving, travelling, trekking, wandering, wayfaring

peremptory 1. absolute, binding, categorical, commanding, compelling, decisive, final, imperative, incontrovertible, irrefutable, obligatory, undeniable 2. arbitrary, assertive, authoritative, autocratic, bossy (*Inf.*), dictatorial, dogmatic, domineering, high-handed, imperious, intolerant, overbearing

perennial 1. abiding, chronic, constant, continual, continuing, enduring, incessant, inveterate, lasting, lifelong, persistent, recurrent, unchanging 2. ceaseless, deathless, eternal, everlasting, immortal, imperishable, never-ending, permanent, perpetual, unceasing, undying, unfailing, uninterrupted

perfect *adj.* 1. absolute, complete, completed, consummate, entire, finished, full, out-and-out, sheer, unadulterated, unalloyed, unmitigated, utter, whole 2. blameless, clean, excellent, faultless, flawless, ideal, immaculate, impeccable, pure, splendid, spotless, sublime, superb, superlative, supreme, unblemished, unmarred, untarnished 3. accurate, close, correct, exact, faithful, precise, right, spot-on (*Brit. inf.*), strict, true, unerring 4. accomplished, adept, experienced, expert, finished, masterly, polished, practised, skilful, skilled ~*v.* 5. accomplish, achieve, carry out, complete, consummate, effect, finish, fulfil, perform, realize 6. ameliorate, cultivate, develop, elaborate, hone, improve, polish, refine

Antonyms *adj.* bad, damaged, defective, deficient, faulty, flawed, impaired, imperfect, impure, incomplete, inferior, partial, poor, ruined, spoiled, unfinished, unskilled, worthless ~*v.* mar

perfection 1. accomplishment, achievement, achieving, completion, consummation, evolution, fulfilment, realization 2. completeness, exactness, excellence, exquisiteness, faultlessness, integrity, maturity, perfectness, precision, purity, sublimity, superiority, wholeness 3. acme, crown, ideal, paragon

perfectionist formalist, precisian, precisionist, purist, stickler

perfectly 1. absolutely, altogether, completely, consummately, entirely, fully, quite, thoroughly, totally, utterly, wholly 2. admirably, exquisitely, faultlessly, flawlessly, ideally, impeccably, superbly, superlatively, supremely, to perfection, wonderfully

Antonyms (*sense 1*) inaccurately, incompletely, mistakenly, partially (*sense 2*) badly, defectively, faultily, imperfectly, poorly

perfidious corrupt, deceitful, dishonest, disloyal, double-dealing, double-faced, faithless, false, recreant (*Archaic*), traitorous, treacherous, treasonous, two-faced, unfaithful, untrustworthy

perfidy betrayal, deceit, disloyalty, double-dealing, duplicity, faithlessness, falsity, infidelity, perfidiousness, treachery, treason

perforate bore, drill, hole, honeycomb, penetrate, pierce, punch, puncture

perforce by force of circumstances, by necessity, inevitably, necessarily, needs must, of necessity, unavoidably, willy-nilly, without choice

perform 1. accomplish, achieve, act, bring

about, carry out, complete, comply with, discharge, do, effect, execute, fulfil, function, observe, pull off, satisfy, transact, work 2. act, appear as, depict, enact, play, present, produce, put on, render, represent, stage

performance 1. accomplishment, achievement, act, carrying out, completion, conduct, consummation, discharge, execution, exploit, feat, fulfilment, work 2. acting, appearance, exhibition, gig (*Inf.*), interpretation, play, portrayal, presentation, production, representation, show 3. action, conduct, efficiency, functioning, operation, practice, running, working 4. *Inf.* act, behaviour, bother, business, carry-on (*Inf., chiefly Brit.*), fuss, pother, rigmarole, to-do

performer actor, actress, artiste, play-actor, player, Thespian, trouper

perfume aroma, attar, balminess, bouquet, cologne, essence, fragrance, incense, niff (*Brit. sl.*), odour, redolence, scent, smell, sweetness

perfunctory automatic, careless, cursory, heedless, inattentive, indifferent, mechanical, negligent, offhand, routine, sketchy, slipshod, slovenly, stereotyped, superficial, unconcerned, unthinking, wooden

Antonyms ardent, assiduous, attentive, careful, diligent, keen, spirited, thorough, thoughtful, zealous

perhaps as the case may be, conceivably, feasibly, for all one knows, it may be, maybe, perchance (*Archaic*), possibly

peril danger, exposure, hazard, insecurity, jeopardy, menace, pitfall, risk, uncertainty, vulnerability

Antonyms certainty, impregnability, invulnerability, safety, security, surety

perilous chancy (*Inf.*), dangerous, exposed, fraught with danger, hairy (*Sl.*), hazardous, parlous (*Archaic*), precarious, risky, threatening, unsafe, unsure, vulnerable

perimeter ambit, border, borderline, boundary, bounds, circumference, confines, edge, limit, margin, periphery

Antonyms central part, centre, core, heart, hub, middle, nucleus

period 1. interval, season, space, span, spell, stretch, term, time, while 2. aeon, age, course, cycle, date, days, epoch, era, generation, season, stage, term, time, years

periodic at fixed intervals, cyclic, cyclical, every once in a while, every so often, infrequent, intermittent, occasional, periodical, recurrent, regular, repeated, seasonal, spasmodic, sporadic

periodical *n.* journal, magazine, monthly, organ, paper, publication, quarterly, review, serial, weekly

peripatetic ambulant, itinerant, migrant, mobile, nomadic, roaming, roving, travelling, vagabond, vagrant, wandering

peripheral 1. beside the point, borderline, incidental, inessential, irrelevant, marginal, minor, secondary, superficial, tangential, unimportant 2. exterior, external, outer, outermost, outside, perimetric, surface

periphery ambit, border, boundary, brim, brink, circumference, edge, fringe, hem, outer edge, outskirts, perimeter, rim, skirt, verge

periphrastic circuitous, circumlocutory, pleonastic, prolix, roundabout, tautological, verbose, wordy

perish 1. be killed, be lost, decease, die, expire, lose one's life, pass away 2. be destroyed, collapse, decline, disappear, fall, go under, vanish 3. decay, decompose, disintegrate, moulder, rot, waste, wither

perishable decaying, decomposable, destructible, easily spoilt, liable to rot, short-lived, unstable

Antonyms durable, lasting, long-life, long-lived, non-perishable

perjure (oneself) bear false witness, commit perjury, forswear, give false testimony, lie under oath, swear falsely

perjured deceitful, false, forsworn, lying, mendacious, perfidious, traitorous, treacherous, untrue, untruthful

perjury bearing false witness, false oath, false statement, false swearing, forswearing, giving false testimony, lying under oath, oath breaking, violation of an oath, wilful falsehood

perk benefit, bonus, dividend, extra, fringe benefit, icing on the cake, perquisite, plus

perk up brighten, buck up (*Inf.*), cheer up, liven up, look up, pep up, rally, recover, recuperate, revive, take heart

perky animated, bouncy, bright, bright-eyed and bushy-tailed (*Inf.*), bubbly, buoyant, cheerful, cheery, chirpy (*Inf.*), gay, genial, in fine fettle, jaunty, lively, spirited, sprightly, sunny, upbeat (*Inf.*), vivacious

permanence constancy, continuance, continuity, dependability, durability, duration, endurance, finality, fixedness, fixity, immortality, indestructibility, lastingness, perdurability (*Rare*), permanency, perpetuity, stability, survival

permanent abiding, constant, durable, enduring, eternal, everlasting, fixed, immovable, immutable, imperishable, indestructible, invariable, lasting, long-lasting, per-

ennial, perpetual, persistent, stable, steadfast, unchanging, unfading
Antonyms brief, changing, ephemeral, finite, fleeting, impermanent, inconstant, momentary, mortal, passing, short-lived, temporary, transitory, variable

permeable absorbent, absorptive, penetrable, pervious, porous, spongy

permeate charge, diffuse throughout, fill, filter through, imbue, impregnate, infiltrate, pass through, penetrate, percolate, pervade, saturate, seep through, soak through, spread throughout

permissible acceptable, admissible, allowable, all right, authorized, kosher (*Inf.*), lawful, legal, legit (*Sl.*), legitimate, licit, O.K. *or* okay (*Inf.*), permitted, proper, sanctioned
Antonyms banned, forbidden, illegal, illicit, prohibited, unauthorized, unlawful

permission allowance, approval, assent, authorization, consent, dispensation, freedom, go-ahead (*Inf.*), green light, leave, liberty, licence, permit, sanction, sufferance, tolerance

permissive acquiescent, easy-going, easy-oasy (*Sl.*), forbearing, free, indulgent, latitudinarian, lax, lenient, liberal, open-minded, tolerant
Antonyms authoritarian, denying, domineering, forbidding, grudging, rigid, strict

permit 1. *v.* admit, agree, allow, authorize, consent, empower, enable, endorse, endure, entitle, give leave *or* permission, grant, let, license, own, sanction, suffer, tolerate, warrant 2. *n.* authorization, liberty, licence, pass, passport, permission, sanction, warrant

permutation alteration, change, shift, transformation, transmutation, transposition

pernicious bad, baleful, baneful (*Archaic*), damaging, dangerous, deadly, deleterious, destructive, detrimental, evil, fatal, harmful, hurtful, injurious, maleficent, malevolent, malicious, malign, malignant, noisome, noxious, offensive, pestilent, poisonous, ruinous, venomous, wicked

pernickety 1. careful, carping, difficult to please, exacting, fastidious, finicky, fussy, hairsplitting, nice, nit-picking (*Inf.*), overprecise, painstaking, particular, picky (*Inf.*), punctilious 2. detailed, exacting, fiddly, fine, tricky
Antonyms (*sense 1*) careless, easy to please, haphazard, heedless, inattentive, lax, slack, slapdash, slipshod, sloppy, uncritical (*sense 2*) easy, simple

peroration closing remarks, conclusion, recapitulation, recapping (*Inf.*), reiteration, summing-up

perpendicular at right angles to, on end, plumb, straight, upright, vertical

perpetrate be responsible for, bring about, carry out, commit, do, effect, enact, execute, inflict, perform, wreak

perpetual 1. abiding, endless, enduring, eternal, everlasting, immortal, infinite, lasting, never-ending, perennial, permanent, sempiternal (*Literary*), unchanging, undying, unending 2. ceaseless, constant, continual, continuous, endless, incessant, interminable, never-ending, perennial, persistent, recurrent, repeated, unceasing, unfailing, uninterrupted, unremitting
Antonyms brief, ephemeral, fleeting, impermanent, momentary, passing, short-lived, temporary, transitory

perpetuate continue, eternalize, immortalize, keep alive, keep going, keep up, maintain, preserve, sustain
Antonyms abolish, destroy, end, forget, ignore, put an end to, stamp out, suppress

perplex 1. baffle, befuddle, beset, bewilder, confound, confuse, dumbfound, flummox, mix up, muddle, mystify, nonplus, puzzle, stump 2. complicate, encumber, entangle, involve, jumble, mix up, snarl up, tangle, thicken

perplexing baffling, bewildering, complex, complicated, confusing, difficult, enigmatic, hard, inexplicable, intricate, involved, knotty, labyrinthine, mysterious, mystifying, paradoxical, puzzling, strange, taxing, thorny, unaccountable, weird

perplexity 1. bafflement, bewilderment, confusion, incomprehension, mystification, puzzlement, stupefaction 2. complexity, difficulty, inextricability, intricacy, involvement, obscurity 3. difficulty, dilemma, enigma, fix (*Inf.*), knotty problem, mystery, paradox, puzzle, snarl

perquisite benefit, bonus, dividend, extra, fringe benefit, icing on the cake, perk (*Brit. inf.*), plus

per se as such, by definition, by itself, by its very nature, essentially, in essence, in itself, intrinsically, of itself

persecute 1. afflict, be on one's back (*Sl.*), distress, dragoon, harass, hassle (*Inf.*), hound, hunt, ill-treat, injure, maltreat, martyr, molest, oppress, pursue, torment, torture, victimize 2. annoy, badger, bait, bother, pester, tease, vex, worry
Antonyms accommodate, back, calm, coddle, comfort, console, cosset, humour, indulge, leave alone, let alone, mollycoddle, pamper, pet, spoil, support

perseverance constancy, dedication, determination, diligence, doggedness, endurance, indefatigability, persistence, pertinacity, purposefulness, resolution, sedulity, stamina, steadfastness, tenacity

persevere be determined *or* resolved, carry on, continue, endure, go on, hang on, hold fast, hold on (*Inf.*), keep going, keep on *or* at, maintain, persist, plug away (*Inf.*), pursue, remain, stand firm, stick at *or* to
Antonyms be irresolute, dither (*Chiefly Brit.*), end, falter, give in, give up, hesitate, quit, shillyshally (*Inf.*), swither (*Scot.*), throw in the towel, vacillate, waver

persiflage badinage, banter, chaff, frivolity, pleasantry, raillery, repartee, teasing, wit, wittiness, wordplay

persist 1. be resolute, continue, hold on (*Inf.*), insist, persevere, stand firm 2. abide, carry on, continue, endure, keep up, last, linger, remain

persistence constancy, determination, diligence, doggedness, endurance, grit, indefatigability, perseverance, pertinacity, pluck, resolution, stamina, steadfastness, tenacity, tirelessness

persistent 1. assiduous, determined, dogged, enduring, fixed, immovable, indefatigable, obdurate, obstinate, persevering, pertinacious, resolute, steadfast, steady, stiff-necked, stubborn, tenacious, tireless, unflagging 2. constant, continual, continuous, endless, incessant, interminable, never-ending, perpetual, relentless, repeated, unrelenting, unremitting
Antonyms (*sense 1*) changeable, flexible, irresolute, tractable, yielding (*sense 2*) inconstant, intermittent, irregular, occasional, off-and-on, periodic

person 1. being, body, human, human being, individual, living soul, soul 2. **in person** bodily, in the flesh, oneself, personally

persona assumed role, character, façade, face, front, mask, part, personality, public face, role

personable affable, agreeable, amiable, attractive, charming, good-looking, handsome, likable *or* likeable, nice, pleasant, pleasing, presentable, winning
Antonyms disagreeable, sullen, surly, ugly, unattractive, unpleasant, unsightly

personage big noise (*Inf.*), big shot (*Inf.*), celeb (*Inf.*), celebrity, dignitary, luminary, megastar (*Inf.*), notable, personality, public figure, somebody, V.I.P., well-known person, worthy

personal 1. exclusive, individual, intimate, own, particular, peculiar, private, privy, special 2. bodily, corporal, corporeal, exterior, material, physical 3. derogatory, disparaging, insulting, nasty, offensive, pejorative, slighting

personality 1. character, disposition, identity, individuality, make-up, nature, psyche, temper, temperament, traits 2. attraction, attractiveness, character, charisma, charm, dynamism, likableness *or* likeableness, magnetism, pleasantness 3. celeb (*Inf.*), celebrity, famous name, household name, megastar (*Inf.*), notable, personage, star, well-known face, well-known person

personally 1. alone, by oneself, independently, in person, in the flesh, on one's own, solely 2. for oneself, for one's part, from one's own viewpoint, in one's own view 3. individualistically, individually, privately, specially, subjectively

personate act, depict, do (*Inf.*), enact, feign, imitate, impersonate, play-act, portray, represent

personification embodiment, epitome, image, incarnation, likeness, portrayal, recreation, representation, semblance

personify body forth, embody, epitomize, exemplify, express, image (*Rare*), incarnate, mirror, represent, symbolize, typify

personnel employees, helpers, human resources, liveware, members, men and women, people, staff, workers, work force

perspective 1. angle, attitude, broad view, context, frame of reference, objectivity, outlook, overview, proportion, relation, relative importance, relativity, way of looking 2. outlook, panorama, prospect, scene, view, vista

perspicacious acute, alert, astute, aware, clear-sighted, clever, discerning, keen, observant, penetrating, perceptive, percipient, sagacious, sharp, sharp-witted, shrewd

perspicacity acumen, acuteness, discernment, discrimination, insight, keenness, penetration, perceptiveness, percipience, perspicaciousness, perspicuity, sagaciousness, sagacity, sharpness, shrewdness, smarts (*Sl., chiefly U.S.*), suss (*Sl.*), wit

perspicuity clarity, clearness, comprehensibility, distinctness, explicitness, intelligibility, limpidity, limpidness, lucidity, plainness, precision, straightforwardness, transparency

perspicuous clear, comprehensible, crystal-clear, distinct, easily understood, explicit, intelligible, limpid, lucid, obvious, plain, self-evident, straightforward, transparent, unambiguous, understandable

perspiration exudation, moisture, sweat, wetness

perspire be damp, be wet, drip, exude, glow, pour with sweat, secrete, sweat, swelter

persuade 1. actuate, advise, allure, bring round (*Inf.*), coax, counsel, entice, impel, incite, induce, influence, inveigle, prevail upon, prompt, sway, talk into, urge, win over 2. cause to believe, convert, convince, satisfy
Antonyms deter, discourage, dissuade, forbid, prohibit

persuasion 1. blandishment, cajolery, conversion, enticement, exhortation, inducement, influencing, inveiglement, wheedling 2. cogency, force, persuasiveness, potency, power, pull (*Inf.*) 3. belief, certitude, conviction, credo, creed, faith, firm belief, fixed opinion, opinion, tenet, views 4. camp, cult, denomination, faction, party, school, school of thought, sect, side

persuasive cogent, compelling, convincing, credible, effective, eloquent, forceful, impelling, impressive, inducing, influential, logical, moving, plausible, sound, telling, touching, valid, weighty, winning
Antonyms feeble, flimsy, illogical, implausible, incredible, ineffective, invalid, unconvincing, unimpressive, weak

pert 1. bold, brash, cheeky, flip (*Inf.*), flippant, forward, fresh (*Inf.*), impertinent, impudent, lippy (*U.S. & Canad. sl.*), insolent, presumptuous, pushy (*Inf.*), sassy (*U.S. inf.*), saucy, smart 2. brisk, dapper, daring, dashing, gay, jaunty, lively, nimble, perky, smart, spirited, sprightly

pertain appertain, apply, be appropriate, bear on, befit, belong, be part of, be relevant, concern, refer, regard, relate

pertinacious bull-headed, determined, dogged, headstrong, inflexible, intractable, mulish, obdurate, obstinate, persevering, persistent, perverse, pig-headed, relentless, resolute, self-willed, stiff-necked, strong-willed, stubborn, tenacious, unyielding, wilful

pertinent admissible, *ad rem,* applicable, apposite, appropriate, apropos, apt, fit, fitting, germane, material, pat, proper, relevant, suitable, to the point, to the purpose
Antonyms discordant, foreign, immaterial, inappropriate, incongruous, irrelevant, unfitting, unrelated, unsuitable

pertness audacity, brashness, brass (*Inf.*), bumptiousness, cheek (*Inf.*), cheekiness, chutzpah (*U.S. & Canad. inf.*), cockiness, effrontery, forwardness, front, impertinence, impudence, insolence, presumption, rudeness, sauciness

perturb 1. agitate, alarm, bother, discompose, disconcert, discountenance, disquiet, disturb, faze, fluster, ruffle, trouble, unnerve, unsettle, upset, vex, worry 2. confuse, disarrange, disorder, muddle, unsettle

perturbed agitated, alarmed, anxious, disconcerted, disquieted, disturbed, fearful, flurried, flustered, ill at ease, nervous, restless, shaken, troubled, uncomfortable, uneasy, upset, worried
Antonyms assured, at ease, comfortable, composed, cool, impassive, relaxed, unperturbed, unruffled

perusal browse, check, examination, inspection, look through, read, scrutiny, study

peruse browse, check, examine, inspect, look through, read, run one's eye over, scan, scrutinize, study, work over

pervade affect, charge, diffuse, extend, fill, imbue, infuse, overspread, penetrate, percolate, permeate, spread through, suffuse

pervasive common, extensive, general, inescapable, omnipresent, permeating, pervading, prevalent, rife, ubiquitous, universal, widespread

perverse 1. abnormal, contradictory, contrary, delinquent, depraved, deviant, disobedient, froward, improper, incorrect, miscreant, rebellious, refractory, troublesome, unhealthy, unmanageable, unreasonable 2. contrary, contumacious, cross-grained, dogged, headstrong, intractable, intransigent, obdurate, wilful, wrong-headed 3. contrary, mulish, obstinate, pig-headed, stiff-necked, stubborn, unyielding, wayward 4. cantankerous, churlish, crabbed, cross, fractious, ill-natured, ill-tempered, peevish, petulant, spiteful, stroppy (*Brit. sl.*), surly
Antonyms accommodating, agreeable, amiable, complaisant, cooperative, flexible, good-natured, malleable, obedient, obliging

perversion 1. aberration, abnormality, debauchery, depravity, deviation, immorality, kink (*Brit. inf.*), kinkiness (*Sl.*), unnaturalness, vice, vitiation, wickedness 2. corruption, distortion, falsification, misinterpretation, misrepresentation, misuse, twisting

perversity contradictiveness, contradictoriness, contrariness, contumacy, frowardness, intransigence, obduracy, refractoriness, waywardness, wrong-headedness

pervert *v.* 1. abuse, distort, falsify, garble, misconstrue, misinterpret, misrepresent, misuse, twist, warp 2. corrupt, debase, debauch, degrade, deprave, desecrate, initiate, lead astray, subvert ~*n.* 3. debauchee, degenerate, deviant, weirdo *or* weirdie (*Inf.*)

perverted aberrant, abnormal, corrupt, debased, debauched, depraved, deviant, distorted, evil, immoral, impaired, kinky (*Sl.*), misguided, pervy (*Sl.*), sick, twisted, unhealthy, unnatural, vicious, vitiated, warped, wicked

pessimism cynicism, dejection, depression, despair, despondency, distrust, gloom, gloominess, gloomy outlook, glumness, hopelessness, melancholy, the hump (*Brit. inf.*)

pessimist cynic, defeatist, doomster, gloom merchant (*Inf.*), kill-joy, melancholic, misanthrope, prophet of doom, wet blanket (*Inf.*), worrier

pessimistic bleak, cynical, dark, dejected, depressed, despairing, despondent, distrustful, downhearted, fatalistic, foreboding, gloomy, glum, hopeless, melancholy, misanthropic, morose, resigned, sad

Antonyms assured, bright, buoyant, cheerful, cheery, encouraged, exhilarated, hopeful, in good heart, optimistic, sanguine

pest 1. annoyance, bane, bore, bother, drag (*Inf.*), gall, irritation, nuisance, pain (*Inf.*), pain in the arse (*Taboo inf.*), pain in the neck (*Inf.*), thorn in one's flesh, trial, vexation 2. bane, blight, bug, curse, epidemic, infection, pestilence, plague, scourge

pester aggravate (*Inf.*), annoy, badger, bedevil, bend someone's ear (*Inf.*), be on one's back (*Sl.*), bother, bug (*Inf.*), chivvy, disturb, drive one up the wall (*Sl.*), fret, get at, get in one's hair (*Inf.*), get on one's nerves (*Inf.*), harass, harry, hassle (*Inf.*), irk, nag, pick on, plague, ride (*Inf.*), torment, worry

pestilence 1. Black Death, epidemic, pandemic, plague, visitation 2. affliction, bane, blight, cancer, canker, curse, scourge

pestilent 1. annoying, bothersome, galling, irksome, irritating, plaguy (*Inf.*), tiresome, vexing 2. corrupting, deleterious, destructive, detrimental, evil, harmful, injurious, pernicious, ruinous, vicious 3. catching, contagious, contaminated, diseased, disease-ridden, infected, infectious, plague-ridden, tainted

pestilential 1. annoying, dangerous, deleterious, destructive, detrimental, evil, foul, harmful, hazardous, injurious, pernicious, ruinous, troublesome 2. catching, contagious, contaminated, deadly, disease-ridden, infectious, malignant, noxious, pestiferous, poisonous, venomous

pet[1] *n.* 1. apple of one's eye, blue-eyed boy (*Inf.*), darling, favourite, idol, jewel, treasure ~*adj.* 2. cherished, dearest, dear to one's heart, favoured, favourite, particular, preferred, special 3. domesticated, house, house-broken, house-trained (*Brit.*), tame, trained ~*v.* 4. baby, coddle, cosset, mollycoddle, pamper, spoil 5. caress, fondle, pat, stroke 6. *Inf.* canoodle (*Sl.*), cuddle, kiss, neck (*Inf.*), smooch (*Inf.*), snog (*Brit. sl.*)

pet[2] bad mood, bate (*Brit. sl.*), huff, ill temper, miff (*Inf.*), paddy (*Brit. inf.*), paddywhack (*Brit. inf.*), pique, pout, sulk, sulks, tantrum, temper

peter out come to nothing, die out, dwindle, ebb, evaporate, fade, fail, give out, run dry, run out, stop, taper off, wane

petite dainty, delicate, dinky (*Brit. inf.*), elfin, little, slight, small

petition 1. *n.* address, appeal, application, entreaty, invocation, memorial, plea, prayer, request, round robin, solicitation, suit, supplication 2. *v.* adjure, appeal, ask, beg, beseech, call upon, crave, entreat, plead, pray, press, solicit, sue, supplicate, urge

petrified 1. fossilized, ossified, rocklike 2. aghast, appalled, dazed, dumbfounded, frozen, horrified, numb, scared shitless (*Taboo sl.*), scared stiff, shit-scared (*Taboo sl.*), shocked, speechless, stunned, stupefied, terrified, terror-stricken

petrify 1. calcify, fossilize, harden, set, solidify, turn to stone 2. amaze, appal, astonish, astound, confound, dumbfound, horrify, immobilize, paralyse, stun, stupefy, terrify, transfix

pettifoggery cheating, corruption, deceit, deception, dishonesty, double-dealing, duplicity, fraud, gerrymandering, jobbery, swindling

pettifogging captious, casuistic, cavilling, equivocating, hairsplitting, insignificant, mean, niggling, nit-picking (*Inf.*), paltry, petty, piddling (*Inf.*), quibbling, sophistical, sophisticated, subtle

pettish cross, fractious, fretful, grumpy, huffy, ill-humoured, irritable, liverish, peevish, petulant, querulous, ratty (*Brit. & N.Z. inf.*), sulky, tetchy, thin-skinned, touchy, waspish

petty 1. contemptible, inconsiderable, inessential, inferior, insignificant, little, measly (*Inf.*), negligible, nickel-and-dime (*U.S. sl.*), paltry, piddling (*Inf.*), slight, small, trifling, trivial, unimportant 2. cheap, grudging, mean, mean-minded, shabby, small-minded, spiteful, stingy, ungenerous 3. inferior, junior, lesser, lower, minor, secondary, subordinate

Antonyms (*sense 1*) consequential, considerable, essential, important, major, momentous, significant (*sense 2*) broad-minded, generous, liberal, magnanimous, open-minded, tolerant

petulance bad temper, crabbiness, ill humour, irritability, peevishness, pettishness, pique, pouts, querulousness, spleen, sulkiness, sullenness, waspishness

petulant bad-tempered, captious, cavilling, crabbed, cross, crusty, fault-finding, fret~

ful, huffy, ill-humoured, impatient, irritable, moody, peevish, perverse, pouting, querulous, ratty (*Brit. & N.Z. inf.*), snappish, sour, sulky, sullen, ungracious, waspish
Antonyms affable, cheerful, congenial, easy-going, even-tempered, good-humoured, good-natured, happy, patient, smiling

phantasm 1. apparition, eidolon, ghost, phantom, revenant, shade (*Literary*), spectre, spirit, spook (*Inf.*), wraith 2. chimera, figment, figment of the imagination, hallucination, illusion, vision

phantasmagoric, phantasmagorical chimerical, dreamlike, hallucinatory, illusory, Kafkaesque, kaleidoscopic, nightmarish, phantasmal, psychedelic, surreal, unreal

phantasmal chimerical, delusory, fancied, fanciful, ghostlike, ghostly, illusory, imaginary, imagined, phantasmagoric, phantasmagorical, phantomlike, shadowy, spectral, unreal, wraithlike

phantasy *see* FANTASY

phantom 1. apparition, eidolon, ghost, phantasm, revenant, shade (*Literary*), spectre, spirit, spook (*Inf.*), wraith 2. chimera, figment, figment of the imagination, hallucination, illusion, vision

pharisaic, pharisaical canting, formal, goody-goody, holier-than-thou, hypocritical, insincere, Pecksniffian, pietistic, sanctimonious, self-righteous

pharisaism cant, false piety, hypocrisy, insincerity, lip service, pietism, religiosity, sanctimoniousness, self-righteousness

pharisee canter, dissembler, dissimulator, fraud, humbug, hypocrite, phoney *or* phony (*Inf.*), pietist, whited sepulchre

phase aspect, chapter, condition, development, juncture, period, point, position, stage, state, step, time

phase out axe (*Inf.*), close, deactivate, dispose of gradually, ease off, eliminate, pull out, remove, replace, run down, taper off, terminate, wind down, wind up, withdraw
Antonyms activate, begin, create, establish, form, initiate, open, set up, start

phenomenal exceptional, extraordinary, fantastic, marvellous, miraculous, notable, outstanding, prodigious, remarkable, sensational, singular, uncommon, unique, unparalleled, unusual, wondrous (*Archaic or literary*)
Antonyms average, common, mediocre, ordinary, poor, run-of-the-mill, second-rate, unexceptional, unremarkable, usual

phenomenon 1. circumstance, episode, event, fact, happening, incident, occurrence 2. exception, marvel, miracle, nonpareil, prodigy, rarity, sensation, sight, spectacle, wonder

philander coquet, court, dally, flirt, fool around (*Inf.*), toy, trifle, womanize (*Inf.*)

philanderer Casanova, dallier, Don Juan, flirt, gallant, gay dog, ladies' man, lady-killer (*Inf.*), Lothario, playboy, stud (*Sl.*), trifler, wolf (*Inf.*), womanizer (*Inf.*)

philanthropic alms-giving, altruistic, beneficent, benevolent, benignant, charitable, eleemosynary, gracious, humane, humanitarian, kind, kind-hearted, munificent, public-spirited
Antonyms egoistic, mean, miserly, niggardly, penurious, selfish, self-seeking, stingy

philanthropist alms-giver, altruist, benefactor, contributor, donor, giver, humanitarian, patron

philanthropy alms-giving, altruism, beneficence, benevolence, benignity, bounty, brotherly love, charitableness, charity, generosity, humanitarianism, kind-heartedness, largess *or* largesse, liberality, munificence, open-handedness, patronage, public-spiritedness

philippic condemnation, denunciation, diatribe, fulmination, harangue, invective, obloquy, stream of abuse, tirade, vituperation

philistine 1. *n.* barbarian, boor, bourgeois, Goth, ignoramus, lout, lowbrow, vulgarian, yahoo 2. *adj.* anti-intellectual, boorish, bourgeois, crass, ignorant, lowbrow, tasteless, uncultivated, uncultured, uneducated, unrefined

philosopher dialectician, logician, mahatma, metaphysician, sage, seeker after truth, theorist, thinker, wise man

philosophical, philosophic 1. abstract, erudite, learned, logical, rational, sagacious, theoretical, thoughtful, wise 2. calm, collected, composed, cool, impassive, imperturbable, patient, resigned, sedate, serene, stoical, tranquil, unruffled
Antonyms (*sense 1*) factual, illogical, irrational, practical, pragmatic, scientific (*sense 2*) emotional, hot-headed, impulsive, perturbed, rash, restless, upset

philosophy 1. aesthetics, knowledge, logic, metaphysics, rationalism, reason, reasoning, thinking, thought, wisdom 2. attitude to life, basic idea, beliefs, convictions, doctrine, ideology, principle, tenets, thinking, values, viewpoint, *Weltanschauung*, world-view 3. composure, coolness, dispassion, equanimity, resignation, restraint, self-possession, serenity, stoicism

phlegmatic apathetic, bovine, cold, dull,

frigid, heavy, impassive, indifferent, lethargic, listless, lymphatic, matter-of-fact, placid, sluggish, stoical, stolid, undemonstrative, unemotional, unfeeling
Antonyms active, alert, animated, emotional, energetic, excited, hyper (*Inf.*), lively, passionate

phobia aversion, detestation, dislike, distaste, dread, fear, hatred, horror, irrational fear, loathing, obsession, overwhelming anxiety, repulsion, revulsion, terror, thing (*Inf.*)
Antonyms bent, fancy, fondness, inclination, liking, love, partiality, passion, penchant, soft spot

phone *n.* 1. blower (*Inf.*), telephone 2. bell (*Brit. sl.*), buzz (*Inf.*), call, ring (*Inf., chiefly Brit.*), tinkle (*Brit. inf.*) ~*v.* 3. buzz (*Inf.*), call, get on the blower (*Inf.*), give someone a bell (*Brit. sl.*), give someone a buzz (*Inf.*), give someone a call, give someone a ring (*Inf., chiefly Brit.*), give someone a tinkle (*Brit. inf.*), make a call, ring (up) (*Inf., chiefly Brit.*), telephone

phoney 1. *adj.* affected, assumed, bogus, counterfeit, ersatz, fake, false, forged, imitation, pseudo (*Inf.*), put-on, sham, spurious, trick 2. *n.* counterfeit, fake, faker, forgery, fraud, humbug, impostor, pretender, pseud (*Inf.*), sham
Antonyms authentic, bona fide, genuine, original, real, sincere, unaffected, unassumed, unfeigned

photograph 1. *n.* image, likeness, photo (*Inf.*), picture, print, shot, slide, snap (*Inf.*), snapshot, transparency 2. *v.* capture on film, film, get a shot of, record, shoot, snap (*Inf.*), take, take a picture of, take (someone's) picture

photographic accurate, cinematic, detailed, exact, faithful, filmic, graphic, lifelike, minute, natural, pictorial, precise, realistic, retentive, visual, vivid

phrase 1. *n.* expression, group of words, idiom, locution, motto, remark, saying, tag, utterance, way of speaking 2. *v.* couch, express, formulate, frame, present, put, put into words, say, term, utter, voice, word

phraseology choice of words, diction, expression, idiom, language, parlance, phrase, phrasing, speech, style, syntax, wording

physical 1. bodily, carnal, corporal, corporeal, earthly, fleshly, incarnate, mortal, somatic, unspiritual 2. material, natural, palpable, real, sensible, solid, substantial, tangible, visible

physician doc (*Inf.*), doctor, doctor of medicine, general practitioner, G.P., healer, M.D., medic (*Inf.*), medical practitioner, medico (*Inf.*), sawbones (*Sl.*), specialist

physiognomy clock (*Brit. sl.*), countenance, dial (*Brit. sl.*), face, features, look, phiz (*Sl.*), phizog (*Sl.*), visage

physique body, build, constitution, figure, form, frame, make-up, shape, structure

pick *v.* 1. choose, decide upon, elect, fix upon, hand-pick, mark out, opt for, select, settle upon, sift out, single out, sort out 2. collect, cull, cut, gather, harvest, pluck, pull 3. have no appetite, nibble, peck at, play *or* toy with, push the food round the plate 4. foment, incite, instigate, provoke, start 5. break into, break open, crack, force, jemmy, open, prise open 6. **pick one's way** be tentative, find *or* make one's way, move cautiously, tread carefully, work through ~*n.* 7. choice, choosing, decision, option, preference, selection 8. choicest, *crème de la crème,* elect, elite, flower, pride, prize, the best, the cream, the tops (*Sl.*)
Antonyms (*sense 1*) cast aside, decline, discard, dismiss, reject, spurn, turn down

pick at carp, cavil, criticize, find fault, get at, nag, pick holes, pick to pieces, quibble

picket *n.* 1. pale, paling, palisade, peg, post, stake, stanchion, upright 2. demonstrator, flying picket, picketer, protester 3. guard, lookout, patrol, scout, sentinel, sentry, spotter, vedette (*Military*), watch ~*v.* 4. blockade, boycott, demonstrate 5. corral (*U.S.*), enclose, fence, hedge in, palisade, pen in, rail in, shut in, wall in

pickings booty, earnings, gravy (*Sl.*), ill-gotten gains, loot, plunder, proceeds, profits, returns, rewards, spoils, yield

pickle *n.* 1. *Inf.* bind (*Inf.*), difficulty, dilemma, fix (*Inf.*), hot water (*Inf.*), jam (*Inf.*), predicament, quandary, scrape (*Inf.*), spot (*Inf.*), tight spot 2. *Brit. inf.* little horror, mischief, mischief maker, monkey, naughty child, rascal ~*v.* 3. cure, keep, marinade, preserve, steep

pick-me-up bracer (*Inf.*), drink, pick-up (*Sl.*), refreshment, restorative, roborant, shot in the arm (*Inf.*), stimulant, tonic

pick on badger, bait, blame, bully, goad, hector, tease, torment

pick out 1. choose, cull, hand-pick, select, separate the sheep from the goats, single out, sort out 2. discriminate, distinguish, make distinct, make out, notice, perceive, recognize, tell apart

pick-up *n.* 1. acceleration, response, revving (*Inf.*), speed-up 2. change for the better, gain, improvement, rally, recovery, revival, rise, strengthening, upswing, upturn

pick up *v.* 1. gather, grasp, hoist, lift, raise, take up, uplift 2. buy, come across, find, garner, happen upon, obtain, purchase, score (*Sl.*) 3. gain, gain ground, get better, improve, make a comeback (*Inf.*), mend, perk up, rally, recover, take a turn for the better 4. call for, collect, get, give someone a lift, go to get, uplift (*Scot.*) 5. acquire, get the hang of (*Inf.*), learn, master 6. *Sl.* apprehend, arrest, bust (*Inf.*), collar (*Inf.*), do (*Sl.*), feel one's collar (*Sl.*), lift (*Sl.*), nab (*Inf.*), nail (*Inf.*), nick (*Sl., chiefly Brit.*), pinch (*Inf.*), pull in (*Brit. sl.*), run in (*Sl.*), take into custody

picky captious, carping, cavilling, choosy, critical, dainty, fastidious, fault-finding, finicky, fussy, nice, particular, pernickety (*Inf.*)

picnic 1. excursion, *fête champêtre,* outdoor meal, outing 2. *Inf.* breeze (*U.S. & Canad. inf.*), cakewalk (*Inf.*), child's play (*Inf.*), cinch (*Sl.*), duck soup (*U.S. sl.*), piece of cake (*Brit. inf.*), pushover (*Sl.*), snap (*Inf.*), walkover (*Inf.*)

pictorial expressive, graphic, illustrated, picturesque, representational, scenic, striking, vivid

picture *n.* 1. delineation, drawing, effigy, engraving, illustration, image, likeness, painting, photograph, portrait, portrayal, print, representation, similitude, sketch 2. account, depiction, description, image, impression, re-creation, report 3. carbon copy, copy, dead ringer (*Sl.*), double, duplicate, image, likeness, living image, lookalike, replica, ringer (*Sl.*), spit (*Inf., chiefly Brit.*), spit and image (*Inf.*), spitting image (*Inf.*), twin 4. archetype, embodiment, epitome, essence, living example, perfect example, personification 5. film, flick (*Sl.*), motion picture, movie (*U.S. inf.*) ~*v.* 6. conceive of, envision, image, see, see in the mind's eye, visualize 7. delineate, depict, describe, draw, illustrate, paint, photograph, portray, render, represent, show, sketch

picturesque attractive, beautiful, charming, colourful, graphic, pretty, quaint, scenic, striking, vivid

Antonyms commonplace, drab, dull, everyday, inartistic, unattractive, uninteresting

piddling chickenshit (*U.S. sl.*), crappy (*Sl.*), derisory, fiddling, insignificant, little, measly (*Inf.*), Mickey Mouse (*Sl.*), nickel-and-dime (*U.S. sl.*), paltry, petty, piffling, poxy (*Sl.*), puny, trifling, trivial, unimportant, useless, worthless

Antonyms considerable, important, major, significant, sizable, substantial, tidy (*Inf.*), useful, valuable

piebald black and white, brindled, dappled, flecked, mottled, pied, speckled, spotted

piece *n.* 1. allotment, bit, chunk, division, fraction, fragment, length, morsel, mouthful, part, portion, quantity, scrap, section, segment, share, shred, slice 2. case, example, instance, occurrence, sample, specimen, stroke 3. article, bit (*Inf.*), composition, creation, item, production, study, work, work of art 4. **go to pieces** break down, crack up (*Inf.*), crumple, disintegrate, fall apart, lose control, lose one's head 5. **in pieces** broken, bust (*Inf.*), damaged, disintegrated, in bits, in smithereens, ruined, shattered, smashed 6. **of a piece** alike, analogous, consistent, identical, of the same kind, similar, the same, uniform ~*v.* 7. *Often with* **together** assemble, compose, fix, join, mend, patch, repair, restore, unite

pièce de résistance *chef-d'oeuvre,* jewel, masterpiece, masterwork, showpiece

piecemeal 1. *adv.* at intervals, bit by bit, by degrees, by fits and starts, fitfully, intermittently, little by little, partially, slowly 2. *adj.* fragmentary, intermittent, interrupted, partial, patchy, spotty, unsystematic

pied dappled, flecked, irregular, motley, mottled, multicoloured, parti-coloured, piebald, spotted, streaked, varicoloured, variegated

pier *n.* 1. jetty, landing place, promenade, quay, wharf 2. buttress, column, pile, piling, pillar, post, support, upright

pierce 1. bore, drill, enter, impale, penetrate, perforate, prick, probe, puncture, run through, spike, stab, stick into, transfix 2. comprehend, discern, discover, fathom, grasp, realize, see, understand 3. *Fig.* affect, cut, cut to the quick, excite, hurt, move, pain, rouse, sting, stir, strike, thrill, touch, wound

piercing 1. *Usually of sound* ear-splitting, high-pitched, loud, penetrating, sharp, shattering, shrill 2. alert, aware, keen, penetrating, perceptive, perspicacious, probing, quick-witted, searching, sharp, shrewd 3. *Usually of weather* arctic, biting, bitter, cold, freezing, frosty, keen, nipping, nippy, numbing, raw, wintry 4. acute, agonizing, excruciating, exquisite, fierce, intense, painful, powerful, racking, severe, sharp, shooting, stabbing

Antonyms (*sense 1*) inaudible, low, low-pitched, mellifluous, quiet, soundless (*sense 2*) obtuse, slow, slow-witted, thick, unperceptive

piety devotion, devoutness, dutifulness, duty, faith, godliness, grace, holiness, piousness, religion, reverence, sanctity, veneration

piffle balderdash, balls (*Taboo sl.*), bilge (*Inf.*), bosh (*Inf.*), bull (*Sl.*), bullshit (*Taboo sl.*), bunk (*Inf.*), bunkum *or* buncombe (*Chiefly U.S.*), cobblers (*Brit. taboo sl.*), codswallop (*Brit. sl.*), crap (*Sl.*), drivel, eyewash (*Inf.*), garbage (*Inf.*), guff (*Sl.*), hogwash, hokum (*Sl., chiefly U.S. & Canad.*), hooey (*Sl.*), horsefeathers (*U.S. sl.*), hot air (*Inf.*), moonshine, nonsense, pap, poppycock (*Inf.*), rot, rubbish, shit (*Taboo sl.*), tarradiddle, tommyrot, tosh (*Sl., chiefly Brit.*), trash, tripe (*Inf.*), twaddle

piffling chickenshit (*U.S. sl.*), crappy (*Sl.*), derisory, fiddling, insignificant, little, measly (*Inf.*), Mickey Mouse (*Sl.*), nickel-and-dime (*U.S. sl.*), paltry, petty, piddling (*Inf.*), poxy (*Sl.*), puny, trifling, trivial, unimportant, useless, worthless

pig 1. boar, grunter, hog, piggy, piglet, porker, shoat, sow, swine 2. *Inf.* animal, beast, boor, brute, glutton, greedy guts (*Sl.*), guzzler, hog (*Inf.*), slob (*Sl.*), sloven, swine

pigeon 1. bird, culver (*Archaic*), cushat, dove, squab 2. *Sl.* dupe, fall guy (*Inf.*), gull (*Archaic*), mug (*Brit. sl.*), sitting duck, sucker (*Sl.*), victim 3. *Brit. inf.* baby (*Sl.*), business, concern, lookout (*Inf.*), responsibility, worry

pigeonhole *n.* 1. compartment, cubbyhole, cubicle, locker, niche, place, section 2. *Inf.* category, class, classification, slot (*Inf.*) ~*v.* 3. defer, file, postpone, put off, shelve 4. catalogue, characterize, classify, codify, compartmentalize, label, slot (*Inf.*), sort

piggish 1. boorish, crude, gluttonous, greedy, hoggish, piggy, rude, swinish, voracious 2. *Inf.* hoggish, mean, obstinate, pigheaded, possessive, selfish, stubborn

pig-headed bull-headed, contrary, cross-grained, dense, froward, inflexible, mulish, obstinate, perverse, self-willed, stiff-necked, stubborn, stupid, unyielding, wilful, wrong-headed

Antonyms agreeable, amiable, complaisant, cooperative, flexible, obliging, open-minded, tractable

pigment colorant, colour, colouring, colouring matter, dye, dyestuff, paint, stain, tincture, tint

pile[1] *n.* 1. accumulation, assemblage, assortment, collection, heap, hoard, mass, mound, mountain, stack, stockpile 2. *Inf.* big bucks (*Inf., chiefly U.S.*), big money, bomb (*Brit. sl.*), fortune, megabucks (*U.S. & Canad. sl.*), mint, money, packet (*Sl.*), pot, pretty penny (*Inf.*), tidy sum (*Inf.*), wad (*U.S. & Canad. sl.*), wealth 3. *Often plural Inf.* a lot, great deal, ocean, oodles (*Inf.*), quantity, stacks 4. building, edifice, erection, structure ~*v.* 5. accumulate, amass, assemble, collect, gather, heap, hoard, load up, mass, stack, store 6. charge, crowd, crush, flock, flood, jam, pack, rush, stream

pile[2] beam, column, foundation, pier, piling, pillar, post, support, upright

pile[3] down, fibre, filament, fur, hair, nap, plush, shag, surface

piles haemorrhoids

pile-up accident, collision, crash, multiple collision, smash, smash-up (*Inf.*)

pilfer appropriate, blag (*Sl.*), cabbage (*Brit. sl.*), embezzle, filch, knock off (*Sl.*), lift (*Inf.*), nick (*Sl., chiefly Brit.*), pinch (*Inf.*), purloin, rifle, rob, snaffle (*Brit. inf.*), snitch (*Sl.*), steal, swipe (*Sl.*), take, thieve, walk off with

pilgrim crusader, hajji, palmer, traveller, wanderer, wayfarer

pilgrimage crusade, excursion, expedition, hajj, journey, mission, tour, trip

pill 1. bolus, capsule, pellet, pilule, tablet 2. **the pill** oral contraceptive 3. *Sl.* bore, drag (*Inf.*), nuisance, pain (*Inf.*), pain in the neck (*Inf.*), pest, trial

pillage *v.* 1. depredate (*Rare*), despoil, freeboot, loot, maraud, plunder, raid, ransack, ravage, reive (*Dialect*), rifle, rob, sack, spoil (*Archaic*), spoliate, strip ~*n.* 2. depredation, devastation, marauding, plunder, rapine, robbery, sack, spoliation 3. booty, loot, plunder, spoils

pillar 1. column, pier, pilaster, piling, post, prop, shaft, stanchion, support, upright 2. leader, leading light (*Inf.*), mainstay, rock, supporter, tower of strength, upholder, worthy

pillory *v.* brand, cast a slur on, denounce, expose to ridicule, heap *or* pour scorn on, hold up to shame, lash, show up, stigmatize

pilot 1. *n.* airman, aviator, captain, conductor, coxswain, director, flier, guide, helmsman, leader, navigator, steersman 2. *v.* conduct, control, direct, drive, fly, guide, handle, lead, manage, navigate, operate, shepherd, steer 3. *adj.* experimental, model, test, trial

pimp 1. *n.* bawd (*Archaic*), go-between, pander, panderer, procurer, white-slaver, whoremaster (*Archaic*) 2. *v.* live off immoral earnings, procure, sell, solicit, tout

pimple boil, papule (*Pathol.*), plook (*Scot.*), pustule, spot, swelling, zit (*Sl.*)

pin *v.* 1. affix, attach, fasten, fix, join, secure 2. fix, hold down, hold fast, immobilize, pinion, press, restrain

pinch *v.* 1. compress, grasp, nip, press,

squeeze, tweak 2. chafe, confine, cramp, crush, hurt, pain 3. afflict, be stingy, distress, economize, oppress, pinch pennies, press, scrimp, skimp, spare, stint 4. *Inf.* blag (*Sl.*), cabbage (*Brit. sl.*), filch, knock off (*Sl.*), lift (*Inf.*), nick (*Sl., chiefly Brit.*), pilfer, purloin, rob, snaffle (*Brit. inf.*), snatch, snitch (*Sl.*), steal, swipe (*Sl.*) 5. *Inf.* apprehend, arrest, bust (*Inf.*), collar (*Inf.*), do (*Sl.*), feel one's collar (*Sl.*), lift (*Sl.*), nab (*Inf.*), nail (*Inf.*), nick (*Sl., chiefly Brit.*), pick up (*Sl.*), pull in (*Brit. sl.*), run in (*Sl.*), take into custody ~*n.* 6. nip, squeeze, tweak 7. bit, dash, jot, mite, small quantity, *soupçon,* speck, taste 8. crisis, difficulty, emergency, exigency, hardship, necessity, oppression, pass, plight, predicament, pressure, strait, stress

Antonyms (*sense 3*) be extravagant, blow (*Sl.*), fritter away, spend like water, squander, waste (*sense 5*) free, let go, let out, release, set free

pinchbeck 1. *n.* counterfeit, fake, imitation, paste, phoney *or* phony (*Inf.*), sham 2. *adj.* artificial, bogus, counterfeit, ersatz, fake, imitation, pseudo (*Inf.*), spurious

pinched careworn, drawn, gaunt, haggard, peaky, starved, thin, worn

Antonyms blooming, chubby, fat, glowing, hale and hearty, healthy, plump, radiant, ruddy, well-fed

pin down 1. compel, constrain, force, make, press, pressurize 2. designate, determine, home in on, identify, locate, name, pinpoint, specify 3. bind, confine, constrain, fix, hold, hold down, immobilize, nail down, tie down

pine 1. *Often with* **for** ache, carry a torch for, covet, crave, desire, eat one's heart out over, hanker, hunger for, long, lust after, sigh, thirst for, wish, yearn 2. decay, decline, droop, dwindle, fade, flag, languish, peak, sicken, sink, waste, weaken, wilt, wither

pinion *v.* bind, chain, confine, fasten, fetter, immobilize, manacle, pin down, shackle, tie

pink[1] 1. *n.* acme, best, height, peak, perfection, summit 2. *adj.* flesh, flushed, reddish, rose, roseate, rosy, salmon

pink[2] incise, notch, perforate, prick, punch, scallop, score

pinnacle 1. acme, apex, apogee, crest, crown, eminence, height, meridian, peak, summit, top, vertex, zenith 2. belfry, cone, needle, obelisk, pyramid, spire, steeple

pinpoint define, distinguish, get a fix on, home in on, identify, locate, spot

pint ale, beer, jar (*Brit. inf.*), jug (*Brit. inf.*)

pint-size diminutive, little, midget, miniature, pygmy *or* pigmy, pocket, small, teensy-weensy, teeny-weeny, tiny, wee

pioneer *n.* 1. colonist, colonizer, explorer, frontiersman, settler 2. developer, founder, founding father, innovator, leader, trailblazer ~*v.* 3. create, develop, discover, establish, initiate, instigate, institute, invent, launch, lay the groundwork, map out, open up, originate, prepare, show the way, start, take the lead

pious 1. dedicated, devoted, devout, God-fearing, godly, holy, religious, reverent, righteous, saintly, spiritual 2. goody-goody, holier-than-thou, hypocritical, pietistic, religiose, sanctimonious, self-righteous, unctuous

Antonyms (*sense 1*) impious, irreligious, irreverent, ungodly, unholy (*sense 2*) humble, meek, sincere

pipe *n.* 1. conduit, conveyor, duct, hose, line, main, passage, pipeline, tube 2. briar, clay, meerschaum 3. fife, horn, tooter, whistle, wind instrument ~*v.* 4. cheep, peep, play, sing, sound, tootle, trill, tweet, twitter, warble, whistle 5. bring in, channel, conduct, convey, siphon, supply, transmit

pipe down belt up (*Sl.*), be quiet, button it (*Sl.*), button one's lip (*Sl.*), hold one's tongue, hush, put a sock in it (*Brit. sl.*), quieten down, shush, shut one's mouth, shut up (*Inf.*), silence

pipe dream castle in the air, chimera, daydream, delusion, dream, fantasy, notion, reverie, vagary

pipeline 1. conduit, conveyor, duct, line, passage, pipe, tube 2. **in the pipeline** brewing, coming, getting ready, in process, in production, on the way, under way

pipe up have one's say, make oneself heard, put one's oar in, raise one's voice, speak, speak up, volunteer

pipsqueak creep (*Sl.*), nobody, nonentity, nothing (*Inf.*), squirt (*Inf.*), upstart, whippersnapper

piquancy 1. bite (*Inf.*), edge, flavour, kick (*Inf.*), pungency, relish, sharpness, spice, spiciness, tang, zest 2. colour, excitement, interest, pep, pizzazz *or* pizazz (*Inf.*), raciness, spirit, vigour, vitality, zip (*Inf.*)

piquant 1. acerb, biting, highly-seasoned, peppery, pungent, savoury, sharp, spicy, stinging, tangy, tart, with a kick (*Inf.*), zesty 2. interesting, lively, provocative, racy, salty, scintillating, sparkling, spirited, stimulating

Antonyms banal, bland, boring, dull, insipid, mild, tame, uninteresting

pique *n.* 1. annoyance, displeasure, grudge, huff, hurt feelings, irritation, miff (*Inf.*), offence, resentment, umbrage, vexation, wounded pride ~*v.* 2. affront, annoy, displease, gall, get (*Inf.*), incense, irk, irritate, miff (*Inf.*), mortify, nark (*Brit., Aust., & N.Z. sl.*), nettle, offend, peeve (*Inf.*), provoke, put out, put someone's nose out of joint (*Inf.*), rile, sting, vex, wound 3. arouse, excite, galvanize, goad, kindle, provoke, rouse, spur, stimulate, stir, whet 4. *With* **on** *or* **upon** *Of oneself* congratulate, flatter, plume, preen, pride

piracy buccaneering, freebooting, hijacking, infringement, plagiarism, rapine, robbery at sea, stealing, theft

pirate *n.* 1. buccaneer, corsair, filibuster, freebooter, marauder, raider, rover, sea robber, sea rover, sea wolf 2. cribber (*Inf.*), infringer, plagiarist, plagiarizer ~*v.* 3. appropriate, borrow, copy, crib (*Inf.*), lift (*Inf.*), plagiarize, poach, reproduce, steal

piratical buccaneering, criminal, dishonest, felonious, fraudulent, lawless, pillaging, plundering, rapacious, thieving, unprincipled, wolfish

pirouette *n./v.* pivot, spin, turn, twirl, whirl

pit *n.* 1. abyss, cavity, chasm, coal mine, crater, dent, depression, dimple, excavation, gulf, hole, hollow, indentation, mine, pockmark, pothole, trench ~*v.* 2. *Often with* **against** match, oppose, put in opposition, set against 3. dent, dint, gouge, hole, indent, mark, nick, notch, pockmark, scar

pitch *v.* 1. bung (*Brit. sl.*), cast, chuck (*Inf.*), fling, heave, hurl, launch, lob (*Inf.*), sling, throw, toss 2. erect, fix, locate, place, plant, put up, raise, settle, set up, station 3. flounder, lurch, make heavy weather, plunge, roll, toss, wallow, welter 4. dive, drop, fall headlong, stagger, topple, tumble ~*n.* 5. angle, cant, dip, gradient, incline, slope, steepness, tilt 6. degree, height, highest point, level, point, summit 7. harmonic, modulation, sound, timbre, tone 8. line, patter, sales talk, spiel (*Inf.*) 9. field of play, ground, park (*U.S. & Canad.*), sports field

pitch-black dark, ebony, inky, jet, jet-black, pitch-dark, raven, sable, unlit

pitch-dark black, dark, pitch-black, pitchy, Stygian, unilluminated, unlit

pitch in 1. chip in (*Inf.*), contribute, cooperate, do one's bit, help, join in, lend a hand, participate 2. begin, fall to, get busy, get cracking (*Inf.*), plunge into, set about, set to, tackle

pitch into assail, assault, attack, get stuck into (*Inf.*), lace into, light into (*Inf.*), sail into (*Inf.*), tear into (*Inf.*)

pitch on *or* **upon** choose, decide on, determine, elect, light on, opt for, pick, plump for, select, single out

pitchy black, coal-black, dark, ebony, inky, jet, jetty, moonless, pitch-black, raven, sable, unilluminated, unlighted

piteous affecting, deplorable, dismal, distressing, doleful, grievous, harrowing, heartbreaking, heart-rending, lamentable, miserable, mournful, moving, pathetic, pitiable, pitiful, plaintive, poignant, sad, sorrowful, woeful, wretched

pitfall 1. banana skin (*Inf.*), catch, danger, difficulty, drawback, hazard, peril, snag, trap 2. deadfall, downfall, pit, snare, trap

pith 1. core, crux, essence, gist, heart, heart of the matter, kernel, marrow, meat, nub, point, quintessence, salient point, the long and the short of it 2. consequence, depth, force, import, importance, matter, moment, power, significance, strength, substance, value, weight

pithy brief, cogent, compact, concise, epigrammatic, expressive, finely honed, forceful, laconic, meaningful, pointed, short, succinct, terse, to the point, trenchant
Antonyms diffuse, garrulous, long, long-winded, loquacious, prolix, verbose, wordy

pitiable deplorable, dismal, distressing, doleful, grievous, harrowing, lamentable, miserable, mournful, pathetic, piteous, poor, sad, sorry, woeful, wretched

pitiful 1. deplorable, distressing, grievous, harrowing, heartbreaking, heart-rending, lamentable, miserable, pathetic, piteous, pitiable, sad, woeful, wretched 2. abject, base, beggarly, contemptible, despicable, dismal, inadequate, insignificant, low, mean, measly, miserable, paltry, scurvy, shabby, sorry, vile, worthless
Antonyms (*sense 1*) amusing, cheerful, cheering, comical, funny, happy, heartening, laughable, merry (*sense 2*) adequate, admirable, honourable, laudable, praiseworthy, significant, valuable

pitiless brutal, callous, cold-blooded, cold-hearted, cruel, hardhearted, harsh, heartless, implacable, inexorable, inhuman, merciless, relentless, ruthless, uncaring, unfeeling, unmerciful, unsympathetic
Antonyms caring, compassionate, kind, merciful, relenting, responsive, soft-hearted, sparing

pittance allowance, chicken feed (*Sl.*), drop, mite, modicum, peanuts (*Sl.*), portion, ration, slave wages, trifle

pitted blemished, dented, eaten away, holey, indented, marked, pockmarked, pocky, potholed, riddled, rough, rutty, scarred, scratched

pity *n.* 1. charity, clemency, commiseration, compassion, condolence, fellow feeling, forbearance, kindness, mercy, quarter, sympathy, tenderness, understanding 2. bummer (*Sl.*), crime (*Inf.*), crying shame, misfortune, regret, sad thing, shame, sin 3. **take pity on** feel compassion for, forgive, have mercy on, melt, pardon, put out of one's misery, relent, reprieve, show mercy, spare ~*v.* 4. bleed for, commiserate with, condole with, feel for, feel sorry for, grieve for, have compassion for, sympathize with, weep for

Antonyms (*sense 1*) anger, apathy, brutality, cruelty, disdain, fury, hard-heartedness, indifference, inhumanity, mercilessness, pitilessness, ruthlessness, scorn, severity, unconcern, wrath

pivot *n.* 1. axis, axle, fulcrum, spindle, swivel 2. centre, focal point, heart, hinge, hub, kingpin ~*v.* 3. revolve, rotate, spin, swivel, turn, twirl 4. be contingent, depend, hang, hinge, rely, revolve round, turn

pivotal central, climactic, critical, crucial, decisive, determining, focal, vital

pixie brownie, elf, fairy, peri, sprite

placard advertisement, *affiche,* bill, poster, public notice, sticker

placate appease, assuage, calm, conciliate, humour, mollify, pacify, propitiate, satisfy, soothe, win over

placatory appeasing, conciliatory, designed to please, pacificatory, peacemaking, propitiative

place *n.* 1. area, location, locus, point, position, site, situation, spot, station, venue, whereabouts 2. city, district, hamlet, locale, locality, neighbourhood, quarter, region, town, vicinity, village 3. grade, position, rank, station, status 4. appointment, berth (*Inf.*), billet (*Inf.*), employment, job, position, post 5. abode, apartment, domicile, dwelling, flat, home, house, manor, mansion, pad (*Sl.*), property, residence, seat 6. accommodation, room, space, stead 7. affair, charge, concern, duty, function, prerogative, responsibility, right, role 8. **in place of** as an alternative to, as a substitute for, in exchange for, in lieu of, instead of, taking the place of 9. **put (someone) in his place** bring down, cut down to size, humble, humiliate, make (someone) eat humble pie, make (someone) swallow his pride, mortify, take down a peg (*Inf.*) 10. **take place** befall, betide, come about, come to pass (*Archaic*), go on, happen, occur, transpire (*Inf.*) ~*v.* 11. bung (*Brit. sl.*), deposit, dispose, establish, fix, install, lay, locate, plant, position, put, rest, set, settle, situate, stand, station, stick (*Inf.*) 12. arrange, class, classify, grade, group, order, rank, sort 13. associate, identify, know, put one's finger on, recognize, remember, set in context 14. allocate, appoint, assign, charge, commission, entrust, give

placement 1. arrangement, deployment, disposition, distribution, emplacement, installation, locating, location, ordering, positioning, stationing 2. appointment, assignment, employment, engagement

placid calm, collected, composed, cool, equable, even, even-tempered, gentle, halcyon, imperturbable, mild, peaceful, quiet, self-possessed, serene, still, tranquil, undisturbed, unexcitable, unfazed (*Inf.*), unmoved, unruffled, untroubled

Antonyms agitated, disturbed, emotional, excitable, impulsive, passionate, rough, temperamental, tempestuous

plagiarism appropriation, borrowing, copying, cribbing (*Inf.*), infringement, lifting (*Inf.*), piracy, theft

plagiarize appropriate, borrow, crib (*Inf.*), infringe, lift (*Inf.*), pirate, steal, thieve

plague *n.* 1. contagion, disease, epidemic, infection, pandemic, pestilence 2. *Fig.* affliction, bane, blight, calamity, cancer, curse, evil, scourge, torment, trial 3. *Inf.* aggravation (*Inf.*), annoyance, bother, hassle (*Inf.*), irritant, nuisance, pain (*Inf.*), pest, problem, thorn in one's flesh, vexation ~*v.* 4. afflict, annoy, badger, bedevil, be on one's back (*Sl.*), bother, disturb, fret, get in one's hair (*Inf.*), get on one's nerves (*Inf.*), harass, harry, hassle (*Inf.*), haunt, molest, pain, persecute, pester, tease, torment, torture, trouble, vex

plaguy annoying, disagreeable, harassing, impossible, irksome, irritating, provoking, troublesome, trying, vexing, wretched

plain *adj.* 1. apparent, clear, comprehensible, distinct, evident, legible, lucid, manifest, obvious, patent, transparent, unambiguous, understandable, unmistakable, visible 2. artless, blunt, candid, direct, downright, forthright, frank, guileless, honest, ingenuous, open, outspoken, sincere, straightforward, upfront (*Inf.*) 3. common, commonplace, everyday, frugal, homely, lowly, modest, ordinary, simple, unaffected, unpretentious, workaday 4. austere, bare, basic, discreet, modest, muted, pure, restrained, severe, simple, Spartan, stark, unadorned, unembellished, unornamented, unpatterned, unvarnished 5. ill-favoured, no oil painting (*Inf.*), not beautiful, not striking, ordinary, ugly, unalluring, unattractive, unlovely, unprepossessing 6. even, flat, level, plane, smooth ~*n.* 7. flatland, grassland, llano, lowland, mesa, open country, plateau, prairie, steppe, tableland

Antonyms (*sense 1*) ambiguous, complex,

concealed, deceptive, difficult, disguised, hidden, illegible, incomprehensible, inconspicuous, indiscernible, indistinct, obscure, vague, veiled (*sense 2*) circuitous, indirect, meandering, rambling, roundabout (*sense 3*) affected, distinguished, egotistic, ostentatious, pretentious, sophisticated, worldly (*sense 4*) adorned, decorated, fancy, ornate (*sense 5*) attractive, beautiful, comely, good-looking, gorgeous, handsome (*sense 6*) bumpy, not level, uneven

plain-spoken blunt, candid, direct, downright, explicit, forthright, frank, open, outright, outspoken, straightforward, unequivocal, upfront (*Inf.*)
Antonyms diplomatic, discreet, evasive, guarded, indirect, reticent, subtle, tactful, thoughtful

plaintive disconsolate, doleful, grief-stricken, grievous, heart-rending, melancholy, mournful, pathetic, piteous, pitiful, rueful, sad, sorrowful, wistful, woebegone, woeful

plan *n.* 1. contrivance, design, device, idea, method, plot, procedure, programme, project, proposal, proposition, scenario, scheme, strategy, suggestion, system 2. blueprint, chart, delineation, diagram, drawing, illustration, layout, map, representation, scale drawing, sketch ~*v.* 3. arrange, concoct, contrive, design, devise, draft, formulate, frame, invent, organize, outline, plot, prepare, represent, scheme, think out 4. aim, contemplate, envisage, foresee, intend, mean, propose, purpose

plane *n.* 1. flat surface, level surface 2. condition, degree, footing, level, position, stratum 3. aeroplane, aircraft, jet ~*adj.* 4. even, flat, flush, horizontal, level, plain, regular, smooth, uniform ~*v.* 5. glide, sail, skate, skim, volplane

planetary 1. earthly, mundane, sublunary, tellurian, terrene, terrestrial 2. aberrant, erratic, journeying, moving, travelling, vacillating, variable, wandering

plangent clangorous, deep-toned, loud, mournful, plaintive, resonant, resounding, reverberating, ringing, sonorous

plant *n.* 1. bush, flower, herb, shrub, vegetable, weed 2. factory, foundry, mill, shop, works, yard 3. apparatus, equipment, gear, machinery ~*v.* 4. implant, put in the ground, scatter, seed, set out, sow, transplant 5. establish, fix, found, imbed, insert, institute, lodge, root, set, settle

plaque badge, brooch, cartouch(e), medal, medallion, panel, plate, slab, tablet

plaster *n.* 1. gypsum, mortar, plaster of Paris, stucco 2. adhesive plaster, bandage, dressing, Elastoplast (*Trademark*), sticking plaster ~*v.* 3. bedaub, besmear, coat, cover, daub, overlay, smear, spread

plastic *adj.* 1. compliant, docile, easily influenced, impressionable, malleable, manageable, pliable, receptive, responsive, tractable 2. ductile, fictile, flexible, mouldable, pliable, pliant, soft, supple, tensile 3. *Sl.* artificial, false, meretricious, phoney *or* phony (*Inf.*), pseudo (*Inf.*), sham, specious, spurious, superficial, synthetic
Antonyms (*sense 1*) intractable, rebellious, recalcitrant, refractory, unmanageable, unreceptive (*sense 2*) brittle, hard, inflexible, rigid, stiff, unbending, unyielding (*sense 3*) authentic, genuine, natural, real, sincere, true

plasticity flexibility, malleability, pliability, pliableness, suppleness, tractability

plate *n.* 1. dish, platter, trencher (*Archaic*) 2. course, dish, helping, portion, serving 3. layer, panel, sheet, slab 4. illustration, lithograph, print ~*v.* 5. anodize, coat, cover, electroplate, face, gild, laminate, nickel, overlay, platinize, silver

plateau 1. highland, mesa, table, tableland, upland 2. level, levelling off, stability, stage

platform 1. dais, podium, rostrum, stage, stand 2. manifesto, objective(s), party line, policy, principle, programme, tenet(s)

platitude 1. banality, bromide, cliché, commonplace, hackneyed saying, inanity, stereotype, trite remark, truism 2. banality, dullness, inanity, insipidity, triteness, triviality, vapidity, verbiage

platitudinous banal, clichéd, commonplace, corny (*Sl.*), hack, hackneyed, overworked, set, stale, stereotyped, stock, tired, trite, truistic, vapid, well-worn

platonic *All of love* ideal, idealistic, intellectual, nonphysical, spiritual, transcendent

platoon company, group, outfit (*Inf.*), patrol, squad, squadron, team

platter charger, dish, plate, salver, tray, trencher (*Archaic*)

plaudit *Usually plural* acclaim, acclamation, applause, approbation, approval, clapping, commendation, congratulation, hand, kudos, ovation, praise, round of applause

plausible believable, colourable, conceivable, credible, fair-spoken, glib, likely, persuasive, possible, probable, reasonable, smooth, smooth-talking, smooth-tongued, specious, tenable, verisimilar
Antonyms genuine, illogical, implausible, impossible, improbable, inconceivable, incredible, real, unbelievable, unlikely

play *v.* 1. amuse oneself, caper, engage in games, entertain oneself, fool, frisk, frolic, gambol, have fun, revel, romp, sport, trifle 2. be in a team, challenge, compete, contend against, participate, rival, take on, take part, vie with 3. act, act the part of, execute, impersonate, perform, personate, portray, represent, take the part of 4. bet, chance, gamble, hazard, punt (*Chiefly Brit.*), risk, speculate, take, wager 5. **play ball** *Inf.* collaborate, cooperate, go along, play along, reciprocate, respond, show willing 6. **play by ear** ad lib, extemporize, improvise, rise to the occasion, take it as it comes 7. **play for time** delay, drag one's feet (*Inf.*), filibuster, hang fire, procrastinate, stall, temporize 8. **play the fool** act the goat (*Inf.*), clown, clown around, horse around (*Inf.*), lark (about) (*Inf.*), mess about, monkey around, skylark (*Inf.*) 9. **play the game** *Inf.* conform, follow the rules, go along with, keep in step, play by the rules, play fair, toe the line ~*n.* 10. comedy, drama, dramatic piece, entertainment, farce, masque, performance, piece, radio play, show, soap opera, stage show, television drama, tragedy 11. amusement, caper, diversion, entertainment, frolic, fun, gambol, game, jest, pastime, prank, recreation, romp, sport 12. gambling, gaming 13. action, activity, elbowroom, exercise, give (*Inf.*), latitude, leeway, margin, motion, movement, operation, range, room, scope, space, sweep, swing 14. action, activity, employment, function, operation, transaction, working 15. foolery, fun, humour, jest, joking, lark (*Inf.*), prank, sport, teasing

play around dally, fool around, mess around, philander, take lightly, trifle, womanize

playboy gay dog, ladies' man, lady-killer (*Inf.*), lover boy (*Sl.*), man about town, philanderer, pleasure seeker, rake, roué, socialite, womanizer

play down gloss over, make light of, make little of, minimize, set no store by, soft-pedal (*Inf.*), underplay, underrate

player 1. competitor, contestant, participant, sportsman, sportswoman, team member 2. actor, actress, entertainer, performer, Thespian, trouper 3. artist, instrumentalist, musician, music maker, performer, virtuoso

playful 1. cheerful, coltish, frisky, frolicsome, gay, impish, joyous, kittenish, larkish (*Inf.*), lively, merry, mischievous, puckish, rollicking, spirited, sportive, sprightly, vivacious 2. arch, coy, flirtatious, good-natured, humorous, jesting, jokey, joking, roguish, teasing, tongue-in-cheek, waggish

Antonyms despondent, gloomy, grave, morose, sedate, serious

playmate chum (*Inf.*), companion, comrade, friend, neighbour, pal (*Inf.*), playfellow

play on *or* **upon** abuse, capitalize on, exploit, impose on, milk, profit by, take advantage of, trade on, turn to account, utilize

plaything amusement, bauble, game, gewgaw, gimcrack, pastime, toy, trifle, trinket

play up 1. accentuate, bring to the fore, call attention to, emphasize, highlight, magnify, point up, stress, turn the spotlight on, underline 2. *Brit. inf.* be painful, be sore, bother, give one gyp (*Brit. & N.Z. sl.*), give one trouble, hurt, pain, trouble 3. *Brit. inf.* be awkward, be bolshie (*Brit. inf.*), be cussed (*Inf.*), be disobedient, be stroppy (*Brit. sl.*), give trouble, misbehave 4. *Brit. inf.* be on the blink (*Sl.*), be wonky (*Brit. sl.*), malfunction, not work properly 5. **play up to** *Inf.* bootlick (*Inf.*), brown-nose (*Taboo sl.*), butter up, curry favour, fawn, flatter, get in with, ingratiate oneself, kiss (someone's) ass (*U.S. & Canad. taboo sl.*), pander to, suck up to (*Inf.*), toady

play with 1. amuse oneself with, flirt with, string along, toy with, trifle with 2. fiddle with (*Inf.*), fidget with, fool around, interfere with, jiggle, mess about, waggle, wiggle

playwright dramatist, dramaturge, dramaturgist

plea 1. appeal, begging, entreaty, intercession, overture, petition, prayer, request, suit, supplication 2. *Law* action, allegation, cause, suit 3. apology, claim, defence, excuse, explanation, extenuation, justification, pretext, vindication

plead 1. appeal (to), ask, beg, beseech, crave, entreat, implore, importune, petition, request, solicit, supplicate 2. adduce, allege, argue, assert, maintain, put forward, use as an excuse

pleasant 1. acceptable, agreeable, amusing, delectable, delightful, enjoyable, fine, gratifying, lovely, nice, pleasing, pleasurable, refreshing, satisfying, welcome 2. affable, agreeable, amiable, charming, cheerful, cheery, congenial, engaging, friendly, genial, good-humoured, likable *or* likeable, nice

Antonyms awful, cold, disagreeable, distasteful, horrible, horrid, impolite, miserable, offensive, repulsive, rude, unfriendly, unlikable *or* unlikeable, unpleasant

pleasantry badinage, banter, bon mot, good-natured remark, jest, joke, josh (*Sl., chiefly U.S. & Canad.*), quip, sally, witticism

please 1. amuse, charm, cheer, content, delight, entertain, give pleasure to, gladden, gratify, humour, indulge, rejoice, satisfy, suit, tickle, tickle pink (*Inf.*) 2. be inclined, choose, desire, like, opt, prefer, see fit, want, will, wish
Antonyms anger, annoy, depress, disgust, displease, dissatisfy, grieve, incense, offend, provoke, sadden, vex

pleased chuffed (*Brit. sl.*), contented, delighted, euphoric, glad, gratified, happy, in high spirits, over the moon (*Inf.*), pleased as punch (*Inf.*), rapt, satisfied, thrilled, tickled, tickled pink (*Inf.*)

pleasing agreeable, amiable, amusing, attractive, charming, delightful, engaging, enjoyable, entertaining, gratifying, likable *or* likeable, pleasurable, polite, satisfying, winning
Antonyms boring, disagreeable, dull, monotonous, rude, unattractive, unlikable *or* unlikeable, unpleasant

pleasurable agreeable, congenial, delightful, diverting, enjoyable, entertaining, fun, good, gratifying, lovely, nice, pleasant, welcome

pleasure 1. amusement, bliss, comfort, contentment, delectation, delight, diversion, ease, enjoyment, gladness, gratification, happiness, jollies (*Sl.*), joy, recreation, satisfaction, solace 2. choice, command, desire, inclination, mind, option, preference, purpose, will, wish
Antonyms abstinence, anger, disinclination, displeasure, duty, labour, misery, necessity, obligation, pain, sadness, sorrow, suffering, unhappiness

plebeian 1. *adj.* base, coarse, common, ignoble, low, lowborn, lower-class, mean, non-U (*Brit. inf.*), proletarian, uncultivated, unrefined, vulgar, working-class 2. *n.* commoner, common man, man in the street, peasant, pleb, prole (*Derogatory sl., chiefly Brit.*), proletarian
Antonyms aristocratic, cultivated, highborn, high-class, patrician, polished, refined, upper-class, well-bred

plebiscite ballot, poll, referendum, vote

pledge *n.* 1. assurance, covenant, oath, promise, undertaking, vow, warrant, word, word of honour 2. bail, bond, collateral, deposit, earnest, gage, guarantee, pawn, security, surety 3. health, toast ~*v.* 4. contract, engage, give one's oath (word, word of honour), promise, swear, undertake, vouch, vow 5. bind, engage, gage (*Archaic*), guarantee, mortgage, plight 6. drink the health of, drink to, toast

plenary 1. absolute, complete, full, sweeping, thorough, unconditional, unlimited, unqualified, unrestricted 2. *Of assemblies, councils, etc.* complete, entire, full, general, open, whole

plenipotentiary ambassador, emissary, envoy, legate, minister

plenitude 1. abundance, bounty, copiousness, cornucopia, excess, plenteousness, plenty, plethora, profusion, wealth 2. amplitude, completeness, fullness, repletion

plenteous 1. abundant, ample, bounteous (*Literary*), bountiful, copious, generous, inexhaustible, infinite, lavish, liberal, overflowing, plentiful, profuse 2. bumper, fertile, fruitful, luxuriant, plentiful, productive, prolific

plentiful 1. abundant, ample, bounteous (*Literary*), bountiful, complete, copious, generous, inexhaustible, infinite, lavish, liberal, overflowing, plenteous, profuse 2. bumper, fertile, fruitful, luxuriant, plenteous, productive, prolific
Antonyms deficient, inadequate, insufficient, scant, scarce, skimpy, small, sparing, sparse

plenty 1. abundance, enough, fund, good deal, great deal, heap(s) (*Inf.*), lots (*Inf.*), mass, masses, mine, mountain(s), oodles (*Inf.*), pile(s) (*Inf.*), plethora, quantities, quantity, stack(s), store, sufficiency, volume 2. abundance, affluence, copiousness, fertility, fruitfulness, luxury, opulence, plenitude, plenteousness, plentifulness, profusion, prosperity, wealth

pleonasm circuitousness, circumlocution, convolution, periphrasis, redundancy, repetition, tautology, verbiage, verbosity, wordiness

pleonastic circuitous, circumlocutory, convoluted, periphrastic, prolix, redundant, repetitious, superfluous, tautological, verbose, wordy

plethora excess, glut, overabundance, profusion, superabundance, superfluity, surfeit, surplus
Antonyms dearth, deficiency, lack, scarcity, shortage, want

pliability 1. bendability, ductility, elasticity, flexibility, malleability, mobility, plasticity, pliancy 2. adaptability, amenability, compliance, docility, impressionableness, susceptibility, tractableness

pliable 1. bendable, bendy, ductile, flexible, limber, lithe, malleable, plastic, pliant, supple, tensile 2. adaptable, compliant, docile, easily led, impressionable, influenceable, manageable, persuadable, pliant, receptive, responsive, susceptible, tractable, yielding
Antonyms headstrong, inflexible, intractable, obdurate, obstinate, rigid, stiff,

stubborn, unadaptable, unbending, unyielding, wilful

pliant 1. bendable, bendy, ductile, flexible, lithe, plastic, pliable, supple, tensile 2. adaptable, biddable, compliant, easily led, impressionable, influenceable, manageable, persuadable, pliable, susceptible, tractable, yielding

plight[1] *n.* case, circumstances, condition, difficulty, dilemma, extremity, hole (*Sl.*), hot water (*Inf.*), jam (*Inf.*), perplexity, pickle (*Inf.*), predicament, scrape (*Inf.*), situation, spot (*Inf.*), state, straits, tight spot, trouble

plight[2] *v.* contract, covenant, engage, guarantee, pledge, promise, propose, swear, vouch, vow

plod 1. clump, drag, lumber, slog, stomp (*Inf.*), tramp, tread, trudge 2. drudge, grind (*Inf.*), grub, labour, peg away, persevere, plough through, plug away (*Inf.*), slog, soldier on, toil

plot[1] *n.* 1. cabal, conspiracy, covin (*Law*), intrigue, machination, plan, scheme, stratagem 2. action, narrative, outline, scenario, story, story line, subject, theme, thread ~*v.* 3. cabal, collude, conspire, contrive, hatch, intrigue, machinate, manoeuvre, plan, scheme 4. calculate, chart, compute, draft, draw, locate, map, mark, outline 5. brew, conceive, concoct, contrive, cook up (*Inf.*), design, devise, frame, hatch, imagine, lay, project

plot[2] *n.* allotment, area, ground, lot, parcel, patch, tract

plough *v.* 1. break ground, cultivate, dig, furrow, ridge, till, turn over 2. *Usually with* **through** cut, drive, flounder, forge, plod, plunge, press, push, stagger, surge, wade 3. *With* **into** bulldoze, career, crash, hurtle, plunge, shove, smash

ploy contrivance, device, dodge, gambit, game, manoeuvre, move, ruse, scheme, stratagem, subterfuge, tactic, trick, wile

pluck[1] *n.* backbone, balls (*Taboo sl.*), ballsiness (*Taboo sl.*), boldness, bottle (*Brit. sl.*), bravery, courage, determination, grit, guts (*Inf.*), hardihood, heart, intrepidity, mettle, nerve, resolution, spirit, spunk (*Inf.*)

pluck[2] *v.* 1. collect, draw, gather, harvest, pick, pull out *or* off 2. catch, clutch, jerk, pull at, snatch, tug, tweak, yank 3. finger, pick, plunk, strum, thrum, twang

plucky ballsy (*Taboo sl.*), bold, brave, courageous, daring, doughty, feisty (*Inf., chiefly U.S. & Canad.*), game, gritty, gutsy (*Sl.*), hardy, have-a-go (*Inf.*), heroic, intrepid, mettlesome, spirited, spunky (*Inf.*), undaunted, unflinching, valiant

Antonyms afraid, chicken (*Sl.*), cowardly, dastardly, dispirited, lifeless, scared, spineless, spiritless, timid, yellow (*Inf.*), weary

plug *n.* 1. bung, cork, spigot, stopper, stopple 2. cake, chew, pigtail, quid, twist, wad 3. *Inf.* advert (*Brit. inf.*), advertisement, good word, hype, mention, publicity, puff, push ~*v.* 4. block, bung, choke, close, cork, cover, fill, pack, seal, stop, stopper, stopple, stop up, stuff 5. *Inf.* advertise, build up, hype, mention, promote, publicize, puff, push, write up 6. *Sl.* blow away (*Sl., chiefly U.S.*), gun down, pick off, pop, pot, put a bullet in, shoot 7. *With* **along** *or* **away** *Inf.* drudge, grind (*Inf.*), labour, peg away, plod, slog, toil

plum *Fig.* 1. *n.* bonus, cream, find, pick, prize, treasure 2. *adj.* best, choice, first-class, prize

plumb *n.* 1. lead, plumb bob, plummet, weight ~*adv.* 2. perpendicularly, up and down, vertically 3. bang, exactly, precisely, slap, spot-on (*Brit. inf.*) ~*v.* 4. delve, explore, fathom, gauge, go into, measure, penetrate, probe, search, sound, unravel

plume 1. *n.* aigrette, crest, feather, pinion, quill 2. *v. With* **on** *or* **upon** congratulate oneself, pat oneself on the back, pique oneself, preen oneself, pride oneself

plummet crash, descend, dive, drop down, fall, nose-dive, plunge, stoop, swoop, tumble

plump[1] *adj.* beefy (*Inf.*), burly, buxom, chubby, corpulent, dumpy, fat, fleshy, full, obese, podgy, portly, roly-poly, rotund, round, stout, tubby, well-covered, well-upholstered (*Inf.*)

Antonyms anorexic, bony, emaciated, lanky, lean, scrawny, skinny, slender, slim, sylphlike, thin

plump[2] *v.* 1. drop, dump, fall, flop, sink, slump 2. *With* **for** back, choose, come down in favour of, favour, opt for, side with, support ~*adj.* 3. abrupt, direct, downright, forthright, plain, unqualified, unreserved

plunder 1. *v.* despoil, devastate, loot, pillage, raid, ransack, ravage, rifle, rob, sack, spoil, steal, strip 2. *n.* booty, ill-gotten gains, loot, pillage, prey, prize, rapine, spoils, swag (*Sl.*)

plunge *v.* 1. cast, descend, dip, dive, douse, drop, fall, go down, immerse, jump, nose-dive, pitch, plummet, sink, submerge, swoop, throw, tumble 2. career, charge, dash, hurtle, lurch, rush, tear ~*n.* 3. descent, dive, drop, fall, immersion, jump, submersion, swoop

plurality 1. diversity, multiplicity, numerousness, profusion, variety 2. bulk, majority, mass, most, nearly all, overwhelming number, preponderance

plus 1. *prep.* added to, and, coupled with, with, with the addition of 2. *adj.* added, additional, add-on, extra, positive, supplementary 3. *n. Inf.* advantage, asset, benefit, bonus, extra, gain, good point, icing on the cake, perk (*Brit. inf.*), surplus

plush costly, de luxe, lavish, luxurious, luxury, opulent, palatial, rich, ritzy (*Sl.*), sumptuous

Antonyms cheap, cheap and nasty, inexpensive, ordinary, plain, spartan

plutocrat capitalist, Croesus, Dives, fat cat (*Sl., chiefly U.S.*), magnate, millionaire, moneybags (*Sl.*), rich man, tycoon

ply[1] 1. carry on, exercise, follow, practise, pursue, work at 2. employ, handle, manipulate, swing, utilize, wield 3. assail, beset, besiege, bombard, harass, importune, press, urge

ply[2] fold, layer, leaf, sheet, strand, thickness

poach appropriate, encroach, hunt *or* fish illegally, infringe, intrude, plunder, rob, steal, steal game, trespass

pock blemish, flaw, mark, pimple, pockmark, pustule, scar, spot

pocket *n.* 1. bag, compartment, hollow, pouch, receptacle, sack ~*adj.* 2. abridged, compact, concise, little, miniature, pint-size(d) (*Inf.*), portable, potted (*Inf.*), small ~*v.* 3. appropriate, cabbage (*Brit. sl.*), filch, help oneself to, lift (*Inf.*), pilfer, purloin, snaffle (*Brit. inf.*), steal, take 4. accept, bear, brook, endure, put up with (*Inf.*), stomach, swallow, take, tolerate

pockmark blemish, pit, pock, scar

pod *n./v.* hull, husk, shell, shuck

podgy chubby, chunky, dumpy, fat, fleshy, fubsy (*Archaic or dialect*), plump, roly-poly, rotund, short and fat, squat, stout, stubby, stumpy, tubby

podium dais, platform, rostrum, stage

poem lyric, ode, rhyme, song, sonnet, verse

poet bard, lyricist, maker (*Archaic*), rhymer, versifier

poetic elegiac, lyric, lyrical, metrical, rhythmical, songlike

poetry metrical composition, poems, poesy (*Archaic*), rhyme, rhyming, verse

po-faced disapproving, humourless, narrow-minded, prim, prudish, puritanical, solemn, stolid, strait-laced

poignancy 1. emotion, emotionalism, evocativeness, feeling, pathos, piteousness, plaintiveness, sadness, sentiment, tenderness 2. bitterness, intensity, keenness, piquancy, pungency, sharpness

poignant 1. affecting, agonizing, bitter, distressing, harrowing, heartbreaking, heart-rending, intense, moving, painful, pathetic, sad, touching, upsetting 2. acute, biting, caustic, keen, penetrating, piercing, pointed, sarcastic, severe 3. acrid, piquant, pungent, sharp, stinging, tangy

point *n.* 1. dot, full stop, mark, period, speck, stop 2. location, place, position, site, spot, stage, station 3. apex, end, nib, prong, sharp end, spike, spur, summit, tine, tip, top 4. bill, cape, foreland, head, headland, ness (*Archaic*), promontory 5. circumstance, condition, degree, extent, position, stage 6. instant, juncture, moment, time, very minute 7. aim, design, end, goal, intent, intention, motive, object, objective, purpose, reason, use, usefulness, utility 8. burden, core, crux, drift, essence, gist, heart, import, main idea, marrow, matter, meaning, nub, pith, proposition, question, subject, text, theme, thrust 9. aspect, detail, facet, feature, instance, item, nicety, particular 10. aspect, attribute, characteristic, peculiarity, property, quality, respect, side, trait 11. score, tally, unit 12. **beside the point** immaterial, incidental, inconsequential, irrelevant, not to the purpose, off the subject, out of the way, pointless, unimportant, without connection 13. **to the point** applicable, apposite, appropriate, apropos, apt, brief, fitting, germane, pertinent, pithy, pointed, relevant, short, suitable, terse ~*v.* 14. bespeak, call attention to, denote, designate, direct, indicate, show, signify 15. aim, bring to bear, direct, level, train 16. barb, edge, sharpen, taper, whet

point-blank 1. *adj.* abrupt, blunt, categorical, direct, downright, explicit, express, plain, straight-from-the-shoulder, unreserved 2. *adv.* bluntly, brusquely, candidly, directly, explicitly, forthrightly, frankly, openly, overtly, plainly, straight, straightforwardly

pointed 1. acicular, acuminate, acute, barbed, cuspidate, edged, mucronate, sharp 2. accurate, acute, biting, cutting, incisive, keen, penetrating, pertinent, sharp, telling, trenchant

pointer 1. guide, hand, indicator, needle 2. advice, caution, hint, information, recommendation, suggestion, tip, warning

pointless absurd, aimless, fruitless, futile, inane, ineffectual, irrelevant, meaningless, nonsensical, senseless, silly, stupid, unavailing, unproductive, unprofitable, useless, vague, vain, worthless

Antonyms appropriate, beneficial, desirable, fitting, fruitful, logical, meaningful, productive, profitable, proper, sensible, to the point, useful, worthwhile

point of view 1. angle, orientation, outlook, perspective, position, standpoint 2. approach, attitude, belief, judgment, opinion, slant, view, viewpoint, way of looking at it

point out allude to, bring up, call attention to, identify, indicate, mention, remind, reveal, show, specify

point up accent, accentuate, emphasize, make clear, stress, underline

poise 1. *n.* aplomb, assurance, calmness, composure, cool (*Sl.*), coolness, dignity, elegance, equanimity, equilibrium, grace, presence, presence of mind, sang-froid, savoir-faire, self-possession, serenity 2. *v.* balance, float, hang, hang in midair, hang suspended, hold, hover, position, support, suspend

poised 1. calm, collected, composed, debonair, dignified, graceful, nonchalant, self-confident, self-possessed, serene, suave, together (*Inf.*), unfazed (*Inf.*), unruffled, urbane 2. all set, in the wings, on the brink, prepared, ready, standing by, waiting

Antonyms (*sense 1*) agitated, annoyed, discomposed, disturbed, excited, irritated, ruffled, worked up

poison *n.* 1. bane, toxin, venom 2. bane, blight, cancer, canker, contagion, contamination, corruption, malignancy, miasma, virus ~*v.* 3. adulterate, contaminate, envenom, give (someone) poison, infect, kill, murder, pollute 4. corrupt, defile, deprave, pervert, subvert, taint, undermine, vitiate, warp ~*adj.* 5. deadly, lethal, poisonous, toxic, venomous

poisonous 1. baneful (*Archaic*), deadly, fatal, lethal, mephitic, mortal, noxious, toxic, venomous, virulent 2. baleful, baneful (*Archaic*), corruptive, evil, malicious, noxious, pernicious, pestiferous, pestilential, vicious

poke *v.* 1. butt, dig, elbow, hit, jab, nudge, prod, punch, push, shove, stab, stick, thrust 2. butt in, interfere, intrude, meddle, nose, peek, poke one's nose into (*Inf.*), pry, put one's two cents in (*U.S. sl.*), snoop (*Inf.*), tamper 3. **poke fun at** chaff, jeer, make a mock of, make fun of, mock, rib (*Inf.*), ridicule, send up (*Brit. inf.*), take the mickey (*Inf.*), take the piss (out of) (*Taboo sl.*), tease ~*n.* 4. butt, dig, hit, jab, nudge, prod, punch, thrust

poky confined, cramped, incommodious, narrow, small, tiny

Antonyms capacious, commodious, large, open, roomy, spacious, wide

polar 1. Antarctic, Arctic, cold, extreme, freezing, frozen, furthest, glacial, icy, terminal 2. beacon-like, cardinal, guiding, leading, pivotal 3. antagonistic, antipodal, antithetical, contradictory, contrary, diametric, opposed, opposite

polarity ambivalence, contradiction, contrariety, dichotomy, duality, opposition, paradox

pole[1] bar, mast, post, rod, shaft, spar, staff, standard, stick

pole[2] 1. antipode, extremity, limit, terminus 2. **poles apart** at opposite ends of the earth, at opposite extremes, incompatible, irreconcilable, miles apart, widely separated, worlds apart

polemic 1. *n.* argument, controversy, debate, dispute 2. *adj.* argumentative, contentious, controversial, disputatious, polemical

polemics argument, argumentation, contention, controversy, debate, disputation, dispute

police *n.* 1. boys in blue (*Inf.*), constabulary, fuzz (*Sl.*), law enforcement agency, police force, the law (*Inf.*), the Old Bill (*Sl.*) ~*v.* 2. control, guard, keep in order, keep the peace, patrol, protect, regulate, watch 3. *Fig.* check, monitor, observe, oversee, supervise

policeman bobby (*Inf.*), bogey (*Sl.*), constable, cop (*Sl.*), copper (*Sl.*), flatfoot (*Sl.*), fuzz (*Sl.*), gendarme (*Sl.*), officer, peeler (*Obsolete Brit. sl.*), pig (*Sl.*), rozzer (*Sl.*)

policy 1. action, approach, code, course, custom, guideline, line, plan, practice, procedure, programme, protocol, rule, scheme, stratagem, theory 2. discretion, good sense, prudence, sagacity, shrewdness, wisdom

polish *v.* 1. brighten, buff, burnish, clean, furbish, rub, shine, smooth, wax 2. brush up, correct, cultivate, emend, enhance, finish, improve, perfect, refine, touch up ~*n.* 3. brightness, brilliance, finish, glaze, gloss, lustre, sheen, smoothness, sparkle, veneer 4. varnish, wax 5. *Fig.* breeding, class (*Inf.*), elegance, finesse, finish, grace, politesse, refinement, style, suavity, urbanity

polished 1. bright, burnished, furbished, glassy, gleaming, glossy, shining, slippery, smooth 2. *Fig.* civilized, courtly, cultivated, elegant, finished, genteel, polite, refined, sophisticated, urbane, well-bred 3. accomplished, adept, expert, faultless, fine, flawless, impeccable, masterly, outstanding, professional, skilful, superlative

Antonyms (*sense 1*) dark, dull, matt, rough (*sense 2*) inelegant, uncivilized, uncultivated, unrefined, unsophisticated (*sense 3*) amateurish, inept, inexpert, unaccomplished, unskilled

polish off 1. consume, down, eat up, finish, put away, shift (*Inf.*), swill, wolf 2. blow away (*Sl., chiefly U.S.*), bump off (*Inf.*), dispose of, do away with, do in (*Sl.*), eliminate, get rid of, kill, liquidate, murder, take out (*Sl.*)

polite 1. affable, civil, complaisant, courteous, deferential, gracious, mannerly, obliging, respectful, well-behaved, well-mannered 2. civilized, courtly, cultured, elegant, genteel, polished, refined, urbane, well-bred
Antonyms crude, discourteous, ill-mannered, impertinent, impolite, impudent, insulting, rude, uncultured, unrefined

politic 1. artful, astute, canny, crafty, cunning, designing, ingenious, intriguing, Machiavellian, scheming, shrewd, sly, subtle, unscrupulous 2. advisable, diplomatic, discreet, expedient, in one's best interests, judicious, prudent, sagacious, sensible, tactful, wise

politician legislator, Member of Parliament, M.P., office bearer, politico (*Inf., chiefly U.S.*), public servant, statesman

politics 1. affairs of state, civics, government, government policy, political science, polity, statecraft, statesmanship 2. Machiavellianism, machination, power struggle, *Realpolitik*

poll *n.* 1. figures, returns, tally, vote, voting 2. ballot, canvass, census, count, Gallup Poll, (public) opinion poll, sampling, survey ~*v.* 3. register, tally 4. ballot, canvass, interview, question, sample, survey

pollute 1. adulterate, befoul, contaminate, dirty, foul, infect, make filthy, mar, poison, smirch, soil, spoil, stain, taint 2. besmirch, corrupt, debase, debauch, defile, deprave, desecrate, dishonour, profane, sully, violate
Antonyms (*sense 1*) clean, cleanse, decontaminate, disinfect, purge, sanitize, sterilize (*sense 2*) esteem, honour

pollution adulteration, contamination, corruption, defilement, dirtying, foulness, impurity, taint, uncleanness, vitiation

poltroon caitiff (*Archaic*), chicken (*Sl.*), coward, craven, cur, dastard (*Archaic*), recreant (*Archaic*), skunk (*Inf.*), yellow-belly (*Sl.*)

polychromatic many-coloured, many-hued, multicoloured, of all the colours of the rainbow, polychrome, rainbow, varicoloured, variegated

pomp 1. ceremony, éclat, flourish, grandeur, magnificence, pageant, pageantry, parade, solemnity, splendour, state 2. display, grandiosity, ostentation, pomposity, show, vainglory

pomposity 1. affectation, airs, arrogance, flaunting, grandiosity, haughtiness, pompousness, portentousness, presumption, pretension, pretentiousness, self-importance, vainglory, vanity 2. bombast, fustian, grandiloquence, loftiness, magniloquence, rant, turgidity

pompous 1. affected, arrogant, bloated, grandiose, imperious, magisterial, ostentatious, overbearing, pontifical, portentous, pretentious, puffed up, self-important, showy, supercilious, vainglorious 2. boastful, bombastic, flatulent, fustian, grandiloquent, high-flown, inflated, magniloquent, orotund, overblown, turgid, windy
Antonyms direct, humble, modest, natural, plain-spoken, self-effacing, simple, succinct, unaffected, unpretentious

pond dew pond, duck pond, fish pond, lochan (*Scot.*), millpond, pool, small lake, tarn

ponder brood, cerebrate, cogitate, consider, contemplate, deliberate, examine, excogitate, give thought to, meditate, mull over, muse, puzzle over, reflect, ruminate, study, think, weigh

ponderous 1. bulky, cumbersome, cumbrous, heavy, hefty, huge, massive, unwieldy, weighty 2. awkward, clumsy, elephantine, graceless, heavy-footed, laborious, lumbering 3. dreary, dull, heavy, laboured, lifeless, long-winded, pedantic, pedestrian, plodding, prolix, stilted, stodgy, tedious, verbose
Antonyms (*senses 1 & 2*) graceful, handy, light, light-footed, little, small, tiny, weightless

poniard bodkin (*Archaic*), dagger, dirk, misericord (*Archaic*), stiletto

pontifical 1. apostolic, ecclesiastical, papal, prelatic 2. bloated, condescending, dogmatic, imperious, magisterial, overbearing, pompous, portentous, pretentious, self-important

pontificate declaim, dogmatize, expound, hold forth, lay down the law, pontify, preach, pronounce, sound off

pooh-pooh belittle, brush aside, deride, disdain, dismiss, disregard, make little of, play down, scoff, scorn, slight, sneer, sniff at, spurn, turn up one's nose at (*Inf.*)
Antonyms exalt, extol, glorify, praise

pool[1] 1. lake, mere, pond, puddle, splash, tarn 2. swimming bath, swimming pool

pool[2] *n.* 1. collective, combine, consortium, group, syndicate, team, trust 2. bank, funds, jackpot, kitty, pot, stakes ~*v.* 3. amalgamate, combine, join forces, league, merge, put together, share

poor 1. badly off, broke (*Inf.*), destitute, dirt-poor (*Inf.*), down and out, flat broke

(*Inf.*), hard up (*Inf.*), impecunious, impoverished, indigent, in need, in want, necessitous, needy, on one's beam-ends, on one's uppers, on the rocks, penniless, penurious, poverty-stricken, short, skint (*Brit. sl.*), stony-broke (*Brit. sl.*), without two pennies to rub together (*Inf.*) 2. deficient, exiguous, inadequate, incomplete, insufficient, lacking, meagre, measly, miserable, niggardly, pitiable, reduced, scant, scanty, skimpy, slight, sparse, straitened 3. below par, chickenshit (*U.S. sl.*), crappy (*Sl.*), faulty, feeble, inferior, low-grade, mediocre, piss-poor (*Taboo sl.*), poxy (*Sl.*), rotten (*Inf.*), rubbishy, second-rate, shabby, shoddy, sorry, substandard, unsatisfactory, valueless, weak, worthless 4. bad, bare, barren, depleted, exhausted, fruitless, impoverished, infertile, sterile, unfruitful, unproductive 5. hapless, ill-fated, luckless, miserable, pathetic, pitiable, unfortunate, unhappy, unlucky, wretched 6. humble, insignificant, lowly, mean, modest, paltry, plain, trivial

Antonyms (*sense 1*) affluent, comfortable (*Inf.*), prosperous, rich, wealthy, well-heeled (*Inf.*), well-off (*Inf.*) (*sense 2*) abundant, adequate, ample, complete, dense, plentiful, satisfactory, sufficient, thick (*sense 3*) excellent, exceptional, first-class, first-rate, satisfactory, superior, valuable (*sense 4*) fertile, fruitful, productive, teeming, yielding (*sense 5*) fortunate, happy, lucky, successful

poorly 1. *adv.* badly, crudely, inadequately, incompetently, inexpertly, inferiorly, insufficiently, meanly, shabbily, unsatisfactorily, unsuccessfully 2. *adj. Inf.* ailing, below par, ill, indisposed, off colour, out of sorts, rotten (*Inf.*), seedy (*Inf.*), sick, under the weather (*Inf.*), unwell

Antonyms (*sense 1*) acceptably, adequately, competently, expertly, satisfactorily, sufficiently, well (*sense 2*) fit, hale and hearty, healthy, in good health, in the pink, well

pop *v.* 1. bang, burst, crack, explode, go off, report, snap 2. *Often with* **in, out,** *etc. Inf.* appear, call, come *or* go suddenly, drop in (*Inf.*), leave quickly, nip in (*Brit. inf.*), nip out (*Brit. inf.*), visit 3. *Esp. of eyes* bulge, protrude, stick out 4. insert, push, put, shove, slip, stick, thrust, tuck ~*n.* 5. bang, burst, crack, explosion, noise, report 6. *Inf.* fizzy drink, lemonade, soda water, soft drink

pope Bishop of Rome, Holy Father, pontiff, Vicar of Christ

popinjay buck (*Archaic*), coxcomb (*Archaic*), dandy, fop, jackanapes, peacock, swell (*Inf.*)

poppycock babble, balderdash, balls (*Taboo sl.*), baloney (*Inf.*), bilge (*Inf.*), bosh (*Inf.*), bull (*Sl.*), bullshit (*Taboo sl.*), bunk (*Inf.*), bunkum *or* buncombe (*Chiefly U.S.*), cobblers (*Brit. taboo sl.*), crap (*Sl.*), drivel, eyewash (*Inf.*), garbage (*Inf.*), gibberish, gobbledegook (*Inf.*), guff (*Sl.*), hogwash, hokum (*Sl., chiefly U.S. & Canad.*), hooey (*Sl.*), horsefeathers (*U.S. sl.*), hot air (*Inf.*), moonshine, nonsense, pap, piffle (*Inf.*), rot, rubbish, shit (*Taboo sl.*), tommyrot, tosh (*Sl., chiefly Brit.*), trash, tripe (*Inf.*), twaddle

populace commonalty, crowd, general public, hoi polloi, inhabitants, Joe (and Eileen) Public (*Sl.*), Joe Six-Pack (*U.S. sl.*), masses, mob, multitude, people, rabble, throng

popular 1. accepted, approved, celebrated, famous, fashionable, favoured, favourite, in, in demand, in favour, liked, sought-after, well-liked 2. common, conventional, current, general, prevailing, prevalent, public, standard, stock, ubiquitous, universal, widespread

Antonyms (*sense 1*) despised, detested, disliked, hated, loathed, unaccepted, unpopular (*sense 2*) infrequent, rare, uncommon, unusual

popularity acceptance, acclaim, adoration, approval, celebrity, currency, esteem, fame, favour, idolization, lionization, recognition, regard, renown, reputation, repute, vogue

popularize disseminate, familiarize, give currency to, give mass appeal, make available to all, simplify, spread, universalize

popularly commonly, conventionally, customarily, generally, ordinarily, regularly, traditionally, universally, usually, widely

populate colonize, inhabit, live in, occupy, people, settle

population citizenry, community, denizens, folk, inhabitants, natives, people, populace, residents, society

populous crowded, heavily populated, overpopulated, packed, populated, swarming, teeming, thronged

pore[1] *v.* brood, contemplate, dwell on, examine, go over, peruse, ponder, read, scrutinize, study, work over

pore[2] *n.* hole, opening, orifice, outlet, stoma

pornographic blue, dirty, filthy, indecent, lewd, obscene, offensive, prurient, salacious, smutty

pornography dirt, erotica, filth, indecency, obscenity, porn (*Inf.*), porno (*Inf.*), smut

porous absorbent, absorptive, penetrable, permeable, pervious, spongy
Antonyms impenetrable, impermeable, impervious, nonporous

port *Nautical* anchorage, harbour, haven, roads, roadstead, seaport

portable compact, convenient, easily carried, handy, light, lightweight, manageable, movable, portative

portal door, doorway, entrance, entrance way, entry, gateway, way in

portend adumbrate, augur, bespeak, betoken, bode, foreshadow, foretell, foretoken, forewarn, harbinger, herald, indicate, omen, point to, predict, presage, prognosticate, promise, threaten, vaticinate (*Rare*), warn of

portent augury, foreboding, foreshadowing, forewarning, harbinger, indication, omen, premonition, presage, presentiment, prognostic, prognostication, sign, threat, warning

portentous 1. alarming, crucial, fateful, forbidding, important, menacing, minatory, momentous, ominous, significant, sinister, threatening 2. amazing, astounding, awe-inspiring, extraordinary, miraculous, phenomenal, prodigious, remarkable, wondrous (*Archaic or literary*) 3. bloated, elephantine, heavy, pompous, ponderous, pontifical, self-important, solemn

porter[1] baggage attendant, bearer, carrier

porter[2] caretaker, concierge, doorman, gatekeeper, janitor

portion *n.* 1. bit, fraction, fragment, morsel, part, piece, scrap, section, segment 2. allocation, allotment, allowance, division, lot, measure, parcel, quantity, quota, ration, share 3. helping, piece, serving 4. cup, destiny, fate, fortune, lot, luck ~*v.* 5. allocate, allot, apportion, assign, deal, distribute, divide, divvy up (*Inf.*), dole out, parcel out, partition, share out

portly ample, beefy (*Inf.*), bulky, burly, corpulent, fat, fleshy, heavy, large, obese, overweight, plump, rotund, stout, tubby (*Inf.*)

portrait 1. image, likeness, painting, photograph, picture, portraiture, representation, sketch 2. account, characterization, depiction, description, portrayal, profile, thumbnail sketch, vignette

portray 1. delineate, depict, draw, figure, illustrate, limn, paint, picture, render, represent, sketch 2. characterize, depict, describe, paint a mental picture of, put in words 3. act the part of, play, represent

portrayal characterization, delineation, depiction, description, impersonation, interpretation, performance, picture, rendering, representation

pose *v.* 1. arrange, model, position, sit, sit for 2. *Often with* **as** feign, impersonate, masquerade as, pass oneself off as, pretend to be, profess to be, sham 3. affect, attitudinize, posture, put on airs, show off (*Inf.*), strike an attitude 4. advance, posit, present, propound, put, put forward, set, state, submit ~*n.* 5. attitude, bearing, mien (*Literary*), position, posture, stance 6. act, affectation, air, attitudinizing, façade, front, mannerism, masquerade, posturing, pretence, role

poser brain-teaser (*Inf.*), conundrum, enigma, knotty point, problem, puzzle, question, riddle, teaser, tough one, vexed question

poseur attitudinizer, exhibitionist, hot dog (*Chiefly U.S.*), impostor, mannerist, masquerader, poser, posturer, self-publicist, show-off (*Inf.*)

posh classy (*Sl.*), elegant, exclusive, fashionable, grand, high-class, high-toned, la-di-da (*Inf.*), luxurious, luxury, ritzy (*Sl.*), smart, stylish, swanky (*Inf.*), swish (*Inf., chiefly Brit.*), top-drawer, up-market, upper-class

posit advance, assert, assume, postulate, predicate, presume, propound, put forward, state, submit

position *n.* 1. area, bearings, locale, locality, location, place, point, post, reference, site, situation, spot, station, whereabouts 2. arrangement, attitude, disposition, pose, posture, stance 3. angle, attitude, belief, opinion, outlook, point of view, slant, stance, stand, standpoint, view, viewpoint 4. circumstances, condition, pass, plight, predicament, situation, state, strait(s) 5. caste, class, consequence, eminence, importance, place, prestige, rank, reputation, standing, station, stature, status 6. berth (*Inf.*), billet (*Inf.*), capacity, duty, employment, function, job, occupation, office, place, post, role, situation ~*v.* 7. arrange, array, dispose, fix, lay out, locate, place, put, set, settle, stand, stick (*Inf.*)

positive 1. absolute, actual, affirmative, categorical, certain, clear, clear-cut, conclusive, concrete, decisive, definite, direct, explicit, express, firm, incontrovertible, indisputable, real, unequivocal, unmistakable 2. assured, certain, confident, convinced, sure 3. assertive, cocksure, decided, dogmatic, emphatic, firm, forceful, opinionated, peremptory, resolute, stubborn 4. beneficial, constructive, effective, efficacious, forward-looking, helpful, practical, productive, progressive, useful 5. *Inf.* absolute, complete, consummate, out-and-out, perfect, rank, thorough, thoroughgoing, unmitigated, utter

Antonyms (*sense 1*) contestable, disputable, doubtful, inconclusive, indecisive, indefinite, uncertain (*sense 2*) not confident, unassured, uncertain, unconvinced, unsure (*sense 3*) diffident, open-minded, receptive, retiring, timid, unassertive, unobtrusive (*sense 4*) conservative, detrimental, harmful, impractical, reactionary, unhelpful, useless

positively absolutely, assuredly, categorically, certainly, definitely, emphatically, firmly, surely, undeniably, unequivocally, unmistakably, unquestionably, with certainty, without qualification

possess 1. be blessed with, be born with, be endowed with, enjoy, have, have to one's name, hold, own 2. acquire, control, dominate, hold, occupy, seize, take over, take possession of 3. bewitch, consume, control, dominate, enchant, fixate, influence, mesmerize, obsess, put under a spell

possessed bedevilled, berserk, bewitched, consumed, crazed, cursed, demented, enchanted, frenetic, frenzied, hag-ridden, haunted, maddened, obsessed, raving, under a spell

possession 1. control, custody, hold, occupancy, occupation, ownership, proprietorship, tenure, title 2. *Plural* assets, belongings, chattels, effects, estate, goods and chattels, property, things, wealth 3. colony, dominion, protectorate, province, territory

possessive acquisitive, controlling, covetous, dominating, domineering, grasping, jealous, overprotective, selfish

possibility 1. feasibility, likelihood, plausibility, potentiality, practicability, workableness 2. chance, hazard, hope, liability, likelihood, odds, probability, prospect, risk 3. *Often plural* capabilities, potential, potentiality, promise, prospects, talent

possible 1. conceivable, credible, hypothetical, imaginable, likely, potential 2. attainable, doable, feasible, on (*Inf.*), practicable, realizable, viable, within reach, workable 3. hopeful, likely, potential, probable, promising

Antonyms impossible, impracticable, improbable, inconceivable, incredible, unfeasible, unimaginable, unlikely, unobtainable, unreasonable, unthinkable

possibly 1. God willing, haply (*Archaic*), maybe, mayhap (*Archaic*), peradventure (*Archaic*), perchance (*Archaic*), perhaps 2. at all, by any chance, by any means, in any way

post[1] 1. *n.* column, newel, pale, palisade, picket, pillar, pole, shaft, stake, standard, stock, support, upright 2. *v.* advertise, affix, announce, display, make known, pin up, proclaim, promulgate, publicize, publish, put up, stick up

post[2] *n.* 1. appointment, assignment, berth (*Inf.*), billet (*Inf.*), employment, job, office, place, position, situation 2. beat, place, position, station ~*v.* 3. assign, establish, locate, place, position, put, situate, station

post[3] *n.* 1. collection, delivery, mail, postal service ~*v.* 2. dispatch, mail, send, transmit 3. advise, brief, fill in on (*Inf.*), inform, notify, report to

poster advertisement, *affiche,* announcement, bill, notice, placard, public notice, sticker

posterior *adj.* 1. after, back, behind, hind, hinder, rear 2. ensuing, following, later, latter, subsequent

posterity 1. children, descendants, family, heirs, issue, offspring, progeny, scions, seed (*Chiefly biblical*) 2. future, future generations, succeeding generations

posthaste at once, before one can say Jack Robinson, directly, double-quick, full tilt, hastily, hotfoot, pdq (*Sl.*), promptly, pronto (*Inf.*), quickly, speedily, straightaway, swiftly

postmortem *n.* analysis, autopsy, dissection, examination, necropsy

postpone adjourn, defer, delay, hold over, put back, put off, put on the back burner (*Inf.*), shelve, suspend, table, take a rain check on (*U.S. & Canad. inf.*)

Antonyms advance, bring forward, call to order, carry out, go ahead with

postponement adjournment, deferment, deferral, delay, moratorium, respite, stay, suspension

postscript addition, afterthought, afterword, appendix, P.S., supplement

postulate advance, assume, hypothesize, posit, predicate, presuppose, propose, put forward, suppose, take for granted, theorize

posture *n.* 1. attitude, bearing, carriage, disposition, mien (*Literary*), pose, position, set, stance 2. circumstance, condition, mode, phase, position, situation, state 3. attitude, disposition, feeling, frame of mind, inclination, mood, outlook, point of view, stance, standpoint ~*v.* 4. affect, attitudinize, do for effect, hot-dog (*Chiefly U.S.*), make a show, pose, put on airs, show off (*Inf.*), try to attract attention

posy bouquet, boutonniere, buttonhole, corsage, nosegay, spray

potbellied bloated, corpulent, distended, fat, obese, overweight, paunchy

potbelly beer belly (*Inf.*), corporation (*Inf.*), gut, paunch, pot, spare tyre (*Brit. sl.*), spread (*Inf.*)

potency authority, capacity, control, effectiveness, efficacy, energy, force, influence, might, muscle, potential, power, puissance, strength, sway, vigour

potent 1. efficacious, forceful, mighty, powerful, puissant, strong, vigorous 2. cogent, compelling, convincing, effective, forceful, impressive, persuasive, telling 3. authoritative, commanding, dominant, dynamic, influential, powerful
Antonyms impotent, ineffective, unconvincing, weak

potentate emperor, king, mogul, monarch, overlord, prince, ruler, sovereign

potential 1. *adj.* budding, dormant, embryonic, future, hidden, inherent, latent, likely, possible, promising, undeveloped, unrealized 2. *n.* ability, aptitude, capability, capacity, possibility, potentiality, power, the makings, what it takes (*Inf.*), wherewithal

potentiality ability, aptitude, capability, capacity, likelihood, potential, promise, prospect, the makings

pother bother, carry-on (*Inf., chiefly Brit.*), commotion, disturbance, flap (*Inf.*), fuss, hoo-ha, lather (*Inf.*), ruction (*Inf.*), stew (*Inf.*), tizzy (*Inf.*), to-do

potion brew, concoction, cup, dose, draught, elixir, mixture, philtre, tonic

potpourri collection, combination, gallimaufry, hotchpotch, medley, *mélange,* miscellany, mixture, motley, pastiche, patchwork, salmagundi

potter dabble, fiddle (*Inf.*), footle (*Inf.*), fribble, fritter, mess about, poke along, tinker

pottery ceramics, earthenware, stoneware, terra cotta

potty 1. barmy (*Sl.*), crackers (*Brit. sl.*), crackpot (*Inf.*), crazy, daft (*Inf.*), dippy (*Sl.*), dotty (*Sl., chiefly Brit.*), eccentric, foolish, loopy (*Inf.*), oddball (*Inf.*), off one's chump (*Sl.*), off one's trolley (*Sl.*), off-the-wall (*Sl.*), out to lunch (*Inf.*), silly, soft (*Inf.*), touched, up the pole (*Inf.*), wacko (*Sl.*) 2. footling (*Inf.*), insignificant, petty, piddling (*Inf.*), trifling, trivial

pouch bag, container, pocket, poke (*Dialect*), purse, sack

pounce 1. *v.* ambush, attack, bound onto, dash at, drop, fall upon, jump, leap at, snatch, spring, strike, swoop, take by surprise, take unawares 2. *n.* assault, attack, bound, jump, leap, spring, swoop

pound[1] 1. batter, beat, belabour, clobber (*Sl.*), hammer, pelt, pummel, strike, thrash, thump 2. bray (*Dialect*), bruise, comminute, crush, powder, pulverize, triturate 3. din into, drub into, drum into, hammer into 4. *With* **out** bang, beat, hammer, thump 5. clomp, march, stomp (*Inf.*), thunder, tramp 6. beat, palpitate, pitapat, pulsate, pulse, throb

pound[2] *n.* compound, enclosure, pen, yard

pour 1. decant, let flow, spill, splash 2. course, emit, flow, gush, run, rush, spew, spout, stream 3. bucket down (*Inf.*), come down in torrents, pelt (down), rain, rain cats and dogs (*Inf.*), rain hard *or* heavily, sheet, teem 4. crowd, stream, swarm, teem, throng

pout 1. *v.* glower, look petulant, look sullen, lour *or* lower, make a moue, mope, pull a long face, purse one's lips, sulk, turn down the corners of one's mouth 2. *n.* glower, long face, *moue,* sullen look

pouting bad-tempered, cross, huffy, ill-humoured, long-faced, moody, moping, morose, peevish, petulant, sulky, sullen

poverty 1. beggary, destitution, distress, hand-to-mouth existence, hardship, indigence, insolvency, necessitousness, necessity, need, pauperism, pennilessness, penury, privation, want 2. dearth, deficiency, insufficiency, lack, paucity, scarcity, shortage 3. aridity, bareness, barrenness, deficiency, infertility, meagreness, poorness, sterility, unfruitfulness
Antonyms (*sense 1*) affluence, comfort, luxury, opulence, richness, wealth (*sense 2*) abundance, plethora, sufficiency (*sense 3*) fecundity, fertility, fruitfulness, productiveness

poverty-stricken bankrupt, beggared, broke (*Inf.*), destitute, dirt-poor (*Inf.*), distressed, down and out, flat broke (*Inf.*), impecunious, impoverished, indigent, needy, on one's beam-ends, on one's uppers, penniless, penurious, poor, short, skint (*Brit. sl.*), stony-broke (*Brit. sl.*), without two pennies to rub together (*Inf.*)

powder *n.* 1. dust, fine grains, loose particles, pounce, talc ~*v.* 2. crush, granulate, grind, pestle, pound, pulverize 3. cover, dredge, dust, scatter, sprinkle, strew

powdery chalky, crumbling, crumbly, dry, dusty, fine, friable, grainy, granular, loose, pulverized, sandy

power 1. ability, capability, capacity, competence, competency, faculty, potential 2. brawn, energy, force, forcefulness, intensity, might, muscle, potency, strength, vigour, weight 3. ascendancy, authority, bottom, command, control, dominance, domination, dominion, influence, mastery, rule, sovereignty, supremacy, sway 4. authority,

authorization, licence, prerogative, privilege, right, warrant
Antonyms (*sense 1*) inability, incapability, incapacity, incompetence (*sense 2*) enervation, feebleness, impotence, listlessness, weakness

powerful 1. energetic, mighty, potent, robust, stalwart, strapping, strong, sturdy, vigorous 2. authoritative, commanding, controlling, dominant, influential, prevailing, puissant, sovereign, supreme 3. cogent, compelling, convincing, effective, effectual, forceful, forcible, impressive, persuasive, striking, telling, weighty

powerfully forcefully, forcibly, hard, mightily, strongly, vigorously, with might and main

powerless 1. debilitated, disabled, etiolated, feeble, frail, helpless, impotent, incapable, incapacitated, ineffectual, infirm, paralysed, prostrate, weak 2. defenceless, dependent, disenfranchised, disfranchised, ineffective, subject, tied, unarmed, vulnerable
Antonyms (*sense 1*) able-bodied, fit, healthy, lusty, powerful, robust, strong, sturdy

powwow 1. *n.* chinwag (*Brit. inf.*), confab (*Inf.*), confabulation, conference, congress, consultation, council, discussion, get-together (*Inf.*), huddle (*Inf.*), meeting, palaver, parley, seminar, talk 2. *v.* confab (*Inf.*), confer, discuss, get together, go into a huddle (*Inf.*), meet, palaver, parley, talk

practicability advantage, feasibility, operability, possibility, practicality, use, usefulness, value, viability, workability

practicable achievable, attainable, doable, feasible, performable, possible, viable, within the realm of possibility, workable
Antonyms beyond the bounds of possibility, impossible, out of the question, unachievable, unattainable, unfeasible, unworkable

practical 1. applied, efficient, empirical, experimental, factual, functional, pragmatic, realistic, utilitarian 2. businesslike, down-to-earth, everyday, hard-headed, matter-of-fact, mundane, ordinary, realistic, sensible, workaday 3. doable, feasible, practicable, serviceable, sound, useful, workable 4. accomplished, efficient, experienced, proficient, qualified, seasoned, skilled, trained, veteran, working
Antonyms (*senses 1, 2, & 3*) impossible, impracticable, impractical, inefficient, speculative, theoretical, unpractical, unrealistic, unsound, unworkable, useless (*sense 4*) inefficient, inexperienced, unaccomplished, unqualified, unskilled, untrained

practically 1. all but, almost, basically, close to, essentially, fundamentally, in effect, just about, nearly, to all intents and purposes, very nearly, virtually, well-nigh 2. clearly, matter-of-factly, rationally, realistically, reasonably, sensibly, unsentimentally, with common sense

practice 1. custom, habit, method, mode, praxis, routine, rule, system, tradition, usage, use, usual procedure, way, wont 2. discipline, drill, exercise, preparation, rehearsal, repetition, study, training, workout 3. action, application, effect, exercise, experience, operation, use 4. business, career, profession, vocation, work

practise 1. discipline, drill, exercise, go over, go through, polish, prepare, rehearse, repeat, study, train, warm up, work out 2. apply, carry out, do, follow, live up to, observe, perform, put into practice 3. carry on, engage in, ply, pursue, specialize in, undertake, work at

practised able, accomplished, experienced, expert, proficient, qualified, seasoned, skilled, trained, versed
Antonyms amateurish, bungling, incompetent, inexperienced, inexpert, unqualified, unskilled, untrained

pragmatic businesslike, down-to-earth, efficient, hard-headed, matter-of-fact, practical, realistic, sensible, utilitarian
Antonyms airy-fairy, idealistic, impractical, inefficient, starry-eyed, stupid, theoretical, unprofessional, unrealistic

praise *n.* 1. acclaim, acclamation, accolade, applause, approbation, approval, cheering, commendation, compliment, congratulation, encomium, eulogy, good word, kudos, laudation, ovation, panegyric, plaudit, tribute 2. adoration, devotion, glory, homage, thanks, worship ~*v.* 3. acclaim, admire, applaud, approve, cheer, compliment, congratulate, crack up (*Inf.*), cry up, eulogize, extol, honour, laud, pay tribute to, sing the praises of 4. adore, bless, exalt, give thanks to, glorify, magnify (*Archaic*), pay homage to, worship

praiseworthy admirable, commendable, creditable, estimable, excellent, exemplary, fine, honourable, laudable, meritorious, worthy
Antonyms condemnable, deplorable, despicable, discreditable, disgraceful, dishonourable, ignoble, reprehensible

prance 1. bound, caper, cavort, dance, frisk, gambol, jump, leap, romp, skip, spring, trip 2. parade, show off (*Inf.*), stalk, strut, swagger, swank (*Inf.*)

prank antic, caper, escapade, frolic, jape, lark (*Inf.*), practical joke, skylarking (*Inf.*), trick

prate babble, blather, boast, brag, chatter, drivel, gab (*Inf.*), gas (*Inf.*), go on and on, jaw (*Sl.*), rabbit (on) (*Brit. inf.*), shoot off one's mouth (*Sl.*), waffle (*Inf., chiefly Brit.*), witter on (*Inf.*), yak (*Sl.*)

prattle babble, blather, blether, chatter, clack, drivel, gabble, jabber, patter, rabbit (on) (*Brit. inf.*), rattle on, run off at the mouth (*Sl.*), run on, twitter, waffle (*Inf., chiefly Brit.*), witter (*Inf.*)

pray 1. offer a prayer, recite the rosary, say one's prayers 2. adjure, ask, beg, beseech, call upon, crave, cry for, entreat, implore, importune, invoke, petition, plead, request, solicit, sue, supplicate, urge

prayer 1. communion, devotion, invocation, litany, orison, supplication 2. appeal, entreaty, petition, plea, request, suit, supplication

preach 1. address, deliver a sermon, evangelize, exhort, orate 2. admonish, advocate, exhort, harangue, lecture, moralize, sermonize, urge

preacher clergyman, evangelist, minister, missionary, parson, revivalist

preachify drone on, go on and on, harangue, hold forth, lecture, moralize, prose, sermonize

preachy canting, didactic, edifying, holier-than-thou, homiletic, moralizing, pharisaic, pietistic, pontifical, religiose, sanctimonious, self-righteous

preamble exordium, foreword, introduction, opening move, opening statement *or* remarks, overture, preface, prelude, proem, prolegomenon

precarious chancy (*Inf.*), dangerous, dicey (*Inf., chiefly Brit.*), dodgy (*Brit., Aust., & N.Z. inf.*), doubtful, dubious, hairy (*Sl.*), hazardous, insecure, perilous, risky, shaky, slippery, touch and go, tricky, uncertain, unreliable, unsafe, unsettled, unstable, unsteady, unsure

Antonyms certain, dependable, reliable, safe, secure, stable, steady

precaution 1. insurance, preventative measure, protection, provision, safeguard, safety measure 2. anticipation, care, caution, circumspection, foresight, forethought, providence, prudence, wariness

precede antecede, antedate, come first, forerun, go ahead of, go before, head, herald, introduce, lead, pave the way, preface, take precedence, usher

precedence antecedence, lead, pre-eminence, preference, primacy, priority, rank, seniority, superiority, supremacy

precedent *n.* antecedent, authority, criterion, example, exemplar, instance, model, paradigm, pattern, previous example, prototype, standard

preceding above, aforementioned, aforesaid, anterior, earlier, foregoing, former, past, previous, prior

precept 1. behest, canon, command, commandment, decree, dictum, direction, instruction, law, mandate, order, ordinance, principle, regulation, rule, statute 2. axiom, byword, dictum, guideline, maxim, motto, principle, rule, saying

precinct 1. bound, boundary, confine, enclosure, limit 2. area, district, quarter, section, sector, zone

precincts borders, bounds, confines, district, environs, limits, milieu, neighbourhood, purlieus, region, surrounding area

precious 1. adored, beloved, cherished, darling, dear, dearest, favourite, idolized, loved, prized, treasured, valued 2. choice, costly, dear, expensive, exquisite, fine, high-priced, inestimable, invaluable, priceless, prized, rare, recherché, valuable 3. affected, alembicated, artificial, chichi, fastidious, overnice, overrefined, twee (*Brit. inf.*)

precipice bluff, brink, cliff, cliff face, crag, height, rock face, sheer drop, steep

precipitate *v.* 1. accelerate, advance, bring on, dispatch, expedite, further, hasten, hurry, press, push forward, quicken, speed up, trigger 2. cast, discharge, fling, hurl, launch, let fly, send forth, throw ~*adj.* 3. breakneck, headlong, plunging, rapid, rushing, swift, violent 4. frantic, harum-scarum, hasty, heedless, hurried, ill-advised, impetuous, impulsive, indiscreet, madcap, precipitous, rash, reckless 5. abrupt, brief, quick, sudden, unexpected, without warning

precipitous 1. abrupt, dizzy, falling sharply, high, perpendicular, sheer, steep 2. abrupt, careless, harum-scarum, hasty, heedless, hurried, ill-advised, precipitate, rash, reckless, sudden

précis 1. *n.* abridgment, abstract, *aperçu*, compendium, condensation, digest, outline, résumé, rundown, sketch, summary, synopsis 2. *v.* abridge, abstract, compress, condense, outline, shorten, summarize, sum up

precise 1. absolute, accurate, actual, clear-cut, correct, definite, exact, explicit, express, fixed, literal, particular, specific, strict, unequivocal 2. careful, ceremonious, exact, fastidious, finicky, formal, inflexible, meticulous, nice, particular, prim, punctilious, puritanical, rigid, scrupulous, stiff, strict

Antonyms (*sense 1*) ambiguous, careless, equivocal, incorrect, indefinite, indistinct, inexact, loose, vague (*sense 2*) flexible, haphazard, inexact, informal, relaxed, unceremonious

precisely absolutely, accurately, bang, correctly, exactly, just, just so, literally, neither more nor less, plumb (*Inf.*), slap (*Inf.*), smack (*Inf.*), square, squarely, strictly

precision accuracy, care, correctness, definiteness, exactitude, exactness, fidelity, meticulousness, nicety, particularity, preciseness, rigour

preclude check, debar, exclude, forestall, hinder, inhibit, make impossible, make impracticable, obviate, prevent, prohibit, put a stop to, restrain, rule out, stop

precocious advanced, ahead, bright, developed, forward, quick, smart

Antonyms backward, dense, dull, retarded, slow, underdeveloped, unresponsive

preconception bias, notion, preconceived idea *or* notion, predisposition, prejudice, prepossession, presumption, presupposition

precondition essential, must, necessity, prerequisite, requirement, *sine qua non*

precursor 1. forerunner, harbinger, herald, messenger, usher, vanguard 2. antecedent, forebear, forerunner, originator, pioneer, predecessor

precursory antecedent, introductory, preceding, prefatory, preliminary, preparatory, previous, prior

predatory 1. carnivorous, hunting, predacious, rapacious, raptorial, ravening 2. despoiling, greedy, marauding, pillaging, plundering, rapacious, ravaging, thieving, voracious, vulturine, vulturous

predecessor 1. antecedent, forerunner, precursor, previous (former, prior) job holder 2. ancestor, antecedent, forebear, forefather

predestination destiny, doom, election (*Theology*), fate, foreordainment, foreordination, lot, necessity, predetermination

predestine doom, fate, foreordain, mean, predestinate, predetermine, pre-elect, preordain

predetermined agreed, arranged in advance, cut and dried (*Inf.*), decided beforehand, fixed, prearranged, preplanned, set, settled, set up

predicament corner, dilemma, emergency, fix (*Inf.*), hole (*Sl.*), hot water (*Inf.*), jam (*Inf.*), mess, pickle (*Inf.*), pinch, plight, quandary, scrape (*Inf.*), situation, spot (*Inf.*), state, tight spot

predicate 1. affirm, assert, aver, avouch, avow, contend, declare, maintain, proclaim, state 2. connote, imply, indicate, intimate, signify, suggest 3. *With* **on** *or* **upon** base, build, establish, found, ground, postulate, rest

predict augur, divine, forebode, forecast, foresee, foretell, portend, presage, prognosticate, prophesy, soothsay, vaticinate (*Rare*)

predictable anticipated, calculable, certain, expected, foreseeable, foreseen, likely, reliable, sure, sure-fire (*Inf.*)

Antonyms out of the blue, surprising, unexpected, unforeseen, unlikely, unpredictable

prediction augury, divination, forecast, prognosis, prognostication, prophecy, soothsaying, sortilege

predilection bag (*Sl.*), bias, cup of tea (*Inf.*), fancy, fondness, inclination, leaning, liking, love, partiality, penchant, predisposition, preference, proclivity, proneness, propensity, taste, tendency, weakness

predispose affect, bias, dispose, incline, induce, influence, lead, make (one) of a mind to, prejudice, prepare, prime, prompt, sway

predisposed agreeable, amenable, given to, inclined, liable, minded, prone, ready, subject, susceptible, willing

predisposition bent, bias, disposition, inclination, likelihood, penchant, potentiality, predilection, proclivity, proneness, propensity, susceptibility, tendency, willingness

predominance ascendancy, control, dominance, dominion, edge, greater number, hold, leadership, mastery, paramountcy, preponderance, supremacy, sway, upper hand, weight

predominant ascendant, capital, chief, controlling, dominant, important, leading, main, notable, paramount, preponderant, prevailing, prevalent, primary, prime, principal, prominent, ruling, sovereign, superior, supreme, top-priority

Antonyms inferior, minor, secondary, subordinate, unimportant, uninfluential

predominate be most noticeable, carry weight, get the upper hand, hold sway, outweigh, overrule, overshadow, preponderate, prevail, reign, rule, tell

pre-eminence distinction, excellence, paramountcy, predominance, prestige, prominence, renown, superiority, supremacy, transcendence

pre-eminent chief, consummate, distinguished, excellent, foremost, incomparable, matchless, outstanding, paramount, peerless, predominant, renowned, superior, supreme, transcendent, unequalled, unrivalled, unsurpassed

pre-eminently above all, by far, conspicuously, eminently, emphatically, exceptionally, far and away, incomparably, inimitably, matchlessly, notably, *par excellence,* particularly, second to none, signally, singularly, strikingly, superlatively, supremely

pre-empt acquire, anticipate, appropriate, arrogate, assume, seize, take over, usurp

preen 1. *Of birds* clean, plume 2. array, deck out, doll up (*Sl.*), dress up, prettify, primp, prink, spruce up, titivate, trig (*Archaic or dialect*), trim 3. **preen oneself (on)** congratulate oneself, pique oneself, plume oneself, pride oneself

preface 1. *n.* exordium, foreword, introduction, preamble, preliminary, prelude, proem, prolegomenon, prologue 2. *v.* begin, introduce, launch, lead up to, open, precede, prefix

prefatory antecedent, introductory, opening, precursory, prefatorial, preliminary, prelusive, prelusory, preparatory, proemial, prolegomenal

prefer 1. adopt, be partial to, choose, desire, elect, fancy, favour, go for, incline towards, like better, opt for, pick, plump for, select, single out, wish, would rather, would sooner 2. file, lodge, place, present, press, put forward 3. advance, aggrandize, elevate, move up, promote, raise, upgrade

preferable best, better, choice, chosen, favoured, more desirable, more eligible, superior, worthier

Antonyms average, fair, ineligible, inferior, mediocre, poor, second-rate, undesirable

preferably as a matter of choice, by choice, first, in *or* for preference, much rather, much sooner, rather, sooner, willingly

preference 1. bag (*Sl.*), choice, cup of tea (*Inf.*), desire, election, favourite, first choice, option, partiality, pick, predilection, selection, top of the list 2. advantage, favoured treatment, favouritism, first place, precedence, pride of place, priority

preferential advantageous, better, favoured, partial, partisan, privileged, special, superior

preferment advancement, dignity, elevation, exaltation, promotion, rise, upgrading

prefigure 1. adumbrate, foreshadow, foretoken, indicate, intimate, portend, presage, shadow forth, suggest 2. consider, fancy, imagine, picture, presuppose

pregnancy gestation, gravidity

pregnant 1. big *or* heavy with child, enceinte, expectant, expecting (*Inf.*), gravid, in the club (*Brit. sl.*), in the family way (*Inf.*), in the pudding club (*Sl.*), preggers (*Brit. inf.*), with child 2. charged, eloquent, expressive, loaded, meaningful, pointed, significant, suggestive, telling, weighty 3. creative, imaginative, inventive, original, seminal 4. abounding in, abundant, fecund, fertile, fraught, fruitful, full, productive, prolific, replete, rich in, teeming

prehistoric 1. earliest, early, primeval, primitive, primordial 2. ancient, antediluvian, antiquated, archaic, out of date, out of the ark (*Inf.*)

prejudge anticipate, forejudge, jump to conclusions, make a hasty assessment, presume, presuppose

prejudice *n.* 1. bias, jaundiced eye, partiality, preconceived notion, preconception, prejudgment, warp 2. bigotry, chauvinism, discrimination, injustice, intolerance, narrow-mindedness, racism, sexism, unfairness 3. damage, detriment, disadvantage, harm, hurt, impairment, loss, mischief ~*v.* 4. bias, colour, distort, influence, jaundice, poison, predispose, prepossess, slant, sway, warp 5. damage, harm, hinder, hurt, impair, injure, mar, spoil, undermine

prejudiced biased, bigoted, conditioned, discriminatory, influenced, intolerant, jaundiced, narrow-minded, one-sided, opinionated, partial, partisan, prepossessed, unfair

Antonyms fair, impartial, just, neutral, not bigoted, not prejudiced, open-minded, unbiased

prejudicial counterproductive, damaging, deleterious, detrimental, disadvantageous, harmful, hurtful, inimical, injurious, undermining, unfavourable

preliminary 1. *adj.* exploratory, first, initial, initiatory, introductory, opening, pilot, precursory, prefatory, preparatory, prior, qualifying, test, trial 2. *n.* beginning, first round, foundation, groundwork, initiation, introduction, opening, overture, preamble, preface, prelims, prelude, preparation, start

prelude beginning, commencement, curtain-raiser, exordium, foreword, intro (*Inf.*), introduction, overture, preamble, preface, preliminary, preparation, proem, prolegomenon, prologue, start

premature 1. abortive, early, embryonic, forward, green, immature, incomplete, predeveloped, raw, undeveloped, unfledged, unripe, unseasonable, untimely 2. *Fig.*

hasty, ill-considered, ill-timed, impulsive, inopportune, overhasty, precipitate, previous (*Inf.*), rash, too soon, untimely

prematurely 1. before one's time, too early, too soon, untimely 2. at half-cock, half-cocked, overhastily, precipitately, rashly, too hastily, too soon

premeditated aforethought, calculated, conscious, considered, contrived, deliberate, intended, intentional, planned, prepense, studied, wilful
Antonyms accidental, inadvertent, unintentional, unplanned, unpremeditated, unwitting

premeditation deliberation, design, determination, forethought, intention, malice aforethought, planning, plotting, prearrangement, predetermination, purpose

premier *n.* 1. chancellor, head of government, P.M., prime minister ~*adj.* 2. arch, chief, first, foremost, head, highest, leading, main, primary, prime, principal, top 3. earliest, first, inaugural, initial, original

premiere debut, first night, first performance, first showing, opening

premise *v.* assume, hypothesize, posit, postulate, predicate, presuppose, state

premises building, establishment, place, property, site

premiss, premise argument, assertion, assumption, ground, hypothesis, postulate, postulation, presupposition, proposition, supposition, thesis

premium 1. bonus, boon, bounty, fee, percentage (*Inf.*), perk (*Brit. inf.*), perquisite, prize, recompense, remuneration, reward 2. appreciation, regard, stock, store, value 3. **at a premium** beyond one's means, costly, expensive, hard to come by, in great demand, in short supply, like gold dust, not to be had for love or money, rare, scarce, valuable

premonition apprehension, feeling, feeling in one's bones, foreboding, forewarning, funny feeling (*Inf.*), hunch, idea, intuition, misgiving, omen, portent, presage, presentiment, sign, suspicion, warning

preoccupation 1. absence of mind, absent-mindedness, absorption, abstraction, brown study, daydreaming, engrossment, immersion, inattentiveness, musing, oblivion, pensiveness, prepossession, reverie, woolgathering 2. bee in one's bonnet, concern, fixation, hang-up (*Inf.*), hobby-horse, *idée fixe,* obsession, pet subject

preoccupied absent-minded, absorbed, abstracted, caught up in, distracted, distrait, engrossed, faraway, heedless, immersed, in a brown study, intent, lost in, lost in thought, oblivious, rapt, taken up, unaware, wrapped up

preordain destine, doom, fate, map out in advance, predestine, predetermine

preparation 1. development, getting ready, groundwork, preparing, putting in order 2. alertness, anticipation, expectation, foresight, precaution, preparedness, provision, readiness, safeguard 3. *Often plural* arrangement, measure, plan, provision 4. composition, compound, concoction, medicine, mixture, tincture 5. homework, prep (*Inf.*), revision, schoolwork, study, swotting (*Brit. inf.*)

preparatory 1. basic, elementary, introductory, opening, prefatory, preliminary, preparative, primary 2. **preparatory to** before, in advance of, in anticipation of, in preparation for, prior to

prepare 1. adapt, adjust, anticipate, arrange, coach, dispose, form, groom, make provision, make ready, plan, practise, prime, put in order, train, warm up 2. brace, fortify, gird, ready, steel, strengthen 3. assemble, concoct, construct, contrive, draw up, fashion, fix up, get up (*Inf.*), make, produce, put together, turn out 4. accoutre, equip, fit, fit out, furnish, outfit, provide, supply

prepared 1. all set, arranged, fit, in order, in readiness, planned, primed, ready, set 2. able, disposed, inclined, minded, of a mind, predisposed, willing

preparedness alertness, fitness, order, preparation, readiness

preponderance ascendancy, bulk, dominance, domination, dominion, extensiveness, greater numbers, greater part, lion's share, mass, power, predominance, prevalence, superiority, supremacy, sway, weight

preponderant ascendant, dominant, extensive, foremost, greater, important, larger, paramount, predominant, prevailing, prevalent, significant

preponderate dominate, hold sway, outnumber, predominate, prevail, reign supreme, rule

prepossessed biased, inclined, partial, partisan, predisposed, prejudiced

prepossessing alluring, amiable, appealing, attractive, beautiful, bewitching, captivating, charming, engaging, fair, fascinating, fetching, glamorous, good-looking, handsome, inviting, likable *or* likeable, lovable, magnetic, pleasing, striking, taking, winning
Antonyms disagreeable, displeasing, objectionable, offensive, repulsive, ugly, unattractive, uninviting, unlikable *or* unlikeable

prepossession 1. absorption, engrossment, preoccupation 2. bias, inclination, liking, partiality, predilection, predisposition, prejudice

preposterous absurd, asinine, bizarre, crazy, excessive, exorbitant, extravagant, extreme, foolish, impossible, incredible, insane, irrational, laughable, ludicrous, monstrous, nonsensical, out of the question, outrageous, ridiculous, senseless, shocking, unreasonable, unthinkable

prerequisite 1. *adj.* called for, essential, imperative, indispensable, mandatory, necessary, needful, obligatory, of the essence, required, requisite, vital 2. *n.* condition, essential, imperative, must, necessity, precondition, qualification, requirement, requisite, *sine qua non*

prerogative advantage, authority, birthright, choice, claim, droit, due, exemption, immunity, liberty, perquisite, privilege, right, sanction, title

presage *n.* 1. augury, auspice, forecast, forewarning, harbinger, intimation, omen, portent, prediction, prognostic, prognostication, prophecy, sign, warning 2. apprehension, boding, feeling, foreboding, intuition, misgiving, premonition, presentiment ~*v.* 3. divine, feel, foresee, have a feeling, intuit, sense 4. adumbrate, augur, betoken, bode, forebode, foreshadow, foretoken, omen, point to, portend, signify, warn 5. forecast, foretell, forewarn, predict, prognosticate, prophesy, soothsay, vaticinate (*Rare*)

prescience clairvoyance, foreknowledge, foresight, precognition, prevision (*Rare*), second sight

prescient clairvoyant, discerning, divinatory, divining, far-sighted, foresighted, mantic, perceptive, prophetic, psychic

prescribe appoint, assign, command, decree, define, dictate, direct, enjoin, establish, fix, impose, lay down, ordain, order, require, rule, set, specify, stipulate

prescript command, dictate, dictum, direction, directive, edict, instruction, law, mandate, order, ordinance, precept, regulation, requirement, rule

prescription 1. direction, formula, instruction, recipe 2. drug, medicine, mixture, preparation, remedy

prescriptive authoritarian, dictatorial, didactic, dogmatic, legislating, preceptive, rigid

presence 1. attendance, being, companionship, company, existence, habitation, inhabitance, occupancy, residence 2. closeness, immediate circle, nearness, neighbourhood, propinquity, proximity, vicinity 3. air, appearance, aspect, aura, bearing, carriage, comportment, demeanour, ease, mien (*Literary*), personality, poise, self-assurance 4. apparition, eidolon, ghost, manifestation, revenant, shade (*Literary*), spectre, spirit, supernatural being, wraith

presence of mind alertness, aplomb, calmness, composure, cool (*Sl.*), coolness, imperturbability, level-headedness, phlegm, quickness, sang-froid, self-assurance, self-command, self-possession, wits

present[1] *adj.* 1. contemporary, current, existent, existing, extant, immediate, instant, present-day 2. accounted for, at hand, available, here, in attendance, near, nearby, ready, there, to hand ~*n.* 3. here and now, now, present moment, the time being, this day and age, today 4. **at present** at the moment, just now, now, nowadays, right now 5. **for the present** for a while, for the moment, for the nonce, for the time being, in the meantime, not for long, provisionally, temporarily

present[2] *v.* 1. acquaint with, introduce, make known 2. demonstrate, display, exhibit, give, mount, put before the public, put on, show, stage 3. adduce, advance, declare, expound, extend, hold out, introduce, offer, pose, produce, proffer, put forward, raise, recount, relate, state, submit, suggest, tender 4. award, bestow, confer, donate, entrust, furnish, give, grant, hand out, hand over, offer, proffer, put at (someone's) disposal ~*n.* 5. benefaction, boon, bounty, donation, endowment, favour, gift, grant, gratuity, hand-out, largess *or* largesse, offering, prezzie (*Inf.*)

presentable acceptable, becoming, decent, fit to be seen, good enough, not bad (*Inf.*), O.K. *or* okay (*Inf.*), passable, proper, respectable, satisfactory, suitable, tolerable
Antonyms below par, not good enough, not up to scratch, poor, rubbishy, unacceptable, unpresentable, unsatisfactory

presentation 1. award, bestowal, conferral, donation, giving, investiture, offering 2. appearance, arrangement, delivery, exposition, production, rendition, staging, submission 3. demonstration, display, exhibition, performance, production, representation, show 4. coming out, debut, introduction, launch, launching, reception

presentiment anticipation, apprehension, expectation, fear, feeling, foreboding, forecast, forethought, hunch, intuition, misgiving, premonition, presage

presently anon (*Archaic*), before long, by and by, erelong (*Archaic or poetic*), in a minute, in a moment, in a short while, pretty soon (*Inf.*), shortly, soon

preservation conservation, defence, keeping, maintenance, perpetuation, protection, safeguarding, safekeeping, safety, salvation, security, storage, support, upholding

preserve *v.* 1. care for, conserve, defend, guard, keep, protect, safeguard, save, secure, shelter, shield 2. continue, keep, keep up, maintain, perpetuate, retain, sustain, uphold 3. conserve, keep, put up, save, store *~n.* 4. area, domain, field, realm, specialism, sphere 5. *Often plural* confection, confiture, conserve, jam, jelly, marmalade, sweetmeat 6. game reserve, reservation, reserve, sanctuary
Antonyms (*sense 1*) assail, assault, attack, leave unprotected, turn out (*sense 2*) abandon, discontinue, drop, end, give up (*sense 3*) blow (*Sl.*), consume, fritter away, spend, squander, waste

preside administer, be at the head of, be in authority, chair, conduct, control, direct, govern, head, lead, manage, officiate, run, supervise

press *v.* 1. bear down on, compress, condense, crush, depress, force down, jam, mash, push, reduce, squeeze, stuff 2. calender, finish, flatten, iron, mangle, put the creases in, smooth, steam 3. clasp, crush, embrace, encircle, enfold, fold in one's arms, hold close, hug, squeeze 4. compel, constrain, demand, enforce, enjoin, force, insist on 5. beg, entreat, exhort, implore, importune, petition, plead, pressurize, sue, supplicate, urge 6. afflict, assail, beset, besiege, disquiet, harass, plague, torment, trouble, vex, worry 7. **be pressed** be hard put, be pushed (hurried, rushed, (*Inf.*)), be short of 8. cluster, crowd, flock, gather, hasten, herd, hurry, mill, push, rush, seethe, surge, swarm, throng *~n.* 9. **the press** a. Fleet Street, fourth estate, journalism, news media, newspapers, the papers b. columnists, correspondents, gentlemen of the press, journalists, journos (*Sl.*), newsmen, photographers, pressmen, reporters 10. bunch, crowd, crush, flock, herd, horde, host, mob, multitude, pack, push (*Inf.*), swarm, throng 11. bustle, demand, hassle (*Inf.*), hurry, pressure, strain, stress, urgency

pressing burning, constraining, crucial, exigent, high-priority, imperative, important, importunate, serious, urgent, vital
Antonyms dispensable, regular, routine, unimportant, unnecessary

pressure 1. compressing, compression, crushing, force, heaviness, squeezing, weight 2. coercion, compulsion, constraint, force, influence, obligation, power, sway 3. adversity, affliction, burden, demands, difficulty, distress, exigency, hassle (*Inf.*), heat, hurry, load, press, strain, stress, urgency

prestige authority, bottom, Brownie points, cachet, celebrity, credit, distinction, eminence, esteem, fame, honour, importance, influence, kudos, regard, renown, reputation, standing, stature, status, weight

prestigious celebrated, eminent, esteemed, exalted, great, illustrious, important, imposing, impressive, influential, notable, prominent, renowned, reputable, respected
Antonyms humble, lowly, minor, obscure, unimportant, unimpressive, unknown

presumably apparently, doubtless, doubtlessly, in all likelihood, in all probability, it would seem, likely, most likely, on the face of it, probably, seemingly

presume 1. assume, believe, conjecture, guess (*Inf., chiefly U.S. & Canad.*), infer, posit, postulate, presuppose, suppose, surmise, take for granted, take it, think 2. dare, go so far, have the audacity, make bold, make so bold, take the liberty, undertake, venture 3. bank on, count on, depend, rely, trust

presumption 1. assurance, audacity, boldness, brass (*Inf.*), brass neck (*Brit. inf.*), cheek (*Inf.*), chutzpah (*U.S. & Canad. inf.*), effrontery, forwardness, front, gall (*Inf.*), impudence, insolence, neck (*Inf.*), nerve (*Inf.*), presumptuousness, temerity 2. anticipation, assumption, belief, conjecture, guess, hypothesis, opinion, premiss, presupposition, supposition, surmise 3. basis, chance, grounds, likelihood, plausibility, probability, reason

presumptive 1. assumed, believed, expected, hypothetical, inferred, supposed, understood 2. believable, conceivable, credible, likely, plausible, possible, probable, reasonable, verisimilar

presumptuous arrogant, audacious, bigheaded (*Inf.*), bold, conceited, foolhardy, forward, insolent, overconfident, overfamiliar, overweening, presuming, pushy (*Inf.*), rash, too big for one's boots, uppish (*Brit. inf.*)
Antonyms bashful, humble, modest, retiring, shy, timid, unassuming

presuppose accept, assume, consider, imply, posit, postulate, presume, suppose, take as read, take for granted, take it

presupposition assumption, belief, hypothesis, preconceived idea, preconception, premiss, presumption, supposition, theory

pretence 1. acting, charade, deceit, deception, fabrication, fakery, faking, falsehood, feigning, invention, make-believe, sham,

simulation, subterfuge, trickery 2. affectation, appearance, artifice, display, façade, hokum (*Sl., chiefly U.S. & Canad.*), posing, posturing, pretentiousness, show, veneer 3. claim, cloak, colour, cover, excuse, façade, garb, guise, mask, masquerade, pretext, ruse, semblance, show, veil, wile
Antonyms (*sense 1*) actuality, fact, reality (*sense 2*) candour, frankness, honesty, ingenuousness, openness

pretend 1. affect, allege, assume, counterfeit, dissemble, dissimulate, fake, falsify, feign, impersonate, make out, pass oneself off as, profess, put on, sham, simulate 2. act, imagine, make believe, make up, play, play the part of, suppose 3. allege, aspire, claim, lay claim, profess, purport

pretended alleged, avowed, bogus, counterfeit, fake, false, feigned, fictitious, imaginary, ostensible, phoney *or* phony (*Inf.*), pretend (*Inf.*), professed, pseudo (*Inf.*), purported, sham, so-called, spurious

pretender aspirant, claimant, claimer

pretension 1. aspiration, assertion, assumption, claim, demand, pretence, profession 2. affectation, airs, conceit, hypocrisy, ostentation, pomposity, pretentiousness, self-importance, show, showiness, snobbery, snobbishness, vainglory, vanity

pretentious affected, assuming, bombastic, conceited, exaggerated, extravagant, flaunting, grandiloquent, grandiose, highfalutin (*Inf.*), high-flown, high-sounding, hollow, inflated, magniloquent, mannered, ostentatious, overambitious, pompous, puffed up, showy, snobbish, specious, vainglorious
Antonyms modest, natural, plain, simple, unaffected, unassuming, unpretentious

preternatural abnormal, anomalous, extraordinary, inexplicable, irregular, marvellous, miraculous, mysterious, odd, peculiar, strange, supernatural, unaccountable, unearthly, unnatural, unusual

pretext affectation, alleged reason, appearance, cloak, cover, device, excuse, guise, mask, ploy, pretence, red herring, ruse, semblance, show, simulation, veil

prettify adorn, deck out, decorate, doll up (*Sl.*), do up, embellish, garnish, gild, ornament, pretty up, tart up (*Brit. sl.*), titivate, trick out, trim

pretty *adj.* 1. appealing, attractive, beautiful, bonny, charming, comely, cute, fair, good-looking, graceful, lovely, personable 2. bijou, dainty, delicate, elegant, fine, neat, nice, pleasing, tasteful, trim *~adv.* 3. *Inf.* fairly, kind of (*Inf.*), moderately, quite, rather, reasonably, somewhat
Antonyms plain, ugly, unattractive, unshapely, unsightly

prevail 1. be victorious, carry the day, gain mastery, overcome, overrule, prove superior, succeed, triumph, win 2. abound, be current (prevalent, widespread), exist generally, obtain, predominate, preponderate 3. *Often with* **on** *or* **upon** bring round, convince, dispose, incline, induce, influence, persuade, prompt, sway, talk into, win over

prevailing 1. common, current, customary, established, fashionable, general, in style, in vogue, ordinary, popular, prevalent, set, usual, widespread 2. dominant, influential, main, operative, predominating, preponderating, principal, ruling

prevalence 1. acceptance, commonness, common occurrence, currency, frequency, pervasiveness, popularity, profusion, regularity, ubiquity, universality 2. ascendancy, hold, mastery, predominance, preponderance, primacy, rule, sway

prevalent 1. accepted, common, commonplace, current, customary, established, everyday, extensive, frequent, general, habitual, popular, rampant, rife, ubiquitous, universal, usual, widespread 2. ascendant, compelling, dominant, governing, powerful, predominant, prevailing, successful, superior
Antonyms (*sense 1*) confined, infrequent, limited, localized, rare, restricted, uncommon, unusual

prevaricate beat about the bush, beg the question, cavil, deceive, dodge, equivocate, evade, flannel (*Brit. inf.*), give a false colour to, hedge, lie, palter, quibble, shift, shuffle, stretch the truth, tergiversate
Antonyms be blunt, be direct, be frank, be straightforward, come straight to the point, not beat about the bush

prevarication cavilling, deceit, deception, equivocation, evasion, falsehood, falsification, lie, misrepresentation, pretence, quibbling, tergiversation, untruth

prevaricator Ananias, deceiver, dissembler, dodger, equivocator, evader, fibber, hypocrite, liar, pettifogger, quibbler, sophist

prevent anticipate, avert, avoid, balk, bar, block, check, counteract, defend against, foil, forestall, frustrate, hamper, head off, hinder, impede, inhibit, intercept, nip in the bud, obstruct, obviate, preclude, restrain, stave off, stop, thwart, ward off
Antonyms allow, encourage, help, incite, permit, support, urge

prevention 1. anticipation, avoidance, deterrence, elimination, forestalling, obviation, precaution, preclusion, prophylaxis, safeguard, thwarting 2. bar, check, deterrence, frustration, hindrance, impediment, interruption, obstacle, obstruction, stoppage

preventive, preventative *adj.* 1. hampering, hindering, impeding, obstructive 2. counteractive, deterrent, inhibitory, precautionary, prophylactic, protective, shielding ~*n.* 3. block, hindrance, impediment, obstacle, obstruction 4. deterrent, neutralizer, prevention, prophylactic, protection, protective, remedy, safeguard, shield

previous 1. antecedent, anterior, earlier, erstwhile, ex-, foregoing, former, one-time, past, preceding, prior, quondam, sometime 2. *Inf.* ahead of oneself, precipitate, premature, too early, too soon, untimely
Antonyms (*sense 1*) consequent, following, later, subsequent, succeeding

previously at one time, a while ago, before, beforehand, earlier, formerly, heretofore, hitherto, in advance, in anticipation, in days *or* years gone by, in the past, once, then, until now

prey *n.* 1. game, kill, quarry 2. dupe, fall guy (*Inf.*), mark, mug (*Brit. sl.*), target, victim ~*v.* 3. devour, eat, feed upon, hunt, live off, seize 4. blackmail, bleed (*Inf.*), bully, exploit, intimidate, take advantage of, terrorize, victimize 5. burden, distress, hang over, haunt, oppress, trouble, weigh down, weigh heavily, worry

price *n.* 1. amount, asking price, assessment, bill, charge, cost, damage (*Inf.*), estimate, expenditure, expense, face value, fee, figure, outlay, payment, rate, valuation, value, worth 2. consequences, cost, penalty, sacrifice, toll 3. bounty, compensation, premium, recompense, reward 4. **at any price** anyhow, cost what it may, expense no object, no matter what the cost, regardless, whatever the cost 5. **beyond price** inestimable, invaluable, of incalculable value, precious, priceless, treasured, without price ~*v.* 6. assess, cost, estimate, evaluate, put a price on, rate, value

priceless 1. beyond price, cherished, costly, dear, expensive, incalculable, incomparable, inestimable, invaluable, irreplaceable, precious, prized, rare, rich, treasured, worth a king's ransom 2. *Inf.* absurd, amusing, comic, droll, funny, hilarious, killing (*Inf.*), rib-tickling, ridiculous, riotous, side-splitting
Antonyms cheap, cheapo (*Inf.*), common, inexpensive, worthless

pricey, pricy costly, dear, exorbitant, expensive, extortionate, high-priced, over the odds (*Brit. inf.*), steep (*Inf.*)

prick *v.* 1. bore, impale, jab, lance, perforate, pierce, pink, punch, puncture, stab 2. bite, itch, prickle, smart, sting, tingle 3. cut, distress, grieve, move, pain, stab, touch, trouble, wound 4. *Usually with* **up** point, raise, rise, stand erect ~*n.* 5. cut, gash, hole, perforation, pinhole, puncture, wound 6. gnawing, pang, prickle, smart, spasm, sting, twinge

prickle *n.* 1. barb, needle, point, spike, spine, spur, thorn 2. chill, formication, goose flesh, paraesthesia (*Medical*), pins and needles (*Inf.*), smart, tickle, tingle, tingling ~*v.* 3. itch, smart, sting, tingle, twitch 4. jab, nick, prick, stick

prickly 1. barbed, brambly, briery, bristly, spiny, thorny 2. crawling, itchy, pricking, prickling, scratchy, sharp, smarting, stinging, tingling 3. bad-tempered, cantankerous, edgy, fractious, grumpy, irritable, liverish, peevish, pettish, petulant, ratty (*Brit. & N.Z. inf.*), shirty (*Sl., chiefly Brit.*), snappish, stroppy (*Brit. sl.*), tetchy, touchy, waspish 4. complicated, difficult, intricate, involved, knotty, thorny, ticklish, tricky, troublesome, trying

pride *n.* 1. *amour-propre,* dignity, honour, self-esteem, self-respect, self-worth 2. arrogance, bigheadedness (*Inf.*), conceit, egotism, haughtiness, hauteur, hubris, loftiness, *morgue,* presumption, pretension, pretentiousness, self-importance, self-love, smugness, snobbery, superciliousness, vainglory, vanity 3. boast, gem, jewel, pride and joy, prize, treasure 4. delight, gratification, joy, pleasure, satisfaction 5. best, choice, cream, elite, flower, glory, pick ~*v.* 6. be proud of, boast, brag, congratulate oneself, crow, exult, flatter oneself, glory in, pique, plume, preen, revel in, take pride, vaunt
Antonyms (*sense 1*) humility, meekness, modesty

priest churchman, clergyman, cleric, curate, divine, ecclesiastic, father, father confessor, holy man, man of God, man of the cloth, minister, padre (*Inf.*), pastor, vicar

priestly canonical, clerical, ecclesiastic, hieratic, pastoral, priestlike, sacerdotal

prig goody-goody (*Inf.*), Holy Joe (*Inf.*), Holy Willie (*Inf.*), Mrs Grundy, old maid (*Inf.*), pedant, prude, puritan, stuffed shirt (*Inf.*)

priggish goody-goody (*Inf.*), holier-than-thou, narrow-minded, pedantic, prim, prudish, puritanical, self-righteous, self-satisfied, smug, starchy (*Inf.*), stiff, stuffy

prim demure, fastidious, formal, fussy, old-maidish (*Inf.*), particular, precise, priggish, prissy (*Inf.*), proper, prudish, puritanical,

schoolmarmish (*Brit. inf.*), starchy (*Inf.*), stiff, strait-laced
Antonyms carefree, casual, easy-going, informal, laid-back, relaxed

primacy ascendancy, command, dominance, dominion, leadership, pre-eminence, superiority, supremacy

prima donna diva, leading lady, star

primal 1. earliest, first, initial, original, primary, prime, primitive, primordial, pristine 2. central, chief, first, greatest, highest, main, major, most important, paramount, prime, principal

primarily 1. above all, basically, chiefly, especially, essentially, for the most part, fundamentally, generally, largely, mainly, mostly, on the whole, principally 2. at first, at *or* from the start, first and foremost, initially, in the beginning, in the first place, originally

primary 1. best, capital, cardinal, chief, dominant, first, greatest, highest, leading, main, paramount, prime, principal, top 2. aboriginal, earliest, initial, original, primal, primeval, primitive, primordial, pristine 3. basic, beginning, bog-standard (*Inf.*), elemental, essential, fundamental, radical, ultimate, underlying 4. elementary, introductory, rudimentary, simple
Antonyms (*sense 1*) inferior, lesser, lowest, subordinate, supplementary, unimportant (*sense 4*) ensuing, following, later, secondary, subsequent, succeeding

prime *adj.* 1. best, capital, choice, excellent, first-class, first-rate, grade A, highest, quality, select, selected, superior, top 2. basic, bog-standard (*Inf.*), earliest, fundamental, original, primary, underlying 3. chief, leading, main, predominant, pre-eminent, primary, principal, ruling, senior ~*n.* 4. best days, bloom, flower, full flowering, height, heyday, maturity, peak, perfection, zenith 5. beginning, morning, opening, spring, start ~*v.* 6. break in, coach, fit, get ready, groom, make ready, prepare, train 7. brief, clue in (*Inf.*), clue up (*Inf.*), fill in (*Inf.*), gen up (*Brit. inf.*), give someone the lowdown (*Inf.*), inform, notify, tell

primeval, primaeval ancient, earliest, early, first, old, original, prehistoric, primal, primitive, primordial, pristine

primitive 1. earliest, early, elementary, first, original, primary, primeval, primordial, pristine 2. barbarian, barbaric, crude, rough, rude, rudimentary, savage, simple, uncivilized, uncultivated, undeveloped, unrefined 3. childlike, naive, simple, undeveloped, unsophisticated, untrained, untutored
Antonyms (*sense 1*) advanced, later, modern (*sense 2*) civilized, comfortable, developed, elaborate, refined (*sense 3*) adult, developed, mature, sophisticated, trained, tutored

primordial 1. earliest, first, prehistoric, primal, primeval, primitive, pristine 2. basic, elemental, fundamental, original, radical

primp be in full fig (*Sl.*), deck out, doll up (*Sl.*), dress up, fig up (*Sl.*), gussy up (*Sl.*), prank, preen, prink, put on one's best bib and tucker (*Inf.*), put on one's gladrags (*Sl.*)

prince lord, monarch, potentate, ruler, sovereign

princely 1. bounteous, bountiful, generous, gracious, lavish, liberal, magnanimous, munificent, open-handed, rich 2. august, dignified, grand, high-born, imperial, imposing, lofty, magnificent, majestic, noble, regal, royal, sovereign, stately

principal *adj.* 1. capital, cardinal, chief, controlling, dominant, essential, first, foremost, highest, key, leading, main, most important, paramount, pre-eminent, primary, prime, strongest ~*n.* 2. boss (*Inf.*), chief, director, head, leader, master, ruler, superintendent 3. dean, director, head (*Inf.*), headmaster, headmistress, head teacher, master, rector 4. assets, capital, capital funds, money 5. first violin, lead, leader, star
Antonyms auxiliary, inferior, minor, subordinate, subsidiary, supplementary, weakest

principally above all, chiefly, especially, first and foremost, for the most part, in the main, largely, mainly, mostly, particularly, predominantly, primarily

principle 1. assumption, axiom, canon, criterion, dictum, doctrine, dogma, ethic, formula, fundamental, golden rule, law, maxim, moral law, precept, proposition, rule, standard, truth, verity 2. attitude, belief, code, credo, ethic, morality, opinion, tenet 3. conscience, integrity, morals, probity, rectitude, scruples, sense of duty, sense of honour, uprightness 4. **in principle** ideally, in essence, in theory, theoretically

principled conscientious, correct, decent, ethical, high-minded, honourable, just, moral, righteous, right-minded, scrupulous, upright, virtuous

prink adorn, deck, doll up (*Sl.*), dress to kill (*Inf.*), dress up, dress (up) to the nines (*Inf.*), fig up (*Sl.*), groom, gussy up (*Sl.*), prank, preen, primp, titivate, trick out

print *v.* 1. engrave, go to press, impress, imprint, issue, mark, publish, put to bed (*Inf.*), run off, stamp ~*n.* 2. book, magazine, newspaper, newsprint, periodical, printed matter, publication, typescript 3. **in print** a. in black and white, on paper, on the streets, out, printed, published b. available, current, in the shops, obtainable, on the market, on the shelves 4. **out of print** no longer published, o.p., unavailable, unobtainable 5. copy, engraving, photo (*Inf.*), photograph, picture, reproduction 6. characters, face, font (*Chiefly U.S.*), fount, lettering, letters, type, typeface

prior 1. aforementioned, antecedent, anterior, earlier, foregoing, former, preceding, pre-existent, pre-existing, previous 2. **prior to** before, earlier than, preceding, previous to

priority first concern, greater importance, precedence, pre-eminence, preference, prerogative, rank, right of way, seniority, superiority, supremacy, the lead

priory abbey, cloister, convent, monastery, nunnery, religious house

prison can (*Sl.*), choky (*Sl.*), clink (*Sl.*), confinement, cooler (*Sl.*), dungeon, gaol, glasshouse (*Military inf.*), jail, jug (*Sl.*), lockup, nick (*Brit. sl.*), penal institution, penitentiary (*U.S.*), poky *or* pokey (*U.S. & Canad. sl.*), pound, quod (*Sl.*), slammer (*Sl.*), stir (*Sl.*)

prisoner 1. con (*Sl.*), convict, jailbird, lag (*Sl.*) 2. captive, detainee, hostage, internee

prissy fastidious, finicky, fussy, old-maidish (*Inf.*), overnice, precious, prim, prim and proper, prudish, schoolmarmish (*Brit. inf.*), squeamish, strait-laced

pristine 1. earliest, first, former, initial, original, primal, primary, primeval, primitive, primordial 2. immaculate, new, pure, uncorrupted, undefiled, unspoiled, unsullied, untouched, virgin, virginal

privacy 1. isolation, privateness, retirement, retreat, seclusion, separateness, sequestration, solitude 2. clandestineness, concealment, confidentiality, secrecy

private *adj.* 1. clandestine, closet, confidential, covert, hush-hush (*Inf.*), in camera, inside, off the record, privy (*Archaic*), secret, unofficial 2. exclusive, individual, intimate, own, particular, personal, reserved, special 3. independent, nonpublic 4. concealed, isolated, not overlooked, retired, secluded, secret, separate, sequestered, solitary, withdrawn 5. **in private** behind closed doors, confidentially, in camera, in secret, personally, privately ~*n.* 6. enlisted man (*U.S.*), private soldier, squaddie *or* squaddy (*Brit. sl.*), tommy (*Brit. inf.*), Tommy Atkins (*Brit. inf.*)
Antonyms (*sense 1*) disclosed, known, official, open, public, revealed (*sense 2*) common, general, open, public, unlimited, unrestricted (*sense 3*) bustling, busy, frequented, outgoing, sociable, unsecluded

privation destitution, distress, hardship, indigence, lack, loss, misery, necessity, need, neediness, penury, poverty, suffering, want

privilege advantage, benefit, birthright, claim, concession, due, entitlement, franchise, freedom, immunity, liberty, prerogative, right, sanction

privileged 1. advantaged, elite, entitled, favoured, honoured, indulged, powerful, ruling, special 2. allowed, empowered, exempt, free, granted, licensed, sanctioned, vested 3. *Of information* confidential, exceptional, inside, not for publication, off the record, privy, special

privy *adj.* 1. *With* **to** apprised of, aware of, cognizant of, hip to (*Sl.*), informed, in on, in the know (*Inf.*), wise to (*Sl.*) 2. *Archaic* confidential, hidden, hush-hush (*Inf.*), off the record, personal, private, secret ~*n.* 3. bog (*Sl.*), closet, earth closet, latrine, lavatory, outside toilet, *pissoir*

prize[1] *n.* 1. accolade, award, honour, premium, reward, trophy 2. haul, jackpot, purse, stakes, windfall, winnings 3. aim, ambition, conquest, desire, gain, goal, hope 4. booty, capture, loot, pickings, pillage, plunder, spoil(s), trophy ~*adj.* 5. award-winning, best, champion, first-rate, outstanding, top, topnotch (*Inf.*), winning

prize[2] *v.* appreciate, cherish, esteem, hold dear, regard highly, set store by, treasure, value

prizefighter boxer, bruiser (*Inf.*), fighter, pug (*Sl.*), pugilist

prizefighting boxing, fighting, pugilism, the noble art *or* science, the prize ring, the ring

probability chance(s), expectation, liability, likelihood, likeliness, odds, presumption, prospect

probable apparent, credible, feasible, likely, most likely, odds-on, on the cards, ostensible, plausible, possible, presumable, presumed, reasonable, seeming, verisimilar

probably as likely as not, doubtless, in all likelihood, in all probability, likely, maybe, most likely, perchance (*Archaic*), perhaps, possibly, presumably
Antonyms doubtful, improbable, not likely, unlikely

probation apprenticeship, examination, initiation, novitiate, test, trial, trial period

probe *v.* 1. examine, explore, go into, investigate, look into, query, research, scrutinize, search, sift, sound, test, verify, work over 2. explore, feel around, poke, prod ~*n.* 3. detection, examination, exploration, inquest, inquiry, investigation, research, scrutiny, study

probity equity, fairness, fidelity, goodness, honesty, honour, integrity, justice, morality, rectitude, righteousness, sincerity, trustworthiness, truthfulness, uprightness, virtue, worth

problem *n.* 1. can of worms (*Inf.*), complication, difficulty, dilemma, disagreement, dispute, disputed point, doubt, hard nut to crack (*Inf.*), point at issue, predicament, quandary, trouble 2. brain-teaser (*Inf.*), conundrum, enigma, poser, puzzle, question, riddle, teaser ~*adj.* 3. delinquent, difficult, intractable, uncontrollable, unmanageable, unruly

problematic chancy (*Inf.*), debatable, doubtful, dubious, enigmatic, moot, open to doubt, problematical, puzzling, questionable, tricky, uncertain, unsettled
Antonyms beyond question, certain, clear, definite, indisputable, settled, undebatable, unquestionable

procedure action, conduct, course, custom, form, formula, method, modus operandi, operation, performance, plan of action, policy, practice, process, routine, scheme, step, strategy, system, transaction

proceed 1. advance, carry on, continue, get going, get on with, get under way with, go ahead, go on, make a start, move on, press on, progress, set in motion 2. arise, come, derive, emanate, ensue, flow, follow, issue, originate, result, spring, stem
Antonyms (*sense 1*) break off, cease, discontinue, end, get behind, halt, leave off, pack in (*Brit. inf.*), retreat, stop

proceeding 1. act, action, course of action, deed, measure, move, occurrence, procedure, process, step, undertaking, venture 2. *Plural* account, affairs, annals, archives, business, dealings, doings, matters, minutes, records, report, transactions

proceeds earnings, gain, income, produce, products, profit, receipts, returns, revenue, takings, yield

process *n.* 1. action, course, course of action, manner, means, measure, method, mode, operation, performance, practice, procedure, proceeding, system, transaction 2. advance, course, development, evolution, formation, growth, movement, progress, progression, stage, step, unfolding 3. *Law* action, case, suit, trial ~*v.* 4. deal with, dispose of, fulfil, handle, take care of 5. alter, convert, prepare, refine, transform, treat

procession 1. cavalcade, column, cortege, file, march, motorcade, parade, train 2. course, cycle, run, sequence, series, string, succession, train

proclaim advertise, affirm, announce, blaze (abroad), blazon (abroad), circulate, declare, enunciate, give out, herald, indicate, make known, profess, promulgate, publish, shout from the housetops (*Inf.*), show, trumpet
Antonyms conceal, hush up, keep back, keep secret, suppress, withhold

proclamation announcement, declaration, decree, edict, manifesto, notice, notification, promulgation, pronouncement, pronunciamento, publication

proclivity bent, bias, disposition, facility, inclination, leaning, liableness, penchant, predilection, predisposition, proneness, propensity, tendency, weakness

procrastinate adjourn, be dilatory, dally, defer, delay, drag one's feet (*Inf.*), gain time, play a waiting game, play for time, postpone, prolong, protract, put off, retard, stall, temporize
Antonyms advance, expedite, get on with, hasten, hurry (up), proceed, speed up

procreate beget, breed, bring into being, engender, father, generate, mother, produce, propagate, reproduce, sire

procure acquire, appropriate, buy, come by, earn, effect, find, gain, get, get hold of, lay hands on, manage to get, obtain, pick up, purchase, score (*Sl.*), secure, win

procurer bawd (*Archaic*), madam, pander, panderer, pimp, procuress, white-slaver, whoremaster (*Archaic*)

prod *v.* 1. dig, drive, elbow, jab, nudge, poke, prick, propel, push, shove 2. egg on, goad, impel, incite, motivate, move, prompt, rouse, spur, stimulate, stir up, urge ~*n.* 3. boost, dig, elbow, jab, nudge, poke, push, shove 4. goad, poker, spur, stick 5. boost, cue, prompt, reminder, signal, stimulus

prodigal *adj.* 1. excessive, extravagant, immoderate, improvident, intemperate, profligate, reckless, spendthrift, squandering, wanton, wasteful 2. bounteous, bountiful, copious, exuberant, lavish, luxuriant, profuse, sumptuous, superabundant, teeming ~*n.* 3. big spender, profligate, spendthrift, squanderer, wastrel
Antonyms (*sense 1*) economical, frugal, miserly, parsimonious, sparing, stingy, thrifty, tight (*sense 2*) deficient, lacking, meagre, scanty, scarce, short, sparse

prodigality 1. abandon, dissipation, excess, extravagance, immoderation, intemperance, profligacy, recklessness, squandering, wantonness, waste, wastefulness 2. abundance, amplitude, bounteousness, bounty, copiousness, cornucopia, exuberance, horn of plenty, lavishness, luxuriance, plenteousness, plenty, profusion, richness, sumptuousness

prodigious 1. colossal, enormous, giant, gigantic, huge, immeasurable, immense, inordinate, mammoth, massive, monstrous, monumental, stupendous, tremendous, vast 2. abnormal, amazing, astounding, exceptional, extraordinary, fabulous, fantastic (*Inf.*), flabbergasting (*Inf.*), impressive, marvellous, miraculous, phenomenal, remarkable, staggering, startling, striking, stupendous, unusual, wonderful

Antonyms negligible, normal, ordinary, small, tiny, unexceptional, unimpressive, unremarkable, usual

prodigy 1. brainbox, child genius, genius, mastermind, talent, whiz (*Inf.*), whiz kid (*Inf.*), wizard, wonder child, wunderkind 2. marvel, miracle, one in a million, phenomenon, rare bird (*Inf.*), sensation, wonder 3. abnormality, curiosity, freak, grotesque, monster, monstrosity, mutation, spectacle

produce *v.* 1. compose, construct, create, develop, fabricate, invent, make, manufacture, originate, put together, turn out 2. afford, bear, beget, breed, bring forth, deliver, engender, furnish, give, render, supply, yield 3. bring about, cause, effect, generate, give rise to, make for, occasion, provoke, set off 4. advance, bring forward, bring to light, demonstrate, exhibit, offer, present, put forward, set forth, show 5. direct, do, exhibit, mount, present, put before the public, put on, show, stage 6. *Geometry* extend, lengthen, prolong, protract ~*n.* 7. crop, fruit and vegetables, greengrocery, harvest, product, yield

producer 1. director, impresario, *régisseur* 2. farmer, grower, maker, manufacturer

product 1. artefact, commodity, concoction, creation, goods, invention, merchandise, produce, production, work 2. consequence, effect, fruit, issue, legacy, offshoot, outcome, result, returns, spin-off, upshot, yield

production 1. assembly, construction, creation, fabrication, formation, making, manufacture, manufacturing, origination, preparation, producing 2. direction, management, presentation, staging

productive 1. creative, dynamic, energetic, fecund, fertile, fruitful, generative, inventive, plentiful, producing, prolific, rich, teeming, vigorous 2. advantageous, beneficial, constructive, effective, fruitful, gainful, gratifying, profitable, rewarding, useful, valuable, worthwhile

Antonyms barren, poor, sterile, unfertile, unfruitful, unproductive, unprofitable, useless

productivity abundance, mass production, output, production, productive capacity, productiveness, work rate, yield

profane *adj.* 1. disrespectful, godless, heathen, idolatrous, impious, impure, irreligious, irreverent, pagan, sacrilegious, sinful, ungodly, wicked 2. lay, secular, temporal, unconsecrated, unhallowed, unholy, unsanctified, worldly 3. abusive, blasphemous, coarse, crude, filthy, foul, obscene, vulgar ~*v.* 4. abuse, commit sacrilege, contaminate, debase, defile, desecrate, misuse, pervert, pollute, prostitute, violate, vitiate

Antonyms clean, decorous, holy, proper, religious, respectful, reverent, sacred, spiritual

profanity abuse, blasphemy, curse, cursing, execration, foul language, four-letter word, impiety, imprecation, irreverence, malediction, obscenity, profaneness, sacrilege, swearing, swearword

profess 1. acknowledge, admit, affirm, announce, assert, asseverate, aver, avow, certify, confess, confirm, declare, maintain, own, proclaim, state, vouch 2. act as if, allege, call oneself, claim, dissemble, fake, feign, let on, make out, pretend, purport, sham

professed 1. avowed, certified, confirmed, declared, proclaimed, self-acknowledged, self-confessed 2. alleged, apparent, ostensible, pretended, purported, self-styled, so-called, *soi-disant,* supposed, would-be

professedly 1. allegedly, apparently, by one's own account, falsely, ostensibly, purportedly, supposedly, under the pretext of 2. admittedly, avowedly, by open declaration, confessedly

profession 1. business, calling, career, employment, line, line of work, métier, occupation, office, position, sphere, vocation, walk of life 2. acknowledgment, affirmation, assertion, attestation, avowal, claim, confession, declaration, statement, testimony, vow

professional 1. *adj.* ace (*Inf.*), adept, competent, crack (*Sl.*), efficient, experienced, expert, finished, masterly, polished, practised, proficient, qualified, skilled, slick, trained 2. *n.* adept, authority, buff (*Inf.*), dab hand (*Brit. inf.*), expert, hotshot (*Inf.*), maestro, master, maven (*U.S.*), past master, pro (*Inf.*), specialist, virtuoso, whiz (*Inf.*), wizard

Antonyms amateurish, incapable, incompetent, inefficient, inept, inexperienced, unpolished, unqualified, unskilled, untrained

professor don (*Brit.*), fellow (*Brit.*), head of faculty, prof (*Inf.*)

proffer extend, hand, hold out, offer, present, propose, propound, submit, suggest, tender, volunteer

proficiency ability, accomplishment, aptitude, competence, craft, dexterity, expertise, expertness, facility, knack, know-how (*Inf.*), mastery, skilfulness, skill, talent

proficient able, accomplished, adept, apt, capable, clever, competent, conversant, efficient, experienced, expert, gifted, masterly, qualified, skilful, skilled, talented, trained, versed
Antonyms bad, incapable, incompetent, inept, unaccomplished, unskilled

profile *n.* 1. contour, drawing, figure, form, outline, portrait, shape, side view, silhouette, sketch 2. biography, characterization, character sketch, sketch, thumbnail sketch, vignette 3. analysis, chart, diagram, examination, graph, review, study, survey, table

profit *n.* 1. *Often plural* bottom line, earnings, emoluments, gain, percentage (*Inf.*), proceeds, receipts, return, revenue, surplus, takings, winnings, yield 2. advancement, advantage, avail, benefit, gain, good, interest, use, value ~*v.* 3. aid, avail, benefit, be of advantage to, better, contribute, gain, help, improve, promote, serve, stand in good stead 4. capitalize on, cash in on (*Inf.*), exploit, learn from, make capital of, make good use of, make the most of, put to good use, rake in (*Inf.*), reap the benefit of, take advantage of, turn to advantage *or* account, use, utilize 5. clean up (*Inf.*), clear, earn, gain, make a good thing of (*Inf.*), make a killing (*Inf.*), make money

profitable 1. commercial, cost-effective, fruitful, gainful, lucrative, money-making, paying, remunerative, rewarding, worthwhile 2. advantageous, beneficial, economic, expedient, fruitful, productive, rewarding, serviceable, useful, valuable, worthwhile
Antonyms disadvantageous, fruitless, unremunerative, unrewarding, useless, vain, worthless

profiteer 1. *n.* exploiter, racketeer 2. *v.* exploit, fleece, make a quick buck (*Sl.*), make someone pay through the nose, overcharge, racketeer, skin (*Sl.*), sting (*Inf.*)

profitless bootless, fruitless, futile, idle, ineffective, ineffectual, pointless, thankless, to no purpose, unavailing, unproductive, unprofitable, unremunerative, useless, vain, worthless

profligacy 1. abandon, corruption, debauchery, degeneracy, depravity, dissipation, dissoluteness, dolce vita, immorality, laxity, libertinism, licentiousness, promiscuity, unrestraint, wantonness 2. excess, extravagance, improvidence, lavishness, prodigality, recklessness, squandering, waste, wastefulness

profligate *adj.* 1. abandoned, corrupt, debauched, degenerate, depraved, dissipated, dissolute, immoral, iniquitous, libertine, licentious, loose, promiscuous, shameless, unprincipled, vicious, vitiated, wanton, wicked, wild 2. extravagant, immoderate, improvident, prodigal, reckless, spendthrift, squandering, wasteful ~*n.* 3. debauchee, degenerate, dissipater, libertine, rake, reprobate, roué 4. prodigal, spendthrift, squanderer, waster, wastrel
Antonyms (*sense 1*) chaste, decent, moral, principled, pure, upright, virginal, virtuous

profound 1. abstruse, deep, discerning, erudite, learned, penetrating, philosophical, recondite, sagacious, sage, serious, skilled, subtle, thoughtful, weighty, wise 2. abysmal, bottomless, cavernous, deep, fathomless, yawning 3. abject, acute, deeply felt, extreme, great, heartfelt, heartrending, hearty, intense, keen, sincere 4. absolute, complete, consummate, exhaustive, extensive, extreme, far-reaching, intense, out-and-out, pronounced, thoroughgoing, total, unqualified, utter
Antonyms imprudent, insincere, shallow, slight, stupid, superficial, thoughtless, uneducated, uninformed, unknowledgeable, unwise

profoundly abjectly, acutely, deeply, extremely, from the bottom of one's heart, greatly, heartily, intensely, keenly, seriously, sincerely, thoroughly, very

profundity 1. acuity, acumen, depth, erudition, insight, intelligence, learning, penetration, perceptiveness, perspicacity, perspicuity, sagacity, wisdom 2. depth, extremity, intensity, seriousness, severity, strength

profuse 1. abundant, ample, bountiful, copious, luxuriant, overflowing, plentiful, prolific, teeming 2. excessive, extravagant, exuberant, fulsome, generous, immoderate, lavish, liberal, open-handed, prodigal, unstinting
Antonyms (*sense 1*) deficient, inadequate, meagre, scanty, scarce, skimpy, sparse (*sense 2*) frugal, illiberal, moderate, provident, thrifty

profusion abundance, bounty, copiousness, cornucopia, excess, extravagance, exuberance, glut, lavishness, luxuriance, multitude, oversupply, plenitude, plethora, prodigality, quantity, riot, superabundance, superfluity, surplus, wealth

progenitor 1. ancestor, begetter, forebear, forefather, parent, primogenitor, procreator 2. antecedent, forerunner, instigator, originator, precursor, predecessor, source

progeny breed, children, descendants, family, issue, lineage, offspring, posterity, race, scions, seed (*Chiefly biblical*), stock, young

prognosis diagnosis, expectation, forecast, prediction, prognostication, projection, speculation, surmise

prognostic 1. *adj.* diagnostic, foretelling, indicating, predicting, predictive, prophetic 2. *n.* forecast, indication, omen, portent, preindication, sign, symptom, warning

prognosticate 1. divine, forecast, foretell, predict, presage, prophesy, soothsay, vaticinate (*Rare*) 2. augur, betoken, forebode, foreshadow, harbinger, herald, point to, portend, presage

prognostication expectation, forecast, prediction, prognosis, projection, prophecy, speculation, surmise

programme *n.* 1. agenda, curriculum, line-up, list, listing, list of players, order of events, order of the day, plan, schedule, syllabus, timetable 2. broadcast, performance, presentation, production, show 3. design, order of the day, plan, plan of action, procedure, project, scheme ~*v.* 4. arrange, bill, book, design, engage, formulate, itemize, lay on, line up, list, map out, plan, prearrange, schedule, work out

progress *n.* 1. advance, course, movement, onward course, passage, progression, way 2. advance, advancement, amelioration, betterment, breakthrough, development, gain, gaining ground, growth, headway, improvement, increase, progression, promotion, step forward 3. **in progress** being done, going on, happening, occurring, proceeding, taking place, under way ~*v.* 4. advance, come on, continue, cover ground, forge ahead, gain ground, gather way, get on, go forward, make headway, make one's way, make strides, move on, proceed, travel 5. advance, ameliorate, better, blossom, develop, gain, grow, improve, increase, mature

Antonyms *n.* decline, failure, recession, regression, relapse, retrogression ~*v.* decrease, get behind, lose, lose ground, recede, regress, retrogress

progression 1. advance, advancement, furtherance, gain, headway, movement forward, progress 2. chain, course, cycle, order, sequence, series, string, succession

progressive 1. accelerating, advancing, continuing, continuous, developing, escalating, growing, increasing, intensifying, ongoing 2. advanced, avant-garde, dynamic, enlightened, enterprising, forward-looking, go-ahead, liberal, modern, radical, reformist, revolutionary, up-and-coming

prohibit 1. ban, debar, disallow, forbid, interdict, outlaw, proscribe, veto 2. constrain, hamper, hinder, impede, make impossible, obstruct, preclude, prevent, restrict, rule out, stop

Antonyms allow, authorize, command, consent to, endure, further, give leave, let, license, order, permit, suffer, tolerate

prohibited banned, barred, forbidden, not allowed, proscribed, taboo, *verboten*, vetoed

prohibition 1. constraint, exclusion, forbiddance, interdiction, negation, obstruction, prevention, restriction 2. ban, bar, boycott, disallowance, embargo, injunction, interdict, proscription, veto

prohibitive 1. forbidding, prohibiting, proscriptive, repressive, restraining, restrictive, suppressive 2. *Esp. of prices* beyond one's means, excessive, exorbitant, extortionate, high-priced, preposterous, sky-high, steep (*Inf.*)

project *n.* 1. activity, assignment, design, enterprise, job, occupation, plan, programme, proposal, scheme, task, undertaking, venture, work ~*v.* 2. contemplate, contrive, design, devise, draft, frame, map out, outline, plan, propose, purpose, scheme 3. cast, discharge, fling, hurl, launch, make carry, propel, shoot, throw, transmit 4. beetle, bulge, extend, jut, overhang, protrude, stand out, stick out 5. calculate, estimate, extrapolate, forecast, gauge, predetermine, predict, reckon

projectile bullet, missile, rocket, shell

projection 1. bulge, eaves, jut, ledge, overhang, protrusion, protuberance, ridge, shelf, sill 2. blueprint, diagram, map, outline, plan, representation 3. calculation, computation, estimate, estimation, extrapolation, forecast, prediction, reckoning

proletarian 1. *adj.* cloth-cap (*Inf.*), common, plebeian, working-class 2. *n.* commoner, Joe Bloggs (*Brit. inf.*), man of the people, pleb, plebeian, prole (*Derogatory sl., chiefly Brit.*), worker

proletariat commonalty, commoners, hoi polloi, labouring classes, lower classes, lower orders, plebs, proles (*Derogatory sl., chiefly Brit.*), the common people, the great unwashed (*Inf. & derogatory*), the herd, the masses, the rabble, wage-earners, working class

Antonyms aristo (*Inf.*), aristocracy, gentry, nobility, peerage, ruling class, upper class, upper crust (*Inf.*)

proliferate breed, burgeon, escalate, expand, grow rapidly, increase, multiply, mushroom, run riot, snowball

proliferation build-up, concentration, escalation, expansion, extension, increase, intensification, multiplication, spread, step-up (*Inf.*)

prolific abundant, bountiful, copious, fecund, fertile, fruitful, generative, luxuriant, productive, profuse, rank, rich, teeming
Antonyms barren, fruitless, infertile, sterile, unfruitful, unproductive, unprolific

prolix boring, diffuse, digressive, discursive, dragged out, full of verbiage, lengthy, long, long-drawn-out, long-winded, prolonged, protracted, rambling, spun out, tedious, tiresome, verbose, wordy

prolixity boringness, circuity, diffuseness, discursiveness, long-windedness, maundering, pleonasm, rambling, redundancy, tautology, tediousness, verbiage, verboseness, verbosity, wandering, wordiness

prologue exordium, foreword, introduction, preamble, preface, preliminary, prelude, proem

prolong carry on, continue, delay, drag out, draw out, extend, lengthen, make longer, perpetuate, protract, spin out, stretch
Antonyms abbreviate, abridge, curtail, cut, cut down, shorten, summarize

promenade *n.* **1.** boulevard, esplanade, parade, prom, public walk, walkway **2.** airing, constitutional, saunter, stroll, turn, walk ~*v.* **3.** perambulate, saunter, stretch one's legs, stroll, take a walk, walk **4.** flaunt, parade, strut, swagger

prominence **1.** cliff, crag, crest, elevation, headland, height, high point, hummock, mound, pinnacle, projection, promontory, rise, rising ground, spur **2.** bulge, jutting, projection, protrusion, protuberance, swelling **3.** conspicuousness, markedness, outstandingness, precedence, salience, specialness, top billing, weight **4.** celebrity, distinction, eminence, fame, greatness, importance, name, notability, pre-eminence, prestige, rank, reputation, standing

prominent **1.** bulging, hanging over, jutting, projecting, protruding, protrusive, protuberant, standing out **2.** blatant, conspicuous, easily seen, eye-catching, in the foreground, noticeable, obtrusive, obvious, outstanding, pronounced, remarkable, salient, striking, to the fore, unmistakable **3.** big-time (*Inf.*), celebrated, chief, distinguished, eminent, famous, foremost, important, leading, main, major league (*Inf.*), notable, noted, outstanding, popular, pre-eminent, renowned, respected, top, well-known, well-thought-of
Antonyms (*sense 1*) concave, indented, receding (*sense 2*) inconspicuous, indistinct, insignificant, unnoticeable (*sense 3*) insignificant, minor, secondary, undistinguished, unimportant, unknown, unnotable

promiscuity abandon, amorality, debauchery, depravity, dissipation, immorality, incontinence, laxity, laxness, lechery, libertinism, licentiousness, looseness, permissiveness, profligacy, promiscuousness, sleeping around (*Inf.*), wantonness

promiscuous **1.** abandoned, debauched, dissipated, dissolute, fast, immoral, lax, libertine, licentious, loose, of easy virtue, profligate, unbridled, unchaste, wanton, wild **2.** chaotic, confused, disordered, diverse, heterogeneous, ill-assorted, indiscriminate, intermingled, intermixed, jumbled, mingled, miscellaneous, mixed, motley **3.** careless, casual, haphazard, heedless, indifferent, indiscriminate, irregular, irresponsible, random, slovenly, uncontrolled, uncritical, undiscriminating, unfastidious, unselective
Antonyms (*sense 1*) chaste, decent, innocent, modest, moral, pure, undefiled, unsullied, vestal, virginal, virtuous (*sense 2*) homogeneous, identical, neat, ordered, orderly, organized, shipshape, uniform, unmixed (*sense 3*) careful, critical, discriminating, fastidious, responsible, selective

promise *v.* **1.** assure, contract, cross one's heart, engage, give an undertaking, give one's word, guarantee, pledge, plight, stipulate, swear, take an oath, undertake, vouch, vow, warrant **2.** augur, bespeak, betoken, bid fair, denote, give hope of, hint at, hold a probability, hold out hopes of, indicate, lead one to expect, look like, seem likely to, show signs of, suggest ~*n.* **3.** assurance, bond, commitment, compact, covenant, engagement, guarantee, oath, pledge, undertaking, vow, word, word of honour **4.** ability, aptitude, capability, capacity, flair, potential, talent

promising **1.** auspicious, bright, encouraging, favourable, full of promise, hopeful, likely, propitious, reassuring, rosy **2.** able, gifted, likely, rising, talented, up-and-coming
Antonyms (*sense 1*) discouraging, unauspicious, unfavourable, unpromising

promontory cape, foreland, head, headland, ness (*Archaic*), point, spur

promote **1.** advance, aid, assist, back, boost, contribute to, develop, encourage, forward, foster, further, help, nurture, stimulate, support 2. aggrandize, dignify, elevate, exalt, honour, kick upstairs (*Inf.*), prefer, raise, upgrade 3. advocate, call attention to, champion, endorse, espouse, popularize, prescribe, push for, recommend, speak for, sponsor, support, urge, work for 4. advertise, beat the drum for (*Inf.*), hype, plug (*Inf.*), publicize, puff, push, sell

Antonyms (*sense 1*) discourage, hinder, hold back, impede, obstruct, oppose, prevent (*sense 2*) demote, downgrade, lower *or* reduce in rank

promotion 1. advancement, aggrandizement, elevation, ennoblement, exaltation, honour, move up, preferment, rise, upgrading 2. advancement, advocacy, backing, boosting, cultivation, development, encouragement, espousal, furtherance, progress, support 3. advertising, advertising campaign, ballyhoo (*Inf.*), hard sell, hype, media hype, plugging (*Inf.*), propaganda, publicity, puffery (*Inf.*), pushing

prompt *adj.* 1. early, immediate, instant, instantaneous, on time, pdq (*Sl.*), punctual, quick, rapid, speedy, swift, timely, unhesitating 2. alert, brisk, eager, efficient, expeditious, quick, ready, responsive, smart, willing *~adv.* 3. *Inf.* exactly, on the dot, promptly, punctually, sharp *~v.* 4. cause, impel, incite, induce, inspire, instigate, motivate, move, provoke, spur, stimulate, urge 5. assist, cue, help out, jog the memory, prod, refresh the memory, remind 6. call forth, cause, elicit, evoke, give rise to, occasion, provoke *~n.* 7. cue, help, hint, jog, jolt, prod, reminder, spur, stimulus

Antonyms *adj.* hesitating, inactive, inattentive, inefficient, late, remiss, slack, slow, tardy, unresponsive *~v.* deter, discourage, prevent, restrain, talk out of

prompter 1. autocue, idiot board (*Sl.*), Teleprompter (*Trademark*) 2. agitator, catalyst, gadfly, inspirer, instigator, moving spirit, prime mover

prompting assistance, encouragement, hint, incitement, influence, jogging, persuasion, pressing, pressure, prodding, pushing, reminder, reminding, suggestion, urging

promptly at once, by return, directly, hotfoot, immediately, instantly, on the dot, on time, pdq (*Sl.*), posthaste, pronto (*Inf.*), punctually, quickly, speedily, swiftly, unhesitatingly

promptness alacrity, alertness, briskness, dispatch, eagerness, haste, promptitude, punctuality, quickness, readiness, speed, swiftness, willingness

promulgate advertise, announce, broadcast, circulate, communicate, declare, decree, disseminate, issue, make known, make public, notify, proclaim, promote, publish, spread

prone 1. face down, flat, horizontal, lying down, procumbent, prostrate, recumbent, supine 2. apt, bent, disposed, given, inclined, liable, likely, predisposed, subject, susceptible, tending

Antonyms (*sense 1*) erect, face up, perpendicular, supine, upright, vertical (*sense 2*) averse, disinclined, indisposed, not likely, unlikely

proneness bent, bias, disposition, inclination, leaning, liability, partiality, proclivity, propensity, susceptibility, tendency, weakness

prong point, projection, spike, tine, tip

pronounce 1. accent, articulate, enunciate, say, sound, speak, stress, utter, vocalize, voice 2. affirm, announce, assert, declare, decree, deliver, judge, proclaim

pronounced broad, clear, conspicuous, decided, definite, distinct, evident, marked, noticeable, obvious, striking, strong, unmistakable

Antonyms concealed, hidden, imperceptible, inconspicuous, unapparent, unnoticeable, vague

pronouncement announcement, declaration, decree, dictum, edict, judgment, manifesto, notification, proclamation, promulgation, pronunciamento, statement

pronunciation accent, accentuation, articulation, diction, elocution, enunciation, inflection, intonation, speech, stress

proof *n.* 1. attestation, authentication, certification, confirmation, corroboration, demonstration, evidence, substantiation, testimony, verification 2. *As in* **put to the proof** assay, examination, experiment, ordeal, scrutiny, test, trial 3. *Printing* galley, galley proof, page proof, pull, slip, trial impression, trial print *~adj.* 4. impenetrable, impervious, repellent, resistant, strong, tight, treated 5. **be proof against** hold out against, resist, stand firm against, stand up to, withstand

prop *v.* 1. bolster, brace, buttress, hold up, maintain, shore, stay, support, sustain, truss, uphold 2. lean, rest, set, stand *~n.* 3. brace, buttress, mainstay, stanchion, stay, support, truss

propaganda advertising, agitprop, ballyhoo (*Inf.*), brainwashing, disinformation, hype, information, newspeak, promotion, publicity

propagandist advocate, evangelist, indoctrinator, pamphleteer, promoter, proponent, proselytizer, publicist

propagandize brainwash, convince, indoctrinate, instil, persuade, proselytize

propagate 1. beget, breed, engender, generate, increase, multiply, procreate, produce, proliferate, reproduce 2. broadcast, circulate, diffuse, disseminate, make known, proclaim, promote, promulgate, publicize, publish, spread, transmit
Antonyms (*sense 2*) cover up, hide, hush up, keep under wraps, stifle, suppress, withhold

propagation 1. breeding, generation, increase, multiplication, procreation, proliferation, reproduction 2. circulation, communication, diffusion, dissemination, distribution, promotion, promulgation, spread, spreading, transmission

propel drive, force, impel, launch, push, send, set in motion, shoot, shove, start, thrust
Antonyms check, delay, hold back, pull, slow, stop

propensity aptness, bent, bias, disposition, inclination, leaning, liability, penchant, predisposition, proclivity, proneness, susceptibility, tendency, weakness

proper 1. appropriate, apt, becoming, befitting, fit, fitting, legitimate, meet (*Archaic*), right, suitable, suited 2. *comme il faut*, decent, decorous, *de rigueur*, genteel, gentlemanly, ladylike, mannerly, polite, punctilious, refined, respectable, seemly 3. accepted, accurate, conventional, correct, established, exact, formal, kosher (*Inf.*), orthodox, precise, right 4. characteristic, individual, own, particular, peculiar, personal, respective, special, specific
Antonyms (*senses 1, 2, & 3*) coarse, common, crude, discourteous, impolite, improper, inappropriate, indecent, rude, unbecoming, unconventional, ungentlemanly, unladylike, unorthodox, unrefined, unseemly, unsuitable, wrong

property 1. assets, belongings, building(s), capital, chattels, effects, estate, goods, holdings, house(s), means, possessions, resources, riches, wealth 2. acres, estate, freehold, holding, land, real estate, real property, realty, title 3. ability, attribute, characteristic, feature, hallmark, idiosyncrasy, mark, peculiarity, quality, trait, virtue

prophecy augury, divination, forecast, foretelling, prediction, prognosis, prognostication, revelation, second sight, soothsaying, sortilege, vaticination (*Rare*)

prophesy augur, divine, forecast, foresee, foretell, forewarn, predict, presage, prognosticate, soothsay, vaticinate (*Rare*)

prophet augur, Cassandra, clairvoyant, diviner, forecaster, oracle, prognosticator, prophesier, seer, sibyl, soothsayer

prophetic augural, divinatory, fatidic (*Rare*), foreshadowing, mantic, oracular, predictive, presaging, prescient, prognostic, sibylline, vatic (*Rare*)

propinquity 1. adjacency, closeness, contiguity, nearness, neighbourhood, proximity, vicinity 2. affiliation, affinity, blood, connection, consanguinity, kindred, kinship, relation, relationship, tie, ties of blood

propitiate appease, conciliate, make peace, mollify, pacify, placate, reconcile, satisfy

propitiation appeasement, conciliation, mollification, peacemaking, placation, reconciliation

propitiatory appeasing, assuaging, conciliatory, pacificatory, pacifying, peacemaking, placative, placatory, propitiative, reconciliatory

propitious 1. advantageous, auspicious, bright, encouraging, favourable, fortunate, full of promise, happy, lucky, opportune, promising, prosperous, rosy, timely 2. benevolent, benign, favourably inclined, friendly, gracious, kind, well-disposed

proponent advocate, apologist, backer, champion, defender, enthusiast, exponent, friend, partisan, patron, spokesman, spokeswoman, subscriber, supporter, upholder, vindicator

proportion 1. distribution, ratio, relationship, relative amount 2. agreement, balance, congruity, correspondence, harmony, symmetry 3. amount, cut (*Inf.*), division, fraction, measure, part, percentage, quota, segment, share 4. *Plural* amplitude, breadth, bulk, capacity, dimensions, expanse, extent, magnitude, measurements, range, scope, size, volume

proportional, proportionate balanced, commensurate, comparable, compatible, consistent, correspondent, corresponding, equitable, equivalent, even, in proportion, just
Antonyms different, discordant, disproportionate, dissimilar, incommensurable, incompatible, inconsistent, unequal

proposal bid, design, motion, offer, overture, plan, presentation, proffer, programme, project, proposition, recommendation, scheme, suggestion, tender, terms

propose 1. advance, come up with, present, proffer, propound, put forward, submit, suggest, tender 2. introduce, invite, name, nominate, present, put up, recommend 3. aim, design, have every intention, have in mind, intend, mean, plan, purpose, scheme 4. ask for someone's hand (in marriage), offer marriage, pay suit, pop the question (*Inf.*)

proposition 1. *n.* motion, plan, programme, project, proposal, recommendation, scheme, suggestion 2. *v.* accost, make an improper suggestion, make an indecent proposal, solicit

propound advance, advocate, contend, lay down, postulate, present, propose, put forward, set forth, submit, suggest

proprietor, proprietress deed holder, freeholder, landlady, landlord, landowner, owner, possessor, titleholder

propriety 1. appropriateness, aptness, becomingness, correctness, fitness, rightness, seemliness, suitableness 2. breeding, courtesy, decency, decorum, delicacy, etiquette, good form, good manners, manners, modesty, politeness, protocol, punctilio, rectitude, refinement, respectability, seemliness 3. **the proprieties** accepted conduct, amenities, civilities, etiquette, niceties, rules of conduct, social code, social conventions, social graces, the done thing

Antonyms (*sense 2*) bad form, bad manners, immodesty, impoliteness, indecency, indecorum, indelicacy, vulgarity

propulsion drive, impetus, impulse, impulsion, momentum, motive power, power, pressure, propelling force, push, thrust

prosaic banal, boring, commonplace, dry, dull, everyday, flat, hackneyed, humdrum, matter-of-fact, mundane, ordinary, pedestrian, routine, stale, tame, trite, unimaginative, uninspiring, vapid, workaday

Antonyms entertaining, exciting, extraordinary, fascinating, imaginative, interesting, poetical, unusual

proscribe 1. ban, boycott, censure, condemn, damn, denounce, doom, embargo, forbid, interdict, prohibit, reject 2. attaint (*Archaic*), banish, blackball, deport, exclude, excommunicate, exile, expatriate, expel, ostracize, outlaw

Antonyms (*sense 1*) allow, authorize, endorse, give leave, give permission, license, permit, sanction, warrant

proscription 1. ban, boycott, censure, condemnation, damning, denunciation, dooming, embargo, interdict, prohibition, rejection 2. attainder (*Archaic*), banishment, deportation, ejection, eviction, exclusion, excommunication, exile, expatriation, expulsion, ostracism, outlawry

prosecute 1. *Law* arraign, bring action against, bring suit against, bring to trial, do (*Sl.*), indict, litigate, prefer charges, put in the dock, put on trial, seek redress, sue, summon, take to court, try 2. carry on, conduct, direct, discharge, engage in, manage, perform, practise, work at 3. carry through, continue, follow through, persevere, persist, pursue, see through

proselyte catechumen, convert, initiate, neophyte, new believer, novice, tyro

proselytize bring into the fold, bring to God, convert, evangelize, make converts, persuade, propagandize, spread the gospel, win over

prospect *n.* 1. anticipation, calculation, contemplation, expectation, future, hope, odds, opening, outlook, plan, presumption, probability, promise, proposal, thought 2. landscape, outlook, panorama, perspective, scene, sight, spectacle, view, vision, vista 3. **in prospect** in sight, in store, in the offing, in the wind, in view, on the cards, on the horizon, planned, projected 4. *Sometimes plural* chance, likelihood, possibility ~*v.* 5. explore, go after, look for, search, seek, survey

prospective about to be, anticipated, approaching, awaited, coming, destined, eventual, expected, forthcoming, future, hoped-for, imminent, intended, likely, looked-for, possible, potential, soon-to-be, -to-be, to come, upcoming

prospectus announcement, catalogue, conspectus, list, outline, plan, programme, scheme, syllabus, synopsis

prosper advance, be fortunate, bloom, do well, fare well, flourish, flower, get on, grow rich, make good, make it (*Inf.*), progress, succeed, thrive

prosperity affluence, boom, ease, fortune, good fortune, good times, life of luxury, life of Riley (*Inf.*), luxury, plenty, prosperousness, riches, success, the good life, wealth, well-being

Antonyms adversity, depression, destitution, failure, indigence, misfortune, poverty, shortage, want

prosperous 1. blooming, booming, doing well, flourishing, fortunate, lucky, on the up and up (*Brit.*), palmy, prospering, successful, thriving 2. affluent, in clover (*Inf.*), in the money (*Inf.*), moneyed, opulent, rich, wealthy, well-heeled (*Inf.*), well-off, well-to-do 3. advantageous, auspicious, bright, favourable, good, profitable, promising, propitious, timely

Antonyms defeated, failing, impoverished, inauspicious, poor, unfavourable, unfortunate, unlucky, unpromising, unsuccessful, untimely

prostitute 1. *n.* bawd (*Archaic*), brass (*Sl.*), call girl, camp follower, cocotte, courtesan, fallen woman, *fille de joie,* harlot, hooker

(*U.S. sl.*), hustler (*U.S. & Canad. sl.*), loose woman, moll (*Sl.*), pro (*Sl.*), scrubber (*Brit. & Aust. sl.*), streetwalker, strumpet, tart (*Inf.*), trollop, white slave, whore, working girl (*Facetious sl.*) 2. *v.* cheapen, debase, degrade, demean, devalue, misapply, pervert, profane

prostitution harlotry, harlot's trade, Mrs. Warren's profession, streetwalking, the game (*Sl.*), the oldest profession, vice, whoredom

prostrate *adj.* 1. abject, bowed low, flat, horizontal, kowtowing, procumbent, prone 2. at a low ebb, dejected, depressed, desolate, drained, exhausted, fagged out (*Inf.*), fallen, inconsolable, overcome, spent, worn out 3. brought to one's knees, defenceless, disarmed, helpless, impotent, overwhelmed, paralysed, powerless, reduced ~*v.* 4. *Of oneself* abase, bend the knee to, bow before, bow down to, cast oneself before, cringe, fall at (someone's) feet, fall on one's knees before, grovel, kneel, kowtow, submit 5. bring low, crush, depress, disarm, lay low, overcome, overthrow, overturn, overwhelm, paralyse, reduce, ruin 6. drain, exhaust, fag out (*Inf.*), fatigue, sap, tire, wear out, weary

prostration 1. abasement, bow, genuflection, kneeling, kowtow, obeisance, submission 2. collapse, dejection, depression, depth of misery, desolation, despair, despondency, exhaustion, grief, helplessness, paralysis, weakness, weariness

prosy boring, commonplace, dull, flat, humdrum, long, long-drawn-out, long-winded, monotonous, overlong, pedestrian, prosaic, prosing, stale, tedious, tiresome, unimaginative, uninteresting, wordy

protagonist 1. central character, hero, heroine, lead, leading character, principal 2. advocate, champion, exponent, leader, mainstay, moving spirit, prime mover, standard-bearer, supporter

protean changeable, ever-changing, many-sided, mercurial, multiform, mutable, polymorphous, temperamental, variable, versatile, volatile

protect care for, chaperon, cover, cover up for, defend, foster, give sanctuary, guard, harbour, keep, keep safe, look after, mount *or* stand guard over, preserve, safeguard, save, screen, secure, shelter, shield, stick up for (*Inf.*), support, take under one's wing, watch over

Antonyms assail, assault, attack, betray, endanger, expose, expose to danger, threaten

protection 1. aegis, care, charge, custody, defence, guardianship, guarding, preservation, protecting, safeguard, safekeeping, safety, security 2. armour, barrier, buffer, bulwark, cover, guard, refuge, safeguard, screen, shelter, shield

protective careful, covering, defensive, fatherly, insulating, jealous, maternal, motherly, paternal, possessive, protecting, safeguarding, sheltering, shielding, vigilant, warm, watchful

protector advocate, benefactor, bodyguard, champion, counsel, defender, guard, guardian, guardian angel, knight in shining armour, patron, safeguard, tower of strength

protégé, protégée charge, dependant, discovery, pupil, student, ward

protest *n.* 1. complaint, declaration, demur, demurral, disapproval, dissent, formal complaint, objection, outcry, protestation, remonstrance ~*v.* 2. complain, cry out, demonstrate, demur, disagree, disapprove, expostulate, express disapproval, kick (against) (*Inf.*), object, oppose, remonstrate, say no to, take exception 3. affirm, argue, assert, asseverate, attest, avow, contend, declare, insist, maintain, profess, testify, vow

protestation 1. complaint, disagreement, dissent, expostulation, objection, outcry, protest, remonstrance, remonstration 2. affirmation, asseveration, avowal, declaration, oath, pledge, profession, vow

protester agitator, demonstrator, dissenter, dissident, protest marcher, rebel

protocol 1. code of behaviour, conventions, courtesies, customs, decorum, etiquette, formalities, good form, manners, politesse, propriety, rules of conduct 2. agreement, compact, concordat, contract, convention, covenant, pact, treaty

prototype archetype, example, first, mock-up, model, norm, original, paradigm, pattern, precedent, standard, type

protract continue, drag on *or* out, draw out, extend, keep going, lengthen, prolong, spin out, stretch out

Antonyms abbreviate, abridge, compress, curtail, reduce, shorten, summarize

protracted dragged out, drawn-out, extended, interminable, lengthy, long, long-drawn-out, never-ending, overlong, prolonged, spun out, time-consuming

protrude bulge, come through, extend, jut, obtrude, point, pop (*of eyes*), project, shoot out, stand out, start (from), stick out

protrusion bulge, bump, hump, jut, lump, outgrowth, projection, protuberance, swelling

protuberance bulge, bump, excrescence,

hump, knob, lump, outgrowth, process, projection, prominence, protrusion, swelling, tumour

protuberant beetling, bulbous, bulging, gibbous, hanging over, jutting, popping (*of eyes*), prominent, protruding, protrusive, proud (*Dialect*), swelling, swollen
Antonyms concave, flat, indented, receding, sunken

proud 1. appreciative, content, contented, glad, gratified, honoured, pleased, satisfied, self-respecting, well-pleased 2. arrogant, boastful, conceited, disdainful, egotistical, haughty, high and mighty (*Inf.*), imperious, lordly, narcissistic, orgulous (*Archaic*), overbearing, presumptuous, self-important, self-satisfied, snobbish, snooty (*Inf.*), stuck-up (*Inf.*), supercilious, toffee-nosed (*Sl., chiefly Brit.*), vain 3. exalted, glorious, gratifying, illustrious, memorable, pleasing, red-letter, rewarding, satisfying 4. august, distinguished, eminent, grand, great, illustrious, imposing, magnificent, majestic, noble, splendid, stately
Antonyms abject, ashamed, base, deferential, discontented, displeased, dissatisfied, humble, ignoble, ignominious, lowly, meek, modest, submissive, unassuming, undignified, unobtrusive

provable attestable, demonstrable, evincible, testable, verifiable

prove 1. ascertain, attest, authenticate, bear out, confirm, corroborate, demonstrate, determine, establish, evidence, evince, justify, show, show clearly, substantiate, verify 2. analyse, assay, check, examine, experiment, put to the test, put to trial, test, try 3. be found to be, come out, end up, result, turn out
Antonyms (*sense 1*) discredit, disprove, give the lie to, refute, rule out

proven *adj.* accepted, attested, authentic, certified, checked, confirmed, definite, dependable, established, proved, reliable, tested, tried, trustworthy, undoubted, valid, verified

provenance birthplace, derivation, origin, source

provender 1. feed, fodder, forage 2. comestibles, eatables, eats (*Sl.*), edibles, fare, feed, food, foodstuffs, groceries, grub (*Sl.*), nosebag (*Sl.*), nosh (*Sl.*), provisions, rations, supplies, sustenance, tack (*Inf.*), victuals, vittles (*Obs. or dialect*)

proverb adage, aphorism, apophthegm, byword, dictum, gnome, maxim, saw, saying

proverbial accepted, acknowledged, archetypal, axiomatic, conventional, current, customary, famed, famous, legendary, notorious, self-evident, time-honoured, traditional, typical, unquestioned, well-known

provide 1. accommodate, cater, contribute, equip, furnish, outfit, provision, purvey, stock up, supply 2. add, afford, bring, give, impart, lend, present, produce, render, serve, yield 3. *With* **for** *or* **against** anticipate, arrange for, forearm, get ready, make arrangements, make plans, plan ahead, plan for, prepare for, take measures, take precautions 4. *With* **for** care for, keep, look after, maintain, support, sustain, take care of 5. determine, lay down, require, specify, state, stipulate
Antonyms (*sense 1*) deprive, keep back, refuse, withhold (*sense 3*) disregard, fail to notice, miss, neglect, overlook (*sense 4*) neglect

providence 1. destiny, divine intervention, fate, fortune, God's will, predestination 2. care, caution, discretion, far-sightedness, foresight, forethought, perspicacity, presence of mind, prudence

provident canny, careful, cautious, discreet, economical, equipped, far-seeing, far-sighted, forearmed, foresighted, frugal, prudent, sagacious, shrewd, thrifty, vigilant, well-prepared, wise
Antonyms careless, heedless, improvident, imprudent, negligent, prodigal, profligate, reckless, short-sighted, spendthrift, thoughtless, thriftless, uneconomical, unthrifty, wasteful

providential fortuitous, fortunate, happy, heaven-sent, lucky, opportune, timely, welcome

provider 1. benefactor, donor, giver, source, supplier 2. breadwinner, earner, mainstay, supporter, wage earner

providing, provided *conj.* as long as, contingent upon, given, if and only if, in case, in the event, on condition, on the assumption, subject to, upon these terms, with the proviso, with the understanding

province 1. colony, county, department, dependency, district, division, domain, patch, region, section, territory, tract, turf (*U.S. sl.*), zone 2. *Fig.* area, business, capacity, charge, concern, duty, employment, field, function, line, orbit, part, pigeon (*Brit. inf.*), post, responsibility, role, sphere, turf (*U.S. sl.*)

provincial *adj.* 1. country, hick (*Inf., chiefly U.S. & Canad.*), home-grown, homespun, local, rural, rustic 2. insular, inward-looking, limited, narrow, narrow-minded, parish-pump, parochial, small-minded, small-town (*U.S.*), uninformed, unsophisticated, upcountry ~*n.* 3. country cousin,

hayseed (*U.S. & Canad. inf.*), hick (*Inf., chiefly U.S. & Canad.*), rustic, yokel
Antonyms cosmopolitan, fashionable, polished, refined, sophisticated, urban, urbane

provincialism 1. insularity, lack of sophistication, narrow-mindedness, parochialism, sectionalism 2. dialect, idiom, localism, patois, regionalism, vernacularism

provision 1. accoutrement, catering, equipping, fitting out, furnishing, providing, supplying, victualling 2. arrangement, plan, prearrangement, precaution, preparation 3. *Fig.* agreement, clause, condition, demand, proviso, requirement, rider, specification, stipulation, term

provisional conditional, contingent, interim, limited, pro tem, provisory, qualified, stopgap, temporary, tentative, transitional
Antonyms definite, fixed, permanent

provisions comestibles, eatables, eats (*Sl.*), edibles, fare, feed, food, foodstuff, groceries, grub (*Sl.*), nosebag (*Sl.*), provender, rations, stores, supplies, sustenance, tack (*Inf.*), viands, victuals, vittles (*Obs. or dialect*)

proviso clause, condition, limitation, provision, qualification, requirement, reservation, restriction, rider, stipulation, strings

provocation 1. *casus belli,* cause, grounds, incitement, inducement, instigation, justification, motivation, reason, stimulus 2. affront, annoyance, challenge, dare, grievance, indignity, injury, insult, offence, red rag, taunt, vexation

provocative 1. aggravating (*Inf.*), annoying, challenging, disturbing, galling, goading, incensing, insulting, offensive, outrageous, provoking, stimulating 2. alluring, arousing, erotic, exciting, inviting, seductive, sexy (*Inf.*), stimulating, suggestive, tantalizing, tempting

provoke 1. affront, aggravate (*Inf.*), anger, annoy, chafe, enrage, exasperate, gall, get in one's hair (*Inf.*), get on one's nerves (*Inf.*), hassle (*Inf.*), incense, infuriate, insult, irk, irritate, madden, make one's blood boil, nark (*Brit., Aust., & N.Z. sl.*), offend, pique, piss one off (*Taboo sl.*), put out, rile, try one's patience, vex 2. bring about, bring on *or* down, call forth, cause, draw forth, elicit, evoke, excite, fire, generate, give rise to, incite, induce, inflame, inspire, instigate, kindle, lead to, motivate, move, occasion, precipitate, produce, promote, prompt, rouse, stimulate, stir
Antonyms (*sense 1*) appease, calm, conciliate, mollify, pacify, placate, propitiate, quiet, soothe, sweeten (*sense 2*) abate, allay, assuage, blunt, curb, ease, lessen, lull, mitigate, moderate, modify, relieve, temper

provoking aggravating (*Inf.*), annoying, exasperating, galling, irking, irksome, irritating, maddening, obstructive, offensive, tiresome, vexatious, vexing

prow bow(s), fore, forepart, front, head, nose, sharp end (*Jocular*), stem

prowess 1. ability, accomplishment, adeptness, adroitness, aptitude, attainment, command, dexterity, excellence, expertise, expertness, facility, genius, mastery, skill, talent 2. boldness, bravery, courage, daring, dauntlessness, doughtiness, fearlessness, gallantry, hardihood, heroism, intrepidity, mettle, valiance, valour
Antonyms (*sense 1*) clumsiness, inability, incapability, incompetence, ineptitude, ineptness, inexpertise (*sense 2*) cowardice, faint-heartedness, fear, gutlessness, timidity

prowl cruise, hunt, lurk, move stealthily, nose around, patrol, range, roam, rove, scavenge, skulk, slink, sneak, stalk, steal

proximity adjacency, closeness, contiguity, juxtaposition, nearness, neighbourhood, propinquity, vicinity

proxy agent, attorney, delegate, deputy, factor, representative, substitute, surrogate

prude Grundy, old maid (*Inf.*), prig, puritan, schoolmarm (*Brit. inf.*)

prudence 1. canniness, care, caution, circumspection, common sense, discretion, good sense, heedfulness, judgment, judiciousness, sagacity, vigilance, wariness, wisdom 2. careful budgeting, economizing, economy, far-sightedness, foresight, forethought, frugality, good management, husbandry, planning, precaution, preparedness, providence, saving, thrift

prudent 1. canny, careful, cautious, circumspect, discerning, discreet, judicious, politic, sagacious, sage, sensible, shrewd, vigilant, wary, wise 2. canny, careful, economical, far-sighted, frugal, provident, sparing, thrifty
Antonyms careless, extravagant, heedless, improvident, imprudent, inconsiderate, indiscreet, irrational, rash, thoughtless, unwise, wasteful

prudery Grundyism, old-maidishness (*Inf.*), overmodesty, priggishness, primness, prudishness, puritanicalness, squeamishness, starchiness (*Inf.*), strictness, stuffiness

prudish demure, narrow-minded, old-maidish (*Inf.*), overmodest, overnice, priggish, prim, prissy (*Inf.*), proper, puritanical, schoolmarmish (*Brit. inf.*), squeamish, starchy (*Inf.*), strait-laced, stuffy, Victorian
Antonyms broad-minded, liberal, open-minded, permissive

prune clip, cut, cut back, dock, lop, pare down, reduce, shape, shorten, snip, trim

prurient 1. concupiscent, desirous, hankering, itching, lascivious, lecherous, libidinous, longing, lustful, salacious 2. dirty, erotic, indecent, lewd, obscene, pornographic, salacious, smutty, steamy (*Inf.*), voyeuristic

pry be a busybody, be inquisitive, be nosy (*Inf.*), ferret about, interfere, intrude, meddle, nose into, peep, peer, poke, poke one's nose in *or* into (*Inf.*), snoop (*Inf.*)

prying curious, eavesdropping, impertinent, inquisitive, interfering, intrusive, meddlesome, meddling, nosy (*Inf.*), snooping (*Inf.*), snoopy (*Inf.*), spying

psalm chant, hymn, paean, song of praise

pseud *n.* fraud, humbug, phoney *or* phony (*Inf.*), poser (*Inf.*), trendy (*Brit. inf.*)

pseudo *adj.* artificial, bogus, counterfeit, ersatz, fake, false, imitation, mock, not genuine, phoney *or* phony (*Inf.*), pretended, quasi-, sham, spurious
Antonyms actual, authentic, bona fide, genuine, heartfelt, honest, real, sincere, true, unfeigned

pseudonym alias, assumed name, false name, incognito, nom de guerre, nom de plume, pen name, professional name, stage name

psyche anima, essential nature, individuality, inner man, innermost self, mind, personality, pneuma (*Philos.*), self, soul, spirit, subconscious, true being

psychedelic 1. consciousness-expanding, hallucinatory, hallucinogenic, mind-bending (*Inf.*), mind-blowing (*Inf.*), mind-expanding, psychoactive, psychotomimetic, psychotropic 2. *Inf.* crazy, freaky (*Sl.*), kaleidoscopic, multicoloured, wild

psychiatrist analyst, headshrinker (*Sl.*), psychoanalyser, psychoanalyst, psychologist, psychotherapist, shrink (*Sl.*), therapist

psychic 1. clairvoyant, extrasensory, mystic, occult, preternatural, supernatural, telekinetic, telepathic 2. mental, psychogenic, psychological, spiritual

psychological 1. cerebral, cognitive, intellectual, mental 2. all in the mind, emotional, imaginary, irrational, psychosomatic, subconscious, subjective, unconscious, unreal

psychology 1. behaviourism, science of mind, study of personality 2. *Inf.* attitude, mental make-up, mental processes, thought processes, way of thinking, what makes one tick

psychopath headbanger (*Inf.*), headcase (*Inf.*), insane person, lunatic, madman, maniac, mental case (*Sl.*), nutcase (*Sl.*), nutter (*Brit. sl.*), psychotic, sociopath

psychotic *adj.* certifiable, demented, deranged, insane, lunatic, mad, mental (*Sl.*), *non compos mentis,* off one's chump (head (*Sl.*), rocker (*Sl.*), trolley (*Sl.*)) (*Sl.*), psychopathic, unbalanced

pub *or* **public house** alehouse (*Archaic*), bar, boozer (*Brit., Aust., & N.Z. inf.*), inn, local (*Brit. inf.*), roadhouse, taproom, tavern, watering hole (*Facetious sl.*)

puberty adolescence, awkward age, juvenescence, pubescence, teenage, teens, young adulthood

public *adj.* 1. civic, civil, common, general, national, popular, social, state, universal, widespread 2. accessible, communal, community, free to all, not private, open, open to the public, unrestricted 3. acknowledged, exposed, in circulation, known, notorious, obvious, open, overt, patent, plain, published, recognized 4. important, prominent, respected, well-known ~*n.* 5. citizens, commonalty, community, country, electorate, everyone, hoi polloi, Joe (and Eileen) Public (*Sl.*), Joe Six-Pack (*U.S. sl.*), masses, multitude, nation, people, populace, population, society, voters 6. audience, buyers, clientele, followers, following, patrons, supporters, those interested, trade 7. **in public** *coram populo,* for all to see, in full view, openly, overtly, publicly
Antonyms (*sense 2*) barred, closed, exclusive, inaccessible, personal, private, restricted, unavailable (*sense 3*) hidden, secluded, secret, unknown, unrevealed

publication 1. advertisement, airing, announcement, appearance, broadcasting, declaration, disclosure, dissemination, notification, proclamation, promulgation, publishing, reporting 2. book, booklet, brochure, handbill, hardback, issue, leaflet, magazine, newspaper, pamphlet, paperback, periodical, title

publicity advertising, attention, ballyhoo (*Inf.*), boost, build-up, hype, plug (*Inf.*), press, promotion, public notice, puff, puffery (*Inf.*)

publicize advertise, beat the drum for (*Inf.*), bring to public notice, broadcast, give publicity to, hype, make known, play up, plug (*Inf.*), promote, puff, push, spotlight, spread about, write up
Antonyms conceal, contain, cover up, keep dark, keep secret, smother, stifle, suppress, withhold

public-spirited altruistic, charitable, community-minded, generous, humanitarian, philanthropic, unselfish

publish 1. bring out, issue, print, produce, put out 2. advertise, announce, blow wide open (*Sl.*), broadcast, circulate, communicate, declare, disclose, distribute, divulge, impart, leak, proclaim, promulgate, publicize, reveal, spread

pucker 1. *v.* compress, contract, crease, crinkle, crumple, draw together, furrow, gather, knit, pout, purse, ruckle, ruck up, ruffle, screw up, tighten, wrinkle 2. *n.* crease, crinkle, crumple, fold, ruck, ruckle, wrinkle

puckish frolicsome, impish, mischievous, naughty, playful, roguish, sly, sportive, teasing, waggish, whimsical

pudding afters (*Brit. inf.*), dessert, last course, pud (*Inf.*), second course, sweet

puerile babyish, childish, foolish, immature, inane, infantile, irresponsible, jejune, juvenile, naive, petty, ridiculous, silly, trivial, weak
Antonyms adult, grown-up, mature, responsible, sensible

puff *n.* 1. blast, breath, draught, emanation, flurry, gust, whiff 2. drag (*Sl.*), pull, smoke 3. bulge, bunching, swelling 4. advertisement, commendation, favourable mention, good word, plug (*Inf.*), sales talk ~*v.* 5. blow, breathe, exhale, gasp, gulp, pant, wheeze 6. drag (*Sl.*), draw, inhale, pull at *or* on, smoke, suck 7. *Usually with* **up** bloat, dilate, distend, expand, inflate, swell 8. crack up (*Inf.*), hype, overpraise, plug (*Inf.*), praise, promote, publicize, push

puffed 1. done in (*Inf.*), exhausted, gasping, out of breath, panting, short of breath, spent, winded 2. **puffed up** bigheaded (*Inf.*), full of oneself, high and mighty (*Inf.*), proud, swollen-headed, too big for one's boots
Antonyms (*sense 2*) humble, modest, self-effacing

puffy bloated, distended, enlarged, inflamed, inflated, puffed up, swollen

pugilism boxing, fighting, prizefighting, the noble art *or* science, the prize ring, the ring

pugilist boxer, bruiser (*Inf.*), fighter, prizefighter, pug (*Sl.*)

pugnacious aggressive, antagonistic, argumentative, bellicose, belligerent, choleric, combative, contentious, disputatious, hot-tempered, irascible, irritable, petulant, quarrelsome
Antonyms calm, conciliatory, gentle, irenic, pacific, peaceable, peaceful, peace-loving, placatory, placid, quiet

puke barf (*U.S. sl.*), be nauseated, be sick, chuck (up) (*Sl., chiefly U.S.*), chunder (*Sl., chiefly Aust.*), disgorge, do a technicolour yawn (*Sl.*), heave, regurgitate, retch, spew, throw up (*Inf.*), toss one's cookies (*U.S. sl.*), upchuck (*U.S. sl.*), vomit

pukka authentic, bona fide, genuine, official, proper, real

pull *v.* 1. drag, draw, haul, jerk, tow, trail, tug, yank 2. cull, draw out, extract, gather, pick, pluck, remove, take out, uproot, weed 3. dislocate, rend, rip, sprain, strain, stretch, tear, wrench 4. *Inf.* attract, draw, entice, lure, magnetize 5. **pull apart** *or* **to pieces** attack, blast, criticize, find fault, flay, lambast(e), lay into (*Inf.*), pan (*Inf.*), pick holes in, put down, run down, slam (*Sl.*), slate (*Inf.*), tear into (*Inf.*) 6. **pull oneself together** *Inf.* buck up (*Inf.*), get a grip on oneself, get over it, regain composure, snap out of it (*Inf.*) 7. **pull strings** *Brit. inf.* influence, pull wires (*U.S.*), use one's influence 8. **pull someone's leg** *Inf.* chaff, have (someone) on, joke, make fun of, poke fun at, rag, rib (*Inf.*), tease, twit, wind up (*Brit. sl.*) ~*n.* 9. jerk, tug, twitch, yank 10. attraction, drawing power, effort, exertion, force, forcefulness, influence, lure, magnetism, power 11. *Inf.* advantage, bottom, clout (*Inf.*), influence, leverage, muscle, weight 12. drag (*Sl.*), inhalation, puff
Antonyms *v.* (*sense 1*) drive, nudge, push, ram, shove, thrust (*sense 2*) implant, insert, plant (*sense 4*) deter, discourage, put one off, repel ~*n.* (*sense 9*) nudge, push, shove, thrust

pull down bulldoze, demolish, destroy, raze, remove
Antonyms build, construct, erect, put up, raise, set up

pull in 1. arrive, come in, draw in, draw up, reach, stop 2. attract, bring in, draw 3. *Brit. sl.* arrest, bust (*Inf.*), collar (*Inf.*), feel one's collar (*Sl.*), lift (*Sl.*), nab (*Inf.*), nail (*Inf.*), pinch (*Inf.*), run in (*Sl.*), take into custody 4. clear, earn, gain, gross, make, net, pocket, take home

pull off 1. detach, doff, remove, rip off, tear off, wrench off 2. accomplish, bring off, carry out, crack it (*Inf.*), cut it (*Inf.*), manage, score a success, secure one's object, succeed

pull out abandon, depart, evacuate, leave, quit, rat on, retreat, stop participating, withdraw

pull through come through, get better, get over, pull round, rally, recover, survive, weather

pull up 1. dig out, lift, raise, uproot 2. brake, come to a halt, halt, reach a standstill, stop 3. admonish, bawl out (*Inf.*), carpet (*Inf.*), castigate, chew out (*U.S. & Canad. inf.*), dress down (*Inf.*), give a rocket (*Brit. & N.Z. inf.*), read the riot act, rebuke, reprimand, reprove, take to task, tear into (*Inf.*), tear (someone) off a strip (*Brit. inf.*), tell off (*Inf.*), tick off (*Inf.*)

pulp *n.* 1. flesh, marrow, soft part 2. mash, mush, pap, paste, pomace, semiliquid, semisolid, triturate ~*v.* 3. crush, mash, pulverize, squash, triturate ~*adj.* 4. cheap, lurid, mushy (*Inf.*), rubbishy, sensational, trashy

pulpy fleshy, mushy, pappy, soft, squashy, succulent

pulsate beat, hammer, oscillate, palpitate, pound, pulse, quiver, throb, thud, thump, tick, vibrate

pulse 1. *n.* beat, beating, oscillation, pulsation, rhythm, stroke, throb, throbbing, vibration 2. *v.* beat, pulsate, throb, tick, vibrate

pulverize 1. bray, comminute, crush, granulate, grind, levigate (*Chem.*), mill, pestle, pound, triturate 2. *Fig.* annihilate, blow out of the water (*Sl.*), crush, defeat, demolish, destroy, flatten, lick (*Inf.*), smash, tank (*Sl.*), vanquish, wipe the floor with (*Inf.*), wreck

pummel bang, batter, beat, belt (*Inf.*), clobber (*Sl.*), hammer, knock, lambast(e), pound, punch, rain blows upon, strike, thump

pump *v.* 1. *With* **out** bail out, drain, draw off, drive out, empty, force out, siphon 2. *With* **up** blow up, dilate, inflate 3. drive, force, inject, pour, push, send, supply 4. cross-examine, give (someone) the third degree, grill (*Inf.*), interrogate, probe, question closely, quiz, worm out of

pun double entendre, equivoque, paronomasia (*Rhetoric*), play on words, quip, witticism

punch[1] *v.* 1. bash (*Inf.*), belt (*Inf.*), biff (*Sl.*), bop (*Inf.*), box, clout (*Inf.*), hit, plug (*Sl.*), pummel, slam, slug, smash, sock (*Sl.*), strike, wallop (*Inf.*) ~*n.* 2. bash (*Inf.*), biff (*Sl.*), blow, bop (*Inf.*), clout (*Inf.*), hit, jab, knock, plug (*Sl.*), sock (*Sl.*), thump, wallop (*Inf.*) 3. *Inf.* bite, drive, effectiveness, force, forcefulness, impact, point, verve, vigour

punch[2] *v.* bore, cut, drill, perforate, pierce, pink, prick, puncture, stamp

punch-drunk befuddled, confused, dazed, groggy (*Inf.*), in a daze, knocked silly, punchy (*Inf.*), reeling, slaphappy (*Inf.*), staggering, stupefied, unsteady, woozy (*Inf.*)

punch-up argument, *bagarre,* battle royal, brawl, dingdong, dust-up (*Inf.*), fight, free-for-all (*Inf.*), row, scrap (*Inf.*), set-to (*Inf.*), shindig (*Inf.*), shindy (*Inf.*), stand-up fight (*Inf.*)

punchy aggressive, dynamic, effective, forceful, incisive, lively, spirited, vigorous

punctilio 1. exactitude, finickiness, meticulousness, particularity, precision, punctiliousness, scrupulousness, strictness 2. convention, delicacy, distinction, fine point, formality, nicety, particular, refinement

punctilious careful, ceremonious, conscientious, exact, finicky, formal, fussy, meticulous, nice, particular, precise, proper, scrupulous, strict

punctual early, exact, in good time, on the dot, on time, precise, prompt, punctilious, seasonable, strict, timely
Antonyms behind, behindhand, belated, delayed, late, overdue, tardy, unpunctual

punctuality promptitude, promptness, readiness, regularity

punctuate 1. break, interject, interrupt, intersperse, pepper, sprinkle 2. accentuate, emphasize, lay stress on, mark, point up, stress, underline

puncture *n.* 1. break, cut, damage, hole, leak, nick, opening, perforation, rupture, slit 2. flat, flat tyre ~*v.* 3. bore, cut, impale, nick, penetrate, perforate, pierce, prick, rupture 4. deflate, go down, go flat 5. deflate, discourage, disillusion, flatten, humble, take down a peg (*Inf.*)

pundit buff (*Inf.*), maestro, one of the cognoscenti, (self-appointed) authority *or* expert

pungent 1. acerb, acid, acrid, aromatic, bitter, highly flavoured, hot, peppery, piquant, seasoned, sharp, sour, spicy, stinging, strong, tangy, tart 2. acrimonious, acute, barbed, biting, caustic, cutting, incisive, keen, mordacious, mordant, penetrating, piercing, poignant, pointed, sarcastic, scathing, sharp, stinging, stringent, telling, trenchant, vitriolic
Antonyms bland, dull, inane, mild, moderate, tasteless, unsavoury, unstimulating, weak

punish 1. beat, castigate, chasten, chastise, correct, discipline, flog, give a lesson to, give (someone) the works (*Sl.*), lash, penalize, rap someone's knuckles, scourge, sentence, slap someone's wrist, whip 2. abuse, batter, give (someone) a going-over (*Inf.*), harm, hurt, injure, knock about, maltreat, manhandle, misuse, oppress, rough up

punishable blameworthy, chargeable, convictable, criminal, culpable, indictable

punishing arduous, backbreaking, burdensome, demanding, exhausting, grinding, gruelling, hard, strenuous, taxing, tiring, uphill, wearing
Antonyms cushy (*Inf.*), easy, effortless,

light, simple, undemanding, unexacting, untaxing

punishment 1. chastening, chastisement, comeuppance (*Sl.*), correction, discipline, just deserts, penalty, penance, punitive measures, retribution, sanction, what for (*Inf.*) 2. *Inf.* abuse, beating, hard work, maltreatment, manhandling, pain, rough treatment, slave labour, torture, victimization

punitive in reprisal, in retaliation, punitory, retaliative, retaliatory, revengeful, vindictive

punt *v.* 1. back, bet, gamble, lay, stake, wager ~*n.* 2. bet, gamble, stake, wager 3. backer, better, gambler, punter

punter *n.* 1. backer, better, gambler, punt (*Chiefly Brit.*) 2. *Inf.* bloke (*Brit. inf.*), fellow, guy (*Inf.*), man in the street, person 3. *Inf.* client, customer

puny 1. diminutive, dwarfish, feeble, frail, little, pint-sized (*Inf.*), pygmy *or* pigmy, sickly, stunted, tiny, underfed, undersized, undeveloped, weak, weakly 2. inconsequential, inferior, insignificant, minor, paltry, petty, piddling (*Inf.*), trifling, trivial, worthless

Antonyms (*sense 1*) brawny, burly, healthy, hefty (*Inf.*), husky (*Inf.*), powerful, robust, strong, sturdy, well-built, well-developed

pup *or* **puppy** *Fig.* braggart, cub, jackanapes, popinjay, whelp, whippersnapper, young dog

pupil beginner, catechumen, disciple, learner, neophyte, novice, scholar, schoolboy, schoolgirl, student, trainee, tyro

Antonyms coach, instructor, master, mistress, schoolmaster, schoolmistress, schoolteacher, teacher, trainer, tutor

puppet 1. doll, marionette 2. *Fig.* cat's-paw, creature, dupe, figurehead, gull (*Archaic*), instrument, mouthpiece, pawn, stooge, tool

purchasable 1. bribable, corrupt, corruptible, dishonest, having one's price, unscrupulous, venal 2. available, for sale, in stock, obtainable, on sale, on the market, to be had

purchase *v.* 1. acquire, buy, come by, gain, get, get hold of, invest in, make a purchase, obtain, pay for, pick up, procure, score (*Sl.*), secure, shop for 2. achieve, attain, earn, gain, realize, win ~*n.* 3. acquisition, asset, buy, gain, investment, possession, property 4. advantage, edge, foothold, footing, grasp, grip, hold, influence, lever, leverage, support, toehold

Antonyms *v.* (*sense 1*) hawk, market, merchandise, peddle, retail, sell, trade in, vend ~*n.* (*sense 3*) marketing, sale, selling, vending

purchaser buyer, consumer, customer, vendee (*Law*)

Antonyms dealer, merchant, retailer, salesman, salesperson, saleswoman, seller, shopkeeper, tradesman, vendor

pure 1. authentic, clear, flawless, genuine, natural, neat, perfect, real, simple, straight, true, unalloyed, unmixed 2. clean, disinfected, germ-free, immaculate, pasteurized, sanitary, spotless, squeaky-clean, sterile, sterilized, unadulterated, unblemished, uncontaminated, unpolluted, untainted, wholesome 3. blameless, chaste, guileless, honest, immaculate, impeccable, innocent, maidenly, modest, true, uncorrupted, undefiled, unspotted, unstained, unsullied, upright, virgin, virginal, virtuous 4. absolute, complete, mere, outright, sheer, thorough, unmitigated, unqualified, utter 5. abstract, academic, philosophical, speculative, theoretical

Antonyms (*senses 1 & 2*) adulterated, contaminated, dirty, filthy, flawed, imperfect, impure, infected, insincere, mixed, polluted, tainted (*sense 3*) contaminated, corrupt, defiled, guilty, immodest, immoral, impure, indecent, obscene, sinful, spoiled, unchaste, unclean, untrue (*sense 4*) qualified (*sense 5*) applied, practical

purebred blood, full-blooded, pedigree, thoroughbred

purely absolutely, completely, entirely, exclusively, just, merely, only, plainly, simply, solely, totally, wholly

purgative 1. *n.* aperient (*Medical*), cathartic, depurative, emetic, enema, evacuant, laxative, physic (*Rare*), purge 2. *adj.* aperient (*Medical*), cleansing, depurative, evacuant, laxative, purging

purgatory *As used informally* agony, hell (*Inf.*), hell on earth, misery, murder (*Inf.*), the rack, torment, torture

purge *v.* 1. axe (*Inf.*), clean out, dismiss, do away with, eject, eradicate, expel, exterminate, get rid of, kill, liquidate, oust, remove, rid of, rout out, sweep out, wipe out 2. absolve, cleanse, clear, exonerate, expiate, forgive, pardon, purify, wash ~*n.* 3. cleanup, crushing, ejection, elimination, eradication, expulsion, liquidation, reign of terror, removal, suppression, witch hunt 4. aperient (*Medical*), cathartic, dose of salts, emetic, enema, laxative, physic (*Rare*), purgative (*Medical*)

purify 1. clarify, clean, cleanse, decontaminate, disinfect, filter, fumigate, refine, sanitize, wash 2. absolve, cleanse, excul-

pate, exonerate, lustrate, redeem, sanctify, shrive
Antonyms adulterate, befoul, contaminate, corrupt, defile, foul, infect, pollute, soil, stain, sully, taint, tarnish, vitiate

purist classicist, formalist, pedant, precisian, stickler

puritan 1. *n.* fanatic, moralist, pietist, prude, rigorist, zealot 2. *adj.* ascetic, austere, hidebound, intolerant, moralistic, narrow, narrow-minded, prudish, puritanical, severe, strait-laced, strict

puritanical ascetic, austere, bigoted, disapproving, fanatical, forbidding, narrow, narrow-minded, prim, proper, prudish, puritan, rigid, severe, stiff, strait-laced, strict, stuffy
Antonyms broad-minded, hedonistic, indulgent, latitudinarian, liberal, permissive, tolerant

purity 1. brilliance, clarity, cleanliness, cleanness, clearness, faultlessness, fineness, genuineness, immaculateness, pureness, untaintedness, wholesomeness 2. blamelessness, chasteness, chastity, decency, guilelessness, honesty, innocence, integrity, piety, rectitude, sincerity, virginity, virtue, virtuousness
Antonyms cloudiness, contamination, immodesty, immorality, impurity, unchasteness, vice, wickedness

purlieus 1. borders, confines, environs, fringes, limits, neighbourhood, outskirts, periphery, precincts, suburbs, vicinity 2. *Sometimes singular* hang-out (*Inf.*), haunt, patch, resort, stamping ground, territory

purloin appropriate, blag (*Sl.*), cabbage (*Brit. sl.*), filch, knock off (*Sl.*), lift (*Inf.*), nick (*Sl., chiefly Brit.*), nobble (*Brit. sl.*), pilfer, pinch (*Inf.*), prig (*Brit. sl.*), rob, snaffle (*Brit. inf.*), snitch (*Sl.*), steal, swipe (*Sl.*), thieve, walk off with

purport *v.* 1. allege, assert, claim, declare, maintain, pose as, pretend, proclaim, profess 2. betoken, convey, denote, express, imply, import, indicate, intend, mean, point to, signify, suggest ~*n.* 3. bearing, drift, gist, idea, implication, import, meaning, significance, spirit, tendency, tenor 4. aim, design, intent, intention, object, objective, plan, purpose

purpose *n.* 1. aim, design, function, idea, intention, object, point, principle, reason 2. aim, ambition, aspiration, design, desire, end, goal, hope, intention, object, objective, plan, project, scheme, target, view, wish 3. constancy, determination, firmness, persistence, resolution, resolve, single-mindedness, steadfastness, tenacity, will 4. advantage, avail, benefit, effect, gain, good, outcome, profit, result, return, use, utility 5. **on purpose** by design, deliberately, designedly, intentionally, knowingly, purposely, wilfully, wittingly ~*v.* 6. aim, aspire, commit oneself, contemplate, decide, design, determine, have a mind to, intend, make up one's mind, mean, meditate, plan, propose, resolve, set one's sights on, think to, work towards

purposeful decided, deliberate, determined, firm, fixed, immovable, positive, resolute, resolved, settled, single-minded, steadfast, strong-willed, tenacious, unfaltering
Antonyms aimless, faltering, irresolute, purposeless, undecided, undetermined, vacillating, wavering

purposeless aimless, empty, goalless, motiveless, needless, pointless, senseless, uncalled-for, unnecessary, useless, vacuous, wanton

purposely by design, calculatedly, consciously, deliberately, designedly, expressly, intentionally, knowingly, on purpose, wilfully, with intent
Antonyms accidentally, by accident, by chance, by mistake, inadvertently, unconsciously, unintentionally, unknowingly, unwittingly

purse *n.* 1. money-bag, pouch, wallet 2. coffers, exchequer, funds, means, money, resources, treasury, wealth, wherewithal 3. award, gift, present, prize, reward ~*v.* 4. close, contract, knit, pout, press together, pucker, tighten, wrinkle

pursuance bringing about, carrying out, discharge, doing, effecting, execution, following, performance, prosecution, pursuing

pursue 1. accompany, attend, chase, dog, follow, give chase to, go after, harass, harry, haunt, hound, hunt, hunt down, plague, run after, shadow, stalk, tail (*Inf.*), track 2. aim for, aspire to, desire, have as one's goal, purpose, seek, strive for, try for, work towards 3. adhere to, carry on, continue, cultivate, hold to, keep on, maintain, persevere in, persist in, proceed, see through 4. apply oneself, carry on, conduct, engage in, perform, ply, practise, prosecute, tackle, wage, work at 5. chase after, court, make up to (*Inf.*), pay attention to, pay court to, set one's cap at, woo
Antonyms avoid, eschew, fight shy of, flee, give (someone *or* something) a wide berth, keep away from, run away from, shun, steer clear of

pursuit 1. chase, hunt, hunting, inquiry, quest, search, seeking, tracking, trail, trailing 2. activity, hobby, interest, line, occupation, pastime, pleasure, vocation

purvey 1. cater, deal in, furnish, provide, provision, retail, sell, supply, trade in, victual 2. communicate, make available, pass on, publish, retail, spread, transmit

purview 1. ambit, compass, confine(s), extent, field, limit, orbit, province, range, reach, scope, sphere 2. comprehension, ken, overview, perspective, range of view, understanding

push *v.* 1. depress, drive, poke, press, propel, ram, shove, thrust 2. elbow, jostle, make *or* force one's way, move, shoulder, shove, squeeze, thrust 3. egg on, encourage, expedite, hurry, impel, incite, persuade, press, prod, speed (up), spur, urge 4. advertise, boost, cry up, hype, make known, plug (*Inf.*), promote, propagandize, publicize, puff 5. browbeat, coerce, constrain, dragoon, encourage, exert influence on, influence, oblige ~*n.* 6. butt, jolt, nudge, poke, prod, shove, thrust 7. *Inf.* ambition, determination, drive, dynamism, energy, enterprise, get-up-and-go (*Inf.*), go (*Inf.*), gumption (*Inf.*), initiative, pep, vigour, vitality 8. *Inf.* advance, assault, attack, charge, effort, offensive, onset, thrust 9. **the push** *Sl.* discharge, dismissal, kiss-off (*Sl., chiefly U.S. & Canad.*), marching orders (*Inf.*), one's books (*Inf.*), one's cards, the boot (*Sl.*), the (old) heave-ho (*Inf.*), the order of the boot (*Sl.*), the sack (*Inf.*)

Antonyms *v.* (*sense 1*) drag, draw, haul, jerk, pull, tow, trail, tug, yank (*sense 3*) deter, discourage, dissuade, put off ~*n.* (*sense 6*) jerk, pull, tug, yank

pushed *Often with* **for** hurried, in difficulty, pressed, rushed, short of, tight, under pressure, up against it (*Inf.*)

pushing 1. ambitious, determined, driving, dynamic, enterprising, go-ahead, on the go, purposeful, resourceful 2. assertive, bold, brash, bumptious, forward, impertinent, intrusive, presumptuous, pushy (*Inf.*), self-assertive

push off beat it (*Sl.*), depart, get lost (*Inf.*), go away, hit the road (*Sl.*), hook it (*Sl.*), launch, leave, light out (*Inf.*), make oneself scarce (*Inf.*), shove off (*Inf.*), slope off, take off (*Inf.*)

pushover 1. breeze (*U.S. & Canad. inf.*), cakewalk (*Inf.*), child's play (*Inf.*), cinch (*Sl.*), doddle (*Brit. sl.*), duck soup (*U.S. sl.*), picnic (*Inf.*), piece of cake (*Brit. inf.*), walkover (*Inf.*) 2. chump (*Inf.*), easy *or* soft mark (*Inf.*), easy game (*Inf.*), mug (*Brit. sl.*), soft touch (*Sl.*), stooge (*Sl.*), sucker (*Sl.*), walkover (*Inf.*)

Antonyms (*sense 1*) challenge, hassle (*Inf.*), ordeal, test, trial, undertaking

pushy aggressive, ambitious, bold, brash, bumptious, forceful, loud, obnoxious, obtrusive, offensive, officious, presumptuous, pushing, self-assertive

Antonyms diffident, inoffensive, meek, mousy, quiet, reserved, retiring, self-effacing, shy, timid, unassertive, unassuming, unobtrusive

pusillanimous abject, chicken-hearted, cowardly, craven, faint-hearted, fearful, feeble, gutless (*Inf.*), lily-livered, recreant (*Archaic*), spineless, timid, timorous, weak, yellow (*Inf.*)

Antonyms bold, brave, courageous, daring, dauntless, fearless, gallant, heroic, intrepid, plucky, valiant, valorous

pussyfoot 1. creep, prowl, slink, steal, tiptoe, tread warily 2. beat about the bush, be noncommittal, equivocate, flannel (*Brit. inf.*), hedge, hum and haw, prevaricate, sit on the fence, tergiversate

pustule abscess, blister, boil, fester, gathering, pimple, ulcer, zit (*Sl.*)

put 1. bring, deposit, establish, fix, lay, place, position, rest, set, settle, situate 2. commit, condemn, consign, doom, enjoin, impose, inflict, levy, subject 3. assign, constrain, employ, force, induce, make, oblige, require, set, subject to 4. express, phrase, pose, set, state, utter, word 5. advance, bring forward, forward, offer, posit, present, propose, set before, submit, tender 6. cast, fling, heave, hurl, lob, pitch, throw, toss

put across *or* **over** communicate, convey, explain, get across, get through, make clear, make oneself understood, spell out

put aside *or* **by** 1. cache, deposit, keep in reserve, lay by, salt away, save, squirrel away, stockpile, store, stow away 2. bury, discount, disregard, forget, ignore

putative alleged, assumed, commonly believed, imputed, presumed, presumptive, reported, reputed, supposed

put away 1. put back, replace, return to (its) place, tidy away 2. deposit, keep, lay in, put by, save, set aside, store away 3. certify, commit, confine, institutionalize, lock up 4. consume, devour, eat up, gobble, gulp down, wolf down 5. destroy, do away with, put down, put out of its misery, put to sleep

put-down barb, dig, disparagement, gibe, humiliation, knock (*Inf.*), one in the eye (*Inf.*), rebuff, sarcasm, slight, sneer, snub

put down 1. enter, inscribe, log, record, set down, take down, transcribe, write down 2. crush, quash, quell, repress, silence, stamp out, suppress 3. *With* **to** ascribe, attribute, impute, set down 4. destroy, do away with, put away, put out of its misery, put to sleep 5. *Sl.* condemn, crush, deflate, dismiss, disparage, humiliate, mortify, reject, shame, slight, snub

put forward advance, introduce, move, nominate, prescribe, present, press, proffer, propose, recommend, submit, suggest, tender

put off 1. defer, delay, hold over, postpone, put back, put on the back burner (*Inf.*), reschedule, take a rain check on (*U.S. & Canad. inf.*) 2. abash, confuse, discomfit, disconcert, dismay, distress, faze, nonplus, perturb, rattle (*Inf.*), throw (*Inf.*), unsettle 3. discourage, dishearten, dissuade
Antonyms (*sense 3*) egg on, encourage, incite, persuade, prompt, push, spur, urge

put on 1. change into, don, dress, get dressed in, slip into 2. affect, assume, fake, feign, make believe, play-act, pretend, sham, simulate 3. do, mount, present, produce, show, stage 4. add, gain, increase by 5. back, bet, lay, place, wager
Antonyms (*sense 1*) cast off, doff, remove, shed, slip off, slip out of, take off, throw off, undress

put out 1. anger, annoy, confound, disturb, exasperate, harass, irk, irritate, nettle, perturb, provoke, vex 2. blow out, douse, extinguish, quench, smother, snuff out, stamp out 3. bother, discomfit, discommode, discompose, disconcert, discountenance, disturb, embarrass, impose upon, incommode, inconvenience, put on the spot, trouble, upset 4. bring out, broadcast, circulate, issue, make known, make public, publish, release

putrefy corrupt, decay, decompose, deteriorate, go bad, rot, spoil, stink, taint

putrescent decaying, decomposing, going bad, rotting, stinking

putrid bad, contaminated, corrupt, decayed, decomposed, fetid, foul, off, olid, putrefied, rancid, rank, reeking, rotten, rotting, spoiled, stinking, tainted
Antonyms clean, fresh, pure, sweet, uncontaminated, untainted, wholesome

put through accomplish, achieve, bring off, carry through, conclude, do, effect, execute, manage, pull off, realize

put up 1. build, construct, erect, fabricate, raise 2. accommodate, board, entertain, give one lodging, house, lodge, take in 3. float, nominate, offer, present, propose, put forward, recommend, submit 4. advance, give, invest, pay, pledge, provide, supply 5. **put up to** egg on, encourage, goad, incite, instigate, prompt, put the idea into one's head, urge 6. **put up with** *Inf.* abide, bear, brook, endure, lump (*Inf.*), pocket, stand, stand for, stomach, suffer, swallow, take, tolerate
Antonyms (*sense 1*) demolish, destroy, flatten, knock down, level, pull down, raze, tear down (*sense 6*) not stand for, object to, oppose, protest against, reject, take exception to

put-upon abused, beset, exploited, harried, imposed upon, inconvenienced, overworked, put-out, saddled, taken advantage of, taken for a fool, taken for granted, troubled

puzzle *v.* 1. baffle, beat (*Sl.*), bewilder, confound, confuse, flummox, mystify, nonplus, perplex, stump 2. ask oneself, brood, cudgel *or* rack one's brains, mull over, muse, ponder, study, think about, think hard, wonder 3. *Usually with* **out** clear up, crack, crack the code, decipher, figure out, find the key, get it, get the answer, resolve, see, solve, sort out, suss (out) (*Sl.*), think through, unravel, work out ~*n.* 4. brain-teaser (*Inf.*), conundrum, enigma, labyrinth, maze, mystery, paradox, poser, problem, question, question mark, riddle, teaser 5. bafflement, bewilderment, confusion, difficulty, dilemma, perplexity, quandary, uncertainty

puzzled at a loss, at sea, baffled, beaten, bewildered, clueless, confused, doubtful, flummoxed, in a fog, lost, mixed up, mystified, nonplussed, perplexed, stuck, stumped, without a clue

puzzlement bafflement, bewilderment, confusion, disorientation, doubt, doubtfulness, mystification, perplexity, questioning, surprise, uncertainty, wonder

puzzling abstruse, ambiguous, baffling, bewildering, beyond one, enigmatic, full of surprises, hard, incomprehensible, inexplicable, involved, knotty, labyrinthine, misleading, mystifying, oracular, perplexing, unaccountable, unclear, unfathomable
Antonyms clear, comprehensible, easy, evident, intelligible, lucid, manifest, obvious, patent, plain, simple, unambiguous, unequivocal, unmistakable

pygmy, pigmy *n.* 1. dwarf, homunculus, Lilliputian, manikin, midget, shrimp (*Inf.*), Tom Thumb 2. cipher, lightweight (*Inf.*), mediocrity, nobody, nonentity, pipsqueak (*Inf.*), small fry ~*adj.* 3. baby, diminutive, dwarf, dwarfish, elfin, Lilliputian, midget, miniature, minuscule, pocket, pygmean, small, stunted, teensy-weensy, teeny-weeny, tiny, undersized, wee

pyromaniac arsonist, firebug (*Inf.*), fire raiser, incendiary

quack 1. *n.* charlatan, fake, fraud, humbug, impostor, mountebank, phoney *or* phony (*Inf.*), pretender, quacksalver (*Archaic*) 2. *adj.* counterfeit, fake, fraudulent, phoney *or* phony (*Inf.*), pretended, sham

quaff bend the elbow (*Inf.*), bevvy (*Dialect*), carouse, down, drink, gulp, guzzle, imbibe, swallow, swig (*Inf.*), tope

quaggy boggy, fenny, marshy, miry, muddy, mushy, paludal, soft, soggy, squelchy, swampy, yielding

quagmire 1. bog, fen, marsh, mire, morass, quicksand, slough, swamp 2. difficulty, dilemma, entanglement, fix (*Inf.*), imbroglio, impasse, jam (*Inf.*), muddle, pass, pickle (*Inf.*), pinch, plight, predicament, quandary, scrape (*Inf.*)

quail blanch, blench, cower, cringe, droop, faint, falter, flinch, have cold feet (*Inf.*), quake, recoil, shake, shrink, shudder, tremble

quaint 1. bizarre, curious, droll, eccentric, fanciful, fantastic, odd, old-fashioned, original, peculiar, queer, rum (*Brit. sl.*), singular, strange, unusual, whimsical 2. antiquated, antique, artful, charming, gothic, ingenious, old-fashioned, old-world, picturesque
Antonyms fashionable, modern, new, normal, ordinary, up-to-date

quake convulse, move, pulsate, quail, quiver, rock, shake, shiver, shudder, throb, totter, tremble, vibrate, waver, wobble

qualification 1. ability, accomplishment, aptitude, attribute, capability, capacity, eligibility, endowment(s), fitness, quality, skill, suitability, suitableness 2. allowance, caveat, condition, criterion, exception, exemption, limitation, modification, objection, prerequisite, proviso, requirement, reservation, restriction, rider, stipulation

qualified 1. able, accomplished, adept, capable, certificated, competent, efficient, equipped, experienced, expert, fit, knowledgeable, licensed, practised, proficient, skilful, talented, trained 2. bounded, circumscribed, conditional, confined, contingent, equivocal, guarded, limited, modified, provisional, reserved, restricted
Antonyms (*sense 1*) amateur, apprentice, self-styled, self-taught, trainee, uncertificated, unqualified, untrained (*sense 2*) categorical, outright, unconditional, unequivocal, whole-hearted

qualify 1. capacitate, certify, commission, condition, empower, endow, equip, fit, ground, permit, prepare, ready, sanction, train 2. abate, adapt, assuage, circumscribe, diminish, ease, lessen, limit, mitigate, moderate, modify, modulate, reduce, regulate, restrain, restrict, soften, temper, vary 3. characterize, describe, designate, distinguish, modify, name
Antonyms (*sense 1*) ban, debar, disqualify, forbid, preclude, prevent

quality 1. aspect, attribute, characteristic, condition, feature, mark, peculiarity, property, trait 2. character, constitution, description, essence, kind, make, nature, sort 3. calibre, distinction, excellence, grade, merit, position, pre-eminence, rank, standing, status, superiority, value, worth 4. *Obsolete* aristocracy, gentry, nobility, ruling class, upper class

qualm 1. anxiety, apprehension, compunction, disquiet, doubt, hesitation, misgiving, regret, reluctance, remorse, scruple, twinge *or* pang of conscience, uncertainty, uneasiness 2. agony, attack, nausea, pang, queasiness, sickness, spasm, throe (*Rare*), twinge

quandary bewilderment, cleft stick, delicate situation, difficulty, dilemma, doubt, embarrassment, impasse, perplexity, plight, predicament, puzzle, strait, uncertainty

quantity 1. aggregate, allotment, amount, lot, number, part, portion, quota, sum, total 2. bulk, capacity, expanse, extent, greatness, length, magnitude, mass, measure, size, volume

quarrel *n.* 1. affray, altercation, argument, *bagarre,* brawl, breach, broil, commotion, contention, controversy, difference (of opinion), disagreement, discord, disputation, dispute, dissension, dissidence, disturbance, feud, fight, fracas, fray, misunderstanding, row, scrap (*Inf.*), shindig (*Inf.*), shindy (*Inf.*), skirmish, spat, squabble, strife, tiff, tumult, vendetta, wrangle ~*v.* 2. altercate, argue, bicker, brawl, clash, differ, disagree, dispute, fall out (*Inf.*), fight, row, spar, squabble, wrangle 3. carp,

cavil, complain, decry, disapprove, find fault, object to, take exception to
Antonyms (*sense 1*) accord, agreement, concord (*sense 2*) agree, get on *or* along (with)

quarrelsome argumentative, belligerent, cat-and-dog (*Inf.*), choleric, combative, contentious, cross, disputatious, fractious, ill-tempered, irascible, irritable, peevish, petulant, pugnacious, querulous
Antonyms easy-going, equable, even-tempered, placid

quarry aim, game, goal, objective, prey, prize, victim

quarter *n.* 1. area, direction, district, locality, location, neighbourhood, part, place, point, position, province, region, side, spot, station, territory, zone 2. clemency, compassion, favour, forgiveness, leniency, mercy, pity ~*v.* 3. accommodate, billet, board, house, install, lodge, place, post, put up, station

quarters abode, accommodation, barracks, billet, cantonment (*Military*), chambers, digs (*Brit. inf.*), domicile, dwelling, habitation, lodging, lodgings, post, residence, rooms, shelter, station

quash 1. beat, crush, destroy, extinguish, extirpate, overthrow, put down, quell, quench, repress, squash, subdue, suppress 2. annul, cancel, declare null and void, invalidate, nullify, overrule, overthrow, rescind, reverse, revoke, set aside, void

quasi- 1. almost, apparently, partly, seemingly, supposedly 2. apparent, fake, mock, near, nominal, pretended, pseudo-, seeming, semi-, sham, so-called, synthetic, virtual, would-be

quaver 1. *v.* flicker, flutter, oscillate, pulsate, quake, quiver, shake, shudder, thrill, tremble, trill, twitter, vibrate, waver 2. *n.* break, quiver, shake, sob, throb, tremble, trembling, tremor, trill, vibration, warble

queasy 1. bilious, giddy, green around the gills (*Inf.*), groggy (*Inf.*), ill, indisposed, nauseated, off colour, queer, sick, sickish, squeamish, uncomfortable, unwell, upset 2. anxious, concerned, fidgety, ill at ease, restless, troubled, uncertain, uneasy, worried

queen 1. consort, monarch, ruler, sovereign 2. diva, doyenne, ideal, idol, mistress, model, perfection, prima donna, star

queenly grand, imperial, majestic, noble, regal, royal, stately

queer *adj.* 1. abnormal, anomalous, atypical, curious, disquieting, droll, eerie, erratic, extraordinary, funny, odd, outlandish, *outré,* peculiar, remarkable, rum (*Brit. sl.*), singular, strange, uncanny, uncommon, unconventional, unnatural, unorthodox, unusual, weird 2. doubtful, dubious, fishy (*Inf.*), irregular, mysterious, puzzling, questionable, shady (*Inf.*), suspicious 3. dizzy, faint, giddy, light-headed, queasy, reeling, uneasy 4. crazy, demented, eccentric, idiosyncratic, irrational, mad, odd, touched, unbalanced, unhinged ~*v.* 5. bodge (*Inf.*), botch, endanger, harm, impair, imperil, injure, jeopardize, mar, ruin, spoil, thwart, wreck
Antonyms *adj.* believable, common, conventional, customary, natural, normal, ordinary, orthodox, rational, regular, straight, unexceptional, unoriginal ~*v.* aid, boost, enhance, help

quell 1. conquer, crush, defeat, extinguish, overcome, overpower, put down, quash, squelch, stamp out, stifle, subdue, suppress, vanquish 2. allay, alleviate, appease, assuage, calm, compose, deaden, dull, mitigate, moderate, mollify, pacify, quiet, silence, soothe

quench 1. check, crush, destroy, douse, end, extinguish, put out, smother, snuff out, squelch, stifle, suppress 2. allay, appease, cool, sate, satiate, satisfy, slake

querulous cantankerous, captious, carping, censorious, complaining, critical, cross, discontented, dissatisfied, fault-finding, fretful, grouchy (*Inf.*), grumbling, hard to please, irascible, irritable, murmuring, peevish, petulant, plaintive, ratty (*Brit. & N.Z. inf.*), sour, testy, tetchy, touchy, waspish, whining
Antonyms contented, easy to please, equable, placid, uncomplaining, uncritical, undemanding

query *v.* 1. ask, enquire, question 2. challenge, disbelieve, dispute, distrust, doubt, mistrust, suspect ~*n.* 3. demand, doubt, hesitation, inquiry, objection, problem, question, reservation, scepticism, suspicion

quest *n.* adventure, crusade, enterprise, expedition, exploration, hunt, journey, mission, pilgrimage, pursuit, search, voyage

question *v.* 1. ask, catechize, cross-examine, enquire, examine, grill (*Inf.*), interrogate, interview, investigate, probe, pump (*Inf.*), quiz, sound out 2. call into question, cast doubt upon, challenge, controvert, disbelieve, dispute, distrust, doubt, impugn, mistrust, oppose, query, suspect ~*n.* 3. examination, inquiry, interrogation, investigation 4. argument, confusion, contention, controversy, debate, difficulty, dispute, doubt, dubiety, misgiving, problem, query, uncertainty 5. issue, motion, point, point at issue, proposal, proposition, subject, theme, topic **6. in question** at issue, in doubt, open to debate, under discussion **7. out of the question** impossible, inconceivable, not to be thought of, unthinkable

Antonyms (*senses 1 & 3*) answer, reply (*sense 2*) accept, believe, buy (*Sl.*), swallow (*Inf.*), take on trust

questionable arguable, controversial, controvertible, debatable, disputable, dodgy (*Brit., Aust., & N.Z. inf.*), doubtful, dubious, dubitable, equivocal, fishy (*Inf.*), iffy (*Inf.*), moot, paradoxical, problematical, shady (*Inf.*), suspect, suspicious, uncertain, unproven, unreliable

Antonyms authoritative, certain, incontrovertible, indisputable, straightforward, unequivocal

queue chain, concatenation, file, line, order, progression, sequence, series, string, succession, train

quibble 1. *v.* carp, cavil, equivocate, evade, pretend, prevaricate, shift, split hairs **2.** *n.* artifice, cavil, complaint, criticism, duplicity, equivocation, evasion, nicety, niggle, objection, pretence, prevarication, protest, quirk, shift, sophism, subterfuge, subtlety

quibbling ambiguous, carping, caviling, critical, equivocal, evasive, hair-splitting, jesuitical, niggling, nit-picking (*Inf.*), overnice, sophistical

quick 1. active, brief, brisk, cursory, expeditious, express, fast, fleet, hasty, headlong, hurried, pdq (*Sl.*), perfunctory, prompt, quickie (*Inf.*), rapid, speedy, sudden, swift **2.** agile, alert, animated, energetic, flying, keen, lively, nimble, spirited, sprightly, spry, vivacious, winged **3.** able, acute, adept, adroit, all there (*Inf.*), apt, astute, bright, clever, deft, dexterous, discerning, intelligent, nimble-witted, perceptive, quick on the uptake (*Inf.*), quick-witted, receptive, sharp, shrewd, skilful, smart **4.** abrupt, curt, excitable, hasty, impatient, irascible, irritable, passionate, petulant, testy, touchy **5.** *Archaic* alive, animate, existing, live, living, viable

Antonyms calm, deliberate, dull, gradual, heavy, inactive, inexpert, lazy, lethargic, long, maladroit, patient, restrained, slow, sluggish, stupid, unintelligent, unresponsive, unskilful

quicken 1. accelerate, dispatch, expedite, hasten, hurry, impel, precipitate, speed **2.** activate, animate, arouse, energize, excite, galvanize, incite, inspire, invigorate, kindle, refresh, reinvigorate, resuscitate, revitalize, revive, rouse, stimulate, strengthen, vitalize, vivify

quickly abruptly, apace, at a rate of knots (*Inf.*), at *or* on the double, at speed, briskly, expeditiously, fast, hastily, hell for leather (*Inf.*), hotfoot, hurriedly, immediately, instantly, pdq (*Sl.*), posthaste, promptly, pronto (*Inf.*), quick, rapidly, soon, speedily, swiftly, with all speed

Antonyms carefully, eventually, slowly, sluggishly, unhurriedly

quick-tempered choleric, excitable, fiery, hot-tempered, impatient, impulsive, irascible, irritable, petulant, quarrelsome, ratty (*Brit. & N.Z. inf.*), shrewish, splenetic, testy, tetchy, waspish

Antonyms cool, dispassionate, phlegmatic, placid, slow to anger, tolerant

quick-witted alert, astute, clever, keen, perceptive, sharp, shrewd, smart

Antonyms dull, obtuse, slow, slow-witted, stupid, thick (*Inf.*), unperceptive

quid pro quo compensation, equivalent, exchange, interchange, reprisal, retaliation, substitution, tit for tat

quiescent calm, dormant, in abeyance, inactive, latent, motionless, peaceful, placid, quiet, resting, serene, silent, smooth, still, tranquil, unagitated, undisturbed, unmoving, unruffled

quiet *adj.* **1.** dumb, hushed, inaudible, low, low-pitched, noiseless, peaceful, silent, soft, soundless **2.** calm, contented, gentle, mild, motionless, pacific, peaceful, placid, restful, serene, smooth, tranquil, untroubled **3.** isolated, private, retired, secluded, secret, sequestered, undisturbed, unfrequented **4.** conservative, modest, plain, restrained, simple, sober, subdued, unassuming, unobtrusive, unpretentious **5.** collected, docile, even-tempered, gentle, imperturbable, meek, mild, phlegmatic, reserved, retiring, sedate, shy, unexcitable ~*n.* **6.** calmness, ease, peace, quietness, repose, rest, serenity, silence, stillness, tranquillity

Antonyms *adj.* (*sense 1*) deafening, ear-splitting, high-decibel, high-volume, loud, noisy, stentorian (*sense 2*) agitated, alert, excitable, exciting, frenetic, troubled, turbulent, violent (*sense 3*) bustling, busy, crowded, exciting, fashionable, lively, popular, vibrant (*sense 4*) blatant, brash, bright, conspicuous, glaring, loud, obtrusive, ostentatious, pretentious, showy (*sense 5*) excitable, excited, high-spirited, impatient, loquacious, passionate, restless, talkative, verbose, violent ~*n.* (*sense 6*) activity, bustle, commotion, din, disturbance, noise, racket

quieten *v.* allay, alleviate, appease, assuage, blunt, calm, compose, deaden, dull,

hush, lull, mitigate, mollify, muffle, mute, palliate, quell, quiet, shush (*Inf.*), silence, soothe, stifle, still, stop, subdue, tranquillize
Antonyms aggravate, exacerbate, intensify, provoke, upset, worsen

quietly 1. confidentially, dumbly, in a low voice *or* whisper, in an undertone, inaudibly, in hushed tones, in silence, mutely, noiselessly, privately, secretly, silently, softly, without talking 2. calmly, contentedly, dispassionately, meekly, mildly, patiently, placidly, serenely, undemonstratively 3. coyly, demurely, diffidently, humbly, modestly, unassumingly, unobtrusively, unostentatiously, unpretentiously

quietness calm, calmness, hush, peace, placidity, quiescence, quiet, quietude, repose, rest, serenity, silence, still, stillness, tranquillity

quietus clincher (*Inf.*), *coup de grâce,* death, deathblow, demise, end, final blow, finish

quilt bedspread, comforter (*U.S.*), counterpane, coverlet, duvet, eiderdown

quintessence core, distillation, essence, extract, gist, heart, kernel, lifeblood, marrow, pith, soul, spirit

quip *n.* badinage, *bon mot,* counterattack, gibe, jest, joke, pleasantry, repartee, retort, riposte, sally, wisecrack (*Inf.*), witticism

quirk aberration, caprice, characteristic, eccentricity, fancy, fetish, foible, habit, *idée fixe,* idiosyncrasy, kink, mannerism, oddity, peculiarity, singularity, trait, vagary, whim

quirky capricious, curious, eccentric, fanciful, idiosyncratic, odd, offbeat, peculiar, rum (*Brit. sl.*), singular, unpredictable, unusual, whimsical

quisling betrayer, collaborator, fifth columnist, Judas, renegade, traitor, turncoat

quit *v.* 1. abandon, abdicate, decamp, depart, desert, exit, forsake, go, leave, pull out, relinquish, renounce, resign, retire, step down (*Inf.*), surrender, take off (*Inf.*), withdraw 2. abandon, cease, conclude, discontinue, drop, end, give up, halt, stop, suspend ~*adj.* 3. absolved, acquitted, clear, discharged, exculpated, exempt, exonerated, free, released, rid of
Antonyms (*sense 2*) complete, continue, finish, go on with, see through

quite 1. absolutely, completely, considerably, entirely, fully, in all respects, largely, perfectly, precisely, totally, wholly, without reservation 2. fairly, moderately, rather, reasonably, relatively, somewhat, to a certain extent, to some degree 3. in fact, in reality, in truth, really, truly

quiver 1. *v.* agitate, convulse, oscillate, palpitate, pulsate, quake, quaver, shake, shiver, shudder, tremble, vibrate 2. *n.* convulsion, oscillation, palpitation, pulsation, shake, shiver, shudder, spasm, throb, tic, tremble, tremor, vibration

quixotic absurd, chimerical, chivalrous, dreamy, fanciful, fantastical, idealistic, imaginary, impracticable, impractical, impulsive, mad, romantic, unrealistic, unworldly, Utopian, visionary, wild

quiz 1. *n.* examination, investigation, questioning, test 2. *v.* ask, catechize, examine, grill (*Inf.*), interrogate, investigate, pump (*Inf.*), question

quizzical arch, bantering, curious, derisive, inquiring, mocking, questioning, sardonic, supercilious, teasing

quondam bygone, earlier, ex-, foregoing, former, late, one-time, past, previous, retired, sometime

quota allocation, allowance, assignment, cut (*Inf.*), part, portion, proportion, ration, share, slice, whack (*Inf.*)

quotation 1. citation, cutting, excerpt, extract, passage, quote (*Inf.*), reference, selection 2. *Commerce* bid price, charge, cost, estimate, figure, price, quote (*Inf.*), rate, tender

quote adduce, attest, cite, detail, extract, instance, name, paraphrase, proclaim, recall, recite, recollect, refer to, repeat, retell

quotidian 1. daily, diurnal 2. common, commonplace, customary, everyday, habitual, ordinary, regular, routine

R

rabble 1. canaille, crowd, herd, horde, mob, swarm, throng 2. *Derogatory* canaille, commonalty, commoners, common people, crowd, dregs, hoi polloi, lower classes, lumpenproletariat, masses, peasantry, populace, proletariat, riffraff, scum, the great unwashed (*Inf. & derogatory*), trash (*Chiefly U.S. & Canad.*)
Antonyms (*sense 2*) aristocracy, bourgeoisie, elite, gentry, high society, nobility, upper classes

rabble-rouser agitator, demagogue, firebrand, incendiary, stirrer (*Inf.*), troublemaker

Rabelaisian bawdy, broad, coarse, earthy, extravagant, exuberant, gross, lusty, raunchy (*Sl.*), robust, satirical, uninhibited, unrestrained

rabid 1. hydrophobic, mad 2. berserk, crazed, frantic, frenzied, furious, infuriated, mad, maniacal, raging, violent, wild 3. bigoted, extreme, fanatical, fervent, intemperate, intolerant, irrational, narrow-minded, zealous
Antonyms (*sense 3*) half-hearted, moderate, wishy-washy (*Inf.*)

race[1] 1. *n.* chase, competition, contention, contest, dash, pursuit, rivalry 2. *v.* barrel (along) (*Inf., chiefly U.S. & Canad.*), burn rubber (*Inf.*), career, compete, contest, dart, dash, fly, gallop, hare (*Brit. inf.*), hasten, hurry, run, run like mad (*Inf.*), speed, tear, zoom

race[2] blood, breed, clan, ethnic group, family, folk, house, issue, kin, kindred, line, lineage, nation, offspring, people, progeny, seed (*Chiefly biblical*), stock, tribe, type

racial ethnic, ethnological, folk, genealogical, genetic, national, tribal

rack *n.* 1. frame, framework, stand, structure 2. affliction, agony, anguish, misery, pain, pang, persecution, suffering, torment, torture ~*v.* 3. afflict, agonize, crucify, distress, excruciate, harass, harrow, oppress, pain, torment, torture 4. force, pull, shake, strain, stress, stretch, tear, wrench

racket 1. babel, ballyhoo (*Inf.*), clamour, commotion, din, disturbance, fuss, hubbub, hullabaloo, noise, outcry, pandemonium, row, shouting, tumult, uproar 2. criminal activity, fraud, illegal enterprise, scheme 3. *Sl.* business, game (*Inf.*), line, occupation

rackety blaring, boisterous, clamorous, disorderly, noisy, rowdy, uproarious

racy 1. animated, buoyant, dramatic, energetic, entertaining, exciting, exhilarating, heady, lively, sexy (*Inf.*), sparkling, spirited, stimulating, vigorous, zestful 2. distinctive, piquant, pungent, rich, sharp, spicy, strong, tangy, tart, tasty 3. bawdy, blue, broad, immodest, indecent, indelicate, naughty, near the knuckle (*Inf.*), off colour, risqué, smutty, spicy (*Inf.*), suggestive

raddled broken-down, coarsened, dilapidated, dishevelled, haggard, run-down, tattered, the worse for wear, unkempt

radiance 1. brightness, brilliance, effulgence, glare, gleam, glitter, glow, incandescence, light, luminosity, lustre, resplendence, shine 2. delight, gaiety, happiness, joy, pleasure, rapture, warmth

radiant 1. beaming, bright, brilliant, effulgent, gleaming, glittering, glorious, glowing, incandescent, luminous, lustrous, resplendent, shining, sparkling, sunny 2. beaming, beatific, blissful, delighted, ecstatic, gay, glowing, happy, joyful, joyous, rapt, rapturous
Antonyms (*sense 1*) black, dark, dull, gloomy, sombre (*sense 2*) disconsolate, gloomy, joyless, miserable, sad, sombre, sorrowful

radiate 1. diffuse, disseminate, emanate, emit, give off *or* out, gleam, glitter, pour, scatter, send out, shed, shine, spread 2. branch out, diverge, issue, spread out

radiation emanation, emission, rays

radical *adj.* 1. basic, constitutional, deep-seated, essential, fundamental, innate, native, natural, organic, profound, thoroughgoing 2. complete, drastic, entire, excessive, extreme, extremist, fanatical, revolutionary, severe, sweeping, thorough, violent ~*n.* 3. extremist, fanatic, militant, revolutionary
Antonyms *adj.* insignificant, minor, superficial, token, trivial ~*n.* conservative, moderate, reactionary

raffish 1. bohemian, careless, casual, dashing, devil-may-care, disreputable, jaunty, rakish, sporty, unconventional 2. coarse, flash (*Inf.*), garish, gaudy, gross, loud, meretricious, showy, tasteless, tawdry, trashy, uncouth, vulgar

raffle draw, lottery, sweep, sweepstake

ragamuffin gamin, guttersnipe, scarecrow (*Inf.*), street arab, tatterdemalion (*Rare*), urchin

ragbag 1. confusion, hotchpotch, jumble, medley, miscellany, mixture, omnium-gatherum, potpourri 2. *Inf.* frump, scarecrow (*Inf.*), scruff (*Inf.*), slattern, sloven, slut, trollop

rage *n.* 1. agitation, anger, frenzy, fury, high dudgeon, ire, madness, mania, obsession, passion, rampage, raving, vehemence, violence, wrath 2. craze, enthusiasm, fad (*Inf.*), fashion, latest thing, mode, style, vogue ~*v.* 3. be beside oneself, be furious, blow a fuse (*Sl., chiefly U.S.*), blow one's top, blow up (*Inf.*), chafe, crack up (*Inf.*), fly off the handle (*Inf.*), foam at the mouth, fret, fume, go off the deep end (*Inf.*), go up the wall (*Sl.*), rant and rave, rave, see red (*Inf.*), seethe, storm, throw a fit (*Inf.*) 4. be at its height, be uncontrollable, rampage, storm, surge
Antonyms *n.* (*sense 1*) acceptance, calmness, equanimity, gladness, good humour, joy, pleasure, resignation ~*v.* (*sense 3*) accept, keep one's cool, remain unruffled, resign oneself to, stay calm

ragged 1. contemptible, down at heel, frayed, in holes, in rags, in tatters, mean, poor, rent, scraggy, shabby, shaggy, tattered, tatty, threadbare, torn, unkempt, worn-out 2. crude, jagged, notched, poor, rough, rugged, serrated, uneven, unfinished 3. broken, desultory, disorganized, fragmented, irregular, uneven
Antonyms (*sense 1*) fashionable, smart, well-dressed

raging beside oneself, boiling mad (*Inf.*), doing one's nut (*Brit. sl.*), enraged, fit to be tied (*Sl.*), fizzing (*Scot.*), foaming at the mouth, frenzied, fuming, furious, incensed, infuriated, mad, raving, seething

rags 1. castoffs, old clothes, tattered clothing, tatters 2. **in rags** down at heel, out at elbow, ragged, seedy, shabby, tattered
Antonyms finery, gladrags, Sunday best

raid 1. *n.* attack, break-in, descent, foray, hit-and-run attack, incursion, inroad, invasion, irruption, onset, sally, seizure, sortie, surprise attack 2. *v.* assault, attack, break into, descend on, fall upon, forage (*Military*), foray, invade, pillage, plunder, reive (*Dialect*), rifle, sack, sally forth, swoop down upon

raider attacker, forager (*Military*), invader, marauder, plunderer, reiver (*Dialect*), robber, thief

rail *v.* abuse, attack, blast, castigate, censure, complain, criticize, fulminate, inveigh, lambast(e), put down, revile, scold, tear into (*Inf.*), upbraid, vituperate, vociferate

railing balustrade, barrier, fence, paling, rails

raillery badinage, banter, chaff, irony, jesting, joke, joking, josh (*Sl., chiefly U.S. & Canad.*), kidding (*Inf.*), mockery, persiflage, pleasantry, repartee, ridicule, satire, sport, teasing

rain *n.* 1. cloudburst, deluge, downpour, drizzle, fall, precipitation, raindrops, rainfall, showers 2. deluge, flood, hail, shower, spate, stream, torrent, volley ~*v.* 3. bucket down (*Inf.*), come down in buckets (*Inf.*), drizzle, fall, pelt (down), pour, rain cats and dogs (*Inf.*), shower, teem 4. deposit, drop, fall, shower, sprinkle 5. bestow, lavish, pour, shower

rainy damp, drizzly, showery, wet
Antonyms arid, dry, fine, sunny

raise 1. build, construct, elevate, erect, exalt, heave, hoist, lift, move up, promote, put up, rear, set upright, uplift 2. advance, aggravate, amplify, augment, boost, enhance, enlarge, escalate, exaggerate, heighten, hike (up) (*Inf.*), increase, inflate, intensify, jack up, magnify, put up, reinforce, strengthen 3. advance, aggrandize, elevate, exalt, prefer, promote, upgrade 4. activate, arouse, awaken, cause, evoke, excite, foment, foster, incite, instigate, kindle, motivate, provoke, rouse, set on foot, stir up, summon up, whip up 5. bring about, cause, create, engender, give rise to, occasion, originate, produce, provoke, start 6. advance, bring up, broach, introduce, moot, put forward, suggest 7. assemble, collect, form, gather, get, levy, mass, mobilize, muster, obtain, rally, recruit 8. breed, bring up, cultivate, develop, grow, nurture, produce, propagate, rear 9. abandon, end, give up, lift, relieve, relinquish, remove, terminate
Antonyms begin, calm, cut, decrease, demolish, depress, destroy, diminish, drop, establish, lessen, let down, level, lower, quash, quell, reduce, ruin, sink, soothe, start, suppress, wreck

rake[1] *v.* 1. collect, gather, remove, scrape up 2. break up, harrow, hoe, scour, scrape, scratch 3. *With* **up** *or* **together** assemble, collect, dig up, dredge up, gather, scrape together 4. comb, examine, hunt, ransack, scan, scour, scrutinize, search 5. graze, scrape, scratch 6. enfilade, pepper, sweep

rake[2] *n.* debauchee, dissolute man, lech *or* letch (*Inf.*), lecher, libertine, playboy, profligate, rakehell (*Archaic*), roué, sensualist, voluptuary
Antonyms ascetic, celibate, monk, puritan

rakish[1] abandoned, debauched, depraved, dissipated, dissolute, immoral, lecherous, licentious, loose, prodigal, profligate, sinful, wanton

rakish[2] breezy, dapper, dashing, debonair, devil-may-care, flashy, jaunty, natty (*Inf.*), raffish, smart, snazzy (*Inf.*), sporty

rally[1] *v.* 1. bring *or* come to order, reassemble, re-form, regroup, reorganize, unite ~*n.* 2. regrouping, reorganization, reunion, stand ~*v.* 3. assemble, bond together, bring *or* come together, collect, convene, gather, get together, marshal, mobilize, muster, organize, round up, summon, unite ~*n.* 4. assembly, conference, congregation, congress, convention, convocation, gathering, mass meeting, meeting, muster ~*v.* 5. come round, get better, get one's second wind, improve, perk up, pick up, pull through, recover, recuperate, regain one's strength, revive, take a turn for the better ~*n.* 6. comeback (*Inf.*), improvement, recovery, recuperation, renewal, resurgence, revival, turn for the better
Antonyms *v.* (*sense 3*) disband, disperse, separate, split up (*sense 5*) deteriorate, fail, get worse, relapse, take a turn for the worse, worsen ~*n.* (*sense 6*) collapse, deterioration, relapse, turn for the worse

rally[2] chaff, make fun of, mock, poke fun at, ridicule, send up (*Brit. inf.*), take the mickey out of (*Inf.*), taunt, tease, twit

ram *v.* 1. butt, collide with, crash, dash, drive, force, hit, impact, run into, slam, smash, strike 2. beat, cram, crowd, drum, force, hammer, jam, pack, pound, stuff, tamp, thrust

ramble *v.* 1. amble, drift, perambulate, peregrinate, range, roam, rove, saunter, straggle, stravaig (*Scot. & northern English dialect*), stray, stroll, traipse (*Inf.*), walk, wander 2. meander, snake, twist and turn, wind, zigzag 3. babble, chatter, digress, expatiate, maunder, rabbit (on) (*Brit. inf.*), rattle on, run off at the mouth (*Sl.*), waffle (*Inf., chiefly Brit.*), wander, witter on (*Inf.*) ~*n.* 4. excursion, hike, perambulation, peregrination, roaming, roving, saunter, stroll, tour, traipse (*Inf.*), trip, walk

rambler drifter, hiker, roamer, rover, stroller, walker, wanderer, wayfarer

rambling 1. circuitous, desultory, diffuse, digressive, disconnected, discursive, disjointed, incoherent, irregular, long-winded, periphrastic, prolix, wordy 2. irregular, sprawling, spreading, straggling, trailing
Antonyms (*sense 1*) coherent, concise, direct, to the point

ramification 1. branch, development, divarication, division, excrescence, extension, forking, offshoot, outgrowth, subdivision 2. complication, consequence, development, result, sequel, upshot

ramify 1. branch, divaricate, divide, fork, separate, split up 2. become complicated, multiply, thicken

ramp grade, gradient, incline, inclined plane, rise, slope

rampage *v.* 1. go ape (*Sl.*), go apeshit (*Sl.*), go berserk, rage, run amuck, run riot, run wild, storm, tear ~*n.* 2. destruction, frenzy, fury, rage, storm, tempest, tumult, uproar, violence 3. **on the rampage** amuck, berserk, destructive, out of control, raging, rampant, riotous, violent, wild

rampant 1. aggressive, dominant, excessive, flagrant, on the rampage, out of control, out of hand, outrageous, raging, rampaging, riotous, unbridled, uncontrollable, ungovernable, unrestrained, vehement, violent, wanton, wild 2. epidemic, exuberant, luxuriant, prevalent, profuse, rank, rife, spreading like wildfire, unchecked, uncontrolled, unrestrained, widespread 3. *Heraldry* erect, rearing, standing, upright

rampart barricade, bastion, breastwork, bulwark, defence, earthwork, embankment, fence, fort, fortification, guard, parapet, security, stronghold, wall

ramshackle broken-down, crumbling, decrepit, derelict, dilapidated, flimsy, jerry-built, rickety, shaky, tottering, tumbledown, unsafe, unsteady
Antonyms solid, stable, steady, well-built

rancid bad, fetid, foul, frowsty, fusty, musty, off, putrid, rank, rotten, sour, stale, strong-smelling, tainted
Antonyms fresh, pure, undecayed

rancorous acrimonious, bitter, hostile, implacable, malevolent, malicious, malign, malignant, resentful, spiteful, splenetic, venomous, vindictive, virulent

rancour animosity, animus, antipathy, bad blood, bitterness, enmity, grudge, hate, hatred, hostility, ill feeling, ill will, malevolence, malice, malignity, resentfulness, resentment, spite, spleen, venom

random 1. accidental, adventitious, aimless, arbitrary, casual, chance, desultory, fortuitous, haphazard, hit or miss, incidental, indiscriminate, purposeless, spot, stray, unplanned, unpremeditated 2. **at random** accidentally, adventitiously, aimlessly, arbitrarily, by chance, casually,

haphazardly, indiscriminately, irregularly, purposelessly, randomly, unsystematically, willy-nilly
Antonyms definite, deliberate, intended, planned, premeditated, specific

randy amorous, aroused, concupiscent, horny (*Sl.*), hot, lascivious, lecherous, lustful, raunchy (*Sl.*), satyric, sexually excited, sexy (*Inf.*), turned-on (*Sl.*)

range *n.* 1. ambit, amplitude, area, bounds, compass, confines, distance, domain, extent, field, latitude, limits, orbit, pale, parameters (*Inf.*), province, purview, radius, reach, scope, span, sphere, sweep 2. chain, file, line, rank, row, sequence, series, string, tier 3. assortment, class, collection, gamut, kind, lot, order, selection, series, sort, variety ~*v.* 4. align, arrange, array, dispose, draw up, line up, order 5. arrange, bracket, catalogue, categorize, class, classify, file, grade, group, pigeonhole, rank 6. aim, align, direct, level, point, train 7. cruise, explore, ramble, roam, rove, straggle, stray, stroll, sweep, traverse, wander 8. extend, fluctuate, go, reach, run, stretch, vary between

rangy gangling, lanky, leggy, long-legged, long-limbed

rank[1] *n.* 1. caste, class, classification, degree, dignity, division, echelon, grade, level, nobility, order, position, quality, sort, standing, station, status, stratum, type 2. column, file, formation, group, line, range, row, series, tier ~*v.* 3. align, arrange, array, class, classify, dispose, grade, line up, locate, marshal, order, position, range, sort

rank[2] 1. abundant, dense, exuberant, flourishing, lush, luxuriant, productive, profuse, strong-growing, vigorous 2. bad, disagreeable, disgusting, fetid, foul, fusty, gamy, mephitic, musty, noisome, noxious, off, offensive, olid, pungent, putrid, rancid, revolting, stale, stinking, strong-smelling, yucky *or* yukky (*Sl.*) 3. absolute, arrant, blatant, complete, downright, egregious, excessive, extravagant, flagrant, glaring, gross, rampant, sheer, thorough, total, undisguised, unmitigated, utter 4. abusive, atrocious, coarse, crass, filthy, foul, gross, indecent, nasty, obscene, outrageous, scurrilous, shocking, vulgar

rank and file 1. lower ranks, men, other ranks, private soldiers, soldiers, troops 2. body, general public, Joe (and Eileen) Public (*Sl.*), Joe Six-Pack (*U.S. sl.*), majority, mass, masses

rankle anger, annoy, chafe, embitter, fester, gall, get one's goat (*Sl.*), get on one's nerves (*Inf.*), irk, irritate, piss one off (*Taboo sl.*), rile

ransack 1. comb, explore, go through, rake, rummage, scour, search, turn inside out 2. despoil, gut, loot, pillage, plunder, raid, ravage, rifle, sack, strip

ransom *n.* 1. deliverance, liberation, redemption, release, rescue 2. money, payment, payoff, price ~*v.* 3. buy (someone) out (*Inf.*), buy the freedom of, deliver, liberate, obtain *or* pay for the release of, redeem, release, rescue, set free

rant 1. *v.* bellow, bluster, cry, declaim, rave, roar, shout, spout (*Inf.*), vociferate, yell 2. *n.* bluster, bombast, diatribe, fanfaronade (*Rare*), harangue, philippic, rhetoric, tirade, vociferation

rap *v.* 1. crack, hit, knock, strike, tap 2. bark, speak abruptly, spit 3. *Sl., chiefly U.S.* chat, confabulate, converse, discourse, talk 4. blast, carpet (*Inf.*), castigate, censure, chew out (*U.S. & Canad. inf.*), criticize, give a rocket (*Brit. & N.Z. inf.*), knock (*Inf.*), lambast(e), pan (*Inf.*), read the riot act, reprimand, scold, tick off (*Inf.*) ~*n.* 5. blow, clout (*Inf.*), crack, knock, tap 6. *Sl., chiefly U.S.* chat, colloquy, confabulation, conversation, dialogue, discourse, discussion, talk 7. *Sl.* blame, censure, chiding, punishment, rebuke, responsibility, sentence

rapacious avaricious, extortionate, grasping, greedy, insatiable, marauding, plundering, predatory, preying, ravenous, usurious, voracious, wolfish

rapacity avarice, avidity, cupidity, graspingness, greed, greediness, insatiableness, predatoriness, rapaciousness, ravenousness, usury, voraciousness, voracity, wolfishness

rape *n.* 1. outrage, ravishment, sexual assault, violation 2. depredation, despoilment, despoliation, pillage, plundering, rapine, sack, spoliation 3. abuse, defilement, desecration, maltreatment, perversion, violation ~*v.* 4. outrage, ravish, sexually assault, violate 5. despoil, loot, pillage, plunder, ransack, sack, spoliate

rapid brisk, expeditious, express, fast, fleet, flying, hasty, hurried, pdq (*Sl.*), precipitate, prompt, quick, quickie (*Inf.*), speedy, swift
Antonyms deliberate, gradual, leisurely, slow, tardy, unhurried

rapidity alacrity, briskness, celerity, dispatch, expedition, fleetness, haste, hurry, precipitateness, promptitude, promptness, quickness, rush, speed, speediness, swiftness, velocity

rapidly apace, at speed, briskly, expeditiously, fast, hastily, hotfoot, hurriedly, in a hurry, in a rush, in haste, like a shot, pdq (*Sl.*), posthaste, precipitately, promptly, pronto (*Inf.*), quickly, speedily, swiftly, with dispatch

rapine depredation, despoilment, despoliation, looting, marauding, pillage, plunder, ransacking, rape, robbery, sack, seizure, spoliation, theft

rapport affinity, bond, empathy, harmony, interrelationship, link, relationship, sympathy, tie, understanding

rapprochement détente, reconcilement, reconciliation, restoration of harmony, reunion, softening
Antonyms antagonism, dissension, exacerbation, falling-out, quarrel, resumption of hostilities, schism

rapscallion blackguard, black sheep, cad, disgrace, good-for-nothing, knave (*Archaic*), ne'er-do-well, rascal, rogue, scally (*Northwest English dialect*), scallywag (*Inf.*), scamp, scoundrel, wastrel

rapt 1. absorbed, carried away, engrossed, enthralled, entranced, fascinated, gripped, held, intent, preoccupied, spellbound 2. bewitched, blissful, captivated, charmed, delighted, ecstatic, enchanted, enraptured, rapturous, ravished, transported
Antonyms bored, detached, left cold, unaffected, uninterested, uninvolved, unmoved

rapture beatitude, bliss, cloud nine (*Inf.*), delectation, delight, ecstasy, enthusiasm, euphoria, exaltation, felicity, happiness, joy, ravishment, rhapsody, seventh heaven, spell, transport

rapturous blissful, delighted, ecstatic, enthusiastic, euphoric, exalted, happy, in seventh heaven, joyful, joyous, on cloud nine (*Inf.*), overjoyed, over the moon (*Inf.*), rapt, ravished, rhapsodic, transported

rare[1] 1. exceptional, few, infrequent, out of the ordinary, recherché, scarce, singular, sparse, sporadic, strange, thin on the ground, uncommon, unusual 2. admirable, choice, excellent, exquisite, extreme, fine, great, incomparable, peerless, superb, superlative 3. invaluable, precious, priceless, rich
Antonyms abundant, bountiful, common, frequent, habitual, manifold, many, plentiful, profuse, regular

rare[2] bloody, half-cooked, half-raw, undercooked, underdone

rarefied 1. elevated, exalted, high, lofty, noble, spiritual, sublime 2. clannish, cliquish, esoteric, exclusive, occult, private, select

rarefy attenuate, clarify, purify, refine, sublimate, subtilize, thin out

rarely 1. almost never, hardly, hardly ever, infrequently, little, once in a blue moon, once in a while, only now and then, on rare occasions, scarcely ever, seldom 2. exceptionally, extraordinarily, finely, notably, remarkably, singularly, uncommonly, unusually
Antonyms commonly, frequently, often, regularly, usually

raring athirst, avid, champing at the bit (*Inf.*), desperate, eager, enthusiastic, impatient, keen, longing, ready, willing, yearning

rarity 1. curio, curiosity, find, gem, one-off, pearl, treasure 2. infrequency, scarcity, shortage, singularity, sparseness, strangeness, uncommonness, unusualness 3. choiceness, excellence, exquisiteness, fineness, incomparability, incomparableness, peerlessness, quality, superbness 4. invaluableness, preciousness, pricelessness, richness, value, worth

rascal blackguard, caitiff (*Archaic*), devil, disgrace, good-for-nothing, imp, knave (*Archaic*), miscreant, ne'er-do-well, pickle (*Brit. inf.*), rake, rapscallion, reprobate, rogue, scally (*Northwest English dialect*), scallywag (*Inf.*), scamp, scoundrel, varmint (*Inf.*), villain, wastrel, wretch

rascally bad, base, crooked, dishonest, disreputable, evil, good-for-nothing, low, mean, reprobate, scoundrelly, unscrupulous, vicious, villainous, wicked

rash[1] adventurous, audacious, brash, careless, foolhardy, harebrained, harum-scarum, hasty, headlong, headstrong, heedless, helter-skelter, hot-headed, ill-advised, ill-considered, impetuous, imprudent, impulsive, incautious, indiscreet, injudicious, madcap, precipitate, premature, reckless, thoughtless, unguarded, unthinking, unwary, venturesome
Antonyms canny, careful, cautious, considered, premeditated, prudent, well thought out

rash[2] 1. eruption, outbreak 2. epidemic, flood, outbreak, plague, series, spate, succession, wave

rashness adventurousness, audacity, brashness, carelessness, foolhardiness, hastiness, heedlessness, indiscretion, precipitation, recklessness, temerity, thoughtlessness

rasp *n.* 1. grating, grinding, scrape, scratch ~*v.* 2. abrade, excoriate, file, grind, rub, sand, scour, scrape 3. grate (upon), irk, irritate, jar (upon), rub (someone) up the wrong way, set one's teeth on edge, wear upon

rasping *or* **raspy** creaking, croaking, croaky, grating, gravelly, gruff, harsh, hoarse, husky, jarring, rough, scratchy

rate[1] *n.* 1. degree, percentage, proportion, ratio, relation, scale, standard 2. charge, cost, dues, duty, fee, figure, hire, price, tariff, tax, toll 3. gait, measure, pace, speed, tempo, time, velocity 4. class, classification, degree, grade, position, quality, rank, rating, status, value, worth 5. **at any rate** anyhow, anyway, at all events, in any case, nevertheless ~*v.* 6. adjudge, appraise, assess, class, classify, consider, count, esteem, estimate, evaluate, grade, measure, rank, reckon, regard, value, weigh 7. be entitled to, be worthy of, deserve, merit 8. *Sl.* admire, esteem, respect, think highly of, value

rate[2] bawl out (*Inf.*), berate, blame, carpet (*Inf.*), castigate, censure, chew out (*U.S. & Canad. inf.*), chide, criticize severely, give a rocket (*Brit. & N.Z. inf.*), haul over the coals (*Inf.*), read the riot act, rebuke, reprimand, reprove, roast (*Inf.*), scold, take to task, tear into (*Inf.*), tear (someone) off a strip (*Inf.*), tell off (*Inf.*), tongue-lash, upbraid

rather 1. a bit, a little, fairly, kind of (*Inf.*), moderately, pretty (*Inf.*), quite, relatively, slightly, somewhat, sort of (*Inf.*), to some degree, to some extent 2. a good bit, noticeably, significantly, very 3. instead, more readily, more willingly, preferably, sooner

ratify affirm, approve, authenticate, authorize, bear out, bind, certify, confirm, consent to, corroborate, endorse, establish, sanction, sign, uphold, validate
Antonyms abrogate, annul, cancel, reject, repeal, repudiate, revoke

rating[1] class, classification, degree, designation, estimate, evaluation, grade, order, placing, position, rank, rate, standing, status

rating[2] chiding, dressing down (*Inf.*), lecture, piece of one's mind, rebuke, reprimand, reproof, roasting (*Inf.*), row (*Inf.*), scolding, telling-off (*Inf.*), ticking-off (*Inf.*), tongue-lashing, wigging (*Brit. sl.*)

ratio arrangement, correlation, correspondence, equation, fraction, percentage, proportion, rate, relation, relationship

ration *n.* 1. allotment, allowance, dole, helping, measure, part, portion, provision, quota, share 2. *Plural* commons (*Brit.*), food, provender, provisions, stores, supplies ~*v.* 3. *With* **out** allocate, allot, apportion, deal, distribute, dole, give out, issue, measure out, mete, parcel out 4. budget, conserve, control, limit, restrict, save

rational 1. enlightened, intelligent, judicious, logical, lucid, realistic, reasonable, sagacious, sane, sensible, sound, wise 2. cerebral, cognitive, ratiocinative, reasoning, thinking 3. all there (*Inf.*), balanced, *compos mentis*, in one's right mind, lucid, normal, of sound mind, sane
Antonyms insane, irrational, unreasonable, unsound

rationale exposition, grounds, logic, motivation, philosophy, principle, *raison d'être*, reasons, theory

rationalize 1. account for, excuse, explain away, extenuate, justify, make allowance for, make excuses for, vindicate 2. apply logic to, elucidate, reason out, resolve, think through 3. make cuts, make more efficient, streamline, trim

rattle *v.* 1. bang, clatter, jangle 2. bounce, jar, jiggle, jolt, jounce, shake, vibrate 3. *With* **on** blether, cackle, chatter, gabble, gibber, jabber, prate, prattle, rabbit (on) (*Brit. inf.*), run on, witter (*Inf.*), yak (away) (*Sl.*) 4. *Inf.* discomfit, discompose, disconcert, discountenance, disturb, faze, frighten, perturb, put (someone) off his stride, put (someone) out of countenance, scare, shake, upset 5. *With* **off** list, recite, reel off, rehearse, run through, spiel off (*Inf.*)

ratty angry, annoyed, crabbed, cross, impatient, irritable, short-tempered, snappy, testy, tetchy, touchy

raucous grating, harsh, hoarse, husky, loud, noisy, rasping, rough, strident
Antonyms dulcet, mellifluous, quiet, smooth, sweet

ravage 1. *v.* demolish, desolate, despoil, destroy, devastate, gut, lay waste, leave in ruins, loot, pillage, plunder, ransack, raze, ruin, sack, shatter, spoil, wreak havoc on, wreck 2. *n. Often plural* damage, demolition, depredation, desolation, destruction, devastation, havoc, pillage, plunder, rapine, ruin, ruination, spoliation, waste

rave *v.* 1. babble, be delirious, fume, go mad (*Inf.*), rage, rant, roar, run amuck, splutter, storm, talk wildly, thunder 2. *With* **about** *Inf.* be delighted by, be mad about (*Inf.*), be wild about (*Inf.*), cry up, enthuse, gush, praise, rhapsodize ~*n.* 3. *Inf.* acclaim, applause, encomium, praise 4. *Also* **rave-up** *Brit. sl.* affair, bash (*Inf.*), beano (*Brit. sl.*), blow-out (*Sl.*), celebration, do (*Inf.*), party 5. *Brit. sl.* craze, fad, fashion, vogue ~*adj.* 6. *Inf.* ecstatic, enthusiastic, excellent, favourable, laudatory

ravenous 1. famished, starved, starving, very hungry 2. avaricious, covetous, devouring, ferocious, gluttonous, grasping, greedy, insatiable, insatiate, predatory, rapacious, ravening, voracious, wolfish
Antonyms full, glutted, sated, satiated

ravine canyon, clough (*Dialect*), defile,

flume, gap (*U.S.*), gorge, gulch (*U.S.*), gully, linn (*Scot.*), pass

raving berserk, crazed, crazy, delirious, frantic, frenzied, furious, hysterical, insane, irrational, mad, out of one's mind, rabid, raging, wild

ravish 1. captivate, charm, delight, enchant, enrapture, entrance, fascinate, overjoy, spellbind, transport 2. abuse, outrage, rape, sexually assault, violate

ravishing beautiful, bewitching, charming, dazzling, delightful, drop-dead (*Sl.*), enchanting, entrancing, gorgeous, lovely, radiant, stunning (*Inf.*)

raw 1. bloody (*of meat*), fresh, natural, uncooked, undressed, unprepared 2. basic, coarse, crude, green, natural, organic, rough, unfinished, unprocessed, unrefined, unripe, untreated 3. abraded, chafed, grazed, open, scratched, sensitive, skinned, sore, tender 4. callow, green, ignorant, immature, inexperienced, new, undisciplined, unpractised, unseasoned, unskilled, untrained, untried 5. bare, blunt, brutal, candid, frank, naked, plain, realistic, unembellished, unvarnished 6. biting, bitter, bleak, chill, chilly, cold, damp, freezing, harsh, parky (*Brit. inf.*), piercing, unpleasant, wet

Antonyms (*sense 1*) baked, cooked, done (*sense 2*) finished, prepared, refined (*sense 4*) experienced, practised, professional, skilled, trained (*sense 5*) embellished, gilded

ray 1. bar, beam, flash, gleam, shaft 2. flicker, glimmer, hint, indication, scintilla, spark, trace

raze 1. bulldoze, demolish, destroy, flatten, knock down, level, pull down, remove, ruin, tear down, throw down 2. delete, efface, erase, excise, expunge, extinguish, extirpate, obliterate, rub out, scratch out, strike out, wipe out

re about, anent (*Scot.*), apropos, concerning, in respect of, on the subject of, regarding, respecting, with reference to, with regard to

reach *v.* 1. arrive at, attain, get as far as, get to, land at, make 2. contact, extend to, get (a) hold of, go as far as, grasp, stretch to, touch 3. amount to, arrive at, attain, climb to, come to, drop, fall, move, rise, sink 4. *Inf.* hand, hold out, pass, stretch 5. communicate with, contact, establish contact with, find, get, get hold of, get in touch with, get through to, make contact with ~*n.* 6. ambit, capacity, command, compass, distance, extension, extent, grasp, influence, jurisdiction, mastery, power, range, scope, spread, stretch, sweep

react 1. acknowledge, answer, reply, respond 2. act, behave, conduct oneself, function, operate, proceed, work

reaction 1. acknowledgment, answer, feedback, reply, response 2. compensation, counteraction, counterbalance, counterpoise, recoil 3. conservatism, counter-revolution, obscurantism, the right

reactionary 1. *adj.* blimpish, conservative, counter-revolutionary, obscurantist, rightist 2. *n.* Colonel Blimp, conservative, counter-revolutionary, die-hard, obscurantist, rightist, right-winger

Antonyms (*senses 1 & 2*) leftist, progressive, radical, reformist, revolutionary, socialist

read 1. glance at, look at, peruse, pore over, refer to, run one's eye over, scan, study 2. announce, declaim, deliver, recite, speak, utter 3. comprehend, construe, decipher, discover, interpret, perceive the meaning of, see, understand 4. display, indicate, record, register, show

readable 1. clear, comprehensible, decipherable, intelligible, legible, plain, understandable 2. easy to read, enjoyable, entertaining, enthralling, gripping, interesting, pleasant, worth reading

Antonyms (*sense 1*) illegible, incomprehensible, indecipherable, unintelligible, unreadable (*sense 2*) badly-written, boring, dull, heavy, heavy going, pretentious, turgid, unreadable

readily 1. cheerfully, eagerly, freely, gladly, lief (*Rare*), promptly, quickly, voluntarily, willingly, with good grace, with pleasure 2. at once, easily, effortlessly, hotfoot, in no time, pdq (*Sl.*), quickly, right away, smoothly, speedily, straight away, unhesitatingly, without delay, without demur, without difficulty, without hesitation

Antonyms hesitatingly, reluctantly, slowly, unwillingly, with difficulty

readiness 1. fitness, maturity, preparation, preparedness, ripeness 2. aptness, eagerness, gameness (*Inf.*), inclination, keenness, willingness 3. adroitness, dexterity, ease, facility, handiness, promptitude, promptness, quickness, rapidity, skill 4. in **readiness** all set, at *or* on hand, at the ready, fit, prepared, primed, ready, set, waiting, waiting in the wings

reading 1. examination, inspection, perusal, review, scrutiny, study 2. homily, lecture, lesson, performance, recital, rendering, rendition, sermon 3. conception, construction, grasp, impression, interpretation, treatment, understanding, version 4. book-learning, edification, education, erudition, knowledge, learning, scholarship

ready *adj.* 1. all set, arranged, completed,

fit, in readiness, organized, prepared, primed, ripe, set 2. agreeable, apt, dis~posed, eager, game (*Inf.*), glad, happy, have-a-go (*Inf.*), inclined, keen, minded, predisposed, prone, willing 3. acute, adroit, alert, apt, astute, bright, clever, deft, dex~terous, expert, handy, intelligent, keen, perceptive, prompt, quick, quick-witted, rapid, resourceful, sharp, skilful, smart 4. about, close, in danger of, liable, likely, on the brink of, on the point of, on the verge of 5. accessible, at *or* on hand, at one's finger~tips, at the ready, available, close to hand, convenient, handy, near, on call, on tap (*Inf.*), present ~*n.* 6. **at the ready** in readi~ness, poised, prepared, ready for action, waiting ~*v.* 7. arrange, equip, fit out, get ready, make ready, order, organize, prepare, set

Antonyms *adj.* disinclined, distant, hesi~tant, immature, inaccessible, inexpert, late, loath, reluctant, slow, unavailable, un~equipped, unfit, unhandy, unprepared, un~willing

real absolute, actual, authentic, bona fide, certain, essential, existent, factual, genu~ine, heartfelt, honest, intrinsic, legitimate, positive, right, rightful, sincere, true, unaf~fected, unfeigned, valid, veritable

Antonyms affected, counterfeit, fake, faked, false, feigned, imaginary, imitation, insincere

realistic 1. businesslike, common-sense, down-to-earth, hard-headed, level-headed, matter-of-fact, practical, pragmatic, ra~tional, real, sensible, sober, unromantic, unsentimental 2. authentic, faithful, genu~ine, graphic, lifelike, natural, naturalistic, representational, true, true to life, truthful

Antonyms fanciful, idealistic, impractical, unrealistic

reality 1. actuality, authenticity, certainty, corporeality, fact, genuineness, materiality, realism, truth, validity, verisimilitude, ver~ity 2. **in reality** actually, as a matter of fact, in actuality, in fact, in point of fact, in truth, really

realization 1. appreciation, apprehension, awareness, cognizance, comprehension, conception, consciousness, grasp, imagina~tion, perception, recognition, understand~ing 2. accomplishment, achievement, carrying-out, completion, consummation, effectuation, fulfilment

realize 1. appreciate, apprehend, be cogni~zant of, become aware of, become conscious of, catch on (*Inf.*), comprehend, conceive, grasp, imagine, recognize, take in, twig (*Brit. inf.*), understand 2. accomplish, ac~tualize, bring about, bring off, bring to fruition, carry out *or* through, complete, consummate, do, effect, effectuate, fulfil, incarnate, make concrete, make happen, perform, reify 3. acquire, bring *or* take in, clear, earn, gain, get, go for, make, net, obtain, produce, sell for

really absolutely, actually, assuredly, cat~egorically, certainly, genuinely, in actual~ity, indeed, in fact, in reality, positively, surely, truly, undoubtedly, verily, without a doubt

realm 1. country, domain, dominion, em~pire, kingdom, land, monarchy, principal~ity, province, state 2. area, branch, depart~ment, field, orbit, patch, province, region, sphere, territory, turf (*U.S. sl.*), world, zone

reap acquire, bring in, collect, cut, derive, gain, garner, gather, get, harvest, obtain, win

rear[1] 1. *n.* back, back end, end, rearguard, stern, tail, tail end 2. *adj.* aft, after (*Nauti~cal*), back, following, hind, hindmost, last, trailing

Antonyms *n.* bow, forward end, front, nose, stem, vanguard ~*adj.* foremost, for~ward, front, leading

rear[2] *v.* 1. breed, bring up, care for, culti~vate, educate, foster, grow, nurse, nurture, raise, train 2. elevate, hoist, hold up, lift, raise, set upright 3. build, construct, erect, fabricate, put up 4. loom, rise, soar, tower

reason *n.* 1. apprehension, brains, compre~hension, intellect, judgment, logic, mental~ity, mind, ratiocination, rationality, rea~soning, sanity, sense(s), sound mind, soundness, understanding 2. aim, basis, cause, design, end, goal, grounds, impetus, incentive, inducement, intention, motive, object, occasion, purpose, target, warrant, why and wherefore (*Inf.*) 3. apologia, apol~ogy, argument, case, defence, excuse, ex~planation, exposition, ground, justification, rationale, vindication 4. bounds, limits, moderation, propriety, reasonableness, sense, sensibleness, wisdom 5. **in** *or* **within reason** in moderation, proper, reasonable, sensible, warrantable, within bounds, within limits ~*v.* 6. conclude, deduce, draw conclusions, infer, make out, ratiocinate, resolve, solve, syllogize, think, work out 7. *With* **with** argue, bring round (*Inf.*), de~bate, dispute, dissuade, expostulate, move, persuade, prevail upon, remonstrate, show (someone) the error of his ways, talk into *or* out of, urge, win over

Antonyms (*sense 1*) emotion, feeling, in~stinct, sentiment

reasonable 1. advisable, arguable, believ~able, credible, intelligent, judicious, justi~fiable, logical, plausible, practical, rational,

reasoned, sane, sensible, sober, sound, tenable, well-advised, well thought-out, wise 2. acceptable, average, equitable, fair, fit, honest, inexpensive, just, moderate, modest, O.K. *or* okay (*Inf.*), proper, right, tolerable, within reason
Antonyms impossible, irrational, unfair, unintelligent, unreasonable, unsound

reasoned clear, judicious, logical, sensible, systematic, well expressed, well presented, well thought-out

reasoning 1. analysis, cogitation, deduction, logic, ratiocination, reason, thinking, thought 2. argument, case, exposition, hypothesis, interpretation, proof, train of thought

reassure bolster, buoy up, cheer up, comfort, encourage, hearten, inspirit, put *or* set one's mind at rest, relieve (someone) of anxiety, restore confidence to

rebate allowance, bonus, deduction, discount, reduction, refund

rebel *v.* 1. man the barricades, mutiny, resist, revolt, rise up, take to the streets, take up arms 2. come out against, defy, disobey, dissent, refuse to obey 3. flinch, recoil, show repugnance, shrink, shy away *~n.* 4. insurgent, insurrectionary, mutineer, resistance fighter, revolutionary, revolutionist, secessionist 5. apostate, dissenter, heretic, nonconformist, schismatic *~adj.* 6. insubordinate, insurgent, insurrectionary, mutinous, rebellious, revolutionary

rebellion 1. insurgence, insurgency, insurrection, mutiny, resistance, revolt, revolution, rising, uprising 2. apostasy, defiance, disobedience, dissent, heresy, insubordination, nonconformity, schism

rebellious 1. contumacious, defiant, disaffected, disloyal, disobedient, disorderly, insubordinate, insurgent, insurrectionary, intractable, mutinous, rebel, recalcitrant, revolutionary, seditious, turbulent, ungovernable, unruly 2. difficult, incorrigible, obstinate, recalcitrant, refractory, resistant, unmanageable
Antonyms dutiful, loyal, obedient, patriotic, subordinate, subservient

rebirth new beginning, regeneration, reincarnation, renaissance, renascence, renewal, restoration, resurgence, resurrection, revitalization, revival

rebound *v.* 1. bounce, recoil, resound, return, ricochet, spring back 2. backfire, boomerang, misfire, recoil *~n.* 3. bounce, comeback, kickback, repercussion, return, ricochet

rebuff 1. *v.* brush off (*Sl.*), check, cold-shoulder, cut, decline, deny, discourage, put off, refuse, reject, repulse, resist, slight, snub, spurn, turn down 2. *n.* brushoff (*Sl.*), check, cold shoulder, defeat, denial, discouragement, knock-back (*Sl.*), opposition, refusal, rejection, repulse, slight, snub, the (old) heave-ho (*Inf.*), thumbs down
Antonyms *v.* encourage, lead on (*Inf.*), submit to, welcome *~n.* come-on (*Inf.*), encouragement, thumbs up, welcome

rebuke 1. *v.* admonish, bawl out (*Inf.*), berate, blame, carpet (*Inf.*), castigate, censure, chew out (*U.S. & Canad. inf.*), chide, dress down (*Inf.*), give a rocket (*Brit. & N.Z. inf.*), haul (someone) over the coals (*Inf.*), lecture, read the riot act, reprehend, reprimand, reproach, reprove, scold, take to task, tear into (*Inf.*), tear (someone) off a strip (*Inf.*), tell off (*Inf.*), tick off (*Inf.*), upbraid 2. *n.* admonition, blame, castigation, censure, dressing down (*Inf.*), lecture, reprimand, reproach, reproof, reproval, row, telling-off (*Inf.*), ticking-off (*Inf.*), tongue-lashing, wigging (*Brit. sl.*)
Antonyms *v.* applaud, approve, commend, compliment, congratulate, laud, praise *~n.* commendation, compliment, laudation, praise

rebut confute, defeat, disprove, invalidate, negate, overturn, prove wrong, quash, refute

rebuttal confutation, defeat, disproof, invalidation, negation, refutation

recalcitrant contrary, contumacious, defiant, disobedient, insubordinate, intractable, obstinate, refractory, stubborn, uncontrollable, ungovernable, unmanageable, unruly, unwilling, wayward, wilful
Antonyms amenable, compliant, docile, obedient, submissive

recall *v.* 1. bring *or* call to mind, call *or* summon up, evoke, look *or* think back to, mind (*Dialect*), recollect, remember, reminisce about 2. abjure, annul, call back, call in, cancel, countermand, nullify, repeal, rescind, retract, revoke, take back, withdraw *~n.* 3. annulment, cancellation, nullification, recision, repeal, rescindment, rescission, retraction, revocation, withdrawal 4. memory, recollection, remembrance

recant abjure, apostatize, deny, disavow, disclaim, disown, forswear, recall, renege, renounce, repudiate, retract, revoke, take back, unsay, withdraw
Antonyms insist, maintain, profess, reaffirm, reiterate, repeat, restate, uphold

recapitulate epitomize, go over again, outline, recap (*Inf.*), recount, reiterate, repeat, restate, review, run over, run through again, summarize, sum up

recede 1. abate, draw back, ebb, fall back, go back, regress, retire, retreat, retrocede, retrogress, return, subside, withdraw 2. decline, diminish, dwindle, fade, lessen, shrink, sink, wane

receipt 1. acknowledgment, counterfoil, proof of purchase, sales slip, stub, voucher 2. acceptance, delivery, receiving, reception, recipience 3. *Plural* gains, gate, income, proceeds, profits, return, takings

receive 1. accept, accept delivery of, acquire, be given, be in receipt of, collect, derive, get, obtain, pick up, take 2. apprehend, be informed of, be told, gather, hear, perceive 3. bear, be subjected to, encounter, experience, go through, meet with, suffer, sustain, undergo 4. accommodate, admit, be at home to, entertain, greet, meet, take in, welcome

recent contemporary, current, fresh, happening (*Inf.*), late, latter, latter-day, modern, new, novel, present-day, up-to-date, young

Antonyms ancient, antique, earlier, early, former, historical, old

recently currently, freshly, lately, latterly, newly, not long ago, of late

receptacle container, holder, repository

reception 1. acceptance, admission, receipt, receiving, recipience 2. acknowledgment, greeting, reaction, recognition, response, treatment, welcome 3. do (*Inf.*), entertainment, function, levee, party, soirée

receptive 1. alert, bright, perceptive, quick on the uptake (*Inf.*), responsive, sensitive 2. accessible, amenable, approachable, favourable, friendly, hospitable, interested, open, open-minded, open to suggestions, susceptible, sympathetic, welcoming

Antonyms biased, narrow-minded, prejudiced, unreceptive, unresponsive

recess 1. alcove, bay, cavity, corner, depression, hollow, indentation, niche, nook, oriel 2. *Plural* bowels, depths, heart, innards (*Inf.*), innermost parts, penetralia, reaches, retreats, secret places 3. break, cessation of business, closure, holiday, intermission, interval, respite, rest, vacation

recession decline, depression, downturn, drop, slump

Antonyms boom, upturn

recherché arcane, choice, esoteric, exotic, far-fetched, rare, refined

recipe 1. directions, ingredients, instructions, receipt (*Obsolete*) 2. formula, method, modus operandi, prescription, procedure, process, programme, technique

reciprocal alternate, complementary, correlative, corresponding, equivalent, exchanged, give-and-take, interchangeable, interdependent, mutual, reciprocative, reciprocatory

Antonyms one-way, unilateral, unreciprocated

reciprocate 1. barter, exchange, feel in return, interchange, reply, requite, respond, return, return the compliment, swap, trade 2. be equivalent, correspond, equal, match

recital account, description, detailing, enumeration, narration, narrative, performance, reading, recapitulation, recitation, rehearsal, relation, rendering, repetition, statement, story, tale, telling

recitation lecture, narration, passage, performance, piece, reading, recital, rendering, telling

recite declaim, deliver, describe, detail, do one's party piece (*Inf.*), enumerate, itemize, narrate, perform, recapitulate, recount, rehearse, relate, repeat, speak, tell

reckless careless, daredevil, devil-may-care, foolhardy, harebrained, harum-scarum, hasty, headlong, heedless, ill-advised, imprudent, inattentive, incautious, indiscreet, irresponsible, madcap, mindless, negligent, overventuresome, precipitate, rash, regardless, thoughtless, wild

Antonyms careful, cautious, heedful, mindful, observant, responsible, thoughtful, wary

reckon 1. add up, calculate, compute, count, enumerate, figure, number, tally, total 2. account, appraise, consider, count, deem, esteem, estimate, evaluate, gauge, hold, judge, look upon, rate, regard, think of 3. assume, believe, be of the opinion, conjecture, expect, fancy, guess (*Inf., chiefly U.S. & Canad.*), imagine, suppose, surmise, think 4. *With* **with** cope, deal, face, handle, settle accounts, treat 5. *With* **with** anticipate, bargain for, bear in mind, be prepared for, expect, foresee, plan for, take cognizance of, take into account 6. *With* **on** *or* **upon** bank, calculate, count, depend, hope for, rely, take for granted, trust in 7. **to be reckoned with** consequential, considerable, important, influential, powerful, significant, strong, weighty

reckoning 1. adding, addition, calculation, computation, count, counting, estimate, summation, working 2. account, bill, charge, due, score, settlement 3. doom, judgment, last judgment, retribution

reclaim get *or* take back, recapture, recover, redeem, reform, regain, regenerate, reinstate, rescue, restore, retrieve, salvage

recline be recumbent, lay (something) down, lean, lie (down), loll, lounge, repose, rest, sprawl, stretch out

Antonyms get up, rise, sit up, stand, stand up, stand upright

recluse anchoress, anchorite, ascetic, eremite, hermit, monk, solitary

reclusive ascetic, cloistered, eremitic, hermitic, hermit-like, isolated, monastic, recluse, retiring, secluded, sequestered, solitary, withdrawn

Antonyms gregarious, sociable

recognition 1. detection, discovery, identification, recall, recollection, remembrance 2. acceptance, acknowledgment, admission, allowance, appreciation, avowal, awareness, cognizance, concession, confession, notice, perception, realization, respect, understanding 3. acknowledgment, appreciation, approval, gratitude, greeting, honour, salute

recognize 1. identify, know, know again, make out, notice, place, recall, recollect, remember, spot 2. accept, acknowledge, admit, allow, appreciate, avow, be aware of, concede, confess, grant, own, perceive, realize, respect, see, understand 3. acknowledge, appreciate, approve, greet, honour, salute

Antonyms (*sense 2*) be unaware of, forget, ignore, overlook

recoil *v.* 1. jerk back, kick, react, rebound, resile, spring back 2. balk at, draw back, falter, flinch, quail, shrink, shy away 3. backfire, boomerang, go wrong, misfire, rebound *~n.* 4. backlash, kick, reaction, rebound, repercussion

recollect call to mind, mind (*Dialect*), place, recall, remember, reminisce, summon up

recollection impression, memory, mental image, recall, remembrance, reminiscence

recommend 1. advance, advise, advocate, counsel, enjoin, exhort, prescribe, propose, put forward, suggest, urge 2. approve, commend, endorse, praise, put in a good word for, speak well of, vouch for 3. make attractive (acceptable, appealing, interesting)

Antonyms argue against, disapprove of, reject, veto

recommendation 1. advice, counsel, proposal, suggestion, urging 2. advocacy, approbation, approval, blessing, commendation, endorsement, favourable mention, good word, plug (*Inf.*), praise, reference, sanction, testimonial

recompense *v.* 1. pay, remunerate, reward 2. compensate, indemnify, make amends for, make good, make restitution for, make up for, pay for, redress, reimburse, repay, requite, satisfy *~n.* 3. amends, compensation, damages, emolument, indemnification, indemnity, meed (*Archaic*), pay, payment, remuneration, reparation, repayment, requital, restitution, return, reward, satisfaction, wages

reconcilable 1. compatible, congruous, consistent 2. appeasable, conciliatory, forgiving, peaceable, placable

reconcile 1. accept, accommodate, get used, make the best of, put up with (*Inf.*), resign, submit, yield 2. appease, bring to terms, conciliate, make peace between, pacify, placate, propitiate, re-establish friendly relations between, restore harmony between, reunite 3. adjust, compose, harmonize, patch up, put to rights, rectify, resolve, settle, square

reconciliation 1. appeasement, conciliation, détente, pacification, propitiation, *rapprochement,* reconcilement, reunion, understanding 2. accommodation, adjustment, compromise, harmony, rectification, settlement

Antonyms alienation, antagonism, break-up, estrangement, falling-out, separation

recondite abstruse, arcane, cabbalistic, concealed, dark, deep, difficult, esoteric, hidden, involved, mysterious, mystical, obscure, occult, profound, secret

Antonyms exoteric, simple, straightforward

recondition do up (*Inf.*), fix up (*Inf., chiefly U.S. & Canad.*), overhaul, remodel, renew, renovate, repair, restore, revamp

reconnaissance exploration, inspection, investigation, observation, patrol, recce (*Sl.*), reconnoitring, scan, scouting, scrutiny, survey

reconnoitre case (*Sl.*), explore, get the lie of the land, inspect, investigate, make a reconnaissance (of), observe, patrol, recce (*Sl.*), scan, scout, scrutinize, see how the land lies, spy out, survey

reconsider change one's mind, have second thoughts, reassess, re-evaluate, re-examine, rethink, review, revise, take another look at, think again, think better of, think over, think twice

reconstruct 1. reassemble, rebuild, recreate, re-establish, reform, regenerate, remake, remodel, renovate, reorganize, restore 2. build up, build up a picture of, deduce, piece together

record *n.* 1. account, annals, archives, chronicle, diary, document, entry, file, journal, log, memoir, memorandum, memorial, minute, register, report 2. documentation, evidence, memorial, remembrance, testimony, trace, witness 3. background, career, curriculum vitae, history, performance, track record (*Inf.*) 4. album, black disc, disc, EP, forty-five, gramophone record, LP, platter (*U.S. sl.*), recording, release, seventy-eight, single, vinyl 5. **off the record** confidential, confidentially, in confidence, in private, not for publication, private, sub rosa, under the rose, unofficial, unofficially ~*v.* 6. chalk up (*Inf.*), chronicle, document, enrol, enter, inscribe, log, minute, note, preserve, put down, put on file, put on record, register, report, set down, take down, transcribe, write down 7. contain, give evidence of, indicate, read, register, say, show 8. cut, lay down (*Sl.*), make a recording of, put on wax (*Inf.*), tape, tape-record, video, video-tape, wax (*Inf.*)

recorder annalist, archivist, chronicler, clerk, diarist, historian, registrar, scorekeeper, scorer, scribe

recording cut (*Inf.*), disc, gramophone record, record, tape, video

recount delineate, depict, describe, detail, enumerate, give an account of, narrate, portray, recite, rehearse, relate, repeat, report, tell, tell the story of

recoup 1. make good, recover, redeem, regain, retrieve, win back 2. compensate, make redress for, make up for, refund, reimburse, remunerate, repay, requite, satisfy

recourse alternative, appeal, choice, expedient, option, refuge, remedy, resort, resource, way out

recover 1. find again, get back, make good, recapture, reclaim, recoup, redeem, regain, repair, repossess, restore, retake, retrieve, take back, win back 2. bounce back, come round, convalesce, feel oneself again, get back on one's feet, get better, get well, heal, improve, mend, pick up, pull through, rally, recuperate, regain one's health *or* strength, revive, take a turn for the better

Antonyms (*sense 1*) abandon, forfeit, lose (*sense 2*) deteriorate, go downhill, relapse, take a turn for the worse, weaken, worsen

recovery 1. convalescence, healing, improvement, mending, rally, recuperation, return to health, revival, turn for the better 2. amelioration, betterment, improvement, rally, rehabilitation, restoration, revival, upturn 3. recapture, reclamation, redemption, repair, repossession, restoration, retrieval

recreation amusement, distraction, diversion, enjoyment, entertainment, exercise, fun, hobby, leisure activity, pastime, play, pleasure, refreshment, relaxation, relief, sport

recrimination bickering, counterattack, countercharge, mutual accusation, name-calling, quarrel, retaliation, retort, squabbling

recruit *v.* 1. draft, enlist, enrol, impress, levy, mobilize, muster, raise, strengthen 2. engage, enrol, gather, obtain, procure, proselytize, round up, take on, win (over) 3. augment, build up, refresh, reinforce, renew, replenish, restore, strengthen, supply ~*n.* 4. apprentice, beginner, convert, greenhorn (*Inf.*), helper, initiate, learner, neophyte, novice, proselyte, rookie (*Inf.*), trainee, tyro

Antonyms (*sense 1*) dismiss, fire, lay off, make redundant, sack (*Inf.*)

rectify 1. adjust, amend, correct, emend, fix, improve, make good, mend, put right, redress, reform, remedy, repair, right, square 2. *Chem.* distil, purify, refine, separate

rectitude 1. correctness, decency, equity, goodness, honesty, honour, incorruptibility, integrity, justice, morality, principle, probity, righteousness, scrupulousness, uprightness, virtue 2. accuracy, correctness, exactness, justice, precision, rightness, soundness, verity

Antonyms (*sense 1*) baseness, corruption, dishonesty, dishonour, immorality, scandalousness

recumbent flat, flat on one's back, horizontal, leaning, lying, lying down, prone, prostrate, reclining, resting, stretched out, supine

recuperate convalesce, get back on one's feet, get better, improve, mend, pick up, recover, regain one's health

recur 1. come again, come and go, come back, happen again, persist, reappear, repeat, return, revert 2. be remembered, come back, haunt one's thoughts, return to mind, run through one's mind

recurrent continued, cyclical, frequent, habitual, periodic, recurring, regular, repeated, repetitive

Antonyms isolated, one-off

recycle reclaim, reprocess, reuse, salvage, save

red *adj.* 1. cardinal, carmine, cherry, coral, crimson, gules (*Heraldry*), maroon, pink, rose, ruby, scarlet, vermeil, vermilion, wine 2. bay, carroty, chestnut, flame-coloured, flaming, foxy, reddish, sandy, titian 3. blushing, embarrassed, florid, flushed, rubicund, shamefaced, suffused 4. blooming, glowing, healthy, roseate, rosy, ruddy 5. bloodshot, inflamed, red-rimmed 6. bloodstained, bloody, ensanguined (*Literary*), gory, sanguine ~*n.* 7. colour, redness 8. **in the red** *Inf.* bankrupt, in arrears, in debit, in debt, in deficit, insolvent, on the rocks, overdrawn, owing money, showing a loss 9. **see red** *Inf.* be *or* get very angry, be beside oneself with rage (*Inf.*), become enraged, blow a fuse (*Sl., chiefly U.S.*), blow one's top, boil, crack up (*Inf.*), fly off the handle (*Inf.*), go mad (*Inf.*), go off one's head (*Sl.*), go off the deep end (*Inf.*), go up the wall (*Sl.*), lose one's rag (*Sl.*), lose one's temper, seethe

red-blooded hearty, lusty, manly, robust, strong, vigorous, virile, vital

redden blush, colour (up), crimson, flush, go red, suffuse

redeem 1. buy back, reclaim, recover, recover possession of, regain, repossess, repurchase, retrieve, win back 2. cash (in), change, exchange, trade in 3. abide by, acquit, adhere to, be faithful to, carry out, discharge, fulfil, hold to, keep, keep faith with, make good, meet, perform, satisfy 4. absolve, rehabilitate, reinstate, restore to favour 5. atone for, compensate for, defray, make amends for, make good, make up for, offset, outweigh, redress, save 6. buy the freedom of, deliver, emancipate, extricate, free, liberate, pay the ransom of, ransom, rescue, save, set free

redemption 1. reclamation, recovery, repossession, repurchase, retrieval 2. discharge, exchange, fulfilment, performance, quid pro quo, trade-in 3. amends, atonement, compensation, expiation, reparation 4. deliverance, emancipation, liberation, ransom, release, rescue, salvation

red-handed bang to rights (*Sl.*), (in) flagrante delicto, in the act, with one's fingers *or* hand in the till (*Inf.*), with one's pants down (*U.S. sl.*)

redolent 1. aromatic, fragrant, odorous, perfumed, scented, sweet-smelling 2. evocative, remindful, reminiscent, suggestive

redoubtable awful, doughty, dreadful, fearful, fearsome, formidable, mighty, powerful, resolute, strong, terrible, valiant

redound 1. conduce, contribute, effect, lead to, militate for, tend 2. accrue, come back, ensue, rebound, recoil, reflect, result

redress *v.* 1. compensate for, make amends (reparation, restitution) for, make up for, pay for, put right, recompense for 2. adjust, amend, balance, correct, ease, even up, mend, put right, rectify, reform, regulate, relieve, remedy, repair, restore the balance, square ~*n.* 3. aid, assistance, correction, cure, ease, help, justice, rectification, relief, remedy, satisfaction 4. amends, atonement, compensation, payment, quittance, recompense, reparation, requital, restitution

reduce 1. abate, abridge, contract, curtail, cut down, debase, decrease, depress, dilute, diminish, impair, lessen, lower, moderate, shorten, slow down, tone down, truncate, turn down, weaken, wind down 2. bankrupt, break, impoverish, pauperize, ruin 3. bring, bring to the point of, conquer, drive, force, master, overpower, subdue, vanquish 4. be *or* go on a diet, diet, lose weight, shed weight, slenderize (*Chiefly U.S.*), slim, trim 5. bring down the price of, cheapen, cut, discount, lower, mark down, slash 6. break, bring low, degrade, demote, downgrade, humble, humiliate, lower in rank, lower the status of, take down a peg (*Inf.*)

Antonyms augment, defend, elevate, enhance, enlarge, exalt, extend, heighten, increase, promote

redundant 1. *de trop,* excessive, extra, inessential, inordinate, supererogatory, superfluous, supernumerary, surplus, unnecessary, unwanted 2. diffuse, padded, periphrastic, pleonastic, prolix, repetitious, tautological, verbose, wordy

Antonyms essential, necessary, needed, vital

reek *v.* 1. hum (*Sl.*), pong (*Brit. inf.*), smell, smell to high heaven, stink 2. be characterized by, be permeated by, be redolent of 3. *Dialect* fume, give off smoke *or* fumes, smoke, steam ~*n.* 4. effluvium, fetor, mephitis, niff (*Brit. sl.*), odour, pong (*Brit. inf.*), smell, stench, stink 5. *Dialect* exhalation, fumes, smoke, steam, vapour

reel 1. falter, lurch, pitch, rock, roll, stagger, stumble, sway, totter, waver, wobble 2. go round and round, revolve, spin, swim, swirl, twirl, whirl

refer 1. advert, allude, bring up, cite, hint, invoke, make mention of, make reference, mention, speak of, touch on 2. direct, guide, point, recommend, send 3. apply, consult, go, have recourse to, look up, seek information from, turn to 4. apply, be directed to, belong, be relevant to, concern, pertain, relate 5. accredit, ascribe, assign, attribute, credit, impute, put down to 6. commit, consign, deliver, hand over, pass on, submit, transfer, turn over

referee 1. *n.* adjudicator, arbiter, arbitrator, judge, ref (*Inf.*), umpire 2. *v.* adjudicate, arbitrate, judge, mediate, umpire

reference 1. allusion, citation, mention, note, quotation, remark 2. applicability, bearing, concern, connection, consideration, regard, relation, respect 3. certification, character, credentials, endorsement, good word, recommendation, testimonial

referendum plebiscite, popular vote, public vote

refine 1. clarify, cleanse, distil, filter, process, purify, rarefy 2. civilize, cultivate, elevate, hone, improve, perfect, polish, temper

refined 1. civil, civilized, courtly, cultivated, cultured, elegant, genteel, gentlemanly, gracious, ladylike, polished, polite, sophisticated, urbane, well-bred, well-mannered 2. cultured, delicate, discerning, discriminating, exact, fastidious, fine, nice, precise, punctilious, sensitive, sublime, subtle 3. clarified, clean, distilled, filtered, processed, pure, purified

Antonyms boorish, coarse, common, ill-bred, impure, inelegant, uncultured, ungentlemanly, unladylike, unmannerly, unrefined

refinement 1. clarification, cleansing, distillation, filtering, processing, purification, rarefaction, rectification 2. fine point, fine tuning, nicety, nuance, subtlety 3. breeding, civility, civilization, courtesy, courtliness, cultivation, culture, delicacy, discrimination, elegance, fastidiousness, fineness, finesse, finish, gentility, good breeding, good manners, grace, graciousness, polish, politeness, politesse, precision, sophistication, style, taste, urbanity

reflect 1. echo, give back, imitate, mirror, reproduce, return, throw back 2. bear out, bespeak, communicate, demonstrate, display, evince, exhibit, express, indicate, manifest, reveal, show 3. cogitate, consider, contemplate, deliberate, meditate, mull over, muse, ponder, ruminate, think, wonder

reflection 1. counterpart, echo, image, mirror image 2. cerebration, cogitation, consideration, contemplation, deliberation, idea, impression, meditation, musing, observation, opinion, perusal, pondering, rumination, study, thinking, thought, view 3. aspersion, censure, criticism, derogation, imputation, reproach, slur

reflective cogitating, contemplative, deliberative, meditative, pensive, pondering, reasoning, ruminative, thoughtful

reform *v.* 1. ameliorate, amend, better, correct, emend, improve, mend, rebuild, reclaim, reconstitute, reconstruct, rectify, regenerate, rehabilitate, remodel, renovate, reorganize, repair, restore, revolutionize 2. clean up one's act (*Inf.*), get back on the straight and narrow (*Inf.*), get it together (*Inf.*), get one's act together (*Inf.*), go straight (*Inf.*), mend one's ways, pull one's socks up (*Brit. inf.*), shape up (*Inf.*), turn over a new leaf ~*n.* 3. amelioration, amendment, betterment, correction, improvement, rectification, rehabilitation, renovation

refractory cantankerous, contentious, contumacious, difficult, disobedient, disputatious, headstrong, intractable, mulish, obstinate, perverse, recalcitrant, stiff-necked, stubborn, uncontrollable, uncooperative, unmanageable, unruly, wilful

refrain[1] *v.* abstain, avoid, cease, desist, do without, eschew, forbear, give up, kick (*Inf.*), leave off, renounce, stop

refrain[2] *n.* burden, chorus, melody, song, tune

refresh 1. brace, breathe new life into, cheer, cool, enliven, freshen, inspirit, reanimate, reinvigorate, rejuvenate, revitalize, revive, revivify, stimulate 2. brush up (*Inf.*), jog, prod, prompt, renew, stimulate 3. renew, renovate, repair, replenish, restore, top up

refreshing bracing, cooling, different, fresh, inspiriting, invigorating, new, novel, original, revivifying, stimulating, thirst-quenching

Antonyms enervating, exhausting, soporific, tiring, wearisome

refreshment 1. enlivenment, freshening, reanimation, renewal, renovation, repair, restoration, revival, stimulation 2. *Plural* drinks, food and drink, snacks, titbits

refrigerate chill, cool, freeze, keep cold

refuge asylum, bolt hole, harbour, haven, hide-out, protection, resort, retreat, sanctuary, security, shelter

refugee displaced person, émigré, escapee, exile, fugitive, runaway

refulgent bright, brilliant, gleaming, irradiant, lambent, lustrous, radiant, resplendent, shining

refund 1. *v.* give back, make good, pay back, reimburse, repay, restore, return 2. *n.* reimbursement, repayment, return

refurbish clean up, do up (*Inf.*), fix up (*Inf., chiefly U.S. & Canad.*), mend, overhaul, re-equip, refit, remodel, renovate, repair, restore, revamp, set to rights, spruce up

refusal 1. defiance, denial, knockback (*Sl.*), negation, no, rebuff, rejection, repudiation, thumbs down 2. choice, consideration, opportunity, option

refuse[1] *v.* abstain, decline, deny, reject, repel, repudiate, say no, spurn, turn down, withhold

Antonyms accept, agree, allow, approve, consent, give, permit

refuse[2] *n.* dreck (*Sl., chiefly U.S.*), dregs, dross, garbage, junk (*Inf.*), leavings, lees, litter, offscourings, rubbish, scum, sediment, sweepings, trash, waste

refute confute, counter, discredit, disprove, give the lie to, negate, overthrow, prove false, rebut, silence

Antonyms confirm, prove, substantiate

regain 1. get back, recapture, recoup, recover, redeem, repossess, retake, retrieve, take back, win back 2. get back to, reach again, reattain, return to

regal fit for a king *or* queen, kingly, magnificent, majestic, noble, princely, proud, queenly, royal, sovereign

regale amuse, delight, divert, entertain, feast, gratify, ply, refresh, serve

regard *v.* 1. behold, check, check out (*Inf.*), clock (*Brit. sl.*), eye, eyeball (*U.S. sl.*), gaze at, get a load of (*Inf.*), look closely at, mark, notice, observe, remark, scrutinize, take a dekko at (*Brit. sl.*), view, watch 2. account, adjudge, believe, consider, deem, esteem, estimate, hold, imagine, judge, look upon, rate, see, suppose, think, treat, value, view 3. apply to, be relevant to, concern, have a bearing on, have to do with, interest, pertain to, relate to 4. attend, heed, listen to, mind, note, pay attention to, respect, take into consideration, take notice of ~*n.* 5. attention, heed, interest, mind, notice 6. account, affection, attachment, care, concern, consideration, deference, esteem, honour, love, note, reputation, repute, respect, store, sympathy, thought 7. aspect, detail, feature, item, matter, particular, point, respect 8. gaze, glance, look, scrutiny, stare 9. bearing, concern, connection, reference, relation, relevance 10. *Plural* best wishes, compliments, devoirs, good wishes, greetings, respects, salutations

regardful attentive, aware, careful, considerate, dutiful, heedful, mindful, observant, respectful, thoughtful, watchful

regarding about, apropos, as regards, as to, concerning, in *or* with regard to, in re, in respect of, in the matter of, on the subject of, re, respecting, with reference to

regardless 1. *adj.* disregarding, heedless, inattentive, inconsiderate, indifferent, neglectful, negligent, rash, reckless, remiss, unconcerned, unmindful 2. *adv.* anyway, come what may, despite everything, for all that, in any case, in spite of everything, nevertheless, no matter what, nonetheless
Antonyms *adj.* heedful, mindful, regardful

regenerate breathe new life into, change, inspirit, invigorate, reawaken, reconstruct, re-establish, reinvigorate, rejuvenate, renew, renovate, reproduce, restore, revive, revivify, uplift
Antonyms become moribund, decline, degenerate, stagnate, stultify

regime administration, establishment, government, leadership, management, reign, rule, system

regiment *v.* bully, control, discipline, order, organize, regulate, systematize

region 1. area, country, district, division, expanse, land, locality, part, patch, place, province, quarter, section, sector, territory, tract, turf (*U.S. sl.*), zone 2. domain, field, province, realm, sphere, world 3. area, locality, neighbourhood, range, scope, vicinity

regional district, local, parochial, provincial, sectional, zonal

register *n.* 1. annals, archives, catalogue, chronicle, diary, file, ledger, list, log, memorandum, record, roll, roster, schedule ~*v.* 2. catalogue, check in, chronicle, enlist, enrol, enter, inscribe, list, note, record, set down, sign on *or* up, take down 3. be shown, bespeak, betray, display, exhibit, express, indicate, manifest, mark, read, record, reflect, reveal, say, show 4. *Inf.* come home, dawn on, get through, have an effect, impress, make an impression, sink in, tell

regress backslide, degenerate, deteriorate, ebb, fall away *or* off, fall back, go back, lapse, lose ground, recede, relapse, retreat, retrocede, retrogress, return, revert, wane
Antonyms advance, improve, progress, wax

regret 1. *v.* bemoan, be upset, bewail, deplore, feel remorse for, feel sorry for, grieve, lament, miss, mourn, repent, rue, weep over 2. *n.* bitterness, compunction, contrition, disappointment, grief, lamentation, pang of conscience, penitence, remorse, repentance, ruefulness, self-reproach, sorrow
Antonyms *v.* be happy, be satisfied, feel satisfaction, rejoice ~*n.* callousness, contentment, impenitence, lack of compassion, pleasure, satisfaction

regretful apologetic, ashamed, contrite, disappointed, mournful, penitent, remorseful, repentant, rueful, sad, sorrowful, sorry

regrettable deplorable, disappointing, distressing, ill-advised, lamentable, pitiable, sad, shameful, unfortunate, unhappy, woeful, wrong

regular 1. common, commonplace, customary, daily, everyday, habitual, normal, ordinary, routine, typical, unvarying, usual 2. consistent, constant, established, even, fixed, ordered, periodic, rhythmic, set, stated, steady, systematic, uniform 3. dependable, efficient, formal, methodical, orderly, standardized, steady, systematic 4. balanced, even, flat, level, smooth, straight, symmetrical, uniform 5. approved, bona fide, classic, correct, established, formal, official, orthodox, prevailing, proper, sanctioned, standard, time-honoured, traditional
Antonyms abnormal, disorderly, erratic,

exceptional, inconsistent, inconstant, infrequent, irregular, occasional, rare, uncommon, unconventional, uneven, unmethodical, unusual, varied

regulate adjust, administer, arrange, balance, conduct, control, direct, fit, govern, guide, handle, manage, moderate, modulate, monitor, order, organize, oversee, rule, run, settle, superintend, supervise, systematize, tune

regulation *n.* 1. adjustment, administration, arrangement, control, direction, governance, government, management, modulation, supervision, tuning 2. commandment, decree, dictate, direction, edict, law, order, ordinance, precept, procedure, requirement, rule, standing order, statute *~adj.* 3. customary, mandatory, normal, official, prescribed, required, standard, usual

regurgitate barf (*U.S. sl.*), chuck (up) (*Sl., chiefly U.S.*), chunder (*Sl., chiefly Aust.*), disgorge, puke (*Sl.*), sick up (*Inf.*), spew (out *or* up), throw up (*Inf.*), vomit

rehabilitate 1. adjust, redeem, reform, reintegrate, save 2. clear, convert, fix up (*Inf., chiefly U.S. & Canad.*), make good, mend, rebuild, recondition, reconstitute, reconstruct, re-establish, reinstate, reinvigorate, renew, renovate, restore

rehash 1. *v.* alter, change, make over, rearrange, refashion, rejig (*Inf.*), reshuffle, reuse, rework, rewrite 2. *n.* new version, rearrangement, reworking, rewrite

rehearsal 1. drill, going-over (*Inf.*), practice, practice session, preparation, reading, rehearsing, run-through 2. account, catalogue, description, enumeration, list, narration, recital, recounting, relation, telling

rehearse 1. act, drill, go over, practise, prepare, ready, recite, repeat, run through, study, train, try out 2. delineate, depict, describe, detail, enumerate, go over, list, narrate, recite, recount, relate, review, run through, spell out, tell, trot out (*Inf.*)

reign *n.* 1. ascendancy, command, control, dominion, empire, hegemony, influence, monarchy, power, rule, sovereignty, supremacy, sway *~v.* 2. administer, be in power, command, govern, hold sway, influence, occupy *or* sit on the throne, rule, wear the crown, wield the sceptre 3. be rampant, be rife, be supreme, hold sway, obtain, predominate, prevail

reimburse compensate, indemnify, pay back, recompense, refund, remunerate, repay, restore, return, square up

rein *n.* 1. brake, bridle, check, control, curb, harness, hold, restraint, restriction 2. **give (a) free rein (to)** free, give a blank cheque (to), give a free hand, give carte blanche, give (someone) his head, give way to, indulge, let go, remove restraints *~v.* 3. bridle, check, control, curb, halt, hold, hold back, limit, restrain, restrict, slow down

reincarnation metempsychosis, rebirth, transmigration of souls

reinforce augment, bolster, buttress, emphasize, fortify, harden, increase, prop, shore up, stiffen, strengthen, stress, supplement, support, toughen, underline

Antonyms contradict, undermine, weaken

reinforcement 1. addition, amplification, augmentation, enlargement, fortification, increase, strengthening, supplement 2. brace, buttress, prop, shore, stay, support 3. *Plural* additional *or* fresh troops, auxiliaries, reserves, support

reinstate bring back, recall, re-establish, rehabilitate, replace, restore, return

reiterate do again, iterate, recapitulate, repeat, restate, retell, say again

reject 1. *v.* bin, cast aside, decline, deny, despise, disallow, discard, eliminate, exclude, jettison, jilt, rebuff, refuse, renounce, repel, repudiate, repulse, say no to, scrap, spurn, throw away *or* out, turn down, veto 2. *n.* castoff, discard, failure, flotsam, second

Antonyms *v.* accept, agree, allow, approve, permit, receive, select *~n.* prize, treasure

rejection brushoff (*Sl.*), denial, dismissal, elimination, exclusion, knock-back (*Sl.*), rebuff, refusal, renunciation, repudiation, the (old) heave-ho (*Inf.*), thumbs down, veto

Antonyms acceptance, affirmation, approval, selection

rejoice be glad (happy, overjoyed), celebrate, delight, exult, glory, joy, jump for joy, make merry, revel, triumph

Antonyms be sad (unhappy, upset), grieve, lament, mourn

rejoicing celebration, cheer, delight, elation, exultation, festivity, gaiety, gladness, happiness, joy, jubilation, merrymaking, revelry, triumph

rejoin answer, come back with, reply, respond, retort, return, riposte

rejoinder answer, comeback (*Inf.*), counter, counterattack, reply, response, retort, riposte

rejuvenate breathe new life into, give new life to, make young again, reanimate, refresh, regenerate, reinvigorate, renew, restore, restore vitality to, revitalize, revivify

relapse *v.* 1. backslide, degenerate, fail, fall back, lapse, regress, retrogress, revert, slip back, weaken 2. deteriorate, fade, fail, sicken, sink, weaken, worsen *~n.* 3. backsliding, fall from grace, lapse, recidivism, regression, retrogression, reversion 4. deterioration, recurrence, setback, turn for the worse, weakening, worsening

Antonyms *v.* (*sense 2*) get better, improve, rally, recover ~*n.* (*sense 4*) improvement, rally, recovery, turn for the better

relate 1. chronicle, describe, detail, give an account of, impart, narrate, present, recite, recount, rehearse, report, set forth, tell 2. ally, associate, connect, coordinate, correlate, couple, join, link 3. appertain, apply, bear upon, be relevant to, concern, have reference to, have to do with, pertain, refer

Antonyms (*sense 2*) detach, disconnect, dissociate, divorce (*sense 3*) be irrelevant to, be unconnected, have nothing to do with

related 1. accompanying, affiliated, agnate, akin, allied, associated, cognate, concomitant, connected, correlated, interconnected, joint, linked 2. agnate, akin, cognate, consanguineous, kin, kindred

Antonyms separate, unconnected, unrelated

relation 1. affiliation, affinity, consanguinity, kindred, kinship, propinquity, relationship 2. kin, kinsman, kinswoman, relative 3. application, bearing, bond, comparison, connection, correlation, interdependence, link, pertinence, reference, regard, similarity, tie-in 4. account, description, narration, narrative, recital, recountal, report, story, tale

relations 1. affairs, associations, communications, connections, contact, dealings, interaction, intercourse, liaison, meetings, rapport, relationship, terms 2. clan, family, kin, kindred, kinsfolk, kinsmen, relatives, tribe

relationship affair, affinity, association, bond, communications, conjunction, connection, correlation, exchange, kinship, liaison, link, parallel, proportion, rapport, ratio, similarity, tie-up

relative *adj.* 1. allied, associated, comparative, connected, contingent, corresponding, dependent, proportionate, reciprocal, related, respective 2. applicable, apposite, appropriate, appurtenant, apropos, germane, pertinent, relevant 3. *With* **to** corresponding to, in proportion to, proportional to ~*n.* 4. connection, kinsman, kinswoman, member of one's *or* the family, relation

relatively comparatively, in *or* by comparison, rather, somewhat, to some extent

relax 1. abate, diminish, ease, ebb, lessen, let up, loosen, lower, mitigate, moderate, reduce, relieve, slacken, weaken 2. be *or* feel at ease, calm, chill out (*Sl., chiefly U.S.*), laze, let oneself go (*Inf.*), let one's hair down (*Inf.*), lighten up (*Sl.*), loosen up, put one's feet up, rest, soften, take it easy, take one's ease, tranquillize, unbend, unwind

Antonyms alarm, alert, heighten, increase, intensify, tense, tighten, work

relaxation 1. amusement, enjoyment, entertainment, fun, leisure, pleasure, recreation, refreshment, rest 2. abatement, diminution, easing, lessening, let-up (*Inf.*), moderation, reduction, slackening, weakening

relay *n.* 1. relief, shift, turn 2. communication, dispatch, message, transmission ~*v.* 3. broadcast, carry, communicate, hand on, pass on, send, spread, transmit

release *v.* 1. deliver, discharge, disengage, drop, emancipate, extricate, free, let go, let out, liberate, loose, manumit, set free, turn loose, unbridle, unchain, undo, unfasten, unfetter, unloose, unshackle, untie 2. absolve, acquit, dispense, excuse, exempt, exonerate, let go, let off 3. break, circulate, disseminate, distribute, issue, launch, make known, make public, present, publish, put out, unveil ~*n.* 4. acquittal, deliverance, delivery, discharge, emancipation, freedom, liberation, liberty, manumission, relief 5. absolution, acquittance, dispensation, exemption, exoneration, let-off (*Inf.*) 6. announcement, issue, offering, proclamation, publication

Antonyms *v.* detain, engage, fasten, hold, imprison, incarcerate, keep, suppress, withhold ~*n.* detention, imprisonment, incarceration, internment

relegate 1. demote, downgrade 2. assign, consign, delegate, entrust, pass on, refer, transfer 3. banish, deport, eject, exile, expatriate, expel, oust, throw out

relent 1. acquiesce, be merciful, capitulate, change one's mind, come round, forbear, give in, give quarter, give way, have pity, melt, show mercy, soften, unbend, yield 2. die down, drop, ease, fall, let up, relax, slacken, slow, weaken

Antonyms (*sense 1*) be unyielding, give no quarter, remain firm, show no mercy (*sense 2*) increase, intensify, strengthen

relentless 1. cruel, fierce, grim, hard, harsh, implacable, inexorable, inflexible, merciless, pitiless, remorseless, ruthless, uncompromising, undeviating, unforgiving, unrelenting, unstoppable, unyielding 2. incessant, nonstop, persistent, punishing, sustained, unabated, unbroken, unfaltering, unflagging, unrelenting, unrelieved, unremitting, unstoppable

Antonyms (*sense 1*) compassionate, forgiving, merciful, submissive, yielding

relevant admissible, *ad rem,* applicable, apposite, appropriate, appurtenant, apt, fitting, germane, material, pertinent, proper, related, relative, significant, suited, to the point, to the purpose
Antonyms beside the point, extraneous, extrinsic, immaterial, inapplicable, inappropriate, irrelevant, unconnected, unrelated

reliable certain, dependable, faithful, honest, predictable, regular, reputable, responsible, safe, sound, stable, staunch, sure, tried and true, true, trustworthy, trusty, unfailing, upright
Antonyms irresponsible, undependable, unreliable, untrustworthy

reliance assurance, belief, confidence, credence, credit, dependence, faith, trust

relic fragment, keepsake, memento, remembrance, remnant, scrap, souvenir, survival, token, trace, vestige

relief 1. abatement, alleviation, assuagement, balm, comfort, cure, deliverance, ease, easement, mitigation, palliation, release, remedy, solace 2. aid, assistance, help, succour, support, sustenance 3. break, breather (*Inf.*), diversion, let-up (*Inf.*), refreshment, relaxation, remission, respite, rest

relieve 1. abate, allay, alleviate, appease, assuage, calm, comfort, console, cure, diminish, dull, ease, mitigate, mollify, palliate, relax, salve, soften, solace, soothe 2. aid, assist, bring aid to, help, succour, support, sustain 3. give (someone) a break *or* rest, stand in for, substitute for, take over from, take the place of 4. deliver, discharge, disembarrass, disencumber, exempt, free, release, unburden 5. break, brighten, interrupt, let up on (*Inf.*), lighten, slacken, vary
Antonyms (*sense 1*) aggravate, exacerbate, heighten, intensify, worsen

religious 1. churchgoing, devotional, devout, divine, doctrinal, faithful, god-fearing, godly, holy, pious, pure, reverent, righteous, sacred, scriptural, sectarian, spiritual, theological 2. conscientious, exact, faithful, fastidious, meticulous, punctilious, rigid, rigorous, scrupulous, unerring, unswerving
Antonyms (*sense 1*) godless, infidel, irreligious, rational, secular, unbelieving

relinquish abandon, abdicate, cast off, cede, desert, drop, forgo, forsake, give up, hand over, lay aside, leave, let go, quit, release, renounce, repudiate, resign, retire from, surrender, vacate, waive, withdraw from, yield

relish *v.* 1. appreciate, delight in, enjoy, fancy, like, look forward to, luxuriate in, prefer, revel in, savour, taste ~*n.* 2. appetite, appreciation, enjoyment, fancy, fondness, gusto, liking, love, partiality, penchant, predilection, stomach, taste, zest 3. appetizer, condiment, sauce, seasoning 4. flavour, piquancy, savour, smack, spice, tang, taste, trace
Antonyms *v.* be unenthusiastic about, dislike, loathe ~*n.* (*sense 2*) dislike, distaste, loathing

reluctance aversion, backwardness, disinclination, dislike, disrelish, distaste, hesitancy, indisposition, loathing, repugnance, unwillingness

reluctant averse, backward, disinclined, grudging, hesitant, indisposed, loath, recalcitrant, slow, unenthusiastic, unwilling
Antonyms eager, enthusiastic, inclined, keen, willing

rely bank, be confident of, be sure of, bet, count, depend, have confidence in, lean, reckon, repose trust in, swear by, trust

remain abide, be left, cling, continue, delay, dwell, endure, go on, last, linger, persist, prevail, rest, stand, stay, stay behind, stay put (*Inf.*), survive, tarry, wait
Antonyms depart, go, leave

remainder balance, butt, dregs, excess, leavings, oddment, relic, remains, remnant, residue, residuum, rest, stub, surplus, tail end, trace, vestige(s)

remaining abiding, extant, lasting, left, lingering, outstanding, persisting, residual, surviving, unfinished

remains 1. balance, crumbs, debris, detritus, dregs, fragments, leavings, leftovers, oddments, odds and ends, pieces, relics, remainder, remnants, residue, rest, scraps, traces, vestiges 2. body, cadaver, carcass, corpse

remark *v.* 1. animadvert, comment, declare, mention, observe, pass comment, reflect, say, state 2. espy, heed, make out, mark, note, notice, observe, perceive, regard, see, take note *or* notice of ~*n.* 3. assertion, comment, declaration, observation, opinion, reflection, statement, thought, utterance, word 4. acknowledgment, attention, comment, consideration, heed, mention, notice, observation, recognition, regard, thought

remarkable conspicuous, distinguished, extraordinary, famous, impressive, miraculous, notable, noteworthy, odd, outstanding, phenomenal, pre-eminent, prominent, rare, signal, singular, strange, striking, surprising, uncommon, unusual, wonderful
Antonyms banal, common, commonplace, everyday, insignificant, mundane, ordi-

nary, unexceptional, unimpressive, unsurprising, usual

remediable corrigible, curable, medicable, repairable, soluble, solvable, treatable

remedy *n.* 1. antidote, counteractive, cure, medicament, medicine, nostrum, panacea, physic (*Rare*), relief, restorative, specific, therapy, treatment 2. antidote, corrective, countermeasure, panacea, redress, relief, solution ~*v.* 3. alleviate, assuage, control, cure, ease, heal, help, mitigate, palliate, relieve, restore, soothe, treat 4. ameliorate, correct, fix, put right, rectify, redress, reform, relieve, repair, set to rights, solve

remember bear in mind, call to mind, call up, commemorate, keep in mind, look back (on), recall, recognize, recollect, reminisce, retain, summon up, think back
Antonyms disregard, forget, ignore, neglect, overlook

remembrance 1. anamnesis, memory, mind, recall, recognition, recollection, regard, reminiscence, retrospect, thought 2. commemoration, keepsake, memento, memorial, monument, relic, remembrancer (*Archaic*), reminder, souvenir, testimonial, token

remind awaken memories of, bring back to, bring to mind, call to mind, call up, jog one's memory, make (someone) remember, prompt, put in mind, refresh one's memory

reminisce go over in the memory, hark back, live in the past, look back, recall, recollect, remember, review, think back

reminiscence anecdote, memoir, memory, recall, recollection, reflection, remembrance, retrospection, review

reminiscent evocative, redolent, remindful, similar, suggestive

remiss careless, culpable, delinquent, derelict, dilatory, forgetful, heedless, inattentive, indifferent, lackadaisical, lax, neglectful, negligent, regardless, slack, slapdash, slipshod, sloppy (*Inf.*), slothful, slow, tardy, thoughtless, unmindful
Antonyms attentive, careful, diligent, painstaking, scrupulous

remission 1. absolution, acquittal, amnesty, discharge, excuse, exemption, exoneration, forgiveness, indulgence, pardon, release, reprieve 2. abatement, abeyance, alleviation, amelioration, decrease, diminution, ebb, lessening, let-up (*Inf.*), lull, moderation, reduction, relaxation, respite, suspension

remit *v.* 1. dispatch, forward, mail, post, send, transmit 2. cancel, desist, forbear, halt, repeal, rescind, stop 3. abate, alleviate, decrease, diminish, dwindle, ease up, fall away, mitigate, moderate, reduce, relax, sink, slacken, soften, wane, weaken 4. defer, delay, postpone, put off, put on the back burner (*Inf.*), shelve, suspend, take a rain check on (*U.S. & Canad. inf.*) ~*n.* 5. authorization, brief, guidelines, instructions, orders, terms of reference

remittance allowance, consideration, fee, payment

remnant balance, bit, butt, end, fragment, hangover, leftovers, oddment, piece, remainder, remains, residue, residuum, rest, rump, scrap, shred, stub, survival, tail end, trace, vestige

remonstrance complaint, expostulation, grievance, objection, petition, protest, protestation, reprimand, reproof

remonstrate argue, challenge, complain, dispute, dissent, expostulate, object, protest, take exception, take issue

remorse anguish, bad *or* guilty conscience, compassion, compunction, contrition, grief, guilt, pangs of conscience, penitence, pity, regret, repentance, ruefulness, self-reproach, shame, sorrow

remorseful apologetic, ashamed, chastened, conscience-stricken, contrite, guilt-ridden, guilty, penitent, regretful, repentant, rueful, sad, self-reproachful, sorrowful, sorry

remorseless 1. inexorable, relentless, unrelenting, unremitting, unstoppable 2. callous, cruel, hard, hardhearted, harsh, implacable, inhumane, merciless, pitiless, ruthless, savage, uncompassionate, unforgiving, unmerciful

remote 1. backwoods, distant, far, faraway, far-off, godforsaken, inaccessible, in the middle of nowhere, isolated, lonely, off the beaten track, outlying, out-of-the-way, secluded 2. alien, extraneous, extrinsic, foreign, immaterial, irrelevant, outside, removed, unconnected, unrelated 3. doubtful, dubious, faint, implausible, inconsiderable, meagre, negligible, outside, poor, slender, slight, slim, small, unlikely 4. abstracted, aloof, cold, detached, distant, faraway, indifferent, introspective, introverted, removed, reserved, standoffish, unapproachable, uncommunicative, uninterested, uninvolved, withdrawn
Antonyms (*sense 1*) adjacent, central, close, near, nearby, neighbouring (*sense 2*) intrinsic, related, relevant (*sense 3*) considerable, good, likely, strong (*sense 4*) alert, attentive, aware, gregarious, interested, involved, outgoing, sociable

removal 1. abstraction, dislodgment, dismissal, displacement, dispossession, ejection, elimination, eradication, erasure, expulsion, expunction, extraction, purging, stripping, subtraction, taking off, uprooting, withdrawal 2. departure, flitting (*Scot. & northern English dialect*), move, relocation, transfer

remove 1. abolish, abstract, amputate, carry off *or* away, delete, depose, detach, dethrone, discharge, dislodge, dismiss, displace, do away with, doff, efface, eject, eliminate, erase, excise, expel, expunge, extract, get rid of, give the bum's rush (*Sl.*), move, oust, purge, relegate, shed, show one the door, strike out, take away, take off, take out, throw out, throw out on one's ear (*Inf.*), transfer, transport, unseat, wipe out, withdraw 2. depart, flit (*Scot. & northern English dialect*), move, move away, quit, relocate, shift, transfer, transport, vacate 3. *Fig.* assassinate, bump off (*Sl.*), dispose of, do away with, do in (*Sl.*), eliminate, execute, get rid of, kill, liquidate, murder, take out (*Sl.*)

Antonyms (*sense 1*) appoint, don, insert, install, join, link, place, put, put back, put in, put on, replace, set

remunerate compensate, indemnify, pay, recompense, redress, reimburse, repay, requite, reward

remuneration compensation, earnings, emolument, fee, income, indemnity, meed (*Archaic*), pay, payment, profit, recompense, reimbursement, reparation, repayment, retainer, return, reward, salary, stipend, wages

remunerative economic, gainful, lucrative, moneymaking, paying, profitable, recompensing, rewarding, rich, worthwhile

renaissance, renascence awakening, new birth, new dawn, reappearance, reawakening, rebirth, re-emergence, regeneration, renewal, restoration, resurgence, resurrection, revival

renascent reanimated, reawakening, reborn, redivivus (*Rare*), re-emerging, renewed, resurgent, resurrected, reviving

rend 1. break, burst, cleave, crack, dissever, disturb, divide, fracture, lacerate, pierce, pull, rip, rive, rupture, separate, sever, shatter, smash, splinter, split, sunder (*Literary*), tear, tear to pieces, wrench 2. afflict, anguish, break, distress, hurt, lacerate, pain, pierce, stab, torment, wound, wring

render 1. contribute, deliver, furnish, give, hand out, make available, pay, present, provide, show, submit, supply, tender, turn over, yield 2. display, evince, exhibit, manifest, show 3. exchange, give, return, swap, trade 4. cause to become, leave, make 5. act, depict, do, give, interpret, perform, play, portray, present, represent 6. construe, explain, interpret, put, reproduce, restate, transcribe, translate 7. cede, deliver, give, give up, hand over, relinquish, surrender, turn over, yield 8. give back, make restitution, pay back, repay, restore, return

rendezvous *n.* 1. appointment, assignation, date, engagement, meeting, tryst (*Archaic*) 2. gathering point, meeting place, place of assignation, trysting-place (*Archaic*), venue ~*v.* 3. assemble, be reunited, collect, come together, converge, gather, get together, join up, meet, muster, rally

rendition 1. arrangement, delivery, depiction, execution, interpretation, performance, portrayal, presentation, reading, rendering, version 2. construction, explanation, interpretation, reading, transcription, translation, version

renegade 1. *n.* apostate, backslider, betrayer, defector, deserter, dissident, mutineer, outlaw, rebel, recreant (*Archaic*), runaway, traitor, turncoat 2. *adj.* apostate, backsliding, disloyal, dissident, mutinous, outlaw, rebel, rebellious, recreant (*Archaic*), runaway, traitorous, unfaithful

renege, renegue back out, break a promise, break one's word, default, go back, repudiate, welsh (*Sl.*)

renew begin again, breathe new life into, bring up to date, continue, extend, fix up (*Inf., chiefly U.S. & Canad.*), mend, modernize, overhaul, prolong, reaffirm, recommence, recreate, re-establish, refit, refresh, refurbish, regenerate, rejuvenate, renovate, reopen, repair, repeat, replace, replenish, restate, restock, restore, resume, revitalize, transform

renounce abandon, abdicate, abjure, abnegate, abstain from, cast off, decline, deny, discard, disclaim, disown, eschew, forgo, forsake, forswear, give up, leave off, quit, recant, reject, relinquish, renege, repudiate, resign, retract, spurn, swear off, throw off, waive, wash one's hands of

Antonyms assert, avow, claim, maintain, reassert

renovate do up (*Inf.*), fix up (*Inf., chiefly U.S. & Canad.*), modernize, overhaul, recondition, reconstitute, recreate, refit, reform, refurbish, rehabilitate, remodel, renew, repair, restore, revamp

renown acclaim, celebrity, distinction, eminence, fame, glory, honour, illustriousness, lustre, mark, note, reputation, repute, stardom

renowned acclaimed, celebrated, distinguished, eminent, esteemed, famed, famous, illustrious, notable, noted, well-known

Antonyms forgotten, little-known, neglected, obscure, unknown

rent[1] 1. *n.* fee, hire, lease, payment, rental, tariff 2. *v.* charter, hire, lease, let
rent[2] 1. breach, break, chink, crack, flaw, gash, hole, opening, perforation, rip, slash, slit, split, tear 2. breach, break, cleavage, discord, dissension, disunity, division, faction, rift, rupture, schism, split
renunciation abandonment, abdication, abjuration, abnegation, abstention, denial, disavowal, disclaimer, eschewal, forswearing, giving up, rejection, relinquishment, repudiation, resignation, spurning, surrender, waiver
repair[1] *v.* 1. compensate for, fix, heal, make good, make up for, mend, patch, patch up, put back together, put right, recover, rectify, redress, renew, renovate, restore, restore to working order, retrieve, square ~*n.* 2. adjustment, darn, mend, overhaul, patch, restoration 3. condition, fettle, form, nick (*Inf.*), shape (*Inf.*), state
Antonyms *v.* damage, destroy, harm, ruin, wreck
repair[2] 1. betake oneself, go, head for, leave for, move, remove, retire, set off for, withdraw 2. have recourse, resort, turn
reparable corrigible, curable, recoverable, rectifiable, remediable, restorable, retrievable, salvageable
reparation amends, atonement, compensation, damages, indemnity, propitiation, recompense, redress, renewal, repair, requital, restitution, satisfaction
repartee badinage, banter, bon mot, persiflage, pleasantry, raillery, riposte, sally, wit, witticism, wittiness, wordplay
repast collation, food, meal, nourishment, refection, spread (*Inf.*), victuals
repay 1. compensate, make restitution, pay back, recompense, refund, reimburse, remunerate, requite, restore, return, reward, settle up with, square 2. avenge, even *or* settle the score with, get back at, get even with (*Inf.*), get one's own back on (*Inf.*), hit back, make reprisal, reciprocate, retaliate, return the compliment, revenge
repeal 1. *v.* abolish, abrogate, annul, cancel, countermand, declare null and void, invalidate, nullify, obviate, recall, rescind, reverse, revoke, set aside, withdraw 2. *n.* abolition, abrogation, annulment, cancellation, invalidation, nullification, rescinding, rescindment, rescission, revocation, withdrawal
Antonyms *v.* confirm, enact, introduce, pass, ratify, reaffirm, validate ~*n.* confirmation, enactment, introduction, passing, ratification, reaffirmation, validation
repeat 1. *v.* duplicate, echo, iterate, quote, recapitulate, recite, redo, rehearse, reiterate, relate, renew, replay, reproduce, rerun, reshow, restate, retell 2. *n.* duplicate, echo, recapitulation, reiteration, repetition, replay, reproduction, rerun, reshowing
repeatedly again and again, frequently, many a time and oft (*Archaic or poetic*), many times, often, over and over, time after time, time and (time) again
repel 1. beat off, check, confront, decline, drive off, fight, hold off, keep at arm's length, oppose, parry, put to flight, rebuff, refuse, reject, repulse, resist, ward off 2. disgust, give one the creeps (*Inf.*), gross out (*U.S. sl.*), make one shudder, make one sick, nauseate, offend, put one off, revolt, sicken, turn one off (*Inf.*), turn one's stomach
Antonyms attract, delight, draw, entrance, fascinate, invite, please, submit
repellent 1. abhorrent, abominable, cringe-making (*Brit. inf.*), discouraging, disgusting, distasteful, hateful, horrid, loathsome, nauseating, noxious, obnoxious, obscene, odious, offensive, off-putting (*Brit. inf.*), repugnant, repulsive, revolting, sickening, yucky *or* yukky (*Sl.*) 2. impermeable, proof, repelling, resistant
repent atone, be ashamed, be contrite, be sorry, deplore, feel remorse, lament, regret, relent, reproach oneself, rue, see the error of one's ways, show penitence, sorrow
repentance compunction, contrition, grief, guilt, penitence, regret, remorse, sackcloth and ashes, self-reproach, sorriness, sorrow
repentant apologetic, ashamed, chastened, contrite, penitent, regretful, remorseful, rueful, self-reproachful, sorry
repercussion backlash, consequence, echo, rebound, recoil, result, reverberation, sequel, side effect
repertory collection, list, range, repertoire, repository, stock, store, supply
repetition duplication, echo, iteration, reappearance, recapitulation, recital, recurrence, redundancy, rehearsal, reiteration, relation, renewal, repeat, repetitiousness, replication, restatement, return, tautology
repetitious long-winded, pleonastic, prolix, redundant, tautological, tedious, verbose, windy, wordy
repetitive boring, dull, mechanical, monotonous, recurrent, samey (*Inf.*), tedious, unchanging, unvaried
rephrase paraphrase, put differently, recast, reword, say in other words
repine brood, complain, eat one's heart out, fret, grieve, grumble, lament, languish, moan, mope, murmur, sulk
replace follow, oust, put back, re-establish,

reinstate, restore, stand in lieu of, substitute, succeed, supersede, supplant, supply, take over from, take the place of

replacement double, fill-in, proxy, stand-in, substitute, successor, surrogate, understudy

replenish fill, furnish, make up, provide, refill, reload, renew, replace, restock, restore, stock, supply, top up
Antonyms consume, drain, empty, exhaust, use up

replete abounding, brimful, brimming, charged, chock-full, crammed, filled, full, full to bursting, full up, glutted, gorged, jammed, jam-packed, sated, satiated, stuffed, teeming, well-provided, well-stocked
Antonyms bare, barren, empty, famished, hungry, lacking, starving, wanting

repletion completeness, fullness, glut, overfullness, plethora, satiation, satiety, superfluity, surfeit

replica carbon copy, copy, duplicate, facsimile, imitation, model, reproduction
Antonyms original

replicate ape, copy, duplicate, follow, mimic, recreate, reduplicate, repeat, reproduce

reply 1. *v.* acknowledge, answer, come back, counter, echo, make answer, react, reciprocate, rejoin, respond, retaliate, retort, return, riposte, write back 2. *n.* acknowledgment, answer, comeback (*Inf.*), counter, counterattack, echo, reaction, reciprocation, rejoinder, response, retaliation, retort, return, riposte

report *n.* 1. account, announcement, article, communication, communiqué, declaration, description, detail, dispatch, information, message, narrative, news, note, paper, piece, recital, record, relation, statement, story, summary, tale, tidings, version, word, write-up 2. gossip, hearsay, rumour, talk 3. character, eminence, esteem, fame, regard, reputation, repute 4. bang, blast, boom, crack, crash, detonation, discharge, explosion, noise, reverberation, sound ~*v.* 5. air, announce, bring word, broadcast, circulate, communicate, cover, declare, describe, detail, document, give an account of, inform of, mention, narrate, note, notify, pass on, proclaim, publish, recite, record, recount, relate, relay, state, tell, write up 6. appear, arrive, be present, clock in *or* on, come, present oneself, show up (*Inf.*), turn up

reporter announcer, correspondent, hack (*Derogatory*), journalist, journo (*Sl.*), newscaster, newshound (*Inf.*), newspaperman, newspaperwoman, pressman, writer

repose[1] *n.* 1. ease, inactivity, peace, quiet, quietness, quietude, relaxation, respite, rest, restfulness, sleep, slumber, stillness, tranquillity 2. aplomb, calmness, composure, dignity, equanimity, peace of mind, poise, self-possession, serenity, tranquillity ~*v.* 3. drowse, lay down, lie, lie down, lie upon, recline, relax, rest, rest upon, sleep, slumber, take it easy, take one's ease

repose[2] confide, deposit, entrust, invest, lodge, place, put, store

repository archive, depository, depot, emporium, magazine, receptacle, store, storehouse, treasury, vault, warehouse

reprehensible bad, blameworthy, censurable, condemnable, culpable, delinquent, discreditable, disgraceful, errant, erring, ignoble, objectionable, opprobrious, remiss, shameful, unworthy
Antonyms acceptable, admirable, forgivable, laudable, pardonable, praiseworthy, unobjectionable

represent 1. act for, be, betoken, correspond to, equal, equate with, express, mean, serve as, speak for, stand for, substitute for, symbolize 2. embody, epitomize, exemplify, personify, symbolize, typify 3. delineate, denote, depict, describe, designate, evoke, express, illustrate, outline, picture, portray, render, reproduce, show, sketch 4. describe as, make out to be, pass off as, pose as, pretend to be 5. act, appear as, assume the role of, enact, exhibit, perform, play the part of, produce, put on, show, stage

representation 1. account, delineation, depiction, description, illustration, image, likeness, model, narration, narrative, picture, portrait, portrayal, relation, resemblance, sketch 2. body of representatives, committee, delegates, delegation, embassy 3. exhibition, performance, play, production, show, sight, spectacle 4. *Often plural* account, argument, explanation, exposition, expostulation, remonstrance, statement

representative *n.* 1. agent, commercial traveller, rep, salesman, traveller 2. archetype, embodiment, epitome, exemplar, personification, type, typical example 3. agent, commissioner, councillor, delegate, depute (*Scot.*), deputy, member, member of parliament, M.P., proxy, spokesman, spokeswoman ~*adj.* 4. archetypal, characteristic, emblematic, evocative, exemplary, illustrative, symbolic, typical 5. chosen, delegated, elected, elective
Antonyms (*sense 4*) atypical, extraordinary, uncharacteristic

repress bottle up, chasten, check, control,

crush, curb, hold back, hold in, inhibit, keep in check, master, muffle, overcome, overpower, quash, quell, restrain, silence, smother, stifle, subdue, subjugate, suppress, swallow
Antonyms encourage, express, free, give free rein to, let out, liberate, release, support

repression authoritarianism, censorship, coercion, constraint, control, despotism, domination, inhibition, restraint, subjugation, suppression, tyranny

repressive absolute, authoritarian, coercive, despotic, dictatorial, harsh, oppressive, severe, tough, tyrannical
Antonyms democratic, liberal, libertarian

reprieve *v.* 1. grant a stay of execution to, let off the hook (*Sl.*), pardon, postpone *or* remit the punishment of 2. abate, allay, alleviate, mitigate, palliate, relieve, respite ~*n.* 3. abeyance, amnesty, deferment, pardon, postponement, remission, stay of execution, suspension 4. abatement, alleviation, let-up (*Inf.*), mitigation, palliation, relief, respite

reprimand 1. *n.* admonition, blame, castigation, censure, dressing-down (*Inf.*), flea in one's ear (*Inf.*), lecture, rebuke, reprehension, reproach, reproof, row, talking-to (*Inf.*), telling-off (*Inf.*), ticking-off (*Inf.*), tongue-lashing, wigging (*Brit. sl.*) 2. *v.* admonish, bawl out (*Inf.*), blame, carpet (*Inf.*), castigate, censure, check, chew out (*U.S. & Canad. inf.*), chide, dress down (*Inf.*), give a rocket (*Brit. & N.Z. inf.*), give (someone) a row (*Inf.*), haul over the coals (*Inf.*), lecture, rap over the knuckles, read the riot act, rebuke, reprehend, reproach, reprove, scold, send one away with a flea in one's ear (*Inf.*), take to task, tear into (*Inf.*), tear (someone) off a strip (*Brit. inf.*), tell off (*Inf.*), tick off (*Inf.*), tongue-lash, upbraid
Antonyms *n.* commendation, compliment, congratulations, praise ~*v.* applaud, commend, compliment, congratulate, praise

reprisal an eye for an eye, counterstroke, requital, retaliation, retribution, revenge, vengeance

reproach 1. *v.* abuse, bawl out (*Inf.*), blame, blast, carpet (*Inf.*), censure, chew out (*U.S. & Canad. inf.*), chide, condemn, criticize, defame, discredit, disparage, find fault with, give a rocket (*Brit. & N.Z. inf.*), lambast(e), read the riot act, rebuke, reprehend, reprimand, reprove, scold, tear into (*Inf.*), tear (someone) off a strip (*Brit. inf.*), take to task, upbraid 2. *n.* abuse, blame, blemish, censure, condemnation, contempt, disapproval, discredit, disgrace, dishonour, disrepute, ignominy, indignity, obloquy, odium, opprobrium, scorn, shame, slight, slur, stain, stigma

reproachful abusive, admonitory, castigatory, censorious, condemnatory, contemptuous, critical, disappointed, disapproving, fault-finding, reproving, scolding, upbraiding

reprobate 1. *adj.* abandoned, bad, base, corrupt, damned, degenerate, depraved, dissolute, hardened, immoral, incorrigible, profligate, shameless, sinful, unprincipled, vile, wicked 2. *n.* asshole (*U.S. & Canad. taboo sl.*), asswipe (*U.S. & Canad. taboo sl.*), bad egg (*Old-fashioned inf.*), bastard (*Offensive*), blackguard, bugger (*Taboo sl.*), cocksucker (*Taboo sl.*), degenerate, evildoer, miscreant, mother (*Taboo sl., chiefly U.S.*), motherfucker (*Taboo sl., chiefly U.S.*), ne'er-do-well, outcast, pariah, profligate, rake, rakehell (*Archaic*), rascal, roué, scoundrel, scumbag (*Sl.*), shit (*Taboo sl.*), sinner, son-of-a-bitch (*Sl., chiefly U.S. & Canad.*), turd (*Taboo sl.*), villain, wastrel, wretch, wrongdoer 3. *v.* condemn, damn, denounce, disapprove of, frown upon, reprehend, vilify

reproduce 1. copy, duplicate, echo, emulate, imitate, match, mirror, parallel, print, recreate, repeat, replicate, represent, transcribe 2. breed, generate, multiply, procreate, produce young, proliferate, propagate, spawn

reproduction 1. breeding, generation, increase, multiplication, procreation, proliferation, propagation 2. copy, duplicate, facsimile, imitation, picture, print, replica
Antonyms (*sense 2*) original

reproof admonition, blame, castigation, censure, chiding, condemnation, criticism, dressing-down (*Inf.*), rebuke, reprehension, reprimand, reproach, reproval, scolding, ticking-off (*Inf.*), tongue-lashing, upbraiding
Antonyms commendation, compliment, encouragement, praise

reprove abuse, admonish, bawl out (*Inf.*), berate, blame, carpet (*Inf.*), censure, check, chew out (*U.S. & Canad. inf.*), chide, condemn, give a rocket (*Brit. & N.Z. inf.*), read the riot act, rebuke, reprehend, reprimand, scold, take to task, tear into (*Inf.*), tear (someone) off a strip (*Brit. inf.*), tell off (*Inf.*), tick off (*Inf.*), upbraid
Antonyms applaud, commend, compliment, encourage, praise

repudiate abandon, abjure, cast off, cut off, deny, desert, disavow, discard, disclaim, disown, forsake, reject, renounce, rescind, retract, reverse, revoke, turn one's back on, wash one's hands of

Antonyms accept, acknowledge, admit, assert, avow, defend, own, proclaim, ratify

repugnance abhorrence, antipathy, aversion, disgust, dislike, disrelish, distaste, hatred, loathing, odium, reluctance, repulsion, revulsion

repugnant 1. abhorrent, abominable, disgusting, distasteful, foul, hateful, horrid, loathsome, nauseating, objectionable, obnoxious, odious, offensive, repellent, revolting, sickening, vile, yucky *or* yukky (*Sl.*) 2. adverse, antagonistic, antipathetic, averse, contradictory, hostile, incompatible, inconsistent, inimical, opposed

Antonyms agreeable, attractive, compatible, pleasant, unobjectionable

repulse *v.* 1. beat off, check, defeat, drive back, fight off, rebuff, repel, throw back, ward off 2. disdain, disregard, give the cold shoulder to, rebuff, refuse, reject, snub, spurn, turn down ~*n.* 3. check, defeat, disappointment, failure, reverse 4. cold shoulder, knock-back (*Sl.*), rebuff, refusal, rejection, snub, spurning, the (old) heave-ho (*Inf.*)

repulsion abhorrence, aversion, detestation, disgust, disrelish, distaste, hatred, loathing, odium, repugnance, revulsion

repulsive abhorrent, abominable, disagreeable, disgusting, distasteful, forbidding, foul, hateful, hideous, horrid, loathsome, nauseating, objectionable, obnoxious, obscene, odious, offensive, repellent, revolting, sickening, ugly, unpleasant, vile

Antonyms appealing, attractive, delightful, enticing, lovely, pleasant

reputable creditable, estimable, excellent, good, honourable, honoured, legitimate, of good repute, reliable, respectable, trustworthy, upright, well-thought-of, worthy

Antonyms cowboy (*Inf.*), disreputable, fly-by-night, shady (*Inf.*), unreliable, untrustworthy

reputation character, credit, distinction, eminence, esteem, estimation, fame, honour, name, opinion, renown, repute, standing, stature

repute celebrity, distinction, eminence, esteem, estimation, fame, name, renown, reputation, standing, stature

reputed accounted, alleged, believed, considered, deemed, estimated, held, ostensible, putative, reckoned, regarded, rumoured, said, seeming, supposed, thought

reputedly allegedly, apparently, ostensibly, seemingly, supposedly

request 1. *v.* appeal for, apply for, ask (for), beg, beseech, call for, demand, desire, entreat, petition, pray, put in for, requisition, seek, solicit, sue for, supplicate 2. *n.* appeal, application, asking, begging, call, demand, desire, entreaty, petition, prayer, requisition, solicitation, suit, supplication

Antonyms command, order

require 1. crave, depend upon, desire, have need of, lack, miss, need, stand in need of, want, wish 2. ask, beg, beseech, bid, call upon, command, compel, constrain, demand, direct, enjoin, exact, insist upon, instruct, oblige, order, request 3. call for, demand, entail, involve, necessitate, take

required called for, compulsory, demanded, essential, mandatory, necessary, needed, obligatory, prescribed, recommended, requisite, set, unavoidable, vital

Antonyms elective, noncompulsory, not necessary, not vital, optional, unimportant, voluntary

requirement demand, desideratum, essential, lack, must, necessity, need, precondition, prerequisite, qualification, requisite, *sine qua non*, specification, stipulation, want

requisite 1. *adj.* called for, essential, indispensable, mandatory, necessary, needed, needful, obligatory, prerequisite, required, vital 2. *n.* condition, desideratum, essential, must, necessity, need, precondition, prerequisite, requirement, *sine qua non*

requisition *n.* 1. application, call, demand, request, summons 2. appropriation, commandeering, occupation, seizure, takeover ~*v.* 3. apply for, call for, demand, put in for, request 4. appropriate, commandeer, occupy, seize, take over, take possession of

requital amends, compensation, payment, recompense, redress, reimbursement, remuneration, repayment, restitution, return, reward

requite compensate, give in return, give tit for tat, make amends, make good, make restitution, pay, reciprocate, recompense, redress, reimburse, remunerate, repay, respond, retaliate, return, return like for like, reward, satisfy

rescind abrogate, annul, cancel, countermand, declare null and void, invalidate, obviate, overturn, quash, recall, repeal, retract, reverse, revoke, set aside, void

Antonyms confirm, enact, implement, reaffirm, support, uphold, validate

rescission abrogation, annulment, cancellation, invalidation, recall, repeal, rescindment, retraction, reversal, revocation, setting aside, voidance

rescue 1. *v.* deliver, extricate, free, get out, liberate, recover, redeem, release, salvage, save, save the life of, set free 2. *n.* deliverance, extrication, liberation, recovery, re-

demption, release, relief, salvage, salvation, saving
Antonyms (*sense 1*) abandon, desert, leave, leave behind, lose

research 1. *n.* analysis, delving, examination, experimentation, exploration, fact-finding, groundwork, inquiry, investigation, probe, scrutiny, study 2. *v.* analyse, consult the archives, do tests, examine, experiment, explore, investigate, look into, make inquiries, probe, scrutinize, study, work over

resemblance affinity, analogy, closeness, comparability, comparison, conformity, correspondence, counterpart, facsimile, image, kinship, likeness, parallel, parity, sameness, semblance, similarity, similitude
Antonyms difference, disparity, dissimilarity, heterogeneity, unlikeness, variation

resemble bear a resemblance to, be like, be similar to, duplicate, echo, favour (*Inf.*), look like, mirror, parallel, put one in mind of, remind one of, take after

resent be angry about, bear a grudge about, begrudge, be in a huff about, be offended by, dislike, feel bitter about, grudge, harbour a grudge against, have hard feelings about, object to, take amiss, take as an insult, take exception to, take offence at, take umbrage at
Antonyms accept, approve, be content with, be pleased by, feel flattered by, like, welcome

resentful aggrieved, angry, bitter, embittered, exasperated, grudging, huffish, huffy, hurt, in a huff, incensed, indignant, in high dudgeon, irate, jealous, miffed (*Inf.*), offended, peeved (*Inf.*), piqued, put out, revengeful, unforgiving, wounded
Antonyms content, flattered, gratified, pleased, satisfied

resentment anger, animosity, bitterness, displeasure, fury, grudge, huff, hurt, ill feeling, ill will, indignation, ire, irritation, malice, pique, rage, rancour, umbrage, vexation, wrath

reservation 1. condition, demur, doubt, hesitancy, proviso, qualification, rider, scepticism, scruple, stipulation 2. enclave, homeland, preserve, reserve, sanctuary, territory, tract

reserve *v.* 1. conserve, hang on to, hoard, hold, husband, keep, keep back, lay up, preserve, put by, retain, save, set aside, stockpile, store, withhold 2. bespeak, book, engage, prearrange, pre-engage, retain, secure 3. defer, delay, keep back, postpone, put off, withhold ~*n.* 4. backlog, cache, capital, fall-back, fund, hoard, reservoir, savings, stock, stockpile, store, supply 5. park, preserve, reservation, sanctuary, tract 6. aloofness, constraint, coolness, formality, modesty, reluctance, reservation, restraint, reticence, secretiveness, shyness, silence, taciturnity ~*adj.* 7. alternate, auxiliary, extra, fall-back, secondary, spare, substitute

reserved 1. booked, engaged, held, kept, restricted, retained, set aside, spoken for, taken 2. aloof, cautious, close-mouthed, cold, cool, demure, formal, modest, prim, restrained, reticent, retiring, secretive, shy, silent, standoffish, taciturn, unapproachable, uncommunicative, undemonstrative, unforthcoming, unresponsive, unsociable 3. bound, destined, fated, intended, meant, predestined
Antonyms (*senses 1 & 2*) ardent, demonstrative, forward, open, sociable, uninhibited, unreserved, warm

reservoir 1. basin, lake, pond, tank 2. container, holder, receptacle, repository, store, tank 3. accumulation, fund, pool, reserves, source, stock, stockpile, store, supply

reshuffle 1. *n.* change, interchange, realignment, rearrangement, redistribution, regrouping, reorganization, restructuring, revision, shake-up (*Inf.*) 2. *v.* change around, change the line-up of, interchange, realign, rearrange, redistribute, regroup, reorganize, restructure, revise, shake up (*Inf.*)

reside 1. abide, dwell, hang out (*Inf.*), have one's home, inhabit, live, lodge, remain, settle, sojourn, stay 2. abide, be intrinsic to, be vested, consist, dwell, exist, inhere, lie, rest with
Antonyms (*sense 1*) holiday in, visit

residence 1. abode, domicile, dwelling, flat, habitation, home, house, household, lodging, pad (*Sl.*), place, quarters 2. hall, manor, mansion, palace, seat, villa 3. occupancy, occupation, sojourn, stay, tenancy

resident 1. *n.* citizen, denizen, indweller, inhabitant, local, lodger, occupant, tenant 2. *adj.* dwelling, inhabiting, living, local, neighbourhood, settled
Antonyms *n.* nonresident, visitor ~*adj.* nonresident, visiting

residual leftover, net, nett, remaining, unconsumed, unused, vestigial

residue balance, dregs, excess, extra, leftovers, remainder, remains, remnant, residuum, rest, surplus

resign 1. abandon, abdicate, cede, forgo, forsake, give in one's notice, give up, hand over, leave, quit, relinquish, renounce, step down (*Inf.*), surrender, turn over, vacate, yield 2. **resign oneself** accept, acquiesce, bow, give in, give up, reconcile, submit, succumb, yield

resignation 1. abandonment, abdication, departure, leaving, notice, relinquishment, renunciation, retirement, surrender 2. acceptance, acquiescence, compliance, endurance, forbearing, fortitude, nonresistance, passivity, patience, submission, sufferance

Antonyms (*sense 2*) defiance, dissent, kicking up a fuss, protest, resistance

resigned acquiescent, compliant, long-suffering, patient, stoical, subdued, submissive, unprotesting, unresisting

resilient 1. bouncy, elastic, flexible, plastic, pliable, rubbery, springy, supple, whippy 2. bouncy, buoyant, feisty (*Inf., chiefly U.S. & Canad.*), hardy, irrepressible, quick to recover, strong, tough

Antonyms (*sense 1*) flaccid, inflexible, limp, rigid, stiff (*sense 2*) delicate, effete, sensitive, sickly, weak

resist 1. battle, be proof against, check, combat, confront, contend with, counteract, countervail, curb, defy, dispute, fight back, hinder, hold out against, oppose, put up a fight (against), refuse, repel, stand up to, struggle against, thwart, weather, withstand 2. abstain from, avoid, forbear, forgo, keep from, leave alone, prevent oneself from, refrain from, refuse, turn down

Antonyms (*sense 1*) accept, acquiesce, give in, submit, succumb, surrender, welcome, yield (*sense 2*) enjoy, give in to, indulge in, surrender to

resistance battle, combat, contention, counteraction, defiance, fight, fighting, hindrance, impediment, intransigence, obstruction, opposition, refusal, struggle

Resistance freedom fighters, guerrillas, irregulars, maquis, partisans, underground

resistant 1. hard, impervious, insusceptible, proof against, strong, tough, unaffected by, unyielding 2. antagonistic, combative, defiant, dissident, hostile, intractable, intransigent, opposed, recalcitrant, unwilling

resolute bold, constant, determined, dogged, firm, fixed, immovable, inflexible, obstinate, persevering, purposeful, relentless, set, stalwart, staunch, steadfast, strong-willed, stubborn, tenacious, unbending, undaunted, unflinching, unshakable, unshaken, unwavering

Antonyms doubtful, irresolute, undecided, undetermined, unresolved, unsteady, weak

resolution 1. boldness, constancy, courage, dedication, determination, doggedness, earnestness, energy, firmness, fortitude, obstinacy, perseverance, purpose, relentlessness, resoluteness, resolve, sincerity, staunchness, staying power, steadfastness, stubbornness, tenacity, willpower 2. aim, decision, declaration, determination, intent, intention, judgment, motion, purpose, resolve, verdict 3. answer, end, finding, outcome, settlement, solution, solving, sorting out, unravelling, upshot, working out

resolve *v.* 1. agree, conclude, decide, design, determine, fix, intend, make up one's mind, purpose, settle, undertake 2. answer, clear up, crack, elucidate, fathom, find the solution to, suss (out) (*Sl.*), work out 3. banish, clear up, dispel, explain, remove 4. analyse, anatomize, break down, clear, disentangle, disintegrate, dissect, dissolve, liquefy, melt, reduce, separate, solve, split up, unravel 5. alter, change, convert, metamorphose, transform, transmute ~*n.* 6. conclusion, decision, design, intention, objective, project, purpose, resolution, undertaking 7. boldness, courage, determination, earnestness, firmness, resoluteness, resolution, steadfastness, willpower

Antonyms (*sense 7*) cowardice, half-heartedness, indecision, vacillation, wavering

resonant booming, echoing, full, resounding, reverberant, reverberating, rich, ringing, sonorous, vibrant

resort *v.* 1. avail oneself of, bring into play, employ, exercise, fall back on, have recourse to, look to, make use of, turn to, use, utilize 2. frequent, go, haunt, head for, repair, visit ~*n.* 3. haunt, holiday centre, refuge, retreat, spot, tourist centre, watering place (*Brit.*) 4. alternative, chance, course, expedient, hope, possibility, recourse, reference

resound echo, fill the air, re-echo, resonate, reverberate, ring

resounding booming, echoing, full, powerful, resonant, reverberating, rich, ringing, sonorous, sounding, vibrant

resource 1. ability, capability, cleverness, ingenuity, initiative, inventiveness, quick-wittedness, resourcefulness, talent 2. hoard, reserve, source, stockpile, supply 3. appliance, contrivance, course, device, expedient, means, resort

resourceful able, bright, capable, clever, creative, imaginative, ingenious, inventive, quick-witted, sharp, talented

Antonyms fushionless (*Scot.*), gormless (*Brit. inf.*), unimaginative, uninventive

resources assets, capital, funds, holdings, materials, means, money, property, reserves, riches, supplies, wealth, wherewithal

respect *n.* 1. admiration, appreciation, approbation, consideration, deference, esteem, estimation, honour, recognition, regard, reverence, veneration 2. aspect, characteristic, detail, facet, feature, matter, particular, point, sense, way 3. bearing, connection, reference, regard, relation 4. *Plural* compliments, devoirs, good wishes, greetings, regards, salutations ~*v.* 5. admire, adore, appreciate, defer to, esteem, have a good *or* high opinion of, honour, look up to, recognize, regard, revere, reverence, set store by, show consideration for, think highly of, value, venerate 6. abide by, adhere to, attend, comply with, follow, heed, honour, notice, obey, observe, pay attention to, regard, show consideration for
Antonyms *n.* (*sense 1*) contempt, disdain, disregard, disrespect, irreverence, scorn ~*v.* abuse, disregard, disrespect, ignore, neglect, scorn

respectable 1. admirable, decent, decorous, dignified, estimable, good, honest, honourable, proper, reputable, respected, upright, venerable, worthy 2. ample, appreciable, considerable, decent, fair, fairly good, goodly, presentable, reasonable, sizable, substantial, tidy (*Inf.*), tolerable
Antonyms (*sense 1*) dishonourable, disreputable, ignoble, impolite, improper, indecent, unrefined, unworthy (*sense 2*) paltry, poor, small

respectful civil, courteous, courtly, deferential, dutiful, gracious, humble, mannerly, obedient, polite, regardful, reverent, reverential, self-effacing, solicitous, submissive, well-mannered

respective corresponding, individual, own, particular, personal, relevant, separate, several, specific, various

respite 1. break, breather (*Inf.*), breathing space, cessation, halt, hiatus, intermission, interruption, interval, let-up (*Inf.*), lull, pause, recess, relaxation, relief, rest 2. adjournment, delay, moratorium, postponement, reprieve, stay, suspension

resplendent beaming, bright, brilliant, dazzling, effulgent, gleaming, glittering, glorious, irradiant, luminous, lustrous, radiant, refulgent (*Literary*), shining, splendid

respond acknowledge, act in response, answer, come back, counter, react, reciprocate, rejoin, reply, retort, return
Antonyms ignore, remain silent, turn a blind eye

response acknowledgment, answer, comeback (*Inf.*), counterattack, counterblast, feedback, reaction, rejoinder, reply, retort, return, riposte

responsibility 1. accountability, amenability, answerability, care, charge, duty, liability, obligation, onus, trust 2. authority, importance, power 3. blame, burden, culpability, fault, guilt 4. conscientiousness, dependability, level-headedness, maturity, rationality, reliability, sensibleness, soberness, stability, trustworthiness

responsible 1. at the helm, carrying the can (*Inf.*), in authority, in charge, in control 2. accountable, amenable, answerable, bound, chargeable, duty-bound, liable, subject, under obligation 3. authoritative, decision-making, executive, high, important 4. at fault, culpable, guilty, to blame 5. adult, conscientious, dependable, level-headed, mature, rational, reliable, sensible, sober, sound, stable, trustworthy
Antonyms irresponsible, unaccountable, unconscientious, undependable, unreliable, untrustworthy

responsive alive, awake, aware, forthcoming, impressionable, open, perceptive, quick to react, reactive, receptive, sensitive, sharp, susceptible, sympathetic
Antonyms apathetic, impassive, insensitive, silent, unresponsive, unsympathetic

rest[1] *n.* 1. calm, doze, forty winks (*Inf.*), idleness, inactivity, kip (*Brit. sl.*), leisure, lie-down, motionlessness, nap, refreshment, relaxation, relief, repose, siesta, sleep, slumber, snooze (*Inf.*), somnolence, standstill, stillness, tranquillity, zizz (*Brit. inf.*) 2. **at rest** asleep, at a standstill, at peace, calm, dead, motionless, peaceful, resting, sleeping, still, stopped, tranquil, unmoving 3. break, breather (*Inf.*), breathing space, cessation, halt, holiday, interlude, intermission, interval, lull, pause, respite, stop, time off, vacation 4. haven, lodging, refuge, retreat, shelter 5. base, holder, prop, shelf, stand, support, trestle ~*v.* 6. be at ease, be calm, doze, drowse, have a snooze (*Inf.*), have forty winks (*Inf.*), idle, kip (*Brit. sl.*), laze, lie down, lie still, nap, put one's feet up, refresh oneself, relax, sit down, sleep, slumber, snooze (*Inf.*), take a nap, take it easy, take one's ease, zizz (*Brit. inf.*) 7. be supported, lay, lean, lie, prop, recline, repose, sit, stand, stretch out 8. break off, cease, come to a standstill, desist, discontinue, halt, have a break, knock off (*Inf.*), stay, stop, take a breather (*Inf.*) 9. base, be based, be founded, depend, found, hang, hinge, lie, rely, reside, turn
Antonyms *v.* keep going, slog away (*Inf.*), work ~*n.* activity, bustle, work

rest[2] 1. *n.* balance, excess, leftovers, others, remainder, remains, remnants, residue, residuum, rump, surplus 2. *v.* be left, continue being, go on being, keep, remain, stay

restful calm, calming, comfortable, languid, pacific, peaceful, placid, quiet, relaxed, relaxing, serene, sleepy, soothing, tranquil, tranquillizing, undisturbed, unhurried
Antonyms agitated, busy, disturbing, restless, uncomfortable, unrelaxed

restitution amends, compensation, indemnification, indemnity, recompense, redress, refund, reimbursement, remuneration, reparation, repayment, requital, restoration, return, satisfaction

restive agitated, edgy, fidgety, fractious, fretful, ill at ease, impatient, jittery (*Inf.*), jumpy, nervous, on edge, recalcitrant, refractory, restless, uneasy, unquiet, unruly
Antonyms at ease, calm, content, peaceful, relaxed, satisfied, serene, tranquil

restless 1. active, bustling, changeable, footloose, hurried, inconstant, irresolute, moving, nomadic, roving, transient, turbulent, unsettled, unstable, unsteady, wandering 2. agitated, anxious, disturbed, edgy, fidgeting, fidgety, fitful, fretful, ill at ease, jumpy, nervous, on edge, restive, sleepless, tossing and turning, troubled, uneasy, unquiet, unruly, unsettled, worried
Antonyms comfortable, composed, easy, quiet, relaxed, restful, steady, undisturbed

restlessness 1. activity, bustle, hurry, hurry-scurry, inconstancy, instability, movement, transience, turbulence, turmoil, unrest, unsettledness 2. agitation, ants in one's pants (*Sl.*), anxiety, disquiet, disturbance, edginess, fitfulness, fretfulness, heebie-jeebies (*Sl.*), inquietude, insomnia, jitters (*Inf.*), jumpiness, nervousness, restiveness, uneasiness, worriedness

restoration 1. reconstruction, recovery, refreshment, refurbishing, rehabilitation, rejuvenation, renewal, renovation, repair, revitalization, revival 2. recovery, re-establishment, reinstallation, reinstatement, replacement, restitution, return
Antonyms (*sense 1*) demolition, scrapping, wrecking (*sense 2*) abolition, overthrow

restore 1. fix, mend, rebuild, recondition, reconstruct, recover, refurbish, rehabilitate, renew, renovate, repair, retouch, set to rights, touch up 2. bring back to health, build up, reanimate, refresh, rejuvenate, revitalize, revive, revivify, strengthen 3. bring back, give back, hand back, recover, re-establish, reinstate, replace, retrocede, return, send back 4. reconstitute, re-enforce, reimpose, reinstate, reintroduce
Antonyms (*sense 1*) demolish, scrap, wreck (*sense 2*) make worse, sicken, weaken (*sense 4*) abolish, abrogate, repeal, rescind

restrain 1. bridle, check, confine, constrain, contain, control, curb, curtail, debar, govern, hamper, handicap, harness, hinder, hold, hold back, inhibit, keep, keep under control, limit, muzzle, prevent, rein, repress, restrict, straiten, subdue, suppress 2. arrest, bind, chain, confine, detain, fetter, hold, imprison, jail, lock up, manacle, pinion, tie up
Antonyms (*sense 1*) assist, encourage, help, incite, urge on (*sense 2*) free, liberate, release

restrained 1. calm, controlled, mild, moderate, muted, reasonable, reticent, self-controlled, soft, steady, temperate, undemonstrative 2. discreet, quiet, subdued, tasteful, unobtrusive
Antonyms (*sense 1*) fiery, hot-headed, intemperate, unrestrained, wild (*sense 2*) garish, loud, over-the-top, self-indulgent, tasteless

restraint 1. coercion, command, compulsion, confines, constraint, control, curtailment, grip, hindrance, hold, inhibition, limitation, moderation, prevention, restriction, self-control, self-discipline, self-possession, self-restraint, suppression 2. arrest, bondage, bonds, captivity, chains, confinement, detention, fetters, imprisonment, manacles, pinions, straitjacket 3. ban, boycott, bridle, check, curb, embargo, interdict, limit, limitation, rein, taboo
Antonyms (*sense 1*) excess, immoderation, intemperance, licence, self-indulgence (*sense 2*) freedom, liberty

restrict bound, circumscribe, confine, contain, cramp, demarcate, hamper, handicap, hem in, impede, inhibit, keep within bounds *or* limits, limit, regulate, restrain, straiten
Antonyms broaden, encourage, foster, free, promote, widen

restriction check, condition, confinement, constraint, containment, control, curb, demarcation, handicap, inhibition, limitation, regulation, restraint, rule, stipulation

result *n.* 1. conclusion, consequence, decision, development, effect, end, event, fruit, issue, outcome, product, reaction, sequel, termination, upshot ~*v.* 2. appear, arise, derive, develop, emanate, ensue, eventuate, flow, follow, happen, issue, spring, stem, turn out 3. *With* **in** culminate, end, finish, pan out (*Inf.*), terminate, wind up
Antonyms (*sense 1*) beginning, cause, germ, origin, outset, root, source

resume 1. begin again, carry on, continue, go on, proceed, recommence, reinstitute,

reopen, restart, take up *or* pick up where one left off 2. assume again, occupy again, reoccupy, take back, take up again
Antonyms (*sense 1*) cease, discontinue, stop

résumé abstract, digest, epitome, précis, recapitulation, review, rundown, summary, synopsis

resumption carrying on, continuation, fresh outbreak, new beginning, re-establishment, renewal, reopening, restart, resurgence

resurgence rebirth, recrudescence, re-emergence, renaissance, renascence, resumption, resurrection, return, revival

resurrect breathe new life into, bring back, raise from the dead, reintroduce, renew, restore to life, revive

resurrection comeback (*Inf.*), raising *or* rising from the dead, reappearance, rebirth, renaissance, renascence, renewal, restoration, resurgence, resuscitation, return, return from the dead, revival
Antonyms burial, demise, killing off

resuscitate breathe new life into, bring round, bring to life, give artificial respiration to, give the kiss of life, quicken, reanimate, renew, rescue, restore, resurrect, revitalize, revive, revivify, save

retain 1. absorb, contain, detain, grasp, grip, hang *or* hold onto, hold, hold back, hold fast, keep, keep possession of, maintain, preserve, reserve, restrain, save 2. bear in mind, impress on the memory, keep in mind, memorize, recall, recollect, remember 3. commission, employ, engage, hire, pay, reserve
Antonyms (*sense 1*) let go, lose, release, use up (*sense 2*) forget

retainer 1. attendant, dependant, domestic, flunky, footman, henchman, lackey, servant, supporter, valet, vassal 2. advance, deposit, fee

retaliate even the score, exact retribution, get back at, get even with (*Inf.*), get one's own back (*Inf.*), give as good as one gets (*Inf.*), give one a taste of one's own medicine, give tit for tat, hit back, make reprisal, pay one back in one's own coin, reciprocate, return like for like, strike back, take an eye for an eye, take revenge, wreak vengeance
Antonyms accept, submit, turn the other cheek

retaliation an eye for an eye, a taste of one's own medicine, counterblow, counterstroke, reciprocation, repayment, reprisal, requital, retribution, revenge, tit for tat, vengeance

retard arrest, brake, check, clog, decelerate, defer, delay, detain, encumber, handicap, hinder, hold back *or* up, impede, obstruct, set back, slow down, stall
Antonyms accelerate, advance, expedite, hasten, speed, speed up, stimulate

retch barf (*U.S. sl.*), be sick, chuck (up) (*Sl., chiefly U.S.*), chunder (*Sl., chiefly Aust.*), disgorge, do a technicolour yawn (*Sl.*), gag, heave, puke (*Sl.*), regurgitate, spew, throw up (*Inf.*), toss one's cookies (*U.S. sl.*), upchuck (*U.S. sl.*), vomit

reticence quietness, reserve, restraint, secretiveness, silence, taciturnity, uncommunicativeness, unforthcomingness

reticent close-mouthed, mum, quiet, reserved, restrained, secretive, silent, taciturn, tight-lipped, uncommunicative, unforthcoming, unspeaking
Antonyms candid, communicative, expansive, frank, open, talkative, voluble

retinue aides, attendants, cortege, entourage, escort, followers, following, servants, suite, train

retire 1. be pensioned off, (be) put out to grass (*Inf.*), give up work, stop working 2. absent oneself, betake oneself, depart, exit, go away, leave, remove, withdraw 3. go to bed, go to one's room, go to sleep, hit the sack (*Sl.*), kip down (*Brit. sl.*), turn in (*Inf.*) 4. decamp, ebb, fall back, give ground, give way, pull back, pull out, recede, retreat, withdraw

retirement loneliness, obscurity, privacy, retreat, seclusion, solitude, withdrawal

retiring bashful, coy, demure, diffident, humble, meek, modest, quiet, reclusive, reserved, reticent, self-effacing, shrinking, shy, timid, timorous, unassertive, unassuming
Antonyms audacious, bold, brassy, forward, gregarious, outgoing, sociable

retort 1. *v.* answer, answer back, come back with, counter, rejoin, reply, respond, retaliate, return, riposte 2. *n.* answer, comeback (*Inf.*), rejoinder, reply, response, riposte

retouch brush up, correct, finish, improve, recondition, renovate, restore, touch up

retract 1. draw in, pull back, pull in, reel in, sheathe 2. abjure, cancel, deny, disavow, disclaim, disown, recall, recant, renege, renounce, repeal, repudiate, rescind, reverse, revoke, take back, unsay, withdraw 3. back out of, go back on, renege on

retreat *v.* 1. back away, depart, draw back, ebb, fall back, give ground, go back, leave, pull back, recede, recoil, retire, shrink, turn tail, withdraw ~*n.* 2. departure, ebb, evacuation, flight, retirement, withdrawal 3. asylum, den, haunt, haven, hideaway,

privacy, refuge, resort, retirement, sanctuary, seclusion, shelter
Antonyms *v.* advance, engage, move forward *~n.* (*sense 2*) advance, charge, entrance

retrench curtail, cut, cut back, decrease, diminish, economize, husband, lessen, limit, make economies, pare, prune, reduce, save, tighten one's belt, trim

retrenchment contraction, cost-cutting, curtailment, cut, cutback, economy, pruning, reduction, rundown, tightening one's belt
Antonyms expansion, investment

retribution an eye for an eye, compensation, justice, Nemesis, punishment, reckoning, recompense, redress, repayment, reprisal, requital, retaliation, revenge, reward, satisfaction, vengeance

retrieve fetch back, get back, recall, recapture, recoup, recover, redeem, regain, repair, repossess, rescue, restore, salvage, save, win back

retrograde 1. *adj.* backward, declining, degenerative, deteriorating, downward, inverse, negative, regressive, relapsing, retreating, retrogressive, reverse, waning, worsening 2. *v.* backslide, decline, degenerate, deteriorate, go downhill (*Inf.*), regress, relapse, retreat, retrogress, revert, wane, worsen

retrogress 1. backslide, decline, deteriorate, go back, go downhill (*Inf.*), regress, relapse, retrocede, retrograde, return, revert, worsen 2. drop, ebb, fall, go back, lose ground, recede, retire, retreat, sink, wane, withdraw

retrospect afterthought, hindsight, recollection, re-examination, remembrance, reminiscence, review, survey
Antonyms anticipation, foresight

return *v.* 1. come back, come round again, go back, reappear, rebound, recoil, recur, repair, retreat, revert, turn back 2. carry back, convey, give back, put back, re-establish, reinstate, remit, render, replace, restore, retrocede, send, send back, take back, transmit 3. give back, pay back, reciprocate, recompense, refund, reimburse, repay, requite 4. bring in, earn, make, net, repay, yield 5. answer, come back (with), communicate, rejoin, reply, respond, retort 6. choose, elect, pick, vote in 7. announce, arrive at, bring in, come to, deliver, render, report, submit *~n.* 8. homecoming, reappearance, rebound, recoil, recrudescence, recurrence, retreat, reversion 9. re-establishment, reinstatement, replacement, restoration 10. advantage, benefit, gain, income, interest, proceeds, profit, revenue, takings, yield 11. compensation, meed (*Archaic*), reciprocation, recompense, reimbursement, reparation, repayment, requital, retaliation, reward 12. account, form, list, report, statement, summary 13. answer, comeback (*Inf.*), rejoinder, reply, response, retort, riposte
Antonyms *v.* (*sense 1*) depart, disappear, go away, leave (*senses 2 & 3*) hold, keep, leave, remove, retain (*sense 4*) lose *~n.* (*sense 8*) departure, leaving (*sense 9*) removal

revamp do up (*Inf.*), fix up (*Inf., chiefly U.S. & Canad.*), give a face-lift to, overhaul, patch up, recondition, refit, refurbish, rehabilitate, renovate, repair, restore

reveal 1. announce, betray, blow wide open (*Sl.*), broadcast, communicate, disclose, divulge, give away, give out, impart, leak, let on, let out, let slip, make known, make public, proclaim, publish, tell 2. bare, bring to light, display, exhibit, expose to view, lay bare, manifest, open, show, uncover, unearth, unmask, unveil
Antonyms conceal, cover up, hide, keep quiet about

revel *v.* 1. *With* **in** bask, crow, delight, drool, gloat, indulge, joy, lap up, luxuriate, rejoice, relish, savour, take pleasure, thrive on, wallow 2. carouse, celebrate, go on a spree, live it up (*Inf.*), make merry, paint the town red (*Inf.*), push the boat out (*Brit. inf.*), rave (*Brit. sl.*), roister, whoop it up (*Inf.*) *~n.* 3. *Often plural* bacchanal, beano (*Brit. sl.*), carousal, carouse, celebration, debauch, festivity, gala, jollification, merrymaking, party, rave (*Brit. sl.*), rave-up (*Brit. sl.*), saturnalia, spree
Antonyms (*sense 1*) abhor, be uninterested in, dislike, hate, have no taste for

revelation announcement, betrayal, broadcasting, communication, disclosure, discovery, display, exhibition, exposé, exposition, exposure, giveaway, leak, manifestation, news, proclamation, publication, telling, uncovering, unearthing, unveiling

reveller carouser, celebrator, merrymaker, partygoer, pleasure-seeker, roisterer

revelry beano (*Brit. sl.*), carousal, carouse, celebration, debauch, debauchery, festivity, fun, jollification, jollity, merrymaking, party, rave (*Brit. sl.*), rave-up (*Brit. sl.*), roistering, saturnalia, spree

revenge 1. *n.* an eye for an eye, reprisal, requital, retaliation, retribution, satisfaction, vengeance, vindictiveness 2. *v.* avenge, even the score for, get one's own back for (*Inf.*), hit back, make reprisal for, repay, requite, retaliate, take an eye for an eye for, take revenge for, vindicate

revengeful bitter, implacable, malevolent, malicious, malignant, merciless, pitiless, resentful, spiteful, unforgiving, unmerciful, vengeful, vindictive

revenue gain, income, interest, proceeds, profits, receipts, returns, rewards, takings, yield
Antonyms expenditure, expenses, outgoings

reverberate echo, rebound, recoil, re-echo, resound, ring, vibrate

reverberation 1. echo, rebound, recoil, re-echoing, reflection, resonance, resounding, ringing, vibration 2. *Fig. Usually plural* consequences, effects, repercussions, results

revere adore, be in awe of, defer to, exalt, have a high opinion of, honour, look up to, put on a pedestal, respect, reverence, think highly of, venerate, worship
Antonyms deride, despise, hold in contempt, scorn, sneer at

reverence 1. *n.* admiration, adoration, awe, deference, devotion, high esteem, homage, honour, respect, veneration, worship 2. *v.* admire, adore, be in awe of, hold in awe, honour, pay homage to, respect, revere, venerate, worship
Antonyms (*sense 1*) contempt, contumely, derision, disdain, scorn

reverent adoring, awed, decorous, deferential, devout, humble, loving, meek, pious, respectful, reverential, solemn, submissive
Antonyms cheeky, disrespectful, flippant, impious, irreverent, mocking, sacrilegious

reverie absent-mindedness, abstraction, brown study, castles in the air *or* Spain, daydream, daydreaming, inattention, musing, preoccupation, trance, woolgathering

reverse *v.* 1. invert, transpose, turn back, turn over, turn round, turn upside down, upend 2. alter, annul, cancel, change, countermand, declare null and void, invalidate, negate, obviate, overrule, overset, overthrow, overturn, quash, repeal, rescind, retract, revoke, set aside, undo, upset 3. back, backtrack, back up, go backwards, move backwards, retreat *~n.* 4. antithesis, contradiction, contrary, converse, inverse, opposite 5. back, flip side, other side, rear, underside, verso, wrong side 6. adversity, affliction, blow, check, defeat, disappointment, failure, hardship, misadventure, misfortune, mishap, repulse, reversal, setback, trial, vicissitude *~adj.* 7. back to front, backward, contrary, converse, inverse, inverted, opposite
Antonyms *v.* (*sense 2*) carry out, enforce, implement, validate (*sense 3*) advance, go forward, move forward *~n.* (*sense 5*) forward side, front, obverse, recto, right side

revert backslide, come back, go back, hark back, lapse, recur, regress, relapse, resume, return, take up where one left off

review *v.* 1. go over again, look at again, reassess, recapitulate, reconsider, re-evaluate, re-examine, rethink, revise, run over, take another look at, think over 2. call to mind, look back on, recall, recollect, reflect on, remember, summon up 3. assess, criticize, discuss, evaluate, examine, give one's opinion of, inspect, judge, read through, scrutinize, study, weigh, write a critique of *~n.* 4. analysis, examination, perusal, report, scrutiny, study, survey 5. commentary, critical assessment, criticism, critique, evaluation, judgment, notice, study 6. journal, magazine, periodical 7. another look, fresh look, reassessment, recapitulation, reconsideration, re-evaluation, re-examination, rethink, retrospect, revision, second look 8. *Military* display, inspection, march past, parade, procession

reviewer arbiter, commentator, connoisseur, critic, essayist, judge

revile abuse, asperse, bad-mouth (*Sl., chiefly U.S. & Canad.*), calumniate, defame, denigrate, knock (*Inf.*), libel, malign, reproach, rubbish (*Inf.*), run down, scorn, slag (off) (*Sl.*), slander, smear, traduce, vilify, vituperate

revise 1. alter, amend, change, correct, edit, emend, modify, reconsider, redo, re-examine, revamp, review, rework, rewrite, update 2. go over, memorize, reread, run through, study, swot up (*Brit. inf.*)

revision 1. alteration, amendment, change, correction, editing, emendation, modification, re-examination, review, rewriting, updating 2. homework, memorizing, rereading, studying, swotting (*Brit. inf.*)

revitalize breathe new life into, bring back to life, reanimate, refresh, rejuvenate, renew, restore, resurrect, revivify

revival awakening, quickening, reanimation, reawakening, rebirth, recrudescence, refreshment, renaissance, renascence, renewal, restoration, resurgence, resurrection, resuscitation, revitalization, revivification
Antonyms disappearance, extinction, falling off, suppression

revive animate, awaken, breathe new life into, bring back to life, bring round, cheer, come round, comfort, invigorate, quicken, rally, reanimate, recover, refresh, rekindle, renew, renovate, restore, resuscitate, revitalize, rouse, spring up again

Antonyms die out, disappear, enervate, exhaust, tire out, weary

revivify breathe new life into, give new life to, inspirit, invigorate, reanimate, refresh, renew, restore, resuscitate, revive

revoke abolish, abrogate, annul, call back, cancel, countermand, declare null and void, disclaim, invalidate, negate, nullify, obviate, quash, recall, recant, renege, renounce, repeal, repudiate, rescind, retract, reverse, set aside, take back, withdraw

Antonyms confirm, endorse, implement, maintain, put into effect, uphold

revolt *n.* 1. defection, insurgency, insurrection, mutiny, putsch, rebellion, revolution, rising, sedition, uprising ~*v.* 2. defect, mutiny, rebel, resist, rise, take to the streets, take up arms (against) 3. disgust, give one the creeps (*Inf.*), gross out (*U.S. sl.*), make one's flesh creep, nauseate, offend, repel, repulse, shock, sicken, turn off (*Inf.*), turn one's stomach

revolting abhorrent, abominable, appalling, cringe-making (*Brit. inf.*), disgusting, distasteful, foul, horrible, horrid, loathsome, nasty, nauseating, nauseous, noisome, obnoxious, obscene, offensive, repellent, repugnant, repulsive, shocking, sickening, yucky *or* yukky (*Sl.*)

Antonyms agreeable, attractive, delightful, fragrant, palatable, pleasant

revolution *n.* 1. coup, coup d'état, insurgency, mutiny, putsch, rebellion, revolt, rising, uprising 2. drastic *or* radical change, innovation, metamorphosis, reformation, sea change, shift, transformation, upheaval 3. circle, circuit, cycle, gyration, lap, orbit, rotation, round, spin, turn, wheel, whirl

revolutionary *n.* 1. insurgent, insurrectionary, insurrectionist, mutineer, rebel, revolutionist ~*adj.* 2. extremist, insurgent, insurrectionary, mutinous, radical, rebel, seditious, subversive 3. avant-garde, different, drastic, experimental, fundamental, ground-breaking, innovative, new, novel, progressive, radical, thoroughgoing

Antonyms (*senses 1 & 2*) counter-revolutionary, loyalist, reactionary (*sense 3*) conservative, conventional, mainstream, minor, traditional, trivial

revolve 1. circle, go round, gyrate, orbit, rotate, spin, turn, twist, wheel, whirl 2. consider, deliberate, meditate, mull over, ponder, reflect, ruminate, study, think about, think over, turn over (in one's mind)

revulsion abhorrence, abomination, aversion, detestation, disgust, distaste, loathing, odium, recoil, repugnance, repulsion

Antonyms attraction, desire, fascination, liking, pleasure

reward *n.* 1. benefit, bonus, bounty, compensation, gain, honour, meed (*Archaic*), merit, payment, premium, prize, profit, recompense, remuneration, repayment, requital, return, wages 2. comeuppance (*Sl.*), desert, just deserts, punishment, requital, retribution ~*v.* 3. compensate, honour, make it worth one's while, pay, recompense, remunerate, repay, requite

Antonyms *n.* (*sense 1*) fine, penalty, punishment ~*v.* (*sense 3*) fine, penalize, punish

rewarding advantageous, beneficial, economic, edifying, enriching, fruitful, fulfilling, gainful, gratifying, pleasing, productive, profitable, remunerative, satisfying, valuable, worthwhile

Antonyms barren, boring, fruitless, unproductive, unprofitable, unrewarding, vain

reword express differently, paraphrase, put another way, put in other words, recast, rephrase

rewrite correct, edit, emend, recast, redraft, revise, touch up

rhetoric 1. eloquence, oratory 2. bombast, fustian, grandiloquence, hot air (*Inf.*), hyperbole, magniloquence, pomposity, rant, verbosity, wordiness

rhetorical 1. bombastic, declamatory, flamboyant, flashy, florid, flowery, grandiloquent, high-flown, high-sounding, hyperbolic, magniloquent, oratorical, pompous, pretentious, showy, silver-tongued, verbose, windy 2. linguistic, oratorical, stylistic, verbal

rhyme *n.* 1. ode, poem, poetry, song, verse 2. **rhyme or reason** logic, meaning, method, plan, sense ~*v.* 3. chime, harmonize, sound like

rhythm accent, beat, cadence, flow, lilt, measure (*Prosody*), metre, movement, pattern, periodicity, pulse, swing, tempo, time

rhythmic, rhythmical cadenced, flowing, harmonious, lilting, melodious, metrical, musical, periodic, pulsating, throbbing

ribald bawdy, blue, broad, coarse, earthy, filthy, gross, indecent, licentious, naughty, near the knuckle (*Inf.*), obscene, off colour, Rabelaisian, racy, raunchy (*Sl.*), risqué, rude, scurrilous, smutty, vulgar

Antonyms chaste, decent, decorous, genteel, inoffensive, polite, proper, refined, tasteful

ribaldry bawdiness, billingsgate, coarseness, earthiness, filth, grossness, indecency, licentiousness, naughtiness, obscenity, raciness, rudeness, scurrility, smut, smuttiness, vulgarity

rich 1. affluent, filthy rich, flush (*Inf.*), loaded (*Sl.*), made of money (*Inf.*), moneyed, opulent, propertied, prosperous, rolling (*Sl.*), stinking rich (*Inf.*), wealthy, well-heeled (*Inf.*), well-off, well-to-do **2.** abounding, full, productive, well-endowed, well-provided, well-stocked, well-supplied **3.** abounding, abundant, ample, copious, exuberant, fecund, fertile, fruitful, full, lush, luxurious, plenteous, plentiful, productive, prolific **4.** beyond price, costly, elaborate, elegant, expensive, exquisite, fine, gorgeous, lavish, palatial, precious, priceless, splendid, sumptuous, superb, valuable **5.** creamy, delicious, fatty, flavoursome, full-bodied, heavy, highly-flavoured, juicy, luscious, savoury, spicy, succulent, sweet, tasty **6.** bright, deep, gay, intense, strong, vibrant, vivid, warm **7.** deep, dulcet, full, mellifluous, mellow, resonant **8.** amusing, comical, funny, hilarious, humorous, laughable, ludicrous, ridiculous, risible, side-splitting

Antonyms (*sense 1*) destitute, impoverished, needy, penniless, poor (*sense 2*) lacking, poor, scarce, wanting (*sense 3*) barren, poor, unfertile, unfruitful, unproductive (*sense 4*) cheap, cheapo (*Inf.*), inexpensive, valueless, worthless (*sense 5*) bland, dull (*sense 6*) dull, insipid, weak (*sense 7*) high-pitched

riches abundance, affluence, assets, fortune, gold, money, opulence, plenty, property, resources, richness, substance, treasure, wealth

Antonyms dearth, indigence, lack, need, paucity, poverty, scantiness, scarcity, want

richly **1.** elaborately, elegantly, expensively, exquisitely, gorgeously, lavishly, luxuriously, opulently, palatially, splendidly, sumptuously **2.** amply, appropriately, fully, in full measure, properly, suitably, thoroughly, well

rickety broken, broken-down, decrepit, derelict, dilapidated, feeble, flimsy, frail, imperfect, infirm, insecure, jerry-built, precarious, ramshackle, shaky, tottering, unsound, unsteady, weak, wobbly

rid **1.** clear, deliver, disabuse, disburden, disembarrass, disencumber, free, lighten, make free, purge, relieve, unburden **2. get rid of** dispense with, dispose of, do away with, dump, eject, eliminate, expel, give the bum's rush (*Sl.*), jettison, remove, shake off, throw away *or* out, unload, weed out

riddance clearance, clearing out, deliverance, disposal, ejection, elimination, expulsion, freedom, release, relief, removal

riddle[1] brain-teaser (*Inf.*), Chinese puzzle, conundrum, enigma, mystery, poser, problem, puzzle, rebus, teaser

riddle[2] *v.* **1.** honeycomb, pepper, perforate, pierce, puncture **2.** corrupt, damage, fill, impair, infest, mar, permeate, pervade, spoil **3.** bolt, filter, screen, sieve, sift, strain, winnow ~*n.* **4.** filter, screen, sieve, strainer

ride *v.* **1.** control, handle, manage, sit on **2.** be borne (carried, supported), float, go, journey, move, progress, sit, travel **3.** dominate, enslave, grip, haunt, oppress, tyrannize over ~*n.* **4.** drive, jaunt, journey, lift, outing, spin (*Inf.*), trip, whirl (*Inf.*)

ridicule **1.** *n.* banter, chaff, derision, gibe, irony, jeer, laughter, mockery, raillery, sarcasm, satire, scorn, sneer, taunting **2.** *v.* banter, caricature, chaff, deride, humiliate, jeer, lampoon, laugh at, laugh out of court, laugh to scorn, make a fool of, make fun of, make one a laughing stock, mock, parody, poke fun at, pooh-pooh, satirize, scoff, send up (*Brit. inf.*), sneer, take the mickey out of (*Inf.*), take the piss (out of) (*Taboo sl.*), taunt

ridiculous absurd, comical, contemptible, derisory, farcical, foolish, funny, hilarious, inane, incredible, laughable, ludicrous, nonsensical, outrageous, preposterous, risible, silly, stupid, unbelievable

Antonyms bright, clever, intelligent, logical, prudent, rational, reasonable, sagacious, sane, sensible, serious, smart, solemn, well-thought-out, wise

rife abundant, common, current, epidemic, frequent, general, plentiful, prevailing, prevalent, raging, rampant, teeming, ubiquitous, universal, widespread

riffraff *canaille,* dregs of society, hoi polloi, rabble, ragtag and bobtail, scum, undesirables

rifle *v.* burgle, despoil, go through, gut, loot, pillage, plunder, ransack, rob, rummage, sack, strip

rift **1.** breach, break, chink, cleavage, cleft, crack, cranny, crevice, fault, fissure, flaw, fracture, gap, opening, space, split **2.** alienation, breach, difference, disagreement, division, estrangement, falling out (*Inf.*), quarrel, schism, separation, split

rig *v.* **1.** accoutre, equip, fit out, furnish, kit out, outfit, provision, supply, turn out **2.** arrange, doctor, engineer, fake, falsify, fiddle with (*Inf.*), fix (*Inf.*), gerrymander, juggle, manipulate, tamper with, trump up ~*n.* **3.** accoutrements, apparatus, equipage, equipment, fitments, fittings, fixtures, gear, machinery, outfit, tackle

right *adj.* **1.** equitable, ethical, fair, good, honest, honourable, just, lawful, moral, proper, righteous, true, upright, virtuous **2.** accurate, admissible, authentic, correct, exact, factual, genuine, precise, satisfactory, sound, spot-on (*Brit. inf.*), true, unerring, valid, veracious 3. advantageous, appropriate, becoming, *comme il faut,* convenient, deserved, desirable, done, due, favourable, fit, fitting, ideal, opportune, proper, propitious, rightful, seemly, suitable 4. all there (*Inf.*), balanced, *compos mentis,* fine, fit, healthy, in good health, in the pink, lucid, normal, rational, reasonable, sane, sound, unimpaired, up to par, well 5. conservative, reactionary, Tory 6. absolute, complete, out-and-out, outright, pure, real, thorough, thoroughgoing, utter ~*adv.* 7. accurately, aright, correctly, exactly, factually, genuinely, precisely, truly 8. appropriately, aptly, befittingly, fittingly, properly, satisfactorily, suitably 9. directly, immediately, instantly, promptly, quickly, straight, straightaway, without delay 10. bang, exactly, precisely, slap-bang (*Inf.*), squarely 11. absolutely, all the way, altogether, completely, entirely, perfectly, quite, thoroughly, totally, utterly, wholly 12. ethically, fairly, honestly, honourably, justly, morally, properly, righteously, virtuously 13. advantageously, beneficially, favourably, for the better, fortunately, to advantage, well ~*n.* 14. authority, business, claim, due, freedom, interest, liberty, licence, permission, power, prerogative, privilege, title 15. equity, good, goodness, honour, integrity, justice, lawfulness, legality, morality, propriety, reason, rectitude, righteousness, truth, uprightness, virtue 16. **by rights** equitably, in fairness, justly, properly 17. **to rights** arranged, in order, straight, tidy ~*v.* 18. compensate for, correct, fix, put right, rectify, redress, repair, settle, set upright, sort out, straighten, vindicate

Antonyms *adj.* (*sense 1*) bad, dishonest, immoral, improper, indecent, unethical, unfair, unjust, wrong (*sense 2*) counterfeit, erroneous, fake, false, fraudulent, illegal, illicit, inaccurate, incorrect, inexact, invalid, mistaken, questionable, uncertain, unlawful, untruthful, wrong (*sense 3*) disadvantageous, inappropriate, inconvenient, undesirable, unfitting, unseemly, unsuitable, wrong (*sense 4*) abnormal, unsound (*sense 5*) left, leftist, left-wing, liberal, radical, right-on (*Inf.*), socialist ~*adv.* (*sense 7*) inaccurately, incorrectly (*sense 8*) improperly (*sense 9*) incompletely, indirectly, slowly (*sense 13*) badly, poorly, unfavourably ~*n.* (*sense 15*) badness, dishonour, evil, immorality, impropriety ~*v.* (*sense 18*) make crooked, topple

right away at once, directly, forthwith, immediately, instantly, now, posthaste, promptly, pronto (*Inf.*), right off, straightaway, straight off (*Inf.*), this instant, without delay, without hesitation

righteous blameless, equitable, ethical, fair, good, honest, honourable, just, law-abiding, moral, pure, squeaky-clean, upright, virtuous

Antonyms bad, corrupt, dishonest, dishonourable, evil, false, guilty, immoral, improper, indecent, insincere, sinful, unethical, unfair, unjust, unprincipled, unrighteous, unscrupulous, unseemly, wicked

righteousness blamelessness, equity, ethicalness, faithfulness, goodness, honesty, honour, integrity, justice, morality, probity, purity, rectitude, uprightness, virtue

rightful authorized, bona fide, de jure, due, just, lawful, legal, legitimate, proper, real, suitable, true, valid

rigid adamant, austere, exact, fixed, harsh, inflexible, intransigent, invariable, rigorous, set, severe, stern, stiff, strict, stringent, unalterable, unbending, uncompromising, undeviating, unrelenting, unyielding

Antonyms bending, elastic, flexible, indulgent, lax, lenient, limber, lissom(e), merciful, mobile, pliable, pliant, soft, supple, tolerant, yielding

rigmarole balderdash, bother, carry-on (*Inf., chiefly Brit.*), gibberish, hassle (*Inf.*), jargon, nonsense, palaver, performance (*Inf.*), red tape, to-do, trash, twaddle

rigorous 1. austere, challenging, demanding, exacting, firm, hard, harsh, inflexible, rigid, severe, stern, strict, stringent, tough 2. accurate, conscientious, exact, meticulous, nice, painstaking, precise, punctilious, scrupulous, thorough 3. bad, bleak, extreme, harsh, inclement, inhospitable, severe

Antonyms (*sense 1*) easy, flexible, friendly, genial, gentle, humane, indulgent, kind, lax, lenient, loose, merciful, mild, permissive, relaxed, soft, sympathetic, tolerant, weak (*sense 2*) careless, half-hearted, haphazard, imperfect, inaccurate, incorrect, inexact, loose, negligent, slapdash, sloppy, slovenly, unscrupulous (*sense 3*) agreeable, mild, pleasant

rigour 1. asperity, austerity, firmness, hardness, hardship, harshness, inflexibility, ordeal, privation, rigidity, sternness, strictness, stringency, suffering, trial 2. accuracy, conscientiousness, exactitude, exactness, meticulousness, preciseness, precision, punctiliousness, thoroughness

rig-out apparel, clobber (*Brit. sl.*), clothing, costume, dress, garb, gear (*Inf.*), get-up

(*Inf.*), habit, outfit, raiment (*Archaic or poetic*), togs

rig out 1. accoutre, equip, fit, furnish, kit out, outfit, set up 2. array, attire, clothe, costume, dress, kit out

rig up arrange, assemble, build, cobble together, construct, erect, fix up, improvise, put together, put up, set up, throw together

rile aggravate (*Inf.*), anger, annoy, bug (*Inf.*), gall, get one's back up, get one's goat (*Sl.*), get on one's nerves (*Inf.*), get under one's skin (*Inf.*), irk, irritate, nark (*Brit., Aust., & N.Z. sl.*), nettle, peeve (*Inf.*), pique, piss one off (*Taboo sl.*), provoke, rub one up the wrong way, try one's patience, upset, vex

rim border, brim, brink, circumference, edge, flange, lip, margin, verge

rind crust, epicarp, husk, integument, outer layer, peel, skin

ring[1] *n.* 1. band, circle, circuit, halo, hoop, loop, round 2. arena, circus, enclosure, rink 3. association, band, cabal, cartel, cell, circle, clique, combine, coterie, crew (*Inf.*), gang, group, junta, knot, mob, organization, syndicate ~*v.* 4. circumscribe, encircle, enclose, encompass, gird, girdle, hem in, seal off, surround

ring[2] *v.* 1. chime, clang, peal, resonate, resound, reverberate, sound, toll 2. buzz (*Inf.*), call, phone, telephone ~*n.* 3. chime, knell, peal 4. buzz (*Inf.*), call, phone call

rinse 1. *v.* bathe, clean, cleanse, dip, splash, wash, wash out, wet 2. *n.* bath, dip, splash, wash, wetting

riot *n.* 1. anarchy, commotion, confusion, disorder, disturbance, donnybrook, fray, lawlessness, mob violence, quarrel, row, street fighting, strife, tumult, turbulence, turmoil, upheaval, uproar 2. boisterousness, carousal, excess, festivity, frolic, high jinks, jollification, merrymaking, revelry, romp 3. display, extravaganza, flourish, show, splash 4. **run riot a.** be out of control, break *or* cut loose, go wild, let oneself go, raise hell, rampage, throw off all restraint **b.** grow like weeds, grow profusely, luxuriate, spread like wildfire ~*v.* 5. fight in the streets, go on the rampage, raise an uproar, rampage, run riot, take to the streets 6. carouse, cut loose, frolic, go on a binge (*Inf.*), go on a spree, make merry, paint the town red (*Inf.*), revel, roister, romp

riotous 1. anarchic, disorderly, insubordinate, lawless, mutinous, rampageous, rebellious, refractory, rowdy, tumultuous, ungovernable, unruly, uproarious, violent 2. boisterous, loud, luxurious, noisy, orgiastic, rambunctious (*Inf.*), roisterous, rollicking, saturnalian, side-splitting, unrestrained, uproarious, wanton, wild
Antonyms calm, civilized, disciplined, gentle, lawful, mild, obedient, orderly, peaceful, quiet, restrained, well-behaved

rip 1. *v.* be rent, burst, claw, cut, gash, hack, lacerate, rend, score, slash, slit, split, tear 2. *n.* cleavage, cut, gash, hole, laceration, rent, slash, slit, split, tear

ripe 1. fully developed, fully grown, mature, mellow, ready, ripened, seasoned 2. accomplished, complete, finished, in readiness, perfect, prepared, ready 3. auspicious, favourable, ideal, opportune, right, suitable, timely
Antonyms (*sense 1*) green, immature, undeveloped, unripe (*sense 2*) imperfect, incomplete, unaccomplished, unfinished, unfit, unprepared (*sense 3*) disadvantageous, inappropriate, inconvenient, inopportune, unfavourable, unfitting, unseemly, unsuitable, untimely

ripen burgeon, come of age, come to fruition, develop, get ready, grow ripe, make ripe, mature, prepare, season

rip-off cheat, con (*Inf.*), con trick (*Inf.*), daylight robbery (*Inf.*), exploitation, fraud, robbery, scam (*Sl.*), sting (*Inf.*), swindle, theft

rip off cabbage (*Brit. sl.*), cheat, con (*Inf.*), cozen, defraud, diddle (*Inf.*), dupe, filch, fleece, gyp (*Sl.*), knock off (*Sl.*), lift (*Inf.*), pilfer, pinch (*Inf.*), rob, skin (*Sl.*), steal from, stiff (*Sl.*), swindle, swipe (*Sl.*), thieve, trick

riposte 1. *n.* answer, comeback (*Inf.*), counterattack, rejoinder, repartee, reply, response, retort, return, sally 2. *v.* answer, come back, reciprocate, rejoin, reply, respond, retort, return

rise *v.* 1. arise, get out of bed, get to one's feet, get up, rise and shine, stand up, surface 2. arise, ascend, climb, enlarge, go up, grow, improve, increase, intensify, levitate, lift, mount, move up, soar, swell, wax 3. advance, be promoted, climb the ladder, get on, get somewhere, go places (*Inf.*), progress, prosper, work one's way up 4. appear, become apparent, crop up, emanate, emerge, eventuate, flow, happen, issue, occur, originate, spring, turn up 5. mount the barricades, mutiny, rebel, resist, revolt, take up arms 6. ascend, climb, get steeper, go uphill, mount, slope upwards ~*n.* 7. advance, ascent, climb, improvement, increase, upsurge, upswing, upturn, upward turn 8. advancement, aggrandizement, climb, progress, promotion 9. acclivity, ascent, elevation, hillock, incline, rising ground, upward slope 10. increment, pay increase, raise (*U.S.*) 11. **give rise to** bring about, bring on, cause, effect, produce, provoke, result in

Antonyms *v.* abate, abbreviate, abridge, condense, curtail, decline, decrease, descend, diminish, drop, dwindle, fall, lessen, plunge, reduce, shrink, sink, wane ~*n.* blip, decline, decrease, downswing, downturn, drop, fall

risible absurd, amusing, comical, droll, farcical, funny, hilarious, humorous, laughable, ludicrous, rib-tickling (*Inf.*), ridiculous, side-splitting

risk 1. *n.* chance, danger, gamble, hazard, jeopardy, peril, pitfall, possibility, speculation, uncertainty, venture 2. *v.* chance, dare, endanger, expose to danger, gamble, hazard, imperil, jeopardize, put in jeopardy, take a chance on, venture

risky chancy (*Inf.*), dangerous, dicey (*Inf., chiefly Brit.*), dodgy (*Brit., Aust., & N.Z. inf.*), fraught with danger, hazardous, perilous, precarious, touch-and-go, tricky, uncertain, unsafe

Antonyms certain, reliable, safe, secure, stable, sure

risqué bawdy, blue, daring, immodest, improper, indelicate, naughty, near the knuckle (*Inf.*), off colour, Rabelaisian, racy, ribald, suggestive

rite act, ceremonial, ceremony, communion, custom, form, formality, liturgy, mystery, observance, ordinance, practice, procedure, ritual, sacrament, service, solemnity, usage

ritual *n.* 1. ceremonial, ceremony, communion, liturgy, mystery, observance, rite, sacrament, service, solemnity 2. convention, custom, form, formality, habit, ordinance, practice, prescription, procedure, protocol, red tape, routine, stereotype, tradition, usage ~*adj.* 3. ceremonial, ceremonious, conventional, customary, formal, habitual, prescribed, procedural, routine, stereotyped

rival *n.* 1. adversary, antagonist, challenger, competitor, contender, contestant, emulator, opponent 2. compeer, equal, equivalent, fellow, match, peer ~*adj.* 3. competing, competitive, conflicting, emulating, opposed, opposing ~*v.* 4. be a match for, bear comparison with, come up to, compare with, compete, contend, emulate, equal, match, measure up to, oppose, seek to displace, vie with

Antonyms *n.* (*sense 1*) ally, friend, helper, supporter ~*v.* (*sense 4*) aid, back, help, support

rivalry antagonism, competition, competitiveness, conflict, contention, contest, duel, emulation, opposition, struggle, vying

riveting absorbing, arresting, captivating, engrossing, enthralling, fascinating, gripping, hypnotic, spellbinding

road 1. avenue, course, direction, highway, lane, motorway, path, pathway, roadway, route, street, thoroughfare, track, way 2. *Nautical* anchorage, roadstead

roam drift, meander, peregrinate, prowl, ramble, range, rove, stravaig (*Scot. & northern English dialect*), stray, stroll, travel, walk, wander

roar *v.* 1. bawl, bay, bell, bellow, clamour, crash, cry, howl, rumble, shout, thunder, vociferate, yell 2. bust a gut (*Inf.*), crack up (*Inf.*), guffaw, hoot, laugh heartily, split one's sides (*Inf.*) ~*n.* 3. bellow, clamour, crash, cry, howl, outcry, rumble, shout, thunder, yell 4. belly laugh (*Inf.*), guffaw, hoot

rob bereave, burgle, cheat, con (*Inf.*), defraud, deprive, despoil, dispossess, do out of (*Inf.*), gyp (*Sl.*), hold up, loot, mug (*Inf.*), pillage, plunder, raid, ransack, rifle, rip off (*Sl.*), sack, skin (*Sl.*), steam (*Inf.*), stiff (*Sl.*), strip, swindle

robber bandit, brigand, burglar, cheat, con man (*Inf.*), fraud, highwayman, looter, mugger (*Inf.*), pirate, plunderer, raider, stealer, swindler, thief

robbery burglary, depredation, embezzlement, filching, fraud, hold-up, larceny, mugging (*Inf.*), pillage, plunder, raid, rapine, rip-off (*Sl.*), spoliation, stealing, steaming (*Inf.*), stick-up (*Sl., chiefly U.S.*), swindle, theft, thievery

robe *n.* 1. costume, gown, habit, vestment 2. bathrobe, dressing gown, housecoat, negligee, peignoir, wrapper ~*v.* 3. apparel (*Archaic*), attire, clothe, drape, dress, garb

robot android, automaton, machine, mechanical man

robust 1. able-bodied, athletic, brawny, fit, hale, hardy, healthy, hearty, husky (*Inf.*), in fine fettle, in good health, lusty, muscular, powerful, Ramboesque, rude, rugged, sinewy, sound, staunch, stout, strapping, strong, sturdy, thickset, tough, vigorous, well 2. boisterous, coarse, earthy, indecorous, raunchy (*Sl.*), raw, roisterous, rollicking, rough, rude, unsubtle 3. commonsensical, down-to-earth, hard-headed, practical, pragmatic, realistic, sensible, straightforward

Antonyms delicate, feeble, frail, hothouse (*Inf., often disparaging*), infirm, refined, sickly, slender, unfit, unhealthy, unsound, weak, weedy (*Inf.*), wimpish *or* wimpy (*Inf.*)

rock[1] 1. boulder, stone 2. anchor, bulwark, cornerstone, foundation, mainstay, protection, support, tower of strength

rock[2] 1. lurch, pitch, reel, roll, sway, swing,

toss, wobble 2. astonish, astound, daze, dumbfound, jar, set one back on one's heels (*Inf.*), shake, shock, stagger, stun, surprise

rocky[1] 1. boulder-strewn, craggy, pebbly, rough, rugged, stony 2. adamant, firm, flinty, hard, rocklike, rugged, solid, steady, tough, unyielding

rocky[2] 1. doubtful, rickety, shaky, uncertain, undependable, unreliable, unstable, unsteady, weak, wobbly 2. *Inf.* dizzy, ill, sick, sickly, staggering, tottering, unsteady, unwell, weak, wobbly

rod bar, baton, birch, cane, crook, dowel, mace, pole, sceptre, shaft, staff, stick, switch, wand

rogue blackguard, charlatan, cheat, con man (*Inf.*), crook (*Inf.*), deceiver, devil, fraud, knave (*Archaic*), mountebank, ne'er-do-well, rapscallion, rascal, reprobate, scally (*Northwest English dialect*), scamp, scoundrel, scumbag (*Sl.*), sharper, swindler, villain

roguish 1. criminal, crooked, deceitful, deceiving, dishonest, fraudulent, knavish, raffish, rascally, shady (*Inf.*), swindling, unprincipled, unscrupulous, villainous 2. arch, cheeky, coquettish, frolicsome, impish, mischievous, playful, puckish, sportive, waggish

roister 1. carouse, celebrate, frolic, go on a spree, live it up (*Inf.*), make merry, paint the town red (*Inf.*), push the boat out (*Brit. inf.*), rave (*Brit. sl.*), revel, rollick, romp, whoop it up (*Inf.*) 2. bluster, boast, brag, show off (*Inf.*), strut, swagger

role 1. character, impersonation, part, portrayal, representation 2. capacity, duty, function, job, part, position, post, task

roll *v.* 1. elapse, flow, go past, go round, gyrate, pass, pivot, reel, revolve, rock, rotate, run, spin, swivel, trundle, turn, twirl, undulate, wheel, whirl 2. bind, coil, curl, enfold, entwine, envelop, furl, swathe, twist, wind, wrap 3. even, flatten, level, press, smooth, spread 4. boom, drum, echo, grumble, resound, reverberate, roar, rumble, thunder 5. billow, lurch, reel, rock, sway, swing, toss, tumble, wallow, welter 6. lumber, lurch, reel, stagger, swagger, sway, waddle ~*n.* 7. cycle, gyration, reel, revolution, rotation, run, spin, turn, twirl, undulation, wheel, whirl 8. ball, bobbin, cylinder, reel, scroll, spool 9. annals, catalogue, census, chronicle, directory, index, inventory, list, record, register, roster, schedule, scroll, table 10. billowing, lurching, pitching, rocking, rolling, swell, tossing, undulation, wallowing, waves 11. boom, drumming, growl, grumble, resonance, reverberation, roar, rumble, thunder

rollick caper, cavort, frisk, galumph (*Inf.*), gambol, make merry, revel, romp

rollicking[1] *adj.* boisterous, carefree, cavorting, devil-may-care, exuberant, frisky, frolicsome, hearty, jaunty, jovial, joyous, lively, merry, playful, rip-roaring (*Inf.*), romping, spirited, sportive, sprightly, swashbuckling
Antonyms cheerless, despondent, dull, gloomy, lifeless, melancholy, morose, sad, sedate, serious, unhappy

rollicking[2] *n.* dressing-down (*Inf.*), lecture, reprimand, roasting (*Inf.*), scolding, telling-off (*Inf.*), ticking off (*Inf.*), tongue-lashing, wigging (*Brit. sl.*)

roly-poly buxom, chubby, fat, overweight, plump, podgy, pudgy, rotund, rounded, tubby

romance *n.* 1. affair, *affaire* (*du coeur*), affair of the heart, amour, attachment, intrigue, liaison, love affair, passion, relationship 2. adventure, charm, colour, excitement, exoticness, fascination, glamour, mystery, nostalgia, sentiment 3. fairy tale, fantasy, fiction, idyll, legend, love story, melodrama, novel, story, tale, tear-jerker (*Inf.*) 4. absurdity, exaggeration, fabrication, fairy tale, falsehood, fiction, flight of fancy, invention, lie, tall story (*Inf.*), trumped-up story ~*v.* 5. be economical with the truth, exaggerate, fantasize, let one's imagination run away with one, lie, make up stories, stretch the truth, tell stories

romantic *adj.* 1. amorous, fond, lovey-dovey, loving, mushy (*Inf.*), passionate, sentimental, sloppy (*Inf.*), soppy (*Brit. inf.*), tender 2. charming, colourful, exciting, exotic, fascinating, glamorous, mysterious, nostalgic, picturesque 3. dreamy, high-flown, idealistic, impractical, quixotic, starry-eyed, unrealistic, utopian, visionary, whimsical 4. chimerical, exaggerated, extravagant, fabulous, fairy-tale, fanciful, fantastic, fictitious, idyllic, imaginary, imaginative, improbable, legendary, made-up, unrealistic, wild ~*n.* 5. Don Quixote, dreamer, idealist, romancer, sentimentalist, utopian, visionary
Antonyms *adj.* cold-hearted, insensitive, practical, realistic, unaffectionate, unimpassioned, uninspiring, unloving, unromantic, unsentimental

romp *v.* 1. caper, cavort, cut capers, frisk, frolic, gambol, have fun, make merry, revel, roister, rollick, skip, sport 2. **romp home** *or* **in** run away with it, walk it (*Inf.*), win by a mile (*Inf.*), win easily, win hands down ~*n.* 3. caper, frolic, lark (*Inf.*)

rook *v.* bilk, cheat, cozen, clip (*Sl.*), defraud, diddle (*Inf.*), do (*Sl.*), fleece, gyp (*Sl.*), mulct, overcharge, rip off (*Sl.*), skin (*Sl.*), stiff (*Sl.*), sting (*Inf.*), swindle

room 1. allowance, area, capacity, compass, elbowroom, expanse, extent, latitude, leeway, margin, play, range, scope, space, territory, volume 2. apartment, chamber, office 3. chance, occasion, opportunity, scope

roomy ample, broad, capacious, commodious, extensive, generous, large, sizable, spacious, wide
Antonyms bounded, confined, cramped, narrow, small, tiny, uncomfortable

root[1] *n.* 1. radicle, radix, rhizome, stem, tuber 2. base, beginnings, bottom, cause, core, crux, derivation, essence, foundation, fountainhead, fundamental, germ, heart, mainspring, nub, nucleus, occasion, origin, seat, seed, source, starting point 3. *Plural* birthplace, cradle, family, heritage, home, origins, sense of belonging 4. **root and branch** completely, entirely, finally, radically, thoroughly, totally, to the last man, utterly, wholly, without exception ~*v.* 5. anchor, become established, become settled, embed, entrench, establish, fasten, fix, ground, implant, moor, set, stick, take root

root[2] burrow, delve, dig, ferret, forage, hunt, nose, poke, pry, rootle, rummage

rooted confirmed, deep, deeply felt, deep-seated, entrenched, established, firm, fixed, ingrained, radical, rigid

root out 1. *Also* **root up** abolish, cut out, destroy, dig up by the roots, do away with, efface, eliminate, eradicate, erase, exterminate, extirpate, get rid of, remove, tear out by the roots, uproot, weed out 2. bring to light, dig out, discover, dredge up, produce, turn up, unearth

rope *n.* 1. cable, cord, hawser, line, strand 2. **the rope** capital punishment, halter, hanging, lynching, noose 3. **know the ropes** be an old hand, be experienced, be knowledgeable, know all the ins and outs, know one's way around, know the score (*Inf.*), know what's what, know where it's at (*Sl.*) ~*v.* 4. bind, fasten, hitch, lash, lasso, moor, pinion, tether, tie

rope in drag in, engage, enlist, inveigle, involve, persuade, talk into

ropy, ropey 1. deficient, inadequate, indifferent, inferior, mediocre, of poor quality, poor, sketchy, substandard 2. *Inf.* below par, off colour, poorly (*Inf.*), rough (*Inf.*), sickish, under the weather (*Inf.*), unwell

roseate 1. blooming, blushing, pink, pinkish, red, rose-coloured, rosy, rubicund, ruddy 2. idealistic, overoptimistic, rose-coloured, unrealistic, utopian

roster agenda, catalogue, inventory, list, listing, register, roll, rota, schedule, scroll, table

rostrum dais, platform, podium, stage

rosy 1. pink, red, roseate, rose-coloured 2. blooming, blushing, flushed, fresh, glowing, healthy-looking, radiant, reddish, roseate, rubicund, ruddy 3. auspicious, bright, cheerful, encouraging, favourable, hopeful, optimistic, promising, reassuring, roseate, rose-coloured, sunny
Antonyms (*sense 2*) ashen, colourless, grey, pale, pallid, sickly, wan, white (*sense 3*) cheerless, depressing, discouraging, dismal, dull, gloomy, hopeless, miserable, pessimistic, unhappy, unpromising

rot *v.* 1. corrode, corrupt, crumble, decay, decompose, degenerate, deteriorate, disintegrate, fester, go bad, moulder, perish, putrefy, spoil, taint 2. decline, degenerate, deteriorate, languish, waste away, wither away ~*n.* 3. blight, canker, corrosion, corruption, decay, decomposition, deterioration, disintegration, mould, putrefaction, putrescence 4. balderdash, balls (*Taboo sl.*), bilge (*Inf.*), bosh (*Inf.*), bull (*Sl.*), bullshit (*Taboo sl.*), bunk (*Inf.*), bunkum *or* buncombe (*Chiefly U.S.*), claptrap (*Inf.*), cobblers (*Brit. taboo sl.*), codswallop (*Brit. sl.*), crap (*Sl.*), drivel, eyewash (*Inf.*), flapdoodle (*Sl.*), garbage (*Chiefly U.S.*), guff (*Sl.*), hogwash, hokum (*Sl., chiefly U.S. & Canad.*), horsefeathers (*U.S. sl.*), hot air (*Inf.*), moonshine, nonsense, pap, piffle (*Inf.*), poppycock (*Inf.*), rubbish, shit (*Taboo sl.*), stuff and nonsense, tommyrot, tosh (*Sl., chiefly Brit.*), tripe (*Inf.*), twaddle

rotary gyratory, revolving, rotating, rotational, rotatory, spinning, turning

rotate 1. go round, gyrate, pirouette, pivot, reel, revolve, spin, swivel, turn, wheel 2. alternate, follow in sequence, interchange, switch, take turns

rotation 1. gyration, orbit, pirouette, reel, revolution, spin, spinning, turn, turning, wheel 2. alternation, cycle, interchanging, sequence, succession, switching

rotten 1. bad, corroded, corrupt, crumbling, decayed, decaying, decomposed, decomposing, disintegrating, festering, fetid, foul, mouldering, mouldy, perished, putrescent, putrid, rank, sour, stinking, tainted, unsound 2. bent (*Sl.*), corrupt, crooked (*Inf.*), deceitful, degenerate, dishonest, dishonourable, disloyal, faithless, immoral, mercenary, perfidious, treacherous, untrustworthy, venal, vicious 3. *Inf.* base, contemptible, despicable, dirty, disagreeable, filthy, mean, nasty, scurrilous, shitty (*Taboo sl.*), unpleasant, vile, wicked 4. *Inf.* bad, deplorable, disappointing, regrettable, un-

fortunate, unlucky **5.** *Inf.* chickenshit (*U.S. sl.*), crummy (*Sl.*), duff (*Brit. inf.*), ill-considered, ill-thought-out, inadequate, inferior, lousy (*Sl.*), low-grade, of a sort *or* of sorts, poor, poxy (*Sl.*), punk, ropy *or* ropey (*Brit. inf.*), sorry, substandard, unac~ceptable, unsatisfactory **6.** *Inf.* bad, below par, ill, off colour, poorly (*Inf.*), ropy *or* ropey (*Brit. inf.*), rough (*Inf.*), sick, under the weather (*Inf.*), unwell
Antonyms (*sense 1*) fresh, good, pure, wholesome (*sense 2*) decent, honest, hon~ourable, moral, scrupulous, trustworthy (*sense 3*) sweet

rotter bad lot, blackguard, blighter (*Brit. inf.*), bounder (*Old-fashioned Brit. sl.*), cad (*Brit. inf.*), cocksucker (*Taboo sl.*), cur, louse (*Sl.*), rat (*Inf.*), scumbag (*Sl.*), stinker (*Sl.*), swine

rotund **1.** bulbous, globular, orbicular, round, rounded, spherical **2.** chubby, cor~pulent, fat, fleshy, heavy, obese, plump, podgy, portly, roly-poly, rounded, stout, tubby **3.** full, grandiloquent, magniloquent, orotund, resonant, rich, round, sonorous
Antonyms (*sense 2*) angular, gaunt, lank, lanky, lean, scrawny, skinny, slender, slight, slim, thin

roué debauchee, dirty old man (*Sl.*), lech *or* letch (*Inf.*), lecher, libertine, profligate, rake, sensualist, wanton

rough *adj.* **1.** broken, bumpy, craggy, ir~regular, jagged, rocky, rugged, stony, un~even **2.** bristly, bushy, coarse, dishevelled, disordered, fuzzy, hairy, shaggy, tangled, tousled, uncut, unshaven, unshorn **3.** agi~tated, boisterous, choppy, inclement, squally, stormy, tempestuous, turbulent, wild **4.** bearish, bluff, blunt, brusque, churlish, coarse, curt, discourteous, ill-bred, ill-mannered, impolite, inconsiderate, indelicate, loutish, rude, unceremonious, uncivil, uncouth, uncultured, ungracious, unmannerly, unpolished, unrefined, untu~tored **5.** boisterous, cruel, curt, drastic, ex~treme, hard, harsh, nasty, rowdy, severe, sharp, tough, unfeeling, unjust, unpleas~ant, violent **6.** *Inf.* below par, ill, not a hundred per cent (*Inf.*), off colour, poorly (*Inf.*), ropy *or* ropey (*Brit. inf.*), rotten (*Inf.*), sick, under the weather (*Inf.*), un~well, upset **7.** cacophonous, discordant, grating, gruff, harsh, husky, inharmonious, jarring, rasping, raucous, unmusical **8.** ar~duous, austere, hard, rugged, spartan, tough, uncomfortable, unpleasant, unre~fined **9.** basic, crude, cursory, formless, hasty, imperfect, incomplete, quick, raw, rough-and-ready, rough-hewn, rudimenta~ry, shapeless, sketchy, unfinished, unpol~ished, unrefined, untutored **10.** crude, raw, rough-hewn, uncut, undressed, unhewn, unpolished, unprocessed, unwrought **11.** amorphous, approximate, estimated, foggy, general, hazy, imprecise, inexact, sketchy, vague ~*n.* **12.** draft, mock-up, outline, pre~liminary sketch, suggestion **13.** *Inf.* bruiser, bully boy, casual, lager lout, ned (*Sl.*), roughneck (*Sl.*), rowdy, ruffian, thug, tough ~*v.* **14.** **rough out** adumbrate, block out, delineate, draft, outline, plan, sketch, sug~gest **15.** **rough up** bash up (*Inf.*), batter, beat the living daylights out of (*Inf.*), beat up, do over (*Brit., Aust., & N.Z. sl.*), knock about *or* around, maltreat, manhandle, mistreat, thrash
Antonyms (*sense 1*) even, level, regular, smooth, unbroken (*sense 2*) smooth, soft (*sense 3*) calm, gentle, quiet, smooth, tran~quil (*sense 4*) civil, considerate, courteous, courtly, delicate, elegant, graceful, gra~cious, pleasant, polite, refined, smooth, so~phisticated, urbane, well-bred, well-mannered (*sense 5*) gentle, just, kind, mild, pleasant, quiet, soft (*sense 7*) harmonious, smooth (*sense 8*) comfortable, cushy (*Inf.*), easy, pleasant, soft (*sense 9*) complete, de~tailed, finished, perfected, polished, re~fined, specific (*sense 10*) smooth (*sense 11*) exact, perfected, specific

rough-and-ready adequate, cobbled to~gether, crude, improvised, makeshift, pro~visional, sketchy, stopgap, thrown together, unpolished, unrefined

rough-and-tumble **1.** *n.* affray (*Law*), brawl, donnybrook, dust-up (*Inf.*), fight, fracas, melee *or* mêlée, punch-up (*Brit. inf..*), roughhouse (*Sl.*), scrap (*Inf.*), scrim~mage, scuffle, shindig (*Inf.*), shindy (*Inf.*), struggle **2.** *adj.* boisterous, disorderly, hap~hazard, indisciplined, irregular, rough, rowdy, scrambled, scrambling

roughhouse **1.** *n.* boisterousness, brawl, brawling, disorderliness, disturbance, horseplay, rough behaviour, row, rowdi~ness, rowdyism, skylarking (*Inf.*) **2.** *v.* brawl, handle roughly, ill-treat, kick up a row (*Inf.*), knock about *or* around, maltreat, manhandle, mistreat, paw, skylark (*Inf.*)

roughneck bruiser (*Inf.*), bully boy, heavy (*Sl.*), rough (*Inf.*), rowdy, ruffian, thug, tough

round *adj.* **1.** annular, ball-shaped, bowed, bulbous, circular, curved, curvilinear, cy~lindrical, discoid, disc-shaped, globular, orbicular, ring-shaped, rotund, rounded, spherical **2.** complete, entire, full, solid, unbroken, undivided, whole **3.** ample, bounteous, bountiful, considerable, gener~ous, great, large, liberal, substantial **4.** am~

ple, fleshy, full, full-fleshed, plump, roly-poly, rotund, rounded 5. full, mellifluous, orotund, resonant, rich, rotund, sonorous 6. blunt, candid, direct, frank, outspoken, plain, straightforward, unmodified ~*n.* 7. ball, band, circle, disc, globe, orb, ring, sphere 8. bout, cycle, sequence, series, session, succession 9. division, lap, level, period, session, stage, turn 10. ambit, beat, circuit, compass, course, routine, schedule, series, tour, turn 11. bullet, cartridge, discharge, shell, shot ~*v.* 12. bypass, circle, circumnavigate, encircle, flank, go round, skirt, turn

roundabout *adj.* circuitous, circumlocutory, devious, discursive, evasive, indirect, meandering, oblique, periphrastic, tortuous
Antonyms direct, straight, straightforward

roundly bitterly, bluntly, fiercely, frankly, intensely, outspokenly, rigorously, severely, sharply, thoroughly, vehemently, violently

round off bring to a close, cap, close, complete, conclude, crown, finish off, put the finishing touch to, settle
Antonyms begin, commence, initiate, open, start

round on abuse, attack, bite (someone's) head off (*Inf.*), have a go at (*Brit. sl.*), lose one's temper with, retaliate, snap at, turn on, wade into

roundup 1. assembly, collection, gathering, herding, marshalling, muster, rally 2. *Inf.* collation, summary, survey

round up assemble, bring together, collect, drive, gather, group, herd, marshal, muster, rally

rouse 1. arouse, awaken, call, get up, rise, wake, wake up 2. agitate, anger, animate, arouse, bestir, disturb, excite, exhilarate, galvanize, get going, incite, inflame, instigate, move, prod, provoke, startle, stimulate, stir, whip up

rousing brisk, electrifying, exciting, exhilarating, inflammatory, inspiring, lively, moving, spirited, stimulating, stirring, vigorous
Antonyms boring, dreary, dull, lifeless, sluggish, spiritless, unenergetic, wearisome, wishy-washy (*Inf.*)

rout 1. *n.* beating, debacle, defeat, disorderly retreat, drubbing, headlong flight, hiding (*Inf.*), licking (*Inf.*), overthrow, overwhelming defeat, pasting (*Sl.*), ruin, shambles, thrashing 2. *v.* beat, chase, clobber (*Sl.*), conquer, crush, cut to pieces, defeat, destroy, dispel, drive off, drub, lick (*Inf.*), overpower, overthrow, put to flight, put to rout, scatter, tank (*Sl.*), thrash, throw back in confusion, wipe the floor with (*Inf.*), worst

route 1. *n.* avenue, beat, circuit, course, direction, itinerary, journey, passage, path, road, round, run, way 2. *v.* convey, direct, dispatch, forward, send, steer

routine *n.* 1. custom, formula, grind (*Inf.*), groove, method, order, pattern, practice, procedure, programme, usage, way, wont 2. *Inf.* act, bit (*Inf.*), line, performance, piece, spiel (*Inf.*) ~*adj.* 3. conventional, customary, everyday, familiar, habitual, normal, ordinary, standard, typical, usual, wonted, workaday 4. boring, clichéd, dull, hackneyed, humdrum, mind-numbing, predictable, run-of-the-mill, shtick (*Sl.*), tedious, tiresome, unimaginative, uninspired, unoriginal
Antonyms *adj.* abnormal, different, exceptional, irregular, special, unusual

rove cruise, drift, gad about, gallivant, meander, ramble, range, roam, stravaig (*Scot. & northern English dialect*), stray, stroll, traipse (*Inf.*), wander

rover bird of passage, drifter, gadabout (*Inf.*), gypsy, itinerant, nomad, rambler, ranger, rolling stone, stroller, transient, traveller, vagrant, wanderer

row[1] bank, column, file, line, queue, range, rank, sequence, series, string, tier

row[2] *n.* 1. altercation, *bagarre,* brawl, commotion, controversy, dispute, disturbance, falling-out (*Inf.*), fracas, fray, fuss, noise, quarrel, racket, ruckus (*Inf.*), ruction (*Inf.*), rumpus, scrap (*Inf.*), shindig (*Inf.*), shindy (*Inf.*), shouting match (*Inf.*), slanging match (*Brit.*), squabble, tiff, trouble, tumult, uproar 2. castigation, dressing-down (*Inf.*), flea in one's ear (*Inf.*), lecture, reprimand, reproof, rollicking (*Brit. inf.*), talking-to (*Inf.*), telling-off (*Inf.*), ticking-off (*Inf.*), tongue-lashing ~*v.* 3. argue, brawl, dispute, fight, scrap (*Inf.*), spar, squabble, wrangle

rowdy 1. *adj.* boisterous, disorderly, loud, loutish, noisy, obstreperous, rough, unruly, uproarious, wild 2. *n.* brawler, casual, hooligan, lager lout, lout, ned (*Sl.*), rough (*Inf.*), ruffian, tearaway (*Brit.*), tough, troublemaker, yahoo, yob *or* yobbo (*Brit. sl.*)
Antonyms *adj.* decorous, gentle, law-abiding, mannerly, orderly, peaceful, refined

royal 1. imperial, kinglike, kingly, monarchical, princely, queenly, regal, sovereign 2. august, grand, impressive, magnificent, majestic, splendid, stately, superb, superior

rub *v.* 1. abrade, caress, chafe, clean, fray, grate, knead, massage, polish, scour, scrape, shine, smooth, stroke, wipe 2. ap~

ply, put, smear, spread 3. **rub up the wrong way** aggravate (*Inf.*), anger, annoy, bug (*Inf.*), get in one's hair (*Inf.*), get one's goat (*Sl.*), get on one's nerves (*Inf.*), get under one's skin (*Inf.*), irk, irritate, nark (*Brit., Aust., & N.Z. sl.*), peeve (*Inf.*), piss one off (*Taboo sl.*), vex ~*n.* 4. caress, kneading, massage, polish, shine, stroke, wipe 5. catch, difficulty, drawback, hindrance, hitch, impediment, obstacle, problem, snag, trouble

rubbish 1. crap (*Sl.*), debris, dreck (*Sl., chiefly U.S.*), dregs, dross, flotsam and jetsam, garbage (*Chiefly U.S.*), grot (*Sl.*), junk (*Inf.*), litter, lumber, offal, offscourings, refuse, scrap, trash, waste 2. balderdash, balls (*Taboo sl.*), bilge (*Inf.*), bosh (*Inf.*), bull (*Sl.*), bullshit (*Taboo sl.*), bunkum *or* buncombe (*Chiefly U.S.*), claptrap (*Inf.*), cobblers (*Brit. taboo sl.*), codswallop (*Brit. sl.*), crap (*Sl.*), drivel, eyewash (*Inf.*), flapdoodle (*Sl.*), garbage (*Chiefly U.S.*), gibberish, guff (*Sl.*), havers (*Scot.*), hogwash, hokum (*Sl., chiefly U.S. & Canad.*), horsefeathers (*U.S. sl.*), hot air (*Inf.*), moonshine, nonsense, pap, piffle (*Inf.*), poppycock (*Inf.*), rot, shit (*Taboo sl.*), stuff and nonsense, tommyrot, tosh (*Sl., chiefly Brit.*), tripe (*Inf.*), twaddle

rubbishy brummagem, cheap, gimcrack, paltry, shoddy, tatty, tawdry, throwaway, trashy, twopenny, twopenny-halfpenny, valueless, worthless

rubicund blushing, florid, flushed, pink, reddish, roseate, rosy, ruddy

rub out 1. cancel, delete, efface, erase, excise, expunge, obliterate, remove, wipe out 2. *U.S. sl.* assassinate, blow away (*Sl., chiefly U.S.*), bump off (*Sl.*), butcher, dispatch, do in (*Inf.*), eliminate (*Sl.*), hit (*Sl.*), kill, knock off (*Sl.*), murder, slaughter, slay, take out (*Sl.*), waste (*Inf.*)

ruction altercation, brawl, commotion, dispute, disturbance, fracas, fuss, quarrel, racket, row, rumpus, scrap (*Inf.*), scrimmage, shindig (*Inf.*), shindy (*Inf.*), storm, to-do, trouble, uproar

ruddy 1. blooming, blushing, florid, flushed, fresh, glowing, healthy, radiant, red, reddish, rosy, rosy-cheeked, rubicund, sanguine, sunburnt 2. crimson, pink, red, reddish, roseate, ruby, scarlet

Antonyms (*sense 1*) anaemic, ashen, colourless, grey, pale, pallid, sickly, wan, white

rude 1. abrupt, abusive, blunt, brusque, cheeky, churlish, curt, discourteous, disrespectful, ill-mannered, impertinent, impolite, impudent, inconsiderate, insolent, insulting, offhand, peremptory, short, uncivil, unmannerly 2. barbarous, boorish, brutish, coarse, crude, graceless, gross, ignorant, illiterate, loutish, low, oafish, obscene, rough, savage, scurrilous, uncivilized, uncouth, uncultured, uneducated, ungracious, unpolished, unrefined, untutored, vulgar 3. artless, crude, inartistic, inelegant, makeshift, primitive, raw, rough, rough-hewn, roughly-made, simple 4. abrupt, harsh, sharp, startling, sudden, unpleasant, violent

Antonyms (*sense 1*) civil, considerate, cordial, courteous, courtly, decent, gentlemanly, gracious, ladylike, mannerly, polite, respectful, sociable, urbane, well-bred (*sense 2*) artful, civilized, cultured, educated, elegant, learned, polished, refined, urbane (*sense 3*) even, finished, shapely, smooth, well-made

rudimentary basic, early, elementary, embryonic, fundamental, immature, initial, introductory, primary, primitive, undeveloped, vestigial

Antonyms advanced, complete, developed, higher, later, mature, refined, secondary, sophisticated, supplementary

rudiments basics, beginnings, elements, essentials, first principles, foundation, fundamentals

rue bemoan, be sorry for, bewail, deplore, grieve, kick oneself for, lament, mourn, regret, repent, reproach oneself for, sorrow for, weep over

rueful conscience-stricken, contrite, dismal, doleful, grievous, lugubrious, melancholy, mournful, penitent, pitiable, pitiful, plaintive, regretful, remorseful, repentant, sad, self-reproachful, sorrowful, sorry, woebegone, woeful

Antonyms cheerful, delighted, glad, happy, joyful, pleased, unrepentant

ruffian bruiser (*Inf.*), brute, bully, bully boy, casual, heavy (*Sl.*), hoodlum, hooligan, lager lout, miscreant, ned (*Sl.*), rascal, rogue, rough (*Inf.*), roughneck (*Sl.*), rowdy, scoundrel, thug, tough, villain, wretch, yardie

ruffle 1. derange, disarrange, discompose, dishevel, disorder, mess up, rumple, tousle, wrinkle 2. agitate, annoy, confuse, disconcert, disquiet, disturb, faze, fluster, harass, hassle (*Inf.*), irritate, nettle, peeve (*Inf.*), perturb, put out, rattle (*Inf.*), shake up (*Inf.*), stir, torment, trouble, unnerve, unsettle, upset, vex, worry

Antonyms (*sense 2*) appease, calm, comfort, compose, console, ease, mollify, solace, soothe

rugged 1. broken, bumpy, craggy, difficult, irregular, jagged, ragged, rocky, rough, stark, uneven 2. furrowed, leathery, lined, rough-hewn, strong-featured, weather-beaten, weathered, worn, wrinkled 3. austere, crabbed, dour, gruff, hard, harsh, rough, rude, severe, sour, stern, surly 4. barbarous, blunt, churlish, crude, graceless, rude, uncouth, uncultured, unpolished, unrefined 5. arduous, demanding, difficult, exacting, hard, harsh, laborious, rigorous, stern, strenuous, taxing, tough, trying, uncompromising 6. beefy (*Inf.*), brawny, burly, hale, hardy, husky (*Inf.*), muscular, Ramboesque, robust, strong, sturdy, tough, vigorous, well-built

Antonyms (*sense 1*) even, gentle, level, regular, smooth, unbroken (*sense 2*) delicate, pretty, refined, smooth, unmarked, youthful (*sense 4*) civil, courteous, cultivated, cultured, elegant, polished, polite, refined, subtle, urbane, well-bred (*sense 5*) agreeable, easy, gentle, mild, pleasant, simple, soft, tender, uncomplicated, unexacting (*sense 6*) delicate, feeble, fragile, frail, infirm, sickly, skinny, soft, weak

ruin *n.* 1. bankruptcy, breakdown, collapse, crackup (*Inf.*), crash, damage, decay, defeat, destitution, destruction, devastation, disintegration, disrepair, dissolution, downfall, failure, fall, havoc, insolvency, nemesis, overthrow, ruination, subversion, the end, undoing, Waterloo, wreck, wreckage ~*v.* 2. bankrupt, break, bring down, bring to nothing, bring to ruin, crush, defeat, demolish, destroy, devastate, impoverish, lay in ruins, lay waste, overthrow, overturn, overwhelm, pauperize, raze, shatter, smash, total (*Sl.*), trash (*Sl.*), wreak havoc upon, wreck 3. blow (*Sl.*), bodge (*Inf.*), botch, cock up (*Brit. sl.*), damage, disfigure, fuck up (*Offens. taboo sl.*), injure, make a mess of, mangle, mar, mess up, screw up (*Inf.*), spoil, undo

Antonyms *n.* creation, preservation, success, triumph, victory ~*v.* build, construct, create, enhance, enrich, improve, keep, mend, preserve, repair, restore, save, start, strengthen, submit to, succumb to, support, surrender to, yield to

ruinous 1. baleful, baneful (*Archaic*), calamitous, catastrophic, crippling, deadly, deleterious, destructive, devastating, dire, disastrous, extravagant, fatal, immoderate, injurious, murderous, noxious, pernicious, shattering, wasteful, withering 2. broken-down, decrepit, derelict, dilapidated, in ruins, ramshackle, ruined

rule *n.* 1. axiom, canon, criterion, decree, dictum, direction, guide, guideline, law, maxim, order, ordinance, precept, principle, regulation, ruling, standard, tenet 2. administration, ascendancy, authority, command, control, direction, domination, dominion, empire, government, influence, jurisdiction, leadership, mastery, power, regime, reign, supremacy, sway 3. condition, convention, custom, form, habit, order *or* way of things, practice, procedure, routine, tradition, wont 4. course, formula, method, policy, procedure, way 5. **as a rule** customarily, for the most part, generally, mainly, normally, on the whole, ordinarily, usually ~*v.* 6. administer, be in authority, be in power, be number one (*Inf.*), command, control, direct, dominate, govern, guide, hold sway, lead, manage, preside over, regulate, reign, wear the crown 7. adjudge, adjudicate, decide, decree, determine, establish, find, judge, lay down, pronounce, resolve, settle 8. be customary (pre-eminent, prevalent, superior), hold sway, obtain, predominate, preponderate, prevail

rule out ban, debar, dismiss, disqualify, eliminate, exclude, forbid, leave out, obviate, preclude, prevent, prohibit, proscribe, reject

Antonyms allow, approve, authorize, let, license, order, permit, sanction

ruler 1. commander, controller, crowned head, emperor, empress, governor, head of state, king, leader, lord, monarch, potentate, prince, princess, queen, sovereign 2. measure, rule, straight edge, yardstick

ruling *n.* 1. adjudication, decision, decree, finding, judgment, pronouncement, resolution, verdict ~*adj.* 2. commanding, controlling, dominant, governing, leading, regnant, reigning, upper 3. chief, current, dominant, main, predominant, pre-eminent, preponderant, prevailing, prevalent, principal, regnant, supreme

Antonyms (*sense 3*) auxiliary, inferior, least, minor, secondary, subordinate, subsidiary, unimportant

rum curious, dodgy (*Brit., Aust., & N.Z. inf.*), funny, odd, peculiar, queer, singular, strange, suspect, suspicious, unusual, weird

rumbustious boisterous, clamorous, disorderly, exuberant, loud, noisy, obstreperous, refractory, robust, rough, rowdy, unmanageable, unruly, uproarious, wayward, wild, wilful

ruminate brood, chew over, cogitate, consider, contemplate, deliberate, meditate, mull over, muse, ponder, reflect, revolve, think, turn over in one's mind, weigh

rummage delve, examine, explore, hunt, ransack, root, rootle, search

rumour 1. *n.* bruit (*Archaic*), buzz, canard,

dirt (*U.S. sl.*), gossip, hearsay, news, report, story, talk, tidings, whisper, word 2. *v.* bruit, circulate, gossip, noise abroad, pass around, publish, put about, report, say, tell, whisper

rump arse (*Taboo sl.*), ass (*U.S. & Canad. taboo sl.*), backside (*Inf.*), bottom, bum (*Brit. sl.*), buns (*U.S. sl.*), butt (*U.S. & Canad. inf.*), buttocks, croup, derrière (*Euphemistic*), haunch, hindquarters, jacksy (*Brit. sl.*), posterior, rear, rear end, seat, tail (*Inf.*)

rumple crease, crinkle, crumple, crush, derange, dishevel, disorder, mess up, pucker, ruffle, screw up, scrunch, tousle, wrinkle

rumpus brouhaha, commotion, confusion, disruption, disturbance, furore, fuss, kerfuffle (*Inf.*), noise, row, shindig (*Inf.*), shindy (*Inf.*), tumult, uproar

run *v.* 1. barrel (along) (*Inf., chiefly U.S. & Canad.*), bolt, career, dart, dash, gallop, hare (*Brit. inf.*), hasten, hie, hotfoot, hurry, jog, leg it (*Inf.*), lope, race, rush, scamper, scramble, scud, scurry, speed, sprint 2. abscond, beat a retreat, beat it (*Sl.*), bolt, clear out, cut and run (*Inf.*), decamp, depart, do a runner (*Sl.*), escape, flee, fly the coop (*U.S. & Canad. inf.*), leg it (*Inf.*), make a run for it, make off, scarper (*Brit. sl.*), show a clean pair of heels, skedaddle (*Inf.*), slope off, take a powder (*U.S. & Canad. sl.*), take flight, take it on the lam (*U.S. & Canad. sl.*), take off (*Inf.*), take to one's heels 3. course, glide, go, move, pass, roll, skim, slide 4. bear, carry, convey, drive, give a lift to, manoeuvre, operate, propel, transport 5. go, operate, ply 6. function, go, operate, perform, tick, work 7. administer, be in charge of, boss (*Inf.*), carry on, conduct, control, coordinate, direct, handle, head, lead, look after, manage, mastermind, operate, oversee, own, regulate, superintend, supervise, take care of 8. continue, extend, go, last, lie, proceed, range, reach, stretch 9. cascade, discharge, flow, go, gush, issue, leak, move, pour, proceed, spill, spout, stream 10. dissolve, fuse, go soft, liquefy, melt, turn to liquid 11. be diffused, bleed, lose colour, mix, spread 12. come apart, come undone, ladder, tear, unravel 13. be current, circulate, climb, creep, go round, spread, trail 14. display, feature, print, publish 15. be a candidate, challenge, compete, contend, put oneself up for, stand, take part 16. bootleg, deal in, ship, smuggle, sneak, traffic in 17. **run for it** abscond, bolt, cut and run (*Inf.*), decamp, do a bunk (*Brit. sl.*), do a runner (*Sl.*), escape, flee, fly, fly the coop (*U.S. & Canad. inf.*), make a break for it, make off, scarper (*Brit. sl.*), scram (*Inf.*), show a clean pair of heels, skedaddle (*Inf.*), take a powder (*U.S. & Canad. sl.*), take flight, take it on the lam (*U.S. & Canad. sl.*), take off ~*n.* 18. dash, gallop, jog, race, rush, sprint, spurt 19. drive, excursion, jaunt, journey, joy ride (*Inf.*), lift, outing, ride, round, spin (*Inf.*), trip 20. chain, course, cycle, passage, period, round, season, sequence, series, spell, streak, stretch, string 21. category, class, kind, order, sort, type, variety 22. application, demand, pressure, rush 23. ladder, rip, snag, tear 24. course, current, direction, drift, flow, motion, movement, passage, path, progress, stream, tendency, tenor, tide, trend, way 25. coop, enclosure, pen 26. **in the long run** at the end of the day, eventually, in the end, in the final analysis, in time, ultimately, when all is said and done 27. **on the run a.** at liberty, escaping, fugitive, in flight, on the lam (*U.S. sl.*), on the loose **b.** defeated, falling back, fleeing, in flight, in retreat, retreating, running away **c.** at speed, hastily, hurriedly, hurrying, in a hurry, in a rush, in haste

Antonyms (*sense 1*) crawl, creep, dawdle, walk (*sense 2*) remain, stay (*sense 8*) cease, stop

run across bump into, chance upon, come across, come upon, encounter, meet, meet with, run into

run after chase, follow, give chase, pursue

runaway *n.* 1. absconder, deserter, escapee, escaper, fugitive, refugee, truant ~*adj.* 2. escaped, fleeing, fugitive, loose, out of control, uncontrolled, wild 3. easily won, easy, effortless

run away 1. abscond, beat it (*Sl.*), bolt, clear out, cut and run (*Inf.*), decamp, do a bunk (*Brit. sl.*), do a runner (*Sl.*), escape, flee, fly the coop (*U.S. & Canad. inf.*), hook it (*Sl.*), make a run for it, run off, scarper (*Brit. sl.*), scram (*Inf.*), show a clean pair of heels, skedaddle (*Inf.*), take a powder (*U.S. & Canad. sl.*), take flight, take it on the lam (*U.S. & Canad. sl.*), take off, take to one's heels 2. *With* **with a.** abduct, abscond, elope **b.** abscond, make off, pinch (*Inf.*), run off, snatch, steal **c.** romp home, walk it (*Inf.*), win by a mile (*Inf.*), win easily, win hands down

rundown briefing, outline, précis, recap (*Inf.*), résumé, review, run-through, sketch, summary, synopsis

run-down 1. below par, debilitated, drained, enervated, exhausted, fatigued, out of condition, peaky, tried, under the weather (*Inf.*), unhealthy, weak, weary, worn-out 2. broken-down, decrepit, dilapi-

dated, dingy, ramshackle, seedy, shabby, tumble-down, worn-out
Antonyms (*sense 1*) fighting fit, fine, fit, fit as a fiddle, full of beans (*Inf.*), healthy, well

run down 1. curtail, cut, cut back, decrease, drop, pare down, reduce, trim 2. debilitate, exhaust, sap the strength of, tire, undermine the health of, weaken 3. asperse, bad-mouth (*Sl., chiefly U.S. & Canad.*), belittle, criticize adversely, decry, defame, denigrate, disparage, knock (*Inf.*), put down, revile, rubbish (*Inf.*), slag (off) (*Sl.*), speak ill of, vilify 4. hit, knock down, knock over, run into, run over, strike

run-in altercation, argument, brush, confrontation, contretemps, dispute, dust-up (*Inf.*), encounter, face-off (*Sl.*), fight, quarrel, row, set-to (*Inf.*), skirmish, tussle

run in 1. break in gently, run gently 2. *Sl.* apprehend, arrest, bust (*Inf.*), collar (*Inf.*), feel one's collar (*Sl.*), jail, lift (*Sl.*), nab (*Inf.*), nail (*Inf.*), pick up, pinch (*Inf.*), pull in (*Brit. sl.*), take into custody, take to jail, throw in jail

run into 1. bump into, collide with, crash into, dash against, hit, ram, strike 2. be beset by, be confronted by, bump into, chance upon, come across, come upon, encounter, meet, meet with, run across

runner 1. athlete, harrier, jogger, miler, sprinter 2. courier, dispatch bearer, errand boy, messenger 3. offshoot, shoot, sprig, sprout, stem, stolon (*Bot.*), tendril

running *adj.* 1. constant, continuous, incessant, in succession, on the trot (*Inf.*), perpetual, together, unbroken, unceasing, uninterrupted 2. flowing, moving, streaming ~*n.* 3. administration, charge, conduct, control, coordination, direction, leadership, management, organization, regulation, superintendency, supervision 4. functioning, maintenance, operation, performance, working 5. competition, contention, contest

runny diluted, flowing, fluid, liquefied, liquid, melted, streaming, watery

run off 1. bolt, clear out, cut and run (*Inf.*), decamp, do a runner (*Sl.*), escape, flee, fly the coop (*U.S. & Canad. inf.*), hook it (*Sl.*), make off, run away, scarper (*Brit. sl.*), show a clean pair of heels, skedaddle (*Inf.*), take a powder (*U.S. & Canad. sl.*), take flight, take it on the lam (*U.S. & Canad. sl.*), take to one's heels 2. churn out (*Inf.*), duplicate, print, produce 3. bleed, drain, flow away, siphon, tap 4. *With* **with** a. lift (*Inf.*), make off, pinch (*Inf.*), purloin, run away, steal, swipe (*Sl.*) b. abscond, elope, run away

run-of-the-mill average, banal, common, commonplace, fair, mediocre, middling, modest, ordinary, passable, tolerable, undistinguished, unexceptional, unexciting, unimpressive
Antonyms excellent, exceptional, extraordinary, marvellous, out of the ordinary, splendid, unusual

run out 1. be exhausted, cease, close, come to a close, dry up, end, expire, fail, finish, give out, peter out, terminate 2. *With* **of** be cleaned out, be out of, exhaust one's supply of, have no more of, have none left, have no remaining 3. *With* **on** *Inf.* abandon, desert, forsake, leave high and dry, leave holding the baby, leave in the lurch, rat (*Inf.*), run away from

run over 1. hit, knock down, knock over, run down, strike 2. brim over, overflow, spill, spill over 3. check, examine, go over, go through, rehearse, reiterate, review, run through, survey

run through 1. impale, pierce, spit, stab, stick, transfix 2. blow (*Sl.*), dissipate, exhaust, fritter away, spend like water, squander, throw away, waste 3. go over, practise, read, rehearse, run over 4. check, examine, go through, look over, review, run over, survey

rupture *n.* 1. breach, break, burst, cleavage, cleft, crack, fissure, fracture, rent, split, tear 2. altercation, breach, break, bust-up (*Inf.*), contention, disagreement, disruption, dissolution, estrangement, falling-out (*Inf.*), feud, hostility, quarrel, rift, schism, split 3. *Medical* hernia ~*v.* 4. break, burst, cleave, crack, fracture, puncture, rend, separate, sever, split, tear 5. break off, cause a breach, come between, disrupt, dissever, divide, split

rural agrarian, agrestic, agricultural, Arcadian, bucolic, countrified, country, hick (*Inf., chiefly U.S. & Canad.*), pastoral, rustic, sylvan, upcountry
Antonyms city, cosmopolitan, town, urban

ruse artifice, blind, deception, device, dodge, hoax, imposture, manoeuvre, ploy, sham, stratagem, subterfuge, trick, wile

rush *v.* 1. accelerate, barrel (along) (*Inf., chiefly U.S. & Canad.*), bolt, burn rubber (*Inf.*), career, dart, dash, dispatch, expedite, fly, hasten, hotfoot, hurry, hustle, lose no time, make haste, make short work of, press, push, quicken, race, run, scramble, scurry, shoot, speed, speed up, sprint, stampede, tear ~*n.* 2. charge, dash, dispatch, expedition, haste, hurry, race, scramble, speed, stampede, surge, swiftness, urgency ~*v.* 3. attack, capture, charge, overcome, storm, take by storm ~*n.* 4. assault, charge, onslaught, push, storm, surge ~*adj.* 5. brisk, cursory, emergency, expedi-

tious, fast, hasty, hurried, prompt, quick, rapid, swift, urgent
Antonyms (*sense 1*) dally, dawdle, delay, procrastinate, slow down, tarry, wait (*sense 5*) careful, detailed, leisurely, not urgent, slow, thorough, unhurried

rust *n.* 1. corrosion, oxidation ~*v.* 2. corrode, oxidize ~*n.* 3. blight, mildew, mould, must, rot ~*v.* 4. atrophy, decay, decline, deteriorate, go stale, stagnate, tarnish

rustic *adj.* 1. agrestic, Arcadian, bucolic, countrified, country, pastoral, rural, sylvan, upcountry 2. artless, homely, homespun, plain, simple, unaffected, unpolished, unrefined, unsophisticated 3. awkward, boorish, churlish, cloddish, clodhopping (*Inf.*), clownish, coarse, crude, graceless, hick (*Inf., chiefly U.S. & Canad.*), loutish, lumpish, maladroit, rough, uncouth, uncultured, unmannerly ~*n.* 4. boor, bumpkin, clod, clodhopper (*Inf.*), clown, country boy, country cousin, countryman, countrywoman, hayseed (*U.S. & Canad. inf.*), hick (*Inf., chiefly U.S. & Canad.*), hillbilly, Hodge, peasant, son of the soil, swain (*Archaic*), yokel
Antonyms *adj.* cosmopolitan, courtly, elegant, grand, polished, refined, sophisticated, urban, urbane ~*n.* city slicker, cosmopolitan, courtier, sophisticate, townee, townsman

rustle 1. *v.* crackle, crepitate, crinkle, susurrate (*Literary*), swish, whish, whisper, whoosh 2. *n.* crackle, crepitation, crinkling, susurration *or* susurrus (*Literary*), rustling, whisper

rusty 1. corroded, oxidized, rust-covered, rusted 2. chestnut, coppery, reddish, reddish-brown, russet, rust-coloured 3. cracked, creaking, croaking, croaky, hoarse 4. ancient, antiquated, antique, dated, old-fashioned, outmoded, out of date, passé 5. deficient, impaired, not what it was, out of practice, sluggish, stale, unpractised, weak

rut *n.* 1. furrow, gouge, groove, indentation, pothole, score, track, trough, wheelmark 2. dead end, groove, habit, humdrum existence, pattern, routine, system ~*v.* 3. cut, furrow, gouge, groove, hole, indent, mark, score

ruthless adamant, barbarous, brutal, callous, cruel, ferocious, fierce, hard, hard-hearted, harsh, heartless, inexorable, inhuman, merciless, pitiless, relentless, remorseless, savage, severe, stern, unfeeling, unmerciful, unpitying, unrelenting, without pity
Antonyms compassionate, forgiving, gentle, humane, kind, lenient, merciful, pitying, sparing

ruttish 1. in heat, in rut, in season, sexually excited 2. aroused, horny (*Sl.*), lascivious, lecherous, lewd, libidinous, lustful, randy (*Inf., chiefly Brit.*), salacious

S

sable *adj.* black, dark, dusty, ebon (*Poetic*), ebony, jet, jetty, raven, sombre

sabotage 1. *v.* cripple, damage, destroy, disable, disrupt, incapacitate, sap the foundations of, subvert, throw a spanner in the works (*Brit. inf.*), undermine, vandalize, wreck 2. *n.* damage, destruction, disruption, subversion, treachery, treason, wrecking

sac bag, bladder, bursa, cyst, pocket, pod, pouch, vesicle

saccharine cloying, honeyed, maudlin, mawkish, nauseating, oversweet, sentimental, sickly, soppy (*Brit. inf.*), sugary, syrupy (*Inf.*), treacly

sack[1] 1. *v.* axe (*Inf.*), discharge, dismiss, fire (*Inf.*), give (someone) his books (*Inf.*), give (someone) his cards, give (someone) his marching orders, give (someone) the boot (*Sl.*), give (someone) the elbow, kick out (*Inf.*), kiss off (*Sl., chiefly U.S. & Canad.*) 2. *n.* **the sack** discharge, dismissal, termination of employment, the axe (*Inf.*), the boot (*Sl.*), the chop (*Brit. sl.*), the (old) heave-ho (*Inf.*), the order of the boot (*Sl.*), the push (*Sl.*)

sack[2] 1. *v.* demolish, depredate (*Rare*), despoil, destroy, devastate, lay waste, loot, maraud, pillage, plunder, raid, ravage, rifle, rob, ruin, spoil, strip 2. *n.* depredation, despoliation, destruction, devastation, looting, pillage, plunder, plundering, rape, rapine, ravage, ruin, waste

sack[3] *n.* **hit the sack** bed down, go to bed, hit the hay (*Inf.*), retire, turn in (*Inf.*)

sackcloth and ashes compunction, contrition, grief, hair shirt, mortification, mourning, penitence, remorse, repentance

sacred 1. blessed, consecrated, divine, hallowed, holy, revered, sanctified, venerable 2. inviolable, inviolate, invulnerable, protected, sacrosanct, secure 3. ecclesiastical, holy, religious, solemn
Antonyms lay, nonspiritual, profane, secular, temporal, unconsecrated, worldly

sacrifice 1. *v.* forego, forfeit, give up, immolate, let go, lose, offer, offer up, surrender 2. *n.* burnt offering, destruction, hecatomb, holocaust (*Rare*), immolation, loss, oblation, renunciation, surrender, votive offering

sacrificial atoning, expiatory, oblatory, propitiatory, reparative

sacrilege blasphemy, desecration, heresy, impiety, irreverence, mockery, profanation, profaneness, profanity, violation
Antonyms piety, respect, reverence

sacrilegious blasphemous, desecrating, godless, impious, irreligious, irreverent, profane, ungodly, unholy

sacrosanct hallowed, inviolable, inviolate, sacred, sanctified, set apart, untouchable

sad 1. blue, cheerless, dejected, depressed, disconsolate, dismal, doleful, down, downcast, down in the dumps (*Inf.*), down in the mouth (*Inf.*), gloomy, glum, grief-stricken, grieved, heavy-hearted, low, low-spirited, lugubrious, melancholy, mournful, pensive, sick at heart, sombre, triste (*Archaic*), unhappy, wistful, woebegone 2. calamitous, dark, depressing, disastrous, dismal, grievous, harrowing, heart-rending, lachrymose, moving, pathetic, pitiable, pitiful, poignant, sorry, tearful, tragic, upsetting 3. bad, deplorable, dismal, distressing, grave, lamentable, miserable, regrettable, serious, shabby, sorry, to be deplored, unfortunate, unhappy, unsatisfactory, wretched
Antonyms blithe, cheerful, cheery, chirpy (*Inf.*), fortunate, glad, good, happy, in good spirits, jolly, joyful, joyous, light-hearted, merry, pleased

sadden aggrieve, bring tears to one's eyes, cast a gloom upon, cast down, dash, deject, depress, desolate, dispirit, distress, grieve, make blue, make one's heart bleed, upset

saddle *v.* burden, charge, encumber, load, lumber (*Brit. inf.*), task, tax

sadistic barbarous, beastly, brutal, cruel, fiendish, inhuman, perverse, perverted, ruthless, savage, vicious

sadness bleakness, cheerlessness, dejection, depression, despondency, dolefulness, dolour (*Poetic*), gloominess, grief, heavy heart, melancholy, misery, mournfulness, poignancy, sorrow, sorrowfulness, the blues, the dumps (*Inf.*), the hump (*Brit. inf.*), tragedy, unhappiness, wretchedness

safe *adj.* 1. all right, free from harm, impregnable, in safety, intact, O.K. *or* okay (*Inf.*), out of danger, out of harm's way, protected, safe and sound, secure, undamaged, unharmed, unhurt, unscathed 2.

harmless, innocuous, nonpoisonous, non~toxic, pure, tame, unpolluted, wholesome 3. cautious, circumspect, conservative, de~pendable, discreet, on the safe side, pru~dent, realistic, reliable, sure, tried and true, trustworthy, unadventurous 4. certain, im~pregnable, risk-free, riskless, secure, sound ~*n.* 5. coffer, deposit box, repository, safe-deposit box, strongbox, vault
Antonyms (*sense 1*) at risk, damaged, en~dangered, imperilled, insecure, jeopardized, put at risk, put in danger, threatened (*sense 2*) baneful, dangerous, harmful, haz~ardous, hurtful, injurious, noxious, perni~cious, unsafe (*sense 3*) imprudent, incau~tious, reckless, risky, unsafe

safe-conduct authorization, licence, pass, passport, permit, safeguard, warrant

safeguard 1. *v.* defend, guard, look after, preserve, protect, screen, shield, watch over 2. *n.* aegis, armour, bulwark, convoy, de~fence, escort, guard, protection, security, shield, surety

safekeeping care, charge, custody, guardi~anship, keeping, protection, supervision, surveillance, trust, tutelage, ward

safely in one piece, in safety, safe and sound, securely, with impunity, without risk, with safety

safety assurance, cover, immunity, impreg~nability, protection, refuge, sanctuary, se~curity, shelter

sag *v.* 1. bag, bulge, cave in, dip, droop, drop, fall, fall unevenly, give way, hang loosely, seat (*of skirts, etc.*), settle, sink, slump, swag 2. decline, droop, fall, flag, slide, slip, slump, wane, weaken, wilt ~*n.* 3. decline, depression, dip, downturn, drop, fall, slip, slump

saga adventure, chronicle, epic, narrative, *roman-fleuve,* soap opera, story, tale, yarn

sagacious able, acute, apt, astute, canny, clear-sighted, discerning, downy (*Brit. sl.*), far-sighted, fly (*Sl.*), insightful, intelligent, judicious, knowing, long-headed, percep~tive, perspicacious, sage, sharp, sharp-witted, shrewd, smart, wise

sagacity acuteness, astuteness, canniness, discernment, foresight, insight, judicious~ness, knowingness, penetration, perspicac~ity, prudence, sapience, sense, sharpness, shrewdness, understanding, wisdom

sage 1. *adj.* acute, canny, discerning, intel~ligent, judicious, learned, perspicacious, politic, prudent, sagacious, sapient, sen~sible, wise 2. *n.* authority, elder, expert, guru, mahatma, man of learning, master, Nestor, philosopher, pundit, savant, Solo~mon, Solon, wise man

sail *v.* 1. cast *or* weigh anchor, embark, get under way, hoist the blue peter, put to sea, set sail 2. captain, cruise, go by water, navigate, pilot, ride the waves, skipper, steer, voyage 3. drift, float, fly, glide, scud, shoot, skim, skirr, soar, sweep, wing 4. *Inf. With* **in** *or* **into** assault, attack, begin, be~labour, fall upon, get going, get to work on, lambast(e), set about, tear into (*Inf.*)

sailor hearty (*Inf.*), Jack Tar, lascar, leatherneck (*Sl.*), marine, mariner, matelot (*Sl., chiefly Brit.*), navigator, salt, sea dog, seafarer, seafaring man, seaman, tar (*Inf.*)

saintly angelic, beatific, blameless, blessed, devout, full of good works, god-fearing, godly, holy, pious, religious, righteous, sainted, saintlike, sinless, virtuous, worthy

sake 1. account, advantage, behalf, benefit, consideration, gain, good, interest, profit, regard, respect, welfare, wellbeing 2. aim, cause, end, motive, objective, principle, purpose, reason

salacious bawdy, blue, carnal, concupis~cent, erotic, indecent, lascivious, lecherous, lewd, libidinous, lickerish (*Archaic*), lust~ful, obscene, pornographic, prurient, ribald, ruttish, smutty, steamy (*Inf.*), wanton

salary earnings, emolument, income, pay, remuneration, stipend, wage, wages

sale 1. auction, deal, disposal, marketing, selling, transaction, vending 2. buyers, consumers, customers, demand, market, outlet, purchasers 3. **for sale** available, in stock, obtainable, on offer, on sale, on the market

salient arresting, conspicuous, important, jutting, marked, noticeable, outstanding, projecting, prominent, pronounced, pro~truding, remarkable, signal, striking

sallow anaemic, bilious, jaundiced-looking, pale, pallid, pasty, peely-wally (*Scot.*), sickly, unhealthy, wan, yellowish
Antonyms glowing, healthy-looking, radi~ant, rosy, ruddy

sally *v.* 1. erupt, go forth, issue, rush, set out, surge ~*n.* 2. *Military* foray, incursion, offensive, raid, sortie, thrust 3. *Fig.* bon mot, crack (*Inf.*), jest, joke, quip, retort, riposte, smart remark, wisecrack (*Inf.*), witticism 4. escapade, excursion, frolic, jaunt, trip

salt *n.* 1. flavour, relish, savour, seasoning, taste 2. **with a grain** *or* **pinch of salt** cynically, disbelievingly, doubtfully, scep~tically, suspiciously, with reservations 3. *Fig.* Attic wit, bite, dry humour, liveliness, piquancy, punch, pungency, sarcasm, sharpness, wit, zest, zip (*Inf.*) 4. mariner, sailor, sea dog, seaman, tar (*Inf.*) ~*adj.* 5. brackish, briny, saline, salted, salty

salt away accumulate, amass, bank, cache,

hide, hoard up, lay by, lay in, lay up, put by, save, save for a rainy day, stash away (*Inf.*), stockpile

salty 1. brackish, briny, over-salted, saline, salt, salted 2. colourful, humorous, lively, piquant, pungent, racy, sharp, snappy (*Inf.*), spicy, tangy, tart, witty, zestful

salubrious beneficial, good for one, healthful, health-giving, healthy, invigorating, salutary, wholesome

salutary 1. advantageous, beneficial, good, good for one, helpful, practical, profitable, timely, useful, valuable 2. healthful, healthy, salubrious

salutation address, greeting, obeisance, salute, welcome

salute *v.* 1. accost, acknowledge, address, doff one's cap to, greet, hail, kiss, pay one's respects to, salaam, welcome 2. acknowledge, honour, pay tribute *or* homage to, present arms, recognize, take one's hat off to (*Inf.*) ~*n.* 3. address, greeting, kiss, obeisance, recognition, salaam, salutation, tribute

salvage *v.* glean, recover, redeem, rescue, restore, retrieve, save

salvation deliverance, escape, lifeline, preservation, redemption, rescue, restoration, saving
Antonyms condemnation, damnation, doom, downfall, hell, loss, perdition, ruin

salve *n.* balm, cream, dressing, emollient, liniment, lotion, lubricant, medication, ointment, unguent

same *adj.* 1. aforementioned, aforesaid, selfsame, very 2. alike, corresponding, duplicate, equal, equivalent, identical, indistinguishable, interchangeable, synonymous, twin 3. changeless, consistent, constant, invariable, unaltered, unchanged, unfailing, uniform, unvarying 4. **all the same a.** after all, anyhow, be that as it may, in any event, just the same, nevertheless, nonetheless, still **b.** immaterial, not worth mentioning, of no consequence, unimportant
Antonyms altered, different, dissimilar, diverse, inconsistent, miscellaneous, other, variable

sameness consistency, identicalness, identity, indistinguishability, lack of variety, likeness, monotony, oneness, predictability, repetition, resemblance, similarity, standardization, tedium, uniformity

sample 1. *n.* cross section, example, exemplification, illustration, indication, instance, model, pattern, representative, sign, specimen 2. *v.* experience, inspect, partake of, taste, test, try 3. *adj.* illustrative, pilot, representative, specimen, test, trial

sanctify absolve, anoint, bless, cleanse, consecrate, hallow, purify, set apart

sanctimonious canting, false, goody-goody (*Inf.*), holier-than-thou, hypocritical, pharisaical, pi (*Brit. sl.*), pietistic, pious, priggish, self-righteous, self-satisfied, smug, Tartuffian *or* Tartufian, too good to be true, unctuous

sanction *n.* 1. allowance, approbation, approval, authority, authorization, backing, confirmation, countenance, endorsement, O.K. *or* okay (*Inf.*), ratification, stamp *or* seal of approval, support 2. *Often plural* ban, boycott, coercive measures, embargo, penalty ~*v.* 3. allow, approve, authorize, back, countenance, endorse, entitle, lend one's name to, permit, support, vouch for 4. confirm, ratify, warrant
Antonyms *n.* (*sense 1*) ban, disapproval, embargo, prohibition, proscription, refusal, veto (*sense 2*) approbation, approval, authority, authorization, dispensation, licence, permission ~*v.* ban, boycott, disallow, forbid, refuse, reject, veto

sanctity 1. devotion, godliness, goodness, grace, holiness, piety, purity, religiousness, righteousness, sanctitude, spirituality 2. inviolability, sacredness, solemnity

sanctuary 1. altar, church, Holy of Holies, sanctum, shrine, temple 2. asylum, haven, protection, refuge, retreat, shelter 3. conservation area, national park, nature reserve, reserve

sanctum 1. Holy of Holies, sanctuary, shrine 2. den, private room, refuge, retreat, study

sane 1. all there (*Inf.*), *compos mentis,* in one's right mind, in possession of all one's faculties, lucid, mentally sound, normal, of sound mind, rational 2. balanced, judicious, level-headed, moderate, reasonable, sensible, sober, sound
Antonyms bonkers (*Sl., chiefly Brit.*), crackpot (*Inf.*), crazy, daft (*Inf.*), foolish, insane, loony (*Sl.*), loopy (*Inf.*), mad, mentally ill, *non compos mentis,* nuts (*Sl.*), off one's head (*Sl.*), off one's trolley (*Sl.*), out to lunch (*Inf.*), round the bend *or* twist (*Sl.*), stupid, unreasonable, unsound, up the pole (*Inf.*)

sang-froid aplomb, calmness, composure, cool (*Sl.*), cool-headedness, coolness, equanimity, imperturbability, indifference, nonchalance, phlegm, poise, self-possession, unflappability (*Inf.*)

sanguinary bloodied, bloodthirsty, bloody, cruel, fell (*Archaic*), flowing with blood, gory, grim, merciless, murderous, pitiless, ruthless, savage

sanguine 1. animated, assured, buoyant, cheerful, confident, hopeful, in good heart, lively, optimistic, spirited 2. florid, red, rubicund, ruddy
Antonyms (*sense 1*) despondent, dispirited, down, gloomy, heavy-hearted, melancholy, pessimistic (*sense 2*) anaemic, ashen, pale, pallid, peely-wally (*Scot.*)

sanitary clean, germ-free, healthy, hygienic, salubrious, unpolluted, wholesome

sanity 1. mental health, normality, rationality, reason, right mind (*Inf.*), saneness, stability 2. common sense, good sense, judiciousness, level-headedness, rationality, sense, soundness of judgment
Antonyms craziness, dementia, folly, insanity, lunacy, madness, mental derangement, mental illness, senselessness, stupidity

sap[1] *n.* 1. animating force, essence, lifeblood, vital fluid 2. *Inf.* charlie (*Brit. inf.*), chump (*Inf.*), drip (*Inf.*), dweeb (*U.S. sl.*), fool, gull (*Archaic*), idiot, jerk (*Sl., chiefly U.S. & Canad.*), muggins (*Brit. sl.*), nerd *or* nurd (*Sl.*), nincompoop, ninny, nitwit (*Inf.*), noddy, noodle, numskull *or* numbskull, oaf, plonker (*Sl.*), prat (*Sl.*), Simple Simon, simpleton, twit (*Inf.*), wally (*Sl.*), weakling, wet (*Brit. inf.*)

sap[2] *v.* bleed, deplete, devitalize, drain, enervate, erode, exhaust, rob, undermine, weaken, wear down

sapience acuity, acuteness, discernment, insight, mother wit, nous (*Brit. sl.*), perspicacity, sagacity, sense, shrewdness, suss (*Sl.*), understanding, wisdom

sapient acute, canny, discerning, discriminating, intelligent, judicious, knowing, long-headed, perspicacious, sagacious, sage, shrewd, wise, would-be-wise

sarcasm bitterness, causticness, contempt, cynicism, derision, irony, mockery, mordancy, satire, scorn, sneering, venom, vitriol

sarcastic acerb, acerbic, acid, acrimonious, backhanded, bitchy (*Inf.*), biting, caustic, contemptuous, cutting, cynical, derisive, disparaging, ironical, mocking, mordacious, mordant, sardonic, sarky (*Brit. inf.*), satirical, sharp, sneering, taunting, vitriolic

sardonic bitter, cynical, derisive, dry, ironical, jeering, malevolent, malicious, malignant, mocking, mordacious, mordant, sarcastic, sneering, wry

Satan Apollyon, Beelzebub, Lord of the Flies, Lucifer, Mephistopheles, Old Nick (*Inf.*), Old Scratch (*Inf.*), Prince of Darkness, The Devil, The Evil One

satanic accursed, black, demoniac, demoniacal, demonic, devilish, diabolic, evil, fiendish, hellish, infernal, inhuman, iniquitous, malevolent, malignant, wicked
Antonyms benevolent, benign, divine, godly, holy

sate 1. indulge to the full, satiate, satisfy, slake 2. cloy, glut, gorge, overfill, saturate, sicken, surfeit, weary

satellite *n.* 1. communications satellite, moon, sputnik 2. *Fig.* attendant, dependant, follower, hanger-on, lackey, minion, parasite, retainer, sidekick (*Sl.*), sycophant, vassal *~adj.* 3. *Fig.* client, dependent, puppet, subordinate, tributary, vassal

satiate 1. cloy, glut, gorge, jade, nauseate, overfill, stuff 2. sate, satisfy, slake, surfeit

satiety 1. overindulgence, saturation, surfeit 2. fullness, gratification, repletion, satiation, satisfaction

satire burlesque, caricature, irony, lampoon, parody, pasquinade, raillery, ridicule, sarcasm, send-up (*Brit. inf.*), skit, spoof (*Inf.*), takeoff (*Inf.*), travesty, wit

satirical, satiric biting, bitter, burlesque, caustic, censorious, cutting, cynical, incisive, ironical, mocking, mordacious, mordant, pungent, Rabelaisian, sarcastic, sardonic, taunting, vitriolic

satirize abuse, burlesque, censure, criticize, deride, hold up to ridicule, lampoon, lash, parody, pillory, ridicule, send up (*Brit. inf.*), take off (*Inf.*), travesty

satisfaction 1. comfort, complacency, content, contentedness, contentment, ease, enjoyment, gratification, happiness, peace of mind, pleasure, pride, repletion, satiety, well-being 2. achievement, appeasing, assuaging, fulfilment, gratification, resolution, settlement 3. amends, atonement, compensation, damages, indemnification, justice, recompense, redress, reimbursement, remuneration, reparation, requital, restitution, settlement, vindication
Antonyms (*senses 1 & 2*) annoyance, discontent, displeasure, dissatisfaction, frustration, grief, injury, misgivings, pain, shame, unhappiness

satisfactory acceptable, adequate, all right, average, competent, fair, good enough, passable, sufficient, suitable, up to standard, up to the mark
Antonyms bad, below par, inadequate, insufficient, leaving a lot to be desired, mediocre, not up to scratch (*Inf.*), poor, substandard, unacceptable, unsatisfactory, unsuitable

satisfied at ease, complacent, content, contented, convinced, easy in one's mind, hap~

py, like the cat that swallowed the canary (*Inf.*), pacified, positive, smug, sure

satisfy 1. appease, assuage, content, feed, fill, gratify, indulge, mollify, pacify, pander to, please, quench, sate, satiate, slake, surfeit 2. answer, be enough (adequate, sufficient), come up to expectations, do, fill the bill (*Inf.*), fulfil, meet, qualify, serve, serve the purpose, suffice 3. assure, convince, dispel (someone's) doubts, persuade, put (someone's) mind at rest, quiet, reassure 4. answer, comply with, discharge, fulfil, meet, pay (off), settle, square up 5. atone, compensate, indemnify, make good, make reparation for, recompense, remunerate, requite, reward

Antonyms (*senses 1, 2, 3 & 4*) annoy, displease, dissatisfy, dissuade, exasperate, fail to meet, fail to persuade, frustrate, give cause for complaint

satisfying cheering, convincing, filling, gratifying, pleasing, pleasurable, satisfactory

saturate douse, drench, drouk (*Scot.*), imbue, impregnate, ret (*used of flax, etc.*), seep, soak, souse, steep, suffuse, waterlog, wet through

saturated drenched, dripping, droukit *or* drookit (*Scot.*), soaked, soaked to the skin, soaking (wet), sodden, sopping (wet), waterlogged, wet through, wringing wet

saturnine dour, dull, gloomy, glum, grave, heavy, morose, phlegmatic, sedate, sluggish, sombre, taciturn, uncommunicative

sauce *n.* audacity, backchat (*Inf.*), brass (*Inf.*), brass neck (*Brit. inf.*), cheek (*Inf.*), cheekiness, disrespectfulness, front, impertinence, impudence, insolence, lip (*Sl.*), neck (*Inf.*), nerve (*Inf.*), rudeness

sauciness backchat (*Inf.*), brass (*Inf.*), brazenness, cheek (*Inf.*), flippancy, impertinence, impudence, insolence, lip (*Sl.*), pertness, rudeness, sauce (*Inf.*)

saucy 1. cheeky (*Inf.*), disrespectful, flip (*Inf.*), flippant, forward, fresh (*Inf.*), impertinent, impudent, insolent, lippy (*U.S. & Canad. sl.*), pert, presumptuous, rude, sassy (*U.S. inf.*), smart-alecky (*Inf.*) 2. dashing, gay, jaunty, natty (*Inf.*), perky, rakish, sporty

saunter 1. *v.* amble, dally, linger, loiter, meander, mosey (*Inf.*), ramble, roam, rove, stravaig (*Scot. & northern English dialect*), stroll, take a stroll, tarry, wander 2. *n.* airing, amble, breather, constitutional, perambulation, promenade, ramble, stroll, turn, walk

savage *adj.* 1. feral, rough, rugged, uncivilized, uncultivated, undomesticated, untamed, wild 2. barbarous, beastly, bestial, bloodthirsty, bloody, brutal, brutish, cruel, devilish, diabolical, ferocious, fierce, harsh, inhuman, merciless, murderous, pitiless, ravening, ruthless, sadistic, vicious 3. in a state of nature, nonliterate, primitive, rude, unspoilt ~*n.* 4. autochthon, barbarian, heathen, indigene, native, primitive 5. barbarian, bear, boor, lout, roughneck (*Sl.*), yahoo, yob (*Brit. sl.*), yobbo (*Brit. sl.*) 6. beast, brute, fiend, monster ~*v.* 7. attack, lacerate, mangle, maul, tear into (*Inf.*)

Antonyms *adj.* balmy, civilized, cultivated, domesticated, gentle, humane, kind, merciful, mild, refined, restrained, tame ~*v.* acclaim, celebrate, praise, rave about (*Inf.*)

savagery barbarity, bestiality, bloodthirstiness, brutality, cruelty, ferocity, fierceness, inhumanity, ruthlessness, sadism, viciousness

savant authority, intellectual, mahatma, master, mastermind, philosopher, sage, scholar

save 1. bail (someone) out, come to (someone's) rescue, deliver, free, liberate, recover, redeem, rescue, salvage, set free 2. be frugal, be thrifty, collect, economize, gather, hide away, hoard, hold, husband, keep, keep up one's sleeve (*Inf.*), lay by, put aside for a rainy day, put by, reserve, retrench, salt away, set aside, store, tighten one's belt (*Inf.*), treasure up 3. conserve, guard, keep safe, look after, preserve, protect, safeguard, screen, shield, take care of 4. hinder, obviate, prevent, rule out, spare

Antonyms (*senses 1 & 3*) abandon, condemn, discard, endanger, expose, imperil, risk, threaten (*sense 2*) be extravagant, blow (*Sl.*), consume, fritter away, spend, splurge, squander, use, use up, waste

saving 1. *adj.* compensatory, extenuating, qualifying, redeeming 2. *n.* bargain, discount, economy, reduction

savings fall-back, fund, nest egg, provision for a rainy day, reserves, resources, store

saviour defender, deliverer, friend in need, Good Samaritan, guardian, knight in shining armour, liberator, preserver, protector, redeemer, rescuer, salvation

Saviour, Our *or* The Christ, Jesus, Messiah, Redeemer

savoir-faire accomplishment, address, diplomacy, discretion, finesse, poise, social graces, social know-how (*Inf.*), tact, urbanity

savour *n.* 1. flavour, piquancy, relish, smack, smell, tang, taste, zest 2. distinctive quality, excitement, flavour, interest, salt, spice, zest ~*v.* 3. *Often with* **of** bear the hallmarks, be indicative, be suggestive, partake, show signs, smack, suggest, verge on 4. appreciate, delight in, drool, enjoy, enjoy to the full, gloat over, like, luxuriate in, partake, relish, revel in, smack one's lips over

savoury 1. agreeable, appetizing, dainty, delectable, delicious, full-flavoured, good, luscious, mouthwatering, palatable, piquant, rich, scrumptious (*Inf.*), spicy, tangy, tasty, toothsome 2. decent, edifying, honest, reputable, respectable, wholesome
Antonyms disreputable, distasteful, insipid, nasty, tasteless, unappetizing, unpalatable, unpleasant, unsavoury, wersh (*Scots.*)

saw adage, aphorism, apophthegm, axiom, byword, dictum, gnome, maxim, proverb, saying

saw-toothed crenate (*Bot., Zool.*), dentate, denticulate (*Biol.*), notched, serrate, serrated

say *v.* 1. add, affirm, announce, assert, asseverate, come out with (*Inf.*), declare, give voice *or* utterance to, maintain, mention, pronounce, put into words, remark, speak, state, utter, voice 2. answer, disclose, divulge, give as one's opinion, make known, reply, respond, reveal, tell 3. allege, bruit, claim, noise abroad, put about, report, rumour, suggest 4. deliver, do, orate, perform, read, recite, rehearse, render, repeat 5. assume, conjecture, dare say, estimate, guess, hazard a guess, imagine, judge, presume, suppose, surmise 6. communicate, convey, express, give the impression that, imply 7. **go without saying** be accepted, be a matter of course, be obvious, be self-evident, be taken as read, be taken for granted, be understood 8. **to say the least** at the very least, to put it mildly, without any exaggeration ~*n.* 9. crack (*Inf.*), turn (chance, opportunity) to speak, voice, vote 10. authority, clout (*Inf.*), influence, power, sway, weight

saying adage, aphorism, apophthegm, axiom, byword, dictum, gnome, maxim, proverb, saw, slogan

say-so 1. assertion, asseveration, assurance, dictum, guarantee, word 2. agreement, authority, authorization, consent, O.K. *or* okay (*Inf.*), permission, sanction

scalding blistering, boiling, burning, piping hot, searing

scale[1] *n.* 1. calibration, degrees, gamut, gradation, graduated system, graduation, hierarchy, ladder, pecking order (*Inf.*), progression, ranking, register, seniority system, sequence, series, spectrum, spread, steps 2. proportion, ratio 3. degree, extent, range, reach, scope, way ~*v.* 4. ascend, clamber, climb, escalade, mount, surmount 5. adjust, proportion, prorate (*Chiefly U.S.*), regulate

scale[2] *n.* flake, lamina, layer, plate, squama (*Biol.*)

scaly flaky, furfuraceous (*Medical*), scabrous, scurfy, squamous *or* squamose (*Biol.*), squamulose

scamp devil, imp, knave (*Archaic*), mischief-maker, monkey, pickle (*Brit. inf.*), prankster, rascal, rogue, scallywag (*Inf.*), scapegrace, toe-rag (*Sl.*), tyke (*Inf.*), whippersnapper, wretch

scamper beetle, dart, dash, fly, hasten, hie (*Archaic*), hurry, romp, run, scoot, scurry, scuttle, sprint

scan check, check out (*Inf.*), clock (*Brit. sl.*), con (*Archaic*), examine, eyeball (*U.S. sl.*), get a load of (*Inf.*), glance over, investigate, look one up and down, look through, recce (*Sl.*), run one's eye over, run over, scour, scrutinize, search, size up (*Inf.*), skim, survey, sweep, take a dekko at (*Brit. sl.*), take stock of

scandal 1. crime, crying shame (*Inf.*), disgrace, embarrassment, offence, sin, wrongdoing 2. calumny, defamation, detraction, discredit, disgrace, dishonour, ignominy, infamy, obloquy, offence, opprobrium, reproach, shame, stigma 3. abuse, aspersion, backbiting, dirt, dirty linen (*Inf.*), gossip, rumours, skeleton in the cupboard, slander, talk, tattle

scandalize affront, appal, cause a few raised eyebrows (*Inf.*), disgust, horrify, offend, outrage, shock

scandalmonger calumniator, defamer, destroyer of reputations, gossip, muckraker, tattle, tattler, traducer

scandalous 1. atrocious, disgraceful, disreputable, highly improper, infamous, monstrous, odious, opprobrious, outrageous, shameful, shocking, unseemly 2. defamatory, gossiping, libellous, scurrilous, slanderous, untrue
Antonyms decent, kind, laudatory, proper, reputable, respectable, seemly, unimpeachable, upright

scant bare, barely sufficient, deficient, inadequate, insufficient, limited, little, minimal, sparse
Antonyms abundant, adequate, ample, full, generous, plentiful, satisfactory, sufficient

scanty bare, deficient, exiguous, inadequate, insufficient, meagre, narrow, poor, restricted, scant, short, skimpy, slender, sparing, sparse, thin

scapegoat fall guy (*Inf.*), whipping boy

scapegrace bad lot (*Inf.*), good-for-nothing, limb of Satan, ne'er-do-well, rascal, rogue, scallywag (*Inf.*), scamp, the despair of

scar 1. *n.* blemish, cicatrix, injury, mark, wound 2. *v.* brand, damage, disfigure, mark, traumatize

scarce at a premium, deficient, few, few and far between, infrequent, in short supply, insufficient, rare, seldom met with, uncommon, unusual, wanting
Antonyms abundant, ample, common, commonplace, frequent, numerous, plenteous, plentiful, sufficient

scarcely 1. barely, hardly, only just, scarce (*Archaic*) 2. by no means, definitely not, hardly, not at all, on no account, under no circumstances

scarcity dearth, deficiency, infrequency, insufficiency, lack, paucity, poverty, rareness, shortage, undersupply, want
Antonyms abundance, excess, glut, superfluity, surfeit, surplus

scare 1. *v.* affright (*Archaic*), alarm, daunt, dismay, frighten, give (someone) a fright, give (someone) a turn (*Inf.*), intimidate, panic, put the wind up (someone) (*Inf.*), shock, startle, terrify, terrorize 2. *n.* alarm, alert, fright, panic, shock, start, terror

scared fearful, frightened, panicky, panic-stricken, petrified, scared shitless (*Taboo sl.*), shaken, shit-scared (*Taboo sl.*), startled, terrified

scaremonger alarmist, Calamity Jane, doom merchant (*Inf.*), prophet of doom, spreader of despair and despondency

scarper abscond, beat a hasty retreat, beat it (*Sl.*), clear off (*Inf.*), cut and run (*Inf.*), decamp, depart, disappear, do a bunk (*Brit. sl.*), flee, go, hook it (*Sl.*), make off, make oneself scarce (*Inf.*), run away, run for it, scram (*Inf.*), skedaddle (*Inf.*), slope off, take flight, take oneself off, take to one's heels, vamoose (*Sl., chiefly U.S.*)

scary alarming, bloodcurdling, chilling, creepy (*Inf.*), frightening, hair-raising, hairy (*Sl.*), horrendous, horrifying, intimidating, shocking, spine-chilling, spooky (*Inf.*), terrifying, unnerving

scathing belittling, biting, brutal, caustic, critical, cutting, harsh, mordacious, mordant, sarcastic, savage, scornful, searing, trenchant, vitriolic, withering

scatter 1. broadcast, diffuse, disseminate, fling, litter, shower, sow, spread, sprinkle, strew 2. disband, dispel, disperse, dissipate, disunite, put to flight, separate
Antonyms assemble, cluster, collect, congregate, converge, rally, unite

scatterbrain bird-brain (*Inf.*), butterfly, featherbrain, flibbertigibbet, grasshopper mind, madcap

scatterbrained bird-brained (*Inf.*), careless, empty-headed, featherbrained, forgetful, frivolous, giddy, goofy (*Inf.*), inattentive, irresponsible, madcap, scatty (*Brit. inf.*), silly, slaphappy (*Inf.*), thoughtless

scattering few, handful, scatter, smatter, smattering, sprinkling

scenario master plan, outline, résumé, rundown, scheme, sequence of events, sketch, story line, summary, synopsis

scene 1. display, drama, exhibition, pageant, picture, representation, show, sight, spectacle, tableau 2. area, locality, place, position, setting, site, situation, spot, whereabouts 3. backdrop, background, location, *mise en scène,* set, setting 4. act, division, episode, incident, part, stage 5. carry-on (*Inf., chiefly Brit.*), commotion, confrontation, display of emotion, drama, exhibition, fuss, performance, row, tantrum, to-do, upset 6. landscape, panorama, prospect, view, vista 7. *Inf.* arena, business, environment, field of interest, milieu, world

scenery 1. landscape, surroundings, terrain, view, vista 2. *Theatre* backdrop, décor, flats, *mise en scène,* set, setting, stage set

scenic beautiful, breathtaking, grand, impressive, panoramic, picturesque, spectacular, striking

scent *n.* 1. aroma, bouquet, fragrance, niff (*Brit. sl.*), odour, perfume, redolence, smell 2. spoor, track, trail ~*v.* 3. be on the track *or* trail of, detect, discern, get wind of (*Inf.*), nose out, recognize, sense, smell, sniff, sniff out

scented aromatic, fragrant, odoriferous, perfumed, redolent, sweet-smelling

sceptic agnostic, cynic, disbeliever, doubter, doubting Thomas, Pyrrhonist, scoffer, unbeliever

sceptical cynical, disbelieving, doubtful, doubting, dubious, hesitating, incredulous, mistrustful, questioning, quizzical, scoffing, unbelieving, unconvinced
Antonyms believing, certain, convinced, credulous, dogmatic, free from doubt, of fixed mind, sure, trusting, undoubting, unquestioning

scepticism agnosticism, cynicism, disbelief, doubt, incredulity, Pyrrhonism, suspicion, unbelief

schedule 1. *n.* agenda, calendar, catalogue, inventory, itinerary, list, list of appointments, plan, programme, timetable 2. *v.* appoint, arrange, be due, book, organize, plan, programme, slot (*Inf.*), time

schematic diagrammatic, diagrammatical, graphic, illustrative, representational

schematize arrange, catalogue, categorize, classify, file, grade, methodize, order, pigeonhole, put into order, regulate, sort, standardize, systematize, systemize, tabulate

scheme *n.* 1. contrivance, course of action, design, device, plan, programme, project, proposal, strategy, system, tactics, theory 2. arrangement, blueprint, chart, codification, diagram, disposition, draft, layout, outline, pattern, schedule, schema, system 3. conspiracy, dodge, game (*Inf.*), intrigue, machinations, manoeuvre, plot, ploy, ruse, shift, stratagem, subterfuge ~*v.* 4. contrive, design, devise, frame, imagine, lay plans, plan, project, work out 5. collude, conspire, intrigue, machinate, manoeuvre, plot, wheel and deal (*Inf.*)

schemer conniver, deceiver, intriguer, Machiavelli, plotter, slyboots (*Inf.*), wangler (*Inf.*), wheeler-dealer (*Inf.*)

scheming artful, calculating, conniving, cunning, deceitful, designing, duplicitous, foxy, Machiavellian, slippery, sly, tricky, underhand, wily
Antonyms above-board, artless, guileless, honest, ingenuous, naive, straightforward, trustworthy, undesigning

schism breach, break, discord, disunion, division, rift, rupture, separation, splintering, split

schismatic, schismatical *adj.* discordant, dissentient, dissenting, dissident, heretical, heterodox, seceding, separatist, splinter

scholar 1. academic, bookworm, egghead (*Inf.*), intellectual, man of letters, savant 2. disciple, learner, pupil, schoolboy, schoolgirl, student

scholarly academic, bookish, erudite, intellectual, learned, lettered, scholastic, studious, well-read
Antonyms lowbrow, middlebrow, philistine, unacademic, uneducated, unintellectual, unlettered

scholarship 1. accomplishments, attainments, book-learning, education, erudition, knowledge, learning, lore 2. bursary, exhibition, fellowship

scholastic 1. academic, bookish, learned, lettered, literary, scholarly 2. pedagogic, pedantic, precise

school *n.* 1. academy, alma mater, college, department, discipline, faculty, institute, institution, seminary 2. adherents, circle, class, clique, denomination, devotees, disciples, faction, followers, following, group, pupils, schism, sect, set 3. creed, faith, outlook, persuasion, school of thought, stamp, way of life ~*v.* 4. coach, discipline, drill, educate, indoctrinate, instruct, prepare, prime, train, tutor, verse

schooling 1. book-learning, education, formal education, teaching, tuition 2. coaching, drill, grounding, guidance, instruction, preparation, training

schoolteacher dominie (*Scot.*), instructor, pedagogue, schoolmarm (*Inf.*), schoolmaster, schoolmistress

science 1. body of knowledge, branch of knowledge, discipline 2. art, skill, technique

scientific accurate, controlled, exact, mathematical, precise, systematic

scintillate blaze, coruscate, flash, give off sparks, gleam, glint, glisten, glitter, sparkle, twinkle

scintillating animated, bright, brilliant, dazzling, ebullient, exciting, glittering, lively, sparkling, stimulating, witty

scion 1. child, descendant, heir, offspring, successor 2. branch, graft, offshoot, shoot, slip, sprout, twig

scoff[1] belittle, deride, despise, flout, gibe, jeer, knock (*Inf.*), laugh at, make light of, make sport of, mock, poke fun at, pooh-pooh, revile, ridicule, scorn, scout (*Archaic*), slag (off) (*Sl.*), sneer, take the piss (out of) (*Taboo sl.*), taunt, twit

scoff[2] 1. *v.* bolt, cram, devour, gobble (up), gollop, gorge (cram, stuff) oneself on, gulp down, guzzle, make a pig of oneself on (*Inf.*), put away, wolf 2. *n.* chow (*Inf.*), eats (*Sl.*), fare, feed, food, grub (*Sl.*), meal, nosh (*Sl.*), nosh-up (*Brit. sl.*), rations

scold 1. *v.* bawl out (*Inf.*), berate, blame, bring (someone) to book, carpet (*Inf.*), castigate, censure, chew out (*U.S. & Canad. inf.*), chide, find fault with, give a rocket (*Brit. & N.Z. inf.*), give (someone) a dressing-down (row, talking-to (*Inf.*)), go on at, haul (someone) over the coals (*Inf.*), have (someone) on the carpet (*Inf.*), lecture, nag, rate, read the riot act, rebuke, remonstrate with, reprimand, reproach, reprove, take (someone) to task, tear into (*Inf.*), tear (someone) off a strip (*Brit. inf.*), tell off (*Inf.*), tick off (*Inf.*), upbraid, vituperate 2. *n.* nag, shrew, termagant (*Rare*), Xanthippe
Antonyms *v.* acclaim, applaud, approve, commend, compliment, extol, laud, praise

scolding dressing-down (*Inf.*), (good) talking-to (*Inf.*), lecture, piece of one's mind, rebuke, row, telling-off (*Inf.*), ticking-off (*Inf.*), tongue-lashing, wigging (*Brit. sl.*)

scoop *n.* 1. dipper, ladle, spoon 2. coup, exclusive, exposé, inside story, revelation, sensation ~*v.* 3. *Often with* **up** clear away, gather up, lift, pick up, remove, sweep up *or* away, take up 4. bail, dig, dip, empty, excavate, gouge, hollow, ladle, scrape, shovel

scoot bolt, dart, dash, run, scamper, scurry, scuttle, skedaddle (*Inf.*), skirr, skitter, sprint, zip

scope ambit, area, capacity, compass, confines, elbowroom, extent, field of reference, freedom, latitude, liberty, opportunity, orbit, outlook, purview, range, reach, room, space, span, sphere

scorch blacken, blister, burn, char, parch, roast, sear, shrivel, singe, wither

scorching baking, boiling, broiling, burning, fiery, flaming, red-hot, roasting, searing, sizzling, sweltering, torrid, tropical, unbearably hot

score *n.* 1. grade, mark, outcome, points, record, result, total 2. **the score** *Inf.* the facts, the reality, the setup (*Inf.*), the situation, the truth 3. *Plural* a flock, a great number, an army, a throng, crowds, droves, hosts, hundreds, legions, lots, masses, millions, multitudes, myriads, swarms, very many 4. account, basis, cause, ground, grounds, reason 5. a bone to pick, grievance, grudge, injury, injustice, wrong 6. **pay off old scores** avenge, get even with (*Inf.*), get one's own back (*Inf.*), give an eye for an eye, give like for like *or* tit for tat, give (someone) a taste of his own medicine, hit back, pay (someone) back (in his own coin), repay, requite, retaliate 7. account, amount due, bill, charge, debt, obligation, reckoning, tab (*U.S. inf.*), tally, total ~*v.* 8. achieve, amass, chalk up (*Inf.*), gain, make, notch up (*Inf.*), win 9. count, keep a tally of, keep count, record, register, tally 10. crosshatch, cut, deface, gouge, graze, indent, mar, mark, nick, notch, scrape, scratch, slash 11. *With* **out** *or* **through** cancel, cross out, delete, obliterate, put a line through, strike out 12. *Music* adapt, arrange, orchestrate, set 13. gain an advantage, go down well with (someone), impress, make a hit (*Inf.*), make an impact *or* impression, make a point, put oneself across, triumph

score off be one up on (*Inf.*), get the better of, have the laugh on, humiliate, make a fool of, make (someone) look silly, worst

scorn 1. *n.* contempt, contemptuousness, contumely, derision, despite, disdain, disparagement, mockery, sarcasm, scornfulness, slight, sneer 2. *v.* be above, consider beneath one, contemn, curl one's lip at, deride, disdain, flout, hold in contempt, look down on, make fun of, reject, scoff at, scout (*Archaic*), slight, sneer at, spurn, turn up one's nose at (*Inf.*)

Antonyms *n.* acceptance, admiration, affection, esteem, high regard, respect, tolerance, toleration, veneration, worship ~*v.* accept, admire, esteem, look favourably on, respect, revere, tolerate, venerate, worship

scornful contemptuous, contumelious, defiant, derisive, disdainful, haughty, insolent, insulting, jeering, mocking, sarcastic, sardonic, scathing, scoffing, slighting, sneering, supercilious, withering

scornfully contemptuously, disdainfully, dismissively, scathingly, slightingly, with a sneer, with contempt, with disdain, witheringly, with lip curled

scot-free clear, safe, scatheless (*Archaic*), undamaged, unharmed, unhurt, uninjured, unpunished, unscathed, without a scratch

Scots Caledonian, Scottish

scoundrel asshole (*U.S. & Canad. taboo sl.*), asswipe (*U.S. & Canad. taboo sl.*), bad egg (*Old-fashioned inf.*), bastard (*Offensive*), blackguard, bugger (*Taboo sl.*), caitiff (*Archaic*), cheat, cocksucker (*Taboo sl.*), dastard (*Archaic*), good-for-nothing, heel (*Sl.*), incorrigible, knave (*Archaic*), miscreant, mother, motherfucker (*Taboo sl., chiefly U.S.*), ne'er-do-well, rascal, reprobate, rogue, rotter (*Sl., chiefly Brit.*), scally (*Northwest English dialect*), scamp, scapegrace, scumbag (*Sl.*), shit (*Taboo sl.*), son-of-a-bitch (*Sl., chiefly U.S. & Canad.*), swine, turd (*Taboo sl.*), vagabond, villain, wretch

scour[1] abrade, buff, burnish, clean, cleanse, flush, furbish, polish, purge, rub, scrub, wash, whiten

scour[2] beat, comb, forage, go over with a fine-tooth comb, hunt, look high and low, rake, ransack, search

scourge *n.* 1. affliction, bane, curse, infliction, misfortune, penalty, pest, plague, punishment, terror, torment, visitation 2. cat, cat-o'-nine-tails, lash, strap, switch, thong, whip ~*v.* 3. beat, belt (*Inf.*), cane, castigate, chastise, discipline, flog, horsewhip, lash, lather (*Inf.*), leather, punish, take a strap to, tan (someone's) hide (*Sl.*), thrash, trounce, wallop (*Inf.*), whale, whip 4. afflict, curse, excoriate, harass, plague, terrorize, torment

Antonyms *n.* (*sense 1*) benefit, blessing, boon, favour, gift, godsend

scout *v.* 1. case (*Sl.*), check out, investigate, make a reconnaissance, nark (*Brit., Aust., & N.Z. sl.*), observe, probe, recce (*Sl.*), reconnoitre, see how the land lies, spy, spy out, survey, watch 2. *Often with* **out, up,** *or* **around** cast around for, ferret out, hunt for, look for, rustle up, search for, search out, seek, track down ~*n.* 3. advance guard, escort, lookout, outrider, precursor, reconnoitrer, vanguard 4. recruiter, talent scout

scowl 1. *v.* frown, glower, grimace, look daggers at, lour *or* lower 2. *n.* black look, dirty look, frown, glower, grimace

scrabble clamber, claw, dig, grope, paw, scramble, scrape, scratch

scraggy 1. angular, bony, emaciated, gangling, gaunt, lanky, lean, rawboned, scrawny, skinny, undernourished 2. draggletailed (*Archaic*), grotty (*Sl.*), lank, meagre, rough, scanty, scruffy, tousled, unkempt

scram abscond, beat it (*Sl.*), bugger off (*Taboo sl.*), clear off (*Inf.*), depart, disappear, fuck off (*Offens. taboo sl.*), get lost (*Inf.*), go away, hook it (*Sl.*), leave, make oneself scarce (*Inf.*), make tracks, quit, scarper (*Brit. sl.*), scoot, skedaddle (*Inf.*), slope off, take oneself off, vamoose (*Sl., chiefly U.S.*)

scramble *v.* 1. clamber, climb, crawl, move with difficulty, push, scrabble, struggle, swarm 2. contend, hasten, jockey for position, jostle, look lively *or* snappy (*Inf.*), make haste, push, run, rush, strive, vie ~*n.* 3. climb, trek 4. commotion, competition, confusion, free-for-all (*Inf.*), hassle (*Inf.*), hustle, melee *or* mêlée, muddle, race, rat race, rush, struggle, tussle

scrap[1] *n.* 1. atom, bit, bite, crumb, fragment, grain, iota, mite, modicum, morsel, mouthful, part, particle, piece, portion, remnant, sliver, snatch, snippet, trace 2. junk, off cuts, waste 3. **on the scrap heap** discarded, ditched (*Sl.*), jettisoned, put out to grass (*Inf.*), redundant, written off 4. *Plural* bits, leavings, leftovers, remains, scrapings ~*v.* 5. abandon, break up, chuck (*Inf.*), demolish, discard, dispense with, ditch (*Sl.*), drop, get rid of, jettison, junk (*Inf.*), shed, throw away *or* out, throw on the scrapheap, toss out, trash (*Sl.*), write off

Antonyms *v.* bring back, recall, re-establish, reinstall, reinstate, restore, return

scrap[2] 1. *n.* argument, *bagarre,* battle, brawl, disagreement, dispute, dust-up (*Inf.*), fight, quarrel, row, scrimmage, scuffle, set-to (*Inf.*), shindig (*Inf.*), shindy (*Inf.*), squabble, tiff, wrangle 2. *v.* argue, barney (*Inf.*), bicker, come to blows, fall out (*Inf.*), fight, have a shouting match (*Inf.*), have words, row, spar, squabble, wrangle

scrape *v.* 1. abrade, bark, graze, rub, scratch, scuff, skin 2. grate, grind, rasp, scratch, screech, set one's teeth on edge, squeak 3. clean, erase, file, remove, rub, scour 4. pinch, save, scrimp, skimp, stint 5. **scrape by, in,** *or* **through** barely make it, cut it fine (*Inf.*), get by (*Inf.*), have a close shave (*Inf.*), struggle ~*n.* 6. *Inf.* awkward *or* embarrassing situation, difficulty, dilemma, distress, fix (*Inf.*), mess, plight, predicament, pretty pickle (*Inf.*), spot (*Inf.*), tight spot, trouble

scrape together amass, dredge up, get hold of, glean, hoard, muster, rake up *or* together, save

scrappy bitty, disjointed, fragmentary, incomplete, perfunctory, piecemeal, sketchy, thrown together

scraps bits, leavings, leftovers, remains, scrapings

scratch *v.* 1. claw, cut, damage, etch, grate, graze, incise, lacerate, make a mark on, mark, rub, score, scrape 2. annul, cancel, delete, eliminate, erase, pull out, stand down, strike off, withdraw ~*n.* 3. blemish, claw mark, gash, graze, laceration, mark, scrape 4. **up to scratch** acceptable, adequate, capable, competent, satisfactory, sufficient, up to snuff (*Inf.*), up to standard ~*adj.* 5. haphazard, hastily prepared, impromptu, improvised, rough, rough-and-ready

scrawl doodle, scrabble, scratch, scribble, squiggle, writing

scrawny angular, bony, gaunt, lanky, lean, macilent (*Rare*), rawboned, scraggy, skeletal, skin-and-bones (*Inf.*), skinny, thin, undernourished

scream *v.* 1. bawl, cry, holler (*Inf.*), screech, shriek, shrill, sing out, squeal, yell 2. *Fig.* be conspicuous, clash, jar, shriek ~*n.* 3. howl, outcry, screech, shriek, wail, yell, yelp 4. *Inf.* card (*Inf.*), caution (*Inf.*), character (*Inf.*), comedian, comic, entertainer, hoot (*Inf.*), joker, laugh, riot (*Sl.*), sensation, wag, wit

screech cry, scream, shriek, squawk, squeal, yelp

screen *v.* 1. cloak, conceal, cover, hide, mask, shade, shroud, shut out, veil 2. defend, guard, protect, safeguard, shelter, shield 3. cull, evaluate, examine, filter, gauge, grade, process, riddle, scan, sieve, sift, sort, vet 4. broadcast, present, put on, show ~*n.* 5. awning, canopy, cloak, concealment, cover, guard, hedge, mantle, shade, shelter, shield, shroud 6. mesh, net, partition, room divider

screw *v.* 1. tighten, turn, twist, work in 2. contort, contract, crumple, distort, pucker, wrinkle 3. *Inf.* bring pressure to bear on, coerce, constrain, force, hold a knife to (someone's) throat, oppress, pressurize, put the screws on (*Inf.*), squeeze 4. *Inf. Often with* **out of** bleed, extort, extract, wrest, wring

screwed up anxious, apprehensive, confused, edgy, in a mess, keyed up, mixed up, nervous, neurotic, on edge, strung up (*Inf.*), tense, uptight (*Inf.*), wired (*Sl.*), worked up, worried

screw up 1. contort, contract, crumple, distort, knit, knot, pucker, wrinkle 2. *Inf.* bitch (up) (*Sl.*), bodge (*Inf.*), botch, bungle, cock up (*Brit. sl.*), fuck up (*Offens. taboo sl.*), louse up (*Sl.*), make a hash of (*Inf.*), make a mess *or* muck-up of (*Sl.*), mess up, mishandle, mismanage, queer (*Inf.*), spoil

screwy batty (*Sl.*), cracked (*Sl.*), crackers (*Brit. sl.*), crackpot (*Inf.*), crazy, dotty (*Sl., chiefly Brit.*), eccentric, loopy (*Inf.*), nutty (*Sl.*), odd, oddball (*Inf.*), off one's trolley (*Sl.*), off-the-wall (*Sl.*), outré, out to lunch (*Inf.*), queer (*Inf.*), round the bend (*Brit. sl.*), rum (*Brit. sl.*), up the pole (*Inf.*), wacko (*Sl.*), weird

scribble *v.* dash off, doodle, jot, pen, scratch, scrawl, write

scribe amanuensis, clerk, copyist, notary (*Archaic*), penman (*Rare*), scrivener (*Archaic*), secretary, writer

scrimmage affray (*Law*), *bagarre,* bovver (*Brit. sl.*), brawl, disturbance, dust-up (*Inf.*), fight, fray, free-for-all (*Inf.*), melee *or* mêlée, riot, row, scrap (*Inf.*), scuffle, set-to (*Inf.*), shindig (*Inf.*), shindy (*Inf.*), skirmish, squabble, struggle

scrimp be frugal, curtail, economize, limit, pinch, pinch pennies, reduce, save, scrape, shorten, skimp, stint, straiten

script 1. calligraphy, hand, handwriting, letters, longhand, penmanship, writing 2. book, copy, dialogue, libretto, lines, manuscript, text, words

Scripture Holy Bible, Holy Scripture, Holy Writ, The Bible, The Book of Books, The Good Book, The Gospels, The Scriptures, The Word, The Word of God

scroll inventory, list, parchment, roll

Scrooge cheapskate (*Inf.*), meanie *or* meany (*Inf., chiefly Brit.*), miser, money-grubber (*Inf.*), niggard, penny-pincher (*Inf.*), skinflint, tight-arse (*Taboo sl.*), tight-ass (*U.S. taboo sl.*), tightwad (*U.S. & Canad. sl.*)

scrounge beg, blag (*Sl.*), bum (*Inf.*), cadge, forage for, freeload (*Sl.*), hunt around (for), mooch (*Sl.*), sorn (*Scot.*), sponge (*Inf.*), touch (someone) for (*Sl.*), wheedle

scrounger bum (*Inf.*), cadger, freeloader (*Sl.*), parasite, sorner (*Scot.*), sponger (*Inf.*)

scrub *v.* 1. clean, cleanse, rub, scour 2. *Inf.* abandon, abolish, call off, cancel, delete, discontinue, do away with, drop, forget about, give up

scrubby insignificant, meagre, paltry, scrawny, spindly, stunted, underdeveloped, undersized

scruff 1. nape, scrag (*Inf.*) 2. *Inf.* ragamuffin, ragbag (*Inf.*), scarecrow, sloven, tatterdemalion (*Rare*), tramp

scruffy disreputable, draggletailed (*Archaic*), frowzy, ill-groomed, mangy, messy, ragged, run-down, scrubby (*Brit. inf.*), seedy, shabby, slatternly, sloppy (*Inf.*), slovenly, sluttish, squalid, tattered, tatty, ungroomed, unkempt, untidy
Antonyms chic, dapper, natty, neat, soigné *or* soignée, spruce, tidy, well-dressed, well-groomed, well-turned-out

scrumptious appetizing, delectable, delicious, exquisite, inviting, luscious, magnificent, moreish (*Inf.*), mouthwatering, succulent, yummy (*Sl.*)

scrunch champ, chew, crumple, crunch, crush, mash, ruck up, squash

scruple 1. *v.* balk at, be loath, be reluctant, demur, doubt, falter, have misgivings about, have qualms about, hesitate, stick at, think twice about, vacillate, waver 2. *n.* caution, compunction, difficulty, doubt, hesitation, misgiving, perplexity, qualm, reluctance, second thoughts, squeamishness, twinge of conscience, uneasiness

scrupulous careful, conscientious, exact, fastidious, honourable, meticulous, minute, moral, nice, painstaking, precise, principled, punctilious, rigorous, strict, upright
Antonyms amoral, careless, dishonest, inexact, reckless, slapdash, superficial, uncaring, unconscientious, unscrupulous, unprincipled, without scruples

scrutinize analyse, dissect, examine, explore, inquire into, inspect, investigate, peruse, pore over, probe, research, scan, search, sift, study, work over

scrutiny analysis, close study, examination, exploration, inquiry, inspection, investigation, perusal, search, sifting, study

scud blow, fly, haste, hasten, race, sail, shoot, skim, speed

scuffle 1. *v.* clash, come to blows, contend, exchange blows, fight, grapple, jostle, struggle, tussle 2. *n.* affray (*Law*), *bagarre,* barney (*Inf.*), brawl, commotion, disturbance, fight, fray, ruck (*Sl.*), ruckus (*Inf.*), ruction (*Inf.*), rumpus, scrap (*Inf.*), scrimmage, set-to (*Inf.*), shindig (*Inf.*), shindy (*Inf.*), skirmish, tussle

sculpture *v.* carve, chisel, cut, fashion, form, hew, model, mould, sculp, sculpt, shape

scum 1. algae, crust, dross, film, froth, impurities, offscourings, scruff 2. *Fig.* *canaille,* dregs of society, dross, lowest of the low, rabble, ragtag and bobtail, riffraff, rubbish, trash (*Chiefly U.S. & Canad.*)

scupper defeat, demolish, destroy, disable, discomfit, overthrow, overwhelm, put paid to, ruin, torpedo, undo, wreck

scurrility abusiveness, billingsgate, coarseness, grossness, indecency, infamousness, invective, obloquy, obscenity, offensiveness, scurrilousness, vituperation

scurrilous abusive, coarse, defamatory, foul, foul-mouthed, gross, indecent, infamous, insulting, low, obscene, offensive, Rabelaisian, ribald, salacious, scabrous, scandalous, slanderous, vituperative, vulgar

Antonyms civilized, decent, polite, proper, refined, respectful

scurry 1. *v.* beetle, dart, dash, fly, hurry, race, scamper, scoot, scud, scuttle, skim, sprint, whisk 2. *n.* bustle, flurry, scampering, whirl

Antonyms *v.* amble, mooch (*Sl.*), mosey (*Inf.*), saunter, stroll, toddle, wander

scurvy *adj.* abject, bad, base, contemptible, despicable, dishonourable, ignoble, low, low-down (*Inf.*), mean, pitiful, rotten, scabby (*Inf.*), shabby, sorry, vile, worthless

scuttle beetle, bustle, hare (*Brit. inf.*), hasten, hurry, run, rush, scamper, scoot, scramble, scud, scurry, scutter (*Brit. inf.*)

sea *n.* 1. main, ocean, the briny (*Inf.*), the deep, the drink (*Inf.*), the waves 2. *Fig.* abundance, expanse, mass, multitude, plethora, profusion, sheet, vast number 3. **at sea** adrift, astray, at a loss, at sixes and sevens, baffled, bewildered, confused, disoriented, lost, mystified, puzzled, upset ~*adj.* 4. aquatic, briny, marine, maritime, ocean, ocean-going, oceanic, pelagic, salt, saltwater, seagoing

seafaring marine, maritime, nautical, naval, oceanic

seal *v.* 1. bung, close, cork, enclose, fasten, make airtight, plug, secure, shut, stop, stopper, stop up, waterproof 2. assure, attest, authenticate, confirm, establish, ratify, stamp, validate 3. clinch, conclude, consummate, finalize, settle, shake hands on (*Inf.*) 4. *With* **off** board up, fence off, isolate, put out of bounds, quarantine, segregate ~*n.* 5. assurance, attestation, authentication, confirmation, imprimatur, insignia, notification, ratification, stamp

seam *n.* 1. closure, joint, suture (*Surgery*) 2. layer, lode, stratum, vein 3. furrow, line, ridge, scar, wrinkle

seamy corrupt, dark, degraded, disagreeable, disreputable, low, nasty, rough, sordid, squalid, unpleasant, unwholesome

sear blight, brand, burn, cauterize, desiccate, dry up *or* out, scorch, seal, shrivel, sizzle, wilt, wither

search *v.* 1. cast around, check, comb, examine, explore, ferret, frisk (*Inf.*), go over with a fine-tooth comb, inquire, inspect, investigate, leave no stone unturned, look, look high and low, probe, pry, ransack, rifle through, rummage through, scour, scrutinize, seek, sift, turn inside out, turn upside down ~*n.* 2. examination, exploration, going-over (*Inf.*), hunt, inquiry, inspection, investigation, pursuit, quest, researches, rummage, scrutiny 3. **in search of** hunting for, in need of, in pursuit of, looking for, making enquiries concerning, on the lookout for, on the track of, seeking

searching *adj.* close, intent, keen, minute, penetrating, piercing, probing, quizzical, severe, sharp, thorough

Antonyms cursory, perfunctory, peripheral, sketchy, superficial

seasickness *mal de mer*

season *n.* 1. division, interval, juncture, occasion, opportunity, period, spell, term, time, time of year ~*v.* 2. colour, enliven, flavour, lace, leaven, pep up, salt, salt and pepper, spice 3. acclimatize, accustom, anneal, discipline, habituate, harden, inure, mature, prepare, toughen, train 4. mitigate, moderate, qualify, temper

seasonable appropriate, convenient, fit, opportune, providential, suitable, timely, welcome, well-timed

seasoned battle-scarred, experienced, hardened, long-serving, mature, old, practised, time-served, veteran, weathered, well-versed

Antonyms callow, green, inexperienced, new, novice, unpractised, unseasoned, unskilled

seasoning condiment, dressing, flavouring, relish, salt and pepper, sauce, spice

seat *n.* 1. bench, chair, pew, settle, stall, stool, throne 2. axis, capital, centre, cradle, headquarters, heart, hub, location, place, site, situation, source, station 3. base, bed, bottom, cause, footing, foundation, ground, groundwork 4. abode, ancestral hall, house, mansion, residence 5. chair, constituency, incumbency, membership, place ~*v.* 6. accommodate, cater for, contain, have room *or* capacity for, hold, sit, take 7. deposit, fix, install, locate, place, set, settle, sit

seating accommodation, chairs, places, room, seats

secede apostatize, break with, disaffiliate,

leave, pull out, quit, resign, retire, separate, split from, withdraw

secession apostasy, break, defection, disaffiliation, seceding, split, withdrawal

secluded cloistered, cut off, isolated, lonely, off the beaten track, out-of-the-way, private, reclusive, remote, retired, sequestered, sheltered, solitary, tucked away, unfrequented

Antonyms accessible, busy, frequented, open, public, sociable

seclusion concealment, hiding, isolation, privacy, purdah, remoteness, retirement, retreat, shelter, solitude

second[1] *adj.* 1. following, next, subsequent, succeeding 2. additional, alternative, extra, further, other, repeated 3. inferior, lesser, lower, secondary, subordinate, supporting 4. double, duplicate, reproduction, twin ~*n.* 5. assistant, backer, helper, supporter ~*v.* 6. advance, aid, approve, assist, back, encourage, endorse, forward, further, give moral support to, go along with, help, promote, support

second[2] *n.* flash, instant, jiffy (*Inf.*), minute, moment, sec (*Inf.*), split second, tick (*Brit. inf.*), trice, twinkling, twinkling of an eye, two shakes of a lamb's tail (*Inf.*)

secondary 1. derivative, derived, indirect, resultant, resulting, second-hand 2. consequential, contingent, inferior, lesser, lower, minor, second-rate, subordinate, unimportant 3. alternate, auxiliary, backup, extra, fall-back, relief, reserve, second, subsidiary, supporting

Antonyms cardinal, chief, head, larger, main, major, more important, only, original, preceding, primary, prime, principal, superior

second childhood caducity, dotage, senility

second class *adj.* déclassé, indifferent, inferior, mediocre, outclassed, second-best, second-rate, undistinguished, uninspiring

second-hand 1. *adj.* handed down, hand-me-down (*Inf.*), nearly new, reach-me-down (*Inf.*), used 2. *adv.* at second-hand, indirectly, on the grapevine (*Inf.*)

second in command depute (*Scot.*), deputy, number two, right-hand man, successor designate

secondly in the second place, next, second

second-rate bush-league (*Aust. & N.Z. inf.*), cheap, cheap and nasty (*Inf.*), commonplace, dime-a-dozen (*Inf.*), inferior, low-grade, low-quality, mediocre, piss-poor (*Taboo sl.*), poor, rubbishy, shoddy, substandard, tacky (*Inf.*), tawdry, tinhorn (*U.S. sl.*), two-bit (*U.S. & Canad. sl.*)

Antonyms a cut above (*Inf.*), choice, de luxe, excellent, fine, first-class, first-rate, good quality, high-class, quality, superior

secrecy 1. concealment, confidentiality, huggermugger (*Rare*), mystery, privacy, retirement, seclusion, silence, solitude, surreptitiousness 2. clandestineness, covertness, furtiveness, secretiveness, stealth

secret *adj.* 1. backstairs, camouflaged, cloak-and-dagger, close, closet (*Inf.*), concealed, conspiratorial, covered, covert, disguised, furtive, hidden, hole-and-corner (*Inf.*), hush-hush (*Inf.*), reticent, shrouded, undercover, underground, under wraps, undisclosed, unknown, unpublished, unrevealed, unseen 2. abstruse, arcane, cabbalistic, clandestine, classified, cryptic, esoteric, mysterious, occult, recondite 3. hidden, out-of-the-way, private, retired, secluded, unfrequented, unknown 4. close, deep, discreet, reticent, secretive, sly, stealthy, underhand ~*n.* 5. code, confidence, enigma, formula, key, mystery, recipe, skeleton in the cupboard 6. **in secret** behind closed doors, by stealth, huggermugger (*Archaic*), in camera, incognito, secretly, slyly, surreptitiously

Antonyms *adj.* apparent, candid, disclosed, exoteric, frank, manifest, obvious, open, overt, public, straightforward, unconcealed, visible, well-known

secret agent cloak-and-dagger man, nark (*Brit., Aust., & N.Z. sl.*), spook (*U.S. & Canad. inf.*), spy, undercover agent

secrete[1] bury, cache, conceal, cover, disguise, harbour, hide, screen, secure, shroud, stash (*Inf.*), stash away (*Inf.*), stow, veil

Antonyms bare, display, exhibit, expose to view, leave in the open, reveal, show, uncover, unmask, unveil

secrete[2] emanate, emit, extravasate (*Medical*), extrude, exude, give off

secretion discharge, emission, excretion, extravasation (*Medical*), exudation

secretive cagey (*Inf.*), clamlike, close, cryptic, deep, enigmatic, playing one's cards close to one's chest, reserved, reticent, tight-lipped, uncommunicative, unforthcoming, withdrawn

Antonyms candid, communicative, expansive, forthcoming, frank, open, unreserved

secretly behind closed doors, behind (someone's) back, clandestinely, confidentially, covertly, furtively, in camera, in confidence, in one's heart, in one's inmost thoughts, in secret, on the q.t. (*Inf.*), on the sly, privately, quietly, stealthily, surreptitiously, unobserved

sect camp, denomination, division, faction,

group, party, schism, school, school of thought, splinter group, wing

sectarian 1. *adj.* bigoted, clannish, cliquish, doctrinaire, dogmatic, exclusive, factional, fanatic, fanatical, hidebound, insular, limited, narrow-minded, parochial, partisan, rigid 2. *n.* adherent, bigot, disciple, dogmatist, extremist, fanatic, partisan, true believer, zealot

Antonyms *adj.* broad-minded, catholic, free-thinking, liberal, non-sectarian, open-minded, tolerant, unbigoted, unprejudiced

section *n.* 1. component, cross section, division, fraction, fragment, instalment, part, passage, piece, portion, sample, segment, slice, subdivision 2. *Chiefly U.S.* area, department, district, region, sector, zone

sectional divided, exclusive, factional, local, localized, partial, regional, separate, separatist

sector area, category, district, division, part, quarter, region, stratum, subdivision, zone

secular civil, earthly, laic, laical, lay, non-spiritual, profane, state, temporal, worldly

Antonyms divine, holy, religious, sacred, spiritual, theological

secure *adj.* 1. immune, impregnable, out of harm's way, protected, safe, sheltered, shielded, unassailable, undamaged, unharmed 2. dependable, fast, fastened, firm, fixed, fortified, immovable, stable, steady, tight 3. assured, certain, confident, easy, reassured, sure 4. absolute, conclusive, definite, in the bag (*Inf.*), reliable, solid, steadfast, tried and true, well-founded ~*v.* 5. acquire, come by, gain, get, get hold of, land (*Inf.*), make sure of, obtain, pick up, procure, score (*Sl.*), win possession of 6. attach, batten down, bolt, chain, fasten, fix, lash, lock, lock up, make fast, moor, padlock, rivet, tie up 7. assure, ensure, guarantee, insure

Antonyms *adj.* endangered, ill-at-ease, insecure, loose, not fastened, precarious, unassured, uncertain, uneasy, unfixed, unprotected, unsafe, unsound, unsure ~*v.* endanger, give up, imperil, leave unguaranteed, let (something) slip through (one's) fingers, loose, lose, unloose, untie

security 1. asylum, care, cover, custody, immunity, preservation, protection, refuge, retreat, safekeeping, safety, sanctuary 2. defence, guards, precautions, protection, safeguards, safety measures, surveillance 3. assurance, certainty, confidence, conviction, ease of mind, freedom from doubt, positiveness, reliance, sureness 4. collateral, gage, guarantee, hostage, insurance, pawn, pledge, surety

Antonyms (*senses 1, 2 & 3*) exposure, insecurity, jeopardy, uncertainty, vulnerability

sedate calm, collected, composed, cool, decorous, deliberate, demure, dignified, earnest, grave, imperturbable, middle-aged, placid, proper, quiet, seemly, serene, serious, slow-moving, sober, solemn, staid, tranquil, unflappable (*Inf.*), unruffled

Antonyms agitated, excitable, excited, flighty, impassioned, jumpy, nervous, undignified, uninhibited, unsteady, wild

sedative 1. *adj.* allaying, anodyne, calmative, calming, lenitive, relaxing, sleep-inducing, soothing, soporific, tranquillizing 2. *n.* anodyne, calmative, downer *or* down (*Sl.*), narcotic, opiate, sleeping pill, tranquillizer

sedentary desk, desk-bound, inactive, motionless, seated, sitting, torpid

Antonyms active, mobile, motile, moving, on the go (*Inf.*)

sediment deposit, dregs, grounds, lees, precipitate, residuum, settlings

sedition agitation, disloyalty, incitement to riot, rabble-rousing, subversion, treason

seditious disloyal, dissident, insubordinate, mutinous, rebellious, refractory, revolutionary, subversive, treasonable

seduce 1. betray, corrupt, debauch, deflower, deprave, dishonour, ruin (*Archaic*) 2. allure, attract, beguile, deceive, decoy, ensnare, entice, inveigle, lead astray, lure, mislead, tempt

seduction 1. corruption, defloration, ruin (*Archaic*) 2. allure, enticement, lure, snare, temptation

seductive alluring, attractive, beguiling, bewitching, captivating, come-hither (*Inf.*), come-to-bed (*Inf.*), enticing, flirtatious, inviting, irresistible, provocative, ravishing, sexy (*Inf.*), siren, specious, tempting

seductress Circe, enchantress, *femme fatale,* Lorelei, siren, temptress, vamp (*Inf.*)

sedulous assiduous, busy, conscientious, constant, diligent, industrious, laborious, painstaking, persevering, persistent, tireless, unflagging, unremitting

see[1] *v.* 1. behold, catch a glimpse of, catch sight of, check, check out (*Inf.*), clock (*Brit. sl.*), descry, discern, distinguish, espy, eyeball (*U.S. sl.*), get a load of (*Sl.*), glimpse, heed, identify, lay *or* clap eyes on (*Inf.*), look, make out, mark, note, notice, observe, perceive, recognize, regard, sight, spot, take a dekko at (*Brit. sl.*), view, witness 2. appreciate, catch on (*Inf.*), comprehend, fathom, feel, follow, get, get the drift of, get the hang of (*Inf.*), grasp, know, make out, realize, take in, understand 3. ascertain, determine, discover, find out, investigate, learn, make enquiries, refer to 4. ensure, guarantee, make certain, make sure, mind, see to it, take care 5. consider, decide, deliberate, give some thought to, judge, make up one's mind, mull over, reflect, think over 6. confer with, consult, encounter, interview, meet, receive, run into, speak to, visit 7. accompany, attend, escort, lead, show, usher, walk 8. consort *or* associate with, court, date (*Inf., chiefly U.S.*), go out with, go steady with (*Inf.*), keep company with, walk out with (*Obsolete*) 9. anticipate, divine, envisage, foresee, foretell, imagine, picture, visualize

see[2] *n.* bishopric, diocese

see about 1. attend to, consider, deal with, give some thought to, look after, see to, take care of 2. investigate, look into, make enquiries, research

seed 1. egg, egg cell, embryo, germ, grain, kernel, ovule, ovum, pip, spore 2. beginning, germ, inkling, nucleus, source, start, suspicion 3. *Fig.* children, descendants, heirs, issue, offspring, progeny, race, scions, spawn, successors 4. **go *or* run to seed** decay, decline, degenerate, deteriorate, go downhill (*Inf.*), go to pieces, go to pot, go to rack and ruin, go to waste, let oneself go, retrogress

seedy 1. crummy (*Sl.*), decaying, dilapidated, down at heel, faded, grotty (*Sl.*), grubby, mangy, manky (*Scot. dialect*), old, rundown, scruffy, shabby, sleazy, slovenly, squalid, tatty, unkempt, worn 2. *Inf.* ailing, ill, off colour, out of sorts, peely-wally (*Scot.*), poorly (*Inf.*), sickly, under the weather (*Inf.*), unwell
Antonyms (*sense 1*) classy, elegant, fashionable, high-toned, posh (*Inf., chiefly Brit.*), ritzy (*Sl.*), smart, swanky (*Inf.*), swish (*Inf., chiefly Brit.*), top-drawer, upmarket

see eye to eye accord, agree, click, coincide, concur, correspond, fit, get along, get on (together), harmonize, speak the same language

seeing *conj.* as, inasmuch as, in view of the fact that, since

seek 1. be after, follow, go gunning for, go in pursuit (quest, search) of, hunt, inquire, look for, pursue, search for 2. aim, aspire to, attempt, endeavour, essay, have a go (*Inf.*), strive, try 3. ask, beg, entreat, inquire, invite, petition, request, solicit

seem appear, assume, give the impression, have the *or* every appearance of, look, look as if, look like, look to be, pretend, sound like, strike one as being

seeming *adj.* apparent, appearing, illusory, ostensible, outward, quasi-, specious, surface

seemingly apparently, as far as anyone could tell, on the face of it, on the surface, ostensibly, outwardly, to all appearances, to all intents and purposes

seemly appropriate, becoming, befitting, *comme il faut,* decent, decorous, fit, fitting, in good taste, meet (*Archaic*), nice, proper, suitable, suited, the done thing
Antonyms improper, inappropriate, indecorous, in poor taste, out of keeping, out of place, unbecoming, unbefitting, unseemly, unsuitable

see over inspect, look round, see round, tour

seep bleed, exude, leach, leak, ooze, percolate, permeate, soak, trickle, weep, well

seepage exudation, leak, leakage, oozing, percolation

seer augur, predictor, prophet, sibyl, soothsayer

seesaw *v.* alternate, fluctuate, go from one extreme to the other, oscillate, pitch, swing, teeter

seethe 1. boil, bubble, churn, ferment, fizz, foam, froth 2. be in a state (*Inf.*), be livid (furious, incensed), breathe fire and slaughter, foam at the mouth, fume, get hot under the collar (*Inf.*), rage, see red (*Inf.*), simmer, storm 3. be alive with, swarm, teem

see-through diaphanous, filmy, fine, flimsy, gauzy, gossamer, sheer, thin, translucent, transparent

see through *v.* 1. be undeceived by, be wise to (*Inf.*), fathom, get to the bottom of, have (someone's) number (*Inf.*), not fall for, penetrate 2. **see (something *or* someone) through** help out, keep at, persevere (with), persist, see out, stay to the bitter end, stick by, stick out (*Inf.*), support

see to arrange, attend to, be responsible for, do, look after, manage, organize, sort out, take care of, take charge of

segment bit, compartment, division, part, piece, portion, section, slice, wedge

segregate discriminate against, dissociate, isolate, separate, set apart, single out
Antonyms amalgamate, desegregate, join together, mix, unify, unite

segregation apartheid (*in South Africa*), discrimination, isolation, separation

seize 1. catch up, clutch, collar (*Inf.*), fasten, grab, grasp, grip, lay hands on, snatch, take 2. apprehend, catch, get, grasp, nab (*Inf.*), nail (*Inf.*) 3. abduct, annex, appropriate, arrest, capture, commandeer, con-

fiscate, hijack, impound, take by storm, take captive, take possession of
Antonyms hand back, free, let go, let pass, loose, release, relinquish, set free, turn loose

seizure 1. abduction, annexation, apprehension, arrest, capture, commandeering, confiscation, grabbing, taking 2. attack, convulsion, fit, paroxysm, spasm

seldom hardly ever, infrequently, not often, occasionally, once in a blue moon (*Inf.*), rarely, scarcely ever
Antonyms again and again, frequently, many a time, much, often, over and over again, time after time, time and again

select *v.* 1. choose, opt for, pick, prefer, single out, sort out *~adj.* 2. choice, excellent, first-class, first-rate, hand-picked, picked, posh (*Inf., chiefly Brit.*), preferable, prime, rare, recherché, selected, special, superior, topnotch (*Inf.*) 3. cliquish, elite, exclusive, limited, privileged
Antonyms *v.* eliminate, reject, turn down *~adj.* cheap, indifferent, indiscriminate, inferior, ordinary, random, run-of-the-mill, second-rate, shoddy, substandard, unremarkable

selection 1. choice, choosing, option, pick, preference 2. anthology, assortment, choice, collection, line-up, medley, miscellany, potpourri, range, variety

selective careful, discerning, discriminating, discriminatory, eclectic, particular
Antonyms all-embracing, careless, desultory, indiscriminate, unselective

self-assurance assertiveness, confidence, positiveness, self-confidence, self-possession

self-centred egotistic, inward looking, narcissistic, self-absorbed, selfish, self-seeking, wrapped up in oneself

self-confidence aplomb, confidence, high morale, nerve, poise, self-assurance, self-reliance, self-respect

self-confident assured, confident, fearless, poised, secure, self-assured, self-reliant, sure of oneself

self-conscious affected, awkward, bashful, diffident, embarrassed, ill at ease, insecure, nervous, out of countenance, shamefaced, sheepish, uncomfortable

self-control calmness, cool, coolness, restraint, self-discipline, self-mastery, self-restraint, strength of mind *or* will, willpower

self-denial abstemiousness, asceticism, renunciation, self-abnegation, selflessness, self-sacrifice, unselfishness

self-esteem *amour-propre,* confidence, faith in oneself, pride, self-assurance, self-regard, self-respect, vanity

self-evident axiomatic, clear, incontrovertible, inescapable, manifestly *or* patently true, obvious, undeniable, written all over (something)

self-government autonomy, democracy, home rule, independence, self-determination, self-rule, sovereignty

self-important arrogant, big-headed, bumptious, cocky, conceited, overbearing, pompous, presumptuous, pushy (*Inf.*), strutting, swaggering, swollen-headed

self-indulgence dissipation, excess, extravagance, incontinence, intemperance, self-gratification, sensualism

selfish egoistic, egoistical, egotistic, egotistical, greedy, looking out for number one (*Inf.*), mean, mercenary, narrow, self-centred, self-interested, self-seeking, ungenerous
Antonyms altruistic, benevolent, considerate, generous, magnanimous, philanthropic, self-denying, selfless, self-sacrificing, ungrudging, unselfish

selfless altruistic, generous, magnanimous, self-denying, self-sacrificing, ungrudging, unselfish

self-possessed collected, confident, cool, cool as a cucumber (*Inf.*), poised, self-assured, sure of oneself, together (*Sl.*), unruffled

self-possession aplomb, composure, confidence, cool (*Sl.*), poise, sang-froid, self-command, unflappability (*Inf.*)

self-reliant able to stand on one's own two feet (*Inf.*), capable, independent, self-sufficient, self-supporting
Antonyms dependent, helpless, reliant, relying on

self-respect *amour-propre,* dignity, faith in oneself, morale, one's own image, pride, self-esteem

self-restraint abstemiousness, forbearance, patience, self-command, self-control, self-discipline, willpower

self-righteous complacent, goody-goody (*Inf.*), holier-than-thou, hypocritical, pharisaic, pi (*Brit. sl.*), pietistic, pious, priggish, sanctimonious, self-satisfied, smug, superior, too good to be true

self-sacrifice altruism, generosity, self-abnegation, self-denial, selflessness

self-satisfaction complacency, contentment, ease of mind, flush of success, glow of achievement, pride, self-approbation, self-approval, smugness

self-satisfied complacent, flushed with success, like a cat that has swallowed the cream *or* the canary, pleased with oneself, proud of oneself, puffed up, self-congratulatory, smug, well-pleased

self-seeking *adj.* acquisitive, calculating, careerist, fortune-hunting, gold-digging, looking out for number one (*Inf.*), mercenary, on the make (*Sl.*), opportunistic, out for what one can get, self-interested, selfish, self-serving

self-styled *soi-disant,* professed, quasi-, self-appointed, so-called, would-be

self-willed cussed (*Inf.*), headstrong, intractable, obstinate, opinionated, pig-headed, refractory, stiff-necked, stubborn, stubborn as a mule, ungovernable, wilful

sell 1. barter, dispose of, exchange, put up for sale, trade 2. be in the business of, deal in, handle, hawk, market, merchandise, peddle, retail, stock, trade in, traffic in, vend 3. gain acceptance for, promote, put across 4. *Inf. With* **on** convert to, convince of, get (someone) hooked on, persuade of, talk (someone) into, win (someone) over to 5. betray, deliver up, give up, sell down the river (*Inf.*), sell out (*Inf.*), surrender
Antonyms (*senses 1 & 2*) acquire, get, invest in, obtain, pay for, procure, purchase, shop for

seller agent, dealer, merchant, purveyor, rep, representative, retailer, salesman, saleswoman, shopkeeper, supplier, tradesman, traveller, vendor

selling 1. business, commercial transactions, dealing, trading, traffic 2. marketing, merchandising, promotion, salesmanship

sell out 1. be out of stock of, dispose of, get rid of, run out of, sell up 2. *Inf.* betray, break faith with, double-cross (*Inf.*), fail, give away, play false, rat on (*Inf.*), sell down the river (*Inf.*), stab in the back

semblance air, appearance, aspect, bearing, façade, figure, form, front, guise, image, likeness, mask, mien, pretence, resemblance, show, similarity, veneer

semidarkness dusk, gloaming (*Scot. or poetic*), gloom, half-light, murk, twilight, waning light

seminal *Fig.* creative, formative, ground-breaking, imaginative, important, influential, innovative, original, productive

seminary academy, college, high school, institute, institution, school

send 1. communicate, consign, convey, direct, dispatch, forward, remit, transmit 2. cast, deliver, fire, fling, hurl, let fly, propel, shoot 3. *With* **off, out,** *etc.* broadcast, discharge, emit, exude, give off, radiate 4. *Sl.* charm, delight, electrify, enrapture, enthrall, excite, intoxicate, move, please, ravish, stir, thrill, titillate, turn (someone) on (*Sl.*) 5. **send (someone) packing** discharge, dismiss, give (someone) the bird (*Inf.*), give (someone) the brushoff (*Sl.*), send away, send (someone) about his *or* her business, send (someone) away with a flea in his *or* her ear (*Inf.*)

send for call for, demand, order, request, summon

sendoff departure, farewell, going-away party, leave-taking, start, valediction

send-up imitation, mickey-take (*Inf.*), mockery, parody, satire, skit, spoof (*Inf.*), take-off (*Inf.*)

send up burlesque, imitate, lampoon, make fun of, mimic, mock, parody, satirize, spoof (*Inf.*), take off (*Inf.*), take the mickey out of (*Inf.*), take the piss out of (*Taboo sl.*)

senile decrepit, doddering, doting, failing, imbecile, in one's dotage, in one's second childhood

senility caducity, decrepitude, dotage, infirmity, loss of one's faculties, second childhood, senescence, senile dementia

senior *adj.* elder, higher ranking, major (*Brit.*), older, superior
Antonyms inferior, junior, lesser, lower, minor, subordinate, younger

senior citizen elder, O.A.P., old *or* elderly person, old age pensioner, pensioner, retired person

seniority eldership, longer service, precedence, priority, rank, superiority

sensation 1. awareness, consciousness, feeling, impression, perception, sense, tingle 2. agitation, commotion, crowd puller (*Inf.*), excitement, furore, hit (*Inf.*), scandal, stir, surprise, thrill, vibes (*Sl.*), wow (*Sl., chiefly U.S.*)

sensational 1. amazing, astounding, breathtaking, dramatic, electrifying, exciting, hair-raising, horrifying, lurid, melodramatic, revealing, scandalous, sensationalistic, shock-horror (*Facetious*), shocking, spectacular, staggering, startling, thrilling, yellow (*of the press*) 2. *Inf.* boffo (*Sl.*), brill (*Inf.*), brilliant, chillin' (*U.S. sl.*), cracking (*Brit. inf.*), crucial (*Sl.*), def (*Sl.*), excellent, exceptional, fabulous (*Inf.*), first class, impressive, jim-dandy (*Sl.*), marvellous, mean (*Sl.*), mega (*Sl.*), mind-blowing (*Inf.*), out of this world (*Inf.*), smashing (*Inf.*), sovereign, superb, topping (*Brit. sl.*)
Antonyms boring, commonplace, dull, humdrum, in good taste, mediocre, ordinary, prosaic, run-of-the-mill, understated, undramatic, unexaggerated, unexciting

sense *n.* 1. faculty, feeling, sensation, sensibility 2. appreciation, atmosphere, aura, awareness, consciousness, feel, impression, intuition, perception, premonition, presentiment, sentiment 3. definition, denotation, drift, gist, implication, import, interpretation, meaning, message, nuance, purport, significance, signification, substance 4. *Sometimes plural* brains (*Inf.*), clear-headedness, cleverness, common sense, discernment, discrimination, gumption (*Brit. inf.*), intelligence, judgment, mother wit, nous (*Brit. sl.*), quickness, reason, sagacity, sanity, sharpness, smarts (*Sl., chiefly U.S.*), tact, understanding, wisdom, wit(s) 5. advantage, good, logic, point, purpose, reason, use, value, worth ~*v.* 6. appreciate, apprehend, be aware of, discern, divine, feel, get the impression, grasp, have a feeling in one's bones (*Inf.*), have a funny feeling (*Inf.*), have a hunch, just know, notice, observe, perceive, pick up, realize, suspect, understand

Antonyms *n.* (*sense 4*) bêtise (*Rare*), folly, foolishness, idiocy, nonsense, silliness, stupidity ~*v.* be unaware of, fail to grasp *or* notice, miss, misunderstand, overlook

senseless 1. absurd, asinine, crazy, daft (*Inf.*), fatuous, foolish, goofy (*Inf.*), half-witted, idiotic, illogical, imbecilic, inane, incongruous, inconsistent, irrational, ludicrous, mad, meaningless, mindless, moronic, nonsensical, pointless, ridiculous, silly, simple, stupid, unintelligent, unreasonable, unwise 2. anaesthetized, cold, deadened, insensate, insensible, numb, numbed, out, out cold, stunned, unconscious, unfeeling

Antonyms conscious, intelligent, meaningful, rational, reasonable, sensible, sensitive, useful, valid, wise, worthwhile

sensibility 1. responsiveness, sensitiveness, sensitivity, susceptibility 2. *Often plural* emotions, feelings, moral sense, sentiments, susceptibilities 3. appreciation, awareness, delicacy, discernment, insight, intuition, perceptiveness, taste

Antonyms deadness, insensibility, insensitivity, lack of awareness, numbness, unconsciousness, unperceptiveness, unresponsiveness

sensible 1. canny, discreet, discriminating, down-to-earth, far-sighted, intelligent, judicious, matter-of-fact, practical, prudent, rational, realistic, reasonable, sagacious, sage, sane, shrewd, sober, sound, well-reasoned, well-thought-out, wise 2. *Usually with* **of** acquainted with, alive to, aware, conscious, convinced, mindful, observant, sensitive to, understanding 3. appreciable, considerable, discernable, noticeable, palpable, perceptible, significant, tangible, visible

Antonyms (*senses 1 & 2*) blind, daft (*Inf.*), foolish, idiotic, ignorant, injudicious, insensible, insensitive, irrational, senseless, silly, stupid, unaware, unmindful, unreasonable, unwise

sensitive 1. acute, delicate, easily affected, fine, impressionable, keen, perceptive, precise, reactive, responsive, sentient, susceptible 2. delicate, easily upset (hurt, offended), irritable, temperamental, tender, thin-skinned, touchy, umbrageous (*Rare*)

Antonyms approximate, callous, hard, hardened, imprecise, inexact, insensitive, obtuse, thick-skinned, tough, uncaring, unfeeling, unperceptive

sensitivity delicacy, reactiveness, reactivity, receptiveness, responsiveness, sensitiveness, susceptibility

sensual 1. animal, bodily, carnal, epicurean, fleshly, luxurious, physical, unspiritual, voluptuous 2. erotic, lascivious, lecherous, lewd, libidinous, licentious, lustful, randy (*Inf., chiefly Brit.*), raunchy (*Sl.*), sexual, sexy (*Inf.*), steamy (*Inf.*), unchaste

sensualist *bon vivant,* bon viveur, epicure, epicurean, hedonist, pleasure-lover, sybarite, voluptuary

sensuality animalism, carnality, eroticism, lasciviousness, lecherousness, lewdness, libidinousness, licentiousness, prurience, salaciousness, sexiness (*Inf.*), voluptuousness

sensuous epicurean, gratifying, hedonistic, lush, pleasurable, rich, sensory, sumptuous, sybaritic

Antonyms abstemious, ascetic, celibate, plain, self-denying, Spartan

sentence 1. *n.* condemnation, decision, decree, doom, judgment, order, pronouncement, ruling, verdict 2. *v.* condemn, doom, mete out justice to, pass judgment on, penalize

sententious 1. aphoristic, axiomatic, brief, compact, concise, epigrammatic, gnomic, laconic, pithy, pointed, short, succinct, terse 2. canting, judgmental, moralistic, pompous, ponderous, preachifying (*Inf.*), sanctimonious

sentient conscious, feeling, live, living, reactive, sensitive

sentiment 1. emotion, sensibility, soft-heartedness, tender feeling, tenderness 2. *Often plural* attitude, belief, feeling, idea, judgment, opinion, persuasion, saying, thought, view, way of thinking 3. emotionalism, mawkishness, overemotionalism, romanticism, sentimentality, slush (*Inf.*)

sentimental corny (*Sl.*), dewy-eyed, drippy (*Inf.*), emotional, gushy (*Inf.*), impressionable, maudlin, mawkish, mushy (*Inf.*), nostalgic, overemotional, pathetic, roman-

tic, schmaltzy (*Sl.*), simpering, sloppy (*Inf.*), slushy (*Inf.*), soft-hearted, tearful, tear-jerking (*Inf.*), tender, touching, weepy (*Inf.*)
Antonyms commonsensical, dispassionate, down-to-earth, earthy, hard-headed, practical, realistic, undemonstrative, unemotional, unfeeling, unromantic, unsentimental

sentimentality bathos, corniness (*Sl.*), emotionalism, gush (*Inf.*), mawkishness, mush (*Inf.*), nostalgia, play on the emotions, romanticism, schmaltz (*Sl.*), sloppiness (*Inf.*), slush (*Inf.*), sob stuff (*Inf.*), tenderness

sentinel *or* **sentry** guard, lookout, picket, watch, watchman

separable detachable, distinguishable, divisible, scissile, severable

separate *v.* 1. break off, cleave, come apart, come away, come between, detach, disconnect, disentangle, disjoin, divide, keep apart, remove, sever, split, sunder, uncouple 2. discriminate between, isolate, put on one side, segregate, single out, sort out 3. bifurcate, break up, disunite, diverge, divorce, estrange, go different ways, part, part company, set at variance *or* at odds, split up *~adj.* 4. detached, disconnected, discrete, disjointed, divided, divorced, isolated, unattached, unconnected 5. alone, apart, autonomous, distinct, independent, individual, particular, single, solitary
Antonyms *v.* amalgamate, combine, connect, join, link, merge, mix, unite *~adj.* affiliated, alike, connected, interdependent, joined, similar, unified, united

separated apart, broken up, disassociated, disconnected, disunited, divided, living apart, parted, put asunder, separate, split up, sundered

separately alone, apart, independently, individually, one at a time, one by one, personally, severally, singly
Antonyms as a group, as one, collectively, in a body, in concert, in unison, jointly, together

separation 1. break, detachment, disconnection, disengagement, disjunction, dissociation, disunion, division, gap, segregation, severance 2. break-up, divorce, estrangement, farewell, leave-taking, parting, rift, split, split-up

septic festering, infected, poisoned, pussy, putrefactive, putrefying, putrid, suppurating, toxic

sepulchral 1. cheerless, dismal, funereal, gloomy, grave, lugubrious, melancholy, morbid, mournful, sad, sombre, Stygian, woeful 2. deep, hollow, lugubrious, reverberating, sonorous

sepulchre burial place, grave, mausoleum, sarcophagus, tomb, vault

sequel conclusion, consequence, continuation, development, end, follow-up, issue, outcome, payoff (*Inf.*), result, upshot

sequence arrangement, chain, course, cycle, order, procession, progression, series, succession

sequestered cloistered, isolated, lonely, out-of-the-way, private, quiet, remote, retired, secluded, unfrequented

seraphic angelic, beatific, blissful, celestial, divine, heavenly, holy, pure, sublime

serene 1. calm, composed, imperturbable, peaceful, placid, sedate, tranquil, undisturbed, unruffled, untroubled 2. bright, clear, cloudless, fair, halcyon, unclouded
Antonyms (*sense 1*) agitated, anxious, disturbed, excitable, flustered, perturbed, troubled, uptight (*Inf.*)

serenity 1. calm, calmness, composure, peace, peacefulness, peace of mind, placidity, quietness, quietude, stillness, tranquillity 2. brightness, clearness, fairness

serf bondsman, helot, liegeman, servant, slave, thrall, varlet (*Archaic*), vassal, villein

series arrangement, chain, course, line, order, progression, run, sequence, set, string, succession, train

serious 1. grave, humourless, long-faced, pensive, sedate, sober, solemn, stern, thoughtful, unsmiling 2. deliberate, determined, earnest, genuine, honest, in earnest, resolute, resolved, sincere 3. crucial, deep, difficult, far-reaching, fateful, grim, important, momentous, no laughing matter, of moment *or* consequence, pressing, significant, urgent, weighty, worrying 4. acute, alarming, critical, dangerous, grave, severe
Antonyms capricious, carefree, flighty, flippant, frivolous, insignificant, insincere, jolly, joyful, light-hearted, minor, slight, smiling, trivial, uncommitted, undecided, unimportant

seriously 1. all joking aside, earnestly, gravely, in all conscience, in earnest, no joking (*Inf.*), sincerely, solemnly, thoughtfully, with a straight face 2. acutely, badly, critically, dangerously, distressingly, gravely, grievously, severely, sorely

seriousness 1. earnestness, gravitas, gravity, humourlessness, sedateness, sobriety, solemnity, staidness, sternness 2. danger, gravity, importance, moment, significance, urgency, weight

sermon 1. address, exhortation, homily 2.

dressing-down (*Inf.*), harangue, lecture, talking-to (*Inf.*)

serpentine coiling, crooked, meandering, sinuous, snaking, snaky, tortuous, twisting, winding

serrated notched, sawlike, sawtoothed, serrate, serriform (*Biol.*), serrulate, toothed

serried assembled, close, compact, dense, massed, phalanxed

servant attendant, domestic, drudge, help, helper, lackey, liegeman, maid, menial, retainer, servitor (*Archaic*), skivvy (*Chiefly Brit.*), slave, varlet (*Archaic*), vassal

serve 1. aid, assist, attend to, be in the service of, be of assistance, be of use, help, minister to, oblige, succour, wait on, work for **2.** act, attend, complete, discharge, do, fulfil, go through, observe, officiate, pass, perform **3.** answer, answer the purpose, be acceptable, be adequate, be good enough, content, do, do duty as, do the work of, fill the bill (*Inf.*), function as, satisfy, suffice, suit **4.** arrange, deal, deliver, dish up, distribute, handle, present, provide, purvey, set out, supply

service *n.* **1.** advantage, assistance, avail, benefit, help, ministrations, supply, use, usefulness, utility **2.** check, maintenance, overhaul, servicing **3.** business, duty, employ, employment, labour, office, work **4.** ceremony, function, observance, rite, worship ~*v.* **5.** check, fine tune, go over, maintain, overhaul, recondition, repair, tune (up)

serviceable advantageous, beneficial, convenient, dependable, durable, efficient, functional, hard-wearing, helpful, operative, practical, profitable, usable, useful, utilitarian

Antonyms impractical, inefficient, unserviceable, unusable, useless, worn-out

servile abject, base, bootlicking (*Inf.*), craven, cringing, fawning, grovelling, humble, low, mean, menial, obsequious, slavish, submissive, subservient, sycophantic, toadying, toadyish, unctuous

servility abjection, baseness, bootlicking (*Inf.*), fawning, grovelling, meanness, obsequiousness, self-abasement, slavishness, submissiveness, subservience, sycophancy, toadyism, unctuousness

serving *n.* helping, plateful, portion

servitude bondage, bonds, chains, enslavement, obedience, serfdom, slavery, subjugation, thraldom, thrall, vassalage

session assembly, conference, congress, discussion, get-together (*Inf.*), hearing, meeting, period, seminar, sitting, term

set[1] *v.* **1.** aim, apply, deposit, direct, embed, fasten, fix, install, lay, locate, lodge, mount, park (*Inf.*), place, plant, plonk, plump, position, put, rest, seat, situate, station, stick, turn **2.** agree upon, allocate, appoint, arrange, assign, conclude, decide (upon), designate, determine, establish, fix, fix up, name, ordain, regulate, resolve, schedule, settle, specify **3.** arrange, lay, make ready, prepare, spread **4.** adjust, coordinate, rectify, regulate, synchronize **5.** cake, condense, congeal, crystallize, gelatinize, harden, jell, solidify, stiffen, thicken **6.** allot, decree, impose, lay down, ordain, prescribe, specify **7.** decline, dip, disappear, go down, sink, subside, vanish ~*n.* **8.** attitude, bearing, carriage, fit, hang, position, posture, turn **9.** *mise-en-scène,* scene, scenery, setting, stage set, stage setting ~*adj.* **10.** agreed, appointed, arranged, customary, decided, definite, established, firm, fixed, prearranged, predetermined, prescribed, regular, scheduled, settled, usual **11.** artificial, conventional, formal, hackneyed, rehearsed, routine, standard, stereotyped, stock, traditional, unspontaneous **12.** entrenched, firm, hard and fast, hardened, hidebound, immovable, inflexible, rigid, strict, stubborn **13.** *With* **on** *or* **upon** bent, determined, intent, resolute

Antonyms (*sense 12*) flexible, free, open, open-minded, undecided

set[2] *n.* **1.** band, circle, class, clique, company, coterie, crew (*Inf.*), crowd, faction, gang, group, outfit, posse (*Inf.*), schism, sect **2.** assemblage, assortment, batch, collection, compendium, coordinated group, kit, outfit, series

set about 1. address oneself to, attack, begin, get cracking (*Inf.*), get down to, get to work, get weaving (*Inf.*), make a start on, put one's shoulder to the wheel (*Inf.*), roll up one's sleeves, sail into (*Inf.*), set to, start, tackle, take the first step, wade into **2.** assail, assault, attack, belabour, lambast(e), mug (*Inf.*), sail into (*Inf.*)

set against 1. balance, compare, contrast, juxtapose, weigh **2.** alienate, disunite, divide, drive a wedge between, estrange, make bad blood, make mischief, oppose, set at cross purposes, set at odds, set by the ears (*Inf.*), sow dissension

set aside 1. keep, keep back, put on one side, reserve, save, select, separate, set apart, single out **2.** abrogate, annul, cancel, discard, dismiss, nullify, overrule, overturn, quash, reject, render null and void, repudiate, reverse

setback bit of trouble, blow, bummer (*Sl.*), check, defeat, disappointment, hitch, hold-up, misfortune, rebuff, reverse, upset

set back delay, hinder, hold up, impede, retard, slow

set off 1. depart, embark, leave, sally forth, set out, start out 2. detonate, explode, ignite, kick-start, light, set in motion, touch off, trigger off 3. bring out the highlights in, enhance, show off, throw into relief

set on assail, assault, attack, fall upon, fly at, go for, incite, instigate, let fly at, pitch into (*Inf.*), pounce on, sail into (*Inf.*), set about, sic, spur on, urge

set out 1. arrange, array, describe, detail, display, dispose, elaborate, elucidate, exhibit, explain, expose to view, lay out, present, set forth 2. begin, embark, get under way, hit the road (*Sl.*), sally forth, set off, start out, take to the road

setting backdrop, background, context, frame, locale, location, *mise en scène,* mounting, perspective, scene, scenery, set, site, surround, surroundings

settle 1. adjust, dispose, order, put into order, regulate, set to rights, straighten out, work out 2. choose, clear up, complete, conclude, decide, dispose of, put an end to, reconcile, resolve 3. *Often with* **on** *or* **upon** agree, appoint, arrange, choose, come to an agreement, confirm, decide, determine, establish, fix 4. allay, calm, compose, lull, pacify, quell, quiet, quieten, reassure, relax, relieve, sedate, soothe, tranquillize 5. alight, bed down, come to rest, descend, land, light, make oneself comfortable 6. dwell, inhabit, live, make one's home, move to, put down roots, reside, set up home, take up residence 7. colonize, found, people, pioneer, plant, populate 8. acquit oneself of, clear, discharge, liquidate, pay, quit, square (up) 9. decline, fall, sink, subside

Antonyms (*sense 4*) agitate, bother, discompose, disquieten, disturb, rattle, trouble, unsettle, upset

settlement 1. adjustment, agreement, arrangement, completion, conclusion, confirmation, disposition, establishment, resolution, termination, working out 2. clearance, clearing, defrayal, discharge, liquidation, payment, satisfaction 3. colonization, colony, community, encampment, hamlet, outpost, peopling

settler colonist, colonizer, frontiersman, immigrant, pioneer, planter

set-to argument, argy-bargy (*Brit. inf.*), barney (*Inf.*), brush, disagreement, dust-up (*Inf.*), fight, fracas, quarrel, row, scrap (*Inf.*), slanging match (*Brit.*), spat, squabble, wrangle

setup arrangement, circumstances, conditions, organization, regime, structure, system

set up 1. arrange, begin, compose, establish, found, initiate, install, institute, make provision for, organize, prearrange, prepare 2. back, build up, establish, finance, promote, put some beef into (*Inf.*), strengthen, subsidize 3. assemble, build, construct, elevate, erect, put together, put up, raise

set upon ambush, assail, assault, attack, beat up, fall upon, go for, lay into (*Inf.*), mug (*Inf.*), put the boot in (*Sl.*), set about, turn on

sever 1. bisect, cleave, cut, cut in two, detach, disconnect, disjoin, disunite, divide, part, rend, separate, split, sunder 2. abandon, break off, dissociate, dissolve, put an end to, terminate

Antonyms attach, connect, continue, fix together, join, link, maintain, unite, uphold

several *adj.* assorted, different, disparate, distinct, divers (*Archaic*), diverse, indefinite, individual, manifold, many, particular, respective, single, some, sundry, various

severe 1. austere, cruel, Draconian, drastic, hard, harsh, inexorable, iron-handed, oppressive, pitiless, relentless, rigid, strict, unbending, unrelenting 2. cold, disapproving, dour, flinty, forbidding, grave, grim, serious, sober, stern, strait-laced, tight-lipped, unsmiling 3. acute, bitter, critical, dangerous, distressing, extreme, fierce, grinding, inclement, intense, violent 4. ascetic, austere, chaste, classic, forbidding, functional, plain, restrained, severe, simple, Spartan, unadorned, unembellished, unfussy 5. arduous, demanding, difficult, exacting, fierce, hard, punishing, rigorous, stringent, taxing, tough, unrelenting 6. astringent, biting, caustic, cutting, harsh, mordacious, mordant, satirical, scathing, unsparing, vitriolic

Antonyms (*senses 1, 2, 3, 5 & 6*) affable, clement, compassionate, easy, genial, gentle, kind, lax, lenient, manageable, mild, minor, moderate, relaxed, temperate, tractable (*sense 4*) embellished, fancy, ornamental, ornate

severely 1. harshly, rigorously, sharply, sternly, strictly, with an iron hand, with a rod of iron 2. acutely, badly, critically, dangerously, extremely, gravely, hard, sorely

severity austerity, gravity, hardness, harshness, plainness, rigour, seriousness, severeness, sternness, strictness, stringency, toughness

sex 1. gender 2. *Inf.* coition, coitus, copulation, fornication, going to bed (with someone), intimacy, lovemaking, nookie (*Sl.*), rumpy-pumpy (*Sl.*), (sexual) intercourse, sexual relations, the other (*Inf.*) 3. desire, facts of life, libido, reproduction, sexuality, the birds and the bees (*Inf.*)

sex appeal allure, desirability, glamour, it (*Inf.*), magnetism, oomph (*Inf.*), seductiveness, sensuality, sexiness (*Inf.*), voluptuousness

sexless androgynous, asexual, epicene, hermaphrodite, neuter, nonsexual, parthenogenetic

sexual 1. carnal, coital, erotic, intimate, of the flesh, sensual, sexy 2. genital, procreative, reproductive, sex, venereal

sexual intercourse bonking (*Inf.*), carnal knowledge, coition, coitus, commerce (*Archaic*), congress, consummation, copulation, coupling, fucking (*Taboo*), mating, nookie (*Sl.*), penetration, rumpy-pumpy (*Sl.*), screwing (*Taboo*), shagging (*Taboo*), the other (*Inf.*), union

sexuality bodily appetites, carnality, desire, eroticism, lust, sensuality, sexiness (*Inf.*), virility, voluptuousness

sexy arousing, beddable, bedroom, come-hither (*Inf.*), cuddly, erotic, flirtatious, inviting, kissable, naughty, provocative, provoking, seductive, sensual, sensuous, slinky, suggestive, titillating, voluptuous

shabby 1. dilapidated, down at heel, faded, frayed, having seen better days, mean, neglected, poor, ragged, run-down, scruffy, seedy, tattered, tatty, the worse for wear, threadbare, worn, worn-out 2. cheap, contemptible, despicable, dirty, dishonourable, ignoble, low, low-down (*Inf.*), mean, rotten (*Inf.*), scurvy, shameful, shoddy, ungentlemanly, unworthy
Antonyms fair, generous, handsome, honourable, in mint condition, neat, new, praiseworthy, smart, well-dressed, well-kempt, well-kept, well-to-do, worthy

shack cabin, dump (*Inf.*), hovel, hut, lean-to, shanty, shiel (*Scot.*), shieling (*Scot.*)

shackle *n.* 1. *Often plural* bond, chain, fetter, gyve (*Archaic*), handcuff, hobble, iron, leg-iron, manacle, rope, tether ~*v.* 2. bind, chain, fetter, handcuff, hobble, manacle, pinion, put in irons, secure, tether, tie, trammel 3. constrain, embarrass, encumber, hamper, hamstring, impede, inhibit, limit, obstruct, restrain, restrict, tie (someone's) hands

shade *n.* 1. coolness, dimness, dusk, gloom, gloominess, obscurity, screen, semidarkness, shadiness, shadow, shadows 2. **put into the shade** eclipse, make pale by comparison, outclass, outshine, overshadow 3. blind, canopy, cover, covering, curtain, screen, shield, veil 4. colour, hue, stain, tinge, tint, tone 5. amount, dash, degree, difference, gradation, hint, nuance, semblance, suggestion, suspicion, trace, variety 6. apparition, eidolon, ghost, manes, phantom, shadow, spectre, spirit ~*v.* 7. cast a shadow over, cloud, conceal, cover, darken, dim, hide, mute, obscure, protect, screen, shadow, shield, shut out the light, veil

shadow *n.* 1. cover, darkness, dimness, dusk, gathering darkness, gloaming (*Scot. or poetic*), gloom, obscurity, protection, shade, shelter 2. hint, suggestion, suspicion, trace 3. eidolon, ghost, image, phantom, remnant, representation, spectre, vestige 4. blight, cloud, gloom, sadness ~*v.* 5. cast a shadow over, darken, overhang, screen, shade, shield 6. dog, follow, spy on, stalk, tail (*Inf.*), trail

shadowy 1. crepuscular, dark, dim, dusky, funereal, gloomy, indistinct, murky, obscure, shaded, shady, tenebrious, tenebrous 2. dim, dreamlike, faint, ghostly, illusory, imaginary, impalpable, intangible, nebulous, obscure, phantom, spectral, undefined, unreal, unsubstantial, vague, wraithlike

shady 1. bosky (*Literary*), bowery, cool, dim, leafy, shaded, shadowy, umbrageous 2. *Inf.* crooked, disreputable, dodgy (*Brit., Aust., & N.Z. inf.*), dubious, fishy (*Inf.*), questionable, shifty, slippery, suspect, suspicious, unethical, unscrupulous, untrustworthy
Antonyms (*sense 1*) bright, exposed, open, out in the open, sunlit, sunny, unshaded (*sense 2*) above-board, ethical, honest, honourable, reputable, respectable, straight, trustworthy, upright

shaft 1. handle, pole, rod, shank, stem, upright 2. beam, gleam, ray, streak 3. barb, cut, dart, gibe, sting, thrust

shaggy hairy, hirsute, long-haired, rough, tousled, unkempt, unshorn
Antonyms close-cropped, crew-cut, cropped, flat-woven, neatly-trimmed, shorn, short-haired, short-piled, smooth

shake *v.* 1. bump, fluctuate, jar, joggle, jolt, jounce, oscillate, quake, quiver, rock, shiver, shudder, sway, totter, tremble, vibrate, waver, wobble 2. brandish, flourish, wave 3. *Often with* **up** agitate, churn, convulse, rouse, stir 4. discompose, distress, disturb, frighten, intimidate, move, rattle (*Inf.*), shock, unnerve, upset 5. impair, pull the rug out from under (*Inf.*), undermine, weaken ~*n.* 6. agitation, convulsion, disturbance, jar, jerk, jolt, jounce, pulsation, quaking, shiver, shock, shudder, trembling, tremor, vibration 7. *Inf.* instant, jiffy (*Inf.*), moment, second, tick (*Brit. inf.*), trice

shake off dislodge, elude, get away from,

get rid of, get shot of (*Sl.*), give the slip, leave behind, lose, rid oneself of, throw off

shake up agitate, churn (up), disturb, mix, overturn, reorganize, shock, stir (up), turn upside down, unsettle, upset

shaky 1. all of a quiver (*Inf.*), faltering, insecure, precarious, quivery, rickety, tottering, trembling, tremulous, unstable, unsteady, weak, wobbly 2. dubious, iffy (*Inf.*), questionable, suspect, uncertain, undependable, unreliable, unsound, unsupported

Antonyms dependable, firm, secure, stable, steady, strong

shallow 1. *adj. Fig.* empty, flimsy, foolish, frivolous, idle, ignorant, meaningless, puerile, simple, skin-deep, slight, superficial, surface, trivial, unintelligent 2. *n. Often plural* bank, flat, sandbank, sand bar, shelf, shoal

Antonyms *adj.* analytical, comprehensive, deep, in-depth, meaningful, penetrating, perceptive, profound, searching, serious, thoughtful, weighty ~*n.* abyss, deep, depth, chasm, gorge, gulf, pit, void

sham 1. *n.* counterfeit, feint, forgery, fraud, hoax, humbug, imitation, impostor, imposture, phoney *or* phony (*Inf.*), pretence, pretender, pseud (*Inf.*), wolf in sheep's clothing 2. *adj.* artificial, bogus, counterfeit, ersatz, false, feigned, imitation, mock, phoney *or* phony (*Inf.*), pretended, pseud (*Inf.*), pseudo (*Inf.*), simulated, spurious, synthetic 3. *v.* affect, assume, counterfeit, fake, feign, imitate, play possum, pretend, put on, simulate

Antonyms *n.* master, original, the genuine article, the real McCoy (*or* McKay), the real thing ~*adj.* authentic, bona fide, genuine, legitimate, natural, real, sound, true, unfeigned, veritable

shambles anarchy, chaos, confusion, disarray, disorder, disorganization, havoc, madhouse, mess, muddle

shambling awkward, clumsy, lumbering, lurching, shuffling, ungainly, unsteady

shambolic anarchic, at sixes and sevens, chaotic, confused, disordered, disorganized, inefficient, in total disarray, muddled, topsy-turvy, unsystematic

shame *n.* 1. blot, contempt, degradation, derision, discredit, disgrace, dishonour, disrepute, ill repute, infamy, obloquy, odium, opprobrium, reproach, scandal, skeleton in the cupboard, smear 2. abashment, chagrin, compunction, embarrassment, humiliation, ignominy, loss of face, mortification, shamefacedness 3. **put to shame** disgrace, eclipse, outclass, outdo, outstrip, show up, surpass ~*v.* 4. abash, confound, disconcert, disgrace, embarrass, humble, humiliate, mortify, reproach, ridicule, take (someone) down a peg (*Inf.*) 5. blot, debase, defile, degrade, discredit, dishonour, smear, stain

Antonyms *n.* (*sense 1*) credit, distinction, esteem, glory, honour, pride, renown, self-respect (*sense 2*) brass neck (*Brit. inf.*), brazenness, cheek, shamelessness, unabashedness ~*v.* acclaim, credit, do credit to, enhance the reputation of, honour, make proud

shamefaced 1. bashful, blushing, diffident, hesitant, modest, shrinking, shy, timid 2. abashed, ashamed, chagrined, conscience-stricken, contrite, discomfited, embarrassed, humiliated, mortified, red-faced, remorseful, sheepish

shameful 1. atrocious, base, dastardly, degrading, disgraceful, dishonourable, ignominious, indecent, infamous, low, mean, outrageous, reprehensible, scandalous, unbecoming, unworthy, vile, wicked 2. blush-making (*Inf.*), cringe-making (*Brit. inf.*), degrading, embarrassing, humiliating, mortifying, shaming

Antonyms admirable, creditable, estimable, exemplary, honourable, laudable, right, worthy

shameless abandoned, audacious, barefaced, brash, brazen, corrupt, depraved, dissolute, flagrant, hardened, immodest, improper, impudent, incorrigible, indecent, insolent, profligate, reprobate, unabashed, unashamed, unblushing, unprincipled, wanton

shanty bothy (*Scot.*), cabin, hovel, hut, lean-to, shack, shed, shiel (*Scot.*), shieling (*Scot.*)

shape *n.* 1. build, configuration, contours, cut, figure, form, lines, make, outline, profile, silhouette 2. frame, model, mould, pattern 3. appearance, aspect, form, guise, likeness, semblance 4. condition, fettle, health, kilter, state, trim ~*v.* 5. create, fashion, form, make, model, mould, produce 6. accommodate, adapt, convert, define, develop, devise, frame, guide, modify, plan, prepare, regulate, remodel

shapeless amorphous, asymmetrical, battered, embryonic, formless, indeterminate, irregular, misshapen, nebulous, undeveloped, unstructured

Antonyms comely, curvaceous, elegant, graceful, neat, trim, well-formed, well-proportioned, well-turned

shapely comely, curvaceous, elegant, graceful, neat, sightly, trim, well-formed, well-proportioned, well-turned

shape up be promising, come on, develop, look good, proceed, progress, turn out

share 1. *v.* apportion, assign, distribute, divide, go Dutch (*Inf.*), go fifty-fifty (*Inf.*), go halves, parcel out, partake, participate, receive, split, use in common 2. *n.* allotment, allowance, contribution, cut (*Inf.*), division, due, lot, part, portion, proportion, quota, ration, whack (*Inf.*)

sharp *adj.* 1. acute, cutting, honed, jagged, keen, knife-edged, knifelike, pointed, razor-sharp, serrated, sharpened, spiky 2. abrupt, distinct, extreme, marked, sudden 3. alert, apt, astute, bright, clever, discerning, knowing, long-headed, observant, penetrating, perceptive, quick, quick-witted, ready, subtle 4. artful, crafty, cunning, dishonest, fly (*Sl.*), shrewd, sly, smart, unscrupulous, wily 5. acute, distressing, excruciating, fierce, intense, painful, piercing, severe, shooting, sore, stabbing, stinging, violent 6. clear, clear-cut, crisp, distinct, well-defined 7. *Inf.* chic, classy (*Sl.*), dressy, fashionable, natty (*Inf.*), smart, snappy, stylish, trendy (*Inf.*) 8. acerb, acrimonious, barbed, biting, bitter, caustic, cutting, harsh, hurtful, mordacious, mordant, sarcastic, sardonic, scathing, severe, trenchant, vitriolic 9. acerb, acerbic, acetic, acid, acrid, burning, hot, piquant, pungent, sour, tart, vinegary ~*adv.* 10. exactly, on the dot, on time, precisely, promptly, punctually 11. abruptly, suddenly, unexpectedly, without warning

Antonyms *adj.* (*sense 1*) blunt, dull, edgeless, pointed, rounded, unsharpened (*sense 2*) even, gentle, gradual, moderate, progressive (*sense 3*) dim, dull-witted, dumb (*Inf.*), slow, slow-on-the-uptake, stupid (*sense 4*) artless, guileless, ingenuous, innocent, naive, simple, undesigning (*sense 6*) blurred, fuzzy, ill-defined, indistinct, unclear (*sense 8*) amicable, courteous, friendly, gentle, kindly, mild (*sense 9*) bland, mild, tasteless ~*adv.* (*sense 10*) approximately, more or less, roughly, round about, vaguely (*sense 11*) bit by bit, gently, gradually, slowly

sharpen edge, grind, hone, put an edge on, strop, whet

shatter 1. break, burst, crack, crush, crush to smithereens, demolish, explode, implode, pulverize, shiver, smash, split 2. blast, blight, bring to nought, demolish, destroy, disable, exhaust, impair, overturn, ruin, torpedo, wreck 3. break (someone's) heart, crush, devastate, dumbfound, knock the stuffing out of (someone) (*Inf.*), upset

shattered all in (*Sl.*), clapped out (*Aust. & N.Z. inf.*), crushed dead beat (*Inf.*), dead tired (*Inf.*), devastated, dog-tired (*Inf.*), done in (*Inf.*), drained, exhausted, jiggered (*Inf.*), knackered (*Sl.*), ready to drop, spent, tired out, weary, worn out, zonked (*Sl.*)

shattering crushing, devastating, overwhelming, paralysing, severe, stunning

shave *v.* 1. crop, pare, plane, shear, trim 2. brush, graze, touch

shed *v.* 1. afford, cast, diffuse, drop, emit, give, give forth, pour forth, radiate, scatter, shower, spill, throw 2. cast off, discard, exuviate, moult, slough

sheen brightness, burnish, gleam, gloss, lustre, patina, polish, shine, shininess

sheepish abashed, ashamed, chagrined, embarrassed, foolish, mortified, self-conscious, shamefaced, silly, uncomfortable

Antonyms assertive, audacious, bold, brash, brass-necked (*Brit. inf.*), brazen, confident, intractable, obdurate, unabashed, unapologetic, unblushing, unembarrassed

sheer 1. abrupt, headlong (*Archaic*), perpendicular, precipitous, steep 2. absolute, arrant, complete, downright, out-and-out, pure, rank, thoroughgoing, total, unadulterated, unalloyed, unmitigated, unqualified, utter 3. *Of fabrics* diaphanous, fine, gauzy, gossamer, seethrough, thin, transparent

Antonyms (*sense 1*) gentle, gradual, horizontal, moderate, slanting, sloping (*sense 3*) coarse, heavy, impenetrable, opaque, thick

sheet 1. coat, film, folio, lamina, layer, leaf, membrane, overlay, pane, panel, piece, plate, slab, stratum, surface, veneer 2. area, blanket, covering, expanse, stretch, sweep

shell *n.* 1. carapace, case, husk, pod ~*v.* 2. husk, shuck 3. attack, barrage, blitz, bomb, bombard, strafe, strike ~*n.* 4. chassis, frame, framework, hull, skeleton, structure

shell out ante up (*Inf., chiefly U.S.*), disburse, expend, fork out (*Sl.*), give, hand over, lay out (*Inf.*), pay out

shelter 1. *v.* cover, defend, guard, harbour, hide, protect, safeguard, seek refuge, shield, take in, take shelter 2. *n.* asylum, cover, covert, defence, guard, haven, protection, refuge, retreat, roof over one's head, safety, sanctuary, screen, security, shiel (*Scot.*), umbrella

Antonyms *v.* endanger, expose, hazard, imperil, lay open, leave open, make vulnerable, risk, subject

sheltered cloistered, conventual, ensconced, hermitic, isolated, protected, quiet, reclusive, retired, screened, secluded, shaded, shielded, withdrawn

Antonyms exposed, laid bare, made public, open, public, unconcealed, unprotected, unsheltered

shelve defer, dismiss, freeze, hold in abeyance, hold over, lay aside, mothball, pigeonhole, postpone, put aside, put off, put on ice, put on the back burner (*Inf.*), suspend, table (*U.S.*), take a rain check on (*U.S. & Canad. inf.*)

shepherd *v.* conduct, convoy, guide, herd, marshal, steer, usher

shield *n.* 1. buckler, escutcheon (*Heraldry*), targe (*Archaic*) 2. aegis, bulwark, cover, defence, guard, protection, rampart, safeguard, screen, shelter, ward (*Archaic*) ~*v.* 3. cover, defend, guard, protect, safeguard, screen, shelter, ward off

shift *v.* 1. alter, budge, change, displace, fluctuate, move, move around, rearrange, relocate, remove, reposition, swerve, switch, transfer, transpose, vary, veer 2. *As in* **shift for oneself** assume responsibility, contrive, devise, fend, get along, look after, make do, manage, plan, scheme, take care of ~*n.* 3. about-turn, alteration, change, displacement, fluctuation, modification, move, permutation, rearrangement, removal, shifting, switch, transfer, veering 4. artifice, contrivance, craft, device, dodge, equivocation, evasion, expedient, move, resource, ruse, stratagem, subterfuge, trick, wile

shiftless aimless, good-for-nothing, idle, incompetent, indolent, inefficient, inept, irresponsible, lackadaisical, lazy, slothful, unambitious, unenterprising

shifty contriving, crafty, deceitful, devious, duplicitous, evasive, fly-by-night (*Inf.*), furtive, scheming, slippery, sly, tricky, underhand, unprincipled, untrustworthy, wily

Antonyms dependable, guileless, honest, honourable, open, reliable, trustworthy, upright

shillyshally *v.* be irresolute *or* indecisive, dilly-dally (*Inf.*), dither (*Chiefly Brit.*), falter, fluctuate, haver (*Brit.*), hem and haw, hesitate, seesaw, swither (*Scot.*), vacillate, waver, yo-yo (*Inf.*)

shimmer 1. *v.* dance, gleam, glisten, phosphoresce, scintillate, twinkle 2. *n.* diffused light, gleam, glimmer, glow, incandescence, iridescence, lustre, phosphorescence, unsteady light

shin *v.* ascend, clamber, climb, scale, scramble, swarm

shine *v.* 1. beam, emit light, flash, give off light, glare, gleam, glimmer, glisten, glitter, glow, radiate, scintillate, shimmer, sparkle, twinkle 2. be conspicuous (distinguished, outstanding, pre-eminent), excel, stand out, stand out in a crowd, star 3. brush, buff, burnish, polish, rub up ~*n.* 4. brightness, glare, gleam, lambency, light, luminosity, radiance, shimmer, sparkle 5. glaze, gloss, lustre, patina, polish, sheen

shining 1. beaming, bright, brilliant, effulgent, gleaming, glistening, glittering, luminous, radiant, resplendent, shimmering, sparkling 2. *Fig.* brilliant, celebrated, conspicuous, distinguished, eminent, glorious, illustrious, leading, outstanding, splendid

shiny agleam, bright, burnished, gleaming, glistening, glossy, lustrous, nitid (*Poetic*), polished, satiny, sheeny

shipshape Bristol fashion, businesslike, neat, orderly, spick-and-span, tidy, trig (*Archaic or dialect*), trim, uncluttered, well-ordered, well-organized, well-regulated

shirk avoid, bob off (*Brit. sl.*), body-swerve (*Scot.*), dodge, duck (out of) (*Inf.*), evade, get out of, scrimshank (*Brit. military sl.*), shun, sidestep, skive (*Brit. sl.*), slack

shirker clock-watcher, dodger, gold brick (*U.S. sl.*), idler, malingerer, quitter, scrimshanker (*Brit. military sl.*), shirk, skiver (*Brit. sl.*), slacker

shiver[1] *v.* 1. palpitate, quake, quiver, shake, shudder, tremble ~*n.* 2. flutter, *frisson,* quiver, shudder, thrill, tremble, trembling, tremor 3. **the shivers** chattering teeth, chill, goose flesh, goose pimples, the shakes (*Inf.*)

shiver[2] *v.* break, crack, fragment, shatter, smash, smash to smithereens, splinter

shivery chilled, chilly, cold, quaking, quivery, shaking, shuddery, trembly

shoal sandbank, sand bar, shallow, shelf

shock *v.* 1. agitate, appal, astound, disgust, disquiet, give (someone) a turn (*Inf.*), gross out (*U.S. sl.*), horrify, jar, jolt, nauseate, numb, offend, outrage, paralyse, revolt, scandalize, shake, shake out of one's complacency, shake up (*Inf.*), sicken, stagger, stun, stupefy, traumatize, unsettle ~*n.* 2. blow, bolt from the blue, bombshell, breakdown, collapse, consternation, distress, disturbance, prostration, state of shock, stupefaction, stupor, trauma, turn (*Inf.*), upset 3. blow, clash, collision, encounter, impact, jarring, jolt

shocking abominable, appalling, atrocious, detestable, disgraceful, disgusting, disquieting, distressing, dreadful, foul, frightful, ghastly, hellacious (*U.S. sl.*), hideous, horrible, horrifying, loathsome, monstrous, nauseating, obscene, odious, offensive, outrageous, repulsive, revolting, scandalous, sickening, stupefying, unspeakable

Antonyms admirable, decent, delightful,

excellent, expected, fine, first-rate, gratifying, honourable, laudable, marvellous, pleasant, praiseworthy, satisfying, unsurprising, wonderful

shoddy cheap-jack (*Inf.*), cheapo (*Inf.*), inferior, junky (*Inf.*), poor, rubbishy, second-rate, slipshod, tacky (*Inf.*), tatty, tawdry, trashy
Antonyms accurate, careful, considerate, craftsman-like, excellent, fastidious, fine, first-rate, meticulous, noble, quality, superlative, well-made

shoemaker bootmaker, cobbler, souter (*Scot.*)

shoot[1] *v.* 1. bag, blast (*Sl.*), blow away (*Sl., chiefly U.S.*), bring down, hit, kill, open fire, pick off, plug (*Sl.*), pump full of lead (*Sl.*), zap (*Sl.*) 2. discharge, emit, fire, fling, hurl, launch, let fly, project, propel 3. barrel (along) (*Inf., chiefly U.S. & Canad.*), bolt, burn rubber (*Inf.*), charge, dart, dash, flash, fly, hurtle, race, rush, scoot, speed, spring, streak, tear, whisk, whiz (*Inf.*)

shoot[2] 1. *n.* branch, bud, offshoot, scion, slip, sprig, sprout, twig 2. *v.* bud, burgeon, germinate, put forth new growth, sprout

shop boutique, emporium, hypermarket, market, mart, store, supermarket

shore 1. *n.* beach, coast, foreshore, lakeside, sands, seaboard (*Chiefly U.S.*), seashore, strand (*Poetic*), waterside 2. *adj.* littoral

shore (up) augment, brace, buttress, hold, prop, reinforce, strengthen, support, underpin

short *adj.* 1. abridged, brief, compendious, compressed, concise, curtailed, laconic, pithy, sententious, succinct, summary, terse 2. diminutive, dumpy, fubsy (*Archaic or dialect*), little, low, petite, small, squat, wee 3. brief, fleeting, momentary, short-lived, short-term 4. *Often with* **of** deficient, inadequate, insufficient, lacking, limited, low (on), meagre, poor, scant, scanty, scarce, short-handed, slender, slim, sparse, tight, wanting 5. abrupt, blunt, brusque, crusty, curt, discourteous, gruff, impolite, offhand, sharp, terse, testy, uncivil 6. direct, straight 7. *Of pastry* brittle, crisp, crumbly, friable ~*adv.* 8. abruptly, by surprise, suddenly, unaware, without warning 9. **cut short** abbreviate, arrest, butt in, curtail, cut in on, dock, halt, interrupt, reduce, stop, terminate 10. **fall short** be inadequate, disappoint, fail, fall down on (*Inf.*), not come up to expectations *or* scratch (*Inf.*) 11. **in short** briefly, in a nutshell, in a word, in essence, to come to the point, to cut a long story short, to put it briefly 12. **short of a.** apart from, except, other than, unless **b.** deficient in, in need of, lacking, low (on), missing, wanting
Antonyms *adj.* (*sense 1*) diffuse, lengthy, long, long-drawn-out, long-winded, prolonged, rambling, unabridged, verbose, wordy (*sense 2*) big, high, lanky, lofty, tall (*sense 3*) extended, long, long-term (*sense 4*) abundant, adequate, ample, bountiful, copious, inexhaustible, plentiful, sufficient, well-stocked (*sense 5*) civil, courteous, polite ~*adv.* (*sense 8*) bit by bit, gently, gradually, little by little, slowly

shortage dearth, deficiency, deficit, failure, inadequacy, insufficiency, lack, leanness, paucity, poverty, scarcity, shortfall, want
Antonyms abundance, adequate amount, excess, overabundance, plethora, profusion, sufficiency, surfeit, surplus

shortcoming defect, drawback, failing, fault, flaw, foible, frailty, imperfection, weakness, weak point

shorten abbreviate, abridge, curtail, cut, cut back, cut down, decrease, diminish, dock, lessen, prune, reduce, trim, truncate, turn up
Antonyms draw out, elongate, expand, extend, increase, lengthen, make longer, prolong, protract, spin out, stretch

short-lived brief, ephemeral, fleeting, impermanent, passing, short, temporary, transient, transitory

shortly 1. anon (*Archaic*), any minute now, before long, erelong (*Archaic or poetic*), in a little while, presently, soon 2. abruptly, curtly, sharply, tartly, tersely 3. briefly, concisely, in a few words, succinctly

short-sighted 1. myopic, near-sighted 2. careless, ill-advised, ill-considered, impolitic, impractical, improvident, imprudent, injudicious, unthinking

short-staffed below strength, short-handed, undermanned, understaffed

short-tempered choleric, fiery, hot-tempered, impatient, irascible, peppery, quick-tempered, ratty (*Brit. & N.Z. inf.*), testy, touchy

shot[1] *n.* 1. discharge, lob, pot shot, throw 2. ball, bullet, lead, pellet, projectile, slug 3. marksman, shooter 4. *Inf.* attempt, chance, conjecture, crack (*Inf.*), effort, endeavour, essay, go (*Inf.*), guess, opportunity, stab (*Inf.*), surmise, try, turn 5. **by a long shot a.** by far, easily, far and away, indubitably, undoubtedly, without doubt **b.** by any means, in any circumstances, on any account 6. **have a shot** *Inf.* attempt, have a go (bash (*Inf.*), crack (*Inf.*), stab (*Inf.*)) (*Inf.*), tackle, try, try one's luck 7. **like a shot** at once, eagerly, immediately, like a flash, quickly, unhesitatingly 8. **shot in the arm**

Inf. boost, encouragement, fillip, impetus, lift, stimulus

shot[2] *adj.* iridescent, moiré, opalescent, watered

shoulder *n.* 1. **give (someone) the cold shoulder** cut (*Inf.*), ignore, ostracize, put down, rebuff, shun, snub 2. **put one's shoulder to the wheel** *Inf.* apply oneself, buckle down to (*Inf.*), exert oneself, get down to, make every effort, set to work, strive 3. **rub shoulders with** *Inf.* associate with, consort with, fraternize with, hobnob with, mix with, socialize with 4. **shoulder to shoulder** as one, in cooperation, in partnership, in unity, jointly, side by side, together, united 5. **straight from the shoulder** candidly, directly, frankly, man to man, outright, plainly, pulling no punches (*Inf.*), straight, unequivocally, with no holds barred ~*v.* 6. accept, assume, bear, be responsible for, carry, take on, take upon oneself 7. elbow, jostle, press, push, shove, thrust

shoulder blade scapula

shout 1. *n.* bellow, call, cry, roar, scream, yell 2. *v.* bawl, bay, bellow, call (out), cry (out), holler (*Inf.*), hollo, raise one's voice, roar, scream, yell

shout down drown, drown out, overwhelm, silence

shove *v.* crowd, drive, elbow, impel, jostle, press, propel, push, shoulder, thrust

shovel *v.* convey, dredge, heap, ladle, load, move, scoop, shift, spoon, toss

shove off bugger off (*Taboo sl.*), clear off (*Inf.*), depart, fuck off (*Offens. taboo sl.*), go away, leave, push off (*Inf.*), scram (*Inf.*), slope off, take oneself off, vamoose (*Sl., chiefly U.S.*)

show *v.* 1. appear, be visible, blow wide open (*Sl.*), disclose, display, divulge, evidence, evince, exhibit, indicate, make known, manifest, present, register, reveal, testify to 2. assert, clarify, demonstrate, elucidate, evince, explain, instruct, point out, present, prove, teach 3. accompany, attend, conduct, escort, guide, lead 4. accord, act with, bestow, confer, grant ~*n.* 5. array, demonstration, display, exhibition, expo (*Inf.*), exposition, fair, manifestation, pageant, pageantry, parade, representation, sight, spectacle, view 6. affectation, air, appearance, display, illusion, likeness, ostentation, parade, pose, pretence, pretext, profession, semblance 7. entertainment, presentation, production

Antonyms (*senses 1 & 2*) be invisible, conceal, deny, disprove, gainsay (*Archaic or literary*), hide, keep secret, mask, obscure, refute, suppress, veil, withhold

showdown breaking point, clash, climax, confrontation, crisis, culmination, *dénouement,* exposé, face-off (*Sl.*), moment of truth

shower *n.* 1. *Fig.* barrage, deluge, fusillade, plethora, rain, stream, torrent, volley 2. *Brit. sl.* bunch of layabouts, crew, rabble ~*v.* 3. deluge, heap, inundate, lavish, load, pour, rain, spray, sprinkle

showing *n.* 1. demonstration, display, exhibition, presentation, staging 2. account of oneself, appearance, demonstration, impression, performance, show, track record 3. evidence, representation, statement

showman entertainer, impresario, performer, publicist, stage manager

show-off boaster, braggadocio, braggart, egotist, exhibitionist, hot dog (*Chiefly U.S.*), peacock, poseur, swaggerer

show off 1. advertise, demonstrate, display, exhibit, flaunt, parade, spread out 2. boast, brag, hot-dog (*Chiefly U.S.*), make a spectacle of oneself, shoot a line (*Inf.*), swagger

show up 1. expose, highlight, lay bare, pinpoint, put the spotlight on, reveal, unmask 2. appear, be conspicuous, be visible, catch the eye, leap to the eye, stand out 3. *Inf.* embarrass, let down, mortify, put to shame, shame, show in a bad light 4. *Inf.* appear, arrive, come, make an appearance, put in an appearance, turn up

showy brash, flamboyant, flash (*Inf.*), flashy, garish, gaudy, loud, ostentatious, over the top (*Inf.*), pompous, pretentious, splashy (*Inf.*), tawdry, tinselly

Antonyms discreet, low-key, muted, quiet, restrained, subdued, tasteful, unobtrusive

shred *n.* 1. bit, fragment, piece, rag, ribbon, scrap, sliver, snippet, tatter 2. *Fig.* atom, grain, iota, jot, particle, scrap, trace, whit

shrew ballbreaker (*Sl.*), dragon (*Inf.*), fury, harridan, nag, scold, spitfire, termagant (*Rare*), virago, vixen, Xanthippe

shrewd acute, artful, astute, calculated, calculating, canny, clever, crafty, cunning, discerning, discriminating, far-seeing, far-sighted, fly (*Sl.*), intelligent, keen, knowing, long-headed, perceptive, perspicacious, sagacious, sharp, sly, smart, wily

Antonyms artless, dull, gullible, imprudent, ingenuous, innocent, naive, obtuse, slow-witted, stupid, trusting, undiscerning, unsophisticated, unworldly

shrewdly artfully, astutely, cannily, cleverly, far-sightedly, knowingly, perceptively, perspicaciously, sagaciously, with all one's wits about one, with consummate skill

shrewdness acumen, acuteness, astuteness, canniness, discernment, grasp, judgment, penetration, perspicacity, quick wits, sagacity, sharpness, smartness, suss (*Sl.*)

shrewish bad-tempered, complaining, discontented, fault-finding, ill-humoured, ill-natured, ill-tempered, nagging, peevish, petulant, quarrelsome, scolding, sharp-tongued, vixenish

shriek *v./n.* cry, holler, howl, scream, screech, squeal, wail, whoop, yell

shrill acute, ear-piercing, ear-splitting, high, high-pitched, penetrating, piercing, piping, screeching, sharp

Antonyms deep, dulcet, mellifluous, silver-toned, soft, soothing, sweet-sounding, velvety, well-modulated

shrink 1. contract, decrease, deflate, diminish, drop off, dwindle, fall off, grow smaller, lessen, narrow, shorten, shrivel, wither, wrinkle 2. cower, cringe, draw back, flinch, hang back, quail, recoil, retire, shy away, wince, withdraw

Antonyms (*sense 1*) balloon, dilate, distend, enlarge, expand, increase, inflate, mushroom, stretch, swell (*sense 2*) attack, challenge, confront, embrace, face, receive, welcome

shrivel 1. burn, dry (up), parch, scorch, sear 2. dehydrate, desiccate, dwindle, shrink, wilt, wither, wizen, wrinkle

shrivelled desiccated, dried up, dry, sere (*Archaic*), shrunken, withered, wizened, wrinkled

shroud *v.* 1. blanket, cloak, conceal, cover, envelop, hide, screen, swathe, veil ~*n.* 2. cerecloth, cerement, covering, grave clothes, winding sheet 3. cloud, mantle, pall, screen, veil

shudder 1. *v.* convulse, quake, quiver, shake, shiver, tremble 2. *n.* convulsion, quiver, spasm, trembling, tremor

shuffle 1. drag, scrape, scuff, scuffle, shamble 2. confuse, disarrange, disorder, intermix, jumble, mix, rearrange, shift 3. *Usually with* **off** *or* **out of** beat about the bush, beg the question, cavil, dodge, equivocate, evade, flannel (*Brit. inf.*), gloss over, hedge, prevaricate, pussyfoot (*Inf.*), quibble

shun avoid, body-swerve (*Scot.*), cold-shoulder, elude, eschew, evade, fight shy of, give (someone *or* something) a wide berth, have no part in, keep away from, shy away from, steer clear of

shut 1. bar, close, draw to, fasten, push to, seal, secure, slam 2. *With* **in, out,** *etc.* cage, confine, enclose, exclude, impound, imprison, pound, wall off *or* up

Antonyms open, throw wide, unbar, unclose, undo, unfasten, unlock

shut down cease, cease operating, close, discontinue, halt, shut up, stop, switch off

shut out 1. bar, black, blackball, debar, exclude, keep out, lock out, ostracize 2. block out, conceal, cover, hide, mask, screen, veil

shuttle *v.* alternate, commute, go back and forth, go to and fro, ply, seesaw, shunt

shut up 1. bottle up, box in, cage, confine, coop up, immure, imprison, incarcerate, intern, keep in 2. *Inf.* be quiet, fall silent, button it (*Sl.*), button one's lip (*Sl.*), gag, hold one's tongue, hush, keep one's trap shut (*Sl.*), muzzle, pipe down (*Sl.*), put a sock in it (*Brit. sl.*), silence

shy[1] 1. *adj.* backward, bashful, cautious, chary, coy, diffident, distrustful, hesitant, modest, mousy, nervous, reserved, reticent, retiring, self-conscious, self-effacing, shrinking, suspicious, timid, wary 2. *v.* *Sometimes with* **off** *or* **away** balk, buck, draw back, flinch, quail, rear, recoil, start, swerve, take fright, wince

Antonyms *adj.* assured, bold, brash, cheeky, confident, fearless, forward, pushy (*Inf.*), rash, reckless, self-assured, self-confident, unsuspecting, unwary

shy[2] *v.* cast, chuck (*Inf.*), fling, hurl, lob (*Inf.*), pitch, propel, send, sling, throw, toss

shyness bashfulness, diffidence, lack of confidence, modesty, mousiness, nervousness, reticence, self-consciousness, timidity, timidness, timorousness

sibyl Cassandra, oracle, prophetess, Pythia, pythoness, seer

sick 1. green around the gills (*Inf.*), ill, nauseated, nauseous, puking (*Sl.*), qualmish, queasy 2. ailing, diseased, feeble, indisposed, laid up (*Inf.*), on the sick list (*Inf.*), poorly (*Inf.*), under the weather, under par (*Inf.*), unwell, weak 3. *Inf.* black, ghoulish, macabre, morbid, sadistic 4. *Inf. Often with* **of** blasé, bored, disgusted, displeased, fed up, jaded, revolted, satiated, tired, weary

Antonyms (*senses 1 & 2*) able-bodied, fine, fit, fit and well, fit as a fiddle, hale and hearty, healthy, robust, tranquil, untroubled, unworried, up to par, well

sicken 1. disgust, gross out (*U.S. sl.*), make one's gorge rise, nauseate, repel, revolt, turn one's stomach 2. ail, be stricken by, contract, fall ill, go down with, show symptoms of, take sick

sickening cringe-making (*Brit. inf.*), disgusting, distasteful, foul, loathsome, nauseating, nauseous, noisome, offensive, putrid, repulsive, revolting, stomach-turning (*Inf.*), vile, yucky *or* yukky (*Sl.*)

Antonyms curative, delightful, health-giving, heartening, inviting, marvellous, mouth-watering, pleasant, salutary, tempting, therapeutic, wholesome, wonderful

sickly 1. ailing, bilious, bloodless, delicate, faint, feeble, indisposed, infirm, in poor health, lacklustre, languid, pallid, peaky, pining, unhealthy, wan, weak 2. bilious (*Inf.*), cloying, mawkish, nauseating, revolting (*Inf.*), syrupy (*Inf.*)

sickness 1. barfing (*U.S. sl.*), nausea, queasiness, (the) collywobbles (*Sl.*), puking (*Sl.*), vomiting 2. affliction, ailment, bug (*Inf.*), complaint, disease, disorder, illness, indisposition, infirmity, malady

side *n.* 1. border, boundary, division, edge, limit, margin, part, perimeter, periphery, rim, sector, verge 2. aspect, face, facet, flank, hand, part, surface, view 3. angle, light, opinion, point of view, position, slant, stand, standpoint, viewpoint 4. camp, cause, faction, party, sect, team 5. *Brit. sl.* airs, arrogance, insolence, pretentiousness *~adj.* 6. flanking, lateral 7. ancillary, incidental, indirect, lesser, marginal, minor, oblique, roundabout, secondary, subordinate, subsidiary *~v.* 8. *Usually with* **with** ally with, associate oneself with, befriend, favour, go along with, join with, second, support, take the part of, team up with (*Inf.*)

Antonyms *n.* (*sense 1*) centre, core, heart, middle *~adj.* central, essential, focal, fundamental, key, main, middle, primary, principal *~v.* counter, oppose, stand against, withstand

sidelong *adj.* covert, indirect, oblique, sideways

side-splitting farcical, hilarious, hysterical, rollicking, uproarious

sidestep avoid, body-swerve (*Scot.*), bypass, circumvent, dodge, duck (*Inf.*), elude, evade, find a way round, skip, skirt

sidetrack deflect, distract, divert, lead off the subject

sideways 1. *adv.* crabwise, edgeways, laterally, obliquely, sidelong, sidewards, to the side 2. *adj.* oblique, side, sidelong, slanted

sidle creep, edge, inch, slink, sneak, steal

siesta catnap, doze, forty winks (*Inf.*), kip (*Brit. sl.*), nap, rest, sleep, snooze (*Inf.*), zizz (*Brit. inf.*)

sieve 1. *n.* colander, riddle, screen, sifter, strainer, tammy cloth 2. *v.* bolt, remove, riddle, separate, sift, strain

sift 1. bolt, filter, pan, part, riddle, separate, sieve 2. analyse, examine, fathom, go through, investigate, pore over, probe, research, screen, scrutinize, work over

sigh *v.* 1. breathe, complain, grieve, lament, moan, sorrow, sough, suspire (*Archaic*) 2. *Often with* **for** eat one's heart out over, languish, long, mourn, pine, yearn

sight *n.* 1. eye, eyes, eyesight, seeing, vision 2. appearance, apprehension, eyeshot, field of vision, ken, perception, range of vision, view, viewing, visibility 3. display, exhibition, pageant, scene, show, spectacle, vista 4. *Inf.* blot on the landscape (*Inf.*), eyesore, fright (*Inf.*), mess, monstrosity, spectacle 5. **catch sight of** descry, espy, glimpse, recognize, spot, view *~v.* 6. behold, discern, distinguish, make out, observe, perceive, see, spot

sign *n.* 1. clue, evidence, gesture, giveaway, hint, indication, manifestation, mark, note, proof, signal, spoor, suggestion, symptom, token, trace, vestige 2. board, notice, placard, warning 3. badge, character, cipher, device, emblem, ensign, figure, logo, mark, representation, symbol 4. augury, auspice, foreboding, forewarning, omen, portent, presage, warning, writing on the wall *~v.* 5. autograph, endorse, initial, inscribe, set one's hand to, subscribe 6. beckon, gesticulate, gesture, indicate, signal, use sign language, wave

signal 1. *n.* beacon, cue, flare, gesture, go-ahead (*Inf.*), green light, indication, indicator, mark, sign, token 2. *adj.* conspicuous, distinguished, eminent, exceptional, extraordinary, famous, memorable, momentous, notable, noteworthy, outstanding, remarkable, significant, striking 3. *v.* beckon, communicate, gesticulate, gesture, give a sign to, indicate, motion, nod, sign, wave

sign away abandon, dispose of, forgo, give up all claim to, lose, relinquish, renounce, surrender, transfer, waive

significance 1. force, implication(s), import, meaning, message, point, purport, sense, signification 2. consequence, consideration, importance, impressiveness, matter, moment, relevance, weight

significant 1. denoting, eloquent, expressing, expressive, indicative, knowing, meaning, meaningful, pregnant, suggestive 2. critical, important, material, momentous, noteworthy, serious, vital, weighty

Antonyms immaterial, inconsequential, insignificant, irrelevant, meaningless, nit-picking, nugatory, of no consequence, paltry, petty, trivial, unimportant, worthless

signify 1. announce, be a sign of, betoken, communicate, connote, convey, denote, evidence, exhibit, express, imply, indicate, intimate, matter, mean, portend, proclaim, represent, show, stand for, suggest, symbolize 2. *Inf.* be of importance *or* significance, carry weight, count, matter

sign on *or* **up** 1. contract with, enlist, enrol, join, join up, register, volunteer 2. employ, engage, hire, put on the payroll, recruit, take into service, take on, take on board (*Inf.*)

silence *n.* 1. calm, hush, lull, noiselessness, peace, quiescence, quiet, stillness 2. dumbness, muteness, reticence, speechlessness, taciturnity, uncommunicativeness ~*v.* 3. cut off, cut short, deaden, extinguish, gag, muffle, quell, quiet, quieten, stifle, still, strike dumb, subdue, suppress
Antonyms *n.* babble, bawling, cacophony, chatter, clamour, din, garrulousness, hubbub, loquaciousness, murmuring, noise, prattle, racket, shouting, sound, speech, talk, talking, tumult, uproar, verbosity, whispering, yelling ~*v.* amplify, broadcast, champion, disseminate, encourage, foster, make louder, promote, promulgate, publicize, rouse, spread, support, ungag

silent 1. hushed, muted, noiseless, quiet, soundless, still, stilly (*Poetic*) 2. dumb, mum, mute, nonvocal, not talkative, speechless, struck dumb, taciturn, tongue-tied, uncommunicative, unspeaking, voiceless, wordless 3. aphonic (*Phonetics*), implicit, implied, tacit, understood, unexpressed, unpronounced, unspoken

silently as quietly as a mouse (*Inf.*), dumbly, inaudibly, in silence, mutely, noiselessly, quietly, soundlessly, speechlessly, without a sound, wordlessly

silhouette 1. *n.* delineation, form, outline, profile, shape 2. *v.* delineate, etch, outline, stand out

silky silken, sleek, smooth, velvety

silly *adj.* 1. absurd, asinine, brainless, childish, dopy (*Sl.*), dozy (*Brit. inf.*), fatuous, foolhardy, foolish, frivolous, giddy, goofy (*Inf.*), idiotic, immature, imprudent, inane, inappropriate, irresponsible, meaningless, pointless, preposterous, puerile, ridiculous, senseless, stupid, unwise, witless 2. *Inf.* benumbed, dazed, groggy (*Inf.*), in a daze, muzzy, stunned, stupefied ~*n.* 3. *Inf.* clot (*Brit. inf.*), duffer (*Inf.*), dweeb (*U.S. sl.*), goose (*Inf.*), ignoramus, nerd *or* nurd (*Sl.*), ninny, nitwit (*Inf.*), plonker (*Sl.*), prat (*Sl.*), silly-billy (*Inf.*), simpleton, twit (*Inf.*), wally (*Sl.*)
Antonyms *adj.* acute, aware, bright, clever, intelligent, mature, perceptive, profound, prudent, reasonable, sane, sensible, serious, smart, thoughtful, well thought-out, wise

silt 1. *n.* alluvium, deposit, ooze, residue, sediment, sludge 2. *v.* *Usually with* **up** choke, clog, congest, dam

silver 1. *adj.* argent (*Poetic*), pearly, silvered, silvery 2. *n.* silver plate, silverware

similar alike, analogous, close, comparable, congruous, corresponding, homogenous, homogeneous, in agreement, much the same, resembling, uniform
Antonyms antithetical, clashing, contradictory, contrary, different, disparate, dissimilar, diverse, heterogeneous, irreconcilable, opposite, unalike, unrelated, various, varying

similarity affinity, agreement, analogy, closeness, comparability, concordance, congruence, correspondence, likeness, point of comparison, relation, resemblance, sameness, similitude
Antonyms antithesis, contradictoriness, difference, disagreement, discordance, discrepancy, disparity, dissimilarity, diversity, heterogeneity, incomparability, irreconcilability, unalikeness, variation, variety

similarly by the same token, correspondingly, in like manner, likewise

simmer *v. Fig.* be angry (agitated, tense, uptight) (*Inf.*), boil, burn, fume, rage, see red (*Inf.*), seethe, smart, smoulder

simmer down calm down, collect oneself, contain oneself, control oneself, cool off *or* down, get down off one's high horse (*Inf.*), grow quieter, unwind (*Inf.*)

simper grimace, smile affectedly (coyly, self-consciously), smirk, titter

simpering *adj.* affected, coy, self-conscious

simple 1. clear, easy, easy-peasy (*Sl.*), elementary, intelligible, lucid, manageable, plain, straightforward, uncomplicated, understandable, uninvolved 2. classic, clean, natural, plain, Spartan, unadorned, uncluttered, unembellished, unfussy 3. elementary, pure, single, unalloyed, unblended, uncombined, undivided, unmixed 4. artless, childlike, frank, green, guileless, ingenuous, innocent, naive, natural, simplistic, sincere, unaffected, unpretentious, unsophisticated 5. bald, basic, direct, frank, honest, naked, plain, sincere, stark, undeniable, unvarnished 6. homely, humble, lowly, modest, rustic, unpretentious 7. brainless, credulous, dense, dumb (*Inf.*), feeble, feeble-minded, foolish, half-witted, moronic, obtuse, shallow, silly, slow, stupid, thick
Antonyms (*senses 1 & 3*) advanced, complex, complicated, convoluted, difficult, elaborate, highly developed, intricate, involved, refined, sophisticated (*senses 2, 4 & 6*) artful, contrived, elaborate, extravagant, fancy, flashy, fussy, intricate, ornate,

smart, sophisticated, worldly, worldly-wise (*sense 7*) astute, bright, clever, intelligent, knowing, on the ball, quick, quick on the uptake, quick-witted, sharp, smart, wise

simple-minded 1. a bit lacking (*Inf.*), addle-brained, backward, brainless, dead from the neck up (*Inf.*), dim-witted, feeble-minded, foolish, idiot, idiotic, moronic, retarded, simple, stupid 2. artless, natural, unsophisticated

simpleton berk (*Brit. sl.*), blockhead, booby, charlie (*Brit. inf.*), coot, dickhead (*Sl.*), dipstick (*Brit. sl.*), divvy (*Brit. sl.*), dolt, dope (*Inf.*), dork (*Sl.*), dullard, dunce, dweeb (*U.S. sl.*), fool, fuckwit (*Taboo sl.*), geek (*Sl.*), gonzo (*Sl.*), goose (*Inf.*), greenhorn (*Inf.*), idiot, imbecile (*Inf.*), jackass, jerk (*Sl., chiefly U.S. & Canad.*), moron, nerd *or* nurd (*Sl.*), nincompoop, ninny, nitwit (*Inf.*), numskull *or* numbskull, oaf, plank (*Brit. sl.*), schmuck (*U.S. sl.*), Simple Simon, stupid (*Inf.*), twerp *or* twirp (*Inf.*), twit (*Inf., chiefly Brit.*), wally (*Sl.*)

simplicity 1. absence of complications, clarity, clearness, ease, easiness, elementariness, obviousness, straightforwardness 2. clean lines, lack of adornment, modesty, naturalness, plainness, purity, restraint 3. artlessness, candour, directness, guilelessness, innocence, lack of sophistication, naivety, openness
Antonyms (*sense 1*) complexity, complicatedness, difficulty, intricacy, lack of clarity (*sense 2*) decoration, elaborateness, embellishment, fanciness, fussiness, ornateness, ostentation (*sense 3*) brains, craftiness, cunning, deviousness, guile, insincerity, knowingness, sharpness, slyness, smartness, sophistication, wariness, wisdom, worldliness

simplify abridge, decipher, disentangle, facilitate, make intelligible, reduce to essentials, streamline

simplistic naive, oversimplified

simply 1. clearly, directly, easily, intelligibly, modestly, naturally, plainly, straightforwardly, unaffectedly, unpretentiously, without any elaboration 2. just, merely, only, purely, solely 3. absolutely, altogether, completely, really, totally, unreservedly, utterly, wholly

simulate act, affect, assume, counterfeit, fabricate, feign, imitate, make believe, pretend, put on, reproduce, sham

simulated 1. artificial, fake, imitation, man-made, mock, pseudo (*Inf.*), sham, substitute, synthetic 2. artificial, assumed, feigned, insincere, make-believe, phoney *or* phony (*Inf.*), pretended, put-on

simultaneous at the same time, coinciding, concurrent, contemporaneous, synchronous

simultaneously all together, at the same time, concurrently, in chorus, in concert, in the same breath, in unison, together

sin 1. *n.* crime, damnation, error, evil, guilt, iniquity, misdeed, offence, sinfulness, transgression, trespass, ungodliness, unrighteousness, wickedness, wrong, wrongdoing 2. *v.* err, fall, fall from grace, go astray, lapse, offend, transgress, trespass (*Archaic*)

sincere artless, bona fide, candid, earnest, frank, genuine, guileless, heartfelt, honest, natural, no-nonsense, open, real, serious, straightforward, true, unaffected, unfeigned, upfront (*Inf.*), wholehearted
Antonyms affected, artful, artificial, deceitful, deceptive, dishonest, false, feigned, hollow, insincere, phoney *or* phony (*Inf.*), pretended, put on, synthetic, token, two-faced

sincerely earnestly, genuinely, honestly, in all sincerity, in earnest, in good faith, really, seriously, truly, wholeheartedly

sincerity artlessness, bona fides, candour, frankness, genuineness, good faith, guilelessness, honesty, probity, seriousness, straightforwardness, truth, wholeheartedness

sinecure cushy number (*Inf.*), gravy train (*Sl.*), money for jam *or* old rope (*Inf.*), soft job (*Inf.*), soft option

sinewy athletic, brawny, lusty, muscular, powerful, robust, strong, sturdy, vigorous, wiry

sinful bad, corrupt, criminal, depraved, erring, guilty, immoral, iniquitous, irreligious, morally wrong, ungodly, unholy, unrighteous, wicked
Antonyms beatified, blessed, chaste, decent, free from sin, godly, holy, honest, honourable, immaculate, moral, pure, righteous, sinless, spotless, unblemished, upright, virtuous, without sin

sing 1. carol, chant, chirp, croon, make melody, pipe, trill, vocalize, warble, yodel 2. *Sl., chiefly U.S.* betray, blow the whistle (on) (*Inf.*), fink (on) (*Sl., chiefly U.S.*), grass (*Brit. sl.*), inform (on), peach (*Sl.*), rat (on) (*Inf.*), shop (*Sl., chiefly Brit.*), spill one's guts (*Sl.*), spill the beans (*Inf.*), squeal (*Sl.*), tell all, turn in (*Inf.*) 3. buzz, hum, purr, whine, whistle

singe burn, char, scorch, sear

singer balladeer, cantor, chanteuse (*Fem.*), chorister, crooner, minstrel, soloist, songster, songstress, troubadour, vocalist

single *adj.* 1. distinct, individual, lone, one, only, particular, separate, singular, sole, solitary, unique 2. free, unattached, unmarried, unwed 3. exclusive, individual, separate, simple, unblended, uncompounded, undivided, unmixed, unshared ~*v.* 4. *Usually with* **out** choose, cull, distinguish, fix on, pick, pick on *or* out, put on one side, select, separate, set apart, winnow

single-handed alone, by oneself, independently, on one's own, solo, unaided, unassisted, without help

single-minded dedicated, determined, dogged, fixed, hellbent (*Inf.*), monomaniacal, steadfast, stubborn, tireless, undeviating, unswerving, unwavering

singly individually, one at a time, one by one, separately

sing out call (out), cooee, cry (out), halloo, holler (*Inf.*), make oneself heard, shout, shout ahoy, yell

singsong *adj.* droning, monotone, monotonous, repetitious, toneless

singular 1. conspicuous, eminent, exceptional, notable, noteworthy, outstanding, prodigious, rare, remarkable, uncommon, unique, unparalleled 2. atypical, curious, eccentric, extraordinary, odd, oddball (*Inf.*), out-of-the-way, outré, peculiar, puzzling, queer, strange, unusual, wacko (*Sl.*) 3. individual, separate, single, sole

Antonyms common, common or garden, commonplace, conventional, everyday, familiar, normal, routine, run-of-the-mill, unexceptional, unremarkable, usual

singularity 1. abnormality, curiousness, extraordinariness, irregularity, oddness, peculiarity, queerness, strangeness 2. eccentricity, idiosyncrasy, oddity, particularity, peculiarity, quirk, twist

singularly conspicuously, especially, exceptionally, extraordinarily, notably, outstandingly, particularly, prodigiously, remarkably, surprisingly, uncommonly, unusually

sinister baleful, dire, disquieting, evil, forbidding, injurious, malevolent, malign, malignant, menacing, ominous, threatening

Antonyms auspicious, benevolent, benign, calming, encouraging, good, heartening, heroic, honourable, just, noble, promising, propitious, reassuring, righteous, upright, worthy

sink *v.* 1. cave in, decline, descend, dip, disappear, droop, drop, drown, ebb, engulf, fall, founder, go down, go under, lower, merge, plummet, plunge, sag, slope, submerge, subside 2. abate, collapse, drop, fall, lapse, relapse, retrogress, slip, slump, subside 3. decay, decline, decrease, degenerate, depreciate, deteriorate, die, diminish, dwindle, fade, fail, flag, go downhill (*Inf.*), lessen, weaken, worsen 4. bore, dig, drill, drive, excavate, lay, put down 5. be the ruin of, defeat, destroy, finish, overwhelm, ruin, scupper (*Brit. sl.*), seal the doom of 6. be reduced to, debase oneself, lower oneself, stoop, succumb

Antonyms (*senses 1, 2 & 3*) arise, ascend, climb, enlarge, go up, grow, improve, increase, intensify, move up, rise, rise up, swell, wax

sink in be understood, get through to, make an impression, penetrate, register (*Inf.*), take hold of

sinless faultless, guiltless, immaculate, innocent, pure, unblemished, uncorrupted, undefiled, unsullied, virtuous, without fault, without sin

sinner evildoer, malefactor, miscreant, offender, reprobate, transgressor, trespasser (*Archaic*), wrongdoer

sinuous coiling, crooked, curved, curvy, lithe, mazy, meandering, serpentine, supple, tortuous, undulating, winding

sip 1. *v.* sample, sup, taste 2. *n.* drop, swallow, taste, thimbleful

siren charmer, Circe, *femme fatale,* Lorelei, seductress, temptress, vamp (*Inf.*), witch

sissy 1. *n.* baby, coward, jessie (*Scot. sl.*), milksop, milquetoast (*U.S.*), mollycoddle, mummy's boy, namby-pamby, pansy, sisspot (*Inf.*), softy (*Inf.*), weakling, wet (*Brit. inf.*), wimp (*Inf.*) 2. *adj.* cowardly, effeminate, feeble, namby-pamby, sissified (*Inf.*), soft (*Inf.*), unmanly, weak, wet (*Brit. inf.*), wimpish *or* wimpy (*Inf.*)

sit 1. be seated, perch, rest, settle, take a seat, take the weight off one's feet 2. assemble, be in session, convene, deliberate, meet, officiate, preside 3. accommodate, contain, have space for, hold, seat

site 1. *n.* ground, location, place, plot, position, setting, spot 2. *v.* install, locate, place, position, set, situate

sitting *n.* congress, consultation, get-together (*Inf.*), hearing, meeting, period, session

situation 1. locale, locality, location, place, position, seat, setting, site, spot 2. ball game (*Inf.*), case, circumstances, condition, kettle of fish (*Inf.*), plight, scenario, state, state of affairs, status quo, the picture (*Inf.*) 3. rank, sphere, station, status 4. berth (*Inf.*), employment, job, office, place, position, post

sixth sense clairvoyance, feyness, intuition, second sight

sizable considerable, decent, decent-sized,

goodly, large, largish, respectable, substantial, tidy (*Inf.*)

size amount, bigness, bulk, dimensions, extent, greatness, hugeness, immensity, largeness, magnitude, mass, measurement(s), proportions, range, vastness, volume

size up appraise, assess, evaluate, eye up, get (something) taped (*Brit. inf.*), get the measure of, take stock of

sizzle crackle, frizzle, fry, hiss, spit, sputter

skedaddle abscond, beat a hasty retreat, bolt, decamp, disappear, do a bunk (*Brit. sl.*), flee, hook it (*Sl.*), hop it (*Brit. sl.*), run away, scarper (*Brit. sl.*), scoot, scram (*Inf.*), scurry away, scuttle away, vamoose (*Sl., chiefly U.S.*)

skeletal cadaverous, emaciated, fleshless, gaunt, hollow-cheeked, lantern-jawed, skin-and-bone (*Inf.*), wasted, worn to a shadow

skeleton *Fig.* bare bones, bones, draft, frame, framework, outline, sketch, structure

sketch 1. *v.* block out, delineate, depict, draft, draw, outline, paint, plot, portray, represent, rough out 2. *n.* delineation, design, draft, drawing, outline, plan, skeleton

sketchily cursorily, hastily, imperfectly, incompletely, patchily, perfunctorily, roughly

sketchy bitty, cobbled together, crude, cursory, inadequate, incomplete, outline, perfunctory, rough, scrappy, skimpy, slight, superficial, unfinished, vague

Antonyms complete, detailed, full, thorough

skewwhiff askew, aslant, cockeyed (*Inf.*), crooked, out of true, squint (*Inf.*), tilted

skilful able, accomplished, adept, adroit, apt, clever, competent, dexterous, experienced, expert, handy, masterly, practised, professional, proficient, quick, ready, skilled, trained

Antonyms amateurish, awkward, bungling, cack-handed, clumsy, cowboy (*Inf.*), ham-fisted, incompetent, inept, inexperienced, inexpert, maladroit, slapdash, unaccomplished, unqualified, unskilful, unskilled

skill ability, accomplishment, adroitness, aptitude, art, cleverness, competence, craft, dexterity, experience, expertise, expertness, facility, finesse, handiness, ingenuity, intelligence, knack, proficiency, quickness, readiness, skilfulness, talent, technique

Antonyms awkwardness, brute force, cack-handedness, clumsiness, gaucheness, ham-fistedness, inability, incompetence, ineptitude, inexperience, lack of finesse, maladroitness, unhandiness

skilled able, accomplished, a dab hand at (*Brit. inf.*), experienced, expert, masterly, practised, professional, proficient, skilful, trained

Antonyms amateurish, cowboy (*Inf.*), inexperienced, inexpert, uneducated, unprofessional, unqualified, unskilled, untalented, untrained

skim 1. cream, separate 2. brush, coast, dart, float, fly, glide, sail, soar 3. *Usually* ***with through*** glance, run one's eye over, scan, skip (*Inf.*), thumb *or* leaf through

skimp be mean with, be niggardly, be sparing with, cut corners, pinch, scamp, scant, scrimp, stint, withhold

Antonyms act as if one had money to burn, be extravagant, be generous with, be prodigal, blow (*Sl.*), fritter away, lavish, overspend, pour on, splurge, squander, throw money away

skimpy exiguous, inadequate, insufficient, meagre, miserly, niggardly, scant, scanty, short, sparse, thin, tight

skin *n.* 1. fell, hide, integument, pelt, tegument 2. casing, coating, crust, film, husk, membrane, outside, peel, rind 3. **by the skin of one's teeth** by a hair's-breadth, by a narrow margin, by a whisker (*Inf.*), narrowly, only just 4. **get under one's skin** aggravate (*Inf.*), annoy, get in one's hair (*Inf.*), get on one's nerves (*Inf.*), grate on, irk, irritate, needle (*Inf.*), nettle, piss one off (*Taboo sl.*), rub up the wrong way ~*v.* 5. abrade, bark, excoriate, flay, graze, peel, scrape

skin-deep artificial, external, meaningless, on the surface, shallow, superficial, surface

skinflint meanie *or* meany (*Inf., chiefly Brit.*), miser, niggard, penny-pincher (*Inf.*), Scrooge, tight-arse (*Taboo sl.*), tight-ass (*U.S. taboo sl.*), tightwad (*U.S. & Canad. sl.*)

skinny emaciated, lean, macilent (*Rare*), scraggy, skeletal, skin-and-bone (*Inf.*), thin, twiggy, undernourished

Antonyms beefy (*Inf.*), broad in the beam (*Inf.*), fat, fleshy, heavy, obese, plump, podgy, portly, stout, tubby

skip *v.* 1. bob, bounce, caper, cavort, dance, flit, frisk, gambol, hop, prance, trip 2. eschew, give (something) a miss, leave out, miss out, omit, pass over, skim over 3. *Inf.* cut (*Inf.*), dog it *or* dog off (*Dialect*), miss, play truant from, wag (*Dialect*)

skirmish 1. *n.* affair, affray (*Law*), battle, brush, clash, combat, conflict, contest, dust-up (*Inf.*), encounter, engagement, fracas, incident, scrap (*Inf.*), scrimmage, set-to (*Inf.*), spat, tussle 2. *v.* clash, collide, come to blows, scrap (*Inf.*), tussle

skirt *v.* 1. border, edge, flank, lie alongside 2. *Often with* **around** *or* **round** avoid, body-swerve (*Scot.*), bypass, circumvent, detour, evade, steer clear of ~*n.* 3. *Often plural* border, edge, fringe, hem, margin, outskirts, periphery, purlieus, rim

skit burlesque, parody, sketch, spoof (*Inf.*), takeoff (*Inf.*), travesty, turn

skittish excitable, fickle, fidgety, frivolous, highly strung, jumpy, lively, nervous, playful, restive

Antonyms calm, composed, demure, laid-back, placid, relaxed, sober, staid, steady, unexcitable, unfazed (*Inf.*), unflappable, unruffled

skive *v.* bob off (*Brit. sl.*), dodge, gold-brick (*U.S. sl.*), idle, malinger, scrimshank (*Brit. military sl.*), shirk, skulk, slack

skiver dodger, do-nothing, gold brick (*U.S. sl.*), idler, loafer, scrimshanker (*Brit. military sl.*), shirker, slacker

skulduggery double-dealing, duplicity, fraudulence, machinations, shenanigan(s) (*Inf.*), swindling, trickery, underhandedness, unscrupulousness

skulk creep, lie in wait, loiter, lurk, pad, prowl, slink, sneak

sky *n.* 1. azure (*Poetic*), empyrean (*Poetic*), firmament, heavens, upper atmosphere, vault of heaven, welkin (*Archaic*) 2. **to the skies** excessively, extravagantly, fulsomely, highly, immoderately, inordinately, profusely

slab chunk, hunk, lump, piece, portion, slice, wedge, wodge (*Brit. inf.*)

slack *adj.* 1. baggy, easy, flaccid, flexible, lax, limp, loose, not taut, relaxed 2. asleep on the job (*Inf.*), easy-going, idle, inactive, inattentive, lax, lazy, neglectful, negligent, permissive, remiss, slapdash, slipshod, tardy 3. dull, inactive, quiet, slow, slow-moving, sluggish ~*n.* 4. excess, give (*Inf.*), leeway, looseness, play, room ~*v.* 5. bob off (*Brit. sl.*), dodge, flag, idle, neglect, relax, shirk, skive (*Brit. sl.*), slacken

Antonyms *adj.* (*sense 1*) inflexible, rigid, stiff, strained, stretched, taut, tight (*senses 2 & 3*) active, bustling, busy, concerned, diligent, exacting, fast-moving, hard, hard-working, hectic, meticulous, stern, strict

slacken (off) abate, decrease, diminish, drop off, ease (off), lessen, let up, loosen, moderate, reduce, relax, release, slack off, slow down, tire

slacker dodger, do-nothing, gold brick (*U.S. sl.*), good-for-nothing, idler, layabout, loafer, passenger, scrimshanker (*Brit. military sl.*), shirker, skiver (*Brit. sl.*)

slag (off) *v.* abuse, berate, criticise, deride, insult, lambast(e), malign, mock, slam, slander, slang, slate

slake assuage, gratify, quench, sate, satiate, satisfy

slam 1. bang, crash, dash, fling, hurl, smash, throw, thump 2. *Sl.* attack, blast, castigate, criticize, damn, excoriate, lambast(e), pan (*Inf.*), pillory, shoot down (*Inf.*), slate (*Inf.*), tear into (*Inf.*), vilify

slander 1. *n.* aspersion, backbiting, calumny, defamation, detraction, libel, misrepresentation, muckraking, obloquy, scandal, smear 2. *v.* backbite, blacken (someone's) name, calumniate, decry, defame, detract, disparage, libel, malign, muckrake, slur, smear, traduce, vilify

Antonyms *n.* acclaim, acclamation, approval, laudation, praise, tribute ~*v.* acclaim, applaud, approve, compliment, eulogize, laud, praise, sing the praises of

slanderous abusive, calumnious, damaging, defamatory, libellous, malicious

slang *v.* abuse, berate, call names, hurl insults at, insult, inveigh against, malign, rail against, revile, vilify, vituperate

slanging match altercation, argument, argy-bargy (*Brit. inf.*), barney (*Inf.*), battle of words, ding-dong, quarrel, row, set-to (*Inf.*), spat

slant *v.* 1. angle off, bend, bevel, cant, heel, incline, lean, list, shelve, skew, slope, tilt ~*n.* 2. camber, declination, diagonal, gradient, incline, pitch, rake, ramp, slope, tilt ~*v.* 3. angle, bias, colour, distort, twist, weight ~*n.* 4. angle, attitude, bias, emphasis, leaning, one-sidedness, point of view, prejudice, viewpoint

slanting angled, aslant, asymmetrical, at an angle, bent, canted, cater-cornered (*U.S. inf.*), diagonal, inclined, oblique, on the bias, sideways, slanted, slantwise, sloping, tilted, tilting

slap *n.* 1. bang, blow, chin (*Sl.*), clout (*Inf.*), cuff, deck (*Sl.*), lay one on (*Sl.*), smack, spank, wallop (*Inf.*), whack 2. **a slap in the face** affront, blow, humiliation, insult, put-down, rebuff, rebuke, rejection, repulse, snub ~*v.* 3. bang, clap, clout (*Inf.*), cuff, hit, spank, strike, whack 4. *Inf.* daub, plaster, plonk, spread ~*adv.* 5. *Inf.* bang, directly, exactly, plumb (*Inf.*), precisely, slap-bang (*Inf.*), smack (*Inf.*)

slapdash careless, clumsy, disorderly, haphazard, hasty, hurried, last-minute, messy, negligent, perfunctory, slipshod, sloppy (*Inf.*), slovenly, thoughtless, thrown-together, untidy

Antonyms careful, conscientious, fastidious, meticulous, ordered, orderly, painstaking, precise, punctilious, thoughtful, tidy

slap down bring to heel, put (someone) in his place, rebuke, reprimand, restrain, squash

slaphappy 1. casual, haphazard, happy-go-lucky, hit-or-miss (*Inf.*), irresponsible, nonchalant 2. dazed, giddy, punch-drunk, reeling, woozy (*Inf.*)

slapstick *n.* buffoonery, farce, horseplay, knockabout comedy

slap-up elaborate, excellent, first-rate, fit for a king, lavish, luxurious, magnificent, no-expense-spared, princely, splendid, sumptuous, superb

slash *v.* 1. cut, gash, hack, lacerate, rend, rip, score, slit ~*n.* 2. cut, gash, incision, laceration, rent, rip, slit ~*v.* 3. cut, drop, lower, reduce

slashing aggressive, biting, brutal, ferocious, harsh, savage, searing, vicious

slate *v.* berate, blame, blast, castigate, censure, criticize, excoriate, haul over the coals (*Inf.*), lambas(t)e, lay into (*Inf.*), pan (*Inf.*), pitch into (*Inf.*), rail against, rap (someone's) knuckles, rebuke, roast (*Inf.*), scold, slam (*Sl.*), slang, take to task, tear into (*Inf.*), tear (someone) off a strip (*Inf.*)

slattern drab (*Archaic*), sloven, slut, trollop

slatternly bedraggled, dirty, draggletailed (*Archaic*), frowzy, slipshod, sloppy (*Inf.*), slovenly, sluttish, unclean, unkempt, untidy

slaughter *n.* 1. blood bath, bloodshed, butchery, carnage, extermination, holocaust, killing, liquidation, massacre, murder, slaying ~*v.* 2. butcher, destroy, do to death, exterminate, kill, liquidate, massacre, murder, put to the sword, slay, take out (*Sl.*) 3. *Inf.* blow out of the water (*Sl.*), crush, defeat, hammer (*Inf.*), lick (*Inf.*), overwhelm, rout, tank (*Sl.*), thrash, trounce, undo, vanquish, wipe the floor with (*Inf.*)

slaughterhouse abattoir, butchery, shambles

slave 1. *n.* bondservant, bondsman, drudge, scullion (*Archaic*), serf, servant, skivvy (*Chiefly Brit.*), slavey (*Brit. inf.*), varlet (*Archaic*), vassal, villein 2. *v.* drudge, grind (*Inf.*), skivvy (*Brit.*), slog, sweat, toil, work one's fingers to the bone

slaver dribble, drool, salivate, slobber

slavery bondage, captivity, enslavement, serfdom, servitude, subjugation, thraldom, thrall, vassalage

Antonyms emancipation, freedom, liberty, manumission, release

slavish 1. abject, base, cringing, despicable, fawning, grovelling, low, mean, menial, obsequious, servile, submissive, sycophantic 2. conventional, imitative, second-hand, unimaginative, uninspired, unoriginal

Antonyms assertive, creative, domineering, imaginative, independent, inventive, masterful, original, radical, rebellious, revolutionary, self-willed, wilful

slay 1. annihilate, assassinate, butcher, destroy, dispatch, do away with, do in (*Sl.*), eliminate, exterminate, kill, massacre, mow down, murder, rub out (*U.S. sl.*), slaughter 2. *Inf.* amuse, be the death of (*Inf.*), impress, make a hit with (*Inf.*), wow (*Sl., chiefly U.S.*)

sleazy crummy, disreputable, low, run-down, seedy, sordid, squalid, tacky (*Inf.*)

sleek glossy, lustrous, shiny, smooth, well-fed, well-groomed

Antonyms badly groomed, bedraggled, dishevelled, frowzy, ill-nourished, in poor condition, ratty (*Inf.*), rough, shaggy, sloppy, slovenly, unkempt

sleep 1. *v.* be in the land of Nod, catnap, doze, drop off (*Inf.*), drowse, hibernate, kip (*Brit. sl.*), nod off (*Inf.*), rest in the arms of Morpheus, slumber, snooze (*Inf.*), snore, take a nap, take forty winks (*Inf.*), zizz (*Brit. inf.*) 2. *n.* beauty sleep (*Inf.*), dormancy, doze, forty winks (*Inf.*), hibernation, kip (*Brit. sl.*), nap, repose, rest, shuteye (*Sl.*), siesta, slumber(s), snooze (*Inf.*), zizz (*Brit. inf.*)

sleepiness doziness, drowsiness, heaviness, lethargy, somnolence, torpor

sleepless 1. disturbed, insomniac, restless, unsleeping, wakeful 2. alert, unsleeping, vigilant, watchful, wide awake

sleeplessness insomnia, wakefulness

sleepwalker noctambulist, somnambulist

sleepwalking noctambulation, noctambulism, somnambulation, somnambulism

sleepy 1. drowsy, dull, heavy, inactive, lethargic, sluggish, slumbersome, somnolent, torpid 2. dull, hypnotic, inactive, quiet, sleep-inducing, slow, slumberous, somnolent, soporific

Antonyms active, alert, animated, attentive, awake, boisterous, bustling, busy, energetic, lively, restless, thriving, wakeful, wide-awake

sleight of hand adroitness, artifice, dexterity, legerdemain, manipulation, prestidigitation, skill

slender 1. lean, narrow, slight, slim, svelte, sylphlike, willowy 2. inadequate, inconsiderable, insufficient, little, meagre, scant, scanty, small, spare 3. faint, feeble, flimsy, fragile, poor, remote, slight, slim, tenuous, thin, weak

Antonyms ample, appreciable, bulky, chubby, considerable, fat, generous, good, heavy, large, podgy, solid, stout, strong, substantial, tubby, well-built

sleuth detective, dick (*Sl., chiefly U.S.*), gumshoe (*U.S. sl.*), private eye (*Inf.*), (private) investigator, sleuthhound (*Inf.*), tail (*Inf.*)

slice 1. *n.* cut, helping, piece, portion, segment, share, sliver, wedge 2. *v.* carve, cut, divide, sever

slick *adj.* 1. glib, meretricious, plausible, polished, smooth, sophistical, specious 2. adroit, deft, dexterous, dextrous, polished, professional, sharp, skilful ~*v.* 3. make glossy, plaster down, sleek, smarm down (*Brit. inf.*), smooth

Antonyms *adj.* amateur, amateurish, clumsy, crude, inexpert, unaccomplished, unpolished, unprofessional, unskilful

slide *v.* 1. coast, glide, glissade, skim, slip, slither, toboggan, veer 2. **let slide** forget, gloss over, ignore, let ride, neglect, pass over, push to the back of one's mind, turn a blind eye to

slight *adj.* 1. feeble, inconsiderable, insignificant, insubstantial, meagre, measly, minor, modest, negligible, paltry, scanty, small, superficial, trifling, trivial, unimportant, weak 2. delicate, feeble, fragile, lightly-built, slim, small, spare ~*v.* 3. affront, cold-shoulder, despise, disdain, disparage, give offence *or* umbrage to, ignore, insult, neglect, put down, scorn, show disrespect for, snub, treat with contempt ~*n.* 4. affront, contempt, discourtesy, disdain, disregard, disrespect, inattention, indifference, insult, neglect, rebuff, slap in the face (*Inf.*), snub, (the) cold shoulder

Antonyms *adj.* appreciable, considerable, great, heavy, important, large, muscular, noticeable, obvious, significant, solid, strong, sturdy, substantial, well-built ~*v.* compliment, flatter, praise, speak well of, treat considerately ~*n.* compliment, flattery, praise

slighting belittling, derogatory, disdainful, disparaging, disrespectful, insulting, offensive, scornful, supercilious, uncomplimentary

slightly a little, marginally, on a small scale, somewhat, to some extent *or* degree

slim *adj.* 1. lean, narrow, slender, slight, svelte, sylphlike, thin, trim 2. faint, poor, remote, slender, slight ~*v.* 3. diet, lose weight, reduce, slenderize (*Chiefly U.S.*)

Antonyms *adj.* broad, bulky, chubby, fat, good, heavy, muscular, obese, overweight, strong, sturdy, tubby, well-built, wide ~*v.* build oneself up, put on weight

slimy 1. clammy, glutinous, miry, mucous, muddy, oozy, viscous 2. creeping, grovelling, obsequious, oily, servile, smarmy (*Brit. inf.*), soapy (*Sl.*), sycophantic, toadying, unctuous

sling *v.* 1. cast, chuck (*Inf.*), fling, heave, hurl, lob (*Inf.*), shy, throw, toss 2. dangle, hang, suspend, swing

slink creep, prowl, pussyfoot (*Inf.*), skulk, slip, sneak, steal

slinky clinging, close-fitting, feline, figure-hugging, sinuous, skintight, sleek

slip[1] *v.* 1. glide, skate, slide, slither 2. fall, lose one's balance, miss *or* lose one's footing, skid, trip (over) 3. conceal, creep, hide, insinuate oneself, sneak, steal 4. *Sometimes with* **up** blunder, boob (*Brit. sl.*), err, go wrong, make a mistake, miscalculate, misjudge, mistake 5. break away from, break free from, disappear, escape, get away, get clear of, take French leave 6. **let slip** blurt out, come out with (*Inf.*), disclose, divulge, give away, leak, let out (*Inf.*), let the cat out of the bag, reveal ~*n.* 7. bloomer (*Brit. inf.*), blunder, boob (*Brit. sl.*), error, failure, fault, faux pas, imprudence, indiscretion, mistake, omission, oversight, slip of the tongue, slip-up (*Inf.*) 8. **give (someone) the slip** dodge, elude, escape from, evade, get away from, lose (someone), outwit, shake (someone) off

slip[2] *n.* 1. piece, sliver, strip 2. cutting, offshoot, runner, scion, shoot, sprig, sprout

slippery 1. glassy, greasy, icy, lubricious (*Rare*), perilous, skiddy (*Inf.*), slippy (*Inf. or dialect*), smooth, unsafe, unstable, unsteady 2. crafty, cunning, devious, dishonest, duplicitous, evasive, false, foxy, shifty, sneaky, treacherous, tricky, two-faced, unpredictable, unreliable, untrustworthy

slipshod careless, casual, loose, slapdash, sloppy (*Inf.*), slovenly, unsystematic, untidy

slit 1. *v.* cut (open), gash, impale, knife, lance, pierce, rip, slash, split open 2. *n.* cut, fissure, gash, incision, opening, rent, split, tear

slither *v.* glide, skitter, slide, slink, slip, snake, undulate

sliver *n.* flake, fragment, paring, shaving, shred, slip, splinter

slob boor, churl, lout, oaf, yahoo, yob (*Brit. sl.*)

slobber *v.* dribble, drivel, drool, salivate, slabber (*Dialect*), slaver, water at the mouth

slobbish messy, slatternly, sloppy (*Inf.*), slovenly, unclean, unkempt, untidy

slog *v.* 1. hit, hit for six, punch, slosh (*Brit.*

sl.), slug, sock (*Sl.*), strike, thump, wallop (*Inf.*) 2. apply oneself to, labour, peg away at, persevere, plod, plough through, slave, toil, tramp, trek, trudge, work ~*n.* 3. effort, exertion, hike, labour, struggle, tramp, trek, trudge

slogan catch-phrase, catchword, jingle, motto, rallying cry

slop *v.* overflow, slosh (*Inf.*), spatter, spill, splash, splatter

slop around *or* **about** flop, loaf, lollop, lounge, shamble, shuffle, slouch, slump, sprawl, veg out (*Sl., chiefly U.S.*)

slope *v.* 1. drop away, fall, incline, lean, pitch, rise, slant, tilt ~*n.* 2. brae (*Scot.*), declination, declivity, descent, downgrade (*Chiefly U.S.*), gradient, inclination, incline, ramp, rise, scarp, slant, tilt ~*v.* 3. *With* **off, away,** *etc.* creep, make oneself scarce, skulk, slink, slip, steal

sloping bevelled, cant, inclined, inclining, leaning, oblique, slanting

sloppy 1. sludgy, slushy, splashy, watery, wet 2. *Inf.* amateurish, careless, clumsy, hit-or-miss (*Inf.*), inattentive, messy, slipshod, slovenly, unkempt, untidy, weak 3. banal, gushing, mawkish, mushy (*Inf.*), overemotional, sentimental, slushy (*Inf.*), soppy (*Brit. inf.*), trite, wet (*Brit. inf.*)

slosh *v.* 1. flounder, plash, pour, shower, slap, slop, splash, spray, swash, wade 2. *Brit. sl.* bash (*Inf.*), belt (*Inf.*), biff (*Sl.*), hit, punch, slog, slug, sock (*Sl.*), strike, swipe (*Inf.*), thwack, wallop (*Inf.*)

slot *n.* 1. aperture, channel, groove, hole, slit, vent 2. *Inf.* niche, opening, place, position, space, time, vacancy ~*v.* 3. adjust, assign, fit, fit in, insert, pigeonhole

sloth faineance, idleness, inactivity, indolence, inertia, laziness, slackness, slothfulness, sluggishness, torpor

slothful do-nothing (*Inf.*), fainéant, idle, inactive, indolent, inert, lazy, skiving (*Brit. sl.*), slack, sluggish, torpid, workshy

slouch *v.* droop, loll, slump, stoop

slouching awkward, loutish, lumbering, shambling, uncouth, ungainly

slovenly careless, disorderly, heedless, loose, negligent, slack, slapdash, slatternly, slipshod, sloppy (*Inf.*), unkempt, untidy

Antonyms careful, clean, conscientious, disciplined, methodical, meticulous, neat, orderly, shipshape, smart, soigné *or* soignée, tidy, trim, well-groomed, well-ordered

slow *adj.* 1. creeping, dawdling, deliberate, easy, lackadaisical, laggard, lagging, lazy, leaden, leisurely, loitering, measured, plodding, ponderous, slow-moving, sluggardly, sluggish, tortoise-like, unhurried 2. backward, behind, behindhand, delayed, dilatory, late, long-delayed, tardy, unpunctual 3. gradual, lingering, long-drawn-out, prolonged, protracted, time-consuming 4. behind the times, boring, conservative, dead, dead-and-alive (*Brit.*), dull, inactive, one-horse (*Inf.*), quiet, slack, sleepy, sluggish, stagnant, tame, tedious, uneventful, uninteresting, unproductive, unprogressive, wearisome 5. blockish, bovine, braindead (*Inf.*), dense, dim, dozy (*Brit. inf.*), dull, dull-witted, dumb (*Inf.*), obtuse, retarded, slow on the uptake (*Inf.*), slow-witted, stupid, thick, unresponsive 6. *With* **to** averse, disinclined, hesitant, indisposed, loath, reluctant, unwilling ~*v.* 7. *Often with* **up** *or* **down** brake, check, curb, decelerate, delay, detain, handicap, hold up, lag, reduce speed, rein in, relax, restrict, retard, slacken (off), spin out

Antonyms *adj.* (*senses 1, 2, 3 & 4*) action-packed, animated, brisk, eager, exciting, fast, hectic, hurried, interesting, lively, precipitate, prompt, quick, quickie (*Inf.*), quick-moving, sharp, speedy, stimulating, swift (*sense 5*) bright, clever, intelligent, perceptive, quick, quick-witted, sharp, smart ~*v.* accelerate, advance, aid, boost, help, pick up speed, quicken, speed up

slowly at a snail's pace, at one's leisure, by degrees, gradually, inchmeal, in one's own (good) time, leisurely, ploddingly, steadily, taking one's time, unhurriedly, with leaden steps

sludge dregs, mire, muck, mud, ooze, residue, sediment, silt, slime, slop, slush

sluggish dull, heavy, inactive, indolent, inert, lethargic, lifeless, listless, phlegmatic, slothful, slow, slow-moving, torpid, unresponsive

Antonyms animated, brisk, dynamic, energetic, enthusiastic, fast, free-flowing, full of life, industrious, lively, swift, vigorous

sluggishness apathy, drowsiness, dullness, heaviness, indolence, inertia, languor, lassitude, lethargy, listlessness, slothfulness, somnolence, stagnation, torpor

sluice *v.* cleanse, drain, drench, flush, irrigate, wash down, wash out

slumber *v.* be inactive, doze, drowse, kip (*Brit. sl.*), lie dormant, nap, repose, sleep, snooze (*Inf.*), zizz (*Brit. inf.*)

slummy decayed, overcrowded, run-down, seedy, sleazy, sordid, squalid, wretched

slump *v.* 1. collapse, crash, decline, deteriorate, fall, fall off, go downhill (*Inf.*), plummet, plunge, reach a new low, sink, slip ~*n.* 2. collapse, crash, decline, depreciation, depression, downturn, drop, failure, fall, falling-off, low, recession, reverse, stagnation, trough ~*v.* 3. bend, droop, hunch, loll, sag, slouch

Antonyms *v.* advance, boom, develop, expand, flourish, grow, increase, prosper, thrive ~*n.* advance, boom, boost, development, expansion, gain, growth, improvement, increase, upsurge, upswing, upturn

slur *n.* affront, aspersion, blot, brand, calumny, discredit, disgrace, innuendo, insinuation, insult, reproach, smear, stain, stigma

slut drab (*Archaic*), scrubber (*Brit. & Aust. sl.*), slattern, sloven, tart, trollop

sly *adj.* 1. artful, astute, clever, conniving, covert, crafty, cunning, devious, foxy, furtive, guileful, insidious, scheming, secret, shifty, stealthy, subtle, underhand, wily 2. arch, impish, knowing, mischievous, roguish ~*n.* 3. **on the sly** behind (someone's) back, covertly, like a thief in the night, on the q.t. (*Inf.*), on the quiet, privately, secretly, surreptitiously, underhandedly, under the counter (*Inf.*)

Antonyms *adj.* above-board, artless, direct, frank, honest, guileless, ingenuous, open, straightforward, trustworthy ~*n.* above-board, candidly, forthrightly, on the level, openly, overtly, publicly

smack *v.* 1. box, clap, cuff, hit, pat, slap, sock (*Sl.*), spank, strike, tap ~*n.* 2. blow, crack, slap 3. **smack in the eye** blow, rebuff, repulse, setback, slap in the face, snub ~*adv.* 4. *Inf.* directly, exactly, plumb, point-blank, precisely, right, slap (*Inf.*), squarely, straight

smack of bear the stamp of, be redolent of, be suggestive *or* indicative of, betoken, have all the hallmarks of, reek of, smell of, suggest, testify to

small 1. diminutive, immature, Lilliputian, little, mini, miniature, minute, petite, pint-sized (*Inf.*), pocket-sized, puny, pygmy *or* pigmy, slight, teensy-weensy, teeny, teeny-weeny, tiny, undersized, wee, young 2. insignificant, lesser, minor, negligible, paltry, petty, trifling, trivial, unimportant 3. inadequate, inconsiderable, insufficient, limited, meagre, measly, scant, scanty 4. humble, modest, small-scale, unpretentious 5. base, grudging, illiberal, mean, narrow, petty, selfish 6. **make (someone) feel small** chagrin, disconcert, humble, humiliate, make (someone) look foolish, mortify, put down (*Sl.*), show up (*Inf.*), take down a peg or two (*Inf.*)

Antonyms (*sense 1*) ample, big, colossal, enormous, great, huge, immense, massive, mega (*Sl.*), sizable, vast (*senses 2, 3 & 4*) appreciable, considerable, generous, grand, important, large-scale, major, powerful, serious, significant, substantial, urgent, vital, weighty

small-minded bigoted, envious, grudging, hidebound, intolerant, mean, narrow-minded, petty, rigid, ungenerous

Antonyms broad-minded, far-sighted, generous, liberal, open, open-minded, tolerant, unbigoted

small-time insignificant, minor, no-account (*U.S. inf.*), of no account, of no consequence, petty, piddling (*Inf.*), unimportant

smarmy bootlicking (*Inf.*), bowing and scraping, crawling, fawning, fulsome, greasy, ingratiating, obsequious, oily, servile, slimy, smooth, soapy (*Sl.*), suave, sycophantic, toadying, unctuous

smart[1] *adj.* 1. acute, adept, agile, apt, astute, bright, brisk, canny, clever, ingenious, intelligent, keen, nimble, quick, quick-witted, ready, sharp, shrewd 2. chic, elegant, fashionable, fine, modish, natty (*Inf.*), neat, snappy, spruce, stylish, trendy (*Brit. inf.*), trim, well turned-out 3. effective, impertinent, nimble-witted, pointed, ready, saucy, smart-alecky (*Inf.*), witty 4. brisk, cracking (*Inf.*), jaunty, lively, quick, spanking, spirited, vigorous

Antonyms (*sense 1*) daft (*Inf.*), dense, dim-witted (*Inf.*), dull, dumb (*Inf.*), foolish, idiotic, moronic, slow, stupid, thick, unintelligent (*sense 2*) dowdy, dull, fogeyish, naff (*Brit. sl.*), old-fashioned, out-moded, out-of-date, passé, scruffy, sloppy, uncool, unfashionable, untrendy (*Brit. inf.*) (*sense 3*) modest, polite, respectful, restrained, unobtrusive

smart[2] 1. *v.* burn, hurt, pain, sting, throb, tingle 2. *adj.* hard, keen, painful, piercing, resounding, sharp, stinging 3. *n.* burning sensation, pain, pang, smarting, soreness, sting

smart aleck clever-clogs (*Inf.*), clever Dick (*Inf.*), know-all (*Inf.*), smartarse (*Sl.*), smarty boots (*Inf.*), smarty pants (*Inf.*), wise guy (*Inf.*)

smarten beautify, groom, put in order, put to rights, spruce up, tidy

smash *v.* 1. break, collide, crash, crush, demolish, disintegrate, pulverize, shatter, shiver ~*n.* 2. accident, collision, crash, pile-up (*Inf.*), smash-up (*Inf.*) ~*v.* 3. defeat, destroy, lay waste, overthrow, ruin, total (*Sl.*), trash (*Sl.*), wreck ~*n.* 4. collapse, defeat, destruction, disaster, downfall, failure, ruin, shattering

smashing boffo (*Sl.*), brill (*Inf.*), brilliant (*Inf.*), chillin' (*U.S. sl.*), cracking (*Brit. inf.*), crucial (*Sl.*), def (*Sl.*), excellent, exhilarating, fab (*Inf., chiefly Brit.*), fabulous

(*Inf.*), fantastic (*Inf.*), first-class, first-rate, great (*Inf.*), jim-dandy (*Sl.*), magnificent, marvellous, mean (*Sl.*), mega (*Sl.*), out of this world (*Inf.*), sensational (*Inf.*), sovereign, stupendous, super (*Inf.*), superb, superlative, terrific (*Inf.*), topping (*Brit. sl.*), wonderful, world-class
Antonyms appalling, average, awful, bad, boring, crap (*Sl.*), disappointing, disgraceful, disgusting, dreadful, dreary, dull, hideous, horrible, mediocre, ordinary, rotten, run-of-the-mill, sickening, terrible, unexciting, uninspired, vile

smattering bit, dash, elements, modicum, rudiments, smatter, sprinkling

smear *v.* **1.** bedaub, bedim, besmirch, blur, coat, cover, daub, dirty, patch, plaster, rub on, smirch, smudge, soil, spread over, stain, sully ~*n.* **2.** blot, blotch, daub, smirch, smudge, splotch, streak ~*v.* **3.** asperse, besmirch, blacken, calumniate, drag (someone's) name through the mud, malign, sully, tarnish, traduce, vilify ~*n.* **4.** calumny, defamation, libel, mudslinging, slander, vilification, whispering campaign

smell *n.* **1.** aroma, bouquet, fragrance, niff (*Brit. sl.*), odour, perfume, redolence, scent, whiff ~*v.* **2.** get a whiff of, nose, scent, sniff ~*n.* **3.** fetor, niff (*Brit. sl.*), pong (*Brit. inf.*), stench, stink ~*v.* **4.** be malodorous, hum (*Sl.*), niff (*Brit. sl.*), pong (*Brit. inf.*), reek, stink, stink to high heaven (*Inf.*), whiff (*Brit. sl.*)

smelly evil-smelling, fetid, foul, foul-smelling, high, malodorous, mephitic, niffy (*Brit. sl.*), noisome, olid, pongy (*Brit. inf.*), putrid, reeking, stinking, stinky (*Inf.*), strong, strong-smelling, whiffy (*Brit. sl.*)

smirk *n.* grin, leer, simper, smug look, sneer

smitten **1.** afflicted, beset, laid low, plagued, struck **2.** beguiled, bewitched, bowled over (*Inf.*), captivated, charmed, enamoured, infatuated, swept off one's feet

smoky begrimed, black, caliginous (*Archaic*), grey, grimy, hazy, murky, reeky, smoke-darkened, sooty, thick

smooth *adj.* **1.** even, flat, flush, horizontal, level, plain, plane, unwrinkled **2.** glossy, polished, shiny, silky, sleek, soft, velvety **3.** calm, equable, glassy, mirror-like, peaceful, serene, tranquil, undisturbed, unruffled **4.** agreeable, bland, mellow, mild, pleasant, soothing **5.** debonair, facile, glib, ingratiating, persuasive, silky, slick, smarmy (*Brit. inf.*), suave, unctuous, urbane **6.** easy, effortless, flowing, fluent, frictionless, regular, rhythmic, steady, unbroken, uneventful, uniform, uninterrupted, untroubled, well-ordered ~*v.* **7.** flatten, iron, level, plane, polish, press **8.** allay, alleviate, appease, assuage, calm, ease, extenuate, facilitate, iron out the difficulties of, mitigate, mollify, palliate, pave the way, soften
Antonyms *adj.* (*senses 1 & 2*) abrasive, bumpy, coarse, irregular, jagged, lumpy, rough, sharp, uneven (*sense 3*) agitated, edgy, excitable, disturbed, nervous, ruffled, troubled, troublesome, turbulent, uneasy ~*v.* aggravate, exacerbate, hamper, hinder, intensify, make worse, roughen

smoothness **1.** evenness, flushness, levelness, regularity, unbrokenness **2.** silkiness, sleekness, smooth texture, softness, velvetiness **3.** calmness, glassiness, placidity, serenity, stillness, unruffled surface **4.** glibness, oiliness, smarminess (*Brit. inf.*), suavity, urbanity **5.** ease, efficiency, effortlessness, felicity, finish, flow, fluency, polish, rhythm, slickness, smooth running

smother *v.* **1.** choke, extinguish, snuff, stifle, strangle, suffocate **2.** conceal, hide, keep back, muffle, repress, stifle, suppress **3.** be swimming in, cocoon, cover, envelop, heap, inundate, overwhelm, shower, shroud, surround ~*n.* **4.** fug (*Chiefly Brit.*), smog

smoulder *Fig.* be resentful, boil, burn, fester, fume, rage, seethe, simmer, smart under

smudge **1.** *v.* blacken, blur, daub, dirty, mark, smear, smirch, soil **2.** *n.* blemish, blot, blur, smear, smut, smutch

smug complacent, conceited, holier-than-thou, priggish, self-opinionated, self-righteous, self-satisfied, superior

smuggler bootlegger, contrabandist, gentleman, moonshiner (*U.S.*), rum-runner, runner, trafficker, wrecker

smutty bawdy, blue, coarse, crude, dirty, filthy, improper, indecent, indelicate, lewd, obscene, off colour, pornographic, prurient, racy, raunchy (*U.S. sl.*), risqué, salacious, suggestive, vulgar

snack bite, bite to eat, break, elevenses (*Brit. inf.*), light meal, nibble, refreshment(s), titbit

snag **1.** *n.* catch, complication, difficulty, disadvantage, downside, drawback, hitch, inconvenience, obstacle, problem, stumbling block, the rub **2.** *v.* catch, hole, rip, tear

snaky **1.** convoluted, serpentine, sinuous, tortuous, twisting, writhing **2.** crafty, insidious, perfidious, sly, treacherous, venomous

snap *v.* **1.** break, come apart, crack, give way, separate **2.** bite, bite at, catch, grip, nip, seize, snatch **3.** bark, flare out, flash, fly off the handle at (*Inf.*), growl, jump down (someone's) throat (*Inf.*), lash out at, retort, snarl, speak sharply 4. click, crackle, pop 5. **snap one's fingers at** cock a snook at (*Brit.*), defy, flout, pay no attention to, scorn, set at naught, wave two fingers at (*Sl.*) 6. **snap out of it** cheer up, get a grip on oneself, get over, liven up, perk up, pull oneself together (*Inf.*), recover ~*n.* 7. crackle, fillip, flick, pop 8. bite, grab, nip 9. *Inf.* energy, get-up-and-go (*Inf.*), go (*Inf.*), liveliness, pep, pizzazz *or* pizazz (*Inf.*), vigour, zip (*Inf.*) ~*adj.* 10. abrupt, immediate, instant, on-the-spot, sudden, unpremeditated

snappy 1. apt to fly off the handle (*Inf.*), cross, edgy, hasty, impatient, irritable, like a bear with a sore head (*Inf.*), quick-tempered, ratty (*Brit. & N.Z. inf.*), snappish, tart, testy, tetchy, touchy, waspish 2. chic, dapper, fashionable, modish, natty (*Inf.*), smart, stylish, trendy (*Brit. inf.*), up-to-the-minute, voguish 3. **look snappy** be quick, buck up (*Inf.*), get a move on (*Inf.*), get one's skates on, hurry (up), look lively, make haste

snap up avail oneself of, grab, grasp, nab (*Inf.*), pounce upon, seize, swoop down on, take advantage of

snare 1. *v.* catch, entrap, net, seize, springe, trap, trepan (*Archaic*), wire 2. *n.* catch, gin, net, noose, pitfall, springe, trap, wire

snarl[1] *v.* complain, growl, grumble, mumble, murmur, show its teeth (*of an animal*)

snarl[2] *v. Often with* **up** complicate, confuse, embroil, enmesh, entangle, entwine, muddle, ravel, tangle

snarl-up confusion, entanglement, muddle, tangle, (traffic) jam

snatch 1. *v.* catch up, clutch, gain, grab, grasp, grip, make off with, pluck, pull, rescue, seize, take, win, wrench, wrest 2. *n.* bit, fragment, part, piece, smattering, snippet, spell

snazzy attractive, dashing, flamboyant, flashy, jazzy (*Inf.*), raffish, ritzy (*Sl.*), showy, smart, sophisticated, sporty, stylish, swinging (*Sl.*), with it (*Inf.*)

sneak *v.* 1. cower, lurk, pad, sidle, skulk, slink, slip, smuggle, spirit, steal 2. *Inf.* grass on (*Brit. sl.*), inform on, peach (*Sl.*), shop (*Sl., chiefly Brit.*), sing (*Sl., chiefly U.S.*), spill one's guts (*Sl.*), tell on (*Inf.*), tell tales ~*n.* 3. informer, snake in the grass, telltale ~*adj.* 4. clandestine, furtive, quick, secret, stealthy, surprise

sneaking 1. hidden, private, secret, suppressed, unavowed, unconfessed, undivulged, unexpressed, unvoiced 2. intuitive, nagging, niggling, persistent, uncomfortable, worrying 3. contemptible, furtive, mean, sly, sneaky, surreptitious, two-faced, underhand

sneaky base, contemptible, cowardly, deceitful, devious, dishonest, disingenuous, double-dealing, furtive, low, malicious, mean, nasty, shifty, slippery, sly, snide, unreliable, unscrupulous, untrustworthy

sneer 1. *v.* curl one's lip, deride, disdain, gibe, hold in contempt, hold up to ridicule, jeer, laugh, look down on, mock, ridicule, scoff, scorn, sniff at, snigger, turn up one's nose (*Inf.*) 2. *n.* derision, disdain, gibe, jeer, mockery, ridicule, scorn, snidery, snigger

snide cynical, disparaging, hurtful, ill-natured, insinuating, malicious, mean, nasty, sarcastic, scornful, shrewish, sneering, spiteful, unkind

sniff *v.* breathe, inhale, smell, snuff, snuffle

sniffy condescending, contemptuous, disdainful, haughty, supercilious, superior

snigger giggle, laugh, smirk, sneer, snicker, titter

snip *v.* 1. clip, crop, cut, dock, nick, nip off, notch, shave, trim ~*n.* 2. bit, clipping, fragment, piece, scrap, shred, snippet 3. *Inf.* bargain, giveaway, good buy, steal (*Inf.*)

snippet fragment, part, particle, piece, scrap, shred, snatch

snivel blubber, cry, girn (*Scot. & northern English dialect*), gripe (*Inf.*), grizzle (*Inf., chiefly Brit.*), mewl, moan, sniffle, snuffle, weep, whimper, whine, whinge (*Inf.*)

snobbery airs, arrogance, condescension, pretension, pride, side (*Brit. sl.*), snobbishness, snootiness (*Inf.*), uppishness (*Brit. inf.*)

snobbish arrogant, condescending, high and mighty (*Inf.*), high-hat (*Inf., chiefly U.S.*), hoity-toity (*Inf.*), patronizing, pretentious, snooty (*Inf.*), stuck-up (*Inf.*), superior, toffee-nosed (*Sl., chiefly Brit.*), uppish (*Brit. inf.*), uppity
Antonyms down to earth, humble, modest, natural, unassuming, unostentatious, unpretentious, without airs

snoop interfere, poke one's nose in (*Inf.*), pry, spy

snooper busybody, meddler, nosy parker (*Inf.*), Paul Pry, pry, snoop (*Inf.*), stickybeak (*Aust. inf.*)

snooze 1. *v.* catnap, doze, drop off (*Inf.*), drowse, kip (*Brit. sl.*), nap, nod off (*Inf.*), take forty winks (*Inf.*) 2. *n.* catnap, doze, forty winks (*Inf.*), kip (*Brit. sl.*), nap, siesta

snub 1. *v.* cold-shoulder, cut (*Inf.*), cut dead (*Inf.*), give (someone) the brush-off (*Sl.*), give (someone) the cold shoulder, humble, humiliate, mortify, put down, rebuff, shame, slight 2. *n.* affront, brushoff (*Sl.*), humiliation, insult, put-down, slap in the face

snug 1. comfortable, comfy (*Inf.*), cosy, homely, intimate, sheltered, warm 2. close, compact, neat, trim

snuggle cuddle, nestle, nuzzle

soak *v.* 1. bathe, damp, drench, immerse, infuse, marinate (*Cookery*), moisten, penetrate, permeate, saturate, seep, steep, wet 2. *With* **up** absorb, assimilate, drink in, take up *or* in

soaking drenched, dripping, droukit *or* drookit (*Scot.*), saturated, soaked, soaked to the skin, sodden, sopping, streaming, waterlogged, wet through, wringing wet

soar 1. ascend, fly, mount, rise, tower, wing 2. climb, escalate, rise, rocket, shoot up
Antonyms descend, dive, drop down, fall, nose-dive, plummet, plunge, swoop

sob *v.* bawl, blubber, boohoo, cry, greet (*Scot. or archaic*), howl, shed tears, snivel, weep

sober *adj.* 1. abstemious, abstinent, moderate, on the wagon (*Inf.*), temperate 2. calm, clear-headed, cold, composed, cool, dispassionate, grave, level-headed, lucid, peaceful, practical, rational, realistic, reasonable, sedate, serene, serious, solemn, sound, staid, steady, unexcited, unruffled 3. dark, drab, plain, quiet, severe, sombre, subdued ~*v.* 4. *Usually with* **up** bring (someone) back to earth, calm down, clear one's head, come *or* bring to one's senses, give (someone) pause for thought, make (someone) stop and think
Antonyms *adj.* (*sense 1*) bevvied (*Dialect*), blitzed (*Sl.*), blotto (*Sl.*), bombed (*Sl.*), drunk, flying (*Sl.*), fu' (*Scot.*), guttered (*Sl.*), had one too many, inebriated, intoxicated, merry (*Brit. inf.*), paralytic (*Inf.*), pie-eyed (*Sl.*), pissed (*Taboo sl.*), plastered, sloshed (*Sl.*), smashed (*Sl.*), steamboats (*Sl.*), steaming (*Sl.*), tiddly (*Sl., chiefly Brit.*), tight (*Inf.*), tipsy, tired and emotional (*Euphemistic*), wasted (*Sl.*), wrecked (*Sl.*), zonked (*Sl.*) (*senses 2 & 3*) bright, excessive, flamboyant, flashy, frivolous, garish, gaudy, giddy, happy, immoderate, imprudent, injudicious, irrational, light, lighthearted, lively, sensational, unrealistic ~*v.* become intoxicated, get drunk

sobriety 1. abstemiousness, abstinence, moderation, nonindulgence, self-restraint, soberness, temperance 2. calmness, composure, coolness, gravity, level-headedness, reasonableness, restraint, sedateness, seriousness, solemnity, staidness, steadiness

so-called alleged, ostensible, pretended, professed, self-styled, *soi-disant,* supposed

sociability affability, companionability, congeniality, conviviality, cordiality, friendliness, gregariousness, neighbourliness

sociable accessible, affable, approachable, companionable, conversable, convivial, cordial, familiar, friendly, genial, gregarious, neighbourly, outgoing, social, warm
Antonyms antisocial, boorish, businesslike, cold, distant, formal, introverted, reclusive, standoffish, stiff, tense, uncommunicative, unfriendly, unsociable, withdrawn

social *adj.* 1. collective, common, communal, community, general, group, organized, public, societal 2. companionable, friendly, gregarious, neighbourly, sociable ~*n.* 3. do (*Inf.*), gathering, get-together (*Inf.*), party

socialize be a good mixer, entertain, fraternize, get about *or* around, get together, go out, mix

society 1. civilization, culture, humanity, mankind, people, population, social order, the community, the general public, the public, the world at large 2. camaraderie, companionship, company, fellowship, friendship 3. association, brotherhood, circle, club, corporation, fellowship, fraternity, group, guild, institute, league, order, organization, sisterhood, union 4. beau monde, elite, gentry, *haut monde,* high society, polite society, the country set, the nobs (*Sl.*), the smart set, the swells (*Inf.*), the toffs (*Brit. sl.*), the top drawer, upper classes, upper crust (*Inf.*)

sodden boggy, drenched, droukit *or* drookit (*Scot.*), marshy, miry, saturated, soaked, soggy, sopping, waterlogged

soft 1. creamy, cushioned, cushiony, doughy, elastic, gelatinous, pulpy, quaggy, spongy, squashy, swampy, yielding 2. bendable, ductile (*of metals*), elastic, flexible, impressible, malleable, mouldable, plastic, pliable, supple, tensile 3. downy, feathery, fleecy, flowing, fluid, furry, like a baby's bottom (*Inf.*), rounded, silky, smooth, velvety 4. balmy, bland, caressing, delicate, diffuse, dim, dimmed, dulcet, faint, gentle, light, low, mellifluous, mellow, melodious, mild, murmured, muted, pale, pastel, pleasing, quiet, restful, shaded, soft-toned, soothing, subdued, sweet, temperate, twilight, understated, whispered 5. compassionate, gentle, kind, pitying, sensitive, sentimental, sympathetic, tender, tenderhearted 6. easy-going, indulgent, lax, lenient, liberal, overindulgent, permissive, spineless, weak 7. *Inf.* comfortable, cushy (*Inf.*), easy, easy-peasy (*Sl.*), undemanding 8. effeminate, flabby, flaccid, limp, namby-pamby, out of condition, out

of training, overindulged, pampered, podgy, weak 9. *Inf.* a bit lacking (*Inf.*), daft (*Inf.*), feeble-minded, foolish, silly, simple, soft in the head (*Inf.*), soppy (*Brit. inf.*)
Antonyms (*senses 1, 2 & 3*) abrasive, coarse, firm, grating, hard, inflexible, irritating, rigid, rough, solid, stiff, tough, unyielding (*sense 4*) bright, garish, gaudy, glaring, hard, harsh, loud, noisy, strident, unpleasant (*sense 6*) austere, harsh, no-nonsense, stern, strict

soften abate, allay, alleviate, appease, assuage, calm, cushion, diminish, ease, lessen, lighten, lower, melt, mitigate, moderate, modify, mollify, muffle, palliate, quell, relax, soothe, still, subdue, temper, tone down, turn down

soften up conciliate, disarm, melt, soft-soap (*Inf.*), weaken, win over, work on

softhearted charitable, compassionate, generous, indulgent, kind, sentimental, sympathetic, tender, tenderhearted, warm-hearted
Antonyms callous, cold, cruel, hard, hard-hearted, heartless, insensitive, uncaring, unkind, unsympathetic

soft pedal de-emphasize, go easy (*Inf.*), moderate, play down, tone down

soft spot fondness, liking, partiality, weakness

soggy dripping, heavy, moist, mushy, pulpy, saturated, soaked, sodden, sopping, spongy, waterlogged

soil[1] *n.* 1. clay, dirt, dust, earth, ground, loam 2. country, land, region, terra firma

soil[2] *v.* bedraggle, befoul, begrime, besmirch, defile, dirty, foul, maculate (*Literary*), muddy, pollute, smear, smirch, spatter, spot, stain, sully, tarnish

sojourn 1. *n.* rest, stay, stop, stopover, visit 2. *v.* abide, dwell, lodge, reside, rest, stay, stop, tarry

solace 1. *n.* alleviation, assuagement, comfort, consolation, relief 2. *v.* allay, alleviate, comfort, console, mitigate, soften, soothe

soldier enlisted man (*U.S.*), fighter, GI (*U.S. inf.*), man-at-arms, military man, redcoat, serviceman, squaddie *or* squaddy (*Brit. sl.*), Tommy (*Brit. inf.*), trooper, warrior

sole alone, exclusive, individual, one, one and only, only, single, singular, solitary

solecism bloomer (*Brit. inf.*), blunder, boo-boo (*Inf.*), breach of etiquette, cacology, faux pas, gaffe, gaucherie, impropriety, incongruity, indecorum, lapse, mistake

solely alone, completely, entirely, exclusively, merely, only, single-handedly, singly

solemn 1. earnest, glum, grave, portentous, sedate, serious, sober, staid, thoughtful 2. august, awe-inspiring, ceremonial, ceremonious, dignified, formal, grand, grave, imposing, impressive, majestic, momentous, stately 3. devotional, hallowed, holy, religious, reverential, ritual, sacred, sanctified, venerable
Antonyms (*senses 1 & 2*) bright, cheerful, chirpy (*Inf.*), comical, frivolous, genial, happy, informal, jovial, light-hearted, merry, relaxed, unceremonious (*sense 3*) irreligious, irreverent, unholy

solemnity 1. earnestness, grandeur, gravitas, gravity, impressiveness, momentousness, portentousness, sacredness, sanctity, seriousness 2. *Often plural* celebration, ceremonial, ceremony, formalities, observance, proceedings, rite, ritual

solemnize celebrate, commemorate, honour, keep, observe

solicit ask, beg, beseech, canvass, crave, entreat, implore, importune, petition, plead for, pray, seek, supplicate

solicitous anxious, apprehensive, attentive, careful, caring, concerned, eager, earnest, troubled, uneasy, worried, zealous

solicitude anxiety, attentiveness, care, concern, considerateness, consideration, regard, worry

solid *adj.* 1. compact, concrete, dense, firm, hard, massed, stable, strong, sturdy, substantial, unshakable 2. genuine, good, pure, real, reliable, sound 3. agreed, complete, continuous, unalloyed, unanimous, unbroken, undivided, uninterrupted, united, unmixed 4. constant, decent, dependable, estimable, law-abiding, level-headed, reliable, sensible, serious, sober, trusty, upright, upstanding, worthy
Antonyms (*sense 1*) broken, crumbling, decaying, flimsy, gaseous, hollow, liquid, permeable, precarious, shaky, unstable, unsteady, unsubstantial (*sense 2*) impure, unreliable, unsound (*sense 3*) at odds, divided, mixed, split, undecided (*sense 4*) flighty, irresponsible, unreliable, unsound, unstable, unsteady

solidarity accord, camaraderie, cohesion, community of interest, concordance, esprit de corps, harmony, like-mindedness, singleness of purpose, soundness, stability, team spirit, unanimity, unification, unity

solidify cake, coagulate, cohere, congeal, harden, jell, set

solitary *adj.* 1. desolate, hidden, isolated, lonely, out-of-the-way, remote, retired, secluded, sequestered, unfrequented, unvisited 2. alone, lone, single, sole 3. cloistered, companionless, friendless, hermitical, lonely, lonesome, reclusive, unsociable,

unsocial ~*n.* 4. hermit, introvert, loner (*Inf.*), lone wolf, recluse
Antonyms *adj.* (*sense 1*) bustling, busy, frequented, public, well-frequented (*senses 2 & 3*) companionable, convivial, cordial, gregarious, one of a group, outgoing, sociable, social ~*n.* extrovert, mixer, socialite

solitude 1. isolation, loneliness, privacy, reclusiveness, retirement, seclusion 2. *Poetic* desert, emptiness, waste, wasteland, wilderness

solution 1. answer, clarification, elucidation, explanation, explication, key, resolution, result, solving, unfolding, unravelling 2. blend, compound, emulsion, mix, mixture, solvent, suspension (*Chem.*) 3. disconnection, dissolution, liquefaction, melting

solve answer, clarify, clear up, crack, decipher, disentangle, elucidate, explain, expound, get to the bottom of, interpret, resolve, suss (out) (*Sl.*), unfold, unravel, work out

sombre dark, dim, dismal, doleful, drab, dull, dusky, funereal, gloomy, grave, joyless, lugubrious, melancholy, mournful, obscure, sad, sepulchral, shadowy, shady, sober
Antonyms bright, cheerful, chirpy (*Inf.*), colourful, dazzling, effusive, full of beans, garish, gaudy, genial, happy, lively, sunny, upbeat (*Inf.*)

somebody *n.* big noise (*Inf.*), big shot (*Inf.*), big wheel (*Sl.*), bigwig (*Inf.*), celeb (*Inf.*), celebrity, dignitary, heavyweight (*Inf.*), household name, luminary, megastar (*Inf.*), name, notable, personage, person of note, public figure, star, superstar, V.I.P.
Antonyms also-ran, cipher, lightweight (*Inf.*), menial, nobody, nonentity, nothing (*Inf.*)

someday eventually, one day, one of these (fine) days, sooner or later, ultimately

somehow by fair means or foul, by hook or (by) crook, by some means or other, come hell or high water (*Inf.*), come what may, one way or another

sometimes at times, every now and then, every so often, from time to time, now and again, now and then, occasionally, off and on, once in a while, on occasion
Antonyms always, consistently, constantly, continually, eternally, ever, everlastingly, evermore, forever, invariably, perpetually, unceasingly, without exception

somnolent comatose, dozy, drowsy, half-awake, heavy-eyed, nodding off (*Inf.*), sleepy, soporific, torpid

song air, anthem, ballad, canticle, canzonet, carol, chant, chorus, ditty, hymn, lay, lyric, melody, number, pop song, psalm, shanty, strain, tune

song and dance ado, commotion, flap (*Inf.*), fuss, hoo-ha, kerfuffle (*Inf.*), performance (*Inf.*), pother, shindig (*Inf.*), shindy (*Inf.*), stir, to-do

sonorous full, grandiloquent, high-flown, high-sounding, loud, orotund, plangent, resonant, resounding, rich, ringing, rounded, sounding

soon anon (*Archaic*), any minute now, before long, betimes (*Archaic*), erelong (*Archaic or poetic*), in a little while, in a minute, in a short time, in the near future, shortly

soothe allay, alleviate, appease, assuage, calm, calm down, compose, ease, hush, lull, mitigate, mollify, pacify, quiet, relieve, settle, smooth down, soften, still, tranquillize
Antonyms aggravate (*Inf.*), agitate, annoy, disquiet, disturb, exacerbate, excite, get on one's nerves (*Inf.*), hassle (*Inf.*), increase, inflame, irritate, rouse, stimulate, upset, vex, worry

soothing balsamic, calming, demulcent, easeful, emollient, lenitive, palliative, relaxing, restful

soothsayer augur, diviner, foreteller, prophet, seer, sibyl

sophisticated 1. blasé, citified, cosmopolitan, cultivated, cultured, jet-set, refined, seasoned, urbane, worldly, worldly-wise, world-weary 2. advanced, complex, complicated, delicate, elaborate, highly-developed, intricate, multifaceted, refined, subtle
Antonyms basic, naive, old-fashioned, plain, primitive, simple, uncomplicated, unrefined, unsophisticated, unsubtle, unworldly

sophistication finesse, poise, savoir-faire, *savoir-vivre*, urbanity, worldliness, worldly wisdom

sophistry casuistry, fallacy, quibble, sophism

soporific 1. *adj.* hypnotic, sedative, sleep-inducing, sleepy, somniferous (*Rare*), somnolent, tranquillizing 2. *n.* anaesthetic, hypnotic, narcotic, opiate, sedative, tranquillizer

soppy corny (*Sl.*), daft (*Inf.*), drippy (*Inf.*), gushy (*Inf.*), lovey-dovey, mawkish, overemotional, schmaltzy (*Sl.*), sentimental, silly, slushy (*Inf.*), soft (*Inf.*), weepy (*Inf.*)

sorcerer enchanter, mage (*Archaic*), magician, magus, necromancer, sorceress, warlock, witch, wizard

sorcery black art, black magic, charm, divination, enchantment, incantation, magic, necromancy, spell, witchcraft, witchery, wizardry

sordid 1. dirty, filthy, foul, mean, seamy, seedy, sleazy, slovenly, slummy, squalid, unclean, wretched 2. backstreet, base, debauched, degenerate, degraded, despicable, disreputable, low, shabby, shameful, vicious, vile 3. avaricious, corrupt, covetous, grasping, mercenary, miserly, niggardly, selfish, self-seeking, ungenerous, venal
Antonyms blameless, clean, decent, fresh, honourable, noble, pure, spotless, squeaky-clean, unblemished, undefiled, unsullied, upright

sore *adj.* 1. angry, burning, chafed, inflamed, irritated, painful, raw, reddened, sensitive, smarting, tender 2. annoying, distressing, grievous, harrowing, severe, sharp, troublesome 3. acute, critical, desperate, dire, extreme, pressing, urgent 4. afflicted, aggrieved, angry, annoyed, cross, grieved, hurt, irked, irritated, pained, peeved (*Inf.*), resentful, stung, upset, vexed ~*n.* 5. abscess, boil, chafe, gathering, inflammation, ulcer

sorrow *n.* 1. affliction, anguish, distress, grief, heartache, heartbreak, misery, mourning, regret, sadness, unhappiness, woe 2. affliction, blow, bummer (*Sl.*), hardship, misfortune, trial, tribulation, trouble, woe, worry ~*v.* 3. agonize, bemoan, be sad, bewail, eat one's heart out, grieve, lament, moan, mourn, weep
Antonyms *n.* bliss, delight, elation, exaltation, exultation, gladness, good fortune, happiness, joy, lucky break, pleasure ~*v.* celebrate, delight, exult, jump for joy, rejoice, revel

sorrowful affecting, afflicted, dejected, depressed, disconsolate, dismal, distressing, doleful, grievous, harrowing, heartbroken, heart-rending, heavy-hearted, lamentable, lugubrious, melancholy, miserable, mournful, painful, piteous, rueful, sad, sick at heart, sorry, tearful, unhappy, woebegone, woeful, wretched

sorry 1. apologetic, conscience-stricken, contrite, guilt-ridden, in sackcloth and ashes, penitent, regretful, remorseful, repentant, self-reproachful, shamefaced 2. disconsolate, distressed, grieved, melancholy, mournful, sad, sorrowful, unhappy 3. commiserative, compassionate, full of pity, moved, pitying, sympathetic 4. abject, base, deplorable, dismal, distressing, mean, miserable, paltry, pathetic, piteous, pitiable, pitiful, poor, sad, shabby, vile, wretched
Antonyms (*sense 1*) impenitent, not contrite, shameless, unapologetic, unashamed, unremorseful, unrepentant (*sense 2*) cheerful, delighted, elated, happy, joyful (*sense 3*) compassionless (*Rare*), heartless, indifferent, uncompassionate, unconcerned, unmoved, unpitying, unsympathetic

sort *n.* 1. brand, breed, category, character, class, denomination, description, family, genus, group, ilk, kind, make, nature, order, quality, race, species, stamp, style, type, variety 2. **out of sorts** crotchety, down in the dumps (*Inf.*), down in the mouth (*Inf.*), grouchy (*Inf.*), in low spirits, mopy, not up to par, not up to snuff (*Inf.*), off colour, poorly (*Inf.*), under the weather (*Inf.*) 3. **sort of** as it were, in part, moderately, rather, reasonably, slightly, somewhat, to some extent ~*v.* 4. arrange, assort, catalogue, categorize, choose, class, classify, distribute, divide, file, grade, group, order, put in order, rank, select, separate, systematize, tabulate

sort out 1. clarify, clear up, organize, put *or* get straight, resolve, tidy up 2. pick out, put on one side, segregate, select, separate, sift

so-so *adj.* adequate, average, fair, fair to middling (*Inf.*), indifferent, middling, moderate, not bad (*Inf.*), O.K. *or* okay (*Inf.*), ordinary, passable, respectable, run-of-the-mill, tolerable, undistinguished

soul 1. animating principle, essence, intellect, life, mind, psyche, reason, spirit, vital force 2. being, body, creature, individual, man, mortal, person, woman 3. embodiment, epitome, essence, incarnation, personification, quintessence, type 4. animation, ardour, courage, energy, feeling, fervour, force, inspiration, nobility, vitality, vivacity

soulful eloquent, expressive, heartfelt, meaningful, mournful, moving, profound, sensitive

soulless 1. callous, cold, cruel, harsh, inhuman, unfeeling, unkind, unsympathetic 2. dead, lifeless, mechanical, soul-destroying, spiritless, uninteresting

sound[1] *n.* 1. din, noise, report, resonance, reverberation, tone, voice 2. drift, idea, implication(s), impression, look, tenor 3. earshot, hearing, range ~*v.* 4. echo, resonate, resound, reverberate 5. appear, give the impression of, look, seem, strike one as being 6. announce, articulate, declare, enunciate, express, pronounce, signal, utter

sound[2] *adj.* 1. complete, entire, firm, fit, hale, hale and hearty, healthy, intact, perfect, robust, solid, sturdy, substantial, undamaged, unhurt, unimpaired, uninjured, vigorous, well-constructed, whole 2. correct, fair, just, level-headed, logical, orthodox, proper, prudent, rational, reasonable, reli-

able, responsible, right, right-thinking, sensible, true, trustworthy, valid, well-founded, well-grounded, wise 3. established, orthodox, proven, recognized, reliable, reputable, safe, secure, solid, solvent, stable, tried-and-true 4. deep, peaceful, unbroken, undisturbed, untroubled
Antonyms (*sense 1*) ailing, damaged, flimsy, frail, light, shaky, sketchy, superficial, unbalanced, unstable, weak (*senses 2 & 3*) fallacious, faulty, flawed, incompetent, irrational, irresponsible, specious, unreliable, unsound, unstable (*sense 4*) broken, fitful, shallow, troubled

sound[3] *v.* 1. fathom, plumb, probe 2. examine, inspect, investigate, test

sound[4] *n.* 1. channel, passage, strait 2. arm of the sea, fjord, inlet, voe

sound out canvass, examine, probe, pump, question, see how the land lies

sour *adj.* 1. acerb, acetic, acid, acidulated, bitter, pungent, sharp, tart, unpleasant 2. bad, curdled, fermented, gone off, rancid, turned, unsavoury, unwholesome 3. acrid, acrimonious, churlish, crabbed, cynical, disagreeable, discontented, embittered, grouchy (*Inf.*), grudging, ill-natured, ill-tempered, jaundiced, peevish, tart, ungenerous, waspish ~*v.* 4. alienate, disenchant, embitter, envenom, exacerbate, exasperate, turn off (*Inf.*)
Antonyms *adj.* (*sense 1*) agreeable, bland, mild, pleasant, savoury, sugary, sweet (*sense 2*) fresh, unimpaired, unspoiled (*sense 3*) affable, amiable, congenial, friendly, genial, good-humoured, good-natured, good-tempered, pleasant, warm-hearted ~*v.* enhance, improve, strengthen

source 1. author, begetter, beginning, cause, commencement, derivation, fount, fountainhead, origin, originator, rise, spring, wellspring 2. authority, informant

sourpuss crosspatch (*Inf.*), grouser, grump (*Inf.*), killjoy, misery (*Brit. inf.*), shrew

souse drench, dunk, immerse, marinate (*Cookery*), pickle, soak, steep

souvenir keepsake, memento, relic, remembrancer (*Archaic*), reminder, token

sovereign *n.* 1. chief, emperor, empress, king, monarch, potentate, prince, queen, ruler, shah, supreme ruler, tsar ~*adj.* 2. absolute, chief, dominant, imperial, kingly, monarchal, paramount, predominant, principal, queenly, regal, royal, ruling, supreme, unlimited 3. effectual, efficacious, efficient, excellent

sovereignty ascendancy, domination, kingship, primacy, supremacy, supreme power, suzerainty, sway

sow broadcast, disseminate, implant, inseminate, lodge, plant, scatter, seed

space 1. amplitude, capacity, elbowroom, expanse, extension, extent, leeway, margin, play, room, scope, spaciousness, volume 2. blank, distance, gap, interval, lacuna, omission 3. duration, interval, period, span, time, while 4. accommodation, berth, place, seat

spaceman *or* **spacewoman** astronaut, cosmonaut

spacious ample, broad, capacious, comfortable, commodious, expansive, extensive, huge, large, roomy, sizable, uncrowded, vast
Antonyms close, confined, cramped, crowded, limited, narrow, poky, restricted, small

spadework donkey-work, groundwork, labour, preparation

span *n.* 1. amount, distance, extent, length, reach, spread, stretch 2. duration, period, spell, term ~*v.* 3. arch across, bridge, cover, cross, extend across, link, range over, traverse, vault

spank *v.* belt (*Inf.*), cuff, give (someone) a hiding (*Inf.*), put (someone) over one's knee, slap, slipper (*Inf.*), smack, tan (*Sl.*), wallop (*Inf.*), whack

spanking *adj.* 1. brisk, energetic, fast, invigorating, lively, quick, smart, snappy, vigorous 2. *Inf.* brand-new, fine, gleaming, smart

spar *v.* argue, bicker, dispute, exchange blows, fall out (*Inf.*), have a tiff, lead a cat-and-dog life, row, scrap (*Inf.*), skirmish, spat (*U.S.*), squabble, wrangle, wrestle

spare *adj.* 1. additional, emergency, extra, free, going begging, in excess, in reserve, leftover, odd, over, superfluous, supernumerary, surplus, unoccupied, unused, unwanted 2. gaunt, lank, lean, macilent (*Rare*), meagre, slender, slight, slim, wiry 3. economical, frugal, meagre, modest, scanty, sparing 4. **go spare** *Brit. sl.* become angry (distracted, distraught, enraged, mad, (*Inf.*), upset), blow one's top (*Inf.*), do one's nut (*Brit. sl.*), go mental (*Sl.*), go up the wall (*Sl.*), have *or* throw a fit (*Inf.*) ~*v.* 5. afford, allow, bestow, dispense with, do without, give, grant, let (someone) have, manage without, part with, relinquish 6. be merciful to, deal leniently with, go easy on (*Inf.*), have mercy on, leave, let off (*Inf.*), pardon, refrain from, release, relieve from, save from
Antonyms *adj.* (*sense 1*) allocated, designated, earmarked, in use, necessary, needed, set aside, spoken for (*sense 2*) corpulent, fat, flabby, fleshy, generous, heavy,

large, plump ~*v.* (*sense 6*) afflict, condemn, damn, destroy, hurt, punish, show no mercy to

spare time free time, leisure, odd moments, time on one's hands, time to kill

sparing careful, chary, cost-conscious, economical, frugal, money-conscious, prudent, saving, thrifty
Antonyms extravagant, lavish, liberal, open-handed, prodigal, spendthrift

spark *n.* 1. flare, flash, flicker, gleam, glint, scintillation, spit 2. atom, hint, jot, scintilla, scrap, trace, vestige ~*v.* 3. *Often with* **off** animate, excite, inspire, kick-start, kindle, precipitate, prod, provoke, rouse, set in motion, set off, start, stimulate, stir, touch off, trigger (off)

sparkle *v.* 1. beam, coruscate, dance, flash, gleam, glint, glisten, glister (*Archaic*), glitter, glow, scintillate, shimmer, shine, spark, twinkle, wink 2. bubble, effervesce, fizz, fizzle ~*n.* 3. brilliance, coruscation, dazzle, flash, flicker, gleam, glint, radiance, spark, twinkle 4. animation, brio, dash, élan, gaiety, life, panache, spirit, vim (*Sl.*), vitality, vivacity, zip (*Inf.*)

sparse few and far between, meagre, scanty, scarce, scattered, sporadic
Antonyms crowded, dense, lavish, lush, luxuriant, numerous, plentiful, thick

spartan 1. abstemious, ascetic, austere, bleak, disciplined, extreme, frugal, plain, rigorous, self-denying, severe, stern, strict, stringent 2. bold, brave, courageous, daring, dauntless, doughty, fearless, hardy, heroic, intrepid, resolute, unflinching, valorous

spasm 1. contraction, convulsion, paroxysm, throe (*Rare*), twitch 2. access, burst, eruption, fit, frenzy, outburst, seizure

spasmodic convulsive, erratic, fitful, intermittent, irregular, jerky, sporadic

spate deluge, flood, flow, outpouring, rush, torrent

spatter bespatter, bestrew, daub, dirty, scatter, soil, speckle, splash, splodge, spray, sprinkle

speak 1. articulate, communicate, converse, discourse, enunciate, express, make known, pronounce, say, state, talk, tell, utter, voice 2. address, argue, declaim, deliver an address, descant, discourse, harangue, hold forth, lecture, plead, speechify, spiel (*Inf.*), spout 3. *With* **of** advert to, allude to, comment on, deal with, discuss, make reference to, mention, refer to

speaker lecturer, mouthpiece, orator, public speaker, spieler (*Inf.*), spokesman, spokesperson, spokeswoman, word-spinner

speak for act for *or* on behalf of, appear for, hold a brief for, hold a mandate for, represent

speaking *adj.* eloquent, expressive, moving, noticeable, striking

speak out *or* **up** 1. make oneself heard, say it loud and clear, speak loudly 2. have one's say, make one's position plain, sound off, speak one's mind, stand up and be counted

speak to 1. accost, address, apostrophize, direct one's words at, talk to 2. admonish, bring to book, dress down (*Inf.*), lecture, rebuke, reprimand, scold, tell off (*Inf.*), tick off (*Inf.*), warn

spearhead *v.* be in the van, blaze the trail, head, initiate, launch, lay the first stone, lead, lead the way, pioneer, set in motion, set off

special 1. distinguished, especial, exceptional, extraordinary, festive, gala, important, memorable, momentous, out of the ordinary, red-letter, significant, uncommon, unique, unusual 2. appropriate, certain, characteristic, distinctive, especial, individual, particular, peculiar, precise, specialized, specific 3. chief, main, major, particular, primary
Antonyms common, everyday, general, humdrum, mediocre, multi-purpose, normal, ordinary, routine, run-of-the-mill, undistinctive, undistinguished, unexceptional, unspecialized, usual

specialist *n.* authority, buff (*Inf.*), connoisseur, consultant, expert, hotshot (*Inf.*), master, maven (*U.S.*), professional, whiz (*Inf.*)

speciality bag, claim to fame, distinctive *or* distinguishing feature, forte, métier, *pièce de résistance,* special, specialty

species breed, category, class, collection, description, genus, group, kind, sort, type, variety

specific *adj.* 1. clear-cut, definite, exact, explicit, express, limited, particular, precise, unambiguous, unequivocal 2. characteristic, distinguishing, especial, peculiar, special
Antonyms approximate, common, general, hazy, imprecise, non-specific, uncertain, unclear, vague, woolly

specification condition, detail, item, particular, qualification, requirement, stipulation

specify be specific about, cite, define, designate, detail, enumerate, indicate, individualize, itemize, mention, name, particularize, spell out, stipulate

specimen copy, embodiment, example, exemplar, exemplification, exhibit, individual, instance, model, pattern, proof, representative, sample, type

specious casuistic, deceptive, fallacious, misleading, plausible, sophistic, sophistical, unsound

speck 1. blemish, blot, defect, dot, fault, flaw, fleck, mark, mote, speckle, spot, stain 2. atom, bit, dot, grain, iota, jot, mite, modicum, particle, shred, tittle, whit

speckled brindled, dappled, dotted, flecked, freckled, mottled, speckledy, spotted, spotty, sprinkled, stippled

spectacle 1. display, event, exhibition, extravaganza, pageant, parade, performance, show, sight 2. curiosity, laughing stock, marvel, phenomenon, scene, sight, wonder

spectacular 1. *adj.* breathtaking, daring, dazzling, dramatic, eye-catching, fantastic (*Inf.*), grand, impressive, magnificent, marked, remarkable, sensational, splendid, staggering, striking, stunning (*Inf.*) 2. *n.* display, extravaganza, show, spectacle
Antonyms *adj.* easy, everyday, modest, ordinary, plain, run-of-the-mill, simple, unimpressive, unostentatious, unspectacular

spectator beholder, bystander, eyewitness, looker-on, observer, onlooker, viewer, watcher, witness
Antonyms contestant, contributor, partaker, participant, participator, party, player

spectral eerie, ghostly, incorporeal, insubstantial, phantom, shadowy, spooky (*Inf.*), supernatural, uncanny, unearthly, weird, wraithlike

spectre apparition, eidolon, ghost, phantom, presence, shade (*Literary*), shadow, spirit, vision, wraith

speculate 1. cogitate, conjecture, consider, contemplate, deliberate, hypothesize, meditate, muse, scheme, suppose, surmise, theorize, wonder 2. gamble, have a flutter (*Inf.*), hazard, play the market, risk, take a chance with, venture

speculation 1. conjecture, consideration, contemplation, deliberation, guess, guesswork, hypothesis, opinion, supposition, surmise, theory 2. gamble, gambling, hazard, risk

speculative 1. abstract, academic, conjectural, hypothetical, notional, suppositional, tentative, theoretical 2. chancy (*Inf.*), dicey (*Inf., chiefly Brit.*), hazardous, risky, uncertain, unpredictable

speech 1. communication, conversation, dialogue, discussion, intercourse, talk 2. address, discourse, disquisition, harangue, homily, lecture, oration, spiel (*Inf.*) 3. articulation, dialect, diction, enunciation, idiom, jargon, language, lingo (*Inf.*), parlance, tongue, utterance, voice

speechless 1. dumb, inarticulate, mum, mute, silent, tongue-tied, unable to get a word out (*Inf.*), wordless 2. *Fig.* aghast, amazed, astounded, dazed, dumbfounded, dumbstruck, shocked, thunderstruck

speed *n.* 1. acceleration, celerity, expedition, fleetness, haste, hurry, momentum, pace, precipitation, quickness, rapidity, rush, swiftness, velocity ~*v.* 2. barrel (along) (*Inf., chiefly U.S. & Canad.*), belt (along) (*Sl.*), bomb (along), bowl along, burn rubber (*Inf.*), career, dispatch, exceed the speed limit, expedite, flash, gallop, get a move on (*Inf.*), go hell for leather (*Inf.*), go like a bat out of hell (*Sl.*), go like the wind, hasten, hurry, lose no time, make haste, press on, put one's foot down (*Inf.*), quicken, race, rush, sprint, step on it (*Inf.*), tear, urge, zoom 3. advance, aid, assist, boost, expedite, facilitate, further, help, impel, promote
Antonyms *n.* delay, slowness, sluggishness, tardiness ~*v.* crawl, creep, dawdle, delay, hamper, hinder, hold up, retard, slow, take one's time, tarry

speed up accelerate, gather momentum, get moving, get under way, increase, increase the tempo, open up the throttle, put one's foot down (*Inf.*), put on speed
Antonyms brake, decelerate, reduce speed, rein in, slacken (off), slow down

speedy expeditious, express, fast, fleet, fleet of foot, hasty, headlong, hurried, immediate, nimble, pdq (*Sl.*), precipitate, prompt, quick, quickie (*Inf.*), rapid, summary, swift, winged
Antonyms dead slow and stop, delayed, dilatory, late, leisurely, lingering, long-drawn-out, plodding, slow, sluggish, tardy, unhurried, unrushed

spell[1] *n.* bout, course, interval, patch, period, season, stint, stretch, term, time, tour of duty, turn

spell[2] *n.* 1. abracadabra, charm, conjuration, exorcism, incantation, sorcery, witchery 2. allure, bewitchment, enchantment, fascination, glamour, magic, trance

spell[3] *v.* amount to, augur, herald, imply, indicate, mean, point to, portend, presage, promise, signify, suggest

spellbound bemused, bewitched, captivated, charmed, enthralled, entranced, fascinated, gripped, hooked, mesmerized, possessed, rapt, transfixed, transported, under a spell

spelling orthography

spell out 1. clarify, elucidate, explicate, make clear *or* plain, make explicit, specify 2. discern, make out, puzzle out

spend 1. disburse, expend, fork out (*Sl.*),

lay out, pay out, shell out (*Inf.*), splash out (*Brit. inf.*) 2. blow (*Sl.*), consume, deplete, dispense, dissipate, drain, empty, exhaust, fritter away, run through, squander, use up, waste 3. apply, bestow, concentrate, devote, employ, exert, invest, lavish, put in, use 4. fill, occupy, pass, while away

Antonyms (*senses 1 & 2*) hoard, invest, keep, put aside, put by, save, store

spendthrift 1. *n.* big spender, prodigal, profligate, spender, squanderer, waster, wastrel 2. *adj.* extravagant, improvident, prodigal, profligate, wasteful

Antonyms *n.* meanie *or* meany (*Inf., chiefly Brit.*), miser, penny-pincher (*Inf.*), Scrooge, skinflint, tight-arse (*Taboo sl.*), tight-ass (*U.S. taboo sl.*), tightwad (*U.S. & Canad. sl.*) ~*adj.* careful, economical, frugal, parsimonious, provident, prudent, sparing, thrifty

spent *adj.* 1. all in (*Sl.*), burnt out, bushed (*Inf.*), clapped out (*Aust. & N.Z. inf.*), dead beat (*Inf.*), debilitated, dog-tired (*Inf.*), done in *or* up (*Inf.*), drained, exhausted, fagged (out) (*Inf.*), knackered (*Sl.*), played out (*Inf.*), prostrate, ready to drop (*Inf.*), shattered (*Inf.*), tired out, weakened, wearied, weary, whacked (*Brit. inf.*), worn out, zonked (*Inf.*) 2. consumed, expended, finished, gone, used up

spew barf (*U.S. sl.*), belch forth, chuck (up) (*Sl., chiefly U.S.*), chunder (*Sl., chiefly Aust.*), disgorge, do a technicolour yawn (*Sl.*), puke (*Sl.*), regurgitate, spit out, throw up (*Inf.*), toss one's cookies (*U.S. sl.*), upchuck (*U.S. sl.*), vomit

sphere 1. ball, circle, globe, globule, orb 2. capacity, compass, department, domain, employment, field, function, pale, patch, province, range, rank, realm, scope, station, stratum, territory, turf (*U.S. sl.*), walk of life

spherical globe-shaped, globular, orbicular, rotund, round

spice *n.* 1. relish, savour, seasoning 2. colour, excitement, gusto, kick (*Inf.*), pep, piquancy, tang, zap (*Sl.*), zest, zip (*Inf.*)

spick-and-span clean, fresh as paint, immaculate, impeccable, in apple-pie order (*Inf.*), neat as a new pin, shipshape, spotless, spruce, tidy, trim

spicy 1. aromatic, flavoursome, hot, piquant, pungent, savoury, seasoned, tangy 2. *Inf.* broad, hot (*Inf.*), improper, indecorous, indelicate, off-colour, racy, ribald, risqué, scandalous, sensational, suggestive, titillating, unseemly

spiel 1. *v.* expatiate on, hold forth, lecture, recite, speechify, spout (*Inf.*) 2. *n.* harangue, patter, pitch, recital, sales patter, sales talk, speech

spike *n.* 1. barb, point, prong, spine ~*v.* 2. impale, spear, spit, stick 3. block, foil, frustrate, render ineffective, thwart

spill *v.* 1. discharge, disgorge, overflow, overturn, scatter, shed, slop over, spill *or* run over, throw off, upset 2. **spill the beans** *Inf.* betray a secret, blab, blow the gaff (*Brit. sl.*), give the game away, grass (*Brit. sl.*), inform, let the cat out of the bag, shop (*Sl., chiefly Brit.*), sing (*Sl., chiefly U.S.*), spill one's guts (*Sl.*), split (*Sl.*), squeal (*Sl.*), talk out of turn, tattle, tell all ~*n.* 3. *Inf.* accident, cropper (*Inf.*), fall, tumble

spin *v.* 1. birl (*Scot.*), gyrate, pirouette, reel, revolve, rotate, turn, twirl, twist, wheel, whirl 2. concoct, develop, invent, narrate, recount, relate, tell, unfold 3. be giddy, be in a whirl, grow dizzy, reel, swim, whirl ~*n.* 4. gyration, revolution, roll, twist, whirl 5. **(flat) spin** *Inf.* agitation, commotion, flap (*Inf.*), panic, state (*Inf.*), tiz-woz (*Inf.*), tizzy (*Inf.*) 6. *Inf.* drive, hurl (*Scot.*), joy ride (*Inf.*), ride, turn, whirl

spindly attenuated, gangling, gangly, lanky, leggy, spidery, spindle-shanked, twiggy

spine 1. backbone, spinal column, vertebrae, vertebral column 2. barb, needle, quill, rachis, ray, spike, spur

spine-chilling bloodcurdling, eerie, frightening, hair-raising, horrifying, scary (*Inf.*), spooky (*Inf.*), terrifying

spineless chickenshit (*U.S. sl.*), cowardly, faint-hearted, feeble, gutless (*Inf.*), inadequate, ineffective, irresolute, lily-livered, soft, spiritless, squeamish, submissive, vacillating, weak, weak-kneed (*Inf.*), weak-willed, without a will of one's own, yellow (*Inf.*)

Antonyms ballsy (*Taboo sl.*), bold, brave, courageous, gritty, strong, strong-willed

spin out amplify, delay, drag out, draw out, extend, lengthen, pad out, prolong, prolongate, protract

spiral 1. *adj.* circular, cochlear, cochleate (*Biol.*), coiled, corkscrew, helical, scrolled, voluted, whorled, winding 2. *n.* coil, corkscrew, curlicue, gyre (*Literary*), helix, screw, volute, whorl

spirit *n.* 1. air, breath, life, life force, psyche, soul, vital spark 2. attitude, character, complexion, disposition, essence, humour, outlook, quality, temper, temperament 3. animation, ardour, backbone, balls (*Taboo sl.*), ballsiness (*Taboo sl.*), brio, courage, dauntlessness, earnestness, energy, enterprise, enthusiasm, fire, force, gameness, grit, guts (*Inf.*), life, liveliness, mettle, resolution, sparkle, spunk (*Inf.*), stout~

heartedness, vigour, warmth, zest 4. motivation, resolution, resolve, will, willpower 5. atmosphere, feeling, gist, humour, tenor, tone 6. essence, intent, intention, meaning, purport, purpose, sense, substance 7. *Plural* feelings, frame of mind, humour, mood, morale 8. apparition, eidolon, ghost, phantom, shade (*Literary*), shadow, spectre, spook (*Inf.*), sprite, vision ~*v.* 9. *With* **away** *or* **off** abduct, abstract, carry, convey, make away with, purloin, remove, seize, snaffle (*Brit. inf.*), steal, whisk

spirited active, animated, ardent, bold, courageous, energetic, feisty (*Inf., chiefly U.S. & Canad.*), game, have-a-go (*Inf.*), high-spirited, lively, mettlesome, plucky, sparkling, sprightly, spunky (*Inf.*), vigorous, vivacious
Antonyms apathetic, bland, calm, dispirited, dull, feeble, half-hearted, lacklustre, lifeless, low-key, spiritless, timid, token, unenthusiastic, weary

spiritless apathetic, dejected, depressed, despondent, dispirited, droopy, dull, lacklustre, languid, lifeless, listless, low (*Inf.*), melancholic, melancholy, mopy, torpid, unenthusiastic, unmoved

spirits alcohol, firewater, liquor, strong liquor, the hard stuff (*Inf.*)

spiritual devotional, divine, ethereal, ghostly, holy, immaterial, incorporeal, nonmaterial, otherworldly, pure, religious, sacred
Antonyms concrete, corporeal, material, nonspiritual, palpable, physical, substantial, tangible

spit 1. *v.* discharge, eject, expectorate, hiss, spew, splutter, sputter, throw out 2. *n.* dribble, drool, saliva, slaver, spittle, sputum

spite *n.* 1. animosity, bitchiness (*Sl.*), gall, grudge, hate, hatred, ill will, malevolence, malice, malignity, pique, rancour, spitefulness, spleen, venom 2. **in spite of** despite, (even) though, in defiance of, notwithstanding, regardless of ~*v.* 3. annoy, discomfit, gall, harm, hurt, injure, needle (*Inf.*), nettle, offend, pique, provoke, put out, put (someone's) nose out of joint (*Inf.*), vex
Antonyms *n.* benevolence, big-heartedness, charity, compassion, generosity of spirit, goodwill, kindliness, kindness, love, warm-heartedness ~*v.* aid, benefit, encourage, go along with, help, please, serve, support

spiteful barbed, bitchy (*Inf.*), catty (*Inf.*), cruel, ill-disposed, ill-natured, malevolent, malicious, malignant, nasty, rancorous, shrewish, snide, splenetic, venomous, vindictive

spitting image clone, (dead) ringer (*Sl.*), double, likeness, living image, lookalike, picture, replica, spit (*Inf., chiefly Brit.*), spit and image (*Inf.*)

splash *v.* 1. bespatter, shower, slop, slosh (*Inf.*), spatter, splodge, spray, spread, sprinkle, squirt, strew, wet 2. bathe, dabble, paddle, plunge, wade, wallow 3. batter, break, buffet, dash, plash, plop, smack, strike, surge, wash 4. blazon, broadcast, flaunt, headline, plaster, publicize, tout, trumpet ~*n.* 5. burst, dash, patch, spattering, splodge, touch 6. *Inf.* display, effect, impact, sensation, splurge, stir 7. **make a splash** be ostentatious, cause a stir, cut a dash, go overboard (*Inf.*), go to town, splurge

splash out be extravagant, lash out (*Inf.*), push the boat out (*Brit. inf.*), spare no expense, spend, splurge

spleen acrimony, anger, animosity, animus, bad temper, bile, bitterness, gall, hatred, hostility, ill humour, ill will, malevolence, malice, malignity, peevishness, pique, rancour, resentment, spite, spitefulness, venom, vindictiveness, wrath

splendid 1. admirable, brilliant, exceptional, glorious, grand, heroic, illustrious, magnificent, outstanding, rare, remarkable, renowned, sterling, sublime, superb, supreme 2. costly, dazzling, gorgeous, imposing, impressive, lavish, luxurious, magnificent, ornate, resplendent, rich, splendiferous (*Facetious*), sumptuous, superb 3. boffo (*Sl.*), brill (*Inf.*), chillin' (*U.S. sl.*), cracking (*Brit. inf.*), crucial (*Sl.*), def (*Sl.*), excellent, fantastic (*Inf.*), fine, first-class, glorious, great (*Inf.*), marvellous, mean (*Sl.*), mega (*Sl.*), sovereign, topping (*Brit. sl.*), wonderful 4. beaming, bright, brilliant, glittering, glowing, lustrous, radiant, refulgent
Antonyms beggarly, depressing, disgusting, distressed, drab, dull, ignoble, ignominious, lacklustre, low, mean, mediocre, miserable, ordinary, pathetic, plain, poor, poverty-stricken, rotten, run-of-the-mill, sombre, sordid, squalid, tarnished, tawdry, undistinguished, unexceptional

splendour brightness, brilliance, ceremony, dazzle, display, éclat, effulgence, glory, gorgeousness, grandeur, lustre, magnificence, majesty, pomp, radiance, refulgence, renown, resplendence, richness, show, solemnity, spectacle, stateliness, sumptuousness
Antonyms dullness, ignominy, lacklustreness, meanness, ordinariness, plain-

ness, poverty, simplicity, sobriety, squalor, tawdriness

splenetic acid, bitchy (*Inf.*), choleric, churlish, crabbed, crabby, cross, envenomed, fretful, irascible, irritable, morose, peevish, petulant, rancorous, ratty (*Brit. & N.Z. inf.*), sour, spiteful, sullen, testy, tetchy, touchy

splice *v.* braid, entwine, graft, interlace, intertwine, intertwist, interweave, join, knit, marry, mesh, plait, unite, wed, yoke

splinter 1. *n.* chip, flake, fragment, needle, paring, shaving, sliver 2. *v.* break into smithereens, disintegrate, fracture, shatter, shiver, split

split *v.* 1. bifurcate, branch, break, break up, burst, cleave, come apart, come undone, crack, disband, disunite, diverge, fork, gape, give way, go separate ways, open, part, pull apart, rend, rip, separate, slash, slit, snap, splinter 2. allocate, allot, apportion, carve up, distribute, divide, divvy up (*Inf.*), dole out, halve, parcel out, partition, share out, slice up 3. *With* **on** *Sl.* betray, give away, grass (*Brit. sl.*), inform on, peach (*Sl.*), shop (*Sl., chiefly Brit.*), sing (*Sl., chiefly U.S.*), spill one's guts (*Sl.*), squeal (*Sl.*) ~*n.* 4. breach, crack, damage, division, fissure, gap, rent, rip, separation, slash, slit, tear 5. breach, break, break-up, difference, discord, disruption, dissension, disunion, divergence, division, estrangement, partition, rift, rupture, schism ~*adj.* 6. ambivalent, bisected, broken, cleft, cracked, divided, dual, fractured, ruptured, twofold

split up break up, disband, divorce, go separate ways, part, part company, separate

spoil *v.* 1. blemish, blow (*Sl.*), damage, debase, deface, destroy, disfigure, harm, impair, injure, mar, mess up, ruin, scar, total (*Sl.*), trash (*Sl.*), undo, upset, wreck 2. baby, cocker (*Rare*), coddle, cosset, indulge, kill with kindness, mollycoddle, overindulge, pamper, spoon-feed 3. addle, become tainted, curdle, decay, decompose, go bad, go off (*Brit. inf.*), mildew, putrefy, rot, turn 4. **spoiling for** bent upon, desirous of, eager for, enthusiastic about, keen to, looking for, out to get (*Inf.*), raring to

Antonyms (*sense 1*) augment, conserve, enhance, improve, keep, preserve, save (*sense 2*) be strict with, deprive, ignore, pay no attention to, treat harshly

spoils boodle (*Sl., chiefly U.S.*), booty, gain, loot, pickings, pillage, plunder, prey, prizes, rapine, swag (*Sl.*)

spoilsport damper, dog in the manger, kill-joy, misery (*Brit. inf.*), party-pooper (*U.S. sl.*), wet blanket (*Inf.*)

spoken expressed, oral, phonetic, put into words, said, told, unwritten, uttered, verbal, viva voce, voiced, by word of mouth

sponger bloodsucker (*Inf.*), cadge (*Brit.*), cadger, freeloader (*Sl.*), hanger-on, leech, parasite, scrounger (*Inf.*)

spongy absorbent, cushioned, cushiony, elastic, light, porous, springy

sponsor 1. *n.* angel (*Inf.*), backer, godparent, guarantor, patron, promoter 2. *v.* back, finance, fund, guarantee, lend one's name to, patronize, promote, put up the money for, subsidize

spontaneous extempore, free, impromptu, impulsive, instinctive, natural, unbidden, uncompelled, unconstrained, unforced, unpremeditated, unprompted, voluntary, willing

Antonyms arranged, calculated, contrived, deliberate, forced, mannered, orchestrated, planned, prearranged, premeditated, preplanned, stage-managed, studied

spontaneously extempore, freely, impromptu, impulsively, instinctively, off one's own bat, off the cuff (*Inf.*), of one's own accord, on impulse, quite unprompted, voluntarily

spoof *n.* 1. burlesque, caricature, lampoon, mockery, parody, satire, send-up (*Brit. inf.*), take-off (*Inf.*), travesty 2. bluff, canard, deception, game, hoax, joke, leg-pull (*Brit. inf.*), prank, trick

spooky chilling, creepy (*Inf.*), eerie, frightening, ghostly, mysterious, scary (*Inf.*), spine-chilling, supernatural, uncanny, unearthly, weird

spoon-feed baby, cosset, featherbed, mollycoddle, overindulge, overprotect, spoil, wrap up in cotton wool (*Inf.*)

sporadic infrequent, intermittent, irregular, isolated, occasional, on and off, random, scattered, spasmodic

Antonyms consistent, frequent, recurrent, regular, set, steady, systematic

sport *n.* 1. amusement, diversion, entertainment, exercise, game, pastime, physical activity, play, recreation 2. badinage, banter, frolic, fun, jest, joking, josh (*Sl., chiefly U.S. & Canad.*), kidding (*Inf.*), merriment, mirth, raillery, teasing 3. buffoon, butt, derision, fair game, game, laughing stock, mockery, plaything, ridicule ~*v.* 4. *With* **with** amuse oneself, dally, flirt, fool, play, take advantage of, toy, treat lightly *or* cavalierly, trifle 5. *Inf.* display, exhibit, show off, wear 6. caper, disport, frolic, gambol, play, romp

sporting fair, game (*Inf.*), gentlemanly, sportsman-like

Antonyms unfair, unsporting, unsportsmanlike

sportive coltish, frisky, frolicsome, full of beans (*Inf.*), full of fun, gamesome, gay, joyous, kittenish, lively, merry, playful, prankish, rollicking, skittish, sprightly

sporty 1. casual, flashy, gay, informal, jaunty, jazzy (*Inf.*), loud, raffish, rakish, showy, snazzy (*Inf.*), stylish, trendy (*Brit. inf.*) 2. athletic, energetic, hearty, outdoor

spot *n.* 1. blemish, blot, blotch, daub, discoloration, flaw, mark, pimple, plook (*Scot.*), pustule, scar, smudge, speck, speckle, stain, taint, zit (*Sl.*) 2. locality, location, place, point, position, scene, site, situation 3. *Inf.* bit, little, morsel, splash 4. *Inf.* difficulty, hot water (*Inf.*), mess, plight, predicament, quandary, tight spot, trouble ~*v.* 5. catch sight of, descry, detect, discern, espy, identify, make out, observe, pick out, recognize, see, sight 6. besmirch, blot, dirty, dot, fleck, mark, mottle, scar, smirch, soil, spatter, speckle, splodge, splotch, stain, sully, taint, tarnish

spotless above reproach, blameless, chaste, clean, faultless, flawless, gleaming, immaculate, impeccable, innocent, irreproachable, pure, shining, snowy, unblemished, unimpeachable, unstained, unsullied, untarnished, virgin, virginal, white
Antonyms besmirched, bespattered, blemished, defiled, dirty, filthy, flawed, impure, messy, notorious, reprehensible, soiled, spotted, stained, sullied, tainted, tarnished, unchaste, untidy

spotlight *Fig.* 1. *v.* accentuate, draw attention to, feature, focus attention on, give prominence to, highlight, illuminate, point up, throw into relief 2. *n.* attention, fame, interest, limelight, notoriety, public attention, public eye

spot-on accurate, correct, exact, hitting the nail on the head (*Inf.*), on the bull's-eye (*Inf.*), precise, punctual (to the minute), right, unerring

spotted dappled, dotted, flecked, mottled, pied, polka-dot, specked, speckled

spotty 1. blotchy, pimpled, pimply, plooky-faced (*Scot.*), poor-complexioned 2. erratic, fluctuating, irregular, patchy, sporadic, uneven

spouse better half (*Humorous*), companion, consort, helpmate, her indoors (*Brit. sl.*), husband, mate, partner, significant other (*U.S. inf.*), wife

spout *v.* 1. discharge, emit, erupt, gush, jet, shoot, spray, spurt, squirt, stream, surge 2. *Inf.* declaim, expatiate, go on (*Inf.*), hold forth, orate, pontificate, rabbit (on) (*Brit. inf.*), ramble (on), rant, speechify, spiel (*Inf.*), talk

sprawl *v.* flop, loll, lounge, ramble, slouch, slump, spread, straggle, trail

spray[1] *v.* 1. atomize, diffuse, scatter, shower, sprinkle ~*n.* 2. drizzle, droplets, fine mist, moisture, spindrift, spoondrift 3. aerosol, atomizer, sprinkler

spray[2] *n.* bough, branch, corsage, floral arrangement, shoot, sprig

spread *v.* 1. be displayed, bloat, broaden, dilate, expand, extend, fan out, open, open out, sprawl, stretch, swell, unfold, unfurl, unroll, widen 2. escalate, multiply, mushroom, proliferate 3. advertise, blazon, broadcast, bruit, cast, circulate, cover, diffuse, disseminate, distribute, make known, make public, proclaim, promulgate, propagate, publicize, publish, radiate, scatter, shed, strew, transmit 4. arrange, array, cover, furnish, lay, prepare, set ~*n.* 5. advance, advancement, development, diffusion, dispersion, dissemination, escalation, expansion, increase, proliferation, spreading, suffusion, transmission 6. compass, extent, period, reach, span, stretch, sweep, term 7. *Inf.* array, banquet, blowout (*Sl.*), feast, repast
Antonyms *v.* (*sense 3*) contain, control, curb, hold back, hold in, repress, restrain, stifle

spree bacchanalia, beano (*Brit. sl.*), bender (*Inf.*), binge (*Inf.*), carousal, carouse, debauch, fling, jag (*Sl.*), junketing, orgy, revel, splurge

sprightly active, agile, airy, alert, animated, blithe, brisk, cheerful, energetic, frolicsome, gay, jaunty, joyous, lively, nimble, perky, playful, spirited, sportive, spry, vivacious
Antonyms dull, inactive, lethargic, sedentary, sluggish, torpid, unenergetic

spring *v.* 1. bounce, bound, hop, jump, leap, rebound, recoil, vault 2. *Often with* **from** arise, be derived, be descended, come, derive, descend, emanate, emerge, grow, issue, originate, proceed, start, stem 3. *With* **up** appear, burgeon, come into existence *or* being, develop, mushroom, shoot up ~*n.* 4. bound, buck, hop, jump, leap, saltation, vault 5. bounce, bounciness, buoyancy, elasticity, flexibility, give (*Inf.*), recoil, resilience, springiness 6. beginning, cause, fount, fountainhead, origin, root, source, well, wellspring ~*adj.* 7. *Of the season* springlike, vernal

springy bouncy, buoyant, elastic, flexible, resilient, rubbery, spongy

sprinkle *v.* dredge, dust, pepper, powder, scatter, shower, spray, strew

sprinkling admixture, dash, dusting, few, handful, scatter, scattering, smattering, sprinkle

sprint *v.* barrel (along) (*Inf., chiefly U.S. & Canad.*), dart, dash, go at top speed, hare (*Brit. inf.*), hotfoot, put on a burst of speed, race, scamper, shoot, tear, whiz (*Inf.*)

sprite apparition, brownie, dryad, elf, fairy, goblin, imp, leprechaun, naiad, nymph, Oceanid (*Greek myth.*), peri, pixie, spirit, sylph

sprout *v.* bud, develop, germinate, grow, push, shoot, spring, vegetate

spruce as if one had just stepped out of a bandbox, dainty, dapper, elegant, natty (*Inf.*), neat, smart, soigné *or* soignée, trig (*Archaic or dialect*), trim, well-groomed, well turned out
Antonyms bedraggled, disarrayed, dishevelled, frowsy, messy, rumpled, uncombed, unkempt, untidy

spruce up groom, have a wash and brush-up (*Brit.*), smarten up, tidy, titivate

spry active, agile, alert, brisk, nimble, nippy (*Brit. inf.*), quick, ready, sprightly, supple
Antonyms awkward, decrepit, doddering, inactive, lethargic, slow, sluggish, stiff

spunk backbone, balls (*Taboo sl.*), ballsiness (*Taboo sl.*), bottle (*Brit. sl.*), courage, gameness, grit, gumption (*Inf.*), guts (*Inf.*), mettle, nerve, pluck, resolution, spirit, toughness

spur *v.* 1. animate, drive, goad, impel, incite, press, prick, prod, prompt, stimulate, urge ~*n.* 2. goad, prick, rowel 3. impetus, impulse, incentive, incitement, inducement, motive, stimulus 4. **on the spur of the moment** impetuously, impromptu, impulsively, on impulse, on the spot, unpremeditatedly, unthinkingly, without planning, without thinking

spurious artificial, bogus, contrived, counterfeit, deceitful, ersatz, fake, false, feigned, forged, imitation, mock, phoney *or* phony (*Inf.*), pretended, pseudo (*Inf.*), sham, simulated, specious, unauthentic
Antonyms authentic, bona fide, genuine, honest, kosher (*Inf.*), legitimate, real, sound, unfeigned, valid

spurn cold-shoulder, contemn, despise, disdain, disregard, put down, rebuff, reject, repulse, scorn, slight, snub, turn one's nose up at (*Inf.*)
Antonyms embrace, grasp, seize, take up, welcome

spurt 1. *v.* burst, erupt, gush, jet, shoot, spew, squirt, surge 2. *n.* access, burst, fit, rush, spate, surge

spy *n.* 1. double agent, fifth columnist, foreign agent, mole, nark (*Brit., Aust., & N.Z. sl.*), secret agent, secret service agent, undercover agent ~*v.* 2. *Usually with* **on** follow, keep under surveillance, keep watch on, shadow, tail (*Inf.*), trail, watch 3. catch sight of, descry, espy, glimpse, notice, observe, set eyes on, spot

spying *n.* espionage, secret service

squabble 1. *v.* argue, bicker, brawl, clash, dispute, fall out (*Inf.*), fight, have words, quarrel, row, scrap (*Inf.*), spar, wrangle 2. *n.* argument, *bagarre,* barney (*Inf.*), difference of opinion, disagreement, dispute, fight, row, scrap (*Inf.*), set-to (*Inf.*), spat, tiff

squad band, company, crew, force, gang, group, team, troop

squalid broken-down, decayed, dirty, disgusting, fetid, filthy, foul, low, nasty, poverty-stricken, repulsive, run-down, seedy, sleazy, slovenly, slummy, sordid, unclean, yucky *or* yukky (*Sl.*)
Antonyms attractive, clean, genial, hygienic, in good condition, pleasant, salubrious, spick-and-span, spotless, tidy, well-kempt, well looked-after

squally blustery, gusty, inclement, rough, stormy, tempestuous, turbulent, wild, windy

squalor decay, filth, foulness, meanness, sleaziness, slumminess, squalidness, wretchedness
Antonyms beauty, cleanliness, fine condition, luxury, neatness, order, pleasantness, splendour

squander be prodigal with, blow (*Sl.*), consume, dissipate, expend, fritter away, frivol away, lavish, misspend, misuse, run through, scatter, spend, spend like water, throw away, waste
Antonyms be frugal, be thrifty, economize, keep, put aside for a rainy day, save, store

square *Fig. v.* 1. *Often with* **with** accord, agree, conform, correspond, fit, harmonize, match, reconcile, tally 2. *Sometimes with* **up** balance, clear (up), discharge, liquidate, make even, pay off, quit, satisfy, settle 3. accommodate, adapt, adjust, align, even up, level, regulate, suit, tailor, true (up) 4. *Sl.* bribe, buy off, corrupt, fix (*Inf.*), rig, suborn ~*adj..* 5. aboveboard, decent, equitable, ethical, fair, fair and square, genuine, honest, just, kosher (*Inf.*), on the level (*Inf.*), on the up and up, straight, straightforward, upfront (*Inf.*), upright 6. *Inf.* behind the times, bourgeois, conservative, conventional, old-fashioned, out of date, straight (*Sl.*), strait-laced, stuffy ~*n.* 7. *Inf.* antediluvian, back number (*Inf.*), conservative, die-hard, dinosaur, fuddy-duddy

(*Inf.*), old buffer (*Brit. inf.*), (old) fogy, stick-in-the-mud (*Inf.*), traditionalist
Antonyms *adj.* (*sense 6*) fashionable, in vogue, modern, modish, stylish, trendy (*Brit. inf.*), voguish

squash *v.* 1. compress, crush, distort, flatten, mash, pound, press, pulp, smash, stamp on, trample down 2. annihilate, crush, humiliate, put down (*Sl.*), put (someone) in his (*or* her) place, quash, quell, silence, sit on (*Inf.*), suppress

squashy mushy, pappy, pulpy, soft, spongy, yielding

squawk *v.* 1. cackle, crow, cry, hoot, screech, yelp 2. *Inf.* complain, kick up a fuss (*Inf.*), protest, raise Cain (*Sl.*), squeal (*Inf., chiefly Brit.*)

squeak *v.* peep, pipe, shrill, squeal, whine, yelp

squeal *n.* 1. scream, screech, shriek, wail, yell, yelp, yowl ~*v.* 2. scream, screech, shout, shriek, shrill, wail, yelp 3. *Sl.* betray, blab, grass (*Brit. sl.*), inform on, peach (*Sl.*), rat on (*Inf.*), sell (someone) down the river (*Inf.*), shop (*Sl., chiefly Brit.*), sing (*Sl., chiefly U.S.*), snitch (*Sl.*), spill one's guts (*Sl.*), tell all 4. *Inf.* complain, kick up a fuss (*Inf.*), moan, protest, squawk (*Inf.*)

squeamish 1. delicate, fastidious, finicky, nice (*Rare*), particular, prissy (*Inf.*), prudish, punctilious, scrupulous, strait-laced 2. nauseous, qualmish, queasy, queer, sick, sickish
Antonyms bold, brassy, brazen, coarse, earthy, immodest, indifferent, strong-stomached, tough, wanton

squeeze *v.* 1. clutch, compress, crush, grip, nip, pinch, press, squash, wring 2. cram, crowd, force, jam, jostle, pack, press, ram, stuff, thrust, wedge 3. clasp, cuddle, embrace, enfold, hold tight, hug 4. bleed (*Inf.*), bring pressure to bear on, extort, lean on (*Inf.*), milk, oppress, pressurize, put the screws on (*Inf.*), put the squeeze on (*Inf.*), wrest ~*n.* 5. clasp, embrace, handclasp, hold, hug 6. congestion, crowd, crush, jam, press, squash

squire *v.* accompany, attend, companion, escort

squint askew, aslant, awry, cockeyed, crooked, oblique, off-centre, skew-whiff (*Inf.*)
Antonyms aligned, even, horizontal, in line, level, perpendicular, plum, square, straight, true, vertical

squirm agonize, fidget, flounder, shift, twist, wiggle, wriggle, writhe

stab *v.* 1. bayonet, cut, gore, impale, injure, jab, knife, pierce, puncture, run through, spear, stick, thrust, transfix, wound 2. **stab in the back** betray, break faith with, deceive, do the dirty on (*Brit. sl.*), double-cross (*Inf.*), give the Judas kiss to, inform on, let down, play false, sell, sell out (*Inf.*), slander ~*n.* 3. gash, incision, jab, puncture, rent, thrust, wound 4. ache, pang, prick, twinge 5. **make a stab at** attempt, endeavour, essay, give it one's best shot (*Inf.*), have a go (crack (*Inf.*), shot (*Inf.*), stab (*Inf.*)) (*Inf.*), try, try one's hand at, venture

stability constancy, durability, firmness, permanence, solidity, soundness, steadfastness, steadiness, strength
Antonyms changeableness, fickleness, fragility, frailty, inconstancy, instability, unpredictability, unreliability, unsteadiness

stable abiding, constant, deep-rooted, durable, enduring, established, fast, firm, fixed, immovable, immutable, invariable, lasting, permanent, reliable, secure, sound, staunch, steadfast, steady, strong, sturdy, sure, unalterable, unchangeable, unwavering, well-founded
Antonyms changeable, deteriorating, erratic, excitable, fickle, frail, inconstant, insecure, irresolute, mercurial, mutable, over-emotional, shaky, shifting, temperamental, uncertain, unpredictable, unreliable, unstable, unsteady, variable, volatile, wavering

stack 1. *n.* clamp (*Brit. agriculture*), cock, heap, hoard, load, mass, mound, mountain, pile 2. *v.* accumulate, amass, assemble, bank up, heap up, load, pile, stockpile

staff *n.* 1. employees, lecturers, officers, organization, personnel, teachers, team, workers, work force 2. cane, crook, pole, prop, rod, sceptre, stave, wand

stage 1. *n.* division, juncture, lap, leg, length, level, period, phase, point, step 2. *v.* arrange, do, engineer, give, lay on, mount, orchestrate, organize, perform, play, present, produce, put on

stagger *v.* 1. falter, hesitate, lurch, reel, sway, teeter, totter, vacillate, waver, wobble 2. amaze, astonish, astound, bowl over (*Inf.*), confound, dumbfound, flabbergast, give (someone) a shock, nonplus, overwhelm, shake, shock, strike (someone) dumb, stun, stupefy, surprise, take (someone) aback, take (someone's) breath away, throw off balance 3. alternate, overlap, step, zigzag

stagnant brackish, motionless, quiet, sluggish, stale, standing, still
Antonyms active, clear, flowing, fresh, lively, moving, pure, running, thriving, unpolluted

stagnate decay, decline, deteriorate, fester,

go to seed, idle, languish, lie fallow, rot, rust, stand still, vegetate

staid calm, composed, decorous, demure, grave, quiet, sedate, self-restrained, serious, sober, solemn, steady

Antonyms adventurous, capricious, demonstrative, exuberant, flighty, giddy, indecorous, lively, rowdy, sportive, wild

stain *v.* 1. blemish, blot, colour, dirty, discolour, dye, mark, smirch, soil, spot, tarnish, tinge 2. besmirch, blacken, contaminate, corrupt, defile, deprave, disgrace, drag through the mud, sully, taint ~*n.* 3. blemish, blot, discoloration, dye, smirch, spot, tint 4. blemish, blot on the escutcheon, disgrace, dishonour, infamy, reproach, shame, slur, stigma

stake[1] *n.* 1. pale, paling, palisade, picket, pole, post, spike, stave, stick ~*v.* 2. brace, prop, secure, support, tether, tie up 3. *Often with* **out** define, delimit, demarcate, lay claim to, mark out, outline, reserve

stake[2] *n.* 1. ante, bet, chance, hazard, peril, pledge, risk, venture, wager 2. claim, concern, interest, investment, involvement, share ~*v.* 3. bet, chance, gamble, hazard, imperil, jeopardize, pledge, put on, risk, venture, wager

stale 1. decayed, dry, faded, fetid, flat, fusty, hard, insipid, musty, old, sour, stagnant, tasteless 2. antiquated, banal, cliché-ridden, common, commonplace, drab, effete, flat, hackneyed, insipid, old hat, overused, platitudinous, repetitious, stereotyped, threadbare, trite, unoriginal, worn-out

Antonyms crisp, different, fresh, imaginative, innovative, lively, new, novel, original, refreshing

stalemate deadlock, draw, impasse, standstill, tie

stalk *v.* 1. creep up on, follow, haunt, hunt, pursue, shadow, tail (*Inf.*), track 2. flounce, march, pace, stride, strut

stall *v.* beat about the bush (*Inf.*), equivocate, hedge, play for time, prevaricate, stonewall, temporize

stalwart athletic, beefy (*Inf.*), brawny, daring, dependable, hefty (*Inf.*), husky (*Inf.*), indomitable, intrepid, lusty, manly, muscular, redoubtable, robust, rugged, sinewy, staunch, stout, strapping, strong, sturdy, valiant, vigorous

Antonyms faint-hearted, feeble, frail, infirm, namby-pamby, puny, shilpit (*Scot.*), sickly, timid, weak

stamina energy, force, grit, indefatigability, lustiness, power, power of endurance, resilience, resistance, staying power, strength, vigour

stammer *v.* falter, hem and haw, hesitate, pause, splutter, stumble, stutter

stamp *v.* 1. beat, crush, trample 2. engrave, fix, impress, imprint, inscribe, mark, mould, print 3. betray, brand, categorize, exhibit, identify, label, mark, pronounce, reveal, show to be, typecast ~*n.* 4. brand, cast, earmark, hallmark, imprint, mark, mould, signature 5. breed, cast, character, cut, description, fashion, form, kind, sort, type

stamp collecting philately

stampede *n.* charge, flight, rout, rush, scattering

stamp out crush, destroy, eliminate, eradicate, extinguish, extirpate, put down, put out, quell, quench, scotch, suppress

stance 1. bearing, carriage, deportment, posture 2. attitude, position, stand, standpoint, viewpoint

stanch, staunch arrest, check, dam, halt, plug, stay, stem, stop

stand *v.* 1. be upright, be vertical, erect, mount, place, position, put, rank, rise, set 2. be in force, belong, be situated *or* located, be valid, continue, exist, halt, hold, obtain, pause, prevail, remain, rest, stay, stop 3. abide, allow, bear, brook, cope with, countenance, endure, experience, handle, put up with (*Inf.*), stomach, submit to, suffer, support, sustain, take, thole (*Dialect*), tolerate, undergo, wear (*Brit. sl.*), weather, withstand ~*n.* 4. halt, rest, standstill, stay, stop, stopover 5. attitude, determination, firm stand, opinion, position, stance, standpoint 6. base, booth, bracket, dais, frame, grandstand, place, platform, rack, rank, stage, staging, stall, stance (*Chiefly Scot.*), support, table

standard[1] *n.* 1. average, benchmark, canon, criterion, example, gauge, grade, guide, guideline, measure, model, norm, par, pattern, principle, requirement, rule, sample, specification, touchstone, type, yardstick 2. *Often plural* code of honour, ethics, ideals, moral principles, morals, principles ~*adj.* 3. accepted, average, basic, customary, normal, orthodox, popular, prevailing, regular, set, staple, stock, typical, usual 4. approved, authoritative, classic, definitive, established, official, recognized

Antonyms *adj.* abnormal, atypical, exceptional, extraordinary, irregular, singular, strange, unauthorised, uncommon, unconventional, unofficial, unusual

standard[2] *n.* banner, colours, ensign, flag, pennant, pennon, streamer

standardize assimilate, bring into line, institutionalize, mass-produce, regiment, stereotype

stand by 1. back, befriend, be loyal to, champion, defend, stick up for (*Inf.*), support, take (someone's) part, uphold 2. be prepared, wait, wait in the wings

stand for 1. betoken, denote, exemplify, indicate, mean, represent, signify, symbolize 2. *Inf.* bear, brook, endure, lie down under (*Inf.*), put up with, suffer, tolerate, wear (*Brit. inf.*)

stand in for cover for, deputize for, do duty for, hold the fort for, replace, represent, substitute for, take the place of, understudy

standing *n.* 1. condition, credit, eminence, estimation, footing, position, rank, reputation, repute, station, status 2. continuance, duration, existence, experience ~*adj.* 3. fixed, lasting, permanent, perpetual, regular, repeated 4. erect, perpendicular, rampant (*Heraldry*), upended, upright, vertical

standoffish aloof, cold, distant, haughty, remote, reserved, unapproachable, unsociable

Antonyms affable, approachable, congenial, cordial, friendly, open, sociable, warm

stand out attract attention, be highlighted, be prominent (conspicuous, distinct, obvious, striking), be thrown into relief, bulk large, catch the eye, leap to the eye, project, stare one in the face (*Inf.*), stick out a mile (*Inf.*)

standpoint angle, point of view, position, post, stance, station, vantage point, viewpoint

stand up for champion, come to the defence of, defend, side with, stick up for (*Inf.*), support, uphold

stand up to brave, confront, defy, endure, oppose, resist, tackle, withstand

staple *adj.* basic, chief, essential, fundamental, key, main, predominant, primary, principal

star 1. *n.* celeb (*Inf.*), celebrity, draw, idol, lead, leading man *or* lady, luminary, main attraction, megastar (*Inf.*), name 2. *adj.* brilliant, celebrated, illustrious, leading, major, paramount, principal, prominent, talented, well-known

starchy ceremonious, conventional, formal, precise, prim, punctilious, stiff, stuffy

stare *v.* gape, gawk, gawp (*Brit. sl.*), gaze, goggle, look, ogle, rubberneck (*Sl.*), watch

stark *adj.* 1. absolute, arrant, bald, bare, blunt, consummate, downright, entire, flagrant, out-and-out, palpable, patent, pure, sheer, simple, unalloyed, unmitigated, utter 2. austere, bare, barren, bleak, cold, depressing, desolate, drear (*Literary*), dreary, forsaken, godforsaken, grim, hard, harsh, plain, severe, solitary, unadorned ~*adv.* 3. absolutely, altogether, clean, completely, entirely, quite, utterly, wholly

stark-naked buck naked (*Sl.*), in a state of nature, in one's birthday suit (*Inf.*), in the altogether (*Inf.*), in the buff (*Inf.*), in the raw (*Inf.*), naked, naked as the day one was born (*Inf.*), nude, stark, starkers (*Inf.*), stripped, unclad, undressed, without a stitch on (*Inf.*)

start *v.* 1. appear, arise, begin, come into being, come into existence, commence, depart, first see the light of day, get on the road, get under way, go ahead, hit the road (*Inf.*), issue, leave, originate, pitch in (*Inf.*), sally forth, set off, set out 2. activate, embark upon, engender, enter upon, get going, initiate, instigate, kick off (*Inf.*), kick-start, make a beginning, open, originate, put one's hand to the plough (*Inf.*), set about, set in motion, start the ball rolling, take the first step, take the plunge (*Inf.*), trigger, turn on 3. begin, create, establish, father, found, inaugurate, initiate, institute, introduce, launch, lay the foundations of, pioneer, set up 4. blench, flinch, jerk, jump, recoil, shy, twitch ~*n.* 5. beginning, birth, commencement, dawn, first step(s), foundation, inauguration, inception, initiation, kickoff (*Inf.*), onset, opening, opening move, outset 6. advantage, edge, head start, lead 7. backing, break (*Inf.*), chance, helping hand, introduction, opening, opportunity, sponsorship 8. convulsion, jar, jump, spasm, twitch

Antonyms *v.* (*senses 1, 2 & 3*) abandon, bring to an end, call it a day (*Inf.*), cease, conclude, delay, desist, end, finish, give up, put aside, put off, quit, stop, switch off, terminate, turn off, wind up ~*n.* (*sense 5*) cessation, conclusion, dénouement, end, finale, finish, outcome, result, stop, termination, turning off, wind-up

startle agitate, alarm, amaze, astonish, astound, frighten, give (someone) a turn (*Inf.*), make (someone) jump, scare, shock, surprise, take (someone) aback

startling alarming, astonishing, astounding, extraordinary, shocking, staggering, sudden, surprising, unexpected, unforeseen

starving faint from lack of food, famished, hungering, hungry, ravenous, ready to eat a horse (*Inf.*), sharp-set, starved

stash *v.* cache, hide, hoard, lay up, put aside for a rainy day, salt away, save up, secrete, stockpile, stow

state[1] *v.* 1. affirm, articulate, assert, asseverate, aver, declare, enumerate, explain, expound, express, present, propound, put, report, say, specify, utter, voice ~*n.* 2. case, category, circumstances, condition, mode, pass, plight, position, predicament, shape, situation, state of affairs 3. attitude, frame of mind, humour, mood, spirits 4. ceremony, dignity, display, glory, grandeur, majesty, pomp, splendour, style 5. *Inf.* bother, flap (*Inf.*), panic, pother, tiz-woz (*Inf.*), tizzy (*Inf.*) 6. **in a state** *Inf.* agitated, all steamed up (*Sl.*), anxious, distressed, disturbed, flustered, het up, panic-stricken, ruffled, upset, uptight (*Inf.*)

state[2] *n.* body politic, commonwealth, country, federation, government, kingdom, land, nation, republic, territory

stately august, ceremonious, deliberate, dignified, elegant, grand, imperial, imposing, impressive, lofty, majestic, measured, noble, pompous, regal, royal, solemn
Antonyms common, humble, lowly, modest, simple, undignified, undistinguished, unimpressive

statement account, announcement, communication, communiqué, declaration, explanation, proclamation, recital, relation, report, testimony, utterance

static changeless, constant, fixed, immobile, inert, motionless, stagnant, stationary, still, unmoving, unvarying
Antonyms active, dynamic, kinetic, lively, mobile, moving, travelling, varied

station *n.* 1. base, depot, headquarters, location, place, position, post, seat, situation 2. appointment, business, calling, employment, grade, occupation, position, post, rank, situation, sphere, standing, status ~*v.* 3. assign, establish, fix, garrison, install, locate, post, set

stationary at a standstill, fixed, inert, moored, motionless, parked, standing, static, stock-still, unmoving
Antonyms changeable, changing, inconstant, mobile, moving, shifting, travelling, unstable, variable, varying, volatile

statuesque dignified, imposing, Junoesque, majestic, regal, stately

stature consequence, eminence, high station, importance, prestige, prominence, rank, size, standing

status condition, consequence, degree, distinction, eminence, grade, position, prestige, rank, standing

statute act, decree, edict, enactment, ordinance, regulation, rule

staunch constant, dependable, faithful, firm, immovable, loyal, reliable, resolute, sound, stalwart, steadfast, stout, strong, sure, tried and true, true, true-blue, trustworthy, trusty

stave off avert, evade, fend off, foil, hold off, keep at arm's length, keep at bay, parry, ward off

stay[1] *v.* 1. abide, continue, delay, establish oneself, halt, hang around (*Inf.*), hover, linger, loiter, pause, put down roots, remain, reside, settle, sojourn, stand, stay put, stop, tarry, wait 2. *Often with* **at** be accommodated at, lodge, put up at, sojourn, visit 3. adjourn, defer, discontinue, hold in abeyance, hold over, prorogue, put off, suspend 4. *Archaic* arrest, check, curb, delay, detain, hinder, hold, impede, obstruct, prevent ~*n.* 5. holiday, sojourn, stop, stopover, visit 6. deferment, delay, halt, pause, postponement, remission, reprieve, stopping, suspension
Antonyms *v.* (*sense 1*) abandon, depart, exit, go, leave, move on, pass through, quit, withdraw

stay[2] *n.* brace, buttress, prop, reinforcement, shoring, stanchion, support

staying power endurance, stamina, strength, toughness

steadfast constant, dedicated, dependable, established, faithful, fast, firm, fixed, immovable, intent, loyal, persevering, reliable, resolute, single-minded, stable, stalwart, staunch, steady, unfaltering, unflinching, unswerving, unwavering
Antonyms capricious, faint-hearted, faltering, fickle, flagging, half-hearted, inconstant, irresolute, uncommitted, undependable, unreliable, unstable, vacillating, wavering

steady *adj.* 1. firm, fixed, immovable, safe, stable, substantial, unchangeable, uniform 2. balanced, calm, dependable, equable, having both feet on the ground, imperturbable, level-headed, reliable, sedate, sensible, serene, serious-minded, settled, sober, staid, staunch, steadfast 3. ceaseless, confirmed, consistent, constant, continuous, even, faithful, habitual, incessant, nonstop, persistent, regular, rhythmic, unbroken, unfaltering, unfluctuating, uninterrupted, unremitting, unvarying, unwavering ~*v.* 4. balance, brace, secure, stabilize, support 5. compose *or* calm oneself, cool down, sober (up), get a grip on oneself
Antonyms *adj.* careless, changeable, faltering, fickle, fluctuating, half-hearted, inconsistent, infrequent, insecure, intermittent, in two minds, irregular, occasional, sporadic, uncommitted, unconscientious, undependable, unpredictable, unreliable, unsettled, unstable, unsteady, vacillating, wavering ~*v.* agitate, shake, tilt, upset, worry

steal 1. appropriate, be light-fingered, blag (*Sl.*), cabbage (*Brit. sl.*), embezzle, filch, half-inch (*Old-fashioned sl.*), heist (*U.S. sl.*), lift (*Inf.*), misappropriate, nick (*Sl., chiefly Brit.*), peculate, pilfer, pinch (*Inf.*), pirate, plagiarize, poach, prig (*Brit. sl.*), purloin, shoplift, snitch (*Sl.*), swipe (*Sl.*), take, thieve, walk *or* make off with 2. creep, flit, insinuate oneself, slink, slip, sneak, tiptoe

stealing embezzlement, larceny, misappropriation, pilferage, pilfering, plagiarism, robbery, shoplifting, theft, thievery, thieving

stealth furtiveness, secrecy, slyness, sneakiness, stealthiness, surreptitiousness, unobtrusiveness

stealthy clandestine, covert, furtive, secret, secretive, skulking, sly, sneaking, sneaky, surreptitious, underhand

steel *v.* brace, fortify, grit one's teeth, harden, make up one's mind

steep[1] *adj.* 1. abrupt, headlong, precipitous, sheer 2. *Inf.* excessive, exorbitant, extortionate, extreme, high, overpriced, stiff, uncalled-for, unreasonable

Antonyms (*sense 1*) easy, gentle, gradual, moderate, slight (*sense 2*) fair, moderate, reasonable

steep[2] *v.* 1. damp, drench, imbrue (*Rare*), immerse, macerate, marinate (*Cookery*), moisten, soak, souse, submerge 2. fill, imbue, infuse, permeate, pervade, saturate, suffuse

steer 1. administer, be in the driver's seat, conduct, control, direct, govern, guide, handle, pilot 2. **steer clear of** avoid, body-swerve (*Scot.*), circumvent, eschew, evade, give a wide berth to, sheer off, shun

steersman cox, coxswain, helmsman, pilot, wheelman (*U.S.*)

stem[1] 1. *n.* axis, branch, peduncle, shoot, stalk, stock, trunk 2. *v. Usually with* **from** arise, be caused (bred, brought about, generated) by, derive, develop, emanate, flow, issue, originate

stem[2] *v.* bring to a standstill, check, contain, curb, dam, hold back, oppose, resist, restrain, stanch, staunch, stay (*Archaic*), stop, withstand

stench foul odour, mephitis, niff (*Brit. sl.*), noisomeness, pong (*Brit. inf.*), reek, stink, whiff (*Brit. sl.*)

step *n.* 1. footfall, footprint, footstep, gait, impression, pace, print, stride, trace, track, walk 2. act, action, deed, expedient, manoeuvre, means, measure, move, procedure, proceeding 3. **take steps** act, intervene, move in, prepare, take action, take measures, take the initiative 4. advance, advancement, move, phase, point, process, progression, stage 5. degree, level, rank, remove 6. doorstep, round, rung, stair, tread 7. **in step** coinciding, conforming, in harmony (agreement, conformity, unison), in line 8. **out of step** erratic, incongruous, in disagreement, out of harmony, out of line, out of phase, pulling different ways 9. **watch one's step** be discreet (canny, careful, cautious), be on one's guard, have one's wits about one, look out, mind how one goes, mind one's p's and q's, take care, take heed, tread carefully ~*v.* 10. move, pace, tread, walk

step down abdicate, bow out, give up, hand over, leave, pull out, quit, resign, retire

step in become involved, chip in (*Inf.*), intercede, intervene, take action, take a hand

step up accelerate, augment, boost, escalate, increase, intensify, raise, speed up, up

stereotype 1. *n.* formula, mould, pattern, received idea 2. *v.* categorize, conventionalize, dub, pigeonhole, standardize, take to be, typecast

stereotyped banal, cliché-ridden, conventional, corny (*Sl.*), hackneyed, mass-produced, overused, platitudinous, played out, stale, standard, standardized, stock, threadbare, tired, trite, unoriginal

sterile 1. abortive, bare, barren, dry, empty, fruitless, infecund, unfruitful, unproductive, unprofitable, unprolific 2. antiseptic, aseptic, disinfected, germ-free, sterilized

Antonyms (*sense 1*) fecund, fertile, fruitful, productive, prolific (*sense 2*) contaminated, dirty, germ-ridden, infected, insanitary, unhygienic, unsterile

sterilize autoclave, disinfect, fumigate, purify

sterling authentic, excellent, fine, first-class, genuine, pure, real, sound, standard, substantial, superlative, true

stern austere, authoritarian, bitter, cruel, drastic, flinty, forbidding, frowning, grim, hard, harsh, inflexible, relentless, rigid, rigorous, serious, severe, steely, strict, unrelenting, unsparing, unyielding

Antonyms amused, approachable, compassionate, flexible, friendly, gentle, kind, lenient, liberal, permissive, soft, sympathetic, tolerant, warm

stick[1] *v.* 1. adhere, affix, attach, bind, bond, cement, cleave, cling, fasten, fix, fuse, glue, hold, hold on, join, paste, weld 2. dig, gore, insert, jab, penetrate, pierce, pin, poke, prod, puncture, spear, stab, thrust, transfix 3. *With* **out, up,** *etc.* bulge, extend, jut, obtrude, poke, project, protrude, show 4. *Inf.* deposit, drop, fix, install, lay, place, plant, plonk, position, put, set, store, stuff

5. be bogged down, become immobilized, be embedded, catch, clog, come to a standstill, jam, lodge, snag, stop 6. linger, persist, remain, stay 7. *Sl.* abide, bear up under, endure, get on with, stand, stomach, take, tolerate 8. **stick it out** *Inf.* bear, endure, grin and bear it (*Inf.*), last out, put up with (*Inf.*), see it through, see through to the bitter end, soldier on, take it (*Inf.*), weather 9. **stick up for** *Inf.* champion, defend, stand up for, support, take the part *or* side of, uphold

stick² *n.* 1. baton, birch, cane, crook, pole, rod, sceptre, staff, stake, switch, twig, wand 2. *Inf.* dinosaur, fuddy-duddy (*Inf.*), (old) fogy, pain (*Inf.*), prig, stick-in-the-mud (*Inf.*) 3. *Brit. sl.* abuse, blame, criticism, flak (*Inf.*), hostility, punishment

stick at 1. continue, keep at, persevere in, persist, plug away at (*Inf.*), see (something) through 2. balk, be conscience-stricken, be deterred by, demur, doubt, hesitate, pause, recoil, scruple, shrink from, stop at

stick-in-the-mud Colonel Blimp, conservative, die-hard, dinosaur, fuddy-duddy (*Inf.*), (old) fogy, reactionary, sobersides, stick (*Inf.*)

stickler fanatic, fusspot (*Brit. inf.*), hard taskmaster, maniac (*Inf.*), martinet, nut (*Sl.*), pedant, perfectionist, purist

stick to adhere to, cleave to, continue in, honour, keep, persevere in, remain loyal (faithful, true), stick at

sticky 1. adhesive, claggy (*Dialect*), clinging, gluey, glutinous, gooey (*Inf.*), gummy, syrupy, tacky, tenacious, viscid, viscous 2. *Inf.* awkward, delicate, difficult, discomforting, embarrassing, hairy (*Sl.*), nasty, painful, thorny, tricky, unpleasant 3. clammy, close, humid, muggy, oppressive, sultry, sweltering

stiff 1. brittle, firm, hard, hardened, inelastic, inflexible, rigid, solid, solidified, taut, tense, tight, unbending, unyielding 2. artificial, austere, ceremonious, chilly, cold, constrained, forced, formal, laboured, mannered, pompous, priggish, prim, punctilious, standoffish, starchy (*Inf.*), stilted, uneasy, unnatural, unrelaxed, wooden 3. arthritic, awkward, clumsy, creaky (*Inf.*), crude, graceless, inelegant, jerky, rheumaticky (*Inf.*), ungainly, ungraceful, unsupple 4. arduous, difficult, exacting, fatiguing, formidable, hard, laborious, tough, trying, uphill 5. austere, cruel, drastic, extreme, great, hard, harsh, heavy, inexorable, oppressive, pitiless, rigorous, severe, sharp, strict, stringent 6. brisk, fresh, powerful, strong, vigorous
Antonyms (*senses 1 & 3*) bendable, ductile, elastic, flexible, limber, lissom(e), lithe, pliable, pliant, supple, yielding (*sense 2*) casual, easy, informal, laid-back, natural, relaxed, spontaneous, unceremonious, unofficial

stiffen brace, coagulate, congeal, crystallize, harden, jell, reinforce, set, solidify, starch, tauten, tense, thicken

stiff-necked boneheaded (*Sl.*), contumacious, haughty, obstinate, opinionated, stubborn, uncompromising, unreceptive

stifle 1. asphyxiate, choke, smother, strangle, suffocate 2. check, choke back, cover up, curb, extinguish, hush, muffle, prevent, repress, restrain, silence, smother, stop, suppress

stigma blot, brand, disgrace, dishonour, imputation, mark, reproach, shame, slur, smirch, spot, stain

stigmatize brand, cast a slur upon, defame, denounce, discredit, label, mark, pillory

still 1. *adj.* at rest, calm, hushed, inert, lifeless, motionless, noiseless, pacific, peaceful, placid, quiet, restful, serene, silent, smooth, stationary, stilly (*Poetic*), tranquil, undisturbed, unruffled, unstirring 2. *v.* allay, alleviate, appease, calm, hush, lull, pacify, quiet, quieten, settle, silence, smooth, smooth over, soothe, subdue, tranquillize 3. *conj.* but, for all that, however, nevertheless, notwithstanding, yet 4. *n. Poetic* hush, peace, quiet, silence, stillness, tranquillity
Antonyms *adj.* active, agitated, astir, bustling, busy, humming, lively, moving, noisy, restless, turbulent ~*v.* aggravate, agitate, exacerbate, increase, inflame, rouse, stir up ~*n.* bustle, clamour, hubbub, noise, uproar

stilted artificial, bombastic, constrained, forced, grandiloquent, high-flown, high-sounding, inflated, laboured, pedantic, pompous, pretentious, stiff, unnatural, wooden
Antonyms flowing, fluid, free, natural, spontaneous, unaffected, unpretentious

stimulant analeptic, bracer (*Inf.*), energizer, excitant, pep pill (*Inf.*), pick-me-up (*Inf.*), restorative, reviver, tonic, upper (*Sl.*)
Antonyms calmant, depressant, downer (*Sl.*), sedative, tranquilliser

stimulate animate, arouse, encourage, fan, fire, foment, goad, impel, incite, inflame, instigate, prod, prompt, provoke, quicken, rouse, spur, turn on (*Sl.*), urge, whet

stimulating exciting, exhilarating, galvanic, inspiring, intriguing, provocative, provoking, rousing, stirring, thought-provoking

Antonyms boring, dull, mind-numbing, unexciting, unimaginative, uninspiring, uninteresting, unstimulating

stimulus encouragement, fillip, goad, incentive, incitement, inducement, provocation, shot in the arm (*Inf.*), spur

sting *v.* 1. burn, hurt, pain, smart, tingle, wound 2. anger, gall, incense, inflame, infuriate, nettle, pique, provoke, rile 3. *Inf.* cheat, defraud, do (*Sl.*), fleece, overcharge, rip off (*Sl.*), skin (*Sl.*), stiff (*Sl.*), swindle, take for a ride (*Inf.*)

stingy 1. avaricious, cheeseparing, close-fisted, covetous, illiberal, mean, mingy (*Brit. inf.*), miserly, near, niggardly, parsimonious, penny-pinching (*Inf.*), penurious, scrimping, tight-arse (*Taboo sl.*), tight-arsed (*Taboo sl.*), tight as a duck's arse (*Taboo sl.*), tight-ass (*U.S. taboo sl.*), tight-assed (*U.S. taboo sl.*), tightfisted, ungenerous 2. inadequate, insufficient, meagre, measly (*Inf.*), mouldy (*Inf.*), on the small side, scant, scanty, skimpy, small

stink *v.* 1. offend the nostrils, pong (*Brit. inf.*), reek, stink to high heaven (*Inf.*), whiff (*Brit. sl.*) 2. *Sl.* be held in disrepute, be no good, be offensive, be rotten (abhorrent, bad, detestable), have a bad name ~*n.* 3. fetor, foulness, foul odour, malodour, noisomeness, pong (*Brit. inf.*), stench 4. *Sl.* brouhaha, commotion, deal of trouble (*Inf.*), disturbance, fuss, hubbub, row, rumpus, scandal, stir, to-do, uproar, upset

stinker 1. bounder (*Old-fashioned Brit. sl.*), cad (*Brit. inf.*), cocksucker (*Taboo sl.*), cur, dastard (*Archaic*), heel, nasty piece of work (*Inf.*), rotter (*Sl., chiefly Brit.*), scab, scoundrel, sod (*Sl.*), swine 2. affliction, beast, difficulty, fine how-do-you-do (*Inf.*), horror, impediment, plight, poser, predicament, problem, shocker

stinking 1. fetid, foul-smelling, ill-smelling, malodorous, mephitic, niffy (*Brit. sl.*), noisome, olid, pongy (*Brit. inf.*), reeking, smelly, whiffy (*Brit. sl.*) 2. *Inf.* contemptible, disgusting, low, low-down (*Inf.*), mean, rotten, shitty (*Taboo sl.*), unpleasant, vile, wretched 3. *Sl.* bevvied (*Dialect*), blitzed (*Sl.*), blotto (*Sl.*), bombed (*Sl.*), boozed, canned (*Sl.*), drunk, drunk as a lord, flying (*Sl.*), intoxicated, legless (*Inf.*), lit up (*Sl.*), out of it (*Sl.*), out to it (*Aust. & N.Z. sl.*), paralytic (*Inf.*), pissed (*Taboo sl.*), plastered (*Sl.*), smashed (*Sl.*), sozzled (*Inf.*), steamboats (*Sl.*), steaming (*Sl.*), stewed (*Sl.*), stoned (*Sl.*), wasted (*Sl.*), wrecked (*Sl.*), zonked (*Sl.*)

stint 1. *n.* assignment, bit, period, quota, share, shift, spell, stretch, term, time, tour, turn 2. *v.* begrudge, be sparing (frugal, mean, mingy (*Brit. inf.*), parsimonious), economize, hold back, save, scrimp, skimp on, spoil the ship for a ha'porth of tar, withhold

stipulate agree, contract, covenant, engage, guarantee, insist upon, lay down, lay down *or* impose conditions, make a point of, pledge, postulate, promise, require, settle, specify

stipulation agreement, clause, condition, contract, engagement, precondition, prerequisite, provision, proviso, qualification, requirement, restriction, rider, settlement, *sine qua non,* specification, term

stir *v.* 1. agitate, beat, disturb, flutter, mix, move, quiver, rustle, shake, tremble 2. *Often with* **up** animate, arouse, awaken, excite, incite, inflame, instigate, kindle, prod, prompt, provoke, quicken, raise, rouse, spur, stimulate, urge 3. affect, electrify, excite, fire, inspire, move, thrill, touch 4. bestir, be up and about (*Inf.*), budge, exert oneself, get a move on (*Inf.*), get moving, hasten, look lively (*Inf.*), make an effort, mill about, move, shake a leg (*Inf.*) ~*n.* 5. activity, ado, agitation, bustle, commotion, disorder, disturbance, excitement, ferment, flurry, fuss, movement, to-do, tumult, uproar

Antonyms *v.* (*senses 2 & 3*) check, curb, dampen, inhibit, restrain, stifle, suppress, throw cold water on (*Inf.*)

stirring animating, dramatic, emotive, exciting, exhilarating, heady, impassioned, inspiring, intoxicating, lively, moving, rousing, spirited, stimulating, thrilling

stock *n.* 1. array, assets, assortment, cache, choice, commodities, fund, goods, hoard, inventory, merchandise, range, reserve, reservoir, selection, stockpile, store, supply, variety, wares 2. *Animals* beasts, cattle, domestic animals, flocks, herds, horses, livestock, sheep 3. ancestry, background, breed, descent, extraction, family, forebears, house, line, lineage, line of descent, parentage, pedigree, race, strain, type, variety 4. *Money* capital, funds, investment, property 5. **take stock** appraise, estimate, review the situation, see how the land lies, size up (*Inf.*), weigh up ~*adj.* 6. banal, basic, commonplace, conventional, customary, formal, hackneyed, ordinary, overused, regular, routine, run-of-the-mill, set, standard, staple, stereotyped, traditional, trite, usual, worn-out ~*v.* 7. deal in, handle, keep, sell, supply, trade in 8. *With* **up** accumulate, amass, buy up, gather, hoard, lay in, put away, replenish, save, store (up), supply 9. equip, fill, fit out, furnish, kit out, provide with, provision, supply

stocky chunky, dumpy, mesomorphic, solid, stubby, stumpy, sturdy, thickset

stodgy 1. filling, heavy, leaden, starchy, substantial 2. boring, dull, dull as ditchwater, formal, fuddy-duddy (*Inf.*), heavy going, ho-hum, laboured, staid, stuffy, tedious, turgid, unexciting, unimaginative, uninspired
Antonyms (*sense 1*) appetizing, fluffy, insubstantial, light (*sense 2*) animated, exciting, fashionable, fresh, interesting, light, lively, readable, stimulating, trendy (*Brit. inf.*), up-to-date

stoical calm, cool, dispassionate, impassive, imperturbable, indifferent, long-suffering, philosophic, phlegmatic, resigned, stoic, stolid

stoicism acceptance, calmness, dispassion, fatalism, forbearance, fortitude, impassivity, imperturbability, indifference, long-suffering, patience, resignation, stolidity

stolid apathetic, bovine, doltish, dozy (*Brit. inf.*), dull, heavy, lumpish, obtuse, slow, stupid, unemotional, wooden
Antonyms acute, animated, bright, emotional, energetic, excitable, intelligent, interested, lively, passionate, sharp, smart

stomach *n.* 1. abdomen, belly, breadbasket (*Sl.*), gut (*Inf.*), inside(s) (*Inf.*), paunch, pot, potbelly, spare tyre (*Inf.*), tummy (*Inf.*) 2. appetite, desire, inclination, mind, relish, taste *~v.* 3. abide, bear, endure, put up with (*Inf.*), reconcile *or* resign oneself to, submit to, suffer, swallow, take, tolerate

stony *Fig.* adamant, blank, callous, chilly, expressionless, frigid, hard, harsh, heartless, hostile, icy, indifferent, inexorable, merciless, obdurate, pitiless, unfeeling, unforgiving, unresponsive

stooge 1. *n.* butt, dupe, fall guy (*Inf.*), foil, henchman, lackey, patsy (*Sl., chiefly U.S. & Canad.*), pawn, puppet 2. *v. Inf.* flit, fly, hang about (*Inf.*), meander, mooch (*Sl.*), mosey (*Inf.*), move, wander

stoop *v.* 1. be bowed *or* round-shouldered, bend, bow, crouch, descend, duck, hunch, incline, kneel, lean, squat 2. *Often with* to condescend, deign, demean oneself, descend, lower oneself, resort, sink, vouchsafe *~n.* 3. bad posture, droop, round-shoulderedness, sag, slouch, slump

stop *v.* 1. axe (*Inf.*), be over, break off, bring *or* come to a halt, bring *or* come to a standstill, call it a day (*Inf.*), cease, come to an end, conclude, cut out (*Inf.*), cut short, desist, discontinue, draw up, end, finish, halt, leave off, pack in (*Brit. inf.*), pause, peter out, pull up, put an end to, quit, refrain, run down, run its course, shut down, stall, terminate 2. arrest, bar, block, break, bung, check, close, forestall, frustrate, hinder, hold back, impede, intercept, interrupt, obstruct, plug, prevent, rein in, repress, restrain, seal, silence, staunch, stem, suspend 3. break one's journey, lodge, put up, rest, sojourn, stay, tarry *~n.* 4. cessation, conclusion, discontinuation, end, finish, halt, standstill 5. break, rest, sojourn, stay, stopover, visit 6. bar, block, break, check, control, hindrance, impediment, plug, stoppage 7. depot, destination, halt, stage, station, termination, terminus
Antonyms *v.* (*senses 1 & 3*) advance, begin, commence, continue, get going, get under way, give the go ahead, go, institute, keep going, kick off (*Inf.*), keep on, proceed, set in motion, set off, start (*sense 2*) assist, boost, encourage, expedite, facilitate, further, hasten, promote, push *~n.* (*sense 4*) beginning, commencement, kick-off (*Inf.*), start (*sense 6*) boost, encouragement, incitement

stopgap 1. *n.* improvisation, makeshift, resort, shift, substitute, temporary expedient 2. *adj.* emergency, impromptu, improvised, makeshift, provisional, rough-and-ready, temporary

stoppage 1. abeyance, arrest, close, closure, cutoff, deduction, discontinuance, halt, hindrance, lay-off, shutdown, standstill, stopping 2. blockage, check, curtailment, interruption, obstruction, occlusion, stopping up

store *v.* 1. accumulate, deposit, garner, hoard, husband, keep, keep in reserve, lay by *or* in, lock away, put aside, put aside for a rainy day, put by, put in storage, reserve, salt away, save, stash (*Inf.*), stock, stockpile *~n.* 2. abundance, accumulation, cache, fund, hoard, lot, mine, plenty, plethora, provision, quantity, reserve, reservoir, stock, stockpile, supply, wealth 3. chain store, department store, emporium, market, mart, outlet, shop, supermarket 4. depository, repository, storehouse, storeroom, warehouse 5. **set store by** appreciate, esteem, hold in high regard, prize, think highly of, value

storm *n.* 1. blast, blizzard, cyclone, gale, gust, hurricane, squall, tempest, tornado, whirlwind 2. *Fig.* agitation, anger, clamour, commotion, disturbance, furore, hubbub, outbreak, outburst, outcry, passion, roar, row, rumpus, stir, strife, tumult, turmoil, violence *~v.* 3. assail, assault, beset, charge, rush, take by storm *~n.* 4. assault, attack, blitz, blitzkrieg, offensive, onset, onslaught, rush *~v.* 5. bluster, complain, fly off the handle (*Inf.*), fume, rage, rant, rave, scold, thunder 6. flounce, fly, rush, stalk, stamp, stomp (*Inf.*)

stormy blustering, blustery, boisterous, dirty, foul, gusty, inclement, raging, rough, squally, tempestuous, turbulent, wild, windy

story 1. account, anecdote, chronicle, fictional account, history, legend, narration, narrative, novel, recital, record, relation, romance, tale, urban legend, version, yarn 2. *Inf.* falsehood, fib, fiction, lie, pork pie (*Brit. sl.*), porky (*Brit. sl.*), untruth, white lie 3. article, feature, news, news item, report, scoop

storyteller anecdotist, author, bard, chronicler, fabulist, narrator, novelist, raconteur, romancer, spinner of yarns

stout 1. big, bulky, burly, corpulent, fat, fleshy, heavy, obese, on the large *or* heavy side, overweight, plump, portly, rotund, substantial, tubby 2. able-bodied, athletic, beefy (*Inf.*), brawny, hardy, hulking, husky (*Inf.*), lusty, muscular, robust, stalwart, strapping, strong, sturdy, substantial, thickset, tough, vigorous 3. bold, brave, courageous, dauntless, doughty, fearless, gallant, intrepid, lion-hearted, manly, plucky, resolute, valiant, valorous

Antonyms (*senses 1 & 2*) feeble, flimsy, frail, insubstantial, lanky, lean, puny, skin-and-bones (*Inf.*), skinny, slender, slight, slim (*sense 3*) cowardly, faint-hearted, fearful, irresolute, shrinking, soft, spineless, timid, weak

stouthearted ballsy (*Taboo sl.*), bold, brave, courageous, dauntless, doughty, fearless, great-hearted, gutsy (*Sl.*), heroic, indomitable, intrepid, lion-hearted, plucky, spirited, stalwart, valiant, valorous

stow bundle, cram, deposit, jam, load, pack, put away, secrete, stash (*Inf.*), store, stuff, tuck

straggle drift, lag, loiter, ramble, range, roam, rove, spread, stray, string out, trail, wander

straggly aimless, disorganized, drifting, irregular, loose, rambling, random, spreading, spread out, straggling, straying, untidy

straight *adj.* 1. direct, near, short, undeviating, unswerving 2. aligned, erect, even, horizontal, in line, level, perpendicular, plumb, right, smooth, square, true, upright, vertical 3. blunt, candid, downright, forthright, frank, honest, outright, plain, point-blank, straightforward, unqualified, upfront (*Inf.*) 4. above board, accurate, authentic, decent, equitable, fair, fair and square, honest, honourable, just, law-abiding, reliable, respectable, trustworthy, upright 5. arranged, in order, neat, orderly, organized, put to rights, shipshape, sorted out, tidy 6. consecutive, continuous, non-stop, running, solid, successive, sustained, through, uninterrupted, unrelieved 7. *Sl.* bourgeois, conservative, conventional, orthodox, square (*Inf.*), traditional 8. neat, pure, unadulterated, undiluted, unmixed ~*adv.* 9. as the crow flies, at once, directly, immediately, instantly 10. candidly, frankly, honestly, in plain English, point-blank, pulling no punches (*Inf.*), with no holds barred

Antonyms *adj.* (*sense 1*) circuitous, indirect, roundabout, winding, zigzag (*sense 2*) askew, bent, crooked, curved, skewwhiff (*Brit. inf.*), twisted, uneven (*sense 3*) ambiguous, cryptic, equivocal, evasive, indirect, vague (*sense 4*) bent (*Sl.*), crooked (*Inf.*), dishonest, dishonourable, shady (*Inf.*), unlawful (*sense 5*) confused, disorderly, disorganized, in disarray, messy, untidy (*sense 6*) broken, discontinuous, interrupted, non-consecutive (*sense 7*) *Sl.* cool, fashionable, trendy (*Brit. inf.*), voguish

straightaway at once, directly, immediately, instantly, now, on the spot, right away, straightway (*Archaic*), there and then, this minute, without any delay, without more ado

straighten arrange, neaten, order, put in order, set *or* put to rights, smarten up, spruce up, tidy (up)

straighten out become clear, clear up, correct, disentangle, put right, rectify, regularize, resolve, settle, sort out, unsnarl, work out

straightforward 1. above board, candid, direct, forthright, genuine, guileless, honest, open, sincere, truthful, upfront (*Inf.*) 2. clear-cut, easy, easy-peasy (*Sl.*), elementary, routine, simple, uncomplicated, undemanding

Antonyms complex, complicated, confused, convoluted, devious, disingenuous, roundabout, shady, sharp, unclear, unscrupulous

strain[1] *v.* 1. distend, draw tight, extend, stretch, tauten, tighten 2. drive, exert, fatigue, injure, overexert, overtax, overwork, pull, push to the limit, sprain, tax, tear, tire, twist, weaken, wrench 3. bend over backwards (*Inf.*), break one's neck (*Inf.*), bust a gut (*Inf.*), do one's damnedest (*Inf.*), endeavour, give it one's all (*Inf.*), give it one's best shot (*Inf.*), go all out for (*Inf.*), go for broke (*Sl.*), go for it (*Inf.*), knock oneself out (*Inf.*), labour, make an all-out effort (*Inf.*), make a supreme effort, rupture oneself (*Inf.*), strive, struggle 4. filter, percolate, purify, riddle, screen, seep, separate, sieve, sift ~*n.* 5. effort, exertion, force, injury, pull, sprain, struggle, tautness, tension, tensity (*Rare*), wrench 6. anxiety, burden, pressure, stress, tension 7. *Often plural* air, lay, measure (*Poetic*), melody, song, theme, tune

Antonyms *v.* (*senses 2 & 3*) idle, loose, pamper, relax, rest, slacken, take it easy, yield ~*n.* (*senses 5 & 6*) ease, effortlessness, lack of tension, relaxation

strain[2] *n.* 1. ancestry, blood, descent, extraction, family, lineage, pedigree, race, stock 2. streak, suggestion, suspicion, tendency, trace, trait 3. humour, manner, spirit, style, temper, tone, vein, way

strained artificial, awkward, constrained, difficult, embarrassed, false, forced, laboured, put on, self-conscious, stiff, tense, uncomfortable, uneasy, unnatural, unrelaxed

Antonyms comfortable, natural, relaxed

straitened difficult, distressed, embarrassed, limited, reduced, restricted

strait-laced moralistic, narrow, narrow-minded, of the old school, old-maidish (*Inf.*), overscrupulous, prim, proper, prudish, puritanical, strict, Victorian

Antonyms broadminded, earthy, immoral, loose, relaxed, uninhibited, unreserved

straits *n. Sometimes singular* 1. crisis, difficulty, dilemma, distress, embarrassment, emergency, extremity, hardship, hole (*Sl.*), mess, panic stations (*Inf.*), pass, perplexity, plight, predicament, pretty *or* fine kettle of fish (*Inf.*) 2. channel, narrows, sound

strand *n.* fibre, filament, length, lock, rope, string, thread, tress, twist, wisp

stranded 1. aground, ashore, beached, cast away, grounded, marooned, wrecked 2. *Fig.* abandoned, helpless, high and dry, homeless, left in the lurch, penniless

strange 1. abnormal, astonishing, bizarre, curious, eccentric, exceptional, extraordinary, fantastic, funny, irregular, marvellous, mystifying, odd, oddball (*Inf.*), off-the-wall (*Sl.*), out-of-the-way, outré, peculiar, perplexing, queer, rare, remarkable, rum (*Brit. sl.*), singular, unaccountable, uncanny, uncommon, unheard of, weird, wonderful 2. alien, exotic, foreign, new, novel, outside one's experience, remote, unexplored, unfamiliar, unknown, untried 3. *Often with* **to** a stranger to, ignorant of, inexperienced, new to, unaccustomed, unpractised, unseasoned, unused, unversed in 4. awkward, bewildered, disoriented, ill at ease, lost, out of place, uncomfortable

Antonyms (*senses 1 & 2*) accustomed, common, commonplace, conventional, familiar, habitual, ordinary, regular, routine, run-of-the-mill, standard, typical, unexceptional, usual, well-known (*sense 3*) accustomed, familiar, habitual (*sense 4*) at ease, at home, comfortable, relaxed

stranger alien, foreigner, guest, incomer, new arrival, newcomer, outlander, unknown, visitor

strangle 1. asphyxiate, choke, garrotte, smother, strangulate, suffocate, throttle 2. gag, inhibit, repress, stifle, suppress

strap *n.* 1. belt, leash, thong, tie ~*v.* 2. bind, buckle, fasten, lash, secure, tie, truss 3. beat, belt (*Inf.*), flog, lash, scourge, whip

strapping beefy (*Inf.*), big, brawny, burly, hefty (*Inf.*), hulking, husky (*Inf.*), powerful, robust, stalwart, sturdy, well-built, well set-up

stratagem artifice, device, dodge, feint, intrigue, manoeuvre, plan, plot, ploy, ruse, scheme, subterfuge, trick, wile

strategic 1. cardinal, critical, crucial, decisive, important, key, vital 2. calculated, deliberate, diplomatic, planned, politic, tactical

strategy approach, grand design, manoeuvring, plan, planning, policy, procedure, programme, scheme

stratum 1. bed, layer, level, lode, seam, stratification, table, tier, vein 2. bracket, caste, category, class, estate, grade, group, level, rank, station

stray *v.* 1. deviate, digress, diverge, get off the point, get sidetracked, go off at a tangent, ramble 2. be abandoned *or* lost, drift, err, go astray, lose one's way, meander, range, roam, rove, straggle, wander ~*adj.* 3. abandoned, homeless, lost, roaming, vagrant 4. accidental, chance, erratic, freak, odd, random, scattered

streak *n.* 1. band, layer, line, slash, smear, strip, stripe, stroke, vein 2. dash, element, strain, touch, trace, vein ~*v.* 3. band, daub, fleck, slash, smear, striate, stripe 4. barrel (along) (*Inf., chiefly U.S. & Canad.*), burn rubber (*Inf.*), dart, flash, fly, hurtle, move like greased lightning (*Inf.*), speed, sprint, sweep, tear, whistle, whiz (*Inf.*), zoom

stream 1. *n.* bayou, beck, brook, burn, course, creek (*U.S.*), current, drift, flow, freshet, outpouring, rill, river, rivulet, run, rush, surge, tide, tideway, torrent, tributary, undertow 2. *v.* cascade, course, emit, flood, flow, glide, gush, issue, pour, run, shed, spill, spout

streamer banner, colours, ensign, flag, gonfalon, pennant, pennon, ribbon, standard

streamlined efficient, modernized, organized, rationalized, sleek, slick, smooth, smooth-running, time-saving, well-run

street 1. avenue, boulevard, lane, road, roadway, row, terrace, thoroughfare 2. **(right) up one's street** acceptable, compatible, congenial, familiar, one's cup of tea (*Inf.*), pleasing, suitable, to one's liking, to one's taste

strength 1. backbone, brawn, brawniness, courage, firmness, fortitude, health, lustiness, might, muscle, robustness, sinew, stamina, stoutness, sturdiness, toughness 2. cogency, concentration, effectiveness, efficacy, energy, force, intensity, potency, power, resolution, spirit, vehemence, vigour, virtue (*Archaic*) 3. advantage, anchor, asset, mainstay, security, strong point, succour, tower of strength
Antonyms (*senses 1 & 2*) debility, feebleness, frailty, impotence, infirmity, powerlessness, weakness (*sense 3*) Achilles heel, chink in one's armour, defect, failing, flaw, shortcoming, weakness

strengthen 1. animate, brace up, consolidate, encourage, fortify, give new energy to, harden, hearten, invigorate, nerve, nourish, rejuvenate, restore, stiffen, toughen 2. augment, bolster, brace, build up, buttress, confirm, corroborate, enhance, establish, give a boost to, harden, heighten, increase, intensify, justify, reinforce, steel, substantiate, support
Antonyms crush, debilitate, destroy, dilute, enervate, render impotent, sap, subvert, undermine, weaken

strenuous 1. arduous, demanding, exhausting, hard, Herculean, laborious, taxing, toilsome, tough, tough going, unrelaxing, uphill 2. active, bold, determined, eager, earnest, energetic, persistent, resolute, spirited, strong, tireless, vigorous, zealous
Antonyms easy, effortless, relaxed, relaxing, undemanding, unenergetic, untaxing

stress *n.* 1. emphasis, force, importance, significance, urgency, weight 2. anxiety, burden, hassle (*Inf.*), nervous tension, oppression, pressure, strain, tautness, tension, trauma, worry 3. accent, accentuation, beat, emphasis ~*v.* 4. accentuate, belabour, dwell on, emphasize, harp on, lay emphasis upon, point up, repeat, rub in, underline, underscore

stretch *v.* 1. cover, extend, put forth, reach, spread, unfold, unroll 2. distend, draw out, elongate, expand, inflate, lengthen, pull, pull out of shape, rack, strain, swell, tighten ~*n.* 3. area, distance, expanse, extent, spread, sweep, tract 4. bit, period, run, space, spell, stint, term, time

strew bestrew, disperse, litter, scatter, spread, sprinkle, toss

stricken affected, afflicted, hit, injured, laid low, smitten, struck, struck down

strict 1. austere, authoritarian, firm, harsh, no-nonsense, rigid, rigorous, severe, stern, stringent 2. accurate, close, exact, faithful, meticulous, particular, precise, religious, scrupulous, true 3. absolute, complete, perfect, total, utter
Antonyms (*sense 1*) easy-going, easy-oasy (*Sl.*), flexible, laid-back (*Inf.*), lax, mild, moderate, soft, tolerant

stricture animadversion, bad press, blame, censure, criticism, flak (*Inf.*), rebuke, stick (*Sl.*)

strident clamorous, clashing, discordant, grating, harsh, jangling, jarring, rasping, raucous, screeching, shrill, stridulant, stridulous, unmusical, vociferous
Antonyms calm, dulcet, gentle, harmonious, mellifluous, mellow, quiet, soft, soothing, sweet

strife animosity, battle, bickering, clash, clashes, combat, conflict, contention, contest, controversy, discord, dissension, friction, quarrel, rivalry, row, squabbling, struggle, warfare, wrangling

strike *v.* 1. bang, beat, box, buffet, chastise, chin (*Sl.*), clobber (*Sl.*), clout (*Inf.*), clump (*Sl.*), cuff, deck (*Sl.*), hammer, hit, knock, lambast(e), lay a finger on (*Inf.*), lay one on (*Sl.*), pound, punch, punish, slap, smack, smite, sock (*Sl.*), thump, wallop (*Inf.*) 2. be in collision with, bump into, clash, collide with, come into contact with, dash, hit, knock into, run into, smash into, touch 3. drive, force, hit, impel, thrust 4. affect, come to, come to the mind of, dawn on *or* upon, hit, impress, make an impact on, occur to, reach, register (*Inf.*), seem 5. *Sometimes with* **upon** come upon *or* across, discover, encounter, find, happen *or* chance upon, hit upon, light upon, reach, stumble upon *or* across, turn up, uncover, unearth 6. affect, assail, assault, attack, deal a blow to, devastate, fall upon, hit, invade, set upon, smite 7. achieve, arrange, arrive at, attain, effect, reach 8. down tools, mutiny, revolt, walk out

strike down afflict, bring low, deal a deathblow to, destroy, kill, ruin, slay, smite

strike out 1. *Also* **strike off, strike through** cancel, cross out, delete, efface, erase, excise, expunge, remove, score out 2. begin, get under way, set out, start out

striking astonishing, conspicuous, dazzling, drop-dead (*Sl.*), extraordinary, forcible, impressive, memorable, noticeable, out of the ordinary, outstanding, stunning (*Inf.*), wonderful

Antonyms average, dull, indifferent, undistinguished, unexceptional, unextraordinary, unimpressive, uninteresting

string *n.* 1. cord, fibre, twine 2. chain, file, line, procession, queue, row, sequence, series, strand, succession ~*v.* 3. festoon, hang, link, loop, sling, stretch, suspend, thread 4. *With* **out** disperse, extend, fan out, lengthen, protract, space out, spread out, straggle

string along 1. *Often with* **with** agree, assent, collaborate, go along with 2. *Also* **string on** bluff, deceive, dupe, fool, hoax, kid (*Inf.*), play fast and loose with (someone) (*Inf.*), play (someone) false, put one over on (someone) (*Inf.*), take (someone) for a ride (*Inf.*)

stringent binding, demanding, exacting, inflexible, rigid, rigorous, severe, strict, tight, tough

Antonyms equivocal, flexible, inconclusive, lax, loose, relaxed, slack, unrigorous, vague

strings *Fig.* catches (*Inf.*), complications, conditions, obligations, prerequisites, provisos, qualifications, requirements, riders, stipulations

stringy chewy, fibrous, gristly, sinewy, tough, wiry

strip[1] *v.* 1. bare, denude, deprive, despoil, dismantle, divest, empty, gut, lay bare, loot, peel, pillage, plunder, ransack, rob, sack, skin, spoil 2. disrobe, unclothe, uncover, undress

strip[2] *n.* band, belt, bit, fillet, piece, ribbon, shred, slip, swathe, tongue

striped banded, barred, striated, stripy

stripling adolescent, boy, fledgling, hobbledehoy (*Archaic*), lad, shaver (*Inf.*), young fellow, youngster, youth

strive attempt, bend over backwards (*Inf.*), break one's neck (*Inf.*), bust a gut (*Inf.*), compete, contend, do all one can, do one's best, do one's damnedest (*Inf.*), do one's utmost, endeavour, exert oneself, fight, give it one's all (*Inf.*), give it one's best shot (*Inf.*), go all out (*Inf.*), go for broke (*Sl.*), go for it (*Inf.*), knock oneself out (*Inf.*), labour, leave no stone unturned, make an all-out effort (*Inf.*), make every effort, rupture oneself (*Inf.*), strain, struggle, toil, try, try hard

stroke *n.* 1. accomplishment, achievement, blow, feat, flourish, hit, knock, move, movement, pat, rap, thump 2. apoplexy, attack, collapse, fit, seizure, shock ~*v.* 3. caress, fondle, pat, pet, rub

stroll 1. *v.* amble, make one's way, mooch (*Sl.*), mosey (*Inf.*), promenade, ramble, saunter, stooge (*Sl.*), stretch one's legs, take a turn, toddle, wander 2. *n.* airing, breath of air, constitutional, excursion, promenade, ramble, turn, walk

strong 1. athletic, beefy (*Inf.*), brawny, burly, capable, hale, hardy, healthy, Herculean, lusty, muscular, powerful, robust, sinewy, sound, stalwart, stout, strapping, sturdy, tough, virile 2. aggressive, brave, courageous, determined, feisty (*Inf., chiefly U.S. & Canad.*), firm in spirit, forceful, hard as nails, hard-nosed (*Inf.*), high-powered, plucky, resilient, resolute, resourceful, self-assertive, steadfast, stout-hearted, tenacious, tough, unyielding 3. acute, dedicated, deep, deep-rooted, eager, fervent, fervid, fierce, firm, intense, keen, severe, staunch, vehement, violent, zealous 4. clear, clear-cut, cogent, compelling, convincing, distinct, effective, formidable, great, marked, overpowering, persuasive, potent, redoubtable, sound, telling, trenchant, unmistakable, urgent, weighty, well-established, well-founded 5. Draconian, drastic, extreme, forceful, severe 6. durable, hard-wearing, heavy-duty, on a firm foundation, reinforced, sturdy, substantial, well-armed, well-built, well-protected 7. bold, bright, brilliant, dazzling, glaring, loud, stark 8. biting, concentrated, heady, highly-flavoured, highly-seasoned, hot, intoxicating, piquant, pungent, pure, sharp, spicy, undiluted

Antonyms (*senses 1, 2, 3, 4, 5 & 6*) characterless, delicate, faint-hearted, feeble, frail, ineffectual, lacking drive, namby-pamby, puny, slight, spineless, timid, unassertive, uncommitted, unimpassioned, weak (*sense 7*) dull, insipid, pale, pastel, washed-out (*sense 8*) bland, mild, tasteless, vapid, weak

strong-arm *adj.* aggressive, bullying, coercive, forceful, high-pressure, terror, terrorizing, threatening, thuggish, violent

stronghold bastion, bulwark, castle, citadel, fastness, fort, fortress, keep, refuge

strong-minded determined, firm, independent, iron-willed, resolute, strong-willed, unbending, uncompromising

strong point advantage, asset, forte, long suit (*Inf.*), métier, speciality, strength, strong suit

stroppy awkward, bloody-minded (*Brit. inf.*), cantankerous, destructive, difficult, obstreperous, perverse, quarrelsome, uncooperative, unhelpful

structure *n.* 1. arrangement, configuration, conformation, construction, design, fabric, form, formation, interrelation of parts, make, make-up, organization 2. building, construction, edifice, erection, pile ~*v.* 3. arrange, assemble, build up, design, organize, put together, shape

struggle *v.* 1. bend over backwards (*Inf.*), break one's neck (*Inf.*), bust a gut (*Inf.*), do one's damnedest (*Inf.*), exert oneself, give it one's all (*Inf.*), give it one's best shot (*Inf.*), go all out (*Inf.*), go for broke (*Sl.*), go for it (*Inf.*), knock oneself out (*Inf.*), labour, make an all-out effort (*Inf.*), make every effort, rupture oneself (*Inf.*), strain, strive, toil, work, work like a Trojan ~*n.* 2. effort, exertion, grind (*Inf.*), labour, long haul, pains, scramble, toil, work ~*v.* 3. battle, compete, contend, fight, grapple, lock horns, scuffle, wrestle ~*n.* 4. battle, brush, clash, combat, conflict, contest, encounter, hostilities, skirmish, strife, tussle

strung up a bundle of nerves (*Inf.*), edgy, jittery (*Inf.*), keyed up, nervous, on edge, on tenterhooks, tense, twitchy (*Inf.*), under a strain, uptight (*Inf.*), wired (*Sl.*)

strut *v.* parade, peacock, prance, stalk, swagger

stub *n.* butt, counterfoil, dog-end (*Inf.*), end, fag end (*Inf.*), remnant, stump, tail, tail end

stubborn bull-headed, contumacious, cross-grained, dogged, dour, fixed, headstrong, inflexible, intractable, mulish, obdurate, obstinate, opinionated, persistent, pig-headed, recalcitrant, refractory, self-willed, stiff-necked, tenacious, unbending, unmanageable, unshakable, unyielding, wilful

Antonyms biddable, compliant, docile, flexible, half-hearted, irresolute, malleable, manageable, pliable, pliant, tractable, vacillating, wavering, yielding

stubby 1. chunky, dumpy, fubsy (*Archaic or dialect*), short, squat, stocky, stumpy, thickset 2. bristling, bristly, prickly, rough, stubbly

stuck 1. cemented, fast, fastened, firm, fixed, glued, joined 2. *Inf.* at a loss, at a standstill, at one's wits' end, baffled, beaten, bereft of ideas, nonplussed, stumped, up against a brick wall (*Inf.*) 3. *Sl. With* **on** crazy about, for, *or* over (*Inf.*), enthusiastic about, hung up on (*Sl.*), infatuated, keen, mad, obsessed with, wild about (*Inf.*) 4. **get stuck into** *Inf.* get down to, make a start on, set about, tackle

stuck-up arrogant, big-headed (*Inf.*), conceited, condescending, haughty, high and mighty (*Inf.*), hoity-toity (*Inf.*), patronizing, proud, snobbish, snooty (*Inf.*), swollen-headed, toffee-nosed (*Sl., chiefly Brit.*), uppish (*Brit. inf.*), uppity (*Inf.*)

stud *v.* bejewel, bespangle, dot, fleck, ornament, spangle, speckle, spot, sprinkle

student apprentice, disciple, learner, observer, pupil, scholar, trainee, undergraduate

studied calculated, conscious, deliberate, intentional, planned, premeditated, purposeful, well-considered, wilful

Antonyms impulsive, natural, spontaneous, spur-of-the-moment, unplanned, unpremeditated

studio atelier, workshop

studious academic, assiduous, attentive, bookish, careful, diligent, eager, earnest, hard-working, intellectual, meditative, reflective, scholarly, sedulous, serious, thoughtful

Antonyms careless, frivolous, idle, inattentive, indifferent, lazy, loafing, negligent, unacademic, unintellectual, unscholarly

study *v.* 1. apply oneself (to), bone up on (*Inf.*), burn the midnight oil, cogitate, con (*Archaic*), consider, contemplate, cram (*Inf.*), examine, go into, hammer away at, learn, lucubrate (*Rare*), meditate, mug up (*Brit. sl.*), ponder, pore over, read, read up, swot (up) (*Brit. inf.*) 2. analyse, deliberate, examine, investigate, look into, peruse, research, scrutinize, survey, work over ~*n.* 3. academic work, application, book work, cramming (*Inf.*), learning, lessons, reading, research, school work, swotting (*Brit. inf.*), thought 4. analysis, attention, cogitation, consideration, contemplation, examination, inquiry, inspection, investigation, perusal, review, scrutiny, survey

stuff *v.* 1. compress, cram, crowd, fill, force, jam, load, pack, pad, push, ram, shove, squeeze, stow, wedge 2. gobble, gorge, gormandize, guzzle, make a pig of oneself (*Inf.*), overindulge, pig out (*Sl.*), sate, satiate ~*n.* 3. belongings, bits and pieces, clobber (*Brit. sl.*), effects, equipment, gear, goods and chattels, impedimenta, junk, kit, luggage, materials, objects, paraphernalia, possessions, tackle, things, trappings 4. cloth, fabric, material, raw material, textile 5. essence, matter, pith, quintessence, staple, substance 6. balderdash, baloney (*Inf.*), bosh (*Inf.*), bunk (*Inf.*), bunkum, claptrap (*Inf.*), foolishness, humbug, nonsense, poppycock (*Inf.*), rot, rubbish, stuff and nonsense, tommyrot, tripe (*Inf.*), twaddle, verbiage

stuffing 1. filler, kapok, packing, quilting, wadding 2. farce, farcemeat, forcemeat

stuffy 1. airless, close, fetid, frowsty, fuggy, heavy, muggy, oppressive, stale, stifling, suffocating, sultry, unventilated 2. conventional, deadly, dreary, dull, fusty, humour-

less, musty, old-fashioned, old-fogyish, pompous, priggish, prim, prim and proper, staid, stilted, stodgy, strait-laced, uninteresting
Antonyms (*sense 1*) airy, breezy, cool, draughty, fresh, gusty, pleasant, well-ventilated

stumble 1. blunder about, come a cropper (*Inf.*), fall, falter, flounder, hesitate, lose one's balance, lurch, reel, slip, stagger, trip 2. *With* **on** *or* **upon** blunder upon, chance upon, come across, discover, encounter, find, happen upon, light upon, run across, turn up 3. falter, fluff (*Inf.*), stammer, stutter

stumbling block bar, barrier, difficulty, hindrance, hurdle, impediment, obstacle, obstruction, snag

stump *v.* 1. baffle, bewilder, bring (someone) up short, confound, confuse, dumbfound, flummox, foil, mystify, nonplus, outwit, perplex, puzzle, stop, stymie 2. clomp, clump, lumber, plod, stamp, stomp (*Inf.*), trudge

stumped at a loss, at one's wits' end, at sea, baffled, brought to a standstill, floored (*Inf.*), flummoxed, in despair, nonplussed, perplexed, stymied, uncertain which way to turn

stump up chip in (*Inf.*), come across with (*Inf.*), contribute, cough up (*Inf.*), donate, fork out (*Sl.*), hand over, pay, shell out (*Inf.*)

stumpy chunky, dumpy, fubsy (*Archaic or dialect*), heavy, short, squat, stocky, stubby, thick, thickset

stun *Fig.* amaze, astonish, astound, bewilder, confound, confuse, daze, dumbfound, flabbergast (*Inf.*), hit (someone) like a ton of bricks (*Inf.*), knock out, knock (someone) for six (*Inf.*), overcome, overpower, shock, stagger, strike (someone) dumb, stupefy, take (someone's) breath away

stung angered, exasperated, goaded, hurt, incensed, nettled, piqued, resentful, roused, wounded

stunned *Fig.* astounded, at a loss for words, bowled over (*Inf.*), dazed, devastated, dumbfounded, flabbergasted (*Inf.*), gobsmacked (*Brit. sl.*), numb, shocked, staggered, struck dumb

stunner beauty, charmer, dazzler, dish (*Inf.*), dolly (*Sl.*), eyeful (*Inf.*), glamour puss, good-looker, heart-throb, honey (*Inf.*), knockout (*Inf.*), looker (*Inf., chiefly U.S.*), lovely (*Sl.*), peach (*Inf.*), sensation, smasher (*Inf.*), wow (*Sl., chiefly U.S.*)

stunning beautiful, brilliant, dazzling, devastating (*Inf.*), drop-dead (*Sl.*), gorgeous, great (*Inf.*), heavenly, impressive, lovely, marvellous, out of this world (*Inf.*), ravishing, remarkable, sensational (*Inf.*), smashing (*Inf.*), spectacular, striking, wonderful
Antonyms average, dreadful, horrible, mediocre, ordinary, plain, poor, rotten, run-of-the-mill, ugly, unattractive, unimpressive, uninspiring, unremarkable

stunt *n.* act, deed, exploit, feat, feature, gest (*Archaic*), *tour de force,* trick

stunted diminutive, dwarfed, dwarfish, little, small, tiny, undersized

stupefaction amazement, astonishment, awe, wonder, wonderment

stupefy amaze, astound, bewilder, confound, daze, dumbfound, knock senseless, numb, shock, stagger, stun

stupendous amazing, astounding, breathtaking, brilliant, colossal, enormous, fabulous (*Inf.*), fantastic (*Inf.*), gigantic, huge, marvellous, mega (*Sl.*), mind-blowing (*Inf.*), mind-boggling (*Inf.*), out of this world (*Inf.*), overwhelming, phenomenal, prodigious, sensational (*Inf.*), staggering, stunning (*Inf.*), superb, surpassing belief, surprising, tremendous (*Inf.*), vast, wonderful, wondrous (*Archaic or literary*)
Antonyms average, diminutive, mediocre, modest, ordinary, petty, puny, tiny, unexciting, unimpressive, unremarkable, unsurprising

stupid 1. Boeotian, braindead (*Inf.*), brainless, cretinous, deficient, dense, dim, doltish, dopey (*Inf.*), dozy (*Brit. inf.*), dull, dumb (*Inf.*), foolish, gullible, half-witted, moronic, naive, obtuse, simple, simple-minded, slow, slow on the uptake (*Inf.*), slow-witted, sluggish, stolid, thick, thickheaded, unintelligent, witless, woodenheaded (*Inf.*) 2. asinine, crackbrained, daft (*Inf.*), futile, half-baked (*Inf.*), idiotic, ill-advised, imbecilic, inane, indiscreet, irrelevant, irresponsible, laughable, ludicrous, meaningless, mindless, nonsensical, pointless, puerile, rash, senseless, short-sighted, trivial, unintelligent, unthinking 3. dazed, groggy, in a daze, insensate, punch-drunk, semiconscious, senseless, stunned, stupefied
Antonyms astute, brainy, bright, brilliant, clear-headed, clever, intelligent, lucid, on the ball (*Inf.*), prudent, quick, quick on the uptake, quick-witted, realistic, reasonable, sensible, sharp, shrewd, smart, thoughtful, well thought-out, wise

stupidity 1. asininity, brainlessness, denseness, dimness, dopiness (*Sl.*), doziness (*Brit. inf.*), dullness, dumbness (*Inf.*), feeble-mindedness, imbecility, lack of brain, lack of intelligence, naivety, obtuseness, puerility, simplicity, slowness, thick-headedness, thickness 2. absurdity, bêtise (*Rare*), fatuity, fatuousness, folly, foolhardiness, foolishness, futility, idiocy, impracticality, inanity, indiscretion, ineptitude, irresponsibility, ludicrousness, lunacy, madness, pointlessness, rashness, senselessness, silliness

stupor coma, daze, inertia, insensibility, lethargy, numbness, stupefaction, torpor, trance, unconsciousness

sturdy athletic, brawny, built to last, determined, durable, firm, flourishing, hardy, hearty, lusty, muscular, powerful, resolute, robust, secure, solid, stalwart, staunch, steadfast, stouthearted, substantial, thick-set, vigorous, well-built, well-made

Antonyms feeble, flimsy, frail, infirm, irresolute, puny, rickety, skinny, uncertain, unsubstantial, weak, weakly

stutter *v.* falter, hesitate, speak haltingly, splutter, stammer, stumble

Stygian black, caliginous (*Archaic*), dark, dreary, gloomy, Hadean, hellish, infernal, sombre, Tartarean, tenebrous

style *n.* 1. cut, design, form, hand, manner, technique 2. fashion, mode, rage, trend, vogue 3. approach, custom, manner, method, mode, way 4. *bon ton,* chic, cosmopolitanism, dash, dressiness (*Inf.*), élan, elegance, fashionableness, flair, grace, panache, polish, refinement, savoir-faire, smartness, sophistication, stylishness, taste, urbanity 5. affluence, comfort, ease, elegance, gracious living, grandeur, luxury 6. appearance, category, characteristic, genre, kind, pattern, sort, spirit, strain, tenor, tone, type, variety 7. diction, expression, mode of expression, phraseology, phrasing, treatment, turn of phrase, vein, wording ~*v.* 8. adapt, arrange, cut, design, dress, fashion, shape, tailor 9. address, call, christen, denominate, designate, dub, entitle, label, name, term

stylish à la mode, chic, classy (*Sl.*), dapper, dressy (*Inf.*), fashionable, in fashion, in vogue, modish, natty (*Inf.*), polished, smart, snappy, snazzy (*Inf.*), trendy (*Brit. inf.*), urbane, voguish, well turned-out

Antonyms badly-tailored, naff (*Brit. sl.*), old-fashioned, out-moded, out-of-date, passé, scruffy, shabby, slovenly, tacky, tawdry, unfashionable, unstylish, untrendy (*Brit. inf.*)

stymie balk, confound, defeat, flummox, foil, frustrate, hinder, mystify, nonplus, puzzle, snooker, spike (someone's) guns, stump, throw a spanner in the works (*Brit. inf.*), thwart

suave affable, agreeable, bland, charming, civilized, cool (*Inf.*), courteous, debonair, diplomatic, gracious, obliging, pleasing, polite, smooth, smooth-tongued, sophisticated, svelte, urbane, worldly

subconscious *adj.* hidden, inner, innermost, intuitive, latent, repressed, subliminal, suppressed

Antonyms aware, conscious, knowing, sensible, sentient

subdue 1. beat down, break, conquer, control, crush, defeat, discipline, gain ascendancy over, get the better of, get the upper hand over, get under control, humble, master, overcome, overpower, overrun, put down, quell, tame, trample, triumph over, vanquish 2. check, control, mellow, moderate, quieten down, repress, soften, suppress, tone down

Antonyms (*sense 2*) agitate, arouse, awaken, incite, provoke, stir up, waken, whip up

subdued 1. chastened, crestfallen, dejected, downcast, down in the mouth, grave, out of spirits, quiet, repentant, repressed, restrained, sad, sadder and wiser, serious, sobered, solemn 2. dim, hushed, low-key, muted, quiet, shaded, sober, soft, subtle, toned down, unobtrusive

Antonyms bright, cheerful, enthusiastic, happy, lively, loud, strident, vivacious

subject *n.* 1. affair, business, field of enquiry *or* reference, issue, matter, object, point, question, subject matter, substance, theme, topic 2. case, client, guinea pig (*Inf.*), participant, patient, victim 3. citizen, dependant, liegeman, national, subordinate, vassal ~*adj.* 4. at the mercy of, disposed, exposed, in danger of, liable, open, prone, susceptible, vulnerable 5. conditional, contingent, dependent 6. answerable, bound by, captive, dependent, enslaved, inferior, obedient, satellite, subjugated, submissive, subordinate, subservient ~*v.* 7. expose, lay open, make liable, put through, submit, treat

subjective biased, emotional, idiosyncratic, instinctive, intuitive, nonobjective, personal, prejudiced

Antonyms concrete, detached, disinterested, dispassionate, impartial, impersonal, objective, open-minded, unbiased

subjugate bring (someone) to his knees, bring to heel, bring under the yoke, conquer, crush, defeat, enslave, hold sway over, lick (*Inf.*), master, overcome, overpower, overthrow, put down, quell, reduce, rule over, subdue, suppress, tame, vanquish

sublimate 1. channel, divert, redirect, transfer, turn 2. elevate, exalt, heighten, refine

sublime elevated, eminent, exalted, glorious, grand, great, high, imposing, lofty, magnificent, majestic, noble, transcendent
Antonyms bad, commonplace, lowly, mundane, ordinary, poor, ridiculous, worldly

submerge deluge, dip, drown, duck, dunk, engulf, flood, immerse, inundate, overflow, overwhelm, plunge, sink, swamp

submerged drowned, immersed, subaquatic, subaqueous, submarine, submersed, sunk, sunken, undersea, underwater

submission 1. acquiescence, assent, capitulation, giving in, surrender, yielding 2. compliance, deference, docility, meekness, obedience, passivity, resignation, submissiveness, tractability, unassertiveness 3. argument, contention, proposal 4. entry, handing in, presentation, submitting, tendering

submissive abject, accommodating, acquiescent, amenable, biddable, bootlicking (*Inf.*), compliant, deferential, docile, dutiful, humble, ingratiating, lowly, malleable, meek, obedient, obeisant, obsequious, passive, patient, pliant, resigned, subdued, tractable, uncomplaining, unresisting, yielding
Antonyms awkward, difficult, disobedient, headstrong, intractable, obstinate, stubborn, uncooperative, unyielding

submit 1. accede, acquiesce, agree, bend, bow, capitulate, comply, defer, endure, give in, hoist the white flag, knuckle under, lay down arms, put up with (*Inf.*), resign oneself, stoop, succumb, surrender, throw in the sponge, toe the line, tolerate, yield 2. commit, hand in, present, proffer, put forward, refer, table, tender 3. advance, argue, assert, claim, contend, move, propose, propound, put, state, suggest, volunteer

subnormal cretinous, E.S.N., feebleminded, imbecilic, mentally defective, moronic, retarded, simple, slow

subordinate *adj.* 1. dependent, inferior, junior, lesser, lower, minor, secondary, subject, subservient 2. ancillary, auxiliary, subsidiary, supplementary ~*n.* 3. aide, assistant, attendant, dependant, inferior, junior, second, subaltern, underling
Antonyms *adj.* central, essential, greater, higher, key, main, necessary, predominant, senior, superior, vital ~*n.* boss (*Inf.*), captain, chief, commander, head, leader, master, principal, senior, superior

subordination inferior *or* secondary status, inferiority, servitude, subjection, submission

sub rosa behind closed doors, in camera, in secret, in strict confidence, secretly

subscribe 1. chip in (*Inf.*), contribute, donate, give, offer, pledge, promise 2. acquiesce, advocate, agree, consent, countenance, endorse, support

subscription annual payment, contribution, donation, dues, gift, membership fee, offering

subsequent after, consequent, consequential, ensuing, following, later, succeeding, successive
Antonyms antecedent, earlier, erstwhile, former, on-time, past, preceding, previous, prior

subsequently afterwards, at a later date, consequently, in the aftermath (of), in the end, later

subservient 1. abject, bootlicking (*Inf.*), deferential, inferior, obsequious, servile, slavish, subject, submissive, sycophantic, truckling 2. accessory, ancillary, auxiliary, conducive, helpful, instrumental, serviceable, subordinate, subsidiary, useful
Antonyms (*sense 1*) bolshie, bossy, disobedient, domineering, overbearing, overriding, rebellious, superior, wilful

subside 1. abate, decrease, de-escalate, diminish, dwindle, ease, ebb, lessen, let up, level off, melt away, moderate, peter out, quieten, recede, slacken, wane 2. cave in, collapse, decline, descend, drop, ebb, lower, settle, sink
Antonyms grow, escalate, heighten, increase, inflate, intensify, mount, rise, soar, swell, tumefy, wax

subsidence 1. decline, descent, ebb, settlement, settling, sinking 2. abatement, decrease, de-escalation, diminution, easing off, lessening, slackening

subsidiary aiding, ancillary, assistant, auxiliary, contributory, cooperative, helpful, lesser, minor, secondary, serviceable, subordinate, subservient, supplemental, supplementary, useful
Antonyms central, chief, head, key, leading, main, major, primary, principal, vital

subsidize finance, fund, promote, put up the money for, sponsor, support, underwrite

subsidy aid, allowance, assistance, contribution, financial aid, grant, help, stipend, subvention, support

subsist be, continue, eke out an existence, endure, exist, keep going, last, live, make ends meet, remain, stay alive, survive, sustain oneself

subsistence aliment, existence, food, keep, livelihood, living, maintenance, provision, rations, support, survival, sustenance, upkeep, victuals

substance 1. body, element, fabric, material, stuff, texture 2. burden, essence, gist, gravamen (*Law*), import, main point, matter, meaning, pith, significance, subject, sum and substance, theme 3. actuality, concreteness, entity, force, reality 4. affluence, assets, estate, means, property, resources, wealth

substandard damaged, imperfect, inadequate, inferior, second-rate, shoddy, unacceptable

substantial 1. ample, big, considerable, generous, goodly, important, large, significant, sizable, tidy (*Inf.*), worthwhile 2. bulky, durable, firm, hefty, massive, solid, sound, stout, strong, sturdy, well-built 3. actual, existent, material, positive, real, true, valid, weighty
Antonyms (*senses 1 & 2*) feeble, frail, inadequate, inconsiderable, infirm, insignificant, insubstantial, jerry-built, lightweight, meagre, niggardly, poor, rickety, skimpy, small, weak (*sense 3*) fictitious, imaginary, imagined, insubstantial, nonexistent, unreal

substantially essentially, in essence, in essentials, in substance, in the main, largely, materially, to a large extent

substantiate affirm, attest to, authenticate, bear out, confirm, corroborate, establish, prove, support, validate, verify
Antonyms confute, contradict, controvert, disprove, expose, invalidate, negate, prove false, rebut, refute

substitute *v.* 1. change, commute, exchange, interchange, replace, swap (*Inf.*), switch 2. *With* **for** act for, be in place of, cover for, deputize, double for, fill in for, hold the fort for, relieve, stand in for, take over ~*n.* 3. agent, depute (*Scot.*), deputy, equivalent, expedient, locum, locum tenens, makeshift, proxy, relief, replacement, representative, reserve, stand-by, stopgap, sub, supply, surrogate, temp (*Inf.*), temporary ~*adj.* 4. acting, additional, alternative, fall-back, proxy, replacement, reserve, second, surrogate, temporary

substitution change, exchange, interchange, replacement, swap (*Inf.*), switch

subterfuge artifice, deception, deviousness, dodge, duplicity, evasion, excuse, machination, manoeuvre, ploy, pretence, pretext, quibble, ruse, shift, stall, stratagem, trick

subtle 1. deep, delicate, discriminating, ingenious, nice, penetrating, profound, refined, sophisticated 2. delicate, faint, implied, indirect, insinuated, slight, understated 3. artful, astute, crafty, cunning, designing, devious, intriguing, keen, Machiavellian, scheming, shrewd, sly, wily
Antonyms artless, blunt, crass, direct, downright, guileless, heavy-handed, lacking finesse, obvious, overwhelming, simple, straightforward, strong, tactless, unsophisticated, unsubtle

subtlety 1. acumen, acuteness, cleverness, delicacy, discernment, fine point, intricacy, nicety, refinement, sagacity, skill, sophistication 2. discernment, discrimination, finesse, penetration 3. artfulness, astuteness, craftiness, cunning, deviousness, guile, slyness, wiliness

subtract deduct, detract, diminish, remove, take away, take from, take off, withdraw
Antonyms add, add to, append, increase by, supplement

suburbs dormitory area (*Brit.*), environs, faubourgs, neighbourhood, outskirts, precincts, purlieus, residential areas, suburbia

subversive 1. *adj.* destructive, incendiary, inflammatory, insurrectionary, overthrowing, perversive, riotous, seditious, treasonous, underground, undermining 2. *n.* deviationist, dissident, fifth columnist, insurrectionary, quisling, saboteur, seditionary, seditionist, terrorist, traitor

subvert 1. demolish, destroy, invalidate, overturn, raze, ruin, sabotage, undermine, upset, wreck 2. confound, contaminate, corrupt, debase, demoralize, deprave, pervert, poison, vitiate

succeed 1. arrive (*Inf.*), be successful, come off (*Inf.*), crack it (*Inf.*), cut it (*Inf.*), do all right for oneself (*Inf.*), do the trick (*Inf.*), flourish, gain one's end, get to the top, make good, make it (*Inf.*), prosper, thrive, triumph, turn out well, work 2. be subsequent, come next, ensue, follow, result, supervene 3. *Usually with* **to** accede, assume the office of, come into, come into possession of, enter upon, inherit, replace, take over
Antonyms (*sense 1*) be unsuccessful, collapse, come a cropper (*Inf.*), fail, fall flat, fall short, flop (*Inf.*), not make the grade, not manage to (*sense 2*) be a precursor of, come before, go ahead of, go before, pave the way, precede

succeeding ensuing, following, next, subsequent, successive
Antonyms antecedent, earlier, former, preceding, previous, prior

success 1. ascendancy, eminence, fame, favourable outcome, fortune, happiness, hit (*Inf.*), luck, prosperity, triumph 2. best seller, big name, celebrity, hit (*Inf.*), market leader, megastar (*Inf.*), sensation,

smash hit (*Inf.*), somebody, star, V.I.P., winner
Antonyms collapse, dead duck (*Sl.*), disaster, downfall, failure, fiasco, flop (*Inf.*), loser, misfortune, nobody, no-hoper, washout

successful acknowledged, at the top of the tree, best-selling, booming, efficacious, favourable, flourishing, fortunate, fruitful, lucky, lucrative, moneymaking, out in front (*Inf.*), paying, profitable, prosperous, rewarding, thriving, top, unbeaten, victorious, wealthy
Antonyms defeated, failed, ineffective, losing, luckless, uneconomic, unprofitable, unsuccessful, useless

successfully famously (*Inf.*), favourably, in triumph, swimmingly, victoriously, well, with flying colours

succession 1. chain, continuation, course, cycle, flow, order, procession, progression, run, sequence, series, train 2. **in succession** consecutively, one after the other, one behind the other, on the trot (*Inf.*), running, successively 3. accession, assumption, elevation, entering upon, inheritance, taking over 4. descendants, descent, line, lineage, race

successive consecutive, following, in a row, in succession, sequent, succeeding

succinct brief, compact, compendious, concise, condensed, gnomic, in a few well-chosen words, laconic, pithy, summary, terse, to the point
Antonyms circuitous, circumlocutory, diffuse, discursive, long-winded, prolix, rambling, verbose, wordy

succour 1. *v.* aid, assist, befriend, comfort, encourage, foster, give aid and encouragement to, help, minister to, nurse, relieve, render assistance to, support 2. *n.* aid, assistance, comfort, help, relief, support

succulent juicy, luscious, lush, mellow, moist, mouthwatering, rich

succumb capitulate, die, fall, fall victim to, give in, give way, go under, knuckle under, submit, surrender, yield
Antonyms beat, conquer, get the better of, master, overcome, rise above, surmount, triumph over

sucker butt, cat's paw, dupe, easy game *or* mark (*Inf.*), fool, mug (*Brit. sl.*), nerd *or* nurd (*Sl.*), pushover (*Sl.*), sap (*Sl.*), sitting duck (*Inf.*), victim

suck up to brown-nose (*Taboo sl.*), butter up, curry favour with, dance attendance on, fawn on, flatter, get on the right side of, ingratiate oneself with, keep in with (*Inf.*), kiss (someone's) ass (*U.S. & Canad. taboo sl.*), lick (someone's) boots, pander to, play up to (*Inf.*), toady, truckle, worm oneself into (someone's) favour

sudden abrupt, hasty, hurried, impulsive, quick, rapid, rash, swift, unexpected, unforeseen, unusual
Antonyms anticipated, deliberate, expected, foreseen, gentle, gradual, slow, unhasty

suddenly abruptly, all at once, all of a sudden, on the spur of the moment, out of the blue (*Inf.*), unexpectedly, without warning

sue 1. *Law* bring an action against (someone), charge, have the law on (someone) (*Inf.*), indict, institute legal proceedings against (someone), prefer charges against (someone), prosecute, summon, take (someone) to court 2. appeal for, beg, beseech, entreat, petition, plead, solicit, supplicate

suffer 1. ache, agonize, be affected, be in pain, be racked, feel wretched, go through a lot (*Inf.*), grieve, have a thin *or* bad time, hurt 2. bear, endure, experience, feel, go through, put up with (*Inf.*), support, sustain, tolerate, undergo 3. appear in a poor light, be handicapped, be impaired, deteriorate, fall off, show to disadvantage 4. *Archaic* allow, let, permit

suffering *n.* affliction, agony, anguish, discomfort, distress, hardship, martyrdom, misery, ordeal, pain, torment, torture

suffice answer, be sufficient (adequate, enough), content, do, fill the bill (*Inf.*), meet requirements, satisfy, serve

sufficient adequate, competent, enough, enow (*Archaic*), satisfactory
Antonyms deficient, inadequate, insufficient, meagre, not enough, poor, scant, short, sparse

suffocate asphyxiate, choke, smother, stifle, strangle

suffrage ballot, consent, franchise, right to vote, voice (*Fig.*), vote

suffuse bathe, cover, flood, imbue, infuse, mantle, overspread, permeate, pervade, spread over, steep, transfuse

suggest 1. advise, advocate, move, offer a suggestion, prescribe, propose, put forward, recommend 2. bring to mind, connote, evoke, put one in mind of 3. hint, imply, indicate, insinuate, intimate, lead one to believe

suggestion 1. motion, plan, proposal, proposition, recommendation 2. breath, hint, indication, insinuation, intimation, suspicion, trace, whisper

suggestive 1. *With* **of** evocative, expressive, indicative, redolent, reminiscent 2. bawdy, blue, immodest, improper, indecent, indelicate, off colour, provocative, prurient, racy, ribald, risqué, rude, smutty, spicy (*Inf.*), titillating, unseemly

suit *v.* 1. agree, agree with, answer, be acceptable to, become, befit, be seemly, conform to, correspond, do, go with, gratify, harmonize, match, please, satisfy, tally 2. accommodate, adapt, adjust, fashion, fit, modify, proportion, tailor ~*n.* 3. addresses, appeal, attentions, courtship, entreaty, invocation, petition, prayer, request 4. *Law* action, case, cause, industrial tribunal, lawsuit, proceeding, prosecution, trial 5. clothing, costume, dress, ensemble, habit, outfit 6. **follow suit** accord with, copy, emulate, run with the herd, take one's cue from

suitability appropriateness, aptness, fitness, opportuneness, rightness, timeliness

suitable acceptable, applicable, apposite, appropriate, apt, becoming, befitting, convenient, cut out for, due, fit, fitting, in character, in keeping, opportune, pertinent, proper, relevant, right, satisfactory, seemly, suited

Antonyms discordant, inapposite, inappropriate, incorrect, inopportune, jarring, out of character, out of keeping, unbecoming, unfitting, unseemly, unsuitable, unsuited

suite 1. apartment, collection, furniture, rooms, series, set 2. attendants, entourage, escort, followers, retainers, retinue, train

suitor admirer, beau, follower (*Obsolete*), swain (*Archaic*), wooer, young man

sulk be in a huff, be put out, brood, have the hump (*Brit. inf.*), look sullen, pout

sulky aloof, churlish, cross, disgruntled, huffy, ill-humoured, in the sulks, moody, morose, perverse, petulant, put out, querulous, resentful, sullen, vexed

sullen brooding, cheerless, cross, dismal, dull, gloomy, glowering, heavy, moody, morose, obstinate, out of humour, perverse, silent, sombre, sour, stubborn, surly, unsociable

Antonyms amiable, bright, cheerful, cheery, chirpy (*Inf.*), genial, good-humoured, good-natured, pleasant, sociable, sunny, warm, warm-hearted

sullenness glumness, heaviness, ill humour, moodiness, moroseness, sourness, sulkiness, sulks

sully befoul, besmirch, blemish, contaminate, darken, defile, dirty, disgrace, dishonour, pollute, smirch, spoil, spot, stain, taint, tarnish

sultry 1. close, hot, humid, muggy, oppressive, sticky, stifling, stuffy, sweltering 2. amorous, come-hither (*Inf.*), erotic, passionate, provocative, seductive, sensual, sexy (*Inf.*), voluptuous

Antonyms (*sense 1*) cool, fresh, invigorating, refreshing

sum aggregate, amount, entirety, quantity, reckoning, score, sum total, tally, total, totality, whole

summarily arbitrarily, at short notice, expeditiously, forthwith, immediately, on the spot, peremptorily, promptly, speedily, swiftly, without delay, without wasting words

summarize abridge, condense, encapsulate, epitomize, give a rundown of, give the main points of, outline, précis, put in a nutshell, review, sum up

summary 1. *n.* abridgment, abstract, compendium, digest, epitome, essence, extract, outline, précis, recapitulation, résumé, review, rundown, summing-up, synopsis 2. *adj.* arbitrary, brief, compact, compendious, concise, condensed, cursory, hasty, laconic, perfunctory, pithy, succinct

summit acme, apex, crest, crown, crowning point, culmination, head, height, peak, pinnacle, top, zenith

Antonyms base, bottom, depths, foot, lowest point, nadir

summon 1. arouse, assemble, bid, call, call together, cite, convene, convoke, invite, rally, rouse, send for 2. *Often with* **up** call into action, draw on, gather, invoke, mobilize, muster

sumptuous costly, dear, de luxe, expensive, extravagant, gorgeous, grand, lavish, luxurious, magnificent, opulent, plush (*Inf.*), posh (*Inf., chiefly Brit.*), rich, ritzy (*Sl.*), splendid, splendiferous (*Facetious*), superb

Antonyms austere, basic, cheap, frugal, inexpensive, meagre, mean, miserly, plain, shabby, wretched

sum up 1. close, conclude, put in a nutshell, recapitulate, review, summarize 2. estimate, form an opinion of, get the measure of, size up (*Inf.*)

sun 1. *n.* daystar (*Poetic*), eye of heaven, Helios (*Greek myth*), Phoebus (*Greek myth*), Phoebus Apollo (*Greek myth*), Sol (*Roman myth*) 2. *v.* bake, bask, sunbathe, tan

sunburnt bronzed, brown, brown as a berry, burnt, like a lobster, peeling, red, ruddy, scarlet, tanned

sundry assorted, different, divers (*Archaic*), miscellaneous, several, some, varied, various

sunk all washed up (*Inf.*), done for (*Inf.*), finished, lost, on the rocks, ruined, up the creek without a paddle (*Inf.*)

sunken 1. concave, drawn, haggard, hollow, hollowed 2. at a lower level, below ground, buried, depressed, immersed, lower, recessed, submerged

sunless bleak, cheerless, cloudy, dark, depressing, gloomy, grey, hazy, overcast, sombre

sunny 1. bright, brilliant, clear, fine, luminous, radiant, summery, sunlit, sunshiny, unclouded, without a cloud in the sky 2. *Fig.* beaming, blithe, buoyant, cheerful, cheery, chirpy (*Inf.*), genial, happy, joyful, light-hearted, optimistic, pleasant, smiling
Antonyms cloudy, depressing, doleful, down in the dumps, dreary, dreich (*Scot.*), dull, gloomy, miserable, morbid, murky, overcast, rainy, shaded, shadowy, sunless, unsmiling, wet, wintry

sunrise aurora (*Poetic*), break of day, cockcrow, dawn, daybreak, daylight, dayspring (*Poetic*), sunup

sunset close of (the) day, dusk, eventide, gloaming (*Scot. or poetic*), nightfall, sundown

super boffo (*Sl.*), brill (*Inf.*), chillin' (*U.S. sl.*), cracking (*Brit. inf.*), crucial (*Sl.*), def (*Sl.*), excellent, glorious, incomparable, jim-dandy (*Sl.*), magnificent, marvellous, matchless, mean (*Sl.*), mega (*Sl.*), out of this world (*Inf.*), outstanding, peerless, sensational (*Inf.*), smashing (*Inf.*), sovereign, superb, terrific (*Inf.*), topnotch (*Inf.*), topping (*Brit. sl.*), wonderful

superannuated aged, antiquated, decrepit, discharged, obsolete, old, past it (*Inf.*), pensioned off, put out to grass (*Inf.*), retired, senile, unfit

superb admirable, boffo (*Sl.*), breathtaking, brill (*Inf.*), chillin' (*U.S. sl.*), choice, excellent, exquisite, fine, first-rate, gorgeous, grand, magnificent, marvellous, mega (*Sl.*), of the first water, splendid, splendiferous (*Facetious*), superior, topping (*Brit. sl.*), unrivalled, world-class
Antonyms awful, bad, disappointing, dreadful, inferior, mediocre, pathetic, poor quality, run-of-the-mill, terrible, third-rate, uninspired, woeful

supercilious arrogant, condescending, contemptuous, disdainful, haughty, high and mighty (*Inf.*), hoity-toity (*Inf.*), imperious, insolent, lofty, lordly, overbearing, patronizing, proud, scornful, snooty (*Inf.*), stuck-up (*Inf.*), toffee-nosed (*Sl., chiefly Brit.*), uppish (*Brit. inf.*), vainglorious
Antonyms deferential, generous, humble, meek, modest, obsequious, self-effacing, submissive, warm-hearted, unassuming, unpretentious

superficial 1. exterior, external, on the surface, peripheral, shallow, skin-deep, slight, surface 2. casual, cosmetic, cursory, desultory, hasty, hurried, inattentive, nodding, passing, perfunctory, sketchy, slapdash 3. empty, empty-headed, frivolous, lightweight, shallow, silly, trivial 4. apparent, evident, ostensible, outward, seeming
Antonyms complete, comprehensive, deep, detailed, earnest, exhaustive, in depth, major, penetrating, probing, profound, serious, substantial, thorough

superficiality emptiness, lack of depth, lack of substance, shallowness, triviality

superficially apparently, at first glance, externally, on the surface, ostensibly, to the casual eye

superfluity excess, exuberance, glut, plethora, redundancy, superabundance, surfeit, surplus

superfluous excess, excessive, extra, in excess, left over, needless, on one's hands, pleonastic (*Rhetoric*), redundant, remaining, residuary, spare, superabundant, supererogatory, supernumerary, surplus, surplus to requirements, uncalled-for, unnecessary, unneeded, unrequired
Antonyms called for, essential, imperative, indispensable, necessary, needed, requisite, vital, wanted

superhuman 1. herculean, heroic, phenomenal, prodigious, stupendous, valiant 2. divine, paranormal, preternatural, supernatural

superintend administer, control, direct, handle, inspect, look after, manage, overlook, oversee, run, supervise

superintendence care, charge, control, direction, government, guidance, inspection, management, supervision, surveillance

superintendent administrator, chief, conductor, controller, director, governor, inspector, manager, overseer, supervisor

superior *adj.* 1. better, grander, greater, higher, more advanced (expert, extensive, skilful), paramount, predominant, preferred, prevailing, surpassing, unrivalled 2. a cut above (*Inf.*), admirable, choice, de luxe, distinguished, excellent, exceptional, exclusive, fine, first-class, first-rate, good, good quality, high calibre, high-class, of the first order, world-class 3. airy, condescending, disdainful, haughty, lofty, lordly, patronizing, pretentious, snobbish, stuck-up (*Inf.*), supercilious ~*n.* 4. boss (*Inf.*), chief, director, manager, principal, senior, supervisor
Antonyms *adj.* (*senses 1 & 2*) average, inferior, less, lesser, lower, mediocre, not as good, ordinary, poorer, second-class, second-rate, substandard, unremarkable,

worse ~*n.* assistant, dogsbody, inferior, junior, lackey, minion, subordinate, underling

superiority advantage, ascendancy, excellence, lead, predominance, pre-eminence, preponderance, prevalence, supremacy

superlative *adj.* consummate, crack (*Sl.*), excellent, greatest, highest, magnificent, matchless, of the first water, of the highest order, outstanding, peerless, supreme, surpassing, transcendent, unparalleled, unrivalled, unsurpassed
Antonyms appalling, average, dreadful, easily outclassed, inferior, ordinary, poor, rotten, run-of-the-mill, undistinguished, unexceptional, uninspired, unspectacular

supernatural abnormal, dark, ghostly, hidden, miraculous, mysterious, mystic, occult, paranormal, phantom, preternatural, psychic, spectral, supranatural, uncanny, unearthly, unnatural

supernumerary excess, excessive, extra, in excess, odd, redundant, spare, superfluous, surplus, unrequired

supersede annul, displace, oust, overrule, remove, replace, set aside, supplant, supplement, suspend, take over, take the place of, usurp

supervise administer, be on duty at, be responsible for, conduct, control, direct, handle, have *or* be in charge of, inspect, keep an eye on, look after, manage, oversee, preside over, run, superintend

supervision administration, auspices, care, charge, control, direction, guidance, instruction, management, oversight, stewardship, superintendence, surveillance

supervisor administrator, boss (*Inf.*), chief, foreman, gaffer (*Inf., chiefly Brit.*), inspector, manager, overseer, steward, superintendent

supervisory administrative, executive, managerial, overseeing, superintendent

supine 1. flat, flat on one's back, horizontal, prone, prostrate, recumbent 2. apathetic, careless, heedless, idle, incurious, indifferent, indolent, inert, languid, lazy, lethargic, listless, lymphatic, negligent, passive, slothful, sluggish, spineless, spiritless, torpid, uninterested

supplant displace, oust, overthrow, remove, replace, supersede, take over, take the place of, undermine, unseat

supple bending, elastic, flexible, limber, lissom(e), lithe, loose-limbed, plastic, pliable, pliant
Antonyms awkward, creaky (*Inf.*), firm, graceless, inflexible, rigid, stiff, taut, unbending, unsupple, unyielding

supplement 1. *n.* added feature, addendum, addition, add-on, appendix, codicil, complement, extra, insert, postscript, pull-out, sequel 2. *v.* add, augment, complement, extend, fill out, reinforce, supply, top up

supplementary accompanying, additional, add-on, ancillary, auxiliary, complementary, extra, secondary, supplemental

suppliant 1. *adj.* begging, beseeching, craving, entreating, imploring, importunate, on bended knee 2. *n.* applicant, petitioner, suitor, supplicant

supplication appeal, entreaty, invocation, petition, plea, pleading, prayer, request, solicitation, suit

supply *v.* 1. afford, cater to *or* for, come up with, contribute, endow, fill, furnish, give, grant, minister, outfit, produce, provide, purvey, replenish, satisfy, stock, store, victual, yield ~*n.* 2. cache, fund, hoard, quantity, reserve, reservoir, source, stock, stockpile, store 3. *Usually plural* equipment, food, foodstuff, items, materials, necessities, provender, provisions, rations, stores

support *v.* 1. bear, bolster, brace, buttress, carry, hold, hold up, prop, reinforce, shore up, sustain, underpin, uphold 2. be a source of strength to, buoy up, cherish, encourage, finance, foster, fund, keep, look after, maintain, nourish, provide for, strengthen, subsidize, succour, sustain, take care of, underwrite 3. advocate, aid, assist, back, boost (someone's) morale, champion, defend, espouse, forward, go along with, help, promote, second, side with, stand behind, stand up for, stick up for (*Inf.*), take (someone's) part, take up the cudgels for, uphold 4. attest to, authenticate, bear out, confirm, corroborate, document, endorse, lend credence to, substantiate, verify 5. bear, brook, countenance, endure, put up with (*Inf.*), stand (for), stomach, submit, suffer, thole (*Dialect*), tolerate, undergo ~*n.* 6. abutment, back, brace, foundation, lining, pillar, post, prop, shore, stanchion, stay, stiffener, underpinning 7. aid, approval, assistance, backing, blessing, championship, comfort, encouragement, espousal, friendship, furtherance, help, loyalty, moral support, patronage, promotion, protection, relief, succour, sustenance 8. keep, livelihood, maintenance, subsistence, sustenance, upkeep 9. backbone, backer, comforter, mainstay, prop, second, stay, supporter, tower of strength
Antonyms *v.* (*sense 2*) live off, sponge off (*senses 3, 4 & 5*) challenge, contradict,

deny, go against, hinder, hold out against, oppose, refute, reject, stab in the back, turn one's back on, undermine, walk away from ~*n.* (*senses 7 & 9*) antagonist, burden, denial, encumbrance, hindrance, impediment, opposition, refutation, rejection, undermining

supporter adherent, advocate, ally, apologist, champion, co-worker, defender, fan, follower, friend, helper, henchman, patron, protagonist, sponsor, upholder, well-wisher
Antonyms adversary, antagonist, challenger, competitor, foe, opponent, rival

supportive caring, encouraging, helpful, reassuring, sympathetic, understanding

suppose 1. assume, calculate (*U.S. dialect*), conjecture, dare say, expect, guess (*Inf., chiefly U.S. & Canad.*), imagine, infer, judge, opine, presume, presuppose, surmise, take as read, take for granted, think 2. believe, conceive, conclude, conjecture, consider, fancy, hypothesize, imagine, postulate, pretend

supposed 1. accepted, alleged, assumed, hypothetical, presumed, presupposed, professed, putative, reputed, rumoured 2. *With* **to** expected, meant, obliged, ought, required

supposedly allegedly, at a guess, avowedly, by all accounts, hypothetically, ostensibly, presumably, professedly, purportedly, theoretically
Antonyms absolutely, actually, certainly, in actuality, in fact, really, surely, truly, undoubtedly, without a doubt

supposition conjecture, doubt, guess, guesswork, hypothesis, idea, notion, postulate, presumption, speculation, surmise, theory

suppress 1. beat down, check, clamp down on, conquer, crack down on, crush, drive underground, extinguish, overpower, overthrow, put an end to, quash, quell, quench, snuff out, stamp out, stop, subdue, trample on 2. censor, conceal, contain, cover up, curb, hold in *or* back, hold in check, keep secret, muffle, muzzle, repress, restrain, silence, smother, stifle, withhold
Antonyms encourage, foster, further, incite, inflame, promote, rouse, spread, stimulate, stir up, whip up

suppression check, clampdown, crackdown, crushing, dissolution, elimination, extinction, inhibition, prohibition, quashing, smothering, termination

suppurate discharge, fester, gather, maturate, ooze, weep

supremacy absolute rule, ascendancy, dominance, domination, dominion, lordship, mastery, paramountcy, predominance, pre-eminence, primacy, sovereignty, supreme authority, sway

supreme cardinal, chief, crowning, culminating, extreme, final, first, foremost, greatest, head, highest, incomparable, leading, matchless, paramount, peerless, predominant, pre-eminent, prevailing, prime, principal, sovereign, superlative, surpassing, top, ultimate, unsurpassed, utmost
Antonyms least, least successful, lowest, most inferior, most minor, most subordinate, most trivial, poorest, worst

sure 1. assured, certain, clear, confident, convinced, decided, definite, free from doubt, persuaded, positive, satisfied 2. accurate, dependable, effective, foolproof, honest, indisputable, infallible, never-failing, precise, reliable, sure-fire (*Inf.*), tried and true, trustworthy, trusty, undeniable, undoubted, unerring, unfailing, unmistakable, well-proven 3. assured, bound, guaranteed, ineluctable, inescapable, inevitable, irrevocable 4. fast, firm, fixed, safe, secure, solid, stable, staunch, steady
Antonyms distrustful, dodgy (*Brit., Aust., & N.Z. inf.*), doubtful, dubious, fallible, iffy (*Inf.*), insecure, sceptical, touch-and-go, unassured, uncertain, unconvinced, undependable, uneasy, unreliable, unsure, untrustworthy, vague

surely assuredly, beyond the shadow of a doubt, certainly, come what may, definitely, doubtlessly, for certain, indubitably, inevitably, inexorably, undoubtedly, unquestionably, without doubt, without fail

surety 1. bail, bond, deposit, guarantee, indemnity, insurance, pledge, safety, security, warranty 2. bondsman, guarantor, hostage, mortgagor, sponsor

surface *n.* 1. covering, exterior, façade, face, facet, outside, plane, side, skin, superficies (*Rare*), top, veneer 2. **on the surface** apparently, at first glance, ostensibly, outwardly, superficially, to all appearances, to the casual eye ~*adj.* 3. apparent, exterior, external, outward, superficial ~*v.* 4. appear, come to light, come up, crop up (*Inf.*), emerge, materialize, rise, transpire

surfeit 1. *n.* excess, glut, overindulgence, plethora, satiety, superabundance, superfluity 2. *v.* cram, fill, glut, gorge, overfeed, overfill, satiate, stuff
Antonyms *n.* dearth, deficiency, insufficiency, lack, scarcity, shortage, shortness, want

surge 1. *v.* billow, eddy, gush, heave, rise, roll, rush, swell, swirl, tower, undulate, well forth 2. *n.* billow, breaker, efflux, flood, flow, gush, intensification, outpouring, roller, rush, swell, uprush, upsurge, wave

surly bearish, brusque, churlish, crabbed, cross, crusty, curmudgeonly, grouchy (*Inf.*), gruff, ill-natured, morose, perverse, sulky, sullen, testy, uncivil, ungracious
Antonyms agreeable, cheerful, cheery, genial, good-natured, happy, pleasant, sunny

surmise 1. *v.* come to the conclusion, conclude, conjecture, consider, deduce, fancy, guess, hazard a guess, imagine, infer, opine, presume, speculate, suppose, suspect 2. *n.* assumption, conclusion, conjecture, deduction, guess, hypothesis, idea, inference, notion, possibility, presumption, speculation, supposition, suspicion, thought

surmount conquer, exceed, master, overcome, overpower, overtop, pass, prevail over, surpass, triumph over, vanquish

surpass beat, best, eclipse, exceed, excel, go one better than (*Inf.*), outdo, outshine, outstrip, override, overshadow, top, tower above, transcend

surpassing exceptional, extraordinary, incomparable, matchless, outstanding, phenomenal, rare, supreme, transcendent, unrivalled

surplus 1. *n.* balance, excess, remainder, residue, superabundance, superfluity, surfeit 2. *adj.* excess, extra, in excess, left over, odd, remaining, spare, superfluous, unused
Antonyms *n.* dearth, deficiency, deficit, insufficiency, lack, paucity, shortage, shortfall ~*adj.* deficient, falling short, inadequate, insufficient, lacking, limited, scant, scanty, scarce

surprise *v.* 1. amaze, astonish, astound, bewilder, bowl over (*Inf.*), confuse, disconcert, flabbergast (*Inf.*), leave open-mouthed, nonplus, stagger, stun, take aback 2. burst in on, catch in the act *or* red-handed, catch napping, catch unawares *or* off-guard, come down on like a bolt from the blue, discover, spring upon, startle ~*n.* 3. amazement, astonishment, bewilderment, incredulity, stupefaction, wonder 4. bolt from the blue, bombshell, eye-opener (*Inf.*), jolt, revelation, shock, start (*Inf.*)

surprised amazed, astonished, at a loss, caught on the hop (*Brit. inf.*), caught on the wrong foot (*Inf.*), disconcerted, incredulous, nonplussed, open-mouthed, speechless, startled, taken aback, taken by surprise, thunderstruck, unable to believe one's eyes

surprising amazing, astonishing, astounding, extraordinary, incredible, marvellous, remarkable, staggering, startling, unexpected, unlooked-for, unusual, wonderful

surrender *v.* 1. abandon, cede, concede, deliver up, forego, give up, part with, relinquish, renounce, resign, waive, yield 2. capitulate, give in, give oneself up, give way, lay down arms, quit, show the white flag, submit, succumb, throw in the towel, yield ~*n.* 3. capitulation, delivery, relinquishment, renunciation, resignation, submission, yielding
Antonyms *v.* defy, fight (on), make a stand against, oppose, resist, stand up to, withstand

surreptitious clandestine, covert, fraudulent, furtive, secret, sly, sneaking, stealthy, unauthorized, underhand, veiled
Antonyms blatant, conspicuous, frank, honest, manifest, obvious, open, overt, unconcealed, undisguised

surrogate *n.* deputy, proxy, representative, stand-in, substitute

surround 1. close in on, encircle, enclose, encompass, envelop, environ, fence in, girdle, hem in, ring 2. *Military* besiege, invest (*Rare*), lay siege to

surrounding nearby, neighbouring

surroundings background, environment, environs, location, milieu, neighbourhood, setting

surveillance care, control, direction, inspection, observation, scrutiny, superintendence, supervision, vigilance, watch

survey *v.* 1. contemplate, examine, eye up, inspect, look over, observe, recce (*Sl.*), reconnoitre, research, review, scan, scrutinize, study, supervise, view 2. appraise, assess, estimate, eye up, measure, plan, plot, prospect, size up, take stock of, triangulate ~*n.* 3. examination, inquiry, inspection, overview, perusal, random sample, review, scrutiny, study

survive be extant, endure, exist, hold out, keep body and soul together (*Inf.*), last, live, live on, outlast, outlive, pull through, remain alive, subsist

susceptibility liability, predisposition, proneness, propensity, responsiveness, sensitivity, suggestibility, vulnerability, weakness

susceptible 1. *Usually with* **to** disposed, given, inclined, liable, open, predisposed, prone, subject, vulnerable 2. alive to, easily moved, impressionable, receptive, responsive, sensitive, suggestible, tender
Antonyms immune, incapable, insensible, insusceptible, invulnerable, resistant, unaffected by, unmoved by, unresponsive

suspect *v.* 1. distrust, doubt, harbour suspicions about, have one's doubts about, mistrust, smell a rat (*Inf.*) 2. believe, conclude, conjecture, consider, fancy, feel, guess, have a sneaking suspicion, hazard a

guess, speculate, suppose, surmise, think probable ~*adj.* 3. dodgy (*Brit., Aust., & N.Z. inf.*), doubtful, dubious, fishy (*Inf.*), iffy (*Inf.*), open to suspicion, questionable
Antonyms *v.* accept, be certain, be confident of, believe, buy (*Sl.*), have faith in, know, swallow (*Inf.*), think innocent, trust ~*adj.* above suspicion, innocent, reliable, straightforward, trustworthy, trusty

suspend 1. append, attach, dangle, hang, swing 2. adjourn, arrest, cease, cut short, debar, defer, delay, discontinue, hold off, interrupt, lay aside, pigeonhole, postpone, put off, shelve, stay, withhold
Antonyms (*sense 2*) carry on, continue, reestablish, reinstate, restore, resume, return

suspense 1. anticipation, anxiety, apprehension, doubt, expectancy, expectation, indecision, insecurity, irresolution, tension, uncertainty, wavering 2. **in suspense** anxious, in an agony of doubt, keyed up, on edge, on tenterhooks

suspenseful cliffhanging, exciting, gripping, hair-raising, spine-chilling, thrilling

suspension abeyance, adjournment, break, breaking off, deferment, delay, disbarment, discontinuation, interruption, moratorium, postponement, remission, respite, stay

suspicion 1. bad vibes (*Sl.*), chariness, distrust, doubt, dubiety, funny feeling (*Inf.*), jealousy, lack of confidence, misgiving, mistrust, qualm, scepticism, wariness 2. **above suspicion** above reproach, blameless, honourable, like Caesar's wife, pure, sinless, unimpeachable, virtuous 3. conjecture, guess, gut feeling (*Inf.*), hunch, idea, impression, notion, supposition, surmise 4. glimmer, hint, shade, shadow, *soupçon,* strain, streak, suggestion, tinge, touch, trace

suspicious 1. apprehensive, distrustful, doubtful, jealous, leery (*Sl.*), mistrustful, sceptical, suspecting, unbelieving, wary 2. dodgy (*Brit., Aust., & N.Z. inf.*), doubtful, dubious, fishy (*Inf.*), funny, irregular, of doubtful honesty, open to doubt *or* misconstruction, queer, questionable, shady (*Inf.*), suspect
Antonyms (*sense 1*) believing, credulous, gullible, open, trustful, trusting, unsuspecting, unsuspicious (*sense 2*) above board, beyond suspicion, not open to question, open, straight, straightforward, unquestionable, upright

sustain 1. bear, carry, keep from falling, keep up, support, uphold 2. bear, bear up under, endure, experience, feel, suffer, undergo, withstand 3. aid, assist, comfort, foster, help, keep alive, nourish, nurture, provide for, relieve 4. approve, confirm, continue, keep alive, keep going, keep up, maintain, prolong, protract, ratify 5. endorse, uphold, validate, verify

sustained constant, continuous, nonstop, perpetual, prolonged, steady, unremitting
Antonyms broken, discontinuous, intermittent, irregular, periodic, spasmodic, sporadic

sustenance 1. aliment, comestibles, daily bread, eatables, edibles, food, nourishment, provender, provisions, rations, refection, refreshments, victuals 2. livelihood, maintenance, subsistence, support

svelte 1. graceful, lissom(e), lithe, slender, slinky, sylphlike, willowy 2. polished, smooth, sophisticated, urbane

swagger 1. *v.* bluster, boast, brag, bully, gasconade (*Rare*), hector, hot-dog (*Chiefly U.S.*), parade, prance, show off (*Inf.*), strut, swank (*Inf.*) 2. *n.* arrogance, bluster, braggadocio, display, gasconade (*Rare*), ostentation, pomposity, show, showing off (*Inf.*), swank (*Inf.*), swashbuckling

swallow *v.* 1. absorb, consume, devour, down (*Inf.*), drink, eat, gulp, ingest, swig (*Inf.*), swill, wash down 2. *Often with* **up** absorb, assimilate, consume, engulf, envelop, overrun, overwhelm, use up, waste 3. choke back, hold in, repress 4. *Inf.* accept, believe, buy (*Sl.*), fall for

swamp *n.* 1. bog, everglade(s) (*U.S.*), fen, marsh, mire, morass, moss (*Scot. & northern English dialect*), quagmire, slough ~*v.* 2. capsize, drench, engulf, flood, inundate, overwhelm, sink, submerge, swallow up, upset, wash over, waterlog 3. beset, besiege, deluge, flood, inundate, overload, overwhelm, snow under

swampy boggy, fenny, marish (*Obsolete*), marshy, miry, quaggy, waterlogged, wet

swank *v.* 1. give oneself airs, hot-dog (*Chiefly U.S.*), posture, put on side (*Brit. sl.*), show off (*Inf.*), swagger ~*n.* 2. attitudinizer, braggadocio, hot dog (*Chiefly U.S.*), poser, poseur, show-off (*Inf.*), swankpot (*Inf.*), swashbuckler 3. boastfulness, display, ostentation, show, swagger, vainglory

swanky de luxe, exclusive, expensive, fancy, fashionable, flash, flashy, glamorous, glitzy (*Sl.*), gorgeous, grand, lavish, luxurious, ostentatious, plush (*Inf.*), plushy (*Inf.*), posh (*Inf., chiefly Brit.*), rich, ritzy (*Sl.*), showy, smart, stylish, sumptuous, swank (*Inf.*), swish (*Inf., chiefly Brit.*)
Antonyms discreet, humble, inconspicuous, low-key, low-profile, modest, subdued, unassuming, unostentatious, unpretentious

swap, swop *v.* bandy, barter, exchange, interchange, switch, trade, traffic

swarm *n.* 1. army, bevy, concourse, crowd, drove, flock, herd, horde, host, mass, multitude, myriad, shoal, throng ~*v.* 2. congregate, crowd, flock, mass, stream, throng 3. *With* **with** abound, be alive (infested, overrun), bristle, crawl, teem

swarthy black, brown, dark, dark-complexioned, dark-skinned, dusky, swart (*Archaic*), tawny

swashbuckling bold, daredevil, dashing, flamboyant, gallant, mettlesome, roisterous, spirited, swaggering

swastika fylfot

swathe bandage, bind, bundle up, cloak, drape, envelop, enwrap, fold, furl, lap, muffle up, sheathe, shroud, swaddle, wrap

sway *v.* 1. bend, fluctuate, incline, lean, lurch, oscillate, rock, roll, swing, wave 2. affect, control, direct, dominate, govern, guide, induce, influence, persuade, prevail on, win over ~*n.* 3. ascendency, authority, clout (*Inf.*), command, control, dominion, government, influence, jurisdiction, power, predominance, rule, sovereignty 4. **hold sway** predominate, prevail, reign, rule, run

swear 1. affirm, assert, asseverate, attest, avow, declare, depose, give one's word, pledge oneself, promise, state under oath, take an oath, testify, vow, warrant 2. be foul-mouthed, blaspheme, curse, cuss (*Inf.*), imprecate, take the Lord's name in vain, turn the air blue (*Inf.*), utter profanities 3. *With* **by** depend on, have confidence in, rely on, trust

swearing bad language, blasphemy, cursing, cussing (*Inf.*), foul language, imprecations, malediction, profanity

swearword curse, cuss (*Inf.*), expletive, four-letter word, oath, obscenity, profanity

sweat *n.* 1. diaphoresis (*Medical*), exudation, perspiration, sudor (*Medical*) 2. *Inf.* agitation, anxiety, distress, flap (*Inf.*), panic, strain, worry 3. *Inf.* backbreaking task, chore, drudgery, effort, labour, toil ~*v.* 4. break out in a sweat, exude moisture, glow, perspire 5. *Inf.* agonize, be on pins and needles (*Inf.*), be on tenterhooks, chafe, fret, lose sleep over, suffer, torture oneself, worry 6. **sweat it out** *Inf.* endure, see (something) through, stay the course, stick it out (*Inf.*)

sweaty clammy, drenched (bathed, soaked) in perspiration, glowing, perspiring, sticky, sweating

sweep *v.* 1. brush, clean, clear, remove 2. career, flounce, fly, glance, glide, hurtle, pass, sail, scud, skim, tear, zoom ~*n.* 3. arc, bend, curve, gesture, move, movement, stroke, swing 4. compass, extent, range, scope, span, stretch, vista 5. draw, lottery, raffle, sweepstake

sweeping 1. all-embracing, all-inclusive, bird's-eye, broad, comprehensive, extensive, global, radical, thoroughgoing, wide, wide-ranging 2. across-the-board, blanket, exaggerated, indiscriminate, overdrawn, overstated, unqualified, wholesale
Antonyms constrained, limited, minor, modest, narrow, qualified, restricted, token, trifling, unimportant

sweet *adj.* 1. cloying, honeyed, luscious, melting, saccharine, sugary, sweetened, syrupy, toothsome, treacly 2. affectionate, agreeable, amiable, appealing, attractive, beautiful, charming, cute, delightful, engaging, fair, gentle, kind, likable *or* likeable, lovable, sweet-tempered, taking, tender, unselfish, winning, winsome 3. beloved, cherished, darling, dear, dearest, pet, precious, treasured 4. aromatic, balmy, clean, fragrant, fresh, new, perfumed, pure, redolent, sweet-smelling, wholesome 5. dulcet, euphonic, euphonious, harmonious, mellow, melodious, musical, silver-toned, silvery, soft, sweet-sounding, tuneful 6. **sweet on** enamoured of, gone on (*Sl.*), head over heels in love with, infatuated by, in love with, keen on, obsessed *or* bewitched by, taken with, wild *or* mad about (*Inf.*) ~*n.* 7. afters (*Brit. inf.*), dessert, pudding, sweet course 8. *Usually plural* bonbon, candy (*U.S.*), confectionery, sweetie, sweetmeats
Antonyms *adj.* (*sense 1*) acerbic, acetic, acid, bitter, savoury, sharp, sour, tart, vinegary (*senses 2, 3 & 4*) bad-tempered, disagreeable, fetid, foul, grouchy (*Inf.*), grumpy, hated, ill-tempered, loathsome, nasty, noisome, objectionable, obnoxious, rank, stinking, unappealing, unattractive, unlovable, unpleasant, unwanted (*sense 5*) cacophonous, discordant, grating, harsh, shrill, strident, unharmonious, unmusical, unpleasant

sweeten 1. honey, sugar, sugar-coat 2. alleviate, appease, mollify, pacify, soften up, soothe, sugar the pill

sweetheart admirer, beau, beloved, boyfriend, darling, dear, flame (*Inf.*), follower (*Obsolete*), girlfriend, inamorata, inamorato, leman (*Archaic*), love, lover, steady (*Inf.*), suitor, swain (*Archaic*), sweetie (*Inf.*), truelove, valentine

sweet-scented ambrosial, aromatic, fragrant, perfumed, sweet-smelling
Antonyms fetid, foul-smelling, malodorous, niffy (*Brit. sl.*), noisome, olid, pongy

(*Brit. inf.*), smelly, stinking, stinky (*Inf.*), whiffy (*Brit. sl.*)

swell *v.* 1. balloon, become bloated *or* distended, become larger, be inflated, belly, billow, bloat, bulge, dilate, distend, enlarge, expand, extend, fatten, grow, increase, protrude, puff up, rise, round out, tumefy, well up 2. add to, aggravate, augment, enhance, heighten, intensify, mount, surge ~*n.* 3. billow, rise, surge, undulation, wave 4. *Inf.* beau, blade (*Archaic*), cockscomb (*Inf.*), dandy, fashion plate, fop, nob (*Sl.*), toff (*Brit. sl.*) ~*adj.* 5. *Inf.* de luxe, exclusive, fashionable, grand, plush *or* plushy (*Inf.*), posh (*Inf., chiefly Brit.*), ritzy (*Sl.*), smart, stylish

Antonyms *v.* become smaller, contract, decrease, deflate, diminish, ebb, fall, go down, lessen, reduce, shrink, wane ~*adj.* common, grotty (*Sl.*), ordinary, plebeian, poor, run down, seedy, shabby, sordid, tatty, unimpressive, vulgar

swelling *n.* blister, bruise, bulge, bump, dilation, distension, enlargement, inflammation, lump, protuberance, puffiness, tumescence

sweltering airless, baking, boiling, burning, hot, humid, oppressive, roasting, scorching, steaming, stifling, sultry, torrid

swerve *v.* bend, deflect, depart from, deviate, diverge, incline, sheer off, shift, skew, stray, swing, turn, turn aside, veer, wander, wind

swift abrupt, expeditious, express, fast, fleet, fleet-footed, flying, hurried, nimble, nippy (*Brit. inf.*), pdq (*Sl.*), prompt, quick, quickie (*Inf.*), rapid, ready, short, short-lived, spanking, speedy, sudden, winged

Antonyms lead-footed, lingering, plodding, ponderous, slow, sluggish, tardy, tortoise-like, unhurried

swiftly apace, as fast as one's legs can carry one, (at) full tilt, double-quick, fast, hotfoot, hurriedly, in less than no time, nippily (*Brit. inf.*), posthaste, promptly, pronto (*Inf.*), rapidly, speedily, without losing time

swiftness alacrity, celerity, dispatch, expedition, fleetness, promptness, quickness, rapidity, speed, speediness, velocity

swill *v.* 1. bend the elbow (*Inf.*), bevvy (*Dialect*), consume, drain, drink (down), gulp, guzzle, imbibe, pour down one's gullet, quaff, swallow, swig (*Inf.*), toss off 2. *Often with* **out** drench, flush, rinse, sluice, wash down, wash out ~*n.* 3. hogwash, mash, mush, pigswill, scourings, slops, waste

swimmingly as planned, cosily, effortlessly, like a dream, like clockwork, smoothly, successfully, very well, with no trouble, without a hitch

swindle 1. *v.* bamboozle (*Inf.*), bilk (of), cheat, con, cozen deceive, defraud, diddle (*Inf.*), do (*Sl.*), dupe, fleece, hornswoggle (*Sl.*), overcharge, pull a fast one (on someone) (*Inf.*), put one over on (someone) (*Inf.*), rip (someone) off (*Sl.*), rook (*Sl.*), skin (*Sl.*), stiff (*Sl.*), sting (*Inf.*), take (someone) for a ride (*Inf.*), take to the cleaners (*Inf.*), trick 2. *n.* con trick (*Inf.*), deceit, deception, double-dealing, fiddle (*Brit. inf.*), fraud, imposition, knavery, racket, rip-off (*Sl.*), roguery, scam (*Sl.*), sharp practice, sting (*Inf.*), swizz (*Brit. inf.*), swizzle (*Brit. inf.*), trickery

swindler charlatan, cheat, chiseller (*Inf.*), confidence man, con man (*Inf.*), fraud, impostor, knave (*Archaic*), mountebank, rascal, rogue, rook (*Sl.*), shark, sharper, trickster

swing *v.* 1. be pendent, be suspended, dangle, hang, move back and forth, suspend 2. fluctuate, oscillate, rock, sway, vary, veer, vibrate, wave 3. *Usually with* **round** curve, pivot, rotate, swivel, turn, turn on one's heel, wheel ~*n.* 4. fluctuation, oscillation, stroke, sway, swaying, vibration 5. **in full swing** animated, at its height, lively, on the go (*Inf.*), under way

swingeing daunting, Draconian, drastic, excessive, exorbitant, harsh, heavy, huge, oppressive, punishing, severe, stringent

swinging dynamic, fashionable, full of go *or* pep (*Inf.*), groovy (*Dated sl.*), happening (*Inf.*), hip (*Sl.*), in the swim (*Inf.*), lively, trendy (*Brit. inf.*), up-to-date, up to the minute, with it (*Inf.*)

swipe *v.* 1. chin (*Sl.*), clip (*Inf.*), deck (*Sl.*), fetch (someone) a blow, hit, lash out at, lay one on (*Sl.*), slap, slosh (*Brit. sl.*), sock (*Sl.*), strike, wallop (*Inf.*) ~*n.* 2. blow, clip (*Inf.*), clout (*Inf.*), clump (*Sl.*), cuff, slap, smack, wallop (*Inf.*) ~*v.* 3. *Sl.* appropriate, cabbage (*Brit. sl.*), filch, lift (*Inf.*), make off with, nick (*Sl., chiefly Brit.*), pilfer, pinch (*Inf.*), purloin, snaffle (*Brit. inf.*), steal

swirl *v.* agitate, boil, churn, eddy, spin, surge, twirl, twist, whirl

swish *adj.* de luxe, elegant, exclusive, fashionable, grand, plush *or* plushy (*Inf.*), posh (*Inf., chiefly Brit.*), ritzy (*Sl.*), smart, sumptuous, swell (*Inf.*)

switch *v.* 1. change, change course, deflect, deviate, divert, exchange, interchange, rearrange, replace by, shift, substitute, swap (*Inf.*), trade, turn aside ~*n.* 2. about-turn, alteration, change, change of direction, exchange, reversal, shift, substitution, swap (*Inf.*) ~*v.* 3. lash, swish, twitch, wave, whip

swivel *v.* pirouette, pivot, revolve, rotate, spin, swing round, turn

swollen bloated, distended, dropsical, edematous, enlarged, inflamed, oedematous, puffed up, puffy, tumescent, tumid

swollen-headed bigheaded (*Inf.*), bumptious, cocky, full of oneself, proud, puffed up, self-important, too big for one's boots, vain, vainglorious

swoop 1. *v.* descend, dive, pounce, rush, stoop, sweep 2. *n.* descent, drop, lunge, plunge, pounce, rush, stoop, sweep

swop *see* SWAP

sword 1. blade, brand (*Archaic*), trusty steel 2. **cross swords** argue, come to blows, dispute, fight, spar, wrangle 3. **the sword** aggression, arms, butchery, death, massacre, military might, murder, slaying, violence, war

swot *v.* apply oneself to, bone up on (*Inf.*), burn the midnight oil, cram (*Inf.*), get up (*Inf.*), lucubrate (*Rare*), mug up (*Brit. sl.*), pore over, revise, study, toil over, work

sybarite epicure, epicurean, hedonist, playboy, sensualist, voluptuary

sybaritic epicurean, hedonistic, Lucullan, luxurious, luxury-loving, pleasure-loving, self-indulgent, sensual, voluptuous

sycophancy adulation, bootlicking (*Inf.*), cringing, fawning, flattery, grovelling, kowtowing, obsequiousness, servility, slavishness, toadyism, truckling

sycophant apple polisher (*U.S. sl.*), ass-kisser (*U.S. & Canad. taboo sl.*), bootlicker (*Inf.*), brown-noser (*Taboo sl.*), cringer, fawner, flatterer, hanger-on, lickspittle, parasite, slave, sponger, toadeater (*Rare*), toady, truckler, yes man

sycophantic all over (someone) (*Inf.*), arse-licking (*Taboo sl.*), bootlicking (*Inf.*), cringing, fawning, flattering, grovelling, ingratiating, obsequious, parasitical, servile, slavish, slimy, smarmy (*Brit. inf.*), time-serving, toadying, unctuous

syllabus course of study, curriculum

sylphlike graceful, lithe, slender, svelte, willowy

symbol badge, emblem, figure, image, logo, mark, representation, sign, token, type

symbolic, symbolical allegorical, emblematic, figurative, representative, significant, token, typical

symbolize betoken, body forth, connote, denote, exemplify, mean, personify, represent, signify, stand for, typify

symmetrical balanced, in proportion, proportional, regular, well-proportioned

Antonyms asymmetrical, disorderly, irregular, lopsided, unbalanced, unequal, unsymmetrical

symmetry agreement, balance, correspondence, evenness, form, harmony, order, proportion, regularity

sympathetic 1. affectionate, caring, commiserating, compassionate, concerned, condoling, feeling, interested, kind, kindly, pitying, responsive, supportive, tender, understanding, warm, warm-hearted 2. *Often with* to agreeable, approving, encouraging, favourably disposed, friendly, in sympathy with, pro, well-disposed 3. agreeable, appreciative, companionable, compatible, congenial, friendly, like-minded, responsive, well-intentioned

Antonyms apathetic, callous, cold, cold-hearted, disdainful, disinterested, indifferent, inhumane, insensitive, scornful, steely, uncaring, uncompassionate, uncongenial, unfeeling, uninterested, unmoved, unresponsive, unsympathetic

sympathetically appreciatively, feelingly, kindly, perceptively, responsively, sensitively, understandingly, warm-heartedly, warmly, with compassion, with feeling, with interest

sympathize 1. bleed for, commiserate, condole, empathize, feel for, feel one's heart go out to, grieve with, have compassion, offer consolation, pity, share another's sorrow 2. agree, be in accord, be in sympathy, go along with, identify with, side with, understand

Antonyms disagree, disregard, fail to understand, have no feelings for, misunderstand, mock, oppose, reject, scorn

sympathizer condoler, fellow traveller, partisan, protagonist, supporter, well-wisher

sympathy 1. commiseration, compassion, condolence(s), empathy, pity, tenderness, thoughtfulness, understanding 2. affinity, agreement, congeniality, correspondence, fellow feeling, harmony, rapport, union, warmth

Antonyms (*sense 1*) callousness, coldness, disdain, hard-heartedness, indifference, insensitivity, lack of feeling *or* understanding *or* sympathy, pitilessness, scorn (*sense 2*) antagonism, disapproval, hostility, opposition, resistance, unfriendliness

symptom expression, indication, mark, note, sign, syndrome, token, warning

symptomatic characteristic, indicative, suggestive

synonymous equal, equivalent, identical, identified, interchangeable, one and the same, similar, tantamount, the same

synopsis abridgment, abstract, *aperçu*, compendium, condensation, conspectus, digest, epitome, outline, outline sketch, précis, résumé, review, rundown, summary

synthesis 1. amalgamation, coalescence, combination, integration, unification, welding 2. amalgam, blend, combination, composite, compound, fusion, meld, union

synthetic artificial, ersatz, fake, man-made, manufactured, mock, pseudo (*Inf.*), sham, simulated
Antonyms authentic, genuine, kosher (*Inf.*), natural, real

system 1. arrangement, classification, combination, coordination, organization, scheme, setup (*Inf.*), structure 2. fixed order, frame of reference, method, methodology, modus operandi, practice, procedure, routine, technique, theory, usage 3. definite plan, logical process, method, methodicalness, orderliness, regularity, systematization

systematic businesslike, efficient, methodical, orderly, organized, precise, standardized, systematized, well-ordered
Antonyms arbitrary, cursory, disorderly, disorganized, haphazard, indiscriminate, random, slapdash, unbusinesslike, unmethodical, unpremeditated, unsystematic

systematize arrange, classify, dispose, make uniform, methodize, organize, put in order, rationalize, regulate, schematize, standardize, tabulate

T

tab flag, flap, label, marker, sticker, tag, ticket

tabby banded, brindled, streaked, striped, stripy, wavy

table *n.* 1. bench, board, counter, slab, stand 2. board, diet, fare, food, spread (*Inf.*), victuals 3. flat, flatland, mesa, plain, plateau, tableland 4. agenda, catalogue, chart, diagram, digest, graph, index, inventory, list, plan, record, register, roll, schedule, synopsis, tabulation ~*v.* 5. enter, move, propose, put forward, submit, suggest

tableau picture, representation, scene, spectacle

tableland flat, flatland, mesa, plain, plateau, table

taboo 1. *adj.* anathema, banned, beyond the pale, disapproved of, forbidden, frowned on, not allowed, not permitted, outlawed, prohibited, proscribed, ruled out, unacceptable, unmentionable, unthinkable 2. *n.* anathema, ban, disapproval, interdict, prohibition, proscription, restriction
Antonyms *adj.* acceptable, allowed, permitted, sanctioned

tabulate arrange, catalogue, categorize, chart, classify, codify, index, list, order, range, systematize, tabularize

tacit implicit, implied, inferred, silent, taken for granted, undeclared, understood, unexpressed, unspoken, unstated, wordless
Antonyms explicit, express, spelled-out, spoken, stated

taciturn aloof, antisocial, close-lipped, cold, distant, dumb, mute, quiet, reserved, reticent, silent, tight-lipped, uncommunicative, unforthcoming, withdrawn
Antonyms blethering, chatty, communicative, forthcoming, garrulous, loquacious, open, outgoing, prattling, sociable, talkative, unreserved, verbose, voluble, wordy

tack *n.* 1. drawing pin, nail, pin, staple, thumbtack (*U.S.*), tintack 2. approach, bearing, course, direction, heading, line, method, path, plan, procedure, tactic, way ~*v.* 3. affix, attach, fasten, fix, nail, pin, staple 4. baste, stitch 5. add, annex, append, attach, tag

tackle *n.* 1. accoutrements, apparatus, equipment, gear, implements, outfit, paraphernalia, rig, rigging, tools, trappings 2. block, challenge, stop ~*v.* 3. apply oneself to, attempt, begin, come *or* get to grips with, deal with, embark upon, engage in, essay, get stuck into (*Inf.*), have a go at (*Inf.*), have a stab at (*Inf.*), set about, take on, try, turn one's hand to, undertake, wade into 4. block, bring down, challenge, clutch, confront, grab, grasp, halt, intercept, seize, stop, take hold of, throw

tacky 1. adhesive, gluey, gummy, sticky, wet 2. *Inf.* cheap, messy, naff (*Brit. sl.*), nasty, seedy, shabby, shoddy, sleazy, tasteless, tatty, vulgar

tact address, adroitness, consideration, delicacy, diplomacy, discretion, finesse, judgment, perception, savoir-faire, sensitivity, skill, thoughtfulness, understanding
Antonyms awkwardness, clumsiness, gaucherie, heavy-handedness, indiscretion, insensitivity, lack of consideration, lack of discretion, tactlessness

tactful careful, considerate, delicate, diplomatic, discreet, judicious, perceptive, polished, polite, politic, prudent, sensitive, subtle, thoughtful, understanding
Antonyms awkward, clumsy, gauche, inconsiderate, indiscreet, insensitive, tactless, tasteless, thoughtless, undiplomatic, unsubtle, untoward

tactic 1. approach, course, device, line, manoeuvre, means, method, move, ploy, policy, scheme, stratagem, tack, trick, way 2. *Plural* campaign, generalship, manoeuvres, plans, strategy

tactical adroit, artful, clever, cunning, diplomatic, foxy, politic, shrewd, skilful, smart, strategic
Antonyms blundering, clumsy, gauche, impolitic, inept

tactician brain (*Inf.*), campaigner, coordinator, director, general, mastermind, planner, strategist

tactless blundering, boorish, careless, clumsy, discourteous, gauche, harsh, impolite, impolitic, imprudent, inconsiderate, indelicate, indiscreet, inept, injudicious, insensitive, maladroit, rough, rude, sharp, thoughtless, uncivil, undiplomatic, unfeeling, unkind, unsubtle
Antonyms considerate, diplomatic, discreet, polite, subtle, tactful

tag *n.* 1. docket, flag, flap, identification, label, mark, marker, note, slip, sticker, tab, ticket ~*v.* 2. earmark, flag, identify, label, mark, ticket 3. add, adjoin, affix, annex, append, fasten, tack 4. *With* **on** *or* **along** accompany, attend, dog, follow, shadow, tail (*Inf.*), trail 5. call, christen, dub, label, name, nickname, style, term

tail *n.* 1. appendage, conclusion, empennage, end, extremity, rear end, tailpiece, train 2. file, line, queue, tailback, train 3. *Of hair* braid, pigtail, plait, ponytail, tress 4. *Inf.* arse (*Taboo sl.*), ass (*U.S. & Canad. taboo sl.*), backside (*Inf.*), behind (*Inf.*), bottom, bum (*Brit. sl.*), buns (*U.S. sl.*), butt (*U.S. & Canad. inf.*), buttocks, croup, derrière (*Euphemistic*), jacksy (*Brit. sl.*), posterior, rear (*Inf.*), rear end, rump 5. **turn tail** cut and run, escape, flee, hook it (*Sl.*), make off, retreat, run away, run for it (*Inf.*), run off, scarper (*Brit. sl.*), show a clean pair of heels, skedaddle (*Inf.*), take off (*Inf.*), take to one's heels ~*v.* 6. *Inf.* dog the footsteps of, follow, keep an eye on, shadow, stalk, track, trail

tail off *or* **away** decrease, die out, drop, dwindle, fade, fall away, peter out, wane
Antonyms grow, increase, intensify, wax

tailor 1. *n.* clothier, costumier, couturier, dressmaker, garment maker, outfitter, seamstress 2. *v.* accommodate, adapt, adjust, alter, convert, cut, fashion, fit, modify, mould, shape, style, suit

tailor-made 1. cut to fit, fitted, made to measure, made to order 2. custom-made, ideal, just right, perfect, right, right up one's street (*Inf.*), suitable

taint *v.* 1. adulterate, blight, contaminate, corrupt, dirty, foul, infect, poison, pollute, soil, spoil 2. besmirch, blacken, blemish, blot, brand, damage, defile, disgrace, dishonour, muddy, ruin, shame, smear, smirch, stain, stigmatize, sully, tarnish, vitiate ~*n.* 3. black mark, blemish, blot, blot on one's escutcheon, defect, demerit, disgrace, dishonour, fault, flaw, shame, smear, smirch, spot, stain, stigma 4. contagion, contamination, infection, pollution
Antonyms *v.* clean, cleanse, decontaminate, disinfect, purify

take *v.* 1. abduct, acquire, arrest, capture, carry off, catch, clutch, ensnare, entrap, gain possession of, get, get hold of, grasp, grip, have, help oneself to, lay hold of, obtain, receive, secure, seize, win 2. abstract, appropriate, blag (*Sl.*), cabbage (*Brit. sl.*), carry off, filch, misappropriate, nick (*Sl., chiefly Brit.*), pinch (*Inf.*), pocket, purloin, run off with, steal, swipe (*Sl.*), walk off with 3. book, buy, engage, hire, lease, pay for, pick, purchase, rent, reserve, select 4. abide, bear, brave, brook, endure, go through, pocket, put up with (*Inf.*), stand, stomach, submit to, suffer, swallow, thole (*Scot.*), tolerate, undergo, weather, withstand 5. consume, drink, eat, imbibe, ingest, inhale, swallow 6. accept, adopt, assume, enter upon, undertake 7. do, effect, execute, have, make, perform 8. assume, believe, consider, deem, hold, interpret as, perceive, presume, receive, regard, see as, think of as, understand 9. be efficacious, do the trick (*Inf.*), have effect, operate, succeed, work 10. bear, bring, carry, cart, convey, ferry, fetch, haul, tote (*Inf.*), transport 11. accompany, bring, conduct, convoy, escort, guide, lead, usher 12. attract, become popular, captivate, charm, delight, enchant, fascinate, please, win favour 13. call for, demand, necessitate, need, require 14. deduct, eliminate, remove, subtract 15. accept, accommodate, contain, have room for, hold 16. *Sl.* bilk, cheat, con (*Inf.*), deceive, defraud, do (*Sl.*), dupe, fiddle (*Inf.*), gull (*Archaic*), pull a fast one on (*Inf.*), stiff (*Sl.*), swindle ~*n.* 17. catch, gate, haul, proceeds, profits, receipts, return, revenue, takings, yield
Antonyms add, avoid, decline, dismiss, dodge, eschew, fail, flop (*Inf.*), free, give, give back, give in, give way, hand over, ignore, let go, put, refuse, reject, release, restore, return, scorn, send, spurn, surrender, yield

take aback astonish, astound, bewilder, disconcert, flabbergast (*Inf.*), floor (*Inf.*), nonplus, stagger, startle, stun, surprise

take back 1. disavow, disclaim, recant, renege, renounce, retract, unsay, withdraw 2. get back, recapture, reclaim, reconquer, regain, repossess, retake 3. accept back, exchange, give one a refund for

take down 1. make a note of, minute, note, put on record, record, set down, transcribe, write down 2. depress, drop, haul down, let down, lower, pull down, remove, take off 3. demolish, disassemble, dismantle, level, raze, take apart, take to pieces, tear down 4. deflate, humble, humiliate, mortify, put down (*Sl.*)

take in 1. absorb, assimilate, comprehend, digest, grasp, understand 2. comprise, contain, cover, embrace, encompass, include 3. accommodate, admit, let in, receive 4. *Inf.* bilk, cheat, con (*Inf.*), cozen, deceive, do (*Sl.*), dupe, fool, gull (*Archaic*), hoodwink, mislead, pull the wool over (someone's) eyes (*Inf.*), stiff (*Sl.*), swindle, trick

takeoff 1. departure, launch, liftoff 2. *Inf.* caricature, imitation, lampoon, mocking, parody, satire, send-up (*Brit. inf.*), spoof (*Inf.*), travesty

take off 1. discard, divest oneself of, doff, drop, peel off, remove, strip off 2. become airborne, leave the ground, lift off, take to the air 3. *Inf.* abscond, beat it (*Sl.*), decamp, depart, disappear, go, hit the road (*Sl.*), hook it (*Sl.*), leave, set out, slope off, split (*Sl.*), strike out 4. *Inf.* caricature, hit off, imitate, lampoon, mimic, mock, parody, satirize, send up (*Brit. inf.*), spoof (*Inf.*), take the piss (out of) (*Taboo sl.*), travesty

take on 1. employ, engage, enlist, enrol, hire, retain 2. acquire, assume, come to have 3. accept, address oneself to, agree to do, have a go at (*Inf.*), tackle, undertake 4. compete against, contend with, enter the lists against, face, fight, match oneself against, oppose, pit oneself against, vie with 5. *Inf.* break down, get excited, get upset, give way, make a fuss

takeover change of leadership, coup, incorporation, merger

take over assume control of, become leader of, come to power, gain control of, succeed to, take command of

take to 1. flee to, head for, make for, man, run for 2. become friendly, be pleased by, be taken with, conceive an affection for, get on with, like, warm to 3. have recourse to, make a habit of, resort to

take up 1. adopt, assume, become involved in, engage in, start 2. begin again, carry on, continue, follow on, go on, pick up, proceed, recommence, restart, resume 3. absorb, consume, cover, extend over, fill, occupy, use up

taking *adj.* 1. attractive, beguiling, captivating, charming, compelling, delightful, enchanting, engaging, fascinating, fetching (*Inf.*), intriguing, likable *or* likeable, pleasing, prepossessing, winning 2. *Inf.* catching, contagious, infectious ~*n.* 3. *Plural* earnings, gain, gate, income, pickings, proceeds, profits, receipts, returns, revenue, take, yield

Antonyms (*sense 1*) abhorrent, loathsome, offensive, repulsive, unattractive, unpleasant

tale 1. account, anecdote, *conte,* fable, fiction, legend, narration, narrative, novel, relation, report, romance, saga, short story, spiel (*Inf.*), story, urban legend, yarn (*Inf.*) 2. cock-and-bull story (*Inf.*), fabrication, falsehood, fib, lie, rigmarole, rumour, spiel (*Inf.*), tall story (*Inf.*), untruth

talent ability, aptitude, bent, capacity, endowment, faculty, flair, forte, genius, gift, knack, parts, power

talented able, artistic, brilliant, gifted, well-endowed

talisman amulet, charm, fetish, juju, lucky charm, mascot, periapt (*Rare*)

talk *v.* 1. articulate, chat, chatter, communicate, converse, crack (*Scot.*), express oneself, gab (*Inf.*), give voice to, gossip, natter, prate, prattle, rap (*Sl.*), say, speak, spout, utter, verbalize, witter (*Inf.*) 2. chew the rag *or* fat (*Sl.*), confabulate, confer, have a confab (*Inf.*), hold discussions, negotiate, palaver, parley 3. blab, crack, give the game away, grass (*Brit. sl.*), inform, reveal information, shop (*Sl., chiefly Brit.*), sing (*Sl., chiefly U.S.*), spill one's guts (*Sl.*), spill the beans (*Inf.*), squeak (*Inf.*), squeal (*Sl.*), tell all ~*n.* 4. address, discourse, disquisition, dissertation, harangue, lecture, oration, sermon, speech 5. blather, blether, chat, chatter, chitchat, conversation, crack (*Scot.*), gab (*Inf.*), gossip, hearsay, jaw (*Sl.*), natter, rap (*Sl.*), rumour, tittle-tattle 6. colloquy, conclave, confab (*Inf.*), confabulation, conference, congress, consultation, dialogue, discussion, meeting, negotiation, palaver, parley, seminar, symposium 7. argot, dialect, jargon, language, lingo (*Inf.*), patois, slang, speech, words

talkative big-mouthed (*Sl.*), chatty, effusive, gabby (*Inf.*), garrulous, gossipy, long-winded, loquacious, mouthy, prolix, verbose, voluble, wordy

Antonyms quiet, reserved, reticent, silent, taciturn, tight-lipped, uncommunicative, unforthcoming

talk big bluster, boast, brag, crow, exaggerate, vaunt

talker chatterbox, conversationalist, lecturer, orator, speaker, speechmaker

talking-to criticism, dressing-down (*Inf.*), lecture, rap on the knuckles, rebuke, reprimand, reproach, reproof, row, scolding, slating (*Inf.*), telling-off (*Inf.*), ticking-off (*Inf.*), wigging (*Brit. sl.*)

Antonyms acclaim, approbation, commendation, encouragement, praise

talk into bring round (*Inf.*), convince, persuade, prevail on *or* upon, sway, win over

tall 1. big, elevated, giant, high, lanky, lofty, soaring, towering 2. *Inf.* absurd, embellished, exaggerated, far-fetched, implausible, incredible, overblown, preposterous, steep (*Brit. inf.*), unbelievable 3. *Inf.* demanding, difficult, exorbitant, hard, unreasonable, well-nigh impossible

Antonyms (*sense 1*) fubsy (*Archaic or dialect*), short, small, squat, stumpy, tiny, wee (*sense 2*) accurate, believable, easy, plausible, realistic, reasonable, true, unexaggerated

tally *v.* 1. accord, agree, coincide, concur, conform, correspond, fit, harmonize, jibe

(*Inf.*), match, parallel, square, suit 2. compute, count up, keep score, mark, reckon, record, register, total ~*n.* 3. count, mark, reckoning, record, running total, score, total 4. counterfoil, counterpart, duplicate, match, mate, stub
Antonyms (*sense 1*) clash, conflict, contradict, differ, disagree

tame *adj.* 1. amenable, broken, cultivated, disciplined, docile, domesticated, gentle, obedient, tractable 2. fearless, unafraid, used to human contact 3. compliant, docile, manageable, meek, obedient, spiritless, subdued, submissive, unresisting 4. bland, boring, dull, flat, humdrum, insipid, lifeless, prosaic, tedious, unexciting, uninspiring, uninteresting, vapid, wearisome ~*v.* 5. break in, domesticate, gentle, house-train, make tame, pacify, train 6. break the spirit of, bridle, bring to heel, conquer, curb, discipline, enslave, humble, master, repress, subdue, subjugate, suppress 7. mitigate, mute, soften, soft-pedal (*Inf.*), subdue, temper, tone down, water down
Antonyms *adj.* aggressive, argumentative, exciting, feral, ferocious, frenzied, hot, interesting, lively, obdurate, savage, stimulating, strong-willed, stubborn, undomesticated, unmanageable, untamed, wild ~*v.* arouse, incite, intensify, make fiercer

tamper 1. alter, damage, fiddle (*Inf.*), fool about (*Inf.*), interfere, intrude, meddle, mess about, monkey around, muck about (*Brit. sl.*), poke one's nose into (*Inf.*), tinker 2. bribe, corrupt, fix (*Inf.*), get at, influence, manipulate, rig

tang 1. aroma, bite, flavour, odour, piquancy, reek, savour, scent, smack, smell, taste 2. hint, suggestion, tinge, touch, trace, whiff

tangible actual, concrete, corporeal, definite, discernible, evident, manifest, material, objective, palpable, perceptible, physical, positive, real, solid, substantial, tactile, touchable
Antonyms abstract, disembodied, ethereal, immaterial, impalpable, imperceptible, indiscernible, insubstantial, intangible, theoretical, unreal

tangle *n.* 1. coil, confusion, entanglement, jam, jungle, knot, mass, mat, mesh, ravel, snarl, twist, web 2. complication, entanglement, fix (*Inf.*), imbroglio, labyrinth, maze, mess, mix-up ~*v.* 3. coil, confuse, entangle, interlace, interlock, intertwist, interweave, jam, kink, knot, mat, mesh, ravel, snarl, twist 4. *Often with* with come into conflict, come up against, contend, contest, cross swords, dispute, lock horns 5. catch, drag into, embroil, enmesh, ensnare, entangle, entrap, implicate, involve
Antonyms (*sense 3*) disentangle, extricate, free, straighten out, unravel, untangle

tangled 1. entangled, jumbled, knotted, knotty, matted, messy, scrambled, snarled, tousled, twisted 2. complex, complicated, confused, convoluted, involved, knotty, messy, mixed-up

tangy acerb, biting, briny, fresh, piquant, pungent, sharp, spicy, tart

tantalize baffle, balk, disappoint, entice, frustrate, keep (someone) hanging on, lead on, make (someone's) mouth water, provoke, taunt, tease, thwart, titillate, torment, torture

tantamount as good as, commensurate, equal, equivalent, synonymous, the same as

tantrum bate (*Brit. sl.*), fit, flare-up, hysterics, ill humour, outburst, paddy (*Brit. inf.*), paroxysm, storm, temper, wax (*Inf., chiefly Brit.*)

tap[1] 1. *v.* beat, drum, knock, pat, rap, strike, touch 2. *n.* beat, knock, light blow, pat, rap, touch

tap[2] *n.* 1. faucet (*U.S.*), spigot, spout, stopcock, valve 2. bung, plug, spile, stopper 3. bug (*Inf.*), listening device 4. **on tap a.** *Inf.* at hand, available, in reserve, on hand, ready **b.** on draught ~*v.* 5. bleed, broach, drain, draw off, open, pierce, siphon off, unplug 6. draw on, exploit, make use of, milk, mine, put to use, turn to account, use, utilize 7. bug (*Inf.*), eavesdrop on, listen in on

tape *n.* 1. band, ribbon, strip ~*v.* 2. bind, seal, secure, stick, wrap 3. record, tape-record, video

taper 1. come to a point, narrow, thin 2. *With* off decrease, die away, die out, dwindle, fade, lessen, reduce, subside, thin out, wane, weaken, wind down
Antonyms (*sense 2*) grow, increase, intensify, step up, strengthen, swell, widen

tardiness belatedness, delay, dilatoriness, lateness, procrastination, slowness, unpunctuality

tardy backward, behindhand, belated, dawdling, dilatory, late, loitering, overdue, procrastinating, retarded, slack, slow, sluggish, unpunctual

target 1. aim, ambition, bull's-eye, end, goal, intention, mark, object, objective 2. butt, quarry, scapegoat, victim

tariff 1. assessment, duty, excise, impost, levy, rate, tax, toll 2. bill of fare, charges, menu, price list, schedule

tarnish 1. *v.* befoul, blacken, blemish, blot,

darken, dim, discolour, drag through the mud, dull, lose lustre *or* shine, rust, smirch, soil, spot, stain, sully, taint 2. *n.* blackening, black mark, blemish, blot, discoloration, rust, smirch, spot, stain, taint
Antonyms *v.* brighten, enhance, gleam, polish up, shine

tarry abide, bide, dally, dawdle, delay, dwell, hang around (*Inf.*), linger, lodge, loiter, lose time, pause, remain, rest, sojourn, stay, take one's time, wait
Antonyms hasten, hurry, move on, rush, scoot, step on it (*Inf.*)

tart[1] 1. pastry, pie, tartlet 2. call girl, fallen woman, *fille de joie,* floozy (*Sl.*), harlot, hooker (*U.S. sl.*), loose woman, prostitute, scrubber (*Brit. & Aust. sl.*), slag (*Brit. sl.*), slut, streetwalker, strumpet, trollop, whore, woman of easy virtue, working girl (*Facetious sl.*)

tart[2] 1. acerb, acid, acidulous, astringent, bitter, piquant, pungent, sharp, sour, tangy, vinegary 2. acrimonious, astringent, barbed, biting, caustic, crusty, cutting, harsh, mordacious, mordant, nasty, scathing, sharp, short, snappish, testy, trenchant, vitriolic, wounding
Antonyms (*sense 1*) honeyed, sugary, sweet, syrupy, toothsome (*sense 2*) agreeable, delightful, gentle, kind, pleasant

task *n.* 1. assignment, business, charge, chore, duty, employment, enterprise, exercise, job, labour, mission, occupation, toil, undertaking, work 2. **take to task** bawl out (*Inf.*), blame, blast, carpet (*Inf.*), censure, chew out (*U.S. & Canad. inf.*), criticize, give a rocket (*Brit. & N.Z. inf.*), lambast(e), lecture, read the riot act, reprimand, reproach, reprove, scold, tear into (*Inf.*), tear (someone) off a strip (*Brit. inf.*), tell off (*Inf.*), upbraid ~*v.* 3. assign to, charge, entrust 4. burden, exhaust, load, lumber (*Brit. inf.*), oppress, overload, push, saddle, strain, tax, test, weary

taste *n.* 1. flavour, relish, savour, smack, tang 2. bit, bite, dash, drop, morsel, mouthful, nip, sample, sip, *soupçon,* spoonful, swallow, titbit, touch 3. appetite, bent, desire, fancy, fondness, inclination, leaning, liking, palate, partiality, penchant, predilection, preference, relish 4. appreciation, cultivation, culture, discernment, discrimination, elegance, grace, judgment, perception, polish, refinement, sophistication, style 5. correctness, decorum, delicacy, discretion, nicety, politeness, propriety, restraint, tact, tactfulness ~*v.* 6. differentiate, discern, distinguish, perceive 7. assay, nibble, relish, sample, savour, sip, test, try 8. have a flavour of, savour of, smack 9. come up against, encounter, experience, feel, have knowledge of, know, meet with, partake of, undergo
Antonyms *n.* bawdiness, blandness, blueness, coarseness, crudeness, disinclination, dislike, distaste, hatred, impropriety, indelicacy, insipidity, lack of discernment, lack of judgment, loathing, mawkishness, obscenity, tackiness (*Inf.*) tactlessness, tastelessness, unsubtlety ~*v.* fail to achieve, fail to discern, miss, remain ignorant of

tasteful aesthetically pleasing, artistic, beautiful, charming, cultivated, cultured, delicate, discriminating, elegant, exquisite, fastidious, graceful, handsome, harmonious, in good taste, polished, refined, restrained, smart, stylish
Antonyms brash, flashy, garish, gaudy, inelegant, loud, objectionable, offensive, showy, sick, tacky (*Inf.*), tasteless, tawdry, twee, uncultured, unrefined, vulgar

tasteless 1. bland, boring, dull, flat, flavourless, insipid, mild, stale, tame, thin, uninspired, uninteresting, vapid, watered-down, weak 2. cheap, coarse, crass, crude, flashy, garish, gaudy, graceless, gross, impolite, improper, indecorous, indelicate, indiscreet, inelegant, low, naff (*Brit. sl.*), rude, tacky (*Inf.*), tactless, tawdry, uncouth, unseemly, vulgar
Antonyms (*sense 1*) appetizing, delectable, delicious, flavoursome, savoury, scrumptious (*Inf.*), tasty (*sense 2*) elegant, graceful, refined, tasteful

tasty appetizing, delectable, delicious, flavourful, flavoursome, full-flavoured, good-tasting, luscious, palatable, sapid, savoury, scrumptious (*Inf.*), toothsome, yummy (*Sl.*)
Antonyms bland, flavourless, insipid, tasteless, unappetizing, unsavoury

tatter 1. bit, piece, rag, scrap, shred 2. **in tatters** down at heel, in rags, in shreds, ragged, ripped, tattered, threadbare, torn

tattle 1. *v.* babble, blab, blather, blether, chat, chatter, gossip, jabber, natter, prate, prattle, spread rumours, talk idly, tell tales, tittle-tattle, yak (*Sl.*) 2. *n.* babble, blather, blether, chat, chatter, chitchat, gossip, hearsay, idle talk, jabber, prattle, small talk, tittle-tattle, yak (*Sl.*), yap (*Sl.*)

tattler bigmouth (*Sl.*), gossip, quidnunc, rumourmonger, scandalmonger, talebearer, taleteller, telltale

taunt 1. *v.* deride, flout, gibe, guy (*Inf.*), insult, jeer, mock, provoke, reproach, revile, ridicule, sneer, take the piss (out of) (*Taboo sl.*), tease, torment, twit, upbraid 2. *n.* barb, censure, cut, derision, dig, gibe, in~

sult, jeer, provocation, reproach, ridicule, sarcasm, teasing

taut 1. flexed, rigid, strained, stressed, stretched, tense, tight 2. *Nautical* in good order, neat, orderly, shipshape, spruce, tidy, tight, trim, well-ordered, well-regulated
Antonyms (*sense 1*) loose, relaxed, slack

tautological iterative, pleonastic, prolix, redundant, repetitious, repetitive, verbose

tautology iteration, pleonasm, prolixity, redundancy, repetition, repetitiousness, repetitiveness, verbiage, verbosity

tavern alehouse (*Archaic*), bar, boozer (*Brit., Aust., & N.Z. inf.*), hostelry, inn, pub (*Inf., chiefly Brit.*), public house, taproom, watering hole (*Facetious sl.*)

tawdry brummagem, cheap, cheap-jack (*Inf.*), flashy, gaudy, gimcrack, glittering, meretricious, naff (*Brit. sl.*), plastic (*Sl.*), raffish, showy, tacky (*Inf.*), tasteless, tatty, tinsel, tinselly, vulgar
Antonyms elegant, graceful, plain, refined, simple, stylish, tasteful, unflashy, unostentatious, well-tailored

tax *n.* 1. assessment, charge, contribution, customs, dŭty, excise, imposition, impost, levy, rate, tariff, tithe, toll, tribute 2. burden, demand, drain, load, pressure, strain, weight ~*v.* 3. assess, charge, demand, exact, extract, impose, levy a tax on, rate, tithe 4. burden, drain, enervate, exhaust, load, make heavy demands on, overburden, push, put pressure on, sap, strain, stretch, task, try, weaken, wear out, weary, weigh heavily on 5. accuse, arraign, blame, charge, impeach, impugn, incriminate, lay at one's door
Antonyms (*sense 5*) acquit, clear, exculpate, exonerate, vindicate

taxing burdensome, demanding, enervating, exacting, heavy, onerous, punishing, sapping, stressful, tiring, tough, trying, wearing, wearisome
Antonyms easy, easy-peasy (*Sl.*), effortless, light, unburdensome, undemanding

teach advise, coach, demonstrate, direct, discipline, drill, edify, educate, enlighten, give lessons in, guide, impart, implant, inculcate, inform, instil, instruct, school, show, train, tutor

teacher coach, dominie (*Scot.*), don, educator, guide, guru, handler, instructor, lecturer, master, mentor, mistress, pedagogue, professor, schoolmaster, schoolmistress, schoolteacher, trainer, tutor

team *n.* 1. band, body, bunch, company, crew, gang, group, line-up, posse (*Inf.*), set, side, squad, troupe 2. pair, span, yoke ~*v.* 3. *Often with* **up** band together, cooperate, couple, get together, join, link, unite, work together, yoke

teamwork collaboration, concert, cooperation, coordination, esprit de corps, fellowship, harmony, joint action, unity

tear *v.* 1. claw, divide, lacerate, mangle, mutilate, pull apart, rend, rip, rive, run, rupture, scratch, sever, shred, split, sunder 2. barrel (along) (*Inf., chiefly U.S. & Canad.*), belt (*Sl.*), bolt, burn rubber (*Inf.*), career, charge, dart, dash, fly, gallop, hurry, race, run, rush, shoot, speed, sprint, zoom 3. grab, pluck, pull, rip, seize, snatch, wrench, wrest, yank ~*n.* 4. hole, laceration, mutilation, rent, rip, run, rupture, scratch, split

tearaway daredevil, delinquent, good-for-nothing, hooligan, madcap, rough (*Inf.*), roughneck (*Sl.*), rowdy, ruffian, tough

tearful 1. blubbering, crying, in tears, lachrymose, sobbing, weeping, weepy (*Inf.*), whimpering 2. distressing, dolorous, harrowing, lamentable, mournful, pathetic, pitiable, pitiful, poignant, sad, sorrowful, upsetting, woeful

tears 1. blubbering, crying, distress, lamentation, mourning, pain, regret, sadness, sobbing, sorrow, wailing, weeping, whimpering, woe 2. **in tears** blubbering, crying, distressed, sobbing, visibly moved, weeping, whimpering

tease aggravate (*Inf.*), annoy, badger, bait, bedevil, bother, chaff, gibe, goad, guy (*Inf.*), lead on, mock, needle (*Inf.*), pester, plague (*Inf.*), provoke, rag, rib (*Inf.*), ridicule, take the piss (out of) (*Taboo sl.*), tantalize, taunt, torment, twit, vex, wind up (*Brit. sl.*), worry

technique 1. approach, course, fashion, manner, means, method, mode, modus operandi, procedure, style, system, way 2. address, adroitness, art, artistry, craft, craftsmanship, delivery, execution, facility, knack, know-how (*Inf.*), performance, proficiency, skill, touch

tedious annoying, banal, boring, deadly dull, drab, dreary, dreich (*Scot.*), dull, fatiguing, ho-hum (*Inf.*), humdrum, irksome, laborious, lifeless, long-drawn-out, mind-numbing, monotonous, prosaic, prosy, soporific, tiring, unexciting, uninteresting, vapid, wearisome
Antonyms enjoyable, enthralling, exciting, exhilarating, imaginative, inspiring, interesting, quickly finished, short, stimulating

tedium banality, boredom, deadness, drabness, dreariness, dullness, ennui, lifelessness, monotony, routine, sameness, tediousness, the doldrums
Antonyms challenge, excitement, exhila-

ration, fascination, interest, liveliness, stimulation

teem[1] abound, be abundant, bear, be crawling with, be full of, be prolific, brim, bristle, burst at the seams, overflow, produce, pullulate, swarm

teem[2] belt (*Sl.*), bucket down (*Inf.*), lash, pelt (down), pour, rain cats and dogs (*Inf.*), sheet, stream

teeming[1] abundant, alive, brimful, brimming, bristling, bursting, chock-a-block, chock-full, crawling, fruitful, full, numerous, overflowing, packed, replete, swarming, thick
Antonyms deficient, lacking, short, wanting

teeming[2] belting (*Sl.*), bucketing down (*Inf.*), lashing, pelting, pouring, sheeting, streaming

teenage adolescent, immature, juvenile, youthful

teenager adolescent, boy, girl, juvenile, minor, youth

teeny diminutive, microscopic, miniature, minuscule, minute, teensy-weensy, teeny-weeny, tiny, wee

teeter balance, pivot, rock, seesaw, stagger, sway, totter, tremble, waver, wobble

teetotaller abstainer, nondrinker, Rechabite

telegram cable, radiogram, telegraph, telex, wire (*Inf.*)

telegraph *n.* 1. tape machine (*Stock Exchange*), teleprinter, telex 2. cable, radiogram, telegram, telex, wire (*Inf.*) ~*v.* 3. cable, send, telex, transmit, wire (*Inf.*)

telepathy mind-reading, sixth sense, thought transference

telephone 1. *n.* blower (*Inf.*), handset, line, phone 2. *v.* buzz (*Inf.*), call, call up, dial, get on the blower (*Inf.*), give (someone) a bell (*Brit. sl.*), give (someone) a buzz (*Inf.*), give (someone) a call, give (someone) a ring (*Inf., chiefly Brit.*), give (someone) a tinkle (*Brit. inf.*), phone, put a call through to, ring (*Inf., chiefly Brit.*)

telescope *n.* 1. glass, spyglass ~*v.* 2. concertina, crush, squash 3. abbreviate, abridge, capsulize, compress, condense, consolidate, contract, curtail, cut, shorten, shrink, tighten, trim, truncate
Antonyms (*sense 3*) amplify, draw out, elongate, extend, flesh out, lengthen, protract, spread out

television gogglebox (*Brit. sl.*), idiot box (*Sl.*), receiver, small screen (*Inf.*), telly (*Brit. inf.*), the box (*Brit. inf.*), the tube (*Sl.*), TV, TV set

tell *v.* 1. acquaint, announce, apprise, communicate, confess, disclose, divulge, express, impart, inform, let know, make known, mention, notify, proclaim, reveal, say, speak, state, utter 2. authorize, bid, call upon, command, direct, enjoin, instruct, order, require, summon 3. chronicle, depict, describe, give an account of, narrate, portray, recount, rehearse, relate, report 4. comprehend, discern, discover, make out, see, understand 5. differentiate, discern, discriminate, distinguish, identify 6. carry weight, count, have *or* take effect, have force, make its presence felt, register, take its toll, weigh 7. calculate, compute, count, enumerate, number, reckon, tally

telling considerable, decisive, effective, effectual, forceful, forcible, impressive, influential, marked, potent, powerful, significant, solid, striking, trenchant, weighty
Antonyms easily ignored, inconsequential, indecisive, ineffectual, insignificant, light-weight, minor, negligible, slight, trivial, unimportant

tell off bawl out (*Inf.*), berate, carpet (*Inf.*), censure, chew out (*U.S. & Canad. inf.*), chide, give (someone) a piece of one's mind, give (someone) a rocket (*Brit. & N.Z. inf.*), haul over the coals (*Inf.*), lecture, read the riot act, rebuke, reprimand, reproach, reprove, scold, take to task, tear into (*Inf.*), tear (someone) off a strip (*Brit. inf.*), tick off (*Inf.*), upbraid

temerity assurance, audacity, boldness, brass neck (*Brit. inf.*), chutzpah (*U.S. & Canad. inf.*), effrontery, foolhardiness, forwardness, front, gall (*Inf.*), heedlessness, impudence, impulsiveness, intrepidity, nerve (*Inf.*), pluck, rashness, recklessness

temper *n.* 1. attitude, character, constitution, disposition, frame of mind, humour, mind, mood, nature, temperament, tenor, vein 2. bad mood, bate (*Brit. sl.*), fit of pique, fury, gall, paddy (*Brit. inf.*), passion, rage, tantrum, wax (*Inf., chiefly Brit.*) 3. anger, annoyance, heat, hot-headedness, ill humour, irascibility, irritability, irritation, passion, peevishness, petulance, resentment, surliness 4. calm, calmness, composure, cool (*Sl.*), coolness, equanimity, good humour, moderation, self-control, tranquillity ~*v.* 5. abate, admix, allay, assuage, calm, lessen, mitigate, moderate, mollify, palliate, restrain, soften, soft-pedal (*Inf.*), soothe, tone down 6. anneal, harden, strengthen, toughen
Antonyms *n.* (*sense 3*) contentment, good will, pleasant mood (*sense 4*) agitation, anger, bad mood, excitability, foul humour, fury, grumpiness, indignation, irascibility, irritation, pique, vexation, wrath ~*v.* (*sense*

5) aggravate, arouse, excite, heighten, intensify, provoke, stir (*sense 6*) soften

temperament 1. bent, cast of mind, character, complexion, constitution, disposition, frame of mind, humour, make-up, mettle, nature, outlook, personality, quality, soul, spirit, stamp, temper, tendencies, tendency 2. anger, excitability, explosiveness, hot-headedness, impatience, mercurialness, moodiness, moods, petulance, volatility

temperamental 1. capricious, easily upset, emotional, erratic, excitable, explosive, fiery, highly strung, hot-headed, hypersensitive, impatient, irritable, mercurial, moody, neurotic, passionate, petulant, sensitive, touchy, volatile 2. congenital, constitutional, inborn, ingrained, inherent, innate, natural 3. erratic, inconsistent, inconstant, undependable, unpredictable, unreliable
Antonyms calm, constant, cool-headed, dependable, easy-going, even-tempered, level-headed, phlegmatic, reliable, stable, steady, unexcitable, unflappable, unperturbable

temperance 1. continence, discretion, forbearance, moderation, restraint, self-control, self-discipline, self-restraint 2. abstemiousness, abstinence, prohibition, sobriety, teetotalism
Antonyms crapulence, excess, immoderation, intemperance, overindulgence, prodigality

temperate 1. agreeable, balmy, calm, clement, cool, fair, gentle, mild, moderate, pleasant, soft 2. calm, composed, dispassionate, equable, even-tempered, mild, moderate, reasonable, self-controlled, self-restrained, sensible, stable 3. abstemious, abstinent, continent, moderate, sober
Antonyms excessive, extreme, harsh, immoderate, inclement, inordinate, intemperate, prodigal, severe, torrid, uncontrolled, undisciplined, unreasonable, unrestrained, wild

tempest 1. cyclone, gale, hurricane, squall, storm, tornado, typhoon 2. commotion, disturbance, ferment, furore, storm, tumult, upheaval, uproar
Antonyms (*sense 2*) calm, peace, quiet, serenity, stillness, tranquillity

tempestuous 1. agitated, blustery, boisterous, breezy, gusty, inclement, raging, squally, stormy, turbulent, windy 2. agitated, boisterous, emotional, excited, feverish, flaming, furious, heated, hysterical, impassioned, intense, passionate, stormy, turbulent, uncontrolled, violent, wild
Antonyms (*sense 2*) calm, peaceful, quiet, serene, still, tranquil, undisturbed, unruffled

temple church, holy place, place of worship, sanctuary, shrine

tempo beat, cadence, measure (*Prosody*), metre, pace, pulse, rate, rhythm, speed, time

temporal 1. carnal, civil, earthly, fleshly, lay, material, mortal, mundane, profane, secular, sublunary, terrestrial, worldly 2. evanescent, fleeting, fugacious, fugitive, impermanent, momentary, passing, short-lived, temporary, transient, transitory

temporarily briefly, fleetingly, for a little while, for a moment, for a short time, for a short while, for the moment, for the nonce, for the time being, momentarily, pro tem

temporary brief, ephemeral, evanescent, fleeting, fugacious, fugitive, here today and gone tomorrow, impermanent, interim, momentary, passing, pro tem, *pro tempore,* provisional, short-lived, transient, transitory
Antonyms durable, enduring, eternal, everlasting, long-lasting, long-term, permanent

temporize be evasive, delay, equivocate, gain time, hum and haw, play a waiting game, play for time, procrastinate, stall, tergiversate

tempt 1. allure, appeal to, attract, coax, decoy, draw, entice, inveigle, invite, lead on, lure, make one's mouth water, seduce, tantalize, whet the appetite of, woo 2. bait, dare, fly in the face of, provoke, risk, test, try
Antonyms (*sense 1*) deter, discourage, dissuade, hinder, inhibit, put off

temptation allurement, appeal, attraction, attractiveness, bait, blandishments, coaxing, come-on (*Inf.*), decoy, draw, enticement, inducement, invitation, lure, pull, seduction, snare, tantalization

tempting alluring, appetizing, attractive, enticing, inviting, mouthwatering, seductive, tantalizing
Antonyms off-putting (*Brit. inf.*), unappetizing, unattractive, undesirable, uninviting, untempting

tenable arguable, believable, defendable, defensible, justifiable, maintainable, plausible, rational, reasonable, sound, viable
Antonyms indefensible, insupportable, unjustifiable, untenable

tenacious 1. clinging, fast, firm, forceful, immovable, iron, strong, tight, unshakable 2. retentive, unforgetful 3. adamant, determined, dogged, firm, immovable, inflexible, intransigent, obdurate, obstinate, persistent, pertinacious, resolute, staunch,

steadfast, stiff-necked, strong-willed, stubborn, sure, unswerving, unyielding 4. coherent, cohesive, solid, strong, tough 5. adhesive, clinging, gluey, glutinous, mucilaginous, sticky
Antonyms (*sense 3*) changeable, flexible, irresolute, vacillating, wavering, yielding

tenacity 1. fastness, firmness, force, forcefulness, power, strength 2. firm grasp, retention, retentiveness 3. application, determination, diligence, doggedness, firmness, inflexibility, intransigence, obduracy, obstinacy, perseverance, persistence, pertinacity, resoluteness, resolution, resolve, staunchness, steadfastness, strength of purpose, strength of will, stubbornness 4. coherence, cohesiveness, solidity, solidness, strength, toughness 5. adhesiveness, clingingness, stickiness
Antonyms (*sense 1*) looseness, powerlessness, slackness, weakness

tenancy 1. holding, lease, occupancy, occupation, possession, renting, residence 2. incumbency, period of office, tenure, time in office

tenant holder, inhabitant, leaseholder, lessee, occupant, occupier, renter, resident

tend[1] 1. be apt, be biased, be disposed, be inclined, be liable, be likely, gravitate, have a leaning, have an inclination, have a tendency, incline, lean, trend 2. aim, bear, be conducive, conduce, contribute, go, head, influence, lead, make for, move, point

tend[2] attend, care for, cater to, control, cultivate, feed, guard, handle, keep, keep an eye on, look after, maintain, manage, minister to, nurse, nurture, protect, see to, serve, take care of, wait on, watch, watch over
Antonyms disregard, ignore, neglect, overlook, shirk

tendency 1. bent, disposition, inclination, leaning, liability, partiality, penchant, predilection, predisposition, proclivity, proneness, propensity, readiness, susceptibility 2. bearing, bias, course, direction, drift, drive, heading, movement, purport, tenor, trend, turning

tender[1] 1. breakable, delicate, feeble, fragile, frail, soft, weak 2. callow, green, immature, impressionable, inexperienced, new, raw, sensitive, unripe, vulnerable, wet behind the ears (*Inf.*), young, youthful 3. affectionate, amorous, benevolent, caring, compassionate, considerate, fond, gentle, humane, kind, loving, merciful, pitiful, sentimental, softhearted, sympathetic, tenderhearted, warm, warm-hearted 4. emotional, evocative, moving, poignant, romantic, touching 5. complicated, dangerous, difficult, risky, sensitive, ticklish, touchy, tricky 6. aching, acute, bruised, inflamed, irritated, painful, raw, sensitive, smarting, sore
Antonyms advanced, brutal, cold-hearted, cruel, elderly, experienced, grown-up, hard, hard-hearted, inhuman, insensitive, leathery, mature, pitiless, seasoned, sophisticated, strong, tough, uncaring, unkind, unsympathetic, worldly, worldly-wise

tender[2] *v.* 1. extend, give, hand in, offer, present, proffer, propose, put forward, submit, suggest, volunteer ~*n.* 2. bid, estimate, offer, proffer, proposal, submission, suggestion 3. currency, medium, money, payment, specie

tenderhearted affectionate, benevolent, benign, caring, compassionate, considerate, fond, gentle, humane, kind, kind-hearted, kindly, loving, merciful, mild, responsive, sensitive, sentimental, softhearted, sympathetic, warm, warm-hearted

tenderness 1. delicateness, feebleness, fragility, frailness, sensitiveness, sensitivity, softness, vulnerability, weakness 2. callowness, greenness, immaturity, impressionableness, inexperience, newness, rawness, sensitivity, vulnerability, youth, youthfulness 3. affection, amorousness, attachment, benevolence, care, compassion, consideration, devotion, fondness, gentleness, humaneness, humanity, kindness, liking, love, mercy, pity, sentimentality, softheartedness, sympathy, tenderheartedness, warm-heartedness, warmth 4. ache, aching, bruising, inflammation, irritation, pain, painfulness, rawness, sensitiveness, sensitivity, smart, soreness
Antonyms (*sense 3*) cruelty, hardness, harshness, indifference, insensitivity, unkindness

tenebrous dark, dim, dingy, dusky, gloomy, murky, obscure, shadowy, shady, sombre, Stygian, sunless, unlit

tenet article of faith, belief, canon, conviction, creed, doctrine, dogma, maxim, opinion, precept, principle, rule, teaching, thesis, view

tenor aim, burden, course, direction, drift, evolution, intent, meaning, path, purport, purpose, sense, substance, tendency, theme, trend, way

tense *adj.* 1. rigid, strained, stretched, taut, tight 2. anxious, apprehensive, edgy, fidgety, jittery (*Inf.*), jumpy, keyed up, nervous, on edge, overwrought, restless, strained, strung up (*Inf.*), twitchy (*Inf.*), under pressure, uptight (*Inf.*), wired (*Sl.*), wound up (*Inf.*), wrought up 3. exciting, moving,

nerve-racking, stressful, worrying ~*v.* 4. brace, flex, strain, stretch, tauten, tighten
Antonyms *adj.* boring, calm, collected, cool-headed, dull, easy-going, flaccid, flexible, limp, loose, pliant, relaxed, self-possessed, serene, unconcerned, uninteresting, unruffled, unworried ~*v.* loosen, relax, slacken

tension 1. pressure, rigidity, stiffness, straining, stress, stretching, tautness, tightness 2. anxiety, apprehension, edginess, hostility, ill feeling, nervousness, pressure, restlessness, strain, stress, suspense, the jitters (*Inf.*), unease
Antonyms (*sense 2*) calmness, peacefulness, relaxation, restfulness, serenity, tranquillity

tentative 1. conjectural, experimental, indefinite, provisional, speculative, unconfirmed, unsettled 2. backward, cautious, diffident, doubtful, faltering, hesitant, timid, uncertain, undecided, unsure
Antonyms (*sense 1*) conclusive, decisive, definite, final, fixed, resolved, settled (*sense 2*) assured, bold, certain, confident, unhesitating

tenuous 1. doubtful, dubious, flimsy, insignificant, insubstantial, nebulous, questionable, shaky, sketchy, slight, weak 2. attenuated, delicate, fine, gossamer, slim
Antonyms (*sense 1*) significant, solid, sound, strong, substantial

tenure holding, incumbency, occupancy, occupation, possession, proprietorship, residence, tenancy, term, time

tepid 1. lukewarm, slightly warm, warmish 2. apathetic, cool, half-arsed, half-assed (*U.S. & Canad. sl.*), half-hearted, indifferent, lukewarm, unenthusiastic
Antonyms (*sense 2*) animated, eager, enthusiastic, excited, keen, passionate, vibrant, zealous

tergiversate 1. apostatize, change sides, defect, desert, go over to the other side, renege, turn traitor 2. beat about the bush, blow hot and cold (*Inf.*), dodge, equivocate, fence, hedge, prevaricate, pussyfoot (*Inf.*), vacillate

term *n.* 1. appellation, denomination, designation, expression, locution, name, phrase, title, word 2. duration, interval, period, season, space, span, spell, time, while 3. course, session 4. bound, boundary, close, conclusion, confine, culmination, end, finish, fruition, limit, terminus ~*v.* 5. call, denominate, designate, dub, entitle, label, name, style

terminal *adj.* 1. bounding, concluding, extreme, final, last, limiting, ultimate, utmost 2. deadly, fatal, incurable, killing, lethal, mortal ~*n.* 3. boundary, end, extremity, limit, termination, terminus 4. depot, end of the line, station, terminus
Antonyms (*sense 1*) beginning, commencing, first, initial, introductory, opening

terminate abort, axe (*Inf.*), bring *or* come to an end, cease, close, complete, conclude, cut off, discontinue, end, expire, finish, issue, lapse, put an end to, result, run out, stop, wind up
Antonyms begin, commence, inaugurate, initiate, instigate, introduce, open, start

termination abortion, cessation, close, completion, conclusion, consequence, cut-off point, discontinuation, effect, end, ending, expiry, finale, finis, finish, issue, result, wind-up
Antonyms beginning, commencement, inauguration, initiation, opening, start

terminology argot, cant, jargon, language, lingo (*Inf.*), nomenclature, patois, phraseology, terms, vocabulary

terminus 1. boundary, close, end, extremity, final point, goal, limit, target, termination 2. depot, end of the line, garage, last stop, station

terms 1. language, manner of speaking, phraseology, terminology 2. conditions, particulars, premises (*Law*), provisions, provisos, qualifications, specifications, stipulations 3. charges, fee, payment, price, rates 4. footing, position, relations, relationship, standing, status 5. **come to terms** be reconciled, come to an agreement, come to an understanding, conclude agreement, learn to live with, reach acceptance, reach agreement

terrain country, going, ground, land, landscape, topography

terrestrial 1. *adj.* earthly, global, mundane, sublunary, tellurian, terrene, worldly 2. *n.* earthling, earthman, earthwoman, human

terrible 1. bad, dangerous, desperate, extreme, serious, severe 2. *Inf.* abhorrent, abysmal, awful, bad, beastly (*Inf.*), dire, dreadful, duff (*Brit. inf.*), foul, frightful, godawful (*Sl.*), hateful, hideous, loathsome, obnoxious, obscene, odious, offensive, poor, repulsive, revolting, rotten (*Inf.*), shitty (*Taboo sl.*), unpleasant, vile 3. appalling, awful, dread, dreaded, dreadful, fearful, frightful, gruesome, harrowing, hellacious (*U.S. sl.*), horrendous, horrible, horrid, horrifying, monstrous, shocking, terrifying, unspeakable
Antonyms (*sense 1*) harmless, insignificant, mild, moderate, paltry, small (*sense 2*) admirable, brilliant, delightful, excellent, fine, great, magic, noteworthy, pleasant, remarkable, super, superb, terrific,

very good, wonderful (*sense 3*) calming, comforting, encouraging, reassuring, settling, soothing

terribly awfully (*Inf.*), decidedly, desperately, exceedingly, extremely, gravely, greatly, much, seriously, thoroughly, very

terrific 1. awesome, awful, dreadful, enormous, excessive, extreme, fearful, fierce, gigantic, great, harsh, horrific, huge, intense, monstrous, severe, terrible, tremendous 2. *Inf.* ace (*Inf.*), amazing, boffo (*Sl.*), breathtaking, brill (*Inf.*), brilliant, chillin' (*U.S. sl.*), cracking (*Brit. inf.*), excellent, fabulous (*Inf.*), fantastic (*Inf.*), fine, great (*Inf.*), jim-dandy (*Sl.*), magnificent, marvellous, mean (*Sl.*), outstanding, sensational (*Inf.*), smashing (*Inf.*), sovereign, stupendous, super (*Inf.*), superb, topping (*Brit. sl.*), very good, wonderful
Antonyms appalling, awful, bad, calming, comforting, dreadful, encouraging, harmless, hideous, insignificant, lousy (*Sl.*), mediocre, mild, moderate, paltry, reassuring, rotten (*Inf.*), settling, shocking, soothing, terrible, uninspired, unpleasant

terrified alarmed, appalled, awed, dismayed, frightened, frightened out of one's wits, horrified, horror-struck, intimidated, panic-stricken, petrified, scared, scared shitless (*Taboo sl.*), scared stiff, scared to death, shit-scared (*Taboo sl.*), shocked, terror-stricken

terrify alarm, appal, awe, dismay, fill with terror, frighten, frighten out of one's wits, horrify, intimidate, make one's blood run cold, make one's flesh creep, make one's hair stand on end, petrify, put the fear of God into, scare, scare to death, shock, terrorize

territory area, bailiwick, country, district, domain, land, patch, province, region, sector, state, terrain, tract, turf (*U.S. sl.*), zone

terror 1. alarm, anxiety, awe, consternation, dismay, dread, fear, fear and trembling, fright, horror, intimidation, panic, shock 2. bogeyman, bugbear, devil, fiend, monster, scourge

terrorize 1. browbeat, bully, coerce, intimidate, menace, oppress, strong-arm (*Inf.*), threaten 2. alarm, appal, awe, dismay, fill with terror, frighten, frighten out of one's wits, horrify, inspire panic in, intimidate, make one's blood run cold, make one's flesh creep, make one's hair stand on end, petrify, put the fear of God into, scare, scare to death, shock, strike terror into, terrify

terse 1. aphoristic, brief, clipped, compact, concise, condensed, crisp, elliptical, epigrammatic, gnomic, incisive, laconic, neat, pithy, sententious, short, succinct, summary, to the point 2. abrupt, brusque, curt, short, snappy
Antonyms ambiguous, chatty, circumlocutory, confused, discursive, lengthy, long-winded, polite, rambling, roundabout, vague, verbose, wordy

test 1. *v.* analyse, assay, assess, check, examine, experiment, investigate, prove, put to the proof, put to the test, research, try, try out, verify, work over 2. *n.* analysis, assessment, attempt, catechism, check, evaluation, examination, investigation, ordeal, probation, proof, research, trial

testament 1. last wishes, will 2. attestation, demonstration, earnest, evidence, exemplification, proof, testimony, tribute, witness

testicles balls (*Taboo sl.*), bollocks *or* ballocks (*Taboo sl.*), cojones (*U.S. taboo sl.*), family jewels (*Sl.*), nuts (*Taboo sl.*), rocks (*U.S. taboo sl.*)

testify affirm, assert, asseverate, attest, bear witness, certify, corroborate, declare, depone (*Scots Law*), depose (*Law*), evince, give testimony, show, state, swear, vouch, witness
Antonyms belie, contradict, controvert, disprove, dispute, gainsay (*Archaic or literary*), oppose

testimonial certificate, character, commendation, credential, endorsement, recommendation, reference, tribute

testimony 1. affidavit, affirmation, attestation, avowal, confirmation, corroboration, declaration, deposition, evidence, information, profession, statement, submission, witness 2. corroboration, demonstration, evidence, indication, manifestation, proof, support, verification

testy bad-tempered, cantankerous, captious, crabbed, cross, fretful, grumpy, impatient, irascible, irritable, liverish, peevish, peppery, petulant, quarrelsome, quick-tempered, ratty (*Brit. & N.Z. inf.*), short-tempered, snappish, snappy, splenetic, sullen, tetchy, touchy, waspish

tetchy bad-tempered, cantankerous, captious, crabbed, cross, fretful, grumpy, impatient, irascible, irritable, liverish, peevish, peppery, petulant, quarrelsome, quick-tempered, ratty (*Brit. & N.Z. inf.*), short-tempered, snappish, snappy, splenetic, sullen, testy, touchy, waspish

tête-à-tête 1. *n.* chat, confab (*Inf.*), cosy chat, parley, private conversation, private word, talk 2. *adv.* in private, intimately, privately

tether *n.* 1. bond, chain, fastening, fetter, halter, lead, leash, restraint, rope, shackle

2. at the end of one's tether at one's wits' end, at the limit of one's endurance, exasperated, exhausted, finished, out of patience ~*v.* 3. bind, chain, fasten, fetter, leash, manacle, picket, restrain, rope, secure, shackle, tie

text 1. body, contents, main body, matter 2. wording, words 3. *Bible* paragraph, passage, sentence, verse 4. argument, matter, motif, subject, theme, topic 5. reader, reference book, source, textbook

texture character, composition, consistency, constitution, fabric, feel, grain, make, quality, structure, surface, tissue, weave

thank express gratitude, say thank you, show gratitude, show one's appreciation

thankful appreciative, beholden, grateful, indebted, obliged, pleased, relieved
Antonyms thankless, unappreciative, ungrateful

thankless 1. fruitless, unappreciated, unprofitable, unrequited, unrewarding, useless 2. inconsiderate, unappreciative, ungracious, ungrateful, unmindful, unthankful
Antonyms (*sense 1*) fruitful, productive, profitable, rewarding, useful, worthwhile (*sense 2*) appreciative, grateful, thankful

thanks 1. acknowledgment, appreciation, Brownie points, credit, gratefulness, gratitude, recognition, thanksgiving 2. **thanks to** as a result of, because of, by reason of, due to, owing to, through

thaw defrost, dissolve, liquefy, melt, soften, unfreeze, warm
Antonyms chill, congeal, freeze, harden, solidify, stiffen

theatrical 1. dramatic, dramaturgic, melodramatic, scenic, Thespian 2. actorly, actressy, affected, artificial, camp (*Inf.*), ceremonious, dramatic, exaggerated, hammy (*Inf.*), histrionic, mannered, ostentatious, overdone, pompous, showy, stagy, stilted, unreal
Antonyms (*sense 2*) natural, plain, simple, straightforward, unaffected, unassuming, unexaggerated, unpretentious, unsophisticated

theft embezzlement, fraud, larceny, pilfering, purloining, rip-off (*Sl.*), robbery, stealing, swindling, thievery, thieving

theme 1. argument, burden, idea, keynote, matter, subject, subject matter, text, thesis, topic 2. leitmotiv, motif, recurrent image, unifying idea 3. composition, dissertation, essay, exercise, paper

theological divine, doctrinal, ecclesiastical, religious

theorem deduction, dictum, formula, hypothesis, principle, proposition, rule, statement

theoretical abstract, academic, conjectural, hypothetical, ideal, impractical, notional, pure, speculative
Antonyms applied, experiential, factual, practical, realistic

theorize conjecture, formulate, guess, hypothesize, project, propound, speculate, suppose

theory 1. assumption, conjecture, guess, hypothesis, presumption, speculation, supposition, surmise, thesis 2. philosophy, plan, proposal, scheme, system
Antonyms certainty, experience, fact, practice, reality

therapeutic ameliorative, analeptic, beneficial, corrective, curative, good, healing, remedial, restorative, salubrious, salutary, sanative
Antonyms adverse, damaging, destructive, detrimental, harmful

therapy cure, healing, remedial treatment, remedy, treatment

therefore accordingly, as a result, consequently, ergo, for that reason, hence, so, then, thence, thus, whence

thesaurus dictionary, encyclopedia, repository, storehouse, treasury, wordbook

thesis 1. composition, disquisition, dissertation, essay, monograph, paper, treatise 2. contention, hypothesis, idea, line of argument, opinion, proposal, proposition, theory, view 3. area, subject, theme, topic 4. assumption, postulate, premise, proposition, statement, supposition, surmise

thick *adj.* 1. broad, bulky, deep, fat, solid, substantial, wide 2. close, clotted, coagulated, compact, concentrated, condensed, crowded, deep, dense, heavy, impenetrable, opaque 3. abundant, brimming, bristling, bursting, chock-a-block, chock-full, covered, crawling, frequent, full, numerous, packed, replete, swarming, teeming 4. blockheaded, braindead (*Inf.*), brainless, dense, dim-witted (*Inf.*), dopey (*Inf.*), dozy (*Brit. inf.*), dull, insensitive, moronic, obtuse, slow, slow-witted, stupid, thick-headed 5. dense, heavy, impenetrable, soupy 6. distorted, guttural, hoarse, husky, inarticulate, indistinct, throaty 7. broad, decided, distinct, marked, pronounced, rich, strong 8. *Inf.* buddy-buddy (*Sl., chiefly U.S. & Canad.*), chummy (*Inf.*), close, confidential, devoted, familiar, friendly, hand in glove, inseparable, intimate, matey *or* maty (*Brit. inf.*), on good terms, pally (*Inf.*), palsy-walsy (*Inf.*), well in (*Inf.*) 9. **a bit thick** excessive, over the score (*Inf.*), too much, unfair, unjust, unreasonable ~*n.* 10. centre, heart, middle, midst

Antonyms (*sense 1*) narrow, slight, slim, thin (*sense 2*) clear, diluted, runny, thin, watery, weak (*sense 3*) bare, clear, devoid of, empty, free from, sparse, thin (*sense 4*) articulate, brainy (*Inf.*), bright, clever, intellectual, intelligent, quick-witted, sharp, smart (*sense 5*) clear, thin (*sense 6*) articulate, clear, distinct, sharp, shrill, thin (*sense 7*) faint, slight, vague, weak (*sense 8*) antagonistic, distant, hostile, unfriendly

thicken cake, clot, coagulate, condense, congeal, deepen, gel, inspissate (*Archaic*), jell, set

Antonyms dilute, thin, water down, weaken

thicket brake, clump, coppice, copse, covert, grove, spinney (*Brit.*), wood, woodland

thickhead berk (*Brit. sl.*), blockhead, bonehead (*Sl.*), charlie (*Brit. inf.*), clot (*Brit. inf.*), dickhead (*Sl.*), dimwit (*Inf.*), dipstick (*Brit. sl.*), divvy (*Brit. sl.*), dolt, dope (*Inf.*), dork (*Sl.*), dummy (*Sl.*), dunce, dunderhead, dweeb (*U.S. sl.*), fathead (*Inf.*), fool, fuckwit (*Taboo sl.*), geek (*Sl.*), gonzo (*Sl.*), idiot, imbecile, lamebrain (*Inf.*), moron, nerd *or* nurd (*Sl.*), numskull *or* numbskull, pillock (*Brit. sl.*), pinhead (*Sl.*), plank (*Brit. sl.*), plonker (*Sl.*), prat (*Sl.*), prick (*Derogatory sl.*), twit (*Inf., chiefly Brit.*), wally (*Sl.*)

thickheaded blockheaded, braindead (*Inf.*), brainless, dense, dim-witted (*Inf.*), doltish, dopey (*Inf.*), dozy (*Brit. inf.*), idiotic, moronic, obtuse, slow, slow-witted, stupid, thick

thickset 1. beefy (*Inf.*), brawny, bulky, burly, heavy, muscular, powerfully built, stocky, strong, stubby, sturdy, well-built 2. closely packed, dense, densely planted, solid, thick

Antonyms angular, bony, gangling, gaunt, lanky, rawboned, scraggy, scrawny, weedy (*Inf.*)

thick-skinned callous, case-hardened, hard-boiled (*Inf.*), hardened, impervious, insensitive, stolid, tough, unfeeling, unsusceptible

Antonyms concerned, feeling, sensitive, tender, thin-skinned, touchy

thief bandit, burglar, cheat, cracksman (*Sl.*), crook (*Inf.*), embezzler, housebreaker, larcenist, mugger (*Inf.*), pickpocket, pilferer, plunderer, purloiner, robber, shoplifter, stealer, swindler

thieve blag (*Sl.*), cabbage (*Brit. sl.*), cheat, embezzle, filch, half-inch (*Old-fashioned sl.*), knock off (*Sl.*), lift (*Inf.*), misappropriate, nick (*Sl., chiefly Brit.*), peculate, pilfer, pinch (*Inf.*), plunder, poach, purloin, rip off (*Sl.*), rob, run off with, snitch (*Sl.*), steal, swindle, swipe (*Sl.*)

thievery banditry, burglary, crookedness (*Inf.*), embezzlement, larceny, mugging (*Inf.*), pilfering, plundering, robbery, shoplifting, stealing, theft, thieving

thievish crooked (*Inf.*), dishonest, fraudulent, larcenous, light-fingered, predatory, rapacious, sticky-fingered (*Inf.*), thieving

thimbleful capful, dab, dash, dram, drop, jot, modicum, nip, pinch, sip, *soupçon*, spoonful, spot, taste, toothful

thin *adj.* 1. attenuate, attenuated, fine, narrow, threadlike 2. delicate, diaphanous, filmy, fine, flimsy, gossamer, see-through, sheer, translucent, transparent, unsubstantial 3. bony, emaciated, lank, lanky, lean, light, macilent (*Rare*), meagre, scraggy, scrawny, skeletal, skinny, slender, slight, slim, spare, spindly, thin as a rake, undernourished, underweight 4. deficient, meagre, scanty, scarce, scattered, skimpy, sparse, wispy 5. dilute, diluted, rarefied, runny, watery, weak, wishy-washy (*Inf.*) 6. feeble, flimsy, inadequate, insufficient, lame, poor, scant, scanty, shallow, slight, superficial, unconvincing, unsubstantial, weak ~*v.* 7. attenuate, cut back, dilute, diminish, emaciate, prune, rarefy, reduce, refine, trim, water down, weaken, weed out

Antonyms (*sense 1*) heavy, thick (*sense 2*) bulky, dense, heavy, strong, substantial, thick (*sense 3*) bulky, corpulent, fat, heavy, obese, stout (*sense 4*) abundant, adequate, plentiful, profuse (*sense 5*) concentrated, dense, strong, thick, viscous (*sense 6*) adequate, convincing, strong, substantial

thing 1. affair, article, being, body, circumstance, concept, entity, fact, matter, object, part, portion, something, substance 2. act, deed, event, eventuality, feat, happening, incident, occurrence, phenomenon, proceeding 3. apparatus, contrivance, device, gadget, implement, instrument, machine, means, mechanism, tool 4. aspect, detail, facet, factor, feature, item, particular, point, statement, thought 5. *Plural* baggage, belongings, bits and pieces, clobber (*Brit. sl.*), clothes, effects, equipment, gear, goods, impedimenta, luggage, odds and ends, paraphernalia, possessions, stuff 6. *Inf.* attitude, bee in one's bonnet, fetish, fixation, hang-up (*Inf.*), *idée fixe*, mania, obsession, phobia, preoccupation, quirk

think *v.* 1. believe, conceive, conclude, consider, deem, determine, esteem, estimate, guess (*Inf., chiefly U.S. & Canad.*), hold, imagine, judge, reckon, regard, suppose, surmise 2. brood, cerebrate, chew over (*Inf.*), cogitate, consider, contemplate, deliberate, have in mind, meditate, mull over, muse, ponder, reason, reflect, revolve, ruminate, turn over in one's mind, weigh up 3. call to mind, recall, recollect, remember 4. anticipate, envisage, expect, foresee, imagine, plan for, presume, suppose 5. **think better of** change one's mind about, decide against, go back on, have second thoughts about, reconsider, repent, think again, think twice about 6. **think much of** admire, attach importance to, esteem, have a high opinion of, hold in high regard, rate (*Sl.*), respect, set store by, think highly of, value 7. **think nothing of** consider unimportant, have no compunction about, have no hesitation about, regard as routine, set no store by, take in one's stride ~*n.* 8. assessment, consideration, contemplation, deliberation, look, reflection

thinkable conceivable, feasible, imaginable, likely, possible, reasonable, within the bounds of possibility
 Antonyms absurd, impossible, inconceivable, not on (*Inf.*), out of the question, unlikely, unreasonable, unthinkable

thinker brain (*Inf.*), intellect (*Inf.*), mahatma, mastermind, philosopher, sage, theorist, wise man

thinking 1. *n.* assessment, conclusions, conjecture, idea, judgment, opinion, outlook, philosophy, position, reasoning, theory, thoughts, view 2. *adj.* contemplative, cultured, intelligent, meditative, philosophical, ratiocinative, rational, reasoning, reflective, sophisticated, thoughtful

think over chew over (*Inf.*), consider, consider the pros and cons of, contemplate, give thought to, mull over, ponder, reflect upon, turn over in one's mind, weigh up

think up come up with, concoct, contrive, create, devise, dream up, imagine, improvise, invent, manufacture, trump up, visualize

thin-skinned easily hurt, hypersensitive, quick to take offence, sensitive, soft, susceptible, tender, touchy, vulnerable
 Antonyms callous, hard, heartless, insensitive, obdurate, stolid, thick-skinned, tough, unfeeling

third-rate bad, cheap-jack, chickenshit (*U.S. sl.*), duff (*Brit. inf.*), indifferent, inferior, low-grade, mediocre, of a sort *or* of sorts, poor, poor-quality, ropy *or* ropey (*Brit. inf.*), shoddy

thirst *n.* 1. craving to drink, drought, dryness, thirstiness 2. appetite, craving, desire, eagerness, hankering, hunger, keenness, longing, lust, passion, yearning, yen (*Inf.*)
 Antonyms (*sense 2*) apathy, aversion, disinclination, dislike, distaste, loathing, revulsion

thirsty 1. arid, dehydrated, dry, parched 2. athirst, avid, burning, craving, desirous, dying, eager, greedy, hankering, hungry, itching, longing, lusting, thirsting, yearning

thorn 1. barb, prickle, spike, spine 2. affliction, annoyance, bane, bother, curse, hassle (*Inf.*), irritant, irritation, nuisance, pest, plague, scourge, torment, torture, trouble
 Antonyms (*sense 2*) balm, benefaction, blessing, comfort, manna, solace, succour

thorny 1. barbed, bristling with thorns, bristly, pointed, prickly, sharp, spiky, spinous, spiny 2. awkward, difficult, harassing, hard, irksome, problematic(al), sticky (*Inf.*), ticklish, tough, troublesome, trying, unpleasant, upsetting, vexatious, worrying

thorough *or* **thoroughgoing** 1. all-embracing, all-inclusive, assiduous, careful, complete, comprehensive, conscientious, efficient, exhaustive, full, in-depth, intensive, leaving no stone unturned, meticulous, painstaking, scrupulous, sweeping 2. absolute, arrant, complete, deep-dyed (*Usu. derogatory*), downright, entire, out-and-out, outright, perfect, pure, sheer, total, unmitigated, unqualified, utter
 Antonyms careless, cursory, half-hearted, haphazard, imperfect, incomplete, lackadaisical, partial, sloppy, superficial

thoroughbred *adj.* blood, full-blooded, of unmixed stock, pedigree, pure-blooded, purebred
 Antonyms crossbred, crossed, half-breed, hybrid, mongrel, of mixed breed

thoroughfare access, avenue, highway, passage, passageway, road, roadway, street, way

thoroughly 1. assiduously, carefully, completely, comprehensively, conscientiously, efficiently, exhaustively, from top to bottom, fully, inside out, intensively, leaving no stone unturned, meticulously, painstakingly, scrupulously, sweepingly, through and through, throughout 2. absolutely, completely, downright, entirely, perfectly, quite, totally, to the full, utterly, without reservation
 Antonyms carelessly, cursorily, half-heartedly, haphazardly, imperfectly, incompletely, in part, lackadaisically, partly, sloppily, somewhat, superficially

though 1. *conj.* albeit, allowing, although, despite the fact that, even if, even supposing, even though, granted, notwithstanding, tho' (*U.S. or poetic*), while 2. *adv.* all the same, for all that, however, nevertheless, nonetheless, notwithstanding, still, yet

thought 1. brainwork, cerebration, cogitation, consideration, contemplation, deliberation, introspection, meditation, musing, reflection, regard, rumination, thinking 2. assessment, belief, concept, conception, conclusion, conjecture, conviction, estimation, idea, judgment, notion, opinion, thinking, view 3. attention, consideration, heed, regard, scrutiny, study 4. aim, design, idea, intention, notion, object, plan, purpose 5. anticipation, aspiration, dream, expectation, hope, prospect 6. dash, jot, little, small amount, *soupçon,* touch, trifle, whisker (*Inf.*) 7. anxiety, attentiveness, care, compassion, concern, kindness, regard, solicitude, sympathy, thoughtfulness

thoughtful 1. attentive, caring, considerate, helpful, kind, kindly, solicitous, unselfish 2. astute, canny, careful, cautious, circumspect, deliberate, discreet, heedful, mindful, prudent, wary, well thought-out 3. contemplative, deliberative, in a brown study, introspective, lost in thought, meditative, musing, pensive, rapt, reflective, ruminative, serious, studious, thinking, wistful
Antonyms cold-hearted, extrovert, flippant, heedless, impolite, inconsiderate, insensitive, irresponsible, neglectful, rash, selfish, shallow, superficial, thoughtless, uncaring, unthinking

thoughtless 1. impolite, inconsiderate, indiscreet, insensitive, rude, selfish, tactless, uncaring, undiplomatic, unkind 2. absent-minded, careless, foolish, heedless, ill-considered, imprudent, inadvertent, inattentive, injudicious, mindless, neglectful, negligent, rash, reckless, regardless, remiss, silly, slapdash, slipshod, stupid, unmindful, unobservant, unthinking
Antonyms attentive, considerate, considered, diplomatic, intelligent, prudent, smart, tactful, thoughtful, unselfish, well-advised, well thought-out, wise

thraldom bondage, enslavement, serfdom, servitude, slavery, subjection, subjugation, thrall, vassalage

thrall 1. bondage, enslavement, serfdom, servitude, slavery, subjection, subjugation, thraldom, vassalage 2. bondservant, bondsman, serf, slave, subject, varlet (*Archaic*), vassal

thrash 1. beat, belt (*Inf.*), birch, cane, chastise, clobber (*Sl.*), drub, flagellate, flog, give (someone) a (good) hiding (*Inf.*), hide (*Inf.*), horsewhip, lambast(e), leather, lick (*Inf.*), paste (*Sl.*), punish, scourge, spank, take a stick to, tan (*Sl.*), whip 2. beat, beat (someone) hollow (*Brit. inf.*), blow out of the water (*Sl.*), clobber (*Sl.*), crush, defeat, drub, hammer (*Inf.*), lick (*Inf.*), maul, overwhelm, paste (*Sl.*), rout, run rings around (*Inf.*), slaughter (*Inf.*), tank (*Sl.*), trounce, wipe the floor with (*Inf.*) 3. flail, heave, jerk, plunge, squirm, thresh, toss, toss and turn, writhe

thrashing 1. beating, belting (*Inf.*), caning, chastisement, drubbing, flogging, hiding (*Inf.*), lashing, pasting (*Sl.*), punishment, tanning (*Sl.*), whipping 2. beating, defeat, drubbing, hammering (*Inf.*), hiding (*Inf.*), mauling, pasting (*Sl.*), rout, trouncing

thrash out argue out, debate, discuss, have out, resolve, settle, solve, talk over

thread *n.* 1. cotton, fibre, filament, line, strand, string, yarn 2. course, direction, drift, motif, plot, story line, strain, tenor, theme, train of thought ~*v.* 3. ease, inch, loop, meander, pass, pick (one's way), squeeze through, string, wind

threadbare 1. down at heel, frayed, old, ragged, scruffy, shabby, tattered, tatty, used, worn, worn-out 2. clichéd, cliché-ridden, common, commonplace, conventional, corny (*Sl.*), familiar, hackneyed, overused, stale, stereotyped, stock, tired, trite, well-worn
Antonyms (*sense 1*) brand-new, good, new, smart, unused, well-preserved (*sense 2*) different, fresh, new, novel, original, unconventional, unfamiliar, unusual

threat 1. commination, intimidatory remark, menace, threatening remark, warning 2. foreboding, foreshadowing, omen, portent, presage, warning, writing on the wall 3. danger, hazard, menace, peril, risk

threaten 1. endanger, imperil, jeopardize, put at risk, put in jeopardy 2. be imminent, be in the air, be in the offing, forebode, foreshadow, hang over, impend, loom over, portend, presage, warn 3. browbeat, bully, cow, intimidate, lean on (*Sl.*), make threats to, menace, pressurize, terrorize, warn
Antonyms defend, guard, protect, safeguard, shelter, shield

threatening 1. bullying, cautionary, comminatory, intimidatory, menacing, minatory, terrorizing, warning 2. baleful, forbidding, grim, inauspicious, ominous, sinister
Antonyms (*sense 2*) auspicious, bright, comforting, encouraging, favourable, promising, propitious, reassuring

threesome triad, trilogy, trine, trinity, trio, triple, triplet, triplex, triptych, triumvirate, triune, troika

threnody coronach (*Scot. & Irish*), dirge, elegy, funeral ode, keen, lament, monody, requiem

threshold 1. door, doorsill, doorstep, doorway, entrance, sill 2. beginning, brink, dawn, inception, opening, outset, start,

starting point, verge 3. lower limit, minimum
Antonyms (*sense 2*) close, decline, end, finish, twilight

thrift carefulness, economy, frugality, good husbandry, parsimony, prudence, saving, thriftiness
Antonyms carelessness, extravagance, prodigality, profligacy, recklessness, squandering, waste

thriftless extravagant, improvident, imprudent, lavish, prodigal, profligate, spendthrift, unthrifty, wasteful
Antonyms careful, economical, frugal, provident, prudent, sparing, thrifty

thrifty careful, economical, frugal, parsimonious, provident, prudent, saving, sparing
Antonyms extravagant, free-spending, generous, improvident, prodigal, spendthrift, wasteful

thrill *n.* 1. adventure, buzz (*Sl.*), charge (*Sl.*), flush of excitement, glow, kick (*Inf.*), pleasure, sensation, stimulation, tingle, titillation 2. flutter, fluttering, quiver, shudder, throb, tremble, tremor, vibration ~*v.* 3. arouse, electrify, excite, flush, get a charge (*Sl.*), get a kick (*Inf.*), glow, move, send (*Sl.*), stimulate, stir, tingle, titillate 4. flutter, quake, quiver, shake, shudder, throb, tremble, vibrate
Antonyms (*sense 1*) boredom, dreariness, dullness, ennui, monotony, tedium

thrilling 1. electrifying, exciting, gripping, hair-raising, rip-roaring (*Inf.*), riveting, rousing, sensational, sexy (*Inf.*), stimulating, stirring 2. quaking, shaking, shivering, shuddering, trembling, vibrating
Antonyms boring, dreary, dull, monotonous, quiet, staid, tedious, uninteresting, unmoving

thrive advance, bloom, boom, burgeon, develop, do well, flourish, get on, grow, grow rich, increase, prosper, succeed, wax
Antonyms decline, droop, fail, languish, perish, shrivel, stagnate, wane, wilt, wither

thriving blooming, booming, burgeoning, developing, doing well, flourishing, going strong, growing, healthy, prosperous, successful, wealthy, well
Antonyms ailing, bankrupt, failing, impoverished, languishing, on the rocks, poverty-stricken, unsuccessful, withering

throaty deep, gruff, guttural, hoarse, husky, low, thick

throb 1. *v.* beat, palpitate, pound, pulsate, pulse, thump, vibrate 2. *n.* beat, palpitation, pounding, pulsating, pulse, thump, thumping, vibration

throe 1. convulsion, fit, pain, pang, paroxysm, spasm, stab 2. *Plural* agony, anguish, pain, suffering, torture, travail 3. **in the throes of** agonized by, anguished by, in the midst of, in the pangs of, in the process of, struggling with, suffering from, toiling with, wrestling with

throng 1. *n.* assemblage, concourse, congregation, crowd, crush, horde, host, jam, mass, mob, multitude, pack, press, swarm 2. *v.* bunch, congregate, converge, cram, crowd, fill, flock, hem in, herd, jam, mill around, pack, press, swarm around, troop
Antonyms *v.* break up, disband, dispel, disperse, scatter, separate, spread out

throttle *v.* 1. choke, garrotte, strangle, strangulate 2. control, gag, inhibit, silence, stifle, suppress

through *prep.* 1. between, by, from end to end of, from one side to the other of, in and out of, past 2. as a consequence *or* result of, because of, by means of, by virtue of, by way of, using, via, with the help of 3. during, in, in the middle of, throughout 4. *With* **with** at the end of, done, finished, having completed, having had enough of ~*adj.* 5. completed, done, ended, finished, terminated, washed up (*Inf.*) ~*adv.* 6. **through and through** altogether, completely, entirely, fully, thoroughly, totally, to the core, unreservedly, utterly, wholly
Antonyms *adv.* moderately, more or less, partially, partly, somewhat, to some extent

throughout all over, all the time, all through, during the whole of, everywhere, for the duration of, from beginning to end, from end to end, from start to finish, from the start, over the length and breadth of, right through, the whole time, through the whole of

throw *v.* 1. cast, chuck (*Inf.*), fling, heave, hurl, launch, lob (*Inf.*), pitch, project, propel, put, send, shy, sling, toss 2. *Inf.* astonish, baffle, confound, confuse, disconcert, dumbfound, faze, put one off one's stroke, throw off, throw one off one's stride, throw out 3. bring down, dislodge, fell, floor, hurl to the ground, overturn, unseat, upset ~*n.* 4. cast, fling, heave, lob (*Inf.*), pitch, projection, put, shy, sling, toss 5. *Inf.* attempt, chance, essay, gamble, hazard, try, venture, wager

throwaway *adj.* careless, casual, offhand, passing, understated

throw away 1. axe (*Inf.*), bin (*Inf.*), cast off, chuck (*Inf.*), discard, dispense with, dispose of, ditch (*Sl.*), dump (*Inf.*), get rid of, jettison, junk (*Inf.*), reject, scrap, throw out 2. blow (*Sl.*), fail to exploit, fritter away, lose, make poor use of, squander, waste
Antonyms (*sense 1*) conserve, keep, preserve, rescue, retain, retrieve, salvage, save

throw off 1. abandon, cast off, discard, drop, free oneself of, rid oneself of, shake off 2. elude, escape from, evade, get away from, give (someone) the slip, leave behind, lose, outdistance, outrun, shake off, show a clean pair of heels to 3. confuse, disconcert, disturb, faze, put one off one's stroke, throw (*Inf.*), throw one off one's stride, unsettle, upset

throw out 1. bin (*Inf.*), cast off, chuck (*Inf.*), discard, dismiss, dispense with, ditch (*Sl.*), dump (*Inf.*), eject, evict, expel, get rid of, give the bum's rush (*Sl.*), jettison, junk (*Inf.*), kick out (*Inf.*), kiss off (*Sl., chiefly U.S. & Canad.*), oust, reject, relegate, scrap, show one the door, throw away, turf out (*Brit. inf.*), turn down 2. confuse, disconcert, disturb, put one off one's stroke, throw (*Inf.*), throw one off one's stride, unsettle, upset 3. diffuse, disseminate, emit, give off, put forth, radiate

throw over abandon, break with, chuck (*Inf.*), desert, discard, drop (*Inf.*), finish with, forsake, jilt, leave, quit, split up with, walk out on (*Inf.*)

throw up 1. abandon, chuck (*Inf.*), give up, jack in, leave, quit, relinquish, renounce, resign from, step down from (*Inf.*) 2. bring forward, bring to light, bring to notice, bring to the surface, produce, reveal 3. *Inf.* barf (*U.S. sl.*), be sick, bring up, chuck (up) (*Sl., chiefly U.S.*), chunder (*Sl., chiefly Aust.*), disgorge, do a technicolour yawn (*Sl.*), heave, puke (*Sl.*), regurgitate, retch, spew, toss one's cookies (*U.S. sl.*), upchuck (*U.S. sl.*), vomit 4. jerry-build, run up, slap together, throw together

thrust *v.* 1. butt, drive, elbow *or* shoulder one's way, force, impel, jam, plunge, poke, press, prod, propel, push, ram, shove, urge 2. jab, lunge, pierce, stab, stick ~*n.* 3. drive, lunge, poke, prod, push, shove, stab 4. impetus, momentum, motive force, motive power, propulsive force

thud *n./v.* clonk, clump, clunk, crash, knock, smack, thump, wallop (*Inf.*)

thug assassin, bandit, bruiser (*Inf.*), bully boy, cutthroat, gangster, heavy (*Sl.*), hooligan, killer, mugger (*Inf.*), murderer, robber, ruffian, tough

thumb *n.* 1. pollex 2. **all thumbs** butter-fingered (*Inf.*), cack-handed (*Inf.*), clumsy, ham-fisted (*Inf.*), inept, maladroit 3. **thumbs down** disapproval, negation, no, rebuff, refusal, rejection 4. **thumbs up** acceptance, affirmation, approval, encouragement, go-ahead (*Inf.*), green light, O.K. *or* okay (*Inf.*), yes ~*v.* 5. hitch (*Inf.*), hitch-hike 6. *Often with* **through** browse through, flick through, flip through, glance at, leaf through, riffle through, run one's eye over, scan the pages of, skim through, turn over 7. dog-ear, finger, handle, mark 8. **thumb one's nose at** be contemptuous of, cock a snook at, deride, flout, jeer at, laugh at, laugh in the face of, mock, ridicule, show contempt for, show disrespect to

thumbnail *adj.* brief, compact, concise, pithy, quick, short, succinct

thump 1. *n.* bang, blow, clout (*Inf.*), clunk, crash, knock, punch, rap, smack, thud, thwack, wallop (*Inf.*), whack 2. *v.* bang, batter, beat, belabour, chin (*Sl.*), clobber (*Sl.*), clout (*Inf.*), crash, deck (*Sl.*), hit, knock, lambast(e), lay one on (*Sl.*), pound, punch, rap, smack, strike, thrash, throb, thud, thwack, wallop (*Inf.*), whack

thumping colossal, elephantine, enormous, excessive, exorbitant, gargantuan, gigantic, great, huge, humongous *or* humungous (*U.S. sl.*), impressive, mammoth, massive, monumental, terrific, thundering (*Sl.*), titanic, tremendous, whopping (*Inf.*)
Antonyms inconsequential, insignificant, meagre, measly (*Inf.*), negligible, paltry, petty, piddling (*Inf.*), trifling, trivial

thunder *n.* 1. boom, booming, cracking, crash, crashing, detonation, explosion, pealing, rumble, rumbling ~*v.* 2. blast, boom, clap, crack, crash, detonate, explode, peal, resound, reverberate, roar, rumble 3. bark, bellow, declaim, roar, shout, yell 4. curse, denounce, fulminate, rail, threaten, utter threats

thundering decided, enormous, excessive, great, monumental, remarkable, unmitigated, utter

thunderous booming, deafening, ear-splitting, loud, noisy, resounding, roaring, tumultuous

thunderstruck aghast, amazed, astonished, astounded, bowled over (*Inf.*), dazed, dumbfounded, flabbergasted (*Inf.*), floored (*Inf.*), flummoxed, gobsmacked (*Brit. sl.*), knocked for six (*Inf.*), left speechless, nonplussed, open-mouthed, paralysed, petrified, rooted to the spot, shocked, staggered, struck dumb, stunned, taken aback

thus 1. as follows, in this fashion (manner, way), like so, like this, so, to such a degree 2. accordingly, consequently, ergo, for this reason, hence, on that account, so, then, therefore

thwack 1. *v.* bash (*Inf.*), beat, chin (*Sl.*), clout (*Inf.*), deck (*Sl.*), flog, hit, lambast(e), lay one on (*Sl.*), smack, thump, wallop (*Inf.*), whack 2. *n.* bash (*Inf.*), blow, clout (*Inf.*), smack, thump, wallop (*Inf.*), whack

thwart baffle, balk, check, defeat, foil, frus-

trate, hinder, impede, obstruct, oppose, outwit, prevent, stop, stymie
Antonyms aggravate, aid, assist, encourage, exacerbate, facilitate, hasten, help, intensify, support

tic jerk, spasm, twitch

tick[1] *n.* 1. clack, click, clicking, tap, tapping, ticktock 2. *Brit. inf.* flash, half a mo (*Brit. inf.*), instant, jiffy (*Inf.*), minute, moment, sec (*Inf.*), second, shake (*Inf.*), split second, trice, twinkling, two shakes of a lamb's tail (*Inf.*) 3. dash, mark, stroke ~*v.* 4. clack, click, tap, ticktock 5. check off, choose, indicate, mark, mark off, select 6. **what makes someone tick** drive, motivation, motive, *raison d'être*

tick[2] account, credit, deferred payment, the slate (*Brit. inf.*)

ticket 1. card, certificate, coupon, pass, slip, token, voucher 2. card, docket, label, marker, slip, sticker, tab, tag

tickle *Fig.* amuse, delight, divert, entertain, excite, gratify, please, thrill, titillate
Antonyms annoy, bore, bother, irritate, pester, trouble, vex, weary

ticklish awkward, critical, delicate, difficult, nice, risky, sensitive, thorny, touchy, tricky, uncertain, unstable, unsteady

tick off 1. check off, mark off, put a tick at 2. *Inf.* bawl out (*Inf.*), berate, carpet (*Inf.*), censure, chew out (*U.S. & Canad. inf.*), chide, give a rocket (*Brit. & N.Z. inf.*), haul over the coals (*Inf.*), lecture, read the riot act, rebuke, reprimand, reproach, reprove, scold, take to task, tear into (*Inf.*), tear (someone) off a strip (*Brit. inf.*), tell off (*Inf.*), upbraid

tide 1. course, current, ebb, flow, stream, tideway, undertow 2. course, current, direction, drift, movement, tendency, trend

tide over aid, assist, bridge the gap, help, keep one going, keep one's head above water, keep the wolf from the door, see one through

tidings advice, bulletin, communication, gen (*Brit. inf.*), greetings, information, intelligence, latest (*Inf.*), message, news, report, word

tidy *adj.* 1. businesslike, clean, cleanly, methodical, neat, ordered, orderly, shipshape, spick-and-span, spruce, systematic, trig (*Archaic or dialect*), trim, well-groomed, well-kept, well-ordered 2. *Inf.* ample, considerable, fair, generous, good, goodly, handsome, healthy, large, largish, respectable, sizable, substantial ~*v.* 3. clean, groom, neaten, order, put in order, put in trim, put to rights, spruce up, straighten
Antonyms (*sense 1*) careless, dirty, dishevelled, disordered, disorderly, filthy, in disarray, messy, scruffy, sloppy, slovenly, unbusinesslike, unkempt, unmethodical, unsystematic, untidy (*sense 2*) inconsiderable, insignificant, little, small, tiny (*sense 3*) dirty, dishevel, disorder, mess, mess up

tie *v.* 1. attach, bind, connect, fasten, interlace, join, knot, lash, link, make fast, moor, rope, secure, tether, truss, unite 2. bind, confine, hamper, hinder, hold, limit, restrain, restrict 3. be even, be neck and neck, draw, equal, match ~*n.* 4. band, bond, connection, cord, fastening, fetter, joint, knot, ligature, link, rope, string 5. affiliation, affinity, allegiance, bond, commitment, connection, duty, kinship, liaison, obligation, relationship 6. encumbrance, hindrance, limitation, restraint, restriction 7. dead heat, deadlock, draw, stalemate 8. *Brit.* contest, fixture, game, match
Antonyms free, loose, release, separate, undo, unfasten, unhitch, unknot, untie

tie-in association, connection, coordination, hook-up, liaison, link, relation, relationship, tie-up

tie in be relevant, come in, connect, coordinate, fit in, have bearing, link, relate

tier bank, echelon, file, layer, level, line, order, rank, row, series, storey, stratum

tie-up association, connection, coordination, hook-up, liaison, link, linkup, relation, relationship, tie-in

tie up 1. attach, bind, pinion, restrain, tether, truss 2. lash, make fast, moor, rope, secure 3. engage, engross, keep busy, occupy 4. bring to a close, conclude, end, finish off, settle, terminate, wind up, wrap up (*Inf.*)

tiff 1. difference, disagreement, dispute, falling-out (*Inf.*), petty quarrel, quarrel, row, scrap (*Inf.*), squabble, words 2. bad mood, fit of ill humour, fit of pique, huff, ill humour, pet, sulk, tantrum, temper

tight 1. close, close-fitting, compact, constricted, cramped, fast, firm, fixed, narrow, rigid, secure, snug, stiff, stretched, taut, tense 2. hermetic, impervious, proof, sealed, sound, watertight 3. harsh, inflexible, rigid, rigorous, severe, stern, strict, stringent, tough, uncompromising, unyielding 4. close, grasping, mean, miserly, niggardly, parsimonious, penurious, sparing, stingy, tight-arse (*Taboo sl.*), tight-arsed (*Taboo sl.*), tight as a duck's arse (*Taboo sl.*), tight-ass (*U.S. taboo sl.*), tight-assed (*U.S. taboo sl.*), tightfisted 5. dangerous, difficult, hazardous, perilous, precarious, problematic, sticky (*Inf.*), ticklish, tough, tricky, troublesome, worrisome 6. close, even, evenly-balanced, near, well-matched 7. *Inf.* bevvied (*Dialect*), blitzed (*Sl.*), blotto (*Sl.*), bombed (*Sl.*), drunk, flying (*Sl.*), half cut (*Brit. sl.*), half seas over (*Brit. inf.*), inebriated, in one's cups, intoxicated, legless (*Inf.*), lit up (*Sl.*), out of it (*Sl.*), out to it (*Aust. & N.Z. sl.*), paralytic (*Inf.*), pickled (*Inf.*), pie-eyed (*Sl.*), pissed (*Taboo sl.*), plastered (*Sl.*), smashed (*Sl.*), sozzled (*Inf.*), steamboats (*Sl.*), steaming (*Sl.*), stewed (*Sl.*), stoned (*Sl.*), three sheets in the wind (*Sl.*), tiddly (*Sl., chiefly Brit.*), tipsy, under the influence (*Inf.*), wasted (*Sl.*), wrecked (*Sl.*), zonked (*Sl.*)

Antonyms (*sense 1*) lax, loose, relaxed, slack, spacious (*sense 2*) loose, open, porous (*sense 3*) easy, easy-going, generous, lax, lenient, liberal, relaxed, soft, undemanding (*sense 4*) abundant, extravagant, generous, lavish, munificent, open, prodigal, profuse, spendthrift (*sense 5*) easy (*sense 6*) easy, landslide, overwhelming, runaway, uneven (*sense 7*) sober

tighten close, constrict, cramp, fasten, fix, narrow, rigidify, screw, secure, squeeze, stiffen, stretch, tauten, tense

Antonyms ease off, let out, loosen, relax, slacken, unbind, weaken

tightfisted close, close-fisted, grasping, mean, mingy (*Brit. inf.*), miserly, niggardly, parsimonious, penurious, sparing, stingy, tight, tight-arse (*Taboo sl.*), tight-arsed (*Taboo sl.*), tight as a duck's arse (*Taboo sl.*), tight-ass (*U.S. taboo sl.*), tight-assed (*U.S. taboo sl.*)

tight-lipped close-lipped, close-mouthed, mum, mute, quiet, reserved, reticent, secretive, silent, taciturn, uncommunicative, unforthcoming

till[1] cultivate, dig, plough, turn over, work

till[2] cash box, cash drawer, cash register

tilt *v.* 1. cant, heel, incline, lean, list, slant, slope, tip 2. attack, break a lance, clash, contend, cross swords, duel, encounter, fight, joust, overthrow, spar *~n.* 3. angle, cant, inclination, incline, list, pitch, slant, slope 4. *Medieval history* clash, combat, duel, encounter, fight, joust, lists, set-to (*Inf.*), tournament, tourney 5. **(at) full tilt** for dear life, full force, full speed, headlong, like a bat out of hell (*Sl.*), like the clappers (*Brit. inf.*)

timber beams, boards, forest, logs, planks, trees, wood

timbre colour, quality of sound, resonance, ring, tonality, tone, tone colour

time *n.* 1. age, chronology, date, duration, epoch, era, generation, hour, interval, period, season, space, span, spell, stretch, term, while 2. instance, juncture, occasion, point, stage 3. allotted span, day, duration, life, life span, lifetime, season 4. heyday, hour, peak 5. *Mus.* beat, measure, metre, rhythm, tempo 6. **all the time** always, at all times, constantly, continually, continuously, ever, for the duration, perpetually, throughout 7. **at one time a.** for a while, formerly, hitherto, once, once upon a time, previously **b.** all at once, at the same time, simultaneously, together 8. **at times** every now and then, every so often, from time to time, now and then, occasionally, once in a while, on occasion, sometimes 9. **behind the times** antiquated, dated, obsolete, old-fashioned, old hat, outdated, outmoded, out of date, out of fashion, out of style, passé, square (*Inf.*) 10. **for the time being** for now, for the moment, for the nonce, for the present, in the meantime, meantime, meanwhile, pro tem, temporarily 11. **from time to time** at times, every now and then, every so often, now and then, occasionally, once in a while, on occasion, sometimes 12. **in good time a.** early, on time, with time to spare **b.** quickly, rapidly, speedily, swiftly, with dispatch 13. **in no time** apace, before one knows it, before you can say Jack Robinson, in an instant, in a trice (flash, jiffy (*Inf.*), moment), in two shakes of a lamb's tail (*Inf.*), quickly, rapidly, speedily, swiftly 14. **in time a.** at the appointed time, early, in good time, on schedule, on time, with time to spare **b.** by and by, eventually, one day, someday, sooner or later, ultimately 15. **on time** in good time, on the dot, punctually 16. **time and again** frequently, many times, often, on many occasions, over and over again, repeatedly, time after time *~v.* 17. clock, control, count, judge, measure, regulate, schedule, set

time-honoured age-old, ancient, conventional, customary, established, fixed, long-established, old, traditional, usual, venerable

timeless abiding, ageless, ceaseless, changeless, deathless, endless, enduring, eternal, everlasting, immortal, immutable, imperishable, indestructible, lasting, permanent, persistent, undying

Antonyms ephemeral, evanescent, momentary, mortal, passing, temporal, temporary, transitory

timely appropriate, at the right time, convenient, judicious, opportune, prompt, propitious, punctual, seasonable, suitable, well-timed

Antonyms ill-timed, inconvenient, inopportune, late, tardy, unseasonable, untimely

timeserver hypocrite, opportunist, self-seeker, trimmer, Vicar of Bray, weathercock

timetable agenda, calendar, curriculum, diary, list, order of the day, programme, schedule

timeworn 1. aged, ancient, broken-down, decrepit, dog-eared, lined, ragged, run-down, shabby, the worse for wear, weathered, worn, wrinkled 2. ancient, clichéd, dated, hackneyed, hoary, old hat, out of date, outworn, passé, stale, stock, threadbare, tired, trite, well-worn

timid afraid, apprehensive, bashful, cowardly, coy, diffident, faint-hearted, fearful, irresolute, modest, mousy, nervous, pusillanimous, retiring, shrinking, shy, timorous

Antonyms aggressive, arrogant, ballsy (*Taboo sl.*), bold, brave, confident, daring, fearless, fierce, forceful, forward, presumptuous, self-assured, self-confident, shameless, unabashed

timorous afraid, apprehensive, bashful, cowardly, coy, diffident, faint-hearted, fearful, frightened, irresolute, mousy, nervous, pusillanimous, retiring, shrinking, shy, timid, trembling

Antonyms assertive, assured, audacious, bold, confident, courageous, daring, fearless

tincture 1. *n.* aroma, colour, dash, flavour, hint, hue, seasoning, shade, smack, *soupçon,* stain, suggestion, tinge, tint, touch, trace 2. *v.* colour, dye, flavour, scent, season, stain, tinge, tint

tinge *n.* 1. cast, colour, dye, shade, stain, tincture, tint, wash 2. bit, dash, drop, pinch, smack, smattering, *soupçon,* sprinkling, suggestion, touch, trace ~*v.* 3. colour, dye, imbue, shade, stain, suffuse, tinge, tint

tingle 1. *v.* have goose pimples, itch, prickle, sting, tickle 2. *n.* goose pimples, itch, itching, pins and needles (*Inf.*), prickling, quiver, shiver, stinging, thrill, tickle, tickling

tinker *v.* dabble, fiddle (*Inf.*), meddle, mess about, monkey, muck about (*Brit. sl.*), play, potter, toy

tinsel *adj.* brummagem, cheap, flashy, gaudy, meretricious, ostentatious, pinchbeck, plastic (*Sl.*), sham, showy, specious, superficial, tawdry, trashy

tint *n.* 1. cast, colour, hue, shade, tone 2. dye, rinse, stain, tincture, tinge, wash 3. hint, shade, suggestion, tinge, touch, trace ~*v.* 4. colour, dye, rinse, stain, tincture, tinge 5. affect, colour, influence, taint, tinge

tiny diminutive, dwarfish, infinitesimal, insignificant, Lilliputian, little, microscopic, mini, miniature, minute, negligible, petite, pint-sized (*Inf.*), puny, pygmy *or* pigmy, slight, small, teensy-weensy, teeny-weeny, trifling, wee

Antonyms colossal, enormous, extra-large, gargantuan, giant, gigantic, great, huge, immense, mammoth, massive, monstrous, titanic, vast

tip[1] 1. *n.* apex, cap, crown, end, extremity, head, peak, point, summit, top 2. *v.* cap, crown, finish, surmount, top

tip[2] *v.* 1. cant, capsize, incline, lean, list, overturn, slant, spill, tilt, topple over, upend, upset 2. *Brit.* ditch (*Sl.*), dump, empty, pour out, unload ~*n.* 3. *Brit.* dump, midden (*Dialect*), refuse heap, rubbish heap

tip[3] *n.* 1. baksheesh, gift, gratuity, perquisite, *pourboire* 2. *Also* **tip-off** clue, forecast, gen (*Brit. inf.*), hint, information, inside information, pointer, suggestion, warning, word, word of advice ~*v.* 3. remunerate, reward 4. *Also* **tip off** advise, caution, forewarn, give a clue, give a hint, suggest, tip (someone) the wink (*Brit. inf.*), warn

tipple 1. *v.* bend the elbow (*Inf.*), bevvy (*Dialect*), drink, imbibe, indulge (*Inf.*), quaff, swig, take a drink, tope 2. *n.* alcohol, booze (*Inf.*), drink, John Barleycorn, liquor, poison (*Inf.*)

tippler bibber, boozer (*Inf.*), drinker, drunk, drunkard, inebriate, soak (*Sl.*), sot, sponge (*Inf.*), toper

tipsy elevated (*Inf.*), fuddled, happy (*Inf.*), mellow, merry (*Brit. inf.*), slightly drunk, tiddly (*Sl., chiefly Brit.*), woozy (*Inf.*)

tirade abuse, denunciation, diatribe, fulmination, harangue, invective, lecture, outburst, philippic

tire 1. drain, droop, enervate, exhaust, fag (*Inf.*), fail, fatigue, flag, jade, knacker (*Sl.*), sink, take it out of (*Inf.*), wear down, wear out, weary, whack (*Brit. inf.*) 2. aggravate (*Inf.*), annoy, bore, exasperate, get on one's nerves (*Inf.*), harass, hassle (*Inf.*), irk, irritate, piss one off (*Taboo sl.*), weary

Antonyms (*sense 1*) energize, enliven, exhilarate, invigorate, liven up, pep up, refresh, restore, revive

tired 1. all in (*Sl.*), asleep *or* dead on one's feet (*Inf.*), clapped out (*Aust. & N.Z. inf.*), dead beat (*Inf.*), dog-tired (*Inf.*), done in (*Inf.*), drained, drooping, drowsy, enervated, exhausted, fagged (*Inf.*), fatigued, flagging, jaded, knackered (*Sl.*), ready to drop, sleepy, spent, weary, whacked (*Brit. inf.*), worn out, zonked (*Sl.*) 2. *With* **of** annoyed with, bored with, exasperated by, fed up with, irked by, irritated by, pissed off with (*Taboo sl.*), sick of, weary of 3. clichéd, conventional, corny (*Sl.*), familiar, hack-

neyed, old, outworn, stale, stock, threadbare, trite, well-worn
Antonyms energetic, enthusiastic about, fond of, fresh, full of beans, innovative, keen on, lively, original, refreshed, rested, wide-awake

tireless determined, energetic, indefatigable, industrious, resolute, unflagging, untiring, unwearied, vigorous
Antonyms drained, exhausted, fatigued, flagging, tired, weak, weary, worn out

tiresome annoying, boring, dull, exasperating, flat, irksome, irritating, laborious, monotonous, tedious, trying, uninteresting, vexatious, wearing, wearisome
Antonyms exhilarating, inspiring, interesting, refreshing, rousing, stimulating

tiring arduous, demanding, enervative, exacting, exhausting, fatiguing, laborious, strenuous, tough, wearing, wearying

tiro *see* TYRO

tissue 1. fabric, gauze, mesh, structure, stuff, texture, web 2. paper, paper handkerchief, wrapping paper 3. accumulation, chain, collection, combination, concatenation, conglomeration, fabrication, mass, network, pack, series, web

titan colossus, giant, leviathan, ogre, superman

titanic Brobdingnagian, colossal, elephantine, enormous, giant, gigantic, herculean, huge, humongous *or* humungous (*U.S. sl.*), immense, jumbo (*Inf.*), mammoth, massive, mighty, monstrous, mountainous, prodigious, stupendous, towering, vast

titbit *bonne bouche,* choice item, dainty, delicacy, goody, juicy bit, morsel, scrap, snack, treat

tit for tat an eye for an eye, as good as one gets, a tooth for a tooth, blow for blow, like for like, measure for measure, retaliation

tithe *n.* 1. assessment, duty, impost, levy, tariff, tax, tenth, toll, tribute ~*v.* 2. assess, charge, levy, rate, tax 3. give up, pay, pay a tithe on, render, surrender, turn over

titillate arouse, excite, interest, provoke, stimulate, tantalize, tease, thrill, tickle, turn on (*Sl.*)

titillating arousing, exciting, interesting, lewd, lurid, provocative, sensational, stimulating, suggestive, teasing, thrilling

titivate doll up (*Sl.*), do up (*Inf.*), make up, prank, preen, primp, prink, refurbish, smarten up, tart up (*Brit. sl.*), touch up

title *n.* 1. caption, heading, inscription, label, legend, name, style 2. appellation, denomination, designation, epithet, handle (*Sl.*), moniker *or* monicker (*Sl.*), name, nickname, nom de plume, pseudonym, sobriquet, term 3. championship, crown, laurels 4. claim, entitlement, ownership, prerogative, privilege, right ~*v.* 5. call, designate, label, name, style, term

titter chortle (*Inf.*), chuckle, giggle, laugh, snigger, te-hee, tee-hee

tittle atom, bit, dash, drop, grain, iota, jot, mite, particle, scrap, shred, speck, whit

tittle-tattle 1. *n.* babble, blather, blether, cackle, chatter, chitchat, clishmaclaver (*Scot.*), dirt (*U.S. sl.*), gossip, hearsay, idle chat, jaw (*Sl.*), natter, prattle, rumour, twaddle, yackety-yak (*Sl.*), yatter (*Inf.*) 2. *v.* babble, blather, blether, cackle, chat, chatter, chitchat, gossip, jaw (*Sl.*), natter, prattle, witter (*Inf.*), yak (*Sl.*), yatter (*Inf.*)

titular honorary, in name only, nominal, puppet, putative, so-called, theoretical, token
Antonyms actual, effective, functioning, real, true

toady 1. *n.* apple polisher (*U.S. sl.*), asskisser (*U.S. & Canad. taboo sl.*), bootlicker (*Inf.*), brown-noser (*Taboo sl.*), crawler (*Sl.*), creep (*Sl.*), fawner, flatterer, flunkey, groveller, hanger-on, jackal, lackey, lickspittle, minion, parasite, spaniel, sycophant, truckler, yes man 2. *v.* be obsequious to, bow and scrape, brown-nose (*Taboo sl.*), butter up, crawl, creep, cringe, curry favour with, fawn on, flatter, grovel, kiss (someone's) ass (*U.S. & Canad. taboo sl.*), kiss the feet of, kowtow to, lick (someone's) boots, pander to, suck up to (*Inf.*)
Antonyms (*sense 2*) confront, defy, oppose, rebel, resist, stand against, withstand

toast[1] *v.* brown, grill, heat, roast, warm

toast[2] *n.* 1. compliment, drink, health, pledge, salutation, salute, tribute 2. darling, favourite, heroine ~*v.* 3. drink to, drink (to) the health of, pledge, salute

to-do agitation, bother, brouhaha, bustle, commotion, disturbance, excitement, flap (*Inf.*), furore, fuss, hoo-ha, performance (*Inf.*), quarrel, ruction (*Inf.*), rumpus, stir, tumult, turmoil, unrest, upheaval, uproar

together *adv.* 1. as a group, as one, cheek by jowl, closely, collectively, hand in glove, hand in hand, in a body, in concert, in cooperation, in unison, jointly, mutually, shoulder to shoulder, side by side 2. all at once, as one, at one fell swoop, at the same time, concurrently, contemporaneously, en masse, in unison, simultaneously, with one accord 3. consecutively, continuously, in a row, in succession, one after the other, on end, successively, without a break, without interruption 4. *Inf.* arranged, fixed, ordered, organized, settled, sorted out, straight, to rights ~*adj.* 5. *Sl.* calm, composed, cool, stable, well-adjusted, well-balanced, well-organized

Antonyms (*sense 1*) alone, apart, independently, individually, one at a time, one by one, separately, singly

toil 1. *n.* application, donkey-work, drudgery, effort, elbow grease (*Inf.*), exertion, graft (*Inf.*), hard work, industry, labour, pains, slog, sweat, travail 2. *v.* bend over backwards (*Inf.*), break one's neck (*Inf.*), bust a gut (*Inf.*), do one's damnedest (*Inf.*), drag oneself, drudge, give it one's all (*Inf.*), give it one's best shot (*Inf.*), go for broke (*Sl.*), go for it (*Inf.*), graft (*Inf.*), grind (*Inf.*), grub, knock oneself out (*Inf.*), labour, make an all-out effort (*Inf.*), push oneself, rupture oneself (*Inf.*), slave, slog, strive, struggle, sweat (*Inf.*), work, work like a dog, work like a Trojan, work one's fingers to the bone

Antonyms (*sense 1*) idleness, inactivity, indolence, inertia, laziness, sloth, torpor

toilet 1. ablutions (*Military inf.*), bathroom, bog (*Sl.*), can (*U.S. & Canad. sl.*), closet, convenience, crapper (*Taboo sl.*), gents (*Brit. inf.*), john (*Sl., chiefly U.S. & Canad.*), khazi (*Sl.*), ladies' room, latrine, lavatory, little boy's room (*Inf.*), little girl's room (*Inf.*), loo (*Brit. inf.*), outhouse, *pissoir,* powder room, privy, urinal, washroom, water closet, W.C. 2. ablutions, bathing, dressing, grooming, toilette

toilsome arduous, backbreaking, difficult, fatiguing, hard, herculean, laborious, painful, severe, strenuous, taxing, tedious, tiresome, tough, wearisome

token *n.* 1. badge, clue, demonstration, earnest, evidence, expression, index, indication, manifestation, mark, note, proof, representation, sign, symbol, warning 2. keepsake, memento, memorial, remembrance, reminder, souvenir ~*adj.* 3. hollow, minimal, nominal, perfunctory, superficial, symbolic

tolerable 1. acceptable, allowable, bearable, endurable, sufferable, supportable 2. acceptable, adequate, all right, average, fair, fairly good, fair to middling, good enough, indifferent, mediocre, middling, not bad (*Inf.*), O.K. *or* okay (*Inf.*), ordinary, passable, run-of-the-mill, so-so (*Inf.*), unexceptional

Antonyms (*sense 1*) insufferable, intolerable, unacceptable, unbearable, unendurable (*sense 2*) awful, bad, dreadful, rotten

tolerance 1. broad-mindedness, charity, forbearance, indulgence, lenity, magnanimity, open-mindedness, patience, permissiveness, sufferance, sympathy 2. endurance, fortitude, hardiness, hardness, resilience, resistance, stamina, staying power, toughness 3. fluctuation, play, swing, variation

Antonyms (*sense 1*) bigotry, discrimination, intolerance, narrow-mindedness, prejudice, sectarianism

tolerant 1. broad-minded, catholic, charitable, fair, forbearing, latitudinarian, liberal, long-suffering, magnanimous, open-minded, patient, sympathetic, unbigoted, understanding, unprejudiced 2. complaisant, easy-going, easy-oasy (*Sl.*), free and easy, indulgent, kind-hearted, lax, lenient, permissive, soft

Antonyms authoritarian, biased, bigoted, despotic, dictatorial, dogmatic, illiberal, intolerant, narrow-minded, prejudiced, repressive, rigid, sectarian, stern, strict, tyrannical, uncharitable

tolerate abide, accept, admit, allow, bear, brook, condone, countenance, endure, indulge, permit, pocket, put up with (*Inf.*), receive, sanction, stand, stomach, submit to, suffer, swallow, take, thole (*Scot.*), turn a blind eye to, undergo, wink at

Antonyms ban, disallow, disapprove, forbid, outlaw, preclude, prohibit, veto

toleration 1. acceptance, allowance, condonation, endurance, indulgence, permissiveness, sanction, sufferance 2. freedom of conscience, freedom of worship, religious freedom

toll[1] *v.* 1. chime, clang, knell, peal, ring, sound, strike 2. announce, call, signal, summon, warn ~*n.* 3. chime, clang, knell, peal, ring, ringing, tolling

toll[2] 1. assessment, charge, customs, demand, duty, fee, impost, levy, payment, rate, tariff, tax, tribute 2. cost, damage, inroad, loss, penalty

tomb burial chamber, catacomb, crypt, grave, mausoleum, sarcophagus, sepulchre, vault

tombstone gravestone, headstone, marker, memorial, monument

tome book, title, volume, work

tomfool 1. *n.* ass, berk (*Brit. sl.*), blockhead, charlie (*Brit. inf.*), chump (*Inf.*), clown, dickhead (*Sl.*), dipstick (*Brit. sl.*), divvy (*Brit. sl.*), dolt, dork (*Sl.*), dweeb (*U.S. sl.*), fool, fuckwit (*Taboo sl.*), geek (*Sl.*), gonzo (*Sl.*), idiot, nerd *or* nurd (*Sl.*), nincompoop, ninny, nitwit (*Inf.*), numskull *or* numbskull, oaf, pillock (*Brit. sl.*), plank (*Brit. sl.*), plonker (*Sl.*), prat (*Sl.*), prick (*Derogatory sl.*), simpleton, twit (*Inf., chiefly Brit.*), wally (*Sl.*) 2. *adj.* asinine, crackbrained, crazy, daft (*Inf.*), foolish, halfwitted, harebrained, idiotic, inane, rash, senseless, silly, stupid

tomfoolery 1. buffoonery, childishness, clowning, fooling around (*Inf.*), foolishness, horseplay, idiocy, larks (*Inf.*), messing around (*Inf.*), shenanigans (*Inf.*), silliness, skylarking (*Inf.*), stupidity 2. balderdash, baloney (*Inf.*), bilge (*Inf.*), bosh (*Inf.*), bunk (*Inf.*), bunkum *or* buncombe (*Chiefly U.S.*), claptrap (*Inf.*), hogwash, hooey (*Sl.*), inanity, nonsense, poppycock (*Inf.*), rot, rubbish, stuff and nonsense, tommyrot, tosh (*Sl., chiefly Brit.*), trash, twaddle
Antonyms demureness, gravity, heaviness, reserve, sedateness, seriousness, sobriety, solemnity, sternness

tone *n.* 1. accent, emphasis, force, inflection, intonation, modulation, pitch, strength, stress, timbre, tonality, volume 2. air, approach, aspect, attitude, character, drift, effect, feel, frame, grain, manner, mood, note, quality, spirit, style, temper, tenor, vein 3. cast, colour, hue, shade, tinge, tint ~*v.* 4. blend, go well with, harmonize, match, suit

tone down dampen, dim, mitigate, moderate, modulate, play down, reduce, restrain, soften, soft-pedal (*Inf.*), subdue, temper

tone up freshen, get in shape, get into condition, invigorate, limber up, shape up, sharpen up, trim, tune up

tongue 1. argot, dialect, idiom, language, lingo (*Inf.*), parlance, patois, speech, talk, vernacular 2. articulation, speech, utterance, verbal expression, voice

tongue-lashing dressing-down (*Inf.*), lecture, rebuke, reprimand, reproach, reproof, scolding, slating (*Inf.*), talking-to (*Inf.*), telling-off (*Inf.*), ticking-off (*Inf.*), wigging (*Brit. sl.*)

tongue-tied at a loss for words, dumb, dumbstruck, inarticulate, mute, speechless, struck dumb
Antonyms articulate, chatty, effusive, garrulous, loquacious, talkative, verbose, voluble, wordy

tonic analeptic, boost, bracer (*Inf.*), cordial, fillip, livener, pick-me-up (*Inf.*), refresher, restorative, roborant, shot in the arm (*Inf.*), stimulant

too 1. also, as well, besides, further, in addition, into the bargain, likewise, moreover, to boot 2. excessively, exorbitantly, extremely, immoderately, inordinately, over-, overly, unduly, unreasonably, very

tool *n.* 1. apparatus, appliance, contraption, contrivance, device, gadget, implement, instrument, machine, utensil 2. agency, agent, intermediary, means, medium, vehicle, wherewithal 3. cat's-paw, creature, dupe, flunkey, hireling, jackal, lackey, minion, pawn, puppet, stooge (*Sl.*) ~*v.* 4. chase, cut, decorate, ornament, shape, work

toothsome agreeable, appetizing, dainty, delectable, delicious, luscious, mouthwatering, nice, palatable, savoury, scrumptious (*Inf.*), sweet, tasty, tempting, yummy (*Sl.*)

top *n.* 1. acme, apex, apogee, crest, crown, culmination, head, height, high point, meridian, peak, pinnacle, summit, vertex, zenith 2. cap, cork, cover, lid, stopper 3. first place, head, highest rank, lead 4. **blow one's top** *Inf.* blow up (*Inf.*), do one's nut (*Brit. sl.*), explode, fly into a temper, fly off the handle (*Inf.*), go spare (*Brit. sl.*), have a fit (*Inf.*), lose one's temper, see red (*Inf.*), throw a tantrum 5. **over the top** a bit much (*Inf.*), excessive, going too far, immoderate, inordinate, over the limit, too much, uncalled-for ~*adj.* 6. best, chief, crack (*Inf.*), crowning, culminating, dominant, elite, finest, first, foremost, greatest, head, highest, lead, leading, pre-eminent, prime, principal, ruling, sovereign, superior, topmost, upper, uppermost ~*v.* 7. cap, cover, crown, finish, garnish, roof, tip 8. ascend, climb, crest, reach the top of, scale, surmount 9. be first, be in charge of, command, head, lead, rule 10. beat, best, better, eclipse, exceed, excel, go beyond, outdo, outshine, outstrip, surpass, transcend
Antonyms *n.* base, bottom, foot, nadir, underneath, underside ~*adj.* amateurish, bottom, incompetent, inept, inferior, least, lower, lowest, second-rate, unknown, unranked, worst ~*v.* be at the bottom of, fail to equal, fall short of, not be as good as

topic issue, matter, point, question, subject, subject matter, text, theme, thesis

topical 1. contemporary, current, newsworthy, popular, up-to-date, up-to-the-minute 2. local, parochial, regional, restricted

topmost dominant, foremost, highest, leading, loftiest, paramount, principal, supreme, top, upper, uppermost
Antonyms base, basic, bottom, bottommost, last, lowest, undermost

topple 1. capsize, collapse, fall, fall headlong, fall over, keel over, knock down, knock over, overbalance, overturn, tip over, totter, tumble, upset 2. bring down, bring low, oust, overthrow, overturn, unseat
Antonyms (*sense 1*) ascend, build, mount, rise, tower

topsy-turvy chaotic, confused, disarranged, disorderly, disorganized, inside-out, jumbled, messy, mixed-up, untidy, upside-down

Antonyms neat, ordered, orderly, organized, shipshape, systematic, tidy

torment *v.* 1. afflict, agonize, crucify, distress, excruciate, harrow, pain, rack, torture 2. aggravate (*Inf.*), annoy, bedevil, bother, chivvy, devil (*Inf.*), harass, harry, hassle (*Inf.*), hound, irritate, nag, persecute, pester, plague, provoke, tease, trouble, vex, worry ~*n.* 3. agony, anguish, distress, hell, misery, pain, suffering, torture 4. affliction, annoyance, bane, bother, harassment, hassle (*Inf.*), irritation, nag, nagging, nuisance, pain in the neck (*Inf.*), persecution, pest, plague, provocation, scourge, thorn in one's flesh, trouble, vexation, worry

Antonyms *v.* comfort, delight, ease, encourage, make happy, put at ease, reassure, soothe ~*n.* bliss, comfort, ease, ecstasy, encouragement, happiness, joy, reassurance, rest

torn *adj.* 1. cut, lacerated, ragged, rent, ripped, slit, split 2. divided, in two minds (*Inf.*), irresolute, split, uncertain, undecided, unsure, vacillating, wavering

tornado cyclone, gale, hurricane, squall, storm, tempest, twister (*U.S. inf.*), typhoon, whirlwind, windstorm

torpid apathetic, benumbed, dormant, drowsy, dull, fainéant, inactive, indolent, inert, lackadaisical, languid, languorous, lazy, lethargic, listless, lymphatic, motionless, numb, passive, slothful, slow, slow-moving, sluggish, somnolent, stagnant

torpor accidie, acedia, apathy, dormancy, drowsiness, dullness, inactivity, inanition, indolence, inertia, inertness, languor, laziness, lethargy, listlessness, numbness, passivity, sloth, sluggishness, somnolence, stagnancy, stupor, torpidity

Antonyms animation, energy, get-up-and-go (*Inf.*), go, liveliness, pep, vigour

torrent cascade, deluge, downpour, effusion, flood, flow, gush, outburst, rush, spate, stream, tide

torrid 1. arid, blistering, boiling, broiling, burning, dried, dry, fiery, flaming, hot, parched, parching, scorched, scorching, sizzling, stifling, sultry, sweltering, tropical 2. ardent, erotic, fervent, flaming, hot, intense, passionate, sexy (*Inf.*), steamy (*Inf.*)

tortuous 1. bent, circuitous, convoluted, crooked, curved, indirect, mazy, meandering, serpentine, sinuous, twisted, twisting, winding, zigzag 2. ambiguous, complicated, convoluted, cunning, deceptive, devious, indirect, involved, mazy, misleading, roundabout, tricky

Antonyms (*sense 2*) candid, direct, honest, ingenuous, open, reliable, straightforward, upright

torture 1. *v.* afflict, agonize, crucify, distress, excruciate, harrow, lacerate, martyr, pain, persecute, put on the rack, rack, torment 2. *n.* affliction, agony, anguish, distress, hell, laceration, martyrdom, misery, pain, pang(s), persecution, rack, suffering, torment

Antonyms (*sense 1*) alleviate, comfort, console, ease, mollify, relieve, salve, solace, soothe (*sense 2*) amusement, bliss, delight, enjoyment, happiness, joy, pleasure, well-being

toss *v.* 1. cast, chuck (*Inf.*), fling, flip, hurl, launch, lob (*Inf.*), pitch, project, propel, shy, sling, throw 2. agitate, disturb, jiggle, joggle, jolt, rock, roll, shake, thrash, tumble, wriggle, writhe 3. heave, labour, lurch, pitch, roll, wallow ~*n.* 4. cast, fling, lob (*Inf.*), pitch, shy, throw

tot[1] *n.* 1. ankle-biter (*Aust. sl.*), baby, child, infant, little one, mite, rug rat (*Sl.*), sprog (*Sl.*), toddler, wean (*Scot.*) 2. dram, finger, measure, nip, shot (*Inf.*), slug, snifter (*Inf.*), toothful

tot[2] *v.* add up, calculate, count up, reckon, sum (up), tally, total

total 1. *n.* aggregate, all, amount, entirety, full amount, mass, sum, totality, whole 2. *adj.* absolute, all-out, arrant, complete, comprehensive, consummate, deep-dyed (*Usu. derogatory*), downright, entire, full, gross, integral, out-and-out, outright, perfect, sheer, sweeping, thorough, thorough-going, unconditional, undisputed, undivided, unmitigated, unqualified, utter, whole 3. *v.* add up, amount to, come to, mount up to, reach, reckon, sum up, tot up

Antonyms *n.* individual amount, part, subtotal ~*adj.* conditional, fragmentary, incomplete, limited, mixed, part, partial, qualified, restricted, uncombined ~*v.* deduct, subtract

totalitarian authoritarian, despotic, dictatorial, monolithic, one-party, oppressive, tyrannous, undemocratic

Antonyms autonomous, democratic, egalitarian, popular, self-governing

totality 1. aggregate, all, entirety, everything, sum, total, whole 2. completeness, entireness, fullness, wholeness

totally absolutely, completely, comprehensively, consummately, entirely, fully, perfectly, quite, thoroughly, unconditionally, unmitigatedly, utterly, wholeheartedly, wholly

Antonyms incompletely, in part, partially, partly, somewhat, to a certain extent

totter falter, lurch, quiver, reel, rock, shake, stagger, stumble, sway, teeter, tremble, walk unsteadily, waver

touch *n.* 1. feel, feeling, handling, palpation, physical contact, tactility 2. blow, brush, caress, contact, fondling, hit, pat, push, stroke, tap 3. bit, dash, detail, drop, hint, intimation, jot, pinch, smack, small amount, smattering, *soupçon,* speck, spot, suggestion, suspicion, taste, tincture, tinge, trace, whiff 4. direction, effect, hand, influence 5. approach, characteristic, handiwork, manner, method, style, technique, trademark, way 6. ability, adroitness, art, artistry, command, craft, deftness, facility, flair, knack, mastery, skill, virtuosity 7. acquaintance, awareness, communication, contact, correspondence, familiarity, understanding ~*v.* 8. brush, caress, contact, feel, finger, fondle, graze, handle, hit, lay a finger on, palpate, pat, push, strike, stroke, tap 9. abut, adjoin, be in contact, border, brush, come together, contact, converge, graze, impinge upon, meet 10. affect, disturb, get through to, get to (*Inf.*), have an effect on, impress, influence, inspire, make an impression on, mark, melt, move, soften, stir, strike, upset 11. be a party to, concern oneself with, consume, deal with, drink, eat, get involved in, handle, have to do with, partake of, use, utilize 12. *With* **on** allude to, bring in, cover, deal with, mention, refer to, speak of 13. bear upon, concern, have to do with, interest, pertain to, regard 14. be a match for, be in the same league as, be on a par with, come near, come up to, compare with, equal, hold a candle to (*Inf.*), match, parallel, rival 15. arrive at, attain, come to, reach

touch-and-go close, critical, dangerous, hairy (*Sl.*), hazardous, near, nerve-racking, parlous, perilous, precarious, risky, sticky (*Inf.*), tricky

touched 1. affected, disturbed, impressed, melted, moved, softened, stirred, swayed, upset 2. barmy (*Sl.*), batty (*Sl.*), bonkers (*Sl., chiefly Brit.*), crackpot (*Inf.*), crazy, cuckoo (*Inf.*), daft (*Inf.*), loopy (*Inf.*), not all there, not right in the head, nuts (*Sl.*), nutty (*Sl.*), nutty as a fruitcake (*Sl.*), off one's rocker (*Sl.*), off one's trolley (*Sl.*), out to lunch (*Inf.*), soft in the head (*Inf.*), up the pole (*Inf.*)

touchiness bad temper, crabbedness, fretfulness, grouchiness (*Inf.*), irascibility, irritability, peevishness, pettishness, petulance, surliness, testiness, tetchiness, ticklishness

touching affecting, emotive, heartbreaking, melting, moving, pathetic, piteous, pitiable, pitiful, poignant, sad, stirring, tender

touch off 1. fire, ignite, light, put a match to, set off 2. arouse, begin, cause, foment, give rise to, initiate, provoke, set in motion, spark off, trigger (off)

touchstone criterion, gauge, measure, norm, par, standard, yardstick

touch up 1. finish off, perfect, put the finishing touches to, round off 2. brush up, enhance, fake (up), falsify, give a face-lift to, gloss over, improve, patch up, polish up, renovate, retouch, revamp, titivate, whitewash (*Inf.*)

touchy bad-tempered, captious, crabbed, cross, easily offended, grouchy (*Inf.*), grumpy, irascible, irritable, oversensitive, peevish, pettish, petulant, querulous, quick-tempered, ratty (*Brit. & N.Z. inf.*), splenetic, surly, testy, tetchy, thin-skinned, ticklish

Antonyms affable, cheerful, easy-going, genial, good-humoured, imperious, indifferent, insensitive, light-hearted, pleasant, sunny, sweet, thick-skinned, unconcerned

tough *adj.* 1. cohesive, durable, firm, hard, inflexible, leathery, resilient, resistant, rigid, rugged, solid, stiff, strong, sturdy, tenacious 2. brawny, fit, hard as nails, hardened, hardy, resilient, seasoned, stalwart, stout, strapping, strong, sturdy, vigorous 3. hard-bitten, pugnacious, rough, ruffianly, ruthless, vicious, violent 4. adamant, callous, exacting, firm, hard, hard-boiled (*Inf.*), hard-nosed (*Inf.*), inflexible, intractable, merciless, obdurate, obstinate, refractory, resolute, severe, stern, strict, stubborn, unbending, unforgiving, unyielding 5. arduous, baffling, difficult, exacting, exhausting, hard, intractable, irksome, knotty, laborious, perplexing, puzzling, strenuous, thorny, troublesome, uphill 6. *Inf.* bad, hard cheese (*Brit. sl.*), hard lines (*Brit. inf.*), hard luck, lamentable, regrettable, too bad (*Inf.*), unfortunate, unlucky ~*n.* 7. bravo, bruiser (*Inf.*), brute, bully, bully boy, heavy (*Sl.*), hooligan, rough (*Inf.*), roughneck (*Sl.*), rowdy, ruffian, thug

Antonyms accommodating, benign, civilized, compassionate, considerate, delicate, easy, easy-peasy (*Sl.*), flexible, flimsy, fragile, gentle, humane, indulgent, kind, lenient, merciful, mild, simple, soft, sympathetic, tender, unexacting, weak

tour *n.* 1. excursion, expedition, jaunt, journey, outing, peregrination, progress, trip 2. circuit, course, round ~*v.* 3. explore, go on the road, go round, holiday in, journey, sightsee, travel round, travel through, visit

tourist excursionist, globetrotter, holiday-maker, journeyer, sightseer, traveller, tripper, voyager

tournament 1. competition, contest, event,

match, meeting, series 2. *Medieval* joust, the lists, tourney

tousle disarrange, disarray, dishevel, disorder, mess up, ruffle, rumple, tangle

tow *v.* drag, draw, haul, lug, pull, trail, trawl, tug

towards 1. en route for, for, in the direction of, in the vicinity of, on the road to, on the way to, to 2. about, concerning, for, regarding, with regard to, with respect to 3. almost, close to, coming up to, getting on for, just before, nearing, nearly, not quite, shortly before

tower *n.* 1. belfry, column, obelisk, pillar, skyscraper, steeple, turret 2. castle, citadel, fort, fortification, fortress, keep, refuge, stronghold ~*v.* 3. ascend, be head and shoulders above, dominate, exceed, loom, mount, overlook, overtop, rear, rise, soar, surpass, top, transcend

towering 1. colossal, elevated, extraordinary, gigantic, great, high, imposing, impressive, lofty, magnificent, outstanding, paramount, prodigious, soaring, striking, sublime, superior, supreme, surpassing, tall, transcendent 2. burning, excessive, extreme, fiery, immoderate, inordinate, intemperate, intense, mighty, passionate, vehement, violent

toxic baneful (*Archaic*), deadly, harmful, lethal, noxious, pernicious, pestilential, poisonous, septic
Antonyms harmless, invigorating, nonpoisonous, nontoxic, safe, salubrious

toy *n.* 1. doll, game, plaything 2. bauble, gewgaw, knick-knack, trifle, trinket ~*v.* 3. amuse oneself, dally, fiddle (*Inf.*), flirt, fool (about *or* around), play, sport, trifle, wanton

trace *n.* 1. evidence, indication, mark, record, relic, remains, remnant, sign, survival, token, vestige 2. bit, dash, drop, hint, iota, jot, shadow, *soupçon,* suggestion, suspicion, tincture, tinge, touch, trifle, whiff 3. footmark, footprint, footstep, path, slot, spoor, track, trail ~*v.* 4. ascertain, detect, determine, discover, ferret out, find, follow, hunt down, pursue, search for, seek, shadow, stalk, track, trail, unearth 5. chart, copy, delineate, depict, draw, map, mark out, outline, record, show, sketch

track *n.* 1. footmark, footprint, footstep, mark, path, scent, slipstream, slot, spoor, trace, trail, wake 2. course, flight path, line, orbit, path, pathway, road, track, trajectory, way 3. line, permanent way, rail, rails 4. **keep track of** follow, keep an eye on, keep in sight, keep in touch with, keep up to date with, keep up with, monitor, oversee, watch 5. **lose track of** lose, lose sight of, misplace ~*v.* 6. chase, dog, follow, follow the trail of, hunt down, pursue, shadow, stalk, tail (*Inf.*), trace, trail

track down apprehend, bring to light, capture, catch, dig up, discover, expose, ferret out, find, hunt down, run to earth, sniff out, trace, unearth

trackless empty, pathless, solitary, uncharted, unexplored, unfrequented, untrodden, unused, virgin

tracks 1. footprints, impressions, imprints, tyremarks, tyreprints, wheelmarks 2. **make tracks** beat it (*Sl.*), depart, disappear, get going, get moving, go, head off, hit the road (*Sl.*), leave, set out, split (*Sl.*), take off (*Inf.*) 3. **stop in one's tracks** bring to a standstill, freeze, immobilize, petrify, rivet to the spot, stop dead, transfix

tract[1] area, district, estate, expanse, extent, lot, plot, quarter, region, stretch, territory, zone

tract[2] booklet, brochure, disquisition, dissertation, essay, homily, leaflet, monograph, pamphlet, tractate, treatise

tractable 1. amenable, biddable, compliant, controllable, docile, governable, manageable, obedient, persuadable, submissive, tame, willing, yielding 2. ductile, fictile, malleable, plastic, pliable, pliant, tensile, tractile, workable
Antonyms defiant, headstrong, obstinate, refractory, stiff-necked, stubborn, unruly, wilful

traction adhesion, drag, draught, drawing, friction, grip, haulage, pull, pulling, purchase, resistance

trade *n.* 1. barter, business, buying and selling, commerce, dealing, exchange, traffic, transactions, truck 2. avocation, business, calling, craft, employment, job, line, line of work, métier, occupation, profession, pursuit, skill 3. deal, exchange, interchange, swap 4. clientele, custom, customers, market, patrons, public ~*v.* 5. bargain, barter, buy and sell, deal, do business, exchange, have dealings, peddle, traffic, transact, truck 6. barter, exchange, swap, switch

trader broker, buyer, dealer, marketeer, merchandiser, merchant, purveyor, seller, supplier

tradesman 1. dealer, merchant, purveyor, retailer, seller, shopkeeper, supplier, vendor 2. artisan, craftsman, journeyman, skilled worker, workman

tradition convention, custom, customs, established practice, folklore, habit, institution, lore, praxis, ritual, unwritten law, usage

traditional accustomed, ancestral, conven-

tional, customary, established, fixed, folk, historic, long-established, old, oral, time-honoured, transmitted, unwritten, usual
Antonyms avant-garde, contemporary, ground-breaking, innovative, modern, new, novel, off-the-wall (*Sl.*), original, revolutionary, unconventional, unusual

traduce abuse, asperse, bad-mouth (*Sl., chiefly U.S. & Canad.*), blacken, calumniate, decry, defame, denigrate, deprecate, depreciate, detract, disparage, drag through the mud, knock (*Inf.*), malign, misrepresent, revile, rubbish (*Inf.*), run down, slag (off) (*Sl.*), slander, smear, speak ill of, vilify

traducer abuser, asperser, calumniator, defamer, denigrator, deprecator, detractor, disparager, slanderer, smearer, vilifier

traffic *n.* 1. coming and going, freight, movement, passengers, transport, transportation, vehicles 2. barter, business, buying and selling, commerce, communication, dealing, dealings, doings, exchange, intercourse, peddling, relations, trade, truck ~*v.* 3. bargain, barter, buy and sell, deal, do business, exchange, have dealings, have transactions, market, peddle, trade, truck

tragedy adversity, affliction, bummer (*Sl.*), calamity, catastrophe, disaster, grievous blow, misfortune
Antonyms fortune, happiness, joy, prosperity, success

tragic anguished, appalling, awful, calamitous, catastrophic, deadly, dire, disastrous, dismal, doleful, dreadful, fatal, grievous, heartbreaking, heart-rending, ill-fated, ill-starred, lamentable, miserable, mournful, pathetic, pitiable, ruinous, sad, shocking, sorrowful, unfortunate, woeful, wretched
Antonyms agreeable, beneficial, cheerful, comic, fortunate, glorious, happy, joyful, lucky, satisfying, worthwhile

trail *v.* 1. dangle, drag, draw, hang down, haul, pull, stream, tow 2. chase, follow, hunt, pursue, shadow, stalk, tail (*Inf.*), trace, track 3. bring up the rear, dawdle, drag oneself, fall behind, follow, hang back, lag, linger, loiter, straggle, traipse (*Inf.*) 4. dangle, droop, extend, hang, straggle ~*n.* 5. footprints, footsteps, mark, marks, path, scent, slipstream, spoor, trace, track, wake 6. beaten track, footpath, path, road, route, track, way 7. appendage, stream, tail, train

trail away *or* **off** decrease, die away, diminish, dwindle, fade away *or* out, fall away, grow faint, grow weak, lessen, peter out, shrink, sink, subside, tail off, taper off, weaken

train *v.* 1. coach, discipline, drill, educate, guide, improve, instruct, prepare, rear, rehearse, school, teach, tutor 2. exercise, improve, prepare, work out 3. aim, bring to bear, direct, focus, level, line up, point ~*n.* 4. chain, concatenation, course, order, progression, sequence, series, set, string, succession 5. caravan, column, convoy, file, procession 6. appendage, tail, trail 7. attendants, cortege, court, entourage, followers, following, household, retinue, staff, suite

trainer coach, handler

training 1. coaching, discipline, education, grounding, guidance, instruction, schooling, teaching, tuition, tutelage, upbringing 2. body building, exercise, practice, preparation, working-out

traipse 1. *v.* drag oneself, footslog, slouch, trail, tramp, trudge 2. *n.* long walk, slog, tramp, trek, trudge

trait attribute, characteristic, feature, idiosyncrasy, lineament, mannerism, peculiarity, quality, quirk

traitor apostate, back-stabber, betrayer, deceiver, defector, deserter, double-crosser (*Inf.*), fifth columnist, informer, Judas, miscreant, quisling, rebel, renegade, snake in the grass (*Inf.*), turncoat
Antonyms defender, loyalist, patriot, supporter

traitorous apostate, disloyal, double-crossing (*Inf.*), double-dealing, faithless, false, perfidious, renegade, seditious, treacherous, treasonable, unfaithful, untrue
Antonyms constant, faithful, loyal, patriotic, staunch, steadfast, true, trusty

trajectory course, flight, flight path, line, path, route, track

trammel 1. *n.* bar, block, bond, chain, check, clog, curb, fetter, handicap, hindrance, impediment, obstacle, rein, shackle, stumbling block 2. *v.* bar, block, capture, catch, check, clog, curb, enmesh, ensnare, entrap, fetter, hamper, handicap, hinder, impede, net, restrain, restrict, snag, tie
Antonyms *v.* advance, assist, expedite, facilitate, foster, further, promote, support

tramp *v.* 1. footslog, hike, march, ramble, range, roam, rove, slog, trek, walk, yomp 2. march, plod, stamp, stump, toil, traipse (*Inf.*), trudge, walk heavily 3. crush, stamp, stomp (*Inf.*), trample, tread, walk over ~*n.* 4. bag lady (*Chiefly U.S.*), bum (*Inf.*), derelict, dosser (*Brit. sl.*), down-and-out, drifter, hobo (*Chiefly U.S.*), vagabond, vagrant 5. hike, march, ramble, slog, trek 6. footfall, footstep, stamp, tread

trample 1. crush, flatten, run over, squash, stamp, tread, walk over 2. do violence to, encroach upon, hurt, infringe, ride roughshod over, show no consideration for, violate

trance abstraction, daze, dream, ecstasy, hypnotic state, muse, rapture, reverie, spell, stupor, unconsciousness

tranquil at peace, calm, composed, cool, pacific, peaceful, placid, quiet, restful, sedate, serene, still, undisturbed, unexcited, unperturbed, unruffled, untroubled
Antonyms agitated, busy, confused, disturbed, excited, hectic, restless, troubled

tranquillity ataraxia, calm, calmness, composure, coolness, equanimity, hush, imperturbability, peace, peacefulness, placidity, quiet, quietness, quietude, repose, rest, restfulness, sedateness, serenity, stillness
Antonyms agitation, commotion, confusion, disturbance, excitement, noise, restlessness, turmoil, upset

tranquillize calm, compose, lull, pacify, quell, quiet, relax, sedate, settle one's nerves, soothe
Antonyms agitate, confuse, distress, disturb, harass, perturb, ruffle, trouble, upset

tranquillizer barbiturate, bromide, downer (*Sl.*), opiate, red (*Sl.*), sedative

transact accomplish, carry on, carry out, conclude, conduct, discharge, do, enact, execute, handle, manage, negotiate, perform, prosecute, see to, settle, take care of

transaction 1. action, affair, bargain, business, coup, deal, deed, enterprise, event, matter, negotiation, occurrence, proceeding, undertaking 2. *Plural* affairs, annals, doings, goings-on (*Inf.*), minutes, proceedings, record

transcend eclipse, exceed, excel, go above, go beyond, leave behind, leave in the shade (*Inf.*), outdo, outrival, outshine, outstrip, outvie, overstep, rise above, surpass

transcendence, transcendency ascendancy, excellence, greatness, incomparability, matchlessness, paramountcy, pre-eminence, sublimity, superiority, supremacy

transcendent consummate, exceeding, extraordinary, incomparable, matchless, peerless, pre-eminent, second to none, sublime, superior, transcendental, unequalled, unique, unparalleled, unrivalled

transcribe 1. copy out, engross, note, reproduce, rewrite, set out, take down, transfer, write out 2. interpret, render, translate, transliterate 3. record, tape, tape-record

transcript carbon, carbon copy, copy, duplicate, manuscript, note, notes, record, reproduction, transcription, translation, transliteration, version

transfer 1. *v.* carry, change, consign, convey, displace, hand over, make over, move, pass on, relocate, remove, shift, translate, transmit, transplant, transport, transpose, turn over 2. *n.* change, displacement, handover, move, relocation, removal, shift, transference, translation, transmission, transposition

transfigure alter, apotheosize, change, convert, exalt, glorify, idealize, metamorphose, transform, transmute

transfix 1. engross, fascinate, halt *or* stop in one's tracks, hold, hypnotize, mesmerize, paralyse, petrify, rivet the attention of, root to the spot, spellbind, stop dead, stun 2. fix, impale, pierce, puncture, run through, skewer, spear, spit, transpierce
Antonyms (*sense 1*) bore, fatigue, tire, weary

transform alter, change, convert, make over, metamorphose, reconstruct, remodel, renew, revolutionize, transfigure, translate, transmogrify (*Jocular*), transmute

transformation alteration, change, conversion, metamorphosis, radical change, renewal, revolution, revolutionary change, sea change, transfiguration, transmogrification (*Jocular*), transmutation

transfuse permeate, pervade, spread over, suffuse

transgress be out of order, break, break the law, contravene, defy, disobey, do *or* go wrong, encroach, err, exceed, fall from grace, go astray, go beyond, infringe, lapse, misbehave, offend, overstep, sin, trespass, violate

transgression breach, contravention, crime, encroachment, error, fault, infraction, infringement, iniquity, lapse, misbehaviour, misdeed, misdemeanour, offence, peccadillo, sin, trespass, violation, wrong, wrongdoing

transgressor criminal, culprit, delinquent, evildoer, felon, lawbreaker, malefactor, miscreant, offender, sinner, trespasser, villain, wrongdoer

transience brevity, briefness, ephemerality, evanescence, fleetingness, fugacity, fugitiveness, impermanence, momentariness, shortness, transitoriness

transient brief, ephemeral, evanescent, fleeting, flying, fugacious, fugitive, here today and gone tomorrow, impermanent, momentary, passing, short, short-lived, short-term, temporary, transitory
Antonyms abiding, constant, durable, enduring, eternal, imperishable, long-lasting, long-term, permanent, perpetual, persistent, undying

transit *n.* 1. carriage, conveyance, crossing, motion, movement, passage, portage, shipment, transfer, transport, transportation, travel, traverse 2. alteration, change, changeover, conversion, shift, transition 3. **in transit** during passage, en route, on the journey, on the move, on the road, on the way, while travelling ~*v.* 4. cross, journey, move, pass, travel, traverse

transition alteration, change, changeover, conversion, development, evolution, flux, metamorphosis, metastasis, passage, passing, progression, shift, transit, transmutation, upheaval

transitional changing, developmental, fluid, intermediate, passing, provisional, temporary, transitionary, unsettled

transitory brief, ephemeral, evanescent, fleeting, flying, fugacious, here today and gone tomorrow, impermanent, momentary, passing, short, short-lived, short-term, temporary, transient

Antonyms abiding, enduring, eternal, everlasting, lasting, long-lived, long-term, permanent, perpetual, persistent, undying

translate 1. construe, convert, decipher, decode, interpret, paraphrase, render, transcribe, transliterate 2. elucidate, explain, make clear, paraphrase, put in plain English, simplify, spell out, state in layman's language 3. alter, change, convert, metamorphose, transfigure, transform, transmute, turn 4. carry, convey, move, remove, send, transfer, transplant, transport, transpose

translation 1. construction, decoding, gloss, interpretation, paraphrase, rendering, rendition, transcription, transliteration, version 2. elucidation, explanation, paraphrase, rephrasing, rewording, simplification 3. alteration, change, conversion, metamorphosis, transfiguration, transformation, transmutation 4. conveyance, move, removal, transference, transposition

translator interpreter, linguist, metaphrast, paraphrast

translucent clear, diaphanous, limpid, lucent, pellucid, semitransparent

transmigration journey, metempsychosis, migration, movement, passage, rebirth, reincarnation, travel

transmission 1. carriage, communication, conveyance, diffusion, dispatch, dissemination, remission, sending, shipment, spread, transfer, transference, transport 2. broadcasting, dissemination, putting out, relaying, sending, showing 3. broadcast, programme, show

transmit 1. bear, carry, communicate, convey, diffuse, dispatch, disseminate, forward, hand down, hand on, impart, pass on, remit, send, spread, take, transfer, transport 2. broadcast, disseminate, put on the air, radio, relay, send, send out

transmute alchemize, alter, change, convert, metamorphose, remake, transfigure, transform

transparency 1. clarity, clearness, diaphaneity, diaphanousness, filminess, gauziness, limpidity, limpidness, pellucidity, pellucidness, sheerness, translucence, translucency, transparence 2. apparentness, distinctness, explicitness, obviousness, patentness, perspicuousness, plainness, unambiguousness, visibility 3. candidness, directness, forthrightness, frankness, openness, straightforwardness 4. photograph, slide

Antonyms (*sense 1*) ambiguity, cloudiness, murkiness, obscurity, opacity, unclearness, vagueness

transparent 1. clear, crystal clear, crystalline, diaphanous, filmy, gauzy, limpid, lucent, lucid, pellucid, seethrough, sheer, translucent, transpicuous 2. apparent, as plain as the nose on one's face (*Inf.*), distinct, easy, evident, explicit, manifest, obvious, patent, perspicuous, plain, recognizable, unambiguous, understandable, undisguised, visible 3. candid, direct, forthright, frank, open, plain-spoken, straight, straightforward, unambiguous, unequivocal

Antonyms ambiguous, cloudy, deceptive, disingenuous, hidden, muddy, mysterious, opaque, thick, turbid, uncertain, unclear, vague

transpire 1. *Inf.* arise, befall, chance, come about, come to pass (*Archaic*), happen, occur, take place, turn up 2. become known, be disclosed, be discovered, be made public, come out, come to light, emerge

transplant displace, relocate, remove, resettle, shift, transfer, uproot

transport *v.* 1. bear, bring, carry, convey, fetch, haul, move, remove, run, ship, take, transfer 2. banish, deport, exile, sentence to transportation 3. captivate, carry away, delight, electrify, enchant, enrapture, entrance, move, ravish, spellbind ~*n.* 4. conveyance, transportation, vehicle 5. carriage, conveyance, removal, shipment, shipping, transference, transportation 6. cloud nine (*Inf.*), enchantment, euphoria, heaven, rapture, seventh heaven 7. bliss, delight, ecstasy, happiness, ravishment

Antonyms (*sense 6*) blues (*Inf.*), depression, despondency, doldrums, dumps (*Inf.*), melancholy

transpose alter, change, exchange, interchange, move, rearrange, relocate, reorder, shift, substitute, swap (*Inf.*), switch, transfer

transverse athwart, crossways, crosswise, diagonal, oblique

trap *n.* 1. ambush, gin, net, noose, pitfall, snare, springe, toils 2. ambush, artifice, deception, device, ruse, stratagem, subterfuge, trick, wile ~*v.* 3. catch, corner, enmesh, ensnare, entrap, snare, take 4. ambush, beguile, deceive, dupe, ensnare, inveigle, trick

trapped ambushed, at bay, beguiled, caught, cornered, cut off, deceived, duped, ensnared, in a tight corner, in a tight spot, inveigled, netted, snared, stuck (*Inf.*), surrounded, tricked, with one's back to the wall

trappings accoutrements, adornments, decorations, dress, equipment, finery, fittings, fixtures, fripperies, furnishings, gear, livery, ornaments, panoply, paraphernalia, raiment (*Archaic or poetic*), things, trimmings

trash 1. balderdash, balls (*Taboo sl.*), bilge (*Inf.*), bosh (*Inf.*), bull (*Sl.*), bullshit (*Taboo sl.*), bunkum *or* buncombe (*Chiefly U.S.*), cobblers (*Brit. taboo sl.*), crap (*Sl.*), drivel, eyewash (*Inf.*), foolish talk, garbage (*Inf.*), guff (*Sl.*), hogwash, hokum (*Sl., chiefly U.S. & Canad.*), horsefeathers (*U.S. sl.*), hot air (*Inf.*), inanity, moonshine, nonsense, pap, piffle (*Inf.*), poppycock (*Inf.*), rot, rubbish, shit (*Taboo sl.*), tommyrot, tosh (*Sl., chiefly Brit.*), tripe (*Inf.*), trumpery, twaddle 2. dreck (*Sl., chiefly U.S.*), dregs, dross, garbage, junk (*Inf.*), litter, offscourings, refuse, rubbish, sweepings, waste

Antonyms (*sense 1*) logic, reason, sense, significance

trashy brummagem, catchpenny, cheap, cheap-jack (*Inf.*), chickenshit (*U.S. sl.*), crappy (*Sl.*), flimsy, inferior, meretricious, of a sort *or* of sorts, poxy (*Sl.*), rubbishy, shabby, shoddy, tawdry, thrown together, tinsel, worthless

Antonyms A1 *or* A-one (*Inf.*), excellent, exceptional, first-class, first-rate, outstanding, superlative

trauma agony, anguish, damage, disturbance, hurt, injury, jolt, ordeal, pain, shock, strain, suffering, torture, upheaval, upset, wound

traumatic agonizing, damaging, disturbing, hurtful, injurious, painful, scarring, shocking, upsetting, wounding

Antonyms calming, healing, helpful, relaxing, therapeutic, wholesome

travail *n.* 1. distress, drudgery, effort, exertion, grind (*Inf.*), hardship, hard work, labour, pain, slavery, slog, strain, stress, suffering, sweat, tears, toil 2. birth pangs, childbirth, labour, labour pains ~*v.* 3. drudge, grind (*Inf.*), labour, slave, slog, suffer, sweat, toil

travel *v.* 1. cross, go, journey, make a journey, make one's way, move, proceed, progress, ramble, roam, rove, take a trip, tour, traverse, trek, voyage, walk, wander, wend 2. be transmitted, carry, get through, move ~*n.* 3. *Usually plural* excursion, expedition, globetrotting, journey, movement, passage, peregrination, ramble, tour, touring, trip, voyage, walk, wandering

traveller 1. excursionist, explorer, globetrotter, gypsy, hiker, holiday-maker, journeyer, migrant, nomad, passenger, tourist, tripper, voyager, wanderer, wayfarer 2. agent, commercial traveller, rep, representative, salesman, travelling salesman

travelling *adj.* itinerant, migrant, migratory, mobile, moving, nomadic, peripatetic, restless, roaming, roving, touring, unsettled, wandering, wayfaring

traverse 1. bridge, cover, cross, cut across, go across, go over, make one's way across, negotiate, pass over, ply, range, roam, span, travel over, wander 2. balk, contravene, counter, counteract, deny, frustrate, go against, hinder, impede, obstruct, oppose, thwart 3. check, consider, examine, eye, inspect, investigate, look into, look over, pore over, range over, review, scan, scrutinize, study

travesty 1. *n.* burlesque, caricature, distortion, lampoon, mockery, parody, perversion, send-up (*Brit. inf.*), sham, spoof (*Inf.*), takeoff (*Inf.*) 2. *v.* burlesque, caricature, deride, distort, lampoon, make a mockery of, make fun of, mock, parody, pervert, ridicule, send up (*Brit. inf.*), sham, spoof (*Inf.*), take off (*Inf.*)

treacherous 1. deceitful, disloyal, double-crossing (*Inf.*), double-dealing, duplicitous, faithless, false, perfidious, recreant (*Archaic*), traitorous, treasonable, unfaithful, unreliable, untrue, untrustworthy 2. dangerous, deceptive, hazardous, icy, perilous, precarious, risky, slippery, slippy (*Inf. or dialect*), tricky, unreliable, unsafe, unstable

Antonyms dependable, faithful, loyal, reliable, safe, true, trustworthy

treachery betrayal, disloyalty, double-cross (*Inf.*), double-dealing, duplicity, faithlessness, infidelity, perfidiousness, perfidy, stab in the back, treason

Antonyms allegiance, dependability, faithfulness, fealty, fidelity, loyalty, reliability

tread *v.* 1. hike, march, pace, plod, stamp,

step, stride, tramp, trudge, walk **2.** crush underfoot, squash, trample **3.** bear down, crush, oppress, quell, repress, ride roughshod over, subdue, subjugate, suppress **4.** **tread on someone's toes** affront, annoy, bruise, disgruntle, get someone's back up, hurt, hurt someone's feelings, infringe, injure, irk, offend, vex ~*n.* **5.** footfall, footstep, gait, pace, step, stride, walk

treason disaffection, disloyalty, duplicity, lese-majesty, mutiny, perfidy, sedition, subversion, traitorousness, treachery
Antonyms allegiance, faithfulness, fealty, fidelity, loyalty, patriotism

treasonable disloyal, false, mutinous, perfidious, seditious, subversive, traitorous, treacherous, treasonous
Antonyms dependable, faithful, loyal, patriotic, reliable, trustworthy

treasure *n.* **1.** cash, fortune, funds, gold, jewels, money, riches, valuables, wealth **2.** apple of one's eye, darling, gem, jewel, nonpareil, paragon, pearl, precious, pride and joy, prize ~*v.* **3.** adore, cherish, dote upon, esteem, hold dear, idolize, love, prize, revere, value, venerate, worship **4.** accumulate, cache, collect, garner, hoard, husband, lay up, salt away, save, stash (away) (*Inf.*), store up

treasury **1.** bank, cache, hoard, repository, store, storehouse, vault **2.** assets, capital, coffers, exchequer, finances, funds, money, resources, revenues

treat *n.* **1.** banquet, celebration, entertainment, feast, gift, party, refreshment **2.** delight, enjoyment, fun, gratification, joy, pleasure, satisfaction, surprise, thrill ~*v.* **3.** act towards, behave towards, consider, deal with, handle, look upon, manage, regard, use **4.** apply treatment to, attend to, care for, doctor, medicate, nurse **5.** buy for, entertain, feast, foot *or* pay the bill, give, lay on, pay for, provide, regale, stand (*Inf.*), take out, wine and dine **6.** be concerned with, contain, deal with, discourse upon, discuss, go into, touch upon **7.** bargain, come to terms, confer, have talks, make terms, negotiate, parley

treatise disquisition, dissertation, essay, exposition, monograph, pamphlet, paper, study, thesis, tract, work, writing

treatment **1.** care, cure, healing, medication, medicine, remedy, surgery, therapy **2.** action towards, behaviour towards, conduct, dealing, handling, management, manipulation, reception, usage

treaty agreement, alliance, bargain, bond, compact, concordat, contract, convention, covenant, entente, pact

trek **1.** *n.* expedition, footslog, hike, journey, long haul, march, odyssey, safari, slog, tramp **2.** *v.* footslog, hike, journey, march, plod, range, roam, rove, slog, traipse (*Inf.*), tramp, trudge, yomp

tremble **1.** *v.* oscillate, quake, quiver, rock, shake, shake in one's shoes, shiver, shudder, teeter, totter, vibrate, wobble **2.** *n.* oscillation, quake, quiver, shake, shiver, shudder, tremor, vibration, wobble

tremendous **1.** appalling, awesome, awful, colossal, deafening, dreadful, enormous, fearful, formidable, frightful, gargantuan, gigantic, great, huge, immense, mammoth, monstrous, prodigious, stupendous, terrible, terrific, titanic, towering, vast, whopping (*Inf.*) **2.** *Inf.* ace (*Inf.*), amazing, boffo (*Sl.*), brill (*Inf.*), brilliant, chillin' (*U.S. sl.*), cracking (*Brit. inf.*), excellent, exceptional, extraordinary, fabulous (*Inf.*), fantastic (*Inf.*), great, incredible, jim-dandy (*Sl.*), marvellous, mean (*Sl.*), sensational (*Inf.*), sovereign, super (*Inf.*), terrific (*Inf.*), topping (*Brit. sl.*), wonderful
Antonyms appalling, average, awful, diminutive, dreadful, little, mediocre, minuscule, minute, ordinary, rotten, run-of-the-mill, so-so, small, terrible, tiny

tremor **1.** agitation, quaking, quaver, quiver, quivering, shake, shaking, shiver, tremble, trembling, trepidation, vibration, wobble **2.** earthquake, quake (*Inf.*), shock

tremulous aflutter, afraid, agitated, agog, anxious, aquiver, excited, fearful, frightened, jittery (*Inf.*), jumpy, nervous, quavering, quivering, quivery, scared, shaking, shivering, timid, trembling, vibrating, wavering

trench channel, cut, ditch, drain, earthwork, entrenchment, excavation, fosse, furrow, gutter, pit, trough, waterway

trenchant **1.** acerbic, acid, acidulous, acute, astringent, biting, caustic, cutting, hurtful, incisive, keen, mordacious, mordant, penetrating, piquant, pointed, pungent, sarcastic, scathing, severe, sharp, tart, vitriolic **2.** driving, effective, effectual, emphatic, energetic, forceful, potent, powerful, strong, vigorous **3.** clear, clear-cut, crisp, distinct, distinctly defined, explicit, salient, unequivocal, well-defined
Antonyms (*sense 1*) appeasing, kind, mollifying, soothing (*sense 3*) ill-defined, indistinct, nebulous, obscure, unclear, vague, woolly

trend *n.* **1.** bias, course, current, direction, drift, flow, inclination, leaning, tendency **2.** craze, fad (*Inf.*), fashion, look, mode, rage, style, thing, vogue ~*v.* **3.** bend, flow, head, incline, lean, run, stretch, swing, tend, turn, veer

trendsetter arbiter of taste, avant-gardist, leader of fashion, pacemaker, pacesetter

trendy 1. *adj.* fashionable, flash (*Inf.*), in (*Sl.*), in fashion, in vogue, latest, modish, now (*Inf.*), stylish, up to the minute, voguish, with it (*Inf.*) 2. *n.* poser (*Inf.*), pseud (*Inf.*)

trepidation agitation, alarm, anxiety, apprehension, blue funk (*Inf.*), butterflies (*Inf.*), cold feet (*Inf.*), cold sweat (*Inf.*), consternation, dismay, disquiet, disturbance, dread, emotion, excitement, fear, fright, jitters (*Inf.*), nervousness, palpitation, perturbation, quivering, shaking, the heebie-jeebies (*Sl.*), trembling, tremor, uneasiness, worry
Antonyms aplomb, calm, composure, confidence, coolness, equanimity, self-assurance

trespass *v.* 1. encroach, infringe, intrude, invade, obtrude, poach 2. *Archaic* offend, sin, transgress, violate, wrong ~*n.* 3. encroachment, infringement, intrusion, invasion, poaching, unlawful entry, wrongful entry 4. breach, crime, delinquency, error, evildoing, fault, infraction, iniquity, injury, misbehaviour, misconduct, misdeed, misdemeanour, offence, sin, transgression, wrongdoing

trespasser 1. infringer, interloper, intruder, invader, poacher, unwelcome visitor 2. *Archaic* criminal, delinquent, evildoer, malefactor, offender, sinner, transgressor, wrongdoer

tress braid, curl, lock, pigtail, plait, ringlet

triad threesome, trilogy, trine, trinity, trio, triple, triplet, triptych, triumvirate, triune

trial *n.* 1. assay, audition, check, dry run (*Inf.*), examination, experience, experiment, probation, proof, test, testing, test-run 2. contest, hearing, industrial tribunal, judicial examination, litigation, tribunal 3. attempt, crack (*Inf.*), effort, endeavour, go (*Inf.*), shot (*Inf.*), stab (*Inf.*), try, venture, whack (*Inf.*) 4. adversity, affliction, burden, cross to bear, distress, grief, hardship, hard times, load, misery, ordeal, pain, suffering, tribulation, trouble, unhappiness, vexation, woe, wretchedness 5. bane, bother, drag (*Inf.*), hassle (*Inf.*), irritation, nuisance, pain in the arse (*Taboo inf.*), pain in the neck (*Inf.*), pest, plague (*Inf.*), thorn in one's flesh, vexation ~*adj.* 6. experimental, exploratory, pilot, probationary, provisional, testing

tribe blood, caste, clan, class, division, dynasty, ethnic group, family, gens, house, people, race, seed (*Chiefly biblical*), sept, stock

tribulation adversity, affliction, bad luck, blow, bummer (*Sl.*), burden, care, cross to bear, curse, distress, grief, hardship, hassle (*Inf.*), heartache, ill fortune, misery, misfortune, ordeal, pain, reverse, sorrow, suffering, trial, trouble, unhappiness, vexation, woe, worry, wretchedness
Antonyms blessing, bliss, ease, good fortune, happiness, joy, pleasure, rest

tribunal bar, bench, court, hearing, industrial tribunal, judgment seat, judicial examination, trial

tribute 1. accolade, acknowledgment, applause, commendation, compliment, encomium, esteem, eulogy, gift, gratitude, honour, laudation, panegyric, praise, recognition, respect, testimonial 2. charge, contribution, customs, duty, excise, homage, impost, offering, payment, ransom, subsidy, tax, toll
Antonyms (*sense 1*) blame, complaint, condemnation, criticism, disapproval, reproach, reproof

trice flash, instant, jiffy (*Inf.*), minute, moment, second, shake (*Inf.*), split second, tick (*Brit. inf.*), twinkling, twinkling of an eye, two shakes of a lamb's tail (*Inf.*)

trick *n.* 1. artifice, canard, con (*Sl.*), deceit, deception, device, dodge, feint, fraud, gimmick, hoax, imposition, imposture, manoeuvre, ploy, ruse, scam (*Sl.*), sting (*Inf.*), stratagem, subterfuge, swindle, trap, wile 2. antic, cantrip (*Scot.*), caper, device, feat, frolic, gag (*Inf.*), gambol, jape, joke, juggle, legerdemain, leg-pull (*Brit. inf.*), practical joke, prank, put-on (*Sl.*), sleight of hand, stunt 3. art, command, craft, device, expertise, gift, hang (*Inf.*), knack, know-how (*Inf.*), secret, skill, technique 4. characteristic, crotchet, foible, habit, idiosyncrasy, mannerism, peculiarity, practice, quirk, trait 5. **do the trick** *Inf.* be effective *or* effectual, have effect, produce the desired result, work ~*v.* 6. bamboozle (*Inf.*), cheat, con (*Inf.*), deceive, defraud, delude, dupe, fool, gull (*Archaic*), have (someone) on, hoax, hoodwink, impose upon, kid (*Inf.*), mislead, pull the wool over (someone's) eyes, put one over on (someone) (*Inf.*), stiff (*Sl.*), sting (*Inf.*), swindle, take in (*Inf.*), trap

trickery cheating, chicanery, con (*Inf.*), deceit, deception, dishonesty, double-dealing, fraud, funny business, guile, hanky-panky (*Inf.*), hoax, hokum (*Sl., chiefly U.S. & Canad.*), imposture, jiggery-pokery (*Inf., chiefly Brit.*), monkey business (*Inf.*), pretence, skulduggery (*Inf.*), swindling
Antonyms artlessness, candour, directness, frankness, honesty, openness, straightforwardness, uprightness

trickle 1. *v.* crawl, creep, dribble, drip, drop, exude, ooze, percolate, run, seep, stream 2. *n.* dribble, drip, seepage

trick out *or* **up** adorn, array, attire, bedeck, deck out, doll up (*Sl.*), do up (*Inf.*), dress up, get up (*Inf.*), ornament, prank, prink

trickster cheat, chiseller (*Inf.*), con man (*Inf.*), deceiver, fraud, hoaxer, impostor, joker, practical joker, pretender, swindler

tricky 1. complicated, delicate, difficult, knotty, problematic, risky, sticky (*Inf.*), thorny, ticklish, touch-and-go 2. artful, crafty, cunning, deceitful, deceptive, devious, foxy, scheming, slippery, sly, subtle, wily
Antonyms (*sense 1*) clear, easy, obvious, simple, straightforward, uncomplicated (*sense 2*) above board, artless, direct, genuine, honest, ingenuous, open, sincere, truthful

trifle *n.* 1. bagatelle, bauble, child's play (*Inf.*), gewgaw, knick-knack, nothing, plaything, toy, triviality 2. bit, dash, drop, jot, little, pinch, spot, touch, trace ~*v.* 3. amuse oneself, coquet, dally, dawdle, flirt, fritter, idle, mess about, palter, play, toy, wanton, waste, waste time

trifler dilettante, good-for-nothing, idler, layabout, loafer, ne'er-do-well, skiver (*Brit. sl.*), waster

trifling empty, footling (*Inf.*), frivolous, idle, inconsiderable, insignificant, measly, minuscule, negligible, nickel-and-dime (*U.S. sl.*), paltry, petty, piddling (*Inf.*), puny, shallow, silly, slight, small, tiny, trivial, unimportant, valueless, worthless
Antonyms considerable, crucial, important, large, major, serious, significant, vital, weighty

trigger *v.* activate, bring about, cause, elicit, generate, give rise to, produce, prompt, provoke, set in motion, set off, spark off, start
Antonyms bar, block, hinder, impede, inhibit, obstruct, prevent, repress, stop

trim *adj.* 1. compact, dapper, natty (*Inf.*), neat, nice, orderly, shipshape, smart, soigné *or* soignée, spick-and-span, spruce, tidy, trig (*Archaic or dialect*), well-groomed, well-ordered, well turned-out 2. fit, shapely, sleek, slender, slim, streamlined, svelte, willowy ~*v.* 3. barber, clip, crop, curtail, cut, cut back, dock, even up, lop, pare, prune, shave, shear, tidy 4. adorn, array, beautify, bedeck, deck out, decorate, dress, embellish, embroider, garnish, ornament, trick out 5. adjust, arrange, balance, distribute, order, prepare, settle ~*n.* 6. adornment, border, decoration, edging, embellishment, frill, fringe, garnish, ornamentation, piping, trimming 7. condition, fettle, fitness, form, health, order, repair, shape (*Inf.*), situation, state 8. clipping, crop, cut, pruning, shave, shearing, tidying up, trimming 9. array, attire, dress, equipment, gear, trappings
Antonyms (*sense 1*) disarrayed, disorderly, messy, scruffy, shabby, sloppy, ungroomed, unkempt, untidy

trimming 1. adornment, border, braid, decoration, edging, embellishment, festoon, frill, fringe, garnish, ornamentation, piping 2. *Plural* accessories, accompaniments, appurtenances, extras, frills, garnish, ornaments, paraphernalia, trappings 3. *Plural* brash, clippings, cuttings, ends, parings, shavings

trinity threesome, triad, trilogy, trine, trio, triple, triplet, triptych, triumvirate, triune

trinket bagatelle, bauble, bibelot, gewgaw, gimcrack, kickshaw, knick-knack, nothing, ornament, piece of bric-a-brac, toy, trifle

trio threesome, triad, trilogy, trine, trinity, triple, triplet, triptych, triumvirate, triune

trip *n.* 1. errand, excursion, expedition, foray, jaunt, journey, outing, ramble, run, tour, travel, voyage 2. bloomer (*Brit. inf.*), blunder, boob (*Brit. sl.*), error, fall, false move, false step, faux pas, indiscretion, lapse, misstep, slip, stumble ~*v.* 3. blunder, boob (*Brit. sl.*), err, fall, go wrong, lapse, lose one's balance, lose one's footing, make a false move, make a faux pas, miscalculate, misstep, slip, slip up (*Inf.*), stumble, tumble 4. catch out, confuse, disconcert, put off one's stride, throw off, trap, unsettle 5. go, ramble, tour, travel, voyage 6. caper, dance, flit, frisk, gambol, hop, skip, spring, tread lightly 7. *Inf.* get high (*Inf.*), get stoned (*Sl.*), take drugs, turn on (*Sl.*) 8. activate, engage, flip, pull, release, set off, switch on, throw, turn on

tripe balderdash, balls (*Taboo sl.*), bilge (*Inf.*), bosh (*Inf.*), bull (*Sl.*), bullshit (*Taboo sl.*), bunkum *or* buncombe (*Chiefly U.S.*), claptrap (*Inf.*), cobblers (*Brit. taboo sl.*), crap (*Sl.*), drivel, eyewash (*Inf.*), foolish talk, garbage (*Inf.*), guff (*Sl.*), hogwash, hokum (*Sl., chiefly U.S. & Canad.*), horsefeathers (*U.S. sl.*), hot air (*Inf.*), inanity, moonshine, nonsense, pap, piffle (*Inf.*), poppycock (*Inf.*), rot, rubbish, shit (*Taboo sl.*), tommyrot, tosh (*Sl., chiefly Brit.*), trash, trumpery, twaddle

triple 1. *adj.* threefold, three times as much, three-way, tripartite 2. *n.* threesome, triad, trilogy, trine, trinity, trio, triplet, triumvirate, triune 3. *v.* increase threefold, treble, triplicate

triplet threesome, triad, trilogy, trine, trinity, trio, triple, triumvirate, triune

tripper excursionist, holiday-maker, journeyer, sightseer, tourist, voyager

trite banal, bromidic, clichéd, common, commonplace, corny (*Sl.*), dull, hack, hackneyed, ordinary, pedestrian, routine, run-of-the-mill, stale, stereotyped, stock, threadbare, tired, uninspired, unoriginal, worn
Antonyms exciting, fresh, interesting, new, novel, original, out-of-the-ordinary, uncommon, unexpected, unfamiliar

triturate beat, bray, bruise, comminute, crush, grind, masticate, pound, powder, pulverize

triumph *n.* 1. elation, exultation, happiness, joy, jubilation, pride, rejoicing 2. accomplishment, achievement, ascendancy, attainment, conquest, coup, feat, hit (*Inf.*), mastery, sensation, smash (*Inf.*), smash-hit (*Inf.*), success, *tour de force,* victory, walkover (*Inf.*) ~*v.* 3. *Often with* **over** best, carry the day, come out on top (*Inf.*), dominate, flourish, get the better of, overcome, overwhelm, prevail, prosper, subdue, succeed, take the honours, thrive, vanquish, win 4. celebrate, crow, drool, exult, gloat, glory, jubilate, rejoice, revel, swagger
Antonyms (*sense 2*) catastrophe, defeat, disaster, failure, fiasco, flop (*Inf.*), washout (*Inf.*) (*sense 3*) come a cropper (*Inf.*), fail, fall, flop (*Inf.*), lose

triumphant boastful, celebratory, cock-a-hoop, conquering, dominant, elated, exultant, glorious, jubilant, proud, rejoicing, successful, swaggering, triumphal, undefeated, victorious, winning
Antonyms beaten, defeated, embarrassed, humbled, humiliated, shamed, unsuccessful

trivia details, minutiae, petty details, trifles, trivialities
Antonyms basics, brass tacks (*Inf.*), core, essentials, fundamentals, nitty-gritty (*Inf.*), rudiments

trivial chickenshit (*U.S. sl.*), commonplace, everyday, frivolous, incidental, inconsequential, inconsiderable, insignificant, little, meaningless, minor, negligible, nickel-and-dime (*U.S. sl.*), paltry, petty, puny, slight, small, trifling, trite, unimportant, valueless, worthless
Antonyms considerable, crucial, essential, important, profound, serious, significant, uncommon, unusual, vital, weighty, worthwhile

triviality 1. frivolity, inconsequentiality, insignificance, littleness, meaninglessness, negligibility, paltriness, pettiness, slightness, smallness, triteness, unimportance, valuelessness, worthlessness 2. detail, no big thing, no great matter, nothing, petty detail, technicality, trifle
Antonyms (*sense 1*) consequence, essential, importance, rudiment, significance, value, worth

trivialize belittle, laugh off, make light of, minimize, play down, scoff at, underestimate, underplay, undervalue

trollop fallen woman, floozy (*Sl.*), harlot, hussy, loose woman, prostitute, scrubber (*Brit. & Aust. sl.*), slag (*Brit. sl.*), slattern, slut, streetwalker, strumpet, tart (*Inf.*), wanton, whore, working girl (*Facetious sl.*)

troop *n.* 1. assemblage, band, bevy, body, bunch (*Inf.*), company, contingent, crew (*Inf.*), crowd, drove, flock, gang, gathering, group, herd, horde, multitude, pack, posse (*Inf.*), squad, swarm, team, throng, unit 2. *Plural* armed forces, army, fighting men, men, military, servicemen, soldiers, soldiery ~*v.* 3. crowd, flock, march, parade, stream, swarm, throng, traipse (*Inf.*)

trophy award, bays, booty, cup, laurels, memento, prize, souvenir, spoils

tropical hot, humid, lush, steamy, stifling, sultry, sweltering, torrid
Antonyms arctic, chilly, cold, cool, freezing, frosty, frozen, parky (*Brit. inf.*)

trot *v.* 1. canter, go briskly, jog, lope, run, scamper ~*n.* 2. brisk pace, canter, jog, lope, run 3. **on the trot** *Inf.* consecutively, in a row, in succession, one after the other, without break, without interruption

trot out bring forward, bring up, come out with, drag up, exhibit, recite, rehearse, reiterate, relate, repeat

troubadour balladeer, jongleur, lyric poet, minstrel, poet, singer

trouble *n.* 1. agitation, annoyance, anxiety, bummer (*Sl.*), disquiet, distress, grief, hardship, hassle (*Inf.*), heartache, irritation, misfortune, pain, sorrow, suffering, torment, tribulation, vexation, woe, worry 2. agitation, bother (*Inf.*), commotion, discontent, discord, disorder, dissatisfaction, disturbance, hassle (*Inf.*), row, strife, tumult, unrest 3. ailment, complaint, defect, disability, disease, disorder, failure, illness, malfunction, upset 4. bother, concern, danger, difficulty, dilemma, dire straits, hassle (*Inf.*), hot water (*Inf.*), mess, nuisance, pest, pickle (*Inf.*), predicament, problem, scrape (*Inf.*), spot (*Inf.*), tight spot 5. attention, bother, care, effort, exertion, inconvenience, labour, pains, struggle, thought, work ~*v.* 6. afflict, agitate, annoy, bother, discompose, disconcert, disquiet, distress, disturb, faze, fret, grieve, harass, hassle (*Inf.*), inconvenience, pain, perplex, perturb, pester, plague, sadden, torment, upset, vex, worry 7. be concerned, bother, burden, discomfort, discommode, disturb, impose upon, incommode, inconvenience, put out 8. exert oneself, go to the effort of, make an effort, take pains, take the time

Antonyms *n.* agreement, comfort, contentment, convenience, ease, facility, good fortune, happiness, harmony, peace, pleasure, tranquillity, unity *~v.* appease, avoid, be unharassed, calm, dodge, ease, mollify, please, relieve, soothe

troublemaker *agent provocateur,* agitator, firebrand, incendiary, instigator, meddler, mischief-maker, rabble-rouser, stirrer (*Inf.*), stormy petrel

Antonyms appeaser, arbitrator, conciliator, pacifier, peace-maker

troublesome 1. annoying, arduous, bothersome, burdensome, demanding, difficult, harassing, hard, importunate, inconvenient, irksome, irritating, laborious, oppressive, pestilential, plaguy (*Inf.*), taxing, tiresome, tricky, trying, upsetting, vexatious, wearisome, worrisome, worrying 2. disorderly, insubordinate, rebellious, recalcitrant, refractory, rowdy, turbulent, uncooperative, undisciplined, unruly, violent

Antonyms agreeable, calming, congenial, disciplined, eager-to-please, easy, obedient, simple, soothing, pleasant, undemanding, well-behaved

trough 1. crib, manger, water trough 2. canal, channel, depression, ditch, duct, flume, furrow, gully, gutter, trench, watercourse

trounce beat, blow out of the water (*Sl.*), clobber (*Sl.*), crush, defeat heavily *or* utterly, drub, give a hiding (*Inf.*), give a pasting (*Sl.*), hammer (*Inf.*), lick (*Inf.*), make mincemeat of, overwhelm, paste (*Sl.*), rout, run rings around (*Inf.*), slaughter (*Inf.*), tank (*Sl.*), thrash, walk over (*Inf.*), wipe the floor with (*Inf.*)

troupe band, cast, company

trouper actor, artiste, entertainer, performer, player, theatrical, thespian

truancy absence, absence without leave, malingering, shirking, skiving (*Brit. sl.*)

truant *n.* 1. absentee, delinquent, deserter, dodger, malingerer, runaway, shirker, skiver (*Brit. sl.*), straggler 2. *~adj.* absent, absent without leave, A.W.O.L., missing, skiving (*Brit. sl.*) *~v.* 3. absent oneself, bob off (*Brit. sl.*), desert, dodge, go missing, malinger, play truant, run away, shirk, skive (*Brit. sl.*), wag (*Dialect*)

truce armistice, break, ceasefire, cessation, cessation of hostilities, intermission, interval, let-up (*Inf.*), lull, moratorium, peace, respite, rest, stay, treaty

truck *n.* 1. commercial goods, commodities, goods, merchandise, stock, stuff, wares 2. barter, business, buying and selling, commerce, communication, connection, contact, dealings, exchange, relations, trade, traffic *~v.* 3. bargain, barter, buy and sell, deal, do business, exchange, have dealings, negotiate, swap, trade, traffic, transact business

truckle bend the knee, bow and scrape, concede, cringe, crouch, defer, fawn, give in, give way, knuckle under, kowtow, lick (someone's) boots, pander to, stoop, submit, toady, yield

truculent aggressive, antagonistic, bad-tempered, bellicose, belligerent, combative, contentious, cross, defiant, fierce, hostile, ill-tempered, itching *or* spoiling for a fight (*Inf.*), obstreperous, pugnacious, scrappy (*Inf.*), sullen, violent

Antonyms agreeable, amiable, civil, co-operative, gentle, good-natured, peaceable, placid

trudge 1. *v.* clump, drag oneself, footslog, hike, lumber, march, plod, slog, stump, traipse (*Inf.*), tramp, trek, walk heavily, yomp 2. *n.* footslog, haul, hike, march, slog, traipse (*Inf.*), tramp, trek, yomp

true *adj.* 1. accurate, actual, authentic, bona fide, correct, exact, factual, genuine, legitimate, natural, precise, pure, real, right, truthful, valid, veracious, veritable 2. confirmed, constant, dedicated, devoted, dutiful, faithful, fast, firm, honest, honourable, loyal, pure, reliable, sincere, staunch, steady, true-blue, trustworthy, trusty, unswerving, upright 3. accurate, correct, exact, on target, perfect, precise, proper, spot-on (*Brit. inf.*), unerring *~adv.* 4. honestly, rightly, truthfully, veraciously, veritably 5. accurately, correctly, on target, perfectly, precisely, properly, unerringly 6. **come true** become reality, be granted, be realized, come to pass, happen, occur

Antonyms (*sense 1*) abnormal, artificial, atypical, bogus, counterfeit, erroneous, fake, false, fictional, fictitious, illegitimate, imaginary, inaccurate, incorrect, made-up, make-believe, phoney *or* phony (*Inf.*), pretended, self-styled, spurious, unofficial, untrue, untruthful (*sense 2*) deceitful, disloyal, faithless, false, treacherous, unreliable, untrue, untrustworthy (*sense 3*) askew, awry, erroneous, inaccurate, incorrect, untrue

true-blue confirmed, constant, dedicated, devoted, dyed-in-the-wool, faithful, loyal, orthodox, staunch, trusty, uncompromising, unwavering

truism axiom, bromide, cliché, commonplace, platitude, stock phrase, trite saying

truly 1. accurately, authentically, beyond doubt, beyond question, correctly, exactly, factually, genuinely, in actuality, in fact, in reality, in truth, legitimately, precisely, really, rightly, truthfully, veraciously, veritably, without a doubt 2. confirmedly, constantly, devotedly, dutifully, faithfully, firmly, honestly, honourably, loyally, sincerely, staunchly, steadily, with all one's heart, with dedication, with devotion 3. exceptionally, extremely, greatly, indeed, of course, really, to be sure, verily, very

Antonyms (*sense 1*) doubtfully, falsely, fraudulently, inaccurately, incorrectly, mistakenly

trumped-up concocted, contrived, cooked-up (*Inf.*), fabricated, fake, false, falsified, invented, made-up, manufactured, phoney *or* phony (*Inf.*), untrue

Antonyms actual, authentic, bona fide, genuine, real, sound, true, veritable

trumpery *n.* 1. balderdash, balls (*Taboo sl.*), bilge (*Inf.*), bosh (*Inf.*), bull (*Sl.*), bullshit (*Taboo sl.*), bunkum *or* buncombe (*Chiefly U.S.*), claptrap (*Inf.*), cobblers (*Brit. taboo sl.*), crap (*Sl.*), drivel, eyewash (*Inf.*), foolishness, foolish talk, garbage (*Inf.*), guff (*Sl.*), hogwash, hokum (*Sl., chiefly U.S. & Canad.*), horsefeathers (*U.S. sl.*), hot air (*Inf.*), idiocy, inanity, moonshine, nonsense, pap, piffle (*Inf.*), poppycock (*Inf.*), rot, rubbish, shit (*Taboo sl.*), stuff, tommyrot, tosh (*Sl., chiefly Brit.*), trash, tripe (*Inf.*), twaddle 2. bagatelle, bauble, gewgaw, kickshaw, knick-knack, toy, trifle, trinket ~*adj.* 3. brummagem, cheap, flashy, meretricious, nasty, rubbishy, shabby, shoddy, tawdry, trashy, trifling, useless, valueless, worthless

trumpet *n.* 1. bugle, clarion, horn 2. bay, bellow, call, cry, roar 3. **blow one's own trumpet** boast, brag, crow, sing one's own praises, vaunt ~*v.* 4. advertise, announce, broadcast, crack up (*Inf.*), extol, noise abroad, proclaim, publish, shout from the rooftops, sound loudly, tout (*Inf.*)

Antonyms *v.* conceal, hide, hush up, keep secret, make light of, play down, soft pedal (*Inf.*)

trump up concoct, contrive, cook up (*Inf.*), create, fabricate, fake, invent, make up, manufacture

truncate abbreviate, clip, crop, curtail, cut, cut short, dock, lop, pare, prune, shorten, trim

Antonyms drag out, draw out, extend, lengthen, prolong, protract, spin out, stretch

truncheon baton, club, cudgel, staff

trunk 1. bole, stalk, stem, stock 2. body, torso 3. proboscis, snout 4. bin, box, case, casket, chest, coffer, crate, kist (*Scot. & northern English dialect*), locker, portmanteau

truss *v.* 1. bind, bundle, fasten, make fast, pack, pinion, secure, strap, tether, tie ~*n.* 2. beam, brace, buttress, joist, prop, shore, stanchion, stay, strut, support 3. *Medical* bandage, support 4. bale, bundle, package, packet

trust *n.* 1. assurance, belief, certainty, certitude, confidence, conviction, credence, credit, expectation, faith, hope, reliance 2. duty, obligation, responsibility 3. care, charge, custody, guard, guardianship, protection, safekeeping, trusteeship ~*v.* 4. assume, believe, expect, hope, presume, suppose, surmise, think likely 5. bank on, believe, count on, depend on, have faith in, lean on, pin one's faith on, place confidence in, place one's trust in, place reliance on, rely upon, swear by, take at face value 6. assign, command, commit, confide, consign, delegate, entrust, give, put into the hands of, sign over, turn over

Antonyms *n.* distrust, doubt, fear, incredulity, lack of faith, mistrust, scepticism, suspicion, uncertainty, wariness ~*v.* be sceptical of, beware, disbelieve, discredit, distrust, doubt, lack confidence in, lack faith in, mistrust, suspect

trustful, trusting confiding, credulous, gullible, innocent, naive, optimistic, simple, unguarded, unsuspecting, unsuspicious, unwary

Antonyms cagey (*Inf.*), cautious, chary, distrustful, guarded, on one's guard, suspicious, wary

trustworthy dependable, ethical, honest, honourable, level-headed, mature, principled, reliable, reputable, responsible, righteous, sensible, staunch, steadfast, to be trusted, true, trusty, truthful, upright

Antonyms deceitful, dishonest, disloyal, irresponsible, treacherous, undependable, unethical, unprincipled, unreliable, untrustworthy

trusty dependable, faithful, firm, honest, reliable, responsible, solid, staunch, steady, straightforward, strong, true, trustworthy, upright

Antonyms dishonest, irresolute, irresponsible, undependable, unfaithful, unreliable

truth 1. accuracy, actuality, exactness, fact, factuality, factualness, genuineness, legitimacy, precision, reality, truthfulness, va-

lidity, veracity, verity 2. candour, constancy, dedication, devotion, dutifulness, faith, faithfulness, fidelity, frankness, honesty, integrity, loyalty, naturalism, realism, uprightness 3. axiom, certainty, fact, law, maxim, proven principle, reality, truism, verity
Antonyms deceit, deception, delusion, dishonesty, error, fabrication, falsehood, falsity, fiction, inaccuracy, invention, legend, lie, make-believe, myth, old wives' tale, untruth

truthful accurate, candid, correct, exact, faithful, forthright, frank, honest, literal, naturalistic, plain-spoken, precise, realistic, reliable, sincere, straight, straightforward, true, trustworthy, upfront (*Inf.*), veracious, veritable
Antonyms deceptive, dishonest, fabricated, false, fictional, fictitious, inaccurate, incorrect, insincere, lying, made-up, untrue, untruthful

truthless deceitful, deceptive, dishonest, faithless, false, fraudulent, insincere, lying, mendacious, perjured, treacherous, untrue, untrustworthy

try *v.* 1. aim, attempt, bend over backwards (*Inf.*), break one's neck (*Inf.*), bust a gut (*Inf.*), do one's best, do one's damnedest (*Inf.*), endeavour, essay, exert oneself, give it one's all (*Inf.*), give it one's best shot (*Inf.*), go for broke (*Sl.*), go for it (*Inf.*), have a go (crack (*Inf.*), shot (*Inf.*), stab (*Inf.*), whack (*Inf.*)) (*Inf.*), knock oneself out (*Inf.*), make an all-out effort (*Inf.*), make an attempt, make an effort, rupture oneself (*Inf.*), seek, strive, struggle, undertake 2. appraise, check out, evaluate, examine, experiment, inspect, investigate, prove, put to the test, sample, taste, test 3. afflict, annoy, inconvenience, irk, irritate, pain, plague, strain, stress, tax, tire, trouble, upset, vex, weary 4. adjudge, adjudicate, examine, hear ~*n.* 5. attempt, crack (*Inf.*), effort, endeavour, essay, go (*Inf.*), shot (*Inf.*), stab (*Inf.*), whack (*Inf.*) 6. appraisal, evaluation, experiment, inspection, sample, taste, test, trial

trying aggravating (*Inf.*), annoying, arduous, bothersome, difficult, exasperating, fatiguing, hard, irksome, irritating, stressful, taxing, tiresome, tough, troublesome, upsetting, vexing, wearisome
Antonyms calming, easy, no bother, no trouble, painless, simple, straightforward, undemanding

try out appraise, check out, evaluate, experiment with, inspect, put into practice, put to the test, sample, taste, test

tsar, czar autocrat, despot, emperor, head, leader, overlord, ruler, sovereign, tyrant

tubby chubby, corpulent, fat, obese, overweight, paunchy, plump, podgy, portly, roly-poly, stout

tuck *v.* 1. fold, gather, insert, push ~*n.* 2. fold, gather, pinch, pleat 3. *Inf.* comestibles, eats (*Sl.*), food, grub (*Sl.*), nosebag (*Sl.*), nosh (*Sl.*), scoff (*Sl.*), tack (*Inf.*), victuals, vittles (*Obs. or dialect*)

tuck in 1. bed down, enfold, fold under, make snug, put to bed, swaddle, wrap up 2. chow down (*Sl.*), eat heartily, get stuck in (*Inf.*)

tuft bunch, clump, cluster, collection, knot, shock, topknot, tussock

tug 1. *v.* drag, draw, haul, heave, jerk, lug, pull, tow, wrench, yank 2. *n.* drag, haul, heave, jerk, pull, tow, traction, wrench, yank

tuition education, instruction, lessons, schooling, teaching, training, tutelage, tutoring

tumble 1. *v.* drop, fall, fall end over end, fall headlong, fall head over heels, flop, lose one's footing, pitch, plummet, roll, stumble, topple, toss, trip up 2. *n.* collapse, drop, fall, flop, headlong fall, plunge, roll, spill, stumble, toss, trip

tumble-down crumbling, decrepit, dilapidated, disintegrating, falling to pieces, ramshackle, rickety, ruined, shaky, tottering
Antonyms durable, firm, solid, sound, stable, sturdy, substantial, well-kept

tumid 1. bloated, bulging, distended, enlarged, inflated, protuberant, puffed up, puffy, swollen, tumescent 2. bombastic, flowery, fulsome, fustian, grandiloquent, grandiose, high-flown, inflated, magniloquent, orotund, overblown, pompous, pretentious, sesquipedalian, stilted, turgid

tumour cancer, carcinoma (*Pathol.*), growth, lump, neoplasm (*Medical*), sarcoma (*Medical*), swelling

tumult ado, affray (*Law*), agitation, altercation, bedlam, brawl, brouhaha, clamour, commotion, din, disorder, disturbance, excitement, fracas, hubbub, hullabaloo, outbreak, pandemonium, quarrel, racket, riot, row, ruction (*Inf.*), stir, stramash (*Scot.*), strife, turmoil, unrest, upheaval, uproar
Antonyms calm, hush, peace, quiet, repose, serenity, silence, stillness

tumultuous agitated, boisterous, clamorous, confused, disorderly, disturbed, excited, fierce, hectic, irregular, lawless, noisy, obstreperous, passionate, raging, restless, riotous, rowdy, rumbustious, stormy, tur-

bulent, unrestrained, unruly, uproarious, violent, vociferous, wild
Antonyms calm, hushed, peaceful, quiet, restful, serene, still, tranquil

tune *n.* 1. air, melody, melody line, motif, song, strain, theme 2. agreement, concert, concord, consonance, euphony, harmony, pitch, sympathy, unison 3. attitude, demeanour, disposition, frame of mind, mood 4. **call the tune** be in charge (command, control), call the shots (*Sl.*), command, dictate, govern, lead, rule, rule the roost 5. **change one's tune** change one's mind, do an about-face, have a change of heart, reconsider, take a different tack, think again ~*v.* 6. adapt, adjust, attune, bring into harmony, harmonize, pitch, regulate
Antonyms (*sense 2*) clashing, conflict, contention, disagreement, discord, discordance, disharmony, disunity, friction

tuneful catchy, consonant (*Music*), easy on the ear (*Inf.*), euphonic, euphonious, harmonious, mellifluous, melodic, melodious, musical, pleasant, symphonic
Antonyms cacophonous, clashing, discordant, dissonant, harsh, jangly, tuneless, unmelodious

tuneless atonal, cacophonous, clashing, discordant, dissonant, harsh, unmelodic, unmelodious, unmusical
Antonyms harmonious, melodious, musical, pleasing, sonorous, symphonic, tuneful

tunnel 1. *n.* burrow, channel, hole, passage, passageway, shaft, subway, underpass 2. *v.* burrow, dig, dig one's way, excavate, mine, penetrate, scoop out, undermine

turbid clouded, cloudy, confused, dense, dim, dreggy, foggy, foul, fuzzy, hazy, impure, incoherent, muddled, muddy, murky, opaque, roiled, thick, unclear, unsettled

turbulence agitation, boiling, commotion, confusion, disorder, instability, pandemonium, roughness, storm, tumult, turmoil, unrest, upheaval
Antonyms calm, peace, quiet, repose, rest, stillness

turbulent 1. agitated, blustery, boiling, choppy, confused, disordered, foaming, furious, raging, rough, tempestuous, tumultuous, unsettled, unstable 2. agitated, anarchic, boisterous, disorderly, insubordinate, lawless, mutinous, obstreperous, rebellious, refractory, riotous, rowdy, seditious, tumultuous, unbridled, undisciplined, ungovernable, unruly, uproarious, violent, wild
Antonyms (*sense 1*) calm, glassy, peaceful, quiet, smooth, still, unruffled

turf 1. clod, divot, grass, green, sod, sward 2. **the turf** horse-racing, racecourse, racetrack, racing, the flat

turf out banish, bounce (*Sl.*), cast out, chuck out (*Inf.*), discharge, dismiss, dispossess, eject, evict, expel, fire (*Inf.*), fling out, give one the bum's rush (*Sl.*), give one the sack (*Inf.*), kick out (*Inf.*), kiss off (*Sl., chiefly U.S. & Canad.*), oust, relegate, sack (*Inf.*), show one the door, throw out

turgid 1. bloated, bulging, congested, distended, inflated, protuberant, puffed up, puffy, swollen, tumescent, tumid 2. bombastic, flowery, fulsome, fustian, grandiloquent, grandiose, high-flown, inflated, magniloquent, orotund, ostentatious, overblown, pompous, pretentious, sesquipedalian, stilted, tumid, windy

turmoil agitation, bedlam, brouhaha, bustle, chaos, commotion, confusion, disarray, disorder, disturbance, ferment, flurry, hubbub, noise, pandemonium, row, stir, strife, trouble, tumult, turbulence, upheaval, uproar, violence
Antonyms calm, peace, quiet, repose, rest, serenity, stillness, tranquillity

turn *v.* 1. circle, go round, gyrate, move in a circle, pivot, revolve, roll, rotate, spin, swivel, twirl, twist, wheel, whirl 2. change course, change position, go back, move, return, reverse, shift, swerve, switch, veer, wheel 3. arc, come round, corner, go round, negotiate, pass, pass around, take a bend 4. adapt, alter, become, change, convert, divert, fashion, fit, form, metamorphose, mould, mutate, remodel, shape, transfigure, transform, transmute 5. become rancid, curdle, go bad, go off (*Brit. inf.*), go sour, make rancid, sour, spoil, taint 6. appeal, apply, approach, go, have recourse, look, resort 7. nauseate, sicken, upset 8. apostatize, bring round (*Inf.*), change one's mind, change sides, defect, desert, go over, influence, persuade, prejudice, prevail upon, renege, retract, talk into 9. construct, deliver, execute, fashion, frame, make, mould, perform, shape, write 10. **turn tail** beat a hasty retreat, bolt, cut and run (*Inf.*), flee, hook it (*Sl.*), run away, run off, show a clean pair of heels, take off (*Inf.*), take to one's heels ~*n.* 11. bend, change, circle, curve, cycle, gyration, pivot, reversal, revolution, rotation, spin, swing, turning, twist, whirl 12. bias, direction, drift, heading, tendency, trend 13. bend, change of course, change of direction, curve, departure, deviation, shift 14. chance, crack (*Inf.*), fling, go, opportunity, period, round, shift, shot (*Inf.*), spell, stint, succession, time, try, whack (*Inf.*) 15. airing, circuit, constitutional, drive, excursion, jaunt, outing, promenade, ride, saunter, spin (*Inf.*), stroll, walk 16. affinity, aptitude, bent, bias, flair, gift, inclination, knack, leaning, propensity, talent 17. cast, fashion, form, format, guise, make-up, manner, mode, mould, shape, style, way 18. act, action, deed, favour, gesture, service 19. bend, distortion, twist, warp 20. *Inf.* fright, scare, shock, start, surprise 21. **by turns** alternately, in succession, one after another, reciprocally, turn and turn about 22. **to a turn** correctly, exactly, just right, perfectly, precisely

turncoat apostate, backslider, defector, deserter, rat (*Inf.*), recreant (*Archaic*), renegade, seceder, tergiversator, traitor

turn down 1. diminish, lessen, lower, muffle, mute, quieten, reduce the volume of, soften 2. abstain from, decline, rebuff, refuse, reject, repudiate, say no to, spurn, throw out
Antonyms (*sense 1*) amplify, augment, boost, increase, raise, strengthen, swell, turn up (*sense 2*) accede, accept, acquiesce, agree, receive, take

turn in 1. go to bed, go to sleep, hit the sack (*Sl.*), retire for the night 2. deliver, give back, give up, hand in, hand over, return, submit, surrender, tender

turning bend, crossroads, curve, junction, side road, turn, turn-off

turning point change, climacteric, crisis, critical moment, crossroads, crux, decisive moment, moment of decision, moment of truth

turn-off branch, exit, side road, turn, turning

turn off 1. branch off, change direction, depart from, deviate, leave, quit, take another road, take a side road 2. cut out, kill, put out, shut down, stop, switch off, turn out, unplug 3. *Inf.* alienate, bore, disenchant, disgust, displease, gross out (*U.S. sl.*), irritate, lose one's interest, nauseate, offend, put off, repel, sicken

turn on 1. activate, energize, ignite, kick-start, put on, set in motion, start, start up, switch on 2. balance, be contingent on, be decided by, depend, hang, hinge, pivot, rest 3. assail, assault, attack, fall on, lose one's temper with, round on 4. *Sl.* arouse, arouse one's desire, attract, excite, please, stimulate, thrill, titillate, work up 5. *Sl.* get high (*Inf.*), get stoned (*Sl.*), take drugs, trip (*Inf.*) 6. *Sl.* expose, get one started with, inform, initiate, introduce, show
Antonyms (*sense 1*) cut out, put out, shut off, stop, switch off, turn off

turnout 1. assemblage, assembly, attendance, audience, congregation, crowd, gate, number, throng 2. amount produced, output, outturn (*Rare*), production, production quota, productivity, turnover, volume, yield 3. array, attire, costume, dress, equipage, equipment, gear (*Inf.*), get-up (*Inf.*), outfit, rigout (*Inf.*)

turn out 1. put out, switch off, turn off, unplug 2. bring out, fabricate, finish, make, manufacture, process, produce, put out 3. axe (*Inf.*), banish, cashier, cast out, deport, discharge, dismiss, dispossess, drive out, drum out, evict, expel, fire (*Inf.*), give one the sack (*Inf.*), give the bum's rush (*Sl.*), kick out (*Inf.*), kiss off (*Sl., chiefly U.S. & Canad.*), oust, put out, relegate, sack (*Inf.*), show one the door, throw out, turf out (*Brit. inf.*), unseat 4. clean out, clear, discharge, empty, take out the contents of 5. become, come about, come to be, come to light, crop up (*Inf.*), develop, emerge, end up, eventuate, evolve, happen, prove to be, result, transpire (*Inf.*), work out 6. accoutre, apparel (*Archaic*), attire, clothe, dress, fit, outfit, rig out 7. appear, assemble, attend, be present, come, gather, go, put in an appearance, show up (*Inf.*), turn up

turnover 1. business, flow, output, outturn (*Rare*), production, productivity, volume, yield 2. change, coming and going, movement, replacement

turn over 1. capsize, flip over, keel over, overturn, reverse, tip over, upend, upset 2. activate, crank, press the starter button, set going, set in motion, start up, switch on, switch on the ignition, warm up 3. assign, commend, commit, deliver, give over, give up, hand over, pass on, render, surrender, transfer, yield 4. consider, contemplate, deliberate, give thought to, mull over, ponder, reflect on, revolve, ruminate about, think about, think over, wonder about 5. break up, dig, plough

turn up 1. appear, arrive, attend, come, put in an appearance, show (*Inf.*), show one's face, show up (*Inf.*) 2. appear, become known, be found, bring to light, come to light, come to pass, come up with, crop up (*Inf.*), dig up, disclose, discover, expose, find, pop up, reveal, transpire, unearth 3. amplify, boost, enhance, increase, increase the volume of, intensify, make louder, raise
Antonyms (*sense 2*) disappear, evaporate, fade, hide, vanish (*sense 3*) diminish, lessen, lower, reduce, soften, turn down

turpitude badness, baseness, corruption, criminality, degeneracy, depravity, evil, foulness, immorality, iniquity, nefariousness, sinfulness, viciousness, vileness, villainy, wickedness

tussle 1. *v.* battle, brawl, contend, fight,

grapple, scrap (*Inf.*), scuffle, struggle, vie, wrestle 2. *n. bagarre,* battle, bout, brawl, competition, conflict, contention, contest, fight, fracas, fray, punch-up (*Brit. inf.*), scrap (*Inf.*), scrimmage, scuffle, set-to (*Inf.*), shindig (*Inf.*), shindy (*Inf.*), struggle

tutelage care, charge, custody, dependence, education, guardianship, guidance, instruction, patronage, preparation, protection, schooling, teaching, tuition, wardship

tutor 1. *n.* coach, educator, governor, guardian, guide, guru, instructor, lecturer, master, mentor, preceptor, schoolmaster, teacher 2. *v.* coach, direct, discipline, drill, edify, educate, guide, instruct, lecture, school, teach, train

tutorial 1. *n.* individual instruction, lesson, seminar 2. *adj.* coaching, guiding, instructional, teaching

TV gogglebox (*Brit. sl.*), idiot box (*Sl.*), receiver, small screen (*Inf.*), television, television set, telly (*Brit. inf.*), the box (*Brit. inf.*), the tube (*Sl.*), TV set

twaddle 1. *n.* balderdash, balls (*Taboo sl.*), bilge (*Inf.*), blather, bosh (*Inf.*), bull (*Sl.*), bullshit (*Taboo sl.*), bunkum *or* buncombe (*Chiefly U.S.*), chatter, claptrap (*Inf.*), cobblers (*Brit. taboo sl.*), crap (*Sl.*), drivel, eyewash (*Inf.*), foolish talk, gabble, garbage (*Inf.*), gobbledegook (*Inf.*), gossip, guff (*Sl.*), hogwash, hokum (*Sl., chiefly U.S. & Canad.*), horsefeathers (*U.S. sl.*), hot air (*Inf.*), inanity, moonshine, nonsense, pap, piffle (*Inf.*), poppycock (*Inf.*), rigmarole, rot, rubbish, shit (*Taboo sl.*), tattle, tommyrot, tosh (*Sl., chiefly Brit.*), trash, tripe (*Inf.*), trumpery, verbiage, waffle (*Inf., chiefly Brit.*) 2. *v.* blather, chatter, gabble, gossip, prattle, rattle on, talk nonsense, talk through one's hat, tattle, waffle (*Inf., chiefly Brit.*)

tweak *v./n.* jerk, nip, pinch, pull, squeeze, twist, twitch

twee bijou, cute, dainty, precious, pretty, quaint, sentimental, sweet

twiddle 1. adjust, fiddle (*Inf.*), finger, jiggle, juggle, monkey with (*Inf.*), play with, twirl, wiggle 2. **twiddle one's thumbs** be idle, be unoccupied, do nothing, have nothing to do, malinger, mark time, sit around

twig[1] branch, offshoot, shoot, spray, sprig, stick, withe

twig[2] catch on (*Inf.*), comprehend, fathom, find out, get, grasp, make out, rumble (*Brit. inf.*), see, tumble to (*Inf.*), understand

twilight *n.* 1. dimness, dusk, evening, gloaming (*Scot. or poetic*), half-light, sundown, sunset 2. decline, ebb, last phase ~*adj.* 3. crepuscular, darkening, dim, evening 4. declining, dying, ebbing, final, last

Antonyms climax, crowning moment, dawn, daybreak, height, morning, peak, sunrise, sunup

twin 1. *n.* clone, corollary, counterpart, double, duplicate, fellow, likeness, lookalike, match, mate, ringer (*Sl.*) 2. *adj.* corresponding, double, dual, duplicate, geminate, identical, matched, matching, paired, parallel, twofold 3. *v.* couple, join, link, match, pair, yoke

twine *n.* 1. cord, string, yarn 2. coil, convolution, interlacing, twist, whorl 3. knot, snarl, tangle ~*v.* 4. braid, entwine, interlace, interweave, knit, plait, splice, twist, twist together, weave 5. bend, coil, curl, encircle, loop, meander, spiral, surround, twist, wind, wrap, wreathe

twinge bite, gripe, pain, pang, pinch, prick, sharp pain, spasm, stab, stitch, throb, throe (*Rare*), tic, tweak, twist, twitch

twinkle *v.* 1. blink, coruscate, flash, flicker, gleam, glint, glisten, glitter, scintillate, shimmer, shine, sparkle, wink ~*n.* 2. blink, coruscation, flash, flicker, gleam, glimmer, glistening, glittering, light, scintillation, shimmer, shine, spark, sparkle, wink 3. flash, instant, jiffy (*Inf.*), moment, second, shake (*Inf.*), split second, tick (*Brit. inf.*), trice, twinkling, two shakes of a lamb's tail (*Inf.*)

twinkling 1. blink, coruscation, flash, flashing, flicker, gleam, glimmer, glistening, glittering, scintillation, shimmer, shining, sparkle, twinkle, wink 2. flash, instant, jiffy (*Inf.*), moment, second, shake (*Inf.*), split second, tick (*Brit. inf.*), trice, twinkle, two shakes of a lamb's tail (*Inf.*)

twirl *v.* 1. gyrate, pirouette, pivot, revolve, rotate, spin, turn, turn on one's heel, twiddle, twist, wheel, whirl, wind ~*n.* 2. gyration, pirouette, revolution, rotation, spin, turn, twist, wheel, whirl 3. coil, spiral, twist

twist *v.* 1. coil, corkscrew, curl, encircle, entwine, intertwine, screw, spin, swivel, twine, weave, wind, wrap, wreathe, wring 2. contort, distort, screw up 3. rick, sprain, turn, wrench 4. alter, change, distort, falsify, garble, misquote, misrepresent, pervert, warp 5. squirm, wriggle, writhe 6. **twist someone's arm** bully, coerce, force, persuade, pressurize, talk into ~*n.* 7. coil, curl, spin, swivel, twine, wind 8. braid, coil, curl, hank, plug, quid, roll 9. change, development, revelation, slant, surprise, turn, variation 10. arc, bend, convolution, curve, meander, turn, undulation, zigzag 11. defect, deformation, distortion, flaw, imperfection, kink, warp 12. jerk, pull, sprain, turn, wrench 13. aberration, bent, characteristic, crotchet, eccentricity, fault, foible, idiosyncrasy, oddity, peculiarity, proclivity, quirk, trait 14. confusion, entanglement, kink, knot, mess, mix-up, ravel, snarl, tangle 15. **round the twist** *Brit. sl.* barmy (*Sl.*), batty (*Sl.*), bonkers (*Sl., chiefly Brit.*), crazy, cuckoo (*Inf.*), daft (*Inf.*), insane, loopy (*Inf.*), mad, not all there, not right in the head, nuts (*Sl.*), nutty (*Sl.*), nutty as a fruitcake (*Sl.*), off one's rocker (*Sl.*), off one's trolley (*Sl.*), out to lunch (*Inf.*), up the pole (*Inf.*)

Antonyms hold stationary, hold steady, hold still, straighten, uncoil, unravel, unroll, untwist, unwind

twister cheat, chiseller (*Inf.*), con man (*Inf.*), crook (*Inf.*), deceiver, fraud, rogue, swindler, trickster

twit[1] *v.* banter, berate, blame, censure, deride, jeer, make fun of, scorn, taunt, tease, upbraid

twit[2] airhead (*Sl.*), ass, berk (*Brit. sl.*), blockhead, charlie (*Brit. inf.*), chump (*Inf.*), clown, dickhead (*Sl.*), dipstick (*Brit. sl.*), divvy (*Brit. sl.*), dope (*Inf.*), dork (*Sl.*), dweeb (*U.S. sl.*), fool, fuckwit (*Taboo sl.*), geek (*Sl.*), gonzo (*Sl.*), halfwit, idiot, jerk (*Sl., chiefly U.S. & Canad.*), juggins (*Brit. inf.*), nerd *or* nurd (*Sl.*), nincompoop, ninny, nitwit (*Inf.*), numskull *or* numbskull, oaf, pillock (*Brit. sl.*), plank (*Brit. sl.*), plonker (*Sl.*), prat (*Sl.*), prick (*Derogatory sl.*), schmuck (*U.S. sl.*), silly-billy (*Inf.*), simpleton, twerp *or* twirp (*Inf.*), wally (*Sl.*)

twitch 1. *v.* blink, flutter, jerk, jump, pluck, pull, snatch, squirm, tug, yank 2. *n.* blink, flutter, jerk, jump, pull, spasm, tic, tremor, twinge

twitter *v.* 1. chatter, cheep, chirp, chirrup, trill, tweet, warble, whistle 2. chatter, giggle, prattle, simper, snigger, titter ~*n.* 3. call, chatter, cheep, chirp, chirrup, cry, song, trill, tweet, warble, whistle 4. agitation, anxiety, bustle, dither (*Chiefly Brit.*), excitement, flurry, fluster, flutter, nervousness, tizzy (*Inf.*), whirl

two-edged ambiguous, ambivalent, backhanded, double-edged, equivocal

two-faced deceitful, deceiving, dissembling, double-dealing, duplicitous, false, hypocritical, insincere, Janus-faced, perfidious, treacherous, untrustworthy

Antonyms artless, candid, frank, genuine, honest, ingenuous, sincere, trustworthy

tycoon baron, big cheese (*Sl., old-fashioned*), big noise (*Inf.*), capitalist, captain of industry, fat cat (*Sl., chiefly U.S.*), financier, industrialist, magnate, merchant prince, mogul, plutocrat, potentate, wealthy businessman

type 1. breed, category, class, classification, form, genre, group, ilk, kidney, kind, order, sort, species, stamp, strain, subdivision, variety 2. case, characters, face, fount, print, printing 3. archetype, epitome, essence, example, exemplar, model, norm, original, paradigm, pattern, personification, prototype, quintessence, specimen, standard

typhoon cyclone, squall, storm, tempest, tornado, tropical storm

typical archetypal, average, characteristic, classic, conventional, essential, illustrative, in character, indicative, in keeping, model, normal, orthodox, representative, standard, stock, true to type, usual

Antonyms atypical, exceptional, out of keeping, out of the ordinary, singular, uncharacteristic, unconventional, unexpected, unique, unrepresentative, unusual

typify characterize, embody, epitomize, exemplify, illustrate, incarnate, personify, represent, sum up, symbolize

tyrannical absolute, arbitrary, authoritarian, autocratic, coercive, cruel, despotic, dictatorial, domineering, high-handed, imperious, inhuman, magisterial, oppressive, overbearing, overweening, peremptory, severe, tyrannous, unjust, unreasonable

Antonyms democratic, easy-going, lax, lenient, liberal, reasonable, tolerant, understanding

tyrannize browbeat, bully, coerce, dictate, domineer, enslave, have (someone) under one's thumb, intimidate, oppress, ride roughshod over, rule with an iron hand, subjugate, terrorize

tyranny absolutism, authoritarianism, autocracy, coercion, cruelty, despotism, dictatorship, harsh discipline, high-handedness, imperiousness, oppression, peremptoriness, reign of terror, unreasonableness

Antonyms democracy, ease, laxity, leniency, liberality, mercy, relaxation, tolerance, understanding

tyrant absolutist, authoritarian, autocrat, bully, despot, dictator, Hitler, martinet, oppressor, slave-driver

tyro apprentice, beginner, catechumen, greenhorn (*Inf.*), initiate, learner, neophyte, novice, novitiate, pupil, student, trainee

U

ubiquitous all-over, ever-present, everywhere, omnipresent, pervasive, universal

ugly 1. hard-favoured, hard-featured, homely (*Chiefly U.S.*), ill-favoured, misshapen, no oil painting (*Inf.*), not much to look at, plain, unattractive, unlovely, unprepossessing, unsightly 2. disagreeable, disgusting, distasteful, frightful, hideous, horrid, monstrous, objectionable, obscene, offensive, repugnant, repulsive, revolting, shocking, terrible, unpleasant, vile 3. baleful, dangerous, forbidding, menacing, ominous, sinister, threatening 4. angry, bad-tempered, dark, evil, malevolent, nasty, spiteful, sullen, surly
Antonyms agreeable, attractive, auspicious, beautiful, friendly, good-humoured, good-looking, good-natured, gorgeous, handsome, likable *or* likeable, lovely, peaceful, pleasant, pretty, promising

ulcer abscess, boil, fester, gathering, gumboil, peptic ulcer, pustule, sore

ulcerous cankered, cankerous, festering, furunculous (*Pathology*), suppurative, ulcerative

ulterior concealed, covert, hidden, personal, secondary, secret, selfish, undisclosed, unexpressed
Antonyms apparent, declared, manifest, obvious, overt, plain

ultimate *adj.* 1. conclusive, decisive, end, eventual, extreme, final, furthest, last, terminal 2. extreme, greatest, highest, maximum, most significant, paramount, superlative, supreme, topmost, utmost 3. basic, elemental, fundamental, primary, radical ~*n.* 4. culmination, epitome, extreme, greatest, height, peak, perfection, summit, the last word

ultimately after all, at last, basically, eventually, finally, fundamentally, in due time, in the end, sooner or later

ultra *adj.* excessive, extreme, fanatical, immoderate, rabid, radical, revolutionary

ultramodern advanced, ahead of its time, avant-garde, futuristic, modernistic, neoteric (*Rare*), progressive, way-out (*Inf.*)

ululate bawl, cry, howl, keen, lament, moan, mourn, sob, wail, weep

umbrage anger, chagrin, displeasure, grudge, high dudgeon, huff, indignation, offence, pique, resentment, sense of injury
Antonyms amity, cordiality, good will, harmony, pleasure, understanding

umbrella 1. brolly (*Brit. inf.*), gamp (*Brit. inf.*) 2. aegis, agency, cover, patronage, protection

umpire 1. *n.* adjudicator, arbiter, arbitrator, judge, moderator, ref (*Inf.*), referee 2. *v.* adjudicate, arbitrate, call (*Sport*), judge, mediate, moderate, referee

umpteen a good many, a thousand and one, considerable, countless, ever so many, millions, n, numerous, very many

unabashed blatant, bold, brazen, confident, unawed, unblushing, unconcerned, undaunted, undismayed, unembarrassed
Antonyms abashed, embarrassed, humbled, mortified, shame-faced, sheepish

unable impotent, inadequate, incapable, ineffectual, no good, not able, not equal to, not up to, powerless, unfit, unfitted, unqualified
Antonyms able, adept, adequate, capable, competent, effective, potent, powerful

unabridged complete, full-length, uncondensed, uncut, unexpurgated, unshortened, whole

unacceptable disagreeable, displeasing, distasteful, improper, inadmissible, insupportable, objectionable, offensive, undesirable, unpleasant, unsatisfactory, unwelcome
Antonyms acceptable, agreeable, delightful, desirable, pleasant, pleasing, welcome

unaccompanied a cappella (*Music*), alone, by oneself, lone, on one's own, solo, unescorted

unaccomplished 1. incomplete, unachieved, uncompleted, undone, unfinished, unperformed 2. inexpert, lacking finesse, uncultivated, unskilful, unskilled

unaccountable 1. baffling, incomprehensible, inexplicable, inscrutable, mysterious, odd, peculiar, puzzling, strange, unexplainable, unfathomable, unintelligible 2. astonishing, extraordinary, uncommon, unheard-of, unusual, unwonted 3. clear, exempt, free, not answerable, not responsible, unliable
Antonyms (*sense 1*) accountable, comprehensible, explicable, intelligible, understandable

unaccounted-for lost, missing, not explained, not taken into consideration, not understood, unexplained

unaccustomed 1. *With* to a newcomer to, a novice at, green, inexperienced, not given to, not used to, unfamiliar with, unpractised, unused to, unversed in 2. new, out of the ordinary, remarkable, special, strange, surprising, uncommon, unexpected, unfamiliar, unprecedented, unusual, unwonted
Antonyms (*sense 1*) experienced, given to, habituated, practised, seasoned, used to, well-versed (*sense 2*) accustomed, familiar, ordinary, regular, usual

unadorned plain, restrained, severe, simple, stark, straightforward, unembellished, unornamented, unvarnished

unadvised 1. careless, hasty, heedless, ill-advised, imprudent, inadvisable, indiscreet, injudicious, rash, reckless, unwary, unwise 2. ignorant, in the dark, unaware, uninformed, unknowing, unsuspecting, unwarned

unaffected[1] artless, genuine, honest, ingenuous, naive, natural, plain, simple, sincere, straightforward, unassuming, unpretentious, unsophisticated, unspoilt, unstudied, without airs
Antonyms affected, assumed, designing, devious, insincere, mannered, pretentious, put-on, snobbish, sophisticated

unaffected[2] aloof, impervious, not influenced, proof, unaltered, unchanged, unimpressed, unmoved, unresponsive, unstirred, untouched
Antonyms affected, changed, concerned, disrupted, hard-hit, influenced, interested, responsive, sympathetic, touched

unafraid confident, daring, dauntless, fearless, intrepid, unfearing, unshakable
Antonyms afraid, alarmed, anxious, fearful, frightened, scared

unalterable fixed, fixed as the laws of the Medes and the Persians, immovable, immutable, invariable, permanent, steadfast, unchangeable, unchanging
Antonyms alterable, changeable, changing, flexible, mutable, variable

unanimity accord, agreement, assent, chorus, concert, concord, concurrence, consensus, harmony, like-mindedness, one mind, unison, unity
Antonyms difference, disagreement, discord, disunity, division, variance

unanimous agreed, agreeing, at one, common, concerted, concordant, harmonious, in agreement, in complete accord, like-minded, of one mind, united
Antonyms differing, discordant, dissident, disunited, divided, schismatic, split

unanimously by common consent, nem. con., unitedly, unopposed, with one accord, without exception, without opposition

unanswerable 1. absolute, conclusive, incontestable, incontrovertible, indisputable, irrefutable, unarguable, undeniable 2. insoluble, insolvable, unascertainable, unexplainable, unresolvable

unanswered disputed, ignored, in doubt, open, undecided, undenied, unnoticed, unrefuted, unresolved, unsettled, up in the air, vexed

unappetizing distasteful, insipid, off-putting (*Brit. inf.*), tasteless, unappealing, unattractive, uninteresting, uninviting, unpalatable, unpleasant, unsavoury, vapid
Antonyms agreeable, appealing, appetizing, attractive, interesting, palatable, savoury, tasty, toothsome

unapproachable 1. aloof, chilly, cool, distant, frigid, offish (*Inf.*), remote, reserved, standoffish, unfriendly, unsociable, withdrawn 2. inaccessible, out of reach, out-of-the-way, remote, un-get-at-able (*Inf.*), unreachable
Antonyms (*sense 1*) affable, approachable, congenial, cordial, friendly, sociable

unapt 1. inapplicable, inapposite, inappropriate, inapt, out of character, out of keeping, out of place, unfit, unfitted, unsuitable 2. backward, dim, dim-witted (*Inf.*), dull, incompetent, slow, stupid, thick 3. averse, disinclined, loath, not prone, reluctant, undisposed, unlikely, unwilling

unarmed assailable, defenceless, exposed, helpless, open, open to attack, unarmoured, unprotected, weak, weaponless, without arms
Antonyms armed, equipped, fortified, protected, ready, strengthened

unasked 1. gratuitous, spontaneous, unbidden, undemanded, undesired, uninvited, unprompted, unrequested, unsought, unwanted 2. off one's own bat, of one's own accord, voluntarily, without prompting

unassailable 1. impregnable, invincible, invulnerable, secure, well-defended 2. absolute, conclusive, incontestable, incontrovertible, indisputable, irrefutable, positive, proven, sound, undeniable
Antonyms (*sense 2*) debatable, doubtful, dubious, inconclusive, uncertain, unfounded, unproven, unsound

unassertive backward, bashful, diffident, meek, mousy, retiring, self-effacing, timid, timorous, unassuming
Antonyms aggressive, assertive, confident, feisty (*Inf., chiefly U.S. & Canad.*), forceful, overbearing, pushy (*Inf.*)

unassuming diffident, humble, meek, modest, quiet, reserved, retiring, self-

effacing, simple, unassertive, unobtrusive, unostentatious, unpretentious
Antonyms assuming, audacious, conceited, ostentatious, overconfident, presumptuous, pretentious

unattached 1. autonomous, free, independent, nonaligned, unaffiliated, uncommitted 2. a free agent, available, by oneself, footloose and fancy-free, not spoken for, on one's own, single, unengaged, unmarried
Antonyms (*sense 1*) affiliated, aligned, attached, committed, dependent, implicated, involved

unattended 1. abandoned, disregarded, ignored, left alone, not cared for, unguarded, unwatched 2. alone, on one's own, unaccompanied, unescorted

unauthorized illegal, unapproved, unconstitutional, under-the-table, unlawful, unofficial, unsanctioned, unwarranted
Antonyms authorized, constitutional, lawful, legal, official, sanctioned, warranted

unavailing abortive, bootless, fruitless, futile, idle, ineffective, ineffectual, of no avail, pointless, to no purpose, unproductive, unsuccessful, useless, vain
Antonyms effective, fruitful, productive, rewarding, successful, useful, worthwhile

unavoidable bound to happen, certain, compulsory, fated, ineluctable, inescapable, inevitable, inexorable, necessary, obligatory, sure

unaware heedless, ignorant, incognizant, oblivious, unconscious, unenlightened, uninformed, unknowing, unmindful, unsuspecting
Antonyms attentive, aware, conscious, informed, knowing, mindful

unawares 1. aback, abruptly, by surprise, off guard, on the hop (*Brit. inf.*), suddenly, unexpectedly, unprepared, without warning 2. accidentally, by accident, by mistake, inadvertently, mistakenly, unconsciously, unintentionally, unknowingly, unwittingly
Antonyms deliberately, forewarned, knowingly, on purpose, on the lookout, prepared, wittingly

unbalanced 1. asymmetrical, irregular, lopsided, not balanced, shaky, unequal, uneven, unstable, unsymmetrical, wobbly 2. barking (*Sl.*), barking mad (*Sl.*), crazy, demented, deranged, disturbed, eccentric, erratic, insane, irrational, loopy (*Inf.*), lunatic, mad, *non compos mentis,* not all there, not the full shilling (*Inf.*), off one's trolley (*Sl.*), out to lunch (*Inf.*), touched, unhinged, unsound, unstable, up the pole (*Inf.*) 3. biased, inequitable, one-sided, partial, partisan, prejudiced, unfair, unjust
Antonyms (*sense 1*) balanced, equal, even, stable, symmetrical

unbearable insufferable, insupportable, intolerable, oppressive, too much (*Inf.*), unacceptable, unendurable
Antonyms acceptable, bearable, endurable, supportable, tolerable

unbeatable indomitable, invincible, more than a match for, unconquerable, unstoppable, unsurpassable

unbeaten 1. triumphant, unbowed, undefeated, unsubdued, unsurpassed, unvanquished, victorious, winning 2. new, untouched, untried, untrodden, virgin

unbecoming 1. ill-suited, inappropriate, incongruous, unattractive, unbefitting, unfit, unflattering, unsightly, unsuitable, unsuited 2. discreditable, improper, indecorous, indelicate, offensive, tasteless, unseemly
Antonyms (*sense 2*) becoming, decent, decorous, delicate, proper, seemly

unbelief atheism, disbelief, distrust, doubt, incredulity, scepticism
Antonyms belief, credence, credulity, faith, trust

unbelievable astonishing, beyond belief, far-fetched, implausible, impossible, improbable, inconceivable, incredible, outlandish, preposterous, questionable, staggering, unconvincing, unimaginable, unthinkable
Antonyms authentic, believable, credible, likely, plausible, possible, probable, trustworthy

unbeliever agnostic, atheist, disbeliever, doubting Thomas, infidel, sceptic

unbelieving disbelieving, distrustful, doubtful, doubting, dubious, incredulous, sceptical, suspicious, unconvinced
Antonyms believing, convinced, credulous, trustful, undoubting, unsuspicious

unbend 1. be informal, calm down, chill out (*Sl., chiefly U.S.*), cool it (*Sl.*), ease up, let it all hang out (*Sl.*), let oneself go, let up, lighten up (*Sl.*), loosen up, relax, slacken, slow down, take it easy, unbutton (*Inf.*), unwind 2. put straight, straighten, uncoil, uncurl

unbending 1. aloof, distant, formal, inflexible, reserved, rigid, stiff, uptight (*Inf.*) 2. firm, hard-line, intractable, resolute, severe, strict, stubborn, tough, uncompromising, unyielding
Antonyms (*sense 1*) approachable, at ease, flexible, friendly, outgoing, relaxed, sociable

unbiased disinterested, dispassionate, equitable, even-handed, fair, impartial,

just, neutral, objective, open-minded, unprejudiced
Antonyms biased, bigoted, partial, prejudiced, slanted, swayed, unfair, unjust

unbidden 1. free, spontaneous, unforced, unprompted, voluntary, willing 2. unasked, uninvited, unwanted, unwelcome

unbind free, loosen, release, set free, unbridle, unchain, undo, unfasten, unfetter, unloose, unshackle, untie, unyoke
Antonyms bind, chain, fasten, fetter, restrain, shackle, tie, yoke

unblemished flawless, immaculate, impeccable, perfect, pure, spotless, unflawed, unspotted, unstained, unsullied, untarnished
Antonyms blemished, flawed, imperfect, impure, stained, sullied, tarnished

unblinking 1. calm, cool, emotionless, impassive, unemotional, unfaltering, unwavering 2. fearless, steady, unafraid, unflinching, unshrinking

unblushing amoral, bold, brazen, forward, immodest, shameless, unabashed, unashamed, unembarrassed

unborn 1. awaited, embryonic, expected, *in utero* 2. coming, future, hereafter, latter, subsequent, to come

unbosom admit, confess, confide, disburden, disclose, divulge, get (something) off one's chest (*Inf.*), get (something) out of one's system, lay bare, let out, reveal, spill one's guts about (*Sl.*), tell, unburden
Antonyms conceal, cover up, guard, hold back, suppress, withhold

unbounded absolute, boundless, endless, immeasurable, infinite, lavish, limitless, unbridled, unchecked, unconstrained, uncontrolled, unlimited, unrestrained, vast
Antonyms bounded, confined, constrained, curbed, limited, restricted

unbreakable armoured, durable, indestructible, infrangible, lasting, nonbreakable, resistant, rugged, shatterproof, solid, strong, toughened
Antonyms breakable, brittle, delicate, flimsy, fragile, frangible

unbridled excessive, intemperate, licentious, rampant, riotous, unchecked, unconstrained, uncontrolled, uncurbed, ungovernable, ungoverned, unrestrained, unruly, violent, wanton

unbroken 1. complete, entire, intact, solid, total, unimpaired, whole 2. ceaseless, constant, continuous, endless, incessant, progressive, serried, successive, uninterrupted, unremitting 3. deep, fast, profound, sound, undisturbed, unruffled, untroubled 4. unbowed, unsubdued, untamed
Antonyms (*sense 1*) broken, cracked, damaged, fragmented, in pieces, shattered (*sense 2*) erratic, fitful, intermittent, interrupted, irregular, occasional, off-and-on, uneven

unburden 1. disburden, discharge, disencumber, ease the load, empty, lighten, relieve, unload 2. come clean (*Inf.*), confess, confide, disclose, get (something) off one's chest (*Inf.*), lay bare, make a clean breast of, reveal, spill one's guts about (*Sl.*), tell all, unbosom

uncalled-for gratuitous, inappropriate, needless, undeserved, unjust, unjustified, unnecessary, unprovoked, unwarranted, unwelcome
Antonyms appropriate, deserved, just, justified, necessary, needed, provoked, warranted

uncanny 1. creepy (*Inf.*), eerie, eldritch (*Poetic*), mysterious, preternatural, queer, spooky (*Inf.*), strange, supernatural, unearthly, unnatural, weird 2. astonishing, astounding, exceptional, extraordinary, fantastic, incredible, inspired, miraculous, prodigious, remarkable, singular, unheard-of, unusual

uncaring indifferent, negligent, unconcerned, unfeeling, uninterested, unmoved, unresponsive, unsympathetic

unceasing ceaseless, constant, continual, continuing, continuous, endless, incessant, never-ending, nonstop, perpetual, persistent, unending, unfailing, unremitting
Antonyms fitful, intermittent, irregular, occasional, periodic, spasmodic, sporadic

uncertain 1. ambiguous, chancy, conjectural, doubtful, iffy (*Inf.*), incalculable, indefinite, indeterminate, indistinct, questionable, risky, speculative, undetermined, unforeseeable, unpredictable 2. ambivalent, doubtful, dubious, hazy, in two minds, irresolute, unclear, unconfirmed, undecided, undetermined, unfixed, unresolved, unsettled, unsure, up in the air, vacillating, vague 3. changeable, erratic, fitful, hesitant, iffy (*Inf.*), inconstant, insecure, irregular, precarious, unpredictable, unreliable, vacillating, variable, wavering
Antonyms certain, clear, clear-cut, decided, definite, firm, fixed, known, positive, predictable, resolute, settled, sure, unambiguous, unhesitating, unvarying, unwavering

uncertainty ambiguity, bewilderment, confusion, dilemma, doubt, dubiety, hesitancy, hesitation, inconclusiveness, indecision, irresolution, lack of confidence, misgiving, mystification, perplexity, puzzlement, qualm, quandary, scepticism, state of suspense, unpredictability, vagueness

Antonyms assurance, certainty, confidence, decision, predictability, resolution, sureness, trust

unchangeable changeless, constant, fixed, immovable, immutable, inevitable, invariable, irreversible, permanent, stable, steadfast, strong, unalterable
Antonyms changeable, inconstant, irregular, mutable, shifting, unstable, variable, wavering

unchanging abiding, changeless, constant, continuing, enduring, eternal, immutable, imperishable, lasting, permanent, perpetual, unchanged, unfading, unvarying

uncharitable cruel, hardhearted, insensitive, mean, merciless, stingy, unchristian, unfeeling, unforgiving, unfriendly, ungenerous, unkind, unsympathetic
Antonyms charitable, feeling, friendly, generous, kind, merciful, sensitive, sympathetic

uncharted not mapped, strange, undiscovered, unexplored, unfamiliar, unknown, unplumbed, virgin

unchaste depraved, dissolute, fallen, immodest, immoral, impure, lewd, loose, promiscuous, unvirtuous, wanton
Antonyms chaste, decent, innocent, modest, moral, pure, virtuous

uncivil bad-mannered, bearish, boorish, brusque, churlish, discourteous, disrespectful, gruff, ill-bred, ill-mannered, impolite, rude, surly, uncouth, unmannerly
Antonyms civil, courteous, mannerly, polished, polite, refined, respectful, well-bred, well-mannered

uncivilized 1. barbarian, barbaric, barbarous, illiterate, primitive, savage, wild 2. beyond the pale, boorish, brutish, churlish, coarse, gross, philistine, uncouth, uncultivated, uncultured, uneducated, unmannered, unpolished, unsophisticated, vulgar

unclad bare, buck naked (*Sl.*), in one's birthday suit (*Inf.*), in the altogether (*Inf.*), in the buff (*Inf.*), in the raw (*Inf.*), naked, naked as the day one was born (*Inf.*), nude, starkers (*Inf.*), stripped, unclothed, undressed, with nothing on, without a stitch on (*Inf.*)

unclean contaminated, corrupt, defiled, dirty, evil, filthy, foul, impure, nasty, polluted, scuzzy (*Sl., chiefly U.S.*), soiled, spotted, stained, sullied, tainted
Antonyms clean, faultless, flawless, pure, spotless, unblemished, unstained, unsullied

unclear ambiguous, bleary, blurred, confused, dim, doubtful, faint, fuzzy, hazy, ill-defined, indefinite, indeterminate, indiscernible, indistinct, indistinguishable, misty, muffled, obscure, out of focus, shadowy, undefined, unintelligible, vague, weak
Antonyms clear, defined, determinate, discernible, distinct, distinguishable, evident, intelligible

uncomfortable 1. awkward, causing discomfort, cramped, disagreeable, hard, ill-fitting, incommodious, irritating, painful, rough, troublesome 2. awkward, confused, discomfited, disquieted, distressed, disturbed, embarrassed, ill at ease, out of place, self-conscious, troubled, uneasy
Antonyms (*sense 2*) at ease, comfortable, easy, relaxed, serene, untroubled

uncommitted floating, free, free-floating, neutral, nonaligned, nonpartisan, not involved, (sitting) on the fence, unattached, uninvolved

uncommon 1. bizarre, curious, few and far between, infrequent, novel, odd, out of the ordinary, peculiar, queer, rare, scarce, singular, strange, unfamiliar, unusual 2. distinctive, exceptional, extraordinary, incomparable, inimitable, notable, noteworthy, outstanding, rare, remarkable, singular, special, superior, unparalleled, unprecedented
Antonyms (*sense 1*) common, familiar, frequent, regular, routine, usual (*sense 2*) average, banal, commonplace, everyday, humdrum, mundane, ordinary, run-of-the-mill

uncommonly 1. hardly ever, infrequently, not often, occasionally, only now and then, rarely, scarcely ever, seldom 2. exceptionally, extremely, particularly, peculiarly, remarkably, strangely, unusually, very

uncommunicative close, curt, guarded, reserved, reticent, retiring, secretive, short, shy, silent, taciturn, tight-lipped, unforthcoming, unresponsive, unsociable, withdrawn
Antonyms chatty, communicative, forthcoming, garrulous, loquacious, responsive, talkative, voluble

uncompromising decided, die-hard, firm, hard-line, inexorable, inflexible, intransigent, obdurate, obstinate, rigid, steadfast, stiff-necked, strict, stubborn, tough, unbending, unyielding

unconcern aloofness, apathy, detachment, indifference, insouciance, lack of interest, nonchalance, remoteness, uninterest, uninterestedness

unconcerned 1. aloof, apathetic, cool, detached, dispassionate, distant, incurious, indifferent, oblivious, uninterested, uninvolved, unmoved, unsympathetic 2. blithe, callous, carefree, careless, easy, insouciant, nonchalant, not bothered, relaxed, serene,

unperturbed, unruffled, untroubled, unworried
Antonyms (*sense 1*) avid, curious, eager, interested, involved (*sense 2*) agitated, anxious, concerned, distressed, perturbed, uneasy, worried

unconditional absolute, arrant, categorical, complete, downright, entire, explicit, full, out-and-out, outright, plenary, positive, thoroughgoing, total, unlimited, unqualified, unreserved, unrestricted, utter
Antonyms conditional, limited, partial, qualified, reserved, restricted

uncongenial antagonistic, antipathetic, disagreeable, discordant, displeasing, distasteful, incompatible, not one's cup of tea (*Inf.*), unharmonious, uninviting, unpleasant, unsuited, unsympathetic
Antonyms affable, agreeable, compatible, congenial, genial, harmonious, pleasant, pleasing, sympathetic

unconnected 1. detached, disconnected, divided, independent, separate 2. disconnected, disjointed, illogical, incoherent, irrelevant, meaningless, nonsensical, not related, unrelated
Antonyms (*sense 2*) coherent, connected, intelligible, logical, meaningful, related, relevant

unconquerable 1. indomitable, invincible, unbeatable, undefeatable, unyielding 2. enduring, ingrained, innate, insurmountable, inveterate, irrepressible, irresistible, overpowering

unconscionable 1. amoral, criminal, unethical, unfair, unjust, unprincipled, unscrupulous 2. excessive, exorbitant, extravagant, extreme, immoderate, inordinate, outrageous, preposterous, unreasonable

unconscious 1. blacked out (*Inf.*), comatose, dead to the world (*Inf.*), insensible, knocked out, numb, out, out cold, senseless, stunned 2. blind to, deaf to, heedless, ignorant, in ignorance, lost to, oblivious, unaware, unknowing, unmindful, unsuspecting 3. accidental, inadvertent, unintended, unintentional, unpremeditated, unwitting 4. automatic, gut (*Inf.*), inherent, innate, instinctive, involuntary, latent, reflex, repressed, subconscious, subliminal, suppressed, unrealized
Antonyms (*sense 1*) alert, awake, aware, conscious, responsive, sensible (*sense 3*) calculated, conscious, deliberate, intentional, planned, studied, wilful

uncontrollable beside oneself, carried away, frantic, furious, irrepressible, irresistible, like one possessed, mad, strong, ungovernable, unmanageable, unruly, violent, wild

uncontrolled boisterous, furious, lacking self-control, out of control, out of hand, rampant, riotous, running wild, unbridled, unchecked, uncurbed, undisciplined, ungoverned, unrestrained, unruly, unsubmissive, untrammelled, violent
Antonyms contained, controlled, disciplined, restrained, subdued, submissive

unconventional atypical, bizarre, bohemian, different, eccentric, far-out (*Sl.*), freakish, idiosyncratic, individual, individualistic, informal, irregular, nonconformist, odd, oddball (*Inf.*), offbeat, off-the-wall (*Sl.*), original, out of the ordinary, outré, uncustomary, unorthodox, unusual, wacko (*Sl.*), way-out (*Inf.*)
Antonyms conventional, normal, ordinary, orthodox, proper, regular, typical, usual

unconvincing dubious, feeble, fishy (*Inf.*), flimsy, hard to believe, implausible, improbable, inconclusive, lame, questionable, specious, suspect, thin, unlikely, unpersuasive, weak
Antonyms believable, conclusive, convincing, credible, likely, persuasive, plausible, probable

uncoordinated all thumbs, awkward, bumbling, bungling, butterfingered (*Inf.*), clodhopping (*Inf.*), clumsy, graceless, heavy-footed, inept, lumbering, maladroit, ungainly, ungraceful

uncounted countless, infinite, innumerable, legion, multitudinous, myriad, numberless, unnumbered, untold

uncouth awkward, barbaric, boorish, clownish, clumsy, coarse, crude, gawky, graceless, gross, ill-mannered, loutish, lubberly, oafish, rough, rude, rustic, uncivilized, uncultivated, ungainly, unrefined, unseemly, vulgar
Antonyms civilized, courteous, cultivated, elegant, graceful, refined, seemly, well-mannered

uncover 1. bare, lay open, lift the lid, open, show, strip, take the wraps off, unwrap 2. blow wide open (*Sl.*), bring to light, disclose, discover, divulge, expose, lay bare, make known, reveal, unearth, unmask
Antonyms clothe, conceal, cover, cover up, drape, dress, hide, keep under wraps, suppress

uncritical easily pleased, indiscriminate, undiscerning, undiscriminating, unexacting, unfussy, unperceptive, unselective, unthinking
Antonyms critical, discerning, discriminating, fastidious, fussy, perceptive, selective

unctuous 1. fawning, glib, gushing, ingratiating, insincere, obsequious, oily, plausible, slick, smarmy (*Brit. inf.*), smooth, suave, sycophantic 2. greasy, oily, oleaginous, slippery, slithery

undaunted bold, brave, courageous, dauntless, fearless, gallant, gritty, indomitable, intrepid, not discouraged, nothing daunted, not put off, resolute, steadfast, undeterred, undiscouraged, undismayed, unfaltering, unflinching, unshrinking

undeceive be honest with, correct, disabuse, disillusion, enlighten, open (someone's) eyes (to), put (someone) right, set (someone) straight, shatter (someone's) illusions

undecided 1. ambivalent, dithering (*Chiefly Brit.*), doubtful, dubious, hesitant, in two minds, irresolute, swithering (*Scot.*), torn, uncertain, uncommitted, unsure, wavering 2. debatable, iffy (*Inf.*), indefinite, in the balance, moot, open, pending, tentative, unconcluded, undetermined, unsettled, up in the air, vague
Antonyms certain, committed, decided, definite, determined, resolute, resolved, settled, sure

undecipherable crabbed, cryptic, hieroglyphic, illegible, impenetrable, incomprehensible, indecipherable, indistinct, undistinguishable, unreadable, unrecognizable

undefended defenceless, exposed, naked, open to attack, unarmed, unfortified, unguarded, unprotected, vulnerable, wide open
Antonyms armed, defended, fortified, guarded, protected

undefiled chaste, clean, clear, flawless, immaculate, impeccable, pure, sinless, spotless, squeaky-clean, unblemished, unsoiled, unspotted, unstained, unsullied, virginal
Antonyms blemished, defiled, flawed, impure, sinful, soiled, spotted, stained, sullied

undefined 1. formless, hazy, indefinite, indistinct, shadowy, tenuous, vague 2. imprecise, indeterminate, inexact, unclear, unexplained, unspecified
Antonyms (*sense 2*) clear, defined, definite, determinate, exact, explicit, precise, specified

undemonstrative aloof, cold, contained, distant, formal, impassive, reserved, restrained, reticent, stiff, stolid, unaffectionate, uncommunicative, unemotional, unresponsive, withdrawn
Antonyms affectionate, demonstrative, emotional, expressive, friendly, outgoing, overemotional, unreserved, warm

undeniable beyond (a) doubt, beyond question, certain, clear, evident, incontestable, incontrovertible, indisputable, indubitable, irrefutable, manifest, obvious, patent, proven, sound, sure, unassailable, undoubted, unquestionable
Antonyms debatable, deniable, doubtful, dubious, questionable, uncertain, unproven

undependable capricious, changeable, erratic, fickle, inconsistent, inconstant, irresponsible, treacherous, uncertain, unpredictable, unreliable, unstable, untrustworthy, variable

under *prep.* 1. below, beneath, on the bottom of, underneath 2. directed by, governed by, inferior to, junior to, reporting to, secondary to, subject to, subordinate to, subservient to 3. belonging to, comprised in, included in, subsumed under *~adv.* 4. below, beneath, down, downward, lower, to the bottom
Antonyms (*senses 1 & 4*) above, over, up, upper, upward

underclothes lingerie, smalls (*Inf.*), underclothing, undergarments, underlinen, underthings, underwear, undies (*Inf.*), unmentionables (*Humorous*)

undercover clandestine, concealed, confidential, covert, hidden, hush-hush (*Inf.*), intelligence, private, secret, spy, surreptitious, underground
Antonyms manifest, open, overt, plain, unconcealed, visible

undercurrent 1. crosscurrent, rip, rip current, riptide, tideway, underflow, undertow 2. atmosphere, aura, drift, feeling, flavour, hidden feeling, hint, murmur, overtone, sense, suggestion, tendency, tenor, tinge, trend, undertone, vibes (*Sl.*), vibrations

undercut 1. sacrifice, sell at a loss, sell cheaply, undercharge, underprice, undersell 2. cut away, cut out, excavate, gouge out, hollow out, mine, undermine

underdog fall guy (*Inf.*), little fellow (*Inf.*), loser, victim, weaker party

underestimate belittle, hold cheap, minimize, miscalculate, misprize, not do justice to, rate too low, sell short (*Inf.*), set no store by, think too little of, underrate, undervalue
Antonyms exaggerate, inflate, overdo, overestimate, overrate, overstate

undergo bear, be subjected to, endure, experience, go through, stand, submit to, suffer, sustain, weather, withstand

underground *adj.* 1. below ground, below the surface, buried, covered, subterranean

2. clandestine, concealed, covert, hidden, secret, surreptitious, undercover 3. alternative, avant-garde, experimental, radical, revolutionary, subversive ~*n.* **the underground** 4. the metro, the subway, the tube (*Brit.*) 5. partisans, the Maquis, the Resistance

undergrowth bracken, brambles, briars, brush, brushwood, scrub, underbrush, underbush, underwood

underhand clandestine, crafty, crooked (*Inf.*), deceitful, deceptive, devious, dishonest, dishonourable, fraudulent, furtive, secret, secretive, sly, sneaky, stealthy, surreptitious, treacherous, underhanded, unethical, unscrupulous
Antonyms above board, frank, honest, honourable, legal, open, outright, principled, scrupulous

underline 1. italicize, mark, rule a line under, underscore 2. accentuate, bring home, call *or* draw attention to, emphasize, give emphasis to, highlight, point up, stress
Antonyms (*sense 2*) gloss over, make light of, minimize, play down, soft-pedal (*Inf.*), underrate

underling flunky, hireling, inferior, lackey, menial, minion, nonentity, retainer, servant, slave, subordinate, understrapper

underlying 1. concealed, hidden, latent, lurking, veiled 2. basal, basic, elementary, essential, fundamental, intrinsic, primary, prime, radical, root

undermine 1. dig out, eat away at, erode, excavate, mine, tunnel, undercut, wear away 2. debilitate, disable, impair, sabotage, sap, subvert, threaten, weaken
Antonyms (*sense 2*) buttress, fortify, promote, reinforce, strengthen, sustain

underpinning 1. base, footing, foundation, groundwork, substructure, support 2. *Plural* backbone, basis, foundation, ground, support

underprivileged badly off, deprived, destitute, disadvantaged, impoverished, in need, in want, needy, poor

underrate belittle, discount, disparage, fail to appreciate, misprize, not do justice to, set (too) little store by, underestimate, undervalue
Antonyms exaggerate, overestimate, overprize, overrate, overvalue

undersell 1. cut, mark down, reduce, slash, undercharge, undercut 2. play down, understate

undersized atrophied, dwarfish, miniature, pygmy *or* pigmy, runtish, runty, small, squat, stunted, teensy-weensy, teeny-weeny, tiny, underdeveloped, underweight
Antonyms big, colossal, giant, huge, massive, oversized, overweight

understand 1. appreciate, apprehend, be aware, catch on (*Inf.*), comprehend, conceive, cotton on (*Inf.*), discern, fathom, follow, get, get the hang of (*Inf.*), get to the bottom of, grasp, know, make head or tail of (*Inf.*), make out, penetrate, perceive, realize, recognize, savvy (*Sl.*), see, take in, tumble to (*Inf.*), twig (*Brit. inf.*) 2. assume, be informed, believe, conclude, gather, hear, learn, presume, suppose, take it, think 3. accept, appreciate, be able to see, commiserate, show compassion for, sympathize with, tolerate

understanding *n.* 1. appreciation, awareness, comprehension, discernment, grasp, insight, intelligence, judgment, knowledge, penetration, perception, sense 2. belief, conclusion, estimation, idea, interpretation, judgment, notion, opinion, perception, view, viewpoint 3. accord, agreement, common view, gentlemen's agreement, meeting of minds, pact ~*adj.* 4. accepting, compassionate, considerate, discerning, forbearing, forgiving, kind, kindly, patient, perceptive, responsive, sensitive, sympathetic, tolerant
Antonyms *n.* (*sense 1*) ignorance, incomprehension, insensitivity, misapprehension, misunderstanding, obtuseness (*sense 3*) aloofness, coldness, disagreement, dispute ~*adj.* inconsiderate, insensitive, intolerant, obtuse, rigid, strict, unfeeling, unsympathetic

understood 1. implicit, implied, inferred, tacit, unspoken, unstated 2. accepted, assumed, axiomatic, presumed, taken for granted

understudy *n.* double, fill-in, replacement, reserve, stand-in, sub, substitute

undertake 1. agree, bargain, commit oneself, contract, covenant, engage, guarantee, pledge, promise, stipulate, take upon oneself 2. attempt, begin, commence, embark on, endeavour, enter upon, set about, tackle, take on, try

undertaker funeral director, mortician (*U.S.*)

undertaking 1. affair, attempt, business, effort, endeavour, enterprise, game, operation, project, task, venture 2. assurance, commitment, pledge, promise, solemn word, vow, word, word of honour

undertone 1. low tone, murmur, subdued voice, whisper 2. atmosphere, feeling, flavour, hint, suggestion, tinge, touch, trace, undercurrent, vibes (*Sl.*)

undervalue depreciate, hold cheap, look down on, make light of, minimize, mis-

judge, misprize, set no store by, underestimate, underrate
Antonyms exaggerate, overestimate, overrate, overvalue

underwater submarine, submerged, sunken, undersea

under way afoot, begun, going on, in motion, in operation, in progress, started

underwear lingerie, smalls (*Inf.*), underclothes, underclothing, undergarments, underlinen, underthings, undies (*Inf.*), unmentionables (*Humorous*)

underweight emaciated, half-starved, puny, skin and bone (*Inf.*), skinny, undernourished, undersized

underworld 1. criminal element, criminals, gangland (*Inf.*), gangsters, organized crime 2. abode of the dead, Hades, hell, infernal region, nether regions, nether world, the inferno

underwrite 1. back, finance, fund, guarantee, insure, provide security, sponsor, subsidize 2. countersign, endorse, initial, sign, subscribe 3. agree to, approve, consent, O.K. *or* okay (*Inf.*), sanction

undesigned accidental, fortuitous, inadvertent, not meant, unintended, unintentional, unpremeditated

undesirable disagreeable, disliked, distasteful, dreaded, objectionable, obnoxious, offensive, out of place, repugnant, (to be) avoided, unacceptable, unattractive, unpleasing, unpopular, unsavoury, unsuitable, unwanted, unwelcome, unwished-for
Antonyms acceptable, agreeable, appealing, attractive, desirable, inviting, pleasing, popular, welcome

undeveloped embryonic, immature, inchoate, in embryo, latent, potential, primordial (*Biol.*)

undignified beneath one, beneath one's dignity, improper, inappropriate, indecorous, inelegant, infra dig (*Inf.*), lacking dignity, unbecoming, ungentlemanly, unladylike, unrefined, unseemly, unsuitable
Antonyms appropriate, becoming, decorous, dignified, elegant, proper, refined, seemly, suitable

undisciplined disobedient, erratic, fitful, obstreperous, uncontrolled, unpredictable, unreliable, unrestrained, unruly, unschooled, unsteady, unsystematic, untrained, wayward, wild, wilful
Antonyms controlled, disciplined, obedient, predictable, reliable, restrained, steady, trained

undisguised blatant, complete, evident, explicit, genuine, manifest, obvious, open, out-and-out, overt, patent, thoroughgoing, transparent, unconcealed, unfeigned, unmistakable, utter, wholehearted
Antonyms concealed, covert, disguised, feigned, hidden, secret

undisputed accepted, acknowledged, beyond question, certain, conclusive, freely admitted, incontestable, incontrovertible, indisputable, irrefutable, not disputed, recognized, sure, unchallenged, uncontested, undeniable, undoubted, unquestioned
Antonyms deniable, disputed, doubtful, dubious, inconclusive, questioned, uncertain

undistinguished commonplace, everyday, indifferent, mediocre, no great shakes (*Inf.*), nothing to write home about (*Inf.*), ordinary, pedestrian, prosaic, run-of-the-mill, so-so (*Inf.*), unexceptional, unexciting, unimpressive, unremarkable
Antonyms distinguished, exceptional, exciting, extraordinary, impressive, notable, outstanding, remarkable, striking

undisturbed 1. not moved, quiet, uninterrupted, untouched, without interruption 2. calm, collected, composed, equable, even, motionless, placid, sedate, serene, tranquil, unagitated, unbothered, unfazed (*Inf.*), unperturbed, unruffled, untroubled
Antonyms (*sense 1*) confused, disordered, interfered with, interrupted, moved, muddled (*sense 2*) agitated, bothered, busy, disturbed, excited, flustered, nervous, perturbed, troubled, upset

undivided combined, complete, concentrated, concerted, entire, exclusive, full, solid, thorough, unanimous, undistracted, united, whole, wholehearted

undo 1. disengage, disentangle, loose, loosen, open, unbutton, unfasten, unlock, untie, unwrap 2. annul, cancel, invalidate, neutralize, nullify, offset, reverse, wipe out 3. bring to naught, defeat, destroy, impoverish, invalidate, mar, overturn, quash, ruin, shatter, subvert, undermine, upset, wreck

undoing 1. collapse, defeat, destruction, disgrace, downfall, humiliation, overthrow, overturn, reversal, ruin, ruination, shame 2. affliction, blight, curse, fatal flaw, misfortune, the last straw, trial, trouble, weakness

undone[1] incomplete, left, neglected, not completed, not done, omitted, outstanding, passed over, unattended to, unfinished, unfulfilled, unperformed
Antonyms accomplished, attended to, complete, done, finished, fulfilled, performed

undone[2] betrayed, destroyed, forlorn, hapless, overcome, prostrate, ruined, wretched

undoubted acknowledged, certain, definite, evident, incontrovertible, indisputable, indubitable, obvious, sure, undisputed, unquestionable, unquestioned

undoubtedly assuredly, beyond a shadow of (a) doubt, beyond question, certainly, definitely, doubtless, of course, surely, undeniably, unmistakably, unquestionably, without doubt

undreamed of astonishing, inconceivable, incredible, miraculous, undreamt, unexpected, unforeseen, unheard-of, unimagined, unsuspected, unthought-of

undress 1. *v.* disrobe, divest oneself of, peel off (*Sl.*), shed, strip, take off one's clothes 2. *n.* disarray, dishabille, nakedness, nudity

undue disproportionate, excessive, extravagant, extreme, immoderate, improper, inordinate, intemperate, needless, overmuch, too great, too much, uncalled-for, undeserved, unnecessary, unseemly, unwarranted
Antonyms appropriate, due, fitting, justified, necessary, proper, suitable, well-considered

undulate billow, heave, ripple, rise and fall, roll, surge, swell, wave

unduly disproportionately, excessively, extravagantly, immoderately, improperly, inordinately, out of all proportion, overly, overmuch, unjustifiably, unnecessarily, unreasonably
Antonyms duly, justifiably, moderately, ordinately, properly, proportionately, reasonably

undying constant, continuing, deathless, eternal, everlasting, immortal, imperishable, indestructible, inextinguishable, infinite, perennial, permanent, perpetual, sempiternal (*Literary*), undiminished, unending, unfading
Antonyms ephemeral, finite, fleeting, impermanent, inconstant, momentary, mortal, perishable, short-lived

unearth 1. dig up, disinter, dredge up, excavate, exhume 2. bring to light, discover, expose, ferret out, find, reveal, root up, turn up, uncover

unearthly 1. eerie, eldritch (*Poetic*), ghostly, haunted, nightmarish, phantom, spectral, spooky (*Inf.*), strange, uncanny, weird 2. ethereal, heavenly, not of this world, preternatural, sublime, supernatural 3. abnormal, absurd, extraordinary, ridiculous, strange, ungodly (*Inf.*), unholy (*Inf.*), unreasonable

uneasiness agitation, alarm, anxiety, apprehension, apprehensiveness, disquiet, doubt, dubiety, misgiving, nervousness, perturbation, qualms, suspicion, trepidation, worry
Antonyms calm, composure, cool, ease, peace, quiet, serenity

uneasy 1. agitated, anxious, apprehensive, discomposed, disturbed, edgy, ill at ease, impatient, jittery (*Inf.*), nervous, on edge, perturbed, restive, restless, troubled, twitchy (*Inf.*), uncomfortable, unsettled, upset, wired (*Sl.*), worried 2. awkward, constrained, insecure, precarious, shaky, strained, tense, uncomfortable, unstable 3. bothering, dismaying, disquieting, disturbing, troubling, upsetting, worrying
Antonyms at ease, calm, comfortable, relaxed, tranquil, unfazed (*Inf.*), unflustered, unperturbed, unruffled

uneconomic loss-making, nonpaying, non-profit-making, nonviable, unprofitable
Antonyms economic, money-making, productive, profitable, remunerative, viable

uneducated 1. ignorant, illiterate, unlettered, unread, unschooled, untaught 2. benighted, lowbrow, uncultivated, uncultured
Antonyms (*sense 1*) educated, informed, instructed, literate, schooled, taught, tutored

unembellished austere, bald, bare, functional, modest, plain, severe, simple, spartan, stark, unadorned, unornamented, unvarnished

unemotional apathetic, cold, cool, impassive, indifferent, listless, passionless, phlegmatic, reserved, undemonstrative, unexcitable, unfeeling, unimpressionable, unresponsive
Antonyms demonstrative, emotional, excitable, feeling, passionate, responsive, sensitive

unemployed idle, jobless, laid off, on the dole (*Brit. inf.*), out of a job, out of work, redundant, resting (*of an actor*), workless

unending ceaseless, constant, continual, endless, eternal, everlasting, incessant, interminable, never-ending, perpetual, unceasing, unremitting

unendurable insufferable, insupportable, intolerable, more than flesh and blood can stand, unbearable
Antonyms bearable, endurable, sufferable, supportable, tolerable

unenthusiastic apathetic, blasé, bored, half-arsed, half-assed (*U.S. & Canad. sl.*), half-hearted, indifferent, lukewarm, neutral, nonchalant, unimpressed, uninterested, unmoved, unresponsive
Antonyms ardent, eager, enthusiastic, excited, interested, keen, passionate

unenviable disagreeable, painful, thank-

less, uncomfortable, undesirable, unpleasant
Antonyms agreeable, attractive, desirable, enviable, pleasant

unequal 1. different, differing, disparate, dissimilar, not uniform, unlike, unmatched, variable, varying 2. *With* **to** found wanting, inadequate, insufficient, not up to 3. asymmetrical, disproportionate, ill-matched, irregular, unbalanced, uneven
Antonyms (*sense 1*) equal, equivalent, identical, like, matched, similar, uniform

unequalled beyond compare, incomparable, inimitable, matchless, nonpareil, paramount, peerless, pre-eminent, second to none, supreme, transcendent, unmatched, unparalleled, unrivalled, unsurpassed, without equal

unequivocal absolute, certain, clear, clear-cut, decisive, definite, direct, evident, explicit, incontrovertible, indubitable, manifest, plain, positive, straight, unambiguous, uncontestable, unmistakable
Antonyms ambiguous, doubtful, equivocal, evasive, indecisive, noncommittal, vague

unerring accurate, certain, exact, faultless, impeccable, infallible, perfect, sure, unfailing

unethical dirty, dishonest, dishonourable, disreputable, illegal, immoral, improper, shady (*Inf.*), underhand, under-the-table, unfair, unprincipled, unprofessional, unscrupulous, wrong
Antonyms ethical, honest, honourable, legal, moral, proper, scrupulous, upright

uneven 1. bumpy, not flat, not level, not smooth, rough 2. broken, changeable, fitful, fluctuating, intermittent, irregular, jerky, patchy, spasmodic, unsteady, variable 3. asymmetrical, lopsided, not parallel, odd, out of true, unbalanced 4. disparate, ill-matched, one-sided, unequal, unfair
Antonyms (*sense 1*) even, flat, level, plane, smooth

uneventful boring, commonplace, dull, ho-hum (*Inf.*), humdrum, monotonous, ordinary, quiet, routine, tedious, unexceptional, unexciting, uninteresting, unmemorable, unremarkable, unvaried
Antonyms eventful, exceptional, exciting, interesting, memorable, momentous, remarkable

unexampled unequalled, unheard-of, unique, unmatched, unparalleled, unprecedented

unexceptional common or garden (*Inf.*), commonplace, conventional, insignificant, mediocre, normal, ordinary, pedestrian, run-of-the-mill, undistinguished, unimpressive, unremarkable, usual
Antonyms distinguished, exceptional, impressive, notable, noteworthy, outstanding, remarkable, significant, unusual

unexpected abrupt, accidental, astonishing, chance, fortuitous, not bargained for, out of the blue, startling, sudden, surprising, unanticipated, unforeseen, unlooked-for, unpredictable
Antonyms anticipated, awaited, expected, foreseen, normal, planned, predictable

unexpressive blank, emotionless, expressionless, impassive, inexpressive, inscrutable, vacant

unfailing 1. bottomless, boundless, ceaseless, continual, continuous, endless, inexhaustible, never-failing, persistent, unflagging, unlimited 2. certain, constant, dependable, faithful, infallible, loyal, reliable, staunch, steadfast, sure, tried and true, true
Antonyms (*sense 2*) disloyal, fallible, inconstant, uncertain, unfaithful, unreliable, unsure, untrustworthy

unfair 1. arbitrary, biased, bigoted, discriminatory, inequitable, one-sided, partial, partisan, prejudiced, unjust 2. crooked (*Inf.*), dishonest, dishonourable, uncalled-for, unethical, unprincipled, unscrupulous, unsporting, unwarranted, wrongful
Antonyms (*sense 2*) ethical, fair, honest, just, principled, scrupulous

unfaithful 1. deceitful, disloyal, faithless, false, false-hearted, perfidious, recreant (*Archaic*), traitorous, treacherous, treasonable, unreliable, untrustworthy 2. adulterous, faithless, fickle, inconstant, two-timing (*Inf.*), unchaste, untrue 3. distorted, erroneous, imperfect, imprecise, inaccurate, inexact, unreliable, untrustworthy
Antonyms (*sense 1*) constant, faithful, loyal, steadfast, true, trustworthy (*sense 3*) accurate, exact, perfect, precise, reliable

unfaltering firm, indefatigable, persevering, resolute, steadfast, steady, tireless, unfailing, unflagging, unflinching, unswerving, untiring, unwavering

unfamiliar 1. alien, curious, different, little known, new, novel, out-of-the-way, strange, unaccustomed, uncommon, unknown, unusual 2. *With* **with** a stranger to, inexperienced in, unaccustomed to, unacquainted, unconversant, uninformed about, uninitiated in, unpractised in, unskilled at, unversed in
Antonyms accustomed, acquainted, average, common, commonplace, conversant, everyday, experienced, familiar, knowl-

edgeable, normal, unexceptional, well-known, well-versed

unfashionable antiquated, behind the times, dated, obsolete, old-fashioned, old hat, out, outmoded, out of date, out of fashion, passé, square (*Inf.*), unpopular
Antonyms à la mode, fashionable, modern, popular, stylish, trendy (*Brit. inf.*)

unfasten detach, disconnect, let go, loosen, open, separate, uncouple, undo, unlace, unlock, untie

unfathomable 1. bottomless, immeasurable, unmeasured, unplumbed, unsounded 2. abstruse, baffling, deep, esoteric, impenetrable, incomprehensible, indecipherable, inexplicable, profound, unknowable

unfavourable 1. adverse, bad, contrary, disadvantageous, hostile, ill-suited, infelicitous, inimical, low, negative, poor, unfortunate, unfriendly, unsuited 2. inauspicious, inopportune, ominous, threatening, unlucky, unpromising, unpropitious, unseasonable, untimely, untoward
Antonyms (*sense 1*) amicable, approving, favourable, friendly, positive, warm, well-disposed

unfeeling 1. apathetic, callous, cold, cruel, hardened, hardhearted, heartless, inhuman, insensitive, pitiless, stony, uncaring, unsympathetic 2. insensate, insensible, numb, sensationless
Antonyms (*sense 1*) benevolent, caring, concerned, feeling, gentle, humane, kind, sensitive, sympathetic

unfeigned genuine, heartfelt, natural, pure, real, sincere, unaffected, unforced, wholehearted

unfettered free, unbridled, unchecked, unconfined, unconstrained, unrestrained, unshackled, untrammelled

unfinished 1. deficient, half-done, imperfect, incomplete, in the making, lacking, unaccomplished, uncompleted, undone, unfulfilled, wanting 2. bare, crude, natural, raw, rough, sketchy, unpolished, unrefined, unvarnished
Antonyms (*sense 2*) finished, flawless, perfected, polished, refined, smooth, varnished

unfit 1. ill-equipped, inadequate, incapable, incompetent, ineligible, no good, not cut out for, not equal to, not up to, unprepared, unqualified, untrained, useless 2. ill-adapted, inadequate, inappropriate, ineffective, not designed, not fit, unsuitable, unsuited, useless 3. debilitated, decrepit, feeble, flabby, in poor condition, out of kelter, out of shape, out of trim, unhealthy
Antonyms (*senses 1 & 2*) able, acceptable, capable, competent, equipped, qualified, ready, suitable (*sense 3*) fit, healthy, in good condition, strong, sturdy, well

unflagging constant, fixed, indefatigable, persevering, persistent, staunch, steady, tireless, unceasing, undeviating, unfailing, unfaltering, unremitting, untiring, unwearied

unflappable calm, collected, composed, cool, impassive, imperturbable, level-headed, not given to worry, self-possessed, unfazed (*Inf.*), unruffled
Antonyms excitable, flappable, hot-headed, nervous, temperamental, twitchy (*Inf.*), volatile

unflattering 1. blunt, candid, critical, honest, uncomplimentary, warts and all 2. not shown in the best light, not shown to advantage, plain, unattractive, unbecoming, unprepossessing

unfledged callow, green, immature, inexperienced, raw, undeveloped, untried, young

unflinching bold, constant, determined, firm, immovable, resolute, stalwart, staunch, steadfast, steady, unfaltering, unshaken, unshrinking, unswerving, unwavering
Antonyms cowed, faltering, scared, shaken, shrinking, wavering

unfold 1. disentangle, expand, flatten, open, spread out, straighten, stretch out, undo, unfurl, unravel, unroll, unwrap 2. *Fig.* clarify, describe, disclose, divulge, explain, illustrate, make known, present, reveal, show, uncover 3. bear fruit, blossom, develop, evolve, expand, grow, mature

unforeseen abrupt, accidental, out of the blue, startling, sudden, surprise, surprising, unanticipated, unexpected, unlooked-for, unpredicted
Antonyms anticipated, envisaged, expected, foreseen, intended, predicted

unforgettable exceptional, extraordinary, fixed in the mind, impressive, memorable, never to be forgotten, notable, striking

unforgivable deplorable, disgraceful, indefensible, inexcusable, shameful, unjustifiable, unpardonable, unwarrantable
Antonyms allowable, excusable, forgivable, justifiable, pardonable, venial

unfortunate 1. adverse, calamitous, disastrous, ill-fated, ill-starred, inopportune, ruinous, unfavourable, untoward 2. cursed, doomed, hapless, hopeless, luckless, out of luck, poor, star-crossed, unhappy, unlucky, unprosperous, unsuccessful, wretched 3. deplorable, ill-advised, inappropriate, infelicitous, lamentable, regrettable, unbecoming, unsuitable
Antonyms (*senses 1 & 3*) appropriate, op-

portune, suitable, tactful, timely (*sense 2*) auspicious, felicitous, fortuitous, fortunate, happy, lucky, successful

unfounded baseless, fabricated, false, groundless, idle, spurious, trumped up, unjustified, unproven, unsubstantiated, vain, without basis, without foundation
Antonyms attested, confirmed, factual, justified, proven, substantiated, verified

unfrequented deserted, godforsaken, isolated, lone, lonely, off the beaten track, remote, sequestered, solitary, uninhabited, unvisited

unfriendly 1. aloof, antagonistic, chilly, cold, disagreeable, distant, hostile, ill-disposed, inhospitable, not on speaking terms, quarrelsome, sour, surly, uncongenial, unneighbourly, unsociable 2. alien, hostile, inauspicious, inhospitable, inimical, unfavourable, unpropitious
Antonyms affable, amiable, auspicious, congenial, convivial, friendly, hospitable, propitious, sociable, warm

unfruitful barren, fruitless, infecund, infertile, sterile, unproductive, unprofitable, unprolific, unrewarding
Antonyms abundant, fecund, fertile, fruitful, productive, profuse, prolific, rewarding

ungainly awkward, clumsy, gangling, gawky, inelegant, loutish, lubberly, lumbering, slouching, uncoordinated, uncouth, ungraceful
Antonyms attractive, comely, elegant, graceful, pleasing

ungodly 1. blasphemous, corrupt, depraved, godless, immoral, impious, irreligious, profane, sinful, vile, wicked 2. *Inf.* dreadful, horrendous, intolerable, outrageous, unearthly, unholy (*Inf.*), unreasonable, unseemly

ungovernable rebellious, refractory, uncontrollable, unmanageable, unrestrainable, unruly, wild

ungracious bad-mannered, churlish, discourteous, ill-bred, impolite, offhand, rude, uncivil, unmannerly
Antonyms affable, civil, courteous, gracious, mannerly, polite, well-mannered

ungrateful heedless, ingrate (*Archaic*), selfish, thankless, unappreciative, unmindful, unthankful
Antonyms appreciative, aware, grateful, mindful, thankful

unguarded 1. careless, foolhardy, heedless, ill-considered, impolitic, imprudent, incautious, indiscreet, rash, thoughtless, uncircumspect, undiplomatic, unthinking, unwary 2. defenceless, open to attack, undefended, unpatrolled, unprotected, vulnerable 3. artless, candid, direct, frank, guileless, open, straightforward
Antonyms (*sense 1*) cagey (*Inf.*), careful, cautious, diplomatic, discreet, guarded, prudent, wary

unhallowed 1. not sacred, unblessed, unconsecrated, unholy, unsanctified 2. damnable, evil, godless, irreverent, profane, sinful, wicked

unhandy 1. awkward, bumbling, bungling, clumsy, fumbling, heavy-handed, incompetent, inept, inexpert, maladroit, unskilful 2. awkward, cumbersome, hampering, ill-arranged, ill-contrived, inconvenient, unwieldy

unhappy 1. blue, crestfallen, dejected, depressed, despondent, disconsolate, dispirited, down, downcast, gloomy, long-faced, melancholy, miserable, mournful, sad, sorrowful 2. cursed, hapless, ill-fated, ill-omened, luckless, unfortunate, unlucky, wretched 3. awkward, clumsy, gauche, ill-advised, ill-timed, inappropriate, inept, infelicitous, injudicious, malapropos, tactless, unsuitable, untactful
Antonyms (*sense 1*) cheerful, chirpy (*Inf.*), content, exuberant genial good-humoured, happy, joyful, light-hearted, overjoyed, over the moon (*Inf.*), satisfied (*senses 2 & 3*) apt, becoming, fortunate, lucky, prudent, suitable, tactful

unharmed in one piece (*Inf.*), intact, safe, safe and sound, sound, undamaged, unhurt, uninjured, unscarred, unscathed, untouched, whole, without a scratch
Antonyms damaged, harmed, hurt, impaired, injured, scarred, scathed

unhealthy 1. ailing, delicate, feeble, frail, infirm, in poor health, invalid, poorly (*Inf.*), sick, sickly, unsound, unwell, weak 2. deleterious, detrimental, harmful, insalubrious, insanitary, noisome, noxious, unwholesome 3. bad, baneful (*Archaic*), corrupt, corrupting, degrading, demoralizing, morbid, negative, undesirable
Antonyms (*senses 1 & 2*) beneficial, fit, good, healthy, robust, salubrious, salutary, well, wholesome (*sense 3*) desirable, moral, positive

unheard-of 1. little known, obscure, undiscovered, unfamiliar, unknown, unregarded, unremarked, unsung 2. inconceivable, never before encountered, new, novel, singular, unbelievable, undreamed of, unexampled, unique, unprecedented, unusual 3. disgraceful, extreme, offensive, outlandish, outrageous, preposterous, shocking, unacceptable, unthinkable

unheeded disobeyed, disregarded, forgot-

ten, ignored, neglected, overlooked, unfollowed, unnoticed, unobserved, untaken
Antonyms heeded, noted, noticed, obeyed, observed, regarded, remembered

unheralded out of the blue, surprise, unacclaimed, unannounced, unexpected, unforeseen, unnoticed, unproclaimed, unpublicized, unrecognized, unsung

unhesitating 1. implicit, resolute, steadfast, unfaltering, unquestioning, unreserved, unswerving, unwavering, wholehearted 2. immediate, instant, instantaneous, prompt, ready, without delay
Antonyms (*sense 1*) diffident, hesitant, irresolute, questioning, tentative, uncertain, unsure, wavering

unhinge 1. confound, confuse, craze, derange, disorder, distemper (*Archaic*), drive out of one's mind, madden, unbalance, unsettle 2. detach, disconnect, disjoint, dislodge, remove

unholy 1. base, corrupt, depraved, dishonest, evil, heinous, immoral, iniquitous, irreligious, profane, sinful, ungodly, vile, wicked 2. *Inf.* appalling, awful, dreadful, horrendous, outrageous, shocking, unearthly, ungodly (*Inf.*), unnatural, unreasonable
Antonyms (*sense 1*) devout, faithful, godly, holy, pious, religious, saintly, virtuous

unhoped-for beyond one's wildest dreams, incredible, like a dream come true, out of the blue, surprising, unanticipated, unbelievable, undreamed of, unexpected, unimaginable, unlooked-for

unhurried calm, deliberate, easy, easy-going, leisurely, sedate, slow, slow and steady, slow-paced
Antonyms brief, cursory, hasty, hectic, hurried, quick, rushed, speedy, swift

unidentified anonymous, mysterious, nameless, unclassified, unfamiliar, unknown, unmarked, unnamed, unrecognized, unrevealed
Antonyms classified, familiar, identified, known, marked, named, recognized

unification alliance, amalgamation, coalescence, coalition, combination, confederation, federation, fusion, merger, union, uniting

uniform *n.* 1. costume, dress, garb, habit, livery, outfit, regalia, regimentals, suit *~adj.* 2. consistent, constant, equable, even, regular, smooth, unbroken, unchanging, undeviating, unvarying 3. alike, equal, identical, like, same, selfsame, similar
Antonyms *adj.* (*sense 2*) changeable, changing, deviating, inconsistent, irregular, uneven, variable

uniformity 1. constancy, evenness, homogeneity, invariability, regularity, sameness, similarity 2. drabness, dullness, flatness, lack of diversity, monotony, sameness, tedium

unify amalgamate, bind, bring together, combine, confederate, consolidate, federate, fuse, join, merge, unite
Antonyms alienate, disconnect, disjoin, disunite, divide, separate, sever, split

unimaginable beyond one's wildest dreams, fantastic, impossible, inconceivable, incredible, indescribable, ineffable, mind-boggling (*Inf.*), unbelievable, unheard-of, unthinkable

unimaginative banal, barren, commonplace, derivative, dry, dull, hackneyed, lifeless, matter-of-fact, ordinary, pedestrian, predictable, prosaic, routine, tame, uncreative, uninspired, unoriginal, unromantic, usual
Antonyms creative, different, exciting, fresh, ground-breaking, imaginative, innovative, inventive, original, unhackneyed, unusual

unimpassioned calm, collected, composed, controlled, cool, dispassionate, impassive, moderate, rational, sedate, temperate, tranquil, undemonstrative, unemotional, unmoved

unimpeachable above reproach, beyond criticism, beyond question, blameless, faultless, impeccable, irreproachable, perfect, unassailable, unblemished, unchallengeable, unexceptionable, unquestionable
Antonyms blameworthy, faulty, imperfect, reprehensible, reproachable, shameful

unimpeded free, open, unblocked, unchecked, unconstrained, unhampered, unhindered, unrestrained, untrammelled
Antonyms blocked, checked, constrained, hampered, hindered, impeded, restrained

unimportant immaterial, inconsequential, insignificant, irrelevant, low-ranking, minor, nickel-and-dime (*U.S. sl.*), not worth mentioning, nugatory, of no account, of no consequence, of no moment, paltry, petty, slight, trifling, trivial, worthless
Antonyms essential, grave, important, major, significant, urgent, vital, weighty

uninhabited abandoned, barren, desert, deserted, desolate, empty, unoccupied, unpopulated, unsettled, untenanted, vacant, waste

uninhibited 1. candid, frank, free, free and easy, informal, instinctive, liberated, natural, open, relaxed, spontaneous, unrepressed, unreserved, unselfconscious 2. free, unbridled, unchecked, unconstrained,

uncontrolled, uncurbed, unrestrained, unrestricted
Antonyms bashful, careful, checked, constrained, controlled, curbed, demure, hampered, inhibited, modest, restrained, self-conscious, shy, uptight (*Inf.*)

uninspired banal, commonplace, dull, humdrum, indifferent, ordinary, prosaic, stale, stock, unexciting, unimaginative, uninspiring, uninteresting, unoriginal
Antonyms brilliant, different, exciting, imaginative, inspired, interesting, original, outstanding

unintelligent braindead (*Inf.*), brainless, dense, dozy (*Brit. inf.*), dull, empty-headed, foolish, gormless (*Brit. inf.*), obtuse, slow, stupid, thick, unreasoning, unthinking
Antonyms bright, clever, intelligent, sharp, smart, thinking

unintelligible double Dutch (*Brit. inf.*), illegible, inarticulate, incoherent, incomprehensible, indecipherable, indistinct, jumbled, meaningless, muddled, unfathomable
Antonyms clear, coherent, comprehensible, intelligible, legible, lucid, understandable

unintentional accidental, casual, fortuitous, inadvertent, involuntary, unconscious, undesigned, unintended, unpremeditated, unthinking, unwitting
Antonyms conscious, deliberate, designed, intended, intentional, premeditated, voluntary, wilful

uninterested apathetic, blasé, bored, distant, impassive, incurious, indifferent, listless, unconcerned, uninvolved, unresponsive
Antonyms alert, concerned, curious, enthusiastic, interested, involved, keen, responsive

uninteresting boring, commonplace, drab, dreary, dry, dull, flat, ho-hum (*Inf.*), humdrum, mind-numbing, monotonous, tedious, tiresome, unenjoyable, uneventful, unexciting, uninspiring, wearisome
Antonyms absorbing, compelling, enjoyable, exciting, gripping, inspiring, interesting, intriguing, stimulating

uninterrupted constant, continual, continuous, nonstop, peaceful, steady, sustained, unbroken, undisturbed, unending

uninvited not asked, not invited, unasked, unbidden, unwanted, unwelcome

uninviting disagreeable, offensive, off-putting (*Brit. inf.*), repellent, repulsive, unappealing, unappetizing, unattractive, undesirable, unpleasant, untempting, unwelcoming
Antonyms agreeable, appealing, appetizing, attractive, desirable, inviting, pleasant, tempting, welcoming

union 1. amalgam, amalgamation, blend, combination, conjunction, fusion, junction, mixture, synthesis, uniting 2. alliance, association, Bund, coalition, confederacy, confederation, federation, league 3. accord, agreement, concord, concurrence, harmony, unanimity, unison, unity 4. coition, coitus, copulation, coupling, intercourse, marriage, matrimony, nookie (*Sl.*), rumpy-pumpy (*Sl.*), the other (*Inf.*), wedlock

unique 1. lone, one and only, only, single, solitary, sui generis 2. incomparable, inimitable, matchless, nonpareil, peerless, unequalled, unexampled, unmatched, unparalleled, unrivalled, without equal

unison accord, accordance, agreement, concert, concord, cooperation, harmony, unanimity, unity
Antonyms disagreement, discord, disharmony, dissension, dissidence, dissonance

unit 1. assembly, detachment, entity, group, section, system, whole 2. component, constituent, element, item, member, module, part, piece, portion, section, segment 3. measure, measurement, module, quantity

unite 1. amalgamate, blend, coalesce, combine, confederate, consolidate, couple, fuse, incorporate, join, link, marry, meld, merge, unify, wed 2. ally, associate, band, close ranks, club together, cooperate, join forces, join together, league, pool, pull together
Antonyms break, detach, disunite, divide, divorce, part, separate, sever, split

united 1. affiliated, allied, banded together, collective, combined, concerted, in partnership, leagued, pooled, unified 2. agreed, in accord, in agreement, like-minded, of like mind, of one mind, of the same opinion, one, unanimous

unity 1. entity, integrity, oneness, singleness, undividedness, unification, union, wholeness 2. accord, agreement, assent, concord, concurrence, consensus, harmony, peace, solidarity, unanimity, unison
Antonyms disagreement, discord, disunity, division, factionalism, heterogeneity, ill will, independence, individuality, infighting, multiplicity, separation, strife

universal all-embracing, catholic, common, ecumenical, entire, general, omnipresent, total, unlimited, whole, widespread, worldwide

universality all-inclusiveness, completeness, comprehensiveness, entirety, generality, generalization, totality, ubiquity

universally always, everywhere, in all cases, in every instance, invariably, uniformly, without exception

universe cosmos, creation, everything, macrocosm, nature, the natural world

unjust biased, inequitable, one-sided, partial, partisan, prejudiced, undeserved, unfair, unjustified, unmerited, wrong, wrongful
Antonyms equitable, ethical, fair, impartial, just, justified, right, unbiased

unjustifiable indefensible, inexcusable, outrageous, unacceptable, unforgivable, unjust, unpardonable, unwarrantable, wrong

unkempt bedraggled, blowzy, disarranged, disarrayed, dishevelled, disordered, frowzy, messy, rumpled, scruffy, shabby, shaggy, slatternly, sloppy (*Inf.*), slovenly, sluttish, tousled, uncombed, ungroomed, untidy
Antonyms neat, presentable, soigné *or* soignée, spruce, tidy, trim, well-groomed

unkind cruel, hardhearted, harsh, inconsiderate, inhuman, insensitive, malicious, mean, nasty, spiteful, thoughtless, uncaring, uncharitable, unchristian, unfeeling, unfriendly, unsympathetic
Antonyms benevolent, caring, charitable, considerate, generous, kind, soft-hearted, sympathetic, thoughtful

unknown 1. alien, concealed, dark, hidden, mysterious, new, secret, strange, unrecognized, unrevealed, untold 2. anonymous, nameless, uncharted, undiscovered, unexplored, unidentified, unnamed 3. humble, little known, obscure, undistinguished, unfamiliar, unheard-of, unrenowned, unsung
Antonyms (*sense 3*) celebrated, distinguished, familiar, known, recognized, renowned, well-known

unladylike coarse, ill-bred, impolite, indelicate, rude, uncivil, ungracious, unmannerly, unrefined
Antonyms civil, delicate, gracious, ladylike, mannerly, polite, refined, seemly

unlamented unbemoaned, unbewailed, undeplored, unmissed, unmourned, unregretted, unwept

unlawful actionable, against the law, banned, criminal, forbidden, illegal, illegitimate, illicit, outlawed, prohibited, unauthorized, under-the-table, unlicensed

unleash free, let go, let loose, release, unbridle, unloose, untie

unlettered ignorant, illiterate, uneducated, unlearned, unschooled, untaught, untutored
Antonyms educated, learned, literate, schooled, taught, tutored

unlike contrasted, different, dissimilar, distinct, divergent, diverse, ill-matched, incompatible, not alike, opposite, unequal, unrelated
Antonyms compatible, equal, like, matched, related, similar

unlikely 1. doubtful, faint, improbable, not likely, remote, slight, unimaginable 2. implausible, incredible, questionable, unbelievable, unconvincing

unlimited 1. boundless, countless, endless, extensive, great, illimitable, immeasurable, immense, incalculable, infinite, limitless, unbounded, vast 2. absolute, all-encompassing, complete, full, total, unconditional, unconstrained, unfettered, unqualified, unrestricted
Antonyms (*sense 1*) bounded, circumscribed, confined, constrained, finite, limited, restricted

unload disburden, discharge, dump, empty, lighten, off-load, relieve, unburden, unlade, unpack

unlock free, let loose, open, release, unbar, unbolt, undo, unfasten, unlatch

unlooked-for chance, fortuitous, out of the blue, surprise, surprising, unanticipated, undreamed of, unexpected, unforeseen, unhoped-for, unpredicted, unthought-of

unloved disliked, forsaken, loveless, neglected, rejected, spurned, uncared-for, uncherished, unpopular, unwanted
Antonyms adored, beloved, cherished, liked, loved, popular, precious, wanted

unlucky 1. cursed, disastrous, hapless, luckless, miserable, unfortunate, unhappy, unsuccessful, wretched 2. doomed, ill-fated, ill-omened, ill-starred, inauspicious, ominous, unfavourable, untimely
Antonyms (*sense 1*) blessed, favoured, fortunate, happy, lucky, prosperous

unman daunt, demoralize, discourage, dispirit, emasculate, enervate, enfeeble, intimidate, psych out (*Inf.*), unnerve, weaken

unmanageable 1. awkward, bulky, cumbersome, difficult to handle, inconvenient, unhandy, unwieldy 2. difficult, fractious, intractable, obstreperous, out of hand, refractory, stroppy (*Brit. sl.*), uncontrollable, unruly, wild
Antonyms (*sense 2*) amenable, compliant, docile, easy, manageable, submissive, tractable, wieldy

unmanly 1. camp (*Inf.*), effeminate, feeble, sissy, soft (*Inf.*), weak, womanish 2. abject, chicken-hearted, cowardly, craven, dishonourable, ignoble, weak-kneed (*Inf.*), yellow (*Inf.*)

unmannerly badly behaved, bad-mannered, discourteous, disrespectful, ill-bred, ill-mannered, impolite, misbehaved, rude, uncivil, uncouth

Antonyms civil, courteous, mannerly, polite, respectful, well-behaved, well-bred, well-mannered

unmarried bachelor, celibate, maiden, single, unattached, unwed, unwedded, virgin

unmask bare, bring to light, disclose, discover, expose, lay bare, reveal, show up, uncloak, uncover, unveil

unmatched beyond compare, consummate, incomparable, matchless, paramount, peerless, second to none, supreme, unequalled, unparalleled, unrivalled, unsurpassed

unmentionable disgraceful, disreputable, forbidden, frowned on, immodest, indecent, obscene, scandalous, shameful, shocking, taboo, unspeakable, unutterable

unmerciful brutal, cruel, hard, heartless, implacable, merciless, pitiless, relentless, remorseless, ruthless, uncaring, unfeeling, unsparing
Antonyms beneficent, caring, feeling, humane, merciful, pitying, sparing, tender-hearted

unmethodical confused, desultory, disorderly, haphazard, irregular, muddled, orderless, random, systemless, unorganized, unsystematic

unmindful careless, forgetful, heedless, inattentive, indifferent, lax, neglectful, negligent, oblivious, remiss, slack, unheeding
Antonyms alert, attentive, aware, careful, heedful, mindful, regardful, watchful

unmistakable blatant, certain, clear, conspicuous, decided, distinct, evident, glaring, indisputable, manifest, obvious, palpable, patent, plain, positive, pronounced, sure, unambiguous, unequivocal
Antonyms ambiguous, dim, doubtful, equivocal, hidden, mistakable, obscure, uncertain, unclear, unsure

unmitigated 1. grim, harsh, intense, oppressive, persistent, relentless, unabated, unalleviated, unbroken, undiminished, unmodified, unqualified, unredeemed, unrelieved 2. absolute, arrant, complete, consummate, deep-dyed (*Usu. derogatory*), downright, out-and-out, outright, perfect, rank, sheer, thorough, thoroughgoing, utter

unmoved 1. fast, firm, in place, in position, steady, unchanged, untouched 2. cold, dry-eyed, impassive, indifferent, unaffected, unfeeling, unimpressed, unresponsive, unstirred, untouched 3. determined, firm, inflexible, resolute, resolved, steadfast, undeviating, unshaken, unwavering
Antonyms (*sense 1*) shifted, touched, transferred (*sense 2*) affected, concerned, impressed, moved, persuaded, stirred, swayed, touched (*sense 3*) adaptable, flexible, shaken, wavering

unnatural 1. aberrant, abnormal, anomalous, irregular, odd, perverse, perverted, unusual 2. bizarre, extraordinary, freakish, outlandish, queer, strange, supernatural, unaccountable, uncanny 3. affected, artificial, assumed, contrived, factitious, false, feigned, forced, insincere, laboured, mannered, phoney *or* phony (*Inf.*), self-conscious, stagy, stiff, stilted, strained, studied, theatrical 4. brutal, callous, cold-blooded, evil, fiendish, heartless, inhuman, monstrous, ruthless, savage, unfeeling, wicked
Antonyms (*senses 1 & 2*) normal, ordinary, typical (*sense 3*) genuine, honest, natural, sincere, unaffected, unfeigned, unpretentious (*sense 4*) caring, humane, loving, warm

unnecessary dispensable, expendable, inessential, needless, nonessential, redundant, supererogatory, superfluous, surplus to requirements, uncalled-for, unneeded, unrequired, useless
Antonyms essential, indispensable, necessary, needed, required, vital

unnerve confound, daunt, demoralize, disarm, disconcert, discourage, dishearten, dismay, dispirit, faze, fluster, frighten, intimidate, psych out (*Inf.*), rattle (*Inf.*), shake, throw off balance, unhinge, unman, upset
Antonyms arm, brace, encourage, hearten, nerve, steel, strengthen, support

unnoticed disregarded, ignored, neglected, overlooked, undiscovered, unheeded, unobserved, unperceived, unrecognized, unremarked, unseen
Antonyms discovered, heeded, noted, noticed, observed, perceived, recognized, remarked

unobtrusive humble, inconspicuous, keeping a low profile, low-key, meek, modest, quiet, restrained, retiring, self-effacing, subdued, unassuming, unnoticeable, unostentatious, unpretentious
Antonyms assertive, blatant, bold, conspicuous, eccentric, eye-catching, getting in the way, high-profile, noticeable, obtrusive, outgoing, prominent

unoccupied 1. empty, tenantless, uninhabited, untenanted, vacant 2. at leisure, disengaged, idle, inactive, unemployed

unofficial informal, personal, private, unauthorized, unconfirmed, wildcat

unorthodox abnormal, heterodox, irregular, off-the-wall (*Sl.*), unconventional, uncustomary, unusual, unwonted
Antonyms conventional, customary, es-

tablished, orthodox, sound, traditional, usual

unpaid 1. due, not discharged, outstanding, overdue, owing, payable, unsettled 2. honorary, unsalaried, voluntary

unpalatable bitter, disagreeable, displeasing, distasteful, horrid, offensive, repugnant, unappetizing, unattractive, uneatable, unpleasant, unsavoury
Antonyms agreeable, appetizing, attractive, eatable, palatable, pleasant, pleasing, savoury, tasteful

unparalleled beyond compare, consummate, exceptional, incomparable, matchless, peerless, rare, singular, superlative, unequalled, unique, unmatched, unprecedented, unrivalled, unsurpassed, without equal

unpardonable deplorable, disgraceful, indefensible, inexcusable, outrageous, scandalous, shameful, unforgivable, unjustifiable

unperturbed calm, collected, composed, cool, placid, poised, self-possessed, tranquil, undismayed, unfazed (*Inf.*), unflustered, unruffled, untroubled, unworried
Antonyms anxious, dismayed, flustered, perturbed, ruffled, troubled, worried

unpleasant abhorrent, bad, disagreeable, displeasing, distasteful, horrid, ill-natured, irksome, nasty, objectionable, obnoxious, repulsive, troublesome, unattractive, unlikable *or* unlikeable, unlovely, unpalatable
Antonyms agreeable, congenial, delicious, good-natured, likable *or* likeable, lovely, nice, pleasant

unpolished 1. crude, rough, rude, sketchy, unfashioned, unfinished, unworked 2. uncivilized, uncouth, uncultivated, uncultured, unrefined, unsophisticated, vulgar

unpopular avoided, detested, disliked, not sought out, out in the cold, out of favour, rejected, shunned, unattractive, undesirable, unloved, unwanted, unwelcome
Antonyms desirable, favoured, liked, loved, popular, wanted, welcome

unprecedented abnormal, exceptional, extraordinary, freakish, new, novel, original, remarkable, singular, unexampled, unheard-of, unparalleled, unrivalled, unusual

unpredictable chance, changeable, doubtful, erratic, fickle, fluky (*Inf.*), iffy (*Inf.*), inconstant, random, unforeseeable, unreliable, unstable, variable
Antonyms certain, constant, dependable, foreseeable, predictable, reliable, stable, steady, unchanging

unprejudiced balanced, even-handed, fair, fair-minded, impartial, just, nonpartisan, objective, open-minded, unbiased, uninfluenced
Antonyms biased, bigoted, influenced, narrow-minded, partial, prejudiced, unfair, unjust

unpremeditated extempore, impromptu, impulsive, offhand, off the cuff (*Inf.*), spontaneous, spur-of-the-moment, unplanned, unprepared

unprepared 1. half-baked (*Inf.*), ill-considered, incomplete, not thought out, unfinished, unplanned 2. caught napping, caught on the hop (*Brit. inf.*), surprised, taken aback, taken off guard, unaware, unready, unsuspecting 3. ad-lib, extemporaneous, improvised, off the cuff (*Inf.*), spontaneous

unpretentious homely, honest, humble, modest, plain, simple, straightforward, unaffected, unassuming, unimposing, unobtrusive, unostentatious, unspoiled
Antonyms affected, assuming, brash, conceited, flaunting, inflated, obtrusive, ostentatious, pretentious, showy

unprincipled amoral, corrupt, crooked, deceitful, devious, dishonest, immoral, tricky, unconscionable, underhand, unethical, unprofessional, unscrupulous
Antonyms decent, ethical, honest, honourable, moral, righteous, scrupulous, upright, virtuous

unproductive 1. bootless, fruitless, futile, idle, ineffective, inefficacious, otiose, unavailing, unprofitable, unremunerative, unrewarding, useless, vain, valueless, worthless 2. barren, dry, fruitless, sterile, unprolific
Antonyms (*sense 1*) effective, fruitful, profitable, remunerative, rewarding, useful, worthwhile (*sense 2*) abundant, fertile, fruitful, productive, prolific

unprofessional 1. improper, lax, negligent, unethical, unfitting, unprincipled, unseemly, unworthy 2. amateur, amateurish, cowboy (*Inf.*), incompetent, inefficient, inexperienced, inexpert, slapdash, slipshod, untrained
Antonyms (*sense 2*) adept, competent, efficient, experienced, expert, professional, skilful

unpromising adverse, discouraging, doubtful, gloomy, inauspicious, infelicitous, ominous, unfavourable, unpropitious

unprotected defenceless, exposed, helpless, naked, open, open to attack, pregnable, unarmed, undefended, unguarded, unsheltered, unshielded, vulnerable

Antonyms defended, guarded, immune, protected, safe, secure, shielded

unqualified 1. ill-equipped, incapable, incompetent, ineligible, not equal to, not up to, unfit, unprepared 2. categorical, downright, outright, unconditional, unmitigated, unreserved, unrestricted, without reservation 3. absolute, arrant, complete, consummate, deep-dyed (*Usu. derogatory*), downright, out-and-out, outright, thorough, thoroughgoing, total, utter

unquestionable absolute, beyond a shadow of doubt, certain, clear, conclusive, definite, faultless, flawless, incontestable, incontrovertible, indisputable, indubitable, irrefutable, manifest, patent, perfect, self-evident, sure, undeniable, unequivocal, unmistakable

Antonyms ambiguous, doubtful, dubious, inconclusive, questionable, uncertain, unclear

unravel 1. disentangle, extricate, free, separate, straighten out, undo, unknot, untangle, unwind 2. clear up, explain, figure out (*Inf.*), get straight, get to the bottom of, interpret, make out, puzzle out, resolve, solve, suss (out) (*Sl.*), work out

unreadable 1. crabbed, illegible, undecipherable 2. badly written, dry as dust, heavy going, turgid

unreal 1. chimerical, dreamlike, fabulous, fanciful, fictitious, illusory, imaginary, make-believe, phantasmagoric, storybook, visionary 2. hypothetical, immaterial, impalpable, insubstantial, intangible, mythical, nebulous 3. artificial, fake, false, insincere, mock, ostensible, pretended, seeming, sham

Antonyms authentic, bona fide, genuine, real, realistic, sincere, true, veritable

unrealistic 1. half-baked (*Inf.*), impracticable, impractical, improbable, quixotic, romantic, starry-eyed, theoretical, unworkable 2. non-naturalistic, unauthentic, unlifelike, unreal

Antonyms (*sense 1*) practical, pragmatic, probable, realistic, sensible, unromantic, workable

unreasonable 1. excessive, exorbitant, extortionate, extravagant, immoderate, steep (*Inf.*), too great, uncalled-for, undue, unfair, unjust, unwarranted 2. arbitrary, biased, blinkered, capricious, erratic, headstrong, inconsistent, opinionated, quirky 3. absurd, far-fetched, foolish, illogical, irrational, mad, nonsensical, preposterous, senseless, silly, stupid

Antonyms (*sense 1*) fair, just, justified, moderate, reasonable, temperate, warranted (*sense 2*) fair-minded, flexible, open-minded (*sense 3*) logical, rational, sensible, wise

unrefined 1. crude, raw, unfinished, unpolished, unpurified, untreated 2. boorish, coarse, inelegant, rude, uncultured, unsophisticated, vulgar

unregenerate 1. godless, impious, profane, sinful, unconverted, unreformed, unrepentant, wicked 2. hardened, intractable, obdurate, obstinate, recalcitrant, refractory, self-willed, stubborn

Antonyms (*sense 1*) converted, godly, pious, reformed, regenerate, repentant, virtuous

unrelated 1. different, dissimilar, not kin, not kindred, not related, unconnected, unlike 2. beside the point, extraneous, inapplicable, inappropriate, irrelevant, not germane, unassociated, unconnected

unrelenting 1. cruel, implacable, inexorable, intransigent, merciless, pitiless, relentless, remorseless, ruthless, stern, tough, unsparing 2. ceaseless, constant, continual, continuous, endless, incessant, perpetual, steady, unabated, unbroken, unremitting, unwavering

unreliable 1. disreputable, irresponsible, not conscientious, treacherous, undependable, unstable, untrustworthy 2. deceptive, delusive, erroneous, fake, fallible, false, implausible, inaccurate, mistaken, specious, uncertain, unconvincing, unsound

Antonyms (*sense 1*) conscientious, dependable, regular, reliable, responsible, stable, trustworthy (*sense 2*) accurate, infallible

unremitting assiduous, constant, continual, continuous, diligent, incessant, indefatigable, perpetual, relentless, remorseless, sedulous, unabated, unbroken, unceasing, unwavering, unwearied

unrepentant abandoned, callous, hardened, impenitent, incorrigible, not contrite, obdurate, shameless, unregenerate, unremorseful, unrepenting

Antonyms ashamed, contrite, penitent, remorseful, repentant, rueful, sorry

unreserved 1. demonstrative, extrovert, forthright, frank, free, open, open-hearted, outgoing, outspoken, uninhibited, unrestrained, unreticent 2. absolute, complete, entire, full, total, unconditional, unlimited, unqualified, wholehearted, without reservation

Antonyms demure, inhibited, modest, reserved, restrained, reticent, shy, undemonstrative

unresolved doubtful, moot, open to question, pending, problematical, unanswered, undecided, undetermined, unsettled, unsolved, up in the air, vague, yet to be decided

unrest 1. agitation, disaffection, discontent, discord, dissatisfaction, dissension, protest, rebellion, sedition, strife, tumult, turmoil, upheaval 2. agitation, anxiety, disquiet, distress, perturbation, restlessness, trepidation, uneasiness, worry
Antonyms calm, contentment, peace, relaxation, repose, rest, stillness, tranquillity

unrestrained abandoned, boisterous, free, immoderate, inordinate, intemperate, natural, unbounded, unbridled, unchecked, unconstrained, uncontrolled, unhindered, uninhibited, unrepressed
Antonyms checked, constrained, frustrated, hindered, inhibited, repressed, restrained

unrestricted 1. absolute, free, free-for-all (*Inf.*), freewheeling (*Inf.*), open, unbounded, uncircumscribed, unhindered, unlimited, unregulated 2. clear, open, public, unobstructed, unopposed

unrivalled beyond compare, incomparable, matchless, nonpareil, peerless, supreme, unequalled, unexcelled, unmatched, unparalleled, unsurpassed, without equal

unruffled 1. calm, collected, composed, cool, peaceful, placid, sedate, serene, tranquil, undisturbed, unfazed (*Inf.*), unflustered, unmoved, unperturbed 2. even, flat, level, smooth, unbroken

unruly disobedient, disorderly, fractious, headstrong, insubordinate, intractable, lawless, mutinous, obstreperous, rebellious, refractory, riotous, rowdy, turbulent, uncontrollable, ungovernable, unmanageable, wayward, wild, wilful
Antonyms amenable, biddable, docile, governable, manageable, obedient, orderly, tractable

unsafe dangerous, hazardous, insecure, perilous, precarious, risky, threatening, treacherous, uncertain, unreliable, unsound, unstable
Antonyms certain, harmless, reliable, safe, secure, sound, stable, sure

unsaid left to the imagination, tacit, undeclared, unexpressed, unspoken, unstated, unuttered, unvoiced

unsanitary dirty, filthy, germ-ridden, infected, insalubrious, insanitary, sordid, squalid, unclean, unhealthy, unhygienic

unsatisfactory deficient, disappointing, displeasing, inadequate, insufficient, mediocre, not good enough, not up to par, not up to scratch (*Inf.*), pathetic, poor, unacceptable, unsuitable, unworthy, weak
Antonyms acceptable, adequate, passable, pleasing, satisfactory, sufficient, suitable

unsavoury 1. distasteful, nasty, objectionable, obnoxious, offensive, repellent, repugnant, repulsive, revolting, unpleasant 2. disagreeable, distasteful, nauseating, sickening, unappetizing, unpalatable
Antonyms appetizing, palatable, pleasant, savoury, tasteful, tasty, toothsome

unscathed in one piece, safe, sound, unharmed, unhurt, uninjured, unmarked, unscarred, unscratched, untouched, whole

unscrupulous conscienceless, corrupt, crooked (*Inf.*), dishonest, dishonourable, exploitative, immoral, improper, knavish, roguish, ruthless, unconscientious, unconscionable, unethical, unprincipled
Antonyms ethical, honest, honourable, moral, principled, proper, scrupulous, upright

unseasonable ill-timed, inappropriate, inopportune, mistimed, out of keeping, unsuitable, untimely

unseat 1. throw, unhorse, unsaddle 2. depose, dethrone, discharge, dismiss, displace, oust, overthrow, remove

unseemly discreditable, disreputable, improper, inappropriate, indecorous, indelicate, in poor taste, out of keeping, out of place, unbecoming, unbefitting, undignified, unrefined, unsuitable
Antonyms acceptable, appropriate, becoming, decorous, fitting, proper, refined, seemly, suitable

unseen concealed, hidden, invisible, lurking, obscure, undetected, unnoticed, unobserved, unobtrusive, unperceived, veiled

unselfish altruistic, charitable, devoted, disinterested, generous, humanitarian, kind, liberal, magnanimous, noble, self-denying, selfless, self-sacrificing

unsettle agitate, bother, confuse, discompose, disconcert, disorder, disturb, faze, fluster, perturb, rattle (*Inf.*), ruffle, throw (*Inf.*), throw into confusion (disorder, uproar), throw off balance, trouble, unbalance, unnerve, upset

unsettled 1. disorderly, insecure, shaky, unstable, unsteady 2. changeable, changing, inconstant, uncertain, unpredictable, variable 3. agitated, anxious, confused, disturbed, flustered, on edge, perturbed, restive, restless, shaken, tense, troubled, uneasy, unnerved, wired (*Sl.*) 4. debatable, doubtful, moot, open, undecided, undetermined, unresolved 5. due, in arrears, outstanding, owing, payable, pending 6. uninhabited, unoccupied, unpeopled, unpopulated

unshakable absolute, constant, firm, fixed, immovable, resolute, staunch, steadfast,

sure, unassailable, unswerving, unwavering, well-founded
Antonyms insecure, shaky, uncertain, unsure, wavering, wobbly

unshaken calm, collected, composed, impassive, unaffected, unalarmed, undaunted, undismayed, undisturbed, unfazed (*Inf.*), unmoved, unperturbed, unruffled

unsheltered exposed, open, out in the open, unprotected, unscreened, unshielded

unsightly disagreeable, hideous, horrid, repulsive, revolting (*Inf.*), ugly, unattractive, unpleasant, unprepossessing
Antonyms agreeable, attractive, beautiful, comely, handsome, pleasing, prepossessing, pretty

unskilful awkward, bungling, clumsy, cowboy (*Inf.*), fumbling, incompetent, inept, inexpert, maladroit, unhandy, unpractised, unworkmanlike

unskilled amateurish, cowboy (*Inf.*), inexperienced, uneducated, unprofessional, unqualified, untalented, untrained
Antonyms adept, expert, masterly, professional, qualified, skilled, talented

unsociable chilly, cold, distant, hostile, inhospitable, introverted, reclusive, retiring, standoffish, uncongenial, unforthcoming, unfriendly, unneighbourly, unsocial, withdrawn
Antonyms congenial, convivial, friendly, gregarious, hospitable, neighbourly, outgoing, sociable

unsolicited free-will, gratuitous, spontaneous, unasked for, uncalled-for, unforced, uninvited, unrequested, unsought, unwelcome, voluntary, volunteered

unsophisticated 1. artless, childlike, guileless, inexperienced, ingenuous, innocent, naive, natural, unaffected, untutored, unworldly 2. plain, simple, straightforward, uncomplex, uncomplicated, uninvolved, unrefined, unspecialized 3. genuine, not artificial, pure, unadulterated
Antonyms (*sense 2*) advanced, complex, complicated, elegant, esoteric, intricate, sophisticated

unsound 1. ailing, defective, delicate, deranged, diseased, frail, ill, in poor health, unbalanced, unhealthy, unhinged, unstable, unwell, weak 2. defective, erroneous, fallacious, false, faulty, flawed, ill-founded, illogical, invalid, shaky, specious, unreliable, weak 3. flimsy, insecure, not solid, rickety, shaky, tottering, unreliable, unsafe, unstable, unsteady, wobbly
Antonyms (*sense 3*) reliable, safe, solid, sound, stable, steady, strong, sturdy, substantial

unsparing 1. abundant, bountiful, generous, lavish, liberal, munificent, open-handed, plenteous, prodigal, profuse, ungrudging, unstinting 2. cold-blooded, hard, harsh, implacable, inexorable, relentless, rigorous, ruthless, severe, stern, stringent, uncompromising, unforgiving, unmerciful

unspeakable 1. beyond description, beyond words, inconceivable, indescribable, ineffable, inexpressible, overwhelming, unbelievable, unimaginable, unutterable, wonderful 2. abominable, appalling, awful, bad, dreadful, evil, execrable, frightful, heinous, hellacious (*U.S. sl.*), horrible, loathsome, monstrous, odious, repellent, shocking, too horrible for words

unspoiled, unspoilt 1. intact, perfect, preserved, unaffected, unblemished, unchanged, undamaged, unharmed, unimpaired, untouched 2. artless, innocent, natural, unaffected, unassuming, unstudied, wholesome
Antonyms (*sense 1*) affected, blemished, changed, damaged, harmed, impaired, imperfect, spoilt, touched

unspoken 1. assumed, implicit, implied, left to the imagination, not put into words, not spelt out, tacit, taken for granted, undeclared, understood, unexpressed, unspoken, unstated 2. mute, silent, unsaid, unuttered, voiceless, wordless
Antonyms (*sense 1*) clear, declared, explicit, expressed, spoken, stated

unstable 1. insecure, not fixed, precarious, rickety, risky, shaky, tottering, unsettled, unsteady, wobbly 2. capricious, changeable, erratic, fitful, fluctuating, inconsistent, inconstant, irrational, temperamental, unpredictable, unsteady, untrustworthy, vacillating, variable, volatile
Antonyms (*sense 2*) consistent, constant, level-headed, predictable, rational, reliable, stable, steady, trustworthy

unsteady 1. infirm, insecure, precarious, reeling, rickety, shaky, tottering, treacherous, unsafe, unstable, wobbly 2. changeable, erratic, flickering, flighty, fluctuating, inconstant, irregular, temperamental, unreliable, unsettled, vacillating, variable, volatile, wavering

unstinted abundant, ample, bountiful, full, generous, large, lavish, liberal, plentiful, prodigal, profuse

unsubstantial 1. airy, flimsy, fragile, frail, inadequate, light, slight, thin 2. erroneous, full of holes, ill-founded, superficial, tenuous, unsound, unsupported, weak 3. dreamlike, fanciful, illusory, imaginary, immaterial, impalpable, visionary

unsubstantiated open to question, unat-

tested, unconfirmed, uncorroborated, unestablished, unproven, unsupported
Antonyms attested, confirmed, corroborated, established, proven, substantiated, supported

unsuccessful 1. abortive, bootless, failed, fruitless, futile, ineffective, unavailing, unproductive, useless, vain 2. balked, defeated, foiled, frustrated, hapless, ill-starred, losing, luckless, unfortunate, unlucky
Antonyms (*sense 1*) flourishing, fruitful, productive, prosperous, remunerative, successful, thriving, useful, worthwhile (*sense 2*) fortunate, lucky, triumphant, victorious, winning

unsuitable improper, inapposite, inappropriate, inapt, incompatible, incongruous, ineligible, infelicitous, out of character, out of keeping, out of place, unacceptable, unbecoming, unbefitting, unfitting, unseasonable, unseemly, unsuited
Antonyms acceptable, apposite, appropriate, apt, compatible, eligible, fitting, proper, suitable

unsullied clean, immaculate, impeccable, pristine, pure, spotless, squeaky-clean, stainless, unblackened, unblemished, uncorrupted, undefiled, unsoiled, untainted, untarnished, untouched

unsung anonymous, disregarded, neglected, unacclaimed, unacknowledged, uncelebrated, unhailed, unhonoured, unknown, unnamed, unrecognized

unsure 1. insecure, lacking in confidence, unassured, unconfident 2. distrustful, doubtful, dubious, hesitant, in a quandary, irresolute, mistrustful, sceptical, suspicious, unconvinced, undecided
Antonyms assured, certain, confident, convinced, decided, persuaded, resolute, sure

unsurpassed consummate, exceptional, incomparable, matchless, nonpareil, paramount, peerless, second to none, superlative, supreme, transcendent, unequalled, unexcelled, unparalleled, unrivalled, without an equal

unsuspecting confiding, credulous, gullible, inexperienced, ingenuous, innocent, naive, off guard, trustful, trusting, unconscious, unsuspicious, unwarned, unwary

unswerving constant, dedicated, devoted, direct, firm, resolute, single-minded, staunch, steadfast, steady, true, undeviating, unfaltering, unflagging, untiring, unwavering

unsympathetic apathetic, callous, cold, compassionless (*Rare*), cruel, hard, harsh, heartless, indifferent, insensitive, soulless, stony-hearted, uncompassionate, unconcerned, unfeeling, unkind, unmoved, unpitying, unresponsive
Antonyms caring, compassionate, concerned, kind, pitying, sensitive, supportive, sympathetic, understanding

unsystematic chaotic, confused, disorderly, disorganized, haphazard, irregular, jumbled, muddled, random, slapdash, unmethodical, unorganized, unplanned, unsystematized

untamed barbarous, feral, fierce, not broken in, savage, unbroken, uncontrollable, undomesticated, untameable, wild

untangle clear up, disentangle, explain, extricate, solve, straighten out, unravel, unsnarl
Antonyms complicate, confuse, enmesh, entangle, jumble, muddle, puzzle, snarl, tangle

untarnished bright, burnished, clean, glowing, immaculate, impeccable, polished, pure, shining, spotless, squeaky-clean, unblemished, unimpeachable, unsoiled, unspotted, unstained, unsullied

untenable fallacious, flawed, groundless, illogical, indefensible, insupportable, shaky, unreasonable, unsound, unsustainable, weak
Antonyms justified, logical, rational, reasonable, sensible, supported, unarguable, uncontestable, valid, verifiable, well-grounded

unthinkable 1. absurd, illogical, impossible, improbable, not on (*Inf.*), out of the question, preposterous, unlikely, unreasonable 2. beyond belief, beyond the bounds of possibility, implausible, inconceivable, incredible, insupportable, unbelievable, unimaginable

unthinking 1. blundering, inconsiderate, insensitive, rude, selfish, tactless, thoughtless, undiplomatic 2. careless, heedless, impulsive, inadvertent, instinctive, mechanical, negligent, oblivious, rash, senseless, unconscious, unmindful, vacant, witless
Antonyms (*sense 2*) careful, conscious, deliberate, heedful, mindful, sensible, witting

untidy bedraggled, chaotic, cluttered, disarrayed, disorderly, higgledy-piggledy (*Inf.*), jumbled, littered, messy, muddled, muddly, mussy (*U.S. inf.*), rumpled, shambolic, slatternly, slipshod, sloppy (*Inf.*), slovenly, topsy-turvy, unkempt
Antonyms methodical, neat, orderly, presentable, ship-shape, spruce, systematic, tidy, well-kept

untie free, loosen, release, unbind, unbridle, undo, unfasten, unknot, unlace

untimely awkward, badly timed, early, ill-timed, inappropriate, inauspicious, inconvenient, inopportune, mistimed, premature, unfortunate, unseasonable, unsuitable
Antonyms appropriate, auspicious, convenient, fortunate, opportune, seasonable, suitable, timely, welcome, well-timed

untiring constant, dedicated, determined, devoted, dogged, incessant, indefatigable, patient, persevering, persistent, staunch, steady, tireless, unfaltering, unflagging, unremitting, unwearied

untold 1. indescribable, inexpressible, undreamed of, unimaginable, unspeakable, unthinkable, unutterable 2. countless, incalculable, innumerable, measureless, myriad, numberless, uncountable, uncounted, unnumbered 3. hidden, private, secret, undisclosed, unknown, unpublished, unrecounted, unrelated, unrevealed

untouched 1. intact, safe and sound, undamaged, unharmed, unhurt, uninjured, unscathed, without a scratch 2. dry-eyed, indifferent, unaffected, unconcerned, unimpressed, unmoved, unstirred
Antonyms (*sense 2*) affected, concerned, impressed, moved, softened, stirred, touched

untoward 1. annoying, awkward, disastrous, ill-timed, inconvenient, inimical, irritating, troublesome, unfortunate, vexatious 2. adverse, contrary, inauspicious, inopportune, unfavourable, unlucky, untimely 3. improper, inappropriate, indecorous, out of place, unbecoming, unfitting, unseemly, unsuitable

untrained amateur, green, inexperienced, raw, uneducated, unpractised, unqualified, unschooled, unskilled, untaught, untutored
Antonyms educated, experienced, expert, qualified, schooled, skilled, taught, trained

untried in the experimental stage, new, novel, unattempted, unessayed, unproved, untested

untroubled calm, composed, cool, peaceful, placid, sedate, serene, steady, tranquil, unagitated, unconcerned, undisturbed, unfazed (*Inf.*), unflappable (*Inf.*), unflustered, unperturbed, unruffled, unstirred, unworried
Antonyms agitated, anxious, concerned, disturbed, flustered, perturbed, ruffled, troubled, worried

untrue 1. deceptive, dishonest, erroneous, fallacious, false, inaccurate, incorrect, lying, misleading, mistaken, sham, spurious, untruthful, wrong 2. deceitful, disloyal, faithless, false, forsworn, inconstant, perfidious, traitorous, treacherous, two-faced, unfaithful, untrustworthy 3. deviant, distorted, inaccurate, off, out of line, out of true, wide
Antonyms (*sense 1*) accurate, correct, factual, right, true (*sense 2*) constant, dependable, faithful, honest, honourable, loyal, truthful, virtuous

untrustworthy capricious, deceitful, devious, dishonest, disloyal, fair-weather, faithless, false, fickle, fly-by-night (*Inf.*), not to be depended on, slippery, treacherous, tricky, two-faced, undependable, unfaithful, unreliable, untrue, untrusty
Antonyms dependable, faithful, honest, loyal, reliable, reputable, steadfast, true, trustworthy, trusty

untruth 1. deceitfulness, duplicity, falsity, inveracity (*Rare*), lying, mendacity, perjury, truthlessness, untruthfulness 2. deceit, fabrication, falsehood, falsification, fib, fiction, lie, pork pie (*Brit. sl.*), porky (*Brit. sl.*), prevarication, story, tale, trick, whopper (*Inf.*)

untruthful crooked (*Inf.*), deceitful, deceptive, dishonest, dissembling, false, fibbing, hypocritical, lying, mendacious
Antonyms candid, honest, sincere, true, truthful, veracious

untutored 1. ignorant, illiterate, uneducated, unlearned, unschooled, untrained, unversed 2. artless, inexperienced, simple, unpractised, unrefined, unsophisticated

unused 1. fresh, intact, new, pristine, untouched 2. *With* to a stranger to, inexperienced in, new to, not ready for, not up to, unaccustomed to, unfamiliar with, unhabituated to 3. available, extra, left, leftover, remaining, unconsumed, unexhausted, unutilized

unusual abnormal, atypical, bizarre, curious, different, exceptional, extraordinary, notable, odd, out of the ordinary, phenomenal, queer, rare, remarkable, singular, strange, surprising, uncommon, unconventional, unexpected, unfamiliar, unwonted
Antonyms average, banal, commonplace, conventional, everyday, familiar, normal, routine, traditional, typical, unremarkable, usual

unutterable beyond words, extreme, indescribable, ineffable, overwhelming, unimaginable, unspeakable

unvarnished bare, candid, frank, honest, naked, plain, pure, pure and simple, simple, sincere, stark, straightforward, unadorned, unembellished

unveil bare, bring to light, disclose, divulge, expose, lay bare, lay open, make known, make public, reveal, uncover

Antonyms cloak, conceal, cover, disguise, hide, mask, obscure, veil

unwanted *de trop,* going begging, outcast, rejected, superfluous, surplus to requirements, unasked, undesired, uninvited, unneeded, unsolicited, unwelcome, useless
Antonyms desired, necessary, needed, useful, wanted, welcome

unwarranted gratuitous, groundless, indefensible, inexcusable, uncalled-for, unjust, unjustified, unprovoked, unreasonable, wrong

unwary careless, hasty, heedless, imprudent, incautious, indiscreet, rash, reckless, thoughtless, uncircumspect, unguarded, unwatchful
Antonyms cautious, chary, circumspect, discreet, guarded, prudent, wary, watchful

unwavering consistent, dedicated, determined, immovable, resolute, single-minded, staunch, steadfast, steady, undeviating, unfaltering, unflagging, unshakable, unshaken, unswerving, untiring

unwelcome 1. excluded, rejected, unacceptable, undesirable, uninvited, unpopular, unwanted, unwished for 2. disagreeable, displeasing, distasteful, thankless, undesirable, unpleasant
Antonyms acceptable, agreeable, desirable, pleasant, pleasing, popular, wanted, welcome

unwell ailing, ill, indisposed, in poor health, off colour, out of sorts, poorly (*Inf.*), sick, sickly, under the weather (*Inf.*), unhealthy
Antonyms fine, healthy, robust, sound, well

unwholesome 1. deleterious, harmful, insalubrious, junk (*Inf.*), noxious, poisonous, tainted, unhealthy, unnourishing 2. bad, corrupting, degrading, demoralizing, depraving, evil, immoral, maleficent, perverting, wicked 3. anaemic, pale, pallid, pasty, sickly, wan
Antonyms (*sense 1*) beneficial, germ-free, healthy, hygienic, salubrious, sanitary, wholesome (*sense 2*) edifying, moral

unwieldy 1. awkward, burdensome, cumbersome, inconvenient, unhandy, unmanageable 2. bulky, clumsy, hefty, massive, ponderous, ungainly, weighty

unwilling averse, demurring, disinclined, grudging, indisposed, laggard (*Rare*), loath, not in the mood, opposed, reluctant, resistant, unenthusiastic
Antonyms amenable, compliant, disposed, eager, enthusiastic, inclined, voluntary, willing

unwind 1. disentangle, slacken, uncoil, undo, unravel, unreel, unroll, untwine, untwist 2. calm down, let oneself go, loosen up, quieten down, relax, sit back, slow down, take a break, take it easy, wind down

unwise asinine, foolhardy, foolish, ill-advised, ill-considered, ill-judged, impolitic, improvident, imprudent, inadvisable, inane, indiscreet, injudicious, irresponsible, rash, reckless, senseless, short-sighted, silly, stupid
Antonyms discreet, judicious, politic, prudent, responsible, sensible, shrewd, wise

unwitting 1. ignorant, innocent, unaware, unconscious, unknowing, unsuspecting 2. accidental, chance, inadvertent, involuntary, undesigned, unintended, unintentional, unmeant, unplanned
Antonyms (*sense 2*) conscious, deliberate, designed, intended, intentional, knowing, meant, planned, witting

unwonted atypical, extraordinary, infrequent, out of the ordinary, peculiar, rare, seldom seen, singular, unaccustomed, uncommon, uncustomary, unexpected, unfamiliar, unheard-of, unusual

unworldly 1. abstract, celestial, metaphysical, nonmaterialistic, religious, spiritual, transcendental 2. green, idealistic, inexperienced, innocent, naive, raw, trusting, unsophisticated 3. ethereal, extraterrestrial, otherworldly, unearthly

unworthy 1. *With* of beneath the dignity of, improper, inappropriate, out of character, out of place, unbecoming, unbefitting, unfitting, unseemly, unsuitable 2. base, contemptible, degrading, discreditable, disgraceful, dishonourable, disreputable, ignoble, shameful 3. ineligible, not deserving of, not fit for, not good enough, not worth, undeserving
Antonyms (*sense 3*) commendable, creditable, deserving, eligible, fit, honourable, meritorious, worthy

unwritten 1. oral, unrecorded, vocal, word-of-mouth 2. accepted, conventional, customary, tacit, traditional, understood, unformulated

unyielding adamant, determined, firm, hardline, immovable, inexorable, inflexible, intractable, obdurate, obstinate, relentless, resolute, rigid, staunch, steadfast, stiff-necked, stubborn, tough, unbending, uncompromising, unwavering
Antonyms adaptable, compliant, compromising, cooperative, flexible, movable, tractable, yielding

up-and-coming ambitious, eager, go-getting (*Inf.*), on the make (*Sl.*), promising, pushing

upbeat *adj.* buoyant, cheerful, cheery, encouraging, favourable, forward-looking, heartening, hopeful, looking up, optimistic, positive, promising, rosy

upbraid admonish, bawl out (*Inf.*), berate, blame, carpet (*Inf.*), castigate, censure, chew out (*U.S. & Canad. inf.*), chide, condemn, dress down (*Inf.*), excoriate, give (someone) a rocket (*Brit. & N.Z. inf.*), lecture, read the riot act, rebuke, reprimand, reproach, reprove, scold, take to task, tear into (*Inf.*), tear (someone) off a strip (*Brit. inf.*), tell off (*Inf.*), tick off (*Inf.*)

upbringing breeding, bringing-up, care, cultivation, education, nurture, raising, rearing, tending, training

update amend, bring up to date, modernize, renew, revise

upgrade advance, ameliorate, better, elevate, enhance, improve, promote, raise
Antonyms decry, degrade, demote, denigrate, downgrade, lower

upheaval cataclysm, disorder, disruption, disturbance, eruption, overthrow, revolution, turmoil, violent change

uphill *adj.* 1. ascending, climbing, mounting, rising 2. arduous, difficult, exhausting, gruelling, hard, laborious, punishing, Sisyphean, strenuous, taxing, tough, wearisome
Antonyms (*sense 1*) descending, downhill, lowering

uphold advocate, aid, back, champion, defend, encourage, endorse, hold to, justify, maintain, promote, stand by, stick up for (*Inf.*), support, sustain, vindicate

upkeep 1. conservation, keep, maintenance, preservation, repair, running, subsistence, support, sustenance 2. expenditure, expenses, oncosts (*Brit.*), operating costs, outlay, overheads, running costs

uplift *v.* 1. elevate, heave, hoist, lift up, raise 2. advance, ameliorate, better, civilize, cultivate, edify, improve, inspire, raise, refine, upgrade *~n.* 3. advancement, betterment, cultivation, edification, enhancement, enlightenment, enrichment, improvement, refinement

upper 1. high, higher, loftier, top, topmost 2. elevated, eminent, greater, important, superior
Antonyms bottom, inferior, junior, low, lower

upper-class aristocratic, blue-blooded, highborn, high-class, noble, patrician, top-drawer, well-bred

upper hand advantage, ascendancy, control, dominion, edge, mastery, superiority, supremacy, sway, whip hand

uppermost 1. highest, loftiest, most elevated, top, topmost, upmost 2. chief, dominant, foremost, greatest, leading, main, paramount, predominant, pre-eminent, primary, principal, supreme
Antonyms bottom, bottommost, humblest, least, lowermost, lowest, lowliest, slightest

uppish affected, arrogant, cocky, conceited, high and mighty (*Inf.*), hoity-toity (*Inf.*), overweening, presumptuous, putting on airs, self-important, snobbish, stuck-up (*Inf.*), supercilious, toffee-nosed (*Sl., chiefly Brit.*), uppity (*Inf.*)
Antonyms diffident, humble, lowly, meek, obsequious, servile, unaffected, unassertive

uppity bigheaded (*Inf.*), bumptious, cocky, conceited, full of oneself, impertinent, on one's high horse (*Inf.*), overweening, self-important, swanky (*Inf.*), uppish (*Brit. inf.*)

upright 1. erect, on end, perpendicular, straight, vertical 2. *Fig.* above board, conscientious, ethical, faithful, good, high-minded, honest, honourable, incorruptible, just, principled, righteous, straightforward, true, trustworthy, unimpeachable, virtuous
Antonyms (*sense 1*) flat, horizontal, lying, prone, prostrate, supine (*sense 2*) corrupt, devious, dishonest, dishonourable, unethical, unjust, untrustworthy, wicked

uprightness fairness, faithfulness, goodness, high-mindedness, honesty, incorruptibility, integrity, justice, probity, rectitude, righteousness, straightforwardness, trustworthiness, virtue

uprising disturbance, insurgence, insurrection, mutiny, outbreak, putsch, rebellion, revolt, revolution, rising, upheaval

uproar *bagarre,* brawl, brouhaha, clamour, commotion, confusion, din, furore, hubbub, hullabaloo, hurly-burly, mayhem, noise, outcry, pandemonium, racket, riot, ruckus (*Inf.*), ruction (*Inf.*), rumpus, turbulence, turmoil

uproarious 1. clamorous, confused, disorderly, loud, noisy, riotous, rowdy, tempestuous, tumultuous, turbulent, wild 2. convulsive (*Inf.*), hilarious, hysterical, killing (*Inf.*), rib-tickling, rip-roaring (*Inf.*), screamingly funny, side-splitting, very funny 3. boisterous, gleeful, loud, rollicking, unrestrained
Antonyms (*sense 1*) inaudible, low-key, orderly, peaceful, quiet, still (*sense 2*) morose, mournful, sad, serious, sorrowful, tragic

uproot 1. deracinate, dig up, extirpate, grub up, pull out by the roots, pull up, rip up, root out, weed out 2. deracinate, disorient, displace, exile 3. destroy, do away with, eliminate, eradicate, extirpate, remove, wipe out

ups and downs changes, ebb and flow, fluctuations, moods, vicissitudes, wheel of fortune

upset *v.* 1. capsize, knock over, overturn, spill, tip over, topple over 2. change, disorder, disorganize, disturb, mess up, mix up, put out of order, spoil, turn topsy-turvy 3. agitate, bother, discompose, disconcert, dismay, disquiet, distress, disturb, faze, fluster, grieve, hassle (*Inf.*), perturb, ruffle, throw (someone) off balance, trouble, unnerve 4. be victorious over, conquer, defeat, get the better of, overcome, overthrow, triumph over, win against the odds ~*n.* 5. defeat, reverse, shake-up (*Inf.*), sudden change, surprise 6. bug (*Inf.*), complaint, disorder, disturbance, illness, indisposition, malady, queasiness, sickness 7. agitation, bother, discomposure, disquiet, distress, disturbance, hassle (*Inf.*), shock, trouble, worry ~*adj.* 8. capsized, overturned, spilled, tipped over, toppled, tumbled, upside down 9. disordered, disturbed, gippy (*Sl.*), ill, poorly (*Inf.*), queasy, sick 10. agitated, bothered, confused, disconcerted, dismayed, disquieted, distressed, disturbed, frantic, grieved, hassled (*Inf.*), hurt, overwrought, put out, ruffled, troubled, worried 11. at sixes and sevens, chaotic, confused, disarrayed, disordered, in disarray *or* disorder, messed up, muddled, topsy-turvy 12. beaten, conquered, defeated, overcome, overthrown, vanquished

upshot conclusion, consequence, culmination, end, end result, event, finale, issue, outcome, payoff (*Inf.*), result, sequel

upside down 1. bottom up, inverted, on its head, overturned, upturned, wrong side up 2. *Inf.* chaotic, confused, disordered, higgledy-piggledy (*Inf.*), in confusion (chaos, disarray, disorder), jumbled, muddled, topsy-turvy

upstanding 1. ethical, good, honest, honourable, incorruptible, moral, principled, true, trustworthy, upright 2. firm, hale and hearty, hardy, healthy, robust, stalwart, strong, sturdy, upright, vigorous
Antonyms (*sense 1*) bad, corrupt, dishonest, false, immoral, unethical, unprincipled, untrustworthy (*sense 2*) delicate, feeble, frail, infirm, puny, unhealthy, weak

upstart arriviste, nobody, *nouveau riche,* parvenu, social climber, status seeker

uptight anxious, edgy, nervy (*Brit. inf.*), on edge, on the defensive, prickly, tense, uneasy, wired (*Sl.*), withdrawn

up-to-date all the rage, current, fashionable, happening (*Inf.*), in, in vogue, modern, newest, now (*Inf.*), stylish, trendy (*Brit. inf.*), up-to-the-minute, with it (*Inf.*)
Antonyms antiquated, dated, *démodé,* obsolete, old fashioned, outmoded, out of date, passé

upturn *n.* advancement, boost, improvement, increase, recovery, revival, rise, upsurge, upswing

urban city, civic, inner-city, metropolitan, municipal, oppidan (*Rare*), town

urbane civil, civilized, cosmopolitan, courteous, cultivated, cultured, debonair, elegant, mannerly, polished, refined, smooth, sophisticated, suave, well-bred, well-mannered
Antonyms boorish, clownish, discourteous, gauche, impolite, rude, uncivilized, uncouth, uncultured

urbanity charm, civility, courtesy, culture, elegance, grace, mannerliness, polish, refinement, sophistication, suavity, worldliness

urchin brat, gamin, guttersnipe, mudlark (*Sl.*), ragamuffin, street Arab, waif, young rogue

urge *v.* 1. appeal to, beg, beseech, entreat, exhort, implore, plead, press, solicit 2. advise, advocate, champion, counsel, insist on, push for, recommend, support 3. compel, constrain, drive, egg on, encourage, force, goad, hasten, impel, incite, induce, instigate, press, prompt, propel, push, spur, stimulate ~*n.* 4. compulsion, desire, drive, fancy, impulse, itch, longing, thirst, wish, yearning, yen (*Inf.*)
Antonyms *v.* (*senses 1 & 2*) caution, deter, discourage, dissuade, remonstrate, warn ~*n.* aversion, disinclination, distaste, indisposition, reluctance, repugnance

urgency exigency, extremity, gravity, hurry, imperativeness, importance, importunity, necessity, need, pressure, seriousness, stress

urgent 1. compelling, critical, crucial, immediate, imperative, important, instant, not to be delayed, pressing, top-priority 2. clamorous, earnest, importunate, insistent, intense, persistent, persuasive
Antonyms apathetic, casual, feeble, half-hearted, lackadaisical, low-priority, minor, perfunctory, trivial, unimportant, weak

urinate leak (*Sl.*), make water, micturate, pass water, pee (*Sl.*), piddle (*Inf.*), piss (*Taboo sl.*), spend a penny (*Brit. inf.*), tinkle (*Brit. inf.*), wee (*Inf.*), wee-wee (*Inf.*)

usable at one's disposal, available, current, fit for use, functional, in running order, practical, ready for use, serviceable, utilizable, valid, working

usage 1. control, employment, handling, management, operation, regulation, running, treatment, use 2. convention, custom, form, habit, matter of course, method, mode, practice, procedure, regime, routine, rule, tradition, wont

use *v.* 1. apply, avail oneself of, bring into play, employ, exercise, exert, find a use for, make use of, operate, ply, practise, profit by, put to use, turn to account, utilize, wield, work 2. act towards, behave towards, deal with, exploit, handle, manipulate, misuse, take advantage of, treat 3. consume, exhaust, expend, run through, spend, waste ~*n.* 4. application, employment, exercise, handling, operation, practice, service, treatment, usage, wear and tear 5. advantage, application, avail, benefit, good, help, mileage (*Inf.*), point, profit, service, usefulness, utility, value, worth 6. custom, habit, practice, usage, way, wont 7. call, cause, end, necessity, need, object, occasion, point, purpose, reason

used cast-off, hand-me-down (*Inf.*), nearly new, not new, reach-me-down (*Inf.*), second-hand, shopsoiled, worn
Antonyms brand-new, fresh, intact, new, pristine, unused

used to accustomed to, at home in, attuned to, familiar with, given to, habituated to, hardened to, in the habit of, inured to, tolerant of, wont to

useful advantageous, all-purpose, beneficial, effective, fruitful, general-purpose, helpful, of help, of service, of use, practical, profitable, salutary, serviceable, valuable, worthwhile
Antonyms inadequate, ineffective, unbeneficial, unhelpful, unproductive, useless, vain, worthless

useless 1. bootless, disadvantageous, fruitless, futile, hopeless, idle, impractical, ineffective, ineffectual, of no use, pointless, profitless, unavailing, unproductive, unworkable, vain, valueless, worthless 2. *Inf.* hopeless, incompetent, ineffectual, inept, no good, stupid, weak
Antonyms (*sense 1*) advantageous, effective, fruitful, practical, productive, profitable, useful, valuable, workable, worthwhile

use up absorb, burn up, consume, deplete, devour, drain, exhaust, finish, fritter away, run through, squander, swallow up, waste

usher *n.* 1. attendant, doorkeeper, escort, guide, usherette ~*v.* 2. conduct, direct, escort, guide, lead, pilot, show in *or* out, steer 3. *Usually with* in bring in, herald, inaugurate, initiate, introduce, launch, open the door to, pave the way for, precede, ring in

usual accustomed, common, constant, customary, everyday, expected, familiar, fixed, general, habitual, normal, ordinary, regular, routine, standard, stock, typical, wonted
Antonyms exceptional, extraordinary, new, novel, off-beat, out of the ordinary, peculiar, rare, singular, strange, uncommon, unexpected, unhackneyed, unique, unorthodox, unusual

usually as a rule, as is the custom, as is usual, by and large, commonly, for the most part, generally, habitually, in the main, mainly, mostly, most often, normally, on the whole, ordinarily, regularly, routinely

usurp appropriate, arrogate, assume, commandeer, infringe upon, lay hold of, seize, take, take over, wrest

utility advantageousness, avail, benefit, convenience, efficacy, fitness, point, practicality, profit, service, serviceableness, use, usefulness

utilize appropriate, avail oneself of, employ, have recourse to, make the most of, make use of, profit by, put to use, resort to, take advantage of, turn to account, use

utmost *adj.* 1. chief, extreme, greatest, highest, maximum, paramount, pre-eminent, supreme 2. extreme, farthest, final, last, most distant, outermost, remotest, uttermost ~*n.* 3. best, greatest, hardest, highest, most

Utopia bliss, Eden, Erewhon, Garden of Eden, heaven, ideal life, paradise, perfect place, seventh heaven, Shangri-la

Utopian 1. *adj.* airy, chimerical, dream, fanciful, fantasy, ideal, idealistic, illusory, imaginary, impractical, perfect, romantic, visionary 2. *n.* Don Quixote, dreamer, idealist, romanticist, visionary

utter[1] *v.* 1. articulate, enunciate, express, pronounce, put into words, say, speak, verbalize, vocalize, voice 2. declare, divulge, give expression to, make known, proclaim, promulgate, publish, reveal, state

utter[2] *adj.* absolute, arrant, complete, consummate, deep-dyed (*Usu. derogatory*), downright, entire, out-and-out, outright, perfect, sheer, stark, thorough, thoroughgoing, total, unmitigated, unqualified

utterance 1. announcement, declaration, expression, opinion, remark, speech, statement, words 2. articulation, delivery, ejaculation, expression, verbalization, vocalization, vociferation

utterly absolutely, completely, entirely, extremely, fully, perfectly, thoroughly, totally, to the core, wholly

uttermost extreme, farthest, final, last, outermost, remotest, utmost

V

vacancy 1. job, opening, opportunity, position, post, room, situation 2. absent-mindedness, abstraction, blankness, inanity, inattentiveness, incomprehension, incuriousness, lack of interest, vacuousness 3. emptiness, gap, space, vacuum, void

vacant 1. available, disengaged, empty, free, idle, not in use, to let, unemployed, unengaged, unfilled, unoccupied, untenanted, void 2. absent-minded, abstracted, blank, dreaming, dreamy, expressionless, idle, inane, incurious, thoughtless, unthinking, vacuous
Antonyms (*sense 1*) busy, engaged, full, inhabited, in use, occupied, taken (*sense 2*) animated, engrossed, expressive, lively, reflective, thoughtful

vacate depart, evacuate, give up, go away, leave, leave empty, move out of, quit, relinquish possession of, withdraw

vacillate be irresolute *or* indecisive, blow hot and cold (*Inf.*), dither (*Chiefly Brit.*), fluctuate, haver, hesitate, keep changing one's mind, oscillate, reel, rock, shilly-shally (*Inf.*), sway, swither (*Scot.*), waver

vacillating hesitant, in two minds (*Inf.*), irresolute, oscillating, shillyshallying (*Inf.*), uncertain, unresolved, wavering

vacillation dithering (*Chiefly Brit.*), fluctuation, hesitation, inconstancy, indecisiveness, irresoluteness, irresolution, shillyshallying (*Inf.*), unsteadiness, wavering

vacuity 1. blankness, emptiness, inanity, incognizance, incomprehension, vacuousness 2. emptiness, nothingness, space, vacuum, void

vacuous 1. blank, inane, stupid, uncomprehending, unintelligent, vacant 2. empty, unfilled, vacant, void

vacuum emptiness, free space, gap, nothingness, space, vacuity, void

vagabond 1. *n.* bag lady (*Chiefly U.S.*), beggar, bum (*Inf.*), down-and-out, hobo (*U.S.*), itinerant, knight of the road, migrant, nomad, outcast, rascal, rover, tramp, vagrant, wanderer, wayfarer 2. *adj.* destitute, down and out, drifting, fly-by-night (*Inf.*), footloose, homeless, idle, itinerant, journeying, nomadic, rootless, roving, shiftless, vagrant, wandering

vagary caprice, crotchet, fancy, humour, megrim (*Archaic*), notion, whim, whimsy

vagrant 1. *n.* bag lady (*Chiefly U.S.*), beggar, bird of passage, bum (*Inf.*), hobo (*U.S.*), itinerant, person of no fixed address, rolling stone, tramp, wanderer 2. *adj.* itinerant, nomadic, roaming, rootless, roving, unsettled, vagabond
Antonyms *adj.* established, fixed, purposeful, rooted, settled

vague amorphous, blurred, dim, doubtful, fuzzy, generalized, hazy, ill-defined, imprecise, indefinite, indeterminate, indistinct, lax, loose, nebulous, obscure, shadowy, uncertain, unclear, unknown, unspecified, woolly
Antonyms clear, clear-cut, definite, distinct, exact, explicit, lucid, precise, specific, well-defined

vaguely absent-mindedly, dimly, evasively, imprecisely, in a general way, obscurely, slightly, through a glass darkly, vacantly

vagueness ambiguity, impreciseness, inexactitude, lack of preciseness, looseness, obscurity, undecidedness, woolliness
Antonyms clarity, clearness, definition, exactness, obviousness, preciseness, precision

vain 1. arrogant, bigheaded (*Inf.*), cocky, conceited, egotistical, inflated, narcissistic, ostentatious, overweening, peacockish, pleased with oneself, proud, self-important, stuck-up (*Inf.*), swaggering, swanky (*Inf.*), swollen-headed (*Inf.*), vainglorious 2. abortive, empty, fruitless, futile, hollow, idle, nugatory, pointless, senseless, time-wasting, trifling, trivial, unavailing, unimportant, unproductive, unprofitable, useless, worthless 3. **be vain** have a high opinion of oneself, have a swelled head (*Inf.*), have one's head turned, think a lot of oneself, think oneself it (*Inf.*), think oneself the cat's whiskers *or* pyjamas (*Sl.*) 4. **in vain** bootless, fruitless(ly), ineffectual(ly), to no avail, to no purpose, unsuccessful(ly), useless(ly), vain(ly), wasted, without success
Antonyms (*sense 1*) bashful, humble, meek, modest, self-deprecating (*sense 2*) fruitful, profitable, serious, successful, useful, valid, worthwhile, worthy

valediction adieu, farewell, goodbye, leave-taking, sendoff (*Inf.*), *vale*

valedictory *adj.* farewell, final, parting

valetudinarian *adj.* delicate, feeble, frail, hypochondriac, infirm, in poor health, invalid, sickly, weakly

valiant bold, brave, courageous, dauntless, doughty, fearless, gallant, heroic, indomitable, intrepid, lion-hearted, plucky, redoubtable, stouthearted, valorous, worthy
Antonyms cowardly, craven, fearful, shrinking, spineless, timid, weak

valid 1. acceptable, binding, cogent, conclusive, convincing, efficacious, efficient, good, just, logical, powerful, sound, substantial, telling, weighty, well-founded, well-grounded 2. authentic, bona fide, genuine, in force, lawful, legal, legally binding, legitimate, official
Antonyms (*sense 1*) baseless, bogus, fallacious, false, illogical, sham, spurious, unacceptable, unfounded, unrealistic, unrecognized, untrue, weak (*sense 2*) illegal, inoperative, invalid, unlawful, unofficial

validate authenticate, authorize, certify, confirm, corroborate, endorse, legalize, make legally binding, ratify, set one's seal on *or* to, substantiate

validity 1. cogency, force, foundation, grounds, point, power, soundness, strength, substance, weight 2. authority, lawfulness, legality, legitimacy, right

valley coomb, cwm (*Welsh*), dale, dell, depression, dingle, glen, hollow, strath (*Scot.*), vale

valorous bold, brave, courageous, dauntless, doughty, fearless, gallant, heroic, intrepid, lion-hearted, plucky, valiant

valour boldness, bravery, courage, derring-do (*Archaic*), doughtiness, fearlessness, gallantry, heroism, intrepidity, lion-heartedness, spirit
Antonyms cowardice, dread, fear, timidity, trepidation, weakness

valuable *adj.* 1. costly, dear, expensive, high-priced, precious 2. beneficial, cherished, esteemed, estimable, held dear, helpful, important, prized, profitable, serviceable, treasured, useful, valued, worthwhile, worthy ~*n.* 3. *Usually plural* heirloom, treasure(s)
Antonyms *adj.* (*sense 1*) cheap, cheapo (*Inf.*), chickenshit (*U.S. sl.*), crappy (*Sl.*), inexpensive, worthless (*sense 2*) insignificant, pointless, silly, trifling, trivial, unimportant, useless, worthless

value *n.* 1. cost, equivalent, market price, monetary worth, rate 2. advantage, benefit, desirability, help, importance, merit, profit, serviceableness, significance, use, usefulness, utility, worth 3. *Plural* code of behaviour, ethics, (moral) standards, principles ~*v.* 4. account, appraise, assess, compute, estimate, evaluate, price, put a price on, rate, set at, survey 5. appreciate, cherish, esteem, hold dear, hold in high regard *or* esteem, prize, regard highly, respect, set store by, treasure
Antonyms *n.* (*sense 2*) insignificance, unimportance, uselessness, worthlessness ~*v.* disregard, have no time for, hold a low opinion of, underestimate, undervalue

valued cherished, dear, esteemed, highly regarded, loved, prized, treasured

valueless miserable, no good, of no earthly use, of no value, unsaleable, useless, worthless

vamoose bugger off (*Taboo sl.*), clear off (*Inf.*), decamp, do a bunk (*Brit. sl.*), fuck off (*Offens. taboo sl.*), go away, hook it (*Sl.*), make off, make oneself scarce (*Inf.*), run away, scarper (*Brit. sl.*), scram (*Inf.*), skedaddle (*Inf.*), take flight, take oneself off

vanguard advance guard, cutting edge, forefront, forerunners, front, front line, front rank, leaders, spearhead, trailblazers, trendsetters, van
Antonyms back, rear, rearguard, stern, tail, tail end

vanish become invisible, be lost to sight, die out, disappear, disappear from sight *or* from the face of the earth, dissolve, evanesce, evaporate, exit, fade (away), melt (away)
Antonyms appear, arrive, become visible, come into view, materialize, pop up

vanity 1. affected ways, airs, arrogance, bigheadedness (*Inf.*), conceit, conceitedness, egotism, narcissism, ostentation, pretension, pride, self-admiration, self-love, showing off (*Inf.*), swollen-headedness (*Inf.*), vainglory 2. emptiness, frivolity, fruitlessness, futility, hollowness, inanity, pointlessness, profitlessness, triviality, unproductiveness, unreality, unsubstantiality, uselessness, worthlessness
Antonyms (*sense 1*) humility, meekness, modesty, self-abasement, self-deprecation (*sense 2*) importance, value, worth

vanquish beat, blow out of the water (*Sl.*), clobber (*Sl.*), conquer, crush, defeat, get the upper hand over, lick (*Inf.*), master, overcome, overpower, overwhelm, put down, put to flight, put to rout, quell, reduce, repress, rout, run rings around (*Inf.*), subdue, subjugate, tank (*Sl.*), triumph over, undo, wipe the floor with (*Inf.*)

vapid 1. bland, dead, flat, flavourless, insipid, lifeless, milk-and-water, stale, tasteless, unpalatable, watery, weak, wishy-washy (*Inf.*) 2. boring, colourless, dull, flat, limp, tame, tedious, tiresome, uninspiring, uninteresting

vapour breath, dampness, exhalation, fog, fumes, haze, miasma, mist, smoke, steam

variable capricious, chameleonic, changeable, fickle, fitful, flexible, fluctuating, inconstant, mercurial, mutable, protean, shifting, temperamental, uneven, unstable, unsteady, vacillating, wavering
Antonyms constant, firm, fixed, settled, stable, steady, unalterable, unchanging

variance 1. difference, difference of opinion, disagreement, discord, discrepancy, dissension, dissent, divergence, inconsistency, lack of harmony, strife, variation 2. **at variance** at loggerheads, at odds, at sixes and sevens (*Inf.*), conflicting, in disagreement, in opposition, out of harmony, out of line
Antonyms (*sense 1*) accord, agreement, congruity, correspondence, harmony, similarity, unison

variant 1. *adj.* alternative, derived, different, divergent, exceptional, modified 2. *n.* alternative, derived form, development, modification, sport (*Biol.*), variation

variation alteration, break in routine, change, departure, departure from the norm, deviation, difference, discrepancy, diversification, diversity, innovation, modification, novelty, variety
Antonyms dullness, monotony, sameness, tedium, uniformity

varied assorted, different, diverse, heterogeneous, manifold, miscellaneous, mixed, motley, sundry, various
Antonyms homogeneous, repetitive, similar, standardized, uniform, unvarying

variegated diversified, many-coloured, motley, mottled, parti-coloured, pied, streaked, varicoloured

variety 1. change, difference, discrepancy, diversification, diversity, many-sidedness, multifariousness, variation 2. array, assortment, collection, cross section, intermixture, medley, miscellany, mixture, multiplicity, range 3. brand, breed, category, class, kind, make, order, sort, species, strain, type
Antonyms (*sense 1*) homogeneity, invariability, monotony, similarity, similitude, uniformity

various assorted, different, differing, disparate, distinct, divers (*Archaic*), diverse, diversified, heterogeneous, manifold, many, many-sided, miscellaneous, several, sundry, varied, variegated
Antonyms alike, equivalent, matching, same, similar, uniform

varnish *v.* adorn, decorate, embellish, gild, glaze, gloss, japan, lacquer, polish, shellac

vary alter, alternate, be unlike, change, depart, differ, disagree, diverge, diversify, fluctuate, intermix, modify, permutate, reorder, transform

varying changing, different, distinct, distinguishable, diverse, fluctuating, inconsistent
Antonyms consistent, fixed, monotonous, regular, settled, unchanging, unvarying

vassal bondman, bondservant, bondsman, liegeman, retainer, serf, slave, subject, thrall, varlet (*Archaic*)

vassalage bondage, dependence, serfdom, servitude, slavery, subjection, thraldom

vast astronomical, boundless, colossal, elephantine, enormous, extensive, gigantic, ginormous (*Inf.*), great, huge, humongous *or* humungous (*U.S. sl.*), illimitable, immeasurable, immense, limitless, mammoth, massive, measureless, mega (*Sl.*), monstrous, monumental, never-ending, prodigious, sweeping, tremendous, unbounded, unlimited, vasty (*Archaic*), voluminous, wide
Antonyms bounded, limited, microscopic, narrow, negligible, paltry, puny, small, tiny, trifling

vault[1] *v.* bound, clear, hurdle, jump, leap, spring

vault[2] *n.* 1. arch, ceiling, roof, span 2. catacomb, cellar, crypt, mausoleum, tomb, undercroft 3. depository, repository, strongroom ~*v.* 4. arch, bend, bow, curve, overarch, span

vaulted arched, cavernous, domed, hemispheric

vaunt boast about, brag about, crow about, exult in, flaunt, give oneself airs about, make a display of, make much of, parade, prate about, show off, talk big about (*Inf.*)

veer be deflected, change, change course, change direction, sheer, shift, swerve, tack, turn

vegetate 1. be inert, deteriorate, exist, go to seed, idle, languish, loaf, moulder, stagnate, veg out (*Sl., chiefly U.S.*) 2. burgeon, germinate, grow, shoot, spring, sprout, swell
Antonyms (*sense 1*) accomplish, develop, grow, participate, perform, react, respond

vehemence ardour, eagerness, earnestness, emphasis, energy, enthusiasm, fervency, fervour, fire, force, forcefulness, heat, impetuosity, intensity, keenness, passion, verve, vigour, violence, warmth, zeal
Antonyms apathy, coolness, indifference, inertia, lethargy, listlessness, passivity, stoicism, torpor

vehement ardent, eager, earnest, emphatic, enthusiastic, fervent, fervid, fierce, flaming,

forceful, forcible, impassioned, impetuous, intense, passionate, powerful, strong, violent, zealous
Antonyms apathetic, calm, cool, dispassionate, half-hearted, impassive, lukewarm, moderate

vehicle *Fig.* apparatus, channel, means, means of expression, mechanism, medium, organ

veil 1. *v.* cloak, conceal, cover, dim, disguise, hide, mantle, mask, obscure, screen, shield 2. *n.* blind, cloak, cover, curtain, disguise, film, mask, screen, shade, shroud
Antonyms *v.* disclose, display, divulge, expose, lay bare, reveal, uncover, unveil

veiled concealed, covert, disguised, hinted at, implied, masked, suppressed

vein 1. blood vessel, course, current, lode, seam, stratum, streak, stripe 2. dash, hint, strain, streak, thread, trait 3. attitude, bent, character, faculty, humour, mode, mood, note, style, temper, tenor, tone, turn

velocity celerity, fleetness, impetus, pace, quickness, rapidity, speed, swiftness

velvety delicate, downy, mossy, smooth, soft, velutinous, velvet-like

venal bent (*Sl.*), corrupt, corruptible, crooked (*Inf.*), dishonourable, grafting (*Inf.*), mercenary, prostituted, purchasable, rapacious, simoniacal, sordid, unprincipled
Antonyms honest, honourable, incorruptible, law-abiding, principled, upright

vendetta bad blood, blood feud, feud, quarrel

veneer *n. Fig.* appearance, façade, false front, finish, front, gloss, guise, mask, pretence, semblance, show

venerable august, esteemed, grave, honoured, respected, revered, reverenced, sage, sedate, wise, worshipped
Antonyms callow, discredited, disdained, disgraced, dishonourable, disreputable, green, ignominious, immature, inexperienced, inglorious, scorned, young, youthful

venerate adore, esteem, hold in awe, honour, look up to, respect, revere, reverence, worship
Antonyms deride, dishonour, disregard, execrate, mock, scorn, spurn

veneration adoration, awe, deference, esteem, respect, reverence, worship

vengeance 1. an eye for an eye, avenging, lex talionis, reprisal, requital, retaliation, retribution, revenge, settling of scores 2. **with a vengeance a.** forcefully, furiously, vehemently, violently **b.** and no mistake, extremely, greatly, to the full, to the utmost, with no holds barred
Antonyms (*sense 1*) absolution, acquittal, exoneration, forbearance, forgiveness, mercy, pardon, remission

vengeful avenging, implacable, punitive, rancorous, relentless, retaliatory, revengeful, spiteful, thirsting for revenge, unforgiving, vindictive

venial allowable, excusable, forgivable, insignificant, minor, pardonable, slight, trivial

venom 1. bane, poison, toxin 2. acidity, acrimony, bitterness, gall, grudge, hate, ill will, malevolence, malice, maliciousness, malignity, rancour, spite, spitefulness, spleen, virulence
Antonyms (*sense 2*) benevolence, charity, compassion, favour, good will, kindness, love, mercy

venomous 1. baneful (*Archaic*), envenomed, mephitic, noxious, poison, poisonous, toxic, virulent 2. baleful, hostile, malicious, malignant, rancorous, savage, spiteful, vicious, vindictive, virulent
Antonyms (*sense 1*) harmless, nonpoisonous, nontoxic, nonvenomous (*sense 2*) affectionate, benevolent, compassionate, forgiving, harmless, loving, magnanimous

vent 1. *n.* aperture, duct, hole, opening, orifice, outlet, split 2. *v.* air, come out with, discharge, emit, empty, express, give expression to, give vent to, pour out, release, utter, voice
Antonyms *v.* bottle up, curb, hold back, inhibit, quash, quell, repress, stifle, subdue

ventilate *Fig.* air, bring out into the open, broadcast, debate, discuss, examine, make known, scrutinize, sift, talk about

venture *v.* 1. chance, endanger, hazard, imperil, jeopardize, put in jeopardy, risk, speculate, stake, wager 2. advance, dare, dare say, hazard, make bold, presume, stick one's neck out (*Inf.*), take the liberty, volunteer 3. *With* **out, forth,** *etc.* embark on, go, plunge into, set out ~*n.* 4. adventure, chance, endeavour, enterprise, fling, gamble, hazard, jeopardy, project, risk, speculation, undertaking

venturesome adventurous, bold, courageous, daredevil, daring, doughty, enterprising, fearless, intrepid, plucky, spirited

veracious accurate, credible, dependable, ethical, factual, faithful, frank, genuine, high-principled, honest, reliable, straightforward, true, trustworthy, truthful, veridical

veracity accuracy, candour, credibility, exactitude, frankness, honesty, integrity, precision, probity, rectitude, trustworthiness, truth, truthfulness, uprightness

verbal literal, oral, spoken, unwritten, verbatim, word-of-mouth

verbally by word of mouth, orally

verbatim exactly, precisely, to the letter, word for word

verbiage circumlocution, periphrasis, pleonasm, prolixity, redundancy, repetition, tautology, verbosity

verbose circumlocutory, diffuse, garrulous, long-winded, periphrastic, pleonastic, prolix, tautological, windy, wordy
Antonyms brief, brusque, concise, curt, quiet, reticent, short, succinct, terse, untalkative

verbosely at great length, at undue length, long-windedly, wordily

verbosity garrulity, logorrhoea, long-windedness, loquaciousness, prolixity, rambling, verbiage, verboseness, windiness, wordiness

verdant flourishing, fresh, grassy, green, leafy, lush

verdict adjudication, conclusion, decision, finding, judgment, opinion, sentence

verge 1. *n.* border, boundary, brim, brink, edge, extreme, limit, lip, margin, roadside, threshold 2. *v.* approach, border, come near

verification authentication, confirmation, corroboration, proof, substantiation, validation

verify attest, attest to, authenticate, bear out, check, confirm, corroborate, prove, substantiate, support, validate
Antonyms deny, discount, discredit, dispute, invalidate, nullify, undermine, weaken

verisimilitude authenticity, colour, credibility, likeliness, likeness, plausibility, realism, resemblance, semblance, show of

verminous alive, crawling, flea-ridden, lousy, rat-infested

vernacular 1. *adj.* colloquial, common, indigenous, informal, local, mother, native, popular, vulgar 2. *n.* argot, cant, dialect, idiom, jargon, native language, parlance, patois, speech, vulgar tongue

versatile adaptable, adjustable, all-purpose, all-round, flexible, functional, handy, many-sided, multifaceted, protean, resourceful, variable
Antonyms fixed, inflexible, invariable, limited, one-sided, unadaptable

versed accomplished, acquainted, competent, conversant, experienced, familiar, knowledgeable, practised, proficient, qualified, seasoned, skilled, well informed, well up in (*Inf.*)
Antonyms callow, green, ignorant, inexperienced, new, raw, unacquainted, unfledged, unpractised, unschooled, unskilled, unversed

version 1. account, adaptation, exercise, interpretation, portrayal, reading, rendering, side, translation 2. design, form, kind, model, style, type, variant

vertex acme, apex, apogee, crest, crown, culmination, extremity, height, pinnacle, summit, top, zenith

vertical erect, on end, perpendicular, upright
Antonyms flat, horizontal, level, plane, prone

vertigo dizziness, giddiness, light-headedness, loss of equilibrium, swimming of the head

verve animation, brio, dash, élan, energy, enthusiasm, force, get-up-and-go (*Inf.*), gusto, life, liveliness, pep, punch (*Inf.*), sparkle, spirit, vigour, vim (*Sl.*), vitality, vivacity, zeal, zip (*Inf.*)
Antonyms apathy, disdain, half-heartedness, indifference, inertia, lack of enthusiasm, languor, lethargy, lifelessness, reluctance, torpor

very *adv.* 1. absolutely, acutely, awfully (*Inf.*), decidedly, deeply, eminently, exceedingly, excessively, extremely, greatly, highly, jolly (*Brit.*), noticeably, particularly, profoundly, really, remarkably, superlatively, surpassingly, terribly, truly, uncommonly, unusually, wonderfully ~*adj.* 2. actual, appropriate, exact, express, identical, perfect, precise, real, same, selfsame, unqualified 3. bare, mere, plain, pure, sheer, simple

vessel 1. barque (*Poetic*), boat, craft, ship 2. container, pot, receptacle, utensil

vest *v.* 1. *With* **in** *or* **with** authorize, be devolved upon, bestow, confer, consign, empower, endow, entrust, furnish, invest, lodge, place, put in the hands of, settle 2. apparel, bedeck, clothe, cover, dress, envelop, garb, robe

vestibule anteroom, entrance hall, foyer, hall, lobby, porch, portico

vestige evidence, glimmer, hint, indication, relic, remainder, remains, remnant, residue, scrap, sign, suspicion, token, trace, track

vestigial imperfect, incomplete, nonfunctional, rudimentary, surviving, undeveloped
Antonyms complete, developed, functional, perfect, practical, useful

vet *v.* appraise, check, check out, examine, give (someone *or* something) the once-over (*Inf.*), investigate, look over, pass under review, review, scan, scrutinize, size up (*Inf.*)

veteran 1. *n.* master, old hand, old stager, old-timer, past master, past mistress, pro

(*Inf.*), trouper, warhorse (*Inf.*) 2. *adj.* adept, battle-scarred, expert, long-serving, old, proficient, seasoned

Antonyms *n.* apprentice, beginner, freshman, initiate, neophyte, novice, recruit, tyro

veto 1. *v.* ban, boycott, disallow, forbid, give the thumbs down to, interdict, kill (*Inf.*), negative, prohibit, put the kibosh on (*Sl.*), refuse permission, reject, rule out, turn down 2. *n.* ban, boycott, embargo, interdict, nonconsent, prohibition

Antonyms *v.* approve, endorse, O.K. *or* okay (*Inf.*), pass, ratify ~*n.* approval, endorsement, go-ahead (*Inf.*), ratification

vex afflict, aggravate (*Inf.*), agitate, annoy, bother, bug (*Inf.*), displease, distress, disturb, exasperate, fret, gall, get on one's nerves (*Inf.*), grate on, harass, hassle (*Inf.*), irritate, molest, nark (*Brit., Aust., & N.Z. sl.*), needle (*Inf.*), nettle, offend, peeve (*Inf.*), perplex, pester, pique, plague, provoke, put out, rile, tease, torment, trouble, upset, worry

Antonyms allay, appease, comfort, console, gratify, hush, mollify, please, quiet, soothe

vexation 1. aggravation (*Inf.*), annoyance, displeasure, dissatisfaction, exasperation, frustration, irritation, pique 2. bother, difficulty, hassle (*Inf.*), headache (*Inf.*), irritant, misfortune, nuisance, problem, thorn in one's flesh, trouble, upset, worry

vexatious afflicting, aggravating (*Inf.*), annoying, bothersome, burdensome, disagreeable, disappointing, distressing, exasperating, harassing, irksome, irritating, nagging, plaguy (*Archaic*), provoking, teasing, tormenting, troublesome, trying, unpleasant, upsetting, worrisome, worrying

Antonyms agreeable, balmy, calming, comforting, pleasant, reassuring, relaxing, soothing

vexed 1. afflicted, aggravated (*Inf.*), agitated, annoyed, bothered, confused, displeased, distressed, disturbed, exasperated, fed up, hacked (off) (*U.S. sl.*), harassed, irritated, miffed (*Inf.*), nettled, out of countenance, peeved (*Inf.*), perplexed, pissed off (*Taboo sl.*), provoked, put out, riled, ruffled, tormented, troubled, upset, worried 2. contested, controversial, disputed, moot, much debated

viable applicable, feasible, operable, practicable, usable, within the bounds of possibility, workable

Antonyms hopeless, impossible, impracticable, inconceivable, out of the question, unthinkable, unworkable

vibes atmosphere, aura, emanation, emotions, feelings, reaction, response, vibrations

vibrant 1. aquiver, oscillating, palpitating, pulsating, quivering, trembling 2. alive, animated, colourful, dynamic, electrifying, full of pep (*Inf.*), responsive, sensitive, sparkling, spirited, vivacious, vivid

vibrate fluctuate, judder (*Inf.*), oscillate, pulsate, pulse, quiver, resonate, reverberate, shake, shiver, sway, swing, throb, tremble, undulate

vibration juddering (*Inf.*), oscillation, pulsation, pulse, quiver, resonance, reverberation, shaking, throb, throbbing, trembling, tremor

vicarious acting, at one remove, commissioned, delegated, deputed, empathetic, indirect, substituted, surrogate

vice 1. corruption, degeneracy, depravity, evil, evildoing, immorality, iniquity, profligacy, sin, turpitude, venality, wickedness 2. blemish, defect, failing, fault, imperfection, shortcoming, weakness

Antonyms (*sense 1*) honour, morality, virtue (*sense 2*) attainment, gift, good point, strong point, talent

vice versa contrariwise, conversely, in reverse, the other way round

vicinity area, district, environs, locality, neck of the woods (*Inf.*), neighbourhood, precincts, propinquity, proximity, purlieus

vicious 1. abandoned, abhorrent, atrocious, bad, barbarous, corrupt, cruel, dangerous, debased, degenerate, degraded, depraved, diabolical, ferocious, fiendish, foul, heinous, immoral, infamous, monstrous, profligate, savage, sinful, unprincipled, vile, violent, wicked, worthless, wrong 2. backbiting, bitchy (*Inf.*), cruel, defamatory, malicious, mean, rancorous, slanderous, spiteful, venomous, vindictive

Antonyms complimentary, docile, friendly, gentle, good, honourable, kind, playful, tame, upright, virtuous

viciousness 1. badness, corruption, cruelty, depravity, ferocity, immorality, profligacy, savagery, wickedness 2. bitchiness (*Sl.*), malice, rancour, spite, spitefulness, venom

Antonyms (*sense 2*) gentleness, goodness, good will, graciousness, kindness, mercy, virtue

vicissitude alteration, alternation, change, fluctuation of fortune, mutation, one of life's ups and downs (*Inf.*), revolution, shift, variation

victim 1. casualty, fatality, injured party, martyr, sacrifice, scapegoat, sufferer 2. dupe, easy prey, fall guy (*Inf.*), gull (*Archaic*), innocent, patsy (*Sl., chiefly U.S. &*

Canad.), sitting duck (*Inf.*), sitting target, sucker (*Sl.*)
Antonyms (*sense 1*) survivor (*sense 2*) assailant, attacker, culprit, guilty party, offender

victimize 1. discriminate against, have a down on (someone) (*Inf.*), have it in for (someone) (*Inf.*), have one's knife into (someone), persecute, pick on 2. cheat, deceive, defraud, dupe, exploit, fool, gull (*Archaic*), hoodwink, prey on, swindle, take advantage of, use

victor champ (*Inf.*), champion, conquering hero, conqueror, first, prizewinner, top dog (*Inf.*), vanquisher, winner
Antonyms also-ran, dud (*Inf.*), failure, flop (*Inf.*), loser, vanquished

victorious champion, conquering, first, prizewinning, successful, triumphant, vanquishing, winning
Antonyms beaten, conquered, defeated, failed, losing, overcome, unsuccessful, vanquished

victory conquest, laurels, mastery, success, superiority, the palm, the prize, triumph, win
Antonyms defeat, failure, loss

victuals bread, comestibles, eatables, eats (*Sl.*), edibles, food, grub (*Sl.*), meat, nosebag (*Sl.*), nosh (*Sl.*), provisions, rations, stores, supplies, tack (*Inf.*), viands, vittles (*Obsolete*)

vie be rivals, compete, contend, contest, match oneself against, strive, struggle

view *n.* 1. aspect, landscape, outlook, panorama, perspective, picture, prospect, scene, spectacle, vista 2. range *or* field of vision, sight, vision 3. *Sometimes plural* attitude, belief, conviction, feeling, impression, judgment, notion, opinion, point of view, sentiment, thought, way of thinking 4. contemplation, display, examination, inspection, look, recce (*Sl.*), scan, scrutiny, sight, survey, viewing 5. **with a view to** in order to, in the hope of, so as to, with the aim *or* intention of ~*v.* 6. behold, check, check out (*Inf.*), clock (*Brit. sl.*), contemplate, examine, explore, eye, eyeball (*U.S. sl.*), gaze at, get a load of (*Inf.*), inspect, look at, observe, recce (*Sl.*), regard, scan, spectate, stare at, survey, take a dekko at (*Brit. sl.*), watch, witness 7. consider, deem, judge, look on, regard, think about

viewer observer, one of an audience, onlooker, spectator, TV watcher, watcher

viewpoint angle, frame of reference, perspective, point of view, position, slant, stance, standpoint, vantage point, way of thinking

vigilance alertness, attentiveness, carefulness, caution, circumspection, observance, watchfulness

vigilant alert, Argus-eyed, attentive, careful, cautious, circumspect, keeping one's eyes peeled *or* skinned (*Inf.*), on one's guard, on one's toes, on the alert, on the lookout, on the qui vive, on the watch, sleepless, unsleeping, wakeful, watchful, wide awake
Antonyms careless, inattentive, lax, neglectful, negligent, remiss, slack

vigorous active, brisk, dynamic, effective, efficient, energetic, enterprising, flourishing, forceful, forcible, full of energy, hale, hale and hearty, hardy, healthy, intense, lively, lusty, powerful, Ramboesque, red-blooded, robust, sound, spanking, spirited, strenuous, strong, virile, vital, zippy (*Inf.*)
Antonyms apathetic, effete, enervated, feeble, frail, inactive, indolent, lethargic, lifeless, spiritless, torpid, weak, weedy (*Inf.*), wimpish *or* wimpy (*Inf.*), wishy-washy

vigorously all out, eagerly, energetically, forcefully, hammer and tongs, hard, like mad (*Sl.*), lustily, strenuously, strongly, with a vengeance, with might and main

vigour activity, animation, balls (*Taboo sl.*), brio, dash, dynamism, energy, force, forcefulness, gusto, health, liveliness, might, oomph (*Inf.*), pep, power, punch (*Inf.*), robustness, snap (*Inf.*), soundness, spirit, strength, verve, vim (*Sl.*), virility, vitality, zip (*Inf.*)
Antonyms apathy, feebleness, fragility, frailty, impotence, inactivity, inertia, infirmity, lethargy, sluggishness, weakness

vile 1. abandoned, abject, appalling, bad, base, coarse, contemptible, corrupt, debased, degenerate, degrading, depraved, despicable, disgraceful, evil, humiliating, ignoble, impure, loathsome, low, mean, miserable, nefarious, perverted, shocking, sinful, ugly, vicious, vulgar, wicked, worthless, wretched 2. disgusting, foul, horrid, loathsome, nasty, nauseating, noxious, obscene, offensive, repellent, repugnant, repulsive, revolting, sickening, yucky *or* yukky (*Sl.*)
Antonyms agreeable, chaste, cultured, delicate, genteel, honourable, lovely, marvellous, noble, pleasant, polite, pure, refined, righteous, splendid, sublime, upright, worthy

vileness coarseness, corruption, degeneracy, depravity, dreadfulness, enormity, evil, foulness, heinousness, noxiousness, offensiveness, outrage, profanity, turpitude, ugliness, wickedness

vilification abuse, aspersion, calumniation,

calumny, contumely, defamation, denigration, disparagement, invective, mudslinging, scurrility, vituperation

vilify abuse, asperse, bad-mouth (*Sl., chiefly U.S. & Canad.*), berate, calumniate, debase, decry, defame, denigrate, disparage, knock (*Inf.*), malign, pull to pieces (*Inf.*), revile, rubbish (*Inf.*), run down, slag (off) (*Sl.*), slander, smear, speak ill of, traduce, vilipend (*Rare*), vituperate
Antonyms adore, commend, esteem, exalt, glorify, honour, praise, revere, venerate

villain 1. blackguard, caitiff (*Archaic*), criminal, evildoer, knave (*Archaic*), libertine, malefactor, miscreant, profligate, rapscallion, reprobate, rogue, scoundrel, wretch 2. antihero, baddy (*Inf.*) 3. devil, monkey, rascal, rogue, scallywag (*Inf.*), scamp
Antonyms (*senses 2 & 3*) angel, goody, hero, heroine, idol

villainous atrocious, bad, base, blackguardly, criminal, cruel, debased, degenerate, depraved, detestable, diabolical, evil, fiendish, hateful, heinous, ignoble, infamous, inhuman, mean, nefarious, outrageous, ruffianly, scoundrelly, sinful, terrible, thievish, vicious, vile, wicked
Antonyms angelic, good, heroic, humane, moral, noble, righteous, saintly, virtuous

villainy atrocity, baseness, crime, criminality, delinquency, depravity, devilry, iniquity, knavery, rascality, sin, turpitude, vice, wickedness

vindicate 1. absolve, acquit, clear, defend, do justice to, exculpate, excuse, exonerate, free from blame, justify, rehabilitate 2. advocate, assert, establish, maintain, support, uphold
Antonyms (*sense 1*) accuse, blame, condemn, convict, incriminate, punish, reproach

vindication apology, assertion, defence, exculpating, exculpation, excuse, exoneration, justification, maintenance, plea, rehabilitation, substantiation, support

vindictive full of spleen, implacable, malicious, malignant, rancorous, relentless, resentful, revengeful, spiteful, unforgiving, unrelenting, vengeful, venomous
Antonyms forgiving, generous, magnanimous, merciful, relenting, unvindictive

vintage 1. *n.* collection, crop, epoch, era, generation, harvest, origin, year 2. *adj.* best, choice, classic, mature, prime, rare, ripe, select, superior, venerable

violate 1. break, contravene, disobey, disregard, encroach upon, infract, infringe, transgress 2. abuse, assault, befoul, debauch, defile, desecrate, dishonour, invade, outrage, pollute, profane, rape, ravish
Antonyms (*sense 1*) honour, obey, respect, uphold (*sense 2*) defend, honour, protect, respect, revere, set on a pedestal

violation 1. abuse, breach, contravention, encroachment, infraction, infringement, transgression, trespass 2. defilement, desecration, profanation, sacrilege, spoliation

violence 1. bestiality, bloodshed, bloodthirstiness, brutality, brute force, cruelty, destructiveness, ferocity, fierceness, fighting, force, frenzy, fury, murderousness, passion, rough handling, savagery, strong-arm tactics (*Inf.*), terrorism, thuggery, vehemence, wildness 2. boisterousness, power, raging, roughness, storminess, tumult, turbulence, wildness 3. abandon, acuteness, fervour, force, harshness, intensity, severity, sharpness, vehemence

violent 1. berserk, bloodthirsty, brutal, cruel, destructive, fiery, flaming, forcible, furious, headstrong, homicidal, hot-headed, impetuous, intemperate, maddened, maniacal, murderous, passionate, powerful, raging, Ramboesque, riotous, rough, savage, strong, tempestuous, uncontrollable, ungovernable, unrestrained, vehement, vicious, wild 2. blustery, boisterous, devastating, full of force, gale force, powerful, raging, ruinous, strong, tempestuous, tumultuous, turbulent, wild 3. acute, agonizing, biting, excruciating, extreme, harsh, inordinate, intense, outrageous, painful, severe, sharp
Antonyms calm, composed, gentle, mild, peaceful, quiet, rational, sane, serene, unruffled, well-behaved

V.I.P. big name, big noise (*Inf.*), big shot (*Inf.*), bigwig (*Inf.*), celebrity, leading light (*Inf.*), lion, luminary, man *or* woman of the hour, notable, personage, public figure, somebody, star

virago ballbreaker (*Sl.*), battle-axe (*Inf.*), fury, harridan, scold, shrew, termagant (*Rare*), vixen, Xanthippe

virgin 1. *n.* damsel (*Archaic*), girl, maid (*Archaic*), maiden (*Archaic*), vestal, virgo intacta 2. *adj.* chaste, fresh, immaculate, maidenly, modest, new, pristine, pure, snowy, uncorrupted, undefiled, unsullied, untouched, unused, vestal, virginal
Antonyms *adj.* contaminated, corrupted, defiled, dirty, impure, polluted, spoiled, used

virginal celibate, chaste, fresh, immaculate, maidenly, pristine, pure, snowy, spotless, uncorrupted, undefiled, undisturbed, untouched, virgin, white

virginity chastity, maidenhead, maidenhood

virile forceful, lusty, macho, male, manlike, manly, masculine, potent, Ramboesque, red-blooded, robust, strong, vigorous
Antonyms camp (*Inf.*), effeminate, emasculate, feminine, impotent, unmanly, weak, weedy (*Inf.*), wimpish *or* wimpy (*Inf.*)

virility machismo, manhood, masculinity, potency, vigour
Antonyms effeminacy, femininity, impotence, softness, unmanliness, weakness

virtual essential, implicit, implied, in all but name, indirect, potential, practical, tacit, unacknowledged

virtually as good as, effectually, for all practical purposes, in all but name, in effect, in essence, nearly, practically, to all intents and purposes

virtue 1. ethicalness, excellence, goodness, high-mindedness, incorruptibility, integrity, justice, morality, probity, quality, rectitude, righteousness, uprightness, worth, worthiness 2. advantage, asset, attribute, credit, good point, good quality, merit, plus (*Inf.*), strength 3. chastity, honour, innocence, morality, purity, virginity 4. **by virtue of** as a result of, by dint of, by reason of, in view of, on account of, owing to, thanks to
Antonyms (*sense 1*) corruption, debauchery, depravity, dishonesty, dishonour, evil, immorality, sin, sinfulness, vice, turpitude (*sense 2*) drawback, failing, frailty, shortcoming, weak point (*sense 3*) promiscuity, unchastity

virtuosity brilliance, craft, éclat, expertise, finish, flair, mastery, panache, polish, skill

virtuoso 1. *n.* artist, genius, grandmaster, maestro, magician, master, master hand, maven (*U.S.*) 2. *adj.* bravura (*Music*), brilliant, dazzling, masterly

virtuous 1. blameless, ethical, excellent, exemplary, good, high-principled, honest, honourable, incorruptible, moral, praiseworthy, pure, righteous, squeaky-clean, upright, worthy 2. celibate, chaste, clean-living, innocent, pure, spotless, virginal
Antonyms (*sense 1*) corrupt, debauched, depraved, dishonest, evil, immoral, sinful, unrighteous, vicious, wicked (*sense 2*) impure, loose, promiscuous, unchaste

virulence 1. deadliness, harmfulness, hurtfulness, infectiousness, injuriousness, malignancy, noxiousness, poisonousness, toxicity, virulency 2. acrimony, antagonism, bitterness, hatred, hostility, ill will, malevolence, malice, poison, rancour, resentment, spite, spleen, venom, viciousness, vindictiveness

virulent 1. baneful (*Archaic*), deadly, infective, injurious, lethal, malignant, pernicious, poisonous, septic, toxic, venomous 2. acrimonious, bitter, envenomed, hostile, malevolent, malicious, rancorous, resentful, spiteful, splenetic, venomous, vicious, vindictive
Antonyms (*sense 1*) harmless, innocuous, nonpoisonous, nontoxic (*sense 2*) amiable, benign, compassionate, kind, magnanimous, sympathetic, warm

viscous adhesive, clammy, gelatinous, gluey, glutinous, gooey (*Inf.*), gummy, mucilaginous, sticky, syrupy, tenacious, thick, treacly, viscid

visible anywhere to be seen, apparent, clear, conspicuous, detectable, discernible, discoverable, distinguishable, evident, in sight, in view, manifest, not hidden, noticeable, observable, obvious, palpable, patent, perceivable, perceptible, plain, to be seen, unconcealed, unmistakable
Antonyms concealed, hidden, imperceptible, invisible, obscured, unnoticeable, unseen

vision 1. eyes, eyesight, perception, seeing, sight, view 2. breadth of view, discernment, farsightedness, foresight, imagination, insight, intuition, penetration, prescience 3. castle in the air, concept, conception, daydream, dream, fantasy, idea, ideal, image, mental picture, pipe dream 4. apparition, chimera, delusion, eidolon, ghost, hallucination, illusion, mirage, phantasm, phantom, revelation, spectre, wraith 5. dream, feast for the eyes, perfect picture, picture, sight, sight for sore eyes, spectacle

visionary *adj.* 1. dreaming, dreamy, idealistic, quixotic, romantic, starry-eyed, with one's head in the clouds 2. chimerical, delusory, fanciful, fantastic, ideal, idealized, illusory, imaginary, impractical, prophetic, speculative, unreal, unrealistic, unworkable, utopian *~n.* 3. daydreamer, Don Quixote, dreamer, enthusiast (*Archaic*), idealist, mystic, prophet, romantic, seer, theorist, utopian, zealot
Antonyms *adj.* actual, mundane, pragmatic, real, realistic, unimaginary *~n.* cynic, pessimist, pragmatist, realist

visit *v.* 1. be the guest of, call in, call on, drop in on (*Inf.*), go to see, inspect, look (someone) up, pay a call on, pop in (*Inf.*), stay at, stay with, stop by, take in (*Inf.*) 2. afflict, assail, attack, befall, descend upon, haunt, smite, trouble 3. *With* **on** *or* **upon** bring down upon, execute, impose, inflict, wreak *~n.* 4. call, sojourn, stay, stop

visitation 1. examination, inspection, visit 2. bane, blight, calamity, cataclysm, catastrophe, disaster, infliction, ordeal, punishment, scourge, trial

visitor caller, company, guest, visitant

vista panorama, perspective, prospect, view

visual 1. ocular, optic, optical 2. discernible, observable, perceptible, visible
Antonyms (*sense 2*) imperceptible, indiscernible, invisible, out of sight, unnoticeable, unperceivable

visualize conceive of, conjure up a mental picture of, envisage, imagine, picture, see in the mind's eye

vital 1. basic, cardinal, essential, fundamental, imperative, indispensable, necessary, radical, requisite 2. critical, crucial, decisive, important, key, life-or-death, significant, urgent 3. animated, dynamic, energetic, forceful, full of the joy of living, lively, sparky, spirited, vibrant, vigorous, vivacious, zestful 4. alive, animate, generative, invigorative, life-giving, live, living, quickening
Antonyms (*sense 1*) dispensable, inessential, nonessential, unnecessary (*sense 2*) minor, trivial, unimportant (*sense 3*) apathetic, lethargic, listless, uninvolved (*sense 4*) dead, dying, inanimate, moribund

vitality animation, brio, energy, exuberance, go (*Inf.*), life, liveliness, lustiness, pep, robustness, sparkle, stamina, strength, vigour, vim (*Sl.*), vivaciousness, vivacity
Antonyms apathy, inertia, lethargy, listlessness, sluggishness, weakness

vitiate 1. blemish, devalue, harm, impair, injure, invalidate, mar, spoil, undermine, water down 2. blight, contaminate, corrupt, debase, defile, deprave, deteriorate, pervert, pollute, sully, taint

vitiation 1. deterioration, devaluation, dilution, impairment, marring, reduction, spoiling, undermining 2. adulteration, contamination, corruption, debasement, degradation, perversion, pollution, sullying

vitriolic *Fig.* acerbic, acid, bitchy (*Inf.*), bitter, caustic, destructive, dripping with malice, envenomed, sardonic, scathing, venomous, virulent, withering

vituperate abuse, asperse, berate, blame, castigate, censure, cry down, denounce, excoriate, find fault with, rail against, rate, reproach, revile, run down, slang, slate (*Inf.*), tear into (*Inf.*), upbraid, vilify

vituperation abuse, billingsgate, blame, castigation, censure, fault-finding, flak (*Inf.*), invective, obloquy, rebuke, reprimand, reproach, scurrility, tongue-lashing, vilification
Antonyms acclaim, approval, commendation, eulogy, flattery, praise, tribute

vituperative abusive, belittling, calumniatory, censorious, defamatory, denunciatory, derogatory, harsh, insulting, malign, opprobrious, sardonic, scurrilous, withering

vivacious animated, bubbling, cheerful, chirpy (*Inf.*), ebullient, effervescent, frolicsome, full of life, gay, high-spirited, jolly, light-hearted, lively, merry, scintillating, sparkling, sparky, spirited, sportive, sprightly, upbeat (*Inf.*), vital
Antonyms boring, dull, languid, lifeless, listless, melancholy, spiritless, unenthusiastic

vivacity animation, brio, ebullience, effervescence, energy, gaiety, high spirits, life, liveliness, pep, quickness, sparkle, spirit, sprightliness
Antonyms apathy, ennui, fatigue, heaviness, inertia, languor, lethargy, listlessness, weariness

vivid 1. bright, brilliant, clear, colourful, glowing, intense, rich 2. distinct, dramatic, graphic, highly-coloured, lifelike, memorable, powerful, realistic, sharp, sharply-etched, stirring, strong, telling, true to life 3. active, animated, dynamic, energetic, expressive, flamboyant, lively, quick, spirited, striking, strong, vigorous
Antonyms colourless, cool, drab, dull, lifeless, nondescript, ordinary, pale, pastel, quiet, routine, run-of-the-mill, sombre, unclear, unmemorable, unremarkable, vague

vividness 1. brightness, brilliancy, glow, life, radiance, resplendence, sprightliness 2. clarity, distinctness, graphicness, immediacy, intensity, realism, sharpness, strength

vixen *Fig.* ballbreaker (*Sl.*), fury, harpy, harridan, hellcat, scold, shrew, spitfire, termagant (*Rare*), virago, Xanthippe

viz. namely, that is to say, to wit, videlicet

vocabulary dictionary, glossary, language, lexicon, wordbook, word hoard, words, word stock

vocal *adj.* 1. articulate, articulated, oral, put into words, said, spoken, uttered, voiced 2. articulate, blunt, clamorous, eloquent, expressive, forthright, frank, free-spoken, noisy, outspoken, plain-spoken, strident, vociferous
Antonyms (*sense 2*) inarticulate, quiet, reserved, reticent, retiring, shy, silent, uncommunicative

vocation business, calling, career, employment, job, life's work, life work, métier, mission, office, post, profession, pursuit, role, trade

vociferous clamant, clamorous, loud, loudmouthed (*Inf.*), noisy, obstreperous,

outspoken, ranting, shouting, strident, uproarious, vehement, vocal
Antonyms hushed, muted, noiseless, quiet, silent, still

vogue *n.* 1. craze, custom, *dernier cri,* fashion, last word, mode, style, the latest, the rage, the thing (*Inf.*), trend, way 2. acceptance, currency, fashionableness, favour, popularity, prevalence, usage, use ~*adj.* 3. fashionable, in, modish, now (*Inf.*), popular, prevalent, trendy (*Brit. inf.*), up-to-the-minute, voguish, with it (*Inf.*)

voice *n.* 1. articulation, language, power of speech, sound, tone, utterance, words 2. decision, expression, part, say, view, vote, will, wish 3. agency, instrument, medium, mouthpiece, organ, spokesman, spokesperson, spokeswoman, vehicle ~*v.* 4. air, articulate, assert, come out with (*Inf.*), declare, divulge, enunciate, express, give expression *or* utterance to, put into words, say, utter, ventilate

void *adj.* 1. bare, clear, drained, emptied, empty, free, tenantless, unfilled, unoccupied, vacant 2. *With* **of** destitute, devoid, lacking, without 3. dead, ineffective, ineffectual, inoperative, invalid, nonviable, nugatory, null and void, unenforceable, useless, vain, worthless ~*n.* 4. blank, blankness, emptiness, gap, lack, opening, space, vacuity, vacuum, want ~*v.* 5. discharge, drain, eject, eliminate (*Physiol.*), emit, empty, evacuate 6. abnegate, cancel, invalidate, nullify, rescind
Antonyms *adj.* (*sense 1*) abounding, complete, filled, full, occupied, replete, tenanted

volatile airy, changeable, erratic, explosive, fickle, flighty, gay, giddy, inconstant, lively, mercurial, sprightly, temperamental, unsettled, unstable, unsteady, up and down (*Inf.*), variable, whimsical
Antonyms calm, consistent, constant, cool-headed, dependable, inert, reliable, self-controlled, settled, sober, stable, steady

volition choice, choosing, determination, discretion, election, free will, option, preference, purpose, resolution, will

volley *n.* barrage, blast, bombardment, burst, cannonade, discharge, explosion, fusillade, hail, salvo, shower

volubility fluency, garrulity, gift of the gab, glibness, loquaciousness, loquacity

voluble articulate, blessed with the gift of the gab, fluent, forthcoming, glib, loquacious, talkative
Antonyms hesitant, inarticulate, reticent, succinct, taciturn, terse, tongue-tied, unforthcoming

volume 1. aggregate, amount, body, bulk, capacity, compass, cubic content, dimensions, mass, quantity, total 2. book, publication, title, tome, treatise

voluminous ample, big, billowing, bulky, capacious, cavernous, copious, full, large, massive, prolific, roomy, vast
Antonyms inadequate, insufficient, scanty, skimpy, slight, small, tiny

voluntarily by choice, freely, lief (*Rare*), of one's own accord, of one's own free will, on one's own initiative, willingly, without being asked, without prompting

voluntary discretional, discretionary, free, gratuitous, honorary, intended, intentional, optional, spontaneous, uncompelled, unconstrained, unforced, unpaid, volunteer, willing
Antonyms automatic, conscripted, forced, instinctive, involuntary, obligatory, unintentional

volunteer *v.* advance, let oneself in for (*Inf.*), need no invitation, offer, offer one's services, present, proffer, propose, put forward, put oneself at (someone's) disposal, step forward, suggest, tender
Antonyms begrudge, deny, keep, refuse, retain, withdraw, withhold

voluptuary *n. bon vivant,* epicurean, hedonist, luxury-lover, playboy, pleasure seeker, profligate, sensualist, sybarite

voluptuous 1. epicurean, hedonistic, licentious, luxurious, pleasure-loving, self-indulgent, sensual, sybaritic 2. ample, buxom, curvaceous (*Inf.*), enticing, erotic, full-bosomed, provocative, seductive, shapely, well-stacked (*Brit. sl.*)
Antonyms (*sense 1*) abstemious, ascetic, celibate, rigorous, self-denying, Spartan

voluptuousness carnality, curvaceousness (*Inf.*), licentiousness, opulence, seductiveness, sensuality, shapeliness

vomit *v.* barf (*U.S. sl.*), belch forth, be sick, bring up, chuck (up) (*Sl., chiefly U.S.*), chunder (*Sl., chiefly Aust.*), disgorge, do a technicolour yawn (*Sl.*), eject, emit, heave, puke (*Sl.*), regurgitate, retch, sick up (*Inf.*), spew out *or* up, throw up (*Inf.*), toss one's cookies (*U.S. sl.*), upchuck (*U.S. sl.*)

voracious avid, devouring, gluttonous, greedy, hungry, insatiable, omnivorous, prodigious, rapacious, ravening, ravenous, uncontrolled, unquenchable
Antonyms moderate, sated, satisfied, self-controlled, temperate

voracity avidity, eagerness, greed, hunger, rapacity, ravenousness

vortex eddy, maelstrom, whirlpool

votary adherent, aficionado, believer, devotee, disciple, follower

vote *n.* 1. ballot, franchise, plebiscite, poll, referendum, right to vote, show of hands, suffrage ~*v.* 2. ballot, cast one's vote, elect, go to the polls, opt, return 3. *Inf.* declare, judge, pronounce, propose, recommend, suggest

vouch *Usually with* **for** affirm, answer for, assert, asseverate, attest to, back, certify, confirm, give assurance of, go bail for, guarantee, stand witness, support, swear to, uphold

vouchsafe accord, cede, condescend to give, confer, deign, favour (someone) with, grant, yield

vow 1. *v.* affirm, consecrate, dedicate, devote, pledge, promise, swear, undertake solemnly 2. *n.* oath, pledge, promise, troth (*Archaic*)

voyage *n.* crossing, cruise, journey, passage, travels, trip

vulgar 1. blue, boorish, cheap and nasty, coarse, common, crude, dirty, flashy, gaudy, gross, ill-bred, impolite, improper, indecent, indecorous, indelicate, low, nasty, naughty, off colour, ribald, risqué, rude, suggestive, tasteless, tawdry, uncouth, unmannerly, unrefined 2. general, native, ordinary, unrefined, vernacular
Antonyms aristocratic, classical, decorous, elegant, genteel, high-brow, polite, refined, sophisticated, tasteful, upper-class, well-mannered

vulgarian arriviste, boor, churl, *nouveau riche,* parvenu, philistine, upstart

vulgarity bad taste, coarseness, crudeness, crudity, gaudiness, grossness, indecorum, indelicacy, lack of refinement, ribaldry, rudeness, suggestiveness, tastelessness, tawdriness
Antonyms decorum, gentility, good breeding, good manners, good taste, refinement, sensitivity, sophistication, tastefulness

vulnerable accessible, assailable, defenceless, exposed, open to attack, sensitive, susceptible, tender, thin-skinned, unprotected, weak, wide open
Antonyms guarded, immune, impervious, insensitive, invulnerable, thick-skinned, unassailable, well-protected

W

wacky crazy, daft (*Inf.*), eccentric, erratic, goofy (*Inf.*), irrational, loony (*Sl.*), nutty (*Sl.*), odd, oddball (*Inf.*), off-the-wall (*Sl.*), outré, screwy (*Inf.*), silly, unpredictable, wacko (*Sl.*), wild, zany

wad ball, block, bundle, chunk, hunk, lump, mass, plug, roll

wadding filler, lining, packing, padding, stuffing

waddle rock, shuffle, sway, toddle, totter, wobble

wade 1. ford, paddle, splash, walk through 2. *With* **through** drudge, labour, peg away, plough through, toil, work one's way 3. *With* **in** *or* **into** assail, attack, get stuck in (*Inf.*), go for, launch oneself at, light into (*Inf.*), set about, tackle, tear into (*Inf.*)

waffle 1. *v.* blather, jabber, prate, prattle, rabbit (on) (*Brit. inf.*), verbalize, witter on (*Inf.*) 2. *n.* blather, jabber, padding, prating, prattle, prolixity, verbiage, verbosity, wordiness

waft 1. *v.* bear, be carried, carry, convey, drift, float, ride, transmit, transport 2. *n.* breath, breeze, current, draught, puff, whiff

wag[1] 1. *v.* bob, flutter, nod, oscillate, quiver, rock, shake, stir, vibrate, waggle, wave, wiggle 2. *n.* bob, flutter, nod, oscillation, quiver, shake, toss, vibration, waggle, wave, wiggle

wag[2] *n.* card (*Inf.*), clown, comedian, comic, humorist, jester, joker, wit

wage 1. *n. Also* **wages** allowance, compensation, earnings, emolument, fee, hire, pay, payment, recompense, remuneration, reward, stipend 2. *v.* carry on, conduct, engage in, practise, proceed with, prosecute, pursue, undertake

wager 1. *n.* bet, flutter (*Brit. inf.*), gamble, pledge, punt (*Chiefly Brit.*), stake, venture 2. *v.* bet, chance, gamble, hazard, lay, pledge, punt (*Chiefly Brit.*), put on, risk, speculate, stake, venture

waggish amusing, comical, droll, facetious, funny, humorous, impish, jesting, jocose, jocular, merry, mischievous, playful, puckish, risible, sportive, witty

waggle 1. *v.* flutter, oscillate, shake, wag, wave, wiggle, wobble 2. *n.* flutter, oscillation, shake, wag, wave, wiggle, wobble

waif foundling, orphan, stray

wail 1. *v.* bawl, bemoan, bewail, cry, deplore, grieve, howl, keen, lament, ululate, weep, yowl 2. *n.* complaint, cry, grief, howl, keen, lament, lamentation, moan, ululation, weeping, yowl

wait 1. *v.* abide, bide one's time, cool one's heels, dally, delay, hang fire, hold back, hold on (*Inf.*), linger, mark time, pause, remain, rest, stand by, stay, tarry 2. *n.* delay, entr'acte, halt, hold-up, interval, pause, rest, stay
Antonyms (*sense 1*) depart, go, go away, leave, move off, quit, set off, take off (*Inf.*)

waiter, waitress attendant, server, steward, stewardess

wait on *or* **upon** attend, minister to, serve, tend

waive abandon, defer, dispense with, forgo, give up, postpone, put off, refrain from, relinquish, remit, renounce, resign, set aside, surrender
Antonyms claim, demand, insist, maintain, press, profess, pursue, uphold

waiver abandonment, abdication, disclaimer, giving up, relinquishment, remission, renunciation, resignation, setting aside, surrender

wake[1] *v.* 1. arise, awake, awaken, bestir, come to, get up, rouse, rouse from sleep, stir 2. activate, animate, arouse, awaken, enliven, excite, fire, galvanize, kindle, provoke, quicken, rouse, stimulate, stir up ~*n.* 3. deathwatch, funeral, vigil, watch
Antonyms (*sense 1*) catnap, doze, drop off (*Inf.*), hibernate, nod off (*Inf.*), sleep, snooze (*Inf.*), take a nap

wake[2] aftermath, backwash, path, slipstream, track, trail, train, wash, waves

wakeful 1. insomniac, restless, sleepless, unsleeping 2. alert, alive, attentive, heedful, observant, on guard, on the alert, on the lookout, on the qui vive, unsleeping, vigilant, wary, watchful
Antonyms (*sense 2*) asleep, dormant, dozing, dreamy, drowsy, heedless, inattentive, off guard, sleepy

waken activate, animate, arouse, awake, awaken, be roused, come awake, come to, enliven, fire, galvanize, get up, kindle, quicken, rouse, stimulate, stir
Antonyms be inactive, doze, lie dormant, nap, repose, sleep, slumber, snooze (*Inf.*)

wale contusion, mark, scar, streak, stripe, weal, welt, wheal

walk *v.* 1. advance, amble, foot it, go, go by shanks's pony (*Inf.*), go on foot, hike, hoof it (*Sl.*), march, move, pace, perambulate, promenade, saunter, step, stride, stroll, traipse (*Inf.*), tramp, travel on foot, trek, trudge 2. accompany, convoy, escort, take ~*n.* 3. constitutional, hike, march, perambulation, promenade, ramble, saunter, stroll, traipse (*Inf.*), tramp, trek, trudge, turn 4. carriage, gait, manner of walking, pace, step, stride 5. aisle, alley, avenue, esplanade, footpath, lane, path, pathway, pavement, promenade, sidewalk, trail 6. area, arena, calling, career, course, field, line, métier, profession, sphere, trade, vocation

walker footslogger, hiker, pedestrian, rambler, wayfarer

walkout industrial action, protest, stoppage, strike

walk out 1. flounce out, get up and go, leave suddenly, storm out, take off (*Inf.*) 2. down tools, go on strike, stop work, strike, take industrial action, withdraw one's labour 3. *With* **on** abandon, chuck (*Inf.*), desert, forsake, jilt, leave, leave in the lurch, pack in (*Inf.*), run away from, throw over

Antonyms (*sense 3*) be loyal to, defend, remain, stand by, stay, stick with, support, uphold

walkover breeze (*U.S. & Canad. inf.*), cakewalk (*Inf.*), child's play (*Inf.*), cinch (*Sl.*), doddle (*Brit. sl.*), duck soup (*U.S. sl.*), easy victory, picnic (*Inf.*), piece of cake (*Inf.*), pushover (*Sl.*), snap (*Inf.*)

Antonyms drudgery, effort, grind (*Inf.*), labour, ordeal, strain, struggle, trial

wall 1. divider, enclosure, panel, partition, screen 2. barricade, breastwork, bulwark, embankment, fortification, palisade, parapet, rampart, stockade 3. barrier, block, fence, hedge, impediment, obstacle, obstruction 4. **go to the wall** *Inf.* be ruined, collapse, fail, fall, go bust (*Inf.*), go under 5. **drive up the wall** *Sl.* aggravate (*Inf.*), annoy, dement, derange, drive crazy (*Inf.*), drive insane, exasperate, get on one's nerves (*Inf.*), infuriate, irritate, madden, piss one off (*Taboo sl.*), send off one's head (*Sl.*), try

wallet case, holder, notecase, pocketbook, pouch, purse

wallop *v.* 1. batter, beat, belt (*Inf.*), buffet, chin (*Sl.*), clobber (*Sl.*), deck (*Sl.*), hit, lambast(e), lay one on (*Sl.*), paste (*Sl.*), pound, pummel, punch, slug, smack, strike, thrash, thump, whack 2. beat, best, blow out of the water (*Sl.*), clobber (*Sl.*), crush, defeat, drub, hammer (*Inf.*), lick (*Inf.*), rout, run rings around (*Inf.*), thrash, trounce, vanquish, wipe the floor with (*Inf.*), worst ~*n.* 3. bash, belt (*Inf.*), blow, haymaker (*Sl.*), kick, punch, slug, smack, thump, thwack, whack

wallow 1. lie, roll about, splash around, tumble, welter 2. flounder, lurch, stagger, stumble, wade 3. bask, delight, glory, indulge oneself, luxuriate, relish, revel, take pleasure

Antonyms (*sense 3*) abstain, avoid, do without, eschew, forgo, give up, refrain

wan 1. anaemic, ashen, bloodless, cadaverous, colourless, discoloured, ghastly, livid, pale, pallid, pasty, sickly, washed out, waxen, wheyfaced, white 2. dim, faint, feeble, pale, weak

Antonyms (*sense 1*) blooming, bright, flourishing, glowing, healthy, roseate, rosy, rubicund, ruddy, vibrant

wand baton, rod, sprig, stick, twig, withe, withy

wander *v.* 1. cruise, drift, knock about *or* around, meander, mooch around (*Sl.*), peregrinate, ramble, range, roam, rove, straggle, stravaig (*Scot. & northern English dialect*), stray, stroll, traipse (*Inf.*) 2. depart, deviate, digress, divagate (*Rare*), diverge, err, get lost, go astray, go off at a tangent, go off course, lapse, lose concentration, lose one's train of thought, lose one's way, swerve, veer 3. babble, be delirious, be incoherent, ramble, rave, speak incoherently, talk nonsense ~*n.* 4. cruise, excursion, meander, peregrination, ramble, traipse (*Inf.*)

Antonyms (*sense 2*) comply, conform, fall in with, follow, run with the pack, toe the line

wanderer bird of passage, drifter, gypsy, itinerant, nomad, rambler, ranger, rolling stone, rover, stroller, traveller, vagabond, vagrant, voyager

wandering drifting, homeless, itinerant, migratory, nomadic, peripatetic, rambling, rootless, roving, strolling, travelling, vagabond, vagrant, voyaging, wayfaring

wanderlust itchy feet (*Inf.*), restlessness, urge to travel

wane *v.* 1. abate, atrophy, decline, decrease, die out, dim, diminish, draw to a close, drop, dwindle, ebb, fade, fade away, fail, lessen, sink, subside, taper off, weaken, wind down, wither ~*n.* 2. abatement, atrophy, decay, declension, decrease, diminution, drop, dwindling, ebb, fading, failure, fall, falling off, lessening, sinking, subsidence, tapering off, withering 3. **on the wane** at its lowest ebb, declining, dropping, dwindling, dying out, ebbing, fading, less-

ening, obsolescent, on its last legs, on the decline, on the way out, subsiding, tapering off, weakening, withering
Antonyms *v.* blossom, brighten, develop, expand, grow, improve, increase, rise, strengthen, wax ~*n.* advancement, development, expansion, growth, increase, rise, strengthening, waxing

wangle arrange, bring off, contrive, engineer, fiddle (*Inf.*), finagle (*Inf.*), fix (*Inf.*), manipulate, manoeuvre, pull off, scheme, work (*Inf.*)

want *v.* 1. covet, crave, desire, eat one's heart out over, feel a need for, hanker after, have a fancy for, have a yen for (*Inf.*), hope for, hunger for, long for, need, pine for, require, thirst for, wish, yearn for 2. be able to do with, be deficient in, be short of, be without, call for, demand, fall short in, have need of, lack, miss, need, require, stand in need of ~*n.* 3. appetite, craving, demand, desire, fancy, hankering, hunger, longing, necessity, need, requirement, thirst, wish, yearning, yen (*Inf.*) 4. absence, dearth, default, deficiency, famine, insufficiency, lack, paucity, scantiness, scarcity, shortage 5. destitution, indigence, need, neediness, pauperism, penury, poverty, privation
Antonyms *v.* be sated, detest, dislike, enjoy, hate, have, loathe, own, possess, reject, spurn, surfeit ~*n.* abundance, adequacy, comfort, ease, excess, luxury, plenty, surplus, sufficiency, wealth

wanting 1. absent, incomplete, lacking, less, missing, short, shy 2. defective, deficient, disappointing, faulty, imperfect, inadequate, inferior, leaving much to be desired, not good enough, not up to expectations, not up to par, patchy, poor, sketchy, substandard, unsound
Antonyms adequate, complete, enough, full, replete, satisfactory, saturated, sufficient

wanton *adj.* 1. abandoned, dissipated, dissolute, fast, immoral, lecherous, lewd, libertine, libidinous, licentious, loose, lustful, of easy virtue, promiscuous, rakish, shameless, unchaste 2. arbitrary, cruel, evil, gratuitous, groundless, malevolent, malicious, motiveless, needless, senseless, spiteful, uncalled-for, unjustifiable, unjustified, unprovoked, vicious, wicked, wilful 3. careless, devil-may-care, extravagant, heedless, immoderate, intemperate, lavish, outrageous, rash, reckless, unrestrained, wild ~*n.* 4. Casanova, debauchee, Don Juan, gigolo, harlot, lech *or* letch (*Inf.*), lecher, libertine, loose woman, profligate, prostitute, rake, roué, scrubber (*Brit. & Aust. sl.*), slag (*Brit. sl.*), slut, strumpet, tart (*Inf.*), trollop, voluptuary, whore, woman of easy virtue ~*v.* 5. debauch, dissipate, revel, riot, sleep around (*Inf.*), wench (*Archaic*), whore 6. fritter away, misspend, squander, throw away, waste
Antonyms (*sense 1*) overmodest, priggish, prim, prudish, puritanical, rigid, strait-laced, stuffy, Victorian (*sense 2*) called-for, excusable, justified, legitimate, motivated, provoked, warranted (*sense 3*) cautious, circumspect, guarded, inhibited, moderate, prudent, reserved, restrained, temperate

war 1. *n.* armed conflict, battle, bloodshed, combat, conflict, contention, contest, enmity, fighting, hostilities, hostility, strife, struggle, warfare 2. *v.* battle, campaign against, carry on hostilities, clash, combat, conduct a war, contend, contest, fight, make war, strive, struggle, take up arms, wage war
Antonyms *n.* accord, armistice, cease-fire, co-existence, compliance, co-operation, harmony, peace, peace-time, treaty, truce ~*v.* call a ceasefire, co-exist, co-operate, make peace

warble 1. *v.* chirp, chirrup, quaver, sing, trill, twitter 2. *n.* call, chirp, chirrup, cry, quaver, song, trill, twitter

war cry battle cry, rallying cry, slogan, war whoop

ward 1. area, district, division, precinct, quarter, zone 2. apartment, cubicle, room 3. charge, dependant, minor, protégé, pupil 4. care, charge, custody, guardianship, keeping, protection, safekeeping

warden administrator, caretaker, curator, custodian, guardian, janitor, keeper, ranger, steward, superintendent, warder, watchman

warder, wardress custodian, gaoler, guard, jailer, keeper, prison officer, screw (*Sl.*), turnkey (*Archaic*)

ward off avert, avoid, beat off, block, deflect, fend off, forestall, keep at arm's length, keep at bay, parry, repel, stave off, thwart, turn aside, turn away
Antonyms accept, admit, allow, embrace, permit, receive, take in, welcome

wardrobe 1. closet, clothes cupboard, clothes-press 2. apparel, attire, clothes, collection of clothes, outfit

warehouse depository, depot, stockroom, store, storehouse

wares commodities, goods, lines, manufactures, merchandise, produce, products, stock, stuff

warfare armed conflict, armed struggle, arms, battle, blows, campaigning, clash of arms, combat, conflict, contest, discord,

fighting, hostilities, passage of arms, strategy, strife, struggle, war
Antonyms accord, amity, armistice, cessation of hostilities, conciliation, harmony, peace, treaty, truce

warily cagily (*Inf.*), carefully, cautiously, charily, circumspectly, distrustfully, gingerly, guardedly, suspiciously, vigilantly, watchfully, with care
Antonyms carelessly, hastily, heedlessly, irresponsibly, rashly, recklessly, thoughtlessly, unwarily

wariness alertness, attention, caginess (*Inf.*), care, carefulness, caution, circumspection, discretion, distrust, foresight, heedfulness, mindfulness, prudence, suspicion, vigilance, watchfulness
Antonyms carelessness, heedlessness, inattention, mindlessness, negligence, oblivion, recklessness, thoughtlessness

warlike aggressive, bellicose, belligerent, bloodthirsty, combative, hawkish, hostile, inimical, jingoistic, martial, militaristic, military, pugnacious, sabre-rattling, unfriendly, warmongering
Antonyms amicable, conciliatory, friendly, nonbelligerent, pacific, peaceable, peaceful, placid, unwarlike

warlock conjurer, enchanter, magician, necromancer, sorcerer, witch, wizard

warm *adj.* 1. balmy, heated, lukewarm, moderately hot, pleasant, sunny, tepid, thermal 2. affable, affectionate, amiable, amorous, cheerful, congenial, cordial, friendly, genial, happy, hearty, hospitable, kindly, likable *or* likeable, loving, pleasant, tender 3. animated, ardent, cordial, earnest, effusive, emotional, enthusiastic, excited, fervent, glowing, heated, intense, keen, lively, passionate, spirited, stormy, vehement, vigorous, violent, zealous 4. irascible, irritable, passionate, quick, sensitive, short, touchy 5. *Inf.* dangerous, disagreeable, hazardous, perilous, tricky, uncomfortable, unpleasant ~*v.* 6. heat, heat up, melt, thaw, warm up 7. animate, awaken, excite, get going, interest, make enthusiastic, put some life into, rouse, stimulate, stir, turn on (*Sl.*)
Antonyms *adj.* aloof, apathetic, chilly, cold, cool, distant, freezing, half-hearted, hostile, icy, phlegmatic, remote, standoffish, uncaring, unenthusiastic, unfriendly, unwelcoming ~*v.* alienate, chill, cool, cool down, depress, freeze, sadden

warm-blooded ardent, earnest, emotional, enthusiastic, excitable, fervent, impetuous, lively, passionate, rash, spirited, vivacious

warm-hearted affectionate, compassionate, cordial, generous, kind-hearted, kindly, loving, sympathetic, tender, tender-hearted
Antonyms callous, cold, cold-hearted, hard, hard-hearted, harsh, heartless, insensitive, mean, merciless, unfeeling, unsympathetic

warmonger belligerent, hawk, jingo, militarist, sabre-rattler

warmth 1. heat, hotness, warmness 2. animation, ardour, eagerness, earnestness, effusiveness, enthusiasm, excitement, fervency, fervour, fire, heat, intensity, passion, spirit, transport, vehemence, vigour, violence, zeal, zest 3. affability, affection, amorousness, cheerfulness, cordiality, happiness, heartiness, hospitableness, kindliness, love, tenderness
Antonyms aloofness, apathy, austerity, chill, chilliness, cold, cold-heartedness, coldness, coolness, hard-heartedness, hostility, iciness, indifference, insincerity, lack of enthusiasm, sternness, remoteness

warn admonish, advise, alert, apprise, caution, forewarn, give fair warning, give notice, inform, make (someone) aware, notify, put one on one's guard, summon, tip off

warning 1. *n.* admonition, advice, alarm, alert, augury, caution, caveat, foretoken, hint, notice, notification, omen, premonition, presage, sign, signal, threat, tip, tip-off, token, word, word to the wise 2. *adj.* admonitory, cautionary, monitory, ominous, premonitory, threatening

warp 1. *v.* bend, contort, deform, deviate, distort, misshape, pervert, swerve, turn, twist 2. *n.* bend, bent, bias, contortion, deformation, deviation, distortion, kink, perversion, quirk, turn, twist

warrant *n.* 1. assurance, authority, authorization, carte blanche, commission, guarantee, licence, permission, permit, pledge, sanction, security, warranty ~*v.* 2. affirm, answer for, assure, attest, avouch, certify, declare, guarantee, pledge, secure, stand behind, underwrite, uphold, vouch for 3. approve, authorize, call for, commission, demand, deserve, empower, entail, entitle, excuse, give ground for, justify, license, necessitate, permit, require, sanction

warrantable accountable, allowable, defensible, justifiable, lawful, necessary, permissible, proper, reasonable, right
Antonyms indefensible, uncalled-for, undue, unjustifiable, unnecessary, reasonable, unwarrantable, wrong

warranty assurance, bond, certificate, contract, covenant, guarantee, pledge

warring at daggers drawn, at war, belligerent, combatant, conflicting, contending, embattled, fighting, hostile, opposed

warrior champion, combatant, fighter, fighting man, gladiator, man-at-arms, soldier

wary alert, attentive, cagey (*Inf.*), careful, cautious, chary, circumspect, distrustful, guarded, heedful, leery (*Sl.*), on one's guard, on the lookout, on the qui vive, prudent, suspicious, vigilant, watchful, wide-awake

Antonyms careless, foolhardy, imprudent, negligent, rash, reckless, remiss, unguarded, unsuspecting, unwary

wash *v.* 1. bath, bathe, clean, cleanse, launder, moisten, rinse, scrub, shampoo, shower, wet 2. *With* **away** bear away, carry off, erode, move, sweep away, wash off 3. *Inf.* bear scrutiny, be convincing, be plausible, carry weight, hold up, hold water, stand up, stick 4. **wash one's hands of** abandon, accept no responsibility for, give up on, have nothing to do with, leave to one's own devices *~n.* 5. ablution, bath, bathe, cleaning, cleansing, laundering, rinse, scrub, shampoo, shower, washing 6. ebb and flow, flow, roll, surge, sweep, swell, wave 7. coat, coating, film, layer, overlay, screen, stain, suffusion

washed out 1. blanched, bleached, colourless, etiolated, faded, flat, lacklustre, mat, pale 2. all in (*Sl.*), clapped out (*Aust. & N.Z. inf.*), dead on one's feet (*Inf.*), dog-tired (*Inf.*), done in (*Inf.*), drained, drawn, exhausted, fatigued, haggard, knackered (*Sl.*), pale, spent, tired-out, wan, weary, worn-out, zonked (*Sl.*)

Antonyms (*sense 2*) alert, chirpy, energetic, full of pep (*Inf.*), lively, perky, refreshed, sprightly, zippy (*Inf.*)

washout 1. disappointment, disaster, dud (*Inf.*), failure, fiasco, flop (*Inf.*), mess 2. failure, incompetent, loser

Antonyms (*sense 1*) conquest, feat, success, triumph, victory, winner

washy attenuated, diluted, feeble, insipid, overdiluted, thin, watered-down, watery, weak, wishy-washy (*Inf.*)

waspish bad-tempered, cantankerous, captious, crabbed, crabby, cross, crotchety (*Inf.*), fretful, grumpy, ill-tempered, irascible, irritable, liverish, peevish, peppery, pettish, petulant, ratty (*Brit. & N.Z. inf.*), snappish, splenetic, testy, tetchy, touchy, waxy (*Inf., chiefly Brit.*)

Antonyms affable, agreeable, cheerful, easy-going, genial, good-humoured, good-natured, jovial, pleasant

waste *v.* 1. blow (*Sl.*), dissipate, fritter away, frivol away (*Inf.*), lavish, misuse, run through, squander, throw away 2. atrophy, consume, corrode, crumble, debilitate, decay, decline, deplete, disable, drain, dwindle, eat away, ebb, emaciate, enfeeble, exhaust, fade, gnaw, perish, sap the strength of, sink, undermine, wane, wear out, wither 3. despoil, destroy, devastate, lay waste, pillage, rape, ravage, raze, ruin, sack, spoil, total (*Sl.*), trash (*Sl.*), undo, wreak havoc upon *~n.* 4. dissipation, expenditure, extravagance, frittering away, loss, lost opportunity, misapplication, misuse, prodigality, squandering, unthriftiness, wastefulness 5. desolation, destruction, devastation, havoc, ravage, ruin 6. debris, dregs, dross, garbage, leavings, leftovers, litter, offal, offscourings, refuse, rubbish, scrap, sweepings, trash 7. desert, solitude, void, wasteland, wild, wilderness *~adj.* 8. leftover, superfluous, supernumerary, unused, unwanted, useless, worthless 9. bare, barren, desolate, devastated, dismal, dreary, empty, uncultivated, uninhabited, unproductive, wild 10. **lay waste** depredate (*Rare*), despoil, destroy, devastate, pillage, rape, ravage, raze, ruin, sack, spoil, wreak havoc upon

Antonyms *v.* build, conserve, defend, develop, economize, husband, increase, preserve, protect, rally, restore, save, strengthen *~n.* economy, frugality, good housekeeping, saving, thrift *~adj.* arable, developed, fruitful, habitable, in use, necessary, needed, productive, utilized, verdant

wasteful extravagant, improvident, lavish, prodigal, profligate, ruinous, spendthrift, thriftless, uneconomical, unthrifty

Antonyms economical, frugal, money-saving, parsimonious, penny-wise, provident, sparing, thrifty

wasteland desert, void, waste, wild, wilderness

waster drone, good-for-nothing, idler, layabout, loafer, loser, malingerer, ne'er-do-well, shirker, skiver (*Brit. sl.*), wastrel

wastrel 1. prodigal, profligate, spendthrift, squanderer 2. drone, good-for-nothing, idler, layabout, loafer, loser, malingerer, ne'er-do-well, shirker, skiver (*Brit. sl.*), waster

watch *v.* 1. check, check out (*Inf.*), clock (*Brit. sl.*), contemplate, eye, eyeball (*U.S. sl.*), gaze at, get a load of (*Inf.*), look, look at, look on, mark, note, observe, pay attention, peer at, regard, see, stare at, take a dekko at (*Brit. sl.*), view 2. attend, be on the alert, be on the lookout, be vigilant, be wary, be watchful, keep an eye open (*Inf.*), look out, take heed, wait 3. guard, keep, look after, mind, protect, superintend, take care of, tend ~*n.* 4. chronometer, clock, pocket watch, timepiece, wristwatch 5. alertness, attention, eye, heed, inspection, lookout, notice, observation, supervision, surveillance, vigil, vigilance, watchfulness

watchdog 1. guard dog 2. custodian, guardian, inspector, monitor, protector, scrutineer

watcher looker-on, lookout, observer, onlooker, spectator, spy, viewer, witness

watchful alert, attentive, circumspect, guarded, heedful, observant, on one's guard, on the lookout, on the qui vive, on the watch, suspicious, vigilant, wary, wide awake

Antonyms careless, inattentive, reckless, thoughtless, unaware, unguarded, unmindful, unobservant, unwary

watchfulness alertness, attention, attentiveness, caution, cautiousness, circumspection, heedfulness, vigilance, wariness

Antonyms carelessness, heedlessness, inattention, indiscretion, irresponsibility, neglect, recklessness, thoughtlessness

watchman caretaker, custodian, guard, security guard, security man

watch out be alert, be careful, be on one's guard, be on the alert, be on (the) watch, be vigilant, be watchful, have a care, keep a sharp lookout, keep a weather eye open, keep one's eyes open, keep one's eyes peeled *or* skinned (*Inf.*), look out, mind out, watch oneself

watch over defend, guard, keep safe, look after, preserve, protect, shelter, shield, stand guard over

watchword 1. countersign, magic word, password, shibboleth 2. battle cry, byword, catch phrase, catchword, maxim, motto, rallying cry, slogan

water *n.* 1. Adam's ale *or* wine, aqua, H_2O 2. **hold water** bear examination *or* scrutiny, be credible (logical, sound), make sense, pass the test, ring true, work 3. **of the first water** excellent, of the best, of the best quality, of the finest quality, of the highest degree, of the highest grade ~*v.* 4. damp, dampen, douse, drench, flood, hose, irrigate, moisten, soak, souse, spray, sprinkle 5. add water to, adulterate, dilute, put water in, thin, water down, weaken

water down 1. add water to, adulterate, dilute, put water in, thin, water, weaken 2. adulterate, mitigate, qualify, soften, tone down, weaken

Antonyms (*sense 1*) fortify, purify, strengthen, thicken

waterfall cascade, cataract, chute, fall, force (*Northern English dialect*), linn (*Scot.*)

watertight 1. sound, waterproof 2. airtight, firm, flawless, foolproof, impregnable, incontrovertible, sound, unassailable

Antonyms defective, flawed, leaky, questionable, shaky, tenuous, uncertain, unsound, weak

watery 1. aqueous, damp, fluid, humid, liquid, marshy, moist, soggy, squelchy, wet 2. rheumy, tear-filled, tearful, weepy 3. adulterated, dilute, diluted, flavourless, insipid, runny, tasteless, thin, washy, watered-down, waterish, weak, wishy-washy (*Inf.*)

Antonyms concentrated, condensed, dense, fortified, solid, strong, thick

wave *v.* 1. brandish, flap, flourish, flutter, move to and fro, oscillate, quiver, ripple, shake, stir, sway, swing, undulate, wag, waver, wield 2. beckon, direct, gesticulate, gesture, indicate, sign, signal ~*n.* 3. billow, breaker, comber, ridge, ripple, roller, sea surf, swell, undulation, unevenness 4. current, drift, flood, ground swell, movement, outbreak, rash, rush, stream, surge, sweep, tendency, trend, upsurge

waver 1. be indecisive, be irresolute, be unable to decide, be unable to make up one's mind, blow hot and cold (*Inf.*), dither (*Chiefly Brit.*), falter, fluctuate, hesitate, hum and haw, seesaw, shillyshally (*Inf.*), swither (*Scot.*), vacillate 2. flicker, fluctuate, quiver, reel, shake, sway, totter, tremble, undulate, vary, wave, weave, wobble

Antonyms be decisive, be determined, be of fixed opinion, be resolute, determine, resolve, stand firm

wax *v.* become fuller, become larger, develop, dilate, enlarge, expand, fill out, get bigger, grow, increase, magnify, mount, rise, swell

Antonyms contract, decline, decrease, diminish, dwindle, fade, lessen, narrow, shrink, wane

waxen anaemic, ashen, bloodless, colourless, ghastly, pale, pallid, wan, white, whitish

way 1. approach, course of action, fashion, manner, means, method, mode, plan, practice, procedure, process, scheme, system, technique 2. access, avenue, channel, course, direction, highway, lane, path, pathway, road, route, street, thoroughfare, track, trail 3. elbowroom, opening, room, space 4. distance, journey, length, stretch, trail 5. advance, approach, journey, march, passage, progress 6. characteristic, conduct, custom, habit, idiosyncrasy, manner, nature, personality, practice, style, trait, usage, wont 7. aspect, detail, feature, particular, point, respect, sense 8. aim, ambition, choice, demand, desire, goal, pleasure, will, wish 9. *Inf.* circumstance, condition, fettle, shape (*Inf.*), situation, state, status 10. forward motion, headway, movement, passage, progress 11. **by the way** by the bye, en passant, incidentally, in parenthesis, in passing 12. **give way a.** break down, cave in, collapse, crack, crumple, fall, fall to pieces, give, go to pieces, subside **b.** accede, acknowledge defeat, acquiesce, back down, concede, make concessions, withdraw, yield 13. **under way** afoot, begun, going, in motion, in progress, moving, on the go (*Inf.*), on the move, started

wayfarer bird of passage, globetrotter, Gypsy, itinerant, journeyer, nomad, rover, traveller, trekker, voyager, walker, wanderer

wayfaring *adj.* drifting, itinerant, journeying, nomadic, peripatetic, rambling, roving, travelling, voyaging, walking, wandering

waylay accost, ambush, attack, catch, hold up, intercept, lie in wait for, pounce on, set upon, surprise, swoop down on

way-out 1. advanced, avant-garde, bizarre, crazy, eccentric, experimental, far-out (*Sl.*), freaky (*Sl.*), oddball (*Inf.*), offbeat, off-the-wall (*Sl.*), outlandish, outré, progressive, unconventional, unorthodox, wacko (*Sl.*), weird, wild 2. amazing, brilliant, excellent, fantastic (*Inf.*), great (*Inf.*), marvellous, sensational (*Inf.*), tremendous (*Inf.*), wonderful

ways and means ability, capability, capacity, course, funds, methods, procedure, reserves, resources, tools, way, wherewithal

wayward capricious, changeable, contrary, contumacious, cross-grained, disobedient, erratic, fickle, flighty, froward, headstrong, inconstant, incorrigible, insubordinate, intractable, mulish, obdurate, obstinate, perverse, rebellious, refractory, self-willed, stubborn, undependable, ungovernable, unmanageable, unpredictable, unruly, wilful

Antonyms complaisant, compliant, dependable, good-natured, malleable, manageable, obedient, obliging, predictable, reliable, submissive, tractable

weak 1. anaemic, debilitated, decrepit, delicate, effete, enervated, exhausted, faint, feeble, fragile, frail, infirm, languid, puny, shaky, sickly, spent, tender, unsound, unsteady, wasted, weakly 2. cowardly, impotent, indecisive, ineffectual, infirm, irresolute, namby-pamby, pathetic, powerless, soft, spineless, timorous, weak-kneed (*Inf.*) 3. distant, dull, faint, imperceptible, low, muffled, poor, quiet, slight, small, soft 4. deficient, faulty, inadequate, lacking, pathetic, poor, substandard, under-strength, wanting 5. feeble, flimsy, hollow, inconclusive, invalid, lame, pathetic, shallow, slight, unconvincing, unsatisfactory 6. defenceless, exposed, helpless, unguarded, unprotected, unsafe, untenable, vulnerable, wide open 7. diluted, insipid, milk-and-water, runny, tasteless, thin, under-strength, waterish, watery, wishy-washy (*Inf.*)

Antonyms able, capable, conclusive, convincing, effective, energetic, firm, flavoursome, forceful, hardy, healthy, hefty, intoxicating, invulnerable, mighty, obvious, potent, powerful, safe, secure, solid, strong, substantial, tasty, tough, trustworthy, uncontrovertible, valid, well-defended

weaken 1. abate, debilitate, depress, diminish, droop, dwindle, ease up, enervate, fade, fail, flag, give way, impair, invalidate, lessen, lower, mitigate, moderate, reduce, sap, sap the strength of, soften up, temper, tire, undermine, wane 2. adulterate, cut, debase, dilute, thin, thin out, water down

Antonyms boost, enhance, grow, improve, increase, invigorate, revitalize, strengthen

weakling coward, doormat (*Sl.*), drip (*Inf.*), jellyfish (*Inf.*), jessie (*Scot. sl.*), milksop, mouse, sissy, wet (*Brit. inf.*), wimp (*Inf.*)

weakness 1. debility, decrepitude, enervation, faintness, feebleness, fragility, frailty, impotence, infirmity, irresolution, powerlessness, vulnerability 2. Achilles heel, blemish, chink in one's armour, defect, deficiency, failing, fault, flaw, imperfection, lack, shortcoming 3. fondness, inclination, liking, partiality, passion, penchant, predilection, proclivity, proneness, soft spot

Antonyms advantage, aversion, dislike, forte, hardiness, hatred, health, impregnability, loathing, potency, power, stamina, strength, strong point, sturdiness, validity, vigour, virtue, vitality

weal contusion, mark, ridge, scar, streak, stripe, wale, welt, wheal

wealth 1. affluence, assets, big bucks (*Inf., chiefly U.S.*), big money, capital, cash, estate, fortune, funds, goods, lucre, means, megabucks (*U.S. & Canad. sl.*), money, opulence, pelf, possessions, pretty penny (*Inf.*), property, prosperity, resources, riches, substance, tidy sum (*Inf.*), wad (*U.S. & Canad. sl.*) 2. abundance, bounty, copiousness, cornucopia, fullness, plenitude, plenty, profusion, richness, store

Antonyms dearth, deprivation, destitution, indigence, lack, need, paucity, penury, poverty, scarcity, shortage, want, wretchedness

wealthy affluent, comfortable, filthy rich,

flush (*Inf.*), in the money (*Inf.*), loaded (*Sl.*), made of money (*Inf.*), moneyed, on Easy Street (*Inf.*), opulent, prosperous, quids in (*Sl.*), rich, rolling in it (*Sl.*), stinking rich (*Sl.*), well-heeled (*Inf.*), well-off, well-to-do
Antonyms broke (*Inf.*), deprived, destitute, dirt-poor (*Inf.*), down and out, flat broke (*Inf.*), impoverished, indigent, needy, penniless, poor, poverty-stricken, short, skint (*Brit. sl.*), without two pennies to rub together (*Inf.*)

wear *v.* **1.** bear, be clothed in, be dressed in, carry, clothe oneself, don, dress in, have on, put on, sport (*Inf.*) **2.** display, exhibit, fly, show **3.** abrade, consume, corrode, deteriorate, erode, fray, grind, impair, rub, use, wash away, waste **4.** bear up, be durable, endure, hold up, last, stand up **5.** annoy, drain, enervate, exasperate, fatigue, get on one's nerves (*Inf.*), harass, irk, pester, tax, undermine, vex, weaken, weary **6.** *Brit. sl.* accept, allow, brook, countenance, fall for, permit, put up with (*Inf.*), stand for, stomach, swallow (*Inf.*), take ~*n.* **7.** employment, mileage (*Inf.*), service, use, usefulness, utility **8.** apparel, attire, clothes, costume, dress, garb, garments, gear (*Inf.*), habit, outfit, things **9.** abrasion, attrition, corrosion, damage, depreciation, deterioration, erosion, friction, use, wear and tear
Antonyms (*sense 9*) conservation, maintenance, preservation, repair, upkeep

wear down **1.** abrade, be consumed, consume, corrode, erode, grind down, rub away **2.** chip away at (*Inf.*), fight a war of attrition against, overcome gradually, reduce, undermine

weariness drowsiness, enervation, exhaustion, fatigue, languor, lassitude, lethargy, listlessness, prostration, tiredness
Antonyms drive, energy, freshness, get-up-and-go (*Inf.*), liveliness, stamina, vigour, vitality, zeal, zest

wearing exasperating, exhausting, fatiguing, irksome, oppressive, taxing, tiresome, tiring, trying, wearisome
Antonyms easy, effortless, light, no bother, painless, refreshing, stimulating, undemanding

wearisome annoying, boring, bothersome, burdensome, dull, exasperating, exhausting, fatiguing, humdrum, irksome, mind-numbing, monotonous, oppressive, pestilential, prosaic, tedious, troublesome, trying, uninteresting, vexatious, wearing
Antonyms agreeable, delightful, enjoyable, exhilarating, interesting, invigorating, pleasurable, refreshing, stimulating

wear off **1.** abate, decrease, diminish, disappear, dwindle, ebb, fade, lose effect, lose strength, peter out, subside, wane, weaken **2.** abrade, disappear, efface, fade, rub away
Antonyms grow, increase, intensify, magnify, persist, reinforce, step up, strengthen, wax

wear out **1.** become useless, become worn, consume, deteriorate, erode, fray, impair, use up, wear through **2.** enervate, exhaust, fag out (*Inf.*), fatigue, frazzle (*Inf.*), knacker (*Sl.*), prostrate, sap, tire, weary
Antonyms (*sense 2*) buck up (*Inf.*), energize, invigorate, pep up, perk up, refresh, revitalize, stimulate, strengthen

weary *adj.* **1.** all in (*Sl.*), asleep *or* dead on one's feet (*Inf.*), clapped out (*Aust. & N.Z. inf.*), dead beat (*Inf.*), dog-tired (*Inf.*), done in (*Inf.*), drained, drooping, drowsy, enervated, exhausted, fagged (*Inf.*), fatigued, flagging, jaded, knackered (*Sl.*), ready to drop, sleepy, spent, tired, wearied, whacked (*Brit. inf.*), worn out, zonked (*Sl.*) **2.** arduous, enervative, irksome, laborious, taxing, tiresome, tiring, wearing, wearisome **3.** bored, browned-off (*Inf.*), discontented, fed up, impatient, indifferent, jaded, sick (*Inf.*), sick and tired (*Inf.*) ~*v.* **4.** burden, debilitate, drain, droop, enervate, fade, fag (*Inf.*), fail, fatigue, grow tired, sap, take it out of (*Inf.*), tax, tire, tire out, wear out **5.** annoy, become bored, bore, exasperate, have had enough, irk, jade, make discontented, plague, sicken, try the patience of, vex
Antonyms *adj.* amused, energetic, excited, exciting, forebearing, fresh, full of beans (*Inf.*), full of get-up-and-go (*Inf.*), invigorated, invigorating, lively, original, patient, refreshed, refreshing, stimulated ~*v.* amuse, enliven, excite, interest, invigorate, refresh, revive, stimulate

weather *n.* **1.** climate, conditions **2.** **under the weather** **a.** ailing, below par, ill, indisposed, nauseous, not well, off-colour, out of sorts, poorly (*Inf.*), seedy (*Inf.*), sick **b.** crapulent, crapulous, drunk, flying (*Sl.*), groggy (*Inf.*), hung over (*Inf.*), inebriated, intoxicated, one over the eight (*Sl.*), the worse for drink, three sheets in the wind (*Inf.*), under the influence (*Inf.*) ~*v.* **3.** expose, harden, season, toughen **4.** bear up against, brave, come through, endure, get through, live through, make it (*Inf.*), overcome, pull through, resist, ride out, rise above, stand, stick it out (*Inf.*), suffer, surmount, survive, withstand
Antonyms (*sense 4*) cave in, collapse, fail, fall, give in, go under, succumb, surrender, yield

weave **1.** blend, braid, entwine, fuse, incorporate, interlace, intermingle, intertwine, introduce, knit, mat, merge, plait, twist, unite 2. build, construct, contrive, create, fabricate, make, make up, put together, spin 3. crisscross, move in and out, weave one's way, wind, zigzag 4. **get weaving** *Inf.* get a move on, get going, get one's finger out (*Brit. inf.*), get under way, hurry, make a start, shake a leg (*Sl.*), start

web 1. cobweb, spider's web 2. interlacing, lattice, mesh, net, netting, network, screen, tangle, toils, weave, webbing

wed 1. become man and wife, be married to, espouse, get hitched (*Sl.*), get married, join, make one, marry, splice (*Inf.*), take as one's husband, take as one's wife, take to wife, tie the knot (*Inf.*), unite 2. ally, blend, coalesce, combine, commingle, dedicate, fuse, interweave, join, link, marry, merge, unify, unite, yoke
Antonyms (*sense 2*) break up, disunite, divide, divorce, part, separate, sever, split

wedding espousals, marriage, marriage ceremony, nuptial rite, nuptials, wedlock

wedge 1. *n.* block, chock, chunk, lump, wodge (*Brit. inf.*) 2. *v.* block, cram, crowd, force, jam, lodge, pack, ram, split, squeeze, stuff, thrust

wedlock marriage, matrimony

wee diminutive, insignificant, itsy-bitsy (*Inf.*), Lilliputian, little, microscopic, miniature, minuscule, minute, negligible, pygmy *or* pigmy, small, teeny, teensy-weensy, teeny-weeny, tiny

weed out dispense with, eliminate, eradicate, extirpate, get rid of, remove, root out, separate out, shed, uproot

weedy feeble, frail, ineffectual, namby-pamby, nerdy *or* nurdy (*Sl.*), puny, skinny, thin, undersized, weak, weak-kneed (*Inf.*)

weekly by the week, every week, hebdomadal, hebdomadally, hebdomadary, once a week

weep bemoan, bewail, blub (*Sl.*), blubber, boohoo, complain, cry, greet (*Scot. or archaic*), keen, lament, moan, mourn, shed tears, snivel, sob, ululate, whimper, whinge (*Inf.*)
Antonyms be glad, celebrate, delight, exult, joy, rejoice, revel, triumph

weepy 1. *adj.* blubbering, close to tears, crying, lachrymose, on the verge of tears, sobbing, tearful, weeping, whimpering 2. *n.* tear-jerker (*Inf.*)

weigh 1. have a weight of, measure the weight of, put on the scales, tip the scales at (*Inf.*) 2. apportion, deal out, dole out, measure 3. consider, contemplate, deliberate upon, evaluate, examine, eye up, give thought to, meditate upon, mull over, ponder, reflect upon, study, think over 4. be influential, carry weight, count, cut any ice (*Inf.*), have influence, impress, matter, tell 5. bear down, burden, oppress, prey

weigh down bear down, burden, depress, get down, oppress, overburden, overload, press down, trouble, weigh upon, worry
Antonyms alleviate, ease, hearten, help, lift, lighten, refresh, relieve, unburden

weight *n.* 1. avoirdupois, burden, gravity, heaviness, heft (*Inf.*), load, mass, poundage, pressure, tonnage 2. ballast, heavy object, load, mass 3. burden, load, millstone, oppression, pressure, strain 4. greatest force, main force, onus, preponderance 5. authority, bottom, clout (*Inf.*), consequence, consideration, efficacy, emphasis, impact, import, importance, influence, moment, persuasiveness, power, significance, substance, value ~*v.* 6. add weight to, ballast, charge, freight, increase the load on, increase the weight of, load, make heavier 7. burden, encumber, handicap, impede, oppress, overburden, weigh down 8. bias, load, unbalance

weighty 1. burdensome, cumbersome, dense, heavy, hefty (*Inf.*), massive, ponderous 2. consequential, considerable, critical, crucial, forcible, grave, important, momentous, portentous, serious, significant, solemn, substantial 3. backbreaking, burdensome, crushing, demanding, difficult, exacting, onerous, oppressive, taxing, worrisome, worrying
Antonyms (*sense 2*) frivolous, immaterial, incidental, inconsequential, insignificant, minor, petty, trivial, unimportant

weird bizarre, creepy (*Inf.*), eerie, eldritch (*Poetic*), far-out (*Sl.*), freakish, ghostly, grotesque, mysterious, odd, outlandish, queer, spooky (*Inf.*), strange, supernatural, uncanny, unearthly, unnatural
Antonyms common, mundane, natural, normal, ordinary, regular, typical, usual

weirdo, weirdie crackpot (*Inf.*), crank (*Inf.*), eccentric, freak (*Inf.*), headbanger (*Inf.*), headcase (*Inf.*), loony (*Sl.*), nut (*Sl.*), nutcase (*Sl.*), nutter (*Brit. sl.*), oddball (*Inf.*), queer fish (*Brit. inf.*)

welcome *adj.* 1. acceptable, accepted, agreeable, appreciated, delightful, desirable, gladly received, gratifying, pleasant, pleasing, pleasurable, refreshing, wanted 2. at home, free, invited, under no obligation ~*n.* 3. acceptance, entertainment, greeting, hospitality, reception, salutation ~*v.* 4. accept gladly, bid welcome, embrace, greet, hail, meet, offer hospitality to, receive, receive with open arms, roll out the red carpet for, usher in

Antonyms (*sense 1*) disagreeable, excluded, rebuffed, rejected, unacceptable, undesirable, unpleasant, unwanted, unwelcome (*sense 3*) cold shoulder, exclusion, ostracism, rebuff, rejection, slight, snub (*sense 4*) exclude, rebuff, refuse, reject, slight, snub, spurn, turn away

weld 1. *v.* bind, bond, braze, cement, connect, fuse, join, link, solder, unite 2. *n.* bond, joint, juncture, seam

welfare advantage, benefit, good, happiness, health, interest, profit, prosperity, success, wellbeing

well[1] *adv.* 1. agreeably, capitally, famously (*Inf.*), happily, in a satisfactory manner, nicely, pleasantly, satisfactorily, smoothly, splendidly, successfully 2. ably, adeptly, adequately, admirably, conscientiously, correctly, effectively, efficiently, expertly, proficiently, properly, skilfully, with skill 3. accurately, attentively, carefully, closely 4. comfortably, flourishingly, prosperously 5. correctly, easily, fairly, fittingly, in all fairness, justly, properly, readily, rightly, suitably 6. closely, completely, deeply, fully, intimately, personally, profoundly, thoroughly 7. approvingly, favourably, glowingly, graciously, highly, kindly, warmly 8. abundantly, amply, completely, considerably, fully, greatly, heartily, highly, substantially, sufficiently, thoroughly, very much 9. **as well** also, besides, in addition, into the bargain, to boot, too 10. **as well as** along with, at the same time as, in addition to, including, over and above *~adj.* 11. able-bodied, fit, hale, healthy, hearty, in fine fettle, in good health, robust, sound, strong, up to par 12. advisable, agreeable, bright, fine, fitting, flourishing, fortunate, good, happy, lucky, pleasing, profitable, proper, prudent, right, satisfactory, thriving, useful

Antonyms *adv.* badly, coldly, disapprovingly, gracelessly, ham-fistedly, inadequately, incompetently, incorrectly, ineptly, inexpertly, poorly, slightly, sloppily, somewhat, unfairly, unjustly, unkindly, unskilfully, unsympathetically, vaguely, wrongly *~adj.* ailing, below par, feeble, frail, going badly, ill, improper, infirm, poorly, run-down, sick, sickly, under-the-weather, unfitting, unsatisfactory, unsuccessful, unwell, weak, wrong

well[2] *n.* 1. fount, fountain, pool, source, spring, waterhole 2. bore, hole, pit, shaft 3. fount, mine, repository, source, wellspring *~v.* 4. exude, flow, gush, jet, ooze, pour, rise, run, seep, spout, spring, spurt, stream, surge, trickle

well-balanced 1. graceful, harmonious, proportional, symmetrical, well-proportioned 2. judicious, level-headed, rational, reasonable, sane, sensible, sober, sound, together (*Sl.*), well-adjusted

Antonyms (*sense 2*) erratic, insane, irrational, neurotic, unbalanced, unreasonable, unsound, unstable, volatile

well-bred 1. aristocratic, blue-blooded, gentle, highborn, noble, patrician, well-born 2. civil, courteous, courtly, cultivated, cultured, gallant, genteel, gentlemanly, ladylike, mannerly, polished, polite, refined, sophisticated, urbane, well-brought-up, well-mannered

Antonyms (*sense 2*) bad-mannered, base, coarse, discourteous, ill-bred, rude, uncivilized, uncouth, uncultured, vulgar

well-favoured attractive, beautiful, bonny, comely, fair, good-looking, handsome, lovely, nice-looking, pretty

well-fed 1. healthy, in good condition, well-nourished 2. chubby, fat, fleshy, plump, podgy, portly, rotund, rounded, stout

well-groomed dapper, neat, smart, soigné *or* soigneé, spruce, tidy, trim, well-dressed, well turned out

well-known celebrated, familiar, famous, illustrious, notable, noted, popular, renowned, widely known

well-nigh all but, almost, just about, more or less, nearly, next to, practically, virtually

well-off 1. comfortable, flourishing, fortunate, lucky, successful, thriving 2. affluent, comfortable, flush (*Inf.*), loaded (*Sl.*), moneyed, prosperous, rich, wealthy, well-heeled (*Inf.*), well-to-do

Antonyms (*sense 2*) badly off, broke (*Inf.*), destitute, dirt-poor (*Inf.*), down and out, flat broke (*Inf.*), hard up (*Inf.*), impoverished, indigent, needy, on the rocks (*Inf.*), penniless, poor, poverty-stricken, short, without two pennies to rub together (*Inf.*)

wellspring 1. fount, fountainhead, origin, source, wellhead 2. fount, fund, mine, repository, reserve, reservoir, source, supply, well

well-thought-of admired, esteemed, highly regarded, of good repute, reputable, respected, revered, venerated

Antonyms abhorred, derided, despised, disdained, reviled, scorned, spurned

well-to-do affluent, comfortable, flush (*Inf.*), loaded (*Sl.*), moneyed, prosperous, rich, wealthy, well-heeled (*Inf.*), well-off

Antonyms bankrupt, broke (*Inf.*), destitute, hard up (*Inf.*), indigent, insolvent, needy, poor, ruined

well-worn banal, commonplace, hackneyed, overused, stale, stereotyped, threadbare, timeworn, tired, trite

welt contusion, mark, ridge, scar, streak, stripe, wale, weal, wheal

welter *v.* 1. flounder, lie, roll, splash, tumble, wade, wallow, writhe 2. billow, heave, pitch, roll, surge, swell, toss ~*n.* 3. confusion, hotchpotch, jumble, mess, muddle, tangle, web

wend direct one's course, go, make for, move, proceed, progress, travel

wet *adj.* 1. aqueous, damp, dank, drenched, dripping, humid, moist, moistened, saturated, soaked, soaking, sodden, soggy, sopping, waterlogged, watery, wringing wet 2. clammy, dank, drizzling, humid, misty, pouring, raining, rainy, showery, teeming 3. *Brit. inf.* effete, feeble, foolish, ineffectual, irresolute, namby-pamby, nerdy *or* nurdy (*Sl.*), silly, soft, spineless, timorous, weak, weedy (*Inf.*) 4. **wet behind the ears** *Inf.* born yesterday, callow, green, immature, inexperienced, innocent, naive, new, raw ~*n.* 5. clamminess, condensation, damp, dampness, humidity, liquid, moisture, water, wetness 6. damp weather, drizzle, rain, rains, rainy season, rainy weather 7. *Brit. inf.* drip (*Inf.*), milksop, weakling, weed (*Inf.*), wimp (*Inf.*) ~*v.* 8. damp, dampen, dip, douse, drench, humidify, irrigate, moisten, saturate, soak, splash, spray, sprinkle, steep, water

Antonyms *adj.* arid, bone-dry, dried, dry, fine, hardened, parched, set, sunny ~*n.* dryness, dry weather, fine weather ~*v.* dehydrate, desiccate, dry, parch

wetness clamminess, condensation, damp, dampness, humidity, liquid, moisture, sogginess, water, wet

whack *v.* 1. bang, bash (*Inf.*), beat, belabour, belt (*Inf.*), box, buffet, chin (*Sl.*), clobber (*Sl.*), clout (*Inf.*), cuff, deck (*Sl.*), hit, lambast(e), lay one on (*Sl.*), rap, slap, slug, smack, sock (*Sl.*), strike, thrash, thump, thwack, wallop (*Inf.*) ~*n.* 2. bang, bash (*Inf.*), belt (*Inf.*), blow, box, buffet, clout (*Inf.*), cuff, hit, rap, slap, slug, smack, sock (*Sl.*), stroke, thump, thwack, wallop (*Inf.*), wham 3. *Inf.* allotment, bit, cut (*Inf.*), part, portion, quota, share 4. *Inf.* attempt, bash (*Inf.*), crack (*Inf.*), go (*Inf.*), shot (*Inf.*), stab (*Inf.*), try, turn

whacking big, elephantine, enormous, extraordinary, giant, gigantic, great, huge, humongous *or* humungous (*U.S. sl.*), large, mammoth, monstrous, prodigious, tremendous, whopping (*Inf.*)

wham bang, bash (*Inf.*), blow, concussion, impact, slam, smack, thump, thwack, wallop (*Inf.*), whack, whang

wharf dock, jetty, landing stage, pier, quay

wheal contusion, mark, ridge, scar, streak, stripe, wale, weal

wheedle butter up, cajole, charm, coax, court, draw, entice, flatter, inveigle, persuade, talk into, worm

wheel *n.* 1. circle, gyration, pivot, revolution, roll, rotation, spin, turn, twirl, whirl 2. **at the wheel** at the helm, driving, in charge, in command, in control, in the driving seat, steering ~*v.* 3. circle, gyrate, orbit, pirouette, revolve, roll, rotate, spin, swing, swivel, turn, twirl, whirl

wheeze *v.* 1. breathe roughly, catch one's breath, cough, gasp, hiss, rasp, whistle ~*n.* 2. cough, gasp, hiss, rasp, whistle 3. *Brit. sl.* expedient, idea, plan, ploy, ruse, scheme, stunt, trick, wrinkle (*Inf.*) 4. *Inf.* anecdote, chestnut (*Inf.*), crack (*Sl.*), gag (*Inf.*), joke, old joke, one-liner (*Sl.*), story

whereabouts location, position, site, situation

wherewithal capital, equipment, essentials, funds, means, money, ready (*Inf.*), ready money, resources, supplies

whet 1. edge, file, grind, hone, sharpen, strop 2. animate, arouse, awaken, enhance, excite, incite, increase, kindle, pique, provoke, quicken, rouse, stimulate, stir

Antonyms (*sense 2*) blunt, dampen, deaden, depress, dull, numb, smother, stifle, subdue, suppress

whiff *n.* 1. aroma, blast, breath, draught, gust, hint, niff (*Brit. sl.*), odour, puff, scent, smell, sniff ~*v.* 2. breathe, inhale, puff, smell, smoke, sniff, waft 3. *Brit. sl.* hum (*Sl.*), niff (*Brit. sl.*), pong (*Brit. inf.*), reek, stink

whim caprice, conceit, craze, crotchet, fad (*Inf.*), fancy, freak, humour, impulse, notion, passing thought, quirk, sport, sudden notion, urge, vagary, whimsy

whimper 1. *v.* blub (*Sl.*), blubber, cry, grizzle (*Inf., chiefly Brit.*), mewl, moan, pule, snivel, sob, weep, whine, whinge (*Inf.*) 2. *n.* moan, snivel, sob, whine

whimsical capricious, chimerical, crotchety, curious, droll, eccentric, fanciful, fantastic, fantastical, freakish, funny, mischievous, odd, peculiar, playful, quaint, queer, singular, unusual, waggish, weird

whine *n.* 1. cry, moan, plaintive cry, sob, wail, whimper 2. beef (*Sl.*), complaint, gripe (*Inf.*), grouch (*Inf.*), grouse, grumble, moan ~*v.* 3. beef (*Sl.*), bellyache (*Sl.*), bleat, carp, complain, cry, gripe (*Inf.*), grizzle (*Inf., chiefly Brit.*), grouch (*Inf.*), grouse, grumble, kvetch (*U.S. sl.*), moan, sob, wail, whimper, whinge (*Inf.*)

whiner complainer, fault-finder, grouch

(*Inf.*), grouser, grumbler, malcontent, moaner, whinger (*Inf.*)

whip *v.* 1. beat, birch, cane, castigate, flagellate, flog, give a hiding (*Inf.*), lambast(e), lash, leather, lick (*Inf.*), punish, scourge, spank, strap, switch, tan (*Sl.*), thrash 2. exhibit, flash, jerk, produce, pull, remove, seize, show, snatch, whisk 3. *Inf.* dart, dash, dive, flit, flounce, fly, rush, shoot, tear, whisk 4. *Inf.* beat, best, blow out of the water (*Sl.*), clobber (*Sl.*), conquer, defeat, drub, hammer (*Inf.*), lick (*Inf.*), outdo, overcome, overpower, overwhelm, rout, run rings around (*Inf.*), take apart (*Sl.*), thrash, trounce, wipe the floor with (*Inf.*), worst 5. agitate, compel, drive, foment, goad, hound, incite, instigate, prick, prod, provoke, push, spur, stir, urge, work up 6. beat, whisk ~*n.* 7. birch, bullwhip, cane, cat-o'-nine-tails, crop, horsewhip, knout, lash, rawhide, riding crop, scourge, switch, thong

whipping beating, birching, caning, castigation, flagellation, flogging, hiding (*Inf.*), lashing, leathering, punishment, spanking, tanning (*Sl.*), the strap, thrashing

whip up agitate, arouse, excite, foment, incite, inflame, instigate, kindle, provoke, rouse, stir up, work up

whirl *v.* 1. circle, gyrate, pirouette, pivot, reel, revolve, roll, rotate, spin, swirl, turn, twirl, twist, wheel 2. feel dizzy, reel, spin ~*n.* 3. birl (*Scot.*), circle, gyration, pirouette, reel, revolution, roll, rotation, spin, swirl, turn, twirl, twist, wheel 4. confusion, daze, dither (*Chiefly Brit.*), flurry, giddiness, spin 5. flurry, merry-go-round, round, series, succession 6. agitation, bustle, commotion, confusion, flurry, hurly-burly, stir, tumult, uproar 7. **give (something) a whirl** *Inf.* attempt, have a bash (crack (*Inf.*), go (*Inf.*), shot (*Inf.*), stab (*Inf.*), whack (*Inf.*)) (*Inf.*), try

whirlwind 1. *n.* dust devil, tornado, waterspout 2. *adj.* hasty, headlong, impetuous, impulsive, lightning, quick, quickie (*Inf.*), rapid, rash, short, speedy, swift
Antonyms (*sense 2*) calculated, cautious, considered, deliberate, measured, prudent, slow, unhurried

whisk *v.* 1. brush, flick, sweep, whip, wipe 2. barrel (along) (*Inf., chiefly U.S. & Canad.*), burn rubber (*Inf.*), dart, dash, fly, hasten, hurry, race, rush, shoot, speed, sweep, tear 3. beat, fluff up, whip ~*n.* 4. brush, flick, sweep, whip, wipe 5. beater

whisky barley-bree (*Scot.*), bourbon, John Barleycorn, malt, rye, Scotch, usquebaugh

whisper *v.* 1. breathe, murmur, say softly, speak in hushed tones, utter under the breath 2. gossip, hint, insinuate, intimate, murmur, spread rumours 3. hiss, murmur, rustle, sigh, sough, susurrate (*Literary*), swish ~*n.* 4. hushed tone, low voice, murmur, soft voice, undertone 5. hiss, murmur, rustle, sigh, sighing, soughing, susurration *or* susurrus (*Literary*), swish 6. breath, fraction, hint, shadow, suggestion, suspicion, tinge, trace, whiff 7. *Inf.* buzz, dirt (*U.S. sl.*), gossip, innuendo, insinuation, report, rumour, word
Antonyms (*sense 1*) bawl, bellow, clamour, roar, shout, thunder, yell

whit atom, bit, crumb, dash, drop, fragment, grain, iota, jot, least bit, little, mite, modicum, particle, piece, pinch, scrap, shred, speck, trace

white 1. ashen, bloodless, ghastly, grey, pale, pallid, pasty, wan, waxen, wheyfaced 2. grey, grizzled, hoary, silver, snowy 3. clean, immaculate, impeccable, innocent, pure, spotless, squeaky-clean, stainless, unblemished, unsullied
Antonyms (*senses 2 & 3*) black, blackish, blemished, dark, dirty, impure, soiled, stained, tarnished

white-collar clerical, executive, nonmanual, office, professional, salaried

whiten blanch, bleach, blench, etiolate, fade, go white, pale, turn pale
Antonyms blacken, colour, darken

whitewash 1. *n.* camouflage, concealment, cover-up, deception, extenuation 2. *v.* camouflage, conceal, cover up, extenuate, gloss over, make light of, suppress
Antonyms *v.* disclose, expose, lay bare, reveal, uncover, unmask, unveil

whittle 1. carve, cut, hew, pare, shape, shave, trim 2. consume, destroy, eat away, erode, reduce, undermine, wear away

whole *adj.* 1. complete, entire, full, in one piece, integral, total, unabridged, uncut, undivided 2. faultless, flawless, good, in one piece, intact, inviolate, mint, perfect, sound, unbroken, undamaged, unharmed, unhurt, unimpaired, uninjured, unmutilated, unscathed, untouched 3. able-bodied, better, cured, fit, hale, healed, healthy, in fine fettle, in good health, recovered, robust, sound, strong, well ~*adv.* 4. in one, in one piece ~*n.* 5. aggregate, all, everything, lot, sum total, the entire amount, total 6. ensemble, entirety, entity, fullness, piece, totality, unit, unity 7. **on the whole a.** all in all, all things considered, by and large, taking everything into consideration **b.** as a rule, for the most part, generally, in the main, in general, mostly, predominantly
Antonyms *adj.* ailing, broken, cut, damaged, diseased, divided, fragmented, ill, in-

complete, in pieces, partial, sick, sickly, under-the-weather, unwell ~*n.* bit, component, constituent, division, element, fragment, part, piece, portion

wholehearted committed, complete, dedicated, determined, devoted, earnest, emphatic, enthusiastic, genuine, heartfelt, hearty, real, sincere, true, unfeigned, unqualified, unreserved, unstinting, warm, zealous

Antonyms cool, grudging, half-hearted, insincere, qualified, reserved, unreal

wholesale 1. *adj.* all-inclusive, broad, comprehensive, extensive, far-reaching, indiscriminate, mass, sweeping, wide-ranging 2. *adv.* all at once, comprehensively, extensively, indiscriminately, on a large scale, without exception

Antonyms *adj.* confined, discriminate, limited, partial, restricted, selective

wholesome 1. beneficial, good, healthful, health-giving, healthy, helpful, hygienic, invigorating, nourishing, nutritious, salubrious, salutary, sanitary, strengthening 2. clean, decent, edifying, ethical, exemplary, honourable, improving, innocent, moral, nice, pure, respectable, righteous, squeaky-clean, uplifting, virtuous, worthy

Antonyms blue, corrupt, degrading, dirty, dishonest, evil, filthy, immoral, lewd, obscene, pernicious, pornographic, putrid, rotten, tasteless, trashy, unhealthy, unhygienic, unprincipled, unwholesome

wholly 1. all, altogether, completely, comprehensively, entirely, fully, heart and soul, in every respect, one hundred per cent (*Inf.*), perfectly, thoroughly, totally, utterly 2. exclusively, only, solely, without exception

Antonyms (*sense 1*) in part, incompletely, moderately, partially, partly, relatively, slightly, somewhat

whoop cheer, cry, halloo, holler (*Inf.*), hoot, hurrah, scream, shout, shriek, yell

whopper 1. colossus, crackerjack (*Inf.*), giant, jumbo (*Inf.*), leviathan, mammoth, monster 2. big lie, fable, fabrication, falsehood, tall story (*Inf.*), untruth

whopping big, elephantine, enormous, extraordinary, giant, gigantic, great, huge, humongous *or* humungous (*U.S. sl.*), large, mammoth, massive, monstrous, prodigious, tremendous, whacking (*Inf.*)

whore *n.* 1. brass (*Sl.*), call girl, cocotte, courtesan, demimondaine, demirep (*Rare*), fallen woman, *fille de joie,* harlot, hooker (*U.S. sl.*), hustler (*U.S. & Canad. sl.*), lady of the night, loose woman, prostitute, scrubber (*Brit. & Aust. sl.*), slag (*Brit. sl.*), streetwalker, strumpet, tart (*Inf.*), trollop, woman of easy virtue, woman of ill repute, working girl (*Facetious sl.*) ~*v.* 2. be on the game (*Sl.*), hustle (*U.S. & Canad. sl.*), prostitute oneself, sell one's body, sell oneself, solicit, walk the streets 3. fornicate, lech *or* letch (*Inf.*), sleep around (*Inf.*), wanton, wench (*Archaic*), womanize

whorehouse bagnio, bordello, brothel, cathouse (*U.S. sl.*), disorderly house, house of ill fame *or* repute, house of prostitution, knocking-shop (*Brit. sl.*)

whorl coil, corkscrew, helix, spiral, swirl, twist, vortex

wicked 1. abandoned, abominable, amoral, atrocious, bad, black-hearted, corrupt, debased, depraved, devilish, dissolute, egregious, evil, fiendish, flagitious, foul, guilty, heinous, immoral, impious, iniquitous, irreligious, maleficent, nefarious, scandalous, shameful, sinful, unprincipled, unrighteous, vicious, vile, villainous, worthless 2. arch, impish, incorrigible, mischievous, naughty, rascally, roguish 3. acute, agonizing, awful, crashing, destructive, dreadful, fearful, fierce, harmful, injurious, intense, mighty, painful, severe, terrible 4. bothersome, difficult, distressing, galling, offensive, troublesome, trying, unpleasant 5. *Sl.* adept, adroit, deft, expert, masterly, mighty, outstanding, powerful, skilful, strong

Antonyms benevolent, ethical, good, harmless, honourable, innocuous, mannerly, mild, moral, noble, obedient, pleasant, principled, virtuous, well-behaved, wholesome

wide *adj.* 1. ample, broad, catholic, comprehensive, distended, encyclopedic, expanded, expansive, extensive, far-reaching, general, immense, inclusive, large, sweeping, vast 2. away, distant, off, off course, off target, remote 3. dilated, distended, expanded, fully open, outspread, outstretched 4. ample, baggy, capacious, commodious, full, loose, roomy, spacious ~*adv.* 5. as far as possible, completely, fully, right out, to the furthest extent 6. astray, nowhere near, off course, off target, off the mark, out

Antonyms *adj.* closed, confined, constricted, cramped, limited, narrow, restricted, shut, strict, tight ~*adv.* barely, narrowly, partially, partly

wide-awake 1. conscious, fully awake, roused, wakened 2. alert, aware, heedful, keen, observant, on one's toes, on the alert, on the ball (*Inf.*), on the qui vive, vigilant, wary, watchful

Antonyms (*sense 2*) distracted, dreamy, heedless, inattentive, negligent, oblivious, preoccupied, unaware, unobservant

wide-eyed credulous, green, impressionable, ingenuous, innocent, naive, simple, trusting, unsophisticated, unsuspicious, wet behind the ears (*Inf.*)

widen broaden, dilate, enlarge, expand, extend, open out *or* up, open wide, spread, stretch

Antonyms compress, constrict, contract, cramp, diminish, narrow, reduce, shrink, tighten

wide-open 1. fully extended, fully open, gaping, outspread, outstretched, splayed, spread 2. at risk, defenceless, exposed, in danger, in peril, open, susceptible, unprotected, vulnerable 3. anybody's guess (*Inf.*), indeterminate, uncertain, unpredictable, unsettled, up for grabs (*Inf.*)

widespread broad, common, epidemic, extensive, far-flung, far-reaching, general, pervasive, popular, prevalent, rife, sweeping, universal, wholesale

Antonyms confined, exclusive, limited, local, narrow, rare, sporadic, uncommon

width breadth, compass, diameter, extent, girth, measure, range, reach, scope, span, thickness, wideness

wield 1. brandish, employ, flourish, handle, manage, manipulate, ply, swing, use 2. apply, be possessed of, command, control, exercise, exert, have, have at one's disposal, hold, maintain, make use of, manage, possess, put to use, utilize

wife better half (*Humorous*), bride, helpmate, helpmeet, her indoors (*Brit. sl.*), little woman (*Inf.*), mate, old lady (*Inf.*), old woman (*Inf.*), partner, significant other (*U.S. inf.*), spouse, (the) missis *or* missus (*Inf.*), woman (*Inf.*)

wiggle *v./n.* jerk, jiggle, shake, shimmy, squirm, twitch, wag, waggle, writhe

wild *adj.* 1. feral, ferocious, fierce, savage, unbroken, undomesticated, untamed 2. free, indigenous, native, natural, uncultivated 3. desert, deserted, desolate, empty, godforsaken, trackless, uncivilized, uncultivated, uninhabited, unpopulated, virgin 4. barbaric, barbarous, brutish, ferocious, fierce, primitive, rude, savage, uncivilized 5. boisterous, chaotic, disorderly, impetuous, lawless, noisy, riotous, rough, rowdy, self-willed, turbulent, unbridled, uncontrolled, undisciplined, unfettered, ungovernable, unmanageable, unrestrained, unruly, uproarious, violent, wayward 6. blustery, choppy, furious, howling, intense, raging, rough, tempestuous, violent 7. dishevelled, disordered, straggly, tousled, unkempt, untidy, windblown 8. at one's wits' end, berserk, beside oneself, crazed, crazy, delirious, demented, excited, frantic, frenzied, hysterical, irrational, mad, maniacal, rabid, raving 9. extravagant, fantastic, flighty, foolhardy, foolish, giddy, ill-considered, impracticable, imprudent, madcap, outrageous, preposterous, rash, reckless 10. *Inf.* agog, avid, crazy (*Inf.*), daft (*Inf.*), eager, enthusiastic, excited, mad (*Inf.*), nuts (*Sl.*), potty (*Brit. inf.*) ~*adv.* 11. **run wild** a. grow unchecked, ramble, spread, straggle b. abandon all restraint, cut loose, go on the rampage, kick over the traces, rampage, run free, run riot, stray ~*n.* 12. *Often plural* back of beyond (*Inf.*), desert, middle of nowhere (*Inf.*), uninhabited area, wasteland, wilderness

Antonyms *adj.* advanced, broken, calm, careful, controlled, disciplined, domesticated, friendly, genteel, gentle, lawful, logical, mild, ordered, orderly, peaceful, polite, practical, quiet, realistic, restrained, self-controlled, tame, thoughtful, unenthusiastic, uninterested, well-behaved, well thought-out (*senses 2 & 3*) civilized, cultivated, farmed, inhabited, planted, populated, urban

wilderness 1. desert, jungle, waste, wasteland, wild 2. clutter, confused mass, confusion, congeries, jumble, maze, muddle, tangle, welter

wildlife flora and fauna

wile 1. artfulness, artifice, cheating, chicanery, craft, craftiness, cunning, fraud, guile, slyness, trickery 2. *Usually plural* artifice, contrivance, device, dodge, imposition, lure, manoeuvre, ploy, ruse, stratagem, subterfuge, trick

wilful 1. adamant, bull-headed, determined, dogged, froward, headstrong, inflexible, intractable, intransigent, mulish, obdurate, obstinate, persistent, perverse, pig-headed, refractory, self-willed, stiff-necked, stubborn, uncompromising, unyielding 2. conscious, deliberate, intended, intentional, purposeful, volitional, voluntary, willed

Antonyms (*sense 1*) biddable, complaisant, compromising, docile, flexible, good-natured, obedient, pliant, tractable, yielding (*sense 2*) accidental, involuntary, uncalculated, unconscious, unintentional, unplanned, unwitting

will *n.* 1. choice, decision, determination, discretion, option, prerogative, volition 2. declaration, last wishes, testament 3. choice, decision, decree, desire, fancy, inclination, mind, pleasure, preference, wish 4. aim, determination, intention, purpose, resolution, resolve, willpower 5. attitude, disposition, feeling 6. **at will** as one pleases, as one thinks fit, as one wishes, at one's desire (discretion, inclination, pleasure, whim, wish) ~*v.* 7. bid, bring about, cause, command, decree, determine, direct, effect, ordain, order, resolve 8. choose, desire, elect, opt, prefer, see fit, want, wish 9. bequeath, confer, give, leave, pass on, transfer

willing agreeable, amenable, compliant, consenting, content, desirous, disposed, eager, enthusiastic, favourable, game (*Inf.*), happy, inclined, in favour, in the mood, nothing loath, pleased, prepared, ready, so-minded
Antonyms averse, disinclined, grudging, loath, indisposed, not keen, reluctant, unenthusiastic, unwilling

willingly by choice, cheerfully, eagerly, freely, gladly, happily, of one's own accord, of one's own free will, readily, voluntarily, with all one's heart, without hesitation, with pleasure
Antonyms grudgingly, hesitantly, involuntarily, reluctantly, unwillingly

willingness agreeableness, agreement, consent, desire, disposition, enthusiasm, favour, good will, inclination, volition, will, wish
Antonyms aversion, disagreement, disinclination, hesitation, loathing, reluctance, unwillingness

willowy graceful, limber, lissom(e), lithe, slender, slim, supple, svelte, sylphlike

willpower determination, drive, firmness of purpose *or* will, fixity of purpose, force *or* strength of will, grit, resolution, resolve, self-control, self-discipline, single-mindedness
Antonyms apathy, hesitancy, indecision, irresolution, languor, lethargy, shilly-shallying (*Inf.*), torpor, uncertainty, weakness

willy-nilly 1. *adv.* necessarily, *nolens volens,* of necessity, perforce, whether desired or not, whether one likes it or not, whether or no 2. *adj.* inevitable, irrespective of one's wishes, necessary, unavoidable

wilt 1. become limp *or* flaccid, droop, sag, shrivel, wither 2. diminish, dwindle, ebb, fade, fail, flag, languish, lose courage, melt away, sag, sink, wane, weaken, wither

wily arch, artful, astute, cagey (*Inf.*), crafty, crooked, cunning, deceitful, deceptive, designing, fly (*Sl.*), foxy, guileful, intriguing, scheming, sharp, shifty, shrewd, sly, tricky, underhand
Antonyms artless, above-board, candid, dull, guileless, honest, ingenuous, naive, simple, straightforward

win *v.* 1. achieve first place, achieve mastery, be victorious, carry all before one, carry the day, come first, conquer, finish first, gain victory, overcome, prevail, succeed, take the prize, triumph 2. accomplish, achieve, acquire, attain, bag (*Inf.*), catch, collect, come away with, earn, gain, get, net, obtain, pick up, procure, receive, secure 3. *Often with* **over** allure, attract, bring *or* talk round, carry, charm, convert, convince, disarm, induce, influence, persuade, prevail upon, sway ~*n.* 4. *Inf.* conquest, success, triumph, victory
Antonyms *v.* fail, fall, forfeit, lose, miss, suffer defeat, suffer loss ~*n.* beating, defeat, downfall, failure, loss, washout (*Inf.*)

wince 1. *v.* blench, cower, cringe, draw back, flinch, quail, recoil, shrink, start 2. *n.* cringe, flinch, start

wind[1] 1. *n.* air, air-current, blast, breath, breeze, current of air, draught, gust, zephyr 2. *Inf.* clue, hint, inkling, intimation, notice, report, rumour, suggestion, tidings, warning, whisper 3. babble, blather, bluster, boasting, empty talk, gab (*Inf.*), hot air, humbug, idle talk, talk, verbalizing 4. breath, puff, respiration 5. *Inf.* flatulence, flatus, gas 6. **get** *or* **have the wind up** *Inf.* be afraid (alarmed, frightened, scared), fear, take fright 7. **in the wind** about to happen, approaching, close at hand, coming, imminent, impending, in the offing, near, on the cards (*Inf.*), on the way 8. **put the wind up** *Inf.* alarm, discourage, frighten, frighten off, scare, scare off

wind[2] *v.* 1. coil, curl, encircle, furl, loop, reel, roll, spiral, turn around, twine, twist, wreathe 2. bend, curve, deviate, meander, ramble, snake, turn, twist, zigzag ~*n.* 3. bend, curve, meander, turn, twist, zigzag

windbag bigmouth (*Sl.*), blether (*Scot.*), blowhard (*Inf.*), boaster, bore, braggart, bullshit artist (*Taboo sl.*), bullshitter (*Taboo sl.*), gasbag (*Inf.*), gossip, loudmouth (*Inf.*), prattler

wind down cool off, decline, diminish, dwindle, lessen, reduce, relax, slacken, subside, taper off, unwind
Antonyms accelerate, amplify, escalate, expand, heat up, increase, intensify, magnify, step up

winded breathless, gasping for breath, out of breath, out of puff, panting, puffed, puffed out

windfall bonanza, find, godsend, jackpot, manna from heaven, stroke of luck
Antonyms bad luck, disaster, infelicity, misadventure, mischance, misfortune, mishap

winding 1. *n.* bend, convolution, curve, meander, turn, twist, undulation 2. *adj.* anfractuous, bending, circuitous, convoluted, crooked, curving, flexuous, indirect, me-

andering, roundabout, serpentine, sinuous, spiral, tortuous, turning, twisting
Antonyms *adj.* direct, even, level, plumb, smooth, straight, undeviating, unswerving

wind-up close, conclusion, culmination, dénouement, end, finale, finish, termination

wind up 1. bring to a close, close, close down, conclude, end, finalize, finish, liquidate, settle, terminate, tie up the loose ends (*Inf.*), wrap up 2. *Inf.* excite, make nervous, make tense, put on edge, work up 3. *Inf.* be left, end one's days, end up, find oneself, finish up
Antonyms (*sense 1*) begin, commence, embark on, initiate, instigate, institute, open, start

windy 1. blowy, blustering, blustery, boisterous, breezy, gusty, inclement, squally, stormy, tempestuous, wild, windswept 2. boastful, bombastic, diffuse, empty, garrulous, long-winded, loquacious, meandering, pompous, prolix, rambling, turgid, verbose, wordy 3. *Sl.* afraid, chicken (*Sl.*), chickenshit (*U.S. sl.*), cowardly, fearful, frightened, nervous, scared, timid
Antonyms (*sense 1*) becalmed, calm, motionless, smooth, still, windless (*sense 2*) modest, quiet, reserved, restrained, reticent, shy, taciturn, unforthcoming (*sense 3*) bold, brave, courageous, daring, fearless, gallant, unafraid, undaunted

wing *n.* 1. organ of flight, pennon (*Poetic*), pinion (*Poetic*) 2. arm, branch, cabal, circle, clique, coterie, faction, group, grouping, schism, section, segment, set, side 3. adjunct, annexe, ell, extension ~*v.* 4. fly, glide, soar 5. fleet, fly, hasten, hurry, race, speed, zoom 6. clip, hit, nick, wound

wink *v.* 1. bat, blink, flutter, nictate, nictitate 2. flash, gleam, glimmer, sparkle, twinkle ~*n.* 3. blink, flutter, nictation 4. flash, gleam, glimmering, sparkle, twinkle 5. instant, jiffy (*Inf.*), moment, second, split second, twinkling

wink at allow, blink at, condone, connive at, disregard, ignore, overlook, pretend not to notice, put up with (*Inf.*), shut one's eyes to, tolerate, turn a blind eye to

winkle out dig out, dislodge, draw out, extract, extricate, force out, prise out, smoke out, worm out

winner champ (*Inf.*), champion, conquering hero, conqueror, first, master, vanquisher, victor

winning 1. alluring, amiable, attractive, bewitching, captivating, charming, cute, delectable, delightful, disarming, enchanting, endearing, engaging, fascinating, fetching, likable *or* likeable, lovely, pleasing, prepossessing, sweet, taking, winsome 2. conquering, successful, triumphant, victorious
Antonyms (*sense 1*) disagreeable, irksome, offensive, repellent, tiresome, unappealing, unattractive, uninteresting, unpleasant

winnings booty, gains, prize(s), proceeds, profits, spoils, takings

winnow comb, cull, divide, fan, part, screen, select, separate, separate the wheat from the chaff, sift, sort out

winsome agreeable, alluring, amiable, attractive, bewitching, captivating, charming, comely, cute, delectable, disarming, enchanting, endearing, engaging, fair, fascinating, fetching, likable *or* likeable, pleasant, pleasing, pretty, sweet, taking, winning

wintry 1. brumal, chilly, cold, freezing, frosty, frozen, harsh, hibernal, hiemal, icy, snowy 2. bleak, cheerless, cold, desolate, dismal
Antonyms balmy, bright, mild, pleasant, summery, sunny, tepid, warm

wipe *v.* 1. brush, clean, dry, dust, mop, rub, sponge, swab 2. clean off, erase, get rid of, remove, rub off, take away, take off ~*n.* 3. brush, lick, rub, swab

wipe out annihilate, blot out, blow away (*Sl., chiefly U.S.*), destroy, efface, eradicate, erase, expunge, exterminate, extirpate, kill to the last man, massacre, obliterate, take out (*Sl.*)

wiry 1. lean, sinewy, strong, tough 2. bristly, kinky, stiff
Antonyms (*sense 1*) fat, feeble, flabby, fleshy, frail, podgy, puny, spineless, weak

wisdom astuteness, circumspection, comprehension, discernment, enlightenment, erudition, foresight, insight, intelligence, judgment, judiciousness, knowledge, learning, penetration, prudence, reason, sagacity, sapience, sense, smarts (*Sl., chiefly U.S.*), sound judgment, understanding
Antonyms absurdity, bêtise (*Rare*), daftness (*Inf.*), folly, foolishness, idiocy, injudiciousness, nonsense, senselessness, silliness, stupidity

wise 1. aware, clever, clued-up (*Inf.*), discerning, enlightened, erudite, informed, intelligent, judicious, knowing, perceptive, politic, prudent, rational, reasonable, sagacious, sage, sapient, sensible, shrewd, sound, understanding, well-advised, well-informed 2. **put wise** *Sl.* alert, apprise, clue in *or* up (*Inf.*), inform, let (someone) into the secret, notify, tell, tip off, warn
Antonyms daft (*Inf.*), foolish, injudicious, rash, silly, stupid, unintelligent, unwise

wisecrack 1. *n.* barb, funny (*Inf.*), gag

(*Inf.*), jest, jibe, joke, pithy remark, quip, sardonic remark, smart remark, witticism 2. *v.* be facetious, jest, jibe, joke, quip, tell jokes

wish *v.* 1. aspire, covet, crave, desiderate, desire, hanker, hope, hunger, long, need, set one's heart on, sigh for, thirst, want, yearn 2. bid, greet with 3. ask, bid, command, desire, direct, instruct, order, require ~*n.* 4. aspiration, desire, hankering, hope, hunger, inclination, intention, liking, longing, thirst, urge, want, whim, will, yearning 5. bidding, command, desire, order, request, will
Antonyms (*sense 4*) aversion, disinclination, dislike, distaste, loathing, reluctance, repulsion, revulsion

wishy-washy bland, feeble, flat, ineffective, ineffectual, insipid, jejune, tasteless, thin, vapid, watered-down, watery, weak

wisp piece, shred, snippet, strand, thread, twist

wispy attenuate, attenuated, delicate, diaphanous, ethereal, faint, fine, flimsy, fragile, frail, gossamer, insubstantial, light, thin, wisplike

wistful contemplative, disconsolate, dreaming, dreamy, forlorn, longing, meditative, melancholy, mournful, musing, pensive, reflective, sad, thoughtful, yearning

wit 1. badinage, banter, drollery, facetiousness, fun, humour, jocularity, levity, pleasantry, raillery, repartee, wordplay 2. card (*Inf.*), comedian, epigrammatist, *farceur,* humorist, joker, punster, wag 3. acumen, brains, cleverness, common sense, comprehension, discernment, ingenuity, insight, intellect, judgment, mind, nous (*Brit. sl.*), perception, practical intelligence, reason, sense, smarts (*Sl., chiefly U.S.*), understanding, wisdom
Antonyms dullness, folly, foolishness, gravity, humourlessness, ignorance, lack of perception, obtuseness, seriousness, silliness, sobriety, solemnity, stupidity

witch crone, enchantress, magician, necromancer, occultist, sorceress

witchcraft enchantment, incantation, magic, necromancy, occultism, sorcery, sortilege, spell, the black art, the occult, voodoo, witchery, witching, wizardry

withdraw 1. draw back, draw out, extract, pull out, remove, take away, take off 2. abjure, disavow, disclaim, recall, recant, rescind, retract, revoke, take back, unsay 3. absent oneself, back out, cop out (*Sl.*), depart, detach oneself, disengage, drop out, fall back, go, leave, make oneself scarce (*Inf.*), pull back, pull out, retire, retreat, secede
Antonyms (*senses 1 & 3*) advance, forge ahead, go on, move forward, persist, press on, proceed, progress

withdrawal 1. extraction, removal 2. abjuration, disavowal, disclaimer, recall, recantation, repudiation, rescission, retraction, revocation 3. departure, disengagement, exit, exodus, retirement, retreat, secession

withdrawn 1. aloof, detached, distant, introverted, quiet, reserved, retiring, shrinking, shy, silent, taciturn, timorous, uncommunicative, unforthcoming 2. hidden, isolated, out-of-the-way, private, remote, secluded, solitary
Antonyms boisterous, bustling, busy, easily accessible, extrovert, forward, friendly, gregarious, open, outgoing, sociable

wither 1. blast, blight, decay, decline, desiccate, disintegrate, droop, dry, fade, languish, perish, shrink, shrivel, wane, waste, wilt 2. abash, blast, humiliate, mortify, put down, shame, snub
Antonyms (*sense 1*) bloom, blossom, develop, flourish, increase, prosper, succeed, thrive, wax

withering 1. blasting, blighting, devastating, humiliating, hurtful, mortifying, scornful, snubbing 2. deadly, death-dealing, destructive, devastating, killing, murderous, slaughterous

withhold 1. check, conceal, deduct, hide, hold back, keep, keep back, keep secret, refuse, repress, reserve, resist, restrain, retain, sit on (*Inf.*), suppress 2. *With* **from** forbear, keep oneself, refrain, stop oneself
Antonyms (*sense 1*) accord, expose, give, grant, hand over, let go, release, relinquish, reveal

with it fashionable, happening (*Inf.*), in (*Inf.*), latest (*Inf.*), modern, modish, progressive, stylish, swinging (*Sl.*), trendy (*Brit. inf.*), up-to-date, up-to-the-minute, vogue

withstand 1. bear, brave, combat, confront, cope with, defy, endure, face, grapple with, hold off, hold out against, oppose, put up with (*Inf.*), resist, stand up to, suffer, take, take on, thwart, tolerate, weather 2. endure, hold *or* stand one's ground, hold out, remain firm, stand, stand fast, stand firm
Antonyms capitulate, falter, give in, give way, relent, succumb, surrender, weaken, yield

witless asinine, braindead (*Inf.*), crackpot (*Inf.*), crazy, daft (*Inf.*), dozy (*Brit. inf.*), dull, empty-headed, foolish, goofy (*Inf.*), halfwitted, idiotic, imbecilic, inane, loopy

(*Inf.*), moronic, obtuse, rattlebrained (*Sl.*), senseless, silly, stupid, unintelligent

witness *n.* 1. beholder, bystander, eyewitness, looker-on, observer, onlooker, spectator, viewer, watcher 2. attestant, corroborator, deponent, testifier 3. **bear witness a.** depone, depose, give evidence, give testimony, testify b. attest to, bear out, be evidence of, be proof of, betoken, confirm, constitute proof of, corroborate, demonstrate, evince, prove, show, testify to, vouch for ~*v.* 4. attend, be present at, look on, mark, note, notice, observe, perceive, see, view, watch 5. attest, authenticate, bear out, bear witness, confirm, corroborate, depone, depose, give evidence, give testimony, testify 6. countersign, endorse, sign

wits 1. acumen, astuteness, brains (*Inf.*), cleverness, comprehension, faculties, ingenuity, intelligence, judgment, nous (*Brit. sl.*), reason, sense, smarts (*Sl., chiefly U.S.*), understanding 2. **at one's wits' end** at a loss, at the end of one's tether, baffled, bewildered, in despair, lost, stuck (*Inf.*), stumped

witticism bon mot, clever remark, epigram, one-liner (*Sl.*), play on words, pleasantry, pun, quip, repartee, riposte, sally, witty remark

witty amusing, brilliant, clever, droll, epigrammatic, facetious, fanciful, funny, gay, humorous, ingenious, jocular, lively, original, piquant, sparkling, waggish, whimsical
Antonyms boring, dull, humourless, stupid, tedious, tiresome, unamusing, uninteresting, witless

wizard 1. conjurer, enchanter, mage (*Archaic*), magician, magus, necromancer, occultist, shaman, sorcerer, thaumaturge (*Rare*), warlock, witch 2. ace (*Inf.*), adept, buff (*Inf.*), expert, genius, hotshot (*Inf.*), maestro, master, maven (*U.S.*), prodigy, star, virtuoso, whiz (*Inf.*), whizz kid (*Inf.*), wiz (*Inf.*)

wizardry conjuration, enchantment, magic, necromancy, occultism, sorcery, sortilege, the black art, voodoo, witchcraft, witchery, witching

wizened dried up, gnarled, lined, sere (*Archaic*), shrivelled, shrunken, withered, worn, wrinkled
Antonyms bloated, plump, rounded, smooth, swollen, turgid

wobble *v.* 1. quake, rock, seesaw, shake, sway, teeter, totter, tremble, vibrate, waver 2. be unable to make up one's mind, be undecided, dither (*Chiefly Brit.*), fluctuate, hesitate, shillyshally (*Inf.*), swither (*Scot.*), vacillate, waver ~*n.* 3. quaking, shake, tremble, tremor, unsteadiness, vibration

wobbly rickety, shaky, teetering, tottering, unbalanced, uneven, unsafe, unstable, unsteady, wonky (*Brit. sl.*)

woe adversity, affliction, agony, anguish, burden, curse, dejection, depression, disaster, distress, gloom, grief, hardship, heartache, heartbreak, melancholy, misery, misfortune, pain, sadness, sorrow, suffering, trial, tribulation, trouble, unhappiness, wretchedness
Antonyms bliss, elation, felicity, fortune, happiness, joy, jubilation, pleasure, prosperity, rapture

woebegone blue, chapfallen, cheerless, crestfallen, dejected, disconsolate, doleful, downcast, downhearted, down in the mouth (*Inf.*), forlorn, funereal, gloomy, grief-stricken, hangdog, long-faced, lugubrious, miserable, mournful, sad, sorrowful, troubled, wretched

woeful 1. afflicted, agonized, anguished, calamitous, catastrophic, cruel, deplorable, disastrous, disconsolate, dismal, distressing, doleful, dreadful, gloomy, grieving, grievous, harrowing, heartbreaking, heart-rending, lamentable, miserable, mournful, pathetic, piteous, pitiable, pitiful, plaintive, sad, sorrowful, tragic, unhappy, wretched 2. abysmal, appalling, awful, bad, deplorable, disappointing, disgraceful, dreadful, duff (*Brit. inf.*), feeble, godawful (*Sl.*), hopeless, inadequate, lousy (*Sl.*), mean, miserable, paltry, pathetic, pitiable, pitiful, poor, rotten (*Inf.*), shitty (*Taboo sl.*), shocking, sorry, terrible, wretched
Antonyms (*sense 1*) carefree, cheerful, chirpy (*Inf.*), contented, delighted, glad, happy, jolly, joyful, jubilant, light-hearted (*sense 2*) abundant, ample, bountiful, enviable, extensive, generous, lavish, luxurious, profuse, prosperous

wolf *n.* 1. *Fig.* devil, fiend, killer, mercenary, pirate, predator, robber, savage, shark 2. *Inf.* Casanova, Don Juan, lady-killer, lech *or* letch (*Inf.*), lecher, Lothario, philanderer, seducer, womanizer ~*v.* 3. *With* **down** bolt, cram, devour, gobble, gollop, gorge, gulp, pack away (*Inf.*), pig out (*Sl.*), scoff (*Sl.*), stuff
Antonyms *v.* bite, nibble, nip, peck, pick at

wolfish avaricious, fierce, gluttonous, greedy, insatiable, predatory, rapacious, ravenous, savage, voracious

woman 1. bird (*Sl.*), chick (*Sl.*), dame (*Sl.*), female, gal (*Sl.*), girl, lady, lass, lassie (*Inf.*), maid (*Archaic*), maiden (*Archaic*), miss, she, wench (*Facetious*) 2. chambermaid, char (*Inf.*), charwoman, domestic, female servant, handmaiden, housekeeper,

lady-in-waiting, maid, maidservant 3. *Inf.* bride, girl, girlfriend, ladylove, mate, mistress, old lady (*Inf.*), partner, significant other (*U.S. inf.*), spouse, sweetheart, wife
Antonyms (*sense 1*) bloke (*Brit. inf.*), boy, chap (*Inf.*), gentleman, guy (*Inf.*), lad, laddie, male, man

womanizer Casanova, Don Juan, ladykiller, lech *or* letch (*Inf.*), lecher, Lothario, philanderer, seducer, wolf (*Inf.*)

womanly female, feminine, ladylike, matronly, motherly, tender, warm

wonder *n.* 1. admiration, amazement, astonishment, awe, bewilderment, curiosity, fascination, stupefaction, surprise, wonderment 2. curiosity, marvel, miracle, nonpareil, phenomenon, portent, prodigy, rarity, sight, spectacle, wonderment ~*v.* 3. ask oneself, be curious, be inquisitive, conjecture, cudgel one's brains (*Inf.*), doubt, inquire, meditate, ponder, puzzle, query, question, speculate, think 4. be amazed (astonished, awed, dumbstruck), be flabbergasted (*Inf.*), boggle, gape, gawk, marvel, stand amazed, stare

wonderful 1. amazing, astonishing, astounding, awe-inspiring, awesome, extraordinary, fantastic, incredible, marvellous, miraculous, odd, peculiar, phenomenal, remarkable, staggering, startling, strange, surprising, unheard-of, wondrous (*Archaic or literary*) 2. ace (*Inf.*), admirable, boffo (*Sl.*), brill (*Inf.*), brilliant, chillin' (*U.S. sl.*), cracking (*Brit. inf.*), excellent, fabulous (*Inf.*), fantastic (*Inf.*), great (*Inf.*), jim-dandy (*Sl.*), magnificent, marvellous, mean (*Sl.*), outstanding, sensational (*Inf.*), smashing (*Inf.*), sovereign, stupendous, super (*Inf.*), superb, terrific, tiptop, topping (*Brit. sl.*), tremendous
Antonyms abominable, appalling, average, awful, bad, common, commonplace, depressing, dire, dreadful, frightful, grim, hellacious (*U.S. sl.*), indifferent, lousy (*Sl.*), mediocre, miserable, modest, ordinary, paltry, rotten, run-of-the-mill, terrible, uninteresting, unpleasant, unremarkable, usual, vile

wonky 1. groggy (*Inf.*), infirm, shaky, unsteady, weak, wobbly, woozy (*Inf.*) 2. askew, awry, out of alignment, skewwhiff (*Brit. inf.*), squint (*Inf.*)

wont 1. *adj.* accustomed, given, in the habit of, used 2. *n.* custom, habit, practice, rule, use, way

wonted 1. accustomed, given, habituated, in the habit of, used 2. accustomed, common, conventional, customary, familiar, frequent, habitual, normal, regular, usual

woo chase, court, cultivate, importune, pay court to, pay one's addresses to, pay suit to, press one's suit with, pursue, seek after, seek the hand of, seek to win, solicit the good will of, spark (*Rare*)

wood 1. *Also* **woods** coppice, copse, forest, grove, thicket, trees, woodland 2. **out of the wood(s)** clear, home and dry (*Brit. sl.*), in the clear, out of danger, safe, safe and sound, secure 3. planks, timber

wooded forested, sylvan (*Poetic*), timbered, tree-clad, tree-covered, woody

wooden 1. ligneous, made of wood, of wood, timber, woody 2. awkward, clumsy, gauche, gawky, graceless, inelegant, maladroit, rigid, stiff, ungainly 3. blank, colourless, deadpan, dull, emotionless, empty, expressionless, glassy, lifeless, spiritless, unemotional, unresponsive, vacant 4. inflexible, obstinate, rigid, stiff, unbending, unyielding 5. dense, dim, dim-witted (*Inf.*), dozy (*Brit. inf.*), dull, dull-witted, obtuse, slow, stupid, thick, witless, woodenheaded (*Inf.*) 6. dull, muffled
Antonyms (*senses 2 & 4*) agile, comely, elegant, flexible, flowing, graceful, lissom(e), nimble, supple

wool 1. fleece, hair, yarn 2. **dyed in the wool** confirmed, diehard, fixed, hardened, inflexible, inveterate, settled, unchangeable, uncompromising, unshakable 3. **pull the wool over someone's eyes** bamboozle (*Inf.*), con (*Sl.*), deceive, delude, dupe, fool, hoodwink, kid (*Inf.*), lead (someone) up the garden path (*Inf.*), pull a fast one (on someone) (*Inf.*), put one over on (*Sl.*), take in (*Inf.*), trick

woolgathering absent-mindedness, abstraction, building castles in the air, daydreaming, dreaming, inattention, musing, preoccupation, reverie
Antonyms alertness, attention, awareness, concentration, heed, observation, thoughtfulness, vigilance, watchfulness

woolly *adj.* 1. fleecy, flocculent, hairy, made of wool, shaggy, woollen 2. blurred, clouded, confused, foggy, fuzzy, hazy, ill-defined, indefinite, indistinct, muddled, nebulous, unclear, vague
Antonyms (*sense 2*) clear, clear-cut, definite, distinct, exact, obvious, precise, sharp, well-defined

woozy befuddled, bemused, confused, dazed, dizzy, nauseated, rocky (*Inf.*), tipsy, unsteady, wobbly

word *n.* 1. brief conversation, chat, chitchat, colloquy, confab (*Inf.*), confabulation, consultation, discussion, talk, tête-à-tête 2. brief statement, comment, declaration, expression, remark, utterance 3. expression, locution, name, term, vocable 4. account, advice, bulletin, communication, communiqué, dispatch, gen (*Brit. inf.*), information, intelligence, intimation, latest (*Inf.*), message, news, notice, report, tidings 5. command, go-ahead (*Inf.*), green light, order, signal 6. affirmation, assertion, assurance, guarantee, oath, parole, pledge, promise, solemn oath, solemn word, undertaking, vow, word of honour 7. bidding, command, commandment, decree, edict, mandate, order, ukase (*Rare*), will 8. countersign, password, slogan, watchword 9. **in a word** briefly, concisely, in a nutshell, in short, succinctly, to put it briefly, to sum up ~*v.* 10. couch, express, phrase, put, say, state, utter

wording choice of words, language, mode of expression, phraseology, phrasing, terminology, words

wordplay punning, puns, repartee, wit, witticisms

words 1. lyrics, text 2. altercation, angry exchange, angry speech, argument, barney (*Inf.*), bickering, disagreement, dispute, falling-out (*Inf.*), quarrel, row, run-in (*Inf.*), set-to (*Inf.*), squabble

wordy diffuse, discursive, garrulous, long-winded, loquacious, pleonastic, prolix, rambling, verbose, windy
Antonyms brief, concise, laconic, pithy, short, succinct, terse, to the point

work *n.* 1. drudgery, effort, elbow grease (*Facetious*), exertion, grind (*Inf.*), industry, labour, slog, sweat, toil, travail (*Literary*) 2. business, calling, craft, duty, employment, job, line, livelihood, métier, occupation, office, profession, pursuit, trade 3. assignment, chore, commission, duty, job, stint, task, undertaking 4. achievement, composition, creation, handiwork, *oeuvre*, opus, performance, piece, production 5. art, craft, skill, workmanship 6. **out of work** idle, jobless, on the dole (*Brit. inf.*), on the street, out of a job, unemployed ~*v.* 7. drudge, exert oneself, labour, peg away, slave, slog (away), sweat, toil 8. be employed, be in work, do business, earn a living, have a job 9. act, control, direct, drive, handle, manage, manipulate, move, operate, ply, use, wield 10. function, go, operate, perform, run 11. cultivate, dig, farm, till 12. fashion, form, handle, knead, make, manipulate, mould, process, shape 13. be agitated, convulse, move, twitch, writhe 14. *Often with* **up** arouse, excite, move, prompt, provoke, rouse, stir 15. accomplish, achieve, bring about, carry out, cause, contrive, create, effect, encompass, execute, implement 16. force, make one's way, manoeuvre, move, progress 17. *Inf.* arrange, bring off, contrive, exploit, fiddle (*Inf.*), fix (*Inf.*), handle, manipulate, pull off, swing (*Inf.*)
Antonyms *n.* (*sense 1*) ease, leisure, relaxation, rest (*sense 2*) entertainment, hobby, holiday, play, recreation, retirement, spare time, unemployment (*sense 3*) child's play (*Inf.*) ~*v.* (*sense 7*) have fun, mark time, play, relax, skive (*Brit. sl.*), take it easy (*sense 10*) be broken, be out of order (*sense 15*) counteract, nullify, prevent, reverse (*sense 16*) remain

workable doable, feasible, possible, practicable, practical, viable
Antonyms hopeless, impractical, impossible, inconceivable, unattainable, unthinkable, unworkable, useless

workaday common, commonplace, everyday, familiar, humdrum, mundane, ordinary, practical, prosaic, routine, run-of-the-mill
Antonyms atypical, different, exciting, extraordinary, rare, special, uncommon, unfamiliar, unusual

worker artisan, craftsman, employee, hand, labourer, proletarian, tradesman, wage earner, working man, working woman, workman

working *n.* 1. action, functioning, manner, method, mode of operation, operation, running 2. *Plural* diggings, excavations, mine, pit, quarry, shaft ~*adj.* 3. active, employed, in a job, in work, labouring 4. functioning, going, operative, running 5. effective, practical, useful, viable

workman artificer, artisan, craftsman, employee, hand, journeyman, labourer, mechanic, operative, tradesman, worker

workmanlike, workmanly adept, careful, efficient, expert, masterly, painstaking, professional, proficient, satisfactory, skilful, skilled, thorough
Antonyms amateurish, botchy, careless, clumsy, cowboy (*Inf.*), incompetent, slapdash, slipshod, unprofessional, unskilful

workmanship art, artistry, craft, craftsmanship, execution, expertise, handicraft, handiwork, manufacture, skill, technique, work

work-out drill, exercise, exercise session, practice session, training, training session, warm-up

work out 1. accomplish, achieve, attain, win 2. calculate, clear up, figure out, find out, puzzle out, resolve, solve, suss (out) (*Sl.*) 3. arrange, construct, contrive, develop, devise, elaborate, evolve, form, formulate, plan, put together 4. be effective, flourish, go as planned, go well, prosper, prove satisfactory, succeed 5. come out, develop, evolve, go, happen, pan out (*Inf.*), result, turn out 6. do exercises, drill, exercise, practise, train, warm up 7. add up to, amount to, come to, reach, reach a total of

works 1. factory, mill, plant, shop, workshop 2. canon, *oeuvre*, output, productions, writings 3. actions, acts, deeds, doings 4. action, guts (*Inf.*), innards (*Inf.*), insides (*Inf.*), machinery, mechanism, movement, moving parts, parts, workings

workshop 1. atelier, factory, mill, plant, shop, studio, workroom, works 2. class, discussion group, seminar, study group

work up agitate, animate, arouse, enkindle, excite, foment, generate, get (someone) all steamed up (*Sl.*), incite, inflame, instigate, move, rouse, spur, stir up, wind up (*Inf.*)

world 1. earth, earthly sphere, globe 2. everybody, everyone, humanity, humankind, human race, man, mankind, men, the public, the race of man 3. cosmos, creation, existence, life, nature, universe 4. heavenly body, planet, star 5. area, domain, environment, field, kingdom, province, realm, sphere, system 6. age, days, epoch, era, period, times 7. **for all the world** exactly, in every respect, in every way, just as if, just like, precisely, to all intents and purposes 8. **on top of the world** *Inf.* beside oneself with joy, cock-a-hoop, ecstatic, elated, exultant, happy, in raptures, on cloud nine (*Inf.*), overjoyed, over the moon (*Inf.*) 9. **out of this world** *Inf.* excellent, fabulous (*Inf.*), fantastic (*Inf.*), great (*Inf.*), incredible, indescribable, marvellous, superb, unbelievable, wonderful

worldly 1. carnal, earthly, fleshly, lay, mundane, physical, profane, secular, sublunary, temporal, terrestrial 2. avaricious, covetous, grasping, greedy, materialistic, selfish, worldly-minded 3. blasé, cosmopolitan, experienced, knowing, politic, sophisticated, urbane, well versed in the ways of the world, worldly-wise
Antonyms (*sense 1*) divine, ethereal, heavenly, immaterial, noncorporeal, spiritual, transcendental, unworldly (*sense 2*) moral, nonmaterialistic, unworldly (*sense 3*) ingenuous, innocent, naive, unsophisticated, unworldly

worldwide general, global, international, omnipresent, pandemic, ubiquitous, universal
Antonyms confined, insular, limited, local, narrow, national, parochial, provincial, restricted

worn 1. frayed, ragged, shabby, shiny, tattered, tatty, the worse for wear, threadbare 2. careworn, drawn, haggard, lined, pinched, wizened 3. exhausted, fatigued, jaded, played-out (*Inf.*), spent, tired, tired out, wearied, weary, worn-out

worn-out 1. broken-down, clapped out (*Brit., Aust., & N.Z. inf.*), decrepit, done, frayed, moth-eaten, on its last legs, ragged, run-down, shabby, tattered, tatty, threadbare, used, used-up, useless, worn 2. all in (*Sl.*), clapped out (*Aust. & N.Z. inf.*), dead *or* out on one's feet (*Inf.*), dog-tired (*Inf.*), done in (*Inf.*), exhausted, fatigued, fit to drop, jiggered (*Dialect*), knackered (*Sl.*), played-out, prostrate, spent, tired, tired out, weary, zonked (*Sl.*)
Antonyms (*sense 2*) fresh, refreshed, relaxed, renewed, rested, restored, revived, strengthened

worried afraid, anxious, apprehensive, bothered, concerned, distracted, distraught, distressed, disturbed, fearful, fretful, frightened, ill at ease, nervous, on edge, overwrought, perturbed, tense, tormented, troubled, uneasy, unquiet, upset, wired (*Sl.*)
Antonyms calm, fearless, peaceful, quiet, tranquil, unafraid, unconcerned, unfazed (*Inf.*), unworried

worrisome 1. bothersome, disquieting, distressing, disturbing, irksome, perturbing, troublesome, upsetting, vexing, worrying 2. anxious, apprehensive, fretful, insecure, jittery (*Inf.*), nervous, uneasy

worry *v.* 1. agonize, annoy, badger, be anxious, bother, brood, disquiet, distress, disturb, feel uneasy, fret, harass, harry, hassle (*Inf.*), hector, importune, irritate, make anxious, perturb, pester, plague, tantalize, tease, torment, trouble, unsettle, upset, vex 2. attack, bite, gnaw at, go for, harass, harry, kill, lacerate, savage, tear ~*n.* 3. annoyance, bother, care, hassle (*Inf.*), irritation, pest, plague, problem, torment, trial, trouble, vexation 4. annoyance, anxiety, apprehension, care, concern, disturbance, fear, irritation, misery, misgiving, perplexity, torment, trepidation, trouble, unease, vexation, woe
Antonyms *v.* be apathetic, be unconcerned, be unperturbed, calm, comfort, console, solace, soothe ~*n.* calm, comfort, consolation, peace of mind, reassurance, serenity, solace, tranquillity

worsen aggravate, damage, decay, decline, degenerate, deteriorate, exacerbate, get worse, go downhill (*Inf.*), go from bad to worse, retrogress, sink, take a turn for the worse
Antonyms ameliorate, better, enhance, improve, mend, recover, rectify, upgrade

worship 1. *v.* adore, adulate, deify, exalt, glorify, honour, idolize, laud, love, praise, pray to, put on a pedestal, respect, revere, reverence, venerate 2. *n.* adoration, adulation, deification, devotion, exaltation, glorification, glory, homage, honour, laudation, love, praise, prayer(s), regard, respect, reverence

Antonyms *v.* blaspheme, deride, despise, disdain, dishonour, flout, mock, revile, ridicule, scoff at, spurn

worst *v.* beat, best, blow out of the water (*Sl.*), clobber (*Sl.*), conquer, crush, defeat, gain the advantage over, get the better of, lick (*Inf.*), master, overcome, overpower, overthrow, run rings around (*Inf.*), subdue, subjugate, undo, vanquish, wipe the floor with (*Inf.*)

worth 1. aid, assistance, avail, benefit, credit, desert(s), estimation, excellence, goodness, help, importance, merit, quality, usefulness, utility, value, virtue, worthiness 2. cost, price, rate, valuation, value

Antonyms (*sense 1*) futility, insignificance, paltriness, triviality, unworthiness, uselessness, worthlessness, wretchedness

worthless 1. chickenshit (*U.S. sl.*), futile, ineffectual, insignificant, inutile, meaningless, measly, miserable, nickel-and-dime (*U.S. sl.*), no use, nugatory, paltry, pointless, poor, poxy (*Sl.*), rubbishy, trashy, trifling, trivial, unavailing, unimportant, unusable, useless, valueless, wretched 2. abandoned, abject, base, contemptible, depraved, despicable, good-for-nothing, ignoble, useless, vile

Antonyms consequential, decent, effective, fruitful, honourable, important, noble, precious, productive, profitable, significant, upright, useful, valuable, worthwhile, worthy

worthwhile beneficial, constructive, expedient, gainful, good, helpful, justifiable, productive, profitable, useful, valuable, worthy

Antonyms inconsequential, pointless, trivial, unimportant, unworthy, useless, vain, valueless, wasteful, worthless

worthy 1. *adj.* admirable, commendable, creditable, decent, dependable, deserving, estimable, excellent, good, honest, honourable, laudable, meritorious, praiseworthy, reliable, reputable, respectable, righteous, upright, valuable, virtuous, worthwhile 2. *n.* big shot (*Inf.*), bigwig (*Inf.*), dignitary, luminary, notable, personage

Antonyms *adj.* demeaning, disreputable, dubious, ignoble, undeserving, unproductive, untrustworthy, unworthy, useless ~*n.* member of the rank and file, nobody, pleb, punter (*Inf.*)

wound *n.* 1. cut, damage, gash, harm, hurt, injury, laceration, lesion, slash 2. anguish, distress, grief, heartbreak, injury, insult, offence, pain, pang, sense of loss, shock, slight, torment, torture, trauma ~*v.* 3. cut, damage, gash, harm, hit, hurt, injure, irritate, lacerate, pierce, slash, wing 4. annoy, cut (someone) to the quick, distress, grieve, hurt, hurt the feelings of, mortify, offend, pain, shock, sting, traumatize

wraith apparition, eidolon, ghost, phantom, revenant, shade (*Literary*), spectre, spirit, spook (*Inf.*)

wrangle 1. *v.* altercate, argue, bicker, brawl, contend, disagree, dispute, fall out (*Inf.*), fight, have words, quarrel, row, scrap, spar, squabble 2. *n.* altercation, angry exchange, argy-bargy (*Brit. inf.*), *bagarre,* barney (*Inf.*), bickering, brawl, clash, contest, controversy, dispute, falling-out (*Inf.*), quarrel, row, set-to (*Inf.*), slanging match (*Brit.*), squabble, tiff

wrap 1. *v.* absorb, bind, bundle up, cloak, cover, encase, enclose, enfold, envelop, fold, immerse, muffle, pack, package, roll up, sheathe, shroud, surround, swathe, wind 2. *n.* cape, cloak, mantle, shawl, stole

Antonyms *v.* disclose, open, strip, uncover, unfold, unpack, unwind, unwrap

wrapper case, cover, envelope, jacket, packaging, paper, sheath, sleeve, wrapping

wrap up 1. bundle up, enclose, enwrap, giftwrap, pack, package 2. dress warmly, muffle up, put warm clothes on, wear something warm 3. *Sl.* be quiet, be silent, button it (*Sl.*), button one's lip (*Sl.*), hold one's tongue, put a sock in it (*Brit. sl.*), shut one's face (*Brit. sl.*), shut one's mouth (*Sl.*), shut one's trap (*Sl.*), shut up 4. *Inf.* bring to a close, conclude, end, finish off, polish off, round off, terminate, tidy up, wind up

wrath anger, choler, displeasure, exasperation, fury, indignation, ire, irritation, passion, rage, resentment, temper

Antonyms amusement, contentment, delight, enjoyment, gladness, gratification, happiness, joy, pleasure, satisfaction

wrathful angry, beside oneself with rage, displeased, enraged, furious, incensed, indignant, infuriated, irate, on the warpath (*Inf.*), raging, wroth (*Archaic*)

Antonyms amused, calm, contented, delighted, glad, gratified, happy, joyful, pleased, satisfied

wreak 1. bring about, carry out, cause, create, effect, execute, exercise, inflict, visit, work 2. express, give free rein to, give vent to, gratify, indulge, unleash, vent

wreath band, chaplet, coronet, crown, festoon, garland, loop, ring

wreathe adorn, coil, crown, encircle, enfold, entwine, envelop, enwrap, festoon, intertwine, interweave, surround, twine, twist, wind, wrap, writhe

wreck *v.* 1. blow (*Sl.*), break, cock up (*Brit. sl.*), dash to pieces, demolish, destroy, devastate, fuck up (*Offens. taboo sl.*), mar, play havoc with, ravage, ruin, screw up (*Inf.*), shatter, smash, spoil, total (*Sl.*), trash (*Sl.*), undo 2. founder, go *or* run aground, run onto the rocks, shipwreck, strand ~*n.* 3. derelict, hulk, shipwreck, sunken vessel 4. desolation, destruction, devastation, disruption, mess, overthrow, ruin, undoing
Antonyms *v.* build, conserve, create, fulfil, make possible, preserve, reconstruct, save, salvage ~*n.* conservation, creation, formation, fulfilment, preservation, restoration, salvage, saving

wreckage debris, fragments, hulk, pieces, remains, rubble, ruin, wrack

wrench *v.* 1. force, jerk, pull, rip, tear, tug, twist, wrest, wring, yank 2. distort, rick, sprain, strain ~*n.* 3. jerk, pull, rip, tug, twist, yank 4. sprain, strain, twist 5. ache, blow, pain, pang, shock, upheaval, uprooting 6. adjustable spanner, shifting spanner, spanner

wrest extract, force, pull, seize, strain, take, twist, win, wrench, wring

wrestle battle, combat, contend, fight, grapple, scuffle, strive, struggle, tussle

wretch 1. asshole (*U.S. & Canad. taboo sl.*), asswipe (*U.S. & Canad. taboo sl.*), bad egg (*Old-fashioned inf.*), bastard (*Offensive*), blackguard, bugger (*Taboo sl.*), cocksucker (*Taboo sl.*), cur, good-for-nothing, miscreant, mother (*Taboo sl., chiefly U.S.*), motherfucker (*Taboo sl., chiefly U.S.*), outcast, profligate, rascal, rat (*Inf.*), rogue, rotter (*Sl., chiefly Brit.*), ruffian, scoundrel, scumbag (*Sl.*), shit (*Taboo sl.*), son-of-a-bitch (*Sl., chiefly U.S. & Canad.*), swine, turd (*Taboo sl.*), vagabond, villain, worm 2. poor thing, unfortunate

wretched 1. abject, brokenhearted, cheerless, comfortless, crestfallen, dejected, deplorable, depressed, disconsolate, dismal, distressed, doleful, downcast, forlorn, funereal, gloomy, hapless, hopeless, melancholy, miserable, pathetic, pitiable, pitiful, poor, sorry, unfortunate, unhappy, woebegone, woeful, worthless 2. calamitous, deplorable, inferior, miserable, paltry, pathetic, poor, sorry, worthless 3. base, contemptible, crappy (*Sl.*), despicable, low, low-down (*Inf.*), mean, paltry, poxy (*Sl.*), scurvy, shabby, shameful, vile
Antonyms admirable, carefree, cheerful, contented, decent, enviable, excellent, flourishing, fortunate, great, happy, jovial, light-hearted, noble, prosperous, splendid, successful, thriving, untroubled, wonderful, worthy

wriggle *v.* 1. jerk, jiggle, squirm, turn, twist, wag, waggle, wiggle, writhe 2. crawl, slink, snake, twist and turn, worm, zigzag 3. crawl, dodge, extricate oneself, manoeuvre, sneak, talk one's way out, worm ~*n.* 4. jerk, jiggle, squirm, turn, twist, wag, waggle, wiggle

wring 1. coerce, extort, extract, force, screw, squeeze, twist, wrench, wrest 2. distress, hurt, lacerate, pain, pierce, rack, rend, stab, tear at, wound

wrinkle[1] 1. *n.* corrugation, crease, crinkle, crow's-foot, crumple, fold, furrow, gather, line, pucker, rumple 2. *v.* corrugate, crease, crinkle, crumple, fold, furrow, gather, line, pucker, ruck, rumple
Antonyms *v.* even out, flatten, iron, level, press, smooth, straighten, unfold

wrinkle[2] device, dodge, gimmick, idea, plan, ploy, ruse, scheme, stunt, tip, trick, wheeze (*Brit. sl.*)

writ court order, decree, document, summons

write author (*Nonstandard*), commit to paper, compose, copy, correspond, create, draft, draw up, indite, inscribe, jot down, pen, put down in black and white, put in writing, record, scribble, set down, take down, tell, transcribe

write off 1. cancel, cross out, disregard, forget about, give up for lost, score out, shelve 2. *Inf.* crash, damage beyond repair, destroy, smash up, total (*Sl.*), trash (*Sl.*), wreck

writer author, columnist, essayist, hack, littérateur, man of letters, novelist, penman, penny-a-liner (*Rare*), penpusher, scribbler, scribe, wordsmith

writhe contort, distort, jerk, squirm, struggle, thrash, thresh, toss, twist, wiggle, wriggle

writing 1. calligraphy, chirography, hand, handwriting, penmanship, print, scrawl, scribble, script 2. book, composition, document, letter, opus, publication, title, work 3. belles-lettres, letters, literature

wrong *adj.* 1. erroneous, fallacious, false, faulty, inaccurate, incorrect, in error, mistaken, off beam (*Inf.*), off target, out, unsound, untrue, wide of the mark 2. bad, blameworthy, criminal, crooked, dishonest, dishonourable, evil, felonious, illegal, illicit, immoral, iniquitous, reprehensible, sinful, under-the-table, unethical, unfair, unjust, unlawful, wicked, wrongful 3. funny, improper, inappropriate, inapt, incongruous, incorrect, indecorous, infelicitous, malapropos, not done, unacceptable, unbecoming, unconventional, undesirable, unfitting, unhappy, unseemly, unsuitable 4. amiss, askew, awry, defective, faulty, not working, out of commission, out of order 5. inside, inverse, opposite, reverse ~*adv.* 6. amiss, askew, astray, awry, badly, erroneously, inaccurately, incorrectly, mistakenly, wrongly 7. **go wrong** a. come to grief (*Inf.*), come to nothing, fail, fall through, flop (*Inf.*), miscarry, misfire b. boob (*Brit. sl.*), err, go astray, make a mistake, slip up (*Inf.*) c. break down, cease to function, conk out (*Inf.*), fail, go kaput (*Inf.*), go on the blink (*Sl.*), go phut (*Inf.*), malfunction, misfire d. err, fall from grace, go astray, go off the straight and narrow (*Inf.*), go to the bad, lapse, sin ~*n.* 8. abuse, bad *or* evil deed, crime, error, grievance, immorality, inequity, infraction, infringement, iniquity, injury, injustice, misdeed, offence, sin, sinfulness, transgression, trespass, unfairness, wickedness 9. **in the wrong** at fault, blameworthy, guilty, in error, mistaken, off beam (*Inf.*), off course, off target, to be blamed ~*v.* 10. abuse, cheat, discredit, dishonour, harm, hurt, ill-treat, ill-use, impose upon, injure, malign, maltreat, misrepresent, mistreat, oppress, take advantage of

Antonyms *adj.* accurate, appropriate, apt, becoming, commendable, correct, ethical, fair, fitting, godly, honest, honourable, just, laudable, lawful, legal, moral, praiseworthy, precise, proper, righteous, rightful, seemly, sensible, square, suitable, true, upright, virtuous ~*adv.* accurately, correctly, exactly, precisely, properly, squarely, truly ~*n.* decency, fairness, favour, good, good deed, goodness, good turn, high-mindedness, honesty, lawfulness, legality, morality, propriety, virtue ~*v.* aid, do a favour, help, support, treat well

wrongdoer criminal, culprit, delinquent, evildoer, lawbreaker, malefactor, miscreant, offender, sinner, transgressor, trespasser (*Archaic*), villain

wrongful blameworthy, criminal, dishonest, dishonourable, evil, felonious, illegal, illegitimate, illicit, immoral, improper, reprehensible, under-the-table, unethical, unfair, unjust, unlawful, wicked

Antonyms ethical, fair, honest, honourable, just, lawful, legal, legitimate, moral, proper, rightful

wrong-headed 1. bull-headed, contrary, cross-grained, dogged, froward, inflexible, intransigent, mulish, obdurate, obstinate, perverse, pig-headed, refractory, self-willed, stubborn, wilful 2. erroneous, fallacious, false, faulty, incorrect, in error, misguided, mistaken, off target, unsound, wrong

wrought-up agitated, animated, aroused, at fever pitch, beside oneself, excited, inflamed, keyed up, moved, overwrought, roused, stirred, strung up (*Inf.*), worked-up, wound up (*Inf.*)

wry 1. askew, aslant, awry, contorted, crooked, deformed, distorted, off the level, skewwhiff (*Brit. inf.*), twisted, uneven, warped 2. droll, dry, ironic, mocking, mordacious, pawky (*Scot.*), sarcastic, sardonic

Antonyms (*sense 1*) aligned, even, level, smooth, straight, unbent

X·Y·Z

Xmas Christmas, Christmastide, festive season, Noel, Yule (*Archaic*), Yuletide (*Archaic*)

X-rays Röntgen rays (*Old name*)

yahoo barbarian, beast, boor, brute, churl, lout, philistine, roughneck (*Sl.*), rowdy, savage, yob *or* yobbo (*Brit. sl.*)

yak 1. *v.* blather, chatter, gab (*Inf.*), gossip, jabber, jaw (*Sl.*), rabbit (on) (*Brit. inf.*), run on, spout, tattle, waffle (*Inf., chiefly Brit.*), witter on (*Inf.*), yap (*Inf.*) 2. *n.* blather, chat, chinwag (*Brit. inf.*), confab (*Inf.*), gossip, hot air (*Inf.*), jaw (*Sl.*), waffle (*Inf., chiefly Brit.*), yackety-yak (*Sl.*), yammer (*Inf.*)

yank *v./n.* hitch, jerk, pull, snatch, tug, wrench

yap *v.* 1. yammer (*Inf.*), yelp, yip (*Chiefly U.S.*) 2. *Inf.* babble, blather, chatter, go on, gossip, jabber, jaw (*Sl.*), prattle, rabbit (on) (*Brit. inf.*), run off at the mouth (*Sl.*), spout, talk, tattle, waffle (*Inf., chiefly Brit.*)

yardstick benchmark, criterion, gauge, measure, par, standard, touchstone

yarn *n.* 1. fibre, thread 2. *Inf.* anecdote, cock-and-bull story (*Inf.*), fable, story, tale, tall story

yawning cavernous, chasmal, gaping, vast, wide, wide-open

yearly annual, annually, every year, once a year, per annum

yearn ache, covet, crave, desire, eat one's heart out over, hanker, have a yen for (*Inf.*), hunger, itch, languish, long, lust, pant, pine, set one's heart upon

years 1. age, dotage, old age, second childhood, senescence, senility 2. days, generation(s), lifetime, span, time

yell 1. *v.* bawl, holler (*Inf.*), howl, scream, screech, shout, shriek, squeal 2. *n.* cry, howl, scream, screech, shriek, whoop
Antonyms *v.* mumble, murmur, mutter, say softly, whisper

yelp cry, yammer (*Inf.*), yap, yip (*Chiefly U.S.*), yowl

yen *n.* craving, desire, hankering, hunger, itch, longing, passion, thirst, yearning

yes man ass-kisser (*U.S. & Canad. taboo sl.*), bootlicker (*Inf.*), bosses' lackey, company man, crawler (*Sl.*), creature, minion, sycophant, timeserver, toady

yet 1. as yet, so far, thus far, until now, up to now 2. however, nevertheless, notwithstanding, still 3. additionally, as well, besides, further, in addition, into the bargain, moreover, over and above, still, to boot 4. already, just now, now, right now, so soon

yield *v.* 1. afford, bear, bring forth, bring in, earn, furnish, generate, give, net, pay, produce, provide, return, supply ~*n.* 2. crop, earnings, harvest, income, output, produce, profit, return, revenue, takings ~*v.* 3. abandon, abdicate, admit defeat, bow, capitulate, cave in (*Inf.*), cede, cry quits, give in, give up the struggle, give way, knuckle under, lay down one's arms, part with, raise the white flag, relinquish, resign, resign oneself, submit, succumb, surrender, throw in the towel 4. accede, agree, allow, bow, comply, concede, consent, go along with, grant, permit
Antonyms *v.* appropriate, attack, combat, commandeer, consume, counterattack, defy, grab, hold on to, hold out, keep, lose, maintain, oppose, reserve, resist, retain, seize, struggle, use, use up ~*n.* consumption, input, loss

yielding 1. accommodating, acquiescent, biddable, compliant, docile, easy, flexible, obedient, pliant, submissive, tractable 2. elastic, pliable, quaggy, resilient, soft, spongy, springy, supple, unresisting
Antonyms (*sense 1*) dogged, headstrong, mulish, obstinate, opinionated, perverse, stiff-necked, stubborn, tenacious, wilful

yob, yobbo heavy (*Sl.*), hoodlum, hooligan, lout, rough (*Inf.*), roughneck (*Sl.*), rowdy, ruffian, thug, tough, yahoo

yoke *n.* 1. bond, chain, coupling, ligament, link, tie 2. bondage, burden, enslavement, helotry, oppression, serfdom, service, servility, servitude, slavery, thraldom, vassalage ~*v.* 3. bracket, connect, couple, harness, hitch, join, link, tie, unite

yokel boor, bucolic, clodhopper (*Inf.*), (country) bumpkin, country cousin, countryman, hayseed (*U.S. & Canad. inf.*), hick (*Inf., chiefly U.S. & Canad.*), hillbilly, hind (*Obsolete*), peasant (*Inf.*), rustic

young *adj.* 1. adolescent, callow, green, growing, immature, infant, in the springtime of life, junior, juvenile, little, unfledged, youthful 2. at an early stage, early, fledgling, new, newish, not far advanced,

recent, undeveloped ~*n.* 3. babies, brood, family, issue, litter, little ones, offspring, progeny
Antonyms *adj.* adult, advanced, aged, developed, elderly, experienced, full-grown, grown-up, mature, old, ripe, senior, venerable ~*n.* adult, grown-up, parent

youngster boy, cub, girl, juvenile, kid (*Inf.*), lad, lass, pup (*Inf., chiefly Brit.*), teenager, teenybopper (*Sl.*), urchin, young adult, young hopeful, young person, young shaver (*Inf.*), young 'un (*Inf.*), youth

youth 1. adolescence, boyhood, early life, girlhood, immaturity, juvenescence, salad days, young days 2. adolescent, boy, kid (*Inf.*), lad, shaveling (*Archaic*), stripling, teenager, young man, young shaver (*Inf.*), youngster 3. teenagers, the rising generation, the young, younger generation, young people
Antonyms adult, adulthood, age, grown-up, later life, manhood, maturity, OAP, old age, pensioner, senior citizen, the aged, the elderly, the old, womanhood

youthful 1. boyish, childish, girlish, immature, inexperienced, juvenile, pubescent, puerile, young 2. active, fresh, spry, vigorous, young at heart, young looking
Antonyms adult, aged, ageing, ancient, careworn, decaying, decrepit, elderly, grown-up, hoary, old, over the hill, mature, senile, senior, tired, waning, weary

yowl *v.* bawl, bay, caterwaul, cry, give tongue, howl, screech, squall, ululate, wail, yell

yucky, yukky beastly, dirty, disgusting, foul, grotty (*Sl.*), horrible, messy, mucky, revolting (*Inf.*), unpleasant

zany 1. *adj.* clownish, comical, crazy, eccentric, funny, goofy (*Inf.*), kooky (*U.S. inf.*), loony (*Sl.*), madcap, oddball (*Inf.*), nutty (*Sl.*), wacko (*Sl.*), wacky (*Sl.*) 2. *n.* buffoon, clown, comedian, jester, joker, merry-andrew, nut (*Sl.*), screwball (*Sl., chiefly U.S. & Canad.*), wag

zeal ardour, devotion, eagerness, earnestness, enthusiasm, fanaticism, fervency, fervour, fire, gusto, keenness, militancy, passion, spirit, verve, warmth, zest
Antonyms apathy, coolness, indifference, passivity, stoicism, torpor, unresponsiveness

zealot bigot, enthusiast, extremist, fanatic, fiend (*Inf.*), maniac, militant

zealous afire, ardent, burning, devoted, eager, earnest, enthusiastic, fanatical, fervent, fervid, impassioned, keen, militant, passionate, rabid, spirited
Antonyms apathetic, cold, cool, half-hearted, indifferent, lackadaisical, lacklustre, languorous, listless, low-key, sceptical, torpid, unenthusiastic, unimpassioned

zenith acme, apex, apogee, climax, crest, height, high noon, high point, meridian, peak, pinnacle, summit, top, vertex
Antonyms base, bottom, depths, lowest point, nadir, rock bottom

zero 1. cipher, naught, nil, nothing, nought 2. bottom, lowest point *or* ebb, nadir, nothing, rock bottom

zero hour appointed hour, crisis, moment of decision, moment of truth, turning point, vital moment

zero in (on) aim, bring to bear, concentrate, converge, direct, focus, home in, level, pinpoint, train

zest 1. appetite, delectation, enjoyment, gusto, keenness, relish, zeal, zing (*Inf.*) 2. charm, flavour, interest, kick (*Inf.*), piquancy, pungency, relish, savour, smack, spice, tang, taste
Antonyms abhorrence, apathy, aversion, disinclination, distaste, indifference, lack of enthusiasm, loathing, repugnance, weariness

zing animation, brio, dash, energy, go (*Inf.*), life, liveliness, oomph (*Inf.*), pep, pizzazz *or* pizazz (*Inf.*), spirit, vigour, vitality, zest, zip (*Inf.*)

zip 1. *n. Fig.* brio, drive, energy, get-up-and-go (*Inf.*), go (*Inf.*), gusto, life, liveliness, oomph (*Inf.*), pep, pizzazz *or* pizazz (*Inf.*), punch (*Inf.*), sparkle, spirit, verve, vigour, vim (*Sl.*), vitality, zest, zing (*Inf.*) 2. *v.* barrel (along) (*Inf., chiefly U.S. & Canad.*), burn rubber (*Inf.*), dash, flash, fly, hurry, rush, shoot, speed, tear, whiz (*Inf.*), zoom
Antonyms apathy, indifference, inertia, laziness, lethargy, listlessness, sloth, sluggishness

zone area, belt, district, region, section, sector, sphere

zoom *v.* barrel (along) (*Inf., chiefly U.S. & Canad.*), burn rubber (*Inf.*), buzz, dash, dive, flash, fly, hare (*Brit. inf.*), hum (*Sl.*), hurtle, pelt, rip (*Inf.*), rush, shoot, speed, streak, tear, whirl, whiz (*Inf.*), zip (*Inf.*)

Classical and Foreign Words and Phrases

Abbreviations - L. Latin; G. Greek; F. French; It. Italian; Ger. German.

à bas [F.] down with.
ab initio [L.] from the beginning.
ab ovo [L.] from the beginning.
absit omen [L.] may there be no ill omen.
accouchement [F.] childbirth, confinement.
à cheval [F.] on horseback, astride.
à deux [F.] of, for two persons.
ad hoc [L.] for this special object.
ad hominem [L.] to the man.
ad infinitum [L.] to infinity.
ad interim [L.] in the meanwhile.
ad majorem Dei gloriam [L.] for the greater glory of God.
ad nauseam [L.] to the point of disgust.
ad referendum [L.] for consideration.
ad rem [L.] to the point.
adsum [L.] I am here; present!
ad valorem [L.] according to value.
affaire d'amour [F.] a love affair.
affaire d'honneur [F.] an affair of honour, a duel.
affaire du coeur [F.] an affair of the heart.
a fortiori [L.] with stronger reason.
agent provocateur [F.] a police or secret service spy.
aide mémoire [F.] memorandum; summary.
à la carte [F.] picking from the bill of fare; *see* **table d'hote**.
à la française [F.] in the French style.
à la mode [F.] in the fashion.
al dente [It.] cooked so as to be firm when eaten.
al fresco [It.] in the open air.
alma mater [L.] benign mother; the term is used by former students in referring to their university.
alter ego [L.] another self, a close friend.
alto relievo [It.] high relief.
amende honorable [F.] apology.
amor patriae [L.] love of country.
amour propre [F.] self-esteem.
ancien régime [F.] the old order.
anglice [L.] in English.
anno Domini [L.] in the year of our Lord.
anno regni [L.] in the year of the reign.
anno urbis conditae [L.] (**A.U.C.**) in the year from the time of the building of the City (Rome).
annus mirabilis [L.] year of wonder.
ante meridiem [L.] before noon.
aperçu [F.] summary; insight.
à propos [F.] to the point.
arrière-pensée [F.] mental reservation.
arrivederci [It.] goodbye.
au contraire [F.] on the contrary.
au courant [F.] fully acquainted (with).
au fait [F.] fully informed; expert.
au fond [F.] fundamentally; essentially.
au naturel [F.] naked; uncooked or plainly cooked.
au revoir [F.] good-bye, till we meet again.
auf wiedersehen [Ger.] good-bye, till we meet again.
auto da fé [Portuguese] act of faith, the public burning of heretics.

beau geste [F.] noble or gracious act.
beau idéal [F.] ideal excellence, imagined state of perfection.
beau monde [F.] fashionable world.
bel esprit [F.] a man of wit.
bête noire [F.] an object of special detestation, pet aversion.
billet doux [F.] a love-letter.
blitzkrieg [Ger.] lightning war.
bona fide [L.] in good faith.
bonhomie [F.] good nature.
bonjour [F.] good-morning, good-day.
bon marché [F.] cheaply.
bonne bouche [F.] titbit.
bonsoir [F.] good-evening, good-night.
bon ton [F.] good breeding.

carpe diem [L.] enjoy the present day.
carte blanche [F.] full powers.
casus belli [L.] something which involves war.
cause célèbre [F.] famous lawsuit or controversy.
ça va sans dire [F.] that is a matter of course.
caveat emptor [L.] let the buyer beware.
cave canem [L.] beware of the dog.
c'est la vie [F.] that's life.
chacun à son gout [F.] every one to his taste.
ceteris paribus [L.] other things being equal.
chef-d'oeuvre [F.] masterpiece.
cherchez la femme [F.] look for the woman; there is a woman at the bottom of the business.
che sarà, sarà [It.] what will be, will be.
ciao [It.] hello, goodbye.
ci-devant [F.] former.
cogito, ergo sum [L.] I think, therefore I am.
comme il faut [F.] as it should be.
compos mentis [L.] sane.
compte rendu [F.] a report.

con amore [It.] with love, earnestly.
concierge [F.] a porter or doorkeeper.
coram populo [L.] in the presence of the people, openly.
corpus delicti [L.] the substance of the offence; the body of the victim of murder.
corrigenda [L.] things to be corrected.
coup d'état [F.] a stroke of policy, a sudden decisive political move, an abuse of authority.
coup de foudre [F.] sudden amazing event.
coup de grâce [F.] a finishing blow.
coup de théâtre [F.] a theatrical effect, a sudden change in a situation.
cui bono? [L.] for whose benefit is it? (i.e. the crime - in a law-case).
cum grano salis [L.] with a grain of salt, with reservation.

de facto [L.] actually, in fact.
Dei gratia [L.] by the grace of God.
de jure [L.] in law, by right.
de mortuis nil nisi bonum [L.] say nothing but good about the dead.
de novo [L.] anew.
Deo gratias [L.] thanks to God.
Deo volente [L.] (**D.V.**) God willing.
de profundis [L.] out of the depths. (The first words of the Latin version of Psalm 130.)
de rigueur [F.] indispensable, obligatory.
dernier cri [F.] latest fashion.
de trop [F.] superfluous, intrusive.
deus ex machina [L.] literally, a god out of the (theatrical) machine, i.e. a too obvious device in the plot of a play or story.
dies non [L.] a day on which judges do not sit.
Dieu et mon droit [F.] God and my right; motto of the British crown.
disjecta membra [L.] the scattered remains.
distingué [F.] of distinguished appearance.
distrait [F.] absent-minded.
dolce far niente [It.] pleasant idleness.
double entendre [F.] double meaning.
douceur [F.] a tip, a bribe.
dramatis personae [L.] the characters in a drama.

ecce homo! [L.] behold the man! (Spoken by Pilate; St. John, c.19, v.5.)
embarras de richesses [F.] perplexing wealth.
emeritus [L.] retired from office.
éminence grise [F.] person who wields power unofficially or behind the scenes.
en famille [F.] with one's family; at home; informally.
enfant terrible [F.] literally, "a terrible child."
en fête [F.] on holiday, in a state of festivity.
en masse [F.] in a body.
en passant [F.] in passing, by the way.
en rapport [F.] in sympathy with.
en règle [F.] in due order.
en route [F.] on the way; march!
entente cordiale [F.] friendly understanding between two nations.
entre nous [F.] between ourselves.
e pluribus unum [L.] one out of many. (Motto of the U.S.A.)
erratum (*pl.* **errata**) [L.] error.
esprit de corps [F.] team-spirit.
eureka! (**heureka**) [G.] I have found it! (The exclamation of Archimedes.)
ex cathedra [L.] from the chair of office, hence, authoritatively.
exeat [L.] literally, "let him go out"; formal leave of absence.
exempli gratia [L.] (**e.g.**) for example.
exeunt omnes [L.] all go out.
exit [L.] goes out.
ex libris [L.] from the books ... (followed by the name of the owner).
ex officio [L.] by virtue of his office.
ex parte [L.] on one side, partisan.

facile princeps [L.] an easy first.
fait accompli [F.] a thing done.
faut de mieux [F.] for lack of anything better.
faux pas [F.] a false step, a mistake.
felo de se [L.] a suicide, literally, a "felon of himself."
femme fatale [F.] seductive woman.
festina lente [L.] hasten slowly.
fête champêtre [F.] a rural festival.
feu de joie [F.] a bonfire; gun salute.
fiat lux [L.] let there be light.
fidei defensor [L.] defender of the faith.
fille de joie [F.] prostitute.
fin de siècle [F.] end of the 19th century; decadent.
finis [L.] the end.
flagrante delicto [L.] in the very act, red-handed.
folie de grandeur [F.] delusions of grandeur.
fons et origo [L.] the source and origin.

gaudeamus igitur [L.] let us then rejoice.
gendarme [F.] one of the *gendarmerie*, a body of armed police in France.

haute couture [F.] high fashion.
haute cuisine [F.] high-class cooking.
hic jacet [L.] here lies.
honi soit qui mal y pense [Old F.] shame to him who thinks ill of it.
horribile dictu [L.] horrible to relate.
hors de combat [F.] out of condition to fight.

ibidem (abbreviated as **ib;** or **ibid;**) [L.] in the same place.
ich dien [Ger.] I serve.
idée fixe [F.] an obsession, monomania.
id est [L.] (usually **i.e.**) that is.
idem [L.] the same.
ignis fatuus [L.] a will-o'-the-wisp.
imprimatur [L.] literally, "let it be printed", a licence to print, sanction.
in camera [L.] in a (judge's private) room.
in extremis [L.] at the point of death.
infra dignitatem [L.] (**infra dig.**) below one's dignity.
in loco parentis [L.] in the place of a parent.
in medias res [L.] into the midst of things.
in memoriam [L.] to the memory of.
in perpetuum [L.] for ever.
in re [L.] in the matter of.
in situ [L.] in its original position.
in statu quo [L.] in the former state.
inter alia [L.] among other things.
in toto [L.] entirely.
in vino veritas [L.] in wine the truth (comes out).
ipse dixit [L.] "he himself said it"; his unsupported word.
ipsissima verba [L.] the very words.
ipso facto [L.] by the fact itself.

je ne sais quoi [F.] "I don't know what", a something or other.
jeu d'esprit [F.] a witticism.
joie de vivre [F.] joy of living; ebullience.

laissez faire [F.] policy of inaction.
lapsus linguae [L.] a slip of the tongue.
lares et penates [L.] household gods.
leitmotif [Ger.] a theme used to indicate a person, idea, etc. in opera, etc.
lèse-majesté [F.] high treason.
l'état, c'est moi [F.] I am the state. (Saying of Louis XIV).
lettre de cachet [F.] a sealed letter; a royal warrant for imprisonment.
locum tenens [L.] "one occupying the place", a deputy or substitute.

magnum opus [L.] a great work.
mal à propos [F.] ill-timed.
mal de mer [F.] sea-sickness.
malentendu [F.] a misunderstanding.
manqué [F.] potential; would-be.
mariage de convenance [F.] a marriage from motives of interest rather than love.
mauvaise honte [F.] false modesty, bashfulness.
mauvais quart d'heure [F.] a brief unpleasant experience.
mea culpa [L.] by my fault.
memento mori [L.] remember death.
ménage à trois [F.] sexual arrangement involving a married couple and the lover of one of them.
mens sana in corpore sano [L.] a sound mind in a sound body.
mésalliance [F.] marriage with someone of lower social status.
meum et tuum [L.] mine and thine.
mirabile dictu [L.] wonderful to relate.
mise en scène [F.] scenic setting.
modus operandi [L.] manner of working.
mot juste [F.] the exact right word.
moue [F.] a disdainful or pouting look.
multum in parvo [L.] much in little.
mutatis mutandis [L.] with the necessary changes.

née [F.] "born", her maiden name being; e.g. *Mrs. Brown née Smith.*
nemine contradicente [L.] (often as **nem.con.**) without opposition.
nemo me impune lacessit [L.] no one hurts me with impunity.
ne plus ultra [L.] nothing further; the uttermost point.
nihil obstat [L.] there is no obstacle.
nil desperandum [L.] despair of nothing.
noblesse oblige [F.] nobility imposes obligations.
nolens volens [L.] whether he will or not.
noli me tangere [L.] don't touch me.
nom de guerre [F.] an assumed name. (**nom de plume** is hardly used in French.)
non compos mentis [L.] insane.
non sequitur [L.] it does not follow.
nota bene [L.] (**N.B.**) note well.
nous avons changé tout cela [F.] we have changed all that.
nouveau riche [F.] one newly enriched, an upstart.
nulli secundus [L.] second to none.

obiit [L.] he (or she) died.
obiter dictum [L.] (*pl.* **obiter dicta**) something said by the way.

on dit [F.] they say; a rumour.
ora pro nobis [L.] pray for us.
O tempora! O mores! [L.] literally, "O the times! O the manners!"; what dreadful times and doings.

pace [L.] by leave of.
par avion [F.] by aeroplane (of mail sent by air).
par excellence [F.] pre-eminently.
pari passu [L.] with equal pace; together.
passim [L.] here and there, everywhere.
pax vobiscum [L.] peace be with you.
peccavi [L.] I have sinned.
per ardua ad astra [L.] through difficulties to the stars.
persona non grata [L.] unacceptable or unwelcome person.
post hoc, ergo propter hoc [L.] after this, therefore because of this (a fallacy in reasoning.)
pour encourager les autres [F.] in order to encourage the others.
prima facie [L.] at a first view.
primus inter pares [L.] first among equals.
pro patria [L.] for one's country.
pro tempore [L.] for the time being.

quis custodiet ipsos custodes? [L.] who will guard the guards?
qui vive? [F.] who goes there?
quod erat demonstrandum [L.] **(Q.E.D.)** which was to be proved.
quot homines, tot sententiae [L.] as many men as there are opinions.
quo vadis? [L.] whither goest thou?

rara avis [L.] a rare bird, something prodigious.
reductio ad absurdum [L.] a reducing to the absurd.
répondez s'il vous plait [F.] **(R.S.V.P.)** please reply.
requiescat in pace [L.] **(R.I.P.)** may he (or she) rest in peace.
rus in urbe [L.] the country in the town.

sans peur et sans reproche [F.] without fear and without reproach.
sans souci [F.] without care.
sauve qui peut [F.] save himself who can - the cry of disorderly retreat.
semper fidelis [L.] always faithful.
seriatim [L.] in order.
sic [L.] thus. Often used to call attention to some quoted mistake.
sic transit gloria mundi [L.] so passes the glory of the world.
sine die [L.] without date, indefinitely postponed.
si monumentum requiris, circumspice [L.] if you seek (his) monument, look around you. (The inscription on the architect Wren's tomb in St. Paul's.)
sine qua non [L.] an indispensable condition.
soi-disant [F.] so-called; self-styled.
status quo [L.] "the state in which", the pre-existing state of affairs.
stet [L.] let it stand.
Sturm und Drang [Ger.] storm and stress.
sub judice [L.] under consideration.
sub rosa [L.] "under the rose", secretly.
sub voce [L.] under that heading.
sursum corda [L.] lift up your hearts (to God).

table d'hôte [F.] general guest-table, meal at a fixed price.
tant mieux [F.] so much the better.
tant pis [F.] so much the worse.
tempore [L.] in the time of.
tempus fugit [L.] time flies.
terra firma [L.] solid earth.
terra incognita [L.] unexplored land or area of study.
tour de force [F.] a feat of strength or skill.
tout de suite [F.] at once.
tout ensemble [F.] the whole taken together, the general effect.
tout le monde [F.] all the world, everyone.

ubique [L.] everywhere.
ultima Thule [L.] the utmost boundary or limit.
ultra vires [L.] beyond one's powers.

vade in pace [L.] go in peace.
vade mecum [L.] go with me; a constant companion, work of reference.
vale [L.] farewell.
veni, vidi, vici [L.] I came, I saw, I conquered.
ventre à terre [F.] belly to the ground; at high speed.
verbum sapienti satis [L.] **(verb.sap.)** a word is enough for a wise man.
via media [L.] a middle course.
videlicet [L.] **(viz.)** namely, to wit.
volente Deo [L.] God willing.

Weltschmerz [Ger.] world-weariness; sentimental pessimism.

Zeitgeist [Ger.] the spirit of the times.

Group Names and Collective Nouns

barren of mules
bevy of quails
bevy of roes
brace or lease of bucks
brood or covey of grouse
brood of hens or chickens
building or clamour of rooks
bunch, company or knob of wigeon (in the water)
bunch, knob or spring of teal
cast of hawks
cete of badgers
charm of goldfinches
chattering of choughs
clowder of cats
colony of gulls (breeding)
covert of coots
covey of partridges
cowardice of curs
desert of lapwings
dopping of sheldrakes
down or husk of hares
drove or herd of cattle (kine)
exaltation of larks
fall of woodcocks
field or string of racehorses
flight of wigeon (in the air)
flight or dule of doves
flight of swallows
flight of dunlins
flight, rush, bunch or knob of pochards
flock or flight of pigeons
flock of sheep
flock of swifts
flock or gaggle of geese
flock, congregation, flight or volery of birds
gaggle of geese (on the ground)
gang of elk
haras (stud) of horses
herd of antelopes
herd of buffaloes
herd, sedge or siege of cranes
herd of curlews
herd of deer
herd of giraffes
herd or tribe of goats
herd or pod of seals
herd or bevy of swans
herd of ponies
herd of swine
hill of ruffs
host of sparrows
kindle of kittens
labour of moles
leap of leopards
litter of cubs
litter of pups or pigs
litter of whelps
murmuration of starlings
muster of peacocks
nest of rabbits
nye or nide of pheasants
pace or herd of asses
pack of grouse
pack, mute or cry of hounds
pack, rout or herd of wolves
paddling of ducks
plump, sord or sute of wildfowl
pod of whiting
pride or troop of lions
rag of colts
richesse of martens
run of poultry
school or run of whales
school or gam of porpoises
sedge or siege of bitterns
sedge or siege of herons
shoal or glean of herrings
shoal, draught, haul, run or catch of fish
shrewdness of apes
skein of geese (in flight)
skulk of foxes
sleuth of bears
sord or sute of mallards
sounder of boars
sounder or dryft of swine
stand or wing of plovers
stud of mares
swarm of insects
swarm or grist of bees, or flies
swarm or cloud of gnats
tok of capercailzies
team of ducks (in flight)
troop of kangaroos
troop of monkeys
walk or wisp of snipe
watch of nightingales
yoke, drove, team or herd of oxen

Signs of the Zodiac

Aquarius • Aries • Cancer • Capricorn • Gemini • Leo
Libra • Pisces • Sagittarius • Scorpio • Taurus • Virgo

Characters in Classical Mythology

Achilles
Actaeon
Adonis
Aeneas
Agamemnon
Ajax
Amazons
Andromeda
Antigone
Aphrodite
Apollo
Arachne
Ares
Argonauts
Ariadne
Artemis
Atalanta
Athena / Athene
Atlas
Aurora
Bacchus
Bellona
Boreas
Cassandra
Cassiopeia
centaurs
Charon
Charybdis
Chimaera
Circe
Cronus
Cupid
Cybele
Cyclopes
Daedalus
Demeter
Diana
Dido
Dionysus
dryads
Echidna
Electra
Eros
Eurydice
Galatea
Ganymede
Gorgons
griffin / gryphon
Hades
hamadryads
Harpies
Hebe
Hecate
Hector
Hecuba
Helen
Hephaestus
Hera
Heracles / Hercules
Hermaphroditus
Hermes
Hydra
Icarus
Iris
Janus
Jason
Jocasta
Juno
Jupiter
Leda
Mars
Medea
Medusa
Mercury
Midas
Minerva
Minotaur
Muses
Narcissus
Nemesis
Neptune
Nereids
Niobe
Oceanids
Odysseus
Oedipus
oreads
Orestes
Orion
Orpheus
Pallas
Pan
Pandora
Paris
Pegasus
Penelope
Persephone
Perseus
Phoebus
Pleiades
Pluto
Poseidon
Priam
Prometheus
Psyche
Pygmalion
Remus
Romulus
Saturn
satyrs
Selene
sibyl
Sirens
Sisyphus
Sphinx
Tantalus
Tiresias
Titans
Triton
Uranus
Venus
Vulcan
Zeus

Months in the French Revolutionary Calendar

Brumaire • Floréal • Frimaire • Fructidor • Germinal • Messidor
Nivôse • Pluviôse • Prairial • Thermidor • Vendémiaire • Ventôse

Months in the Hebrew Calendar

Adar • Av • Elul • Heshvan • Iyar • Kislev
Nisan • Shevat • Sivan • Tammuz • Tevet • Tishri

Planets of the Solar System

Earth • Jupiter • Mars • Mercury • Neptune
Pluto • Saturn • Uranus • Venus

Chemical Elements

actinium
aluminium
americium
antimony
argon
arsenic
astatine
barium
berkelium
beryllium
bismuth
boron
bromine
cadmium
caesium
calcium
californium
carbon
cerium
chlorine
chromium
cobalt
copper
curium
dysprosium
einsteinium
erbium
europium
fermium
fluorine
francium
gadolinium
gallium
germanium
gold
hafnium
hahnium
helium
holmium
hydrogen
indium
iodine
iridium
iron
krypton
lanthanum
lawrencium
lead
lithium
lutetium
magnesium
manganese
mendelevium
mercury
molybdenum
neodymium
neon
neptunium
nickel
niobium
nitrogen
nobelium
osmium
oxygen
palladium
phosphorus
platinum
plutonium
polonium
potassium
praseodymium
proactinium
promethium
radium
radon
rhenium
rhodium
rubidium
ruthenium
rutherfordium
samarium
scandium
selenium
silicon
silver
sodium
strontium
sulphur
tantalum
technetium
tellurium
terbium
thallium
thorium
thulium
tin
titanium
tungsten
uranium
vanadium
xenon
ytterbium
zinc
zirconium

Books of the Bible (including the Apocrypha)

Acts of the Apostles
Amos
Baruch
Chronicles
Colossians
Corinthians
Daniel
Daniel and Susanna
Daniel, Bel, and the Snake
Deuteronomy
Ecclesiastes
Ecclesiasticus
Ephesians
Esdras
Esther
Exodus
Ezekiel
Ezra
Galatians
Genesis
Habbakuk
Haggai
Hebrews
Hosea
Isaiah
James
Jeremiah
Job
Joel
John
Jonah
Joshua
Jude
Judges
Judith
Kings
Lamentations
Leviticus
Luke
Maccabees
Malachi
Manasseh
Mark
Matthew
Micah
Nahum
Nehemiah
Numbers
Obadiah
Peter
Philemon
Philippians
Proverbs
Psalms
Revelations
Romans
Ruth
Samuel
Solomon
Song of Songs
Song of the Three
Thessalonians
Timothy
Titus
Tobit
Zechariah
Zephaniah